THE DICTIONARY OF NATIONAL BIOGRAPHY

Founded in 1882 by

GEORGE SMITH

EDITED BY

Sir LESLIE STEPHEN

AND

Sir SIDNEY LEE

From the Earliest Times to 1900

VOLUME XIII

MASQUERIER——MYLES

Published since 1917 by the

OXFORD UNIVERSITY PRESS

LONDON : GEOFFREY CUMBERLEGE

Oxford University Press, Amen House, London E.C.4

GLASGOW NEW YORK TORONTO MELBOURNE WELLINGTON
BOMBAY CALCUTTA MADRAS CAPE TOWN

Geoffrey Cumberlege, Publisher to the University

Reprinted at the Oxford University Press 1921–1922
from plates furnished by Messrs. Spottiswoode & Co.
and again 1937–1938, 1949–1950

PRINTED IN GREAT BRITAIN

NOTE

In reprinting the twenty-two volumes of the main Dictionary in 1921–2 and again in 1937–8 it seemed best to leave the text unaltered. The bulk of the corrections hitherto received or collected by the present Publishers is insignificant when compared with the magnitude of the work, and would not justify the issue of a 'new edition' purporting to supersede the editions now in the libraries and in private hands. The collection and classification of such corrections for future use is, however, being steadily carried on; and students of biography are invited to communicate their discoveries to the Publishers.

Two changes have been made in reprinting:—

1. The lists of Contributors originally prefixed to each of the sixty-six volumes, and later combined in twenty-two lists, have been combined in one list which is now printed in Volume 1 only.

2. In using the main Dictionary (to 1900) it is necessary to remember that it is in *two* alphabetical series: Vols. 1–21, and the supplementary Vol. 22, in which were added lives of persons who had died too late for inclusion in their places (as well as lives of some who had been accidentally omitted). It has been sought to mitigate the inconvenience arising from this by adding to the index at the end of each volume those names, occurring in Vol. 22, which belong to the same part of the alphabet. These 'supplementary' names are added at the bottom of each page. It is thus possible to ascertain, by reference to a single volume, whether any person (who died before 1901) is or is not in the 22-volume Dictionary.

The opportunity has been taken, in accordance with the wishes of the donors, to commemorate upon each title-page the name of the munificent Founder.

CONTENTS OF VOLS. 1–22

Note.—*Vols.* 1–21, *as originally issued* 1885–1890, *were edited by Sir Leslie Stephen; Vols.* 22–26, 1890–1891, *by Sir Leslie Stephen and Sir Sidney Lee; Vols.* 27–66, 1891–1901, *by Sir Sidney Lee.*

DICTIONARY

OF

NATIONAL BIOGRAPHY

MASQUERIER, JOHN JAMES (1778–1855), painter, is stated to have been born at Chelsea in October 1778, the son of French parents, his mother's name being Barbot, and on both sides descended from French refugee protestant families. Louis Masquerier, a goldsmith in Coventry Street, Haymarket, at the beginning of the eighteenth century, whose widow, Madeleine Touchet, married Reynolds Grignion, was possibly a relative [see under GRIGNION, CHARLES, 1717–1810]. According to the account given in the 'Gentleman's Magazine' (1855, pt. i. p. 540), Masquerier had two elder brothers, who sought their fortunes in America, and a sister. Masquerier studied at the Royal Academy and painted a portrait of himself as a boy (in the collection of Baroness Burdett Coutts), which was shown to George III, and gained for him a travelling allowance from the Royal Academy, which enabled him to go to Paris to study. About 1789 he settled with his mother in the Champs-Elysées, while he studied painting under François Vincent at the Tuileries. He was painting in this school at the time of the murder of the Swiss Guards on 10 Aug. 1792, and narrowly escaped with his life. Masquerier made sketches from personal observation of many events of the French revolution, such as the murder of the Princesse de Lamballe and the trial of the king, and was acquainted with some leading notabilities. In 1793, when the arrest was imminent of all English residents in France, he and his mother determined to escape from Paris. His mother was, however, arrested and imprisoned with Helen Maria Williams [q. v.] and others. She owed her life and liberty only to the fall of Robespierre and the events of the 10 Thermidor. Masquerier returned to London, and subsequently entered the studio of John Hoffner, R.A. [q.v.], many of whose pictures he completed. In 1793 he visited the Isle of Wight, where he was the guest of John Wilkes [q. v.] In 1795 he began his professional career as an artist, and in 1796 exhibited for the first time at the Royal Academy, sending a portrait and 'The Incredulity of St. Thomas;' the latter formed the altar-piece of the chapel (once the hall of the house of Lord-chief-justice Jeffreys [q. v.]) in Duke Street, Westminster. In 1800 Masquerier revisited Paris, and claimed, through the interest of Madame Tallien, whose portrait he painted, to have made a drawing of Napoleon Bonaparte as first consul. He certainly brought to England sketches and notes, and with the help of Charles Turner [q. v.] and Henry Bernard Chalon very hurriedly painted in his London studio a picture of 'Napoleon reviewing the Consular Guards in the Court of the Tuileries,' which he exhibited in Piccadilly in 1801 (in the collection of Baroness Burdett Coutts). This picture attracted large crowds on the assumption that it was the first authentic likeness of Napoleon exhibited in England (ALFRED WHITMAN, in *Strand Mag.* xxxvi. 113–15). 'Peter Porcupine' (William Cobbett [q. v.]) accused him of being an alien spy and emissary of Napoleon. Masquerier rebutted the scandal by producing the register of his birth at Chelsea. Masquerier continued to paint and exhibit portraits, which reached in twenty-eight years a total of over four hundred. He also occasionally sent to the Royal Academy a subject picture, such as 'The Fortune Teller' (1800), 'Petrarch and Laura '(1803), 'January and May' (1808). In 1814 he fetched his mother from Paris, and provided for her maintenance in England. It was probably on this journey that he painted a portrait of Emma, lady Hamilton [q. v.]

In the following year he visited the field of Waterloo and made a painting of 'La Belle Alliance' (in the collection of Baroness Burdett Coutts). He also drew a portrait of Napoleon's guide, J. B. Coster. In 1823 he retired from his profession, having amassed a comfortable fortune, and settled at Brighton, where he resided for the remainder of his life. He revisited Paris in 1850, and in 1851 made a tour in Germany with Henry Crabb Robinson [q. v.] Masquerier still painted occasionally after his retirement; in 1831 he exhibited 'A Marriage in the Church of St. Germain l'Auxerrois, Paris,' and in 1838 'Buonaparte and Marie Louise viewing the Tomb of Charles the Bold at Bruges.' He died at Brighton on 13 March 1855. His remaining pictures, sketch-books, &c., became the property of a relative, Mr. D. E. Forbes, and were sold by auction at Christie's on 19 Jan. 1878. A number of his sketch-books were in the possession of his friend, Baroness Burdett Coutts.

Among the notabilities painted by him were Miss Mellon and Miss O'Neil (both in the collection of Baroness Burdett Coutts), and Warren Hastings (engraved by S. Freeman for Cadell's 'Portraits'), besides many of his personal friends and relations. Masquerier was popular in cultivated and intellectual society, numbering among his friends Sir Francis Burdett, bart. [q. v.], and his daughter, Baroness Burdett Coutts. He was also on intimate terms with Henry Crabb Robinson [q. v.], and Michael Faraday [q. v.], who never forgot some early assistance which Masquerier rendered him. Campbell, the poet, described Masquerier as 'a pleasant little fellow, with French vivacity' (see Beattie, *Life of Campbell*). Masquerier painted his own portrait more than once. He married in 1812 Rachel, widow of Dr. Robert Eden Scott, professor of moral philosophy at Aberdeen, daughter of Duncan Forbes, esq., of Thainstone; she died in 1850, leaving no children.

[Gent. Mag. 1855, new ser. xliii. 540; Ottley's Dict. of Recent and Living Painters; Redgrave's Dict. of Artists; Diaries of Henry Crabb Robinson; information from Baroness Burdett Coutts and George Scharf, esq., C.B.] L. C.

MASSEREENE, Earl of. [See Skeffington, Clotworthy, second Earl, 1742–1805.]

MASSEREENE, Viscounts. [See Clotworthy, Sir John, first Viscount, *d.* 1665; Skeffington, Sir John, second Viscount, *d.* 1695.]

MASSEY, Sir EDWARD (1619?–1674?), major-general, was the fifth son of John Massey of Coddington, Cheshire, and Anne, daughter of Richard Grosvenor of Eaton (Ormerod, *Hist. of Cheshire*, ed. 1882, ii. 729, 732). The story that Edward Massey served as an apprentice on London Bridge and ran away to Holland seems improbable, but he may have been in the Low Countries as a 'soldier of fortune' before the outbreak of the first Scottish war in 1639, by which date he had returned to England (Clarendon, *Hist. of Rebellion*, ed. 1888, bk. vii. § 158). Massey then took service in Charles's army as captain of pioneers in Colonel William Legge's regiment (*ib.*) At the commencement of the English civil war in 1642 Massey joined the king at York, but, dissatisfied with his preferment, went over to the parliament, and became lieutenant-colonel in a foot regiment under Henry Grey, first earl of Stamford [q. v.], (Peacock, *Army Lists of the Roundheads and Cavaliers*, p. 27). He was present at Worcester (23 Sept. 1642), after which his regiment was sent to Hereford and to Gloucester, where the Earl of Stamford was appointed governor (December 1642). The Earl of Stamford soon afterwards marched west against Hopton, and Massey was left behind as deputy-governor with one regiment.

From this time until 1645 Massey played an important part in the war in the west, first in defending Gloucester from royalist attacks, and secondly in using that city as a basis from which to conquer the surrounding country. The first royalist attack took place before Massey had been in command many weeks. On 7 Jan. 1643 Prince Rupert appeared before Gloucester, summoned and prepared to storm the city, but withdrew next day to Oxford. Massey now tried to strengthen his position by seizing the places of strength in the neighbourhood. He took Sudeley Castle, the seat of Lord Chandos, on 29 Jan., but abandoned it a few days later, after Rupert had stormed Cirencester (2 Feb.) In March a Welsh army, under Lord Herbert, advanced to Highnam, expecting to be joined by Rupert in a combined attack on Gloucester. On 23 March an attack was made on the Welsh troops at Highnam, in which Massey himself took part; and the next day, with the aid of Waller, the Welsh were defeated and Highnam taken, nearly fifteen hundred prisoners being led into Gloucester. Massey then took Tewkesbury, and, with Waller, tried unsuccessfully to prevent Prince Maurice crossing the Severn at Upton Bridge; they were beaten at Ripple Field on 12 April 1643 (Corbet, 'Historical Relation' in *Bibliotheca Glouc.* p. 33). Still attempting to make Gloucester secure on the western side, Massey and Waller took Hereford, and cleared the eastern side of that county. Massey now became governor of Gloucester.

The defeat of Waller at Roundway Down (13 July 1643), followed by the surrender of Bristol, exposed Gloucester to greater danger. The sole force at Massey's command consisted of two regiments of foot and two hundred horse, and a few trained bands and reformadoes—in all some fifteen hundred men. As the king's intention of besieging Gloucester became apparent, Massey opened negotiations with the royalists, either to gain time or possibly with the real intention of handing the city over to the king (see WARBURTON, *Prince Rupert*, ii. 278, 280; CLARENDON, *Hist. of Rebellion*, bk. vii. § 158; GARDINER, *Hist. of the Great Civil War*, i. 233). On 10 Aug. the king's army appeared before the walls, and the siege continued till 5 Sept., when it was raised on the Earl of Essex's approach. The general supplied the town with ammunition (of which only three barrels remained at the end of the siege), but was unable to leave any troops behind. On 15 Sept. the thanks of both houses of parliament and a sum of 1,000*l.* were voted to Massey (*Commons' Journals*, iii. 241; cf. GARDINER, *Hist. of Great Civil War*, vol. i. chap. x.; *Notes and Queries*, 8th ser. v. 164–5; WASHBOURN'S *Bibliotheca Gloucestrensis*). Massey, now anxious to act on the offensive, vainly sought to get either supplies from parliament or another commission in the army. During October 1643 the royalists were gradually surrounding Gloucester, and frequent skirmishes took place, especially with Sir John Wintour's garrison in the Forest of Dean, at Berkeley, and Brookthorpe Hill, where Massey was beaten. A vain attempt was made by the royalists in mid-winter to win Gloucester through the expected treachery of Captain Backhouse, who acted throughout with cognisance of Massey (CORBET, *Relation*, ut supra, p. 78). In March 1644 the command of the royalist forces in Herefordshire and the neighbourhood was given to Colonel Nicholas Mynne. In April 1644 Massey was reinforced and able to act on the offensive, attacking the royalists in Herefordshire and taking Westbury, Newnham (garrisoned by Sir John Wintour's troops), and Beverston Castle, and shortly afterwards Malmesbury and Tewkesbury. Lydney and Berkeley alone remained to the king in Gloucestershire, but Massey's deficiency in men and money hampered his movements.

In the early summer of 1644 Massey was again able to take the field against Mynne, who was planning a combined attack by the Herefordshire and Gloucestershire royalists on the city. The design failed, however, owing to the defeat and death of Mynne at Eldersfield (August 1644) (*ib.* p. 111). In September Massey destroyed Beachley Camp and took Monmouth (24 Sept.) Massey could not garrison the places he had won, and Beachley was reoccupied by the royalists; but Massey returned on 14 Oct., and, after a desperate struggle, in which Massey's head-piece was knocked off by the butt-end of a musket, succeeded in dislodging the enemy, killing thirty and capturing as many as 230 (*ib.* p. 127).

Rupert now made another attack on the counties round Gloucester, and Massey failed to take Sir John Winter's house, near Lydney, which was, however, soon deserted by the royalists and fired. He was beaten by Rupert at Ledbury on 22 April 1645, but on 26 May took Evesham. He was made general of the Western Association on 24 May (*Lords' Journals*, vii. 393), *i.e.* of the forces raised by the five counties of Cornwall, Devon, Somerset, Dorset, and Wilts.

During the campaigns of 1645 and 1646 Massey co-operated with Fairfax in the reduction of the west. He joined Fairfax in July 1645 near Taunton, routed General Porter at Ilminster on 9 July, and took part in the storming of Bridgwater (CARTE, *Original Letters*, i. 131; SPRIGGE, *Anglia Rediviva*, pp. 70, 77). He was afterwards sent to Taunton, apparently to prevent Goring from marching northwards. Throughout the rest of the year and the winter of 1645–6 he remained in Somerset and Devonshire, blocking the king's garrisons, especially Barnstaple, and taking Warham and other places. In July 1646 he took his seat in parliament as member for Gloucester, and on 20 Oct. his brigade was disbanded at Devizes by order of both houses (LUDLOW, *Memoirs*, ed. 1722, ii. 181). In the struggle between the parliament and the army, the presbyterian leaders endeavoured to make use of Massey's skill and popularity, and during the summer of 1647 he became one of the leaders of the city against the army, along with Waller and Poyntz; was named commander-in-chief of the city forces; and on 30 July joined the presbyterian committee of safety. On 2 April 1647 parliament appointed Massey lieutenant-general of horse, under Skippon, in the army intended to be sent to Ireland. But the officers of the new model were disinclined to serve under him, some alleging that he was 'a profane man, and unfit for a command,' the real objection being that he was 'not of the faction which they call the army' (WALLER, *Vindication*, p. 84). The army on 16 June on its arrival in London impeached him and ten others on the ground of their designing to raise a new civil war (for charges see *Old Parliamentary Hist.* xvi. 70, 116), and on the approach of the army to London Massey fled to Holland. On 9 Aug., together with Poyntz, he published an apology explaining their flight and justifying their action (RUSHWORTH, *Collections*, vii. 765). Massey, although summoned to appear in parliament before 16 Oct. 1647 and answer the charges, did not return to take his seat till early in September 1648. From that time till his exclusion by Pride's Purge (6 Dec.) he sat and voted with the presbyterians. On 12 Dec. he was imprisoned with Waller, but escaped on 18 Jan. from St. James's to Holland (*ib.* vii. 1394; CLARENDON, *Hist. of Rebellion*, xi. 208; *Clarendon State Papers*, i. 464).

Massey now definitely took service under the king, and spent some time at the Hague and later at Breda. He was one of the few English royalists whom the Scots allowed to attend on Charles II. In preparation for Charles's invasion he was appointed lieutenant-general and second in command of a regiment of horse to be raised by the Duke of Buckingham (HEATH, *Chronicle*, ed. 1663, pp. 505, 529). Massey was made governor of Kirkcaldy; he kept the bridge five miles east of Stirling with a brigade of horse against Cromwell, and took part in the battle of Inverkeithing on 20 July 1651 (WHITELOCK, p. 472). When Charles marched into England, Massey preceded him, and vainly attempted to induce the Lancashire presbyterians, with whom he had some personal influence, to join the king (CLARENDON, *Hist. of Rebellion*, xiii. § 58). He took part in the skirmish at Warrington Bridge, and on 29 Aug. tried in vain to hold Upton Bridge against Lambert. In the fight Massey was injured, and was therefore unable to take part in the battle of Worcester (3 Sept.); he, however, accompanied Charles in his flight as far as Droitwich, where he fell behind and threw himself on the protection of Lady Stamford at Broadgate, Leicestershire (*ib.* xiii. §§ 73, 136; CARY, *Memorials of Civil War*, pp. 376, 381). When sufficiently recovered he was moved to London for trial, and, after making an ineffectual attempt to escape, was lodged in the Tower (November 1651). He escaped, however, in August 1652, and fled to Holland (CLARENDON, *Hist. of Rebellion*, xiii. § 137), and for some years worked, as one of the leaders of the presbyterian party, to bring about the return of Charles. In spite of plotting and negotiating, Massey was looked upon with distrust by the royalists. Sir Walter Strickland wrote of him in December 1649: 'And truly I have not yet seen a man thrust himself into a business with less advantage than he did. It seems that he had rather play at a small game than stand out' (CARY, *Memorials of Civil War*, ii. 203). Hyde also wrote of Massey as 'a wonderfully vain and weak man' (*Clarendon State Papers*, iii. 144). Massey seems, however, to have been useful to Charles in negotiations with the English presbyterians. He visited England in 1654 and 1656 on this business, and again after Oliver Cromwell's death. In 1655 he was in Denmark (*Clarendon State Papers*, in the Bodleian, iii. 67), and in 1657 mention is made of his possible employment by the Spaniards (*ib.* p. 399). In 1659 Massey was busy round Gloucester preparing for a rising, but was betrayed by Sir Richard Willis and was taken. He escaped at Nympsfield Hill on 31 July 1659 (CLARENDON, *Hist. of Rebellion*, xvi. §§ 25, 31, 37). In January 1660 Charles empowered him to renew his attempts on Gloucester, and appointed him governor. Massey, after conferring with General Monck in London, arrived in the city in March (*Clarendon State Papers*, iii. 646, 647), and represented it in the Convention parliament (cf. THURLOE, vii. 854, 865, 872, 877). After the Restoration he was rewarded by knighthood (*Hist. MSS. Comm.* 5th Rep. p. 199), and on 16 May by a vote of 1,000*l.*, which was increased by a second vote of 3,000*l.* on 19 Dec. (*Commons' Journals*, viii. 215). In September he was appointed governor of Jamaica, but did not go thither, as he was elected M.P. for Gloucester in April 1661. In 1665 he was appointed one of the commissioners of prizes (*ib.* 1664–5, p. 245), and during the Dutch war was commander of auxiliary troops to be raised by himself (*ib.* 1665–6, p. 520). He continued to sit in parliament until his death, which took place, according to Le Neve, in Ireland either towards the end of 1674 or the beginning of 1675 (LE NEVE, *Pedigrees of Knights*, pp. 51–2; *Names of Members returned to serve in Parliament*, i. 523; *Accounts and Papers*, vol. lxii.) He was unmarried.

Massey, as a strong presbyterian and a pronounced enemy of independency, was opposed to Charles I on religious rather than on political grounds. He was straightforward and honest (none of the charges brought against him have been proved), and of great personal bravery. He had also the power of winning the confidence of those about him. In person he was of a 'middle stature,' with 'brown hair' and 'sanguine complexion' (*A New Hue and Cry after Major-General Massey and some others*, London, 1652). Portraits of him appear in Ricraft's 'Survey of

England's Champions' (ed. 1647, chap. xv.), and with the 'Verses on the Siege of Gloucester and Colonel Massey,' 1647.

[Bibliotheca Gloucestrensis, ed. Washbourn, Gloucester, 1825, containing reprints of the most important tracts, &c., relating to Massey's governorship of Gloucester, including reprint of Corbet's Historical Relation of the Military Government of Gloucester, originally printed in 1645. For Massey's pedigree, Ormerod's History of Cheshire; for letters Cal. State Papers, Dom. 1644 and 1645. Other authorities are referred to in the text.] G. N. R.

MASSEY, EYRE, first BARON CLARINA (1719–1804), general, born on 24 May 1719, was fifth son of Colonel Hugh Massey of Duntryleague, co. Limerick, and his wife Elizabeth, fourth daughter of the Right Hon. George Evans, father of George, first baron Carbery. His eldest brother was Hugh, first lord Massey. In a memorial of his services (*Home Office Papers*, Ireland, vol. ccccxl.) he states that he 'purchased a pair of colours' in the 27th foot in 1739, and went with the regiment to the West Indies as lieutenant of the grenadiers. The 27th foot, of which General William Blakeney (afterwards Lord Blakeney [q. v.]) was colonel, was at Porto Bello, with Admiral Vernon, in 1739, and the few survivors returned home in December 1740. The English military records show the dates of Massey's commissions in the 27th foot as ensign, 25 Jan. 1741; hitherto 3 Nov. 1741 (*Home Office Mil. Entry Book*, xviii. 47, 243). Massey served with his regiment in Scotland in 1745–1746, and was made captain-lieutenant, and captain in the regiment by the Duke of Cumberland, apparently in 1747 (*ib.*), captain 24 May 1751, and major 10 Dec. 1755. In 1757 he went out to North America as a major 46th foot, of which he became lieutenant-colonel in 1758, and the year after commanded the regiment in the expedition to Niagara, succeeding to the command of the king's troops when Brigadier-general Prideaux was killed. Massey states (*Memorial*, ut supra) that as Sir William Johnson [q. v.] was in command of a large body of Indians, who were lukewarm in our cause, he waived the chief command in favour of Johnson. Massey commanded in the action at La Belle Famille, where with five hundred of the 46th and some Indians he routed eighteen hundred French regulars and Canadians, together with five hundred Indians, taking all the French officers but one prisoners. This action took place in view of Fort Niagara, which surrendered immediately afterwards, leaving the whole region of the Upper Ohio in possession of the English (PARKMAN, ii. 247). This was the first time at which Indians, according to Massey, were beaten in this war (*Memorial*, ut supra). Massey was transferred to his old regiment, the 27th Inniskillings, at his own request, and commanded the grenadiers of the army in the advance on Montreal in 1760. He commanded a battalion of grenadiers at the capture of Martinique in 1761, and at the conquest of Havana in 1762. He was several times severely wounded (*ib.*) He commanded the 27th—'the Enniskillen Regiment' he styles it in his letters—at New York and Quebec in 1763–9, and afterwards in Ireland. He was appointed colonel of the regiment on 19 Feb. 1773. As a major-general he went out to Nova Scotia in 1776, and commanded the troops at Halifax for four years. Later he held command at Cork. A plan of his for the defence of Cork in 1780 is in British Museum Add. MS. 33178, f. 240.

For many following years he appears to have remained unemployed. In some letters to General Sir John Vaughan about 1793–4 (*Egerton MS.* 2137, ff. 76, 93, 140), Massey relates his disappointments in not obtaining a command (as lieutenant-general), and his vexations at the appointment by the Marquis of Buckingham, the lord-lieutenant, of 'Popish children' (Master Talbot, aged eight, Master Skerritt, aged nine, and others), to ensigncies in his regiment. 'Indeed, my dear brother grenadier, my heart is broke.' The carrying of the standards taken at Martinique in 1794 in state to St. Paul's appears to have greatly roused his ire. 'We had no such honours paid to our noble and brave commander, General Monckton!' Later in 1794 he writes in quite a jubilant strain, having obtained the Cork command, which he held until his promotion to full general in 1796. The command was a critical one, seeing, among other causes, the difficulties with new regiments, which the government persisted in 'drafting' in defiance of their recruiting engagements. He quelled a mutiny of two thousand of these young troops at Spike Island in 1795, 'which was near being a very serious business, but by General Massey's exertions they laid down their arms' (see *Mil. Library*, vol. viii.) In a letter to the Duke of Portland, dated 9 Nov. 1800, the Marquis Cornwallis states that Massey had 'most strongly urged upon him' that his wife should be made a peeress in her own right, as a reward for his own 'long and faithful services as a soldier and his zealous loyalty as a subject' (*Cornwallis Correspondence*, iii. 301). Massey was raised to the peerage of Ireland on 27 Dec. 1800, under the title of Baron Clarina of Elm Park, co. Limerick. He died a full general, colonel of the 27th Inniskilling foot, marshal of the army in Ireland, and governor of Limerick and of the Royal Hospital, Kilmainham, on 17 May 1804, aged 85.

Massey married Catherine, sister of Robert Clements, first earl of Leitrim, by whom he had four children. Two of his successors in the title—his second and only surviving son, Nathaniel William, second baron, who died a major-general on the staff in the West Indies in 1810, and his great-grandson, the fourth baron (*d.* 1897), who served in the 95th regiment in the Crimea and the Indian mutiny—rose to general's rank.

[Burke's and Foster's Peerages, under 'Clarina' and 'Massy;' Lodge's Peerage, vii. 162; Memorial of Services, Home Office Papers, Ireland, vol. ccccxl.; see also Printed Calendars of Home Office Papers from 1770; Parkman's Montcalm and Wolfe, London, 1884; Brit. Mil. Library, vol. viii. 1799.] H. M. C.

MASSEY, JOHN (1651?–1715), catholic divine, born about 1651, was son (according to the entry in the Oxford matriculation register) of John Massey, 'pleb.,' of Bristol, Somerset. His father is said to have been a presbyterian minister, at one time settled in Wiltshire. Becoming clerk at Magdalen College, Oxford, in 1666, he matriculated there on 26 Nov. 1669, at the age of eighteen, and graduated B.A. from Magdalen Hall in 1673. Meanwhile in 1672 he was elected a fellow of Merton, proceeded M.A. on 29 Jan. 1675–1676, and was senior proctor in 1684. After the accession of James II he became a Roman catholic. Dodd states that for several years he had 'entertained some thoughts that way, by the instructions he received under' Obadiah Walker, master of University College. Walker's influence, or that of Philip Ellis (see *Ellis Correspondence*), secured him in October 1686 the deanery of Christ Church, which had been vacant since Fell's death in June, and of which Aldrich and Parker had had expectations. Burnet asserts that Massey 'had neither the gravity, the learning, nor the age that was suitable to such a dignity,' and Macaulay is equally depreciatory; but Dodd describes him as 'well skilled in the classics, and much esteemed for his talent in preaching.' It is expressly stated in the king's letter granting him a dispensation from the oaths that he had not taken priest's orders. He fitted up a catholic chapel in Canterbury quadrangle, and James heard mass in it when staying at the deanery in September 1687. Massey, like Walker, was appointed a magistrate for Oxfordshire, and there was talk, according to Luttrell, of a mandamus being sent to the university to make him a D.D. Had this idea been carried out, he would have been not merely the first deacon dean, but the first deacon D.D. He was one of the six founders of the Oxford Chemical Society in 1683, and he is styled 'mon bon ami' by the scholarly Abbé de Longuerue, to whom, in proof of the perfidy of James's ministers, he related a curious story of his receiving what falsely purported to be a royal order, countersigned by Sunderland, for the expulsion of the eighty students of Christ Church, unless they embraced Romanism. Massey says he went up to London to remonstrate, whereupon James disclaimed all knowledge of the order, and commended him for not obeying it.

After the arrival of William III in England Massey left Oxford for London before daybreak on 30 Nov. 1688, in company with Thomas Deane, a fellow of University, who had also become a catholic, and secretly embarked for France. He repaired to St. Germain, was admitted on 17 Sept. 1692 as a student at Douay, was ordained priest, and returning to Paris, resided in the Oratorian seminary of St. Magloire till 1696, when he became chaplain to the English Conceptionist nunnery, or the convent of Blue Nuns, in Paris. In this obscure post he remained till his death on 11 Aug. 1715.

[Wood's Fasti Oxon. ed. Bliss, ii. 348, 393; Dodd's Church Hist.; Luttrell's Diary; Gutch's Collectanea Curiosa; Burnet's Hist. of his Own Time; Longueruana, Berlin, 1754; Brodrick's Memorials of Merton, Oxford, 1885; Macaulay's Hist. of England, chap. vi.; T. F. Knox's Diaries of Douai, London, 1878; Foster's Alumni Oxon. 1500–1715; Welch's Alumni Westmonasterienses, p. 28; Bloxam's Reg. of Magdalen Coll. Oxford, ii. 75.] J. G. A.

MASSEY, WILLIAM (1691–1764?), miscellaneous writer and translator, born in January 1691 of quaker parents, learnt Latin, Greek, and French at a private grammar school kept by William Thompson at Nottingham, and afterwards took lessons in Hebrew from one Knobs, clerk of the parish of St. Gregory, Norwich. In 1712 he became Latin usher in a boarding-school at Half-farthing-house, Wandsworth, Surrey, kept by Richard Scoryer, after whose death in 1714 he continued in the same employment for about a year under Scoryer's successor, Edward Powell, a noted writing-master and accountant. Subsequently he conducted a boarding-school of his own for many years at Wandsworth, and it was much patronised by the Society of Friends. Dr. Birch notes that on 24 March 1764 Massey was seized with the dead palsy on his right side, and under date 28 Aug. following he adds: 'I visited him at his house on Cambridge Heath, near Hackney, and found him very ill of the stone, added to the palsy.' Probably he died shortly afterwards.

He was the author of: 1. 'Musa Parænetica, or a Tractate of Christian Epistles, on sundry occasions, in verse,' London, 1717, 8vo; reprinted 1746. 2. 'Synopsis Sacerrima, or an Epitome of the Holy Scriptures, in English verse,' London, 1719, 8vo; reprinted 1801. 3. 'Pietas Promota, sive Collectio Novissima Verba Multorum illius Sectæ, qui apud Anglos vulgò Quakeri appellantur, exhibens. . . . Linguâ vernaculâ olim . . . conscripta . . . jam verò . . . latinè reddita,' London, 1737, 12mo. Translated from Tomkins's 'Piety Promoted.' 4. 'Adhortatio Pathetica . . . being a translation of Benjamin Holme's Serious Call into Latin,' London, 1747, 8vo. 5. 'Humanæ Vitæ Œconomia: sive Instituta ad formandos Hominum Mores. Primùm Anglicè à Roberto Dodsley conscripta. Nunc Latinè reddita,' London, 1752, 8vo. 6. 'Tully's Compendious Treatise of Old Age; intitled Cato Major . . . translated into English, with copious notes,' London, 1753, 8vo. 7. 'Corruptæ Latinitatis Index, or a Collection of Barbarous Words and Phrases which are found in the works of the most celebrated Writers in Latin,' London, 1755, 8vo. 8. 'Ovid's Fasti . . . translated into English verse, with explanatory notes,' London, 1757, 8vo. 9. 'Remarks upon Milton's Paradise Lost, Historical, Geographical, Critical, and Explanatory,' London, 1761, 12mo. 10. 'The Origin and Progress of Letters; an Essay,' 2 pts. London, 1763, 8vo. The second part of this curious book, treating of caligraphy, contains particulars not elsewhere recorded of the lives of celebrated English penmen, 'with the titles and characters of the books that they published both from the Rolling and Letter-Press.'

[Addit. MS. 6211, ff. 123, 127; Ayscough's Cat. of MSS. p. 749; Lowndes's Bibl. Man. (Bohn), p. 1509; Massey's Origin and Progress of Letters, pp. 115–18, and Dr. Birch's MS. notes; Notes and Queries, 2nd ser. ii. 310, 311; Smith's Cat. of Friends' Books, ii. 157; Watt's Bibl. Brit.] T. C.

MASSEY, WILLIAM NATHANIEL (1809–1881), member of parliament and historian, son of William Massey, was born in 1809, and was a member of the Clarina family. He was called to the bar in 1844, and became recorder of Portsmouth in 1852 and of Plymouth in 1855. In the same year he was returned to parliament in the liberal interest as member for Newport in the Isle of Wight, and sat for that borough until 1857, when the moderate liberal party in Manchester, while inviting Mr. Robert Lowe to oppose Gibson and Bright in that city, extended a similar invitation to Massey to contest Salford against Sir Elkanah Armitage. Massey, wiser than Lowe, responded to the summons, and gained the seat with an ease astonishing to all who were not acquainted with the personal unpopularity of his opponent. His return for so important a borough made him a person of consequence; he was already under-secretary for the home department, and although he lost this appointment on Lord Palmerston's resignation in 1858, he was elected chairman of committees after the dissolution of the following year. He continued to sit for Salford until 1863, when he succeeded Mr. Samuel Laing as financial member of the government of India, a position which he held until 1868. He possessed high qualifications for this important post, but his efficiency in it, as well as in the chair of the house in committee, was thought to be impaired by his constitutional indolence. He was made a privy-councillor on his return to England, was elected for Tiverton in 1872, and sat until his death, but took no prominent part in politics, and did not again hold office. He died in Chester Square on 25 Oct. 1881. He was a devoted follower of Lord Palmerston, and both by conviction and temperament averse to political innovation. He was personally popular both in the house and among his constituents; his abilities were considerable, his legal and financial knowledge extensive, but he lacked energy and ambition. He wrote an essay on legal reform entitled 'Common Sense *versus* Common Law;' but his only important literary performance is an unfinished history of the reign of George III, extending to the peace of Amiens, 4 vols. London, 1855–1863 (2nd edit. 1865). In writing this book he had the assistance of the extensive materials collected by Mr. E. H. Locker for his intended biography of George II; his style is lucid, and his general treatment of the subject sensible and impartial; but he is devoid of all distinctive characteristics, and exhibits the qualities neither of a picturesque nor of a philosophic historian.

[Annual Register, 1881; Times, 27 Oct. 1881; private information.] R. G.

MASSIE, JAMES WILLIAM (1799–1869), independent minister, born in Ireland in 1799, was educated by Dr. David Bogue [q. v.], and began his ministry as a missionary in India. After labouring there from 1822 until 1839, he returned home, and was pastor in Perth, Dublin, and Salford, but subsequently removed to London, where he became secretary to the Home Missionary Society.

He was an advocate of free trade, the anti-slavery movement, and an ardent member of the union and emancipation societies that were formed during the civil war in America. Massie visited America several times, on the last occasion as one of the deputation appointed to convey to ministers there the address adopted at the ministerial anti-slavery conference held in the Free Trade Hall, Manchester, on 3 June 1863. He was also frequently in Ireland in connection with 're-vival work.'

Massie died in Kingstown, near Dublin, on 8 May 1869. He was married, and left a son, Milton, and two daughters. He was D.D., LL.D., and a member of the Royal Irish Academy. His portrait by Wageman was engraved by Holl (Evans, *Cat. of Engraved Portraits*, ii. 274).

Besides numerous pamphlets and sermons Massie published: 1. 'Continental India,' 2 vols. 8vo, London, 1840. 2. 'Recollections of a Tour: a Summer Ramble in Belgium, Germany, and Switzerland,' 8vo, London, 1846. 3. 'The Evangelical Alliance; its Origin and Development,' 8vo, London, 1847. 4. 'The American Crisis, in relation to the Anti-Slavery Cause,' 8vo, London, 1862. 5. 'America: the Origin of her present Conflict; her Prospect for the Slave, and her Claim for Anti-Slavery Sympathy; illustrated by Incidents of Travel . . . in . . . 1863 throughout the United States,' 8vo, London, 1864.

[Massie's Works; Cooper's Regist. and Mag. of Biog. 1869, i. 472, ii. 54; Appleton's Cyclop. of Amer. Biog.] G. G.

MASSIE, JOSEPH (*d.* 1784), writer on trade and finance, united a profound knowledge of the economic literature of the sixteenth and seventeenth centuries with a keen interest in the economic difficulties of his own time. He formed a collection of some fifteen hundred treatises, extending from 1557 to 1763, and the study of these served to make him upon the whole a discriminating critic, though he was too much inclined to judge events of his own day in the light of the past. The catalogue of his collection, dated 1764, is Lansdowne MS. 1049 in the British Museum, and affords much valuable information regarding economic bibliography. His chief aim was to establish 'commercial knowledge upon fixed principles,' and he devoted a great portion of his time to the compilation of statistics, which traversed the vague contemporary impression that British trade was declining, and illustrate in an important manner the gradual expansion and relative distribution of our industries and commerce during the middle of the last century. His schemes met apparently with little encouragement either from the public or from the statesmen to whom he dedicated his works, for he had ceased to write, or at least to publish, twenty years before his death, which took place in Holborn on 1 Nov. 1784 (*Gent. Mag.* 1784, pt. ii. p. 876).

Massie's writings, exclusive of tables of calculations published in single folio sheets, are: 1. 'An Essay on the Governing Causes of the Natural Rate of Interest, wherein the Sentiments of Sir W. Petty and Mr. Locke on that head are considered,' 8vo, London, 1750. He here refutes the notion of Locke that the rate of interest depends on the abundance of money by showing, as Hume did two years later in his 'Essay on Interest,' that the rate of interest really depends on the abundance and scarcity of disposable capital compared with the demands of the borrowers and the rate of profit. To Hume is usually assigned the credit of having been the first to point out the fallacy of Locke's opinion. 2. 'Calculations of Taxes for a Family of each Rank, Degree, or Class, for One Year,' 8vo, London, 1756; 2nd edit. 1761. 3. 'Observations on Mr. Fauquier's "Essay on Ways and Means for Raising Money for the Support of the Present War,"' 8vo, London, 1756 [see Fauquier, Francis]. Fauquier's project was a moderate house tax, which Massie deprecated (cf. No. 6). 4. 'Ways and Means for Raising the Extraordinary Supplies to carry on the War for Seven Years, pt. i.,' 8vo, London, 1757. A collection of valuable statistics on the growth of English trade during the first half of the eighteenth century, prefaced by an apparently serious proposal to impose a tax on bachelors and widowers. 5. 'Considerations on the Leather Trades of Great Britain,' 8vo, London, 1757. 6. 'The Proposal, commonly called Sir Matthew Decker's Scheme, for one General Tax upon Houses, laid open,' 8vo, London, 1757. Decker's project was the repeal of all existing taxes and the substitution of a single graduated house tax, so completely freeing trade from artificial restraint. Massie criticises this early plea for abolition of customs by simply demonstrating the fact that it was opposed to the first principles of protection, on which subject he shared the views of the majority (see under No. 13 and art. Decker). 7. 'A Letter to Bourchier Cleave [*sic*] . . . concerning his Calculations of Taxes,' 8vo, London, 1757. Massie demonstrates that the taxes could not amount to anything like half the sum as stated by B. Cleeve [q. v.] in his 'Letter to Lord Chesterfield,' 1756. 8. 'Facts which shew the Necessity of Establishing a Regular Method for the Punctual, Frequent, and Certain Payment of Seamen employed in the Royal Navy,' 4to, London, 1758. 9. 'Reasons humbly offered against laying any farther British Duties on Wrought Silks,' 4to, London, 1758. 10. 'A Plan for the Establishment of Charity Houses for Exposed or Deserted Women and Girls; Observations concerning the Foundling Hospital; Considerations relating to the Poor and Poor's Laws,' 4to, London, 1758. Of this important work, which inveighs against the old law of settlement and advocates a national rather than a parochial settlement for the poor, a full account is given in Dr. Cunningham's 'Growth of England,' ii. 384–7. 11. 'Farther Observations concerning the Foundling Hospital,' 4to, London, 1759. 12. 'A State of the British Sugar Colony Trade,' 4to, London, 1759. 13. 'A Representation concerning the Knowledge of Commerce as a National Concern, pointing out the proper Means of Promoting such Knowledge in this Kingdom,' 4to, London, 1760. England, he maintained, had nothing to apprehend, but everything to gain, from the publication of facts and statistics relative to commerce. He therefore proposed to divide his historical account of every branch of manufacture into sixteen heads, under one or other of which fragments of information might be classified, in the hope that the whole account would sooner or later be made sufficiently complete. In the same work he attributes the retention of British industries to four causes: (1) Possession of better materials; (2) Natural advantages in regard to labour and navigation; (3) Superior skill and spirit, the latter due to the secure enjoyment of liberty and property; (4) Protection from foreign manufactures. 14. 'Observations relating to the Coin of Great Britain,' 4to, London, 1760. 15. 'Brief Observations concerning the Management of the War,' 2nd edit. 8vo, London, 1761. 16. 'An Historical Account of the Naval Power of France,' 4to, London, 1762. 17. 'Observations relating to British and Spanish Proceedings,' 4to, London, 1762. 18. 'Observations on the new Cyder Tax, so far as the same may affect our Woollen Manufacturies,' &c., fol. London, 1764; another edition, in 4to, the same year. He opposed the tax strongly on the ground that it would denude Devonshire of its population and strengthen the tendency for the woollen manufacture to migrate from the cider counties into Yorkshire. His 'Memorandum to the Land-holders of England, 1768,' is in Additional MS. 33056, f. 285, in the British Museum.

In the Breadalbane sale at Edinburgh in 1866 was an almost complete set of Massie's tracts, bound up together as a thick quarto volume; a similar set (if it be not this identical one) is at present in Dr. Cunningham's possession.

[Cunningham's Growth of English Industry and Commerce in Modern Times, ii. 426, and elsewhere; McCulloch's Lit. Pol. Econ. pp. 251, 330–1; Coquelin and Guillaumin's Dict. de l'Économie Politique, ii. 144; Roscher's Pol. Econ. i. 150; Notes and Queries, 3rd ser. v. 241, ix. 119.] G. G.

MASSINGBERD, FRANCIS CHARLES (1800–1872), chancellor of Lincoln, the son of Francis Massingberd, rector of Washingborough, near Lincoln, and Elizabeth, his wife, youngest daughter of William Burrell Massingberd of Ormsby Hall, was born at his father's rectory, 3 Dec. 1800, and baptised 30 Dec. After preparatory education at a school at Eltham, Kent, he entered Rugby School under Dr. Wooll in 1814. He matriculated at Magdalen College, Oxford, and was elected a demy, 23 July 1818. He gained a second class in *literæ humaniores*, and graduated B.A. 5 Dec. 1822, M.A. 26 June 1825. He was ordained deacon by Edward Legge, bishop of Oxford, 13 June 1824, and priest by Bishop Tomline [q. v.] of Lincoln, 5 Sept. 1825, and was instituted to the family living of South Ormsby, Lincolnshire, on 9 Dec. of that year. He had during the previous summer, together with his friend William Ralph Churton [q. v.], accompanied Dr. Arnold, head-master of Rugby, in a visit to Italy, undertaken by Arnold to determine the line of Hannibal's passage over the Alps, and to explore the battlefields of his campaign, for the purposes of his 'Roman History.' When settled at Ormsby he devoted himself assiduously to the care of his parish, containing a scattered rural population, whom he watched over with fatherly solicitude. He rebuilt Driby church, and thoroughly restored that at Ormsby, erected a new rectory on a better site, and built schools, which he had originally started in a kitchen. In 1840, at the request of his lifelong friend, Edward Churton [q. v.], who revised the proofs during his absence from England, he undertook the 'English History of the leaders of the Reformation,' as one of the series known as the 'Englishman's Library,' of which Churton was the editor. It was published in 1842, and reached a fourth edition in 1866. Written from a distinctly high-church point of view, it affords a clear, temperate, and on the whole trustworthy narrative of the events of the period, and is free from sectarian bitterness. The style is pleasing, and it may still be read with profit. In 1841 he visited Italy, and spent two winters in Rome on account of his health. He delighted to tell how, 'Polybius in hand,' he walked over the battlefield of Thrasimene, which he had surveyed with Arnold seventeen years before. He was back at Ormsby in 1844. In 1846 he declined an offer from Bishop Phillpotts [q. v.] of Exeter to exchange into that diocese with the prospect of appointment to the first vacant archdeaconry. He was collated to the prebendal stall of Thorngate in Lincoln Cathedral by Bishop Kaye, 15 May 1847, and was made chancellor and canon residentiary by Bishop Jackson, 11 Dec. 1862.

From an early period he had been a strenuous advocate for the revival of the deliberative functions of convocation. In 1833 he published 'Reasons for a Session of Convocation,' and when that object was attained he was one of its most active members, first as proctor for the parochial clergy in 1857, and subsequently, in 1868, for the chapter. He frequently sat on committees and drew up their reports, and took a large share in the debates, proving himself a persuasive, if prolix, speaker. As chancellor of Lincoln he directed his efforts to the increase of the practical efficiency of the cathedral. Together with other minor reforms, he was the first to institute an afternoon nave sermon, and during successive Lents he delivered courses of lectures on the prayer-book and on church history. He died in London of congestion of the lungs on 5 Dec. 1872, and was buried at South Ormsby.

On 15 Jan. 1839 he married at Putney Church Fanny, eldest daughter of William Baring, esq., M.P., and granddaughter of Sir Francis Baring, bart. [q. v.] He left two sons: Francis Burrell, captain 5th lancers; and William Oswald, at one time rector of Ormsby. He was a typical high churchman of the school of John Keble, and in politics was a strong tory.

Besides many occasional sermons, pamphlets, letters, and printed speeches on ecclesiastical subjects, of which a catalogue is given in Bloxam's 'Magdalen College Register' (vii. 273), his chief literary works, apart from his 'English leaders of the Reformation' (1842), were: 1. 'The Educational and Missionary Work of the Church in the Eighteenth Century,' 1857. 2. 'The Law of the Church and the Law of the State,' 1859. 3. 'Lectures on the Prayer Book,' 1864. 4. 'Sermons on Unity, with an Essay on Religious Societies,' 1868, 8vo.

[Bloxam's Magdalen College Register, vii. 272–279; private information.] E. V.

MASSINGER, PHILIP (1583–1640), dramatist, was son of Arthur Massinger, a member of an old Salisbury family, who was confidential servant or house-steward at Wilton to Henry Herbert, second earl of Pembroke [q. v.], and retained the post under his first master's son, William, third earl [q. v.], the patron and friend of Shakespeare. The elder Massinger is certainly identical with the Arthur Massinger who graduated B.A. from St. Alban Hall, Oxford, in 1571 (M.A. 1577), and became fellow of Merton in 1572; he was subsequently M.P. for Weymouth and Melcombe Regis (1588–9 and 1593) and for Shaftesbury in 1601. In 1587 his master, who regarded him highly, recommended him for the office of examiner in 'the court of the marches toward South Wales,' and in 1597 he was conducting the negotiations for a marriage between Lord Pembroke's son and a daughter of Lord Burghley (*Notes and Queries*, 1st ser. iii. 52; cf. *Sydney Papers*, ii. 93). 'Many years he happily spent in the service of your honourable house, and died a servant to it,' wrote Philip Massinger (1624), when dedicating his 'Bondman' to Philip Herbert. He seems to have died in 1606 (Foster, *Alumni Oxon.* 1500–1714, p. 1004; Brodrick, *Memorials of Merton College*, p. 270). Walter, a brother of the elder Massinger, was also a student at St. Alban Hall about 1572.

Philip, perhaps named after Sir Philip Sidney, brother of the second Earl of Pembroke's wife [see Herbert, Mary], was baptised at St. Thomas's, Salisbury, on 24 Nov. 1583. Gifford supposes him to have been a page at Wilton in his youth, and Wood conjectures that he was supported at the university by Henry Herbert, second earl of Pembroke, until he offended his patron by adopting the Roman catholic religion, but of his religious conversion little is known. On 14 May 1602, 'Philip Messinger,' described as a Salisbury man and son of a gentleman, was entered at St. Alban Hall, Oxford, where his father and uncle had already been educated. According to Wood, 'he applied his mind more to poetry and romances for about four years or more than to logic and philosophy,' and he left Oxford in 1606 without taking a degree, probably at the time of his father's death.

Coming to London, Massinger seems to have sought the society of writers for the stage, and soon made a reputation for himself as a playwright. The extent of his work it is difficult to define. Many of his dramas are lost, and in accordance with the custom of the time he wrote in association with his friends very much that he did not publicly claim. External evidence proves that Nathaniel Field and Robert Daborne were among his collaborators, and that with Fletcher he formed at an early period a close literary partnership. Internal evidence suggests that he and Cyril Tourneur produced together the 'Second Maiden's Tragedy' as early as 1611. Dekker joined him in the 'Virgin Martyr' in 1620. Traces of Massinger's hand have been doubtfully suggested in such early works of Beaumont and Fletcher as the 'Scornful Lady,' written about 1610, 'Cupid's Revenge,' acted in January 1611–12, and the 'Captain,' written very early in 1613; but there is little likelihood of Massinger's connection with Fletcher until late in 1613. From about that year Fletcher and Massinger wrote regularly in conjunction until Fletcher's death in 1625. Third or fourth pens occasionally joined them. Sir Aston Cokayne [q. v.] thrice in his poems mentions the friendship subsisting between Fletcher and Massinger, and their association in dramatic composition [see FLETCHER, JOHN, 1579–1625], but the editions of Fletcher's works, which contain most of their joint efforts, ignore Massinger's name altogether. For some years Fletcher and Massinger were connected with the same company of actors. Both, with Field, joined the king's men in 1616. At the end of 1623 Massinger temporarily transferred his services to the Cockpit company (queen's men, i.e. Lady Elizabeth's), and for them he wrote, apparently for the first time unaided, three pieces, the 'Parliament of Love,' the 'Bondman,' and the 'Renegado.' After Fletcher's death in 1625 he rejoined the king's men. In 1627 his 'Great Duke of Florence' was prepared for another company (the queen's servants). There is no other indication of Massinger's connection with any but the king's company at the period, and consequently, with the exception of about a year and a half (1623–5), Massinger may be regarded as writing from 1616 to his death on 18 March 1639–40 for that company alone.

Massinger's literary friends included James Smith (1605–1667), editor of 'Musarum Deliciæ,' whom Massinger, according to Wood, habitually called his son (WOOD, iii. 776). With the Herbert family he maintained friendly relations to the end. Aubrey describes him as servant to Philip, the fourth earl, and in receipt of a pension of 30*l.* or 40*l.* from his master. In 1624 he dedicated his 'Bondman' to Earl Philip, and he chose Robert Dormer, earl of Carnarvon, as sponsor for his best-known comedy, 'A New Way to Pay Old Debts,' in 1633, on the ground that 'I was born a devoted servant to the thrice noble family of your incomparable lady,' the daughter of Earl Philip. In 1634 Massinger wrote 'verses on the death of Charles, Lord Herbert, [third] son to Philip, [fourth] Earl of Pembroke' (*Brit. Mus. MS. Reg.* 18 A xx.) Other men of eminence took notice of him, he tells us, and were patrons of his 'humble studies' (*Unnatural Combat*, Ded.) Among them was Sir Warham St. Leger, to whose son Walter he dedicated his 'Unnatural Combat' (1639). He acknowledged that he had 'tasted of the bounty' of 'Sir Robert Wiseman of Thorrell's Hall in Essex' (*Great Duke*, Ded.), and of Sir Francis Foljambe and Sir Thomas Bland (*Maid of Honour*, Ded.) His friend Sir Aston Cokayne brought his work to the notice of his uncle, Lord Mohun of Okehampton, to whom Massinger dedicated his 'Emperor of the East.'

His political views, like those of his patron Earl Philip, inclined to the popular party. In the 'Bondman,' 1623, he clearly denounced Buckingham under the disguise of Gisco (i. 1), and supported the Herberts in their quarrel with James I's favourite. Thinly veiled reflections on current politics figure in 'Believe as you List,' the 'Emperor of the East,' and the 'Maid of Honour.' On 11 Jan. 1630–1 Sir Henry Herbert [q. v.] refused a license to an unnamed play of Massinger 'because it did contain dangerous matter, as the deposing of Sebastian, king of Portugal, by Philip [the second], and there being a peace sworn betwixt the kings of England and Spain.' This piece seems to have been an early draft of 'Believe as you List.' According to his own account he made a very narrow income out of his literary pursuits.

He died suddenly in his house on the Bankside, Southwark, near the Globe Theatre, in the middle of March 1639–40. 'He went to bed well, and was dead before morning: whereupon his body, being accompanied by comedians, was buried about the middle of that ch. yard belonging to St. Saviour's Church there, commonly called the Bullhead ch. yard,' on 18 March 1639–40 (WOOD, *Athenæ*, ed. Bliss). According to the entry of burial in the parish register he was a 'stranger,' that is a non-parishioner (*Notes and Queries*, 1st ser. x. 206). Cokayne says that he was buried in the same grave as Fletcher. The theory that Massinger was converted to Roman catholicism in middle life depends on the catholic tone of many passages in his 'Renegado' and the 'Virgin Martyr,' which he wrote with Dekker, but the proofs are by no means conclusive.

Massinger was married, and left a widow, who at one time resided at Cardiff, and received from the Earl of Pembroke, according to Aubrey, the pension bestowed on her husband. She seems to have had children. Miss Henrietta Massinger, claiming to be a direct descendant, died on 4 Aug. 1762 (*London Mag.* 1762). A portrait was engraved by Worthington after Thurston. Other engraved portraits by Grignion, T. Cross, and H. Robinson are extant (EVANS, *Cat.* Nos. 7027 and 1914).

Massinger wrote fifteen plays unaided—tragedies, tragi-comedies, and comedies—and thence his characteristics as a dramatist are best deduced. Several of his plots are borrowed from Cervantes, and the influence of Spanish and Italian models is often apparent in both matter and manner. But in the masterly working-out of his plots and in his insight into stage requirements he has hardly an equal among his contemporaries either at home or abroad. His characters, as in Italian comedy, are to a great extent conventional. The tyrant grovelling at the feet of a mistress who glories in her power over him; that mistress boasting of her very questionable virtue, and consumed with a desire of forcing all within her sphere to feel and acknowledge the power of her beauty; the pert page and the flippant waiting-woman, are familiar figures in his pages. His men are generally under the influence of one ruling passion, which, paralysing all their mental powers, leads to the catastrophe. 'For the most part,' wrote Hazlitt, an unfriendly critic, 'his villains are a sort of "lusus naturæ;" his impassioned characters are like drunkards or madmen; their conduct is extreme and outrageous, their motives unaccountable and weak.' Generally speaking, he gives an impression of hardness, and seldom deviates into tender pathos. But his most characteristic trait is a peculiarly corrupt tone of thought, even in his heroines when they are intended as models of virtue. Their morality lies entirely in obedience to outward observances, and in no inner principle. Purity is not to be found in his world, and his obscenity seems often purposeless. The warning in his 'Roman Actor,' i. 3, that his portrayal of evil was intended to convey a wholesome reproof to the evil-minded, is unconvincing.

Massinger's language is generally full and flowing, with more of a rhetorical than a dramatic character. In a contemporary poem 'On the Time-Poets' (*Choyce Drollery*, 1656) it is said of him that his

> Easy Pegasus will amble o'er
> Some threescore miles of Fancy in an hour.

He wrote, according to Charles Lamb, 'with that equability of all the passions which made his English style the purest and most free from violent metaphors and harsh constructions of any of the dramatists who were his contemporaries.' Coleridge declares that Massinger's style is 'differenced in the smallest degree possible from animated conversation by the vein of poetry.' He often substitutes description for action, and is hardly ever carried away by his situations. He has consequently few passages of the highest poetical beauty. On the other hand, he seldom sinks into the trivial, and his sustained and even flow of language sometimes rises into very solemn eloquence, tinged with a melancholy which suggests a sermon. 'No author repeats himself oftener or with less ceremony than Massinger' (GIFFORD). A list of more than a thousand of repeated phrases and expressions, not counting the commonest, is given in 'Englische Studien' (v. 1, vii. 1, x. 3). This habit enables us to recognise Massinger's hand in anonymous or joint plays, and is especially useful in tracing the work of his early life, before his metrical characteristics, which are an adequate test of his later productions, became distinctive.

In his early work he introduces very much prose and rhyme, but in his later work he confines himself to blank verse. His blank verse shows a larger proportion of run-on lines and double endings in harmonious union than any contemporary author. Cartwright and Tourneur have more run-on lines, but not so many double endings. Fletcher has more double endings, but very few run-on lines. Shakespeare and Beaumont alone exhibit a somewhat similar metrical style.

I. PLAYS BY MASSINGER ALONE (in approximate chronological order).—1. 'The Duke of Milan,' 4to, 1623; acted by the king's men at Blackfriars; probably written about 1618; partly founded on Josephus's 'History of the Jews' (xv. 4), and slightly on Guicciardini's 'History' (xv. c. iv.) There is a striking resemblance between the painting of the corpse in this play and in the 'Second Maiden's Tragedy' and the 'Revenger's Tragedy.' A *réchauffé* of it and Fenton's 'Mariamne' by Cumberland was played at Covent Garden 10 Nov. 1779. It was revived at Drury Lane, with Edmund Kean in the title-rôle, 9 March 1816. 2. 'The Unnatural Combat,' 4to, 1639; acted by the king's men at the Globe, probably about 1619. It is one of Massinger's most characteristic, but at the same time least pleasing, productions. 3. 'The Bondman,' 4to, 1624; licensed 3 Dec. 1623, and played at the Cockpit; partly founded on Plutarch. It was revived, 1 March 1661, when Pepys saw it; at Drury Lane 8 June 1719; and, altered by Cumberland, at Covent Garden 13 Oct. 1779. 4. 'The Renegado,' 4to, 1630;

licensed 17 April 1624; played by the queen's men. 5. 'The Parliament of Love' was first printed by Gifford from an imperfect manuscript in 1805; licensed for the Cockpit 3 Nov. 1624. It was entered on the 'Stationers' Registers' 29 June 1660, and ascribed to W. Rowley. 6. 'A New Way to Pay Old Debts,' 4to, 10 Nov. 1632, a comedy; acted by the queen's men at the Phœnix. There is an allusion to the taking of Breda, July 1625. Mr. Fleay dates it before May 1622; but it probably belongs to 1625 or 1626. No entries by Sir Henry Herbert are known between 10 Feb. 1625 and 22 Jan. 1626. The first two acts contain passages in Fletcher's peculiar metre, but his contributions must have been slight (he died in August 1625). This comedy retained its popularity longer than any other of Massinger's plays, and kept possession of the stage even into the present century. Genest notices thirteen revivals between 1748 and 1827. 7. 'The Roman Actor,' 4to, 1629; played at Blackfriars by the king's men; licensed 11 Oct. 1626, and written immediately before, as it alludes to a terrible storm which swept over London during the same autumn. Massinger calls it the most perfect birth of his Minerva; revived after thirty years at Lincoln's Inn Fields 13 June 1722, and at Drury Lane in 1796 and (in one act) in 1822. 8. 'The Maid of Honour,' 4to, 1632, was played by the queen's men at the Phœnix. It is probably a recast of an older play by Massinger. Fulgentio, the king's favourite, can only refer to Buckingham. It was altered by Kemble and produced at Drury Lane 27 Jan. 1785, with Kemble and Mrs. Siddons in the chief parts. 9. 'The Picture,' 4to, 1630; licensed 8 June 1629. An altered version, by the Rev. H. Bate Dudley [q. v.], was produced at Covent Garden 8 Nov. 1783. The plot bears some resemblance to the mediæval story of the 'Wright's Chaste Wife' (Early English Text Soc. 1866), but was doubtless taken by Massinger from Bandello's 'Novelle' (21 Nov.), through Painter's 'Palace of Pleasure' (28 Nov.) Musset borrowed from the same story of Bandello the plot of his 'Barberini' (*Notes and Queries*, 5th ser. vii. 81, 160). Bandello doubtless himself derived the tale from the 'Gesta Romanorum' (cap. lxiv.) 10. 'The Great Duke of Florence,' 4to, 1635, was licensed 5 July 1627 for the queen's servants. 11. 'The Emperor of the East,' 4to, 19 Nov. 1631; licensed 4 March 1631 for the king's men. There is a curious parallel between a passage in act iv. 4 and one in Molière's 'Malade Imaginaire' (1673), act iii. (the last few lines in Toinette's first long speech) (*ib.* 3rd ser. viii. 348). 12. 'Believe as you List;' entered on the 'Stationers' Registers' 1653. This was the play sent back by Herbert 11 Jan. 1631 because it contained dangerous matter. It was discovered in manuscript in 1844, and printed for the Percy Society in 1848. 13. 'The City Madam,' 8vo, 1658; licensed 25 May 1632. It has lately been doubted whether this play was Massinger's, but the parallel passages connecting it with Massinger's work, the characterisation, and the metre equally exclude the idea of participation, on the part of Jonson or any other. It was revived for Baddeley's benefit at Drury Lane 29 April 1783. 14. 'The Guardian,' published 1655 by Moseley, together with 'A Very Woman' (by Massinger and Fletcher, see below) and the 'Bashful Lover.' It was licensed for the king's men 31 Oct. 1633; performed at court 12 Jan. 1634; and was 'well liked.' 15. 'The Bashful Lover,' published as above, licensed 9 May 1636. The play has an allusion to the death of Wallenstein, 25 Feb. 1634. Revived at Covent Garden, 30 May 1798, as 'Disinterested Love.'

II. Plays by Massinger and others.—In these plays Massinger's hand can only be detected by internal evidence of style, characterisation, and metre. Fletcher was Massinger's collaborateur in each of those numbered 1 to 20, but in a few cases other hands are also visible. Those marked † are by Fletcher and Massinger alone, and first appeared in the 1647 folio of Beaumont and Fletcher's 'Works.'

1. 'The Honest Man's Fortune.' An undated letter, addressed to Philip Henslowe by Field, Daborne, and Massinger, mentions that the three were engaged with Fletcher on a play for Henslowe. Fletcher did not probably begin to write for Henslowe before the burning of the Globe, on 29 June 1613, and the letter was probably drawn up soon after that event. The balance of evidence seems to identify the play mentioned with the 'Honest Man's Fortune,' acted by the Lady Elisabeth's men in 1613, and reallowed for the king's men on 8 Feb. 1624–5 by Sir Henry Herbert, whose copy of that date is in the Dyce Library. It was first printed in the 1647 folio edition of Beaumont and Fletcher's works. Act iii. must be pronounced Massinger's (cf. III. i. 120, and *Two Noble Kinsmen*, I. i. 118). Act v. is undoubtedly Fletcher's.

2. 'Thierry and Theodoret' (printed in 1621) and 3. 'The Bloody Brother' (printed in 1639) were by Massinger, Field, Fletcher, and another author. They were probably written in 1613 or 1614. The fourth author wrote act iv. 1 of the 'Bloody Brother' and act iii. 2 of 'Thierry and Theodoret,' and the grammatical peculiarities of those passages

suggest Wilkins. Massinger's share in the 'Bloody Brother' is act i. and act v. 1; in 'Thierry and Theodoret' it is act i. 2, act ii. 1, 3, and act iv. 2.

4†. 'The Knight of Malta.' Massinger's share is act iii. 2, 3, iv. 1, and perhaps a part of v. 2. As Burbage and Field acted together in this play, it was probably produced after the latter had joined the king's men in 1616.

5†. 'The Queen of Corinth' (written about 1617). Massinger wrote act i. and act v. Field perhaps aided Fletcher in this piece.

6. 'Barnavelt,' by Fletcher and Massinger (first printed in Bullen's 'Old Plays,' vol. ii. 1881), played August 1619. Massinger's share is i. 1, 2, ii. 1, iii. 2, 3, 5, iv. 4, 5, v. 1 (down to 'Enter Provost'); thirty-four parallel passages connect it with Massinger's undoubted work.

7. 'Henry VIII,' in the form which has come down to us, was probably not written earlier than 1617. It is doubtless by Massinger and Fletcher (*Transactions of the New Shakspere Soc.* 1884).

8. 'The Two Noble Kinsmen,' 4to, 1634, is in the present writer's opinion entirely by Massinger and Fletcher (*ib.* for 1882). Massinger's share is i., ii. 1, iii. 1, 2, iv. 3, v. 1 (except the opening eighteen lines), 3, 4. The numerous parallel passages connecting this play with the rest of Massinger's work, and the characterisation, especially of the female characters, are decisive as to Massinger's participation.

9†. 'The Custom of the Country.' It is mentioned in Sir Henry Herbert's 'Office-Book,' 22 Nov. 1628, as an old play. It is founded on Cervantes's 'Persiles and Sigismunda,' and is partly a literal translation from the Spanish novel; even the original names are retained in the drama. Massinger's share is ii. 1, 2, 3, 4, iii. 4, 5, iv. 1, 2, v. 1, 2, 3, 4.

10. 'The Elder Brother,' printed as by Fletcher only, 4to, 29 March 1637, and by him and Beaumont in 1651, was probably revised generally by Massinger; it is preserved in a contemporary manuscript, Egerton MS. 1994. Massinger's share is i. 1, 2, v. 1, 2. The plot is like that of Calderon's 'De una causa dos efectos.'

11†. 'The Sea Voyage' was licensed 22 June 1622. Massinger's share is ii. 1, 2, iii. 1 (from 'Enter Rosellia'), v. 1, 2, 3, 4.

12†. 'The Double Marriage,' probably produced about 1620. Massinger's share is i. 1, iii. 1, iv. 1, 2, v. 2 (to 'Enter Pandulpho'), v. 3.

13†. 'The Beggar's Bush,' performed at court at Christmas 1622. Massinger's share is i. 1, 2, 3, v. 1 (latter part of the scene), and 2 (first part of the scene). There are few of the parallel passages characteristic of Massinger, and those only in the scenes here ascribed to him.

14†. 'The False One,' probably produced about 1620. Massinger's share is acts i. and v.

15†. 'The Prophetess,' licensed 14 May 1622. Massinger's share is ii., iv., v. 1, 2. The plot is based on Plutarch and Lucan.

16†. 'The Little French Lawyer,' probably written not later than 1620. A duel between Villiers, the favourite's brother, and Mr. Rich took place in 1619. The seconds also fought, and this is spoken of as a new custom, and explained by Mr. Rich 'having new come out of France.' Massinger's part is i., iii. 1, v. 1 (from 'Enter Cleremont'). There are traces of his hand in other scenes, but the above are the only ones that have parallel passages connecting them with Massinger (fifteen in number). The plot is from the 'Spanish Rogue,' ii. 4.

17†. 'The Lovers' Progress,' licensed as 'Cleander,' 9 May 1634. It is probably an alteration of the 'Wandering Lovers,' licensed 6 Dec. 1623. Massinger's share is i. 1, 2 (to 'Enter Malfort'), ii. 2, iii. 4 and 6 (the last two speeches), acts iv. and v. Founded on Daudiguier's 'Lysandre et Caliste.'

18†. 'The Spanish Curate,' licensed 24 Oct. 1622. Massinger's part is i., iii. 3, iv. 1, 4, v. 1, 3. Founded on Cespedes's 'Gerardo, the Unfortunate Spaniard' (English translation by Leonard Digges, 1622).

19†. 'The Fair Maid of the Inn,' licensed 22 Jan. 1626. The idea is taken from Cervantes's 'La illustre Fregona,' but only in a general way. Massinger's share is i., iii. 2, v. 3. Mr. Fleay gives a great part of the play to Jonson, but adduces no evidence.

20. 'A Very Woman, or the Prince of Tarent;' published by Moseley, 1655, in one volume with the 'Guardian' and the 'Bashful Lover;' licensed 6 June 1634. It was entered as Massinger's on the 'Stationers' Registers,' 9 Sept. 1653, but is partly by Fletcher. Massinger's share is i., ii. 1, 2, 3 (down to 'Enter Pedro'), iv. 1 and 3. The lost plays—the 'Woman's Plot,' acted 1621–2, and the 'Spanish Viceroy,' acted 20 Dec. 1624, without Herbert's license—may possibly be early versions of this piece.

In the following plays there are no traces of Fletcher's hand, and the names of Massinger's collaborators are determined with less certainty: 21. 'The Second Maiden's Tragedy,' licensed by Sir George Buck 31 Oct. 1611, and acted by the king's men. Massinger's hand is traceable in the first two acts, and Tourneur's in the last three. Tourneur in the 'Revenger's Tragedy' and Massinger in the 'Duke of Milan' have situations similar to the painting of the lady's corpse in this play. The underplot is taken from Cervantes's 'Curious Impertinent,' and in the first two acts, which are ascribed to Massinger, there are passages literally taken from the novel. The play must have been written after the execution of Ravaillac, 27 May 1610, to which an allusion is made. A manuscript copy in a scribe's hand is extant in the Lansdowne collection (from the Warburton MSS.) The title suggests that Massinger and his coadjutor were emulating the success of Beaumont and Fletcher's 'Maid's Tragedy.'

22. 'Love's Cure, or the Martial Maid,' fol. 1647. The date must be after 1622, from the allusion to the Muscovite ambassador and the renewal of the war between Holland and Spain, 1622. Massinger's share is i., iv., v. 1, 2. Fleay supposes this play to be an alteration from an old one by Beaumont and Fletcher. There is no trace of Fletcher in the play, nor is there anything in it reminding us of Beaumont. Mr. A. H. Bullen suggests Middleton as the probable coadjutor of Massinger, but in 1623 these dramatists were writing for different companies.

23. 'The Fatal Dowry,' 4to, 1632, by Field and Massinger. The latter's share is i., iii. (down to 'Enter Noval Junior'), iv. 2, 3, 4, v. 1, 2. The date is with all probability supposed to be before Richard Burbage's death in 1619, when Field retired from the stage. Rowe plundered this play in his 'Fair Penitent,' which was acted with much success by Betterton in 1703 (Genest, ii. 281-290), and gave up his original intention of editing Massinger in order that his theft might not be discovered.

24. 'The Virgin Martyr,' 4to, 1621; licensed 6 Oct. 1620 by Sir George Buck. Massinger's share is i., iii. 1, 2, iv. 3, v. 2; the rest is Dekker's. Partly founded on the story of the martyr Dorothea. It was revived at Drury Lane 27 Feb. 1668, and at Richmond in 1715 in an altered version by Griffin.

In 1656 there was published, as the joint work of Massinger, Middleton, and Rowley, an excellent comedy called 'The Old Law.' The fact that 1599, when Massinger was fifteen, has been plausibly argued to be the date of its composition, renders Massinger's responsibility for it doubtful. Internal evidence gives no support to Massinger's claim to part authorship, and it is probable that he merely gave it very slight revision at a late revival (see Middleton, Thomas; and Middleton, *Works*, ed. Bullen, vol. i. p. xv).

III. Plays alleged to be Lost.—Many plays in which Massinger was solely or jointly concerned are lost, several of them being destroyed in manuscript by the carelessness of Warburton's cook. In a few cases the titles of the pieces suggest that they were identical with extant plays known by other names. The titles (those destroyed by Warburton's cook being distinguished by an asterisk) are as follows: 1. 'The Forced Lady,' given in Warburton's list with a second title as 'Minerva's Sacrifice.' It was licensed 23 Nov. 1629, and entered on the 'Stationers' Registers,' 9 Sept. 1653. This play may possibly be identical with the extant 'Queen of Corinth.' 2. 'The Noble Choice, or the Orator.' A play was licensed as 'The Orator' 10 Jan. 1635, and there is an entry in the 'Stationers' Registers,' 9 Sept. 1653, 'The Noble Choice, or the Orator.' This may be the 'Elder Brother.' 3. 'The Wandering Lovers;' licensed for the king's men 6 Dec. 1623, is probably the original form of 'Cleander,' licensed 9 May 1634, which is in all likelihood the folio play of the 'Lovers' Progress.' 4.* 'Philengo and Hippolito;' entered on the 'Stationers' Registers' 9 Sept. 1653. 5.* 'Antonio and Vallia;' entered on the 'Stationers' Registers' 29 June 1660. 6. 'The Tyrant,' entered on the 'Stationers' Registers,' 1660, has been supposed to be another title for the 'Second Maiden's Tragedy.' It has also been identified with the 'King and Subject,' licensed 5 June 1638, in which King Charles marked a passage as 'too insolent, and to be changed.' Fleay identifies this play with the 'Double Marriage,' for which he has two further titles, the 'Unfortunate Piety,' or the 'Italian Nightpiece,' licensed 13 June 1631. 7.* 'The Woman's Plot,' acted at court 1621–2; entered on the 'Stationers' Registers,' 9 Sept. 1653, as 'The Very Woman, or the Woman's Plot.' 8.* 'The Spanish Viceroy' was acted without license in 1624. It is probably the same play as the 'Honour of Women,' licensed 6 May 1628. Both this and the preceding piece may possibly be drafts of the extant piece, 'A Very Woman' (see above). 9. 'The Judge;' licensed 6 June 1627. Mr. Fleay supposes this to be a recast of the 'Fatal Dowry.' 10. 'Alexius, or the Chaste Lover;' licensed 25 Sept. 1639. In Warburton's list the title is 'Alexius, or the Chaste Gallant.' 11.* 'The Fair Anchoress of Pausilippo;' licensed 26 Jan. 1640; entered on the 'Stationers' Registers,' 9 Sept. 1653, as 'The Prisoner, or the Fair Anchoress.'

Poole, in his 'English Parnassus,' notes that he has used Massinger's 'Secretary' for purposes of quotation. No such work is now known. It may have been either a play or a compilation resembling a 'Complete Writer,' of which many contemporary examples are known (*Notes and Queries*, 5th ser. v. 429).

No edition of Massinger attempts to give his productions complete. It would be impossible to do so without editing Beaumont, Massinger, and Fletcher in one work. The time for undertaking such an arduous task has almost come, and it would be of immense use in clearing up the relations between these three authors. The principal collected editions of Massinger are: 1. Coxeter's edition, 4 vols. 8vo, published 1759, and reissued 1761, with an introduction by Davies. 2. 'Dramatic Works of Philip Massinger,' in 4 vols. complete, revised and corrected, with notes, critical and explanatory, by J. Monck Mason, London, 1779. 3. 'The Plays of Philip Massinger,' with notes, critical and explanatory, by William Gifford, 4 vols. 8vo, London, 1805, 1813. This remains the chief edition. 4. 'The Dramatic Works of Massinger and Ford,' with an introduction by Hartley Coleridge, 1 vol. royal 8vo, London, 1840. 5. 'The Plays of Philip Massinger,' from the text of William Gifford, with the addition of the tragedy, 'Believe as you List,' edited by Lieutenant-colonel Cunningham, London, 1867. Selections from Massinger, edited by Arthur Symons, have appeared in the 'Mermaid Series' (1887–9).

[Hazlitt's Bibliography of Old English Literature; Hazlitt's Collections and Notes; Ward's History of the Drama; Fleay's History of the Stage; Fleay's Biog. History of the English Drama; Genest's Account of the English Stage, vi. 119–24, and vii. 683–98; Aubrey's Natural Hist. of Wiltshire, ed. Britton, p. 91; Hoare's History of Salisbury; Wood's Athenæ Oxon. ed. Bliss, ii. 654; Transactions of the New Shakspere Society, 1882 seq.; 'Beaumont, Fletcher, and Massinger,' by the present writer, in Englische Studien, v. 74, vii. 66, viii. 39, ix. 209, x. 383; Zeitschrift für vergleichende Litteraturgeschichte, vi. 3, new ser.; Anglia; Macaulay's Study of Francis Beaumont; Arber's Transcript of the Stationers' Registers; Halliwell's Dictionary of Old Plays; Mr. Leslie Stephen's Hours in a Library, ii. 141–76 (an interesting critical paper); Mr. S. R. Gardiner on 'Massinger's Political Views' in Contemporary Review, August 1876; art. John Fletcher.] R. B–e.

MASSON, FRANCIS (1741–1805), gardener and botanist, was born at Aberdeen in August 1741. Making his way to London he seems to have obtained some appointment at the Royal Gardens, Kew, for in 1771 or 1772 he was selected by Aiton, the superintendent, as the fittest person to undertake a journey to the Cape for the purpose of collecting plants and bulbs. Masson was the first collector thus sent out by the authorities at Kew.

Making Cape Town his headquarters, he undertook at least three separate journeys into the interior, the first extending from 10 Dec. 1772 to 18 Jan. 1773; the second, in company with Thunberg, the Swedish naturalist, lasted from 11 Sept. 1773 to 29 Jan. 1774; while the third was begun 26 Sept. and brought to an end on 28 Dec. 1774. Having for the time thoroughly supplied the wants of the gardens from that locality, Masson was sent on a like errand in 1776 to the Canaries, Azores, Madeira, and the West Indies, more especially to St. Christopher. He returned to England in 1781, and remained at home till 1783, when he was despatched to Portugal and Madeira. In 1786, when once more sent out to the Cape, he confined his botanical excursions, by the advice of Sir Joseph Banks, to a circuit of forty miles round Cape Town. He remained there till 1795, when the anticipation of political disturbances drove him home.

Masson spent some two years in England with his friends, and prepared and published in 1796 his well-known book, 'Stapeliæ Novæ, or . . . new Species of that Genus discovered in the Interior Parts of Africa.' The work was issued in four fasciculi (imp. fol.), and contains many charming coloured plates. In 1798 he set out for North America, where he died at Montreal, about Christmas 1805.

Many plants now common in conservatories were first brought to this country by Masson. The genus *Massonia* was named after him by Linnæus.

In addition to his work already mentioned, two papers by Masson appeared in the 'Philosophical Transactions:' 1. 'An Account of three Journeys from Cape Town to the Southern Parts of Africa,' 1776. 2. 'An Account of the Island of St. Miguel,' 1778. Two papers standing under his name in the Royal Society's list are descriptions of orchidaceous plants sent home by him, which were written by J. Bellenden Ker [q. v.] A collection of his plants and drawings is preserved in the botanical department of the British Museum (Natural History).

A portrait of Masson in oils hangs in the Linnean Society's rooms at Burlington House.

[Rees's Cyclop.; Chalmers's Biog. Dict.; Journ. of Bot.] B. B. W.

MASSON, GEORGE JOSEPH GUSTAVE (1819–1888), educational writer, was born in London on 9 March 1819. His father had served under Napoleon I, and survived the retreat from Moscow; his mother was of English origin. Gustave (he invariably dropped his first two names) was educated at Tours, was exempted from military service as eldest son of a widow, and was awarded the diploma of 'Bachelier ès Lettres' by the Université de France on 8 Aug. 1837. After some ten years of literary struggle in Paris, he came to England as tutor to the two sons of Captain Trotter of the Woodlands, Harrow, and was in 1855 appointed by Dr. Vaughan, head-master of Harrow School, French master there. He proved himself a good organiser, and took a prominent part in the life of the school. He was from 1869 Vaughan librarian and published a catalogue (1st edit. 1877, 2nd edit. 1887).

Masson was an author and translator on a large scale, writing many books on French literature and history, and editing with much success numerous French classics for English students. He was at the same time a frequent contributor to the 'Athenæum,' and supplied the notes on French literature to the 'Saturday Review' from soon after its foundation until 1880. He gave up his Harrow mastership in the autumn of 1888, and died a few weeks later (29 Aug.) at Ewhurst, Surrey, while on a visit to Sir Henry Doulton; he was buried in Harrow churchyard. By his wife, whose maiden name was Janet Clarke, and whom he married in 1843, he left two sons and two daughters.

Masson's chief works are: 1. 'Introduction to the History of French Literature,' Edinburgh, 1860. 2. 'La Lyre Française,' London, 1867, an excellent French anthology, forming a volume of the 'Golden Treasury' series. 3. 'Early Chronicles of Europe: France' [1879]. 4. 'The Huguenots: a Sketch of their History from the beginning of the Reformation to the Death of Louis XIV' [1881]. 5. 'Richelieu' [1884]. 6. 'Mazarin' [1886], based on Chéruel's great work on the 'History of France during the Minority of Louis XIV,' and forming, with Nos. 3, 5, and 7, volumes in the 'Home Library' of the Society for Promoting Christian Knowledge. 7. 'The Dawn of European Literature—French Literature,' 1888. 8. 'Mediæval France from the Reign of Hugues Capet to the beginning of the Sixteenth Century,' 1888; an inadequate compilation, not free from serious blunders.

His translations include, from the English: 1. Sir W. Baker's 'Discovery of Albert Nyanza,' 1868. 2. 'New Voyage to the Sources of the Nile,' 1869. And from the French: 3. P. Janet's 'Matérialisme,' 1865. 4. Caro's 'George Sand,' Sorel's 'Montesquieu,' Say's 'Turgot,' and Simon's 'Victor Cousin,' in the series of 'Grands Écrivains Français.' 5. George Sand's 'François le Champi,' 1879.

Among his educational works are: 1. 'A Chronological and Historical Atlas of the Middle Ages,' 1849, fol. 2. 'Class Book of French Literature,' Edinburgh, 1861. 3. 'A Compendious Dictionary of the French Language,' 1874. 4. Various adaptations of A. Brachet's 'Public School French Grammar,' 1876, &c. 5. 'Choice Readings from French History,' with notes, 1880. Masson also edited seven volumes of 'French Classics' for the Clarendon Press, Oxford, 1866; many single plays by Molière, Racine, Corneille, Musset, Piron, Lemercier, Collin d'Harleville, Villemain, Mélesville et Duveyrier, and Victor Hugo; Voltaire's 'Siècle de Louis XIV,' 1875; Thierry's 'Lettres sur l'Histoire de France,' 1885, and 'Récits des Temps Mérovingiens,' 1887; Xavier de Maistre's 'Voyage autour de ma Chambre,' and various works by Madame de Staël.

[Times, 31 Aug. and 1 Sept. 1888; Athenæum, 2 Sept. 1888; Saturday Review, 9 Sept. 1888; Annual Register, 1888, p. 169; Harrovian, 4 Oct. 1888; Brit. Mus. Cat.; materials kindly supplied by Masson's daughter, Mrs. Horley, and by Mr. B. P. Lascelles, librarian at Harrow school.] T. S.

MASSUE DE RUVIGNY, HENRI DE, second MARQUIS DE RUVIGNY, EARL OF GALWAY (1648–1720), born on 9 April 1648 at his father's house in the Faubourg St. Germain, Paris, was the eldest son of Henri de Massue, marquis de Ruvigny and Raineval, a French general of repute, deputy-general of the Huguenots at the court of Versailles, sometime ambassador at the English court, and uncle of Rachel, wife of Lord William Russell. He entered the army at an early age, and saw service first in Portugal, being present at the siege of the Fort de la Garda. From 1672 to 1675 he served in the war against Germany as aide-de-camp to Marshal Turenne. He obtained the approbation of that general, and after the battle of Eusheim in October 1674 was recommended by him to Louis XIV for the command of the regiment of Cornas. On Turenne's death at Salzburg in 1675 he is said (LE GENDRE, *Vie de Pierre du Bosc*, Épître Dedicatoire) to have displayed great tact at a critical moment in reconciling the claims of Generals Lorges and Vaubrun to the chief command of the army. His connection with the Russell family furnishing a plausible pretext for the appointment, he was early in 1678 sent by Louis to England to endeavour, by intriguing with the leaders of the opposition, to detach Charles II from the Dutch alliance. The object of his mission was well known to Danby, but Ruvigny showed much address in the management of the business, and by co-operating with Barillon succeeded in arranging a secret understanding between Charles and Louis. In the same year he was chosen to succeed his father as deputy-general of the Huguenots. His election gave great satisfaction to his co-religionists, especially to such as had been inclined to regard his father's conduct as somewhat timid. He laboured zealously, but unsuccessfully, to avert their persecution, and after the revocation of the edict of Nantes in 1685 he declined Louis's well-meant offer of exceptional treatment for himself; and following the example of his father, who, foreseeing the course of events, had prudently in 1680 obtained letters of naturalisation as an English subject, he accompanied him and his brother, Pierre, lord de la Caillemotte, to England in January 1688, being as a special favour allowed to take with him what personal property he liked.

In July 1689 his father, who had estalished himself at Greenwich, died, and in July 1690 his brother, La Caillemotte, was killed at the battle of the Boyne. The event determined Ruvigny, and he entered the English service as a major-general of horse, though by doing so he forfeited his fine estates in Champagne and Picardy. He was appointed colonel of the Huguenot cavalry, in succession to the Duke of Schomberg, and in May 1691 he proceeded to Ireland. He joined the army under Ginkell at Mullingar, and at the council of war before Athlone gave his voice in favour of forcing the passage of the Shannon. At the battle of Aughrim, 12 July 1691, he commanded the horse of the second line, consisting of his own corps and the royal (or Oxford) regiment of horse guards, and by his spirited attack at a critical moment contributed largely to the victory of the English arms. During the march on Galway he was stationed at Athenry with General Scravenmore and three thousand horse as a corps of observation. He served at the siege of Limerick, and assisted at the negotiations for its capitulation.

After taking part in the festivities at Dublin, he returned to England in November, but on 27 Feb. 1692 he was appointed, though with no higher title than that of major-general, commander-in-chief of the forces in Ireland. He proceeded thither in March, but much of his time that year was spent in England on military business, chiefly in connection with the abortive expedition against St. Malo, of which he had been appointed second in command. On 25 Nov. he was created Viscount Galway and Baron Portarlington, in recognition of his services at the battle of Aughrim, and shortly afterwards received a grant *in custodiam*, made absolute 26 June 1696, of the forfeited estates of Sir Patrick Trant, situated chiefly in the Queen's County, and amounting to more than fifty-eight thousand English acres.

In April 1693 he left Ireland to join the army in Flanders, and arrived there in time to command the English and Huguenot horse at the battle of Landen. He displayed conspicuous bravery in covering William's retreat at the bridge of Neerhespen. He was apparently wounded in the action, and it is stated by St.-Simon (*Mémoires*, ed. 1873, i. 95), who was present at the battle, that he was made prisoner by the French, but immediately liberated in order to avoid the necessity of consigning him to the galleys as a traitor. In November he was appointed, with the rank of lieutenant-general, commander-in-chief of the English auxiliary forces in Piedmont, with credentials as envoy extraordinary to the court of Turin. But, says a contemporary, 'il n'y va qu'à regret et par pure obeissance au Roy' (*Hist. MSS. Comm.* 7th Rep. p. 215). He left London early in December with a considerable sum of money for the relief of the distressed Vaudois, and proceeding through Switzerland for the purpose of raising recruits, he arrived at Turin in March 1694. His position was a difficult one. An excellent officer, he was no match for Victor Amadeus in diplomacy, and though not without his suspicions as to the intrigues of the duke with France, he was completely deceived by his protestations of loyalty to the alliance, and by the readiness with which at his request he granted religious toleration to the Vaudois. The capture of the fort of S. Giorgio and the meeting of a protestant synod at Vigliano to regulate the morals of the army, in which he sat as an elder, were the chief events of the year. The winter was passed in completing his arrangements for the next year's campaign. According to his instructions he was anxious to co-operate with the fleet by an attack on Marseilles, but was compelled to acquiesce in the siege of Casale. The sudden surrender of that fortress surprised him, but his suspicions were set at rest by the apparent sincerity of the duke in renewing the grand alliance. He grumbled at wasted time and neglected opportunities, but even the pilgrimage of the duke to Loretto did not strike him as particularly mysterious; and it was only in August 1696, when the duke threw off the mask and announced his intention of concluding a treaty with France, that he realised how completely he had been duped. He at once withdrew into the Milanese, and was successful in intercepting the subsidy intended for the duke. During September he took part in the defence of Valenza, but after the recognition of the neutrality of the Italian peninsula on 7 Oct. he retired with the English contingent to Flanders, and on 11 Jan. 1697 returned to England. A present which the Duke of Savoy wished to make him of his portrait set in diamonds he declined. He had already forfeited his estates in France, and shortly before the peace of Ryswick he was deprived by Louis of a considerable sum of money which his father had entrusted to the care of President Harlay.

On 6 Feb. 1697 he was appointed by the king's command lord justice of Ireland *ad interim*. On 12 May he was advanced to the rank of Earl of Galway, and two days later he was joined with the Marquis of Winchester and Lord Villiers in a commission as lords justices of Ireland; but the latter being occupied as plenipotentiary at Ryswick, and the former being of little importance, the conduct of affairs rested chiefly with him and the lord chancellor, John Methuen [q. v.] On 31 May Galway and the Marquis of Winchester landed at Dublin, and were sworn in on the same day. Galway's government of Ireland from February 1697 to April 1701 marks an important period in the history of that country, for it was during his government that the parliament of England asserted its right to make laws binding on Ireland, and that the first acts of the penal code were passed. As the devoted servant of King William, Galway would have preferred to steer an even and impartial course, and so far as his personal influence went it was exerted in moderating the violence of political and religious faction. But he was better fitted for the camp than for the council-chamber. His inability to speak English fluently naturally placed him at a disadvantage, and though his bearing was always courteous and conciliatory, his influence in affairs of state was really very small. His devotion to William's interest, his indifference to party politics, his high personal character, his perfect unselfishness, his discretion and tolerant disposition, were the chief reasons that influenced his appointment. For himself he seems to have liked Ireland and the Irish people. During his residence there, and in the intervals of official business, he devoted himself to the improvement of his estates. By the liberal encouragement he offered them to settle on his land he established a flourishing colony of protestant refugees at Portarlington. He also built and endowed two churches, in one of which the liturgy in French was used till the beginning of the nineteenth century, and two schools, which were for a long time the most fashionable in Ireland. He was extremely charitable, and though a protestant of a pronounced type, he was so far unwilling to reap any personal advantage from his religion that he not merely maintained the two grandsons of Lord Clanmalier at Eton, but expressed his intention of resigning their grandfather's estate to them on condition that they conformed to the law by becoming protestants. But in 1700 he was deprived of all his estates by the Act of Resumption. Personally he was not much affected by his loss, but William, who felt keenly for him, gave him a pension of 1,000*l.* a year, and made him general of the Dutch forces, and colonel of the blue regiment of foot-guards. In April 1701 he obtained permission to retire from the government of Ireland. In July he accompanied Marlborough to Holland, and, after visiting the king at Loo, he was sent to the elector of Cologne on a diplomatic mission connected with the formation of the grand alliance. On his return to England, upon William's death, he took up his residence at a small house called Rookley, near Winchester, in the neighbourhood of his cousin, Lady Russell. He was troubled with gout, and, feeling himself growing infirm, he was anxious to retire from active employment, but in June 1704 he was appointed, with the rank of general, to succeed the Duke of Schomberg as commander of the English forces in Portugal.

He arrived at Lisbon on 10 Aug. At Almeida he inspected the troops, and, finding the commissariat defective, he opposed an autumn campaign in Spain. His opinion was overruled, but was justified by the speedy retreat of the army from want of provisions. During the winter he was busily occupied in preparations for a new frontier campaign in the spring, and in furnishing the Prince of Hesse with additional forces for the defence of Gibraltar. The campaign of 1705 opened with the invasion of Estremadura. Galway's plan for an immediate attack on Badajoz being rejected, the spring was consumed in the capture of Valenza and Albuquerque. In the autumn Badajoz was attacked, and on 2 Oct. the siege began under his direction, but while superintending the erection of a battery his right hand was shattered by a shot from the fortress. He was compelled to retire, and the command devolved upon Baron Fagel, who raised the siege. Fever and irritation at Fagel's conduct rendered his condition so critical that he was compelled to solicit a pass from Marshal Tessé to proceed to Olivença. Tessé not only complied with his request, but sent his own physicians to attend on him, and in November he began to recover. In the following spring, 1706, he was anxious to take advantage of Tessé's attempt to recapture Barcelona to advance straight on Madrid. The scheme, though a bold one, was approved by Marlborough and the English ministers, but the Portuguese interposed so many obstacles that it was only by a singular admixture of firmness and address that he accomplished his purpose. Though so weak that he had to be lifted on horseback he drove the Duke of Berwick from the Guadiana to the Henares, wrested from him eight thousand Spanish troops and a hundred pieces of artillery, besides an immense amount of ammunition and provisions, and reduced the fortresses of Alcantara and Ciudad Rodrigo. On 27 June he entered Madrid, and for six weeks maintained his position there. On 6 Aug. he was joined by King Charles at Guadalaxara, but meanwhile reinforcements had reached Berwick, the Spaniards had returned to their allegiance to the Bourbons, and the opportunity created by Galway had passed away. Finding it impossible to reoccupy Madrid, Galway, after spending a month at Chinchon, determined to fall back on Valencia. The retreat was conducted by him in a masterly fashion, and on 28 Sept. he gained the Valencian frontier without much loss. Perceiving the importance of occupying Madrid, he was anxious to renew the attempt in the following spring. At a council of war on 15 Jan. 1707 his plan, which had already been sanctioned by the English ministry, was approved by a majority of the generals, but King Charles, acting on the sinister advice of Noyelles, refused to adopt it, and shortly afterwards withdrew, with the Dutch and Spanish troops, to Barcelona. Though greatly weakened by this defection, Galway, who had recently been appointed commander-in-chief of all the English forces in Spain, was confirmed in his original intention by expectation of assistance from Lisbon. But feeling it necessary to provide in the first place for the defence of Valencia, he opened the campaign by destroying the French magazines on the Murcian frontier. At Villena he heard that Berwick, expecting to be joined by Orléans, was marching towards Almanza. With the unanimous concurrence of the generals he determined to attack before the junction was effected. Considering his great inferiority, the resolution was a daring one, but an offensive policy had been determined upon, and an offensive policy, all things being considered, was probably the best course that could have been taken. He was compelled to yield the right to the Portuguese, but otherwise his arrangements for the battle were made with care, and in order to strengthen his cavalry he adopted the novel plan of interposing battalions of foot. The battle was lost through the cowardice of the Portuguese cavalry. Galway himself received a sabre wound near his right eye, which, depriving him of sight, obliged him to quit the field. But undismayed by his defeat, and after making what arrangements he could for the defence of Valencia, he retired into Catalonia, in order 'to make up another army,' and within less than five months after his defeat he was able to take the field with 14,600 well-equipped troops. He was unable to avert the fall of Lerida, but his energy had saved the situation. He had long desired to be relieved from his post. He had lost an arm and an eye, and had become partially deaf. In December his wish was complied with, but the English ministers, in order to mark their approbation of his conduct, appointed him envoy extraordinary to the court of Lisbon, and commander-in-chief of the English forces in Portugal. He sailed on 8 Feb. 1708 for Lisbon. During that year the state of his health confined him entirely to his diplomatic duties, but in 1709, though disapproving strongly of Fronteira's determination to attack the Marquis de Bay, he commanded the English contingent at the battle on the Caya. He displayed great personal bravery. His horse was shot under him, and he narrowly escaped capture. But age and his infirmities pressed heavily upon him, and he was glad when he was recalled in the following year.

He returned to England shortly after the accession of Harley and the tories to power. In January 1711 the management of the war in Spain formed the subject of several acrimonious debates in the House of Lords. On 11 Jan. a motion censuring Galway for fighting the battle of Almanza was carried by sixty-four to forty-three, and a subsequent motion, 'that the Earl of Galway, in yielding the post of her Majesty's troops to the Portuguese in Spain, acted contrary to the honour of the imperial crown of Great Britain,' by sixty-four to forty-four. The votes were a mere party manœuvre, and cannot be held to affect either the wisdom or unwisdom of Galway's conduct at Almanza. On his return to England he retired to Rookley, and about the same time resigned his colonelcy of the Dutch guards. In 1715 it was felt advisable, in view of the Jacobite rising, to place the government of Ireland in firm hands. Accordingly on 23 Aug. the Duke of Grafton and Galway were appointed lords justices. They landed at Dublin on 1 Nov., but the parliament, which assembled a few days later, showed itself so distinctly loyal as to remove all anxiety from the government. On 11 Dec. it in a measure repaired the old wrong done to Galway by voting him a military pension of 500*l.* a year in addition to his civil pension of 1,000*l.* With the appointment of Lord Townshend as viceroy in January 1716 Galway's term of office came to an end. He returned to England in February, and spent the remainder of his life at Rookley. He died on 3 Sept. 1720, during a visit to his cousin, Lady Russell, at Stratton House, and was buried at Micheldever churchyard on 6 Sept., the grave never closing over a braver and more modest soldier. Galway was unmarried, and the bulk of his property passed by will to Lady Russell. On his death his British titles became extinct, but the marquisate of Ruvigny and Raineval passed to his nephew, Pierre David, one of whose sons came to England, and was a colonel in the royal engineers. It is from him that the present Marquis de Ruvigny and Raineval, and Philip Louis de Ruvigny, count d'Arcis, are descended. The Ruvigny estates in France were conferred by Louis XIV on Cardinal Polignac in 1711.

An admirable mezzotint by Simon, from a picture by De Graves, appeared in 1704. 'He is,' wrote Macky about 1700, 'one of the finest gentlemen in the army, with a head fitted for the cabinet as well as the camp; is very modest, vigilant, and sincere; a man of honour and honesty, without pride or affectation; wears his own hair, is plain in his dress and manners.'

[D. C. A. Agnew's Life of the Earl of Galway, Edinburgh, 1864, and the carefully written memoir in the same author's Protestant Exiles from France, i. 144–219, London, 1871, are the chief sources of information. For special information regarding his career as a Frenchman may be added St.-Simon's Mémoires, ed. Paris, 1873; Haag's La France Protestante, art. 'Massue;' Benoit's Hist. de l'Édit de Nantes, iv. 358; Mignet's Négociations relatifs à la Succession d'Espagne, vol. iv. in Collection de Documents Inédits; Copies and Extracts of some Letters written to and from the Earl of Danby in the years 1676, 1677, and 1678, published by his Grace's direction, London, 1710; Duke of Leeds Official Corresp., Additional MS. 28054; Dalrymple's Memoirs of Great Britain and Ireland; Savile Correspondence (Camden Society); Temple's Memoirs, p. 321; Burnet's Own Time; Weiss's Hist. des Réfugiés Protestants de France, of which a translation was published at Edinburgh in 1854. For the campaign in Ireland the following may be usefully consulted: G. Story's Impartial History and Continuation of the Wars in Ireland, London, 1693; Dumont de Bostaquet's Mémoires inédits, Paris, 1864, quoted by Macaulay as the Dumont MS.; O'Kelly's Macariæ Excidium (Irish Archæol. Society); An Exact Journal of the Victorious Progress of General Ginkell, London, 1691; R. Kane's Campaigns of William III; Hist. MSS. Comm. 4th Rep. pp. 321, 323, 324. For the campaign in Savoy: Galway's Letters in Cox's Original Correspondence of the Duke of Shrewsbury have been supplemented by Memoirs of the Transactions in Savoy during this War, London, 1697; State Papers, Savoy and Sardinia, No. 31 in the Public Record Office; Addit. MSS. British Museum, 19771, 21494 f. 45, 28879 f. 47. For the period of his government of Ireland: The State Papers, Ireland, in the Public Record Office, are unfortunately very scanty, and have been utilised in Froude's English in Ireland; but Grimblot's Letters of William III and Vernon's Letters illustrative of the Reign of William III furnish additional and confirmatory information. To them may be added Dr. Burridge's Short View of the Present State of Ireland, Dublin, 1708; History of the Ministerial Conduct of the Chief Governors of Ireland from 1688 to 1753, London, 1754; The Case of the Forfeitures in Ireland fairly stated, London, 1700; Jus Regium, or the King's Right to Grant Forfeitures, in Collection of State Tracts published during the reign of William III, ii. 731, the author of which appears to have been Dr. E. Burridge. For matters relating to military appointments and the disbandment of the army Addit. MSS. 9716 and 9718; and for miscellaneous information Addit. MSS. 28053 f. 400, 28218 f. 29, 28881 f. 411, 28882 f. 59, 28883 f. 344, 28885 f. 249; Hist. MSS. Comm. 3rd Rep. p. 193, 7th Rep. p. 806. In regard to his conduct in Spain the Hon. A. Parnell's War of the Succession in Spain is distinctly the most valuable authority; Abel Boyer's Annals of the Reign of Queen Anne supplies impartial and trustworthy contemporary information; An Impartial Enquiry into the Management of the War in Spain, London, 1712 (reprinted in 1726 with a new title-page, 'The History of the Last War in Spain from 1702 to 1710'), is based on the Annals, and may have been written by Boyer himself; the Godolphin Official Corresp., Addit. MSS. 28056 and 28057, includes many letters from Galway, and some useful information is contained in the Leake Papers, Addit. MSS. 5441 and 5443; Griffet's Recueil de Lettres pour servir à l'Histoire Militaire du Règne de Louis XIV; De Quincey's Histoire Militaire du Règne de Louis le Grand, and H. Reynald's Succession d'Espagne deserve to be consulted; Cobbett's Parliamentary History, vi. 936, furnishes a full account of the debates in the House of Lords on the management of the war. Gleanings more or less valuable are to be found in the Duke of Berwick's Memoirs; Mémoires et Lettres du Comte de Tessé; Marlborough's Letters and Despatches; Kemble's State Papers; Cole's Memoirs; Richard Hill's Diplomatic Corresp.; Private Corresp. of the Duchess of Marlborough; Addit. MSS. 7077 f. 156, 15170 f. 197, 15866 f. 138, 15895 ff. 41, 54, 15916 f. 21, 16467 f. 191, 20966 f. 37, 21136 ff. 45, 59, 22200, 22231 f. 97, 22880 f. 23, 29587 f. 91, 29588 f. 400; Hist. MSS. Comm. 8th Rep., Duke of Marlborough's MSS., 9th Rep. p. 467, 10th Rep. pt. i. p. 521, pt. iv. p. 340, pt. v. pp. 182, 511, 11th Rep. pt. iv. pp. 331–4, pt. v. pp. 297–9, 12th Rep. App. pt. v., Duke of Rutland's MSS. vol. ii. For general information reference should be made to the histories of Burnet, Harris, Kennet, Tindal, Stanhope, Macaulay, and Burton. Luttrell's Diary often supplies information not noted elsewhere. Some personal details are in Lady Russell's Letters and in the works of St. Evremond. For special information on one or two points the writer of the article is indebted to the present Marquis de Ruvigny. Galway's letters are almost entirely in French. The writing is legible and the style agreeable. After the loss of his right hand at Badajoz he employed an amanuensis, but signed his letters with his left hand.] R. D.

MASTER, RICHARD, M.D. (*d.* 1588), physician, was a younger son of Robert Master of Streetend, in the parish of Willesborough, Kent. On 29 Oct. 1533, being fellow of All Souls' College, Oxford, he graduated B.A., proceeding M.A. on 11 May 1537. He was converted from popery by the perusal of the works of Heinrich Bullinger. He seems to have been personally acquainted with Rudolph Walther when Walther visited England in 1537, and Master subsequently corresponded with him. About 1539 he accepted a benefice in the church of England, but soon afterwards resigned it to the patron because he considered himself ill qualified for the function of a good clergyman. He then betook himself to medical studies at Oxford, and was admitted M.B. with license to practise in 1545 (FOSTER, *Alumni Oxon.* 1500–1714, iii. 986). In 1547 he migrated to Christ Church, proceeded M.D. on 29 July 1555, and was incorporated at Cambridge in 1571. About 1549 he was seized with a fever, which confined him to his bed for more than eighteen months. He was carried in a litter into Kent for a change of air, but while there had a quartan ague of three months' continuance. Admitted fellow of the College of Physicians on 17 March 1553, he was censor in 1556, 1557, 1558, and 1560, elect in 1558, president in 1561, and consiliarius in 1564 and 1583. By patent dated 26 June 1559 he was constituted physician to Queen Elizabeth, with the yearly fee of 100*l.* On 13 March 1562–3 he was made prebendary of York (LE NEVE, *Fasti*, ed. Hardy, iii. 188), and on 6 Jan. 1564–5 the queen by letters patent, for the consideration of 590*l.* 16*s.* 4*d.*, granted to him and his heirs the reversion of the site of the late monastery of Cirencester, and of the lands thereto belonging. He was present with the queen at Oxford in September 1566, and was moderator of the physic act kept there before her.

Master died at his house in Silver Street, St. Olave, London, in the enjoyment of a high reputation for professional skill, in January 1587–8 (cf. his will registered in P. C. C. 34, Rutland). His wife was Elizabeth, eldest daughter of John Fulnetby of Fulnetby, Lincolnshire (HERVEY, *Visitation of Suffolk*, ed. Howard, i. 307), by whom he had seven sons. The eldest son, George (*b.* 1556?), of St. John's College, Oxford, and Lincoln's Inn, M.P. for Cirencester in 1586 and 1588, was father of Sir William Master [see under MASTER, WILLIAM]. Thomas (1560–1628), B.D., master of the Temple 1601, was canon of Lichfield 1613, and archdeacon of Salop 1614. Robert (1565–1625), D.C.L., was principal of Alban Hall 1599–1603, chancellor of Rochester and Lichfield, and M.P. for Cricklade 1601. Henry (*b.* 1566), M.A., was principal of Alban Hall 1603–1614.

Some of Master's letters in Latin and English are among the Lansdowne MSS. in the British Museum (xix. 83, xlvi. 38, cxxi. 19).

[Visitation of Gloucestershire, 1623 (Harl. Soc.), p. 111; Burke's Landed Gentry, 1886; Cooper's Athenæ Cantabr. ii. 20; Munk's Coll. of Phys. 1878, i. 52; Wood's Fasti (Bliss), i. 122, 143; Lansd. MS. 984, f. 64; Foster's Alumni Oxon. 1500–1714.] G. G.

MASTER, STREYNSHAM (1682–1724), captain in the navy, was the only son of James Master of East Langdon in Kent, by Joyce, only daughter of Sir Christopher Turner, baron of the exchequer. James Master's father, Sir Edward Master (*d.* 1648), married Audry, eldest daughter and coheiress of Robert Streynsham (HASTED, *Hist. of Kent*, ii. 803), by whom he had fifteen children, including, besides James, Sir Streynsham Master, governor of Madras [see LANGHORNE, SIR WILLIAM]. The name Streynsham is still common in the family (*Manchester School Register*, Chetham Soc., ii. 33, 263). Master entered the navy under the care of Captain George Byng, afterwards Viscount Torrington [q. v.], who had married his sister, Margaret. He was serving with him as a midshipman of the Ranelagh in 1704, was promoted to be a lieutenant of the Ranelagh, and was severely wounded in the leg by the explosion at the capture of Gibraltar. On 5 July 1709 he was promoted by Byng, then commander-in-chief in the Mediterranean, to command the Fame, and on 22 March 1709–10 he was posted by Sir John Norris to the Ludlow Castle. In 1712 he was captain of the Ormonde in the Mediterranean; in 1716 and 1717 of the Dragon in the Baltic with Norris and Byng. In March 1718 he was appointed to the Superbe, one of the fleet which went out to the Mediterranean with Byng. In the battle of Cape Passaro, 31 July 1718, Master's share was exceptionally brilliant. The Superbe and Kent together engaged the Real Felipe, the Spanish flagship, till, having beaten her to a standstill, she was boarded and taken by a party from the Superbe, led by Thomas Arnold (1679–1737) [q. v.], her first lieutenant. Master was probably the first 'private captain who ever had the honour of making a commander-in-chief of so high a rank his prisoner.' Captain John Macbride [q. v.] had a similar honour off Cape St. Vincent in 1780, as also had Captain Israel Pellew at Trafalgar. After his return to England Master had no further service, dying of a fever, 22 June 1724. He had married, only four months before, Elizabeth, only daughter and heiress of Richard, son of Sir Henry Oxenden, first baronet, but left no issue (Wotton, *Baronetage*, 1771, ii. 428). At the end of last century his portrait was in the possession of Edmund Turner, F.R.S., of Panton House, Lincolnshire.

[Charnock's Biog. Nav. iv. 24; Memoirs relating to the Lord Torrington (Camden Soc.); commission and warrant books in the Public Record Office.] J. K. L.

MASTER, THOMAS (1603–1643), divine, son of William Master, rector of Cote, near Cirencester in Gloucestershire, was born at Cote in 1603. He was educated at Cirencester grammar school under Henry Topp, 'a noted master,' and 'ripened for the university' at Winchester College, where he obtained a scholarship in 1617. He entered New College, Oxford, in 1622, at the age of nineteen, became perpetual fellow in 1624, and graduated B.A. 1625, M.A. 1629, and B.D. 30 Jan. 1640–1. After 1629 he took holy orders, and in 1637 became rector of Wykeham, Lincolnshire, a sinecure office. Wood states that he was esteemed 'a vast scholar, a general artist and linguist, a noted poet, and a most florid preacher.' His contemporary Michael Woodward, afterwards warden of New College, wrote the words 'summæ spei' against his name in the college list of fellows. He assisted Edward Herbert, lord Herbert of Cherbury [q. v.], in collecting materials for his 'Life of Henry VIII,' and in turning this and other of Herbert's works into Latin. Four volumes of Herbert's manuscript history, largely in his handwriting, are preserved in Jesus College library. He died near Louth, of a 'malignant fever,' on 31 Aug. 1643, and was buried in the outer chapel of New College. There is an epitaph upon him among Lord Herbert's 'Occasional Verses.' He was author of: 1. 'Mensa Lubrica Montgom. illustriss. Domino D. Edwardo Baroni de Cherbury,' 1641, a poem in Latin and English on the game of shovel-board. Wood prints the English version in eighty-four lines. It was printed along with Sir Henry Savile's 'Oration to Queen Elizabeth' in 1658 and 1690. 2. 'Μονοστροφικὰ εἰς τὴν τοῦ Χριστοῦ σταύρωσιν,' composed in 1633, and printed along with 'Mensa Lubrica' in 1658. It was translated into Latin by Henry Jacob of Merton College, and into English verse by Abraham Cowley; Bishop Huntingford, in his 'Apology for his Monostrophics' (p. 30), says: 'Few remains of the ancient Greek lyrics are superior to Master's "Ode on the Crucifixion" either in spirit, imagery, or harmony. 3. 'Monarchia Britannica sub Elizabetha, Jacobo: in Oratione quam pro more habuit 1642 Thomas Master, Nov. Coll. Soc., in Capella vi. Kal. Aprilis,' Oxford, 1661, 4to, 1681, 8vo. A letter by Dr. John Lamphire [q. v.] accompanies Master's oration. 4. 'Tho. Masteri Μακαρίτου Novi Coll. quondam Socii Iter Boreale ad ipsius patrem Gulielmum Masterum Cotiæ in Agro Glocestrensi Pastorem,' 1675, 4to. This was written in 1637 in prose and verse, and published by the companion of the journey, George Ent [q. v.] The journey was to Louth, near Wykeham in Lincolnshire. 5. 'The Virgin Mary. A sermon preached in Saint Mary's College (vulgo New College), Oxon., March the 25th, 1641,' London, 1710, 8vo. A note to this sermon speaks of Master's memory as 'still pretious.' The sermon occurs again in a collection entitled 'Conjugal Duty set forth,' &c., London, 1732. Wood mentions poems on 'Carolus Redux,' 1623, 'Ad Regem Carolum,' 1625, on Bishop Lake 1626, on Ben Jonson 1637, and on Vaulx as existing in manuscript.

[Information supplied by the Warden of New College; Wood's Athenæ Oxon. iii. 83; Life, pp. 86, 165; Fasti, ii. 35, 335; Brit. Mus. Cat.; Clark's Register of the University of Oxford, iii. 443; Kirby's Winchester Scholars; Foster's Alumni Oxon.] R. B.

MASTER, WILLIAM (1627–1684), divine, was the second son of Sir William Master (*d.* 1662), knt., of Cirencester, Gloucestershire, and of his wife Alice, daughter of

Edward Eastcourt of Salisbury. The father, son of George and grandson of Dr. Richard Master [q. v.], was admitted a member of the Inner Temple in November 1612, knighted by James I at Newmarket on 3 Dec. 1622, elected M.P. for Cirencester on 20 Jan. 1623–4, and was high sheriff for the county of Gloucester in 1627. At the outbreak of the civil war he maintained a horseman and arms for the service of the parliament, but soon after (2 Feb. 1642), when the town was taken by the king's forces, Prince Rupert and Prince Maurice were both quartered in his house, and he was forced to sign warrants for contributions to the royal garrison. The king spent the night of 8–9 Aug. 1642 in his house, while on his way from Oxford to Bristol. In August 1644 Sir William submitted to all ordinances of parliament, but on 31 Oct. of the same year entertained the king for one night on his route from Bath to Oxford. His estate was accordingly sequestered. In March 1646–1647 he begged to compound, having taken the covenant and the negative oath. He was still in difficulties as to his assessment in 1652, at which time he states that he was the father of twelve children. He died on 3 March 1661–2, aged 61, his wife having predeceased him on 5 Sept. 1660.

William was born at Cirencester, and baptised on 7 Sept. 1627. He matriculated from Christ Church, Oxford, on 2 April 1647, graduated B.A. on 7 Nov. 1650, by order of the parliamentary visitors of the university, was admitted bachelor-fellow of Merton College in 1651, and was M.A. on 19 Nov. 1652. Soon after he became vicar of Preston, near Cirencester, of which place his father was patron, and while there, on Ascension day 1658, performed the ceremony of marriage between George Bull [q. v.] (afterwards bishop of St. Davids) and Bridget, daughter of Alexander Gregory, incumbent of Cirencester, according to the form prescribed in the Book of Common Prayer, although that usage was forbidden under penalty at the time. He was admitted rector of Woodford in Essex on 13 Feb. 1660–1, was prebendary of Chamberlainwood at St. Paul's from 17 July 1663 till 1666, and was admitted to that of Cadington Major on 14 Feb. 1666–7. For a year, from 3 July 1666, he was rector of Southchurch, Essex, and from 29 April 1671 till his death rector of St. Vedast, Foster Lane, London, with the church of St. Michael Quern. Master died in London, and was buried in the chancel of Woodford Church on 6 Sept. 1684. He married at Woodford, on 18 May 1665, Susanna, daughter of the Rev. Job Yate, rector of Rodmarton in Gloucestershire. At the time of his death his three children, Richard, Thomas, and Elizabeth, were all under age. He left landed property in Essex, in Wiltshire, and at Preston, near Cirencester. He desired that the impropriate tithes of Preston, which he had from his father upon trust, should be purchased from his nephew, Thomas of Cirencester, when his lease was out, and devoted partly to the repair of the vicarage house at Preston and to the better maintenance of the vicar, and partly to the preaching of sermons in Oxford, and providing assistance in money and books for the 'post masters and young scholars' of Merton College. His grandson William, son of his eldest son Richard, baptised in December 1715, was educated at Winchester College, and became fellow of New College, Oxford, in 1736.

Under the pseudonym of 'A Student in Theologie' Master published 'Λόγοι Εὔκαιροι, Essayes and Observations, Theologicall and Morall. Wherein many of the Humours and Diseases of the Age are Discovered,' to which was added 'Drops of Myrrhe, or Meditations and Prayers, fitted to Divers of the preceding Arguments,' London, 1654. In the dedication to his parents he speaks of his studies being 'much of another nature.' The work is not without merit; a high standard of morality is combined with a humorous and easy style.

JOHN MASTER, born at Cirencester, and baptised there on 25 Sept. 1637, probably William's youngest brother, matriculated at Christ Church, Oxford, on 20 July 1654 (B.A. 3 Feb. 1656–7, M.A. from St. Mary Hall, 25 June 1659, M.B. and M.D. from Christ Church 4 July 1672), and was admitted honorary fellow of the College of Physicians on 30 Sept. 1680. He assisted his intimate friend Dr. Thomas Willis [q. v.] in his medical publications.

[Visitation of Gloucestershire (Harl. Soc.), p. 111; Members admitted to the Inner Temple, p. 202; Atkyns's Gloucestershire, pp. 180, 318; Parliaments of England, pt. i. p. 457; Iter Carolinum (Gutch, Collect. Curiosa, ii. 431, 438); Cal. of State Papers, Dom. Ser. 1646–7, pp. 532–533; Cal. of Committee for Compounding, pp. 85, 1143–4; Cal. of Committee for the Advance of Money, p. 1383; Newcourt's Repertorium, i. 128–129, 566, ii. 535; Kennett's Reg. p. 380; Wood's Athenæ (Bliss), iv. cols. 148–9; Le Neve's Fasti (Hardy), ii. 371, 376; Lysons's Environs, iv. 279; Nelson's Life of Bull, p. 38; Reg. of Visitors of Univ. Oxon. p. 488; Foster's Alumni, 1500–1714 and 1715–1886; Kirby's Winchester Scholars, p. 235; will (Hare, 116) at Somerset House; Munk's Coll. of Phys. i. 410; Washbourn's Bibliotheca Gloucestrensis, clxxxv; Rudder's Gloucestershire, passim; Cirencester Par. Reg. per the vicar.] B. P.

MASTERS, Mrs. MARY (*d.* 1759?), poetess, was of humble birth, and her genius was 'always discountenanced by her parents.' She seems to have been known to most of the *literati* of the day; and Dr. Johnson, whom she occasionally visited, is said to have revised her volumes and 'illuminated them here and there with a ray of his own genius' (Boswell, edit. Croker, 1860, p. 743). In her 'Familiar Letters and Poems upon several Occasions' (London, 1755) there are three 'Short Ejaculations,' the first of which, the well-known, ''Tis religion that can give Sweetest pleasures while we live,' has been adopted in most hymnals. The original consists of six lines only; two more were added in Rippon's 'Selection' (1787), and the eight lines divided into two stanzas, in which form the hymn is now known. An ejaculation for use 'At the Altar,' and beginning, 'O my ador'd Redeemer! deign to be,' is sometimes met with. She is spoken of as 'chaste, moral, and religious,' and 'an agreeable and ingenious writer' (*Monthly Review*, 1st ser. xiii. 155). She is supposed to have died about 1759 (Croker, p. 78, *n.*)

[Holland's Psalmists of Great Britain, ii. 202; Julian's Dictionary of Hymnology, i. 718; W. Garrett Horder in Sunday Magazine, April 1889.] J. C. H.

MASTERS, ROBERT (1713–1798), historian of Corpus Christi College, Cambridge, born in Norfolk in 1713, was son of Thomas Master (*d.* 1680), by his wife Elizabeth, daughter of Sir Thomas Dyke of Sussex. Sir William Master of Cirencester was his grandfather [see under Master, William]. He was admitted at Corpus Christi College in 1731; graduated B.A. in 1734, M.A. in 1738, B.D. in 1746; and was fellow and tutor of the college from 1738 to 1750. On 14 May 1752 he was elected fellow of the Society of Antiquaries (Gough, *Chron. List*, p. 11). He continued to reside in college till he was presented by that society to the rectory of Landbeach, Cambridgeshire, in 1756. Mawson, bishop of Ely [q. v.], collated him to the vicarage of Linton, which he resigned for that of Waterbeach in 1759. This latter benefice he, by the bishop's leave, resigned in 1784 to his son William, for whom he built a house. He was in the commission of the peace for Cambridgeshire, and acted as deputy to William Compton, LL.D., chancellor of the diocese of Ely, who resided abroad. In 1797 he resigned the living of Landbeach in favour of Thomas Cooke Burroughes, senior fellow of Caius College, who, immediately upon his presentation, married Mary, Masters's second daughter. Masters continued to reside in the parsonage with his son-in-law and daughter until his death on 5 July 1798. He was buried at Landbeach, where a monument was erected to his memory.

About 1757 Masters married a granddaughter of one of his predecessors at Landbeach, and daughter of John Cory, rector of Impington and Waterbeach. She died on 29 Aug. 1764, leaving a son William, who died rector of Waterbeach in 1794, and two daughters, viz. Anne, married to the Rev. Andrew Sprole, and Mary, wife of the Rev. T. C. Burroughes.

His principal work is: 'The History of the College of Corpus Christi and the Blessed Virgin Mary (commonly called Bene't) in the University of Cambridge, from its foundation to the present time,' pt. i. Cambridge, at the university press, 1753, 4to. This was followed in 1755 by the second part, containing the lives of members of the college, with an appendix of documents. An edition of the work, 'with additional matter and a continuation' by John Lamb, D.D. [q. v.], master of Corpus Christi College, appeared at Cambridge in 1831, 4to, but the original edition is superior to its successor in biographical and other respects.

Masters's other works are: 1. 'A List of the Names, Counties, Times of Admission, Degrees, &c., of all that are known to have been Members of Corpus Christi College in Cambridge,' 1749, 4to, and subsequently appended to the history of the college. 2. 'Some Remarks on Mr. Walpole's Historic Doubts on the Life and Reign of King Richard III,' 1771. In 'Archæologia,' ii. 198; also printed separately, London, 1772, 4to. 3. 'Memoirs of the Life and Writings of Thomas Baker, B.D., of St. John's College in Cambridge, from the papers of Dr. Zachary Grey, with a Catalogue of his MS. Collections,' Cambridge, 1784, 8vo. 4. 'Account of some Stone Coffins and Skeletons found on making some alterations and repairs in Cambridge Castle,' 1785. In 'Archæologia,' viii. 63. 5. 'Account of an Antient Painting on Glass,' representing the pedigree of the Stewart family, 1786. In 'Archæologia,' viii. 321. 6. 'Catalogue of the Pictures in the Public Library and Colleges in the University of Cambridge' [1790], 12mo. 7. 'A Short Account of the Parish of Waterbeach, in the Diocese of Ely, by a late Vicar,' sine loco, 1795, 8vo, with a slight sketch of Denney Abbey. Only twenty-five copies printed for private circulation. 8. 'Collectanea de Landbeach,' incorporated in the Rev. William Keatinge Clay's 'History of Landbeach,' printed for the Cambridge Antiquarian Society, 1861.

A portrait of Masters, from a drawing by the Rev. Thomas Kerrich, was engraved by Facius in 1796.

[Addit. MSS. 5852 ff. 107 b, 118, 5876 ff. 137, 200, 5886 f. 18; Gough's British Topography; Clay's Landbeach, pp. 118, 124; Clay's Waterbeach, p. 69; Gent. Mag. 1798, pp. 634, 720; Lamb's Hist. of Corpus Christi College, p. 395; Lowndes's Bibl. Man. (Bohn), p. 1511; Nichols's Illustr. of Lit.; Nichols's Lit. Anecd. iii. 479–84, vol. vii. pt. i. p. 256, pt. ii. p. 626, viii. 448; Warburton's Walpole, ii. 412, 426.] T. C.

MASTERTOWN, CHARLES (1679–1750), presbyterian divine, born in Scotland, probably in Linlithgowshire, on 23 March 1679, was educated at Edinburgh University, where he graduated M.A. as 'Carolus Masterton' on 28 June 1697, the same day as Ebenezer Erskine [q. v.] On 1 June 1703 he presented himself to the general synod of Ulster at Antrim, with his license from Linlithgow presbytery, and was 'allow'd to preach within the bounds' of the synod. Accepting a call from the congregation of Connor, co. Antrim, he was ordained there by Antrim presbytery on 17 May 1704. For nearly nineteen years he ministered at Connor with increasing repute as an able preacher and sound divine. It is remarkable that in 1718 he headed a protest against the general synod's resolution removing John Abernethy (1680–1740) [q. v.], the non-subscribing leader, to Dublin, a resolution which Abernethy disobeyed.

The irregular installation of Samuel Haliday [q. v.] at First Belfast in 1720, alienated several members of both presbyterian congregations in that town. On 4 July 1721 a subscription for building a third meeting-house was begun, and by help from Scotland (two pews in the gallery were set apart for 'Scottish strangers') the new structure, on the next plot of ground to the two others [see MacBride, John], was completed in 1722. Mastertown was called to the pastorate in October 1722, and installed at Third Belfast on 20 Feb. 1723 by Belfast presbytery. His successor at Connor was not ordained till 18 March 1724, the congregation insisting that Mastertown, and not a non-subscriber, should preside. On 18 June 1723 he was elected moderator of the general synod at Dungannon. His position was a difficult one. The non-subscription controversy was now in active progress. His immediate neighbours, Haliday and James Kirkpatrick [q. v.], had unwisely used every effort to restrain the flow of Scottish aid to the new congregation. Yet they announced their intention of presenting themselves at his communion on 30 Feb. 1724. The proposal was treated by Mastertown's session as an 'attempt to disturb,' and this was resented by Haliday and Kirkpatrick as a formal exclusion. The general synod's action removed the first and second congregations in 1725 into another presbytery (Antrim), and that presbytery was excluded from the synod's jurisdiction in 1726. The two ministers thus excluded 'convened the whole town,' causing 'a dreadful ferment.' Mastertown pursued his course calmly and with firmness, and built up a congregation which for over a hundred years stood alone in Belfast as the representative of orthodoxy in connection with the general synod. He attended the general synod in 1745, but by next year was incapacitated from preaching. William Laird was appointed his assistant and successor on 16 Sept. 1747. Mastertown died on 15 July 1750. His only child, Susan, married John Poaug in 1725; her descendants are numerous and influential. Mastertown wrote and printed his name thus; in the synodical records it appears as 'Masterton,' a form adopted by Reid and Killen.

His polemical publications show great ability. His brief catechetical treatise on the doctrine of the Trinity originated in lectures at Connor, repeated at Belfast, and presents the pith of much reading and thought in a form remarkably lucid and compact. On vexed points he usually follows Edmund Calamy, D.D. [q. v.]; he chiefly controverts Samuel Clarke (1675–1729) [q. v.]; but the treatise is more expository than polemic, and has hardly been excelled in its own line.

Mastertown published: 1. 'An Apology for the Northern Presbyterians in Ireland . . . requiring Subscription to the Westminster Confession . . . in Answer to the Seasonable Advice [by Abernethy],' &c., Glasgow, 1723, 4to (preface by Samuel Hemphill [q. v.]). 2. 'Christian Liberty founded on Gospel Truth,' &c., Belfast, 1725, 12mo (against Abernethy; reprinted 1753 with No. 6). 3. 'A Short Reply to the Postscript to Mr. Abernethy's Defence . . . by the three Dublin Ministers,' &c., Dublin, 1726, 8vo (against Nathaniel Weld, Joseph Boyse [q.v.], and Richard Choppin). 4. 'The Doctrine of the Holy Trinity explained and asserted from the Holy Scriptures,' &c., Belfast [November, 1728], 12mo (for date, cf. Reid, p. 220); reprinted, Edinburgh, 1729; 4th edit. London, 1734 (preface and Greek notes by Abraham Taylor, D.D., of Deptford); another 4th edit. Belfast, 1745, 12mo; Northampton, 1776 (preface by John Ryland); London, 1827, 12mo (with 'The Catholic Doctrine of the Trinity,' by William Jones, of Nayland [q. v.]); Edinburgh, 1880, 16mo (with 'Memoir' by Mastertown's great-grandson, the Rev. Hope Masterton Waddell of Dublin). 5. 'The great importance of the Scripture Doctrine of the ever-blessed Trinity,' &c., Belfast, 1745, 8vo.

[Waddell's Memoir, 1880; Cat. of Edinburgh Graduates, 1858, p. 158; Reid's Hist. Presb. Church in Ireland (Killen), 1867, iii. 158 sq.; Benn's Hist. of Belfast, 1877, i. 410 sq.; Witherow's Hist. and Lit. Memorials of Presbyterianism in Ireland, 1879, i. 256 sq.; Killen's Hist. Congr. Presb. Church in Ireland, 1886, pp. 86, 100; Ramsey's Early Hist. of Belfast, 1889, p. 33; Records of General Synod of Ulster, 1890, i. 71, 82, 471; Anderson's Early Belfast Printed Books, 1890.] A. G.

MATCHAM, GEORGE (1753-1833), traveller, only son of Simon Matcham, superintendent of the marine of the East India Company, and senior member in council of the presidency of Bombay, was born in 1753, and educated at Charterhouse School. Entering the civil service of the East India Company, he subsequently became their resident at Baroche. On its cession to the Mahrattas in 1783 Matcham retired from the service. He had already travelled much in the East, and now made his way to England by an overland route, much of which he had previously explored. It included Persia, Arabia, Egypt, Asia Minor, Turkey, Greece, the Greek Islands, Hungary, and other countries. Attended only by Arabs, he rode on horseback from Bagdad to Pera; he kept journals of his travels, and an account of a journey from Aleppo to Bagdad was published with the second edition of James Capper's 'Observations on the Passage to India,' London, 1784, and bound up with Eyles Irwin's 'Voyage up the Red Sea.' During his tour he became acquainted with many persons of note, including the emperor Joseph II. In 1785 he finally settled in England, where he devoted himself to the pursuits of a country gentleman; in 1802 he patented an apparatus for preserving vessels in danger of shipwreck, and made several communications to the government on various public improvements. Some of his views are embodied in his privately printed volumes, 'Anecdotes of a Croat' (*Gent. Mag.* 1833, i. 276) and 'Parental Chitchat,' 1826. He died on 3 Feb. 1833. In 1785 Matcham married Catherine, daughter of the Rev. Edmund Nelson, and sister of Admiral Lord Nelson, by whom he had five daughters and three sons.

The eldest son, George Matcham (1789-1877), born in 1789, was educated at St. John's College, Cambridge, where he graduated LL.B. in 1814, and LL.D. in 1820. In the same year he was admitted advocate in Doctors' Commons. He became chairman of the Wiltshire quarter sessions in 1836, and contributed accounts of the hundreds of Downton and Frustfield to Hoare's 'Modern History of Wilts,' London, 1825, &c. On 6 Nov. 1861 he contributed to the 'Times' 'Notes on the Character of Admiral Lord Nelson,' which were reprinted in the same year, together with 'Observations on No. ccxxi. of the "Quarterly Review"' (referred to in Stanhope's *Life of Pitt*, iv. 329 note, ed. 1862). He died on 18 Jan. 1877, leaving a son and two daughters by his wife Harriet, eldest daughter and heiress of William Eyre of Newhouse, whom he had married in 1817.

[Works in British Museum Library; Law Mag. and Review, 27 May 1877; Gent. Mag. 1833, i. 276; List of East India Company's Servants, 1782; Bengal Cal. 1788.] A. F. P.

MATHER, INCREASE, D.D. (1639-1723), president of Harvard College, the youngest son of Richard Mather [q. v.], was born in 1639 at Dorchester, Massachusetts, and graduated M.A. at Harvard in 1656, and became fellow. In 1657 he came to England, and from Lancashire proceeded to Dublin, where his brother Samuel [q. v.] was then settled. Entering Trinity College, he was admitted M.A. in 1658; with his graduation exercises 'the scholars were so pleased that they humm'd him, which was a compliment to which he was a stranger in his education in New England' (Calamy). Possibly it was an Irish custom of compliment, for at Cambridge, in 1623, 'they hummed' in sign of 'distast' (Heywood and Wright, *Cambridge Univ. Transactions*, 1854, ii. 315). He was chosen fellow of Trinity, but did not accept the appointment. Returning to England, he was substitute, on full salary, for John Howe [q. v.], at Great Torrington, Devonshire, till May 1659. He was then invited to Guernsey by Colonel Bingham, the governor; and preached for some time at Castle Cornet and St. Peter's Port. He removed to Gloucester at the end of the year as assistant to James Forbes (1629?-1712) [q. v.], but returned to Guernsey shortly before the Restoration. On the appointment of Sir Hugh Pollard as governor he left Guernsey rather than conform; declining on the same ground a valuable English living. He returned to New England, and became minister of the New North Church, Boston, Massachusetts, where he was ordained on 27 May 1664. Mather is sometimes called the last of the ejected nonconformists (a distinction which belongs to Nathan Denton [q. v.], who was buried on 13 Oct. 1720); he was the last survivor of those included in Calamy's lists, but though officiating as a preacher he had no regular ministerial status at the date of the Uniformity Act.

His career in New England was one of great eminence. He presided at the Boston synod of 1680, and wrote the preface to the confession of faith then agreed upon. When Charles II, in October 1683, called upon the colony of Massachusetts to surrender its charter, Mather attended a public meeting of the freemen of Boston, and procured a unanimous refusal. He was elected president of Harvard College in 1684, having previously been rector. On the issue of James II's declaration for liberty of conscience (1687), Mather was deputed by the New England ministers to convey an address of thanks. He embarked for England on 7 April 1688, as the accredited agent from the colony, and was graciously received by James. On the arrival of William, Mather was introduced to him by Philip, fourth baron Wharton; he obtained the removal of Sir Edmund Andros [q. v.], governor of New England, gained an enlarged charter for Massachusetts colony, and embarking on 29 March 1692 with Sir William Phipps, the new governor, reached Boston on 14 May, and received the thanks of the colonial assembly on 8 June. He was made D.D. In 1701 he resigned the presidency of Harvard College, owing to the requirement of residence. He remained in his Boston charge, retaining his vigour till he had passed his eightieth year. He died on 23 Aug. 1723, and had a public funeral. His portrait, engraved by Hopwood 'from an original painting in the possession of Mr. Townsend, Holborn,' is given by Palmer, 'Nonconformist's Memorial,' 1802, ii. 245.

Calamy gives two lists (with few dates), of Increase Mather's many publications, most of them being sermons and religious pieces. Among those published in London are: 1. 'A Discourse concerning the Mystery of Israel's Salvation,' &c., 1669, 8vo. 2. 'Some Important News about Conversion,' &c., 1674, 8vo. 3. 'A Brief History of the War with the Indians,' &c., 1676, 4to. 4. 'De Successu Evangelii apud Indos,' &c., 1688, 12mo. 5. 'Cases of Conscience concerning Witchcraft,' &c., 1693, 4to. 6. 'A Further Account of . . . New England Witches,' &c., 1693, 4to; reprinted, 1862, 12mo. 7. 'Two plain and practical Discourses', &c., 1699, 12mo. 8. 'The Order of the Churches in New England,' &c., 1700, 12mo. In the 'Philosophical Transactions Abridged,' 1714, vi. 85, is his 'Account of several Observations made in New England in 1712.'

Mather married the daughter of John Cotton (whose widow his father married), and had seven daughters and three sons. The eldest son, COTTON MATHER (1663–1728), D.D. (Glasgow, 1710) and F.R.S. (1714), who was born at Boston, Massachusetts, on 12 Feb. 1663, entered Harvard College at the age of twelve, and became a master of many languages, including Iroquois; from May 1684, as minister at Boston, he was a leading spirit in civil as well as ecclesiastical matters; he was the author of 383 publications; his most curious piece, which does little credit either to his understanding or his charity, is (1) 'The Wonders of the Invisible World, being an Account of the Trial of several Witches,' &c., 1693, 4to; his most valuable work is (2) 'Magnalia Christi Americana, or An Ecclesiastical History of New England,' &c., 1702, fol., in which the information, indispensable though often imperfect, is overloaded with ill-regulated pedantry; he died at Boston on 13 Feb. 1728; his third wife was Lydia, daughter of Samuel Lee (1625–1691) [q. v.]

Increase Mather's younger sons were Nathaniel Mather (*d.* 17 Oct. 1688, aged 19); and Samuel Mather, presbyterian minister at Witney, Oxfordshire, author of 'A Discourse concerning the Godhead of the Holy Ghost,' 1719, 8vo, and other tracts.

[Memoirs, with preface by Calamy, 1725 (portrait); Cotton Mather's Magnalia Christi Americana, 1702, iv. 137; Calamy's Account, 1713, p. 317; Calamy's Continuation, 1727, i. 494 sq.; Samuel Mather's Life of Cotton Mather, 1729; Hutchinson's Hist. of Massachusets-Bay, 1765, pp. 337 sq., 388 sq.] A. G.

MATHER, NATHANAEL (1631–1697), congregationalist divine, second son of Richard Mather [q. v.], was born at Much Woolton, Lancashire, on 20 March 1630–1. In 1635 his father took him to New England, where he graduated M.A. at Harvard College in 1647. He finished his studies in England, probably returning with his brother Samuel [q. v.] in 1650. He was assistant to George Mortimer at Harberton, Devonshire (a sequestered vicarage), and succeeded him there in 1655. In 1656 he was presented by the Protector to the sequestered vicarage of Barnstaple, Devonshire, in which the vicar, Martin Blake, B.D., was reinstated at the Restoration. Mather then went over to Holland, and for some years was pastor of the English Church at Rotterdam. On the death of his brother Samuel, he succeeded him (1671) as minister at New Row, Dublin. In the troubled year 1688 he left Ireland, and became pastor of the independent church in Paved Alley, Lime Street, London, vacant by the death of John Collins (1632?–1687) [q. v.] He joined the 'happy union' of 1691, but was a leader in its disruption, owing to the alleged heresies of Daniel Williams, D.D. [q. v.] On the withdrawal of William Bates, D.D. [q. v.] (who sided with Williams), from the Pinners' Hall lectureship, Mather was appointed (1694) in his place. He died on 26 July 1697, and was buried at Bunhill Fields, where a long Latin inscription was placed upon his tombstone; a still longer Latin epitaph is in Isaac Watts's Lyric Poems,' 1709, pp. 300 sq. He was of tall stature, and a dignified preacher.

He published: 1. 'The Righteousness of God through Faith,' &c., Oxford, 1694, 4to (his first lectures at Pinners' Hall). Posthumous were: 2. 'The Lawfulness of a Pastor's acting in other Churches,' &c., 1698, 12mo. 3. 'Twenty-three select Sermons . . . at Pinners' Hall,' &c., 1701, 8vo.

[Calamy's Account, 1713, p. 238; Calamy's Continuation, 1727, i. 257 sq.; Walker's Sufferings of the Clergy, 1714, ii. 196, 216; Wilson's Dissenting Churches of London, 1808, i. 231; Armstrong's Appendix to Martineau's Ordination Service, 1829, p. 80; Nelson's Bull, p. 262.] A. G.

MATHER, RICHARD (1596–1669), congregational divine, son of Thomas and Margaret Mather, was born in 1596 at a house still standing in Mather Lane, Lowton, in the parish of Winwick, Lancashire. His parents were of good family, reduced by 'unhappy mortgages.' At Winwick grammar school he was under William Horrocke, a good but severe master, who dissuaded his father from apprenticing the lad to a Roman catholic merchant. When but fifteen he was appointed master of Winwick school by Sir Peter Legh, the patron, but in 1612 he became the first master of a school newly established by the inhabitants of Toxteth Park, near Liverpool. Here he lodged in the family of Edward Aspinwall, a cultured puritan landowner. He heard puritan sermons and read puritan divinity, attaining definite religious convictions in 1614. His school flourished and attracted pupils from a distance. Jeremiah Horrocks [q. v.] is said to have been his scholar, but this seems impossible. To improve his qualifications he went to Oxford, and joined Brasenose College on 9 May 1618. It seems probable that his school was suspended while a chapel was being built at Toxteth. His stay at Oxford was cut short by a call from the Toxteth people 'to instruct, not so much their children as themselves.' He preached his first sermon there on 30 Nov. 1618, and was soon afterwards (certainly before March 1619) ordained by Thomas Morton [q. v.], bishop of Chester, who had formed a high estimate of his religious character. His age suggests that he was only ordained deacon; at a later date, when he had come to think episcopal ordination 'superstition,' he tore the parchment certificate. For nearly fifteen years he pursued his ministry at Toxteth with growing repute. He married a lady whose father long withheld his consent, through dislike to 'non-conformable puritans.' After this (1624), he lived in a house he had bought at Much Woolton, three miles off, but he preached at Toxteth twice each Sunday and often on holy days, held a fortnightly lecture at Prescot, and, at the request of the mayor, took part in 1629 in monthly sermons at Liverpool. William Gellibrand, the puritan minister of Warrington, on hearing him preach, said, 'Call him Matter; for, believe it, this man hath substance in him.' This pun shows that the first vowel in Mather was short. John Bridgeman [q. v.], Morton's successor, suspended him in August 1633 for disusing the ceremonies, but restored him in November at the instance of influential friends. The suspension led Mather to define his views of church government, which became essentially congregational. In 1634 he was again suspended, by the visitors of Richard Neale or Neile [q. v.], then archbishop of York; efforts for his restoration proved hopeless when it transpired that he had never worn a surplice. In the following year he resolved to emigrate to New England, after consulting several meetings of Lancashire puritans, and receiving encouraging letters from the Boston ministers, John Cotton and Thomas Hooker [q. v.]

Mather with his family left Warrington for Bristol on 16 April 1635. On 23 May they went on board the James, but the vessel did not sail till 4 June. They got away from Milford on 22 June, and reached Boston harbour on Sunday 16 Aug. landing next day. Mather's journal of the voyage is a graphic and interesting narrative.

After staying a few months in Boston, he had overtures from three New England settlements, and at length accepted a call from Dorchester, Massachusetts, where a congregational church was constituted, with Mather as 'teacher,' on 23 Aug. 1636. In this charge he remained till his death, though solicited to return to Lancashire during the Commonwealth period. He became an influential leader in the church councils of New England congregationalism. At the Cambridge synod of 1648, held for the purpose of checking the introduction of presbyterianism, three alternative schemes of congregational polity were proposed, and though one of these carried the authority of John Cotton, Mather's plan, generally known as the 'Cambridge platform,' was adopted. It provided for an associate congregationalism, with occasional but not constant synods. His health was remarkably good, and he never called in a physician, though in his latter years he became deaf, in 1662 one of his eyes failed him, and from 1667 he had several attacks of stone. After presiding at a council of churches in Boston, 13-16 April 1669, he was seized with a violent fit of this disorder, and returned to Dorchester, where he died on 22 April 1669. He married first, on 29 Sept. 1624, Katherine (*d.* 1655), daughter of Edmund Hoult of Bury, Lancashire; among his six sons by her were Samuel [q.v.], Nathanael [q.v.], Eleazar (*b.* 1637; minister at Northampton, Connecticut; *d.* 24 July 1669, aged 32), and Increase [q.v.] He married secondly, on 26 Aug. 1656, Sarah, whose first husband was named Story, and whose second husband was John Cotton (*d.* 23 Dec. 1652). She died before Mather.

He published: 1. 'An Answer of the . . . Churches in New England, unto nine Propositions,' &c., 1643, 4to. 2. 'Church-Government and Church-Covenant discvssed in an Answer to two-and-thirty Questions,' &c., 1643, 4to. (these two tracts on church government were written by Mather in 1639, and published in London in the name of the Elders of the New England churches). 3. 'A modest . . . Ansvver to Mr. Charles Herle against the Independancy of Churches,' London, 1644, 4to. 4. 'A Reply to Mr. Rutherford, or a . . . Defence of . . . Answer to . . . Herle,' &c., 1647, 4to. 5. 'An Heart-melting Exhortation . . . to their dear countrey-men of Lancashire,' &c., 1650, 12mo. (written exclusively by Mather, though bearing also the name of William Thompson of Braintree, Massachusetts, *d.* 10 Dec. 1666). 6. 'A Catechisme,' &c., 1650, 8vo. 7. 'A Treatise of Justification,' &c., Cambridge, New England, 1652, 4to. 8. 'A Farewell Exhortation to the Church . . . of Dorchester,' &c., Cambridge [Massachusetts], 1657, 4to. 9. 'A Plea for the Churches of New England,' &c., 1660. 10. 'A Defence of the Synod at Boston in . . . 1662,' &c., Cambridge [Massachusetts], 1664, 4to (in conjunction with J. Mitchell). 11. 'A Brief Relation . . . of the Lord's Work among the Indians,' &c., 4to (no date or place; copy in Dr. Williams's Library). He had a hand with John Eliot [q.v.] and Thomas Weld in the preparation of the 'Bay Psalm Book,' 1640; and prepared for press a series of sermons on 2 Peter and a 'Defence' of New England churches against William Rathband [q.v.]; he wrote part of 'An Answer to Twelve Questions,' &c., 1712, 16mo, published by Increase Mather.

[The Life and Death of . . . Richard Mather, 1670, reprinted 1850, is by an anonymous friend, whose accuracy is vouched for by Increase Mather; Journal of Richard Mather (Dorchester Antiquarian and Historical Society), 1850; Clarke's Lives of Eminent Persons, 1683, i. 126 sq.; Wood's Athenæ Oxon. (Bliss), iii. 832 sq.; Cotton Mather's Magnalia Christi Americana, 1702, iii. 122 sq.; Brook's Lives of the Puritans, 1813, iii. 152, 426 sq. 440 sq.; Sprague's Annals of the American Pulpit, 1857, i. 75 sq.; Beamont's Winwick [1876], pp. 75 sq.; Dexter's Congregationalism [1879]; V. D. Davis's Ancient Chapel of Toxteth Park, 1884, pp. 6 sq. (cf. Davis's 'Richard Mather's Voyage to America,' in *Unitarian Herald*, 15, 22, 29, Aug. 1884).] A. G.

MATHER, ROBERT COTTON, LL.D. (1808-1877), missionary, son of James Mather, congregational minister, was born at New Windsor, Manchester, on 8 Nov. 1808, and educated at the Edinburgh and Glasgow universities and Homerton College. After his ordination at Lendal Chapel, York, on 1 June 1833, he went to India as an agent of the London Missionary Society. He had the pastorate of the Union Chapel, Calcutta, for a few months, then removed to Benares, where he remained until May 1838, when he settled at Mirzapore. There he established a new mission, and in course of time gathered a flourishing Christian community, built schools and churches, founded the orphan school press, and started and edited a monthly journal in Hindustani. He was an excellent preacher in the native languages of Northern India, a successful administrator of the important mission which he founded, and an influential member of various associations of missionaries in India. He revised and edited the entire Bible in Hindustani, and in recognition of this work the university of Glasgow conferred on him the degree of LL.D. in 1862. He wrote many tracts and treatises in Hindu and Urdu, and among his English writings is one on 'Christian Missions in India,' London, 1858. He edited Sherring's 'Indian Church during the Great Rebellion,' 1859. He returned to England in 1873, after forty years' work in India, and subsequently published a commentary on the New Testament in Hindustani. At the time of his death, which took place at Torrington Park, Finchley, London, on 21 April 1877, he was engaged on a commentary on the Old Testament in the same language. His wife Elizabeth, born Sewell, 'church member of Hew Court Chapel, Carey Street, London,' was an industrious author, and published a Hindustani dictionary of the Bible. After Mather's death she joined the female mission at Mirzapore, and died 29 March 1879. Their youngest son, Dr. C. B. Mather, is now medical missionary in Tanganyika, Central Africa.

[Congregational Year Book, 1878, p. 325; Athenæum, 28 April 1877; Brit. Mus. Cat.; private information.] C. W. S.

MATHER, SAMUEL (1626–1671), congregationalist divine, eldest son of Richard Mather [q. v.], was born at Much Woolton, Lancashire, on 13 May 1626. His father took him in 1635 to New England, where he was educated at Harvard College, graduated M.A. in 1643, and became fellow. He was the first fellow of Harvard who had graduated there. Having already become a preacher, he returned to England, and in 1650 was made one of the chaplains of Magdalen College, Oxford, under the presidency of Thomas Goodwin [q. v.], the independent. He is said to have been incorporated M.A.; of this there is no record in the register. He frequently preached at St. Mary's. In 1653 he resigned his chaplaincy, having been appointed to attend the parliamentary commissioners to Scotland. He was at Leith, according to Calamy, for two years, exercising his ministry, but without regular charge. Returning to England, he is said to have been incorporated M.A. at Cambridge; he went over to Ireland soon after with Henry Cromwell. He was incorporated M.A. of Trinity College, Dublin, in 1654, and appointed one of the senior fellows. On 5 Dec. 1656 he was ordained in St. Nicholas's Church, Dublin, by Samuel Winter [q. v.], provost of Trinity, Timothy Taylor [q. v.] of Carrickfergus, and Thomas Jenner of Drogheda [see under Jenner, Thomas], all congregationalists. He was morning preacher at St. Nicholas's, and preached once in six weeks as chaplain to the lord-deputy. Wood commends him for his civility to episcopal divines; he declined to act on commissions for displacing them in Munster and Dublin. At the Restoration he was suspended (October 1660) for sermons against the revival of the ceremonies. Crossing to England he obtained the perpetual curacy of Burtonwood, Lancashire, a poor chapelry with a wooden chapel, in the parish of Warrington. From this he was ejected by the Uniformity Act of 1662. He went back to Dublin and gathered a congregation, which met at his house till a meeting-house was erected in New Row. He was arrested on 18 Sept., and imprisoned on 20 Sept. 1664 for preaching at a private conventicle, but soon released. A pressing call came to him from Boston, Massachusetts, which he declined. He died at Dublin on 29 Oct. 1671, and was buried in St. Nicholas's Church. He married a sister of Sir John Stephens.

He published: 1. 'A Wholesome Caveat for a Time of Liberty,' &c., 1652, 4to. 2. 'A Defence of the Protestant Religion,' &c., Dublin, 1671, 4to. Posthumous were: 3. 'An Irenicum: or an Essay for Union among Reformers,' &c., 1680, 4to. 4. 'The Figures or Types of the Old Testament,' &c., Dublin, 1683, 4to (both published by his brother Nathaniel). He wrote also a 'Discourse' against Valentine Greatrakes [q. v.], the 'miraculous conformist,' but it was 'not allow'd to be printed' (Calamy).

[Wood's Athenæ Oxon. (Bliss), iii. 941 sq.; Cotton Mather's Magnalia Christi Americana, 1702, iv. 136, 143; Calamy's Account, 1713, pp. 415 sq.; Armstrong's Appendix to Martineau's Ordination Service, 1829, pp. 79 sq.; Bloxam's Registers of Magd. Coll. Oxford, 1857, ii. 134 sq.; Catalogue of Dublin Graduates, 1869.] A. G.

MATHER, WILLIAM (*fl.* 1695), author of 'The Young Man's Companion,' was born at Bedford, and was a grandson of a mayor of Hull. He was a churchman, but about 1661 he and his wife joined the quakers. He became a teacher, and kept a private school in Bedford. He also held an appointment as surveyor of highways, and wrote a pamphlet 'On Repairing and Mending the Highways,' 1696, in which he is described as 'late surveyor.' Besse, under 'Bedfordshire,' mentions that one William Mather was imprisoned in 1683 on a writ in the ecclesiastical court.

Mather's chief work, 'The Young Man's Companion,' published 1681, contains, in very small compass, information on nearly every practical subject. It became extremely popular, and ran through twenty-four editions. To the fourth edition, 1695, are added some verses, and fourteen chapters written by Mather's son Samuel, a clever young man, who died at the age of twenty-two. The twelfth, eighteenth, and twenty-fourth editions received successively further additions and alterations.

Mather also wrote 'An Instrument from that Little Stone cut out of the Mountain without Hands, to break in pieces that great Image,' &c., 1694; and another pamphlet called 'A Novelty,' on women's preaching, and disapproving of the women's meetings for discipline, then just established in the society. He is also probably the author of 'A Brief Character of the Antient and Christian Quakers,' London, 1695.

About 1695 Mather began to be dissatisfied with quakerism. In 1700 he published a broadside with cut 'Of the Quakers despising the Holy Scriptures,' and an answer to Wyeth's 'Switch for the Snake.' In the following year he published 'A Vindication of William Mather and his Wife, who, having lived about forty years professed Quakers, have now renounced that persuasion and returned to the Communion of the Church of England.' In this he states that he had no personal quarrel with the quakers.

[Mather's published works; Smith's Catalogue.] C. F. S.

MATHETES, Welsh biblical scholar. [See Jones, John, 1821?-1878.]

MATHEW. [See also Matthew.]

MATHEW, THEOBALD (1790-1856), apostle of temperance, was the fourth son of James Mathew and his wife Anne, daughter of George Whyte of Cappawhyte, in co. Tipperary. The father acted as agent for his kinsman, the first Lord Llandaff, and resided at the family seat, Thomastown Castle, near Cashel, where Theobald was born on 10 Oct. 1790. The boy was deeply religious, and at an early age resolved to become a priest. He was first sent to the catholic academy at Kilkenny, then under Patrick Magrath, whence he passed in 1807 to the college of Maynooth. He left, after a short stay, to join the small convent of Franciscans of the capuchin order or grey friars in Dublin, and having passed through the usual noviciate was ordained by Archbishop Murray in 1841.

The Irish Franciscans had suffered heavily in the penal times, and the order in the beginning of the century was represented by a few priests scattered through the towns of catholic Ireland. The special mission of the followers of St. Francis is to minister to the needs of the poor in towns:

Bernardus valles, colles Benedictus amabat,
Oppida Franciscus.

Shortly after he was ordained, Father Mathew was sent to Cork to take charge of a small chapel known as the 'Little Friary.' The church was hidden away among narrow lanes, the congregation was small and very poor, there was no endowment, and the accommodation for the priest in charge was of the humblest description. The poverty of the city and surrounding country was deplorable. There was no poor law, and the charity of the well-to-do was constantly taxed to save the destitute from starvation. For the education of catholics there was no state aid, and individual effort accomplished little. Amidst so much that was discouraging the young priest set to work patiently and courageously. He soon won the confidence and affection of the people of Cork. His success as a preacher was remarkable. Though possessing few oratorical gifts, he was master of the art of pathetic exhortation. But his high character was the source of his chief influence. A resolute will and an impetuous temper were well held in subjection beneath his gentle and courteous manner.

Mathew opened a free school for boys, whom he taught himself, and it was soon crowded. He also established a school for poor girls, and induced many catholic ladies to assist him by taking classes. To deal with the wretchedness about him he formed a society on the plan of those of St. Vincent de Paul, of young men of respectable position, who visited the poor and distributed alms.

From the strife of politicians and religious controversialists Father Mathew personally kept aloof. He was fond of the saying, 'We should bear with each other as God bears with us all.' What was said of him at a later period was true during his whole career. 'He is almost the only man that I have met with in Ireland,' says Thackeray, in his 'Sketch Book,' 'who, speaking of public matters, did not talk as a partisan. It was impossible on hearing him to know, but from previous acquaintance with his character, whether he was whig, tory, catholic or protestant.' He lost no opportunity of setting an example of forbearance. Some deplorable quarrels had taken place at the graveside, from the claims of a few too zealous clergymen of the establishment to read the burial service at the funerals of catholics. The difficulty was promptly met by Father Mathew, who dedicated a cemetery to the use of all denominations. In the centre he raised a plain cross, beneath which he now lies. He commenced the building of a church for his order, which remained unfinished at his death. It was recently completed in honour of the centenary of his birth.

After labouring for nearly a quarter of a century in the southern city, inspiring universal confidence among his fellow citizens, he was appealed to by some of his nonconformist friends to place himself at the head of their temperance society. After a long interval of doubt he agreed, and on 10 April 1838 signed the pledge of total abstinence, using the characteristic words, 'Here goes—in the name of the Lord.'

The new doctrine was accepted with enthusiasm by his fellow countrymen. The people of the south flocked in thousands to Cork to become his disciples. The strange influence he exercised over others was regarded by devout catholics as a divine endowment.

He was invited to visit the principal cities

of Ireland, and even in the north he was received with respect, and with entire confidence in his sincerity and singleness of purpose. A marvellous reform was made in the habits of his disciples, who numbered, it was said, nearly half the adult population of Ireland. The duties on Irish spirits fell from 1,434,573*l.* in 1839 to 852,418*l.* in 1844. Statistics showed an extraordinary diminution in crime. The judges in their charges attributed the unusual peace of the country to temperance. At the summer assizes in Cork in 1844, and in the following spring assize, the calendar contained the name of one prisoner.

In 1843 Father Mathew came to London. His meetings, despite some opposition from roughs, were held successfully. Society offered its homage. He met the members of the administration, and was treated with great kindness by Sir Robert Peel. 'H. B.' (John Doyle [q. v.]) bore testimony to his popularity by one of his famous sketches, where the good friar appears administering the pledge to 'a rare batch' of all the leading people of the time.

Mrs. Carlyle, in a letter to her husband of 9 August 1843, thus describes one of the meetings she attended (Froude, *Letters and Memorials of Jane Welsh Carlyle*, i. 220-4): 'I found my youthful enthusiasm rise higher and higher as I got on the ground and saw the thousands of people all hushed into awful silence, with not a single exception that I saw—the only religious meeting I have ever seen in Cockneyland which had not plenty of scoffers at its heels. . . . Father Mathew took me to the front of the platform to see him give the pledge. From one to two hundred took it, and all the tragedies I have ever seen, melted into one, could not have given me such emotion as that scene did. There were faces of both men and women that will haunt me while I live; faces exhibiting such concentrated wretchedness, making, you would have said, its last deadly struggle with the powers of darkness. . . . When I went to bed I could not sleep; the faces I had seen haunted me, and Father Mathew's smile.' The pride and happiness of Irishmen at the change in the national ways were unbounded, and the hope of future prosperity for a people, 'sober, regenerate, and free,' was universal. But a great calamity was impending—the famine—a disaster destined to check the social regeneration of the people, to overwhelm the Old Ireland for which Father Mathew had laboured; and to bring into existence a new country which should know him only by tradition.

He saw early the misery that was coming, and bent all his energies to save the lives of the peasantry. His appeals for help to English and American friends were most generously met. The government was guided much by his advice, and after the second year of dearth few deaths were directly traceable to starvation, but meanwhile the loss of life had been appalling. In the midst of the labours which the famine brought upon him, the great honour of his life was offered him, He was named by the clergy of the diocese for the vacant bishopric of Cork. The choice was not ratified by the Vatican. He was perhaps considered in Rome to have erred from an excess of the love of his neighbour. A pension was granted to him in the same year by the kind interposition of Lord John Russell; this, together with a public subscription, relieved him of liabilities incurred in organising his temperance associations, and founding temperance clubs and libraries throughout the country.

In 1848 it became apparent that he was overworked. He disregarded symptoms which showed that rest was needed, and suffered from an attack of paralysis, and though he seemed to have speedily recovered, he was never restored to his former vigour. But his activity of mind and love of his work remained the same. He had had pressing invitations to follow his flying countrymen to America, and, against the anxious advice of his relatives and friends, he determined to go. He reached New York in July 1849, and was received by the mayor and citizens as their guest. He was invited to Washington, and by a resolution unanimously carried in congress he was admitted to a seat in the floor of the house. The same honour was paid him in the senate. He travelled to all the principal cities. He preached in the catholic churches to large congregations, and afterwards held his temperance meetings. His strength was failing, but he was sustained by the enthusiasm for doing good, which never left him to the end of his days. The memory of his labours in the United States is preserved in numerous societies called after his name.

A second illness, more severe than the first, compelled him to yield, and he was at length prevailed upon to come home. He returned to Ireland in 1851. During his short stay in Dublin on his way to Cork, he was received with much kindness by Archbishop Cullen, who informed him that it had been proposed in Rome to raise him to the rank of a bishop. But his health rendered the discharge of any active duties of the episcopacy impossible, and on this ground he was allowed to decline the honour. In Cork he was welcomed with all the old warmth, but he had become aged and enfeebled, and though willing as ever to labour, he was compelled gradually to relinquish all active employment. He passed the greater part of the following years with his brother Charles who lived near Cork, and to whom and to whose family he was most tenderly attached. He died at Queenstown on 8 Dec. 1856. The citizens of Cork erected to his memory a statue, which is one of the most successful works of his countryman Foley, and his centenary was celebrated in 1890 by the same community. Another statue, erected to his memory in Sackville or O'Connell Street, Dublin, was unveiled on 8 Feb. 1893. A portrait by E. D. Leahy is in the National Portrait Gallery, London.

Father Mathew was of middle height, well formed, and remarkably handsome. His complexion was pale, with hair dark and abundant, and eyes of the softest blue. His expression, somewhat stern and sombre in repose, was remarkable, when animated, for its gentleness and sweetness.

[A life by John Francis Maguire was published in 1863 (London, 8vo), 2nd edit. 1864 (New York, 1864). Other biographies are by James Birmingham (Dublin, 1840), by S. R. Wells (New York, 1867), and F. J. Mathew (London, 1890). A life in French by J. H. Olivier appeared at Bar-le-Duc, 1878, and one in Dutch by C. S. A. van Scheltema.] J. C. M.

MATHEWS. [See also MATTHEWS.]

MATHEWS, CHARLES (1776–1835), actor, the seventh son of James Mathews, bookseller and Wesleyan local preacher, and his wife Elizabeth, was born 28 June 1776 at 18 Strand, London, a house pulled down on the erection of Hungerford Bridge. The family name, Matthews, was changed by his grandfather, also a bookseller, on inheriting a small estate, subsequently lost. Mathews, who claimed when a child to have been dandled by Garrick, was sent first to St. Martin's free school, where he developed a taste for mimicry, and afterwards to Merchant Taylors'. At a French school near Bedford Street, Strand, kept by a Madame Cottrell, which he attended in the evening, he met Robert William Elliston [q. v.], to whose Pyrrhus, in a school representation of Philips's 'Distressed Mother,' he played Phœnix. Other parts in tragedy and comedy were essayed at private theatres. After an unsatisfactory interview with Charles Macklin [q. v.], then very old, he played as an amateur, at the Richmond Theatre, Richmond to the Richard III of his friend Litchfield, and Bowkett in the 'Son-in-Law,' while at Canterbury he appeared as Richmond and Old Doyley in 'Who's the Dupe?' He also played on a solitary occasion, at Sadler's Wells, David Dunder in 'Ways and Means.' He wrote for periodicals, contributing to the 'Ladies' Magazine,' and sub-editing the 'Thespian Magazine.' At the suggestion of Hitchcock, the historian of the Irish stage, who offered him an engagement from Daly, manager of the Theatre Royal, Dublin, he induced his father to cancel his indentures, and went to Dublin, arriving 3 June 1794. Daly failed to redeem Hitchcock's promises, and Mathews, after appearing on 19 June for the benefit of Mrs. Wells (afterwards Mrs. Sumbell) as Jacob in the 'Chapter of Accidents,' and Lingo in the 'Agreeable Surprise,' found himself compelled to remain, at a salary of a guinea a week, as a walking gentleman. As a musician, a dancer, and a mimic he made some impression in Dublin, Cork, and Limerick, but he fumed under the inferiority of the characters allotted to him, which included Paris in 'Romeo and Juliet,' the Sexton in 'Much Ado about Nothing,' Albany in 'Lear,' Guildenstern, and the like. In more than one character he was hissed. While at Limerick he had a narrow escape from drowning. Quitting Dublin with Montague Talbot, a tragedian, in September 1795, with the intention of retiring from the stage, he was driven by stress of weather to Swansea. Here he acted with sufficient success to be reconciled to the stage, and to remain in Wales two years, playing a round of comic characters. On 19 Sept. 1797, on a salary of twelve shillings a week, he married, at Swansea, Eliza Kirkham Strong, a teacher in a school.

Applications to Tate Wilkinson of the York circuit were ultimately successful, and Mathews joined his new manager at Pontefract. He was at this time very tall, so thin that his early friends addressed him as 'Stick,' and, as Wilkinson said, a hiss would blow him off the stage; he had a face set awry, which Wilkinson persisted in regarding as a consequence of paralysis. He appeared as Silky in the 'Road to Ruin' and his favourite part of Lingo, and visited York, Leeds, and other towns, making at first little headway. Wilkinson recommended him to quit the stage, declaring that nature had interposed an insurmountable barrier between him and comic excellence. Mathews persisted, refusing no part, however small, and was rewarded by becoming one of the most popular actors that ever appeared on the circuit. Through his travels he had won high social reputation. In 1801 Mathews lost his eldest brother, William, a barrister, who died of yellow fever at Tobago; he was seriously hurt by a portion of the Wakefield stage falling upon him, and on 25 May 1802 his wife, the author of a volume of poems and some unsuccessful novels, died of consumption. On 28 March 1803 Mathews married in York Anne Jackson, an actress, half-sister of Frances Maria Kelly [q. v.] Mrs. Mathews accompanied her husband to the Haymarket, where she played Emma in 'Peeping Tom,' 20 May 1803, and many other characters, and was, 1 July 1809, the original Fanny in 'Killing no Murder.' After some negotiations with George Colman the younger [q. v.], Mathews appeared at the Haymarket, 16 May 1803, as Jabal in 'The Jew' and as Lingo. His first original part was Old Wiggins in Allingham's farce, 'Mrs. Wiggins.' His first conspicuous triumph was obtained, 25 July, as Risk, a comic servant, in 'Love laughs at Locksmiths,' by Arthur Griffinhoofe, otherwise George Colman. He was, during the season, the original Dr. Cranium in Boaden's 'Maid of Bristol,' and played Tag in the 'Spoil'd Child,' Sadi in the 'Mountaineers,' Verdun in 'Lovers' Vows,' Tom in 'Peeping Tom,' Scout in the 'Village Lawyer,' Zekiel Homespun in the 'Heir-at-Law,' Ollapod in the 'Poor Gentleman,' Motley in 'Dead Alive,' Darby in the 'Poor Soldier,' Diggory in 'All the World's a Stage,' Sir Abel Handy in 'Speed the Plough,' Fluellen in 'King Henry V,' and many other parts. Croaker in the 'Good-natured Man' was the great part of the following season, in which also he was the original Triangle, a schoolmaster, in Thomas Dibdin's 'Guilty or Not Guilty.' After visiting Liverpool he appeared for the first time at Drury Lane, 18 Sept. 1804, as Don Manuel in 'She would and she would not.' He played here Sir Peter Teazle, Lissardo in the 'Wonder,' Thomas Appletree in the 'Recruiting Officer,' Weazle in the 'Wheel of Fortune,' &c., and was the original Lampedo in the 'Honeymoon.' His acting left the impression that he was unsuited to a large theatre. In the 'Village, or the World's Epitome'—Haymarket, 18 July 1805, an unprinted comedy by Cherry, acted but twice—Mathews played Timothy Anvil. This piece led to a scrimmage between Mathews and his manager, Elliston, followed by a newspaper controversy and a reconciliation. On 15 Aug. Mathews was Abrahamides in the 'Tailors,' on an occasion when the real tailors in the audience, indignant at the light in which they were presented, caused a riot. Early in the Haymarket season, on 12 June 1806, in 'Catch him who can,' by Theodore Hook, Mathews played Philip, a comic servant, who assumes many disguises. At Drury Lane meanwhile, he was the original Plod in Kenney's 'False Alarms,' 12 Jan. 1807, and played on the 28th in Miss Lee's ill-starred comedy, 'The Assignation.' He was also seen as Clown in the 'Winter's Tale,' Periwinkle in 'A bold Stroke for a Wife,' and Eunice in the 'Dramatist.' A great variety of characters followed at the Haymarket. Mathews was the original Flutterman in Kenney's 'Ella Rosenberg,' Drury Lane, 19 Nov. 1807. About this time he was disabled, while pigeon-shooting, by the bursting of a fowling-piece. In 'Plot and Counterplot, or the Portrait of Michael Cervantes,' by Charles Kemble, he was the original Hernandez, 30 June 1808, played Scapin in the 'Cheats of Scapin,' with additions, Clod in the 'Young Quaker,' and gave an imitation of 'Hippisley's Drunken Man.' He also, according to the 'Memoirs' by his wife, played Sir Fretful Plagiary, winning high praise from Leigh Hunt. After the destruction by fire of Drury Lane he accompanied the burnt-out actors to the Lyceum, where he played, 21 April 1809, as Joe Thresher in Leigh's 'Grieving is a Folly,' and repeated Sir Fretful Plagiary. As Buskin, an actor, in Hook's 'Killing no Murder,' Haymarket, 1 July 1809, he assumed once more a variety of characters, and was, with Liston, responsible for the success of a piece that Larpent, the reader of plays, had mutilated and sought to suppress. In this Mrs. Mathews played Miss Nancy. Old Rapid in 'A Cure for the Heartache' and Sir Anthony Absolute were among the parts he now assumed. During his country tours Mathews began, with the aid of his wife, the series of 'At Homes' by which he is best remembered. The first, called 'The Mail Coach, or Rambles in Yorkshire,' with songs by James Smith, was seen at Hull 12 April 1808. Like its successors, it consisted of recitations, songs, imitations, ventriloquy, &c., and was received with signal favour. At the Lyceum with the Drury Lane company, 4 Jan. 1810, he was Touchstone for the first time, on the 12th Gripe in the 'Confederacy,' and on the 23rd Mawworm in the 'Hypocrite.' In Pocock's farce, 'Hit or Miss,' 26 Feb., he made a great name as Dick Cypher, a member of the Four-in-Hand Club. He also played Lord Ogleby in the 'Clandestine Marriage.' Old Mirabel in the 'Inconstant' followed at the Haymarket, and he was the original Crastinus in Eyre's 'High Life in the City,' 25 July, and Artaxominous in 'Bombastes Furioso,' 7 Aug. With the Drury Lane company he was excellent, 19 Jan. 1811, as Mingle, an innkeeper, in Millingen's musical farce, 'The Beehive.' Sensible that he was not seen to advantage in a large theatre, he retired from the Drury Lane company at the close of the season, and was seen only once at the Haymarket, 16 Oct. Refusing offers from Elliston, he revisited, in company with Incledon at first and subsequently alone, Portsmouth, Liverpool, Dublin, York, and various other towns. Edinburgh, where he appeared 4 April 1812, received him with enthusiasm, and was counted by him 'an annuity for the future.' On 15 May he was again in London, residing at King's Road, Fulham, and reappearing at the Haymarket, playing Bob Acres, Jerry Sneak, Colonel Feignwell, &c., and augmenting his reputation as the original Somno, a servant, in the 'Sleepwalker' of Oulton, 15 June. On 12 Oct. he made, as Buskin, what was practically his first appearance at Covent Garden, and played, 20 Nov., his great original character of Flexible in Kenney's 'Love, Law, and Physic.'

He played Falstaff for the first time, 15 July 1814, at the Haymarket, a curious and not too successful experiment, which, however, was repeated at Covent Garden. A 'spill' from a tilbury, in which he was driving with Daniel Terry [q. v.], caused him trouble and pecuniary loss, and resulted in permanent lameness. His acting consisted more and more of imitations, and he even played Macheath in imitation of Incledon. His entertainment, 'Mail Coach Adventures,' was given at Covent Garden for his benefit, and followed by imitations of many leading actors. The 'Actor of all Work' of George Colman, Haymarket, 13 Aug. 1817, was written expressly to show Mathews as Multiple in successive assumptions. In the winter of 1817–18 he accompanied Frederick Yates [q. v.] to France. This journey formed the subject of his second 'At Home,' written by James Smith [q. v.] and John Poole [q. v.], and entitled 'The Trip to Paris.' It was given 8 March 1819 at the Theatre Royal English Opera House, otherwise the Lyceum. The old Scotch lady which it introduced was one of his most popular creations. During this season Mathews removed to his well-known residence, Ivy Cottage, Kentish Town, the lease of which he had bought. Here his son, Charles James Mathews [q. v.], built for him a gallery, to which he transferred the collection of pictures now the property of the Garrick Club and of books. From this time forward most years witnessed the production of a new 'At Home,' the intermediate periods being spent in fulfilling country engagements. 'Country Cousins,' 1820, 'Adventures in Air, Earth, and Water,' 1821. 'The Youthful Days of Mr. Mathews,' 1822, followed each other at the Lyceum. Among his friends at this period were Coleridge and Charles and Mary Lamb. In August 1822 Mathews started for New York, where he arrived 5 Sept., making his first appearance in Baltimore, 23 Sept., in his 'Trip to Paris.' He subsequently played in the regular drama Lord Duberly in the 'Heir-at-Law,' Solomon Gundy in 'Who Wants a Guinea?' Goldfinch in the 'Road to Ruin,' &c. As Goldfinch and Monsieur Tonson he appeared in New York. His artistic and social successes were equal, though he was more popular as an actor than as an entertainer; and he wrote jubilantly to his wife concerning his triumphs. After playing in Philadelphia and other towns he returned to New York, and was sufficiently ill-advised to play Othello. This representation was given once more at Liverpool, where he arrived in June 1823. A little later he appeared at the Lyceum in comedy, playing Monsieur Tonson, Caleb Quotem, &c., and in one of the 'monodramatic' pieces in which he was successful, 'The Polly Packet.' The 'Trip to America' was the subject of his next entertainment, Lyceum, 25 March 1824. In this he imitated various types of Americans, black and white, causing some little irritation in the United States, from which he afterwards suffered. 'Mr. Mathews's Memorandum-Book' followed in 1825, 'Mr. Mathews's Invitations' in 1826, and 'Home Circuit, or London Gleanings,' in 1827. On 31 Dec. 1827 he reappeared at Drury Lane as Sir Fretful Plagiary in the 'Critic' and Buskin in 'Killing no Murder.' During the following season he entered conjointly with Yates on the management of the Adelphi, which opened 29 Sept. 1828 with Beazeley's 'Wanted a Partner,' an occasional piece, in which Mathews personated various would-be partners with Yates in management. As Caleb Pipkin in Buckstone's 'May Queen' he sang a song composed by his son, C. J. Mathews. He was still at the height of his reputation, but his health was failing, and he was extremely irritable. At the Adelphi he recommenced in 1829 his 'At Homes,' which he delivered often, but not always, in conjunction with Yates. In the autumn of 1829 the two actors played in Paris, where Mathews was much praised and likened to Potier, an eminent comedian. In 1833, as the result of unwise speculations, he found himself compelled to resign his cottage in Kentish Town, and became anxious to dispose of his pictures, nearly four hundred in number. An effort to sell them to the Garrick Club failed at the time, and an exhibition of them at the Queen's Bazaar in Oxford Street was unremunerative. In 1836, however, they were purchased by the Garrick

Club through the generosity of a member, John Rowland Durrant.

At 101 Great Russell Street, to which Mathews now removed, he began in earnest an autobiography, previously attempted and ultimately abandoned. In 1834 he was again in New York, where he appeared in his entertainment 'A Trip to America.' A riot was anticipated, but was avoided, and damages were obtained in a suit against the 'Philadelphia Gazette,' which attacked and libelled him. Owing to a failure of voice his performances were few, and he arrived in Liverpool 10 March 1835. Illness now afflicted him, and he was with some difficulty carried to Plymouth, where in lodgings in Cocker Street he died on the morning of his fifty-ninth birthday, 28 June 1835. His body was interred in a vault in St. Andrew's Church, Plymouth. Mrs. Mathews, who had retired from the stage in 1810, survived her husband, whose 'Memoirs' she edited, and wrote 'Anecdotes of Actors, with other Desultory Recollections, &c.,' 8vo, 1844, and 'Tea-Table Talk, Ennobled Actresses, and other Miscellanies,' 2 vols. 8vo, 1857. She died, 12 Oct. 1869, at Chelsea Villa, Fulham.

Without rising into the highest rank as an actor, Mathews was in his way inimitable. He had genuine power as a comedian, and as a mimic he had no equal. He would take upon himself characters such as Coleridge or Curran, and wear for an hour not only the manner but apparently the intellectual gait of the man, and this with no apparent opportunity of preparation. To this gift Lord Byron bears testimony.

So great was his power in this direction that judges, statesmen, councillors feared and mistrusted him. Unlike his great predecessor, Samuel Foote [q. v.], he did 'his spiriting gently,' and even at royal bidding declined to imitate afresh those whose feelings had been hurt. Exclusive of his assumptions in his 'At Homes,' he must have played near four hundred different parts, many of them original. A nervous, irritable man, he shrank honestly from observation, and was silent in the presence of those he did not esteem. Affectionate and loyal in disposition, fond of home and yet not averse from congenial company, expensive in tastes, improvident, generous, and easily beguiled, he was a type of the actor of popular acceptation. Leigh Hunt, who calls him a man of genius in his way, praises his moderation, but charges him with restlessness, and says his principal excellence is as 'officious valets and humorous old men.' His Sir Fretful Plagiary Hunt regards as perfect. Mathews had the power of losing in the characters he took almost all trace of his own individuality, and could even disguise his voice. His Lying Valet, Risk in 'Love laughs at Locksmiths,' Don Manuel in 'She would and she would not,' and Old Philpot in the 'Citizen' are a few among many parts in which he won warmest commendation.

Horace Smith says: 'There was but one Charles Mathews in the world—there never can be such another! Mimics, buffoons, jesters, wags, and even admirable comedians we shall never want; but what are the best of them compared to him?' In the Mathews collection now in the Garrick Club are numerous portraits, among which may be signalled portraits by De Wilde as Sir Fretful Plagiary, Somno in 'The Sleepwalker,' as Matthew Daw in 'The School for Friends,' and as Buskin in 'Killing no Murder;' and by Harlowe in four different characters. Clint shows him as Flexible in a scene from 'Love, Law, and Physic,' introducing also Liston, Blanchard, and Emery. Very many portraits of Mathews, principally in character, appear in his wife's 'Memoirs' of him. Paintings of him and of his wife by Masquerier belonged to the Baroness Burdett Coutts, and two portraits of Mrs. Mathews are also in the Garrick Club. Many of Mathews's 'At Homes' have been published, and are valued for the illustrations.

[The chief authority for the life of Mathews consists of the Memoirs by his wife, 4 vols. 8vo, 1839, some dates in which may be corrected by Genest's Account of the English Stage. A continuation of the Memoirs of Charles Mathews, 2 vols. 8vo, was issued in Philadelphia in 1839, and is almost unknown in England. The early portions of the Memoirs are by Mathews himself. Wightwick contributed in 1833 'Recollections of Charles Mathews' to Fraser's Magazine. A full account of his entertainments is given in 'The Manager's Note-book,' which appeared in Bentley's Miscellany; and single entertainments are described in the New Monthly Magazine and many other periodicals. Biographies appear in the Georgian Era, Oxberry's Dramatic Biography, vol. v., and Thespian Dictionary. See also Peake's Colman, Dunlap's Cooke, Bernard's Recollections, &c., Barham's Hook, the Life of C. M. Young, by Julian Young, Records of a Veteran, &c., Dibdin's Edinburgh Stage, and Lowe's Bibliographical Account of English Theatrical Literature.]

J. K.

MATHEWS, CHARLES JAMES (1803–1878), actor and dramatist, son of Charles Mathews [q. v.], was born in Basnett Street, Liverpool, on 26 Dec. 1803, and christened at St. Helen's Church, York. After attending preliminary schools at Hackney and Fulham, he went to Merchant Taylors', where he boarded with the Rev. Thomas Cherry, the head-master, who is said to have taken a strong dislike to him. Mathews was then removed to a private school in the Clapham Road, kept by Richardson the lexicographer, where he formed friendships with John Mitchell Kemble and Julian Young, and was one of Richardson's assistants in copying extracts for the dictionary. On 4 May 1819 he was articled to Augustus Pugin [q. v.] as an architect, and designed the picture gallery for his father's cottage in Kentish Town, where he subsequently met Byron, Scott, Moore, Coleridge, Colman, Lamb, Leigh Hunt, the Smiths, Campbell, and other men of eminence. In company with his master he visited York, Oxford, and various country towns, executing sketches, some of which were inserted in architectural works.

A visit with Pugin to Paris, in which he saw the principal French comedians, fostered a lurking disposition towards the stage, and he made after his return his first appearance as an amateur at the Lyceum Theatre on 26 April 1822, playing, under the name of M. Perlet, Dorival, a comedian in 'Le Comédien d'Etampes,' a French piece subsequently adapted by him under the title of 'He would be an Actor,' singing a song as M. Emile of the Porte Saint-Martin Theatre, and acting in his own name as Werther in the 'Sorrows of Werther,' by John Poole, in which his mother took the part of Charlotte. His imitations of French actors were received with much favour. His father urged him to adopt the stage, but he liked his profession. Refusing a renewed invitation to join John Nash [q. v.], the architect, he went over in 1823 to Ireland, when his articles had expired, for the purpose of building for Lord Blessington a house at Mountjoy Forest, co. Tyrone. Very little progress, or none at all, was made with the scheme. Mathews stayed hunting, shooting, fishing, &c., and discussing details of the house, never to be built, and then accepted an invitation from his patron to accompany him to Italy. In Naples he stayed a year at the Palazzo Belvedere, the party including his host and hostess, Miss Power, the sister of Lady Blessington, and Count D'Orsay, with whom he had a misunderstanding almost leading to a duel. His imitations of Italian life and manners were the delight of a fashionable world, English and foreign. Madden, in his 'Life of Blessington,' describes him at the period as an admirable sketcher and a close student of his profession, 'full of humour, vivacity, and drollery, but gentlemanlike withal, marvellously mercurial, always in motion,' but steady and well conducted.

After a couple of years spent in Wales as architect to a Welsh iron and coal company at Coed Talwn, North Wales, where he built Hartsheath Hall, an inn, a bridge, and some cottages, he entered the employ of Nash, but kept on an office in Parliament Street as a practising architect. His leisure time he occupied in writing songs and trifling pieces for the theatre. Among the latter were 'Pongwong,' 'Pyramus and Thisbe,' 'Truth,' 'My Wife's Mother,' 'The Wolf and the Lamb,' and 'The Court Jesters.' On 30 April 1827, in company with D'Egville, he started once more, on an allowance from his father, for Italy. Milan and Venice were visited, and in the former city the travellers, who exhibited some paintings, were admitted members of the academy. From Trieste they proceeded to Florence, where Mathews caught the small-pox. At the Palazzo San Clementi Lord Normanby had erected a private theatre, in which Mathews played comic characters, such as Peter in 'Romeo and Juliet,' Launcelot Gobbo, and Falstaff in the 'First Part of King Henry IV.' From Rome, where Mathews suffered much from malaria, they returned to Venice, and at the close of 1830 Mathews arrived home on crutches. Five years of a desultory life, spent in visiting at the houses of noblemen and the like, followed, and included his acceptance of the post of district surveyor at Bow.

His father's failure put an end to this idle career, and on 28 Sept. 1835 he turned his theatrical abilities to account, and, in conjunction with Yates, opened the Adelphi Theatre. The first piece was 'Mandrin,' an adaptation by Mathews of a well-known French melodrama. The speculation failed, and Mathews retired from management. On 6 Nov. 1835 he appeared at the Olympic in his own piece, the 'Humpbacked Lover,' in which he played George Rattleton, and in a farce by Leman Rede, called 'The Old and Young Stagers,' Liston, who recited a prologue, being the old stager, and Mathews the young. His performance was fashionable, though his success was not triumphant.

On 18 July 1838, at Kensington Church, he married his manager, Madame Vestris [see Mathews, Lucia Elizabeth]. A visit to America which followed was unsuccessful. Mathews then reappeared at the Olympic in 'Patter *versus* Clatter,' to the end a favourite piece. On 30 Sept. 1839 Mathews and his wife opened Covent Garden with an elaborate revival of 'Love's Labour's Lost,' the company including Robert Keeley, Bartley, Meadows, Anderson, Mrs. Nisbett, and Mrs. Humby. This was a failure. 'Love' by Sheridan Knowles followed, introducing Miss Ellen Tree, with little better result, and Mathews found himself involved in debts from which he was unable to free himself. The 'Beggar's Opera,' with Harrison as Macheath and Madame Vestris as Lucy Lockett, was more successful, and the 'Merry Wives of Windsor,' with Mathews as Slender and Mrs. Nisbett and Madame Vestris as the wives, proved a draw. During the period in which he held possession of Covent Garden he produced over a hundred plays, operas, interludes, farces, melodramas, and pantomimes, including 'Hamlet,' 'Romeo and Juliet,' the 'School for Scandal,' 'A Midsummer-Night's Dream,' given seventy times, the 'Rivals,' 'Twelfth Night,' an alteration of the 'Spanish Curate,' &c. Among the novelties were Leigh Hunt's 'Legend of Florence,' 7 Feb. 1840, given thirteen times; the 'Baronet,' a comedy by Haynes Bayly, hissed from the stage; the 'Bride of Messina,' subsequently known as 'John of Procida,' by Sheridan Knowles, 19 Sept. 1840; the 'Greek Boy,' a musical afterpiece by Samuel Lover [q. v.]; the 'White Milliner;' Boucicault's 'London Assurance,' in which Mathews played Dazzle; 'Old Maids,' by Sheridan Knowles, a failure; and several farces, some of them, as 'You can't marry your Grandmother,' 'He would be an Actor,' &c., his own works. Charles Kemble accepted an engagement and reappeared. On 2 Nov. 1841 Adelaide Kemble appeared as Norma, with a success that drew on Mathews the attention of the proprietors of Covent Garden, who pressed him for arrears of rent, and so sealed his ruin. His management finished on 30 April 1842. An arrest for debt followed, and Mathews was lodged in the Queen's Bench, whence, after an act of bankruptcy, he was released, under conditions with regard to his creditors that deprived him of all chance of shaking off the burden. A flight to Paris was followed by a fresh bankruptcy.

In October 1842 Mathews and his wife were engaged for Drury Lane by Macready, but they soon quarrelled with him, and transferred their services to the Haymarket. There they appeared 14 Nov. 1842, respectively as Charles Surface and Lady Teazle. On 29 Aug. 1843 Mathews made a great hit as Giles in Planché's 'Who's your Friend?' and 6 Feb. 1844 a still greater success as Sir Charles Coldstream in 'Used up.' On 22 Feb. 1843 Mathews, with his wife, made his first appearance in Edinburgh, playing Mr. Charles Swiftly in 'One Hour' and in 'Patter *versus* Clatter.' After performing at the Surrey and at the Princess's, and in various country towns, Mathews opened the Lyceum 18 Oct. 1847 with the 'Light Dragoons,' the 'Two Queens,' and the 'Pride of the Market,' the company including Harley, Buckstone, Leigh Murray, Charles Selby, and Mrs. Stirling. For seven years the theatre was remuneratively conducted, without enabling Mathews to get free from debt, and a whip upon the part of some friends and a 'bumper' public benefit followed unavailingly a new bankruptcy. Management was resigned, and Mathews, after playing in the country, was lodged for a month, beginning 4 July 1856, as a common prisoner in Lancaster Castle.

On 8 Aug. following his wife died, and Mathews, a year later, after playing at Drury Lane, where he was acting-manager, revisited America, where he met and married his second wife, who survived him, Mrs. (Lizzie) Davenport, an actress at Burton's Theatre, New York. He played sixty nights at Burton's Theatre. In October 1858, with his wife as Lady Gay Spanker, he reappeared at the Haymarket as Dazzle in 'London Assurance.' He played a round of his favourite characters, including, for the first time, Paul Pry and Goldfinch in the 'Road to Ruin.' In 1860–1 he was again at Drury Lane, where he played Will Wander in a wild melodrama adapted by himself, and called 'The Savannah,' and on 25 Nov. 1861 appeared with his wife at the concert-room (then called the Bijou Theatre) in Her Majesty's Theatre in an entertainment called 'Mr. and Mrs. Mathews at Home,' illustrated by pictures by John O'Connor, from sketches by Mathews. 'My Wife and I,' and a burlesque by H. J. Byron, the 'Sensation Fork, or the Maiden, the Maniac, and the Midnight Murderers,' were also given. In 1863 he was again at the Haymarket, and the same year played in Paris, at the Théâtre des Variétés, in 'Un Anglais Timide,' a French version of 'Cool as a Cucumber.' This experiment was repeated in the autumn of 1865, when, at the Vaudeville, he played in 'L'Homme Blasé' ('Used up'). Both engagements were successful, but were not renewed, though Mathews in July 1867 played 'Un Anglais Timide' at the St. James's, for the benefit of Ravel, and gave 'Cool as a Cucumber' the same night at the Olympic. Between these performances Mathews had acted at the St. James's in 'Woodcock's Little Game' and in 'Adventures of a Love-Letter,' his own adaptation of M. Sardou's 'Pattes de Mouche.' A scheme for a journey round the world led to a benefit at Covent Garden, 4 Jan. 1870, in which, in scenes from various plays, the principal actors of the day took part, and a dinner at Willis's Rooms on the 10th, over which Mathews, contrary to custom, presided. Mathews himself played, on the 4th, his favourite character of Puff in the second act of the 'Critic,' Mrs. Mathews appearing as Tilburina.

On 9 April 1870 he made his first appearance at the Theatre Royal, Melbourne, in 'Patter *versus* Clatter' and 'Married for Money.' Various parts were played, and Ballarat, Sydney, and Adelaide were visited, the Australian trip ending 31 Jan. 1871, when he set sail for Auckland. He gave there a performance of 'Used up' and 'Cool as a Cucumber' at 11 A.M. on 7 Feb., and sailed three hours later for Honolulu, where he acted for one night. On the 12th he arrived at San Francisco, where he performed, then proceeded to New York, and fulfilled a six weeks' engagement. A tour in the United States and Canada followed, and on 1 June 1872 he took, at Wallack's Theatre, New York, as Sir Simon Simple in H. J. Byron's 'Not such a Fool as he looks,' his farewell of America. On 7 Oct. 1872 he appeared at the Gaiety Theatre, London, in 'A Curious Case' and the 'Critic.' A second engagement at the same house began 26 May 1873, and a third, 29 Sept. of the same year. In 1874 he was again at the Gaiety, and 13 Sept. 1875 produced there his own adaptation, 'My Awful Dad' ('Un Père Prodigue'). This was his last new part. The periods between these performances had been spent in the country. In November 1875 he went to India, and played at Calcutta before the Prince of Wales. In 1876 he was again at the Gaiety, and in 1877 at the Opera Comique, where, in the 'Liar' and the 'Cosy Couple,' he reappeared 2 June 1877. In 1878 he started on a country tour with a company under the management of Miss Sarah Thorne. On 8 June he made his last appearance, playing at Stalybridge in 'My Awful Dad.' He died 24 June, at the Queen's Hotel in Manchester. His body was removed to 59 Belgrave Road, S.W., his last London residence, and was on the 29th buried in Kensal Green cemetery.

Mathews played some 240 characters, very many of them in his own pieces. His most conspicuous successes were obtained in light comedy and farce. Passion and pathos seemed wholly alien from his nature, and even on those occasions when he obtained the most flattering homage an actor can receive he found himself compelled to speak words of gratitude, he remained 'cool as a cucumber,' conveying sometimes the idea that the seriousness of those around him perplexed as much as it pleased him. The motto of the dial was held to apply to him in acting—'Horas non numero nisi serenas.' He was, within limits, an admirable comedian. In his early days he was a model of grace, brightness, and elegance. George H. Lewes tells how the youth of the day were wont to worship him, and says of his Affable Hawk that its artistic merit was so great 'that it almost became an offence against morality, by investing a swindler with irresistible charms, and making the very audacity of deceit a source of pleasurable sympathy.' Lewes saw M. Got in the same part, and says that he prefers Mathews. Lewes owns, however, that Mathews was 'utterly powerless in the manifestation of all the powerful emotions: rage, scorn, pathos, dignity, vindictiveness, tenderness, and wild mirth are all beyond his means. He cannot even laugh with animal heartiness. He sparkles; he never explodes.' Mathews had, however, airiness, finesse, aplomb, and, in spite of an occasional tendency to jauntiness, repose and good breeding, which are rare on the English stage, and he had powers of observation and gifts of mimicry. His popularity was indescribable, and at times embarrassing. His frequent imprisonment and the class of parts he played gained him a character he did not wholly deserve of 'a gay dog.' He was not at all the reckless character popularly supposed, was the least possible of a *gourmet*, and was a little shy in the presence of strangers. His greatest parts were Sir Charles Coldstream in 'Used up,' Affable Hawk in 'A Game of Speculation,' Lavater, the hero of 'Cool as a Cucumber,' Puff in the 'Critic,' and the Chorus in Planché's 'Golden Fleece.'

Of Mathews's plays, mostly adaptations, no full catalogue seems to be in existence. A list of his own pieces and of those in which he had appeared was contributed to the 'London Figaro,' whence it was, with additions, transferred as an appendix to Mr. Dickens's 'Life of Mathews.' Such of the plays as are printed are included in Lacy's 'Acting Edition' and the collections of Cumberland, Webster, &c. The British Museum collection is meagre. In the 'Chain of Events,' a drama in eight acts, Mathews collaborated with Slingsby Lawrence (Lewes, *Actors*). With the exception of this piece and the 'Savannah,' a four-act melodrama, in which he was seen at Drury Lane, his plays were generally in three acts or less. His three-act pieces included 'Black Domino,' 'Dead for a Ducat,' 'Married for Money,' 'Milliner to the King,' 'Match for a King,' and 'Soft Sex.' In two acts are 'Aggravating Sam,' 'Bachelor of Arts,' 'Carlo,' 'Court Jester,' 'Impudent Puppy,' 'Kill him again,' 'My Awful Dad,' 'My Wife's Mother,' 'Pong-wong,' 'Serve him Right,' 'Striking Likeness,' 'Take that Girl away,' 'Who killed

Cock Robin?' In one act he wrote 'Cousin German,' 'Cherry and Blue,' 'Dowager,' 'He would be an Actor,' 'Humpbacked Lover,' 'His Excellency,' 'Little Toddlekins,' 'Mathews & Co.,' 'Methinks I see my Father,' 'My Mother's Maid,' 'My Usual Luck,' 'Nothing to Wear,' 'Patter *v.* Clatter,' 'Paul Pry Married and Settled,' 'Pyramus and Thisbe,' 'Ringdoves,' 'Too Kind by Half,' 'Two in the Morning,' 'Wolf and the Lamb,' 'Why did you Die?' 'You're Another.' Many of these are trifles, intended to serve a temporary purpose, and more than one is now forgotten. Into all the pieces in which he played he put sometimes so much that it is difficult to say where he is to be credited with collaboration. He translated 'Cool as a Cucumber' into French as 'Un Anglais Timide,' Paris, 1864, 12mo. One or two of his pieces were translated into German. He also wrote a 'Lettre aux Auteurs Dramatiques de la France,' London, 1852. A translation of this was published the same year. The burlesques which were a feature in the Lyceum management are dealt with in the biography of his wife. A complete gallery of brilliant sketches of Mathews in various characters is exhibited in the Garrick Club. The costumes are innumerable, but it is not especially difficult to trace the same man under each disguise.

[The Life of Charles James Mathews, chiefly autobiographical, with selections from his correspondence and letters, edited by Charles Dickens, 2 vols. 1879, is the principal authority. His early life is depicted in the Memoirs of Charles Mathews by Anne Mathews. Personal information, backed up by files of the Literary Gazette, the Athenæum, and the Sunday Times, has been used. See also Mr. Clark Russell's Representative Actors, G. H. Lewes's Actors and Acting, the New Monthly Magazine, and Dibdin's Edinburgh Stage.] J. K.

MATHEWS, LUCIA ELIZABETH or **ELIZABETTA**, also known as Madame Vestris (1797–1856), actress, the daughter of Gaetano Stefano Bartolozzi [q. v.] and his wife, Theresa Jansen, daughter of a dancing-master of Aix-la-Chapelle, was born in January 1797 at 72 Dean Street, Soho, London, or, according to another and improbable account, in Naples. She received rudimentary education at Manor Hall, Fulham Road, and learned music with Dr. Jay and Domenico Corri [q. v.] She married, 28 Jan. 1813, at St. Martin's Church, Auguste Armand Vestris (*d.* 1825), a dancer and ballet-master at the King's Theatre, the witnesses being Gaetano Bartolozzi, Lucy Elizabeth Tomkins, and Cecilia Voilet. Possessor of 'one of the most luscious of low voices,' great sprightliness and vivacity, a beautiful face, and 'an almost faultless figure,' she took at first to Italian opera, making her appearance, 20 July 1815, at the King's Theatre, as Proserpina in Peter Winter's 'Il Ratto di Proserpina.' Her success was immediate; she was said to possess a perfect contralto voice, a correct harmonious expression, to appear about eighteen, and to have 'a countenance expressive rather of modest loveliness than of any very marked passion' (*Theatrical Inquisitor and Monthly Mirror*, vii. 57). Her training was, however, deficient, and her voice needed cultivation. The following year she reappeared as Proserpina, and played in Winter's 'Zaira,' 17 Feb. 1816, Martini's 'Cosa Rara,' Mozart's 'Così fan tutte,' and Susanna in his 'Nozze di Figaro.' In the winter she acted at the Italian Opera, Paris, at the Théâtre Français, where she enacted Camille to the Horace of Talma, and at other theatres. Her husband, who had been arrested for debt and cleared himself by bankruptcy, and who had full occasion to doubt her fidelity, deserted her while in Paris, and was never reunited to her. Her first appearance on the English stage (non-Italian) was made at Drury Lane, 19 Feb. 1820, as Lilla, a part created by Signora Storache, in Cobb's 'Siege of Belgrade.' On 25 March, for one night only, she was Caroline in Prince Hoare's 'Prize;' on 5 April Artaxerxes in the opera of that name, translated from Metastasio; on 18 May as Adela in Cobb's 'Haunted Tower;' and on 30 May caught the town as Don Giovanni in Moncrieff's 'Giovanni in London,' transferred by Elliston from the Olympic. On 4 Nov. she played Macheath in the 'Beggar's Opera,' and 28 Nov. was the original Monsel in 'Justice, or the Caliph and the Cobler.' Little Pickle in the 'Spoil'd Child,' Rose Sydney in 'Secrets worth knowing,' Edmund in the 'Blind Boy,' and Effie Deans in the 'Heart of Midlothian' were among the parts taken in this second season. On 19 June 1821 she played Macheath at Covent Garden, apparently for one occasion only. At Drury Lane, 22 Dec., she was Giovanni in 'Giovanni in Ireland,' an unsuccessful attempt to obtain an aftermath of the success of 'Giovanni in London.' During the season she played in a version of Scott's 'Pirate,' was Paul in 'Paul and Virginia,' the original Bell in Knight's opera 'The Veteran, or the Farmer's Sons,' 23 Feb. 1822, Betty Blackberry in the 'Farmer,' and Nell in the 'Devil to Pay.' In the summer she was at the Haymarket, where she was the original Lisette in a musical farce called 'Love Letters,' 24 June 1822, and played Patrick, the hero of O'Keeffe's 'Poor Soldier.'

At Drury Lane, Covent Garden, or the Haymarket, with an occasional appearance in Italian opera, she played many comic and some serious parts, among which may be noted Ophelia and Mrs. Oakley. She was at Drury Lane, 19 Dec. 1822, the original Herman in Dimond's 'Tale of Other Times,' played Florella in 'My Grandmother,' Maria in 'A Roland for an Oliver,' Annette in the 'Lord of the Manor,' Letitia Hardy in the 'Belle's Stratagem,' was at Drury Lane, 13 Jan. 1824, the original Pauline in Beazley's opera 'Philandering, or the Rose Queen,' was Ariel to Macready's Prospero, Luciana in the 'Comedy of Errors,' Lydia Languish, Rosalind, Lady Teazle, Mrs. Ford and also Mrs. Page in the 'Merry Wives of Windsor,' Carlos in the 'Duenna,' Hypolita in 'She would and she would not,' Diana Vernon, and Cherubino in the 'Marriage of Figaro.' Her original parts also included Phœbe in 'Paul Pry,' Haymarket, 13 Sept. 1825; Georgette Clairville in ''Twas I,' Covent Garden, 3 Dec. 1825; Fatima, a character introduced by Planché into his adaptation of 'Oberon,' Covent Garden, 12 April 1826; Madame Germance in Pocock's 'Home, Sweet Home,' Covent Garden, 19 March 1829; and Kate O'Brien in Haynes Bayly's 'Perfection, or the Lady of Munster,' Drury Lane, 25 March 1830. In 1825 she sang 'Cherry Ripe' at Vauxhall. On 8 June 1826, at Covent Garden, she performed Macheath, positively, as was announced, 'for the last time.' On 29 March 1828 she, however, repeated it. She played frequently in Ireland and at Liverpool, Manchester, Birmingham, and other places. Genest, who saw her in Bath in 1827–8, says that she did herself no credit by her Hypolita, and was not qualified to play first-rate characters, but was 'one of the best singing actresses that ever appeared.' Her singing in songs such as 'Cherry Ripe,' 'Meet me by moonlight alone,' 'I've been roaming,' 'The Light Guitar,' 'Rise, gentle Moon,' 'Buy a Broom,' &c., delighted town and country, as did her performances in 'breeches' parts, Don Giovanni, Macheath, Cherubino.

On 3 Jan. 1831, Mme. Vestris—according to a prologue by John Hamilton Reynolds, delivered on the occasion, the first female lessee the stage had known—opened the Olympic in partnership with Maria Foote [q. v.], who soon, however, seceded from management. Her opening programme consisted of 'Mary Queen of Scots,' with Miss Foote as the queen; the 'Little Jockey,' also for Miss Foote; 'Clarissa Harlowe,' a burletta, introducing Mrs. Glover; and 'Olympic Revels,' by Planché and Dance, the first of a series of extravaganzas in which Mme. Vestris obtained her greatest triumphs. The mounting and decoration of these were superintended by her and were regarded as models of taste. In 'Olympic Revels' Mme. Vestris made a hit as Pandora, raising the theatre to the height of popularity. Following this came 'Olympic Devils,' 26 Dec. 1831, in which she was Orpheus; the 'Paphian Bower, or Venus and Adonis,' 26 Dec. 1832, in which she was Venus; 'High, Low, Jack, and Game,' 30 Sept. 1833, with Mme. Vestris as Queen of Hearts; the 'Deep, Deep Sea, or Perseus and Andromeda,' in which she was Perseus. She played Calypso in 'Telemachus, or the Island of Calypso,' 26 Dec. 1834; Princess Esmeralda in 'Riquet with the Tuft,' 26 Dec. 1836; Ralph in 'Puss in Boots,' 26 Dec. 1837; and Praise in the 'Drama's Levée,' 16 April 1838. She had meanwhile gathered for the performance of comedy and burlesque a company including Mrs. Orger, Mrs. Humby, Miss Murray, Keeley, Farren, Bland, and Liston, and, after a few years, her future husband [see MATHEWS, CHARLES JAMES], who made his début, 7 Dec. 1835, under her management. After her marriage she started with him for America, received ungenerous treatment, and returned poorer than she went, to reappear at the Olympic as Fleurette in 'Blue Beard,' 1 Jan. 1839. She took her farewell of the Olympic 31 May 1839, and aided her husband in his management of Covent Garden, beginning 30 Sept. 1839. Here she played many musical parts in operas, 'Artaxerxes,' 'Comus,' the 'Marriage of Figaro,' in which she was Cherubino, &c.; played in 'Love's Labour's Lost,' Oberon in 'A Midsummer-Night's Dream,' and was Lucy Lockit in the 'Beggar's Opera.' Her original parts included Catherine in Sheridan Knowles's 'Love,' 1839, Lady Anne in the same writer's 'Old Maids,' 1841, and Grace Harkaway in Boucicault's 'London Assurance,' 4 March 1841. She also produced some of Planché's burlesques: 'The Sleeping Beauty in the Wood,' 20 April 1840, in which she was the Princess Is-a-belle; 'Beauty and the Beast,' 12 April 1841, in which she was Beauty; and the 'White Cat,' 28 March 1842. She was unable, however, to fight against the burden of debt to which Mathews succumbed. At the Haymarket, where, after having played with Macready at Drury Lane, she accepted an engagement under Webster, she was Medea in Planché's 'Golden Fleece,' 24 March 1845, and Suivanta in his 'Golden Branch,' 27 Dec. 1847. She then went with her husband to the Princess's, where she appeared in March 1846, and then undertook the management of the Lyceum, opening in October 1847 with the 'Pride of the Market.' Charles Mathews played his familiar parts, and Mrs. Mathews produced the best remembered of Planché's burlesques. A company including the Leigh Murrays, Selby, Harley, Meadows, Buckstone, Mrs. Fitzwilliam, and Mrs. Stirling, made the house one of the most fashionable in London. William Beverley painted the scenery, and what was long known as the transformation scene was introduced. In April 1848 she played Theseus to the Dædalus of Mathews in Planché's 'Theseus and Ariadne;' on 26 Dec. 1848 was Argus the Brilliant-eyed in his 'King of the Peacocks;' on 9 April 1849 produced the 'Seven Champions of Christendom;' on 26 Dec. 1849 the 'Island of Jewels;' on 1 April 1850 'Cymon and Iphigenia;' on 26 Dec. 1850 was King Charming the First in 'King Charming;' on 21 April 1851 produced the 'Queen of the Frogs;' on 26 Dec. 1851 the 'Prince of Happy Land' ('La Biche au Bois'); on 27 Dec. 1852 was Dame Goldenhead in the 'Good Woman in the Wood;' and 26 Dec. 1853 was Queen Dominantia in 'Once upon a time there were two Kings.'

Her last appearance was for her husband's benefit at the Lyceum, 26 July 1854, in 'Sunshine through Clouds,' an adaptation of 'La Joie fait Peur' of Madame de Girardin. She died, after a long and painful illness, 8 Aug. 1856, and was buried in Kensal Green cemetery. She was responsible for many improvements in stage scenery and effects, and had much taste in costume. As a singer of songs she had no equal on the stage. Had she possessed musical patience and energy, she might, says Chorley in his 'Musical Recollections,' have 'queened it' at the Italian opera. In high comedy she was but moderately successful, and, though her Julia in the 'Rivals' found admirers, her Lady Teazle was generally condemned. Leigh Hunt ascribes to her at the outset tenderness, depth, and subtlety. Her command of these qualities, if ever possessed, was soon lost, and apart from the attraction of a flexible mouth, large lustrous eyes, and a thick crop of dark hair, her chief gifts were archness, fascination, *mutinerie*, a careless acceptance of homage, and a kind of constant confidential appeal to an audience by which she was always spoiled. In pieces such as the 'Carnival Ball,' the 'Loan of a Lover,' 'Naval Engagements,' and 'You can't marry your Grandmother,' she was irresistible. At the Haymarket she was bewitching in the 'Little Devil,' an adaptation from Scribe, and in 'Who's your Friend?' Engraved portraits of Mme. Vestris abound. A picture of her by George Clint, A.R.A., with Liston, Mrs. Glover, and Mr. Williams, in 'Paul Pry,' was exhibited in the National Portrait Gallery in 1868, and is now in the Science and Art Department, South Kensington. One after Clint is in the Mathews collection in the Garrick Club. Her name on her marriage certificate is signed Lucy Bartolozzi. A constant signature in following days was 'Eliza Vestris.'

[The early dramatic career of Mrs. Mathews is given fully in Genest's Account of the English Stage. Some scandalous Memoirs, published in 1839 for the booksellers, are untrustworthy in the main and are almost entirely without dates. Dickens's Life of Charles J. Mathews makes very sparing mention of her; Westland Marston, in his Some Recollections of the Modern Actors, gives some characteristically just and appreciative criticisms, of which full use has been made. Cole's Life and Times of Charles Kean, Marshall's Lives of the most Celebrated Actors and Actresses, Mrs. Baron-Wilson's Our Actresses; the Dramatic and Musical Review, Notes and Queries, 7th ser. vols. i. and xi., the Theatrical Inquisitor, &c., have been consulted.] J. K.

MATHEWS, THOMAS (1676–1751), admiral, eldest son of Colonel Edward Mathews (*d.* 1700), and of Jane, daughter of Sir Thomas Armstrong [q. v.], was born in October 1676 at Llandaff Court, the seat of the family for many generations, now the palace of the bishops of Llandaff. He entered the navy about 1690, on board the Albemarle with Sir Francis Wheler. It is uncertain whether he was in her at the battle of Beachy Head; it is believed that he was at the battle of Barfleur. In 1697 he was a volunteer in the Portland with Captain James Littleton [q. v.], and on 31 Oct. 1699 was promoted by Vice-admiral Aylmer to be a lieutenant of the Boyne, his flagship in the Mediterranean (*Add. MS.* 28124). On 15 March 1699–1700, on the king's direction to the admiralty to appoint Mathews as a lieutenant to the Deal Castle, he was called before the board, and deposed that before he had been appointed by Aylmer to act as a lieutenant, he had been examined and had passed (*Admiralty Minutes*); there is no mention of any certificate. In 1703 he was with Graydon in the West Indies, and was promoted by him to be captain of the Yarmouth. He took post from 24 May 1703. In 1704 he commanded the Kinsale in the Channel, and in October 1708 was appointed to the Gloucester, from which he was moved shortly afterwards to the Chester, a new ship of 50 guns. In the spring of 1709 the Chester was attached to the Channel fleet under Lord Berkeley, when it fell in, on the Soundings, with the little squadron of Du Guay Trouin. Trouin himself in the Achille escaped, though with difficulty; but his prize, the Bristol, was regained, and the Gloire, overtaken by the Chester, was brought to action and captured (LAUGHTON, *Studies in Naval History*, p. 322). In 1710 the Chester was part of the force under Commodore George Martin for the reduction of Nova Scotia, and covered the main attack; when Martin went home, Mathews remained as senior officer, and the following summer joined the fleet under Sir Hovenden Walker [q. v.] at Boston. The Chester was then sent to convoy some transports to New York, and, having been a good deal shattered in a heavy gale, was afterwards ordered to make the best of her way to England.

For the next few years Mathews settled down at Llandaff Court, but in January 1717–18 he was appointed to the Prince Frederick, apparently to wait till the Kent was ready. On 31 March 1718 he took command of the Kent, which went out to the Mediterranean in the fleet under Sir George Byng, afterwards Viscount Torrington [q. v.], and had a distinguished share in the action off Cape Passaro, materially assisting in the capture of the Spanish admiral [cf. MASTER, STREYNSHAM]. After the battle Mathews was detached in command of a small squadron in the more especial object of closely blockading Messina, and intercepting George Camocke [q. v.], rear-admiral in the Spanish service, if he should attempt to escape. In January, however, Camocke did manage to escape in a small boat, and during the next eighteen months the service of the different detachments of the fleet was practically limited to the blockade of Sicily. In the autumn of 1720 Mathews returned to England with the admiral. From 1722 to 1724 he commanded a squadron in the East Indies against the pirates. His efforts, however, were unavailing. The pirates were, indeed, somewhat overawed by the neighbourhood of the king's ships, and their ravages ceased for the time; but their strongholds were unassailable, and they repulsed an attempt on the island of Kolaba, a little to the southward of Bombay, made by the squadron in co-operation with a body of Portuguese troops from Goa.

On his return in 1724 Mathews again settled down to a country life at Llandaff, virtually retired from the service, and was passed over in the promotions to flag rank. The purchase of an estate formerly belonging to the family and the wish to rebuild the house would seem to have determined him to accept the burden together with the emoluments of office; and in 1736 he was appointed commissioner of the navy at Chatham, an employment then understood as distinctly civil. When, however, war with Spain broke out and war with France appeared imminent, Mathews obtained the restoration of his rank, involving promotion at one step, 13 March 1741–2, to be vice-admiral of the red, and his appointment as commander-in-chief in the Mediterranean, and plenipotentiary to the king of Sardinia and the States of Italy.

A man at the age of sixty-six, thus undertaking new duties and the renewal of long-forgotten and imperfect experiences, could scarcely have been expected to succeed without the goodwill and hearty co-operation of his subordinates; and this the government neglected to secure for him. Rear-admiral Lestock [q. v.], then in temporary command in the Mediterranean, had been for some years senior officer in the Medway while Mathews was commissioner at Chatham, and their relations had not been friendly. It was said that Mathews, on accepting the command, stipulated that Lestock should be recalled; and though the matter was perhaps not put thus crudely, we have his own statement to the Duke of Newcastle that 'I took the liberty of giving your Grace my opinion in regard to Mr. Lestock before I left England. I did the same to Lord Winchelsea and Lord Carteret' (Mathews to the Duke of Newcastle, 3 Jan. 1743–4). Lestock, however, was not recalled, and the ill-feeling which showed itself at once on Mathews's arrival was only prevented from breaking out in open quarrel by the fact that Mathews's duties at Turin kept him very much away from the fleet. But they also kept him away from the exercise of the command. He had never been at sea with the fleet, and was a comparative stranger to every officer under his command when the combined fleets of France and Spain sailed from Toulon on 10 Feb. 1743–4, and stood towards the south in a long and straggling line ahead. The English fleet left Hyères roadstead at the same time, closely attending on the allies; but during the 10th they never succeeded in getting into line, though the signal to form line was kept up all the time, and was still up when night fell. Mathews then made the signal to bring to, intending that the several ships should first get into their station; and those in the van and centre so understood it and obeyed it in that sense. Lestock, with the ships of the rear division, brought to where he was, some miles astern, and drifted still further away during the night.

At daybreak on the 11th the rear was separated from the rest of the fleet by a gap which was scarcely lessened during the whole day. Mathews wished to wait for Lestock's ships to close up, but found the allies slipping away to the southward and likely to escape him. This, he quite well understood, was what they wanted to do. Between France and England war had not been declared, and the primary object of the French fleet was to lend its support to the Spanish to break the blockade; if that could be done without fighting, so much the better. But besides that, the French also intended, or Mathews believed that they intended, to make for the Straits of Gibraltar, to join the Brest fleet, and thus the more effectually to cover the invasion to be attempted from Dunkirk [see NORRIS, SIR JOHN, *d.* 1749]. This it was Mathews's obvious duty to prevent. It was therefore impossible for him to allow the allies to get away to the south while he was waiting for Lestock. He was obliged to fight, and at once. About one o'clock he made the signal to engage; and in the Namur, closely followed by Captain James Cornewall [q. v.] in the Marlborough, ran down towards the rear of the allies, and brought the Spanish admiral to close action. In doing this, however, he neglected to haul down the signal for the line of battle; the two signals were flying simultaneously, and, under the existing circumstances, were irreconcilable. No one knew what to do. Those whose heads were clear and hearts were sound did close the enemy and engage [see HAWKE, EDWARD, LORD HAWKE]; but many were muddle-headed, some were perhaps shy, and Lestock —it was averred—was wickedly glad to see his commander-in-chief in difficulties, and would do nothing to help him out. Thus left to themselves, the Namur and Marlborough suffered very severely, and though they beat the Spanish ships opposed to them out of the line, the Marlborough was dismasted and the Namur temporarily disabled.

About five o'clock the French tacked to the assistance of the Spaniards. The ships of the English van thought that the object of this manœuvre was to double on and overwhelm them, and tacked to the northward [see WEST, TEMPLE]. There were no directing signals; the admiral had apparently lost his head, and no one ventured to take his place. A sort of panic set in, and the English fleet fled to the northward, the French appearing to chase them, but in reality intent only on rescuing the Spaniards. The Spaniards even neglected to secure the Marlborough, disabled, deserted, and wellnigh defenceless though she was. They did, however, recapture the Poder, and, content with that and with having saved the Spanish admiral, turned back, steering again to the southward. The English, on the other hand, continued during the night standing to the north; it was only towards daybreak of the 12th that they recovered themselves, and turned to the south, following the enemy in line of battle. The enemy now had no inclination to stay; but several of their ships were disabled and in tow; the Poder, which was the worst, they abandoned to the English, and she was burnt by Mathews's order. Still, the allies' retreat was very much hampered by the other crippled ships, and by nightfall the English fleet, in fair line, was within three or four miles of them, when Mathews again made the signal to bring to. At daybreak on the 13th the enemy was almost out of sight to the south-west; Mathews gave up the chase, and, after trying to get back to Hyères roads, finally reached Port Mahon in the early days of March. His health had been for some time failing, and in August 1744 he was allowed to resign the command and to return home overland.

As the result of the battle the blockade was fairly broken; reinforcements and supplies were sent to the Spanish army in Italy, and the course of the war was turned in favour of the allies. But what specially enraged the people of England was the too evident fact that the English fleet had met a Franco-Spanish fleet of inferior force, and had gained no decisive advantage over it, if, indeed, it had not been worsted. Feeling, both afloat and ashore, ran exceedingly high; and the House of Commons in 1745 passed an address to the king praying that an official inquiry might be held. There were, in consequence, a great many courts-martial; some ten or a dozen captains were tried for misconduct and cashiered. Lestock, who in popular opinion was the main, if not the sole cause of the miscarriage, was acquitted, promoted, and employed again. Mathews was also tried in 1746 on charges preferred against him by Lestock, charges of having taken the fleet into action in an irregular and confused manner, of having neglected to give the necessary orders, of having fled from the enemy, and of having afterwards given up the chase when there was every prospect of being able to bring the enemy to action on advantageous terms. And these charges were all maintained by the evidence. It was alleged in his favour that Mathews had fought bravely; it was proved against him that he had deserted the Marlborough, the Poder, and the Berwick; and after a trial of unprecedented length he was sentenced to be dismissed the service, June 1747. Meantime Mathews was busying himself at Llandaff Court, building a new house in place of the old one, which he had directed to be pulled down while he was in the Mediterranean. And the result of the trial seems to have affected him little. He believed the sentence to be iniquitous, and the outcome of parliamentary faction (cf. WALPOLE, *Letters*, i. 350)—with which, indeed, in its final stage, it seems to have had nothing to do—and he did not regard it as a reflection on his honour. In 1749, feeling himself in failing health, he settled in Bloomsbury Square, London, and there he died 2 Oct. 1751. He was buried in St. George's, Bloomsbury.

Both in his public and private capacities, by his friends and his enemies, Mathews is described as a choleric old man of the traditional John Bull type. 'I dare to say,' wrote Walpole to Mann, 'Mathews believes that Providence lives upon beef and pudding, loves prize-fighting and bull-baiting, and drinks fog to the health of Old England' (*ib.* i. 207); and again, speaking of the debate in 1745 in the House of Commons, 'Mathews remains in the light of a hot, brave, imperious, dull, confused fellow' (*ib.* i. 350). Horace Mann [q. v.], who felt personally injured by the diplomatic mission which had been added to Mathews's naval duties, and who stood aghast at the way in which the neutrality of Naples had been won [see MARTIN, WILLIAM, 1696?–1756], wrote: ''Tis wonderful how void Admiral Mathews is of common sense, good manners, or knowledge of the world. He understands nothing but Yes or No, and knows no medium' (DORAN, *Mann and Manners*, i. 157); and again: 'Mathews has sent me a ridiculous note wrote by the claw of a great lobster, by way of thanks for a present I sent him of some Cedrati and Marzolini cheeses, which are more delicate than our cream cheeses in England. "I am much oblig[d] to you for y[r] kinde present. the sweetmeats is good; so, sayes sume of my Gentlm[n] is the cheeses. but its to good for me. I love nothing after the French fashion"' (*ib.*) As a matter of fact, however, Mathews's writing and spelling were much better than those of most naval officers or country squires of the time; and while Walpole and his correspondents spoke of him as 'Il Furibondo,' irascible in temper and brutal in manners, those who knew him well described him as hot-tempered indeed, and sometimes brusque, but warm-hearted, kindly, and affectionate; a clear-sighted magistrate, a capable farmer, and a keen sportsman.

He was twice married: first in 1705 to Henrietta, daughter of S. Burgess of Antigua; she died about 1740, leaving issue one son, Thomas, a major in the army; secondly, about 1745, to Millicent, daughter of Rawdon Powell of Glamorganshire. His portrait, painted during his residence at Chatham, is in the Painted Hall at Greenwich. It represents him in the laced blue coat with red facings and the red waistcoat affected by naval officers before the prescription of uniform, and gives the idea of being a good likeness. It has been engraved.

[A memoir in the Red Dragon, the National Magazine of Wales (December 1884), vi. 481, is written with familiar knowledge of the family history, by a connection of the family, who has also kindly supplied some further particulars. That in Charnock's Biog. Nav. iii. 252, is very imperfect. Official letters and minutes of the courts-martial in the Public Record Office; Low's Hist. of the Indian Navy, i. 101 et seq.; Beatson's Nav. and Mil. Memoirs, vol. i.; Doran's Mann and Manners at the Court of Florence, vol. i. freq.; Walpole's Letters (Cunningham), vol. i. freq.; Troude's Batailles Navales de la France, i. 291; Rivière's La Marine française sous le Règne de Louis XV, p. 175; Brun's Guerres maritimes de la France, Port de Toulon, tom. i. livres x. et xi.; Vida de D. Juan Josef Navarro, por D. Josef de Vargas y Ponce. The charge and finding of the court-martial have been published; so also has the correspondence between Mathews and Lestock after the battle; and there are many pamphlets relating to the Mediterranean command, mostly scurrilous and worthless; a fairly complete set of them is in the library of the Royal United Service Institution.]

J. K. L.

MATHIAS, BENJAMIN WILLIAMS (1772–1841), divine, born on 12 Nov. 1772, was only surviving child of Benjamin Mathias, a native of Haverfordwest, Pembrokeshire, who settled in Dublin about 1760 as a woollen cloth manufacturer. Both his parents died when he was about ten. Entering Trinity College, Dublin, on 3 Oct. 1791, he was elected scholar in 1794, and graduated B.A. in 1796, M.A. in 1799 (*College Register*, where the name of his father is given as 'Henry'). In 1797 he was ordained to the curacy of Rathfryland, co. Down, and in 1805 became chaplain of Bethesda Chapel, Dorset Street, Dublin, an appointment which he was compelled to resign through ill-health in May 1835. In doctrine he was a moderate Calvinist. Mathias died in Merrion Avenue, Dublin, on 30 May 1841, and was buried in the cemetery of Mount Jerome. His congregation erected a tablet to his memory in Bethesda Chapel and a monument in the cemetery. In January 1804 he married a daughter of Mr. Stewart of Wilmont, co. Down, by whom he had a family.

Mathias, who was an eloquent preacher, wrote: 1. 'An Inquiry into the Doctrines of the Reformation and of the United Church of England and Ireland, respecting the Ruin and Recovery of Mankind,' 2 pts. 8vo, Dublin, 1814, which evoked replies by W. Eames in 1817, and a 'Clergyman of the Church of England' in 1818. 2. 'Vindiciæ Laicæ, or the Right of the Laity to the unrestricted Reading of the Sacred Scriptures vindicated,' 8vo, Dublin, 1827. 3. 'A Compendious History of the Council of Trent,' 8vo, Dublin, 1832. 4. 'Popery not Catholicism, in Two Parts,' 8vo, Liverpool, 1851, edited by his son, the Rev. W. B. Stewart Mathias. Part ii. is a reprint of 'Vindiciæ Laicæ.'

His portrait, engraved after Martin Cregan, R.H.A., by J. Horsburgh, was prefixed to his 'Twenty-one Sermons,' 8vo, Dublin, 1838.

[Information from the Rev. John W. Stubbs, D.D.; Brief Memorials of the Rev. B. W. Mathias, 8vo, Dublin, 1842.] G. G.

MATHIAS, THOMAS JAMES (1754?–1835), satirist and Italian scholar, belonged to a family connected with the English court, several members of which are mentioned in the fragments of the 'Journal' of Charlotte Burney (*Early Diary of Frances Burney*, ii. 306–12). His father, Vincent Mathias, subtreasurer in the queen's household and treasurer of Queen Anne's Bounty, died 15 June 1782, aged 71; his mother, Marianne, daughter of Alured Popple, secretary to the board of trade and governor of Bermuda, was born 8 Nov. 1724 and died 6 Jan. 1799 (*Gent. Mag.* 1782 pt. ii. p. 311, 1799 pt. i. p. 82). He is said to have been educated at Eton, and the long passage in the notes to the 'Pursuits of Literature' appears to corroborate this statement, but he was entered at Trinity College, Cambridge, on 2 July 1770, at the age of sixteen, as coming from the school at Kingston-on-Thames kept by the Rev. Richard Woodeson. He took an ægrotat degree in 1774 and proceeded M.A. in 1777, having gained, as a middle bachelor, in 1775 one of the members' prizes for the best dissertation in Latin prose, and in 1776, as a senior bachelor, another of the same prizes. He was admitted scholar of his college on 26 April 1771, elected as a minor fellow in 1776—the Latin letter which he sent to the electing fellows for their suffrages on this occasion is given in Nichols's 'Literary Anecdotes,' ii. 676–8—became major fellow in 1776, and acted as third, second, and first sublector respectively in 1777–8, 1779, and 1780. Latin exercises, written by him in 1775 and 1776, probably as tests for a fellowship, are preserved at the British Museum, and in 1779 he printed a Latin oration which he had delivered in the chapel of his college at Trinitytide. While at college he was very intimate with Spencer Perceval, afterwards prime minister, and a letter from one of Perceval's sons speaks of Mathias as his father's private tutor at Cambridge. In 1782 he succeeded to the post of sub-treasurer to the queen, when he probably quitted Cambridge; he afterwards became her treasurer, and about 1812 he appears to have been librarian at Buckingham Palace. For many years he lived in London on the emoluments of these posts, and engaged in literary pursuits, but his edition of the works of Gray in 1814 proved a severe loss to him, and would have been still more disastrous but for the assistance of the authorities at Pembroke College, Cambridge, under whose auspices it was undertaken, and by whom many copies were purchased. It was published at the enormous price of seven guineas, and consequently had no sale, so that most of the volumes were locked up in a warehouse for years. His straitened means, combined with an 'alarming stroke and attack' (*Madame d'Arblay's Diary*, vii. 307), decided him to make his way to Italy 'on a desperate experiment of health.' Southey met him at Paris in May 1817, when he was 'outward bound' (*Letters*, iv. 437–8); and he remained in Southern Italy, 'in love with the climate and the language,' for the rest of his life. When Sir Walter Scott was at Naples in his last illness, Mathias contributed to his 'comfort and amusement,' and a description of him in his lodgings in an old palace on the Pizzofalcone is given by N. P. Willis in his 'Pencillings by the Way,' i. 100–2. Another account of his life in Italy is given in the 'Athenæum,' 22 Aug. 1835, p. 650). He was a royal associate of the Royal Society of Literature, and so long as its funds allowed he was in receipt of one of its pensions. He died at Naples in August 1835. His books and manuscripts were sold by R. H. Evans in 1820 and 1837. He was at one time the owner of a picture of his family by Hogarth (Dobson, *Hogarth*, ed. 1891, p. 346). He was elected F.R.S. in March 1795, and F.S.A. in January 1795.

The first dialogue of the 'Pursuits of Literature' came out in May 1794, the second and third in June 1796, and the fourth in July 1797. The 'fifth edition, revised and corrected,' was published in 1798, and in the same year there appeared three editions of 'Translations of the passages quoted in the Pursuits of Literature.' The eleventh edition, 'again revised, and with the citations translated,' is dated in 1801, and the sixteenth issue bore the date of 1812. All the impressions were anonymous, and the writer was long unknown. Dawson Turner, who possessed letters addressed to the unknown author, with the answers of Mathias, which are now No. 22976 of the Addit. MSS. in the British Museum, wrote that the authorship 'was scarcely made a secret by the family after Mathias went to Italy' (*Notes and Queries*, 1st ser. iii. 276). Rumour asserted that he was aided in the composition by Bishop W. L. Mansel [q. v.], while Gilbert Wakefield, says Rogers, 'used to say he was certain that Rennell and Glynn assisted in it' (*Table Talk of Samuel Rogers*, p. 135), but these suggestions can now be dismissed from consideration. The poem contained some slashing lines scattered among a mass of affected criticism, and as its sole idea was to ridicule those trading on literature, it soon proved wanting in life. George Steevens called it 'a peg to hang the notes on,' and these were often of portentous length, though Rogers thought them 'rather piquant.' De Quincey, in his 'Essay on Parr,' speaks of it as marred by 'much licence of tongue, much mean and impotent spite, and by a systematic pedantry without parallel in literature,' and he might have added, by the shameless puffing of his own works by Mathias. Cobbett, who shared many of his prejudices, called it a 'matchless poem,' but Dr. Wolcot dubbed him 'that miserable imp Mathias.' Among the writers most severely satirised were Payne Knight, Parr, Godwin, 'Monk' Lewis, and Joseph Warton for his edition of Pope's 'Works;' but Mathias was often obliged to soften or to expunge his criticisms. In Parr's 'Works' (viii. 59–82) are several eulogistic letters subsequently addressed to him by Mathias.

A satire of such recklessness naturally provoked attacks. Among them were: 1. 'The Egotist, or Sacred Scroll. A Familiar Dialogue between the Author of the "Pursuits of Literature" and Octavius,' 1798. 2. 'The Progress of Satire, an Essay in Verse. With Notes containing Remarks on the "Pursuits of Literature,"' 2nd ed. 1798. Supplement, with 'Remarks on the Pursuer of Literature's Defence,' 1799. Anonymous, but by William Boscawen. 3. 'Impartial Strictures on the "Pursuits of Literature," and particularly a Vindication of the Romance of "The Monk,"' 1798. 4. 'The Sphinx's Head Broken, or a Poetical Epistle with Notes to Thomas James M*th**s, by Andrew Œdipus, an injured Author,' 1798. 5. 'The Literary Census, a Satirical Poem, with Notes, including Free and Candid Strictures on the "Pursuits of Literature." By Thomas Dutton,' 1798. 6. 'Remarks on the "Pursuits of Literature,"' Cambridge, 1798. Anonymous, by John Mainwaring. This provoked from Mathias 'A Letter to the Author of "Remarks," &c., which purported to be written by "A Country Gentleman, formerly of the University of Cambridge."' 7. 'An Examination of the Merits and Tendency of the "Pursuits of Literature,"' by W. Burdon, Newcastle-upon-Tyne, 1799. Nearly the whole of these works censured the malignity and partiality of the criticisms of Mathias, and some of them reflected on his personal appearance. He was small and swarthy, with a face like that of Sir Francis Burdett.

Satire always had charms for Mathias. So early as 1780 he published anonymously 'An Heroic Address in Prose to the Rev. Richard Watson [afterwards Bishop Watson] on his late Discourse to the Clergy of the Archdeaconry of Ely,' in which Watson had expressed the hope of supplying some day a 'more exact survey of the deserts of Arabia and Tartary,' and 'An Heroic Epistle [in verse] to the Rev. Richard Watson,' which passed into two editions and provoked 'An Answer to the Heroic Epistle.' The success of the 'Pursuits of Literature' tempted him into politics. He attacked Sheridan with great coarseness in 'The Political Dramatist' in November 1795 [anon.], 1796; a second edition of which came out in 1796, with a postscript in prose, also published separately, of 'Remarks on the Declaration of the Whig Club, 23 Jan. 1796.' The curious correspondence between the Earl and Countess of Jersey and Dr. Randolph on the missing letters of the Prince of Wales drew from him 'An Equestrian Epistle in Verse to the Earl of Jersey' [anon.], 1796, and 'An Epistle in Verse to Dr. Randolph' [anon.], 1796; also issued as 'A Pair of Epistles in Verse' [anon.], 1796, with 'An Appendix to the Pair of Epistles' [anon.], 1796. The presence in England of the 'numerous emigrant French priests and others of the Church of Rome' caused him to write a foolish 'Letter to the Marquis of Buckingham. By a Layman,' 1796. The tories were praised and Fox with his whig followers condemned in 'An Imperial Epistle from Kien Long, Emperor of China, to George III in 1794;' 2nd edit. 1796; 4th edit. 1798. In 1797 he ventured upon 'An Address to Mr. Pitt on some parts of his Administration' [anon.], 1797; and in 1799 there appeared four editions, also anonymous, of 'The Shade of Alexander Pope on the Banks of the Thames. A Satirical Poem on the Residence of Henry Grattan at Twickenham.' This occasioned 'A Vindication of Pope and Grattan from the Attack of an Anonymous Defamer. By W.

Burdon,' 1799; and eight severe lines by Grattan printed in Wrangham's 'Catalogue of his English Library,' pp. 409-10. An ephemeral production by Mathias was called 'Pandolpho Attonito, or Lord Galloway's Poetical Lamentation on the Removal of the Armchairs from the Pit of the Opera House' [anon.], 1800; and next year he produced a volume of 'Prose on Various Occasions collected from the Newspapers' [anon.], 1801.

Mathias was a devoted admirer of Gray the poet and of Dr. Robert Glynn [q. v.] One of his first works was 'Runic Odes imitated from the Norse Tongue in the manner of Mr. Gray,' 1781, republished in London in 1790 in 'Odes English and Latin,' in 1798, and at New York in 1806 in a collection called 'The Garden of Flowers.' In 1814 he edited, at a ruinous expense, 'The Works of Thomas Gray, with Mason's Memoir. To which are subjoined Extracts from the Author's Original Manuscripts,' 1814, 2 vols. 4to. The second volume contained his 'Observations on the Writings and Character of Mr. Gray,' also issued separately in 1815. His knowledge of Gray's appearance and habits was derived from Nicholls, of whom he wrote in 'A Letter occasioned by the Death of the Rev. Norton Nicholls, with Italian Ode to him,' pp. 30. A few copies were printed for private circulation, and it was inserted in the 'Gentleman's Magazine,' 1810, pt. ii. pp. 346-51; his 'Works of Gray' (1814), i. 515-35; his 'Observations on the Writings and Character of Gray,' 1815; 'Correspondence of Gray and Nicholls,' 1843, pp. 3-28; in 'Poesie Liriche,' 1810; and in Nichols's 'Illustrations of Literature,' v. 65-83; while the Italian 'Canzone' to Nicholls was printed separately in 1807. Nicholls left his books to Mathias and a considerable sum of money in the event, which did not take place, of his surviving a near relation of his own. With the assistance of Dr. Glynn, who gave him some Chatterton manuscripts, he compiled 'An Essay on the Evidence relating to the Poems attributed to Thomas Rowley,' 1783; 2nd edit. 1784. In 1782 he brought out an anonymous 'Elysian Interlude in Prose and Verse of Rowley and Chatterton in the Shades,' in which Chatterton described the success of the poems, the means by which they were concocted, and the strife over their authenticity. His unpublished volume of 'Odes English and Latin,' 1798, contained, as pt. i., 'The Runic Odes,' and as pt. ii. many Latin poems, among which were verses to Thomas Orde as governor of the Isle of Wight, an ode to Bishop Mansel on his neglecting a parrot, and an address on Lord Holland's villa near Margate: all three had been printed separately, and were afterwards included in 'Odæ Latinæ,' 1810. He printed privately at Rome in 1818 and at Naples in 1819 several 'Lyrica Sacra excerpta ex Hymnis Ecclesiæ Antiquis,' which were reprinted, with an appendix, by Frederick Martin at Norwich in January 1835. Mathias also printed privately a few copies of a Latin elegy taken from that on Netley Abbey by George Keate [q. v.], and of the ballad of Hardyknute with a commentary. There are letters to him in 'Notes and Queries,' 2nd ser. x. 41-2, 283-4, xii. 221, and from him in Nichols's 'Illustrations of Literature,' viii. 214, 312-14.

Mathias was probably instructed in Italian at Cambridge by Agostino Isola, and he ranks as the best English scholar in that language since the time of Milton. He was the author of 'Poesie Liriche' and of 'Canzoni Toscane,' each of which went through many editions, and of 'Canzoni' on Nicholls, Sir William Drummond, and Lord Guilford. He edited the works of numerous Italian authors, among whom were Gravina, Tiraboschi, and Menzini; published a collection in three volumes of 'Lyrics from Italian Poets,' 1802, 1808, and 1819; and letters in Italian on the study of its literature, a new edition of which was published by L. P. at Naples in 1834. The English works which he translated into Italian included Akenside's 'Naiads,' Armstrong's 'Art of Health,' Beattie's 'Minstrel,' Mason's 'Caractacus' and 'Sappho,' Milton's 'Lycidas,' Spenser's 'Fairy Queen,' and Thomson's 'Castle of Indolence.' In Wrangham's 'English Library,' pp. 348-9, is an unpublished Italian sonnet by him.

[Gent. Mag. 1782 pt. ii. p. 360, 1835 pt. i. p. 524, pt. ii. pp. 550-2; Croker Papers, ii. 371; Dyce's Table Talk of Samuel Rogers, pp. 134-6, 323; Biog. Dict. of Living Authors, 1816, pp. 227-8; De Quincey's Works, ed. 1890, v. 88-9, 142; Smith's Cobbett, i. 244-5; Brydges's Restituta, iv. 250; Lockhart's Scott, ed. 1838, vii. 340; Wordsworth's Scholæ Acad. pp. 153, 360; Halkett and Laing's Anonymous Lit. i. 43, ii. 1389, iii. 1848, 2038, 2232; Notes and Queries, 8th ser. v. 284; information from Mr. W. Aldis Wright, of Trinity College, Cambridge.] W. P. C.

MATILDA (*d.* 1083), queen of William the Conqueror, was the daughter of Baldwin V, called of Lisle, count of Flanders, by his second wife, Adela, daughter of Robert, and sister of Henry I, kings of France. She was a descendant of Alfred or Ælfred [q. v.], king of the West Saxons, through his daughter Ælfthryth, wife of Count Baldwin II (*d.* 918). William, then duke of Normandy, sought her in marriage in 1049, and the marriage was forbidden by the council of Rheims held in that year by Pope Leo IX, the prohibition evidently being grounded on some nearness of kin (LABBE, *Concilia*, xix. 741). The relationship between Matilda and William has never been made out certainly. Of the various theories on the subject that best worth consideration is that the impediment arose from the marriage contract between Richard III, William's uncle, and Matilda's mother, Adela, although the marriage was not completed (see *Spicilegium*, iii. 390; PALGRAVE, *England and Normandy*, iii. 264; *Norman Conquest*, iii. 657). A rival but less satisfactory theory is that Matilda, as well as William, was descended from Rolf, for William, called Caput-stupæ, or Tow-head, count of Poitou, is said, on the strength of a vague statement by an anonymous writer, to have been the father of Adela or Adelais, wife of Hugh Capet, great-grandfather of Matilda (DUCHESNE, *Rerum Gallicarum Scriptores*, iii. 344, and *Life and Times of St. Anselm*, i. 419). Against this may be urged that Helgald, who wrote at least a century earlier than the anonymous writer, and was a friend of King Robert, Hugh's son, says that Robert used to declare that his mother Adelais was of Italian family. It is alleged that Helgald's words may be interpreted as meaning that Robert was sprung from Italy by his father's side, but the Italian genealogy of Hugh is baseless (RICHER, lib. i. c. 5, and *Recueil des Historiens*, x. pref. i–xviii). If Hugh married a daughter of William Towhead, it is hard to see why William IV, duke of Aquitaine, should have opposed Hugh's accession to the throne; for on this supposition Hugh would have been his brother-in-law. If, however, such a relationship existed between them, it is strange that neither Ademar of Chabanois nor Peter of Maillezais, nor indeed any other chronicler should notice it. It is therefore unlikely that Matilda was descended from Rolf through the wife of Hugh Capet. (For opinions on both sides see *Recueil*, ix. 273 *n.*, x. 74, 99 *n.*, xi. 130 *n.*; *L'Art de Vérifier*, x. 95; *Guardian*, 28 Nov. 1883, p. 1803, 19 Dec. p. 1919, 30 Jan. 1884, p. 176.)

The belief that Matilda was already the wife of Gerbod, advocate of the abbey of St. Bertin, near St. Omer, and that she had by him two or three children, one of whom was Gundrada, afterwards wife of William of Warrenne, earl of Surrey, is erroneous, and was founded on some charters of Lewes Priory, which have been proved to be untrustworthy (see GUNDRADA DE WARENNE; *Monasticon*, v. 12, 14. Stapleton argued that Gundrada was the daughter of Matilda by Gerbod, and that the prohibition of the marriage of Matilda and William was due to the fact that Gerbod was then alive, *Archæological Journal*, iii. sq.; Blaauw in answer asserted that Matilda was a maid when she married William, and made Gundrada a child of that marriage, *Archæologia*, 1847, xxxii. 108 sq.; Freeman accepted the alleged marriage to Gerbod as proved, *Norman Conquest*, iii. 86, 645–53; Mr. Chester Waters pointed out that the marriage was a fiction, and that Gundrada was not the daughter either of Matilda or William, *Academy*, 28 Dec. 1878, and 24 May 1879, and so far he was followed by Mr. M. Rule, *Life and Times of St. Anselm*, i. 419, and, finally, Freeman owned that he was mistaken, and summed up the case against the alleged marriage in a paper on the 'Parentage of Gundrada' in *English Historical Review*, 1888, xii. 680–701). According to another story, Matilda wished to marry Brihtric, a Gloucestershire thegn, who came on an embassy to Bruges, but was rejected by him; and that she afterwards when queen of England took vengeance on him for his refusal (*Cont.* WACE, *Chroniques Anglo-Normandes*, i. 73; *Monasticon*, ii. 60; ELLIS, *Introduction to Domesday*, ii. 55) is unworthy of belief (*Norman Conquest*, iii, 83, iv. 761-4). In spite of the papal prohibition, Matilda was married to William, probably in 1053 (*Chronicon Turonense* ap. *Recueil des Historiens*, xi. 348) at Eu, whence William brought her to Rouen, where she was received with much rejoicing. An idle legend records that she at first refused William's offer, declaring that she would never marry a bastard; that William rode secretly to Bruges, caught her as she was coming out of church, and beat and kicked her; and that she thereupon took to her bed, and told her father that she would marry none but the duke (*ib.*)

Malger, archbishop of Rouen, and Lanfranc [q. v.], then prior of Bec, severely blamed William for this marriage, on the old ground that Matilda was too nearly related to him, and it is said that Normandy was laid under an interdict (WILLIAM OF JUMIÈGES, vii. c. 26; WILLIAM OF MALMESBURY, *Gesta Regum*, iii. c. 267; *Vita Lanfranci*, p. 288; WACE, l. 9659). The matter was not settled until the Lateran Council of 1059, when Nicolas II granted a dispensation for the marriage. As her share in the atonement required from her and her husband, Matilda built the abbey of the Holy Trinity for nuns at Caen; the church, of which the eastern part only can be the work of the foundress, was consecrated 18 June 1066 (*Norman Conquest*, iii. 107 *n.*) A curious though untrustworthy story represents her as talking much with Earl Harold [see HAROLD II, *d.* 1066] during his visit to the Norman court, and persuading him to promise to marry one of her daughters (SNORRO ap. LAING, iii. 76). When William was preparing to invade England, she presented him with a ship for his own use, called the Mora, and had placed on the prow a golden image of a boy, with his right hand pointing towards England, and his left holding an ivory horn to his lips (*Brevis Relatio*, p. 22).

During William's absence on the invasion of England, Matilda ruled Normandy successfully, being assisted by a council, at the head of which was Roger de Beaumont [see under BEAUMONT, ROBERT DE, *d.* 1118]. Her regency ended with the return of William to Normandy in March 1067, and was resumed in conjunction with her eldest son, Robert, on her husband's departure in the following December. Early the next year William sent men of high rank to conduct her to England, whither she came accompanied by a large number of nobles and ladies, and bringing as the chief of her chaplains Guy, bishop of Amiens, who had already written his poem on William's victory (ORDERIC, p. 510). At Whitsuntide, 11 May, she was crowned and anointed queen by Aldred [q. v.], archbishop of York, at Westminster (*ib.*; *A.-S. Chronicle* an. 1067, Worcester version). Later in the year she bore her fourth son, Henry, afterwards Henry I [q. v.], it is said at Selby in Yorkshire. She appears to have resided much in Normandy, and to have been occupied in the affairs of the duchy. In 1070 she and her son Robert joined in requesting Lanfranc to accept the archbishopric of Canterbury. William FitzOsbern was in December sent over from England by the king to help Matilda in the regency of Normandy; he marched at the queen's desire to uphold the cause of her brother's widow and son in Flanders against Robert the Frisian (WILLIAM OF JUMIÈGES, viii. 14). Matilda was deeply afflicted by the death of her brother and nephew and by the troubles that war brought upon her native land (ORDERIC, p. 527). When her son Robert was in exile, having quarrelled with his father in 1079, she sent him large quantities of gold and silver and other valuable things without her husband's knowledge, for she was very rich. William found it out and reproached her, but she pleaded her love for her son. William ordered that the messenger whom she employed in the business should be blinded, but, warned by the queen's friends, the man escaped to the monastery of St. Evroul, where at the queen's request the abbot received him (*ib.* p. 571). About this time she sent gifts to a famous hermit in Germany who was held to be a prophet, requesting him to pray for her husband and Robert and tell her what should befall them, which he did (*ib.*) On the death of her kinsman the holy Simon de Valois, count of Crepy, at Rome in 1082, she sent gifts to adorn his tomb ('Mabillon,' *Acta Sanctorum*, viii. 374); and at this time rendered some help to William, bishop of Durham, in his scheme for substituting monks for canons in his church (*Hist. Dunelm. Eccl.* iv. c. 2). She died in Normandy on 3 Nov. 1083, after an illness of some length, and was buried in her church at Caen. Her tomb was richly adorned, and bore an epitaph, recorded by Orderic (p. 648); it was restored in 1819, and is in the middle of the choir.

Matilda was handsome in person and noble in disposition (WILLIAM OF JUMIÈGES, vii. c. 21), of great ability, a faithful and helpful wife, and an affectionate mother; she was religious and liberal to the poor, and was followed to the grave by many whom she had befriended. Her husband felt her death keenly, and is said to have mourned for her the rest of his life (WILLIAM OF MALMESBURY, iii. 273, who records, without believing it, a foolish story, that William having been unfaithful to her, she had his mistress hamstrung, and was for so doing beaten to death with a bridle). She bore her husband four sons—Robert, who succeeded his father in the duchy; Richard, who met his death while hunting in the New Forest; and William and Henry, who both became kings—and five, or perhaps six, daughters: Cecilia, dedicated as a nun in childhood in her mother's church at Caen in 1066, professed in 1075, became abbess in 1113, and died in 1127; Constance, married to Alan of Brittany in 1086, and died in 1090; Adelaide, probably betrothed to Earl Harold, and died in youth; Adela, married to Stephen of Blois in 1080, and died in 1137; perhaps an Agatha, possibly promised to Edwin, earl of Mercia, and betrothed to Alfonso of Spain, who died unmarried, with a character for sanctity; and a Matilda (see on Matilda's children, *Norman Conquest*, iii. 666 sqq. with full references). She made her son Henry her heir in England (ORDERIC, p. 510; FREEMAN, *William Rufus*, i. 195), and bequeathed her crown and other ornaments of state to her church at Caen. Besides her abbey there, she founded the abbey of St. Mary de Pré at Rouen (*Monasticon*, vi. 1106), and gave rich gifts to Cluny (*Cluny Charters*, ii. 72) and St. Evroul (ORDERIC, p. 603). At Abingdon, however, she appears as a spoiler; she probably robbed the English abbey in order to enrich a Norman house with its treasures (*Historia de Abingdon*, i. 485, 491).

[Freeman's Norman Conquest, vols. iii. iv., contain full notices of Matilda. For story of a marriage to Gerbod, Norman Conquest, iii. App. O. 651–65 (2nd edit.), corrected by Engl. Hist. Review, 1888, xii. 680–701; Archæol. Journal,

iii. 1 sq.; Archæologia, 1847, xxxii. 108; Sir G.F. Duckett's Sussex Archæol. Collections, 1878, p. 114, and Charters and Records of Cluny, i. 1, 43, 49, ii. 72; Chester Waters in Academy, 28 Dec. 1878, 24 May 1879, and his Gundrada de Warrenne; Green's Lives of the Princesses, i. 4; Rule's Life and Times of St. Anselm, i. 415–421. For impediment to marriage: Norman Conquest, u.s.; Rule's St. Anselm, i. 419; Palgrave's England and Normandy, iii. 264; D'Achery's Spicilegium, iii. 390; Labbe's Concilia, xix. 741, ed. Cossart; Richer, vol. i. c. 5, ed. Pertz; Rer. Gall. Scriptt. iii. 344; Helgald's Vita Roberti ap. Recueil des Historiens, x. 99, see also Pref. i–xviii, and 74, ix. 273 *n.*, xi. 130 *n.*; L'Art de Vérifier les Dates, x. 95; Guardian, 28 Nov. 1883, p. 1803, 19 Dec. p. 1919, 30 Jan. 1884; Will. of Jumièges, vol. vii. c. 26, vol. viii. c. 32 (Duchesne); Orderic, pp. 510, 527, 571, 603, 648 (Duchesne); Will. of Poitiers and Brevis Relatio, ap. Scriptt. Rerum. Gest. Will. I, pp. 22, 155, 167, ed. Giles; Will. of Malmesbury's Gesta Regum, vol. iii. cc. 234, 267, 273 (Rolls Ser. ii. 291, 327, 331, 332), Vita Lanfranci ap. B. Lanf. Op. i. 288, 293, ed Giles; Alberic ap. Recueil, xi. 361; Chron. Turon. ap. Recueil, xi. 348; Wace's Roman de Rou, l. 6959 sq., ed. Pluquet; Anglo-Sax. Chron. ann. 1067, 1083; Dugdale's Monasticon, ii. 60, iii. 485, v. 12, 14, vi. 1100; Ellis's Introd. to Domesday, i. 6, 7, 328, 393, ii. 55; Laing's Sea Kings, iii. 76; Hist. Dunelm. Eccl. vol. iv. c. 2, ap. Symeon of Durham (Rolls Ser.), i. 121; Turner's Cotman's Antiq. of Normandy, i. 27; Pignot's Ordre de Cluni, ii. 503, iii. 34; Liber de Hyda, pp. 286, 296 (Rolls Ser.); Neustria Pia, p. 625; Gallia Christiana, xi. 61; Hist. Monast. de Abingdon, i. 485, 491 (Rolls Ser).] W. H.

MATILDA, MAUD, MAHALDE, MOLD (1080–1118), first wife of Henry I, king of England [q. v.], was a daughter of Malcolm III, king of Scots, and Margaret, grand-daughter of Eadmund Ironside [see MARGARET, SAINT]. She was probably born in the autumn of 1080, as her godfather was Robert, duke of Normandy, who was in Scotland then, and, so far as is known, at no other time. She was baptised Eadgyth (Edith), but Matilda or Maud, in various forms, is the name by which she is known in history. Her education was entrusted to her mother's sister Christina, who was a nun at either Romsey or Wilton. Christina compelled the girl to wear a nun's black veil, as a protection against 'the brutality of the Normans, which was then raging;' according to another account, it was the abbess who made her wear it for fear of William Rufus. 'I trembled under my aunt's rod,' said Matilda long afterwards; 'when I threw off the veil, she tormented and insulted me with sharp blows and shameful words, so that in her presence I wore it, groaning and shuddering, but whenever I could get out of her sight I flung it on the ground and trode it under foot.' Once Malcolm came to visit his daughter, found her wearing the veil, and pulled it off angrily, swearing that he intended her not for a nun, but for the wife of Count Alan, i.e. Alan II. of Richmond; and it seems that he took her back with him to Scotland. This was apparently in 1093. Before the end of that year, Alan, Malcolm, and Margaret were all dead, and Donald, the new king of Scots, drove Margaret's children out of his realm. Matilda seems to have found a shelter in England by the help of her uncle, Eadgar the Ætheling [see EDGAR ATHELING]. Earl William of Warren sought her hand, but it was reserved for a loftier bridegroom. Henry I was no sooner king (August 1100) than he set himself to win the attachment of his English subjects in various ways, and among others by a marriage with Matilda, the child of 'Margaret the good queen, king Eadward's cousin, and of the right kingly kin of England.' She was quite willing to marry him, but objections were raised against the marriage of one who, being known to have worn the black veil, was supposed to be a professed nun. Matilda went straight to Archbishop Anselm [see ANSELM, SAINT] and told him her story; he and an assembly of bishops, nobles, and clergy, decided, after careful inquiry, that the story was true, that she had never taken the vows, and was therefore free to marry. Matilda received their verdict 'with a happy face,' and on 11 Nov. (1100) she was married and crowned by Anselm in Westminster Abbey. Her first child seems to have been born at Winchester, at the end of July or beginning of August 1101 (WACE, *Roman de Rou*, ed. Pluquet, vv. 15453–5), and to have died an infant. A daughter, Matilda [see MATILDA, 1102–1167], was born in London (W. FITZSTEPHEN, in ROBERTSON, *Materials for Hist. Becket*, iii. 13) before 5 Aug. 1102, and a son, William, before 5 Aug. 1103 (GERV. CANT., ed. Stubbs, i. 91–2). In that year Matilda persuaded Duke Robert of Normandy to give up the pension from England secured to him by his treaty with Henry in 1101. In 1105, when Henry exacted heavy sums from the English clergy, they begged the queen to intercede for them; she burst into tears, but dared not meddle in the matter. She kept up an affectionate correspondence with Anselm throughout his exile (1103–6), and when he came back in autumn 1106 she gave him an eager welcome; 'neither worldly business nor worldly pleasure could keep her from hastening to every place through which he was to pass,' hurrying to prepare him a lodging, and to be always the first to meet him. In 1111 she was present at the translation of St. Ethelwold's relics at Winchester. On 28 Dec. 1116 she was with

Henry at the consecration of St. Albans Abbey Church (Rog. Wendover, ed. Coxe, ii. 193). She died at Westminster on 1 May 1118, and was buried in the abbey. Westminster had been her abode for many years; soon after the birth of her son she had ceased to follow the wanderings of her husband's court. It is possible that she accompanied him in one visit to Normandy, in 1105–6 (*Ann. Winton.* a. 1107; the date, as regards her, must be a year too late); but in later years, while he was 'busy elsewhere,' she stayed at home. Like her mother, she was very pious, wearing a hair shirt, going barefoot round the churches in Lent, and devoting herself especially to the care of lepers, washing their feet and kissing their scars, besides building a hospital for them at St. Giles-in-the-Fields, London (Matt. Paris, *Chron. Maj.* ed. Luard, ii. 144; *Monast. Angl.* vol. vi. pt. ii. p. 635). The first Austin priory in England, Holy Trinity, Aldgate (London), was founded by her in 1108 (Hearne, *Will. Newb.* vol. iii. App. p. 690). Another of her good works was the construction of two bridges, with a causeway between them, over the two branches of the river Lea, near Stratford, instead of the dangerous passage of Old Ford; she gave the maintenance of these bridges in charge to the nuns of Barking, with a grant of land to provide funds for the purpose (*Abbr. Placit.* 6 *Edw. II.* p. 316). In her convent days she had 'learned and practised the literary art,' and six letters written by her to Anselm (Ans. *Epp.* l. iii. epp. 55, 93, 96, 119, l. iv. epp. 74, 76), as well as one to Pope Paschal II (Migne, *Patrol.* vol. 163, cols. 466–7) display a scholarship unusual among laymen, and probably still more among women, in her day. Another of her correspondents was the learned Bishop Hildebert of Le Mans, who had probably made her acquaintance in England in 1099, and who wrote to her several friendly letters (Hildeb. Cenom. *Epp.* l. i. epp. 7, 9, l. iii. ep. 12, ed. Migne, vol. 171), and two highly complimentary poetical addresses (*ib.* vol. 171, cols. 1408, 1443–5). He sings of her beauty; William of Malmesbury thought her merely 'not ill-favoured.' She was a warm patroness of verse and song; she gave lavishly to musical clerks, to scholars, poets, and strangers of all sorts, who were drawn to her court by the fame of her bounty, and who spread her praises far and wide. On the other hand, the tenants on her estates were too often fleeced by her bailiffs in order to provide funds for this ill-regulated generosity. Yet in English tradition she is emphatically 'Mold the good queen.' Not only was the Confessor's prophecy of the re-grafting of the 'green tree' (*Vita Edw. Conf.* ed. Luard, p. 431) fulfilled through her marriage and her children; Robert of Gloucester over and over again ascribes to her a direct, personal, and most beneficial influence on the condition of England under Henry I, and finally declares that 'the goodness that she did here to England cannot all be here written, nor by any man understood.'

[English Chronicle, ed. Thorpe; Eadmer's Historia Novorum, ed. Rule; William of Malmesbury's Gesta Regum, ed. Stubbs, vol. ii.; Annals of Winchester, in Annales Monastici, ed. Luard, vol. ii.; Robert of Gloucester, ed. Wright, vol. ii., all in Rolls Series; Ordericus Vitalis, in Duchesne's Hist. Norm. Scriptt.; Herman of Tournay, De Restauratione Tornacensis Ecclesiæ, in D'Achéry's Spicilegium, vol. ii.; Freeman's William Rufus, vol. ii. App. EE and WW; Strickland's Queens of England, vol. i.] K. N.

MATILDA of Boulogne (1103?–1152), wife of Stephen, king of England, was the only child of Eustace III, count of Boulogne, and his wife, Mary, daughter of Malcolm III, king of Scots, and Margaret, sister of Eadgar the Ætheling. The marriage of Eustace and Mary took place soon after that of Mary's sister [see Matilda, 1080–1118] with the English king, Henry I, and Matilda of Boulogne was probably born about 1103. Before 1125 Henry gave her in marriage to his favourite nephew, Stephen of Blois, whom he had endowed with large possessions in England and Normandy. Eustace also held considerable estates in England, and these, as well as the county of Boulogne, had passed to Matilda by his death shortly before her marriage. The possession of Boulogne gave her husband command over the shortest passage between Gaul and England, and thus enabled Stephen, on Henry's death in December 1135, to seize the English crown before its destined heiress, the Empress Matilda (1102–1167) [q. v.] could enforce her claim. On Easter day, 22 March 1136, his wife was crowned at Westminster. When the barons rose against him in 1138, she besieged one of them, Walkelyn Maminot, in Dover castle by land, while a squadron of ships from Boulogne blockaded him by sea till he was driven to surrender. In the spring of 1139, she reconciled her husband with her uncle David I, king of Scots [q. v.]; the terms of the treaty were settled between her and David's son, Henry [q. v.], at Durham, 9 April. When at the close of the year civil war began on the empress's landing in England, the queen exerted herself to gain the alliance of France; she went over sea with her eldest son, Eustace, and in February 1140 secured his investiture as duke of the Normans and his betrothal with the

French king's sister Constance, whom she brought back with her to England. In 1141, when Stephen had been made prisoner at the battle of Lincoln, and a council met at Winchester (7 April) under his brother, bishop Henry [see Henry of Blois], to acknowledge the empress as lady of England, the queen sent a clerk of her household with a letter to the assembly, entreating for her husband's restoration. This appeal having failed, she endeavoured to negotiate with the empress for his release, but in vain. Meanwhile, however, she was busy, in concert with Stephen's favourite captain, William of Ypres, rallying the king's scattered partisans, and gathering a host, which now advanced wasting, plundering, slaughtering all before it, almost to the gates of London, where the empress had set up her court and was making herself so unpopular that the citizens drove her out at the queen's approach. Matilda of Boulogne established her headquarters in London, obtained an interview with bishop Henry at Guildford, and persuaded him to return to his natural allegiance. When the empress besieged him at Winchester, she was speedily besieged in her turn by 'the king's queen with all her strength' (*Engl. Chron.* a. 1140) so effectually that she was driven to withdraw. Her half-brother, Robert, earl of Gloucester [q. v.], was captured in the retreat, and the next six months were spent in negotiations between his wife and the queen for his release in exchange for Stephen. Matilda herself took charge of the captive earl, putting him under no physical restraint, but merely leading him about in her train, till the exchange was effected, November 1141. Stephen and Matilda re-entered London together, and on Christmas-day they both 'wore their crowns' in Canterbury Cathedral. In 1147 Matilda shared with William of Ypres the task of mediation between Stephen and Archbishop Theobald, whose appointment to Canterbury ten years before had been partly owed to her influence. In 1148–9 she resided chiefly at Canterbury, to superintend the building of Faversham Abbey, which she and Stephen had founded on land obtained from William of Ypres in exchange for her manor of Lillechurch, Kent. At the end of April 1152 she fell sick at Hedingham Castle, Essex; she sent for her confessor, Ralph, prior of Holy Trinity, Aldgate, and died three days later, 3 May. She was buried in Faversham Abbey.

In 1136 or 1137 Matilda and her husband had founded, for the souls of her father 'and of our children,' a preceptory of Knights Templars at Cowley in Oxfordshire. In 1142 she founded a Cistercian abbey on her lands at Coggeshall in Essex. The Hospital of St. Katharine by the Tower of London was established by her in 1148, on land acquired by exchange with the canons of Trinity, Aldgate, for the souls of two of her children, Baldwin and Matilda, who were buried in Trinity Church. This younger Matilda was born in 1134, and betrothed in 1136 to Count Waleran of Meulan. Three children survived: Eustace, who died in August 1153; William, who became by marriage Earl of Warenne, but died childless in 1160; and Mary, who was devoted as an infant to the religious life, and was brought up first in the nunnery of Stratford, then in a cell founded for her by her mother, at Lillechurch, and afterwards (probably on the transfer of Lillechurch to William of Ypres in 1148) removed to Romsey, where she became abbess. On her brother William's death Henry II recognised her as heiress of Boulogne, and obtained a papal dispensation for her marriage with Matthew, son of the Count of Flanders. She died in 1182, leaving two daughters, through the younger of whom, Matilda, the county of Boulogne ultimately passed to the house of Brabant.

[William of Malmesbury, vol. ii.; Gervase of Canterbury, vol. i., ed. Stubbs; Henry of Huntingdon, ed. Arnold; Chronicles of Stephen, &c., vols. i. iii. iv., ed. Howlett (all in Rolls Series); Continuation of Florence of Worcester, ed. Thorpe (Engl. Hist. Soc.); Hist. of Holy Trinity, Aldgate, in App. to William of Newburgh, ed. Hearne, vol. iii.; Vita Theobaldi & Chronicon Beccense, in Lanfranc's Works, ed. Giles, vol. i.; Ordericus Vitalis, in Duchesne, Historiæ Normannorum Scriptores; Monasticon Anglicanum, vols. iv. v. vi.; Strickland's Queens of England, vol. i.; Everett Green's Princesses of England, vol. i.] K. N.

MATILDA, MAUD, MOLD, ÆTHELIC, AALIZ (1102–1167), empress, daughter of Henry I, king of England, and his first wife, Matilda (1080–1118) [q. v.], was born in London (Will. FitzStephen, in *Mater. for Hist. of Becket*, iii. 13) in 1102 (Gerv. Cant. i. 91–2). The 'English Chronicle' (a. 1127) calls her 'Æthelic,' and John of Hexham calls her 'Aaliz' and 'Adela' (Twysden, cols. 266, 269). Gervase, however, says that she was named Matilda after her mother; and by that name, in its various forms, she is known. At Whitsuntide 1109 her father accepted a proposal for her marriage with the German king, Henry V. Early next spring she was sent into Germany, under the care of Bishop Burchard of Cambrai and Roger FitzRichard, and with a dowry of ten thousand marks. At Easter, 10 April, she was betrothed at Utrecht to Henry V in person, and on 8 May she was crowned at Mainz by the Archbishop of Cöln, the Archbishop of Trier holding her 'reverently' in his arms. Henry dismissed all her English attendants, and had her carefully trained in the German language and manners. On 6 or 7 Jan. 1114 (Flor. Worc. a. 1114; Sim. Durham, a. 1114; *Ann. Hildesheim*, a. 1110) he married her and had her crowned again at Mainz. As Robert of Torigni says that 'once and again, in the city of Romulus, the imperial diadem was placed on her head by the supreme pontiff' (*Contin.* Will. Jumièges, p. 306), she may have accompanied her husband to his crowning at Rome in 1111. She certainly went with him to Italy in 1116 (Ekkehard, a. 1116, in Pertz, vi. 250); and he seems to have left her there as his representative during part of the winter of 1118, when she and the chancellor decided a law-case at Castrocaro, near Forlì, 14 Nov. (Mittarelli, *Ann. Camaldul.* iii. 178). On 22 May 1125 she was present at her husband's death at Utrecht. Her father at once summoned her back to his own court; she joined him in Normandy, and in September 1126 returned with him to England. The emperor when dying had placed his sceptre in her hands, as if bequeathing to her his dominions—where, indeed, she was so much beloved, that some of the princes of the empire followed her over sea to demand her back as their sovereign; a demand to which she would gladly have acceded. But Henry of England had other plans for the daughter who was now his only legitimate child. At Christmas 1126 he made his barons and bishops swear that if he should die without lawful son, they would acknowledge her as lady of England and Normandy. According to William of Malmesbury, he in return swore that he would not give her in marriage to anyone outside his realm. In spite, however, of this promise, of her own reluctance, and of the general resentment of his subjects, he sent her over sea soon after Whitsuntide 1127, under the care of Brian FitzCount [q.v.] and her half-brother, Robert, earl of Gloucester [q.v.], with instructions to the Archbishop of Rouen to make arrangements for her marriage with Geoffrey Plantagenet, son of the Count of Anjou. A year later, on the octave of Whitsunday, 17 June 1128, the wedding was solemnised in Le Mans Cathedral by the Bishop of Avranches (cf. *Hist. Gaufredi Ducis*, in Marchegay, *Chron. des Comtes d'Anjou*, pp. 234–6; Ord. Vit. p. 889; *Acta Pontif. Cenoman.*, in Mabillon, *Vet. Anal.* p. 321; and Green, *Princesses*, i. 107).

Matilda's first husband had been thirty years older than herself; the second was ten years younger—a boy scarce fifteen, the heir of an upstart race whose territory, insignificant in extent, was so placed as to make their hostility a perpetual thorn in the side of the ruler of Normandy, until it was bought off with Matilda's hand. The empress and her boy-husband soon quarrelled; and in July 1129 Geoffrey, now Count of Anjou, drove his wife out of his dominions. She withdrew to Rouen (Sim. Durham, a. 1129), and remained there till July 1131, when she went with her father to England. Geoffrey soon afterwards sent a message to recall her; a council held at Northampton, 8 Sept., decided that she should return to him, and the barons renewed their homage to her as her father's heir. Thenceforth community of political interest seems to have kept the ill-matched couple on friendly terms. Their first child was born at Le Mans on 5 March 1133 [see Henry II], and the king immediately caused his barons to swear fealty to Matilda for the third time, as well as to her infant son (Rog. Howden, ed. Stubbs, i. 187). Another son, Geoffrey, was born at Rouen on 1 June 1134 (*Chron. S. Albin. Andeg.* a. 1134, in Marchegay, *Eglises d'Anjou*). Matilda remained in Normandy with her father till the autumn of 1135, when a quarrel broke out between him and Geoffrey; she now sided with her husband, and went back to Angers after parting in anger from the king. On 1 Dec. Henry died. Matilda at once re-entered Normandy to claim her inheritance; the border-districts submitted to her, but England chose her cousin Stephen for its king, and Normandy soon adopted England's choice. Matilda appealed at Rome against Stephen for his breach of his oath to her; the case was tried before Innocent II early in 1136, but she obtained no redress (cf. 'Historia Pontificalis,' in Pertz, *Mon. Germ. Hist.* xx. 543–4; Gilb. Foliot, *Ep.* p. lxxix; and Round, *Geoffrey de Mandeville*, App. B). She, however, maintained her position at Argentan, and there her third child, William, was born, 21 July 1136 (*ib.* a. 1136). On 2 Oct. she brought a body of troops to reinforce Geoffrey at the siege of Le Sap; but Geoffrey was disabled by a wound, and they were compelled to retreat. Matilda now devoted herself to stirring up opposition to Stephen in England through her brother Earl Robert, her great-uncle David [q.v.], king of Scots, and other friends of her father. On 30 Sept. 1139 she landed, with Robert and a hundred and forty knights, at Arundel. Her stepmother, Queen Adeliza, received her into the castle; Stephen besieged her there, but soon allowed her to join her brother at Bristol. The barons of the west rallied round her; she removed to Gloucester, and there, in February 1141, Stephen was brought captive to her feet. She sent him in chains to Bristol Castle, and set out on a triumphal progress towards Winchester. A message to its bishop, Henry [see HENRY OF BLOIS], that if he joined her she would honour him as chief of her councillors, but if not, she would 'lead all the host of England against him at once,' brought him to a meeting with her at Wherwell, Hampshire, on 2 March. Next day she was solemnly welcomed into the city and the cathedral. From Winchester she proceeded to Wilton, Reading, Oxford, and St. Albans. On 8 April a council held at Winchester, under the direction of Bishop Henry, acknowledged her as 'Lady of England and Normandy;' and at midsummer she entered London and took up her abode at Westminster. But she overrated the security of her triumph. She took the title of queen without waiting to be crowned (*Monast. Anglic.* i. 44; GREEN, *Princesses*, vol. i. app. iii.; ROUND, *Geoff. Mandeville*, pp. 63–7); she confiscated lands and honours more ruthlessly than Stephen himself; she offended the barons who came to offer her their homage by the haughty coldness of her demeanour; she turned a deaf ear to the appeals of Stephen's wife and brother in his behalf and that of his children; she scornfully rejected a petition from the citizens of London for a renewal of 'King Eadward's laws,' demanded from them a heavy subsidy, and when they remonstrated, drove them from her presence with a torrent of abuse. The consequence was that they rose in arms and drove her out of their city. She fled to Oxford; but soon afterwards, hearing that Bishop Henry had renewed his allegiance to Stephen, she set off to try conclusions with him at Winchester. She established herself in the castle, and after vainly calling upon the bishop to rejoin her, rallied her forces to besiege him in his palace of Wolvesey. 'The king's queen with all her strength,' however, soon blockaded the city so effectually that the empress and her troops were in danger of starving. On 14 Sept. they cut their way out, but with such heavy loss that Matilda was separated from all her adherents save Brian FitzCount, with whom she rode first to Ludgershall and then to Devizes. There, half dead with fatigue, and still in terror of pursuit, she laid herself on a bier, and, bound to it with ropes as if she were a corpse, was carried thus into Gloucester. In the winter she returned to Oxford; in the spring (1142) she moved to Devizes, and thence, at mid-Lent, she sent messengers asking her husband to come to her aid. Geoffrey refused to come unless fetched by Earl Robert in person; so in June Robert went over sea, leaving his sister in Oxford Castle under the protection of the other leaders of her party, who swore to guard the town from attack until his return. Stephen, however, outgeneralled them, and on 26 Sept. stormed Oxford and laid siege to the castle. Its garrison were on the verge of starvation, when one night just before Christmas, the empress and three faithful knights clad themselves in white robes, dropped down over the castle wall upon the frozen river at its foot, passed unseen and unheard over the freshly fallen snow right through Stephen's camp, fled on foot as far as Abingdon, and by daybreak were safe at Wallingford. There Matilda met her brother and her eldest son. Her cause, however, was lost, though she remained in England five years longer, residing, it seems, chiefly at Gloucester or Bristol; in September 1146 she was once more at Devizes (STAPLETON, *Mag. Rot. Scacc. Norm.* vol. ii. p. lxx). Early in 1148 she went back to Normandy (GERV. CANT. i. 133), which Geoffrey was now holding by right of conquest. In 1150 the husband and wife seem to have conjointly ceded the duchy to their son Henry; but the cession was not formally complete till next summer, when it was ratified by King Louis of France. Peter de Langtoft (ed. Wright, i. 466) says that Matilda accompanied her husband to the French court on this occasion; but she was certainly not with him when he died, on the way home, 7 Sept. 1151.

Thenceforth Matilda seems to have lived entirely in Normandy. After her son's accession to the English crown, December 1154, she took up her abode in a palace which her father had built beside the minster of Notre-Dame des Prés, near Rouen. The Normans held her in great esteem for her works of piety and charity, and for the influence which she was known to exercise over her royal son. In England, where the haughtiness of her conduct had never been forgiven, this influence was regarded with suspicion (W. MAP, *De Nugis Curial.* ed. Wright, p. 227); but it seems to have been exercised chiefly for good. It probably helped to guide the young king's first steps in the reorganisation of his realm; for his mother was the one person with whom he took counsel before sailing for England in December 1154. In September 1155 she induced him to give up a rash scheme for the invasion of Ireland. In 1162 she tried to dissuade him from making Thomas Becket archbishop of Canterbury (*Materials for Hist. Becket*, v. 410). In the quarrel between Henry and Thomas she was constantly employed as mediatrix, and showed considerable fairness and skill in dealing with the case (*ib.* v. 142, 145–50, 161, 194–5, 361, 421, 423). Two letters of hers are extant; one, written in 1166–7 at the pope's request, beseeching Thomas to be reconciled with the king (*ib.* vi. 128–9); the other, of uncertain date, is addressed to Louis of France, and pleads for a cessation of his hostilities against Henry (Duchesne, *Hist. Franc. Scriptt.* iv. 722). Matilda had a dangerous illness in 1160. She died, after much suffering from fever and decay of strength, at Notre-Dame des Prés, early in the morning of 10 Sept. 1167. On her deathbed she took the veil as a nun of Fontevraud (Geoff. Vigeois, in Labbe, *Nova Biblioth.* ii. 317). Archbishop Rotrou of Rouen and Bishop Arnulf of Lisieux officiated at her burial before the high altar in the abbey church of Bec—the resting place which she had, despite her father's remonstrances, chosen for herself thirty-three years before (*Cont. W. Jumièges*, p. 306). In 1263 the church, and with it Matilda's tomb, was destroyed by fire. In 1282, when the church had been restored, search was made for her remains, and they were found, wrapped in an ox-hide (*Chron. Becc.* ed. Porée, p. 129). The new tomb in which they were reburied was stripped of its ornaments by the English soldiers who sacked Bec in 1421 (*ib.* p. 91). In 1684 a brass plate, with a long inscription, was placed over the grave by the brethren of St. Maur, who had lately come into possession of the abbey (Ducarel, *Anglo-Norm. Antiquities*, p. 89). This, too, perished in 1793, and the church itself was demolished in 1841. The leaden coffin of the empress, however, was re-discovered in 1846, and next year her remains were translated to what her father in 1134 had told her was their only fitting abode, the cathedral church of Rouen (*Revue de Rouen*, 1847, pp. 43–4, 699).

Twice in her life—in 1134 and again in 1160—Matilda had made careful testamentary arrangements for the distribution of her wealth to the poor, and to various hospitals, churches, and monasteries, of which Bec was chief. Her final dispositions included a large bequest for the completion of a stone bridge which she had begun to build over the Seine at Rouen. She founded several religious houses, and was a benefactress to many more. A little settlement of anchorites at Radmore in Staffordshire, on land granted by her in 1142, grew under her fostering care into a Cistercian monastery, which Henry II removed to Stoneleigh, Warwickshire, in 1155 (*Monast. Angl.* v. 446). Stanley Abbey sprang from a small Cistercian house founded at Lockwell, Wiltshire as a cell to Quarr, Isle of Wight, by her son Henry, acting in her name and his own, in 1149 or 1150 (*ib.* pp. 563–4). The origin of another English house of the same order, Bordesley, Worcestershire, has been ascribed to her; but this is doubtful (*ib.* pp. 407, 409–10). A chapel of Notre-Dame du Vœu at Cherbourg, founded by William the Conqueror, formed the nucleus of an Austin priory which she established at some time between 1132 and 1150 (Du Monstier, *Neustria Pia*, p. 813; *Gallia Christiana*, vol. xi. instr. col. 229). A Cistercian house bearing the same name, but also known as Valasse, near Lillebonne, was built between 1148 and 1157, the result of a vow which she had made when blockaded in Oxford in 1142 (Du Monstier, pp. 851–2). A Premonstratensian priory at Silly-en-Gouffern, near Argentan, was built on land given by her between 1151 and 1161 (cf. *ib.* pp. 830–1, and R. Torigni, a. 1167); and in the last year of her life she founded a Cistercian abbey at La Noë, near Evreux (*Gallia Christ.* vol. xi. instr. col. 133; the date there given to the foundation-charter is disproved by internal evidence). In Matilda's later years the harsh and violent temper which had marred one period of her career seems to have been completely mastered by the real nobleness of character which had gained for her, as a mere girl, the esteem of her first husband and the admiration of his subjects, and which even in her worst days had won and kept for her the devotion of men like Robert of Gloucester, Miles of Hereford, and Brian FitzCount. Arnulf of Lisieux (*Opera*, ed. Giles, p. 41) called her 'a woman who had nothing of the woman in her;' but the words were evidently meant as praise, not blame. One German chronicler gives her the title which English writers give to her mother, 'the good Matilda' (*Chron. Repkav.*, in Mencken, *Rer. Germ. Scriptt.* vol. iii. col. 357). Germans, Normans, and English are agreed as to her beauty. The sole existing portrait of her is that on her great seal; a majestic figure, seated, robed and crowned, and holding in her right hand a sceptre terminating in a lily-flower. This seal had been made for her in Germany, before her husband's coronation at Rome; its legend is 'Matilda, by God's grace Queen of the Romans.' The style which she commonly used in her charters was 'Matilda the Empress, King Henry's daughter;' during her struggle with Stephen, 1141–7, she sometimes added the title 'Lady of the English;' that of 'Queen of the English' occurs only twice, early in 1141 (Round, *Geoff. Mandeville*, pp. 70–7). As Matthew Paris says (*Chron. Maj.* i. 435), the significance of her life was summed up in the epitaph graven on her tomb: 'Here lies Henry's daughter, wife and mother; great by birth—greater by marriage—but greatest by motherhood.'

[English Chronicle, ed. Thorpe; Henry of Huntingdon, ed. Arnold; William of Malmesbury's Historia Novella, ed. Stubbs (Gesta Regum, vol. ii.); Draco Normannicus, Gesta Stephani, and Robert of Torigni's Chronicle, ed. Howlett (Chronicles of Stephen, &c., vols ii–iv.); Gervase of Canterbury, ed. Stubbs, vol. i.; Robertson's Materials for History of Becket, vols. iii. v. vi., all in Rolls Series; Florence of Worcester, ed. Thorpe, vol. ii. (English Historical Society); Ordericus Vitalis, and Robert of Torigni's Continuation of William of Jumièges, in Duchesne, Historiæ Normannorum Scriptores; W. de Gray Birch's Charters of Empress Matilda, in Journal of Archæological Association, vol. xxxi.; Round's Geoffrey de Mandeville; Mrs. Everett Green's Princesses of England, vol. i.]

K. N.

MATILDA, Duchess of Saxony (1156–1189), third child and eldest daughter of Henry II, king of England, and his wife, Eleanor of Aquitaine [q. v.], was born in 1156 (R. Diceto, i. 302), and baptised in the church of Holy Trinity, Aldgate, by Archbishop Theobald of Canterbury ('Hist. Trinity, Aldgate,' in *App.* to Hearne's *W. Newburgh*, iii. 706). In 1160 the queen took her daughter to join the king in Normandy (R. Torigni, p. 207); they seem to have brought her back with them in January 1163. Early in 1165 an embassy came from the emperor, Frederic Barbarossa, to ask in marriage two of Henry's daughters, one for Frederic's son, the other for his cousin, Henry the Lion, duke of Saxony. The former of these proposals came to nothing; the second was accepted for Matilda, who then accompanied her mother on another visit to Normandy, whence they returned in the autumn of 1166 (*ib.* pp. 224, 225, 233, dating the return a year too late). The earliest extant register of English tenants-in-chivalry and their holdings, still preserved in the 'Red' and 'Black' 'Books of the Exchequer,' was probably compiled with a view to the assessment of the aid levied by the king for his daughter's marriage. Early in 1167 the duke sent envoys to fetch his bride. She sailed from Dover about Michaelmas, was accompanied by her mother to Normandy, and thence proceeded, probably after Christmas, to Germany (Gerv. Cant. i. 205; R. Diceto, i. 330; Eyton, *Itin. Hen. II*, p. 109). The duke met her at Minden, and there they were married by Bishop Werner in the cathedral church, 1 Feb. 1168 ('Chron. Episc. Mindens.,' quoted in Leibnitz's *Orig. Guelf.* iii. 69).

Henry the Lion was twenty-seven years older than his child-bride; he had been married long before she was born, and divorced from his first wife in 1162. First cousin to the emperor, he was Duke of Bavaria, Saxony, and Brunswick; 'from the Elbe to the Rhine, from the Hartz to the sea,' all was his. Brunswick was his home; there the new-married couple held their wedding-feast (*Ann. Stadens.*, Pertz, xvi. 346); and there their first child, Richenza, was born during her father's absence on pilgrimage in 1172 (Arn. Lubeck in Pertz, xxi. 116). Two sons were born in the next eight years. In January 1180 (Böhmer, *Regesta Reg. Roman.* p. 140) a quarrel which had long been smouldering between the duke and the emperor ended in Henry's condemnation, by a diet at Würzburg, to forfeiture of all his territories (*Gesta Hen.* i. 249; Rog. Howden, ii. 201). He refused to submit, and Frederic laid siege to Brunswick just as Matilda had given birth within its walls to her third son. She appealed to the emperor's chivalry; he sent her a tun of wine, and raised the siege ('Chron. Laudun.,' with a wrong date, in *Rer. Gall. Scriptt.* xviii. 703). At the end of November 1181 the duke submitted, and abjured his country for three years (*Ann. Palidens.*, Pertz, xvi. 96; Arn. Lubeck, *ib.* xxi. 142). Frederic secured to Matilda the revenues of her dower-lands, and offered to let her dwell on them in peace, but she preferred to go with her husband to her father's court (*Gesta Hen.* i. 288). Their daughter and two of their sons accompanied them; the third, Lothar, was left in Germany (R. Diceto, ii. 13). They reached Argentan in the summer of 1182 (cf. *Gesta Hen.* i. 288, and Eyton, *Itin. Hen. II*, p. 248), and there soon afterwards their fourth son was born (*Gesta Hen.* l. c.) On 12 June 1184 Matilda went to England (*ib.* p. 312), and in that year her fifth son, William, was born at Winchester (*ib.* p. 313; R. Diceto, ii. 22). In November she was in London with her husband; at Christmas both were at Windsor with the king (*Gesta Hen.* i. 319, 333). In 1185, the three years having expired, and Henry II having obtained for his son-in-law the restitution of the allodial lands of Brunswick, Matilda returned thither with her husband and sons (*ib.* pp. 322, 334; Arn. Lubeck, Pertz, xxi. 156). In the spring of 1189 the emperor bade Henry the Lion either accompany him on crusade, or go into exile again till his return. Henry again sought refuge in England (*Gesta Hen.* ii. 62); Matilda remained with her children at Brunswick, and there died, 28 June (*Ann. Stederburg.*, Pertz, xvi. 221), or 13 July (R. Diceto, ii. 65).

Two original portraits of her exist in the church of St. Blasius at Brunswick; one, a picture representing her marriage, painted early in the thirteenth century; the other, a recumbent figure carved in stone upon her tomb. Both are engraved in Leibnitz's 'Origines Guelficæ' (vol. iii. pl. iii. and xiv.) She seems to have been tall and handsome. The troubadour Bertrand de Born wrote two love-songs in which he celebrates her under the name of Elena (RAYNOUARD, *Poésies des Troubadours*, iii. 135, 137, v. 81; CLÉDAT, *Bert. de Born*, pp. 79, 81). Her husband returned to Brunswick after Frederic's death, and dying there in 1195 was buried at her right hand, 'choosing to sleep beside her in death as in life' (*Ann. Stederburg*, PERTZ, xvi. 231). His people revered her as 'a most religious woman, whose memory is of note before God and man, whose good works and sweet disposition enhanced the lustre of the long royal line whence she sprang; a woman of profound piety, of wondrous sympathy for the afflicted, of much almsgiving and many prayers' (ARN. LUBECK, PERTZ, xxi. 116). Her eldest child, Richenza, is said by some writers to have married Waldemar II, king of Denmark; but it is clear that this is a mistake (see SCHEID's note in *Orig. Guelf.* iii. 172), and that Richenza is identical with the daughter whom the English chroniclers call Matilda, who was left in Normandy with her grandparents in 1185, returned to England with them in 1186 (*Gesta Hen.* i. 345), was married, first, in 1189, to Geoffrey of Perche (*ib.* ii. 73), and secondly, between 1200 and 1205, to Ingelram III of Coucy, and died before 1210 (LEIBNITZ, *Orig. Guelf.* iii. 174–5, 583–5). The eldest son, Henry, assumed the title of Duke of Saxony on his father's death, became count palatine of the Rhine in 1196, and died in 1227, leaving only two daughters. His brother Otto, nominated by his uncle Richard I as Earl of York in 1190, and Count of Poitou in 1196, was chosen emperor in 1198, crowned at Rome in 1209, and died childless in 1218. Lothar died in 1190. The boy born at Argentan in 1182 is never heard of again; doubtless he died in infancy. Matilda's youngest child, the English-born William 'of Winchester,' died in 1213, leaving by his wife, Helen, daughter of Waldemar I of Denmark, a son named Otto, who became sole heir male of the family on the death of his uncle Henry in 1227, and from whom sprang the ducal house of Brunswick and Luneburg, and the present royal house of England.

[The original authorities are given above. Ralph de Diceto, Gervase of Canterbury, the Gesta Henrici, Roger of Howden, and Robert of Torigni (Chronicles of Stephen, &c., vol. iv.) are in the Rolls Series; the German chronicles referred to are in Pertz, Monumenta Germaniæ Historica, vols. xvi. and xxi. The modern works consulted are Mrs. Everett Green's Princesses of England, vol. i.; the Origines Guelficæ, compiled by Leibnitz and edited by Scheid; and L'Art de vérifier les Dates, vol. xvi.] K. N.

MATON, ROBERT (1607–1653?), divine, was the second son of William Maton of North Tidworth, Wiltshire, and his wife Thomazin, daughter of William Hayter of Langford. He was born in 1607, probably at North Tidworth, but the registers previous to 1700 have been destroyed. He entered as a commoner at Wadham College, Oxford, in Michaelmas term 1623, aged about sixteen, matriculated 3 Nov. 1626, proceeded B.A. 25 Oct. 1627, and M.A. 10 June 1630 (GARDINER). Taking holy orders he was presented to a living, but in what county is uncertain. Wood (*Athenæ Oxon.*) says that he was always at heart a 'millenary,' but that he never made public his views until the rebellion, in which he saw a possibility of their fulfilment. He published in 1642 'Israel's Redemption, or the Propheticall History of our Saviour's Kingdom on Earth,' &c., and 'Gog and Magog, or the Battle of the Great Day of God Almightie,' London, 1642; 2nd edit. 1646. The former work led him into some controversy, and in 1644 a reply, entitled 'Chiliasto Mastix, or the Prophecies . . . vindicated from the Misinterpretations of the Millenaries, and specially of Mr. Maton,' &c., was published at Rotterdam by Alexander Petrie, minister of the Scots church there. Maton remained an ardent believer in the literal meaning of scriptural prophecy, and in 1646 he published, in reply to Petrie, 'Israel's Redemption Redeemed, or the Jewes generall and miraculous Conversion to the Faith of the Gospel, and Returne into their owne Land; and our Saviour's Personall Reigne on Earth cleerly proved.' He endeavours here to show the 'proper sense of the plagues contained under the Trumpets and Vialls.' Wood wrongly says (*ib.* iii. 409) that Petrie wrote a second reply. Maton's book was republished (London, 1652) under a new title, 'Christ's Personall Reigne on Earth One Thousand Yeares. . . . The Manner, Beginning, and Continuation of His Reigne clearly proved by many plain Texts of Scripture,' &c. It was again republished as 'A Treatise of the Fifth Monarchy' (1655), with a portrait of Maton by Cross (GRANGER). Though not apparently openly connected with the Fifth-monarchy men, Maton was doubtless in sympathy with them. Of his death we have no record.

[Wood's Athenæ Oxon. ed. Bliss, iii. 409; Granger's Biog. Hist. of England, iii. 52; Steven's Hist. of the Scottish Church in Rotterdam, Edinburgh, 1832, pp. 12–14; Gardiner's Registers of Wadham Coll. Oxford, pp. 70–1; Sir Thomas Phillipps's Visitatio Heraldica Com. Wilt., 1828, catalogued under 'Wilts,' for Maton's pedigree.] C. F. S.

MATON, WILLIAM GEORGE, M.D. (1774–1835), physician, son of George Maton, a wine merchant, was born at Salisbury, 31 Jan. 1774. He was sent to the free grammar school of his native city, and early showed some taste for natural history. In July 1790 he entered at Queen's College, Oxford, and while there gave much time to botany, and acquired the friendship of Dr. John Sibthorp [q. v.], the professor of that subject. On 18 March 1794 he was elected a fellow of the Linnean Society, and thus came to know Sir James Edward Smith [q. v.] the botanist. He published several papers in the 'Transactions'—one in vol. iii. on a freshwater shell, Tellina rivalis; another in vol. v., 'Observations on the Orcheston Long Grass;' a third (vol. vii.), with Mr. Rackett, 'An Historical Account of Testaceological Writers,' and 'A Descriptive Catalogue of British Testacea;' a fifth (vol. x.), 'On Testacea from Rio de la Plata.' He became vice-president of the society; and the members showed their regard for him by calling a woodpecker, a shell-fish, and a genus of plants after him. In the 'London Medical Journal,' vol. v., he published a paper on cinchona, in which he describes his discovery of the alkaline principle of the bark. He also worked at history; wrote an account of a conventual seal found at Salisbury in the 'Gentleman's Magazine' for 1792, and parts of the 'Salisbury Guide,' and Hutchins's 'History of Dorset,' as well as a paper on Stonehenge in the 'Archæologia' for 1794. In that year he graduated B.A. at Oxford, and in 1797 M.A. In 1797 he published at Salisbury, in two volumes, 'Observations relative chiefly to the Natural History, Picturesque Scenery, and Antiquities of the Western Counties of England, made chiefly in the Years 1794 and 1796.' This is a record of travels in Dorset, Devonshire, Cornwall, and Somerset. The plants and the antiquities are pleasantly described, while the author seems to have been very sensible to the charms of landscape. In Cornwall he did not forget to inquire about the Cornish language, but could not find a single person who could speak it, and concluded that it was extinct. The first tour was made with his friend Charles Hatchett, F.R.S., and Mr. Rackett the botanist. On his return from the second he began medical study at the Westminster Hospital, and 11 July 1798 graduated M.B. at Oxford, and 15 April 1801 M.D. He was elected a fellow of the College of Physicians of London 30 Sept. 1802, became Gulstonian lecturer in 1803, censor 1804, 1813, and 1824, treasurer 1814 to 1820, and Harveian orator 1815. He was physician to the Westminster Hospital 1800–8. He published three papers in the 'Transactions of the College of Physicians:' 'On Superfœtation' (vol. iv.); 'Some Account of a Rash liable to be mistaken for Scarlatina;' 'On a case of Chorea in an Aged Person cured by Musk.' They do not show much depth of medical attainment.

During the Weymouth season Maton used to practise in that town. One day as he was walking there an equerry summoned him to Queen Charlotte, who asked him to name a specimen of *Arundo* (now *Calamagrostis*) *Epigejos*, which one of the princesses fond of botany had obtained. He named the plant, and acquired the confidence of the royal family. In 1816 he was appointed physician extraordinary to Queen Charlotte, and in 1820 attended the Duke of Kent in his last illness. He afterwards became physician to the duchess and to the infant Princess Victoria. His practice increased, and was only exceeded by that of Sir Henry Halford [q. v.] In his holidays he travelled abroad. His father, who died in 1816, proved to be deeply in debt, and before 1827 Maton paid all that was owing to the amount of 20,000*l.* The mayor and corporation of Salisbury, in testimony of his honourable conduct, on this occasion gave him the freedom of their city in a gold box. He bought a country seat near Downton, Wiltshire, but six months later became very ill and died 30 March 1835 at his house in Spring Gardens, London. A portrait of him hangs in the dining-room of the College of Physicians, and a good engraving of a drawing of him is the frontispiece of Dr. Paris's 'Life.'

[J. A. Paris's Biographical Sketch of William George Maton, M.D., London, 1838; Munk's Coll. of Phys. iii. 6; Works.] N. M.

MATTHEW. [See also MATHEW.]

MATTHEW PARIS (*d.* 1259), historian. [See PARIS.]

MATTHEW WESTMINSTER, imaginary historian. [See WESTMINSTER.]

MATTHEW, TOBIE or TOBIAS (1546–1628), archbishop of York, was the son of John Matthew of Ross, Herefordshire, and his wife Eleanor Crofton of Ludlow. He was born at Bristol in 1546, and gave many books to his native city when archbishop (Godwin, *De Præsulibus Angliæ*, 1516). He received his early education at Wells and matriculated at Oxford as a probationer of University College in 1559. He graduated B.A. in February 1563-4. In February 1564-5 he was a member of Christ Church, and he proceeded M.A. in July 1566, being then student of that house. He was ordained in the same year, 'at which time he was much respected for his great learning, eloquence, sweet conversation, friendly disposition, and the sharpness of his wit' (Wood, *Athenæ Oxonienses*). When Queen Elizabeth visited the university in the same year he took part in a 'disputation in philosophy' before her in St. Mary's Church on 3 Sept., arguing in favour of an elective as against an hereditary monarchy. When the queen left Christ Church on her departure from Oxford, he bade her farewell in an eloquent oration (*Elizabethan Oxford*, Oxford Historical Society). His handsome presence and his ready wit attracted the queen's notice. 'He was one of a proper person (such people, *cæteris paribus* and sometimes *cæteris imparibus*, were preferred by the queen) and an excellent Preacher' (Fuller, *Church History*, p. 133). The queen continued her favour to him throughout her life (Thoresby, *Vicaria Leodiensis*, gives many instances), and was equally kind to his wife, on whom she bestowed 'a fragment of an unicorn's horn.' On 2 Nov. 1569 he was unanimously elected public orator of the university, and held the office till August 1572. In 1570 he was appointed a canon of Christ Church, on 28 Nov. 1572 archdeacon of Bath, on 15 May 1572 prebendary of Teynton Regis in the cathedral of Salisbury, and 'being much famed for his admirable way of preaching he was made one of the queen's chaplains in ordinary' (Wood, *Athenæ Oxon.*) On 17 July 1572 he was elected president of St. John's College, which had then an intimate connection with Christ Church. He was the fifth president since the foundation seventeen years before, and he had to struggle with the difficulties of a poor and divided college. In 1573 he endeavoured, on the score of poverty, to win release from the annual obligation to elect scholars from Merchant Taylors' School (Wilson, *History of Merchant Taylors' School*). In 1576 he was appointed dean of Christ Church, and resigned the headship of St. John's on 8 May 1577. He took the degree of B.D. 10 Dec. 1573, and D.D. June 1574. On 14 July 1579 he was nominated vice-chancellor of the university by Robert Dudley, earl of Leicester, then chancellor. When Campion published his 'Decem Rationes' in 1581, Matthew's was the first answer from Oxford. In a Latin sermon before the university, 9 Oct. 1581, he defended the Reformation, appealing chiefly to the teaching of Christ and primitive Christianity, and refraining from either quoting or defending Luther. In June 1583 he became precentor of Salisbury, but resigned in the following February. He was installed as dean of Durham 31 Aug. 1583, and resigned the deanery of Christ Church early in 1584. He was inducted as vicar of Bishop's Wearmouth on 28 May 1590.

While dean of Durham, Matthew acted as a political agent of the government in the north, and was a vigorous pursuer of recusants. Through him the queen's advisers frequently received information on the condition of Scotland ('a court and kingdom as full of welters and uncertainties as the moon is of changes,' Tobie Matthew to Walsingham, 15 Jan. 1593, *Cal. State Papers*). He was none the less active as an orator, and his services as preacher were eagerly sought all over the county palatine. 'Yet for all his pains in preaching he neglected not his proper episcopal acts of visitation, confirmation, ordination, &c. . . . he confirmed sometimes five hundred, sometimes a thousand at a time; yea, so many that he hath been forced to betake himself to his bed for refreshment. At Hartlepool he was forced to confirm in the churchyard.' In 1595 he was promoted to the bishopric of Durham. A letter of his successor in the deanery to Cecil (16 Jan. 1597, *ib.*) gives a graphic picture of the condition of the great northern diocese at the time. In the bishopric five hundred ploughs had decayed within fifty years. Of eight thousand acres lately in tillage not eight score were then tilled, and the people were driven into the coast towns. In Northumberland great villages were dispeopled, and there was no man to withstand the enemy's attack. The misery had arisen through decay of tillage. Amid the confusion recusancy held up its head. Matthew sat in the court of high commission and examined the offenders, but they were obstinate. The remedies suggested for the condition of Northumberland (June 1602, *ib.*) show the difficulties against which he had to contend. The bishop, it is proposed in this paper, should compel his incumbents to be resident and preach, and the queen's farmers of taxes who hold Hexham, Holy Island, Bamborough, and Tynemouth, and leave churches either wholly unprovided, or supplied with mean curates, ought to be forced to support preachers. The bishop seems gradually to have brought about an improvement; he was most energetic in discharge of his duties, and constantly sent up lists of recusants and examinations of suspected persons. His services were recognised by James I no less than by his predecessor; he took a prominent part in the Hampton Court conference, and preached at the close before the king, who greatly admired his sermons (cf. STRYPE, *Whitgift*, App. pp. 236–8).

On 18 April 1606 he was appointed archbishop of York, on the death of Dr. Matthew Hutton, whom he had succeeded also at Durham. In the primacy his political activity increased. He was named on the commission for 'examining and determining all controversies in the north' (21 July 1609, *ib.*) He was given the custody of the Lady Arabella Stuart, and it was from his house that she escaped in June 1611. He preached the sermon on the opening of parliament in 1614. In the same year, when the lords refused to meet the commons in conference on the impositions, and sixteen bishops voted in the majority, Matthew alone voted for conferring with the lower house. If the letter in 'Cabala' is genuine (see below), this was not the only occasion on which he opposed the royal policy. During his last years he retired from political life, and was excused attendance at parliament, 1624–6, on account of his age and infirmities. In 1624 he gave up York House to the king for Buckingham, in exchange for certain Yorkshire manors.

As early as 1607 rumours of his death were abroad (J. Chamberlain to Dudley Carleton, *ib.* 30 Dec. 1607), and he was supposed to encourage them. 'He died yearly,' says Fuller (*Church History*, p. 133), 'in report, and I doubt not but that in the Apostle's sense he died daily in his mortifying meditations.' In 1616 one of these reports caused considerable mirth at the expense of the avaricious archbishop of Spalato, who applied to the king for the see which he supposed to be vacant (GARDINER, *Hist. of Engl.* iv. 285). Matthew died on 29 March 1628, and was buried in York Minster, where his tomb stands (the effigy now separate) in the south side of the presbytery.

Matthew, though renowned in his day as a preacher and divine, was a statesman quite as much as a prelate. The advisers of Elizabeth and James felt that they could rely upon him to watch and guard the northern shires. None the less was he a diligent bishop and a pious man. 'He had an admirable talent for preaching, which he never suffered to lie idle, but used to go from one town to another to preach to crowded audiences. He kept an exact account of the sermons which he preached after he was preferred; by which it appears that he preached, when dean of Durham, 721; when bishop of that diocese, 550; when archbishop of York, 721; in all, 1992' (GRANGER, *Biographical History*, i. 342). He was noted for his humour. 'He was of a cheerful spirit,' says Fuller, 'yet without any trespass on episcopal gravity, there lying a real distinction between facetiousness and nugacity. None could condemn him for his pleasant wit, though often he would condemn himself, as so habited therein he could as well be as not be merry, and not take up an innocent jest as it lay in the way of his discourse' (*Church History*, p. 133).

He married Frances, daughter of William Barlow (*d.* 1568) [q. v.], sometime bishop of Chichester, and widow of Matthew Parker, second son of the archbishop. She was 'a prudent and a provident matron' (*ib.*), gave his library of over three thousand volumes to the cathedral of York, and 'is memorable likewise for having a bishop to her father, an archbishop to her father-in-law, four bishops to her brethren, and an archbishop to her husband' (CAMDEN, *Britannia*). She died 10 May 1629. Their brilliant son, Sir Tobie [q. v.], was a great trouble to his father. Two younger sons were named John and Samuel, and there were two daughters (HUNTER, *Chorus Vatum*, Addit. MS. 24490, f. 234).

His portrait in the hall of Christ Church, Oxford, shows him as a small, meagre man, with moustache and beard turning grey.

Matthew published 'Piissimi et eminentissimi viri Tobiæ Matthew Archiepiscopi olim Eboracensis concio apologetica adversus Campianum. Oxoniæ excudebat Leonardus Lichfield impensis Ed. Forrest an. Dom. 1638.' There is a manuscript in late sixteenth-century hand in the Bodleian. The sermon seems to have been largely circulated in manuscript, though it was not printed till ten years after the archbishop's death. Matthew is also credited with 'A Letter to James I' (*Cabala*, i. 108). This is a severe indictment of the king's proposed toleration and of the prince's journey into Spain. The writer declares that the king was taking to himself a liberty to throw down the laws of the land at pleasure, and threatens divine judgments. The letter is unsigned and undated, and, in default of evidence of authorship, it seems improbable that Matthew was the writer. Thoresby attributes it to George Abbot.

'I have been informed that he had several things lying by him worthy of the press, but what became of them after his death I know not, nor anything to the contrary, but that they came into the hands of his son, Sir Tobie' (WOOD, *Athenæ Oxon.*)

[For the degrees and university offices held by Matthew the Reg. of Univ. of Oxford, ed. Boase and Clark (Oxford Hist. Soc.) For later life: St. John's College MSS.; Wood's Athenæ Oxon.; Fuller's Church Hist.; Godwin, De Præsulibus Angliæ; H. B. Wilson's Hist. of Merchant Taylors' School; Granger's Biog. Hist.; Camden's Britannia; Le Neve's Lives of Bishops since the Reformation; Wrangham's Zouch, ii. 160; Thoresby's Vicaria Leodiensis, pp. 155 sq. (largely from the archbishop's manuscript diary). The Calendars of State Papers afford many illustrations of the archbishop's political and private life.] W. H. H.

MATTHEW, Sir TOBIE (1577–1655), courtier, diplomatist, and writer, was born at Salisbury on 3 Oct. 1577, 'a little after three of the clock in the afternoon' (Thoresby, *Vicaria Leodiensis*, 1724, p. 174), his father, Tobie or Tobias Matthew [q. v.], afterwards archbishop of York, being at that time dean of Christ Church, Oxford, where Wood states, erroneously, that Tobie was born. He matriculated from Christ Church 13 March 1589-90, and graduated B.A. 5 June 1594, M.A. 5 July 1597. While still at Oxford the advantages of 'pregnant parts' and 'a good tutor' combined to render him a 'noted orator and disputant,' and his father conceived the greatest hopes of him from his vivacity (Wood). The same quality made him a welcome guest at the houses of the great, and as early as 1595 he acted the esquire's part in Essex's 'Device' on the queen's day (Rowland Whyte to Sir Robert Sidney, *Sidney Papers*, i. 362). In 1596 he had a severe illness, aggravated by a misunderstanding with his father, who was inclined to be severe and exacting (*Cal. State Papers*, Dom. 1595–1597, p. 168). In 1598 he was staying with young Throgmorton in France (Chamberlain, *Letters*, Camd. Soc., p. 10); later in the year the domestic atmosphere was again troubled owing to Tobie's debts. On 15 May 1599 he was admitted of Gray's Inn. On 3 Oct. 1601 he entered parliament as member for Newport, Cornwall, and about the same time laid the foundation of an intimacy with Francis Bacon, which only terminated with the latter's death in 1626. In March 1603 he undertook to deliver a letter from Bacon to James I, and Bacon describes him as a very worthy and rare young gentleman. On 25 March 1604 he re-entered parliament as member for St. Albans, *vice* Sir Francis Bacon, who elected to serve for Ipswich (*Returns of Memb. of Parl.* i. 444). In 1604, in accordance with a wish that he had long entertained, he resolved to visit Italy, having 'often heard of the antiquities and other curiosities of' that country. But his parents refused their consent. His mother, who was puritanically inclined, and seems to have early suspected his bias towards Roman catholicism, was most reluctant to lose sight of him, and offered to settle her fortune on him if he would stay in England and marry. But deceitfully announcing that he intended to go to France only, he obtained his parents' permission, on the express condition that he did not stay long abroad, and on no account visited either Italy or Spain. With a license to travel for three years, dated 3 July 1604 (*Cal. State Papers*, Dom. 1603–1610, p. 128), he sailed for France early in the following year, and once out of England he did not stop until he reached Florence. While there he was surprised and touched by a kind letter from his father, begging him to return after satisfying his curiosity, and urging him to be true to the protestant religion. His protestant principles were, he says, at that time in no need of confirmation, but soon after this he met in Florence some English catholics, especially Sir George Petre and Robert Cansfield; and from one Partridge, nephew of Sir Henry Western, he received a sensational account of the liquefaction of the blood of St. Januarius—protestant testimony to the miracle, which was confirmed by that of another protestant, the Earl of Suffolk's eldest son. Subsequently Matthew moved to Siena, that he might 'be with Italians only, in order to learn their language,' and thence he went to Naples, and finally to Rome. At Rome he visited the famous jesuit Robert Parsons [q. v.], partly, as he says, out of curiosity, and partly 'out of respect to one who might possibly do him an injury.' Parsons at once set about converting him, and recommended him to read William Reynolds's 'masterly "Reprehension of Dr. Whitaker."' At the same time he was most courteously received by Cardinal Pinelli, his conversion being evidently regarded as a foregone conclusion. He returned to Florence in an unsettled state, kept aloof from the little English colony, and lived 'freely and dissolutely' in a small house in a retired part of the town. During the spring of 1606 he was much impressed by the Florentine observance of Lent. He resolved impulsively to reform his life and change his religion, and was received into the Roman catholic communion at the close of March by Father Lelio Ptolomei, an Italian jesuit, whom he had frequently heard preach during Lent. He remained abroad for about six months after his conversion, and then set out for England, where he arrived, by way of France and Flanders, in September. He took up his abode in a French ordinary near the Tower of London, and at first kept his conversion secret, but subsequently communicated it to Sir Robert Cecil through Bacon, and simultaneously changed his lodging to Fleet Street. It devolved upon Bacon to make known his backsliding to Bancroft, archbishop of Canterbury, who promptly undertook his reconversion. He had many conferences with the archbishop, but they only ended in his being committed a close prisoner to the Fleet, where he was detained six months. He was, however, allowed free converse with his friends, 'who sought to recover him,' and was, moreover, put in good hope of further liberty. Among those who visited him were Thomas Morton [q. v.], afterwards bishop of Durham, of whom he had a bad opinion, Sir Edwin Sandys, on whose vanity he enlarges, Sir Henry Goodyear, John Donne the poet, Richard Martin, and Captain Whitelock, who called St. Paul a widgeon, and was generally so blasphemous that his hearer momentarily expected his annihilation, but was 'yet so witty as would almost tempt a man to forgive him, in spight of his heart and judgment.' Bacon wrote him a letter during his imprisonment on his seduction, laying stress upon 'the extreme effects of superstition in this last gunpowder treason.' The high opinion entertained by Bacon of Matthew's literary judgment is shown by his submitting to him at this time the rough sketch of his 'In felicem memoriam Elizabethæ,' thus commencing a practice which he appears to have continued to the last (MATTHEW, *Letters*, p. 22). Another of Tobie's interviewers was Bishop Andrewes, and before the close of 1607 Alberico Gentili [q. v.] was sent by the renegade's father, as a last resource, to try and bring him back. Early in 1608, owing to a severe outbreak of the plague, Matthew was allowed to leave the prison on parole, and on 7 Feb. 1607–8 the combined influence of his father, Bacon, and Cecil (who had previously had a dispute with, but was now reconciled to him), procured his release from the Fleet. He was transferred to the charge of a messenger of state, who was made responsible for his appearance. Two months later he obtained the king's leave to go abroad.

He left England not to return for ten years. He seems to have first gone to Brussels, and thence to Madrid. There he appears in 1609 to have been in the train of Sir Robert Shirley (WINWOOD, *Memorials*, iii. 104, 128), and thither in the same year Bacon sent him his 'Advancement of Learning,' and the key to his famous cipher, about which he requests secrecy. In February 1610 Bacon sent him his 'De Sapientia Veterum,' and in the following year he was at Venice with his friend Mr. Gage (*ib.* iii. 384), through whom he became acquainted with Edward Norgate [q. v.] the illuminer. Sir Dudley Carleton met him there in 1612, 'so broken with travel' that the name 'Il vecchio' was applied to him (*Court and Times of James I*, i. 195). From 1611 onwards he missed no opportunity of urging Salisbury and others to obtain him permission to return home, if only as a recognition of his exemplary conduct while abroad; but the king turned a deaf ear to his importunities. In 1614 he was ordained priest at Rome by Cardinal Bellarmine (FOLEY). After this he probably returned to Madrid, where he possessed some influence and a wide circle of acquaintance. In 1616 his father, the archbishop, wrote to the newly converted Thomas Howard, second earl of Arundel [q. v.], deploring his son's recusancy, and entreating the earl by his judicious advice to persuade him, 'yea, to press him,' to take a proper view of his duty 'towards his king and his father, as well as his God.' This would seem at first sight to imply that Tobie was in England, but his return was, it is almost certain, deferred until the following year, when influence which he had brought to bear upon Buckingham procured the king's consent (cf. *State Papers*, Dom. 1610–18, p. 465). He landed at Dover in May 1617, and was seen by Chamberlain on the 18th of that month at Winwood's house. Soon afterwards he went to Bacon at Gorhambury, and in August was entertained by Thomas Wilbraham at Townsend, near Nantwich, during the king's stay at that mansion. By October he was settled in London, and was observed to pay nightly visits to Gondomar (*ib.* p. 489). At this time, says Wood, he was generally allowed to be a person of wit and polite behaviour, and 'a very compleat gentleman,' remarkably conversant with foreign affairs. From London in 1618 he issued an Italian translation of Bacon's essays, entitled 'Saggi morali del Signore Francesco Bacono, cavagliero inglese, gran cancelliero d'Inghilterra. Con vn altro suo trattato della sapienza degli antichi,' London, 8vo. A dedicatory letter to Cosmo, grand duke of Tuscany, contains a fine eulogy of Bacon. On Bacon's impeachment, Matthew wrote him a letter which Bacon compared to 'old gold' (MATTHEW, *Letters*, p. 69; cf. SPEDDING, xiv. 286–7). A second edition of Matthew's translation appeared in 1619 and a third in 1621. The second edition ('curante Andrea Cioli') contains the essay 'On Seditions and Troubles,' which was not printed in English till 1625.

Though Matthew had now been nearly two years in England, he had not taken the oath of allegiance. The king was displeased at his constant refusal, and in January 1618–

1619 he was ordered to leave the kingdom. He went to Brussels, whence in February he wrote to Bacon on Spanish affairs (SPEDDING, xiv. 20). Two translations occupied the next year of his exile. The first was 'The Confession of the Incomparable Doctour, S. Augustine, translated into English: Together with a Large Preface, which it will much import to be read over first; that so the book itself may both profit and please the reader more.' It was very sharply answered by Matthew Sutcliffe [q. v.], dean of Exeter, in his vituperative 'Unmasking of a Masse Monger,' London, 1626, in which frank allusion is made to the alleged libertinism of Tobie's youth. Another translation, issued anonymously in 1620, but undoubtedly by Matthew (Peacham's ascription, in *Truth of our Time*, p. 102, being corroborated by internal evidence), was entitled 'A Relation of the Death of the most illustrious Lord, Sigr Troilo Sauelli, a baron of Rome, who was there beheaded in the castle of Sant Angelo, on the 18 of Aprill 1592.' Another edition, 'more correct,' appeared in 12mo in 1663, entitled 'The Penitent Bandito,' and signed by Sir T. M., knight, to which in the British Museum copy is added the author's name in full in Anthony à Wood's handwriting.

In the meantime Lord Bristol's influence was being exerted to procure Matthew's permanent return. On 29 Dec. 1621 he landed at Dover, and after a short delay was permitted to proceed to London. In May 1622 he dined with Gondomar; in June, at the instance of Buckingham's mother, he sustained the catholic cause against Dr. Wright in a disputation before the king (*Diary of Walter Yonge*, Camd. Soc. p. 60). He had the goodwill of Buckingham (see his *Letters to the Duke*, ap. Goodman, ii. 267–70), and seems to have exerted himself to obtain that of the king, as in 1622 he acquainted the government with a scheme for erecting titular Roman catholic bishoprics in England, and the project was accordingly nipped in the bud. In 1623 he was rewarded with the confidence of the king, who despatched him to Madrid to advise Charles and Buckingham, and he amused the prince by penning a flattering and witty, but somewhat licentious, description of the beauties of the infanta's mind and person (copied in *Harl. MS.* 1576). The Prince of Wales, in a postscript to a letter from Buckingham to the king (dated 20 June 1623), related how 'littel prittie Tobie Matthew' came to entreat them to send to the king what he called 'a pictur of the Infanta's drawen in black and white:' 'We pray you let none lafe at it but yourselfe and honnest Kate [the Duchess of Buckingham]. He thinkes he hath hitt the naille of the head, but you will fynd it foolishest thing that ever you saw' (*ib.* 6987). In a letter to her lord, dated 16 July, 'honnest Kate' deplores that 'she hath not seen the picktur Toby Mathus ded. . . . I do immagen what a rare pesce it is being of his doing.' On 8 Aug. he wrote from Madrid a letter of comfort to the duchess, assuring her that the duke continued supreme 'in the prince's heart' (GOODMAN, *Court of James I*, ii. 303). While in Spain Matthew had some sharp rallies with a rival wit, Archie [see ARMSTRONG, ARCHIBALD] (Chamberlain to Sir Dudley Carleton, ap. *Court and Times of James I*, ii. 423). It does not appear that he greatly assisted the negotiations, but shortly before the prince's departure he sent a memorandum to the catholic king, protesting as strongly as was feasible against the 'voto' of the 'theologi' (*Cabala*, 1691, p. 303). On his return he attended the court with assiduity, and on 20 Oct. 1623 he was knighted by the king at Royston, 'for what service,' says Chamberlain, 'God knows' (NICHOLS, *Progresses of James I*, iv. 931; METCALFE, *Book of Knights*, p. 181). These marks of royal favour led his parents to relent and invite him to York. At his father's house there he relates how 'it happened that there came by accident, if not by designe, a kind of lustie knott, if it might not rather goe for a little colledge, of certaine eminent Clergiemen,' by whom he found himself inveigled into controversial discussion. Provoked at last to a warm utterance of his views, he states 'it was strange to see how they wrung their hands, and their whites of eyes were turned up, and their devout sighes were sent abroad to testifie their grief that I would utter myself after that manner.' During these two years (1622–3) he had much serious talk with the archbishop, who derived what consolation he could from the fact that his son was content to read such protestant manuals as he put before him. Sir Tobie even cherished the hope of making a proselyte of his father. On his mother's fervent puritanism he could make little impression, and his filial piety suffered in consequence. 'My mother,' he wrote, upon her death in May 1629, 'went out of the world calling for her silkes and toyes and trinketts, more like an ignorant childe of foure yeares than like a talking scripturist of almost foure score' (NELIGAN). His father on his death in 1628 is stated to have left him in his will only a piece of plate of twenty marks, having in his lifetime given him over 14,000*l.* (WILLIS, *Cathedrals* (York), p. 53).

In 1624 Sir Tobie was selected one of the eighty-four 'Essentials,' or original working members, of the abortive Academe Royal, of which the scheme had just been completed by Edmund Bolton [q. v.] In June 1625 he was at Boulogne, whence he wrote an interesting letter to the Duchess of Buckingham, describing Henrietta Maria in enthusiastic terms which rival those of his previous 'picture' of the infanta (*Cabala*, p. 302). A considerable portion of the next few years Sir Tobie spent abroad, probably either in Paris or in Brussels. It is said that in 1625, at Sir Tobie's special request, Bacon added his 'Essay on Friendship' to the series in commemoration of their long intimacy. On his death in the following year he bequeathed Matthew 30*l.* to buy a ring.

At the court of the new king Sir Tobie became more openly identified with the catholics, among whom he was sometimes known as Father Price. A secular priest of this name, described as 'long a prisoner in Newgate,' is included in Gee's list of 190 Romish priests and jesuits resident about London in March 1624 ('Foot out of the Snare,' printed in SOMERS, *Tracts*, 1810, iii. 87, 91).

In September 1633 a lying report was spread by Lodowick Bowyer to the effect that he had died at Gravesend, and that compromising correspondence from Laud to the pope had been found upon him (*Hist. MSS. Comm.* 11th Rep. App. vii. 185). Later in the year he accompanied Strafford to Ireland in the capacity of secretary, but was soon back again in London, and his influence there at the moment was vividly depicted by the French ambassador. 'The cleverest of the Catholic seminarists,' he writes, 'is Tobie Matthew, a man of parts, active, influential, an excellent linguist; he penetrates cabinets, he insinuates himself into all kinds of affairs, and knows the temper and purpose of those who govern the kingdom, especially of the Lord Treasurer, whom he manages so skilfully that he is able to realise all his schemes in favour of Spain.... He is a man, "sans intéret particulier, qui ne travaille que pour l'honneur et pour sa passion, qui est le soulagement et l'avancement des catholiques."' He was described as well affected to France, if only that country would aid him in his design, the means indicated being: 1. By interposing to obtain the same oath of allegiance for England as for Ireland, a project approved by the pope. 2. By establishing seminaries in France. 3. By subsidising a certain number of missionary priests, both from the ranks of jesuits, Benedictines, and seculars ('Relation par M. de Fontenay au retour de son ambassade d'Angleterre,' June 1634, ap. RANKE, *Hist. of England*, v. 448). In July 1636 Matthew was on a visit to Lord Salisbury at Hatfield; in October 1637 he got the credit (wrongly as subsequently appeared) of being chief instrument in the conversion of Lady Newport, whereupon 'the king did use such words . . . that the fright reduced Don Tobiah to such perplexity that I find he will make a very ill man to be a martyr; but now the dog doth again wag his tail' (Lord Conway to Earl of Strafford, *Strafford Corresp.* ii. 125). The queen's influence was in fact a guarantee to Matthew of a position at court, which if ill defined was so considerable as to prove a serious grievance to puritans of all shades. In 1639 a political squib, entitled 'Reasons that Ship and Conduct Money ought to be paid,' suggests that Sir Tobie was an abettor of the 'Popish plot' and, with Sir John Wintour and the queen-mother, was making a laughing-stock of the country (cf. *Cal. State Papers*, Dom. 1639–40, p. 246). Habernfeld and Boswell followed this up next year in their 'Particular Discovery of the Plot against King Kingdom and Protestant Religion,' in which he is described as a 'jesuited priest' and 'a most dangerous man, to whom a bed was never so dear that he would rest his head thereon, refreshing his body with sleep in a chair, neither day nor night spared his machinations; a man principally noxious . . . . who flies to all banquets and feasts, called or not called, never quiet, a perpetual motion; thrusting himself into all conversations of superiors, he urgeth conferences familiarly that he may fish out the minds of men. These discoveries he communicates to the Pope's Legate, but the most secret things to Cardinal Barberini [in whose pay it was assevered he had been for many years] or the Pope himself' (RUSHWORTH, *Hist. Collections*, p. 1322). Prynne wrote of him in a similar vein as a papal spy and missionary sent to reclaim England. It was therefore only to be expected that in October 1640 he should be apprehended, or that (16 Nov. 1640) the House of Commons should join the lords in petitioning for his banishment. It is said that he voluntarily renounced the court and retired to reside at the English College (the House of Tertians) in Ghent. There he occupied himself in writing an account of his conversion, considered as the central feature of his life. This work, entitled 'A True Historicall Relation of the Conversion of Sir Tobie Matthews to the Holie Catholic Fayth, with the Antecedents and Consequents thereof,' 1640, and consisting of 234 pages of manuscript, was unfortunately never printed. It is stated to have been for many years an heirloom in a Roman catholic family in Cork; it was for some time in the possession of the Rev. Alban Butler [q. v.], who published an abridgment (in which for the original phrasing is substituted the decorous prose of the last century) in the form of an octavo pamphlet (thirty-seven pages) in 1795. It passed into the hands of Dr. W. C. Neligan, who printed thirty-five copies of a 'Brief Description of a Curious MS.,' consisting of a number of brief and tantalising extracts. To the 'Relation' he states was appended 'Posthumus, or the Survivour' (twenty-one pages), signed and dated 1640, in which Sir Tobie strenuously denied that he was in receipt of a pension either from Barberini or the pope.

For the rest of his life he would seem to have stayed, with few interruptions, at Ghent. In 1650, however, he went to Brussels, and tried, without success, to obtain a canonry there (*Cal. Clar. State Papers*, ii. 60). He died at the English College, Ghent, on 13 Oct. 1655, and was buried in a vault beneath the college, with the plain inscription on his coffin, 'Hic jacet D. Tobias Matthæi.' There is no evidence that he was an actual member of the Society of Jesus, but he very probably received as a benefactor a diploma of aggregation to the merits and prayers of the society. His will, making a valuable bequest to the jesuits, is preserved in the English College at Rome (*Collect. Topog. et Geneal.* v. 87).

When Lord Thomas Fairfax once found Sir Tobie's father very melancholy and inquired the reason of his grace's pensiveness, the archbishop replied, 'My lord, I have great reason of sorrow with respect of my sons; one of whom has wit and no grace, another grace but no wit, and the third neither grace nor wit.' Sir Tobie's father merely expressed the universal opinion with regard to his eldest son's possession of wit, while the denial of grace was probably merely official, and was so echoed by Fuller, who says of the son that 'having all his father's name and many of his natural parts, he had few of his moral virtues and fewer of his spiritual graces.' Less qualified is Harrington's portrait of him as 'likely for learning, memory, sharpness of wit, and sweetness of behaviour.' His character, like that of Sir Kenelm Digby, Endymion Porter, and other highly cultivated contemporaries, presents some interesting contrasts. A zealous catholic, he was no pietist. Despite his being the most 'Italianate' Englishman of his time, he seems to have been a thoroughly loyal subject, though his ubiquity, his subtle and secret manner, together with his exotic graces, his knowledge of foreign courts and of the Spanish and Italian tongues, caused him to be regarded by many as a dangerous schemer (cf. SUCKLING's introduction of him into his *Session of the Poets*, 'whispering nothing in somebody's ear'). He was a sedulous courtier, who had the gift of gossip and a finger in all court intrigues, about which he was a sure informant; he was moreover an esteemed virtuoso, who bought pictures and articles of vertu for Buckingham and other English nobles. By Horace Walpole, Sir Tobie is described contemptuously as 'one of those heteroclite animals who finds his place anywhere.' He certainly had no title to a place and a woodcut in the 'Anecdotes of Painting,' in which Walpole gave him a niche on the mistaken assumption that the 'Picture of the Infanta' was drawn not on letter-paper but on canvas. In this error (which he demonstrated himself in a subsequent edition) he was followed by Granger and others. Besides the rough woodcut of Matthew in Walpole's 'Anecdotes,' an engraved portrait in which he appears in company with Jean Petitot, the Genevese, and Johann Hans Torrentius, the Dutch artist, was executed while he was in Rome (EVANS, *Cat. of Engraved Portraits*, p. 227).

The work most frequently associated with Matthew's name appeared five years after his death, under the title 'A Collection of Letters made by Sr Tobie Mathews, K^t^., with a Character of the most excellent Lady, Lucy Countess of Carleile: to which are added many Letters of his own to several Persons of Honour who were contemporary with him. For Henry Herringman, at the sign of the Anchor, 1660.' Prefixed are a portrait engraved by J. Gammon and an epistle dedicatory, signed by John Donne, son of the poet. The scheme of the collection is the inverse of James Howell's, its object being, not to illustrate history or biography, but to exhibit specimens of epistolary composition. The author in most instances has taken pains to remove names and dates, and such particulars as might serve to identify persons. Letters from Bacon, Digby, Carleton, and Dr. Donne are given under the names of the writers, but the majority are headed after this fashion: 'One friend gives another many thanks for the service which he did him with his Lord.' Some were doubtless from originals in his possession. Others were by himself, and are characterised by the sprightliness and ingenuity of the writer. The collection includes Matthew's eulogy on Lucy Hay, countess of Carlisle [q. v.], to whose interest at court Sir Tobie was very greatly indebted.

Other works attributed to Matthew by Wood and Dod, but not extant, and probably never published, are: 1. 'A Rich Cabinet of Precious Jewels.' 2. 'The Benefit of Washing the Head every Morning with Cold Water' (he is said to have practised the habit of dipping his head every morning as a corrective to his frequent vigils). 3. 'The History of the Times (Opus Imperfectum).' 4. 'The Life of St. Theresa' [1623].

An answer to Suckling's witty

> Out upon it I have loved
> Three whole days together,

and commencing

> Say, but did you love so long
> In troth I needs must blame you,

is headed 'Sir Toby Matthews,' but the poet very possibly only borrows the name for an interlocutor, as he borrows that of Carew and others.

[The chief authority for Matthew's life is the abridgment of his own Historical Relation, by Alban Butler, which has been mentioned above; a brief summary of its contents is given by Dr. Joseph Hunter in the Chorus Vatum Anglicanorum (Add. MS. 24490, ff. 319–24). With this should be compared Neligan's Brief Description of a Curious MS., in which a number of extracts from the original are pieced together without any attempt at editing; it is reprinted, without alteration, as an appendix to W. H. Smith's Bacon and Shakespeare, 1856. Wood's account of Sir Tobie (Athenæ, ed. Bliss, iii. 401), justly described by Hunter as not in his best style, has been followed by Dod (Church History, 1742, iii. 59, 60) and by Granger (Biog. Hist. of England, 1779, ii. 203–4, 357), with some embellishments, apparently his own, such as that 'Sir T. was often a spy upon such companies as he was admitted into upon the foot of an agreeable companion; and with the most vacant countenance would watch for intelligence to send to Rome.' See also Foster's Alumni Oxon. 1500–1714, and Gray's Inn Register, p. 97; Birch's Queen Elizabeth, i. 314, ii. 150, 182, 226, 270, 304; Spedding's Bacon, passim; Nichols's Progresses of James I, iv. 930; Court and Times of James I, ii. 225, 267, 270, 281, 302, &c.; Chamberlain's Letters, Camden Soc. pp. 1, 2, 10, 120, 133; Lodge's Illustrations, 1838, iii. 199, 291; Peacham's Truth of Our Time, p. 102; Hacket's Life of Williams, 1715, p. 135; Sidney Papers, i. 362; Strafford Correspondence, ii. 125, 149; Lister's Life of Clarendon, iii. 54; Sir John Harrington's Brief View of the State of the Church of England; Suckling's Works, ed. Hazlitt, i. 9, 59; Prynne's Rome's Masterpiece, 1643, p. 19; Fuller's Church Hist. 1845, vi. 62 n.; Commons' Journals, 16 Nov. 1640; Gardiner's Hist. of England, v. 60, viii. 239; Foley's English Prov. of Soc. of Jesus, vii. 493; Notes and Queries, 3rd ser. iii. 329, iv. 159, ix. 350, 5th ser. xii. 43; Gent. Mag. 1830 i. 205, 1839 ii. 272; Bromley's Engraved Portraits; Evans's Cat. of Engraved Portraits, No. 7043; Halkett and Laing's Dict. of Anon. and Pseudon. Lit. cols. 1882 and 2126; Harl. MS. 6987; Lansd. MS. 984, ff. 106–8; Addit. MS. 5503, passim; Calendars of State Papers, Dom. Ser. 1595, and following years passim, especially 1595–7 pp. 361, 437, 1598–1601 pp. 54, 95, 97, 1601–3 p. 134, 1610–18 pp. 24, 530; Owen's Epigrams, 3rd Coll. 391.] T. S.

MATTHEWS. [See also MATHEWS.]

MATTHEWS, HENRY (1789–1828), judge and traveller, fifth son of John Matthews [q.v.], of Belmont, Herefordshire, born in 1789, received his education at Eton, and afterwards became a fellow of King's College, Cambridge, where he graduated B.A. in 1812, and M.A. in 1815. In 1817 he left England for the continent on account of ill-health, and on his return he published his well-known 'Diary of an Invalid, being the Journal of a Tour in pursuit of health; in Portugal, Italy, Switzerland, and France, in the years 1817, 1818, and 1819,' London (two editions), 1820, 8vo. This work attracted much popular favour; it was reprinted, 2 vols. 1822, 8vo, and reached a fifth edit. London, 1835, 8vo.

In 1821, having been previously called to the bar, he was appointed advocate-fiscal of Ceylon, and fulfilled the duties of that office till October 1827, when he was promoted to the judicial bench on the vacancy occasioned by the death of Sir Hardinge Giffard [q. v.] He died in Ceylon on 20 May 1828, and was interred in St. Peter's Church, in the Fort of Colombo.

By his marriage with Emma, daughter of William Blount, esq., of Orleton Manor, Herefordshire, he had an only son, Henry Matthews, Q.C., M.P. for East Birmingham, and home secretary in Lord Salisbury's administration, 1886–92, who was created Viscount Llandaff in 1895.

[Gent. Mag. 1828, ii. 647; Graduati Cantabr.; Lowndes's Bibl. Man. (Bohn), p. 1518; Walford's County Families, 1892, p. 705.] T. C.

MATTHEWS, JOHN (1755–1826), physician and poet, baptised 30 Oct. 1755, was the only surviving child of William Matthews of Burton, in Linton, Herefordshire, who died 29 Aug. 1799, by his wife Jane, daughter of Philip Hoskyns of Bernithen Court, Herefordshire, who died 20 May 1768. Both were buried in Linton churchyard. He matriculated from Merton College, Oxford, on 14 Feb. 1772, and graduated B.A. 1778, M.A. 1779, M.B. 1781, and M.D. 1782. On 30 Sept. 1782 he was a candidate for the College of Physicians, and a year later he became a fellow. From 20 April 1781 to his resignation in 1783 he was physician to St.

George's Hospital, London, and in 1784 he delivered the Gulstonian lectures, after which he withdrew to his native county. Matthews then acquired the estate of Clehonger, near Hereford, and built on it in 1788–90 the present mansion of Belmont, situated on the banks of the Wye, and adorned with extensive lawns and plantations. A sapling planted by him in 1788 is famous as Colonel Matthews's oak, and is marked by a cast-iron tablet. Its trunk is 22 feet in circumference, and it contains 140 feet of timber (Murray, *Hereford Handbook*, p. 315). For the rest of his life he took a leading part in county affairs. He acted as mayor of Hereford in 1793, and was senior alderman and magistrate for twenty years. He was also colonel of the first regiment of Hereford militia, chairman of quarter sessions, and member for the county from 31 March 1803 to 1806. After a protracted illness he died at Belmont on 15 Jan. 1826, when a monument to his memory was placed in the south aisle of Clehonger Church. Matthews married at Marcle, Herefordshire, on 9 Nov. 1778, Elizabeth, daughter and heiress of Arthur Ellis, who died 7 Nov. 1823, aged 66. They had issue eight sons and six daughters, and among their sons were Charles Skynner Matthews, the friend of Byron, and Henry Matthews [q. v.], author of 'The Diary of an Invalid.'

Matthews was a man of versatile disposition and generous tastes, which frequently occasioned him pecuniary loss. His works are anonymous. The best-known of them, a very ineffective parody of Pope's 'Eloisa,' which was long attributed to Porson (Watson, *Life of Porson*, pp. 289–92), is 'Eloisa en Dishabille: being a New Version of that Lady's celebrated Epistle to Abelard, done into familiar English metre by a Lounger,' 1780. It was reprinted in 1801, and again in 1822, when the bookseller put on the title-page that it was 'ascribed to Porson.' Matthews wrote 'A Sketch from the Landscape: a Didactic Poem, addressed to R. Payne Knight,' 1794, an attack which Knight, in the Advertisement to the second edition of the 'Landscape,' stigmatised as 'a sort of doggerel ode' and 'a contemptible publication.' The 'Fables from La Fontaine, in English Verse,' published by Matthews in 1820, were marked by sprightliness, but not infrequently offended through diffuseness and partisan allusions to the politics of the day. He composed many fugitive pieces in prose and verse.

[Duncumb's Herefordshire, ii. 387–8, 402, iii. 174, 215; Gent. Mag. 1826, pt. i. p. 368; Moore's Lord Byron, ed. 1846, p. 129; Foster's Alumni Oxon.; Munk's Coll. of Phys. 2nd ed. ii. 332–3; Robinson's Hereford Mansions, pp. 66, 181.]

W. P. C.

MATTHEWS or **MATHEWS, LEMUEL** (*fl.* 1661–1705), archdeacon of Down, younger son of Marmaduke Matthews [q. v.], was born at Swansea in 1644, and matriculated from Lincoln College, Oxford, on 25 May 1661 (Foster, *Alumni*, 1500–1714). He proceeded M.A. before 1667 (see *Elegie* on Jeremy Taylor). Soon after leaving Oxford Jeremy Taylor, bishop of Down, Connor, and Dromore, made Matthews his chaplain, and presented him to the rectory of Lenavy (now Glenavy), co. Antrim (see Reeves, *Ecclesiastical Antiquities of Down, Connor, and Dromore*, p. 47). At the bishop's death in 1667 Matthews published 'A Pandarique Elegie upon the Death of the R. R. Father in God Jeremy, late Lord Bishop of Doune, Connor, and Dromore.' On 26 Oct. 1666 he was collated to the prebend of Carncastle, co. Antrim (installed 5 Jan. 1667). He obtained on 2 Nov. 1674 the archdeaconry of Down, and in 1690 was made chancellor, or vicar-general, of Down and Connor. In this position he acquired almost entire control of the diocese, the bishop, Thomas Hacket, D.D., being non-resident (*Lansdowne MS.* 446, fol. 126). Matthews used his influence for his own advantage. He held altogether nine livings, and was accused of simony in obtaining Archdeacon Baynard's resignation in order to collate his nephew, Philip Matthews, M.A., to the archdeaconry of Connor in 1689, and of illegally presenting John Francis to the prebend of Down in 1690 or 1691. Matthews was attainted with other protestant clergymen by James II's Irish parliament of 1689.

In February 1694 a special visitation was held (22 Feb.–17 April 1694) at Lisburn by a royal commission to inquire into the misdemeanours of Matthews and others. The commission was executed by Anthony Dopping [q. v.], bishop of Meath, and William King [q. v.], bishop of Derry, and they found Matthews guilty of maintenance, in a suit between John M'Neale, dean of Down, and a Mr. Major, of non-residence and neglect of various duties. Suits were also commenced against him by Talbot Keen for non-payment of proxy money, non-exhibition of his collative title, and non-residence on the rectories attached to his archdeaconry. He was suspended from all offices during the pleasure of the crown. He immediately agitated for his restoration, and addressed a series of appeals—fourteen in all—to Lord-chancellors Cox, Freeman, and Phipps in succession, and to King William, and Queen

Anne (MANT, *Church of Ireland*, ii. 43). In 'A Letter to the Right Reverend William [King], Lord Bishop of Derry,' printed in 1703, he protested that he had resided for nineteen years in Lisburn 'neer the center' of his archdeaconry, and had spent much on several other parishes.

After he had presented a petition to Sir Richard Cox on 3 Sept. 1703, the judges on 4 Dec. reported their opinion that he should be allowed a commission of delegates. Delays followed, and Matthews set forth, early in 1704, his claim to such a commission in two pamphlets, one called 'Demonstrations that the Lord Chancellor of Ireland is bound by the Statute and Common Law, and also by his Commission and Oath as Lord Chancellor, to grant a Commission of Delegates;' and the other, 'The Argument of Archdeacon Mathews' [Dublin], 1704. In reply to further appeals, Sir Richard Cox at the end of 1704 summoned all parties concerned to appear in the exchequer chamber on 20 Jan. 1705. Matthews subsequently printed 'A Brief of the Printed Argument of Archdeacon Mathews on his Petition to the Lord Chancellor of Ireland,' n.d., and on 5 June 1705 he presented a new petition to the house of peers in Dublin. The lords, in an address on 16 June to the Duke of Ormonde, lord-lieutenant, prayed that he should be relieved (*Add. MS.* 21132, fol. 30, indexed '*Samuel* Mathews').

Matthews had adherents, notably John Pooley, D.D., bishop of Raphoe, who adds to his autograph, in a copy of Matthews's 'Argument,' the words 'sent me Nov[ber] [1]704 by the ill-treated author, Archde. Mathews' (cf. COTTON, *Fasti Eccles. Hib.* v. 240). Matthews's tracts were not generally offered for sale, but seem to have been distributed among his friends (*ib.*) They are consequently now very rare. Cotton says that Matthews was restored to his prebend, but not to his archdeaconry. He died unmarried after 1705. By what university he was created doctor of divinity does not appear.

[Cotton's Fasti Eccles. Hib. iii. 231–3, 241, 257, 271, v. 241, 242; Mant's Hist. of the Church of Ireland, ii. 42–3 (s. n. *Leonard* Matthews); Cat. of the Library of Trinity Coll. Dublin; Killen's Ecclesiastical Hist. of Ireland, 1875, ii. 183; Reid's Hist. of the Presbyterian Church in Ireland, ed. Killen, 1867, ii. 438, 439; Lansdowne MS. No. 446, ff. 124–8.] C. F. S.

MATTHEWS, MARMADUKE (1606–1683?), Welsh nonconformist, was the son of Matthew Matthews (or Mathew Jones?) of Swansea, where he was born in 1606. He matriculated at All Souls' College, Oxford, on 20 Feb. 1623–4, and proceeded B.A. on 25 Feb. 1624–5, and M.A. on 5 July 1627 (FOSTER, *Alumni Oxon.*) In 1636 Laud, in the annual account of his province (*Lambeth MSS.* vol. 943; cf. DR. REES, *Nonconformity in Wales*, pp. 35–6), notes that he was vicar of Penmain in Gower, and was 'preaching against all holy-days.' He was 'inhibited' by the Bishop of St. Davids, and when proceedings were begun against him in the court of high commission, he fled to New England. He visited the West Indies, and finally became a 'teaching-elder' of the church of Maldon in New England. In 1658 he was induced by his friend and patron Colonel Philip Jones [q. v.], who chiefly supported his wife and family during his exile, to return to Swansea. He was appointed the minister of the parish of St. John's, Swansea, from which place he was ejected in 1662. He afterwards preached, by the connivance of the magistrates, 'in a little chapel at the end of the town,' and under the indulgence granted by Charles II to nonconformists in 1672, he took out a license to preach as an independent in his own house at Swansea (REES, op. cit. p. 177). He died there about 1683. In his old age he was supported by his children, 'of whom two or three were sober conformists' (CALAMY, *Account*, ed. 1713, ii. 732); one of them, Lemuel, is separately noticed. Perhaps Edward Matthews, who matriculated at New Inn Hall, Oxford, on 11 July 1634, aged 19, and is described as a son of Matthew Jones of Swansea, was a younger brother of Matthews.

Marmaduke was author of 'The Messiah Magnified by the Mouthes of Babes in America,' London, 1659, 8vo. It is dedicated to Philip, Lord Jones.

[Rees's Nonconformity in Wales, pp. 35, 36, 53–4, 177; Calamy's Account, ut supra; Foster's Alumni Oxonienses, 1500–1714; Matthews' Messiah Magnified, Ded.] D. LL. T.

MATTHEWS, THOMAS, translator of the Bible, pseudonym for John Rogers (1500?–1555) [q. v.]

MATTHEWS, THOMAS (1805–1889), actor and pantomimist, born 17 Oct. 1805, entered as a boy the office of the 'Independent Whig,' subsequently known after other changes as the 'Sunday Times.' After appearing at the Olympic Theatre he went to Sadler's Wells, where, on the retirement of Grimaldi in 1828, he appeared, 26 Dec. 1829, as clown in a pantomime called 'The Hag of the Forest.' Upon the revival of 'Mother Goose' he played clown for fifty nights, after being coached by Grimaldi. He then appeared at Covent Garden in successive years in 'Puss in Boots,' 'Old Mother Hubbard,' 'Whittington and his Cat,' and 'Gammer

Gurton.' At Drury Lane he created a sensation by imitating Duvernay in 'La Cachuca.' His Orson was also a hit. Engaged by Macready at 3*l.* per week, 20 July 1837, he reappeared at Covent Garden, where he brought out 'Fair Rosamond,' and danced a mock bayadère dance. He visited Scotland and played in Edinburgh and elsewhere, and returned to the Olympic in Nelson Lee's pantomime 'Riddle me, Riddle me Ree;' then went to Paris, where, August 1842, he superintended the production at the Variétés of a pantomime called 'Arlequin.' Théophile Gautier speaks of his get-up as of 'a rare fantasy,' and praises his parody of the 'Cachuca' (*L'Art Dramatique en France*, ii. 260).

In 1843 he played at Drury Lane in Planché's 'Fortunio,' was seen in ballet at Vauxhall with the Paynes and Rosina Wright in 1847, was clown in 1848 in 'Harlequin Lord Lovel' at the Surrey, was at the Marylebone in 1851, and in the following year was at Drury Lane in Blanchard's 'Dame Durden and the Droll Days of the Merry Monarch.' In other pantomimes at the Adelphi, Drury Lane, Covent Garden, and in the country, he was familiarly known, singing constantly the songs of 'Hot Codlings,' 'Tippitywitchet,' and the 'Life of a Clown,' the last composed for him by Balfe. In 1859 he gave an entertainment. After this he played at Drury Lane in the burlesque introductions to various pantomimes. His last appearance was at Drury Lane in 1865 in 'Hop o' my Thumb.' He then retired. After being bedridden for four months he died at Brighton, 4 March 1889, and was buried in Brighton cemetery. He was the last of the old-fashioned clowns, sang in approved fashion, transmitted the traditions of Grimaldi, was a prudent man, and was much respected.

[Personal recollections; Era newspaper, 9 March 1889; Era Almanack, various years; Scott and Howard's Life of E.L. Blanchard; Daily News, 11 March 1889; Theatrical Times, i. 274; Dramatic and Musical Review, various years; Pollock's Macready's Reminiscences.] J. K.

MATTHIAS. [See MATHIAS.]

MATTHIESSEN, AUGUSTUS (1831–1870), chemist and physicist, was born in London on 2 Jan. 1831. His father, who died while Matthiessen was quite young, was a merchant. A paralytic seizure during infancy produced a permanent and severe twitching of Matthiessen's right hand. Notwithstanding the taste for chemistry which he displayed as a boy, he was, upon leaving school, sent by his guardians to learn farming with a Dorset farmer, as being the only occupation suited to his condition. His inclination was then towards a business career, but becoming interested in agricultural chemistry, then in its earliest infancy in this country, he immediately, on coming of age, went to Giessen, where he studied under Will and Buff, and graduated Ph.D. From 1853 he spent nearly four years under the direction of Bunsen at Heidelberg, and by means of his electrolytic method isolated the metals calcium and strontium in the pure state for the first time. In Kirchhoff's laboratory he studied the electrical conductivity first of the new metals, and then of many others. His results were published in Poggendorff's 'Annalen' and the 'Philosophical Magazine' for 1857. He returned to London in 1857 with a thorough knowledge of the methods of physics and of inorganic chemistry, and studied organic chemistry with Hofmann at the Royal College of Chemistry. The work done under Hofmann's direction was not important, but it led the way to Matthiessen's considerable researches on the opium alkaloids of later years. Matthiessen soon fitted up a laboratory on his own account at No. 1 Torrington Place, where he began a series of investigations on the physical properties of pure metals and alloys which has become classical.

The preparation of copper of the greatest conducting power possible had become a question of great practical importance in connection with telegraphy. Matthiessen showed that the discrepancies of previous observations and the low conductivity of certain samples of the metal supposed to be pure were due to the presence of minute quantities of other elements. He embodied his results both in a report presented in 1860 to the government committee appointed to inquire into the subject, and in a conjoint paper with Holzmann, published in the 'Philosophical Transactions.' In 1861 he became a fellow, and afterwards a member of the council of the Royal Society. In 1862 he was elected to the lectureship on chemistry at St. Mary's Hospital, a post which he held till 1868. During 1862–5 he undertook important voluntary work for the British Association committee on electrical standards, and in the latter year constructed for them ten standards and several copies of these, made from various metals and alloys. In 1867 he summarised his work on the constitution of alloys in a lecture given before the Chemical Society (*Chem. Soc. Journ.* 1867, p. 201). Besides pointing out a remarkable difference in the behaviour of tin, lead, zinc, and cadmium in alloys from that of other metals, he made two general suggestions of great importance: first, that small amounts of impurity in a metal do not by their direct action produce the remarkable changes in physical properties to which their presence corresponds, but that they cause the metal with which they are alloyed to assume an allotropic form; and secondly, that in most cases alloys must be considered as 'solidified solutions.' In 1868 Matthiessen was appointed lecturer on chemistry at St. Bartholomew's Hospital in conjunction with Professor Odling; on the latter's resignation in 1870 he became sole lecturer. In 1869 he was awarded a royal medal by the Royal Society 'for his researches on the electric and other physical and chemical properties of metals and their alloys.' Besides his other work he had a large private practice as a consulting chemist, and from January 1869 to June 1870 was one of the editors of the 'Philosophical Magazine.' In 1870 he was appointed examiner to the university of London. On 6 Oct. of the same year he committed suicide, his mind having given way under severe nervous strain. At the time of his death he was occupied with the experiments on the chemical nature of pure cast-iron, of the committee appointed to inquire into which he was a member, and also with experiments with a view to the construction of a standard pyrometer.

The 'Royal Society's Catalogue' contains a list of thirty-eight papers published by Matthiessen alone, and of twenty-three published conjointly with Von Bose, Burnside, Carey Foster, Hockin, Holzmann, Russell, Szcepanowski, Vogt, and Wright. The most important appeared in the 'Philosophical Transactions' and 'Proceedings' of the Royal Society, the 'British Association Reports,' 'Journal of the Chemical Society,' and 'Philosophical Magazine,' from which many were reprinted in foreign periodicals. Matthiessen's researches show remarkable acuteness, experimental skill, and conscientiousness, together with a distinct power of generalisation. That with his physical defect he should have accomplished so much delicate and exact work is a proof of rare perseverance. Matthiessen bore a high personal character among his contemporaries.

[Besides the sources already quoted, see Times, 8 Oct. 1870; Nature, ii. 475, 517; Pharmaceutical Journal, [3] i. 317; Chemical News, xxii. 189; Journ. Chem. Soc. 1870, p. 615; American Journal of Science, [3] i. 73; Proc. Roy. Soc. xviii. 111.] P. J. H.

MATTOCKS, ISABELLA (1746–1826), actress, was the daughter of a low comedian named Lewis Hallam, who acted at the older theatre in Goodman's Fields (not to be confounded with the Goodman's Fields theatre), of which his brother William Hallam, founder of a theatrical 'dynasty' in America, was manager. At this house, sometimes known as the New Wells, Leman Street, Goodman's Fields, there were three Hallams, Hallam sen., Lewis Hallam, and George Hallam (Genest), besides a Mrs. Hallam. The relations of the various members of this family, or families of this name, have received much attention in America, but nothing very definite is known. The 'New Monthly Magazine' for 1826, in a eulogistic article full of errors, speaks of the Hallam killed by Macklin as her father, which he was not. He does not appear even to have been her grandfather. Mrs. Hallam, who became in America by marriage a Mrs. Douglass, was a relative of Rich of Covent Garden, and was the mother of Isabella Hallam. Left behind by her father and mother upon their departure for America, Isabella was educated by her aunt, Mrs. Barrington, also an actress. She is said to have played at Covent Garden, when four-and-a-half years old, the part of the Parish Girl in 'What d'ye Call It?' and, not long after, the child in 'Coriolanus.' Her first traceable appearance is, however, given vaguely by Genest, 1752–3, at Covent Garden, as the Duke of York in 'King Richard III.' On 14 Feb. she was Page in the 'Orphan' to the Monimia of Mrs. Bellamy, 10 Dec. 1754; the child in 'Coriolanus,' assigned to Thomas Sheridan, 19 Feb. 1757; Page in 'Rover.' Mattocks, subsequently her husband (*d.* 1804), appeared for the first time at Covent Garden as Macheath, 1 Nov. 1757, and on the 5th Miss Hallam played the Boy in 'King Henry V.' On 22 April 1757 she was Robin in the 'Merry Wives of Windsor,' her aunt, Mrs. Barrington, being Mrs. Page. On 10 April 1761, for Barrington's benefit, she played Juliet to the Romeo of Ross. She was announced as 'a young gentlewoman, being her first appearance (as a woman).' She repeated this performance 22 April 1762. In 1762–3 she was regularly engaged, playing Dorinda in the '(Beaux) Stratagem,' Isabella in the 'Wonder,' Isabinda in the 'Busy Body,' Parisatis in the 'Rival Queens,' the Princess in 'King Henry V,' Serena in the 'Orphan,' Selima in 'Tamerlane,' Sylvia in the 'Recruiting Officer,' Narcissa in 'Love's Last Shift,' Angelica in the 'Constant Couple,' the Lady in 'Comus,' and Miss Hoyden, and being the original Lucinda in Bickerstaffe's 'Love in a Village,' 8 Dec. 1762. Teresia in the 'Squire of Alsatia,' Isabella in 'Wit without Money,' Nysa in 'Midas' were added to her repertory the following season, in which also she was, 9 Dec. 1763, the original Nancy in Murphy's 'What we must all come to.' On 29 Oct. 1764 she played Cordelia for the first time, and was subsequently Lady Harriet in the 'Funeral,' was the original Lady Julia in Arne's 'Guardian Outwitted,' 12 Dec. 1764, the original Theodosia in Bickerstaffe's 'Maid of the Mill,' 31 July 1765, and 19 Feb. Polly in the same play.

On 24 April 1765, for her own benefit, as Mrs. Mattocks late Miss Hallam, she played the Lady in 'Comus' and Sophy in the 'Musical Lady' of George Colman, not previously seen at Covent Garden. On 2 May she was the original Elvira in the 'Spanish Lady,' attributed to Hull, her husband playing Worthy. A few days later she played Maria in the 'Citizen.' Until her retirement in 1808 she remained at Covent Garden, of which she became a chief support. In the seasons of 1784–5 and 1785-6 she was apparently not engaged, and in the summers of 1772–5 inclusive, and probably in very many others, she played an extensive range of characters in Liverpool, where her husband became manager of a theatre. She played also with him at Portsmouth, where he was for a time a manager. On 22 June she made her first appearance at the Haymarket, playing for the first time Mrs. Oakley to the Oakley of Pope. Among the characters entrusted to her at Covent Garden were Hermione, Lucia in 'Cato,' Rosetta in 'Love in a Village,' Lucy Lockit, Phædra in 'Amphitryon,' Roxana, Octavia in 'All for Love,' Statira, Elvira in 'Spanish Friar,' Clarissa in 'Lionel and Clarissa,' Julia in 'Two Gentlemen of Verona,' Leonora in 'Revenge,' Miss Prue, Charlotte Rusport, Celia in 'As you like it,' Queen in 'Richard III,' Lydia Languish, Æmilia in 'Othello,' Audrey, and Tilburina. In Liverpool she was seen, among many other parts both tragic and comic, as Monimia in the 'Orphan,' Portia in the 'Merchant of Venice,' Angelica in 'Love for Love,' Constance in 'King John,' Julia in the 'Rivals,' Rosalind, Imogen, and Helena in 'All's well that ends well.' Her original parts at Covent Garden were numerous. She was, 6 Dec. 1765, the first Amelia in 'Summer's Tale,' a three-act musical comedy by Cumberland, whose first acted piece it was. Her singing saved it, and it was reduced to two acts and rechristened 'Amelia,' 3 Dec. 1766; Fanny, the heroine of the 'Accomplished Maid,' a translation by Toms of 'La Buona Figliuola;' Priscilla in Bickerstaffe's 'Love in the City,' 21 Feb. 1767, in which she acted 'inimitably;' Gertrude in the 'Royal Merchant,' 14 Dec. 1767, founded by Hull on the 'Beggar's Bush' of Beaumont and Fletcher; Olivia in the 'Good-natured Man,' 29 Jan. 1768; Aspasia in 'Cyrus,' adapted by John Hoole, 3 Dec. 1768; Honour in 'Tom Jones,' 14 Jan. 1769, translated from the 'Tom Jones' of Poinsinet, given in Paris at the Théâtre des Italiens four years previously; Lettice in Colman's 'Man and Wife,' 7 Oct. 1769; Lucy Waters in Cumberland's 'Brothers,' 2 Dec. 1769. Genest in error assigns to her Sophia, which was played by Mrs. Yates; Albina in Mason's 'Elfrida,' 21 Nov. 1772; Jenny in O'Hara's 'Two Misers,' 21 Jan. 1775; Daraxa in 'Edward and Eleonora,' 18 March 1775, altered from Thomson by Hull; Louisa in the 'Duenna,' 21 Nov. 1775; Priscilla Tomboy in the 'Romp,' 28 March 1778; Mrs. Racket in the 'Belle's Stratagem,' 22 Feb. 1780; Sophy in Mrs. Cowley's 'Which is the Man,' 9 Feb. 1782; Olivia in Mrs. Cowley's 'A Bold Stroke for a Husband,' 25 Feb. 1783; Lady Tremor in Mrs. Inchbald's 'Such things are,' 10 Feb. 1787; Betty Blackberry in Colman's 'Farmer,' 31 Oct. 1787; Marchioness Merida in Mrs. Inchbald's 'Child of Nature,' 28 Nov. 1788; Lady Peckham in the 'School for Arrogance,' 4 Feb. 1791, Holcroft's adaptation of 'Le Glorieux' of Destouches; Mrs. Warren in Holcroft's 'Road to Ruin,' 18 Feb. 1792; Miss Vortex in Morton's 'Cure for the Heartache,' 10 Jan. 1797; Miss Lucretia McTab in the younger Colman's 'Poor Gentleman,' 11 Feb. 1801; Camilla in 'Monk' Lewis's 'Rugantino,' 18 Oct. 1805. Her last original parts were Mrs. Trot in Morton's 'Town and Country,' 10 March 1807, and Lady Wrangle in 'Too Friendly by Half,' 29 Oct. 1807, an unprinted and anonymous piece. On 7 June 1808, for her benefit, Mrs. Mattocks appeared for the last time, playing Flora in the 'Wonder,' Cooke recited Garrick's 'Ode,' and Mrs. Mattocks then took her leave of the public in a prose address which was found 'very affecting.' She claimed to have been on the stage (Covent Garden) fifty-eight years. During later years her salary had been reduced. After the death of her husband, ruined by his Liverpool management, Mrs. Mattocks settled a portion on her daughter, retired to Kensington, and confided to her son-in-law, a barrister named Hewson, the management of her fortune of 6,000*l.*, which before her premature death he spent. On 24 May 1813 a benefit was given her at the Opera House, in which Mrs. Jordan, Quick, Fawcett, Palmer, Benham, &c., took part. She delivered a further address. The sum realised, amounting to 1,092*l.*, was invested in an annuity for the actress, with some reversion for her daughter. She died 25 June 1826, at Kensington. An indifferent performer in tragedy and a second-rate singer in opera, Mrs. Mattocks rose to the front rank in comedy. In light and genteel comedy she obtained a distinct success, but her triumph was in chambermaids. Her best parts were Betty Hint in the 'Man of the World,' Mrs. Racket, Mrs. Brittle, Betty Blackberry, Camilla in 'Rugantino,' Mrs. Placid, Mrs. Cockletop in 'Modern Antiques,' and Lucretia MacTab. The 'Theatrical Biography' of 1772 credits her with ability to realise her parts, with sensibility, a pleasing person, and an agreeable voice. It says that she eloped to France to marry her husband, who was more of a singer than an actor, more than hints that the marriage was unhappy, and states that Mrs. Mattocks was closely intimate with Robert Bensley [q. v.] O'Keeffe says that her talents were of the first order, and associates her Betty Blackberry with Edwin's Jemmy Jumps as a treat of the highest order. He speaks also of Mattocks as a gentleman, and *point-device* beloved and respected. Boaden declares that Mrs. Mattocks left no successor on the English stage, and the 'Monthly Mirror' speaks of Mrs. Davenport as vastly her inferior. With Quick and Lewis she formed an irresistible trio. She was a good hand at reciting the prologues of Miles, Peter Andrews, and others, and Anthony Pasquin, after some severe strictures, says in his 'Children of Thespis:'

Her Peckhams, her Flirts, and her Adelaides charm me,
And her epilogue-speaking can gladden and warm me.

Portraits of her by De Wilde as Lady Restless in 'All in the Wrong' and by Dupont as Louisa in the 'Duenna' are in the Garrick Club.

[Seilhamer's History of the American Theatre, Philadelphia, privately printed; Genest's Account of the English Stage; Theatrical Biography, 1772; Monthly Mirror, 18 June 1808; New Monthly Magazine; Boaden's Life; Mrs. Inchbald's Life of Kemble; Bernard's Reminiscences; O'Keeffe's Memoirs; Georgian Era; Clark Russell's Representative Actors; Thespian Dict.; Dunlap's Hist. of the American Theatre; Gilliland's Dramatick Mirror.] J. K.

MATURIN, CHARLES ROBERT (1782–1824), novelist and dramatist, was born in Dublin in 1782. His family, of French extraction, had settled in Ireland on the revocation of the edict of Nantes; his great-grandfather, Peter, was dean of Killala from 1724 to 1741. His grandfather, Gabriel James Maturin, who became archdeacon of Tuam in 1733, succeeded Swift in the deanery of St. Patrick's in 1745, and dying 9 Nov. 1746 was buried in St. Patrick's Cathedral (COTTON, *Fasti Eccl. Hib.* ii. 105). His father held an important post under government. From a child Maturin was remarkable for a taste for theatricals and a general love of dress and display. He distinguished himself at Trinity College, where he obtained a scholarship in 1798, and graduated B.A. in 1800, but discontinued his university career on marrying, at the age of twenty, Henrietta, daughter of Thomas Kingsbury, afterwards archdeacon of Killala. Entering the church, he became curate, first of Loughrea, and afterwards of St. Peter's, Dublin. His stipend was slender, and he was partly supported by his father until the latter's sudden dismissal from office on a charge of malversation. His innocence was eventually established, and he obtained another appointment, but in the meanwhile the family were reduced to great embarrassment. Maturin set up a school in addition to his curacy, and also betook himself to literature, successively producing three romances: 'The Fatal Revenge, or the Family of Montorio,' 1807; 'The Wild Irish Boy,' 1808; and 'The Milesian Chief,' 1812. These works, which appeared under the pseudonym of Dennis Jasper Murphy, attracted considerable attention, though none reached a second edition at the time, and Maturin was unable to dispose of the copyright of any of them except 'The Milesian Chief,' which Colburn bought for 80*l.* Scott, however, reviewed 'Montorio' with appreciation, and paid 'The Milesian Chief' the higher compliment of imitating it in 'The Bride of Lammermoor.' About 1813 Maturin's imprudence in becoming security for an unfaithful friend compelled him to give up his house, and consequently his school. In these desperate circumstances he had recourse to Scott, sending him the manuscript of 'Bertram,' a tragedy which he had already offered unsuccessfully to a Dublin theatre. Scott, some time in 1814, recommended the play to Kemble as 'one which will either succeed greatly or be damned gloriously.' Kemble having declined it, Scott next submitted it to Byron, who first imitated Scott's example in sending the author 50*l.* from his own purse, and then introduced the play to Kean. Kean, after some hesitation, accepted it, and it was produced at Drury Lane on 9 May 1816, and ran for twenty-two nights, bringing Maturin 1,000*l.*, while the printed play sold at the then exorbitant charge of 4*s.* 6*d.* a copy, and ran through seven editions within the year (GENEST, *History of the English Stage*, viii. 532–3). The only dissonant note was the hostile criticism of Coleridge, who was mortified that his own play had not been preferred for representation.

Maturin came to London, and was duly lionised, but he wanted conduct and knowledge of the world; 'deluged' Murray with manuscripts for the 'Quarterly,' of which only a review of Sheil's 'Apostate'—said to have given Gifford unspeakable trouble to rewrite—could be accepted, and was only prevented by the earnest remonstrances of Scott from retorting upon Coleridge. His next tragedy, 'Manuel,' was produced at Drury Lane on 8 March 1817, with Kean again in the title-rôle, and was acted five times; 'Fredolfo,' another tragedy, followed at Covent Garden on 12 May 1817, with Macready as Wadenberg. Both these pieces, though inferior, should hardly have been utter failures with the audiences that had applauded 'Bertram,' but they were unlucky. The first entirely depended upon Kean, whose dissatisfaction with his part paralysed his powers. Maturin received nothing from the performance of either, and though Murray allowed him the entire profit of the printed edition, the publisher protested against Byron's proposal to divide the proceeds of his 'Siege of Corinth' and 'Parisina' between Maturin and Coleridge with such energy, that the idea had to be given up. Another tragedy, 'Osmyn,' entrusted to Kean for his opinion, was lost or destroyed while in the actor's possession.

Maturin returned to novel-writing, and 'Women, or Pour et Contre,' appeared in 1818, and in 1820 his masterpiece, 'Melmoth the Wanderer.' 'The Albigenses' was published in 1824, the year of his death. In the same year he had printed 'Six Sermons on the Errors of the Roman Catholic Church,' and in 1821 he had allowed his name to be prefixed to 'The Universe,' a long poem in blank verse, really written, as would appear, by the Rev. James Wills [q. v.] His last years were a struggle with ill-health, as well as embarrassment. He died at Dublin on 30 Oct. 1824, his death, it is alleged, being hastened by taking a wrong medicine. His literary remains and correspondence are said—though the statement appears hardly credible—to have been destroyed by one of his sons, the Rev. William Maturin [q. v.], who was offended at his father's connection with the theatre. The loss was no doubt considerable, though it is impossible that Maturin should have corresponded with Balzac as represented, and very improbable that he corresponded with Goethe. Another son, Edward (1812–1881), emigrated to the United States, became professor of Greek in the college of South Carolina, subsequently lived in New York, published several romances and poems, and revised the translation of St. Mark's Gospel for the American Bible Union.

Maturin himself condemned all his early writings as deficient in reality. 'The characters, situations, and language are drawn merely from imagination; my limited acquaintance with life denied me any other resource.' This objection, however, does not lie against the most celebrated among them, for 'Montorio' belongs to a species of novel where everything that is not plagiarism must be invention, and where the accurate portrayal of life is absolutely excluded. The merits of the school of Mrs. Radcliffe may be variously estimated, but its productions must be judged by their own laws, and every condition of these is fulfilled by 'Montorio.' 'The Wild Irish Boy,' on the other hand, is in the main an extravagant caricature of modern life; and 'The Milesian Chief' is an unsuccessful mixture of both styles. 'Women,' in some measure a religious novel, is also remarkable as the only one of the author's novels which affords any insight into the Irish society of his time, or from which much can be learned respecting his own opinions. In 'Melmoth' the author returns to the manner of 'Montorio' with matured powers, and the advantage of an impressive conception. Melmoth himself is hardly a creation, he is rather a compound of 'Faust' and 'The Wandering Jew;' yet the sentiment of supernatural awe is successfully evoked, and would be still more potent but for the extreme confusion and involution of the narrative. 'Melmoth' had great influence on the rising romantic school of France, and was half imitated, half parodied, in a sequel by Balzac, whose combination of it with the popular German story of 'The Bottle Imp' has given hints to Mr. Stevenson. 'The Albigenses,' Maturin's last novel, is in some respect his best. It is full of eloquent passages, and though defective as a picture of actual life and manners, is not wanting in poetical truth. The three tragedies, especially 'Bertram,' exhibit real poetical feeling, and by the aid of spirited declamation and theatrical illusion might conceivably succeed for a time on the stage; but they will not bear serious criticism. The controversial discourses are rather platform addresses than sermons, but sufficiently effective to justify Maturin's contemporary reputation as a popular preacher. Of the nature of his literary talent he says himself: 'If I possess any talent, it is that of darkening the gloomy, and of deepening the sad; of painting life in extremes, and representing those struggles of passion when the soul trembles on the verge of the unlawful and the unhallowed.' He might in addition have credited himself with eloquence and reproached himself with a lack of artistic instinct and constructive skill. Miss Jewsbury also truly observes that his horrors are too purely physical. As a man he fully developed the propensity to extremes which he attributes to himself as a writer; he appears to have had no idea of measure or conduct in life; every trait recorded of him, from his extravagant expenditure to his amazing portrait and the rouge he forced upon his unwilling wife, witnesses to a morbid passion for display; but this was a genuine manifestation of character, not affectation but eccentricity.

[The principal authority for Maturin's life and writings is the anonymous memoir, with bibliography, prefixed to the most recent edition of Melmoth (1892). See also Webb's Compendium of Irish Biography; Read's Irish Cabinet; Mr. Saintsbury's critique in Tales of Mystery; Irish Quarterly Rev. March 1852; Planché's Portraits Littéraires; Smiles's Memoir of John Murray; Watts's Life of Alaric A. Watts; Appleton's Cyclopædia of American Biography.]
R. G.

MATURIN, WILLIAM (1803-1887), divine, son of Charles Robert Maturin [q. v.], born at Dublin in 1803, was educated at Dublin University, where he graduated B.A. in the spring commencement 1831, and accumulated the degrees of M.A., B.D., and D.D. at the summer commencement 1866 (*Cat. Dubl. Grad.* p. 378). After serving for some years a curacy in Dublin, Maturin was presented in 1844 by William Le Fanu to the perpetual curacy of Grangegorman. A high churchman formed by the movement of Pusey and Newman, his unreserved expression of his views led Archbishop Whately and others to neglect him, so that in spite of his great talents as a preacher and his exemplary and most successful devotion to parochial details, he remained all his life merely incumbent of All Saints, Grangegorman, with an income never exceeding 100*l.* a year, though about 1860 his friends obtained for him the additional post of librarian in Archbishop Marsh's library, Dublin. In England he would have been considered a thoroughly moderate man, but to the Irish evangelical masses he always appeared as little removed from a papist, and to a large section in Dublin his name was a term of theological reproach. In his personal character Maturin was most distinguished. After speaking of the great qualities of his sermons, Professor Mahaffy says of Maturin: 'He was a grim Dantesque sort of man, with deep affection for his family and friends hidden under a severe exterior. He was perfectly certain and clear in his views—a quality rare in modern preachers and fatal to modern preaching; his simple and burning words reflected the zeal of his spirit. . . . I saw him crush by his fiery words a mob of young men, who came to disturb his service on Protestant principles, and drive them cowed and slinking from his church. They had victoriously broken up a service in another church the previous Sunday.'

Maturin died at Alma House, Monkstown, on 30 June 1887, and after lying in state for four days before the altar was buried in All Saints' Church on 4 July, when many distinguished churchmen stood by his grave.

Besides several pamphlets, single sermons, and addresses to the Irish Church Society, Maturin issued 'Six Lectures on the Events of Holy Week,' Oxford, 1860, 8vo; and in 1888 was published posthumously 'The Blessedness of the Dead in Christ,' a collection of twenty-four of his sermons, London, 8vo.

[Athenæum, 1887, ii. 54 (9 July); Irish Times, 4 and 5 July 1887; Dublin Daily Express, 2 July 1887; Brit. Mus. Cat.] T. S.

MATY, MATTHEW (1718-1776), physician, writer, and principal librarian of the British Museum, son of Paul Maty, was born at Montfort, near Utrecht, on 17 May 1718. His father was a protestant refugee from Beaufort in Provence, who settled in Holland and became minister of the Walloon church at Montfort, and subsequently catechist at the Hague, but was dismissed from his benefices and excommunicated by synods at Campen and the Hague in 1730 for maintaining, in a letter on 'The Mystery of the Trinity' to De la Chappelle, that the Son and Holy Spirit are two finite beings created by God, and at a certain time united to him (Mosheim, *Institutes of Eccles. Hist.* 1863, iii. 484, and *Dissert. ad Hist. Eccles. pert.*, ii. 390, 582). After ineffectual protest against the decision of the synods, the elder Maty sought refuge in England, but was unable to find patronage there, and had to return to the Hague, whence his enemies drove him to Leyden. He was living in Leyden with his brother Charles Maty, compiler of a greatly esteemed 'Dictionnaire géographique universel' (1701 and 1723, 4to, Amsterdam), in 1751, being then seventy years of age (Bruys, *Mémoires*, 1751, i. 171-204). He subsequently returned to England, and lived with his son in London, where he died on 21 March 1773 (*Gent. Mag.* 1773, p. 155, s.v. Matty).

Matthew was entered at Leyden University on 31 March 1732, and graduated Ph.D. in 1740, the subject for his inaugural dissertation (which shows Montesquieu's influence) being 'Custom.' A French version of the Latin original, greatly modified and improved, appeared at Utrecht in 1741 under the title 'Essai sur l'Usage,' and attracted some attention. He also graduated M.D. at Leyden, 11 Feb. 1740, with a parallel dissertation, 'De Consuetudinis Efficacia in Corpus Humanum.' In 1741 he came over to London and set up in practice as a physician. He frequented a club which numbered Drs. Parsons, Templeman, Watson, and Fothergill among its members, and met every fortnight in St. Paul's Churchyard, but soon began to devote his best energies to literature. He commenced in 1750 the publication of the bi-monthly 'Journal Britannique,' which was printed at the Hague, and gave an account in French of the chief productions of the English press. The 'Journal,' which had a considerable circulation in the Low Countries, on the Rhine, and at Paris, Geneva, Venice, and Rome, as well as in England, became in Maty's hands an instrument of ingenious eulogy; and it continued to illustrate, in Gibbon's words, 'the taste, the knowledge, and the judgment of Maty' until December 1755, by which time it had introduced him to a very wide circle of literary friends. He had been elected F.R.S. on 19 Dec. 1751, and in 1753, upon the establishment of the British Museum, he was nominated, together with James Empson, an under-librarian, the appointment being confirmed in June 1756. On 1 March 1760 he unsuccessfully applied to the Duke of Newcastle for the post of secretary to the Society of Arts; but he was in March 1762 elected foreign secretary of the Royal Society, in succession to Dr. James Parsons, whose *éloge* was written by him (it is printed in *Lit. Anecd.* v. 474–89). He was at this time member of a literary society which included Jortin, Wetstein, Ralph Heathcote, De Missy, and Dr. Thomas Birch. On the resignation of the post by Birch (who died a few months later and left him his executor), Maty was, 30 Nov. 1765, appointed secretary of the Royal Society. He was in the same year admitted a licentiate of the College of Physicians.

Finally, in 1772, on the death of Dr. Gowin Knight [q. v.], Maty was nominated his successor as principal librarian of the British Museum. The courtesy with which Maty had hitherto discharged the duties of a cicerone is praised by Grosley (1765), but in his capacity as chief librarian he placed, like his predecessor, every difficulty in the way of visitors, who, after obtaining tickets, were hurried silently through Montagu House in a regulation period of thirty minutes (HUTTON, *Journey to England*, pp. 187–96). He bought a number of valuable books for the Museum at Anthony Askew's sale in 1775.

Maty died on 2 July 1776. The trying disease to which he succumbed had troubled him for nearly ten years; it was primarily due to an ulcerated intestine. A short account of his illness and of the appearance of his dead body, examined on 3 July 1776, was contributed by Drs. Hunter and Henry Watson to vol. lxvii. pt. ii. pp. 608–13 of the 'Philosophical Transactions.' He was twice married: first to Elizabeth Boisragon, by whom he had a son Paul Henry, who is separately noticed, and three daughters, of whom Louisa (*d.* 1809) married Rogers (1732–1795), only son of John Jortin [q. v.], and Elizabeth married Obadiah Justamond, F.R.S., surgeon of Westminster Hospital, and translator of Abbé Raynal's 'History of the East and West Indies,' and secondly to Mary Deners. His books were sold in 1777 by Benjamin White.

Without striking talent, Maty was a man of ability, who was always on good terms with those best able to contribute to his advancement. Gibbon, looking about in 1760 for a discriminating critic and judge of his first performance, 'The Essay on the Study of Literature,' pitched upon Maty, whom he knew as the 'candid and pleasing' reviewer of the 'Journal Britannique,' and described as 'one of the last disciples of the school of Fontenelle.' Gibbon subsequently revised the 'Essay' in accordance with his correspondent's friendly advice. Maty corrected the proof-sheets of the work previous to its appearance in the following year, and inserted 'an elegant and flattering epistle to the author, composed with so much art, that in case of defeat his favourable report might have been ascribed to the indulgence of a friend for the rash attempt of a young English gentleman.' Though generally of so conciliatory a disposition, Maty was one of the few persons against whom Dr. Johnson harboured resentment. When his name was mentioned in 1756 by Dr. William Adams [q. v.] as a suitable assistant in the projected review of literature, Johnson's sole comment was, 'The little black dog! I'd throw him into the Thames first.' Maty had earned the doctor's dislike by a very disingenuous allusion in his 'Journal' to Johnson's relations with Chesterfield (a patron of his own); he had also commented on Johnson's 'foiblesse de faire connoître ses principes de politique et religion' in his 'Dictionary,' and was a strong partisan of the unacceptable De Moivre

(De Morgan in *Notes and Queries*, 2nd ser. iv. 341). He was in frequent intercourse with Sloane and other scientific men, was an earnest advocate of inoculation, and when doubts of its complete efficacy were entertained experimented on himself. A portrait of Maty was by his own order engraved after his death by Bartolozzi to be given to his friends. Of these a hundred copies were struck off and the plate destroyed. An oil portrait by Bartholomew Dupan in the board room at the British Museum depicts a young man with a refined and amiable face.

Maty's chief works are: 1. 'Ode sur la Rebellion en Écosse,' 8vo, Amsterdam, 1746. 2. 'Essai sur le Caractère du Grand Medecin, ou Eloge Critique de Mr. Herman Boerhaave,' 8vo, Cologne, 1747. 3. 'Authentic Memoirs of the Life of Richard Mead, M.D.,' 12mo, London, 1755. Expanded from the memoir in the 'Journal Britannique.'

At the time of his death Maty had nearly finished the 'Memoirs of the Earl of Chesterfield,' which were completed by his son-in-law Justamond, and prefixed to the earl's 'Miscellaneous Works,' 2 vols. 4to, 1777. Maty had been one of Chesterfield's executors. He completed for the press Thomas Birch's 'Life of John Ward,' published in 1766, and translated from the French 'A Discourse on Inoculation, read before the Royal Academy of Sciences at Paris, 24 April 1754, by Mr. La Condamine,' with a preface, postscript, and notes, 1765, 8vo, and 'New Observations on Inoculation, by Dr. Garth, Professor of Medicine at Paris,' 1768. Maty's contributions to the 'Philosophical Transactions' are enumerated in Watt's 'Bibl. Britannica.' Some French verses by him on the death of the Comte de Gisors are given in the 'Gentleman's Magazine,' 1758, p. 435.

[Chalmers's Biog. Dict.; Munk's Coll. of Phys. ii. 265–7; Nichols's Anecdotes of Bowyer, p. 607; Lit. Anecd. iii. 257–8, and vols. ii. iv. and v. passim; Edwards's Founders of the British Museum, pp. 337, 342–4; Hume's Letters, ed. Birkbeck Hill, pp. 94–5; Hutchinson's Biog. Medica, ii. 133; Éloy's Dict. Hist. de la Medecine, 1778, iii. 194; Thomson's Hist. of the Royal Society, App. xlvi; De Morgan's Budget of Paradoxes, 1872, p. 17; London Magazine, xxv. 302; Gent. Mag. 1776 p. 191, 1778 p. 319; Rees's Cyclopædia, vol. xxiii.; English Cyclopædia, iv. 153; Gibbon's Memoirs, 1827, i. 105–7, 202; Philosophical Trans. vol. lxvii.; Boswell's Johnson, ed. G. B. Hill, i. 384; Apologie de la Conduite et de la Doctrine de Sr Paul Maty, Utrecht, 1730; Add. MS. 28539, f. 259, and 32903, f. 29.] T. S.

MATY, PAUL HENRY (1745–1787), assistant-librarian of the British Museum, son of Matthew Maty [q. v.], was born in London in 1745. He was admitted a king's scholar at Westminster in 1758, and was elected in 1763 to Trinity College, Cambridge, whence he graduated B.A. in 1767 and M.A. in 1770 (*Grad. Cantabr.* s.v. 'Matty'). He was nominated to one of the travelling fellowships of his college, and passed three years abroad, after which he was appointed chaplain to David Murray, lord Stormont (afterwards second Earl of Mansfield) [q. v.], English ambassador at the court of France. He vacated his fellowship in 1775 by his marriage to a daughter of Joseph Clerke of Wethersfield, Essex, sister to Captain Charles Clerke [q. v.], the successor to Captain Cook. In the following year doubts conceived as to the consistency of the Thirty-nine Articles, especially on such points as predestination and original sin, compelled him to refrain from seeking any further ecclesiastical appointment; his scruples, which evince a tendency to Arianism, were printed in full in the 'Gentleman's Magazine' for October 1777. Fortunately for him, however, he obtained, upon his father's death in July 1776, the situation of an assistant-librarian in the British Museum, and in 1782 was promoted to be under-librarian in the department of natural history and antiquities. He also succeeded in 1776 to the foreign secretaryship of the Royal Society, of which he had been elected a member 13 Feb. 1772 (Thomson), and on 30 Nov. 1778, on the withdrawal of Dr. Horsley, he became principal secretary. In this capacity he threw himself with unexplained and ungovernable heat into the controversy which raged about the virtual dismissal of Dr. Charles Hutton [q. v.] from the post of foreign secretary by the president, Sir Joseph Banks. In a pamphlet entitled 'An History of the instances of Exclusion from the Royal Society . . . with Strictures on the formation of the Council and other instances of the despotism of Sir Joseph Banks, the present President, and of his incapacity for his high office' (1784), he proposed that, as a means of protest against the president, the dissatisfied minority should form themselves into a solid phalanx, and resolutely oppose any admission whatsoever into the society, a proposal from which all moderate supporters of Maty's views dissented. Having tried in vain to organise a regular opposition under Horsley, Maty resigned his office on 25 March 1784, and his resignation helped to restore peace to the society (Weld, *Hist. of Roy. Soc.* ii. 160 sq.; Kippis, *Observations on the late Contests in the Roy. Soc.*) As secretary and an officer of the society he was not called upon to take any active part in the dissension, but here, as elsewhere, 'his vivacity outran his judgment.' The loss of his office involved a reduction of income which he could ill afford, and he was not highly successful in the attempt which he made to replace it by giving instruction in classical and modern languages.

He had commenced in January 1782 a 'New Review,' which aimed at giving a bird's-eye view of foreign publications, and he continued this considerable work, almost unassisted, down to September 1786. As a reviewer Gibbon speaks of him as the 'angry son' who wielded the rod of criticism with but little of 'the tenderness and reluctance' of his father. Horace Walpole speaks of some of his comments as 'pert and foolish' (cf. *Canons of Criticism extracted from the Beauties of Maty's Review*). A kindly man, though cantankerous and utterly devoid of his father's complaisance, Maty made strong friendships and strong enmities. He died of asthma on 16 Jan. 1787, and was buried in Bunhill Fields. He left his widow and young son (aged 10) in very poor circumstances. The child was educated at the expense of Dr. Burney, but died while at school. A medallion by James Tassie in the Scottish National Portrait Gallery depicts Maty's shaven face, bald prominent forehead, and protruding lower lip.

Three works appeared from Maty's hand bearing the date of the year of his death: 1. 'A General Index to the Philosophical Transactions,' vols. i–lxx. 4to, which he had prepared some time previously. 2. A translation of Riesbeck's 'Travels through Germany, in a Series of Letters,' 3 vols. 8vo (see *Monthly Review*, lxxvi. 608). 3. A French translation of the text to the first volume of 'Gemmæ Marlburienses,' to accompany the Latin of James Bryant, for which Maty received 100*l.* and a copy of the work (cf. Brunet, *Manuel*, 1861, ii. 1528). A volume of sermons delivered in the Ambassador's Chapel at Paris during the years 1774, 1775, and 1776, in which some of Secker's sermons were inadvertently included, was published in 1788. Bishop Horsley, Dean Layard, and Dr. Southgate were responsible for the editing.

[Gent. Mag. 1787, i. 92; Nichols's Lit. Anecd. iii. 259, 261, 623, iv. 97, v. passim, and Lit. Illustr. iv. 833; Watt's Bibl. Britannica; Chalmers's Biog. Dict.; Welch's Queen's Scholars, p. 380; D'Arblay's Memoirs, iii. 303; Green's Diary of a Lover of Lit. 1810, pp. 162, 169, 173; Gibbon's Memoirs; Lindsey's Historical View of the Unitarian Doctrine, 1783, pp. 515–25; Rutt's Memoirs of Priestley, i. 406, 407; Add. MS. 33977; An Authentic Narrative of the Dissensions and Debates in the Roy. Soc. 1784.] T. S.

MAUCLERK, WALTER (*d.* 1248), bishop of Carlisle, first appears as a royal clerk in 1202, when he was presented to the church of the Trinity at Falaise. Afterwards he also received two parts of Croxton, Lincolnshire, in 1205; Nimeton (probably Nympton), Devonshire, 1207; a moiety of Catfield, Norfolk, in 1212; and on 16 Sept. 1213 Mylor, Cornwall (*Cal. Rot. Pat.* 14, 49*b*, 74, 93, 103). In 1205 he appears as bailiff of the county of Lincoln. In June 1210 he was sent on a mission to Ireland, and again in October 1212 was sent over to take charge of the exchequer there (Sweetman, *Cal. Documents relating to Ireland*, i. 401, 441, 443). In 1215 he was sent to Rome to urge the royal complaints against the barons (*Fœdera*, i. 120). In 1219 he was a justice itinerant for the counties of Lincoln, Nottingham, and Derby, and was employed with the sheriff for the collection of royal dues and in the collection of fines (cf. Shirley, *Royal Letters*, i. 20, 28, 36). In 1220 he appears as prebend of Woodburgh, Southwell (Le Neve, iii. 488). He was a justice of the forest in 1221, and next year was sheriff of Cumberland and constable of Carlisle.

In August 1223 Mauclerk was elected bishop of Carlisle, but as this had been done without the royal permission assent was withheld till 27 Oct. (*Cal. Rot. Claus.* i. 560, 573). In Oct. 1224 he was appointed to go on an embassy to Germany, and set out in the following January. His mission was to treat for the king's marriage with a daughter of Leopold of Austria, and with the Archbishop of Cologne. Three letters from Mauclerk reporting on the progress of his embassy have been preserved (Shirley, i. 249–54, 259, 260). These letters have been sometimes confused with a later mission in 1235, but cf. *Fœdera*, i. 275, orig. edit. and Pauli, *Geschichte*, iii. 549 *n.* 2). While at Cologne Mauclerk dedicated a 'capsa' in the Church of the Apostles there. In January 1227 Mauclerk was sent on an embassy to the court of Brittany to negotiate a marriage for Henry. This mission was concerned with the troubles in France consequent on the minority of Louis IX. The moment seemed advantageous for pressing the English king's claims to his ancestral possessions, but the mission failed of its object, because the French nobles had in the meantime made terms with the regent Blanche (Matt. Paris, iii. 123; *Ann. Mon.* iii. 203; iv. 420). Mauclerk was back in England by Easter. He seems to have been treasurer before 27 May 1227, when he witnesses a charter in this capacity (cf. Giraldus Cambrensis, vii. 232–4). Foss, however, states that he was not made treasurer till July 1232. Early in 1233 he was expelled from his office through the influence of Peter des Roches, bishop of Winchester, and fined 100*l.* Mauclerk determined to appeal to the pope, and in October was on his way to leave England when he was violently stopped at Dover; on an appeal to the king by the other bishops he was released, and allowed to go to Flanders. The 'Chronicle of Lanercost' alleges that this voluntary exile was on account of the injuries done to his church, and that for the same cause Carlisle was under interdict on 27 Nov. 1233, the first Sunday in Advent. Mauclerk was pardoned at the intercession of Archbishop Edmund, and soon recovered the royal favour. Stephen de Segrave [q. v.] endeavoured, on his fall in 1234, to excuse himself under the plea that Mauclerk, as the higher authority, was really responsible. In 1235 Mauclerk was sent to negotiate a marriage for the king with the daughter of Simon, count of Ponthieu, but without success, and in April of the same year was engaged on a mission to the Emperor Frederick (Shirley, i. 469). In 1236 he witnessed the confirmation of the charters. In 1239 he was one of the sponsors for the king's son Edward. Mauclerk was also present at the meeting of the bishops on the state of the churches in 1241. He was one of the councillors during Henry's absence in France in 1243, and governor of the kingdom while Henry was in Wales in 1245, on which account he was excused from attendance at the council of Lyons. In 1248 he resigned his bishopric and became a Dominican at Oxford 29 June (*Ann. Mon.* iii. 170, but *Wykes*, iv. 94, gives the date as 24 June). He died on 28 Oct. following. The writer of the 'Flores Historiarum' gives a not too favourable character of Mauclerk. He says that the bishop had resigned his see in his old age out of a feeling that he had owed it rather to royal favour than to his learning and character. 'This is he whom fortune ofttimes raised up only to dash down; who imprudently concerned himself with the royal policy, that he had neither the power nor will to carry out; who negotiated unsuitable alliances for the king in Scotland and Ponthieu.' He further alleges, with monkish jealousy, that it was Mauclerk who obtained for the Dominicans, perhaps by bribery, the unheard-of privilege that no friar might legitimately leave that order for another. Mauclerk is, however, said to have made a good end, thus hoping to avert the sinister omen of his surname. Mauclerk had a brother, R., prior of Reading, whom John wanted to make abbot of St. Albans in 1215 (*Cal. Rot Pat.* p. 140). Two nephews of his are also mentioned, Arnhale (Shirley, i. 68) and Ralph, who in 1231 was made prior of Carlisle (*Chron. Lanercost*, p. 41).

[Matthew Paris; Annales Monastici; Shirley's Royal and Historical Letters; Flores Historiarum, ii. 350–1 (all these in the Rolls Ser.); Chron. Lanercost (Bannatyne Club); Foss's Judges of England. ii. 404–6; Scriptt. Ord. Prædicatorum, i, 120–1; Le Neve's Fasti, iii. 232, 458.] C. L. K.

MAUD. [See Matilda.]

MAUDE, THOMAS (1718–1798), minor poet and essayist, belonged to the ancient family of Maude of Alverthorpe and Wakefield, Yorkshire (Burke, *Commoners*, ii. 84). He was born in Downing Street, Westminster, during May 1718 (cf. *Gent. Mag.* 1841, pt. i. p. 597, and pt. ii. p. 36), and entered the medical profession. In 1755 he was appointed surgeon on board the Barfleur, commanded by Lord Harry Powlett [q. v.] Maude's favourable evidence at a court-martial before which Lord Harry was tried at Portsmouth in October 1755 was so highly valued by his commander that upon his succession as sixth and last Duke of Bolton in 1765 he appointed Maude steward of his Yorkshire estates. This post he held, residing at Bolton Hall, Wharfedale, until the death of the duke in 1794. He then retired to Burley Hall, near Ottley, where he died unmarried in December 1798, aged 80 (*York Courant*, Monday, 14 Jan. 1799). He was buried in Wensley churchyard; lines from the 'Deserted Village' are engraved on his tomb (*Notes and Queries*, 4th ser. viii. 230).

Maude's accomplishments were inconsiderable, but he was esteemed for his love of 'letters and of man.' His verses are mainly descriptive of the Yorkshire dales. He contributed to Grose's 'Antiquities' the information about Bolton Castle and Wensleydale. Grose, who was his friend, quotes from 'Wharfedale' in illustration of Aysgarth Bridge. William Paley [q. v.], the divine, also visited Maude at Bolton (*ib.* 2nd ser. viii. 407).

His works are: 1. 'Wensleydale, or Rural Contemplations; a Poem,' 1772, 4to; 3rd edition, London, 1780; 4th edition, Richmond, Yorkshire, 1816. Published for the benefit of Leeds General Infirmary. 2. 'An Account of the Cowthorpe Oak, near Weatherby, Yorks,' 1774. See 'Opuscula Botanica,' vol. clxiv. 3. 'Verbeia, or Wharfedale; a Poem descriptive and didactic,' 1782, 4to. 4. 'Viator; a Journey from London to Scarborough by way of York; a Poem, with notes historical and topographical,' 1782, 4to 5. 'The Invitation, or Urbanity; a Poem

1791, 4to. 6. 'The Reaper; a collection of Essays, &c.,' some of which were originally published in the 'York Courant,' 1797. Enlarged and printed for the benefit of the Ottley and Burley Sunday-schools, 2 vols. 8vo, York, 1798, but never published in consequence of the author's death. The second volume ends abruptly at p. 100. Two copies only were issued, of which one, with manuscript notes by W. Blanchard, the printer, is in the British Museum.

[Authorities stated above; Notes and Queries, 2nd ser. viii. 291, 4th ser. viii. 230, and xii. 233; Gent. Mag. 1799, i. 79, 163, 191; Martin's Bibl. Cat. of Privately Printed Books, p. 195, where Maude's last work is given as by '— Mander, Esq.'] C. F. S.

MAUDSLAY, HENRY (1771–1831), engineer, son of Henry Maudslay, was born at Woolwich 22 Aug. 1771, and entered the arsenal, where his father, a native of Clapham, Yorkshire, who served in the royal artillery from 1756 to 1776, was an artificer. He became a very expert workman, and at the age of eighteen entered the employment of Bramah, who was then engaged in devising machines for the manufacture of his well-known locks. According to James Nasmyth (Smiles, *Industrial Biography*, p. 205) it was Maudslay who suggested to Bramah the self-tightening leather collar for the hydraulic press, in place of the cupped leather shown in the specification of his patent of 1795 (No. 2045).

A dispute about wages led Maudslay to leave Bramah in 1798; and setting up in business as an engineer on his own account, he took premises at No. 64 Wells Street, Oxford Street. In 1802 he removed to a larger house, No. 75 Margaret Street, and his business increased rapidly (cf. rate-books of the parish of Marylebone). He was employed by the elder Brunel to construct his machinery for making ships' blocks, afterwards erected at Portsmouth dockyard. In 1805 he took out a patent (No. 2872) for printing calico, and another in 1808 (No. 3117) relating to the same subject. In conjunction with Bryan Donkin he patented in 1806 (No. 2948) a differential motion for raising weights, applicable also to driving lathes. In 1807 he patented (No. 3050) an arrangement of steam engine known as a 'table engine,' which, with some modifications, continued for forty years or thereabouts to be a favourite type for engines of small power. In 1810 he removed to Westminster Bridge Road, where the works have remained ever since. In 1812 he patented (No. 3538), in conjunction with Robert Dickinson, a method of purifying water on board ship by blowing air through it. Some time afterwards the firm was known as Henry Maudslay & Co., and subsequently Mr. Joshua Field was taken into partnership. In conjunction with Mr. Field, Maudslay patented in 1824 (No. 5021) a method of regulating the supply of water to boilers at sea, and preventing the formation of brine in the boilers. The firm devoted their attention especially to marine engines, in which Maudslay and his partners made many important improvements. He devoted great attention to the improvement of the lathe, and an account of his labours in this direction may be found in Gregory's 'Mechanics,' 2nd edit. 1807, ii. 471. Maudslay's original screw-cutting lathe, made about the end of the last century, at which Sir Joseph Whitworth worked during the time he was in Maudslay's employment, is still in existence. Among other specimens of his skill may be mentioned the measuring machine, divided so as to register a ten thousandth of an inch, which was made about the same time as the lathe. Whitworth afterwards adopted the principle of Maudslay's apparatus in his 'millionth measuring machine.' These relics were shown at the Naval Exhibition in 1891. In a chapter on 'The Introduction of the Slide Principle in Tools and Machines,' contributed by Nasmyth to Buchanan on 'Millwork,' ed. 1840, he says, p. 401: 'It would be blamable indeed (after having endeavoured to set forth the vast advantages which have been conferred on the mechanical world, and therefore on mankind generally, by the invention and introduction of the slide-rest) were I to suppress the name of that admirable individual to whom we are indebted for this powerful agent towards the attainment of mechanical perfection. I allude to the late Henry Maudslay, engineer, of London, whose useful life was enthusiastically devoted to the grand object of improving our means of producing perfect workmanship and machinery. To him we are certainly indebted for the slide-rest. . . . The indefatigable care which he took in inculcating and diffusing among his workmen, and mechanical men generally, sound ideas of practical knowledge, and refined views of construction, has rendered, and ever will continue to render, his name identified with all that is noble in the ambition of a lover of mechanical perfection.' Among Maudslay's pupils and workmen may be named Joseph Whitworth, James Nasmyth, Richard Roberts, Joseph Clements, Samuel Seaward, and William Muir.

Maudslay died at Lambeth on 14 Feb. 1831, and was buried in Woolwich churchyard, where he is commemorated by a cast-iron monument, bearing a number of inscriptions relating to his father and mother, his wife

Sarah (*d.* 29 March 1828, aged 66), and many of his children and grandchildren.

The eldest son, THOMAS HENRY MAUDSLAY (1792–1864), became a member of his father's firm, and by his commercial ability greatly contributed to its progress. His firm constructed the engines for the ships of the royal navy for more than a quarter of a century. He gave evidence before a select committee of the House of Commons on steam navigation in 1831. He purchased the estate of Banstead Park, Surrey, but died at Knight's Hill, Norwood, on 23 April 1864, and was buried at Woolwich. He was twice married (*Mechanics' Magazine*, 29 April 1864; *Gent. Mag.* 1864, i. 808; inscriptions on the father's tomb).

The third son, JOSEPH MAUDSLAY (1801–1861), engineer, originally intended for a shipbuilder, was apprenticed to William Pitcher of Northfleet, but he subsequently joined his father's engineering business at Lambeth, in which he took a prominent position. In 1827 he patented an oscillating engine in which the slide valves were worked by an eccentric, and many engines were made upon that plan. He was elected a member of the Institution of Civil Engineers in 1833. In conjunction with Joshua Field he took out a patent in 1839 for a double-cylinder marine engine, which came into extensive use. His early training as a shipbuilder led him to take great interest in marine propulsion, and in 1841–2 his firm made the engines for the Rattler, the first screw-steamer built for the admiralty, which was afterwards employed in the trials of various forms of screw propellers. The screw was driven direct without the intervention of gearing. In 1848 he patented a feathering screw propeller, which was fitted in 1850 in three vessels belonging to the Screw Steam Shipping Company. Another of his inventions was the direct-acting annular cylinder screw engine, which formed the subject of a paper read by him before the Institution of Naval Architects in 1860. He died on 25 Sept. 1861 (*Mechanics' Magazine*, 11 Oct. 1861 p. 250, 29 Nov. 1861 p. 351; ALBAN, *High Pressure Steam Engine*, p. 208).

[Smiles's Industrial Biography, pp. 198–235; W. Walker's Distinguished Men of Science, 1862, p. 129; Vincent's Records of Woolwich, v. 213; Autobiography of James Nasmyth.] R. B. P.

MAUDUIT, ISRAEL (1708–1787), political pamphleteer, was born, it is believed at Bermondsey, London, in 1708. He was descended from a family of French protestants who settled at Exeter early in the seventeenth century. His father, Isaac Mauduit, the first dissenting minister at the chapel of St. John's or King John's Court, Bermondsey, died 8 April 1718, aged 55; his mother, Elizabeth, died 10 March 1713, aged 41. Both were buried, with several of their infant children, in Bermondsey Church. Israel was educated for the dissenting ministry in the nonconformist school at Taunton, and afterwards travelled abroad with several other young men of the same opinions. He preached for a time at the Hague and in other protestant chapels at home and abroad, but afterwards became a partner in a woollen-draper's business in Lime Street, London, with his brother Jaspar, and with James Wright, who had married Jaspar's only child by his first wife. During the rebellion of 1745 the firm executed a government contract without retaining any profit from the transaction. In 1763 Israel was appointed customer of Southampton. Jaspar was agent in England for the province of Massachusetts Bay, but, as the business was managed by Israel, a majority of the council voted for appointing the latter to the agency (HUTCHINSON, *Massachusetts Bay*, 1828, pp. 105, 416–418). Governor Bernard, however, induced them to reverse their decision, and Jaspar remained in his post for a time, though Israel was appointed about 1763. So long as Governor Hutchinson and Lieutenant-governor Oliver were in America the agency was held by him, and when the petition for their removal from the governorship of Massachusetts came before the privy council, he applied to be heard on their behalf by counsel. The application was granted. Wedderburn argued their case, and during the proceedings made his celebrated attack on Benjamin Franklin. For some years after the outbreak of war with the American colonies he was not in sympathy with the colonists, and he withheld from them a fund for propagating the gospel among the subjects of the crown. In March 1778 he declared for American independence, and produced to Hutchinson 'a printed sheet of his own composing' in support of that view. On 6 May 1787 he was chosen to succeed Richard Jackson [q. v.] as governor of the Dissenters' Society for the Propagation of the Gospel in Foreign Parts, but only lived to attend one board meeting. He was elected F.R.S. on 13 June 1751.

Mauduit died at Clement's Lane, Lombard Street, London, on 14 June 1787, when his library was sold by John Walker of Paternoster Row. A bachelor, possessed of an ample fortune, he entertained at his house many friends, among whom were Baron Maseres and Dr. Heberden. Miss Hawkins calls him 'a gentleman of the old school' and a good classical scholar, and she quotes his punning motto, 'Deus me audit.' His portrait, painted by M. Chamberlin in 1751 for Benjamin Lethieullier, was engraved by Thomas Holloway for the 'European Magazine' (1787, pt. i. pp. 383–4, pt. ii. pp. 6–8).

Mauduit wrote: 1. 'Letter to the Right Hon. Lord B——y, being an Enquiry into the merits of his Defence of Minorca' [anon.], 1757, which brought out in reply, 'A Full Answer to a Libel, entitled A Letter to Lord B——y,' 1757. 2. 'Considerations on the present German War' [anon.], 1760; 6th edit. 1761. This pamphlet, which attracted many answers, came out under the countenance of Lord Hardwicke, and was defended in parliament (10 Dec. 1761) by Charles Yorke. According to Horace Walpole it was 'shrewdly and ably written, having more operation in working a change on the minds of men than perhaps ever fell to the lot of a pamphlet,' as, after its publication, England remained neutral on the differences between the various German states. Walpole says that its author received a place, others assert that a pension, varying in amount from 200*l.* to 600*l.* a year, was bestowed on him for life. 3. 'Occasional Thoughts on the present German War' [anon.], 1761; 4th edit., with additions, 1762. This also was answered in several pamphlets. 4. 'The Plain Reasoner, or Further Considerations on the present German War' [anon.], 1761. 5. 'The Parallel, the substance of two Speeches supposed to have been made in the Closet by two different Ministers, some time before a late demise, on the renewal of our Prussian Treaty' [anon.], 1762. 6. 'An Apology for the Life and Actions of General Wolfe, in reply to a pamphlet called "A Counter-Address to the Public"' [anon.], 1765; twenty-five copies only printed. 7. 'Some Thoughts on the Method of Improving the advantages accruing to Great Britain from the Northern Colonies' [anon.], 1765. 8. 'Short View of the History of the Colony of Massachusetts Bay' [anon.], 1769; 2nd edit. by Israel Mauduit, 1774; 4th edit. 1776. 9. 'Short View of the History of the New England Colonies,' 1769, attributed to him by Allibone. 10. 'Case of the Dissenting Ministers, with Copy of the Bill for their Relief,' 1772; 4th edit. 1772, and printed at Boston, New England, in 1773. This pamphlet, in favour of releasing them from subscription to the Thirty-nine Articles, provoked a printed letter to Mauduit in reply. 11. 'Letters of Hutchinson and Oliver,' printed at Boston, and remarks thereon by Israel Mauduit, 1774; 2nd edit. 1774. 12. 'Remarks upon General Howe's Account of his Proceedings on Long Island, in the "Extraordinary Gazette" of 10 Oct. 1776' [anon.], 1776; 2nd edit. 1778. Very sarcastic on the general's dilatoriness. 13. 'Observations upon the Conduct of S—r W—m H—e at the White Plains, as related in the "Gazette" of 30 Dec. 1776' [anon.], 1779. 14. 'Strictures on the Philadelphia Mischianza, or Triumph upon leaving America unconquered' [anon.], 1779. 15. 'Three Letters to Lieutenant-General Sir William Howe' [anon.], 1781. 16. 'Three Letters to Lord Viscount Howe, with Remarks on the Attack at Bunker's Hill' [anon.], 1781.

Mauduit wrote 'Some Observations upon an American Wasps'-Nest' (*Phil. Trans.* 1775, pp. 205–8), which was translated into German in the 'Hamburg Magazine,' vol. xxiv.

[Halkett and Laing's Anon. Lit. i. 486, ii. 1414, iii. 1790, 1797, 1856, 2160, 2377, 2588; Rich's Bibl. Americana, i. 150, 173, 268, 277, 297–8; Gent. Mag. 1787, pt. i. p. 549; Thomas Hutchinson's Diary, passim; Franklin's Works, ed. Sparks, iv. 447, viii. 104; Walpole's George III. ed. 1845, i. 33–4, 111; Manning and Bray's Surrey, i. 209; Nichols's Lit. Anecdotes, iii. 667, viii. 465; Parton's Franklin, i. 578–86; Haag's France Protestante, vii. 336; L. M. Hawkins's Anecdotes, 1822, pp. 7, 166–9.] W. P. C.

MAUDUIT, WILLIAM, Earl of Warwick (1220–1268), was son of William Mauduit of Hanslape, whose great-grandfather of the same name was chamberlain to Henry I. William Mauduit (*d.* 1257) fought in the barons' war against John, during which his castle of Hanslape was taken and destroyed by Fawkes de Breauté on 28 Nov. 1215. He was present on the same side at Lincoln on 20 May 1217. In 1233 he had to give his son as a hostage to the king, but was taken into favour next year. He died in April 1257, leaving by his wife Alice, daughter of Waleran, earl of Warwick, one son, William, and a daughter Isabella. William Mauduit was thirty-six years old at his father's death. On the death of John de Plessis, second husband of his cousin Margaret, countess of Warwick, Mauduit became Earl of Warwick, on 4 April 1263, in right of his mother, and in the same year was summoned to the Welsh war under that title. In the barons' war he at first sided with Simon de Montfort, but afterwards joined the king. In April 1264 he was surprised at Warwick Castle by John Giffard [q. v.], taken prisoner with his wife, and imprisoned at Kenilworth. He had to pay nineteen hundred marks for his ransom. He was hereditary chamberlain to the king. Mauduit died on 8 Jan. 1268, having married Alice, daughter of Gilbert de Segrave. He left no children, and the earldom of Warwick consequently passed to his sister's son, William Beauchamp, who was father of Guy de Beauchamp [q. v.]

[Matthew Paris; Flores Historiarum (both in Rolls Ser.); Dugdale's Baronage, i. 398–9; Doyle's Official Baronage, iii. 577.] C. L. K.

MAUDUITH or **MANDUIT, JOHN** (*fl.* 1310), astronomer, was a fellow of Merton College, Oxford, and is supposed to have been elected about 1305. He is said to have resided at Merton as late as 1346; the name of Maudit occurs as bursar in 1311. Mauduith had a great reputation as a physician, astronomer, and theologian. Leland says that his mathematical tables were still well known to students in his time. Richard de Bury [q. v.] was a patron of his. Mauduith or Mauduit is no doubt the correct form of his name, the variety Manduit, given by Tanner and others, is probably an error. Mauduith's Tables are contained in Laud. MS. Misc. 674, f. 69, 'Tabule Mawdith facte in Oxon. 1310,' and f. 72, 'Maudith. Tabula ascensionis signorum in arculo obliquo Oxon., cujus latitudo est 51 grad. et 50 min. verificata Oxon. A.D. 1310.' In MS. Univ. Camb. Gg. vi. 3, f. 45, there is 'Parvus Tractatus editus a magistro Johanne Mauduth super quattuor tabulis mirabiliter inventis in civitate Oxon. MCCCX.' Inc.: 'Quia scientia astronomiæ.' The four tables are: 1. 'De chorda et arcu recto et verso, et umbris.' 2. 'De arcu æquinoctiali elevato, et horis et arcu diei.' 3. 'De altitudine stellarum, et arcu diurno stellæ, et distantia ab æquinoctio.' 4. 'De ascensionibus regionis triæ.' The first of these tables explains Leland's reference to a 'Libellus de chorda recta et umbra.' This manuscript may also contain some other small tracts by him. Mauduith is likewise said to have written a treatise, 'De doctrina Theologica,' inc.: 'Legimus in scripturis sacris.' He left 40*s.* to the university, to be kept in S. Frideswide's chest (*Munimenta Academica*, i. 10, Rolls. Ser.)

[Leland's De Scriptt. p. 329; Bale, v. 70; Pits, p. 455; Tanner's Bibl. Brit.-Hib. p. 506; Brodrick's Memorials of Merton College, pp. 193–4 (Oxf. Hist. Soc.); information kindly supplied by Mr. F. Jenkinson, Cambridge University Library.] C. L. K.

MAUGER (*d.* 1212), bishop of Worcester, of illegitimate birth, was physician to Richard I (Diceto), and archdeacon of Evreux. He was elected bishop of Worcester in August 1199, but his election was annulled by Pope Innocent III on the ground of his illegitimacy. Against this decision he pleaded in person before the pope, who was so favourably impressed by him that he confirmed the election, issued a decretal on his behalf (*Innocentii Decretalium Collectio*, tit. iv.), and consecrated him at Rome on 4 June 1200. On his return to England he was enthroned at Worcester, and reverently replaced in the church the bones of Bishop Wulfstan (*d.* 1095), which had been disturbed by his predecessor, Bishop John, of Coutances (*d.* 1198). Very many miracles followed this act. On 17 April 1202 the cathedral and other buildings were burnt. Apparently in order to raise funds to repair this disaster, the bishop and monks applied for the canonisation of Wulfstan, and satisfactory proof of the miracles having been given, their request was granted the following year. Mauger obtained a judgment subjecting the Abbey of Evesham to his jurisdiction, but the judgment was reversed by the pope. In 1207 Pope Innocent wrote to him and to the bishops of London and Ely bidding them urge King John to submit to the see of Rome, threatening him with an interdict, which they were to publish if he would not give way. They had an interview with John, and, their entreaties being in vain, pronounced the interdict on 23 March 1208. After this Mauger fled the kingdom secretly in company with the Bishop of Hereford, and his possessions were confiscated. At the king's bidding he returned with the bishops of London and Ely in the hope of an accommodation, but failed to persuade John, and after eight weeks returned to France. Innocent sent him and the other two bishops another letter bidding them pronounce the king's excommunication. They hesitated to obey, and sent the letter to the bishops remaining in England. Meanwhile they were blamed by some for having fled, and it was said that they lived in comfort, having left their flocks defenceless (Wendover, iii. 224). In 1209 Mauger and the bishops of London and Ely were again sent for by the king, who commissioned the chief justiciar, Geoffrey Fitz-Peter [q. v.], to arrange a reconciliation. The bishops landed in September, and discussed terms with the justiciar and other magnates at Canterbury. Mauger received back his manors and 100*l.* as an instalment of his losses. As, however, the king would not make full restitution, the negotiations fell through, and he and the two other bishops returned to France. He resided at the abbey at Pontigny, and died there on 1 July 1212, having before his death assumed the monastic habit.

[Ann. Monast.—Margam, i. 29, Tewkesbury, i. 56, Waverley, ii. 261, 267, Worcester, iv. 390, 391, 396, 401 (Rolls Ser.); Wendover, iii. 224, 238 (Engl. Hist. Soc.); R. de Diceto, ii. 168 (Rolls Ser.); Gervase of Cant. ii. 107 (Rolls Ser.); Inno-

centii Regest. x. ep. 113, xi. ep. 211, ap. Migne's Patrol. vol. ccxv. cols. 1208, 1526; Decret. Collect. tit. iv. ap. Patrol. vol. ccxvi. cols. 1193–5.]
W. H.

MAUGHAM, ROBERT (*d.* 1862), first secretary to the Incorporated Law Society, was admitted a solicitor in 1817, after serving his articles with Mr. Barrow of Threadneedle Street. In 1825 he urged, in conjunction with Bryan Holme, the formation of the Incorporated Law Society. He became secretary of a committee to report on the scheme, and the formal establishment of the society (1827) and its incorporation (1831) were the outcome of his labours. He continued to act as secretary and solicitor to the society during the rest of his life. He endeavoured in other ways to advance the interests of his profession, and was the author of several treatises which obtained a wide popularity. In 1830 he founded the 'Legal Observer,' of which he continued sole proprietor and editor until 1856, when it was merged in the 'Solicitors' Journal and Reporter.' He did much to promote the Attorneys and Solicitors Acts (1843 and 1860), and he was examined by the select committee on legal education (1846). In 1856 the members of the Law Society subscribed 600*l.* for a testimonial to him. He died on 16 July 1862, and was buried on 22 July at Nunhead cemetery.

Maugham's best-known works are: 1. 'A Treatise on the Principles of the Usury Laws; with Disquisitions on the Arguments adduced against them by Mr. Bentham and other Writers, and a Review of the Authorities in their Favour,' London, 1824, 8vo. See also the 'Pamphleteer,' vol. xxiii. 2. 'A Treatise on the Laws of Literary Property, comprising the Statutes and Cases relating to Books, Manuscripts, Lectures,' &c., London, 1828, 8vo. He published also: 3. 'A Treatise on the Law of Attornies,' &c., London, 1825, 8vo. 4. 'A Complete Collection of the Statutes and Rules and Orders of Court relating to Attornies,' &c., London, 1839, 8vo.

[Solicitors' Journal and Reporter, vi. 699, 727; Report from Select Committee on Legal Education, 1846, pp. 158–68.] W. A. S. H.

MAULE, FOX, second Baron Panmure (of the United Kingdom), and eventually eleventh Earl of Dalhousie (in the peerage of Scotland) (1801–1874), was the eldest son of William Maule, first baron Panmure [q. v.] His mother was Patricia Heron, daughter of Gilbert Gordon of Halleaths, N.B. Born on 22 April 1801 at Brechin Castle, Forfarshire, he was educated at the Charterhouse under Dr. Russell, and entered the army at the usual age, but after twelve years' service retired as captain from the 79th highlanders in 1831–2. He was known as a spendthrift in youth. He sat in the House of Commons in the liberal interest in 1835–7 as M.P. for Perthshire, and afterwards represented the Elgin burghs, 1838–41, and the borough of Perth from the latter date until 1852, when his father's death raised him to the peerage. He was one of the under-secretaries of state in Lord Melbourne's ministry in 1835–41, and vice-president of the board of trade for a few months in the last-named year. He became secretary at war on 6 July 1846 in Lord John Russell's administration, and remained in office until 6 Feb. 1852. When Lord Palmerston formed an administration in February 1855, Panmure took office as secretary for war, and it was thus under his direction that the Crimean war reached its termination. Although he was in no way responsible for the errors for which his predecessor in the department, the Duke of Newcastle, was so freely blamed by the press, all Panmure's acts were rigorously scrutinized. While holding office he addressed a despatch to the military authorities in the Crimea, asking them to pay special attention to his nephew, a young officer named Dowbiggin; and the despatch gave birth to a long popular phrase, 'Take care of Dowb.' Panmure was one of the few Scottish noblemen who supported the free church at the date of the disruption of 1843. In December 1860 he succeeded to the earldom of Dalhousie on the death of his cousin, James Andrew Ramsay, tenth earl and first marquis of Dalhousie [see Ramsay]. In the following year, by royal licence, he assumed the additional name of Ramsay, as head of the ancient house of Dalhousie. He was a knight of the Scottish order of the Thistle, a knight grand cross of the Bath (civil division), a privy councillor, keeper of the privy seal of Scotland, lord-lieutenant of Forfarshire, a commissioner of the royal military asylum, and a governor of the Charterhouse. He married in 1831 Montagu Abercromby, daughter of George, second Lord Abercromby, but died without issue on 6 July 1874, when the earldom passed to his cousin, George Ramsay, admiral R.N., the barony of Panmure becoming extinct.

[Burke's Peerage; The Panmure Papers, ed. Sir George Douglas and Sir George Dalhousie Ramsay, 2 vols. 1908.] E. W.

MAULE, HARRY, titular Earl of Panmure (*d.* 1734), was the third son of George, second earl of Panmure, by his wife Lady Jean Campbell, eldest daughter of John, earl of Loudon, lord high chancellor of Scotland. In his youth he travelled on the continent, and spent much of his time at the courts of England and France. He was a member of the convention of estates in 1689, but left that assembly when he found it was determined to declare that James II had forfeited the crown. He joined eagerly in the rising of 1715, and with his brother, James, fourth earl of Panmure, fought at the indecisive battle of Sheriffmuir. The earl was taken prisoner by the royal troops, but was afterwards rescued by his brother under circumstances of great peril. This stirring incident is commemorated in the Jacobite ballad on the battle. In 1716 Maule was obliged to fly to Holland, where he devoted his leisure to the study of the civil and canon laws. Both before and after his return to Scotland he corresponded largely with the leading adherents of the Jacobite cause and other prominent men. From the leading Jacobites of the day he was constantly receiving news-letters, of a number of which abstracts are given in 'Historical Manuscripts Commission,' 1st Rep. App. pp. 117–19. His latter years were spent in his castle of Kelly, where he occupied himself in historical pursuits, and both he and his brother made extensive collections of chronicles, chartularies, and documents bearing on the history of Scotland, all of which are preserved in the library at Brechin Castle (*Hist. MSS. Comm.* 2nd Rep. p. 186). He appears to have been a nonjuror, and had much correspondence on religious topics with the Rev. James Greenshields, an episcopalian clergyman of Edinburgh, who had been thrown into prison for using the English prayer book. Sometimes he was styled Earl of Panmure, a title to which he would have succeeded on his brother's death but for the attainder. He died at Edinburgh in June 1734, and was buried in Holyrood Abbey.

He married, first, in 1695, Lady Mary Fleming, only daughter of William, fifth earl of Wigton; and secondly in 1704 Anne, second daughter of the Hon. Patrick Lindsay of Kilburnie, and sister of John, first viscount Garnock. Among the children by his first wife was James Maule, who assisted him in his historical researches, and who died unmarried on 16 April 1729. Among the issue of the second marriage was John Maule, who became a member of parliament and one of the barons of the court of exchequer in Scotland, and who died unmarried on 2 July 1781.

Maule was the author of 'Registrum de Panmure. Records of the Families of Maule, De Valoniis, Brechin, and Brechin-Barclay, united in the line of the Barons and Earls of Panmure. Compiled by the Hon. Harry Maule of Kelly, A.D. 1733. Edited by John Stuart, LL.D.,' with illustrations and facsimiles, 2 vols. 1874, 4to. Prefixed to this magnificent work, of which only 150 copies were privately printed, is a portrait of the author in armour, engraved from the original at Dalhousie Castle.

[Memoir by Stuart prefixed to the Registrum de Panmure; Douglas's Peerage of Scotland (Wood), ii. 355.] T. C.

MAULE, JAMES, fourth Earl of Panmure (1659?–1723), Jacobite, was the eldest son of George, second earl of Panmure, by Lady Jean Campbell, eldest daughter of John, earl of Loudoun. He succeeded to the earldom on the death of his brother George, third earl, 1 Feb. 1686, having previously been known as of Ballumbie, Forfarshire. In his early years he travelled on the continent, and in 1684 served as a volunteer at the siege of Luxemburg. After succeeding to the earldom, he was named a privy councillor by James II, but he opposed the policy of the king in favour of the catholics, and was consequently removed 10 March 1687. Nevertheless at the revolution he remained faithful to the king, even after the latter's flight to France. In January 1689 he went to London, and his father-in-law, the Duke of Hamilton, earnestly pressed him to join the Prince of Orange, but he declined to do so. At the convention of the estates at Edinburgh in March he opposed the recognition of William and Mary, and when the vote went against him, retired to his own house (Balcarres, *Memoirs*, p. 25), and henceforth ceased to attend the meetings of the estates.

Panmure was mentioned by the Duke of Perth to the Jacobite, Nathaniel Hooke [q. v.], 3 July 1705, as one to be relied on (Hooke, *Correspondence*, i. 229), and in a memoir given to MM. De Torcy and De Chamillart, at Fontainebleau, 17 Oct., is referred to as one of the richest men of Scotland, and wholly devoted to the king of England (*ib.* p. 404). The proposal for a union between Scotland and England, especially that part of the treaty which provided for the election of representative peers, was strongly distasteful to Panmure, and still further confirmed his Jacobite convictions. At the time of Hooke's second visit to Scotland in 1707, he is mentioned as one to whom the 'king's' letter was to be shown (*ib.* ii. 141), and the Pretender himself wrote him a private letter expressing his confidence in his loyalty (*Registrum de Panmure*, ii. 346).

On the outbreak of the rebellion in 1715 Panmure proclaimed James Francis Edward king at the Cross of Brechin and afterwards joined the forces of Mar with about five hundred men (PATTEN, *History of the Rebellion*, pt. ii. p. 95.) At the battle of Sheriffmuir, on 31 Nov. his regiment formed part of the second line (*ib.* p. 53), and he was taken prisoner, but was rescued by his brother and his servants (*ib.* p. 60; Preface to *Registrum de Panmure*, vol. i. p. xlix). After the landing of the Pretender, Panmure entertained him on the way south at Brechin Castle, 9 Jan. 1716, and on the prince's flight in February escaped to the continent. By a letter dated from Avignon 8 April 1716, he received from the prince the order of the Thistle (*ib.* ii. 352). On 30 June he was attainted by parliament, and his estates confiscated. They were the most valuable of all the confiscated estates, their annual rental being 3,456*l.*, and they were sold to the York Building Company for 60,400*l.*

Panmure twice declined the government's offer to restore his estates on his returning and taking the oath of allegiance to the house of Hanover. After travelling in Italy and elsewhere, he finally settled in Paris. In 1720 he paid a visit to the town of Maule in France, which enabled him to establish the connection of his family with the Maules and Valoniis of Normandy ('Journal of a Journey by the Earl of Panmure, and Mr. James Maule, his nephew, from Paris to Maule in 1720,' in *Registrum de Panmure*, vol. i. pp. civ–cx). He died at Paris 11 April 1723 (O.S.) By his wife, Lady Margaret Hamilton, daughter of William, third duke of Hamilton, he left no issue. In 1717 an act was passed by parliament to enable George I to make such provision and settlement upon his wife as she would have been entitled to had her husband been dead. She died 6 Dec. 1731. There is an engraving of Panmure in the 'Registrum de Panmure,' by Harry Maule [q. v.], from the original painting at Brechin Castle.

The bulk of the Panmure estates were purchased in 1764 from the York Building Company for 49,157*l.* 18*s.* 4*d.* by William Maule, son of Harry Maule of Kelly [q. v.], and nephew of the fourth Earl of Panmure, who on 6 April 1743 was created Earl of Panmure of Forth, and Viscount Maule of Whitchurch, in the peerage of Ireland. With his death, 1 Jan. 1782, this title also became extinct, but on 9 Sept. the title of Baron Panmure of Brechin and Navar was conferred on the Hon. William Ramsay, eldest son of the eighth earl of Dalhousie, who thereupon assumed the name and arms of Maule [see MAULE, WILLIAM RAMSAY, first LORD PANMURE].

[Registrum de Panmure, ed. Stuart, 1874; Jervise's Lands of the Lindsays; Jervise's Memorials of Angus Mearns; Balcarres's Memoirs (Bannatyne Club); Patten's History of the Rebellion; Hooke's Correspondence (Roxburghe Club); Douglas's Scottish Peerage (Wood), ii. 355.] T. F. H.

MAULE, PATRICK, first EARL OF PANMURE (*d.* 1661), was the son of Patrick Maule of Panmure, Forfarshire, and Margaret, daughter of John Erskine of Dun, the reformer. He succeeded to the estate on the death of his father in 1605, but before that time had made his appearance at court, and accompanied James I to London in 1603, being then appointed a gentleman of the bedchamber. He had charters of the barony and teinds of Panmure in 1610 and 1619. After the death of James I, in 1625, he was continued in his office as gentleman of the bedchamber, and was made keeper of the palace and park of Eltham, and sheriff of Forfarshire. He gained the confidence of Charles I during his long term of service at the court, and became one of that monarch's special favourites. There is ample evidence afforded by his letters to his nephew, Alexander Erskine of Dun, that Maule did his best to bring about a reconciliation between the king and the covenanters. Throughout the troubles in which Charles I was involved Maule adhered to him with unshaken fidelity, and he espoused the cause of Charles II, fighting bravely in his defence. His faithfulness was recognised by his being raised to the peerage on 2 Aug. 1646, with the title of Baron Maule of Brechin and Navar and Earl of Panmure. His loyalty provoked the resentment of Cromwell, and by the Act of Grace and Pardon he was fined in the exorbitant sum of 10,000*l.* sterling (afterwards reduced to 4,000*l.*), while his son, Henry Maule, was mulcted in the penalty of 2,500*l.* These fines were paid in 1655. Maule died on 22 Dec. 1661, and was buried in the family vault at Panbride, Forfarshire. He was thrice married, his first wife being Frances, daughter of Sir Edward Stanhope of Grimston, Yorkshire, who was the mother of his two sons, George, second earl of Panmure, and Henry Maule of Balmakelly, Kincardineshire. His two daughters by this wife were Jean, married to the second Earl of Northesk, and Elizabeth, married to the second Earl of Kinghorne, and ancestress of the Earls of Strathmore. His second wife was Mary Waldrum, maid of honour to Queen Henrietta Maria; and his third wife was Lady Mary Erskine, daughter of John, earl of Mar, and widow of William, sixth earl Marischal, but by neither of these had he issue.

[Millar's Roll of Eminent Burgesses of Dundee, p. 144; Registrum de Panmure; Taylor's Great Historic Families of Scotland, ii. 300; Hist. MSS. Comm. 5th Rep. p. 637; Nichols's Progresses of James I, i. 597, 600, ii. 440, 610.]

A. H. M.

MAULE, Sir WILLIAM HENRY (1788–1858), judge, was born at Edmonton in Middlesex on 25 April 1788. His father, Henry Maule, was a medical practitioner; his mother's maiden name was Hannah Rawson. She was of a quaker family of Leeds. Maule received his early education at a private school kept by his uncle, John Maule, rector of Greenford, Middlesex, 'an excellent scholar and a great brute' (*Greville Memoirs*, ii. 101). Among his schoolfellows was Charles Greville [q. v.], who describes him as 'a very clever boy.' In October 1806 Maule entered at Trinity College, Cambridge. In the mathematical tripos of 1810 he was senior wrangler, his number of marks being far above all his competitors. He also obtained the first Smith's prize. In October 1811 he was elected a fellow of Trinity. After taking his degree he remained for some time at Cambridge as a mathematical 'coach.' Among his pupils was Edward Ryan, afterwards chief justice of Calcutta, who continued his intimate friend for life. Another of his Cambridge friends was Charles Babbage [q. v.], who acknowledges assistance received from him in his mathematical investigations. In Michaelmas term 1810 Maule became a student at Lincoln's Inn. While still a student he was offered and declined the professorship of mathematics at Haileybury College. In 1814 he was called to the bar, took chambers at 3 Essex Court, Temple, and joined the Oxford circuit. His progress at the bar was not at first rapid, but he gradually obtained a reputation as a commercial lawyer, and a considerable commercial business, being considered one of the best authorities on questions of marine insurance. He became a king's counsel in Easter term 1833. In 1835 he was appointed counsel to the Bank of England, then a most lucrative office, in succession to Sir James Scarlett, who had been appointed chief baron. In the spring of 1837 Maule was leading counsel for the sitting member in the Carlow county election petition, and conducted the case to a successful issue with marked ability. This led to his being returned for Carlow borough in the liberal interest at the general election in August of that year. In March 1839 he was appointed a baron of the exchequer in succession to Baron Bolland and was knighted, and in Michaelmas term following he was transferred to the common pleas on the death of Mr. Justice Vaughan. He continued a member of that court till June 1855, when he resigned on account of ill-health. Shortly afterwards he was sworn of the privy council, and acted as a member of the judicial committee till his death on 16 Jan. 1858. He was not married.

Maule was an excellent judge, combining knowledge of the law with common sense, courtesy, and ingenuity in defeating technicalities. Both at the bar and on the bench he was distinguished for his ironical humour. Of the latter a well-known instance is his speech at the Warwick assizes in pronouncing sentence of one day's imprisonment on a poor man convicted of bigamy. The prisoner's first wife, who had deserted him, lived with another man, and Maule pointed out to the prisoner the various steps which the law as it then stood required him to take in order to obtain a divorce at an expense of about 1,000*l*. His ironical observations sometimes misled country juries.

A drawing by George Richmond, R.A., belongs to Trinity College, Cambridge.

[Law Magazine and Law Review, vol. v.; Foss's Judges of England, ix. 223; Emma Leathley's Early Life of Sir W. H. Maule]. J. D. F.

MAULE, WILLIAM RAMSAY, Lord Panmure of Brechin and Navar, Forfarshire, (1771–1852), second son of George Ramsay, eighth earl of Dalhousie, by his wife Elizabeth, daughter of Andrew Glen, and niece and heiress of James Glen of Longcroft, Stirlingshire, was born on 27 Oct. 1771. His father's maternal uncle, General William Maule of Kelly, created Earl of Panmure in the Irish peerage in 1743 [cf. Maule, Patrick, and Maule, James], died unmarried in 1782, and left his property to his nephew, the eighth Earl of Dalhousie, with remainder to Dalhousie's second son, William. Dalhousie died in 1787, when William succeeded to the estates of Panmure and adopted the name of Maule. In 1789 he purchased a cornetcy in the 11th dragoons, and afterwards raised an independent company of foot, which was disbanded in 1791. On 25 April 1796 he was elected M.P. for the county of Forfar, but at another election later in the year was defeated by Sir David Carnegie, on whose death he was again elected, in June 1805, and continued to hold his seat during eight following parliaments, and until he was called to the House of Lords. He was throughout a steady adherent of Fox, whose personal friend he was, and a supporter of the whig party. On 9 Sept. 1831 he was raised to the peerage of Great Britain, with the title of Baron Panmure. As a young man he was devoted to the turf, and many of his practical jokes at race meetings were long recounted in Scotland. He had been one of the most dissipated and extravagant, even of the Scottish gentry of his younger days, and survived them, thanks to a constitution of extraordinary strength and a fortune of vast resources. He preserved late into this century the habits and passions—scandalous and unconcealed—which had, except in his case, passed away with the last. He was devoted to his friends so long as they remained complaisant, and violent and implacable to all who thwarted him. His uncontrollable temper alienated him from nearly all his family in his latter years, yet he performed many unostentatious acts of charity. In politics he was a liberal, and his views were invariably humane; in private life he was an immovable despot. He died at Brechin Castle, Forfarshire, 13 April 1852. He married, on 1 Dec. 1794, Patricia Heron (*d.* 11 May 1821), daughter of Gilbert Gordon of Halleaths, by whom he had three sons and seven daughters. The eldest son and heir, Fox Maule, became eleventh earl of Dalhousie [see Maule, Fox]. Panmure's second wife, whom he married in 1822, was Miss Elizabeth Barton, by whom he had no issue.

[Douglas's Peerage of Scotland; Gent. Mag. 1852, i. 515; Daily News, 16 April 1852; Annual Register, 1852; Sir C. E. Adam's Political State of Scotland in the Eighteenth Cent. p. 147; Times, 16 April 1852.] J. A. H.

MAULEVERER, Sir **THOMAS** (*d.* 1655), regicide, was son of Sir Richard Mauleverer, knt., of Allerton Mauleverer, Yorkshire, by his second wife, Katharine, daughter of Sir Ralph Bourchier, knt. (Thoresby, *Ducatus Leodiensis*, ed. Whitaker, pp. 118, 190). He was admitted of Gray's Inn on 22 Oct. 1617, and during the Long parliament sat for Boroughbridge, Yorkshire. Though he signed the petition of the Yorkshire gentry (28 July 1640) against the oppressive billeting of soldiers (*Cal. State Papers*, Dom. 1640, p. 523), Charles, hoping to gain his interest in the county, which was considerable, made him a baronet on 2 Aug. 1641. Mauleverer, however, preferred to take sides with the parliament, for whose service he raised two regiments of foot and a troop of horse (*Commons' Journals*, iii. 68). His conduct, always brutal and vindictive, was on one occasion brought before the notice of the house (*ib.* iii. 125; *Lords' Journals*, vi. 54). In 1643 he fought under Fairfax at the battle of Atherton Moor, and just escaped being made prisoner (*Life of Duke of Newcastle*, by the Duchess, ed. Firth, p. 376). Having represented to the parliament that he had expended in their behalf some 15,000*l.*, it was resolved in October 1647 to allow him 1,000*l.* out of the excise in part satisfaction of his arrears, while a committee was appointed to consider how the remainder might be paid (*Commons' Journals*, v. 323, 330, 362, 374). Upon being placed on the commission to try the king he attended every day, and signed the warrant. He was also a committee man for the East Riding of Yorkshire. Mauleverer died about June 1655 (*Administration Act Book, P.C.C.* 1655, f. 126). He married, first, Mary, daughter of Sir Richard Hutton [q. v.], justice of the common pleas, by whom he had no issue; and secondly, Elizabeth (*d.* 1653), daughter of Thomas Wilbraham, of Woodhey, Cheshire, by whom he had a son, Richard, and two daughters, Grace (1622–1646), married in 1644 to Colonel Thomas Scot, M.P., the regicide, and Elizabeth, wife of Richard Beverley. In 1654 he engaged himself to Susanna Raylton, a widow of Fulham, but the marriage does not appear to have taken place. Though dead, he was ordered at the Restoration to be excepted out of the bill of pardon as to pains and penalties (*Commons' Journals*, viii. 61).

His son, Richard Mauleverer (1623?–1675), royalist, born about 1623, was admitted of Gray's Inn on 12 July 1641 (*Harl. MS.* 1912, f. 128), and on the king's coronation day, 27 March 1645, was knighted in Christ Church, Oxford (Symonds, *Diary*, Camden Soc., p. 162). In 1649 he was fined 3,287*l.* 13*s.* 4*d.* for being in arms against the parliament in both wars, and in 1650 the estate settled on him by his father was ordered to be sequestered (*Cal. of Committee for Compounding*, pt. iii. p. 2030). In 1654 he was declared to be an outlaw. He was out in Lord Wilmot's rising in 1655 (*Cal. State Papers*, Dom. 1655, passim), was taken prisoner, and confined at Chester, whence he escaped in the most daring fashion on 26 March (Thurloe, *State Papers*, iii. 304), and reached the Hague in June (*Nicholas Papers*, Camden Soc., vol. ii.) His wife was allowed by Cromwell to occupy the house at Allerton Mauleverer, but the commissioners for Yorkshire had to complain of her activity on the king's side (Thurloe, v. 185). Mauleverer returned to London in 1659, and was forthwith committed to prison, but was liberated on giving security in September (*Cal. State Papers*, Dom. 1659–60, pp. 44, 179), and was one of the first who flocked to the king at Breda before the restoration (Pepys, *Diary*, 3rd ed. i. 60). Charles confirmed him in his titles and estates, and in April 1660 appointed him gentleman of the privy chamber (*Cal. State Papers*, Dom. 1659-62). On 8 April 1661 he was elected M.P. for Boroughbridge, which he represented until his death. In 1663 he was nominated a commissioner to put in execution the laws against regrators, forestallers, and engrossers of corn, and sellers of live fat cattle contrary to the act, and was empowered to receive all forfeitures incurred for five years to come (*ib.* 1663-4, pp. 372, 642). He was captain in the horse regiment commanded by Charles, lord Gerard of Brandon (*ib.* 1665-6, p. 577), and in the same year was reconstituted a commissioner for licensing and regulating hackney coaches (*ib.* 1666-7, p. 358). Mauleverer was buried in Westminster Abbey on 25 July 1675. By his marriage, on 10 July 1642, to Anne, daughter of Sir Robert Clerke, knt., of Pleshey, Essex, he had issue.

His eldest son, Sir Thomas Mauleverer (1643?-1687), born about 1643, represented Boroughbridge in parliament from 14 March 1678-9 until his death. In 1678 he was second to Sir Henry Goodricke in a duel, and ran his adversary through the body; and in 1685 he had a command of a troop in Monmouth's rebellion. Reresby says he was hated as a reputed papist (*Memoirs*, ed. Cartwright, pp. 152, 292). He sold his estate of Armley Hall, Yorkshire, to the widow of Sir William Ingleby of Ripley in the same county. He was buried on 13 Aug. 1687 in Westminster Abbey. With his wife Catherine, daughter of Sir Miles Stapilton of Myton, Yorkshire, he lived very unhappily, and after his death she married her cousin, John Hopton of Ingerskill there, and died without issue on 31 Jan. 1704 (*Yorkshire Archæolog. and Topogr. Journal*, v. 456).

There was also John Mauleverer (*d.* 1650), eldest son of John Mauleverer of Lettwell, Yorkshire, by Margaret, daughter of John Lewis of Marr, in that county (*ib.* xi. 86, 457; cf. also *Administration Act Book, P. C. C.* 1651, f. 29). He was among the first of the Yorkshire gentry to declare for the parliament, became a colonel in the army, and after the disgrace of Sir John Hotham and his son was made governor of Hull. There is a curious letter from Ferdinando, lord Fairfax, to him, dated 13 June 1646, thanking him for not allowing Mrs. Hotham, who had made certain inconvenient demands for the restitution of property which Fairfax desired to keep, to search Sir John Hotham's house at Hull (*Hist. MSS. Comm.* 9th Rep. p. 438). In May 1650 he was appointed colonel of one of the five regiments of foot for the war in Scotland (*Cal. State Papers*, Dom. 1650, pp. 95, 141), but he died from fatigue at Edinburgh in December following. Cromwell wrote to Speaker Lenthall, asking parliament to make adequate provision for Mauleverer's 'sad widow (Dorcas) and seven small children' (*Letters and Speeches*, ed. Carlyle, 1882, v. 242-3). After receiving a report from the committee of the army, the house ordered Mauleverer's debts to be paid, and voted 100*l.* for his widow's immediate relief, and on 20 July 1652 passed a resolution for settling lands in Scotland of 400*l.* a year on her, her children, and their heirs (*Commons' Journals*, vi. 575-6, vii. 155-6).

The Colonel James Mauleverer alluded to in Rushworth's 'Historical Collections' (pt. ii. vol. i. p. 216) was apparently a brother of the above Colonel John Mauleverer, and, like him, was a staunch parliamentarian. On 11 March 1642-3 he was commissioned by the Earl of Essex to raise a troop of horse in Yorkshire, an order renewed by parliament on 10 May (*Lords' Journals*, vi. 40). He may have been the 'Col. Mauleverer' who was killed at the first siege of Pontefract Castle on 1 March 1645; another Colonel Maleverer, however, was present with his regiment of foot at the third siege of Pontefract in 1649 (*Surtees Soc. Miscellanies*, App. pp. 15, 100, 101, 110).

[Noble's Lives of the English Regicides, ii. 34; Chester's Registers of Westminster Abbey, pp. 140, 146, 186; Yorkshire Archæolog. and Topogr. Journal, vi. 93-4, viii. 440.] G. G.

MAULEY, PETER DE (*d.* 1241), favourite of King John, was a Poitevin noble, who left his inheritance to his brother Aymer, and entered the service of King John. According to the account preserved in Hemingburgh (i. 232), he was employed by John to murder Arthur of Brittany, but no contemporary writer mentions him by name in this connection. He received a grant of land in December 1202 (Hardy, *Rot. Normanniæ*, p. 66), and is mentioned in the king's service in 1205 (*Rot. Lit. Pat.* 25 *b*), and his name is of frequent occurrence in the Close and Patent Rolls during the remainder of John's reign. Hemingburgh states that he was rewarded for his share in Arthur's murder with the hand of Isabel, heiress of the barony of Mulgres, and daughter of Robert de Turnham. Turnham's lands were granted to Mauley on 25 April 1214 (*ib.* p. 113). Matthew Paris mentions him as one of John's evil counsellors in 1211 (ii. 533). In 1214 he served with John in Poitou (*Rot. Lit. Pat.* p. 112), and in the following year was entrusted with the charge of Corfe Castle (*ib.* p. 128), where he had custody of much treasure and various important prisoners. On 26 June 1216 he was made sheriff of the counties of Somerset and Dorset (*ib.* p. 189). Mauley retained charge of both the castle and the counties during the first years of Henry III. On 7 May 1220 he was summoned to come from Corfe to the coronation, and bring with him the king's brother Richard and the regalia (*Rot. Lit. Claus.* i. 417 *b*). In February 1221 he joined with Falkes de Breauté [q. v.] in supporting William, earl of Albemarle, at Biham. He was arrested during the summer, and forced to resign his castles. This was on a charge of treason, in having promised to hand over Eleanor, sister of Arthur of Brittany, to the king of France (Coventry, ii. 260; *Ann. Mon.* iii. 75). He, however, made his peace with the king in the autumn, and next year received the charge of Sherborne Castle. Dugdale says he died in 1222, but the 'Chronicon de Melsa' states that he survived his wife, who died apparently after 1235 (i. 105, ii. 59), and Matthew Paris, in referring to his death in 1241, speaks of him as 'natione Pictaviensis diuque in clientela regis Johannis educatus et ditatus' (iv. 89; but see also *Excerpta e Rot. Finium*, pp. 364, 379, 409, and *Calendarium Genealogicum*, i. 278). It was probably he, and not his son, who supported Randulph Blundevill, earl of Chester, in 1224 (Matt. Paris, iii. 83), was one of the sponsors for Henry's son Edward in 1239, and in 1241, going on the crusade with William de Fortibus, earl of Albemarle, died in the Holy Land during the same year. He built Mulgrave Castle, near Whitby, and was a benefactor of Meaux Abbey, where he endowed a chapel in memory of his wife. He left a son Peter, who succeeded him, and was followed by six others of the same name. Peter III (*d.* 1309) was summoned to parliament in 1295, and served in the wars of Edward I in Wales, Scotland, and Gascony. His brother Edmund, who was killed at Bannockburn, was steward to Edward II and a friend of Piers Gaveston (*Chron. Edw. I and II*, i. 215, 272–273, ii. 42, 183). Peter VIII succeeded his grandfather, Peter VI, in 1383, and died without issue, when the barony fell into abeyance. The present Lord de Mauley is of a modern creation, though he descends from the old barons in the female line.

[Matt. Paris; Walter of Coventry's Memoriale; Annales Monastici; Chronicon de Melsa (all in Rolls Ser.); Dugdale's Baronage, i. 733; other authorities as quoted.] C. L. K.

MAUND, BENJAMIN (1790–1863), botanical writer, was born in 1790, and for many years carried on the combined business of a chemist, bookseller, printer, and publisher at Bromsgrove, Worcestershire. He became a fellow of the Linnean Society in 1827, and served for several years on botanical committees of the Worcestershire Natural History Society. About 1852 Maund retired from business, and resided first at Folkestone and afterwards at Sandown, Isle of Wight, where he died, 21 April 1863.

A great lover of flowers and gardening, he sought to spread a taste for these subjects by starting a monthly publication, 'The Botanic Garden' (4to, London), in 1825. The work consisted of coloured plates, with descriptive letterpress, and with it were issued, in parts also, 'The Auctarium of the Botanic Garden,' 'The Floral Register,' 'The Fruitist,' and 'A Dictionary of English and Latin Terms used in Botanical Descriptions,' by J. S. Henslow. The whole work ran to thirteen volumes, and was finished in 1850. It was in part reissued as 'The Botanic Garden and Fruitist,' 3 vols. 4to, London, 1851–4, and another edition in 12 vols., edited by J. C. Niven, appeared in 1878. A similar but more extended work, 'The Botanist . . . conducted by B. Maund,' 4to, London, was initiated in 1837, and ended in 1846. In conjunction with W. Holl, Maund edited the first volume of the 'Naturalist,' 8vo, London, 1837. The original drawings for 'The Botanic Garden' are preserved in the botanical department of the British Museum (natural history).

[Proc. Linn. Soc. Lond. 1863–4, p. xxx; Journ. of Bot. xxvii. 371; Papers and Proc. Worcestershire Natural Hist. Soc. circa 1834; Brit. Mus. Cat.] B. B. W.

MAUNDER, SAMUEL (1785–1849), compiler, born in 1785, belonged to a Devonshire family settled near Barnstaple. His sister married William Pinnock [q. v.], the well-known projector of the educational 'Catechisms,' which were published in eighty-three parts between 1837 and 1849. Maunder took part in their preparation, although Pinnock's name alone appears on their title-page. The two were also partners in a publishing business in London, and published for two or three years the 'Literary Gazette.' Under his own name Maunder compiled and issued numerous dictionaries, chiefly for educational purposes. They were very useful in their day and had a large sale. Maunder died at his house in Gibson Square, Islington, on 30 April 1849. His portrait was painted by an American artist named Waugh in the preceding year. William Jerdan [q. v.], who knew Maunder, says he was an honourable and worthy man in every relation of life.

The following is a list of his works: 1. 'The Little Lexicon, or Multum in Parvo of the English Language,' 1st edit. 1825, 16mo; 5th edit. revised and enlarged, 1845. 2. 'Treasury of Knowledge and Library of Reference,' 1st edit. 1830, 12mo, 2 pts.; 18th edit. enlarged, 1848; new edit. 1859, revised by B. B. Woodward, assisted by J. Morris and W. Hughes. 3. 'Biographical Treasury,' 1st edit. 1838; 5th edit. with supplement 1845; seven posthumous editions, besides two of the works reconstructed and brought down to date of publication (1873 and 1882), by W. L. R. Cates. 4. 'The Scientific and Literary Treasury, a new and Popular Encyclopædia of the Belles Lettres,' 1st edit. 1841, 12mo; 5th edit. 1848; besides two editions revised and re-written by J. Yate-Johnson, 1866 and 1880. 5. 'The Treasury of History, comprising a general introductory Outline of universal History and separate Histories of every principal Nation,' 1844; 'new edit. revised and brought down to present date by G. W. Cox,' 1864. 6. 'The Universal Class-Book, a new Series of Reading Lessons for Every Day in the Year,' 1st edit. 1844, 8vo; 3rd edit. 1847. 7. 'The Little Gazetteer, or Geographical Dictionary in Miniature. To which is added a population table, and a list of the Cities, Boroughs, &c., of England and Wales, &c.,' London, 1845? 8. 'The Treasury of Natural History, or a Popular Dictionary of Animated Nature. To which are added a Syllabus of Practical Taxidermy and a Glossarial Appendix,' 1st edit. 1848; 6th edit. revised and supplemented by T. S. Cobbold, 1862; new edit., revised and corrected by E. W. H. Houldsworth, 1874. 9. 'The Treasury of Geography,' designed and commenced by S.M., continued and completed by W. Hughes, 1856 and 1860, London and Bungay.

Maunder also prepared a school edition of R. Montgomery's 'Omnipresence of the Deity,' a revised edition of Shakespeare's plays, 1851, and of 'Geography and History,' by E. R., 1859, 22nd edit.

[Literary Gazette, 2 Dec. 1848, 5 May 1849 (copied by Gent. Mag. vol. xxxi., and elsewhere); Leisure Hour, xii. 261–3; information kindly supplied by G. W. Maunder, esq.; Brit. Mus. Cat.] G. Le G. N.

MAUNDRELL, HENRY (1665–1701), oriental traveller, son of Robert Maundrell of Compton Bassett, near Calne, Wiltshire, was baptised there 23 Dec. 1665. His family had been of good position in the county, but his father is described in the Oxford University books as 'pleb.' He matriculated 4 April 1682, and entered Exeter College as batler on 27 Sept., graduating B.A. 1685, M.A. 1688, and B.D., by decree, 1697. On 30 June 1686 he was elected Sarum fellow of his college, and became full fellow on 28 June 1697. He was ordained in the English church and probably remained for some time at Oxford, as in November 1689 he was summoned to London by Bishop Trelawny to answer his questions on the recent scandals in his college. These quarrels may have induced him to accept the curacy of Bromley in Kent, which he served from 1689 to 1695. On 20 Dec. 1695 Maundrell was elected, by plurality of votes, by the Company of Levant Merchants as chaplain to their factory at Aleppo, and on 15 Jan. 1695–6 the sum of 20*l*. was granted to him to buy books for its library. He is said to have left England at once and to have passed through Germany, making a short stay at Frankfort, where he conversed with Job Ludolphus, who suggested to him several points of topography in the Holy Land which required elucidation. His friends at Richmond, where his uncle, Sir Charles Hedges [q. v.], had a house on the Green, were left with regret, but he found at Aleppo an English colony, about forty in number, whom he highly praises, and he performed daily service every morning to a devout and large congregation. His celebrated journey to Jerusalem was begun, with fourteen other residents from the settlement, on 26 Feb. 1696–7. They arrived in the holy city on 25 March, the day before Good Friday in the Latin style, and left on Easter Monday (29 March) for Jordan and Bethlehem, but returned again on 2 April. Their second departure from Jerusalem was on 15 April, and the day of their return to the factory was about 20 May. He died, presumably of fever, at Aleppo early in 1701. The date of the vacancy at the chaplaincy by his death is entered on the company's minutes on 15 May 1701. A tombstone in the Richmond burial-ground to Henry Maundrell, gent., who died in 1847, calls him 'a descendant of the Rev. Henry Maundrell, formerly curate of this parish,' the traveller.

His narrative of the expedition, entitled 'A Journey from Aleppo to Jerusalem at Easter A.D. 1697,' was printed at Oxford in 1703, with dedications to Sprat, bishop of Rochester, whom he had probably met at Bromley, and to Hedges. It consisted of sixteen pages unpaged, partly of corrections and additions which had come too late for incorporation in the text, then 142 pages of narrative, and lastly, seven pages with two letters from him to Osborn, also a fellow of Exeter College. A second edition came out in 1707, and a third issue, with 'An Account of the Author's Journey [April 1699] to the

Banks of Euphrates at Beer and to Mesopotamia,' appeared in 1714. Hedges had given the manuscript to the university without any restrictions, and when the third impression was required he was asked for Maundrell's 'inscriptions and some other improvements' in his possession, but he declined, as the authorities had 'not sent him so much as one copy for his former present,' an omission, says Hearne, not to be imputed to Aldrich, who had supervised the impressions (*Collections*, ed. Doble, iii. 117). Numerous impressions came out in later years, and it was issued in 1810 in a volume with Bishop Robert Clayton's 'Journal from Grand Cairo to Mount Sinai,' and with the remarks of Joseph Pitts on the Mahometans, to which was prefixed Maundrell's print, 'from an original drawing' belonging to Richard Dagley. It was also included in the collections of Harris, Pinkerton, and Moore, in the 'World Displayed,' vol. xi., and in H. G. Bohn's 'Early Travels in Palestine,' edited by Thomas Wright in 1848. A French translation appeared at Utrecht in 1705 and at Paris in 1706. A Dutch translation was inserted in 'Kanaan en d'omleggende Landen,' Leeuwarden, 1717, pp. 455–520; a rendering from French into German, by Louis Fr. Vischer, was published at Hamburg in 1737, and it formed part of volume i. of Paulus's 'Collection,' issued at Jena in 1792. The journals of his companion, Richard Chiswell (1673–1751) [q. v.], and a copy of Maundrell's 'Journey, with a few manuscript notes, are in British Museum Addit. MSS. 10623–4.

Maundrell is entitled to considerable praise as a judicious and careful traveller, but it is insinuated in the Rawlinson MSS. ii. 81, that he had taken one of his views from the 'Histoire et Voyage de la Terre Sainte par Père Jaques Goujon' (Lyon, 1671), and Alexander Drummond in his 'Travels' (1754) censures some of his suggestions. He was also the author of 'A Sermon preach'd before the Company of Levant Merchants at St. Peter Poor, Dec. 15, 1695,' and an inscription from Syria, sent by him to Bishop Lloyd of Worcester, is illustrated with critical observations in Samuel Jebb's 'Bibliotheca Literaria' (1722), pp. 2–6.

[Boase's Exeter Coll. pp. 82–7, 213, 229; Foster's Alumni Oxon.; Dunkin's Bromley, p. 27; Pearson's Levant Chaplains, pp. 18, 24–5, 58; Addit. MS. 24107, Brit. Mus. (with many letters from Hedges to Maundrell); Biog. Univ.; information from the Rev. Vincent F. Ransome of Compton Bassett.] W. P. C.

MAUNSELL, ANDREW (*d.* 1595), bibliographer and publisher, was at the beginning of Elizabeth's reign probably a member of the Drapers' or Grocers' Company, but as early as 1578 he undertook, in addition to his other business, the publication and sale of books, although he did not join the Stationers' Company (Arber, *Stationers' Reg.* ii. 28). On 6 Nov. 1578 he obtained a license to publish a work entitled, 'The State of Swearinge and Swearers' (*ib.* p. 340), and until 1595 he was busily occupied in selling or publishing books, chiefly theological (cf. *ib.* pp. 381, 402). In 1583 he joined with H. Denham, T. Chard, and W. Broome, in bringing out in folio a translation by Anthony Martin [q. v.] of Peter Martyr's 'Commonplaces,' and he undertook the publication of many works by Archbishop Bancroft's well-known chaplain, Thomas Rogers [q. v.] He at first dwelt at the sign of the Parrot in St. Paul's Churchyard, but by 1595 had removed to Lothbury. His device was a pelican with its offspring, rising out of the flames, which was formerly employed by Richard Jugge [q. v.], and his motto was 'Pro lege, rege, grege.' He took a genuine interest in his profession, and finding the need of a general catalogue of English printed books, set about preparing one. Nothing quite similar had been previously attempted in this country, although Bale had made efforts in the direction in his 'Scriptores.' Maunsell designed a catalogue in three parts, the first embracing divinity, the second, science in all its branches with music, and the third, literature, including logic, law, and history. The entries were arranged under authors' surnames, but many general headings, like 'Sermons' or 'Music,' were introduced, and gave the work something of the character of a subject-index. The first two parts were alone completed, and both appeared in folio in 1595. The first part, entered on the 'Stationers' Register' 8 May 1595, was entitled 'The First Part of the Catalogue of English Printed Bookes: which concerneth such Matters of Divinite as have bin either written in oure Tongue or translated out of some other Language, and have bin published to the Glory of God and Edification of the Church of Christ in England. Gathered into Alphabet and suche Method as it is by Andrew Maunsell . . . London, printed by John Windet for Andrew Maunsell,' fol. This is dedicated to Queen Elizabeth, and there follow the dedication addresses to the members of the Stationers' Company, and to 'the reverend divines and lovers of divine books.' Mannsell warns the latter that he has omitted the works 'of fugitive papistes' or printed attacks on the existing government. Both defects are supplied in manuscript by a contemporary in a copy of the catalogue in Trinity

College Library, Cambridge. The continuation of the catalogue was called 'The Seconde Parte of the Catalogue of English printed Bookes eyther Written in oure own Tongue or translated out of any other Language: which concerneth the Sciences Mathematicall, as Arithmeticke, Geometrie, Astronomie, Astrologie, Musick, the Arte of Warre and Nauigation, And also of Physick and Surgerie, London, by James Roberts, for Andrew Maunsell,' 1595. The dedication, addressed to Robert Devereux, second earl of Essex [q. v.], is signed 'Andrew Maunsell, Bookseller,' and there follow letters to the 'professors' of mathematics and physic, and to the Stationers' Company and booksellers in general. Francis Meres [q. v.] makes familiar reference to Maunsell's 'Catalogue' in his 'Palladis Tamia,' 1598. The promised third part failed to appear, probably owing to Maunsell's death late in 1595. The 'Catalogue' of William London [q. v.] of 1658 ultimately superseded Maunsell's labours.

Another Andrew Maunsell or Mansell, apparently the elder Maunsell's son, was admitted to the freedom of the Stationers' Company on 6 Dec. 1613 (Arber, iii. 684), and on 4 May 1614 obtained a license to publish 'A Fooles Bolt is soone Shot.'

[Maunsell's Cat.; Growoll and Eames: Three Centuries of English booktrade bibliography, New York, 1903, pp. 20–30, 107–8; Sinker's Cat. of Trin. Coll. Library, Cambridge; Brit. Mus. Cat. of Books before 1640.] S. L.

MAUNSELL, JOHN (*d.* 1265), keeper of the great seal. [See Mansel.]

MAUNSFIELD, MAUNNESFELD, MAMMESFELD, or MAYMYSFELD, HENRY de (*d.* 1328), chancellor of the university of Oxford, was educated at Oxford, and became fellow of Merton College. In 1283, according to Wood, he filled with glass at his own expense all the side windows of the chancel of the old collegiate church of St. John the Baptist in Merton College, putting his monogram on several of them. He was chancellor of the university in 1309, and again in 1311, appointing William Gifford his *locum tenens* (Wood, *Fasti*, pp. 18, 327). In the latter year he was professor of theology and rector of Flintham, Nottinghamshire (Tanner, p. 519), and he attended a provincial council about the Templars, held in York Minster (Brodrick, *Merton College*, 180).

On 17 Dec. 1314 he was elected dean of Lincoln (Willis, *Cathedrals*, iii. 76; Le Neve, ii. 32); he was collated to the prebend of Asgarby, Lincoln, in 1316, and was elected bishop of Lincoln in 1319; the latter office he declined (Brodrick, p. 181). In 1324 he was canon of Carlisle, and in 1328 he died, his will being proved on 6 Dec.

Pits, p. 863, Tanner, p. 519, Fabricius, ii. 223, and Brodrick all attribute to Maunsfield a commentary on Boethius, preserved in New College library (No. cclxiv. i) (Coxe, *Cat. Codicum*). The work was, however, by William of Wheatley [q. v.] (see Fabricius, ii. 171; Tanner, p. 760), and was merely dedicated by Wheatley to Maunsfield.

[Authorities quoted.] A. F. P.

MAUNY, Sir WALTER, afterwards Baron de Manny (*d.* 1372). [See Manny.]

MAURICE (*d.* 1107), bishop of London, chaplain and chancellor to William the Conqueror, was appointed by him to the see of London, vacated by the death of Hugh of Orival, at the memorable council held at Gloucester (Christmas 1085–6). At the same time two other royal chaplains, William Beaufeu [q. v.] and Robert de Limesey were appointed respectively to the sees of Thetford and Chester (Lichfield) (Symeon Dunelm. ii. 213). Maurice was consecrated by Lanfranc at Winchester, 5 April 1086, having been previously ordained priest by him at Chichester, 19 March (*Epp. Lanfranc*, p. 24). Maurice was an early friend of Ranulf Flambard (*ib.* p. 135), and his moral character was, like Flambard's, open to grave reproach. Sober with regard to other pleasures, according to William of Malmesbury, his fondness for the female sex was carried to an extent unbefitting a bishop. He excused his licentiousness as a medical prescription, essential to his health (Malmesbury, *Gesta Pontiff.* p. 145). He attended William Rufus's first court at Westminster at Christmas 1087 (Henry of Huntingdon, p. 211; Freeman, *William Rufus*, i. 19). In 1094 he had a controversy with Anselm as to his right as metropolitan to consecrate the newly built church of Harrow, in the diocese of London, which by the verdict of Wulfstan of Worcester, then 'one and alone of the ancient fathers of the English,' was decided in favour of the primate (Eadmer, p. 22; *Anselmi Epp.* iii. 19; Freeman, u. s. p. 440). In the absence of Anselm, Maurice, as the highest suffragan of his province, crowned Henry I at Westminster, 5 Aug. 1100 (Hoveden, i. 157; Henry of Huntingdon, p. 233; Orderic, p. 783 b; Freeman, ii. 350), and witnessed the charter he put forth (Stubbs, *Select Charters*, p. 98; Freeman, u. s. p. 358). He also attended the council at Westminster, 29 Sept. 1102, as one of Anselm's assessors (Malmesbury, p. 118; Symeon Dunelm. ii. 235). The chief work which signalised the episcopate of Maurice was the commencement of his cathedral church of St. Paul's, on a scale that rendered it ultimately the vastest of all the cathedrals of England, by which, and by the general efficiency of his rule, his faulty moral character, 'vir moribus non usquequaque probatissimis,' was held by his contemporaries to be atoned for (MALMESBURY, p. 145). He died 26 Sept. 1107.

[Symeon of Durham, i. 135, ii. 213, 235; Hoveden, i. 157, 160, 164, ii. 213, 235, 239; William of Malmesbury's Gesta Pontiff. pp. 118, 145; Henry of Huntingdon, pp. 208, 211, 233, 236, 316; Diceto, i. 211, 218, 233; Matt. Paris's Hist. Angl. i. 32, 308.] E. V.

MAURICE (*fl.* 1210), epigrammatist, generally styled MORGANENSIS and MORGANIUS, was a native of Glamorgan. Giraldus Cambrensis, who describes him as a resident in Glamorgan and calls him 'vir bonus et copiose litteratus,' says he was the brother of Clement, abbot of Neath, and narrates a vision attributed to him ('De Principis Instructione,' dist. iii. cap. 28, in *Giraldi Camb. Opera*, Rolls ed. viii. 310). According to Bale (1st ed. fol. 98 *a*), he wrote a volume of epigrams (cf. GIRALDUS loc. cit.) and several works 'in patrio sermone.'

Maurice is probably to be identified with MEURYG (*fl.* 1250), treasurer of Llandaff, who is said (in *Iolo MSS.* pp. 222, 638), on the authority of Iago ab Dewi [q. v.], to have been the author of 'Y Cwtta Cyfarwydd,' and of a 'History of the whole Isle of Britain,' a 'Book of Proverbs,' 'Rules of Welsh Poetry,' 'Welsh Theology,' and a Welsh translation of the Gospel of St. John (with a commentary). Iago ab Dewi declares that the last work was at Abermarlais, Carmarthenshire, a century before his time. No trace of these works has, it is believed, been found. The existing copy of 'Y Cwtta Cyfarwydd' (*Hengwrt MS.* 34; cf. the extracts in *Iolo MSS.* p. 336, and *Y Cymmrodor*, ix. 325) was written about 1445, and according to the Glamorgan tradition of the seventeenth century, by Gwilym Tew, the poet (*Arch. Cambr.* for 1869, p. 218); but it may of course have been largely copied from an older manuscript. Meuryg is improbably said (in WILLIAMS, *Eminent Welshmen*, s.v., but on what authority is unknown) to have died in 1290; the date is far too late.

[Works cited as above; Owen's Pembrokeshire, pt. i. p. 232, pt. ii. note(s).] D. LL. T.

MAURICE, PRINCE (1620–1652), the third son of Frederick V, elector palatine of the Rhine, and Elizabeth, daughter of James I, was born on 25 Dec. 1620 (or on 6 Jan.), at the castle of Custrin during Elizabeth's flight from Prague after the battle of the White Mountain (19 Nov. 1620) (WARBURTON, *Prince Rupert*, i. 40; MRS. GREEN, *Lives of the Princesses of England*, v. 353). At first Maurice was placed under the care of the electress of Brandenburg, his mother's sister-in-law, but soon removing to Holland, he and his elder brother Rupert were in 1637 sent to learn the art of war in the army of the Prince of Orange (*Cal. State Papers*, Dom. 1637, pp. 128, 201, 206, 235). They showed considerable bravery at the siege of Breda in 1638 (WARBURTON, i. 80). In the same year Maurice, with his brother Edward, was sent to a French university, and he remained there till the end of 1639 (*Cal. State Papers*, Dom. 1639, p. 39). He then returned to Holland, and possibly studied at Leyden (see satire on Maurice in WEBB, *Civil War in Herefordshire*, i. 286). In December 1640 he served in Banier's army till June 1641, being present at the siege of Amberg in January 1641 (*Cal. State Papers*, Dom. 1640, pp. 294, 430, 469). Maurice soon afterwards joined Rupert at the Hague, and the brothers crossed over to England. They landed at Tynemouth in August 1642 (*ib.* 1642, p. 11; WARBURTON, i. 109, 110), and they remained in England till July 1646.

During the early days of the civil war Rupert and Maurice were together. They were present at the raising of the standard at Nottingham (22 Aug. 1642), and were zealous in raising troops for the king. They were consequently declared traitors by the parliament (MAY, *Breviary*, ed. Maseres, i. 53). Marching west with the main army, Maurice was present at the skirmish at Powick Bridge, being 'slightly wounded on the head' (23 Sept. 1642) (Pyne's 'Narrative' in WARBURTON, i. 465; *Cal. State Papers*, Dom. 1642, p. 395); and still following the fortunes of his brother, he took part in the capture of Cirencester, 2 Feb. 1643 (WASHBOURN, *Bibliotheca Gloucestrensis*, p. 171). A month later Maurice separated from Rupert, and was given independent command, being on 2 March commissioned to protect Gloucestershire, and to levy money for that purpose (BLACK, *Oxford Docquets*, p. 13). The chief part of his work was to check the victorious progress of William Waller in those parts (CLARENDON, *Hist. of the Rebellion*, ed. 1888, bk. vii. §§ 29, 30). On 11 April 1643 Waller was beaten in a skirmish at Little Dean; and on the next day Maurice succeeded in crossing the Severn, and defeated Waller and Massey at Ripple Field, on their return from the capture of Tewkesbury (WEBB, i. 252; WASHBOURN, p. 33). Maurice was now called away to help the king to raise the siege of Reading, but shortly returned to the west as lieutenant-general under the Marquis of

Hertford. In the skirmish with some of Waller's troops at Chewton Mendip (10 June 1643) he received 'two shrewd hurts in his head' (CLARENDON, *Hist.* bk. vii. §§ 101, 102). He was also present at the battle of Lansdowne (5 July), after which he retired towards Devizes, and, with the Marquis of Hertford, made his way through the enemy's line to Oxford to obtain reinforcements and ammunition, with the help of which Waller was beaten at Roundway Down (13 July) (*ib.* bk. vii. §§ 104–10; WARBURTON, ii. 227, 233). Maurice joined Rupert in the siege of Bristol, and after its fall sided with his brother in the quarrel with the Marquis of Hertford about the appointment of governor of the city (*ib.* ii. 236 sqq., 269; CLARENDON, *Hist.* bk. vii. §§ 124–55).

Maurice, with the Earl of Carnarvon, was now sent back to the south-west, where he remained in command till December 1644. During August 1643 nearly all Dorset was won, Dorchester (4 Aug.) and other places being gradually reduced; but owing to the license of Maurice's troops, and a dispute about the appointment of a governor of Weymouth, a quarrel broke out between him and Carnarvon, which led to the prince being sent into Devonshire (*ib.* bk. vii. §§ 192, 199; GARDINER, *Hist. of the Great Civil War*, i. 231), where he at once set about the reduction of the parliamentary garrisons. Exeter surrendered to him on 4 Sept. 1643 and Dartmouth on 6 Oct., and even Plymouth seemed likely to be won (DUGDALE, *Diary*; CLARENDON, *Hist.* bk. vii. §§ 296, 297; RUSHWORTH, *Historical Collections*, v. 273). The siege of this town was, however, delayed by Maurice's illness, of the nature of 'a slow fever with great dejection of strength,' which kept him inactive at Milton from the middle of October for about one month (WARBURTON, ii. 307, 326). On his recovery Maurice continued his attack on Plymouth, but without real success, and the design was abandoned. He was directed to march through the southern counties on London, and in February 1644 was commissioned to act as lieutenant-general in all the counties south of the Thames except Hampshire (BLACK, *Oxford Docquets*, p. 140). In March he was ordered to advance eastwards (*Cal. State Papers*, Dom. 1644, pp. 57, 75). Accordingly, in the same month he laid siege to Lyme without success, and withdrew on the approach of the Earl of Essex (15 June 1644). This failure and waste of time after his ill-success at Plymouth did much to lessen Maurice's reputation (CLARENDON, *Hist.* bk. viii. § 92). He now retired west before Essex, and on 26 July his troops were reviewed by the king at Crediton, after which he joined Charles at Exeter, and with the main army followed Essex into Cornwall, his troops forming the advanced guard (*Cal. State Papers*, Dom. 1644, pp. 304, 407). Maurice was present at Lostwithiel with five thousand foot and two thousand five hundred horse, and signed the letter for a treaty sent by the Earl of Brentford and Forth and other officers to the Earl of Essex (SYMONDS, *Diary*, pp. 45, 53, 56–8; CLARENDON, *Hist.* bk. viii. § 105). After the surrender of Essex's army, Maurice's Cornish troops refused to march east with the king, and were sent home, the prince accompanying Charles to meet Waller. Maurice failed to take Taunton and Bridgewater, and was responsible for the failure of the attempt to surprise Waller on 18 Oct. (GARDINER, i. 497). He was present at the second battle of Newbury, 27 Oct., and took up his position on Speen Hill, which was stormed by Skippon and Balfour (CLARENDON, *Hist.* bk. viii. §§ 154, 159). After the battle he retired to Oxford, and on 7 Nov. returned to relieve Donnington Castle (SYMONDS, *Diary*, pp. 147, 148).

Maurice was now appointed to fill Prince Rupert's place in Wales, but without the title of president. In December 1644 he accordingly resigned his command in the west, and was made major-general of Worcestershire, Shropshire, Herefordshire, and Monmouthshire (WEBB, ii. 126). Leaving Oxford on 14 Jan. 1645 he took up his position at Worcester, and set about the task of reducing these counties to order. The plundering of Maurice's troops, an increase in taxation, and the rise of the Clubmen aggravated the prevailing discontent and rendered organisation impossible. He himself complained of want of power and (29 Jan.) asked for the enlargement of his commission. His soldiers also were deserting (*Arch. Cambrensis*, 'Maurice's Diary,' i. 39; WEBB, ii. 129; WARBURTON, iii. 53, 60).

As both Shrewsbury and Chester were in danger, Maurice left Worcester, and on 5 Feb. reached the former town. On the 14th he marched towards Chester; Shrewsbury was lost on the 22nd. The parliamentary troops were now gathering round Maurice in Chester, but he was relieved by the arrival of Prince Rupert (17 March) (WEBB, ii. 141), and the siege of Beeston Castle was raised. On the approach of the Scottish army Rupert and Maurice retreated towards Hereford (*Cal. State Papers*, Dom. 1645, pp. 375, 402), and the latter, probably after returning to Worcester, marched again towards Chester (*ib.* p. 404), whence he proceeded to Oxford to escort the king's train of artillery to Rupert at Hereford. Oliver Cromwell was sent against him and delayed his arrival at Oxford (*ib.* p. 419; GARDINER, ii. 157). But, joined by Rupert, he entered the city on 4 May, and on the 7th marched west with the king (*Cal. State Papers,* Dom. 1645, p. 458; WEBB, ii. 185; SYMONDS, *Diary,* p. 164). For some time Maurice seems to have remained with the king; he was present at the storming of Leicester (30 May), and at Naseby (14 June) he fought with Rupert on the right wing (CLARENDON, *Hist.* bk. ix. § 39). He then returned to Worcester, awaiting the attack of the Scottish army, which was expected to lay siege to the city (7 July) (WARBURTON, iii. 133). On 15 Sept. Maurice joined the king at Bromyard and marched with him to raise the siege of Hereford (SYMONDS, *Diary,* p. 239; WEBB, ii. 223); and again joined Charles at Chirk on 28 Sept. (*ib.* p. 244), but four days later he marched towards Worcester (*ib.* p. 245), and on 13 Oct. was joined by Rupert. Maurice remained faithful to his brother during his disgrace, without losing favour with the king (*ib.* p. 271; WARBURTON, iii. 189). He went with him to Belvoir Castle and to Newark, after which he returned to the west, and on 13 Nov. was with Rupert in Worcester (SYMONDS, *Diary,* p. 263). A little later the two again joined the king at Oxford (WHITELOCKE, *Memorials,* p. 187). They were in the city during the siege, and on its surrender (22 June 1646) were granted special terms on condition of their not approaching within twenty miles of London (WARBURTON, iii. 230), but this condition was held to have been broken, and on 26 June parliament voted that they should leave England within ten days (*ib.* iii. 235; *Old Parliamentary Hist.* xiv. 473). Accordingly, on July 8, Maurice crossed over from Dover to Holland, Rupert having sailed three days before to Calais.

Maurice served in the army of the Prince of Orange in Flanders, and was joined by Prince Rupert in 1648, in which year he began his career of piracy in the Channel and adventure on the sea. In January 1649 he resolved to join Rupert in a voyage to the West Indies. On the journey he visited Kinsale, and leaving Ireland in the autumn of 1649, crossed to Portugal. Thence he proceeded by way of Toulon to Africa, Cape Verd Isles, and the river Gambia, where in March 1652 he hoisted his vice-admiral's flag on an English prize named the Friendship, which was renamed the Defiance (WARBURTON, iii. 542). Afterwards Maurice and Rupert sailed to the West Indies, and on 14 Sept. 1652, in a storm off the Anagadas, Maurice was lost with three of the four ships ('Narrative' in WARBURTON, vol. iii. ch. ii. and iii. 544; *Cal. State Papers,* Dom. 1652–3, p. 522).

Prince Maurice does not seem to have shared in any way the capacity of his elder brother; as a soldier he was personally brave, but without power of strategy or discipline; he had much of Rupert's rashness, but not apparently his power of commanding men; he 'understood very little more of the war than to fight very stoutly when there was occasion;' and he carried to excess Rupert's disregard of the civil and political aspects of the English civil war. Perhaps the best trait in his character is his affection for, and fidelity to his brother (CLARENDON, *Hist.* bk. vii. §§ 85, note).

A portrait by Mytens is at Hampton Court, and two by Vandyck belong to the Earl of Craven.

[Mrs. Green's Lives of the Princesses of England; Warburton's Memoirs of Prince Rupert and the Cavaliers, 1849; Webb's Memorials of the Civil War in Herefordshire, 1879; Diary of Richard Symonds (Camden Society), 1859; Clarendon's Great Rebellion; Bibliotheca Gloucestrensis, ed. Washbourn, 1825, and the Calendars of State Papers.] G. N. R.

MAURICE, FREDERICK DENISON (1805–1872), divine, born at Normanston, near Lowestoft, on 29 Aug. 1805, was the fifth child of Michael Maurice, by Priscilla (Hurry), daughter of a Yarmouth merchant. Michael Maurice, educated for the dissenting ministry, had become a unitarian before leaving the Hackney academy in 1787, and had sacrificed the prospects of an estate rather than abandon his opinions. In 1792 he was elected evening preacher at the chapel at Hackney in which Priestley preached in the mornings. He married in 1794, and took pupils from 1801 to 1812 at Normanston manor-house. In 1812 he moved to Clifton, and a year later to Frenchay, near Bristol. Frederick had three elder sisters: Elizabeth, Mary, and Anne (*b.* 1795, 1797, and 1799), and four younger: Emma, his special friend (*b.* 1807), Priscilla (*b.* 1810), and twin sisters (born at Frenchay), Lucilla, who became Mrs. Powell, and Esther, who in 1844 married Julius Hare. The family also included a nephew and niece of Mrs. Maurice: Edmund Cobb Hurry, who died on 18 Oct. 1814, and Anne, who married Alfred Hardcastle on 3 Jan. 1815, and died the same year in her first confinement. The illness and death of their cousins greatly affected the three elder sisters, and led to a change in their religious opinions. They became Calvinists; Elizabeth joined the church of England, and Anne the baptists. Anne and Mary took for their guide John Foster (1770–1843) [q. v.] the essayist. Their mother followed the daughters after long perplexity. Painful religious controversies thus divided the family while Frederick was still a child. As he came to understand the state of the case he received strong and permanent impressions. A profound desire for religious unity, and the conviction that a 'society founded upon opinions had no real cohesion' (F. MAURICE, *Life*, ii. 276), were embodied in all his teaching. Maurice was educated by his father in puritan principles. He read no fictions, except, apparently, Miss Edgeworth; he studied the Bible and Neal's 'History of the Puritans,' and attended meetings of the Anti-Slavery Society, the Bible Society, and similar institutions. He was a thoroughly 'good boy,' industrious and truthful; he cared little for games, read in time a good deal of miscellaneous literature, and had ambitions of rivalling Brougham, Sir Francis Burdett, and Joseph Hume, then the idols of the radicals (*ib.* p. 31). A letter written at the age of ten shows that he must have been very precocious, and perhaps a little self-conscious.

His mother finally abandoned unitarianism in 1821. Maurice, who had been intended by his father for the ministry, had by this time revolted against unitarianism and the narrowness of the dissenters generally (*Life*, i. 175). To escape from the difficulties of his position he resolved to become a barrister. Thomas Clarkson, son of the philanthropist, offered to take him as a legal pupil gratuitously. He wished to gain the wider culture obtainable at the universities, although his friends generally regarded them with dislike, and chose Cambridge, because no test was there imposed upon the students at entrance. He began residence at Trinity College, Cambridge, in the October term of 1823. He attended Julius Hare's lectures upon the Greek drama and Plato. Hare saw little of him personally, but recognised his remarkable aptitude for metaphysics. His private tutor was Frederick Field (1801–1885) [q. v.] He spoke at the Union, was one of the founders of the well-known 'Apostles' Club,' and formed a close intimacy with John Sterling, also a favourite pupil of Hare. With Sterling he migrated in October 1825 to Trinity Hall, where the fellowships were tenable by barristers and given for a law degree. He kept the terms for the LL.B. degree. He went to London to read for the bar in the long vacation of 1826, and in the following term returned for the examination, and took a first-class in the 'civil law classes' for 1826–7. He would have had a fair chance of election to a fellowship at Trinity Hall, but he felt himself unable to make the subscriptions then necessary for a degree, and at once took his name off the books, saying that he would not 'hang a bribe round his neck to lead his conscience.'

Although shy and reserved, Maurice had become an intellectual leader among his ablest contemporaries. While still at Cambridge he with his friend Whitmore edited the 'Metropolitan Quarterly Magazine,' which first appeared in November 1825, and lived through four numbers. He wrote several articles, attacking Bentham sharply, praising Byron, Wordsworth, Shelley, De Quincey, Scott, Keats, and Southey, and expressing unqualified admiration for Coleridge, at this time his chief guide in philosophy. Maurice contributed to the 'Westminster Review' in 1827 and 1828, and joined the debating society of which J. S. Mill was a member (*Autobiography*, pp. 123–9). The society had originated in a discussion with Owen's disciples. Maurice opposed both the Benthamites and the tories. In January 1828 he contributed some 'Sketches of Contemporary Authors' to the 'Athenæum,' just started by James Silk Buckingham [q. v.] He and some friends bought the 'London Literary Chronicle,' which he edited from 1 May following. On 30 July it was amalgamated with the 'Athenæum,' which was purchased from Buckingham, Maurice continuing to be editor. The paper was in favour of reform. Maurice's own articles, however, were strongly anti-Benthamite. He wrote warmly in support of the constitutional party in Spain. Some sons of Spanish exiles had been pupils of his father. He dissuaded Sterling, however, from joining the rash expedition in 1830. The 'Athenæum' did not pay under his management, and he was dispirited by home troubles. His father had lost much money by investments in Spanish bonds. He was no longer able to take pupils. The family had to move into a smaller house in Southampton, where they now lived. His sister Elizabeth became for a time companion to Mr. Gladstone's sister. She died in April 1839 (*Life*, i. 264). Mary decided to be a schoolmistress. Emma soon became dangerously ill. Frederick Maurice gave up his editorship, returned home, taught his sisters, and wrote for the 'Athenæum.' He gradually made up his mind to take orders, and resolved to go to Oxford, where Jacobson, a friend of Sterling (p. 179), then tutor of Exeter, had arranged that he should be allowed to count his Cambridge terms. He entered Exeter in the beginning of 1830, hoping to pay his expenses by a novel upon which he was now employed, with the warm encouragement of his sister Emma. There were delays in disposing of it, and he was only enabled to keep the last term of

1830 by a small legacy, though Jacobson had offered to advance his expenses (*ib.* i. 112).

At Oxford Maurice joined an 'Essay Society,' on the model of the Apostles', and made the acquaintance of Mr. Gladstone and of James Bruce, afterwards eighth Earl of Elgin [q. v.] Bruce introduced him to the writings of Thomas Erskine (1788–1870) [q. v.] of Linlathen. He was much interested by the religious excitement in Irving's congregation and the alleged miracles, but he was not personally acquainted with the leaders of the Oxford movement. On 29 March 1831 he was baptised as a member of the church of England. He spent the next three months by the deathbed of his sister Emma. She died on 9 July 1832, having, it is said, had much influence upon the development of his mind. Her papers, with those of her sister Anne, who died in 1826, were published as 'Memorials of Two Sisters.' He took a second class in November 1831. After spending some time with A. J. Stephenson, incumbent of Lympsham, Somerset, to prepare for holy orders, he was ordained by the Bishop of Lichfield on 26 Jan. 1834 to the curacy of Bubbenhall, near Leamington. His story, 'Eustace Conway,' for which he received 100*l.* (*ib.* i. 124), was published soon afterwards. Coleridge, as Sterling told him, praised it warmly, though it had little commercial success. He never met Coleridge personally (*ib.* i. 178). He also published a pamphlet, 'Subscription no Bondage,' of which Southey said in 1836 (*ib.* vi. 292) that he 'never read an abler treatise,' against the measure then proposed for abolishing subscription to the Thirty-nine Articles in the universities. He argued that the declaration of bonâ fide membership of the church of England imposed upon graduates at Cambridge was really more stringent than the Oxford subscription to the articles, which he interpreted as only implying acceptance of them as the terms of university teaching. He had changed his mind by 1853 (*ib.* ii. 154) on finding that this subscription was not generally made in this sense, and afterwards strongly advocated the abolition of the tests. At Bubbenhall he also began for the 'Encyclopædia Metropolitana' an article upon 'Moral and Metaphysical Philosophy,' the completion and revision of which in later editions occupied much of his attention through life.

In January 1836 he became chaplain to Guy's Hospital. Here he lectured the students twice a week upon moral philosophy. His sister Priscilla kept house for him, and he had a pupil, afterwards a warm friend, (Sir) Edward Strachey. He saw few friends except Sterling, but occasionally met Carlyle and others. His relation to Carlyle became more antagonistic. He felt bound to insist upon points of difference, which Carlyle preferred to pass over (*ib.* i. 250), and they agreed enough to make the differences painful (see Maurice's criticisms upon Carlyle's 'pantheism,' *Life*, i. 276–82). In 1836 he declined an offer of the tutorship at Downing, where the new master, Thomas Worsley, dreamt of 'making theology and Christian philosophy the centre of all studies' (*ib.* i. 207). At the end of the year he allowed himself to be named as candidate for the chair of political economy at Oxford. The appointment was supported without his knowledge by the leaders of the Oxford movement. His pamphlet upon subscription had been shown (*ib.* i. 182) to Newman and Pusey, who approved the aim, if not the spirit. Maurice, however, had been profoundly alienated by Pusey's tracts upon baptism, representing a theology radically opposed to his own. His second 'Letter to a Quaker' (published early in 1837) dealt with baptism, and showed his previous supporters that they had mistaken his position. They decided at once to vote against him, and his name was withdrawn.

In June 1837 Maurice visited Hare at Hurstmonceaux, where he met Sterling and Anna Barton, sister of Sterling's wife, and already known to him. He now became engaged to her, and they were married by Sterling at Clifton on 7 Oct. following. During the first ten months of 1837 Maurice was publishing the 'Letters to a Quaker.' They were addressed to his friend Samuel Clark (1810–1875), then a quaker, and afterwards a clergyman. They were collected at the end of the year as 'The Kingdom of Christ.' The publication was the signal for the beginning of a series of attacks from the religious press, which lasted for the rest of his life, and caused great pain to a man of a singularly sensitive nature. The book contains a very full statement of his fundamental convictions, which were opposed to the tenets of all the chief parties in the church. His philosophical position was not easily grasped by the average mind, and if he was often misrepresented and attacked with unjustifiable bitterness, it must be admitted that he condemned very unsparingly the favourite doctrines of his opponents.

In September 1839 Maurice became one of the editors of a newly founded 'Educational Magazine.' The progress of chartism and Owenism had increased his deep interest in national education. A grant of 20,000*l.* previously given was increased to 30,000*l.* in 1839, with a condition of government inspection. Maurice's chief contention was that the school system should not be transferred from the church to the state. He became sole editor of the magazine in 1840, and was contented with the agreement made by government with the National Society in that year. The magazine, which had not paid its way, was abandoned in the spring of 1841.

In June 1840 Maurice was elected professor of English literature and history at King's College, London. His lectures were rather above the heads of his boyish hearers. They dealt with general principles to the exclusion of dates and facts, and he was too sensitive and gentle to enforce order upon lads not very accessible to appeals to their (assumed) feelings as gentlemen. But he stimulated the more thoughtful minds, and attracted the strong personal devotion of many of his hearers.

Maurice took a strong interest in the religious questions of the day. He warmly supported the foundation of the Jerusalem bishopric, which to Newman and his friends was a great offence, Maurice holding that it recognised the catholicity of the church, which was really denied by the external unity of 'popery.' He defended his position in an answer to a pamphlet by William Palmer of Magdalen, who had attacked protestantism on the occasion. When, on the other hand, Pusey was suspended from preaching at Oxford in 1843, Maurice earnestly protested against the measure in a letter to Lord Ashley (afterwards Shaftesbury), who had presided over an anti-tractarian meeting. In 1844 W.G. Ward was attacked for his book upon the 'Ideal of a Christian Church,' and Maurice again protested vigorously against the statute which deprived Ward of his degree in 'Two Letters to a Non-resident Member of Convocation.' These discussions led incidentally to some later controversies.

Sterling's wife died on 18 April 1843; Sterling himself died on 18 Sept. 1844; and Mrs. Maurice, who had been greatly shocked by her sister's death, on 25 March 1845. She left two sons. Maurice was deeply affected by these calamities. He ever afterwards reproached himself with having been unduly harsh towards Sterling's change of belief, although they had always retained their mutual affection, and he could not bear even to read Hare's 'Life' of his friend.

At the end of 1843 Hare expressed his hopes that Maurice might succeed to the principalship of King's College and the preachership to Lincoln's Inn, both of which were to be vacated by the appointment of Lonsdale to the bishopric of Lichfield. In reply Maurice described himself as so unpopular with both of the chief parties in the church, that if he became principal of King's College the professors would all resign, and the college be reduced to a third or a fourth of its numbers. He felt that he must always hold a subordinate position in the church. Jelf became principal of King's College. In July 1845 Maurice was appointed Boyle lecturer by the Archbishop of York and the Bishop of London, and in August Warburton lecturer by the Archbishop of Canterbury. The Warburton lectures were the substance of his book on 'The Epistle to the Hebrews,' 1846, which contains an answer to Newman's 'Theory of Development,' and the Boyle lectures were developed into 'The Religions of the World,' 1847. The appointments, as his son thinks (i. 521), were due to his support of the Jerusalem bishopric scheme, and the favour of two archbishops might imply that he was a 'safe' man. When in 1846 a theological department was founded at King's College, he became one of the professors, upon Jelf's nomination. In June 1846 he was elected chaplain of Lincoln's Inn, with a salary of 300*l.* a year, and resigned the chaplaincy at Guy's Hospital, where his labours had tried his health (*Life*, i. 361). At Lincoln's Inn Maurice had to conduct a daily morning prayer, and a full service on Sunday afternoon. He very soon attracted an intelligent audience, including many young barristers. Among them were Thomas Hughes [see SUPPL.] and Mr. J. M. Ludlow. Charles Kingsley had become known to him in 1844, and all were soon devoted friends.

In 1848 he founded Queen's College, with the help of other professors at King's College. His sister Mary, who had set up a school at Southampton, had been led and had led him to take an interest in governesses, and the new institution was especially intended to meet their wants. (For an account of the college see an article by Lady Stanley of Alderley in the *Nineteenth Century* for August 1879.)

On 12 Nov. 1844 Julius Hare had married Esther, Maurice's younger sister, and on 4 July 1849 Maurice married Georgiana, daughter of Francis Hare-Naylor [q.v.], half-sister of Julius Hare. Meanwhile Maurice's position had been profoundly affected by the revolutionary movements of 1848. Maurice and his friends agreed with the chartists and radicals that great changes were urgently needed, but held that the substitution of genuine Christianity for the secularist doctrines supplied the only sound foundation for a reconstruction of society. Maurice was the spiritual leader of the 'Christian Socialists,' as they came to be called, and, though often against his will, was induced also to preside ever many of their practical endeavours. He edited, with Mr. Ludlow, their first organ, called 'Politics for the People,' which was apparently first suggested by Julius Hare. It lasted through seventeen weekly numbers, of which the first appeared on 6 May 1848. Among the contributors were many distinguished men, including Kingsley, Arthur Stanley, Helps, S. G. Osborne, Conington, and Whately. It reached a circulation of two thousand, but did not pay its expenses. It led to friendly relations with some of the chartist leaders. After its death weekly meetings, which had been held by the chief writers at Maurice's house, were continued and increased in numbers. From this was also developed at the end of 1848 a weekly class for the study of the Bible, which extended Maurice's influence with many rising young men. 'Conferences' were held with the working classes during 1849, when Maurice presided, and was generally well received. A visit of Mr. Ludlow to Paris to examine the 'Associations Ouvrières' and the publication of Mayhew's 'London Labour and the London Poor' helped to draw the attention of the friends to co-operation. At the beginning of 1850 they started a tailors' association, and other associations were afterwards formed. A society for the promotion of such associations was founded. A 'central board,' consisting of the managers of the separate associations, met for business purposes, and a 'council of promoters,' with Maurice for its head, acted as referees and general advisers. A series of tracts upon 'Christian Socialism' was issued, none of them without the sanction of Maurice, who intervened decisively on occasion. He suppressed a tract in which Lord Goderich had defended the movement on democratic grounds (*Life*, ii. 125, &c.) The 'Christian Socialist' was started as an organ of the party on 2 Nov. 1850, and at the beginning of 1852 became the 'Journal of Association.' Maurice objected to it at starting, and only contributed a few articles (*ib.* ii. 55, 88, 96). The associations formed by the Christian Socialists failed after a time, while those founded independently by working men in the north ultimately succeeded. The causes cannot be considered here. The Christian Socialists in any case secured one very important result by obtaining in 1852 the passage of the act which gave a legal status to co-operative bodies. Their advocacy of the movement had also a very great influence in obtaining recognition of the principle of co-operation among the more educated classes.

Maurice had meanwhile been growing in disfavour with the chief religious parties. An absurd outcry had been made about the Sterling Club, founded for purely social purposes by Sterling's friends (*ib.* i. 516, 532). The publication of Hare's 'Life of Sterling' had made his heterodoxy known, and Maurice, Manning, the Wilberforces, and others who had joined the club, were accused of infidelity. Maurice's 'Christian Socialism' was represented as implying the acceptance of all manner of atheistic and immoral revolutionary doctrines. He was fiercely attacked by Croker in the 'Quarterly Review' for September 1851. Jelf, as principal of King's College, called upon him for an explanation. Jelf said that unless Maurice disavowed Kingsley (who was wrongly suspected of contributing to the freethinking 'Leader') he would be identified with Kingsley, who was identified with Holyoake, who was identified with Tom Paine, and concluded by suggesting resignation of his professorships as an alternative to disavowal. Jelf accepted Maurice's denial of the more extravagant charges; but the council of King's College appointed a committee of inquiry. The committee reported decisively in Maurice's favour, with some expression of regret that his name had been 'mixed up' with other publications 'of questionable tendency,' and after some further explanations the affair dropped for the time. The publication of his 'Theological Essays' in 1853 produced a new attack. Jelf brought before the council the passage in which Maurice defended his doctrine (which had already been incidentally brought forward in the discussion of Ward's 'Ideal') that the popular belief in the endlessness of future punishment was superstitious, and not sanctioned by the strictest interpretation of the articles. 'Eternity,' he maintained, has nothing to do with time or indefinite duration. After a long correspondence with Jelf, a meeting of the council on 27 Oct. 1853 voted that Maurice's doctrines were dangerous, and that his continuance of his connection with the college would be detrimental. Mr. Gladstone moved as an amendment that 'competent theologians' should be appointed to examine Maurice's writings, hoping that some *formula concordiæ* might be arranged. The amendment, however, was lost. Maurice was much hurt by Jelf's decision that he should not even finish his course of lectures. He challenged the council to say which of the articles condemned his teaching, but they prudently declined to continue the discussion. Maurice's son mentions some circumstances tending to show unfairness in the procedure, and Jelf had advertised in the 'Record,' Maurice's chief assailant, that Maurice's orthodoxy was under consideration, and that he hoped that the requirements of the paper would be satisfied.

Maurice upon resigning received many warm expressions of sympathy and approval from his friends and old pupils, including Lord Tennyson's fine poem. The benchers of Lincoln's Inn declined his offer to resign the chaplaincy. He resigned the chairmanship of the committee of Queen's College, but consented to retain his lectureship if he should be unanimously requested to do so. A minority objecting he resigned, but in 1856 resumed the position, all opposition having been withdrawn. The public feeling was strongly with him, though perhaps the popular objections to everlasting punishment did not quite coincide with his own.

The failure of the Christian Socialist associations had suggested the importance of improving the education of the artisan class. Some lectures had been given during 1853 at the 'Hall of Association.' In February 1854 Maurice drew up a scheme for a Working Men's College, partly suggested by a 'People's College' founded at Sheffield in 1842. During the remainder of the year he gave lectures in its behalf at various places. On 30 Oct. he delivered an inaugural address at St. Martin's Hall, and the college started with over 130 pupils, in Red Lion Square, moving successively to Great Ormond Street and to Crowndale Road, N.W. Maurice became principal, and took an active part both in teaching and superintending during the rest of his life in London. Many distinguished men became gratuitous lecturers, and similar colleges were started in other towns. Both teachers and pupils were of many religious persuasions. In 1855 two French gentlemen of strongly revolutionary principles were excluded from the council. Some difficulties afterwards arose about the 'Sunday question.' Maurice, though carefully avoiding anything like a sectarian system, desired to give an essentially Christian character to the college. He had Bible classes both in connection with the college and outside of it, where he encouraged the freest discussion of all questions.

During the King's College controversy H. L. Mansel [q. v.] had written a pamphlet against Maurice's theories, which had been noticed by Maurice in his 'Old Testament Sermons.' A short correspondence between them only showed the absence of any common ground (*Life*, ii. 311). When Mansel in 1858 delivered his Bampton lectures, Maurice was profoundly moved by their assertion of a principle diametrically opposite to his own. He wrote a reply, called 'What is Revelation?' A very sharp controversy followed, which occasionally led to unfortunate imputations on both sides. As Maurice assumed as the centre of his whole teaching a 'knowledge of God' in a sense in which, according to Mansel, such knowledge was demonstrably impossible, any compromise or approximation was out of the question. Arthur Stanley, Mr. Goldwin Smith, and Mr. Chretien took Maurice's side in Oxford.

In July 1860 Maurice was appointed to the chapel of St. Peter's, Vere Street, by Mr. William Cowper, then chief commissioner of the board of works. The appointment was attacked by the 'Record,' and an address, signed by about twenty clergymen, was sent to the Bishop of London (Tait), protesting against his institution. A counter-address, with 332 clerical and 487 lay signatures, congratulating him upon the 'tardy recognition' of his services to the church, showed that the prejudices against him were now confined to a few determined antagonists. Mr. Ludlow, Mr. Llewellyn Davies, and Dean Hook had been the chief promoters, and among the signatures were those of Mr. Gladstone, Lord Tennyson, and Bishop Thirlwall. His position, however, was not free from trouble. Bishop Colenso had been an old friend, and (as bishop-designate of Natal) had greatly touched Maurice by dedicating a volume of sermons to him during the King's College controversy. When preparing his book upon the Pentateuch in 1862, he consulted Maurice and showed him the proof-sheets. Maurice was shocked by the tendency of the book. He told Colenso that many people would think that he ought to resign his bishopric. Colenso replied that many people thought that Maurice had no business to hold his living. Maurice had been alarmed by decisions (reversed on appeal) in the cases of Heath and Wilson, which would condemn his own teaching. He now determined to resign, thinking that as an unbeneficed clergyman he would be able to assert more forcibly his adherence to its formularies, whereas his legal ejection from his living might cause a schism. His intention became known, and excited many protests. He found that he was supposed to be resigning because he had doubts as to subscribing the articles. Bishop Tait declared that he could hardly accept the resignation; but Maurice was at last only withheld by the suggestion that he was acting unfairly to Colenso, who had confided in him, and would be injured by the resignation. He agreed to be guided by the advice of the bishop, and retained the living. The misunderstanding, however, caused a falling off of the congregation, who were puzzled by his scrupulosity (*ib.* ii. 553). In 1863 he replied to

Colenso in a series of letters called 'The Claims of the Bible and Science,' and some estrangement followed (*ib.* ii. 485), which made him decline to meet Colenso at the house of a common friend. On 25 Oct. 1866 Maurice was elected to the Knightbridge professorship of 'casuistry, moral theology, and moral philosophy' at Cambridge, vacant by the death of John Grote [q. v.] The election was all but unanimous, and Maurice was warmly received at Cambridge, where, at any rate, there were no doubts of his sufficient orthodoxy. He remained principal of the Working Men's College, though he had to give up his constant attendance. He retained the Vere Street Chapel, with which no parish work was connected, but the labour of a weekly journey to perform the services tried his strength, which was already showing symptoms of decline. He resigned it in October 1869 under medical orders. In 1870 he agreed to serve on the commission upon contagious diseases, and came up weekly from Cambridge to the meetings. At the same time he accepted St. Edward's, Cambridge (in the gift of Trinity Hall), a position which gave no income and little parish work, but which involved regular preaching. He was also giving his professorial lectures, and seeing as much as he could of the undergraduates personally. He had never spared his strength, and by 1870 his health was visibly breaking down. Yet at the beginning of July 1871 the Bishop of London (Jackson) induced him to accept the Cambridge preachership at Whitehall. He preached in November and December 1871 and January 1872, besides preaching two university sermons in November. At Christmas he became seriously ill. He afterwards struggled through a little work. On 30 March he was able to sign a letter resigning St. Edward's. He was exceedingly weak, and suffered from mental depression. On 1 April 1872 he became unconscious, after, with a great effort, pronouncing a blessing, and died.

A proposal was made that he should be buried in Westminster Abbey, but his family agreed unanimously that such a funeral would have been contrary to his wishes. He was buried at Highgate (5 April) in a vault where his father, mother, and sisters had been laid. A bust is in Cambridge University Library. A portrait by Miss Hayward is in the National Portrait Gallery, London; other portraits, by Lowes Dickenson, are at the Working Men's College in Crowndale Road and at Queen's College, London.

Maurice was rather below middle height, but a singularly noble and expressive countenance gave dignity to his appearance. His voice and manner in conducting divine service were especially reverent and impressive. He suffered from severe illnesses, partly due to overwork (*Life*, ii. 288), but behaved like a man in strong health. He rose early, often saw his friends at breakfast, and afterwards worked till his dinner-time, unless interrupted by business (*ib.* pp. 6, 30), dictating most of his writing. His manuscripts were elaborately corrected and rewritten.

Maurice's character was most fascinating. Kingsley called him the 'most beautiful human soul' he had known; and an early friend (*ib.* i. 38) says that he was the 'most saintlike,' or, if he 'dared to use the words,' the most Christlike individual he had ever met. Those who knew him well would generally agree in the opinion. He was exceedingly gentle and courteous in personal intercourse, beloved by his servants, and an easy victim to begging impostors. He was absolutely unworldly, shrinking from preferment when it was within his reach, as in previous days he had frankly uttered the convictions which then made preferment impossible. He had an even excessively scrupulous sense of honour, and throughout his life was devoted exclusively to setting forth what he held to be the truth. He was at times moved to vehement indignation, and could be very sharp in controversy; some natural irritability joined with his keen sense of the importance of certain truths, and with the consciousness that, from whatever cause, his meaning was very liable to be misconceived. His sensitiveness and extreme diffidence sometimes gives an impression of rather exaggerated humility, though the sincerity of his feeling is beyond a doubt. A certain want of practical capacity only increased the devotion of his friends by the sense that he needed protection against rougher natures. They looked up to him with the reverence due to a great spiritual teacher. Whatever the value of his philosophy, he was among the first of the clergy to perceive the full importance of the great social movement of his time, and in spite of much practical failure rendered great service in raising the general tone of feeling upon such questions. The long continuance of a persecution from religious opponents, which embittered much of his life, is easily explicable, but not the less lamentable.

Maurice constantly protested against being identified with any party. He had early left a sect, based upon dogma, because he thought that the national church represented the vital principle of Christian unity, and rested on a spiritual fact instead of the intellectual acceptance of defined opinions. If, however, he did not belong to a 'party,' he held very distinctive doctrines and an intimate circle of sympathetic friends, and to outsiders this looked like being the head of a party. He condemned in the strongest terms the characteristic theories of the 'high' and 'low' church, and, although it included many of his warmest friends, those also of the 'broad church' party. The 'broad church,' first so called by W. J. Conybeare [q. v.], appeared to him to reduce Christianity to a mere *caput mortuum*, by abandoning all disputed doctrines and mysteries. He stood to them in the relation in which the 'Cambridge Platonists,' his nearest analogues in the Anglican church, stood to Locke and Tillotson. According to the definition of his early master (Coleridge) he was emphatically a 'Platonist' as opposed to an 'Aristotelian,' and has been regarded by theological opponents (see Dr. Rigg, *Anglican Theology*, 3rd edition, pp. 244–345) as substantially a neo-Platonist. The peculiarity which divided him from the mystics was his strong conviction of the necessity of an historical element in theology. A mystic appears, in any case to ordinary common sense, as unintelligible, and Maurice's distinctions (e.g. between 'eternal' and 'everlasting') seemed mere evasions to uncongenial minds. They were equally perplexed by his statements as to the worthlessness of mere dogmas or opinions considered as such, and their infinite value when considered as divine revelations of truth. His catholic interest in all religious beliefs, and sympathetic appreciation of their value, seemed to imply an excessive intellectual ingenuity in reconciling apparent contradictions. The effort to avoid a harsh dogmatic outline gives an indistinctness to his style, if not to his thought, and explains why some people held him, as he says himself, to be a 'muddy mystic.' The value of his theological teaching will therefore be estimated very differently as the critic belongs to a school more or less in sympathy with his philosophical tendencies. But no fair reader can doubt that he was a man of most generous nature, of wide sympathies, and of great insight and subtlety of thought, and possessed of wide learning. Such qualities are compatible with much confusion of thought, but are too rare to be overlooked or undervalued.

A bibliography of Maurice's writings, by Mr. G. J. Gray, was published by Messrs. Macmillan in 1885. His works, omitting a few occasional sermons, are: 1. 'Eustace Conway, or the Brother and Sister, a novel,' 1834. 2. 'Subscription no Bondage,' 1835. 3. 'The Kingdom of Christ, or Hints to a Quaker respecting the Principle, Constitution, and Ordinances of the Catholic Church,' 1838; 2nd enlarged edition, 1842; 3rd edition, 1883. 4. 'Has the Church or the State power to Educate the Nation?' (a course of lectures), 1839. 5. 'Reasons for not joining a Party in the Church; a Letter to S. Wilberforce,' 1841. 6. 'Three Letters to the Rev. W. Palmer' (on the Jerusalem bishopric), 1842. 7. 'Right and Wrong Methods of supporting Protestantism' (letter to Lord Ashley), 1843. 8. 'Christmas Day, and other Sermons,' 1843. 9. 'The New Statute and Dr. Ward,' 1845. 10. 'Thoughts on the Rule of Conscientious Subscription,' 1845. 11. 'The Epistle to the Hebrews' (Warburtonian lectures), with preface on Newman's 'Theory of Development,' 1846. 12. 'Letter on the Attempt to Defeat the Nomination of Dr. Hampden,' 1847. 13. 'Thoughts on the Duty of a Protestant on the present Oxford Election,' 1847. 14. 'The Religions of the World, and their Relations to Christianity' (Boyle lectures), 1847. 15. 'The Lord's Prayer' (nine sermons), 1848; with the succeeding in 1880. 16. 'Queen's College, London; its Objects and Methods,' 1848. 17. 'The Prayer Book, considered especially in reference to the Romish System' (nineteen sermons at Lincoln's Inn), 1849, 1857, and with the preceding in 1880. 18. 'The Church a Family' (twelve sermons at Lincoln's Inn), 1850. 19. 'Queen's College, London' (in reply to the 'Quarterly Review'), 1850. 20. 'The Old Testament' (nineteen sermons at Lincoln's Inn), 1851 (second edition as 'Patriarchs and Lawgivers of the Old Testament,' 1855). 21. 'Sermons on the Sabbath Day, on the Character of the Warrior, and on the Interpretation of History,' 1853. 22. 'Theological Essays,' 1853 (a second edition in 1854 with new preface and concluding essay). 23. 'The word Eternal and the Punishment of the Wicked' (letter to Dr. Jelf), 1853. 24. 'The Prophets and Kings of the Old Testament' (sermons at Lincoln's Inn), 1853. 25. 'The Doctrine of Sacrifice deduced from the Scriptures,' 1854. 26. 'Ecclesiastical History of the First and Second Centuries,' 1854. 27. 'The Unity of the New Testament, a Synopsis of the First Three Gospels, and the Epistles of St. James, St. Jude, St. Peter, and St. Paul,' 1854. 28. 'Learning and Working' (six lectures at Willis's Rooms), with 'Rome and its Influence on Modern Civilisation' (four lectures at Edinburgh), 1855. 29. 'The Epistles of St. John: a Series of Lectures on Christian Ethics,' 1857. 30. 'The Eucharist' (five sermons), 1857. 31. 'The Gospel of St. John' (sermons), 1857. 32. 'The Indian Mutiny' (five sermons),

1857. 33. 'What is Revelation?' (with letters on the Bampton lectures of Dr. Mansel), 1859. 34. 'Sequel to the Enquiry, What is Revelation?' 1860. 35. 'Lectures on the Apocalypse,' 1861. 36. 'Dialogues ... on Family Worship,' 1862. 37. 'Claims of the Bible and of Science' (upon the Colenso controversy), 1863. 38. 'The Gospel of the Kingdom of Heaven' (eighteen lectures on the Gospel according to St. Luke), 1864. 39. 'The Conflict of Good and Evil in our Day' (twelve letters to a missionary), 1864. 40. 'The Workman and the Franchise; Chapters from English History on the Representation and Education of the People,' 1866. 41. 'Casuistry, Moral Philosophy, and Moral Theology' (inaugural lecture at Cambridge), 1866. 42. 'The Commandments considered as Instruments of National Reformation,' 1866. 43. 'The Ground and Object of Hope for Mankind' (four university sermons), 1867. 44. 'The Conscience, Lectures on Casuistry,' 1868. 45. 'Social Morality' (lectures at Cambridge), 1869. 46. 'Moral and Metaphysical Philosophy,' 2 vols. 8vo, 1871–2. Maurice wrote the article 'Moral and Metaphysical Philosophy' for the 'Encyclopædia Metropolitana.' This was expanded into three volumes, published in the series called the second edition of the 'Encyclopædia.' The first, upon 'Ancient Philosophy,' appeared in 1850; the second, upon the 'Philosophy of the First Six Centuries,' in 1853; and the third, upon 'Mediæval Philosophy,' containing the period from the fifth to the fourteenth century, in 1857. A continuation, upon 'Modern Philosophy,' containing the period from the fourteenth century to the French revolution, appeared in 1862. The four are combined in this work; the first volume containing the three first periods, and the second the fourth period. 47. 'Sermons preached in Country Churches,' 1873. 48. 'The Friendship of Books, and other Lectures' (edited by Mr. Thomas Hughes), 1874.

[Life of Frederick Denison Maurice, chiefly told in his own Letters, edited by his son, Frederick Maurice, 1884. See also Caroline Fox's Memories of Old Friends, 2nd edit. 1882, i. 299, ii. 54–5, 63, 86, 113, 119, 170, 195, 217, 230, 233; Memorials of J. McLeod Campbell, 1877, passim; Mill's Autobiography, pp. 152–4; Froude's Carlyle, and Life in London, i. 39, 40, 125, 409; A. J. Ross's Life of Bishop Ewing, pp. 434, 518, 576, &c.; Life of Charles Kingsley, passim; Liddon's Life of Pusey; Mozley's Reminiscences; The Working Men's College 1854–1904, edit. the rev. J. Llewelyn Davies, 1904.] L. S.

MAURICE, GODFREY (*d.* 1598), Franciscan. [See Jones, John.]

MAURICE, HENRY (1648–1691), divine, born in 1648, was son of Thomas Maurice, perpetual curate of Llangristiolus, Anglesey. He was grandson of Henry Perry [q. v.], the Welsh scholar (Wood, *Athenæ Oxon.* ed. Bliss, i. 667). After attending Beaumaris grammar school, he matriculated on 20 May 1664 from Jesus College, Oxford, and graduated B.A. on 28 Jan. 1667–8, M.A. in 1671, B.D. in 1679, and D.D. in 1683 (Foster, *Alumni Oxon.* 1500–1714, iii. 991). His learning and brightness attracted the notice of Sir Leoline Jenkins [q. v.], then principal of the college, and he was elected to a fellowship. About 1669 he took, at the request of the college, the curacy of Cheltenham, Gloucestershire, where, says Wood, being provoked by some 'malapert Socinians, he managed a controversy with them in writing so successfully that he gained to himself great reputation.' In 1671 he returned to college. When Jenkins was sent as plenipotentiary to Cologne in 1673, Maurice accompanied him as chaplain. During the three years that he remained abroad he took every opportunity of increasing his knowledge by learning modern languages and conversing with eminent scholars. On his return to England he lived in the family of Jenkins at Doctors' Commons and in college until 1680, when he became domestic chaplain to Sancroft; he continued in that office till June 1691, though he did not sympathise in the archbishop's refusal to take the oath of allegiance to William. Under the patronage of Sancroft he received the treasurership of Chichester, in which he was installed on 7 Jan. 1681, the rectory of Chevening, Kent, which he held from 1681 until 1685, and in 1684 the sinecure rectory of Llandrillo-yn-Rhôs, Denbighshire (Thomas, *St. Asaph*, p. 551). In April 1685 he was presented to the richly endowed rectory of Newington, Oxfordshire. By the clergy of the diocese of Oxford he was chosen in October 1689 to be their representative in the convocation held at Westminster in the following November, and he fully justified their choice. On 18 July 1691 he was elected Lady Margaret professor of divinity at Oxford (Le Neve, *Fasti*, ed. Hardy, iii. 519), in right of which office he was installed prebendary of Worcester (*ib.* iii. 85). Maurice died suddenly on 30 Oct. 1691 at his house near Newington, and was buried in the chancel of the church there on 6 Nov. He was unmarried, and his estate was administered to by his sister, Elizabeth Clancey, a widow (*Administration Act Book*, P. C. C. 1691, f. 224). A monument was erected to his memory in Jesus College chapel (Wood, *Colleges and Halls*, ed. Gutch, i. 588).

Both Wood and Hearne praise Maurice's fine scholarship, solid judgment, ready wit, and blameless life. He was an eloquent extempore preacher and a learned controversialist, being especially well versed in canon law. He wrote: 1. 'A Vindication of the Primitive Church and Diocesan Episcopacy, in Answer to Mr. Baxter's Church History of Bishops,' &c. [anon.], 8vo, London, 1682. To this Baxter rejoined the same year in his 'True History of Councils enlarged and defended,' and appended to his book a reply called 'Diocesan Churches not yet discovered in the Primitive Times,' by the anonymous author of a tract entitled 'No Evidence for Diocesan Churches,' 1681, whose arguments Maurice had also assailed. 2. 'The Antithelemite; or an Answer to certain Quæres by the D[uke] of B[uckingham], and to the Considerations of an unknown Author concerning Toleration' [anon.], 4to, London, 1685. 3. 'The Project for repealing the Penal Laws and Tests, with the honourable means used to effect it,' &c. [anon.], 4to [London, 1688], a satirical tract, secretly printed, on James's efforts to introduce Roman catholicism. 4. 'Doubts concerning the Roman Infallibility' [anon.], 4to, London, 1688 (reprinted in Bishop Gibson's collection, called 'A Preservative against Popery,' edit. 1738, vol. i., and edit. 1848, vol. iv.) 5. 'Letter to a Member of the House of Commons concerning the Bishops lately in the Tower, and now under Suspension' [anon.], 4to, London, 1689. 6. 'Remarks from the Country upon the two Letters relating to the Convocation and Alterations in the Liturgy' [anon.], 4to, London, 1689. 7. 'The Lawfulness of taking the new Oaths asserted' [anon.], 4to, London, 1689. 8. 'A Defence of Diocesan Episcopacy, in Answer to a Book of Mr. David Clarkson . . . entituled "Primitive Episcopacy,"' 8vo, London, 1691; 2nd edit. 1700. Maurice also published in 1682 a sermon preached before the king at Whitehall on 30 Jan. 1681-2, which was reprinted in 1744. He was the reputed author of 'Animadversions on Dr. Burnet's "History of the Rights of Princes,"' 4to, London, 1682, which elicited an 'Answer' from Burnet in the same year. Maurice was an intimate friend of Henry Wharton, a fellow-chaplain at Lambeth, whom he assisted in the composition of the 'Defence of Pluralities,' 1692.

In 1688 Maurice was bitterly attacked by an anonymous Roman catholic writer in 'Some Reasons tender'd to impartial People why Dr. Henry Maurice ought not to be traduc'd as the Licenser of the Pamphlet entituled "A plain Answer to a Popish Priest, questioning the Orders of the Church of England,"' appended to 'Twenty-one Conclusions further demonstrating the Schism of the Church of England,' 4to, Oxford.

[Wood's Athenæ Oxon. (Bliss), iv. 326; Williams's Eminent Welshmen, 1852, pp. 317-18; Lansd. MS. p. 987, ff. 129, 147; Hearne's Remarks and Collections (Oxford Hist. Soc.), i. 99, 214, ii. 60; Notes and Queries, 4th ser. iv. 337.]
G. G.

MAURICE, JAMES WILKES (1775-1857), rear-admiral, was born at Devonport on 10 Feb. 1775. He entered the navy in 1789 as 'able seaman' on board the Inspector sloop, and in 1793 was midshipman of the Powerful, which convoyed a fleet of Indiamen to the Cape of Good Hope. He afterwards served in the Cambridge, Concorde, and Royal George, all in the Channel and off Brest; and on 3 April 1797 was promoted to be lieutenant of the Glory. In 1799 he was moved to the Canada, and in September 1802 was appointed to the Centaur, going out to the West Indies with Commodore Samuel Hood (1762-1814) [q. v.] In her he was present at the reduction of St. Lucia, Tobago, Demerara, and Essequibo; and was landed, 26 Nov. 1803, at the destruction of a battery at Petite Anse d'Arlet in Martinique, when he was severely wounded by the explosion of the magazine. When the Diamond Rock, Martinique (see M'CORMICK, *Voyages of Discovery*, &c., ii. 190) was occupied, armed, and commissioned as a 'sloop of war,' 3 Feb. 1804, Maurice was appointed to the command, and his promotion was confirmed by the admiralty to 7 May 1804. For more than a year Maurice held this rock, a thorn in the sides of the French at Martinique; and yielded to an attack in force by a detachment of Villeneuve's fleet, 31 May-2 June 1805, only when his ammunition was exhausted. In the three days the English lost two men killed and one wounded; the loss of the French, on the other hand, was severe, but has never been exactly stated. Maurice estimated it at seventy killed and wounded of the landing party alone, exclusive of those on board the ships and gunboats. Maurice was tried by court-martial for the loss of his post, but was honourably acquitted, and highly complimented on his conduct (JAMES, iii. 244-5, 349; CHEVALIER, p. 148). He returned to England in August, and was immediately appointed to the Savage brig, which after two years in the Channel was sent out to the West Indies. There, in the autumn of 1808, he was appointed by Sir Alexander Cochrane governor of Marie Galante, which had been seized in the previous March. On 18 Jan. 1809 he was advanced to post rank.

In October 1809 he was compelled by ill-health to return to England, and in July 1810 he was appointed governor of the island of Anholt, in the Baltic, which had been captured, without difficulty, in May 1809, by a small squadron under the command of Captain Aiskew Paffard Hollis [q. v.] The island had been found most useful as a depôt of trade and as a station for communicating with the continent, and when Maurice was appointed it was understood that neither Bonaparte nor the Danes would lose any opportunity of recapturing it. It was garrisoned by about four hundred marines, under the command of Captain Torrens. As long as the weather remained open the English cruisers secured it from attack, as, afterwards, did the severity of the winter. As soon as the water was open an attempt was made by the Danes to retake it. Twelve gunboats convoyed the Danish transports, and in the early morning of 27 March 1811, in darkness and fog, a force of a thousand men was landed about four miles from the fort. The enemy were ignorant that the Tartar frigate and Sheldrake brig had arrived from England the day before; the Danish troops advanced gallantly to the assault, driving in the advanced parties of the English, while the gunboats opened a lively fire on the sea defences. The approach of the Tartar put another complexion on the matter. The gunboats withdrew; a small schooner attached to the island took up a position on the enemy's flank, and drove them from behind the sandhills, while the direct fire from the fort was well sustained and deadly. Finding no retreat open to them, the Danes on the north side, to the number of 543, surrendered at discretion; the rest fled to the west end of the island, where, temporarily guarded by the reefs, they managed to get on board the gunboats and transports. These, however, were pursued and scattered by the English ships; four of them were captured; one was sunk (James, v. 222). The loss to the Danes was very severe; but Maurice's conduct, splendid as it undoubtedly was, was much exaggerated in popular estimation. The decisive support of the Tartar and Sheldrake was ignored or unknown; the force of the Danes was magnified; and the garrison of barely four hundred men was described as defeating and capturing a force of ten times its numbers (O'Byrne). Maurice retained his governorship till September 1812. He had no further employment, and was retired with the rank of rear-admiral on 1 Oct. 1846. He died at Stonehouse on 4 Sept. 1857 in his eighty-third year.

Maurice married, in October 1814, Miss Sarah Lyne of Plymouth, but was left a widower in the following June.

[Marshall's Roy. Nav. Biog. v. (Suppl. pt. i.) 434; O'Byrne's Dict. of Naval Biog.; Gent. Mag. 1857, pt. ii. p. 569; James's Naval Hist. (edit. of 1860); Chevalier's Hist. de la Marine française sous le Consulat et l'Empire.] J. K. L.

MAURICE, THOMAS (1754–1824), oriental scholar and historian, came of an ancient Welsh family which claimed connection with the princes of Powis, and descent from Eineon (*fl.* 1093) [q. v.] His father, Thomas, was articled to a West India merchant, made several voyages to the West Indies, and after a three years' settlement at Jamaica opened an academy at Clapham, and married an elderly lady with some property. In 1737 he was elected head-master of a school at Hertford belonging to Christ's Hospital. His first wife had died, and Thomas, the eldest of six children by a second, was born at Hertford in 1754. His father died in 1763 and his mother married an Irish methodist, who is said to have treated her badly, while Thomas was sent to Christ's Hospital, thence to Ealing, and subsequently, through his mother's influence, to Kingswood School, Bath. Taking chambers in the Inner Temple, he found the study of classical and English literature more attractive than that of law, and under the tuition of Dr. Samuel Parr [q. v.], at Stanmore, devoted himself to classics. On 6 May 1774 he matriculated from St. John's College, Oxford, migrated after a year to University College, and graduated B.A. in 1778 and M.A. in 1808. While at Oxford he published a translation of the Œdipus Tyrannus, for which Dr. Johnson wrote a preface (Hill, *Boswell*, iii. 370 *n.* 2) and some English poems. He was ordained by Bishop Lowth on leaving Oxford and became curate of Woodford, Essex; he was also, through the influence of Dr. Johnson, offered the curacy of Bosworth. In 1785 he relinquished his curacy for the chapel of Epping, and about the same time purchased the chaplaincy of the 97th regiment, which was disbanded soon afterwards, and Maurice received half-pay for the rest of his life. In 1798 he was presented by Earl Spencer to the vicarage of Wormleighton, Warwickshire; in the same year he became assistant keeper of manuscripts in the British Museum, and in 1804, on the presentation of the lord-chancellor, vicar of Cudham, Kent. All these offices he retained until his death. In 1800 he obtained, through Bishop Tomline [q. v.], the pension which had been enjoyed by Cowper. Maurice died on 30 March 1824 in his apartments at the British Museum. In 1786 he married the daughter of Thomas Pearce, a captain in the service of the East India Company; she died in 1790.

Maurice was on intimate terms with many of the foremost of his contemporaries. He was an industrious student, a voluminous author, and one of the first to popularise a knowledge of the history and religions of the east; but Byron, in his 'English Bards and Scotch Reviewers,' described Maurice as 'dull,' and his poem on 'Richmond Hill' as 'the petrifactions of a plodding brain.' His principal works are: 1. 'Poems and Miscellaneous Pieces,' 1779, 4to. 2. 'Westminster Abbey, an elegiac poem,' 1784, 4to; another edition with other poems was published in 1813, 8vo. 3. 'Indian Antiquities,' 7 vols. 1793–1800, 8vo; another edition 1794–1800 and 1806. 4. 'History of Hindostan,' 2 vols. 1795–8, 4to; 2nd edition, 3 vols. 1820. 5. 'Sanscreet Fragments,' 1798. 6. 'A Dissertation on the Oriental Trinities,' 1800, 8vo, extracted from the 4th and 5th volumes of the 'Indian Antiquities.' 7. 'Poems: epistolary, lyric, and elegiacal,' 1800, 8vo. 8. 'Modern History of Hindostan,' 2 vols. 1802–10, 8vo. 9. 'The Crisis of Britain,' 1803, 4to; a poem addressed to Pitt. 10. 'Select Poems,' 1803, 8vo. 11. 'A Vindication of the Modern History of Hindostan,' 1805, 8vo. 12. 'Elegy on the late Rt. Hon. W. Pitt' [1806], 8vo. 13. 'The Fall of the Mogul: a Tragedy,' 1806. 14. 'Richmond Hill, a descriptive and historical Poem,' 1807. 15. 'Brahminical Fraud Detected,' 1812, 8vo; another edition, entitled 'The Indian Sceptic Refuted,' 1813, 8vo. 16. 'Observations connected with Astronomy,' 1816, 4to; another edition, 1816, 8vo. 17. 'Memoirs,' 1819–22, 8vo. He also published numerous other poems, several of them being odes on the deaths of well-known persons.

[Memoirs of the Author of Indian Antiquities; Brit. Mus. Cat.; Gent. Mag. 1824, i. 467–72; Georgian Era; Nichols's Lit. Illustrations, ii. 661, 663, 848, viii. 187; Lit. Anecdotes, iii. 242; Hill's Boswell, iii. 370 *n.* 2; Foster's Alumni Oxon. 1714–1886; Watt's Bibl. Brit.; Biographical Dictionary of Living Authors.]

A. F. P.

MAURICE, WILLIAM (*fl.* 1640–1680), Welsh antiquary, was a gentleman of good family and landed property, and lived at Cevnybraich, in the parish of Llansilin, Denbighshire, where he built a library in which he spent most of his time studying Welsh literature. He was an industrious collector and transcriber of Welsh manuscripts, and his collection is preserved at Wynnstay; a chronological account of the civil war in North Wales from his notebook was published in the 'Archæologia Cambrensis,' i. 33–41. He died between 1680 and 1690.

[Archæologia Cambrensis, i. 33–41; Williams's Eminent Welshmen, p. 318.] A. F. P.

MAVOR, WILLIAM FORDYCE (1758–1837), compiler of educational works, was born on 1 Aug. 1758 at New Deer, Aberdeenshire. In 1775 he became an assistant in a school at Burford, Oxfordshire, and he subsequently taught a school at Woodstock. After instructing the children of the Duke of Marlborough in writing, he obtained a title for holy orders in 1781. In 1789 the duke gave him the vicarage of Hurley, Berkshire, which he retained until his death; and in the same year the degree of LL.D. was conferred upon him by the university of Aberdeen. He was afterwards presented by the duke to the rectory of Stonesfield, Oxfordshire, which he exchanged in 1810 for the rectory of Bladon-with-Woodstock. On 12 July of that year he was licensed by the bishop to the head-mastership of Woodstock grammar school. In 1808 he was elected mayor of Woodstock, and served the office ten times. He died on 29 Dec. 1837, and was buried at Woodstock, where there is a tablet to his memory.

Mavor was a successful compiler of educational books, many of which, particularly 'The English Spelling Book,' 1801, passed through numerous editions. He also invented a system of shorthand, which he explained in a treatise entitled 'Universal Stenography,' 8vo, 1779 (2nd edit. 1785, and several later editions).

His other writings are: 1. 'The Springs of Parnassus, or Poetic Miscellanies,' 8vo, 1779. 2. 'Poetical Cheltenham Guide,' 12mo, 1781. 3. 'The Geographical Magazine,' 2 vols. 4to, 1781, published under the name of Martyn. 4. 'Dictionary of Natural History,' 2 vols. fol. 1784, issued under the same pseudonym. 5. 'Elegy to the Memory of Captain James King,' 4to, London 1785. 6. 'Blenheim, a poem, to which is added a Blenheim Guide,' 4to, 1787. 7. 'New Description of Blenheim,' 8vo, 1789 (many subsequent editions). A French version appeared in 1791. At page 124 Mavor states that he had for several years been making collections for a history of Woodstock, which, however, never appeared. 8. 'Vindiciæ Landavenses, or Strictures on the Bishop of Landaff's Charge' (Bishop Watson), 4to, 1792. 9. 'Poems,' 8vo, 1793. 10. 'Appendix to the Eton Latin Grammar,' 12mo, 1796. 11. 'The Youth's Miscellany, or a Father's Gift to his Children,' 12mo, 1797 (reprinted in 2 vols. 1805 and 1814). 12. 'Historical Account of the most celebrated Voyages, Travels, and Discoveries from the time of Columbus to the present period,' 25 vols. 12mo, 1798–1802. 13. 'The British Tourists, or Traveller's Pocket Companion through England, Wales, Scotland, and Ireland,' 6 vols. 12mo, 1798–1800, a series of tours by various authors. The third edition, 1809, contained a reprint, with alterations and omissions, of Mavor's 'Tour in Wales in 1805,' which had been published anonymously by Sir Richard Phillipps in 1806, and in that form is now rare. 14. 'The British Nepos, or . . . Lives of Illustrious Britons,' 12mo, 1798 (many editions). 15. 'Elements of Natural History,' 12mo, 1799. 16. 'The Young Gentleman's and Lady's Magazine,' 2 vols. 12mo, 1799. 17. 'Natural History,' 12mo, London, 1800 (2nd edit. 1801). 18. 'The Lady's and Gentleman's Botanical Pocket Book,' 12mo, 1800. 19. 'A Selection of the Lives of Plutarch,' abridged, 12mo, 1800. 20. 'The Modern Traveller, with illustrative notes,' 4 vols. 12mo, 1800. 21. 'Classical English Poetry for the use of young persons,' 12mo, 1801, edited in conjunction with Samuel Jackson Pratt. 22. 'The New Speaker, or English Class Book,' 12mo, 1801. 23. 'Universal History, ancient and modern . . . to the General Peace of 1801,' 25 vols. 18mo, 1802–1804. 24. 'The History of Greece,' 2 vols. 12mo, 1804. 25. 'The History of Rome,' 3 vols. 12mo, 1804. 26. 'The History of England,' 2 vols. 12mo, 1804. 27. 'Proverbs, or the Wisdom of all Nations,' 12mo, 1804. 28. 'Holmes's Art of Rhetoric made easy,' improved, 12mo, 1807. 29. 'A Circle of the Arts and Sciences,' 12mo, 1808. 30. 'The Eton Latin Grammar, with explanatory notes,' 12mo, 1809. 31. 'General View of the Agriculture of Berkshire,' 8vo, London 1809, undertaken for the board of agriculture. 32. 'The Mother's Catechism; or first principles of Knowledge,' 12mo, 1809. 33. 'Catechism of General Knowledge,' 12mo, 1809. 34. 'The Catechism of Health,' 12mo, 1809. 35. 'Collection of Catechisms,' 2 vols. 12mo, 1810. 36. 'General Collection of Voyages and Travels,' 28 vols. 12mo, London 1810. 37. 'The Garland: a selection of short poems . . . a new edition,' 12mo, London 1812. 38. 'Catechism of the Biography of some of the more eminent Britons,' 12mo, London 1820. 39. 'Catechism of the History of Scotland and of Ireland . . . with an Appendix respecting Wales,' 12mo, London 1820. Mavor also published a new edition of Blackwall's 'Introduction to the Classics,' 12mo, 1809, abridged Bourgoanne's 'State of Spain,' 12mo, 1812, and edited with notes and a glossary Thomas Tusser's 'Five Hundred Points of Good Husbandrie,' 4to, 1812. To a selection from his works—'Miscellanies,' Oxford, 1829—was prefixed his portrait, engraved in mezzotint by C. Turner, A.R.A., after Saxon.

[Gent. Mag. 1838 i. 434–5, 1841 ii. 252; Marshall's Early Hist. of Woodstock Manor; Notes and Queries, passim; Brit. Mus. Cat.] G. G.

MAWBEY, Sir JOSEPH (1730–1798), politician, born at Ravenstone, in a house partly in Derbyshire and partly in Leicestershire, on 2 Dec. 1730, was fourth son and youngest child of John Mawbey, who died 4 Sept. 1754, aged 61, by his first wife, Martha, daughter of Thomas Pratt, who died in September 1737. Both were buried at Ravenstone, where Joseph erected in 1764, on the north wall of the chancel, a mural monument to the memory of his parents and ancestors. When about ten years old he was removed to Surrey by his uncle, Joseph Pratt, chief owner of a distillery at Vauxhall, to be trained for the ministry of the English church, but in consequence of the serious illness of another nephew of Pratt, a partner in the distillery, he was taken into the business at the age of seventeen, and carried it on for many years with his brother John. On his uncle's death in 1754, Joseph Mawbey inherited considerable property in Surrey and established himself as a landed proprietor. He was sheriff of the county in 1757, bought the estate of Botleys in Chertsey in 1763, on which he built a large house, and for about twenty-seven years acted, on the whole with considerable success, as chairman of the Surrey quarter sessions. From 1761 to 1768 and from 1768 to 1774 he sat for Southwark, Henry Thrale, Johnson's friend, being his colleague from 1765. In 1774 he contested the county of Surrey, but through the coalition of the interests of four other candidates he was defeated, though 1,390 votes were given for him. On a chance vacancy in June 1775 he was at the head of the poll; he was in the same position in 1780, when he incurred the odium of some of his whig supporters through his refusal to coalesce with Admiral Keppel; and in April 1784 he was returned without a contest. Originally in opposition to toryism, he became a supporter of Pitt; after 1790, however, he ceased to sit in parliament. By his first friends in politics he was created a baronet (30 July 1765), and another distinction on which he plumed himself was his friendship with Speaker Onslow. He died at Botleys, 16 June 1798, and was buried in the family vault in the chancel of Chertsey Church, where his wife and several of his children had preceded him. He married in August 1760 Elizabeth, only surviving daughter of his cousin, Richard Pratt of Vauxhall, and on her brother's death in 1766 she succeeded to considerable property. She died at Botleys, 19 Aug. 1790, having had nine children, four of whom were then alive. The second and last baronet was Sir Joseph Mawbey, who died 28 Aug. 1817. The estate of

Botleys was sold by his trustees in 1822. Several members of the family of Pratt were buried at Lambeth, and a monument was erected by Mawbey to their memory in 1779. His portrait by R. E. Pine, a three-quarter length, with table covered with 'votes' and with a book in his left hand lettered 'Sidney' and opened at 'On Government,' was engraved by John Dixon. An engraving of him by T. Holloway appeared in the 'European Magazine,' March 1787.

Mawbey, though leaning for many years to the side of the whigs, professed to be above party, and so was ridiculed by the wits of either side. Walpole calls him 'vain, noisy, and foolish.' Among the best-known lines in the 'Rolliad' are those referring to Speaker Cornwall's 'unhappy fate' who hears

Fox, North, and Burke, but hears Sir Joseph too.

Other passages in the same poem allude to his voice, his knowledge 'in grain,' and to the fact that

Sir Joseph is as witty as he's good.

The last of the translations of Lord Belgrave's quotation in the 'Political Miscellanies' at the end of the 'Rolliad' is assigned to him, and he is introduced by Gillray into his caricatures of ancient music (10 May 1787) and 'A Pig in a Poke' (10 Dec. 1788). On 14 Nov. 1768 Wilkes presented a petition through him, and numerous speeches by him on the proceedings against Wilkes are reported in Sir Henry Cavendish's 'Debates.' He was author of 'The Battle of Epsom. A New Ballad' [anon.], 1763, on a meeting convened to return an address of thanks for the recent peace; the first production printed by Wilkes at his private press, and it was reprinted for sale at Guildford and in London in the same year. He is also credited with some 'Reflections on the French Revolution.' For many years he was a contributor in prose and verse to the 'Gentleman's Magazine,' the chief of his communications being 'Account of Elections for Surrey,' 1788, pt. ii. pp. 975, 1052–3, and 'Account of Thomas, or "Hesiod" Cooke,' 1791, pt. ii. and 1792, pt. i. A road-certificate which he had given when late in life caused him so much trouble that he printed 'A Letter to the Magistrates of Surrey' in vindication of his conduct, which is given in the 'Gentleman's Magazine,' 1797, pt. i. pp. 379–80, and an account of an unfortunate altercation with Richard Wyatt is in the 'Westminster Magazine,' February 1773, p. 157. A volume of 'Miscellaneous Pieces, by Leonard Howard, Rector of St. George's, Southwark,' 1765, was dedicated to Mawbey, who wrote a letter to Howard, which is inserted in the 'Gentleman's Magazine,' 1797, pt. ii. pp. 742–3. Several letters by him belong to the Marquis of Lansdowne (*Hist. MSS. Comm.* 6th Rep. App. p. 240).

[Gent. Mag. 1790 pt. ii. pp. 649, 748, 769, 1798 pt. i. p. 543, pt. ii. p. 622; European Mag. 1787, pt. i. pp. 139–40; Leicestershire Collections in Bibl. Topogr. Britannica, viii. 1397-1408 (by himself); Nichols's Leicestershire, vol. iii. pt. ii. pp. 931–9; Manning and Bray's Surrey, iii. 222–223, 234–5, 488–9, 513; Admiral Keppel's Life, ii. 286–8; Wright and Evans on Gillray's Caricatures, pp. 20, 27; J. C. Smith's Portraits, i. 212–213; Walpole's George III, iii. 260–1, 275–6, 281, 318, 400, iv. 293; Notes and Queries, 2nd ser. ix. 342, 452, 4th ser. i. 581, xi. 485, xii. 119, 458, 513.] W. P. C.

MAWE, JOHN (1764–1829), mineralogist, was born in Derbyshire in 1764. In early life he appears to have spent fifteen years at sea. About the end of the century he made a tour of most of the mines in England and Scotland, collecting minerals for the cabinet of the king of Spain.

In August 1804 he started on a voyage to Rio de la Plata. He had reached Cadiz when war broke out between England and Spain, and he was blockaded in the town where he was taken ill and nearly died. He sailed from Cadiz in March 1805 for Montevideo, and on reaching that town was imprisoned as an English spy. He procured his liberty soon after, but was interned, and did not obtain his release till the capture of Montevideo by General Beresford in 1806. He accompanied the expedition under General Whitelocke to Buenos Ayres, and on his return to Montevideo purchased a schooner and sailed to Brazil, putting in at various ports on the way. He was well received in Brazil by the prince regent, Dom Pedro, who gave him permission to visit the diamond mines of Minas Geraes and other parts of the interior during 1809–10, and also granted him access to the government archives.

Mawe returned to London in 1811, and opening a shop in the Strand, close to Somerset House, became well known as a practical mineralogist. He died in London on 26 Oct. 1829. A tablet to his memory is in Castleton church, Derbyshire. The business was afterwards carried on by James Tennant [q. v.] the mineralogist.

Mawe's principal work was the account of his South American voyage, 'Travels in the Interior of Brazil,' 4to, London, 1812; Philadelphia, 1816; 2nd edit. 8vo, 1823. He also wrote: 1. 'The Mineralogy of Derbyshire,' 8vo, London, 1802. 2. 'A Treatise on Diamonds and Precious Stones,' 8vo,

London, 1813; 2nd ed. 1823. 3. 'A Catalogue of Minerals,' 12mo, London, 1815. 4. 'A Descriptive Catalogue of Minerals,' &c., 8vo, London, 1816; 4th edit. 12mo, London, 1821; reissued in 1823. 5. 'Familiar Lessons on Mineralogy and Geology,' 12mo, London, 1819; 10th edit. 12mo, 1828. 6. 'Amateur Lapidary's Guide,' 3rd edit. 8vo, London, 1823; 12mo, London, 1827. 7. 'Instructions for the use of the Blow-pipe and Chemical Tests,' 4th edit. 12mo, London, 1825. 8. 'The Voyager's Companion or Shell-Collector's Pilot,' 16mo, London, 1821; 4th edit. 1825. 9. 'The Linnæan System of Conchology,' 8vo, London, 1823. He edited the 2nd edit. of 'Wodarch's Introduction to . . . Conchology,' 8vo, London, 1822, and wrote a paper on 'The Occurrence of Diamonds, &c., in Brazil' for Gilbert's 'Annalen' lix. (1818), besides one 'On the Tourmaline and Apatite of Devonshire' for the 'Quart. Journ. of Science,' iv. (1818). He appears also to have issued at some time 'Directions to Captains of Ships, Officers, and Travellers; particularly to those engaged in the South Sea Fishery' (for collecting shells). A manuscript paper 'On a Gold Mine in South America' is preserved in the library of the Geological Society.

[Appleton's Cyclop. of American Biog.; Mawe's Works, Nos. 1, 8, and Travels in Brazil. Rose and others wrongly give his christian name as Joseph.] B. B. W.

MAWE or MAW, LEONARD (*d.* 1629), bishop of Bath and Wells, son of Simon Mawe, gentleman, of Rendlesham, Suffolk, by his wife Margery, daughter and co-heiress of Thomas Wyld of Yorkshire, by his wife Alice, daughter and heiress of John Jago of Suffolk (Wood), was born at Rendlesham, and educated at Cambridge, where he was admitted fellow of Peterhouse in 1595, and having proceeded M.A. was incorporated at Oxford in 1599. He was proctor of the university of Cambridge, 1609, was chosen master of Peterhouse, 1617, and vice-chancellor, 1621. He held a prebend at Wells, and was chaplain to Charles, prince of Wales. When Charles was in Spain in 1623, King James sent Mawe and Matthew Wren [q. v.], afterwards bishop of Ely, along with other officers and attendants, to join him, charging the chaplains to fit up a room chapel-wise, hold prayers twice a day, and generally so to manage as to commend the English service to the Spaniards (Gardiner). Mawe and the rest set sail on 3 April. During his journey through Spain he had a fall from his mule, 'lighting on his head and shoulders' (Wynn). The prince was obliged to send orders that the greater part of the company was to return to England without coming on to Madrid, and Mawe returned through France. As a reward for his services he was appointed master of Trinity College by patent in 1625. Before he left Peterhouse he gave 300*l.* for covering the roof of the chapel then being built there with lead. As master of Trinity College he did much towards freeing that foundation from a heavy debt (Fuller). He used all his influence to secure the election of the Duke of Buckingham as chancellor of the university in 1626, urging the members of his college to vote unanimously for the duke (*Original Letters*). In 1628 he received the see of Bath and Wells, being elected 24 June, and consecrated at Croydon 7 Sept. He died on 2 Sept. 1629 at Chiswick, and was buried in the church there. He was 'a good scholar, a grave preacher, a mild man, and one of gentle deportment' (Fuller). There is a portrait of him in the palace at Wells.

[Wood's Fasti Oxon. vol. i. col. 282, ed. Bliss; Registrum Univ. Oxon. II. i. 355 (Oxf. Hist. Soc.); Fuller's Worthies, ii. 333; Le Neve's Fasti, i. 146, iii. 621, 669, 699, ed. Hardy; State Papers, ed. Hardwicke, i. 406; Cal. State Papers, Chas. I, Dom. 1627, p. 448; Sir Richard Wynn's Account of the Journey of Prince Charles ap. App. to Historia Ric. II. ed. Hearne; notices of the Spanish journey, though without mention of Mawe's name, also in Verney Papers (Camden Soc.); Ellis's Original Letters, vol. iii. pt. i. p. 229; Gardiner's Prince Charles and the Spanish Marriage, ii. 330, 337 (History of England, v. 35, 43); Willis and Clark's Architectural History of Cambridge, i. 42; Godwin, De Præsulibus Angliæ, p. 392.] W. H.

MAWSON, MATTHIAS (1683-1770), bishop of Ely, was born in August 1683, his father being a prosperous brewer at Chiswick, Middlesex. He was educated at St. Paul's School, whence he was admitted in 1701 to Corpus Christi College, Cambridge. He graduated B.A. 1704, M.A. 1708, B.D. 1716, D.D. 1725, and was elected a fellow of his society in 1707, and a moderator in the university in 1708. On 6 Oct. 1724 he was chosen master of his college, and held the office till 20 Feb. 1744. Soon after his appointment he was presented by Bishop Green to the rectory of Conington in Cambridgeshire, and afterwards to that of Hadstock in Essex; the latter he held for many years. In 1730 and 1731 he was vice-chancellor of the university, and signalised his term of office by several useful reforms. Academic exercises were made more stringent and orderly; capricious migration from college to college was checked; and the practice of exhuming bodies from the neighbouring churchyard, for dissection by students of medicine, was prohibited.

After refusing the bishopric of Gloucester in 1734, Dr. Mawson was consecrated bishop of Llandaff, 18 Feb. 1738–9. This diocese he administered for two years, and in 1740 was translated to Chichester. Thence, on the death of Sir Thomas Gooch in 1754, he was translated to Ely, where he remained for the rest of his life. He died unmarried at his house in Kensington Square, 23 Nov. 1770, aged eighty-seven years and three months, having been 'active and healthy to a very little time before his death' (*Cole MSS.* xlvii. 86). He was buried in his cathedral of Ely, and a monument was erected to his memory by his chaplain and executor, Dr. Warren, under the second window of the north aisle of the choir. A drawing of it, with the inscription and arms (party per bend sinister, ermine and ermines, a lion rampant, or, impaling those of the diocese) is preserved by Cole (*ib.*)

Bishop Mawson's official income and his inheritance of the fortune made by his brother in the family business gave him great wealth, and Cole expatiates on his liberality. To King's College, Cambridge, he lent some 6,000*l.* or 7,000*l.* for their new buildings. At Ely he 'gave 1,000*l.* in money, with the painting of the east window, and intended to pave the choir with white marble at his own expense' (*ib.* xxiii. ff. 64–5). He also endowed his old college in 1754 with property sufficient to found twelve scholarships, amounting to 400*l.* per annum in all (Potts, *Liber Scholasticus*, 1843, p. 99.)

Mawson's published works consist only of single sermons, preached at anniversary gatherings, and the like, and a speech made before the gentlemen of Sussex, at Lewes, 11 Oct. 1745, on the occasion of the Jacobite rising.

[Authorities quoted; Masters's History of C. C. C. C., 1753, pp. 195 sqq.; Nichols's Lit. Anecd. iv. 459 *n.*; Nichols's Lit. Illustrations, viii. 537; Le Neve's Fasti. ii. 255, &c.; Faulkner's Kensington, p. 398; Gardiner's Admission Registers of St. Paul's School. Some letters of Bishop Mawson to the Duke of Newcastle will be found in the Additional and Egerton MSS. 32694 sqq.] J. H. L.

MAXEY, ANTHONY (*d.* 1618), dean of Windsor, apparently a native of Essex, was educated on the foundation at Westminster School (Welch, *Alumni Westmon.* ed. 1852, p. 54), whence he was elected to Trinity College, Cambridge, on 18 April 1578 (*College Admission Register*), and graduated B.A. in 1581, M.A. in 1585, B.D. in 1594, and D.D. in 1608 (*University Register*), but he failed to obtain a fellowship at Trinity. James I, out of admiration for his florid pulpit eloquence and dislike of tobacco, made him his chaplain, and on 21 June 1612 appointed him dean of Windsor and registrar of the order of the Garter (Le Neve, *Fasti*, ed. Hardy, iii. 375). Maxey was a simonist of the first water. He offered money to Sir Henry Hobart [q. v.] for preferment (letter in *Tanner MS.* cclxxxiii. 195), and two months before his death made the highest bid for the vacant see of Norwich (*Cal. State Papers*, Dom. 1611–18, p. 532). He died on 3 May 1618, and was buried in the church of St. Martin-in-the-Fields, London, his wife having predeceased him without issue. By will he made liberal provision for his poor kinsfolk and servants, but 'unto Roger my cooke, beinge verye lewde in his tongue, and besides corrupting my clarke, Roberte Berrye, with tobacco and drinckinge,' he bequeathed nothing, 'neyther in money nor mourninge cloke.' He left his books, or as many as the authorities cared to take, to 'our publique library,' presumably that of the university of Cambridge (will registered in P. C. C. 47, Meade).

Maxey published three sermons preached before the king, with the title 'The Churches Sleepe' and 'The Golden Chaine of Mans Saluation, and the fearefull point of hardening,' 3 pts. 8vo, London, 1606; 3rd edit. 1607. Other editions with additional sermons, were issued in1610, 1614, 1619, and 1634.

[Information from J. Willis Clark, esq, and William White, esq.; Cole MS. xlv. 295; Cat. of Books in Brit. Mus. to 1640; Hackman's Cat. of Tanner MSS. p. 1022; Cat. of Harsnett Library, Colchester, p. 110.] G. G.

MAXFIELD, THOMAS (*d.* 1616), Roman catholic priest, born at Chesterton Hall, of an old Staffordshire family, was son of William Maxfield, mentioned in the 'Hatfield MSS.' (i. 576, iv. 272) as a recusant in Staffordshire who was at liberty in 1592; at the time of his birth his mother and father were both prisoners for recusancy. In early youth he was sent to the English seminary at Douay, where he arrived on 16 March 1603. He was compelled to return to England in 1610 on account of ill-health, but recovered, and in 1614 was again at Douay, where he was ordained on the presentation of Dr. Matthew Kellison [q. v.], the president of the college. He was sent on a mission to England in 1615, but had not landed three months before he was arrested, on a visit to Gatehouse prison, where, after examination, he was confined for some months. On 24 June 1616 he attempted to escape by means of a cord from his window, but on reaching the ground was seized and placed in a more secure and disagreeable cell. On 26 June he was tried at Newgate, and offered pardon if he would take the oath of allegiance; he refused, and, in spite of the intercession of the Spanish ambassador, was executed on 1 July. A few days before his trial he wrote a letter to Dr. Kellison; it is still preserved in Douay College, and was printed in Challoner's 'Martyrs.'

Challoner supplies a somewhat fanciful picture of Maxfield in prison. Granger (i. 376) supposes him to be one of the 'Jesuits and priests in council' depicted in a print in the second volume of the 'Vox Populi' by Thomas Scott.

[Douai Diaries, i. 21, 35; Coppie d'une lettre envoyée d'Angleterre au Seminaire des Anglois à Douai, Douay, 1616; Vita et Martyrium D. Thomæ Maxfildæi, Douay, 1617; Brevis Narratio Martyrii Thomæ Maxfeildii, printed in vol. i. of the Miscellany of the Abbotsford Club from the Balfour MSS. in the Advocates' Library; Hist. MSS. Comm., Hatfield House MSS. iv. 272; Challoner's Martyrs to the Roman Catholic Faith, ii. 68–77, and Modern British Martyrology, iii. 57–64; Granger's Biog. Hist. i. 376; Dod's Church Hist. ii. 378.] A. F. P.

MAXFIELD, THOMAS (*d.* 1784), Wesleyan, a native of Bristol, of humble origin, was converted by John Wesley during his first visit to the city in 1739. The 'conversion' took place on 1 May. In March 1740 he was travelling with Charles Wesley, and remained with him 'for a year or two.' At the conference of 1766 Wesley spoke of Maxfield as the first layman who 'desired to help him as a son in the gospel,' but in his last journal Joseph Humphreys is said to have been 'the first lay preacher that assisted me in England in the year 1738' (Southey, *Life of Wesley*, i. 511; cf. Tyerman, *Life and Times of John Wesley*, i. 276 *n.*, and New, *Life of Lady Huntingdon*, i. 32).

Maxfield seems early to have gained the confidence of Charles's brother John, who on 21 April 1741 wrote: 'I am not clear that brother Maxfield should not expound at Greyhound Lane; nor can I as yet do without him' (Wesley, *Works*, xii. 102; Tyerman, i. 369–70). In 1742, when Wesley left London, he gave Maxfield the charge of the Foundery Society, directing him to pray with the members and give them suitable advice. Maxfield soon passed from praying to preaching, and Lady Huntingdon, who was a constant attendant at the chapel, was impressed by his talents, and 'exhorted him to expound the scriptures.' Many shared Lady Huntingdon's admiration, but others complained to Wesley that Maxfield had usurped the sacred office without being called to it. Wesley hastened back to London, deeply displeased. His mother deprecated his anger, and asserted that Maxfield was 'surely called of God to preach.' After Wesley heard Maxfield he decided the dispute in his favour, and became a convert to lay preaching.

In June 1745 Maxfield, while preaching in Cornwall, was pressed for the navy, but the captain to whom he was taken refused to have him on board, and he was thrown into prison at Penzance. When about to be released he was handed over to the military authorities through the intervention of the Rev. William Borlase of Ludgvan, who was very hostile to the methodists. Wesley, who was preaching in the neighbourhood, rode over on the 19th to Crowan Church-town, where Maxfield was confined, and examined the warrant; and on the 21st attended the meeting of the justices at Marazion, by whom Maxfield was given over to the military (Wesley, *Journal*, 1745). He served in the army for several years. After his discharge he was at Wesley's request ordained at Bath by Dr. Barnard, bishop of Derry. From this time he was one of Wesley's chief assistants, as well as an assistant chaplain to the Countess of Huntingdon.

Maxfield, however, was ambitious, and soon created dissatisfaction in the minds of the more sober methodists. As early as 1760 he encouraged 'the select band in London . . . who professed to be entirely sanctified,' who saw visions and 'began to have a contempt for those who had not.' At the conference of 1761 Maxfield silenced his accusers (Wesley, *Works*, iii. 120), but Wesley wrote to him subsequently respecting the complaints made of his views, and Maxfield defended his position.

At the beginning of 1762 Wesley wrote to his brother Charles: 'If Thos. Maxfield continue as he is, it is impossible he should long continue with us.' About the same time Fletcher of Madeley, who was well acquainted with Maxfield, asserted that 'spiritual pride, stubbornness, party spirit, uncharitableness, prophetic mistakes — in short, every sinew of enthusiasm is now at work among them [i.e. Maxfield and his friends].' In the course of the year the crisis became more acute. Maxfield had adopted a prediction made by George Bell, a fellow-minister, sharing his mystical opinions that the world would end on 28 Feb. 1763. Wesley openly preached against him on 23 Jan., but with little effect. 'All this time,' he writes, Maxfield 'was continually spiriting up all with whom I was intimate against me; he told them I was not capable of teaching them, and insinuated that none was but himself' (WESLEY, *Journal*, 7 Jan. 1763). Whether Maxfield was or was not one of the 'two or three' of Bell's friends whom Wesley met and tried to convince of the falsity of the prophecy does not appear. He subsequently denied his own belief in it, and charged Wesley himself with sharing in it.

Maxfield's conduct rendered a schism in the society inevitable. In February 1763 he practically told Wesley 'You take too much upon you.' He was deaf to all Wesley's arguments respecting the danger of separation (WESLEY, *Works*, xii. 116–17), and on 28 April he fully and finally separated himself from Wesley, taking Bell and about two hundred others with him. He was now chosen preacher by a society in Snow's Fields, whence he removed two or three years later to Ropemakers' Alley, Moorfields. There he had a large congregation. He finally set up in Princes Street, Moorfields, where he preached till about 1767. From the time of his secession Maxfield became Wesley's worst enemy. 'He spake all manner of evil of me, his father, his friend, his greatest earthly benefactor.'

In February 1770 he met Wesley once more at the Countess of Huntingdon's house in Portland Row, where he preached against the doctrine of Christian perfection, of which he had formerly been a zealous upholder. Two years later he professed to desire a reunion. Wesley saw him, but his confidence in him was not restored (TYERMAN, iii. 115).

In 1778 Maxfield published a pamphlet charging the Wesleys with turning the hearts of the people from Whitefield during his absence in America, and John Wesley replied with 'A Letter to the Rev. Thomas Maxfield, occasioned by a late Publication.' In 1779 there was more talk of reunion. Charles Wesley insisted that an acknowledgment on Maxfield's part of his 'fault' was a needful preliminary. Wesley still expressed much personal affection for him (*ib.* p. 296, from *Methodist Magazine*, 1826 and 1789), but nothing came of the negotiations. Wesley, nevertheless, visited Maxfield in his last illness, and preached in his chapel (WESLEY, *Works*, iv. 132). Maxfield died at his house in Moorfields on 18 March 1784.

He married Elizabeth Branford, a lady of means, who was one of Whitefield's earliest followers. She died on 23 Nov. 1777, and left a family.

Maxfield was a man of some ability, and an eloquent preacher. Fletcher of Madeley wrote to Charles Wesley, a few months after his secession: 'I believe him sincere; and though obstinate and suspicious, I am persuaded he has a true desire to know the will and live the life of God' (TYERMAN, ii. 464).

A portrait of Maxfield 'preaching' was twice painted by T. Beach, and engraved in one case by P. Dawe, and in the other by Houston. A third portrait of him 'with his wife and family' was executed in 1772 (BROMLEY, *Catalogue of Portraits*, p. 365).

Maxfield published: 1. 'A Short Account of Mr. Murgetroyd during the Last Month of his Life,' &c., Bath, 1771. 2. 'A Short Account of the Particular Circumstances of the Life and Death of William Davies, who was Executed 11 Dec. 1776, with his Speech at Tyburn,' &c., London, 1776. 3. 'A Short Account of God's Dealings with Mrs. Elizabeth Maxfield' (his wife), 1778, 8vo. This contains three letters to her from Whitefield, dated 16 Jan. 1738, 16 Nov. 1738 (from Kilrush), and 3 Nov. 1739 (Philadelphia). 4. 'A Short Account of the Circumstances that Happened the Last Seven Days before the Death of T. Sherwood,' 1778. Also 'A Collection of Psalms and Hymns extracted from various Authors,' 1778, 12mo; and a sermon, 'Christ the Great Gift of God and the Nature of Faith in Him,' 1769.

[Tyerman's Life of Wesley, 3 vols. passim; Larrabee's Wesley and his Coadjutors, ed. Tefft, i. 217–19, 264; Jackson's Life of Charles Wesley, ii. 207, 218; New's Memorials of the Countess of Huntingdon, pp. 32–4, 226; Overton's John Wesley, pp. 163–4; Bogue and Bennett's Hist. Prot. Dissenters, 2nd edit. ii. 35; Wilson's Dissenting Churches, iv. 283; Gent. Mag. 1784, i. 239; Brit. Mus. Cat.] G. LE G. N.

MAXSE, SIR HENRY BERKELEY FITZHARDINGE (1832–1883), governor of Heligoland, the son of James Maxse (*d.* 1864) of Effingham Hill, Surrey, and Caroline, daughter of the fifth Earl of Berkeley, was born in 1832, and entered the army on 1 June 1849 as a lieutenant in the grenadier guards, changing on 11 June 1852 to the 13th light dragoons, and on 6 July to the 21st foot. He became captain in the Coldstream guards on 29 Dec. 1854, and in the same year was ordered to the Crimea; he served throughout the war on the staff of the Earl of Cardigan, was present at the Alma, Balaclava (where he was wounded), and the siege of Sebastopol, and won the Crimean medal and clasps, besides Turkish medals and the decoration of the fifth class of the Medjidie. In 1855 he became a major. In 1863 he was promoted to be lieutenant-colonel in the army, out of which he sold on 22 Dec. 1873. In 1863 he went to Heligoland as lieutenant-governor, and was appointed governor in February 1864. His long tenure of the government was an eventful one for the island. The reformed constitution was established in 1868, the gaming-tables were abolished in 1870, and Maxse had to face the consequent financial difficulties and complaints of the islanders. Under him also Heligoland was joined by telegraph cable to the mainland. In 1881 Maxse became governor of Newfoundland, but never really settled there. He died at St. John's on 10 Sept. 1883.

Maxse was a good German scholar, and published an English translation of Prince Bismarck's 'Letters to his Wife and Sisters, 1844 to 1870.' He was fond of acting. He was popular in Germany. where he spent his yearly vacations, and married a daughter of Herr von Rudloff.

[Colonial Office List, 1882; Times, 11 Sept. 1883; Burke's Knightage, 1883.] C. A. H.

MAXWELL, CAROLINE ELIZABETH SARAH, Lady Stirling (1808–1887), poet and novelist. [See Norton.]

MAXWELL, Sir GEORGE CLERK (1715–1784). [See Clerk-Maxwell.]

MAXWELL, JAMES (*fl.* 1600–1640), author, born in 1581, was the only son of William Maxwell of Little Airds, and grandson of William Maxwell of Kirkconnell, Kirkcudbrightshire, man-at-arms to James V of Scotland, and also in the service of his queen, Mary of Guise, and of his daughter, Mary Queen of Scots, from her childhood. He was great-great-grandson of Robert, second lord Maxwell, laird of Kirkconnell, from whose second son, Thomas, the Maxwell family of Kirkconnell descended. He was educated at Edinburgh University, where he graduated M.A. 29 July 1600 (*Cat. of Edinb. Graduates*, p. 18), and afterwards went abroad. While in France in 1600 Maxwell wrote in Latin 'Tyrannidi-graphia Ecclesiæ militantis secundum Danielis Prophetiam,' &c., dedicating it to Edinburgh University, whither he sent it, but it was lost on the way (cf. 'A Catalogue of the Author's Exercises and Essaies, &c.,' in *Admirable and Notable Prophecies*). Subsequently he lived for a time in London (*The Golden Art*, Ded.), but again returned to the continent. On 30 April 1631 he wrote from Brussels to Archbishop Laud, complaining of threats of assassination because he would not forsake protestantism. The emperor (Ferdinand II) had, he declared, commanded his presence at court, and offered him spiritual preferment, with the office of imperial antiquary and genealogist, and a pension of a thousand crowns after the death of Sebastian Tegnangel. He 'would rather live poor at home than gather riches abroad by change of religion or sinister employments,' and as he had matters of moment to impart to the king, he desired to return to England soon. In recompense for the many books written by him in defence of the church of England against the puritans, and towards finishing one on the king's genealogy, he solicited the gift of some lay prebend (*Cal. State Papers*, Dom. Ser. 1631–3, p. 25). The appeal was probably unavailing.

Maxwell dealt in his publications with religion, history, genealogy, and antiquarian research, as well as poetry. His style, which was curiously bombastic and nearly allied to that of Sir Thomas Urquhart [q. v.], earned from Laud the name of 'Mountebank Maxwell.' Among his most curious productions is a poem entitled 'Carolanna, That is to say, a Poeme in honovr of ovr King Charles—James, Qveene Anne, And Prince Charles: But principally in honour of the immortall memory of our late noble & good Queene of *Albion* and *Vnion*,' London, by Edw: Allde [1614], 4to (Brit. Mus.) Maxwell here writes under the pseudonym of James Anneson, a play upon the names of the king, queen, and their son. Another very rare work of his is 'The Laudable Life, and Deplorable Death, of our late peerlesse Prince Henry. Briefly represented. Together with some other Poemes, in honor both of our most gracious Soueraigne King *James* his auspicious entrie to this Crowne, and also of his most hopefull Children, Prince *Charles* and Princesse *Elizabeths* happy entrie into this world,' London, by E. Allde, for T. Pauier, 1612, 4to, entered at Stationers' Hall 28 Nov. (Brit. Mus.) The principal poem consists of forty-four six-line stanzas, and is succeeded by 'Peerelesse Prince Henries Epitaph in his owne foure *Languages*' (English, French, Latin, and Greek) (cf. Brydges, *Restituta*, iii. 477–80, and his *British Bibl.* iv. 30–6).

He also published: 1. 'The Golden Legend, or the Mirrour of Religious Men and Godly Matrones, concerning Abraham, Isaac, Jacob, and their Wives,' &c., London, 1611, 8vo. 2. 'The Golden Art, or The right way of Enriching. . . . Very profitable for all such persons in citie or countrie as doe desire to get, increase, conserue, and vse goods with a good conscience,' London, 1611, 4to (Brit. Mus.) 3. 'Queene Elizabeths Looking-glasse of Grace and Glory, wherein may be seen the fortune of the faithfull: that is to say, the wrastling, victory, and reward, or the combat, conquest, and Crowne of Gods children,' &c., London, by E. Allde, 1612, 12mo (Brit. Mus.) 4. 'Jamesanna, or a Pythagoricall play at

Cardes, representing the Excellency and vtilitie of Vnion and Concord, with the incommodities of diuision and discorde, dedicated to the most hopefull Prince Charles,' 1612 (?) 5. 'A Speedy Passage to Heaven, or a perfect direction for every Christian to walk in the right path of true holinesse, containing an explanation of the tenne Commandments, the creede, and our Lords Prayer, with divers other godly prayers,' London, 1612, 8vo. 6. 'A Christian Almanacke, needefull and true for all countryes, persons and times, faithfully calculated by the course of holy Scripture,' London, 1612, 8vo. 7. 'Two Genealogical Tables or Pedigrees of the two most noble Princes *Fredericke* Prince Palatine, and the Lady *Elizabeth* his wife, shewing their Lineall discent equally, first from *Robert* the Emperour, and Prince Palatine, and *Elizabeth* the Empresse his Wife, in the 9 and 10 Degrees, and then from Edward the 3, the most victorious King of England, and Queene *Philippa* his Wife in the 11 Degree.' 8. 'A Monvment of Remembrance erected in Albion, in honour of the magnificent Departvre from Brittannie, and honorable receiuing in Germany, namely at Heidelberge, of the two most noble Princes Fredericke and Elizabeth. . . . Both of them being almost in one and the same degree of lineall descent from 25 Emperours of the East and West, of Romanes, Greekes, and Germans, and from 30 Kings of diuers countries,' London, 1613, 4to (Brit. Mus.) 9. 'Admirable and Notable Prophecies, vttered in former time by 24. famous Romain-Catholickes, concerning the Church of *Romes* defection, Tribulation, and reformation. Written first in Latine, & now published in the English tongue, both by James Maxwell, a Researcher of Antiquities,' London, by Ed: Allde, 1615, 4to (Brit. Mus.) 10. 'A New Eightfold Probation of the Chvrch of Englands Divine Constitvtion, prooved by many Pregnant arguments to be much more complete than any Geneuian in the world against the contrary assertion of the fifty-three petitioner-preachers of Scotland in their petition presented to the Kings most excellent Majesty,' London, 1617 (Brit. Mus.) 11. 'A Demonstrative Defence, or Tenfold Probation of the Doctrine of the Church of England tovching one of the most important points of our Creed, . . . which is of our Sauiours descending into hell after death to binde and subdue Sathan,' &c., London, 1617, 4to, usually bound up with No. 10 (Brit. Mus.) 12. 'Herodian of Alexandria, His History of Twenty Roman Cæsars and Emperors (of his Time), &c. Interpreted out of the Greeke Originall,' London, 1629, 4to (Brit. Mus.); another edit. 1635, 12mo (Brit. Mus.) 13. 'Emblema Animæ, or Morall Discourses reflecting upon Humanitie, by John Du Plessis, Cardinal Richelieu, translated into English,' London, 1635 (Brit. Mus.)

Besides the above Maxwell prepared a catalogue, printed in more than one of his books, of twenty-two works 'not as yet published.' They include many religious treatises on controversial topics, some royal genealogies and panegyrics, a poem on the antiquity of the city of London, tracts on fortune-telling and astrology, 'A Centurie of most noble Questions in Philosophie,' &c., and 'James-anna, or the Patterne of a Perfect Cittie.' The list in 'Carolanna' of works consecrated 'to the immortal memorie of two most noble Brittannish Queenes' contains fifteen more pretentious and fanciful Latin titles of works 'partly written,' among which are: 'Monarchæmeros, Panalbion,' 'Sapientia Cæsarum, seu Manuale Magnatum,' 'Carolidon,' 'Albion-Ibera,' 'Tuba Austriaca,' 'Charilaus seu Philolaus,' 'Rota Fortunæ Aulicorum.'

A second James Maxwell was appointed by Charles I, on 1 Nov. 1629, gentleman-usher of the black rod and custodian of Windsor Little Park (*Lords' Journals*, vii. 7 *b*; GARDINER, *Hist. of England*, vii. 75, ix. 235, 289, 346; TIGHE and DAVIS, *Annals of Windsor*, ii. 178–80; *Cal. State Papers*, 1638–9, p. 586). He held those offices until 1644. Laud remained in custody at this Maxwell's house for ten weeks (1640–1), and was escorted by Maxwell in his own coach to the Tower on 1 March 1641 (*Troubles and Tryals*, p. 174). The archbishop in his diary acknowledges Maxwell's kindness (*ib.*) On 3 June 1644 he was granted leave to go into Scotland 'about his affaires,' and his goods were ordered not to be seized for assessment upon his house near Charing Cross until his return (*Lords' Journals*, vi. 575 *a*).

A third James Maxwell was in attendance, as groom of the bedchamber, on Charles I at Holmby House in 1647 (JESSE, *Mem. of Court of England during the Stuarts*, ii. 117; WOOD, *Athenæ*, iii. 1116, iv. 16). He advanced the king large sums of money, for which jewels were pledged him and afterwards sold (*Cal. State Papers*, Dom. Ser. 1629–31, pp. 11, 99, 173, 174), and he was granted land in Derbyshire (*ib.* 17 June 1631, p. 81) and mines in the Peak country, where he carried on the manufacture of iron by a new process. He was also granted a patent for the manufacture of pipe-clay (*ib.* 1638–9 p. 248, 1639 pp. 384, 513). His brother, Robert Maxwell, was serjeant-at-arms to the House of Commons. This James Maxwell married the widow of one Ryther of Kingston-upon-Thames, surveyor of the stables to

James I, whose daughter, afterwards Jane Whorwood [q. v.], was a strong partisan of Charles I (see Wood, *Athenæ Oxon.* vol. i. p. xxviii; *Cal. State Papers*, Dom. Ser. 1638, p. 256).

It is very doubtful whether either of these Maxwells is to be identified with a fourth James Maxwell of Innerwick, son of John Maxwell of Kirkhouse by Jean Murray, sister of John, first earl of Annandale, who was in 1646 created a peer by the title of Earl of Dirletoun (Douglas, *Peerage*, ed. Wood, i. 418). The latter was, according to Douglas, a gentleman of the king's bedchamber under James I and Charles I; he enjoyed a pension for keeping a light upon the isle of May, and by his wife Elizabeth de Boussoyne was father of two daughters, of whom the younger, Lady Diana, married Charles Cecil, viscount Cranbourne, and was mother of James, third earl of Salisbury [q. v.]

[Fraser's Book of Caerlaverock, i. 600–1; Nichols's Progresses of James I, ii. 507–8; Hist. MSS. Comm. 5th Rep. p. 650; Cal. State Papers, 1631–3 pp. 128, 265, 1638–9 p. 567; Lowndes's Bibl. Manual, iii. 1522; Halkett and Laing's Dict. of Anon. and Pseudon. Lit. i. 310; Bodl. Libr. Cat.; Hazlitt's Handbook to Pop. Lit. 1st ser. 1867, p. 384; Hazlitt's Bibl. Coll. Suppl. 3rd ser. pp. 66, 67; Hunter's Chorus Vatum, Add. MS. 24489, f. 249; Notes and Queries, 8th ser. v. 284.] C. F. S.

MAXWELL, JAMES (1708?–1762), of Kirkconnel, Jacobite, born about 1708, was eldest son of William Maxwell of Kirkconnel, Kirkcudbrightshire, by Janet, daughter of George Maxwell of Carnsalloch, Dumfriesshire, and widow of Colonel John Douglas of Stenhouse. On 21 Aug. 1721 he entered the Catholic College of Douay, of which he was a specially distinguished student. After completing his studies he returned to Scotland in 1728. Like the majority of the Maxwells, the family were hereditary adherents of the Stuarts; and when the father heard in 1745 that his son had joined the Young Chevalier he expressed his supreme satisfaction, and added that if he lost his life in the cause it would be well spent. The only information obtainable regarding Maxwell's connection with the rebellion is that which may be gathered from references in his own 'Narrative of Charles Prince of Wales's Expedition to Scotland in the Year 1745,' written in France after his escape from the battle of Culloden, and printed by the Maitland Club in 1841. In it he states that he was in a position to know 'the most material things that were transacted in the council, though not a member of it,' and that he was an 'eye-witness of the greatest part of what happened in the field.' The probability is that he was attached in some capacity to the staff of the prince, or employed in some kind of secretarial duties. After his return to Scotland in 1750 he built, with bricks made on his estate, the modern portion of Kirkconnel House. The estate of Carnsalloch, which he inherited on the death of his mother in 1755, he sold to Alexander Johnstone, a merchant in London, and purchased the estate of Moble. He died 23 July 1762. By his wife Mary, youngest daughter of Thomas Riddle of Swinburne Castle, Northumberland, he had three sons: James, who succeeded him; William, and Thomas. William in September 1792 started a subscription in London for the French, citing the Corsica subscription as a precedent. His house being mobbed on the day the promoters were to meet, Maxwell slipped away unobserved, and Horne Tooke received the arrivals in his own house, where money was raised and an order for arms sent to Birmingham. In December 1792 he joined the French revolutionary national guard, as a member of which he was present at the execution of Louis XVI in 1793. He afterwards settled as a physician in Dumfries, and died at Edinburgh on 13 Oct. 1834 (Alger, *Englishmen in French Revolution*, pp. 77–8).

[Preface to Narrative of Charles, Prince of Wales's Expedition in 1745 (Maitland Club); Anderson's Scottish Nation; Mackerlie's Lands and their Owners in Galloway, v. 219–20.] T. F. H.

MAXWELL, JAMES (1720–1800), 'Poet in Paisley,' was born at Auchenback, parish of Mearns, Renfrewshire, on 9 May 1720. At the age of twenty he went to England as a packman, became a weaver, and was at various times clerk, usher, schoolmaster, and stone-breaker. In 1787 he became the recipient of a charity in the gift of the town council of Paisley, which he enjoyed till his death in the spring of 1800 (council records). He was one of the most prolific rhymers of his day, usually designating himself 'Poet in Paisley,' and on some of his title-pages adding to his name the letters S.D.P., meant to signify 'student of divine poetry.' He rarely rises above doggerel. A bibliography of his works, comprising fifty-two separate publications, is given in Brown's 'Paisley Poets,' i. 17–23. His chief works are: 1. 'Divine Miscellanies,' Birmingham, 1756. 2. 'Hymns and Spiritual Songs,' London, 1759. 3. 'A new Version of the whole Book of Psalms in Metre,' Glasgow, 1773, in which he exemplifies his objection to the employment of the organ in church by paraphrasing all references to instrumental music in worship so as to suit his own views. 4. A rhymed autobiography of himself, written in his seventy-sixth year, Paisley, 1795.

[William Motherwell in Paisley Magazine, 1828; Brown's Paisley Poets, i. 14-26; Autobiography as above; Holland's Psalmists of Great Britain, where specimens of his psalms are printed.] J. C. H.

MAXWELL, JAMES CLERK (1831-1879), first professor of experimental physics at Cambridge, was born in Edinburgh 13 Nov. 1831. His father, who died in 1856, was John Clerk, brother of Sir George Clerk, of Penicuik in Midlothian. John Clerk adopted the surname of Maxwell on succeeding to an estate in Kircudbrightshire, which had come into the family by a marriage with a Miss Maxwell. Clerk Maxwell's mother was Frances, daughter of Robert Cay, of Charlton, Northumberland. His early childhood was passed in his father's country house of Glenlair, near Dalbeattie. In 1839 his mother died, and two years later Maxwell became a pupil at the Edinburgh Academy, and in 1847 entered the university of Edinburgh, attending lectures on mathematics, natural philosophy, chemistry, and mental philosophy. He had already, at the age of fifteen, communicated to the Royal Society of Edinburgh a paper 'On the Description of Oval Curves' (*Proc. Roy. Soc. Edin.* 1846, vol. ii.) A second paper 'On the Theory of Rolling Curves' (*Trans. Roy. Soc. Edin.* vol. xvi. pt. v.), was read in 1849, and a third 'On the Equilibrium of Elastic Solids' (*Trans. Roy. Soc. Edin.* vol. xx. pt. i.), in 1850. The last paper was the outcome of a visit paid in 1848 to Nicol, the inventor of Nicol's prism, who showed him the beautiful chromatic effects exhibited by unannealed glass in polarised light. It occurred to Maxwell to study by their aid the strains set up in an elastic substance such as gelatine when subject to stress, and to compare his experimental results with theory. In obtaining his theory Maxwell discarded the hypotheses of Navier and Poisson as to the action between the molecules of an elastic body, since they had led to results inconsistent with experiment, and starting afresh arrived at equations which, as he states, had been already obtained in a different way by Stokes and Candy. They had also been given in 1837 by Green, who based his work on the fundamental principle of the conservation of energy.

In October 1850 Maxwell left Edinburgh for Cambridge, entering as an undergraduate at Peterhouse, but in December of the same year he migrated to Trinity; Dr. Thompson, afterwards master, was his tutor. He became a pupil of the great 'coach,' Hopkins, in 1851, and in April 1852 was elected a scholar of his college. He graduated in 1854 as second wrangler, the senior being Dr. Routh of Peterhouse, with whom he was bracketed as first Smith's prizeman. In 1855 he was elected a fellow of Trinity, and was placed on the staff of lecturers. During the next year he was appointed professor of natural philosophy in Marischal College, Aberdeen. The college was amalgamated in 1860 with King's College, to form the university of Aberdeen, and Maxwell vacated his chair, but almost immediately afterwards became professor of natural philosophy in King's College, London. This post he resigned in 1865, retiring to private life at Glenlair, but in 1871 he was induced to come forward as a candidate for the new chair of experimental physics, which the university proposed to found at Cambridge. He was elected without opposition, and delivered his inaugural lecture 25 Oct. 1871.

The Duke of Devonshire, the chancellor, had just offered to present the university with a physical laboratory, and Maxwell's first work was to arrange the details of the plans and to superintend the building. The laboratory was opened in June 1874. The work of the professorship occupied him during term time for the next five years; the long vacation was usually spent at Glenlair. While staying there during the summer of 1879, he became seriously ill, and returned to Cambridge in October, only to succumb to a painful malady on 5 Nov. of the same year, at the early age of forty-eight.

In 1858 he married Katherine Mary Dewar, daughter of the principal of Marischal College.

Maxwell's power as an original investigator, of which he gave the first proofs at the age of fifteen, was signally illustrated shortly after he obtained his fellowship at Trinity. A paper on 'Faraday's Lines of Force' was read before the Cambridge Philosophical Society on 10 Dec. 1855 and on 11 Feb. 1856 (*Camb. Phil. Soc. Trans.* vol. x. pt. i.), and contains the germs of much of his future work. He had read Faraday's 'Experimental Researches,' and set himself 'not to attempt,' quoting his own words, 'to establish any physical theory of a science in which I have hardly a single experiment, but to show how by a strict application of the ideas and methods of Faraday, the connection of the very different order of phenomena which he has discovered, may be placed before the mathematical mind.' Following a suggestion of Sir William Thomson (now Lord Kelvin), he worked his endeavour out by the aid of analogies with corresponding phenomena in hydrodynamics and heat. In later papers the ideas here originated received further development. Meanwhile other phenomena were interesting him. He had already (1855) written on the theory of colours in relation to colour-blindness, and in a paper on 'Experiments on Colour as Perceived by the Eye' (*Phil. Trans. Roy. Soc. Edin.* vol. xxi. pt. ii.), he had investigated the effects of combinations of various colours by means of the rapid rotation of discs coloured differently in different parts. Maxwell's colour-top is now well known. The main results of his work on colour are summed up in his paper 'On the Theory of Compound Colours,' read before the Royal Society 22 March 1860 (*Phil. Trans.* 1860). His instrument, the colour-box, by which he investigated the effect of mixing in given proportions light taken from different parts of the spectrum, is first described, and then it is shown that any given colour sensation may be produced by combinations in due proportion of rays taken from three parts of the spectrum, and also that if we select three definite rays as standards, all other colours may be produced by proper combinations of these. In the most general case it may be that, to produce a given colour, we should have to subtract a certain amount of the third colour C, from the two other colours A and B, taken arbitrarily. This would mean that the effect of mixing the given colours, and a proper amount of C, just matches the mixture of A and B, but it is further shown that there are *three primary* colours by arithmetical addition of which, in proper proportions, any other colour may be produced. Probably these three different elements of colours correspond to three different sensations in the eye, and a body appears to us of a definite colour because it excites these sensations each in its proper proportion. The experiments tended to confirm the conclusion that colour-blindness is due to the absence of one of the three primary sensations. For this work Maxwell was awarded the Rumford medal of the Royal Society 30 Nov. 1860.

Meanwhile Maxwell had been engaged on his essay 'On the Stability of Motion of Saturn's Rings,' which gained the Adams prize in 1857. Laplace had shown that the ring could not be solid, for if so it would be unstable, the slightest displacement of its centre from the centre of the planet would originate a motion, which would ultimately destroy the whole.

Maxwell considered the effect of loading the ring at one or more points, and showed that if the load were great enough we could account for the motion on known laws, but if this were so, the load must be so great, that it would be visible as a satellite, and this is not the case. There then remained the assumption that the ring is fluid, or else consists of a large number of very small separate solid particles. Either of these hypotheses was proved to give a possible form of motion, and the latter in all probability is the nature of the ring.

It may have been the discrete particles of Saturn's rings that led Maxwell to study the kinetic theory of gases. According to this theory, the pressure which a gas exerts is due to the impact of its molecules on the walls of the enclosing vessel; the temperature depends on the average energy of the motion. This had been clearly pointed out by Herapath in 1847, and in 1848 Joule, assuming that all the molecules of the gas possessed the same velocity of agitation, determined the relation between the velocity and the pressure, and calculated the former for hydrogen and other gases at a definite pressure and temperature. Clausius in 1857 and 1859 extended the work, making the same hypothesis as to the velocity of the individual molecules, and introduced the idea of the mean free path.

Maxwell's first papers on the subject appeared in the 'Philosophical Magazine' (January and July 1860). He pointed out that the velocities of the different molecules, even if equal to start with, would become unequal immediately in consequence of the collisions. He therefore devised the statistical method of treating the problem. On this method the whole number of molecules are divided into a series of groups, the velocities of all the molecules constituting a group, being the same within narrow limits, and the average velocity of each group is considered. He also found the law connecting this average velocity with the number of molecules in the group, and showed that when a state of permanence, that is of uniform temperature, has been reached, in the case either of a single gas or of a mixture, the average energy of agitation is the same throughout. From these considerations and on the supposition that the mean energy of agitation measures the temperature, the laws of Gay Lussac and Charles are deduced. The theory of diffusion had been given by Herapath, Maxwell extended it, and by applying similar reasoning to the diffusion of the momentum and the diffusion of the energy, explained the phenomena of viscosity and of conduction of heat respectively. The law of Dulong and Petit connecting the specific heat and the molecular weight was shown to follow, but difficulties of a serious nature were met with when the theory was applied to deduce the elation between the specific heats of a gas at constant pressure and volume respectively.

These difficulties led Maxwell to abandon the hypothesis of collisions between hard spherical molecules, and to attack the problem on the assumption of action of a more general character between the particles. This is done in his paper 'On the Dynamical Theory of Gases' (*Phil. Trans.* 1866). Some of his conclusions he had attempted to verify by direct experiments, which are described in the Bakerian lecture 'On the Viscosity of Air and other Gases' (*Phil. Trans.* 1866).

The theorem as to the distribution of velocity in a gas was extended by Boltzmann (*Vienna Proceedings*, 1871–2), and still further by Maxwell in a paper 'On Boltzmann's Theorem' (*Camb. Phil. Soc. Trans.* 1878). Various objections have been urged against the theorem, and it seems now to be established that in the most general form given to it in his last paper, it does not hold (see Bryan, 'On our Knowledge of Thermodynamics,' *Brit. Assoc. Report*, 1891, where the points at issue are clearly stated). Another paper on the same subject, 'On Stresses in Rarefied Gases arising from Inequalities in Temperature' (*Phil. Trans.* 1879), deals among other things with the theory of Mr. Crookes's beautiful instrument, the radiometer.

In Maxwell's collected papers are to be found many others which have a bearing on the constitution of matter and on the theory of gases. Among them may be mentioned his lecture before the British Association at Bradford (*Nature*, vol. viii.) on 'Molecules;' and another lecture before the Chemical Society (*ib.* vol. xi.) on the 'Dynamical Evidence for the Molecular Constitution of Bodies;' his articles in the 'Encyclopædia Britannica' on 'Atom,' 'Attraction,' 'Capillary Action,' 'Diffusion,' 'Constitution of Bodies,' and other subjects; together with his review of Van der Waal's important work 'On the Continuity of the Gaseous and Liquid States' (*Nature*, vol. x.)

But the researches for which Maxwell is best known are those dealing with electricity and magnetism. These commenced with the paper in 1856 on Faraday's lines of force. The next published paper of importance was that on 'Physical Lines of Force' (*Phil. Mag.* 1861, 1862). It was Maxwell's view that electrical and magnetic effects do not arise from the attractions of electric or magnetic matter distributed over the surfaces of conductors or magnetic bodies, but are the means by which changes of some unknown description in the ether which fills space or in some of its properties become known to us. In consequence of these changes energy is stored up in the ether, and electrical or magnetic forces are one form of the manifestation of changes in the distribution of the energy. The experiments of Quincke on electric stress and of Kerr on electro-optics have shown the reality of this stress in the ether, while the theory of Poynting enables us to understand one method by which the energy may travel from place to place. The paper we are now considering describes a mechanism which would have properties in many respects analogous to those possessed by the electro-magnetic medium, though it does not pretend to be a complete representation of the actual condition of the ether.

Similar ideas, though in a far more general form, are developed in the great paper 'On a Dynamical Theory of the Electromagnetic Field,' read before the Royal Society, 8 Dec. 1864 (*Phil. Trans.* vol. clv.) In it Maxwell took the important and novel step of applying dynamical equations in the generalised form given to them by Lagrange to the problems of electro-magnetism, in dealing with which 'we are led to the conception of a complicated mechanism capable of a vast variety of motions, but at the same time so connected that the motion of one part depends, according to definite relations, on the motion of other parts. . . . Such a mechanism must be subject to the laws of dynamics.' Electro-magnetic action is shown to travel through space at a definite rate in waves, and these waves consist of disturbances which are transverse to the direction in which the waves are propagated. In this respect then they resemble waves of light. Moreover, it is found by experiment that the velocity of the electro-magnetic waves in air and in many other media is the same as that of light, and thus the electro-magnetic theory of light becomes possible. The experiments in Maxwell's time were indirect, though so far as they went conclusive enough. We owe it to the genius of Hertz that we are now able to measure directly the velocity of electro-magnetic waves and to show that they are propagated, and can undergo reflection, refraction, and polarisation exactly like waves of light, and we now feel able to say that the two are the same in character; they differ merely, as do the bass and treble notes of a musical instrument, in the rapidity with which they are executed. In light waves periodic changes in the ether are taking place at the rate of some five hundred billions per second; the most rapid electro-magnetic changes we have yet produced are some few millions per second. The laws of these vibrations, when they are completely known, will give us the secret of the ether, and will enable some disciple of Clerk Maxwell to take that step which the master himself in his 'Electricity and Magnetism' confessed himself unable to take, and to explain the mechanism at one time of light, electricity, and magnetism. The paper on the electromagnetic field was in time expanded into the great 'Treatise on Electricity and Magnetism,' published in 1873, on the second edition of which Maxwell was at work at the time of his death.

But it is not only on the theoretical side of electricity that advance is due to Maxwell. He realised, like Lord Kelvin, that a carefully thought-out system of measurement was essential for its progress, and that accurate experiment was needed to form a foundation for his theory. Maxwell became a member of the newly formed electrical standards committee of the British Association in 1862, and was one of the sub-committee appointed to construct the standard of resistance. The necessary experiments were carried out in his own laboratory at King's College, and the results, which have been so fruitful to electrical science, are recorded in the 'Reports' of the committee for 1863 and 1864. The 'Report' for 1863 contains an appendix by Maxwell and Fleeming Jenkin 'On the Elementary Relations between Electrical Measurements,' in which the fundamental principles involved are stated with unrivalled accuracy and clearness.

Another important series of experiments, those on the velocity of propagation of electro-magnetic waves, is described in the paper 'On a method of making a direct Comparison of Electrostatic with Electro-magnetic Force; with a Note on the Velocity of Light' (*Phil. Trans.* vol. clviii). Maxwell's numbers showed that this velocity was nearly that of light; more recent work has proved that the two are, within the limits of error of very exact experiments, identical.

The theory Maxwell formulated is day by day gaining more and more acceptance; the foremost physicists throughout the world are engaged in working at it, and in developing ideas, the germs of which may nearly all be traced in the 'Electricity and Magnetism' or in the paper on the 'Electro-magnetic Field.'

Besides the books already mentioned Maxwell published in 1879 the 'Electrical Researches' of Henry Cavendish, written between 1771 and 1781; edited from the original manuscripts in the possession of the Duke of Devonshire, K.G.; he also wrote a text-book of 'Heat' and a small treatise on dynamics called 'Matter and Motion.' After his death an elementary treatise on 'Electricity,' which was left unfinished, was completed and published by Professor Garnett. Among his other papers are some on 'Geometrical Optics,' which contain important results, and several published mostly in the 'Transactions of the Royal Society of Edinburgh,' 'On Reciprocal Figures and Diagrams of Force.' A memorial edition of his scientific papers, undertaken by a committee appointed soon after his death, was edited by Mr. W. D. Niven, and was issued from the Cambridge University Press in 1890, 4to.

As a man Maxwell was loved and honoured by all who knew him; to his pupils he was the kindest and most sympathetic of teachers, to his friends he was the most charming of companions; brimful of fun, the life and soul of a Red Lion dinner at the British Association meetings, yet in due season grave and thoughtful, with a keen interest in problems that lay outside the domain of his own work, and throughout his life a stern foe to all that was superficial or untrue. On religious questions his beliefs were strong and deeply rooted; the words which close his lecture on molecules, expressing his faith in 'Him, who in the beginning created not only the heaven and the earth, but the material of which heaven and earth consist,' have often been quoted.

There is a bust by Boehm in the Cavendish Laboratory, and also a portrait painted by his cousin, Miss Wedderburn. The bust was executed after his death from G. J. Stodart's engraving, which forms the frontispiece to his works; and a portrait by Mr. Lowes Dickenson, based on the same engraving, was presented to Trinity College by the subscribers to the memorial fund.

By his will he left funds to found a studentship in experimental physics open to members of the university of Cambridge. This was carried out in 1890, when, by the death of Mrs. Maxwell, the university came into possession of the property.

[Life by Professor Lewis Campbell of St. Andrews, and Professor Garnett, his Demonstrator at the Cavendish Laboratory, 1882.]

R. T. G.

MAXWELL, Sir **JOHN** of Terregles, Master of Maxwell, and afterwards fourth Baron Herries (1512?–1583), partisan of Mary Queen of Scots, second son of Robert, fifth baron Maxwell [q. v.], by Janet Douglas, daughter of Sir William Douglas of Drumlanrig, Dumfriesshire, was born about 1512, and was educated at Sweetheart Abbey, Kirkcudbrightshire (document at Terregles, quoted in Sir William Fraser's *Book of Caerlaverock*, i. 497). As tutor to his nephews, and presumptive heir to them and his brother, he was for some time known as the Master of Maxwell. While his father and brother were prisoners in England in 1545, he with great valour held the castle of Lochmaben, and refused to deliver it up. In 1547 he married Agnes Herries, eldest daughter and coheiress with her two sisters of William, third baron Herries. To win her hand he had to enter into complicated intrigues against her guardian, the Earl of Arran, who designed to marry her to his son, Lord John Hamilton. Although related to her within the prohibited degrees, he neglected to obtain a papal dispensation for the marriage, but on 26 May 1555 an absolution and grace of dispensation was granted him.

On 20 March 1551–2 the Master of Maxwell was appointed to succeed his brother Robert, sixth baron Maxwell, as warden of the west marches (*Reg. P. C. Scotl.* i. 121); but on 29 Aug. 1553 resigned the office on the ground that he had come under deadly feud with various clans of the marches (*ib.* p. 143). It was therefore transferred to his uncle, James Douglas of Drumlanrig. In 1559 the master was committed by the queen regent to the castle of Edinburgh for declaring that he would to the uttermost of his power 'assist the preachers and the congregation' (Knox, i. 319), but on 1 Aug. he made his escape (*Cal. State Papers*, For. Ser. 1558–9, entry 1107). On the 15th Knox advised Cecil to comfort him with 'favourable writings,' as his assistance would be invaluable to their cause (*Works*, vi. 69). From this time Maxwell gave strenuous support to the reformed party. He was one of the commission who signed the treaty with Elizabeth at Berwick, 7 Feb. 1559–60; he signed the band of 20 April following to defend the liberty of the Evangel, and for the expulsion of the French from Scotland (*ib.* ii. 63); and on 27 Jan. 1560–1 he subscribed the Book of Discipline (*ib.* p. 129).

After the return of Queen Mary to Scotland, Maxwell on 4 Sept. 1561 was reappointed warden of the west marches (*Reg. P. C. Scotl.* i. 157). Henceforth his attitude towards the reformed party was uncertain; for while he continued nominally a protestant, his political sympathies, like those of Secretary Maitland, were with the queen. He had been on terms of special friendship with Knox, who never lost respect for him, and refers to him as 'a man stout and wittie' (*Works*, i. 459), and as of 'great judgment and experience' (*ib.* ii. 351); but on account of a letter written by Knox in October 1563 in reference to the mass, the master gave Knox 'a discharge of the familiarity which before was great betwixt them' (*ib.* p. 399). Still the master did not break with Moray even when he rose in rebellion at the time of the Darnley marriage in 1565, and endeavoured to prevent the queen going to extremities against him. When Moray retreated westwards from Edinburgh, the master had an interview with him at Hamilton, after which he endeavoured without success to mediate an arrangement with the queen. On Moray passing southwards into Dumfries he entertained him in his house (*ib.* p. 512); but when the queen expressed her determination to revenge herself on Moray, he declined to arrest him and advised him to pass into England. The queen on Moray's retirement committed to the master the charge of guarding the borders, and returned to Edinburgh (Herries, *Memoirs*, p. 72). On 1 Jan. 1565–6 an act was also passed absolving him from all charges of treason that had been made against him (*Reg. P. C. Scotl.* i. 415). On the queen's escape from Holyrood, after the murder of Rizzio, the master joined her with a strong force at Dunbar, and henceforth may be reckoned one of her staunchest supporters. At the end of 1566 he became Baron Herries. Sir James Balfour states that he was created Baron Herries at the baptism of Prince James, 17 Dec.; but according to a decision of the House of Lords, 23 June 1858, no new peerage was created in his person, and he was merely called to the peerage in right of his wife. He also acquired from his wife's sisters their share in their father's estates, and on 8 May 1566 a charter of Terregles was granted to him and his wife and their heirs, and failing these to his heirs male. The charter was confirmed by parliament on 19 April 1567.

Herries was one of the assize who acquitted Bothwell of the murder of Darnley, and excused himself for doing so merely on the ground that in the indictment the murder was stated wrongly to have been done on the 9th instead of on the morning of the 10th Feb. (Herries, *Memoirs*, p. 87). He was, however, rather an enemy than a friend of Bothwell; and Sir James Melville states that when rumours reached Herries of the queen's intention to marry Bothwell, he besought her on his knees to eschew 'sic utter wrak and inconvenientis as that wuld bring on' (*Memoirs*, p. 175). Still he remained faithful to the queen when the marriage resulted in disaster to her. Although not present at Carberry, he subscribed the band at Dumbarton on her behalf; and such was the faith in his honesty and ability that the queen's lords entrusted to him the management of her cause, and advised Throckmorton that communications from Elizabeth in reference to means of aiding her should be sent to him' (*Cal. State Papers*, For. Ser. 1566–8, entry 1613). Throckmorton informed Cecil that Herries was 'the cunning horse-leech and the wisest of the whole faction; but, as the Queen of Scots says of him, there is nobody can be sure of him' (*ib.* entry 1615). For a time he declined to have any conference with Moray so long as the queen was imprisoned, and he refused to permit the herald to proclaim the regency of Moray at Glasgow. On 14 Oct. 1567 he came to Edinburgh and gave in his acknowledgment of the regent's authority, but, as would appear from the letter of the Bishop of St. Andrews to him (8 Oct. *ib.* entry 1761), the submission was merely nominal. At the meeting of parliament in December, he made a remarkable speech to the effect that those who, in view of the queen's refusal to give up Bothwell, had 'sequestered' her in Lochleven had done the 'duty of noble men,' and that therefore Argyll, Huntly, and others, ought to give in their acknowledgment to the king's party, as he and others had done (Robertson, *Hist. of Scotl.* 5th ed. ii. 385–6). Notwithstanding these specious professions he subscribed the band for the queen's deliverance from Lochleven, joined her standard immediately after her escape, and fought for her at Langside, where he had the command of the horse (13 May 1568).

It was to Herries that Mary entrusted herself when her cause was lost. When flight to Dumbarton was impossible, she sought refuge in his territories; but, probably in doubt also as to the strength of his loyalty, she finally decided, in opposition to his strong persuasions, to seek personally the assistance of Elizabeth. On 16 May Herries and the queen crossed the Solway into England, and on the 25th he was sent by her to Elizabeth to solicit for her an interview that she might explain her position (Labanoff, ii. 81, 84). Elizabeth, however, declined to see her, or to interfere in her behalf, or to permit her to leave the country until she had cleared her reputation. Whether at the instance of Mary or not, Herries thereupon seems to have suggested a compromise. He told Sir Francis Knollys [q. v.] that he 'misliked not' that Mary 'should be bridled in her regiment by assistance of the noblemen of her realm in consideration of her rashness and foul marriage with the Earl of Bothwell' (28 July, Anderson, iv. 112–13); and Middlemore was under the impression that he desired that the 'regent with the noblemen should still bear rule, but under the direction of the Queen of England' (13 July, *Cal. State Papers*, For. Ser. 1566–8, entry 2350).

At a meeting of the estates on 19 Aug. 1568 Herries was formally forfeited, but proceedings against him were suspended pending the result of the proposed conference in England. The regent also intended to have demolished his castle, but the laird of Drumlanrig having stated that it was the intention of Herries himself to pull it down and build a new one, the regent, scorning to be 'a barrowman to his old walls,' allowed it to stand (Herries, *Memoirs*, p. 106). Herries was chosen by Mary one of her commissioners to the conferences in England, sharing the chief responsibility with the Bishop of Ross. On 1 Dec. he made a vehement speech against the regent and the Scottish commissioners, affirming that some of them had themselves foreknowledge of the murder.

After Moray's return to Scotland in the spring of 1569 Herries joined the Hamiltons in an attempted revolt; and on coming to Edinburgh to arrange terms for an agreement he was on 16 April warded in the castle (*Diurnal of Occurrents*, p. 144), on the ground that he had advised the Duke of Chatelherault not to take the oath to the regent (Herries, *Memoirs*, p. 114). On 5 July he deemed it advisable to inform Elizabeth (*Cal. State Papers*, For. Ser. 1569–71, entry 314) and Cecil (*ib.* entry 315) that he had not 'dealt doubly in the cause of his mistress,' nor had been 'committed to ward with his own will.' At the same time he gave 'good words' to the regent, who, however, distrusting his intentions, detained him in prison, and it was only after the regent's assassination that Kirkcaldy set him free. There can scarcely be any doubt that he was at least indirectly concerned in the Norfolk conspiracy (cf. Murdin, *State Papers*; and *Cal. Hatfield MSS.* pt. i. passim).

Shortly after obtaining his liberty Herries joined the queen's lords at Linlithgow, when it was determined to assemble at Edinburgh on 8 April. They so far carried out their purpose; but further serious results were frustrated by Morton, on whose advice (April 25, *Cal. State Papers*, For. Ser. 1569–71, entry 849) Sussex caused a diversion by advancing across the borders into the territories of the Maxwells. At Morton's request the lands of Lord Maxwell were spared, but those of Herries and the Johnstones were devastated (Scrope, 9 May, *ib.* entry 907). The shelter given by Herries to the English rebel Leonard Dacres led to further proceedings against him; and finally finding himself exposed to two fires—those of Elizabeth and the regent—he resolved to attempt a compromise by coming to terms with Elizabeth, and promising to employ his 'will and power in her service' (Sussex, 10 Sept. *ib.* entry 1249).

To preserve Elizabeth's good will he refrained from assisting the Hamiltons against the regent in the following February; but he earnestly entreated her to 'take some good order for the restitution of Queen Mary, or her party would utterly despair of her goodness, and seek the aid of some other prince' (*ib.* entry 1581). On 17 May 1571 he eluded the forces sent to watch him by Morton, and joined Kirkcaldy in the castle of Edinburgh (*ib.* entry 1710), but shortly afterwards returned home (*ib.* entry 1721), his purpose having been merely to assist in mediating an agreement with Morton (*ib.* entry 1726). On 7 June he, however, again returned to Edinburgh to attend a parliament of the queen's party on the 12th (Calderwood, iii. 78, 91). On 21 Aug. he informed Elizabeth that 'he must do as the others do,' unless Elizabeth showed some disposition to interfere on behalf of the queen of Scots (*ib.* entry 1934); and when finally he became convinced that Elizabeth would not interfere, he saw that Mary's cause was hopeless, and some time before the capture of the castle came to terms with the regent.

Along with his relative, Lord Maxwell, who laid claim to the earldom of Morton, Herries took an active part in the scheme for depriving Morton in 1578 of the regency (Moysie, *Memoirs*, p. 2). He was one of those sent by the king and council to Morton on 15 March to demand the delivery of the castle of Edinburgh (*ib.* p. 3), and was chosen a member of the new privy council after Morton's resignation. On Morton's return to power he for some time held aloof from him, but on 8 Sept. was nominated with seven other noblemen to proceed on 20 Sept. to Stirling to assist the king in the adoption of measures for 'the repose and quietness of the troubled commonwealth' (*Reg. P. C. Scotl.* iii. 26). On 21 Jan. 1578–9 he presented a discourse to the king on the management of the west borders (*ib.* pp. 77–82), and shortly afterwards he was appointed to succeed his nephew, Lord Maxwell, as warden (*ib.* p. 76). On 21 Aug. 1579 he was succeeded as warden by his hereditary enemy, Johnstone of Johnstone (*ib.* p. 207). On the execution of Morton in 1581 Herries, true to his Marian sympathies, became one of the most strenuous supporters of Lennox. After the raid of Ruthven in August 1582, he joined Lennox in Edinburgh, and was one of the nobles sent by Lennox to ask a private conference with the king, but had to return with a message that Lennox must leave Scotland. Herries died suddenly on Sunday, 20 Jan. 1582–3, at Edinburgh, 'in time of the afternoon preaching,' in 'an upper chamber in William Fowler's lodging,' where, feeling too ill to go to the preaching, he had gone to 'see the boys bicker' (Calderwood, viii. 232). He was interred in the choir of the church of Terregles. By his wife Agnes Herries he had four sons and seven daughters. The sons were: William, fifth baron Herries [q. v.]; Sir Robert of Spottes; Edward, commendator of Dundrennan and laird of Lamington; and John of Newlaw. The daughters were: Elizabeth, lady Lochinvar; Margaret, first countess of Lothian; Agnes, lady Amisfield; Mary, lady Yester; Sarah, lady Johnstone; Grizel, lady Bombie; and Nicolas, lady Lag.

[Histories of Knox, Buchanan, Leslie, Calderwood, and Spotiswood; Herries's Memoirs (Abbotsford Club); History of James the Sext, Sir James Melville's Memoirs, Diurnal of Occurrents, and Moysie's Memoirs (all Bannatyne Club); The Proceedings of the Commissioners at Westminster in Anderson's Collections and Goodall's Examination; Cal. State Papers, For. Ser. Reign of Elizabeth, and Scott. Ser.; Reg. P. C. Scotl. vols. i–iii.; Murdin's State Papers; Cal. Hatfield MSS.; Sir William Fraser's Book of Caerlaverock, i. 497–570; Douglas's Scottish Peerage (Wood), ii. 318–319.]
T. F. H.

MAXWELL, JOHN, seventh or eighth Baron Maxwell and also Earl of Morton (1553–1593), second son of Robert, sixth baron Maxwell, by his wife Lady Beatrix Douglas, second daughter of James, third earl of Morton, was born 24 April 1553, about six months after the death of his father. His elder brother, Robert, died young. He was brought up under the guardianship of Sir John Maxwell of Terregles, afterwards fourth Baron Herries [q. v.], through whose influence he became a supporter of Queen Mary. At the Perth convention, 30 July 1569, he voted for the queen's divorce from Bothwell (*Reg. P. C. Scotl.* ii. 4). He was suspected of having given support and shelter to the English rebel Leonard Dacres. Consequently his territories were in the spring of 1570 invaded by the English under Lord Scrope, who in April had two successful skirmishes with him, taking on each occasion about a hundred prisoners (*Cal. State Papers*, For. Ser. 1569–71, entry 835). Morton also on the 25th advised that Scrope should make an inroad on Maxwell's country and that of Lord Herries to prevent them coming to Edinburgh (*ib.* entry 849). This led to a remonstrance from Kirkcaldy, who in a letter to Randolph asserted that Maxwell had not left the king's obedience or had to do with the English rebels (27 April, *ib.* entry 854). To this Randolph replied that he had not only maintained the queen of England's rebels, but had spoiled her subjects (1 May, *ib.* entry

875). Although Scrope, at Morton's request, at first spared the lands of Maxwell (9 May, *ib.* entry 907), it was discovered that he was subsequently in communication with Dacres, and his castles as well as those of Lord Herries were accordingly demolished on 22 Aug. (*ib.* entry 1213). It was rumoured in the spring of 1571 that Maxwell and Herries were marching to the relief of Paisley, then held by the Hamiltons and besieged by the regent (*ib.* entry 1561), but they did not arrive in time to prevent its capture (Scrope, 22 Feb. *ib.* entry 1567). On 10 May Maxwell, with a large force, entered Edinburgh in company with Herries (*ib.* entry 1710), but they both returned home on the 23rd (*ib.* entry 1721). Shortly afterwards they, however, again entered Edinburgh to attend the parliament of Queen Mary's party on 12 June (Calderwood, iii. 78, 91).

Maxwell, having come to terms with Morton before the fall of the castle in 1573, was in August 1573 made warden of the west marches, the castle of Lochmaben being also delivered to him on 26 Oct. His claims to the earldom of Morton aroused, however, the jealousy of the regent. Probably this was at least the indirect cause why, after he had, in May 1577, demitted the office of warden (*Reg. P. C. Scotl.* ii. 613), he was on 13 July committed to ward in the prison of Edinburgh and subsequently sent to Blackness. On the fall of Morton he was on 13 March 1577–8 discharged of his ward (*ib.* p. 677), and on the 25th he was reappointed warden (*ib.* pp. 677–678). He was also chosen a member of the new privy council. In January 1578–9 he was succeeded as warden by his kinsman Lord Herries (*ib.* iii. 76). Subsequently his connection with the Armstrongs and other border raiders brought him under the displeasure of the government. On 13 July 1579 he gave caution to enter into ward in Dundee (*ib.* p. 195), and on 27 Oct. that he would remain in Blackness (*ib.* p. 232); but on 11 Dec. was permitted to return home (*ib.* p. 245). After the imprisonment of Morton in 1581 he was on 29 April reappointed warden (*ib.* p. 376). On Morton's execution on 5 June he obtained, as representative of his mother, daughter of the third earl, a charter of the earldom of Morton, erected anew in his favour, a grant being also made to him of certain of Morton's forfeited estates, the charter and grant being ratified by parliament on 19 Nov. (*Acta Parl. Scot.* iii. 262). After the raid of Ruthven and the overthrow of Lennox, he was, on 12 Nov. 1582, denounced rebel and put to the horn for not appearing to give advice in regard to the quieting of the borders (*Reg. P. C. Scotl.* iii. 528), and on the 19th he was succeeded in the wardenship by Johnstone of Johnstone (*ib.* p. 531). He arrived in Edinburgh on the 30th to assist Lennox in a project for capturing the city and Holyrood Palace, but the strict watch kept by Colonel Stewart and others foiled their purpose (Calderwood, iii. 691).

Maxwell soon incurred the displeasure of the king's favourite, the Earl of Arran, on account of a refusal to exchange with him the lands of Pollok and Maxwellhaugh. In January 1585 the attainder of the earldom of Morton was rescinded in favour of Archibald, earl of Angus. His title was thus indirectly menaced. For certain comparatively minor offences he was on 26 Feb. denounced a rebel (*Reg. P. C. Scotl.* iii. 725), and on 10 April the gift and infeftment to him of the earldom of Morton and its adjuncts was revoked, and declared to have been null from the beginning (*ib.* p. 734). To revenge himself on Arran, Maxwell therefore entered into communication with the banished lords, and, accompanying them from the borders with a large force, enabled them on 1 Nov. to obtain possession of Stirling Castle and drive Arran from power. After the nobles had entered the town, the border followers of Maxwell took advantage of the opportunity to seize their horses, 'not respecting friend or foe' (Calderwood, iv. 390). This outrage was, however, probably covered by the act passed on 10 Dec. granting entire indemnity to Lord Maxwell and his servants for all their doings within the realm from April 1569. Maxwell was also at the same time chosen a member of the privy council.

Hardly had the act of indemnity been passed when Maxwell again exposed himself to the penalties of the law by causing mass to be celebrated on 24, 25, and 26 Dec. in the college of Lincluden, near Dumfries. On being summoned to answer for his conduct by the privy council, he offered himself for trial, but was committed to the castle of Edinburgh (*ib.* p. 489). On 22 March he was freed on giving caution in a hundred thousand merks to repair to the burgh of Edinburgh, and keep ward there until freed by the king (*Reg. P. C. Scotl.* iv. 55), and shortly afterwards, at the command of the king, he left the country (Calderwood, iv. 489). In April he returned from Spain without the king's license (*ib.* p. 547), but on the 13th gave caution in 1,000*l.* to appear before the assembly in May to 'answer anent religion' (*Reg. P. C. Scotl.* iv. 62). On 14 May he again gave caution to remain within the burgh of Edinburgh and four miles round (*ib.* p. 77). On 4 Oct. he was released from the horn while on the king's service in the west march (*ib.* p. 109); but the king remained distrustful of him, and on 14 April 1587 he undertook to go abroad and not to return without the king's license (*ib.* p. 159). In June he was superseded as warden by Lord Herries (*ib.* p. 188), and on 29 July the earldom of Morton was ratified by parliament to the Earl of Angus.

Maxwell was closely connected with the intrigues of Lord Claud Hamilton [q.v.] for a Spanish invasion (cf. TEULET, *Relations Politiques*, v. 453; CALDERWOOD, v. 14, 24, 27). In April 1588 he returned to Scotland without license, and began to assemble his followers to be in readiness to assist the Spaniards either in Scotland or England (*ib.* iv. 678). On 25 April an act was passed against resetting or harbouring him, and in May the king took the field against him in person (*Reg. P. C. Scotl.* iv. 286–92). Maxwell had fortified and garrisoned the castle of Lochmaben, but on the king's arrival at Dumfries he left it in charge of a lieutenant and went on board his ship. So hotly, however, was he pursued by Sir William Stewart that he was forced to take to his boat and go on shore, where on the 5th he was captured in a hut (CALDERWOOD, iv. 678). After being conveyed to Dumfries, he was brought by the king—who committed the government of the district to Angus, the new earl of Morton—to Edinburgh, where he was warded in a private house under the custody of Sir William Stewart (*ib.* p. 679). To attend the arrival of the queen (*ib.* v. 59) he was in September released from imprisonment on giving caution in 100,000*l.* Scots to do nothing 'tending to the trouble or alteration of the state of religion presently professed and by law established' (*Reg. P. C. Scotl.* iv. 412). On 11 July 1592 he was appointed warden of the west march under the title of Earl of Morton (*ib.* p. 767); but on the 12th an act was passed declaring that the designation of Earl of Morton applied to him in the last acts shall not prejudice William, earl of Morton, lord Dalkeith (*ib.* p. 768; cf. DOUGLAS, WILLIAM, sixth or seventh EARL OF MORTON).

On 26 Jan. 1592–3 Morton subscribed the confession of faith before the presbytery of Edinburgh (CALDERWOOD, v. 222); but his small respect for presbyterian devotions was evidenced on 2 Feb. by his personal encounter with the rival Earl of Morton in reference to the possession of a pew in the kirk of Edinburgh. They were, however, 'parted, without sword drawn, by the provost, and convoyed to their lodgings' (*ib.*) Notwithstanding his act of conformity an advertisement against him and other 'Spanish factioners' was, on 17 Feb., affixed to the Tolbooth. He was slain on 7 Dec. following at Dryfe Sands, in an encounter with the forces of the laird of Johnstone. Having a commission of lieutenancy for Johnstone's apprehension, he was proceeding at the head of two thousand men to lay siege to Johnstone's house of Lochwood, when he was caught in an ambush and put to flight. He is said to have been struck from his horse by Johnstone himself, and killed as he lay helpless on the ground (MOYSIE, p. 110; CALDERWOOD, v. 290). The body lay unburied till February 1597–8, when on the 14th an order of council was made for the burial of him and the Earl of Moray (the 'Bonnie Earl,' slain by Huntly) 'in the accustomed places of their predecessors within twenty days' (*Reg. P. C. Scotl.* v. 445). Spotiswood describes Maxwell as 'a nobleman of great spirit, humane, courteous, and more learned than noblemen commonly are, but aspiring and ambitious of rule.' By his wife, Lady Elizabeth Douglas, daughter of the seventh earl of Angus, he had three sons and four daughters. The sons were: John, eighth or ninth baron [q. v.]; Robert, ninth or tenth baron, and afterwards earl of Nithsdale; and James of Kirkconnel and Springkell, master of Maxwell. The daughters were: Elizabeth, married to John Maxwell, baron Herries; Margaret, to John Wallace of Craigie; Jean, unmarried; and Agnes to William Douglas of Penzerie.

[Histories of Calderwood and Spotiswood; Herries's Memoirs (Abbotsford Club); History of James the Sext, Diurnal of Occurrents, and Moysie's Memoirs (all Bannatyne Club); Cal. State Papers, For. Ser. Reign of Elizabeth, and Scott. Ser.; Reg. P. C. Scotl. vols. ii–v.; Sir William Fraser's Book of Caerlaverock, i. 223–99; Douglas's Scottish Peerage (Wood), ii. 317–18.]

T. F. H.

MAXWELL, JOHN, eighth or ninth BARON MAXWELL (1586?–1612), eldest son of John, seventh or eighth baron Maxwell [q.v.], by his wife Lady Elizabeth Douglas, was born about 1586 and was served heir to his father 10 March 1596–7. His guardian was William Maxwell, fifth baron Herries [q. v.] A combination of circumstances tended to foster in him a peculiar lawlessness; he had the death of his father at the hand of Johnstone to revenge; he was at feud with the Douglases, earls of Morton, regarding that earldom; and his hereditary faith was catholic. He was thus in perpetual conflict with the government, and special acts had constantly to be passed by the council to hold him in restraint. On 27 June 1598 he attended a convention of estates for the rooting out of deadly feuds (*Reg. P. C. Scotl.* v. 462), and on 6 March 1598–9 promised, in presence of the king and council, to appear on the 22nd and give 'ane resoluit answer' anent subscribing an assurance to the laird of Johnstone, and in the meantime not to repair within the bounds of Nithsdale or shire of Dumfries (*ib.* p. 535). On the 22nd Lord Hamilton undertook under a bond of 5,000*l.* to keep Maxwell in his company, without permitting him to go to Nithsdale, and to enter him before the king and council on 6 June (*ib.* p. 719). On 15 Sept. it was ordained, for the better quieting of the west march, that Maxwell should be warded in Edinburgh Castle, and that the laird of Johnstone should also still be retained in ward (*ib.* vi. 31). It would appear that he was not warded, for, being on 18 Nov. summoned to appear before the council to answer for the obedience of his men, he failed to do so (*ib.* p. 851). On 30 April 1600 he and Johnstone were charged by open proclamation at the cross of Dumfries to subscribe within six hours a bond of mutual assurance, Maxwell being required, should he refuse, to find caution in 10,000*l.* within six days to depart the realm within forty days (*ib.* p. 105). As he failed to appear he was on 27 June denounced a rebel (*ib.* p. 121), but on 21 July he gave caution in ten thousand merks to repair within forty-eight hours to the house of John, marquis of Hamilton, and there remain six months, or at least not to visit Nithsdale, Annandale, or Galloway without the king's authority (*ib.* p. 658). On 21 May 1601 he was charged to answer for a new design against Johnstone (*ib.* p. 240); on 15 Feb. 1601–2 he was again charged to answer for his misdeeds (*ib.* p. 352), and on 3 March he signed a band for the better observance of the king's peace (*ib.* p. 356). On 11 July he appeared before the council, but on his refusing to subscribe an assurance to Johnstone, he was on the 16th warded in the castle of Edinburgh (*ib.* p. 419). Besides his constant plots against Johnstone, he had for some time countenanced popish practices in Dumfries and elsewhere; and Calderwood states that, a little before Maxwell's imprisonment, 'John Hamilton the apostate taught in Maxwell's gallery publicly' (*History*, vi. 146). Consequently at the ensuing assembly in November he was included among those nobles for whose 'confirmation in the truth' special provision was made, a minister being appointed to attend on him for this purpose so long as he remained in the castle of Edinburgh (*ib.* p. 166). On 29 Nov. 1602 it was declared that, as he still refused to subscribe an assurance to Johnstone, he should not be released till he found caution in twenty thousand merks to repair to certain places and remain there till 1 March, the time appointed for his going abroad, but on 12 Jan. he made his escape and returned to his own country (*Reg. P. C. Scotl.* vi. 831).

On 18 April 1605 Maxwell appeared before the council and expressed his readiness, 'without submission or other ceremony, to take the laird of Johnstone by the hand and to be reconciled to him' (*ib.* vii. 38). Consequently, on 11 June they joined hands before the council in token of reconciliation (*ib.* p. 58), and on the 25th he gave in a 'letter of Slains' to the laird of Johnstone for the murder of his father (*ib.* p. 64). Hardly was his feud with Johnstone settled, when his claims on the earldom of Morton led to the proposal for a duel between him and William Douglas, eldest son of the laird of Drumlanrig, which, on 6 March 1606, was stopped by order of the council (*ib.* p. 187). At the Linlithgow convention of the clergy on 10 Dec. it was recommended that the king should order Lord Maxwell to reside in Leith for the benefit of instruction from the clergy (Calderwood, vi. 608). His residence was apparently fixed in Edinburgh, for on 9 Jan. 1607 the council had to make regulations for the better keeping of the peace in Edinburgh between him and the Marquis of Hamilton, it being provided that they should not appear on the streets at the same time (*Reg. P. C. Scotl.* vii. 295). Meantime the feud between him and the Earl of Morton was gradually reaching a crisis. On 23 May 1607 they subscribed an assurance that there was no feud between them, but only some civil actions which they meant to pursue 'according to law' (*ib.* p. 370); but on 29 July Maxwell, to avoid quarrels between him and Morton, was charged not to come to Edinburgh to attend the meeting of parliament (*ib.* p. 420); and on 8 Aug. he was denounced a rebel for not appearing before the council for sending a challenge to Morton, and was required not to send any further challenge on pain of treason (*ib.* p. 425). On 19 Aug. the king sent a letter to the council directing that Maxwell, for his 'youthful riot and insolence,' should be committed to the castle of Edinburgh (*ib.* p. 539); and after excuses had, on 24 Sept., been heard for his conduct, effect was given to the king's request (*ib.* p. 441). In answer to a petition for his liberty, the council on 5 Nov. ordained that he be detained in ward till he submitted the differences between him and the Earl of Morton to the council (*ib.* viii. 2); but on the night of 4 Dec.

he, with the aid of a fellow-prisoner, Sir James Maconell, made his escape (cf. *ib.* p. 17; CALDERWOOD, vi. 686; and deposition of Sir James Maconell in PITCAIRN, *Criminal Trials*, iii. 10–11). A warrant was immediately issued for his apprehension (*ib.* p. 19), and also a proclamation against resetting him (*ib.* p. 20); on 17 Dec. he was denounced as a rebel (*ib.* p. 24); on the 30th a commission was given to the captain of the guard for his pursuit (*ib.* p. 29); and on 12 Jan. a summons of forfeiture was libelled against him (*ib.* p. 33). He continued, however, to defy all the edicts, and evaded all efforts to capture him, notwithstanding that on 9 Feb. the whole company of the guard was ordered to proceed to Dumfries, and either apprehend him and other rebels, or put them out of the country (*ib.* p. 48). His perilous position, instead of inducing him to surrender, drove him to desperation; and, knowing that he must either be captured or leave the country, he resolved, before bidding farewell to Scotland, to have at least revenge on his father's murderer, Johnstone. He therefore sent Johnstone a message, thanking him for holding aloof from his pursuit, and asking for a conference with him for the final settlement of their differences, each to be accompanied by only one attendant. While Johnstone and Maxwell were conferring together, Maxwell's attendant began a quarrel with Johnstone's attendant, and shot him with a pistol. Johnstone shouted 'Treason!' and turned to see 'what the matter meant,' whereupon Maxwell immediately fired at him from behind and shot him dead (CALDERWOOD, vi. 704). On 9 April a new proclamation was therefore made for Maxwell's pursuit (*Reg. P. C. Scotl.* viii. 70); and all skippers were warned against carrying him forth of the realm under pain of death (*ib.* p. 70), a royal proclamation being also, on 28 April, issued for his capture dead or alive (*ib.* p. 83). Nevertheless, so faithful were his followers that he succeeded for some months in evading the most strenuous efforts to capture him, and ultimately made good his escape to the continent. The sympathy of the people with his misfortunes was indicated in the ballad 'Lord Maxwell's Lament.'

In his absence Maxwell was, by the parliament of June 1609, found guilty of three separate charges of treason: the slaughter of two Johnstones in 1602; breaking his ward in Edinburgh Castle in December 1607; and the murder of the laird of Johnstone under trust in April 1608; and was condemned to death and the loss of his honours and estates (*ib.* pp. 805–9; *Acta Parl. Scot.* iv. 414–19; PITCAIRN, *Criminal Trials*, iii. 32–41). In March 1612 he returned to Scotland (CALDERWOOD, vii. 165), and a commission for his pursuit having been issued on 4 July (*Reg. P. C. Scotl.* ix. 359), he was apprehended in Caithness, and, after being brought by sea to Leith, was on 10 Sept. warded in the gaol of Edinburgh (CALDERWOOD, vii. 165). For some time no further proceedings were taken against him, but the Johnstones having on 21 April sent in a petition for his execution (*Reg. P. C. Scotl.* x. 29), an order was issued by the council on 10 May that the sentence passed against him in his absence should be carried out. He was accordingly, on the 21st, beheaded at the market-cross of Edinburgh. 'He died comfortless,' writes Calderwood, 'having none of the ministers present to pray for him, or to make exhortation to him or the people. He desired them not; neither was he content to receive information from them touching his religion' (*History*, vii. 177). His body was interred by Mark Ker in the abbey of Newbattle. By his wife, Lady Margaret Hamilton, only daughter of John, first marquis of Hamilton, he left no issue. The title and estates were, on 13 Oct. 1618, restored to his brother Robert, who also was, on 29 Aug. 1620, invested with the title of Earl of Nithsdale in lieu of that of Earl of Morton, with precedency of the former title.

[Reg. P. C. Scotl. vols. v–x.; Histories of Calderwood and Spotiswood; Letters of John Colville (Bannatyne Club); Pitcairn's Criminal Trials; Sir William Fraser's Book of Caerlaverock, i. 300–24; Douglas's Scottish Peerage (Wood) ii. 319–20.]

T. F. H.

MAXWELL, JOHN (1590?–1647), archbishop of Tuam, son of Maxwell of Cavens, Kirkcudbrightshire, was born about 1590. He was educated at St. Andrews, where he was laureated M.A. on 29 July 1611. In 1615 he was presented to the crown living of Mortlach, Banffshire. He removed in 1622 to Edinburgh, where he successively held four charges. On 18 July 1622 he was elected by the town council to the charge of the New or High Church; he was transferred on 25 Nov. 1625 to the Trinity College Church; on 14 Dec. he was elected by the town council to the second charge in the Old Church, or St. Giles's, and admitted on 27 Jan. 1626; he was promoted in the same year (after 14 Aug.) to the first charge.

Maxwell soon distinguished himself as an advocate for the restoration of liturgical forms in the Scottish church. He had influence at court through his cousin, James

Maxwell of Innerwick (afterwards Earl of Dirleton) [see under MAXWELL, JAMES]. In 1629, by command of Charles I, he waited on Laud, to explain the views of the Scottish hierarchy in reference to a book of common prayer. Laud and Charles were in favour of bringing the Anglican prayer-book into use throughout the three kingdoms. Maxwell reported that the Scottish bishops believed there would be less opposition to a service-book framed in Scotland, though on the English model. In 1630 Maxwell was in correspondence with Henry Leslie [q. v.], then dean of Down, about the presbyterian irregularities of Robert Blair (1593–1666) [q. v.], and other Scottish clergymen who had migrated to the north of Ireland. He carried to the court an account, derived from Leslie, of Blair's alleged teaching respecting physical convulsions as requisites of religious revival. In consequence of this report, Robert Echlin [q. v.], bishop of Down and Connor, suspended Blair in 1631, and deposed him and his friends in 1632. Maxwell, according to Blair's sarcasm, 'was then gaping for a bishopric.' He was raised to the bishopric of Ross on 26 April 1633, and consecrated between 15 June and 18 July following, while Charles was in Scotland. The king granted him on 19 March 1634 a yearly pension of 166*l.*, adding on 20 Oct. 1634 a grant of the priory of Bewlie or Beauly, Inverness-shire, and on 26 July 1636 a mortification of certain kirks and chaplaincies. He was also made a privy councillor, and in 1636 an extraordinary lord of session.

It is conjectured that Maxwell took part in the compilation of the 'canons and constitutions ecclesiastical,' authorised by the king in 1635 and published in 1636. In conjunction with James Wedderburn, bishop of Dumblane, he certainly had a chief hand in drawing up the new service-book for Scotland, subsequently revised by Laud, Juxon, and Wren. On its introduction by order (13 June 1637) of the Scottish privy council, Maxwell at once brought it into use in his cathedral at Fortrose. In December 1637, in consequence of the opposition to the service-book, the privy council sent the lord high treasurer (John, first earl of Traquair) to London for instructions. Traquair urged that the service-book be withdrawn. Laud would have had him superseded as lord high treasurer by Maxwell. The service-book was in use at Fortrose till 11 March 1638, when 'certane scolleris cam pertlie in to the kirk and took wp thir haill seruice bookis, and careit them doun to the Ness with ane coill of fyre, thair to haue brynt them altogidder. Bot there fell out ane suddant schour, that befoir thay culd wyn to the Ness the coill wes drounit out. The scolleris seing this, thay rave thame all in blaidis, dispytfullie, and kest them in the sea' (SPALDING, *Trubles*, i. 87). Maxwell preached a short sermon without common prayer, took horse, rode south in disguise, and went straight to London to the king. In November 1638, on the eve of the meeting of the general assembly at Glasgow, he was at Hamilton, with Walter Whitford, bishop of Brechin. He was one of the six prelates who signed the declinature addressed to the general assembly, and on this and other grounds was deposed and excommunicated (13 Dec.) by the assembly. Maxwell was charged with bowing to the altar, wearing cope and rochet, using 'the English liturgy' for the past two years in his house and cathedral, ordaining deacons, giving absolution, fasting on Friday, and travelling and card-playing on Sunday. His accusers described him as 'a perfect pattern of a proud prelate.' In August 1639 Maxwell and five other bishops signed a protestation against the general assembly as unlawful, and appealing to an assembly of the clergy lawfully convened. Charles proposed to confer on Maxwell the bishopric of Elphin, but Wentworth had promised it to Henry Tilson. The day after the death (26 Nov. 1639) of Archbishop Spotiswood, Maxwell, in terms of the deceased primate's will, gave the manuscript of his history into the king's own hand at Whitehall. Spotiswood had made Maxwell his executor, and recommended him as his successor in the primacy.

In 1640 Maxwell went over to Ireland, where he was made D.D. by Trinity College, Dublin, and appointed on 12 Oct. 1640 bishop of Killala and Achonry by royal patent, in room of Archibald Adair, deprived 18 May for favouring the covenant. According to Patrick Adair, Maxwell came 'in a disguised habit' to Raphoe, co. Donegal, 'about a fortnight before the rebellion' of 1641. Here, with Bishops Henry Leslie and John Leslie (1571–1671) [q. v.], he conferred with Cullenan, Roman catholic bishop of Raphoe. On the outbreak of the rebellion he was driven by the rebels from his palace at Killala, co. Mayo. Fleeing with his wife, three children, and neighbours, the company, numbering about a hundred, was attacked at the bridge of Shruel, co. Mayo, when several were killed and the bishop stripped, wounded, and left for dead. Rescued by Barnabas O'Brien, sixth earl of Thomond [q. v.], he took refuge in the town of Galway, but the townsmen rose against the garrison, and his life was again in peril. He removed to Dublin, where he encouraged his friends by his zealous preaching. Ultimately he made his way to the king at Oxford and acted as royal chaplain. On 30 Aug. 1645 he was appointed to the archbishopric of Tuam, in succession to Richard Boyle (*d.* 1644–5) [q. v.] He returned to Dublin, and in August 1646 signed the address of thanks by eighty Dublin divines to Ormonde, the lord-lieutenant, for the protection he had accorded them in the use of the prayer-book. When the news reached him at Dublin of the surrender of Charles by the Scottish army (30 Jan. 1647), he retired to his closet and was found dead on his knees on 14 Feb. 1647. His age was about 55. He was buried in Christ Church Cathedral. He married Elizabeth Innes, by whom he had four sons, John, David, James, and Robert, and four daughters, Anne, Janet, Elizabeth, and Rachel.

Grub considers Maxwell 'the greatest Scottish prelate of the reign of Charles,' and maintains that his merits 'have never been sufficiently acknowledged, even by the writers most favourable to monarchy and episcopacy.' He had learning and character, and shone as a preacher. His publications, after he left Scotland, were in vindication of the cause he was not strong enough to uphold. They were: 1. 'Episcopacy not Abjured in his Majesties Realm of Scotland,' &c., 1641, 4to. 2. 'An Answer to a Gentleman who desired of a Divine some Reasons by which it might appear how inconsistent Presbyteriall Government is with Monarchie,' &c., 1644, 4to. 3. 'Sacro-sancta Regum Majestas, or the Sacred Prerogative of Christian Kings,' &c., Oxford, 1644, 4to (published under the initials I. A.; answered in the 'Lex Rex,' 1644, of Samuel Rutherford [q. v.]). 4. 'The Burthen of Issachar, or the Tyrannical Power and Practises of the Presbyteriall Government in Scotland,' &c., Oxford, 1646, 4to (anon.; ascribed to Maxwell by Robert Baillie, D.D. [q. v.], who answered it in his 'Historicall Vindication,' 1646; it was reprinted as 'Presbytery Displayed,' &c., 1703, 4to). Wood mentions the ascription to Maxwell of the 'Lysimachus Nicanor,' 1640, of John Corbet (1603–1641) [q. v.]

[Cotton's Fasti Eccl. Hib. iv. 68, 86 *n.*; Hew Scott's Fasti Eccles. Scoticanæ; Ware's Works (Harris), 1764, i. 617, 653, ii. 359; Mant's Hist. of the Church of Ireland, 1840, i. 563, 584; Acts of General Assembly, 1843, p. 10; Memoirs of Robert Blair, 1844, pp. 87 sq.; Spalding's Memorialls of the Trubles, 1850, i. 87; Grub's Eccles. Hist. of Scotl. 1850, ii. 338, 366, 377, iii. 32 sq., 61, 89 sq.; Adair's True Narrative, ed. Killen, 1866, pp. 33, 62; Stewart's History, ed. Killen, 1866, p. 314; Reid's Hist. Presb. Church in Ireland, ed. Killen, 1867, i. 134, 270; Strafford's Letters, ii. 369.] A. G.

MAXWELL, JOHN HALL (1812–1866), agriculturist, eldest son of William Maxwell of Dargavel, Renfrewshire, who died in 1847, by Mary, eldest daughter of John Campbell of Possil, near Glasgow, was born in Queen Street, Glasgow, in February 1812, and called to the Scottish bar in 1835. He practised his profession until 1845, when he succeeded Sir Charles Gordon of Grimkin as secretary to the Highland Agricultural Society. At this time the number of members was 2,620, and the funds of the society amounted to 34,000*l.*; when he retired there were 4,200 members, and the finances had risen to 50,000*l.* The annual shows under his management displayed great improvements in the quantity and quality of stock, and in the workmanship of agricultural implements. He paid great attention to the collection of agricultural statistics respecting stock and crops, and for this and other services was, on 5 Feb. 1856, created a C.B. On his own estate at Dargavel he effected, at great expense, many improvements, especially in the reclamation of waste land. On 17 Jan. 1866 he was presented with one thousand guineas and a service of plate. He died at his residence, Torr Hall, near Paisley, on 25 Aug. 1866. He married, 3 Aug. 1843, Eliza Anne Margaret, eldest daughter of Thomas Williams of Southwick Crescent, Hyde Park, London.

[Law Times, 1866, xli. 763; Saddle and Sirloin, by the Druid, Part North, 1870, pp. 3–6; Irving's Book of Scotsmen, 1881, p. 342.]
G. C. B.

MAXWELL, Sir MURRAY (1775–1831), captain in the navy, third son of James Maxwell, a captain in the 42nd regiment, third son of Sir Alexander Maxwell of Monreith, Wigtownshire, second baronet (Foster, *Baronetage*), was born in the parish of Penninghame, near Newton Stewart, on 10 Sept. 1775. This date is given in the certificate of baptism annexed to his passing certificate in the Public Record Office. On 10 Sept. 1790 he entered the navy on board the Juno, with Captain (afterwards Sir) Samuel Hood [q. v.], and served in her till March 1794, when he followed Hood to the Aigle. In November 1794 he was moved into the Nemesis, and was still in her when she was captured at Smyrna on 9 Dec. 1795. He afterwards joined the Blenheim, and a few months later the Princess Royal, in which he returned to England, and passed his examination, 7 Sept. 1796. On 10 Oct. 1796 he was promoted to be lieutenant, and again, 15 Dec. 1802, to be commander of the Cyane sloop in the West Indies. In her he was present at the reduction of St. Lucia, and was appointed by Hood acting captain of the Centaur, bearing his broad pennant. He had thus an important part in the capture of Tobago, Demerara, and Essequibo in July and September 1803, and of Berbice and Surinam in April 1804. His commission as captain was confirmed to 4 Aug. 1803. In 1805 he commanded the Galatea in the West Indies, and in 1807 was appointed to the Alceste, a 38-gun frigate, in which 'he rendered his name conspicuous by the dashing nature of his services in the Mediterranean.' On 4 April 1808, being off Cadiz, with the Mercury and Grasshopper brig in company, he dispersed a flotilla of twenty gunboats, sank two of them, drove their convoy on shore, and afterwards boarded and brought off seven. On the coast of Italy he assisted at the destruction of several armed vessels and martello towers. On 22 May 1810 he landed a party of men near Fréjus, stormed a 2-gun battery, spiked the guns, broke the carriages, blew up the magazine, and threw the shot into the sea. A few days later the Alceste's boats attacked a flotilla of French coasting vessels, captured four, drove two on shore, and compelled the others to put back.

In the spring of 1811 he was in the Adriatic, under the orders of Captain James Brisbane [q. v.], and in the autumn had for some months a semi-independent command there. On 28 Nov. he was lying at Lissa, in company with the Active and Unité, when 'three suspicious sail' were signalled as in sight from the hill. Maxwell immediately put to sea, and on the morning of the 29th sighted three French frigates. Towards noon the smallest of the three separated from her consorts; she was chased, and in the evening was captured by the Unité. The other two were engaged by the Alceste and Active [see Gordon, Sir James Alexander], Maxwell telegraphing 'Remember the battle of Lissa' [see Hoste, Sir William]. After a sharp action of about an hour and a half, one of the French frigates, the Pauline, fled; the other, the Pomone, defended herself for half an hour longer, and then, having lost her main and mizen masts, surrendered. Neither the Alceste nor Active was able to chase the Pauline, which got into Brindisi. Her captain was severely punished by Napoleon (James, v. 262; Troude, iv. 146, 149; Chevalier, iii. 391). In 1812 Maxwell was appointed to the Dædalus, in which he sailed for India in charge of a fleet of Indiamen. On 2 July 1813 the Dædalus was wrecked off the coast of Ceylon. Maxwell returned to England, and, being acquitted of all blame, was nominated a C.B. in 1815.

In October he was again appointed to the Alceste, at the desire of Lord Amherst [see Amherst, William Pitt, Earl Amherst], going out as ambassador to the emperor of China. The Alceste sailed from Spithead on 9 Feb. 1816, and anchored off the Pei-ho on 28 July. Lord Amherst landed on 9 Aug., directing the ship to meet him at Canton, whither he proposed to travel overland from Pekin. Maxwell took the opportunity of exploring the Gulf of Pechili, the west coast of Corea—till then unknown except by hearsay, and drawn on the chart by imagination—and the Loo-Choo Islands. The results were afterwards ably described by Captain Basil Hall [q. v.] of the Lyra brig, then in company with the Alceste, in his 'Account of a Voyage of Discovery to the Western Coast of Corea and the Great Loo-Choo Island,' 1818, 4to. The Alceste arrived off the mouth of the Canton river on 2 Nov., and Maxwell, unable to get any satisfactory answer to his application for a pass, determined to go up the river without one. As he approached the Bocca Tigris, a mandarin came on board and ordered him to anchor at once; if he attempted to go on, the batteries would sink the ship. Maxwell sent back an angry answer, and the Alceste passed on, scattering the war-junks which attempted to stop her, and silencing the batteries for the time by a single well-directed broadside. Without further molestation she arrived at Whampoa, where Lord Amherst re-embarked on 21 Jan. 1817. The Lyra was sent to Calcutta with despatches for the governor-general, and the Alceste, pursuing her voyage by herself, entered the Straits of Gaspar on the morning of 18 Feb.

These straits, exceedingly dangerous even now, were then little more than explored, and the charts were very imperfect. About eight o'clock the ship struck on a rock about three miles from Pulo Leat. It was at once found that she had sustained fatal injuries. Everyone was landed on the island, together with such stores as time permitted, but on the third day the wreck was taken possession of by swarms of Malay pirates, who threatened the encampment on shore. On the morning of the 19th Lord Amherst and his staff had been sent on to Batavia in two boats, under the command of Lieutenant Henry Parkyns Hoppner, a son of John Hoppner the artist. Some two hundred men remained on this inhospitable island, without clothes, with a very scanty supply of food, and beset by ferocious savages. The perfect order preserved has always been justly considered one of the splendid triumphs of discipline over brute instinct. They were relieved on 3 March by the arrival of the East India Company's ship Ternate, sent by Amherst from Batavia. Henry (afterwards Sir Henry) Ellis, an attaché of the embassy, who returned in the Ternate, wrote in his journal: 'Participation of privation and equal distribution of comfort had lightened the weight of suffering to all, and I found the universal sentiment to be an enthusiastic admiration of the temper, energy, and arrangements of Captain Maxwell. . . . His look was confidence, and his orders were felt to be security.' At Batavia a ship was chartered to convey to England both the embassy and the officers and ship's company of the Alceste. Touching at St. Helena, Maxwell was presented to Napoleon, who referred to the capture of the Pomone. 'Your government,' he said, 'must not blame you for the loss of the Alceste, for you took one of my frigates.' (The Alceste was also one of his frigates; she had been captured by Sir Samuel Hood off Rochefort on 25 Sept. 1806.) On his arrival in England in August 1817 Maxwell was tried by court-martial, and not only 'most fully acquitted,' but specially complimented for 'the most zealous and officer-like manner' in which he had conducted himself in the difficult and intricate navigation, and for 'his coolness, self-collection,' and exertions after the ship struck. Lord Amherst appeared as a witness in his behalf. On 27 May 1818 Maxwell was knighted. He was elected F.R.S., 18 Feb. 1819, and on 20 May 1819 was presented by the East India Company with 1,500*l.* in reward of the services rendered by him to the embassy and in compensation for the loss he had sustained in the wreck.

In 1821–2 he was captain of the Bulwark, bearing the flag of Sir Benjamin Hallowell (afterwards Carew) at Chatham, and in 1823 of the Briton on the South American station. In May 1831 he was appointed lieutenant-governor of Prince Edward's Island, and was preparing for his departure when he died suddenly on 26 June 1831.

He married about 1798 Grace Callander, daughter of Colonel Waugh of the 57th regiment, and had issue a daughter and one son, John Balfour, who died an admiral on the retired list in 1874. The latter possessed a portrait of Sir Murray by Martin Cregan.

Of Maxwell's six brothers three were in the army, two in the navy. Of these last, John, a captain of 1810, died in command of the Aurora frigate in 1826. Keith, born about 1774, a lieutenant of 1794, was specially promoted to be commander in 1801 for his brilliant and successful gallantry in cutting out the French 20-gun corvette Chevrette from under the batteries of Camaret Bay, on the night of 21–2 July (James, iii. 138; Troude, iii. 255). He was promoted to be captain in 1804, and died in 1823.

[Marshall's Roy. Nav. Biog. iv. (vol. ii. pt. ii.) 797, 884, and vi. (Suppl. pt. ii.) 94; O'Byrne's Nav. Biog. Dict. s.n. 'Maxwell, John Balfour;' James's Naval Hist. (edit. of 1860); Ellis's Journ. of the Proceedings of the late Embassy to China (1817); McLeod's Narrative of a Voyage in H.M. late ship Alceste (1817), with a portrait of Maxwell. The story of the loss of the Alceste is popularly told in Maria Hack's Winter Evenings, or Tales of Travellers.] J. K. L.

MAXWELL, ROBERT, fifth Baron Maxwell (*d.* 1546), was descended from a family which, probably originally from England, settled in Scotland at Maccuswell or Maxwell, on the Tweed, near Kelso, in or before the reign of David I. Ewen Maccuswel of Caerlaverock, Dumfriesshire, assisted Malcolm Canmore at the siege of Alnwick in 1093, and it is with Dumfriesshire and Galloway that the subsequent history of the Maxwells is chiefly associated. Sir Herbert Maxwell won special renown for his defence of the castle of Caerlaverock against the army of Edward I in 1300, and in the subsequent wars its possession was frequently in dispute. The lordship of Maxwell dates from about 1428. The fifth baron was the eldest son of John, fourth baron, killed at Flodden, 9 Sept. 1513, his mother being Agnes, daughter of Sir Alexander Stewart of Garlies, ancestor of the Earls of Galloway. He was returned heir to his father on 4 Nov. 1513. At the time of Flodden he was admiral of a fleet, which it was proposed to send to France, but which on the voyage was driven back, and arrived at Kirkcudbright on the day after the battle. Maxwell immediately afterwards seized Lochmaben; and on 26 Nov. he was appointed captain and keeper of Thrieve. On the forfeiture of Lord Home in 1516 he acquired part of his lands, and in the following year was made warden of the west marches.

After the return of the Earl of Angus, husband of the queen, to Scotland, Maxwell became one of the queen's party. He was concerned in the removal of the young king from Stirling to Edinburgh, 26 July 1524; was on 18 Aug. made lord provost of Edinburgh; took part in the scheme for the king's nominal assumption of the government in November, with the advice of his mother; and was one of the council appointed assist her in the government. The queen's divorce from Angus changed the attitude of Maxwell as well as other nobles towards her; and on the king attaining his majority, fourteen years, 21 June 1526, Maxwell became one of the council appointed to assist

Angus in the guardianship of the king and management of affairs. He was in company with the king at Melrose Bridge on 25 July, when an unsuccessful attempt was made by the Douglases to get possession of him. The same year he was appointed steward of Kirkcudbright and keeper of Thrieve. On the escape of the king from Falkland Palace to Stirling in July 1528, Maxwell separated himself from the party of Angus, and was chosen one of the new council. Having accompanied the king to Edinburgh he was again made lord provost of the city, and on 26 Aug. frustrated an attempt of Angus to take possession of it (*Diurnal of Occurrents*, p. 11). He was one of the jurors on the trial of Angus, and on his forfeiture received a portion of his lands. Like most of the southern nobles, Maxwell gave his indirect countenance to the border raiders, and not unfrequently engaged in raids on his own account. In 1528 he had been compelled by Angus to make compensation to the English for burning Netherby, and this probably was the reason of his hostility to Angus. In the following year, when the king determined to make a progress southwards for the chastisement of the raiders, it was deemed advisable to place Maxwell and other sympathisers with them in ward in the castle of Edinburgh, but after the king's return they were released on giving pledges for their allegiance. The execution of John Armstrong [q. v.], who was partly under his protection, was specially distasteful to Maxwell, but he afterwards became reconciled to the king, and on 17 Nov. 1533 was appointed an extraordinary lord of session. During an excursion into England in 1536 he burned Penrith. The same year he was appointed one of the regents during the absence of King James on his matrimonial expedition to France; and after the death of the king's first wife, Madeline of France, was sent in December 1537 with other ambassadors to conclude a treaty of marriage with Mary of Guise.

Maxwell as high admiral commanded an expedition to the Orkneys in 1540. He joined the army which assembled on the Borough Muir of Edinburgh in October 1542, and having in vain urged that battle should be given to the English, he after its disbandment took the principal part in raising a force for a new expedition. In command of ten thousand men he proceeded to the western borders, but just before the encounter with the English at Solway Moss a warrant was produced by Oliver Sinclair, authorising him to assume the chief command. Such confusion and discontent thereupon resulted that scarce any resistance was made to the English, Maxwell alone strenuously endeavouring to induce his men to make a stand. On being 'admonished to take horse,' he answered, 'Nay, I will rather abide here the chance which it shall please God to send me, than to go home and there to be hanged.' 'So,' says Calderwood, 'he remained on foot, and was taken when the multitude fled' (*History*, i. 14). Along with other captive nobles he was sent to London, but the death of James V shortly afterwards somewhat changed Henry's policy. The captive nobles were permitted to return to Scotland on paying a ransom, and on entering into a bond to aid the English king—by force if necessary—in his scheme for a marriage of Prince Edward with the young queen, Mary Stuart, an essential preliminary being the recognition of Henry's overlordship. Maxwell, who perhaps more than any other Scottish noble had been inveterate in his hostility to England, must have only consented to serve the interests of Henry from desperation. Nevertheless he now, while Beaton was in prison, took occasion to show his hostility to him by proposing and getting passed an act that all should have liberty to read the Bible in the Scots and English tongue, provided that 'na man dispute or hold opinions under the pains contenit in the actis of parliament' (*Acta Parl. Scot.* ii. 45). Along with Lord Somerville he was one of the chief agents of Angus in his intrigues with Henry. On the last day of October 1543 Maxwell and Somerville were captured by the Abbot of Paisley, while proceeding with letters to the Earls of Cassilis and Glencairn, Maxwell being sent to the castle of Edinburgh (*Diurnal of Occurrents*, p. 29). On obtaining his liberty he joined Lennox in the castle of Glasgow, and was taken prisoner at its capture, 1 April 1544, but was set at liberty on 3 May following, on the approach of the English fleet to Leith roads, lest his friends or followers should take part with the English. Having now excited the suspicions of Henry as to his fidelity, he was taken prisoner and sent to the Tower. Thereupon he offered to serve under the Earl of Hertford, with a red cross on his armour as a symbol of his devotion to England; and in October 1545 he was allowed to return to Scotland, on delivering the castle of Caerlaverock into English keeping. Early in November his castles were captured by Beaton, and he was conveyed a prisoner to Dumfries; but having affirmed that he had only made terms with Henry in fear of his life, he on 12 Jan. 1545–6 received a remission, and was at the same time made chief justice of Annandale. On 3 June 1546 he was appointed warden of the west marches. He died on 9 July of the same year. By his first wife, Janet, daughter of Sir William Douglas of Drumlanrig, he had two sons—Robert, sixth baron Maxwell, and Sir John Maxwell of Terregles, fourth baron Herries [q. v.]—and a daughter, Margaret, married, first, to Archibald, sixth earl of Angus, and secondly to Sir William Baillie of Lamington. By his second wife, Lady Agnes Stewart, daughter of James, earl of Buchan, and widow of Adam, second earl of Bothwell, he had no issue.

[Histories of Buchanan, Leslie, and Calderwood; Diurnal of Occurrents (Bannatyne Club); State Papers, Henry VIII; Cal. Hamilton Papers, vol. i.; Sir William Fraser's Book of Caerlaverock, i. 172–209; Douglas's Scottish Peerage (Wood), ii. 316–17.] T. F. H.

MAXWELL, ROBERT (1695–1765), writer on agriculture, eldest son of James Maxwell of Arkland, Kirkpatrick-Durham, Kircudbrightshire, by his wife Margaret, daughter of Robert Neilson of Barncaillie, in the same parish, was born at Arkland in 1695. The Maxwells had been settled at Arkland since the beginning of the seventeenth century, and the Neilsons, descended from the house of Craigcaffie, Wigton, had been proprietors of Barncaillie since 1537. After receiving an education 'becoming his rank,' Maxwell engaged in agriculture, and about 1723 took on a lease of four periods of nineteen years a farm of 130 acres, all arable, at Cliftonhall, near Edinburgh, the rent of which, paid in money, was 50*l.* From this time he devoted himself to the improvement of agriculture, and during the first half of the eighteenth century he probably did more than any other to introduce or encourage the practice of new methods. If he did not initiate he was one of the earliest and most active members of the Society of Improvers in the Knowledge of Agriculture in Scotland, which was established at Edinburgh on 8 June 1723. In 1739 he proposed to the Society for the Propagation of Christianity in Scotland a scheme for the application of certain funds in their possession to the education of boys in the new principles of agriculture. The society invited him to give a full account of the uses of the root crops which he proposed to grow, and the Society of Improvers encouraged him, but the scheme fell through. Meanwhile Maxwell had taken the largest share of the work of the Society of Improvers. He wrote 'not a little that was laid before them,' and replied to most of the inquiries which were sent in from all parts of the country. He had besides the management of his own farm, where he appears to have paid more attention to experiments than to making a profit, and he supervised improvements on the estates of the great land proprietors. Among those who availed themselves of his advice and assistance was John, second earl of Stair. In 1743 he published 'Select Transactions of the Society of Improvers,' &c., Edinburgh, 8vo. This valuable work, a large portion of which consists of Maxwell's contributions, contains many suggestions which were then new to Scotland, such as the efficacy and the mode of burning clay or subsoil, the method of cutting seed potatoes and of planting them, the rotation of crops, root crops, and the enclosing of land, in addition to much useful information on the agriculture and manufactures of Scotland. On the dissolution of the Society of Improvers, in consequence of the death of nearly all its founders, Maxwell transferred his energies to the Edinburgh Society for the Encouragement of Arts, Sciences, Manufactures, and Agriculture, which took its place.

In 1745 Maxwell succeeded his father in the estate of Arkland, but by this time he had exhausted his somewhat slender resources. He had to surrender the lease of his farm at Cliftonhall, and in 1749 he became insolvent. At the instance of his creditors Arkland was sold, 9 Jan. 1750, for 10,304*l.* Scots to John Coltart of Areeming.

After this period Maxwell earned his living by acting as land valuer and supervisor of improvements, while his wife probably became a shopkeeper 'betwixt James's and Wardrop's Courts in the north side of the Lawn Market at Edinburgh' (Advertisement in the *Practical Beemaster*, 2nd edit. 1750). He did not, however, relax his efforts for the improvement of agriculture. He had before this time endeavoured to obtain the establishment of a lectureship or a class in agriculture at Edinburgh University, and Lord Stair and the Society of Improvers had been favourable to the scheme. Unable, however, to accomplish this design, Maxwell, 'without the patronage of any public body, and encouraged by individuals only,' gave public lectures on agriculture in Edinburgh in 1756. His lectures, probably the first of the kind delivered in Great Britain, were attended by many of the farmers and landowners in the district, and he was strongly urged to publish them. Two of them were printed in the 'Practical Husbandman, being a Collection of Miscellaneous Papers on Husbandry,' Edinburgh, 1757, 8vo. He died at Renfrew, in the house of his son-in-law, James King, on 17 May 1765.

Maxwell married Margaret, daughter of Bailie Montgomery of Edinburgh, who predeceased him, leaving six daughters.

In addition to the works mentioned above, Maxwell probably edited and wrote parts of 'A Treatise concerning the Manner of Fallowing of Ground, &c., by the Society for Improving in the Knowledge of Agriculture,' Edinburgh, 1724, 8vo. He also published 'The Practical Beemaster,' &c., Edinburgh, 1747, 8vo; 2nd edit. 1750; reprinted in John Reid's 'Scots Gardiner,' Edinburgh, 1756.

[Select Transactions of the Society of Improvers, passim; Thomas Murray's Literary History of Galloway, 2nd edit. pp. 167–74; M'Kerlie's Lands and their Owners in Galloway, iv. 227, 303.] W. A. S. H.

MAXWELL, WILLIAM, fifth BARON HERRIES (*d.* 1603), was the eldest son of John, fourth baron Herries [q. v.], by his wife Agnes, daughter of the third Baron Herries. While still Master of Herries he was, on 15 Oct. 1580, elected a gentleman of the chamber (*Reg. P. C. Scotl.* iii. 323). On 26 Jan. 1582–3 he was chosen a member of the privy council in place of his father, who died on the 20th (*ib.* p. 548). On 9 June 1587 he became warden of the west march (*ib.* iv. 188). On 31 Jan. following he was, however, denounced a rebel for not entering before the council certain of his dependents charged with oppression and depredations (*ib.* p. 244), and on 5 Feb. was again summoned to appear before the council on 5 March (*ib.* p. 248). On the 20th the general assembly also handed in a complaint against him and others for attending mass in Dumfries (CALDERWOOD, iv. 657); but already on 16 Feb. he had made his submission to the king (*ib.* p. 677). On 3 March he was therefore released from the horn (*Reg. P. C. Scotl.* iv. 258); and on the 5th he came under an obligation neither to hear nor suffer mass to be said within his wardening, and also to repair to the kirk of Dumfries for the hearing of the sermons (*ib.* p. 259). On 1 Aug. 1588 he was appointed a commissioner for executing the act against the Spanish Armada.

About 14 Oct. 1595 Herries, to avenge the slaughter of John, seventh or eighth baron Maxwell [q. v.] in 1593, came in command of about three hundred of the Maxwells to Lockerbie to attack the Johnstones, but the latter had much the best of the encounter, many of the Maxwells being slain, and others taken prisoner (MOYSIE, *Memoirs*, pp. 124–5; CALDERWOOD, v. 385). On 8 March 1595–6 he appeared before the council, and protested that by his assurance to Sir James Johnstone he should not be answerable for certain Maxwells, and that he did not include in the assurance any of the Johnstones who had taken part in the late conflict (*Reg. P. C. Scotl.* v. 280). On 7 July he was denounced a rebel for not appearing to give his advice regarding the quieting of the borders (*ib.* p. 300). Shortly thereafter he was warded in Edinburgh Castle, but on the 24th was released on promising to give caution within three days to keep good rule (*ib.* p. 741). On 22 March 1598–9 he was charged, under pain of rebellion, to appear before the council on 6 June to underlie such order as would be given him for the quieting of the west march (*ib.* p. 543). He failed to do so, and was subsequently imprisoned in Tantallon Castle, but on promising to make his men answerable to justice, he was released on 11 Sept. (*ib.* vi. 31). On 20 Nov. he and others were required to submit their feud with the laird of Johnstone to arbitration (*ib.* p. 46), which he agreed to do, but protested that he should 'reserve his duty of blood and friendship to the Lord Maxwell,' and the king admitted his protest (*ib.* p. 91). On 17 June he was temporarily reappointed warden of the west march, in succession to Sir John Carmichael, who had a short time previously been murdered (*ib.* p. 117), and on 5 July the keeping of the castle of Lochmaben was given to him (*ib.* p. 128); but on 13 Aug. the wardency was conferred on Sir James Johnstone (*ib.* p. 155). This provoked the jealousy of the Maxwells, and on 20 May 1601 Herries was charged to answer for a new design against Johnstone (*ib.* p. 240). On 20 Nov. he and others in Dumfries were denounced for contravening the acts of parliament 'against saying and hearing mass and entertaining priests,' and were summoned before the council on 17 Dec. (*ib.* p. 312), with which summons they complied (*ib.* p. 327). On his appearance he was, however, warded in Edinburgh Castle for not entering James Murray to answer for the slaughter of Sir James Carmichael (*ib.* p. 316), but on 8 Jan. he was released on giving surety to repair to the burgh of Edinburgh and there remain during the king's pleasure (*ib.* p. 712). On 9 Feb. he appeared, and bound himself not to harbour John Hamilton and other jesuits, and to defend and support the minister of Dumfries in his office and in the discipline of the kirk (*ib.* p. 352). On the 28th he came under an obligation not to assist Lord Maxwell and his rebellious accomplices (*ib.* p. 355). In May 1602 the assembly of the kirk decided that he should be placed in charge of a minister for his better instruction and confirmation in the truth, in case he repaired to Edinburgh; but it was reported in November that he had stayed only a short time in Edinburgh (CALDERWOOD, vi. 163, 166). He died on 11 Oct. of the following year. By his wife, Catherine Ker, sister of Mark, first earl of Lothian, he had five sons—John, sixth baron Herries, Sir William of Gribton, Sir Robert of Sweetheart, Edward, and James—and two daughters: Elizabeth, lady Urchell, and Margaret, lady Parton.

[Reg. P. C. Scotl. vols. iii–vi.; Histories of Calderwood and Spotiswood; Moysie's Memoirs (Bannatyne Club); Sir William Fraser's Book of Caerlaverock, i. 571, 584; Douglas's Scottish Peerage (Wood), ii. 320.] T. F. H.

MAXWELL, WILLIAM, fifth EARL OF NITHSDALE (1676–1744), Jacobite, eldest son of Robert, fourth earl, by Lady Lucy Douglas, was born in 1676. On 26 May 1696 he was returned heir to his father. He was in 1699 in Paris, where on 2 March he signed a marriage contract with Lady Winifred Herbert, fifth and youngest daughter of William, first marquis of Powis. Doubtless while in Paris he paid homage to the exiled sovereign at St. Germains. He also maintained the hereditary attachment of his family to the church of Rome; and in 1703 some of the presbyterian ministers assembled a number of countrymen and attacked his house of Terregles, on pretence of searching it for jesuits and priests. The case came before the justiciary court on 1 Feb. 1704, and he was deprived of the office of hereditary steward of Kirkcudbright. He was mentioned in the Duke of Perth's 'Instructions' in 1704 as a Jacobite, and as having interest in Nithsdale and Galloway (HOOKE, *Correspondence*, i. 229); and in a Jacobite 'Memoir' of 3 Jan. 1707 as puissant and a catholic (*ib.* ii. 201). He was also one of the nobles who in 1707 signed an agreement for a rising (*ib.* p. 238). On 20 Nov. 1712, in view of eventualities resulting from his support of the Stuart cause, he signed a contract disposing of his estates to his eldest son, and reserving to himself only a life-rent.

In October 1715 Nithsdale, along with Viscount Kenmure [see GORDON, WILLIAM, sixth VISCOUNT KENMURE], joined the English Jacobites under Derwentwater. He is the 'Willie' of the Jacobite song, 'Kenmure's up and awa, Willie.' Few or none of his own dependents joined him, and at the battle of Preston he was one of the commanders of the gentlemen volunteers. He was taken prisoner at the battle, and sent to the Tower of London. At his trial in January following he, like Kenmure, made a rather abject declaration of penitence, excusing his consent to join the rebels on the ground that, having been summoned by the government to Edinburgh, he was, on account of his feeble health, afraid to risk the possibility of imprisonment. His humiliating protestations were of no avail, and he was sentenced to be beheaded on 24 Feb. along with the other Jacobite nobles, Kenmure, Derwentwater, Carnwath, Widdrington, and Nairn. The last three were reprieved. The Countess of Nithsdale, after a difficult journey to London, succeeded in gaining entrance to the palace of St. James, and threw herself at the king's feet beseeching mercy for her husband, but her importunities were fruitless. Determined, however, not to be baffled, she obtained access to her husband in the Tower, accompanied by some ladies, on the night before the day fixed for the execution, and, disguising him in a hood and cloak, deceived the guards and enabled him to leave the prison with her. He was conveyed to Dover disguised in a livery coat by a servant of the Venetian ambassador, and there he hired a small boat, which conveyed him to Calais. The king on learning his escape merely said that it was 'the best thing a man in his condition could have done.' The House of Lords, on 21 Jan. 1723, decided that only the life-rent of his estates was forfeited, but his honours were attainted. Nithsdale joined the Chevalier in Rome, and died there 20 March 1744. His wife, who wrote a narrative of his escape, published in the 'Transactions of the Society of Antiquaries of Scotland,' vol. i., set sail for Bruges on 19 July 1716, and joined her husband at Rome, where she died in May 1749. They had one son, William, commonly called Lord Maxwell, to whom his estates passed, and a daughter, Anne, married to Lord Bellew.

Kneller painted portraits of both the earl and countess: that of the former belongs to the Earl of Kintore, and that of the countess to the present Baron Herries. There are engravings of the earl and countess, from originals at Terregles, in Sir William Fraser's 'Book of Caerlaverock.'

[Histories of the Rebellion in 1715 by Patten, Rae, and Chambers; Hooke's Correspondence (Roxburghe Club); Narrative by Lady Winifred Maxwell in Transactions of the Society of Antiquaries of Scotland, vol. i.; Hepworth Dixon's Her Majesty's Tower, ii. 385–403 (a detailed account of the escape); Jesse's Pretenders and their Adherents, pp. 69–77; State Trials, xv. 762–806; Sir William Fraser's Book of Caerlaverock, i. 414–53; Douglas's Scottish Peerage (Wood), ii. 320–1.] T. F. H.

MAXWELL, WILLIAM (1732–1818), friend of Dr. Johnson, born 24 Aug. 1732, was eldest son of John Maxwell of Falkland, in Donagh parish, co. Monaghan, archdeacon of Clogher 1762–83, by his first wife, Isabella, daughter of the Rev. John Leavens of Ardee, co. Louth. He was admitted a pensioner at Trinity College, Dublin, where he was elected scholar in 1750 and graduated B.A. 1752, M.A. 1755, B.D. and D.D. 1777 (Todd, *Graduates*, p. 381). His health suffered through study, and he travelled abroad with his relative, Lord Farnham, until it was re-established. About 1755 he was introduced to Johnson by George Grierson, the government printer at Dublin. For several years he was assistant preacher at the Temple Church when the Rev. Gregory Sharpe, D.D., was master; in 1775, through the favour of his relative, the Hon. Henry Maxwell, bishop of Meath, he obtained the rectory of Mount Temple, co. Westmeath. On his return to Ireland, Johnson, who had been for many years his 'social friend,' and always 'spoke of him with a very kind regard,' took an affecting leave of him. His house at Falkland was of considerable size, with a good library, the relics of which are preserved at Trough Lodge, the seat of the Ancketills. When he was required to reside more regularly on his benefice, he resigned the rectory, and about 1780 removed to Bath, allowing the house at Falkland to fall into ruins. It is, however, asserted that he was there at the time of the rebellion, and that the rebels fired into his bedroom to kill him. He died at Bennett Street, Bath, 3 Sept. 1818, and was buried in Walcot Church, where his widow erected to his memory an enormous monument, with the family escutcheon and the motto, 'Je suis prêt.' His first wife was Anne, eldest daughter of William Burrell Massingberd of Ormsby, Lincolnshire, whom he married on 6 Dec. 1777, and by whom he had four children. Three of them died without issue; the youngest, Anne, married at Queen Square Chapel, Bath, on 21 Jan. 1818, Henry Francis Lyte [q.v.], and died at Berry Head, Brixham, Devonshire, 7 Jan. 1856. Maxwell's first wife died at Bath, and some time later he married in Ireland Miss Jane Ellis, who died without issue 21 May 1847, aged 82, and was buried by her husband's side in Walcot Church. He left by his will bequests for the better education of the poor at Donagh; on the old school-house at Glaslough in that parish was placed an inscription to the effect that it was built in 1821 from his last designs. Two oval portraits in pastel of the first Mrs. Maxwell and her son, both dated 1784 and signed by Sir Thomas Lawrence, and one of Dr. Maxwell, not dated or signed, are in the possession of Miss Hogg.

Maxwell was very proud of his friendship with Johnson, copying him 'in wig, general appearance, and in manner.' He furnished Boswell with considerable collectanea (in which some of the doctor's best sayings are embodied) on Johnson's life before 1770. The greater part of them were inserted in Boswell, 1st edit. i. 336–45, but some further anecdotes were given by him in the additions to the second edition. He is said to have written some political pamphlets, one on the Falkland Islands, and another addressed to Pitt on taxation as it affected Ireland.

[Gent. Mag. 1819, pt. i. p. 92; Monkland's Literature of Bath, Supplement, pp. 7–8; Shirley's Monaghan, pp. 160–2, 299; J. Silvester's Walcot Church, p. 47; Isaac Taylor's Family Pen, i. 298–300; Boswell, ed. Croker, 1831, i. 373, ed. Hill, ii. 116; T. Hutchinson's Diary i. 430; information from his great-grandson, Mr. H. Maxwell Lyte, C.B.] W. P. C.

MAXWELL, WILLIAM HAMILTON (1792–1850), Irish novelist, born at Newry, co. Down, in 1792 (*Register of Matriculations, Trinity College, Dublin*), was son of James Maxwell, merchant, a descendant of the Maxwells of Caerlaverock, who had come from Nithsdale to Ireland. His mother was a daughter of William Hamilton, of good family. Maxwell was educated at Dr. Henderson's school, and on 7 Dec. 1807, at the age of fifteen, entered Trinity College, Dublin. Though he wasted his time, he is said to have graduated with some distinction. He is probably identical with the William 'Henry' Maxwell who proceeded B.A. in 1812. Maxwell appears to have previously entered the army. According to the 'Army List,' 1813, 'Hamilton Maxwell' obtained a captaincy in the 42nd foot on 14 May 1812. He seems to have subsequently transferred himself to the 88th regiment (*Illustrated London News*, 25 Jan. 1851; cf. *Army List*, 1815, p. 659). He was present in the Peninsular campaigns and at Waterloo.

On the disbanding of the forces he returned to Newry and spent some years desultorily, reading, hunting, and shooting. Having anticipated his future income by confirming for ready money certain leases granted by his father as tenant for life, and being baulked in his expectation of an aunt's fortune by an informality in her will, he applied for a commission in the Spanish service in South America, but the friend who was to have obtained it for him inopportunely died. Shortly afterwards he mended his fortunes by marriage, and took holy orders. In 1820 the Archbishop of Armagh gave him the rectory of Ballagh in Connemara, a place destitute of congregation, but abounding in game. In retirement, at a shooting-lodge at Ballycroy, he wrote his first novel, 'O'Hara,' which was issued anonymously, and met with no success. He seems to have become unsettled once more; but the Marquis of Sligo, with whom he was on friendly terms, gave him a house rent free to retain him at Ballagh. His 'Wild Sports of the West,' published in 1832, brought him some reputation as a sporting and military novelist, and earned the praises of Professor Wilson in 'Noctes Ambrosianæ' (November 1832) as the work of a true sportsman. He next published his best-known work, 'Stories from Waterloo,' for which Colburn gave him 300*l*. Besides contributing to 'Bentley's Miscellany' and the 'Dublin University Magazine,' Maxwell wrote a variety of sketches and novels, chiefly on sporting or military subjects. He also wrote a 'Life of the Duke of Wellington,' which was afterwards repeatedly reissued by other hands, sometimes in a condensed form. His 'History of the Rebellion in 1798' was avowedly meant as a corrective to Madden's 'Lives of United Irishmen.' Maxwell is said to have been deprived of his living in 1844 for non-residence (COTTON). He made no provision for the future, and after spending several years in ill-health and distress he retired to Musselburgh, near Edinburgh, where he died on 29 Dec. 1850.

Maxwell, who was clever and sociable, wrote rapidly, and originated the rollicking style of fiction which reached its height in Lever's 'Harry Lorrequer.' In appearance he was tall and good-looking. There is a portrait and a eulogy of him in the 'Dublin University Magazine,' xviii. 220.

Besides editing the 'Military and Naval Almanack' for 1840, and contributing to a volume on 'Sporting' (London, 1838) by 'Nimrod' (i.e. Charles James Apperley), Maxwell published the following: 1. 'O'Hara, or 1798,' an historical novel, 1825. 2. 'Wild Sports of the West, with Legendary Tales and Local Sketches,' 2 vols. London, 1832. 3. 'The Field Book, or Sports and Pastimes of the United Kingdom,' London, 1833. 4. 'Stories of Waterloo,' London, 1834. 5. 'The Dark Lady of Doona;' a novel, London, 1834 (in Leitch Ritchie's 'Library of Romance'). 6. 'My Life,' a novel in 3 vols., London, 1835, afterwards, in 1838, appearing as 'The Adventures of Captain Blake,' in 1 vol., of which there were various later editions. 7. 'The Bivouac, or Stories of the Peninsular War,' 3 vols., London, 1837. 8. 'The Victories of the British Armies,' 2 vols., London, 1839. 9. 'Life of the Duke of Wellington,' 3 vols., London, 1839–41. 10. 'The Expedition of Major ap Owen to the Lakes of Killarney,' contributed to the 'Picnic Papers' by various hands, and edited by C[harles] D[ickens], London, 1841. 11. 'Rambling Recollections of a Soldier of Fortune,' Dublin, 1842. 12. 'The Fortunes of Hector O'Halloran and his Man, Mark Antony O'Toole,' with illustrations by John Leech, London, 1842–3. 13. 'Wanderings in the Highlands and Islands, with Sketches taken on the Scottish Border,' being a sequel to 'Wild Sports of the West,' 2 vols., London, 1844. 14. 'Peninsular Sketches,' by actors on the scene, edited by W. H. Maxwell, 2 vols., London, 1845. 15. 'Hints to a Soldier on Service,' 2 vols., London, 1845. 16. 'History of the Irish Rebellion in 1798, with Memoirs of the Union and Emmet's Insurrection in 1803,' London, 1845. 17. 'Captain O'Sullivan, or Adventures, Civil, Military, and Matrimonial, by a Gentleman on half-pay,' 3 vols., London, 1846. 18. 'Hillside and Border Tales (Sketches), with Legends of the Cheviots and Lammermuir,' 2 vols., London, 1847. 19. 'Barry O'Linn, or Luck is Everything;' a novel in 3 vols., London, 1848. 20. 'The Irish Movements: their Rise, Progress, and certain Termination, with a few broad Hints to Patriots and Pikemen,' London, 1848. 21. 'Erin-go-bragh, or Irish Life Pictures,' 2 vols., London, 1859 (edited, with a biographical sketch, by Dr. Maginn). 22. 'Terence O'Shaughnessy's First Attempt to get Married,' published in 'Bentley's Miscellany,' and afterwards republished in 'Tales from Bentley,' London, 1859. There is no reason to believe that 'The Hamilton Wedding; a Humorous Poem on the Marriage of Lady Susan,' Lanark, 1833, ascribed to Maxwell in the British Museum Catalogue, is really by him.

[Besides authorities mentioned, see Webb's Compendium of Irish Biog.; Gent. Mag. 1851 pt. i. p. 674; Times, 16 Jan. 1851; Globe, 15 Jan. 1851.] T. B. S.

MAXWELL, SIR WILLIAM STIRLING, BART. (1818–1878), historian. [See STIRLING-MAXWELL.]

MAXWELL-INGLIS, MRS. MARGARET (1774–1843), Scottish poetess. [See INGLIS.]

MAY. [See also MEY.]

MAY, BAPTIST (1629–1698), keeper of the privy purse to Charles II, born in 1629, is believed to have been a son of Sir Humphrey May [q. v.] by his first wife, Jane (*d.* 1615), sister of Sir William Uvedale (*Harl. MS.* 5801, f. 147 *b*), and to have been named after his uncle by marriage, Baptist Hicks or

Hickes, first viscount Campden [q. v.] His name, however, does not appear in a family pedigree, and his claim to be a son of Sir Humphrey is ignored by John Nichols in his 'Leicestershire,' and by Lord Braybrooke in his note on the May family in Pepys's 'Diary' (1854, ii. 242). Baptist was probably educated in France, and there doubtless first became known to Charles II. In 1648 he was, with his relative Charles May, in attendance upon the Duke of York while at sea (*Cal. of Clarendon Papers*, i. 445); in 1654 he appears in a list of the duke's creditors (*ib.* ii. 304). In August 1660 Charles appointed him registrar in the court of chancery (*Cal. State Papers*, Dom. s.a. p. 213). May showed his gratitude by rendering himself indispensable to the king in his private pleasures. With Rochester, the Killigrews, Henry Savile, and Sir Fleetwood Sheppard [q. v.], he generally attended those select parties which enlivened the evenings of Charles in the apartments of his mistresses. Wood seems to include him in his denunciation of Sheppard as a debauchee and an atheist, while Pepys calls him roundly a 'court pimp.' He was certainly a frequent and lavish entertainer of the king and his friends at his lodgings, first at Whitehall and afterwards at St. James's, and he seems to have rivalled William Chiffinch [q. v.], the king's closet keeper, in the attentions which he showed the king. He was rewarded in 1665 by a grant of 'several parcels of ground in Pall Mall Fields for building thereon a square of thirteen or fourteen great and good houses,' and of the highway from Charing Cross to St. James's (*ib.* 1665, p. 204). In April 1665 he sailed with the Duke of York in the Royal Charles against the Dutch (*ib.* p. 321), and in the same year he was appointed keeper of the privy purse, in succession to Viscount Fitzharding. Large sums of money passed through his hands, and, like William Chiffinch and his brother, he developed a taste for valuable pictures, possessing, among others, a fine portrait of Moll Davis playing a guitar, by Sir Peter Lely. He also kept a fine stud of horses. In Easter week 1675 he rode his horse 'Thumper' against the king's 'topping horse Blew Cap.' In April 1680 two of his horses ran matches at Newmarket, and in October 1682 his 'Whim' was a winner (MUIR, *Olde Newmarkitt Calendar*, p. 21). He was made clerk of the works under Sir Christopher Wren at Windsor Castle, and undertook extensive alterations and repairs there in 1671. Evelyn speaks of him as a friend, and in January of this year May supported Lely's and Evelyn's recommendation of Grinling Gibbons to the king, with the result that Gibbons found ample employment at Windsor. May had been returned for Midhurst, vice Sir John Lewkenor, deceased, in 1670 (*Returns of Members of Parl.* i. 529, 564, 567). His duties as chief bribery agent of the court had long previously familiarised him with the usages of the House of Commons. His skill was conspicuous in 1669, when, under Buckingham's direction, he prepared the passage of a bill for the king's divorce; at the last moment, however, to his no small embarrassment, Charles told him 'it would not do' (BURNET, *Own Time*, i. 262). Burnet attributes his undoubtedly great influence over Charles to an exact similarity between his tastes and those of his master. May did not, however, share the king's predilections for a French paid policy and the church of Rome. He seems to have fallen from favour before Charles's death, and retired to Windsor, for which borough he was returned to parliament in 1690, together with Sir Christopher Wren, but the election was declared void by order of the house dated 17 May 1690 (*Commons' Journals*, x. 350, 419). He was returned for Thetford, vice William Harbord, a few days later. May died in London on 2 May 1698. His portrait is said by Walpole to have been introduced on the ceiling of St. George's Hall, Windsor, by Verrio, who represents the courtier in a periwig as a spectator of Christ healing the sick. His name is still commemorated by 'Babmaes Mews' at the top of Wells Street, St. James's. In 'New Remarks of London' (1732) 'Bab's Meuse or Bab's Mays Meuse' is entered as being in Jermyn Street. In Pine's map, 1742, it is figured as 'Babmay's mewse,' and so also in Horwood's map, 1792.

May is stated by Le Neve to have been unmarried, but to have left issue natural. A son Charles was under age on 23 Jan. 1688–1689, when his father made his will. A Baptist May, possibly another son, was residing by the High Bridge, Hammersmith, in 1739, and was a trustee of the pews in the church there. He was in 1739 also appointed 'yeoman of the king's carriages,' a post which he held until 1758 (FAULKNER, *Hammersmith*).

[Dict. of Architecture, v. 52; Evelyn's Diary, i. 382, ii. 53, 54; Walpole's Anecdotes, 1849, p. 553; Le Neve's Pedigrees of Knights, p. 349; Steinman's Mrs. Myddelton, p. 55; Rowland Davies's Diary (Camden Soc.), pp. 21, 83, 84, 85; Tighe and Davis's Annals of Windsor, 1858, ii. 449; Fisher's Tombs in St. Paul's, 1684, p. 103; Wood's Athenæ Oxon. ed. Bliss, iv. 628; Granger's Biog. Hist. iv. 186; Contin. of Lord Clarendon's Life, 1759, pp. 338, 355, 438; Luttrell's Brief Relation; Notes and Queries, 5th ser. v. 393, 6th ser. x. 525; Burnet's History of his own Time, i. 262, 470, 604; Strickland's Queens of

England, v. 594; Wheatley and Cunningham's London, art. 'Babmaes Mews;' Add. MS. 23199, f. 33.] T. S.

MAY, GEORGE AUGUSTUS CHICHESTER (1815–1892), Irish judge, born at Belfast in 1815, was son of Edward May, rector of Belfast, by Elizabeth, eldest daughter of William Sinclair of Fort-William, co. Antrim. He was educated at Shrewsbury School and at Magdalene College, Cambridge, where he graduated B.A. in classical honours in 1838, proceeded M.A. in 1841, and was elected fellow. Called to the Irish bar in Hilary term 1844, he soon acquired considerable practice in chancery, and was made Q.C. in 1865. In 1867 he edited the first volumes of the Irish 'Law Reports.' In 1873 he was elected a bencher of the kings' inns, and in the following year was appointed legal adviser at Dublin Castle. On 27 Nov. 1875 he was made attorney-general by Mr. Disraeli, and on 8 Feb. 1877 was created lord-chief-justice of Ireland, and sworn of the privy council. On 1 Jan. 1878 he was transferred to the high court of justice as president of the queen's bench division and constituted an *ex officio* lord justice of appeal, retaining the title of lord chief justice of Ireland. In this capacity he should have presided at the trial of Charles Stewart Parnell and his confederates in the conspiracy against payment of rent in 1880–1, but having (6 Dec.) dismissed a motion for the postponement of the trial, he was loudly accused of partiality by the partisans of the traversers, and in consequence did not sit during the subsequent proceedings. Owing to failing health he resigned in 1887. He died on 15 Aug. 1892. May was a learned, painstaking, and impartial judge. He married in 1853 Olivia, fourth daughter (*d.* 1876) of Sir Matthew Barrington, bart., and had issue.

[Irish Law Times, 15 Jan. 1887; Royal Kalendar, 1866; Law Times, 20 Aug. 1892; Times, 12 and 30 Nov., 6 and 11 Dec. 1880, and 17 Aug. 1892; Dublin Gazette, 3 Dec. 1875, 9 Feb. 1877; Thom's Irish Almanac, 1871–8; Burke's Peerage and Baronetage; Haydn's Book of Dignities, ed. Ockerby.] J. M. R.

MAY, Sir HUMPHREY (1573–1630), statesman, born in 1573, was fourth son of Richard May, citizen and merchant taylor of London, and of Mayfield, Sussex, by his wife Mary Hillersden (Nichols, *Leicestershire*, iv. 548; Dallaway, *Rape of Chichester*, p. 114). He matriculated at Oxford from St. John's College on 25 Oct. 1588, graduated B.A. on 3 March 1591–2, and became student of the Middle Temple in 1592 (Foster, *Alumni Oxon.* 1500–1714, iii. 993). In February 1604 he was groom of the king's privy chamber (*Cal. State Papers*, Dom. 1603–10, p. 86). He was M.P. for Beeralston from October 1605 to 1611, Westminster in 1614, Lancaster in 1621–2, Leicester in 1624–5, Lancaster in 1625, and Leicester in 1626, and again in 1628–9. His conciliatory disposition commended him to the favour of James I and Charles I, but he possessed much real ability and considerable knowledge of affairs; while in parliament he displayed conspicuous talent as debater and tactician. On 26 Nov. 1607 he was granted a part reversion of the clerkship of the council of the Star-chamber, a grant renewed on 17 July 1609 (*ib.* pp. 384, 530). With his wife he had a grant, with survivorship, of a pension of 16*s.* a day on 23 May 1611 (*ib.* p. 33); and on 5 Aug. he was awarded two hundred marks per annum 'for official services' (*ib.* p. 67); and on 10 Dec. the grant in reversion of a clerkship of the signet (*ib.* p. 99). In January 1612–1613 he was knighted at Newmarket (Metcalfe, *Book of Knights*, p. 164).

His influence at court was now very great. 'Sir Hum. May can make any suitor, be they never so honest, disliked by the king,' writes John Cusack to Sir Ralph Winwood on 11 Nov. 1615 (*Cal. State Papers*, Dom. 1611–1618, p. 327). In January 1618 he was appointed surveyor of the court of wards (*ib.* p. 514); and on 9 March following, by the mediation of the lord chamberlain (Lord Pembroke) and the Countess of Bedford with Buckingham, was appointed chancellor of the duchy of Lancaster (*ib.* 1611–18 p. 525, 1623–5 p. 553). On 6 March 1624–5 he was admitted a member of Gray's Inn (Foster, *Register*), and on the ensuing 28 March he became a privy councillor. On May chiefly fell the onerous and often hopeless task of defending Charles and Buckingham in the House of Commons from the attacks of the opposition. In July 1625 he supported Sir Edwin Sandys in arguing against the committal of Richard Montague [q. v.] for the opinions expressed in his book entitled 'Appello Cæsarem.' When on 7 July it became known that the king had determined to ask for a further collection of tonnage and poundage, May, foreseeing the vigorous resistance which would be made, resolved to keep back the proposed motion until he had sent Sir John Eliot to remonstrate with Buckingham. On 6 Aug. he strove to justify Buckingham's foreign policy in the debate initiated by Sir Francis Seymour. Meanwhile, in private, he was vigorously remonstrating with the duke on the rashness of his policy (cf. *Cal. State Papers*, Dom. 1627–8, p. 375). In the heated debate which arose on 22 March 1628 on the misgovernment of the kingdom he could only plead on the part of the cabinet that the house should forgive and forget. On 3 June, when Eliot in his great speech on the king's foreign policy declared that 'to this French war the Palatinate had been sacrificed,' May hastily arose to interrupt him. Eliot, however, was encouraged with cries of 'Go on!' from every side. 'If he goes on,' retorted May, 'I hope that I may myself go out;' but he remained to listen.

In February 1629 the goods of John Rolle, a member of the house, were seized for his refusal to pay tonnage and poundage. The question of privilege was raised in the commons on 19 Feb., and the custom-house officers were brought to the bar. It was May who alone with the feeble Sir John Coke [q. v.] sustained the weight of the defence of the government. He declared that it had never been heard 'till this parliament' that a member 'should have his goods privileged against the king, and he is not yet satisfied that he ought.' Later on he protested against obedience to the king's commands being counted as a delinquency. 'When that is done his crown is at stake.' When on 21 Feb. the committee declared by resolution that a member of the house ought to have privilege for his goods as well as for his person, May asked whether it was meant that he ought to have privilege against the king. The committee did its best to avoid a reply. Ultimately (23 Feb.) May endeavoured to effect a compromise between the king and the commons. 'Think,' he vainly pleaded, 'upon some course to have restitution made.'

On 2 March 1629 May with the other privy councillors present did their best to rescue the speaker (Finch) from the violence of those who claimed for the house the right to adjourn itself. Overwork eventually told on him (*ib.* 1629–31, p. 287). In April he resigned the chancellorship of the duchy, and was made vice-chamberlain (*ib.* 1628–1629, p. 524). He wished for the mastership of the rolls, and Charles granted him in 1629 the office in reversion, but he did not live to enjoy it. He died from softening of the brain at his house in St. Martin-in-the-Fields on 9 June 1630 (*Administration Act Book P. C. C.*, 1630), and was buried on the 11th in Westminster Abbey (*Registers*, ed. Chester, pp. 129, 137). He married, first, Jane, sister of Sir William Uvedale, knt., of Wickham Market, Suffolk, who died in childbed of a son, Richard, in May 1615 (Nichols, *Collectanea*, v. 372). On 3 Feb. 1615–16 he married secondly, at Bury St. Edmunds, Judith, daughter of Sir William Poley, knt., of Boxted, Suffolk, by whom he had, with several daughters, two sons, Charles (*b.* 1619), B.A. 1638 of St. John's College, Oxford, and Richard (1621–1644). Lady May died on 9 June 1661, aged about 63 (Hervey, *Visitation of Suffolk*, ed. Howard, i. 285).

May was seated at Carrow Priory, Norfolk, in 1624, and had some church patronage in that county (Blomefield, *Norfolk*, 8vo ed., iv. 81, 131, 530, v. 52). He is also said to have purchased the manor of Froyle, Hampshire, from Sir John Leigh of Stockwell, Surrey (Nichols, viii. 211).

[Gardiner's Hist. of England; Forster's Sir John Eliot; Notes and Queries, 2nd ser. viii. 188; Middlesex County Records (Jeaffreson), iv. 349; Cal. of Clarendon State Papers, vol. i.; Hist. MSS. Comm. 12th Rep.] G. G.

MAY, JOHN (*d.* 1598), bishop of Carlisle, a native of Suffolk, and brother of William May [q. v.], archbishop-elect of York, was matriculated as a pensioner of Queens' College, Cambridge, on 2 May 1544. He was appointed bible-clerk of his college, and in 1549–50 proceeded B.A., being elected fellow in 1550. He commenced M.A. in 1553, and acted as bursar of the college during 1553, 1554, and 1555. At midsummer 1557 he was ordained priest, and on 16 Nov. following he was instituted to the rectory of Aston Sandford, Buckinghamshire, on the presentation of Anne, countess of Oxford, which benefice he resigned in 1558 (Lipscomb, *Buckinghamshire*, i. 47). In 1559 he was elected to the mastership of Catharine Hall. In 1560 he commenced B.D., and was collated to the rectory of Long Stanton St. Michael, Cambridgeshire. In 1562 Archbishop Parker collated him by lapse to the rectory of North Creake, Norfolk; and he held likewise the moiety of the rectory of Darfield, Yorkshire. About 1564 he obtained a canonry of Ely, which he held until May 1582 (Le Neve, *Fasti*, ed. Hardy, i. 361). In 1564 he was created D.D. In 1565 he was nominated one of the Lent preachers at court. On 26 Sept. in that year he was collated by Archbishop Parker to the rectory of St. Dunstan-in-the East, London, which he vacated in January 1573–4. He was admitted to the archdeaconry of the East Riding of Yorkshire by proxy on 3 Aug. 1569, in person on 8 Oct. 1571, and retained it until the end of 1588. He served the office of vice-chancellor of the university for the year commencing November 1569, and was in a commission to visit King's College, Cambridge, which had been thrown into a state of confusion by the conduct of Dr. Philip Baker [q. v.], the provost.

Through the influence of the Earl of Shrewsbury, May was raised to the see of Carlisle, being consecrated on 29 Sept. 1577. He obtained the queen's license to hold his other preferments *in commendam*. His name occurs in a commission issued on 14 May 1578 for the visitation of the church of Durham. From his correspondence with George Talbot, sixth earl Shrewsbury, he appears to have taken a warm interest in Scottish affairs. In a letter to the earl, dated from the episcopal seat, Rose Castle, Cumberland, 3 Dec. 1578, he requests him to write to Robert Dudley, earl of Leicester [q. v.] to back his suit to the queen for the remission of his first-fruits, having been put to excessive charges the last year by hospitality and relieving of the poor in the time of a great dearth in his country. He protested that when his year's account was made at Michaelmas preceding his expenses surmounted the year's revenues of his bishopric, 600*l.*, and he concluded by begging to be excused from attending parliament on account of his poverty. In another letter to the Earl of Shrewsbury, dated 22 July 1587, he writes that he is in debt and danger by reason of the intolerable dearth for want of corn in his country, and on account of process against him out of the exchequer for non-payment of 146*l.* due to the queen for subsidy. On 15 Feb. 1592–3 the queen presented William Holland to the rectory of North Creake, which May still held. Thence arose a suit in the queen's bench, wherein it was held that the rectory might be treated as void by reason of May having been subsequently inducted to Darfield.

May died at Rose Castle on 15 Feb. 1597–8, being about seventy years of age. He was buried at Carlisle, according to the parish register of Dalston, Cumberland, a few hours after his death, which was probably caused by the plague. His wife was Amy, daughter of William Vowel of Creake Abbey, Norfolk, and widow of John Cowel of Lancashire. By her he had issue: John of Shouldham, Norfolk, who married Cordelia, daughter of Martin Bowes of Norfolk; Elizabeth, wife of Richard Bird, D.D.; Alice, wife of Richard Burton of Burton, Yorkshire; and Anne, wife of Richard Pilkington, D.D., rector of Hambleden, Buckinghamshire.

May wrote some plays, now lost, which were acted by the members of Queens' College in 1551 and 1553. He was concerned in the compilation of the statutes given to the university by Elizabeth in 1570. Among the Tanner MSS. in the Bodleian Library are some notes of a sermon which he preached at Paul's Cross the Sunday after St. Bartholomew's day, 1565 (Hackman, *Cat. of Tanner MSS.* p. 1022).

[Cooper's Athenæ Cantabr. ii. 233–4, 549.]

G. G.

MAY, JOHN (*fl.* 1613), economic writer, was appointed deputy aulnager about 1606. He published 'A Declaration of the Estate of Clothing now used within this Realme of England . . . with an Apologie for the Aulneger, shewing the necessarie use of his office,' London, 1613, 4to. In this work, which contains much information useful to the historian, he describes the means by which manufacturers evaded the statutes regulating the woollen trade.

[John Smith's Memoirs of Wool, 1757, i. 91–8; Cunningham's Growth of English Industry and Commerce in Modern Times, 1892, p. 42.]

W. A. S. H.

MAY, THOMAS (1595–1650), poet, eldest son of Sir Thomas May of Mayfield, Sussex, by the daughter of —— Rich of Horndon-on-the-Hill, Essex, born 1595, entered at Sidney Sussex College, Cambridge, on 7 Sept. 1609 as fellow-commoner, and took the degree of B.A. in 1612 (*Biographia Britannica*, p. 3064; Wood, *Athenæ Oxonienses*, iii. 810; Berry, *Sussex Pedigrees*, pp. 36, 56). On 6 Aug. 1615 May was admitted to Gray's Inn (Foster, *Gray's Inn Register*, p. 137). His father having spent his fortune, and sold the family estate, May 'had only an annuity left him, not proportionable to a liberal education.' 'Since his fortune,' continues Clarendon, 'could not raise his mind, he brought his mind down to his fortune by a great modesty and humility in his nature, which was not affected, but very well became an imperfection in his speech, which was great mortification to him, and kept him from entering upon any discourse but in the company of his very friends. His parts of art and nature were very good' (*Life of Edward, Earl of Clarendon*, i. § 33, ed. 1857). Prevented by his defective utterance from practising the law, May devoted himself entirely to literature. He turned first to the stage, and produced a comedy entitled 'The Heir,' acted in 1620 by the company of the revels, printed two years later, and much commended in verses prefixed to it by Thomas Carew. This was followed by another comedy and three classical tragedies, none of which obtained much success. May then betook himself to translating the classics, and published in 1628 a translation of the 'Georgics' of Virgil, and in 1629 a version of some of Martial's 'Epigrams.' His translation of Lucan's 'Pharsalia,' published in 1627, passed through three editions in eight years. May followed it up by composing a continuation of Lucan (1630), both in Latin and English verse, which carried the story down to the death of Cæsar. The translation was unstintingly praised by Ben Jonson, and May was permitted to dedicate his continuation to Charles I. An epigram addressed to May compares his fortunes with those of Lucan:

Thou son of Mercury whose fluent tongue
Made Lucan finish his Pharsalian song,
Thy fame is equal, better is thy fate,
Thou hast got Charles his love, he Nero's hate.
Wit's Recreations, p. 12, 1640.

By the king's command May wrote two narrative poems on the reign of Henry II (1633) and Edward III (1635). Charles gave him other proofs of his favour. In January 1634, at a masque performed by the gentlemen of the Inns of Court before the king, May came into collision with the lord chamberlain, the Earl of Pembroke. Pembroke, who did not know him, broke his staff across his shoulders, but the king called May 'his poet,' and rebuked Pembroke. Next morning Pembroke sent for May, excused himself for his violence, and presented the poet with 50*l.* (*Strafford Papers*, i. 207; *Secret History of James I*, 1811, i. 222). The death of Ben Jonson in August 1637 left vacant the posts of poet-laureate and chronologer to the city of London. Suckling mentions 'Lucan's translator' among the candidates for the first, and the Earls of Dorset and Pembroke and the king himself wrote to the lord mayor recommending May for the second (Suckling, *Works*, ed. Hazlitt, i. 7; *Index to Remembrancia*, pp. 305–6). But D'Avenant was appointed poet-laureate, and the post of chronologer seems to have remained vacant until the appointment of Francis Quarles in February 1639.

Contemporaries attributed to this disappointment May's subsequent adoption of the parliamentary cause during the civil wars. 'Though he had received much countenance and a considerable donative from the king,' says Clarendon, 'upon his majesty's refusing him a small pension, which he had designed and promised to another very ingenious person, whose qualities he thought inferior to his own, he fell from his duty' (*Life*, i. § 32). Wood (*Athenæ Oxon.* ed. Bliss, iii. 810), Winstanley (*Lives of the most famous English Poets*, 1687, p. 164), and Edward Phillips (*Theatrum Poetarum*, 1675, ii. 179) all make the same statement. In a poetical tract, published in 1645, entitled 'The Great Assizes holden in Parnassus by Apollo,' 'Mercurius Aulicus' is represented as bringing the charge of ingratitude against May, a charge which Apollo dismisses as arising from mere malice.

During the war May lived in the parliament'squarters. He was probably the Thomas May of Allhallows the Great, assessed at 40*l.* by the committee for advance of money on 2 Oct. 1644 (*Calendar*, p. 473). On 19 Jan. 1645–6 May and Sadler were appointed by the House of Commons to draw up a declaration 'for vindicating to the world the honour of the parliament, in this great cause of religion and liberty undertaken and maintained by the parliament.' They are styled 'secretaries for the parliament,' promised a salary of 200*l.* a year jointly, and granted 100*l.* at once as a reward for past services (*Commons' Journals*, iv. 410). In 1647 May published his 'History of the Long Parliament' (licensed 7 May 1647; cf. *Commons' Journals*, v. 175). This was followed by the 'Breviary of the History of the Parliament of England,' published in 1650, first in Latin and then in English.

May has been wrongly identified with a certain Thomas May, servant to Mr. John Clement, who was arrested in February 1649 for 'raising false rumours concerning the parliament and general,' and it is hence inferred by Guizot that the poet was towards the end of his life opposed to Cromwell and the independent party (Whitelocke, *Memorials*, 1853, iii. 146; *Cal. State Papers*, Dom. 1649–50 pp. 495, 525, 1650 p. 75; Guizot, *Portraits Politiques des Hommes de différents partis*, p. 114). Up to the time of his death May was still actively employed in the service of the parliament. On 2 July 1650 the council of state ordered that the 'declaration of the parliament of England upon the marching of their army to Scotland be sent to Thomas May to be translated into Latin, that it may be sent into foreign parts' (*Cal. State Papers*, Dom. 1650, p. 228). Personally May was most closely connected with the free-thinking and free-living section of the republican party. 'He became,' says Wood, 'a debauchee *ad omnia*, entertained ill principles as to religion, spoke often very slightly of the holy Trinity, and kept beastly and atheistical company, of whom Thomas Chaloner the regicide was one' (*Athenæ*, iii. 810; cf. *Original Letters and Papers of State addressed to Oliver Cromwell*, ed. by John Nickolls, 1743, p. 43).

May died on 13 Nov. 1650. According to Wood, 'going well to bed, he was therein found next morning dead, occasioned, as some say, by tying his nightcap too close under his fat chin and cheeks, which choked him when he turned on the other side.' Marvell's poem represents him as dying after too jovial an evening:

> As one put drunk into the packet-boat,
> Tom May was hurried hence and did not know't.
> MARVELL, *Poems*, ed. 1681, p. 35.

The council of state ordered May's friends, Chaloner and Henry Marten [q. v.], to arrange for his interment in Westminster Abbey, and voted 100*l.* for the purpose (*Cal. State Papers*, Dom. 1650, p. 432). He was buried 'on the west side of the large south aisle or transept,' and a large monument of white marble erected over his grave, with an epitaph by Marchmont Nedham (WOOD, iii. 811). At the Restoration his body was taken up, by warrant dated 9 Sept. 1660, and buried in a pit in the yard of St. Margaret's Church, Westminster. His monument was taken down and its place filled in 1670 by that of Dr. Thomas Triplet (*ib.*; CHESTER, *Westminster Abbey Registers*, p. 521). A portrait of May, with a laurel-wreath over his head, is prefixed to his 'Breviary of the History of the Parliament of England,' 1655.

May's writings fall under the four heads of plays, poems, translations, and prose works. I. PLAYS.—1. 'The Heir: a Comedy acted by the Company of the Revels, 1620,' 4to, 1622. Reprinted in Dodsley's 'Old Plays,' ed. Hazlitt, vol. xi. This is probably the best of May's dramas (WARD, *Dramatic Literature*, ii. 348). 2. 'The Tragedy of Antigone, the Theban Princess,' 8vo, 1631. Dedicated to Endymion Porter, with a preface on the nature of tragedy and comedy. 3. 'The Tragedy of Julia Agrippina, Empress of Rome,' 12mo, 1639 and 1654. 4. 'The Tragedy of Cleopatra, Queen of Egypt,' 12mo, 1639 and 1654. 5. 'The Old Couple,' 4to, 1658 (Dodsley, vol. xii.) 6. 'Julius Cæsar, a Latin Play.' 'The manuscript is in the possession of Mr. Stephen Jones' (*Biog. Dram.* 1812). Mr. Fleay gives reasons for supposing that the tragedy of 'Nero' (1624) was by May, and holds that 'The Old Couple' was the earliest of May's plays (*Biog. Chron. of the English Drama*, ii. 83, 84).

II. POEMS.—1. 'The Reign of King Henry the Second. Written in seven books. By his Majesty's Command,' 8vo, 1633. 2. 'The Victorious Reign of King Edward the Third.' Written in seven books. By his Majesty's Command,' 8vo, 1635. 3. Miscellaneous verse. A manuscript poem, entitled 'Neptune to King Charles,' is among the 'Domestic State Papers' (*Calendar*, 1627–8, p. 238). Verses by May are prefixed to 'The Tournament of Tottenham,' 4to, 1631, to Alleyn's 'Battles of Crescy and Poitiers,' 1633, and to James Shirley's 'Poems,' 8vo, 1646. He also contributed an elegy to 'Jonsonus Virbius,' 4to, 1638.

III. TRANSLATIONS.—1. 'Lucan's Pharsalia, or the Civil Wars of Rome between Pompey the Great and Julius Cæsar,' 8vo, 1627, 1631, 1635. Verses by Ben Jonson are prefixed, which are also printed in 'Underwoods,' p. xxi. 2. 'Virgil's Georgics, with Annotations on each Book,' 16mo, 1628. 3. 'Selected Epigrams of Martial,' 16mo, 1629. 4. 'John Barclay his Argenis, translated out of Latin into English, the Prose upon his Majesty's Command by Sir Robert le Grys, knight, and the verse by Thomas May, esq.,' 1629, 4to (see *Cal. State Papers*, Dom. 1627–8, pp. 585, 589). 5. 'The Mirror of Minds, or Barclay's Icon Animorum, englished by T. M.,' 12mo, 1631. Dedicated to Lord-treasurer Weston. 6. May's English and Latin continuations of Lucan belong in part to both these classes. 'A Continuation of Lucan's Historicall Poem till the death of Julius Cæsar, by T. M.,' 8vo, 1630, 1633, 1657. 'His supplement to Lucan,' says Clarendon, 'being entirely his own, for the learning, the wit, and the language, may be well looked upon as one of the best dramatic poems in the language' (*Life*. i. 32, ed. 1857). 7. 'Supplementum Lucani, lib. vii.,' Leyden, 1640, 8vo. This is a translation of the foregoing, 'written,' says Wood, 'in so lofty and happy Latin hexameter that he hath attained to much more reputation abroad than he hath lost at home.'

IV. PROSE WORKS.—1. 'A Discourse concerning the Success of former Parliaments,' 4to, 1642. May's name is first attached to the second edition of this pamphlet, 1644. 2. 'The Character of a Right Malignant,' 4to, 1644. 3. 'The Lord George Digby's Cabinet and Dr. Goff's Negotiations,' 4to, 1646. This consists of the correspondence of Lord Digby, captured at Sherburn in October 1645. The 'Observations' prefixed to the letters were the joint work of May and Thomas Sadler (*Commons' Journals*, iv. 410). 4. 'The History of the Parliament of England which began 3 Nov. 1640, with a short and necessary view of some precedent years. Written by Thomas May, Esq., Secretary for the Parliament,' fol. 1647. This was published in May 1647 (*ib.* v. 174). Reprinted by Baron Maseres, with a preface, 1812, 4to, and by the Clarendon press, 8vo, 1854. 5. 'Historiæ Parliamenti Angliæ Breviarium, tribus partibus explicitum,' 12mo, 1650. 6. 'A Breviary of the History of the Parliament of England,' 1650, 12mo; 2nd edit. 1655. This is a translation of the foregoing, and is reprinted by Maseres in 'Select Tracts relating to the Civil Wars in England,' 1815. 7. 'The Changeable Covenant,' 1650, 4to. 8. 'The

Life of a Satirical Puppy called Nim.' By T. M., 8vo, 1657. This is probably attributed to May solely on the evidence of the initials. May's authorship of 2 and 7 is also doubtful.

As a prose writer May's reputation rests on his 'History of the Long Parliament.' It is written in a flowing and elegant style, abounding, like all May's writings, with quotations and parallels from Latin literature. Strafford is compared to Curio, Marie de Medicis to Agrippina. May bases his history on the newspapers and on the official manifestos of the two parties. He keeps himself studiously in the background, avoids, as far as possible, any expression of his own opinion, and is silent about his own reminiscences. He professes to relate facts without rhetoric or invective, to recall to the minds of his readers the judgments passed at the time on the facts he records, and to inform the world of the right nature, causes, and growth of the civil strife. Secret motives or hidden causes he makes no attempt to explain. 'I cannot,' he says, 'search into men's thoughts, but only relate the actions which appeared.' With the partisans of the parliament the book at once became popular. Mrs. Hutchinson, in her life of her husband, praises 'Mr. May's history,' as 'impartially true, saving some little mistakes in his own judgment, and misinformations which some vain people gave of the state, and more indulgence to the king's guilt than can justly be allowed' (*Memoirs of Colonel Hutchinson*, ed. 1885, i. 136).

A century later Warburton recommended May's work to Hurd, as 'written with much judgment, penetration, manliness, and spirit, and with a candour which will greatly increase your esteem when you understand that he wrote by the order of his masters the parliament.' Chatham also advised his nephew to read May's 'History' as being 'a much honester and more instructive book than Clarendon's.' Maseres, who quotes these testimonies, eulogises May's impartiality (*History of the Long Parliament*, ed. 1854, pp. ix, x). But May deserves praise rather for the moderation of his language than for the independence of his views. A comparison of the 'History of the Parliament' with the 'Breviary' shows a remarkable difference both in his style and conclusions. In the 'History' he is the official apologist of the parliament and its original leaders. In the 'Breviary' he is the panegyrist of the army and the independent party. His contemporaries in general justly regarded him as neither impartial nor honest. 'Most servile wit and mercenary pen' is Marvell's scathing verdict. With obvious reference to May, the Duchess of Newcastle alludes to historians of the civil war, who 'were such parasites, that after the king's party was overpowered, the government among the rebels changing from one faction to another, they never missed to exalt highly the merits of the chief commanders of the then prevailing side, comparing some of them to Moses, and some others to all the great and most famous heroes, both Greeks and Romans' (*Life of the Duke of Newcastle*, ed. 1886, p. lix). Guizot, in the account of May, originally prefixed to his translation of the 'History,' criticises his historical works with great severity, speaks of his 'adroit partiality,' and accuses him of misrepresenting the facts by 'omission, palliation, and dissimulation' (*Portraits Politiques des Hommes de différents Partis*, ed. 1874, p. 123).

[Wood's Athenæ Oxonienses; Biographia Britannica, vol. v.; the edition of the Hist. of the Long Parliament, edited by Maseres; and Guizot's Portraits Politiques; authorities cited in the article.] C. H. F.

MAY, Sir THOMAS ERSKINE, Baron Farnborough (1815–1886), constitutional jurist, was born in London on 8 Feb. 1815. He was educated (1826–31) as a private pupil of Dr. Brereton, then head-master, at Bedford grammar school, and in 1831 obtained the post of assistant librarian of the House of Commons. Called to the bar at the Middle Temple on 4 May 1838, he was elected a bencher *honoris causa* of that inn on 21 Nov. 1873. In 1844 he published 'A Practical Treatise on the Law, Privileges, Proceedings, and Usage of Parliament' (London, 8vo, 10th ed., much enlarged in 1893), a work of profound, accurate, and well-digested learning, recognised by parliament as authoritative, and translated into German, French, Italian, Spanish, Japanese, and Hungarian. From 1847 to 1856 he was examiner of petitions for private bills and taxing master for both houses of parliament, from 1856 to 1871 clerk assistant, and from 1871 until shortly before his death clerk of the House of Commons. In 1854 he for the first time reduced to writing the 'Rules, Orders, and Forms of Procedure of the House of Commons,' which were printed by order of parliament. In 1860 he was made C.B., and on 6 July 1866 K.C.B. In 1874 he received from the university of Oxford the honorary degree of D.C.L. He served on the Digest of Law Commission, appointed 22 Nov. 1866, and from 1866 to 1884 was president of the Statute Law Revision Committee. In August 1885 he was sworn of the privy council. He resigned his post at the House of Commons in April 1886, and on the 10th of the following month was raised to the peerage as Baron Farnborough of Farnborough in the county of Southampton. He died at Westminster Palace on the 17th of the same month, and after a public funeral service at St. Margaret's, Westminster, where a window was subsequently dedicated to his memory, was buried on the 24th in the churchyard, Chippenham, Cambridgeshire. His bust, by Mr. Bruce Joy, executed from photographs taken after his death, was unveiled by the speaker in the House of Commons on 6 March 1890.

Erskine May married, on 27 Aug. 1839, Louisa Johanna, only daughter of George Laughton of Fareham, Hampshire, by whom he had no issue. His title is accordingly extinct. He was a most able, faithful, and meritorious public servant, and was universally respected. Besides his great work on parliamentary procedure he published a learned work on 'The Constitutional History of England since the Accession of George III,' 1760–1860, which is worthy to rank with that of Hallam, of which it is in fact a continuation; it has been translated into French and German (London, 1861–3, 2 vols. 8vo; 3rd edit., with supplementary chapter, London, 1871, 3 vols. 8vo). Another large undertaking was his 'Democracy in Europe: A History,' London, 1877, 2 vols. 8vo. He was also the author of a pamphlet entitled 'Remarks and Suggestions with a view to facilitate the Despatch of Public Business in Parliament' (London, 1849, 8vo), another 'On the Consolidation of the Election Laws' (London, 1850, 8vo). May was also a frequent contributor to the later volumes of the 'Penny Cyclopædia,' the 'Edinburgh Review,' the 'Law Magazine,' and other periodicals. A reprint of his article on 'Parliament,' from the 'Penny Cyclopædia,' is in 'Knight's Store of Knowledge,' London, 1841, 8vo. His article on 'The Machinery of Parliamentary Legislation' ('Edinburgh Review,' January 1854) was reprinted in pamphlet form in 1881, London, 8vo.

[The Biograph, January 1882; Times, 18, 25, and 27 May 1886; Ann. Reg. 1886, pt. ii. p. 139; Law Times, lxxxi. 70; Middle Temple Register; Inns of Court Cal. 1878; Men of the Time, 11th edit.; Foster's Peerage, Alumni Oxon. and Men at the Bar; Parl. Papers, House of Commons (1867) [3849] 65; the Statutes, 2nd rev. edit. 1888, Pref.; Chron. Table and Index of Statutes, 1870, Pref.; Adams's Manual of Historical Literature, pp. 482, 525; London Gazette, 10 May 1886.]

J. M. R.

MAY, MEY, or MEYE, WILLIAM (*d.* 1560), archbishop-elect of York, was a native of Suffolk, and elder brother of John May [q. v.], bishop of Carlisle. He was educated at Cambridge, where he graduated LL.B. in 1526, commenced doctor in 1531, and became fellow of Trinity Hall. In 1537 he was elected president of Queens' in succession to Dr. Heynes [q. v.], and not master of Trinity College, as Wood states. During his tenure of the presidency the college acquired the Cambridge house of the Carmelites. The latter, aware of the imminent dissolution of the monasteries, proposed to surrender their buildings to the president and fellows of Queens' College; but this amicable transaction was interrupted by a royal commission directed to May and three others on 17 Aug. 1538 ordering them to receive the surrender of the Carmelite house, and to send an inventory of all the goods to the crown. On 28 Nov. 1541 May purchased of the king's officers all the stone, slate, &c., for 20*l.*, and on 30 Nov. 1544 he bought the site of John Eyre of Bury, to whom it had been granted by the king, but whether on his own account or on behalf of the college is not clear (WILLIS and CLARK, *Architectural Hist. of Cambridge Univ.* ii. 3–6).

May was a vigorous partisan of the Reformation in its early days; in 1532 he was chancellor to Nicholas West, bishop of Ely, became vicar-general to his successor, Bishop Goodrich, and acted as his proxy at his installation in Ely Cathedral on 2 May 1533; in the same year he was Cranmer's vicar-general in Ely (BREWER, *Letters and Papers*, vi. 1340). In July 1534 he was appointed Cranmer's commissary to visit the see of Norwich, and when Bishop Nix declined to appear, May declared him contumacious, and condemned him in penalties for obstinacy. On 27 March 1535 he was instituted to the rectory of Bishops Hatfield, Hertfordshire, on the king's presentation, but held the preferment under a dispensation from the archbishop, not being ordained deacon and priest until the following year. In 1536 he was one of the king's commissioners to visit the diocese of Ely (*Addit. MS.* 5808, f. 130), and in the same year signed, as proctor of the clergy of Ely, the Six Articles. He was one of those commissioned to compose the 'Institution of a Christian Man' in 1537, and on 12 April 1538 he was admitted, on the presentation of Goodrich, to the sinecure rectory of Littlebury, near Saffron Walden in Essex. On 17 Oct. 1540 he was collated to the prebend of Balsham in Cambridgeshire, and on 10 Sept. 1541 he was made by the charter of erection first prebendary of the third stall in Ely Cathedral (WILLIS, *Cathedrals*, iii. 381; LE NEVE, ed. Hardy, i. 356). On 1 Nov. 1545 he was collated to the prebend of Chamberlainewood in St. Paul's Cathedral, and subsequently of Wenlocksbarn. On 16 Jan. 1545–6, May, with Matthew Parker and John Redman, was empowered to inquire into the possessions of the several colleges in Cambridge, and to ascertain how the statutes were kept, and he accompanied Parker to Hampton Court to present a summary of their labours to the king, with the result that the colleges were saved from dissolution. On 8 Feb. 1545–6 he succeeded John Incent as dean of St. Paul's. In August 1546 he and Sir William Petre [q. v.] were despatched to Calais to treat with commissaries of the king of France. Sir William terms his colleague 'a man of the most honest sort, wise, discrete, and well lernyd, and one that shall be very mete to sarve his Majestie many wayes.' In the same year he was on the commission to reform the ecclesiastical laws.

The accession of Edward VI and the more vigorous prosecution of the Reformation brought May into still greater prominence, and there were few ecclesiastical measures in which he was not concerned. In September 1547 he appeared in St. Paul's Cathedral with the other commissioners for the execution of the edict of the council which commanded the destruction of images in churches and the discontinuance of all customs held to be superstitious, not in the cathedral only, but in all its precincts. On 14 Feb. 1548 he sanctioned by his presence the chanting of the litany and the reading of the gospel and epistle in English (*Chronicle of the Grey Friars of London*, ed. Nichols, p. 55); he consented to the abolition of all obits and chantries, though the loss to himself must have been considerable; on the second Sunday in Lent, after a sermon by Miles Coverdale [q. v.], the 'Sacrament of the Altar' in St. Paul's Cathedral was pulled down by May's command, and he administered the communion at a table. In 1547 he became one of the royal visitors, visited in that capacity the dioceses of Salisbury, Exeter, Bristol, Bath and Wells, and Gloucester, and was present at convocation; in the following year he was on the commission for the visitation of the universities of Oxford and Cambridge, and the college of Eton (*Cal. State Papers*, 1547–80, p. 11). He was a strong advocate of liturgical revision, and was on both commissions appointed to confer concerning the ecclesiastical laws (Strype, *Ecclesiastical Memorials*, II. i. 531) and the drawing up of the Book of Common Prayer. In January 1550 he was on a commission against anabaptists, on another to assist the lord keeper, and on a third to try Bonner (cf. Foxe, *Acts and Monuments*, i. 748–800, for a full account of its proceedings). On 12 April 1550 he officiated at the installation by proxy of Ridley as bishop of London, and in the sixth year of Edward he was master of requests.

On Mary's accession May lost all his preferments, including the presidency of Queens' College, which he had hitherto retained, but he lived quietly and unmolested. Willis even states that he was made rector of Pulham in Norfolk in 1557, and had other benefices given him at this time, including the rectory of Long Stanton St. Michael, Cambridgeshire, on 3 Dec. 1557, but this is probably a confusion with another May (cf. *Addit. MS.* 5808, f. 130), for May, in addition to his conduct during Edward's reign, was married, and this would have proved an insuperable bar to preferment in Mary's reign.

The accession of Elizabeth again brought May into favour; on 23 June 1559 he was reinstated in the deanery of St. Paul's, and all his preferments were restored to him, including the presidency of Queens' College; in the same year he was put on the university commission and on the commission for the revision of the prayer-book. Parker in his 'History of Cambridge' wrongly states that he became vice-chancellor in 1560 (cf. *Addit. MS.* 5808, f. 130). On 8 Aug. 1560 by the queen's recommendation he was elected archbishop of York, but died on the same day at London. He was buried in the choir of his deanery, and an epitaph in Latin elegiacs commemorated his virtues until it was defaced by the fire of 1666. His funeral sermon was preached by Grindal.

May is said to have been of a mild and generous character; he was a genuine believer in the doctrines of the reformation, and Elizabeth held him in high esteem. He married the widow of Dr. Heynes, his predecessor in the presidency of Queens' College, and left a daughter seven years old at the date of his death, who became the wife of John Tedcastel of Barking, Essex.

[Addit. MSS. 5808 f. 130, 5813 f. 108, 5842 f. 376, 5884 f. 25; Strype's Annals of the Reformation, Memorials of Cranmer, Lives of Grindal, Parker, and Sir Thomas Smith, and Ecclesiastical Memorials, passim; Brewer's Letters and Papers, vi. 1340; Cal. State Papers, Dom. Ser. 1547–80, For. Ser. 1547–53 p. 63, 1559–60 entry 323 (6); Wriothesley's Chronicle (Camd. Soc.), ii. 17, 114, 146; Machyn's Diary (Camd. Soc.), p. 241; Chronicle of the Grey Friars of London, pp. 55, 58, 69 (Camd. Soc.); Rymer's Fœdera; Eighth Report of Deputy-Keeper of the Records, App. ii. 168; Foxe's Acts and Monuments, v. passim; Burnet's Hist. of the Reformation, passim; Dugdale's Hist. of St. Paul's, ed. Ellis, p. 229; Newcourt's Repertorium, i. 47; Willis's Cathedrals, iii. 381; Cooper's Athenæ Cantabr. i. 207, 553; Wood's Athenæ Oxon.; Fuller's Church Hist. iii. 160, iv. 27, and Hist. of the University of Cambridge; Bass Mullinger's Hist. of Univ. of Cambridge, pp. 110, 151, 174, 176; Willis and Clark's Architectural Hist. of Univ. of Cambridge, ii. 3–6, iii. 336; Le Neve's Fasti, ed. Hardy, i. 356, iii. 314, 446, iii. 114; Milman's Annals of St. Paul's, passim; R. W. Dixon's Church Hist. ii. 493; Wright's Elizabeth, i. 39; Clutterbuck's Hertfordshire, ii. 363; Blomefield's Norfolk, v. 391; Lingard's Hist. of England, v. 309; Notes and Queries, 4th ser. viii. 67, 133; Cardwell's Two Books of Common Prayer; Gasquet and Bishop's Edward VI and Book of Common Prayer; Luckock's Studies in Hist. of the Common Prayer, pp. 13, 24, 122.] A. F. P.

MAYART, Sir SAMUEL (*d.* 1660?), Irish judge, was in 1624 a counsellor-at-law in Dublin. After the death, on 18 Oct. 1624, of Sir Gerald Lother or Lowther, second justice of the Irish common pleas (who must not be confused with Sir Gerard Lowther, chief justice in Ireland [see under Lowther, Sir Richard]), Mayart offered 300*l.* 'to him that shall procure him the said place *modo et forma* as the other held it.' He is described as 'a gentleman not to be excepted against, and of general good repute' (*Cal. State Papers*, Ireland, 1615–25, p. 546). He accordingly received a patent for the office dated 19 Jan. 1625 (*Liber Mun. Hib.* I. ii. 37). In this capacity he is frequently mentioned in the 'Journals of the Irish House of Lords' (1634–48 passim). He was knighted on 5 Nov. 1631 (Metcalfe, *Book of Knights*). In 1643 a pamphlet entitled 'A Declaration how and by what means the Laws and Statutes of England . . . came to be of force in Ireland,' and attributed without ground to Sir Richard Bolton, attracted the notice of the Irish Houses of Parliament. Mayart was employed as an intermediary between the lords and commons (*Journal of the House of Lords*, 1643, pp. 200–10), and soon after published an 'Answer to A Declaration, &c.,' printed in Harris's 'Hibernia,' pt. ii. 1778, from a manuscript in the possession of John Sterne, bishop of Clogher, subsequently presented to Trinity College, Dublin (Harris, *Hibernia*, vol. ii. Preface). A Colonel Mayart is mentioned by Gilbert as taking part against the Irish rebels, but this is more probably the Colonel John Mayart referred to in the 'Cal. State Papers' (Dom. Ser. 1651–2, p. 331, and 1652–3, p. 473). Samuel Mayart is said to have died in 1660.

[Authorities quoted; Smyth's Law Officers of Ireland, pp. 127, 219; Brit. Mus. Cat.; Gilbert's Irish Confederation, iii. 119, iv. 327, v. 123, and Hist. of Affairs in Ireland, ii. 462.] A. F. P.

MAYDESTONE, RICHARD (*d.* 1396), Carmelite. [See Maidstone.]

MAYER, JOHN (1583–1664), biblical commentator, was born in 1583, at Long Melford in Suffolk. He was admitted to Emmanuel College, Cambridge, as a sizar on 2 March 1597, graduated B.A. in 1602, M.A. in 1605, B.D. in 1612, and D.D. 1627. From 1609 to 1631 he was rector of Little Wratting in Suffolk, and from 1631 till his death rector of Raydon, near Hadleigh.

Mayer's life was spent in digesting the work of former commentators on the Bible and adding notes of his own. The publication of his work as it was prepared was hindered 'by the Hierarchicall Government that then was,' and it only began to appear in 1627. The commentary of the whole Bible was published in seven volumes: i., on the Pentateuch, in 1653; ii., on the Historical Books, in 1647; iii., on Job, the Psalms, Proverbs, Ecclesiastes, and Solomon's Song, in 1653 and again in 1659; iv., on the Prophets, in 1652; v., on the Evangelists and the Acts, in 1631; vi., on the Epistles of St. Paul, in 1631; vii., on the Seven Small Epistles, called Catholic, and the Revelation, in 1627 and 1631. The last named was originally issued, under the title of 'Ecclesiastica Interpretatio,' in 1627. The complete work is difficult to obtain, the first volume being especially scarce. But for the delay in publication it would have preceded the commentaries of Diodati and Jackson.

Mayer always suffered from delicate health. He died on 5 March 1663–4, and was buried at Raydon on the 8th. In the chancel of the church is a monument with a long inscription to his memory.

Besides the 'Commentary' he published: 1. 'A Fourfold Resolution,' London, 1609. 2. 'A Patterne for Women,' on Mrs. Lucy Thornton, 'whereunto is annexed a most pithy and persuasive Discourse of the . . . Father Jerome,' London, 1619. 3. 'The English Catechisme, or a Commentarie on the Short Catechisme,' London, 1621; 4th edit. 1630; 5th edit. 1635. An abridged edition, consisting of the questions only, was published in 1630, under the title of 'The English Teacher, or the A, B, C enlarged,' and several times subsequently with slightly varying titles; the 7th edit. appeared in 1639. 4. 'A Treasury of Ecclesiastical Expositions upon the difficult and doubtful Passages of the Scriptures,' London, 1623. 5. 'An Antidote against Popery,' London, 1625, 1627, 1630. 6. 'Praxis Theologica, or the Epistle of the Apostle St. James resolved,' London, 1629. 7. 'Christian Liberty vindicated from grave

Mistakes, occasioning so great Divisions in England,' London, 1647. 8. 'Unity restored to the Church of England,' London, 1661.

At the time of his death Mayer had ready for publication 'The History of the World from the Creation to the year 1648' (Preface to *Unity Restored*). Mention is also made on his memorial stone at Raydon that he left in manuscript 'The Topography of the Three Parts of the World, and the Countries and most famous Cities therein,' and eight sermons on Genesis, and on the Song of Solomon.

[Davy's Athenæ Suffolc. (Addit. MS. 19165, fol. 382*); Darling's Cyclop. Bibliogr.; Spurgeon's Commenting and Commentaries, pp. 10–11; Cole's B.A.'s (Addit. MS. 5885, fol. 51); Harl. MS. 7038, ff. 89, 96; Raydon par. reg. per the Rev. Dennis Coyle; Emmanuel Coll. Admission Reg. per the Master; Melford Terrier, communicated by the Rev. B. S. Fryer.] B. P.

MAYER, JOSEPH (1803–1886), antiquary and collector, son of Samuel Mayer, tanner and currier, was born at Newcastle-under-Lyme, Staffordshire, on 23 Feb. 1803. He was only fourteen when his taste for antiquities was excited by the discovery of an urn containing a quantity of Roman coins. This was in a field, near Little Madeley, Staffordshire. He earned a reward from his grandfather by deciphering the inscriptions, and thence acquired a love for ancient relics which never left him. At the age of twenty he settled in Liverpool as a jeweller and goldsmith, and being successful in business was enabled to indulge his passion for collecting. One of his earliest studies was Greek coins, his cabinet of which he sold to the French government in 1844. His museum ultimately reached great proportions, and embraced Egyptian antiquities, prehistoric and ethnographic curiosities, glass and pottery (especially a remarkable collection of Wedgwood ware); British and Anglo-Saxon antiquities, including W. H. Rolfe's collection and that of Saxon sepulchral remains made by the Rev. Bryan Faussett. Of this collection Mayer printed in 1856 a costly catalogue and history, compiled for him by Charles Roach Smith [q. v.], and entitled 'Inventorium Sepulchrale.' Other sections of the museum contained antique ivories, gems and rings, enamels, miniatures, metal-work, and many other objects. The museum, valued at 80,000*l.*, was presented by Mayer to the corporation of Liverpool in 1867, and now forms part of the public museum in William Brown Street in that town. He had previously disposed of a collection of objects of art relating to the Bonaparte family, but at the death of the owner (Mr. Mather) it was bequeathed to the corporation.

Mayer was a shrewd judge of the genuineness of all kinds of antiquities, but on one occasion was deceived. This was when he purchased some spurious papyri of the gospel of Matthew and other scriptures, concocted by the impostor Simonides, who induced him to publish them at considerable cost in 1861.

He acquired many thousands of drawings, engravings, and autograph letters bearing on the history of art in England. He became the possessor of large portions of the collections of William Upcott [q. v.] and of Thomas Dodd [q. v.], the print dealer and collector. Dodd was befriended in his latter days by Mayer, in whose house he died. These collections are described in 'Temple Bar' for May and July 1876 (reprinted in 'Memoirs of Thomas Dodd, William Upcott, and George Stubbs, R.A.,' 1879).

A number of valuable books were printed wholly or in part at his expense, among them being: 1. 'Sprott's Chronicle, edited by Dr. William Bell,' 1851. 2. 'Anglo-Saxon and Old English Vocabularies,' edited by Thomas Wright, 2 vols. 1857 and 1873; a second edition, edited by P. H. Wülcker, was brought out in 1884. 3. 'Feudal Manuals of English History,' edited by T. Wright, 1872. He assisted largely in the publication of Benjamin Thorpe's 'Diplomatarium Anglicum Ævi Saxonici,' 1865, and he supplied Miss Meteyard [q. v.] with the greater part of the materials for her 'Life of Wedgwood' and 'Group of Englishmen.'

He was one of the founders of the Historic Society of Lancashire and Cheshire, of which he was president from 1866 to 1869. He contributed the following among other papers to its 'Transactions:' 1. 'The Mock Mayor at Newcastle-under-Lyme.' 2. 'Roscoe and the Influence of his Writings on the Fine Arts.' 3. 'Shotwick Church.' 4. 'Liverpool Pottery.' 5. 'The Arming of Levies in the Hundred of Wirral.' 6. 'Addresses as President.' 7. 'The Preparations of the County of Kent to resist the Spanish Armada.' 8. 'On the Art of Pottery.' In 1876 he printed a volume on 'Early Exhibitions of Art in Liverpool, with some Notes for a Memoir of George Stubbs.'

In 1860 he devoted himself to the volunteer movement, and was captain of the Liverpool borough guard. He afterwards raised and clothed at his own expense a corps of volunteers at Bebington, near Birkenhead, Cheshire, where he went to live in 1860. He was for a time chairman of the local board and always a benefactor to the village and neighbourhood. In 1866 he established a free library of twenty thousand volumes in Bebington, and bore the whole cost of management as long as he lived, besides providing for its continuance afterwards. The library stands in public grounds (six acres), which he also dedicated to the use of the people. He was much interested in floriculture, and was accustomed to distribute flowers during the summer months to readers who came to change their books. He founded two scholarships at the Newcastle-under-Lyme high school, and presented drawings and pictures.

He retired from business in 1873, and died unmarried at Pennant House, Bebington, Cheshire, on 19 Jan. 1886, aged 82. His private library, prints and manuscripts were dispersed by auction in 1867.

A marble statue of Mayer, by G. Fontana, was placed by the Liverpool corporation in St. George's Hall in September 1869. His portrait was presented by subscribers to the Bebington Free Library in 1872. Another portrait as a young man, painted by Daniels, is in the Mayer Museum, Liverpool. An engraved portrait is prefixed to 'Inventorium Sepulchrale.'

[Liverpool newspapers, 20 Jan. 1886; Men of the Time, 6th edit.; C. Roach Smith's Retrospections, i. 67; Prefaces to Meteyard's Life of Wedgwood and Group of Englishmen; C. T. Gatty's Catalogues of the Mayer Collection, 1877–82; Gatty's Mayer Collection considered as an Educational Possession, 1877; A Free Village Library, Bebington, 1878; communications from Mr. Rupert Simms, Newcastle-under-Lyme.]

C. W. S.

MAYER, SAMUEL RALPH TOWNSHEND (1840–1880), miscellaneous writer, second son of Samuel Mayer, solicitor, Gloucester, was born at Gloucester in August 1841, and as he grew up bore a remarkable resemblance to the poet Keats. He was a ready and voluminous writer, and for several years a frequent contributor to the Gloucester newspapers, and to many serial publications. Removing to London, he founded and was secretary of the Free and Open Church Association from 1866 till February 1872. He edited the 'Churchman's Shilling Magazine,' the 'Illustrated Review' from January to June 1871, the 'Free and Open Church Advocate,' 3 vols. 1872–7, and was proprietor and editor of the 'St. James's Magazine' in 1875. In conjunction with J. B. Payne he established the Junior Conservative Club in 1870, and was the editor of the first report of the Metropolitan Conservative Working Men's Association, 1868. In 'The Origin and Growth of Sunday Schools in England,' 1878, and 'Who was the Founder of Sunday Schools? Being an Inquiry,' 1880, he attempted to prove that whatever credit belonged to Robert Raikes as the founder of those institutions, equally belonged to the Rev. Thomas Stock. Mayer died at Richmond, Surrey, on 28 May 1880. His wife Gertrude, daughter of John Watson Dalby, whom he married in 1868, was a great favourite with Leigh Hunt and B. W. Procter (Barry Cornwall). She wrote 'Sir Hubert's Marriage,' 3 vols. 1876; 'The Fatal Inheritance and other Stories,' 1878; 'Belmore,' 1880; and with J. C. Paget, 'Afghanistan,' 1878.

Besides the works already mentioned Mayer wrote: 1. 'Amy Fairfax,' a novelette, 1859. 2. 'Fractional Supplement to Hotson's Ready Reckoner,' 1861.

[Academy, 5 June 1880, p. 420; Gloucester Chron. 5 June 1880, p. 4; Gloucester Journal, 5 June 1880, p. 5; Cowden Clarke's Recollections.]

G. C. B.

MAYERNE, Sir THEODORE TURQUET DE, M.D. (1573–1655), physician, son of Louis Turquet de Mayerne, a French protestant historian, of Piedmontese origin, and his wife Louise le Maçon, daughter of Antoine le Maçon, treasurer-at-war in the reigns of Francis I and Henry II of France, was born at Mayerne, near Geneva, 28 Sept. 1573, and had Theodore Beza for his godfather. After school education at Geneva he went to the university of Heidelberg for four years, and thence to Montpellier, where he graduated M.B. in 1596 and M.D. 20 Feb. 1597. He then went to Paris, where, through the influence of Dr. Ribbitz de la Rivière, he became a royal district physician in 1600. He began to give lectures on medicine to such students as would come, chiefly surgeons and apothecaries, and openly used and defended the use of chemical remedies, abhorred by the Galenists. Irritated by an anonymous attack, he published in 1603 'Apologia in qua videre est inviolatis Hippocratis et Galeni legibus remedia chymice preparata, tuto usurpari posse.' This treatise of 120 pages is dedicated to Achilles Harlæus, president of the parliament of Paris, and after a statement of the jealousy with which Mayerne, as a doctor of Montpellier, had been received by the physicians of Paris, and an account of his own education, he goes on to show that the use of chemical remedies was not only in accord with the principles but even with the practice of Hippocrates and Galen. The pamphlet, while expressing just indignation, is moderate in tone and dignified in style. A reply appeared at once: 'Ad famosam Turqueti Apologiam responsio,' which is attributed to the elder Riolanus by Guy Patin, and which is filled with abuse, beginning with a bad pun on 'Turquet,' a cur, quoting several errors of hasty writing, such as 'palatin' for 'palato,' 'salia' for 'sales,' 'balsaurum' for 'balsamus,' and finally charging Mayerne with having injured several patients by his treatment. The College of Physicians in the university of Paris condemned Mayerne's apology by a unanimous vote, 5 Dec. 1603, ordered physicians to refuse to meet him in consultation, and recommended that he should be deprived of his office. He ceased to lecture, but took no further notice of the attack. In 1601 he had accompanied the Duc de Rohan to Spires and to Italy, and his favour at court rose every year. In 1606 he cured an English peer who had come to Paris. This peer took Mayerne to England and presented him to the king, who appointed him physician to the queen. He was incorporated M.D. at Oxford 8 April 1606, and afterwards returned to Paris, where he remained till 1611, when he was called to London early in the summer (*Works*, pp. 76, 90) by letters patent under the great seal, presented by the English ambassador. He was appointed first physician to the king, and the physicians of London, unlike those of Paris, recognised his ability and sought his friendship. He at once sprang into large practice, and went hither and thither to see great men. On 1 Aug. 1611 he examined, at Salisbury, Sir Robert Cecil, who had a tumour on the right side of his abdomen, and other symptoms pointing to cancer of the liver, secondary to an intestinal new growth (*Opera*, ed. Browne, p. 80); on 1 Sept. 1611 Lord Rochester for dyspepsia (*ib.* p. 90); Lord Monteagle's daughter for epilepsy, 22 Jan. 1612, in which year he was also consulted, though not at first, about Prince Henry, and after his death wrote, as a sort of state paper, in both Latin and French: 'Relation veritable de la Maladie, Mort, et Ouverture du Corps de tres Hault et tres illustre Henry, Prince de Valles, decedé a St. James lez Londres le ui de Novembre 1612.' This document gives a full and lucid account of the typhoid fever of which the prince died, and is a valuable monument of the medicine of the time. His account of the illness and death of Isaac Casaubon, 1 July 1614 (*Opera*, p. 144), is also a good illustration of the elaborate and exact method which he always followed in examining and prescribing for his patients. The regimen given by Mayerne is minutely and copiously recorded in each case. French patients often came over to consult him. Dunfermline, Montrose, Balmerino, and other Scots shared the confidence which their king felt in him. James I trusted him implicitly, and was treated by him for renal colic with hæmaturia 12 July 1613, and for an abscess of his arm from a fall, 28 July 1613, at Salisbury, for melancholy, for gout again and again, and for jaundice in 1619 (*Sloane MS.* No. 1679). On 25 June 1616 he was elected a fellow of the College of Physicians of London, and in 1618 wrote the dedication to the king of the first pharmacopœia published by the college. In 1618 he revisited France for a short time, and from 1621 is spoken of as Baron d'Aubonne. He had a house at Aubonne, near Lausanne, in Switzerland. He was knighted at Theobalds 14 July 1624 (Metcalfe, *Book of Knights*).

Mayerne had attended Charles I as a boy (*Sloane MS.* No. 1679), and on his accession was appointed physician to the king and queen, who both regarded him as an old friend. In one of his case-books he has transcribed a long letter from the queen and one from the king: 'Mayerne, pour l'amour de moy allé trouver ma femme C.R.' He drew up a report to the king on a case of supposed poisoning referred to the College of Physicians, 31 May 1632 (Goodall, *Royal College of Physicians*, p. 435), and in 1635 the college at his instance prosecuted a quack named Evans. His leisure was occupied with chemical and physical experiments which he had begun in Paris (*Sloane MSS.* Nos. 2041, 2222). Some of his experiments were pharmacological, and their results are useful to this day, for he brought calomel into use, and first prepared the mercurial lotion known as black-wash. Other experiments related to pigments and enamels. He discovered the purple colour necessary for the carnation tints in enamel painting. He wrote from 1620 to 1646 a large manuscript volume (Sloane MS. No. 2052) entitled 'Pictoria Sculptoria et quæ subalternarum artium,' &c., which contains many trials of pigments (fol. 80), most of them now much faded. He made an ingenious kind of tablet-book, capable of being washed by covering parchment with a resinous compound, and used such a one (*ib.* No. 552) as a scribbling-book, in which he wrote prescriptions in red ink. Only one, dated 14 Dec. 1649, is now legible, as much of the varnish has chipped off. He kept notes of a great many cases, many at length, in twenty-three volumes of the Sloane collection in the British Museum. He usually divides his account of a patient into two parts: (1) Theoria, (2) curatio, and when the curatio is very elaborate he adds, 'recapitulatio ordinis agendorum.' He generally gives the patients' names, except where it was obvious that publication was undesirable, as 'pro Camilla, 15 Jul. 1642;' 'pro Ascanio, 23 Jul. 1642' (*ib.* No. 1998). He often wrote long counsels in reply to letters. The most important of these adversaria are printed in Joseph Browne's edition of his 'Opera Medica' published in 1701. The 'Praxis Medica' published by his godson, Sir Theodore des Vaux, in 1690 contains another series of his medical notes, with a long letter on hæmoptysis to Dr. George Bate [q. v.], dated 10 Nov. 1641. He always wrote in Latin or French, and several spellings of English names in his writings suggest that he was never perfectly familiar with English. A Lady 'Cherosbury,' who thought herself poisoned, was 'Shrewsbury,' and there are numerous similar phonetic attempts. He stayed in London during the great rebellion, and saw many patients. He drew up, 28 Aug. 1644, 'Prophylactica pro Principibus in regia Sti Jacobi habitantibus,' a series of precautions against plague. In the same year he went with Sir Matthew Lister [q. v.] to Exeter, to see Queen Henrietta Maria. His London house was in St. Martin's Lane (addressed letter in *Sloane MS.* No. 2052). After Charles I's execution he was appointed physician to Charles II, and in the same year he retired to Chelsea, where he died 22 March 1655. He bequeathed his library to the College of Physicians, where it was burnt in the great fire. He was twice married, first to Marguerite de Boetslaër, by whom he had two children who died young, and secondly to Elizabeth Joachimi, who bore him two sons and three daughters of whom only one child, Elizabeth, survived him. She married in 1652 Pierre de Caumont, Marquis de Cugnac, and died in childbed at the Hague in 1653, when his descendants became extinct. He was buried, with his wife, mother, and five children, in the church of St. Martin's-in-the-Fields, London, where he had a monument on the north wall of the chancel, with a long Latin inscription written by Sir Theodore des Vaux. He bequeathed 200*l.* to the hospital of Geneva.

Mayerne was a great physician, and the general tone of his writings is enlightened. All physicians who have read much in the works of their predecessors are considerate of old methods and opinions, and this is the explanation of the quantity of mediæval pharmacology to be found in Mayerne's writings. He continued to regard as useful many remedies which had not been proved useless. He was an innovator and a man of new ideas, and for that very reason was perhaps over-anxious to prove his respect for what had long been generally received. His industry in chemistry, shown in his innumerable notes and experiments, explains his prescription of cosmetics for the queen. Her vanity was pleased by them and his experimental curiosity satisfied. No trace of courtly servility is to be found in his writings or is related of him. He adhered throughout life to the principles in which he was brought up, and the universal respect in which he was held by contemporary physicians is further proof of his upright character. A good portrait of him hangs on the staircase of the College of Physicians, and is engraved in Browne's edition of his works. A fine drawing in colours by Rubens is in the British Museum.

[Sloane MSS. in Brit. Mus. Nos. 552, 646, 693, 1512, 1679, 1981, 2019, 2044, 2052–3, 2055, 2086, 2222, cum aliis; Coll. of Phys. MS. Annales, vol. iii.; Joseph Browne's Opera Medica T. T. Mayernii, London, 1700, some copies are dated 1701; Preface to Theodore des Vaux's T. de Mayerne's Praxis Medica, 2nd edit. Geneva, 1692; Theoph. Bonetus's T. T. de Mayerne's Tractatus de Arthritide, London, 1676; Ad famosam Turqueti responsio, Paris, 1603; J. Astruc's Mémoires pour servir à l'Histoire de la Faculté de Medecine de Montpellier, Paris, 1767; C. Goodall's Royal College of Physicians, London, 1684; Philosophical Transactions, 1687 and 1700; J. Aikin's Biog. Memoirs of Medicine, London, 1780; Munk's Coll. of Phys. i. 163; Norman Moore's Last Illness and Death of Henry, Prince of Wales; Walpole's Anecdotes of Painting; Jean Senebier's Histoire Littéraire de Genève, Geneva, 1786, ii. 111; Eugène and Emile Haag's La France Protestante, Paris, 1861, vii, 350, in which is a list of editions of writings attributed to him; Guy Patin's Lettres, vol. i.; Digby's Powder of Sympathy, p. 13.] N. M.

MAYERS, WILLIAM FREDERICK (1831–1878), Chinese scholar, son of the Rev. M. John Mayers, afterwards rector of St. Peter's, Winchester, was born on 7 Jan. 1831 in Tasmania. The father at his son's birth was colonial chaplain, but was subsequently appointed consular chaplain at Marseilles, where Mayers received the chief part of his education. After spending some years as a journalist in New York, Mayers in 1859 went to China as a student-interpreter, accompanying Lord Elgin to Pekin, and, after serving as interpreter to the allied commission charged with the government of Canton, was appointed interpreter to the consulate there. He filled various consular posts at Chinese ports until 1872, when he was made Chinese secretary of legation at Pekin. In the same year he visited England, and in August read a paper on the 'Pathays of Yünan' before the geographical section of the British Association at Brighton. He died on 24 March 1878 at Shanghai of typhus fever.

Mayers was an accomplished Chinese scholar, and his works are monuments 'of his industry and the completeness of his knowledge.' He wrote: 1. 'The Anglo-Chinese Calendar Manual,' 1869, 8vo. 2. 'The Chinese

Reader's Manual,' Lond. 1874, 8vo. 3. 'Treaties between the Empire of China and Foreign Powers,' 1877, 8vo. 4. 'The Chinese Government,' Shanghai, 1878, 8vo. In 1867, with N. B. Dennys and Lieutenant Charles King, he wrote 'The Treaty Ports of China,' and in 1877 translated the 'Pekin Gazette' for that year, Shanghai, 1878, 8vo. His official report on 'The Famine in the Northern Provinces of China' was published as a parliamentary paper. In 1861 he became fellow of the Royal Geographical Society; he was also a member of the Royal Asiatic Society, to whose 'Journal' in 1869 he contributed a paper on the 'Lamaist Septem in Tibet.' He was a constant contributor to periodical publications, especially the 'China Review,' published at Shanghai, and rendered valuable service to the British Museum by procuring for its library one of the few existing copies of the 'Imperial Encyclopedia of Chinese Literature' in 5,020 volumes.

[Works in Brit. Mus. Library; Journal of Royal Asiatic Society; Proceedings of Royal Geographical Society, 1878, pp. 326–7; Times, 6 May 1878.] A. F. P.

MAYHEW, AUGUSTUS SEPTIMUS (1826–1875), author, born in 1826, was seventh and youngest son of Joshua Dorset Joseph Mayhew, attorney, of 26 Carey Street, Lincoln's Inn Fields, London, who died in 1858, and was brother of Henry and Horace Mayhew, both of whom are separately noticed. Like his brothers he devoted himself to literature from an early age, and in conjunction with his brother Henry he produced many popular works of fiction. The best remembered is 'The Greatest Plague of Life, or the Adventures of a Lady in Search of a Good Servant,' 1847, which displays much humour and power of acute observation, but is now chiefly sought after for Cruikshank's excellent plates [see for other joint writings under Mayhew, Henry]. A Dutch version appeared at Amsterdam in 1858. 'Paved with Gold, or the Romance and Reality of the London Streets,' 1857, and 'Faces for Fortunes,' 1865, 3 vols., are the best of his separate writings, which also include 'Kitty Lamere, or a Dark Page in London Life,' 1855; 'The Finest Girl in Bloomsbury,' a serio-comic tale of ambitious love, 1861; 'Blow Hot, Blow Cold,' a love story, 1862.

With Henry Sutherland Edwards he was joint author of six dramatic pieces: 'The Poor Relation,' 1851; 'My Wife's Future Husband,' 1851; 'A Squib for the Fifth of November,' 1851; 'The Goose with the Golden Eggs,' a farce, Strand Theatre, 1 Sept. 1859; 'Christmas Boxes,' a farce, Strand, 1860; and 'The Four Cousins,' a comic drama, Globe Theatre, May 1871. He also wrote for 'The Comic Almanac,' 1845–53, which he edited from 1848–50, and contributed to 'The Boy's Birthday Book,' by Mrs. S. C. Hall and others, 1859.

He resided at 7 Montpelier Row, Twickenham, but died in the Richmond Infirmary, whither he had gone to undergo an operation for hernia, on 25 Dec. 1875. He was buried in Barnes cemetery 30 Dec. He left an only son, Richard Mayhew.

[Academy, 1 Jan. 1876, p. 8; Era, 2 Jan. 1876, p. 15; Hodder's Memories of My Time, 1870, pp. 62–5; Times, 28 Dec. 1875 p. 7, 30 Dec. p. 6.] G. C. B.

MAYHEW, EDWARD (1570–1625), Benedictine. [See Maihew.]

MAYHEW, HENRY (1812–1887), author, was the son of Joshua Dorset Joseph Mayhew, a London attorney, and was born in 1812. He was educated at Westminster School, though not on the foundation (see F. H. Forshall, *Westminster School*, p. 329), but ran away under some sense of ill-usage, and, going to sea, made the voyage to Calcutta. On his return he was articled to his father for three years, but soon abandoned law for literature. His first venture was the publication, along with Gilbert à Beckett, of 'Figaro in London,' a weekly periodical, (1831–39), and in 1832 he started 'The Thief,' the earliest of the great crowd of paste-and-scissors journals. He began his career as a dramatist with 'The Wandering Minstrel,' at the Royal Fitzroy Theatre, 16 Jan. 1834, a one-act farce, in which was introduced the well-known cockney song, 'Villikins and his Dinah.' In 1838 his farce 'But However,' written in collaboration with Henry Baylis, and dedicated to Benjamin Wrench, was produced at the Theatre Royal, Haymarket, 30 Oct. Contrary to general belief, he did not collaborate with his brother Horace [q. v.], but, along with his brother Augustus Septimus [q. v.], he wrote in 1847 'The Greatest Plague of Life,' and a fairy tale, 'The Good Genius; in 1850, 'The Image of his Father' and 'Acting Charades;' and in 1870, 'Ephemerides, or the Comic Almanack;' and with Athol Mayhew he wrote a three-act comedy 'Mont Blanc,' adapted from Labiche and Martin's 'Voyage de M. Perrichon.' He is, however, best known as one of the originators and for a short time joint editor of 'Punch,' in 1841, and as the first to strike out the line of philanthropic journalism which takes the poor of London as its theme. His principal work, in which he was assisted by John Binny and others, was 'London Labour and

London Poor,' a series of articles, anecdotic and statistical, on the petty trades of London, originally appearing in the 'Morning Chronicle.' Two volumes were published in 1851, but their circulation was interrupted by litigation in chancery, and was long suspended, but in March 1856 Mayhew announced its resumption, and a continuation of it appeared in serial monthly parts as 'The Great World of London,' which was ultimately completed and published as 'The Criminal Prisons of London,' in 1862. The last portion of it was by Binny. 'London Labour and the London Poor' appeared in its final form in 1864, and again in 1865, and he published in the same year 'Shops and Companies of London,' and contributed to a work of a similar kind, 'London Characters,' in 1874.

Mayhew had meanwhile spent some years abroad, and had written 'The Rhine' in 1856, and 'The Upper Rhine' in 1858. In 1862 he resided in Germany, principally in Eisenach and Jena. This visit sprang from his desire to make inquiries into the early life of Martin Luther. It resulted in a work in two volumes, full of detailed and practical information on 'German Life and Manners in Saxony' in 1864, and 'The Boyhood of Martin Luther' in 1865. His minor works were: 'What to Teach and How to Teach it,' 1842, 'The Prince of Wales's Library—the Primer,' 1844; both intended as parts of educational series, and both discontinued forthwith; two humorous stories, 'Whom to Marry,' 1848, and 'The Magic of Kindness,' 1849; 'Adventures of the Sandboys Family,' 1851; 'The Mormons,' 1852; 'The Peasant Boy Philosopher,' 1854; 'Living for Appearances,' and 'The Wonders of Science,' 1855. He was also the author of the words of Jonathan Blewitt's song, 'My Wife is a Woman of Mind,' published in 1849. In his later years he wrote 'Young B. Franklin,' 1870, started a shortlived periodical, 'Only once a Year,' at the same time, and in 1871 prepared a report on working men's clubs. He died at Charlotte Street, Bloomsbury, on 25 July 1887, and was buried at Kensal Green.

[Athenæum, 6 Aug. 1887; Times, 27 July 1887; Scott's Life of E. Laman Blanchard, p. 608; Fox Bourne's English Newspapers, ii. 117-20, 155, 238; Brit. Mus. Cat.] J. A. H.

MAYHEW, HORACE (1816-1872), author, younger brother of Henry Mayhew [q. v.], was born in 1816, and, like Henry, early took to literature. He wrote a considerable number of farces and tales, and contributed to current journalism. In 1845 he was one of the brilliant staff of contributors to Cruikshank's 'Table Book.' For a time he was Mark Lemon's sub-editor on the staff of 'Punch.' In December 1847 his 'Plum Pudding Pantomime' was brought out at the Olympic. In 1848 he produced 'Change for a Shilling,' 'Model Men,' 'Model Women,' and an edition of Cruikshank's 'Comic Almanac;' in 1849 'A Plate of Heads,' with Gavarni's drawings; 'The Toothache, imagined by Horace Mayhew and realised by George Cruikshank;' another issue of the 'Comic Almanac,' with Cruikshank's illustrations; and 'Guy Faux.' From 1852, in which year it passed under Douglas Jerrold's editorship, he became a frequent contributor to 'Lloyd's Weekly News.' In 1853 he wrote 'Letters left at the Pastry-cook's.' The death of his father about 1857 left him in easy circumstances, and he wrote little in later years. He was a handsome, captivating man, a brilliant talker and raconteur, and was very popular in society. He married about 1869, but had no children, and on 30 April 1872 he died suddenly at Kensington, of the rupture of a blood-vessel.

[Scott's Life of E. Laman Blanchard, p. 411; George Hodder's Memories of my Time; Athenæum, 4 May 1872; Times, 2 May 1872. A manuscript diary, giving a curious and particular account of Mayhew's daily expenditure, is in the possession of Mr. T. Seccombe.]

J. A. H.

MAYMYSFELD, MAUNNESFELD, or MAUNSFIELD, HENRY DE (*d.* 1328), chancellor of the university of Oxford. [See Maunsfield.]

MAYNARD, EDWARD (1654–1740), antiquary, born at Daventry, Northamptonshire, in 1654, was the son of William Maynard of Daventry. He was educated at Magdalen College, Oxford, and graduated B.A. on 7 July 1674, M.A. 22 May 1677, B.D. 3 Nov. 1688, D.D. 3 March 1690-1. He was fellow of the college 1678–94, and bursar 1687–8. He was expelled by the commissioners of James II in August 1688, on the plea of non-residence (having been for some time chaplain to Lord Digby), but restored on 25 Oct. in the same year (Bloxam, *Magd. Coll. and James II*, passim). Maynard was about eight years (1692–1700?) preacher at Lincoln's Inn. On 15 Nov. 1700 he was installed precentor of Lichfield, and was for forty years canon and precentor of that cathedral. From 1701–6 he was rector of Passenham, Northamptonshire (Bridge, *Northamptonshire*, i. 307), and from 3 April 1696 till his death rector of Boddington in the same county (*ib.* i. 106). He died on 13 April 1740, aged 86, and was buried in Boddington

Church. He married Elizabeth (*d.* 1736), daughter of William Hastings of Hinton.

Maynard edited and published in 1716, fol., the second edition of Dugdale's 'History of St. Paul's Cathedral,' and published two volumes of 'Sermons,' London, 1722-4, 8vo. He bequeathed to Magdalen College his library, which included about twenty volumes on the popish controversy in James II's reign, the sum of 500*l.* and a silver flagon presented to him at Lincoln's Inn in 1700. He also made charitable bequests to Daventry and Boddington and to the Society for the Propagation of the Gospel.

[Bloxam's Reg. of Magdalen Coll. v. (II.), 319, 320; Bridge's Northamptonshire; Wilford's Memorials, 1741, pp. 781-2.] W. W.

MAYNARD, JOHN (*fl.* 1611), lutenist, and, according to Wood, one of the first who used the lyra-viol (*Manuscript Lives*), was probably born in Shropshire. It appears from the preface to 'The Twelve Wonders,' that he belonged at one time to the household of Caux (or Cause) Castle, Shropshire. In 1611 Maynard was lutenist to the school of St. Julian (once the hospital for lepers) in Hertfordshire.

Maynard's volume of songs, of which he appears to have written words and music, was printed by Thomas Snodham for John Brown in 1611. The title runs, 'The Twelve Wonders of the World, set and composed for the Violl de gambo, the Lute, and the Voyce to sing the Verse, all three jointly and none severall; also Lessons for the Lute and Bass-violl to play alone; with some Lessons to play Lyra-wayes alone, or if you will to fill up the parts with another Violl set Lute-waye.' A canon, in eight parts, is on the title-page. Wood quotes some of the verses (*Athenæ*, iii. 892). The work is dedicated to Joan, wife of John Thynne, son and successor to the founder of Longleat. A manuscript organ voluntary by Maynard is in a volume of manuscript music, once in the possession of Richard Clark, and now in the library of the Royal College of Music.

[Grove's Dict. of Music, ii. 241; Chauncy's Hertfordshire, p. 506; authorities cited.] L. M. M.

MAYNARD, SIR JOHN (1592-1658), courtier, presbyterian, and royalist, second son of Sir Henry Maynard of Little Easton, Essex, by Susan, second daughter of Thomas Pierson, gentleman-usher of the Star-chamber, was born in 1592. He entered the Inner Temple in 1610, but does not appear to have been called to the bar. Except that he was 'extremely purblind,' he would have been, says Chamberlain, 'a proper man,' and danced the admired of all beholders in the court masque on Twelfth Night, 1618-19. In July 1622 he was present at the siege of Bergen-op-Zoom, of which he wrote an account to Buckingham (*Hist. MSS. Comm.* 10th Rep. App. p. 107). For Buckingham he composed a masque, performed on 19 Nov. 1623 at York House in the presence of Mendoza, who resented its congratulatory allusions to the return of the prince from Spain. It was again performed in August 1624 at Burley-on-the-Hill, but with no great approbation (NICHOLS, *Progresses of James I*, iii. 521, 941; *Court and Times of James I*, ii. 472).

Maynard entered the House of Commons in January 1623-4 as member for Chippenham, for which borough he also sat in the first parliament of Charles I, at whose coronation he was created a knight of the Bath, and appointed servant of the privy chamber (2 Feb. 1624-5). In Charles's second parliament he represented Calne. He was a partisan of Buckingham, by whom he appears to have been retained as a sort of political pamphleteer. In Buckingham's interest, but without his privity, he published before 1627-8 a 'Discourse' representing him as hostile to Arminianism, and on occasion of the discovery of the Jesuits' College at Clerkenwell (March 1627-8) forged a letter purporting to be from an English jesuit to the father rector at Brussels, in which the duke was made to appear as the 'furious enemy' of the Society of Jesus. The letter was accepted as genuine by all but Buckingham, who detected Maynard's hand, and censured him for some indiscreet allusions to Dulbier's horse. In June 1637 Maynard excited a brawl at a bowling-green by striking Jack Craven with his fist for making default in payment of a debt, and thrashing Lord Powis for interposing. The quarrel was with much ado made up by the lord chamberlain (*Documents relating to the Proceedings against William Prynne*, Camden Soc., p. 80).

On the rupture with the king in June 1642, Maynard adhered to the parliament, and was active in raising troops in Surrey. A contemporary tract (*The Lawes Subversion*, &c., 1648) states that he 'lent 2,100*l.* upon the first propositions,' i.e. in July 1642; and that 'when the army was new moulded (1645), and Sir Thomas Fairfax elected general, he lent 1,000*l.* and procured 3,000*l.* more by his influence upon his friends towards that 8,000*l.* which necessity then required.' These statements, however, are not confirmed by the 'Calendar of the Proceedings of the Committee for the Advance of Money.'

Maynard did not enter the Long parliament until 1647, when he was returned for Lostwithiel, 20 Jan. At heart a royalist, he became conspicuous as a leader of the presbyterian party in the struggle with the army, and was accordingly included in the eleven members charged with disaffection by Fairfax on 16 June 1647. After the outbreak of mob violence, by which, on 26 July, the recent militia ordinance was rescinded, and the command of the London trained bands restored to the lord mayor and corporation, he was readmitted to the House of Commons and placed on the committee of safety [cf. Gayer, Sir John, *d.* 1649, and Glynne, Sir John, 1603–1666]. When the army gained the ascendency, he was charged with unlawfully levying an armed force within the city, was arrested by a general warrant under the speaker's hand, and committed to the Tower (8 Sept.) during pleasure of parliament. An impeachment of high treason followed on 1 Feb. 1647–8. Maynard replied by a letter to the speaker, 4 Feb., in which he refused to make any defence, and claimed to be tried by a jury, citing Magna Charta and the Petition of Right. This claim he reiterated at the bar of the House of Lords on the following day, refusing to kneel or in any way recognise the jurisdiction of the house. He was accordingly fined 500*l.* and remanded to the Tower. Thence he issued several protests against the claim of the House of Lords to jurisdiction over commoners, and on 19 Feb., being again brought to the bar of the House of Lords, he repeated his former tactics, and was again remanded. He remained in the Tower until 3 June, when he was set at liberty, and resumed his seat in the commons. On 27 June he spoke in support of the 'city petition' for a 'personal treaty with his Majesty.' On 27 July he pleaded the cause of John Lilburne [q. v.] in an able speech which procured his release.

Maynard had estates at Walthamstow, Tooting, Bradford, Yorkshire, and Isleham, Cambridgeshire. His town house was 'The Portcullis,' Russell Street, Covent Garden. In 1649 he argued at length in the exchequer chamber before the committee on the scheme for draining the Bedford level, which he opposed as encroaching upon proprietary rights. He also laid (3 July 1653) a petition against the scheme before the commissioners charged with supervising its execution. The petition, with a schedule of exceptions to the act of parliament (1649, c. 29) authorising the work, was published, and elicited 'An Answer to a printed Paper dispersed by Sir John Maynard, entituled the Humble Petition of the Owners and Commoners of the towne of Isleham,' &c., London, 1653. 4to.

Maynard died on 29 July 1658, and was buried in the churchyard of Tooting Graveney. By his wife, Mary, daughter of Sir Thomas Middleton of Stansted Mountfitchet, lord mayor of London (who survived him), he had issue a son, John, who was knighted 7 June 1660, and died 14 May 1664.

There are extant by Maynard: 1. 'The Copy of a Letter addressed to the Father Rector at Brussels, found among some Jesuites taken at London about the third yeere of his Majesty's Raigne. Wherein is manifested that the Jesuites from time to time have been the only Incendiaries and Contrivers of the Miseries and Distractions of this Kingdom,' London, 1643, 4to. Other versions are in Prynne's 'Hidden Works of Darkness,' London, 1646, fol.; Rushworth's 'Historical Collections,' i. 474–6; and 'Camden Society's Miscellany,' ii. and iv. Supplement, note *ad fin.* 2. 'The 'Humble Plea and Protest of Sir John Maynard (a late Member of the hon. House of Commons) to the Speaker of the House of Peeres,' London, February 1647–8, fol. 3. 'England's Champion: or the Just Man's Fortitude manifested in that gallant resolution of Sir John Maynard (late Member of the House of Commons). Being the Copie of his Letter and Protest sent into the Lords, 14 Feb. 1647,' London, 1648 fol. 4. 'A Speech spoken by an hon. Knight in the House of Commons, upon the delivery of the City Petition, being Tuesday, the 27th of June 1648,' London, 1648, 4to. 5. 'A Speech spoken in the hon. House of Commons, by Sir John Maynard, &c. Wherein he hath stated the Case of Lieut.-col. John Lilburne,' &c., London, 1648, 4to; reprinted in 'Parliamentary History,' iii. 959 et seq. 6. 'The Picklock of the old Fenne Project,' London, 1650, 4to (the substance of Maynard's argument in the exchequer chamber against the draining of the Bedford level).

[Baker's Northamptonshire, ii. 190; Visitations of Essex (Harl. Soc.), ii. 679; Wood's Athenæ Oxon. iv. 296; Morant's Essex, ii. 432; Collins's Peerage (Brydges), vi. 284; Manning and Bray's Surrey, iii. 489; Inner Temple Books; Commons' Debates in 1625 (Camden Soc.), p. 108; Returns of Members of Parliament (Official); Nicolas's Hist. Brit. Knighthood, vol. iii., Chron. List, xvi; Metcalfe's Book of Knights, p. 186; Burke's Extinct Baronetage; Le Neve's Pedigrees of Knights (Harl. Soc.), p. 73; Cal. State Papers, Dom. 1623–5 pp. 115, 330, 1628–9 p. 186, 1637 p. 237, 1641–3 p. 505, 1644–5, 1653–1654; Cal. Comm. Advance of Money, Dom. 1642–56, pt. ii. p. 834; Cobbett's State Trials,

iv. 858 et seq.; Comm. Journ. i. 684; Lords' Journ. x. 5, 12–13; Hamilton Papers (Camden Soc.), p. 153; Parl. Hist. iii. 678 *n.*, 777, 839, 843; Whitelocke's Mem. pp. 253, 258–60, 290, 292; Rushworth's Hist. Coll. vi. 570, 612, 652–3, vii. 800–4, 856, 986, 1130; Hist. MSS. Comm. 6th Rep. App. p. 67, 7th Rep. App. p. 687, 8th Rep. App. pt. i. p. 637; Bell's Mem. Civil War (Fairfax Corr.), ii. 365 et seq.; Howldin's 'The Lawes Subversion,' London, 1648, pp. 8 et seq.; 'The Royal Quarrell, or England's Lawes and Liberties Vindicated and Maintained, &c. By Sirraucho' (J. Harris), London, 1648; 'The Grande Designe: or a Discovery of that Forme of Slavery, entended and in part brought upon the free People of England by a powerful Party in Parliament,' &c., London, 1647, 4to; Maseres's Select Tracts, i. 257, 289; Walker's Hist. of Independency, 1648, p. 61; The Kingdome's Weekly Intelligencer, No. 214; Mercur. Brit. No. 1; Lysons's Environs of London, 'Surrey,' p. 500; Gardiner's Hist. of England, vi. 238 *n.*; and Hist of the Great Civil War, iii. 191, 293.] J. M. R.

MAYNARD, JOHN (1600–1665), divine, son of a wealthy yeoman, was baptised at Mayfield, Sussex, on 8 March 1600. The Maynards had been numerous in Mayfield and Rotherfield parishes for many generations. William Maynard, a member of the family, was burned with two of his servants at Lewes in the Marian persecution, 1557. John entered as a commoner at Queen's College, Oxford, 21 June 1616, and graduated B.A. 3 Feb. 1620 as a 'grand compounder.' He removed to Magdalen Hall, and proceeded M.A. 26 June 1622. He was allowed to use 'communis et vulgaris habitus,' instead of his purple gown, 6 July 1622. He owned at the time land in the manor of Sharendon, Mayfield parish (*Sussex Arch. Coll.* xxv. 55).

On taking holy orders Maynard was presented 'by Thomas Maynard and William Peckham, yeomen,' to the living of Mayfield (instituted 31 July 1624). Upon the commencement of the civil wars Maynard avowed himself a puritan, took the covenant, and was chosen one of the Westminster Assembly, which he regularly attended. An entry in the Mayfield parish register, 1646, records his offer 'to give up all the tythes due from the parishioners for the mayntenance of a minister during his absence,' but he adds, 'through their negligence in not providing a fit man for the place, there was no constant minister for some time, and divers changes, so that the register was neglected for divers years.' He preached before the Long parliament on a fast-day (26 Feb. 1644), on 28 Oct. 1646, and again in September 1648 (*Commons' Journals*, iv. 12, vi. 707). In 1654 Maynard was appointed one of the assistants to the commissioners of Sussex for the ejection of scandalous ministers and schoolmasters. Being thus engaged in public affairs, which necessitated absence from his parish, Maynard employed as his assistant Elias Paul D'Aranda, previously curate of Petworth and Patcham, allowing him the tithes of the parish, and reserving only the parsonage house and glebe for himself. On St. Bartholomew's day, 1662, rector and curate were both ejected. The latter became, in 1664, pastor of the French, or Walloon, Church, in the Undercroft of Canterbury Cathedral (Burn, *Hist. of Prot. Refugees*, 1846, p. 45).

Maynard was succeeded by Seyliard, who resigned a year later in favour of Peck (Calamy says with Maynard's approval). Maynard continued to reside at Mayfield until his death, three years after (7 June 1665), and was buried in the churchyard, where his tomb, now much dilapidated, records that 'for forty years he shone a light and glory to his Mayfield flock.' Wood says the library of another John Maynard, whom he confuses with the divine, was sold by auction on 13 June 1687.

He published 'A Sermon preached to the Honorable House of Commons, 26 Feb. 1644,' London, 1645, and 'A Shadow of the Victory of Christ,' preached at St. Margaret's, Westminster, 28 Oct. 1646, printed 1646. He also wrote 'The Young Man's Remembrancer and Old Man's Monitor,' 1669 (Wood). Some of his Mayfield sermons were published after his death by H. Hurst, chaplain to the Countess of Manchester, at the instance, he says, of Maynard's son-in-law, and dedicated to the inhabitants of the parish, London, 1674.

Maynard was three times married. First to Margaret Luck, daughter of his predecessor at Mayfield, whom he married at Wadhurst, 9 Feb. 1625, and who died 2 Oct. 1635. She had two sons, John and Richard, and five daughters, most of whom died young. Secondly, he married, 28 June 1636, at St. Edmund, Lombard Street, Mary Withers, widow, buried at Mayfield, 6 May 1640. A tablet in St. Saviour's, Southwark, records the death of her daughter Margaret, 14 March 1653, aged 13. His third wife was Ann, daughter of Henry Engham. She died 7 Sept. 1670, and was buried in the same grave as her husband at Mayfield.

[Wood's Athenæ Oxon. ed. Bliss, iii. 891; Lower's Sussex Worthies, 1865, p. 234; Sussex Archæol. Coll. iv. 258, xxi. 19, xxv. 55; Calamy and Palmer's Nonconf. Mem. iii. 322; Add. MS. 15852, f. 61, for Maynard's autograph, dated 3 Feb. 1635; registers of Mayfield, per Rev. H. T. Murdoch Kirby.] C. F. S.

MAYNARD, Sir JOHN (1602–1690), judge, son of Alexander Maynard of Tavistock and the Middle Temple, barrister-at-law, by Honora, daughter of Arthur Arscott of Tetcott, Devonshire, was born at the Abbey House, Tavistock, in 1602. His name appears in the matriculation register of Exeter College, Oxford, under date 26 April 1621, which clashes unaccountably with the date of his admission to the degree of B.A., 25 April 1621, given in the 'University Register of Degrees.' In 1619 he entered the Middle Temple; he was called to the bar in November 1626, and was elected a bencher in 1648. A pupil of William Noy [q. v.], afterwards attorney-general, a Devonian, and born in the law, he rapidly acquired a large practice, both on the Western circuit and at Westminster—he argued a reported case in the king's bench in 1628—and was appointed recorder of Plymouth in August 1640. He represented Totnes in both the Short parliament of 1640 and the Long parliament, and from the first took an active part in the business of the house. In December 1640 he was placed on the committee of scrutiny into the conduct of lords-lieutenant of counties, and on that for the discovery of the 'prime promoters' of the new 'canons ecclesiastical' passed in the recent irregular session of convocation. He was also one of the framers of the articles upon which Strafford was impeached, and one of the principal speakers at the trial. He threw himself with great zeal into the affair, and on the passing of the bill of attainder said joyfully to Sir John Bramston, 'Now we have done our work. If we could not have effected this we could have done nothing.' A strong presbyterian, he subscribed and administered to the house the protestation of 3 May 1641 in defence of the protestant religion, and drafted the bill making subscription thereto obligatory on all subjects. In the committee, which sat at Guildhall after the adjournment of the House of Commons which followed the king's attempt to arrest the five members (4 Jan. 1641–2), he made an eloquent speech in defence of parliamentary privilege. In the following May he accepted a deputy-lieutenancy of militia under the parliament, and on 12 June 1643 was nominated a member of the Westminster Assembly of Divines. He took the covenant on 25 Sept. following, and was one of the managers of the impeachment of Laud, January–March 1643–4. With his friend Bulstrode Whitelocke, Maynard attended, by Essex's invitation, a meeting of the anti-Cromwellian faction, held at Essex House in December 1644, to discuss the expediency of taking public action against Cromwell as an 'incendiary.' The idea, which seems to have originated with the Scottish Lord-chancellor Loudon, met with no favour from the English lawyers, and was in consequence abandoned. A curious testimony to Maynard's reputation at this time is afforded by a grant made in his favour by parliament in October 1645 of the books and manuscripts of the late Lord-chief-justice Bankes, with liberty to seize them wherever he might find them. In the House of Commons he was heard with the profoundest respect, while he advocated the abolition of feudal wardships and other salutary legal reforms. He also prospered mightily in his profession, making in the course of the summer circuit of 1647 the unprecedentedly large sum of 700*l.* As a politician he was a strict constitutionalist, protested against the first steps taken towards the deposition of the king, and on the adoption of that policy withdrew from the house as no longer a lawful assembly (November 1648). Nevertheless, on the establishment of the Commonwealth he did not scruple to take the engagement, and held a government brief at the trial of Major Faulconer for perjury in May 1653. Assigned by order of court to advise John Lilburne [q. v.] on his second trial in July 1653, Maynard at first feigned sickness. A repetition of the order, however, elicited from him some exceptions to the indictment which confounded the court and secured Lilburne's acquittal by the jury. The jury were afterwards interrogated by the council of state as to the grounds of their verdict, but refused to disclose them, and Maynard thus escaped censure, and on 9 Feb. 1653–4 was called to the degree of serjeant-at-law. In the following year his professional duty brought him into temporary collision with the government. One Cony, a city merchant, had been arrested by order of the council of state for non-payment of taxes, and Maynard, with Serjeants Thomas Twysden and Wadham Windham, moved on his behalf in the upper bench for a habeas corpus. Their argument on the return, 18 May 1655, amounted in effect to a direct attack on the government as a usurpation, and all three were forthwith, by order of Cromwell, committed to the Tower; they were released on making submission (25 May).

Maynard was among the commissioners appointed to collect the quota of the Spanish war tax of 1657 payable by Devonshire. Carlyle (Cromwell, *Speech* xvi.) is in error in stating that he was a member of Cromwell's House of Lords. He sat in the House of Commons for Plymouth during the parliament of 1656–8, and on the debates on the designation to be given to the 'other' house argued strongly for the revival of the old name (4 Feb. 1657–8). Burnet states, and it is extremely probable, that he was also in favour of the revival of monarchy. On 1 May 1658 he was appointed Protector's serjeant, in which capacity he followed the Protector's bier on the ensuing 23 Nov. On the accession of Richard Cromwell he was made solicitor-general, and in parliament, where he sat for Newtown, Isle of Wight, lent the whole weight of his authority as a constitutional lawyer to prop up the Protector's tottering government. On Richard's abdication and the resuscitation of the Rump, Maynard took no part in parliamentary business until 21 Feb. 1659–60, when he was placed on the committee for drafting the bill to constitute the new council of state. He reported the bill the same day, and was himself voted a member of the council on the 23rd. He sat for Beeralston, Devonshire, in the Convention parliament, was one of the first serjeants called at the Restoration (22 June 1660), and soon afterwards (9 Nov.) was advanced to the rank of king's serjeant and knighted (16 Nov.) With his brother-serjeant, Sir John Glynne [q. v.], he rode in the coronation procession, on 23 April 1661, behind the attorney and solicitor-general, much to the disgust of Pepys, who regarded him as a turncoat.

As king's serjeant, Maynard appeared for the crown at some of the state trials with which the new reign was inaugurated, among others that of Sir Henry Vane [q. v.] in Trinity term 1662. He represented Beeralston in the Pensionary parliament, 1661–79, and sat for Plymouth during the rest of Charles II's reign. He was the principal manager of the abortive impeachment of Lord Mordaunt [q. v.] in 1666–7, and constituted himself counsel for the defence in the proceedings against Lord Clarendon [see Hyde, Edward, Earl of Clarendon] in the following October. He appeared for the House of Lords in the king's bench on the return to Lord Shaftesbury's habeas corpus on 29 June 1677, and sustained its sufficiency on the ground that, though a general warrant for commitment to prison would be invalid if issued by any court but the House of Lords, the king's bench had no jurisdiction to declare it so when issued by that house. In 1678 he made a spirited but ineffectual attempt to secure the conviction of Lord Cornwallis for the brutal murder of a boy in St. James's Park. The severe censure which Lord Campbell passed upon him for his conduct of this case is based upon an entire misapprehension of the facts (see Cobbett, *State Trials*, vi. 1290 et seq., and Lord Campbell, *Lives of the Chancellors*, iv. 20).

In the debate on Danby's impeachment (December 1678) Maynard showed a regrettable disposition to strain the Treason Act (25 Edward III) to his disadvantage, maintaining that its scope might be enlarged by retrospective legislation, which caused Swift to denounce him, in a note to Burnet's 'Own Time' (fol.), i. 441, as 'a knave or a fool for all his law.' On constitutional questions he steered as a rule a wary and somewhat ambiguous course, professing equal solicitude for the royal prerogative and the power and privileges of parliament, acknowledging the existence of a dispensing power, without either defining its limits or admitting that it had none (10 Feb. 1672–3), at one time resisting the king's attempts to adjourn parliament by message from the speaker's chair (February 1677–8), and at another counselling acquiescence in his arbitrary rejection of a duly elected speaker (10–11 March 1678–1679). [See Seymour, Sir Edward.]

Maynard opened the case against Edward Coleman [q. v.] on 27 Nov. 1678, and took part in most of the prosecutions arising out of the supposed popish plot, including the impeachment of Lord Stafford, in December 1680. Lord Campbell's interesting story of his slipping away to circuit without leave during the debate on the Exclusion Bill in the preceding November, 'upon which his son was instructed to inform him that if he did not return forthwith he should be sent for in custody, he being treated thus tenderly in respect of his having been long the father of the House,' is a sheer fabrication (see *Commons' Journal*, ix. 646–68).

Maynard favoured the impeachment of Edward Fitzharris [q. v.], declared its rejection by the House of Lords a breach of privilege (26 March 1681), and took part in the subsequent prosecution in the king's bench. In the action for false imprisonment during his mayoralty brought by Sir William Pritchard against ex-sheriff Papillon on 6 Nov. 1684, an incident in the attack made by the court upon the liberties of the city, Maynard conducted the defence with eminent skill and zeal, though a Jeffreys-ridden jury found a verdict for the plaintiff with 10,000*l.* damages. Summoned to give evidence on behalf of Oates on his trial for perjury in May 1685, and questioned concerning the impeachment of Lord Stafford, Maynard pleaded total inability to swear to his memory in regard to that matter, and was dismissed by Jeffreys with a sneer at his supposed failing powers.

During the reign of James II Maynard represented Beeralston in parliament. He opposed so much of the abortive bill for the preservation of the king's person as proposed to make it high treason to assert by word of mouth the legitimacy of the Duke of Monmouth (June), and likewise the extraordinary supply for the creation of a standing army demanded by the king after the suppression of the western rebellion. Though not, it would seem, a privy councillor, he was summoned, as king's ancient serjeant, to the council held to establish the birth of the Prince of Wales on 22 Oct. 1688, and also to the meeting of the lords spiritual and temporal held on 22 Dec., to confer on the emergency presented by the flight of the king, and as doyen of the bar was presented to the Prince of Orange on his arrival in London. William congratulated him on having outlived so many rivals; Maynard replied: 'And I had like to have outlived the law itself had not your highness come over.'

In the convention which met on 22 Jan. 1688-9, Maynard sat for Plymouth, and in the debate of the 28th on the state of the nation, and the conference with the lords which followed on 2 Feb., argued that James had vacated the throne by his Romanism, and attempted subversion of the constitution, and that as during his life he could have no heir, the choice lay between an alteration of the succession and a regency of indefinite duration. He supported the bill for declaring the convention a parliament on the very frank ground that a dissolution, owing to the ferment among the clergy, would mean the triumph of the tory party. On 5 March he was sworn lord commissioner of the great seal, jointly with Sir Anthony Keck and Sir William Rawlinson. This office did not exclude him from the House of Commons, and he continued to take an active part in its proceedings. On 16 March he moved for leave to introduce a bill for disarming papists; and while professing perfect confidence in the queen, he energetically opposed the bill for vesting the regency in her during William's absence from the realm, the passing of which into law was closely followed by his retirement or removal from office, his last appearance in court being on 14 May 1690. So brief a tenure of office at so advanced an age afforded Maynard little or no opportunity for the display of high judicial powers. As to his merits, however, all parties were agreed; the bench, as Fuller quaintly wrote before the Restoration, 'seeming sick with long longing for his sitting thereon.' Roger North admits that he was 'the best old book lawyer of his time.' Clarendon speaks of his 'eminent parts,' 'great learning,' and 'signal reputation.' Anthony à Wood praises his 'great reading and knowledge in the more profound and perplexed parts of the law,' and his devotion to 'his mother the university of Oxon.' As a politician, his moderation and consistency were generally recognised, though for his part in the impeachments of Strafford and Stafford he was savagely attacked by Roscommon in his 'Ghost of the late House of Commons, 1680-1. Though hardly eloquent, Maynard was a singularly facile and fluent speaker—Roscommon sneers at 'his accumulative hackney tongue'—and could sometimes be crushing in retort. Jeffreys once taxing him in open court with having forgotten his law, he is said to have replied: 'In that case I must have forgotten a great deal more than your lordship ever knew.' He humorously defined advocacy as 'ars bablativa.' Manningham (*Diary*, Camden Soc., p. 157) attributes to him the aphorism, 'Felices essent artes si nulli de eis judicarent nisi artifices' (cf. WARBURTON, *Letters to Hurd*, xci.) He amassed a large fortune, bought the manor of Gunnersbury, and there in 1663 built from designs by Inigo Jones or his pupil Webbe a palace (afterwards the residence of the Princess Amelia, daughter of George II). He died there on 9 Oct. 1690, his body lying in state until the 25th, when it was interred with great pomp in Ealing Church.

Portraits are in the National Portrait Gallery, London, and at Exeter College, Oxford.

Maynard married, first, Elizabeth, daughter of Andrew Henley of Taunton, Somerset, buried in Ealing Church, 4 Jan. 1654-5; secondly, Jane, daughter of Cheney Selhurst of Tenterden, and relict of Edward Austen, buried in Ealing Church in 1668; thirdly, Margaret, daughter of Edward, lord Gorge, and relict (1) of Sir Thomas Fleming of North Stoneham, Hampshire; (2) of Sir Francis Prujean [q. v.], physician to the king; fourthly, Mary, daughter of Ambrose Upton, canon of Christ Church, Oxford, and relict of Sir Charles Vermuyden, M.D. who survived him and remarried Henry Howard, fifth earl of Suffolk and Berkshire. Except by his first wife Maynard had no issue; by her he had one son, Joseph, and four daughters, Elizabeth, Honora, Joan, and Martha. His eldest daughter married Sir Duncumbe Colchester of Westbury, Gloucestershire; the second, Edward Nosworthy of Devonshire; the third, Thomas Leigh of Addington; and the fourth, Sir Edward Gresham, bart. Maynard's son, Joseph, had two daughters, Elizabeth and Mary. The former married Sir Henry Hobart, and was the mother of Henrietta, the celebrated Mrs. Howard, afterwards Countess of Suffolk [see HOWARD, HENRIETTA]. The latter married Thomas, second earl of Stamford. Maynard survived all his children, except his youngest daughter, and devised his estates in trust for his granddaughters and their issue in tail by a will so obscure that to settle the disputes to which it gave rise a private act of parliament was passed in 1694, notwithstanding which it was made the subject of litigation in 1709 (see an inaccurate report of the case in VERNON, *Reports in Chancery*, ii. 644, ed. Raitby).

To Maynard we owe the unique edition of the reports of Richard de Winchedon, being the 'Year-Books of Edward II,' covering substantially the entire reign to Trinity term 1326, together with excerpts from the records of Edward I, printed under the title 'Les Reports des cases argue et adjudge in le Temps del' Roy Edward le Second, et auxy Memoranda del' Exchequer en Temps le Roy Edward le Primer. Solonq; les ancient Manuscripts ore remanent en les Maines de Sir Jehan Maynard Chevalier Serjeant de la Ley al sa tres Excellent Majesty Le Roy Charles le Second. Ovesq; un perfect Table des Matters en les dits Cases de Temps del' Roy Edward le Second, colligee par le mesme Serjeant,' London, 1678–9, fol.

Maynard's manuscript collections in eighty-seven volumes, comprising commonplace books, transcripts of legal records, reports, and other miscellanea (including the 'Reports' of Francis Rodes [q. v.], a variety of readings, and 'The Mirror of Justices') are preserved in Lincoln's Inn Library (see HUNTER, *Catalogue of Lincoln's Inn MSS.* 1838). One of Maynard's opinions was printed in 'London's Liberty' [see under HALE, SIR MATTHEW]. For his speeches at Strafford's trial see Rushworth's 'Historical Collections,' vol. viii. For other of his speeches see Cobbett's 'State Trials,' 'Parliamentary History,' and 'Somers Tracts,' vi. 430. He must be carefully distinguished from his namesake, Sir John Maynard, K.B. (1592–1658) [q. v.], with whom he has been confounded by Lord Campbell.

[Wood's Athenæ Oxon. (Bliss), iv. 292; Fasti, i. 397; Reg. Univ. Oxon. vol. ii. pt. ii. p. 387, iii. 395, vol. iv. Pref. p. vii. note; Lysons's Mag. Brit. vol. vi. pt. i. p. ccvi, pt. ii. pp. 40, 41, 227, 475, 535; Environs of London, ii. 226–35; Le Neve's Pedigrees of Knights (Harl. Soc.); Croke's Reports, ed. Grimston, Car. I, p. 145; Cal. State Papers Dom. 1636–7 p. 6, 1639 pp. 116, 262, 1655 pp. 168–9, 1660–1 p. 477, 1661–2 p. 213; Comm. Journ. ii. 4, iii. 254, iv. 313, 315, vii. 72, viii.; Hist. MSS. Comm. 3rd Rep. App. p. 429, 4th Rep. App. p. 542, 5th Rep. App. pp. 171, 180, 7th Rep. App. p. 462, 9th Rep. pt. i. App. pp. 266, 280, 10th Rep. App. p. 172; Rushworth's Hist. Coll. vols. iii., iv., v., viii. 736; Verney's Notes of the Long Parliament (Camd. Soc.), pp. 34–46, 66–76; Sir John Bramston's Autobiography (Camd. Soc.), p. 75; Whitelocke's Memorials, pp. 39, 50, 59, 116–17, 194, 273, 581, 673; Scobell's Collection of Acts and Ordinances, 1643 c. ii. 1656 c. xii.; Acts of Parliament (in Lincoln's Inn Library), 1650–3, p. 286; Siderfin's Reports, pt. i. pp. 3, 4; Wynne's Serj.-at-Law; Walker's Coronation of Charles II, p. 83; Pepys's Diary, 23 April 1661, 30 March 1668; Parl. Hist. iii. 1128, iv. and v.; Cobbett's State Trials, vols. v–viii. and x.; Howell's State Trials, xii. 123; Clarendon's Rebellion, ed. 1849, bk. x. § 149; Clarendon's Life, ed. 1827, i. 67; Burton's Diary, ii. 183–9, 458–62, 526, iv. 73, 99; Lists of Members of Parliament (Official); Willis's Not. Parl. iii. 272; Baker's Chron. p. 712; Hatton Corresp. (Camd. Soc.), i. 135; Burnet's own Time, ed. 1833 (fol.), i. 441 et seq., 639, 803; Evelyn's Diary, 1–6 Dec. 1680; Inderwick's Interregnum, p. 240; Fox's History of the Early Part of the Reign of James II, p. 145, and Heywood's Vindication thereof, p. 228; Luttrell's Relation of State Affairs, i. 490, 506, ii. 52; Hardy's Cat. of Lords Chancellors; Vernon's Reports in Chancery, ed. Raitby, ii. 95; Collins's Peerage, (Brydges), iii. 157, 367; Edmondson's Baron. Genealog. p. 257; Wotton's Baronetage, vol. iii. pt. i. p. 95; Fuller's Worthies, 'Devonshire;' North's Lives, i. 19; Woolrych's Life of Jeffreys. p. 100 *n.*; Noble's Continuation of Granger's Biog. Hist. of England, 1806, i. 172; Gent. Mag. lix. 585; Atkyns's Gloucestershire, p. 420; Rudder's Gloucestershire, p. 794; Misc. Gen. et Herald. 2nd ser. i. 44, ii. 163, new ser. i. 406, ii. 50, iv. 303; Selby's Genealogist, new ser. iv. 167; Private Act of Parliament for settling the Estates of Sir John Maynard, 5 and 6 William and Mary c. 16, not printed; Forsyth's Hortensius, p. 431; Campbell's Lives of the Chancellors; Foss's Lives of the Judges; Gardiner's Hist. of England, ix. 320, 323, 336.] J. M. R.

MAYNE, CUTHBERT (*d.* 1577), the first seminary priest executed in England, was a native of Youlston, near Barnstaple, Devonshire. At the age of eighteen or nineteen he was made a protestant minister at the instance of his uncle, a conforming priest, who desired to procure for him the succession to his benefice. Being afterwards sent to the university of Oxford, he studied for a time at St. Alban Hall, but was soon chosen chaplain of St. John's College, where he was admitted B.A. 6 April 1566, and commenced M.A. 10 July 1570 (*Oxford Univ. Reg.* ed. Boase, i. 260). He became secretly attached to the Roman catholic faith, and on the invitation of Gregory Martin [q. v.], Edmund Campion [q. v.], and other friends, he proceeded to Douay, where he was admitted into the English College in 1573. He was ordained priest in 1575, and graduated B.D. in the university of Douay on 7 Feb. 1575–6 (*Records of the English Catholics*, i. 5, 7). On 24 April 1576 he was sent with

John Paine to the English mission, and he became chaplain to Francis Tregian, esq., of Wolveden or Golden, in St. Probus's parish, Cornwall, passing as that gentleman's steward. In June 1577 Dr. William Bradbridge, bishop of Exeter, being on his visitation at Truro, prevailed on Sir Richard Greville, the high sheriff, to search Golden House, and there, says Tonkin, the Cornish historian, 'the priest was found concealed under an old tower.' He was imprisoned at Launceston and tried before Sir Roger Manwood [q. v.], chief baron of the exchequer, at the Michaelmas assizes. The act of parliament which made it high treason to receive holy orders abroad had not yet been passed, and it was found difficult to prefer any capital charge against him. Nevertheless, he was tried and condemned to death for denying the queen's spiritual supremacy, saying mass, possessing a printed copy of a bull for a jubilee, and wearing an Agnus Dei. For harbouring the priest, his patron, Sir Francis Tregian, was, by a sentence of premunire, stripped of all his property, and sentenced to perpetual imprisonment. Hallam asserts that Mayne was condemned 'without any charge against him except his religion' (*Constitutional Hist.* ed. 1832, i. 197; cf. *English Historical Review*, i. 144). He was drawn, hanged, and quartered at Launceston on 29 Nov. 1577. Dr. Oliver states that 'the skull of the martyr is religiously kept at Lanherne' in the convent of the Theresian nuns (*Catholic Religion in Cornwall*, p. 2). He was beatified by Pope Leo XIII on 29 Dec. 1886 (*Tablet*, 15 Jan. 1887, pp. 81, 82). His portrait has been engraved.

[A short account of his life, in English, by Cardinal Allen, was published in 1582; and a Latin life of him, in manuscript, is preserved among the archives of the see of Westminster. See also Aquepontanus, Concertatio Eccl. Catholicæ, ii. 50 *b*, iii. 291 *b*; Boase and Courtney's Bibl. Cornubiensis, pp. 343, 1278; Camden's Annals, s.a. 1577; Challoner's Missionary Priests, *n.* 1; Dodd's Church Hist. ii. 91–4; Douay Diaries, p. 431; Estcourt's Question of Anglican Ordination, p. 138 and App. p. lxii; Foster's Alumni Oxon. early series, iii. 995; Gilbert's Cornwall, iii. 370; Granger's Biog. Hist. of England, 5th edit. i. 273; Historia del glorioso Martirio di diciotto Sacerdoti (Macerata, 1585), p. 178; Lansd. MS. 981, f. 136; Lingard's Hist. of England, 1849, vi. 331; Lysons's Cornwall, p. 271; Morris's Troubles of our Catholic Forefathers, i. 64–101; Oliver's Cornwall, pp. 203, 355; Pollen's Acts of English Martyrs, p. 250; Prince's Worthies, 1810, p. 583; Raissius, Catalogus Christi Sacerdotum, p. 7; Records of the English Catholics, ii. 471; Rymer's Fœdera, xv. 791; Simpson's Campion, pp. 49, 73, 93; Stanton's Menology, p. 570; Strype's Works (index); Tablet, 6 Dec. 1890, p. 913; Wood's Fasti Oxon. (Bliss), i. 185.] T. C.

MAYNE, JASPER (1604–1672), archdeacon of Chichester and dramatist, was son of Gasper or Jasper Mayne, 'gent,' and was baptised at Hatherleigh, Devonshire, where the family owned a small property, on 23 Nov. 1604 (par. reg.) He was educated at Westminster, and proceeded to Oxford as a servitor of Christ Church in 1623. He there received much encouragement from the dean, Brian Duppa [q. v.], and was elected a student in 1627. Taking holy orders, he graduated B.A. 1628, M.A. 1631, B.D. 1642, and D.D. 1646. Like his patron, Duppa, Mayne had much literary taste, and was soon known in the university as 'a quaint preacher and noted poet.' When William Herbert, third earl of Pembroke [q. v.], chancellor of the university, died in 1630, he wrote an English elegy (cf. *Corpus Christi Coll. Oxon. MSS.* clxxvi. 3, cccxxviii. 52). English poems by him also figure in the collections of verse issued by the university in 1633 on Charles I's recovery from illness, in 1638 on Queen Henrietta's convalescence after confinement, and in 1643 on the queen's return from the continent. His university friends included William Cartwright [q. v.], the dramatist and divine, also a member of Christ Church, and he contributed commendatory verses to the collected edition of Cartwright's plays and poems, 1651. Meanwhile he mixed in London literary society, and was one of those who wrote 'to the memory of Ben Jonson' in 'Jonsonus Virbius' (1637); and verses by him in honour of Beaumont and Fletcher were first printed in the folio of 1679. He is also, very doubtfully, credited with the admirable elegy superscribed 'I. M. S.,' and prefixed to the 1632 folio of Shakespeare's 'Works.' 'I. M. S.' has been interpreted as 'Jasper Mayne, Student,' but the lines are of far superior quality to any assigned with certainty to Mayne (SHAKESPEARE, *Centurie of Praise*, New Shakspere Soc., pp. 190–4).

Mayne himself attempted playwriting, and in 1639 completed the 'City Match,' a domestic comedy of much sprightliness, although somewhat confused in plot. It was acted both at the court at Whitehall and at the Blackfriars Theatre, and was published at Oxford. Its full title ran: 'The City Match. A Comœdye. Presented to the King and Qveene at White-Hall. Acted since at Black-Friers by his Maiesties Servants. Horat. de Arte Poet. Versibus exponi Tragicis res Comica non vult. Oxford, Printed by Leonard Lichfield, Printer to the University. Anno Dom. M.D.C. XXXIX,' fol. Another edition appeared at Oxford in 1659, and it is included in Dodsley's 'Old Plays.' On 28 Sept. 1668 Pepys saw it performed—the first time 'these thirty years,' he declares—and condemned it as 'but a silly play.' In 1755 William Bromfield revised it, and presented his version to the governors of the Lock Hospital, who secured a representation of it at Drury Lane for the benefit of the charity. Bromfield's revision was issued as 'The Schemers, or the City Match.' In 1828 J. R. Planché constructed out of the 'City Match' and Rowley's 'Match at Midnight' a piece called 'The Merchant's Wedding, or London's Frolics in 1638,' which was performed at Covent Garden 5 Feb. 1828, and was printed. A second dramatic effort by Mayne—a tragi-comedy, entitled 'The Amorous War'—was far more serious, and at most points inferior to its forerunner, but it contained a good lyric, 'Time is a Feathered Thing,' which is reprinted in Henry Morley's 'King and Commons,' p. 53. It was published in 1648, 4to, and in 1658 copies of it were bound up with the 'City Match,' in a volume called 'Two Plaies: The City Match, a Comœdy; and the Amorous Warre, a Tragy Comœdy; both long since written. By J. M. of Ch. Ch. in Oxon. Oxford: Printed by Hen. Hall for Ric. Davis,' 1658, 4to.

Mayne's more distinctly academic work was represented by a translation of Lucian's 'Dialogues,' which he began about 1638 for the entertainment of a distinguished patron, William Cavendish, marquis of Newcastle [q. v.] But the 'barbarous times' of civil war diverted Newcastle's attention from literature, and the book remained incomplete, although it was printed in 1664, with a continuation by Francis Hickes [q. v.], as 'Part of Lucian made English from the originall, in the Yeare 1638, by Iasper Mayne . . . to which are adjoyned these other Dialogues . . . translated by Mr. Francis Hicks '(Oxford, 1664). The volume is dedicated by Mayne to the Marquis of Newcastle. To Donne's 'Paradoxes, Problemes, Essayes, Characters' (1652), Mayne contributed a verse translation of the Latin epigrams, which he entitled 'A Sheaf of Miscellany Epigrams' (pp. 88–103). Other occasional verse attributed to him includes a poem in MS. Harl. 6931, f. 117, 'On Mrs. Anne King's Table Booke of Pictures,' beginning:

> Mine eyes were once blest with the sight;

some manuscript lines signed 'J. M.,' in a copy of Alexander Ross's 'Mel Heliconicum,' 1646, formerly in Sir William Tite's library; an epitaph on some unknown friend, in the British Museum copy of Milton's English and Latin poems, 1646, signed 'J. M. 10ber 1647' (*Times*, 16 July 1868 and following days; *Athenæum*, 1868, ii. 83 sq.; Morley, *King and Commons*, passim; *Notes and Queries*, 4th ser. vol. ii. passim); 'Proteleia Anglo-Batava,' 1641 (Hunter, manuscript *Chorus Vatum*), and 'To the Duke of York on the late Seafight,' 1665, beginning:

> War the supreme decider of a cause,

among Matthew Wilson's manuscripts at Eshton Hall, Yorkshire (*Hist. MSS. Comm.* 3rd Rep. p. 295).

In middle life Mayne definitely abandoned poetry. In 1639 he accepted the college living of Cassington, near Woodstock, but during the civil war he was chiefly in Oxford, and often preached before the king. He is possibly the 'J. M., D.D.,' who published, 30 May 1646, 'The Difference about Church Government ended,' with a dedication to the parliament. The writer argues in favour of the dependence of the church on the state. On 9 Aug. 1646 he preached at Carfax Church 'concerning unity and agreement' (Oxford, 1646, 4to). In 1647 he defended the royalist position in a pamphlet, 'Οχλο-μαχια, or the People's War, in answer to a Letter sent by a person of quality who desired satisfaction' (25 July 1647). He also issued a sermon against false prophets 'shortly after the surrender of the garrison.' This evoked a reply from Francis Cheynell [q. v.], and Mayne vindicated himself from Cheynell's 'causeless aspersions' in a published letter entitled 'A late printed Sermon against False Prophets . . . Vindicated . . .,' 1647. On 3 May 1648 he was summoned before the parliamentary visitors, and 2 Oct. was removed from his studentship (*Register of the Visitors*, ed. Burrows, Camd. Soc., pp. 30–1, 196). He was also ejected from Cassington. At the same time the family estate of Hatherleigh was sequestrated, and Mayne's brother, John, obtained permission to compound on 4 Aug. 1652 (*Cal. Committee for Compounding*, p. 3033). On 30 March 1648 Mayne, however, was presented to the Christ Church living of Pyrton, Oxfordshire, and resided there at intervals for eight years. On 11 Sept. 1652 he took part in a public disputation in the neighbouring church of Watlington with John Pendarves [q. v.], and preached 'a sermon against schism' (1652, 4to), amid much interruption from the friends of his opponent. This he reprinted, with earlier controversial works, in 'Certain Sermons and Letters of Defence and Resolution to some of the late Controversies of our Times,' London, 1653, 4to.

Ejected from Pyrton in 1656, Mayne took

refuge with William Cavendish, earl of Devonshire, and occupied his leisure in disputing on religious topics with Hobbes, the earl's tutor. 'Between them,' says Wood, 'there never was a right understanding.' Aubrey, however, describes Mayne as Hobbes's 'old acquaintance.' On 1 Nov. 1653 Mayne had written from Derbyshire, apparently from Chatsworth, declining Richard Whitlocke's invitation to prefix verses to Whitlocke's forthcoming 'Ζωοτομία,' on the double ground that the rude place in which he was dwelling abated his fancy, and that his published verse had been condemned as unbefitting his profession.

At the Restoration Mayne was reinstated in his benefices, and was appointed a canon of Christ Church, archdeacon of Chichester, and chaplain in ordinary to the king. He preached at Oxford 27 May 1662, when 'his drift was to display the duncery of the university in the late intervall' (Wood), and in the same year he preached in London at the consecration of Herbert Croft [q. v.], bishop of Hereford. Both sermons were published, the latter with a graceful dedication to Mayne's early benefactor, Duppa. In January 1663–4, at a supper given by Dean Fell at Christ Church after the undergraduates had performed a play, Mayne made a speech, declaring that 'he liked well an acting student' (Wood). He died at Oxford on 6 Dec. 1672, and was buried in Christ Church Cathedral. Robert Thynne wrote Latin elegiac verses in his honour. Robert South [q. v.] and John Lamphire [q. v.] were his executors, and by his will he left 500*l.* towards the rebuilding of St. Paul's Cathedral, and 100*l.* to each of his benefices, Cassington and Pyrton. He left nothing to Christ Church, because, according to Wood, 'he had taken some distaste for affronts received from the dean of his college and certain students encouraged by him in their grinning and sauciness towards him.' Though 'accounted a witty and a facetious companion,' he seems to have been addicted to unseasonable practical jokes. He told an old servant that he had left him 'something which would make him drink after his master's death.' The bequest was a red herring.

Besides the works noticed, Wood tentatively assigns to Mayne 'Policy Unveiled, or Maxims and Reasons of State, by J. M., of Oxon.'

[Information kindly supplied by the Rev. T. Vere Bayne, and by the vicars of Cassington and Pyrton; Wood's Athenæ Oxon. ed. Bliss, iii. 971; Wood's Colleges and Halls, ed. Gutch, p. 500; Wood's Life, ed. Andrew Clarke (Oxf. Hist. Soc.), i. 441, ii. 2, 90, 254; Hunter's Chorus Vatum in Addit. MS. 24488, f. 210; Walker's Sufferings of the Clergy, p. 107.] S. L.

MAYNE, JOHN (1759–1836), Scottish poet, was born at Dumfries, 26 March 1759. Educated in the local grammar school, he became a printer in the office of the 'Dumfries Journal.' In 1782 he accompanied his family to Glasgow, where he was engaged for five years in the publishing house of the brothers Foulis. In 1787 he settled in London, first as a printer, and then as proprietor and joint editor of the 'Star,' an evening paper, in which he inserted several of his poems. He had written poetry in Dumfries, and after 1777 he occasionally contributed poems to 'Ruddiman's Weekly Magazine,' Edinburgh. Between 1807 and 1817 several of his lyrics appeared in the 'Gentleman's Magazine.' Although expressing in verse a strong desire to revisit Dumfries, Mayne never realised his wish. He died at Lisson Grove, London, 14 March 1836.

Mayne's 'Siller Gun,' descriptive of a Dumfries wapinschaw (wherein the competitors are members of the corporations, and the prize a silver cannon-shaped tube presented by James VI), consisted of twelve stanzas when it appeared in 1777. Enlarged to two cantos in 1779, and to three and four in 1780 and 1808 respectively, it took final shape in five cantos with notes in 1836. It is vivacious and humorous, conceived and worked in the spirit of 'Peblis to the Play.' Scott considers it superior to anything of Fergusson's and approaching the excellence of Burns (note to *Lady of the Lake*, v. 20). Mayne's 'Hallowe'en,' published in 'Ruddiman's Weekly Magazine,' in November 1780, probably stimulated Burns's brilliant treatment of the same theme (Chambers, *Life and Work of Burns*, i. 154, ed. 1851). 'Logan Braes,' which appeared in the 'Star,' 23 May 1789, is a song so daintily attuned to the old Scottish spirit and manner that Burns, thinking it a vagrant of an early master, appropriated two of its lines in a 'Logan Braes' of his own. 'Glasgow,' a poem of description and characterisation, published in the 'Glasgow Magazine' in December 1783, was favourably noticed in the 'Transactions of the Society of Antiquaries of Scotland,' i. 451, and was enlarged and issued in 1803. In the same year Mayne published a patriotic address entitled 'English, Scots, and Irishmen.'

[Gent. Mag. May 1836; Grant Wilson's Poets and Poetry of Scotland; MacDowall's Dumfries, p. 724; Chambers's Scottish Songs prior to Burns.] T. B.

MAYNE, PERRY (1700?–1761), vice-admiral, was the son of Covill Mayne, captain in the navy, who in 1740 commanded the Lennox, and was senior officer of the small squadron which, on 18 April, captured the Spanish 70-gun ship Princesa (BEATSON, i. 75); he died 25 Aug. 1746 (CHARNOCK, iv. 34). Perry Mayne entered the navy in August 1712, on board the Dolphin, then commanded by his father. After two years and a half in the Dolphin, he was presumably sent to school for another two years and a half; after which, in July 1717, he joined the Strafford, again with his father, with whom he also served in the Prince Frederick, in the Baltic in 1718. He passed his examination, 21 June 1720 (passing certificate), and on 7 July was promoted to be lieutenant of the Ipswich. In June 1721 he was appointed to the Falkland, going out to Jamaica with the broad pennant of Commodore Barrow Harris, who on 22 March 1724–5, two days before his death, promoted him to the command of the Spence sloop. On 24 Sept. 1725 he was advanced by Captain Ellis Brand, the senior officer on the station after Harris's death, to be captain of the Dragon. In 1739 he commanded the Worcester at the reduction of Porto Bello by Vice-admiral Edward Vernon (*d.* 1757) [q. v.], and in 1741 at the unsuccessful attack on Cartagena. On the death of Lord Augustus Fitzroy, 24 May 1741, Mayne was appointed to the Orford, remaining on the West Indian station till he was promoted to be rear-admiral, 23 April 1745. He sailed for England shortly afterwards, but going through the windward passage, the Orford struck on a reef known as the Hogstyes, and was totally lost, happily without loss of life. On arriving in England he was appointed to a command in the Channel fleet, and in January 1745–6 was ordered to preside at the trial of Vice-admiral Richard Lestock [q. v.] On 10 March he was appointed commander-in-chief at the Nore; but during 1746, and till June 1747, he was entirely occupied as president at the trial of Lestock, and afterwards of Admiral Thomas Mathews [q. v.]

During the trial of Lestock the court-martial came into curious collision with the civil law. A Lieutenant Frye of the marines had, two years before, been tried in the West Indies by a court-martial of which Mayne was a member for disobedience and disrespect; for these offences, and for contempt of court, Frye had been cashiered and sentenced to fifteen years' imprisonment, the greater part of which was remitted by the king [see OGLE, SIR CHALONER, *d.* 1750]. In 1746 he brought an action against the members of the court for false imprisonment and ill-treatment, and obtained writs against them—among others, against Mayne, the president, and Captain Rentone, a member of the court-martial then sitting on Lestock. On these writs being served, the court, as a body, passed a resolution complaining of the infringement of the lord high admiral's prerogative by this arrest of the president and a member of a court-martial sitting by direct authority of the admiralty. Corbett, the secretary of the admiralty, replied, fully approving of what Mayne and his colleagues had done, and enclosing a letter from the Duke of Newcastle, to the effect that the king had expressed great displeasure at the insult offered to the court-martial (*Correspondence of John, fourth Duke of Bedford*, i. 105, 108, 111). Thus encouraged, the court passed a resolution amounting to a vote of censure on the lord chief justice, Sir John Willes, who on hearing of it forthwith issued warrants for the arrest of every member of the court, as having insulted the majesty of the law. Mayne and the other members of the court preferred making an abject apology to being arrested. On this the warrants were withdrawn, but in withdrawing them Willes desired that the circumstance might be registered 'as a memorial to the present and future ages.' It seems doubtful whether the lord chief justice had the authority, which he assumed, to arrest the president and members of a legally constituted court sitting in the execution of their office; but as Mayne and his colleagues did not venture to contest it, the case remains on record as a precedent.

On 15 July 1747 Mayne was promoted to be vice-admiral, but had no further service. In February 1757 he retired on a pension equal to his half-pay. He died 5 Aug. 1761.

[Charnock's Biog. Nav. iv. 137; Beatson's Nav. and Mil. Memoirs; offical documents in the Public Record Office.] J. K. L.

MAYNE, SIR RICHARD (1796–1868), police commissioner, fourth son of Edward Mayne, one of the judges of the court of king's bench in Ireland, was born in Dublin on 27 Nov. 1796. He was educated at Trinity College, Dublin, where he graduated B.A. in 1818, and then, proceeding to Trinity College, Cambridge, was incorporated B.A. in 1818, and proceeded M.A. in 1821. He was called to the bar at Lincoln's Inn on 9 Feb. 1822, and went the northern circuit. On the institution of the metropolitan police, 29 Sept. 1829, Colonel (afterwards Sir) Charles Rowan and Mayne were appointed joint-commissioners, and in 1850, on the resignation of the former, the latter became chief commissioner. With his colleague he had to raise, organise, and train a small army, to instruct them in duties hitherto unknown in England, and to teach them to discharge their office with patience and consideration. In addition, a system had to be created dealing with great public gatherings and for controlling street traffic. Great ability, industry, and patience had to be exercised, and much active service by day and night. The number of police ultimately under his command reached about seven thousand men. The portion forming the X Division Mayne originally recruited to take charge of the International Exhibition of 1862. In July 1866, during the Hyde Park riots, Mayne was ill-treated by some of the mob. But his management of the police was very successful during his long tenure of office. For his services he was created a C.B., 29 April 1848, and on the close of the Great Exhibition of 1851 was promoted to be K.C.B. on 25 Oct. He died at 80 Chester Square, London, 26 Dec. 1868, and on 30 Dec. was buried in Kensal Green cemetery, where a monument to his memory was unveiled on 25 Jan. 1871. In 1831 he married Georgiana Marianne Catherine, eldest daughter of Thomas Carvick of Wyke, Yorkshire. She was granted a civil list pension of 150*l.* on 21 April 1870.

His son, Richard Charles Mayne (1835–1892), admiral, was educated at Eton, and entered the navy in 1847. After serving in the Baltic and Black Seas and the Sea of Azof in 1854–5, he went out to New Zealand, where he was wounded in 1863, and commanded the survey expedition to the Straits of Magellan (1866–9). He retired with the rank of rear-admiral on 27 Nov. 1879, and was made a C.B., and on 26 Nov. 1885 was gazetted a retired vice-admiral. After unsuccessfully contesting the parliamentary representation of the Pembroke and Haverfordwest district in the conservative interest in 1885, he was returned in 1886. He died suddenly, after attending a Welsh national banquet at the Mansion House, London, on 29 May 1892. He was author of 'Four Years in British Columbia and Vancouver Island,' 1862, and of 'Sailing Directions for Magellan Straits and Channels leading to the Gulf of Penas,' 1871 (*Times*, 30 May 1892).

[Law Times, 1869, xlvi. 178; Register and Magazine of Biography, 1869, i. 113–15, 358; Times, 28 Dec. 1868 p. 7, 29 Dec. pp. 6, 7; Illustr. London News, 1869 liv. 23, 45, 1871 lviii. 117.]

G. C. B.

MAYNE, SIMON (1612–1661), regicide, baptised at Dinton, Buckinghamshire, 17 Feb. 1611–12, was the son and heir of Simon Mayne of Dinton Hall, Buckinghamshire, who died 13 July 1617, aged 40, and was buried in Dinton Church, where a large monument was erected to his memory. His mother was Coluberry, daughter of Richard Lovelace of Hurley, Berkshire, sister of the first Lord Lovelace and widow of Richard Beke, who died in 1606. She died 10 Jan. 1628–1629, and was also buried in Dinton Church. The family property came to Simon on his father's death, and to qualify himself as a magistrate he became a student at the Inner Temple in November 1630. Mayne was related to many of the chief families that adopted the cause of the parliament, and among his near neighbours were Arthur Goodwin and Sir Richard Ingoldsby [q. v.] He threw in his lot with them, was one of the grand jury of Buckinghamshire which presented an address to Charles I for the dismissal of his army (1642), and acted on the parliamentary committee for Berkshire. On 14 June 1645, after the battle of Naseby, Cromwell stopped at his house, Dinton Hall, and about September 1645, when the then members were 'disabled to sit,' Mayne was returned for the adjoining borough of Aylesbury. He was appointed one of the judges for the trial of Charles I, attended on most days, and signed the warrant for the king's execution. In the 'Mystery of the Good Old Cause' he is said to have been a 'great committee man, wherein he licked his fingers;' and although the latter part of this statement is untrue, he served during the protectorate on the committee for Buckinghamshire. As a regicide he was expressly excepted from the general act of pardon, and he surrendered himself in June 1660 to a serjeant-at-arms. He was tried at the Old Bailey on 13 Oct. 1660, and after a spiritless defence, in which he pleaded that he was ill and acted under coercion, was found guilty and attainted. In the second volume of 'Somers Tracts,' 3rd collection (1751), pp. 196–7, is a pamphlet of 'Considerations humbly tendered by Simon Mayne to show that he was no contriver of that horrid action of the Death of the late King, but merely seduced and drawn into it by the persuasion of others.' So far back as 1635 and 1636 he and his wife had received licenses, 'for notorious sickness,' to eat flesh on fish-days, and after his committal to the Tower of London his illness became fatal. He died there on 13 April 1661 'from gout, with fever and convulsion-fits;' the requisite inquest was held next day, and Sir Edward Nicholas [q. v.] thereupon gave the lieutenant of the Tower a warrant for the delivery of the corpse to his wife 'for interment in the country without ostentation.' Mayne was buried in Dinton Church on 18 April 1661.

The faculty office of the Archbishop of Canterbury granted a license on 21 May 1633 for his marriage to Jane, eldest daughter, then aged 19, of John Burgoyne of

Sutton in Bedfordshire, by his wife Jane, daughter and heiress of William Kempe of Finchingfield, Essex, the marriage to be celebrated at St. Anne, Blackfriars, or St. Faith, London. She died in 1641, and Mayne subsequently married a widow, whose surname is unknown. She survived him many years, and was buried at Dinton, 10 Aug. 1694. The dean and chapter of Rochester and two of his majesty's servants petitioned for parts of his property, and in January 1660–1 Sir Richard Lane obtained a grant of the remainder of the lease of the rectories of Haddenham and Cuddington in Buckinghamshire, which he had forfeited. His son was permitted to enjoy the family estate at Dinton, but his grandson alienated the property.

[Hist. MSS. Comm. 11th Rep. App. pt. vii. p. 2; State Papers, 1660–1, pp. 343–4, 497; Students of Inner Temple, 1877, p. 264; Marriage Licences (Harl. Soc. 1886, vol. xxiv.), p. 33; History of Croke Family, pp. 630, 667, and pedigree No. 34; Smyth's Ædes Hartwellianæ, Addenda, p. 247; Foster's Alumni Oxon.; Lipscomb's Buckinghamshire, ii. 138–40, 147–52; Noble's Regicides, ii. 64–8; Gibbs's Buckinghamshire Occurrences, i. 127, 164, 205, 208; Visitation of Bedfordshire (Harl. Soc. 1884), p. 88; information from the Rev. John Bond, vicar of Dinton.] W. P. C.

MAYNE, WILLIAM (1818–1855), colonel, and brigadier of the Hyderabad contingent, born on 28 Oct. 1818, was second surviving son of the Rev. Robert Mayne of Limpsfield, Surrey, by his wife, Charlotte Cuninghame Graham, daughter of Colonel Graham of St. Lawrence House, near Canterbury. William Mayne, baron Newhaven, was his father's brother (see Burke, *Extinct Peerages*, under 'Mayne'). He joined the East India Company's Military Seminary, Addiscombe, 5 Feb. 1836, and passed his examination 12 June. Appointed ensign, 15 Dec. 1837, he did duty with the 4th Bengal native infantry, and was afterwards posted to the 49th Bengal native infantry at Neemuch. On 29 Nov. 1838 he was specially appointed to serve with the 37th Bengal infantry in the army of the Indus. Two companies of the 27th Bengal infantry and ten of the 37th Bengal infantry were attached to Sir Robert Sale's force. Mayne was appointed detachment-adjutant to these companies, and much distinguished himself at the unsuccessful attack on the fort of Julgar, 3 Oct. 1840. He became lieutenant 2 Nov. 1841. As lieutenant in command of a rissalah (squadron) of the 2nd Shah Soojah's irregular cavalry, or Anderson's horse, he repeatedly signalised himself during the defence, by Sir Robert Sale [q. v.], of Jellalabad, and subsequently with the quartermaster-general's department under General Pollock, and at the capture of Istiliff, 29 Sept. 1842. He was selected by Lord Ellenborough for the adjutancy of the body-guard, as 'among the officers most distinguished in the late war' (*G. O.* 20 Dec. 1842). While second in command of the body-guard, he had a horse killed under him at Maharajpore, 31 Dec. 1843. He was not engaged in the Sikh wars, being in command of the late 5th irregular horse at Bhowapur during the first, and commandant of Lord Dalhousie's bodyguard at the time of the second war. In 1851, while still a captain in the 37th Bengal infantry, he was specially selected by Lord Dalhousie for the command of the Nizam's forces (Hyderabad contingent), and at the head of six thousand of these troops was much employed in suppressing disturbances in the Deccan. The rapidity of Mayne's marches, and the invariable success of his operations, attracted general notice. He was repeatedly thanked by the governor-general in council, particularly for the defeat of a large body of Arabs near Aurungabad, 20 Sept. 1853, and for his conduct on 22 Sept. 1854. On the latter occasion, while investing the fort of Saila, near Hyderabad, he defeated and annihilated a party of Rohillas, who sallied out at dead of night, and attempted to cut their way through the besiegers.

Returning to England at the close of 1854, Mayne was made a brevet-colonel and A.D.C. to the queen. He had just returned to India when a violent attack of dysentery sent him home again. He died at Cairo, 23 Dec. 1855. He married Helen Cunliffe, daughter of Thomas Reed Davidson, Bengal civil service, and niece of Lieutenant-general Sir Robert Cunliffe, by whom he left one child.

[Information supplied by the India office; Gent. Mag. 1856, pt. i. p. 185.] H. M. C.

MAYNE, ZACHARY (1631–1694), religious writer, 'sonne of Richard Maine,' was born in Exeter at the end of 1631, and baptised in St. Petrock's Church, on 1 Jan. 1631–2. He was entered at Christ Church, Oxford, 15 Oct. 1649, but by favour of the parliamentary visitors was soon made demy of Magdalen College. On 6 May 1652 he graduated B.A., although he had resided two or three terms less than the ordinary regulations required. The indulgence was allowed him at the request of Oliver Cromwell, on the recommendation of Thomas Goodwin [q. v.], at that time president of Magdalen College. Mayne was described by Cromwell as 'eminently godly, of able parts, and willing to perform all his exercises.' He was senior collector of the determining bachelors in the following Lent, fellow of Magdalen College in 1652, and M.A. on 6 July 1654. He became a preacher in and near Oxford, and a constant attendant at the weekly independent meeting held by Goodwin, whom Mayne described as 'a very great friend, and as a father.' He was appointed, by Goodwin's influence, on 23 March 1657–8, lecturer at St. Julian's Church in Shrewsbury, where he 'gave no disturbance to the town, but . . . had a fair reception and acceptation.' While there he was inclined at the suggestion of Dr. Henry Hammond [q. v.] to accept ordination from the Bishop of Bangor. The death of Oliver Cromwell in 1658 interrupted the plan. On preaching 'Concerning the Salvability of the Heathen and of Universal Redemption,' in St. Mary's Church, Oxford, in February 1660, he was convened before the vice-chancellor, Dr. Conant, and threatened with expulsion. He retired to London till the following May. His religious opinions vacillated. He is said to have had a leaning towards Socinianism, and to have passed thence to Arianism. His published works distinctly show him to have held Arminian views. Scruples as to his authority prevented him from administering the sacraments while he was an independent preacher. At the Restoration he was expelled from his fellowship, and retired to Dalwood in Dorsetshire, where, about 1671, he became a schoolmaster. He remained there till 19 Jan. 1689–90, when he was made master of the free grammar school in Exeter. In his latter years he conformed to the church (probably as a layman), and enthusiastically welcomed the revolution. He died in Exeter on 11 Nov. 1694, and was buried in the north aisle of St. Peter's Church, Dalwood, where lie also the remains of several of his children. A son, Samuel, of Exeter College (B.A. 1698 and M.A. 1701), proceeded B. Med. from New Inn Hall in 1708, practised medicine in Northampton, and died there in 1750, aged about 73.

Mayne published: 1. 'St. Paul's Travailing Pangs . . . or a Treatise of Justification,' London, 1662. Wood, who had never seen a copy of this rare book, gives it as two. 'J. G.,' who signs the 'Advice to the Reader,' prefixed to the work, was John Goodwin [q. v.] 2. 'The Snare Broken,' Oxford, 1692, 1694, anon., written ten or twelve years previous to publication, in which the author recants Socinian and Arian views, and tries to confute various calumnies. Edmund Elys [q. v.] of Totnes prefixed a Latin epistle, and Francis Lee [q. v.] an English one. 3. 'Sanctification by Faith Vindicated,' London, 1693, with a preface by R. Burscough, rector of Totnes.

He communicated to the Royal Society the description of a waterspout that took place at Topsham, near Exeter, on 7 Aug. 1694 (*Philosophical Transactions*, xix. 28, and in the abridged versions, 1716, ii. 104, and 1809, iv. 12). Two letters by Mayne, dated from Dalwood, 8 Oct. 1669 and 3 May 1671, are printed in the 'Gentleman's Magazine,' 1794, part i. p. 11.

[Foster's Alumni Oxon. 1500–1714; Wood's Athenæ (Bliss), vol. iv. cols. 411–414; Wood's Fasti (Bliss), vol. ii. cols. 169, 182; Bloxam's Reg. of Magdalen Coll. vol. ii. pp. cxvii–cxviii, 75 *n.*; Hutchins's Dorset, ii. 248; Carlyle's Cromwell, 1850, iv. 444; Cal. of State Papers, Dom. Ser. 1657–8, p. 338; Carlisle's Endowed Grammar Schools, i. 317; notice by the Rev. J. Ingle Dredge in Transactions of the Devonshire Association, 1889, p. 498; par. reg. of St. Petrock's, Exeter; information from the Rev. C. Lister James of Dalwood.] B. P.

MAYNWARING. [See also Mainwaring and Manwaring.]

MAYNWARING, ARTHUR (1668–1712), auditor of the imprests. [See Mainwaring.]

MAYNWARING, EVERARD, M.D. (1628–1699?), medical writer, born in 1628, was son of Kenelm Maynwaring, rector of Gravesend, Kent, and was educated at the grammar school there. On 21 June 1645 he was admitted a sizar of St. John's College, Cambridge, and proceeded M.B. on 1 July 1652 (*Reg. of Admissions*, ed. Mayor, pt. i. p. 71). He afterwards visited America, where he formed a lasting friendship with Christopher Lawrence, M.D. of Dublin. At Lawrence's invitation he went to Dublin in 1655 and was there created M.D. on 17 Aug. By September 1663 he had set up in business as 'doctor in physick and hermetick phylosophy' next to the Blue Boar on Ludgate Hill. He had a profound belief in specifics of his own compounding, and considered tobacco smoking productive of diseases such as scurvy, but he was in advance of his time in condemning the use of violent purgatives and indiscriminate bloodletting. During the plague year of 1665 he was entrusted by the society for employing the poor in Middlesex with the care of their pest-house, and he boasted that of eighty patients committed to him he returned fifty-six safe and sound. In 1666 he removed to a house in Clerkenwell Close, and is subsequently found residing in Fetter Lane (1671), Wine Office Court, Fleet Street (November 1678), Old Southampton Buildings by Gray's Inn (January

1690), and lastly in Gray's Inn Lane by King's Gate (1693). His contemporaries regarded him as an empiric, and one of the last acts of his life was to circulate copies of his diplomas at the end of his 'Ignota Febris' (1698). Latterly he fell into poverty, the public having lost faith in the efficacy of his 'catholick medicine.'

Maynwaring wrote: 1. 'Tutela Sanitatis, sive Vita protracta: the Protection of Long Life. . . . With a Treatise of issues. Whereunto is annexed, Bellum necessarium, sive Medicus belligerans: the . . . Physitian reveiwing his Armory,' 8vo, London, 1664. 2. 'Morbus Polyrhizos et Polymorphæus: a Treatise of tbe Scurvy (Antiscorbutick Medecines, etc.),' 2 pts. 8vo, London, 1664-1665; 2nd edit. 1666, 3rd edit. 1669, 4th edit. 1672. 3. 'Solamen Ægrorum, sive Ternarius Medicamentorum chymicorum. Ad omnes fere morbos curandum . . . remedia,' &c., 8vo, London, 1665. 4. 'Nova medendi Ratio: a short . . . Method of Curing. Exemplified by a ternary of Radical Medicines universal in their respective classes,' 4to, London, 1666. 5. 'Tabidorum Narratio: a Treatise of Consumptions,' 8vo, London, 1667; 2nd edit. 1668. 6. 'Useful Discoveries and Practical Observations in some late remarkable Cures of the Scurvy,' 8vo, London, 1668. 7. 'Medicus Absolutus . . . The Compleat Physitian, qualified and dignified. The Rise and Progress of Physick . . . illustrated,' 8vo, London, 1668. 8. 'Vita sana & longa. The Preservation of Health and Prolongation of Life proposed and proved, &c. (The Pharmacopœian Physician's Repository, &c.),' 2 pts. 8vo, London, 1669. 9. 'Praxis Medicorum Antiqua & Nova: the Ancient and Modern Practice of Physick examined,' &c., 4to, London, 1671, in which he attacks many of the fellows of the College of Physicians. 10. 'Historia et Mysterium Luis Venereæ,' 8vo, Frankfort and Hamburg, 1675, also in English as 'The Mystery of the Venereal Lues.' 11. 'Pains afflicting Humane Bodies, their . . . causes. . . . With a Tract of issues and setons,' 8vo, London, 1682. 12. 'The Method and Means of Enjoying Health, Vigour, and Long Life,' 8vo, London, 1683. 13. 'The Test and Tryal of Medicines, and the different Modes of Medical Practice,' 4to, London, 1690. 14. 'Monarchia Microcosmi: the origin, vicissitudes, and period of vital government in man, for a farther discovery of diseases incident to Human Nature (Inquiries into the General Catalogue of Diseases. The Practice of Physick reformed. A brief Account of the Catholick Medicine),' 4 pts. 8vo, London, 1692. 15. 'The Mystery of Curing comprehensively: explained and confirmed by exemplar of the Catholic Medicine,' 4to, London, 1693; 2nd edit. 1694. 16. 'Ignota Febris. Fevers mistaken in notion & practice,' 8vo, London, 1698.

Maynwaring's portrait by R. White, dated 1668, is prefixed to his 'Medicus Absolutus,' 'Vita Sana,' 'Pains,' and the fourth impression of 'Morbus Polyrhizos.'

[Maynwaring's Works; Granger's Biog. Hist. of Engl. 2nd edit. iv. 19-20; Notes and Queries, 3rd ser. ii. 506, iii. 198; Pinks's Clerkenwell (Wood).] G. G.

MAYO, sixth Earl of (1822-1872). [See Bourke, Richard Southwell.]

MAYO, CHARLES (1750-1829), historian, born 7 Dec. 1750 at Beechingstoke, Wiltshire, was son of the Rev. John Mayo, rector of Beechingstoke and vicar of Wilcot, and grandson of the Rev. John Mayo, vicar of Avebury, the brother of Charles Mayo of Hereford. He entered at Queen's College, Oxford, 1767, and graduated M.A. 1774, and B.C.L. 1779. He held the livings of Huish (1775) and Beechingstoke (1779), and was chaplain to the Somerset Hospital, Froxfield, Wiltshire.

He wrote 'A Chronological History of European States (1678-1792),' 1793, a 'Compendious View of Universal History (1753-1802),' 1804, and two volumes of sermons. He founded two scholarships for sons of Wiltshire clergy, to be held at any college at Oxford, and vested the patronage in the trustees of Froxfield Hospital. He died at Beechingstoke 27 Nov. 1829. He was unmarried.

[Hist. of Mayo Family, 1882.] C. H. M.

MAYO, CHARLES (1792-1846), educational reformer, born in London 9 June 1792, was son of Charles Mayo, a solicitor in London, grandson of the Rev. Charles Mayo, M.A., rector of Corringham, Essex, and Castle Frome, Herefordshire, and great-grandson of Charles Mayo of Hereford. Elizabeth Mayo [q. v.] was his sister. He was educated at Merchant Taylors' School and matriculated 25 June 1810, from St. John's College, Oxford. He was elected scholar of St. John's in the same year, and Laudian fellow 26 April 1813, and he graduated B.A. 1814, B.C.L. 1817 and D.C.L. 1822. He was ordained in December 1817, having in the previous August gone to Bridgnorth, Shropshire, as head-master of the grammar school, where he remained two years. Hearing through Mr. Synge of Glanmore Castle, Wicklow, of Pestalozzi's principles of education, he in 1819 joined the latter's establishment at

Yverdun as English chaplain, bringing with him some English pupils. At Yverdun he remained nearly three years, mastering Pestalozzi's principles. Returning to England in April 1822, he resolved to devote his life to their introduction into this country. He at once opened a school at Epsom for the purpose of showing their application to the education of the upper classes, and when, in 1826, the number of boys outgrew the accommodation of the house there, he removed to Cheam, where he continued to carry on his school till his death. The undertaking was very successful; boys' names were entered several years before their school age, and on some occasions immediately upon their births. Among his more distinguished pupils may be reckoned Samuel Waldegrave, bishop of Carlisle; Henry Shepheard, fellow of Oriel, and subsequently master of Cheam school; Henry Richards Luard [q. v.], registrary of Cambridge University; and three sons of Sir Thomas Francis Fremantle, first lord Cottesloe. 'With great earnestness of purpose, in Dr. Mayo's character was combined a sincere and all-absorbing yet somewhat simple piety, which was tinged with the principles of the evangelical revival, while at the same time he was a consistent and loyal son of the Church of England.' Mayo took every opportunity of expounding Pestalozzi's system, and delivered a lecture on his life at the Royal Institution in May 1826. He also took great interest in the foundation and management of the Home and Colonial Training College in Gray's Inn Road, London, which was intended to show the application of Pestalozzianism to elementary education.

Mayo died 23 Feb. 1846, and was buried at Cheam, where a tablet, erected by pupils and friends, speaks of his work as illustrating, 'both in theory and practice, the blessings of an education based upon Intellectual Development, Scriptural Teaching, and Christian Influence.' By his wife Mary, daughter of Edward Walwyn Shepheard, esq., of Great Russell Street, London, he left issue a daughter Mary, and two sons, the Rev. Charles Theodore Mayo, M.A. (1832–1892), vicar of St. Andrew's, Hillingdon, Middlesex, and the Rev. Theodore Mayo, M.A., of Quatford House, Shropshire.

Mayo wrote 'Observations on the Establishment and Direction of Infant Schools,' 1827, and 'Memoirs of Pestalozzi,' 1828, besides numerous school books and sermons.

[Hist. of Mayo Family, 1882.] C. H. M.

MAYO, CHARLES (1767–1858), professor of Anglo-Saxon, born in London 24 March 1767, was second son of HERBERT MAYO, D.D. (1720–1802), by his wife Mary, daughter of George Coldham, surgeon extraordinary to the Prince of Wales. The father (son of Charles Mayo of Hereford) was elected fellow at Brasenose College, Oxford, in 1740 (M.A. 1745, and D.D. 1763), and after serving curacies in the east of London was presented in 1764 to the living of Middleton Cheney, Northamptonshire, which he relinquished the same year to return to the east end of London as rector of St. George's. There he continued till his death. He was J.P. for Middlesex, and treasurer of Raine's Hospital, and was an exemplary parish priest in poor districts at a time not generally noted for spiritual activity.

Charles was admitted to Merchant Taylors' School, 1776, and thence elected to St. John's College, Oxford, 1785, of which society he became fellow in 1788. He graduated M.A. 1793, and B.D. 1796. In 1795 he was elected by the university professor of Anglo-Saxon on the foundation of Dr. Rawlinson, being the first to hold that office, and he occupied it for the allotted space of five years. Dr. Samuel Parr states that his lectures were much applauded. Mayo took holy orders and was Whitehall preacher 1799–1800, and morning lecturer at the old chapel of St. Michael, Highgate, for thirty years. He was elected F.S.A. 1820, F.R.S. 1827, and a governor of Cholmeley School in Highgate 1842. He resided during the greater part of his life at Cheshunt, Hertfordshire, where he inherited in 1824 the manor of Andrewes and Le Motte from his grandmother Rebecca, daughter of Sir John Shaw, bart. He married Louisa, daughter of James Landon, but died without issue 10 Dec. 1858, aged 91 years. He was buried at Cheshunt.

Charles's elder brother, PAGGEN WILLIAM MAYO (1766–1836), was elected to a medical fellowship at St. John's College, Oxford, 6 July 1792, and graduated D.M. in 1795. Elected physician to the Middlesex Hospital 23 Aug. 1793, he was admitted F.R.C.P. 30 Sept. 1796, and was censor 1797, Gulstonian lecturer 1798, and Harveian orator 1807. Resigning his hospital appointment in 1801, he removed from Conduit Street, London, to Doncaster, and eventually to Bridlington, where he died 6 July 1836. He married Charlotte, daughter of the Rev. Stephen Buckle, LL.D., and left issue.

[E. Wilson's History of Middlesex Hospital; Munk's Coll. of Phys.; Hist. of Mayo Family, 1882.] C. H. M.

MAYO, CHARLES (1837–1877), army surgeon, born at Winchester 13 Jan. 1837, was elder son of Charles Mayo, F.R.C.S. (1788–

1876), senior surgeon of Winchester County Hospital, descended from the Rev. John Mayo, vicar of Avebury, Wiltshire, 1712–46. He was elected on the foundation of Winchester College in 1847, and of New College, Oxford, where he became fellow in 1856. He graduated B.A. 1859, M.A. 1863, D.M. 1871, M.R.C.S. 1861, M.R.C.P. 1869. In October 1862 he proceeded to America, where he was staff surgeon-major and medical inspector of the 13th U.S. army corps with Grant's army at the siege of Vicksburg (see his 'Medical Service of the Federal Army' in *Vacation Tourists*, 1862–3).

The next few years he spent partly at Oxford, where he was coroner of the university, 1865–9, and dean of New College, and partly in London as physician to the General Dispensary in Bartholomew Close.

On the breaking out of the Franco-Prussian war in 1870 he entered the medical service of the German army as staff surgeon-major, and was appointed director of the Alice Hospital at Darmstadt, which was built under his superintendence. This hospital was in existence for nine months, and about 700 German and 250 French sick and wounded soldiers were treated in it; the number of deaths was only 51. At the close of the war he received five decorations, and the German ministry of war expressed 'its most thankful acknowledgment for the prudence and untiring energy with which you have built, fitted out, and conducted up to the present time the Alice Hospital.' He was also made a knight of the Hessian order of Philip the Generous. The campaign in Atchin next gave him the opportunity of entering the Dutch medical service, and he was present with the expedition from Holland in the swamps of Sumatra 1873–4, and wrote the account of the war which appeared in the 'Times' of 19 Oct. 1874, and was subsequently reprinted.

Being still unwilling to settle in England he sailed for Fiji as one of the government medical officers in 1875. Here, after suffering much discomfort, he was attacked with acute dysentery, and dying on the voyage to Sydney, was buried at sea, 15 July 1877. He was unmarried.

Mayo was not only a skilful medical man, but a good architect and musician. He wrote a 'History of Wimborne Minster,' 1860; and in 1875 a pamphlet on the 'Organ in New College Chapel.' He also edited the thirteenth edition of the 'Seaman's Medical Guide.'

[Kirby's Winchester Scholars, pp. 220, 322; Foster's Alumni Oxonienses, 1715–1886; Hist. of Mayo Family, 1882.] C. H. M.

MAYO, DANIEL (1672?–1733), presbyterian minister, son of Richard Mayo [q. v.], was born about 1672. He was educated by his father, had the degree of M.A., probably from Glasgow, and finished his studies at Leyden under Hermann Witsius. He settled in London as assistant to Vincent Alsop [q. v.], but removed in 1698 to Kingston-on-Thames, Surrey, where he was pastor of the presbyterian congregation in succession to John Goffe. At Kingston he kept a school, at which Philip Doddridge, D.D. [q. v.] was a pupil (1712–15). On the death in 1714 of Matthew Henry [q. v.], the votes were equal for Mayo and John Barker (1682–1762) [q. v.] as his successor at Mare Street, Hackney. The congregation divided; an influential secession built a new meeting-house for Mayo at the Gravel Pit, Hackney. He now preached both at Kingston and Hackney, having George Smyth (ordained 19 Dec. 1716) as his colleague in both charges. At the Salters' Hall rupture [see Bradbury, Thomas] he went with the subscribers, and in 1723 he resigned Hackney to succeed Jeremiah Smith (*d.* 20 Aug.), one of the four leaders of the subscribing presbyterians, and one of the two pastors at Meeting House Yard, Silver Street, Wood Street. He appears still to have resided at Kingston and kept on his school. In 1724 he was elected a trustee of Dr. Williams's foundations. He preached the funeral sermon (1732) for Edmund Calamy, D.D. [q. v.] He was a good practical preacher, and a strong whig in politics. He died at Kingston on 13 June 1733, aged 61. Funeral sermons were preached by his colleague, Thomas Bures, and by William Harris, D.D. [q. v.] He was succeeded at Kingston from 1723 by Daniel Mayo the younger, probably his son.

He published, besides separate sermons, 1700–32, several being funeral sermons: 1. 'Thomas against Bennet,' &c., 1702, 8vo (anon.; see Bennet, Thomas, D.D. Mayo furnished a preface and postscript, against Bennet, to a reprint, 1703, 8vo, of 'A Treatise of Divine Worship' by William Bradshaw (1571–1618) [q. v.]). 2. 'The Modesty . . . of a High Churchman,' &c., 1707, 8vo (against John Jacques). To the continuation of Matthew Henry's 'Exposition,' 1710, fol., he contributed the notes on 2 Corinthians and 1 and 2 Thessalonians.

[Wilson's Dissenting Churches of London, 1800, iii. 60 sq.; Waddington's Surrey Congregational Hist. 1866, p. 233; James's Hist. Litig. Presb. Chapels, 1867, pp. 669, 680, 697, 708, 709 sq.; Jeremy's Presbyterian Fund, 1885, pp. 124 sq.; Protestant Dissenter's Magazine, 1797, p. 472, 1799, p. 429.] A. G.

MAYO, ELIZABETH (1793 - 1865), educational reformer, sister of Charles Mayo (1792–1846) [q. v.], was born in London 18 June 1793, and on the return of her brother from Switzerland in 1822, joined him at Epsom and subsequently at Cheam, where she remained till 1834, helping him in the instruction of his boys and in applying the principles of Pestalozzi to English education. During this time she wrote the work by which her name is best known, 'Lessons on Objects,' 1831, which was followed by 'Lessons on Shells,' 1832. From 1843 her attention was concentrated upon the work of the Home and Colonial School Society, and for many years she supervised the courses of lessons, wrote model sketches, criticised every week some of the journals kept by the students, and generally superintended the work of the institution. 'Her criticisms were always very direct, often sharp, always clear, going to the very root of the matter, always genial, because never ill-natured or sarcastic.'

Miss Mayo resided for many years at Hampstead, and dying at Malvern 1 Sept. 1865, was buried at Kensal Green cemetery. A tablet in the society's buildings, Gray's Inn Road, London, commemorates her services in having adapted to the English mind and character the principles of Pestalozzi, leavened with evangelical truth.

Besides 'Lessons on Objects' and 'On Shells' she wrote 'Lessons on Scripture Prints,' 1840, 'On Miracles,' 1845, 'On Religious Instruction,' 1849, and 'Model Lessons for Infant Schools,' 1848–50. She also joined her brother in writing 'Practical Remarks on Infant Education,' 1837.

[Hist. of Mayo Family, 1882.] C. H. M.

MAYO, HENRY (1733–1793), dissenting minister, was born in the west of England in 1733, and coming from Plymouth to London in 1756 was admitted to the academy at Mile End Road. Having preached for a short time at Northampton, he became (1762) the pastor of the Independent Congregation in Nightingale Lane, Wapping, London, of which he continued in charge until his death. He held the degrees of D.D. and LL.D., and upon the decease of Dr. Thomas Gibbons [q. v.] in 1785 he was chosen one of the tutors at the Homerton Academy, a post for which he was well qualified. 'He was a very sensible man, a good preacher, and a respectable orator.' In 1763 he was engaged in controversy with Dr. Gill on infant baptism. He frequently met Dr. Johnson at the house of Edward and Charles Dilly, booksellers, in the Poultry. A conversation which he had with Johnson there in 1773 on liberty of conscience is fully reported by Boswell (*Life of Johnson*, ed. Hill, ii. 247–55). 'Dr. Mayo's calm temper and steady perseverance rendered him an admirable subject for the exercise of Dr. Johnson's powerful abilities. He never flinched; but, after reiterated blows, remained seemingly unmoved as at first. The scintillations of Johnson's genius flashed every time he was struck, without his receiving any injury. Hence he obtained the epithet of "The Literary Anvil"' (Boswell).

Mayo died at his house in Wellclose Square 4 April 1793, and was buried in Bunhill Fields. He was twice married, first to Jane Marder, the widow of Mr. Martin, a West India merchant, and secondly to Dame Elizabeth Belfour, and had issue three daughters.

[W. Wilson's MSS. in Dr. Williams's Library; Wilson's Dissenting Churches, ii. 531; Boswell's Johnson, ed. Hill, ii. 252 n, &c.; private information.] C. H. M.

MAYO, HERBERT (1796–1852), physiologist and anatomist, third son of John Mayo [q. v.], was born in Queen Anne Street, London, 3 April 1796. He entered Middlesex Hospital as a surgical pupil 17 May 1814, and was a pupil of Sir Charles Bell [q. v.], 1812–15. He also studied at Leyden, and graduated D.M. in that university. He became house-surgeon at Middlesex Hospital in 1818, and M.R.C.S. in 1819. In August 1822 appeared the first part of the 'Anatomical and Physiological Commentaries,' a work which is remarkable as containing Mayo's assertion of his discovery of the real function of the nerves of the face, and his account of the experiments which proved it. This was the starting-point of an exceedingly bitter and prolonged controversy with Sir Charles Bell, the discoverer of the distinction between sensory and motor nerves. Dr. Whewell, in a letter to the 'London Medical Gazette,' dated 11 Dec. 1837, describes the discovery as having been made by Bell, Mayo, and Majendie, the two latter physiologists having corrected and completed the researches of the former. His claim was stated with more emphasis by Dr. Druitt, who says: 'Mayo was the first in enunciating the positive doctrine that the portio dura is the nerve of voluntary motion for the face, and the fifth nerve, the nerve of common sensation to the same. It is true there are certain passages in Sir Charles Bell's treatise in 1821 which make it difficult to conceive how he could have missed the truth, whilst there are other passages which show positively that he did miss it. Meanwhile Mayo's statement and claim in 1822 were clear, precise, and unmistakable' (DR. R. DRUITT, author of *Surgeon's Vade Mecum*). While lecturer on anatomy in the Medical School, Great Windmill Street, he published on 1 Jan. 1827 the first edition of 'Outlines of Human Physiology,' being heads of lectures delivered at that school. He was surgeon of the Middlesex Hospital from 1827 until 1842, professor of anatomy and surgery to Royal College of Surgeons 1828 and 1829, F.R.S. 1828, F.G.S. 1832, and his name appears in the first list of fellows of the Royal College of Surgeons in 1843. On the establishment of King's College in 1830 he received the appointment of professor of anatomy, and he became professor of physiology and pathological anatomy in 1836. He resided at 19 George Street, Hanover Square.

Mayo's ill-judged and unsuccessful candidature in 1836 for a vacant professorship at University College necessitated his withdrawal from King's College. He thereupon founded the Medical School at the Middlesex Hospital, which has since attained great practical reputation. 'As a teacher he was admirable, bringing forward the leading facts or doctrines without superfluous detail, and illustrating them with impromptu drawings on the black-board, in which he showed great power as a draughtsman. He was an accomplished scholar, profoundly versed in the best English literature and history, of a peculiarly quaint and pithy style of conversation, and he had a great power of attaching the students to him' (*ib.*) In 1843 gradually increasing rheumatic gout reduced him to a state of helplessness, and compelled his retirement from his duties as lecturer on surgery at the Middlesex Hospital, after six years' tenure of the post. Finding relief in Germany from hydropathic treatment, he became physician in a hydropathic establishment at Boppart, and afterwards at Bad Weilbach, where he died 15 May 1852. In the later years of his life he had thrown himself into the hands of the mesmerists, and his work on the 'Truths contained in Popular Superstitions' is an ably written exposition of his views regarding the supposed cause of mesmeric and kindred phenomena. He married Jessica Matilda, daughter of Samuel James Arnold [q. v.], the dramatist, and had issue one son and two daughters.

He published: 1. 'Anatomical and Physiological Commentaries,' 1822–3. 2. 'Course of Dissections for Students,' 1825. 3. 'Outlines of Human Physiology,' four editions, 1827–1837. 4. 'A Series of Engravings of Brain and Spinal Cord in Man,' 1827. 5. 'Observations on Injuries and Diseases of the Rectum,' 1833. 6. 'An Introductory Lecture,' 1834. 7. 'Outlines of Human Pathology,' 1836. 8. 'Management of Organs of Digestion,' 1837 and 1840. 9. 'Powers of the Roots of the Nerves in Health and in Disease,' 1837. 10. 'Philosophy of Living,' 1837 and 1851. 11. 'Treatise on Syphilis,' 1840. 12. 'Nervous System and its Functions,' 1842. 13. 'The Cold Water Cure,' 1845. 14. 'Letters on Truths in Popular Superstitions,' 1848 and 1851. The 'London Medical Gazette' contains many contributions from his pen.

[Hist. of Mayo Family, 1882.] C. H. M.

MAYO, JOHN (1761–1818), physician, son of Thomas Mayo, and grandson of Charles Mayo of Hereford, was born in that city 10 Dec. 1761. He matriculated at Oxford in 1778 from Brasenose College, graduated B.A. 1782, was elected fellow of Oriel College 16 April 1784, and proceeded M.A. 1785, B.M. 1787, and D.M. 1788. He became F.R.C.P. 30 Sept. 1789, and was censor in 1790, 1795, 1804, and 1808, Harveian orator in 1795, elect on 10 April 1807, resigning this last position 6 Oct. 1813. He served as physician to the Foundling Hospital from July 1787 to 1809, physician to the Middlesex Hospital 6 Nov. 1788 until 11 Jan. 1803, and was also physician in ordinary to the Princess of Wales. At a meeting of the board of the Middlesex Hospital, December 1802, it was resolved that Dr. Mayo, 'who had been physician to this hospital with equal advantage to the charity and honour to himself for fourteen years, be solicited to attend the cancer ward as physician extraordinary' (WILSON).

Mayo long divided his time between London and Tunbridge Wells, residing at the latter resort during the summer months. There he enjoyed 'the undisputed lead in medical business and emoluments' (MUNK). On resigning his hospital appointments in 1817, he fixed his permanent abode at Tunbridge Wells, and dying 29 Nov. 1818, was buried at Speldhurst, Kent.

By his first wife, Jane, daughter of Thomas Cock, esq., of Tottenham, he had issue three sons: Thomas [q. v.], subsequently president of the Royal College of Physicians; John, in holy orders; and Herbert [q. v.] His second wife was Frances Lavinia, daughter of William Fellowes, esq., of Ramsey Abbey, M.P. for Sudbury and Andover.

After his death his eldest son published 'Remarks on Insanity, founded on the Practice of J. Mayo, M.D.,' 1817.

[Erasmus Wilson's Hist. of Middlesex Hospital, 1845; Foster's Alumni Oxon. 1715–1886; Munk's Coll. of Phys. ii. 395; Hist. of Mayo Family, 1882.] C. H. M.

MAYO, RICHARD (1631?–1695), ejected divine, was born about 1631. His family seems to have belonged to Hertfordshire. In early life he was at school in London under John Singleton, a puritan divine, and he entered the ministry when very young. During the Commonwealth period he obtained the vicarage of Kingston-on-Thames, Surrey, probably succeeding Edmund Staunton, D.D., in 1648. For several years he also conducted a weekly lecture at St. Mary's, Whitechapel, London. By the uniformity act he was ejected (1662) from his living, but continued to preach in conventicles. He was one of the few who, in 1666, took the oath which exempted from the operation of the Five Miles Act. Towards the end of the reign of Charles II he settled as minister of a presbyterian congregation meeting at Buckingham House, College Hill, Upper Thames Street. After the Toleration Act (1689) his congregation removed to a newly built meeting-house in Salters' Hall Court, Cannon Street. Here in 1694, after the exclusion of Daniel Williams, D.D., from the merchants' lectureship, a new lectureship was established [see HOWE, JOHN]. Mayo was one of the lecturers. He died, after six weeks' illness, on Sunday, 8 Sept. 1695, in his sixty-fifth year. Nathaniel Taylor, his assistant, preached his funeral sermon. He left two sons, Richard Mayo, D.D., who in 1708 was minister of St. Thomas's Hospital, Southwark, and afterwards rector of St. Michael's, Crooked Lane (Watt confuses him with his father); and Daniel Mayo [q. v.]

He published: 1. 'The Life . . . of . . . Edmund Staunton,' 1673, 8vo. 2. 'A Plain Answer to this Question . . . of Secret Prayer,' &c., 1679, 8vo; 1687, 12mo. 3. 'A Present for Servants,' &c., 1693, 8vo. 4. 'The Cause and Cure of Strife and Divisions,' &c., 1695, 4to. Also the notes on the Epistle to the Romans in 'Annotations upon the Holy Bible,' vol. ii. 1685, fol., by Matthew Poole, &c., and sermons in the 'Morning Exercise against Popery,' 1675, 4to; in the 'Continuation,' 1683, 4to, of the practical 'Morning Exercise;' and in the 'Casuistical Morning Exercises,' 1690, 4to.

[Taylor's Funeral Sermon, 1695; Reliquiæ Baxterianæ, 1696, iii. 13; Calamy's Account, 1713, p. 668; Calamy's Continuation, 1727, ii. 972; Wilson's Dissenting Churches of London, 1808, ii. 9 sq.; Williams's Life of Philip Henry, 1825, p. 165; Pike's Ancient Meeting Houses, 1870, pp. 378 sq.] A. G.

MAYO, THOMAS (1790–1871), president of the Royal College of Physicians, eldest son of John Mayo, [q. v.], born in London 24 Jan. 1790, commenced his education under the Rev. John Smith of Eltham, and after eighteen months at Westminster School was transferred to the private tuition of the Rev. George Richards, vicar of Bampton, Oxfordshire. He entered at Oriel College 1807, and obtained a first class *in literis humanioribus* 1811. Dr. Copleston, the provost, recorded that this was the best classical examination he ever heard. Mayo was elected fellow of Oriel 23 April 1813, 'to the attainment of which honour I had pledged myself to my father, provided he would permit me to escape the Foundation of Westminster and its peculiar training, which combined with a very fair proportion of Latin and Greek occasional aerostation in a blanket.'

He graduated M.A. 1814, B.M. 1815, and D.M. in 1818. On his father's death he succeeded to his lucrative practice at Tunbridge Wells, and in 1835 settled in London, residing at 56 Wimpole Street. He became F.R.C.P. 1819, censor of the college 1835, 1839, and 1850, and delivered the Lumleian lectures in 1839 and 1842, the Harveian oration in 1841, and the Croonian lectures in 1853, and was named an elect in 1847. In 1835 he became F.R.S., and in 1841 physician to the Marylebone Infirmary. He was also physician in ordinary to the Duke of Sussex. On 5 January 1857 he was elected president of the Royal College of Physicians, and was annually re-elected until 1862.

'Mayo presided over the college at a most critical period of its history, when it was undergoing those changes in its constitution that were rendered necessary by the Medical Act of 1858 and the amendment of 1860. In the necessary deliberations Mayo, as president, took an active part, and the fellows of the college acknowledged his services by retaining him for another year in his office. In 1862 Mayo withdrew from practice, and resided first at Yarmouth, Isle of Wight, and then with his son at Corsham, Wiltshire, where he died 13 Jan. 1871, and where he was buried.

'Mayo was an accomplished and vigorous writer, an acute and logical thinker, and occupied a high position among his contemporaries. He was an authority on mental diseases (see his Croonian lectures, No. 7 below). In 1860 he delivered a remarkable address at the Royal Institution on the 'Relations of the Public to the Science and Practice of Medicine.'

He twice married; first, Lydia, daughter of John Bill, M.D., of Farley Hall, Staffordshire, and secondly, Susan Mary, widow of Rear-admiral Sir William Symonds, and daughter of the Rev. John Briggs, fellow of Eton College, and had issue (by the first marriage only), Augustus Frederick Mayo, B.A., barrister-at-law, Rev. Robert Mayo, B.A., Charles Thomas Mayo of Corsham, Wiltshire, and four other children.

He published: 1. 'Essay on the Influence of Temperament in Modifying Dyspepsia,' 1831. 2. 'Essay on relation of the Theory of Morals to Insanity,' 1834. 3. 'Elements of the Pathology of the Human Mind,' 1838. 4. 'Harveian Oration,' 1841. 5. 'Clinical Facts and Reflections,' 1847. 6. 'Outlines of Medical Proof,' 1848 and 1850, with 'Sequel,' 1849. 7. 'Medical Testimony in Cases of Lunacy' (Croonian lectures), 1854, with supplement, 1856. 8. 'Medical Examinations and Physicians' Requirements considered,' 1857.

[Munk's Coll. of Phys. iii. 200; Hist. of Mayo Family, 1882.] C. H. M.

MAYOW, MAYOUWE, or **MAYO**, JOHN (1640–1679), physiologist and chemist, 'descended from a genteel family of his name living at Bree in Cornwall' (Wood), was son of William and Elizabeth Mayow. Born on 24 May 1640 (Sloane, 1708, f. 117) in the parish of St. Dunstan-in-the-West, London, he was received as commoner of Wadham College, Oxford, 3 April 1658, and admitted scholar 23 Sept. 1659. On the recommendation of Henry Coventry (1619–1686) [q. v.], who was a former fellow of the college, he was elected on 3 Nov. 1660 (Gardiner, *Registers of Wadham*) to a fellowship at All Souls' College. He graduated B.C.L. 30 May 1665, and D.C.L. 5 July 1670. Mayow obtained the further privilege of studying physic, which exempted him from taking holy orders. It is probable that he was a pupil of Thomas Willis [q. v.], Sedleian professor of natural philosophy, whom he treated in controversy with especial respect, and he certainly came into contact with Richard Lower [q. v.], who was working with Willis.

Mayow practised medicine at Bath in the summer season, and made a careful chemical study of the Bath waters, and published the results as a chapter of his tract 'De Sal-Nitro' (cf. his *Tractatus Quinque*). One of his rivals, Dr. Thomas Guidott [q. v.], denounced his chief conclusions in his 'Discourse of Bathe,' 1676, and suggested at the same time that Mayow had 'ploughed with his heifer' (*Discourse*, p. 12). Mayow was elected F.R.S. 30 Nov. 1678, on the proposition of Hooke, a fact of some importance in connection with the bitter charge of plagiarism made against him by Thomson (*Hist. of the Royal Society*, p. 467). That there is much in common between the fundamental ideas of Hooke (*Micrographia*, 1665, p. 103) and of Mayow with regard to combustion is undeniable, although the two men approached the subject in very different ways; but it must be noted that Hooke brought no charge in this connection against Mayow, and maintained friendly relations with him. 'He died,' says Wood, 'in an apothecaries house bearing the sign of the Anker, in York Street, Covent Garden (having a little before been married, not altogether to his content).' He was buried in the church of St. Paul, Covent Garden, 10 Oct. 1679. Prefixed to the 'Tractatus quinque' is a fine engraved portrait of Mayow. The face is long and thin, the features, and especially the mouth, delicately moulded and expressive.

In 1668 Mayow published his 'Tractatus duo, de Respiratione et de Rachitide,' Oxford, 8vo. The second tract, purely medical, was not of great importance; the subject of the first determined the work of Mayow's life. They were republished at Leyden in 1671, and an English translation of 'De Rachitide,' by W. Tury, appeared under the title 'Ραχιτιδολογία at Oxford, in 1685. The two tracts were meanwhile republished at Oxford in 1674 (with the vice-chancellor's imprimatur, 17 July 1673), together with three fresh essays under the title, 'Tractatus quinque Medico-Physici,' 8vo. The book was dedicated, with a grateful and characteristic preface, to his patron, Coventry, and abstracts were published in the 'Philosophical Transactions of the Royal Society.' The 'Tractatus quinque' were republished at the Hague in 1681, 8vo, under the title 'Opera Omnia,' and at Geneva in 1685. They were translated into Dutch (1684), German (1799), and French (1840).

From the 'numerosa scriptorum turba' of his time Mayow at the outset chooses Descartes as his master in method. He takes his facts from great observers like Boyle, Malpighi, Steno, Willis, and Lower, but above all from personal observation. In the tract on 'Respiration' (1668) he described its mechanism, with the movement of ribs and diaphragm, almost as perfectly as can be done to-day (Heidenhain). He made the capital discovery of the double articulation of the ribs with the spine, and put forward views with regard to the function of the internal intercostals which are still under discussion. The function of breathing is merely, he says, to bring air in contact with the blood, to which it gives up its nitroaerian constituent (oxygen), and from which it carries off the vapours produced by the heating of the blood. He shows that the heart cannot be dilated by the blood fermenting in its cavity (Descartes), but that it is a muscle, whose function is to drive the blood through the lungs and over the body, a view proved experimentally in the following year by Lower (*De Corde*, 1669). The blood carries the nitroaerian constituent to the muscles, and their motion results from the chemical reaction (fermentation) in the muscle with the combustible matter contained therein. The heart, like any other muscle, ceases to act when the nitroaerian particles are no longer supplied to it.

In the 'Tractatus quinque' the subject of the earlier work is developed and treated from a higher point of view, and carefully tested in many details. The chemistry of burning is studied separately before being applied to physiology. The treatise 'On Saltpetre and the Nitroaerian Spirit' develops a theory of combustion on lines closely resembling those followed by Lavoisier in the next century. Saltpetre is recognised as containing a base and an acid, and the acid part is formed from one of the constituents of the air, its nitroaerian particles, the air being composed of these and of another gas, left after combustion and respiration. To produce combustion sulphureous, i.e. inflammable, matter must come into contact with the nitroaerian particles. When antimony is calcined its increase in weight is due to the fixation of these particles; the rusting of metals and the conversion of iron pyrites into a vitriol are due to the same cause. It is too much to say, as some have done, that Mayow proves his case fully. The best evidence of his mental calibre is that he himself distinguishes everywhere between his facts and the hypothesis which he seeks to establish. But the logical consequences of his hypothesis he developes with the greatest acuteness. He is, it is true, misled by the desire to explain everything mechanically (which has dominated physical science since Descartes) into long and useless speculations with regard to the elasticity of the air and of solid bodies, the nature of light and of the sun, &c. But whenever he sees a way of submitting his ideas to the test of experiment, he does so. He proves that a candle burning and a mouse breathing in a closed space act in precisely the same way on the air contained, and diminish its volume and alter its properties. The failure to grasp the notion of compound gases is his true stumbling-block. Yet he recognises the fact that different gases (e.g. air and nitric oxide) exist, and carefully shows that they all follow Boyle's law.

The older tract, 'De Respiratione,' revised, follows 'De Sal-Nitro,' and Mayow next extends his explanation of respiration to the fœtus and the egg. The maternal blood supplies the fœtus not only with nutrition, but with oxygen. The egg, he thinks, contains sufficient air for itself, and probably this air is itself 'pure or vital air,' and not ordinary air. Moreover, as the egg is kept warm and the chick does little work, it needs little respiration. In the tract on 'Muscular Motion and Animal Spirits' he comes to the conclusion that the nitroaerian particles must be identified with the animal spirits of his contemporaries, and that they are separated from the blood in the brain, and thence travel along the nerves to the muscles, where they combine with the combustible matter and cause the muscle to contract by the vehement motion set up in the fibres; an important modification of Descartes's theory. The animal spirits, he declared, must not be confounded with the universal sensitive soul. In the course of the five treatises the most various points are touched on, including the theory of the relation of the saltpetre in the soil with plants (*De Sal-Nitro*, p. 52); the remarkably lucid theory of chemical affinity (*idem*, p. 242); and the mechanical explanation of the act of jumping (*De Motu Musculari*, p. 100).

Mayow stands immeasurably above such men as Willis and Sylvius, with their medley of half-digested Cartesianism and iatrochemistry. He must be classed with Hooke and Boyle, possessing the scientific imagination of the one, the tenacity of the other, and succeeding where Boyle failed. He had the genius to perceive exactly the problems which must be solved before any great advance in chemistry or physiology could be made, to guess at and partly to discover their solutions; and he showed a critical faculty in theory and experiment that is not to be met with in these two sciences until we come to Lavoisier. His premature death retarded the advent of modern chemistry for more than a century (Hoefer, *Hist. de la Chimie*, ii. 262).

By his chief contemporaries, save possibly Lower, Mayow's work met with little understanding; several, like Pechlin, borrow his language, but neither grasp his ideas nor even mention his name. The anatomical discovery with regard to the ribs was alone definitely adopted by the text-books (S. Collins, *Systeme of Anatomy*, 1685, pp 826, 833, 837). It is noteworthy that Stephen Hales [q. v.] repeated some of Mayow's experiments on combustion (*Vegetable Staticks*, 1727, i. 230 et seq.) As soon as Priestley had discovered oxygen, Mayow's works were disinterred. Blumenbach gives them high praise (*Institutiones Physiologicæ*, 1786, p. 114), and he was followed by Yeats, Beddoes, Fourcroy, J. A. Scherer, and A. N. Scherer, who are as a rule more enthusiastic than critical. The development of modern ideas with regard to muscular action again drew attention to Mayow (R. HEIDENHAIN, *Mechanische Leistung*, 1864, p. 8; A. GAMGEE, *Physiological Chemistry*, i. 407).

An engraved portrait is prefixed to Mayow's 'Tractatus Quinque.'

[Besides the sources already quoted: Wood's Athenæ Oxonienses, 1st ed. ii. 474, and ed. Bliss, iii. 1199, and Fasti, ii. 281; Registers of the parishes of St. Dunstan-in-the-West and St. Paul's, Covent Garden; Gardiner's Registers of Wadham College; Catalogue of Library of Royal College of Surgeons; Birch's History of the Royal Society, iii. 384, 442; Jöcher's Gelehrten-Lexicon, 1751, iii. 333; J. N. Pechlin's De aeris et alimenti defectu, 1676, p. 142; G. F. Rodwell, 'On the supposed Nature of Air prior to the Discovery of Oxygen,' Chemical News, xii. 293, xiv. 51; Cuvier's Histoire des Sciences Naturelles, ii. 357–9; Burrows's Worthies of All Souls', p. 204; Gmelin's Geschichte der Chemie, 1798, ii. 112; Hoefer's Histoire de la Chimie and Nouvelle Biographie; Kopp's Geschichte der Chemie, passim, and Beiträge, &c.; K. Sprengel's Geschichte der Arzneykunde, passim; G. D. Yeats's Claims of the Moderns to some Discoveries in Chemistry, 1780; T. Beddoes's Chemical Experiments and Opinions (of Mayow), 1793; J. A. Scherer's Beweis dass J. Mayow vor hundert Jahren den Grund zur antiphlogistischen Chemie u. Physiologie gelegt hat; J. Koellner's Mayow's Schriften aus dem Lateinischen übersetzt nebst einer Vorrede von A. N. Scherer; Gotch's Two Oxford Physiologists (Lower and Mayow), 1907.] P. J. H.

MAZZINGHI, JOSEPH, COUNT (1765–1844), composer, descended from an ancient Corsican family, was the eldest son of Tommaso Mazzinghi, a wine merchant settled in London. According to Cansick, the composer's father, who died in 1775, was violinist at Marylebone Gardens (*St. Pancras Epitaphs*). A Tommaso Mazzinghi published six solos for the violin, London, 1763.

Mazzinghi was born on 25 Dec. 1765 (*Gent. Mag.*) His mother's sister, Cassandra Frederich (afterwards Mrs. Wynne), a pianist, interested herself in his musical training, and he was a pupil of John Christian Bach, and later of Bertolini, Sacchini, and Anfossi. At the age of ten he became organist to the Portuguese Chapel (1775). He is said to have held the post of composer and director of music at the Italian opera from 1785 to 1792 (*Georgian Era*). He may have assisted the advertised directors, Anfossi and Cherubini, at the King's Theatre, Haymarket, but it was not until 9 Jan. 1787 that his connection with the theatre was advertised, when Cimarosa's 'Giannina e Bernardone' was announced, 'under the direction of Signor Mazzinghi,' for 9 Jan. 1787. Several songs in the pasticcio were by him. On 8 Dec. 1787 Paisiello's 'Il Re Teodoro in Venezia' was performed, with Mazzinghi, who had supplied some of the music, at the harpsichord. While holding the office Mazzinghi was not only responsible for alterations of and additions to various Italian operas, but brought out several ballets: 'L'Amour et Psiche' on 6 March 1788, 'Sapho et Phaon,' 'Eliza,' and others. He remained at his post until the King's Theatre was burnt down on 17 June 1789. In 1791 he was director of the Pantheon, the managers of which had succeeded in securing the one license granted for Italian opera. The Pantheon was, in its turn, destroyed by fire on 14 Jan. 1792. On 1 March Mazzinghi conducted at the 'Little Theatre in the Haymarket,' called then Theatre Royal, Paisiello's 'La Locanda.' He had reconstructed the opera, the score of which had been lost in the fire. The new King's Theatre, Haymarket, opened for Italian opera under other direction in 1793.

In the meantime Mazzinghi had set music to Merry's comic opera, 'The Magician no Conjuror,' produced at Covent Garden on 2 Feb. 1792. Other English operas by Mazzinghi were: 'A Day in Turkey,' 1791; 'The Wife of Two Husbands,' 1803; 'The Exile,' the Covent Garden company acting at the Opera House, 1808; 'Free Knights,' with the popular duet, 'When a little farm we keep,' 1810; and in collaboration with Reeve, who wrote the lighter airs, 'Ramah Droog,' 1798; 'The Turnpike Gate,' 1799; 'Paul and Virginia,' 1800; 'The Blind Girl,' 1801; and 'Chains of the Heart,' which gave much pleasure to George III, 1802.

Mazzinghi's concertanti were played at the professional concerts (POHL, *Haydn in London*), and his miscellaneous compositions were popular, especially those for the pianoforte. He taught the pianoforte to many influential pupils, among them the Princess of Wales, afterwards Queen Caroline. He was entrusted with the arrangement of the concerts at Carlton House, and of the Nobility concerts, established in 1791, and held on Sunday evenings at private houses. For fifty-six years Mazzinghi was a member of the Royal Society of Musicians. In about 1790 he entered into partnership with the firm of Goulding, D'Almaine, & Co., who published all his music after that date.

Visiting Italy in 1834, Mazzinghi recovered the title of count. On his return to England he retired to Bath (*Bath Journal*). He died on 15 Jan. 1844 at Downside College, where he had been on a visit to his son. He was buried with some pomp in the vault of the

Chelsea catholic church on the 25th (*Gent. Mag.* 1844, p. 322).

Besides the stage-pieces mentioned above, Mazzinghi published between seventy and eighty pianoforte sonatas; upwards of two hundred airs, &c., for pianoforte, and as many for harp and other instruments; thirty-five or more vocal trios, of which 'The Wreath' is still remembered; and a number of songs. A full list of his music is given in the 'Dictionary of Musicians,' 1827. Much of this mass of work, produced with apparent ease, was musicianly; but the flowing melodies were seldom strikingly original.

[Dictionary of Musicians, 1827, ii. 139; Georgian Era, iv. 524; Pohl's Mozart in London, pp. 30, 177; Haydn in London, pp. 18, 33, 173; Gent. Mag. 1771 p. 524, 1844 i. 322; Bath Journal, 20 Jan. 1844; Musical World, 25 Jan. 1844; Times, 18 Jan. 1844; Thespian Dict.; Grove's Dict. ii. 242.] L. M. M.

MEAD or **MEDE, JOSEPH** (1586–1638), biblical scholar, was born at Berden, Essex, in October 1586. His father, a kinsman of Sir John Mede of Lofts Hall, Essex, died about 1596; his mother married Gower of Nazeing, Essex. Mead was at school at Hoddesdon, Hertfordshire, and Wethersfield, Essex. As a schoolboy his uncle, Richard Mede, a merchant, offered to adopt him; but he preferred study. On a visit to London he bought a copy of Bellarmin's 'Institutiones Linguæ Hebraicæ,' and, though discouraged by his schoolmaster, persisted in teaching himself Hebrew. He was admitted in 1602 at Christ's College, Cambridge; his tutors were Daniel Rogers, B.D., afterwards a noted nonconformist, and William Addison. He graduated M.A. in 1610, and was elected fellow in 1613, through the influence of Lancelot Andrewes [q. v.], then bishop of Ely. More than once he had been passed over, owing to a 'very causeless' suspicion on the part of the master, Valentine Cary [q. v.], that he 'looked too much towards Geneva.' Soon afterwards he was appointed to the Greek lectureship founded by Sir Walter Mildmay, which he held along with his fellowship till his death. In 1618 he proceeded B.D.

By the time he took his master's degree Mead was already a man of encyclopedic information. To his attainments in philology and history he had added mathematics and physics. He was an enthusiastic botanist and a practical anatomist, frequenting the dissections at Caius College. He was fond of astrology, and this took him to Egyptology and kindred topics, including the origin of Semitic religions. His philosophical reading had led him towards pyrrhonism; but he got no comfort from the doctrine that the mind has no cognisance of realities, dealing only with ideas of an external world which may be illusory. From 'these troublesome labyrinths' he escaped by an effort of will, and turned to physics as a reassuring study. But the earlier conflict left its traces on his mental development, and is accountable for some mystical elements which appear in his sacramental and millennial doctrines. Fuller calls him 'most learned in mystical divinity.' His method with his pupils was the encouragement of independent and private study. His powerful memory enabled him largely to dispense with notebooks. He laboured under a difficulty of utterance. Fuller says that 'in private discourse he often smiled out his stammering into silence.' But he preached 'without any considerable hesitation.'

His character was singularly void of ambition. He declined the post of domestic chaplain to Andrewes, and twice refused the provostship of Trinity College, Dublin, for which Ussher was anxious to secure him, in March 1627 and in April 1630. Maintaining a constant converse with men as well as with books, he kept up an extensive correspondence, and he had a keen curiosity for 'foreign intelligence,' paying for weekly letters with news from abroad of the state of learning and religion. One of his agents in this matter seems to have been Samuel Hartlib [q. v.] The extracts from his own letters, printed by Heywood and Wright, are full of university gossip. Other letters, unprinted, show that he made digests of his foreign news for the use of friends. His literary friendships were catholic; his closest intimate was William Chappell [q. v.], a fellow of Christ's and afterwards bishop of Cork; Sir William Boswell [q. v.] introduced his writings to continental scholars. A communicative, he was never an assertive scholar, and declined mere controversy with pertinacious critics like Thomas Hayne [q. v.] His judgments of others were characteristically generous. A tenth of his income went in unostentatious charity.

Mead was no party man. 'I never,' he says, 'found myself prone to change my hearty affections to any one for mere difference in opinion.' His openness of mind is expressed in the maxim, 'I cannot believe that truth can be prejudiced by the discovery of truth.' But his loyal attachment to anglican doctrine and usage, as representing 'the catholick consent of the church in her first ages,' was disturbed by no scruples. On 6 Feb. 1636 he writes strongly to Hartlib against a puritan book, which is evidently one of the Latin treatises of John Bastwick, M.D. [q. v.] Against the presbyterian discipline, the institution of 'lay-elders,' and the use of the term 'minister' in place of presbyter or priest, he argues learnedly in his 'Discourses.' In the same strain are his historical arguments for the reverence due to sacred places, and for the view of the Eucharist as a sacrifice. With the puritans he held the pope to be antichrist; with the high churchmen he admitted that the Roman church teaches the fundamentals of the faith. The points at issue between Calvinists and Lutherans he did not take to be fundamental; but professed himself not 'well versed in the subtilties of those controversies.' He apprehended that the puritan arguments might make way for Socinianism, which would be 'to undermine antichrist with a vengeance.' His warm sympathies were with the object proposed by the unifying schemes of John Durie (1596–1680) [q. v.], with whom he corresponded; but he was not in love with Durie's plan, nor did he think it would commend itself to English acceptance. While inclined to simplify the essentials of communion, he expected better results from an alliance of mutual toleration between churches than from an attempt to frame new terms for a corporate union.

Mead's posthumous fame rests on his 'Clavis Apocalyptica' and kindred writings. He has the merit of perceiving that a thorough determination of the structural character of the Apocalypse must be a preliminary to any sound interpretation of it. He decides that its visions form a connected and chronological sequence; the key to the discrimination of an earlier and later chain of events he finds in Rev. xvii. 18; he makes no claim to write history in advance by help of prophecies which remain for fulfilment. Inferences opposed to his own principles were drawn by others from his apocalyptic writings; there is extant on this subject, from the pen of an anonymous admirer, 'An Apologie, or a Defence of Joseph Mede against the Puritanes' (*Harl. MS.* 6648).

His millennial speculations are based on the theory that the 'day' of judgment is a period of a thousand years, preceded by the resurrection of martyrs and their admission to heaven. He describes it as a period of 'most blissful peace' for the church on earth, but expressly rejects a terrestrial reign of Christ. In reference to the Sabbath question Mead maintains the hallowing of 'one day of seven' to be alone of divine obligation. The last day of the week was fixed by the choice of the Jews, and was not their original choice; the first day is fixed by the choice of Christians. Mead has been regarded as the originator of the rationalistic view of demoniacal possession. It is true that he admits of no distinction between demoniacs and maniacs, but he leaves it, to say the least, an open question whether all maniacs are not possessed. As an expositor of scripture in general, Doddridge well says that Mead 'has a good many original thoughts not to be found anywhere else.'

Till his last year Mead enjoyed strong health. He died on 1 Oct. 1638, and was buried in the inner chapel of his college on 2 Oct. A memorial sermon was preached at St. Mary's on 1 Feb. 1639 by John Alsop, fellow of Christ's and his executor. A Latin epitaph for him by 'G. D.,' 'a reverend person sometime of Cambridge,' is given in the 1672 edition of his 'Works.' He was tall and swarthy, originally spare, but afterwards portly and of a handsome presence, with a sparkling eye. By his will, executed on the day of his death, he left 100*l.* to the poor of Cambridge, smaller sums to his sisters, their children, and a pupil, and the residue, amounting to 300*l.*, besides his books, to his college. Throughout his correspondence (1620–31) he writes his name 'Mead,' occasionally with a flourish which has been mistaken for a final *e*; his handwriting is remarkably firm and distinct. He latinised his surname into 'Medus;' hence, perhaps, the very general adoption of the form 'Mede' by his editors.

He published: 1. 'Clavis Apocalyptica ex innatis et insitis Visionum characteribus,' &c., Cambridge, 1627, 4to, for private circulation, and extremely rare; reprinted, 1632, 4to, 1642, 4to; translated, 'The Key of the Revelation,' &c., 1643, 4to, by Richard More [q. v.], preface by Twisse; another translation, 1833, 8vo, by R. Bransby Cooper. 2. 'In Sancti Joannis Apocalypsin Commentarius,' &c., 1632, 4to, an application of the method explained in the 'Clavis,' with 'Appendix' in reply to Daniel Lawen, a Dutch divine; reprinted and translated with No. 1. 3. 'Of the Name Altar, or Θυσιαστήριον. . . . A Chappel Commonplace, An. 1635,' &c., 1637, 4to (anon.) 4. 'Churches . . . Places for Christian Worship, both in and ever since the Apostles times,' &c., 1638, 4to (Latin dedication to Laud). 5. 'The Reverence of God's House,' &c., 1638, 4to, sermon at St. Mary's, Cambridge, 24 Feb. 1636. Posthumous were: 6. 'The Apostacy of the Latter Times,' &c., 1641, 4to, preface by Twisse; 2nd edit. 1644, 4to; later editions, 1836, 8vo, introduction by Tresham D. Gregg; 1845, 18mo, introduction by J. R. Birks. 7. 'A Paraphrase and Exposition of the Prophesie of Saint Peter,' &c., 1642, 4to (on 2 Peter iii.) 8. 'Daniel's Weekes,' &c., 1643, 4to. 9. 'Dia tribæ. Discourses on divers texts,' &c., 1643, 4to; with part ii. 1648, 4to; pt. iii.

1650, 4to; pt. iv. 1652, 4to, with 'Epistles' and 'Short View of the Author's Life.' 10. 'Opuscula Latina,'&c., 1652, 4to. 11. 'Dissertationum Ecclesiasticarum Triga,' 1653, 4to. His 'Works' were first collected 1648, 4to, 2 parts; enlarged edit. by John Worthington, D.D., 1663–4, fol. 2 vols.; further enlarged by Worthington, with anonymous 'Life,' 1672, fol.; reprinted 1677, fol. Two volumes of his autograph letters, principally to Sir Martin Stutevile, are in Harl. MSS. 389, 390.

[Short View, 1652, of little moment; Life, 1672, the facts are drowned in eulogy; more valuable, so far as they go, are 'Some Additionals,' by another hand; Fuller's Hist. of the University of Cambridge, 1655, p. 92; Fuller's Worthies, 1662, pp. 334 sq.; Middleton's Biographia Evangelica, 1784, iii. 73 sq.; Doddridge's Works, 1804, v. 476; Brook's Lives of the Puritans, 1813, ii. 429 sq.; Neal's Hist. of the Puritans (Toulmin), 1822, ii. 310 sq.; Heywood and Wright's Cambr. Univ. Trans. 1854, ii. 305 sq., 557; Cox's Lit. of the Sabbath Question, 1865, i. 154 sq.; Hunt's Religious Thought in England, 1870, i. 167 sq.; Church's Miraculous Powers, 1750, Preface; information from the master of Christ's College; the Berden parish register does not begin till 1707.] A. G.

MEAD or **MEADE, MATTHEW** (1630?–1699), independent divine, second son of Richard Mead of Mursley, Buckinghamshire, by his wife Joane, was born about 1630 at Leighton Buzzard, Bedfordshire. His epitaph accordingly speaks of him as 'honesta apud Cattieuclanos familia ortus.' In 1648 he was elected scholar, and on 6 Aug. 1649 admitted a fellow of King's College, Cambridge. He resigned on 6 June 1651, Cole says, to avoid expulsion, owing, probably, to refusal of the engagement; but he had gained ill-will by urging the expulsion of Richard Johnson and others. Francis Charlett, rector of Great Brickhill, Buckinghamshire, died in 1653; Mead hoped to succeed him, but the patron, John Duncombe, presented Thomas Clutterbuck. Mead, on the ground that the patron's right had lapsed, obtained a presentation under the great seal. Duncombe appealed to the law, and a verdict for Clutterbuck was given at the Aylesbury assizes. Mead began another suit on the plea of Duncombe's malignancy. Clutterbuck resigned his title, and Duncombe, in July 1655, presented Robert Hocknell, whom the 'commissioners for approbation' (triers) rejected, putting in Mead by aid of a troop of horse. After some violent proceedings, the matter was compromised by Duncombe's agreeing to present William Peirce, a nephew of Hugh Peters [q. v.] Mead now became morning lecturer at Stepney Church (St. Dunstan's), the afternoon lecturer being William Greenhill [q. v.], who held the vicarage. He resided in Gracechurch Street, and was admitted a member, on 28 Dec. 1656, of the congregational church formed at Stepney by Greenhill in 1644. On 22 Jan. 1658 he was appointed by Cromwell to the 'new chapel' at Shadwell (St. Paul's). From Shadwell, as well as from his lectureship, he was displaced at the Restoration, but obtained a lectureship at St. Sepulchre's, Holborn, from which he was ejected by the uniformity act of 1662.

In 1663 he was living at Worcester House, Stepney. Either the Conventicle Act (1664) or the Five Miles Act, which came into operation in 1666, drove him to Holland. He seems to have been in London during the great plague of 1665. On 31 Jan. 1669 he was called to 'exercise his guifts' as assistant to Greenhill at Stepney. He accepted the call on 21 Feb. Shortly after Greenhill's death he was called (13 Oct. 1671) to succeed him as pastor, and was ordained on 14 Dec. 1671 by John Owen, D.D. [q. v.], Joseph Caryl [q. v.], and two others. In 1674 a meeting-house (opened 13 Sept.) was built for him at Stepney; its roof was upheld by four round pine pillars, 'presented to him by the States of Holland;' above the ceiling was an attic with concealed entrance, a hiding-place for the congregation in troubled times. His congregation was the largest in London, and his preaching was much sought after. On 1 May 1674 he instituted a Mayday sermon to the young, which is still continued; he always held a Good Friday service. About 1680 he became the guardian of James Peirce [q. v.], the Exeter heretic, who lived in his house for some years. In December 1682 Sir William Smith with a strong guard invaded his meeting-house, pulled down the pulpit, and broke up the forms. In June 1683 Mead was apprehended on suspicion of complicity in the Rye House plot, and brought before the privy council, when his answers were so satisfactory that the king at once ordered his discharge. He succeeded John Owen in September 1683 as one of the Tuesday morning lecturers (presbyterian and congregational) at the merchants' lecture in Pinners' Hall. Pleading there on one occasion on behalf of poor ministers, he got a collection of 300*l.*, ladies putting their rings and watches into the plates. In 1686 he was again in Holland, preaching at Utrecht; he returned on the issue of James's declaration for liberty of conscience in 1687.

After the revolution galleries were built (25 March 1689) in his meeting-house, and the adjoining residence and garden were settled (16 July) by the congregation on Mead and his heirs 'in consideration for' his sufferings and services. Mead went heartily with the movement initiated (1690) by John Howe [q. v.] for an amalgamation of the presbyterian and congregationalist bodies. The 'happy union' held its meeting at Stepney on 6 April 1691, when Mead preached his famous sermon 'Two Sticks made One' (Ezek. xxxvii. 19). On the rupture of the union (1694) through the alleged heresies of Daniel Williams, D.D. [q. v.], Mead took a moderate part, but remained in the Pinners' Hall lectureship when the presbyterians seceded. When Calamy applied to him (1694) for ordination he declined to act, from no scruples of his own, but for fear of giving umbrage to others. He preached his last sermon on May day 1699, and died on 16 Oct. 1699, aged 70. He was buried in Stepney churchyard; Calamy gives the Latin inscription on his tombstone. Howe preached his funeral sermon. Peirce describes him as a gentleman and a scholar. An elegy on his death, 'Tristiæ Christianæ,' was issued in a folio sheet, 1699. He had thirteen children, of whom Richard Mead, M.D. [q. v.], was the eleventh. An elder son, Samuel, was a fellow-student with Calamy at Utrecht in 1687; published at Utrecht a 'Disputatio,' 1686, 4to, an 'Exercitatio,' 1687, 4to, and an 'Oratio,' 1689, 4to; in 1694 was an evening lecturer at Salters' Hall; was not ordained, and became a chancery practitioner.

Besides separate sermons, 1660–98, including funeral sermons for Thomas Rosewell (1692) and Timothy Cruso [q. v.], he published: 1. ''Εν ὀλίγῳ Χριστιανός, the Almost Christian Discovered,' &c., 1662, 8vo (substance of sermons at St. Sepulchre's, Holborn, in 1661); often reprinted; in Dutch, Utrecht, 1682, 12mo; in Welsh, Merthyr Tydfil, 1825, 12mo. 2. 'Solomon's Prescription for the Removal of the Pestilence,' &c., 1666, 4to; 1667, 12mo (with appendix). 3. 'The Good of Early Obedience,' &c., 1683, 8vo (Mayday sermons). 4. 'The Vision of the Wheels,' &c., 1689, 4to (sermons on Ezekiel). Posthumous were: 5. 'The Young Man's Remembrancer,' &c., 3rd edit. 1701, 8vo (his last two Mayday sermons; often reprinted). 6. 'Original Sermons on the Jews [5]; and on Falling into the Hands of . . . God [12] . . . with a Memoir,' &c., 1836, 12mo (edited from shorthand notes transcribed by James Andrews in 1703 and 1710; the manuscripts, long preserved in the family of Sir Thomas W. Blomefield, bart., are now in the British Museum). He had a hand in the 'English Greek Lexicon,' 1661 8vo. His farewell sermon before ejection was published separately, 1662, 4to and 12mo, and also in the 'Compleat Collection,' 1663, 8vo. He wrote a preface to 'The Life and Death of Nathaniel Mather,' 1689, 8vo. In earlier documents he spelled his name 'Meade,' but used the spelling 'Mead' from about 1679.

Three engraved portraits are known.

[Funeral Sermon by Howe 1699; Calamy's Account, 1713, p. 471; Calamy's Continuation, 1727, ii. 614; Calamy's Own Life, 1830, i. 142, 341 sq.; Walker's Sufferings of the Clergy, 1714, ii. 215, 260; Peirce's Vindication of the Dissenters, 1718, i. 258; Peirce's Remarks, 1719, p. 42; Protestant Dissenter's Magazine, 1799, p. 140; Palmer's Nonconformist's Memorial, 1802, ii. 461 sq.; Wilson's Dissenting Churches of London, 1808, ii. 252, 1810, iii. 31; Toulmin's Historical View, 1814, p. 104; Neal's Hist. of the Puritans (Toulmin), 1822, v. 37; Urwick's Nonconformity in Hertfordshire, 1884, p. 647; Jones's Notes on the Early Days of Stepney Meeting [1887]; Hist. MSS. Comm. 3rd Rep. App. x. 269; Cole's manuscript Hist. of King's College, Cambridge, iii. 201 sq.; A Booke for Church Affaires att Stepny (folio manuscript records from 1644 to present time).] A. G.

MEAD, RICHARD, M.D. (1673–1754), physician, eleventh child of Matthew Mead [q. v.], minister of Stepney, Middlesex, was born in that parish on 11 Aug. 1673. His father was ejected for nonconformity in 1662, but, his private means being large, continued to reside in comfort at Stepney, and educated his thirteen children at home. Richard learnt Latin till ten years old from John Nesbitt, a nonconformist, and from 1683 to 1689 was sent to a private school kept by Thomas Singleton, who was probably a good scholar, as he was at one time second master at Eton, and was certainly a sectary, since he declined to conform in 1662. Mead became a good classic and a consistent whig. He entered at the university of Utrecht in the beginning of the academical year at the end of 1689, and, under the instruction of Grævius for three years, acquired an extended knowledge of classical literature and antiquities. In 1692 he entered at Leyden as a student of medicine, attended the botany lectures of Paul Herman, and became acquainted with Boerhaave, then a young graduate and student of theology. The professor of physic was Archibald Pitcairne [q. v.], the chief of the iatromechanical school, who taught that physiological and pathological processes were the result of physical as distinct from chemical forces. Mead admired his lectures, and in spite of Pitcairne's reserved disposition obtained some private conversations with him.

In 1695, with his eldest brother, who had also belonged to the university of Utrecht, with Dr. Thomas Pellett [q. v.] of Cambridge, and with David Polhill, he travelled in Italy, visiting Turin, Florence, and then Padua, where he graduated M.D. on 16 Aug. 1695. He went on to Rome and Naples, and returned to London in the summer of 1696. A story, probable enough, but with one obvious inaccuracy, relates (*Authentic Memoirs*, 1755, p. 6) that he rediscovered among the lumber of a museum the bronze tablets inlaid with silver known as the Tabula Isiaca. They had been found in the Villa Caffarelli gardens in 1547, were carried with other plunder from Rome to Mantua, and thence to Turin, where Mead, who had heard much of their supposed Egyptian origin and meaning, asked leave to search for them, and was successful in finding them. They have ever since been duly exhibited in the treasury of the archives at Turin, but have lost their supposed interest, having been proved not to be Egyptian, but a Roman forgery of the time of Hadrian (Letter from J. H. Middleton, 30 March 1873).

Mead began practice in 1696 at Stepney, living in the house in which he had been born. To practise legally required a license from the College of Physicians, which he did not obtain, but was probably suffered as being on the outskirts of the jurisdiction. He certainly made no endeavour at concealment, for in 1702 he published 'A Mechanical Account of Poisons,' which excited so much attention that an abstract of it was printed in the 'Philosophical Transactions' for 1703, and in the same year he was elected F.R.S. The hypothesis of the work is a result of the teaching of Pitcairne, to whose school of medical thought Mead at this time belonged, and the subject was partly suggested by some remarks of Herman the botanist and by specimens of venomous snakes which he had shown to his pupils. Mead dissected vipers, and gives an exact account of the mechanism which provides for the erection of the fang when the snake opens its mouth. Quoting the remark of Lucan (*Pharsalia*, ix. 617), 'Pocula morte carent,' he swallowed the poison, and thus confirmed Galen's experiment (*Theriaca*, bk. i.) on fowls, in proof of the fact that puncture is necessary to produce the effect. He thence proceeds to the conclusion that hard particles in the poison mechanically produce in the blood the fatal effect. The rules of treatment laid down are sounder than the argument, which is, however, supported by much learning and many interesting observations. In the same year he communicated to the Royal Society (*Phil. Trans.* 1703) an account of Bonomo's discovery of the *acarus scabiei*, the mite which causes the disease known as itch, up to that time supposed to be a constitutional disorder. It is remarkable that this was then disbelieved in England, though clearly demonstrated in Italy in 1687. In 1704 he published a second iatromechanical treatise on the influence of the sun and moon upon human bodies, 'De imperio Solis ac Lunæ in Corpora Humana et Morbis inde oriundis.' He had mastered Newton's discovery of attraction, and was anxious to show that the heavenly bodies affected the human frame as they affected one another. This work is much shallower than that on poisons. He republished both later in life (1743), the former with many additions, and with a statement surrendering as untenable the mechanical hypothesis.

Mead was elected into the council of the Royal Society in 1705, and again in 1707 and till his death, being vice-president in 1717. On 5 May 1703 he was elected physician to St. Thomas's Hospital, and then went to live in Crutched Friars, in the eastern part of the city of London, whence in 1711 he moved again to Austin Friars to a house vacated by Dr. George Howe [q. v.] Here he was often visited by Dr. John Radcliffe [q. v.], who admired his learning, was pleased by his deference, and gave him much help and countenance. On 4 Dec. 1707 he had been made M.D. at Oxford, and on 25 June 1708 passed the examination, and was admitted a candidate or member of the College of Physicians. He was elected a fellow on 9 April 1716, and was censor in 1716, 1719, and 1724. On 16 Aug. 1711 he was elected anatomy lecturer for four years to the Barber-Surgeons (Young, *Annals of Barber-Surgeons*, p. 375). His practice soon became large, and in 1714 he took Radcliffe's former house in Bloomsbury Square, and was the chief physician of the day (cf. *Spectator*, ed. Morley, p. 671). On 5 Jan. 1715 he resigned his physiciancy at St. Thomas's Hospital, received the thanks of the authorities, and was elected a governor. He was called in to see Queen Anne two days before her death, which he predicted to be imminent, though this was a view of the case which the ministry desired to discourage. His reputation was enhanced under the new dynasty. On 19 Dec. 1717 Hearne wrote in his diary: 'My great friend, Dr. Richard Mead, hath recovered the Princess of Wales (as she is called) when the other physicians had certainly killed her, had their prescriptions been followed. This hath gained Dr. Mead a great reputation at Prince George's court, and Dr. Garth and Dr. Sloane are now out of favour as well as others' (*Diaries*, ii. 56). In 1720 (Letter to Dr. Waller) he removed to Great Ormond Street, where his house occupied the site of the present Hospital for Sick Children. It was standing till a few years ago, and much of the old oak remained on the walls and staircase. The present writer has often seen out-patients there in a wainscotted room which formed part of Mead's library.

Mead's collection of books, of manuscripts, and of statuary, coins, gems, and drawings was the largest formed in his time. It contained more than ten thousand volumes, and after his death sold for 5,518*l.* 10*s.* 11*d.* (NICHOLS, *Literary Anecdotes*, vi. 218); his pictures, coins, and other antiquities realised 10,550*l.* 18*s.* (*Notes and Queries*, 2nd ser. xi. 443). Pope, who was his patient, as he records in the epistle to Bolingbroke,

> I'll do what Mead and Cheselden advise,

has also commemorated his bibliographical tastes (*Epistle*, iv. 10):—

> Rare monkish manuscripts for Hearne alone,
> And books for Mead and butterflies for Sloane.

The poet drank asses' milk by Mead's order (ELWIN, *Pope*, ix. 326), and was interested in his pulvis antilyssis, a powder for curing hydrophobia (*ib.* p. 129). Warton mentions that when Mead objected on critical grounds to the expression 'amor publicus,' Pope could find no better defence than that he could allow a doctor of medicine to understand one Latin word, but not two together. The story is probably as untrue as Warton's suggestion that the description of John Woodward [q. v.] as Mummius in the 'Dunciad' is intended for Mead. His classical attainments were the result of careful training of the best kind, followed by much reading for pleasure in after-life, and were respected by the greatest scholars of the day. He had an enormous circle of friends, but Richard Bentley and Dr. John Freind were the two with whom he was most intimate. His intimacy with the master of Trinity was close and unbroken, and Monk states that 'he was the only friend who in the latter part of Bentley's life possessed any material influence over him' (*Life of Bentley*, ii. 114). He had in 1721 persuaded Edmund Chishull [q. v.] to publish the inscription in boustrophedon found at Sigeum, and Bentley wrote him a long epistle the day after he read the book. It was at his instance that Bentley revised the 'Theriaca' of Nicander, and the copy of Nicander edited by Gorræus given by Mead to Bentley, with the latter's notes and a prefixed Latin epistle to the physician, is preserved in the British Museum (Dr. Monk in *Museum Criticum*, Nos. iii. and iv.) With Dr. Freind his intimacy was still closer; they spent much time together, and though Mead was a whig and Freind a tory, they had many opinions and tastes in common. Both had studied chemistry, but both were at first attached to the mechanical school in medicine. They were elected fellows of the College of Physicians on the same day, and ate sweet cakes together as censors. They were chosen at the same court of the Barber-Surgeons to lecture on anatomy to the company. Both were devoted to classical learning, and they were agreed in the motto of Freind's medal, 'Medecina vetus et nova unam facimus utramque.' Both had read the medical writers of the middle ages as well as those of classical times. Mead enjoyed the 'Schola Salernitana' (Letter to Dr. E. Waller, 19 April 1720), and had the earliest edition of the 'Rosa Anglica' (his copy is now in the library of the Royal Medical and Chirurgical Society), books on which Freind dwells with pleasure in his 'History of Physic.' Mead wrote on 1 Sept. 1716, in reply to a request from Freind, a letter on the treatment of small-pox, and Freind's 'De Purgantibus in secunda Variolarum Confluentium Febre adhibendis Epistola,' 1719, is addressed to Mead, of whom he says in the introduction that they had long been accustomed 'idem sentire atque idem judicare.' When Freind was committed to the Tower at the time of Atterbury's plot, he wrote thence, 'indulgentia Præfecti, in presentia Warderi,' to Mead, 'De quibusdam Variolarum Generibus Epistola,' dated 30 March 1723. Mead visited him in the Tower, and ultimately procured from Walpole, when prescribing for that minister, an order for his release. He had sent Freind Le Clerc's 'History of Medicine,' and asked his opinion of it. The result was the admirable 'History of Physick from the Time of Galen, in a Discourse written to Dr. Mead.' Garth and Arbuthnot, and most of the physicians of his time, except Cheyne and Woodward, were his friends. It is difficult to ascertain whether there is any truth in the story that he fought with Woodward (it is, however, circumstantially narrated in 'Mist's Journal,' 13 June 1719), and that the tiny figures at the gate of the stable-yard in the picture by Virtue of Gresham College (opposite p. 33, JOHN WARD, *Lives of the Professors of Gresham College*; cf. HAWKINS, *Life of Johnson*, p. 245) represent Woodward laying down his sword in submission to Mead.

Numerous dedications were addressed to Mead, some against his will. Smart Lethieullier and Martin Foulkes used to consult with him about antiquities (NICHOLS, *Illustrations*, iii. 636). The Rev. F. Wise addressed him about the Berkshire White Horse in 1738; Nathaniel Cotton [q. v.] on a kind of scarlet fever at St. Albans in 1749. Dr. Davies in 1732 bequeathed to him his papers on Cicero, and he gave them to Thomas, the nephew of Dr. Richard Bentley, in order to complete and bring out an edition of the 'Offices.' They were burnt by accident in Thomas Bentley's lodgings in the Strand, as is stated by Mead in a Latin letter, printed in the third edition of Davies's edition of Cicero, 'De Natura Deorum' (MONK, *Life of Bentley*, ii. 357). Warburton, writing to Dr. Birch, 15 Dec. 1739, of a pamphlet of Crousaz, says: 'I ordered him to send one to Dr. Mead, as a man to whom all people that pretend to letters ought to pay their tribute on account of his great eminence in them and patronage of them.' Lewis Theobald acknowledges his help to him in the preparation of his edition of Shakespeare (NICHOLS, *Illustrations*, ii. 114, 732). William Lauder [q. v.], the literary forger, had received a subscription from him, and when detected wrote on 9 April 1751 a long letter of vain, feeble justification to him. The king of Naples wrote to ask for his works, and in return invited him to his palace, and sent him the first two volumes of Bajardi's book on the 'Antiquities of Herculaneum.' He gave an almost unique copy of Servetus to De Boze, the secretary of the Academy of Inscriptions and Belles-Lettres in Paris. His name occurs in most of the subscription-lists of the historical and other learned books which appeared in his time. He took a large-paper copy when, in 1724, 'The History of his own Time' of his former patient, Bishop Burnet, appeared, and ten copies, five of them on large paper, of his friend John Ward's 'Lives of the Professors of Gresham College.' Endless appeals for influence came to him, and he was the one person who could approach every one, even the Duke of Somerset, who was so difficult of access (*ib.* iv. 249). The Rev. George Kelly, an Irish clergyman, shut up in the Tower for corresponding with Bishop Atterbury, was pardoned by his influence, and writes of him, 'that great and good man, Dr. Mead, to whose intercession I owe my life, and all the liberties allowed me in confinement' (Letter in *ib.* v. 149). He frequented, for social purposes, Rawthmell's Coffee-house in Henrietta Street, Covent Garden, but used to see patients and give opinions on written cases at a given hour at a coffee-house in the city (usually Batson's, against the Royal Exchange) as well as at home, and made many professional journeys into the country in his coach-and-four. He used to drive six horses when he went to his country house near Windsor. The king, Sir Robert Walpole, and most people of fashion consulted him. He was intimate with Sir Isaac Newton, and attended him in his last illness, as he also did Bishop Burnet. His income from practice is stated by his librarian, Mr. Hocker, to have been for many years between five and six thousand pounds, while in one year he received more than seven thousand pounds; but if many fees were paid to him, he also saw numerous patients without fee, and gave money as well as medical advice to many who needed both. With the exception of one aggressive Johnian, he never took a fee from a clergyman.

In 1719, in consequence of the serious epidemic of plague at Marseilles, great alarm was felt in London lest an outbreak should occur. The king was in Hanover, and the lords justices, through Craggs, then secretary of state, desired Mead to draw up a statement concerning the prevention of the plague. He accordingly published in 1720 'A Short Discourse concerning Pestilential Contagion and the Methods to be used to Prevent it.' Seven editions appeared within a year, an eighth, with large additions, in 1722, and a ninth in 1744. The book is lucid and interesting; every one could understand it, and it was effectual in allaying the public alarm. The practical conclusion at which the author arrives is in accordance with the views held by all sanitary authorities at the present day, and is that the isolation in proper places of the sick is more effectual in checking the progress of an epidemic than a general quarantine or than measures of fumigation. George Pye in 1721 and others wrote attacks upon the book. In 1721 he superintended the inoculation, at the request of the Prince of Wales, of seven condemned criminals. All recovered favourably, and this established the practice of inoculation at the time. On 18 Oct. 1723 he delivered the Harveian oration at the College of Physicians. It is for the most part a defence of the position of physicians in Greece and in Rome, showing that they were always honoured and often wealthy in ancient society. He supports his statements by a variety of passages in the classics, and by arguments drawn from representations on coins and medals. Conyers Middleton attacked the oration, and maintained that the physicians of Rome were slaves. Ward replied, and some lesser writers took part in the controversy.

Mead's first wife had died in February 1719. She was Ruth, daughter of John Marsh, a merchant of London; was married in July 1699, and bore eight children, of whom four died in infancy, while three daughters and one son survived her. On 14 Aug. 1724 Mead married Anne, daughter of Sir Rowland Alston of Odell, Bedfordshire. She bore him no children. In 1727 he was appointed physician to George II, and afterwards had Sir Edward Wilmot [q. v.] and Dr. Frank Nicholls [q. v.], his sons-in-law, as his colleagues. His second daughter married Charles Bertie of Uffington, Lincolnshire.

Mead did not write much himself. But he edited in 1724 W. Cowper's 'Myotomia Reformata,' the best general account of the anatomy of the human muscular system of its time, and from 1722 to 1733 he provided the means necessary for a complete edition of De Thou's 'History' in seven volumes, folio. He bought some materials which Thomas Carte [q. v.] had collected from that historian, who was a refugee in France, and paid Buckley to edit the work. On 11 Feb. 1741 he read a paper at the Royal Society on the invention of Samuel Lutton for ventilating the holds of ships, and, in relation to the same subject, wrote in 1749 'A Discourse on Scurvy,' which is chiefly occupied with remarks on that disease as it was observed on Lord Anson's voyage round the world. He urged the value of Lutton's invention on the lords of the admiralty, and after ten years persuaded them to adopt it. He corresponded with Boerhaave, and made him a present of John Wigan's folio edition of Aretæus, when the Leyden professor was preparing his own edition, published in 1735, of that medical writer. He urged Dr. Samuel Jebb in 1729 to undertake an edition of the works of Roger Bacon, which appeared in 1733, and he gave pecuniary help to many lesser literary projects. In 1747 he wrote a preface to Chishull's posthumous 'Travels in Turkey' and published 'De Variolis et Morbillis,' and appended to it a translation of the first treatise on the subject by Muhammad ibn Zacharia al Rhazis, a physician of the ninth century, from an Arabic manuscript at Leyden, of which Boerhaave sent him a copy. The translation was edited by Thomas Hunt, Arabic professor at Oxford, from two versions made for Mead, one by Solomon Negri, a native of Damascus, and the other by John Gagnier. Mead praises Sydenham in these treatises, but adds very little of his own. In 1749 he published 'Medica Sacra, a Commentary on the Diseases mentioned in Scripture,' in which he explains Job's disease as elephantiasis, Saul's as melancholia, Jehoram's as dysentery, Hezekiah's as an abscess, Nebuchadnezzar's as hypochondriasis, and discusses leprosy, palsy, and demoniacal possession. In 1751 he published his last book, 'Monita et Præcepta Medica,' a summary of his practical experience. It is clear that he had not kept copious notes of the many cases he had seen, and hence the grounds of his opinions are not sufficiently clear, and the total of information contained in the book is small. A comparison of the elder William Heberden's [q. v.] 'Commentaries' with Mead's 'Precepts' shows of what permanent value a concise treatise may be when it is based upon a series of observations recorded at the time, and how empty it is when it rests on no such basis. He introduced the method of slowly compressing the abdominal walls during tapping for ascites, or abdominal dropsy, with a view to preventing fainting or collapse.

By a will proved 17 Jan. 1754 Erasmus Lewis [q. v.] made Mead a bequest of 100*l.*; before the end of the same month the doctor was observed to be himself declining in health (Letter of Dr. R. Pococke; Nichols, *Illustrations*, iii. 685), and he died on 16 Feb. 1754 at his house in Great Ormond Street, after an illness of five days only. He was buried 23 Feb. in the Temple Church. Dr. Johnson said, 'Dr. Mead lived more in the broad sunshine of life than almost any man.' The world in which he desired to live was that of learning, the taste for which in every branch began in his boyhood and continued to old age. He was a universal reader, but not a perfect observer in all directions. His natural history was that of a Londoner, as he shows in his account of the scene, familiar to all rustics, of small birds mobbing a hawk. He thinks that the small birds are trying to get away, but that fright prevents them, and fails to observe that their voices and actions are those of exultant pigmies in a crowd safely attacking a common enemy, and not of trembling victims. If, however, he was not an observer of the first order, he brought learning, careful reasoning, and kindly sympathy to the bedside of his patients, and very many sick men must have been the better for his visits. His life was an example of what Aristotle calls *μεγαλοπρέπεια*, the magnificence befitting a great man. Of the many men who have grown rich in professions, few have expended their riches during their lives so generously and so wisely as Mead.

His bust by Roubiliac was given to the College of Physicians by Dr. Askew [q. v.], and stands in the censor's room of the college, which also possesses three portraits of him. A portrait by Allan Ramsay, painted in 1740, was purchased by the trustees of the National Portrait Gallery, London, in June 1857. Another, by Michael Dahl, was lent by Sir M. S. Wilmot, bart., to the second loan exhibition, South Kensington.

He presented the college with a fine marble bust of Harvey, which stands in the library. A beautiful flowering plant is called after him, 'Dodecatheon Meadia,' mentioned by Erasmus Darwin,

Meadia's soft chains five suppliant beaux confers

(*Loves of the Plants*, p. 61), but the footnote is an error, for the name was given by Mark Catesby, and not by Mead himself (Letter from F. Darwin, January 1893). His gold-headed cane, given to him by Radcliffe, is preserved in the College of Physicians.

The best collected editions of Mead's works are 'The Medical Works of Dr. Richard Mead,' 4to, London, 1762, and 'The Medical Works of Richard Mead, M.D.,' 3 vols. 8vo, Edinburgh, 1765. His son Richard, who survived him, married Anne, daughter of William Gore of Thring, Hertfordshire, but left no descendants.

[Authentic Memoirs of the Life of Richard Mead, M.D. London, 1755 (by Matthew Maty [q. v.]); Munk's Coll. of Phys. ii. 40; W. MacMichael's Gold-headed Cane, 2nd ed. 1828, and Lives of British Physicians, 1830; Wheatley and Cunningham's London, passim; Notes and Queries, 7th ser. i. 114; J. Channing's Rhazes de Variolis et Morbillis, London, 1766; J. Freind's Opera Omnia Medica, London, 1733; S. Jebb's Fratris Rogeri Bacon Ordinis Minorum Opus Major, Venice, 1750, Preface; the Sloane MSS. in Brit. Mus. contain a few unimportant autograph letters of Mead; G. Pye's Discourse of the Plague, wherein Dr. Mead's notions are refuted, London, 1721; Caii Spectrum, or Dr. Keye's Charge against Dr. M., London, 1721; Dr. Mead: His Short Discourse explained, or His Account of Pestilential Contagion exploded, London, 1722; Works; Notes and Queries, 8th ser. v. 284.] N. M.

MEAD, ROBERT (1616–1653), poet, son of Robert Mead, a stationer, was born at the Black Lion in Fleet Street in 1616. He was educated at Westminster, and while still a king's scholar contributed commendatory verses (of average merit) to his schoolfellow Abraham Cowley's 'Poetical Blossomes' (1633). He was elected student of Christ Church, whence he matriculated 1 Sept. 1634, and graduated B.A. 11 April 1638, M.A. 22 May 1641. While still an undergraduate he wrote a comedy entitled 'The Combat of Love and Friendship.' The play was acted by the students, but not printed until after Mead's death, when it appeared 'as it hath formerly been presented by the gentlemen of Christ Church in Oxford,' London, 4to, 1654. In 1638 he was one of the contributors to the 'Jonsonus Virbius,' after which he appears to have definitely relinquished literature, and in 1640 was appointed a captain in Charles I's army. He subsequently distinguished himself at the siege of Oxford, took a gallant part in the assault on Abingdon in the spring of 1646, and was one of the commissioners for negotiating the surrender of Oxford to the parliament, 17 May 1646. He was created M.D. on 23 June, the day before the surrender actually took place, but was expelled from his studentship by the parliamentary commission in 1648. He was in Jersey at the time of Charles I's execution, and soon afterwards proceeded to Gottenburg in Sweden as Charles II's agent (*Cal. Clarendon State Papers*, ii. 23, 30). He wrote thence to Secretary Nicholas in February 1650, expressing Queen Christina's dissatisfaction at hearing so little of the king's movements (*Cal. State Papers*, Dom. 1650, pp. 104, 158). He subsequently submitted a diplomatic note from Charles to the queen, and entered actively into Charles's project of visiting Stockholm (*ib.* pp. 610, 611). He did not, however, remain long in Sweden, and in 1651 Lord Inchiquin appears to have sought to engage him as tutor for his son. He travelled, probably with a pupil, up the Rhine ('which failed his expectation much') into Switzerland, and then *via* Strasburg, Spire, Heidelberg, Frankfort, and Mainz to Cologne. He returned to England in the same year, to find his father on his deathbed, and on 21 Feb. 1652–3 he himself fell a victim to a malignant fever. He died in the house in which he had been born in Fleet Street, and was buried in the church of St. Dunstan's-in-the-West. Mead was generally regarded as possessing great literary abilities, though his writings very slenderly support the claim. Wood quotes the bookseller's epistle prefixed to 'The Combat of Love and Friendship,' to the effect that Mead, 'though a little, was a stout and learned man, and excellent in the faculty of poetry and making plays. His eminent general abilities were also such that they have left him a character precious and honourable to our nation.'

Phillips has, entirely without foundation, attributed to Mead an anonymous piece, entitled 'The Costlie Whore, a Comicall Historie,' 1633, 4to, which was reprinted in Mr. A. H. Bullen's 'Old Plays' (1885), iv. 219 sq.

[Wood's Athenæ Oxon. ed. Bliss, i. 342–4; Fasti, i. 468, 500, ii. 3, 98, 210; Hist. and Antiq. ii. 477, 482; Foster's Alumni Oxon. 1500–1714; Welch's Westminster Scholars, pp. 105–6; Fleay's Chron. of English Drama, 1559–1642, ii. 85; Corser's Collect. ii. 498; Langbaine's Dram. Poets, p. 366; Add. MS. 24490, f. 384 (Hunter's Chorus Vatum); Gifford's Ben Jonson, 1846, p. 803; Burrows's Parl. Visit. of Oxford, p. 489; Cal. State Papers, Dom. 1649–51, passim: Baker's Biog. Dram. p. 505; Brit. Mus. Cat.] T. S.

MEAD, WILLIAM (1628–1713), quaker, was born probably in or near London, where he became a wealthy linendraper of Fenchurch Street, and member of the Company of Merchant Taylors. He was captain of a train-band before joining the quakers early in 1670. On 14 Aug. of that year he was present at a crowded meeting in Gracechurch Street, at which William Penn was the preacher. Both were apprehended and committed to Newgate. Their memorable trial, when they boldly defended the right of free worship, began at the Old Bailey on 1 Sept. They were accused of disturbing the peace by unlawfully assembling together by agreement, and pleaded not guilty. The jury, in spite of intimidation, pronounced on 5 Sept. that Penn was not guilty of breaking the law, and that Mead was not guilty at all, but jury and prisoners were committed to Newgate. Penn's father, Admiral Sir William Penn [q. v.], is said by Croese (p. 78) to have paid fines to secure their release. A detailed account of the trial, under the title 'The People's Ancient and Just Liberties asserted,' was published (London, 1670) by Penn and Mead, and it is also related at length by Besse in his 'Sufferings.' Mead afterwards lived at Highgate, and entertained Fox there in 1677. He held a leading position among the quakers, and several times waited upon the king with George Whitehead [q. v.] and others. Mead purchased about 1684 the estate of Goosehays, in Hornchurch parish, Essex, where George Fox was a frequent visitor.

Mead wrote, in conjunction with Whitehead and others, several vindications of 'the people called Quakers.' One of these was delivered to the House of Lords, 21 Feb. 1701. He died at Goosehays 3 April 1713, aged 86, and was buried in the Friends' cemetery at Barking, where a headstone records the fact. He married and lost his first wife, Mary, in 1679. A child, Jonathan, died in 1680. In 1681 he married Sarah Fell, fourth daughter of Judge Thomas and Margaret Fell [q. v.] She was beautiful, an eloquent preacher, a good Hebrew scholar, the executive manager of the large household at Swarthmoor, and the correspondent of Penn and Barclay. She had been sought in marriage by Richard Lower [q. v.], court physician, whose brother Thomas married her sister Mary. Sarah Fell obtained from the king in 1670 the order for the release of her mother (then Mrs. Fox) from prison, which she herself conveyed to Lancaster. She was the first clerk of the Lancashire Women's Quarterly Meeting, and before she left Swarthmoor drew up for her sisters 'Instructions how you may order the business in the Quarterly Women's Meeting Book.' Her account-book of family expenditure and many letters are in the Swarthmoor MSS. She died at Goosehays, 9 June 1714, and was buried with her husband at Barking. To Nathaniel Mead, his 'dear and onely child,' Mead left by will his estates in London, Middlesex, Kent, Essex, and Surrey, and many legacies to the poor among quakers and others. Nathaniel Mead entered the Middle Temple at sixteen, became serjeant-at-law, and was knighted. He sold the Goosehays estate, and died in London in April 1760, aged 76 (*Lond. Chron.* April 1760).

[Webb's Fells of Swarthmoor Hall, 1865; Besse's Sufferings of the Quakers, i. 418, &c.; Fox's Journal, 3rd ed., numerous references; Smith's Cat.; Croese's Hist. of Quakers, 1696; the Yorkshireman, No. lxxx. p. 114; will at Somerset House, P. C. C. Leeds, 85; Swarthmoor MSS. and registers at Devonshire House.]

C. F. S.

MEADE, JOHN (1572–1653), jesuit missionary. [See ALMEIDA.]

MEADE, RICHARD CHARLES FRANCIS, third EARL OF CLANWILLIAM in the peerage of Ireland, and first BARON CLANWILLIAM in the peerage of the United Kingdom (1795–1879), born on 15 Aug. 1795, was the only son of the second earl by his first wife, Caroline, third daughter of Joseph, count Thun. He succeeded to the title in September 1805. After education at Eton he entered the diplomatic service at an early age. In August 1814 he attended Lord Castlereagh, plenipotentiary at the congress of Vienna, and in February of the following year was there with Castlereagh's half-brother, Lord Stewart. He was private secretary to Castlereagh at the foreign office from 5 Jan. 1817 to 11 July 1819, and acted as under-secretary for fifteen months before being formally appointed to the office on 22 Jan. 1822 (cf. BUCKINGHAM, *Memoirs of Court of George IV*, ii. 284). On 12 Aug. he resigned in order to become chef de chancellerie to the Duke of Wellington's mission at the congress of Verona. Clanwilliam served as envoy extraordinary and minister plenipotentiary at Berlin from 1 Feb. 1823 to 25 Dec. 1827, and was created grand cross of the royal Hanoverian Guelphic order (G.C.H.) in 1826. In a letter dated 14 Aug. 1827, from Sir H. Hardinge to the Duke of Wellington, Clanwilliam was described as 'up to his neck' in the preliminary arrangements for the formation of the Goderich ministry, but incredulous as to its duration (*Wellington Correspondence*, iv. 93). On 28 Jan. 1828 he became a peer of the United

Kingdom by the title of Baron Clanwilliam of Tipperary county (cf. Lord Chesterfield, *Diary*, iii. 533). He took little part in public affairs after this date. On 3 Jan. 1830 Wellington wrote to ask him to second the address in the lords; but he does not appear to have consented (*Wellington Correspondence*, vi. 458). The degree of D.C.L. was conferred on him by Oxford University on 11 June 1834.

Clanwilliam died at his house, 32 Belgrave Square, London, on 7 Oct. 1879, having lately returned from Deal Castle, of which he was captain. He married, on 3 July 1830, Lady Elizabeth Herbert (*d.* 20 Sept. 1858), daughter of George, eleventh earl of Pembroke, and had four sons and one daughter. The eldest son, Richard James (1832–1907), succeeded to the peerage, and was a distinguished naval officer. (For a notice of the second son, Sir Robert Henry Meade, see Supplement.)

[Burke's Peerage; G. E. C.'s Peerage, ii. 262; Foster's Peerage and Alumni Oxonienses, 1715–1886; Rush's Diary of the Court of London, 1819–25; Morning Post, 8 Oct. 1879; Illustrated London News, 18 Oct. 1879; Boase's Modern Engl. Biog.] G. Le G. N.

MEADLEY, GEORGE WILSON (1774–1818), biographer, was born at Sunderland, co. Durham, on 1 Jan. 1774. He was an only son; his father died in 1775, and his mother soon afterwards removed with her five children to the adjoining town of Bishop Wearmouth. In 1783 he was placed at the grammar school of Witton-le-Wear, under John Farrer; he had a remarkable memory and a turn for rhyme, which he cultivated till 1791. At the end of 1788 he was apprenticed to Chipchase (afterwards alderman), a banker and general dealer at Durham, where Meadley became an ardent liberal in politics. Leaving Durham in 1793 he remained at home, learning Italian, improving his French, and founding a subscription library at Sunderland (1795) with the help of his old schoolmaster, now rector of Sunderland. In March 1795 he made the acquaintance of William Paley, D.D. [q. v.], then made rector of Bishop Wearmouth. Next year Meadley went on a mercantile voyage to the Levant. He made some stay at Naples, Smyrna, and Constantinople, collected a library of books, fell into the hands of the French on his return voyage, and was for some time a prisoner in Spain. He now learned German, and made mercantile voyages to Danzig (1801) and Hamburg (1803), travelling thence on foot with a friend through north Germany (see accounts in *Monthly Magazine*, xiv. 127 sq., 218 sq., 412 sq.) Disgusted with trade, and having a competence, he devoted himself to a literary life.

Three years after Paley's death (1805) he began to collect materials for his biography, applying, among others, to John Disney, D.D. [q. v.], who introduced him to Thomas Jervis [q. v.] Intercourse with these men led to his adoption of unitarian views. The first edition of his 'Memoirs' of Paley was entirely rewritten before publication, on the advice of a friend who blamed its florid style. When bringing out a second and amended edition he spent the winter (1810–11) in Edinburgh to see it through the press. Here he attended the moral philosophy lectures of Thomas Brown (1778–1820) [q. v.] He wrote several other lives, and projected more; but his biographies were more accurate than judicious. Personally he was amiable, but not prepossessing, and somewhat fanatical in his liberalism.

In 1818 he returned from literary researches in London and the south of England in ill-health. He died unmarried at Bishop Wearmouth on 28 Nov. 1818, and was buried in the churchyard of Holy Trinity, Sunderland. A marble tablet to his memory was placed in the Sunderland Subscription Library. An attempt at the annual meeting (2 Feb. 1819) to have this tablet removed, on the ground of Meadley's religious views, led to an angry local controversy.

He published: 1. 'Memoirs of . . . Paley,' &c., Sunderland, 1809, 8vo; 2nd edit. Edinburgh, 1810, 8vo. 2. 'A Sketch of . . . Proposals for . . . Reform in Parliament,' &c., 1812, 8vo (reprinted by Jeremy Bentham in his 'Plan of Parliamentary Reform,' 1817). 3. 'Memoirs of Algernon Sydney,' &c. 1813, 8vo. 4. 'A Letter to the Bishop of St. David's [Thomas Burgess] . . . by a Lay Seceder,' &c., 1814, 8vo. 5. 'A Second Letter to the Bishop of St. David's. By a Lay Seceder,' &c., 1816, 8vo. To the 'Monthly Repository' he contributed lives of Ann Jebb [see under Jebb, John, M.D.], Robert Clarke, and Robert Waugh, vicar of Bishop Middleham; also some verses, 'The Little Chimney Sweeper,' 'Monthly Repository,' 1818, p. 454. He made collections for the lives of John Hampden and John Disney, D.D., and had ready for press a sketch of the political character of Sir William Jones, and a parallel between Bonaparte and Rienzi.

[Monthly Repository, 1818 p. 772, 1819 pp. 5 sq., 121 sq., 137 sq. (memoir by V. F., i.e. William Turner of Newcastle-on-Tyne), pp. 281 sq., 465; Monthly Magazine, 1819, pp. 86 sq.] A. G.

MEADOWBANK, Lords. [See Maconochie, Allan, 1748–1816, Scottish judge; Maconochie, afterwards Maconochie-Welwood, Alexander, 1777–1861, Scottish judge.]

MEADOWCOURT, RICHARD (1695–1760), divine and writer, son of Richard Meadowcourt, esq., of Worcester, was born in 1695. He matriculated at Merton College, Oxford, on 9 March 1710, graduated B.A. in 1714, and proceeded M.A. in 1718, when he also became fellow. While in residence at Merton he is stated to have had a very elegant garden, the benches of which were adorned by Latin mottoes (*Terræ Filius*, 1726, i. 88, 123). Some specimens are given in Chambers's 'Worcestershire Biography,' p. 260. In 1727 he was presented to the vicarage of Oakley, Buckinghamshire; was instituted canon of Worcester on 15 Oct. 1734, and rector of St. Martin's parish in 1738, and in the latter year also became vicar of Quinton in Gloucestershire. From 1751 until his death he held the vicarage of Lindridge, Worcestershire.

On 1 May 1722 Meadowcourt preached in Merton College chapel a university sermon on 'The Sinful Causes and Fatal Effects of the Practice of Calumny and Defamation in Religious Controversy.' It was published in the same year, 'at the request of several gentlemen,' with a dedication to the Earl of Macclesfield, then lord chancellor. It had reference to the attacks of Bishop Sherlock and Dr. Snape on Bishop Hoadly, and was replied to in a pamphlet entitled 'A Vindication of Dr. Snape and Dr. Sherlock against Mr. Meadowcourt's Attempt to Calumniate and Defame those Gentlemen. . . . By a Member of the Antient Society of Freemasons, with a Postscript relating to Dr. Sherlock's Complaint against the Sermon,' 1722, 8vo. Meadowcourt is here described as 'a sawcy young Preacher, a Fellow of a College, undignified and unpreferred.' Ten other sermons, preached between 1721 and 1753, most of them in Worcester Cathedral, or at Oxford, were published (cf. COOKE, *Preacher's Assistant*, iii. 231). There are some lines by Meadowcourt on Hagley, addressed to Lord Lyttelton, in Nash's 'Worcestershire,' i. 490.

Meadowcourt, who is said to have been greatly esteemed by scholars, died at Worcester on 8 Sept. 1760. He was the author of 'A Critique on Paradise Regained' (1732, 4to) and 'A Critical Dissertation, with Notes,' on the same (1748), besides several small tracts containing critical remarks on the English poets. Meadowcourt, although a sympathetic and a learned critic, is deficient in insight. Newton embodied some of the notes to 'Paradise Regained' in his edition of Milton, in the preface to which he says that Meadowcourt 'likewise transmitted to me a sheet of his manuscript remarks, wherein he hath happily explained a most difficult passage in "Lycidas" [viz. lines 160 and 162, 'Bellerus' and 'Bayona's hold'] better than any man had done before him.' In Coxe's 'Memoirs of Sir R. Walpole' (iii. 137) is a curious extract from a letter, dated 16 April 1733, from Meadowcourt to Delafaye, under-secretary of state, giving an account of the rejoicings at Oxford consequent on the rejection of Walpole's excise scheme.

[Foster's Alumni Oxonienses, 1500–1714; Le Neve's Fasti Eccles. Angl. iii. 87; Gent. Mag. 1760, p. 443; Letters by several Eminent Persons Deceased, ii. 246; Brit. Mus. Cat.; Chalmers's Biog. Dict. xxi. 517, where the dates of Meadowcourt's birth and death are given wrongly.]

G. LE G. N.

MEADOWE, JOHN (1622–1697), ejected minister. [See MEADOWS.]

MEADOWS. [See also MEDOWS.]

MEADOWS, ALFRED (1833–1887), obstetric physician, born at Ipswich on 2 June 1833, was fourth child of Charles Meadows. A brother, Robert (1839–1887), obtained a distinguished position in China as a medical man. Alfred was educated at the grammar school, Ipswich, and later at King's College, London, of which he was first associate and afterwards fellow. He matriculated at the London University in 1853, and after serving as pupil to William Elliston of Ipswich, he entered, in October 1853, the King's College medical school, where he obtained many prizes. In 1856 he was admitted a member of the Royal College of Surgeons of England and a licentiate of the Apothecaries' Hall. He also became a licentiate in midwifery of the Royal College of Surgeons. In 1857 he graduated M.B. of the university of London, and in the following year he became M.D., and in 1862 a member of the Royal College of Physicians of London; but it was not until 1873 that he was elected a fellow of that body. Immediately after obtaining his first qualifications to practice he held the offices of house-physician and resident midwifery assistant at King's College Hospital, and in 1857 he spent the winter in Paris.

Few men held a larger number of appointments than Meadows. The following are some of the more important. In 1860 he was assistant-physician for diseases of women and children at King's College Hospital; from 1863 until his resignation of the post in 1874 he was physician to the Hospital for Women, Soho Square. In 1871 he became physician accoucheur to St. Mary's Hospital, a post he held until his death, and was lecturer in the medical school on the diseases of women and children. He was elected the first president of the British Gynæcological Society on its foundation in 1884, and was a corresponding member of the German, Swedish, and Boston gynæcological societies. In 1878 he attended the crown prince of Sweden while he visited England, and in recognition of his services the king of Sweden, in 1881, made him a commander of the second class of the order of Wasa. He died on Tuesday, 18 April 1887, at his house in George Street, Hanover Square, and is buried at Colnbrook, Buckinghamshire.

Meadows was an active promoter of the Guild of St. Luke. He was an energetic freemason and an officer in grand lodge, and took a leading part in founding the University of London lodge. Sir Edward Sieveking says of him: 'He was an active and energetic man, and he was able to bring to the contested field of practice those qualities which, combined with activity and energy, insured him a large amount of success. He was kind and hospitable in all his social arrangements, a good mechanician, clever in the adoption of means to an end, and skilful in the manipulative details of his department of practice.'

He published 'A Manual of Midwifery,' 3rd edit. London, 1876 (the second edition was translated in 1875 into Japanese and published in 12mo), and, with Dr. Tanner, a work on the diseases of children. He was translator of Bernutz and Goupil's 'Clinical Memoirs on the Diseases of Women' for the New Sydenham Society, vols. i. and ii. 1866. He edited the 'London Medical Review' in 1860.

[British Gynæcological Journal, with portrait, iii. 343; Midland Med. Miscell. and Prov. Med. Journ., Leicester, 1883, with portrait, ii. 65–7; Additional facts kindly contributed by Dr. W. A. Elliston and Mr. R. C. Meadows.] D'A. P.

MEADOWS, DRINKWATER (1799–1869), actor, a native of Yorkshire, or, according to another account, of Wales, born in 1799, joined a theatrical company established in Kendal, and played in various towns in Westmoreland and Yorkshire. Subsequently he became member of a second company, playing in Lincoln, Leicester, Peterborough, and Birmingham, at which last named town he was seen and engaged by Charlton, the manager of the Bath Theatre. Meadows made his first appearance at Bath on 4 Nov. 1817 as Fogrum, Liston's part, in Morton's musical drama 'The Slave.' He played on the 24th Scrub in the 'Beaux' Stratagem,' and on 6 Dec. Clincher, jun., in the 'Constant Couple.' The following season he was Hempseed in the younger Colman's 'X. Y. Z.,' Simon in the 'Rendezvous,' Molino in the 'Blind Boy,' Adam Winterton in the 'Iron Chest,' Solomon Lob in 'Love Laughs at Locksmiths,' and Old Philpot in the 'Citizen;' in 1819–20 Ratcliffe in the 'Heart of Midlothian,' First Gravedigger in 'Hamlet' to Kean's Hamlet, Slender in the 'Merry Wives of Windsor,' Dromio of Syracuse, Clod in the 'Young Quaker,' and in 1820–1 Peter in the 'Stranger,' Laurence in the 'Fate of Calas,' Peter Pastoral, and Interpreter in 'All's well that ends well.' On 28 Sept. 1821 as Scrub he made his first appearance at Covent Garden. Here he played his old characters, replaced Liston, the original Dugald Dalgetty, in Pocock's 'Montrose, or the Children of the Mist,' and was seen as Crabtree in the 'School for Scandal,' and Filch in the 'Beggar's Opera.' In following seasons he was, among other characters, Don Pedro in the 'Wonder,' the original Timothy Quaint in Howard Payne's 'Soldier's Daughter,' Pacheco in 'Brother and Sister,' the original Nimpedo in 'Clari, or the Maid of Milan' (8 May 1823), Fainwou'd in 'Raising the Wind,' Baron Altradoff in the 'Exile,' Blaise in the 'Forest of Bondy, or the Dog of Montargis,' the original Spado in 'Pride shall have a Fall,' attributed to Croly (11 March 1824), Jaquez in the 'Honeymoon,' Sampson in 'Isabella,' Jeffrey in 'Animal Magnetism,' Launcelot Gobbo, Medium in 'Inkle and Yarico,' Stephen in 'Every Man in his Humour,' Baron Piffleberg in 'Of Age Tomorrow,' the original Robin in Poole's 'Scapegoat' (25 Nov. 1825), Simon Pure in 'A Bold Stroke for a Wife,' Shallow in the 'Merry Wives of Windsor,' Squire Richard in Cibber's 'Provoked Husband,' the original Raubvogel in Planché's 'Returned Killed' (31 Oct. 1826), Apothecary in 'Romeo and Juliet,' the original Salewit, a poet, in Planché's 'Merchant's Wedding' (5 Feb. 1828), adapted from 'A City Match' by Jasper Mayne, the original Oliver in Moncrieff's 'Somnambulist' (19 Feb. 1828), Heeltap in the 'Mayor of Garratt,' Marrall in 'A New Way to pay Old Debts,' Thomas Appletree in the 'Recruiting Officer,' the original Bronze in Pocock's 'Home, Sweet Home' (19 March 1829), Tester in the 'Suspicious Husband,' the original Torpid in the 'Night before the Wedding and the Wedding Night' (17 Nov. 1829), and the original Jotham Riddel in 'Wigwam, or the Men of the Wilderness,' founded on the 'Pioneers' of Cooper.

From the close of Genest's 'History' Meadows is not easily traced. At Covent Garden he remained until 1844, being the original Fathom in Sheridan Knowles's 'Hunchback' in 1832, and the following year the original Bartolo in the 'Wife' of the same author. He was on 10 Feb. 1836, at Drury Lane, the original Philippe in Lovell's 'Provost of Bruges,' but returned to Covent Garden, where in September 1842 he made a success as a miserly old clerk in Lovell's 'Love Sacrifice,' played one of the witches in 'Macbeth,' was the original Gallop, a trainer, in Mark Lemon's farce the 'Turf,' and played in Robert Bell's 'Mothers and Daughters.' In 1844 he acted under the Keeley management at the Lyceum (1844–7), and remained under the succeeding management of C. Mathews. At the revival of the 'Merry Wives of Windsor' in December 1848 he was Sir Hugh Evans. After joining the Kean and Keeley management of the Princess's he was the original Boaz in Douglas Jerrold's 'Prisoner of War,' first given at Windsor Castle, under Charles Kean's direction, on 24 Jan. 1851; on 6 March was the original Joe Harrup, a toothless old huntsman, in Boucicault's 'Love in a Maze,' and on 22 Nov. 1852 played 'Shallow' in the 'Merry Wives of Windsor.' He remained at the Princess's under Harris until his retirement in 1862. He died at Prairie Cottage, the Green, Barnes, on 12 June 1869, one account says at the age of seventy-five. A careful, retiring man, shunning publicity, he was much respected and little noticed. A careful, conscientious, and trustworthy actor, he was lacking in inspiration, homely, dry, and quaint in style, and seen to most advantage in eccentric comedy. In a catalogue of actors in the 'Dramatic and Musical Review' of 2 Oct. 1847, with qualifying adjectives he is called 'Meek Meadows.' He was secretary to the Covent Garden Theatrical Fund, and contributed some recollections and other articles to the press. A portrait of him as Raubvogel in 'Returned Killed' is in the Mathews collection in the Garrick Club.

[Genest's Account of the English Stage; Dramatic and Musical Review, various years; Tallis's Dramatic Mag.; New Monthly Mag., various years; Athenæum, 19 June 1869; Era newspaper, 20 June 1869; Cole's Life of Charles Kean; Oxberry's Dramatic Biog. vol. vii.] J. K.

MEADOWS or MEADOWE, JOHN (1622–1697), ejected minister, second son of Daniel Meadowe (1577–1651) of Chattisham, near Ipswich, by his wife, Elizabeth (Smith, *d.* circa 1678), was born at Chattisham on 7 April 1622. He altered his name to Meadows in later life. Sir Philip Meadows [q. v.] was his younger brother. On 26 Feb. 1639–40 he was admitted at Emmanuel College, Cambridge, and graduated B.A. in 1643. He removed to Christ's College on 23 Dec. 1644, having been put into one of the fellowships made vacant by the parliamentary commissioners; he graduated M.A. in 1646. Leaving Cambridge in 1653, he was presented by Humphrey Mosely to the rectory of Ousden, Suffolk (26 Aug. 1653); was ordained by three presbyters at Cheveley, Cambridgeshire, on 17 April 1657, and was approved by the 'commissioners for approbation' (triers) on 7 May 1658. By the uniformity act of 1662 he was ejected on 24 Aug., but retained the rectory and received the profits of the living till Michaelmas, when he removed to Ousden Hall. John Greene, his successor, was not inducted till 8 Aug. 1663. At Ousden Hall he remained till 21 Oct. 1670. In 1672, under the indulgence of that year, he took out licenses as a presbyterian teacher in his own house at Stowmarket, Suffolk, and that of Elizabeth Nelson there. He seems to have been called on to appear at three successive sessions in 1680 for his nonconformity. About 1688 he removed to Bury St. Edmunds, where he had often preached while at Stowmarket. He lived in close fellowship with Samuel Bury [q. v.] the presbyterian minister. Being a man of wealth, Meadows was able to do much for his nonconformist brethren in straitened circumstances, and his liberality had no sectarian bias; he was an occasional communicant at the established church. He died at Bury St. Edmunds in 1696–7 and was buried in the churchyard at Stowmarket on 1 March. His will (proved 7 April 1697) devised property in ten Suffolk parishes; he had also an estate at Wickhambrook, Suffolk, and owned the advowson of the rectory of Witnesham, Suffolk. His portrait as a youth at Cambridge, engraved by A. Fox, is prefixed to the memoir by Edgar Taylor, F.S.A., his descendant. He married, first, in 1653, Anne (*d.* about 1670), daughter of Roger Rant of Swaffham Prior, Cambridgeshire, who brought him an estate at Exning, Suffolk. He married, secondly, in 1675, Sarah (1654–1688), daughter of Benjamin Fairfax (*d.* 1708) of Halesworth, Suffolk, elder brother of John Fairfax (1623–1700) [q.v.] By his second marriage only had he issue—four sons and three daughters. The eldest son JOHN MEADOWS (1676–1757), educated at Caius College, Cambridge; settled (21 Sept. 1701) as presbyterian minister at Needham Market, Suffolk; published 'The Apostolic Rule of Ordination,' &c., 1738, 8vo, and died at Needham on 10 April 1757. The third son, Philip (1679–1752), was mayor of Norwich, 1734.

[Calamy's Account, 1713, p. 641; Taylor's Suffolk Bartholomeans, 1840; Browne's Hist. Congr. Norfolk and Suffolk, 1877, pp. 491, 498, 533.] A. G.

MEADOWS, JOSEPH KENNY (1790–1874), draughtsman, born at Cardigan in South Wales, and baptised on 1 Nov. 1790, was the son of James Meadows, a retired naval officer. Details of his early life are wanting. In 1823 he designed and lithographed the plates for Planché's 'Costume of Shakespeare's Historical Tragedy of King John.' The 'Heads of the People, or Portraits of the English,' published in 1838–40, and to which Thackeray and Douglas Jerrold contributed some of their earliest sketches, established his popularity as an artist. But the chief ambition of his life was to produce an illustrated edition of Shakespeare, and this he accomplished between 1839 and 1843. The wit and graceful fancy of his art here had free scope, and although the designs are often forced and affected, the work was a great success. So popular, indeed, was his conception of Falstaff that a bronze statuette was modelled after it in Germany, and had a large sale. His services were eagerly sought as an illustrator of children's books and fanciful stories, and for many years he was employed on the Christmas numbers of the 'Illustrated London News.' He was one of the first to introduce wood engraving among English publishers as a means of cheap and popular illustration. He painted sometimes in oil, and on two or three occasions he exhibited at the Royal Academy and the Society of British Artists. Many of his best years were passed in intimate friendship with Leigh Hunt, Laman Blanchard, Douglas Jerrold, Dickens, Thackeray, Stanfield, Roberts, and the Landseers.

Meadows married a daughter of John Henning [q. v.] the sculptor, and in 1864 was granted a civil list pension of 80*l.* 'in acknowledgment of his merit as an artist, more especially shown by his illustrations of Shakespeare.' Up to the last he was a hale and vigorous old man. He died, at the age of eighty-four, at 458 King's Road, Chelsea, on 19 Aug. 1874, and was buried in the St. Pancras cemetery at Finchley.

Besides those already mentioned, Meadows illustrated, either wholly or in part, the following among other works: 'The Autobiography of a notorious Legal Functionary (Jack Ketch),' 1836; 'Songs of Home, or Lays of Married Life,' 1840; Hall's 'Book of British Ballads,' 1842; Dean Swift's 'Hints to Servants,' 1843; 'Punch's Complete Letter Writer,' by Douglas Jerrold, 1845; the New Testament, 1847; Mrs. S. C. Hall's 'Midsummer Eve,' 1848; the Brothers Mayhew's 'Magic of Kindness,' in conjunction with George Cruikshank, 1849; 'The Illustrated Byron,' 1854–6; Laman Blanchard's 'Corporation Characters,' 1855; 'Merry Pictures by the Comic Hands of H. K. Browne and others,' 1857; 'Granny's Wonderful Chair, and its Tales of Fairy Times,' by Frances Browne, 1857; 'The Sydenham Sindbad,' 1857; Captain Crawley's 'Backgammon,' 1858; 'Pearls of Shakespeare,' 1860; Greene's 'Winter and Summer at Burton Hall,' 1861; and 'Don Quixote,' 1872.

[Academy, 1874, ii. 360, by Mrs. Heaton; Athenæum, 1874, ii. 326; Art Journal, 1874, p. 306; Bryan's Dictionary of Painters and Engravers, ed. Graves and Armstrong, 1886–9, ii. 767; information from the Rev. W. Cynog Davies, vicar of Cardigan.] R. E. G.

MEADOWS, Sir PHILIP (1626–1718), diplomatist, baptised at Chattisham, Suffolk, on 4 Jan. 1625–6 (Page, *Suffolk*, p. 13), was fifth son of Daniel Meadowe (1571–1651) of Chattisham, by his wife Elizabeth, and grandson of William Meddowe or Meadowe (*d.* 1588), as the name was anciently spelt, of Witnesham. Philip was educated at Queens' College, Cambridge, whence he graduated M.A. In October 1653 he was appointed, on Thurloe's recommendation, Latin secretary to Cromwell's council at a salary of 100*l.*, soon augmented to 200*l.* a year. The appointment was made in order to relieve Milton, who was then receiving 15*s.* 10½*d.* a day from the council, but whose blindness incapacitated him from the full discharge of his duties, and who virtually became henceforth 'Latin secretary extraordinary' (*Cal. State Papers*, Dom. 1653–4, p. 386). The poet would have preferred the appointment of Andrew Marvell (in whose interest he wrote to Bradshaw) as his assistant; but Meadows soon gave complete satisfaction, and henceforth did the bulk of the routine work in the department (Masson, *Milton*, iv. 479, 526, 575–80). In March 1656 he was selected to represent the Lord Protector at Lisbon in respect to the ratification of the treaty between England and Portugal, and he sailed from Portsmouth in the Phœnix, Captain Whetstone, on the 11th of the month (*Cal. State Papers*, Dom. 1655–6, pp. 236, 503–4). Good news received from him in July were qualified by the report that he had been insulted and 'maimed' in the execution of his duty (*ib.*; and cf. *Cal. of Clarendon State Papers*, iii. 154); lands to the value of 100*l.* a year were granted to him by way of compensation; but no confiscated property of precisely the right amount being instantly available, this was commuted by a lump sum of 1,000*l.* Meadows returned from Lisbon in the Phœnix towards the end of November. In February 1657 it was decided to send him as envoy to Frederick III, king of Denmark. His goods were to pass free of customs and excise, and he was to have 400*l.* for preliminary expenses in addition to 1,000*l.* a year salary. A Mr. Sterry was appointed to act as secretary during his absence on two hundred marks a year, and Meadows sailed in the Assistance in August 1657. He arrived at Elsinore in September (THURLOE, p. 509), and was received at Copenhagen about the 20th, his entry and reception being 'more solemn than usual, to the regret of some other ministers residing in the court' (*ib.*) In March 1657–8 he gave a full account to Thurloe of the treaty of Roskild (8 March) between Frederick III and Charles Gustavus of Sweden. Though Denmark lost considerably by the treaty, Cromwell was unwilling to see her absorbed by Sweden, and did what he could to protect her interests. Meadows had an interview with Charles X after the treaty, and described him as perfectly well disposed to the Protector. He presented him with a handsome sword, which Charles swore to use against the house of Austria. The envoy now asked permission to return to England, but was sent to take part as a mediator in negotiations pending between the kings of Sweden and Poland. The task was very delicate, especially as the Polish monarch's sentiments with regard to Cromwell were quite uncertain, and it was soon relinquished.

During the spring of 1658 Meadows was knighted, and was sent as ambassador to the court of Sweden, but he was unable to exert much influence. Cromwell was endeavouring to unite Sweden and Denmark with England, France, and if possible Brandenburg, against Austria and Spain. Charles Gustavus had other views. He recommenced war with Denmark, marched an army across the frozen waters of the Baltic, and before the end of 1658 was bombarding the Danish capital. A witness of these exploits, Meadows remained with Charles before Copenhagen, giving him vague promises of English support as his position grew more and more embarrassing. Brandenburg and the Dutch came to Denmark's aid, and Charles's situation became most precarious. The English fleet under Edward Montague, earl of Sandwich [q. v.], appeared in the Sound in April 1659, and Charles now confidently anticipated support; but Meadows was only empowered to insist upon the *status quo* as defined by the peace of Roskild, and this principle was soon adopted as the basis for an armistice. Meadows, however, returned to England on leave (July 1659) before the terms of the peace were finally enforced, or supplemented and confirmed by the treaty of Copenhagen in 1660. Meadows had been created a knight of the order of the Elephant of Denmark, and by Cromwell a knight-marshal of the palace (1658). At the Restoration his position was untenable, and in February 1660 he was turned out of his lodgings at Whitehall to make room for [Sir] William Temple. Little is heard of him in his retirement until 1677, when he published 'A Narrative of the Principal Actions occurring in the Wars betwixt Sueden and Denmark before and after the Roschild Treaty, with the Counsels and Measures by which those actions were directed, together with a View of the Suedish and other Affairs as they stood in Germany in the year 1675, with relation to England,' London, 12mo, dedicated to the Right Hon. Earl of Bristol. Four years later he published 'A Brief Enquiry into Leagues and Confederacies made betwixt Princes and Nations, with the Nature of their Obligations,' a not very lucid protest against the inconsistency of English foreign policy under Charles II (printed in *Somers Tracts*, 1812, viii. 22). In 1689 appeared his interesting 'Observations concerning the Dominion and Sovereignty of the Seas, being an Abstract of the Marine Affairs of England,' London, 4to. Here, while accepting the general conclusions of Selden's 'Mare Clausum,' the author deprecates a policy of encroachment. He inquires what is meant by 'dominion of the sea,' and what things are incident to such a dominion. He considers England's claim to salutation by the flag and topsail, a practice in which he discovers both inconsistencies and dangers, treats of the exclusion of foreign men-of-war from British waters, and finally of marine jurisdiction, fishing rights, and other subsidiary topics. In 1690 Meadows was exchanging verses and epigrams with John Cotton, and the latter writes: 'In this traffic of poetry I am the great gainer, for Sir Ph. doth exchange (as Glaucus did with Diomedes) χρυσεα χαλκειων' (AUBREY, *Bodleian Letters*, 1813, i. 19).

Restored to favour at the revolution, Meadows was in January 1691–2 appointed commissioner for taking public accounts, and in May 1696 created a member of the original council of trade. He was reappointed commissioner for the promoting of trade in January 1707–8, with a salary of 1,000*l.* a year (*Harl. MS.* 2263, ff. 152, 333). He died, aged 93, on 16 Sept. 1718, and was buried at Hammersmith (*Chron. Regist.* 1718, p. 34).

Meadows married, in April 1661, Constance, second daughter and coheiress of Francis Lucy of Westminster, by whom he had a son and three daughters, of whom Elizabeth married Sir Thomas Powys [q. v.], while a second espoused Richard Dyott, commissioner of stamp duties from 1708 to 1710, in which year he was convicted of fraud and sent to Newgate, but soon afterwards pardoned (see SWIFT, *Journal to Stella*, letter v.) The son, PHILIP MEADOWS (*d.*1757), who was a commissioner of excise from 1698 to 1700, was on 2 July 1700 appointed knight-marshal of the king's household, and formally knighted by William III on 23 Dec. 1700 at Hampton Court; he succeeded Stanhope as envoy to Holland in December 1706, was in 1707 despatched on a special mission to the emperor, and during his absence appointed controller of army accounts (*Cal. State Papers*, Treasury, 1708–14, passim); in November 1708 he presented a memorial to the emperor in favour of the protestants of Silesia, but before his vigorous protest had time to take effect he was succeeded by Lord Raby in August 1709. He subsequently took up his abode at Richmond, and died at Brompton on 5 Dec. 1757, leaving issue by his wife Dorothy, sister of Hugh Boscawen, first viscount Falmouth, three sons and five daughters (*Wentworth Papers*, p. 98; BOYER, *Queen Anne*, 1735, pp. 338, 395). Of these the third son, Philip (1708–1781), deputy-ranger of Windsor Park, married in 1734 Frances, only daughter of William Pierrepoint, viscount Newark, a niece to Lady Mary Wortley Montagu, and was father of Charles, who succeeded to the Kingston estates on the death of the dowager-duchess in 1788, took the name of Pierrepoint, and was on 9 April 1806 created Earl Manvers; and of Sir William Medows [q. v.]

[Gent. Mag. 1824, ii. 518; Burke's Peerage, 1889, p. 923, and Extinct Peerages, p. 428; A. Page's Supplement to the Suffolk Traveller, 1844, p. 74; Thurloe's State Papers, ed. Birch, vi. vii. passim; Cal. State Papers, Dom. Ser. 1653–60, passim; Hist. MSS. Comm. 11th Rep. App. iv. 254, 296, 13th Rep. App. v. 183; Cooper's Memorials of Cambridge, i. 313; Dyer's Modern Europe, iii. 337; Luttrell's Brief Relation, passim; Patrick's Autob. p. 20; Litt. Cromwellii, 1676, passim; Add. MS. 5131, 5132, passim, and 19141, ff. 342–59 (Davy's Suffolk Collections); Brit. Mus. Cat.] T. S.

MEAGER, LEONARD (1624?–1704?), gardener, was for some time in the service of Philip Holmlan of Warkworth, Northamptonshire, who encouraged his experiments in the art of gardening. Although hampered by 'multiplicity of business together with the want of learning,' Meager published, among other works which obtained popularity: 1. 'The English Gardener, or a Sure Guide to Young Planters and Gardeners, in three parts,' &c., London, 1670, 4to; 9th edit. 1699. Republished as 'The Compleat English Gardener,' &c., 10th edit. 'To which is now added a Supplement [by S. G.],' London, 1704, 4to; 11th edit. 1710 (?), 4to. 2. 'The New Art of Gardening; with the Gardener's Almanack,' &c., London, 1697, 12mo; 2nd edit. corrected, 1732.

[English Gardener, 1670, Ep. Ded.; Loudon's Encyclopædia of Gardening, 1822, p. 88; Brit. Mus. Cat.] W. A. S. H.

MEAGHER, THOMAS FRANCIS (1823–1867), Irish nationalist, was born in the city of Waterford on 3 Aug. 1823. His father, Thomas Meagher, a retired merchant, represented the city of Waterford in the House of Commons from August 1847 to March 1857, and was mayor of the city. To a branch of the family settled in the seventeenth century in Tipperary belonged THADDEUS or THADÉE DE MEAGHER (1670–1765), who on leaving Ireland served in the French army, and subsequently, in 1739, became chamberlain to Frederick Augustus II, king of Poland and elector of Saxony. In 1740 the king made him colonel of the 1st battalion of foot guards, in 1744 captain proprietor of the Swiss guards, in 1744 major-general in the Polish army, and in 1752 lieutenant-general. When Frederick the Great crossed into Saxony at the opening of the Seven Years' War in 1756, Meagher was despatched by his master to negotiate terms with the invader. He died in Dresden in May 1765 (*Choix de Correspondance du Marquis de Valori*, ii. 178; CARLYLE, *Frederick the Great*, iv. 551; *Archives of the Royal Saxon War Office*, No. 450 I A; information from J. C. O'Meagher, esq.)

Thomas Francis was educated by the jesuit fathers at Clongowes Wood College, Kildare, and subsequently at Stonyhurst College, Lancashire. In 1844 he went to Dublin with the intention of studying for the bar, but soon abandoned law for the political platform. In spite of his boyish appearance and somewhat affected manners, Meagher quickly established his reputation as a powerful orator at the meetings of the Repeal Association. He made a brilliant speech against the peace resolutions in Conciliation Hall on 28 July 1846, refusing to condemn the use of arms as immoral, and hailing the sword as a sacred weapon (SULLIVAN, *Speeches from the Dock*, pp. 140–1). On being interrupted by John O'Connell he left the meeting with O'Brien, Duffy, Mitchel, and others, and seceded from the association. His speech on the occasion led Thackeray subsequently to dub him 'Meagher of the Sword'—an appellation that adhered to him. He was one of the founders of the Irish Confederation, the first meeting of which took place on 13 Jan. 1847. Meagher unsuccessfully contested the city of Waterford at a by-election in February 1848.

At a meeting of the Irish Confederation on 15 March 1848 Meagher passionately declared that the people were justified in saying to the government: 'If you do not give us a parliament in which to state our wrongs and grievances, we shall state them by arms and force.' For this speech he was arrested on a charge of sedition on 21 March, but was allowed out on bail the following day. Shortly afterwards Meagher, with O'Brien and Holywood, visited Paris in order to present an address of congratulation to the provisional government. The return of the Irish deputation was celebrated by a banquet on 15 April 1848, when Meagher, through the president, presented an Irish tricolor to the citizens of Dublin. On 16 May following he was tried at Dublin before Lord-chief-justice Blackburne for his speech of 15 March. Meagher was defended by Butt, O'Loghlen, and O'Hagan, and the jury being unable to agree were discharged on the following day without giving a verdict. On 21 July Meagher was appointed a member of the war directory of the Irish Confederation, and thereupon accompanied O'Brien in his expedition through Ireland for the purpose of organising the proposed revolution. On the 28th a warrant was issued for his arrest, and a reward of 300*l.* offered for his capture. On the following day Meagher left O'Brien at Ballingarry with the idea of raising an insurrection elsewhere, and thus for a time escaped being captured. Though all chance of success had vanished, Meagher refused to leave the country, and on 13 Aug. he was arrested on a country road in Tipperary and conveyed to Kilmainham gaol on the same day.

Meagher was tried at Clonmel in October 1848 before a special commission, consisting of Lord-chief-justice Blackburne, Lord-chief-justice Doherty, and Mr. Justice Moore. He was defended by Whiteside, Butt, O'Loghlen, and F. Maher. After a trial lasting six days he was found guilty of high treason, with a recommendation to mercy on account of his youth. He was sentenced by Lord-chief-justice Doherty on 23 Oct. to be hanged, drawn, and quartered, but this sentence was subsequently commuted to penal servitude for life, and in July 1849 he was transported to Van Diemen's Land, where he was allowed considerable liberty under a ticket of leave. While there he contributed some reminiscences of 1848 to the Dublin 'Nation.' On 3 Jan. 1852 he gave notice to the district magistrate that he was about to withdraw his parole, and defying the police sent to arrest him, he made his escape, with the aid of P. J. Smyth. After a number of vicissitudes he arrived at New York at the latter end of May, and was presented with a congratulatory address by the corporation and offered a public reception on behalf of the city, which he refused (*Speeches*, pp. 311–17). For the first two years after his arrival in America, Meagher followed the occupation of a public lecturer with considerable success. In September 1855 he was admitted to the New York bar. In January 1854 he had helped Mitchell to found the 'Citizen' newspaper in New York. On 9 April 1856, assisted by James Roche, R. J. Lalor, and John Savage, he published the first number of the 'Irish News' in New York. Meagher wrote a good deal for it at first, including 'Personal Recollections,' but was unfitted for a journalist, and the paper became extinct in July 1860. In 1857 he undertook an exploring expedition to Central America, and upon his return recounted his experiences in a series of lectures. At the outbreak of the civil war Meagher raised a company of Zouaves for the 69th New York volunteers, and served with the army of the North during the first campaign in Virginia. His horse was shot under him at the first battle of Bull Run (21 July 1861). Towards the close of this year Meagher organised the 'Irish Brigade,' and was elected colonel of the first regiment. The command of the entire brigade was subsequently assigned to him, and on 3 Feb. 1862 he was granted the rank of brigadier-general. Meagher took a gallant part in the seven days' battles round Richmond, in the second battle of Bull Run, and in the battle of Antietam, where his horse was again shot under him. At Fredericksburg he received a bullet wound in his leg, and lost the greater part of his men. He led the remnant of the brigade for the last time at Chancellorsville, where its annihilation was completed, and a few days afterwards sent in his resignation, which was officially accepted on 14 May 1863. In the following year he was recommissioned as brigadier-general of volunteers, and appointed to the command of the Etowah district. At the conclusion of the war in 1865 Meagher was nominated by President Johnson secretary of Montana territory, and in September 1866 he became the temporary governor of that territory. While acting in this capacity he fell from a steamboat into the Missouri, and was drowned near Fort Benton, Montana, on 1 July 1867, aged 43. His body was not recovered.

'Meagher of the Sword' was an impulsive and reckless Irishman, a fiery orator, and a brave soldier. Thackeray makes a cutting allusion to him in the 'Battle of Limerick' (stanzas 6 and 16). Personally he was very handsome. Meagher was twice married, and left a widow and an only son. Before leaving Ireland Meagher appears to have given his papers to Duffy (*Young Ireland*, pt. i. p. viii). Assisted by his friend John Savage, Meagher published in 1853 his 'Speeches on the Legislative Independence of Ireland, with Introductory Notes' (and a portrait), New York, 12mo. He was also the author of 'Recollections of Ireland and the Irish;' 'The Last Days of the 69th in Virginia. A Narrative in three Parts . . . with a Portrait,' New York [1862?], 8vo. He contributed the following articles to Harper's 'New Monthly Magazine:' 1. 'Holidays in Costa Rica,' xx. 18–38, 145–64, 304–25. 2. 'The New Route through Chiriqui,' xxii. 198–209. 3. 'Rides through Montana' (left unfinished), xxxv. 568–85.

[A voluminous biography of Meagher, written by his friend Michael Cavanagh, with letters, speeches, and autobiographical fragments and portrait, Worcester, Mass. U.S.A. 1892; Captain W. F. Lyons's Brigadier-General Thomas Francis Meagher, New York, 1870 (with portrait); Meagher's Speeches, 1853; Sir C. G. Duffy's Young Ireland, 1884, pt. i. p. 209, pt. ii. passim; Mitchel's Jail Journal, 1868; Mitchel's History of Ireland, 1869, ii. 400–50; Sullivan's New Ireland, 1878; Sullivan's Speeches from the Dock, 1887, pp. 137–47; Read's Cabinet of Irish Literature, 1880, iv. 54–8; Irish Monthly, xiv. 11–16; In Memoriam Thomas Francis Meagher, Melbourne, 1867; Appleton's Cyclopædia of American Biography, 1888, iv. 283; Webb's Compendium of Irish Biography, 1878, pp. 338–9; Wills's Irish Nation, 1875, iv. 74–8; Annual Register, 1848 passim, 1852 Chron. pp. 81–2; Freeman's Journal, 17 and 18 May 1848, 17–24 Oct. 1848, and 20 July 1867; Notes and Queries, 7th ser. xii. 209; information kindly supplied by D. J. O'Donoghue, esq.] G. F. R. B.

MEANS, JOSEPH CALROW (1801–1879), general baptist minister, was born at 29 Mark Lane, London, on 20 May 1801. His father, John Means, was a wine-merchant in Rood Lane; his mother was Phillis (*d.* 11 Aug. 1814), third daughter of John Simpson, successor of Charles Bulkley [q. v.], as afternoon preacher to the general baptist congregation at Worship Street, Finsbury Square. He was educated from 1814 at the boarding-school of John Evans (1767–1827) [q. v.] In 1818, while in his father's counting-house, he became one of the original teachers of the Worship Street Sunday school. In 1822 he was baptised by immersion at Deptford, and in 1823 he was placed on the committee of the general baptist assembly. Turning his thoughts towards the ministry, he entered (1828) the classical and mathematical classes of the newly opened University College, London, and at the same time studied theology in the general baptist academy under Benjamin Mardon, M.A. (*b.* 18 May 1792, *d.* 15 April 1866), a biblical scholar. In 1829, while still pursuing his studies, he became preacher to the afternoon congregation at Worship Street. His ministry was successful, and his congregation removed (October 1829) to Trinity Place and subsequently to Coles Street, Southwark. He was appointed secretary (1831) to the general baptist assembly, edited (1831–6) the organ of his denomination, the 'General Baptist Advocate,' and in 1834 was elected one of their 'messengers,' a quasi-episcopal office, held for life. In 1836 he preached the annual sermon before the assembly, and made some stir by setting forth an evangelical view of the atonement. At that date the general baptists of the old connexion were unitarians of a somewhat rigid type. Means had to retire from his editorship, and after the publication of his volume on the atonement (1838) his connection with his congregation was severed (1839). He formed a small evening congregation at Worship Street (December 1839), to which he ministered without stipend, supporting himself by literary work and by taking boarders. In 1843 he became minister of the general baptist congregation at Chatham, Kent; his settlement was in the face of great opposition, but proved a very happy one. He was elected headmaster of the Chatham proprietary school, and kept it on when relinquished by the proprietors. In 1855 he succeeded Mardon as minister at Worship Street, and from this time he exerted a paramount influence on the counsels of his denomination. He was never robust, and in later life he suffered greatly from asthma. He retired from the pastoral charge in October 1874, but returned again to many of its duties, and preached the last sermon (23 June 1878) at Worship Street, before the removal of the congregation to new premises in Bethnal Green Road. He died on 6 Feb. 1879. He married in 1837 Louisa (*d.* 1878), daughter of Lieutenant-colonel Hugh Robert Alcock, but had no issue. Firm in his convictions, Means was a man of pure and gentle character; a good scholar, he did his work with accuracy and thoroughness. His contributions to theology were undervalued by his co-religionists; they are marked by considerable power and lucidity. His position was a modified Arianism. His general literary work began in the 'Penny Cyclopædia,' to which he contributed topographical and other articles, including a biography of Lant Carpenter, LL.D. [q. v.] His only published volume is 'Jesus the Mercy Seat; or a Scriptural View of Atonement,' &c., 1838, 16mo. He published a few separate sermons; his addresses as 'messenger,' often valuable for their historical details, are in the 'Proceedings' of the assembly, and some were published separately. He wrote frequently on theological topics in the 'Christian Reformer,' the 'Inquirer,' and in baptist periodicals. He contributed to the 'Biographical Dictionary' of the Society for the Diffusion of Christian Knowledge, and to Dr. William Smith's 'Dictionary of Greek and Roman Biography.'

[Christian Life, 15 Feb. 1879, pp. 78 sq.; Inquirer, 15 Feb. 1879, pp. 98 sq.; Memoir in Proceedings of General Assembly of Gen. Bapt. Churches, 1880; Monthly Repository, 1814, p. 506; Unitarian Herald, 27 April 1866, p. 137; Means's publications and private correspondence; personal recollection.] A. G.

MEARA, DERMOD or DERMITIUS (*fl.* 1610), author and physician, was a native of the district styled Ormonde, in the county of Tipperary, Ireland. He studied at Oxford, where, Wood tells us, 'he was esteemed a good poet.' 'In all my searches,' added Wood, 'I cannot find him matriculated, or that he took a degree.' An earlier Dermitius Meara, who had studied at Paris and Cambridge, supplicated for the degree of B.C.L. 3 July 1514 (*Oxf. Univ. Reg.*, Oxf. Hist. Soc., i. 93). Meara practised as a physician in Ireland with high repute. In 1615 he published at London a panegyrical poem in Latin on the genealogy and career of Thomas Butler, earl of Ormonde and Ossory [q. v.], who had died in the preceding year. The title was 'Ormonius: sive illustrissimi herois ac domini, d. Thomæ Butleri, Ormoniæ et Osoriæ Comitis, Viscomitis de Thurles, Baronis de Arckelo . . . commemoratio, heroico carmine conscripta à Dermitio Meara, Ormoniensi Hyberno et insignissimæ Oxoniensis Academiæ quondam alumno.'

The poem is divided into five books, and occupies 144 pages 12mo. Prefixed are dedications to Thomas Butler and Walter Butler, earls of Ormonde and Ossory, with an epistle to the reader. The volume closes with an 'epicedion' by the author, anagrams, acrostics, and chronograms.

Meara in 1619 published at Dublin a volume (sm. 12mo) entitled 'Pathologia hereditaria generalis sive de morbis hæreditariis tractatus spagyro-dogmaticus. In quo generalis eorundem morborum radix natura et therapeutica indicatio ex utriusque medicinæ fontibus investigatur.' This treatise is in twelve chapters, and ends at page 128 with 'epilogus ad lectorem.' It was dedicated to Sir Oliver St. John, lord-deputy of Ireland, and prefixed to the work are two Latin epigrams by John Kelli, in praise of the author.

The precise date of Meara's death has not been ascertained. Edmund Meara [q. v.] was his son. Harris, in his edition of Ware's 'Works,' 1746, stated that Meara's poem on the Earl of Ormonde was translated into English verse by William Roberts, Ulster king-of-arms in the reign of Charles I. No mention of such a work is to be found either in the known writings of Roberts or in any authentic document at present accessible.

[Wood's Athenæ Oxon. ed. Bliss, ii. 275; Gilbert's Hist. of City of Dublin; W. Roberts's manuscript Hist. of House of Ormonde; Facsimiles of National MSS. of Ireland, 1884, vol. iv.; D'Alton's King James's Irish Army List, p. 75.] J. T. G.

MEARA or O'MEARA, EDMUND (*d.* 1680), physician, son of Dermod or Dermitius Meara [q. v.], was born in Ormond, co. Tipperary, and graduated M.D. at Rheims in 1636. He practised at Ormond and in Dublin, studied medicine at Oxford, where he appears, however, to have taken no degree, and was in December 1664 admitted an honorary fellow of the Royal College of Physicians. He published in 1665 'Examen diatribæ Thomæ Willisii Doctoris Medici et professoris Oxoniensis de Febribus . . . cui accesserunt historiæ aliquot medicæ rariores,' London, 8vo. The work, which contains a fine engraved title, and is dedicated to Sir Kenelm Digby, was keenly resented by Willis's friend and ally, Richard Lower (1631–1691) [q. v.] He at once produced a 'Vindicatio Diatribæ Willisii,' and 'therein,' says Ware, 'handles our Ormondian very coarsely' (*Irish Writers*, p. 190). This was followed by 'Willisius male vindicatus, sive medicus Oxoniensis mendacitatis et inscitiæ detectus,' Dublin, 1667, which was at least inspired by Meara. Lower's animosity was unextinguished in 1669, when in the dedicatory epistle to his 'Tractatus de Corde' he spoke bitterly of the ignoramuses who amused themselves by obstructing scientific progress with their blundering criticisms, 'inter quos summæ proterviæ et stuporis Meara quidam Hybernus, cæteris omnibus palmam præripere videtur.' Meara subsequently practised with much success in Bristol, where he died in 1680. Among his friends was John Maplet [q. v.], who also practised in Bristol, and in some important cases called in Meara for advice. He left three sons: William, who was also a physician, and prefixed a copy of Latin verses to his father's 'Examen;' Edmund, a jesuit; and Francis. Francis, the second son, was named a burgess in James II's charter of 1687 to the town of Wicklow, and was granted a commission of horse in Tyrconnel's regiment in the same year. He was sheriff of co. Wicklow in 1688, and was killed at the battle of the Boyne, being then a major, on 1 July 1690.

[Munk's Coll. of Phys. i. 337; Webb's Compend. of Irish Biog. p. 404; Ware's Irish Writers, p. 190; Wood's Athenæ Oxon. ed. Bliss, ii. 275; Chalmers's Biog. Dict.; D'Alton's James II's Army Lists, pp. 53, 75; Clarke's James II, ii. 400; Eloy's Dict. Hist. de la Médecine, ii. 210; Brit. Mus. Cat.] T. S.

MEARES. [See also MERES.]

MEARES, JOHN (1756?–1809), commander in the navy and voyager, entered the navy in 1771 on board the Cruiser, in the rating of 'captain's servant,' and after serving for nearly seven years, mostly in small ships, passed his examination 17 Sept. 1778, when he was said to be more than twenty-two (passing certificate); the next day he was promoted to the rank of lieutenant. After the peace of 1783 he entered the merchant service and obtained command of a ship for a voyage to India. At Calcutta he formed a company for opening or developing a trade with North-west America, and on 12 March 1786 sailed in the ship Nootka of 200 tons. In September he arrived in Prince William Sound, where he wintered; and having explored part of the neighbouring coast and got together a cargo of furs, he went to Canton. In January 1788 he sailed for Nootka Sound in the ship Felice, arriving there in May. In June he was joined by the Iphigenia, William Douglas master; and after some traffic with the Indians, buying some land and obtaining a promise of free and exclusive trade, he sailed for China in the Felice in September, leaving the Iphigenia and her tender, the North-west America, with orders to winter at the Sandwich Islands.

In 1789 Meares and his partner at Canton despatched two ships, the Argonaut in April, and the Princess Royal in May, to join the Iphigenia in Nootka Sound. The Iphigenia was already there on 6 May, when the Spanish frigate Princesa of 26 guns came in. On the 13th the Princesa was joined by the 16-gun corvette San Carlos; and on the 14th the Spaniards seized the Iphigenia and the North-west America, making Douglas and all his men prisoners. On their arrival later on, the Argonaut and Princess Royal were also seized, the grounds of the aggression being the allegation that the coast and the adjacent seas were Spanish, and that any foreign ship trading there was violating the commercial code of Spain and was guilty of smuggling, if not of piracy.

As soon as the news reached Meares he returned to England, and in a memorial dated 30 April 1790 laid the state of the case before the government. On 13 May the memorial was presented to the House of Commons. The utmost indignation was felt and expressed; satisfaction and reparation were peremptorily demanded from the Spanish government; and as they were not at once given, a very large fleet was assembled, under the command of Lord Howe [see HOWE, RICHARD, EARL HOWE], which is commonly spoken of as 'the Spanish armament of 1790.' Before this material threat the Spanish government acceded to all demands. The political excitement gave an unwonted interest to Meares's voyages and mercantile schemes, and encouraged him to bring out his narrative, under the title of 'Voyages made in the Years 1788 and 1789 from China to the North-west Coast of America: to which are prefixed an Introductory Narrative of a Voyage performed in 1786 from Bengal in the Ship Nootka; Observations on the probable existence of a North-west Passage; and some Account of the Trade between the North-west Coast of America and China, and the latter Country and Great Britain,' 4to, 1790. To this is prefixed a portrait after Beechey.

The publication of this volume led to a warm controversy with George Dixon [q. v.], who immediately brought out 'Remarks on the Voyages of John Meares, Esq.,' 4to, 1790. This was followed by 'An Answer to Mr. George Dixon, late Commander of the Queen Charlotte, by John Meares, Esq.,' 4to, 1791; and this again by 'Further Remarks on the Voyages of John Meares, Esq., in which several important Facts, misrepresented in the said Voyages, relative to Geography and Commerce, are fully substantiated, by George Dixon,' 4to, 1791. By this time the political trouble was at rest, and the quarrel was dropped. It does not appear that Meares had any further service in the navy; but on 26 Feb. 1795 he was promoted to the rank of commander. He died in 1809.

[In addition to the several works named in the text, and the memorial, which was printed in 1790, with the date 1760 in error, there are an Authentic Narrative of all the Facts relative to Nootka Sound (1790), and Official Papers relative to the Dispute, &c. (1790). See also Parliamentary History, vol. xxviii. col. 765 et seq. There is a short and inaccurate notice in Appleton's Cyclopædia of American Biography. In Gent. Mag. 1810, freq. (cf. Notes and Queries, 2nd ser. xii. 138), there is a long discussion of the pedigree of Meares or Mears, a family that settled in Ireland in the time of James I. Whether John Meares belonged to this family or not is unknown.] J. K. L.

MEARNS, DUNCAN, D.D. (1779–1852), professor of theology, was born on 23 Aug. 1779 at the manse of Cluny, Aberdeenshire, of which parish his father, Alexander Mearns, was minister. His mother was Anne, daughter of James Morison of Disblair and Elsick, provost of Aberdeen in 1745. At the age of twelve he entered King's College, Aberdeen, gaining the first bursary. After graduating M.A., March 1795, he entered the Divinity Hall, where he studied under Dr. Gilbert Gerard [q. v.] and Principal George Campbell [q. v.] At the age of twenty he was licensed by the presbytery of Kincardine O'Neil, and the same year (13 Nov. 1799), on the presentation of George, earl of Aberdeen, was ordained assistant and successor to the parish of Tarves, succeeding shortly after to the benefice. He became professor of divinity in King's College, Aberdeen, in succession to Dr. Gilbert Gerard on 12 Oct. 1816. There he carried on the traditions of the chair, and his learning and character quickly made him a leader of the 'moderate' party in the Scottish church during the long and growing controversy with the evangelicals or 'high-flyers.' In 1821 he was chosen moderator of the general assembly, and in 1823 was appointed one of George IV's chaplains for Scotland. During the ten years' conflict that ended in the secession of 1843, his faculty of direct and incisive speech was unsparingly employed in support of the establishment. He died, after a long and painful illness, 2 March 1852, aged 72. Mearns married Eliza Forsyth, by whom he had two sons and six daughters. His younger son, William Mearns, D.D., was minister of Kinneff, and died in 1891. Of his daughters, the eldest, Anne, married Dr. Robert Macpherson (1806–1867), who succeeded him in his chair of theology, and the second, Jane, married Dr. Hercules Scott, professor of moral philosophy, in the university of Aberdeen.

Next to Principal George Campbell Mearns was considered the most learned Scottish divine of his time. He published outlines of the Murray lecture on 'The Knowledge Requisite for the Attainment of Eternal Life' in 1825; and his 'Principles of Christian Evidence Illustrated' (1818), in which he sought to show that the views of Dr. Chalmers were subversive of natural theology, is an interesting exposition of the internal evidence of Christianity. After his death his son edited 'Scripture Characters,' 1853, 2 vols., discourses delivered at King's College, as Murtle lecturer on Practical Religion.

[Hew Scott's Fasti; family knowledge.]

R. M.

MEARS or MAIRS, JOHN (1695?–1767), Irish presbyterian divine, was born at Loughbrickland, co. Down, about 1695, or perhaps earlier. His father was John Mairs, presbyterian minister successively at Loughbrickland, 1687, Longford, 1697, and Newtownards, co. Down, 1707, where he died on 25 Dec. 1718. The spelling Mears is Irish, the pronunciation being Mairs. Mears entered Glasgow University in 1710, graduated M.A. in 1713, and studied divinity under John Simson [q. v.], whose teaching shook his orthodoxy. Early in 1718 he was licensed by Down presbytery, and ordained by the same body on 20 Feb. 1720 at Newtownards, in succession to his father. On the outbreak of the non-subscription controversy in 1720, Mears, who was clerk of Down presbytery, sided strongly with the non-subscribers. In 1722 he made overtures to Francis Hutchinson [q. v.], bishop of Down and Connor, offering to conform to the established church. The matter came before Down presbytery on 22 Nov. 1722, when Mears ascribed his action to a 'temptation of Satan,' and said it would have 'a good effect upon him in making him a more able advocate of the presbyterian cause.' Part of his flock was dissatisfied, and in May 1723 the presbytery erected the minority into a separate congregation. In July 1724 Thomas Nevin [q. v.], presbyterian minister of Downpatrick, brought an action for defamation against Echlin, a layman of the established church at Bangor, co. Down, who had called him an Arian. Mears was present at the Downpatrick assizes when the case came on. The judge asked several episcopal clergymen to explain to the bench what Arianism was; on their declining, Mears volunteered an explanation, on which the judge complimented him (CAMPBELL). In the previous month Mears had himself been accused of Arianism in a pamphlet ('Defence,' &c., 1724), published by Gilbert Kennedy [q. v.] From this charge he vindicated himself in an anonymous contribution to the 'Letter to Kennedy,' 1725, by Samuel Haliday [q. v.] In June 1725 Mears with his congregation were transferred to the Antrim presbytery, excluded from jurisdiction, as non-subscribing, in 1726.

In 1735 he resigned Newtownards to take charge of the small presbyterian congregation at Clonmel, co. Tipperary, where he was installed on 9 April. Here in 1738 he had between seventy and eighty communicants. On 9 Jan. 1740 he was installed minister of a small congregation in Stafford Street, Dublin, which had separated from Capel Street congregation, on 10 Oct. 1738. In December 1740 he preached at Wood Street (and published) a funeral sermon for John Abernethy (1680–1740) [q.v.] In 1762 the Stafford Street congregation amalgamated with that in Wood Street, when Mears became colleague to Samuel Bruce, father of William Bruce (1757–1841) [q.v.] A new meeting-house was built for the united congregation in Strand Street; Mears preached the opening sermon on 22 Jan. 1764. He died on 11 Oct. 1767. Armstrong says 'he died in 1768, about the eighty-fifth year of his age, having been fifty-nine years a minister;' this last statement must be corrected to forty-seven years; he was probably ordained as soon as possible, and therefore born late in 1694 or early in 1695, making his age at death seventy-two. He left one son, who settled in Calcutta, and a daughter, who married John Brown, presbyterian minister at Waterford. A portrait was engraved by R. Hunter.

He was author of: 1. 'A Catechism . . . In three Parts; for the use of Adult Persons,' London, 1732, 12mo, often reprinted, and in general use, as superseding the Westminster 'shorter catechism,' in Irish non-subscribing congregations till the present century; the last edition, Belfast, 1818, 16mo, 'revised and recommended by the Presbytery of Antrim,' is virtually a new catechism on the basis of Mears's. 2. 'A Short Explanation . . . of the Lord's Supper,' Dublin, 1758, 12mo; mainly incorporated in 'Forms of Devotion . . . By J. Leland, J. Duchal, I. Weld, and J. Mears,' Dublin, 1772, 16mo.

[Armstrong's Short Account of the General Fund, 1815, p. 77; Armstrong's Appendix to Martineau's Ordination Service, 1829, pp. 75, 99 sq.; Reid's Hist. Presb. Church in Ireland (Killen), 1867, iii. 131, 166, 184, 191; Witherow's Hist. and Lit. Memorials of Presbyterianism in Ireland, 1880, ii. 26 sq.; Killen's Hist. Congr. Presb. Church in Ireland, 1886, pp. 104, 185, 207 sq.; Irwin's Hist. Presbyterianism in Dublin, 1890, pp. 286 sq.; Records of General Synod of Ulster, 1890, i. 456, 486, 518; Campbell's manuscript Sketches of the Hist. of Presb. in Ireland, 1803.]

A. G.

MEATH, LORDS OF. [See LACY, HUGH DE, first LORD, *d.* 1186; LACY, WALTER, second LORD, *d.* 1241.]

MECHI, JOHN JOSEPH (1802–1880), agriculturist, born in London 22 May 1802, was third son of Giacomo Mechi, a citizen of Bologna, who early in life settled in England, was naturalised, and obtained a post at Kensington Palace in the household of George III. His mother was Elizabeth, daughter of J. Beyer of Poland Street, London. John at the age of sixteen was placed as a clerk in a house in Walbrook in the Newfoundland trade, where he remained ten years. By great care and industry he was enabled in 1828 to set up on his own account as a cutler in a small shop at 130 Leadenhall Street, whence he removed to No. 4 in the same street in 1830. Between 1830 and 1840 he realised a handsome fortune by the 'magic razor strop' which bore his name. After the Crimean war and the extension of the beard movement the sale fell off to the extent of 1,500*l.* a year. On 10 Nov. 1840 he took out a patent for 'improvements in apparatus to be applied to lamps in order to carry off heat and the products of consumption.' This was for the outside shop-window lamps since become so well known. From 1859 to 1869 he was in partnership with Charles Bazan, and then gave up his city business and removed to 112 Regent Street.

In 1841, after attentively studying English farming, he resolved to attempt some improvements in agriculture, and accordingly purchased for 3,400*l.* a farm of about 130 acres at Tiptree Heath, one of the least productive districts in Essex. Here he tried deep drainage and the application of steam power, and persevered until he brought his farm into such a state of productiveness that it realised annually on an average a handsome profit. The press acknowledged the services he had rendered to agricultural science by the introduction of modern processes into his model farm. He was appointed to the shrievalty of London in 1856, and in 1858 elected an alderman of the city. He was a member of the council of the Society of Arts, and was a juror in the department of art and science at the Great Exhibition of 1851 and at the Industrial Exhibition at Paris in 1855. His well-known publication, 'How to Farm Profitably,' 1857, had in various forms a circulation of ten thousand copies.

The failure of the Unity Joint Stock Bank in 1866, of which he was a governor, and an unfortunate connection with the Unity Fire and General Life Assurance Office, caused him such heavy losses that, instead of becoming lord mayor, he was in August 1866 obliged to resign his aldermanic gown. Many bad seasons followed at Tiptree farm, particularly that of 1879, and at last, worn out with diabetes and broken-hearted, Mechi was forced to place his affairs in liquidation on 14 Dec. 1880. He died at Tiptree Hall on 26 Dec. 1880, and was buried in Tiptree Church on 1 Jan. 1881. He married first, in 1823, Fanny Frost, and secondly, in 1846, Charlotte, daughter of Francis Ward of Chillesford, Suffolk. A subscription was made for his widow and daughters.

Mechi was the author of: 1. 'Letters on Agriculture,' 1844. 2. 'A Series of Letters on Agricultural Improvement,' 1845. 3. 'On the Principles which ensure Success in Trade,' 1850; another edition 1856. 4. 'How to Farm Profitably, particularly on Stiff Heavy Clays,' 1857; several editions. 5. 'On the Sewerage of Towns as it affects British Agriculture,' 1860. 6. 'Mr. Mechi's Farm Balance Sheets, also his Lectures and Papers on Farming,' 1867. 7. 'Profitable Farming: Mr. Mechi's Latest Agricultural Sayings and Doings, with Balance Sheets,' 1869. 8. 'Profitable Farming: Being the Second Series of the Sayings and Doings of J. J. Mechi,' 1872. 9. 'How to Farm Profitably: Third Series,' 1876. 10. 'Mr. Mechi's Statement to his Visitors on Agricultural Improvements,' 1878. Some of Mechi's statements were replied to in publications by W. W. Good in 1851 and 1852, and by R. Rolton in 1853.

The 'Tiptree Hall Farm Visitors' Book from 1846 to 1878' is preserved at the British Museum (Add. MS. 30015). It contains the names of persons, including numerous foreigners, who came to visit the farm, and in many cases their notes and observations.

[Times, 28 Dec. 1880, p. 9; City Press, 29 Dec. 1880, p. 5; Men of the Time, 1879, pp. 700–1; Insurance Guardian, 24 Jan. 1881, p. 6; Illustrated London News, 1857 xxx. 337, with portrait, 1857 xxxi. 317, 1881 lxxviii. 37, with portrait; Pictorial World, 29 Jan. 1881, pp. 355, 361, with portrait.] G. C. B.

MEDBOURNE, MATTHEW (*d.* 1679), actor and dramatist, was a distinguished member of the company at the Duke's Theatre. He published (1667) 'St. Cecilie, or the Converted Twins,' a tragedy, dedicated to the queen consort, and (1670, reprinted 1707) 'Tartuffe, or the French Puritan, a Comedy, lately acted at the Theatre Royal, written in French by Molière, and rendered into English with much Addition and Advantage.' The first piece is said on the title-page to have been 'written by E. M.,' but according to Gildon it was supposed to have been the work of Medbourne, and a comparison of the two plays leaves no doubt as to their common origin. An epilogue to 'Tartuffe' by Lord Buckhurst (published in a 'Miscellany' of 1672) was spoken by Medbourne himself. According to an epilogue by Lord Buckhurst, written for the revival of Jonson's 'Every Man in his Humour,' it would appear that Medbourne was the author of ten plays, but no trace of the others remains. Medbourne was a Roman catholic, and his excessive zeal for his religion laid him under suspicion. He was arrested 26 Nov. 1678, upon the information of Titus Oates, and committed to Newgate, where he died 19 March 1679.

[Langbaine's Account of Dram. Poets, p. 366; Baker's Biog. Dram. i. 506.] G. T. D.

MEDE, JOSEPH (1586–1638), biblical scholar. [See Mead.]

MEDHURST, GEORGE (1759–1827), engineer and projector of the atmospheric railway, born at Shoreham, Kent, where he was baptised on 11 Feb. 1759, was son of George and Anne Medhurst. He was brought up as a clockmaker, and carried on business for a time in Pleasant Row, Clerkenwell; but the imposition of a duty on clocks in 1797 inflicted great injury upon his trade, and about 1799 he started as an engineer at Battle Bridge. In the year last mentioned he obtained a patent (No. 2299) for 'a windmill and pumps for compressing air for obtaining motive power.' The sails of the windmill were arranged in the manner now generally followed in the construction of small windmills for pumping water. The pumping machinery shows great ingenuity, a governor being attached to vary the length of stroke of the pump, according to the strength of the wind and the pressure of the air in the reservoir. Medhurst's idea was to avail himself of the wind, whenever it served, to compress large bodies of air for use when required, and he worked steadily at the subject to the end of his life. The specification also contains a description of a small rotary engine to be worked by compressed air. In the following year he patented his 'Æolian engine' (No. 2431), in which he describes other machinery for compressing air, and shows how carriages may be driven upon common roads by compressed air contained in a reservoir underneath the vehicle. He contemplated the establishment of regular lines of coaches, with pumping stations at the end of each stage for replenishing the reservoirs. He also describes an engine worked by gas produced by the explosion in the cylinder of small quantities of gunpowder at regular intervals. He endeavoured to form a company, with a capital of 50,000*l.*, to work this invention, and published a pamphlet 'On the Properties, Power, and Applications of the Æolian Engine, with a Plan of the Particulars for carrying it into Execution,' London, n.d., 8vo, pp. 19. He calculated that a vessel of sixteen cubic feet capacity, containing compressed air of sixteen atmospheres, would suffice to do the work of one horse for an hour.

In 1801 he patented a 'compound crank' for converting rotary into rectilinear motion. It is not quite certain whether the George

Medhurst to whom a patent (No. 2525) for a washing and wringing machine was granted in the same year is identical with the subject of this memoir, as he is described as 'a mathematical instrument maker, of Pentonville.'

About the beginning of the century Medhurst established himself as a machinist and ironfounder at Denmark Street, Soho, where the concern was carried on by his successors until a few years ago. He turned his attention to weighing machines and scales, and was the inventor of the 'equal balance weighing machine,' now in universal use, as well as of the scales which are to be found in almost every retail shop.

Medhurst was the first to suggest the 'pneumatic dispatch,' as it has since been called. This was not patented, his proposals being made public in 'A New Method of Conveying Letters and Goods with great Certainty and Rapidity by Air,' London, 1810. He proposed to convey small parcels or letters in tubes by compressed air, and heavy goods to the weight of a ton and a half through brick tunnels, which the carriage just fitted. In 1812 he published 'Calculations and Remarks tending to prove the Practicability, Effects and Advantages of a Plan for the Rapid Conveyance of Passengers upon an Iron Railway, through a Tube of Thirty Feet in Area, by the Power and Velocity of Air,' London, 1812, 8vo, pp. 19. He argued that an average speed of fifty miles an hour might be attained, and that passengers might be conveyed at a cost of a farthing per mile, and goods at a penny per ton per mile. The passengers were to travel inside the tunnel, but he hints at the possibility of driving a carriage on rails in the open air by means of a piston in a continuous tube between the rails. This was long afterwards known as the atmospheric railway. The subject was further developed in 'A new System of Inland Conveyance for Goods and Passengers capable of being applied and extended throughout the Country, and of Conveying all kinds of Goods and Passengers with the Velocity of Sixty Miles in an Hour,' London, 1827, 8vo, pp. 38. This pamphlet contains several illustrations showing the pumping engines and the details of the valve for opening and closing the longitudinal slit in the tube, a difficulty which has never yet been overcome, and has been the cause of failure of all the atmospheric railways hitherto tried. It does not appear that Medhurst had the opportunity of putting any of his schemes into practice, but he had a very clear conception of the conditions of the problem of atmospheric propulsion. He laid his plans before the post-office authorities, but the reply was not encouraging. He is also said to have invented a one-wheel clock, and to have been the actual inventor of the box-mangle, long known as 'Baker's patent mangle,' though no patent was obtained. Medhurst is occasionally referred to as a Dane, but this arose from the blunder of a French writer, who was misled by the address 'Denmark Street' (see *Mechanics' Magazine*, 1844, xli. 141). Copies of Medhurst's publications are exceedingly rare, but a complete set is to be found in the library of the Institution of Civil Engineers, Westminster.

Medhurst died in September 1827, and was buried at Shoreham on 10 Sept.

[The personal details in the above notice are based upon information supplied by Mr. Thomas Medhurst, grandson of George Medhurst.]

R. B. P.

MEDHURST, WALTER HENRY (1796–1857), missionary, was born in London on 29 April 1796. In the register-book of St. Paul's School, where his admission stands recorded on 27 July 1807, at the age of eleven, his father is described as William Medhurst, innkeeper, of Ross, N.B. After quitting the school he found occupation as a printer, first at Gloucester, and afterwards with the London Missionary Society. In their service, after a few months' study and preparation under Dr. Collison at Hackney College, he embarked for China in September 1816 as a missionary printer. His destination was Malacca. On the way the ship in which he sailed put in at Madras, and there he found a wife to share his labours. While working at the printing-press he made rapid progress in the knowledge of the Malay and Chinese languages, and developed a faculty of preaching. He was accordingly ordained by Dr. W. Milne [q.v.] and his colleagues at Malacca on 27 April 1819. Of wiry frame, good health, and unfailing cheerfulness, he proved a most efficient missionary. Penang and Batavia were the scene of his earlier efforts. At Parapattan he established an orphan asylum. In 1836 he returned for a while to England. There he wrote his 'China, its State and Prospects,' published in 1838, with the view of stimulating interest in Chinese missions, and especially in a new version of the bible in Chinese, a work which, with the co-operation of friends, he was able to accomplish some years later. It is known as the 'Delegates' Version.' In 1838 he went back to Java. Thence, when the ports of Canton, Shanghai, and three others were opened to British merchants by the treaty of 29 Aug. 1842, he moved to Shanghai, and laboured there for fourteen years. On 10 Sept. 1856 he sailed with his wife and family from

Shanghai to England in order to recruit his health. He landed at Southend on 21 Jan. 1857, and was just able to reach London, where he died on the evening of the 24th. He was buried in Abney Park cemetery on 31 Jan.

Medhurst's works were numerous. They exhibit unceasing activity of mind and a remarkable gift for languages. Besides the works mentioned above, he published in Batavia in 1830 an 'English and Japanese Vocabulary,' and in 1842–3 a 'Chinese and English Dictionary,' in two vols. 8vo; at Shanghai he published in 1844 'Chinese Dialogues,' of which a new and enlarged edition was brought out in 1861 by his son, Walter Henry (afterwards Sir Walter) Medhurst [q. v.], and in 1847 a 'Dissertation on the Theology of the Chinese,' besides many lesser tracts.

The coloured frontispiece to his 'China, its State and Prospects' gives a portrait of him in conversation with Choo-Tih-Lang, attended by a Malay boy.

[Inscription on gravestone (No. 17572) in Abney Park cemetery; Gardiner's Admission Registers of St. Paul's School; obituary notice by the Rev. W. C. Milne in the Evangelical Magazine, September 1857; abstract of the same, with some few additional particulars, in the Congregational Year-Book for 1858, p. 215.] J. H. L.

MEDHURST, Sir WALTER HENRY (1822–1885), British consul in China, the son of Dr. Walter Henry Medhurst [q. v.] the missionary, was born in China in 1822, and in October 1840 entered the office of the Chinese secretary to the British superintendency of trade in China. Early in 1841 he was one of a party sent to inspect the newly acquired Hongkong. In August he was attached to Sir Henry Pottinger's suite, and on the renewal of the war was present at the taking of Amoy and Chusan. His knowledge of Chinese attracted the notice of his chief, and from October 1841 to December 1842 he was interpreter to the garrison at Chusan. He received the war medal for his services in this campaign, and was appointed consular interpreter at Shanghai on 7 Oct. 1843, when the ports were first opened for trade under the treaty. From April 1848 till August 1849 he also acted as vice-consul at Amoy. In August 1850 he became Chinese secretary to the superintendent of trade in China, and was also general secretary and registrar from July 1853 to 9 Nov. 1854, when he was appointed consul at Foo-chow-foo. On 21 Dec. 1858 he was transferred to Tang-chow, though he was temporarily employed in the succeeding years both at Foo-chow-foo and Shanghai. When the war broke out in 1861 he again rendered important services to the British troops, and was mentioned in despatches. On 25 Jan. 1864 he became consul at Hankow, and early in 1868 made an energetic stand there in defence of British treaty rights in conjunction with Captain Heneage of the Rodney. On 23 July 1868 he removed to Shanghai to act as consul, and was confirmed on 24 Jan. 1871. On 1 Jan. 1877 he retired, being presented with a testimonial by the Shanghai community, and on 20 March he was knighted. Medhurst was 'a warrior consul,' but he was distinguished for his command of the Chinese language, and his success with the natives gave him a special position among his countrymen.

In 1881 Medhurst threw himself heartily into the formation of the British North Borneo Company, and in its interest in 1882 returned to the East to organise a system of emigration from China into the company's territories. Accordingly for eighteen months he resided in Hongkong, where he was a frequent contributor to the local press. Having returned to England in 1884, he died at Torquay on 26 Dec. 1885. He was the author of the 'Foreigner in Far Cathay,' London, 1872.

[Foreign Office List, 1885; Times, 30 Dec. 1885; Hongkong Daily Press, 31 Dec. 1885.] C. A. H.

MEDINA, Sir JOHN BAPTIST (1659–1710), portrait-painter, born at Brussels in 1659, was son of Medina de Caustanais, a Spanish officer of good family, who married at Brussels and settled there. Medina studied painting at Brussels under François Du Chatel. He married when young at Brussels Joanna Maria Van Dael. He came to England in 1686, and practised for two years as a portrait-painter in London, but finding a munificent patron in the fifth Earl of Leven, he was induced by that nobleman to go to Scotland, where a subscription of 500*l.* was collected in order to enable him to practise at Edinburgh. According to Vertue (Brit. Mus. Add. MS. 23068, f. 35), Medina went with his large family to Scotland, taking with him 'many postures for heads, the draperys painted—only to put the faces to them, cover'd them over with water-colours.' By this means Medina got through a surprising amount of work in a very short time, and the number of portraits for which he received commissions in Scotland fully entitled him to be known as 'the Kneller of the North.' For the Earl of Leven he painted twenty portraits, including three of his patron.

He executed a number of portraits of fellows of the Royal College of Surgeons at Edinburgh, which still remain in Surgeons' Hall there. Many families in Scotland possess portraits by him, among these being a large picture of the Marquis of Argyll and his two sons, and another of George, first duke of Gordon, with his son and daughter. Medina was knighted in 1707 by the Duke of Queensberry, the lord high commissioner in Scotland, and was the last knight made in Scotland before the Act of Union. Medina, when visiting England, drew the illustrations for the edition of Milton's 'Paradise Lost,' published by Jonson in 1705. He also drew a series of illustrations for Ovid's 'Metamorphoses.' According to Vertue (*loc. cit.* f. 28) Medina had an 'exact design, a clever pencil, and good colouring, he drew and painted historical subjects very well, and had a fine taste in landskip, and would have made a good history painter had he lived where suitable encouragement was to be had.' The excellence of some of Medina's portraits is much disguised by the stiffness of his postures. Medina died at Edinburgh on 5 Oct. 1710, and was buried on the north side of Grey Friars churchyard there. His widow survived him, with two sons and four daughters. A portrait of himself is at Florence, presented by the Duke of Gordon, and another, painted in 1708, is in Surgeons' Hall, Edinburgh (engraved in Pinkerton's 'Scottish Gallery'). Two portraits drawn by him of the Earl of Carnwath and Grinling Gibbons, the sculptor, are in the print room at the British Museum. A picture of two of his children by him is in the collection of the Earl of Wemyss.

His son, John Medina (*d.* 1764), also practised as a portrait-painter, and died in Edinburgh on 1 Dec. 1764. The latter's son, JOHN MEDINA (1721–1796), also followed the same profession. He restored the pictures at Holyrood Palace, and made several copies of the 'Ailsa' portrait of Mary Queen of Scots. He resided in London for a short time, and exhibited portraits at the Royal Academy in 1772 and 1773. He died at Edinburgh on 27 Sept. 1796, in his seventy-sixth year.

[Stirling Maxwell's Annals of the Artists of Spain; Walpole's Anecd. of Painting; Brit. Mus. Add. MSS. 23068 and 23072; Redgrave's Dict. of Artists; information from J. M. Gray, esq.]

L. C.

MEDLAND, THOMAS (*d.* 1833), engraver and draughtsman, resided in London for many years, practising both in the line manner and in aquatint; he excelled in landscape work, and was chiefly employed upon topographical plates. He engraved many of those in Farington's 'Views of the Lakes in Cumberland and Westmoreland,' 1789, and 'Cities and Castles of England,' 1791; Harding's 'Shakspeare Illustrated,' 1793; 'The Copperplate Magazine;' Sir G. Staunton's 'Embassy of the Earl of Macartney to China,' 1797; 'Select Views in London and Westminster,' 1800; and Sir W. Gell's 'Topography of Troy,' 1804. Medland's most successful work was a set of illustrations to 'Robinson Crusoe,' from designs by Stothard, 1790, and his largest plate was 'Evening of the Glorious First of June,' after R. Cleveley Among his aquatints may be noticed the series of nineteen plates of Egyptian monuments in the British Museum, after W. Alexander, 1807, and those in Captain Gold's 'Oriental Drawings,' 1806. Medland also practised water-colour painting, and exhibited views of London at the Royal Academy in 1777 and 1779, and later many transcripts of English scenery. When Haileybury College was founded by the East India Company in 1806, Medland appears to have been appointed drawing-master there, and from that time resided in the neighbourhood of Hertford. He continued to send drawings to the Royal Academy up to 1822. He died at Hertford 30 Oct. 1833 (*Gent. Mag.* 1833, ii. 476).

[Redgrave's Dict. of Artists; Graves's Dict. of Artists, 1760–1880; Universal Cat. of Books on Art.]

F. M. O'D.

MEDLEY, HENRY (*d.* 1747), vice-admiral, entered the navy in 1703; was in 1706 a midshipman of the Somerset with Captain Price at the relief of Barcelona; passed his examination on 8 Feb. 1709–10 (passing certificate); and on 5 Sept. 1710 was promoted by Sir John Norris [q. v.] to be lieutenant of the Fame, from which a few months later he was moved into the Stirling Castle. In 1717 he was a lieutenant of the Barfleur, flagship of Sir George Byng in the Baltic. Early in 1720 he was promoted to the command of the Poole fire-ship, and on 17 Feb. 1720–1 was posted into the York. In 1722, while commanding the Leopard in the Mediterranean, he seized a ship named the Revolution, lying within the mole of Genoa, on information of her being in the service of the pretender. He afterwards commanded the Leopard on the coast of Portugal and in the Channel till the end of 1728. From 1731 to 1735 he was employed on the home station; in 1741 he commanded the Nassau in the Channel fleet under Sir John Norris, and in 1742–3–4 was with Norris as captain of the fleet. On 19 June 1744 he was promoted to be rear-admiral of the white, and in the following winter commanded a squadron cruising in the Soundings for the protection of trade.

On 23 April 1745 he was promoted to be vice-admiral, and sent out as commander-in-chief in the Mediterranean. The service was one of blockade and co-operation with the allied armies, who in the winter of 1746-7, having driven the French out of Italy, invaded Provence; but, after an unsuccessful attack on Antibes, were obliged to retire. On 15 July 1747 Medley was advanced to be vice-admiral of the red, but died, probably in ignorance of his latest promotion, on board the Russell, at Vado, on 5 Aug. 1747. His portrait, by John Ellys, has been engraved by John Faber, junior.

[Charnock's Biog. Nav. iv. 93; commission and warrant books and other documents in the Public Record Office.] J. K. L.

MEDLEY, JOHN (1804–1892), first bishop of Fredericton, New Brunswick, son of George Medley of Grosvenor Place, Chelsea, was born 19 Dec. 1804. He was entered in November 1822 at Wadham College, Oxford, whence he graduated B.A. in 1826 in the second class *in literis humanioribus*. In the same year he was ordained deacon, and priest in 1829. He proceeded M.A. in the following year.

For the first three years of his ministry he was curate of Southleigh, Devonshire; in 1831 he became incumbent of St. John's parish, Truro. In 1838 he was transferred to the vicarage of St. Thomas, Exeter, and in 1842 became a prebendary of Exeter Cathedral. Having proceeded D.D. 15 March 1845, on 4 May he was consecrated to the bishopric of Fredericton, New Brunswick. On 11 June he was installed in the partly built cathedral of that city. He had come to a diocese full of dissension and strife, and he met his difficulties with vigour. In the summer of 1848 he returned to England to raise funds for the completion of his cathedral. In subsequent years he only occasionally left his diocese to attend meetings of the bishops in neighbouring dioceses. On 11 June 1879, as oldest bishop in the Dominion, he became metropolitan of Canada in succession to Bishop Oxenden. In the summer of 1889 he attended the Lambeth Pan-Anglican Conference, and was made an honorary LL.D. of Cambridge and D.D. of Durham. He died on 9 Sept. 1892, aged nearly 88.

He was the author of the 'Episcopal Form of Church Government,' 1835; of two volumes of 'Sermons,' 1845; and of a 'Commentary on the Book of Job,' 1860. With the Rev. H. J. Cornish he translated the 'Homilies of St. John Chrysostom on the Corinthians' (vol. iv. of the 'Library of the Fathers,' Oxford, 1838). He also composed a few anthems.

[Dr. W. Q. Ketchum's Life of Medley, St. John's, N.B., 1893; Toronto Mail, 10 Sept. 1892; Colonial Church Chronicle; Foster's Alumni Oxon.] C. A. H.

MEDLEY, SAMUEL (1738–1799), baptist minister and hymn-writer, second son of Guy Medley (*d.* 25 Oct. 1760), was born at Cheshunt, Hertfordshire, on 23 June 1738. His grandfather, Samuel Medley, had been in the diplomatic service, and accompanied the Earl of Kinnoull's embassy to Constantinople in 1729. His father, Guy, had been tutor to the Duke of Montague, and attorney-general of the Isle of St. Vincent; he subsequently kept a school at Cheshunt; married the youngest daughter of William Tonge, a schoolmaster at Enfield; and was an intimate friend of James Hervey (1714–1758) [q. v.] Medley was educated by Tonge, his maternal grandfather, and at the age of fourteen was apprenticed to an oilman in the city of London. In 1755, however, he obtained his freedom on entering the royal navy, from which he was discharged after being severely wounded in the action off Cape Lagos on 18 Aug. 1759, while serving in Admiral Boscawen's squadron. From 1762 to 1766 he kept a flourishing school in King Street, Soho, and became acquainted with Andrew Gifford [q. v.], assistant-librarian at the British Museum and pastor of the particular baptist church in Eagle Street, Holborn, whose church he joined in December 1760. Gifford led him to enter the baptist ministry. He began preaching on 29 Aug. 1766, and on 6 June 1767 he accepted a call to a congregation at Watford, Hertfordshire, which had been without a minister since 1763. Here he was ordained on 13 July 1768. His ministry was successful, and on 11 Nov. 1771 he was invited to the baptist church in Byrom Street, Liverpool. He first visited Liverpool at the end of December, and began his stated ministry in Byrom Street on 15 April 1772.

Medley's career as a preacher in Liverpool was one of remarkable and increasing popularity. His meeting-house was enlarged in 1773, and in 1789 a new and much larger building was erected for him in the same thoroughfare. His old meeting-house was consecrated in 1792 as St. Stephen's Church. Medley did a valuable work among the seamen of the port of Liverpool. His methods, often adapted to gain the ear of this class, exposed him to the criticism of fastidious persons like Gilbert Wakefield; his daughter collected some of his witticisms. Halley, who ranks him as 'a great preacher,' testifies to his 'liberal and catholic spirit.' His high character and disinterested philanthropy are unquestionable. Adult baptism was not an essential for membership in his church, which became practically congregational. He yearly visited London, preaching at the Surrey Tabernacle and that in Tottenham Court Road. After a painful illness he died on 17 July 1799. He married (17 April 1762) Mary, daughter of William Gill, hosier, of Nottingham. His portrait was painted and engraved by his son Samuel [q. v.], for a volume of 'Memoirs,' published by the latter in 1800.

Two of Medley's sermons are printed with his 'Memoirs' (1800); one was translated into Welsh. His hymns, originally printed on single sheets, and in the 'Gospel Magazine' and other publications, were collected in 1. 'Hymns,' &c., Bradford, 1785. 2. 'Hymns on Select Portions of Scripture,' &c., Bristol, 1785 (this is called 2nd edit., but is a smaller and variant collection; it was enlarged 1787). 3. 'Hymns,' 1794. 4. 'The Public Worship and Private Devotion . . . Assisted . . . in Verse,' &c., 1800. Though Halley calls Medley 'a small poet,' Mr. Stevenson speaks of 'the warmth and occasional pathos' of his hymns, of which he specifies twenty as having gained considerable vogue. His daughter Sarah published a volume of 'Original and Miscellaneous Poems,' Liverpool, 1807, and other poems in Liverpool magazines; also a 'Memoir,' 1833, of her father, with appended hymns, ascribed to him, but many of them altered, and some of them by Thomas Kelly (1769–1854).

[Memoirs by Samuel Medley, his son, 1800; Memoirs of Gilbert Wakefield, 1804, i. 208 sq.; Memoirs by Sarah Medley (his daughter), 1833; Thom's Liverpool Churches and Chapels, 1854, pp. 43 sq.; Halley's Lancashire, 1869, ii. 479 sq.; Urwick's Nonconf. in Herts, 1884, pp. 361, 466; Mr. W. R. Stevenson, in Julian's Dict. of Hymnology, 1892, pp. 112, 722.] A. G.

MEDLEY, SAMUEL (1769–1857), painter and one of the founders of University College, London, born on 22 March 1769, was son of Samuel Medley (1738–1799) [q. v.], the baptist minister. Adopting painting as his profession, he exhibited for the first time at the Royal Academy, in 1792 sending 'The Last Supper.' He painted several religious and historical subjects, but latterly devoted himself chiefly to portraiture, in which he gained considerable practice and reputation. In 1805, however, he found his profession injurious to his health, so he abandoned it, and went on the Stock Exchange, where he made a comfortable income, continuing to paint in his leisure hours. Medley was a member of a large baptist community in London, under the Rev. F. A. Cox, with whom, Lord Brougham, and some leading dissenters of education and position, he was associated in founding University College, London, in 1826. He resided for the latter portion of his life at Chatham, where he died on 10 Aug. 1857, and was buried there. Medley married, first, in 1792 Susannah, daughter of George Bowley of Bishopsgate Street, London; secondly, in 1818, Elizabeth, daughter of John Smallshaw of Liverpool. By his first wife he had three sons, William, Guy, and George, and three daughters, of whom the eldest, Susannah, married Henry Thompson, and was mother of Sir Henry Thompson, the eminent surgeon. A large group of portraits, representing 'The Medical Society of London,' painted by Medley, is in the rooms of that society in Chandos Street, Cavendish Square, London; it has been engraved by C. Branwhite [q. v.] Other portraits by him, including one of his father, are in the possession of Sir Henry Thompson, and show a firm, powerful touch; two of them, representing his children, were exhibited at the winter exhibition, Burlington House, 1887.

[Medley's Memoir of the Rev. S. Medley, 1800; Redgrave's Dict. of Artists; Royal Acad. Catalogues; private information.] L. C.

MEDOWS. [See also Meadows.]

MEDOWS, Sir WILLIAM (1738–1813), general, second son of Philip Medows [see under Meadows, Sir Philip], deputy ranger of Richmond Park, and Lady Frances Pierrepont, daughter of the Duke of Kingston, was born on 31 Dec. 1738. He entered the army as an ensign in the 50th regiment in 1756. In 1760 he went with his regiment to join the allied army under Prince Ferdinand of Brunswick, who as Frederick the Great's lieutenant was defending western Germany against the French. Medows remained in Germany till March 1764. In the December of that year he obtained the lieutenant-colonelcy of the 5th regiment of foot, exchanging in September 1773 into the 12th light dragoons. In 1775 Medows again exchanged into the 55th regiment of foot, which was on the point of starting for America, to act against the revolted colonists. He distinguished himself at the battle of Brandywine in 1776, and in an expedition against Santa Lucia in 1778. He returned to England in 1780, and was now made colonel of the 89th regiment. Medows held a high command in the expedition sent out under Commodore Johnstone against the Cape of Good Hope in 1781. A skirmish occurred with the French admiral, Suffren, in Prava Bay on 16 April 1782, and on arriving at the Cape of Good Hope the English found that Suffren had anticipated them and landed such strong reinforcements that an attack would be useless. Johnstone now decided to return to Europe. Medows, however, having heard that the English in the south of India were being hard pressed by Hyder Ali, sultan of Mysore, sailed with three of the ships and a large body of troops to Madras, where he arrived on 13 Feb. 1783. He accompanied Colonel Fullarton in an expedition from Madras against Mysore, but the sudden conclusion of peace soon put a stop to the campaign. In September 1788 Medows received the post of commander-in-chief and governor at Bombay. He remained here till January 1790, when he was transferred to the supreme command at Madras. A war with Tippoo, Hyder Ali's son and successor as sultan of Mysore, had arisen, and Lord Cornwallis [q. v.], the governor-general, now instructed Medows to open the campaign. Starting from Trichinopoli at the head of fifteen thousand men on 15 June 1790, Medows crossed the frontier into Mysore, and advanced in a westerly direction. Karúr and Darapuram were taken and garrisoned in order to maintain communications with Madras, and on 22 July the army arrived at Coimbatore, which was found evacuated by the enemy. The latter place was made the centre of operations, from which detachments sent out by Medows captured the fortresses of Palghaut and Dindigal, and occupied the positions of Erode and Satyamangalam; the two latter with Karúr covering the road to the Gujelhuttey pass, through which Medows hoped to advance against Seringapatam in October. His forces, however, had been much weakened by being distributed over a large extent of territory, and Tippoo was thus able to fall upon the isolated English detachments in detail. On 13 Sept. Colonel Floyd was attacked at Satyamangalam and compelled to retreat. Erode was abandoned; Darapuram was recaptured by the sultan on 8 Oct., and the English were again compelled to concentrate at Coimbatore. Medows now marched out in strong force with the object of bringing on a pitched battle. But the English moved too slowly to come up with their enemy, and at last Tippoo, having outmanœuvred his opponent, crossed into English territory and laid siege to Trichinopoli, the neighbourhood of which was remorselessly ravaged. Medows hurried up to defend the city, which he reached on 14 Dec., and Tippoo now retired to his own country by the north. Medows returned to Madras. Four of the border fortresses of Mysore still remained in English hands; but their campaign had on the whole been a failure. Lord Cornwallis now announced his intention of undertaking sole command of the English army in Mysore. Medows went through the campaigns of 1791–2, but in a strictly subordinate character, and in the planning of operations he had no share. He led the storming party which captured Nandidrug on 19 Oct. 1791, and he commanded the right column in the night attack on the Seringapatam redoubts on 16 Feb. 1792. The latter event was followed by peace. Medows resigned the prize-money (nearly 15,000*l.*) which fell to his share and distributed it among the troops. He left for England in August 1792. On 14 Dec. of that year he was made a knight of the Bath, on 12 Oct. 1793 he was made a lieutenant-general, and in November 1796 he was appointed to the command of the 7th dragoon guards. At the brevet promotion of 1 Jan. 1798 he was made a general and received the post of governor of the Isle of Wight. In 1801 he succeeded Cornwallis for a short space as commander-in-chief in Ireland. He died at Bath on 14 Nov. 1813.

[Philippart's East India Military Calendar; Wilks's History of Mysore; Mill's History of British India; Dodwell and Miles's Alphabetical Lists of East India Company's Civil Servants; Army Lists, passim: Burke's Peerage; Cornwallis Correspondence.] G. P. M-y.

MEDWALL, HENRY (*fl.* 1486), writer of interludes, was chaplain to John Morton [q. v.], who was raised to the see of Canterbury in 1486. The only work of his extant is 'Nature: a goodly interlude of Nature cõpylyd by mayster Henry Medwall, chapleyn to the ryght reverend father in god Johan Morton, somtyme cardynall and archebyshop of Canterbury,' b. l. folio, 36 leaves. It is without date, place, or printer's name, but was probably printed between 1510 and 1520 by John Rastell, the supposed author of the interlude entitled 'The Nature of the Four Elements.' In the British Museum copy, from the Garrick collection, are bound up two duplicate leaves (c. i. and ii.) 'Nature' was produced before Morton in Henry VII's reign, and is thus one of the most ancient of our moralities or moral plays. Bale states that it was translated into Latin. Another interlude not now extant, but ascribed to Medwall, 'Of the Finding of Truth, carried away by Ignorance and Hypocrisy,' was diversified by the introduction of a fool, an innovation which commended it to Henry VIII when it was produced before him at Richmond, Christmas 1516. Apart from this feature the piece was misliked, and the king 'departyd before the end to hys chambre.'

[Collier's Dramatic Poetry, i. 69, ii. 217–24; Warton's Hist. of Poetry, ed. Hazlitt, iii. 189, 292; Ames's Typograph. Antiq. ed. Herbert; Tanner, Bibl. Brit. s.v. Medwallus.] T. S.

MEDWIN, THOMAS (1788–1869), biographer of Shelley, and author of a journal of the 'Conversations of Lord Byron,' was born at Horsham, 20 March 1788 (parish register). He was third son of Thomas Charles Medwin, of a good Sussex family, by Mary, daughter of John Pilfold, and first cousin to Elizabeth Pilfold, the mother of Percy Bysshe Shelley. Medwin was educated at Sion House, Brentford, whither Shelley followed him, and as boys they spent most of their vacations together at Horsham. Medwin entered the army early in life, and on 16 Sept. 1813 became a lieutenant in the 24th dragoon guards. Later on he went with his regiment to India, where he had numerous adventures, probably the basis, more or less slight, of those afterwards described in 'The Angler in Wales.' About this time he published anonymously two short poems, called 'The Pindarries' and 'Sketches in Hindoostan,' but they attracted no notice. From 25 July 1819 he remained for several years on half-pay, with the rank of captain, and, after having apparently served in the 1st life-guards (title-page to *Angler in Wales*) finally quitted the service.

In the autumn of 1821 he went to Italy for his health, and joined the party of literary Englishmen then living in Tuscany. At Pisa Shelley introduced him as his cousin and schoolfellow to Byron [q. v.], who had hired the Palazzo Lanfranchi. Medwin stayed at Pisa from 20 Nov. 1821 until 15 March 1822, and, after a visit to Rome, again from 18 until 28 of the following August, during which time he was constantly in Byron's society and took notes of his talk. On Byron's death in 1824 Medwin, who was then in Switzerland, published a 'Journal of the Conversations of Lord Byron,' and the book excited great interest, being republished in Paris and New York, and translated into French and German before the end of the year. At home it created considerable controversy, especially over the statements made therein in regard to Lady Byron (see article and letter by 'Harroviensis' in *Blackwood's Magazine*, xvi. 530–40), some impugning Medwin's veracity or his recollection, others holding that Byron, with his love of half mystifying confidences, had deliberately misled him (see Moore, *Life*, 1822, æt. 34; and Professor Wilson in *Noctes Ambrosianæ*, xvii. November 1824). Byron's friend, Hobhouse, wrote a pamphlet contradicting some of Medwin's statements. Southey, who had fiercely attacked 'Don Juan' in his 'Vision of Judgment,' and had been roughly handled in the 'Journal,' treated Medwin as an authentic chronicler, and, denouncing the 'impudent lies' in the volume, declared the liar to be Byron, 'and not his blunderbuss, who had only let off what it was charged with' (see Southey, *Correspondence with Catherine Bowles*, edited by Dowden, p. 76; also Southey's letter to the *Courier*, dated Keswick, 8 Dec. 1824).

In 1823 Medwin had brought out a dramatic poem on the subject of the 'Wandering Jew,' published anonymously in London. He spent much of his time travelling on the continent, and in 1825 married, in Italy, Anne, baroness Hamilton of Sweden, by her first marriage Countess of Stainfort or Starnford. By her he had two daughters, who were born in Florence, and afterwards married to Italian noblemen. He soon fell into debt, deserted his wife, and led an unsettled life. But he continued his literary work, and in 1833 wrote a memoir of Shelley, afterwards expanded into a life of the poet. He also made himself a fair classical scholar, and translated the 'Agamemnon' into English verse. He moved about for some time between England and the continent, engaged in various literary schemes, and contributed to the 'Athenæum' and other periodicals. After spending some twenty years in retirement at Heidelberg he returned to Horsham, where he died in his brother's house in the Carfax, on 2 Aug. 1869. His wife, who was born in London on 26 Feb. 1788, died in Siena on 28 June 1868.

His published works are: 1. 'The Pindarries,' a poem, afterwards affixed to the 'Angler in Wales.' 2. 'Sketches in Hindoostan, and other poems.' 3. 'Ahasuerus the Wanderer,' a dramatic legend in six parts, London, 1823. 4. 'Journal of the Conversations of Lord Byron, noted during a residence with his Lordship at Pisa in the years 1821 and 1822,' London, 1824. 5. 'The Agamemnon of Æschylus, translated into English verse,' London, 1832. 6. 'A Memoir of Percy Bysshe Shelley,' published in the 'Shelley Papers,' London, 1833. 7. 'The Angler in Wales, or Days and Nights of Sportsmen,' 2 vols. London, 1834. 8. 'Lady Singleton, or the World as it is,' a novel in 3 vols. London, 1843. 9. 'The Life of Percy Bysshe Shelley,' 2 vols. London, 1847.

[The authorities for Medwin's life are very meagre; Albery's Monthly Illustrated Horsham Journal, September 1869; Horsham Express, 10 Aug. 1869; Dallaway's Hist. of the Western Division of Sussex, edited by Cartwright, vol. ii. pt. ii. p. 368 (obviously wrong as to date of birth); Notes and Queries, 5th ser. v. 161, and 6th ser. vi. 293; Army Lists, 1816, 1820; Brit. Mus. Cat.] T. B. S.

MEDWYN, Lord. [See Forbes, John Hay, 1776–1854, Scottish judge.]

MEE, ANNE (1775?–1851), miniature painter, eldest child of John Foldsone [q. v.], was educated at Madame Pomier's school in Queen Square, Bloomsbury, where she gave early proofs of artistic talent. She began to practise when very young, and her father dying prematurely, she became the sole support of her family. Miss Foldsone received much royal and aristocratic patronage; and Walpole, in his letters to Miss Berry of 1790 and 1791, mentions that she is at Windsor, 'painting portraits of all the princesses to be sent to all the princes upon earth,' and complains that she will not complete commissions for which she has been paid, having (as he has discovered) a mother and eight brothers and sisters to maintain. She married Joseph Mee, a man who 'pretended to both family and fortune, without being possessed of either' (Edwards, *Anecdotes of Painting*, p. 110). The prince regent gave Mrs. Mee much employment in painting portraits of fashionable beauties, and many of these are now at Windsor. Some of her portraits were engraved in the 'Court Magazine,' 'La Belle Assemblée,' and similar periodicals, and in 1812 she commenced a serial publication, 'Gallery of Beauties of the Court of George III,' with her own portrait prefixed, but only a single number was issued. Mrs. Mee exhibited occasionally at the Royal Academy between 1815 and 1837. She died at Hammersmith, 28 May 1851, aged, according to the 'Gentleman's Magazine,' 76, but more probably over 80.

Mrs. Mee's early miniatures are well drawn and executed, but those of her later time, which are on a comparatively large scale, are meretricious in character and of poor quality. A memoir of her, with a portrait engraved by H. R. Cook, appeared in the 'Lady's Monthly Museum,' January 1814. She had a son, A. P. Mee, who practised as an architect, and exhibited at the Royal Academy from 1824 to 1837.

[Redgrave's Dict. of Artists; Graves's Dict. of Artists, 1760–1880; Clayton's English Female Artists, 1876; Gent. Mag. 1851, ii. 202; Notes and Queries, 3rd ser. viii. 289, 424, and 7th ser. v. 368, 494; Correspondence of Horace Walpole, ed. Cunningham, vol. ix.] F. M. O'D.

MEEHAN, CHARLES PATRICK (1812–1890), author and translator, was born at 141 Great Britain Street, Dublin, on 12 July 1812. He received his early education at Ballymahon, co. Longford, the native place of his parents. In 1828 he went to the Irish Catholic College, Rome, where he studied till he was ordained priest in 1834. Returning to Dublin in the same year he was appointed to a curacy at Rathdrum, co. Wicklow. After nine months he was transferred to a curacy at the parish church of Saints Michael and John, Dublin. In that position he continued till his death, which took place on 14 March 1890. Verses by Meehan appeared in the Dublin 'Nation' newspaper under the pseudonym of 'Clericus,' and he wrote many articles in Roman catholic periodicals, some of which were amplified and republished. He was a member of the Royal Irish Academy. Most of Meehan's productions were in connection with Irish and Roman catholic subjects, and intended for popular reading. They principally consisted of translations and historical compilations. His translations included the following: 'History of the Geraldines, Earls of Desmond,' from the Latin of O'Daly [see Daly or O'Daly, Daniel or Dominic], 1847; Manzoni's 'La Monaca di Monza,' a continuation of the 'Promessi Sposi,' 1847; 'Life of Francis Kirwan, Bishop of Killala,' from the Latin of Lynch, 1848; 'Lives of the most Eminent Sculptors and Architects of the Order of Saint Dominic,' from the Italian of Marchese, 2 vols. 1852. Meehan's chief compilations were as follows: 1. 'History of the Confederation of Kilkenny,' 12mo, 1846. 2. 'Rise and Fall of Irish Franciscan Monasteries, and Memoirs of the Irish Hierarchy in the Seventeenth Century,' 1869. 3. 'Fate and Fortunes of Hugh O'Neill, Earl of Tyrone, and Rory O'Donel, Earl of Tyrconnel,' 1870. Of most of these works, all of which appeared at Dublin, cheap editions were published there from time to time, but generally without dates. Meehan edited in 1883 and 1884 Davies's 'Essays,' James's Clarence Mangan's essays and poems, 'Anthologia Germanica,' and translations of Irish songs by Munster authors. He also re-edited Madden's 'Literary Remains of the United Irishmen,' 1887.

[Personal information; Irish Monthly, 1889; Catholic World, September 1890; notes supplied by P. A. Sillard, esq., of Dublin.] J. T. G.

MEEK, Sir JAMES (1778–1856), public servant, born in 1778, entered the public service in the commissariat department in 1798, and was employed by Lord Keith in collecting supplies in Sicily for the Egyptian expedition of 1800. He was afterwards secretary to several flag-officers on the Mediterranean station, and in 1830 was appointed comptroller of the victualling and transport services at the admiralty.

In 1841 he was employed by government to collect information of the cost and supply of agricultural produce at various ports in the north of Europe. His report was printed by command of parliament in the following year, and formed part of the material upon which Sir Robert Peel based his free-trade measure of 1846.

On his retirement from the public service Meek received the honour of knighthood, 3 Feb. 1851. He died at his residence, Ilfracombe, Devonshire, of which county he was in the commission of the peace, on 18 May 1856.

Meek married twice: first, a daughter of Edward Brown, lieutenant R.N.; secondly, in 1852 a daughter of Dr. Grant of Jamaica.

[Royal Kalendar, 1831, 1851; London Gazette, 3 Feb. 1851; Ann. Reg. 1856, App. p. 256; Gent. Mag. 1856, ii. 245; Parl. Papers, H. C., 1842, vol. xl. No. 7.] J. M. R.

MEEKE, Mrs. MARY (*d.* 1816?), novelist, seems to have been the wife of the Rev. Francis Meeke (B.A. Christ's College, Cambridge, 1773, and M.A. 1776), who published a volume of poems in 1782 (*Notes and Queries*, 3rd ser. ii. 229). She began her prolific career as a novelist in 1795, when she published 'Count St. Blancard,' in 3 vols., and continued her labours for more than twenty years. In October 1816 there died at Johnson Hall, Staffordshire, Mary, widow of the Rev. Francis Meeke, who may perhaps be identified with the novelist.

Mrs. Meeke naïvely recommends novelists, before planning a work, to consult their publisher as to how they may best satisfy the prevailing public taste (*Midnight Weddings*, pref.) Personally, she apparently followed this plan with some success. Although her plots are commonplace, and her literary style poor, and her characters only faintly reflect contemporary manners, she had some distinguished readers. Macaulay 'all but knew,' Lady Trevelyan writes, 'Mrs. Meeke's romances by heart,' but, despite his liking for them, he relegated Mrs. Meeke to the position of his favourite among the bad novel-writers, and agreed in his sister's criticism 'that they were one just like another, turning on the fortunes of some young man in a very low rank of life who eventually proves to be the son of a duke' (Trevelyan, *Life of Macaulay*, vol. i.) Miss Mitford was also a reader of Mrs. Meeke's works in her youth, and in her old age re-read at least six of them (*Notes and Queries*, 7th ser. xii. 405).

The titles of the novels published under her own name (all in 3 vols., unless otherwise stated) are: 1. 'Count St. Blancard, or the Prejudiced Judge,' 1795. 2. 'The Abbey of Clugny,' 1795. 3. 'Palmira and Ermance,' 1797. 4. 'Ellesmere,' 1799. 5. 'Which is the Man?' 4 vols. 1801. 6. 'Midnight Weddings,' 1802. 7. 'A Tale of Mystery, or Selina,' 1803. 8. 'Amazement!' 9. 'The Old Wife and Young Husband.' 10. 'Murray House.' 11. 'The Nine Days' Wonder,' 1804. 12. 'Ellen, Heiress of the Castle,' 1807. 13. 'Matrimony the Height of Bliss or Extreme of Misery,' 4 vols. 1811. 14. 'Conscience,' 4 vols. 1814. 15. 'Spanish Campaigns, or the Jew,' 1815. Probably posthumously published were: 16. 'The Veiled Protectress, or the Mysterious Mother,' 1818; another edition, 1819. 17. 'What shall be, shall be,' 1823.

Mrs. Meeke also translated from the French: 'Lobenstein Village,' by Augustus La Fontaine, 4 vols. 1804; 'Julian, or My Father's House,' by Ducray Dumenil, 4 vols. 1807; 'The Unpublished Correspondence of Madame du Deffand,' 1810, 2 vols.; 'Elizabeth, or the Exiles of Siberia,' by Madame de Cottin, 1817. In 1811 she completed the translation by Mrs. Collyer [q. v.] of Klopstock's 'Messiah' (another ed. 1821).

Mrs. Meeke has been identified with the writer who assumed the pseudonym of Gabrielli (*Notes and Queries*, 2nd ser. i. 133) and published: 'The Mysterious Wife,' 1797; 'The Mysterious Husband;' 'Harcourt,' 1799; 'Independence,' 1802; 'Something Odd,' 1804; 'Something Strange,' 1806; 'Laughton Priory,' 1809; and 'Stratagems Defeated,' 1811; all in four volumes excepting 'Something Odd,' which was in three. Miss Mitford assigned to her 'Anecdotes of the Altamont Family.'

[Watt's Bibl. Brit.; Biog. Dict. of Living Authors, 1816.] E. L.

MEEN, HENRY (*d.* 1817), classical scholar, a native of Norfolk, was entered as a sizar at Emmanuel College, Cambridge, on 9 Oct. 1761, and graduated B.A. 1766, M.A. 1769, and B.D. 1776. He became a fellow of his college (cf. *Hist. MSS. Comm.* 10th Rep. App. pt. iv. p. 28). Having been ordained in the English church, he was appointed to a minor canonry in St. Paul's Cathedral; instituted to the rectory of St. Nicholas Cole Abbey, with St. Nicholas Olave, London, on 30 April 1792; and collated on 13 Nov. 1795 as prebendary of Twyford in St. Paul's Cathedral, where he also held the office of lecturer. He obtained no other preferment, and these posts left him ample time for literary pursuits. He died at the rectory, Bread Street Hill, London, 3 Jan. 1817, aged 72. The title of 'Little Meen' was applied to him by George Steevens, who described him as 'confused and irregular in all his undertakings,' possessing much learning but lacking method and constancy of application, so that he was 'always employed without doing anything.'

Meen published, while an undergraduate, a poem in blank verse, called 'Happiness, a Poetical Essay,' London, 1766, which he afterwards wished his friends to forget. In 1780 he 'revised, corrected, and completed, as coadjutor and editor,' the unfinished translation of Apollonius Rhodius, by the Rev. Francis Fawkes [q. v.], and superintended its publication for the widow's benefit. To it he annexed his own independent version of the 'Rape of Helen, or the Origin of the Trojan War,' by Coluthus, which was afterwards included in the 'Works of the Greek and Roman Poets' (vol. v.), the 'British Poets' (vol. lxxxviii.), and in the collections of Anderson (vol. xiii.) and of Chalmers (vol. xx.) His other works were 'A Sermon before the Association of Volunteers,' 1782; 'Remarks on the Cassandra of Lycophron,' 1800, and 'Succisivæ Operæ, or Selections from Ancient Writers, with Translations and Notes,' 1815. Gilbert Wakefield describes him as 'pacific, gentle, unassuming,' and speaks of him in his 'Correspondence with Charles James Fox,' p. 177, as having studied the writings of Lycophron more than any man living. When Meen told Dr. Parr that he purposed undertaking an edition of Lycophron's works, Parr severely remarked that 'many books have been well edited by men who were no scholars.' His criticisms on Lycophron appeared in the 'European Magazine' from 1796 to 1813, but his complete translation was never published, and was sold with his books and manuscripts by Sotheby on 17 March 1817 and four following days. He corrected the proofs of Bishop Percy's 'Blank Verse before Milton,' a work which was destroyed in the fire at the printing-office of Messrs. Nichols, and was employed to collect and pass through the press a volume of poems, entitled 'Alonzo and Cora,' by Mrs. Elizabeth Scot of Edinburgh, which came out in 1801. J. P. Malcolm, when engaged in compiling the 'Londinium Redivivum,' obtained through Meen permission to consult the archives of St. Paul's Cathedral. Many letters from him to Bishop Percy are in Nichols's 'Illustrations of Literature' (vii. 38–68).

[Gent. Mag. 1817, pt. i. pp. 86–7; Le Neve's Fasti, ii. 443; Barker's Parriana, vol. i. p. xxxi, and ii. 636–7; Nichols's Illustr. of Literature, vii. 6–68; Malcolm's Lond. Redivivum, vol. i. Pref. pp. ii, iv, 546–8; information from the Rev. Dr. Phear Emmanuel Coll. Cambr.] W. P. C.

MEESON, ALFRED (1808–1885), architect and surveyor, son of Edward Meeson and Elizabeth Collins, his wife, was born on 4 April 1808 at 67 Aldermanbury, London. He was educated in London, and spent the earlier part of his life in private practice as architect and surveyor in Wakefield, Yorkshire. In 1842 he came to London at the request of Sir Charles Barry [q. v.], to superintend the constructional and engineering details of the new houses of parliament, and continued to act as Barry's confidential assistant until the completion of the work. In 1853 he was appointed engineer in charge of the houses of parliament, with a residence in the building. On the abolition of that post he continued in private practice at 58 Pall Mall. Meeson had a great reputation as a surveyor and consulting engineer, and was employed on the international exhibitions of 1851 and 1862, and on the erection of Covent Garden Theatre, the Albert Hall, and other important public works. He was architect to the first Alexandra Palace on Muswell Hill, and on its destruction by fire was joint architect of the new building. Meeson died unmarried on 12 Jan. 1885, at 4 Harley Road, South Hampstead, London.

[Private information.] L. C.

MEETKERKE, EDWARD (1590–1657), divine, born in St. Botolph, Aldersgate, and baptised in the Dutch Church, Austin Friars, London, on 29 Sept. 1590 (*Registers*, ed. Moens, p. 49), was only son of Sir Adolphus van Meetkerke (1528–1591) of Brussels, ambassador to England from the States-General, by his second wife, Margaret (1549–1594), daughter of John Lichtervelde of Flanders (Berry, *Genealogies*, 'Hertfordshire,' p. 190). He was educated on the foundation at Westminster School, whence he was elected to Christ Church, Oxford, in 1606, and matriculated on 16 Jan. 1606–7 (Foster, *Alumni Oxon.* 1500–1714, iii. 999). He graduated B.A. in 1610, was chosen student, and became 'a most careful tutor' in his college. In 1613 he proceeded M.A., was incorporated M.A. at Cambridge in 1617, and received the B.D. degree at Oxford with license to preach on 19 June 1620. He became D.D. on 26 May 1625. Meetkerke was elected to the regius professorship of Hebrew at Oxford on 8 Nov. 1620 (Le Neve, *Fasti*, iii. 514). He resigned it in 1626 upon being presented to the well-endowed rectory of Easton, Hampshire. On 9 Jan. 1631 he was installed prebendary of Winchester (*ib.* iii. 36). Under the parliament he was deprived of his stall and retired to his rectory, where he died in August 1657, and was buried in the middle of the chancel of the church. Having inherited his father's estate and bought property in Hampshire, he died comparatively rich (cf. his will registered in P. C. C. 322, Ruthen). By his wife Barbara, daughter of the Rev. Dr. More, who survived him, he had a son, Adolf (1628–1664), M.A. of Christ Church, Oxford, and a daughter, Frances, married to Nathaniel Naper or Napier.

There are some poems by Meetkerke in the Oxford collections of 1619 on the death of Anne, queen of James I, and of 1625 on the death of James himself and on the marriage of Charles I. The first-mentioned poem is in Latin; the two latter are in Hebrew.

[Welch's Alumni Westmon. 1852, p. 75; Wood's Fasti Oxon. ed. Bliss, i. 423; Burke's Landed Gentry, 5th ed.; Clutterbuck's Hertfordshire, iii. 572; Cussans's Hertfordshire, 'Odsey Hundred,' p. 166.] G. G.

MEGGOT or **MEGGOTT, RICHARD** (*d.* 1692), dean of Winchester, was a native of Surrey. He was admitted as a pensioner to Queens' College, Cambridge, on 4 March 1650, and graduated B.A. in 1653, M.A. in 1657, and D.D. in 1669. From 17 Nov. 1668 to 1686 he was vicar of Twickenham, being at the same time rector of St. Olave's, Southwark. He was appointed canon of Windsor on 18 July 1677, and on 9 Oct. 1679 he was installed dean of Winchester. As chaplain in ordinary he preached several times before the court at Whitehall, Hampton Court, and Windsor. James II, when at Winchester in September 1685, 'lodged at the dean's (Dr. Meggot)' (Evelyn, *Diary*, ii. 233). Evelyn heard several sermons by Meggot, and especially commends one preached on 7 March 1684 as an 'incomparable sermon . . . on Hebrews xii. 15' (*ib.* ii. 195, cf. ii. 7, 256, 262). He seems to have passed much of his time in London, and to have been on bad terms with the canons at Winchester.

Meggot died on 7 Dec. 1692, and was buried in Windsor Chapel. In the funeral sermon preached on him by Dean Sherlock at Twickenham on 10 Dec. 1692 the preacher said of Meggot: 'He was abundantly furnished with all good learning, both for use and ornament. . . . He had true and clear notions of religion, and he was master of them. He knew why he believed anything, and was neither prejudiced nor imposed on by popular opinions. . . . He was an admirable preacher, not for noise and lungs, but for well-digested, useful, pious discourses, delivered with all that becoming gravity, seriousness, and a commanding elocution, as made them sink deep into the minds of his hearers.' Ten of Meggot's sermons were printed together in 1699. Several of his letters are in Winchester Cathedral library.

Kneller twice painted Meggot's portrait. In one case it was engraved by White, in the other by Loggan. The latter engraving is described as 'fine and very rare.'

[Granger's Biog. Hist. of England, iii. 258; Wilford's Memorials of Eminent Persons, p. 277; Le Neve's Fasti Eccles. Angl. iii. 22, 404; Luard's Grad. Cant. abridged, 1659–1823; Newcourt's Repert. Eccl. Lond. i. 758; Lysons's Environs of London, iii. 585; Wood's Athenæ Oxon. (Bliss), iii. 899, note, iv. 832; Brit. Mus. Cat.; Evans's Cat. Engraved Portraits, pp. 229, 276; information from Queens' College, Cambridge, and from the Dean of Winchester.] G. Le G. N.

MEGGOTT, JOHN (1714–1789), miser. [See Elwes.]

MEIDEL, CHRISTOPHER (*fl.* 1687–1708), quaker, a Norwegian by birth, was educated at Copenhagen. He came to England about 1683 as chaplain to Prince George of Denmark (Bevan), and was appointed minister of the Danish congregation in Wellclose Square, Ratcliffe, in 1687. He was soon troubled in his conscience by the fact that he 'administered the sacrament to persons who were no way bettered thereby,' and consequently he relinquished the charge. About 1696, he began preaching to an independent congregation in Nightingale Lane, East Smithfield, but after holding the post for some years he grew confirmed in his doubts, and eventually joined the quakers (Bevan says about 1699). At the time, he was living at Stratford, and supported his family by manual labour. On 24 Feb. 1701, Meidel took part in a notable dispute at Green's Coffeehouse, Finch Lane, between Benjamin Keach [q. v.], a baptist, and Richard Claridge [q. v.] In November he accompanied Claridge on a series of meetings in Hertfordshire and Buckinghamshire. In September 1705, they attended the burial of a quakeress, which took place in Barking churchyard (by direction of her son), and they protested that she, being unbaptised, or excommunicate, had no need of ceremonies. Meidel addressed a large crowd over her grave, but the vicar's son thrust him out of the churchyard. He again spoke to many hundreds 'by the sign-post of the Anchor and Crow.' The same year Meidel issued 'An Address to my Neighbours and others in and about Stratford, near Bow, Essex, assembled to dance on the 1st of the 3rd month, called Mayday.'

Meidel was soon afterwards imprisoned. On 4 July 1706 he wrote from Chelmsford gaol 'An Address to the Danish and Norwegian Lutheran Church in London.' This is printed in a Danish translation by himself in his Danish rendering of W. Dell's 'Treatise on Baptism,' London, 1706. An English version appeared in 'The Irish Friend.' In it he gives his reasons for joining the society, and takes affectionate leave of his former congregation.

Meidel became a quaker minister, and about 1708 visited Friedrickstadt and other towns in Holstein, where the Friends were suffering persecution. In travelling through France he was arrested, detained at Pont and St. Lys, and finally carried to Paris. There he was brought through the streets chained to other prisoners, and preached repentance to the people standing by, who freely offered him money, which he refused. On 22 Aug. 1708 he wrote to William Sewel [q. v.] from the Grand Châtelet, asking for money to be remitted.

Meidel seems to have died abroad, as the registers at Devonshire House contain no record of his death.

Besides the above translations, Meidel also published both French and Danish versions of Penn's 'Key Opening a Way . . . to Discern the Difference,' &c., in 1701 and 1705 respectively. Of his Danish translation of Barclay's 'Apology,' the Meeting for Sufferings, in a minute, 11 Jan. 1717, ordered five hundred copies to be printed. The earliest edition known is 1738. It was reprinted at Stavanger, 1848. 'Directions to collect matter for a general History of the Progress of Truth in our Age,' fol., 1706, and 'A Preface to the Reader,' inserted in the third part of 'Piety Promoted, in a collection of the dying sayings of many of the people called quakers,' by John Tomkins [q. v.], 1706, 12mo, are also by Meidel.

[Piety Promoted, pt. x. 2nd edit. by J. G. Bevan, 1811, pp. iii–vii.; Journal of Thomas Story, Newcastle, 1747, p. 496; The Irish Friend, Belfast, 1837, No. 5, ii. 36; Smith's Cat. i. 184, ii. 172.] C. F. S.

MEIKLE, ANDREW (1719–1811), millwright and inventor of the thrashing-machine, born in 1719, was son of James Meikle, who went to Holland on behalf of Andrew Fletcher of Salton to gain a knowledge of the art of making pot barley [see Fletcher, Andrew, 1655–1716]. Andrew established himself as a millwright at Houston Mill, near Dunbar, and in 1768, in conjunction with Robert Mackell, obtained a patent (No. 896) for a machine for dressing grain.

Meikle's chief invention was the well-known drum thrashing-machine, which cannot be dated earlier than 1784. Six years before that date he had, however, constructed a completely different thrashing-machine, which seems to have been identical with one patented in 1734 by Michael Menzies [q. v.] A trial of Meikle's first machine took place in February 1778 before a number of farmers in the neighbourhood, who appended their names to a report printed in Wight's 'Present State of Agriculture in Scotland,' ii. 491. Among them was George Rennie of Phantassie, East Lothian, father of John Rennie [q. v.], the engineer, who served an apprenticeship to Meikle. The machine was not successful, and nothing more is heard of it.

About 1784 Francis Kinloch, a gentleman farmer of Gilmerton, East Lothian, while travelling in Northumberland, saw a thrashing-machine at Wark, and on returning home he caused a model to be made. After repeated trials, all of which were unsuccessful, it was sent in 1784 to Meikle's shop, where it was tried at a high velocity and again failed, the machine being destroyed in the experiment. Meikle saw where the fault lay, and conceived the idea of a drum strong enough to run at a great speed, armed with fixed scutchers or beaters, which should beat and not rub out the grain, as the previous machines had done. Kinloch also used a drum, but made in a different way, and a controversy respecting Meikle's indebtedness to Kinloch followed (cf. *Farmers' Magazine*, Edinburgh, December 1811, p. 483; John Shirreff, *Reply to an Address to the Public . . . on . . . the Thrashing-Machine*). It has also been alleged that Meikle only adapted the well-known flax-scutching mill for the purpose of thrashing grain, and it is not unimportant to point out that the words 'scutchers' and 'scutching' are used throughout his specification. J. A. Ransome (*Implements of Agriculture*, p. 146) gives a series of diagrams showing the exact form of the 'beaters,' as they are now called, upon which the efficiency of Meikle's machine depends.

Meikle communicated his ideas to his second son, George, then residing at Alloa, who in February 1786 completed a machine for Mr. Stein, a large distiller and farmer at Kilbeggie, Clackmannanshire. In the following year Andrew Meikle made a machine to be worked by horses for George Rennie. He took out a patent for the invention in 1788 (No. 1645), but it was for England only, no application being made for a Scottish patent, because he had destroyed his right to a valid patent for Scotland by publicly using his invention before making his application. He seems to have commenced the manufacture of thrashing-machines as a business in 1789 (see his advertisement in the *Scots Magazine* for May 1789, p. 211). 'In all its essential parts, and in the principle of its construction, it remains as it came from the hands of its inventor' (Low, *Elements of Practical Agriculture*, 4th edition, p. 188).

A humorous poem in the form of a dialogue between the flail and the thrashing-machine was written and circulated about 1787. The following is a specimen:—

When round my axletree I reel,
Wi' men, wind, nout, or water-wheel,
In twenty minutes, or I'm a deil,
I'll clean mair strae
Than you, if ye will thrash it weel,
In a hail day.

'Nout' is 'neat,' or cattle. The entire poem is printed in the 'Farmers' Magazine,' 1810, xi. 53.

He does not seem to have derived much pecuniary benefit from his invention. In 1809 a subscription for his relief was started by Sir John Sinclair and others, and upwards of 1,500*l.* was raised. A list of the subscriptions is given in the 'Farmers' Magazine' for December 1810, pp. 465, 520, and it appears that only 85*l.* was given in England, of which 21*l.* was subscribed by two of his friends, James Watt and John Rennie.

Meikle was also the inventor of a method of rapidly furling the sails of windmills to prevent damage by sudden squalls (see Brown, *General View of the Agriculture of York*, 1799, p. 61). In Smeaton's 'Reports' (ii. 421) there is a reference to Meikle's proposals for improving the mills at Dalry, near Edinburgh.

He died at Houston Mill on 27 Nov. 1811, aged 92, and was buried in the churchyard at Prestonkirk, near Dunbar, where there is a tombstone to his memory. A copy of the inscription is given by Smiles (*Scots Magazine*, January 1812, p. 79; *Farmers' Magazine*, 1811, xii. 566).

George Meikle (*d.* 1811), son of Andrew, was also a millwright. Besides assisting his father in working out the details of the thrashing-machine he invented a water-raising wheel, which was used in draining the moss of Kincardine in 1787, being adopted in preference to Whitworth's pumping-machine (*Farmers' Magazine*, 1817, xviii. 265). He died on 29 Nov. 1811 (*Scots Magazine*, January 1812, p. 79; *Farmers' Magazine*, 1811, xii. 566).

[Authorities cited; Smiles's Lives of the Engineers, 'Rennie and Smeaton,' ed. 1874, p. 199; Sir John Sinclair's General Report on the Agriculture of Scotland, 1814, i. 228, 400; Correspondence of Sir John Sinclair, i. 414; R. Somerville's Agriculture of East Lothian, 1813, p. 294; John Bailey and George Culley's Agriculture of Northumberland, 1794, p. 48; Notes on the History of the Thrashing Machine in Farmers' Magazine (Edinburgh), iii. 428, iv. 128.] R. B. P.

MEIKLE, JAMES (1730–1799), surgeon and devotional writer, born at Carnwath, in the upper part of Clydesdale, 19 May 1730, was fifth child of George Meikle, a surgeon and druggist of humble means. James, a delicate boy, received little regular education; but he was religiously brought up by his parents, and when about sixteen years old joined the 'Secession,' a body which had separated from the established kirk of Scotland in 1732. A wish to study at Edinburgh for the ministry remained unfulfilled owing to his poverty and the death of his father in February 1748, which left his mother and two sisters dependent on his exertions. He managed to attend some medical lectures at Edinburgh, and returned to Carnwath in 1750, intending as a temporary expedient to practise as a surgeon. But his difficulties grew, and in December 1757 he resolved on entering the royal navy. After passing at Surgeons' Hall in London he was appointed second surgeon's mate to the Portland, a 50-gun ship, in April 1758. Although he was distressed by the abandoned conduct both of the officers and the crew, they grew to respect him. He employed himself much in reading and writing; many of the 'Meditations,' which afterwards appeared in 'The Traveller' and in 'Solitude Sweetened,' being composed at this time. After cruising about on the western coast of France and in the Mediterranean, the Portland was ordered to join the fleet under Admiral Boscawen, and took part in the victory off Cape Lagos, 18 Aug. 1759. His ship being ordered home with the prisoners and for repairs, Meikle reached Spithead on 16 Sept. An application to the admiralty for his supersession was refused, but he was promoted to the rank of first mate, and put to sea again on 22 Oct. He joined the fleet under Admiral Hawke, and took part in the great victory off Belleisle on 20 Nov. After repeated applications he obtained his discharge in February 1762, and immediately returned to Carnwath. He went to Edinburgh for some months in the summer of 1764 to prosecute his professional studies. In July 1789 he was ordained to the eldership in the congregation of Biggar, and continued his devotional writings to the last week of his life, dying rather suddenly on 7 Dec. 1799. In 1779 he married his first wife, who died in 1782; he married again in 1785, and left behind him a widow and five children in very poor circumstances. He was a man of earnest religious feeling, and at the same time of great cheerfulness, a characteristic which the titles of his works would scarcely lead one to expect. In 1797 he published a small volume entitled 'Metaphysical Maxims,' which was reprinted, Edinburgh, 1805, 1807. He left behind him a large number of religious meditations in prose and verse, a selection from which was published by subscription for the benefit of his widow, with the title, 'The Select Remains . . . or Extracts . . . entitled: I. The Monthly Memorial, or a Periodical Interview with the King of Terrors. II. A Secret Survey into the State of the Soul. III. The House of Mourning, or Poems on Melancholy Subjects. IV. The Tomb,' Edinburgh, 1803; 2nd edit., enlarged, 1804. This volume was so well received that it was followed in the same year by 2. 'Solitude Sweetened, or Miscellaneous Meditations on various Religious Subjects,' of which a 7th edit. was published, Edinburgh, 1823. He also wrote: 3. 'The Traveller, or Meditations on various Subjects . . . to which is added, Converse with the World Unseen, with a life of the author by James Peddie, Edinburgh, 1805; 4th edit. Edinburgh, 1816; reprinted, Aberdeen, 1844; and 4. 'Miscellaneous Works . . . containing all his remaining Pieces in Prose intended for Publication,' Edinburgh, 1807. The verses (which he himself preferred to his prose meditations) have little apart from their religious sentiments to recommend them.

[James Peddie's Life prefixed to 'The Traveller;' Christian Magazine for February 1800; Watt's Bibliotheca Britannica, ii. 662.]

W. A. G.

MEILAN, MARK ANTHONY (*fl.* 1812), miscellaneous writer, born about 1743, held at one time a situation in the post-office, which he resigned in order to become 'instructor' in private families in English, bookkeeping, and shorthand, of languages, arts, and sciences. In 1776 he was keeping an academy in Charles Square, Hoxton, but is subsequently found residing at Westminster, St. George's Fields, and Kennington. He took orders, and for some time served the curacy of St. John, Wapping. He submitted tragedies to Garrick and Colman, who declined them on the ground that they contained rather too many reminiscences of Shakespeare and Rowe. At the suggestion of some kind-hearted ladies he printed his dramas by subscription, and prefixed a diverting preface, in which he gives a detailed account of his interviews and correspondence with the 'despots of the drama' (i.e. the managers). He had intended to inflict a second volume upon his subscribers, but found their patience exhausted. In 1809 he was assistant minister of St. Mary, Newington, Surrey, and was apparently alive in 1816 (*Dict. of Living Authors*, 1816). He was married and had a family.

Meilan published: 1. 'Stenography, or Shorthand improved,' 8vo, London, 1764, which professes to be an 'improvement' on Gurney's system. 2. 'Northumberland, a Tragedy,' 8vo, London, 1771. 3. 'The Adventures of Telemachus, an epic poem from the French of Fénelon, with alterations,' in heroic couplets, 2 vols. 8vo, London, 1776; 2nd edit. with plates, 2 vols. 4to, 1792–4. 4. 'Dramatic Works (tragedies entitled "Emilia," "Northumberland," and "The Friends"), published by way of an appeal from the arbitrary decisions of the despots of the drama,' 8vo, London, 1780. 5. 'The Children's Friend,' translated from the French of A. Berquin, 24mo, London, 1786. 6. 'The Friend of Youth . . . consisting of . . . stories, . . . dialogues, and moral dramas,' partly translated from Berquin and other writers, and partly original, 12 vols. 12mo, London, 1788. 7. 'Sermons for Children,' 3 vols. 12mo, London, 1789. 8. 'The Book of Righteousness, or an Elucidation of the . . . Gospel . . . with . . . the Acts,' 12mo, London (1790?). 9. 'Holy Writ familiarized to Juvenile Conceptions,' 4 vols. 12mo, London, 1791. 10. 'An Introduction to the English Language,' 2 vols. 8vo, London, 1803. A portrait of Meilan, surrounded by his 'Works,' is prefixed to the second edition of his 'Telemachus.'

[Meilan's Works; Baker's Biog. Dram. (1812); Westby-Gibson's Bibliography of Shorthand, p. 129.]

G. G.

MEILYR BRYDYDD (i.e. THE POET) (*d.* 1140?), Welsh bard, was the son of Mabon ab Iarddur ap Mor, and dwelt at Trefeilyr, in the parish of Trefdraeth, Anglesey, a township which doubtless took its name from him (LEWYS DWNN, *Heraldic Visitations of Wales*, ii. 128, 139, 266). Three of his poems are preserved in the 'Myvyrian Archaiology' (2nd edit. pp. 140–2), namely: (1) an elegy on Gruffydd ap Cynan (*d.* 1137) [q. v.]; (2) a short poem on the battle of Mynydd Carn (1081), said to have been written in the army of Trahaiarn ap Caradog, there defeated; (3) the poet's death-lay, in which he prays that his bones may be laid in Enlli (Bardsey Island). Meilyr is the first of the 'Gogynfeirdd,' the mediæval bards whose poems can be approximately dated, as distinguished from the 'Cynfeirdd,' the half-mythical poets of the sixth century, of whose genuine work very little can have come down to us. He is the herald of the poetic revival which contact with Norman civilisation and success in arms brought about among the Welsh towards the middle of the twelfth century. From his elegy to Gruffydd ap Cynan we learn that he was 'pencerdd' (chief bard) under that prince ('bum o du gwledig yn lleithiawc' = 'I sat by the monarch's side'—a privilege only enjoyed by the *chief* bard, *Ancient Laws of Wales*, edit. 1841, i. 74). On one occasion, we gather from the same source, he acted as envoy for the court of Aberffraw. His son, Gwalchmai, and his grandsons, Einion and Meilyr, also won renown as poets, and the family was for generations of consequence in Anglesey (Lewys Dwnn, ii. 108, 128, 202, 266; *Record of Carnarvon*, Record edit. pp. 45, 46, 48).

[Myvyrian Archaiology, 2nd edit. pp. 140–2; Stephens's Literature of the Kymry, 2nd edit. pp. 10–15.] J. E. L.

MEL (*d.* 487), Irish saint, is believed by Irish writers and in the district to have been founder of the see of Ardagh, now in co. Longford, a part of the ancient kingdom of Teffia in Meath. The genealogists do not attach him to any great clan, but state only that his father was Conis and his mother Darerca, sister of St. Patrick. Except a visit to Britain, and the foundation of the church and monastery of Ardagh about 454, and the confirmation of St. Brigit, all the events of his life are miraculous or symbolical. St. Brigit turned water into beer for him to drink, he fished for salmon, when visited by St. Patrick, in the puddles of a ploughed field, he prophesied the greatness of Brigit before her birth. The chronicles mention his death in 487, and he is noticed frequently in the lives of St. Patrick and St. Brigit. No early life of him is extant. His feast is kept on 6 Feb.

[J. Colgan's Acta Sanctorum Hiberniæ, Louvain, 1645, vol. i.; Annals of Ulster, ed. W. M. Hennessy, 1887, p. 29; W. Stokes's Tripartite Life of St. Patrick, 1887, vols. i. and ii., and Three Middle-Irish Homilies, Calcutta, 1877, and Life of St. Brigit, pp. 182–200, in Lives of Saints from the Book of Lismore, Oxford, 1890.] N. M.

MELBANCKE, BRIAN (*fl.* 1583), euphuistic writer, was educated at St. John's College, Cambridge, where he graduated B.A. in 1579. In 1583 he described himself as 'Student in Graies Inn,' but his name cannot be found on the books.

He was the author of a book (now rare) entitled 'Philotimus. The Warre betwixt Nature and Fortune,' London, 1583. It is a close imitation of Lyly's 'Euphues,' and the many old proverbs and scraps of verse it contains render it quaint and interesting. On page 53 'Philotimus' alludes to the story of Romeo and Juliet as well known and popular at the time. In an address to the 'Gentlemen students in the Inns of Court and Chancerie, and the University of Cambridge,' Melbancke acknowledges his failings in the use of the English tongue, and remarks that 'if ever I had anything to vaunt . . . it was some small skill in other languages.'

In the registers of St. Olave's, Southwark, under date 3 June 1583, there is the entry, 'Brian Mellebanke and Sara Baker married.'

[Cooper's Athenæ Cantabrigienses, i. 490; Addit. MS. (Cole MS.) 5885, f. 34; Sir Egerton Brydges's Brit. Bibliographer, ii. 438 et seq., where a full account of Philotimus, by J. Haslewood, is given. Ritson includes Melbancke in his Bibl. Poetica, p. 278, on account of the orginal verses scattered through his book.] B. P.

MELBOURNE, Viscounts. [See Lamb, William, second Viscount, 1779–1848; Lamb, Frederick James, third Viscount, 1782–1853.]

MELCOMBE, Baron (1691–1762). [See Dodington, George Bubb.]

MELDOLA, RAPHAEL (1754–1828), Jewish theologian, son of Rabbi Hezekiah Meldola (*d.* 1791), was born at Leghorn in 1754. His forefathers through many generations were eminent rabbis; his grandfather was Raphael Meldola, the author of a collection of responsa called 'Mayim Rabbim.' In 1791 he bewailed the death of his father, to whose memory he dedicated the first-fruit of his literary labours, 'Korban Min'hah' (A Meal Offering), being a Hebrew commentary on the ''abhodah' (i.e. the description of the sacrificial service on the Day of Atonement). The commentary, which is concise and clear, was published in 'Sepher 'abhodath hammikdash' (Additional Service for the Day of Atonement), at Leghorn in 1791. In 1797 a second work of his was published at Leghorn, viz. ''Huppath 'Hathanim' (Laws and Regulations concerning the Conduct of Jews and Jewesses when Engaged or Married); in the Introduction he wittily but sharply depicts the poverty of the rabbis, whose income was as a rule very small. He officiated as 'dayyan' (i.e. judge or assistant rabbi) in the Jewish congregation of Leghorn.

On 7 Oct. 1804 the congregation of the Spanish and Portuguese Jews in London appointed Meldola to the office of ''hakham' or 'rabbi.' The congregation had been without a spiritual chief since 1784. The task of inspiring the London community with fresh life was beset with great difficulties, especially for a minister who could not speak English. But Meldola met with much success. He struggled hard to prevent the children of the poor from attending schools opened for them by conversionists, and endeavoured to maintain the sanctity of the Sabbath. During his pastorate the ancient synagogue of his congregation in Bevis Marks was restored in 1824, and he composed for the occasion of its reopening a Hebrew hymn, 'Kol Rinnah' ('the voice of song'). He died 9 June 1828, and was buried, in accordance with his wish, beside the rabbi David Netto, in the Beth-'holim cemetery at Mile End. His wife Stella died in London 20 July 1857. His son, David Meldola, officiated as dayyan or assistant rabbi in London, where he died 2 March 1853.

In addition to the works named above, Meldola published 'Derekh Emunah' ('The Way of Faith'); in 1848 the introduction and one chapter were edited by his son, David Meldola (London), the former in Hebrew, the latter in an English translation. The book was intended to be a graduated catechism of the Jewish religion.

[Gent. Mag. 1828, pt. ii. p. 377; J. Picciotto's Sketches of Anglo-Jewish History; The Way of Faith (Preface).] M. F.

MELDRUM, GEORGE (1635?–1709), rector of Marischal College, Aberdeen, and professor of divinity in the university of Edinburgh, was 'the fourth son of a family in Aberdeenshire of the old house of Meldrum (Wodrow, *Analecta*, i. 175). At seventeen years of age, and before he had taken the degree of M.A., he was made one of the regents of Marischal College, Aberdeen. On 1 Dec. 1658 he was chosen by the town council to be minister of Aberdeen. After the Restoration he was on 24 Oct. 1662 suspended by the synod till 1 Jan. 1663, for not subscribing canonical obedience (*Ecclesiastical Records of Aberdeen*, Spalding Club, p. 269). Being cited before the council on 10 Dec. 1662, he agreed to comply with the government of the church as 'presently established by archbishops and bishops,' and his case being recommended by the council to the Bishop of St. Andrews, he was restored to his charge (Wodrow, *Sufferings of the Kirk of Scotland*, i. 315–16). He afterwards explained that he only supported episcopacy so far as it was consistent with presbyteries and synods (*ib.*) According to Wodrow he 'showed much zeal against popery, and especially against Dempster the jesuit, and one night was almost assassinated going to see a sick person' (*Analecta*, i. 176). He was ten times elected rector of Marischal College.

In 1681 Meldrum was deprived of his charge for refusing to take the test; but after the Toleration Act of James II he was admitted to the charge of Kilwinning, Ayrshire, some time before 2 Oct. 1688. On 11 Feb. 1692 he was admitted to the collegiate or second charge of the Tron Church, Edinburgh. On 11 Jan. 1698 he was chosen moderator of the general assembly. On 24 Dec. 1701 he was chosen professor of divinity in the university, but accepted office very unwillingly, and only on condition that the presbytery should relieve him from nearly all the routine duties of his pastorate, except preaching on Sunday. He was admitted to the chair on 13 Oct. 1702. According to Wodrow, he 'understood scholastic divinity to a pitch' (*ib.* i. 176), and discharged his professorial duties with great efficiency. On 10 March 1703 he was again elected moderator of the general assembly. This assembly, after several sittings, was abruptly dismissed by the lord high commissioner, James, earl of Seafield, without consulting the moderator, who, however, had sufficient tact to avoid collision with the temporal powers, and concluded with prayer. The occurrence led to an agreement between the church and the government as to the manner of dissolving the assembly in future. Meldrum died on 18 Feb. 1709, in his seventy-fifth year.

Meldrum published: 1. 'Sermon preached in the High Church of Edinburgh, Sunday, 27 April 1690.' 2. 'A Letter to a Friend, giving an Account of all the Treatises that have been published with relation to the present Persecution against the Church of Scotland,' anon. 1692. 3. 'Letter asserting the Lawfulness of Informing against the Vitious and Profane before the Courts of Immorality,' anon. 1701. 4. 'A Letter from a Friend in the City to a Member of Parliament anent Patronage,' anon. 1703. 5. 'Sermon preached before the Lord High Commissioner in New Church, Edinburgh, on 16 May 1703,' 1703. It touched on the evils of patronage and the danger of extending toleration. 6. 'Defence of Sermon,' 1703, in reply to the criticism of Bishop Sage. 7. 'Sermon preached before the Lord High Commissioner, 10 March 1704,' 1704. 8. 'The Danger of Popery discovered, with a Dissuasive from it,' anon. 2nd edit. 1714.

[Wodrow's Analecta and Sufferings of the Kirk of Scotland; Bower's Hist. of the University of Edinburgh; Kennedy's Annals of Aberdeen; Fasti Aberd. and Ecclesiastical Records of Aberdeen (both Spalding Club); Anderson's Fasti Academiæ Mariscallanæ (New Spalding Club); Hew Scott's Fasti Eccles. Scot. i. 59, ii. 182, iii. 467.] T. F. H.

MELDRUM, SIR JOHN (*d.*1645), soldier, claims in the letter which he wrote to Charles I in 1642 to have spent thirty-six years in the service of the king and of his father, and speaks of his 'zeal to your majesty's father's service in Ireland in settling the province of Ulster' (RUSHWORTH, iv. 628). In November 1610 Sir Arthur Chichester wrote from Ireland to the Earl of Salisbury, complaining of one Meldrum, who had brought a letter from the king for a share in the plantation. In spite of this remonstrance James, on 17 April 1611, reminded Chichester of his previous instructions to further the claim of Captain John Meldrum, upon the vacancy of any charge fit for him, and on 13 March 1617 he was granted some land in the county of Fermanagh. Meldrum seems to have been the agent of Lord Balfour of Burley, who had extensive grants both in Fermanagh and Donegal (*Cal. State Papers*, Irish, 1608–10 p. 526, 1611–14 p. 30, 1615–25 p. 152). After serving in the wars in the Low Countries he returned to England, and was knighted at Windsor on 6 Aug. 1622 (METCALFE, *Book of Knights*, p. 180). In the next reign he took part in the expedition to Rochelle, and the war with France (*Cal. State Papers*, Dom. 1627–8, pp. 417, 489). Monro mentions him in his list of Scottish officers serving under Gustavus Adolphus as 'colonel in Spruce to foot' (MONRO, *His Expedition with the worthy Scotch Regiment called Mackay's*, fol. 1637, App. to pt. i).

About 1618 Meldrum purchased from a previous grantee the half-share in a patent for maintaining a lighthouse at Winterton Ness, by means of a tax of a penny a ton on passing ships. The patent was complained against as a grievance in the parliament of 1624, but the king refused to consent to its abolition. In 1635 Meldrum obtained a similar patent for erecting lighthouses on the North and South Foreland, which involved him in controversies with adjacent ports and with Trinity House (*Cal. State Papers*, Dom. 1611-18 pp. 537, 545, 1623-5 pp. 255, 258, 1634–5 pp. 505, 529). The desire to preserve these lucrative privileges was, according to the royalists, the reason which led Meldrum to adopt the service of the parliament during the civil wars. In an acrimonious correspondence exchanged at the siege of Scarborough in 1645, Sir Hugh Cholmley [q. v.] taunted Meldrum with boasting about 'the dazzling light of reformation, all men knowing what lights you study to preserve, which not like seamarks have directed, but like ignes fatui have misled you out of the way of obedience' (*Hist. MSS. Comm.* 10th Rep. vi. 156; cf. HUSBANDS, *Exact Collection*, 4to, 1643, p. 580).

Meldrum asserted that he was guided simply by his hostility to the king's policy in church and state. 'A moderate and well-tempered monarchy' he loved, but 'a Straffordian monarchy' he deemed 'at least cousin-german to, if not worse than, anarchy itself.' In July 1642 Meldrum accepted a commission to assist Sir John Hotham in the defence of Hull. Before actual hostilities began he wrote a bold letter to the king, assailing the policy of Charles, justifying his own conduct. 'When I perceived that no corner in your dominions could afford a good man . . . who did not groan under the exorbitances of the time . . . I could find no better way to do your majesty a more general service than by stopping the course of a civil war . . . as to cast myself into Hull' (RUSHWORTH, iv. 628). He made two sallies against the king's forces, 'the first blood as some say that was shed in these unnatural wars' (*ib.* p. 610). In September Meldrum assisted Sir William Waller in the reduction of Portsmouth (VICARS, *Jehovah Jireh*, p. 161), and served under Essex at Edgehill and at the siege of Reading in April 1643 (*ib.* pp. 161, 193, 308). In June 1643 parliament sent him to be commander-in-chief of the Nottinghamshire forces, and he arrested Captain John Hotham, and stopped his intended treachery (RUSHWORTH, v. 275; *Memoirs of Colonel Hutchinson*, i. 221, ed. 1885). In October Manchester sent Meldrum and four hundred men to reinforce the besieged garrison of Hull. The successful sally of 9 Oct. was commanded by Meldrum, who was wounded in leading it (VICARS, *God's Ark*, p. 39; *Report on the Portland MSS.* i. 138). After the siege of Hull had been raised Meldrum was placed in command of a portion of Manchester's army, with which he captured Gainsborough (December 1643), drove the royalists out of the Isle of Axholme (February 1644), took Cawood Castle and the fort of Airemouth in Yorkshire (May 1643). He also commanded a division of foot in Lord Fairfax's victory at Selby (11 April 1644; VICARS, *God's Ark*, pp. 102, 147, 205, 233, 234; RUSHWORTH, v. 618). At the end of February 1644, however, he had been commanded to besiege Newark, but Prince Rupert raised the siege, and forced Meldrum to make a disadvantageous capitulation (22 March), by which he sacrificed his artillery and the muskets of his men (*ib.* p. 307). Baillie attributes the disaster to 'his own improvidence alone,' but other accounts show that it was mainly caused by the misconduct of his subordinates and the weakness of his forces (*Cal. State Papers*, Dom. 1644, pp. 24, 61, 76; *Life of Colonel Hutchinson*, i. 322;

Letters of Robert Baillie, ed. Laing, ii. 152–158).

It is evident that Meldrum's defeat was not attributed to incapacity, for in May 1644 he was detached with two regiments to secure Manchester, and take command of the Lancashire forces against Prince Rupert. He held Manchester, but could not prevent the loss of Bolton and Liverpool. After the battle of Marston Moor, however, he defeated Rupert's fugitive horse at Ormskirk on 20 Aug., and on 1 Nov. recaptured Liverpool (*Cal. State Papers*, Dom. 1644, pp. 173, 440, 442; Robinson, *Discourse of the War in Lancashire*, pp. 54–9; Ormerod, *Lancashire Civil War Tracts*, p. 204; *Hist. MSS. Comm.* 10th Rep. pt. iv. pp. 73, 95). On 18 Sept. 1644 Meldrum took part in the defeat of Lord Byron before Montgomery Castle. 'Sir John Meldrum,' says Sir William Brereton's letter, 'did with much judgment order and command these forces, and therefore deserves a large share in the honour of this day's success' (Phillips, *Civil War in Wales*, ii. 201). Meldrum, however, bitterly complained that the newspapers gave all the credit of the victory to Brereton (*Cal. State Papers*, Dom. 1644–5, p. 6). In February 1645 he returned to Yorkshire to besiege Scarborough, which was held by Sir Hugh Cholmley for the king. He stormed the town early in February, but was mortally wounded in a sally during May. Parliament voted him 1,500*l.*, and the committee of both kingdoms sent him on 26 May a singularly warm and complimentary letter. But the castle held out till 21 July, and Meldrum seems to have died before it was taken. His will, dated 24 May 1645, was proved on 2 June 1647 (*ib.* pp. 304, 527; Rushworth, vi. 118; Chester, *Westminster Abbey Registers*, p. 137; *Commons' Journals*, iv. 59, 97, 149). Ricraft gives a panegyric on Meldrum in his 'Survey of England's Champions,' 1647, p. 50, and also a portrait. A drawing is among the Sutherland collection in the Bodleian Library (*Catalogue of the Sutherland Collection*, i. 634).

[Numerous letters of Meldrum's are calendared among the Domestic State Papers for 1644 and 1645. The following pamphlets relate to him: The Copy of a Letter sent to the King by Sir John Meldrum, 4to, 1642; A True Relation of the great Victories obtained by the Earl of Manchester and the Lord Fairfax . . . with two Letters concerning the said Victories, the one from the Lord Fairfax, the other from Sir John Meldrum, 4to, 1643; A True Relation of two great Victories, the one by Sir W. Brereton in Cheshire, the other by Sir John Meldrum in Lancashire, 4to, 1644; A Brief Relation of the Siege at Newark, as it was delivered by Lieutenant-colonel Bury, 4to, 1644. Other authorities mentioned in the article.] C. H. F.

MELFORT, first Earl and titular Duke of (1649–1714). [See Drummond, John.]

MELIA, PIUS, D.D. (1800–1883), Roman catholic divine, born at Rome in 1800, became professor of literature in the Jesuits' College there, and afterwards visited Corsica, Tuscany, and other countries as a missionary priest. In 1848 he came to England and took charge of the mission at St. Leonards, whence he was removed to Walthamstow. About fourteen years later he was made almoner of the Italian Benevolent Society, and sought to ameliorate the condition of the poor Italian immigrants to this country, and to prevent the abuses arising from the importation of Italian children. For many years he officiated on Sundays at Brentwood, and also preached to the Italians of London on Sunday afternoons. He was a member of the Pious Society of Missions, and the erection of the Italian church of St. Peter in Hatton Garden, London, was in great measure due to his persevering efforts. He died in London on 25 May 1883, and was buried at St. Mary's, Kensal Green.

He was the author of: 1. 'Doctrines of St. Thomas Aquinas on the Rulers and Members of Christian States, extracted and explained,' London, 1860, 8vo; entitled on the cover 'The Pope, the Prince, and the People.' 2. 'The Origin, Persecution, and Doctrines of the Waldenses, from documents,' London, 1870, 4to. 3. 'Hints and Facts on the Origin of Man, and of his Intellectual Faculties,' London, 1872, 8vo.

[Annual Reg. 1883, p. 152; Tablet, 2 June 1883, p. 873; Times, 1 June 1883, p. 8, col. 4; Weekly Register, 2 June 1883, p. 699.] T. C.

MELITON, MILITON, or MILTON, WILLIAM of (*d.* 1261), Franciscan, was D.D. and fifth master of the Friars Minors at Cambridge about 1250. He was afterwards called to Paris, and was appointed by Innocent IV to finish the 'Summa Theologiæ' of Alexander of Hales in 1252. About 1260 Meliton, Bonaventura, and other distinguished Minorites, at the request of Isabel or Elizabeth, sister of St. Louis, king of France, revised and corrected the rule which she had drawn up for the government of her new nunnery at Longchamp. Meliton died suddenly at Paris in 1261, leaving a reputation for learning and great holiness. His commentaries on Proverbs, Ecclesiastes, the Song of Solomon, Ezekiel, the Twelve Minor Prophets, the Canonical Epistles, and the Apocalypse, are extant among the manuscripts of the National Library at Paris, and his 'Quæstiones de Sacramento' in the library of St. Anthony, Padua. Other works are preserved at Assisi. All or nearly all of these manuscripts date from the thirteenth century—showing that Meliton's popularity, though considerable, was not lasting.

[Monumenta Franciscana, vol. i.; Lanercost Chronicle, p. 70; Bollandists' Acta Sanctorum, sub die 31 Aug. p. 801; Wadding's Annales Minorum, vol. iv.; Supplementum ad Scriptores, p. 324, ed. 1806; Hist. Litt. de la France, xix. 416, xxvi. 403.] A. G. L.

MELL, DAVIS (*fl.* 1650), violinist, born at Wilton near Salisbury 15 Nov. 1604, was son of a servant of William Herbert, third earl of Pembroke [q. v.] He was primarily a clockmaker, and was, until the middle of the seventeenth century, accounted the first violinist in England in point of skill. He may be said to occupy the position of the earliest English violinist of note. Wood says that Mell was 'one of the musick to King Charles I,' and 'had a sweet stroke.' According to the same authority, Mell visited Oxford in March 1657–8, when 'Peter Pett, Will Bull, Ken Digby, and others of Allsoules did give him a very handsome entertainment in the Taverne, called "The Salutation," in St. Marie's Parish. The company did look upon Mr. Mell to have a prodigious hand on the violin, and they thought that no person, as all in London did, could goe beyond him. But when Tho Baltzar [q. v.], an Outlander, came to Oxon in the next yeare, they had other thoughts of Mr. Mell, who tho he played farr sweeter than Baltzar, yet Baltzar's hand was more quick.' Elsewhere Wood describes Mell as 'a well-bred gentleman, and not given to excessive drinking as Baltzar was.' Wood seems to have entertained him at Oxford in August 1658. Mell was conjointly with George Hudson the first 'Master of the Music,' or leader of Charles II's 'four and twenty fiddlers,' a band of twenty-four performers on the violin, tenor, and bass, instituted by the king in 1660 in imitation of Louis XIV's 'vingt-quatre violons du Roi.' He was succeeded in 1661 by Baltzar. Some of Mell's compositions for the instrument are to be found in Christopher Simpson's 'Division Violin,' 1684. In Aubrey's 'Miscellanies' is an account of a child of Davis Mell, who was cured of a crooked back by the touch of a dead hand.

[Hawkins's History of Music, ed. 1875, p. 681; Anthony à Wood's Life and Times (Oxf. Hist. Soc.), i. 241, 257–8; Aubrey's Miscellanies; Hunter's Chorus Vatum in MS. Addit. 24491 f. 550.] E. H-A.

MELLENT, COUNT OF (1104–1166), warrior. [See BEAUMONT, WALERAN DE.]

MELLIS, HUGH (*fl.* 1588), mathematician, had from his youth, as he himself informs us, a natural genius for drawing proportions, maps, cards, buildings, and plates. He attended Dr. Robert Forth at Trinity Hall, Cambridge, and went to the arithmetic lecture in the common school. He left the service of Forth, who afterwards became a master in chancery, about 1564. Subsequently he kept a school for writing and arithmetic at Mayes Gate, near Battle Bridge, in the parish of St. Olave, 'in shorte Southwarke.'

His works are: 1. 'Brief Rules, called Rules of Practize, of Rare, Pleasant, and commodious effect, abridged into a briefer Method than hitherto hath bene published. With diuers other very necessarie Rules, Tables, and Questions, not only profitable for Merchants, but also for Gentlemen and all other occupiers whatsouer;' dedicated to Dr. Robert Forth, it constitutes the third part or addition to Robert Recorde's 'Grounde of Artes, teaching the perfecte Worke and Practise of Arithmetike,' London, 1582. 2. 'A Briefe Instruction and Maner how to keepe Bookes of Accompts after the order of Debitor and Creditor, & as well for proper Accompts partible, &c. . . . Newely augmented and set forth by John Mellis,' London (J. Windet), 1588. In the preface he describes his work as a reissue 'of an auncient old copie printed here in London the 14 of August, 1543,' from the pen of 'Hugh Oldcastle, Scholemaster.' No copy of Oldcastle's edition is known. 3. 'A Short and Plaine Treatise of Arithmeticke in whole numbers comprised into a briefer Method than hetherto hath bin published,' London, 1588, 8vo, ff. 54; annexed to the preceding work.

[Ames's Typogr. Antiq. (Herbert), pp. 743, 1227; De Morgan's Arithmetical Books, pp. 22, 27; Lowndes's Bibl. Man. (Bohn), pp. 1531, 1721; Massey's Origin and Progress of Letters, ii. 16.] T. C.

MELLISH, SIR GEORGE (1814–1877), lord justice of appeal, second son of Edward Mellish, D.D., rector of East Tuddenham, Norfolk, and afterwards dean of Hereford, by his wife Elizabeth Jane, daughter of a prior dean of Hereford, William Leigh of Rushall Hall, Staffordshire, was born at Tuddenham, 19 Dec. 1814. His godfather was George Canning, who was his mother's first cousin. He was educated at Eton, where his name appears in the school lists (pp. 137 *a*, 147 *a*) in 1829, in the middle division, and in 1832 in the sixth form. At school he was a good sculler, but neither an athlete nor a diligent scholar. In 1833 he entered as a commoner at University College, Oxford, but shortly gained an open scholarship on Sir Simon Bennet's foundation. He took a second class in *literæ humaniores* in 1836, and graduated B.A. on 26 Jan. 1837, and M.A. on 24 Oct. 1839. He was a good speaker at the Union, as he had been at the debating society at Eton, but obtained less distinction in the schools than his talents seemed to merit. He became an honorary fellow of his college in 1872, and received the honorary degree of D.C.L. 17 June 1874.

Mellish was admitted a student of the Inner Temple 6 Nov. 1837, and read in the chambers of Spencer Walpole, John Unthank, and Crompton. For eight years he practised as a special pleader, and on 9 June 1848 he was called to the bar and joined the northern circuit. He rapidly obtained a good mercantile business, became a queen's counsel in 1861, and quitted the lead of his circuit after a few years to devote himself to a very heavy leading practice in London. Neither the bent of his mind nor the state of his health fitted him for the strain of nisi prius work, though he appeared for one of the defendants in the prosecution of Overend, Gurney & Co. His forte lay in arguments in banco, in chancery, and in the House of Lords. More than once he refused a puisne judgeship, but in 1870, on the death of Sir George Giffard, he was appointed a lord justice of appeal in chancery, was knighted, and sworn of the privy council. The experiment of appointing a common-law practitioner to so important a post in chancery was bold, but it was justified by its success, and the court, which consisted of him and Lord Justice James, continued for some years to give judgments of the highest importance and value. All his life, however, he had suffered from gout, and in spite of his great fortitude under severe pain in court, he was frequently disabled from work. He died unmarried at his house, 33 Lowndes Square, London, on 15 June 1877. His chief judicial fault was an eager habit of controversially interrupting the arguments of counsel, but his learning was profound, his intellect logical and clear, and his character impartial and amiable.

[For a lengthy estimate of his character by Lord Selborne see Law Mag. and Rev. 4th ser. iii. 62–4. See also G. K. Richards in Law. Mag. 4th ser. iii. 55; Solicitors' Journal, 23 June 1877.]
J. A. H.

MELLITUS (*d.* 624), first bishop of London and third archbishop of Canterbury, was leader of the second band of missionaries sent by Pope Gregory the Great to reinforce Augustine at Canterbury in 601. According to Bæda he was of noble birth (*Hist. Eccles.* lib. ii. cap. 7), and he was styled abbot in Pope Gregory's letters (*Ep.* lib. xi. cap. 54, &c.) It has been suggested that he was abbot either of St. Andrew's on the Cælian Hill, an office previously held by Augustine, or of the church in the Lateran assigned to the Benedictines (Stubbs, *Dict. Christian Biog.*); but the title may merely designate his relation to the band of monks who accompanied him to England (*Ep.* lib. xi. 54, 59, &c.) Extant commendatory letters from the pope, written on behalf of Mellitus and his associates, serve to mark the route which they followed. Gregory's epistles are addressed to the bishops of Vienne, Arles, Lyons, Gap, Toulon, Marseilles, Chalons on the Saone, Metz, Paris, Rouen, Angers, to the kings of the Franks, Theodoric, Theodebert, and Clothair, and to Queen Brunichild (*ib.* lib. xi. 54–62). Those of Mellitus's companions whose names are preserved were Laurentius, who had already been in Britain, Justus, Paulinus, and Rufinianus, who came for the first time. By their hands Gregory sent 'all things necessary for divine worship and the service of the church, namely sacred vessels and altar-cloths, ornaments for the churches, and vestments for the priests and clerks, likewise relics of the holy apostles and martyrs and many books' (*Hist. Eccles.* i. 29). Elmham, writing in the fifteenth century, gives a list of these gifts and books (*Hist. Mon. S. Aug. Cant.* ed. Hardwick, pp. 96 sqq.) Tradition affirms that two copies of the 'Gospels,' one at Corpus College, Cambridge, the other at the Bodleian Library, and a psalter in 'Cott. MS. Vesp.' A. L. (Wanley in Hickes's *Thesaurus*, ii. 172; Bosworth, *A.-S. Gospels*, Pref. p. xi), were brought by Mellitus; but all these manuscripts belong to a later date (*Palæog. Soc. Facsimiles*, vol. ii. pl. 19, p. 33; Macray, *Annals of the Bodleian*, p. 24). Mellitus was further charged with the delivery of a number of letters to Augustine and others of Gregory's friends in Britain. Gregory did not hear from Mellitus as soon as he expected, and he wrote another letter (*Hist. Eccles.* i. 30) asking for news of his journey and giving an answer to Augustine's question on the propriety of using the temples of idols for divine worship. This letter is wrongly dated 17 June; Mellitus did not leave Rome till 22 June (Haddan and Stubbs, iii. 38).

Augustine consecrated Mellitus and Justus bishops (*Hist. Eccles.* ii. 3) between 601 and 604, the year of Augustine's death. Before his consecration Mellitus probably joined either the monastery of St. Peter and St. Paul (afterwards St. Augustine's) or the archiepiscopal community at Christchurch. As bishop he was sent to preach to the province of the East Saxons, which Bæda describes as divided from the kingdom of Kent by the river Thames and bounded on the east by the sea, having London for its metropolis—'a city situated on the bank of the Thames, the mart of many nations resorting to it by land and sea.' The king of the East Saxons was Sabert, the nephew of Æthelbert, king of Kent, and subject to him. Mellitus was thus able to win his support, and when the work of conversion was sufficiently far advanced, King Æthelbert built the church of St. Paul in London, where Mellitus and his successors were to have their episcopal see.

The genuineness of many of the charters in which Mellitus's name occurs is 'more than questionable' (STUBBS, *Dict. of Christian Biog*, s. v.); but to the grant of Tillingham in Essex (KEMBLE, *Codex Dipl.*, No. 982), although bearing marks of later garbling, Bishop Stubbs is willing to assign some measure of authenticity. Tillingham is undoubtedly a very early possession of St. Paul's. Mellitus joined in Archbishop Laurentius's letter to the bishops of the Irish and British churches proposing union, and urging compliance with the customs of the Roman church, and subsequently returned to Rome to attend a council (27 Feb. 610) held, Bæda says, to secure the peace of the monastic order ('de vita monachorum et quiete ordinaturus'). Mellitus brought back the council's decrees to England, besides letters from Pope Boniface IV to Archbishop Laurentius, King Æthelbert, and the whole clergy and people of the English. The decrees and the letters are in all probability lost, though some are extant in fictitious forms. The letter to Æthelbert, almost certainly fictitious (STUBBS, *Dict. of Christian Biog.* s. v.), is preserved in William of Malmesbury (*Gesta Pontiff.* i. §30) and in Eadmer (*Hist. Nov.* ed. Rule, p. 261). It was first produced in 1072 in support of the claims of Canterbury to supremacy over York (HADDAN and STUBBS, iii. 65). Equally spurious is the bull of Boniface IV, dated 27 Feb. 611, in which Mellitus is mentioned (*ib.* p. 67).

Æthelbert's son Eadbald, on his father's death in 616, rejected the new religion. Sabert died at the same time; his sons refused to be converted, and granted free liberty to the people under their government to serve idols. Mellitus for a while pursued his ministrations, subject to the taunts of the young princes, who, watching him celebrate mass, asked for the white bread which he had been wont to give to their father, and which they saw him give to the people. To this he replied that they must first seek salvation through baptism, and he declined to comply with their wishes on any other conditions. He was consequently banished, and went to Kent, where he found Laurentius and Justus in like difficulties. Mellitus and Justus took refuge in Gaul, but Eadbald was soon afterwards converted and recalled them a year later. But the East Saxons remained refractory, and the Londoners refused to receive Mellitus as their bishop. In 619 Laurentius died, and Mellitus succeeded him as archbishop. He never received the pall (*Dict. of Christian Biog.* loc. cit.), but Bæda reports that he received letters of exhortation from Pope Boniface V. These are not extant, though reference seems to have been made to them in 805 (HADDAN and STUBBS, iii. 71, 560).

Mellitus consecrated a church to the Blessed Virgin in the monastery of St. Peter and St. Paul, which had been built by King Eadbald. On the occasion of a great fire in Canterbury, which raged round 'the place of the four crowned martyrs,' he was borne thither by his servants; and Bæda reports that in answer to his fervent prayers a strong wind immediately arose which drew the flames southward and saved the city. He died, after much suffering from gout, on 24 April 624, and was buried, like his predecessors, in the monastery of St. Peter and St. Paul. Legend ascribes the foundation of St. Peter's, Westminster, to Mellitus (LUARD, *Lives of Edward the Confessor*, v. 2057 sqq.), but it is unsupported by any historical evidence. Further details of Mellitus's life, recorded in Elmham, are equally untrustworthy.

Hardy (*Cat. of Materials*, i. 219, 220) supplies a list of manuscript lives which do not add anything but legendary matter to the account of Mellitus given by Bæda, who derived his information from Gregory's letters and from traditions known to Nothelm, a priest of London in the middle of the eighth century.

[See Bæda's Historia Ecclesiastica, bk. i. 29, 30, ii. 3-7; other letters of Pope Gregory in Gregorii Epistolæ, Op. ii. Of modern writers, see Bishop Stubbs on Mellitus in the Dictionary of Christian Biography; and Haddan and Stubbs's Councils and Ecclesiastical Documents, vol. iii.; Kemble's Codex Diplomaticus.] M. B.

MELLON, ALFRED (1820-1867), musician, born in Birmingham, 17 April 1820, became a violinist in the opera and other orchestras, and subsequently leader of the ballet at the Royal Italian Opera, Covent Garden. He held at a later date the post of musical director at the Haymarket and Adelphi Theatres, and afterwards of the Pyne and Harrison English opera company, by whom his opera 'Victorine' was produced at Covent Garden in 1859. He was conductor of the Musical Society, and also of a series of promenade concerts given under his name at Covent Garden. In 1865 he became conductor of the Liverpool Philharmonic Society, and dying 27 March 1867, was buried in Brompton cemetery. He married Miss Woolgar, the well-known actress. He was an excellent musician.

[Grove's Dictionary of Music, ii. 248; Musical Times, May 1867.] J. C. H.

MELLON, HARRIOT, Duchess of St. Albans (1777?–1837), actress, is said to have been born in London 11 Nov. 1777. Her mother, a native of Cork, of peasant descent, was a shopgirl in that city, and was also dresser, wardrobe-keeper, and money-taker in Kena's company, well known in Ireland and Wales. She claimed to have married, on Boxing day 1777, a certain Lieutenant Mathew Mellon of the Madras native infantry, who shortly afterwards deserted her, and has never been traced. Mysterious hints were subsequently dropped by her that the pseudonym hid a person of high rank. She married in 1782 Thomas Entwhistle, leader of the orchestra in Kena's company. Harriot received some education at Ulverstone, Lancashire, where her mother and Entwhistle were jointly engaged in Bibby's company. Here she made her first stage appearance as one of four juvenile mourners around the bier of Juliet. Other juvenile parts followed, and on 16 Oct. 1787, in the barn doing duty for a theatre at Ulverstone, she appeared as Little Pickle in the farce of the 'Spoiled Child.' She subsequently appeared as Priscilla Slowboy in the 'Romp.' On 31 Oct. 1789 she took an older part as Narcissa in 'Inkle and Yarico,' and on 12 Dec. Phœbe in 'As you like it.' She then joined Stanton's company in the midlands, playing for a guinea a week important parts in comedy, including Beatrice, Celia, Lydia Languish, and Letitia Hardy. Her singing and dancing also commanded attention. She was seen by Sheridan, through whom, after some delays, she obtained an engagement at Drury Lane, where she appeared, according to the trustworthy authority of Genest, 31 Jan. 1795, as Lydia Languish. Her beauty and the music of her voice were commended, but her performance was almost a failure. On 15 Oct. 1795 she was Lady Godiva in a revival of O'Keeffe's 'Peeping Tom,' and she played during the season Maria in the 'Spoiled Child,' Lucy in the 'Country Girl,' Maria in 'Twelfth Night,' Blanch in 'King John,' Amanthis in the 'Child of Nature,' and many other parts. In the summer of 1796 she visited Liverpool, where she played an extensive round of characters, including Ophelia, Rosalind, Miranda, Louisa Dudley in the 'West Indian,' Miss Grantham in the 'Liar,' Cherry in the 'Beaux' Stratagem,' and the Page (Cherubin) in the 'Follies of a Day.' At the opening of the Drury Lane season, 20 Sept. 1796, she took again Mrs. Jordan's part of Amanthis in the 'Child of Nature.' She played subsequently Miss Prue in 'Love for Love,' Celia, Maria in 'Twelfth Night,' and Hero in 'Much Ado about Nothing.' Some original parts, including Philotis in the 'Roman Actor' of Massinger, compressed into two acts, and Cicely Copsley in the 'Will' of Reynolds, had already been assigned her. Among the more important parts trusted her in succeeding seasons were Susan in the 'Follies of a Day,' and, 6 Feb. 1800, Estifania in 'Rule a Wife and have a Wife,' Blanch in the 'Iron Chest,' and Albina Mandeville, a 'breeches part,' in which her figure was seen to surpass that of Mrs. Jordan, a former representative. In Allingham's 'Marriage Promise,' 16 April 1803, she was the original Mary. She also played Lady Constant in the 'Way to Keep him,' Olivia in 'A Bold Stroke for a Husband,' and Mrs. Page in the 'Merry Wives of Windsor.' On 31 Jan. 1805 she made a success as the first Volante in Tobin's 'Honeymoon.' Later in the season Mrs. Ford, Angelica in the 'Constant Couple,' Viletta in 'She would and she would not,' and Dorcas in the 'Mock Doctor,' were added to her characters, and she was, 10 Dec. 1806, the heroine of Lamb's ill-starred farce, 'Mr. H——.' Dorinda in the 'Beaux' Stratagem,' Lady Delmar in H. Siddons's 'Time's a Telltale,' Audrey, Nell in the 'Devil to Pay,' Muslin, and Mrs. Candour, the last-named one of her most successful impersonations, followed. On 7 Feb. 1815, as Audrey, she made her last appearance on the stage. While engaged at Drury Lane she had paid frequent summer visits to Liverpool, where she became very popular, and to other provincial towns.

Harriot Mellon was long intimate with Thomas Coutts [q. v.] the banker, said to be the richest man in London, and the connection, which was generally known, caused much unfriendly comment. Early in 1815 Coutts, then eighty years of age, after the death of his first wife, married Harriot Mellon privately at St. Pancras Church. The marriage was publicly announced 2 March 1815. Coutts died 24 Feb. 1822, leaving to his wife the whole of his large fortune. To his children by his first marriage she behaved with much generosity. On 16 June 1827, at her house in Stratton Street, she married William Aubrey de Vere, ninth duke of St. Albans. She died in Stratton Street, 6 Aug. 1837. She was a handsome brunette, with a figure inclining slightly to portliness, great vivacity and animal spirits, generous, ostentatious, and somewhat fiery in temper. As an actress she came in the second line, being eclipsed by Mrs. Jordan. Scott, whom she visited at Abbotsford, regarded her as a kind, friendly woman, 'without either affectation or insolence in the display of her wealth.' Dibdin speaks of her as a great favourite with the public. A portrait of her by Romney was exhibited at Burlington House in 1887. Portraits of her by Sir William Beechey and by Masquerier (as Mrs. Page) belonged to the Baroness Burdett Coutts: the former was engraved by T. Woolnoth. An engraving of her as Cherry was very popular.

[A full but not wholly trustworthy memoir of Mrs. Mellon, by Mrs. Cornwell Harries (afterwards Mrs. Baron Wilson), was published, in 2 vols. 8vo, in 1839, and again in 1886. Scurrilous memoirs of her and her first husband were written with a view principally to extort money. These are fully described in Mr. Lowe's Bibliographical Account of the English Theatre. The Secret Memoirs of Harriott Pumpkin, a Celebrated Actress, &c., is the most infamous of these. It was bought up and destroyed, and copies are scarce and costly. Genest's Account of the English Stage mentions many of her performances, but gives no list. See also Boaden's Life of Mrs. Jordan; Clark Russell's Representative Actors; Dibdin's History of the Stage; the Life of Reynolds; Lockhart's Life of Scott; Notes and Queries, 6th and 7th ser.; Memoir of Charles Mathews; Gent. Mag. for October 1837, and Georgian Era.] J. K.

MELLOR, Sir JOHN (1809–1887), judge, son of John Mellor, a member of an old South Lancashire family, and partner in the firm of Gee, Mellor, Kershaw & Co., who resided at Leicester, and was mayor of the borough and a justice of the peace there, was born at Hollinwood House, Oldham, 1 Jan. 1809. He was educated at the Leicester grammar school, and afterwards under Charles Berry, a unitarian minister of Leicester. Being unwilling to subscribe the Thirty-nine Articles, he abandoned his original intention of entering at Lincoln College, Oxford, and after reading for a time in the office of a Leicester attorney, he entered as a student at the Inner Temple in 1828, read in the chambers of Thomas Chitty for four years, attended John Austin's lectures at University College, and was called to the bar 7 June 1833. He joined the midland circuit, and practised at Leicester borough and Warwick sessions, at assizes, and at the parliamentary bar. After becoming a queen's counsel in 1851 he became leader of the circuit, and also had a fair London practice. From 1849 to 1852 he was recorder of Warwick, and from 1855 to 1861 recorder of Leicester. He stood as a liberal unsuccessfully for Warwick in 1852, and for Coventry in 1857, but late in 1857 he was elected for Great Yarmouth, and at the general election of 1859 was returned for Nottingham. He spoke little in parliament. On 3 Dec. 1861 he succeeded Mr. Justice Hill in the queen's bench and was knighted. He was a member of the special commission which tried the Fenian prisoners at Manchester in 1867 and of the court which tried Arthur Orton, *alias* Castro, for perjury in the Tichborne case in 1873. In June 1879 being troubled with increasing deafness, he retired on a pension and was sworn of the privy council. Thereafter he often attended the judicial committee, went the northern circuit once as commissioner of assize, and frequently acted as an arbitrator in important cases. He died at his house, 16 Sussex Square, Bayswater, on 26 April 1887, and was buried at Dover, where he had lived in his later years, on 30 April. He married in 1833 Elizabeth Cooke, only daughter of William Moseley of Peckham, Surrey, by whom he had eight sons, John William, a queen's counsel, a member of the privy council, judge advocate-general from 1880 to 1885, and chairman of committees in the House of Commons in 1893; James Robert, master of the crown office; and six others. He published two lectures on the 'Christian Church before the Reformation,' 1857, and 'The Life and Times of John Selden,' and a pamphlet advocating the abolition of oaths in courts of law or in parliament in 1882.

[Foss's Judges of England; Law Times, 7 May 1887; Times, 25 April 1887; Solicitors' Journal, 30 April 1887.] J. A. H.

MELMOTH, COURTNEY (1749–1814), miscellaneous writer. [See Pratt, Samuel Jackson.]

MELMOTH, WILLIAM, the elder (1666–1743), religious writer and lawyer, born in 1666, was called to the bar on 29 May 1693. His temperament, even in early life, was meditative and introspective (*Memoir*, pp. 2–3), with a leaning to casuistry, which finds curious expression in some letters which he addressed to his friend John Norris (1657–1711) [q. v.], rector of Bemerton, Wiltshire, when it became necessary to take the oaths to William III (March–May 1693). On 5 June 1699 he was admitted a member of Lincoln's Inn (*Addit. MS.* Brit. Mus. 8127, f. 2). The theology of the government seems to have convinced him of its legitimacy, and about 1705 he entered into an anonymous correspondence with Archbishop Tenison, urging the closing of all theatres as the sole remedy for the depraved stage. He wrote in a similar strain to Defoe, then engaged with his 'Review.' His increasing celebrity as an advocate, however, gradually robbed him of leisure, and, according to his son's statement, he wrote 'The Great Importance of a Religious Life,' his chief work, on Sundays 'in the intervals wrested from the offices of the day.' The remarkable success of this pamphlet was due in a measure to its style, but chiefly to its unaffected hedonistic piety, the whole forming a graceful and ingenious amplification of the theme, 'Man was made for happiness: belief promises this; therefore, belief is best.' He published it anonymously in 1711, and shortly afterwards a collection of prayers and a brief essay on the sacrament. In the edition of 1713 these are added as an appendix to the 'Importance.' The authorship remained a secret during his life, nor did the short character by his son, prefixed to the editions after his death, guide curiosity. John Perceval, first earl of Egmont [q. v.], was generally regarded as the author. Walpole assigned it to him unquestioningly (*Catalogue of Royal and Noble Authors*, 1806, v. 251). Nichols in his edition of Swift (1779) follows Walpole, but corrects the error in 1782 in his 'Anecdotes of Bowyer.' Forty-two thousand copies of the work were sold between 1766 and 1784. It has been often reprinted and translated into French and Welsh.

In June 1719 Melmoth was made a bencher of Lincoln's Inn, and on the death of Thomas Vernon [q. v.] in 1726, he was entrusted, along with Peere-Williams, with the editing of his 'Reports.' In 1730 he was treasurer for the year at Lincoln's Inn. The intended publication of his own 'Reports' he never carried into effect. They are now among the Additional MSS. in the British Museum (8127). Melmoth died on 6 April 1743, and on the 14th was buried in the cloister under the chapel, Lincoln's Inn. After the death of his first wife, whose maiden name was Sambroke, and who seems to have left him some property, he married Catherine, daughter of Samuel Rolt of Bedford, and granddaughter on her mother's side of Dr. Thomas Coxe [q. v.] His son William, by his second wife, is noticed separately.

A portrait, designed by Richardson, is prefixed to the first edition of the 'Great Importance of a Religious Life,' 1711 (Bromley, *Cat.*), and another, by Schiavonetti, to the 'Memoir' written by the son.

[The chief authority for Melmoth's life is the memoir by his son, Memoir of a late eminent Advocate, London, 1796. It contains what is left of his correspondence with Norris, Tenison, and Defoe, and a fragment of a diary. The date of his death is, however, wrongly given as 1748. Later biographies simply follow the Memoir with more or less accuracy. See also Fitzosborne's Letters, 1805; Letters, xi. and lxvii.; Gent. Mag. 1797, pt. i. 586–7; Nichols's Lit. Anecd. 1812, iii. 38–9; Supplement to Swift, ii. 442; Anecdotes of Bowyer, 1782, pp. 381–2; Cooper's edition of the Importance, 1849, Pref. pp. viii, 176; Noble's Continuation of Granger, 1806, iii. 320–1.]

J. A. C.

MELMOTH, WILLIAM, the younger (1710–1799), author and commissioner of bankrupts, son of William Melmoth the elder [q. v.] by his second wife, Catherine Rolt, was born in 1710, most probably in London. He is reported to have studied at Emmanuel College, Cambridge (cf. Cole's manuscript *Athenæ Cantabr.*), and was certainly well educated and a good classical scholar. Bred to the law, he soon abandoned it in order to seek studious quiet in the country. He left London before 1739, and marrying about the same time, settled near Shrewsbury. There he wrote 'Letters on Several Subjects,' his first book, published in 1742, under the pseudonym of Sir Thomas Fitzosborne. His wife, the 'Cleora' of the 'Letters,' was Dorothy, daughter of William King (1685–1763) [q. v.], principal of St. Mary Hall, and she was the subject of his daintiest and most finished effort in verse, the ode written for the third anniversary of their wedding (*Fitzosborne's Letters*, 35). He afterwards contributed many fugitive anonymous essays and verse to the 'World,' but he chiefly occupied himself in his retirement in translating Pliny and Cicero. In 1746 appeared his 'Letters of Pliny the Younger.' The grace and accuracy of the work are remarkable, and partly explain Birch's extravagant praise; Warton placed it among works that are better than their originals. Even Mathias, in his 'Pursuits of Literature' (ed. 1798, p. 355 and note) has a pleasant word for it. A second edition was printed in 1747, a third in 1748. He had meanwhile collected material for a second volume of 'Fitzosborne's Letters,' which he published next year with a translation of the 'De Oratoribus' added to the closing letter. Bowyer brought out the two volumes of 'Letters' together in the same year, in the form that is now familiar. In 1753 he published his translation of Cicero's 'Ad Familiares,' with a careful study of Cicero's character in the running comment. His next work—a translation of the 'De Senectute'—appeared in 1773.

In 1756 Sir John Eardley Wilmot had appointed Melmoth a commissioner of bankrupts, and his letter of thanks, dated 6 Dec. 1756, suggests that the office was more welcome than the easy circumstances of his earlier life would warrant (*Memoirs of Wilmot*, 1802, pp. 9–10). A few years later his wife died, and he broke up his home at Shrewsbury. In 1769 he had settled in Bath. There shortly afterwards he married Mrs. Ogle, a malicious rumour tracing a scene in Garrick's 'Irish Widow' to the circumstances of the engagement. The 'De Senectute' was followed in 1777 by the 'De Amicitia,' with a note on Roman friendship. The 'Travels in Switzerland' of William Coxe [q. v.] consist of letters addressed to Melmoth at this period (1776–9), and in the edition of 1801 Coxe expresses unstinted admiration of the latter as his literary guide (Advert. p. viii). In 1791 Jacob Bryant [q. v.], in his learned and foolish attempt to prove that Rome tolerated every religion except the Christian, attacked Melmoth for asserting in his 'Pliny' that the persecution under Trajan was due not to imperial bigotry, but to the principles of the Roman state. Melmoth vindicated himself in a pamphlet published in 1793, comparing his task, not without fitness, to that of Laberius. His last work was dedicated to his father's memory—the 'Memoir of a late eminent Advocate,' published in 1796. His 'Fitzosborne' reached the tenth edition that year, but in a letter to Wilmot, son of his old patron, he speaks of himself as weak, bedridden, and old. Melmoth was a familiar figure in Bath literary society of the close of the century. Mrs. Thrale described a meeting with him at Mrs. Montagu's in 1780, and drew from Johnson the characteristic snort, 'From the author of "Fitzosborne's Letters" I cannot think myself in much danger. I met him only once, about thirty years ago, and in some small dispute reduced him to whistle' (Boswell, *Life*, ed. G. B. Hill, iii. 422–4, iv. 272 *n.*) An interesting reference to Melmoth is in the 'Notes from the Pocket Book of a late Opium Eater.' 'A lady who had been educated by Melmoth,' writes De Quincey, 'told me about 1813 that she had a trunk full of his manuscripts. As an article of literary gossip this may as well be made known, for some author writing a biographical dictionary may be interested in knowing all that can now be known of Melmoth, and may even wish to examine his manuscripts. . . . For my part I never looked into the "Fitzosborne's Letters" since my boyhood; but the impression I then derived from them was, that Melmoth was a fribble in literature, and one of the "sons of the feeble." Accordingly I shrank myself even from the "sad civility" of asking to look at the manuscripts.' Melmoth was of middle height, spare, with bright, quick eyes, and a deeply lined face. He died at No. 12 Bladud's Buildings, Bath, on 13 May 1799. There is a Latin epitaph on a tablet in Bath Abbey, but Melmoth was buried at Batheaston.

[The Memoir prefixed to the eleventh (1805) edition of Fitzosborne's Letters contains the most satisfactory account of Melmoth. But see also these Letters themselves, passim; Gent. Mag. 1791 ii. 759, 1794 i. 550, 989, 1797 i. 586–7, 1799 i. 261; Europ. Mag. xxxv. 214 (in both of which there are several errors in the dates given to his works); Monthly Review, viii. 340–1, xlix. 109–115, lvii. 461–6, and enlarged ser. xv. 251–2, xxiii. 269–70; Birch's Life of Tillotson, 1752, p. 362; Warton's Essay on Pope, 1782, ii. 325; Works of Pope, 1806, vii. 13; Nichols's Anecdotes, 1812, ii. 193–4, 215, iii. 40–2, iv. 163, v. 414, and Literary Illustrations, i. 613–16; Cole's Athenæ; Pearch's Collection, ii. 142–52; Dodsley's Collection, 1748, i. 185–96; Peach's Historic Houses in Bath, 2nd ser. p. 52; Bryant's Authority of the Scriptures, 1791, pp. 118–25; Brit. Mus. Addit. MS. 32733, f. 411; Autograph Letters, 22, 171.] J. A. C.

MELROSE, Earl of (1563–1637). [See Hamilton, Thomas.]

MELTON, Sir JOHN (*d.* 1640), politician and author, son of Evan Melton, came of a Yorkshire family, and may have been connected with the Meltons of Aston, though the direct line became extinct with Dorothy, only daughter and heiress of Sir John Melton, who died about 1545 (see Poulson, *Holderness*, ii. 199; Hunter, *South Yorkshire*, i. 162; Baker, *Northamptonshire*, i. 672; and *Collectanea Topographica*, passim). Melton was reading law in chambers in 1609 when he published his 'Sixefolde Politician.' In 1616 he contributed commendatory verses to the 'Descriptions' by William Fennor, and in 1620 published his 'Astrologaster.' He was knighted at Whitehall on 4 Nov. 1632. He appears to have increased his means by trading extensively in saltpetre and coal (see *Cal. State Papers*, Dom. 1631–3 pp. 109, 183, and 1638–9 p. 397), and became a personage of some importance. There is a letter from him to James Hay, first earl of Carlisle [q. v.], dated 2 Dec. 1633, preserved in Egerton MS. 2597, f. 166, and another to the Earl of Strafford, dated 4 May 1635, advising him to use his influence to procure the summons of a parliament (*Strafford Letters*, i. 418). In the latter year he was secretary to the council of the north, with an annual salary of 33*l.* 6*s.* 8*d.* In 1640 he was elected M.P. for Newcastle-on-Tyne, but a petition was lodged against his return, and before it was decided Melton died (*Commons' Journals*, 17 Dec. 1640; *Official Returns of Members of Parliament*, i. 491, n. 11). He was buried at Tottenham, and a monument was erected to his memory.

Melton married, apparently in 1634, a lady named Currans, who within the space of twelve months presented him with five children, two sons at the first birth, and at the second, in 1635, two sons and a daughter; the latter event she did not survive (*Cal. State Papers*, Dom. 1635, p. 385).

Melton was author of: 1. 'A Sixefolde Politician . . . together with a Sixefolde Precept of Policy,' 1609, 8vo. This book contains commendatory lines by John Davis, and has been frequently assigned to John Milton's father, but on insufficient grounds; a pun in the first line of the introductory verses would lose its point if the author's name were Milton, not Melton. 2. 'Astrologaster, or the Figure-Caster; rather the Arraignment of Artlesse Astrologers and Fortune-tellers,' 1620, 4to; it is dedicated to Melton's father, Evan, and contains commendatory verses by 'John Hancocke, bachelor of arts and student of Brazenose College, Oxford,' and others by 'John Malin, master of arts and sometime student of Trinity College in Cambridge.' Hunter (*New Illustr. of Shakespeare*, ii. 54) says the 'Astrologaster is now a very curious book, and in its day was no doubt a very useful book.' Copies of both works are preserved in the British Museum Library.

[Works in Brit. Mus. Library; Cal. State Papers, passim; Commons' Journals; Strafford Letters; Egerton MS. 2597; Official Returns of Members of Parliament; Cat. Early Printed Books; Brydges's British Bibliographer, i. 531; Joseph Hunter's New Illustr. of Shakespeare, ii. 54, and his Tract on Milton, pp. 11, 13; Cat. Huth Library; Metcalfe's Book of Knights; Notes and Queries, 1st ser. xii. 420, 4th ser. iv. 476; Lowndes's Bibl. Man.] A. F. P.

MELTON, WILLIAM DE (*d.* 1340), archbishop of York, was born of humble parentage at Melton, in the parish of Welton, near Hull; his parents' names are unknown, but he had a brother Henry, whose son, Sir William de Melton, was his heir. Melton seems to have entered the royal service, and was perhaps employed in some capacity about the person of the young Prince of Wales, for Edward II speaks of Melton as having been in his service from his boyhood (*Fœdera*, ii. 107). Melton is first mentioned in 1299 as rector of Repham, Lincolnshire. In 1300 he was one of the ostiarii of the king's wardrobe, of which department he became comptroller on the accession of Edward II, retaining his office till 1315. In the intervening years Melton received a variety of ecclesiastical preferments. He was rector of Hornsea, Yorkshire, 10 July 1301, Lythe 13 March 1308, Thorpland, Norfolk, 1309, and Spofforth, Yorkshire, 4 Aug. 1310. On 2 Jan. 1305 he received the prebend of Oxton with Cropwell at Southwell, which on 30 July 1309 he exchanged for that of Norwell-Palishall. He was prebendary of Louth, Lincoln, from 1309 to 1317; on 3 May 1309 exchanged a stall at Westbury, Gloucestershire, for one at Beverley; and on 23 March 1310 one at Darlington for that of Driffield, York. He was also dean of St. Martin-le-Grand, London, 27 Aug. 1308, archdeacon of Barnstaple 13 Oct. 1308 to March 1309, and provost of Beverley on 6 Oct. 1309. Soon after the accession of Edward II Melton is mentioned as the king's clerk, and in October 1307 as keeper of the privy seal (*Close Rolls, Edward II*, pp. 3, 42). In January 1308 he accompanied the king on his journey to France, and had charge of the great seal, being apparently at this time the king's secretary (*ib.* p. 57; *Fœdera*, ii. 29). Edward regarded him with special favour, and in May 1310 Melton had temporary charge of the great seal (*Close Rolls, Edward II*, p. 258). On 20 April 1310, and again on 12 Nov. 1312, the king addressed commendatory letters on Melton's behalf to the pope and to certain cardinals (*Fœdera*, ii. 107, 187). In 1312 he was one of the proctors of the northern convocation in refusing an aid to the king (*Letters from the Northern Registers*, 211–12), and on 12 Aug. of that year one of the commissioners from the king to the Cinque ports (*Parl. Writs*, II. ii. 43). On 3 May 1313 he was sent abroad on the royal service (*Fœdera*, ii. 211), and on 1 Aug. was a commissioner for the protection of the Scottish marches.

On 21 Jan. 1316 Melton, being then treasurer of the king's wardrobe, was through royal influence elected archbishop of York (*Flores Historiarum*, iii. 169). The royal assent was given 5 Feb., and letters commendatory to the pope issued three days later (*Fœdera*, ii. 285). Melton at once went abroad, but was detained at Avignon for over eighteen months before he could procure papal confirmation, despite numerous letters addressed by the king on his behalf to the pope and various cardinals (*ib.* ii. 300, 305, 314, 332, 337). The delay seems to have been partly due to the interregnum in the papacy between the death of Clement V and the election of John XXII, but also to intrigues among the cardinals. It was not till 25 Sept. 1317 that Melton was consecrated at Avignon by Pope John XXII (Stubbs, p. 415; 11 Sept. according to Murimuth, p. 26). He returned to England on 24 Nov., and had his cross borne before him through Kent and London to St. Martin-le-Grand (*Chron. Edward I and II*, i. 281). Early in Advent he was at Beverley, but was not enthroned at York till 13 Feb. 1318 (Stubbs, p. 416). The early years of Melton's episcopate were much disturbed through the troubles with the Scots (cf. *Letters from the Northern Registers*, 273–279). On 18 March 1318 he was one of the commissioners to treat with Bruce, and in June one of the keepers of the marches. In the summer of 1319 the Scots broke past the king at Berwick and began to ravage Yorkshire. Melton in conjunction with John Hotham [q. v.] and other northern ecclesiastics mustered what forces they could, and met the Scots at Myton-on-Swale on 12 Sept. The English were utterly routed, and the archbishop and other leaders escaped with difficulty. Melton's banner was saved only by the valour of its bearer. In ridicule of the ecclesiastical soldiers Barbour says this battle was called

> The Chaptour of Mytoun, for thar
> Slane sa many prestis war.

On 19 Jan. 1321 Melton again appears as a commissioner for peace with Scotland (*Fœdera*, ii. 441). On 28 June he attended the meeting held by Earl Thomas of Lancaster and the northern lords at Sherburn in Elmet, but he did not accompany the barons to London, and in the following spring sided with the Despensers against the earl (*Flores Historiarum*, iii. 190, 206). Yet, on the other hand, Melton was on 9 April 1322 censured for inducing his clergy to grant two thousand marks to Thomas of Lancaster (*Parl. Writs*, ii. i. 556); and in 1323 gave his protection to Adam Orleton [q. v.], bishop of Hereford (Blaneforde, p. 141). However, on 7 Aug. 1323 he prohibited the worship of Thomas as unauthorised (*Letters from the Northern Registers*, 323–6).

On 18 June 1323 Melton appears as justiciar for Nottinghamshire, and on 8 Nov. as commissioner to treat with the Scots. On 3 June 1325 he was appointed treasurer of England, an office which he held till January 1327, when he was displaced by the government of the young king, Edward III. Melton refused to be present at Edward's coronation, but he was nevertheless sent on a mission to Scotland in April (*Cal. Pat. Rolls, Edward III*, p. 95). He would indeed seem to have accepted the change of government to the full, for on 24 Feb. he had written to the pope in favour of the canonisation of Thomas of Lancaster (*Letters from the Northern Registers*, 339–342). Melton also officiated at the marriage of Edward to Philippa of Hainault on 24 Jan. 1328. Nevertheless he seems to have entered into the plot of Edmund of Woodstock, earl of Kent [q. v.], in the beginning of 1329, in the belief that Edward II was still alive. The earl's confession distinctly alleges that Melton had promised to contribute 5,000*l.* towards the undertaking (Murimuth, App. p. 255); on the other hand, although Melton was indicted for his share in the plot, he was acquitted, and obtained a writ of conspiracy against his accusers (*Rot. Parl.* ii. 31, 54). After the overthrow of Mortimer, Melton was once more made treasurer on 28 Nov. 1330, but only held office till 1 April following. On 16 Feb. 1331 he was one of the justiciars for enforcing observance of the truce with Scotland, and on 1 Dec. 1332 had power to open parliament at York (*Fœdera*, ii. 802, 848). From 10 Aug. 1333 to 13 Jan. 1334 he was keeper of the great seal during the temporary absence of John de Stratford [q. v.]

This was the end of Melton's official life, but he survived till 1340, when he died on 4 or 5 April at Cawood, and was buried in York Minster, near the font. His tomb was opened during the last century, when his skeleton, about six feet long, was found; the chalice and paten were then removed from the tomb (Drake, *Eboracum*, p. 433). One incident of his episcopal administration was a long dispute with Walter Reynolds [q. v.], archbishop of Canterbury, as to his right to bear the cross in the southern province; on this ground Reynolds opposed Melton's appointment as treasurer in 1325 (*Chron. Edw. I and II*, ii. 283–4). Melton was also involved in a dispute with his chapter as to his rights of visitation, but this was settled in February 1329. Another quarrel, which began in 1328, was with Louis de Beaumont [q. v.], bishop of Durham, as to the rights of visitation in Allertonshire. Beaumont resisted his superior by force, but after excommunication and suspension, the matter was at length compromised in 1331. On Beaumont's death, on 24 Sept. 1333, Melton was engaged in a fresh trouble, for he confirmed and consecrated Robert de Graystanes [q. v.] as bishop, although the pope had provided Richard de Bury [q. v.] to the see, and the king had not given his assent; in the issue Graystanes had to resign. Melton's register, which is very full, is preserved at York; numerous documents are printed in Raine's 'Letters from the Northern Registers,' and many are summarised in the 'Fasti Eboracenses.' Thomas Stubbs describes Melton as charitable and pious, parsimonious to himself, bountiful to the needy, and above all to the religious, as well mendicants as others (*Historians of the Church of York*, ii. 416). Another writer speaks of him as a man faithful in all that was trusted to him, and not corrupted by his long intercourse with the court (*Chron. Edw. I and II*, ii. 284). Melton's episcopate was marked by much progress in the building of York minster; he restored the tomb of St. William, and gave 700*l.* towards the completion of the nave. The west end was erected in his time, and it is probably his statue which occupies the niche over the great doorway. He also fortified the Old Bailey at York. Melton amassed considerable wealth; this was inherited by his nephew, Sir William de Melton (1317–1362), who became the founder of a knightly family at Aston, Yorkshire.

[Chronicles of Edward I and II; Flores Historiarum; Murimuth's Chronicle; Letters from the Northern Registers; Historians of the Church of York; Chron. de Melsa; Annales de Trokelowe, Blaneforde, &c. (all these are in the Rolls Ser.); Robert de Graystanes's Chronicle in Hist. Dunelm. Scriptores Tres (Surtees Soc.); Chron. de Lanercost (Bannatyne Club); Cal. of Close Rolls, Edward II; Cal. of Patent Rolls, Edward III; Rymer's Fœdera, Record ed.; Le Neve's Fasti Eccl. Angl. i. 406, ii. 180, iii. 106, 182, 440, 447; Dixon and Raine's Fasti Eboracenses, pp. 397–437; Foss's Judges of England, iii. 461–3.] C. L. K.

MELTON, WILLIAM DE (*d.* 1528), chancellor of York, a native of Yorkshire, was educated at Cambridge, where he graduated M.A. 1479, B.D. 1490, and D.D. 1496. In 1495 he was master of Michaelhouse, Cambridge, and on 13 Jan. 1495–6 became chancellor of the church of York. He died at the end of 1528, and his will is dated 28 Aug. of that year, from Acklam, Yorkshire. He is supposed to have been buried either there or in York minster. He was famed as a philosopher, divine, and preacher, and was for some time tutor to Fisher (cf. *De Veritate Corporis*, p. 327). Melton was author of a 'Sermo Exhortatorius,' published by Wynkyn de Worde in 1494, a copy of which is in the British Museum Library. His wills and inventories are printed in 'Test. Ebor.' (Surtees Soc.), pp. 251–63.

Melton has been constantly confused with his namesakes William de Melton (*d.* 1340) [q. v.], archbishop of York, and William of Meliton [q. v.] Misled by the identity of name, Wood (*Athenæ Oxon.* i. 49) claimed him for Oxford. Pits, Tanner, and others state that he was a Dominican (which is an additional mistake, because Meliton was a Franciscan, not a Dominican) and chancellor of the university of Paris, and attribute to him numerous works written by Meliton (cf. Sixtus Senensis, *Bibl. Sancta*, iv. 243; Echard, *Scriptores Ord. Prædicatorum*, i. 488; and Sbaralæus, *Supplementum ad Scriptores Trium Ordinum*, pp. 324–5).

There was yet another William de Melton, a Franciscan, who in 1426 preached at York on the subject of miracle plays, and in 1427 went about the country preaching against tithes. He was arrested and brought to Oxford, where he was compelled to recant (*Greyfriars in Oxford*, pp. 86, 259).

[Authorities quoted; Brit. Mus. Cat.; Cooper's Athenæ Cantabr. i. 37; Tanner, p. 521; Le Neve's Fasti, iii. 165; Pits, p. 696; Yorks. Archæol. Journ. viii. 291.] A. F. P.

MELUN, ROBERT DE (*d.* 1167), bishop of Hereford. [See Robert.]

MELVILL, HENRY (1798–1871), canon of St. Paul's, fifth son of Philip Melvill (1762–1811), an officer in the army, who was lieutenant-governor of Pendennis Castle from 1797 till 1811, by his wife Elizabeth Carey (1770–1844), daughter of Peter Dobree of Beauregard, Guernsey, was born in Pendennis Castle, Cornwall, on 14 Sept. 1798, and became a sizar of St. John's College, Cambridge, in October 1817. After migrating to St. Peter's College he passed as second wrangler in 1821, and was a fellow and tutor of his college from 1822 to 1832. He graduated B.A. 1821, M.A. 1824, and B.D. 1836. From 1829 to 1843 he served as incumbent of Camden Chapel, Camberwell, London; was appointed by the Duke of Wellington chaplain to the Tower of London in 1840; was principal of the East India College, Haileybury, from 1843 till the college was closed on 7 Dec. 1857; Golden lecturer at St. Margaret's, Lothbury, 1850–1856; one of the chaplains to Queen Victoria, 13 June 1853; canon residentiary of St. Paul's, 21 April 1856; and rector of Barnes, Surrey, 1863–71. Melvill for many years had the reputation of being 'the most popular preacher in London,' and one of the greatest rhetoricians of his time. First at Camden Chapel, then at St. Margaret's, and later on at St. Paul's, large crowds of people attended his ministrations. His sermon generally occupied three-quarters of an hour, but such was the rapidity of his utterance that he spoke as much in that time as an ordinary preacher would have done in an hour. His delivery was earnest and animated without distinctive gesticulation; his voice was clear and flexible; while his emphatic pronunciation and his hurried manner of speaking impressed the hearers with a conviction of his sincerity. But his sermons lacked simplicity and directness of style, and his ornate phraseology, his happy analogies, smoothly balanced sentences, appealed more directly to the literary than to the spiritual sense. His views were evangelical, and he was a zealous parish priest. He died at the residentiary house, Amen Corner, London, 9 Feb. 1871, and was buried in St. Paul's Cathedral on 15 Feb. He married Margaret Alice, daughter of Peter Dobree of Beauregard, Guernsey. She died 18 April 1878, aged 73, leaving a daughter Edith, who married Clement Alexander Midleton.

Melvill's more important works—all sermons—were: 1. 'Sermons, 1833-8,' 2 vols., 6th edit. 1870. 2. 'Sermons preached before the University of Cambridge,' to which are added two sermons preached in Great St. Mary's, 1836, five editions. 3. 'Four Sermons preached before the University of Cambridge,' 1837, five editions. 4. 'Four Sermons preached before the University of Cambridge,' 1839, three editions. 5. 'Sermons preached at Cambridge,' 1840. 6. 'Sermons on certain of the less prominent Facts and References in Sacred Story,' 1843-5, 2 vols., new edit. 1872. 7. 'Sermons preached on Public Occasions,' 1846. 8. 'The Preacher in Print,' 'The Golden Lectures,' 'Forty-eight Sermons delivered at St. Margaret's Church, Lothbury,' 1850 (published without Melvill's sanction). 9. 'Thoughts appropriate to the Season and the Days: Lectures delivered at St. Margaret's, Lothbury,' 1851. 10. 'A Selection from the Lectures delivered at St. Margaret's, Lothbury,' 1853. 11. 'The Golden Lectures for the Years 1850 to 1855 inclusive,' 1856, 6 vols. 12. 'Selections from the Sermons preached in the Parish Church of Barnes, and in the Cathedral of St. Paul's,' 1872, 2 vols.

[Grant's Metropolitan Pulpit, 1839, ii. 1-21; Diary of H. C. Robinson, 1869, iii. 177-8; Ritchie's London Pulpit, 1858, pp. 60-8; Johnson's Popular Preachers, 1863, pp. 189-201; Hood and Longwill's Preacher's Lantern, 1871, i. 193-207, 257-67, 332-42; The Pulpit, 1830, xiv. 92-3; Roose's Ecclesiastica, 1842, pp. 410-413; The Lamps of the Temple, 3rd edit. 1856, pp. 210-41; Blanch's Parish of Camberwell, 1875, pp. 209-10; Illustrated London News, 1844 iv. 48, with portrait, 1871 lviii. 163; Illustrated News of the World, 6 Sept. 1862, with portrait; Boase and Courtney's Bibl. Cornub. pp. 345-8, 1279-80; Boase's Collect. Cornub. 1890, col. 552; cf. Memoirs of the late Philip Melvill, esq., 1812, 2nd edit. 1815.] G. C. B.

MELVILL, THOMAS (1726-1753), experimental philosopher, was a student of divinity in 1748-9 at the university of Glasgow, where he became intimate with Dr. Alexander Wilson [q. v.] They discussed many philosophic schemes, and experimented together, by means of kites, on the temperature of the air at various altitudes. Melvill then studied optics with the view of verifying Newton's theories. His 'Observations on Light and Colours,' read before the Medical Society of Edinburgh on 3 Jan. and 7 Feb. 1752, showed him to be familiar with the use of the prism for examining coloured flames, and contained a remarkable notice of the peculiar yellow light of burning sodium (*Edinburgh Physical and Literary Essays*, ii. 34). These fundamental experiments in spectrum analysis were not repeated until after seventy years.

In a communication to Dr. Bradley on the 'Cause of the different Refrangibility of the Rays of Light,' dated from Geneva 2 Feb. 1753, and read before the Royal Society on 8 March, Melvill threw out the idea of employing the eclipses of Jupiter's satellites to test possible variations with colour in the velocity of light (*Phil. Trans.* xlviii. 261). A second letter to Bradley of 2 June suggested that the rate of light-travel concerned in aberration might be that in the humours of the eye itself. Melvill died at Geneva in December 1753, at the early age of twenty-seven.

[Edinburgh Phys. and Lit. Essays, ii. 12; Brewster's Edinburgh Journal of Science, x. 5, 1829; Chemical News, v. 251 (Jevons); Priestley's Hist. of Optics, i. 359; Clerke's Popular Hist. of Astronomy, p. 165, 2nd ed.] A. M. C.

MELVILLE, Viscounts. [See Dundas, Henry, first Viscount, 1740-1811; Dundas, Robert Saunders, second Viscount, 1771-1857; Dundas, Henry, third Viscount, 1801-1876.]

MELVILLE or MELVILL, ANDREW (1545-1622), Scottish presbyterian leader and scholar, youngest child of Richard Melvill (*d.* 1547) of Baldovie, Forfarshire, by his wife Gills, daughter of Thomas Abercrombie of Montrose, was born at Baldovie on 1 Aug. 1545. He is described as the ninth son, yet speaks in a letter of 1612 as having outlived his 'fourteen brethren.' The family was attached to the reformed religion. His father was killed at the battle of Pinkie, his mother died soon after, and he was brought up by his eldest brother, Richard (1522-1575), who had married Isabel Scrimgeour. This brother and two others, James and John, subsequently entered the reformed ministry. Andrew was educated first at the Montrose grammar school, and in 1559 entered St. Mary's College, St. Andrews; in the matriculation list his name is given as 'Andreas Mailuile.' His knowledge of Greek, 'quhilk his maisters understood nocht,' created wonder; he had gained it at Montrose (1557–9) under Pierre de Marsiliers, established there as a teacher by John Erskine [q. v.] of Dun. Since Melvill addresses George Buchanan (1506–1582) [q.v.] as 'præceptori suo,' McCrie thinks it possible that Buchanan may have given him 'private instructions' during visits to St. Andrews. There also McCrie places his introduction to Pietro Bizari [q. v.], who in 1565 addressed verses to Melvill as well as to Buchanan.

Having graduated at St. Andrews, he repaired to France in the autumn of 1564, reaching Paris from Dieppe after a roundabout and stormy voyage. He now attained great fluency in Greek, made acquirements in oriental languages, studied mathematics and law, and came under the direct influence of Peter Ramus, whose new methods of teaching he subsequently transplanted to Scotland. From Paris he proceeded in 1566 to Poitiers for further study of law. He was at once made regent in the college of St. Marceon; his skill in Latin verse and in classic oratory gave his college the advantage in literary contests with the rival college of St. Pivareau. Classes were broken up in 1568 during the siege of Poitiers by the Huguenots under Coligny. As a protestant, though not an obtrusive one, Melvill fell under suspicion of sympathy with the besiegers, but he proved his readiness to take part in the defence of the place. He left Poitiers, however, on the raising of the siege, and made his way with some difficulty to Geneva.

Beza received him with open arms, and he was placed forthwith in the vacant chair of humanity in the Genevan academy. Still young (twenty-three) he availed himself of every opportunity of study, frequenting the lectures of his colleagues. At Geneva as early as 1570 he met Joseph Scaliger and Francis Hottoman, who in 1572, after the massacre on St. Bartholomew's day, took up their abode in that city.

Melvill till 1572 did not correspond with his friends in Scotland; his home letters in that year brought him successive appeals, the earliest being from his nephew, James Melville (1556–1614) [q. v.], to devote his powers to raising the standard of education in his own country. In 1573 he published at Basle his first volume of Latin verse, and in the same year obtained his demission from the Genevan Academy. In the spring of 1574 he left Geneva, carrying a commendatory letter from Beza to the Scottish general assembly. At Paris he conducted for some days a public discussion in the Jesuits' College. Alarmed by some words of James Beaton (1517–1603) [q. v.], the refugee archbishop of Glasgow, he left Paris on 30 May 1573, and proceeding by Dieppe, Rye, and London, reached Edinburgh early in July.

Declining a post in the household of the regent, James Douglas, fourth earl of Morton [q. v.], for which he was recommended by Buchanan, Melvill stayed three months with his brother Richard at Baldovie, directing the studies of his nephew James, whom his father committed henceforth wholly to his charge. In the autumn of 1574 he was appointed John Davidson's successor as head of the college of Glasgow which had been closed since Davidson's death in 1572. After spending a couple of days at Stirling, where he was introduced to the youthful James VI, and had some consultation with Buchanan, Melvill settled in Glasgow early in November 1574.

With his appointment 'the literary history of the university of Glasgow properly commences' (McCrie). His plan was twofold, the introduction of an enlarged curriculum, extending over six years, and the training of 'regents,' to whom he might delegate the permanent conduct of special branches of study. Within six years he established four chairs in languages, science, and philosophy, reserving divinity to the principal. To the principalship was annexed on 13 July 1577 the charge of Govan, near Glasgow, where Melvill preached every Sunday. In the same year a royal charter, the 'nova erectio,' confirmed his plan of studies.

Meanwhile Melvill was an active leader in ecclesiastical affairs, and a prime mover in the steps by which the organisation of the Scottish church was definitely cast in a presbyterian mould. Spotiswood (his pupil) represents him as an iconoclast, ascribing to him the design of demolishing the cathedral of Glasgow as a monument of idolatry. This seems a complete misapprehension. Even the outbreak of popular iconoclasm in the early days of Knox was directed only against images and monasteries. The reforming policy was to utilise all churches for protestant worship, the larger ones being sometimes divided for the accommodation of several congregations. Melvill's attack was directed against the remaining forms of episcopacy. The first 'book of discipline' (1561) had permitted a quasi-episcopacy in the shape of 'superintendents.' The convention of Leith (1572) had re-established the hierarchy, though with limited powers. Melvill was appointed (March 1575) on the general assembly's committee for drafting a scheme of church government, which was set forth in the second 'book of discipline,' sanctioned by the general assembly (though not by the state) in 1581. His prominence as an ecclesiastical leader is shown by his being selected by the regent Morton in October 1577 as the first of three deputies to a proposed general council of protestants at Magdeburg. On 24 April 1578 he was for the first time elected moderator of the general assembly.

The second 'book of discipline' discarded every vestige of prelacy, set aside patronage, placed ordination in the hands of the eldership, and established a gradation of church courts. To church courts was assigned a jurisdiction independent of the civil magistrate. On the one hand, the exercise of civil jurisdiction was forbidden to the clergy; on the other, the church court was entitled to instruct the civil magistrate in the exercise of his jurisdiction, according to the divine word. It did not, however, complete the development of the Scottish 'presbytery,' for it recognised no intermediate court between the eldership of the particular congregation and the assembly of the province; though it pointed the way to 'presbyteries' by allowing three or four contiguous congregations to have an eldership in common. Melvill's ecclesiastical polity has been treated as the fruit of his experience of foreign protestantism, especially in Geneva. As regards his grasp of principles this is true. But he did not bring with him from abroad any rigid model to be followed, and the ultimate shape of Scottish presbyterianism was a native growth.

Melvill's ideas of Scottish university reform were not limited to Glasgow. In 1575 he assisted Alexander Arbuthnot (1538–1583) [q. v.], principal of King's College, Aberdeen, in the formation of a new constitution for that university. In 1578 he was appointed by the Scottish parliament a commissioner for the visitation of St. Andrews, the richest and most frequented of the Scottish universities. The plan for its reformation (ratified 11 Nov. 1579) was mainly his; he had the advantage here of working on the lines of a prior scheme drawn up in 1563 by George Buchanan (1506–1582) [q. v.], on which, however, he materially improved. Of the three colleges at St. Andrews, St. Mary's, or the New College (begun 1532, finished 1552), was henceforth reserved for a four years' course of theological studies under five professors.

In October 1580 a royal letter invited the concurrence of the assembly in the translation of Melvill to St. Andrews as principal of St. Mary's. Melvill accepted the appointment in November. Chairs at St. Andrews were at once offered, but in vain, to Thomas Cartwright (1535–1603) [q. v.] and Walter Travers (see letter in FULLER, *Church Hist.* bk. ix. p. 215; internal evidence proves the date). Taking with him his nephew James as professor of oriental languages, Melvill began his work at St. Andrews in December 1580. The new arrangements had displaced several men who had grievances not easily satisfied. The professors of St. Leonard's College delivered inflammatory lectures in fierce defence of the authority of Aristotle, 'owirharled' by Melvill in the name of the new learning. In return he promoted the real study of Aristotle, created a taste for Greek letters, and in philosophy, as in biblical knowledge, superseded the second-hand methods of an effete scholasticism. In September 1581 he paid a visit in Edinburgh with other friends to George Buchanan, whose history was then in the press. Buchanan showed them the epistle dedicatory to the king, which Melvill thought 'obscure in sum places.' Buchanan seems to have accepted Melvill's corrections.

At the general assembly which met at Edinburgh in October 1581, Melvill exhibited fifteen articles of libel against Robert Montgomery (*d.* 1609) [q. v.], who had accepted from Esmé Stuart, first duke of Lennox [q. v.], the see of Glasgow, the revenues, except a small pension, going to Lennox himself. It was this kind of simoniacal arrangement which gave rise to the name of 'tulchan' bishops. The prosecution of Montgomery was resumed at the general assembly which met at St. Andrews, in St. Mary's College, on 24 April 1582, Melvill being moderator. In the face of a royal inhibition, Montgomery was tried, convicted on eight articles, and would have been excommunicated but for his temporary submission. As the submission did not last, the assembly's order for excommunication was carried out by John Davidson (1549?–1603) [q. v.] at Liberton, near Edinburgh. The assembly and the court were now at open war. A special meeting of assembly was convened at Edinburgh on 27 June. Melvill, in his opening sermon, denounced the doctrine of the ecclesiastical supremacy of the crown. He was retained as moderator, and appointed on a commission to wait upon James VI at Perth with a remonstrance and petition. His relatives urged the danger of his errand, but Melvill was fearless. He presented the remonstrance to the king in council. 'Wha,' exclaimed Arran, 'dar subscryve thir treasonable articles?' Melvill replied, 'We dar and will,' and immediately subscribed, followed by the other commissioners.

By the 'raid of Ruthven' (22 Aug. 1582) Lennox and James Stewart, earl of Arran [q. v.], were dislodged, and the party whose ecclesiastical policy was directed by Melvill grasped for a short season the reins of power. Seven of the bishops were ordered by the general assembly in October to be tried before presbyteries; Melvill and Smeton were appointed to examine into the case of Adam Bothwell [q. v.], bishop of Orkney. But on 27 June 1583 James escaped from the hands of the confederated lords, and the bishops were again protected.

In January 1584 Robert Browne [q. v.], the English separatist, arrived at Dundee from Middelburg with a handful of his followers. Making his way to St. Andrews, he obtained from Melvill a commendatory letter to James Lawson [q. v.], minister of St. Giles's, Edinburgh, and settled in the Canongate for a short time, but after quarrelling with the Edinburgh presbytery, returned to England.

Melvill, on 15 Feb. 1584, was summoned before the privy council at Edinburgh to answer for alleged treason in a fast sermon at St. Andrews in June previous. He appeared on 17 Feb. and explained his language, a strong and perhaps ambiguous outcome of his favourite doctrine of the independence of the church. There was no ground for charging him with sedition, nevertheless the privy council determined to proceed with his trial. Next day he read a formal protest against the action of the council in a spiritual matter, claiming to be tried, in the first instance, by an ecclesiastical court at St. Andrews, the scene of the alleged offence. Order was made for his imprisonment in Edinburgh Castle for contempt of court. His friends kept him in hiding. When the place of his proposed incarceration was changed to Blackness Castle, Linlithgowshire, they assisted him to escape, with his brother Roger, to Berwick, where he joined the banished lords of the Ruthven raid. In the following May the royal supremacy in ecclesiastical affairs was established, and the jurisdiction of bishops restored, while Adamson, archbishop of St. Andrew's, suppressed the teaching of theology at St. Mary's College.

From Berwick, in June, Melvill proceeded to London, accompanied by Patrick Forbes (1564–1635) [q. v.], and was soon joined by a number of ministers of his party in flight from Scotland. At the court of Elizabeth he did his best to win friends for the Scottish presbyterians. He was well received at Oxford and Cambridge in July, both by the puritan leaders Rainolds and Whitaker, and by men of letters. Returning to London, he read a Latin lecture on Genesis at the chapel in the Tower, which was exempt from episcopal jurisdiction, and placed by its lieutenant at the disposal of the Scottish ministers. Arran's fall, a preliminary to James's English alliance, led to the return to Scotland of Melvill and his friends. On 4 Nov. 1585, at Stirling, the confederated lords became once more masters of the situation.

The Linlithgow parliament of December 1585 restored the 'peregrine' ministers to their places, but left untouched the reactionary measures of the previous year. A personal contest between James and the presbyterian ministers, headed by Melvill, produced only certain royal 'explanations' of the obnoxious acts. In February 1586 a compromise with episcopacy was agreed on between the more moderate ministers and members of the privy council. At the meeting of the synod of Fife, in April, Adamson was arraigned by James Melvill, evidently acting in concert with his uncle, and a sentence of excommunication was passed, in a manner 'precipitant and irregular' (McCrie). The general assembly in May removed the excommunication and made terms with Adamson; its decree formally divided the kingdom into provincial synods and presbyteries. James ordered Melvill to Baldovie during pleasure, and presently sent him (26 May) on a mission to jesuits north of the Tay. But during the autumn he resumed his academic labours at St. Mary's, although under injunction not to preach except in Latin. He acted as a ruling elder in the kirk-session of St. Andrews. In 1590 he was placed at the head of the university of St. Andrews as its rector.

In June 1587 Melvill was moderator of the general assembly at Edinburgh. At the end of the month James visited St. Mary's College with Du Bartas, the French poet, commanded a lecture from Melvill, and heard an oration by Adamson in support of prelacy. Melvill answered Adamson with great tactical skill, proving his arguments to be derived from Roman catholic authorities. As moderator he convened a special meeting of the general assembly for 6 Feb. 1588, in view of the threatened expedition of the Spanish Armada. James resented the interference. A party, headed by George Gordon, sixth earl of Huntly [q. v.], urged him to open the Scottish ports to the Armada, but a deputation from the assembly, with Melvill's pupil Robert Bruce (1554–1631) [q. v.] as moderator, steadied his purpose; a bond of national defence against Spain was promoted by the presbyterian clergy.

At the coronation of the queen on Sunday, 17 May 1590, only presbyterian ministers officiated, Melvill reciting a Latin poem, which was published by royal command. When Adamson was deposed by the assembly and neglected by James, Melvill met his necessities from his own purse, and by a contribution from his friends. At the same time he insisted on Adamson's recantation as the condition of release from excommunication. Adamson's death (19 Feb. 1592) removed the ablest advocate of episcopacy. The parliament in June 1592 ratified the presbyterian system, confirming, however, the rights of patrons, and not affecting the civil status of bishops, including their right to sit in parliament. Melvill was again moderator of the general assembly at Edinburgh in May 1594. Huntly and other catholic peers left Scotland in 1595, and Melvill used every means in his power to prevent their return. In August 1596 he forced himself into a meeting of the privy council at Falkland to protest against Huntly's proposals. He was excluded, but made himself the spokesman of a deputation to the king in the following month, when he plucked James by the sleeve, calling him 'Gods sillie vassall,' claimed the character of loyal patriotism for the policy of his party, and extorted a promise that the demands of the church should be respected.

The tide now turned against the presbyterian cause. The general assembly convened by James at Perth for 28 Feb. 1597 adopted thirteen articles which gave new power to the king in ecclesiastical affairs, and forbade the clergy to preach on matters of state. Melvill was not present, and his party unsuccessfully challenged the legality of the assembly. In June 1597 James made a visitation of St. Andrews University. Melvill was deprived of the rectorship, a council nominated by the king was entrusted with the government of the university, and all holders of chairs, not being pastors, were prohibited from sitting in church courts, except that one representative (whose election was carefully guarded) was given to the university in the general assembly. Notwithstanding this, Melvill presented himself at the general assembly at Dundee in March 1598. James personally bade him withdraw, and he was compelled to leave the town. By way of amends he was made dean of the faculty of theology in the summer of 1599. He maintained the leadership of his party by assisting at extra-judicial meetings of clergy. One of the most important of these was the conference held at Holyrood House, November 1599, in James's presence, on the admission of bishops to parliament. His personal controversies with James were not limited to verbal altercation. In 1599 James printed the first edition of the 'Basilicon Doron,' consisting of only seven copies. One of them came into Melvill's hands through Sir James Sempill. He extracted propositions from it, and caused them to be censured by the synod of Fife. At Montrose, in March 1600, he again unsuccessfully claimed his right to sit in the assembly; he appears, however, to have been admitted to the assembly of May 1601 at Burntisland. In June 1602, in a sermon at St. Andrews, he condemned the attitude of some of the clergy, and was ordered (11 July) to confine himself within the precincts of his college.

Melvill hailed the accession of James to the English throne with a series of odes, in which he addressed him as 'Scotangle princeps, optime principum.' He was in favour of a legislative union of the two kingdoms. In 1605 nine presbyteries sent their representatives to Aberdeen, and after constituting the general assembly in defiance of the king's messenger adjourned to 28 Sept. Severe measures were taken with the leaders of this meeting, in whose behalf and in behalf of the right of free assembly, Melvill headed a protest (drafted by Patrick Simson) which was offered to the parliament at Perth in August 1606. He was summoned, with his nephew and six other ministers, to appear in London before 15 Sept.

He reached London by 25 Aug.; John Gordon [q. v.], dean of Salisbury, had instructions for him. The ministers were lodged at Kingston-on-Thames, and received at Hampton Court on 20, 22, and 23 Sept. Melvill, who made two uncompromising speeches, each of nearly an hour's length, on behalf of the freedom of assemblies, turned upon the Scottish lord advocate (Thomas Hamilton, afterwards Earl of Melrose [q. v.]), and vituperated him in a Greek phrase. 'By God,' said James, 'it is the devil's name in the Revelation.' After some further parleying, Melvill and his friends were required to attend in the Chapel Royal on Sunday, 28 Sept. Melvill, returning from this service to his lodging, penned a bitter Latin epigram on the accessories of Anglican worship. For this he was brought before the English privy council at Whitehall on 10 Nov. Here he turned the tables upon Archbishop Bancroft, by producing his former publication against James's title to the English crown; and seizing the white sleeves of Bancroft's rochet, he called them 'Romish rags.' At length he was removed, and placed in the custody of John Overal, D.D. [q.v.], then dean of St. Paul's. On 9 March 1607 he was nominally transferred to the custody of Bilson, bishop of Winchester, but permitted to be at large and consort with his Scottish brethren. He was again summoned to the privy council at Whitehall on 26 April, and once more taxed with his epigram. He broke forth into personal and unsparing invective directed against members of the council, lay and clerical. He was sent by water to the Tower. A royal commission on 16 June declared the principalship of St. Mary's College vacant. His confinement was solitary; pen, ink, and paper were forbidden him; he covered the walls of his chamber with Latin verses, scratched with the tongue of his shoe-buckle.

Not till April 1608 was some relaxation allowed, through the good offices of Sir James Sempill. He was indulged with the company of a young nephew and great-nephew, to whom he gave tuition. Meanwhile the authorities of La Rochelle had applied to James for his removal thither as professor of divinity in their college, but the French court had interfered. Melvill at the end of 1608 addressed a copy of conciliatory verses to James, and an apologetic letter to the privy council, on the advice of Archbishop Spotiswood. Among his friendly visitors were Isaac Casaubon [q. v.] and Joseph Hall [q. v.], afterwards bishop of Norwich. He kept up a correspondence with Scotland and with foreign protestants. At length his release was obtained, after several months' negotiation, by Henri de la Tour, duc de Bouillon (*d.* 1623, aged 67), who sought his services for the university of Sédan within his principality. Just before his removal he was seized with fever, and permitted to recruit his health in the neighbourhood of London. He embarked for France from the Tower on 19 April 1611.

By Rouen and Paris Melvill travelled to Sédan, and was installed in the chair of biblical theology, the department of systematic divinity being retained by Daniel Tilenus (1563–1633), who had previously taught both branches. Tilenus was unpopular, and many students had withdrawn to Saumur. Melvill did not find his prospects inviting. In November 1612 he visited Grenoble, on the invitation of De Barsac, treasurer of the parlement of Dauphiné, who offered him a salary to educate his sons, either privately or at the university of Dié. He soon, however, returned to Sédan; but the situation was not made happier by a theological difference with Tilenus, who, compelled to resign, came to England in 1620, and gratified James by writing against the presbyterianism of Scotland.

Melvill, who appears to have been of small stature, had excellent health till 1612, excepting occasional attacks of gravel; he had never used spectacles. In 1616 he speaks of his gout; by 1620 his health was broken. He died at Sédan in 1622; the exact date has not been ascertained. He was unmarried. His faults lay on the surface, but they disqualified him from being a good leader. His ideas were patriotic and statesmanlike, but his action was too little under restraint. Spotiswood spoke of him as 'a blast;' he roused his nation to great issues, heedless of immediate consequences. King James was right in saying that his heart was in his mouth. Unprovoked he was generous, and could be sympathising and even gentle, yet to his closest intimates he was always the candid friend. His letters to his nephew in 1608 on the subject of a second marriage are exceedingly sensible, but there is a touch of asperity in the manner which robs the advice of all suasiveness. In controversy he could never conciliate; his impetuous eloquence was soon roused, when he poured forth without calculation a fierce stream of mordant invective. His polemical epigrams, always exquisite in their form, were corrosive in matter. Yet his spirit was never wanting in dignity, and under reverses he was 'patient, constant, and courageous' (Grub). Of self-seeking he was entirely free.

As a reformer of the Scottish universities Melvill showed real constructive power, and his work was permanent. Foreigners were for the first time attracted to St. Andrews as a seat of liberal learning, others were drawn to Glasgow and Edinburgh. The European repute of the Scottish universities begins with Melvill.

The part which he played in the development of the framework of presbyterianism exhibits similar qualities. Both by helping to perfect its machinery and by inspiring enthusiasm for its polity, he did much to mould that Scottish type of presbyterianism which is often taken as synonymous with presbyterianism itself. But with Melvill the triumph of one form of church government over another was not the main business. His prime object was to make religion, as he understood it, a matter of popular concern, and he judged forms as they appeared to him to help or hinder that result. Theologian as he was, his conception of religion was, in the broad sense, ethical, Christianity being to him a divine guide of conduct for individuals and for nations. Of religious sentimentalism there is no trace (as McCrie has noticed) even in his most confidential correspondence; his life was the outcome of solid and virile conviction, but as regards his personal experiences in religion he observes a manly reticence.

Isaac Walton ranks Melvill as a Latin

poet next to Buchanan. He had more poetic genius than Buchanan, with greater ease and spontaneity. But most of his pieces were fugitive, having a motive quite apart from that of literary fame, and he attempted no great work. His 'Carmen Mosis' takes the highest place among Latin paraphrases of scriptural themes. Of his printed poetical pieces the following list is corrected from McCrie: 1. 'Carmen Mosis,' &c., Basel, 1573, 8vo; reprinted with others of his pieces in 'Delitiæ Poetarum Scotorum,' &c., Amst., 1637, 12mo, vol. ii.. 2. 'Jvlii Cæsaris Scaligeri Poemata,' &c., Geneva, 1575, 8vo (commendatory epigrams by Melvill). 3. 'Στεφανισκιον. Ad Scotiæ Regem, habitum in Coronatione Reginæ,' &c., Edinb., 1590, 4to; reprinted in 'Papers relating to the Marriage of King James VI,' &c. (Bannatyne Club), Edinb., 1828, 4to. 4. 'Carmina Sacra duo,' &c., Geneva, 1590, 12mo (contains his 'Poetica Paraphrasis Cantici Canticorum'). 5. 'Principis Scoti-Britannorvm Natalia,' &c., Edinb., 1594, 4to; also the Hague, 1594, 4to. 6. 'Inscriptiones Historicæ Regvm Scotorvm . . . Ioh. Ionstono . . . Authore . . . Præfixus est Gathelvs, sive de Gentis Origine Fragmentum, Andreæ Melvini,' &c., Amst., 1602, 4to. 7. 'In Obitvm Johannis Wallasii,' &c., Leyden, 1603, 4to (several poems by Melvill). 8. 'Pro supplici Evangelicorum Ministrorum in Anglia . . . Apologia, sive Anti-Tami-Cami-Categoria,' &c. [? 1604]; reprinted in Calderwood's 'Parasynagma Perthense,' &c. [Edinb.], 1620, 4to; and in his 'Altare Damascenum,' 1623, 4to. A reply was written by the poet George Herbert [q. v.] 9. 'Sidera Veteris Ævi,' &c., Saumur, 1611, 4to (by John Johnston; contains two poems by Melvill). 10. 'Comment. in Apost. Acta M. Joannis Malcolmi,' &c., Middelburg, 1615 (verses by Melvill prefixed). 11. 'Duellum Poeticum contendentibus G. Eglisemmio,' &c., Lond. 1618, 8vo (prints and attacks Melvill's 'Cavillum in Aram Regiam,' the epigram on the Chapel Royal). 12. Sir James Sempill's 'Sacriledge Sacredly Handled,' &c., Lond., 1619, 4to, has three epigrams by Melvill. 13. 'Viri clarissimi A. Melvini Musæ,' &c. [Edinb.], 1620, 4to (the appended Life of Adamson, &c., are not by Melvill). 14. 'Ad Serenissimvm Jacobvm Primvm . . . Libellus Supplex,' &c., Lond. 1645, 8vo, by James Melvill, has his uncle's epitaph for him in Latin verse. 15. 'Atlas Major,' &c., Amst., J. Blaeu, 1662, fol. vol. vi. (contains 'Andreæ Melvini Scotiæ Topographia'). 16. Koelman's 'De Diebus Festis,' &c., Utrecht, 1693, has five poems 'ex Musis Andreæ Melvini.' Besides these, a Latin paraphrase of certain psalms was printed by Melvill in 1609, while in the Tower, but no copy is known. In Harl. MSS. 6947 (9) is a 'Paraphrasis Epistolæ ad Hebræos Andreæ Melvini.' Other Latin verses are in the Sempill papers (among the archives of the church of Scotland), and in a collection in the Advocates' Library, Edinburgh. McCrie mentions as generally ascribed to Melvill, 'Nescimus qvid vesper servs vehat. Satyra Menippæa,' &c., 1619, 4to, 1620, 4to; this, according to Lowndes, is by Gaspar Scioppius.

Among his prose publications McCrie mentions: 1. 'Theses Theologicæ de Libero Arbitrio,' &c., Edinb. 1597, 4to. 2. 'Scholastica Diatriba de Rebvs Divinis,' &c., Edinb. 1599, 4to; these two are mere topics for academic disputations. 3. 'Lusus Poetici,' &c., Edinb. 1605, 4to, by David Hume (1560?–1630?) [q. v.], has four letters by Melvill. 4. 'De Adiaphoris. Scoti του τυχοντος Aphorismi,' &c., 1622, 12mo (against conformity to the ceremonies). 5. 'Commentarius in Divinam Pauli Epistolam ad Romanos,' &c., Edinb., 1850, 8vo (edited for the Wodrow Society by W. Lindsay Alexander, D.D., from a transcript by Daniel Demetrius, finished at St. Andrews on 26 July 1601). His 'Answer to the Declaration of certain Intentions set out in the King's Name . . . 7th of Feb. 1585,' was circulated in manuscript, and possibly printed. His 'Answer to Downham's Sermon,' 1608, was widely circulated in manuscript. In the library of Trinity College, Dublin, is a manuscript 'A. Melvinus in cap. 4 Danielis.' To these must be added the manuscript collection of his Latin letters (1608–13) to James Melvill, in the Edinburgh University Library, and the manuscript collection of his letters (1612–16) to Robert Durie of Leyden, in the Advocates' Library, Edinburgh. An answer to Tilenus, 'Scoti του τυχοντος Paraclesis contra Dan. Tileni Silesii Paræenesin,' &c., 1622, is often ascribed to Melvill, but is by Sempill.

McCrie spells the name Melville, and this form occurs in some contemporary documents relating to members of the family. No instance is produced of the use of this spelling by the reformer himself. He writes himself Melvine (1610), Meluill (1616), and Melvin (1617); in Latin invariably Melvinus. His nephew writes of him indifferently as 'Andro Meluill' and 'Andro Meluin.'

[McCrie's Life, 1819 (the edition used in 1856, edited by his son), is a work of close and wide research, and may be safely followed for the facts. Of McCrie's manuscript sources, since printed, the chief are James Melvill's Diary (Bannatyne Club), 1829, and with addition of his Hist. of the Declining Age (Wodrow Soc.), 1842; William Scot's Apologetical Narration

(Wodrow Soc.), 1846; Calderwood's Hist. of the Kirk (Wodrow Soc.), 1842–9. For less favourable views of Melvill's character and policy, see Spotiswood's Hist. of the Church of Scotland (Spottiswoode Soc.), 1847–51; Grub's Eccl. Hist. of Scotland, 1861, vol. ii. See also Gardiner's Hist. of England, vol. i.; Walton's Lives (Zouch), 1796, p. 295. Hew Scott's Fasti Eccles. Scoticanæ adds a few particulars; the biographies in Scots Worthies, 1862, pp. 233 sq., and Anderson's Scottish Nation, 1872, iii. 140 sq., add nothing to McCrie.] A. G.

MELVILLE, ANDREW (1624–1706), soldier of fortune, was born in Scotland in May 1624. His father, John Melville, sprang from a younger branch of the Melville family; his mother was Jane Kelley (Kellie?), her brother being chamberlain to Charles I. Sent to Königsberg university at thirteen to study the languages of northern Europe, Melville escaped to Poland, intending to enter the army, but, seeing no prospect of active employment, he returned to Scotland. There he learned that his parents, ruined by his uncle's debts, had died, and that creditors had seized the entire property. Lord Grey of Werke, who had already taken his brother into his service, promised Andrew a cornetcy, pending which, at the head of other young men also waiting for appointments, he lived by plunder, till captured by peasants and imprisoned for some months. On his release he joined in 1647 the presbyterian troops; but on Charles I being given up he went to France, served with the French army in Flanders, and after a variety of adventures waited on Charles II at Breda, and agreed to join him in Scotland. At the battle of Worcester he was shot in the arm, stripped, and left for dead, but was sheltered for three months by villagers until he recovered from his wounds. He then repaired in disguise to London, and was assisted by a roundhead kinsman (probably George, afterwards earl of Melville) in escaping to Holland. After further privations and perils he joined the Scottish bodyguard of Cardinal de Retz, and next served in the French army. Eventually he linked his fortunes with those of Count Josias Waldeck, with whom he fought for the elector of Brandenburg, the king of Sweden, the elector of Cologne, and the Duke of Celle (Brunswick-Luneburg). The duke sent him to London in 1660 to compliment Charles II on his restoration, and Melville paid a second visit on his own account; but the king, while very affable, professed inability to do anything for him. In 1680 Melville accompanied the Prince of Hanover (afterwards George I) to England, and received the degree of M.D. at Oxford, whither he went with the prince (Wood, *Fasti Oxon.* ii. 379). In 1677, retiring from active service, Melville had been appointed drost (governor or commandant) of Gifhorn. Melville died at Gifhorn in 1706. The church, in which he was probably buried, was burnt down in 1744. He had married in Germany, and had a son who predeceased him, also a daughter, Charlotte Sophia Anna (1670–1724), who in 1690 became the wife of Alexander von Schulenburg-Blumberg, a Hanoverian general.

He was author of an autobiography published as 'Mémoires de M. le Chevalier de Melvill,' Amsterdam, 1704, with a preface eulogising his valour and protestantism.

[Melville's Mémoires; Hermann Schulze's Geschichtliches aus dem Lüneburgischen, Gifhorn, 1877; Allgemeine Deutsche Biographie, Leipzig, 1885; Oettinger's Dict. des Dates, Leipzig, 1869.] J. G. A.

MELVILLE, DAVID, third Earl of Leven and second Earl of Melville (1660–1728), military commander, third son of George, first earl of Melville [q.v.], by his wife, Lady Catherine Leslie, only daughter of Alexander, lord Balgonie, afterwards second earl of Leven, was born on 5 May 1660. On the death of the second Earl of Leven in 1664 without male issue the title was to devolve, after his daughters, first on the second son of John, duke of Rothes, and after him on the second son of the first Earl of Melville. On the death of Leven's two daughters, successively Countesses of Leven in their own right, the Earl of Melville in 1676 applied, on the ground that Rothes had no male issue, that the earldom should be assigned to his second surviving son, David; but to this Rothes objected, and the objection was sustained by the court of session. On the death, however, of Rothes without male issue on 27 July 1681, David Melville assumed the title.

Although in no degree implicated in the Rye House plot, Leven in 1683 accompanied his father to Holland. In 1685 he entered the service of the elector of Brandenburg as captain of horse, and in September 1687 was appointed colonel. At the court of Berlin he acted as a confidential agent to the Prince of Orange, and arranged the meeting at Cleves between him and the elector of Brandenburg. Subsequently at his own expense he raised a regiment of Scottish refugees in Germany and Holland, of which he was appointed colonel, on 7 Sept. 1688, and with which he accompanied the Prince of Orange to England. The regiment was chosen to garrison Plymouth after its surrender.

Leven was selected by William of Orange to be the bearer of his letter to the Scottish convention in March 1689. He was also empowered to raise a regiment of eight hundred men to guard the city until the arrival of the regular troops from England. On the alarm occasioned by the march of Dundee out of Edinburgh, and his interview with the Duke of Gordon at the castle ramparts, Leven ordered the drums to beat, and assembled a sufficient force to restore the confidence of the convention. His own regiment subsequently arrived in Scotland, and in command of it he joined Mackay in his campaigns against Graham of Claverhouse. At Killiecrankie, on 17 July 1689, his regiment occupied a position on the extreme right, and escaping therefore the brunt of the highland charge, remained practically intact when the other troops broke and fled. After Claverhouse received his mortal wound, the fire of Leven's regiment compelled Claverhouse's friends to forego their purpose of carrying him immediately off the field. The steadiness of Leven's regiment amidst general panic and flight was highly estimated by General Mackay, who wrote: 'I had no regiment or troop with me but behaved like the vilest cowards in nature, except Hastings' and my Lord Leven's, whom I must praise to such a degree as I cannot but blame others of whom I expected more' (*Memoirs*, p. 248; cf. MACAULAY, ed. 1883, ii. 59). Leven showed also great coolness and determination in guarding the rear of the retreat to Stirling. He also distinguished himself in the campaign in Ireland.

After the surrender of the castle of Edinburgh by the Duke of Gordon on 14 June 1689, Leven on 23 Aug. obtained a commission as keeper of the castle. In 1692 he served in the campaign in Flanders. Although he took an active part in promoting the succession of Queen Anne in 1702, and in October was appointed a commissioner for the union, he was on 31 Dec. superseded in the command of the castle by William, earl of March. In January 1703 he was, however, constituted major-general of the forces in Scotland. On 20 May 1704 his services were recognised by a gift of the wards which had fallen into the hands of the crown since 1689. The same year he went to London to give his advice on Scottish affairs, probably in connection with the so-called Queensberry plot [see DOUGLAS, JAMES, second DUKE OF QUEENSBERRY]. Simon Fraser of Lovat (1726-1782) [q. v.] asserted that while in Scotland on behalf of the Pretender he had communications with Queensberry, Argyll, and Leven, who he says 'may at this time be styled the triumvirate of Scotland;' but the opinions of the two last were so well known that the Earl of Middleton remarked on his statement that 'he had not been as careful as authors of romances to preserve probability' (quoted in FERGUSON'S *Ferguson the Plotter*, p. 338).

On 17 Oct. 1704 Leven was restored to the command of the castle of Edinburgh; on 7 Aug. 1705 was appointed master of ordnance in Scotland, with a pension of 150*l.*, in addition to the usual salary of 150*l.*; and on 22 March 1706 was appointed commander-in-chief of the forces in Scotland. After the union, which he had taken an active part in promoting, he was chosen a representative peer for Scotland, and he was re-elected till 1710. On the death of his father, on 20 May 1707, he united the title of Earl of Melville to that of Leven. He displayed vigour and activity in suppressing the attempt at a Jacobite rising in 1708, when a large force was placed by Marlborough at his disposal (*Despatches*, iii. 690); but Lockhart testifies that 'he was nowise severe, but rather very civil to all the cavaliers, especially such as were prisoners in the castle of Edinburgh' (*Papers*, i. 91). In 1712 he was deprived of all his offices by the tory administration. He died on 6 June 1728, and was buried at Markinch. Lockhart states that 'in the beginning of his life' Leven 'was so vain and conceity that he became the jest of all sober men,' but admits that 'as he grew older he overcame that folly in part, and from the proudest became the civilest man alive;' and that he 'was a man of good parts and sound judgment,' although 'master of no kind of learning.' He professes, however, to entertain great doubts as to his military abilities (*ib.*) Leven had two sons—George, lord Balgonie and Raith, who died before his father, leaving a son David, fourth earl of Leven and third earl of Melville, who died in 1729, in his twelfth year; and Alexander, fifth earl of Leven and fourth earl of Melville—and two daughters: Mary, married to William, lord Haddo, second earl of Aberdeen, and Margaret, who died in infancy.

[Leven and Melville Papers and Lauder of Fountainhall's Historical Notices (both Bannatyne Club); Lockhart Papers; General Mackay's Memoirs; Harl. MS. 6584; Sir William Fraser's The Melvilles, Earls of Melville, and the Melvilles, Earls of Leven, i. 245-307; Douglas's Scottish Peerage (Wood), ii. 117.] T. F. H.

MELVILLE, ELIZABETH (*fl.* 1603), Scottish poetess. [See COLVILLE.]

MELVILLE, GEORGE, fourth BARON MELVILLE and first EARL OF MELVILLE (1634?-1707), eldest son of John, third baron Melville, by his wife, Anne Erskine of Invertiel, Fifeshire, was born about 1634 (*Leven* *and Melville Papers*, Preface, p. xiii). He succeeded his father in 1643, and in the following year parliament ratified in his favour a charter granted to his father erecting the lands of Monimail and Raith into one barony. After the death of Charles I he seems to have given his support to his son. On 3 Jan. 1654 he was taken prisoner by a party of English horse at St. Andrews and brought to Burntisland (LAMONT, *Diary*, p. 65). In May 1660 he went to London to welcome the king on his restoration (*ib.* p. 145). He seems also to have taken an active part in the sports and pastimes which marked the overthrow of the Cromwellian régime in Scotland as well as in England. Several notices of races in which he had horses running at Cupar Muir occur in Lamont's 'Diary,' pp. 145, 160, 161, 187.

Having paid a visit to the king in London in 1679, Melville was commissioned by him to join the army under Monmouth against the covenanters, which he did a little before the battle of Bothwell Bridge. As his sympathies were presbyterian, he was anxious that a conflict should be avoided, and at the instance of Monmouth, or with his sanction, endeavoured to induce the covenanters to lay down their arms, on the ground that their demands would receive much more favourable consideration than would otherwise be possible. That Melville had at least been consulted in regard to the insurrection schemes connected with the Rye House plot in 1683 can scarcely be doubted, but he was said to 'have thought everything hazardous,' and to have been 'positive in nothing' (FERGUSON, *Ferguson the Plotter*, p. 162; cf. MACAULAY, *Hist.* ed. 1883, ii. 11). On discovery of the plot it was decided to apprehend him, but he escaped from Melville House, and taking boat at Kinghorn to Berwick, went to London. There he endeavoured to obtain an interview with the king, in order to exculpate himself, but without success, and after some dragoons had been sent to his lodgings to apprehend him, he made his escape by aid of a page to Wapping, and thence took boat to Hamburg. According to the letter from a spy to Lord Preston, he arrived there in the same ship as Robert Ferguson, Sir Thomas Armstrong, and others concerned in the plot, and sailed again towards Mecklenburg, without making any stay (*ib.* p. 179). He joined the expatriated gentlemen and nobles at the court of the Prince of Orange, and doubtless was consulted in regard to the expeditions of Argyll and Monmouth, although he does not seem to have accompanied either expedition. On 13 June 1685 his estates were forfeited by parliament.

On account of illness Melville remained in Holland for some time after the Prince of Orange set out on his expedition to England, but arrived in London in time to be sent to represent his interests at the convention of estates in Edinburgh on 14 March 1689. Although he possessed little force of character and only mediocre talents, he was, chiefly on account of his mild disposition and moderate opinions, appointed by William III on 13 May secretary of state for Scotland. The appointment on the whole gave satisfaction even to the episcopalians, for in any case the selection of a presbyterian was inevitable, and the choice seemed to lie between him and Sir James Montgomery (*fl.* 1690) [q. v.], a rabid covenanter. The extremists were of course dissatisfied, and in a pamphlet on the 'Scots Grievance,' the joint work of Montgomery and Ferguson, Melville was ridiculed as 'but a puny in politics,' while it was also asserted that he was 'wholly employed how to engross the considerable places of the kingdom for enriching his family.' The disappointment of Montgomery and others led to the formation of the plot which Montgomery himself revealed to Melville [see MONTGOMERY, SIR JAMES]. In the difficult crisis of Scottish affairs Melville manifested a prudence and discretion which amply justified his appointment. In February 1690 he was appointed commissioner to the Scottish parliament, which established the ecclesiastical constitution of Scotland on a presbyterian basis, and recognised the Calvinism of the Westminster confession as the standard of orthodoxy. The king seems to have hinted to Melville to make such arrangements as he deemed necessary to secure the good will of the presbyterians. So far as the king himself was concerned the questions of chief difficulty were those regarding patronage and the royal supremacy. According to Burnet the king insisted that both should be maintained; but Melville found their abrogation 'so much insisted on' by the presbyterians that he had to write for fresh instructions to the king, who thereupon enlarged them, but 'not such as to warrant what Melville did, for he gave them both up' (*Own Time*, ed. 1838, p. 560). It is undoubtedly true that the king was extremely hostile even to the abolition of patronage, and this on the ground of the vested rights of the proprietors; but Melville met this difficulty by awarding a small compensation to them. Burnet states that the king was so offended by Melville's conduct 'that he lost all the credit he had with him, though the king did not think fit to disown him, or to call him to an account for going beyond his instructions' (*ib.*); but it does not appear that the king even privately intimated to Melville any dissatisfaction with the policy he had pursued.

On 8 April 1690 Melville was created Earl of Melville, Viscount Kirkcaldy, Lord Raith, Monimail, and Balwearie. In January 1691 Sir John Dalrymple, first earl of Stair [q. v.], was appointed joint secretary along with him. This would seem to indicate that while the king was so far satisfied with his services, he had some doubt as to his administrative talents and his power to cope with the new difficulties of the situation. The fact that he was not superseded altogether, indicated a desire to spare his feelings; but on 29 Dec. he exchanged the office of joint secretary for that of lord privy seal. In August 1696 he became president of the privy council, and a member of the committee for the security of the kingdom. On the accession of Queen Anne he was in December 1702 deprived of his offices. He died on 20 May 1707, and was buried in the parish church of Monimail. By his wife, Lady Catherine Leslie, only daughter of Alexander, lord Balgonie, afterwards second earl of Leven, he had eight sons and four daughters. The sons were: Alexander, master of Melville and lord Raith, who predeceased his father in 1698; John, who died young; David, third earl of Leven and fourth earl of Melville [q. v.]; George, James, John (who died young), Charles, and John (who died young). The daughters were: Margaret, married to Robert, fourth lord Balfour, Mary, Anne, and Catherine. An engraving of the Earl of Melville, from the original portrait of Medina, is in Sir William Fraser's 'Earls of Melville.'

[Leven and Melville Papers (Bannatyne Club), containing his political correspondence; Carstares's State Papers; Burnet's Own Time; Ralph's History, ii. 212; Lamont's Diary (Maitland Club); Lauder of Fountainhall's Historical Notices (Bannatyne Club); Douglas's Scottish Peerage (Wood), ii. 114; Sir William Fraser's The Melvilles, Earls of Melville, and the Melvilles, Earls of Leven, i. 194–245.] T. F. H.

MELVILLE, Capt. GEORGE JOHN WHYTE (1821–1878), novelist and poet. [See Whyte-Melville.]

MELVILLE, Sir JAMES (1535–1617), of Hallhill, autobiographer, born in 1535, was the third son of Sir John Melville of Raith [q. v.], by his second wife, Helen Napier. When fourteen years of age he was appointed page to the youthful Mary Queen of Scots, then at the French court. On his way to France in the train of John de Montluc, bishop of Valence, a visit was paid to the coast of Ireland, and Melville was there eagerly sought in marriage by a young Irish lady, who had a priest in readiness. But Melville declined, telling her he was too young and had no means. For three years he remained in the retinue of the bishop, and then entered the service of the constable of France, whom he accompanied to the field against the emperor, and was wounded in 1557 at the battle of St. Quentin, where the constable was made prisoner. In 1559 Melville was introduced by his master to the French king, Henry II, and was sent to Scotland to discover the real designs of Lord James Stewart, the half-brother of Queen Mary, whom Mary of Guise, the queen-dowager of Scotland, charged with aiming at the crown. He carried out his mission successfully, but on his return to France was obliged to withdraw for a short time to the court of the elector palatine. While there he was entrusted with the delicate task of recommending a marriage between Duke John Casimir, the elector's second son, and Queen Elizabeth, and about the same time he proposed marriages between Archduke Charles of Austria and Mary Queen of Scots, and between Charles IX and the second daughter of the Emperor Maximilian. In none of these schemes was he successful.

At the earnest desire of Queen Mary he settled next at the Scottish court, and was appointed a privy councillor and gentleman of the bedchamber. She granted him two yearly pensions of 100*l.* and five hundred merks Scots for life, and these were afterwards confirmed to him by James VI. At first the queen employed his diplomatic talents to win over Queen Elizabeth to her projected marriage with Darnley, and Melville personally ingratiated himself with Elizabeth. On his return from England he vainly attempted to prevent the murder of Rizzio, which from the aspect of affairs at court he clearly foresaw. He was present in Holyrood at the time of the tragedy, but was apparently not a witness. He was made the bearer of the tidings of the birth of Queen Mary's son to Elizabeth, and was present at the baptism of the prince. After the murder of Darnley he tried to dissuade Mary from marrying Bothwell, but only incurred the resentment of that nobleman. He was present at their marriage, which was followed by the queen's deposition and imprisonment, and the coronation of her infant son.

The nobles sent Melville to offer the regency to James Stewart, earl of Moray [q. v.], at Berwick. Through the troublesome period of James's minority he was entrusted with the most delicate diplomatic missions. During the latter portion of Morton's regency he retired from court, but after James began to reign in person he returned, and his counsel and services were always sought by the king, to whom he had been recommended by Queen Mary. James kept him constantly about the court, but Melville declined missions to England, Denmark, and Spain. On the king's return from Denmark with his queen, Melville was knighted, and appointed a privy councillor and gentleman of the bedchamber to Queen Anne; but when in 1603 James succeeded to the English crown and earnestly desired Melville to go with him to London, Melville declined on account of his age. He retired to his estate of Hallhill, formerly Easter Collessie, in Fife, which he acquired from Henry Balnaves. Balnaves had no children of his own, and had adopted Melville as his heir. Here Melville occupied himself in writing the 'Memoirs' of his own life. He paid one visit to the king at London, and was graciously received. He died at Hallhill on 13 Nov. 1617. He married Christina Boswell, and had by her one son, James, who succeeded him, and two daughters—Elizabeth, wife of John Colville, commendator of Culross [see COLVILLE, ELIZABETH], and Margaret, who was the second wife of Sir John Scott of Scotstarvet.

The 'Memoirs' written by Melville form an important contribution to the historic literature of his period. The original manuscript was first discovered in Edinburgh Castle in 1660, and was first published by George Scott of Pitlochie, the author's grandson, in 1683, London, folio. Two impressions were issued (*Notes and Queries*, IV. xii. 86). A second edition appeared in 1735 in octavo, and a reprint of this in 1751 in duodecimo. The latest and best edition is that issued by the Bannatyne Club in 1827. A French translation was published at the Hague in 1694 (2 vols. 8vo), which was reprinted at Lyons in 1695, and at Amsterdam in 1704; while a new French edition was published at Edinburgh in 1745 (3 vols. 8vo), the third of which contained a collection of letters by Queen Mary.

[Memoirs of his own life, by Sir James Melville of Hallhill; Sir W. Fraser's Melvilles of Melville and Leslies of Leven, i. 133–62.]

H. P.

MELVILLE or MELVILL, JAMES (1556–1614), Scottish reformer, nephew of Andrew Melville [q. v.] and son of Richard Melville of Baldovie, minister of Mayton, near Montrose, by Jabel Scrimgeour, sister of the laird of Glasswell, was, according to his own account, born 26 July 1556, although 'Mr. Andrew,' he states, held that he 'was born in anno 1557' (JAMES MELVILLE, *Diary*, Wodrow Society ed., p. 13). After receiving his early education under the care of Mr. Gray, minister of Logie, and at Montrose, he entered as student of St. Leonard's College, St. Andrews, not as he himself states in November 1571, but, according to the roll of entrants, in 1569. He was admitted B.A. in November 1571, but there is no record as to when or where he proceeded M.A. He was a diligent and eager student, and being unable at first to understand the Latin lessons of the regent, William Collace, burst into tears, whereupon the regent undertook to give him lessons in private. Besides attending the usual classes at the university he obtained lessons in music from Alexander Smith, servant to the principal, and 'lovit singing and playing on instruments passing well' (*ib.* p. 29). At St. Andrews he also heard Knox preach his weekly sermons in 1571–2 (*ib.* p. 33).

Melville was originally intended by his father for the law, but in accordance with his own preference for the church he was placed under his uncle Andrew's charge in 1574, and received special instruction from him in Greek and Hebrew. On the appointment of his uncle in October 1574 to be principal of the university of Glasgow he accompanied him thither, and in 1575 was elected one of the regents, the course of instruction in the first year being Greek and logic, and in the second logic and mathematics. He was the first regent in Scotland who read the Greek authors to his class in the original tongue. In 1580, for 'correcting' Mark Alexander Boyd [q. v.], he was assaulted in the kirkyard by Boyd's cousin, Alexander Cunningham, who, when brought before the privy council, was ordered on 29 July to crave pardon publicly in the churchyard on 7 Aug. (*Diary*, p. 70; *Reg. P. C. Scotl.* iii. 296–7).

On the translation in December 1580 of Andrew Melville to be principal of the New College (now St. Mary's), St. Andrews, his nephew accompanied him as professor of Hebrew and oriental languages. He zealously seconded his uncle in his extreme views as to the authority of the kirk and the divine origin of presbyterianism. On the flight of his uncle to England in February 1584, he undertook the charge of his classes in addition to his own, and also the general superintendence of the affairs of the college; but in May of the same year, having learned that Bishop Adamson held a warrant for his apprehension, he escaped to Dundee, whence, disguised as a shipwrecked seaman, he set sail in an open boat for Berwick. After remaining there about a month he resolved to join his uncle and other exiled ministers in London; but at the earnest request of the Earls of Angus and Mar he stayed his journey at Newcastle-on-Tyne, remaining there to preach to the exiled presbyterians. While at Newcastle he drew up an 'Order of Exercise in Doctrine, Prayer, and Discipline' (CALDERWOOD, iv. 150, printed in *Diary*, pp. 173–84); and also a paper on the 'Abuses and Corruptions of the Kirk' (CALDERWOOD, iv. 150–7; *Diary*, pp. 186–93). In November he returned to Berwick, and while there he was, at the instance of the Earl of Arran, prohibited from preaching by the governor, Lord Hunsdon. From Berwick he sent a letter 'to the brethrein of the ministrie of Scotland, who have latelie subscrived to the popish supremacie of the king and ambitious tyrannie of the bishops over their brethern' (CALDERWOOD, iv. 219–36; *Diary*, pp. 200–18). He is also supposed to have been the author of the dialogue 'Zelator, Temporizar, Palemon,' affixed to his uncle's 'Answer to the Declaration of Certain Intentions set out in the King's Name.' On being prohibited from preaching at Berwick he joined the exiled ministers in London. After the capture of the castle of Stirling by the exiled lords, he, in November 1585, returned to Scotland. During the absence of himself and his uncle in England, the New College had been converted by Bishop Adamson from a school of theology into one of arts and philosophy; but by the act of parliament passed at Linlithgow in December all ejected professors were to be restored to their chairs, and on 25 May 1586 the privy council made a special arrangement for settling the disputes between the Melvilles and Bishop Adamson (*Reg. P. C. Scotl.* iv. 74–5).

In April 1586 James Melville, in the opening sermon at the meeting of the synod of Fife, vehemently attacked Bishop Adamson, who 'was sitting at his elbow' (CALDERWOOD, iv. 495), affirming that he threatened the 'wracke and destruction' of the kirk if he 'were not tymouslie and with courage cut off' (*ib.*) The bishop was thereupon excommunicated, but retaliated by sending 'a boy with one or two of his jackmen' to read an excommunication of the Melvilles in the kirk of Edinburgh (*ib.* p. 503). He also gave in an appellation of the sentence of excommunication, which was answered by James Melville (*ib.* pp. 504–47). In consequence of their disputes with Adamson, the Melvilles were on 26 May called before the king and council, who ordained that while Andrew should meanwhile be sent to the north to instruct the jesuits, James 'should attend in his own place for the instruction of the youth committed to his care,' and 'the bishop should teach weekly two lessons of theology within St. Salvator's College' (*Reg. P. C. Scotl.* iv. 74–5).

In 1586 Melville undertook the charge of the parish of Anstruther Wester, Fifeshire, to which he was ordained on 12 Nov.; and on 8 May 1587 he was also presented by James VI to the vicarage of Abercrombie. In 1589 the charge, which had included the two Anstruthers, Pittenweem, Abercrombie, and Kilrenny, was reduced to Anstruther Easter and Kilrenny; and on 6 Oct. 1590 he removed to Kilrenny, where, besides building a manse, he purchased the right to the vicarage and the tithe-fish for the support of himself and his successors. While at Anstruther he in 1588 obtained shelter and relief for a number of distressed sailors from the wrecked Spanish Armada.

Having been appointed moderator of the general assembly on 17 June 1589, Melville, in his sermon preached at the opening of the succeeding assembly in August 1590 on the subject of discipline, took occasion to inveigh against all attempts to establish conformity with the church government in England; and more especially denounced Bishop Adamson, who was then, he said, 'making a book against our discipline.' Yet, when in the spring of 1591 he was sent to conduct the trial of the bishop, and the bishop professed repentance for all his past errors, Melville agreed to recommend his absolution from excommunication (CALDERWOOD, v. 119).

Melville was one of the commissioners appointed by the Edinburgh convention of 17 Dec. 1593 to wait upon the king to have order taken with the excommunicated lords (*ib.* v. 270), and at a meeting held at Edinburgh on 29 Oct. was appointed to be 'speechman' to those named to present a petition to the king at Linlithgow (*ib.* p. 277). But the court party suspected him of having furnished money to the turbulent Earl of Bothwell [see HEPBURN, FRANCIS STEWART], and it was proposed in May 1594 to omit his name from the list of commissioners from the assembly to the king. He requested to be included as a special favour, that he might have an opportunity of clearing himself. When, however, after the commissioners had concluded their business, he brought the matter before the king, not only did the king decline to lay anything to his charge, but in a private interview expressed himself in very flattering terms in regard both to Melville and his uncle. 'So of the strange working of God,' records the gratified Melville, 'I that came to Stirling the traitor returned to Edinburgh a great courtier, yea a cabinet minister' (*Diary*, p. 317).

As further evidence of his trust in the Melvilles, King James invited them to accompany him in October 1594 in his expedition to the north against Bothwell and the catholic earls. While the king was still in the north he sent James Melville to Edinburgh and other powerful towns to collect subscriptions from the presbyterians in payment of the forces raised for the expedition. Afterwards he was, in 1596, a member of various commissions appointed to expostulate with the king for allowing Huntly and Errol to return to Scotland. In November he was also appointed one of a commission to wait on the king to represent that the kirk had developed a 'most dangerous suspicion' of the king's intentions, and to crave for its removal; but the commissioners of the assembly were ordered on the 24th to leave Edinburgh and to depart home to their flocks and congregations within twenty-four hours (*Reg. P. C. Scotl.* v. 333). After the ministers convened by the king at Perth in February 1596–7 had at the king's request declared themselves a lawful assembly, Melville withdrew from the meeting. He also in the synod of Fife opposed, in February 1598, the proposal of the king that ministers should have a vote in parliament, pointing out that the proposal was merely part of a scheme for the furthering of episcopacy, for unless they were bishops or prelates they would not be allowed to vote. Although less choleric than his uncle, and a more skilful tactician, he loyally supported his uncle in all his difficulties, and was equally persistent in his endeavours to thwart the schemes of the king in behalf of episcopacy. On being assured in 1604 that the king hated him 'worse than any man in Scotland, because he crossed all his turns and was a ringleader to others,' he replied to his informer, 'My resolve is this:

> Nec sperans aliquid, nec extimescens
> Exarmaveris impotentis iram.'

In May 1606 Melville was summoned along with his uncle and other ministers to a conference in September with the king in London in regard to the ecclesiastical state of Scotland. After its unsatisfactory termination, and the imprisonment of Andrew Melville in the Tower, 30 April 1607, he was on 6 May permitted to depart from London, but ordered not to proceed further north than Newcastle-on-Tyne, and to confine himself within ten miles of the town during the king's pleasure. At Newcastle various attempts were made to win him over, by offers of high preferment, to the policy of the king, but bribes and threats equally failed to move him. On the death of his wife in 1607 he obtained leave to go to Scotland for a month to take order about his private affairs, but was required to return immediately afterwards and remain at Newcastle. In 1610 a proposal was made to transfer him to Carlisle, but at his earnest request it was not persisted in. The Earl of Dunbar on his way to Scotland, in April of this year, as the king's commissioner, called on him at Newcastle and advised him to 'apply himself to pleasure the king.' Dunbar took Melville with him as far as Berwick-on-Tweed, but, finding him immovable in his resolution not to conform to episcopacy, he left him there with an expression of regret that he was unable in the circumstances to do him any service. Ultimately a proposal was made about the end of 1613 for his return to Scotland, but cares and disappointments had already shattered his health, and he had not proceeded far on his journey to Edinburgh to confer on the subject when a severe attack of illness compelled him to return to Berwick. He died there on 13 Jan. 1613–14.

By his first wife, Elizabeth, daughter of John Dury, minister of Edinburgh, Melville had four sons and three daughters: Ephraim, minister of Pittenweem; Andrew, died young; Andrew, schoolmaster of Hoddesdon; John, minister of Newton; Margaret, Isabel, and Anne. By his second wife, Deborah, daughter of Richard Clerke, vicar of Berwick, whom he married about 1611, he left no issue. The sum total of his personal estate, as stated in his will, was 137*l.* 6*s.* 10*d.*

Melville was author of: 1. A poem entitled 'Description of the Spainyarts Naturall, out of Julius Scaliger, with sum Exhortationes for Warning of Kirk and Countrey,' printed, according to his own account, in 1592, but no copy is now known to exist. 2. 'A Spiritval Propine of a Pastour to his People, Heb. v. 12,' Edinburgh, 1598, printed as a catechism for the use of his people at an expense to himself of four hundred merks (very rare; copy wanting title-page in the Advocates' Library, Edinburgh, and complete copy in the British Museum). 3. A poem called 'The Black Bastill, or a Lamentation of the Kirk of Scotland, compiled by Mr. James Melville, sometime minister at Anstruther, and now confyned in England,' 1611, of which the manuscript was at one time in the possession of Robert Graham, esq., of Redgorton, Perthshire, and an abridgment was published in 1634, and republished in 'Various Pieces of Fugitive Scottish Poetry, principally of the Seventeenth Century,' ed. David Laing, Edinburgh, 1825. 4. A poem of sixty-nine stanzas in the same manuscript entitled 'Thrie may keip Counsell, give Twa be away, or Eusebius, Democritus, Heraclitus.' 5. Also in the same manuscript a translation into English verse of part of the 'Zodiacus Vitæ' of Marcellus Palingenius. 6. 'Ad Serenissimum Jacobum primum Britanniarum Monarcham Ecclesiæ Scoticanæ libellus supplex ἀπολογητικὸς καὶ ὀλοφυρτικὸς, Auctore Jacobo Melvino verbi Dei Ministro, Domini Andreæ Melvini τοῦ πάνυ nepote,' London, 1645, with epitaph on James Melville by Andrew Melville. 7. In the library of the university of Edinburgh is a manuscript volume of the correspondence between Andrew and James Melville while in England [see under MELVILLE, ANDREW, 1545–1622]; and in the Laing collection of the library are transcripts of the correspondence copied under the direction of Dr. M'Crie. 8. A manuscript volume of poems, letters, &c., by James Melville, presented to the Advocates' Library, Edinburgh, in 1822, by Rev. William Blackie, minister of Yetholm, contains (*a*) Sonnet and other short poems, written in 1610 and 1611; (*b*) 'A Preservative from Apostasie, or the Song of Moses, with short notes for the Deduction and Doctrine thereof, translated out of Hebrew and put in metre, first shortly, and then more at length paraphrastically;' (*c*) 'David's Tragique Fall,' in verse, concluding with a paraphrase of the 51st psalm; (*d*) 'The Beliefe of the Singing Soul, or the Song of Songs which is Solomon's, exponed by a large Paraphrase in Metre for Memorie and Meditation;' and (*e*) 'A Meditation of the Love of Christ.' 9. The 'Diary' of James Melville, of which the original manuscript is in the Advocates' Library, Edinburgh, was printed by the Bannatyne Club in 1829 and also by the Wodrow Society in 1842, the latter volume also containing a continuation of the 'Diary' of James Melville (from another manuscript in the Advocates' Library) under the title of a 'True Narrative of the Declyning Aige of the Kirk of Scotland,' 1596–1610. The 'Diary' is invaluable as a record of the ecclesiastical events of the period from the presbyterian point of view, and is the chief authority for the narrative of Calderwood, who has incorporated the bulk of it in his 'History' verbatim.

[James Melville's Diary; Histories of Calderwood, Row, and Spotiswood; Reg. P. C. Scotl.; M'Crie's Life of Andrew Melville; Hew Scott's Fasti Eccles. Scot.] T. F. H.

MELVILLE, SIR JOHN (*d.* 1548), laird of Raith in Fife, was the eldest son of John Melville the younger of Raith and Janet Bonar, his wife, probably a daughter of the neighbouring laird of Rossie. He succeeded his grandfather, William Melville, as laird of Raith in 1502, and was knighted by James IV in the following year, probably on the occasion of that king's marriage in August to Princess Margaret Tudor. He is said to have accompanied James IV to Flodden, but if so he returned in safety, and was more or less actively engaged in the many disputes of the regency during James V's minority. He was appointed master of the artillery for life in October 1526, but a few months later he took part with John, earl of Lennox, in his unsuccessful attempt to free the king from the control of the Earl of Angus, and had to sue to Angus for mercy. Yet within a brief space the Douglases were in exile, and for intercommuning with them Melville had to beg a remission from the crown.

With James V, whose banner he followed in several of his expeditions to the borders and elsewhere, Melville stood in considerable favour, and the king took a personal interest in the staunching of a blood-feud between him and his neighbour, Moultray of Seafield. He was on the juries who tried Janet Douglas, lady Glamis, and Sir James Hamilton of Finnart, respectively for conspiring the death of the king. About 1540 he was made captain of the castle of Dunbar, and had the custody of several important state prisoners.

Melville was early impressed by the principles of the Reformation, and associated himself closely with the movement; and he was one of the three hundred noblemen and gentlemen whom Cardinal Beaton pressed James V to pursue as heretics. During the minority of Queen Mary, Melville was a steady favourer of the policy of the 'English' party in Scotland, who sought to consolidate the interests of the two nations by uniting the crowns in the marriage of Edward VI and Mary. He had a natural son in England, John Melville, with whom he regularly corresponded while the two countries were at war. One of his letters fell into the hands of the Scottish governor, Arran, and he was arrested, carried prisoner to Edinburgh, and, being convicted of treason, was executed there on 13 Dec. 1548. His estates were forfeited, but this forfeiture was rescinded in favour of his widow and children in 1563. Many believed that Melville suffered more on account of his religion than of treachery to the country. John Johnston, D.D. [q. v.], places him among his Scottish heroes (*Heroes ex omni Historia Scotica lectissimi*, 1603, pp. 28, 29). Melville was twice married, first to Margaret, daughter of John Wemyss of that ilk, and secondly to Helen Napier, of the family of Merchiston, and he had a family of nine sons and three daughters. John, the eldest son of his second marriage, succeeded to the family estates; others of his sons were Robert, first lord Melville [q. v.], Sir James Melville of Hallhill [q. v.], Sir Andrew Melville of Garvock, master of the household to Queen Mary, William Melville, commendator of Tungland, and Captain David Melville of Newmill. A daughter of his first marriage, Janet, became the wife of Sir James Kirkcaldy of Grange [q. v.]

[Sir W. Fraser's Melvilles of Melville and Leslies of Leven, i. 38–81.] H. P.

MELVILLE, ROBERT, first BARON MELVILLE (1527–1621), the second son of Sir John Melville of Raith [q. v.] and Helen Napier, was born in 1527. In his youth he entered the service of Mary of Guise, queen-dowager of Scotland, and was afterwards at the French court in the service of Henry II, on whose death in 1559 he returned to Scotland. Throwing in his lot with the lords of the congregation, who were then in conflict with the queen-regent, Melville was sent by them, along with Maitland of Lethington, to beg the assistance of Queen Elizabeth of England. Later he was employed in other diplomatic missions to England, one of which had for its object the marriage of Elizabeth and the Earl of Arran. He joined the opposition to Mary's marriage with Darnley, and for a time took refuge in England, but Mary granted him an early pardon, and sent him as her resident to the English court, the projects of which he faithfully reported. He was instrumental in making peace between Mary and the Earl of Moray, but the murder of Darnley disgusted him, and he withdrew from politics.

Mary, however, after marrying Bothwell, sent him again to Queen Elizabeth to make the most plausible representation of her actions. But Melville, who thoroughly disliked Bothwell, acted more in the interests of the Scottish nobles who were opposing Mary than in those of the queen. About this time she made him keeper of her palace of Linlithgow, and he held this office till 1587. When Melville returned to Scotland, Mary was a captive in Lochleven Castle, but he was permitted to visit her there, and he used all his persuasive energy to induce her to renounce Bothwell, and so save herself and the country. Mary was obdurate, and the nobles, resolving to force her to abdicate, selected Melville to intimate to her their intention. He declined the mission, but seeing their determination he visited Mary privately, and advised her to acquiesce.

When in the following year, 1568, Queen Mary effected her escape, Melville joined her at Hamilton, and was present when she publicly revoked her deed of abdication. At the battle of Langside, Mary's last stand, he was taken prisoner by the regent Moray, but being a non-combatant, and having many friends in the regent's party, he was speedily released and employed in further diplomatic negotiations with Elizabeth. While Mary was a prisoner in England, Melville, who maintained his attachment to her to the end, and was trusted by her, laboured to bring about a reconciliation of all parties. His efforts failed, and hostilities breaking out between her supporters and the friends of the young king, James VI, Melville joined with Kirkcaldy of Grange in his attempt to re-establish the authority of the queen. During the siege of Edinburgh Castle he was declared a traitor and forfeited, and when the castle surrendered in 1573 he fell into the hands of the regent Morton, who would have put him to death with other prominent prisoners had not Elizabeth interposed in his favour. After a year's captivity, spent partly in Holyrood and partly at Lethington, near Haddington, he was liberated, and lived in retirement during the remainder of Morton's government.

In 1580 the influence of Esmé Stuart, duke of Lennox, became paramount at court, and Melville was recalled, his forfeiture rescinded, and in the following year (20 Oct.) the honour of knighthood conferred upon him. At the same time Lord Ruthven, who was created Earl of Gowrie, was lord high treasurer of Scotland, and a few months later Melville was appointed his clerk and treasurer depute. In the Ruthven raid (August 1582) Melville did not participate, but he assisted James to make his escape from the Earl of Gowrie, who shortly afterwards was executed. A year later Melville was appointed a privy councillor. When Queen Mary was lying under sentence of death, he was sent by James, along with the Master of Gray, to entreat Elizabeth to spare Mary's life, and he discharged his mission so fearlessly that Elizabeth threatened his own life, and but for the Master of Gray would have deprived him of his liberty. On his return Melville was commended, and received from James, as a reward, the gift of a wardship worth 1,000*l.*

On the departure of James for Denmark in October 1589 to bring home his bride, Melville was deputed to act as chancellor. He was afterwards sent to pacify disorderly districts in the north and on the borders. In 1593 he again went to England to negotiate with Elizabeth about the relations of the two kingdoms with Spain. In the following year he was admitted as an extraordinary lord of session by the title of Lord Murdocairnie, the name of his seat in Fife. The same year he accompanied King James to the north against Huntly, and remained there for some time with Lennox to restore order. On the appointment in 1586 of the Octavians, who undertook to manage the national finance, Melville ceased to be treasurer depute, but before the expiry of a year the Octavians petitioned for assistance, and Melville, with some others, was directed to help them. When he quitted the office of treasurer Melville was so much out of pocket that he could not meet his own creditors, and had to be protected from them by a special act of parliament, while the court of session was forbidden to entertain any action at law against him.

But old age was now telling upon Melville, and in 1600 he resigned both his offices of privy councillor and lord of session in favour of his son; from time to time he still attended the council meetings, notwithstanding a special dispensation from the king in February 1604, because of 'his age, sickness, and infirmities.' He accompanied James to London in 1603, and when steps were being taken in 1605 for uniting the kingdoms, the Scottish parliament appointed him one of their commissioners. A draft treaty of union was prepared, which Melville signed, but it was not then carried into effect.

Melville's long services were recognised by his creation, on 1 April 1616, as a baron of parliament, with the title of Lord Melville of Monimail, a title derived from his estate of Monimail (now Melville) in Fife, an old residence of Cardinal Beaton. He died in December 1621, aged 94. He was thrice married, first to Katherine, daughter of William Adamson of Craigcrook, a burgess of Edinburgh; secondly, before 1593, to Lady Mary Leslie, daughter of Andrew, earl of Rothes, who died in 1605; and thirdly to Lady Jean Stewart, daughter of Robert, earl of Orkney (who was a natural son of King James V), and widow of Patrick Leslie, first lord Lindores, who survived him. But he had issue only by his first wife, a son Robert, who succeeded him as second baron Melville.

[Sir W. Fraser's Melvilles of Melville and Leslies of Leven, i. 82–124; Memoirs of Sir James Melville of Hallhill, passim; and State Papers, For. and Dom. Ser. 1547–1623, passim.] H. P.

MELVILLE, ROBERT (1723–1809), general and antiquary, son of Andrew Melville, minister of Monimail, Fifeshire, was born on 12 Oct. 1723, passed some time at the grammar school at Leven, and afterwards studied at the universities of Glasgow and Edinburgh. In 1744 he was appointed ensign in the 25th foot (now the king's own Scottish borderers), at that time generally known as the Edinburgh regiment, with which he served in Flanders. When shut up in Ath, after the battle of Fontenoy, he narrowly escaped death by the bursting of a shell. At Val, in 1747, the Edinburgh regiment captured a pair of French colours, which Melville was ordered to carry to the Duke of Cumberland. These colours were in Westminster Hall in 1819 (Higgins, p. 80). Melville was shipwrecked on the French coast on his return from Flanders. He obtained his company in the regiment in 1751, and after having been employed in Scotland recruiting, and as aide-de-camp to his colonel, Lord Panmure, then in command of the forces in North Britain, he was promoted to a majority in the 38th foot on 8 June 1756, and served with that corps at Antigua. As major he commanded the regiment at the reduction of Guadeloupe in 1759, and became lieutenant-governor of the island. He was appointed lieutenant-colonel 38th foot on 14 May 1759, and on the death of Brigadier Crump in 1760 governor of Guadeloupe. On 3 Aug. 1763 he was made governor of the ceded islands (Grenada, the Grenadines, Dominica, St. Vincent, and Tobago) (*Home Office Mil. Entry Book*, xxviii. 41), a post he filled for seven years with great judgment and humanity, and much advantage to the islands (*Calendar Home Office Papers*, 1766–1769, p. 345). Twelve years later, when Tobago was ceded to the French, who had captured it during the American war, Melville, with William (afterwards Sir William) Young, was sent to France on a special mission to solicit certain indulgences from the French government for British settlers in the island, for whom their own government had neglected to make the usual stipulations. On the conclusion of his mission, which was entirely successful, Melville travelled through Switzerland, Italy, and other parts of the continent, examining the sites of great military events, and, guided by Polybius, suggested a new and more obvious route for Hannibal's march across the Alps. He also made a special study of some of the Roman camps in Britain (*Topographica Britannica*, p. 36), while botanical researches deeply interested him. He founded the Botanic Garden at St. Vincent, which was afterwards taken over by the government. He was an honorary LL.D. Edinburgh, F.R.S. London and Edinburgh, F.S.A., author of a paper on 'an ancient sword' in 'Archæologia,' vol. vii., and an active member of the Society of Arts. He was also a member of the board of agriculture, and a very energetic supporter of the Scottish Corporation in London and other Scottish charities.

In 1759 Melville invented a piece of carriage ordnance, intended for a ship gun, which, though shorter than the navy four-pounder and lighter than the navy twelve-pounder, equalled in its cylinder the 8-inch howitzer. It was first manufactured for the navy in 1779 and proved very destructive, especially against timber. Carronades, as the new pieces were called, from the place of manufacture, Carron, Stirlingshire, were used with great effect in the sea-fight between De Grasse and Rodney on 12 April 1782. At that date no less than 429 ships in the navy mounted this class of gun, ranging in calibre from thirty-two to twelve-pounders. They continued in use, mainly in the British and American navies, until the middle of this century (cf. *Notes and Queries*, 1st ser. xi. 247–8; Macpherson, *Annals of Commerce*, 1805, iii. 609; Rees, *Cyclopædia*, s.v. 'Cannon').

Melville, who was long a well-known figure in Edinburgh society, was blind during the last years of his life, owing, as he believed, to injury to the eyes caused by an explosion when he was in command of the outposts at the reduction of Guadeloupe. He died on 29 Aug. 1809, the oldest general in the British army.

[Anderson's Scottish Nation, vol. iii.; Higgins's Hist. Record, 25th King's Own Borderers; Kay's Edinburgh Portraits; Nichols's Illustr. of Literature, viii. 833; Lit. Anecd. viii. 111; Home Office Papers, 1760–5, pp. 66–9.] H. M. C.

MELVIN, JAMES (1795–1853), Latin scholar, was born in Aberdeen, of poor parents, on 21 April 1795. He passed through the grammar school a few years after Byron had left it, during Cromar's rectorship, and was the first bursar of his year at Marischal College, whence he graduated A.M. in 1816. After acting successively as usher at a private school kept by Bisset at Udny, and at Old Aberdeen grammar school under Ewen Maclachlan [q. v.], he became in 1822 a master at the Aberdeen grammar school, and in 1826 he succeeded Cromar as rector. He also became 'lecturer on humanity' (i.e. Latin) at Marischal College, and was created LL.D. by the college in 1834. He formed a wonderful collection of classical and mediæval Latin literature, and became probably the most accomplished Scottish Latinist of his day. An appreciative account of his teaching and personality was contributed to 'Macmillan's Magazine' for January 1864 by a former pupil, Professor David Masson, who, with pardonable exaggeration, compares Melvin as a ruler and inspirer of boys to Thomas Arnold [q. v.] His method of instruction was certainly most dissimilar, being minute, punctilious, and strictly philological. In 1839 and in 1852 he was an unsuccessful candidate for the professorship of Latin at Marischal College. On 18 June 1853 a testimonial in the shape of 300*l.* in a silver snuff-box (souvenir of an inveterate habit) was presented to him by old pupils. Severe application had told upon his health, and he died at his house in Belmont Street, 29 June 1853. He was publicly buried in the town churchyard on 5 July.

'Latin Exercises as dictated by the late James Melvin, LL.D., to which are prefixed Dissertations on a variety of Latin Idioms and Constructions,' was published by the Rev. Peter Calder, rector of Grantown grammar school, in 1857. A supplementary volume or key appeared in 1858, and a third edition, revised by the Rev. J. Pirie, Edinburgh, in 1873, 8vo. Melvin also wrote for use in his school a Latin grammar, which first appeared in 1822, and passed through three editions, and a number of grammatical 'Melviniana' were appended by W. D. Geddes, professor of Greek in Aberdeen University, to his 'Principles of Latinity,' Edinburgh, 1860.

Melvin was said to have been long occupied with a large Latin dictionary, but does not appear to have left any materials. His books (6,984 in number) were presented to Marischal College in September 1856 by his sister and executrix, Agnes Melvin. A stained-glass window in the university library, Aberdeen, represents Melvin in his rectorial robes, in association with Buchanan, Arthur Johnston, and Ruddiman. The device is a beehive and grapes, and the inscription, 'Mel-vinum Natura dedit, gaudete Camenæ' (Geddes, *The Melvin Memorial Window*, 1885).

[Athenæum, 1853, pp. 861–2; Gent. Mag. 1853, ii. 318 (same notice); Macmillan's Mag. January 1864, pp. 225–39; Aberdeen Herald, 2 and 9 July 1853; Anderson's Fasti Academiæ Mariscallanæ, 1889, pp. 527–9; private information.] T. S.

MENASSEH BEN ISRAEL (1604–1657), founder of the Anglo-Jewish community. [See Manasseh.]

MENDES, FERNANDO, M.D. (*d.* 1724), physician, was born of Jewish parentage in the province of Beira, Portugal. He graduated M.D. at Montpellier in December 1667, and became physician to John IV of Portugal. When Catherine of Braganza was on her way to England to become the wife of Charles II, she was attacked during her journey through New Castile with erysipelas, and Mendes was sent to her assistance. He gained such favour with the princess that she made him a member of her household, and desired him to accompany her to England and settle there. Mendes reached this country on 25 Oct. 1669, and was appointed physician in ordinary to the queen. He was one of the many physicians in regular attendance on Charles II in his last illness. By the charter of James II he was created a fellow of the College of Physicians, and was admitted on 12 April 1687, but at the accession of William and Mary his name was removed from the roll. Mendes died in London on 15 Nov. 1724 (*Hist. Reg.* vol. ix., Chron. Diary, p. 48). By his wife, Miss Marques, he had a son James (*d.* 1739), and a daughter Catherine (named after the queen, who acted as godmother), born about 1678 in the royal palace of Somerset House (*Gent. Mag.* 1812, pt. i. p. 22). Moses Mendes [q. v.], the dramatist, was his grandson.

Mendes's only published work was his thesis for the degree of M.D., entitled 'Stadium Apollinare, sive Progymnasmata medica, ad Monspeliensis Apollinis Laurum consequendam,' 4to, Lyons, 1668. Prefixed is his portrait engraved by N. Regnesson. A letter in Portuguese from him to John Mendes da Costa, dated 1663, is among the Additional MSS. in the British Museum (No. 29868, f. i.)

[Barbosa Machado's Bibliotheca Lusitana, ii. 38; Munk's Coll. of Phys. 1878, i. 434; Lysons's Environs, iii. 478; Lindo's Hist. of the Jews; Picciotto's Sketches of Anglo-Jewish Hist. p. 44; Wolf and Jacobs's Bibl. Anglo-Judaica, p. 138; Lists of Coll. of Phys. in Brit. Mus.] G. G.

MENDES, MOSES (*d.* 1758), poet and dramatist, was only son of James Mendes (*d.* 1739), stockbroker, of Mitcham, Surrey, and grandson of Fernando Mendes, M.D. [q. v.] He is said to have received part of his education under Dr. William King at St. Mary Hall, Oxford. Though he once intended to become an advocate in Doctors' Commons, he ultimately saw fit to follow his father's business of stockbroking, by which he made a large fortune, and he acquired a fine estate called St. Andrews at Old Buckenham, Norfolk. He passed for a *bon-vivant* and a wit, was 'of an agreeable behaviour, entertaining in conversation, and had a very pretty turn for poetry.' The poet James Thomson was a frequent visitor at his pleasant house at Mitcham (Lysons, *Environs*, i. 356). In 1744 he made a journey to Ireland, of which he gave a humorous account in a rhymed epistle addressed to a brother-poet, John Ellis. On 19 June 1750 he was created M.A. at Oxford (Foster, *Alumni Oxon.* 1714–1886, iii. 942). He died at Old Buckenham on 4 Feb. 1758 (Probate Act Book, P. C. C. 1758), and was buried there on 8 Feb. By his marriage to Anne Gabrielle, daughter and coheiress of Sir Francis Head, bart., he had two sons, Francis and James Roper, who were authorised to take the surname of Head in lieu of Mendes by royal license dated 11 May 1770, and his grandson, Francis Bond Head [q. v.], was created a baronet on 14 July 1838. Mrs. Mendes married secondly, on 21 March 1760, Captain the Hon. John Roper (1734–1780), and died on 11 Dec. 1771 (Collins, *Peerage*, 1812, vii. 86–7; will of Moses Mendes registered in P. C. C. 47, Hutton).

Mendes wrote verse with facility, and some of his songs are not wanting in grace. His dramatic pieces are: 1. 'The Double Disappointment,' a ballad opera, first performed at Drury Lane on 18 March 1746, and at Covent Garden on 22 March 1759 (Genest, *Hist. of the Stage*, iv. 181). It owed its success to the cleverly drawn characters of two rival lovers, a fortune-hunting Irishman and Frenchman, and was printed in 1755, 12mo, and 1760, 8vo. 2. 'The Chaplet,' a musical entertainment, brought out on 2 Dec. 1749 at Drury Lane, where, thanks to the music by Boyce and the charming acting of Mrs. Clive as Pastora, it had a considerable run (*ib.* iv. 291). It was printed in 8vo in 1749, 1753, 1756, 1759, 1761, and about 1777. 3. 'Robin Hood,' a musical entertainment, which though set to music by Boyce was not so successful. It was produced at Drury Lane on 13 Dec. 1750 (*ib.* iv. 320), and printed in 8vo in 1751. 4. 'The Shepherd's Lottery,' a musical entertainment, acted at Drury Lane on 19 Nov. 1751 without much success, Burney supplying the music (printed in 8vo in 1751 and about 1781). With Paul Whitehead and Dr. Schomberg Mendes produced 'The Battiad,' in two cantos, fol. 1751 (reprinted in Dilly's 'Repository'), a satire on William Battie, M.D. [q.v.] (Nichols, *Lit. Anecd.* iv. 606). The same year he published 'The Seasons, a Poem in imitation of Spenser,' fol. 1751 (reprinted in Richardson and Urquhart's 'Collection' and in Pearch's 'Collection'). In the opening lines he mourns the death of James Thomson. Another imitation of Spenser by Mendes, called 'The Squire of Dames,' appeared in vol. iv. of Dodsley's 'Collection of Poems.' He has also a few miscellaneous pieces in Richardson and Urquhart's 'Collection,' 1767 and 1770; while his translation of Maphæus's continuation of Virgil's 'Æneid' was included in Pearch's 'Collection,' 1775. His humorous epistle to John Ellis, inviting him to supper at the 'Cock,' near the Royal Exchange, was first printed from a copy in manuscript in 'Notes and Queries' (4th ser. vii. 5).

His only prose work was entitled 'Henry and Blanch, or the Revengeful Marriage, a Tale taken from the French of "Gil Blas,"' 4to, 1745; the same story as that of Tancred and Sigismunda, on which Thomson the same year produced a tragedy at Drury Lane.

Mendes's portrait has been engraved by W. Bromley; there is also a bad portrait of him by Hayman.

[European Mag. xxii. 251–2, with portrait; Baker's Biog. Dram. 1812; Wolf and Jacobs's Bibl. Anglo-Judaica, p. 139; Jewish World, 14 Feb. 1873.] G. G.

MENDHAM, JOSEPH (1769–1856), controversialist, born in 1769, was the eldest son of Robert Mendham, formerly a merchant in Walbrook, London, who died at Highgate, Middlesex, 7 April 1810, aged 77, leaving a widow, who died there on 11 Oct. 1812, at the age of seventy-eight. He matriculated at St. Edmund Hall, Oxford, on 27 Jan. 1789, and graduated B.A. 1792, M.A. 1795. In 1793 he was ordained a deacon in the English church, and in 1794 priest. Early in 1795 he accepted the curacy of Sutton Coldfield, Warwickshire. On 15 Dec. in the same year he married Maria, second daughter of the Rev. John Riland, rector of Sutton Coldfield (*d.* 1822), by his wife Ann, daughter of Thomas Hudson of Huddersfield. His sole preferment seems to have been the incumbency of Hill Chapel in Arden, Warwickshire, to which he was licensed on 22 Aug. 1836 (Foster, *Index Ecclesiasticus*). In this district of Warwickshire his whole life was spent, and he died at Sutton Coldfield on 1 Nov. 1856, aged 87. His wife, who was born in 1772, died in 1841. Their only son, the Rev. Robert Riland Mendham, matriculated at Wadham College, Oxford, 12 Nov. 1816, aged 18, took the degrees of B.A. 1820, M.A. 1824, and died at Sutton Coldfield 15 June 1857. Their daughter, Ann Maria Mendham, died 1872. Both were unmarried.

Mendham was well acquainted with ancient and modern languages, especially with Spanish and Italian. He studied the points of controversy between the church of Rome and its protestant opponents, and collected a valuable library of controversial theology. This came to his nephew, the Rev. John Mendham, on whose death his widow placed the books at the disposal of Charles Hastings Collette, solicitor in Lincoln's Inn Fields, by whom a selection was made and presented to the Incorporated Law Society in Chancery Lane, London. These are described in a printed catalogue dated 1871, and in a supplement which was issued in 1874.

Mendham wrote: 1. 'An Exposition of the Lord's Prayer,' 1803. 2. 'Clavis Apostolica, or a Key to the Apostolic Writings,' 1821. This originally appeared in the 'Christian Observer' for 1807. 3. 'Episcopal Oath of Allegiance to the Pope.' By Catholicus [1822]. 4. 'Taxatio Papalis, being an Account of the Tax-books of Rome.' By Emancipatus, 1825; 2nd edit., as 'Spiritual Venality of Rome,' 1836. Preface signed Joseph Mendham. 5. 'Account of Indexes, Prohibitory and Expurgatory, of the Church of Rome,' 1826; 2nd edit., as 'Literary Policy of the Church of Rome exhibited,' 1830; Supplement, 1836; Additional Supplement, 1843; whole work, 1844. 6. 'Some Account of Discussion on Infallibility at Cherry Street Chapel, Birmingham, 30 Sept. and 1 Oct. 1830.' By a Plain Man, 1830. 7. Watson's 'Important Considerations,' 1601; edited, with preface and notes, by Rev. J. Mendham, 1831. 8. 'Life and Pontificate of Saint Pius the Fifth,' 1832; 2nd edit., with Supplement, 1844. 9. 'On the Proposed Papal Cathedral in Birmingham; three Letters between Catholicus Protestans [Mendham] and a Birmingham Catholic,' 1834. 10. 'Address to Inhabitants of Sutton Coldfield on Introduction of Popery into that Parish,' 1834. 11. 'Memoirs of Council of Trent,' 1834; Supplement thereto, 1836. 12. 'Index Librorum Prohibitorum a Sixto V Papa,' 1835. 13. 'Venal Indulgences and Pardons of the Church of Rome,' 1839 (a correction of an error in this volume is given in Hist. MSS. Comm. 12th Rep. App. ix. p. 165). 14. 'Index of Prohibited Books by command of the present Pope Gregory XVI,' 1840. 15. 'Remarks on some parts of the Rev. T. L. Green's Second Letter to Archdeacon Hodson,' 1840. 16. 'Modern Evasions of Christianity,' 1840. 17. 'Services of Church of England vindicated against certain Popular Objections,' 1841. 18. 'Cardinal Allen's Admonition,' 1588; reprinted, with a preface, by Eupator, 1842. 19. 'Acta Concilii Tridentini . . . a Gabriele Cardinale Paleotto descripta,' edited by J. Mendham, 1842. 20. 'Additions to three Minor Works: I. "Spiritual Venality;" II. "Venal Indulgences;" III. "Index by Pope Gregory,"' 1848. 21. 'Declaration of the Fathers of the Councell of Trent' [on attendance at heretical services], edited by Eupator, 1850.

His library at the Incorporated Law Society contains many sermons and pamphlets by him, as well as many copies of the works enumerated above, which have been annotated and prepared for further editions. He contributed to 'Notes and Queries,' the 'Protestant Journal,' and 'Christian Observer.' Many articles by him in the 'Church of England Quarterly Review' have been printed separately.

[Gent. Mag. 1795 pt. ii. p. 1054, 1810 pt. i. p. 397, 1812 pt. ii. p. 495, 1856 pt. ii. p. 780, 1857 pt. i. pp. 218–19; Foster's Alumni Oxon.; Notes and Queries, 2nd ser. ii. 379, 385, 3rd ser. iii. 469; W. K. R. Bedford's Three Hundred Years of a Family Living, 1889, pp. 123–30, 166; Record, 5 Nov. 1856, p. 3; Halkett and Laing's Anon. Literature, i. 778, ii. 1513, iii. 2037–8, 2077, 2417, 2547.] W. P. C.

MENDIP, first Baron (1713–1802), politician. [See Ellis, Welbore.]

MENDOZA, DANIEL (1764–1836), pugilist, of Jewish parentage, was born in the parish of Aldgate, London, in July 1764. His first encounter of any importance was on 17 April 1787, when in twenty minutes on Barnet racecourse he beat Samuel Martin, 'the Bath butcher.' In height about five feet seven inches, with a well-formed chest, strong arms, great courage, and good wind, Mendoza always contrived that his battles should be well contested. His advent was a new feature in the practice of boxing, and his style caused much discussion. There was more neatness than strength in his manner, his blows were deficient in force but given with astonishing quickness, and he struck oftener and stopped more dexterously than any other pugilist. He derived his first scientific knowledge from Richard Humphries, 'the gentleman boxer,' but he so rapidly improved upon his master's system as to stand for years without a rival. No man of his time united the theory of sparring with the practice of boxing so successfully; hence 'the school of Mendoza' marks a period in the history of pugilism.

His third encounter was with Humphries, at Odiham in Hampshire, on 9 Jan. 1788, for 150 guineas a side. The men fought on a stage, in the presence of a vast concourse of people. After twenty-nine minutes Mendoza fell, sprained his foot, and fainted. The result not being considered satisfactory, the antagonists again met on 6 May 1789. The place chosen was Henry Thornton's park, near Stilton, Huntingdonshire, where a building forty-eight feet in diameter was specially erected. Humphries's umpire was Harvey Combe, brewer and alderman, while Sir Thomas Apreece, bart., acted for Mendoza. After a long fight Mendoza was declared the conqueror. At an inn yard in Doncaster the two men met for a third time on 29 Sept. 1790, when five hundred half-guinea tickets were sold. The contest was well sustained, but Humphries, although he fought with great resolution, was again defeated. In 1789 Mendoza had published a small duodecimo entitled 'The Art of Boxing;' during 1791 he was employed in a sparring tour in Ireland. He was then matched to meet William Warr of Bristol. The fight took place at Smitham Bottom, near Croydon, on 14 May 1792. In the fourteenth round Mendoza, from a blow on the jaw, came down with great violence, but recovering himself fought on, and in the twenty-third round was hailed as the conqueror. Warr not being satisfied, the two men again met on Bexley Common on 12 Nov. 1794, when in fifteen minutes Warr was again defeated. On 15 April 1795, at Hornchurch in Essex, in the presence of three thousand spectators, among whom were the Duke of Hamilton, Lord Delaval, and others, Mendoza, for two hundred guineas a side, met John Jackson. In the fifth round the latter caught his opponent by the hair and held him down while he gave him severe blows, a proceeding which was considered unfair. Jackson was a powerful man, and in the ninth round Mendoza, being quite exhausted, gave in.

Subsequently Mendoza became landlord of the Admiral Nelson public-house in Whitechapel, and at times acted as an officer of the sheriff of Middlesex. On 21 March 1806, at Grinstead Green, near Bromley, Kent, he in fifty-three rounds defeated Henry Lee for stakes of fifty guineas. For many years afterwards Mendoza made sparring tours, and appeared in the chief towns in the United Kingdom. In July 1820, on his last appearance 'within the ropes,' he was defeated by Tom Owen, a much younger man. In August 1820 he had a public benefit, and henceforth was seen only now and then in the fives court. He died in Horseshoe Alley, Petticoat Lane, London, 3 Sept. 1836, leaving a wife and eleven children. Aaron Mendoza, a cousin of D. Mendoza, fought Packer, a west-country boxer, at Doncaster, on 29 Sept. 1790.

[Memoirs of the Life of Daniel Mendoza, 1816; Miles's Pugilistica, 1881, i. 71–83, 86–8, 112–13, with portrait; Egan's Boxiana, 1818, i. 253–80, ii. 11, iii. 60–71, 488–90; The Fancy, 1826, i. 46, 184, ii. 341–8; Mendoza's Art of Boxing, 1789; The Odiad, or Battle of Humphries and Mendoza, 1788; Bell's Life in London, 4 Sept. 1836, p. 3, 11 Sept. p. 3.] G. C. B.

MENDOZA Y RIOS, JOSEPH DE (1762–1816), astronomer, born on 15 Sept. 1762 (1764 is sometimes given) in the parish of St. Vincent, Seville, was eldest son of Don Joseph de Mendoza, a noble of Seville, by his wife Doña Maria Romana de Morillo. He was educated at the Royal College of Nobles, Madrid, where he displayed a marked taste for the exact sciences. On 30 April 1774 he was nominated cavalry cadet in the king's regiment of dragoons, but being anxious for a more active life he obtained on 12 April 1776 a lieutenant's commission in the Spanish navy. On 15 Dec. 1777 he sailed for the Philippines on board the Santa Inès, but the ship was taken by two English cruisers, and Mendoza was detained at Cork for a year. He then returned to Cadiz and stayed there until 1781, engaged upon important works, which the war between France, Spain, and England forced him to abandon.

By April 1782 he was captain (by brevet) of the Rosario, and in command of the second division of floating batteries sent against Gibraltar. On 1 Sept. he was gazetted aide-de-camp to the Duke de Crillon, an appointment which he held only a few days, for the attack failed, and he returned to Cadiz at the end of the month. He was made captain-lieutenant ('lieutenant de vaisseau'), and spent his leisure in composing a treatise on navigation.

On 1 Jan. 1786 he became adjutant of the government of the port of Cadiz, and performed the duties until May 1787, when ill-health compelled him to return to Madrid. His treatise on navigation, which was published soon afterwards, brought much renown. The government made him captain of a frigate in 1789, and subsequently placed at his disposal three hundred thousand francs with which to form a maritime library by the purchase in England and France of books and instruments. Mendoza acquitted himself of this task with creditable zeal, and on 1 Feb. 1794 he was made brigadier of the royal navy.

Having been elected fellow of the Royal Society of London on 11 April 1793, he went to England for the purpose of being formally admitted in April 1797 (THOMSON, *Hist. of Roy. Soc.* Append. iv. p. lxiii). Here he made so many friends and met with such liberal patronage, that he was in no hurry to return to Spain. In 1798 he forwarded to the Royal Hydrographic Museum at Madrid a choice collection of books and subjects. At length, determining to make England his home, he sent in his resignation to the Spanish government, and on 21 May 1800 his name was removed from the list of the Spanish navy.

The cost of Mendoza's publications was chiefly defrayed by liberal grants from the East India Company, the commissioners of longitude, the admiralty, and the corporation of Trinity House. Overwork at length told on him. He grew irritable and despondent, and having found in one of his tables a grave miscalculation, he shot himself at Brighton on 3 March 1815. About 1799 he married an Englishwoman, who had nursed him through a long illness, and by her he had two daughters, one of whom, Anna Fermina (1800–1857), became on 19 Jan. 1829 the wife of Sir Patrick Bellew, afterwards Lord Bellew (1798–1866) of Barmeath Castle, Dunleer, co. Louth (BURKE, *Peerage*, 1891, p. 119).

Mendoza by his discoveries completely changed the bases of nautical astronomy. Among other eminent men, M. Biot has borne eloquent testimony to the simplicity and clearness of his methods.

To the 'Philosophical Transactions' for 1797 (pp. 43–122) he contributed a paper entitled 'Recherches sur les principaux problèmes de l'astronomie nautique,' and to the volume for 1801 (pp. 363–74) an elaborate essay, illustrated with diagrams, 'On an Improved Reflecting Circle.'

His other writings are: 1. 'Tratado de Navegacion,' 2 vols. 4to, Madrid, 1787. 2. 'Memoria sobre algunos Métodos nuevos de calcular la Longitud por las distancias lunares,' &c., fol., Madrid, 1795. 3. 'Coleccion de tablas para varios usos de la navegacion,' fol., Madrid, 1800 (another edit., with supplementary tables, by J. J. Martínez de Espinosa y Tacon and J. Sánchez y Cerquero, 2 pts. 4to, Madrid, 1863). 4. 'Tables for Facilitating the Calculations of Nautical Astronomy, . . . and several other Tables, useful in Astronomy and Navigation' ('Appendix, containing Tables for Clearing the Lunar Distances of Refraction and Parallax,' by Henry Cavendish), 2 pts. 4to, London, 1801. 5. 'A Complete Collection of Tables for Navigation and Nautical Astronomy,' 4to, London, 1805, 2nd edit. 2 pts. 4to, London, 1809.

His portrait has been engraved.

[Mendoza et Navarrete, notices biographiques par M. Duflot de Mofras, Paris, 1845; Gent. Mag. 1816, pt. i. p. 372; Evans's Cat. of Engraved Portraits, ii. 277; Houzeau and Lancaster's Bibliographie Générale de l'Astronomie.]

G. G.

MENDS, SIR ROBERT (1767?–1823), commodore, of a Pembrokeshire family, entered the navy in 1779 on board the Culloden with Captain George Balfour, and in her was present at the action off Cape St. Vincent and the relief of Gibraltar in January 1780. Afterwards in the Guadeloupe frigate with Captain Hugh Robinson, he was present in the action off the mouth of the Chesapeake on 16 March 1781, and at the defence of York town, where the Guadeloupe was destroyed, and Mends, then not fourteen (MARSHALL), lost his right arm, besides being wounded in the left knee. On his recovery, he was again with Captain Balfour in the Conqueror, one of the van of the fleet in the battle of Dominica, where he was severely wounded in the head by a splinter. In 1786 he was in the Grampus with Commodore Edward Thompson [q.v.] on the coast of Africa. On 26 Aug. 1789 he was promoted to the rank of lieutenant. He was then for some time in the Childers sloop in the Channel; in 1793 was in the Colossus in the Mediterranean, and was present at the occupation of Toulon; and in 1795, still in the Colossus, was in the action off L'Orient, 23 June, when he was severely burnt by an explosion of powder. On 15 Dec. 1796 he was promoted to be commander, and for the next three years commanded the Diligence sloop on the Jamaica station. He was advanced to post rank on 2 May 1800, and continuing on the same station, successively commanded the Abergavenny, Thunderer, and Quebec frigate, returning to England in the Néréide in September 1802.

In 1805 he was appointed to command the Sea Fencibles of the Dublin district: and in 1808 to the Arethusa frigate, in the bay of Biscay and on the north coast of Spain. On the morning of 6 April 1809 she assisted in the closing scene of the action between the Amethyst and Niemen [see SEYMOUR, SIR MICHAEL, 1768–1834]. The Arethusa's share in it was small; but as Mends was severely wounded in the head by a splinter, it is clear that the statement that to her fire the French made no return (JAMES, *Naval History*, v. 15) is incorrect. In the summer of 1810, in command of a squadron on the coast of Spain, Mends destroyed several French batteries; for which service, in addition to a formal letter of thanks from the Junta of Gallicia, he received the order of the Cross of Victory of the Asturias, and the nominal rank of major-general of the Spanish army. From 1811 to 1814 he was superintendent of the prison hulks in Portsmouth Harbour. On 25 May 1815 he was knighted, on receiving permission to wear the cross of the order of Charles III of Spain; and in April 1816, the pension of 7*l.*, which had been granted him for the loss of his arm, was increased to 300*l.* In June 1821 he was appointed commodore and commander-in-chief on the west coast of Africa, with his broad pennant first in the Iphigénie, and afterwards in the Owen Glendower frigate. He died on board the Owen Glendower at Cape Coast on 4 Sept. 1823.

Mends married in 1802 a daughter of James Butler of Bagshot, and had issue three sons; of whom one, a midshipman of the Owen Glendower, died at Sierra Leone three months after his father; another, James Augustus Mends, died a captain on the retired list, in 1875; the third, George Clarke Mends, was a retired vice-admiral at his death in 1885. Admiral Sir William Robert Mends, G.C.B. (1812–1897), son of Sir Robert's brother, Admiral William Bowen Mends (*d.* 1864), is noticed in the SUPPLEMENT.

[Marshall's Royal Nav. Biog. iii. (vol. ii. pt. i.) 270; O'Byrne's Nav. Biog. Dict. s.n. George Clarke Mends.] J. K. L.

MENKEN, ADAH ISAACS, formerly ADELAIDE MCCORD (1835–1868), actress and writer, the daughter of James McCord, a merchant, was born 15 June 1835 at Chartrain, subsequently known as Milneburg, in the state of Louisiana. Her father died when she was a child, and Adelaide McCord and her younger sister became engaged as the Theodore Sisters at the Opera House, New Orleans. A life in Appleton's 'Cyclopædia of American Biography' makes no mention of the name McCord, says she was born a Jewess, and was called Dolores Adios Fuertes. After dancing at the Tacon Theatre in Havana, she played in various towns in Texas, and is said to have been captured by Red Indians and to have escaped. In New Orleans and Cincinnati she did considerable work as a journalist, and published her first poem. She also taught languages, French, Greek, and Latin, at a ladies' school in the former city. On 3 Aug. 1856 she married Alexander Isaac Menken, a Jew, whose religion she adopted, calling herself thenceforth Adah Isaacs Menken. At the Varieties Theatre, New Orleans, she appeared as an actress in Milman's 'Fazio.' She next played in Cincinnati and Louisville, and accompanied W. H. Crisp's company through the southern states. The intervals of acting were passed in studying sculpture and writing in newspapers. She was divorced from Menken in Nashville. A second marriage, with John C. Heenan, a prize-fighter known as 'The Benicia Boy,' contracted in New York on 3 April 1859, was unhappy. In New York she played at the National and Old Bowery Theatres in dramas such as the 'Soldier's

Daughter' and the 'French Spy,' making her first appearance in June 1859, and she then accompanied James E. Murdoch through the southern states, playing leading business, and essaying even Lady Macbeth. Murdoch suggested to her the expediency of turning to account her fine physique, and on 7 June 1861 she made, at the Green Street Theatre, Albany, her first appearance as Mazeppa. In various American cities, including New York, these performances had much success. In October 1861 she went through a form of marriage with R. H. Newell, known as Orpheus C. Kerr, and, a year later, was divorced from Heenan. In April 1864 she sailed for London, appearing on 3 Oct. as Mazeppa at Astley's Theatre, when she had what might in part be considered a 'succès de scandale.' A failure was experienced when, at the same house, she appeared on 9 Oct. 1865 as Leon in Brougham's 'Child of the Sun.' While in England she contracted intimacies with many men of letters, including Charles Dickens (to whom, by permission, she dedicated in 1868 her volume of poems called 'Infelicia'), Charles Reade, Mr. A. C. Swinburne, and many others. On her visit to Paris, where she appeared on 30 Dec. 1866 at the Gaîté in 'Les Pirates de la Savane' of Bourgeois and Dugué, she became closely associated with the elder Dumas and with Théophile Gautier. She had meanwhile been divorced from Newell, and married on 21 Aug. 1866 James Barclay. In June 1868, while in Paris rehearsing, she was taken ill, and on 10 Aug. died in the Jewish faith. Her remains were buried in the cemetery of Père la Chaise, her tomb bearing the motto 'Thou knowest.' She also published about 1856, under the pseudonym 'Indigena,' a volume of poems entitled 'Memories,' which is not in the British Museum. In December 1858 she gave by desire in the synagogue, Louisville, a sermon on Judaism, a subject on which also she wrote. A new illustrated edition of 'Infelicia' appeared in 1888.

Those favoured with the intimacy of Menken thought highly of her. Her poems have little lyrical quality, but convey pleasant and moving aspirations, to which the conditions of her life imparted added significance. As an actress she had few charms, and her performance of Mazeppa, though it involved some difficulty and risk, is to be regarded rather as a study of physique than as a performance. Many photographs of her are extant. One presenting her in company with Dumas had considerable vogue. A second, showing her with Mr. Swinburne, is less common. An engraved portrait is prefixed to 'Infelicia.' She possessed a good figure, and a face which was strongly marked, and striking rather than handsome.

[Most details as to the life of Menken are derived from the Memoir prefixed to the illustrated edition of her Infelicia, 1888, and from Appleton's Cyclopædia of American Biography. A biography, obviously inspired, prefaces the text of Les Pirates de la Savane, Paris, 1867. The two accounts are contradictory on many points. Some few particulars are obtained from the Era Almanack for 1868, Scott and Howard's E. L. Blanchard, the Theatrical Journal, from personal knowledge, and from private information.] J. K.

MENMUIR, Lord (1552–1598), secretary of state for Scotland. [See Lindsay, John.]

MENNES, Sir **JOHN** (1599–1671), admiral, of a family long settled at Sandwich, was grandson of Matthew Mennes, mayor of Sandwich in 1549–50, 1563–4, 1571–2, and 1587–8 (Boys, *Hist. of Sandwich*, pp. 686, 689, 691, 698), and third son of Andrew Mennes, by his wife Jane, daughter of John Blechenden. The family is described by Hasted (*Hist. of Kent*, iv. 266) as gentle, and Matthew, John's eldest brother, who was made a K.B. at the coronation of Charles I, was described on his matriculation at Oxford in 1608, aged 15, as 'generosi filius.' It appears too that they were connected with the Boyses and Bretts, old Kent families, and nothing sanctions the suggestion that the family was in its origin Scottish, and that the name was Menzies (*Notes and Queries*, 3rd ser. iv. 144). John Mennes was born at Sandwich on 1 March 1598–9, and according to Wood was entered at the age of seventeen as a commoner at Corpus Christi College, Oxford, 'where continuing for some years he did advance himself much in several sorts of learning, especially in humanity and poetry, and something in history' (*Athenæ Oxon.* 1817, iii. 925). His name, however, does not appear in the Oxford matriculation lists, and Wood's statement may be due to some confusion with another John Mynne, Minne (or Mennes), 'eq. aur. fil.,' who matriculated from Corpus on 27 Oct. 1615, aged 17, and may have been son of Sir William Mynne or Mennes, who was knighted on 23 July 1603 (Foster, *Alumni Oxon.* 1500–1714). Sir Alexander Brett, who afterwards commanded a regiment under the Duke of Buckingham at Ré, writing to Nicholas on 15 April 1626, said of Mennes: 'This gentleman was recommended by me unto my Lord Duke for the command of a ship who hath been divers times at sea, first in the Narrow Seas with Sir William Monson [q. v.], in the late king's service, and afterwards with his father-in-law, Captain Chester, into the West Indies with a small ship called the Margaret and John of London, where they were assaulted by two of the king's of Spain's galeons, and after a long and bloody fight, with the loss of a great part of their men, came off with honour [cf. LEDIARD, *Naval History*, p. 465; the fight was off Dominica in 1620]. Likewise to Virginia, and since, he commanded the Seahorse in his Majesty's service; which employments with his own industry have made him fit for command and his king's and country's service' (*State Papers*, Dom. Charles I, xxiv. 87).

During the following years Mennes continued actively employed at sea. In July 1626 he was at Portsmouth, in command of the Espérance prize. From 1628 to 1630 he commanded the Adventure in the North Sea, capturing or detaining Hamburg or Dutch ships laden with prohibited goods for France. On 25 May 1629 he reported to the admiralty that, according to his orders, he had landed the Marquis de Ville at Dunkirk, and had brought back to Dover 'a gentleman who is coming towards his Majesty.' This 'gentleman' is identified by Mr. Sainsbury with Rubens, the celebrated painter (*Notes and Queries*, 2nd ser. viii. 437). In 1630 and 1631 Mennes commanded the Garland in the Narrow Seas. In March 1635 he was appointed to the Red Lion, one of the fleet in the Narrow Seas under the Earl of Lindsey (cf. LEDIARD, p. 524), and on 7 Oct. was moved by Lindsey to the Vanguard, as vice-admiral of the fleet for the guard of the Narrow Seas, under Sir John Penington [q. v.] On 13 Nov., however, Penington ordered him to leave the Vanguard, take command of the Swiftsure, and carry her up the river to Woolwich or Deptford. In the following year he was captain of the Convertine, in the fleet under the Earl of Northumberland. In 1639 he was captain of the Victory, and on 22 Feb. 1639–40 was appointed by Northumberland, then lord high admiral, to raise, command, and exercise a troop of carabineers, to be conducted to the rendezvous when required.

On 28 April 1640 he took his troop to Newcastle, and during the year continued with the army in the north of England. On 8 Dec. Sir John Conyers wrote to Lord Conway that he had orders to send 20,000*l.* to the Scottish army under the care of a discreet captain; 'Jack Mince shall be the man;' on 18 Dec. he wrote to the Earl of Northumberland, 'Captain Mynce has marched today towards Ripon to convoy the money to Croft Bridge.' On 1 Jan. 1640–1 Mennes was asking for his promotion, presumably on account of this service, and during the following months he was in command of Commissary-general Wilmot's regiment of horse, till it was disbanded on 28 Aug. On 25 Feb. 1641–2 he was knighted at Dover, and shortly afterwards was again appointed captain of the Victory under the Earl of Warwick [see RICH, ROBERT, EARL OF WARWICK]. On 2 July Warwick sent him an order to attend a general council on board the James, his flagship. Mennes paid no attention to the order, and 'for this contempt and misdemeanour' Warwick, two days later, 4 July, discharged him from the command of the Victory (*State Papers*, Dom. Charles I, ccccxci. 51, 53; the official account, which differs considerably in its details from that given by CLARENDON, *Hist. of the Rebellion*, Macray's edit. ii. 218).

During the civil war he served with the royalist army. In 1644 he was governor of North Wales for the king, apparently on the appointment of Prince Rupert (*Addit. MS.* 18981; WARBURTON, *Mem. of Prince Rupert*, ii. 371–3, iii. 55; CARTE, *Collection of Original Letters*, &c., i. 49, 54, 67), and in 1645, on the death of Sir John Penington, was named as commander of the king's navy (*ib.* i. 89). In 1648 his estates in Bedfordshire, inherited from his brother, Sir Matthew, were seized, and the rents and arrears detained, he 'being in arms against the parliament' (*Cal. Committee for Advance of Money*, p. 892). He was at that time with Rupert as commander of the Swallow and rear-admiral of the semi-piratical squadron (WARBURTON, iii. 266; CLARENDON, iv. 424), which was finally crushed by Blake in November 1650 [see BLAKE, ROBERT; and RUPERT]. For the next ten years he followed the fortunes of the king, a trusted agent when occasion required (CLARENDON, v. 372; MACRAY, *Cal. Clarendon State Papers*, vol. iii. passim), and whiling away his enforced leisure in writing verses.

At the Restoration Mennes returned to England, and in 1661–2 was commander-in-chief in the Downs and admiral of the Narrow Seas, with his flag in the Henry. On 30 Oct. 1661 he was appointed comptroller of the navy, and on 26 May 1662 he was elected master of the Trinity House. As comptroller, he was necessarily brought into close relationship with Samuel Pepys [q. v.], whose 'Diary' abounds with references to him. These are more favourable than those to most of Pepys's intimate acquaintances. He is, he says, 'most excellent company,' 'doats mightily' on Chaucer, 'seems to know something of chemistry,' and 'hath some judgment in pictures.' On 2 Jan. 1665–6 he 'was in the highest pitch of mirth; and most excellent pleasant company he is, and the best mimic that ever I saw; and certainly would have made an excellent actor, and now would be an excellent teacher of actors.' On 20 Aug. 1666 he was said to be dying, 'which,' says Pepys, 'troubles me mightily, for he is a very good, harmless, honest gentleman, though not fit for business.' On 6 Oct. 1666 Pepys quotes Sir William Coventry as saying that 'besides all the shame and trouble he—Mennes—hath brought on the office, the king had better have given 100,000*l.* than ever have had him there.' And on 4 Jan. 1668–9 he and Lord Brouncker complained to the Duke of York 'that it is but to betray the king to have any business of trust committed to his weakness.' Despite his obvious incapacity, he was still comptroller at the time of his death, 18 Feb. 1670–1. He was buried in the church of St. Olave in the city of London, where there is a mural tablet to his memory. There is also a monument in the parish church of Nonington in Kent (HASTED, iii. 711). There are some 'foolish verses' to him in Denham's 'Poems' (p. 73).

A portrait by Vandyck is in Lord Clarendon's collection at The Grove, Watford. It is engraved in the 1874 edition of the 'Musarum Deliciæ.'

Mennes married, apparently in 1640, Jane, daughter of Thomas Liddell of Ravensworth in Durham, and widow of Robert Anderson (*Cal. State Papers*, Dom. 9 Feb. 1640–1; COLLINS, *Baronetage*, ii. 372). She died without issue on 23 July 1662, at the house of John Boys of Fredville (cf. HASTED, iii. 710; *Topographer*, iii. 154) in Nonington, during the absence of her husband in command of the squadron. She was buried in Nonington Church, where there is a mural tablet to her memory. The expression in Brett's letter, already quoted, as to Mennes's 'father-in-law, Captain Chester,' is unexplained.

By his will, dated 16 May 1669, proved on 9 March 1670–1, Mennes left the bulk of his property to his nephew Francis and niece Mary, son and daughter of his sister, Mary Hammond, then deceased. Several members of the Hammond family are buried in Nonington Church (*ib.* iii. 711). To his niece, Lady Heath, wife of Sir John Heath of Brasted in Kent, he bequeathed 'my great Portugal jewel containing 180 diamonds set in gold,' and to his goddaughter Margaret, daughter of Lady Heath, a small gold cross with seven diamonds. Another niece, 'Mrs. Jane Moyle, wife of Anthony Moyle, Esq.,' and her son, John Moyle, are also mentioned. The name of Mennes has been spelt in an almost countless number of different ways. The spelling here followed is that of his own signature [cf. MYNGS, SIR CHRISTOPHER].

Mennes's verses, chiefly *vers de société*, seem to have caught the fancy of the age, and have been since described as the ideal of wit and mirth, but most of the pieces are coarse. It is, however, difficult to apportion his share of praise or blame, for nothing stands published in his name alone. Where his name does appear it is in conjunction with that of Dr. James Smith (1605–1667) [q. v.], who was probably the more fertile writer of the two, and their joint publications mainly consisted of anthologies of verse, to which many other writers besides themselves were contributors.

The works assigned to Mennes and Smith are: 'Wits Recreations selected from the finest Fancies of Moderne Muses,' first published in 1640, and in five other editions by 1667, with very considerable variations; 'Musarum Deliciæ, or the Muses' Recreation,' 1655 (2nd edit. 1656), and 'Wit Restored in several select Poems, not formerly published,' 1658. These three were collected and edited by Thomas Park, under the title of 'Musarum Deliciæ,' 2 vols. 8vo, 1817, and reissued, with additional notes, by J. C. Hotten, 2 vols. 8vo, 1874. Besides these Mennes was the author, according to Anthony à Wood, of 'Merrie Newes from Epsom Wells,' 4to, 1663, and was one of the writers against Sir William D'Avenant in 'certain verses written by severall of the Authour's friends, to be reprinted with the second edition of Gondibert,' 1653; also, says Wood, of 'divers other poems scattered in other men's works; and he did assist, as I have been credibly informed, Sir John Suckling in the composition of some of his poetry.'

[Memoir by Thomas Park, prefixed to the 1817 edition of Musarum Deliciæ, with some additions in the edition of 1874; Add. MS. 24487, f. 4 (Hunter's Chorus Vatum); Harl. MSS. 818, f. 49, and 1106, f. 118; Charnock's Biog. Nav. i. 61; Duckett's Naval Commissioners, with Historical Notices; Calendars of State Papers, Dom.; Notes and Queries, 1st ser. i. passim; Pepys's Diary, passim; notes kindly furnished by Mr. C. H. Firth.] J. K. L.

MENTEITH, EARLS OF. [See COMYN, WALTER, *d.* 1258; GRAHAM, WILLIAM, seventh EARL, 1591–1661.]

MENTEITH, SIR JOHN DE (*d.* after 1329), Scottish knight, was the younger son of Walter Stewart, earl of Menteith, and of his wife, the daughter and heiress of William Comyn, earl of Menteith, whose marriage brought the Menteith earldom for a time into the house of Stewart (DOUGLAS, *Peerage of*

Scotland, p. 472, ed. 1764). His elder brother was Alexander, earl of Menteith (*Fœdera*, i. 872). He was involved with his brother in the resistance made by the Scots to Edward I's conquest of Scotland in 1296; but while the earl made his submission to the English king (*Ragman Roll*, p. 103, Bannatyne Club), John remained a prisoner in England until the next year. He was confined for thirteen days in Nottingham Castle, along with Edward Comyn of Kilbride, whence he was sent with an escort of fourteen men to join Edward I at Winchelsea (STEVENSON, *Doc. illustrating History of Scotland*, ii. 136). In August Edward released Menteith from prison, on his taking oath and giving security to serve with the king against Philip of France (*Fœdera*, i. 872). He therefore in all probability took part in the campaign of 1297 in Flanders. His history during the next few years is a little puzzling. Late Scottish writers make him out to have joined in the revolt of Wallace and to have taken part in an incursion into Galloway in 1298, in which Wallace took the command (*Relationes Arnaldi Blair*, p. 5, ed. Edinburgh, 1758). The untrustworthy romance of Blind Harry lays stress on the fact that Menteith was the 'gossip' of Wallace (*Henry the Minstrel*, bk. xi. l. 795 sq. ed. Jamieson), and makes Wallace repair to the Lennox early in his revolt, because Menteith was then captain of that district (*ib.* bk. viii. 1595). Moreover authentic documents show that a John of Menteith was ravaging the lands of Edward's partisans in Scotland in 1301, and was sent in 1303 to treat of peace with the English, but refrained from pressing his mission when he discovered the distressed condition to which Edward's Irish troops were reduced (STEVENSON, ii. 437, 453). It seems most probable, considering the constant changes of front that took place among the Scottish nobles, that the John of Menteith who joined Wallace is identical with the John of Menteith pardoned in 1297, but the name is too common to make the identification quite certain. By 1303 the conquest of Scotland had nearly been completed by Edward, and Menteith, if he had held out so long, must again have submitted and been restored to Edward's favour, for on 20 March 1304 Edward, who was then at St. Andrews, appointed him warden of the castle, town, and sheriffdom of Dumbarton (*ib.* ii. 474). It was in this neighbourhood that William Wallace held out after all other resistance in Scotland had been stifled. But Wallace was now rather a fugitive than a belligerent, and great efforts were made to secure his capture. Blind Harry tells a long romance of a 'plot' entered into between Menteith and Aymer de Valence, Edward's general, to secure the person of the hero; but this is unhistorical (*Henry the Minstrel*, bk. xi.) At last one of Wallace's servants, Jack Short, whose brother Wallace had slain, seems to have betrayed him to Menteith, who apprehended him at Glasgow, whither he had gone to visit his mistress (LANGTOFT, ii. 362, Rolls Ser.; ROBERT OF BRUNNE in HEARNE's *Langtoft*, ii. 329; FORDUN, i. 340; WYNTOUN, ii. 370; *Chron. de Lanercost*, p. 203; *Scalachronica*, Maitland Club; *Chron. de Melsa*, ii. 275; *Buik of the Croniclis of Scot.* iii. 199). The Scottish writers denounce Menteith's capture of Wallace as an act of treachery (FORDUN, i. 340; *Henry the Minstrel*, bk. xi. line 812), though it was only his duty as sheriff of Dumbarton to take proper steps to secure the fugitive's apprehension. His act, however, assumes a very grave complexion, if his recent alliance with Wallace could be regarded as certainly established. Lord Hailes (*Annals of Scotland*, i. 281) seeks to disprove any complicity of Menteith in the capture of Wallace, on the ground that it rests on the untrustworthy authority of Blind Harry; but there are many other better writers who closely connect Menteith with the event (see the note in TYTLER, *Hist. of Scotland*, i. 384–387).

Menteith took his captive, loaded with chains, to London. A month after Wallace's death on the scaffold Menteith was nominated one of the representatives of the Scots barons in the parliament of both nations which assembled at London in September. He was chosen a substitute for the Earl of March [see under DUNBAR, AGNES], who had not attended, and was put upon the Scottish council, which was appointed to assist John of Brittany, Edward's nephew, the new regent of Scotland, in the English interest (PALGRAVE, *Doc. illustrating Hist. of Scotland*, p. 293). He was further rewarded with a grant of lands valued at 100*l.* (*ib.* p. 295), and on 1 June Edward ordered that the earldom of Lennox should be conferred on him, while on 15 June he gave him his Dumbarton office for life (*ib.* p. 305). Before October Menteith received his final grants, and was despatched to Scotland on the king's business (*Cal. Doc. Scotland*, iv. 488, 489).

Neither the favour of Edward nor the odium which accrued to the betrayer of Wallace kept Menteith faithful to the English alliance. He was among the Scottish magnates whom Edward appealed to in December 1307 to join him in resisting the revolted Bruce (*Fœdera*, ii. 22). But he had already chosen his part, and, abandoning his newly won earldom of Lennox, henceforth steadfastly adhered to the popular cause. In March 1308 Menteith was among the Scottish magnates who wrote to the king of France on behalf of the national cause (*Acts Parl. Scotland*, i. 13, 99). In 1309 he was sent with Sir Nigel Campbell to treat with Richard de Burgh, earl of Ulster [q. v.], for which purpose he received a safe-conduct, dated 21 Aug., from Edward II (*Fœdera*, ii. 85). His English lands were forfeited for his treason, and were either granted to royal servants or impoverished by heavy fines (*Acts Parl. Scotland*, i. 80, 138). In 1316 he was commissioned with Thomas Randolf to treat on behalf of Robert Bruce for a truce with the English (*Fœdera*, ii. 302). Menteith remained closely attached to the royal court, as is shown by the numerous charters he attested (*Liber de Mailros*, ii. 341, 351, 356; *Liber Sancte Crucis*, pp. 74, 90, 105, 365; *Reg. Dunfermline*, p. 229; *Reg. de Kelso*, p. 365). He was at the Arbroath parliament in April 1320, and signed the letter sent by the barons of Scotland to Pope John XXII (*Acts Parl. Scotland*, i. 15, 114; *Liber Pluscarden*. i. 202). He was then described as 'guardian' of the earldom of Menteith. He was one of the negotiators of the thirteen years' truce between Bruce and the English, signed on 30 May 1323 (*Fœdera*, ii. 521), and was immediately afterwards present at a Scottish council at Berwick in June (*ib.* ii. 524). The last recorded grants to him are in 1329, during the minority of King David Bruce (*Exchequer Rolls of Scotland*, i. 178, 180), one of whose charters he also attested. Later references to John of Menteith probably refer to a knight of the same name who was sheriff of Clackmannan in 1359 (*ib.* i. 570).

[Cal. of Documents relating to Scotland, vols. ii. iii. iv.; Palgrave's Documents relating to Scotland; Acts of Parliament of Scotland, vol. i.; Stevenson's Documents illustrating the Hist. of Scotland; Rymer's Fœdera, Record ed.; Fordun, ed. Skene; Scalachronica (Maitland Club); Chron. de Lanercost (Bannatyne Club); Wallace Papers (Maitland Club); Henry the Minstrel's Wallace, ed. Jamieson, 1869; Douglas's Peerage of Scotland, 1764, p. 473; Anderson's Scottish Nation, iii. 148; Tytler's Hist. of Scotland, vol. i.]

T. F. T.

MENTEITH, MENTET, or MONTEITH, ROBERT (*fl.* 1621–1660), author of 'Histoire des Troubles de la Grande Bretagne,' represented himself in France as one of the Menteiths of Salmonet, descended from the Menteiths of Kerse, and more remotely from the ancient earls of Monteith. According to one account the designation of Salmonet was his own invention: 'The fact was that his father was a mere fisherman or tacksman of fishings (user of a *Salmonnet*) on the Forth at Stirling' (Chambers, *Domestic Annals of Scotland*, ii. 70). There was, however, at one time in Stirlingshire a place called Salmonet, with which his father, Alexander Menteith, a citizen of Edinburgh, may have had some connection. Robert was the third and youngest son. He was educated at the university of Edinburgh, where he graduated M.A. in 1621. Subsequently he became professor of philosophy in the protestant university of Saumur, where he remained four years. In 1629 he was nominated by two ministers of Edinburgh for the professorship of divinity in the university, but his nomination being strongly opposed by three other ministers as well as by the principal and regents, he was not appointed. Having obtained orders from Archbishop Spotiswood, he was in 1630 presented by Charles I to the kirk of Duddingston, and on the 20th he was admitted by warrant from Spotiswood by two or three ministers 'without acquainting the Presbytery' (Calderwood, *History*, viii. 72). Having, however, been discovered in an illicit amour with Anna Hepburn, wife of Sir James Hamilton of Priestfield (Scot, *Staggering State of the Scots Statesmen*, ed. 1872, p. 75), he fled the country, and on 7 Oct. 1633 was denounced a rebel. He himself attributed his retirement from Scotland to the action of the extreme presbyterian party on account of his episcopal leanings.

Menteith went to Paris, and having joined the catholic church obtained the favour of Cardinal Richelieu, and became secretary first to M. de la Port, grand prior of France, and after his death to de Retz, then coadjutor to the Archbishop of Paris, and afterwards cardinal. By de Retz he was made one of the canons of Notre-Dame. Michel de Marolles, who met him at court in 1641, refers to his gentle and agreeable personality and his witty conversation, and adds that never 'was there a man more wise, or more disinterested, or more respected by the legitimate authorities' (*Mémoires*, Amsterdam, 1755, i. 244). He expresses an equally high opinion of his learning and intellectual accomplishments, and makes special mention of the elegant French style of his writings. On the arrest of Cardinal de Retz in the Louvre in December 1652, Menteith was for some time sheltered by Michel de Marolles in his abbey of Baugerais in Touraine (*ib.* p. 367). He died some time before 13 Sept. 1660, when in the privilege for printing his 'Histoire' he is referred to as dead. He had two sons: William of Carruber and Randeford, from whom the Stuart Menteiths of Closeburn are descended; and Robert.

Menteith was the author of: 1. 'Remonstrance très humble faite au sérénissime Prince Charles II, Roi de la Grande Bretagne, sur la conjoncture présente des affaires de sa Majesté,' Paris, 1652 (very rare). 2. 'Histoire des Troubles de la Grande Bretagne; contenant ce qui s'est passé depuis l'année mille six cens trente-trois, jusques à l'année mille six cens quarante six,' Paris, 1661, translated into English by James Ogilvie, 1785. He also wrote a pasquil against Robert Bruce of Kinnaird, formerly minister of Edinburgh. An engraving of his portrait, by P. Mignard, painted at Rome in 1656, is prefixed to his 'Histoire.'

[Scot's Staggering State of the Scots Statesmen; Calderwood's History of the Kirk of Scotland; Bobert Baillie's Letters and Journals; Life of Robert Bruce prefixed to his Sermons; Mémoires de Michel de Marolles; Tallemant's Les Historiettes; Francisque-Michel's Les Écossais en France; Bower's Hist. of Univ. of Edinburgh; Scott's Fasti Eccles. Scot. i. 110–11.] T. F. H.

MENZIES, ARCHIBALD (1754–1842), botanical collector, was born at Weims, Perthshire, on 15 March 1754. His elder brother, William, was employed in the Edinburgh Botanic Garden, and he became a gardener there. Dr. John Hope, then professor of botany, enabled him to go through the training of a surgeon at the university, and after making a botanical tour through the highlands and Hebrides in 1778, he became assistant to a surgeon at Carnarvon. He subsequently entered the navy as assistant-surgeon on board the Nonsuch, under Captain Truscott, and was present at Rodney's victory over the Comte de Grasse on 12 April 1782. On the declaration of peace he was sent to the Halifax station, but in 1786 was engaged as surgeon on board the Prince of Wales, under Lieutenant Colnett, on a fur-trading voyage of discovery to the north-west coast of America. They visited Staten Island, the Sandwich Islands, and China, returning direct from the latter in 1789. In the following year he was chosen as naturalist and surgeon on the Discovery, under Captain George Vancouver, and visited the Cape, King George's Sound, New Zealand, Otaheite, the Sandwich and Galapagos Islands, and North-west America. Vancouver speaks highly of his services in the preface to his account of the voyage, not one man dying from ill-health between the date of the departure of the expedition from the Cape on the way out and that of its return in October 1795. Menzies ascended Wha-ra-rai and Mauna Loa, an active volcano, over thirteen thousand feet in height, in Hawaii, determining their altitude by the barometer, and collected in all the countries visited, especially at Valparaiso and at Nootka Sound. He brought back a great variety of plants, including *Ribes speciosum*, *Araucaria imbricata*, and *Abies Menziesii*, and numerous cryptogams, besides other natural history objects. Vancouver records (*loc. cit.*) that 'for the purpose of preserving such . . . plants as he might deem worthy of a place amongst his Majesty's . . . collection . . . at Kew, a glazed frame was erected on the quarter-deck.' The new species of plants were described by Sir J. E. Smith, Robert Brown, and Sir W. J. Hooker, and Menzies himself gave an account of the voyage in Loudon's 'Magazine of Natural History,' vols. i. and ii. Menzies next served on board the Sanspareil in the West Indies, under Lord Hugh Seymour, but soon after his return he retired from the navy, and practised for some time in London. He died at Ladbroke Terrace, Notting Hill, on 15 Feb. 1842, and was buried at Kensal Green. His wife, by whom he had no family, predeceased him by five years. Having been elected a fellow of the Linnean Society in 1790, Menzies, on the death of A. B. Lambert, became the father of the society. A portrait of him by Eddis is at the society's rooms. His herbarium of grasses, sedges, and cryptogams was bequeathed to the Edinburgh Botanical Garden. Sir J. E. Smith dedicated to him the ericaceous genus *Menziesia*.

Four papers by Menzies are recorded in the Royal Society's Catalogue (iv. 345): 1. Descriptions of three new animals found in the Pacific Ocean (*Echeneis lineata*, *Fasciola clavata*, *Hirudo branchiata*), 'Linnean Transactions,' 1791, i. 187–8. 2. A new arrangement of the genus *Polytrichum*, *ib.* 1798, iv. 63–84. 3. *Polytrichum rubellum* [and] *P. subulatum*, *ib.* 1798, iv. 303–4. 4. Account of an ascent and barometrical measurement of Wha-ra-rai, a mountain in Owhyhee, 'Magazine of Natural History,' 1829, i. 201–208, ii. 435–42.

[Proceedings of the Linnean Soc. i. 139–41; Gent. Mag. 1842, i. 668–9.] G. S. B.

MENZIES, JOHN (1624–1684), Scottish divine and professor, born in 1624, entered Marischal College, Aberdeen, in 1638, and after graduating held the office of regent till 1649. He is said to have been brought up a Roman catholic, but he early connected himself with the reformed church. In 1649 he was ordained and admitted to the second charge of St. Nicolas, Aberdeen, and in the same year was appointed professor of divinity in Marischal College and translated to the Greyfriars Church, which was connected with it. Joining the protesters, he became one of their leaders, and with the rest of that party separated from the church in 1651. Soon after he espoused the interests of Cromwell, and avowed himself an independent. He was processed in consequence by the synod of Aberdeen, but their proceedings against him were stopped by order of the commandant of the English garrison. Cromwell, having put an end to the meetings of the general assembly, called up Menzies and other protesters to London in 1654 to assist in preparing an ordinance for the admission of ministers to parishes in Scotland similar to that of the tryers in England, and Menzies was appointed a tryer for his own part of the country. After a time he lost faith in independency, in reference to which system he said, 'It is dangerous to slip a buckle,' and became again a presbyterian. At the Restoration he refused to conform to episcopacy, but when summoned before the privy council, and threatened with deposition by the bishop and synod if he did not comply before January 1663, he accepted the change and retained his offices. He afterwards took an active part in controversy with the Roman catholics and with the quakers, who had then obtained a footing in the north, and made himself so acceptable to the authorities that he was several times spoken of for a bishopric. The professorship of divinity in King's College, Old Aberdeen, he accepted from the bishop and synod, after some hesitation, in January 1679; but very soon he resigned, and was reinstated in his professorship in Marischal College and in the charge of Greyfriars Church. In 1681 he refused the test imposed by parliament, with many others of the clergy, and was deprived of his office in consequence. The following year, however, he changed his mind, and was continued in his post.

He died 1 Feb. 1684, much troubled in conscience for having fallen into independency, for having conformed to episcopacy, and most of all for having taken the test. He professed penitence for his vacillation, and charged his brother-in-law to publish his declaration to that effect. Menzies was a man of much ability and learning, a zealous controversialist, and a most fervent preacher, but his pliability injured his influence and reputation.

He married Margaret, eldest daughter of Sir W. Forbes of Craigievar, Aberdeenshire, and had one son, whom he survived.

His publications were: 1. 'Papismus Lucifugus,' Aberdeen, 1668. 2. 'Roma Mendax,' London, 1675. 3. 'A Sermon on the Death of Sir Alexander Fraser of Doores,' Edinburgh, 1681.

[Scott's FastiEccl. Scot.; Records of Marisch. Coll.; Wodrow's Hist. and Analecta; Eccles. Rec. of Aberdeen (Spalding Club); Baillie's Letters; Jaffray's Diary.] G. W. S.

MENZIES, JOHN (1756–1843), founder of Blairs College, Kincardineshire, was the last member of an ancient family long settled at Pitfodels, Aberdeenshire, which had always adhered to the Roman catholic faith. He was born on 15 Aug. 1756, a few months after his father's death. The care of his education devolved on his mother, a daughter of the house of Kirkconnel. She resided for some time at Dinant in Belgium, where her son was educated, and, on the breaking up of the Jesuit College there, she applied in 1774 to Bishop Hay, vicar-apostolic of the lowland district of Scotland, for permission to employ the services of Sir Alexander Strachan, the ex-jesuit missionary at Kirkconnel, in completing the education of her son. Hay was compelled, however, to decline the request. It has been said of Menzies that for thirty-seven years he never became aware of distress or difficulty without exerting himself to relieve it. Sir Walter Scott, writing on 30 Jan. 1827, says: 'About three, Pitfoddels called. A bauld crack that auld papist body, and well informed. We got on religion. He is very angry with the Irish demagogues, and a sound well-thinking man' (*Journal*, 1890, i. 349). In the course of that year Menzies conveyed to Bishop Paterson his beautiful estate, with the large mansion-house of Blairs, Kincardineshire, about six miles from Aberdeen. There the college dedicated to St. Mary, for the education of secular priests, was opened 2 June 1829, and the students from the two seminaries of Aquhorties and Lismore were removed to the new institution. Menzies was also a munificent benefactor to the convent of St. Margaret, Edinburgh, opened in 1835. For many years he discharged the duties of convener of Aberdeenshire, and he was a member of the Abbotsford Club, to which he presented 'Extracta e variis Cronicis Scocie,' 1842 (Lowndes, *Bibl. Man.* ed. Bohn, App. p. 38). He died at Greenhill Cottage, near Edinburgh, 11 Oct. 1843.

[Catholic Mag. new ser. (July–December 1843), ii. 295; Catholic Mag. and Review (Birmingham, 1831–2), i. 281 *n.*; Irving's Eminent Scotsmen, p. 348; Hist. of St. Margaret's Convent, Edinburgh, pp. 104–8; Sir W. Scott's Journal, i. 347, ii. 168; Stothert's Catholic Mission in Scotland, p. 129.] T. C.

MENZIES, MICHAEL (*d.* 1766), advocate and inventor, had a younger brother who was sheriff-depute of East Lothian (Hepburn, *Agriculture of East Lothian*, Edinburgh, 1794, p. 147). He was admitted a member of the Faculty of Advocates on 31 Jan. 1719, but the books contain no particulars of his parentage. He probably belonged to the Menzies of Culter-Allers, Lanarkshire (cf. IRVING, *Upper Ward of Lanarkshire*, iii. 145). He was the first to suggest thrashing grain by a machine, and his idea was to imitate the action of the ordinary flail. A number of flails were attached to a horizontal axis, which was moved rapidly to and fro through half a revolution, the grain to be thrashed being placed on either side. He took out a patent for his invention in 1734 (No. 544), and he made a machine, which he brought under the notice of the Society of Improvers in Agriculture, who seemed inclined to think well of it. It is described in the 'Transactions' of that body (Edinburgh, 1743, p. 276), and the report is alluded to in the 'Farmers' Magazine,' Edinburgh, 1816, xvii. 401. It was not a practical success. Menzies also took out a patent in 1750 (No. 653) for a machine for conveying coal from the face of the working to the bottom of the shaft, and in 1761 he obtained another patent (No. 762) for working and draining coal mines. The specifications of these two patents are of very great length, and the machinery is exceedingly complicated. According to Curr's 'Coal Viewer's Companion,' 1797, pp. 33, 35, Menzies's machinery came into use, in part at all events, but the method of raising coals up the shaft was only applicable where a stream of water with a fall of about half the depth of the pit was available. It seems also to have been used at Chatershaugh colliery, on the Wear, in 1753 (cf. GALLOWAY, *Coal Mining*, p. 112), and it is briefly alluded to by R. Bald in his 'Coal Trade of Scotland,' p. 90.

Menzies died at Edinburgh 13 Dec. 1766.

[Scots Magazine, 1766, p. 671; see art. ANDREW MEIKLE.] R. B. P.

MEOPHAM or **MEPEHAM**, SIMON (*d.* 1333), archbishop of Canterbury, was a native of Kent (MURIMUTH, p. 57), and was probably born at the village of Meopham in that county, seven miles west by south of Rochester, from which he derived his name, and where he certainly possessed property. The Meophams seem to have been a numerous clan, or at least many persons entered the ecclesiastical state who took their names from the village. There was Master Richard Meopham, who was archdeacon of Oxford in 1263 and dean of Lincoln in 1273, who spoke up for the rights of the English church at the council of Lyons in 1274, and incurred the disfavour of Pope Gregory X by his boldness (HEMINGBURGH, ii. 3-4). No less than five Meophams, Edmund, Roger, John, Thomas, and William, were ordained by Archbishop Peckham (PECKHAM, *Letters*, iii. 1031-54). One of these, Edmund, was ordained in 1286 sub-deacon on the title of rector of Tunstall, near Sittingbourne, which was in later times the title of Simon to holy orders. He may probably be identical with Edmund, brother of Simon, though this would make him to have attained a very considerable age for the fourteenth century. Simon had, besides Edmund, another brother, named Thomas, who became a friar, and apparently a sister named Joan, the wife of John de la Dene, whose family was of sufficient standing to give its name to the chapel of St. James de la Dene in Meopham parish church. On 25 March 1327 Edmund and Simon Meopham, along with John de la Dene, obtained, on paying a fine of five marks, a license for alienation in mortmain of a messuage, two mills, land and rents in the parishes of East Malling, Northfleet, Meopham, and Hoo (all in Kent), and Barling (Essex), for a chaplain to celebrate divine service daily in the chapel of St. James de la Dene in Meopham Church for the souls of the founders, Joan de la Dene, their parents, kinsfolk, and benefactors (*Cal. Patent Rolls*, 1327-30, p. 62).

Simon Meopham duly proceeded to Oxford, where he is one of the large number of famous men who have been claimed, on no precise documentary evidence, as fellows of Merton College (BRODRICK, *Hist. of Merton Coll.* pp. 209-10, Oxf. Hist. Soc.; WOOD, *Colleges and Halls*, p. 14, ed. Gutch, who both reject the story). In due course he proceeded doctor or master of divinity. He was ordained priest by Archbishop Winchelsea, who conferred on him that same rectory of Tunstall which had some years before been held by Edmund Meopham, and which Simon continued to hold until his election to the archbishopric (WILKINS, ii. 544). He was made prebendary of Llandaff in 1295. He was also a canon of Chichester (MURIMUTH, p. 57; *Cal. Pat. Rolls*, p. 198).

Meopham is described as a man poor in worldly circumstances but rich in virtues (WILKINS, *Concilia*, ii. 540). He took no great part in public affairs, and attained no very distinguished position as a churchman or scholar. Though he numbered him among the mediæval lists of writers, Tanner could not find that he had composed any literary works (see *Bibl. Brit.-Hib.* p. 522). The death of Archbishop Walter Reynolds, on 16 Nov. 1327, opened up to him, however, the unexpected prospect of succession to the throne of Canterbury. An attempt was made by Queen Isabella and Mortimer to procure the appointment of their faithful partisan, Henry Burghersh [q.v.], bishop of Lincoln, and it was at least suggested to the pope that he should be chosen by papal provision. But the more moderate section of the government, Henry of Lancaster and his friends, were strong enough to prevent this, and seem to have hurried on a canonical election with the view of anticipating papal interference. The monks of Christ Church, Canterbury, received a permission to elect, dated 30 Nov., and accompanied by royal letters recommending Meopham to their choice. On 11 Dec. the election was effected, a committee of seven monks acting for the whole body, in accordance with the method 'per viam compromissi' (*Ann. Paul.* p. 338). On 21 Dec. Meopham, who was then in residence at Chichester, accepted the proffered dignity. On 2 Jan. 1328 Edward III gave his consent at Lichfield. On 6 Jan. the archbishop-elect received from Nottingham a safe-conduct for one year on his going to Rome, and on the same day he nominated his brother Edmund and one William of Fishbourne to act as his attorneys during the same period (*Cal. Pat. Rolls*, 1327–30, p. 199). On 18 Jan. he took ship for France at Dover (*Ann. Paul.* p. 338). Some delay now ensued. The English government urged on pope and cardinals the speedy acceptance of Simon as archbishop; but the pope was significantly reminded that if he found difficulties in accepting the chapter's nominee the king would willingly accept his former candidate, the Bishop of Lincoln (Wilkins, ii. 542). John XXII was in no position to offend any one. On 25 May he confirmed the election of Meopham. On 5 June Peter, cardinal-bishop of Palestrina, consecrated Simon bishop in the church of the Dominicans at Avignon. On 9 June the pallium was conferred. Meopham did not hurry home. At last he landed at Dover on 5 Sept., and on 19 Sept. received the temporalities of his see from the king at Lynn.

Meopham seems to have been a weak man, of no great ability, and with but a scanty knowledge of ecclesiastical tradition and propriety. His helplessness is well seen in the curious correspondence between him and the experienced prior of Christ Church, Canterbury, Henry of Eastry [q.v.], who gave him the most elementary advice, in a tone of patronising superiority, especially during the first year of his archbishopric (*Literæ Cantuarienses*, vol. i. passim). But Meopham took a serious view of his office, and strove to do what he could to promote peace and religion, though his minute and litigious care for the rights of his see soon involved him in disputes on every side. He wished to be surrounded by a reputable household, and was laughed at because of the scrupulousness shown by his brothers Edmund and Thomas in gathering together a suitable household of clerks and servants for him. They found, says William Dene, hardly any persons fit for this office in England. They sought for angels rather than men (W. Dene in *Anglia Sacra*, i. 368). But Edmund was soon seized with a mortal illness, and the archbishop, immediately after his interview with the king at Lynn, hurried to London to pay his brother a final visit. On 25 Sept. 1328 Simon took advantage of this to preach a short sermon to the Londoners at St. Paul's, and implore the prayers of the people (*Ann. Paulini*, p. 342). In October Simon attended the Salisbury parliament, where great confusion was produced by the refusal of Earl Henry of Lancaster to attend its deliberations. Civil war seemed threatened between Lancaster and Mortimer. The archbishop with some of his suffragans sought to bring about peace; but Mortimer peremptorily ordered them to cease all negotiations with the recalcitrant earl. The parliament broke up in confusion. Meopham returned to London, where he remained until January 1329, preaching to the people at St. Paul's, and frightening the king by his presence at a meeting of the discontented barons on 18 Dec. The meeting seems to have been but scantily attended, and even the Bishop of Rochester, Haymo Heath, an immediate dependent of the archbishop, incurred Meopham's wrath by refusing to attend. Moreover, Lancaster held aloof until 2 Jan. 1329, when he came sulkily from Waltham and attended another great meeting at St. Paul's, at which he patched up an agreement with the magnates who acted with the archbishop. But the king's uncles deserted Lancaster, and Simon urged strongly on him the need of submission to the king. At last Earl Henry humbled himself, whereupon Simon went with him, the Bishop of London, and the king's brothers to meet the young king at Bedford, where a general reconciliation was effected. Meopham was thus set free to complete the ceremonies incident to his appointment. On 22 Jan. 1329 he was enthroned at Canterbury (*ib.* pp. 343–4). On 4 Feb. he crowned Queen Philippa at London (*Gesta Edwardi, Auctore Bridlingtoniensi*, p. 100). Frightened perhaps by the troubles that followed on his attempt to play the part of mediator, Meopham seems to have carefully abstained from all politics for the rest of his life. His attempt to renew the policy of Stephen Langton had been but a sorry failure.

Thrown back upon the purely ecclesiastical side of his office, Meopham showed considerable activity in holding church councils and visiting his province. The first of his provincial councils was held at St. Paul's on 27 Jan. 1329, which was begun by the archbishop preaching a long sermon to the clergy (*Ann. Paul.* p. 344). The proceedings continued until 10 Feb., on which day the prelates assembled at St. Paul's, where the archbishop solemnly excommunicated those who had taken part in the murder of Bishop Stapleton of Exeter, those who had plundered and burnt the abbeys of St. Edmundsbury and Abingdon, and the other robbers of church property during the troubles incident on the deposition of Edward II. A large number of canons were promulgated, which, in Murimuth's opinion, were arrived at too hastily. It was ordered that no manual work should be done on Good Friday and All Souls' day; that the feast of the Conception of the Virgin should be observed in all churches; and, in order that poor men should be able to bequeath freely their property by will, ordinaries were forbidden to take fees for the probate of testaments dealing with estates of less value than a hundred shillings (Wilkins, ii. 552–4; *Ann. Paul.* pp. 344–5; Murimuth, p. 59).

In 1329 Meopham summoned a convocation of the clergy of his province to Lambeth, which refused to grant any money to the king (*Ann. Paul.* p. 348). In 1330 another council at London forbade any persons from becoming hermits without the permission of their diocesan. In 1332 a council at Mayfield, Sussex, drew up canons for the better observance of Sundays and holy days, the results of which were communicated by Meopham in a circular addressed to his suffragans.

Meopham's zeal for the rights of the church of Canterbury was tempered neither by tact nor by knowledge. In 1329 he refused to institute the Cardinal Annibale de Ceccano, archbishop of Naples, on whom the pope had conferred the church of Maidstone. John XXII grew angry, cited Meopham to the papal curia, and suspended him from his office, but was soon pacified and restored the archbishop (*ib.* p. 347). Meopham now entered into a series of systematic visitations of his province, which soon embroiled him fatally with his suffragans. He began with the see of Rochester, against whose bishop, Haymo Heath, a series of charges was brought, which was investigated by a commission appointed by the archbishop (Wilkins, ii. 556). The bishop was fined and excommunicated, but was soon reconciled to Meopham and became his fast friend. In 1330, when Meopham reopened the frivolous old contention with regard to the right of the Archbishop of York to have his cross borne erect before him in the southern province, the Bishop of Rochester was the only one of the suffragans of Canterbury who gave him any support, and advised him to refuse to appear in parliament until the rights of the primatial see had been duly acknowledged (W. Dene in *Anglia Sacra*, i. 370–1).

Meopham's persistence in his visitations sufficiently explains the lukewarmness of his suffragans in backing up his claims. He visited in succession the dioceses of Chichester, Salisbury, and Bath and Wells. In 1331 he kept his Christmas at Wiveliscombe, and in the spring proposed to proceed with the visitation of Exeter. The Bishop of Exeter, John Grandison [q. v.], had already annoyed Meopham by refusing to attend his council in 1328 because of the enormous expense involved and the great danger incurred in leaving his unruly diocese. Meopham now threatened all sorts of penalties against Grandison and his clerks. Grandison therefore appealed to the pope to prevent Meopham proceeding with his visitation. Meopham took no notice of the appeal, and on 1 June 1332 appeared with a great train before the gates of Exeter. But a body of armed men surrounded the cathedral and cloisters, and prevented the archbishop from effecting an entrance (*Ann. Paul.* pp. 356–7; Murimuth, p. 65). Meopham and his followers remained in the neighbourhood, and a pitched battle was only prevented by the intervention of the king, who persuaded Meopham to desist for a time from holding his visitation. Another provincial council was summoned to London to settle the matter, but the other bishops took up the cause of Grandison, and, by reason of the discord between Meopham and his suffragans, no result was arrived at.

Not content with quarrelling with the pope, the Archbishop of York and the suffragans of his province, Meopham was always on the verge of a quarrel with Henry of Eastry and the monks of Christ Church, and plunged into a hot dispute with the monks of St. Augustine's Abbey at Canterbury. In 1329, while visiting his own diocese, Meopham had required the convent of St. Augustine's to produce the evidence on which were based their claims to the appropriation of a larger number of Kentish churches. The abbot and monks refused to justify their well-known and long-established rights. Prior Eastry strongly advised the archbishop to rather abate his strict legal rights than to get involved in an interminable and costly lawsuit at the papal curia (*Literæ Cantuar.* i. 333–4); but the archbishop was deaf to such judicious counsels. On the failure of the abbot and monks to appear before the archbishop's court, Meopham pronounced them contumacious. The abbey thereupon appealed to the pope, who sent a nuncio, Icherius de Concoreto, canon of Salisbury, to act as judge of the suit. Meopham denounced the judge as prejudiced, and refused to take any part in the case. Early in 1330 the proctor of the abbey, Thomas of Natendon, went with a public notary and a large following to the manor of Slindon in Sussex, where Meopham was then residing, to serve on him a summons to attend the court of the papal commissioner. The archbishop was ill in bed, but his servants beat and insulted the followers of the proctor, breaking the arm of the notary, and carrying on rude horseplay against one of the retinue, whom they beat severely, tied tightly with cords, and drenched with cold water. The proctor himself fled to Petworth, but was brought back and kept prisoner three days before he was allowed to escape.

Meopham protested that he had no knowledge of this outrage, and eight of his suffragans, feeling that they had a common cause with him in his attack on the great monastery, sent strong letters to the pope testifying to his high and honourable character. But the pope was much incensed, and, through the Archbishop of Aquino, pronounced the archbishop guilty. Meanwhile Icherius had, in November 1332, condemned Meopham in England, pronouncing him contumacious for refusing to appear, and awarding the enormous costs of 700*l.* to the monks of St. Augustine's, in whose favour he pronounced judgment (*ib.* i. 511–17). In January 1333 Icherius informed the archbishop that if he did not pay the costs within thirty days he became suspended, and if he did not pay within sixty days, incurred the sentence of excommunication (*ib.* i. 517–19). The archbishop made no sign of submission, and in due course incurred the threatened penalties. Meopham spent the summer, in failing health and great sadness, at his manor of Mayfield, where he was visited by the faithful Bishop of Rochester, whom he told that he was not troubled by his excommunication. He died on 12 Oct. He was buried on 26 Oct. at Canterbury, in the chapel of St. Peter, at the east end of the south aisle of the choir and near the tomb of St. Anselm; but the monks of St. Augustine's boasted that it was in their power to prevent his burial until his body had been formally released from the sentence which the living archbishop had incurred (Thorn, c. 2066). By his will, the executor of which was Master Lawrence Falstof, he left 50*l.* to the monks of his cathedral to buy land, the rent of which was to be appropriated for the expenses of celebrating his anniversary (*Anglia Sacra*, i. 59).

[Wharton's Anglia Sacra, vol. i.; Thorn's Chronica, in Twysden's Decem Scriptores, cc. 2039–66; Wilkins's Concilia, ii. 539–64; Murimuth (Rolls Ser.); Annales Paulini and Canon of Bridlington, in Stubbs's Chron. of Edward I and II (Rolls Ser.); Calendar of Patent Rolls, 1327–30; Literæ Cantuar. vol. i., with Dr. Sheppard's Introduction, pp. lxiv–vi (Rolls Ser.); Hook's Archbishops of Canterbury, iii. 492–518, is inaccurate in some particulars; Le Neve's Fasti Eccl. Angl. i. 17, ed. Hardy; Godwin, De Præsulibus, 1743, pp. 105–6.] T. F. T.

MERBECKE, JOHN (*fl.* 1583), musician and theologian. [See Marbeck.]

MERBURY or **MARBURY, CHARLES** (*fl.* 1581), author, is described by Strype as the son of a dependent 'on the Duchess of Suffolk and the Duke of Suffolk.' The patrons of the father, who are said to have continued a revenue and pension to the son, were probably Richard Bertie [q. v.] and his wife Catharine, whose first husband was Charles Brandon, duke of Suffolk (*d.* 1545). There were no other persons who could claim any connection with the title of Duke or Duchess of Suffolk in Elizabeth's reign. Merbury graduated B.A. at Oxford on 18 March 1569–70, and speaks of studying under 'Master Humfrey,' apparently a reference to Laurence Humphrey [q. v.], president of Magdalen College. In 1571 he entered Gray's Inn, but soon afterwards left England for a long sojourn in Italy, and acquired perfect familiarity with the language. He was a friend of Henry Unton, and on returning home obtained a post in the household of the lord chamberlain, the Earl of Sussex. He was thus often about the court. In 1581 he published a defence of absolute government, which was licensed, after it had been carefully read and approved in manuscript by Thomas Norton (1532–1584) [q. v.] It was entitled: 'A briefe Discourse of Royall Monarchie, as of the best Common Weale: wherein the subiect may beholde the Sacred Majestie of the Princes most Royall Estate: written by Charles Merbury, Gentleman, in duetifull Reuerence of Her Majesties Most Princely Highnesse: Whereunto is added by the same Pen a Collection of Italian Prouerbes in Benefite of such as are studious of that Language,' London, 1581, 4to (by Thomas Vautrollier). A dedication in Italian to Queen Elizabeth is followed by a commendatory address to 'the vertuous reader,' by Henry Unton.

In 1582–3 Merbury was employed on official business in France, probably as a spy. In April and August 1582 he corresponded with Walsingham from Paris and Orleans, and complained of robbery by pirates (*Cal. State Papers*, Dom. Add. 1580–1625, pp. 56–72). In Nov. 1583 he was at La Rochelle, and sent Anthony Bacon [q. v.] the current gossip. In Dec. he wrote to Bacon from Poitiers (Birch, *Elizabeth*, i. 42–4). In Feb. 1593–4 he was granted the clerkship of the faculties (Murdin, 802).

[Foster's Alumni Oxon.; Strype's Annals, iii. i. 104–5.] S. L.

MERCER, ANDREW (1775–1842), poet and topographer, was born in Selkirk in 1775. He was destined for the ministry, and in 1790 entered the university of Edinburgh. Ultimately he gave up theology, studied the fine arts, and endeavoured unsuccessfully to make a living in Edinburgh as a miniature-painter and man of letters. He wrote both in prose and verse for the 'Edinburgh' and 'Scots' magazines, and edited the 'North British Magazine' during its short existence. He subsequently settled in Dunfermline, where he lived by teaching and by drawing patterns for the damask manufacturers. His best-known work is a 'History of Dunfermline from the earliest Records' (Dunfermline, 1828). There was also published in his name an 'Historical and Chronological Table of the Ancient Town of Dunfermline from 1064 to 1834,' which was really an abridgment, with the consent of the author, Mr. E. Henderson, of a manuscript volume entitled 'Annals of Dunfermline from the earliest Records to 1833.' He was the author of a poem on 'Dunfermline Abbey' (Dunfermline, 1819), and a volume of verse, 'Summer Months among the Mountains' (Edinburgh, 1838). A man of considerable ingenuity and scholarship, he lacked steadiness of application, and his last years were clouded by poverty (Chalmers). He died at Dunfermline, 11 June 1842.

[Rogers's Scottish Minstrel, p. 150; Chalmers's Historical and Statistical Account of Dunfermline, 1844, pp. 77, 552; Grant Wilson's Poets and Poetry of Scotland, ii. 531.] J. C. H.

MERCER, HUGH (1726?–1777), American brigadier-general, is described by American biographers as a native of Aberdeen, Scotland, born about 1721, who studied medicine at Aberdeen University. The name 'Hugo Mercer' is among the fourth-year students of 1744 in the 'Album Studiensis' of Marischal College, Aberdeen. His age, probably, was between sixteen and eighteen. The academic records afford no other particulars. Mercer was a surgeon's mate in the Pretender's army, and afterwards went to America in 1747, and settled as a doctor near what is now Mercersburg, Pennsylvania. He is said to have served in the expedition against Fort Du Quesne, under General Edward Braddock [q. v.], and to have been wounded at the Monaghahela 9 July 1756, for which he received a medal from the corporation of Philadelphia. Winthrop Sargent, in his monograph of the expedition, implies uncertainty on this point. Among the provincial officers engaged were two other Mercers, George and John, who were thanked by the burgesses (see *Trans. Hist. Soc. of Philadelphia*, v. 240, 329). Mercer became a lieutenant-colonel of provincials in 1758, and accompanied the expedition under Brigadier-general John Forbes against the new Fort Du Quesne, where he was for several months in command (see Parkman, *Montcalm and Wolfe*, xi. 49, 130–162). Mercer then returned to medical practice, establishing himself at Fredericksburg, Virginia. He organised and drilled the Virginia militia; commanded the minute men at the outbreak of the revolution; was appointed colonel of the 3rd Virginia regiment; and in June 1776, at the desire of Washington, was chosen by congress a brigadier-general, with command of a flying brigade. He accompanied Washington in his retreat through New Jersey. He led the attack on the Hessians at Trenton, and advised the night march on Princeton, in which he led the advance. His horse was disabled while he was attempting to rally his troops, mostly raw militia, and he was himself knocked down with the butt of a musket and bayoneted when on the ground. After several days of severe suffering he died of his wounds 12 Jan. 1777. His funeral was attended by 20,000 people. The St. Andrew Society of Philadelphia raised a monument to him in the Laurel Hill cemetery, and in 1790 congress made provision for the education of his youngest son, Hugh. Mercer County, Kentucky, is named after him.

Mercer had an elder son, John, who died a colonel in the United States army in 1817. The younger, Hugh, died at Fredericksburg, Virginia, in 1853, aged 77. A married daughter, Anna Gordon Patton, died in 1832, aged 58.

[Information kindly supplied by the Registrar of the University of Aberdeen; Parkman's Montcalm and Wolfe, 2 vols. London, 1884;

Beatson's Nav. and Mil. Memoirs, vol. iv.; Bancroft's Hist. United States, vols. iv. and v. (pp. 492–3, account of Princeton); biographical notices are given in Drake's Amer. Biog. and Appleton's Encycl. Amer. Biog., the latter with vignette portrait of Mercer.] H. M. C.

MERCER, JAMES (1734–1804), poet and friend of Beattie, eldest son of Thomas Mercer, a cadet of the Mercer family of Aldie in Perthshire, was born in Aberdeen on 27 Feb. 1733–4. He was a second cousin to Hugh Mercer [q. v.] and of William Mercer, the correspondent of Warren Hastings (see *Add. MSS.* 29168-9 and 29172-3). James was educated at the high school, and afterwards at the Marischal College, Aberdeen, where he acquired a decided taste for Greek literature. Graduating M.A. in 1754, he proceeded to Paris, where his father, who had fought at Culloden and was an exile in the Stuart cause, was then residing. Returning to England on his father's death in 1756, after a brief experience as a volunteer in the disastrous expedition to Cherbourg, Mercer joined a British regiment, and served under Prince Ferdinand of Brunswick through the early campaigns of the seven years' war. He distinguished himself at Minden, and was in 1761 presented by General Graeme with a company in the newly raised queen's regiment, but the corps was reduced on the peace of 1763. Shortly afterwards he purchased a company in the 49th regiment, and served for several years in Ireland. He won the friendship of Michael Cox, archbishop of Cashel, but declined the archbishop's pressing invitation to take orders and a fat living in his gift. In 1770 he purchased a majority in his regiment; in 1772, however, he lost the succession to Sir Henry Calder's lieutenant-colonelcy, and in a fit of disgust sold out of the army. He settled in the neighbourhood of Aberdeen, cultivated the friendship of Dr. Beattie and other literary and learned persons, and travelled for health, chiefly in the south of France. In 1777 he accepted a majority from the Duke of Gordon in the 'Gordon Fencibles,' and at Glasgow, where the regiment was stationed, he maintained intimate relations with Dr. Reid and Sir William Forbes, as well as with the duke and duchess. In 1799 Beattie appointed him one of his executors, together with their common friend, Robert Arbuthnot, kinsman of the well-known doctor. He subsequently settled at Sunny Bank, near Aberdeen, where he died on 27 Nov. 1804 (*Scots Mag.* 1804, ii. 974). Mercer married, on 13 Sept. 1763, Katherine Douglas, a lady of great beauty, and sister of Sylvester Douglas, lord Glenbervie; she died on 3 Jan. 1802.

Mercer produced privately in 179[illegible] what his biographer calls 'the secret of his p[illegible]tical amusements.' A second edition appea[illegible] in 1804, and the third and best edition wa[illegible] published posthumously in 1806, with the title 'Lyric Poems by the late James Mercer, with an Account of the Life of the Author by Lord Glenbervie,' London, 8vo. The volume contains an engraved portrait, by Picart after Irvine, and was praised without stint in the 'Edinburgh Review' (January 1807) and by Sir James Macintosh, who describes the poems as 'everywhere elegant and sometimes charming' (WILSON, *Macintosh*, i. 17).

Beattie described Mercer somewhat exuberantly to the Duchess of Gordon as uniting the wit and wisdom of Montesquieu with the sensibility of Rousseau and the generosity of Tom Jones; in another letter he doubted if six gentlemen in Scotland knew Greek so well as the accomplished major, who is further described as correcting his partiality for French literature by unremitting attention to the best models of antiquity. Mercer does not appear to have composed in Latin or Greek, but in his English verses, of which the 'Ode to Novelty,' quoted by Sir Egerton Brydges (*Censura*, v. 213), is perhaps the least insipid, he seems to have aimed with small success at imitation of Horace. Sir William Forbes, who speaks of him as one of the pleasantest companions he ever met, relates how Mercer when a boy concealed himself in a chest, the lid of which fell down upon him and automatically locked. From the fate of Rogers's 'Italian Bride' he was fortunately delivered, but not until he had been nearly suffocated. A consequent dread of a living tomb caused Mercer to direct that before burial his heart should be pierced with a gold pin.

[Life prefixed to Lyric Poems, 1806; Sir William Forbes's Life of Beattie, 1807, i. 35, ii. 181, iii. 238–42; Gent. Mag. 1808 ii. 1142, 1809 ii. 1204; Brydges's Censura Literaria, ii. 383, v. 209–13; Chalmers's Biog. Dict.; Allibone's Dict. of Engl. Lit. ii. 1266; Irving's Book of Scotsmen, p. 348; Bruce's Eminent Men of Aberdeen, p. 378 *n.*; Brit. Mus. Cat.] T. S.

MERCER, JOHN (1791–1866), calico-printer and chemist, was born on 21 Feb. 1791 at Dean, in the parish of Great Harwood, near Blackburn. His father, Robert Mercer (whose family had been established in the district for at least 250 years), was at the time a hand-loom weaver; he soon after gave up this occupation and took a farm in the neighbourhood of Great Harwood, where John passed his early years. In 1800 Robert Mercer died, leaving his wife and family with small means; at the age

[...]e John became first a bobbin-winder, [...] then a hand-loom weaver. At ten a work[...]an in a print-works taught him reading, writing, and arithmetic. He also learnt to play on several instruments, and gave much time to music, to which he remained keenly sensitive through life. When he served as a militiaman, a few years later, he was known as 'Awkward John,' and he was transferred to the band. In 1807 his future career was decided by seeing on his infant half-brother a dress of an orange-colour, which 'set him all on fire to learn dyeing.' He straightway bought all the dyeing materials he could procure, and, having by a long series of experiments learnt to dye in most colours, he set up in partnership with a man who had suitable premises, and they 'dyed for Great Harwood and the surrounding country;' the material operated on consisting chiefly of the remnants which were at that time the perquisites of the hand-loom weavers. In September 1809 Mercer gave up this business, despite its success, to become an apprentice in the colour-shop of the Oakenshaw print-works on the invitation of the owners, Messrs. Fort Bros. But the jealousy of a foreman prevented him from acquiring any real knowledge of the processes employed; and he therefore, in the following year, accepted the surrender of his indentures offered by his masters, who were forced by commercial distress, due to the Berlin decrees, to reduce their staff. Mercer again became a hand-loom weaver, and invented many ingenious designs in weaving. He also gave much attention to the study of mathematics, in which he was helped by an excise surveyor named Lightfoot. In 1813 he became deeply religious and joined the Wesleyans. In the same year he became engaged to Mary Wolstenholme, whom he married on 17 April 1814.

In 1813 Mercer had resumed work as a dyer, while still continuing to weave, and in 1814 his attention was directed towards chemistry by the 'Chemical Pocket-Book' of James Parkinson, which 'introduced him [he writes] into a new world.' It was this book which led him to his first discovery of importance, a method of fixing orange sulphide of antimony on cotton-cloth; no good orange dye suitable for calico-printing having been previously known. The details of the process were communicated to a firm of printers, and successfully applied, but Mercer received no reward for his services. In 1818 Messrs. Fort Bros. re-engaged Mercer, this time as a chemist in their colour-shop, at a salary of thirty shillings a week. In 1823 Mercer rediscovered and introduced into England a method of applying to cotton-cloth lead chromate, a yellow dye of great importance, originally discovered in France by D. Koechlin, whose patterns had been shown to him. He also discovered the use of certain manganese compounds, which still have considerable importance as bronze dyes, greatly improved the methods of printing indigo, and made many other minor inventions. In 1825 Mercer was taken into partnership by Messrs. Fort Bros., and continued a partner of the firm until its dissolution in 1848. During this period Mercer showed great mental activity, technical discoveries of more or less importance following each other in quick succession from his laboratory.

Mercer took a keen interest in theoretical chemistry, and this interest was greatly stimulated and strengthened by the influence of Dr. Lyon (now Baron) Playfair. The two men became friends in 1841, Playfair being then one of the chemists at Messrs. Thompson's works at Clitheroe. Playfair and a few scientific friends met once a week at Whalley to discuss scientific matters; and it was at one of the Whalley meetings that Mercer propounded the first rational theory of the so-called 'catalytic' action. He read a paper on the subject at the Manchester meeting of the British Association in 1842; and the theory was more fully developed and illustrated by Playfair (*Mem. Chem. Soc.* iii. 348). Certain observations of his made in 1843, and discussed at the Whalley meetings, led Playfair to the discovery of a new class of compounds, the nitro-prussides. In 1847 Mercer joined the Chemical Society (*ib.* iii. 315). In 1848 the Oakenshaw firm decided to dissolve partnership and retire, rather than face the severe competition which had arisen among calico-printers—their determination proceeding chiefly from an unwillingness to manufacture goods of an inferior quality at a cheaper rate. The profits of the undertaking had been considerable, and Mercer was now free to pursue researches sketched out during the busy years. He undertook an investigation on the action of caustic soda, sulphuric acid, and zinc chloride on cotton-cloth, paper, and other materials made from vegetable fibre. These experiments (which were carried out in commercial partnership with Robert Hargreaves of Broadoak, near Accrington, and at his works) led to the discovery of the process known as 'mercerising,' and to the preparation of parchment paper, patented by Mercer in 1850. By treating cotton-cloth with any one of the reagents mentioned, in a solution of a certain concentration, the individual cotton fibres become thicker and shorter, and the strength of the cloth is greatly increased. It also becomes semi-transparent, and dyes far more rapidly than ordinary cloth, this being due to the swelling up of the cell-walls in the fibre (Crum). Owing to the expense of the treatment, the use of mercerised cloth has been hitherto limited to special applications, e.g. the manufacture of 'calico-printers' blankets,' in which increased strength of the fabric is required. In 1851 Mercer, who was one of the jurors of the International Exhibition held in London in that year, and therefore excluded from the ordinary distinctions, was awarded a council medal for the discovery of mercerisation. In 1852 he reluctantly assented to becoming a fellow of the Royal Society. In 1858 he contributed a paper to the meeting of the British Association at Leeds on the reducing action of light on persalts of iron, and their subsequent treatment with potassium ferricyanide, which yields a blue colour, varying in depth according to the intensity of light to which they have been exposed. The experiments were originally made by Mercer in 1828, and had been rediscovered by Robert Hunt [q. v.] The discovery of this photo-chemical action has given rise to many technical applications; Mercer himself proposed to utilise it for recording the intensity of sunlight, and Jordan has since practically carried out this suggestion in an instrument at present employed in meteorological observatories. At the Leeds meeting of the British Association Mercer also read a paper 'On Relations among the Atomic Weights of the Elements;' but he did not succeed in obtaining any results of importance in a field which has since proved fertile in discoveries. In 1859 his wife died, and from this time forward Mercer seems to have given up his scientific work. In 1861 he was placed on the commission of the peace for the county of Lancaster, but was judged by those who knew him to be too merciful for a magistrate (Parnell, *Life*, p. 266). In 1862 he served as a juror for the second international exhibition. A severe cold, brought on by falling into a water-reservoir in 1864, was the cause of a painful disease, of which Mercer died on 30 Nov. 1866. He left behind him two sons and two daughters.

In his private life Mercer was eminently unselfish and lovable. Endowed with the perseverance and business capacity necessary to raise himself from poverty to affluence, he was never grasping; and although he patented some of his inventions, he freely gave away many others, which brought large sums of money to those who profited by them. Through life he took an anxious interest in religion and religious affairs. In 1849 he seceded from the Wesleyans and returned to the established church, but, with characteristic liberality of mind, he continued to give material help to the local Wesleyan institutions. He was an ardent reformer, and was probably much influenced in his views by a short acquaintance with Richard Cobden [q. v.], who, with two partners, acted as the London agent for Messrs. Fort Bros. from 1828 till 1831 (J. Morley, *Life of Cobden*, i. 15–18). In his experimental discoveries Mercer displayed great fertility of invention and a remarkable insight into chemistry. His classical researches on catalytic action, on the constitution of the ferrocyanides and of bleaching powder, and his anticipation of Pasteur's germ theory (communicated in a letter to Playfair), show the true scientific temper. There can be no doubt that had he devoted himself entirely to research he would have been among the most distinguished chemists of the day.

Among Mercer's more important discoveries, besides those already quoted, may be mentioned: (1) the use of potassium ferricyanide and potash for the discharge of indigo (*Mem. Chem. Soc.* iii. 320); (2) the use of arseniates as a substitute for phosphates in the process of 'dunging;' (3) the treatment of woollen fabrics (delaines, &c.) with a weak oxidising agent before printing; (4) the manufacture of sodium stannate and stannite in the dry way; (5) the production of 'sulphated oil' for the Turkey-red process; (6) the discovery of the solubility of cellulose in ammoniacal copper solutions.

[Authorities cited; E. A. Parnell's Life and Labours of John Mercer (compiled from materials supplied by Mercer's family and revised by Lord Playfair); Journ. Chem. Soc. 1867, p. 395 (obituary notice); Report of British Association, Notices and Abstracts, 1842 p. 32, 1858 pp. 57, 59; Journal of Royal Institution, 1852; List of Fellows of the Royal Society, 1853; F. H. Bowman's Structure of the Cotton Fibre, 2nd ed. p. 52; private information from the Rev. A. F. Johnson, who kindly consulted the parish register of Great Harwood; from J. J. Hummel, esq., professor of dyeing at Yorkshire Coll., Leeds; and from E. Bentz, esq., of Owens Coll.]

P. J. H.

MERCER, WILLIAM (1605?–1675?), lieutenant-colonel and poet, was born probably at Methlic, Aberdeenshire, about 1605, his father, John Mercer, being at the time minister of that parish, and being afterwards translated to the church of Slains, where he officiated till his death in 1637. William was a wild youth, and running away from school, served as a soldier in Denmark and Sweden, according to his own account, without pay. He returned to Scotland before 1630, and on 28 June in that year Charles I granted a letter of presentation in favour of 'William Mercer, sone lawfull to Mr. Johnne Mercer, minister at Slaynes, to the parsonage and vicarage of the teyndis, &c., of the kirk and parochine of Glenholme,' &c. Glenholme was a prebend attached to the Chapel Royal of Stirling, but there is nothing to show that Mercer ever occupied the post, although benefices were often conferred on those who held no orders in the church. About 1638 he seems to have served as an officer in Ireland, where he says in his 'Angliæ Speculum' that his 'father's heir' was 'put to sword.' It appears that his elder brother, Robert, master of the grammar school at Ellon in Aberdeenshire, having resigned his office in 1628, and settling in Ireland, as minister of Mullaghbrack, co. Armagh, was with his wife massacred in the Irish rebellion of 1641, leaving three young children. William subsequently obtained through the Earl of Essex a commission as captain of horse in the parliamentary army in England; and while in this service he published his first volume, 'Angliæ Speculum,' in 1646. One of the poems at the end of this work is a petition from Mercer to the lords and commons for arrears of pay, amounting to 900*l.*; and in the journals of the house reference is made more than once to 'Capt. Mercer's petition for arrears.' In 1646 he published elegies on the deaths of his patron, the Earl of Essex, and of his father-in-law, Sir Henry Mervyn, both of whom had died in that year, and about the same time he was promoted to be lieutenant-colonel. In May 1650 Mercer was back in Scotland, once more in the direst straits. The minutes of the general assembly, dated Edinburgh, 23 May 1650, state: 'The Commission of the Generall Assembly, considering the necessitous condition of Lieutenant-Colonell William Mercer, sone to umquhill Mr. Johne Merser, minister at Slaines, doe referre him to the charitable supplie of the Presbyterie of Edinburgh.' At the Restoration Mercer made vows of loyalty to the new monarch. In 1669, when Baron Truro was appointed governor-general of Ireland, Mercer issued 'A Welcom . . . at his Royal entry into the Castle of Dublin.' In 1672 he revisited Scotland, to arrange a marriage between his eldest son and the heiress of the barony of Aldie, and when the negotiations broke down Mercer raised an action of damages for breach of treaty (*Decisions of Court of Session*), and prepared a series of verses eulogising the judges of the court, and appealing for their lordships' favour. An autograph copy of this production, which was not printed, is preserved, with his signature attached, in the Advocates' Library, Edinburgh; the title runs: 'A Compendious Companion of the Lives and Lawes of the Senators of Rome, with the Lives and Lawes of the Senators of the Colledge of Justice, Edingburgh, in familiar Lynes. By a Servant to Mars and a Lover of the Muses, Lie^{vt} Coll^{ll} William Mercer, Edinburgh, 1673,' 4to, 32 pp. Mercer lost his cause, and father and son returned to Ireland. Mercer was alive in 1682, when his 'News from Parnassus' was 'printed by M. W. for the Author,' with a dedication to Charles II. This pamphlet was issued in order to advertise a 'big book,' on which the writer states that he had been occupied for twenty years.

Mercer's writings are mainly valuable for their autobiographical details. The majority of his verses are mere doggerel, and display an inordinate self-conceit. Their titles are: 1. 'Angliæ Speculum, or England's Looking-Glasse, devided into two parts: the First Part containing a Brief Description of these unnatural Wars in England, with some particular persons, fomentors thereof, discovered; the vast Expenses and the Glory of the famous City of London, in maintaining the Protestant Religion, and their Privileges displayed. The Second Part, consisting of several Speeches, Anagrams, Epigrams, Acrosticks, and Sonnets, &c., by C. W. Mercer,' London, printed by T. Paine, &c., 1646, 4to. In some copies there is the simple title 'Angliæ Speculum, or Englands Looking-Glasse. Devided into two parts. By C. W. Mercer. London, printed by Tho. Paine, MDCXLVI.' 2. 'An Elegie in Memorie and at the interring of the bodie of the most famous and truly noble Knight, Sir Henry Mervyn, paterne of all true valour, worth, and arts, who departed this life the 30 of May, and lyes interred at Westminster, Anno Do. 1646. London, printed by James Cox, 1646,' a broadsheet. 3. 'An Elegie upon the Death of the Right Honble., most Noble, worthily Renownend, and truly valiant Lord, Robert, Earle of Essex and Ewe, &c., His Excellency, late Lord General of all the Forces raised by the Parliament of England in Defence of the Protestant Religion, who departed the 14th of September 1646. London, printed by I. C., 1646,' a broadsheet. 4. 'A Welcom in a Poem, to his Excellency, &c., at his Royal entry into the Castle of Dublin' (first title). 'Verbum Sapienti, or Mercer's Muse-making Melody, in a Welcom to his Excellency John, Lord Roberts, Baron of Truro, &c. Dublin, printed by Josiah Windsor, 1669,'

4to (second title). 5. 'News from Parnassus, in the Abstracts and Contents of three Crown'd Chronicles, relating to the three Kingdoms of England, Scotland, and Ireland. In a Poem, divided into two parts: First, to the King; secondly, to the Subjects of the said three Kingdoms. Dedicated to his Majesty. By a Servant to Mars, and a Lover of the Muses, William Mercer. London, printed by M. W. for the Author, 1682,' 8vo. A unique work sold at Laing's sale, which wanted the title-page, but had the date (1632), the name of the printer (J. Wreittoun) and the author's initials, 'W. M.,' appended, is assigned to Mercer. The contents —anagrams, acrostics, &c., on the magistrates of Edinburgh, all in the style of Mercer—are stated to be 'by a soldier's hand.'

Mercer is also credited with 'The Moderate Caualier, or the Soldier's Description of Ireland and of the Country Disease, with Receipts for the same. A Book fit for all Protestant houses in Ireland,' 1675, 4to (Brit. Mus.)

[Mercer's Works; Proceedings of the Society of Antiquaries of Scotland, vol. iii.; Reid's Ireland, vol. i.; Journals of the House of Commons, iii. 10, 346, viii. 291; Morison's Dictionary of Decisions, pp. 3150–3, 12708–12; Scott's Fasti, vi. 613.] G. S-h.

MERCIA, Earl of (*d.* 1057). [See Leofric.]

MERCIANS, Kings of the. [See Penda, 577?–655; Peada, *d.* 656; Wulfhere, *d.* 675; Coenred, *fl.* 704–709; Ceolred, *d.* 716; Ethelbald, *d.* 757; Offa, *d.* 796; Beornwulf, *d.* 826; Wiglaf, *d.* 838; Beorhtwulf, *d.* 852; Burhred, *fl.* 852–874.]

MERCIER, PHILIP (1689–1760), portrait-painter, was born at Berlin in 1689 of French parents. He studied art in the academy of painting there, and also under the court painter, Antoine Pesne. He then visited Italy and France, and finally came to Hanover, where he painted a portrait of Frederick, prince of Wales, and was appointed page of the bedchamber to the prince. About 1716 he came to London, bringing this picture and a recommendation from the prince. His expectation of obtaining employment at the court was not realised until the arrival of the Prince and Princess of Wales in England. He was appointed in 1727 principal painter, and subsequently also librarian to their royal highnesses at their house in Leicester Fields. In 1728 he painted the prince and his sisters, the princesses Anne, Caroline, and Amelia, at full length (all engraved in mezzotint by J. Simon). He also gave the princesses lessons in drawing and painting. About 1737 Mercier fell out of favour with the prince, was dismissed, and retired for a time into the country, but soon resumed practice in Covent Garden as a fashionable portrait-painter, and regained his position in the prince's household. Subsequently he resided for some years at York, until he was induced to go to Oporto in Portugal. There he found so much profit in painting leading merchants, that he sent for his family, intending to settle there. He soon, however, returned to London, and after a visit to Ireland died in London on 18 July 1760, aged 71.

Mercier was a painter whose merit has hardly been sufficiently recognised. In his earlier works he was distinctly an imitator of Watteau, and caught some of his spirit. His portraits and conversation-pieces, which are very pleasing, have sometimes been credited to Hogarth, though they have none of the strength and directness of purpose shown by that great painter. He painted a large number of half-length pictures representing young men or women employed in domestic or rural occupations, or with emblematical meaning; these were frequently drawn from his own children, and many of them were engraved in mezzotint by J. Faber, jun., R. Houston, J. McArdell, and other engravers. Many notable people sat to him, such as Peg Woffington (now at the Garrick Club) and Handel (now in the possession of the Earl of Malmesbury). His small conversation-pieces are to be met with in private collections. At Belton House, Grantham, there is a signed picture, representing John Brownlow, viscount Tyrconnel, and his family in a garden with Mercier sketching them. There are some characteristic drawings by him in the print-room at the British Museum. Mercier executed a few etchings in the style of Watteau, including a group of himself, his wife, and two of his children. His own portrait, painted by himself in 1735, was engraved in mezzotint by J. Faber, jun., and a poor copy was made of this for Walpole's 'Anecdotes of Painting.'

Of his children a son, Philip, became a captain in the Welsh fusiliers, and fort major of the island of Jersey, and died in 1793, aged 54, and a daughter, Charlotte, practised as a painter, her 'Four Ages' being engraved by S. F. Ravenet, but taking to a vicious life, she ended miserably in the workhouse of St. James's, Westminster, on 21 Feb. 1762.

[Walpole's Anecd. of Painting, ed. Wornum; Vertue's MSS. (Brit. Mus. Add. MSS. 23068–23076); Seguier's Dict. of Painters; Chaloner Smith's Brit. Mezzotinto Portraits; Redgrave's Dict. of Artists.] L. C.

MERDDIN, WYLLT (*fl.* 580?), Welsh poet. [See MYRDDIN.]

MEREDITH, EDWARD (1648–1689?), Roman catholic controversialist, was son of Edward Meredith, rector of Landulph, Cornwall, in which county he was born in 1648. He was elected a king's scholar at Westminster School, and was elected to Christ Church, Oxford, in 1665. He left the university without having taken a degree in order to enter into the service of Sir William Godolphin, whom he accompanied on his embassy to Spain in the capacity of secretary. While in Spain he followed the example of his patron by professing himself a Roman catholic. On his return he took part in the current controversy between the Anglican and Roman churches. He was present at the singular conference between Tenison and Andrew Pulton the jesuit on 29 Sept. 1687. Tenison denied Meredith's competency to act as an umpire, one of his objections being that Meredith was converted when very young. The latter replied: 'I know not what the Doctor calls young, but it was not 'till I had gone through one of the best and most careful schools in England, and spent above three years at the university, and as many in Spain.' Some time after the revolution of 1688 Meredith went abroad, and, as Dodd was informed, died in Italy.

His works are: 1. 'Some Remarques upon a late popular piece of Nonsense called Julian the Apostate [by the Rev. Samuel Johnson]. Together with a particular Vindication of His Royal Highness the Duke of York. . . . By a Lover of Truth, Vertue, and Justice,' London, 1682, fol. 2. 'A Journal of Meditations for every Day in the Year. Gathered out of divers Authors. Written first in Latin by N. B., and newly translated into English by E. M.,' 3rd edition, London, 1687, 8vo. 3. 'A Letter to Dr. E. S[tillingfleet] concerning his late Letter to Mr. G[odden] and the Account he gives of it in a Conference between Mr. G. and himself,' London, 1687, 4to. 4. 'Remarks on a late Conference between Andrew Pulton, Jesuit, and Thomas Tenison, D.D.,' London, 1687, 4to. 5. 'Some further Remarks on the late Account given by Dr. Tenison of his Conference with Mr. Pulton, wherein the Doctor's three exceptions against Edward Meredith are examined, &c.,' London, 1688, 4to. James Harrington published anonymously 'A Vindication of Protestant Charity, in answer to some passages in Mr. E. M[eredith's] Remarks on a late Conference,' Oxford, 1688, 4to.

[Boase and Courtney's Bibl. Cornub. p. 348; Dodd's Church Hist. iii. 465; Jones's Popery Tracts, pp. 128, 137, 140, 434; Welch's Alumni Westmon. (Phillimore), p. 161; Wood's Athenæ Oxon. (Bliss), iv. 393, 653; Wood's Autobiog. (Bliss), p. xcv.] T. C.

MEREDITH, RICHARD (1550?–1597), bishop of Leighlin and Ferns, a native of Denbighshire, was a son of Robert Meredith ap Gronw and Margaret his wife, daughter of William John ap Gronw, and was nearly related to Richard Davies [q. v.], bishop of St. David's. He was born about 1550, and about 1568 matriculated at Oxford, probably from White Hall, in 1570 merged in Jesus College, from which he graduated B.A. on 4 March 1572–3, and M.A. on 1 June 1575. In 1578 he became prebendary of the collegiate church of Brecon; rector of Barton, Pembrokeshire, in 1578; vicar of Llanavon Vawr, Brecknockshire, in 1579; cursal prebendary of St. David's and rector of Angle or Nangle, Pembrokeshire, in 1580. In 1584 he was appointed chaplain to Sir John Perrot [q.v.], lord deputy of Ireland, and accompanied him to Dublin. By letters patent dated 13 June 1584 he was appointed dean of St. Patrick's. On 4 May 1586 he was presented to the living of Loughrea in the diocese of Clonfert, and also held the rectory of Killadorie in the diocese of Kildare. On 16 March 1586–7 he obtained license to visit England for four months. In 1589 he was promoted by patent dated 13 April to the see of Leighlin, which had been vacant for two years, and was consecrated by Adam Loftus [q. v.], archbishop of Dublin; he took possession on 30 April, holding his deanery *in commendam*, because the bishopric was not worth 50*l*. a year. Meredith rebuilt the see-house and surrounded it with a strong wall. Soon after Meredith's arrival in Ireland the question of diverting the revenues of St. Patrick's to establish a university at Dublin became the occasion of a bitter quarrel between Loftus and Perrot [see under LOFTUS, ADAM, 1533?–1605]. Meredith sided with Perrot. He consequently shared in the odium which was lavished upon the lord-deputy, and was subsequently accused of complicity in the treasonable designs imputed to his patron (cf. *Cal. State Papers*, Ireland, 1588–92, pp. 313, 350). On 10 June 1590 orders were received for his conveyance to England. He crossed on 9 Aug., was tried in the Star-chamber, fined 2,000*l*., and was a prisoner in the Fleet in March 1590–1. In the following year the fine was remitted on Meredith's granting the queen an annuity of three hundred marks for ten years, which was assigned to the chief baron of the exchequer, chief justice of common pleas, and master of the rolls. On 30 Jan. 1593–4 Meredith was again fined

20*l*. and imprisoned for eight days. His health was now failing, and orders were given that no new dean of St. Patrick's was to be appointed in case of Meredith's death until his fine was paid in full. He died in Dublin on 3 Aug. 1597, and was buried on 7 Aug. by the side of his brother John in St. Patrick's Cathedral, at a spot reserved for members of his family. His heirs erected a handsome monument to his memory, which was defaced in 1688, when James II's troops converted the cathedral into a stable; but a monument of black marble, with an inscription to his memory, has since been erected. By his will, dated 28 July, Meredith left considerable sums to the corporation of Dublin and to his children on condition of their preserving their chastity until marriage.

Meredith married Sarah Batho or Bathow, and had issue by her. His eldest son, Robert, was knighted by Strafford on 6 Sept. 1635, and became privy councillor and chancellor of the Irish exchequer. He and Sir Thomas Rotherham were the only privy councillors who met on 21 Oct. 1641 in obedience to the summons of Lord-justice Parsons upon the first intimation of the rebellion. In 1647 he was appointed with others to take over the government of Ireland, in place of James Butler, first duke of Ormonde [q. v.] Meredith's second son, Thomas, was also knighted, and settled at Dollardstown, co. Meath. His widow remarried Adam Loftus, first viscount Loftus of Ely [q. v.]

Another Richard Meredith (1559–1621), dean of Wells, born in 1559, was admitted scholar of Winchester School in 1573, of New College, Oxford, in 1576, and fellow of New College in 1578, probably graduating B.C.L. on 1 July 1584, and B.D. on 17 Nov. 1606. He became rector of St. Peter and St. Paul, Bath, and of Portishead, Somerset, king's chaplain and dean of Wells in 1607. On 11 and 25 Feb. 1606–7 he preached before the king at Whitehall, and subsequently published the two sermons in a single volume (London, 4to, 1606, by G. Eld for S. Waterson). He died on 15 Aug. 1621, and was buried in Wells Cathedral (cf. Nichols, *Progresses of King James*; Kirby, *Winchester Scholars*; Foster, *Alumni Oxon.* 1500–1714; Wood, *Fasti*, i. 317; Fuller, *Church Hist.* ii. 367).

[Monk Mason's Deanery of St. Patrick's, pp. 175–7; Cal. State Papers, Ireland, 1588–92, 1592–6 passim; Cotton's Fasti Eccl. Hib. ii. 97, 387; Ware's Antiquities, i. 462; Foster's Alumni Oxon. 1500–1714; Wood's Athenæ Oxon. ii. 841; Williams's Eminent Welshmen, pp. 328–9; Bagwell's Ireland under the Tudors, iii. 229–31; Ryan's County of Carlow; Archdall's Peerage, vii. 247.] A. F. P.

MEREDITH, Sir WILLIAM (*d.* 1790), politician, third and last baronet of Henbury, Cheshire, was son of Amos Meredith (1688–1745) of Chester city, by Anne St. John, his second wife. He matriculated at Christ Church, Oxford, on 24 March 1742–3, when aged 18, and was created D.C.L. on 14 April 1749. In 1752 the title and family estates descended to him by the death of his grandfather, Sir William Meredith, the second baronet. He sat in parliament for Wigan from 1754 to 1761, and for Liverpool from 1761 to 1780, when he withdrew from public life, though at the election in 1784 a small number of votes was cast for him. When young he inclined to Jacobitism, but soon became an active whig, and was numbered among the followers of Lord Rockingham. He took a leading part in the proceedings connected with Wilkes, and his speeches are included in the published volumes of Sir Henry Cavendish's shorthand notes of the debates. When the Rockingham ministry was formed, Meredith became a lord of the admiralty (August 1765), and he remained in office for a short time after its fall; but at the close of November 1766 he resigned his post. In the following March he zealously struggled to effect an alliance of the followers of Rockingham with those of George Grenville, and for some years was one of the most active leaders of the opposition. Horace Walpole describes him as 'inflexibly serious and of no clear head; yet practice formed him to a manner of speaking that had weight. He was, I believe, an honest man, though not without personal views.' In 1771 he brought in a bill for repealing a clause in the Nullum Tempus Act, by which rights and titles acquired under grants or letters patent from the crown can be prosecuted with effect within a certain time, and it was carried against the government for some stages, but was ultimately rejected. He was even less successful in his attempt in February 1773 to abolish the subscription to the Thirty-nine Articles which was imposed on members of the universities. Much to his credit he interfered in March 1771, at considerable risk to his own person, to protect Lord North from the violence of the mob, and that minister acknowledged the courtesy by bestowing a benefice on his brother, the Rev. Theophilus Meredith. A little later his position in the house was that of leader of 'a very small squadron' of personal followers, and he was supposed 'by the Rockingham party to lean to the court.' On the dismissal of Charles James Fox, in February 1774, his name was mentioned for the vacant lordship of the treasury, and in the next month he kissed hands 'as comptroller of the household and privy councillor,' when Horace Walpole called him 'that fluctuating patriot who has broken with all parties and at last has dropped anchor at his own interest.' Meredith knew his own faults of character, for in response to some compliments on this promotion he piteously referred to his instability of mind. His reputation was now lost, and when he was ordered by the court not to visit the Duke of Gloucester, the king's brother, he was forced, though his particular friend, to acquiesce in the command. He resigned his post on principle, early in December 1777, only to find that he was treated by both sides with equal contempt.' His career had been marked by great extravagance, and in 1779 he was obliged to sell the family property at Henbury for 24,000*l.* At the dissolution of 1780 he lost his seat in parliament, and dropped into obscurity, but at the close of 1785 it was rumoured that he would be appointed to assist William Eden (afterwards Lord Auckland) [q. v.] in the commercial negotiations at Paris. Meredith died at Lyons, France, 2 Jan. 1790. when it was mentioned that 'the last annuity he sold was to M. Perigeux, the banker, who is probably one of the greatest gainers by his death.' The baronetcy became extinct, for the announcement of his marriage on 17 Nov. 1747 to Miss Cheetham of Mellor, Derbyshire (*Gent. Mag.* 1747, p. 544), was a mistake. He had five sisters: one married the Hon. Frederick Vane; another was the wife of Barlow Trecothick, lord mayor of London; a third married, as her second husband, Lord Frederick Campbell. All his brothers-in-law were prominent politicians. His portrait, a half-length in oval frame, painted by Daniel Gardner, was engraved by Thomas Watson, and published on 10 June 1773.

When Charles Lloyd (1735–1773) [q. v.] published his 'Defence of the Majority in the House of Commons on General Warrants,' it was answered anonymously by Meredith in 'A Reply to the Defence of the Majority,' 1764; 2nd edit. 1765. His other works were: 2. 'The Question stated whether the Freeholders of Middlesex lost their right by voting for Mr. Wilkes. In a Letter from a Member of Parliament to one of his Constituents,' 1769. This was attacked by the Rev. Nathaniel Forster in 'An Answer to a Pamphlet entitled "The Question Stated"' [anon.], 1769; and by Blackstone in 'A Letter to Sir William Meredith,' to which Meredith replied with 3. 'A Letter to Dr. Blackstone, by the Author of "The Question Stated,"' 1770. 4. 'A Letter to the Earl of Chatham on the Quebec Bill' [anon.], 1774, which produced 'A Letter to Sir William Meredith in answer to his last Letter to the Earl of Chatham' [anon.], 1774. 5. 'Punishment of Death. Speech of Sir W. Meredith, 13 May, 1777, in Committee on a Bill creating a new Capital Felony,' 1777; 3rd edit. of sixty thousand copies, 1831–2; 5th edit. 1831–2; another edit. 1833. Meredith is stated to have been 'remarkably averse to punishments that reached the lives of criminals.' 6. 'Historical Remarks on the Taxation of Free States' [anon], London, printed 16 Nov. 1778 (thirty copies only). This was marked by learning and argumentative power.

An account by Meredith of a short tour which he made from Lancashire into Scotland is printed in the 'Gentleman's Magazine,' 1766, pp. 166–9, 209–12; numerous speeches by him are inserted in the same magazine, and in the volume for 1773, pp. 216–17, is a letter from him on religious toleration. His report, assisted by the Hon. Constantine Phipps, afterwards Lord Mulgrave [q. v.], of the speeches in the debate of 27 Feb. 1771, on his bill to repeal a clause in the Nullum Tempus Act, was printed in that year, and embodied in 'Hansard's Parliamentary Debates,' xvii. 6–34. Letters by him are in Albemarle's 'Life of Lord Rockingham,' ii. 64–5, and in 'Hist. MSS. Comm.' 6th Rep. App. p. 240; and John Jebb, M.D., F.R.S., addressed to him 'A Letter on Subscription to the Liturgy and Thirty-nine Articles by an Englishman,' 1772 (see Jebb's Works, i. 223–62).

[Ormerod's Cheshire, ed. 1882, iii. 650, 708; Kimber's Baronetage, iii. 374–5; Gent. Mag. 1790, pt. i. pp. 85–6, 272; Albemarle's Rockingham, ii. 28; Grenville Papers, ii. 261–5, iv. 213, 503; Burke's Extinct Baronetcies, p. 632; Pink's Lancashire Representation, pp. 200–2, 234; Chatham Corresp. iv. 98, 103, 139, 252, 327; Almon's Anecdotes, i. 80–2; Walpole's Corresp. vii. 164; Walpole's George III, i. 350–74, ii. 45, 51–63, 304–7, iii. 163, 309–27, iv. 63–4, 91–2, 116, 273–4, 302–3; Walpole's Last Journals, i. 9–13, 45–7, 60, 185, 243, 392, ii. 170, 327–8; J. C. Smith's Portraits, iv. 1560; Nichols's Lit. Illustr. iii. 188; Nichols's Lit. Anecd. viii. 310; Letters of Junius, Nos. 18, 20.] W. P. C.

MEREDYDD (*d.* 999?), Welsh prince. [See MAREDUDD AB OWAIN.]

MEREDYDD AB BLEDDYN, PRINCE OF POWYS (*d.* 1132). [See MAREDUDD.]

MEREDYTH, first BARON. [See SOMERVILLE, SIR WILLIAM MEREDYTH, 1802–1873.]

MERES, FRANCIS (1565–1647), divine and author, born in 1565, was son of Thomas Meres or Meers of Kirton in Holland, Lincolnshire. The family, whose name was originally written 'Atte Meres,' was of old standing in the Fen district, and in the fifteenth century it supplied Lincolnshire with members of parliament (1428, 1434, 1441) and high sheriffs (1437, 1447, 1468, 1485). Francis doubtless belonged to the branch settled at Aubourn. He claimed kinship with John Meres, high sheriff of the county in 1596, whom he visited at Aubourn, and to whom he was indebted for pecuniary assistance in the early part of his career (*Gods Arithmeticke*, Ded.)

Meres graduated B.A. from Pembroke College, Cambridge, in 1587, and proceeded M.A. in 1591. He was incorporated in the latter degree at Oxford on 10 July 1593. In 1597 he was living in London in Botolph Lane, and developed a strong interest in contemporary English literature. In that year he preferred a 'successlesse suite to Maister Lawrence Meres of Yorke, sometimes of her Maiesties Counsell established for the North' (*ib.*; cf. *Yorks. Record Series*, vol. ii.) John Meres, the high sheriff, appears to have promised him further means of support if he chose to settle at Cambridge. But on 14 July 1602 he became rector of Wing in Rutland, and kept a school there. He retained the living till his death on 29 Jan. 1646–7. His wife Maria died 2 May 1631, aged 54. An only son, Francis, born in 1607 (B.A. Trinity College, Cambridge, 1628), was headmaster of Uppingham School 1641–1669. Meres, when entering his wife's death in his parish register, records her virtues at length both in English and Latin. The son Francis was father of Edward Meres (B.A. 1679 and M.A. 1683, St. John's College, Cambridge), rector of Wing 1688-90.

Meres has been identified with the 'F. M.' who contributed verses to the 'Paradise of Dainty Devices' in 1595. Charles FitzGeoffrey, in addressing to him a Latin poem in his 'Affaniæ,' 1601 (p. 62), describes him as 'theologus et poeta.' But it seems doubtful whether he is the 'Francis Meares' who prefixed a Latin epigram to Randolph's 'Jealous Lover,' 1640. He mainly confined himself to prose. In 1597 he published a sermon entitled 'Gods Arithmeticke,' London (by Richard Iohmes), to which a long and learned 'Epistle Nuncupatorie' to John Meres, the high sheriff, was prefixed (Brit. Mus.) Meres described himself on the title-page as 'Maister of Arts in both Universities and Student in Divinity.'

Meres's second and most interesting publication was a contribution to a series of volumes of collected apophthegms, or sententious reflections on morals, religion, and literature, which was inaugurated by the issue in 1597 of 'Politeuphuia: Wits Commonwealth.' This work was chiefly from the pen of Nicholas Ling, the publisher, although it is commonly assigned to John Bodenham [q. v.] Meres's continuation was entitled 'Palladis Tamia, Wits Treasury; being the second part of Wits Commonwealth,' London, by P. Short for Cuthbert Burbie, 1598. It was entered on the 'Stationers' Register' 7 Sept. 1598. No copy of this edition seems to contain Meres's address 'To the Reader,' which figures in later issues, and seems, on internal grounds, to have been written for the original publication. It promises a third contribution to the series by an eminent scholar.

Meres, who writes euphuistically, and prides himself on his free use of similes, acknowledges obligations to numerous classical writers and to the following English authors: Hugh Broughton, Sir Philip Sidney, Robert Greene, Foxe, Lyly, Sir John Harington, William Warner, Capgrave, and Thomas Playfere [q. v.] The most attractive feature of the volume is 'A Comparative Discourse of our English Poets with the Greek, Latin, and Italian Poets' (ff. 279–89). Meres passes in review all English literary effort from the time of Chaucer to his own day, briefly contrasting each English author with a writer of like character in Latin, Greek, or Italian. In other sections, on 'Bookes,' 'Reading of Bookes,' 'Philosophie,' 'Poets and Poetrie,' he makes casual references to contemporary English authors, and in his section on 'Painting' and 'Music' he supplies a few comments on contemporary English painters and musicians. He thus commemorates in all 125 Englishmen; and his lists of Shakespeare's works, with his commendation of the great dramatist's 'fine filed phrase,' and his account of Marlowe's death are *loci classici* in English literary history. The work was reissued in 1634 as 'Wits Commonwealth, the second part: A Treasurie of Diuine, Moral, and Phylosophical Similes, generally useful, but more particularly for the use of schools,' London, 1634, 12mo. A title-page, engraved by John Droeshout [q. v.], and dated 1636, was prefixed to the unsold copies of this edition, and describes the work as 'Witts Academy. A Treasurie of Goulden Sentences, Similies, and Examples. Set forth cheefely for the benefitt of young Schollers, London, printed for Richard Royston.' The passages dealing with Elizabethan literature were reprinted in Haslewood's 'Critical Essays,' in 'Shakspere Allusion Books' (New Shakspere Soc.), pt. i. pp. 164 sq., 1874, and in Arber's 'English Garner,' ii. 94 sq.

Meanwhile a third volume of the series, of

which 'Palladis Tamia' was the second, appeared in 1599 as 'Wits Theater of the Little World,' for which Nicholas Ling was again responsible. A fourth volume was 'Palladis Palatium. Wisedoms Pallace, or the fourth part of Wits Commonwealth' (London, by G. Elde for Francis Burton, 1604, 8vo); a unique copy belongs to Sir Charles Isham of Lamport. This part is ascribed in the 'Stationers' Registers,' iii. 264, to William Wrednot.

Meres also published translations, probably made through the French, of two religious works by the Spaniard, Luis de Grenada. The first, 'Granados Devotion, exactly teaching how a Man may truely dedicate and deuote himself vnto God,' London (E. Allde for Cuthbert Burbie), 1598, 12mo, was dedicated to Will Sammes of the Middle Temple, from London, 11 May 1598. The second, 'Sinners Guide, A Worke contayning the whole Regiment of Christian Life,' London (R. Field for Edward Blount), 1614, 4to, was dedicated to Sir Thomas Egerton under date 10 May 1598.

Another Francis Meres, with whom the divine is sometimes confused, died in 1557, and belonged to an elder branch of the family. He was son of Thomas, the disinherited elder son of one Sir John Meres, whose younger son, Anthony, founded the Aubourn branch to which the divine belonged. This Francis was father of Anthony (*d.* 1617), a prosperous merchant of Lincoln, whose son, Robert Meres, D.D. (1596–1652), was chancellor of the cathedral of Lincoln (from 1631), vicar of Tempsford, Bedfordshire, and rector of Hougham-cum-Marston. Dr. Robert Meres had a son, Sir Thomas Meres (1635–1715), who was knighted 11 June 1660, was M.P. for Lincoln from 1659 to 1710, and a commissioner of the admiralty from 1679 to 1684. He became prominent as a whig politician. Pepys admired his good sense as a speaker (*Diary*, 2 Jan. 1666–7). On the accession of James II he assumed an attitude of stubborn resistance to the king's policy of religious toleration. At the opening of the first parliament of the reign his name and that of Sir James Trevor were presented for the speakership to the king, who at once chose the latter (Bramston, *Autobiog.* pp. 197, 212). On 1 July 1685 Meres sought to pass through parliament a bill to compel all foreigners settled in England to adopt the English liturgy (*Lives of the Norths*, ed. Jessopp, iii. 180–1). By his wife, Anne, daughter of Sir Erasmus de la Fontaine, he left three sons, Thomas, John, and William. The eldest son was disinherited, and was father of John Meres [q. v.] The second son, Sir John Meres, F.R.S., one of the six clerks in chancery, was high sheriff of Lincolnshire in 1715, and was author of 'The Equity of Parliaments and Publick Faith vindicated, in answer to [Sir Richard Steele's] Crisis of Property, and addressed to the Annuitants' (1720, two editions). He died unmarried in 1736.

[Information kindly supplied by the Rev. C. Boys, rector of Wing; Wood's Fasti Oxon., ed. Bliss, i. 263; E. Peacock's English Church Furniture, 1866, pp. 34–6; A. R. Maddison's Lincolnshire Wills, 1500–1600 pp. 55, 2nd ser. 1600–17 pp. 148–50; E. Deacon's Family of Meres, Bridgeport, Connecticut, U.S.A., 1891; Hunter's Chorus Vatum, in MS. Addit. 24489, p. 265; Brit. Mus. Cat.; information kindly furnished by R. E. Graves, esq., of the British Museum.] S. L.

MERES, JOHN (1698–1761), printer and journalist, son of Thomas, the disinherited eldest son of Sir Thomas Meres (1635–1715) [see under Meres, Francis, *ad fin.*], was born in London in 1698, and apprenticed by his father, on 9 Feb. 1712, to William Stephens, printer. A kinsman, Hugh Meres or Meere, was already in the printing business, and was also a director of the Sun Fire Insurance, for which he printed the 'British Mercury,' and subsequently the 'Historical Register' (1716–38), the estimable precursor of the 'Gentleman's Magazine;' the 'Register' was his private enterprise from 1721 onwards. In October 1719 Hugh Meres commenced issuing a new daily paper, the 'Daily Post' (1719–71), and in September 1722 he started the 'British Journal,' which distinguished itself by its denunciations of the South Sea promoters. Hugh Meres died 19 April 1723, but his business passed entire into the hands of his widow, Cassandra, until her death in February 1726. It passed then into the hands of the daughter's husband, Richard Nutt (1694–1780), who started in December 1727 the 'London Evening Post.' It was this paper, which for a time distanced all its daily rivals, that John Meres came to direct in 1737. Meres, who seems to have become partner in all Nutt's enterprises and ultimately sole manager of them, took up his abode in the Old Bailey, dropped the 'Historical Register,' and devoted himself to the newspaper, which he carried on side by side with the 'Daily Post,' the imprint on both journals being 'printed for John Meres.' He was imprisoned for ten weeks in 1740 for passing some remarks upon an act of parliament dealing with the provision trade, and in 1745 he unwarily exposed himself to Fielding's attacks in the 'Jacobite Journal' by his high-flying and barely concealed Jacobite tendencies. In 1754 the 'Evening Post' published a letter reflecting on the government, and on 10 July

1755 Richard Nutt, the printer, was defendant in an action for libel, was found guilty, sentenced to stand in the pillory, and heavily fined. Ten years later Meres was mulcted 140*l.* for mentioning the name of a nobleman in his paper. Meres died in 1761, and left the business to his son by his wife Sarah Robinson (married 2 June 1732), also named John, by whom the 'Daily Post' was discontinued in 1772. The 'London Evening Post' survived until the death of Nutt in 1780.

Nichols confuses John Meres with WILLIAM MEARS (*fl.* 1722), a London publisher, son of Leonard Meers of Faversham, Kent, mariner. Made free of the Stationers' Company 6 Oct. 1707, he 'opened an office at the Lamb without Temple Bar,' and issued in 1722 an edition of Holinshed's 'Chronicle' at 5*l.*; Defoe's 'Moll Flanders,' 3rd edit.; Ludlow's 'Memoirs;' and Spelman's English works. On 23 Nov. 1732 he was committed to the custody of a messenger for publishing 'A Philosophical Dissertation on Death,' by Count de Passereau and John Morgan (*Gent. Mag.* 1732). William Mears is twice mentioned in Pope's 'Dunciad' (bk. ii. l. 125, and bk. iii. l. 28). He compiled a useful catalogue of English plays (London 1713, 4to, with continuation, 1715), and in 1734 published 'Lives of the Princes of the House of Orange.' His son William was apprenticed to him in 1727.

[The Family of Meres, a paper by Mr. Edward Deacon, Bridgeport, Conn. 1891; Nichols's Lit. Anecd. i. 62, 311–12, iii. 733, viii. 481; Fox Bourne's English Newspapers, i. 53; Knight Hunt's Fourth Estate; Gent. Mag. 1755, p. 826; Lowe's Engl. Theatr. Lit. p. 235.] T. S.

MEREWETHER, HENRY ALWORTH (1780–1864), serjeant-at-law, born in 1780, was eldest son of Henry Merewether of Calne, Wiltshire. A younger brother, Francis (1784–1864), was well known as the rector of Coleorton, a living to which he was presented by his friend Sir George Beaumont in 1816. Henry was educated at Reading school under Dr. Valpy, was called to the bar 5 May 1809, was created serjeant-at-law 25 June 1827, and became king's counsel with patent of precedence in Hilary term 1853. He practised on the western circuit with much success. Merewether was appointed recorder of Reading, and was attorney-general to Adelaide, queen-dowager. He received the degree of D.C.L. from the university of Oxford on 12 June 1839.

He was elected town-clerk of London on 23 June 1842, by a majority of twenty-six votes, in competition with William Pritchard, then high bailiff of Southwark. By accepting this appointment he relinquished an income of over 5,000*l.* at the bar. It is said by those among the corporation who knew him that the office of town-clerk had never been filled with such dignity as in his time. He appeared on behalf of the corporation in the court of chancery and elsewhere on several occasions, and defended their interests with great learning and ability. He resigned the office of town-clerk on 10 Feb. 1859, and died at his family seat, Castlefield, near Calne, Wiltshire, on 22 July 1864, in his eighty-fourth year.

Merewether was twice married, and left several children. His eldest son, Henry Alworth (1812–1877), was recorder of Devizes and a bencher of the Inner Temple. His youngest son, Sir William Lockyer Merewether, is separately noticed.

The serjeant's principal work is 'The History of the Boroughs and Municipal Corporations of the United Kingdom,' written in conjunction with Archibald John Stephens, and published in three octavo volumes in 1835. He also wrote: 1. 'A New System of Police,' 8vo, London, 1816. 2. 'A Sketch of the History of Boroughs, and of the Corporate Right of Election,' 8vo, London, 1822. 3. 'Report of the Case of the Borough of West Looe,' 8vo, London, 1823. 4. 'An Address to the King, the Lords, and Commons on the Representative Constitution of England,' 8vo, London, 1830. 5. 'The Speech . . . at the Bar of the House of Commons against the Bill intituled An Act to make Temporary Provision for the Government of Jamaica,' 8vo, London, 1839. 6. 'The Speech . . . upon the Claim of the Commissioners of Woods and Forests to the Seashore, &c.,' 8vo, London, Dublin, 1850.

[Gent. Mag. 1864, pt. ii. pp. 393–4; City Press, 30 July 1864, p. 4; Foster's Alumni Oxon.; Burke's Landed Gentry, 5th edit., 1871; Haydn's Book of Dignities, 1890, pp. 413, 417; Brit. Mus. Cat.] C. W-H.

MEREWETHER, JOHN (1797–1850), dean of Hereford, son of John Merewether of Blackland, Wiltshire, was born at Marshfield, Gloucestershire, in 1797. His father was a great-grandson of the John Merewether of Devizes (1655–1724) who attended Bishop Ken in his last illness, and whose daughter married William Hawkins, a grandson of Izaac Walton, and author of the 'Short Account of Ken's Life,' 1713. He was a distant cousin of Serjeant Henry Alworth Merewether [q. v.] John matriculated from Queen's College, Oxford, on 18 Oct. 1814, graduated B.A. in 1818, and B.D. and D.D. in 1832. He was ordained priest in 1820 by the Bishop of Salisbury, and served curacies at Gillingham, Dorset, and Hampton, Middlesex. While at Hampton he was instrumental in building a chapel of ease at Hampton Wick, and attracted the favourable notice of the Duke of Clarence, afterwards William IV, then residing at Bushey. He was chaplain to the Duchess of Clarence, afterwards Queen Adelaide, in 1824. In 1828 he was presented by the lord chancellor to the living of New Radnor, and in 1832, on the promotion of the Hon. Edward Grey to the bishopric, he succeeded him as dean of Hereford. On 13 Jan. 1833 William IV appointed him one of the deputy clerks of the closet, and asked Lord Melbourne to have a care for his advancement. In 1836 he was instituted to the vicarage of Madeley, Shropshire, but to his bitter disappointment was passed over again and again as vacancies occurred on the episcopal bench. In 1847 he was a strenuous opponent of the election of Renn Dickson Hampden [q. v.] to the see of Hereford. After a fruitless memorial to the queen, he announced to Lord John Russell, prime minister, in a letter of great length (22 Dec.), his intention of voting against Hampden's election in the chapter meeting, and he received in reply the laconic note: 'Sir, I had the honour to receive your letter of the 22nd inst. in which you intimate to me your intention of violating the law.' Merewether finally refused to affix the seal of the dean and chapter to the document recording the bishop's formal election (see his letter of justification in *Times*, 1 Jan. 1848; cf. Walpole, *Life of Lord John Russell*, 1891, i. 498, and 'The Case of Dr. Hampden,' *Official and Legal Proceedings*, 1848).

Merewether, who was an enthusiastic local antiquary, was elected F.S.A. in 1836, and communicated to the 'Archæologia' accounts of discoveries made during the restoration of Hereford cathedral. In this work he took a leading and most valuable, because strictly conservative, part. In 1843 he issued an interesting 'Statement on the Condition and Circumstances of the Cathedral Church of Hereford,' with notes on the effigies and excellent illustrations of the then condition of the structure. He himself contributed 500*l.* to the restoration fund. He was an active member of the Archæological Institution, in connection with which he did some important work in Wiltshire, commemorated by the posthumous publication in 1851 of the 'Diary of a Dean: being an Account of the Examination of Silbury Hill and of various Barrows and other Earthworks on the Downs of North Wilts.' The plates illustrating human remains, flint implements, pottery, &c., are from Merewether's own drawings. Merewether died at Madeley vicarage on 4 April 1850, and was buried in the lady-chapel of Hereford Cathedral. The five lancet windows at the east end of the minster were fitted with stained glass to his memory with the inscription 'In Memoriam Johannis Merewether, S.T.P. ecclesiæ Heref. decani, quo strenuo fautore huius sacræ ædis restitutio feliciter est inchoata.' By his wife Mary Ann Baker, of Wiley, Wiltshire, Merewether had six sons and three daughters. Mrs. Merewether died on 17 June 1879, aged 71.

[Gent. Mag. 1850, i. 536, 562; G. V. Cox's Recollections, p. 342; Jones's Hereford Cathedral and City, 1858, p. 74; Havergal's Fasti Herefordenses, 1869, p. 41; Ann. Reg. 1850, p. 217; Guardian, 10 April 1850; Illustr. Lond. News, 1850, i. 247 (portrait).] T. S.

MEREWETHER, Sir WILLIAM LOCKYER (1825–1880), Indian military officer and administrator, son of Serjeant Henry Alworth Merewether [q. v.], was born in London on 6 Feb. 1825. Educated at Westminster School, and destined for the military profession, he entered the Bombay army as a second lieutenant in March 1841. He served with the 21st regiment of native infantry during the Sind campaign of 1843, and was present at the battle of Hyderabad. Appointed afterwards to the irregular horse, stationed on the north-west border of Sind, he was recalled to his old regiment for service in the southern Maratha country, but rejoined the frontier force in 1847, eventually (1859) to become its commandant, in succession to General John Jacob [q. v.] His distinguished services during this period of twelve years were numerous. In 1847, with one hundred and thirty-three Sind horsemen, he defeated a body of seven hundred Bhugtis, Baluch marauders who had been proclaimed outlaws, inflicting upon them a severe chastisement, which helped to secure the permanent peace of the frontier. In 1848–9 he was second in command of Sir George Malcolm's detachment of Sind horse, serving with the army of the Punjab, and was present at the siege and surrender of Multán, the battle of Gujrát, and occupation of Pesháwar. In 1856, during General Jacob's absence in Persia, he was left in charge of the Sind frontier, and succeeded in suppressing not only rebellion of tribes, but insubordination of troops under his control. His own small force, though numerically augmented by auxiliary cavalry, had been practically weakened by the accession of untrustworthy soldiers.

Gazetted C.B. in 1860, Merewether was

nominated military secretary to the government of Bombay in 1861, and political agent at Aden in 1865. In the last post he undertook active operations against the Fudhli Arabs, who sought to intercept the supplies of grain and food provided for the garrison by the inhabitants of the interior. These operations, though subsequently approved by government, were, owing to the urgency of the case, carried out by Merewether on his own personal responsibility. It afterwards fell to his lot to negotiate with King Theodore of Abyssinia; and on the outbreak of war with that potentate he took command of the pioneer force despatched from Bombay in September 1867, and rendered other valuable assistance to General Lord Napier, commander-in-chief of the expedition. For these services he was made K.C.S.I., and received the thanks of parliament (1868). Appointed chief commissioner in Sind in June 1867, it was not until July in the following year that he could be spared to take up the appointment. In 1876 he returned home to take his seat in the council of India. He died on 4 Oct. 1880. A generous, open-hearted companion and sincere friend, Merewether was universally popular, and was generally acknowledged to be a true soldier, a shrewd politician, and an enlightened administrator. In 1854 he married Harriett, youngest daughter of J. Dale, esq., of Coleshill, Warwickshire. He left a widow and three sons.

[Annual Register, 1880; Proc. Roy. Geogr. Soc. 1880; Bombay Government Gazette, 1847; private information.] F. J. G.

MERFYN Frych, i.e. Freckled (*d.* 844), Welsh prince, succeeded to the lordship of Anglesey (with, possibly, other adjacent districts), on the failure of the male line of Maelgwn Gwynedd with the death of Hywel, in 825. He was the son of Gwriad ab Elidyr, a descendant of Llywarch Hên [q. v.] According to the twelfth-century poem entitled 'Cyfoesi Myrddin a Gwenddydd ei Chwaer,' he came 'from the land of Manaw' (*Myvyrian Archaiology*, 2nd edit. p. 110), which Skene conjectures to be Manaw Gododin, on the banks of the Forth (*Four Ancient Books of Wales*, i. 94). According to the modern authorities (*Gwentian Brut*; Powel; Warrington; *Cambrian Biography*; Carnhuanawc) he became prince in right of his wife, Esyllt, daughter of Cynan Tindaethwy. But older and better accounts speak of him as the son of Cynan's daughter, who is termed Ethil or Ethellt (*Harl. MS.* 3859, as given in *Cymmrodor*, ix. 169; *Jesus Coll. MS.* 20, as given in *Cymmrodor*, viii. 87). This is more consistent with the Welsh law of inheritance, which in certain cases recognised a claim through a mother, but never one derived from a wife (see the sections treating of 'mamwys' (maternity) in the Record edition of the 'Welsh Laws'). The same authorities which speak of Esyllt as Merfyn's wife call him the son of Nest, daughter of Cadell, the last but one of the princes of Powys of the older line. Jesus Coll. MS. 20 is probably right in making Nest Merfyn's wife and the mother of Rhodri the Great. Many modern writers style Merfyn king of Man, but this is merely an ill-grounded inference from the passage in the 'Cyfoesi' quoted above, which speaks, it should be noted, not of 'ynys,' but of '*tir* Manaw.'

Of Merfyn's reign nothing is known. The traditional name 'Camwri' ('Injustice') given him in one manuscript of the Welsh Laws (*Ancient Laws of Wales*, edit. 1841, i. 342) shows that his rule was not accepted without demur; nevertheless, he founded a family which supplied both North and South Wales with princes until the conquest of Edward I.

[Annales Cambriæ, Rolls ed.; pedigrees in Harl. MS. 3859 and Jesus Coll. MS. 20.] J. E. L.

MERICK. [See Merrick and Meyrick.]

MERITON or **MERYTON, GEORGE,** D.D. (*d.* 1624), dean of York, was born in Hertfordshire, probably at Braughing. His father was a tenant of Thomas Howard, first earl of Suffolk (1561–1626) [q. v.], who inherited estates in Hertfordshire from his mother, and he himself was born under the earl's roof (Meriton, *Epistle to Sermon of Nobilitie*). He was educated at St. John's College, Cambridge, graduated B.A. in 1584–5, M.A. in 1588, and was on 4 July 1589 elected fellow of Queen's College. There he filled the post of junior bursar, 1595–6, senior bursar 1596–7, and proceeded B.D. in 1596, and D.D. in 1601. During his residence at Cambridge he made known his adherence to church establishment by frequent discussions on ceremonies which he held with Thomas Brightman [q. v.] in the chapel of Queen's College. He was collated to the rectory of Hadleigh in Suffolk by Archbishop Whitgift in 1599, and was appointed to the deanery of Bocking (usually held in conjunction with the rectory) on 24 May 1599. He was made dean of Peterborough on 12 June 1612, was chaplain to Anne of Denmark, wife of James I, dean of York on 27 March 1617, and prebendary of Tockerington in the cathedral church of York on 5 March 1617. He resigned Hadleigh in 1618, and dying on 23 Dec. 1624, was buried in York Cathedral.

Meriton married Mary Rands, granddaughter of Henry Rands, bishop of Lincoln, by whom he had several children, whose baptisms are recorded in the registers of Hadleigh.

He published: 1. 'A Sermon of Nobilitie,' London, 1607. 2. 'A Sermon of Repentance,' London, 1607. 3. 'A Sermon preached before the General Assembly at Glasgow,' London, 1611. 4. 'The Christian Man's Assuring House, and a Sinner's Conversion,' London, 1614.

[Dugdale's Visitation of Yorkshire, 1665, p. 107; Lansdowne MS. 984, f. 29; Fuller's Church Hist. 1655, bk. x. p. 49; Newcourt's Repert. ii. 68; Pigot's Hadleigh, pp. 276–7; Drake's Eboracum, pp. 510, 559, 565; Davy's Athenæ Suffolc. (Add. MS. 18165, f. 293).] B. P.

MERITON or MERRITON, GEORGE (1634–1711), legal and miscellaneous writer, born in July 1634, was the eldest son of Thomas Meriton (1606–1652), second son of George Meriton [q. v.], by his wife Grace, daughter of Francis Wright of Bolton-upon-Swale, Yorkshire. He inherited the paternal estate at Castle Leavington, Yorkshire, in 1652, studied law, and became an attorney or 'practiser of the common law' at Northallerton in Yorkshire. On the title-page of his 'Abridgment of the Irish Statutes' he is described as barrister-at-law, but his name cannot be found in the books of the Inns of Court of London or Dublin. After 1684 he left England and went to Ireland, and in the autumn of 1700 had the degree of LL.B. conferred upon him by the university of Dublin. He died in Dublin in 1711. By his wife, Mary, daughter of John Palliser of Kirkby Wiske in Yorkshire, he had five sons and one daughter. His eldest son, Thomas, born in October 1657, was admitted a student of Gray's Inn, London, on 17 June 1675. George, the second son, born in 1660, who entered St. John's College, Cambridge, 13 June 1678, died in Cambridge on 14 Aug. 1680, and was buried in All Saints' Church. John, the third son, born at Kirkby Wiske, was educated at Northallerton and Christ's College, Cambridge (admitted 30 June 1682), and graduated B.A. in 1685. Luke, his father's executor, Charles, and Katherine were mentioned in Meriton's will, made 26 Sept. 1701 and proved 15 March 1711. His wife survived him.

Meriton was 'the truly noble, judicious gentleman, and . . . most esteemed brother . . .' to whom Thomas Meriton [q. v.] the dramatist dedicated his tragedy 'Love and War' in 1658. Although the writer of several books on law, his most noticeable work is a curious humorous poem, 'The Praise of Yorkshire Ale,' the scene of which is laid in Northallerton. To this is added 'A Yorkshire Dialogue in its Pure Natural Dialect,' and 'An Alphabetical Clavis, unfolding the meaning of the Yorkshire Words made use of in the aforegoing Dialogue.' The work, which is of no small merit, was published under the initials 'G. M., gent.,' in London 1683, York 1683, London 1684, York 1685 and 1697. Newsam in his 'Poets of Yorkshire' ascribes it to Giles Morrington, an error repeated in Ingledew's 'History of Northallerton,' p. 387, where the greater part of the poem is given. In Boyne's 'Yorkshire Library' it is ascribed to George Merrington.

Meriton's other published works include: 1. 'Land-Lords Law,' London, 1665, 1669 (3rd edit.), 1681, 1697 (5th edit.) 2. 'A Touchstone of Wills,' London, 1668, 1671, 1674. 3. 'A Guide for Constables, Church-wardens,' &c., London, 1669, 1681 (7th edit.) 4. 'Anglorum Gesta, or a Brief History of England,' London, 1675, 1678. 5. 'A Geographical Description of the World,' London, 1674 (2nd edit.), 1679 (3rd edit.) 6. 'The Parson's Monitor,' London, 1681. 7. 'Nomenclatura Clericalis,' London, 1685. 8. 'A Guide to Surveyors of the High Ways,' London, 1694. 9. 'Immorality, Debauchery, and Profaneness Exposed,' London, 1698 (2nd edit.) 10. 'An Abridgment of the Irish Statutes, from the third Year of the Reign of King Edward II . . . with an Abridgment of English Statutes enacted since Sir Edward Poyning's Law relating to the Kingdom of Ireland,' Dublin, 1700; London, 1724. The work was acknowledgedly used by N. Robbins, who published 'An Exact Abridgment of all the Irish Statutes' in Dublin in 1736. 11. 'An Abridgment of the Act of Parliament for the better Execution of His Majesty's Declaration for the Settlement of . . . Ireland, 14 & 15 Car. II,' Dublin, 1701.

A manuscript, 'Briefe History or Account, shewing howe People did Trafficke in the World before the Invention of Money,' &c., by George Meriton is in the British Museum (Addit. MS. 10401). In 'Notes and Queries,' 3rd ser. v. 480, is ascribed to Meriton the authorship of 'Miscellanea, or a Choice Collection of Wise and Ingenious Sayings,' &c., London, 1694, but this was the work of Guy Miege [q. v.]

[Dugdale's Visitation of Yorkshire, 1665, p. 107; Notes and Queries, 3rd ser. v. 480–1; Dublin Graduates; Le Neve's Monumenta Anglicana, 1680–99, p. 4; Watt's Bibl. Brit.; Marvin's Legal Bibliography; Allibone's Dict. of Engl. Lit.; Lowndes's Bibliographer's Manual; Cat. of Libr.

of Trin. Coll. Dublin; Admission Reg. of Christ's Coll. Cambr. per the master; will in Public Record Office, Dublin; Notes and Queries, 8th ser. v. 284.] B. P.

MERITON, JOHN (1636–1704), divine, was the son of Richard Meriton of Northallerton in Yorkshire, and was born in 1636. He was educated first at a private school at Danby Wiske, and was admitted sizar of St. John's College, Cambridge, on 18 Oct. 1652, but at that time took no degree. On 9 Jan. 1655–6 he was presented, on the recommendation of Oliver Cromwell, lord protector, to the rectory of St. Nicholas Acons, London (*Lambeth MS.* 996, fol. 456). On 14 July 1657 he was incorporated M.A. in the university of Oxford, and became an upholder of the presbyterian form of church government. He was made Sunday lecturer of St. Martin's-in-the-Fields shortly before the Restoration. On 26 Sept. 1660 he was created M.A. of Cambridge by royal mandate, and D.D. in 1669. He signed the 'Humble and Grateful Acknowledgements of many Ministers in and about London' to the king for his concessions expressed in his declaration concerning ecclesiastical affairs in November 1660. On 18 July he was reinstituted to his rectory of St. Nicholas Acons, which he resigned before 1664. The church was burnt in 1666 and not rebuilt. Before the Act of Uniformity came into operation he opposed it strongly, but later on he himself conformed and retained his living. He was appointed to the rectory of St. Michael's, Cornhill, on 28 March 1663, which he held till his death. He was rector of St. Mary Bothaw from 25 June 1666 till 1669; the church was destroyed in the great fire in the former year, and the parish was in 1669 annexed to that of St. Swithin's, London Stone. He was also lecturer of St. Mary-at-Hill from 1661 to 1683. Wood (*Athenæ*, vol. iv. col. 722) speaks of him as having been deprived of the lectureship of St. Olave's, Southwark, 'for fanaticism,' but an inspection of the 'Vestry Minutes' of the parish shows that the lecturer removed in October 1683 was a Thomas Meriton appointed on 24 Sept. 1662.

Meriton was one of the London rectors who remained at his post during the great plague year of 1665, and later on, after the fire of 1666, was very energetic in the arrangements for uniting, rebuilding, and endowing the city churches. Two letters of his to Sancroft on the subject, dated 1670, are in the Bodleian Library (Tanner MSS. xliv. ff. 239, 242). Meriton appears to have been a popular preacher. Pepys (*Diary*, 1849, iii. 333, iv. 45), though he speaks of him as 'the old dunce Meriton,' and 'my old acquaintance, that dull fellow,' went to hear him (11 Nov. 1666 and 19 May 1667), and pronounced that he 'made a good sermon, and hath a strange knack of a grave, serious delivery, which is very agreeable.' Calamy (*Own Life*, ii. 89) was in the habit of hearing him in 1689 when the dissenting meetings were closed, and of sending his father accounts of the sermons.

Meriton died in December 1704, and was buried in the chancel of St. Michael's, Cornhill, on the 11th. His wife Elizabeth predeceased him in December 1680, and a son Thomas in June 1678. The registers of St. Michael's record the baptisms of a daughter Elizabeth on 6 Dec. 1664, and of a son Rowland on 18 Oct. 1674, and the marriages of three daughters and of the son Rowland. The last named, dying in December 1743, was buried at St. Michael's, Cornhill.

He published: 1. 'Curse not the King,' anniversary sermon on the day of humiliation for the 'horrid murder' of Charles I, London, 1660. 2. 'Of Christ's Humiliation,' sermon printed in 'Morning Exercises,' London, 1660 (new ed. 1844, vol. v.); an outline is given in Dunn's 'Divines,' pp. 210–211. 3. 'Religio Militis,' London, 1672. In Wood's 'Fasti' (Bliss), on the authority of Grey, it is stated that he published 'Forms of Prayer for every Day in the Week, for the Use of Families.'

He must not be confused with two contemporaries—an uncle and nephew—of the same name. John Meriton (*b.* 1629), the uncle, son of the Rev. Henry Meriton of Stilton, Huntingdon, graduated B.A. at Magdalene College, Cambridge, in 1648, and M.A. in 1652; became vicar of St. Ives, Huntingdonshire, and chaplain to Henry, earl of Arlington, lord chamberlain, and published: 1. 'The Obligation of a Good Conscience to Civil Obedience,' London, 1670. 2. 'Sermon before the King at Whitehall,' London, 1677.

The third John Meriton (1662–1717), the nephew of the former, was son of Henry Meriton, rector of Oxburgh in Norfolk (1647–1707) and of Boughton in the same county (1677–83), was educated at Gonville and Caius College, Cambridge; became rector of Boughton in 1687, of Caldecote in 1688, and of Oxburgh (on the death of his father) in 1707. He died in 1717. With his father he entered into controversy with the quakers, and took part in a conference between them and some clergymen of the church of England, on 8 Dec. 1698 in West Dereham Church in Norfolk. He published 'An Antidote against the Venom of Quakerism,' London, 1699. Smith (*Bibl. Anti-Quakeriana*, pp. 66–9) gives a list of the pamphlets called forth by the controversy. In the Bodleian

Library (Tanner MS. 22 f. 5) is a letter from him to Dr. Humphrey Prideaux [q. v.] at Norwich (dated from Westminster 18 March 1698–9) respecting a petition against the quakers, which it was in contemplation to present.

[Mayor's Reg. of Admissions to St. John's Coll. Cambr. p. 108; Wood's Fasti (Bliss), vol. ii. col. 206; Dunn's Divines, p. 210; Newcourt's Repertorium, i. 448, 483, 505; Sylvester's Reliq. Baxt. bk. i. pp. 284–5; Kennett's Reg. p. 513; Registers of St. Michael's, Cornhill (Harl. Soc.), pp. 42, 44, 53, 144, 148, 263, 265, 278, 296; Blomefield's Norfolk, vi. 60, 185, 193, 194, vii. 302; Admission Registers of Gonville and Caius College per the Master, and of Magdalene Coll. Cambr. per F. Pattrick, esq.; Cambr. Univ. Reg. per J. W. Clark, esq.] B. P.

MERITON, THOMAS (*fl.* 1658), dramatist, born in 1638, was the second son of Thomas Meriton of Castle Leavington, Yorkshire, and Grace, daughter of Francis Wright of Bolton-on-Swale, and so grandson of George Meriton [q. v.], dean of York, and younger brother of George Meriton [q. v.], author of the 'Praise of Yorkshire Ale.' He was educated at a private school at Danby Wiske, and admitted at the unusual age of four-and-twenty a sizar of St. John's College, Cambridge, 9 May 1662, B.A. 1665, M.A. 1669.

He published two tragedies in 1658, 'Love and War,' dedicated to his brother, George Meriton, and 'The Wandring Lover,' which, according to the title-page, had been 'acted severall times privately at sundry places by the Author and his friends, with great applause.' In the dedication to Francis Wright he mentions the fact that he had also written the 'Several Affairs,' a comedy, and the 'Chast Virgin,' a romance, but that they were only shown to some private friends. 'Happy certainly,' says Langbaine, 'were those men who were not reckoned in the number of his friends.' Langbaine describes him as 'certainly the meanest *Dramatick* writer that ever *England* produc'd.'

[Dugdale's Visitation of Yorkshire (Surtees Society), p. 107; J. E. B. Mayor's Admissions to St. John's College, 1630–1655, pt. i. p. 155; Graduati Cantabr.; Langbaine's Account of English Dram. Poets, p. 367.] G. T. D.

MERIVALE, HERMAN (1806–1874), under-secretary for India, born 8 Nov. 1806, at Cockwood House, Dawlish, Devonshire, was the eldest of twelve children of John Herman Merivale [q. v.] by Louisa Heath, daughter of Joseph Drury [q. v.]

Herman was a boy of extraordinary precocity. He read the Latin accidence when four years old with his grandfather Drury. In January 1817 he was sent to Harrow to the house of his uncle, Henry Joseph Thomas Drury [q. v.] He took a high place and was captain of the school before he was sixteen. He read much in his uncle's library and became, like his father, a good Italian scholar. In the 'Family Memorials' are printed long letters written by the boy to his father upon Tasso's 'Jerusalem Delivered' in 1819, and upon Gibbon's account of the Arian controversy in 1820. He won all the school prizes, and was taken by his father to see Coleridge at Highgate. He was entered at Oriel College, then under Copleston, on 3 Nov. 1823, and began residence with the highest school reputation in January 1824. In 1825 he won an open scholarship at Trinity College, and in the same year was elected to the Ireland scholarship, of which he was the first holder. He took a first class in classical honours in 1827, and in December 1828 was elected to a fellowship at Balliol. He was called to the bar at the Inner Temple in 1832, and practised upon the western circuit. He was highly respected in his profession, and was, when he had a favourable opportunity, a very effective speaker, but his practice was not in proportion to his reputation, perhaps because he was not disposed to the oratorical efforts which are admired at quarter sessions. He was appointed recorder of Falmouth, Helston, and Penzance in 1841. On 2 March 1837 he was elected to the professorship of political economy at Oxford, founded by Henry Drummond [q. v.] in 1825. His predecessors were Senior, Whately, and W. F. Lloyd. He held it for the usual term of five years, and in the last three delivered a course of lectures upon the colonies, which made a great impression. They contained a very able and discriminative criticism of the Wakefield scheme of colonisation, then much discussed, and showed much foresight in pointing out its strong and weak points. The book led to his appointment in 1847 as assistant under-secretary of state for the colonies, and in 1848 he succeeded Sir James Stephen as permanent under-secretary. In 1859 he was transferred to the permanent under-secretaryship for India, with the distinction of C.B., and held the office for his life. Lord Lytton, when resigning the secretaryship for the colonies in June 1859, expressed his gratitude for Merivale's services in the warmest terms. He was held in the highest esteem by all his official colleagues, but the precise nature of the work done by a permanent official is necessarily, for the most part, known only within his office, and in Merivale's case cannot be more precisely specified.

He married at Dawlish, on 29 Oct. 1834, Caroline Penelope, eldest daughter of the

Rev. William Villiers Robinson and sister of Sir George Stamp Robinson. His son, Herman Charles (1839–1906), was well known as a dramatic author. One daughter, Isabella Frances, married William Peere Williams-Freeman. Another daughter, Agnes, married to Mr. Townshend Trench, died in 1872. His grief at the loss affected his health. He died 8 Feb. 1874 at his house, 13 Cornwall Gardens, South Kensington, and was buried in the Fulham cemetery. By his mother's death in the previous year he inherited the family estate of Barton Place. His widow died 11 Aug. 1881. The first Lord Lytton, in a manuscript note upon Merivale's 'Historical Studies' (notice by the dean of Ely), called the author 'one of the most remarkable men he ever met.' His intellectual characteristic was 'massiveness,' and he could be compared 'to no one of less calibre than Macaulay,' with the difference that, whereas 'no one of much merit could form his opinion by Macaulay,' any one, however powerful his mind, 'would form his opinion upon Merivale.' He was a man of great promptitude of judgment, and vigorous, if not combative, in defending it. In politics he was a staunch liberal. In private life he showed a singularly affectionate nature, both in early life to his parents and brothers and sisters and afterwards among his own family and friends. His literary works, except the 'Lectures on Colonisation,' which deal with questions now out of date, were written in the intervals of more absorbing business, and scarcely give a full impression of his powers.

He was made D.C.L. by the university of Oxford in 1870.

His works are: 1. 'The Character of Socrates as drawn from Xenophon and Plato,' &c. (prize essay at Oxford), 1830. 2. 'Introductory Lecture upon Political Economy,' 1837. 3. 'Introduction to the Course upon Colonisation,' 1839. 4. 'Lectures on Colonisation and the Colonies' (delivered in 1839, 1840–1), 1841. 5. 'Reports of Cases in the Queen's Bench' (with A. Davison), 1844. 6. 'Historical Studies,' 1865 (a collection of articles in periodicals). 7. 'Memoirs of Sir Philip Francis,' 1867 (completed from the unfinished work of J. Parkes). 8. 'Life of Sir Henry Lawrence' (1st vol. by Sir Herbert Edwardes, 2nd by Merivale), 1872.

Merivale also wrote sixty-six articles in the 'Edinburgh Review' between 1832 and 1874, upon a great variety of topics, historical, literary, and economical. Between 1827 and 1864 he wrote five articles for the 'Foreign Quarterly,' and between 1853 and 1867 nine for the 'Quarterly Review.' He regularly wrote also till his death in the 'Pall Mall Gazette,' started in 1865.

[Notice by Charles Merivale, D.D., younger brother of Herman Merivale, read before the Devonshire Association at Newton Abbot, 1884, and reprinted. This contains also some obituary notices and a list of contributions to quarterly reviews; Family Memorials compiled by Anna W. Merivale, printed for private circulation, 1884; McCulloch's Literature of Political Economy, 1845, p. 95; Notes and Queries, 5th ser. i. 124.] L. S.

MERIVALE, JOHN HERMAN (1779–1844), scholar and minor poet, only son of John Merivale of Barton Place, Exeter, and Bedford Square, London, by Ann Katencamp or Katenkamp, daughter of a German merchant settled in Exeter, was born in that city on 5 Aug. 1779.

The earliest records of the Merivale family are to be found in the parish registers of Middleton Cheney, Northamptonshire, and there is a tradition that an ancestor fled from religious persecution in France and settled at Middleton Cheney about 1590; the name is, however, found in the parish registers as early as 1558, and it was originally spelt Mervayle.

Samuel Merivale (1715–1771), John Herman's grandfather, was brought up as a baptist; falling under the influence of Dr. Philip Doddridge [q. v.], he became a presbyterian, and began to officiate as 'stated' minister at Sleaford in 1737. In 1743 he received a 'call' to Tavistock, where he went through the formal ceremony of ordination. In 1761 he accepted the post of tutor to the Presbyterian Theological Seminary, founded in that year at Exeter. He died in December 1771. He published 'Daily Devotions for the Closet. To which are added Prayers on particular occasions,' pp. 159; 3rd edit. London, 1796, 12mo; other editions 1812 and 1829, with preface by Lant Carpenter [q. v.] (cf. A. W. Merivale, *Family Memorials*, 1844).

John Herman was himself bred in strict presbyterian principles, so that, though he spent some years at St. John's College, Cambridge, he left without taking a degree. In later life he conformed to the church of England. On 17 Dec. 1798 he entered Lincoln's Inn, where he was called to the bar in Hilary term 1804. In 1811 he published, at the request of the Society for the Diffusion of Knowledge respecting the Punishment of Death and the Improvement of Prison Discipline, 'A Brief Statement of the Proceedings in both Houses of Parliament in the Last and Present Sessions upon the several Bills introduced with a view to the Amendment of the Criminal Law: together with a General Review of the Arguments used in the Debates upon those occasions,'

London, 8vo. He practised in chancery and bankruptcy, and published 'Reports of Cases argued and determined in the High Court of Chancery,' London, 1817–19, 8vo. He sat on the Chancery Commission of 1824, in the report of which he concurred, but expounded a wider scheme of reform in 'A Letter to William Courtenay, Esq., on the Subject of the Chancery Commission,' London, 1827, 8vo.

On 2 Dec. 1831 he was appointed to a commissionership in bankruptcy, which he held until his death, on 25 April 1844. He was buried in the churchyard, Hampstead. Merivale married, on 10 July 1805, Louisa Heath, daughter of the Rev. Joseph Drury [q. v.], head-master of Harrow School, by whom he had six sons and six daughters. His eldest son was Herman Merivale, C.B. [q. v.]; his second son, Charles Merivale, dean of Ely, and historian of the Roman empire, is noticed in the Supplement to this work.

Merivale was an accurate and elegant scholar, accomplished alike in classical and romantic literature. He was Bland's principal collaborator in his 'Collections from the Greek Anthology and from the Pastoral, Elegiac, and Dramatic Poets of Greece,' London, 1813, 8vo. In 1814 he published 'Orlando in Roncesvalles,' London, 8vo, a poem in ottava rima, founded on the 'Morgante Maggiore' of Luigi Pulci, and in 1820 a free translation in the same metre of the first and third cantos of Fortiguerra's 'Ricciardetto.' A collective edition of his 'Poems, Original and Translated,' appeared in 1838, London, 2 vols. 8vo, which includes, besides the before-mentioned pieces, a continuation of Beattie's 'Minstrel,' some translations from Dante, and other miscellanea. When past middle age he learned German, and shortly before his death published felicitous translations, partly reprinted from the 'New Monthly Magazine' for 1840, of 'The Minor Poems of Schiller of the Second and Third Periods,' London, 1844, 8vo.

Merivale was a friend of Byron, who warmly praised both his translations from the Greek and his 'Orlando in Roncesvalles' (see *English Bards and Scotch Reviewers*, 'And ye associate bards,' &c., Moore, *Life of Byron*, ed. 1847, p. 225; and Hodgson, *Memoir of the Rev. Francis Hodgson*, ii. 80). He was a frequent contributor to the 'Quarterly' and other reviews and periodicals. In 1837–8 he published in the 'Gentleman's Magazine' some valuable letters by Walter Moyle [q. v.] He made some collections for a history of Devonshire. Some of his letters to his friend the Rev. Joseph Hunter are preserved in Add. MS. 24871, ff. 145–60.

[Gent. Mag. 1844, pt. ii. p. 96; Lincoln's Inn Reg.; Athenæum, 1844, pp. 285, 407; Quarterly Review, October 1839; Moore's Diary, ed. Lord John Russell, 1854, vi. 320; Chancery Comm. Rep. 1826; London Gazette, 6 Dec. 1831; Brit. Mus. Cat.; Dublin Univ. Mag. 1840, pt. ii. p. 403; Blackwood's Mag. vols. xxxiii. xxxiv.; Transactions of the Devonshire Association, 1884 (art. by Dr. Charles Merivale).] J. M. R.

MERKE, THOMAS (*d.* 1409), bishop of Carlisle, has usually been called Merks, but this form is almost certainly an error. Undoubtedly so are the names Newmarket and Somastre sometimes given to him. The former originated with Bale, who, misled by a slight verbal similarity, confused Merke with Thomas of Newmarket, a Cambridge scholar who wrote on mathematics and rhetoric (Pits, p. 591; *Proceedings of Cambridge Antiquarian Soc.* vol. ii. pt. xiv. p. 18). 'Somastre' is a corruption of his later episcopal title. Merke was educated at Oxford, where he became doctor of divinity, and stood next to the chancellor among the delegates selected in November 1395 to convey to the king the submission of the university touching the rooting out of Lollardy enjoined earlier in that year (Wood, *Antiquities of University of Oxford*, i. 528 (Gutch); Kennett, *Third Letter*, pp. 6–7; Godwin, *De Præsulibus*, p. 766). He is described as a monk of Westminster when, about the beginning of 1397, he was thrust upon the chapter of Carlisle by the pope at the king's request (*ib.* p. 767; *Fœdera*, vii. 844, 848; Adam of Usk, p. 42). The temporalities were restored to him on 18 March (Godwin, *loc. cit.*) His appointment, which connects itself with the close relations between Richard and the abbot and monks of Westminster, was probably the reward of some service to the king; for in little more than a month, about the end of April, he was sent on a mission to the German princes with the Earls of Rutland and Nottingham (Kennett, pp. 34–5; *Fœdera*, vii. 858, viii. 1). Merke was present in the famous September parliament of 1397, was sent by Richard to order Archbishop Arundel not to appear therein, probably had some hand in the proceedings against Thomas, duke of Gloucester, and on 30 Sept. swore obedience on the relics with other prelates to the king (Adam of Usk, p. 9; *Rot. Parl.* iii. 355; *Annales Henrici IV*, p. 314; Stow, *Annals*, p. 321).

On 19 Oct. 1398 Merke was commissioned with the Earl of Salisbury to obtain payment of Queen Isabella's dowry (*Fœdera*, viii. 52). He is coupled by the Monk of Evesham (ed. Hearne, p. 168) and in two manuscript chronicles with Tydeman, bishop of Worcester, also a monk, as ill adviser and boon companion of Richard 'in potationibus et aliis non dicendis' (*Chronique de la Traison*, p. xlv; Hardyng, ed. Ellis, cxciii. 347). These charges do not appear in the 'Annales Ricardi' or in Walsingham. But the latter doubtless included him among the 'certi episcopi' who were the instruments of Richard's extortion. Like Richard and several of his courtiers, Merke sold his favour to the monastery of St. Albans (*Gesta Abbatum*, iii. 454), and there is reason to doubt whether he ever visited his diocese (Kennett, p. 33). He was one of the executors named in Richard's will, made 16 April 1399, on the eve of his journey to Ireland, whither the bishop accompanied him (Nichols, *Royal Wills*, p. 199; *Ann. Ricardi*, p. 250; *Fœdera*, viii. 78–9; Kennett, p. 37). Returning with Richard to Wales, on the news of the landing of Henry of Bolingbroke, Merke was one of the few who remained with him to the last. He is said by a French authority to have joined in advising him to go to Bordeaux, to have insisted at Conway that Northumberland should take an oath that Henry had no designs against Richard, and to have remonstrated against the latter's excessive grief at Flint (*Chronique de la Traison*, pp. 44, 49, 56; cf. Creton in *Archæologia*, xx. 110, 198, 214). According to the English account he was one of the eight for whose lives Richard stipulated when surrendering to Northumberland at Conway (*Ann. Ricardi*, p. 250). At Chester on 19 Aug. they were separated, and the bishop may have been kept in custody for a time (*Chronique de la Traison*, p. 60). Kennett (p. 42) thinks it unlikely that he entered London with Henry, as he would in that case have probably fallen a victim to the popular hatred, like John Slake. Possibly he was committed to the care of the abbot of St. Albans. But he was apparently present in parliament, sitting next to Henry, when Richard's renunciation of the crown was read on 30 Sept., and was summoned on that day to Henry's first parliament, which met on 6 Oct. (*Continuatio Eulogii*, iii. 383; *Archæologia*, xx. 388; *App. to Rep. on Dignity of a Peer*, pp. 766, 768). The bold protest against Henry's treatment of Richard, when all his other friends kept silence, which the contemporary 'Chronique de la Traison' (pp. 70–1) puts into the mouth of Bishop Merke, whom Henry is said to have thrown into prison in consequence, could only have been delivered in the October parliament, if at all. This famous speech passed through Hall and Holinshed into Shakespeare (*Richard II*, act iv. sc. 1). Sir John Hayward, in his 'History of Henry IV,' 1599, expanded it into a florid disquisition on the rights of kings, bristling with quotations from sacred and profane authors. He repeated Hall's assertion that Merke died soon after his condemnation for this speech, 'more by fear than sickness, as one desiring to die by Death's darte, rather than by the Temporal sworde' (p. 281, ed. 1642). In this shape it became a chief weapon in the armoury of the prerogative writers of the seventeenth century, and at the revolution a battle-field of the supporters and opponents of divine right. It was stripped of its embellishments, and rendered very questionable, by the whig researches of Bishop White Kennett [q. v.], in three 'Letters to the Bishop of Carlisle concerning one of his predecessors, Bishop Merks' (1713, 1716, 1717). The authenticity of the speech in its original form rests entirely upon the anti-Lancastrian and confused testimony of the 'Chronique de la Traison,' and it is not mentioned in the other French contemporary authority, the metrical chronicle of Creton, who indeed expressly states that on 30 Sept. not a voice was raised for Richard (*Archæologia*, xx. 99). It cannot be shown that Merke was imprisoned for any speech of his in parliament, and he certainly was not deprived of his bishopric on that account, although an error of Rymer's (*Fœdera*, viii. 106), antedating a document by a whole year, whose detection by Kennett has strangely escaped later historians, has hitherto lent some colour to the charge. He was, indeed, brought up from custody before parliament on 29 Oct., but it was in company with the lords appellant, and for his alleged share in the proceedings against Gloucester, against which charge he eloquently defended himself (*Ann. Hen. IV*, p. 314; cf. Wylie, i. 72). He had been for some time in charge of the abbot of St. Albans, for his protection against the people, and for the same reason, though acquitted, he went back to St. Albans for a time (*Ann. Hen. IV*, u.s.) As on Sunday, 19 Oct., he had performed his profession of obedience and fidelity to the Archbishop of York as his metropolitan, in the archbishop's chapel at Westminster, Kennett's conjecture that he had been committed to custody on the same day (20 Oct.) as the lords appellant may be correct (Kennett, p. 64; Le Neve, *Fasti*, ed. Hardy, p. 236, with incorrect date; Wylie, i. 72). That he chose this time to perform a long-delayed episcopal duty seems to show that he desired to make an appearance at least of submission to the new government. Bishop Stubbs infers that he had been consecrated at Rome (*Registrum Sacrum*). Recovering his liberty, Merke is said to have been present at the meeting on 17 Dec. in the rooms of the Abbot of Westminster, in which, according to the 'Chronique de la Traison' (p. 77), the plot to surprise the king at Windsor on 6 Jan. 1400 was arranged (cf. WAVRIN, 1399–1422, pp. 19, 20). According to Wylie (p. 98), who, however, gives no authority, he was with the conspirators at Cirencester. But this seems irreconcilable with his committal to the Tower on 10 Jan. 1400 (*Fœdera*, viii. 121), and we have a statement that he and Roger Walden, the late archbishop of Canterbury, were taken from the liberties of Westminster (*Chronique de la Traison*, p. 100).

On 28 Jan. the special justices for the trial of treasons and felonies in London and Middlesex were empowered to try any archbishop or bishop, notwithstanding the statute 18 Ed. III, c. 1, reserving such (unless by the king's special command) for other remedy (*Fœdera*, viii. 123; KENNETT, pp. 70 sqq.) The trial of the Bishop of Carlisle had begun on Tuesday, the 27th, according to the record quoted by Kennett (p. 71), and was adjourned to the Wednesday following, when the bishop, after his plea of episcopal privilege had been set aside, was found guilty by a common jury, but judgment was reserved, and he was sent back to the Tower (*ib.*; *Ann. Hen. IV*, p. 330; *Cont. Eulog.* iii. 387; WALSINGHAM, ii. 245; *Chronique de la Traison*, p. 101; ADAM OF USK, p. 42). On 23 June Merke was removed to the custody of the Abbot of Westminster until the king's further pleasure should be known (*Fœdera*, viii. 150). Between the two dates he had been deprived of his bishopric, custody of whose temporalities was granted on 18 Feb. to William Strickland (*Pat.* 1 Hen. IV, p. 5, m. 9). Henry had desired to have Merke degraded and handed over to the secular arm. But his trial not being canonical, Pope Boniface IX had hastened to 'accommodate matters to his own supremacy' by translating Merke to a titular eastern see, and filled up Carlisle by provision, without election by the chapter or consent of the king. He craftily provided Strickland, whose election by the chapter in 1396 he had quashed in favour of Reade, and who was now favoured both by the chapter and the king (KENNETT, p. 102; LE NEVE, iii. 236). The translation was in flat contradiction of his recent undertaking (20 Oct. 1399) not to have recourse to this device in such cases (KENNETT, p. 102). Henry on 15 March wrote him a very strong remonstrance (*Proceedings of Privy Council*, i. 115–117). He got no satisfaction in the matter of the translation, but did not acknowledge the appointment of Strickland as successor until he was elected by the chapter and confirmed by himself (KENNETT, p. 117). It was not until 15 Nov. that he gave Strickland restitution of the temporalities of Carlisle (*Pat.* 2 Hen. IV, p. 1, m. 13, misplaced by RYMER, viii. 106), and on 28 Nov. granted Merke a conditional pardon in consideration of his spiritual capacity (*Fœdera*, viii. 165). On 29 Jan. 1401 Merke surrendered himself at Westminster to the prison of the Marshalsea, and pleading his pardon of 28 Nov., and giving securities for good behaviour, was dismissed (KENNETT, p. 122). Merke had been translated 'ad ecclesiam de Samastone' (*Pat.* 2 Hen. IV, p. 2, m. 11). This see has been variously identified with Samos, Samos in Cephalonia, and Samothrace. But none of these conjectures can be right. Le Quien (*Oriens Christianus*, iii. 1383) takes it to be Salmasa, or Salmastrum, eight days' journey east of Nineveh. But the adjective Samastenus rather points, though not conclusively, to Samosata, and while there was a papal collector for Salmasa (*ib.*), in Samastone there was 'neither Christian clergy nor people.' Moved by the poverty into which Merke thereby fell, Henry, on 21 March 1401, allowed him to solicit benefices from the pope, bishoprics excepted, provided their annual value did not exceed one hundred marks (*Pat.* 2 Hen. IV, p. 2, m. 11; KENNETT, pp. 127–8). The pope, it would seem from a letter written by Merke from Oxford on 7 June 1401, gave him the prebend of Masham, the 'golden prebend' of York, but his claim was disputed (*Letters of Hen. IV*, Rolls Ser., i. 66; cf. FISHER, *Hist. of Masham*, pp. 322, 328–9). On 5 Nov. 1401 Henry gave him permission to accept further 'expectations' of benefices from the pope up to three hundred marks per annum, along with a full pardon (WYLIE, i. 109). It would almost appear, from a passage in Wadding's 'Annales Minorum' (ed. 1734, ix. 256), that Boniface on 6 Nov. 1402 translated Merke from Samastone to some other see, the name of which is not given, but which may be concealed in the 'Millatencus' of Adam of Usk (p. 42). The king himself, on 19 Nov. 1403, presented him to the vicarage of Sturminster Marshall, Dorset (WYLIE, i. 110; HUTCHINS, *Dorsetshire*, ii. 133), and the abbot and convent of Westminster to the rectory of Todenham in Gloucestershire on 13 Aug. 1404 (LE NEVE, iii. 237; KENNETT, p. 138). He acquired the confidence of Wykeham and Arundel, acting occasionally as deputy of the former, and being commissioned by the latter, on 18 Oct. 1405, to perform episcopal functions in the diocese of Winchester during its vacancy (LOWTH, *Life of Wykeham*, p. 247; KENNETT, p. 139). He was returned as a member of the lower house of convocation for the province of Canterbury early in 1406, and opened it as the archbishop's commissary on 10 May with a Latin sermon (*ib.* pp. 139, 140; cf. WILKINS, *Concilia*, iii. 272–273). Merke seems to have been one of the three Englishmen, 'viri non modice auctoritatis,' who were present at Lucca in May 1408, and took sides with the dissenting cardinals against the pope (THEODORIC OF NIEM, *Nemus*, vi. 31). He apparently signed as a witness the appeal of the cardinals at Pisa against Gregory (LABBE, *Concilia*, xi. 2, 2217; HARDOUIN, viii. 101).

Merke died during 1409 (HUTCHINS, ii. 133; GODWIN, p. 766; for the bible given by him to Robert Stonham, vicar of Oakham, see GIBBONS's *Lincoln Wills*, p. 139). He appears in a cowl in an illumination representing the consultation of Richard with his friends at Conway Castle in a manuscript of Creton in the British Museum (Harl. MS. 1319). This is reproduced in Strutt's 'Regal and Ecclesiastical Antiquities' (No. xxiv), and by Mr. Webb in 'Archæologia' (xx. 97).

[Annales Ricardi II et Henrici IV, Walsingham's Historia Anglicana, Eulogium, Wavrin, and Gesta Abbatum S. Albani, in the Rolls Ser.; Adam of Usk, ed. Maunde Thompson, for the Society of Literature; Chronique de la Traison, published by the English Historical Society; Creton in Archæologia, xx. 86–7; Rymer's Fœdera, original edit.; Acts and Proceedings of the Privy Council, ed. Harris Nicolas; Kalendars and Inventories (Record Comm.), ii. 26, 59, 81; Froissart, ed. Kervyn de Lettenhove, xvi. 330–7, 344, 357–9, 365; Pits, De Illustribus Scriptoribus Angliæ, Paris, 1619; Bale's Scriptores, cent. vii. No. 60, ed. Basel, 1559; Raleigh's Prerogative of Parliament, p. 45; Godwin, De Præsulibus Angliæ, ed. Richardson, 1743; Browne Willis's Cathedrals, i. 293, ed. 1742; Fuller's Worthies, Cambridgeshire, p. 153; Brady's Richard II, p. 366, and App. p. 132; Spelman's Concilia, ii. 655; Collier's Ecclesiastical Hist. i. 610; Sandford's Genealogical Hist. p. 268. Much the fullest and most accurate account of Merke is given by White Kennett in his Third Letter, who corrected errors which are repeated by subsequent writers down to Sir James Ramsay in Lancaster and York, 1892, i. 12; Wylie's Hist. of Henry IV; Pauli's Geschichte Englands, v. 637. Other authorities in text.]

J. T–T.

MERLAC, DANIEL OF (*fl.* 1170–1190), astronomer. [See MORLEY.]

MERLE or MORLEY, WILLIAM (*d.* 1347), meteorologist, son of William Merle, is said to have been a fellow of Merton College, Oxford (*Digby MS.* 176, f. 3), but his name does not appear on the extant lists of fellows. He was presented to the rectory of Driby, near Alford, Lincolnshire, by John Harsyk in 1331, was admitted thereto on 13 May in that year, and died in 1347. His connection with Oxford is supported by the fact that some of his observations were made there. Those contained in Digby MS. 176 were prepared for William Reed (*d.* 1385) [q. v.], bishop of Chichester, a former fellow of Merton, who presented this volume to his old college. Mr. Symons suggests that Merle was of French extraction, on the supposition that the name is French and not English. This conjecture seems needless; the modern form of the name may be Morley, as given by Tanner, and in any case Merle is not uncommon in thirteenth and fourteenth century records (cf. *Patent Rolls Edward I.*, sub anno 1283, and *Cal. Documents relating to Scotland*, iii. 257); in Digby MS. 147 the name is spelt Merlee, and in Digby MS. 97 Merla.

Merle wrote: 1. 'Temperies aeris Oxoniæ pro septennio scilicet a Januario MCCCXXXVII ad Januar. MCCCXLIV.' In Digby MS 176, ff. 4–8. This tract is perhaps the oldest systematic record of the weather, which is noted month by month, and in large part day by day. The last date is 8 Jan. 1344. Reference is made both to Lincolnshire and to Oxford. A photographic reproduction of the manuscript, with a translation, was published, under the supervision of Mr. G. J. Symons, in 1891, with the title, 'Consideraciones temperiei pro 7 Annis.' 2. 'De futura aeris intemperie:' incipit 'Hec sunt consideranda ad hoc.' Digby MS. 97, f. 128*b* and Digby MS. 176, f. 3 in the Bodleian Library. 3. 'De prognosticatione aeris. Digby MS. 147, ff. 125–37. A footnote states 'Expletum igitur est opus istud Exon. [? Oxon.] anno domini 1340 per magistrum Willielmum Merlee.'

[Tanner's Bibl. Brit.-Hib., p. 532; R. Plot in Philosophical Transactions, No. 169, 1685; Symons's Preface to the Consideraciones Temperiei; Athenæum, 28 Nov. 1891; Catalogue of Digby MSS.] C. L. K.

MERLIN AMBROSIUS, or MYRDDIN EMRYS, legendary enchanter and bard, is first to be definitely traced in the 'Historia Brittonum' ascribed to Nennius, a work which seems to date from the end of the eighth century (ZIMMER, *Nennius Vindicatus*). Nennius relates that the wise men had told Vortigern that he could not build his castle on Snowdon unless the foundations were sprinkled with the blood of a child that had no father. On a search being made a child whose mother swore that he had no father was by accident discovered at a place called 'Campus Elleti' (perhaps Maesaleg or Bassaleg in Monmouthshire). The child was brought before the king, and proved himself a match for the wise men. Vortigern inquired his name, and the boy answered, 'I am called Ambrosius.' But in response to a further inquiry he added, in manifest contradiction to the first description given of him, 'My father is one of the consuls of the Roman race.' Vortigern thereupon surrendered to him the city on the summit of Mount Heremus, in the province of Guenet (Snowdon in North Wales), and all the western part of Britain. The name Ambrosius is explained as being in the British tongue 'Embries Guletic,' meaning the King Ambrosius (NENNIUS, pp. 31–4).

Geoffrey of Monmouth appears to have perceived the incongruity in Nennius's account, but though he makes use of Welsh legends his main authority seems to be Nennius. Geoffrey first supplies the name Merlin, and represents the child playing with his companion Dabutius at Kaermodin or Caermarthen (of which Merlin or Myrddin is the eponymous hero). He is made to describe his mother as a daughter of the king of Demetia, dwelling with the nuns in the church of St. Peter. Merlin, 'qui et Ambrosius dicebatur,' is then brought before Vortigern, and foretells the king's death and the triumph of Aurelius Ambrosius. Aurelius, when anxious to erect a memorial of his triumph, is advised to consult Merlin. Merlin bids him send for the stones called 'Giants' Dance' out of Ireland, and accordingly the enchanter is despatched with Uther Pendragon [see under ARTHUR] to fetch them. By Merlin's arts the Irish are defeated and the Dance brought over to be set up at Stonehenge. After this Aurelius dies, and is succeeded by Uther Pendragon, who, with the aid of Merlin, is successful in a love-suit to Igern, and so becomes the father of Arthur (GEOFFREY OF MONMOUTH, *Hist. Brit.* vi. 17, viii. 19).

Giraldus Cambrensis, in the 'Itinerarium Cambriæ,' definitely distinguishes between Merlin Ambrosius and another later Merlin Celidonius or Silvester, or Myrddin Wyllt [q. v.] (*Opera*, vi. 133), but makes no addition to the story.

Geoffrey and Giraldus were no doubt familiar with the ancient national legends of Wales, but the extant references to Merlin in Welsh literature are very much later than Giraldus or Geoffrey. In the 'Triads' Merlin Ambrosius, who is distinguished from Myrddin Wyltt (*Myvyrian Archaiology*, pp. 65, 401), is described as the bard of Aurelius Ambrosius, and is named with Taliesin and Myrddin Wyllt as one of the three Christian bards of Britain. In the 'Triads' also figures the legend that Merlin went to sea in a vessel of glass with his nine scientific bards, and was never heard of again. Another Welsh legend, however, represents Merlin as confined with the thirteen treasures of Britain in a glass house in the island of Bardsey, where he lay in an enchanted sleep, from which he was to awake when the time came for the reappearance of Arthur (cf. RHYS, *Hibbert Lectures*, pp. 155–6). A Breton form, which was adopted in many mediæval romances, represents him as sleeping under the spell of Vivien in an enchanted bower in the forest of Broceliande.

Welsh tradition thus recognises two Merlins, Merlin Ambrosius, the bard of Aurelius Ambrosius, and Merlin Silvester, or Myrddin Wyllt, who lived some hundred years later, about 570, in the time of the Cumbrian chief Rhydderch Hael. Stephens, in his 'Literature of the Kymry,' argues that in reality there was but one person, pointing out that Merlin Ambrosius was but a boy when he appears before Vortigern, and that therefore he might well be identical in very old age with Myrddin Wyllt, who was in the service of Rhydderch Hael. Mr. Nash maintains the separation, arguing that Myrddin Wyllt is probably an actual person, and that Merlin Ambrosius was in the original form of the legend no other than Aurelius Ambrosius himself (he is called Guletic, or royal, and Vortigern gives him a province to rule). Mr. Nash would accordingly regard Merlin in his rôle of enchanter as a 'pure work of fiction woven in with the historical threads which belong to the epoch of the Saxon wars in Britain.' From this legendary Merlin the characteristics of prophet and magician were transferred to Myrddin Wyllt at some period previous to the time when Geoffrey wrote. Professor Rhys finds in Merlin or Myrddin Emrys 'an adumbration of a personage who was at once a king and warrior, a great magician and a prophet—in a word, a Zeus of Brythonic paganism.' M. Hersat de la Villemarqué, regarding the whole of the Merlin legends as relating to a single personage, is ready to accept Merlin as a Christian priest and the bard of Aurelius Ambrosius. This last theory, however, depends on giving the extant references in Welsh literature, and especially the 'Triads,' an antiquity and importance which they do not possess. In the legend of Merlin Ambrosius as it has come down to us there are certainly no historical incidents, and some such theory as that given by Mr. Nash appears to be the most acceptable (cf. *Cymmrodor*, xi. 47–9).

Whatever element of reality there may be

in the figure of Merlin would seem to be derived from the more genuine personality of Myrddin Wyllt. In the latter we appear to have preserved the tradition of a famous bard of the sixth century, to whom an air of mystery and romance has been imparted from confusion with the wholly legendary Merlin Ambrosius. The 'Vita Merlini,' which seems to be a genuine work of Geoffrey of Monmouth, is concerned only with the Caledonian Merlin, or Myrddin Wyllt, his connection with the fatal battle of Arderydd in 573, his subsequent insanity, sojourn in the forest, and vaticination. But though there is nothing in this poem which directly relates to the legend of Merlin Ambrosius, M. Gaston Paris is of opinion that its Merlin is intended to be the same with the one who spoke before Vortigern, and that the two Merlins are an invention of Giraldus Cambrensis (*Romania*, xii. 376; cf. *Vita Merlini*, p. 39, ed. Michel). Another suggestion is that the original of Vivien is to be found in the 'Hwimleian or Chwifleian (the female companion) of Merlinus Silvestris' (PRICE, *Literary Remains*, i. 144).

Professor Rhys suggests that the name Merlin represents a form Moridûnjos, meaning 'him of moridunum or the sea-fort,' thus connecting it with Moridunum or Caermarthen (*Hibbert Lectures*, p. 160). Mr. Nash somewhat improbably interprets Merlin in its original form as meaning the son of a nun (or virgin)—Mableian, Mac-leian, Mab-merchleian, which was latinised as Merlinus, Mellinus, Merclinus. Meller is the form applied to the Cumbrian bard in the 'Scotichronicon,' Merlin that of the French romances. In modern Welsh we have Myrddin or Merddin, and in Breton Marzin. This last form M. de la Villemarqué identifies with Marsus the son of Circe, from whom descended, according to fable, a race of magicians. Thus Marzin would signify a wizard, and more particularly one who sprang from the intercourse of a supernatural father with a Christian virgin. This theory does not, however, seem to rest on any sure foundation.

In various forms the Merlin legend is common to Southern Scotland and Cumbria, Wales, Cornwall, and Brittany. Attempts have been made to identify it specially with Scotland (cf. 'The Scottish Origin of the Merlin Myth,' in the *Scottish Review*, No. 40). The legends concerning Myrddin Wyllt are specially connected with Cumbria and Scotland, that of Merlin Ambrosius with Wales. In Breton legend and poetry Marzin appears more simply as a magician of supernatural, if not of diabolic, powers. A fanciful theory has endeavoured to find an historical basis for Merlin and his friend Blaise in Germanus and his companion Lupus (SURTEES, *Merlin and Arthur*).

Geoffrey of Monmouth says that he had translated the prophecies of Merlin out of the original Welsh into Latin by request of Alexander, bishop of Lincoln. This was before 1136, for Ordericus Vitalis, writing about that date, quotes the prophecies (*Hist. Eccl.* xii. 47). Afterwards this work was embodied in the 'Historia Regum Britanniæ' as book vii. of that work. It is to it that Giraldus Cambrensis no doubt alludes when he says that the prophecies of Merlin Ambrosius had long since been published (*Opera*, v. 401). Before 1160 John of Cornwall [q. v.] translated from Cornish into Latin hexameters, at the request of Robert of Warelwast, bishop of Exeter, a 'Merlini Prophetia de septem regibus,' and published it, with an exposition. This poem, which relates to the Norman kings, is printed in the 'Spicilegium Vaticanum' of Carl Greith (pp. 92–106), and in Villemarqué's 'Myrdhin' (pp. 417–22; cf. also *Myrdhin*, pp. 261–76). About 1180 Alanus de Insulis composed a commentary on the 'Prophecy' published by Geoffrey. This treatise was printed at Frankfort 1603, 1608, and 1649. Geoffrey's 'Prophecy' is in part reproduced by Wace and Layamon. William of Newburgh, however, comments on the publication of Merlin's prophecies by Geoffrey as a daring falsehood (i. 4–6, Engl. Hist. Soc.) Nevertheless, the Merlin legend as given by Geoffrey is reproduced by sober historians, from Matthew Paris to Higden. In 1208 appeared the 'Merlínus Spá' of Gunnlang Leifsson, an Icelandic version of the prophecy, which is printed in the 'Annales' of the Society of Northern Antiquaries,' Copenhagen, 1849. During the succeeding three centuries there appeared various prophecies under the name of Merlin. Some of these are specifically attributed to Merlin Silvester, but it is no doubt to the legendary fame of Merlin Ambrosius that they owe their alleged author. Among these prophecies may be mentioned the French work of Richard of Ireland, composed about 1250 for Frederick II (VILLEMARQUÉ, *Myrdhin*, pp. 343–64). Another common prophecy, which appears both in French and English versions, is on the six kings after John (cf. *MS. Univ. Libr. Cambr.* Gg. I. i., *Cotton. MSS.* Julius A. v., and Galba E. ix., and for more exact particulars WARD, *Catalogue of Romances*, i. 293–324). There is also a collection of Yorkist prophecies of Merlin in Cotton. MS. Vesp. E. iv. Finally may be noticed Thomas Heywood's 'Life of Merlin, surnamed Ambrosius. His

Prophecies and Predictions interpreted, and their truth made good by our English Annalls. Being a Chronographical History of all the Kings and Memorable Passages of this Kingdome from Brute to the reigne of our Royall Sovereigne King Charles,' London, 1641. The prophecies also form part of the regular romances of Merlin, and the version of Richard of Ireland is indeed a sort of continuation of the romance.

The romance of Merlin owes its origin to Robert de Borron, who founded his work on Geoffrey of Monmouth. Robert's knowledge was, however, probably oral only, and he adds much of his own composition. His romance ends with the coronation of Arthur, and the later portion probably dates from 1230–50. The great French prose romance which was thus created became very popular; one Messer Zorzi translated it into Italian in 1379, and this version was printed at Venice in 1480, and Florence in 1495; as also at Venice many times in the next century and in 1884. In Spain we have 'El baladro del Sabio Merlin cō suas profecias,' Burgos, 1498, and 'Merlin y demanda del Santo Graal,' Seville, 1500. There was also a German version about 1478, and as it would seem probable a Provençal one. The French romance was printed by Antoine Verard at Paris in 1498 with the prophecies which form the third volume of the romance. Numerous editions appeared during the next thirty years (Graesse, *Trêsor de Livres*, iv. 498). A French version of the romance was edited by M. Gaston Paris for the Société des Anciens Textes Français, 1886. An English version has been published by the Early English Text Society, and Sir Thomas Malory [q. v.] gave the 'Story of Merlin' a permanent place in English literature by borrowing much from Borron's romance and the old prophecies of Merlin for his 'Morte d'Arthur.' Mention may also be made of 'A lytel treatys of the Byrth and Prophecye of Merlin,' printed by Wynkyn de Worde in 1510.

[Nennius's Historia Britonum (Engl. Hist. Soc.); Geoffrey of Monmouth's Historia Regum Britanniæ; Myvyrian Archaiology; Stephens's Literature of the Kymry; Hersat de la Villemarqué's Myrdhin, ou l'Enchanteur Merlin, son histoire, ses œuvres, son influence, and Romans de la Table Ronde; W. D. Nash's Merlin the Enchanter and Merlin the Bard (Early English Text Society), vol. x.; Rhys's Arthurian Legend, and Hibbert Lectures; San Marte's (A. Schulz) Die Sagen von Merlin mit altwälschen, bretagnischen, schottischen und lateinischen Gedichten und Prophezeiungen Merlins; Skene's Four Ancient Books of Wales; Ward's Catalogue of Romances in the British Museum; Michel's Preface to Vita Merlini; M. G. Paris's Preface to Huth Merlin; Romania, xii. 374–6; Revue des questions historiques, v. 559–68, 'Merlin est-il un personnage réel?' by M. D'Arbois de Jubainville; on editions of the Vita Merlini and prophecies, see also art. Geoffrey of Monmouth. Leland's Commentarii de Scriptoribus, pp. 42–8, has a long life of Merlin; see also Tanner's Bibl. Brit.-Hib. pp. 523–5, and Notes and Queries, 8th ser. v. 285.] C. L. K.

MERRET or **MERRETT, CHRISTOPHER** (1614–1695), physician and miscellaneous writer, son of Christopher Merret, was born at Winchcomb, Gloucestershire, on 16 Feb. 1614. In 1631 he was admitted a student of Gloucester Hall, Oxford, and removed to Oriel College about 1633. He graduated B.A. in January 1635, and then, returning to Gloucester Hall, devoted himself to medicine, proceeding M.B. in June 1636, and M.D. in January 1643. Having settled in London, he became a fellow of the Royal College of Physicians in 1651, and in 1654 Gulstonian lecturer. In the same year he was nominated by his friend Dr. William Harvey [q. v.] the first keeper of the library and museum which Harvey had given to the college, and in February of that year Merret had a lease of the college house in Amen Corner at 20*l.* a year, but the rent was remitted in the following June 'in recompense for his pains for looking to the new library.' In his deed of gift in 1656 Harvey allows 20*l.* a year for a librarian. Merret was censor of the college seven times between 1657 and 1670, and is stated by Wood to have come 'into considerable practice.'

William How's 'Phytologia' being out of print, Merret was requested to prepare a book to replace it. Detained in London by his profession, he employed Thomas Willisel [q. v.] for five summers to collect plants for him, and purchased eight hundred figures, which Thomas Johnson [q. v.] had had engraved. These plates are in the British Museum Library (press-mark 441. i. 6), without title-page, but catalogued as 'Plants: a Collection of Figures, with MS. notes by C. Merrett. London, 1670, fol.;' and a note in the book by 'Robert Gray, M.D.,' says that the figures were executed for a new herbal which Johnson had intended to issue. Merret's work was entitled 'Pinax Rerum Naturalium Britannicarum, continens Vegetabilia, Animalia, et Fossilia,' a duodecimo. It was apparently printed in 1666; but the first impression was probably destroyed, either at the printer's or in his own house, in the great fire. Most copies are dated 1667. The zoological and mineralogical parts of this work are little more than lists of names, while the botanical part, though containing over fourteen hundred species, arranged alphabetically, with synonyms from Gerard and Parkinson, and an attempted classification, is so uncritical that it was at once superseded by John Ray's 'Catalogus' and synopses.

During the plague Merret retired into the country, and in his absence the college was broken into and its treasure-chest was emptied. Shortly afterwards the house and the bulk of the library was destroyed in the great fire, and the college thereupon resigned their lease of the Amen Corner site to the dean and chapter of St. Paul's for 550*l.*, giving Merret 50*l.* as compensation, and, having lost their library, thought to dispense with his services. Merret, however, argued that his appointment was for life, and in 1680 applied to the king's bench for a mandamus to the college for his reinstatement. In this he was defeated, and ultimately, in 1681, he was expelled by the college from his fellowship, nominally for non-attendance.

'He died at his house, near the chapel in Hatton Garden . . . 19 August, 1695, and was buried twelve feet deep in the church of St. Andrew's, Holborne' (Wood). Merret was one of the earliest members of the Royal Society, and contributed several papers, chiefly on vegetable physiology, to the 'Philosophical Transactions.' His plants are preserved in the Sloane Herbarium, and his name is commemorated by the genus *Merrettia* of Gray, among the unicellular algæ.

Besides the 'Pinax,' Merret's chief works were: 1. 'Catalogus Librorum, Instrumentorum, . . . in Museo Harveiano,' 4to, 1660. 2. 'A Collection of Acts of Parliament, Charters, Trials at Law, and Judges' Opinions, concerning Grants to the College of Physicians, . . . made by Christopher Merrett, Fellow and Censor,' 4to, 1660. 3. 'The Art of Glass . . . translated into English,' 8vo, 1662, which was privately reprinted in folio at Middle Hill, Worcestershire, in 1826, and edited by Sir T. Phillipps. 4. 'An Account of Freezing made in December and January, 1662' (but containing observations made in 1664, 'there being no frosts in England in 1663'), annexed to Robert Boyle's 'New Experiments . . . touching Cold,' 8vo, 1665, pp. 1–54; and 2nd edit., 4to, 1683, pp. 1–20. 5. 'Antonio Neri, De Arte Vitriariâ libri septem et in eosdem . . . Observationes et Nota,' 12mo, Amsterdam, 1668, his additions equalling the original work in bulk. 6. 'A Short View of the Frauds and Abuses committed by Apothecaries, and of the only Remedy thereof by Physicians making their own Medicines,' 4to, 1669; 2nd edit. 1670. 7. 'Self-conviction, or an Enumeration of the Absurdities and Railings against the College and Physicians in general,' 4to, 1670. 8. 'The Accomplisht Physician, the Honest Apothecary, and the Skilful Chyrurgeon detecting their necessary connexion and dependence on each other. Withall a Discovery of the Quacking Empirick, the Prescribing Surgeon, and the Practising Apothecary,' 4to, 1670. 9. 'Some Observations concerning the Ordering of Urines,' 8vo, 1682.

[Wood's Athenæ Oxon. ed. Bliss, iv. 430–2; Pulteney's Sketches of the Progress of Botany, i. 290–7; Munk's Coll. of Phys. i. 258.]

G. S. B.

MERREY, WALTER (1723–1799), numismatist, of Castle Gate, Nottingham, combined great knowledge of coins and medals with the practical experience of a manufacturer. Impressed with the evils which the scarcity of silver and the circulation of a base copper coinage brought upon the working classes, he signed an association with a number of masters not to offer any man more than 6*d.* worth of copper. In 1789 he published 'Remarks on the Coinage of England, from the Earliest to the Present Times . . . to which is added an Appendix containing Observations upon the Ancient Roman Coinage, and a Description of some Medals and Coins found near Nottingham,' Nottingham, 8vo; 2nd edit. 1794. In this work he attributes the scarcity of silver to the over-valuation of gold, in consequence of which, he alleges, silver was exported. He proposes, therefore, the reduction of the guinea to 20*s.* 6*d.* To illustrate his doctrines he gives an exhaustive sketch of the history of English coinage, in which he shows a wide acquaintance with the works of early writers on currency.

Merrey had a large and valuable collection of coins and medals. He died at Nottingham on 9 Aug. 1799.

[Gent. Mag. 1789 pt. ii. p. 728, 1799 pt. ii. p. 815; Monthly Review, 1791, iv. 234; Bailey's Annals of Nottinghamshire, iv. 175.]

W. A. S. H.

MERRICK, JAMES (1720–1769), poet and scholar, born on 8 Jan. 1719–20, was the second son of John Merrick, M.D., of St. Lawrence, Reading, who died 5 April 1757, aged 87, by his wife Elizabeth, daughter of Richard Lybbe of Hardwick, Oxfordshire, who died 3 April 1764. Both were buried in Caversham Church, Oxfordshire, with many members of their family, who were commemorated in a long Latin inscription by their son James. He was educated at the Reading school, but through some difference between the aldermen and burgesses of the town was not elected, though the head boy, for a scholarship on Sir Thomas White's foundation at St. John's College, Oxford. On 5 July 1736, when aged 16, he was admitted as 'commoner of the third order' at Trinity College, Oxford, and was admitted scholar on 6 June 1737. He graduated B.A. 1739, M.A. 1742, and became probationer-fellow 21 May 1744, full fellow 21 May 1745. Though he was ordained in the English church, and preached occasionally between 1747 and 1749, he was prevented by ill-health from accepting any parochial duty. For some time he dwelt in college, where Lord North and Lord Dartmouth were among his pupils, and towards the close of his life he seems to have lived at Reading. After a long and painful illness he died on 5 Jan. 1769, and was buried near his relatives in Caversham Church. He bequeathed many scarce and valuable books to John Loveday [q. v.] of Williamscote, near Banbury, and 400*l.* to Trinity College. His arms are on the panelling in the college hall.

Merrick wrote: 1. 'The Messiah, a Divine Essay,' Reading, 1734; a schoolboy production. 2. 'The Destruction of Troy, being the sequel of the Iliad, translated from the Greek of Tryphiodorus, with Notes,' Oxford, 1739. Gilbert Wakefield called this translation 'excellent' (*Correspondence with Fox*, p. 139). 3. 'Tryphiodori Ilii excidium. Lacunas aliquot e codice manuscripto explevit et suas annotationes adjecit J. Merrick,' 1741. When this work was edited by F. A. Wernicke at Leipzig in 1819, the annotations of Merrick were reproduced, and it was stated in the preface that a manuscript in the royal library at Berlin, which was believed to be by Merrick, contained some additional notes. These were added as an addendum, pp. 495–8. 4. 'Dissertation on Proverbs, chap. ix. vv. 1–6,' 1744. 5. 'Prayers for a time of Earthquakes and Violent Floods,' 1756. 6. 'An Encouragement to a Good Life,' addressed to some soldiers at Reading, 1759. Granger, in his 'Biographical History,' when treating of John Rawlet, says that nearly ten thousand copies of his tract of the 'Christian Monitor' were distributed by Merrick, chiefly among the soldiers at Reading. 7. 'Poems on Sacred Subjects,' 1763. 8. 'Annotations, Critical and Grammatical, on chap. i. vv. 1–14 of St. John's Gospel, with a Discourse on Studying the Greek Language,' 1764. This was followed by—9. 'Second Part of Annotations on St. John's Gospel, to end of third chapter,' 1767. Merrick's notes on the whole of this gospel passed on his death to Dr. Loveday. 10. 'A Letter to Mr. Joseph Warton, chiefly on the Composition of Greek Indexes,' dated Reading, 11 Oct. 1764. This advocated the compilation and amalgamation of indexes to the principal Greek authors. Twenty-three were finished, others were in progress. Further letters by Merrick to Warton are in Wooll's 'Life of Warton,' pp. 310–12, 326–8. The three indexes by Robert Robinson of Reading to Longinus, Eunapius, and Hierocles, published at Oxford in 1772, and the five indexes in William Etwall's edition of 'Three Dialogues of Plato,' 1771, were compiled on his rules. 11. 'The Psalms Translated or Paraphrased in English Verse,' Reading, 1765. Bishop Lowth characterised this version as 'an admirable work, distinguished by many splendid marks of learning, art, and genius,' but it was justly condemned by Mason in 'Essays on English Church Music,' 1795, pp. 178 et seq., for diffuseness and laxity of rendering. It was often reprinted in London, and selections were published at Halifax (1798) and Ipswich (1815). Several editions, 'divided into stanzas and adapted for devotion,' were published by the Rev. W. D. Tattersall, who also issued in a very expensive form, in 1794, the first volume of an edition 'with new music.' Sixteen psalms from Merrick's version were set to music in 1775 by William Hayes, for use in Magdalen College Chapel, Oxford, a new edition of which, arranged by W. Cross, came out in 1810; and a second set of the same number was musically arranged by Philip Hayes for the same chapel (Bloxam, *Magd. Coll. Reg.* ii. 218, 224). Eighteen of his psalms and three pieces from his volume of 'Poems on Sacred Subjects' are given by Julian as still included in modern hymn-books (*Hymnology*, pp. 725–6). 12. 'Annotations on the Psalms,' 1768. This embodied the comments of Bishop Lowth and of an anonymous writer, presumed to be Archbishop Secker. The latter's remarks on Dr. Sharpe's arguments with respect to psalm cx. produced 'A Letter to the Bishop of Oxford from the Master of the Temple' [i.e. Rev. Gregory Sharpe], 1769. 13. 'Manual of Prayers for Common Occasions,' 1768, the ninth edition of which appeared in 1805; and it was reprinted so lately as 1836. It was also translated into Welsh.

Merrick contributed to the verses which were issued by the university of Oxford on the accession of George III (1761), his marriage (1761), and the birth of his heir (1762), and many poems by him are in the collections of Dodsley, ed. 1766, iv. 173–87, v

143-6, 213-25, vi. 295; Pearch, i. 142-53; Bell's 'Fugitive Poetry,' xii. 52-6, xviii. 158-62; and in Dodsley's 'Museum,' ii. 182-8. Some curious observations by him on a fragment ascribed to Longinus are published by Nathaniel Lardner in the 'Collection of Testimonies of Ancient Heathens on the Truth of the Christian Religion' (*Works*, ed. 1838, vi. 380-1), and John Taylor, LL.D., in the preface to 'Marmor Sandvicense,' 1743, confesses his obligations to him. Many letters to him from Dr. John Ward of Gresham College, London, and one from Bernard de Montfaucon, are in Brit. Mus. Addit. MS. 6226, and some verses by him, taken from a note-book of Dr. Ward (Addit. MS. 6230), are printed in 'Notes and Queries,' 2nd ser. iv. 291. Four English lines of his composition were placed over the debtors' gate of the old county gaol in Castle Street, Reading, and he left behind him in manuscript an account of all the Greek authors, finished to Hypsicles. His contemporaries, Dr. Thomas Hunt, Bishop Lowth, and Thomas Warton, unite in praising his learning and his good feeling. So early in his life as April 1739 he was corresponding on classical subjects with Hermann Samuel Reimar, the Dutch philologist, and there are many references to his 'Notes on Tryphiodorus' in Alberti's last volume of 'Hesychius.' To English readers Merrick is now best known by his bright little poem of 'The Chameleon.'

[Gent. Mag. 1769, p. 54; Coates's Reading, pp. 313, 319, 436-41; Foster's Alumni Oxon.; the Rev. J. Granger's Letters, pp. 17, 393; Doddridge's Letters, ed. 1790, pp. 339, 342, 345; Holland's Psalmists, pp. 209-13; information from the Rev. H. E. D. Blakiston of Trinity College, Oxford.] W. P. C.

MERRICK, RICE (*d.* 1587), historian of Glamorgan, son of Meiric ap Howell of Cottrell in Glamorganshire, resided at that place, being part owner of the manor of St. Nicholas. He was appointed clerk of the peace for the county of Glamorgan by William Herbert, first earl of Pembroke (and subsequently by Henry, the second earl), and held the office until his death on 1 March 1586-7. He was buried in the south aisle of Cowbridge Church, where an inscribed stone was placed over his grave, and a mural tablet bearing his shield was set up close by (these were transcribed by Dineley; see BEAUFORT, *Progress*, ed. 1888, p. 346, and cf. *Arch. Cambr.* 5th ser. vii. 321-322).

Merrick was the author of a small history of Glamorgan (in English), called 'Morganiæ Archaiographia,' of which the only known copy, transcribed between 1660 and 1680, is preserved at Queen's College, Oxford. It was privately printed by Sir Thomas Phillipps at Middlehill in 1825 (fol.), and reproduced, with notes by J. A. Corbett of Cardiff, in 1887 (London, 4to). It contains valuable information about the different methods of administration in the Welsh and English portions of the county, as well as accounts of the ownership and tenure of land. A letter addressed by Merrick to Sir Edward Stradling, and dated from St. Nicholas, 18 Dec. 1574, is printed in the 'Stradling Correspondence,' ed. Traherne, pp. 167-8.

[Merrick's pedigree is given in Arch. Cambr. 3rd ser. viii. 111, 112; cf. also Clark's Genealogies of Glamorgan; Morganiæ Archaiographia, ed. 1887, Introduction, and pp. 43 and 115.] D. LL. T.

MERRIFIELD, CHARLES WATKINS (1827-1884), mathematician, son of John Merrifield of Tavistock, Devonshire, was born in London (or according to some accounts at Brighton) on 20 Oct. 1827. After receiving a good general education he entered the Education Department in 1847 at Whitehall, and was subsequently appointed an examiner. Although called to the bar in January 1851, he did not practise. All his leisure he devoted to mathematics and hydraulics, and especially to naval architecture. In 1858 he published a paper 'On the Geometry of the Elliptic Equation,' which disclosed remarkable aptitude. Important papers on the calculation of elliptic functions followed, and led to his election on 4 June 1863 as fellow of the Royal Society. On 19 March 1866 he was elected member of the London Mathematical Society, became member of the council on 10 Nov. 1870, vice-president 1876-8, president 1878-80, and treasurer until his resignation on 14 Dec. 1882. On the establishment in 1867 of the Royal School of Naval Architecture and Marine Engineering at South Kensington, Merrifield became its first vice-principal, succeeding shortly afterwards to the post of principal. This office he held until 1873, when, on the transference of the school to Greenwich, he returned to the Education Office. From 1864 to 1875 Merrifield was member and secretary of the Royal Institution of Naval Architects, receiving a handsome testimonial on his retirement. He was also a member of the Association for Improvement of Geometrical Teaching, and he sat on many committees of the British Association, being president of Section G at the Brighton meeting of 1875 and at the Glasgow meeting of 1876. He served on various royal commissions, including one on the unseaworthiness of ships in 1869, frequently acted as assessor in the wreck commissioner's court, and was superintendent of the naval museum at South Kensington. After two attacks of paralysis in April 1882 and October 1883 respectively, he died at 45 Church Road, Hove, Brighton, on 1 Jan. 1884, aged 56. Merrifield married Elizabeth Ellen, daughter of John Nicholls of Trekenning, St. Colomb; she died on 23 March 1869 at 23 Scarsdale Villas, South Kensington.

Merrifield's works are: 1. 'Miscellaneous Memoirs on Pure Mathematics,' London, 1861, 8vo. 2. 'A Catalogue of a Collection of Models of Ruled Surfaces,' London, 1872, 8vo. 3. 'Technical Arithmetic,' London, 1872, 8vo. He contributed more than a hundred papers to the 'Transactions of the Institution of Naval Architects,' and numerous others to the 'Philosophical Transactions,' the 'Assurance Magazine,' the 'British Association Reports,' the 'School of Naval Architects Annual,' to the 'Proceedings of the London Mathematical Society,' and various other periodicals. Twenty-eight of his papers are enumerated in the Royal Society's 'Catalogue of Scientific Papers.' Some of his papers on 'the difficult and scientifically interesting subject of sea-waves' were translated into Italian for the 'Revista Marittima,' in which they appear with a footnote bearing testimony to the author's 'extensive knowledge and excellence of style.' He also edited for many years Longman's 'Text-books of Science' series, and on 16 Aug. 1866 contributed a paper to the 'Pall Mall Gazette' on 'The Distress in Cornwall.'

[Works in Brit. Mus. Libr.; Times, 4 Jan. 1884; Athenæum, 5 Jan. 1884; Nature, 17 Jan. 1884 (by J. W. L. Glaisher); Annual Register, 1884, ii. 112; Boase and Courtney's Bibl. Cornub.; Boase's Collectanea Cornub.; Proc. Royal Soc. vol. xxxvi.; Philosophical Trans. passim; Proc. Instit. Naval Architects, vols. v–xxi.; Cat. Scientific Papers, 1800–63 and 1864–73; Proc. London Math. Soc. vols. ii–xii. and vol. xv. App. pp. 281–3.] A. F. P.

MERRIMAN, BRIAN (1757–1808), Irish poet, was born in the parish of Clondagad, barony of Clonderlaw, co. Clare, where his father was a farmer. He became a schoolmaster at Kilclerin in the parish of Feakle, co. Clare, a region so wild that up to 1823 it had no road practicable for any kind of wheeled vehicle. He occasionally acted as resident tutor in the houses of the neighbouring gentry. In 1780 he wrote a poem of two thousand lines, entitled, 'Cuirt an mheadhoin oidhche' ('The Midnight Court'), of which numerous copies exist. That in the British Museum (Egerton 111) is an abridged version of 1024 lines. The poet is walking by the Graney river and falls asleep. Carried off to a fairy assembly, he is arraigned as responsible for the evil state of Ireland. A young woman gives evidence, and denounces the men of Ireland. Brian is convicted as their representative, and is about to be flogged when he awakes. There is sympathetic description of nature, the dialogue contains witty passages, and the versification is smooth. The poem became popular, and circulated in manuscript in Clare and Limerick. It was printed in 1800 as 'Mediæ noctis consilium,' with a curious symbolical frontispiece. A second edition was published in Dublin in 1893, and L. C. Stern printed a text with notes and glossary in 'Zeitschrift für Celtische Philologie,' vol. v. Merriman, who was a good fiddler, died in Limerick in 1808. He is sometimes called MacGillameidhre in manuscripts, but those who spoke Irish only called him Merriman; his true patronymic was probably MacConmara.

[Egerton MS. 111, art. 149, in Brit. Mus., S. H. O'Grady's Cat. of Irish MSS. in Brit. Mus. p. 493; E. O'Reilly in Transactions of Iberno-Celtic Society, Dublin, 1820; J. O. Daly's Pious Miscellany, Dublin, 1868; Poets and Poetry of Munster, 2nd ser. Dublin, 1860.] N. M.

MERRIMAN, NATHANIEL JAMES (1810–1882), bishop of Grahamstown, South Africa, born in 1810, was third son of Thomas Merriman of Marlborough, Wiltshire. His family was of Lancashire origin. Educated at Winchester and Brasenose College, Oxford, where he was Hulme exhibitioner, and graduating B.A. with second-class honours *in literis humanioribus* in 1831 (M.A. 1834), he was ordained deacon in 1832, priest 1833, and became perpetual curate of Over Darwen in Lancashire. In 1841 he moved to the vicarage of Street in Somerset.

In 1848 Merriman accepted an offer of the archdeaconry of Grahamstown made him by Robert Gray [q. v.], bishop of Capetown. At the end of the year he was in Africa; at the beginning of 1849 he had started on his first visitation, often walking long distances on foot. 'He is a very remarkable man,' wrote the bishop in this year; 'his self-denial and energy both of body and mind are greater than in any other man I have ever met with . . . the record of his life for the past year would astonish any one.' In 1850 he offered to undertake a mission to the Kaffirs, in whom he took great interest; and the success of mission work among the natives was largely due to his exertions.

In 1863, at the trial of Bishop Colenso [q. v.], Merriman, as proxy for his clergy, was one of the accusers. When the see of Grahamstown was established out of Capetown (1853), he had declined the bishopric, but on 5 Dec. 1871 he was consecrated the third bishop of the diocese. He was also dean of Capetown. In 1880 he excommunicated Dean Williams of Grahamstown on account of views in sympathy with those of Colenso; yet in the same year he highly praised the latter for his championship of the Zulus (Letter to Aborigines' Protection Society).

His death, on 16 Aug. 1882, was the result of a carriage accident. He married in 1836 Miss Potter, and left a large family; three of his sons were in the service of the Cape government at the time of his death.

He was the author of some lectures on Shakespeare (Grahamstown, 1857–8) and of 'The Kafir, the Hottentot, and the Frontier Farmer,' London, 1854, and 'The Bishop's Ride through Independent Kaffraria to Natal and back,' 1872.

[Cape Argus, 18 Aug. 1882; Crockford's Clerical Directory; Gray's Life of Bishop Gray, passim; Times, 18 Aug. 1882.] C. A. H.

MERRIMAN, SAMUEL, M.D. (1731–1818), physician, born on 29 Dec. 1731 at Marlborough, Wiltshire, was third son of Nathaniel Merriman, grocer there, by his wife Elizabeth Hawkes. Being intended for the medical profession he was sent to Edinburgh in 1748, and graduated there as M.D. in 1753, his thesis 'De Conceptu,' 8vo, Edinburgh, 1753, being of so much value that it was reprinted by William Smellie in the second volume of his 'Thesaurus Medicus' (1779). Merriman first settled as a physician in Bristol, and afterwards removed to Andover, Hampshire; but coming to London in April 1757, he commenced practice in Queen Street, Mayfair, as an apothecary or general practitioner, in partnership with Oakley Halford, who was about to retire. He remained an apothecary for about twenty years, when he acted on his diploma, and practised only as a physician, finally retiring in 1812. His speciality was midwifery. The number of labours which he attended amounted to rather more than ten thousand; in one year alone he attended 362. His leisure was devoted to literature and biblical studies.

Merriman died at his son-in-law's house, 26 Half Moon Street, on 17 Aug. 1818. In 1753 he married one of the daughters and coheiresses of William Dance, surgeon, of Marlborough, and by her, who died in 1780, he had fourteen children; of these one alone, Ann, wife of his nephew Samuel Merriman [q. v.], survived him.

There is an excellent miniature of him painted by Richmond and engraved by Corner.

[Information from John J. Merriman, esq.; Gent. Mag. 1818, pt. ii. p. 180; Lancet, 30 Nov. 1850, p. 610.] G. G.

MERRIMAN, SAMUEL, M.D. (1771–1852), physician, born on 25 Oct. 1771 at Marlborough, Wiltshire, was son of Benjamin (1722–1781), who was eldest son of Nathaniel Merriman of the same place. Samuel's great-grandfather, another Nathaniel, was youngest son of John Merriman (1618–1670), a captain in the army of Cromwell (Waylen, *Hist. of Marlborough*; Rushworth, *Hist. Coll.* vii. 1351; Grove, *Antiquities of Carisbrook Castle*, 1 Dec. 1648; Whitelocke, *Memorials*). His mother, who was his father's second wife, was Mary, eldest daughter of William Hawkes of Marlborough, and niece to Sir Michael Foster [q. v.] the judge. The father Benjamin had a large brewery in Marlborough. He was a man of scientific pursuits, and the author of political and other essays, some of which were inserted in the 'Gentleman's Magazine.' He likewise received medals from the Society of Arts and the Bath Agricultural Society for inventing various machines. Samuel was sent to Marlborough free school, of which in 1783 he was head-boy. In 1784 he arrived in London, and studied medicine under his uncle, Dr. Samuel Merriman [q. v.] After hearing the lectures of Baillie and Cruikshank at the Anatomical Theatre in Great Windmill Street he attended in 1795 the midwifery lectures of Dr. Thynne and the Westminster Lying-in Hospital, but his clinical knowledge of disease was principally obtained by seeing the numerous patients of his cousin William (1766–1800), son of the elder Samuel Merriman [q. v.] In 1807, having become a member of the Society of Apothecaries, he entered into partnership with Mr. Peregrine, to whom he soon resigned the general practice, limiting himself to midwifery alone. In 1808 he was appointed physician-accoucheur to the Westminster General Dispensary, having previously received the honorary degree of M.D. from Marischal College, Aberdeen, for which he was specially examined in London by Dr. Vaughan (afterwards Sir Henry Halford [q. v.]). He resigned the office in 1815, and was appointed consulting physician-accoucheur and subsequently vice-president of the charity. On 17 Aug. 1809 he was elected to the like office at the Middlesex Hospital, where in 1810 he commenced his annual course of lectures on midwifery, and continued them regularly till 1825. In 1822, when his consultation practice as a physician for the diseases of women and children had largely increased, he removed to Brook Street, Grosvenor Square, and he subsequently purchased an estate at Rodborne Cheney, Wiltshire. Merriman resigned his post at the Middlesex Hospital on 7 March

1826, but continued to take a warm interest in the institution, and was one of the treasurers from 1840 until 1845. Of the Royal Medical and Chirurgical Society he was elected treasurer in 1837.

Merriman died in Brook Street on 22 Nov. 1852. He married in 1799 Ann (1778–1831), only surviving daughter of his uncle, Samuel Merriman [q. v.] Their children were two daughters and a son, Samuel William John Merriman, M.D. (1814–1873), consulting physician to the Westminster General Dispensary (1847), physician to the Royal Infirmary for Children (1849), and author of 'Arguments against the Indiscriminate Use of Chloroform in Midwifery,' 8vo, London, 1848, and other treatises.

Merriman published in 1805 a pamphlet in vindication of vaccination entitled 'Observations on some late Attempts to Depreciate the Value and Efficacy of Vaccine Inoculation.' He had taken up his pen to prove the superior excellence of the smallpox inoculation, but as he wrote he found his arguments untenable. Essays and other papers of his were published in the 'London Medical Repository,' the 'London Medical and Physical Journal,' and the 'Medico-Chirurgical Transactions,' but the medical works for which he was best known were his 'Synopsis of the Various Kinds of Difficult Parturition,' 12mo, London, 1814, which passed through several editions, and was translated into Italian, German, and French, and his edition of Dr. M. Underwood's 'Treatise on the Diseases of Children,' 8vo, London, 1827. During his tenure of office as examiner to the Society of Apothecaries (1831–7) he published in 1833, under the title of 'The Validity of "Thoughts on Medical Reform,"' an answer to a pamphlet of that title written, as was understood, by John Allen, M.D. (1771–1843) [q. v.] He also wrote a 'Dissertation on the Retroversion of the Womb,' 8vo, London, 1810.

Merriman illustrated with anecdotes his copies of 'A Picture of the College of Physicians' and Wadd's 'Nugæ Chirurgicæ.' He had also a fine collection of portraits of medical men. Philological subjects much interested him. To the 'Gentleman's Magazine' and 'Notes and Queries,' then recently established, he contributed articles of real value. For the 'London Journal of Medicine' he wrote an historical retrospect of the science and practice of medicine under the title of 'The First of October 1851, by an Octogenarian.'

Several portraits of Merriman were taken at different periods, two of which only have been engraved—one a private plate.

His first cousin, John Merriman (1774–1839), surgeon, born on 26 Oct. 1774 at Marlborough, was son of Nathaniel Merriman by his wife Elizabeth, daughter of Thomas Baverstock of Alton, Hampshire. In 1794 he came to London to complete his medical education, and was admitted member of the Royal College of Surgeons and of the Society of Apothecaries. He soon became associated in business at Kensington with Thomas Hardwick, whose niece Jane, daughter of John Hardwick of Weston, Herefordshire, he married. For many years he was general medical attendant on the Duchess of Kent, the Princess Victoria, and the Princess Sophia, at Kensington Palace; accordingly the Princess Victoria, as soon as she ascended the throne, conferred upon him and his two sons, John (1800–1881) and James Nathaniel (1806–1854), all of whom were in partnership at Kensington, the appointment of apothecary extraordinary to her majesty. He died on 17 June 1839 at Kensington Square (*Gent. Mag.* 1839, pt. ii. p. 204). His portrait was engraved by Newton from a painting by Lucas.

[Information from John J. Merriman, esq.; Lancet, 30 Nov. 1850 pp. 610–15, 682 (with portrait), 27 Nov. 1852 p. 498; Gent. Mag. 1853, pt. i. pp. 207–9 (with list of articles contributed thereto); Georgian Era, ii. 452–3.]

G. G.

MERRIOT, THOMAS (1589–1662), grammarian, born in 1589 at Steeple Langford in Wiltshire, entered Winchester College in 1601, and matriculated at New College, Oxford, on 14 Oct. 1608, where he devoted himself to the study of law, and was fellow from 1610 to 1624, and B.C.L. on 22 Nov. 1615. He taught for some time in the grammar school which then adjoined the college, until he was made vicar of Swalcliffe near Banbury, by the warden and fellows of New College on 15 Jan. 1623–1624. Previous to 1637 he appears to have had misunderstandings with his parishioners, who, in consequence, assessed him at a high rate for ship-money. Against this 'very hard measure' he petitioned the council of state on 10 May 1637. In 1642 his royalist sympathies brought him into difficulties with the parliament, and he was summoned to appear before the House of Commons on 26 July. His living was sequestered by the Westminster assembly, and on his petitioning the Committee for Plundered Ministers, he was granted (31 Aug. 1646) 'a full and legal hearing' by the committee of his own county. He resigned the vicarage of Swalcliffe on 10 March 1658–9 (cf. *Collectanea Topographica et Genealog.* iii. 184, 347). He died at Swalcliffe on 19 July

1662, and was buried in the church, where a brass tablet to his memory still remains.

Merriot was a good latinist and an orator. He taught grammar at Swalcliffe till he was of an advanced age. On some points he dissented from Lily, whose grammar he had studied so assiduously at Winchester. He published: 1. 'Vulgaria, sive Miscellanea prosaica hinc inde decerpta,' Oxford, 1652. 2. 'Adagia Selectissima,' Oxford, 1652. 3. 'Grammaticall Miscellanies,' Oxford, 1660. Wood also mentions 'several Latin copies of verses, dispersed in books.'

[Wood's Athenæ (Bliss), vol. iii. cols. 589–90; Foster's Alumni Oxon. 1500–1714; Kirby's Winchester Scholars, p. 159; Clark's Reg. Univ. Oxf. i. 272, ii. 302, iii. 342; Cal. State Papers, Dom. Ser. 1637, p. 90; Commons' Journals, ii. 692; Hunter's Chorus Vatum, Addit. MS. 24491, v. 437; Minutes of Committee for Plundered Ministers, Addit. MS. 15670 fol. 198; Halkett and Laing's Dict. of Anon. and Pseudon. Lit.; information from the Rev. Dr. Wilkinson of Swalcliffe.] B. P.

MERRITT, HENRY (1822–1877), picture-cleaner and art-critic, the son of Joseph Merritt, a tailor, was born at Oxford on 8 June 1822. He was educated at a charity school, and his early years were passed in considerable poverty, his employment being at one time to collect old-standing debts from members of the university. While filling humble and precarious situations, he found time, however, to copy pictures in the Bodleian and to learn the rudiments of art from Alfred William Delamotte. In 1846 he made his way to London on foot, and in 1847 became acquainted with Mr. G. J. Holyoake. With Mr. Holyoake he lived at Dymoke Lodge and 1 Woburn Buildings for many years, but their relations do not seem to have been invariably harmonious. He wrote in the 'Reasoner,' under the pseudonym 'Christopher,' and soon afterwards contributed to the 'Leader' some papers, which in 1854 were republished in the 'Cabinet of Reason,' with a preface by Holyoake, under the title 'Dirt and Pictures separated in the Works of the Old Masters.' About the same time Merritt was entrusted by Dean Stanley with the task of cleaning the portrait of Richard II belonging to the chapterhouse of Westminster Abbey. He restored it successfully, and was afterwards employed on the portrait of Henry VII in the National Portrait Gallery, on various pictures at Hampton Court, and the battle scenes on the staircases of Marlborough House. His honesty and ability as a judge of old paintings led to his being constantly consulted by the authorities of the National Gallery and Royal Academy, to an acquaintance with Mr. Gladstone and other distinguished persons, and to a friendship with Mr. Ruskin, with whom he was in frequent correspondence. In 1865 Merritt published 'Robert Dalby and his World of Troubles,' an account, in the form of a romance, of his own early life, and the next year he became art-critic to the 'Standard.' Soon afterwards he commenced a story, called 'The Oxford Professor,' which was never completed. He died in July 1877, after considerable suffering, and was buried in the West Brompton cemetery. He married a few weeks before his death.

The above-mentioned works, with selections from Merritt's occasional writings and a memoir by his wife, were edited by Basil Champneys, and were published in London in 1879, 2 vols.

[Works in Brit. Mus.; Memoir by his wife, Anna Lea Merritt, 1879; Holyoake's Sixty Years of an Agitator's Life, ii. 332–47; Notes and Queries, vi. i. 471; Times, 14 July 1877.] A. F. P.

MERRY, ROBERT (1755–1798), dilettante, a direct descendant of Sir Henry Merry, who was knighted by James I in 1621, was born in London in April 1755. His father was governor of Hudson's Bay Company, and his grandfather, Captain Merry, sailing in search of the North-west passage, discovered and gave its name to Merry's Island. His mother was the eldest daughter of Sir John Willes [q. v.], lord chief justice. Merry's education was entrusted to his father's sister, who sent him to Harrow, where his tutor was Dr. Parr, and then to Christ's College, Cambridge, where he was admitted 2 April 1771. He lived irregularly and did not graduate. He studied at Lincoln's Inn, where he had been entered on 5 Nov. 1770, by his father's wish. On the latter's death he immediately purchased a commission in the horse guards. The American war had begun; but after squandering a large part of his fortune on high living and heavy play, he sold out as adjutant of the first troop. He was twenty-five, without a profession, poor, and a disappointment to everybody but himself. He went abroad, and apparently spent some three or four years in travelling in France, the Low Countries, Germany, Switzerland, and Italy. He finally joined the English colony settled in Florence.

He was there in 1784, studying Italian, lounging in the Tribuna, and definitely embarked upon a literary career in the 'Arno,' and in 1785 in the 'Florence Miscellany.' These were collections of verse by Mrs. Piozzi, Greatheed, Parsons, and Merry. 'We wrote them,' says Mrs. Piozzi, in a preface which won Horace Walpole's ironical praise, 'to divert ourselves and to say kind things of each other' (see also Gifford's Introduction to the *Mæviad*, ed. 1795). Merry rapidly became a recognised figure in Florentine society, and a member of the Della Cruscan Academy. But his social success, and above all his superiority as a versifier, quickened the jealousy and ill-will that underlay the fulsome admiration of the 'Miscellany;' his open *liaison* with the Countess Cowper, and the rivalry of the Grand-duke Leopold, made him an easy target for slander, and he had soon the whole English colony about his ears. He stood his ground for a time, then after lampooning his fellow-rhymers, abruptly quitted Florence in the spring of 1787. The 'Miscellany' had kindled curiosity in London, and literary coteries welcomed the poet. On 29 June his 'Adieu and Recall to Love,' signed 'Della Crusca,' appeared in the 'World,' then chiefly conducted by Captain Topham, a fellow-commoner of Merry's at Cambridge, and fellow-officer in the horse guards. 'I read the beautiful lines,' Mrs. Hannah Cowley [q. v.] declares, 'and without rising from the table at which I was sitting answered them.' Her reply, 'The Pen,' signed 'Anna Matilda,' was published in the 'World' of 12 July, and the correspondence thus started rapidly attracted a crowd of imitators, whose performances, welcomed by the 'World' and afterwards by the 'Oracle,' first amused and then revolted public taste. Merry's pseudonym gave its name to the Della Cruscan school, which faithfully exaggerated the worst features of his style—his affectation, incredibly foolish misuse of epithet, metaphor, and alliteration, his frantic efforts at sublimity, his obscurity and tasteless ornament. The best and worst of the poems in the 'World' were reprinted in the 'British Album,' which Bell brought out in 1789. It ran through three editions in the next two years, and the publication of the 'Baviad,' Gifford's satire on it, in 1791 sold a fourth and last. But it was mutual disappointment, as much as Gifford's satire, that ended Della Crusca's and Anna Matilda's sentimental versifying. They wrote, according to Mrs. Cowley's statement, without any knowledge of each other's identity until 1789. Then the ardent enthusiasts upon paper met, but the lady was forty-six, the lover thirty-four, and the only fruit of the meeting was one more poem, 'The Interview,' by Della Crusca, and some regrets in cloudy verse by Anna Matilda. The stream of nonsense flowed on in the newspapers, but Merry's part in it may fairly be said to have here terminated. When he published the 'Laurel of Liberty' next year it was under his own name. Merry had little humour; but if we compare his verses on 'Fontenoy,' 'Werther,' or 'The Close of a Year,' with the address to 'Laura Maria' (Mrs. Robinson), which Gifford quotes, it is not easy to avoid the impression that in the latter, as well as in some other flights in the 'World' and 'Oracle,' he was simply fooling his correspondents to the top of their bent. For the crazy introductions prefixed to the verses, most probably by Bell, the writers themselves can hardly be held responsible (see, for instance, the *World* of 28 Dec. 1787, 3 and 12 Jan. 1788; Brit. Mus. newspapers).

Merry had meanwhile been engaged in other literary ventures. 'Paulina,' a tale in verse, had appeared towards the close of 1787, 'Diversity,' a frigid and elaborate ode, in the following year (*Monthly Rev.* old ser. lxxx. 529–32), and in 1789 the 'Ambitious Vengeance,' a drama, which in plot, character, and situation is a mere travesty of Macbeth, was inserted in the 'British Album.' It was never acted. In the beginning of the same year he wrote the ode for the recovery of the king recited by Mrs. Siddons on 21 April (BOADEN, *Memoirs of Mrs. Siddons*, ii. 277–8). But the events of the 14th July in Paris gave a new direction to his energies, and coloured the rest of his life. Merry did not judge the French revolution, but judged everything by it—his friends, himself, literature, art, all civil and social relations. He went immediately to Paris, visited the Assembly, where he saw 'some disorder, but all from zeal,' and on his return published the 'Laurel of Liberty.' The effort has a certain fire; but Della Crusca's defects are still prominent, and Walpole fastens with glee upon his 'gossamery tears' and 'silky oceans.' He aimed at the laureateship at this time, but his principles, already the talk of the town, made his candidature hopeless; and though the 'World' moved mountains on his behalf, the court was all for Pye. In the summer of 1791 he was again in Paris, presented to the convention a treatise on the 'Nature of a Free Government,' and resumed an acquaintance with the artist David. On 14 July his ode on the 'Fall of the Bastille' was declaimed at a meeting in the Strand of '1,500 English gentlemen,' sympathisers with the French revolution (*Gent. Mag.* lxi. 673, &c.) Three months previously his 'Lorenzo,' a tragedy, had a brief success at Covent Garden (OULTON, *London Theatres*, ii. 81), and in August 1791 he married the well-known actress Elizabeth Brunton (MADAME D'ARBLAY, *Memoirs*, 1842, v. 264).

His wife, the daughter of John Brunton, an actor of some provincial fame, and sister of Louisa, countess of Craven [q. v.], was born in 1769, and in her sixteenth year, as Euphrasia, had carried Bath by storm. The manager Harris brought her to London, and she opened at Covent Garden in 1785 as Horatia, Murphy writing her a prologue. It was a success, but after the first season there was no question of her rivalling Mrs. Siddons, and the public enthusiasm waned. She kept her place, however, and during her short career in London had the chief tragic parts at Covent Garden (list in Genest, vii. 75–6). She had a sweet voice, a refined and graceful manner, but wanted energy. After her marriage—during the winter of 1791–2—she continued to act under her new name; but the outcry of his family—his mother was still alive—forced Merry to withdraw her from the stage in the spring. The complete failure of his play, 'The Magician no Conjuror,' produced at Covent Garden in February 1792, may have made the decision easier. They went together to France, and Merry was in Paris on 10 Aug. and on 2 Sept., but refused an invitation to be present at the trial of the king. Walpole tells a pretty story of his being mistaken by the mob for Abbé Maury, and of his being pursued with the cry 'A la lanterne.' In 1793 he and his wife returned to London, and lived in an unsettled way for the next three years, Merry haunting the clubs, declaiming on freedom and the French revolution, writing epigrams—some of which are very neat—against Pitt and his supporters in the 'Argus' and 'Telegraph,' and, notwithstanding his friend Topham's good-nature, sinking daily deeper into debt. 'Fénelon,' an adaptation of Marie-Joseph Chenier's play, was published in 1795, and the 'Pains of Memory,' a versified reproduction of talks with Rogers, in the following year. He also wrote the epilogue spoken by Mrs. Jordan at the notable performance of the pseudo-Shakespearean 'Vortigern' on 2 April 1796 [see Ireland, Samuel]. Regard for his family still kept his wife reluctantly from the stage; but when Wignell, of the New Theatre, Philadelphia, offered her an engagement in 1796, Merry, to whom life in London was becoming embarrassing, gave his consent, and in October they landed at New York. On 5 Dec. Mrs. Merry appeared in Philadelphia as Juliet, 'perhaps the best Juliet,' Dunlap thinks, 'that was ever seen or heard' (*American Stage*, 1832, p. 158). She acted in New York next year, and afterwards in the chief cities of the union, everywhere leaving her American rivals behind. Merry himself, in 1797, brought out his drama, 'The Abbey of St. Augustine,' at Philadelphia, but for the most part contented himself with the unofficial laureateship which the younger writers—though not without dissentient voices—readily granted to his London reputation. In 1798 he was living in Baltimore, grown fat and very indolent, and still clinging to his faith in the French revolution, upon which he had some vague plans for an epic. The 'Monthly Magazine' for August of that year announces a work by him on American manners, but on 14 Dec., in the morning, while walking in his garden, he fell in an apoplectic fit, and three hours later was dead. His widow married a manager of the Philadelphia and Baltimore Theatres named Warren, and died at Alexandria, Virginia, in 1808 (*Gent. Mag.* 1808, pt. ii. p. 749).

[In addition to the authorities quoted, Monthly Mag. iii. 46, vi. 129, vii. 255–8; European Mag. xxiv. 411–12, prefixed to which is a better engraving of Merry than that of the British Album; Letters of Horace Walpole, 1858, viii. 493–4, ix. pass.; Gifford's Autobiography, and Baviad and Mæviad; Frederick Reynolds's Memoirs, 1826, i. 281, 315, ii. passim; O'Keeffe's Memoirs, ii. 299; Boaden's Memoirs of Kemble, 1825; Mrs. Thrale's Autobiography, 1861, ii. 92–3, 197–206; D'Arblay's Diary and Letters, 1842, v. 264; Anna Matilda, 1788, p. xi; Miss Berry's Correspondence, 1866, i. 252–3; Monthly Review, enlarged ser. iv. 56–62, v. 201–5, 344, xix. 274–7, xxi. 149–5; Gent. Mag. 1799 pt. i. 252–4; Mathias's Pursuits of Literature, 1812, p. 449; Metcalfe's Book of Knights; Brit. Mus. Add. MS. 6675, f. 257; Baker's Biographia Dramatica; Oulton's London Theatres, 1795, ii. 80–1, 107; Thespian Dictionary; Genest, vii. 25, 29–30, 75–76; Appleton's American Biography; Dunlap's American Stage, 1832, pp. 155, 158, 173–7, 213; Griswold's Poets of America, 1856, p. 8 *n.*; Duyckinck's Cyclopædia of American Literature, i. 434; P. W. Clayden's Early Life of Samuel Rogers, passim.] J. A. C.

MERRYFELLOW, DICK (1723–1781), author. [See Gardiner, Richard.]

MERSINGTON, Lord. [See Swinton, Alexander, 1625?–1700.]

MERTON, WALTER de (*d.* 1277), bishop of Rochester and founder of Merton College, Oxford, was by family connected with Basingstoke. His mother was Christina Fitz-Oliver; of his father nothing is known save that his name was William. Foss is no doubt mistaken in identifying him with the William de Merton who was archdeacon of Berkshire, and died about 1239. Walter de Merton probably owed his surname either to Merton being his birthplace, or to having received his education at the priory there. He was afterwards at Oxford, where he is traditionally said to have studied at Mauger Hall, afterwards the Cross Inn, in the Cornmarket. He was probably a pupil of Adam de Marisco, who recommended him to Robert Grosseteste for ordination as subdeacon (*Monumenta Franciscana*, i. 405, Rolls Ser.) This must have been after June 1235, but the first dated reference to him occurs in 1237, in an inquisition of Walter's lands at Basingstoke, where his parents are described as dead; they are known to have been buried at St. Michael's, Basingstoke. Not long after Walter founded a hospital at Basingstoke to their memory; grants to this foundation were confirmed by the king in 1253 and 1262, and it was eventually placed in close relationship with Merton College. In 1237 Merton is spoken of as 'clericus' simply. Afterwards he became a clerk in the royal chancery, and is spoken of as 'clericus noster' in a grant of free-warren for his lands at Maldon in 1249. Merton obtained the living of Sedgefield, Durham, from Nicholas de Farnham [q. v.], between 1241 and 1248. He also held the livings of Potton, Bedfordshire; Stratton; Staindrop, Durham; Haltwistle, Northumberland; Codington, Surrey; Benningbrough, Yorkshire; and Branston, Lincoln (Foss, iii. 129; Hobhouse, p. 45). In August 1256 he was one of the clerks who were acting for Walter de Kirkham [q. v.], bishop of Durham, in his dispute with St. Albans about Conscliffe (Matt. Paris, vi. 326-7, 340). Merton received, on 15 June 1259, the prebend of Kentish Town at St. Paul's, which he afterwards exchanged for that of Holywell or Finsbury (Le Neve, ii. 394, 403). On 4 July 1259 he became prebendary of Exeter, and previously to 1262 was prebendary of Yatesbury, Salisbury, and canon of Wells. He was prothonotary of the chancery, and perhaps it is in this capacity that he had charge of the seal for Henry de Wingham on 7 May 1258, and on 14 March and 6 July 1259. In the former year he was employed in the negotiations with the pope as to the grant of Sicily to Edmond, the king's son. In 1261 the king appointed him chancellor, in place of the baronial official, Nicholas of Ely; probably this was in April, when Hugh Despenser gave way to Philip Basset as justiciar, though the appointment does not seem to have been formally made until 5 July (*Ann. Mon.* iv. 129; *Flores Historiarum*, ii. 470). On 15 Oct. Merton was granted four hundred marks for the support of himself and the chancery. Merton retained his office as chancellor until 12 July 1263, when the baronial party recovered their position, and he was displaced by Nicholas of Ely. In March 1264, owing to his support of the king, some of Merton's prebendal property near London was plundered by the rioters (*Ann. Mon.* iv. 141). After the royal victory in 1265, Merton was not restored to the chancery, but he is mentioned as a justiciar on 10 Dec. 1271 (*Excerpta e Rot. Fin.* ii. 555). On the death of Henry III in November 1272, the council appointed Merton to act as chancellor, and he attests a document in that capacity on 29 Nov. (*Fœdera*, i. 498). The contemporary chronicles, however, speak of him as being appointed in the parliament held at Westminster in January 1273, when he was directed to remain at Westminster till Edward's return to England (*Ann. Mon.* ii. 113, iv. 462). Merton retained his office throughout the regency, but resigned soon after Edward's return to England on 2 Aug. 1274, for in his final statutes for Merton College, which are dated in this month, he styles himself 'quondam cancellarius.' He had previously been elected bishop of Rochester about the end of July, and on 21 Oct. was consecrated by Archbishop Kilwardby at Gillingham (*ib.* iv. 462; *Flores Historiarum*, iii. 44). The Rochester chronicles say that, though Merton was a man of great authority and power, he did no special good to the prior and convent, though he gave them the manors of Cobhambury and Middleton (*ib.*) Merton's episcopate only lasted three years. While fording the Medway his horse stumbled and fell, and though the bishop was rescued by his servants, he died from the effects of the accident two days later on, 27 Oct. 1277 (*Ann. Mon.* iii. 278, iv. 275). The Osney annalist speaks of Merton as a man of liberality and great worldly learning, who had always been very ready in his assistance to the monastic orders, and elsewhere preserves some complimentary verses on his character (*ib.* iv. 259-60, 275). Merton was buried in Rochester Cathedral in the north transept of the choir, near the tomb of St. William; his original monument was much injured in the reign of Edward VI, and in 1598 another was erected in its place by Sir Henry Savile, warden, and the fellows of Merton College, This monument in its turn gave way, in 1852, to a restoration of the original tomb, erected in accordance with the description in the accounts of the bishop's executors, and at the expense of Merton College. Merton's chalice was removed from his tomb to Oxford in 1598. Merton had seven sisters, but no brother; full genealogical tables will be found in Bishop Hobhouse's 'Sketch of the Life of Walter de Merton,' p. 51. His will is summarised by Hobhouse, pp. 44-50. A portrait (engraved by Faber) is in the Bodleian Library, Oxford.

Merton's chief title to fame is the foundation of Merton College, Oxford, and therefore, in a sense, of the collegiate system of the English universities. In 1261 he obtained a charter from Richard de Clare, earl of Gloucester, empowering him to assign his manors at Farley and Malden in Surrey to the priory of Merton, for the support of 'scholars residing at the schools,' an expression which probably means scholars at Oxford. A little later, probably in September 1263, he published a deed of assignation of these and other lands. Under this deed special provision was made for the education of eight nephews under a warden and chaplains; the care of his nephews, who are here spoken of as 'scholares in scholis degentes,' appears indeed to have been the first object of Merton's foundation. On 7 Jan. 1264 there came a regular charter of incorporation, which established the 'House of the Scholars of Merton' at Malden in Surrey, under a warden and bailiffs, with ministers of the altar, and with power to maintain twenty scholars at Oxford or any other place of general learning. During the next few years Merton acquired the site of the present college, together with the advowson of St. John's Church, and other property at Oxford. In 1270 the statutes of 1264 were reissued without any material alteration, but eventually, in August 1274, Merton put forth his final statutes, transferring the warden, bailiffs, and ministers to Oxford, and designating Oxford as the exclusive and permanent home of the scholars. Under these statutes provision was made for such a number of scholars as the college revenues would support, and for their common life as a corporate body under the rule of a superior called the warden. Merton's intention appears to have been to provide for the training of secular clergy, and though he borrowed from monasticism the idea of a corporate life under a common rule and head, he expressly prohibited his scholars from taking vows, and provided that any who entered one of the regular orders should forfeit his scholarship. Above all, the college was to be a place of study, in the first place of philosophy and the liberal arts, and afterwards of theology. The Rochester chronicler describes the college as established for the perpetual sustenance of students 'in arte dialectica et theologia' (*Flores Historiarum*, iii. 44). The establishment of Merton College was the beginning of the true collegiate system, for though the benefactions of William of Durham and of John and Devorguila de Balliol are of earlier date, they did not provide for the formation of regular corporate bodies, and the establishment of University and Balliol colleges followed, and did not precede, that of Merton. At Cambridge, Merton College was avowedly the model of the collegiate system, for when Hugh de Balsham [q. v.] obtained license for the foundation of Peterhouse, it was expressly stated to be for 'studious scholars who shall in everything live together as students in the university of Cambridge, according to the rule of the scholars of Oxford who are called of Merton.' So in the statutes actually drawn up for Peterhouse by Simon Montague in 1284 constant reference is made to the fact that they are 'ad instar aulæ de Merton.' It is needless to add that the system initiated by Walter de Merton has moulded the whole history of both universities, and thus fully justifies the words of Savile's epitaph:—

> Re, unius
> Exemplo, omnium quoquot extant
> Collegiorum, fundatori.

[Annales Monastici; Flores Historiarum (both in Rolls Ser.); Hobhouse's Sketch of the Life of Walter de Merton, 1859; Percival's Foundation Statutes of Merton College; Brodrick's Memorials of Merton College, Oxf. Hist. Soc. (a translation of the statutes of 1274 is given on pp. 317–40); Lyte's Hist. of Univ. of Oxford; Foss's Judges of England, iii. 129–31.] C. L. K.

MERVIN or **MERVYN, AUDLEY** (*d.* 1675), soldier, lawyer, and politician, was second son of Admiral Sir Henry Mervyn of Petersfield, Hampshire, by Christian, daughter of George Touchet, baron Audley and Earl of Castlehaven [q. v.] Mervyn acquired a considerable portion of the lands in Ulster, which his uncle Lord Castlehaven had undertaken to 'plant.' For a time he was captain of a regiment raised by Sir Henry Tichborne and established himself in the castle of Trillick in the county of Tyrone. In 1639–1640 Mervyn was elected member for Tyrone in the House of Commons at Dublin, where, according to Carte, he became 'the most tiresome and continual speech-maker of the puritan party.' On behalf of the commons he in 1641 presented to the peers articles of impeachment against Sir Richard Bolton [q. v.] and others. The speech delivered by Mervyn on this occasion was printed in 1641 and republished in 1764.

Immediately after the commencement of the rising in Ulster in October 1641, Colonel Rory Maguire, M.P. for Fermanagh, who had married Mervyn's sister and was brother of Lord Maguire, apprised Mervyn of the project of the Irish then in arms to employ him to wait upon Charles I with a statement of their grievances and suggestions for a satisfactory settlement. Mervyn, however, associated himself with the English and Scottish settlers in his vicinity, and as lieutenant-colonel to Sir Ralph Gore took an active part against the Irish rebels. A somewhat verbose and egotistical account of his action was on 4 June 1642 addressed by Mervyn to the speaker of the House of Commons in London. By order of that house it was printed at London and sold at 'the Irish warehouse at Stationers' Hall,' and entitled 'An Exact Relation of all such Occurrences as have happened in the several counties of Donegall, Londonderry, Tyrone, and Fermanagh, in the North of Ireland, since the beginning of the Rebellion.' Mervyn received a commission as colonel of one of the British regiments in Ulster, and with others of these commanders waited on the parliament at London in 1643 and on Charles I at Oxford for the purpose of obtaining money and supplies. On 5 July 1643 Mervyn was examined before a select committee of the House of Commons in London, mainly in reference to his relations with Colonel Rory Maguire. This examination, attested by Mervyn's signature, was published with other papers at London in 1643 by order of the House of Commons.

The zeal which Mervyn displayed against the covenant induced Ormonde in 1644 to appoint him governor of the town of Derry. Mervyn, however, soon afterwards took the covenant and excused his conduct to Ormonde on the ground of expediency. Mervyn was accordingly removed from the government of Derry, but continued as a 'British colonel' to command his regiment in its vicinity.

Towards the close of 1648 Mervyn was taken 'insidiously' by parliamentarians in Ulster, and by order of George Monck, afterwards first duke of Albemarle, then in command there, he was sent to London as a prisoner. He appears not to have been long detained, and in June 1649 he co-operated with Sir Robert Stewart against Sir Charles Coote, president of Connaught under the parliament. Coote, in a letter to the council of state at London on 15 Aug. 1649, charged Mervyn with having forged articles purporting to have been authorised by him. Later in the same month Ormonde employed Mervyn and the Bishop of Raphoe to confer with Owen O'Neill, general of the Irish in Ulster, on matters of importance to the interests of Charles II. Influenced probably by the recent arrival of Oliver Cromwell in Ireland with forces of the parliament of England, Mervyn withdrew from the royalist party and came to an arrangement with Coote at Derry.

In June 1658 Mervyn obtained formal admission to the society of King's Inns at Dublin, then under the control of law officers of the Cromwellian government. He soon after took part with Sir Charles Coote and Lord Broghill in the movements in Ireland for the restoration of Charles II. In conjunction with them and their associates Mervyn framed the instrument adopted by the king in reference to legal arrangements for Ireland. Mervyn was knighted, and on 20 Sept. 1660 he received the appointment of chief serjeant-at-law in Ireland. In February 1660–1 he was named as a commissioner for executing the king's declaration from Breda concerning Ireland. He was also made a commissioner to ascertain the value of lands in Ireland let out to 'adventurers' and soldiers, and a trustee for the officers who had served the king before June 1649. On 8 May 1661 Mervyn was chosen speaker of the House of Commons, Dublin, and on his presentation on the 11th of that month in the House of Peers there, he delivered an elaborate and pedantic oration, which was printed. In the same year Mervyn was included among the commissioners elected by parliament to proceed to England concerning arrangements for the settlement of Ireland, and Sir John Temple was appointed to act as deputy-speaker. Mervyn resumed his place at Dublin as speaker in May 1662, and in July of that year delivered a congratulatory address to the Duke of Ormonde, in the presence chamber at Dublin Castle, which was subsequently published. In February 1662–3 Mervyn, on behalf of the House of Commons, Dublin, presented to Ormonde, as viceroy, a series of rules and directions which they proposed should be put in operation in the execution of the act of settlement with a view to promote and secure the interests of protestants in Ireland. These propositions and the mode of Mervyn's advocacy of them were distasteful to the king's advisers in England, and a royal letter was addressed to Ormonde with a grave censure of the proceedings.

Mervyn continued to act as speaker till the termination of the parliament in 1666. In his official capacity as a commissioner in connection with lands he was reputed to have been influenced by pecuniary considerations. He was also suspected of having been connected with a plot against the government in which some members of parliament were believed to be implicated. He died at Dublin on 24 Oct. 1675, and was interred in the church of St. Werburgh in that city.

A sum of 6,000*l.* which Mervyn claimed as due to him for his 'long and faithful service to the protestant interest in Ireland' does not appear to have been received by him or his representatives, although payment of it was strongly recommended by the House of Commons, Dublin, in 1694.

[Carte's Ormonde; Journals Houses of Lords and Commons, Ireland; Acts of Settlement and explanation; Speeches of Audley Mervin; Cox's Hibernia Anglicana; Clarendon's History; Ormonde Archives; Whitelocke's Memorials; Carte Papers; manuscripts of King's Inns, Dublin; Relation of Sir C. Coote's Transactions, 1649; Harris's Writers of Ireland; Fasciculus Mervinensis, 1873; Gilbert's Contemporary History; Hist. of Irish Confederation and Jacobite Narrative, 1892; Case of Roman Catholics, manuscript.] J. T. G.

MERYCK, Sir WILLIAM (*d.* 1668), civilian. [See Meyrick.]

MERYON, CHARLES LEWIS (1783–1877), physician and biographer of Lady Hester Stanhope, son of Lewis Meryon of Rye in Sussex, of an old Huguenot stock, was born on 27 June 1783. He was educated at Merchant Taylors' School (1796–1802), and obtaining a Stuart's exhibition to St. John's College, Oxford, matriculated there on 29 March 1803, and graduated B.A. 1806, M.A. 1809, M.B. and M.D. 1817. He studied medicine at St. Thomas's Hospital under Henry Cline [q. v.], by whose recommendation he was in 1810 engaged to accompany the eccentric Lady Hester Stanhope [q. v.], in the capacity of medical attendant, on a voyage to Sicily and the East. He followed her during her seven years' wanderings, saw her finally settled on Mount Lebanon, and then returned to England for the purpose of taking his medical degrees. Meryon revisited Syria at Lady Hester's request in 1819, when he found that she had completely adopted the usages of the East. A difference with one of his patroness's local medicine men caused his speedy return. He was admitted a candidate of the College of Physicians on 26 June 1820, and a fellow on 25 June 1821. Shortly afterwards he became domestic physician to Sir Gilbert Heathcote, but in 1827, at the earnest request of Lady Hester, he started once more for Syria, in company with his wife and family. They were attacked and plundered en route by a Levantine pirate, and returned to Leghorn, where Mrs. Meryon's fears detained the doctor until 1830. In November of that year they sailed from Marseilles, and arrived at Mount Lebanon about 15 Dec. Lady Hester was then at the zenith of her power, and Meryon subsequently described with the utmost minuteness her complicated oriental environment, her tyranny, and her interminable conversations and cross-questionings, of which he himself was often a victim. Owing to disagreements, chiefly resulting from Lady Hester's avowed intolerance of his wife, Meryon had to leave Mount Lebanon in April 1831, but he paid Lady Hester a fourth and last visit between July 1837 and August 1838. Finally settling in London, he issued there in 1845 his 'Memoirs of the Lady Hester Stanhope, as related by herself in Conversations with her Physician,' 3 vols. 8vo. Despite their diffuseness, the memoirs are excellent reading, contain many curious particulars about persons of note, and only want an index. Though published earlier the 'Memoirs' are in reality a sequel to the scarcely less entertaining 'Travels of Lady Hester Stanhope, forming the completion of her Memoirs narrated by her Physician,' 3 vols. London, 8vo, 1846. The third volume contains a portrait of Meryon in Bedouin dress. Meryon died in London on 11 Sept. 1877, aged ninety-four.

[The Memoirs and Travels of Lady Hester Stanhope, as above; Foster's Alumni Oxon. 1715–1886; Robinson's Merchant Taylors' Reg. ii. 166; Munk's Coll. of Phys. i. 234; Allibone's Dict. Engl. Lit. art. 'Stanhope.'] T. S.

MESSING, RICHARD (*d.* 1462?), bishop of Dromore. [See Misyn.]

MESTON, WILLIAM (1688?–1745), burlesque poet, the son of a blacksmith, was born in the parish of Midmar, Aberdeenshire, about 1688 (the baptismal registers do not date back beyond 1717). His parents sent him to the Marischal College, Aberdeen; and, having made good use of his opportunities, he was elected, when he had finished his university course, one of the doctors of the high school of Aberdeen. Meston was afterwards tutor to George Keith, who became tenth Earl Marischal in 1712, and to his brother James Francis Edward Keith, afterwards field-marshal in the Prussian service; and in 1715, through the interest of the Countess of Marischal (widow of the ninth earl), he was appointed regent of Marischal College. Later in the year, however, Meston joined the family of the Earl Marischal in fighting for the Old Pretender, and was made governor of Dunnottar Castle, Kincardineshire; but when the rising was put down he had for a time to hide among the hills. Afterwards, refusing to comply with the conditions of the Act of Indemnity, he lived in the family of the Countess of Marischal, but her death left him in a destitute condition. He then, in conjunction with his brother Samuel, who was a good Greek scholar, opened an academy at Elgin; but, though the venture was a success, Meston's easy-going habits prevented him from saving money. He afterwards moved his school to Turriff at the invitation of the Countess of Erroll, whose brother, the twelfth Earl of Erroll, had been chancellor of King's College, Aberdeen, when Meston was regent at Marischal College. Meston, who was treated very kindly by the countess, was again successful until, several years afterwards, one of his pupils was nearly killed in a duel. This incident, though Meston was in no way to blame, led to the downfall of his academy. He then tried to establish schools at Montrose and Perth, and afterwards was tutor to the children of Mr. Oliphant of Gask. There he remained some years, until ill-health caused him to go to Peterhead to drink the mineral waters. Subsequently he was again supported by the Countess of Erroll, and finally moving to Aberdeen, was cared for by some relatives until his death there in the spring of 1745. He was buried, without any inscription, in the Spittal churchyard of Old Aberdeen. He seems to have been a good scholar and a wit and pleasant companion; but he was too fond of the bottle. He was a great admirer of Samuel Butler; and in his verses, which are often coarse, he sometimes plagiarises or quotes from his model.

Meston's poems were first published in collected form, with a life, at Edinburgh in 1767, though the book is called 'sixth edition' on the title-page; and they were reprinted, without the Latin pieces, at Aberdeen in 1802. The several poems originally appeared anonymously as follows: 1. 'Phaethon, or the first Fable of the second Book of Ovid's Metamorphoses burlesqu'd,' Edinburgh, 1720. 2. 'The Knight of the Kirk,' Edinburgh, 1723; reprinted in London with corrections in 1728. This, the best of Meston's pieces, and perhaps the best of the imitations of 'Hudibras,' is a satire upon the presbyterians. 3. 'Mob contra Mob, or the Rabblers rabbled,' Edinburgh, 1731. 4. 'Old Mother Grim's Tales, Decade I,' London, 1737. 5. 'Decadem Alteram . . . subjunxit Jodocus Grimmus,' London, 1738. 6. 'Viri humani, salsi et faceti, Gulielmi Sutherlandi . . . Diploma,' n.p. or d., sometimes attributed to Arbuthnot.

[Life in Meston's Poetical Works; Chalmers's Biog. Dict. xxii. 88; Aberdeen University Calendar; P. Buchan's Family of Keith, Earls Marischal of Scotland, 1820; Brit. Mus. and Advocates' Libraries Cat.; Retrospective Review, iii. 329–32; Notes and Queries, 7th ser. x. 21.]

G. A. A.

METCALF, JOHN (1717–1810), commonly known as 'Blind Jack of Knaresborough,' was born at Knaresborough, of poor parents, on 15 Aug. 1717. When six years old he lost his sight as a consequence of a severe attack of small-pox, but his self-confidence was uninjured, and he soon excelled most boys of his age in performances which require activity and daring. He was taught the fiddle, so that he might obtain a subsistence as a strolling musician, then regarded as the sole occupation open to a blind man, 'but Jack Metcalf had more natural taste for the cry of a hound or a harrier.' He became a good rider and swimmer, led nesting and orchard-robbing expeditions, distinguished himself as a diver, a cock-fighter, and in the hunting-field. He was soon known, moreover, as a gallant, as a wag, a successful card-player, and a shrewd dealer in horses. By 1738, when he attained the age of twenty-one, he was barely under six feet two inches in height, extremely robust, and ready-tongued. He rode several races with success, and desired to become a jockey. In 1739 he surprised the country-side by eloping with a publican's daughter named Dorothy Benson, on the night before her marriage with a certain Dickinson, and he married her the next morning, before the disconsolate Dickinson had obtained a clue to her whereabouts. He took a small house at Knaresborough, and seems to have been a model husband, though his exploits grew more and more daring. He walked to London and back, easily outstripping the coach of one of his patrons, Colonel Liddel, on the return journey. In 1745 he became recruiting-sergeant on the king's side, and enlisted 140 Knaresborough men with extraordinary rapidity. Sixty-four of the men were drafted into a company formed by William Thornton, and marched, with Blind Jack playing at their head, to Newcastle, where, by General Wade's orders, they were incorporated in Pulteney's regiment. Metcalf fought at and escaped from the battle of Falkirk. He afterwards fiddled at a ball given at Aberdeen by the Duke of Cumberland, who 'spoke him fair,' and gave him two guineas, and he was present at Culloden. After returning to Knaresborough he engaged in horse-dealing at Harrogate, being an excellent judge of horseflesh, entirely by touch. He also traded in cotton and worsted goods, and did a vigorous stroke of smuggling (chiefly brandy and tea) whenever occasion offered. In 1750 he made good profits out of some military transport work, and in 1754 commenced a new business, setting up a stage-coach between York and Knaresborough, which he conducted himself twice a week in summer and once in winter. He also bought and sold timber and hay in the stack, measuring with his arms and rapidly reducing cubic contents to feet and inches, after a mental process of his own.

Metcalf's travels had given him an unrivalled familiarity with the northern roads. He knew how bad they were, and how their worst features could best be remedied. He now became a pioneer road-maker and bridge-builder, and one of the chief predecessors of Telford and Macadam. In 1765 parliament passed an act authorising the construction of a new turnpike-road between Harrogate and Boroughbridge. Metcalf offered to construct three miles of the proposed road, between Minskip and Fearnsby, and the master-surveyor, Ostler, who knew him well and had the greatest confidence in his abilities, let him the contract. Metcalf devoted himself wholly to the new undertaking. He completed his work with unusual speed and thoroughness, and, encouraged by success, undertook to build a bridge at Boroughbridge, which he again completed satisfactorily. His success led to his constant employment on similar work during a period of more than thirty years. The total mileage of the turnpike-roads constructed by him, involving the building of many bridges, retaining walls, and culverts, was about 180 miles, for which he received not less than 65,000*l.* Among his roads were those between Wakefield and Doncaster, Huddersfield and Halifax, Ashton and Stockport, and Bury and Blackburn. The Huddersfield and Manchester road was carried by him over a bog which had been thought quite impracticable.

In all these undertakings Metcalf took an active personal share. A contemporary writes: 'With the assistance only of a long staff, I have several times met this man traversing the roads, ascending steep and rugged heights, exploring valleys, and investigating their several extents, forms, and situations, so as to answer his designs in the best manner. The plans which he makes and the estimates which he prepares are done in a method peculiar to himself, and of which he cannot well convey the meaning to others. His abilities in this respect are nevertheless so great that he finds constant employment. Most of the roads over the Peak in Derbyshire have been altered by his directions. . . . I have met this blind projector while engaged in making his survey. He was alone as usual, and amongst other conversation I made some enquiries respecting the new road [from Wilmslow to Congleton]. It was really astonishing to hear with what accuracy he described its course and the nature of the different soils through which it was conducted' (Bew, *Observations on Blindness*). He finally relinquished road-making in 1792, and, after an unsuccessful venture in the cotton business, retired to a small farm at Spofforth, near Wetherby. He retained his shrewd mother-wit and resolute spirit to the last, and dying on 26 April 1810, at Follifoot, near Knaresborough, was buried at Spofforth. An epitaph in All Saints churchyard bears a well written inscription in heroic verse (quoted in *Notes and Queries*, 2nd ser. vi. 323). He was ninety-three years of age at the time of his death, and left behind him ninety great-grandchildren. Mrs. Metcalf died at Stockport in 1778.

[The best account of Metcalf, doing full justice to his value as a road-maker, is that in Smiles's Telford, 1867, pp. 74–94 (with portrait and cuts of his birthplace and farm at Spofforth); Life of John Metcalf, York, 1795 (with portrait after J. R. Smith); another edition (with portrait engraved by Pigot), Manchester, 1826; Life of Blind Jack of Knaresborough in Baring-Gould's Yorkshire Oddities, i. 120–76 (mainly based on chap-books); Gent. Mag. 1810, i. 597; Spencer Walpole's Hist. of England, i. 73–4; Memoirs of Literary and Philosophical Society of Manchester, i. 172–4; Hargrove's Hist. of Knaresborough, 1809; Calvert's Hist. of Knaresborough, 1844, p. 104; Boyne's Yorkshire Library, p. 246.] T. S.

METCALFE, CHARLES THEOPHILUS, Baron Metcalfe (1785–1846), provisional governor-general of India, born at the Lecture House, Calcutta, on 30 Jan. 1785, was second son of Thomas Theophilus Metcalfe, then a major in the Bengal army. The father afterwards became a director of the East India Company, and was created a baronet on 21 Dec. 1802. Metcalfe's mother was Susannah Selina Sophia, widow of Major John Smith of the East Indian army, and daughter of John Debonnaire of the Cape of Good Hope. At an early age he was sent to a preparatory school at Bromley in Middlesex, and in January 1796 went to Eton, where he showed remarkable powers of application, and a great distaste for all athletic sports. Leaving Eton on 1 April 1800, he was appointed to a Bengal writership on 13 Oct., and in January 1801 arrived at Calcutta. He was the first student admitted to Lord Wellesley's College of Fort William, where he studied oriental languages with some success. On 3 Dec. 1801 he was nominated assistant to the embassy to the Arab States, an appointment which was cancelled a few days afterwards at his own request for that of assistant to the resident with Dowlut Rao Scindiah. Metcalfe's connection with Scindiah's court was, however, brief, as he soon found that he was unable to agree with Colonel Collins, the resident. On 4 Oct. 1802 Metcalfe became an assistant in the chief secretary's office at Calcutta, and was transferred on 4 April 1803 to a similar position in the governor-general's office. In the summer of 1804 Metcalfe was attached to the headquarters of Lake's army in the capacity of political assistant, and as a volunteer took part in the storming of the fortress of Deeg (24 Dec. 1804). He acted successively as political agent to General Smith and General Dowdeswell, and on 10 Jan. 1806 was received in full durbar by Holkar, with whom a treaty had been concluded a few days previously. Metcalfe was appointed first assistant to the resident at Delhi on 15 Aug. 1806, and in August 1808 was despatched on a special mission to Lahore. After a series of tedious negotiations Metcalfe obtained all that he had demanded of Runjeet Singh, who withdrew his troops to his own side of the Sutlej and concluded a treaty of general amity with the British government at Vmritsur on 25 April 1809. By the adroitness with which he overcame the many difficulties of this mission Metcalfe won for himself a considerable reputation as a diplomatist at the age of twenty-four.

From August 1809 to May 1810 Metcalfe acted as Lord Minto's deputy secretary during the governor-general's visit to Madras, and on 15 May 1810 was appointed acting resident to the court of Dowlut Rao Scindiah. On 25 Feb. 1811 he was promoted to the post of resident at Delhi. By his careful administration the industrial resources of the territory were largely developed, while his scheme for the settlement of Central India largely influenced the policy of the governor-general, Lord Moira (afterwards Marquis of Hastings). In 1816 he refused the post of financial secretary, and on 29 Jan. 1819 became secretary in the secret and political department, and private secretary to the governor-general. Accustomed to an independent command, Metcalfe quickly found his new situation irksome, and on 26 Dec. 1820 was appointed resident at Hyderabad. An attempt made by him to remove the baneful influence of the money-lending firm of William Palmer & Co., which was overshadowing the Nizam's government, brought upon Metcalfe the displeasure of the governor-general, who rejected his scheme for opening a six per cent. loan, guaranteed by the British government, by which the Nizam's huge obligations to Palmer's house and other creditors might be paid off. Soon after Hastings's return to England, where these pecuniary transactions were warmly discussed in the court of proprietors during a six days' debate, the debt due to William Palmer & Co. was discharged, and in less than a year the house became bankrupt.

On the death of his elder brother, Theophilus John, in August 1822 Metcalfe succeeded to the baronetcy. In the following year he was invalided and went to Calcutta, but returned to Hyderabad in 1824. On 26 Aug. 1825 he was appointed resident and civil commissioner in Delhi Territories, and agent to the governor-general for the affairs of Rajpootana. Under his advice the government supported the claims of Bulwunt Singh against the usurpation of his uncle Doorjun Saul, and in January 1826 Bhurtpore was successfully stormed by Lord Combermere, and Doorjun Saul taken prisoner. On 24 Aug. 1827 Metcalfe became a member of the supreme council, which at that time consisted of the governor-general, the commander-in-chief, and two members of the civil service. By a resolution of the court of directors on 14 Dec. 1831, Metcalfe's period of service on the council was extended from five to seven years. He was appointed on the newly created government of Agra on 20 Nov. 1833, but owing to the absence from Bengal of the governor-general (Lord William Bentinck) he was compelled to stay at Calcutta for some time as vice-president of the council and deputy-governor of Bengal. In December 1834 Metcalfe set out for the seat of his government at Allahabad, but no sooner had he got there than he had to return to Calcutta in consequence of Lord William Bentinck's resignation. By virtue of a resolution of the court of directors in December 1833 Metcalfe acted as provisional governor-general during the interval between the departure of Lord William Bentinck and the arrival of Lord Auckland (20 March 1835 to 4 March 1836). The directors wished that Metcalfe should remain in office, but the whig ministry refused to sanction the appointment on the ground that it was not advisable to appoint any servant of the company to the highest office of the Indian government. Before Lord Melbourne had appointed a successor to Lord William Bentinck, there was a ministerial crisis, and Lord Heytesbury [q. v.] was nominated by Sir Robert Peel. But before Lord Heytesbury set out another ministerial crisis occurred, the tory appointment was cancelled, and Lord Auckland was appointed. Metcalfe's short administration is chiefly distinguished by the act of 15 Sept. 1835, which removed the vexatious restrictions on the liberty of the Indian press.

Shortly after the arrival of the new governor-general, Metcalfe was invested with the grand cross of the Bath, 14 March 1836. In the same month (the Agra government having been meanwhile abolished) he was appointed lieutenant-governor of the North-Western Provinces, the headquarters of which were fixed at Agra instead of Allahabad. In filling up the vacant governorship of Madras, Metcalfe was passed over by the directors, who had been greatly displeased by his giving legal sanction to the liberty of the press. In consequence of this slight, Metcalfe resigned his lieutenant-governorship on 1 Jan. 1838 and retired from the service. He reached England in May 1838, and took up his abode at Fern Hill, near Windsor. While making arrangements for contesting Glasgow in the radical interest, Metcalfe was appointed governor of Jamaica (11 July 1839). He was admitted a member of the privy council on 31 July, and on 26 Sept. following was sworn in as governor at Spanish Town. By his conciliatory conduct he speedily effected the reconciliation of the colony to the mother-country, and brought about a better feeling between the proprietors and the emancipated negroes. Having accomplished what he had been sent out to do, Metcalfe resigned his office and returned to England on 2 July 1842. In January 1843 he accepted the government of Canada, and on 30 March following took the oaths at Kingston as governor-general. Owing to the burning question of responsible government and the inflamed state of party spirit in the colony, Metcalfe's position was one of extreme difficulty. His attempts to conciliate all parties displeased the executive council, who were determined to reduce the governor-general to a mere passive instrument in their hands, and were supported in their endeavours by the majority of the representative assembly. In consequence of Metcalfe's refusal to admit their right to be consulted about official appointments, all the members of the council, with one exception, resigned in November 1843. For some time he was without a full council, but after the general election in November 1844, which resulted in a slight majority for the government, he was able to fill up all the vacant places with men of moderate views. Meanwhile, Metcalfe had for a long time been suffering from a malignant growth on his cheek, which at length deprived him of the sight of one eye. Unwilling to leave the government to his successor in a state of embarrassment, he still struggled on at his post. As a 'mark of the Queen's entire approbation and favour' he was created Baron Metcalfe of Fern Hill in the county of Berks on 25 Jan. 1845. Before the year was out he had become physically unfit for work, and having resigned his post he returned to England in December 1845 in a dying state. After patiently enduring still further agony, he died at Malshanger, near Basingstoke, Hampshire, on 5 Sept. 1846. He was buried in the family vault in the parish church of Winkfield, near Fern Hill, where there is a tablet to his memory; the inscription was written by Lord Macaulay.

Metcalfe was an able and sagacious administrator, of unimpeachable integrity and untiring industry. His self-reliance and imperturbable good humour were alike remarkable, though perhaps his undeviating straightforwardness was his most marked characteristic. Metcalfe did not take his seat in the House of Lords. As he never married, the barony became extinct upon his death, while the baronetcy devolved upon his younger brother, Thomas Theophilus Metcalfe, whose grandson, Sir Theophilus John Metcalfe, is separately noticed. A portrait of Metcalfe by John James Masquerier is preserved at Eton College (see *Catalogue of the Third Exhibition of National Portraits at South Kensington in* 1868, No. 154). Another by Say, which has been engraved, hangs in the library of the Oriental Club, Hanover Square, London. A third portrait, by a Canadian artist named Bradish, is in the Court House at Falmouth, Jamaica. There is a bust by E. H. Baily, R.A., in the Metcalfe Hall, Calcutta, an engraving of which by J. C. Armytage forms the frontispiece to the first volume of Kaye's 'Life and Correspondence,' 1858, and there is a statue by the same sculptor in the Central Park, Kingston, Jamaica. A selection of Metcalfe's early papers, Indian council minutes, and colonial despatches has been edited by Sir J. W. Kaye (London, 1855, 8vo). Two of Metcalfe's speeches delivered in the Jamaica legislature have been separately published (London, 1840, 8vo). Metcalfe is said to have published in 1838 a pamphlet on the payment of the national debt, as well as an anonymous pamphlet entitled 'Friendly Advice to the Conservatives' (*Life*, ii. 230). His essay 'On the best Means of acquiring a knowledge of the Manners and Customs of the Natives of India' is printed in the first volume of 'Essays by the Students of the College of Fort William in Bengal,' &c., Calcutta, 1802, 8vo, pp. 75–90.

[Sir J. W. Kaye's Life and Correspondence of Charles, Lord Metcalfe (new and revised ed. 1858); Sir J. W. Kaye's Lives of Indian Officers, 1889, i. 535–660; Marshman's History of India, 1867, vols. ii. and iii.; Gardner's History of Jamaica, 1873, pp. 405–18; MacMullen's History of Canada, 1868, pp. 499–501; E. G. Wakefield's View of Sir Charles Metcalfe's Government of

Canada, 1844; Morgan's Sketches of Celebrated Canadians, 1862, pp. 432–46; Walpole's History of England, 1886, v. 174, 196–9, 215, 225, 235–240; Edinburgh Review, cii. 147–78; North British Review, xxii. 145–78; Times, 9 Sept. 1846; Gent. Mag. 1846, ii. 534–6; Annual Register, 1846, App. to Chron. pp. 282–4; Dodwell and Miles's Bengal Civil Servants, 1839, pp. 324–5; Foster's Baronetage, 1881, p. 427; Notes and Queries, 7th ser. xii. 447; Haydn's Book of Dignities, 1890; London Gazettes; Brit. Mus. Cat.]

G. F. R. B.

METCALFE, FREDERICK (1815–1885), Scandinavian scholar, fifth son of Morehouse Metcalfe of Gainsborough, was born in 1815, and elected scholar of St. John's College, Cambridge, in 1834, whence he graduated B.A. in 1838 as junior optime, with a second class in classics. On 28 Nov. 1844 he was incorporated at Lincoln College, Oxford, where he held a fellowship from 1844 to 1885. In 1845 he graduated M.A. and was ordained deacon, receiving priest's orders in the following year. For a short time he was head-master of Brighton College, and on his return to Oxford in 1849 became bursar of Lincoln College and incumbent of St. Michael's, Oxford, a living in the gift of his college. In 1851 he became sub-rector, and in 1853 Greek lecturer at Lincoln, and in 1855 he graduated B.D. He died on 24 Aug. 1885.

Metcalfe, who was an accomplished Scandinavian scholar, was twice an unsuccessful candidate for the professorship of Anglo-Saxon at Oxford. He frequently spent his summer holidays in Norway, Sweden, or Iceland, and his books had considerable influence in bringing these countries to the notice of the student, the sportsman, and the tourist. His principal works are: 1. 'The Oxonian in Norway,' 1856; 2nd ed. 1857. 2. 'The Oxonian in Thelemarken,' 2 vols. 1858. 3. 'A History of German Literature,' 1858. 4. 'The Oxonian in Iceland,' 1861. 5. 'The Englishman and the Scandinavian,' 1880. He also translated Bekker's 'Charicles' and 'Gallus,' and edited some classical school books.

[Works in Brit. Mus. Libr.; Cat. Cambridge Graduates, 1800–84; Foster's Alumni Oxon. 1715–1886; Oxford Mag. 21 Oct. 1885; Times, 29 Aug. 1885.]

A. F. P.

METCALFE, JAMES (1817–1888), lieutenant-colonel Indian army, a natural son of Lord Metcalfe [see Metcalfe, Charles Theophilus, Baron Metcalfe; cf. *Gent. Mag.* 1846, pt. ii. p. 536], was born in 1817, educated at Addiscombe Military Seminary, and in 1836 was appointed to the late 3rd Bengal native infantry, of which regiment he was adjutant from 1839 to 1846. On the death of his father in the latter year he inherited a fortune of 50,000*l.* (*Gent. Mag.* ut supra). He was aide-de-camp to the Marquis of Dalhousie from 1848 to 1853. On the outbreak of the mutiny he was appointed interpreter to the commander-in-chief. In that capacity, as well as in that of aide-de-camp and commandant at headquarters, he went through the mutiny with Sir Colin Campbell, lord Clyde [q. v.], 'whose side he never quitted from the day he joined him in Calcutta in 1857 until Clyde left Paris for England in 1860' (Shadwell, Preface, i. p. x). Metcalfe was made C.B., with the brevet of lieutenant-colonel, and had the mutiny medal and clasps. He retired in 1861, and died at Harcourt Terrace, London, S.W., 8 March 1888. Metcalfe married in 1852 José Eliza, daughter of Evelyn Meadows Gordon, Bengal civil service.

[Gent. Mag. 1846, pt. ii. pp. 534–6; L. Shadwell's Life of Lord Clyde; Broad Arrow, 17 March 1888.]

H. M. C.

METCALFE, NICHOLAS (1475?–1539), archdeacon of Rochester, and a distinguished patron of learning, was the son of Richard Metcalfe, esq., of Beare Park, in the parish of Aysgarth, Richmondshire, and of 'an ancient and numerous family' (Baker, *Hist. of St. John's College*, p. 109). He was educated at Cambridge, probably at Michaelhouse. He graduated B.A. in 1494, B.D. in 1504, and D.D. in 1507. He appears early to have gained the notice of Fisher, bishop of Rochester, to whom he was chaplain, and through whose influence he was constituted archdeacon of Rochester in 1515. On 30 July 1517 he was presented to the living of Woodham Ferris in Essex, and in the following year was elected master of St. John's College, Cambridge. In this capacity he greatly contributed to the advancement of that society as a home of scholarship and learning, and attracted to it numerous benefactions. Roger Ascham, who was especially indebted to his discerning patronage, describes him as one who 'was parciall to none, but indifferent to all; a master for the whole, a father to every one in that college' (*Scholemaster*, ed. Mayor, p. 160). Baker characterises him as 'a man of equal industry and conduct, skilful in business, and fitted for government' (*Hist. of St. John's College*, p. 85). In common, however, with his patron, Fisher, and other eminent promoters of university reform, Metcalfe could not bring himself to recognise the royal supremacy in matters of doctrine, while he openly opposed Henry's divorce from Catherine. He was accordingly constrained to resign his mastership in 1537, and retired to his living of Woodham Ferris, where he died in 1539. His will, which was proved 16 Oct. 1539, contains bequests of forty shillings to St. John's College for a 'Dirige' and a mass; legacies to his sisters, Elizabeth, Alice, Jane, &c.; the residue being left for the maintenance of poor scholars in Cambridge.

[Baker's Hist. of St. John's College, ed. Mayor; Aschami Epistolæ; Cooper's Athenæ Cantabr. i. 62.] J. B. M.

METCALFE, ROBERT (1590?–1652), fellow of Trinity College, Cambridge, son of Alexander Metcalfe of Beverley, Yorkshire, was educated at the grammar school in that town, and at Michaelmas 1605 his father appears to have received from the corporation the sum of ten shillings 'to the use of his son at Cambridge' (Poulson, *Beverley*, p. 453). On 10 April 1606 Robert was admitted a fellow of St. John's College, and on the festival of St. Mark 1616 he was elected a preacher of the same society. Some time prior to 1645 he succeeded Andrew Byng of St. John's College as regius professor of Hebrew, but at what date is not known. In 1648 he vacated the chair, and was succeeded by Ralph Cudworth [q. v.] His retirement stands apparently in some connection with his election to a fellowship at Trinity in the same year; he was also appointed catechiser and vice-master of the society in October. On 14 Aug. 1646 he was appointed lecturer in Hebrew. Duport, in his 'Epicedia,' speaks of him as a man of singularly retired habits, leading a solitary life among his books in his college chamber (*Musæ Subsecivæ*, p. 492). Nicholas Hookes [q. v.] of Trinity College, who composed two elegies, one Latin and one English, to his memory, and who styles him 'sagax vice-præsul' and 'cardinalis presbyter' (i.e. head of the clerical members of the foundation), says that he was distinguished by his numerous charities, and especially by his liberality to poor deserving students (*Amanda*, pp. 121–3). Metcalfe, however, is chiefly remembered by his benefactions to the grammar school where he received his education. By his will (9 Oct. 1652) he bequeathed to 'three poor scholars of the school of Beverley, for their better maintenance at the university, to every one of them 6*l.* 13*s.* 4*d.*,' with the proviso that 'no son of any of the aldermen, or of any of sufficient ability to maintain their children at the university, should be capable of that maintenance.' To his sister, Prudence Metcalfe, he also bequeathed 20*l.* yearly; to the schoolmaster 10*l.*, and to the 'preacher or lecturer' of Beverley 10*l.*; to St. John's College, 'gratitudinis ergo,' 100*l.*; to the university library 20*l.* His arms, with a few lines respecting him, are in the 'Liber Memorialis' of Trinity College.

[Registers of Trinity College and St. John's College, Cambridge; Baker's Hist. of St. John's College; J. Duport's Musæ Subsecivæ.] J. B. M.

METCALFE, THEOPHILUS (*fl.* 1649), stenographer, was a professional writer and teacher of shorthand, who in 1645 resided in St. Katherine's Court, near the Tower of London. He published a stenographic system based almost entirely on the lines of Thomas Shelton's 'Tachygraphy.' The first edition of his work was entitled 'Radio-Stenography, or Short Writing,' and is supposed to have been published in 1635. A so-called sixth edition appeared at London in 1645, 12mo. It was followed in 1649 by 'A Schoolmaster to Radio-Stenography, explaining all the Rules of the said Art, by way of Dialogue betwixt Master and Scholler, fitted to the weakest capacities that are desirous to learne this Art.' Many editions of the system appeared under the title of 'Short Writing: the most easie, exact, lineall, and speedy Method that hath ever yet been obtained or taught by any in this Kingdome.' On the title-page of the nineteenth edition (1679) it is asserted that 'a young man, that lately lived at Cornhill, learned so well by this book that he wrote out all the Bible in this character.' The statement is repeated on the title-page of the fifty-fifth edition, printed for Edmund Parker at the Bible and Crown in Lombard Street about 1756. In reality these editions, as they are called, were for the most part only small numbers of copies taken from the same plates at different times, the dates being as often altered as the title. These plates were engraved by Frederick Henry Van Hove of Haarlem (*Shorthand*, i. 81, 82). A copy of the Bible written in Metcalfe's system by Dr. William Holder [q. v.], and completed in 1668, is preserved in the British Museum (*Addit. MS.* 30385). Dr. Isaac Watts was also a writer of this system.

A portrait of Metcalfe is prefixed to the so-called sixth edition of his 'Radio-Stenography,' published in 1645.

[Anderson's Hist. of Shorthand, p. 114; Gibson's Bibliography of Shorthand, pp. 12, 96, 129; Granger's Biog. Hist. of England, 5th edit. iii. 194; Journalist, 25 March 1887, p. 381; Levy's Hist. of Shorthand, p. 30; Lewis's Hist. of Shorthand, pp. 65–9; Rockwell's Literature of Shorthand, 2nd edit. p. 109; Shorthand, i. 50, ii. 10, 55.] T. C.

METCALFE, Sir **THEOPHILUS JOHN** (1828–1883), joint-magistrate at Meerut at the outbreak of the Mutiny, born at Delhi 28 Nov. 1828, was eldest son of Sir Thomas Theophilus Metcalfe, fourth baronet, by his second wife, the daughter of J. Browne, of the Bengal Medical Board. The father entered the Bengal Civil Service in 1813; held various appointments in the Delhi territories, and was commissioner and governor-general's agent at Delhi from 1835 to his death in 1853. One of the father's brothers, Sir Theophilus John, second baronet, was president of the select committee at Canton, and died in 1823; another brother, Sir Charles Theophilus, the third baronet, became Lord Metcalfe [q. v.]

The son, Theophilus John, fifth baronet, was intended for the army, and was sent to the East India Company's military college at Addiscombe, but was removed to Haileybury, and in 1848 entered the Bengal civil service, and joined his father at Delhi. Young Metcalfe succeeded to the baronetcy in 1853, and in 1857 was appointed joint-magistrate and deputy-collector, first grade, at Meerut, and deputy-collector at Futtepore. On the morning of 11 May 1857 Metcalfe brought information to the magazine at Delhi that the Meerut (Miráth) mutineers of the previous day were crossing the river to the city (*ib.* ii. 66). Many sinister native traditions attached to the family residence, Metcalfe House, Delhi, which was reputed to have been the tomb of a foster-brother of the Emperor Akhbar. It was one of the first houses that had been gutted by the mutineers, when the library, said to be the finest in India, was burned (cf. Malleson, ii. 408). Metcalfe aided the escape of the European inhabitants, and reached Anson's army at Kurnaul. On 6 June he was at Kurnaul with Mr. Le Bas, joint-magistrate at Delhi, when the guide corps arrived on its march down to join the army before Delhi. He detained the guides to punish some suspected villages, so that the corps was too late for the battle of Budlee-ke-Serai (*ib.* ii. 351). Metcalfe joined the army before Delhi. A brave, resolute man, who seemed to bear a charmed life, and knew every inch of the ground, he was often of great service to the besieging troops. He piloted the cavalry that fell on the enemy's rear at Mejgufghur, and at the assault of 14 Sept. Colonel George Campbell, commanding the 52nd light infantry, reported the 'invaluable assistance' he received from Metcalfe, 'who was at my side throughout the operations, and fearlessly guided me through many intricate streets and turnings to the Jumna Musjid, traversing at least two-thirds of the city, and enabling me to avoid many dangers and difficulties' (*Hist. Rec. 52nd Regt.* 2nd edit. p. 377). After the city fell, Metcalfe, on whose head a price had been set, was foremost in what the historian Malleson calls 'the retributive eagerness of the civilians' (Malleson, ii. 351). He appears to have been intensely hated and feared by the natives (cf. Holmes, p. 387). He was appointed assistant to the agent at Delhi and deputy-collector at Futtepore in 1858, and went home on sick furlough in 1859. Ill-health prevented his return to India. He was made C.B. in 1864, and retired on an invalid pension in 1866. He died in Paris, 10 Nov. 1883, aged 54.

Metcalfe married, first, in 1851, Charlotte, daughter of General (Sir) John Low [q. v.]; she died at Simla in 1855, leaving issue; secondly, in 1876, Katherine Hawkins, daughter of the late James Whitehead Dempster of Dunnichen, Forfarshire.

[Information supplied by the India Office; Ann. Reg. 1857 and 1883, p. 177; Malleson's Indian Mutiny, 6th edit. (1888–9); Holmes's Indian Mutiny, 3rd edit. 1884.] H. M. C.

METEYARD, ELIZA (1816–1879), author, daughter of William Meteyard, surgeon, and his wife Mary, daughter of Zebedee Beckham of Great Yarmouth, was born on 21 June 1816, in Lime Street, Liverpool, in which town her father had been settled for a year. In 1818, on the appointment of her father as surgeon to the Shropshire militia, she was taken to Shrewsbury, and in 1829 removed to Thorpe, near Norwich, where she remained till 1842, when she settled in London. She began literary work in 1833 by assisting her eldest brother, a tithe commissioner, in preparing his reports relating to the eastern counties. She afterwards became a regular contributor of fiction and social articles to the periodical press, writing in 'Eliza Cook's Journal,' the 'People's Journal,' 'Tait's Magazine,' 'Chambers's Journal,' 'Household Words,' 'Country Words,' and other journals. To the first number of 'Douglas Jerrold's Weekly Newspaper' she contributed a leading article to which Jerrold appended the signature of 'Silverpen,' which she afterwards used as her *nom de guerre*. She gained prizes for essays on 'Juvenile Depravity' and 'Omnibus Conductors.' Her first novel was written in 1840 for 'Tait's Magazine,' and republished in 1845 under the title of 'Struggles for Fame,' but her most popular novels were 'Mainstone's House keeper,' 1860, and 'Lady Herbert's Gentlewoman,' 1862. Between 1850 and 1878 she wrote a series of seven or eight charming stories for children. In 1861 she published an interesting volume on the 'Hallowed Spots of Ancient London,' and in 1865–6 her important 'Life of Josiah Wedgwood,' in two volumes. This was followed in 1871 by 'A Group of Englishmen (1795–1815), being Records of the younger Wedgwoods and their Friends.' In 1875 she wrote 'The Wedgwood Handbook, a Manual for Collectors,' and contributed the letterpress descriptions to 'Wedgwood and his Works,' 1873, 'Memorials of Wedgwood,' 1874, 'Choice Examples of Wedgwood Ware,' 1879, and a 'Catalogue of Wedgwood Manufactures.'

She died on 4 April 1879 at Stanley Terrace, Fentiman Road, South Lambeth. For several years she had enjoyed a pension of 100*l.* from the civil list. An excellent likeness of her in a marble medallion executed by G. Fontana, formerly the property of her friend Joseph Mayer [q. v.], who had aided her in bringing out the 'Life of Wedgwood,' is in the Mayer Public Hall at Bebington, near Birkenhead.

[Men of the Time, 10th edit.; C. Roach Smith's Retrospections, 1886, ii. 106; Manchester City News, 12 April 1879; Allibone's Dictionary of Authors, iii. 1271.] C. W. S.

METHOLD, Sir **WILLIAM** (1560?–1620), lord chief baron of the exchequer in Ireland, born about 1560, was eldest son of William Methold of Rushworth and South Pickenham, Norfolk, by Susanna, daughter of George Alington of Swinhope, Lincolnshire, and Rushworth, Norfolk (*Visitations of Norfolk*, Harl. Soc., p. 198). On 20 Feb. 1580–1 he was admitted a member of Lincoln's Inn, in 1608 he was Lent reader of his inn and a bencher, and in 1611 he was made a serjeant. On 16 March 1612 he was appointed chief baron of the exchequer in Ireland and a privy councillor, and was knighted by James I (Metcalfe, *Book of Knights*, p. 163; Smyth, *Law Officers of Ireland*, p. 141). He subsequently became lord chief justice of the king's bench in Ireland, and was appointed a joint keeper of the great seal on 10 April 1619 (*ib.* pp. 26, 217). Methold died on 7 March 1620, and was buried in Christ Church, Dublin. His wife was Margaret, daughter of John Southwell of Barham, Suffolk. By her he had an only daughter, Elizabeth, who on 18 July 1608 married at Dagenham, Essex, Thomas Potts, master of the harehounds to James I and Charles I (Lodge, *Peerage*, ed. Archdall, vi. 14), and after her husband's death suffered so much poverty that the council of state, on 25 May 1655, granted her a pension of 10*s.* a week. Lady Methold survived her husband, and married Sir Thomas Rotheram, knt., one of the privy council of Ireland. She died on 23 Dec. 1640, in the lifetime of her second husband, and was buried in Christ Church, Dublin, on the 26th.

Methold's nephew, William Methold (*d.* 1653), son of Thomas Methold, by Susanna, daughter of Anthony Hogan of Gosthorp, Norfolk, was apprenticed to a merchant at Middleborough. He was on his own petition admitted into the East India Company's service in 1615, and sailed for Surat. He travelled much in India, and visited the diamond mines of Golconda in 1622, being the first Englishman to accomplish the journey. His narrative of his Indian travels, entitled 'Relations of the Kingdome of Golchonda and other neighbouring Nations within the Gulfe of Bengala,' &c., was printed in 1626, when Methold had returned to England, in the fifth volume of Purchas's 'Pilgrims,' pp. 993–1007. Purchas, in the preface, passes a high eulogium on Methold. On 27 June 1628 he was sworn a 'free brother' (i.e. in effect a director) of the East India Company. In 1632 he acted as deputy of Humphrey Leigh as swordbearer of the city of London. In 1633 he was sent by the company to Surat in charge of an important mission to Persia (cf. *Addit. MS.* 11268, p. 46). He probably came home again in 1636. In 1650 he was deputy governor of the East India Company. He died possessed of great wealth on 5 March 1652–3 at his mansion, Hale House, afterwards known as Cromwell House, Kensington, which he had purchased about 1648 of the executors of his first wife's relative Sir William Blake; it was pulled down in 1850 to form a site for the Great Exhibition. He had also bought land in Yorkshire, Wiltshire, and Somerset, and buildings near Charing Cross. He was buried as 'Meathall' on the 10th in Kensington Church (*Register*, Harl. Soc., p. 123). He married twice. By his first wife, Mary Blake, of a Hampshire family, whom he married in 1632–3, he had two sons and three daughters; she was buried at Kensington on 5 Oct. 1652. His second wife was Sarah, daughter of Sir Richard Deane, at one time lord mayor of London, and widow of William Rolfe of Ealing, Middlesex, whom he married on 16 Feb. 1652–3; her will was proved on 8 April 1678. He erected almshouses for six poor women near Hale House, and endowed them with 24*l.* per annum; but they were removed in 1865 by the Metropolitan Railway Company under their statutory powers.

[Notes of much value kindly supplied by E. Chester Waters, esq.; Woolrych's Lives of Eminent Serjeants-at-Law, i. 165–9; Blomefield's

Norfolk, ed. Parkin, vi. 73; Waters's Genealog. Memoirs of the Chesters of Chicheley, ii. 696; Nichols's Herald and Genealogist, vi. 598; Pedigree of the Methwold Family, 4to, 1870, pp. 21–4; Faulkner's Kensington, pp. 331, 370; Lysons's Environs, iii. 180, 186, 228; Jones's Treasures of the Earth, p. 215.] G. G.

METHUEN, JOHN (1650?–1706), lord chancellor of Ireland, was the eldest son of Paul Methuen of Bradford, Wiltshire, clothier, by his wife Grace (*d.* 1676), daughter of John Ashe of Freshford, Somerset. Paul Methuen, eldest son of Anthony Methuen or Methwin (1574–1640), vicar of Frome, by Jean, daughter of Thomas Taylor of Bristol, settled in Bradford between 1620 and 1630, took over the business of his father-in-law, John Ashe, greatly improved the property, became, in the words of his acquaintance, John Aubrey, 'the greatest cloathier of his time,' and amassed a large fortune. At first he issued only a coarse cloth or drugget, but in 1659 he obtained from Holland some spinners who instructed his men in the manufacture of the finer kinds of cloth. In connection with his industry he issued several tokens, some of which are figured in Akerman's 'List of Wiltshire Tokens' (1846). He lived in Pippet Street, Bradford, in a large house which formerly belonged to Sir Edward Rogers of Cannington, comptroller of the household to Queen Elizabeth, and there he died in 1667 (*Wiltshire Archæol. Magazine*, v. 48–378). John matriculated at Oxford University from St. Edmund Hall on 21 April 1665, aged 15. He does not appear to have taken any degree, but was subsequently called to the bar at the Inner Temple, and on 20 June 1685 was appointed a master in chancery, a post which he held during the rest of his life. He was included in the double return made for Devizes at the general election in 1689-90, but his name was taken off the file by an order of the House of Commons on 29 March 1690 (*Journals of the House of Commons*, x. 360). In the following December, however, he obtained the seat upon petition, and continued thenceforth to represent the borough until his death. Methuen became envoy to Portugal in 1691 (LUTTRELL, ii. 225), and was a member of the council of trade from 15 May 1696 to 9 June 1699. In November 1696 he supported the third reading of the bill of attainder against Sir John Fenwick (*Parl. Hist.* v. 1112–15; see also p. 1023 ante). Methuen was appointed lord chancellor of Ireland on 24 Jan. 1697, and took his seat as speaker of the Irish House of Lords on 15 June following (*Journals of the Irish House of Lords*, i. 596). His original patent was dated 11 March 1697, and he was confirmed in the appointment by Anne on 26 July 1702. He was succeeded in his post of envoy to Portugal by his son Paul. Ignorant of the principles of equity, Methuen made an inefficient judge, though Luttrell records under date 13 July 1697 that 'Irish letters say the Lord Chancellor Methwyn has already reformed divers ill practices there, to the great satisfaction of the publick' (iv. 251). He appears to have signally failed in his attempt to manage the Irish parliament (COXE, *Shrewsbury Correspondence*, 1821, pp. 555–7). Methuen was frequently absent from Ireland, and after his return to England in December 1701 he never resumed his judicial duties. In April 1702 he was despatched to Portugal to demand a positive answer from the king whether he would 'recede from his alliance with France and Spain or persist therein' (LUTTRELL, v. 163). Methuen soon afterwards returned to England. The object of his mission was ultimately gained, and a treaty between the allied powers and Portugal was concluded at Lisbon by his son Paul on 16 May 1703. Methuen was succeeded in his post of lord chancellor of Ireland by Sir Richard Cox [q. v.] in July 1703, and in the following month was appointed ambassador extraordinary to Portugal (*ib.* v. 325, 328, 336). He concluded the famous treaty with Portugal, which bore his name, on 27 Dec. 1703. It consisted only of three articles, and by them Dom Pedro agreed to admit into Portugal the woollen manufactures of England, while Anne engaged to grant differential duties in favour of all Portuguese wines imported into England, duties less by one-third than those exacted on the wines of France. It was owing to this treaty that port gradually took the place of Burgundy, which had hitherto been the favourite wine in this country (STANHOPE, *Reign of Queen Anne*, 1870, pp. 111–12). The 'Methuen Treaty' was renewed by the 26th article of the treaty of commerce and navigation of 19 Feb. 1810, and was not finally abrogated until 1836. Methuen died at Lisbon on 2 July 1706. His remains were subsequently brought to England and were buried on 17 Sept. 1708 in Westminster Abbey, where there is a memorial to him and his son Paul by Rysbrack.

Methuen was a staunch whig. He is described by Macky as 'a man of intrigue, but very muddy in his conceptions, and not quickly understood in anything. In his complexion and manners much of a Spaniard: a tall black man' (*Memoirs of the Secret Services of John Macky*, 1733, p. 143), and Swift adds that he was 'a profligate rogue without religion or morals; but cunning enough; yet without abilities of any kind' (*Works*, 1814, x. 313). On the other hand it is asserted that 'he was a person of great parts, much improved by study, travel, and conversation with the best,' and that 'his manly yet easy eloquence shin'd in the House of Commons upon many important and nice occasions' (*Annals of Queen Anne*, 1707, v. 495). Methuen married, in February 1671–2, Mary, daughter of Seacole Chevers of Comerford, Wiltshire, by whom he had, with other issue, an only surviving son, Sir Paul Methuen [q. v.] His only daughter, Isabel, died unmarried, aged 29, and was buried in Westminster Abbey on 12 April 1711. One of his sons was killed in a brawl abroad in 1694 (Luttrell, iii 362). A quantity of Methuen's correspondence is preserved in the Hatton collection (*Hist. MSS. Comm.* 1st Rep. p. 26), and a number of his letters will be found among the Additional Manuscripts in the British Museum (see *Indices to Addit. MSS.* for 1836–53, 1854–75, 1882–7), and in the Spencer and Ormonde collections (*Hist. MSS. Comm.* 2nd Rep. p. 16, 7th Rep. App. i. App. 765, 833, 834). There is a mezzotint engraving of Methuen by Humphreys.

[Luttrell's Brief Historical Relation of State Affairs, 1857; Letters illustrative of the Reign of William III from 1696 to 1708, addressed to the Duke of Shrewsbury by James Vernon, edited by G. P. R. James, 1841; Correspondence of Henry Hyde, Earl of Clarendon, and Laurence Hyde, Earl of Rochester, 1828, vol. ii.; Locke's Letters, ed. 1708, passim; O'Flanagan's Lives of the Lord Chancellors of Ireland, 1870, i. 489–96; Burke's Hist. of the Lord Chancellors of Ireland, 1879, pp. 97–100; Hertslet's Commercial Treaties, 1827 ii. 24–5, 59, 1840 v. 413–14; Granger's Biog. Hist. of England (Noble), ii. 216–17; Chester's Westminster Abbey Registers, 1876, pp. 264, 272, 390; Foster's Peerage, 1883, p. 484; Haydn's Book of Dignities, 1890.] G. F. R. B.

METHUEN, PAUL (*fl.* 1566), Scottish reformer, originally a baker in Dundee, was an early convert to the new doctrines. Although imperfectly educated, his eloquence and intimate acquaintance with scripture enabled him to render such good service to the protestant cause that he became obnoxious both to the prelates and the secret council; and the latter not only issued an order for his apprehension, but also forbade the people to listen to his orations or to harbour him in their houses. Methuen avoided arrest through the intrepidity of Provost Haliburton, and to show their disappointment at his escape, the secret council fined the town of Dundee in the sum of 2,000*l.* During the war between Scotland and England, which began in the autumn of 1556, and continued through the following year, the protestants enjoyed considerable liberty, and their numbers rapidly increased. Methuen, William Harlaw, John Douglas, and John Willock now began to preach with greater publicity in different parts of Scotland. On 10 May 1559 Methuen and other prominent reformers were placed on their trial before the justiciary court at Stirling for usurping the ministerial office, for administering without the consent of their ordinaries the sacrament of the altar in a manner different from that of the catholic church, in the burghs of Dundee and Montrose, and for convening the subjects of the realm in those places, preaching to them erroneous doctrines, and exciting seditions and tumults. Being found guilty, he was 'denounced rebel and put to the horn as fugitive' (Pitcairn, *Ancient Criminal Trials*, i. 406).

He was nominated by the lords of the congregation to the church of Jedburgh, Roxburghshire, 19 July 1560, in which year and the following he was a member of assembly. He was deposed from his incumbency, with some difficulty, towards the end of 1562, for adultery with his servant, and sentence of excommunication was also pronounced against him. Thereupon he fled to England and resumed his ministerial office there. In 1563 it was declared in the assembly that he was 'verie sorrowful for his grievous offence, and wald underly whatever punishment the kirk would lay upon him,' which declaration, on 27 Dec. 1564, 'the haill Assemblie with ane voyce are content to receive.' After an absence of upwards of two years the assembly, on 26 June 1566, ordained his public repentance. He was ordered to appear at the church door of Edinburgh when the second bell rang for public worship, clothed in sackcloth, bareheaded and bare-footed; to stand there until the prayer and psalms were finished; when he was to be brought into the church to hear the sermon, during which he was to be 'placeit in the publick spectakill [stool of repentance] above the peiple.' He was to repeat this procedure at Dundee and Jedburgh, where he had officiated as minister. Methuen went through a part of this discipline, but being overwhelmed with shame, or despairing to regain his lost reputation, he stopped in the midst of it, and again returned to England.

[Athenæum, 26 Dec. 1868, p. 884; Calderwood's Hist. of the Kirk of Scotland (Wodrow Soc.), i. 304, 333, 343, 344, 347, 439, ii. 11, 207, 210, 284, 322, 323; Jervise's Memorials of Angus and the Mearns (Gammack), i. 99, 281, 282; McCrie's Life of Knox (1812), pp. 169,

268, 269, 490; Row's Hist. of the Kirk of Scotland (Wodrow Soc.), pp. 25, 26, 29, 36; Hew Scott's Fasti, vol. i. pt. ii. p. 479; Spotiswood's Hist. of the Church of Scotland (Spottiswoode Soc.), i. 186, 266; Wiltshire Archæological Mag. v. 380 and pedigree.] T. C.

METHUEN, PAUL (*d.* 1667), clothier of Bradford. [See under METHUEN, JOHN.]

METHUEN, SIR PAUL (1672–1757), diplomatist, eldest and only surviving son of John Methuen [q. v.], lord chancellor of Ireland, was born in 1672. When about twenty years old he entered the diplomatic service, and from 1697 to 1705, as envoy to the king of Portugal, he assisted his father in negotiations at Lisbon, where his conduct was much praised by the Hon. Alexander Stanhope, minister at Madrid (STANHOPE, *Spain under Charles II*, p. 132). In July 1705 he accompanied Charles, archduke of Austria and claimant to the Spanish throne, on an expedition to Gibraltar, and at the close of that year was appointed minister at Turin. In 1706 he succeeded his father as ambassador to Portugal and remained there until August 1708, when he obtained leave of absence on account of his election to parliament by the borough of Devizes in Wiltshire. That constituency he represented from 1708 to 1710, and was again elected in 1710 by a double return, but was unseated by the House of Commons. In 1713 he was returned for Brackley, Northamptonshire, and although his name was erased by the house, he was rechosen by that borough at the general election of 1714–15, and represented it continuously until 1747. From November 1709 to December 1710 he held the post of lord of the admiralty, and from October 1714 to April 1717 he served in the same capacity at the treasury. In 1714 Methuen was appointed ambassador to Spain and Morocco, and on 29 Oct. in that year was created a privy councillor. During Stanhope's absence from England in 1716 he acted in his place as secretary of state, and then succeeded to the southern department; but on Townshend's dismissal from office he resigned with Walpole and Pulteney. A plaintive letter from him to Stanhope, in December 1716, sets out that he was writing 'at four in the morning,' after having been at work for eleven hours, and that, if he had any choice, he would much 'rather be a slave in the gallies.' On the return of his friends to power he became, in June 1720, comptroller of the household, a dignity exchanged in 1725 for that of treasurer of the household, which he occupied until 1730. He was, moreover, made a knight of the Bath on the revival of that order by George I in May 1725. Townshend endeavoured in 1730 to obtain his reappointment as secretary of state, but failed in the effort, and from that year Methuen remained out of office. He led the opposition to Bolingbroke's partial pardon, spoke vehemently against Walpole's excise measure, and in December 1741 carried Dr. Lee by four votes as chairman of committees in opposition to Walpole's nominee. He died, unmarried, on 11 April 1757, and was buried near his father in the south aisle of Westminster Abbey, where a memorial by Rysbrach was erected to their memory. His wealth was estimated at 250,000*l.*, of which 50,000*l.* in guineas were found, tied up in bags and sealed, in his house, not having produced any interest for years. Through his liberality all his servants were left with board wages for the rest of their lives.

Horace Walpole, in his 'Observations on Lord Chesterfield's Memoirs,' which are printed in the Philobiblon Soc. vol. xi., calls Methuen 'a dull, formal, romantic braggadochio,' who had returned from Spain with some reputation, and gives some specimens of his coarseness of demeanour; but this criticism was no doubt influenced by Methuen's political action. Lady Mary Wortley Montagu considered him 'handsome and well made, with wit enough, and a romantic turn in his conversation' worthy of Othello. She adds that he was a lover of Madame Kilmansegge (*Letters*, &c. ed. 1861, i. 132), at whom Lady Cowper describes him as 'making sweet eyes' at a party at Madame Montandre's in December 1714 (*Diary*, p. 29). His name twice occurs in Swift's 'Journal to Stella;' the fourth of Gay's 'Epistles on Several Occasions' is addressed to him, and in the epistle to Pope on the completion of the translation of the 'Iliad' Gay speaks of 'Methuen of sincerest mind, as Arthur grave, as soft as womankind.' The dedication by Steele of the seventh volume of the 'Spectator' to him praises his part, as British ambassador, in promoting commerce between England and Portugal, and the military renown which he won while minister at the court of Savoy. It also records his 'most graceful address in horsemanship, the use of the sword, and dancing,' as well as his genial hospitality. Methuen possessed a considerable knowledge of foreign languages and of the best authors in the chief European countries. During his stay abroad he formed a fine collection of pictures, an account of which, given in 'Catalogues of the Collections of Pictures of the Duke of Devonshire, General Guise, and the late Sir Paul Methuen. Strawberry Hill, 1760,' was reproduced in

Thomas Martin's 'English Connoisseur,' 1766, ii. 17–37. He left the pictures to his cousin, Paul Methuen of Corsham House, Wiltshire (cf. Waagen's 'Treasures of Art in Great Britain,' supplementary vol. pp. 394–9). Letters from the Methuens abound in the manuscripts at the British Museum, particularly in Addit. MS. 28056, and in the collections described by the Historical MSS. Commission. Many are printed in Coxe's 'Sir Robert Walpole,' vol. ii., and in the 'Letters and Despatches of Marlborough;' John Hill Burton makes much use of them in the 'History of Queen Anne,' ii. 57–178.

The third volume of Charles King's 'British Merchant,' 1721, is dedicated to Methuen.

[Burke's Peerage; Gent. Mag. 1757, p. 189; Wilts Archæol. Mag. v. 378–83; Britton's Beauties of England, vol. xv. 'Wiltshire,' pp. 510–20; Britton's Corsham House and its Pictures, 1806; Baker's Northamptonshire, i. 570–1; Chester's Westminster Abbey, pp. 272, 390; Neale and Brayley's Westminster Abbey, ii. 251; Coxe's Sir R. Walpole, i. 105–7, 159, 207, 336, 399; Parnell's War of Succession in Spain, pp. 113, 163; Luttrell's Hist. Relation, v. 556, vi. 14, 341; Garth's Dispensary, 1775, canto i. p. 22; Walpole's Letters, i. 100, 284; Walpole's Painting, ed. Wornum, iii. 992.] W. P. C.

METHVEN, first Baron (1495?–1551?). [See Stewart, Henry.]

METHVEN, Lord (1746–1806), Scottish judge. [See Smythe, David.]

MEUDWY MÔN (1806–1889), Welsh miscellaneous writer. [See Jones, Owen.]

MEULAN, Counts of. [See Beaumont, Robert de, *d.* 1118; Beaumont, Waleran de, 1104–1166.]

MEURYG (*fl.* 1250), treasurer of Llandaff. [See Maurice, *fl.* 1210.]

MEVERALL, OTHOWELL, M.D. (1585–1648), physician, was born in 1585 in Derbyshire, and after education at home became a member of Christ's College, Cambridge, where he graduated B.A. In 1608, while living in that college, he had an illness, probably smallpox. The method of treatment then adopted included the closing of all apertures of the sick room, and often resulted in the partial asphyxiation of the patient when almost convalescent. He became insensible and was supposed to be dead. The preparations for his burial by exposing him to fresh air revived him, and he was thus restored to life after a narrow escape from being buried alive. He went to Leyden, and there graduated M.D. on 2 Oct. 1613. On this degree he was incorporated at Cambridge 15 March 1616. He settled in practice in the city of London, and was elected a fellow of the College of Physicians 21 April 1618. He was censor for eight years between 1624 and 1640, was registrar 1639–40, and president 1641–4. His graduation thesis at Leyden is extant in manuscript (information from Dr. Munk), as are the notes of the anatomy lectures which he read at the College of Physicians in November 1628 (Sloane MS. 2614 A). On 28 Dec. 1637 (Young, *Annals of Barber-Surgeons*, p. 367) it was resolved by the court of assistants of the Barber-Surgeons Company that 'Dr. Meverell shalbe Reader of our anatomical lectures at the next publique discection to be held in the new erected Theater;' and 8 Nov. 1638, 'that there shalbe presented as the guift of this Compaine to Mr. Doctor Meverell a peece of plate with the Compaines scutchion ingraven thereon for his paynes in readeing at our last publiqe anatomye in the new Theater before the Lords of his Majesties most honourable privye Councell and others, spectators in the time of those 3 dayes readeings.' The lectures began with a prayer (Sloane MS. 2614 A), beginning, 'Deo autem optimo et maximo æternas agamus gratias.' Then followed an introduction in Latin, then the dissection was carried out under the lecturer's direction, and with his explanations, and at the end he again gave a short address. Its last words were 'vos autem gratias agite chirurgiæ proceribus et anatomiæ magistris his quia dextri et artificiose putridum hoc cadaver dissecaverunt.' In his pocket notebook (*ib.*) he has written below, 'Sic perorabam in theatro anatomico chirurgorum, Londin: 13 April 1638.' He resigned the office at the end of that year. His notebooks show that he was well read in Cicero, and what might not have been expected of a Ciceronian and Grecian he quotes Rhazes as well as Hippocrates and Galen. Some few notes of cases, general notes on diseases, and numerous prescriptions are contained in his notebooks, as well as a rhythmical declamation in Latin on 'The fear of the Lord is the beginning of wisdom.' He died 13 July 1648, and was buried in the church of St. Lawrence Jewry. He left 40*l.* to the College of Physicians, and to several of the fellows a gold ring with the inscription, 'Medici morimur, medicina perennis.' He is to be distinguished from Dr. Andrew Meverell of Trinity College, Cambridge, elected a fellow of the College of Physicians in December 1664, to whom John Pechey's [q. v.] 'Observations on the Therapeutic Value of the Byzantine Cockroach' are addressed.

[Munk's Coll. of Phys. ii. 172; Sloane MSS. in Brit. Mus. 2614 A and B; Hamey's Bustorum aliquot Reliquiæ, manuscript in Library of Coll. of Phys. of London.] N. M.

MEWS, PETER (1619–1706), bishop of Winchester, son of Elisha Mews, was born at Purse Candle, near Sherborne, Dorset, on 25 March 1618–19 (HUTCHINS, *History of Dorset*, 1774, ii. 345). He was sent to Merchant Taylors' School at the charge of his uncle, Dr. Winniffe, then dean of St. Paul's. He was elected scholar of St. John's College, Oxford, 11 June 1637, and graduated B.A. on 13 May 1641, and M.A. in 1645. In 1642 he took service in the force raised by the university for the king's service, and served in his majesty's guards throughout the war, obtaining the rank of captain (GODWIN, *De Præsulibus Angliæ*, ed. Richardson, p. 244). 'He received several times near thirty wounds, and was taken prisoner at Naseby' (*Nicholas Papers*, ii. 19). In 1648 he retired to Holland, and was constantly employed during the Commonwealth as an agent of the royalists, being chiefly employed by his intimate friend, Secretary Nicholas. He was an adept at disguising himself (*ib.* p. 236). In August 1653 Nicholas applied to the Princess of Orange to use her influence to gain him the post of philosophy reader at Breda (*ib.* p. 19), but was assured by Hyde that the place required a man 'that hath not bene a truant from his bookes' (Hyde to Nicholas, 22 Aug. 1653, *Cal. Clarendon State Papers*, ii. 242). The statement that at this time he sent a weekly letter from Leyden to the parliamentarians (Bunce to Ormonde, 27 Nov. 1653, *ib.* p. 27) was unquestionably a slander; as a stout Anglican he was much disliked by the 'presbyterian gang' (Hyde to Nicholas, 16 Jan. 1654, *ib.*) In the winter of 1653–4, when Middleton took command of the insurrection of the highlanders, Mews was designated his secretary, with a special recommendation from Charles II (2 Jan. 1654, *ib.*; BURNET, *Hist. of my own Time*, ed. 1753, ii. 435). He bore a number of letters to the Scots nobility, and it was probably on this mission that he had a narrow escape of being hanged by the rebels (WALKER, *Sufferings of the Clergy*, p. 119; *Hist. MSS. Comm.*, Duke of Hamilton's MSS., 1887, p. 137; *Clarendon State Papers*, passim). Before the end of the year he returned to Holland (*Nicholas Papers*, ii. 93, 138), and shortly afterwards fell out with Hyde, but continued to be intimate with Nicholas, with whom he was in constant correspondence (Hyde to Nicholas, *Clarendon State Papers*, iii. 30, 31, 33; *Nicholas Papers*, ii. passim, especially 275, 311, 329; and *Cal. State Papers*, 1657–8, pp. 341, 358, 366). He again undertook a mission to Scotland in 1655, and sent a gloomy but valuable account of affairs to Nicholas (*Nicholas Papers*, ii. 187). He served also under the Duke of York in Flanders (*Cal. State Papers*; WILSON, *History of Merchant Taylors' School*, p. 729).

The date of his ordination is uncertain, but he is said to have been collated archdeacon of Huntingdon on 19 Nov. 1649, though he was not installed until after the Restoration (CASSAN, *Lives of the Bishops of Winchester*, ii. 188–99). He was also presented, but not instituted, to the rectory of Lambourne, Essex, during the Commonwealth (GRANGER, *Biog. Hist.* iii. 237). On the Restoration he returned to England, and petitioned the king for money to pay debts contracted in the royal service, and to furnish him with books to prosecute his studies at the university (*Cal. State Papers*, September, 1660). He took the degree of D.C.L. on 6 Dec. 1660 (WOOD, *Fasti*, ii. 809). Preferments were rapidly heaped upon him. He was installed archdeacon of Huntingdon on 12 Sept. 1660, and was made vicar of St. Mary's, Reading, where he was active against conventicles (*Cal. State Papers*, 14 and 19 Jan. 1662–3, and 26 Sept. 1667), rector of South Warnborough, Hampshire, and chaplain to the king. In September 1661 he was presented to the rectory of Worplesdon, Surrey. He was readmitted to his fellowship at St. John's College on the special recommendation of the king (29 Dec. 1661, *ib.*) On 30 Oct. 1662 he was installed canon of Windsor, and shortly afterwards canon of St. Davids. He resigned the archdeaconry of Huntingdon in 1665, and on 30 Aug. was made archdeacon of Berkshire. During this period Mews was a constant correspondent of Williamson, who then edited the 'London Gazette.'

On the death of Dr. Richard Baylie, president of St. John's College, Arlington, by the king's command, addressed a letter to the vice-president and fellows, recommending Mews (who had married Baylie's daughter) for the post on account of his 'orthodox learning and sober life' and his loyal service to the crown during the rebellion. A similar letter was sent by the Bishop (Morley) of Winchester (both letters in St. John's College manuscript Register). He was accordingly elected president on 5 Aug. 1667, and on 26 Sept. was admitted, according to the ancient custom, by the dean and canons of Christ Church (JOSEPH TAYLOR, history of the college in *St. John's College MSS.*) At the time of the election he was absent at Breda as one of the royal commissioners to treat for the peace (*Cal. State Papers*, 25 Aug. 1667). During the same year he received the 'golden prebend' of St. Davids, and was made canon of Durham. He was vice-chancellor of the university of Oxford 1669-73, and in 1670 he became dean of Rochester. On 9 Feb. 1672 he was consecrated bishop of Bath and Wells (KENNETT, *Register*, 1728, i. 752). He resigned the presidency of St. John's 3 Oct. 1673, at the expiration of his vice-chancellorship (*St. John's College MSS.*) In his diocese he was 'greatly beloved by the loyal gentry, who were almost unanimous in all elections and public affairs during his residence among them' (HUTCHINS, *Hist. of Dorset*, ii. 345). Early in November 1684 the king gave him the bishopric of Winchester (CASSAN, *Lives of the Bishops of Winchester*, ii. 189). In the next year he was one of the first to offer an energetic resistance to Monmouth (RANKE, *Hist. of England*, iv. 257), and at Sedgmoor his own horses drew the royal cannon to the point whence he himself directed their fire with decisive effect. He received a wound in the battle, from which he suffered for the rest of his life (*Life of Ken*, by a Layman, pp. 282, 409). After the victory he interceded for the lives of the rebels.

In the famous contention between James II and Magdalen College he played an important part (cf. BLOXAM, *Magdalen College and James II*, Oxford Historical Society). As visitor of the college he supported the fellows in their adherence to the statutes, telling them that he 'admired their courage,' and in spite of the king's known wishes he admitted Dr. Hough to the presidency, 16 April 1687, and stoutly defended his action in a letter to Sunderland. At the end of the long contest, 25 Oct. 1688, he restored the ejected fellows, making 'a Latin speech every way becoming his function and character.' 'Never was visitor received with greater joy or with greater favour' (Dr. T. Smith to Sir W. Howard, *ib.* p. 261). Mews was known to approve of the petition of the seven bishops, and was only prevented by illness from taking part in their meeting (MACAULAY). Yet James, in the crisis of the revolution, sought his advice, and was strongly urged by him to call a parliament (*Life of Ken*, p. 476). When William landed, the king thought of taking refuge at Farnham Castle (RERESBY, *Memoirs*, 4to edit. p. 178). Mews took the oaths to William and Mary, and served for a time on the royal commission on toleration, but withdrew when it was proposed to allow the holy eucharist to be administered to communicants sitting (MACAULAY; BIRCH, *Tillotson*, i. 127). On Whit-Sunday 1691 he was, in the absence of Compton, bishop of London, chief consecrator of Tillotson as archbishop.

After the revolution he does not appear to have taken much part in politics. Among the protests of the lords to which his signature is attached are those against an alteration of the marriage laws, 19 Nov. 1689; against confirming the laws passed in the convention, 8 April 1690, and against the expunging of the said protest as an act unprecedented and unconstitutional; against the bill of attainder for Sir John Fenwick, 23 Dec. 1696, and against Montague's bill annulling the privileges of the old East India Company, 1 July 1698 (*Protests of the Lords*, ed. J. E. T. Rogers, i. 89, 97, 98, 128-30, 133-4). He died 9 Nov. 1706, aged 89, and was buried in Winchester Cathedral, where a monument commemorates his fidelity to king and church.

Mews was versatile and energetic. His correspondence shows a clear and acute intellect and considerable political sagacity. The extraordinary lavishness with which his services were rewarded at the Restoration bears witness alike to the value of his past work and the importance that was attached to his future support. His unwearied activity and the *bonhomie* of his manners rendered him a most useful agent of the government of Charles II. At the same time he never subordinated his principles to his partisanship. He was a loyal soldier and a good bishop. An ardent loyalist (one of his sermons before the king was quoted in the defence of Sacheverell), he was firm in resisting the unconstitutional action of James II, to whom he was bound by long ties of personal service. Without being himself learned he was the patron of learned men. Lowth received his first preferment at his hands. While Burnet speaks sneeringly of his obsequiousness and zeal, Wood praises his hospitality, generosity, justice, and frequent preaching. Hearne briefly describes him as 'an old honest Cavalier.'

Mews published: 1. Some laudatory hexameters prefixed to 'Phasaurus sive Libido Vindex,' by T. Snelling, London, Andrew Pennycook, 1650. 2. 'The Ex-ale-tation of Ale (in verse), written by a Learned Pen,' London, 1671. ''Tis said the author was Dr. Peter Mews, bishop of Winchester' (HEARNE, ed. Doble, Oxford Hist. Soc., iii. 219). 3. His 'Articles of Visitation,' 1676 (L. Lichfield, Oxford) and 1679 (no printer's name).

There are portraits of him at Farnham Castle, St. John's and Magdalen colleges, Oxford, and in the National Portrait Gallery, London. The last was engraved by Loggan. He is represented in the robes of prelate of the Garter, and with a black patch covering a scar on the left cheek.

[St. John's College MSS.; Cal. of State Papers, Commonwealth and Charles II; Clarendon Papers; Wilson's Hist. of Merchant Taylors'

School; Cassan's Lives of Bishops of Winchester; Bloxam's Magdalen Coll. Reg.; Walker's Sufferings of the Clergy; Hutchins's Hist. of Dorset; and especially Nicholas Papers (Camd. Soc.), vol. ii.] W. H. H.

MEY, JOHN (*d.* 1456), archbishop of Armagh, was official of the court of Meath, and vicar of the parish churches of Delvin and Kilmessan, co. Meath, before 1444, when he was made by papal provision archbishop of Armagh; he was consecrated on 20 June, and enthroned by the dean, Charles O'Neillan, on 9 July 1444. Like his predecessors, he was much obstructed in the exercise of his primatial rights within the diocese of Dublin, and refused in consequence to attend parliament there. By a deed dated 19 Nov. 1455 Mey, with the consent of his dean and chapter, annexed his mensal tithes of Rathcoole to the choir of St. Anne's Chapel in St. Peter's Church, Drogheda, to which he also added his mensal portion of the tithes in Drummyng Church. About the same time the lord lieutenant, James Butler, earl of Ormonde and Wiltshire [q. v.], appointed Mey his deputy, but the archbishop did not maintain order very successfully. The English government ordered Ormonde to perform the duties himself, and on his refusal directed the Earl of Kildare to supersede him. Mey died in 1456.

[Ware's Ireland, i. 86; Cotton's Fasti, iii. 16; Gams's Series Episcoporum; Cox's Hibernia Anglicana, i. 163–4; Brady's Episcopal Succession, i. 215; Stuart's Armagh, pp. 198–9; Wright's Hist. of Ireland, i. 240.] A. F. P.

MEY, WILLIAM (*d.* 1560), archbishop-elect of York. [See May.]

MEYER, HENRY (1782?–1847), portrait-painter and engraver, was born in London about 1782. He was a nephew of John Hoppner [q. v.], and a pupil of Francesco Bartolozzi [q. v.], in whose dotted manner many of his plates are engraved. He worked also in mezzotint, and painted a considerable number of portraits, both in oil and in water-colours, of which he exhibited twelve at the Royal Academy between 1821 and 1826. He was one of the foundation members of the Society of British Artists, and to the first exhibition in 1824 he sent eight portraits, two sketches in chalk, and no less than forty-three engravings. In 1826 he exhibited a portrait of Charles Lamb, and in 1831 one of Benjamin Webster the actor. He became president of the society in 1828, but retired from it in the following year, and ceased to exhibit after 1833. In the later years of his career he devoted much attention to drawing portraits, and was very successful in his likenesses. He died on 28 May 1847, in his sixty-fifth year.

Meyer's engraved works consist chiefly of portraits, and include those of George IV; Prince Leopold, afterwards king of the Belgians, and the Princess Charlotte, full-lengths after A. E. Chalon, R.A.; Frederick William, duke of Brunswick, after J. P. Zahn; Admiral Viscount Nelson, and Earl Cathcart, after J. Hoppner, R.A.; Admiral Viscount Exmouth, after S. Drummond, A.R.A.; the Marquis of Wellesley, after a miniature by A. Robertson; Lady Leicester, afterwards Lady de Tabley, as 'Hope,' after Sir Thomas Lawrence, P.R.A.; Lord Byron, after a miniature by J. Holmes; Sir John Nicholl, dean of the arches, after W. Owen, R.A.; Miss O'Neill, as 'Belvedera, after A. W. Devis; Charles Mathews, in five characters on one sheet, after G. H. Harlow; Alderman John Boydell, after Gilbert Stuart; Philip James de Loutherbourg, R.A., after John Jackson, R.A.; and Henry Tilson, portrait-painter, after himself. Among his other plates are 'Mary anointing the feet of Jesus,' after W. Hilton, R.A.; 'Sir Roger de Coverley going to Church,' after C. R. Leslie, R.A.; 'The Proposal' (three girls sitting under a tree), and 'Congratulation,' after G. H. Harlow; 'Hesitation,' after S. Drummond, A.R.A.; 'The Approaching Checkmate,' after A. E. Chalon, R.A.; 'Exeter Change,' after J. Northcote, R.A.; 'The Blunt Razor,' after E. Bird, R.A.; 'The Stolen Kiss,' after W. Kidd, R.S.A.; 'The Dancing Bear,' after W. F. Witherington, R.A.; and 'I *will* fight,' after the picture by Philip Simpson in the South Kensington Museum.

[Gent. Mag. 1847, ii. 665; Redgrave's Dict. of Artists of the English School, 1878; Exhibition Catalogues of the Royal Academy, 1821–6; Exhibition Catalogues of the Society of British Artists, 1824–33.] R. E. G.

MEYER, JEREMIAH (1735–1789), miniature-painter, born at Tübingen, Würtemberg, in 1735, was the son of an obscure artist, who brought him to England in 1749. He studied in Shipley's academy in St. Martin's Lane, and during 1757 and 1758 was a pupil of C. F. Zincke [q. v.], to whom he paid 400*l.* for instruction and materials. He practised both in enamel and miniature with great ability, and was for many years without a rival. In 1760 and 1764 Meyer exhibited enamels with the Society of Arts, and in 1761 gained the prize of 20*l.* offered by the society for a profile portrait of the king, to be used for the coinage; engravings from this by MacArdell and others were very popular. He was naturalised in

1762, and in 1764 became enamel-painter to the king, having already been appointed miniature-painter to the queen. Meyer was one of the original directors of the Incorporated Society of Artists, and in 1769 was chosen a foundation member of the Royal Academy. He contributed to the Academy's exhibitions until 1783, sending several portraits of members of the royal family. To Meyer's initiative was due the establishment of the Royal Academy pension fund in 1775. He was a friend of both Romney and Hayley, and brought them together in 1776. Meyer resided for many years in Tavistock Row, Covent Garden, and later at Kew, where he died of a fever on 19 Jan. 1789. He lies close to Gainsborough in Kew churchyard. A mural tablet to his memory, with a medallion portrait and some eulogistic verses by Hayley, is in Kew Church.

Meyer's art was strongly influenced by his study of Reynolds, and his miniatures are unsurpassed for truth and refinement. In private life he was much esteemed, and Hayley, in his 'Essay on Painting,' paid a warm tribute to his merits. He married in 1763 Barbara Marsden, a lady of some artistic talent, who survived him.

An unfinished portrait of Meyer, by N. Dance, R.A., was engraved after his death by W. Pether, and a profile of him is in the set of portraits of artists by D. Pariset, after P. Falconet. A portrait of one of his daughters, in the character of Hebe, painted by Reynolds, has been engraved in mezzotint by J. Jacobé.

[Chalmers's Biog. Dict.; Sandby's Hist. of the Royal Acad.; Redgrave's Dict. of Artists; Hayley's Life of Romney; Edwards's Anecd. of Painting; Lysons's Environs of London, i. 152.]

F. M. O'D.

MEYER, PHILIP JAMES (1732–1820), musician, was born at Strassburg in 1732, of protestant parents, and brought up with a view to the ministry. He was early attracted by music, learnt the organ, and coming accidentally across an old German harp without pedals he mastered that instrument. He embraced music as a profession, and introduced some improvements in the harp, which was then in a transition state previous to its perfection by the mechanical genius of Sebastian Erard. He proceeded to Paris in 1765, and was among the first performers on the pedal harp in that city, where, in 1766, he published his 'Methode sur la vraie manière de jouer la Harpe, avec les règles pour l'accorder,' a pioneer work of considerable merit. He studied German music during this period with Müthel, a pupil of Sebastian Bach. In 1772 he visited England, and was the first person who publicly played the pedal harp in this country, at a concert at the Hanover Square Rooms. His stay in England was a short one. He returned to Paris, and set to music a dramatic piece by Pitra, entitled 'Damète et Zulmis.' Its success procured his introduction to Voltaire, who invited him to compose the music for a serious opera, 'Samson,' but died before the work was completed. Meyer definitely settled in London in 1784. He performed little, but wrote a quantity of harp music, and found distinguished patronage as a teacher. In addition to the 'Methode,' the most considerable of his published works are: 'Two Collections of French Songs for the Harp,' London, 1780; 'Two Sonatas for the Harp, with an Accompaniment for the Pianoforte or two Violins, Viola, and 'Cello' [1800]; 'Irish Melodies arranged as Duets for the Harp and Piano,' 1811; and 'A Collection of Hymns and Psalms arranged for the Harp,' 1815. Meyer died in London 17 Jan. 1820. By the wife whom he married at Strassburg in 1768 Meyer left two sons, Philip James the younger (1770–1849), who was appointed harpist to Queen Adelaide, and wrote numerous works for the harp, and Frederic Charles (1773–1840), who was also a composer and professor of the harp.

[Dictionary of Musicians, 1824; Fétis's Biog. Univ. des Musiciens; Mendel und Reissmann's Musikalisches Conversations-Lexikon, vii. 143; Brit. Mus. Catalogue of Music; information kindly supplied by Mr. Sebastian W. Meyer, grandson of Philip James the younger. Brief notices of Meyer also appear in Biographie degli Artisti, 1846, and Dizionario e Bibliografia, Milan, 1826.]

T. S.

MEYNELL, CHARLES, D.D. (1828–1882), catholic divine, born in 1828, was educated at Sedgley Park, Staffordshire, and at the English College, Rome. For many years he was professor of metaphysics at St. Mary's College, Oscott, and after being attached to the cathedral at Birmingham for a short time he was removed in 1873 to the small mission of Caverswall, North Staffordshire, where he died on 3 May 1882.

He was the author of: 1. 'The "Colenso" Controversy considered from the Catholic Standpoint; being five Letters about Dr. Colenso's work upon the Pentateuch, and the criticisms which it has called forth on either side,' London, 1863, 8vo, written in conjunction with the Rev. James Spencer Northcote. 2. 'Short Sermons on Doctrinal Subjects,' 1866 (two editions). 3. 'Padre Liberatore and the Ontologists: a Review,' London [1868], 8vo. 4. 'Proteus and Amadeus: a Correspondence. Edited by [Sir] Aubrey De Vere,

London, 1878, 8vo; Meynell sustains the part of Amadeus, the assertor and defender of the God of natural reason in the face of modern infidel objections, while the part of Proteus was sustained by Mr. Wilfrid Blunt. 5. 'Sermons for the Spring Quarter,' London, 1883, 8vo, a posthumous publication, edited by Henry Ignatius Dudley Ryder of the Oratory, Birmingham.

[Tablet, 1882 i. 692, 753, 1883 i. 408; Notes and Queries, 8th ser. iv. 451.] T. C.

MEYRICK, SIR GELLY or **GILLY** (1556?–1601), conspirator, was eldest son of Rowland Meyrick [q. v.], bishop of Bangor, by Katherine, daughter of Owain Barret of Gelliswic. After his father's death in 1565 he spent his youth with his mother on the family estate of Hascard in Pembrokeshire. At an early age he became a soldier and served in the Netherlands, receiving in 1583 the grant of a crest as 'a remembrance of his good deserts.' He soon became acquainted with Robert Devereux, second earl of Essex [q. v.], who owned property in Wales, and thus came into intimate relations with many of the Welsh gentry. He attended the earl to Flushing in 1585, and joined in the campaigns under Leicester in the Low Countries in that and the following year. On returning to England Essex conferred on him the office of steward in his household (cf. *Cal. State Papers*, Dom., 1581–90 p. 696, cf. 1591–1594 p. 9). Meyrick went with Essex on the expedition to Portugal in 1589, and two years later accompanied him to Normandy, but sickness prevented Meyrick from taking much part in the campaign which Essex then conducted in behalf of Henry of Navarre. In 1595 he and another of Essex's followers, Henry Lindley, were jointly presented by the crown, at Essex's suit, with nine parks in the duchy of Lancaster and one in the duchy of Cornwall, besides the manor and castle of Wigmore in Herefordshire and the forest and chase of Bringwood (*ib.* 1595–7, pp. 9, 61–2). He thenceforth made Wigmore Castle his chief country residence; his London house was in St. Clement's parish without Temple Bar (cf. SYMONDS, *Diary*, Camden Soc., p. 262). In 1596 Meyrick accompanied Essex on the expedition to Cadiz, serving as lieutenant-colonel in Sir Conyers Clifford's regiment, and also acting as commissioner of stores. Essex knighted him at Cadiz after the capture of the city. On his return in August, Meyrick was officially reported to have brought home as prize '250 India hides,' valued at 125*l.*; but some trifling charges of pilfering in connection with the disposal of the goods captured from the enemy were brought against him by Sir Anthony Ashley [q. v.], and he retaliated by accusing Ashley of far more serious peculations. The quarrel ended in Ashley's committal to prison, and Meyrick was left at peace (*Archæologia*, xxii. 172–189; *Cal. State Papers*, 1595–7, pp. 270–84, 528–36). In 1597 he took part with Essex in the Islands Voyage, and was in command of the Swiftsure. In the earl's disputes with Raleigh in the course of the expedition, Meyrick strongly supported his master, and is credited with embittering the relations between the two leaders (cf. *Archæologia*, xxxiv. 323; EDWARDS, *Ralegh*, i. 223; MARKHAM, *Fighting Veres*, p. 238). In the spring of 1599 Meyrick went to Ireland with Essex, who was then lord-deputy, and he returned with messages from his master in August, a few weeks before Essex himself arrived in London to meet the charges preferred against his Irish administration. In July 1600 Essex was induced to dismiss Meyrick from his office of steward by friends who represented him as a dangerous counsellor, but he was soon reinstated at Essex House. A month later Essex, once more at liberty, was considering suggestions of rebellion with a view to regaining his hold on the government, and Meyrick freely entertained in his master's mansion all who favoured his master's reckless policy. When in January 1600–1 Essex had decided on raising an insurrection in the city, Meyrick armed many of his country friends with muskets and invited them to London; and he gave 40*s.* to the actors of the Globe Theatre on condition that they performed, on the night (Saturday, 6 Feb.) before the day fixed for the outbreak, the play of 'Richard II' (apparently Shakespeare's), in order to excite the feelings of the populace by representing the abdication of an English sovereign on the stage. On the following Sunday (7 Feb.), when Essex left for the city at the head of his armed followers, the defence of Essex House was left in Meyrick's hands, and he acted as gaoler to the members of the privy council who had arrived earlier in the day in order to inquire into Essex's movements and had been locked up in the house. Meyrick defended the house when attacked by the royal troops in the afternoon, and only surrendered at Essex's bidding. He was at once lodged in the Tower, but, unlike his fellow-prisoners, when examined by the council disclosed little. Brought to trial on 5 March, with Sir Charles Davers, Sir Christopher Blount [q. v.], Sir John Davis, and Henry Cuff or Cuffe [q. v.], he declined to admit his guilt, but was convicted and sentenced to death. He declared himself 'not unwilling to die,' and explained that he merely acted under his master's orders. He was hanged at Tyburn on 13 March, together with Cuffe, and suffered 'with a most undaunted resolution.' In a short speech at the gallows he expressed the hope that 'such as had unwarily espoused this unhappy cause' might receive a pardon (*State Trials*, i. 1413–14, 1446–9; *Cal. State Papers*, Dom., 1598–1601 pp. 546–98, 1601–3 pp. 1–2, 11–17). His confiscated goods in Herefordshire were valued at 461*l.* 10*s.* 2*d.*

Meyrick married about 1584 Elizabeth or Margaret, daughter of Ieuan Lewis of Cladestry, Radnorshire, and widow of John Gwyn of Llanelwedd; she inherited the estates of both her father and first husband. By her Meyrick left a son, Roland, and a daughter, Margaret, wife of Sir John Vaughan, earl of Carberry. Both children were subsequently restored in blood, and seem to have been granted out of their father's confiscated estates lands at Lucton and Eyton in Herefordshire. Lady Meyrick died in 1625.

[Lewys Dwnn's Visitation of Wales, 1586–1613, ed. Sir S. R. Meyrick, i. 137; Archæologia, xxii. 172–89 (by Sir S. R. Meyrick); Williams's Eminent Welshmen; Birch's Memoirs of Queen Elizabeth, ii. 463–6, 492–3; Devereux's Earls of Essex: Cecil's Letters to Carew (Camden Soc.), pp. 73–4; Spedding's Life of Bacon, vol. ii.; authorities cited.] S. L.

MEYRICK, JOHN (1538–1599), bishop of Sodor and Man, natural son of Owen ab Huw ab Owen ab Meyric of Bodeon, Anglesey, and Gwenllian, daughter of Evan of Penrhyn Deudraeth, Merionethshire, became scholar of Winchester College in 1550, was admitted scholar of New College, Oxford, in July 1555, and fellow on 5 July 1557. He graduated B.A. on 12 Dec. 1558, M.A. on 26 June 1562, and served as junior proctor in 1565. In 1570 he was presented to the college living of Hornchurch, Essex, and in 1575, on the nomination of Henry Stanley, fourth earl Derby, elected bishop of Sodor and Man, the queen assenting on 5 Nov. and again on 13 April 1576. He was consecrated at Lambeth on 15 April 1576 by Grindal, archbishop of Canterbury, the diocese of York, in which Man is, being then vacant. Meyrick held the bishopric for twenty-three years, but his position involved many hardships which he detailed in a letter to Lord Burghley. He also furnished Camden with an account of the Isle of Man, preserved in Cotton MS. Julius F. 10, part of which is printed in Camden's 'Britannia,' ii. 390. Meyrick died on 7 Nov. 1599.

Two of Meyrick's half-brothers were also educated at Winchester and New College, Oxford. One, William, was admitted scholar of New College, Oxford, on 9 March 1565–6, fellow on 9 March 1567–8, graduating B.C.L. on 28 Jan. 1573–4, and D.C.L. on 5 July 1582, and was subsequently chantor, commissary, and chancellor of Bangor, when he vacated his fellowship, and rector of Llanvechell. He died in 1605. The other, Maurice (1563–1640), was admitted scholar of New College on 31 March 1582, aged 19, and fellow on 31 March 1584, graduated B.A. on 27 Oct. 1585, and M.A. on 2 June 1589, was subsequently steward of New College and registrar of the university, 1600–8; he resigned his fellowship in August 1595. By his wife, Jane, daughter of Lewis Evans, he was father of Sir William Meyrick (*d.* 1668), judge of the prerogative court of Canterbury, who is separately noticed.

[Lansd. MSS. lxiii. 81, 982 f. 274; Cotton MS. Julius F. x. 124; Wood's Athenæ Oxon. ii. 843; Foster's Alumni Oxon. 1500–1714; Tanner's Bibl. Brit.; paper by Sir Samuel Rush Meyrick in Gent. Mag. 1825, i. 403; Camden's Britannia, ii. 390; Le Neve's Fasti; Williams's Eminent Welshmen; Kirby's Winchester Scholars; information kindly supplied by the Warden of New College.] A. F. P.

MEYRICK, Sir JOHN (*d.* 1638), English ambassador to Russia, was the second son of William Meyrick or Merick, at one time of Gloucester, but afterwards of London. The father became one of the original members of the Russia or Muscovy Company, which was founded by Cabot in 1554, and before 1567 seems to have acted as agent of the company in Russia. John's youth was spent at the factory of English merchants at Moscow. In 1584 he became the agent of the London Russia Company at Jaroslavl, and in May 1592 he was filling a like position at Moscow. By 1596 he had been admitted to membership of the London company, and had entered into partnership with his elder brother, Richard, who lived in Leadenhall Street. Through 1596 and 1597 Meyrick forwarded from Russia much political intelligence to Queen Elizabeth, and on 14 March 1598 he reported the Tsar Fedor Ivanovitch's death. In 1600 he came home in the company of Mikulin who was sent as Russian ambassador to England. The new tsar, Boris Godounoff, was anxious to find an English bride for his eldest son, and in February 1601–2 Meyrick was despatched as ambassador to the tsar with instructions to strengthen the friendly relations between the two countries, but to treat the matrimonial proposals evasively. Meyrick was honourably received by the emperor at the Kremlin Palace. He translated Elizabeth's letters to the tsar into Russian in a personal interview, and laid before him a pedigree of the English royal family. Elizabeth (Meyrick declared) had selected a daughter of the Earl of Derby as the tsarevitch's bride; but she was eighteen years old, and seeing that the Russian prince was only thirteen, Meyrick argued that the union was undesirable. Meyrick remained in Russia till June. On the 22nd of that month he had a final audience with the tsar, who promised full protection to English merchants, and sent cordial greetings to Elizabeth, besides entrusting Meyrick with four Russian youths of high birth to be educated in England. Meyrick journeyed home in July. A full account of his embassy, written by himself, is in the British Museum (MS. Cott. Nero B. viii.); it was printed by Sir Samuel Rush Meyrick in the 'Gentleman's Magazine,' 1824, pt. ii. pp. 226 sq.

Meyrick soon returned to Russia. In 1603 he forwarded as a gift to the Bodleian Library, Oxford, two Russian manuscripts—a bible and 'Canones Patrum Muscov.' (Macray, *Annals of the Bodleian Library*, p. 30). In October 1603 his partner and brother, Richard, died in London, and John was described in the dying man's will as 'then residing in Muscovy.' After the death in 1605 of the Tsar Boris, probably by poison, the utmost confusion prevailed at Moscow. An impostor named Demetrius seized the throne, but Meyrick obtained from him protection for English commerce, and when in 1606 Basil IV (Vassily Shuiski) became tsar, Meyrick was again successful in obtaining a renewal of the privileges previously accorded to his fellow-countrymen. Political disturbances compelled Meyrick to remove at times from Moscow to Archangel and Cholmogorü, and late in 1606 he returned to England to report the progress of affairs. He was soon, however, again acting as 'agent' in Russia, but paid another visit to London in 1611. In 1614 he was reappointed English ambassador to the tsar's court, with full powers to use his influence to reduce the anarchy prevailing in the Russian government. Before his departure James knighted him at Greenwich (13 June 1614). He travelled with forty-four persons, and with a large sum of money to be advanced, if need be, to the tsar and his ministers. Meyrick's mission proved successful. Michael, of the house of Romanoff, was securely installed on the throne, and Meyrick took part in the negotiations for bringing to a close the long-standing warfare between Russia and Sweden. In 1615 he journeyed to Staraia-Russa, and met envoys from the two countries, as well as commissioners from Holland, who agreed to take part in the mediation. On 4 March 1616 an armistice for three months was arranged under Meyrick's guidance; on 20 Nov., owing to his intercession with Gustavus Adolphus, the Swedes raised the seige of Narva; and on 27 Feb. 1617 he helped to secure the final peace of Stolbovo, which bore his signature as that of one of the contracting parties. In November 1617 Meyrick came again to England, accompanied by an elaborate embassy from Russia, and bearing rich presents from the tsar to James I. On 19 Oct. 1620 he was reappointed the English envoy at Moscow, and was directed to negotiate a commercial treaty and to recover the money recently lent to the tsar. In 1623 a commercial treaty with Russia—the first of its kind—was duly signed by Meyrick and the tsar's councillors (Rymer, *Fœdera*, xvii. 504). In 1628 he was still in Moscow, and was then governor of the Russia Company. He died ten years later, and was credited at the time with more knowledge of Russia than any other Englishman (cf. Bond, *Russia at the Close of the Sixteenth Century*, Hakluyt Soc., p. 265). In his will he desired that he might be buried in his parish church of St. Andrew Undershaft, if he died in London, and he bequeathed 100*l.* to the Merchant Taylors' Company, with 300*l.* to be lent to scholars of the company's school on their commencing business; he also left legacies to many London parishes and hospitals. His wife Frances, daughter of Sir Francis Cherrie, also a Russia merchant, predeceased him; she had no issue.

[Articles by Sir S. R. Meyrick in Gent. Mag. 1824, pt. ii. pp. 226, 401, 495; Hamel's England and Russia, translated by J. S. Leigh (1854), pp. 374–407; Nichols's Progresses of James I, iii. 6, 440, 766; Early Voyages to Russia and Persia (Hakluyt Soc.), i. 120, ii. 211.] S. L.

MEYRICK, Sir JOHN (*d.* 1659), parliamentary general, was the fifth son of Sir Francis Meyrick of Fleet, in the parish of Monkton, Pembrokeshire, by Anne, daughter of Francis Laugharne of St. Brides in the same county. Bishop Rowland Meyrick [q. v.] was his grandfather. Like his father, who died in 1603, and his uncle, Sir Gelly [q. v.], John adopted a military career. His influence with the Devereux family procured him a troop under Robert Devereux, third earl of Essex [q. v.], whom he accompanied to Flanders in 1620; he fought another campaign in the United Provinces in 1624. In 1625 he served in the expedition against Spain, and it was probably on his return that he received the honour of knighthood. In 1630 he had a subordinate command in General Morgan's regiment in the service of

Gustavus Adolphus, and was wounded before Maestricht in a sally made by the enemy on 17 Aug. 1632 (HEXHAM, *Journal of the Siege*, 1633, p. 40).

He returned to England with the reputation and experience of a professional soldier, cultivated the goodwill of his old patron, Essex, and was on 25 March 1640 elected to the Short parliament for Newcastle-under-Lyme. He was re-elected to the Long parliament on 13 Oct., and on the outbreak of the civil war was assigned a regiment of ten companies, and appointed president of the council of war and serjeant-major-general (adjutant-general) of Essex's army. He confirmed the parliament's selection by making extensive advances of money to the cause, but he probably did the latter an injury by his strong advice to Essex to confine himself to the defensive on 13 Nov. 1642, when the rival forces confronted each other at Turnham Green (WHITELOCKE, pp. 62–6; cf. GARDINER, *Great Civil War*, vol. i.) He fought at Edgehill, and when in 1643 his old companion in arms, William Skippon [q. v.], was preferred to the post of sergeant-major-general, Meyrick was made general of the ordnance, in which capacity he did excellent service before Gloucester, and afterwards at Newbury. During the rest of Essex's career he remained in close relations with his commander, and when, after the fiasco at Lostwithiel, Essex, between despair and dread of ridicule, deserted his army and made off in a small boat for Plymouth, Meyrick was his companion (*ib.* i. 468; RUSHWORTH, v. 701). At Essex's imposing public funeral in September 1646 he bore the gorget on the left side of the pall (*The True Mannor and Forme of Proceeding to the Funerall*, 1646, p. 17). In 1649 Meyrick, who was ultimately conservative in his views, was placed by Cromwell's orders under temporary arrest during the debate as to whether negotiations should be reopened with the king (*Cal. State Papers*, Dom. 1648–9 passim). Henceforth he appears to have taken no prominent part in public affairs, spending the remainder of his life in Pembrokeshire, where he died in 1659. There is a portrait in black armour at Bush, Pembrokeshire, the seat of his branch of the Meyrick family and the home of his descendants, until the death of Thomas Meyrick in 1837 (*Miscellanea Genealog. et Herald.* new ser. ii. 415). He is also represented kneeling, on his father's monument in the Priory Church at Monkton.

By his first wife, Alice, daughter of Sir Edward Fitton of Gawsworth, Cheshire, he had a son named Essex and two daughters; by his second wife, Jane (*d.* 1660), widow of Sir Peter Wyche [q. v.], ambassador at Constantinople, and daughter of William Meredith of Wrexham, Denbighshire, he left no issue.

[Burke's Landed Gentry, p. 919; Dwnn's Heraldic Visitation of Counties Carmarthen, Pembroke, and Cardigan, i. 136; Williams's Eminent Welshmen, p. 333; Clarendon's Hist. of the Rebellion, vii. 26; Whitelocke's Memorials, pp. 116, 232; Gent. Mag. 1825, i. 471; Official Ret. Memb. of Parl. i. 483, 493; Devereux's Lives of the Earls of Essex, ii, 443; List of the Army raised under the command of his Excellency, Robert, earle of Essex, 1642, passim.] T. S.

MEYRICK, ROWLAND (1505–1566), bishop of Bangor, born at Bodargan in the parish of Llangadwaladr, Anglesey, in 1505, was the second son of Meyric ab Llewelyn ab Heylin, by Margaret daughter of Rowland ab Hywl, rector of Aberffraw in the same county. He was named after his maternal grandfather, and, according to Wood, educated 'at St. Edward's Hall (Oxford), a noted place for civilians, sometime situated near St. Edward's Church,' whence he graduated B.C.L. 9 Dec. 1531, and proceeded D.C.L. 17 Feb. 1537–8. He was principal of New Inn Hall from 1534 to 1536. In 1541 he obtained preferment at Eglwysael, and was also made precentor of Llandewy-Velfrey, Pembrokeshire. In 1544 he was collated to the vicarage of Stoke-by-Nayland, Suffolk, and in 1547 was appointed by convocation on a commission to try and obtain the mitigation of the penalty for the non-payment by recusants of the perpetual tenth. About 1547 also he was appointed chancellor of the diocese of Wells, and in 1550 became canon and chancellor of St. David's. In this capacity he took a leading part in the struggle between the chapter and Bishop Robert Ferrar [q. v.] The bishop on his appointment in 1550 found 'great spoil being made of the plate and ornaments of the church,' and the canons combining with barefaced robberies malpractices of the most diverse kind. In a letter to the lord chancellor the bishop accused Meyrick of 'shameless whoredom' (FOXE, *Acts and Monuments*, 1847, vii. 17). Meyrick consequently refused to acknowledge the bishop's authority to make a visitation of the cathedral, and led the chapter in a factious opposition. Articles were exhibited against the bishop, containing 'vague and various accusations of abuse of authority, maintenance of superstition, covetousness, wilful negligence, and folly.' For these crimes Ferrar was on a charge of præmunire committed to prison, whence he was only removed in the next reign to be sent to the stake for another series of offences. Of the bishop's three bitterest enemies, Young and Constantine sought his pardon before his martyrdom in 1555, but Meyrick made no such concession. The accession of Mary, shortly followed by Meyrick's marriage in 1554 to Catherine, daughter of Owen Barret of Gellyswick and Hascard, Pembrokeshire, put a period to Meyrick's advancement, and he was ejected from his canonry at St. David's. On Elizabeth's accession, however, he was, with Dr. Richard Davies and Thomas Young, commissioned to visit the four Welsh dioceses, as well as Hereford and Worcester, and on 21 Dec. 1559 he was consecrated by Parker to the see of Bangor in succession to William Glynn. He took the oath of allegiance on 1 March 1559–1560, and in the same year received a commission from his metropolitan to visit the diocese. The following January, being then on a visit to London, he ordained five priests and five readers in Bow Church. He was shortly afterwards appointed a member of the council of the marches. With his see he held the prebend of Trevlodau and the rectories of Llanddewy-Brefi and Llanddewy-Velfrey, to which he added in 1562 the rectory of Llanbedrog, Carnarvonshire. He died on 24 Jan. 1565–6, and was buried at Bangor, 'on the south side of the altar near the wall, where there was an effigies in brasse, on a flat stone over his grave,' but the monument has long disappeared (Browne Willis; Wood).

Meyrick left four sons: Sir Gelly, who is separately noticed; Francis, Harry, and John. Francis, like his elder brother, served under and was knighted by Essex in Ireland, died in 1603, and was buried in the Priory Church of Monkton, Pembrokeshire, where his monument was destroyed during the civil wars; he was father of Sir John Meyrick (*d.* 1659) [q. v.]

[Wood's Athenæ Oxon. ed. Bliss, ii. 797; Foster's Alumni Oxon. 1500–1714; Godwin, De Præsulibus, p. 627; Le Neve's Fasti Eccl. Anglic.; Camden's Annales, ed. Hearne, i. 49; Hardy's Syllabus of Rymer's Fœdera, pp. 801, 802, 805; Foxe's Acts and Monuments, 1847, vii. passim; Strype's Memorials of Cranmer, pp. 222, 385, Memorials, III. i. 424, ii. 355, 362, Annals, I. i. 248–234, 487, Parker, i. 124, 126, 129, 152; Browne Willis's Survey of Cath. Church of Bangor, 1721, pp. 28, 106; Freeman and Jones's St. David's, p. 331; Kennet's Antiq. Brit. p. 37; Dwnn's Visitations, i. 137; Williams's Eminent Welshmen.] T. S.

MEYRICK, Sir SAMUEL RUSH (1783–1848), antiquary, born on 26 Aug. 1783, was only surviving son of John Meyrick (*d.* 1805), F.S.A., agent, of Great George Street, Westminster, and Peterborough House, Fulham, by Hannah (*d.* 1832), daughter and coheiress of Samuel Rush of Ford House, Hertfordshire, and Chislehurst, Kent. He matriculated at Oxford from Queen's College on 27 June 1800, and graduated B.A. in 1804, M.A. and B.C.L. in 1810, and D.C.L. in 1811 (Foster, *Alumni Oxon.* 1715–1886, iii. 950). By an early marriage he offended his father, who arranged that the property should devolve on his son's children instead of his son. But the early death of Meyrick's only son destroyed the effect of this disposition.

For many years Meyrick practised as an advocate in the ecclesiastical and admiralty courts. He resided at 3 Sloane Terrace, Chelsea, and afterwards at 20 Upper Cadogan Place, where he gradually accumulated a magnificent collection of armour. He was elected F.S.A. in 1810, and for some years frequently contributed to the 'Archæologia,' besides taking an active part in the proceedings of the society.

In 1823 Meyrick became acquainted with James Robinson Planché, and introduced him to Francis Douce. Planché, in his 'Recollections' (i. 54–5), warmly acknowledges the valuable assistance he received from both in his efforts for the reform of theatrical costume. He was afterwards called upon to arrange the Meyrick collection of armour twice for public exhibition, at Manchester in 1857 and at South Kensington in 1868.

About 1827 Meyrick, having vainly endeavoured to purchase the ruins of Goodrich Castle, near Ross, Herefordshire, bought the opposite hill, and, with Edward Blore for his architect, erected thereon a mansion, which he styled Goodrich Court. Rooms were specially constructed for the reception of the armoury.

In 1826 he was consulted by the authorities at the Tower of London as to the arrangement of the national collection of arms and armour (*Gent. Mag.* 1826 pt. ii. pp. 159, 195, 1827 pt. i. pp. 195–6), and in 1828, at the command of George IV, he arranged the collection at Windsor Castle (*ib.* vol. xcviii. pt. i. p. 463). In January 1832 William IV conferred the Hanoverian order upon him for these services, and dubbed him a knight bachelor on 22 Feb. following.

In 1834 he served the office of high sheriff of Herefordshire, and made his year in office conspicuous by the revival of javelin-men, duly harnessed, and other pageantry. During the same year Francis Douce bequeathed him a part of his museum—chiefly ivories and carvings in ivory—of which Meyrick furnished a catalogue to the 'Gentleman's Magazine' in 1836. Meyrick assisted in the formation of the British Archæological Association, and presided over the Gloucester congress in 1846.

Meyrick died at Goodrich Court on 2 April 1848. By his marriage, on 3 Oct. 1803, with Mary, daughter and coheiress of James Parry of Llwyn Hywel, Cardiganshire, he had an only son, Llewelyn (1804–1837), B.C.L., F.S.A., and equerry to the Duke of Sussex, who died unmarried. He left his property to his second cousin, Lieutenant-colonel Augustus Meyrick. About 1871 this gentleman's son and heir sold the armoury and art-treasures at Goodrich, mostly to M. Spitzer of Paris, after offering the entire collection to the government for 50,000*l.* (PLANCHÉ, *Recollections*, ii. 168–72, 268–71). In 1893 the Spitzer collection was dispersed by sale.

Planché gives a pleasing account of Meyrick's love of thoroughness in research, precise ways, and sterling qualities (*ib.* ii. 144–146). His portrait, by H. P. Briggs, was engraved by Skelton (EVANS, *Cat. of Engraved Portraits*, ii. 278).

In 1810 Meyrick published in quarto the 'History and Antiquities of the County of Cardigan,' a very creditable work. In 1812 he made some preparations for a history of the monarchs of Britain prior to 703, on the plan of Dr. Henry's 'History,' but he never finished it. With Captain Charles Hamilton Smith, Meyrick joined in 1814 in the production of a work on the 'Costume of the original Inhabitants of the British Islands, from the earliest periods to the sixth century; to which is added that of the Gothic Nations on the Western Coasts of the Baltic, the Ancestors of the Anglo-Saxons and Anglo-Danes,' fol., London 1815, with twenty-four coloured plates.

Meyrick's great work on arms and armour was published in three quarto volumes in 1824, under the title of 'A Critical Inquiry into antient Armour as it existed in Europe, but particularly in England, from the Norman Conquest to the Reign of King Charles II, with a Glossary of Military Terms of the Middle Ages,' with eighty plates, seventy-two of which are beautifully coloured and illuminated in gold and silver. This laborious work, practically the first on the subject, remains an authority. A second edition, corrected and enlarged by Meyrick, with the assistance of Francis Douce, Albert Way, and other antiquarian friends, was published by Bohn in 1844, with additional but inferior plates. He subsequently promoted an undertaking by Joseph Skelton, F.S.A., entitled 'Engraved Illustrations of Antient Arms and Armour, from the Collection at Goodrich Court, from the Drawings and with the Descriptions of Dr. Meyrick by J. Skelton,' 2 vols. 4to, London 1830. A second edition, containing corrections by Meyrick, was issued by Bohn in 1854.

Meyrick's last important work was his edition of Lewis Dwnn's 'Heraldic Visitations of Wales,' which he undertook in 1840 for the Society for the Publication of Ancient Welsh Manuscripts, and completed in 1846 in two quarto volumes.

He likewise assisted Thomas Dudley Fosbrooke in his 'Encyclopædia of Antiquities,' 1823–5; in 1836 contributed the descriptions to Henry Shaw's 'Specimens of Ancient Furniture;' and was the author of many papers in the 'Gentleman's Magazine' (1822–1839), the 'Analyst,' the 'Cambrian Quarterly Magazine,' the 'Cambrian Archæological Journal,' and Brayley's 'Graphic and Historical Illustrator,' 1834.

[Gent. Mag. 1848, pt. ii. 92–5; Williams's Eminent Welshmen; Allibone's Dict. of English Literature, ii. 1271–2; Lowndes's Bibl. Man. (Bohn) iii. 1541; Spitzer Catalogue.] G. G.

MEYRICK or MERICKE, SIR WILLIAM (*d.* 1668), civilian, son of Maurice Meyrick [see under MEYRICK, JOHN, bishop of Sodor and Man] of Bodeon, Anglesey, by Jane, daughter of Lewis Evans, was admitted scholar of Winchester College in 1608, scholar of New College, Oxford, on 16 July 1614, and fellow on 16 July 1616; he graduated B.C.L. on 18 April 1621, D.C.L. on 30 June 1627. He resigned his fellowship in 1626, and was admitted a member of the College of Advocates on 2 Feb. 1627–8, and practised before the court of high commission. On 28 Sept. 1641 he succeeded Sir Henry Martin [q. v.] as judge of the prerogative court of Canterbury. In 1643 he joined the king at Oxford, whence on 8 May he issued a notice revoking the powers of his deputies at Canterbury. Sir Nathaniel Brent [q. v.] was appointed to succeed him on 10 Jan. 1647–8. At the Restoration Meyrick was reinstated in the prerogative court, and on 8 Nov. 1661 was knighted at Whitehall. He died on 3 Feb. 1667–8, and was succeeded by Sir Leoline Jenkins [q. v.]

[Le Neve's Pedigrees of Knights (Harl. Soc.), p. 146; Reg. Univ. Oxon., ed. Clark, vol. ii. pt. ii. p. 334, pt. iii. p. 403; Wood's Fasti (Bliss), i. 397, 432; Coote's Catalogue of English Civilians; Cal. State Papers, Dom. 1634–5 et seq., 1661–2, p. 110; Hist. of the Troubles of William Laud, c. xi; Lords' Journ. iv. 406 *a*, 409 *a*, vi. 51, ix. 648; Evelyn's Diary, 31 Aug. 1663; Wynne's Life of Sir Leoline Jenkins, p. xvii; Haydn's Book of Dignities, ed. Ockerby; Hist. MSS. Comm. 9th Rep. App. ii.; information kindly supplied by the Warden of New College.]

J. M. R.

MEYRIG (*fl.* 1250), treasurer of Llandaff. [See Maurice.]

MIALL, EDWARD (1809–1881), politician, younger son of Moses Miall, a general merchant, of Portsmouth, by his wife Sarah, daughter of George Rolph, was born at Portsmouth, 8 May 1809. During his childhood his father removed to London, first to Hammersmith, and afterwards to the north of London, and opened a school. After being for a short time a pupil at St. Saviour's grammar school, Edward became, at about the age of sixteen, assistant to his father, and in 1827, when, owing to his father's poverty, the home was broken up, he filled the office of usher, first in the school of a Mr. Saltmarsh of Bocking, near Braintree, and then in that of a Mr. Waddell of Nayland in Suffolk.

At an early date he developed strong religious feeling. At the same time he showed literary propensities, reading English poetry with avidity, and writing numerous verses. Shortly before the death of his father in 1829 he entered the Wymondley Theological Institution, Hertfordshire, subsequently merged in New College, London, and began his preparation for the independent ministry. In the debating society and in the chapel pulpit he distinguished himself by natural eloquence and great fluency, and he accepted, in February 1831, the charge of a congregation at Ware in Hertfordshire, and in 1834 became minister of the Bond Street Chapel, Leicester. He familiarised himself with the condition of the working classes in Leicester, but did not take an active part in politics till 1840.

In November of that year he began his lifelong attacks upon the established church, by taking part in a meeting to express sympathy with William Baines, a member of his congregation, who had been sent to gaol for nonpayment of church rates. He had already planned the foundation of a newspaper to be the special organ of the nonconformist demand for disestablishment, and had acquired journalistic facility by writing for the 'Leicester Mercury.' He now gave up his congregation in Leicester, and after canvassing among English nonconformists for the requisite capital from August 1840 to March 1841, he established the 'Nonconformist,' a weekly publication with the motto and principle of 'The Dissidence of Dissent and the Protestantism of the Protestant Religion.' The first number appeared on 14 April 1841. Miall was appointed editor, and, settling at Stoke Newington, devoted all his energies to the venture. His weekly articles denouncing the state church he subsequently collected for republication as 'The Nonconformist Sketch-Book' (1845, republished in 1867), 'Views of the Voluntary Principle' (1845), and 'Ethics of Nonconformity.' He also opposed the Melbourne administration, denounced the tory party, and attacked aristocratic government. In spite of the silent disfavour of leading dissenters, the circulation of his paper grew, and he gradually acquired real political influence. He was one of that small band of radicals which endeavoured, fruitlessly, to bring the chartist leaders into line with the more established political organisations. He advocated what was practically manhood suffrage, and appealed to the middle classes to join hands with the artisans. Through his support of the Anti-Corn Law League he obtained the acquaintance of Joseph Sturge, and in April 1842 he, with Sturge, Bright, Mursell, and Sharman Crawford, arranged the Birmingham conferences with the chartist leaders, Lovett, O'Brien, and Henry Vincent, to promote the abolition of class legislation. The National Complete Suffrage Union was then founded, and carried on for some years the propaganda for a wider franchise, and the 'Nonconformist' was formally constituted its organ in the press, though after the second Birmingham conference, in December 1842, Miall did not take part in its meetings.

Miall's writings did more than anything else to produce a school of aggressive politicians among dissenters. The foundation of the free church of Scotland greatly encouraged his supporters, and his determined opposition to the compulsory religious education clauses in Graham's Factories Education Bill of 1843 increased his influence. After much effort he procured the assembling of a conference on disestablishment in London on 30 April 1844, when there was established a society called the 'British Anti-State Church Association,' having for its object 'the liberation of religion from all governmental or legislative interference.' It was renamed in 1853 'The Society for the Liberation of Religion from State Patronage and Control.' On behalf of the Association Miall undertook frequent missionary tours in the north of England and in Scotland. In August 1845 he contested Southwark at a by-election, caused by the death of its member, Benjamin Wood. In his election address he declared himself consecrated to the separation of church and state, and advocated complete suffrage, the ballot, equal electoral districts, payment of members, and annual parliaments. He polled one-sixth of the votes of the successful liberal candidate, Sir William Molesworth [q. v.]

At the general election of 1847 he contested Halifax on the principles of his Anti-State

Church Association. He spent no money on his contest. His committees conducted their meetings with prayer, and he startled the electors by discussing with them spiritual topics, but he found himself, with Ernest Jones [q. v.] the chartist, at the bottom of the poll. In 1852, however, he succeeded Sharman Crawford in the representation of Rochdale.

In the House of Commons he was not, except upon questions which bore upon disestablishment, a frequent speaker. He was the advocate of voluntaryism in the debates on the Oxford University Bill, the Canadian Clergy Reserves Bill, the Bill for the Abolition of Church Rates, and the Parliamentary Oaths Bill. In 1853 appeared his 'Bases of Belief, an Examination of Christianity as a Divine Revelation,' which reached a third edition in 1861. Failing health obliged him to visit Switzerland in August 1854.

In 1856 the Liberation Society resolved on a more aggressive policy, and on 27 May Miall, on its behalf, introduced resolutions in the House of Commons in favour of Irish disestablishment. He was defeated by 163 to 93. At the general election of 1857 he lost his seat like many others of the radical party who had opposed Palmerston. Though he soon contested Tavistock and Banbury, he remained out of parliament for twelve years. Lord Salisbury, president of the council, nominated him, however, in June 1858, a member of the royal commission on education, and the work occupied him for nearly three years. He represented the dissenters on the commission, and opposed state education. Accordingly he and Goldwin Smith presented a joint minority report in March 1861, though he also signed the general report. In 1862 he prepared for the Liberation Society a polemical handbook called 'The Title Deeds of the Church of England to her Parochial Endowments,' reprinted from the 'Nonconformist,' being an examination into the history and conditions of the tenure of ecclesiastical endowments from the disestablishment point of view. This reached a sixth edition in 1865. After the sixth triennial conference of the Liberation Society in 1862 he received a testimonial of 5,000*l.* and a service of plate. In 1863 he was the author of the new policy adopted by the Liberation Society, which aimed at inducing the liberal party in the large towns to adopt a programme of disestablishment without qualification. In the autumn of 1866 he carried out a tour of propaganda in Wales. In 1867 he first contested Bradford; but the liberal party was not united, nor were Miall's the views to unite them, and he was defeated by 2,210 votes to 1,807, at a cost of 1,335*l.* He contested the place for a second time on 18 Nov. 1868. William Edward Forster [q.v.] headed the poll and Miall was last, but the second candidate was unseated for bribery, and at the contest for the vacant seat, 12 March 1869, Miall was returned.

In the house he soon found himself in conflict with his colleague, W. E. Forster, whose Education Bill, 1870, was not as hostile to the established church as Miall, who had at length accepted the principle of state education, desired, and the terms in which he denounced the bill on the third reading brought upon him the strong censure of Mr. Gladstone. With the concurrence of the Liberation Society, he gave notice at the end of the session of 1870 to move for a committee on English disestablishment. After addressing numerous meetings during the winter, he brought on his motion on 9 May 1871, and secured 89 votes to 374. He renewed the motion in the former year and in July 1872, but his supporters only numbered 96 on the first occasion and 61 on the second. His contention throughout was that his motion was as much in the interest of the church of England as in that of the voluntary bodies, and that his hostility was not to the church but to what he regarded as the fatal incubus of state patronage.

But his health was failing. In 1873 ten thousand guineas were subscribed for him, and he announced that he would not again contest Bradford. In 1874 he retired from parliament. Almost his last public appearance was at a liberation conference in Manchester in that year. The death of his wife in January 1876 shook him severely, and though he continued to edit the 'Nonconformist,' he lived in retirement. He quitted Honor Oak, near London, where he had lived since 1864, for Sevenoaks in Kent early in 1881, and died there on 29 April 1881. By his wife Louisa, daughter of Edward Holmes of Clayhill, Enfield, whom he married on 25 Jan. 1832, he had two sons—including Arthur, the author of his biography—and three daughters.

Apart from the question of disestablishment Miall had few interests, and sought few distractions. For many years he was a contributor to the 'Illustrated London News,' and on the income from this source, combined with his stipend as editor of the 'Nonconformist,' which was not financially successful, he depended for his livelihood. He was in private life genial, pious, and unassuming, and hardly deserved the reputation for narrowness and bitterness which his public career brought him. As a writer he was fluent, if verbose. In addition to the works above mentioned, and many tracts and printed speeches, his chief publications were: 1. 'The British Churches in relation to the British People,' 1849. 2. 'The Franchise as a means of a People's Training,' 1851. 3. 'An Editor off the Line: Wayside Musings,' 1865. 4. 'Social Influences of the State Church,' 1867.

[His life, by his son Arthur Miall, with a portrait, was published in 1884. See, too, supplement to the Nonconformist, 5 May 1881; Times, 2 May 1881; Monthly Christian Spectator, 1852.] J. A. H.

MICHAEL BLAUNPAYN (*fl.* 1250), also called Michael the Cornishman and Michael the Englishman, Latin poet, was clearly a native of Cornwall, for in his satire he says:

Nam rex Arturus *nos* primos *Cornubienses*.

He is said to have studied at Oxford and Paris, and to have finally become dean of Utrecht. More reasonably, perhaps, he may be conjectured to have been a Cambridge scholar, for he thought fit to recite his satire before the chancellor and masters of that university. Michael boasts of being a better scholar and teacher than his adversary, Henry of Avranches. Henry was a poet who enjoyed the favour of the court, and had reflected on Cornish rusticity. This moved Michael to reply, which he did in a satire that was recited before Hugh, abbot of Westminster, the Dean of St. Paul's, and R. de Mortimer, an official of the Archbishop of Canterbury; afterwards it was again recited before the Bishop of Ely and the chancellor and masters of Cambridge. This poem, in leonine hexameters, is contained in MS. Royal 14, C. xiii. f. 269, and Cotton MS. Titus A. xx. ff. 52–69, in the British Museum, in MS. Bodley O.C. 3041 (Bernard, *Cat. MSS. Angliæ*), and MS. Ff. vi. 13, in the Cambridge University Library. An allusion to the bishop-elect of Winchester fixes its date between 1250 and 1260. In Cotton MS. Vespasian, D. v. f. 149, there are 'Epistolæ et Carmina,' which are ascribed to Michael by Richard James [q. v.] The introductory epistle begins 'Solus et sapiencia.' The poems include verses to various prelates, as Fulk Basset, William Ralegh, and Peter des Roches, and some lines 'De veteri Sarisburie et ecclesie mutatione,' inc. 'Mons Saltisberie.' Camden, in his 'Remaines' (ed. 1674, p. 10), quotes some lines against Normandy, which 'merry Michael the Cornish poet piped on his oaten pipe for England.' They begin:

Nobilis Anglia pocula, prandia donat et æra.

Michael is also credited with a 'Life of St. Birinus' and a 'Historia Normannorum.'

[Tanner's Bibl. Brit.-Hib. 432; Hardy's Cat. Brit. Hist. iii. 125; Warton's Hist. of Poetry, ed. Price, i. cxxxiii, ed. Hazlitt, ii. 48–9; Cotton and Royal MSS.; Hist. Litt. de la France, xviii. 529–30.] C. L. K.

MICHEL, Sir JOHN (1804–1886), field-marshal, was eldest son of General John Michel of Dewlish and Kingston Russell, Dorset, by his second wife, Anne, daughter of the Hon. Henry Fane, M.P., of Fulbeck, Lincolnshire, and granddaughter of the eighth earl of Westmoreland. The father, who had no issue by the first wife, was a subaltern in the 51st foot at the memorable defence of Minorca in 1781, of which he was one of the last survivors, was lieutenant-colonel commanding the 30th light dragoons in 1794–6, and the 14th light dragoons in 1799–1806, and afterwards held a brigade command in Ireland. He died in April 1844, leaving, according to report, considerable wealth (*Gent. Mag.* 1844, pt. i. p. 554).

John, born on 1 Sept. 1804, was educated at Eton. On 3 April 1823 he obtained an ensigncy by purchase in the 57th foot, passing through the 27th to the 64th foot, joining that corps at Gibraltar, and obtaining his lieutenancy in it on 28 April 1825. He purchased an unattached company on 12 Dec. 1826, and on 15 Feb. 1827 exchanged back to the 64th at Gibraltar. On 8 Feb. 1832 he entered the senior department of the Royal Military College, Sandhurst, and on 7 Nov. 1833 passed his examination and received a first certificate. He then rejoined his regiment, and served with it in Ireland until February 1835, when he exchanged to the 3rd buffs in Bengal. He was aide-de-camp to his uncle, General Sir Henry Fane, G.C.B. [see Fane, Sir Henry], while commander-in-chief in India in 1835–40. On 6 May 1840 he was promoted to a majority by purchase in the 6th foot, over the heads of many old officers in the regiment, an appointment which provoked much criticism at the time, and on 15 April 1842, a few weeks after the arrival of the regiment in England, he purchased the lieutenant-colonelcy. He commanded the 6th at home and at the Cape until 1854. He was in command of a brigade during the Kaffir war of 1846–7, and during part of the war of 1852–3 was in command of the 2nd division of the army in the Waterkloof (medal). At the close he was made C.B. 'for distinguished service in the Kaffir wars of 1846–7 and 1851–3.' He became brevet-colonel on 20 Jan. 1854, and was appointed to command the York recruiting district, but exchanged to half-pay 98th foot, on appointment as chief of the staff of the Turkish contingent, with the local rank of major-general in Turkey, a post he held until the end of the Crimean war (2nd class of the Medjidié and Turkish medal). In 1856 he was appointed to a brigade at Fort Beaufort, Cape of Good Hope, at a time of great danger and threatened war, owing to the expected fulfilment in February 1857 of an old Kaffir prophecy of the destruction of the whites.

The danger was hardly over before Michel was ordered to China for a command there. He was shipwrecked in the Transit steamer in the Straits of Sunda on 10 July 1857, and carried to Singapore (*Ann. Reg.* 1857, p. 169). His services were subsequently diverted to India, and he was placed on the Bombay Staff, 18 Feb. 1858. In June 1858 the troops in Rajputana were concentrated at Nusseerábád and Nímach, under Major-general H. G. Roberts, Bombay army, those at Mhow consisting of a brigade under Brigadier Honner. The latter, reinforced from Bombay, were formed into a division, as the Málwá field force, under Michel, the command of the troops in Rajputana being added thereto in August 1858, when Roberts was promoted to the command in Gujarat. Michel became major-general on 26 Oct. 1858. Impressed with the necessity of cutting off from the towns the bodies of rebels under Tantia Topee, Rao Sahib, and other leaders, and compelling them to seek the jungles, Michel adopted a strategy which proved eminently successful, despite serious physical obstacles, for the rains at this season had converted the soil of Málwá into a sea of black mud, and the heat was phenomenal. He distributed his troops in lightly equipped columns at salient points in Rajputana and Málwá, with orders to follow the rebels without intermission. Starting himself from Mhow, Michel came up with Tantia Topee at Beorora on 15 Sept. 1858. Tantia and the cavalry fled, pursued by the British cavalry. The infantry and guns made a stand, but did not await the British onset, and leaving thirty guns behind them, eight thousand well-trained troops were put to flight without the loss of a man. Michel again defeated Tantia at Mingrauli on 9 Oct., marched against Rao Sahib the next day, and defeated him at Sindwaha on 15 Oct.; on 5 Dec. he annihilated one wing of Tantia's force near Saugor, the other escaped and crossed the Narbadá into Nágpur. Other defeats of bodies of rebels followed, and they began to lose heart and creep away to their homes. Between 20 June 1858 and 1 March 1859 the field force traversed an aggregate distance of over three thousand miles, of which Michel himself marched seventeen hundred miles. The operations ended with the capture of Tantia Topee, who was taken by a small column under Brigadier Meade, was at once tried by court-martial, and was hanged on 18 April 1859 for being in arms against the British. The legality of the sentence was questioned, but he was admitted to have been one of the most bloodthirsty of Nana Sahib's advisers (cf. note to MALLESON's *Hist.* 6th edit. v. 265).

Michel, who was made K.C.B. and received the medal, remained in command of the Mhow division until the end of 1859, when he was appointed to the army under Sir James Hope Grant [q. v.], proceeding to the north of China. Michel commanded the 1st division at the action at Sinho (medal and clasp for the Takú Forts), and the occupation of Pekin on 12 Oct. 1860. His division on 18 Oct. burned the summer palace at Pekin, in return for the treacherous treatment by the Chinese of Mr. (afterwards Sir Harry) Parkes [q. v.] and some other captives. At the close of the campaign Michel was made G.C.B. for 'his zeal, skill, and intrepidity.' He was appointed colonel of the 86th royal county Down regiment (since the 2nd Irish rifles) on 19 Aug. 1862, became a lieutenant-general on 25 June 1866, and general on 28 March 1874. He was selected to command the troops in the first 'autumn manœuvres' in the south of England in 1873. In 1875 he was appointed commander of the forces in Ireland, and was sworn of the Irish privy council. He held the Irish command from 1875 to 1880, his social qualities and ample means rendering him extremely popular. He was made a field-marshal on 27 March 1885, and was a J.P. for Dorset. He died at his seat, Dewlish, Dorset, on 23 May 1886, aged 82.

Michel married, on 15 May 1838, Louise Anne, only daughter of Major-general H. Churchill, C.B., then quartermaster-general of the queen's troops in India, by whom he left two sons and three daughters. Michel was an active, spare-built man, somewhat below the middle height, impetuous and warm-hearted, a good sportsman, and a very energetic and capable officer.

[Burke's Landed Gentry, 1886 ed. vol. ii. under 'Michel;' Hart's Army Lists; London Gazettes and Ann. Registers under dates. The best account of Michel's Central Indian campaign is that given by an officer who was present in Blackwood's Mag. August 1860. See also Malleson (6th ed.) and Holmes (3rd ed.), Histories of the Indian Mutiny, Wolseley's Narrative of the Campaign in China in 1860, and Army and Navy Gazette, 25 May 1886.] H. M. C.

MICHELBORNE, Sir EDWARD (*d.* 1611?), adventurer, belonged to the family of the name settled in Hampshire and Sussex. He was captain of a company of foot soldiers in the Low Countries in 1591 (*Addit. MS.* 5753, f. 250), and was continued in the queen's pay till September 1598, but he is not named on any service, except as commanding the Moon in the Islands' Voyage, under the Earl of Essex, in 1597 (Lediard, *Naval Hist.* p. 354). In 1593 he represented Bramber in parliament, and is usually described as of 'Hamondes, Sussex.' In 1599 he served with Essex in Ireland, and was knighted by him at Dublin on 5 Aug. (Metcalfe, *Book of Knights*, p. 210.) On 16 Oct. 1599, Lord Buckhurst, the lord high treasurer, recommended him to the newly formed East India Company as 'principal commander' for their first voyage. The promoters declined, not wishing to employ any gentleman in a place of charge or command in the voyage (C. R. Markham, *Voyages of Sir James Lancaster*, p. ii). A year later Lord Buckhurst wrote again to the same effect, 'using much persuasion to the company,' who resolved as before, praying the lord treasurer 'to give them leave to sort their business with men of their own quality' (*Cal. State Papers*, East Indies, 3 Oct. 1600). Michelborne was, however, permitted to subscribe, and in the list of those to whom the charter was granted his name stands fourth (*ib.* 31 Dec. 1600). In the following February he was implicated in the Earl of Essex's rebellion, and was, in appearance at least, engaged in the detention of the lord keeper and lord chief justice on the 8th (*ib.* Dom. 10 Feb. 1601). On this charge he was exmined before the commissioners (*ib.* 13 March 1601), when he was described as of Clayton, Suffolk. He seems to have been able to clear himself, but the East India Company thought it a favourable opportunity for getting rid of one of their 'gentlemen,' and resolved on 6 July 1601 that he was 'disfranchised out of the freedom and privileges of the fellowship, and utterly disabled from taking any benefit or profit thereby' (*ib.* East Indies).

Three years later, however, Michelborne obtained from the king a license 'to discover the countries of Cathay, China, Japan, Corea, and Cambay, and the islands and countries thereto adjoining, and to trade with the people there, notwithstanding any grant or charter to the contrary' (*ib.* 18 June 1604). On 5 Dec. 1604 he sailed in command of the Tiger, having with him as pilot John Davys [q. v.] of Sandridge. Though nominally undertaken for discovery and trade, plunder seems to have been the object of the voyage. At Bantam, 28 Oct.–2 Nov. 1605, he put a summary check on the insolence of the Dutch (*Voyages and Works of John Davis*, p. 174), but the service which he thus rendered the English merchants was more than counterbalanced by his plundering a richly laden China ship on her way to Java (*ib.* p. 183). The sad death of Davys, the representations of the merchants, and the improbability of further gain, led to his return to England, where he arrived on 9 July 1606. Three years after his departure from Bantam the agent of the company had still to write of the bad effects of his voyage; the position of the English there would be very dangerous, he said, if 'any more such as he be permitted to do as he did' (*Cal. State Papers*, East Indies, 4 Dec. 1608). Michelborne after his return seems to have been settled in or near London (*ib.* 19, 23 Feb. 1608), and to have died about 1611.

A son Edward, born in 1587, matriculated at Christ Church, Oxford, in 1604, and was a student at the Middle Temple in 1606.

[The account of the voyage to the East Indies is given in Purchas his Pilgrimes, vol. i. lib. iii. p. 132. It is reprinted in The Voyages and Works of John Davis, edited for the Hakluyt Soc. by Captain (now Rear-admiral) A. H. Markham; see Foster's Alumni Oxon. and other authorities in the text.] J. K. L.

MICHELBORNE, EDWARD (1565–1626), Latin poet, son of a gentleman of Hampshire, was brought up as a Roman catholic. The family of Michelborne was widely disseminated in Hampshire and Sussex, and from the Sussex branch of Bradhurst sprang John Michelborne [q. v.], the governor of Londonderry (cf. Berry, *Sussex Genealogies*, p. 50). Edward the poet had two brothers, Thomas and Lawrence (Fitzgeffrey, *Affaniæ*, 1601, p. 165). He matriculated at Oxford as a commoner of St. Mary Hall on 27 March 1579, aged 14, and afterwards migrated to Gloucester Hall, but took no degree owing to religious scruples. He appears to have lived most of his life at Oxford, and was, according to Wood, 'the most noted Latin poet in the university.' His compositions, which Wood declares to have been numerous, seem mainly to have been contributed to books by his friends. 'The poets of his time,' writes Wood, 'did mostly submit their labours to his judgment before they were made public.' His closest friends were Charles Fitzgeffrey [q. v.] and Thomas Campion [q. v.] Fitzgeffrey dedicated his 'Affaniæ,' 1601, to him, and inscribed seven other poems in the volume to him, besides printing some complimentary

Latin verses by Michelborne. Four of Campion's 'Latin Epigrams,' 1619, are addressed to him in very affectionate terms (bk. i. nos. 180, 192, bk. ii. nos. 77, 121). Both Campion and Fitzgeffrey lament the modesty which prevented their friend from publishing his verse. Two poems by Michelborne in praise of the author are prefixed to 'The Art of Brachygraphy,' 1597, of Peter Bales [q. v.], and he is a contributor to 'Camdeni Insignia,' 1624. Michelborne died at Oxford on 27 Dec. 1626, and was buried in the church of St. Thomas the Martyr.

Fitzgeffrey inscribes several poems in his 'Affaniæ' to Edward's brothers—three to Thomas (pp. 84, 165), and two to Lawrence (pp. 5, 32), while each brother is the subject of an epigram by Campion (bk. ii. no. 34 on Lawrence and no. 69 on Thomas). Lawrence was residing at Oxford in 1594, although his name does not appear in the university register (*Oxf. Univ. Reg.*, Oxf. Hist. Soc., II. i. 318). Thomas prefixed Latin hexameters —'In Dracum Redivivum Carmen'—to the first edition, and some English stanzas to the second edition of Fitzgeffrey's poem on 'Sir Francis Drake,' 1596. English commendatory verses by him also figure in Thomas Storer's poetic 'Life and Death of Thomas Wolsey, Cardinall,' 1599, and in Sir William Vaughan's 'Golden Grove,' 1608.

[Wood's Fasti Oxon. ed. Bliss, i. 428; Foster's Alumni Oxon.; Ritson's Bibliographia Poetica, pp. 278, 283; Campion's Works, ed. Bullen, pp. 301, 304, 323, 332, 346.] S. L.

MICHELBORNE, MITCHELBURN, or MICHELBURNE, JOHN (1647–1721), governor of Londonderry, son of Abraham Michelborne by his first wife, Penelope, daughter of John Wheeler of Droitwich (see Berry, *Sussex Genealogies*, p. 50), was baptised on 8 Jan. 1647–8 at Horsted Keynes in Sussex. He was of an ancient family long settled there and at Stanmer, and Sir Richard Michelborne of Bradhurst was his grandfather. After serving under Percy Kirke [q. v.] at Tangier between 1680 and 1683, he had a major's commission from the Prince of Orange dated 5 Feb. 1689, and in the same month took part in the attempt on Carrickfergus. He commanded Skeffington's regiment of foot at Cladyford and during the siege of Londonderry. When Governor Baker fell ill on 17 June 1689 he deputed Mitchelburn to act for him, and at his death ten days later named him governor. The two officers had been on bad terms and had even crossed swords, and the author of the 'Londerias' says Mitchelburn was under arrest when his predecessor died; but Walker, Mackenzie, and Ash do not mention this. He was a pall-bearer at Baker's funeral. Though not confirmed by any vote of the officers, Mitchelburn acted as military governor during the rest of the siege; but Walker always signs his name first. About the middle of July Melfort, on behalf of King James, offered Mitchelburn 10,000*l.* if he would procure a surrender, but the governor answered that William was his sovereign, who could reward him without the help of brass money (Letters in *Siege of Derry*, act iv.) He lost his wife and all his children—seven in number—during the siege. After the relief of Londonderry Kirke commissioned Mitchelburn as sole governor, and made him colonel of both Skeffington's and Crofton's regiments, which he fused into one. Mitchelburn commanded this corps at the Boyne, and mustered 664 rank and file after the battle (Story). He served at the long siege of Sligo, of which he took possession 19 Sept. 1691, and of which he was made governor (Harris).

In 1690 the Irish Society voted 100*l.* to Mitchelburn, but he had spent his own money during the siege of Londonderry, and was a heavy loser. He petitioned the English treasury, alleging that 9,570*l.* 16*s.* 8*d.* were due to him and his regiment (*Cal. of Treasury Papers*, 21 April 1691). Various delays and difficulties were interposed, but it appears that some portion of what was due was at length paid to him (Harris, book viii.) He remained permanently at Londonderry, and became alderman. In 1699 he issued a printed statement of his losses, which gave great offence at Londonderry, and he was expelled from his office of alderman (*Corporation Minutes* in Hempton, p. 406). He succeeded in the litigation which followed, and was restored by *mandamus*. A result of the statute 2 Anne, cap. 6, which imposed the sacramental test, was to exclude Mitchelburn's presbyterian opponents from the corporation, and in August 1703 his bill of costs was paid. He made at least two journeys to London on account of his claims, and in 1709 suffered imprisonment for debt in the Fleet.

Mitchelburn originated some well-known Londonderry observances. With Bishop King's leave he placed in the cathedral the French flags which had been taken on 7 May 1689, and in 1713 Bishop Hartstonge allowed him to record the fact in an inscription on the east window (*ib.* p. 410). On 1 Aug. 1718 the red flag, which still adorns the steeple, was hoisted for the first time, as Bishop William Nicolson [q. v.] has recorded (*ib.* p. 411), amid great rejoicings and feastings and with illuminations and salvoes of artillery. On the same day in 1720 Mitchelburn dined with the bishop, and there were more bonfires. By his will, dated 12 July 1721, he bequeathed 50*l.* 'for maintaining the flag on the steeple of Derry.' He died in his own house at the waterside, within sight of the walls which he had defended, on 1 Oct. 1721, and was buried near Adam Murray [q. v.] in Glendermot churchyard, co. Derry. His second wife is believed to have been the daughter of another defender, Captain Michael Cunningham of Prehen, Londonderry. By her Mitchelburn had no issue. A portrait of Mitchelburn in armour, by an unknown artist, is mentioned by Bromley. Mitchelburn's sword is preserved at Caw House, Londonderry, and his saddle, which was also used by Walker, is in possession of the Dublin society of 'Apprentice Boys of Derry,' who use it in their installation ceremonies.

[Lower's Worthies of Sussex; George Walker's True Account of the Siege of Londonderry; John Mackenzie's Narrative of the Siege; Captain Thomas Ash's Narrative of the Siege; Joseph Aickin's Londerias, 1699; George Story's Impartial History; Walter Harris's Life of William III; John Hempton's Siege and History of Londonderry; the Rev. John Graham's Ireland Preserved, containing the 'Siege of Derry,' a contemporary drama, which has been attributed to Mitchelburn; Witherow's Derry and Enniskillen, 3rd edit. 1885; manuscript minutes of Dublin 'Apprentice Boys;' Berry's Sussex Genealogies, p. 50; see arts. Lundy, Robert, and Mackenzie, John, 1648–1696.] R. B-l.

MICHELL. [See also Michel, Mitchel, and Mitchell.]

MICHELL, CHARLES CORNWALLIS (1793–1851), lieutenant-colonel, born in 1793, was baptised Charles Collier Michell, but when serving with the Portuguese artillery the name Cornwallis became attached to him, through some confusion with Cornwall, the name of the county in which he was born, and he never took the trouble to correct the mistake. Sampson Michell, his father, after serving for some years in the British navy, was permitted to enter the Portuguese service. On the invasion of Portugal by the French in 1807 he brought his family to England, and subsequently followed the king to the Brazils, where he died a full admiral in 1809.

Michell entered the Royal Military Academy at Woolwich in 1807 as a cadet, and was commissioned in the royal artillery on 2 Oct. 1809. The following are the dates of his subsequent commissions: lieutenant 16 March 1813; captain 4 Sept. 1817, when he was placed on half-pay; major 5 Jan. 1826; and lieutenant-colonel 23 Nov. 1841.

In 1810 Michell embarked for Gibraltar, and soon afterwards succeeded in getting himself transferred to the scene of active operations in the Peninsula. During the greater part of the war he was in command of a company or battery of Portuguese artillery, to which service he was lent, and he distinguished himself at the siege and capture of Badajoz and at the battles of Vittoria and Toulouse. At the latter engagement his battery was ordered up to cover the advance of some Spanish troops, who could not be induced to leave a hollow road leading to the town of Toulouse. During this advance the driver of the leaders of the first gun was killed. Michell instantly sprang from his horse, vaulted into the vacant saddle, and dashed forward with his guns. According to an eye-witness, he was 'one of the tallest and handsomest men in the Peninsular army. His cap had fallen off, and his appearance, as at full speed he led onwards the foremost gun . . . excited as much interest as admiration.' Towards the close of the battle he was wounded.

Some little time after the entry of the troops into Toulouse, Michell was quartered at the house of Jean Pierre d'Arragon, a retired French royalist officer. Falling in love with the young and beautiful daughter of the house, who was not then fifteen years old, and failing to get the consent of the parents, he obtained the help of several of his senior officers in carrying off and marrying his young bride. Mrs. Michell accompanied her husband in his march back to Portugal, and never saw her parents again.

On the return of the Portuguese army to Lisbon, Michell was attached to the staff of Marshal Beresford, whom he accompanied in 1820 to the Brazils, and thence retired to France. In 1824 he was appointed military drawing master at the Royal Military College, Sandhurst, and in 1825 he obtained the professorship of fortification at the Royal Military Academy at Woolwich. In 1828 he became surveyor-general, civil engineer, and superintendent of works at the Cape of Good Hope. As assistant quartermaster-general in the Caffre war of 1833–4 he devoted 'unwearied labour' to sketching the unknown country through which the troops passed, and he received the Hanoverian order in recognition of his services on this occasion. In 1844 the queen of Portugal conferred on him the order of St. Bento d'Avis, as a reward for his services in the Peninsula and in memory of his father's connection with the Portuguese navy. In 1846 the queen also admitted him to the royal military order of the Tower and the Sword.

After twelve years' employment, the multifarious duties at the Cape began to tell heavily on Michell's health, and in 1848 he was obliged to resign his appointment. Great progress had been made by the department under his charge during these years in pushing forward the roads of the colony.

Michell was a genial companion, and made himself popular everywhere. He was an excellent draughtsman and an accomplished linguist. He died at Eltham on 28 March 1851.

[Colburn's United Service Magazine, 1851.]
L. D.

MICHELL, EDWARD THOMAS (1787–1841), brigadier-general, born in 1787, entered the Royal Military Academy, Woolwich, as a cadet on 27 Jan. 1802, and passed out as second lieutenant royal artillery on 8 Sept. 1803. He became first lieutenant 13 Sept. 1803, second captain 11 Aug. 1811, brevet major 17 March 1814, first captain 20 Aug. 1825, brevet lieutenant-colonel 11 June, and regimental lieutenant-colonel 30 June 1838. He was detached from his company at Gibraltar to Spain in 1810, and commanded a guerilla division in the Sierra de Ronda, and was present at the capture of Ronda, the combats of El Brosque and Bornos, and the night attack and capture of Arcos. He commanded the artillery of the British force occupying Tarifa in 1810–12; was shot through the shoulder at the battle of Barossa, and was much praised for his skilful conduct of the artillery at the final defence of Tarifa in December 1811 (Napier, rev. ed. iv. 60). In 1812 he was engaged at the attack on the forts of Salamanca, the battle of Salamanca, and minor affairs. From December 1813 to May 1814 he served in Holland at Merxem, the bombardment of Antwerp, and the attack on Bergen-op-Zoom. On one occasion in the course of these operations he extinguished a lighted shell that had fallen into a wagonload of ammunition. He volunteered to lead one of the assaulting columns at Bergen-op-Zoom, where he was very severely wounded. He was British commissioner with the Spanish armies during the latter part of the Carlist war, from August 1839 to December 1840, and received the Spanish decorations of St. Fernando, Charles III, and Isabella the Catholic. He was then despatched to Syria, with the rank of brigadier-general, to command the detachments of royal artillery and sappers and miners sent with Admiral Stafford's fleet to assist the Turks in driving the Egyptian army out of Syria. With the other English officers he accompanied the Turks, under General Jochmus, in their advance from Jaffa towards Gaza, and was present at the affair at Medjdel, on 15 Jan. 1841, which compelled the Egyptians to retreat. The English counselled the immediate seizure of Gaza, six miles distant. Jochmus pleaded the bad state of the roads, and two days later news arrived of the convention concluded by Commodore Napier at Alexandria, ending the war.

Michell died, 24 Jan. 1841, of fever caused by sleeping in his wet clothes on the night after the battle of Medjdel. He was buried by the British sappers in a grave in the left flank of the 'Sir Sidney Smith' bastion of the fortress of Jaffa. By permission of the Turkish authorities a large white marble tablet, subscribed for by the British officers who served with him in Syria, was afterwards placed in the interior slope of the parapet facing the grave (see *Naval and Military Gazette*, 7 Sept. 1844).

Michell, who was made C.B. on 19 July 1838, and was in receipt of 300*l.* a year for wounds, was popular with his brother officers and his men. He is described as an open-hearted, frank old soldier, small in stature, with a stoop from the effects of a wound in former days, and a keen, clear eye (Browne, p. 211).

[Kane's Lists Royal Artillery, rev. ed. Woolwich, 1869; Browne's England's Artillerymen, pp. 210–11; Napier's Hist. Peninsular War, vol. iv. rev. ed.; W. P. Hunter's Hist. of the War in Syria; Nav. and Mil. Gaz. 20 Feb. 1841, 7 Sept. 1844]. H. M. C.

MICHELL, Sir FRANCIS (*fl.* 1621), commissioner for enforcing monopolies, born in 1556, was probably of an Essex family. He matriculated at Magdalen Hall, Oxford, about 1574 and seems to have been subsequently employed as private secretary to a succession of noblemen. In a letter to Secretary Conway (February 1626) he speaks of having served 'six great persons' in that capacity, but only gives the name of Lord Burgh, lord deputy of Ireland. He was secretary from 1594 to 1597 to Sir William Russel, lord deputy, and was probably in the employment of William Davison and Lord Salisbury—possibly in the service of the latter he visited Rome, where he was imprisoned by the inquisition. He appears to have performed services in Scotland on behalf of James I before that king's accession to the English throne (*State Papers*, Dom. Ch. I, vol. xxi. No. 105). Doubtless through the favour of one of his patrons he secured (25 May

1603) the grant in reversion of the office of clerk of the market for life. He seems to have returned from abroad, where he had been travelling for six years, about 1611, and subsequently to have lived in Clerkenwell as a justice for Middlesex. There is an entry in the register of St. James, Clerkenwell, dated 16 Aug. 1612, of the marriage of Francis Michell and Sisley Wentworth.

In 1618 the king adopted the policy of extending and more vigorously enforcing existing patents. On 6 April 1618 the original patentee surrendered by agreement the gold and silver thread patent; fresh patents were immediately granted, and a commission was issued for the discovery and punishment of offenders. Michell was appointed a member of this commission, and he and one Henry Tweedy were throughout the subsequent proceedings the acting commissioners. Their duties were to guard against the importation, or unauthorised manufacture, of gold and silver thread, and any two or more of them were granted the power of imprisonment. These powers, however, proved insufficient, and on 20 Oct. 1618 a fuller commission was issued with the name of Sir Giles Mompesson [q. v.] added. Michell had exceeded his authority under the first commission, and now, stimulated by the activity of Mompesson, he exercised his powers corruptly and with considerable harshness for two years, thereby incurring great odium. The result was an outburst of public feeling against the enforcement of the obnoxious patent. A parliamentary committee of inquiry into monopolies reported that the enforcement of the patent involved serious grievances (*Commons' Journals*, i. 540). Michell, who in December 1620 had been knighted, was accordingly committed by the House of Commons to the Tower for contempt in February 1621, and travelled thither 'on foot and bareheaded' (*Cal. State Papers*, Dom. 1621, p. 106). On 6 March 1621 he confessed at the bar of the House of Commons that he had received 100*l.* per annum for executing the commission for gold and silver thread. On 26 April 1621 he was tried at the bar of the House of Lords, the chief accusations against him being that he had erected an office and kept a court and exacted bonds, and that he had taken money in a suit to compound the same (*Journals of the House of Lords*, iii. 88). On 4 May 1621 the lord chief justice sentenced him to degradation from knighthood, a fine of 1,000*l.*, disability to hold or receive any office in future, and imprisonment during the king's pleasure in Finsbury gaol, 'in the same chamber where he provided for others, the tower where he now remains being a prison too worthy of him.' On 23 June the portion of the sentence relating to degradation from knighthood was carried out with all formalities publicly in Westminster Hall, and Michell was proclaimed by the herald as 'no knight but arrant knave.' The king, however, granted the commissioner's petition for release from prison, dated 30 June 1621.

Shortly after his release he petitioned the king for means to live, and at the same time he wrote to Prince Charles and Buckingham begging their support; to the latter he hinted that he was deserving of his especial favour, 'as he [Buckingham] could not but commiserate, knowing wherefore his sufferings were inflicted' (*Cotton MS.* Jul. c. iii. f. 254), but the favourite declined to become a suitor on his behalf. In December 1623 Michell was in trouble for an attack he had made in writing on his old enemies, Lord Coke and Sir Dudley Digges, and narrowly escaped examination before the Star-chamber. At this time he was beset with financial difficulties, and in the same year petitioned the council for protection from his creditors, 'having lost most of his estate in his trouble.' In July 1625 he presented a petition to the commons for release of an unjust information made against him in their house in 1620, and he begged for leave to discourse to a committee the 'slights and practises' then used (*Harl. MS.* 161, f. 33). On the accession of Charles I he represented, in a carefully framed petition, that he had screened the principals (notably Sir Edward Villiers) against whom the attack of the commons had been directed; and the house, he complained, after 'failinge against Cedars then oppressed your supplicant, a poore shrubb, to his utter undoinge' (*State Papers*, Dom. Ch. I, vol. xxi. No. 105). His petitions were ungranted in March 1628, when he wrote to a friend that if it were necessary for him to come to London for the prosecution of his suit 'he will teach his old limbs so weary a tedious journey' (*Cotton MS.* Jul. c. iii. f. 256).

[Cal. State Papers, Ireland and Eliz.; Cal. Carew MS.; Cal. State Papers, Dom. James I, Ch. I; Journals of the House of Lords, vol. iii.; Commons' Journals, vol. i.; Archæologia, vol. xli.; Debate in the House of Lords (Camd. Soc.), v. 107; Gardiner's Hist. of England; A. Wilson's Life and Reign of King James I; Camden's Annals; Reg. of University of Oxford, II. ii. 58; Reg. of St. James's, Clerkenwell (Harl. Soc.)]

W. C–R.

MICHELL, HENRY (1714–1789), scholar, born in 1714 at Lewes, was educated there and at Clare Hall, Cambridge; he graduated B.A. 1735, M.A. 1739, and became fellow of his college. In 1739 he was presented to the rectory of Maresfield in Sussex, and in 1744 to the vicarage of Brighton with the rectory of Bletchingdon united. Here he lived until his death, enjoying ample means, the friendship of many men of note, and the reputation of an accomplished Greek and Latin scholar. He had considerable share in the rapid development of Brighton, and for a short time the Duke of Wellington was among his pupils. Michell died at Brighton on 31 Oct. 1789, and was buried in the parish church, where there is an inscription to his memory. He married in 1747 the only daughter and heiress of the Rev. Francis Reade of Bedford, by whom he had sixteen children. There is a portrait in Nichols's 'Illustrations' (iv. 868), engraved by E. Scott from a miniature painted by Sherriff.

Michell published: 1. 'De Arte Medendi apud Priscos Musicos,' 1766, dedicated to the Earl of Shelburne; of a second edition only, published in 1767, is there a copy in the British Museum. 2. 'De Jure Colonias inter et Metropolin,' 1777. He left with other manuscripts a translation, with notes, of 'Le Dîner du Comte de Boulainvilliers, 1768, par Mons. St. Hiacinte' [i.e. Voltaire].

[Nichols's Lit. Anecd. iv. 447, Illustrations, iv. 866–70; Gent. Mag. 1789, ii. 1055; manuscript note prefixed to the De Arte in Brit. Mus. Libr.; Life of Sir John Eardley Wilmot, p. 187, &c.]

A. F. P.

MICHELL, JOHN (1724–1793), astronomer, was born apparently in 1724. He was described as of Nottinghamshire when he was admitted to Queens' College, Cambridge, on 17 June 1742. He was elected a bible-clerk there on 23 Jan. 1747, and graduated as fourth wrangler in 1748. He was elected to a fellowship in 1749, and proceeded M.A. in 1752, and B.D. in 1761. He served the college offices of lecturer in Hebrew (1751–2, 1759–60, 1762), in arithmetic (1751–2), in geometry (1753–4, 1763), in Greek (1755–6, 1759–60), and was theological censor (1753–5), senior bursar (1756–60), and philosophical censor (1760). From 20 March 1760 till June 1763 he was rector of St. Botolph's, Cambridge, and he resigned his fellowship on 8 April 1764. His membership of the Royal Society dated from 12 June 1760, but his name does not appear in the lists until 1762, in which year he was appointed Woodwardian professor of geology at Cambridge. In 1767 he became rector of Thornhill in Yorkshire, where he resided until his death. His leisure and fortune were devoted to the promotion of science; but he also cultivated music, and was no mean violinist. Although the statement involves some chronological difficulty, there seems no doubt that William Herschel [q. v.] often performed on the violin at his entertainments, which were attended by Priestley, the Hon. Henry Cavendish [q. v.], and other distinguished persons. From him, too, Herschel received his first lessons in speculum-grinding, and a ten-foot reflector turned out by him eventually came into Herschel's possession.

Michell published at Cambridge in 1750 'A Treatise of Artificial Magnets' (2nd edit. 1751, translated into French, 1752), in which he described the mode of making artificial magnets by 'double touch,' and enunciated the law of variation of magnetic action according to the inverse squares of distances. He communicated to the Royal Society his observations of the comet of January 1760, made at Cambridge with a Hadley's quadrant (*Phil. Trans.* li. 466), and shortly afterwards 'Conjectures concerning the Cause, and Observations upon the Phenomena of Earthquakes' (*ib.* p. 566; published separately, London, 1760, 4to), in which he put forward the theory of their origin through the elastic force of subterraneanly generated steam. 'A Recommendation of Hadley's Quadrant for Surveying' followed in 1765 (*ib.* lv. 70), and a 'Proposal of a Method for Measuring Degrees of Longitude upon Parallels of the Equator' in 1767 (*ib.* lvi. 119). 'An Enquiry into the Probable Parallax and Magnitude of the Fixed Stars from the Quantity of Light which they afford us,' read 7 and 14 May 1767 (*ib.* lvii. 234), led him to infer the extreme minuteness of stellar parallax. In the same remarkable paper he argued the overwhelming probability for the physical grouping of the Pleiades, and investigated the possibility of our sun belonging to some similar association. He anticipated, moreover, the detection of the revolutions of double stars, and showed how their relative densities could thence be deduced on the supposition of equal surface-brightness, whatever might be their distances from the earth. He divined, too, the presence of an element in stellar proper motions due to the sun's motion in space, and foresaw that from the amount of this 'secular parallax' might be deduced the distances of the objects affected by it. He finally pointed out the law connecting the visibility of small stars with telescopic aperture, and sought from it guidance as to their distances. Reverting to these problems in 1783 (*ib.* lxxiv. 35), he reaffirmed the binary nature of pairs of stars, but speculated fruitlessly on a supposed retardation of light through the attraction of its corpuscles by the emitting masses.

Michell arrived independently at Boscovich's theory of the constitution of matter (Priestley, *History of Optics*, i. 392), and inferred that the moon reflects less than one-sixth of the light falling upon it. Several communications from him were embodied in Priestley's 'History of Optics.' Shortly before his death he devised a method and completed an apparatus for weighing the earth by means of the torsion-balance, of which he was the original inventor. The appliances in question passed from the hands of William Hyde Wollaston [q. v.] to those of Cavendish, who successfully carried out in 1798 the experiments planned by their constructor (*Phil. Trans.* lxxxviii. 469).

Michell died at Thornhill, Yorkshire, on 21 April 1793, in his sixty-ninth year, leaving an only daughter, who died about 1836, aged upwards of eighty. His scientific instruments were presented after his death to Queens' College, Cambridge.

[English Mechanic, xiii. 310 (a communication from Michell's great-grandson); European Mag. xxiii. 400; Whitaker's Hist. of Leeds, p. 326; Knowledge, xv. 108, 206 (J. R. Sutton); Poggendorff's Biog. Lit. Handwörterbuch; Thomson's Hist. of the Roy. Soc.; Grant's Hist. of Astronomy, p. 543; Clerke's Popular Hist. of Astronomy, p. 22, &c.; Cat. Cambridge Graduates; Gent. Mag. 1793, i. 480; information kindly supplied by the Rev. the President of Queens' College, Cambridge.] A. M. C.

MICHELL or MITCHELL, MATTHEW (*d.* 1752), commodore, was promoted to be lieutenant of the Advice with Captain William Martin [q. v.] on 11 April 1729. He afterwards served in the Royal Oak and Ipswich, and in August 1738 was promoted to the command of the Terrible bomb, employed in the North Sea. In 1740 he commanded the Swift sloop in the Channel; and in June 1740 was posted to the Pearl frigate, one of the squadron which, on 18 Sept. 1740, sailed for the South Seas under the command of Commodore George (afterwards Lord) Anson [q. v.] At Madeira he was moved into the Gloucester of 50 guns, the only ship of force, besides the Centurion, which doubled Cape Horn and reached Juan Fernandez. The sufferings of her crew from scurvy and want of water had been very great, and many men had died. When the few survivors had recovered their health, and with such reinforcements as circumstances permitted, the Gloucester rejoined the commodore off Paita in November 1741, continued with him during the remainder of his cruise on the American coast, and sailed with him for China. The sickness broke out again worse than before, and in a violent storm the ship lost her topmasts and sprang a leak. With jury-topmasts she sailed so badly as to endanger the safety of her consort; she had only sixteen men and eleven boys able, in any way, to do duty, and many of these were sick. She had seven feet of water in the hold, and there were no means of freeing her or of stopping the leak. It was therefore determined to abandon her and set her on fire. Michell, with the miserable remnant of his ship's company, went on in the Centurion to Macao, whence he took a passage home in a Swedish ship. He arrived in England in June 1743, and in October was appointed to the Worcester, in which he joined the fleet under Sir John Norris [q. v.] in January 1743-4. He was afterwards commodore of a small squadron on the coast of Flanders and off Dunkirk, on which service he continued until March 1748, when, on the plea that his private affairs required his presence in England, he was permitted to resign his command. In 1747 he was elected member of parliament for Westbury. He died 'in the prime of life,' 29 April 1752. He married in 1749 Frances, daughter of Mr. Ashfordby of Norfolk Street, London, with whom, it was announced, he received a fortune of 20,000*l.* The name is commonly misspelt Mitchell. The spelling given here is that of his own signature.

[Charnock's Biog. Nav. v. 48; Walters's Voyage Round the World; Beatson's Nav. and Mil. Memoirs, i. 303 and iii. 43; commission and warrant books and official letters in the Public Record Office.] J. K. L.

MICHELL, NICHOLAS (1807–1880), miscellaneous writer, born at Calenick, near Truro, on 4 June 1807, was son of John Michell (1774–1868). The latter, known as the father of the tin trade, was a tin smelter and chemist, and one of the discoverers of tantalite. Nicholas, after attending the Truro grammar school, was employed in the office of his father's smelting works at Calenick, and afterwards in London. He wrote poems from an early age; was encouraged by Thomas Campbell and other literary men, and contributed to the 'Forget-me-not,' the 'Keepsake,' and other annuals. But it was not till after the publication of his 'Ruins of Many Lands' in 1849 that Michell succeeded in attracting much public attention. This work supplies poetical descriptions of nearly all the existing remains of ancient people and kingdoms in the old and new world. His next work, produced in 1853, was the 'Spirits of the Past,' a title altered in a subsequent edition to 'Famous Women and

Heroes.' 'The Poetry of Creation' followed in 1856, and 'Pleasure,' a poem in the heroic measure, appeared in 1859, with sketches and tales introduced. 'The Immortals, or Glimpses of Paradise,' was composed in 1870 in Cornwall, and is the most imaginative of the author's productions. 'Sibyl of Cornwall,' a story in verse, deals with love and adventure, the scene being laid on the north coast of his native county. He also wrote several novels, but these did not obtain so large a circulation as his poems. He died in Tehidy Terrace, Falmouth, 6 April 1880, and was buried in St. Kea churchyard on 12 April.

Michell married, on 3 Aug. 1836, Maria, second daughter of John Waterhouse of Halifax, Yorkshire; she died in Penzance on 9 June 1887, aged 74.

Besides the works already mentioned, Michell was the author of: 1. 'The Siege of Constantinople, with other Poems,' 1831. 2. 'Living Poets and Poetesses, a Biographical and Critical Poem,' 1832. 3. 'An Essay on Woman,' 1833. 4. 'The Saxon's Daughter, a Tale of the Crusades,' 1835. 5. 'The Fatalist, or the Fortunes of Godolphin,' 3 vols. 1840. 6. 'The Traduced, an Historical Romance,' 3 vols. 1842. 7. 'The Eventful Epoch, or the Fortunes of Arthur Clive,' 3 vols. 1846. 8. 'London in Light and Darkness, with all the Author's Minor Poems, now first collected,' 1871. 9. 'The Heart's Great Ruler, a Poem,' and 'Wanderings from the Rhine to the South Sea Islands,' 1874. 10. 'Nature and Life, including all the Miscellaneous Poems with many Original Pieces,' 1878.

A collected edition of his 'Poems' appeared in 1871.

[Men of the West, pt. iv. N. Michell, April 1877, pp. 17–20, with portrait; Boase and Courtney's Bibl. Cornub. 1874–82, pp. 352–4, 1281; Boase's Collect. Cornub. 1890, p. 558.]

G. C. B.

MICHELL, RICHARD (1805–1877), first principal of Hertford College, Oxford, third son of Edward Michell of Bruton and Ann Clements of Wyke Champflower, Somerset, was born at Bruton in 1805, and was educated at Bruton grammar school. He proceeded in 1820 to Wadham College, Oxford, where his uncle, Dr. Richard Michell (1766–1826), was a fellow of some distinction. Obtaining a first-class *in lit. hum.* (B.A. 1824, M.A. 1827, B.D. 1836, and D.D. 1868), Michell became a remarkably successful private tutor. Many of his pupils afterwards distinguished themselves in the learned professions or politics, among them being Lords Selborne and Sherbrooke, Bishops Charles Wordsworth, Fraser, and Pelham, Deans Church and Liddell, and Professor J. A. Froude. At the previously unprecedented age of twenty-four he was appointed an examiner in the school of *lit. hum.*, an office which he frequently held afterwards, and was elected in 1830 fellow of Lincoln College, where he acted as bursar in 1832, and as tutor from 1834 to 1848. In 1839 he was elected in convocation, by a very large majority, the first prælector of logic, on the revival of the public teaching of that subject. This he held for ten years. In 1849 he delivered the Bampton lectures. His subject, 'The Nature and Comparative Value of the Christian Evidences,' he treated with good sense and felicitous diction. In 1849 also Michell was appointed public orator of the university, and he retained that office till his death. His orations delivered at the annual act or encænia, alternately with the professor of poetry, were notable for their excellent latinity and conservative sentiment. They were published in 1878, soon after his death, by his eldest son, Mr. E. B. Michell, with valuable notes. The work forms a sort of running commentary on the history of the university for nearly thirty years. In 1856 Michell became rector of South Moreton, Berkshire, but did not reside there. On the formation of the new hebdomadal council under the act for reforming the university in 1854, Michell was elected to a seat, and retained it by frequent re-elections till 1872.

In 1848 Michell became vice-principal of Magdalen Hall, now Hertford College, of which Dr. John David Macbride [q. v.] was then principal. Michell succeeded William Jacobson [q. v.], afterwards bishop of Chester, who had been appointed regius professor of divinity. The hall, under the guidance of these three remarkable officers, held an important place in the university, and sent forth during the sixty years of its existence many distinguished men, but its very limited staff was too small for its numbers and position. In 1868 Michell succeeded Dr. Macbride in the principalship, and he then began to agitate for the conversion of the hall into a college. The design assumed a definite shape in 1873, was approved by convocation, and the expenses required for passing the bill through parliament paid by subscription among the members of the hall. Before, however, the act was passed Michell received a munificent offer from Mr. T. C. Baring, M.P., to endow the college with a large number of fellowships and scholarships, mostly limited to members of the church of England. This offer was accepted, and the new foundation took the name of Hertford College. He became the first principal of the new college in 1874, and died 29 March 1877.

Michell was in politics a tory of the old school, but by no means inclined to obstruct well-considered projects of reform. In religion he was more or less of the evangelical school. In person he was of a commanding figure. There is a good picture of him in Hertford College, a copy of one by Edis, R.A., presented to Mrs. Michell by her husband's pupils about 1860. In 1841 he married the daughter of Thomas Blair, esq., of Walton Grove, Surrey, by whom he had several children. One daughter, Mary, married the third duke of Sutherland (and subsequently Sir Albert Rollit).

[Personal knowledge; Orationes Crewianæ, 1849–1875; Oxford Univ. Cal. 1892; Foster's Alumni Oxon.] M. B–s.

MICKLE, WILLIAM JULIUS (1735–1788), poet, was born 28 Sept. 1735, at Langholm, Dumfriesshire, where his father, Alexander Meikle, was parish minister from 1717 till 1746 (Hew Scott, *Fasti*, pt. ii. pp. 628–9). His mother was Julian, daughter of Thomas Henderson of Ploughlands, Dalmeny. He was educated at Langholm grammar school till his father, owing to advancing years, arranged for a substitute in his parish and settled in Edinburgh. Here Mickle attended the high school till his fifteenth year, when he became a clerk in an Edinburgh brewery, purchased by his father on the death of a brother-in-law. At the end of six years Mickle was made chief partner, and a little afterwards, on his father's death in 1757, he found himself owner of the brewery under certain restrictions in the interests of the family. Unluckily for his commercial success he trusted servants and attended to literature; he soon became so harassed that a composition with his creditors was necessary; and at length, in 1763, he left business and settled in London as a man of letters.

About 1761 Mickle had contributed anonymously 'Knowledge, an Ode,' and 'A Night Piece' to Donaldson's 'Collection of Poetry,' Edinburgh. He had criticised, to the admiration of his friends, Annet's 'History of the Man after God's own Heart,' and Chalmers says that before the crisis in his business he finished a dramatic piece on the death of Socrates and began a poem on 'Providence.' He had also corresponded under an assumed name with Lord Lyttelton regarding his poetry, and now, when he revealed himself on settling in London, Lyttelton, while advising him to avoid publishing immature work, encouraged him to persevere in literature, and dissuaded him from seeking a post in the West Indies.

Becoming corrector to the Clarendon Press, Oxford, in 1765, Mickle settled to his work. In 1767 he published the longest of his original poems, 'The Concubine,' which was reissued in 1778 as 'Sir Martyn.' A fragmentary tribute to his brother Charles, who died young, was written in 1768. In 1769 he wrote his 'Letter to Mr. Harwood' [see Harwood, Edward, D.D.], and in 1770 produced 'Voltaire in the Shades,' an onslaught on the deists with Hume as an interlocutor. His literary reputation was growing, and when, in 1771, he proposed to publish by subscription a translation of 'Os Lusiadas' of Camoens, he received abundant encouragement. A specimen of Book V, given in the 'Gentleman's Magazine,' in March 1771, and Book I, published separately somewhat later, were so favourably regarded that Mickle resolved to devote his entire time to the translation. He left the Clarendon Press and settled with Mr. Tomkins, a farmer at Forest Hill, near Oxford. Here he completed his task in 1775, and he at once published the translation in London. Besides copiously annotating the 'Lusiad,' Mickle furnished the work with an introduction in defence of 'Commerce,' 'A History of the Discovery of India,' 'A History of the Portuguese Empire in the East,' 'A Life of Camoens,' a dissertation on the 'Lusiad' and a critical excursus on epic poetry. The first edition, on the recommendation of Mickle's friend, Commodore Johnston, was dedicated to the Duke of Buccleuch, whose indifference and insolence (prompted, Mickle thought, by Hume and Adam Smith) led to the suppression of the dedication. A second edition appeared in 1778, to which Mickle added a discussion of the religious beliefs of the Brahmins. It was reprinted in two volumes in 1798, and in three in 1807. It presents Camoens in English much as Pope presents Homer—with freedom of interpretation and considerable license of expansion—but it is true to the spirit of the original, and is a fine poem in itself. It completely superseded Fanshawe's version.

About 1771, while he was engaged on the 'Lusiad,' Mickle, on the suggestion of friends, had written 'The Siege of Marseilles,' a tragedy, which Garrick declined to accept for the stage while admitting its merits as a poem. The Wartons and John Home revised the piece for Garrick's further consideration without success. Harris also declined it, and it was afterwards submitted to Sheridan who never returned it. Mickle inserted an angry note on Garrick in the first edition of his 'Lusiad,' and Boswell and others with some difficulty dissuaded him from writing a new 'Dunciad' with Garrick as hero. A legend relates that afterwards on seeing the actor in 'Lear' he relented, and wished the note were out of his book (Bishop Horne, *Essays*, p. 38, ed. 1808, quoted in Chalmers's 'Life of Mickle' and Boswell's 'Johnson,' ii. 182, ed. Birkbeck Hill).

Mickle gained 1,000*l.* by the 'Lusiad,' but was without regular employment. His friends failed to secure for him a literary pension, and he declined Bishop Lowth's suggestion of taking orders. In 1779 he issued a pamphlet in defence of the East India Company against Adam Smith. In May 1779 Commodore George Johnstone [q. v.] appointed him his secretary in the Romney man-of-war, sailing with a squadron to Portugal. Here Mickle was enthusiastically received. He was made a member of the Royal Academy of Portugal, under the presidency of Prince John, duke of Braganza, who presented him with his portrait. In Lisbon he wrote 'Almada Hill, an epistle from Lisbon'—a fresh and interesting poem —which he published in 1781, after his return to England. He came back as purser of the Brilliant, and in London was appointed joint agent for disposal of the prizes gained by the squadron. The outcome for himself was a handsome competence for life. He paid off debts in Scotland, settled annuities on his sisters, and married (3 June 1781) Mary Tomkins, the farmer's daughter at Forest Hill, with whom he received a substantial addition to his fortune.

Settling at Wheatley, near Oxford, Mickle began to enjoy literary ease. He had in 1772 published an edition of Pearch's 'Collection of Poems,' including in it his own 'Hengist and May' and 'Mary Queen of Scots.' To Evans's 'Old Ballads, historical and narrative, with some of Modern Date' (1777–84), he now contributed his exquisite ballad 'Cumnor Hall,' the haunting beauty of which fascinated Scott (*Introd. to Kenilworth*). He was afterwards troubled by losses due to the failure and death of a banker associated with him in the management of the naval prizes, and he suffered not a little from a protracted chancery suit instituted to recover part of his wife's fortune. But in 1782 he discussed the question of American independence in an allegorical form, showing himself a capable master of travesty and persiflage. This was entitled 'Prophecy of Queen Emma,' and to it was prefixed a clever travesty of critical method in the 'Hints towards the Vindication of the Authenticity of the Poems of Ossian and Rowley.' His last composition was 'Eskdale Braes,' a song on his birthplace written at the suggestion of a friend. He died when visiting at Forest Hill, 28 Oct. 1788, and was buried in the churchyard of the parish. He left one son.

To Mickle has been attributed the Scottish song 'There's na'e luck about the hoose,' which of itself is sufficient to establish a poetical reputation. Internal evidence is rather against the likelihood of his authorship and in favour of that of Jean Adams (1710–1765), but there is no definite external evidence, and the doubt on the subject cannot be resolved.

In 1794 a quarto edition of Mickle's poems was published by subscription for the benefit of his son, with life by John Ireland. In 1807 appeared a corrected and enlarged edition, to which Mickle's friend, John Sim, supplied a biography. Mickle's poems form vol. xvii. of Chalmers's 'English Poets,' 1810, and volume lxvi. of the 'Chiswick Press Poets,' 1822.

[Reed's Memoir of Mickle in the European Mag. 1789; biographies prefixed to the various editions; Lives of Eminent Scotsmen by the Society of Ancient Scots; Mathias's Pursuits of Literature, p. 53; Johnson's Musical Museum, vol. iv. ed. Laing; Chambers's Eminent Scotsmen.] T. B.

MICKLETHWAITE, Sir JOHN, M.D. (1612–1682), physician, son of Thomas Micklethwaite, rector of Cherry Burton, Yorkshire, was born in 1612 and baptised, 23 Aug., in the church of Bishop Burton, three miles from Beverley. He entered at the university of Leyden as a medical student 15 Dec. 1637 (Peacock, *Leyden Students*, p. 68), and took the degree of M.D. at Padua in 1638. He proceeded M.D. by incorporation at Oxford 14 April 1648. On 26 May 1643 he was appointed assistant physician at St. Bartholomew's Hospital to Dr. John Clarke, whose eldest daughter he married, and he was elected physician 13 May 1653. The Long parliament, 12 Feb. 1644, had recommended him for promotion, 'in the place of Dr. Harvey, who hath withdrawn himself from his charge and is retired to the party in arms against the Parliament.' He was elected a fellow of the College of Physicians 11 Nov. 1643, and delivered the Gulstonian lectures in 1644. He was elected censor seven times, was treasurer from 1667 to 1675, and president from 1676 to 1681. When Charles II in 1681 was taken ill at Windsor, he was sent for by order in council, and attained much repute by his treatment of the king, on whose recovery he was knighted. He was physician in ordinary to the king. He died of acute cystitis 29 July 1682, and was buried in the church of St. Botolph, Aldersgate, where his monument, with a long inscription, still remains. His death and achievements were celebrated in a broadside, 'An Elegy to commemorate and lament the Death of the most worthy—Doctor of Physick, Sir John Micklethwaite.' His portrait, representing him in a flowing wig, was given to the College of Physicians by Sir Edmund King [q. v.], and hangs in the dining-room.

[St. Bartholomew's Hospital Manuscript Minute Books; C. Goodall's Historical Account of the College's Proceedings against Empirics, 1684; Elegy published by William Miller at the Guilded Acorn in St. Paul's Churchyard; Munk's Coll. of Phys. i. 237; Notes and Queries, 8th ser. v. 285; Willis's Life of Harvey, p. 175.] N. M.

MIDDIMAN, SAMUEL (1750–1831), engraver, born in 1750, first appears as an exhibitor of landscape drawings at the Incorporated Society of Artists in 1772 and following years, and in 1780 he exhibited drawings at the Royal Academy. He studied engraving under William Byrne [q. v.], and is also said to have had instruction in this art from William Woollett [q. v.] He was employed as an engraver by John Boydell for several years, and engraved for him, in the 'Shakespeare Gallery,' 'As you like it,' act ii. scene 1, after W. Hodges, R.A.; 'Winter's Tale,' act iii. scene 3, after J. Wright, A.R.A.; 'First Part of Henry IV,' act ii. scene 2, after R. Smirke, R.A., and J. Farington, R.A.; and 'As you like it,' act ii. scene 1, after John Boydell. Middiman's chief excellence lay in his engraving of landscape, in which he pursued worthily the course marked out by Woollett and others. His etchings for the early stages in this style were highly esteemed, and, being of an unassuming disposition, he was frequently engaged by other engravers for this preliminary work. Middiman, however, finished with great skill and care many engravings of his own, after well-known artists, most of which appeared in the following publications: 'Select Views in Great Britain,' 1784–92, 53 plates (2nd edit. 1812); 'Picturesque Castles and Abbeys in England and Wales,' 1805–8, 16 plates; and 'Picturesque Views and Antiquities of Great Britain,' 1807–11, 69 plates. A large collection of his engravings in progressive states is in the print room at the British Museum. Middiman died in Cirencester Place, London, on 20 Dec. 1831.

[Dodd's manuscript Hist. of English Engravers (Brit. Mus. Add. MS. 33403); Redgrave's Dict. of Artists; Univ. Cat. of Books on Art; Gent. Mag, 1831, ii. 650 (indexed Middiham).] L. C.

MIDDLEMORE, GEORGE (*d.* 1850), lieutenant-general, received a commission in the 86th foot (now 2nd royal Irish rifles) when that corps was raised as 'General Cuyler's Shropshire Volunteers' in 1793. He was a lieutenant in the regiment in February 1794, and became captain 15 Oct. the same year. He commanded a company in the 86th, and embarked as marines in the Brunswick, 74 guns, Captain Lord Charles Fitzgerald, which served in the Channel with Admiral Cornwallis in 1795, and afterwards with Lord Duncan in the North Sea. He subsequently served with his regiment at the Cape, Madras (it was not at the capture of Seringapatam as sometimes stated), Ceylon, and Bombay, and he accompanied the expedition up the Red Sea to Egypt, where he commanded the grenadier company. With Colonel Ramsay he went on a mission to the Turkish capitan pacha relative to the plots against the Mamelukes. After the return of his regiment to India he served at Madras as aide-de-camp to Sir David Baird [q. v.], with whom he came home. On 14 Sept. 1804 he was promoted to a majority in the 48th foot (now 1st Northampton regiment) at Gibraltar. He served with it in Portugal in 1809, and at the battle of Talavera, when Colonel Donellan was mortally wounded, he commanded it during the greater part of its famous advance to the rescue of the guards (see Napier, rev. ed. ii. 176–7), which 'tended so much to the success of the action' (Gurwood, iii. 370). On that occasion the regiment won its badge of the Star of Brunswick, or 'Coldstream Star.' Wellington recommended him for promotion in the strongest terms: 'He is an excellent officer, and if his conduct then did not, I may say, demand promotion, his good conduct and attention to his duty would warrant it' (*ib.*) Middlemore received the brevet of lieutenant-colonel and a gold medal, and was created C.B., 4 June 1815. He was promoted to lieutenant-colonel 12th garrison battalion, and was subsequently on half-pay thereof through ill-health. He was appointed assistant-quartermaster-general in the Severn district in 1813, and in 1814 inspecting field-officer at Nottingham. He afterwards held a like post at Cork. He became a major-general in 1830, and for five years commanded the troops in the West Indies. In 1836 he was made governor of the island of St. Helena, and held that post at the time of the removal of the remains of Napoleon I in 1840. He was made a lieutenant-general in 1841 and was colonel in succession of the 76th and 48th foot. He died at Tunbridge Wells, 18 Nov. 1850. His son, Lieutenant-colonel R. F. Middlemore (captain, half-pay, 91st foot), was his aide-de-camp at St. Helena.

[Cannon's Hist. Rec. 86th Royal County Down Regt. and Muster-rolls of the same; Napier's Peninsular War, rev. ed., account of Talavera in vol. ii.; Gurwood's Wellington Desp. vol. iii.; Gent. Mag. 1851, pt. i. p. 95. Some letters and memoranda of General Middlemore are printed in Theodore Hook's Life of Sir David Baird, vol. i.] H. M. C.

MIDDLESEX, Earls of. [See Cranfield, Lionel, first Earl, 1575–1645; Sackville, Charles (1638–1706), first Earl, of the second creation.]

MIDDLETON. [See also Myddelton.]

MIDDLETON, CHARLES, second Earl of Middleton and titular Earl of Monmouth (1640?–1719), secretary of state to James II, born about 1640, was eldest son of John, first earl of Middleton [q. v.], by his wife Grizel, daughter of Sir James Durham of Pitkerrow, and widow first of Sir Alexander Fotheringham of Ballindrone, and secondly of Sir Gilbert Ramsay of Balmain. He accompanied his father in his highland campaign against Cromwell in 1653–4, and after his defeat at Lochgarry escaped with him to France. At the Restoration he was appointed by Charles II envoy extraordinary to the court of Vienna. In 1673 he succeeded his father in the earldom of Middleton, but not in the estates, which were all seized by creditors.

Middleton was one of those who in May 1682 accompanied James, duke of York, in the Gloucester frigate, to bring the duchess from Scotland, and when the frigate was wrecked on the Yorkshire coast made his escape in the small boat [see James II of England]. Shortly afterwards he was sworn a member of the Scottish privy council; on 26 Sept. was appointed joint secretary of Scotland with the Earl of Moray; on 11 July 1684 was sworn a privy councillor of England; on the 15th of the same month was admitted an extraordinary lord of session of Scotland; and on 25 Aug. was appointed to succeed Godolphin as secretary of state for England. In February 1686 he resigned the office of extraordinary lord of session in favour of his brother-in-law, Patrick Lyon, first earl of Strathmore [q. v.]

After the accession of King James in 1685 Middleton, who on 15 April was returned member for Winchelsea (*Official Return of Members of Parliament*, i. 556), was entrusted, along with Richard Graham, viscount Preston [q. v.], with the chief management of the House of Commons. By his 'good judgment and lively apprehension' (Burnet, *Own Time*, ed. 1838, p. 384) he succeeded, perhaps as well as any other could, in covering the more glaring errors and defects of the blundering and ill-fated policy of the king. Although his wife was a catholic, he himself 'was without much religion' (*ib.*), and as long as James reigned in England withstood every effort of James to convert him to catholicism. A priest sent by James to instruct him in the principles of the old faith began with transubstantiation, and as a first step in his argument said, 'You believe the Trinity?' upon which Middleton replied, 'Who told you so?' (*ib.* p. 435).

In the first parliament of James, Middleton adopted every possible expedient to secure the support of the commons to the proposal for a standing army, and to overcome the opposition to the infringements of the Test Act; but at the same time he was well aware of the dangers attending the purpose on which the king was bent, and did his utmost to induce him to consent to a compromise. In such circumstances it was probably owing chiefly to his wife's influence with the queen that he was retained in office, but he justified the confidence reposed in him by remaining faithful to James to the last. After the king's sudden withdrawal to Feversham he declined to attend the meeting of the lords and privy council called to consider the steps to be taken in the crisis (Clarke, *Life of James II*, ii. 259). Nevertheless he was one of the four nobles deputed by them to invite the king to return to Whitehall, and was present with him at Whitehall when a message came from the Prince of Orange that James should retire from London. At the king's request he arranged for his withdrawal to Rochester. Subsequently he waited on the king there to surrender the seals of the secreary's office, and endeavoured to induce him to abandon his projected flight and to summon a parliament. It was to him that the king, after making his secret escape, left the paper containing his reasons for 'withdrawing himself from England.'

On the flight of the king Middleton remained in England, but did not come to terms with the new government. He was practically the head of the less extreme section of the Jacobites known as the 'compounders,' and made it his chief aim to set on foot a movement for a restoration, accompanied by guarantees which would have restrained James from persevering in his former fatal policy. How far he sincerely believed in the possibility of restraining him by any guarantees is, however, doubtful. Yet there is no reason to suppose that he had any connection with the earlier plots to effect his restoration by force, although at the time of the threatened invasion of England by France in 1692 an order was emitted on 11 May for committing him on the charge of high treason (LUTTRELL, *Short Relation*, ii. 449). On the 17th he was apprehended in disguise at a quaker's in Goodman's Fields, and after examination by the council was committed to the Tower (*ib.* p. 453). As, however, no evidence was forthcoming against him, he was on 18 Aug. released on bail (*ib.* p. 543), and on 19 Nov. the bail was discharged (*ib.* p. 619).

Early in 1693 Middleton joined the court of St. Germains. Burnet mentions a general belief that he was sent to propose that King James 'should offer to resign his title in favour of his son, and likewise to send him to be bred in England under the direction of a parliament till he should be of age;' but adds that he 'could never hear that he ventured on this advice' (*Own Time*, ed. 1838, p. 598). It would at least appear that some endeavour was made either then or subsequently, and either at the instigation of Middleton or others, to induce William III to consent that the Prince of Wales should succeed him (CLARKE, *Life of James II*, ii. 574); but James objected to this proposal on any conditions (MACPHERSON, *Original Papers*, i. 553). Middleton, however, who had been in communication with the less extreme supporters of the revolution, was specially commissioned to induce James to sign the new declaration, by which he virtually withdrew from his position of absolutism, and renounced his endeavours to restore the catholic religion. He is said to have assured the king that if he signed it, 'those who sent it engaged to restore him in three or four months after' (CLARKE, *Life of James II*, ii. 575). As a pledge of the reality of the new departure, Middleton now succeeded the Earl of Melfort [see DRUMMOND, JOHN, first EARL, and titular DUKE OF MELFORT] as chief adviser of the exiled king, with the title of secretary of state. In consequence of his having joined the court at St. Germains, he was on 23 July 1694 outlawed by the high court of justiciary in Scotland, and on 2 July of the following year forfeited by parliament.

On the death of James II on 6 Sept. 1701, Middleton suggested the omission of the proposed ceremony of proclaiming the young king at St. Germains, on account of the difficulty of proclaiming him there king of France. By the titular James III he was created Earl of Monmouth. James II had on his deathbed earnestly exhorted Middleton to seek refuge from doubt in the catholic church. Middleton had been accustomed to parry the efforts to convert him by asserting that 'a new light never came into the house except through a crack in the tiling' (MACKY, *Secret Memoirs*, p. 239); but he now resolved himself to falsify this maxim by at least outwardly conforming to the king's dying request. Possibly he was chiefly influenced by the consideration that in no other way could he now maintain his position and influence at St. Germains and among the leading Jacobites. In any case he professed his conviction of the insufficiency of protestantism, and retiring for a time from the court of St. Germains, entered a convent in Paris to obtain fuller instruction in the catholic faith. In the will of the late king he had been named one of the council to assist the queen in the guardianship of the young prince, and soon after his return to St. Germains in the summer of 1703 he found abundant occupation in exposing and thwarting the intrigues of Simon Fraser, twelfth lord Lovat [q. v.], in connection with his pretended negotiations for a rising in the highlands. After Lovat's arrival in Paris, Middleton, on 16 Jan. 1704, recommended that he should be at once arrested, sending along with the recommendation a translation of his memorial to the exiled queen, with remarks upon it; Lovat, he wrote, had 'not in some places been as careful as authors of romance to preserve probability' (MACPHERSON, *Original Papers*, i. 652).

Middleton was in a great degree responsible for the abortive expedition of the young prince James to Scotland in 1707, and advised that an attempt should be made to land at Burntisland, on the Firth of Forth. His two sons, Lord Clermont and Charles Middleton, accompanied the expedition, and being captured in the Salisbury, were detained in prison for three years. Subsequently he joined the prince in Flanders, and he also accompanied him to Lorraine, when in the beginning of 1713 he was compelled to leave France. In December 1713 he resigned the office of secretary of state, and returned to St. Germains, where he was appointed great chamberlain to the queen. He died in 1719.

Macky describes Middleton as 'a black man, of a middle stature, with a sanguine complexion, and one of the pleasantest companions in the world.' He also states that he was 'one of the politest gentlemen in Europe; had a great deal of wit mixed with a sound judgment, and a very clear understanding' (*Secret Memoirs*, pp. 238–40), to which Swift adds that Sir W. Temple told him 'he was a very valuable man and a good scholar.' By his wife, Lady Catherine Brudenell, daughter of Robert, second earl of Cardigan, and a zealous catholic and a great favourite of the queen, Middleton had two sons, Lord Clermont and Charles Middleton, both of whom predeceased him, and two, or possibly three, daughters, Elizabeth, married to Edward Drummond, third son of James, duke of Perth, and Mary or Catherine, one of whom was married to Sir John Gifford, knight, and probably to the Count de La Roches or Rothe.

[Burnet's Own Time; Luttrell's Short Relation; Clarke's Life of James II; Macpherson's Original Papers, containing a large number of his letters; Sir John Reresby's Memoirs; Macky's Secret Memoirs; Dalrymple's Memoirs of Great Britain; Klopp's Fall des Hauses Stuart; Macaulay's Hist. of England; Biscoe's Earls of Middleton; Douglas's Scottish Peerage (Wood), ii. 232–3.] T. F. H.

MIDDLETON, CHARLES, first BARON BARHAM (1726–1813), admiral, second son of Robert Middleton, collector of customs at Bo'ness in Linlithgowshire, and of Helen, daughter of Charles Dundas of Arniston, was born at Leith on 14 Oct. 1726. His grandfather, George Middleton, D.D. (*d.* 1726), and his great-grandfather, Alexander Middleton, D.D. (*d.* 1684), were successively principals of King's College, Aberdeen. The last named, Alexander, was younger brother of John, first earl of Middleton [q. v.] Charles Middleton was promoted in 1745 to be lieutenant of the Chesterfield with Captain William Gordon. He seems to have remained in her till the peace and to have then been placed on half-pay. In 1754 he was appointed to the Anson, guardship at Portsmouth, and afterwards employed on convoy service to the West Indies. In 1758 he was promoted to be captain of the Arundel, taking post from 22 May. In 1761 he commanded the Emerald frigate in the West Indies, and cruised with success against the enemy's privateers, many of which he captured or destroyed. For his services in the protection of trade the assembly of Barbados gave him a vote of thanks and a gold-hilted sword. He was afterwards captain of the Adventure on the home station till the peace, and for the following twelve years remained on half-pay.

In 1775 he commanded the Ardent, guardship at Chatham, from which he was moved in November 1776 to the Prince George, and in April 1778 to the Jupiter. In August 1778 he was appointed comptroller of the navy, and held the office till March 1790. He was created a baronet on 23 Oct. 1781; was elected member of parliament for Rochester in 1784, and was promoted to the rank of rear-admiral on 24 Sept. 1787. He became a vice-admiral on 1 Feb. 1793, and admiral on 1 June 1795. In 1794–5 he was one of the lords commissioners of the admiralty under the Earl of Chatham. Ten years later, on the resignation of Lord Melville [see DUNDAS, HENRY, first VISCOUNT MELVILLE], he was appointed first lord of the admiralty (30 April 1805), and raised to the peerage by the title of Baron Barham (1 May 1805). He was a near relation of Melville, and it would seem that the appointment was due to Mr. Pitt's desire to lessen the force of the blow which had struck down his friend. But Barham was now eighty years old, and no longer fit to be at the head of the English navy even in peace, still less during a great war. Later writers have, indeed, commended the promptitude with which, on the morning of 9 July 1805, when he received the news of Villeneuve's approach to Europe, he sent orders to Calder to look out for him to the west of Cape Finisterre (cf. MAHAN, *Influence of Sea Power upon the French Revolution and Empire*, ii. 168–9); but, judging from the character of the man, it would seem more probable that the contingency had been previously discussed by the board, and the course to be adopted had been decided. In any case, his term of office was short: in the administration of January 1806 he had no place. He retired from public affairs, and died on 17 June 1813.

Middleton married, in December 1761, Margaret (cf. CHATTERTON, *Memorials of Lord Gambier*, i. 139), daughter of James Gambier, barrister-at-law, and aunt of James (afterwards Lord) Gambier [q. v.] She died in 1792, leaving one daughter, Diana, married in 1780 to Gerard Noel Edwardes, who in 1798 succeeded to the estates of his maternal uncle, the Earl of Gainsborough, and by royal license assumed the name of Noel. On the death of Lord Barham, Noel, by the terms of the patent, succeeded to the baronetcy, and his wife Diana to the peerage. On her death in 1823, her eldest son, Charles Noel Noel, succeeded to the barony; on the death of his father in 1838 he succeeded also to the baronetcy, and in 1841 was created Earl of Gainsborough.

[Charnock's Biog. Nav. vi. 330; official lists in Public Record Office; Complete Peerage, ed. G. E. C[okayne]; Nicolas's Despatches and Letters of Nelson; Letters and Papers of Charles, Lord Barham, 1758–1813, ed. Laughton (Navy Records Soc.), 1907–8; cf. Lady Chatterton's Memorials of Lord Gambier.] J. K. L.

MIDDLETON, CHRISTOPHER (1560?–1628), translator and poet, may be identical with the Christopher Middleton of Cheshire who matriculated from Brasenose College, Oxford, 12 Dec. 1580, aged 20. A clergyman of the same name, who graduated B.D. from St. John's College, Cambridge, in 1619, was incorporated in that degree at Oxford on 13 July 1619, and was rector of Aston-le-Walls, Northamptonshire, from 1612 till his death there in 1628 (Foster, *Alumni Oxon.* 1500–1714).

Christopher Middleton was the author of: 1. 'A Short Introduction for to Learn to Swimme, gathered out of Master Digbies Booke of the Art of Swimming, and translated into English for the better instruction of those who understand not the Latin tongue, by Christopher Middleton,' 1595, 4to. This was illustrated with woodcuts of persons swimming. It was a translation of the 'De Arte Natandi libri duo,' 1587, of Everard Digby [q. v.] 2. 'The Historie of Heaven: containing the Poetical Fictions of all the Starres in the Firmament, gathered from amongst all the Poets and Astronomers, by Chrystopher Middleton. Printed for him 1596,' 4to (Bodl.) 3. 'The Famous Historie of Chinon of England, with his Strange Adventures for the love of Celestina, daughter to Lewis, King of France; with the worthy Atchivement of Sir Lancelot du Lake, and Sir Tristram du Lions for faire Laura, daughter to Cadar, Earle of Cornewall, beeing all Knights of King Arthur's Round Table. By Chr. Middleton. At London, printed by John Danter for Cuthbert Burbie,' 1597, b.l. 4to, forty-seven leaves. The dedication is by Danter (Brit. Mus.) 4. 'The Legend of Humphrey, Duke of Glocester, by Chr. Middleton. London, printed by E. A. for Nicholas Ling,' 1600, 4to. The author dedicates this poem to Sir Jarvis [i.e. Gervase] Clifton. It is preceded by a Latin hexastichon by Robert Allott, a sonnet by Michael Drayton, and two short poems by John Weever. The poem, consisting of 184 six-line stanzas, is written on the plan of the poems in the 'Mirror for Magistrates,' and 'need not shrink from a comparison with the majority of the poems in that collection.' (There are two copies of the original edition in the Museum and one in the Huth Library.) It is reprinted in the 'Harleian Miscellany' (1813), x. 165.

[Harleian Miscellany, x. 164; Brydges's Censura Literaria, iii. 256; Hazlitt's Warton's Hist. of English Poetry, iv. 208–9, 211; Ames's Typographical Antiquities (Herbert), pp. 1029, 1033, 1342, 1382; Cooper's Athenæ Cantabr. ii. 147; Bibliotheca Anglo-Poetica, p. 216.] R. B.

MIDDLETON, CHRISTOPHER (*d.* 1770), commander in the navy and Arctic voyager, was from about 1720 in the employment of the Hudson's Bay Company, and seems to have been early recognised as a capable servant of the company and a scientific navigator. In a memorial which he addressed to the admiralty, apparently in 1750 (*Captains' Letters*, M. 17), he stated that for several years before 1741 he had commanded a ship which was worth to him, one year with another, 800*l.* As early as 1721 he observed the variation of the magnetic needle at Churchill (*Phil. Trans.* xxxiv. 73); and he claimed 'to have found, from repeated observations, a method of obtaining the true time at sea by taking eight or ten different altitudes of the sun or stars when near the prime vertical, by Mr. Smith's or Mr. Hadley's quadrant,' and to have practised it from about 1737. This is the method of finding the ship time now in daily use at sea, for determining the longitude; whether Middleton found it out himself or not, he must have been one of the first to practise it, for Hadley's quadrant was only introduced at a meeting of the Royal Society in 1731. On 7 April 1737 Middleton was elected a fellow of the Royal Society, as one 'who has communicated to this society several curious observations relating to the variation of the needle in the northern seas, printed in the "Philosophical Transactions"' (information from the society; *Phil. Trans.* xxxvii. 71, 76, xxxviii. 127, xxxix. 270); and in 1741 he was, after several years' solicitation, prevailed on, he says, by Arthur Dobbs [q. v.], who promised him a great reward from the public, or at least an equivalent to his profits in the service of the Hudson's Bay Company, to undertake the discovery of the north-west passage. Dobbs, however, did nothing more than obtain for him a commission from the admiralty as commander in the navy, 5 March 1740–1, and an appointment to the Furnace sloop, with pay, for himself and servant, of 7*s.* 6*d.* a day. Some two months later he sailed for the Arctic seas in company with the Discovery tender, commanded by Lieutenant Moor.

On 27 June he left the Orkneys; made Cape Farewell on 16 July, and the entrance of Hudson's Strait on the 25th. The passage was clear of ice, and on the 31st he was off Carey's Swan's Nest; here he held a council, which agreed that it was too late in the season to attempt any discovery. By 9 Aug. they got into the Churchill River in search of winter quarters, and for the next six weeks they were busily employed in digging docks for the ships, repairing an old fort that was in ruins, and cutting firewood. By the end of September the winter had set in very cold. They were well housed, well clothed, had an ample supply of fuel and plenty of provisions; but the men suffered terribly from scurvy. 'By

March they almost all had it, and several died.' 'In twenty years,' wrote Middleton in June 1742, 'that I have used this voyage, I never heard of, or knew any afflicted with this or any other distemper, before the last and this year.' It does not, however, appear that he had ever before wintered there; and Mr. Barrow has pointed out that the supply of brandy to the men was excessive.

On 20 March, by the observation of an eclipse of Jupiter's satellite No. 1, he calculated the longitude of his position to be 97° W., the true longitude of Fort Churchill being 94° 10′. The error was thus nearly 3°, which, though it would be now considered monstrous, was a mere trifle compared with the enormous errors which were at that date the rule [cf. LEGGE, EDWARD]. On 1 July 1742 the ships left the river and examined the coast to the northward. On 12 July they were off a cape which Middleton named Dobbs; and on the 13th they entered 'an inlet or strait which makes a fair opening.' A short experience of the tides convinced Middleton that it was only a river, and he named it Wager River. The tides showed him that the Frozen Strait was the passage to the sea; but this was choked with ice, and his men were very sickly. On 15 Aug. he held a council, which determined that they ought to bear away for England. On 15 Sept. they arrived at the Orkney Islands, where several of the sick men were put ashore. But most of both crews were 'very much afflicted with the scurvy and otherwise distempered.' After recruiting them as much as possible, Middleton pressed men to take the ships to the Thames, where he arrived on 2 Oct. 1742.

The results of the voyage were mainly negative; but though more might perhaps have been done had not the ships been, as Middleton put it, 'pestered with such a set of rogues, most of them having deserved hanging before they entered with me,' and had not the scurvy raged so terribly among them, Middleton still felt warranted to express a strong opinion that there was no passage to the westward in that direction; that Wager River was a river and not a strait, and that the flood tide came from the eastward through the Frozen Strait. Dobbs took on him to controvert this opinion. Middleton, he alleged, had taken no pains to assure himself whether Wager River was a river or not; or rather, he had in reality found it to be a strait, but concealed the discovery in the interests of the monopolists, his old masters of the Hudson's Bay Company. The admiralty called on Middleton to answer the charges laid against him, which he did publicly in 'A Vindication of the Conduct of Captain Middleton' (1743, 8vo). Dobbs's personal interest, however, was considerable, and the admiralty hesitated as to accepting Middleton's statements; so that, although the war was calling for the services of every capable officer, he was left unemployed for nearly two years. It was not till 8 June 1745 that he was appointed to command the Shark sloop of war. In her he was stationed on the coast of Scotland during the rebellion, and claimed to have rendered exceptional service by his intimate local knowledge. When Scotland was quieted he was sent to the coast of Flanders, under the orders of Commodore Matthew Michell [q.v.] At the peace he was put on half-pay; and though in his memorial he represented the great loss to which he had been subjected, he received neither compensation, nor promotion, nor employment, but remained on the half-pay of his rank, 4*s.*, till his death, 12 Feb. 1770 (*Half-Pay List*).

[Coats's Geography of Hudson's Bay, with an Appendix containing Extracts from the Log of Captain Middleton . . . in 1741–2, edited for the Hakluyt Society by John Barrow; the Vindication and Memorial referred to in the text; the official letters in the Public Record Office, several of which are published by Barrow; see also Phil. Trans. vols. xl. xli. xlii. Besides these there are the pamphlets alternately by Dobbs and Middleton in their controversy. Sir John Barrow, in his Voyages into the Arctic Regions (1818), inclined to the belief that Dobbs was right, and that Middleton was either deceived or was deceiving. But Middleton's correspondence with the admiralty has every appearance of honesty; and his good faith was proved by Moor's subsequent voyage described by Henry Ellis [q.v.], and still more fully afterwards by Sir William Edward Parry [q.v.] J. K. L.

MIDDLETON, CONYERS (1683–1750), divine, born at York or at Richmond, Yorkshire, on 27 Dec. 1683, was son of William Middleton, rector of Hinderwell, near Whitby, Yorkshire, by his second wife, Barbara Place. He was named after his father's friend, a Conyers of Boulby Hall. The father had some independent means, kept a curate at Hinderwell, and lived at York, where his wife died 8 Aug. 1700, and he on 13 Feb. 1713–14. His other children, one son by the first marriage and two by the second, were extravagant, and he passed his later years in terror of bailiffs. Conyers Middleton is said to have been a good son, and was kind to an old woman who had been his father's only servant for some years. He was entered at Trinity College, Cambridge, 19 Jan. 1700, graduated B.A. 1702–3, M.A. 1707, and was elected a fellow of his college in 1706. He was for a short time curate of Trumpington, Cambridge. He was better known for his musical tastes than for excellence in studies, and was afterwards nicknamed 'fiddling Conyers' by Bentley, then master of Trinity. Middleton was one of the thirty fellows who on 6 Feb. 1709–10 petitioned the Bishop of Ely as visitor of Trinity College to take steps against Bentley. Middleton vacated his fellowship a few months later by his marriage to Mrs. Sarah Drake, the rich widow of 'Counsellor Drake' of Cambridge, and daughter of Mr. Morris of Oak Morris in Kent. He held for a short time the small rectory of Coveney in the Isle of Ely, which was in his wife's gift (he was presented to this in 1726, see NICHOLS, *Lit. Anecd.* v. 700). On 3 July 1710 he was one of a party of ten who dined at the Rose Tavern in Cambridge with the members for the university, and drank the health of Sacheverell. They were interrupted by the senior proctor, Richard Laughton, tutor of Clare, who made a formal complaint against them to the heads of houses for disorderly revelling. The authorities treated the complaint as frivolous, but Middleton some time afterwards had to explain that the feast was moderate, and the tavern bill only 1*s.* 6*d.* a head. In 1717 George I visited the university, when the degree of D.D. was conferred upon thirty-two persons, including Middleton. Bentley, as regius professor of divinity, demanded a fee of four guineas from each of the new doctors in addition to the established 'broad-piece.' Middleton, after some dispute, consented to pay, taking Bentley's written promise to return the money if the claim should be finally disallowed. He was then created doctor. Having vainly applied for a return of the fee, he sued for it as a debt in the vice-chancellor's court. After various delays and attempts to make up the quarrel, the vice-chancellor issued a decree (23 Sept. 1718) for Bentley's arrest. Bentley's refusal to submit to this decree led to further proceedings and to his degradation from all his degrees by a grace of the senate on 18 Oct.

Arthur Ashley Sykes [q. v.] soon afterwards published letters protesting against Bentley's degradation, to which a reply was made by Sherlock, who dwelt upon the original demand for fees. Middleton now took up the attack in what he called a 'full and impartial account' of the late proceedings, condemning Bentley's conduct as to the fees and in the management of the college. Middleton showed his great powers as a writer of bitter and plausible invective. Two more pamphlets from Sykes were met by two further replies from Middleton, in which Sykes and other supporters of Bentley were roughly handled, especially for bringing up the old scandal about the dinner at the Rose. The pamphlets were anonymous, and Middleton, being hitherto unknown as a writer, was not suspected until he acknowledged his first tract upon its general success. A final reply, written or dictated by Bentley himself, closed this controversy. Middleton was still keen for revenge. His friend John Colbatch [q. v.], Bentley's most determined opponent, was afraid to give the master a pretext for expelling him from his fellowship. He was glad, however, to supply Middleton with materials for 'On the Present State of Trinity College,' which was published in 1719. Bentley, having immediately obtained powers from the seniority, brought an action against the publisher. Middleton at once issued an advertisement (dated 9 Feb. 1720), claiming the pamphlet as his own. Bentley continued to prosecute the bookseller till Middleton made a declaration of his authorship before witnesses. Bentley then laid an information against him in the king's bench, founded upon a passage in the pamphlet about the impossibility of obtaining redress in 'any proper court of justice in the kingdom.' The proceedings were slow, and meanwhile Middleton took advantage of Bentley's proposals for an edition of the New Testament to attack him in a sharp pamphlet. Bentley replied, using terms of gross abuse directed chiefly against his other enemy, Colbatch, to whom he chose to attribute the authorship. Bentley's reply was condemned by the heads. Colbatch brought an action against him, and Middleton wrote a longer rejoinder, in which he is admitted to have made some very good points, in language far more decent than his opponent's. He is said, on doubtful tradition, to have been helped in the discussion by Charles Ashton [q. v.], master of Jesus College. It has been frequently asserted that his criticisms gave the deathblow to Bentley's project; but Monk shows this to be a 'vulgar error' (MONK, ii. 144, 147–9). Meanwhile, Middleton's case came on in the court of king's bench (Trinity term 1721), and he was found guilty of libel. Sentence was delayed. A few of his friends subscribed towards his expenses, and he obtained the intercession of 'a certain great personage' for a lenient sentence. The chief justice (Pratt) advised the two doctors to avoid scandal by a compromise, and Bentley finally accepted an apology. Middleton, however, had to pay his own costs and the taxed expenses of his opponent, which, as the balance paid by the college was 150*l.*, were probably considerable. His friends, wishing to make him some compensation, induced the senate to pass a grace by 112 to 49 votes (14 Dec. 1721), which made him 'Protobibliothecarius' of the university library, with a salary of 50*l.* This was a new office, created expressly for Middleton, although the king's recent donation of Bishop Moore's library gave a pretext. Middleton in 1723 published a plan for the future arrangement of the books. He took the opportunity of attacking Bentley for retaining some manuscripts (the famous 'Codex Bezæ' among others) in his own house. A dedication to the vice-chancellor also included a phrase, aimed at Bentley, which might be construed as reflecting upon the court of king's bench. Colbatch had vainly recommended its suppression. Bentley immediately appealed to the court, and on 20 June 1723 Middleton was fined 50*l.* and ordered to provide securities for good behaviour for a year. Bentley had finally triumphed by this time in his long warfare with the college and university. Middleton, disgusted at his defeat, and in weak health, went to Italy. On his return he renewed his old suit for the four guineas. Bentley apparently did not oppose him, and in February 1725-6 he at last got back his fee, together with 12*s.* costs. Middleton stayed in Rome during a great part of 1724 and 1725. A silly story—probably a bit of college wit taken seriously—is told in the 'Biographia Britannica,' that Middleton found that the librarian at the Vatican had only heard of Cambridge as a school where boys were prepared for Oxford, and that Middleton, to show his dignity, took an hotel at 400*l.* a year, and injured his fortune by buying antiquities. He did in fact make a collection, of which he afterwards published a description. He sold it to Horace Walpole in 1744 (Walpole, *Letters*, ed. Cunningham, i. 307). Henry Hare, third lord Coleraine [q. v.], also a collector, was his companion on this journey. Another result of his journey was the 'Letter from Rome,' published in 1729, upon the incorporation of pagan beliefs and ceremonies in the catholic church. The argument, as Middleton said in his preface, was old enough, and he only claimed novelty for his mode of statement. It was applauded by the orthodox English divines as an attack upon popery, and its merits of style brought it to a fourth edition in 1741. His first wife died on 19 Feb. 1730-1. In 1731 Middleton was appointed first Woodwardian professor by the executors of the founder, and delivered an inaugural address in Latin, pointing out the services which might be expected from a study of fossils in confirming the history of the deluge. He resigned the chair, however, in 1734, upon his (second) marriage to his cousin Mary, daughter of the Rev. Conyers Place of Dorchester. She died 26 April 1745, aged 38. He had meanwhile got into a controversy with Waterland. Waterland had attacked Matthew Tindal's 'Christianity as old as the Creation' (1730), which marked the culmination of the deist controversy. Middleton published an anonymous 'Letter to Waterland,' urging that apologists placed themselves in a false position by endeavouring to maintain the historical accuracy of every statement in the Bible. He ridiculed some parts of the book of Genesis, and said that Tindal should be answered by proving the utility of a traditional religion, and confuting his *à priori* theories of the 'religion of nature.' This sceptical tendency, really latent in the 'Letter from Rome,' now became obvious. Zachary Pearce [q. v.], afterwards bishop of Rochester, accused him in a 'Reply' of covert infidelity. Middleton's authorship had become known, and he was threatened with a loss of his Cambridge degrees. Middleton replied in two pamphlets, making such explanations as he could. Some time later (1733), however, an anonymous pamphlet by Dr. Williams, the public orator, declared that his books ought to be burnt and himself banished from the university, unless he made a recantation. Middleton made an explanation in a final pamphlet, but for some time remained silent upon theological topics. His letters to Lord Oxford (*Add. MS.* 32457) show that he suspected Oxford of dropping his friendship on account of the suspicions thus cast upon his orthodoxy. He complains that he had 'for many years' been 'a kind of domestic' to the earl, who now recommended some very inferior person to be travelling governor to a young nobleman. Though some overtures of reconciliation followed, their friendship soon ended. He employed himself upon his life of Cicero, which was long regarded as a model of style. Serious imputations, however, have been made upon his literary honesty. He is accused of plagiarism from the 'De tribus luminibus Romanorum,' a scarce work by William Bellenden (*d.* 1633?) [q. v.] It was a compilation, giving Cicero's history in his own words, and most of the impression having been lost at sea, had become very scarce. Middleton, whose book followed a similar plan, had thus all his materials arranged for him, and instead of acknowledging the debt, boasted in the preface of his great labours. Parr, in his famous 'Preface to Bellendenus,' states that after a careful investigation he has been compelled to regard Middleton as guilty of plagiarism. The book was published by subscription in

1741. Middleton had three thousand subscribers, and gained a considerable sum, which, as he says, would enable him to provide for two nieces of about eight years old, left to him by 'an unfortunate brother who had nothing else to leave' (*Works*, i. 397). He also bought from the profits a small estate at Hildersham, six miles from Cambridge, where he turned a 'rude farm' into an 'elegant habitation,' and spent his summers. He was still living at Cambridge, where he met his friends every night at the coffee-house. Gray, who came into residence in 1742, found Middleton's house the only agreeable place for conversation in Cambridge. His house adjoined Caius College, and looked over the senate-house yard. Cole also speaks of his great charm in society.

Middleton returned to his theological controversies by his writings upon the miraculous powers attributed to the Christian church. He published an 'Introductory Discourse' in 1747, followed up by a fuller treatise at the end of 1748. The book denied the credibility of the stories of miracles in periods subsequent to the first age of the church, attacked the character of the narrators, and explained the origin of the narratives by the general credulity of the times in which they arose. The book produced a lively controversy. Hume found that it had eclipsed the volume of essays (published in April 1748), which included his own argument against the credibility of miracles. Gibbon's temporary conversion to catholicism soon afterwards was chiefly due to a perusal of Middleton. The continuity of the claim to miraculous power seemed to him to confirm the later, instead of disproving the earlier stories. Middleton was generally thought to favour the inverse conclusion, although he professed to deny the applicability of his arguments to the first age of the church. The very natural doubts of his sincerity were confirmed by the last volume which he published, an examination of Sherlock's discourses on prophecy (1749–50). Middleton's main position as to the nature of the argument from prophecy might pass for orthodox, but he again attacked the Mosaic account of the fall. Sherlock's book was first published in 1725, in answer to the deist Anthony Collins [q. v.] Middleton declares that he had never read it until he wrote against it, although it had then been a popular treatise for many years. The bookseller Whiston reported, on the authority of Sherlock, that Middleton professed at least to have read the book when presented by its author on the first publication (see CHALMERS, *Biog. Dict.*) Middleton, however, is said to have had a personal cause of offence. In 1737 he tried to obtain the mastership of the Charterhouse. He says at the time (*Misc. Works*, i. 390) that Walpole was in his favour, but that the Duke of Newcastle had obtained the appointment for a friend. Walpole, however, afterwards informed him that his failure had really been caused by Sherlock's declaration that the bishops would be offended by Middleton's appointment. Cole says that he heard this from Middleton himself, and the story is repeated in Bishop Newton's autobiography. Warburton says to Hurd (11 July 1750, *Letters of an Eminent Prelate*, p. 59) that Middleton had been prejudiced against religion 'by the pretended injuries of some churchmen.' Such imputations generally deserve little attention, but it must be admitted that, whatever his personal motives, Middleton was probably one of the few divines who can be fairly accused of conscious insincerity. In a letter to Lord Hervey (see NICHOLS, *Anecdotes*, v. 421) he says that he would like to have some amends (in the shape of preferment) for that 'ugly assent and consent, which no man of sense can approve of.' Except Coveney and the rectory of Hascombe, Surrey, worth 50*l.* a year, to which he was presented by Sir John Frederick in March 1746–7 (*ib.* v. 419, 700), he held no preferment, and is said to have observed that as he had not been trusted (with a bishopric) he was 'at liberty to speak his mind' (*ib.* p. 421). His letters to Hervey show that he was much aggrieved at not obtaining preferment. Warburton said (*ib.* p. 648) that Middleton only went so far as to 'suspend his belief' in regard to revelation (see Middleton's Letters to Warburton in *Misc. Works*, i. 374, 383, 394, which suggested this statement). However his position may be judged from a moral point of view, there can be no doubt that he was far too able a man to be blind to the tendency of his arguments. Not long before his death Middleton married a third wife, Anne, daughter of John Powell of Boughrood, near Radnor. She had lived with Mrs. Trenchard, widow of John Trenchard [q. v.], afterwards married to Thomas Gordon (*d.* 1750) [q. v.] His health was breaking, and while he was preparing a general answer to the critics of the 'Free Enquiry,' he died at Hildersham, 'of a slow hectic fever and disorder in his liver,' on 28 July 1750. He was engaged in a lawsuit with a builder at the time of his death (WALPOLE, *Letters*, ii. 237; *Letters of an Eminent Prelate*, p. 54). Middleton left behind him several manuscripts, some of which appeared in the posthumous collection of his 'Miscellaneous Works.' His papers were left by his widow to Dr. Heberden. Heberden is said to have burnt one paper against the utility of prayer. It is also said that Bolingbroke surreptitiously preserved a copy of this paper, after advising Middleton's executors to destroy it (NICHOLS, *Anecd.* v. 423; WALPOLE, *George II*, 1846, i. 224). The paper, however, which Bolingbroke returned with advice against publication, appears to have been a Latin dissertation upon miracles of a decidedly heterodox kind (Bolingbroke's letter of 11 Sept. 1751, in British Museum *Addit. MS.* 32457, and list of fragments in *Addit. MS.* 32459).

Middleton took some sons of the nobility into his house as pupils. According to Cole, the regular tutors were much annoyed by his encroaching upon their province. His income was about 600*l.* or 700*l.* a year. He is said to have had a share in educating the once famous Mrs. Montagu, granddaughter of his first wife. He was very intimate with John, lord Hervey [q. v.], to whom he dedicated his 'Cicero,' and who was erroneously credited with translations of some of the orations. Middleton's letters to him contained the substance of the treatise upon the Roman senate, and were published, with Hervey's replies, by Dr. Knowles in 1778. Middleton's relations with most of the eminent divines of his day were uncomfortable. He carried on a friendly correspondence with Warburton for a time, and Warburton was blamed (in 1738) for complimenting him in the first volume of the 'Divine Legation' as a 'formidable adversary to the freethinkers.' They afterwards had a dispute about the 'Letters from Rome,' which Middleton defended against Warburton in a postscript to the fourth edition (1741). This put an end to their friendship.

A portrait of Middleton, engraved by Ravenet after J. G. Echardt, is prefixed to his 'Works.' A medal, taken by Giovanni Pozzo at Rome in 1724, was copied by Wedgwood. The original portrait by J. G. Echardt is in the National Portrait Gallery, London. He was athletic in his youth, but injured his health by an injudicious diet, intended to suppress a tendency to corpulence.

Middleton's fame as a writer of pure English has rather faded. Parr declared that he was scarcely excelled by any one but Addison. He seems to have been admired by Landor, who introduces him, with less deviation than usual from historical accuracy, in an imaginary conversation with Magliabecchi. His writings are among the ablest of those produced by the deist controversy, and with Warburton's 'Divine Legation' show the tendency of the discussion to pass into an historical criticism. He touched upon many points raised by modern investigators of the history of religion, without, however, noticing their full significance.

Middleton's works are: 1. 'A full and impartial Account of all the late Proceedings . . . against Dr. Bentley,' 1719. 2. 'Second Part' of the above, 1719. 3. 'Some Remarks upon a Pamphlet entitled "The Case of Dr. Bentley further stated and vindicated" . . .,' 1719. 4. 'A True Account of the Present State of Trinity College in Cambridge under the oppressive rule of their Master, Richard Bentley, late D.D.,' 1720. 5. 'Remarks, paragraph by paragraph, upon the Proposals lately published by Richard Bentley for a new Edition of the Greek Testament and Latin Version,' 1721. 6. 'Some further Remarks . . . containing a full Answer to the Editor's late Defence . . .,' 1721. 7. 'Bibliothecæ Cantabrigiensis ordinandæ Methodus quædam . . .,' 1723. 8. 'De Medicorum apud Veteres Romanos degentium Conditione Dissertatio; quà contra viros celeberrimos Jac. Sponium et Rich. Meadium, M.D., servilem atque ignobilem eam fuisse ostenditur,' 1726. This was in answer to the Harveian oration by Mead, with an appendix by Edmund Chishull [q. v.], and was answered by John Ward [q. v.], Joseph Letherland, and others, to whom Middleton replied in the next: 9. 'Dissertationis . . . contra anonymos quosdam . . . auctores Defensio,' 1727. Middleton wrote an 'Appendix seu Definitiones, pars secunda,' but having met Mead upon friendly terms at the Earl of Oxford's house, suppressed it. It was published in 1761 by Dr. William Heberden the elder [q. v.], with an English letter from Middleton to another opponent, Charles La Motte (see NICHOLS, *Lit. Anecd.* i. 266–8, v. 519–20). 10. 'A Letter from Rome, showing an exact Conformity between Popery and Paganism . . .,' 1729. To the 4th edition in 1741 was added a 'Prefatory Discourse' and 'Postscript.' 11. 'A Letter to Dr. Waterland, containing some Remarks on his "Vindication of Scripture" . . .,' 1731. 12. 'A Defence of the Letter to Dr. Waterland . . .,' 1731. 13. 'Some further Remarks on a Reply to the Defence of the Letter to Dr. Waterland . . .,' 1732. 14. 'Oratio de Novo Physiologiæ explicandæ munere, ex celeberrimi Woodwardi Testamento instituto, habita Cantabrigiæ in Scholis publicis,' 1732. 15. 'Remarks on some Observations addressed to the Author of the Letter to Dr. Waterland,' 1733. 16. 'A Dissertation concerning the Origin of Printing in England; showing that it was first introduced . . . by . . . William Caxton . . .,' 1734–5. The substance of this was reprinted in the 'Origin of Printing,' by Bowyer and Nichols, in 1774; second edition 1776, with appendix 1781.

(For the controversy to which it refers see under ATKYNS, RICHARD; see also NICHOLS, *Anecd.* iii. 171–7.) 17. 'The History of the Life of M. Tullius Cicero,' 2 vols. 4to, 1741; 4th edition in 1750. 18. 'The Epistles of M. T. Cicero to M. Brutus and of Brutus to Cicero . . .,' the Latin with English translation, and a prefatory dissertation in defence of the authenticity of the epistles, 1743. This was in reply to James Tunstall, who had attacked the use of the epistles in the 'Life.' Middleton's opinion was attacked by Markland and others (see NICHOLS, *Anecd.* v. 412–14, note). The opinion of modern critics seems to be generally against him. 19. 'Germana quædam Antiquitatis eruditæ Monumenta . . .,' 1745 (account of the antiquities bought by him in Rome); with an engraving of Middleton by J. Mynde. 20. 'A Treatise on the Roman Senate,' 1747. 21. 'An Introductory Discourse to a larger Work . . . concerning the Miraculous Powers which are supposed to have subsisted in the Christian Church from the earliest ages . . . with a Postscript . . . on an Archidiaconal Charge . . . by the Rev. Dr. Chapman . . .,' 1747. 22. 'Remarks on two Pamphlets' (against the last), 1748. 23. 'A Free Inquiry into the Miraculous Powers,' &c., 1749. 24. 'An Examination of the Lord Bishop of London's Discourses concerning the Use and Intent of Prophecy, with . . . a further Inquiry into the Mosaic account of the Fall,' 1750. 25. 'A Vindication of the Free Inquiry . . . from the Objections of Dr. Dodwell and Mr. Church' (posthumous), 1751. Middleton's 'Miscellaneous Works' were published in 4 vols. 4to in 1752, and in 5 vols. 8vo in 1755. They include all the above except 'The Life of Cicero,' 'Germana Antiquitatis Monumenta,' and the first four pamphlets against Bentley, which are in the quarto but omitted in the octavo edition; and the following, published for the first time: 1. 'Preface to an intended Answer to all the Objections made against the Free Inquiry.' 2. 'Cursory Reflections on the Dispute . . . between St. Peter and St. Paul.' 3. 'Reflections on the Variations . . . among the four Evangelists . . .' 4. 'An Essay on the Gift of Tongues . . .' 5. 'Some short Remarks on a Story . . . concerning St. John . . . and Cerinthus . . .' 6. 'An Essay on the Allegorical and Literal Interpretation of the Creation and Fall of Man.' 7. De Latinarum Literarum Pronunciatione Dissertatio.' 8. A few letters to Warburton and others. Further letters to Warburton in Addit. MS. 32457. In Nichols's 'Anecdotes,' v. 521, a list is given of some other manuscripts of little importance left at his death.

[Biog. Brit.; Nichols's Lit. Anecd. v. 405–23 and elsewhere; a few notices are in Nichols's Illustrations; Monk's Life of Bentley, 1833, i. 253, 287, 373–4, ii. 31, 44, 49, 69–73, 91–6, 130–5, 142, 149–54, 199–202, 209–10 (Monk had before him Middleton's correspondence with Colbatch); Watson's Warburton, 1863, pp. 63, 132–5, 141–2, 258–62, 369–73; Addit. MSS. 32457 (Middleton's miscellaneous correspondence), 32458 (correspondence with Lord Hervey); Notes and Queries, 8th ser. v. 285. Some fragments of earlier letters to Hervey are given in this, and were, it is said, circulated 'all over the nation.' Another copy is in Addit. MS. 5826, f. 21 (Cole's Collection; see also quotations in Nichols's Anecdotes as above); Addit. MS. 32459 (fragments and rough drafts of writings); Cole's Athenæ Cantabr. Addit. MS. 5833, ff. 229–34.]
L. S.

MIDDLETON, DAVID (*d.* 1615), merchant and sea-captain, younger brother of John and Sir Henry Middleton [q. v.], was in 1601 joint commander of a voyage to the West Indies (PURCHAS, iv. 1246). In 1604 he went to the East Indies with his brother Henry, as second captain of the Red Dragon, and is mentioned as having conducted the negotiations with the native kings of Ternate and Tidore. He returned with Henry in May 1606, and on 12 March 1606–7 sailed from Tilbury as captain of the Consent, one of the ships of the third voyage under William Keeling [q. v.] He had with him as master John Davis [q. v.] of Limehouse. The Consent lost sight of her consorts in the Channel, and, as no rendezvous had been given, went on by herself to the Cape of Good Hope. She anchored in Table Bay on 16 July, with her men in good health. Middleton reluctantly proceeded without Keeling, and after touching in St. Augustine's Bay, arrived on 14 Nov. at Bantam, whence after refitting he sailed for the Moluccas. He found the Spaniards personally friendly, but having a monopoly of the commerce; and it was not till March 1607–8 that he could obtain any open permission to trade. He managed, however, to do business privately, and when the permission was withdrawn, within a few days of its being granted, he went to Bangay, and afterwards to Button, where he was well received by the king, and obtained a full cargo of cloves. By 22 May he was back at Bantam, and sailed for England on 15 July.

The voyage, though irregular, had been both speedy and profitable. Middleton was recognised as a capable and fortunate commander, and was at once sent out again in a larger ship, the Expedition, in which he sailed from the Downs on 24 April 1609, Davis being again his master. Again he reached the Cape of Good Hope with his men in good health, and after a stay of only eight days went on to Bantam, where he arrived on 7 Dec. A month later he came to Button, where he entertained the king at a banquet on board; but no trade was to be done, owing to the recent destruction of the storehouses by fire, and he passed on to Bangay. The drunken and dissolute Dutchman domineered over the natives, collected the duties for the king of Ternate, and, keeping for himself as much as he wanted, sent on to the king what he could spare. Middleton, being unable to trade at Bangay, endeavoured to go to the Moluccas. Foul winds compelled him to bear up for Banda, but there the Dutch governor told him plainly that to permit him to buy a nut there was more than his head was worth. He believed that they intended to seize or burn the ship, till he showed them that he was prepared to fight if attacked. At Ceram, after some negotiation, he obtained a full cargo of nutmegs and mace. On his way back to the westward he foiled an attempt of the Dutch to intercept him, and having refitted at Bantam sailed thence on 16 Nov. He arrived in England in the early summer of 1611.

In May 1614 he sailed once more for the East Indies in the Samaritan, with the Thomas and Thomasine under his orders, and arrived at Bantam on 14 Feb. 1614–15. A full cargo was collected, and after sending the smaller vessels to other ports, Middleton, in the Samaritan, sailed for England on 3 April 1615 (*Cal. State Papers*, East Indies, 30 Sept. 1615). But the ship was wrecked on the coast of Madagascar, and though it was at first reported that 'passengers and goods were saved' (*ib.* Captain Pepwell to East India Company, 7 March 1617, read 5 Sept. 1617), the loss seems to have been total. The first report of Middleton's death reached the company on 5 Sept. 1617. No exact news was ever received, but he was registered as dead, and his will proved on 18 April 1618. On 6 Oct. 1624 the court of directors had under consideration a letter in favour of Middleton's son. 'After much reasoning the court called to mind that the captain lost both ship and goods to a very great value, and therefore they gave it for answer that there is nothing due' (*ib.*)

In his will, dated 20 April 1614 (Meade, 31), he names his wife Alice, sons Henry and John, daughter Elizabeth, and mentions a child not yet born, also his wife's sister, Jane Pullybancke. He names, too, his brother Christopher, his sisters and their children, several cousins [see Middleton, Sir Henry] and friends, the bulk of his property being left to his son Henry. Within three weeks of the announcement of the loss of Middleton's ship, his widow had married one Cannon (*ib.*; *Court Minutes*, p. 23, 30 Sept. 1617), who on 4 Dec. 1618, in right of Captain David Middleton, was administrator to Sir Henry Middleton, deceased (*ib.*)

[Purchas his Pilgrimes, i. 226, 238, 524; Calendars of State Papers, East Indies, where, however, there is much confusion between the brothers David and Henry, especially in respect of Alice Middleton.] J. K. L.

MIDDLETON, ERASMUS (1739–1805), author, born in 1739, was son of Erasmus Middleton of Horncastle, Lincolnshire. On 4 June 1767 he matriculated at St. Edmund Hall, Oxford (Forster, *Alumni Oxon.*, 1715–1886, iii. 951), but was expelled from the university in May 1768, along with five other members of the hall, for publicly praying and preaching (*Gent. Mag.* 1768, pp. 225, 410). The affair caused considerable stir at the time, and some pamphleteering (cf. Boswell, *Life of Johnson*, edit. 1848, p. 241; see Macgowan, John). Middleton nevertheless obtained ordination, and subsequently entered himself at King's College, Cambridge, but does not appear to have graduated there. He became in succession minister at Dalkeith, curate of Chelsea, lecturer of St. Benet, Gracechurch Street, and St. Helen, Bishopsgate, curate of St. Margaret's Chapel, Westminster, and in 1804 rector of Turvey, Bedfordshire. He was also chaplain to the Countess of Crawford and Lindsay. He died on 25 April 1805.

Middleton wrote: 1. 'A Letter to A. D., Esq.' [on walking with God], 8vo (Edinburgh), 1772. 2. The theological, philosophical, critical, and poetical branches of a 'New Dictionary of Arts and Sciences,' fol. 1778, an indifferent compilation. 3. 'Biographia Evangelica, or an Historical Account of the Lives and Deaths of the most eminent and evangelical Authors or Preachers both British and Foreign in the several Denominations of Protestants,' 4 vols. 8vo, London, 1779–86, a useful work, written in a singularly uncouth style. 4. 'Versions and Imitations of the Psalms of David,' 8vo, London, 1806, on the title-page of which he is styled B.D. He also published several sermons.

There are two engraved portraits of Middleton, one by A. Smith.

[Gent. Mag. 1805, pt. i. p. 490; Evans's Cat. of Engraved Portraits, ii. 279.] G. G.

MIDDLETON, HENRY (*d.* 1587), printer, was most probably the son of William Middleton [q. v.], the printer, as he was admitted to the freedom of the Stationers' Company on 17 Feb. 1567 by patrimony, without having been an apprentice. He commenced business in partnership with Thomas East near to St. Dunstan's Church in Fleet Street, and on 29 March 1567 they completed their earliest known book, Phaer's 'Regiment of Life.' In 1569 they printed Ovid's 'Invective against Ibis,' translated by Thomas Underdowne, and in 1571, being then located in London Wall, near the sign of the Ship, they issued in a folio volume Vigo's 'Most excellent workes of Chirurgerie.' In 1571 also, they printed the 'Psalms of David' and Fulke's 'Astrologorum Ludus,' and in 1572 Bullinger's 'Common Places of Christian Religion,' Christopher Carlile's 'Discourse, wherein is plainly proved that Peter was never at Rome,' and Dr. John Jones's 'Benefit of the auncient Bathes of Buckstones,' for Luke Harrison, George Bishop, William Jones, and William Norton. In 1572 Middleton left East and set up his press at the sign of the Falcon in Fleet Street, and also opened a shop for the sale of his books in St. Dunstan's Churchyard. The earliest book which bears his name alone is Bull's 'Christian praiers and holy meditations,' printed in 1570, and this was followed in 1572 by Cato's 'Disticha de Moribus;' but more often than not the books which he printed were for Ralph Newbery, John Harrison, George Bishop, Christopher Barker, and other booksellers, by whom he continued to be fully employed. A report on London printing-offices made to the Bishop of London in May 1583 states that he had then three presses at work. The most important books printed by him were the works of Sallust, in Latin, 1573; Gascoigne's 'Glasse of Governement,' 1575; Sir Humphrey Gilbert's 'Discourse of a Discoverie for a new Passage to Cataia,' and Lambard's 'Perambulation of Kent,' 1576; several translations from Calvin; 'The Heidelberg Catechism,' 1578; the Bible and the works of Virgil, both in Latin, Bedford's 'English Medicines,' and Bishop Hooper's 'Certeine expositions upon the Psalmes,' 1580; Laurence Humphrey's 'Jesuitismus,' 1582; Cicero's 'De Officiis' and Sir Thomas Smith's 'De Republica Anglorum,' 1584; Ovid's Metamorphoses,' in Latin, and Archbishop Sandys's 'Sermons,' 1585; and Lambard's 'Duties of Constables,' 1587.

Middleton was admitted into the livery of the Stationers' Company on 1 July 1577, and after having served the office of renter from 1582 to 1584 was elected under-warden in July 1587. He died in September 1587, and his widow appears to have carried on the business until 4 March 1588, when she was forbidden by the company to print anything more 'till such time as the Master, Wardens, and four of the Court of Assistants shall present her name to the High Commissioners for causes ecclesiastical, and that they admit her to be a printer, and governor of a press and printing house, according to a decree of the Star Chamber,' an event which apparently never happened. Middleton used as a device a figure of the Good Shepherd, enclosed within a cartouche, and surrounded by the motto 'Periit et inventa est.'

[Ames's Typogr. Antiq. (Herbert), 1785–90, ii. 1055–63; Arber's Transcript of the Registers of the Company of Stationers of London, i. 344, ii. 474, 865.] R. E. G.

MIDDLETON, Sir HENRY (*d.* 1613), merchant and sea-captain, was the second son of John Middleton of Chester, sheriff in 1570. Robert Middleton, sheriff of Chester in 1518, was probably his grandfather. In his will, he styles Sir Thomas Myddelton [q. v.], lord mayor in 1613–14, 'my loving and good friend.' His elder brother, John, was one of the twenty-four directors of the newly formed East India Company in 1599, and was captain of the Hector when that vessel took part in 1600 under Captain James Lancaster [q. v.] in the first voyage fitted out by the company. He died at Bantam on 10 Feb. 1602–3 (Markham, p. 101). On John's recommendation, 10 Oct. 1600, Henry was appointed purser of the Malice Scourge, afterwards named the Red Dragon, which was engaged in Lancaster's expedition; but before the fleet sailed he was advanced to be a factor for the voyage, 11 Nov., and another purser was appointed, 24 Dec. (Stevens, *Dawn of British Trade to the East Indies*). At Acheen, in June 1602, Lancaster appointed him to the Susan as 'captain and chief-merchant,' and sent him to Priaman (Markham, p. 84). There he obtained a cargo of cloves and pepper, and in December sailed for England (*ib.* p. 98), where he arrived on 21 June 1603 (Corney, p. vi.)

On Lancaster's return, Middleton was appointed to command the second voyage, and on 25 March 1604 he sailed from Gravesend in the Dragon, having also under his command the Hector, Ascension, and Susan [see Keeling, William]. After touching at Maio, one of the Cape Verde islands, they sailed again on 26 April, but being becalmed in the doldrums, they did not sight the Cape of Good Hope till 13 July. Although in the former voyage Middleton had seen the value of lemon juice, he had taken no measures to provide his ships with it.

The men had consequently suffered severely, and, contrary to the company's orders, the fleet was obliged to stop for a month at the Cape. On 19 Dec. they made the coast of Sumatra, and anchored at Bantam on the 23rd, the men being, by this time, again at the last extremity of weakness. On 18 Jan. 1604–5, Middleton, in the Dragon, with the Ascension, went on eastwards, and the Hector and Susan were ordered home with cargoes of pepper. The men were at this time dying fast; twenty-six are named as having died on board the Dragon between leaving Bantam and anchoring at Amboyna on 10 Feb. And just at this time the Dutch seized the island, and so put an end to all chance of trade there. After long debate and with much misgiving, the Ascension and Dragon resolved to separate, the former going to Banda, the latter to the Moluccas. They sailed from Amboyna on 18 Feb., and on 22 March after a tedious voyage the Dragon got off Tidore, where the Portuguese had a settlement, and were supporting the natives in a war with their neighbours at Ternate, who were aided by the Dutch. Middleton's force was too insignificant to permit of his taking any part in the quarrel, which ended in the complete defeat of the Portuguese. The Dutch then threw every possible obstacle in the way of the English trade; and though Middleton managed, here and there, to pick up some cloves, it does not appear that he had anything like a full cargo when, on 24 July, the Dragon anchored again at Bantam. She sailed for England on 6 Oct., and on 19 Dec., standing in for Table Bay, sighted the Hector in the last extremity of distress, almost all her men being dead. Middleton sent men on board to take her into the bay, where they stayed for a month, and where they were joined by the Ascension. They sailed on 16 Jan., and, after touching at St. Helena, anchored in the Downs on 6 May 1606. Middleton's services were promptly recognised. He had pushed his voyage much further than the company had dared to order him, and the profits were very great. He was knighted at Greenwich on 25 May 1606; and ten years later he was still described as 'the thrice worthy general who laid the true foundation of our long desired Cambaya trade' (SIR DUDLEY DIGGES, *The Defence of Trade*, p. 23).

In 1610 Middleton was appointed to command the sixth voyage set forth by the East India company, and sailed from the Downs on 4 April in the Trade's Increase, having in company the Peppercorn, commanded by Nicholas Downton [q. v.], and the Darling. The voyage out was comparatively fortunate, and there was no exceptional sickness when, on 7 Nov., they arrived at Aden. Leaving the Peppercorn there, Middleton, with the Darling, went on to Mocha; but in entering the roadstead, in charge of a native pilot, the Trade's Increase was run ashore, and much of her cargo and stores had to be landed before she could be floated off. The governor, or aga, received Middleton and the merchants with every appearance of friendship; but a few days later, 28 Nov. when a large working party was on shore, he suddenly attacked them, killed eight in the scuffle, and made prisoners of Middleton and the others, to the number of fifty-nine. He then attempted to seize the Darling, which was lying close in shore; but in that the Turks were repulsed with heavy loss. For more than three weeks the prisoners were kept at Mocha, heavily ironed; they were then sent to the bashaw at Sinan (Sana), where they were more humanely treated and allowed to communicate freely with the ships. Downton, who had arrived from Aden in the Peppercorn, proposed making reprisals on the Turkish and Indian trading vessels, but Middleton restrained him, fearing that 'it might prove prejudicial to him and his company.' The bashaw, he said, had promised that they should all be set free at the coming of the westerly winds; if he suspected any breach of faith, he would make his escape. And when he learnt that a fleet of galleys was expected from Suez, and that the aga was negotiating for the hire of some of the larger country ships which Downton had allowed to come to Mocha, Middleton, on 15 May 1611, with fifteen of his men, did make his escape, got on board the Darling, and sent orders to Downton to join him at once with the other ships.

He then, by a strict blockade of the port, compelled the Turks to send back all the men who remained in captivity, and to restore the goods which had been seized on shore, or to pay compensation for the loss, and after refitting at Socotra, he went to Surat, where he arrived on 26 Sept. He found the place closely blockaded by a Portuguese fleet of eighteen frigates, which made communication with the shore difficult, and prevented fresh victuals or refreshments being sent off for the men who were suffering from scurvy. After some skirmishing the prohibition to trade was partially withdrawn; but the governor was in too great dread of the Portuguese to receive the English with any appearance of friendship. He refused them permission to establish a factory, and after a stay of four months ordered them to leave. The merchants on shore were also ordered away, no time being allowed them to get in their debts. On 11 Feb. 1611–12 they sailed for Dabul, but neither there could any trade be done; and Middleton thought himself poorly recompensed by seizing a Portuguese ship of three hundred tons, and taking out of her what she had of 'cloves, cinnamon, wax, and bales of raw China silk—but a mite in comparison to the loss inflicted on the venture by the Portuguese.'

From Dabul he went back to the Red Sea, blockaded Aden and the Straits of Bab-el-Mandeb, and seized several Indian ships by way of reprisals; but learning that the company's fleet of the year (the eighth voyage), under the command of John Saris [q. v.], with whom was Gabriel Towerson [q. v.], had passed into the Red Sea, he went in and joined Saris at Assab. He then demanded from the Turks one hundred thousand pieces of eight as compensation for former injuries and insults, and would probably have forced them to pay but for an angry quarrel between him and Saris, partly about the division of the spoil, and still more, it would seem, about their precedence. Finally they accepted something like a third of their demand from the Indian ships; and so with much ill-feeling, and without 'the usual courtesies,' they separated in the beginning of August 1612, Middleton, with the Peppercorn in company, going to Tecoa, where he joined the Darling on 19 Oct. From Tecoa they went to Bantam, and Middleton proposed to send Downton home in the Trade's Increase with a cargo of pepper, while he himself, in the Peppercorn, should attempt another voyage to the Moluccas. It was found, however, that the Trade's Increase was in need of a very extensive refit; so in the beginning of February 1612–13, Downton sailed for England in the Peppercorn. After a few months the Trade's Increase, while being careened, fell over on her side, became a total wreck, and was maliciously set on fire by the Javanese (Purchas, i. 526, 533; *Cal. State Papers*, East Indies, 9 June 1614; 2 Jan. 1615). Most of the men died from their injuries, and with them Middleton himself, 24 May 1613 (Fuller, *Worthies*, i. 289).

It does not appear that Middleton was married; the entries in the Calendar of State Papers (East Indies) to the contrary effect are certainly erroneous, as is shown by his will (at Somerset House, *Lawe*, 55), dated on board the Trade's Increase 29 March 1610, and proved by Alice, wife of David Middleton, on 22 June 1614. By this, his brother David, and David's son Henry, are left executors and residuary legatees. Mention is made of his brother Christopher; of his three sisters, Katharine Tetlow, Margaret Burre, who has been erroneously named as his daughter (Corney, p. viii; Markham, p. v), and Ursula Fawcet; his niece and god-daughter, Joan Burre; his cousins, John Haylin, Margaret Radford, Jane Hill, and her sister Sarah Hanmer; 'my sister, Alice Middleton' (David's wife), and her daughter Elizabeth; 'my sister, Margery Middleton' (? Christopher's wife); also Sir Thomas Myddelton and his son Thomas, Hugh Myddelton, Captain William Myddelton, Captain Roger Middleton, and his brother William, and Robert Middleton. None of these last are described as relations; but in John's will (*Bolein*, 75), dated 5 March 1600–1, proved by Henry 27 Oct. 1603, Hugh Myddelton is styled cousin; the sisters, Margaret and Ursula, were then unmarried, and two other brothers, Jarrett and Randall, are named, as well as his father, John. David in his will (*Meade*, 31), mentions Robert Middleton also as a cousin.

[The Voyages of Sir James Lancaster to the East Indies, with Abstracts of Journals of Voyages to the East Indies during the Seventeenth Century, edited by C. R. Markham, C.B., F.R.S., for the Hakluyt Society. This contains, besides other notices, a very full abstract of Downton's Journal of the Sixth Voyage. The Voyage of Sir Henry Middleton to Bantam and the Maluco Islands, being the Second Voyage set forth by the Governor and Company of Merchants of London trading into the East Indies. The original edition of this (1606, 8vo), is extremely rare; there is no copy in the British Museum; it was edited for the Hakluyt Society in 1855 by Bolton Corney. See also Purchas his Pilgrimes, i. 179, 185, 247, 703; and Calendars of State Papers, East Indies, where, however, in some cases, it would seem, by the error of the company's clerks, the brothers Henry and David are confused, and David's wife is assigned to Henry.] J. K. L.

MIDDLETON, Sir HUGH (1560?–1631), projector of New River. [See Myddelton.]

MIDDLETON, JANE (1645–1692), court beauty. [See Myddelton.]

MIDDLETON, JOHN, first Earl of Middleton (1619–1674), was the eldest son of Robert Middleton of Caldhame, Kincardineshire, who was killed in his own house by Montrose's soldiers in 1645. His mother was a daughter of Alexander Strachan of Thornton in the same county. The family owned the lands of Middleton, Kincardineshire, from which they took their surname, before the time of William the Lion. The future earl began his career as a pikeman in

Hepburn's regiment in France. He came home to join the army of the covenant, and as major under Montrose distinguished himself by storming the Brig of Dee in June 1639. He afterwards entered the parliamentary army in England, and was conspicuous for his bravery and generosity. He was made lieutenant-general, but resigned his commission when the army was remodelled, and rejoined that of his countrymen. He was second in command at the battle of Philiphaugh in September 1645, when he contributed so much to the victory that the estates gave him twenty-five thousand merks. The following year he pursued Montrose in the north, burnt his castle of Kincardine, and shot twelve of the garrison who had surrendered. When the king ordered Montrose to disband his forces, Middleton was employed by the estates to negotiate conditions. In July 1646 the two commanders had a long conference in a meadow near the river Islay in Angus, when Middleton granted Montrose and his followers more favourable terms than the commission of assembly approved of.

In 1647 he repressed a royalist rising in the north under Huntly. In 1648 he was appointed lieutenant-general of the cavalry in the army raised by the Scottish estates to rescue the king from the hands of the sectaries, and on his march south he received a wound at Mauchline-Muir in dispersing some two thousand ultra-covenanters, who had assembled in arms on the Monday, after a communion, to resist the action of the government in connection with 'the engagement.' Middleton behaved with great bravery at the battle of Preston, but his horse having been shot under him he was taken prisoner and confined at Newcastle. He was afterwards allowed to reside in Berwick, when, as some say, he broke his parole and returned to Scotland. Up till the revolution in the end of 1648 he had been a zealous covenanter, but after that time his ardour cooled. In 1649 he unsuccessfully attempted a rising for Charles II in the highlands, and was allowed to return home on 'giving assurance of his dutiful carriage in time coming.' The general assembly of that year threatened him with excommunication, but having appeared before it and pleaded his own cause, he got leave to sign 'the declaration and acknowledgment' prescribed to those who had taken part in 'the engagement' or 'in the late rebellion in the north.' In 1650 Middleton joined the king on his landing in Scotland, but some months later he and others, resenting the treatment which his majesty received from the government, raised a separate force in the north in his interest. Leslie marched against him, and as Charles urged him to submit, and the estates offered an indemnity, Middleton agreed to terms on the basis of the covenants. The commission of the church, however, was not satisfied, and on a motion made by James Guthrie, minister of Stirling, and carried by votes of elders, resolved on his excommunication. This was opposed by many of the leading ministers, and the committee of estates urged delay; but Guthrie carried out the sentence on the following Sunday. At its next meeting the commission resolved to undo what had been done so rashly, and Middleton, having done penance in sackcloth in the church of Dundee, 12 Jan. 1651, was restored to church communion. After this he took a prominent part in the conflict with Cromwell till the battle of Worcester, when he commanded the cavalry. On that disastrous field, after driving back the enemy, he was wounded, taken prisoner, and sent to the Tower of London. Cromwell wished to have him tried for his life, but he escaped in his wife's clothes and joined the king at Paris.

He was appointed captain-general of the forces that rose for the king in the highlands in the end of 1653, and took command at Dornoch early in 1654. Monck marched against him with a large force, and in July came upon him by surprise near Lochgarry, when his followers were dispersed, and he escaped with difficulty and joined the king at Cologne. Cromwell exempted him from the act of indemnity, and he remained abroad till the Restoration, with the king, or employed by him on missions to various courts. In 1656 Charles had made him an earl. In 1660 he returned to England in the same ship with the king. His peerage was then confirmed by letters patent under the title of Earl of Middleton, Lord Clermont and Fettercairn. He was also appointed commander-in-chief in Scotland, governor of Edinburgh Castle, and lord high commissioner to the Scottish parliament. He arrived at Holyrood in the end of December, having been escorted from Musselburgh by many of the nobles and gentry and a thousand horse.

In January 1661 he opened the Scottish parliament with great state, and soon after passed the acts rescissory, which annulled all the legislation of the previous twenty-three years. In May following he presided at the funeral of Montrose, whose scattered limbs were then collected and buried with all honour in St. Giles's, Edinburgh. He took an active part in the prosecution of Argyll, who was executed on the 27th of the same month, and he is said to have cherished a personal animosity against James Guthrie [q. v.], who had excommunicated him, and who suffered a few days later. In July Middleton went to London and urged the king to restore episcopacy in Scotland. He is said to have received no instructions to change the government of the church, but to have been authorised to sound the Scots on the subject, and he now assured the king that episcopacy was 'desired by the greater and honester part of the nation.' Lauderdale was of a different mind, and this was the beginning of a deadly feud between them, which ended in Middleton's overthrow.

Middleton was again commissioner to the parliament which met in May 1662, and in July of that year was made an extraordinary lord of session. In the end of September following he and the privy council met at Glasgow; and when most of them, it is said, were under the influence of drink, passed the act by which the clergy who refused to conform to episcopacy were deprived of their benefices. In 1663 he was ordered up to London to meet the accusations of Lauderdale, who charged him with many offences, such as withholding letters from the king on public affairs, consenting to measures without his authority, and taking bribes from presbyterians to exempt them from fines. He was deprived of all his offices, and then retired to the house of an old Scottish companion in arms near Guildford in Surrey. The king some years afterwards made him governor of Tangier, where he died in June 1674 (Sloane MS. 3512, f. 79) from the effects of a fall which he met with in a fit of intoxication.

Middleton was one of the most successful of the Scottish soldiers of fortune, and was eminent alike for force of character, personal courage, and ability as a commander. Clarendon says he was 'a man of great honour and courage, and much the best officer they (the Scots) had.' Sir George Mackenzie describes him as of 'heroic aspect, courage, and generosity, manly, eloquent, and as more pitied in his fall than envied in his prosperity.' Baillie, soon after his return to Scotland as royal commissioner, says that 'his wisdom, sobriety, and moderation have been such as make him better beloved, and reputed as fit for that great charge as any other we could have gotten;' but his character, like that of his rival Lauderdale, rapidly deteriorated after that time, and there is every reason to believe that this was due to habitual intemperance.

He married, first, Grizel, daughter of Sir James Durham of Pitkerrow, Forfarshire, and had a son, Charles, second and last earl [q. v.], and two daughters, Lady Grisel who married the ninth earl of Morton, and Lady Helen who married the first earl of Strathmore; secondly, Lady Martha Carey, daughter of the second earl of Monmouth, by whom he had a son John, who died in early life.

[Biscoe's Earls of Middleton; Clarendon's History; Pepys's Diary; Lauderdale Papers (Camd. Soc.); Douglas's Peerage of Scotland; Balfour's Annals; Baillie's Letters; Napier's Life of Montrose; Sir G. Mackenzie's Historical Affairs of Scotland; Wodrow's History.]

G. W. S.

MIDDLETON, JOHN (1827–1856), landscape painter, born at Norwich in 1827, was from early days a student in the Norwich school of landscape painters, working under John Crome [q. v.] and Joseph Stannard [q. v.] He practised almost entirely at Norwich, but was an exhibitor at the Royal Academy and the British Institution in London from 1847 till his death. His landscapes were noted for their effective rendering of the seasons of the year, especially the early spring. Middleton was unfortunately a victim to consumption, of which he died on 11 Nov. 1856, at Surrey Street, Norwich, in his thirtieth year.

[Redgrave's Dict. of Artists; Graves's Dict. of Artists, 1760–1880; Norwich Mercury, 15 Nov. 1856.]

L. C.

MIDDLETON, JOSHUA (1647–1721), quaker, born in 1647, at Darlington, was one of the Silksworth (Durham) Middletons, a younger branch of the Middletons of Belsay Castle, Northumberland. His fifth direct ancestor, Gilbert Middleton, was mayor of Newcastle in 1530. His father, John Middleton (so called in the marriage register, but Gurney in his pedigree has Joshua), was a strict presbyterian, and brought him up with much care. He, however, early joined the quakers, who had attracted at that time many families of importance in the northern counties. Soon after joining the society, Middleton became a minister, and travelled in many parts of England and Scotland, entertaining also at his house Thomas Story [q. v.] and many other travelling friends. He lived first at Raby, near Staindrop, Durham, and afterwards at Newcastle, where he died 27 Jan. 1720–1.

The 'Testimony' of his quarterly meeting speaks of his good example and 'care of the churches.' He was of a peaceable spirit, useful in healing differences.

Middleton married Dorothy, daughter of Timothy and Katherine Draper of Newcastle; she died 27 June 1688. He married secondly, on 9 Sept. 1697, Jane Molleson of London, daughter of Gilbert Molleson of Aberdeen, and sister of Christian Barclay, wife of the apologist.

Middleton's eldest son, Joshua, married Isabella, daughter of John Doubleday of Alnwick Abbey, Northumberland. A second son, John, was burned to death in the Cross Keys Inn, Gracechurch Street, London, he being a lodger there at the time (SMITH, *Catalogue*, ii. 175). A daughter Elizabeth married Peregrine Tyzack of Norwich. Through his youngest daughter, Hannah, Middleton became the ancestor of the Gurneys, Hoares, Frys, and a host of other quaker families. She married, on 21 July 1713, at Norwich, Joseph Gurney of Keswick Hall, Norfolk, brother of John Gurney (1688–1741) [q. v.] Hannah Middleton Gurney was a woman of extraordinary beauty. Her portrait was painted by Richard Houston [q. v.], who published a print (1746?) entitled 'The Fair Quaker,' which became extremely popular as a typical illustration of the costume of the Society of Friends.

[J. Gurney Bevan's Piety Promoted, London, 1811, pp. 306–10; Life of Thomas Story, Newcastle, 1747, pp. 585, 596, 657, 666, 690; Gurney's Record of the House of Gurney (printed for private circulation), London, 1848, pp. 556–61; Smith's Cat.; marriage register at Devonshire House.] C. F. S.

MIDDLETON, MARMADUKE (*d.* 1593), bishop of Waterford and St. Davids, was the second son of Marmaduke Middleton of Cardiganshire (descended from the Middletons of Middleton in Westmoreland) and his wife Isabella, daughter of John Staveley (DWNN, *Heraldic Visitations of Wales*, i. 69, but cf. A. WOOD, *Athenæ Oxon.* ed. Bliss, ii. 830). He was educated at Oxford, but left the university without a degree. Subsequently he went to Ireland, where he became vicar of Coolock in the diocese of Dublin, vicar of Dunboyne, and rector of Killare in the diocese of Meath. On 31 May 1579 he was created bishop of Waterford and Lismore, in succession to Patrick Walsh. His intemperate zeal soon brought him into collision with the citizens. It was impossible for him, Captain Yorke of the Achates averred, to remain thus without special protection (*State Papers*, Irel. Eliz. lxx. 44), and on 7 Dec. Sir William Pelham advised his translation to the see of Ferns (*ib.* lxx. 45). Justly or unjustly, he was charged by the mayor with being a man of bad life, and guilty of plundering the cathedral of Christ Church Neither the lord deputy, Grey, nor the chief government officials believed the charge, and the mayor failing to substantiate his assertions, Middleton was 'acquitted with great credit' (*ib.* lxxviii. 45, lxxxv. 33, 60; *Cal. of Fiants*, Eliz. No. 3743). But the popular feeling ran so strongly against him that it was felt impossible for him to remain at Waterford, and having obtained letters of recommendation to Walsingham from Lord Grey and Archbishop Loftus, he repaired to England, apparently in September 1581. On 30 Nov. 1582 he was translated to the see of St. Davids in Wales, and on 27 April 1583 he was, at his special request, created D.D. of Oxford, convocation allowing the degree in the hope that it might make him 'more willing to promote in the church graduates, and especially Oxford graduates' (*Register of the University of Oxford*, vol. ii. pt. i. p. 145). But his conduct in his new diocese did not escape censure. One of his servants reported that he was dissatisfied with his position, and spoke disrespectfully of the queen and her ministers (*State Papers*, Dom. Eliz. cxc. 40). He quarrelled with Sir John Perrot [q. v.] in an affair of ecclesiastical jurisdiction (*ib.* cxcv. 113); and finally in 1589 he seems to have given so much offence in his diocese as to cause the ecclesiastical commissioners to interfere (*ib.* ccxxviii. 14, 15). The exact nature of the complaint against him is uncertain. By one account (MARTIN MARPRELATE, *A Dialogue. Wherin is plainly layd open the tyrannicall dealing of Lord Bishopps*; *Hay any Worke for Cooper*) he is charged with having had two wives, Elizabeth Gigge and Alice Prime. According to another account (case of the Bishop of Lincoln in RUSHWORTH, *Hist. Coll.* pt. ii. vol. i. p. 428), he had contrived and published a forged will. Browne Willis, who carefully investigated his case (*Addit. MS.* 5840, p. 420), came to the conclusion that he had been guilty of simoniacal practices, of a notorious abuse of a charity, and of a design to alienate some lands of the bishopric with intention of settling them on his son Richard, archdeacon of Cardigan (*Survey of St. Davids*, p. 123). In any case his offence was considered of so grave a nature that after being fined in the court of Star-chamber he was handed over to the high commission court for degradation. He claimed, but was denied, his privilege as a peer not to answer on oath, but upon his honour. The sentence of degradation and deprivation was executed before the high commissioners at Lambeth House, not only by reading it *in scriptis*, but by formally divesting him of his episcopal robes and priestly vestments (PETER HEYLYN, *Examen Historicum*, London, 1659, p. 221). He died apparently on 1 Nov. 1593, and was buried in the royal chapel of St. George at Windsor. Richard Middleton (*d.* 1641) [q. v.] was possibly his son.

[A useful life is included by mistake in Cooper's Athenæ Cantabr. ii. 139. See also Wood's Athenæ

Oxon. ed. Bliss, ii. 830; Lewys Dwnn's Heraldic Visitations of Wales (Welsh MSS. Society, ed. Meyrick), i. 69; Ware's Works, ed. Harris, i. 538; Browne Willis's Survey of St. Davids; Cal. State Papers, Eliz., Ireland, and Dom.; Morrin's Cal. Patent Rolls, ii. 24; Cal. Fiants, Eliz. 3685, 3698, 3743; Martin Marprelate's Hay any Worke for Cooper, and A Dialogue. Wherin is plainly layd open the tyrannicall dealing of Lord Bishopps; Alumni Oxonienses; Register of the University of Oxford; Strype's Annals, iii. 171, 401; Whitgift, pp. 117, 215, 400; Grindal, p. 270; W. M. Brady's State Papers concerning the Irish Church, pp. 37, 39; Dr. Dee's Diary (Camd. Soc.), p. 18.] R. D.

MIDDLETON, PATRICK (1662–1736), Scottish nonjuring divine, born in 1662, studied in St. Leonard's College, St. Andrews; graduated M.A. 20 July 1680, and after ordination became, in 1684, minister of Leslie, in the presbytery of Kirkcaldy. He was deprived by the privy council, 22 Aug. 1689, for not reading the proclamation of the estates and for praying for James II. He was discharged from exercising any part of the clerical function under a severe penalty by the privy council in December 1692 for not praying for William and Mary. In 1716 he had a meeting-house in Skinner's Close, Edinburgh, and was prosecuted, with others, before the lords of justiciary, and being convicted a second time, 19 June 1717, of not praying *nominatim* for George I in terms of the Act of Toleration, he was forbidden to preach or exercise any part of the ministry. He died at Bristol on 25 July 1736.

His works are: 1. 'A Dissertation upon the Power of the Church; In a Middle Way, Betwixt those who screw it up to the highest, with the Papists and Scottish Presbyterians on the one hand; and the Erastians and Followers of Hugo Grotius, who, on the other hand, do wholly reject the Intrinsic Spiritual Authority wherewith Jesus Christ hath vested the Rulers of his Church,' London, 1733, 8vo. 2. 'A Short View of the Evidences upon which the Christian Religion, and the Divine Authority of the Holy Scriptures is established. . . . With a Defence not only of the Usefulness, but also of the Necessity of Divine Revelation; against [Matthew Tindal],' 2 parts, London [1734], 8vo. 3. 'The Case of Abraham's being commanded by God Almighty to offer up his son Isaac in sacrifice, impartially examined and defended, against the Deists and other modern Infidels,' 2nd edit. London, 1740, 8vo. On the title-page he is styled a doctor of divinity, though it does not appear that he took that degree. 4. 'An Enquiry into the Inward Call of the Holy Ministry' (anon.), Cambridge, 1741, 8vo.

[Bodl. Cat. ii. 741; Hist. Reg. 1736, Chron. Diary, p. 44; Political State of Great Britain, lii. 102; Hew Scott's Fasti, ii. 550.] T. C.

MIDDLETON, RICHARD (*fl.* 1280), Franciscan, was no doubt an Englishman, though Dempster (*Hist. Eccl.* xii. 512) calls him a Scot. Fuller (*Church History,* xiv. 25) suggests that he was a native of Middleton Stoney, Oxfordshire, or Middleton Cheyney, Northamptonshire. He is conjectured to have studied at Oxford; he was certainly a scholar at Paris, where he graduated B.D. in 1283, and D.D. soon afterwards (cf. Du Boulay, *Hist. Univ. Paris,* iii. 708). He devoted himself specially to the canon law and theology, and acquired a great name by his disputations. Bonagratia, the then general of the Franciscans, appointed Middleton with others to examine into the doctrines of Peter Olivi in 1278, 1283, and 1288. Middleton was a friend of St. Louis of Toulouse (*d.* 1297); he is supposed to have died about 1307. Marianus Florentius erroneously described him as archbishop of Rheims. Middleton's name is inscribed on the tomb of Joannes Duns Scotus at Cologne as one of the fifteen chief doctors of his order; Duns is alleged to have been a pupil of Middleton. Middleton was known at Paris as 'doctor solidus et copiosus, fundatissimus et authoratus.' At the council of Constance in 1415 his authority was cited in condemnation of Wyclif, and at Basle in 1433 he was quoted by John of Ragusa as 'doctor profundus et magnæ authoritatis in scholis.' In the 1499 (Venice) edition of his commentary on the 'Fourth Book of the Sentences' the following verses are given:

Sacra refert celeber Richardus dogmata quædam,
Quem tenuit Media Villa decora virum.
Hauserunt veteres claro de fonte Ricardi,
Doctoresque novi qui meliora docent.

Middleton wrote: 1. 'Super Sententias Petri Lombardi.' The commentary of Middleton, of which there are numerous manuscripts at Oxford and elsewhere, was written between 1281 and 1285; it was printed complete at Venice, 1489 and 1509, Brescia, 1591; the first book, Venice, 1507, the second and third books, Venice, 1509, and the fourth book only, Venice, 1489, without date, and 1499, and Paris, 1504 and 1512. The statement made by Wadding, that the fourth book was not by Middleton, is an error. 2. 'Quæstiones Quodlibetales,' incipit 'Quæritur utrum Deus sit summe simplex,' MS. Merton College 139, f. 2, Troyes 142, Florence Laurentiana ex Bibl. S. Crucis Plut. xvii. Sin. Cod. vii. 3. 'Quodlibeta tria,' printed in the 1509 edition of the 'Sentences.' 4. 'De gradibus formarum,' MS. Munich 8723. 5. 'Quæstiones disputatæ,' manuscript at Assisi. Middleton is also credited with 6. 'Super epistolas Pauli.' 7. 'Super evangelia.' 8. 'Super distinctiones decreti.' 9. 'De ordine judiciorum.' 10. 'De clavium sacerdotalium potestate.' 11. 'Contra Petrum Joannem Olivum.' 12. 'De Conceptione immaculata Virginis Mariæ,' in verse. 13. 'Expositio super Ave Maria,' which is more probably by Richard or Conrad de Saxonia. To Middleton has incorrectly been assigned the authorship of a treatise, 'In regulam S. Francisci,' and of the 'Quadragesimale' of Francis of Asti. It is also stated in error that he completed the 'Summa' of Alexander of Hales by order of Alexander IV; this was the work of William of Meliton [q. v.], who died in 1261. Three sermons, preached by a Friar Richard at Paris in 1281 and 1283, and now preserved in MS. Bibliothèque Nationale 14947; Nos. 47, 69, and 98, may be by Middleton.

[Tanner's Bibl. Brit.-Hib. pp. 526–7; Wadding's Script. Ord. Min. pp. 207–8; Sbaralea's Suppl. in Script. Ord. Min. pp. 633–5; Hist. Litt. de la France, xxi. 128–32; Little's Grey Friars in Oxford, pp. 214–15 (Oxf. Hist. Soc.), where a full list of manuscripts will be found.] C. L. K.

MIDDLETON, RICHARD (*d.* 1641), divine, was educated at Jesus College, Oxford, where he graduated B.A. on 13 July 1586. Wood conjectures that he was son of Marmaduke Middleton [q.v.], bishop of St. David's. It is probable that he was presented to the vicarage of Llanarthney, Carmarthenshire, in 1588. He was collated to a prebend in the collegiate church of Brecon in 1589, held the archdeaconry of Cardigan from 1589 to 1629, became chaplain in ordinary to Charles, prince of Wales, and was designed vicar of Leeds in 1614 (Thoresby, *Vicaria Leodiensis*, pp. 62, 64). In 1628 he was appointed rector of Eaton, Northamptonshire, being then B.D. He died on 16 Nov. 1641. One Richard Middleton was admitted to the rectory of Stisted, Essex, on 28 Sept. 1619, on the translation of Samuel Harsnet from the see of Chichester to that of Norwich; but his identity with the rector of Eaton is not certain.

Middleton was author of: 1. 'The Carde and Compasse of Life, containing many Passages fit for these Times,' London, 1613, 8vo. 2. 'The Heauenly Progresse,' London, 1617, 8vo. 3. 'The Key of Dauid,' London, 1619, 12mo. On the title-page is his portrait, engraved by R. Elstracke, representing him with a ruff and a great beard (Bromley, *Cat. of Portraits*, p. 54). At the end of the book is another tract by Middleton, also printed in 1619, and entitled 'Goodnes: The blessed Man's Badge, or God's Character stampt on Man's Conscience.'

[Addit. MS. 5876, f. 108; Bodleian Cat.; Bridges's Northamptonshire, ii. 144; Foster's Alumni Oxon. early ser. iii. 1010; Granger's Biog. Hist. of England, 5th edit. ii. 63; Le Neve's Fasti (Hardy), i. 315; Lowndes's Bibl. Man. (Bohn), p. 1545; Newcourt's Repertorium, ii. 562; Watt's Bibl. Brit.; Wood's Fasti Oxon. (Bliss), i. 235.] T. C.

MIDDLETON, THOMAS (1570?–1627), dramatist, was the son of William Middleton, gentleman, and Anne, daughter of William Snow, and was probably born in London, to which both parents belonged. Of his early training nothing is directly known; but his writings, though seldom obtrusively learned (as in 'A Game at Chess,' v. 1), contain plenty of evidence of classical scholarship, and bear, as a whole, the stamp of culture and breeding. Whether or not, however, Middleton studied at either university, he entered, while still a young man, at Gray's Inn, being probably the earlier of two Thomas Middletons admitted there in 1593 and 1596. It is plain that he used his opportunities, and his earlier plays in particular abound with vigorous sketches of legal life at first-hand. His first essays, however, probably belonged to the domain, which was still thought more reputable for a 'gentleman,' of pure literature. The 'Wisdom of Solomon Paraphrased' (1597) and the 'Microcynicon' (1599) have commonly been assigned to Middleton in default of any other qualified claimant with the same name or initials; but the former recalls his acknowledged work only in its metrical fluency, the latter only in the satirical animus of which the fashion had just been set by the 'Virgidemiæ' of Joseph Hall [q. v.]

Middleton's connection with the stage cannot be shown to have begun before 1599, when, according to hardly disputable internal evidence, his 'Old Law' was written in conjunction with William Rowley [q. v.] —to the end his most frequent coadjutor. In 1601–2 he was writing regularly for the 'Admiral's Men,' taking part, according to the system of combined production prevalent in that company, with Munday, Drayton, Webster, and 'others,' in a play called 'Cæsar's Fall,' for which Henslowe on 22 May advanced 5*l.* Seven days later Henslowe paid the four dramatists named 3*l.* for a play called 'Too Harpes,' i.e. 'Two Harpies.' The following autumn we find him receiving 6*l.* in two instalments (21 Oct. and 9 Nov.) for a play of his own, variously called by Henslowe 'The Chester Tragedy' and 'Randowlle earlle of Chester.' In December he was employed to write a prologue and epilogue for Greene's 'Friar Bacon' on its performance at court; and an obscure entry of 2 Oct. further describes him as writing a play, not named, for Lord Worcester's company. In 1602 also his 'Blurt, Master-Constable,' was published, after having been 'sundry times privately acted.' Although the pieces recorded by Henslowe are all lost, their subjects were evidently—like that of 'The Old Law'—taken in name from remote history; and it seems likely that the only other play of Middleton's which shares this feature, 'The Mayor of Quinborough,' was at least sketched at this time.

Within the next few years, however, he had discovered a more congenial path, the comedy of contemporary manners, and to this species the abounding energy, vivacity, and invention of his early maturity were devoted. His prose tracts of 1603–4, 'The Black Book' and 'Father Hubburd's Tales,' are vivid and richly coloured satirical sketches of London life, in the manner of Nashe and Dekker. The publication of not less than six plays of his in 1607–8 shows with what success he worked this vein on the stage. These plays contain, however, much poor and hasty work, as well as a good deal of scattered excellence, and it is likely that Middleton abused his facile powers under the stimulus of popularity. The remainder of his extant plays appeared (so far as their dates are known) at longer intervals, and they include his most powerful work.

Twice in 1613 he was commissioned to take a literary part in public ceremonials. In September he composed speeches for the formal opening of the New River, the work of the public-spirited goldsmith Hugh Myddelton [q. v.] In October he wrote a pageant in celebration of the mayoralty of Sir Thomas Myddelton (29 Oct.), the first of a long series of 'Triumphs' contributed by him for the same annual occasions. Such work was usually entrusted to the city poet, Anthony Munday [q. v.], and although Middleton undertook in each of the cases specified to eulogise men of his own name, he does not appear to have claimed relationship with either, and did not owe his selection to family partiality (cf. Nichols, *London Pageants*, p. 97). On 4 Jan. 1614 he produced the 'Mask of Cupid'—of which nothing is known—for the reception of Somerset and Lady Frances Howard, whose marriage had been celebrated with another masque at court in the previous December. A minute in the 'City Records' (18 Jan.) directs that Middleton be recouped for the 'Mask' as well as for 'other shows lately made' at Merchant Taylors' Hall by him. Middleton's work in this department culminates in the elaborate and effective masque 'The World Tost at Tennis,' performed at court in 1620, and published in July of that year. In the following September Middleton was, on his own petition and as a direct recognition of his services to the city, appointed city chronologer (*City Records*, 6 Sept. 1620), being required 'to collect and set down all memorable acts of this city and occurrences thereof,' with a yearly salary of ten marks (6*l.* 13*s.* 4*d.*) The same 'Records' attest numerous extra payments made to him in connection with this office. His salary was on 20 Nov. raised to 10*l.* On 17 April 1621, 7 May 1622, and 24 April 1623, freedoms were granted him in aid of his labours; on 17 Sept. 1622, 6 Feb. 1623, and 2 Sept. 1623, he received gifts ranging from twenty marks to twenty pounds for special services. Of Middleton's official writings nothing remains. Two manuscript books of his were, however, extant in the last century, and were briefly described by Oldys in his annotations to Langbaine's 'Account of the English Dramatick Poets.' One of them ('Annales') was devoted to specifically civic events (among others the arrest and imprisonment of Bacon), the other ('Middleton's Farrago') to various non-civic, political, and social topics of the day. The latter collection, which was doubtless not a part of his official work, indicates that he followed contemporary affairs with some zest.

Middleton was at the very height of his powers when he produced the 'Changeling,' and probably also the 'Spanish Gipsy,' in 1621–2. In 1624 he ventured on a remarkable political drama called 'A Game at Chess.' The national hatred of Spain had in March of that year found expression in the despatch of six thousand men into Flanders; but the 'peace-making' king had stubbornly resisted to the last, and, despite the ignominious failure (October 1623) of the proposed Spanish match, had taken action with reluctance. To represent the situation on the stage was a matter of some delicacy; and Middleton hit upon the device of disguising the leading politicians of Spain and England in his play under the names of the pieces on a chess-board. He thus did not conceal, but rendered it possible to ignore, the true character of his plot. The play was acted early in August by the king's players for nine days continuously, and excited unparalleled interest: persons accustomed to avoid the theatre crowded to see the protestant play, and the nine performances are said to have produced 1,500*l.* It is significant that

James first heard of the matter from the Spanish ambassador, who complained of a 'very scandalous comedy acted publickly by the king's players,' in which they brought on the stage 'in a rude and dishonourable fashion' both the two kings themselves and Gondomar, the ambassador's predecessor, who had returned to Spain in 1622. James at once took action, and on 12 Aug. sent, through Secretary Conway, an indignant letter to the privy council requiring them to immediately summon and punish the poet and the actors. On 21 Aug. the lords replied that the players on appearing before them had produced an 'original and perfect copy' of the play duly 'seen and allowed' by the master of the revels, Sir H. Herbert. The players were accordingly dismissed with a 'round and sharp reproof,' but forbidden to act any play whatever until the king's pleasure were known, and bound over in 300*l.* bonds to appear when called for. Middleton himself did not obey the summons. The lords informed the king that the poet was 'one Middleton who, shifting out of the way, and not attending the Board as was expected, we have given warrant to a messenger for the apprehending of him.' The search was apparently not at once successful, and on 27 Aug. a warrant was issued to bring Middleton's son Edward, a youth of twenty, before the board. On 30 Aug. he accordingly appeared and his indemnity was formally recognised. A tradition, preserved in a manuscript note by a contemporary hand in Dyce's copy of the play, records that Middleton himself was 'committed to prisson, where hee lay some Tyme, and at last gott oute upon this petition presented to King James'—(six verses follow); but as the 'chief actors' are said to have been likewise imprisoned, which the official documents show was not the case, this statement cannot be relied on. Moreover, the king's resentment had rapidly cooled, and already on 27 Aug. the lord chamberlain wrote to the lord president of the council intimating that 'in consideration of those his poor servants, his Majesty would have their Lordships connive at any common play lycensed by authority, that they shall act as before.' The lords were, it is true, directed to proceed with their investigations into 'the originall roote of this offence;' but it is evident that the inquiry was now little more than academic, and Middleton's punishment, if he suffered any, was probably trivial.

Of the remaining three years of Middleton's life we know only that he wrote in 1626 one more pageant, 'The Triumphes of Health and Prosperity.' At Midsummer 1627 he died, probably in his house at Newington Butts, where he had lived at least four years. He was buried, according to the register of the parish church, on 4 July. Middleton married (according to pedigree in 'Visitation of Surrey,' 1623) Mary, daughter of Edward Morbeck of London, one of the six clerks of chancery, by whom he had one son, Edward, born 1604. She probably died before 1627, and Middleton married again. His second wife, Magdalen, survived him, and applied in the February after his death to the city for pecuniary aid, and received twenty nobles. She is possibly the 'Mrs. Midleton' who was buried at Newington Butts on 18 July 1628.

Of Middleton's relations to his fellow-dramatists little is known. He collaborated repeatedly with Thomas Dekker [q. v.] and with William Rowley [q. v.], in his apprentice days also with Drayton, Webster, and Anthony Munday [q. v.] To Webster's 'Duchess of Malfi' he contributed complimentary verses (1623); but he does not seem to have been highly regarded by his fellow-authors. Jonson not only alluded publicly to 'A Game at Chess' as a 'poor . . . play' (*Staple of News*, iii. 1), but spoke of Middleton himself to Drummond as a 'base fellow' (*Conversations*, § 11). Unlike his successor, Jonson, Middleton evidently gave high satisfaction in his function of 'city chronologer,' and his pageants were admired by his city patrons. He seems also to have been popular with the playgoing public both before and after the civil wars. None of his pieces is known to have failed on the stage. But before the revolution he had fallen, in common with all but one or two of his dramatic contemporaries, into a neglect from which he has been among the last to recover. This is partly due to his striking inequality. A facile and inventive writer, he could turn out an abundance of sufficiently effective work with little effort; but he had little sustained inspiration; he is very great only in single scenes. He is rather prone to repeat motives (e.g. the 'Mayor of Quinborough,' 'A Mad World,' and the 'Spanish Gipsy,' all contain variations of the play within the play); in his earlier plays the same stock types incessantly reappear, and many of them are not only gross but dull. Yet even here he habitually shows keen observation of the London world he knew, and of which he is, on the whole, the most veracious painter, avoiding both the airy extravagance of Dekker and the laborious allusiveness of Jonson. His later plays show more concentrated as well as more versatile power. His habitual occupation with depraved types becomes an artistic method; he creates characters which fascinate without making the smallest appeal to sympathy, tragedy which harrows without rousing either pity or terror, and language which disdains charm, but penetrates by remorseless veracity and by touches of strange and sudden power. While, however, his greatest triumphs are in the region of moral pathology, he could on occasion represent with great force and brilliance fresh and noble types of character, such as Captain Ager (No. 11 below), Pretiosa (No. 13), Phœnix (No. 4), and the 'Roaring Girl' (No. 10).

The writings attributed to Middleton fall into four groups: plays, masques and pageants, miscellaneous verse, and miscellaneous prose. They are enumerated in their presumed chronological order, the titles and dates being those of the first extant editions. Those of which his authorship is doubtful or improbable are marked with an asterisk.

I. Plays.—1. 'The Old Law, or A New Way to please you, by Phil. Massinger, Tho. Middleton, William Rowley,' 4to, 1656. In its present state doubtless largely revised, with the aid of Rowley, whose hand is traceable in several scenes (esp. v. 1), and probably edited by Massinger. But the first version can hardly be dated later than 1599 (cf. iii. 1), and in this version Rowley can hardly have been concerned, while Massinger is out of the question. The play, granting the farcical extravagance of its motive, is highly effective. 2. 'The Mayor of Quinborough,' a comedy, 4to, 1661. A romantic drama, crude in structure and treatment, but finely written. Like No. 1, this play can hardly have been planned later than Middleton's first period; its present state, however, also shows his mature hand. There are striking reminiscences of the 'Tempest' in iv. 3, and of 'Hamlet' in v. 1. The dumb show and chorus (perhaps suggested by 'Pericles') are borrowed from the early drama to symbolise, it would seem, the antiquity of the subject. Raynulph of Chester, i.e. Ranulf Higden [q. v.], author of the 'Polychronicon,' the 'chorus,' was the direct source of the story, as Gower in the case of 'Pericles.' The caricature of a puritan secured the revival and publication of the play after the Restoration. 3. 'Blurt, Master-Constable, or the Spaniards Night-walke,' 4to, 1602. The plot, which contains effective elements, is not quite clearly worked out. Lazarillo is a portrait in Jonson's elaborate manner; Blurt has traces of Dogberry; but the imitation is nowhere close. 4. 'The Phœnix,' 4to, 1607; 1630; licensed for the press 9 May 1607. A felicitous conception, allied both to the Jonsonian humour comedy (a virtuous critic or censor contemplating a corrupt world) and to 'Measure for Measure' (the censor being a prince in disguise), but where Jonson paints follies Middleton paints crimes. 5. 'Michaelmas Terme,' 4to, 1607; 1630; licensed for the press 15 May 1607. A lively and effective comedy of city intrigue. 6. 'A Trick to Catch the Old-One,' 4to, 1608; 1616; licensed for the press 7 Oct. 1607. A highly ingenious and well-constructed plot, the strongest of Middleton's comedies of intrigue. 7. 'The Familie of Love,' 4to, 1608; licensed for the press 12 Oct. 1607. The introduction of the familists merely serves as an opening to a comedy of intrigue of the usual kind; as a representation of manners it has no value except as it reflects the scandal of the time. The play was very successful, and probably contributed much to establish Middleton's reputation, the 'Prologue' describing the author as not yet famous, while the 'Address to the Reader' refers complacently to the applause the play had excited when new. The terms of this address hardly permit us to date the play later than 1605. 8. 'Your Five Gallants,' 4to, n. d. [1608]; licensed for the press 22 March 1608. The play 'The Fyve Wittie Gallants,' entered on the Stationers' Registers under the same date, is doubtless the same. A hasty and loosely constructed comedy of intrigue. 9. 'A Mad World, my Masters,' 4to, 1608; 1640; licensed for the press 4 Oct. 1608. 10. 'The Roaring Girle, by T. Middleton and T. Dekkar' (*sic*), 4to, 1611. Dekker is easily traced in the 'canting' scenes (v. 1), less certainly elsewhere. The original of the heroine was Mary Frith [q. v.]; Middleton, who was strong in moral pathology, has idealised her character in an unexpected and remarkable way, 'but it is the excellency of a writer to leave things better than he finds 'em' (Preface). 11. 'A Faire Quarrell, by Thomas Midleton and William Rowley,' 4to, 1617; 1622. The remainder of the first edition was issued, the same year, 'with new Additions of Mr. Chaugh's and Trimtram's Roaring . . .' The main plot is without a parallel in Middleton's plays for intensity of moral passion. But it is easier to assign it to Middleton, a man of refined sensibility who chose to deal with gross materials, than to Rowley's coarse though gifted nature. The story of Jane and the physician is apparently borrowed in part from Cinthio's 'Hecatommithi,' Novel 5 of Dec. 4 (stories of persons who fall victims to their own plots). 12. 'The Changeling, by

Thomas Midleton (*sic*) and William Rowley,' 4to, 1653. The remainder of this edition was reissued in 1668 with a new title-page, referring to its revival after the Restoration. Sir H. Herbert's 'Office-book' mentioned it as played 4 Jan. 1623 (Malone, *Shakespeare*, iii. 227). The main plot was taken from Reynolds's 'The Triumphs of God's Revenge against . . . Murther,' book i. hist. 4. The extraordinary strength of one scene (iii. 4) has given this play a reputation which as a whole it hardly deserves. This scene, however, shows in the highest degree Middleton's power of producing intense dramatic effects without the aid of sympathetic characters. The play was revived with great success at the Restoration, when it was witnessed by Pepys (23 Feb. 1661). 13. 'The Spanish Gipsie, by Thomas Midleton (*sic*) and William Rowley,' 4to, 1653; 1661. Sir H. Herbert's 'Office-book' mentioned it as acted at court 5 Nov. 1623, under the title 'The Gipsye' (Malone, *Shakespeare*, iii. 227). A significantly emphasised allusion in ii. 1 ('Yes, father, I will play the changeling') makes probable that this play was written as well as acted after No. 12. The two stories here combined (of Pretiosa and Clara) are founded upon two of Cervantes's 'Novelas Ejemplares:' 'La Jitanilla' (A) and 'La Fuerza de la Sangre' (B). The following are the principal modifications: Clara, a mere child in B, is treated with tragic dignity; of the three friends who take part in her capture, Louis is represented, with some absurdity, as engaged to her; Diego is identified with the 'soldier' (unnamed) who in A attacks Don Juan, and is wounded (in A killed) by him. The comic figure, Sancho (due probably to Rowley), is suggested by Clemente, the poet-lover in A. The Hamlet-like device of the play, by which Fernando seeks to 'catch the conscience' of Roderigo, is a characteristic addition of Middleton's. The happy ending of the gipsy story is facilitated by Carducha's confession of her treachery, and by Diego's being only wounded (in A his death is compounded for by a money payment). The time of the action is greatly contracted, and the crisis is brought about by an accident, not, as in B, to Clara's son, but to herself. The story of Alvarez is new. The treatment of the gipsy story is more humorous and vivacious, but much inferior in refined art to A; and the roystering songs bear no resemblance to the charming romances of the original. It is, however, one of Middleton's most attractive plays. 14. 'More Dissemblers besides Women,' 8vo, 1657 (with 'Women Beware Women'); licensed by Sir George Buc before May 1622, when he resigned his office. The arch-dissembler Lactantio is felicitously described by Mr. Swinburne as a 'poetic or romantic Joseph Surface.' 15. 'A Game at Chess,' 4to, n. d. [1624], three editions. There are also three early manuscript copies (British Museum, Bridgewater House, Trinity College, Cambridge). A fourth copy, stated to differ widely from the others, was in the book-market some years ago (*Works*, ed. Bullen, vii. 3), but has now disappeared. Much of the abundant detail, and some of the wit, are drawn from contemporary tracts, especially Scott's 'Vox Populi,' Gee's 'Foot out of the Snare,' and Robinson's 'Anatomy of the English Nunnery at Lisbon.' The piece does not stand high in strictly dramatic qualities: the action is thin, and to a modern reader in parts obscure, but it is written with great satiric brilliance, and abounds with telling dialogue.

The date of the following plays is conjectural: 16. 'A Chast Mayd in Cheape-side,' 4to, 1630. Said on the title-page to have been 'often acted at the Swan on the Bankside, by the lady Elizabeth her servants.' As this company was formed in 1611, and left the Swan in 1613, it has been urged that the play was composed between these years (Fleay). But it was not necessarily composed for the company, nor do we know that the company never performed at the Swan after 1613. The play belongs in character, however, decidedly to the former half of Middleton's career. No other play of his is so rich in humour extracted from situations of unvaried, but by no means insidious, grossness. 17. 'No Wit, No Help like a Woman's,' 8vo, 1657. The play, which was revived in 1638 (iii. 1) by Shirley, is assigned to 1613 by Mr. Bullen on the basis of this passage; but it is hardly safe to press the 'five-and-twenty' years there referred to. It is ingeniously contrived, with a romantic plot of classical rather than Elizabethan type. An adaptation of the play, 'The Counterfeit Bridegroom,' with some new scenes and changed names, appeared after the Restoration (4to, 1677). 18. 'Women Beware Women,' 8vo, 1657 (with 'More Dissemblers besides Women'). The main plot is adapted from the history of Bianca Capello; the minor plot is said by Langbaine (*Account of Dramatick Poets*) to be founded on a romance called 'Hyppolito and Isabella.' This is no doubt the most powerful single play of Middleton's. The main plot is worked out with great mastery, the leading characters are most vividly drawn, and, unattractive as they all are, strikingly illustrate what Middleton could achieve by sheer dramatic force. 19. 'The Witch,' first printed in 1778 from a unique manuscript entitled 'A Tragi-Coomodie called the Witch; long since acted by His Ma[tie's] Servants at the Black-friers,' which passed from the actor Griffin (*b.* 1680) through several hands to Steevens and Malone, and is now in the Bodleian Library. Much of the incident is drawn from Machiavelli's 'Florentine History,' perhaps through the medium of Belleforest, 'Histoires Tragiques,' iv. 73. The play, which is gross without being effective, derives its whole interest from certain points of contact with 'Macbeth.' The same witch-motive is in both plays, and two songs, of which the first lines only are given in 'Macbeth,' are supplied at length in 'The Witch.' It has therefore been suggested either that Middleton was responsible for the witch scenes in 'Macbeth' and for the two songs alluded to in those scenes, or that Shakespeare was a plagiarist of Middleton. But these theories may safely be rejected. The absence of any marks of date in 'The Witch' renders the question difficult, but Middleton's tragic plots belong, with no certain exception, to a period later than 'Macbeth,' and in 'The Witch' he is doubtless, as he is frequently elsewhere, an imitator of Shakespeare. The use of semi-supernatural beings is altogether alien to his realistic manner; and though his witches are largely transformed to vulgar instruments of crime, the figure of Hecate is a significant remnant of a style not his own. As for the two songs in 'The Witch' (iii. 3 and v. 2), the first lines of which are quoted in 'Macbeth' (iii. 5 and iv. 1), the quoted lines, with parts of the continuations, might certainly be allowed to Shakespeare, but Middleton was not incapable of such efforts, and on the other hand, portions of the complete songs can only be his. The whole may fairly be assigned to Middleton, and were probably foisted by stage-managers into the acting edition of 'Macbeth.' 20. 'Anything for a Quiet Life,' 4to, 1662. A not very striking play of intrigue. Mr. Bullen suspects revision by Shirley. 21. 'The Widdow, a Comedie, written by Ben. Johnson, John Fletcher, Tho. Middleton,' 4to, 1652. In a copy possessed by Dyce was a manuscript note, in an old hand, ascribing the play to Middleton 'alone.' There are signs of Jonson, or of a follower of Jonson, in act iv., but the play is no doubt mainly by Middleton.

Of several of Middleton's plays only the titles are known. Such are: 1. 'The Puritan Maid, Modest Wife, and Wanton Widow, by T. Middleton,' entered on the Stationers' Registers, 9 Sept. 1653. 2. 'The Chester Tragedy.' Middleton had also, according to Henslowe, some share in Dekker's 'Honest Whore,' pt. i. 1604; but his share was doubtless slight. A share has also been claimed for him, on grounds of style solely, in 'The Puritan,' printed 1607, 'by W. S.,' and in 'A Match at Midnight,' printed 1633, 'by W. R.' (Bullen and Fleay).

II. Pageants and Masques.—1. 'The Triumphs of Truth: a Solemnity,' &c., celebrating the mayoralty of Sir Thomas Middleton; 'Also his Lordship's Entertainment at the Opening of the New River,' 4to, 1613; two editions. 2. 'Civitatis Amor: an Entertainment,' &c., at Whitehall, on the creation of the Prince of Wales, 4 Nov. 1616, 4to. 3. 'The Tryumphs of Honor and Industry: a Solemnity,' &c., on the mayoralty of George Bowles, 4to, 1617. 4. 'The Inner Temple Masque, or Masque of Heroes, presented, as an Entertainment for many worthy Ladies, by Gentlemen of the same Ancient and Noble House,' 4to, 1619, entered on the Stationers' Registers 10 July 1619, the masque being there dated 1618. 5. 'The Triumphs of Love and Antiquity,' for the mayoralty of Sir W. Cockayn, 4to, 1619. 6. 'The World Tost at Tennis (a Courtly Masque, The Device called): As it hath been divers times Presented . . . by the Prince his Servants,' 4to, 1620. By far the most elaborate and striking of Middleton's masques. Like Jonson's later masques it shows a marked approximation to the drama. 7. 'The Sunne in Aries,' for the mayoralty of Edward Barkham, 4to, 1621. 8. 'An Invention performed for the Service of . . . E. Barkham, L. Mayor,' at an entertainment at his house, Easter 1623[2], first printed by Bullen; manuscript in 'State Papers, Domestic,' vol. cxxix. 9. 'The Triumphs of Honor and Virtue,' for the mayoralty of Peter Proby, 4to, 1622. 10. 'The Triumphs of Integrity,' for the mayoralty of Martin Lumley, 4to, 1623. 11. 'The Triumphs of Health and Prosperity,' for the mayoralty of Cuthbert Hacket, 4to, 1626.

Middleton also wrote a lost masque: 12. 'The Mask of Cupid,' performed at Merchant Taylors' Hall, 4 Jan. 1614. He likewise contributed a speech of sixty lines (Zeal) to Dekker's 'Entertainment to King James on his Passage through the City,' 15 March 1604. Ten minor entertainments—some of which were not previously printed—were published in 1621 under the title, 'Honorable Entertainments compos'de for the Seruice of this Noble Cittie. Some of which were fashion'd for the Entertainment of the Lords of his Maiesties most Honorable Privie Councell upon the Occasion of their late Royall Employment. Inuented by Thomas Middleton, imprinted at London by G.E.' A description of the work, which is believed to be unique, was communicated to the Athenæum by its discoverer, Mr. F. A. Wheeler, on 2 Oct. 1886. It was subsequently sold to an American collector.

III. MISCELLANEOUS VERSE.—1*. 'The Wisdome of Solomon Paraphrased, written by Thomas Middleton,' 4to, 1597. The preliminary address 'To the Gentlemen Readers' shows singular confidence in the work. 2*. 'Microcynicon: Sixe Snarling Satyres,' 8vo, 1599. The introductory stanzas, 'His Defiance to Envy,' are signed 'T. M., gent.;' so that, the work being confessedly unworthy of him, its authenticity rests on a slender basis. The character of the verse in these two pieces is wholly distinct. It is hardly possible to attribute both to the same writer. Mr. Swinburne peremptorily rejects Middleton's authorship of either.

IV. MISCELLANEOUS PROSE. — 1. 'The Blacke Booke,' 4to, 1604; entered on Stationers' Registers 22 March 1604; the Preface signed 'T. M.' Though only signed with initials, this and the following piece bear the stamp of Middleton far more palpably than either of the foregoing. Mr. Fleay assigns all the writings signed 'T. M.' to Thomas Moffat [q. v.], a student of physic. 2. 'Father Hubburd's Tales, or The Ant and the Nightingale,' 4to, 1604. Another edition, in which the second title precedes, and one tale is omitted, appeared in the same year. The 'Address to the Reader' is signed 'T. M.' Entered on Stationers' Registers 3 Jan. 1604. The vivid sketch of a spendthrift heir has many parallels in Middleton's plays (e.g. Nos. 4 and 5). 3*. 'Sir Robert Sherley, sent Ambassador, in the name of the King of Persia, to Sigismund the Third, King of Poland,' &c., 4to, 1609. The dedication is signed 'Thomas Midleton.' A curious pamphlet, consisting mainly of translations of the complimentary speeches and poems lavished upon Sherley at the Polish court. It has some interest as a picture of Polish manners. 4*. 'The Peacemaker: or, Great Britaines Blessing,' 4to, 1618; anonymous, but described in the 'Calendar of Domestic State Papers,' 19 July 1618, as by 'Thomas Middleton.' The dramatist's authorship is very doubtful: the style is totally unlike his. Mr. Bullen supposes that the author attempts to personate the king; but there is no suggestion of this except in the prefixed address, 'To all our True-loving and Peace-embracing Subjects,' nor does the style resemble that of James. It is highly probable that this, with iii. 1, 2, and iv. 3, are due to some more obscure owner or owners of Middleton's not uncommon name. Undoubtedly genuine, however, were the lost writings before named—1, 'Annales;' 2, 'Middleton's Farrago'—which are not known to have been printed.

Middleton's works were never collected in his own day. Attention was first recalled to him by the discovery of 'The Witch' (printed 1778); but Lamb's 'Specimens' first disclosed his rare merits. In 1840 appeared the admirable collected edition of his works by Dyce. This had been long out of print when, in 1886, Mr. A. H. Bullen published what will no doubt remain the final edition, in eight volumes. Five of the best plays (Nos. 6, 12, 13, 16, 18) have been separately edited by Havelock Ellis with an introduction by Mr. A. C. Swinburne in the 'Mermaid Series' (1887).

The only known portrait of Middleton is a rough woodcut prefixed to 'Two New Plays' (i.e. Nos. 14 and 18), 1657. It is reproduced, as an etching, by Bullen, and also in the volume of the 'Mermaid Series.'

[Dyce's and Bullen's Memoirs of Middleton, prefixed to their editions; Ward's Engl. Dram. Lit. ch. vi.; Langbaine's English Dramatick Authors, and Oldys's notes; Rapp's Englisches Theater; Fleay's Shakspereana, vol. xii., and Biographical Chronicle of the English Drama; A. C. Swinburne's 'Middleton' in Nineteenth Century, January 1886, and the 'Mermaid' selection above named.] C. H. H.

MIDDLETON, SIR THOMAS (1550–1631), lord mayor of London. [See MYDDELTON.]

MIDDLETON, SIR THOMAS (1586–1666), parliamentarian. [See MYDDELTON.]

MIDDLETON, THOMAS FANSHAW (1769–1822), bishop of Calcutta, was the only son of Thomas Middleton, rector of Kedleston, Derbyshire, where he was born on 26 Jan. 1769. He entered Christ's Hospital on 21 April 1779, and became a 'Grecian.' Among his schoolfellows were S. T. Coleridge and Charles Lamb, who describes him (*Christ's Hospital Five-and-thirty Years Ago*) as 'a scholar and a gentleman in his teens,' whose manner at school was 'firm, but mild and unassuming.' Middleton was always grateful to Christ's Hospital, and shortly before his death gave a donation of 400*l.* and was elected a governor of the institution. Entering Pembroke College, Cambridge, he graduated B.A. January 1792 as fourth in the list of senior optimes. He became M.A. 1795, D.D. 1808. In March 1792 he was ordained deacon by Dr. Pretyman, bishop of Lincoln, and became curate of Gainsborough, Lincolnshire, where he edited, and in great part wrote, a weekly periodical called 'The Country Spectator.' The first number appeared 9 Oct. 1792, the last on 21 May 1793 (Mozley, *Reminiscences of Oriel, &c.* ii. 414). This periodical—an echo of Addison and Steele—attracted the attention of Dr. John Pretyman, archdeacon of Lincoln, and brother of Bishop Pretyman, and he made Middleton tutor to his sons, first at Lincoln and then at Norwich. In 1795 Middleton was presented by Dr. Pretyman to the rectory of Tansor, Northamptonshire, and in 1802 to the consolidated rectory of Little and Castle Bytham, Lincolnshire. At this time he began his well-known work on the Greek article, being incited by a controversy on this subject, in which Granville Sharp, Wordsworth, master of Trinity, and Calvin Winstanley engaged (1798–1805). The volume appeared in 1808 as 'The Doctrine of the Greek Article applied to the Criticism and the Illustration of the New Testament,' London, 8vo. It was praised in the 'Quarterly Review' (ii. 187 ff.) as a learned and useful work, and went through five editions (2nd edit. 1828, by Professor James Scholefield; 3rd edit. 1833, by H. J. Rose; 1841, 1858). In 1809 Middleton obtained a prebendal stall at Lincoln, and in 1811 exchanged Tansor and Bytham for the vicarage of St. Pancras, London, and the rectory of Puttenham, Hertfordshire. In 1812 he became archdeacon of Huntingdon. On his removal to London in 1811 he undertook the editorship of the 'British Critic' (new series), and took an active part in the proceedings of the Society for Promoting Christian Knowledge. He endeavoured, unsuccessfully, to raise funds for a new church in St. Pancras parish.

The act of 1813 which renewed the charter of the East India Company erected their territories into one vast diocese, with a bishop (of Calcutta) and three archdeacons. The number of Anglican clergy in India was very small. The bishopric, the salary of which was 5,000*l.*, was offered to Middleton. He was consecrated at Lambeth Palace on 8 May 1814, and reached Calcutta on 28 Nov. 1814. Difficulties had been prophesied with the natives on religious grounds, but the bishop's arrival and subsequent visitations created no alarm or disturbance. He found the Bible Society established at Calcutta, but declined an invitation to join it. He had a difficulty (1815) with the presbyterian ministers who were maintained by the court of directors of the East India Company. In 1815 he organised the Free School and the Orphan School at Calcutta, and in May of the same year formed a diocesan committee of the Society for Promoting Christian Knowledge, a society which, when he left England, had placed 1,000*l.* at his disposal in furtherance of its views. On 18 Dec. 1815 he left Calcutta to make his primary visitation, attended by a party of about 450 people. The whole journey was one of about five thousand miles. He had an interview with the nabob of the Carnatic at Madras, traversed Southern India, visited Bombay, Goa, Ceylon, and the Syrian Christians at Cochin. During this visitation, which ended in 1816, the bishop made no heathen converts. His view, frequently expressed, was that the 'fabric of idolatry' in India would never be shaken merely by the preaching of missionaries. He trusted rather to the general diffusion of knowledge and the arts to pave the way for Christianity. The first duty of the Anglican church was to bring the European inhabitants under its influence, and to set up a high standard of moral and religious life. About September 1820 the bishop's house was struck by lightning while the family was at dinner, but no one was injured (*India Gazette*, quoted in *Selections from the Asiatic Journal*, i–xxviii. 399).

On 15 Dec. 1820 Middleton laid the foundation-stone of Bishop's Mission College, on a site within three miles of Calcutta. The establishment of this college was the bishop's favourite scheme. The institution was to consist of a principal and professors, and of students who were afterwards to be provided for as missionaries and schoolmasters in India. On 19 April 1821 the bishop again visited Cochin to ascertain the condition of the Syrian church there, and in December held his third visitation at Calcutta. He died on 8 July 1822 of a fever, in the fifty-fourth year of his age and the ninth of his episcopate. He was buried in Calcutta Cathedral.

The Society for the Propagation of the Gospel, to which he left 500*l.* and five hundred volumes from his library, joined the Society for Promoting Christian Knowledge in subscribing for a monument to him in the nave of St. Paul's Cathedral. This memorial—a marble group by J. G. Lough—represents Bishop Middleton blessing two Indian children kneeling before him. In accordance with Middleton's will all his writings in manuscript were destroyed, including a memoir on the Syrian church. While in India he collected Syriac manuscripts and learnt Hindustani, but gave up the study of Greek. His 'Sermons and Charges' were published, with a memoir, in 1824 by Archdeacon Bonney. Middleton was a fellow of the Royal Society (elected

1814) and a vice-president of the Asiatic Society (1815).

A portrait of Middleton in his robes, engraved by T. A. Dean, forms the frontispiece to vol. i. of the 'Life of T. F. Middleton,' London, 1831, 8vo, by his friend the Rev. C. W. Le Bas. Middleton was a man of handsome and vigorous appearance; his voice was clear and sonorous, and his preaching impressive. Kaye (*Christianity in India*, pp. 312–14) calls him 'a cold and stately formalist' who had 'an overweening sense of the dignity of the episcopal office,' though he admits that the bishop was not actuated by personal vanity, and that the externals of religion had been too much neglected in India before his arrival. Other friends of Middleton found him stiff and proud in his manner (Mozley, *Reminiscences*, vol. ii. Addenda), though, as Charles Lamb expressed it, the 'regni novitas'—the new and imperfectly defined position of the first Anglican bishop of India—perhaps justified his high carriage. As an organiser he was cautious, able, and active, and his successor, Reginald Heber [q. v.], was not a little indebted to him. Some favourite common-sense maxims of Middleton's are collected in the 'Life' by Le Bas, i. 60, 61.

Middleton married in 1797 Elizabeth, eldest daughter of John Maddison of Alvingham, Lincolnshire. His wife survived him, but there were no children of the marriage.

[Life of Middleton by Le Bas; Notes and Queries, 8th ser. v. 285; authorities cited.] W. W.

MIDDLETON, WILLIAM of (*d.* 1261), Franciscan. [See Meliton.]

MIDDLETON or MYDDYLTON, WILLIAM (*fl.* 1541–1547), printer, worked at the sign of the George, next to St. Dunstan's Church in Fleet Street, London. He succeeded to the press which had belonged successively to Richard Pynson [q.v.] and to Robert Redman [q. v.], and which had been carried on after the death of the latter, in October 1540, by his widow, Elizabeth Pickering, until her marriage with Ralph Cholmondeley in 1541. Like his predecessors, Middleton confined himself almost entirely to the production of learned works. The earliest dated books which issued from his press were Richard Whitforde's 'Dyuers holy instrucyons and teachynges very necessarye for the helth of mannes soule,' and the 'Perutilis Tractatus' of John Perkins, a law book in Norman-French, both printed in 1541. About 1542 he printed in folio 'The great boke of statutes cōteynyng all the statutes made in the parlyamentes from the begynnynge of the fyrst yere of the raigne of kynge Edwarde the thyrde tyll the begynnyng of the xxxiiii yere of . . . kyng Henry the viii,' as far as the end of the twenty-first year of Henry VIII, the volume being completed with the acts of the subsequent sessions printed annually by the king's printer, Berthelet. Many other law books issued from his press, including 'The greate abbrydgement of all ye statutes of Englāde,' 1542, Saint Germain's 'Dialogues in English between a Doctor of Divinity and a Student in the Laws of England,' 1543, 'Carta Feodi,' 1543, 'Returna Brevium,' 1543, Littleton's 'Tenures,' 1544, 'Natura Brevium,' 1544, 'Manner of Keeping a Court Baron,' 1544, 'Institutions of the Laws of England,' 1544 and 1547, 'Office of Sheriffs,' 1545, and the 'Book for a Justice of Peace,' and two editions of Sir Anthony Fitzherbert's 'Book of Surveying,' without date. He printed also some medical books, among which were the 'Treasure of Poor Men,' 1543, 'The Seeing of Urines,' 1544, an 'Herbal,' 1546, Carey's 'Hammer for the Stone,' 1546, Borde's 'Breviary of Health,' 1547, and Moulton's 'Mirror or Glass of Health,' undated. Among miscellaneous works his chief productions were the 'Chronycle of Yeres,' 1544, Robert Whittington's translation of the three treatises of Seneca, 'The Form and Rule of Honest Living,' 1546, 'The Mirror or Glass of Manners,' 1547, and 'Remedyes agaynst all casuall chaunces,' 1547, Richard Smythe's 'Defence of the Mass,' 1547, Erasmus's 'Flores Sententiarum,' 1547, and Æsop's 'Fables,' Taverner's 'Garden of Wisdom,' Gosynhyll's 'Praise of all Women,' and John Heywood's 'Foure PP.,' without date. He also reprinted twice in folio the first volume of Pynson's edition of Lord Berners's translation of Froissart's 'Chronicles,' but both of his editions are undated.

Middleton used two devices. The smaller consists of a shield bearing a rebus on his name, with supporters. The larger, of which there are three sizes, has the shield with the rebus hanging from a tree, and supported by two nondescript male and female figures, having at their feet a scroll, which, in the smallest of the three devices, bears the printer's name. Henry Middleton [q. v.] was probably his son.

[Ames's Typogr. Antiq. ed. Dibdin, 1810–19, iii. 547–54.] R. E. G.

MIDDLETON, WILLIAM (1556?–1621), Welsh poet and seaman. [See Myddelton.]

MIDDLETON, WILLIAM (*d.* 1613), protestant controversialist, a native of Shropshire, matriculated as a sizar of Queens' College, Cambridge, in October 1567, proceeded B.A. in 1570–1, and was elected a fellow of his college 28 June 1572 (Searle, *Hist. of Queens' College*, pp. 324–31). The president and fellows in 1574 denied him permission to proceed to the degree of M.A. at Cambridge, and he consequently took that degree at Oxford. But his title to it was not recognised by his Cambridge colleagues, and he was deprived of his fellowship in July 1575, for not having commenced M.A. within the period prescribed by the college statutes. On appealing to Lord Burghley, chancellor of the university, he was restored to his fellowship, but not to his seniority (*Lansdowne MS.* 20, art. 76). He was incorporated M.A. at Cambridge in 1576, proceeded B.D. in 1582, and vacated his fellowship in or about 1590. For many years he held the rectory of Hardwick, Cambridgeshire. It seems that he was elected master of Corpus Christi College, Cambridge, at the end of the reign of Elizabeth, in the room of Dr. Thomas Jegon [q. v.], of whom the queen disapproved, but on the accession of King James Jegon was restored, although Middleton made a fruitless attempt to retain possession (Cooper, *Athenæ Cantabr.* ii. 446). Middleton died on 14 June 1613, and was buried in Hardwick churchyard, where a monument, with an English inscription, was erected to his memory (*Addit. MS.* 5823, f. 180).

Middleton's only known work, although he is said to have written others, is 'Papisto Mastix, or the Protestants Religion defended. Shewing briefeley when the great compound heresie of Poperie first sprange; how it grew peece by peece till Antichrist was disclosed; . . . . and when it shall be cut down and withered,' London, 1606, 4to. It is dedicated to Dr. Humphrey Tendall, master, and to the fellows of Queens' College. The work has the secondary title: 'A Briefe Answere to a Popish Dialogue between two Gentlemen; the one a Papist, the other a Protestant.'

[Addit. MS. 5876, f. 108; Blomefield's Collect. Cantabr. p. 12; Heywood and Wright's Univ. Trans. i. 177–84, 538; Prynne's Trial of Archbishop Laud, pp. 429–31; Cal. of State Papers (Dom. Eliz. 1603–10), p. 8; Tanner's Bibl. Brit. p. 526; Wood's Athenæ Oxon. (Bliss), i. 649.] T. C.

MIDGLEY, ROBERT, M.D. (1655?–1723), alleged author of the 'Turkish Spy,' has been doubtfully identified with a son of Ralph Midgley of Brerehagh in the West Riding of Yorkshire, by Frances, daughter of George Burniston of Potter Newton in the same riding. This man, born in 1653, graduated B.A. at St. John's College, Cambridge, in 1673. The alleged author of the 'Turkish Spy' seems more probably identical with another Robert Midgeley (son of Samuel Midgeley) who, born at Adel, near Leeds, was admitted a sizar of Christ's College, Cambridge, 27 June 1671, aged 16, proceeded M.B. in 1676 and M.D. in 1687, and was admitted (22 Dec. 1687) a candidate of the College of Physicians. He resided in the parish of Bassishaw, London, and was licenser of the press in 1686 and subsequent years. He died on 16 Oct. 1723. Midgley married twice; first, Isabella, daughter of George Neale, M.D., of Leeds (died 17 Feb. 1706–7 and buried in the parish church, Leeds); secondly, Mary, daughter of Admiral Sir John Cox. His nephew Robert Midgley (1684–1761), son of the Rev. Joseph Midgley of Thirsk, Yorkshire (B.A. Trinity Hall, Cambridge, 1703, M.A. in 1733), was master for fifty-three years of Coxwold free school, and author of the 'Compendious Schoolmaster,' to which his portrait is prefixed. He died on 24 May 1761, and has a monument in Husthwaite Church (Nichols, *Lit. Illustrations*, i. 767–9; *Gent. Mag.* 1761; Bromley, *Cat. of Portraits*).

For the English version of 'Plutarch's Morals' (London, 1684–1704, 8vo) Midgley translated the treatise on the cessation of oracles and Plutarch's letter of consolation to his wife. In 1687 he published 'A New Treatise of Natural Philosophy, freed from the Intricacies of the Schools, adorned with many curious Experiments, both Medicinal and Chymical, as also with several Observations useful for the Health of the Body' (London, 12mo). The same year he edited 'The History of the War of Cyprus' (a translation of Antonio Maria Graziani's Latin history of the conquest of Cyprus by the Turks). In 1689 he published a tract entitled 'Popery Banished. With an Account of their [*sic*] base Cheats, especially making the Word of God of no effect,' Edinburgh, 4to. The 'Key to Hudibras,' published by L'Estrange in 1713, is said to have been derived from Midgley.

But Midgley is chiefly remembered as the 'editor' of the celebrated 'Letters writ by a Turkish Spy, who liv'd five and forty years . . . at Paris: giving an Account . . . of the most remarkable transactions of Europe . . . from 1637 to 1682' (London, 1687–93, 8 vols. 8vo; 26th edit. 1770), the composition of the greater part of which is, on very precarious grounds, ascribed to him by Hallam (*Lit. of Europe*, 1839, iv. 554). Mrs. Manley asserted that her father, Roger Manley [q. v.], wrote the first two (and best) volumes; Dunton, in his 'Life and Errors,' asserts that the greater part of the 'Letters' were written by one

Sault, at two guineas a sheet, under the direction of Dr. Midgley, while elsewhere he insinuates that William Bradshaw [q. v.] was the real writer. Midgley certainly owned the copyright of the work previously to 27 Dec. 1693 (NICHOLS, *Lit. Anecd.* i. 413); and that he acquired it as, at least, joint author is a view in which Hallam has received vigorous support. But the theory that Midgley and Bradshaw supplemented and continued Manley, though the one generally held during the eighteenth century, will not suffer investigation (cf. Warton's note to *Pope*, and 'A Letter from W. Bishop to Dr. Charlett on the "Turkish Spy,"' in AUBREY'S *Bodleian Letters*, i. 223).

In 1684 a Genoese named Giovanni Paolo Marana published at Paris a small volume in French entitled the 'Espion Turc.' A second volume followed in 1685, a third in 1686, and a fourth at Amsterdam in 1688. The substance of these four volumes appeared in English in the first volume of the familiar 'Turkish Spy' in 1687. It is practically certain, therefore, that the first volume of the 'Letters' was composed, not by Manley, but by Marana, and it is at least very probable that the Italian was the author of the remainder of the work. This theory, which affords a solution to a perplexed question, has been ably reconciled by Bolton Corney (in the 'Gentleman's Magazine' for 1841) not only with Midgley's possession of the copyright, but with the fact that the last seven volumes appeared first in English and at London. Marana, Corney contends, met with obstacles to publication in France. In Holland, to the freer press of which country he had recourse, his work was held in little esteem. Rhodes, the publisher of the popular English translation of the first volumes, was in frequent communication with Holland, and may well have purchased the inedited manuscript of the last seven volumes. Midgley, it is suggested, advanced the purchase-money and so obtained the copyright. He employed his 'operative' Bradshaw on the translation, which he very slightly edited.

The chief permanent interest of the once popular 'Letters' is derived from the fact that they inaugurated a new species of literary composition. The similar idea of a description of England as if by a foreigner was suggested by Swift as a good and original one in the 'Journal to Stella,' and was utilised by Ned Ward and by many successors, but Montesquieu's 'Lettres Persanes' (1723) is the best classical example. Many subsequent writers, including Charles Lamb, have been under obligations to the 'Letters' (*Notes and Queries*, 1st ser. i. 334, 3rd ser. v. 260, 5th ser. xii. 353; D'ISRAELI, *Curiosities*, 1840, pp. 136–7; CIBBER, *Lives of the Poets*, 1753, iv. 4; *Gent. Mag.* 1840 and 1841 passim; *Brit. Mus. Cat.* under 'Muhammad, the Turkish Spy' pseud.)

[Thoresby's Ducat. Leod. ed. Whitaker, ii. 23, 48; Munk's Coll. of Phys. i. 476; Diary of Abraham de la Pryme (Surtees Soc.), liv. 26, 213; Gent. Mag. 1840 pt. ii. pp. 142, 260, 374, 465, 1841 pt. i. p. 151; Notes and Queries, 5th ser. xii. 353; Boswell's Johnson, ed. Birkbeck Hill, iv. 200; Dunton's Life and Errors, ii. 241, 350; Nichols's Lit. Anecd. i. 413–14, 704, iv. 72; cf. supra BRADSHAW, WILLIAM (*fl.* 1700), and L'ESTRANGE, SIR ROGER, versus finem.]

J. M. R.

MIDLETON, first VISCOUNT (1660?–1728), lord chancellor of Ireland. [See BRODRICK, ALAN.]

MIDNIGHT (MARY). [Pseudonym of NEWBERY, JOHN, q. v., and SMART, CHRISTOPHER, q. v.]

MIEGE, GUY (1644–1718?), miscellaneous writer, born in 1644, was a native of Lausanne. He was educated at the school in that town, and became an 'academist' about 1658. After studying philosophy for over two years, he left Switzerland in January 1660–1, and arriving in London in the following March, was witness of the coronation of Charles II on 23 April. For two years he served the household of the Earl of Elgin. He then obtained the post of under-secretary (in June 1663) to Charles Howard, earl of Carlisle [q. v.], ambassador-extraordinary to Russia, Sweden, and Denmark. He was absent with the embassy from July 1663 till January 1664–5. From the following April till 1668 he travelled in France at his own expense, and while abroad prepared for the press, from notes taken at the time, 'The Relation of the Three Embassies,' published anonymously in London in 1669, with the consent of the Earl of Carlisle. This appeared also in French in Rouen, 1669; Amsterdam and Rouen, 1670; Amsterdam, 1672, 1700; and, with a preface by Prince Galitzen, Paris, 1857; a German edition was published at Frankfort and Leipzig in 1701. A condensed version of the English edition was printed in Harris's 'Navigantium Bibliotheca,' London, 1705, ii. 177–213, and the account of the earl's reception in Moscow (in an abridged form) in Dumont and Roussel's 'Corps Universel Diplomatique,' Suppl. v. 648–9 (Ceremonial Diplomatique, vol. ii.)

In 1678 Miege was living in Panton Street, Leicester Fields, teaching the French language and geography. He is best known by his attempt to rival Chamberlayne's year-book, 'Angliæ Notitia' [see CHAMBERLAYNE, EDWARD], in the 'New State of England.' This he first published in London in 1691 (2nd edit. 1693; 3rd edit. 1699; 4th edit. 1701; 5th edit. 1703 and 1705; 6th edit. 1706). Miege supplied geographical descriptions of England, accounts of the inhabitants, government, religion, courts of justice, &c., with lists of the officers of church and state. The geographical portion was fuller than Chamberlayne's, but the arrangement of subjects inferior, and the lists of officers less accurate. A supplement to 'The New State,' containing an accurate description of North Britain with the Northern and Western Isles, was dated 1709. After the union of England and Scotland the work was enlarged, and the title altered to 'The Present State of Great Britain,' London, 1st edit. 1707; 2nd edit. 1711 (including a description of Ireland); 3rd edit. 1715; 4th edit. 1717; 5th edit. 1723; 6th edit. 1728; 7th edit. 1731; 8th edit. 1737; 9th edit. 1742; 10th edit. 1745; 11th edit. 1748. A French translation, 'L'État présent de la Grande Bretagne,' was published at Amsterdam in 1708 (cf. *Journal des Sçavans*, 1709, p. 801), and a German one, by J. B. Heinzelmann, 'Geist- und weltlicher Staat von Gross-Britannien und Irrland,' at Leipzig in 1718. John Chamberlayne [q. v.], who after his father's death in 1703 continued the publication of the 'Angliæ Notitia,' attacked Miege (preface to 21st edit. 1704) as the plagiarist of his father's work. Miege, who was a devoted adherent of the house of Hanover, and moreover resented Chamberlayne's slights on the dissenters, defended himself in a pamphlet, 'Utrum Horum?' in the following year. Here he assigns political motives for the appearance of his book, and points out subject matter in which he claims the priority of publication. The edition of 1718 was the last bearing Miege's name, and he probably died in that year; those of 1745 and 1748 were professedly continuations by S. Bolton.

His other published works include: 1. 'A New Dictionary, French and English, with another, English and French,' London, 1677. 2. 'A New French Grammar, or a New Method for Learning of the French Tongue,' London, 1678, 1698. 3. 'A Dictionary of Barbarous French . . . taken out of Cotgrave's Dictionary, with some Additions,' London, 1679. 4. 'A New Cosmography, or Survey of the Whole World,' London, 1682. 5. 'L'État présent de l'Europe; suivant les Gazettes et autres Avis,' London, 1682. 6. 'The Present State of Denmark,' London, 1683. 7. 'A Short Dictionary, English and French . . . French and English,' London, 1684; 3rd edit. 1690; the Hague, 1691; 5th edit. 1701, 1703; Rotterdam, 1728 (a different work from the dictionary of 1677). 8. 'Nouvelle Méthode pour apprendre l'Anglais,' London, 1685; reissued in 'Grammaire Anglaise-Française, par Miege et Boyer,' Paris, 1767. 9. 'Nouvelle Nomenclature Française et Anglaise,' London, 1685 (also published with the preceding); and reissued in 'The Great French Dictionary,' pt. i., London, 1688. 10. 'The Grounds of the French Tongue,' London, 1687; reissued in 'The Great French Dictionary,' pt. ii., London, 1688. 11. 'The Great French Dictionary,' London, 1688, a considerable portion of which was afterwards incorporated into Boyer's dictionaries. 12. 'The English Grammar,' 2nd edit. London, 1691. 13. 'A Complete History of the late Revolution' (anon.), London, 1691. 14. 'Miscellanea, or a Choice Collection of Wise and Ingenious Sayings,' London, 1694, reissued under the title of 'Delight and Pastime,' London, 1697.

He also published 'An Historical Map of the Monarchs of England, with their several Effigies,' 'which,' he states, 'has been imitated since,' and contributed largely to the English edition of Moreri's 'Great Historical, Geographical, and Poetical Dictionary,' London, 1694.

He translated into French, Gumble's 'La Vie du Général Monk,' London, 1672, 'Nouvelles Expériences . . . sur l'Eau de Mer dessalée, suivant le secret du Sieur Fitzgrald,' 1684, and 'Additions au Traité de l'Eau de Mer douce . . . avec la lettre de Mr. Boyle,' from Nehemiah Grew [q. v.]; and from French into English, 'The Ancient Sea Laws of Oleron, Wisby, and the Hanse Towns,' which was published in Malynes's 'Consuetudo vel Lex Mercatoria,' London, 1686.

[Miege's Utrum Horum? passim; Bechmann's Litteratur der älteren Reisebeschreibungen, ii. 204–6; Stück's Land und Reisebeschreibungen, p. 62; Boucher de la Richarderie's Bibl. Univ. des Voyages, i. 408; Adelung's Reisenden in Russland, ii. 336; Meiners's Vergleicherung des ältern und neuern Russlands, i. 26; Marvell's Poems, ed. Grosart, xviii.; Notes and Queries, 5th ser. ii. 475, iii. 56–7, x. 11, 7th ser. i. 123–4, 203–4, 462–4, ii. 121–2; Galitzen's preface to Trois Ambassades; Nichols's Lit. Anecd. iv. 71; Hazlitt's Collections and Notes, 1876, p. 290, and Bibl. Coll. and Notes, 3rd ser. Suppl. 1889, p. 68; Watt's Bibl. Brit.; Durey de Noinville's Table Alphabetique; Post-Boy, 30 Aug. to 1 Sept. 1698; Bodl. Libr. Cat.; Cat. of Libr. of Trin. Coll. Dubl.; Cat. of Libr. of Incorp. Law Soc.; Kayser's Bücher Lexicon; information from Arthur Irwin Dasent, esq.] B. P.

MIERS, JOHN (1789–1879), engineer and botanist, was born in London 25 Aug. 1789. His early years were spent in business with his father, John Miers, a jeweller and miniaturist, a good miniature of Robert Burns by whom is extant; but he devoted much attention to mineralogy and chemistry, and his first contributions to science were three papers, published in Thomson's 'Annals of Philosophy,' in 1814, on the composition of azote. In 1818 Lord Cochrane invited Miers to join him in developing the copper and other mineral resources of Chile, and they accordingly sent out a large quantity of machinery; and, in 1819, accompanied by his newly-wedded wife, Miers sailed for Buenos Ayres. He crossed the Pampas and the Cordilleras into Chile, and there devoted his attention to natural history. He made important observations on the geology of the Cordilleras, on earthquakes and on the rising of the coast-line, and collected birds, insects, and plants. Though not a trained botanist, by careful dissection and accurate drawing, he amassed at this time much material for his future work. In 1825 he visited England for a few months, made the acquaintance of Robert Brown and John Lindley, and began the scientific study of botany. During this visit he also prepared his first independent work, 'Travels in Chile and La Plata.' After again crossing South America he settled for some years at Buenos Ayres, where he erected a mint for the government, and then removed to Rio, where he did the same for the Brazilian government, and practised for seven years as an engineer. He returned to England in 1838, settled in London, and devoted himself to working out his botanical materials. He was elected a fellow of the Linnean Society in 1839, and in 1841 published in its 'Transactions' the first of nearly eighty papers, dealing mainly with the description of South American plants. He was elected a fellow of the Royal Society in 1843, and served as a juror in the Brazilian section of the International Exhibition of 1862, for which, and other services to Brazil, he was made grand cross of the order of the Rose. Miers died, 17 Oct. 1879, at Addison Road, Kensington. He bequeathed his fine herbarium of over twenty thousand specimens, together with his voluminous notes and numerous drawings, to the British Museum, his duplicates having been previously presented to the Kew herbarium. A lithographic portrait of Miers is prefixed to the detailed memoir of him by Mr. W. Carruthers in the 'Journal of Botany' for 1880, and a coloured photograph is preserved at the rooms of the Linnean Society. Lindley dedicated to him the genus *Miersia*, a Chilian group of plants.

Besides the 'Travels in Chile and La Plata,' 2 vols. 1825, Miers's chief works are the reissue of his various botanical papers, which were in quarto form, and were mostly illustrated by lithographs made by himself from his own drawings. Of these there are six volumes, viz.: 'Illustrations of South American Plants,' vol. i. 1850, vol. ii. 1857; 'Contributions to Botany,' vol. i. 1861, vol. ii. 1869, and vol. iii., containing his monograph of the order 'Menispermaceæ,' perhaps his most important work, 1871; and 'Apocynaceæ of South America,' 1878. Among these papers, in addition to monographs of many orders and genera, are some dealing with the structure of the seed and its importance in classification, which are of general botanical interest. In the 'Professional Papers of the Royal Engineers,' vol. v. (1842), is a 'Description of the Machinery employed in Deptford Dockyard for spinning Hemp and manufacturing Ropes,' by Miers, illustrated by seventeen double-page quarto plates of the machinery.

[Journal of Botany, 1880, pp. 33–6; Royal Society's Catalogue of Scientific Papers, iv. 382, viii. 402.] G. S. B.

MILBANKE, MARK (1725?–1805), admiral, was the third son of Sir Ralph Milbanke, fourth baronet, of Halnaby, Yorkshire, by his second wife, Anne, daughter of Edward Delavall of South Dissington in Northumberland. Sir Ralph's grandfather, Sir Mark Milbanke (*d.* 1680), had been created a baronet by a patent, dated 7 Aug. 1661, as a reward for the seasonable loans furnished to Charles II when at Breda by his father, Mark (1603–1677), mayor of Newcastle in 1658 and 1672, and a prosperous merchant there. The family, emigrants from Scotland in the reign of Elizabeth, were distinguished locally in Northumberland during the eighteenth century (notes kindly supplied by Miss Bertha Porter). Mark's eldest brother, Ralph, fifth bart. (*d.* 1798), was grandfather of Anne Isabella Milbanke, who in 1815 married Lord Byron the poet.

Milbanke entered the navy in February 1736–7 as a scholar in the academy at Portsmouth, where he remained nearly three years. He afterwards served in the Tilbury, in the Romney with Captain Thomas Grenville [q. v.], and in the Princess Mary with Captain Thomas Smith [q. v.] On 22 March 1743–4 he passed his examination, being apparently, according to his certificate, more than twenty. As his father's first wife died in October 1721 (*Add. MS.* 24121, f. 94), and Mark was the third son of the second wife, he can scarcely have been much above eighteen at the time. On 20 April 1744 he was promoted to be lieutenant of the Anglesea, and in December was appointed to the Royal Sovereign. On 13 Sept. 1746 he was promoted to the command of the Serpent sloop, and on 21 May 1748 was posted to the Inverness frigate. It was for rank only, and during the peace he was on half-pay.

In 1755 he commanded the Romney, and in July 1756 was appointed to the Guernsey of 50 guns, in which in 1758 he went out to the Mediterranean. In the summer of 1759 he was sent on a mission to the emperor of Morocco, the Guernsey being left under the command of the first lieutenant. He was thus absent from his ship in the action off Lagos on 20 Aug. He continued in the Guernsey till the peace in 1763, and then went on half-pay. In 1775–6 he commanded the Barfleur, guard-ship at Portsmouth; in 1777–8 the Princess Royal, and afterwards the Namur, till his promotion to the rank of rear-admiral of the white on 19 March 1779; one of his last important duties as captain was to sit on the court-martial on Admiral Keppel. During the following years he occasionally acted as commander-in-chief at Plymouth, in the room of Lord Shuldham (CHARNOCK, v. 508, vi. 82; BARROW, *Life of Earl Howe*, p. 139). On 26 Sept. 1780 he was advanced to be vice-admiral of the blue, and in the spring of 1782 was appointed to a command in the grand fleet under Lord Howe, with whom he took part in the demonstration in the North Sea, and afterwards in the relief of Gibraltar, and the rencounter off Cape Spartel [see HOWE, RICHARD, EARL]. From 1783 to 1786 he was port-admiral at Plymouth, and during the years 1790–1–2 was commander-in-chief at Newfoundland. On 1 Feb. 1793 he was promoted to the rank of admiral, but had no active command during the war. From 14 Sept. 1799 to 24 March 1803 he was commander-in-chief at Portsmouth. He died on 10 June 1805. He married Miss Mary Webber, and by her had a son Ralph, a captain in the navy, who retired from the active list in 1804, and died 21 Nov. 1823, and two daughters, of whom the youngest married William Huskisson [q. v.]

[Charnock's Biog. Nav. vi. 81; official letters and other documents in the Public Record Office.] J. K. L.

MILBOURN, JOHN (*fl.* 1773–1790), portrait-painter, was a pupil of Francis Cotes, R.A. He was awarded a small premium by the Society of Arts in 1764, and exhibited crayon portraits at the Royal Academy in 1772, 1773, and 1774. Two fancy subjects, 'Courtship' and 'Matrimony,' engraved by T. Gaugain from pictures by Milbourn, were published in 1789.

[Redgrave's Dict. of Artists; Royal Academy Catalogues; Premiums offered by the Society for the Encouragement of Arts, &c., 1764.] F. M. O'D.

MILBOURNE, LUKE (1622–1668), ejected nonconformist divine, was born at Loughborough, Leicestershire, and baptised on St. Luke's day, 18 Oct. 1622. He was educated at Emmanuel College, Cambridge, and graduated M.A. in 1646. He was ordained by Matthew Wren, bishop of Ely, and first settled at King's Lynn, either as curate or schoolmaster. Thence he removed to the perpetual curacy of Honiley, Warwickshire. Being a royalist, he was exposed to much molestation from Cromwell's troops, but found a retreat at Kenilworth Castle, held (1645–60) by Cromwell's officers. His plain speaking on the subject of the execution of Charles I nearly cost him imprisonment. He kept, for the rest of his life, an annual fast on 30 Jan. On the resignation of Ephraim Hewet, or Huit, who went to America, he succeeded him, apparently in 1650, in the donative of Wroxhall (then a hamlet in the parish of Honiley). It was in the gift of the Burgoyne family and worth 6*l.* 13*s.* 4*d.* per annum, but made up to 40*l.* As he could not subscribe the engagement recognising a non-monarchical government (to be taken by 23 March 1650), he expected to have to leave his place, but 'was overlooked.' He had taken the covenant, and his name occurs as Myllbourne in a list of members of the Kenilworth presbyterian classis in 1658. On the passing of the Uniformity Act (1662), he was ejected for nonconformity. He retired to Coventry, and tried to support himself by a school, and by taking boarders for the grammar school, but the authorities interfered with him. He was compelled to leave Coventry, being a corporate town, by the operation of the Five Miles Act, which came into force on 25 March 1666. He removed to Newington Green, where his wife kept a school. He died in 1668, and was buried in the churchyard of St. Michael's, Coventry; the vicar, Samuel Feake, offering interment in the chancel. He had twenty children, of whom four, including Luke Milbourne [q. v.], survived him.

[Thomas Hall's Apologia, 1658; Calamy's Account, 1713, pp. 746 sq.; Calamy's Continuation, 1727, ii. 860 sq.; Brook's Lives of the

Puritans, 1813, iii. 527; Sharp's County of Warwick, 1835, p. 88; Oakley's Kenilworth Castle, 1893.] A. G.

MILBOURNE, LUKE (1649–1720), poet, was the son of Luke Milbourne [q. v.], incumbent of Wroxhall, Warwickshire, where he was born in 1649. His mother's name was Phœbe. Educated at Pembroke Hall, Cambridge, he contributed Latin verses to 'Lacrymæ Cantabrigienses,' 1670, on the death of Henrietta, duchess of Orleans. After graduating he appears to have held chaplaincies to the English merchants at Hamburg and Rotterdam (KENNETT, *Wisdom of Looking Backwards*, 1715, p. 264). He was afterwards at Harwich, and was beneficed in the beginning of William III's reign at Yarmouth. There he associated much with Rowland Davies [q. v.], afterwards dean of Cork, and wrote a lampoon on the town, entitled 'Ostia' (DAVIES, *Journal*, Camd. Soc., passim). In 1688 he had become lecturer of St. Leonard's, Shoreditch, and in 1704 he succeeded Samuel Harris as rector of St. Ethelburga's, London. He is 'the priest of the church of England and rector of a church in the city of London' who, in a published 'Letter' (1713) to Roger Laurence [q. v.], author of 'Lay Baptism Invalid,' refuted the validity of lay baptism by the authority of Calvin and of French protestant writers. His sympathies were generally with the high church party, many of his numerous printed sermons touching upon the martyrdom of Charles I, and enforcing the duty of passive obedience. He supported Dr. Sacheverell, in whose footsteps he would have liked to follow. After listening to one of Milbourne's high-flying sermons in January 1713, Bishop Kennett asked indignantly 'why he did not stay in Holland' and 'why he is suffered to stay in England' (*Wisdom of Looking Backwards*, pp. 13, 332–3). He died in London 15 April 1720 (*Hist. Reg.* 1720; *Chron. Diary*, p. 17).

A son, Thomas Milbourne, was fellow of St. John's College, Cambridge, and died in October 1743.

Milbourne is chiefly remembered on account of his strictures on Dryden's translation of 'Virgil,' and of the retaliation made upon him both by Dryden, and by Pope in Dryden's behalf. Milbourne attempted an English rendering of Virgil before Dryden. According to an advertisement at the close of 'The Comparison of Pindar and Horace: written in French by M. Blondel, Master in Mathematics to the Dauphin. English'd by Sir Edward Sherburn,' and published in 1696, Milbourne had then issued 'The First Book of Virgil's Æneis made English,' 4to. No copy seems now known. Dryden's translation appeared in 1697, and its success inspired Milbourne's attack on it in his 'Notes on Dryden's Virgil, in a Letter to a Friend, with an Essay on the same Poet,' London, 1698. Here, in order to demonstrate his own superiority, Milbourne supplemented coarse criticisms by 'rickety' specimens of his own translation of the first and fourth Eclogues and the first Georgic. Dryden complained in the preface to the 'Fables' (1700) that his critic's scurrility was wholly unprovoked. One of Milbourne's avowed reasons for not sparing Dryden was that Dryden had never spared a clergyman. Dryden replied that if he had fallen foul of the priesthood he had only to ask pardon of good priests, and was afraid Milbourne's 'part of the reparation would come to little.' 'I am satisfied,' he concludes, 'that while he and I live together I shall not be thought the worst poet of the age.' The morals of Milbourne, who, according to Dryden, had lost his living for libelling his parishioners, were severely handled in a poem entitled 'The Pacificator,' 1699 (LUTTRELL, *Collection*). He was subsequently coupled with Sir Richard Blackmore [q. v.] in Pope's 'Art of Criticism' as the type of all that is contemptible in a critic.

Milbourne's other works, apart from thirty-one single sermons and some minor tracts, are: 1. 'A Short Defence of the Order of the Church of England, by a Presbyter of the Diocese of Norwich' (anon.), 1688. 2. 'Mysteries in Religion vindicated, or the Filiation, Deity, and Satisfaction of our Saviour asserted against Socinians and others, with occasional reflections on several late pamphlets, London, 1692, 8vo. 3. A metrical version of 'The Imitation of Christ,' entitled 'The Christian Pattern Paraphrased,' 1697, 8vo. 4. 'The Psalms of David in English Metre,' 1698, 12mo, which deservedly attracted no attention. 5. 'Tom of Bedlam's answer to his Brother, Ben Hoadly,' 1709, 8vo. 6. 'The Moderate Cabal, a Satyr in Verse,' 1710 (anon.) 7. 'The Two Wolves in Lamb's Skins, or Old Eli's sorrowful Lamentations over his two Sons,' 1716, 8vo. 8. 'A Legacy to the Church of England, vindicating her Orders from the Objections of Papists and Dissenters,' 2 vols. London, 1722, 8vo (posthumous).

[Colvile's Worthies of Warwickshire, p. 534; Chalmers's Biog. Dict.; Scott's Dryden, i. 394–7; Elwin and Courthope's Pope, ii. 62, 108, iv. 336; Holland's Psalmists of Britain; Johnson's Life of Dryden; Wroxhall Register; Nichols's Lit. Anecd. ii. 199; Notes and Queries, 1st ser. ix. 563, 3rd ser. x. 27; Halkett and Laing's Dict. of Anonymous Literature; Wheatley and Cunningham's London, ii. 19; a well-written letter of condolence from Milbourne to the Countess of Yarmouth on the loss of her husband in 1683 is in Add. MS. 27448, f. 237.]

MILBURG, MILDBURGA, or MILDBURH (*d.* 722?), saint and abbess, eldest daughter of Merewald, himself a saint and under-king of the Hecani, who inhabited the present Herefordshire (GREEN, *Making of England*, p. 328). Her mother, Eormenburga or Domneva, also a saint, was daughter of Eormenred, under-king of Kent and son of Eadbald [q. v.] Merewald's father was Penda, king of the Mercians. St. Mildred [q. v.] and St. Mildgith were Milburg's sisters. About 680 she built a nunnery at Winwick or Wenlock in Shropshire, and was consecrated abbess there, being the first to introduce the monastic institution into that part of England (STUBBS). While at Stoke, near Wenlock, she was in some danger from a suitor, and was saved by the sudden rising of the river Corf. She is said to have been obeyed by the geese, which she commanded to keep away from her fields, and to have performed other miracles. She died at the age of sixty on 25 June, in or about 722. Her day is 23 Feb. Her house having become forsaken and ruined, Roger of Montgomery, earl of Shrewsbury, rebuilt it about 1080 as a house of the Cluniac order. During the building of the new church the saint's burial-place was discovered either by a boy who, in running over the pavement, broke in the covering of it, or by means of a paper discovered by a workman named Raymond that contained directions as to its position. After the translation of the relics in 1101 vast numbers of people flocked to Wenlock, and many miracles were performed. Churches dedicated to St. Milburg are at Stoke and Beckbury, Shropshire, Wixford, Warwickshire, and Offenham, Worcestershire (PARKER).

[Acta SS. Bolland. Feb. iii. 394–7; Flor. Wig. Geneal. i. 259, 265 (Engl. Hist. Soc.); Will. of Malmesbury's Gesta Regum, i. 78, 267, and Gesta Pontiff. p. 306 (both Rolls Ser.); Hardy's Cat. Mat. i. 274, 275 (Rolls Ser.); Parker's Anglican Church Calendar, p. 263; Dugdale's Monasticon, v. 72; Dict. Chr. Biog. iii. 913, art. by Bishop Stubbs.] W. H.

MILDMAY, SIR HENRY (*d.* 1664?), master of the king's jewel-house, was second son of Humphrey Mildmay (*d.* 1613) of Danbury Place, Essex, by Mary (1560–1633), daughter of Henry Capel of Little Hadham, Hertfordshire (*Visitations of Essex*, Harl. Soc., vol. xiii. pt. i. pp. 252, 452). He was brought up at court, and excelled in all manly exercises. Clarendon terms him a 'great flatterer of all persons in authority, and a spy in all places for them' (*Rebellion*, ed. Macray, iv. 487–8). On 9 Aug. 1617 Mildmay, being then one of the king's sewers, was knighted at Kendal (METCALFE, *Book of Knights*, p. 171). In 1619 he made a wealthy match, through the king's good offices (*Court and Times of James I*, ii. 152), and bought Wanstead House, Essex, of the Marquis of Buckingham, where he entertained James in June of that year (NICHOLS, *Progresses of James I*, iii. 454, 483, 553). In April 1620 he was appointed master of the king's jewel-house (*Cal. State Papers*, Dom. Ser. 1619–23, p. 140), on 8 Aug. following entered Gray's Inn (FOSTER, *Register*, p. 161), and was elected M.P. for Maldon, Essex, of which he became chief steward on 20 Dec. He was chosen one of the tilters before the king on the anniversary of his accession, 24 March 1622 (NICHOLS, iv. 754). On 3 Feb. 1623–4 he was returned to parliament for Westbury, Wiltshire, and on 12 April 1625 again for Maldon, which he continued to represent in the parliament of 1627–8, and the Short and Long parliaments of 1640 (*Members of Parliament, Official Return*, pt. i.) In parliament he took part in the great debate on the foreign policy of the crown, 6 Aug. 1625, when, as a friend of Buckingham, he proposed a vote of money for completing the equipment of the fleet against Spain (GARDINER, *History*, v. 413). On 5 May 1627 the king suspended a statute of Emmanuel College, Cambridge, for the removal of fellows at the time of commencing doctors, or within one year thereafter. Mildmay being anxious, as grandson of Sir Walter Mildmay [q. v.], the founder, to maintain the statute, offered to annex five or six new benefices to the college within six years, and thus obtained its revocation (*Cal. State Papers*, Dom. Ser. 1627–8, p. 165). On 4 Aug. 1630 he was appointed a commissioner for compounding with persons selected for knighthood, and likewise a collector (*ib.* 1629–31, p. 321). In 1639 he accompanied Charles on his expedition to Scotland, and maintained an interesting correspondence with Secretary Windebanke (*ib.* 1639). As deputy-lieutenant of Essex he endeavoured in May 1640 to collect the 'conduct-money' in that county, but found the task little to his liking (*ib.* 1640, p. 163). On 21 April 1641 he voted against the bill for the attainder of Lord Strafford (*Verney Papers*, Camden Soc., p. 59).

Mildmay eventually deserted the king, and was appointed one of the committee of the commons on 9 Sept. 1641 (*Cal. State Papers*, Dom. Ser. 1641–3, p. 201; CLARENDON, i. 386). The parliament, regarding him as an important acquisition, refused, despite its ordinance, to expel him for his notorious peculation (*Declaration of the King concerning the Proceed-*

ings of this Present Parliament, 12 Aug. 1642; Clarendon, i. 228–229), and allowed him to retain his salary as master of the jewel-house (Whitelocke, *Memorials*, ed. 1732, p. 106). He made himself useful by acting as master of the ceremonies to foreign ambassadors, and was an active committeeman for Essex (*ib.* pp. 80, 518, 681). In November 1643 he got into trouble with parliament by saying of Philip, lord Wharton [q. v.], who had raised a regiment for the parliamentary service (*Cal. State Papers*, 1642–44, p. 366) and subsequently became a member of the council of state (*ib.* 1644, p. 561), 'that he had made his peace at Oxon, and therefore was not fit to be entrusted with any public trust' (*Commons' Journals*, iii. 300). After endeavouring to shift the blame on Lord Murray he thought it prudent to absent himself from the house. (It was not he but a cousin Sir Henry Mildmay of Woodham Walters and Moulsham who on 17 June 1645 vainly claimed, by petition, the barony of Fitzwalter; see *Lords' Journals*, vii. 438). From 1645 to 1652 he was a commissioner for the revenue (cf. the warrants signed by him in *Addit. MSS.* 21482, 21506, and *Egerton MS.* 2159). By reason of his wealth Mildmay was one of the hostages left with the Scots in December 1646 (Whitelocke, p. 230). In January 1647–8, on the debate upon the letters of the Scottish commissioners, he made a long speech in praise of Argyll [see Campbell, Archibald, first Marquis of Argyll], and moved that the latter be paid his 10,000*l.*, and the rest of the Scottish debts be continued at interest at 8 per cent. For his 'good service' in Hampshire at the trial of Captain John Burley [q. v.] he received the thanks of parliament on 2 Feb. 1647–8 (Whitelocke, p. 290; Walker, *Hist. of Independency*, edit. 1661, pt. i. p. 79). He was nominated one of the king's judges, and attended on 23 Jan. 1648–9, but abstained from signing the warrant (Nalson, *Trial of Charles I*, edit. 1684, pp. 2, 50, 52). He was a member of the councils of state elected in 1649, 1650, 1651, and 1652, and sat on the committee appointed to consider the formation of a West India Company, and the regulation of the fishing upon the British coasts (*Commons' Journals*, vi. 141, 362, 532, vii. 221). In July 1649 parliament ordered the sum of 2,000*l.* which he had lent to Charles I to be repaid him with interest from the fund accumulated by sales of cathedral lands (*ib.* vi. 264). When, in the summer of 1650, news reached London that Charles II had landed in Scotland, Mildmay, who had often been sent on a commission to inquire into the state of the late king's three younger children, suggested, as a matter of public safety, that they should be immured in Carisbrooke Castle, of which his brother Anthony was governor (Clarendon, v. 335–6; Mrs. Green, *Princesses of England*, vi. 381; Thurloe, *State Papers*, i. 158). Thenceforward he ceased to take a prominent part in affairs, though he signed the remonstrance promoted on 22 Sept. 1656 by Sir Arthur Hesilrige [q. v.] on behalf of the excluded members (Whitelocke, p. 653). When ordered, on 15 May 1660, to attend the committee appointed to consider Charles II's reception, and give an account of the whereabouts of the crowns, robes, sceptres, and jewels belonging to the king, Mildmay attempted to escape abroad, but was seized by Lord Winchelsea at Rye, Sussex, and was excepted out of the bill of pardon as to pains and penalties. On his petition he was ordered to be committed to the custody of the serjeant-at-arms instead of to the Tower. On 1 July 1661 he was brought to the bar of the House of Commons, and after evidence had been produced against him, and he had been made to confess his guilt, he was degraded from his honours and titles. He was likewise sentenced to be drawn every year on the anniversary of the king's sentence (27 Jan.) upon a sledge through the streets to and under the gallows at Tyburn, with a rope about his neck, and so back to the Tower, there to remain a prisoner during his life (*Commons' Journals*, viii. 26, 37, 38, 60, 66, 285, 286; Pepys, *Diary*, ed. Bright, i. 407, 528–9). In a petition to the House of Lords, dated 25 July, he prayed for commiseration, alleging that he was present at the trial only to seek some opportunity of saving the king's life (*Hist. MSS. Comm.* 7th Rep. pp. ix. 150). On 31 March 1664 a warrant was issued for Mildmay's transportation to Tangier, but on account of his feeble health he was allowed a servant (*Cal. State Papers*, Dom. Ser. 1663–1664, pp. 536, 561). He died, after setting out on the journey, between April 1664 and May 1665 at Antwerp (Pepys, iii. 156), where a friend had a picture taken of him as he lay dead, to confute the popular notion that no regicide could die a natural death. It is now in the possession of Sir Henry B. P. St. John Mildmay. Most of his vast accumulations were forfeited to the crown, his estate at Wanstead being granted to James, duke of York. By his marriage, in April 1619, to Anne, daughter and coheiress of William Hallyday, alderman of London, he had two sons, William (*b.* 1623), and Henry, who was admitted of Gray's Inn on 26 April 1656 (Foster, p. 277), and three daughters, Susan, Anne, and Mary. In the British Museum are Mildmay's letters to Sir Thomas Barrington in 1643 (Egerton MSS. 2643, 2647), letter to the parliamentary committee at Southampton in 1645 (Addit. MS. 24860, f. 114), and a guarantee on a loan for pay of troops in Essex in 1643 (Egerton MS. 2651, f. 146); there are also letters of his in the Tanner MSS. in the Bodleian Library (*Lords' Journals*, vols. vi. x).

[Morant's Essex, i. 30, ii. 29; Noble's Lives of the English Regicides; the Traytor's Pilgrimage from the Tower to Tyburn; Bramston's Autobiog. (Camd. Soc.), p. 28; Coxe's Cat. Cod. MSS. Bibl. Bodl. pt. iv. p. 1025.] G. G.

MILDMAY, Sir WALTER (1520?–1589), chancellor of the exchequer, and founder of Emmanuel College, Cambridge, was fourth and youngest son of Thomas Mildmay of Chelmsford, by his wife, Agnes Read. The latter was buried at Chelmsford, 5 Oct. 1557 (Machyn, *Diary*, p. 154). As commissioner for receiving the surrender of the monasteries, the father had made a large fortune. In 1540 he was granted the manor of Moulsham, near Chelmsford, and built there a fine mansion (cf. Nichols's *Progresses of Queen Elizabeth*, ii. 287). He received a general pardon from Queen Mary, 1 Oct. 1553 (*Hist. MSS. Comm.* 5th Rep. p. 307). His eldest son, Sir Thomas (*d.* 1566), auditor of the court of augmentation, which was established in 1537 for controlling the property taken by the crown from the monasteries, was grandfather of Thomas (*d.* 1626), who was created a baronet in 1611, and of Henry (*d.* 1645), who was knighted. The latter claimed, in right of his mother Frances Ratcliffe, daughter of Henry, third baron Fitz-walter, and second earl of Sussex, the barony of Fitzwalter, and his grandson Benjamin (*d.* 1679), on 10 Feb. 1670, was summoned to the House of Lords by that title. Benjamin's two sons, Charles (*d.* 1728) and Benjamin, were in succession Lords Fitz-walter, the latter being further created Viscount Harwich and Earl Fitz-walter in 1730. On his death, in 1756, the earldom became extinct and the barony fell into abeyance (cf. Burke's *Extinct Peerages*, p. 368).

Walter was educated at Christ's College, Cambridge, but apparently took no degree. He subsequently became a student of law at Gray's Inn (1546), and obtained some employment under his father in the court of augmentation. When that court was reconstituted, about 1545, he was made one of its two surveyors-general. During Edward VI's reign Mildmay extended his official connection. On 22 Feb. 1546–7 he was knighted, and on 14 Sept. following prepared, with three others, an inventory of the late king's wardrobe. Sixteen days later he was appointed a commissioner to report upon the crown revenues. In 1548 he acted on commissions for the sale of lands (March) and for the maintenance of such grammar schools as had belonged to the dissolved chantries. After the Duke of Somerset's arrest he was ordered by the privy council, 12 Nov. 1549, to examine the royal palace at Westminster, which had been in the duke's custody, and on 8 March 1550–1 to take charge of the duke's property at Sion House. He received for his services many grants of land in Gloucestershire and Berkshire, some of which he exchanged for manors in Oxfordshire and Northamptonshire; other grants in Cornwall, Essex, and London soon followed. He fixed his country residence at Apethorpe, Northamptonshire, which was granted to him in 1552, and was confirmed to him in 1556. In London he lived in the parish of Great St. Bartholomew's (cf. Strype, *Grindal*, p. 92).

Mildmay soon proved himself a skilful financier. In 1550 he was directed, together with the Earl of Warwick and Sir William Herbert, to examine the accounts of the king's mints, and in 1551 superintended the establishment of a new mint at York. In December 1551 he was a commissioner to inspect the courts which controlled the crown lands. On 2 Jan. 1552 he was commissioned to levy the king's debts; on 21 Nov. to settle with the crown accountants the effect of a fall in the value of money; in December to audit the funds belonging to the king's officers; and in that and the next year he superintended the receipt by the crown of plate, jewels, bells, and the like surrendered by dissolved monasteries or chantries. He was elected M.P. for Maldon on 1 March 1552–3, and for Peterborough on 5 Oct. 1553. Although he was a convinced Calvinist, Queen Mary's accession did not appreciably depress his fortunes, and before her death he was employed on government business. On 9 Jan. 1557–8 he was appointed treasurer of the forces sent to the relief of Calais. He was chosen to represent Northamptonshire in the parliament meeting in January 1557, and represented that constituency till his death.

Under Queen Elizabeth, with whom he regularly exchanged New-Year's gifts, his influence steadily grew. On her accession he was at once made treasurer of her household, and was appointed a member of a small committee of ways and means to supply the empty exchequer. He was soon busily employed in preparing a census of the farms of the royal revenues (22 Dec. 1558), in examining Queen Mary's grants of land, in compounding with those who refused knighthood (28 March 1559), in directing the issue of a new coinage (29 Oct. 1560), and in selling crown lands (May 1563). On 21 April 1566 Sir Richard Sackville, chancellor of the exchequer, died, and Mildmay was appointed in his stead. He was also made auditor of the duchy of Lancaster. Busily occupied in the duties of his offices till his death, he concerned himself little with general politics. As the brother-in-law of Walsingham and the friend of Cecil, he was, however, always heard with attention in the privy council, the Star-chamber, and in parliament. He used what influence he possessed to shield the puritans from the attacks of the bishops, and often urged the queen to intervene on behalf of the protestants in the Low Countries (cf. his discourse in *Cott. MS.* Calig. C. ix. 49). In his speeches in parliament he argued that a liberal grant of subsidies placed the government under an obligation to redress grievances, and thus identified himself with the popular party in the commons.

In 1572 he helped to prepare evidence against the Duke of Norfolk, who, nevertheless, after his condemnation gave him some rich jewels. The affairs of Mary Queen of Scots occasionally occupied his attention. When she arrived in England in 1567 he strongly advised her detention (cf. his opinion in Burnet's *Reformation*, pt. ii. bk. iii. No. xii.) In October 1577 he and Cecil visited her at Chatsworth, after she had announced that she had important secrets to reveal to Elizabeth. In 1586 he went to Fotheringay and informed her of her forthcoming trial, in which he took part as one of the special commissioners. In March 1587 he urged the condemnation of William Davison [q. v.] in the Star-chamber. Although four times nominated an ambassador to Scotland, in 1565, 1580, 1582, and 1583, he was on each occasion detained at home, but when his name was suggested for the office in 1589, James VI expressed great readiness to receive him. Mildmay's illness, however, brought the suggestion to nothing. He died at Hackney on 31 May 1589, and was buried beside his wife in the church of St. Bartholomew the Great in London, where an elaborate monument still exists to his memory. 'The marble panelling and gilded mouldings produce a gorgeous effect.' The decorations are heraldic, but the Latin epitaph merely records names and dates. The tomb was restored in 1865 by Henry Bingham Mildmay, esq. (Norman Moore, *The Church of St. Bartholomew the Great*, pp. 41–2). Epitaphs on Mildmay and Sir John Calthrop were licensed by the Stationers' Company on 29 July 1589. They are not known to be extant.

Mildmay was a man of cultivation and of great piety, with some popular reputation as a believer in second sight. Henry Cæsar [q. v.], dean of Ely, was directed by the Star-chamber to retract a report that he had circulated to the effect that Mildmay had endeavoured to see by conjuration the person of Cardinal Pole after his death. Henry Roberts, in his 'Fames Trumpet Soundinge,' 4to, 1589, mentions a book by Mildmay, and describes it as 'in print now extant.' It was entitled 'A Note to know a Good Man.' Sir John Harington [q. v.], in his 'Orlando Furioso,' bk. xxii. p. 175, gives a stanza in Latin with an English translation; the former he says he derived from Mildmay's Latin poems, which are not otherwise known. A 'memorial' by Mildmay, written for his son Anthony in 1570, consisting of sensible moral precepts, was printed from a manuscript at Apethorpe by the Rev. Arundell St. John Mildmay in 1893. Many of his official letters and papers are at Hatfield or in the state paper office.

His interest in education Mildmay displayed with much effect. On 23 Nov. 1583 he purchased for 550*l.* the site at Cambridge of the dissolved house of the Dominicans or Black Friars, which was situated in what was then called Preachers Street, but is now known as St. Andrews Street. Upon this land, on 11 Jan. 1583–1584 he obtained the queen's license to set up Emmanuel College. The architect was Ralph Symons, and in 1588 the new building was opened with a dedication festival, which Mildmay attended. He installed in the college a master, Laurence Chaderton [q. v.], three fellows, and four scholars; but subsequent benefactions soon increased the fellowships to fourteen and the scholarships to fifty. According to Fuller, Mildmay, on coming to court, after the college was opened was addressed by the Queen with the words: 'Sir Walter, I hear you have erected a puritan foundation,' to which Mildmay replied: 'No, madam; far be it from me to countenance anything contrary to your established laws; but I have set an acorn, which when it becomes an oak, God alone knows what will be the fruit thereof.' His statutes for the government of Emmanuel College bear date 1 Oct. 1585. They are attested by his sons, Anthony and Humphrey, John Hammond, LL.D., William Lewyn, LL.D., Thomas Byng, LL.D., Timothy Bright, M.D., and Edward Downing. Mildmay deprecated perpetual fellowships, and warned the fellows against regarding the college as 'a perpetual abode;' they were to look forward to spreading outside the knowledge they acquired within its walls (cf. *University and College Documents*, iii. 483–526; WILLIS and CLARK'S *Architectural Hist. of Cambridge*, ii. 687 sq.)

Mildmay otherwise showed his interest in education by acting as an original governor of Chelmsford School, founded in 1550–1; by giving an annuity of 52*s.* to Christ's Hospital (10 April 1556); and by bestowing 20*l.* a year on Christ's College, Cambridge (10 March 1568–1569), to be expended on a Greek lectureship, six scholarships and a preachership to be filled by a fellow of the college. He also contributed stone for completing the tower of Great St. Mary's Church, Cambridge, and he helped to found the free-school at Middleton, Lancashire.

There are three portraits of Mildmay at Emmanuel College—one with his wife. A fourth painting is at Moulsham Hall, near Chelmsford, and a fifth at Knole Park, Sevenoaks (H. N. WILLIS, *Pictures at Knole*, 1795, p. 124). There are engravings by J. Faber and E. Harding, and an unsigned plate is known.

Mildmay married Mary, daughter of William Walsingham, by Joyce, daughter of Edmund Denny, baron of exchequer, and sister of Sir Francis Walsingham. She died 16 March 1576. His children were Sir Anthony (see below); Humphrey of Danbury Place, Essex, father of Sir Henry Mildmay [q. v.]; Winifred, wife of Sir William Fitzwilliam of Gains Park, Essex; Martha, wife of Sir William Brouncker; and Christian, wife successively of Charles Barrett of Aveley in Essex, and Sir John Leveson of Kent, knight.

The eldest son, SIR ANTHONY MILDMAY (*d.* 1617), who inherited the family estate of Apethorpe, delivered an oration with much success at Peterhouse, Cambridge, when the queen visited the college 9 Aug. 1564 (NICHOLS'S *Progresses*, i. 173). He entered Gray's Inn in 1579 (*Reg.* ed Foster, p. 55). He was knighted in 1596, when he was appointed ambassador to Henry IV. 'I always knew him,' wrote Chamberlain soon after Mildmay had settled in Paris, 'to be *paucorum hominum*, yet he hath ever showed himself an honourable fast frend where he found vertue and desert' (CHAMBERLAIN, *Letters*, p. 2). The French king complained of Mildmay's ungenial manner and of the coldness with which he listened to the praises of the Earl of Essex. At an interview in March 1597 Henry ordered him out of his chamber and threatened to strike him (BIRCH, *Memoirs*, ii. 305). He returned home later in the year, and declined an invitation to resume the post in 1598. He died on 11 Sept. 1617, and was buried at Apethorpe, where an elaborate monument was erected to his memory (BRIDGES, *Northamptonshire*, ii. 425). A portrait is at Emmanuel College, Cambridge. By his marriage in 1567 with Grace (*d.* 27 July 1620), daughter and co-heiress of Sir Henry Sherington of Lacock, in Wiltshire (cf. *Cal. State Papers*, Dom. 1581–90, p. 35), he left an only child, Mary, who married Francis Fane, first earl of Westmorland, and was mother of Mildmay Fane, second earl of Westmorland [q. v.]

[Visitation of Essex (Harl. Soc.), 1612, pt. i. pp. 251, 452; Cooper's Athenæ Cantabr. ii. 51–5; Bridges's Northamptonshire, ii. 425; Strype's Annals; Froude's Hist.; Mullinger's Hist. of Cambridge University, ii. 310 sq.; Cal. of Hatfield MSS, vols. i–iv.; Hist. MSS. Comm. 10th Rep. pt. iv. (Westmorland MSS.); Hist. MSS. Comm. 5th Rep. p. 507; Wright's Elizabeth.] S. L.

MILDRED or **MILDRYTH** (*d.* 700?), saint and abbess, younger sister of St. Milburg [q. v.], was destined by her mother, Eormenburga or Domneva, to a conventual life; for Eormenburga was then abbess of a nunnery which she had built at Minstre or Minster in the Isle of Thanet, on land given to her by Egbert, king of Kent, as a wergild for her two brothers, St. Ethelbert and St. Ethelred, slain at Eastry with his consent by his counsellor Thunor (THORN ap. *Decem Scriptores*, col. 1906; SYMEON, *Historia Regum*, ap. *Opp.* ii. 3–10). Mildred, who was a girl of excellent disposition, was therefore sent to the nunnery of Chelles, about twelve miles to the east of Paris, to be instructed in ecclesiastical learning. While she was there a kinsman of the abbess Wilcoma wished to marry her; the abbess favoured his suit, and persecuted Mildred for refusing him; she shut Mildred into a hot oven, and kept her there for three hours, but Mildred came out unhurt. On another day the abbess beat her and tore out her hair. Mildred sent her mother a tress of her torn-out hair and a little psalter that she had written for her, with a request that her mother would help her. Eormenburga sent for her, but the abbess would not let her go. However, she escaped, and taking with her some precious relics that she had bought sailed for England. She landed at Ebbsfleet, and the stone on which she stepped on landing was impressed by her foot, and many were healed there. Along with seventy other virgins she became a nun of her mother's house, being blessed by Archbishop Deusdedit (*d.* 663?) [q. v.] (SYMEON), or by his successor Theodore (THORN), and succeeded her mother in the rule of the house. She is supposed to have died about 700, but this is a vague guess, and seems too early. Her festival is 13 July in the Roman calendar. She was succeeded as abbess by Eadburga, who translated her body [see under EADBURGA or BUGGA, *d.* 751]. Minster was destroyed by the Danes in 1011, and its destruction led to a dispute as to the possession of St. Mildred's body. The convent of St. Augustine's, Canterbury, asserted that the place of her burial was known to and kept secret by the people of Thanet, and that it was revealed to their abbot Elfstan, who with Canute's leave, and after the king's return from Rome, translated it to St. Augustine's. There it was more than once moved and worked miracles, the day of her deposition being kept there on 20 Feb. On the other hand, the canons of St. Gregory's, Canterbury, declared that they had the body, that it had been translated to Liming by Eadburga, a daughter of Ethelbert of Kent, and had thence been removed and given to their house by Archbishop Lanfranc. With reference to this dispute Goscelin [q. v.] wrote his 'Libellus contra usurpatores S. Mildrithæ,' and Thorn describes the history of the saint and her relics 'contra Gregorianos corpus beatæ virginis Mildredæ fallaciter usurpantes.' Parker notes churches dedicated to St. Mildred at Preston and Canterbury in Kent, two in London, and another at Whippingham, Isle of Wight, to which must be added one at Oxford now destroyed (*Anglican Church Calendar*, p. 264; WOOD, *City of Oxford*, ii. 94–7). The earliest mention of St. Mildred is, Bishop Stubbs notes, in the attestation of the privilege granted by Wihtred, king of Kent, between 696 and 716, if the document be genuine (*Ecclesiastical Documents*, iii. 240). The charters in which her name occurs, given by Thorn, Elmham, and in the 'Codex Diplomaticus,' are not perhaps sufficiently authoritative to demand references here (see BISHOP STUBBS, as below). Her life has been written by Goscelin, Thorn, and Capgrave.

[Acta SS. Bolland. July, iii. 485–96; Thorn's Chron. of St. Augustine's ap. Decem SS. ed. Twysden; Elmham (Rolls Ser.); Flor. Wig. Geneal. i. 265 (Engl. Hist. Soc.); Symeon of Durham's Gesta Regum, ap. Opp. ii. (Rolls Ser.); William of Malmesbury's Gesta Regum, i. 78, 268, and Gesta Pontiff. pp. 7, 306 (Rolls Ser.); Hardy's Cat. Mat. i. 376–84 (Rolls Ser.); Parker's Anglican Church Calendar; Wood's City of Oxford (Oxf. Hist. Soc.); Dict. Chr. Biog., art. by Bishop Stubbs, with notices of the charters bearing on the subject.] W. H.

MILES. [See also MILLES.]

MILES DE GLOUCESTER, EARL OF HEREFORD (*d.* 1143). [See GLOUCESTER.]

MILES, EDWARD (*d.* 1798), miniature-painter, was a native of Yarmouth, where he began life as an errand-boy to Giles Wakeman, a surgeon in that town. He showed a talent for drawing, which was encouraged by his master, and after receiving sufficient patronage from friends in Yarmouth, he came to London in 1771. He was introduced to and favourably received by Sir Joshua Reynolds, and copied some of his pictures. Miles quickly obtained some repute as a miniature-painter. He first lived in Tavistock Street, Covent Garden, but subsequently removed to Berkeley Street, Berkeley Square, where he obtained much aristocratic patronage. He exhibited at the Royal Academy from 1775 to 1797. In 1792 he was appointed miniature-painter to the Duchess of York, and in 1794 to Queen Charlotte, whose portrait he painted. One of his last works was a portrait of the Emperor Alexander of Russia, which was presented to the Earl of Liverpool. Miles paid frequent visits to Yarmouth, where he died in 1798.

[Redgrave's Dict. of Artists; Palmer's Perlustration of Great Yarmouth, ii. 412.] L. C.

MILES, GEORGE FRANCIS, known as FRANK MILES (1852–1891), painter, born on 22 April 1852, was sixth and youngest son of Robert Henry William Miles, rector of Bingham in Nottinghamshire, by Mary, daughter of the Rev. J. J. Cleaver (afterwards Peach); he was grandson of Philip John Miles, M.P., of Leigh Court, near Bristol. Miles studied art at home, being encouraged by his parents and family, who possessed strong artistic tendencies themselves. There are examples of their skill in art in the church at Bingham. Miles afterwards studied on the continent, and worked for some time in Wales, where he painted a picture, 'An Ocean Coast, Llangravia, Carnarvonshire,' which was well hung in the Royal Academy. He subsequently settled in London, first in Salisbury Street and later in Tite Street, Chelsea. His work soon gained repute, and several pictures found their way into the Royal Academy, one of them, 'A Flower Girl,' being purchased by the Prince of Wales. He had a good practice also as a portrait-painter, painting the Princess of Wales and other members of her family, besides such noted men as Charles Questel, J. L. Dyckmans, Nathan Hughes, and others. But he was best known for a series of pretty portrait studies of female heads, which were reproduced cheaply, and commanded an immense popularity and sale. He was a devoted student of Japanese art, and also of botany, which led him to study the flowers depicted by Japanese artists, and, by ascertaining the places whence they came, to introduce many for the first time into England. Miles was less successful as an artist in later days. He was popular in society, and was about to be married when he was afflicted by a cerebral malady, which proved incurable, and necessitated his removal to Brislington Asylum, near Bristol, on 27 Dec. 1887. A false report of his death was circulated soon after, but he lived on until 15 July 1891. He was buried at Almondsbury, near Bristol.

[Obituary notices in Nottingham Guardian, 2 March 1888, Magazine of Art, April 1888, &c.; private information.] L. C.

MILES, HENRY, D.D. (1698–1763), dissenting minister and scientific writer, was born at Stroud, Gloucestershire, on 2 June 1698. He was educated for the dissenting ministry, probably in London. His first settlement was at Lower Tooting, Surrey, where he succeeded Francis Freeman (*d.* 17 Nov. 1726), a presbyterian. Miles was at this time an independent. He was ordained in 1731. In 1737, still retaining his Tooting charge, he became assistant to Samuel Chandler [q. v.], at the Old Jewry. From this time he ranked as a presbyterian. He held the double appointment till 1744, and for the rest of his life was minister at Tooting only, having John Beesley as his assistant from 1756. In 1743 he was elected a fellow of the Royal Society, and in 1744 he received the degree of D.D. from Aberdeen. His communications to the 'Philosophical Transactions' extend from 1741 to 1753, and relate to natural history, meteorology, and electricity, in which he made new experiments. He gave important assistance to Birch in his edition (1744) of the works of Robert Boyle [q. v.] To his pulpit work, for thirty years, he devoted two days a week, rising between two and three in the morning to write his sermons. He was a friend of Daniel Neal [q. v.], and Nathaniel Lardner [q. v.], and a correspondent of Philip Doddridge [q. v.], to whom he sent some criticisms of his 'Family Expositor.' In private life he bore the character of great amiability. He died on 10 Feb. 1763. His funeral sermon was preached by Philip Furneaux [q. v.] His widow, Emma Miles (*d.* 1790), by deeds of 6 Oct. 1763 and 15 Feb. 1766, settled an endowment of 500*l.* on the ministry at Tooting, and conveyed the meeting-house to trustees for the use of dissenters of 'the presbyterian or independent denomination.' In 1880 the property became the subject of a chancery suit, which was decided on 1 March 1888 in favour of the independents.

[Furneaux's Funeral Sermon, 1763; Stedman's Letters to and from Doddridge, 1790; Wilson's Dissenting Churches of London, 1808, ii. 384; Neal's Hist. of the Puritans, 1822, i. p. xxxi; Humphreys's Correspondence of Doddridge, 1830, vol. iii; Waddington's Surrey Congregational History, 1866, pp. 312 sq.; Attorney-General v. Anderson, 1888.] A. G.

MILES, JOHN (1621–1684), founder of Welsh baptist churches. [See MYLES.]

MILES, SIBELLA ELIZABETH (1800–1882), poetess, born at Falmouth 28 Sept. 1800, was daughter of John Westby Hatfield, auctioneer in West Cornwall, who died at York 13 Jan. 1839, aged 72, by his wife Sibella, who died on 1 June 1832, aged 68. For some years previous to 1833 she kept a girls' boarding-school at Penzance, and occupied her leisure hours with the composition of poetry. On 13 Aug. 1833 she married, at Madron, Cornwall, Alfred Miles, a commander in the royal navy, who was afterwards an assistant in the hydrographic department of the admiralty, and edited two editions (1841 and 1852) of Horsburgh's 'Indian Directory.' He died at Lympston, Devonshire, 28 Nov. 1851, leaving one son, Frederick Arundel Miles, who died 3 June 1862, aged 26, and one daughter, Helen Jane Arundel Miles, a book illustrator. Mrs. Miles died at 54 South Lambeth Road on 29 March 1882.

She wrote: 1. 'The Wanderer of Scandinavia, or Sweden delivered,' in five cantos, 1826, 2 vols. 2. 'Moments of Loneliness, or Prose and Poetic Efforts,' 1829. 3. 'Fruits of Solitude,' 1831. This was dedicated to Sir R. T. Wilson, and a letter from him to her is printed in his 'Essay on Canning's Administration.' 4. 'Essay on the Factory Question' (anon.), 1844. 5. 'Leisure Evenings, or Records of the Past,' 1860. 6. 'The Grotto of Neptune,' 1864. Many of her contributions appeared in the 'Forget-me-Not' for 1825 and subsequent years, the 'Selector or Cornish Magazine,' 1826–8, the 'Oriental Herald' for 1827 and later volumes, and the 'Nautical Magazine' for 1833 onwards. Some poems in 'Original Cornish Ballads,' 1846 (pt. ii.), with the introductory essay, were by her, and she wrote the introduction to 'Te Deum, with illustrations by Helen J. A. Miles' (1877). Her lines on 'St. Michael's Mount, Cornwall,' are quoted in works on West Cornwall.

[Boase and Courtney's Bibl. Cornubiensis; O'Byrne's Naval Biog. Dict.; Ellen C. Clayton's English Female Artists, 1876, ii. 110–11.] W. P. C.

MILES, WILLIAM (1780–1860), major-general Indian army, obtained a cadetship in 1799, becoming on 6 March 1800 ensign, and on 20 March 1800 lieutenant in the 1st Bombay native infantry. He joined his regiment in 1801 at Alexandria, where it formed part of the force sent from India under Sir David Baird to join in the expulsion of the French. On settling in India he took part in operations against Baroda and in 1804 at Bhurtpore. He became captain 27 March 1815, and in the same year was made commandant of the British guard at Baroda. In 1817 he captured the fortified town of Pahlanpore, reinstating the rightful heir and acting for some years as political superintendent of the state. In 1820 he, as political agent with Colonel Barclay's expedition, concluded a treaty with the Rajah of Radhanpore. He became major 21 May 1821, and on 1 May 1824 was appointed lieutenant-colonel 1st Bombay European regiment. In 1826 he concluded a treaty with the chiefs of Suigam, in Gujerat, formerly noted freebooters, who since the treaty have been peaceful cultivators. He was subsequently resident in Kuch and political agent in Gujerat. He became brevet-colonel 1 Dec. 1829, and retired from the command of the 9th Bombay native infantry 28 July 1834. He was promoted major-general 28 Nov. 1854 and died 21 May 1860.

Miles published a translation (London, 1838) of the 'Shajrat Ul Atrak,' or genealogical tree of the Turks and Tartars, a native work, the chief merit of which is said, in the introduction, to reside in the details it furnishes of Ghengis Khan (Ceenghis Khan) and his successors. He also translated for the Oriental Translation Fund 'Ali Kirmānā' Husain's 'History of Hyder Naik,' London [1842], 8vo; and his 'History of the Reign of Tipú Sultan,' London [1844], 8vo.

[Information supplied by the India Office; Hunter's Gazetteer of India; Philippart's East India Military Calendar; Miles's own papers.]
H. M. C.

MILES, WILLIAM AUGUSTUS (1753?–1817), political writer, born 1 July 1753 or 1754, was son of Jefferson Miles, proof-master general (*d.* 1763). The boy, who was ill provided for, ran away from a school near Portsmouth 'in order to espouse the cause of Mr. Wilkes.' After travelling in America he returned to England and was appointed in 1770 to the ordnance office, but soon quarrelled with his superiors and retired, afterwards exposing in the 'Letters of Selim' the abuses of the office. In 1773 he published his 'Letter to Sir John Fielding' [q. v.], with a postscript to D. Garrick, esq., protesting against the suppression of the 'Beggar's Opera.' He thus won the friendship of Garrick, through whose influence he obtained a civil appointment in the navy. He served under Rodney in the West Indies during the American war, was in Newfoundland in 1779, and two years later was a prisoner of war in St. Lucia. Soon after his release he left the service. In August 1782 he was in Dublin, and was corresponding with Lord Temple (just appointed lord-lieutenant), with the view of obtaining political employment. Though backed by the influence of Lord Shelburne, he failed, and in January following went to the continent, settling at Seraing, near Liège, in order to economise and educate his daughter. He became intimate with two successive prince-bishops of Liège. In 1784–5 he published in the 'Morning Post' some letters (signed 'Neptune' and 'Gracchus') in support of Pitt's ministry, and condemning the Prince of Wales and his supporters. Pitt appreciated his assistance, and is said to have employed him as a confidential correspondent. The statesman's latest biographer refers to him as a 'wearisome busybody' (Lord Rosebery, *Pitt*, p. 127).

In September 1785, when on a visit to England, Miles seems to have suggested to Pitt a legacy tax (*Introduction to Correspondence on French Revolution*, note on p. 20), but at least two other persons claimed to have made the same suggestion (Rosebery, *Pitt*, p. 153 *n*). Obliged to remove to Brussels on account of the Liège revolution, he lived there through 1788, still holding confidential relations with the English foreign secretary. In 1789 he made a vain attempt to persuade Pitt to interfere in the affairs of Liège. On 5 March 1790 Miles had an interview with the prime minister, and in July was sent to Paris with a view to inducing the constituent assembly to annul the family compact with Spain. At Paris he came to know Mirabeau, Lebrun, Lafayette (whom he had met during his naval experiences in America), and other leading politicians. In April 1791 he left Paris for London. Pitt offered him a pension of 300*l.* a year for his past services, and he acted as intermediary between the agents of the French republic in London and the ministry, seeking to prevent war. In 1794 he issued a 'Letter to Earl Stanhope on his Political Conduct in reference to the French Revolution,' London, 1794, with notes and postscript, and the 'Letter to the Duke of Grafton,' in which Lafayette was defended from the charges made against him by Burke on 17 March in the House of Commons (*Monthly Review*, vol. xiv.)

In 1795 Miles published anonymously his

'Letter to the Prince of Wales on the subject of the Debts contracted by him since 1787.' This went through thirteen editions. Lord Thurlow moved in the House of Lords for the disclosure of the author's name. Unable thenceforth to obtain employment from Pitt, Miles retired to Froyle in Hampshire. In 1796, in a 'Letter to H. Duncombe, Esq., Member for the County of York,' he answered Burke's 'Letter to a Noble Lord,' the pamphlet reaching a fourth edition within the year.

Miles returned to London early in 1800, but in 1803 retired to a house lent him by his friend Charles Sturt on Brownsea (now called Branksea) Island in Poole Harbour. On the death of Pitt in 1806 he sought employment from the new ministry, and was promised the consul-generalship at Corfu, but the death of Fox prevented the fulfilment of the promise. He now busied himself in writing for the press. In the 'Independent Whig' appeared his 'Letters of Neptune' on parliamentary reform. He also wrote in favour of Burdett's candidature for Westminster in 1807, and contributed to the 'Statesman.' In July Miles obtained through Lord Moira an interview with the Prince of Wales, and in the following year published his 'Letter to the Prince of Wales, with a Sketch of the Prospect before him,' London, 1808, Appendix and notes. It was answered by William Pettmann [q. v.], writing under the pseudonym 'Philopolites.' In 1812 he removed to Hythe, near Southampton, and corresponded with Whitbread, Lord Moira, and other public men. On 23 April 1816 he started for Paris, in order to collect materials for a history of the French revolution, and stayed a month at Chateau Lagrange with Lafayette. He died at Paris on 25 April 1817. Lafayette attended his funeral.

Among Miles's numerous friends, besides those already mentioned, were Horne Tooke, Sir Alexander Ball, Sir John Warren, Andrew Saunders, and Lord Rodney; and he corresponded at different times with Goldsmith, Somers-Cocks, and Pye, the Poet Laureate. His 'Authentic Correspondence with Lebrun,' London, 1796, supplies much valuable information. To Lebrun as to Latude, the celebrated prisoner of the Bastille, he rendered pecuniary assistance. The Letters of 'Neptune' gave Thackeray some hints in the composition of his 'Four Georges,' and his 'Correspondence on the French Revolution, 1789–1817,' edited by his son Charles Popham Miles [see below] in 1890, is of considerable historical value. In addition to the pamphlets already noticed, Miles published: 1. 'Remarks on an Act of Parliament passed in Fifteenth Year of his Majesty's Reign, intituled "An Act for the Encouragement of the Fisheries carried on from Great Britain,"' London, 1779. 2. 'Cursory Reflections on Public Men and Public Measures' (written at Aschaffenburg in 1789, and translated by Lebrun). 3. 'On the Expediency and Justice of Prescribing Bounds to the Russian Empire,' 1791, in which a Suez canal was suggested (see art. in *Times*, 16 Nov. 1855); a copy is in the Imperial Library, St. Petersburg. 4. 'The Conduct of France towards Great Britain Examined.' Appendix and notes, 1793. 5. 'Letter to the Earl of Wycombe on the Present State of Ireland,' London, 1804. He was also the author of two comic operas: 'Summer Amusements, or an Adventure at Margate,' written in conjunction with Miles Peter Andrews [q. v.], and produced at the Haymarket in 1779 with music by Arnold, and 'The Artifice,' in two acts, London, 1780 (dedicated to Sheridan).

He married his first wife in 1772; she died in 1792, leaving a daughter Theodosia (*b.* 1773). In 1803 Miles married Harriet Watkinson of Bristol, who died at Monkwearmouth in 1872. By her he had five sons, of whom three entered the army; Robert Henry (lieutenant-colonel) accompanied M. de Lesseps upon his tour of inspection before the opening of the Suez Canal for traffic, and died at Malta in 1867; Frederick Alexander, translated into Oordoo Pinnock's 'Catechism of Astronomy,' commanded a battery in the Punjaub campaign, 1848–9, and died soon after his return to England; and Rawdon Muir (captain) was killed in the retreat from Cabul in January 1842. The youngest son, Thomas Willoughby, was drowned in his boyhood.

The fourth son, Charles Popham Miles, (1810–1891), divine, after attending Morpeth grammar school and serving in the East India Company's navy as a midshipman, graduated at Caius College, Cambridge, B.A. in 1838, M.A. in 1851, was ordained, in May 1838 became chaplain of the Sailors' Home, Wells Street, London Docks, held several curacies, and in 1843 succeeded Robert Montgomery as incumbent of St. Jude's, Glasgow; after a controversy in 1844 between him and his bishop (Russell of Glasgow), which led to a debate in the House of Lords (Hansard, 3rd ser. cv. 782–840), his benefice was withdrawn from episcopal jurisdiction. While at Glasgow Miles graduated M.D. From 1858 to 1867 he was principal of the Malta Protestant College, and from 1867 to 1883 rector of Monkwearmouth, where he restored the old Saxon church, and laboured with much success. In 1872 he was made hon. canon of Durham. He died when on a visit to Great

Chesterford, Essex, on 10 July 1891, and was buried there. Miles's only daughter was married to M. Richard Waddington, brother of the well-known diplomatist and statesman. He was one of the earliest fellows of the Linnean Society, and wrote a paper on 'The Marine Zoology of the Clyde,' in the 'Annual Report of the British Association.' Besides editing the correspondence of his father in 1890, he published some religious treatises and pamphlets on Scottish episcopacy.

[Manuscript Biographical Memoir (unfinished) by Rev. C. P. Miles; Correspondence of W. A. Miles on the French Revolution, 1789–1817, ed. C. P. Miles, with Introduction, 1890; Brit. Mus. Cat. The correspondence up to 1789 is unpublished. See also Biog. Dramatica, i. 512; Public Characters, ii. 778; Memoirs of Living Authors (1798), vol. ii.; Dict. of Living Authors (1816); private information; Sunderland Daily Echo, 13 July 1891; Sunderland Herald, 15 and 17 July; Newcastle Daily Journal, 15 July; Luard's Grad. Cantabr.; Brit. Mus. Cat.; private information.] G. Le G. N.

MILEY, JOHN, D.D. (1805?–1861), catholic divine, a native of co. Kildare, was born about 1805. He was educated at Maynooth and Rome, in which city he resided from 1833 to 1835, devoting himself chiefly to the study of theology and the history of the papacy. On his return to Ireland in 1835 he was appointed curate of the metropolitan parish, Dublin. He was an ardent admirer of Daniel O'Connell, and warmly defended his attitude on certain politico-religious questions, notably national education and the Catholic Bequest Bill in 1838. He attended the Liberator during his confinement in Richmond Gaol in 1844. He was greatly distressed at the rupture between O'Connell and the young Ireland party, and in December 1846 he laboured hard to effect a reconciliation between him and Smith O'Brien. With the permission of Archbishop Murray he accompanied O'Connell as his private chaplain to Italy in 1847, and by his assiduous devotion did much to alleviate his last sufferings. In obedience to O'Connell's injunction he carried his heart to Rome, and having seen it placed with impressive ceremonies in the church of St. Agatha, he returned with his friend's body to Ireland, and on 4 Aug. preached his funeral sermon in the metropolitan church, Marlborough Street. In 1849 he was appointed rector of the Irish college in Paris, and ten years later became parish priest of Bray, where he died on 18 April 1861. He was an accomplished preacher, well read in ecclesiastical history, and the author of 'Rome under Paganism and the Popes,' 1848; 'History of the Papal States,' 1850; 'Temporal Sovereignty of the Popes,' 1856; 'L'Empereur Napoléon III et la Papauté,' 1859.

[Webb's Compendium of Irish Biography; Fitzpatrick's Correspondence of Daniel O'Connell; Freeman's Journal, 7 Aug. 1847, 19 April 1861.] R. D.

MILL, HENRY (1683?–1771), engineer to the New River Company, eldest son of Andrew and Dorothy Mill, was born in 1683 or 1684. Betham (*Baronetage*, i. 175) says that he was of the family of Mill of Camois Court, Sussex, and according to his epitaph in Breamore Church, near Salisbury, he was a relative of Sir Hugh Myddelton [q. v.] It was probably owing to the latter circumstance that he obtained the appointment about 1720 of engineer to the New River Company. It is probable that he was identical with the Henry Mill who in 1706 obtained a patent (No. 376) for an improvement in carriage springs, and also in 1714 another patent (No. 395) for an apparatus 'for impressing or transcribing of letters singly or progressively one after another, so neat and exact as not to be distinguished from print, very useful in settlements and public records.' The patent contains no description of the apparatus, but it has always been regarded as the first proposal for a type-writer. The engineer's epitaph sets forth that 'his capacity [was] excellent in . . . all the branches of the mathematicks, and other liberal sciences,' and in his will, proved 6 April 1771 (P. C. C. Trevor, fol. 170), he mentions his 'private fancied toys,' a phrase which might well include models of his inventions.

The obituary notice in the 'Gentleman's Magazine' states that he erected waterworks at Northampton, and that he received the freedom of the borough in recognition of his services, but there was no regular water supply at Northampton until the present century, and the municipal records of the town show that in 1722 Henry Mill obtained his freedom by purchase. He was employed by Sir Robert Walpole to carry out the water supply for Houghton Hall, and a well sunk by him is still in use. It has the peculiarity of being provided with a flight of steps leading down to the pumps, which are said to show great ingenuity.

Mill died unmarried at his house in the Strand on 26 Dec. 1771, and he was buried in Breamore Church, near Salisbury, where there is a long epitaph to his memory. The epitaph states that he was 'aged eighty-seven,' but he is entered in the parish register as 'aged 88 years.'

[Gent. Mag. 1771 p. 46, 1779 p. 537, 1780 p. 365; epitaph in Breamore Church, copy kindly supplied by the Rev. E. P. Dew; private communications from the town clerk of Northampton and from W. Freuer, esq., Houghton Hall. The records of the New River Company were destroyed in a fire.] R. B. P.

MILL or **MILLE, HUMPHREY** (*fl.* 1646), verse writer, was probably a younger brother of Thomas Mill or Mille (1604–1650), the son of William Mille of 'Grattam,' Sussex, who matriculated at Queen's College, Oxford, 8 Dec. 1620 (*Oxf. Univ. Reg.*, Oxf. Hist. Soc. II. ii. 385; FOSTER, *Alumni Oxon.* 1500–1714, p. 1013). Humphrey published: 1. 'Poems occasioned by a Melancholy Vision. Or a Melancholy Vision upon Divers Theames enlarged . . . ,' London, 1639, 8vo. This work, which the author describes as 'the first fruits of his poore indeavours in this kinde,' is dedicated to Thomas, earl of Winchelsea. It has an engraved title by Droeshout. 2. 'A Nights Search. Discovering the Nature and Condition of all sorts of Night-Walkers; with their Associates. As also the Life and Death of many of them . . .' London, 1640, 8vo. This is dedicated to the Earl of Essex and contains commendatory lines by the author's brother, Thomas Mill, M.A., Oxford, Thomas Heywood, Thomas Nabbs, Robert Chamberlain, Richard Broome, and others. It has also an engraved title in compartments. 3. 'The Second Part of the Nights Search discovering the Condition of the various Fowles of Night. Or, the Second great Mystery of Iniquity exactly revealed . . . ,' London, 1646, 8vo. This is dedicated to Robert, earl of Warwick, and has an engraved title in compartments, one of which contains a portrait of the author, which is probably that mentioned by Granger (ii. 312).

[Corser's Collect. Anglo-Poet. pt. viii. p. 404.] G. T. D.

MILL, JAMES (*fl.* 1744), Indian colonel, devised a project for the conquest of India, and appears to have submitted it in 1744 to Francis, duke of Lorraine, husband of Maria Theresa of Austria, who at the time was commanding the imperialist army against the Turks. His scheme, which is given in the appendix to Bolt's 'Affairs of Bengal,' sets forth that the Moghul empire was overflowing with gold and silver, and had always been weak and defenceless. It was a miracle that no European nation with a maritime power had attempted the conquest of Bengal. By a single stroke infinite wealth might be acquired, which would counterbalance the mines of Brazil and Peru. The country might be conquered or laid under contribution as easily as the Spaniards conquered the naked Indians of America. A rebel subject named Aliverdi Khan had torn away the three provinces of Bengal, Behar, and Orissa from the Moghul emperor, and had acquired treasure to the amount of 30,000,000*l.* sterling. The provinces were open to the sea, and three ships with fifteen hundred to two thousand regular troops would suffice for the operation. The British government would co-operate for the sake of the plunder and the extension of their trade. The East India Company had better be left alone. No company could keep a secret, and the East India Company was so distracted as to be incapable of any firm resolution. In 1743 'James Mill, esq.,' was appointed captain and second in command of the East India Company's military in Bengal (*Gent. Mag.* 1743, p. 275). Bolt described Mill as a colonel who had served twenty years in India. The India office contains no lists of officers in the employment of the East India Company of so early a date.

[Wheeler's Early Records of British India, p. 269 et seq., on the authority of Bolt's Affairs of Bengal.] H. M. C.

MILL, JAMES (1773–1836), utilitarian philosopher, born 6 April 1773 at Northwater Bridge, in the parish of Logie Pert, Forfarshire, was the son of James Mill, a country shoemaker, by his wife Isabel Fenton, daughter of a farmer in the Kirriemuir district. The father occupied a cottage under a farmer named Barclay, whose family were afterwards friends of the son. The Fentons were supposed to have descended from a higher social position. The neighbours thought that Mrs. Mill gave herself airs on the strength of her origin, and health or temperament made her rather fastidious. She resolved to bring up her eldest son as a gentleman. He had probably shown early promise, and was certainly allowed to devote himself to study instead of following his father's trade. He was sent to the parish school, and was then and afterwards befriended by Mr. Peters, the minister of Logie Pert. He attended the Montrose academy, boarding in the town for 2*s.* 6*d.* a week. He there made friends with his schoolfellow, Joseph Hume (1777–1855) [q. v.], afterwards his political ally. He became known to Sir John Stuart (previously Belsches) of Fettercairn. Sir John, with his wife, Lady Jane (Leslie) daughter of the Earl of Leven and Melville, passed their summers at Fettercairn House, five miles from Northwater Bridge, and their winters at Edinburgh. Lady Jane Stuart was charitable, and is said to have started a fund for educating poor young men for the ministry. James Mill was recommended for the purpose by Peters. He also (the dates are uncertain) acted as tutor to Wilhelmina (*b.* October 1776), the Stuarts' only child, afterwards the object of Scott's early passion, and subsequently wife of Sir William Forbes and mother of James David Forbes [q.v.] Mill, in one capacity or other, spent much time at Fettercairn House, where both Sir James and Lady Jane Stuart became strongly attached to him, and their daughter spoke of him affectionately with 'her last breath.' The patronage of the Stuarts enabled him to study at Edinburgh instead of Aberdeen, for which his father had intended him (Mill to F. Place, 26 Oct. 1817). He entered the university of Edinburgh in 1790, at the then unusually late age of seventeen. He joined in his first session the senior classes in Greek and Latin. He heard the lectures of Dugald Stewart, and long afterwards he told Macvey Napier that neither Pitt nor Fox approached Stewart in eloquence. In 1794 he began his studies in divinity, which lasted through four winters. The library records show that he was interested in philosophy: studying Plato in addition to the ordinary Scottish authorities, and showing some knowledge of French by reading Massillon and Rousseau. He became so good a Greek scholar that in 1818 there was some talk of his standing for the Greek chair in Glasgow (Bain, p. 166), and he was always a keen student of Plato. He made few friends, and did not, like most of his many contemporaries who afterwards distinguished themselves, belong to the Speculative Society. He formed, however, a close intimacy with Thomas Thomson, the distinguished chemist, and his brother. He was licensed to preach on 4 Oct. 1798; and delivered some sermons in his own district, not, it would seem, with much success. He lived partly at home, where a corner of a room was curtained off as his study and bedroom, and held some tutorships. He appears to have been tutor in the family of a Mr. Burnet in Aberdeen; and also in the family of the Marquis of Tweeddale. There is a vague story that he gave up this position in consequence of a slight received at the dinner-table, and resolved to seek his fortunes in London. Another rumour is that he left Scotland in consequence of disappointment at not being appointed minister of Craig. At any rate he went to London in the beginning of 1802 in search of literary employment. He accompanied Sir John Stuart, who was going to attend parliament as member for Kincardineshire. Stuart procured him frequent admission to the gallery of the House of Commons, where he listened to some great debates and became an ardent politician. His friend Thomson wrote a testimonial on his behalf to be shown to John Gifford [q.v.], then editing the 'Anti-Jacobin Review.' Gifford gave him some work, and he gradually found other employment. He undertook to co-operate with Dr. Henry Hunter [q.v.] in rewriting a work called 'Nature Delineated.' One of the publishers interested in this book was Baldwin, who after Hunter's death in October 1802 changed the scheme for a periodical called the 'Literary Journal,' of which Mill became editor. He obtained the co-operation of Thomson and other friends, and the first number appeared at the beginning of 1803. It lasted for three years as a shilling weekly, and through another year a 'second series' appeared as a monthly. During 1805 and for two or three years subsequently Mill also edited the 'St. James's Chronicle.' In 1804 he published a pamphlet upon the bounties on the exportation of grain, and in 1805 a translation of Villers's 'Spirit and Influence of the Reformation of Luther.' He was thus managing to make a living, and writes at the beginning of 1804 that he has been a volunteer for six months, and spent at least twenty-one or twenty-two guineas in consequence. Professor Bain estimates his income during the double editorship at over 500*l.* a year. He therefore thought himself justified in marrying. In 1804 he became engaged to Harriet Burrow, daughter of a widow who managed a lunatic asylum, started by her husband, in Hoxton. They were married on 5 June 1805, and settled in 12 Rodney Terrace, Pentonville, in a house bought by his mother-in-law, for which he paid her 50*l.* a year.

Like many energetic young Scots, Mill managed to keep out of debt by rigid frugality; but the struggle was for a long time a severe one. The loss of his editorships left him no resource except writing articles. He was determined to write a work which might give him a more permanent position. About the end of 1806 he began with this view the composition of a history of India, and the task was far more laborious than he had anticipated. Three years spread into ten. His family was increasing, and he ultimately became the father of nine children, an oversight for which his eldest son apologises. Meanwhile, his relatives in Scotland were distressed. The mother died before his departure to England. His father was paralysed and became bankrupt through imprudence in giving security for a friend. The other son, William, died soon afterwards. The father continued to live in his house with his only other child, May, who married one of his journeymen named Greig, and carried on the business. The father died in 1808, and the Greigs were for a long time very poor, although their two sons ultimately succeeding in establishing a business. Mrs. Greig died in 1837. Her family had an impression that James Mill had not been a good brother, and that the expenses of his education had caused an unjust diminution of his sister's means. They probably exaggerated the prosperity of the brother, who was rising to a good position in English society. Letters to his friends the Barclays, given by Professor Bain, show that Mill did in fact clear off the father's debts, and contributed to his support, besides offering to help the sister's family. Considering his own great difficulties, there seems to be no ground for complaint, and Greig probably made himself disagreeable from the first. Mill was not a man to neglect his duties, but neither was he a man to confer benefits gracefully. The contributions to periodicals, by which he must have supported himself at the time, cannot be identified. He is said to have written in the 'British' and 'Monthly' reviews, and especially in the 'Eclectic,' then an organ of evangelical dissent. Brougham, who may have known him at Edinburgh, helped him in obtaining admission to the 'Edinburgh Review,' for which he wrote some articles from 1808 to 1813. About the same time he formed an important connection with Bentham. The acquaintance had begun in 1808. Mill used to walk from Pentonville to dine with Bentham in Westminster. He soon became Bentham's warmest disciple. Dumont was already known as the promulgator of Benthamism abroad; but Mill was soon his trusted lieutenant for carrying on the propaganda in England. He revised Bentham's writings and took an active part in the radical agitation of which the Benthamites formed the philosophical core. Bentham desired to have his best disciple constantly at hand. In 1810 Mill occupied the house formerly belonging to Milton and afterwards to Hazlitt, which belonged to Bentham and looked upon his garden. It proved to be unhealthy, and was abandoned after a few months. Mill could not find a house nearer than Newington Green, whence he continued his regular pilgrimages to Westminster; but in 1814 Bentham let him another house, 1 Queen Square (changed to 40 Queen Anne's Gate), for 50*l.* a year, afterwards raised to 100*l.* when Mill was able to pay the full value. Here they were immediate neighbours, and met constantly for many years. In the summer of 1809 and later years Mill spent two or three months with his family at Barrow Green House, near Oxted, Surrey, which Bentham had taken for a time; and from 1814 to 1818 the Mills stayed with Bentham at Ford Abbey, near Chard, Somerset, spending there as much as nine or ten months together. The residence with Bentham was of great importance to Mill, and probably was of some pecuniary advantage. A remarkable letter written by Mill to Bentham in 1814 (given fully in BAIN, pp. 136–40) speaks of some difference arising from one of Bentham's fanciful humours. Mill says that he has been proud to receive obligations from Bentham, although it has been 'one of the great purposes of his life to avoid pecuniary obligations,' and he has consequently lived in 'penury.' He has been a gainer by Bentham's hospitality and by the low rent of his house, though not otherwise. He proposes, however, that they should hereafter avoid the danger of too close a connection. By thus preserving their friendship Bentham will have a disciple able and anxious to devote his whole life 'to the propagation of the system.' A reconciliation must have followed; and Mill amply fulfilled his promise to spread the true faith. According to J. S. Mill, James Mill during this period supported his family by writing, while at the same time pursuing the 'History' and being the sole teacher of his children. Some unpublished correspondence with Francis Place [q. v.], whose acquaintance Mill made in 1812, illustrates this period. Place was proposing in 1814 to raise 3,000*l.* for Mill's benefit without his knowledge. The scheme fell through, partly because it was felt that Mill's independence of spirit would prevent his acceptance of the offer. Mill was clearly in great need of money; and Place seems to have made some advances on the expected profits of the 'History.' In December 1814 he was working at it from 5 A.M. to 11 P.M., as he tells Place, a statement slightly exaggerated by Mrs. Mill (see BAIN, p. 162). His ordinary day's work at Ford Abbey lasted with few interruptions from 6 A.M. till 11 P.M.; three hours, from 10 to 1, being devoted to teaching, and a couple of short walks his only relaxation. Mill's early religious opinions appear to have been finally abandoned after his acquaintance with Bentham. In previous writings he had occasionally used the language of at least a qualified belief in Christianity. He now abandoned all theology. According to J. S. Mill, the 'turning-point of his mind was reading Butler's "Analogy"' (*Autobiog.* p. 38). A report given by Professor Bain attributes the final change to his friendship with General Miranda, the South American patriot, who was in England in 1808–10, and was an ardent disciple of Bentham. Although the Bentham circle disbelieved in Christianity, its members observed a studied reticence in their writings.

Mill's scepticism did not interfere with an alliance which he formed with the quaker William Allen (1770–1843) [q. v.] Mill wrote articles for the 'Philanthropist,' published by Allen from 1811 to 1817, in which he had an opportunity of expounding Bentham's principles of law reform; supported the anti-slavery movement, and especially took an active part in the great Bell and Lancaster controversy [see BELL, ANDREW, 1753–1832, and LANCASTER, JOSEPH]. The utilitarians agreed with the dissenters in supporting the Lancasterian institution, which developed into the British and Foreign School Society. It was also taken up by the whigs and the 'Edinburgh Review.' Mill's last article (February 1813) in the 'Edinburgh' was in defence of the system. The National Society was started in November 1811, to educate the poor 'in the principles of the established church,' supported by the tories and the 'Quarterly Review,' and a bitter controversy raged for some time. Mill, with the approval of Bentham (whose 'Church of Englandism' contains a long assault on the National Society), and supported by Allen, Place, and others, resolved in 1813 to start a 'West London Lancasterian Institution' to educate all the children west of Temple Bar on unsectarian principles. A public meeting was held in August 1813 to start the scheme, and about the same time appeared anonymously Mill's 'Schools for all in preference to Schools for Churchmen only.' Many difficulties occurred; but in February 1814 an association was formed to set up a 'Chrestomathic' school for superior education on the same lines. Place thought of Mill for the mastership (PLACE, *Letters*). Bentham offered part of his garden, and wrote his treatise, the 'Chrestomathia,' to expound the principles. Mill was very active in the affair, and was supported by Romilly, Brougham, and Mackintosh; but, after many troubles, it finally dropped in 1820. The chief outcome of this movement was the foundation of the London University. It had been suggested by Thomas Campbell, the poet, to Place, who discussed the plan with Mill in 1825. Mill was a member of the first council, appointed in December 1825; and, with the support of Brougham, Joseph Hume, and Grote, was active in carrying the scheme into effect. He tried to get his friend Thomson for the chair of chemistry; John Austin and M'Culloch, both sound adherents of the school, were the first professors of jurisprudence and political economy. For the chair of philosophy he consented to the election of John Hoppus [q. v.], who, though a dissenting clergyman, believed in Hartley [see under GROTE, GEORGE].

Place, Mill's colleague in this agitation, and the great manager on the radical side in Westminster, became very intimate with Mill, and constantly consulted him in political affairs. Mill himself was an active member of the committee which brought forward Burdett and Kinnaird against Romilly in June 1818. Romilly, although a personal friend of Bentham's, was regarded as too moderate. Mill was much affected by Romilly's death on 2 Nov. following and went to Worthing to offer his help to the family. He took no part in the consequent election, in which Hobhouse, the radical candidate, was defeated by George Lamb.

Mill had meanwhile completed his 'History of India,' which appeared about the beginning of 1818. The purpose with which he had started was fully achieved. His affairs now became prosperous. The 'History' succeeded at once, and has become a standard work. Mill unfortunately left his share of the profits in the hands of the publisher, Baldwin, and though he received the interest during his life, the capital was afterwards lost to his family by Baldwin's bankruptcy. The book, though dry and severe in tone, supplied a want, and contained many interesting reflections upon social questions. He has been accused of unfairness, and his prejudices were undoubtedly strong. His merits, however, met with an unexpected recognition. Although he had condemned the shortcomings of the East India Company, and was known as a radical politician, he was appointed in 1819 to a place in the India House. The knowledge of India displayed in his book was a strong recommendation, and his friends Ricardo and Joseph Hume used all their influence on his behalf. Canning, then president of the board of control, is said to have been in his favour (BAIN, pp. 142, 185). He was appointed on 12 May 1819 'assistant to the examiner of India correspondence,' with a salary of 800*l.* a year; on 10 April 1821 'second assistant to the examiner,' with 1,000*l.* a year, Edward Strachey being first assistant; on 9 April 1823 'assistant examiner,' with 1,200*l.* a year, passing over Strachey; on 1 Dec. 1830 'examiner,' with 1,900*l.* a year, being thus at the head of the office, and on 17 Feb. 1836 his salary was raised to 2,000*l.* a year. Mill had to spend the hours from ten to four at his office, though, as business came irregularly, he had often time to spare for other employments. His son tells us, as may well be believed, that he had great influence with his superiors, and was able to get many of his opinions upon Indian policy adopted in practice. During the inquiries which preceded the renewal of the charter in 1833, Mill was examined at great length before committees of the House of Commons, his evidence upon the revenue system occupying eight days in August 1831, while in the beginning of 1832 he was examined upon the whole administrative and judicial systems. Mill also wrote the despatches in which the company stated its case in the final correspondence with the government. In spite of his dogmatic radicalism in home politics, Mill showed in this discussion that he was not prepared to apply his *à priori* method to India. His official experience had convinced him that the natives were totally unfit for self-government, and that even free trade would not produce a miraculous improvement. He showed remarkable knowledge and power in arguing the case. Mill's situation did not exclude him from continuing to take a very important though not a conspicuous share in political movements. His master, Bentham, was a recluse, difficult of access, growing old, and little acquainted with practical business. Mill therefore became the recognised head of the party. His dearest friend was David Ricardo, first known to him in 1811. Bentham said: 'I was the spiritual father of Mill, and Mill the spiritual father of Ricardo.' It was by Mill's encouragement that Ricardo was induced to publish his 'Political Economy,' and to enter parliament, and Ricardo's sudden death in 1823 affected Mill to a degree which astonished those who had only recognised his sternness. Brougham was also a warm friend of Mill; and though J. S. Mill, who regarded Brougham as a humbug, says that his father kept up the friendship on account of Brougham's powers of carrying out utilitarian principles in practice, it seems that Brougham was really able to fascinate the elder Mill. Mill certainly wrote to Brougham in terms of the warmest admiration, and declares in 1833 (Bain, p. 371), 'the progress of mankind would lose a century by the loss of you.' The Political Economy Club, founded in 1820, arose from some meetings of Mill and others at Ricardo's house for economic discussions. Mill drafted the rules, and was conspicuous from the first in the debates. In the same year he published the 'Elements of Political Economy,' which was the substance of verbal instructions given to his son John. A younger generation was now rising, which looked up to Mill as a leader. Henry Bickersteth [q. v.], afterwards Lord Langdale, was already an intimate. George Grote, John Austin and his brother Charles, William Ellis (1800–1881) [q. v.], Walter Coulson [q. v.], and others were friends of the younger Mill, who sat at the feet of the father, and were sufficiently pugnacious and dogmatic expounders of utilitarian principles. John Black [q. v.], editor of the 'Morning Chronicle,' and Albany Fonblanque [q. v.] of the 'Examiner' represented the party in the press. The 'Morning Chronicle' was for some ten years after 1817 their recognised organ. Fonblanque contributed to it under Black, and afterwards gave a general support to the same side in the 'Examiner.' Mill had been invited by Macvey Napier in 1814 to contribute to the supplement to the 'Encyclopædia Britannica,' and between 1816 and 1823 wrote a number of articles which expounded utilitarianism in the most uncompromising fashion. The most remarkable of these articles, that upon 'Government,' appeared in 1820, and is substantially a terse statement of the radical creed of the time as based upon Benthamite principles. It was regarded, says John Mill (*Autobiog.* p. 104), as a 'masterpiece of political wisdom' by the so-called 'philosophical radicals.' The essays had been twice reprinted in 1825, when Mill says that they had 'become text-books of the young men of the Union at Cambridge' (Bain, p. 292). They were reprinted again in 1828. In 1829 the essay upon 'Government' was attacked by Macaulay in the 'Edinburgh Review.' Mill took no part in the controversy which followed, although his line of reply is given in his 'Fragment on Mackintosh' (edit. 1870, pp. 275–94). He bore no grudge to Macaulay, whose appointment to the Indian council he supported, and they had friendly relations, which induced Macaulay not to reprint the articles during his life.

The starting of the 'Westminster Review' in the beginning of 1824 provided the party with an organ of their own. Mill had long discussed the plan of such a publication with Bentham, and it appears that Bentham was to have provided the funds at starting. Mill's official position prevented him from accepting the editorship, which was divided between Bowring and Southern. The first number contained an article upon the 'Edinburgh Review' by James Mill. It caused the Longmans to decline publishing the new periodical, which was undertaken by Baldwin, and it made a considerable sensation, which secured an encouraging start for the review. It was a vigorous attack upon the Edinburgh reviewers as mere trimmers, courting the favour of the aristocracy, being in fact a radical indictment of the whigs. The attack was carried on by John Mill in the second number, and the 'Quarterly Review' was assailed by James Mill in the fourth. Mill continued to write energetic articles, attacking Southey's 'Book of the Church' in January 1825, denouncing church establishments in April 1826, and in the following October discussing the 'State of the Nation' as an illustration of the incapacity of the governing classes. The review had never paid its way, and Bowring was not in favour with the Mills. Though a Benthamite, he disapproved of the religious part of the creed, and his personal attentions led to his partly superseding Mill in Bentham's favour. The review was increasingly unsatisfactory to the Mills, and James Mill did not write after 1826, except that in July 1830 he was persuaded to contribute a defence of the ballot. In 1828 the review passed into the hands of Colonel Perronet Thompson. In 1827 Mill contributed an article on parliamentary reform to the 'Parliamentary History and Review,' set up by Mr. Marshall of Leeds.

In 1822 Mill took a house at Dorking, where his family spent six months for several successive summers, while he joined them for his six weeks' holiday, and stayed from Friday to Monday. In the first of these holidays he began his 'Analysis of the Human Mind,' which was continued during successive holidays, and finally published in 1829. In 1830 Mill moved from Queen Square to a house in Vicarage Place, Church Street, Kensington. He had moved his summer residence from Dorking to Mickleham. His friends visited him there, and accompanied him on long Sunday walks. Bickersteth took a house at Mickleham, to be near him, and Brougham when chancellor drove down to see him on Sundays, and kept up an affectionate correspondence. J. S. Mill and some of his friends from the India House often joined him, and he continued to be consulted in political matters, especially during the crisis of the Reform Bill, by Place and others. His health was growing weaker, and he suffered much from gout, to which he had long been subject. He was less able to write, although after 1830 he composed the 'Fragment on Mackintosh,' the publication of which was delayed till 1835 on account of Mackintosh's death. His last writings were articles in the 'London Review,' founded by Sir William Molesworth, a recruit gained by the philosophical radicals in 1833, and virtually edited by J. S. Mill. Four articles by James Mill appeared in 1835, the most remarkable of which (in the July number) is a plan of church reform, proposing in substance the abolition of dogmas and ceremonies, and the transformation of the clergy into a body of officials paid by results, and preaching morality and natural theism. The curiously unpractical line of argument shows Mill's entire ignorance of the religious movements outside his own circle. His last writings were an article upon 'The Aristocracy' and a dialogue upon the utility of political economy in the same review for January 1836. Mill had begun to suffer from disease of the lungs, aggravated, it was thought, by the dusty three-hour journeys on the coach-top to Mickleham. In August 1835 he was seized with a hemorrhage from the lungs, and in the following June he was attacked by bronchitis, and died peacefully 23 June 1836, retaining his faculties and spirits to the last. He was buried in Kensington Church. Mill had nine children, who all survived him: (1) John Stuart [q. v.], born in 1806; (2) Wilhelmina Forbes, named after Sir John Stuart's daughter, *d.* 1861; (3) Clara; (4) Harriet; (5) James Bentham, who entered the Indian civil service in 1835, and died 1862; (6) Jane, named after Lady Stuart; (7) Henry, a young man of great promise, called by John the 'noblest and worthiest of us all,' who died of consumption at Falmouth in 1840; (8) Mary; and (9) George Grote, who entered the India House, showed much ability, and died of consumption in 1853. Four of the daughters were married, and three of them, but none of the sons, left children (see Bain, pp. 61, 333). Mill was of middle height, of well-knit figure, and nervous temperament. He had a massive forehead, projecting eyes, and an expressive and mobile face. A portrait from a drawing in possession of Mrs. Grote is prefixed to Professor Bain's 'Life.' He had a strong voice, and was singularly animated and impressive in conversation. To this power was partly due the remarkable influence which he exercised upon all who came in contact with him. His force of character is sufficiently apparent from the struggles by which he achieved independence in spite of many difficulties, and from the ardent devotion of his whole abilities to the propagation of his doctrines. His powerful though rigid and unimaginative intellect was applied to the support and extension of the positions which he shared with Bentham. In jurisprudence he did not go beyond applying the theories already taught by Bentham. His political views were equally those of his master, but his far greater powers of dealing with men enabled him to exert a more potent, direct influence upon the operations of the party, and he cast the theories into a form more immediately applicable. He was more original in the psychological inquiries, to which Bentham had contributed little, although the essential principles are taken for granted in Bentham's ethical speculations. Mill's 'Analysis' is a book of singular merit, from the terse and lucid exposition of a one-sided point of view. He was greatly influenced by Hobbes, Locke, Hume, and by the French writers, such as Condillac, Helvetius, and Cabanis; but his chief master was Hartley, whose theory of association he applied and extended. The book marks a distinct stage in the development of the empirical school, and many of J. S. Mill's logical and ethical doctrines are evidently suggested by the attempt to solve problems to which his father's answers appeared unsatisfactory. The 'Fragment on Mackintosh' is one of the most characteristic expressions of utilitarian morals. In James Mill utilitarianism showed all its most characteristic qualities. The resolution to keep to solid facts, and not to be misled by words; the attempt to treat all problems by a scientific method, the blindness to opposite schemes of metaphysical thought, and the contempt for the mystical and the sentimental apparent in all Mill's writings, explain both the attractions of the doctrine for some temperaments and the repulsion which it aroused in others. In domestic life Mill was a curious example of a man who, while resolutely discharging every duty, somehow made even his virtues unamiable. He seems to have despised his wife, and to have allowed his contempt to appear in his conversation, though in his letters he always refers to her respectfully. He spared no labour in the attempt to teach his children thoroughly, though his habitual repression of his feelings and his constitutional irritability made the task trying on both sides, and the children, though not unhappy, were never at ease in his presence. His son observes (*Autobiog.* p. 47) that he was, 'in the ancient sense of the words,' a stoic in his personal qualities, an epicurean as regarded his standard of morals, and a cynic in that he set little value upon pleasures, and thought that human life was 'a poor thing at best,' after the freshness of early years had decayed.

Mill's works are: 1. 'Essay on the Impolicy of a Bounty on the Exportation of Grain and the Principles which ought to regulate the Commerce of Grain,' 1804. 2. 'Commerce Defended: an Answer to the Arguments by which Mr. Spence, Mr. Cobbett, and others have attempted to prove that Commerce is not the source of National Wealth,' 1808. Spence replied in 'Agriculture the Source of the Wealth of Britain.' 3. 'History of India,' 3 vols. 4to, 1817; 4th edit., 9 vols. 8vo, 1848; 5th edit., ed. with continuation by H. H. Wilson, 10 vols. 8vo, 1858. 4. 'Elements of Political Economy,' 1821; 2nd edit. 1824; 3rd edit. 1826. 5. 'Analysis of the Phenomena of the Human Mind,' 1829, edited by J. S. Mill, with notes by Alexander Bain, Andrew Findlater, and George Grote, 2 vols. 8vo, 1869. 6. 'A Fragment on Mackintosh,' 1835 and 1870.

Between 1816 and 1823 Mill contributed to the supplement of the 'Encyclopædia Britannica' articles upon 'Government,' 'Jurisprudence,' 'Liberty of the Press,' 'Prison and Prison Discipline,' 'Colony,' 'Law of Nations,' and 'Education,' which were reprinted in a separate volume (n. d., see above); and others upon 'Caste,' 'Economists,' 'Beggars,' 'Benefit Societies,' 'Banks for Saving,' which were not collected. A review of the essays of Samuel Bailey [q. v.], originally contributed to the 'Westminster Review' for July 1829, was reprinted as 'The Principles of Toleration' in 1837. A full account of many of Mill's contributions to various periodicals is given in Professor Bain's 'Life of James Mill.'

[James Mill: a Biography, by Professor Bain, 1882, contains a careful account of all the facts. See also Macvey Napier's Correspondence; Life, by A. Bisset, in the Penny Cyclopædia; J. S. Mill's Autobiography; Bowring's Life of Bentham; Personal Life of G. Grote, pp. 21-5. Place's manuscripts in the British Museum have been used by Professor Bain. The writer has to thank Mr. Graham Wallas, who is preparing a life of Place, for communicating other letters.]

L. S.

MILL, JOHN (1645-1707), principal of St. Edmund Hall, Oxford, was born at Hardendale, in the parish of Shap, Westmoreland, in 1645. His father, Thomas, son of John Mill or Milln, of Banton, near Shap, was a weaver. The son was known until 1673 as Milne. Mill matriculated in the university as 'pauper puer' on 14 Oct. 1661, and entered Queen's College, Oxford, in Michaelmas term, on 18 Oct. 1661, as a batler. On 23 June 1663 he was elected tabardar of the college, to be admitted as soon as possible. He proceeded B.A. on 3 May 1666, M.A. 1669, B.D. 1680, D.D. 1681, and his distinction in classics led to his selection as speaker of the 'Oratio Panegyrica' at the opening of the

Sheldonian Theatre on 9 July 1669. He was elected fellow of his college on 17 Oct. 1670. During 1670 he was ordained and became tutor. He was also for some time chaplain to Sir William Palmer of Warden in Bedfordshire, whose daughter Priscilla, he married at Westminster Abbey on 6 May 1684. Her surname does not appear on the register; that of her mother (daughter of Sir John Bramston, 1577–1654 [q. v.]) was substituted in error. In 1676 he was chosen by Dr. Thomas Lamplugh [q. v.], on his promotion to the see of Exeter, to be his chaplain; on 29 Oct. 1677 he was made prebendary of Exeter; in August 1681 was presented by his college to the rectory of Bletchington, Oxfordshire, and about the same time became chaplain in ordinary to Charles II. Mill was a benefactor to his parish. In 1686 he was instrumental in restoring to their proper use the funds and lands of a local charity, which had been misappropriated for some years by the lord of the manor. He drew up an account of the land (glebe and other), rates, and advowson of his parish, with a copy of the original grant to the provost and scholars of Queen's College by Edward III. His manuscript is still preserved by the rector of Bletchington.

Mill vacated his fellowship at Queen's College towards the end of 1682. On the removal of Thomas Crosthwait he was elected principal of St. Edmund Hall, and was admitted on 5 May 1685. He was not popular there, and his duties were chiefly performed by his vice-principal. His political vacillations gained him the nickname of 'Johnny Wind-Mill.' Although upholding the doctrine of passive obedience and non-resistance, he disliked the practical inconveniences of turning nonjuror, and he became the subject of a jingle, sung by the children in the streets of Oxford:

> Wilt thou take the oaths, little Johnny Mill?
> No, no, that I won't, Yes but I will.

In 1694 he was proctor for the clergy of the diocese of Canterbury, in the lower house of convocation. On 14 Aug. 1704 he obtained the fourth prebend at Canterbury, and on 1 Aug. 1705 he resigned his prebend at Exeter.

Mill was seized with apoplexy on the evening of Saturday, 21 June 1707, and, without recovering consciousness, died about 7 A.M. on Monday, 23 June, exactly a fortnight after the appearance of his great work on the New Testament (cf. *Gibson MSS.* 933, f. 42, in Lambeth Palace; *Gent. Mag.* 1801, p. 587). He was buried in the chancel of Bletchington Church, where monuments to his memory and to that of his wife (who had predeceased him on 1 April 1685) are still preserved.

While principal of St. Edmund Hall, Mill continued to prosecute with diligence the great work of his life, his edition of the New Testament in Greek. To this his attention had been first directed by the Savilian professor, Dr. Edward Bernard [q. v.], in 1677; and Dr. John Fell [q. v.], who had previously recognised his abilities, placed all his own notes at Mill's disposal. The printing of the work was commenced at Fell's expense, but on his death in 1686 only fifteen sheets were completed, and the burden of carrying on the work fell on Mill, who also refunded all that Fell had laid out. Hearne at a later date gave Mill some assistance. After thirty years of labour, the work was given to the world on 9 June 1707. It was dedicated to the queen in somewhat fulsome terms, but was the most beautiful edition (fol.) that had hitherto appeared. The text, that of Stephens of 1550, was left untouched, and the various readings were added at the bottom of each page. Mill had collated many valuable manuscripts in England, and procured collations of the principal ones on the continent; the result was a masterpiece of scholarship and critical insight. Prefixed are valuable 'Prolegomena,' divided into three parts; the first treating separately of each book of the New Testament, the second containing the history of the text from the time of the apostles, and the third giving a review of his own labours.

Mill was the first editor of the New Testament who attempted to give a clear and accurate description of the manuscripts used, and was also the first to draw up a genealogy of the editions of the Greek text. The edition met with much adverse criticism. His small acquaintance with the oriental languages was the most fruitful source of error. For references to the Syriac, Arabic, and Ethiopic, he had recourse, as he avows (*Proleg.* 1707, p. clxii), to the Latin translations in Walton's 'Polyglott.' His extracts from the Coptic and Anglo-Saxon, on the contrary, were taken partly from the papers of Thomas Marshall [q. v.], and partly from the communication of Ludovicus Piques, and may be regarded as authentic.

The most famous attack on Mill was that by Dr. Daniel Whitby, who, in his 'Examen variantium lectionum J. Millii,' London, 1709, sought to show that the great number of readings (amounting it is said to over thirty thousand) endangered the authority of the printed text. This view was eagerly taken up by Anthony Collins [q. v.] in his 'Discourse of Free Thinking,' pp. 87–90. Bentley, under the pseudonym 'Phileleutherus Lipsiensis,' vigorously defended his friend Mill in 'Remarks upon a Late Discourse.' Mill's labours on 1 John v. 7, supplied a mass of material for the well-known controversy respecting the authenticity of that text (BURGESS, *Annotationes Millii;* EMLYN, *Full Enquiry*).

In the Bodleian Library is a copy of Mill's Testament, with his own manuscript additions, and some by Hearne. Many of these have been printed in Griesbach's 'Symbolæ criticæ' (i. 245–304).

In 1710 Mill's New Testament was republished in Amsterdam and Rotterdam, in 1723 at Leipzig, and again, in 1746, at Amsterdam, under the supervision of Kuster. Kuster added the readings of thirteen fresh manuscripts, supplied a preface, and inserted Le Clerc's letter on Mill's work to 'C. Junius Optimianus,' which had appeared in vol. xvi. of the 'Bibliothèque Choisie.' The first Dutch edition was regarded by Hearne as 'downright knavery,' but Kuster kept his own notes separate from those of Mill, and some of his collations are more complete. The 'Prolegomena,' with observations by Salthen, were reissued at Königsberg in 1733–4 and 1752.

To Mill are assigned 'Dissertatio de Nilo et Euphrate terræ Sanctæ Terminis,' published in Ugolino's 'Thesaurus Antiquitatum Sacrarum' (Venice, 1744), and the preface to Benson's 'Anglo-Saxon Vocabulary' (HEARNE); the latter is often attributed to Thwaites. He supervised the edition of Malala's 'Chronicle,' published at Oxford in 1690, and thus became the recipient of Bentley's famous 'Letter to Mill,' printed with the 'Chronicle.' Prefixed to a copy of Simon Ford's 'Conflagration of London,' in the Bodleian Library, are some deplorable manuscript verses addressed by Mill, when a young man, to Dr. Thomas Barlow. A large number of Mill's notes for his Greek Testament, together with letters to and from eminent men of the time, are preserved in the library of Queen's College, Oxford. Letters from Mill to H. Wanley, Dr. Covel, and Dr. Hickes, are in the British Museum (Harl. MS. 3780, ff. 97, 98, 156, 157; Addit. MSS. 4253, f. 7, 22, 910, ff. 251, 256), and one from Grabe to Mill is among the Rawlinson MSS. in the Bodleian Library (C. 851, f. 39).

Hearne, who frequently comments on Mill, gives an unpleasing impression of him as a man, though anxious to do him justice as a scholar and generous patron of scholars. According to Kennet (*Lansdowne MS.* 987, f. 187), he was 'a ready extemporare preacher,' but he only published one sermon (1676). Kennet also states that 'he talked and wrote the best Latin of any man in the University, and was the most airy and facetious in conversation—in all respects a bright man.'

Portraits of Mill are in the dining hall of St. Edmund Hall, and in the common room gallery of Queen's College. The painting by P. Berchet has been engraved by Vandergucht. There is a representation of him presenting his Greek Testament to Queen Anne in the 'Oxford Almanack' for 1747, engraved by Vertue.

[Nicolson and Burn's Westmorland and Cumberland, i. 481; Wood's Athenæ (Bliss), vol. iv. cols. 528, 757–8; Wood's Fasti (Bliss), vol. ii. cols. 289, 308, 374, 382; Wood's Antiq. Univ. Oxon. (Gutch), vol. ii. pt. ii. p. 801; Wood's Colleges and Halls (Gutch), p. 665; Hook's Eccles. Biog.; Hearne's Remarks and Collections (Doble, Oxford Hist. Soc.), passim; Le Neve's Fasti (Hardy), i. 425, iii. 594; Chamberlayne's Angliæ Notitia, 1694, p. 145; Hasted's Kent, iv. 610; Biog. Brit.; Nichols's Lit. Anecd. iv. 142; Le Neve's Monumenta Anglicana, 1680–99 p. 65, 1650–1718 (Suppl.) p. 219; Coxe's Cat. of MSS. in Colleges and Halls; Bromley's Cat. of Engraved Portraits. Contemporary notices of the editions of 1707 and of 1710 of the Greek Testament are in Bibliothèque Choisie, vols. xvi. xxi.; Journal des Sçavans (Suppl.), 1708 pp. 255–67, 1711 pp. 18–24; Leipzig Acta Eruditorum, 1708 pp. 1–12, 1710 pp. 421–4; Pfaff's Dissertatio Critica, 1709, pp. 113 et seq.; Nouvelles de la République des Lettres, 1710, pp. 243–53; Trevoux's Mémoires, 1710, pp. 785–807. Accounts of Mill's work are numerous: the best are Pritz's Introductio in lectionem Novi Testamenti, pp. 288–92; Budæus's Isagoge, pp. 1505–6; Hichtel's Exercitatio . . . contra Millium; Bengel's Apparatus Criticus (in his Greek Testament, 1734), pp. 880–1; Walch's Bibliotheca Theologica, iv. 25–8; Le Long's Bibliotheca Sacra, i. 235–239; Scrivener's Introd. to the Criticism of the New Test. pp. 374, 447–80; Michaelis's Introduction (trans. by Marsh), passim; Michaelis's Curæ in Versionem Syriacum, pp. 80–159 (with reference to Mill's errors in oriental versions); see also Bode's Pseudocritica Millio-Bengeliana; Registers of Queen's College, Oxford, kindly communicated by the provost; information from the Rev. R. F. Dale of Bletchington.] B. P.

MILL, JOHN STUART (1806–1873), philosopher, eldest son of James Mill [q. v.], was born on 20 May 1806 at his father's house, 13 Rodney Street, Pentonville, London. He was a singularly precocious child, and was entirely educated by his father, who from the first carried out unflinchingly a severe system of training. The child was set when three years old to learn 'vocables,' or lists of Greek words with the English meanings. By his eighth year he had read many Greek authors, starting with 'Æsop's Fables' and Xenophon's 'Anabasis,' including Herodotus, parts of Lucian, Diogenes Laertius, and six dialogues of Plato. His only other lessons were in arithmetic, but he also read books by himself. From 1810 till 1813 the Mills lived at Newington Green, and the father used to walk before breakfast in the then green lanes round Hornsey. During these walks the child gave accounts of his reading in Gibbon, Robertson, Hume, and (his especial favourite) Watson's 'Philip II' and 'Philip III.' He read Langhorne's 'Plutarch,' Millar's 'English Government,' Mosheim's 'Ecclesiastical History,' Sewel's 'Quakers,' and many voyages, besides a few children's books. In his eighth year he began Latin, and was also employed by his father to teach the younger children, a plan probably suggested by the Lancasterian system then in great favour with the utilitarians. By his twelfth year he had read in Latin much of Virgil, Horace, Livy, Ovid, Terence, and Cicero, and had added to his Greek Homer, Thucydides (read in his eighth, and again in his eleventh year), and parts of the dramatists, orators, and historians, besides Aristotle's 'Rhetoric.' He continued to read English histories, and during his eleventh and twelfth years began to write a history of the Roman government in imitation of Hooke. He had already written some fragmentary 'histories,' and Professor Bain (p. 3) gives a scrap composed when he was six and a half. Between the ages of eight and thirteen he had acquired elementary geometry and algebra 'thoroughly,' and had begun the differential calculus. His father was unable to guide him in the higher mathematics, or in the niceties of classical scholarship. He never practised composition in Greek, and little in Latin (see a Latin letter to his sisters of 1820, given in Bain, p. 21 *n.*) He was pleased with Pope's 'Homer,' Scott's 'Lays,' and Campbell's 'Lyrics,' but did not take to Shakespeare or Spenser. His father made him write English verses as a practice in composition, but he was not destined to be a poet. He was much interested by popular books upon science, though he had no opportunity of experimental inquiry. About twelve he began a serious study of logic, including some of Aristotle, some scholastic treatises, and especially Hobbes's 'Computatio sive Logica,' a book of great authority with his father. He began also to study classical literature for the thoughts as well as for the language. Demosthenes and Plato received especial attention. During 1817 he read the proofs of his father's 'History of India,' and was greatly impressed by the doctrines with which it is 'saturated.' In 1819 he went through a 'complete course of political economy.' His father made him write out a summary of the instructions given during their walks. The notes so made served for the father's treatise. The two afterwards carefully went through Adam Smith and Ricardo (see letter of 30 July 1819 in Bain, pp. 6–9). Before his fourteenth birthday Mill had thus read much classical literature, had seriously studied logic and political economy, had read much history and general literature, and made a good start in mathematics. He records his own achievements as a proof that the years of childhood may be employed to better purpose than usual, and while admitting that his father was a stern and impatient teacher, declares also that the education was never mere 'cram,' but invariably directed to stimulate his powers of thought. Francis Place [q. v.], when staying at Ford Abbey in 1814, reports that John, with his two sisters, were kept at lessons from six to nine, and again from ten to one, and that on one occasion their dinner hour had been put off from one till six because the sisters had made a mistake in a single word, and John had passed their exercise. He says that John is a 'prodigy,' but expects that he will grow up 'morose and selfish' (Place, *Letters*, communicated by Mr. Graham Wallas). Mill was brought up as a thorough agnostic, and says (ungrammatically) that he was one of the very few examples in this country of one who has 'not thrown off religious belief, but never had it' (*Autobiography*, p. 43). It appears, however, that the boy went to church in his infancy, and called Homer and the Bible the 'two greatest books' (Bain, *James Mill*, p. 90).

In May 1820 Mill left London for France, and stayed there until July 1821. He lived with Sir Samuel Bentham [q. v.], partly at the Château Pompignon, between Toulouse and Montauban, and partly in Toulouse, besides making an excursion to the Pyrenees, and ascending the Pic du Midi, Bigorre. From a diary published by Professor Bain, it appears that he studied nine hours a day. He became a thorough French scholar, and acquired an interest in French society and politics which never failed. He continued his studies in mathematics, chemistry, and political economy, learnt some music, and took lessons with less success in dancing, fencing, and riding. He was devoted to walking, and an enthusiastic lover of scenery, but he was never athletic. He took up botany as an amusement while in France, under the influence doubtless of George Bentham [q. v.], Sir Samuel's son, and was always an enthusiastic collector, though not a scientific botanist.

Upon returning to England Mill again became tutor of the younger children. He began to study for the bar, and read Roman law during the winter with John Austin (1790–1859) [q. v.] He gave up any thoughts of the profession upon being appointed (21 May 1823) to a junior clerkship in the examiner's office of the India House under his father. He had 30*l.* a year for the first three years, and afterwards 100*l.* In 1828 he was promoted over the other clerks and made an assistant, with 600*l.* a year. He rose to be third in the office, upon his father's death in 1836, with 1,200*l.* a year. In 1854 an addition of 200*l.* was made to his salary, and on the retirement of his seniors in 1856 he became chief of the office, with 2,000*l.* a year. His position enabled him to devote much time to study and to the composition of laborious works, and he found few drawbacks, except the exclusion from parliament and the confinement to London. He spent his month's holiday at his father's house in the country, and afterwards in excursions, the earlier of which were made on foot.

While reading with Austin, Mill for the first time studied Bentham's doctrines in Dumont's redaction. Reading the 'Traité de Législation,' he says, was a turning-point in his mental history. He afterwards, under the direction of his father, then employed upon his 'Analysis,' studied Condillac, Helvetius, Hartley, and the chief English psychologists. He became known to his father's disciples, especially Grote and Charles Austin [q. v.] In the winter of 1822–3 he formed a society, to which he gave the name 'Utilitarian.' He says (*Autobiography*, p. 79) that he found the name in Galt's 'Annals of the Parish.' The word had been used by Bentham many years before (BENTHAM, *Works*, x. 92, 390), but the name came into popular use as designating the party now gathering round the Mills. The society, which read essays and discussed questions, lasted till 1826, and Mill was active in enlisting recruits, although the number of members never reached ten. Charles Austin had introduced some of his college friends to the Mills, and John, during a brief visit to Cambridge in 1822, had made a great impression by his abilities. His father was vainly urged in 1823 to enter him at the university. Mill soon began to write in the papers, his first publication being a letter to the 'Traveller,' belonging to Colonel Torrens, in defence of one of his father's economical theories. He contributed soon afterwards a series of letters, signed 'Wickliffe,' to the 'Morning Chronicle,' denouncing the prosecution of Richard Carlile [q. v.] When the 'Westminster Review' was started in April 1824, Mill helped his father in assailing the old Quarterlies, and afterwards wrote frequently until 1828. The most remarkable of these writings was a review of Whately's 'Logic' in January 1828, which shows some interesting anticipations of his later theories. During 1825 Mill's chief employment was editing Bentham's 'Treatise upon Evidence.' Besides reducing to unity three masses of manuscripts written independently, Mill had to correct the style, fill up gaps, insert some replies to critics of Dumont's earlier abstract of the treatise, and add dissertations upon speculative questions. The labour, he says, took up his leisure for a year, and he had afterwards to see the five large volumes through the press. The book occupies two volumes in Bentham's collected 'Works,' and it is not only one of the richest in matter of Bentham's books, but one of the best edited. It would be difficult to mention a youth of twenty who ever completed such a task in the intervals of official work. Mill thinks that his editorial labour had a marked effect in improving his own style. During the next three years he contributed to the 'Parliamentary History and Review,' writing articles upon some of the chief political and economical questions of the day. Meanwhile he learnt German, though he never seems to have become a thorough German scholar. He collected 'about a dozen' friends, who met at Grote's house in Threadneedle Street on two mornings in the week from half-past eight till ten. They went steadily through various treatises, including Ricardo, Du Trieu's 'Manuductio ad Logicam,' Hartley, and Mill's 'Analysis,' thoroughly discussing every difficulty raised until each disputant had finally made up his mind. These discussions, which lasted 'some years,' made Mill (as he thought) an independent thinker, and were an admirable exercise in thorough analysis of difficulties. Mill's 'Essays upon Unsettled Questions of Political Economy' were one result. He wrote them about 1830, but could not obtain a publisher till after the success of his 'Logic.' They contain his most original work upon abstract political economy. Among the young men who then cultivated and propagated utilitarian principles, and became afterwards known as the 'philosophical radicals,' were Charles Austin, (Lord) Romilly, William Eyton Tooke (son of the economist), William Ellis (1800–1881) [q.v.], George John Graham (afterwards official assignee of the bankruptcy court, who helped Mill in working out his economical doctrines), J. A. Roebuck [q. v.], and Charles Buller [q. v.] Although sympathising with Bentham and James Mill, they disagreed upon various points both with their leaders and each other, but they appeared to outsiders as a clique. Mill admits that their contempt for 'sentimentalities' and 'vague generalities,' and for poetic culture generally, was excessive, as it naturally made them offensive to others. They came into contact with other young men at a debating society named after the famous Speculative Society at Edinburgh. Some of the utilitarians, led by Charles Austin, had attended the meetings of the Co-operative Society of Owenites in Chancery Lane. They fought a pitched battle, which lasted for three months, in defence of their conflicting opinions. This suggested the formation of the Speculative Society, which was joined by many of the most promising men of the day, including Macaulay, Thirlwall, Praed, Sam Wilberforce, and the Bulwers. The first session was a failure, but in 1826–7 they gained recruits, and sharp debates took place, A. Hayward [q. v.] and Shee (afterwards judge) representing the tories, while Mill and Roebuck, helped by Charles Buller and Cockburn, defended the radical cause. In the seasons of 1828 and 1829 they were joined by Maurice and Sterling, representing the Coleridgean influence. Mill became a friend of both, and in spite of profound differences of opinion was influenced by them in his mental development. He dropped the society in 1829, having abandoned the 'Westminster' in the previous year.

Mill had meanwhile gone through a spiritual crisis, which he compares to the conversion of methodists. It was connected, as he says, with 'a dull state of nerves.' Although he dwells chiefly upon the mental state, it seems to be clear that the pressure to which he had been subjected from his infancy, and the extraordinary labours of his early manhood, in which the work upon Bentham in the previous year was a mere interlude, must have tried his nervous system. In 1836 he had an illness due to 'an obstinate derangement of the brain' (Bain, p. 42), which produced involuntary nervous movements, and to the end of his life there was 'an almost ceaseless spasmodic twitching over one eye.' From this and other attacks it is clear that he had suffered from excessive intellectual strain. The mental crisis, whether the effect, or, as he apparently fancied, the cause of the nervous mental derangement, greatly affected his later development. He suddenly felt that even the full attainment of his political and social aims would fail to give happiness. He concluded that the systematic analysis of his school tended to 'wear away the feelings' by destroying the associations which, in their view, were the cause of all happiness. The 'first ray of light' came from a passage in Marmontel's 'Memoirs.' Marmontel there describes how, upon his father's death, he was inspired by the resolution to make up the loss to his family. Mill learnt that happiness was to be found not in directly pursuing it, but in the pursuit of other ends; and learnt, also, the importance of a steady cultivation of the feelings. In this state of mind he was profoundly attracted by Wordsworth, whose merits he defended against Roebuck at the Speculative Society. He learnt something, too, from Maurice, who introduced him to Coleridge and Goethe. He began to diverge from the stern utilitarianism of his father, who also repelled him by a denial of the rights of women. Macaulay's attack upon James Mill's essay on 'Government' suggested to him the necessity of a more philosophical treatment of politics. In 1829–30 he became acquainted with the St.-Simonians, and was especially impressed by an early work of Auguste Comte, then an avowed follower of St.-Simon. In 1830 he went to Paris upon the revolution, was introduced to Lafayette and to some of the popular leaders, and saw the chiefs of the St.-Simonians. He was thus led to widen and humanise his traditional utilitarianism, and he convinced himself that he could retain all that was ennobling in the 'Freewill' doctrine—the belief, namely, that we can mould our own characters—without abandoning the philosophical theory of determinism. He wrote much in newspapers after his visit to France in 1830, especially in the 'Examiner,' to which he contributed a series of papers on the 'Spirit of the Age' in 1831. Carlyle was attracted by them, and upon coming to London soon afterwards made Mill's acquaintance. They were for some time friends, although Carlyle soon discovered that Mill was not, as he had fancied, a 'new mystic.' In fact, the absence of 'mysticism' in Mill's intellect made the relationship uncongenial, and they gradually drifted apart. Mill had made collections for a history of the French revolution, which were very useful to Carlyle.

Mill now began to put together materials for his most important works. The discussions at Grote's house had suggested to him the composition of a logical treatise. After finishing the economist essays, he again took up the question, was able to frame his theory of the syllogism, and wrote a sketch of his first book. Difficulties, however, stopped him as to the theory of induction, and he put the subject aside for five years. He wrote in 1832 for 'Tait's Magazine' and contributed to the 'Jurist' the article upon 'Endowments,' reprinted in his 'Dissertations.'

In 1830 Mill had been introduced to Mrs. Taylor, his junior by two years. Her husband was a 'drysalter and wholesale druggist' in Mark Lane; and his grandfather had been a neighbour and friend of James Mill at Newington Green. Mill rapidly formed an intimacy with Mrs. Taylor, who profoundly affected the rest of his life. She was an invalid, and obliged to live in the country apart from her husband. Mill visited her regularly in the country, dined with her twice a week in London, and occasionally travelled with her alone. Her husband accepted the situation with singular generosity, and dined out when Mill dined at his house. He was, according to Mill, a man of most honourable character, and regarded with steady affection by his wife, although he could not be her intellectual companion. The relationship between Mill and Mrs. Taylor was, as he intimates (*Autobiog.* p. 229), purely one of friendship. It was, however, inevitable that it should cause some scandal, and it led to difficulties with his family. His father strongly disapproved, and his marriage to her (in 1851) led to a complete estrangement from his mother and sisters. He never spoke of her to his friends or in his family, and the connection was probably the main cause of his complete withdrawal from society in later years. After ceasing to be active in journalism, he was only to be seen by a few intimate friends at the India House, and at monthly meetings of the Political Economy Club. He gives, however, more philosophical and doubtless genuine reasons for his seclusion (*ib.* p. 227). If his own language is to be trusted (see dedication to 'Liberty,' *Dissertations*, ii. 411, and *Autobiography*), Mrs. Taylor's influence upon his intellectual and moral development was of the highest importance, and yet not more important than might be expected from her transcendent abilities. He declares that her excellences of mind and heart were 'unparalleled in any human being he had known or read of.' His friends naturally did not share this opinion; some of them accounted for it by her excellence in echoing his own views. As Professor Bain observes, this is purely conjectural, and Mill generally liked friends with independent views. His vehement hyperboles, however, seem to betray a sense that he could give no tangible proof of their accuracy. From his account of her share in his writings it would seem that she did not influence his logical and scientific theories, but did a great deal to stimulate his enthusiasm upon such questions as liberty, women's rights, and social progress. The opinions, however, advocated in his later writings upon these topics were natural developments of his earlier thought. The only independent work attributed to her is the essay upon the enfranchisement of women in the second volume of the 'Dissertations.' The Reform Bill of 1832 had given power to the whigs, and Mill's great object for some years was to prevent the radicals from becoming a mere left wing of the whig party. From 1832 to 1834 he wrote much in the 'Examiner,' in the 'Monthly Repository,' edited by W. J. Fox, on political and other subjects, and published abstracts of some of Plato's 'Dialogues,' besides adding a short estimate of Bentham to Bulwer's 'England and the English.' His publications, he says, independently of the newspaper articles, would fill a large volume. His party had for some time desired to possess an organ of 'philosophical radicalism' which might take the place of the 'Westminster Review.' The 'London Review' was started by Sir William Molesworth [q.v.] for this purpose. The first number appeared in April 1835, and in April 1836 it was amalgamated with the 'Westminster Review,' which had been bought by Molesworth. Molesworth in 1837 transferred the proprietorship to Mill, who in 1840 transferred it to Mr. Hickson. There was a loss of about 100*l.* a number during Molesworth's proprietorship, and Mill, who paid a subeditor and many contributors, was also a considerable loser. Mill's official position prevented him from being actual editor, but he superintended the review from the first, the ostensible editors being, first, Thomas Falconer (1805–1882) [q.v.], and from about the beginning of 1837 John Robertson, a smart young Scottish journalist. (The dates are not quite clear: see MILL's *Autobiog.* pp. 199, 207; BAIN, pp. 46, 58–9; and *Atlantic Monthly* for January 1892, where are published some interesting letters from Mill to Robertson.)

Mill was at first hampered by the necessity of publishing his father's articles and others by the utilitarians of the older school. When he became freer, after his father's death in 1836, he could give more scope to his own doctrines. He inserted many articles, however, with which he was not in full agreement, the authorship being indicated by letters and editorial *caveats* frequently added. Among the writers were Carlyle, Sterling, Bulwer, Charles Buller, Roebuck, Harriet and James Martineau, Mazzini, W. J. Fox, and Henry Cole. Mill contributed some remarkable essays, some of which are republished in his 'Dissertations.' Among them were an article upon Tocqueville's 'Democracy in America,' a book which greatly affected his political theories; two well-known articles upon Bentham and Coleridge; an article (in the second number, July 1835) which was one of the first to do justice to Tennyson's poetry; and another (July 1837) which gave a warm and, as he thought, a very seasonable welcome to Carlyle's 'French Revolution.' Mill was always anxious to help unrecognised genius. Other articles show his interest in French politics and the gradual development of his political theories, in which his old democratic zeal was tempered by a fear of the danger to individualism. His main practical purpose, however, was to stimulate the flagging energies of the 'philosophical radicals.' He tried to believe that they only required a leader; and he thought that such a leader might be found in Lord Durham, whose Canadian administration he warmly supported in two articles (January and December 1838). The first of these, according to Robertson (*Atlantic Monthly*), greatly injured the sale of the number; but Mill in his 'Autobiography' congratulates himself upon the effect produced upon colonial policy.

Mill's attempt to influence politics ceased with his abandonment of the review and the complete eclipse for the time of the philosophical radicals. He had again taken up his logical speculations in 1837. Whewell's 'History of the Inductive Sciences,' published in that year, gave him needed materials, and he succeeded in elaborating his theory of induction. In spite of his other occupations and a serious illness, which caused six months' leave of absence in 1839, he carried on the work. In the beginning of 1840 he stayed some time at Falmouth, where his favourite brother Henry had gone in consumption (he died 4 April 1840), and saw much of Sterling and the Fox family. In 1841 he finally rewrote the 'Logic,' and at the end of the year offered it to Murray. It was rejected by him, but accepted by J. W. Parker, who finally published it in March 1843. The book had a rapid success, beyond the expectations of its author, and was for many years the standard authority with all who took his side in the main philosophical questions. Mill, in fact, was recognised as the great leader of the empirical as opposed to what he called the intuitional school; and few men have had a more marked influence upon the rising intellect of the time. His chief opponents at the moment were Whewell, to whom he replied in a third edition, and W. G. Ward, who reviewed him at great length in the 'British Critic.' Though diametrically opposed upon important points, Ward and Mill received each other's criticisms with singular candour and good temper.

The later part of the 'Logic' shows the influence of Comte, although Mill is careful to state that his own theory of induction had been independently reached. Mill had been an early student of Comte; he had read every volume of the 'Philosophie' as it appeared; and from 1841 to 1846 they carried on a correspondence at first very intimate and affectionate. (The 'Lettres d'Auguste Comte à John Stuart Mill, 1841-6,' Paris, 1877, throw more light upon Comte's position than upon Mill's, whose letters have not been published.) Mill took part with Grote and Molesworth in supplying Comte with a sum to make up for his loss of official income in 1844. They declined, however, after a second year, to consider the subsidy. Considerable divergences of opinion had shown themselves; Mill's views of the equality of the sexes had led to a warm dispute, and he, though not so strongly as Grote, objected to Comte's doctrines as destructive of liberty. The intercourse ceased, and Mill in later editions of his 'Logic' softened down the high compliments which he had first paid to Comte. Comte's influence, however, upon Mill was clearly very great, especially in his general view of social development.

Mill now contemplated a book to be called 'Ethology,' a theory of human character as preparatory to a theory of social statics. This, however, gradually gave place to a treatise upon political economy, upon which he laboured from the autumn of 1845. He contributed some articles to the 'Edinburgh Review' at this time, and in the winter of 1846–7 wrote a series of leaders in the 'Morning Chronicle,' urging the formation of peasant-proprietorships on waste lands in Ireland. His long familiarity with political economy enabled him to compose his treatise with unusual rapidity; it was finished by the end of 1847 and published early in 1848. While expounding the old doctrines of Ricardo it indicated also the opinions which he shared with Mrs. Taylor, and which entitled them in his view to come 'under the general designation of socialists' (*Autobiog.* p. 231). This, however, must not be understood as including later implications of the word. Mill's theories, to which he gave greater prominence in later editions, are indicated in the chapter upon the 'Probable Future of the Labouring Classes,' which was written at the suggestion, and partly by the inspiration, of Mrs. Taylor (*ib.* p. 245). The 'Political Economy' succeeded more rapidly than the 'Logic;' and the two combined gave the essence of the social and philosophical system of the more educated radicals of the time.

Mill's correspondence now became considerable. He wrote occasional articles, but he began no important work for a time. Mr. Taylor died in July 1849, and in April 1851 Mrs. Taylor became Mill's wife. A serious illness, causing permanent injury to the lungs, forced him to take eight months' holiday in 1854. He rallied, and in 1856 became head of his department in the India House. He drew up a petition in which the company remonstrated against its own extinction, arguing very vigorously against the probable effect upon the natives of the change of system and the evils to be anticipated from making the government of India a prize to be scrambled for by second-rate English officials. On the dissolution of the company at the end of 1858 he retired with a pension of 1,500*l.* a year, declining a seat on the new council. He left England intending to spend the winter in the south of Europe. His wife was taken ill on the journey and died at Avignon of congestion of the lungs. Mill was deeply affected, and for the rest of his life spent half the year in a house which he bought at Avignon to be near his wife's grave. In England he lived at Blackheath. He returned, however, to intellectual work. His last occupation with Mrs. Mill had been the revision of his 'Essay on Liberty' (first written in 1854), the most carefully prepared of his writings. He now published it without further alteration. In 1860 he wrote his essay upon 'Representative Government,' and in the same year revised his 'Utilitarianism' (first written in 1854), which appeared as three articles in 'Fraser's Magazine' in 1861. These books together contain a full, though condensed, exposition of his characteristic political and social views. In 1861 he returned to his metaphysical investigations, having taken up Sir William Hamilton's works for an intended review which soon expanded into a treatise. He read through Hamilton's works thrice and many subsidiary books. Hamilton was taken by Mill as the chief representative of the intuitionists, and the book, which finally appeared in 1865, included an elaborate survey of all the chief points at issue. It produced a very lively controversy. His best-known antagonist was Hamilton's disciple Mansel, whose 'Limits of Religious Thought' he had sharply attacked, and which he pronounced in private to be a 'loathsome book' (BAIN, p. 124). While writing upon Hamilton he contributed to the 'Edinburgh' (October 1863) an article upon John Austin, and to the 'Westminster Review' in 1864 two articles upon Comte, subsequently republished in a separate volume.

The Hamilton book had hardly appeared when Mill was invited to stand for Westminster. He had taken some part in contemporary political discussions by a pamphlet on parliamentary reform (written some years before), and by articles strongly supporting the cause of the union in the American civil war; and in the beginning of 1865 he published popular editions of his 'Political Economy,' 'Liberty,' and 'Representative Government.' He had declined previous requests to become a candidate, but felt bound to accede to a proposal which met his views of independence. It was understood that he should not canvass or spend money, and he had frankly stated his opinions, especially as to the extension of the franchise to women. He took no part in the contest till the last week, when he attended some public meetings and answered questions. He declined to say anything of his religious opinions, but was perfectly frank upon all other topics. When asked whether he had written a passage stating that the English working classes were 'generally liars,' he excited vehement applause by replying simply 'I did.' He was elected in 1865. Mill's immense reputation and his previous seclusion made his parliamentary performance the object of very general curiosity. His first speech was upon the bill for prevention of the cattle diseases (14 Feb. 1866), and gave some offence to the country gentlemen. A speech in favour of the second reading of Mr. Gladstone's Reform Bill (12 April 1866) was highly successful. A weak voice, great rapidity of utterance, and a nervous manner —occasionally producing a prolonged full stop—were unfavourable to oratorical success. But his command of copious and precise language was remarkable, and the general effect was that of reading a highly finished and felicitous essay. Bright and Mr. Gladstone welcomed him with especial cordiality, and he had much influence with both. When the first curiosity had been satiated and some of his utterances (especially that upon Hare's scheme) had provoked conservative antipathies, he showed some irritability, but on the whole retained the ear of the house. His speeches, as the speaker is reported to have said, raised the tone of debate, and his general reputation spread through a wider area. He attended to his duties with singular assiduity, and even provoked the remonstrances of his friends for wasting energy upon mere routine drudgery. Mill chiefly followed Mr. Gladstone in the various parliamentary contests which led finally to the passage of the Reform Bill of 1867. He spoke upon his own favourite schemes, the extension of the franchise to women and the introduction of some system of cumulative voting. After the Hyde Park riots of 1866 he had some influence in persuading the leaders to give up their intention of holding a second meeting in defiance of the government. He helped afterwards to talk out a measure, introduced by the conservative government, for preventing meetings in the parks. He took a strong part in Irish questions, giving offence by denouncing English methods of government upon the suspension of the habeas corpus on 17 Feb. 1866. In 1868 he published a pamphlet upon 'England and Ireland,' and afterwards spoke in the house upon the same topic. While holding a separation to be undesirable for both countries, he proposed to settle the land question by giving a permanent tenure to the tenants, and allowing as an alternative the sale of the landlords' estates to the government. He endeavoured also to procure the establishment of a municipal government for London, and served on a committee which considered the question in 1866. A speech (17 April 1866) in which he urged the duty of paying off the national debt before our coal was exhausted (suggested by a pamphlet of William Stanley Jevons [q. v.]) also made a favourable impression. Another movement in which he took a considerable share during 1866 and 1867 was the attempted prosecution of Governor Eyre for his action in suppressing the Jamaica insurrection. Mill was for a time chairman of the 'Jamaica Committee,' formed to promote the prosecution; he spoke in the house on its behalf, and received a good deal of personal abuse in consequence.

After the dissolution of 1868 Mill lost his seat. The Eyre business had given offence to some of his own party; the feeling against 'theoretical' politicians had been revived by his advocacy of Hare's scheme and other doctrines; and he shocked some supporters by subscribing to the election expenses of Bradlaugh, among other working-class candidates.

His parliamentary duties had not absorbed Mill's whole attention. At the end of 1866 he had written a long address to the students of St. Andrews, by whom he had been elected rector. He brought out a third edition of his 'Hamilton,' with replies to critics. He then edited his father's 'Analysis' in co-operation with Dr. Findlater and his old friend Professor Bain, who had first made his acquaintance in 1839, and who had helped him in the various editions of the 'Logic,' both by criticisms and by supplying him with illustrations. Upon losing his seat he returned to his literary pursuits, intending to divide his time between Avignon and Blackheath. His parliamentary career had greatly increased his correspondence, and brought him into contact with many rising young men. Among his chief friends in later life were Thomas Hare, whose scheme he had adopted, W. T. Thornton, his colleague in the India House, Professor Cairnes, Henry Fawcett, and Mr. John Morley. He wrote for the 'Fortnightly,' then edited by Mr. Morley, various articles, which formed the fourth volume of his 'Dissertations.' He published in 1869 his last book, the 'Subjection of Women,' written in 1861. His step-daughter co-operated in this book, which was partly also the product of conversations with her mother. He speaks of his singular good fortune in drawing such 'another prize in the lottery of life' after the loss of his wife. He had 'several prostrating attacks' after this, but showed great power of recovery. He died 8 May 1873, of a 'local endemic disease.' Three days before his death he had walked fifteen miles on a botanical excursion. Three posthumous 'Essays on Religion' were published by Miss Taylor in 1874: the first two, upon 'Nature' and the 'Utility of Religion,' were written between 1850 and 1858; the last, upon 'Theism,' was written between 1868 and 1870. The fact that he intended to publish the last in 1873 shows that he would not have persevered in the singular reticence upon religious topics which had been the systematic practice of his early associates. It was remarkable that in spite of the obvious bearing of his philosophical treatises, the only sentence which his political antagonists could find to produce odium was the really very orthodox remark (from the 'Examination' of Hamilton), 'To hell I will go' rather than obey an immoral deity. The essay itself betrays an insufficient acquaintance with the philosophy of the subject. Professor Bain thinks that he had never read a book upon theology.

The best impression of Mill's personal appearance is given by the portrait painted by Mr. Watts, of which an etching by Rajon has been published. A bronze statue was erected to his memory upon the Thames Embankment. He was rather tall, slight, ruddy and fair-haired, with a sweet and thoughtful expression. He was always in black, and till his later years wore a dress suit. He had a good constitution, overstrained by his labours. He loved walking and natural scenery. He protested in 1836, as Mr. Ruskin might have done later, against the passage of a railway through the beautiful valley of Mickleham; and it was through his influence that the line of trees, still on the south side of Piccadilly, was saved when the street was widened. He was a founder and active member of the Commons Preservation Society. His astonishing powers of work, shown by his early edition of Bentham's 'Evidence,' enabled him, in spite of a daily six hours at his office (of which Mr. Bain thinks only half were spent upon his necessary duties), to get through immense intellectual labours. He was very temperate, and took nothing between an early breakfast and a plain dinner at six o'clock. His animal appetites were probably below the average intensity, and he underestimated their force in others.

Although Mill's intellect was essentially of the logical order, his emotions were extremely tender and vivid. The severe training of his father directed them mainly into the channel of public spirit. His whole life was devoted to the propagation of principles which he held to be essential to human happiness; and his metaphysical doctrines were valued by him not so much upon purely logical grounds, as by their application to the well-being of his fellows. The affectionate nature shown in his idolatry of his wife appeared in his friendships; though unfortunately his absorption in this passion and his seclusion from society led to difficulties with his family, and checked his sympathies with even so old a friend as Grote. His appreciation of such friends as Hare and Thornton was expressed in terms of even excessive generosity. He was always eager to recognise the merits of an antagonist, or of a still obscure genius. He was liberal in money matters, and offered to guarantee the cost of early writings of Professor Bain and Mr. Herbert Spencer. He could speak sharply at times, especially upon such questions as woman's rights, and was both sensitive and irritable. Yet in published controversy his candour and calmness were conspicuous. When W. T. Thornton was disabled by illness from performing his duties in the India House, and thought of resigning his post, Mill obviated the necessity by doing all Thornton's work in addition to his own for a year. He was the author, as Thornton adds, of nearly all the 'political' despatches from the India House for twenty-three years, and his official writings would fill two large volumes annually. The same qualities mark his intellectual career. Brought up after the strictest sect of the utilitarians, the history of his development is mainly a history of his attempts to widen and humanise their teaching. He adhered, indeed, to the philosophical groundwork of his predecessors, and much of his thought is best understood as an elaboration of his father's principles, intended to supply gaps and correct crudities. Mill thus carried on the traditional teaching of English philosophers on the lines originally laid down by Locke; and for the quarter of a century after the publication was regarded as the leading exponent of its principles. His influence has diminished with the rise of the evolutionist doctrine on his own side and the appearance on the other side of men familiar with Kant and his German successors. Mill's superficial acquaintance with the German writers prevented him from perceiving some weaknesses of his teaching; and his contemporary antagonists, though rather better informed, scarcely recognised defects which have been since pointed out by Thomas Hill Green [q. v.] and others. Whatever the result to his system, he at least did more than any one of his time to stimulate English thought upon such topics.

In political economy Mill built upon the foundations of Ricardo and Malthus. He came to regard the Malthusian principles not as a barrier to progress, but as showing the conditions by which progress could be achieved. His book is throughout governed by a belief in the possibility of great social improvements, combined with a resolution to expose quack remedies and utter unpalatable truths. If he appears to the modern socialist as a follower of Ricardo, he would have been regarded by Ricardo's disciples as a socialist. The purely scientific part of his doctrine retains much value. When his exposition of the 'wage fund' theory was assailed by his friend Thornton, Mill not only made concessions, but, according to Professor Marshall, allowed himself to have fallen into confusions of which he was not really guilty. The same high authority observes that most of Mill's exposition of the theory in the last book of his treatise will stand later inquiry. Mill's political and social doctrines show a similar transition. While ardently sympathising with the aspirations of radicals, he had learnt to regard as the great danger of modern society the tendency of democracies to crush individual development and tyrannise over minorities. No one had a more rooted hatred for all oppression, and his advocacy of the equality of the sexes—whatever the value of the particular measures advocated —showed his chivalrous devotion to the weaker side. The general disparagement of so-called 'individualism' has led for the time to a lower estimate of Mill's services to liberal principles. The final decision as to the soundness of his teaching will not yet be reached. But no historian of the social and political movement in his time can fail to note the extraordinary influence which he exercised for a generation; the purity and energy of his purpose; and his immense services in the encouragement of active speculation, and of the most important movements of his time. It is equally noticeable that no one ever did less to court favour by the slightest compromise of principle.

Among reviews of Mill's writings may be mentioned T. R. Birks's 'Modern Utilitarianism,' 1874; W. L. Courtney's 'Metaphysics of J. S. Mill,' 1879; J. Grote's 'Exploratio Philosophica,' 1865, and 'Examination of the Utilitarian Philosophy,' 1870; Guyau's 'Morale Anglaise Contemporaine,' 1879; Jodl's 'Geschichte der Ethik in der neueren Philosophie,' 1889; F. A. Lange's 'J. S. Mill's Ansichten über die sociale Frage,' &c., 1866; Littré's 'A. Comte et J. S. Mill' [1866]; J. MacCosh's 'Examination of J. S. Mill's Philosophy,' 1866; H. L. Mansel's 'Philosophy of the Conditioned,' 1866; Ribot's 'Psychologie Anglaise Contemporaine,' 1870; Taine's 'Mill et le Positivisme Anglaise,' 1870 (separately, and in 'History of English Literature'); Whewell's 'Of Induction, with special reference to J. S. Mill,' 1889. Mill's 'Wage-fund theory' was criticised by Mr. F. D. Longe in 'Refutation of the Wage-fund,' 1866, and by W. T. Thornton 'On Labour,' 1869. Mill's reply to Thornton, containing a withdrawal of his theory, was originally published in the 'Fortnightly Review' for May 1869, and is given in the 'Dissertations,' vol. iv.

Mill's works are: 1. 'A System of Logic, Ratiocinative and Inductive, being a connected View of the Principles of Evidence and the Methods of Scientific Investigation,' 1843, 2 vols. 8vo. The third edition (1851), the sixth (1866), and the eighth (1872) were carefully revised. A ninth appeared in 1875, and a 'people's edition' in 1884. 2. 'Essays on some Unsettled Questions of Political Economy,' 1844; 2nd edit. 1874. 3. 'Principles of Political Economy,' 2 vols. 8vo, 1848, 1849, 1852, 1857, 1862, 1865. 4. 'On Liberty,' 1859. 5. 'Thoughts on Parliamentary Reform,' 1859 (reprinted in 'Dissertations,' vol. iii.) 6. 'Dissertations and Discussions,' vols i. and ii. in 1859; vol. iii. in 1867; vol. iv. in 1876. 7. 'Considerations on Representative Government,' 1861; 3rd edit. 1865. 8. 'Utilitarianism,' 1863 (reprinted from 'Fraser's Magazine' of 1861). 9. 'Examination of Sir William Hamilton's Philosophy,' 1865 (3rd edit.) 10. 'Auguste Comte and Positivism,' 1865 (from the 'Westminster Review'). 11. 'Inaugural Address at the University of St. Andrews' (delivered 1 Feb. 1867), 1867. 12. 'England and Ireland,' 1868. 13. 'The Subjection of Women,' 1869. 14. 'Chapters and Speeches on the Irish Land Question,' 1870 (reprinted from 'Political Economy' and 'Hansard's Debates'). 15. 'Autobiography,' 1873. 16. 'Three Essays on Religion: Nature, the Utility of Religion, Theism,' 1874. The abstracts of some of Plato's 'Dialogues,' to which Mill refers in his 'Autobiography,' p. 168, appeared in W. J. Fox's 'Monthly Repository' for 1834. The dialogues were the 'Protagoras,' 'Phædrus,' and 'Gorgias.' 'Memorandum on the Improvements in the Administration of India during the last Thirty Years, and the Petition of the East India Company to Parliament' (1858) is by Mill. Mill edited Bentham's 'Rationale of Judicial Evidence,' which first appeared in 1827; and from vols. vi. and vii. in the collective edition of Bentham's 'Works;' and James Mill's 'Analysis of the Phenomena of the Human Mind' in 1869.

[Autobiography, 1867; John Stuart Mill, a Criticism, with Personal Recollections, by Professor Bain, 1882; John Morley's Miscellanies (1877), ii. 239–327 (reminiscences and review of posthumous works); Memories of Old Friends, by Caroline Fox (2nd edit.), 1882, i. 132–68, 173, 177–8, 188–90, 197–206, 291, 300, 309, 333, ii. 27, 56, 97, 313–42 (some excellent descriptions of Mill's conversations in 1840, &c.); Lettres de J. S. Mill (1885) of no great interest, originally published by M. de Laveleye in the Revue Belgique; Memoirs of A. Fonblanque, 1874, ii. 29–33; Life of Blanco White, 1845, ii. 121, 126, 143, 182, 188, 208, 242, 341, 354 (letters to Mill as editor of the London and Westminster Review); Life of J. S. Mill by W. L. Courtney (in Great Writers Series), 1889. The Examiner of 17 May 1873 contained a series of articles, including the personal recollections and estimates of Mill's work by W. T. Thornton (on his official labours), Mr. Herbert Spencer (on his moral qualities), J. E. Cairnes (on his economical speculations), Professor and Mrs. Fawcett (on his influence upon the younger generation, and his political career), Professor Minto (on his literary work), Mr. Fox Bourne, and others.]

L. S.

MILL, WALTER (*d.* 1558), martyr. [See MYLNE.]

MILL, WILLIAM HODGE (1792–1853), orientalist, son of John Mill, a native of Dundee, by his wife Martha, born Hodge, was born 18 July 1792 at Hackney, Middlesex. He was educated chiefly in private under Dr. Belsham, a unitarian preacher, and in 1809 proceeded to Trinity College, Cambridge, where he graduated B.A. as sixth wrangler in 1813, was elected fellow in 1814, and proceeded M.A. in 1816. He took deacon's orders in 1817, and priest's in the following year. Continuing in residence at Cambridge, he appears to have devoted himself especially to oriental studies. In 1820 he was appointed the first principal of Bishop's College, Calcutta, then just founded, under the superintendence of Bishop Thomas Fanshawe Middleton [q.v.] Mill's work there gave satisfaction, and he strenuously pursued his linguistic studies. He not only assisted in the publication of works in Arabic, of which he had already gained some knowledge, but likewise addressed himself to the study of the vernaculars and of Sanskrit, and he cooperated in the work of the Sanskrit and other native colleges. He was also a leading member of the Bengal Asiatic Society (vice-president 1833–7), and appears to have been regularly consulted on all discoveries relating to Sanskrit or Arabic scholarship; he energetically supported the society's 'Journal,' then just founded, his contributions extending from vol. ii. to vol. vi. He also gave valuable assistance by his decipherments of several important inscriptions, then little understood, especially those on the pillars at Allahabad and Bhitari.

Mill's health obliged him to return to Europe in 1838. At his departure an address was voted to him by the Asiatic Society, and his bust placed in the society's rooms. Resuming his theological career, he was appointed in 1839 chaplain to William Howley, archbishop of Canterbury [q. v.], and in the same year Christian advocate on the Hulse foundation at Cambridge. In 1848 he became regius professor of Hebrew in the same university, with a canonry at Ely. His lectures were chiefly on the text of the Psalms. He died 25 Dec. 1853, at Brasted, Kent, a living to which he had been presented by the archbishop in 1843. He was buried in Ely Cathedral on New-year's eve. A portion of a window in the chapel of Trinity College, Cambridge, was subsequently (1862) filled with stained glass to his memory.

His chief work is 'Christa-saṅgitā' (Calcutta, 1831, 8vo; 2nd edition, 1837), a remarkable translation of the Gospel-story into the metre and style of the Sanskrit *purāṇas*; it was originally suggested to Mill by a Hindu pundit, who was the main author of the first canto.

Other works of the same period are a Sanskrit translation of the Sermon on the Mount, and contributions to the Arabic translation of the Anglican prayer-book. His Christian advocate's publication for 1840–4, 'On the attempted Application of Pantheistic Principles to the Criticism of the Gospel,' appeared in two editions, and is mainly directed against the criticism of Strauss. It abounds in illustration from various sources, characteristic of the author's wide reading. Mill also published many theological lectures and sermons.

[Gent. Mag. 1854, i. 205; Journal of Royal Asiatic Society, 1855, vol. xv. Rep. p. ii; Journal of Bengal Asiatic Society; communications from members of Mill's family.] C. B.

MILLAR. [See also MILLER and MÜLLER.]

MILLAR, ANDREW (*fl.* 1503–1508), the first Scottish printer. [See MYLLAR.]

MILLAR, ANDREW (1707–1768), publisher, a native of Scotland, was born in 1707. About 1729 he established himself in the Strand, first near St. Clement's Church, and afterwards at Tonson's old shop, 'The Shakespeare's Head' (re-christened Buchanan's Head), over against Catherine Street, where he speedily realised a handsome fortune. Though no great judge of literature himself, he was careful to surround himself with capable advisers as to the purchase of copyright. His liberality to authors led Johnson to say of him in 1755: 'I respect Millar, sir; he has raised the price of literature' (BOSWELL, *Life of Johnson*, ed. Hill, i. 287). He paid Thomson in 1729 137*l.* 10*s.* for 'Sophonisba' and 'Spring,' and in 1738 105*l.* for the sole right of publishing the 'Seasons.' For Armstrong's 'Œconomy of Love' he gave fifty guineas. Fielding received from him 183*l.* 11*s.* for 'Joseph Andrews' (1742), 600*l.* for 'Tom Jones' (1749), and an additional 100*l.* upon its success (WALPOLE, *Letters*, ed. Cunningham, ii. 163), while 1,000*l.* was allowed for 'Amelia' (1751), of which, thanks to some ingenious devices adopted by Millar, a second edition was called for on the day of publication. Fortunately for Millar, Mallet refused his offer of 3,000*l.* for the copyright of Bolingbroke's 'Works;' the editor had afterwards to borrow money from Millar to get the book printed. On Millar devolved the chief responsibility of conducting Johnson's 'Dictionary' through the press. His patience was sorely tried by Johnson's unpunctuality, and when the last sheet was brought to him he could not help exclaiming 'Thank God I have done with him!' On this being repeated to Johnson he replied, with a smile, 'I am glad that he thanks God for anything.' He was also the publisher of the histories of Robertson and Hume. The latter had much correspondence with Millar, generally of a grumbling or suspicious order. Dr. Alexander Carlyle met Millar in 1763 at the 'Dragon' in Harrogate, a favourite resort of persons of quality. The gentry staying in the house, having failed to take the precaution of ordering newspapers, were dependent upon Millar, 'who had two papers sent to him by every post, and were civil accordingly; and yet when he appeared in the morning in his old, well-worn suit of clothes, they could not help calling him Peter Pamphlet; for the generous patron of Scotch authors, with his city wife and her niece, were sufficiently ridiculous when they came into good company' (*Autobiog.* pp. 434–5). A monument to James Thomson was erected in Westminster Abbey in 1762, the cost being defrayed by the sale of a splendid quarto edition of the poet's works, of which Millar generously relinquished the copyright. In 1767 Millar resigned his business to Thomas Cadell the elder [q. v.], his partner since 1765, and retired to Kew Green, where he died on 8 June 1768; he was buried in Chelsea cemetery. His three children died in infancy. His widow, Jane, remarried Sir Archibald Grant of Monymusk, Aberdeenshire, and died at her house in Pall Mall on 25 Oct. 1788, aged 81. In his will (P. C. C. 250, Secker) Millar left legacies to David Hume and to William and Allen Fielding, sons of Henry Fielding, the novelist.

Among the Additional MSS. in the British Museum are letters from Millar to Sir Hans Sloane (4059), Dr. Thomas Birch, 1736–50 (4314), the Society for Encouragement of Learning, 1736–9 (6190), for which he published, Sir Andrew Mitchell, 1760–4 (6858), and J. Caryll, 1747 (28230, f. 377). His correspondence with Bishop Warburton, whose 'Divine Legation' he published, is in Egerton MS. 1959, f. 15.

[Nichols's Lit. Anecd. iii. 386, and elsewhere; David Hume's Letters, ed. Birkbeck Hill, passim; Knight's Shadows of the Old Booksellers; Timperley's Encyclopædia; Walpole's Letters (Cunningham), ii. 509.] G. G.

MILLAR, JAMES, M.D. (1762–1827), physician and miscellaneous writer, born at Ayr 4 Feb. 1762, distinguished himself in classics and science at Glasgow university. For some years he acted as tutor in Jamaica and afterwards was chaplain at Glasgow university. Removing to Edinburgh, he graduated M.D. and became fellow of the Royal College of Physicians of Edinburgh. He frequently lectured on natural history and chemistry, and was one of the physicians at the Edinburgh Dispensary, where he caught a fever and died 13 July 1827. He left a family ill provided for.

In 1807 Millar published in conjunction with William Vazie 'Observations on the Advantages and Practicability of making Tunnels under Navigable Rivers, particularly applicable to the proposed Tunnel under the Forth,' 8vo, Edinburgh. He also edited the fourth edition of the 'Encyclopædia Britannica,' 20 vols. 4to, Edinburgh, 1810, and the last fifteen volumes of the fifth edition of the same work, 20 vols., 4to, Edinburgh, 1817, and wrote largely in both editions. Millar also planned and edited a more popular dictionary of arts, sciences, and literature, the 'Encyclopædia Edinensis,' 6 vols. 4to, Edinburgh, 1827.

His other publications, which are chiefly based on his articles contributed to the encyclopædias, include: 1. 'A Guide to Botany,' 12mo, Edinburgh, 1819. 2. 'Elements of Chemistry,' 8vo, Edinburgh, 1820. 3. 'Practical Observations on Cold and Warm Bathing, and descriptive Notices of Watering-places in Britain,' 12mo, Edinburgh, 1821.

[Gent. Mag. 1827, pt. ii. pp. 276–7; Biog. Dict. of Living Authors, 1816, p. 233; Watt's Bibl. Brit.; Irving's Book of Scotsmen, p. 351.] G. G.

MILLAR, JOHN (1735–1801), professor of law, was born 22 June 1735 in the parish of Shotts, Lanarkshire, of which his father, James Millar, was minister. His mother was a daughter of Archibald Hamilton of Westburn, Lanarkshire. The elder Millar became minister of Hamilton in 1737; and the son was sent to live with his uncle, John Millar, who lived on the small family estate of Millheugh, Blantyre, near Glasgow. The boy was taught to read by his uncle, and in 1742 was sent to the grammar school of Hamilton. In 1746 he went to Glasgow, where he became a friend of William Morehead, afterwards of Herbertshire, the uncle of Francis Jeffrey. When a little older he lived in college chambers, and dined with his mother's first cousin, William Cullen [q. v.] He became intimate with the famous James Watt (1736–1819) [q. v.], and attended Adam Smith's lectures upon moral philosophy. Millar's description of these lectures is given in Dugald Stewart's 'Life of Smith.' Smith long afterwards showed his esteem for his hearer by sending his cousin, David

Douglas, to study under Millar at Glasgow (STEWART, *Works*, x. 11–13, 80).

Millar had been intended for the ministry, but he had some scruples as to the necessary profession of faith; and his uncle John, who had been a writer to the signet, encouraged him to take to the law. After completing his course at Glasgow he was for two years in the family of Henry Home, lord Kames [q. v.], to whose son he was tutor. He there made the acquaintance of David Hume. Millar became a firm believer in Hume's metaphysical doctrines, and though they were politically opposed, Hume placed his nephew, David Hume (1757–1838) [q. v.], under Millar's charge in 1775 (BURTON, *Hume*, ii. 479–81). Millar became an advocate in 1760, and made a promising start in his profession, but he sacrificed any prospects which he might have had by accepting next year the professorship of law at Glasgow, to which he was appointed, 'through the interest of the guardians of the Duke of Hamilton and at the recommendation of Lord Kames and Adam Smith.' The pay was small, but he had just married Miss Margaret Craig, and preferred a small certainty to the chances of professional success. His duties did not at first preclude him from attending circuits, and he had a reputation for his influence with juries in defending criminals. He was also frequently employed in arbitrations in commercial cases (*Life*, pp. lxxxvii–lxxxix). He devoted himself, however, to his professorial duties and rapidly increased the attendance of students, upon whose fees the salary chiefly depended. He had soon forty students of civil law in place of four or five, and a greater number attended his lectures on government. His predecessor, Hercules Lindsay, had lectured in English, in spite of a protest from the Faculty of Advocates, and Millar attracted students by adhering to this precedent. Unlike many Scottish professors, he never wrote his lectures, but spoke from notes, and continued to modify his lectures materially until his death. He gave half the session to lectures upon civil law, and half to lectures upon jurisprudence generally. He gave additional courses upon government, upon Scottish law, and for some years before his death upon English law. His books (see below) gave the substance of some of his lectures. A general account of the whole course is given by his biographer. He appears to have been a very animated lecturer, commanding the interest of his hearers, and uncompromising in asserting his principles. He took pupils in his house; and on becoming professor was elected a member of the 'Literary Society' of Glasgow, founded in 1752. He practised speaking there regularly, and became one of the leading orators; especially maintaining Hume's theories in opposition to Reid, who held the professorship of moral philosophy at Glasgow from 1763 to 1796. Their controversies did not disturb their friendship.

Millar's whiggism made him conspicuous at a time when Scotland was chiefly in the hands of the tories. He did not scruple to express his hopes that the American struggle might end in the independence, rather than in the conquest of the colonies. He was in favour of parliamentary reform, though he opposed universal suffrage as leading to corruption. He held by the Rockingham whigs and afterwards by Fox. He taught that the power of the crown had made alarming advances, and held that the triumph of Pitt and George III in 1784 had dealt 'a fatal blow to the British Constitution.' His 'Historical View,' published in 1787, was dedicated to Fox, and intended in part to meet the toryism of Hume's history. He was an ardent supporter of the agitation against the slave-trade. He sympathised with the French revolution at its start, and, though he lamented the catastrophes which followed, continued to oppose the war and the 'crusade' advocated by Burke. He was a zealous member of the 'Society of the Friends of the People,' and incurred much odium in consequence. He is said to have refused a 'lucrative place' in order that his independence of an administration whose measures he condemned might not be doubtful (*ib.* p. xcviii). Jeffrey when at Glasgow was forbidden by his father to attend Millar's lectures on account of their whig tendency.

Millar spent much of his time at the small farm of Whitemoss, near Kilbride, about seven miles from Glasgow, which was given to him by his uncle, John Millar. He was there a neighbour of James Baillie, the professor of divinity, with whose children, Joanna [q. v.] and Matthew [q. v.], his own children became intimate. Upon the death of his father and his uncle in 1785 he became proprietor of Millheugh, and here, as at Whitemoss, amused himself by planting and cultivating. He visited England twice: in 1774, when he was at London, Oxford, and Cambridge; and in 1792, when he stayed in London, heard debates, and made the acquaintance of Fox.

Millar was an athletic and temperate man, and appeared to retain his health and spirits, but was weakened by an illness in 1799, and after recovering incautiously exposed himself, and died of pleurisy at Millheugh 30 May 1801.

Millar lost a daughter by consumption in 1791, and his wife in 1795. His eldest son, John, a promising young man, went to the bar, and married the daughter of Dr. Cullen. He published a book upon the 'Law relating to Insurances' in 1787. Ill-health and the unpopularity of the whiggism which he inherited from his father induced him to emigrate in the spring of 1795 to America, where he died soon afterwards from a sunstroke.

Three sons and six daughters survived their father. Of these James became professor of mathematics at Glasgow; the second, William, is separately noticed; the third was a writer to the signet. One daughter was married to James Mylne, professor of moral philosophy at Glasgow, and another to Dr. John Thomson, by whom she was mother of Allan Thomson, professor of surgery at Edinburgh. He left his manuscripts to his eldest son, to Professor Mylne, and to John Craig, his nephew, by whom some were published in 1803.

Millar was a man of strong sense and singularly sanguine temperament; vivacious and fond of argument, consistent in his opinions, and a severe judge of the consistency of others. He was well read in English literature, had strong social and domestic sympathies, was playful and fond of children, and was eminently capable of attracting the affection of friends and pupils, though a little formal in his manners and reserved in expressions of feeling. Among his intimate friends was John Moore [q. v.], the author of 'Zeluco,' and his pupil, the Earl of Lauderdale, upon whose economical speculations he had considerable influence, and to whom he paid an annual visit. There is a medallion portrait of Millar by James Tassie in the Scottish National Portrait Gallery, Edinburgh.

Millar's works are: 1. 'The Origin of the Distinction of Ranks, or an Enquiry into the circumstances which gave rise to influence and authority in the different Members of Society,' London, 4to, 1771. A fourth edition was published at Edinburgh in 1806, with a 'Life' by John Craig. This interesting book shows the influence of Montesquieu, and especially of Hume, whose essay upon 'The Populousness of Ancient Nations' is similar in design. J. F. Maclennan says of it (*Studies in Ancient History*, 1871, p. 420 *n.*): 'The reader will find an admirable review of the facts connected with this matter and with gynaikocracy in Professor Millar's "Origin of Ranks," a work in which Bachofen [author of 'Das Mutterrecht'] has *almost* been anticipated, and that by a treatment of the facts in every sense strictly scientific.' It was translated into German at Leipzig in 1772, and into French by Dominique Joseph Garat, minister of justice, in 1792. 2. 'Historical View of the English Government from the Settlement of the Saxons in Britain to the Accession of the House of Stewart,' 1787; 2nd edit. 1790. A third edition, with additions from his manuscripts, was published in 1803, in 4 vols. 8vo, with the addition to the previous title, 'To which are subjoined some Dissertations connected with the History of the Government from the Revolution to the Present Time.' The first two volumes are the original work. A fourth edition appeared in 1818. The book had a high reputation, and was praised by Jeffrey in the 'Edinburgh Review,' iii. 154–81. Both books were greatly admired by James Mill (Bain, *Mill*, p. 56), and John Stuart Mill acknowledged that there was great similarity between some of Millar's historical speculations and Guizot's (Macvey Napier, *Correspondence*, p. 510). Hallam, in the preface to his 'Middle Ages,' says that the history is pleasing from its 'liberal spirit,' but that Millar is too fond of 'theorising upon an imperfect induction, and very often upon a total misapprehension of particular facts.' It was, however, almost the only book upon the subject when Hallam wrote.

[Life, by John Craig, prefixed to Origin of Ranks, 1806; Scots Mag. 1801, pp. 527–8; A. Carlyle's Autobiog. 1860, p. 492; Life of Lord Minto, 1879, ii. 26; Edinburgh Review, iii. 154–81, iv. 83–92 (articles by Jeffrey upon the 'History' and the 'Life').] L. S.

MILLAR, JOHN, M.D. (1733–1805), medical writer, born in Scotland in 1733, graduated M.D. at Edinburgh. He commenced practice at Kelso, but on being appointed, in August 1774, physician to the Westminster General Dispensary, he settled in Pall Mall, London, and became an active promoter of the Medical Society of London, instituted in 1773. He died on 25 Feb. 1805 in Shepherd Street, Mayfair (*Scots Mag.* 1805, p. 237). By his wife Isabella, sister of Admiral Brisbane, he had two sons (Burke, *Landed Gentry*, 1886, p. 211). John, the eldest, was a lieutenant in the English navy, but died at Revel on 29 May 1804 in command of a 74-gun ship in the service of the emperor of Russia (*Gent. Mag.* 1804, pt. ii. p. 784); the youngest, a ship-surgeon, was drowned in early youth at sea (Millar, *Observations on the Change of Public Opinion*, Pref. p. cxxviii).

Millar was an excellent physician, especially for women and children, but was eccentric and irritable. His chief works are: 1. 'Observations on the Asthma and on the

Hooping Cough,' 8vo, London, 1769 (translated into French by L. Sentex, 8vo, Paris, 1808). 2. 'Observations on the prevailing Diseases in Great Britain,' &c., 4to, London, 1770; another edit. 1798. He announced some 'Additional Observations' on the same subject in 1777. 3. 'Observations on Antimony,' 8vo, London, 1774. 4. 'A Discourse on the Duty of Physicians,' 4to, London, 1776. 5. 'Observations on the Practice in the Medical Department of the Westminster General Dispensary,' &c., 4to, London, 1777. 6. 'Observations on the Management of the Diseases of the Army and Navy during the American War,' &c., 4to, London, 1783, partly in answer to 'Observations,' 1780, by Donald Monro, M.D. [q. v.] 7. 'Observations on the Change of Public Opinion in Religion, Politics, and Medicine; on the Conduct of the War; on the Prevailing Diseases in Great Britain, and on Medical Arrangements in the Army and Navy,' 2 vols. 4to, London [1804]. To Millar the elder Benjamin Rush, M.D., of Philadelphia, addressed his 'Dissertation on the Spasmodic Asthma of Children,' 1770, in which he acknowledges his obligations to Millar's 'excellent treatise' on the subject.

[Gent. Mag. 1805, pt. i. p. 384; Cat. of Libr. of Med. and Chirurg. Soc.] G. G.

MILLAR, WILLIAM (*d.* 1838), lieutenant-general, colonel commandant royal artillery, second son of John Millar (1735–1801) [q. v.], received a direct appointment as second lieutenant royal artillery 24 May 1781. His subsequent commissions were: first lieutenant 1787, captain lieutenant 1794, captain 1799, major (brevet 1805) 1806, lieutenant-colonel 1806, colonel (brevet 4 June) 14 June 1814, major-general 1831, colonel commandant 1834, lieutenant-general 1837. He served eighteen years in the West Indies, and was present at the capture of most of the French islands during the early part of the revolutionary wars. In 1804, on the rebuilding of Woolwich Arsenal after the great fire of 1802, he was appointed assistant to Colonel Fage in the royal carriage department, and was one of the officers to whose skill and indefatigable exertions during the Peninsular war the services were indebted for their material. With mechanical resources which, judged by a later standard, were of the most imperfect description, they poured forth a never failing supply of a quality and excellence which were the admiration of other armies, and at the close of the war led to the French commission of Baron Dupin to inquire into the system that could produce such results. Millar was the originator of the 10-inch and 8-inch shell-guns which formed so large a part of British armaments from 1832 until some years after the Crimean war. He was among the first to perceive the advantages of shell-guns of large calibre; and as early as 1820, that is to say two years before the publication of Paixhans's 'Nouvelle Force Maritime,' brought forward his first 8-inch shell-gun (*Official Catalogue Mus. of Artillery*, p. xxiv). He was appointed inspector-general of artillery in 1827, and director-general of the field-train department in 1833.

Millar died from self-inflicted injuries near Hastings, on 14 March 1838. He had previously exhibited symptoms of suicidal mania. He was married and left a grown-up family.

[Kane's Lists Roy. Artillery, rev. ed., Woolwich, 1869; Official Catalogue Museum of Artillery; Dupin's Voyages dans la Grande-Bretagne; Sir Howard Douglas's Naval Gunnery; Naval and Military Gazette, 17 and 24 March 1838.] H. M. C.

MILLER. [See also MILLAR and MÜLLER.]

MILLER, ANDREW (*d.* 1763), mezzotint engraver, is believed to have been a Scotsman by descent but a native of London, and to have been a pupil of John Faber, jun. [q. v.] The earliest date on his plates is 1737. After practising for a few years in London he went to Dublin and settled there. Miller's portraits, which number more than sixty, are executed in a broad, effective style, and are very scarce; they include Dean Swift, after F. Bindon (1743); the Hon. Robert Boyle, after Kerseboom; Philip, earl of Chesterfield, after Hoare; William, duke of Cumberland, after Hudson; Queen Elizabeth; David Garrick as Richard III, after Hogarth; John Hampden; Archbishop King, after Jervas; Dr. Charles Lucas, after Jones; John, duke of Marlborough, after Kneller; Joe Miller as Teague, after Stoppelaer; Archbishop Ussher, after Lely; Dr. Warburton, after Vandergucht; and George Whitefield, after Jenkin. Some of these are copies of prints by Houbraken, Vertue, and others. Miller also produced a few fancy subjects after Courtin, Rosalba, P. Veronese, &c. His Dublin plates, which are dated from 1743 to 1756, were mostly published by himself 'on Hog Hill, near the Round Church,' and some bear also the address of Michael Ford [q. v.] Miller is said to have shortened his life by intemperance. He died in Dublin in September 1763.

[J. Chaloner Smith's British Mezzotinto Portraits; Bryan's Dict. of Painters and Engravers, ii. 154; J. T. Gilbert's Hist. of Dublin, iii. 318.] F. M. O'D.

MILLER, ANNA, Lady (1741–1781), verse-writer, was the daughter of Edward Riggs, by his wife, Margaret Pigott, of the ancient house of Chetwynd, Shropshire. From her grandfather, Edward Riggs, for many years a member of the Irish House of Commons, and a commissioner of revenue, and a privy councillor in Ireland, she inherited much wealth (cf. *Notes and Queries*, 3rd ser. viii. 192). Her father became a commissioner of customs in London in 1741 (*Gent. Mag.* 1741, p. 387). Horace Walpole describes her mother in 1765 as 'an old rough humourist, who passed for a wit' (*Letters*, vi. 170). Miss Burney characterises Mrs. Riggs as 'mighty merry and facetious' (*Diary*, i. 364). In 1765 Anna married John Miller, a member of a poor Irish family seated at Ballicasey, co. Clare. As a lieutenant in Elliot's light horse, he had served through the seven years' war, but resigned his commission at the peace of 1763. His wife brought him a large fortune, and he, 'full,' according to Walpole, 'of good-natured officiousness,' adopted her maiden surname before his own. At extravagant cost he built a house at Batheaston, near Bath, and laid out a garden, of which Horace Walpole gives a detailed description (*Letters*, v. 20). The expenses incurred soon necessitated a retreat to France, in order to economise. In 1770–1771, Mrs. Miller and her husband made the tour of Italy. In 1776 the sprightly letters that she had sent during her travels to a friend were published anonymously in three volumes, 'Letters from Italy, describing the Manners, Customs, Antiquities, Paintings, &c., of the Country, in 1770–1.' A second edition, in two volumes, appeared in 1777. The book enjoyed some reputation. Horace Walpole, said, however: 'The poor Arcadian patroness does not spell one word of French or Italian right through her three volumes of travel' (*ib.* vi. 332). Boswell met John Miller at dinner at his wife's publishers (C. & E. Dilly) in 1775 and 1776.

Soon after returning to Batheaston, the husband, whose head had been turned, says Walpole, 'with virtu,' was created an Irish baronet (1778), and the wife, henceforth known as Lady Miller, instituted a literary salon at her villa. It bore some resemblance to the later follies of the Della Cruscans, which Gifford satirised in the 'Baviad' [see Merry, Robert]. She invited all persons of wit and fashion in Bath to meet once a fortnight at her house. An antique vase that had been purchased in Italy—it was dug up at Frascati in 1759—was placed on a modern altar decorated with laurel, and each guest was invited to place in the urn an original composition in verse. A committee was appointed to determine the best three productions, and their authors were then crowned by Lady Miller with wreaths of myrtle. The practice was continued until Lady Miller's death. The urn was then purchased by Edwyn Dowding, of Bath, and placed by him in the public park of the town. The society became famous, and was much laughed at. Anthony Morris Storer, writing to George Selwyn, says: 'Their next subject is upon Trifles and Triflers. . . . You may try your hand at an ode, and I do not doubt but you may be crowned with myrtle for your performance' (*George Selwyn and his Contemporaries*, iii. 266). Horace Walpole, in a letter to the Hon. H. S. Conway,' says: 'I am glad you went [to Bath], especially as you escaped being initiated into Mrs. Miller's follies at Bath-Easton' (*Letters*, vii. 163). Miss Burney, while on a visit to Bath in 1780, was introduced to Lady Miller by Mrs. Thrale, and wrote: 'Nothing here is more tonish than to visit Lady Miller. She is a round, plump, coarse-looking dame of about forty, and while all her aim is to appear an elegant woman of fashion, all her success is to seem an ordinary woman in very common life, with fine clothes on' (*Diary*, i. 364).

In 1775 a selection of the compositions was published under the title of 'Poetical Amusements at a Villa near Bath.' The edition was sold out within ten days. A new edition appeared in 1776 with a second volume of poems. Horace Walpole calls the book 'a bouquet of artificial flowers, and ten degrees duller than a magazine' (*Letters*, vi. 169, 178). A third volume was published in 1777, and a fourth in 1781. The profits of the sale were applied to charity. Among the contributors were the Duchess of Northumberland, who wrote on a buttered muffin, Lord Palmerston, Lord Carlisle, Anstey, Mason, David Garrick, Miss Seward, and Lady Miller herself, to whom most of the writers paid extravagant compliments. Dr. Johnson held the collection in high contempt (Hill, *Boswell*, ii. 336). Sir Walter Scott states in his biography of Miss Seward, prefixed to her works (1810), that her poetical power was brought to light by Lady Miller, an obligation that Miss Seward acknowledged in her 'Poem to the Memory of Lady Miller.'

Lady Miller died 24 June 1781, at the Hot Wells, Bristol, and was buried in the Abbey Church, Bath. On her monument by Bacon, erected in 1785, is an epitaph in verse, composed by Miss Seward (cf. *Gent. Mag.* 1781, p. 295, and 1785, pt. ii. p. 746). She left two children, a son and a daughter.

Miss Burney mentions the latter in 1780 as a most beautiful little girl of ten (*Diary*, i. 364).

Sir John Riggs Miller, who inherited his wife's fortune, married, after 1786, the widow of Sir Thomas Davenport. He sat in parliament from 1784 to 1790, as member for Newport in Cornwall, and made various unsuccessful efforts to reform the system of weights and measures. He corresponded on the subject with Talleyrand. Settling in Bloomsbury Square, he became known in London society as an inveterate gossip and newsmonger, and was a well-known figure in many London clubs. He died suddenly on 28 May 1798, and was succeeded in the baronetcy by his son by his first marriage, John Edward Augustus Miller (1770–1825) (cf. *Gent. Mag.* 1798, pt. ii. pp. 626-7, and 1825, pt. ii. p. 286).

Besides the works already mentioned, a volume by Lady Miller entitled 'On Novelty, and on Trifles and Triflers,' appeared in 1778.

[Allibone, ii. 1286; Miss Seward's preface to her Poem in Memory of Lady Miller; Collinson's Somerset, i. 103; Notes and Queries, 2nd ser. v. 495.] E. L.

MILLER, EDWARD (1730–1807), organist and historian of Doncaster, was born at Norwich in 1730. His father was a pavior, and he was put to the same trade, but ran away from home and obtained a musical training from Dr. Burney, who was then at King's Lynn. His brother Thomas is separately noticed. The 'Dictionary of Musicians' (London, 1827) makes the impossible statement that he played the flute in Handel's first oratorios, which were 'Il trionfo del tempo e del disinganno' (1707) and 'La Resurrezione' (1708). The mistake probably arises from the fact that a translation and revision of 'Il trionfo' was produced in 1751 and called 'The Triumph of Time and Truth;' it is possible that Miller played in this oratorio, probably the flute. In 1752 he published 'Six Solos for the German Flute, with remarks on double tonguing' (London). On 25 July 1756 he was elected organist of the church of Doncaster on the recommendation of James Nares [q. v.], and he retained the post until his death, supplementing his resources by giving lessons on the pianoforte. In 1768 he published 'Six Sonatas for the Harpsichord' (London), and in 1771 the work by which he is best known, 'The Institutes of Music, or Easy Instructions for the Harpsichord' (London, n. d., fol.); this work ran into sixteen editions. In 1773 he published 'Twelve Songs' (London), 'Elegies for Voice and Pianoforte' (London), and in 1774 he issued by subscription, under the patronage of the king, 'The Psalms of David set to Music and arranged for every Sunday in the year.' For this work he had over five thousand subscribers. In 1774 Francis Linley [q. v.] was born (blind) at Doncaster, and from an early age studied under Miller. In 1784 Miller published 'Letters in behalf of Professors of Music residing in the Country' (London), a critique of which occurs in the 'Critical Review,' 1784, lvii. 399. It is a plea that poor musicians in the country should benefit as well as those in London by the Handel commemoration festival then in contemplation. In 1786 he was created Mus. Doc. by the university of Cambridge, and in 1787 he published simultaneously in London and Dublin his 'Treatise of Thorough Bass and Composition.' In 1791 he published 'Thoughts on the present performance of Psalmody in the Established Church of England addressed to the Clergy' (London), and in 1792 'A Letter to the Country Spectator in reply to the author of his 9th Number . . . by a Professor of Music' (London and Doncaster), which is a defence of 'Fiddlers.' In 1801 he published 'The Psalms of Watts and Wesley for three Voices for the use of Methodists' (London), and in 1804 'The History and Antiquities of Doncaster and its vicinity with anecdotes of Eminent Men, with a map, &c.' (Doncaster). He was also the author of 'The Tears of Yorkshire on the death of the Most Noble the Marquis of Rockingham' (London, n. d.), and Fétis states that he began a translation of J. J. Rousseau's 'Dictionnaire de la Musique,' of which a few proofs of the first eighteen pages were printed, but no more. He died at Doncaster on 12 Sept. 1807, aged 76.

[J. D. Brown's Biographical Dict. of Musicians, Paisley, 1886; A Dictionary of Musicians, 1827; P. Lichtenthal's Dizionario e Bibliografia della Musica, Milan, 1826; Fétis's Biographie Universelle des Musiciens; Watt's Bibl. Brit.] E. H.-A.

MILLER, GEORGE, D.D. (1764–1848), divine, eldest son of Stephen Miller, general merchant, of Dublin, was born there on 22 Oct. 1764 and was there educated. Among his schoolfellows and early friends were Theobald Wolfe Tone [q. v.] and Charles Kendal Bushe [q. v.], afterwards chief justice of the king's bench, Ireland. In July 1779 he entered Trinity College, where he was elected scholar in 1782, graduated B.A. in 1784, took holy orders and a fellowship, and proceeded M.A. in 1789, graduated B.D. in 1794, and proceeded D.D. in 1799. After a visit to England in 1793, Miller returned to Ireland, married, and thenceforth resided in Dublin, busily occupied in tutorial and literary work until 1803, when he accepted the college living of Derryvullane in the diocese of Clogher. In 1796 he delivered, but did not publish, a course of lectures on the Donnellan foundation 'On the Causes which impeded the further Progress of Christianity.' In 1797 he published a critical edition of Dionysius Longinus 'De Sublimitate,' Dublin, 8vo, 2nd edit. 1820. In 1799 appeared his 'Elements of Natural Philosophy,' Dublin, 8vo, 2nd edit. 1820. An enthusiastic member of the historical society founded by Grattan, he held from 1799 until 1803 the post of assistant professor of modern history, and from 1803 to 1811 that of lecturer on the same subject in the university. His lectures at first attracted but little attention, but grew steadily in popularity, and were afterwards published under the title 'Lectures on the Philosophy of Modern History delivered in the University of Dublin,' Dublin, 1816–28, 8 vols. 8vo. Though hardly justifying their somewhat pretentious title, they are characterised by width of reading, grasp of principle, and methodical arrangement. A free and carefully revised abridgment, entitled 'History Philosophically Illustrated from the Fall of the Roman Empire to the French Revolution,' appeared in 1832, London, 4 vols. 8vo, reprinted 1848–9 and 1852, ed. Bohn.

In 1817 Miller had been appointed headmaster of the Royal School, Armagh, a post which he held until shortly before his death. Miller began life an Arian in theology and a liberal in politics, but was gradually converted to strongly orthodox protestant church and state principles. In 1825 he published an ingenious pamphlet entitled 'Observations on the Doctrines of Christianity in reference to Arianism, illustrating the Moderation of the Established Church, and on the Athanasian Creed, purporting to prove that it is not damnatory, nor metaphysical, nor contradictory,' London, 1825, 8vo; and in 1826 'The Athanasian Creed: with Explanatory Observations,' Dublin, 8vo. In the latter year the celebrated 'Dissertation' by Edward Hawkins (1789-1882) [q.v.] 'On the Use and Importance of Unauthoritative Tradition,' which heralded the rise of the tractarian movement (cf. Newman, *Apologia*, chap. i.), was met by Miller with a learned and ably reasoned defence of the principles of the reformation, entitled 'An Historical Review of the Plea of Tradition as maintained in the Church of Rome: with Strictures on Hawkins's Dissertation,' London, 8vo. He also issued a manifesto against the emancipation of the Roman catholics, entitled 'The Policy of the Roman Catholic Question discussed in a Letter to the Right Hon. W. C. Plunket,' London, 1826, 8vo. In October 1840 he published a trenchant 'Letter to the Rev. E. B. Pusey, D.D., in reference to his Letter to the Lord Bishop of Oxford' (London, 8vo), which perhaps helped to elicit Newman's celebrated 'Tract XC.,' to which he virtually replied in 'A Second Letter to the Rev. E. B. Pusey in reference to his Letter to the Rev. R. W. Jelf, D.D., Canon of Christ Church,' London, September 1841, 8vo (cf. the correspondence between Miller and Professor Sewell in the *Irish Ecclesiastical Journal*, November 1840 et seq.) In 1843 Miller was appointed vicar-general of the diocese of Armagh, of which he had for some time previously been surrogate. His judgments in this capacity were marked by ability and settled some important points on the law of marriage and divorce. He died in Armagh on 6 Oct. 1848, and was buried in St. Mark's churchyard. For the last forty years of his life he had been a strict vegetarian.

Miller was a member of the Royal Irish Academy, in the 'Transactions' of which learned society will be found three papers by him, viz.: 'On the Nature and Limits of Certainty and Probability,' and 'On the Origin and Nature of our Idea of the Sublime,' both in vol. v. (1793), and 'Observations on the Theory of Electric Attraction and Repulsion' (1799). To the 'British Critic,' January 1828, he contributed an article on 'The Irish Reformation of 1826 and 1827;' to Blackwood's 'Edinburgh Magazine,' November 1829, 'Considerations on the Law of Divorce.' He was also a contributor to the 'Irish Ecclesiastical Journal,' 1840–6, and the 'British Magazine,' 1845–6. Besides the treatises and pamphlets above mentioned, Miller published various sermons and the following miscellanea: 1. 'An Examination of the Charters and Statutes of Trinity College, Dublin, in regard to the supposed distinction between the College and the University,' Dublin, 1804, 8vo. 2. 'A Lecture on the Origin and Influences of the Wars of the French Revolution,' Dublin, 1811, 8vo. 3. 'A Letter to the Lord Primate of Ireland on the manner in which Christianity was taught by our Saviour and his Apostles,' London, 1822, 8vo. 4. 'The Temptations of Jesus Christ in the Wilderness explained as symbolically representing the Trials of the Christian Church,' London, 1826, 8vo. 5. 'The Question of the Change of the Sabbath examined, in reference to the Jewish Scriptures, for obviating the inferences both of Jews and of Roman Catholics,' London, 1829, 8vo. 6. 'Examination of the Act to amend the Representation of the People of Ireland in relation to the University of Dublin,' Dublin, 1832, 8vo. 7. 'The Principal Events of Modern History with their Times selected in reference to Modern History Philosophically Illustrated,' Armagh, 1839, 8vo. 8. 'Judgment in the Consistorial Court of Armagh, involving the Question of the Law of Marriage in Ireland,' Armagh, 1840, 8vo. 9. 'Notes on the Opinions of Lord Brougham and Vaux and Lord Campbell on the Law of Marriage in Ireland,' London, 1844, 8vo. 10. 'The Present Crisis of the Church of Ireland considered,' Dublin, 1844, 8vo; 2nd edit. 1845. 11. 'The Case of the Church Education Society of Ireland argued in reply to Dr. Elrington,' London, 1847, 8vo. 12. 'Supplement to the Case of the Church Education Society of Ireland,' &c., London, 1847, 8vo. 13. 'The Law of Ecclesiastical Residences in Ireland,' Dublin, 1848, 8vo.

[A Memoir of Miller is prefixed to vol. iv. of his History Philosophically Illustrated, ed. 1849; cf. Dublin Univ. Mag. xvii. 674–92; Gent. Mag. 1848, pt. ii. p. 551; Notes and Queries, 1st ser. iii. 137, vii. 527, 631, xi. 231, 2nd ser. viii. 50, 4th ser. iii. 187; Castlereagh Corresp. ii. 302; Corresp. of Bishop Jebb and Alexander Knox, i. 374; Dublin Graduates; Webb's Compendium of Irish Biography.] J. M. R.

MILLER, HUGH (1802–1856), man of letters and geologist, son of Hugh Miller by his second wife Harriet, was born at Cromarty on 10 Oct. 1802. His father, who came of a long line of seafaring men of Scandinavian descent, was lost in the Moray Firth with his trading-sloop and all hands on 9 Nov. 1807. His mother was great-granddaughter of Donald Ross or Roy, a sage and seer of Celtic race long remembered in Ross-shire. As a child Hugh was a keen observer of nature and a collector of shells and stones, while he evinced much interest in literature. But when sent to the school of his native burgh he proved incorrigibly self-willed, and left it after a violent personal encounter with the dominie, on whom he revenged himself in some stinging verses. Wild and intractable, he formed his companions into a gang of rovers and orchard robbers; but at the same time he infected some of them with his own love of reading and rhyming, and edited a boyish 'Village Observer,' to which several of them contributed. At seventeen he was apprenticed to a stonemason, abandoned his boyish frowardness, and became an excellent workman. His occupation gave his mind its scientific cast. He saw ripple-marks on the bed of his first quarry; and thus 'the necessity that had made him a quarrier taught him also to be a geologist.' On 11 Nov. 1822 his apprenticeship ceased and he became a journeyman mason. Miller thenceforth pursued his craft in different parts of the highlands and lowlands of Scotland, sometimes in towns—he was in Edinburgh in 1824–5—oftener in the open country. Always observing, reflecting, and writing, he developed a strongly religious temperament, and devotion to the Christian faith became the determining principle of his life. He soon formed the acquaintance of persons of literary taste, among them Dr. Carruthers of the 'Inverness Courier,' and Alexander Stewart, minister of Cromarty. In 1829 he published 'Poems written in the Leisure Hours of a Journeyman Mason,' a volume that attracted the favourable attention of some distant critics, among them Leigh Hunt, but it lacked fire or facility, and he wisely abandoned poetry for prose. He contributed in 1829 'Letters on the Herring Fishery' to the 'Inverness Courier;' they were reprinted separately, and gave promise of much literary capacity.

At thirty-two, in 1834, his reputation in his native town brought him an accountantship in the branch of the Commercial Bank recently established there. On 7 Jan. 1837 he married, after a long courtship, Lydia Falconer Fraser [see Miller, Lydia Falconer], a lady of great mental refinement. He showed some interest in his work at the bank by publishing 'Words of Warning to the People of Scotland,' in which he advocated the continuance of the one-pound-note circulation. But he made his first mark in literature in 1835 when he issued 'Scenes and Legends of the North of Scotland,' the traditions of his native Cromarty, and a little later he contributed largely to Mackay Wilson's 'Tales of the Borders.' But while he thoroughly studied the antiquities of his native town, he did not neglect the geological examination of the neighbouring country which he had begun as a stonemason's apprentice. Geology formed the subject of a chapter in his 'Scenes and Legends.' He explored the fossil fish-beds of the old red sandstone about Cromarty; and when Dr. John Malcolmson and Professor Fleming of Aberdeen visited the town, he met them and discussed geological problems. He soon began to correspond with Murchison and Agassiz, and to collect the materials for a work on the 'Old Red Sandstone.'

Since 1834 Miller had been an intensely interested spectator of the attempts of the Church of Scotland to neutralise the effects of the law of patronage, and to secure to the Scottish people the right of freely electing their pastors. In May 1839 the House of Lords decided that the rights of patronage were 'inconsistent with the exercise of any volition on the part of the people, however expressed.' Miller and others saw that an ecclesiastical reform bill for Scotland was needful to restore the Scottish people's rights, and to rouse popular feeling on the question he published two powerful pamphlets, 'A Letter to Lord Brougham' and 'The Whiggism of the Old School,' 1839, in which he ably stated the popular view. In January 1840 he was offered by the leaders of his party—the non-intrusionists—the editorship of their new organ, the 'Witness,' a bi-weekly newspaper. He accepted the post with diffidence, but, once settled at the editorial desk in Edinburgh, he proved that he was in his right place. He impressed his personality on the paper, and it rapidly attained a very wide circulation. His leading articles, to which he devoted the utmost care, were invariably brilliant and convincing. The movement grew, and Miller's part in it was only second to that of Chalmers. Signatures to non-intrusion petitions increased fivefold. At the general election of 1841 all the Scottish parliamentary candidates, with a single exception, were advocating some popular modification of patronage. In 1843 the disruption came, and the free church, embracing two-thirds of the members of the church of Scotland, was established. In the free church, at the outset, Miller saw an opportunity for realising his ideal of a national church. The free church, reared alongside the establishment (which he at that time held with Chalmers to have become a 'moral nullity'), was to overshadow and absorb it without self-aggrandisement, and by pure moral force. 'The church of the future,' he insisted, 'must be missionary, not political.' But, to his sorrow, the free church, after the death of Chalmers, and under other leaders, abandoned, in his opinion, her high claims by identifying her position with that of a dissenting sect.

Throughout this exciting period science was Miller's relaxation. In 1840 his well-known book on 'The Old Red Sandstone, or New Walks in an Old Field,' appeared serially in the 'Witness,' and was re-published in 1841, with remarkable figures of 'Old Red' fishes from his own pencil. By this work, wrote Buckland, geologists were astonished and delighted. They at once accorded to the old red sandstone, as a formation, an importance scarcely before recognised. His technical ichthyology was based on Agassiz's contemporary researches among the fishes of the 'Old Red,' but it contained important improvements, and the best part of the work was founded entirely on original observation. 'The more I study the fishes of the "Old Red,"' wrote Professor Huxley twenty years afterwards, 'the more I am struck with the patience and sagacity manifested in Hugh Miller's researches, and by the natural insight, which in his case seems to have supplied the place of special anatomical knowledge.' His common sense gave him a grasp of the scientific method in palæontology, while his imagination enabled him to pictorially restore ancient physical geographies.

In 1845, broken down in health by excessive labour, he visited England, and his 'First Impressions of England and its People' appeared in 1846. In 1847 he published 'Footprints of the Creator, or the Asterolepis of Stromness.' This was a reply to the 'Vestiges of Creation,' and a contribution both to Christian apologetics and to palæontology. Many of the fossils described were supplied to Miller by his friend, Robert Dick [q. v.] of Thurso. To the American edition Agassiz affixed a memoir of the writer. The doctrine of development Miller here held to be irreconcilable with the dogmas of Christianity. He argued for the miracle of creation *versus* the law of development, and set himself to prove that the earliest fossils, and more especially the fishes of the 'Old Red,' were as advanced of their kind as those that have lived since or that live now.

In 1848 Miller contributed a geological section to McCrie's work on the Bass Rock, and in 1852 he published his autobiography, 'My Schools and Schoolmasters.' 'Truly I am glad,' wrote Thomas Carlyle to him of this work, 'to condense the bright but indistinct rumour labelled to me by your Name, for years past, into the ruddy-visaged, strong-boned, glowing Figure of a Man which I have got, and bid good speed to, with all my heart! You have, as you undertook to do, painted many things to us; scenes of life, scenes of Nature, which rarely come upon the canvas; and I will add, such Draughtsmen too are extremely uncommon in that and in other walks of painting. There is a right genial fire in the Book, everywhere nobly tempered down into peaceful, radical heat, which is very beautiful to see. Luminous, memorable; all wholesome, strong, and breezy, like the "Old Red Sandstone Mountains" in a sunny summer day.'

Miller's last volume, which received its final corrections on the day of his death, 'The Testimony of the Rocks' (1857) mainly deals, like 'The Footprints,' with the borderland between science and religion. Miller took the six days of creation as synonymous with six periods, and sublimed them into representative visions of the progress of creation. 'Rightly understood,' says Miller, speaking of Genesis, 'I know not a single truth that militates against the minutest or least prominent of its details.'

In the meantime, in 1845, 'The Witness' became the joint property of Miller and his business partner, Robert Fairby, and its sentiments henceforth diverged from those held by the leaders of the free church. In politics Miller was an 'old whig,' or independent liberal—'whig in principle, tory in feeling'—and his political independence gave, in the words of the 'Scotsman,' 'dignity and character to the newspaper press of Scotland.' In education he supported the national, not the sectarian, view, and favoured no such narrow restriction of subjects as some of his co-religionists adopted, and in 'Thoughts on the Education Question' (1850) he outlined a scheme now substantially law. Conscious of the growing power of the masses he advocated, besides education, a moderate extension of the franchise, the abolition of entail, and the curtailment of the game laws. He exposed and denounced the Sutherlandshire clearings and the intolerant refusal of sites to the free church, but he countenanced no vision of clearing the proprietors. To chartism he was hostile, strikes he discouraged, and he accepted a poor law for Scotland with regret, deeming it to have been rendered necessary by the inefficiency of the old church administration of relief. Puritan in temper, he deemed Ireland in need of education and protestantism, and the grant to Maynooth he would gladly have seen converted into a grant to science.

In the words of Dr. John Brown, Miller was the 'inexorable taskmaster' of his own energies, and with characteristic tenacity he worked on at his newspaper or his books when he needed rest. The seeds of the 'stonemasons' disease' had been sown in his constitution in early manhood, and his frame was subsequently weakened by repeated attacks of inflammation of the lungs. Under the strain of bodily illness his intellect suddenly gave way, and on the night of 23 Dec. 1856 he died by his own hand.

Miller's features were rugged, but his calm, grey eyes and pleasing smile softened their austerity. His voice was gentle. Not mixing much in general society, he reckoned himself a working man to the end, but he carried himself with much natural stateliness. There is an early calotype by D. O. Hill, which though not very distinct in its lineaments, and certainly too aggressive in its expression, is more suggestive of Miller's strength of character than any other likeness. A portrait by Bonnar belongs to the family. A bust, by William Brodie, is in the National Portrait Gallery, Edinburgh.

Miller's chief works, other than those mentioned, are: 1. 'The Whiggism of the Old School, as exemplified by the Past History and Present Position of the Church of Scotland,' 1839. 2. 'Memoir of William Forsyth,' 1839. 3. 'The Two Parties in the Church of Scotland exhibited as Missionary and Anti-missionary,' 1841. 4. 'Scenes and Legends of the North of Scotland; or the Traditional History of Cromarty,' 1850. 5. 'The Fossiliferous Deposits of Scotland,' 1854. 6. 'Geology versus Astronomy; or the Conditions and the Periods; being a View of the Modifying Effects of Geologic Discovery on the Old Astronomic Inferences respecting the Plurality of Inhabited Worlds,' Glasgow [1855]. 7. 'Voices from the Rocks; or Proofs of the Existence of Man during the Palæozoic Period,' 1857. 8. 'The Cruise of the Betsy; or a Summer Ramble among the Fossiliferous Deposits of the Hebrides,' ed. by W. S. Symonds, 1858. 9. 'Essays,' ed. by P. Bayne, 1862. 10. 'Tales and Sketches,' ed. Mrs. Miller, 1863. 11. 'Edinburgh and its Neighbourhood, Geological and Historical,' ed. by Mrs. Miller, 1864.

[Life and Letters of Hugh Miller by Peter Bayne, 1871; Miller's My Schools and Schoolmasters; personal knowledge.] H. M.

MILLER, JAMES (1706–1744), playwright, son of John Miller, rector of Compton Valence and Upcerne in Dorset, was born in 1706. He went to Wadham College, Oxford, in 1726, and was to have been bred to business, but entered holy orders. While at Oxford he wrote a satirical comedy, the 'Humours of Oxford,' by which he made many enemies. Some of the characters were thought to be designed for students and heads of the university. On leaving Oxford he was appointed to the lectureship of Trinity Chapel, Conduit Street, and made preacher of the private chapel, Roehampton, Surrey. The 'Humours of Oxford' had been successfully acted at Drury Lane 9 Jan. 1730, on the recommendation of Mrs. Oldfield (who took the part of Clarinda, with Wilks as Gainlove and Cibber as Ape-all), so he took to dramatic writing to enlarge his income (Genest, *Account*, iii. 250). But by this occupation Miller offended the bishop from whom he had expectations, and when soon afterwards he published a satirical poem in which a character appeared that was thought to be intended for the bishop, all his hopes of preferment from that quarter were destroyed.

Several of Miller's plays were performed with considerable success, but in 1737 two of the characters in his comedy 'The Coffee-house' were supposed to be aimed at Mrs. Yarrow and her daughter, who kept Dick's Coffee-house, between the Temple gates. This offended the residents in the Temple, who went in a body to the theatre to damn the piece. Miller denied the charge, but as the engraver of the frontispiece had sketched that very coffee-house he was not believed, and henceforward the templars ruined every piece which they imagined to be written by Miller. He was now dependent on the church, and his high-church principles did not aid his advancement. A large offer was made him by the agents of the ministry, but in vain. However, in 1743 he was presented by Nicholas Carey to the living of Upcerne, Dorset, which his father had held before him. There he prepared an adaptation of Voltaire's 'Mahomet,' which was successfully performed at Drury Lane 25 April 1744. It was not thought to be his, as all his previous plays had been comedies, and the fifth act was, in fact, written by John Hoadly. Miller died on the night of his first benefit, 26 April 1744, at his lodgings in Cheyne Walk. He left a widow and a son and daughter.

The 'Humours of Oxford' is the play that is most entirely his own. The plots of the others are generally taken from the French, chiefly from Molière. Miller wrote several political pamphlets against Sir Robert Walpole, one of which, 'Are these things so?' attracted considerable attention. A volume of sermons was published after his death by his widow.

His principal plays are:—1. 'The Humours of Oxford,' 1730, several editions with a frontispiece drawn by Hogarth. 2. 'Vanelia: or the Amours of the Great: an opera (in three acts) as it is acted by a private company near St. James's' [1732]. This vivacious work, containing twenty-one songs of the Beggar's Opera type, is founded on the amour between the Prince of Wales and a lady named Vane. It was never acted, but rapidly went through six editions. 3. 'The Man of Taste: or the Guardians' [1735], a successful mélange from Molière, played at Drury Lane, March 1735. This piece must be distinguished from a piece also called 'The Man of Taste,' which was published under that title in 1733, being a reissue with a new title of 'Mister Taste, the Poetical Fop: or the Modes of the Court,' a comedy [1732]; an insolent attack on Pope, for which Hogarth designed a satirical frontispiece (cf. Nichols, *Anecdotes of Hogarth*, 1833, p. 176). 4. 'Universal Passion,' 1737. 5. 'The Coffee-house,' 1737. 6. 'Art and Nature,' 1738. 7. 'The Hospital for Fools,' 1739. 8. 'Mahomet the Impostor,' 1744. 9. 'Joseph and his Brethren,' 1744. 10. 'The Picture, or the Cuckold in Conceit,' taken from Molière's 'Cocu Imaginaire,' 1745. 11. 'Harlequin Horace' and other poems. Miller also joined with Henry Baker, F.R.S., in a complete translation of Molière (1739).

[Baker's Biographia Dramatica; Nichols's Lit. Anecd. iii. 142; Notes and Queries, 2nd ser., xii. 293; Cibber's Lives; Genest, x. 157; Hutchings's Dorset; Watt's Bibl. Brit.; Foster's Alumni Oxonienses; Brit. Mus. Cat.] C. O.

MILLER, JAMES (1812–1864), surgeon, born at the manse, Essie, Forfarshire, 2 April 1812, was third son of the Rev. James Miller (1777–1860). His mother was Barbara, daughter of the Rev. Dr. Martin of Monimail in Fife (Hew Scott, *Fasti Eccl. Scotic.* pt. vi. p. 727). He was taught by his father, and in 1824 was sent to St. Andrews University, where in three winter sessions he completed his general education. In 1827 he became a pupil of Dr. Ramsay of Dundee, but later in the same year he was transferred to Mr. Mackenzie of Edinburgh, and entered upon the ordinary course of a medical student. He obtained the license of the Royal College of Surgeons of Edinburgh in 1832, and he was subsequently elected a fellow. He acted for many years as an assistant to Robert Liston [q. v.], and on the removal of that surgeon to London in 1834 Miller succeeded to the more lucrative part of his practice. In 1842 he was appointed professor of surgery in the university of Edinburgh, in succession to Sir Charles Bell [q. v.] In 1848 he was surgeon in ordinary in Scotland to the queen and Prince Albert. He was also surgeon, and later consulting surgeon, to the Royal Infirmary, professor of pictorial anatomy to the School of Design at the Royal Institution, and a fellow of the Royal Society of Edinburgh.

At the disruption of the presbyterian church in Scotland, Miller, like his father, who since 1827 had been minister of Monikie, sided with the free kirk party, and rendered it substantial service by speech and pen. Although he held the position of professor of surgery in Edinburgh, Miller practised both as a physician and as an operating surgeon, and it is rather remarkable that, in spite of his long association with Liston, Miller, even in his youth, was conservative in his methods, only resorting to the knife when all other treatment had failed. He proved himself a dexterous operator, and especially prided himself upon the manner in which he performed lithotomy. In his latter years Miller devoted much of his time to religious and social questions, and became an ardent advocate of temperance. He died on 17 June 1864, and is buried in the Grange cemetery in Edinburgh. In 1836 he married Penelope Garden Campbell Gordon, by whom he had issue.

He was author of: 1. 'Probationary Essay on the Dressing of Wounds,' Edinburgh, 1840; his thesis for the fellowship of the Royal College of Surgeons of Edinburgh. 2. 'Principles of Surgery.' 3. 'Practice of Surgery.' These two works ran concurrently through several editions in Edinburgh and in America. They were edited for America by Dr. Sargent of Philadelphia. They appeared first in 12mo, Edinburgh, 1844 and 1846; 2nd edit. 8vo, 1850 and 1852; 3rd edit. 1853 and 1856. They were finally amalgamated into: 4. 'A System of Surgery,' Edinburgh, 1864. It is by these works that Miller became extensively known as a surgeon outside the university in which he taught. The articles on 'Surgery' in the 7th and 8th editions of the 'Encyclopædia Britannica' were from his pen. He wrote numerous pamphlets and addresses on social, religious, and professional topics.

There is a bust of Miller by Sir John Steell in the Medical Mission House, 56 George Square, Edinburgh.

[Obituary notices in Edinburgh Medical Journal, 1864, x. 92–6, and Medical Times and Gazette, 1864, i. 695, 705; additional information kindly supplied to the writer by Dr. A. G. Miller.] D'A. P.

MILLER, JOHN (*fl.* 1780), architect, studied in Italy, and afterwards practised in London. He exhibited drawings of buildings, mostly in London, in the Royal Academy exhibitions between 1781 and 1787, during which years he resided in Westminster. The date of his death is not known.

He published: 1. Andrea Palladio's 'Elements of Architecture, restored to its Original Perfection, with a Geometrical Explanation of its True Principles of Perspective,' 28 plates, London, circ. 1748, 1759. 2. 'The Country Gentleman's Architect . . . Designs for Cottages, Farm-houses,' &c., 32 plates, London, 1787, 1797, 1800, 1805. 'The Ruins of Pæstum or Posidonia, a Town of Magna Grecia,' 4 plates, London, 1767, is also attributed to him. A drawn 'Map of an Estate of Mr. Stephen Searson. Lying in Wetheringset in the County of Suffolk. Surveyed by John Miller, 1750' (Addit. MS. Brit. Mus. 21057 E), may be his.

[Redgrave's Dict. of Artists; Royal Academy Exhibition Catalogues; Univ. Cat. of Books on Art; information from Wyatt Papworth, esq.] B. P.

MILLER, JOHN, otherwise JOHANN SEBASTIAN MÜLLER (1715?–1790?), draughtsman and engraver, was born at Nuremberg about 1715, and studied there under J. C. Weigel and M. Tyroff. In 1744 he came to England with his brother Tobias, an engraver of architecture, and he passed the remainder of his life in this country, chiefly practising as an engraver. He signed his early works J. S. Müller or J. S. Miller, but after 1760 used the signature of John Miller. In 1759 and 1760 he was living in Maiden Lane, Covent Garden; in 1777 in Dorset Court, near Parliament Street; and in 1789 at 10 Vauxhall Walk, Lambeth.

In the preface to his 'Illustration of the Sexual System' Müller speaks of his own 'early inclination to Botany,' and 'desire of rendering his Profession as an Engraver subservient to the Cultivation of his favourite Science;' but though most of his work is faithful to nature and artistically excellent, Philip Miller [q. v.], Dr. Gowan Knight [q. v.], and Lord Bute are probably largely responsible for its scientific supervision. On 31 March 1759 he issued 'Proposals for publishing one hundred prints, exhibiting a curious Collection of Plants and Insects by John Miller . . . Each Print will contain a Plant coloured from Nature, with the peculiar Insects which feed on [it] . . . The Plants will be classed under their proper Genera, according to the Botanick System of Mr. Miller of Chelsea (who has generously offered his kind assistance). . . . The Insects will be ranged as by Dr. Linnæus in his Systema Naturæ . . . This work will be published in Fifty Numbers, one . . . every Month. Each Number will contain Two . . . plates, with a half-sheet of letter-press, . . . Price Five Shillings. The first number on 10 May . . . If the Proprietor meets with Encouragement . . . he proposes to go through the whole Animal Creation according to the System adapted by Dr. Linnæus.' Of this work, equal if not superior to the previously published 'Plantæ et Papiliones' of Ehret, only ten folio plates were published, with the letter-press to the first eight, the plates bearing date between May 1759 and April 1760.

Richard Weston, in his 'Catalogue of English Authors on Agriculture' (1773), notes, under 1770, that Miller then published 'No. 1' of his 'System of Linnæus explained ... To be compleated in 15 Numbers, one Guinea each. Each Number contains 4 plants coloured and 4 plain.' John Ellis wrote to Linnæus of this undertaking on 28 Dec. 1770, 'There is a valuable work now carrying on upon your system by Mr. John Miller, a German painter and engraver, under the direction of Dr. Gowan Knight, of the British Museum. This will make your system of botany familiar to the ladies, being in English as well as Latin. The figures are well drawn, and very systematically dissected and described. I have desired that he may send to your ambassador for you the two first numbers to know your opinion of it, and if you approve you may get him subscriptions' (*Correspondence of Linnæus*, i. 255). The plates are dated from 1771 to 1776, and in 1777 the work was issued complete in three volumes folio, containing 108 coloured plates, 104 uncoloured, and 109 sheets of letter-press in Latin and English, 'published and sold by the author.' The English title was 'An Illustration of the Sexual System of the Genera Plantarum of Linnæus.' A list of eighty-two subscribers, taking about 125 copies, and including the name of David Garrick, is prefixed, and in the preface are given four letters to the author from Linnæus, in one of which he writes, 'Donum tuum operis immortalis chariori veniet pretio quam, ut id remunerare valeam. Figuræ enim sunt et pulchriores et accuratiores quam ullæ quas vidit mundus a condito orbe.' In Linnæus's own copy of the work, now in the Linnean Society's library, in that in the King's library (36 i. 1–3), in the Banksian copy, at the Natural History Museum, and in that at Kew, formerly belonging to James Lee of the Vineyard, Hammersmith, some plates are proofs before letters.

In 1779 Miller published an octavo edition of the 'Illustration,' with 107 uncoloured plates and a preface containing a letter of encouragement from the younger Linnæus, and promising a second volume to exhibit specific characters. This second volume was not issued until 1789, the delay being stated in the preface to be due to 'a particular engagement.' It is entitled 'An Illustration of the Termini Botanici of Linnæus,' and contains eighty-six uncoloured plates. New title-pages for the folio edition and the first volume of the octavo edition of the 'Illustration' seem to have been issued subsequently, copies at the Natural History Museum bearing the imprint, 'Printed for Robert Faulder, New Bond Street, 1794.' The 'Illustration' was published in German in folio by Konrad Felsing, Darmstadt, 1792, and at Frankfurt-on-Maine, 1804, both coloured; the octavo edition, by Dr. F. G. Weiss, at Frankfurt in 1789, with the plates of the first volume, re-engraved by Charles Goepfert and coloured, in a separate volume, entitled 'Johannis Milleri Tabulæ Iconum centum quatuor plantarum ad illustrationem systematis sexualis Linnæani.'

Meanwhile Miller attempted another ambitious work dealing with new plants. Of this seven folio plates, dated 1780, were published, with a half-sheet of letter-press, but no title. In the botanical department of the Natural History Museum are five volumes, including in all 1072 original coloured drawings, with the manuscript title, 'Drawings of the Leaves, Stalks, and Ramifications of Plants for the purpose of ascertaining their several Species, executed for the Rt. Honble. the Earl of Bute, for the years 1783 and 1784, by John Miller, Author of the Illustration of the Sexual System of Linnæus.' These drawings were not utilised in Lord Bute's great work, 'Botanical Tables' (1785); but all the plates in the nine volumes of that work are also signed by Miller.

Miller engraved numerous plates other than botanic from his own designs; they are somewhat feeble in drawing and treatment, but his plates from compositions by good masters have much merit. To the former class belong 'The Ladies' Lesson,' 1755; frontispiece to Smollett's 'History of England,' 1758; ticket for the marriage of George III, 1761; the Oxford Almanacks for 1763–1765; 'The Passions Personifyed in Familiar Fables;' 'Morning,' a domestic interior, 1766; and 'The Confirmation of Magna Carta by Henry III,' 1780. Of Miller's engravings after other artists, the most important are the plates to Gray's 'Poems,' after R. Bentley, 1753; twelve plates to Milton's 'Paradise Lost,' after Hayman; 'Apollo and Marsyas,' after Claude; 'Moonlight,' after A. van der Neer, 1766; four plates of Roman monuments, after Pannini; 'The Continence of Scipio,' after Vandyck; 'Writing the Billet,' after Pantoja de la Cruz; 'The Repose in Egypt,' after Murillo; and a 'Holy Family,' after Barocci. From Miller's own statement, made in a letter to Van Murr, it appears that the originals of the three last-mentioned prints were painted by himself, and that he sold them to English connoisseurs as genuine works of the masters. Miller produced some excellent prints of antiquities, including four views of the temples at Pæstum, 1767; the whole of the plates in 'Marmora Oxoniensia,' a work on the Arundelian marbles, with text by Chandler, 1763;

and several of those in L. Natter's 'Treatise on the Ancient Method of Engraving on Precious Stones,' 1754. He also engraved portraits of George III and Queen Charlotte, Peter Collinson, F.R.S., John Wilkes, George Edwards the naturalist, after Dandridge; Thomas Gray the poet, after Eccardt (intended to form the frontispiece to his 'Poems,' 1753, but suppressed); and some of those in Smollett's 'History.' He engraved in mezzotint a portrait of William Barrowby, M.D., after F. Hayman. Furthermore he painted landscapes, which, as well as some of his engravings, he exhibited with the Society of Arts and at the Royal Academy from 1762 to 1788. Though the date of his death is unknown, it was probably soon after 1789, and almost certainly before 1794.

Miller engraved his own portrait with that of Linnæus on the frontispiece of his 'Illustration of the Sexual System,' 1777.

He was twice married, and had in all twenty-seven children, two of his sons, JOHN FREDERICK and James Müller or Miller, becoming known as draughtsmen, and as frequent exhibitors of topographical views at the Society of Artists. The former accompanied Sir Joseph Banks and Dr. Solander to Ireland in 1772 as a draughtsman, and published in numbers in 1785 'Various Subjects of Natural History wherein are delineated Birds, Animals, and many curious Plants: with the parts of fructification of each plant, all of which are drawn and coloured from Nature,' London, imp. fol.

[Nagler's Künstler-Lexikon; Mason's Memoirs of Gray, 1814, i. 335; Dodd's manuscript Hist. of English Engravers (Brit. Mus. Add. MS. 38403); Universal Catalogue of Books on Art; Catalogues of the Society of Artists; Bryan's Dict. of Painters and Engravers; Miller's own works.] F. M. O'D.—G. S. B.

MILLER, JOHN CALE, D.D. (1814–1880), evangelical divine, only son of John Miller of Margate, Kent, who held a confidential appointment in connection with the American embassy, was born at Margate 11 Oct. 1814. He was educated at Brompton grammar school, matriculated at Oxford from St. John's College 27 March 1832, and was a scholar of Lincoln College from 1834 to 1836, graduating B.A. 1835, M.A. 1838, and B.D. and D.D. 1857. He was ordained to the curacy of Bexley, Kent, in 1837, was assistant curate of Park Chapel, Chelsea, in 1839, and succeeded Thomas Vores in the sole charge in 1841. His rising reputation as an able and energetic pastor led to his election by the trustees of St. Martin's, Birmingham, to fill the vacancy caused in June 1846 by the resignation of Thomas Moseley. Miller devoted himself energetically to the welfare of Birmingham. A working man's association was established in 1854 on a wider basis than the church educational societies previously in vogue. Hence sprang the working men's parochial mission, a band of working-men missionaries who worked among their neighbours. Miller acquired in a remarkable degree the confidence of the labouring classes, and began in November 1856 in St. Martin's Church special services for them at which he divided the liturgy into three parts so as to obviate iteration and undue length; during the summer season he held open-air services. The tower and spire of St. Martin's Church he restored at a cost of 7,000*l.*, raised by subscription, and for the General Hospital he, in November 1859, organised simultaneous collections on a given Sunday in the churches of Birmingham, by which means the sum of 5,000*l.* was raised, and the first foundations laid of Hospital Sunday. On 7 March 1866 he was presented by the crown to the vicarage of Greenwich, where he remained till his death. His other appointments were select preacher at Oxford 1867, honorary canon of Worcester August 1852, canon and treasurer 31 Oct. 1871 to 1873, canon of Rochester 1873, and examining chaplain to the Bishop of Rochester 1877. He was a member of the London School Board for Greenwich 29 Nov. 1870 to March 1872. On the platform, as in the pulpit, he was a ready speaker, full of passionate energy. He died in Park Place, Maze Hill, East Greenwich, 11 July 1880, and was buried in Shooter's Hill Cemetery on 16 July.

He married in 1836 Elizabeth, daughter of J. A. Edwards of Winchester, and had issue.

The Miller Hospital of Greenwich, grafted upon the Royal Kent Dispensary, was opened in December 1884, as a memorial to Miller.

Miller published much, including: 1. 'Sermons,' 1838. 2. 'Sermons preached at Park Chapel, Chelsea,' 1843. 3. An attack on 'the Tractarian Heresy,' 1850, 5 editions; evoking several printed replies. 4. 'Bible Inspiration Vindicated, an Essay on "Essays and Reviews,"' 1861. 5. 'A Hymn Book for the Church of England Sunday Schools,' 1862, 2 editions. 6. 'Death Words of a Noble Woman [Lady A. F. E. Stanley],' 1876, 2 parts. 7. 'Letters to a Young Clergyman,' 1878.

[John Poland's Records of the Miller Hospital and Royal Kent Dispensary, 1893; Christian Cabinet Illustrated Almanack for 1861, pp. 31–2; Church of England Photograph Portrait Gallery, 1859, portrait No. 35; Drawing-Room Photograph Portrait Gallery, 4th ser. 1860, portrait, No. x.; Davies's Orthodox London, 1874, pp. 199–208; Times, 12, 15, 19, 27 July and 28 Aug. 1880.] G. C. B.

MILLER, JOSEPH or JOSIAS, commonly called Joe Miller (1684–1738), actor and reputed humourist, may have been related to the proprietors of 'Miller's Droll Booth,' which occupied a prominent place in St. Bartholomew's Fair from 1699 to 1731 (Morley, *Bartholomew's Fair*, pp. 263, 280, 319). He first joined the Drury Lane company in the winter season of 1709. On 28 Nov., when Sir Robert Howard's 'Committee' was produced at Drury Lane, he appears to have filled the part of Teague, and was described as 'one who never appeared on the stage before' (Genest, *Hist. Account*, ii. 431). The part was subsequently a favourite one with Miller's admirers; 'though the gentlemen of Ireland would never admit that he had the true brogue, yet he substituted something in the room of it that made his Teague very diverting to an English audience' (Victor). On 3 Dec. 1709 he was Jeremy in Congreve's 'Love for Love,' and on 17 Dec. Clip in 'Vanbrugh's 'Confederacy.' He did not reappear at Drury Lane till the autumn of 1714, and was thenceforth a prominent member of the company. On 4 Feb. 1715 he was Sneak in Charles Johnson's new play 'The County Lasses;' on the 22nd Kate Matchlock in Sir Richard Steele's 'Funeral;' and next day Sir Roger in the initial representation of Gay's 'What d'ye call it?' On 30 April he first appeared in what soon became another of his most popular rôles—Young Clincher in Farquhar's 'Constant Couple.' On 7 May he and Mrs. Cox took a joint benefit, when he figured as Old Wilfull in Cibber's 'Double Gallant,' and he was Cokes in Jonson's 'Bartholomew Fair' on 28 June. During the season of 1715–16 he was Sir Jolly Jumble in Otway's 'Soldier's Fortune' (17 Jan. 1716), Trico in 'Ignoramus' (19 June), Sir Mannerly Shallow in Crowne's 'Country Wit' (12 July), besides filling many inferior parts. On 2 April Brome's 'Jovial Crew' was acted for his benefit, when he doubtless assumed the character of Tallboy, which was always reckoned among his successes. On 27 Oct. 1716 he acted Clodpole in Betterton's 'Amorous Widow' to Colley Cibber's Brittle; on the 30th was Squire Somebody in Farquhar's 'Stage Coach;' on 13 Nov. Lance in Beaumont and Fletcher's 'Wit without Money;' and on 27 Nov. Sir Harry Gubbin in Steele's 'Tender Husband.' On 25 April 1717 he took his benefit as Sir Joseph Wittoll in Congreve's 'Old Bachelor.' A theatre ticket engraved for the occasion, on which a scene from the third act of this play is depicted, has been doubtfully assigned to Hogarth, who was then only nineteen. A copy is in the print room at the British Museum. It is reproduced in 'The Family Joe Miller' in 1848, but is generally regarded as a forgery (Nichols, *Anecdotes of Hogarth*, p. 301).

Miller's chief triumphs in succeeding seasons (1717–1728) were in such parts as Marplot in Mrs. Centlivre's 'Busybody' (29 Oct. 1718), doubtless in succession to Pack; Trinculo in the 'Tempest' (11 Dec.); Foigard in Farquhar's 'Beaux' Stratagem' (16 Dec.); Osric in 'Hamlet' (2 Jan. 1720); Sir William Belfond, an original part, in Shadwell's 'Squire of Alsatia' (20 Sept. 1720); Kastril in Jonson's 'Alchemist' (27 Oct. 1721); Sir Philip Moneylove in Mrs. Centlivre's 'Artifice,' a new piece (2 Oct. 1722); Roderigo in 'Othello' (3 Sept. 1726); Abel Drugger in the 'Alchemist' (20 Oct.); John Moody in Vanbrugh's and Cibber's 'Provoked Husband,' an original part (10 Jan. 1728); and Sir Apish Simple in Fielding's 'Love in Several Masques' (10 Feb.) In 1729—on 7 Jan. and 6 Feb. respectively—he filled parts in two new pieces, Cimon in Cibber's 'Love in a Riddle,' and Brush in Charles Johnson's 'Village Opera.' He was in the same year Dashwell in Johnson's 'Country Lasses,' and Brush in Farquhar's 'Constant Couple' (10 Feb. 1730).

In the autumn of 1731 Miller temporarily left Drury Lane owing to 'some mean economy of the managers' (Davies), and was engaged at Goodman's Fields, where he made a first appearance as Teague in the 'Committee' (3 Jan. 1732). All his favourite rôles followed, including Foigard, in which he took his benefit on 23 March. He was also the First Gravedigger in 'Hamlet' (26 Feb.), Robin in Carey's 'Contrivances' (23 May), and on 10 May he was announced to appear 'for the last time that season' as Ben in 'Love for Love'—a part in which he was an acknowledged 'favourite of the town' (Davies). He returned to Drury Lane in the winter of 1732, and acted Jack Straw in the 'Alchemist' on 19 Jan. 1733. On 23 Sept. 1734 he reappeared as Sir William Belfond in Shadwell's 'Squire of Alsatia.' On 1 Feb. 1737 he created the part of John Cockle the Miller in Dodsley's 'Miller of Mansfield.' Next season he appeared as Pompey in a revival of 'Measure for Measure' (26 Jan. 1738), and was the First Witch in 'Macbeth' five days later. On 23 Feb. 1738 he assumed the rôle of Sir John Cockle at the first performance of Dodsley's 'Sir John Cockle at Court.' On 13 April he took his benefit both as Ben in 'Love for Love' and the 'Miller of Mansfield.' There followed his renderings of Dr. Caius in the 'Merry Wives' (3 May), Lord Sands in 'Henry VIII' (6 May), Colonel Cocade in

James Miller's 'Man of Taste' (13 June), Wittol (16 June), and Teague (19 June). His final appearance was as Abel Drugger (27 June 1738) in the 'Alchemist.' Genest enumerates fifty-nine different characters in a selected list of his parts.

Miller secured a good position at Drury Lane, and was a member of the committee of actors which proposed to rent the theatre of Fleetwood, the lessee, in 1735 (Cibber, *Apology*, ed. Lowe, ii. 262). Victor describes him as 'a natural spirited comedian,' and adds that he long enjoyed a good salary, 'a full proof of the force of his abilities.' Davies calls him a 'lively comic actor.' He was unable to read, and 'his principal object in marrying was to have a wife who was able to read his parts to him.' He is vaguely reported to have been of convivial disposition, and to have spent much time at the Bull's Head in Spring Gardens, Charing Cross, or at the Black Jack in Portsmouth Street, Clare-market. He resided in Clare-market, and, according to very doubtful evidence, at one time himself kept a tavern in the neighbourhood. His boon companions are reported to have included James Spiller, the actor, and Hogarth. Miller died on 16 Aug. 1738, aged 54. The 'Gentleman's Magazine,' 1738, p. 436, describes him as 'Mr. *Joseph* Miller, a celebrated comedian.' Genest asserts, on the other hand, that his christian name was Josias. He was buried in St. Clement's burial-ground, Portugal Street, Clare-market. The inscription on his grave, written by Stephen Duck, described him as 'a tender husband, a sincere friend, a facetious companion, and an excellent comedian,' and emphasised his 'honesty and wit and humour.' The monument, which only gives his christian name as 'Joe,' was restored in 1816 by 'Jarvis Buck, churchwarden,' and was finally destroyed in 1852, when an extension of King's College Hospital was erected on the site of the burial-ground (cf. *Notes and Queries*, 1st ser. v. 485).

His widow, Henrietta Maria, was accorded a benefit at Drury Lane on 14 Dec. 1738, when 'Hamlet' was performed with satisfactory results (cf. Genest, iii. 573).

Miller's chief reputation was made for him, after his death, by John Mottley [q. v.], who was commissioned by a publisher, T. Read, in 1739 to compile a collection of jests, and unwarrantably entitled his work 'Joe Miller's Jests.' Whincop writes in his account of Mottley that 'the book that bears the title of "Joe Miller's Jests" was a collection made by him [i.e. Mottley] from other books, and great part of it supplied by his memory from among stories recollected in his former conversations.' Miller is mentioned as the hero of three of the recorded anecdotes, but the name is introduced without historic justification. The jests are of a homely tone, often lack point, and rarely excite merriment in the modern reader. Most of them are borrowed from earlier collections, none of which were very exhilarating. The full title of the rare first edition ran: 'Joe Miller's Jests; or the Wits Vade-Mecum. Being a Collection of the most Brilliant Jests; the Politest Repartees; the most Elegant Bon-Mots, and most pleasant short Stories in the English Language. First carefully collected in the company, and many of them transcribed from the mouth of the Facetious Gentleman whose name they bear; and now set forth and published by his lamentable friend and former companion, Elijah Jenkins, Esq. Most Humbly Inscribed to those Choice Spirits of the Age, Captain Bodens, Mr. Alexander Pope, Mr. Professor Lacy, Mr. Orator Henley, and Job Baker, the Kettle-Drummer. London: Printed and sold by T. Read in Dogwell Court, White Fryars, Fleet Street. MDCCXXXIX. (Price One Shilling.)' The work in this form contained 247 witticisms. A lithographed facsimile was prepared in 1861 by M. J. Bellars. The number of jests had risen in the third edition, issued in the same year as the first, to 273. A fourth edition appeared in 1740, a fifth in 1742, a sixth in 1743, and a seventh in 1744. The eighth of 1745 supplied large additions, bringing the total of 'The Jests' to 587, and appending for the first time 'a choice collection of moral sentences and of the most pointed and truly valuable epigrams in the British tongue, with the names of the authors to such as are known.' A ninth edition of the work in this enlarged form appeared in 1747, and a tenth in 1751. Others are dated 1762 and 1771, and reissues, perfect and imperfect, often in chapbook form, have repeatedly come from the press both in this country and America until the present time, while Joe Miller's name has long been a synonym for a jest or witty anecdote of ancient flavour. An edition published at New York in 1865 supplies as many as 1,286 jests.

Several engraved portraits are known. One after C. Stoppelaer, dated 1738, as Teague, by Andrew Miller [q. v.]; another by Charles Mosley as Sir Joseph Wittoll (in 'The Jests,' 8th edit. 1745).

[Genest's Account of the Stage, ii. and iii. esp. 544–6; Notes and Queries, passim; Gent. Mag. 1820 pt. ii. 327–8, 487, 1821 pt. i. 321; B. Victor's Hist. of the Stage, i. 12, ii. 66–7; Davies's Dramatic Miscellanies, iii. 369; The

Family Joe Miller, 1848; Brit. Mus. Cat.; Mr. W. C. Hazlitt's Jests New and Old, his Jest Book, and his Studies in Jocular Literature (1890).] S. L.

MILLER, JOSIAH (1832–1880), hymnologist, son of the Rev. Edward Miller, was born at Putney, Surrey, on 8 April 1832. In his fourteenth year he was articled to an engineering surveyor at Westminster, but he afterwards gave up his articles and entered Highbury College, where he studied for the independent ministry. He graduated B.A. in 1853 and M.A. in 1855 at the London University. He was appointed pastor successively at Dorchester in 1855, at Long Sutton, Lincolnshire, in 1860, and at Newark, Nottinghamshire, in 1868. But he relinquished the last charge in order to become secretary of the British Society for the Propagation of the Gospel among the Jews. Subsequently he succeeded the Rev. J. Robinson as secretary to the London City Mission. He died on 22 Dec. 1880, and was buried at Abney Park.

His principal works are: 1. 'Our Hymns: their Authors and Origin. Being Biographical Sketches of the principal Psalm and Hymn Writers (with Notes on their Psalms and Hymns),' London, 1866, 8vo; intended to be a companion to the New Congregational Hymn Book. 2. 'Our Dispensation: or, the place we occupy in the Divine History of the World,' London, 1868, 8vo. 3. 'Singers and Songs of the Church; being Biographical Sketches of the Hymn-Writers in all the principal collections,' 2nd edit. London, 1869, 8vo. 4. 'Christianum Organum; or, the Inductive Method in Scripture and Science. With an Introduction by J. H. Gladstone,' London, 1870, 8vo.

[Congregational Year-Book, 1882, p. 319; Nonconformist, 30 Dec. 1880, p. 1334.] T. C.

MILLER, Mrs. LYDIA FALCONER (1811?–1876), authoress, daughter of an Inverness tradesman named Fraser, who failed in business and retired to Cromarty, was born about 1811. She was educated in Edinburgh, where she moved in literary society, and then returned to live in Cromarty with her mother. Here she first met Hugh Miller [q. v.] in 1831, and being herself clever and well read, was attracted by his talents. In spite of some opposition from her mother, Miller and she became engaged in 1832. They were not, however, married until 7 Jan. 1837, and in the meantime she took a few pupils. When Miller removed to Edinburgh and became editor of the 'Witness,' she gave him considerable assistance in the management of the paper, and occasionally also wrote in it. In 1855, however, a severe illness almost deprived her of the use of her limbs. After her husband's death she helped Mr. Peter Bayne in preparing his biography, and also in editing his works. She died at her son-in-law's manse at Lochinver in Sutherlandshire, 11 March 1876, and was buried in her husband's grave in the Grange cemetery in Edinburgh on 20 March.

Under the name of 'Harriet Myrtle' (a pseudonym also employed by Miss Mary Gillies in 'More Fun for our Little Friends,' 1864), Mrs. Miller wrote numerous stories, principally for the young, of a moral and religious tendency: the 'Story-book of Country Scenes—Spring,' 1845, and the same, 'Summer,' 1846; 'Little Amy's Birthday,' 1846; 'The Man of Snow and other tales,' 1848; 'Pleasures of the Country,' 1851; 'Home and its Pleasures,' 1852; 'The Little Sister,' 1852; 'A Day of Pleasure,' 1853; 'Amusing Tales,' 1853; 'The Water-lily,' 1854; 'The Ocean Child,' 1857; 'A Visit to the New Forest,' 'Always do your Best,' and 'Lizzie Lindsay' in 1859; 'Aunt Maddy's Diamonds,' 1864; 'Country Scenes' and 'Tales of the Four Seasons,' 1866; 'Cats and Dogs,' anecdotes, 1868, 2nd edit. 1873; 'Twilight Stories of Overbury Farm,' 1871; 'The Dog and his Cousins, the Wolf, the Jackal, and the Hyæna,' 1876; 'The Cat and her Cousins, the Lion, Tiger, &c.,' 1877, and some others. She also wrote a novel on the 'disruption' in the Scottish kirk, called 'Passages in the Life of an English Heiress.'

[Bayne's Life of Hugh Miller; Scotsman, 16 and 20 March 1876; Times, 22 and 24 March 1876; Ann. Reg. 1876; Brit. Mus. Cat.; Hamst's Fictitious Names, pp. 84, 90; Cushing's Dict. of Pseudonyms.] J. A. H.

MILLER, PATRICK (1731–1815), projector of steam navigation, third son of William Miller of Glenlee, and Janet (*née* Hamilton) his wife, was born at Glasgow in 1731. He was brother to Sir Thomas Miller [q. v.], lord president of the court of session, Edinburgh. Anderson (*Scottish Nation*, iii. 729) states that he began life 'without a sixpence,' as he often used to boast, and that his early years were spent at sea. His son Patrick says: 'My father was not of any profession, either military or naval. His proper business was that of a banker, by means of which he had accumulated considerable wealth' (*Edinb. Phil. Journ.* 1825, xiii. 83). He was in business in Edinburgh as a merchant in November 1760, as appears from the books of the Bank of Scotland. In one of his letters Miller refers to his partner, Mr. Ramsay of Barnton, and the Edinburgh 'Directory' for

1773-4 contains the entry 'Millar Patrick, Banker, James's Court.' In 1767 he was elected a director of the Bank of Scotland, and in 1790 he became deputy-governor, which office he held until his death. He is said to have rendered valuable service by organising a new system of exchanges on London. He seems to have been a man of active mind, much given to experimenting.

According to James Nasmyth (*Autobiography*, p. 27), Miller was one of the largest shareholders in the Carron Iron Company, and he seems to have taken part in the experiments made there for improving the construction of ordnance. It is frequently stated that he was the inventor of the carronade, so called from the Carron foundry, where they were first cast. But Miller himself never made any claim to the invention, which seems to have been due to General Robert Melville [q. v.] Anderson (*op. cit.*) states that Miller was so much interested in the matter that he fitted out a privateer, the Spitfire, armed with sixteen 18-pounder carronades, but there is no evidence of this, though he may have had a share in the ship. The Spitfire was captured by the Surveillante, and taken into L'Orient 19 April 1779 (see *Edinburgh Advertiser*, May 1779, pp. 313, 317, 340). It is probable that in this engagement carronades were first used in actual warfare [see Melville, Robert, 1723-1809]; the admiralty minute recommending their use in the royal navy was not issued until 16 July 1779.

In 1785 Miller purchased the estate of Dalswinton, Dumfriesshire, in ancient times the seat of the Comyns. He gives an account of the estate, which was in a very bad condition, in Singer's 'Agriculture of Dumfriesshire,' 1812, pp. 549-54. He seems to have gradually retired from active business in Edinburgh, and to have made Dalswinton his home, devoting himself mainly to schemes of agricultural improvement.

He spent much time and money in shipbuilding experiments, his main idea being the construction of ships with two or three hulls, propelled by paddle-wheels placed between the hulls and worked by men from capstans on deck. In January 1786 the Edinburgh, a triple ship upon this plan, was commenced at Leith, and was launched in October of the same year. He published a description of this vessel at Edinburgh in February 1787 in a folio tract entitled 'The Elevation, Section, Plan, and Views of a Triple Vessel with Wheels, with Explanations of the Figures in the Engravings, and a Short Account of the Properties and Advantages of the Invention,' copies of which were sent to all the foreign governments and to the principal public libraries. The Leith Trinity House conferred upon him the freedom of the corporation for this publication in June 1787 (*Scots Mag.* xlix. 309). It has now become rare, but it is reprinted in full in Woodcroft's 'Steam Navigation,' 1848, pp. 21, &c. The drawings were made by Alexander Nasmyth the artist, who was an intimate friend of Miller. On 2 June 1787 he made some experiments on the Firth of Forth with a double vessel, sixty feet long and fourteen and a half feet broad. Another boat of the same kind, said to have cost 3,000*l.*, was launched at Leith in the following year (*Scots Mag.* August 1788, p. 412). The 'Gentleman's Magazine' for December 1788, pt. ii. p. 1069, contains an engraving of the boat from a sketch taken while it was lying in Leith harbour, and Woodcroft (*op. cit.* p. 32) reproduces a drawing made for Miller by Alexander Nasmyth. A model of a double boat made under Miller's directions is preserved in the machinery and inventions department at South Kensington Museum. It appears from Macpherson's 'Annals of Commerce,' iv. 178, that one of these double ships was sent to St. Petersburg, but the frame was so much strained during the voyage that no one cared to venture home in her, and she was accordingly left in Russia.

In his description of his 'triple vessel,' published in 1787, Miller wrote: 'I have reason to believe that the power of the steam engine may be applied to work the wheels. . . . In the course of this summer I intend to make the experiment, and the result, if favourable, shall be communicated to the public.' Accordingly the application of the steam engine as a means of propelling boats subsequently engaged his attention, and on 14 Oct. 1788 he made his celebrated experiment on the lake at Dalswinton House with a double boat, twenty-five feet long and seven feet broad, fitted with a steam engine made by Symington. An extraordinary amount of interest has centred round this trip, which demonstrated for the first time the practicability of steam navigation. James Nasmyth (*Autobiography*, p. 29) says that the boat was made of tinned iron plates. He also states that Robert Burns the poet, then a tenant of Miller's, formed one of the party on board, and that the experiment was witnessed from the shore by Henry Brougham, afterwards Lord Brougham, who was on a visit to Dalswinton House. The presence of Burns has been questioned, and Brougham, in a letter printed in 'Notes and Queries' (5th ser. v. 247), states that he did not visit Dalswinton until many years afterwards.

The experiment is briefly recorded in the 'Scots Magazine' for November 1788, p. 566. At the conclusion of the trials the engine was placed in the library at Dalswinton House, and it is now in the South Kensington Museum. A drawing of the boat from a sketch by Alexander Nasmyth, who formed one of the party, is given in Woodcroft's book (p. 36). Miller made further experiments with a larger boat, for which Symington built another engine, in November and December 1789, in the Forth and Clyde canal.

On 14 April 1790 Miller's friend Robert Cullen (afterwards Lord Cullen), who was acquainted with James Watt, wrote in Miller's behalf to Watt expressing dissatisfaction on Miller's part with the performance of Symington's engines, on account of the great loss of power by friction, and declaring that from what Miller had seen of Boulton and Watt's engines he thought that they might be successfully adapted to the purpose of steam navigation. The letter, which was recently discovered at Soho after a search made at the request of the present writer, is printed in full in the 'Engineer' for November 1893. Watt's reply, dated 24 April 1790, is given by Williamson in his 'Memorials of James Watt,' 1856, p. 219. It was not encouraging; Watt seems to have considered Symington's engines 'as attempts to evade our exclusive privilege.' These letters furnish a sufficient explanation of the abandonment by Miller of experiments which at one time seemed to be full of promise.

Miller seems to have derived some assistance from the suggestions of James Taylor, who was then living in his family as tutor to his sons, and many years afterwards Taylor set up a claim to be regarded as part inventor. A similar claim was also advanced by Symington. The relative amount of credit to be assigned to Miller, Taylor, and Symington has been dealt with fairly and impartially by Woodcroft, by Major-general Miller, in 'A Letter to Bennet Woodcroft vindicating the Right of Patrick Miller to be called the first Inventor of Practical Steam Navigation,' London, 1862, and by Patrick Miller the younger (*Edinb. Phil. Journ.* 1825, xiii. 83, and art. SYMINGTON, WILLIAM).

After abandoning the subject of steam navigation, Miller still paid attention to the improvement of naval architecture, and in May 1796 he obtained a patent (No. 2106) for ships with flat bottoms, of great capacity, and drawing very little water. In calms or light winds they were to be propelled by paddle-wheels, but the specification contains no mention of steam power.

With the poet Burns Miller maintained very agreeable relations. In December 1786 Burns writes: 'An unknown hand left ten guineas for the Ayrshire bard with Mr. Sibbald, which I got. I have since discovered my generous unknown friend to be Patrick Miller, Esq., of Dalswinton.' Several of Burns's letters to Miller, written after the poet became Miller's tenant, are printed in W. Chambers's 'Burns.'

When nearly eighty years of age Miller introduced fiorin grass into Scotland, sending his steward, John Farish, to Ireland, where it had been cultivated with great success, to collect information. His report was published at Dumfries in 1810 under the title of 'Treatise on Fiorin Grass.' Miller's method of cultivating this grass is described at length in the Edinburgh 'Farmers' Magazine,' 1811, xii. 233; 1812, xiii. 3, 21, 203.

He died at Dalswinton House, 9 Dec. 1815, and was buried in Greyfriars churchyard, Edinburgh.

Miller married a Miss Lindsay, by whom he had five children: (1) Patrick, at whose instance Perry in 1794 offered to place Burns on the list of contributors to the 'Morning Chronicle' (CHAMBERS, *Burns*, iv. 18); (2) William, captain in the horse guards, M.P. for Dumfriesshire, 1790, alluded to as 'the sodger youth' in Burns's election ballad, 'The Five Carlines;' (3) Janet, married to John Thomas, eighth earl of Mar and thirteenth lord Erskine (MARSHALL, *Genealogist*, 1878, ii. 80); (4) Jean, married to Leslie Grove Jones, lieutenant-colonel grenadier guards; and (5) Thomas Hamilton, advocate. After the father's death a dispute arose in the family respecting the disposition of his property, and the case reached the House of Lords, by whom it was remitted back to the Edinburgh court of session (see *Journals of House of Lords*, 1818 li. 542, 1822 lv. 465).

There is a portrait of Miller by Alexander Nasmyth, which was lent for exhibition in 1859–60 at the Patent Office Museum, by Miss Gregan of Dumfries; a copy is in the possession of the widow of Bennet Woodcroft. It was engraved in 1862 by Walker and Zobel as one of a group of inventors and men of science. Another, by an unknown artist, was presented to Woodcroft in 1861 by Mrs. Bairnsfather, a granddaughter of Miller, and is now temporarily deposited in the machinery and inventions department, South Kensington Museum. Mrs. Woodcroft also possesses a portrait-medallion by Wedgwood. A medallion by James Tassie is in the National Portrait Gallery, Edinburgh.

[The notice in Anderson's Scottish Nation, iii. 729, was supplied by General W. H. Miller, a grandson, who was collecting materials for a larger memoir, which, however, he did not live to complete; Woodcroft's Steam Navigation embodies the results of a long and painstaking inquiry. The particulars given in Nasmyth's Autobiography are derived from the recollections of his father, Alexander Nasmyth. Mr. J. A. Wenley, treasurer of the Bank of Scotland, has supplied some information. See also Mechanics' Mag. 1845, xlii. 333.] R. B. P.

MILLER, PHILIP (1691–1771), gardener, was born either at Deptford or Greenwich in 1691. His father was a Scotchman, who, after serving for some time as gardener to a gentleman at Bromley, Kent, commenced business as a market gardener near Deptford. Philip on leaving school assisted his father for a short time, but at an early age began business on his own account as a florist on a piece of ground in St. George's Fields, afterwards the site of the King's Bench prison. Here he soon attracted the attention of Sir Hans Sloane and others, and, induced by them to give up his florist's business, he devoted himself to assisting other gardeners, including Ellis, then foreman of the Chelsea Garden. In 1722, the year in which Sloane made his final grant of the Chelsea Garden to the Apothecaries' Company, Ellis was dismissed, and Miller, on Sloane's recommendation, was appointed. The 'Gentleman's Magazine' in announcing his death (xli. 571), Sir J. E. Smith, in Rees's 'Cyclopædia,' and Pulteney, all erroneously state that he succeeded his father. In 1724 he published his first work, a first sketch of the chief work of his life, as 'The Gardener's and Florist's Dictionary, or a Complete System of Horticulture,' in two vols. 8vo, dedicated to the Apothecaries' Company; and by 1728 he had evinced his skill as a cultivator by a paper communicated to the Royal Society (*Philosophical Transactions*, xxxv. 485) on 'A Method of Raising some Exotic Seeds which have been judged almost impossible to be raised in England,' by first germinating them on a bed of tan. Two years later he for the first time described (*ib.* xxxvii. 81) the method, now so well known, of flowering bulbous plants in bottles filled with water. About this time he acted as secretary to a society of a few experienced gardeners who met weekly 'until, a serious difference arising among the members respecting the publishing of some portion of their proceedings and information, they broke up rather abruptly. The opponents of the publication demanded their papers from Miller, who immediately gave them up, having, however, with his usual foresight, taken a copy of each' (JOHN ROGERS, *The Vegetable Cultivator*, 1839). In 1730 he published a thin folio, with twenty-one coloured plates after Van Huysum, entitled 'Catalogus Plantarum . . . quæ in hortis haud procul a Londino . . . propagantur,' which does not bear his name, but has a preface signed by the members of this society.

Of his skill as a gardener Loudon says (*Arboretum Britannicum*, p. 81): 'Miller during his long career had no considerable competitor until he approached the end of it.' He was, however, looked upon with jealousy, as of Scottish birth, and also, it appears (*Gent. Mag.* liii. 332), as employing none but Scotsmen. Though Switzer bears testimony to his 'usual generosity, openness, and freedom,' he is believed to refer to Miller in his 'Gardener's Recreation' as one of the 'northern lads who have invaded the southern provinces.' In 1731 appeared the first volume of his 'magnum opus' ('The Gardener's Dictionary'), of which Linnæus said, 'Non erit lexicon hortulanorum, sed botanicorum.' On 1 April of that year he presented a copy to the Royal Society, 'who returned him their unanimous thanks for that excellent useful work' (*Gent. Mag.* i. 171). The work went through eight editions during his lifetime, and it is said of it that, while before its appearance not more than a thousand species of plants were in cultivation, at Miller's death there were more than five thousand. Trained in the school of Tournefort and Ray, 'it was not without reluctance that he was brought to adopt the system of Linnæus; but he was convinced at length by the arguments of Sir William Watson and Mr. [William] Hudson' (1730–1793) [q. v.] (PULTENEY, ii. 242). He became a correspondent of Linnæus, who several times visited the Chelsea Garden when in England in 1736, and records in his diary for that year that Miller permitted him 'to collect many plants in the garden, and gave [him] several dried specimens collected in South America.' It was not, however, until the seventh edition of the 'Dictionary,' published in 1759, and containing twice as many plants as the first edition, that the Linnean nomenclature was adopted. In the following year he added to the twelfth edition of his 'Gardener's Kalendar' 'a short introduction to the science of botany,' with five plates illustrating the Linnean system. In 1750 the committee of the Apothecaries' Company reported their satisfaction at the 'large number of rare plants, many of them nondescripts,' then in the garden owing to Miller's 'diligence in foreign correspondence' (FIELD and SEMPLE, *Memoirs of the Botanic Garden, Chelsea*, pp. 71–2). In 1751 Miller seems to have conducted some experiments on fertilisation, which are specially interesting as the first notice of the aid of insects in pollination (SACHS, *History of Botany*, English translation, p. 392). As a result of visits paid to Holland between 1723 and 1730, Miller issued in 1758 'The Method of Cultivating Madder, as it is practised by the Dutch in Zealand,' his object being to introduce this industry into England. His numerous correspondents in Siberia, at the Cape, and in North America, and especially Dr. William Houston's collections from the West Indies, led him to plan a series of illustrations of all known genera. This resulted in the issue in numbers between 1755 and 1760 of two volumes containing together three hundred folio plates, drawn from plants in the Chelsea Garden.

Professor Thomas Martyn says of Miller: 'He accumulated no wealth from his respectable connection with the great, or from the numerous editions of his works. He was of a disposition too generous and too careless of money to become rich.' A curious comment on this is afforded by the papers of the Apothecaries' Company. In 1761 Miller asked that a residence might be built for him in the garden, but his request was apparently not granted. At the end of 1766 he drew up a memorandum showing his salary to have been 50*l.* a year, in addition to which he had received 31*l.* as gate-money, while he had to pay 74*l.* wages to under-gardeners and 15*l.* freight on plants, leaving him 8*l.* out of pocket on the year. Shortly afterwards he asked for repayment of 62*l.* disbursed by him, but apparently only received a special grant of 50*l.* (FIELD and SEMPLE). On 28 Dec. 1770 John Ellis wrote to Linnæus: 'Poor Miller, through his obstinacy and impertinence to the Society of Apothecaries, is turned out of the Botanical Garden of Chelsea. I am sorry for it, as he is now 79 years of age: they will allow his stipend, but have chosen another gardener. His vanity was so raised by his voluminous publications that he considered no man to know anything but himself; though Gordon, Aiton, and Lee have been long infinitely superior to him in the nicer and more delicate part of gardening' (*Correspondence of Linnæus*, i. 255). Aiton, and also Forsyth, who succeeded him, were his own pupils, and Forsyth took office with 60*l.* a year, besides 50*l.* for under-gardeners and rooms. Miller died near Chelsea churchyard, 18 Dec. 1771, and was buried on the north side of it, the spot being marked by a flat stone. An obelisk (engraved in the 'Gentleman's Magazine,' 1815, pt. i. p. 409) was erected near it in 1815 by members of the Linnean and Horticultural Societies. The engraved portrait by Maillet, prefixed to the French translation of his 'Dictionary' (Paris, 8 vols. 4to, 1785), is a fancy sketch. He was commemorated by John Martyn in the genus *Milleria* among the Compositæ.

Miller married Mary Kennet of Southwark, whose sister was wife of the botanical draughtsman George Dionysius Ehret [q. v.] Of his two sons, Philip, the elder, worked under him for a time, and then went to the East Indies, where he died; Charles, the younger (*b.* 1739), became in 1762 the first curator of the Cambridge Botanic Garden, went in 1770 to India and Sumatra, returned to England, and dying in London, 6 Oct. 1817, was buried in his father's grave. Miller left a large herbarium, mostly of exotics gathered in the Chelsea Garden, which was purchased by Sir Joseph Banks, and is now in the Natural History Museum.

Pulteney says of Miller: 'By foreigners he was emphatically stiled "Hortulanorum Princeps." He was admitted a member of the Botanical Academy of Florence, and of the Royal Society of London, in which he was occasionally honoured by being chosen of the council. Mr. Miller was the only person I ever knew who remembered to have seen Mr. Ray. I shall not easily forget the pleasure that enlightened his countenance, it so strongly expressed the *Virgilium tantum vidi*, when, in speaking of that revered man, he related to me that incident of his youth' (*Sketches of the Progress of Botany*, ii. 243). Another anecdote of Miller is recorded in Monk's 'Life of Bentley' (p. 653), and in Elwin and Courthope's 'Pope' (iv. 360). Miller, it appears, went to Cambridge to consult Bentley on some classical point, and was hospitably received, but when Miller had made his inquiry the great scholar offered no remark on the subject, but merely bade his questioner drink his wine. Miller persisted in his questioning, and Bentley crying, 'Walker, my hat,' left the room. The scene is alluded to in Pope's 'Dunciad,' bk. iv. l. 273. Many reminiscences of Miller are recorded by John Rogers, gardener at Richmond Palace, in the 'Vegetable Cultivator,' London, 1839, 8vo. Rogers (*d.* 1842) met Miller about three years before the latter's death, and was perhaps the last survivor of his acquaintances.

Miller's chief works were: 1. 'The Gardener's and Florist's Dictionary, or a Complete System of Horticulture,' 2 vols. London, 8vo, 1724. 2. 'Catalogus Plantarum . . . quæ in Hortis haud procul a Londino . . . propagantur,' London, fol., 1730, anonymous.

3. 'Catalogus Plantarum Officinalium quæ in Horto Botanico Chelseyano aluntur,' London, 8vo, 1730. 4. The botanical part of N. Bailey's 'Dictionarium Britannicum,' London, fol., 1730. 5. 'The Gardener's Dictionary,' London, fol., vol. i. 1731, vol. ii. 1739; 2nd ed. 1733, 3rd ed. 1736–7, 8th ed. 1768; corrected by Thomas Martyn [q. v.] as 'The Gardener's and Botanist's Dictionary,' vol. i. 1797, vol. ii. 1804; revised in part as 'Miller's Dictionary of Gardening, Botany, and Agriculture,' London, 4to, 1834; 9th ed., incomplete, London, 8vo, 1835–6; Dutch translation, Leyden, 1745; German, Nuremberg, 1750–8 and 1769–76; and French, Paris, 1785–90. 6. 'The Gardener's Kalendar,' London, 1732, 8vo; 3rd ed., London, 1734; 2nd ed., Dublin, 1735; 12th ed., 'to which is added a short introduction to the . . . science of botany,' London, 1760, 8vo; 15th ed. 1769, 8vo; in German, Göttingen, 1750; in Dutch, Haarlem, 1772. 7. 'The Gardener's Dictionary Abridged,' 3 vols., London, 8vo, 1735–40; 2nd ed. 1741; 5th ed. 1763, 4to; 6th ed., 1771, 4to; German edition, Frankfurt-on-Maine, 1802–3. 8. 'The Method of Cultivating Madder,' London, 1758, 4to. 9. 'Figures of the most beautiful, useful, and uncommon Plants described in the Gardener's Dictionary,' 2 vols., London, 1755–60, fol.; German edition, Nuremberg, 1768–82. He also contributed numerous papers to the 'Philosophical Transactions,' most of which are merely the lists of the fifty dried specimens sent annually to the Royal Society from the Chelsea Garden.

[Pulteney's Sketches of the Progress of Botany, 1790, vol. ii.; Field and Semple's Memoirs of the Botanic Garden, Chelsea, 1878; Rees's Cyclopædia; John Rogers's Vegetable Cultivator, 1839.] G. S. B.

MILLER, RALPH WILLETT (1762–1799), captain in the navy, was born at New York on 24 Jan. 1762. Willett was his mother's family name; his father, a loyalist, lost all his property in the American revolution. At an early age Miller was sent to England; he entered the navy, and in 1778 was serving in the Ardent with Rear-admiral James Gambier (1723–1789) [q. v.] He is said to have been 'in all the actions fought by Admirals Barrington, Rodney, Hood, and Graves, and was three times wounded.' He must have gone to the West Indies in December 1778, in one of the ships under Commodore Hotham [see HOTHAM, WILLIAM, LORD]. On 25 May 1781, just after Hood's action with De Grasse, off Fort Royal of Martinique [see HOOD, SAMUEL, VISCOUNT], he was promoted by Rodney to be lieutenant of the Terrible. In the action off Cape Henry on 5 Sept. 1781, the Terrible received such damage that she had to be abandoned and burnt (BEATSON, *Naval and Military Memoirs*, v. 277). Miller, it seems, joined one of the ships which went back to the West Indies with Hood, and returned to England towards the end of 1782. On 20 Dec. he was appointed to the Fortitude. In 1793 he was a lieutenant of the Windsor Castle in the Mediterranean, and at the evacuation of Toulon was placed, individually, under the orders of Sir W. Sidney Smith [q. v.], for the destruction of the French ships and arsenal (BARROW, *Life of Sir Sidney Smith*, i. 148). He was shortly afterwards moved by Hood into the Victory, and was actively employed in the boats and on shore at the reduction of San Fiorenzo, Bastia, and Calvi. In July 1794 he volunteered to set fire to the French squadron in Golfe Jouan, and was promoted on 1 July to the Poulette, with orders to fit her as a fireship, for that purpose. He made five successive attempts to take her in to the French anchorage, but calms and contrary winds always prevented him. On 12 Jan. 1796 he was posted to the command of the Mignonne, but was moved into the Unité by Sir John Jervis and sent into the Adriatic.

In August 1796, when Commodore Nelson hoisted his broad pennant in the Captain, Miller was selected to be his flag-captain, and was thus in command of the Captain in the battle of Cape St. Vincent [see NELSON, HORATIO, VISCOUNT]. In May 1797 he moved with Nelson to the Theseus, was with him during his command of the inshore squadron off Cadiz through June, and in the disastrous attack on Santa Cruz on 20 July, when he was landed in command of the small-arm men of the Theseus. After Nelson returned to England the Theseus remained with the fleet off Cadiz, but the next year was detached to join Nelson in the Mediterranean, and took an effective part in the battle of the Nile. Miller sent his wife (17 Oct.) a remarkably able description of the battle (NICOLAS, vol. vii. pp. cliv–clx), finishing it in sight of Gibraltar, where he was sent with Sir James Saumarez (afterwards Lord de Saumarez) [q. v.], in charge of the prizes. Towards the end of December the Theseus was again sent to the Levant, and under the orders of Sir Sidney Smith took part in the operations on the coast of Egypt and Syria. Miller was killed on board his ship during the defence of St. Jean d'Acre, by the accidental explosion of some shells on 14 May 1799. 'He had long,' wrote Smith to Lord St. Vincent, 'been in the practice of collecting such of the enemy's shells as fell in the town without bursting, and of sending them back to the enemy better prepared and with evident effect. He had a deposit on board the Theseus ready for service, and more were preparing, when, by an accident for which nobody can account, they exploded at short intervals,' killing and wounding nearly eighty men, wrecking the poop and the after part of the quarter-deck, and setting fire to the ship. The monument in St. Paul's, by Flaxman, was erected to Miller's memory by subscription among his brother officers who fought with him at the Nile and St. Vincent (Nicolas, iv. 276, v. 5; Ross, *Memoirs of Lord de Saumarez*, ii. 305). He left a widow and two daughters.

[Naval Chron. ii. 581; Nicolas's Despatches and Letters of Lord Nelson, ii. 465 and passim (see index at end of vol. vii.); see also Barrow's Life of Sir W. Sidney Smith; commission and warrant books in the Public Record Office.]

J. K. L.

MILLER, Sir THOMAS, Lord Glenlee (1717–1789), lord president of the College of Justice, the second son of William Miller of Glenlee, Kirkcudbrightshire, and of Barskimming, Ayrshire, writer to the signet, by his wife, Janet, eldest daughter of Thomas Hamilton of Shield Hall, was born on 3 Nov. 1717. He matriculated at Glasgow University in November 1730, but did not graduate, and on 21 Feb. 1742, was admitted a member of the Faculty of Advocates. In 1748 he was appointed sheriff-depute of Kirkcudbright, and was elected joint town-clerk of the city of Glasgow. In 1755 he resigned the office of sheriff-depute, and became solicitor of the excise in Scotland. He succeeded Andrew Pringle as solicitor-general on 17 March 1759, and was appointed lord advocate in the place of Robert Dundas the younger of Arniston (1713–1787) [q. v.], who became lord president of the court of session on 30 April 1760. At the general election in April 1761, he was returned to parliament for the Dumfries district of burghs. The only speech which he made in the house is said to have been one in opposition to the repeal of the American Stamp Act, but no speech of his is recorded in the pages of the 'Parliamentary History' (vols. xv. and xvi.) Miller was elected rector of the university of Glasgow in November 1762, and was made lord justice clerk on 14 June 1766 in the place of Sir Gilbert Eliot of Minto, taking the title of Lord Barskimming, which he afterwards changed to that of Lord Glenlee. He succeeded Robert Dundas the younger, of Arniston, as lord president of the College of Justice on 15 Jan. 1788, and was created a baronet on 3 March following. His health, which had been failing some years, soon afterwards gave way, and he died at Barskimming on 27 Sept. 1789, aged 71. He was buried in the family vault at Stair, Ayrshire.

Miller enjoyed a high reputation as a lawyer, and was an industrious and conscientious judge. Burns alludes to him in the 'Vision' as 'an aged judge . . . dispensing good' (Duan i. stanza 20). With the help of five other advocates Miller compiled the 'Decisions of the Court of Session from the beginning of February 1752 to the end of the year 1756' (Edinburgh, 1760, fol.) His able and elaborate report to the Duke of Grafton, dated 23 Oct. 1768, on Lieutenant Ogilvie's case, in which he expressed his opinion that there was no appeal from the court of justiciary to the House of Lords, is preserved in the Record Office (*Scotland MSS.* 1737–70, No. 25).

Miller married, first, on 16 April 1752, Margaret, the eldest daughter of John Murdoch of Rose Bank, provost of Glasgow, by whom he had an only son, Sir William Miller, lord Glenlee [q. v.], and one daughter, Jessie, who became the wife of Mr. John Dunlop. His first wife died on 18 April 1767. He married, secondly, on 7 June 1768, Anne, daughter of John Lockhart of Castlehill, Lanarkshire, by whom he had no issue. She survived him many years, and died at Clifton on 14 Jan. 1817. Portraits of Miller and of his first wife by Sir Joshua Reynolds, and of his second wife by Sir Henry Raeburn, are to be seen in the Scottish National Gallery. There is also a medallion of Miller by James Tassie in the National Scottish Portrait Gallery, Edinburgh. Miller's portrait has been engraved by D. B. Pyet.

[Transactions of the Royal Society of Edinburgh, 1790, vol. ii. pt. i. pp. 63–75; Brunton and Haig's Senators of the College of Justice, 1832, pp. 530–1; Omond's Lord Advocates of Scotland, 1883, ii. 68–73; Anderson's Scottish Nation, 1863, iii. 157; Foster's Members of Parliament, Scotland, 1882, p. 251; Haydn's Book of Dignities, 1890; Foster's Baronetage, 1881, p. 434; Hist. of the Society of Writers to the Signet, 1890, p. 145; Scots Mag. x. 155, 207, xiv. 213, xvii. 269, li. 467.]

G. F. R. B.

MILLER, THOMAS (1731–1804), bookseller, born at Norwich on 14 Aug. 1731, was son of a pavior and brother of Edward Miller [q. v.] He was apprenticed to a grocer, but when he commenced business for himself in 1755 his fondness for reading induced him to combine bookselling with his other trade. Unfortunately he settled in Bungay, Suffolk, where the demand for books was small. Moreover, his sturdy independence lost him the custom of many of the local magnates. His stock of books was very valuable, and he had an extensive collection of engraved portraits, and nearly a complete series of Roman and English silver and brass coins. He published catalogues of his collections in 1782 and 1790. In 1795, when the fashion was very general for tradesmen to circulate provincial halfpennies, he had a die cast, but an accident happening to one of the blocks when only twenty-three pieces were struck off, Miller, like a true antiquary, declined having a fresh one made. This coin (which is very finely engraved, and bears a strong profile likeness of Miller) is known to collectors by the name of the 'Miller halfpenny.' As he was careful into whose hands the impressions went, they soon became very rare. In 1799 he became quite blind, but continued in business until his death, which took place at Bungay on 25 July 1804. His son, William Miller (1769–1844), is separately noticed.

Miller's portrait was engraved by E. Scriven from a miniature by H. Edridge.

[Nichols's Lit. Anecd. iii. 680, viii. 471; Gent. Mag. 1845, i. 102; Timperley's Encycl. of Lit. and Typogr. Anecd., 2nd edit.] G. G.

MILLER, THOMAS (1807–1874), poet and novelist, known as 'the basket-maker,' son of George Miller, a wharfinger, was born at Gainsborough 31 Aug. 1807. During a visit to London the father left his lodgings on the morning of the Burdett riots, 6 April 1810, and was never heard of afterwards. The widow was left in poverty, and the son was bound apprentice to a basket-maker, and resided in Sailors' Alley, Gainsborough, next door to Thomas Cooper the chartist. In 1832, while in the employment of Mr. Watts, basket-maker, Bromley House, Nottingham, he made the acquaintance of Thomas Bailey [q. v.], then editing the 'Good Citizen,' who encouraged him to print 'Songs of the Sea Nymphs,' 1832. This work gained him many friends, and enabled him to start a business on his own account at Swan's Yard, Long Row. About 1835 he came to London, and, working at his trade at 33 Elliott's Row, St. George's Road, Southwark, sent some fancy baskets, in which he had placed verses, to the Countess of Blessington. The verses were appreciated, and from that time Miller's success was assured. His next work, 'A Day in the Woods, a connected series of Tales and Poems,' appeared in 1836, and was followed in 1837 by 'Beauties of the Country,' which was favourably reviewed by the 'Literary Gazette.' Under the auspices of Samuel Rogers he was enabled, about 1841, to commence business as a bookseller at 9 Newgate Street. He was also noticed by W. H. Harrison, then editing 'Friendship's Offering,' who inserted his verses, 'The Desolate Hall,' in the annual for 1838, and gave him two guineas for the well-known lines entitled 'The Fountain,' printed in 1839 and illustrated by an engraving from a painting by Westall. Some of his leisure was employed in writing tales for the 'London Journal.' Later on he removed to Ludgate Hill, and, although always in business, was intimate with many of the best known literary characters. Early in 1874, Disraeli, then prime minister, whom he had met in early life at Lady Blessington's, granted him 100*l.* from the Royal Bounty Fund. He died at 23 New Street, Kennington Park Road, London, 24 Oct. 1874, leaving a son and two daughters. The son died in April 1888, when a public appeal was made for funds to bury him, and to aid in supporting his surviving sister, Ellen Miller.

Miller was the author of upwards of forty-five works; the most important were: 'Royston Gower, or the Days of John King,' a novel in two volumes, 1838; 'Rural Sketches,' 1839, verses in the style of Bloomfield's poetry, simple, picturesque, and cheerful; 'Gideon Giles the Roper,' 1840, second edition, 1841, a tale of humble life rendered interesting by truthful and vigorous delineation; 'Godfrey Malvern, or the Life of an Author,' 2 vols. 1842–3, giving the adventures of a country youth who repaired to London in quest of literary fame and fortune; and a 'History of the Anglo-Saxons from the Earliest Period to the Norman Conquest,' 1848, which went to five editions, although it was adversely criticised in the 'Westminster Review' for July 1856, pp. 253–4. In 1846 he edited the 'Poetical Works of Beattie and W. Collins, with Memoirs,' and in 1849 he wrote 'The Mysteries of London, or Lights and Shadows of London Life,' a work forming vol. v. of G. W. Reynolds' 'Mysteries of London.' He also wrote many books for boys or children.

Other works were: 1. 'Fair Rosamond,' 3 vols. 1839. 2. 'Lady Jane Grey,' 3 vols. 1840. 3. 'Poems,' 1841. 4. 'Poetical Language of Flowers,' 1847. 5. 'Pictures of Country Life and Summer Rambles,' 1847. 6. 'Fortune and Fortitude, a Tale,' 1848. 7. 'A Tale of Old England,' 1849. 8. 'Original Poems for my Children,' 1852; 2nd series, 1852. 9. 'The Village Queen, or Summer in the Country,' 1852. 10. 'Picturesque Sketches of London Past and Present,' 1852. 11. 'Our Old Town,' 1857. 12. 'The Poacher and other Pictures of Country Life,' 1858. 13. 'Birds, Bees, and Blossoms,' 1858. 14. 'English Country Life,' 1859; new edition, 1864. 15. 'British Wolf Hunters,' 1859. 16. 'Sports and Pastimes of Merry England,' 1859. 17. 'Langley on the Lea, or Love and Duty,' 1860. 18. 'Songs for British Riflemen,' 1860. 19. 'Common Wayside Flowers,' 1860. 20. 'Dorothy Dovedale's Trials,' 2 vols. 1864. 21. 'Songs of the Seasons,' 1865. 22. 'My Father's Garden,' 1867. 23. 'Jack of All Trades,' 1867. 24. 'The Gaboon,' 1868. 25. 'Watch the End,' 1869; new edition, 1873. 26. 'The Old Park Road,' 1871.

[Wylie's Old and New Nottingham, 1853, pp. 168, 207-10; Pen and Ink Sketches, 2nd edit. 1847, pp. 205-8; S. T. Hall's Biographical Sketches, 1873, pp. 321-2; T. Cooper's Life, 4th edit. 1873, pp. 1-54; C. Bonnell's Thomas Miller printed in Amcoats & Co.'s Gainsborough Almanack for 1892; Chambers's Cyclop. of English Lit. 1844, ii. 626; Illustrated London News, 1874, lxv. 425; Gent. Mag. 1884, ii. 582; Daily News, 27 Oct. 1874, p. 2; Pall Mall Gazette, 4 April 1888, p. 10.] G. C. B.

MILLER, WILLIAM (1740?-1810?), painter, was born about 1740, and practised in London with considerable repute towards the end of the last century. He exhibited portraits with the Free Society in 1768, and in the following year sent a battle-piece, being then, as stated in the catalogue, on his way to Rome. In 1780 and 1783 Miller contributed to the Society of Artists, of which he became a director, and from 1788 to 1803 to the Royal Academy. He painted historical, poetical, and domestic subjects, somewhat in the style of Mather Brown and Peters, as well as some good portraits. Two of the plates in Boydell's 'Shakespeare,' scenes from 'Romeo and Juliet' and 'Henry VI,' are from pictures by Miller, and many of his other works have been engraved, including three subjects from the story of 'Werther,' by J. Cary and W. Sedgwick; 'Alexander presenting Campaspe to Apelles,' by J. B. Michel; 'The Distracted Damsel,' by V. Picot, 1785; 'The Memorable Address of Louis XVI at the Bar of the National Convention' and 'The Last Moments of Louis XVI,' both by Schiavonetti, 1796; 'Innocent Recreation' and 'Animal Affection,' by J. Godby, 1799; 'Swearing-in of Alderman Newnham as Lord Mayor, 8 Nov. 1782,' by B. Smith, 1801; and a portrait of Comte de Grasse, by J. Walker, 1782. Miller is said to have died about 1810. His 'Swearing-in of Alderman Newnham,' a very well painted picture, is in the Art Gallery of the Corporation of London.

[Nagler's Allgemeines Künstler-Lexikon; Redgrave's Dict. of Artists; Exhibition Catalogues of Society of Artists, &c.] F. M. O'D.

MILLER, WILLIAM (1769-1844), publisher, born at Bungay, Suffolk, on 25 March 1769, was son of Thomas Miller (1731-1804) [q. v.], bookseller. When a youth he evinced a taste for drawing, and was advised by Sir Joshua Reynolds to enter the Royal Academy as a student, but in 1787 he was placed in Hookham's publishing house. In 1790 he commenced business on his own account in Bond Street, London, where the first book which he sent forth was his uncle Dr. Edward Miller's 'Select Portions of the New Version of the Psalms of David, with Music.' A series of publications in large quarto, illustrating the costumes of various countries, with descriptions in English and French, brought him considerable profit. Among his other successful ventures may be mentioned Howlett's 'Views of Lincolnshire,' Stoddart's 'Remarks upon Scotland,' and Forster's edition of the 'Arabian Nights Entertainments,' illustrated by Smirke. In 1804 Miller removed to a larger house in Albemarle Street, where he continued until his retirement from business in 1812, being succeeded by John Murray. During this period he was one of the most popular publishers in London. He took shares in the poems of Sir Walter Scott, and published solely Scott's edition of 'Dryden' in 18 vols. 8vo. He reprinted 'The Antient Drama,' 'British Drama,' 'Shakespeare,' and Blomefield's 'History of Norfolk,' 11 vols, 8vo, and Samuel Richardson's works in nineteen small octavo volumes. The 'Travels' of Viscount Valentia, Sir Richard Colt Hoare's 'Giraldus Cambrensis,' and the same author's 'Ancient History of South Wiltshire,' vol. i., were among his most splendid undertakings. His 'British Gallery' was notable for the excellence of the engravings.

For the copyright of Charles James Fox's 'History of the Reign of James II' Miller paid 4,500*l.*, hitherto the largest sum ever given for literary property. Five thousand copies were printed in demy quarto at 1*l.* 16*s.* by Savage, and 250 copies on royal quarto at 2*l.* 12*s.* 6*d.*, with fifty upon elephant size quarto at 5*l.* 5*s.* by Bulmer. Miller barely cleared his expenses by the speculation.

Having realised a modest competency, Miller took a farm in Hertfordshire, but after a brief experience of country life he removed to Duchess Street, Portland Place, London. He died on 25 Oct. 1844, at Dennington, Suffolk, the residence of his son, the Rev. Stanley Miller.

In 1826 he published two quarto volumes of 'Biographical Sketches of British Characters recently deceased, commencing with the Accession of George the Fourth . . .

with a list of their Engraved Portraits.' He announced, but did not print, a continuation.

There is a good portrait of Miller engraved by E. Scriven, after a painting by T. Phillips, R.A., given in Dibdin's 'Bibliographical Decameron.' Another was drawn from the life on stone by J. D. Engleheart in 1826, and is frequently found inserted in Miller's 'Biographical Sketches.'

[Gent. Mag. 1845, pt. i. pp. 102–3; advertisements at beginning and end of Ames's Typogr. (Herbert & Dibdin), vol. i.; Dibdin's Bibliogr. Decameron; Timperley's Encycl. of Lit. and Typogr. Anecd., 2nd edit.] G. G.

MILLER, SIR WILLIAM, LORD GLENLEE (1755–1846), Scottish judge, born on 12 Aug. 1755, was only son of Sir Thomas Miller [q.v.], lord president of the College of Justice, by his first wife Margaret, eldest daughter of John Murdoch of Rose Bank, provost of Glasgow. Educated at the high school of Edinburgh, he was admitted a member of the Faculty of Advocates on 9 Aug. 1777, and was subsequently appointed principal clerk in the high court of justiciary. At the general election in September 1780 he was returned to the House of Commons for the city of Edinburgh, after a keen contest with Sir Laurence Dundas, but was unseated on petition in the following March (*Journals of the House of Commons*, xxxviii. 315, 316). The only occasion on which he appears to have spoken in the house was on Fox's motion condemning the appointment of Sir Hugh Palliser [q. v.] to Greenwich Hospital (*Parl. Hist.* xxi. 1128–30). On the death of his father in September 1789, he succeeded to the baronetcy. He was appointed a lord of session in the place of Alexander Murray, lord Henderland [q. v.], and took his seat on the bench with the title of Lord Glenlee on 23 May 1795. After nearly forty-five years of judicial work he resigned his post in January 1840 (COCKBURN, *Journal*, i. 251), and died at Barskimming, Ayrshire, on 9 May 1846, aged 90. He was buried in the family vault at Stair, Ayrshire. Miller was a very able man, and had a profound knowledge of jurisprudence, mathematics, and literature. His conversation is said to have been 'full of thought and curious original views.' His appearance was striking: 'the figure was slender; the countenance pale, but with a full dark eye; the features regular, unless when disturbed, as his whole frame often was, by little jerks and gesticulations, as if he was under frequent galvanism; his air and manner polite' (COCKBURN, *Life of Lord Jeffrey*, i. 123–4). Miller was the last Scottish judge who appeared in his wig in the streets, his practice being, before he got so feeble as to require a sedan-chair, 'to walk to court in his wig and long cravat, his silk stockings, and silver buckles, and his cocked hat in his hand' (COCKBURN, *Journal*, i. 251). Guthrie has left a graphic description of the delivery of Miller's judgment in the Auchterarder case (*Autobiog. of Thomas Guthrie*, 1877, pp. 349–50), and an amusing account of a sharp passage of arms between Miller and John Clerk (afterwards lord Eldin) [q. v.] will be found in 'Cockburn's Journal' (ii. 207–10).

Miller married, on 5 Nov. 1778, his cousin Grizel, the daughter of George Chalmers, a large grain merchant in Edinburgh, by whom he had six sons and three daughters. His wife died in Edinburgh on 15 Feb. 1817. He was succeeded in the baronetcy by his grandson, William Miller, the grandfather of the fifth baronet. There is a portrait of Miller in the Parliament House at Edinburgh (PAUL, *Handbook to the Parliament House*, 1884, pp. 49–50), and three etchings of him by Kay will be found in the second volume of 'Original Portraits' (Nos. 285, 300, 312). A full-length portrait of Miller, by Sir Henry Raeburn, was engraved by W. Walker in 1838. His library was sold by auction at Edinburgh on 18 Jan. 1853, and the eleven following days.

His second son, WILLIAM MILLER (*d.* 1815), a lieutenant-colonel of the 1st foot-guards, was mortally wounded at Quatre Bras on 16 June 1815, and died the following day at Brussels, where a monument was erected in the cemetery to his memory. Sir Walter Scott, in his 'Field of Waterloo,' refers to the 'gallant Miller's failing eye, still bent where Albion's banners fly' (*Poetical Works*, 1848, p. 505 and note).

[Kay's Original Portraits and Caricature Etchings, 1877, i. 42, 119, 243, ii. 158, 346–8, 380, 417; Cockburn's Life of Lord Jeffrey, 1852, i. 121–4; Journal of Henry Cockburn, 1874, i. 77, 251–2, ii. 207–10, 267; Brunton and Haig's Senators of the College of Justice, 1832, p. 542; Anderson's Scottish Nation, 1863, iii. 157–8; Gent. Mag. 1846 pt. i. p. 643; Annual Register, 1846, App. to Chron. p. 254; Burke's Peerage, &c. 1890, p. 958; Foster's Members of Parliament, Scotland, 1882, p. 251; Scots Mag. xl. 469, lxxix. 239.] G. F. R. B.

MILLER, WILLIAM (1795–1861), Peruvian general, was born at Wingham, Kent, 2 Dec. 1795, and, like his brother and biographer John Miller, served in the field-train department of the (British) royal artillery, in which he was appointed assistant-commissary 1 Jan. 1811. He landed in the Peninsula in August that year, and made the campaigns of 1811–14, including the sieges of Ciudad Rodrigo, Badajoz, St. Sebastian, and Bayonne. He afterwards served in North America, in the operations in the Chesapeake, and the expedition to New Orleans, and was shipwrecked in the Ranger ordnance transport off Mobile. Returning home at the peace he travelled for two years on the continent, and then went out to La Plata. He made an excursion in the direction of Patagonia; and afterwards crossed the Pampas and Andes to Chili, where with his corps, the Buenos Ayres artillery, he repeatedly distinguished himself in the struggle for Chilian independence. He served as major commanding the marines on board the O'Higgins, 50 guns, in which Lord Cochrane [see Cochrane, Thomas, tenth Earl of Dundonald] hoisted his flag on 22 Dec. 1818. In August 1821 he landed at Pisco, defeated and pursued the Spanish garrison, and assumed the government of Yca. Hearing that Cantereau, a French royalist and one of the ablest of the Spanish generals, was threatening Lima, Miller marched thither to reinforce General San Martin. He was made a general of brigade there in 1823. He became the intimate friend of Simon Bolivar, who was invested with the chief authority in Peru 1 Sept. 1823, and under him he attained the rank of general of division and commander-in-chief of the cavalry. To commemorate Miller's brilliant services at the battle of Juria, 6 Aug. 1824, Bolivar conferred on his regiment the title of 'Húsares de Juria.' The most conspicuous of his many gallant exploits was his charge at the head of these hussars at the battle of Ayacucho, which finally secured the liberties of Chili and Peru, 9 July 1824. He was many times wounded, and at the battle of Pisco nearly lost his life. At the attack on Chiloe a grapeshot passed through one of his thighs, and his right instep was crushed by a cannon-ball. In 1825 he was governor of Potosi, but in 1826 returned to Europe.

He received the freedom of the city of Canterbury and many marks of attention on the continent, notably from the Austrian officers in garrison at Milan. He returned to Peru, and as commander-in-chief put down an insurrection under General Gamarra in 1834; but changing political circumstances banished him from the republic, in which he was then holding the rank of grand-marshal. With Santa Cruz and some other officers he embarked in H.M.S. Samarang, commanded by Captain William Broughton, in February 1839, thus closing his honourable military career of twenty years, during which he had taken part in every battle fought in Chili and Peru in the cause of South American independence. In 1843 he was made British consul-general in the Pacific, a post he held some years. In 1859 he went to Callao, to prefer some unsettled claims against the Peruvian government, which the Peruvian congress unanimously agreed should be paid. But the president, General Castillo, stopped the payment, which proved the crowning disappointment of a chequered life. Miller, who was dangerously ill, expressed a wish to die under the British flag. He was carried on board the Naiad, then in Callao harbour, and there died on 31 Oct. 1861. He was buried in the English cemetery at Bella Vista, all the church bells in Callao tolling, an honour never before paid to any protestant in Peru.

Miller is described as very tall and handsome, of winning address. He was an able officer, and distinguished alike by his conspicuous personal gallantry and his humanity towards his Spanish prisoners.

[Miller's biography from 1817 to 1826, written by his brother John Miller, in 2 vols. 8vo (London, 1827); Clements R. Markham's Hist. of Peru (Chicago, 1892); Basil Hall's Journal in Chili, pt. i. ch. iii.; Appleton's Encycl. Amer. Biog.; Gent. Mag. 1862 pt. i. p. 236; cf. art. Mackenna, John or Juan.] H. M. C.

MILLER, WILLIAM (1810–1872), Scottish poet, was born in Bridgegate, Glasgow, in August 1810, and spent his early years in Parkhead, near Glasgow. Owing to precarious health he discarded his early intention of becoming a doctor, and took to wood-turning. He was actively engaged at his trade in Glasgow till November 1871, when his health failed. A change to Blantyre, near Hamilton, Lanarkshire, was only slightly beneficial, and he returned to Glasgow, where he died 20 Aug. 1872. He was buried in Tollcross graveyard, Glasgow; a monument was placed in the city necropolis.

Miller early contributed to periodicals, and established his poetical reputation by songs published in 'Whistle Binkie' (1832–53). His 'Wee Willie Winkie,' and other nursery and miscellaneous lyrics, in which he delineates the charm of children's mythology and the attractions of rural life, have been widely popular, and gained for him the title of 'Laureate of the Nursery' (Robert Buchanan in *St. Paul's Magazine*, July 1872). He has an easy mastery of the Scottish dialect; his sense of fitting maxim and allegory is quick and trustworthy, and his lyrical effects are much helped by the directness and simplicity of his style. His 'Scottish Nursery Songs and other Poems' appeared in 1863.

[Biography prefixed to Whistle Binkie, vol. ii. ed. 1878; Glasgow Herald, 22 Aug. 1872; Grant Wilson's Poets and Poetry of Scotland.] T. B.

MILLER, WILLIAM (1796–1882), line-engraver, youngest son of George Miller, a descendant of an old quaker family who settled in Edinburgh about 1688, was born in that city on 28 May 1796. He was educated partly in England and partly at the university of Edinburgh, and it was intended that he should enter his father's business of a shawl manufacturer. His early devotion to art led, however, to his being apprenticed in 1811 to William Archibald, an engraver. With him Miller remained four years, and after having done a little work on his own account he, at the end of 1819, went to London, and became a pupil of George Cooke. He returned to Edinburgh in the autumn of 1821 and at once obtained a good practice as a landscape engraver. His first plate for Williams's 'Views in Greece' was finished in 1822, and was followed by eighteen other plates for the same work. In 1824 he completed his first engraving after Turner, 'Clovelly Bay,' which with 'Comb Martin' and 'Portsmouth' appeared in Turner's 'Antiquarian and Picturesque Tour round the South Coast,' 1826. He afterwards engraved some plates for Surtees's 'History of Durham,' 1816–40, and Brown's 'Select Views of the Royal Residences of Scotland,' 1830; but it was as an interpreter of the works of Turner that Miller acquired his fame. The larger plates which he engraved after that master were 'The Grand Canal, Venice' (1837), 'Modern Italy' (1842), issued by the Art Union of London, 'The Rhine, Osterspey and Feltzen' (1853), 'The Piazzetta, Venice' (1854), 'The Bell Rock Lighthouse' (1864), and 'St. Michael's Mount' (1866). Other plates after Turner were the 'Straits of Dover,' 'Great Yarmouth,' 'Stamford,' 'Windsor Castle,' 'Chatham,' 'Carew Castle,' and 'Durham Cathedral,' for the 'Picturesque Views in England and Wales,' 1838; 'The Prince of Orange Landing at Torbay,' 'Modern Italy,' 'The Shipwreck,' 'Spithead,' 'Line Fishing off Hastings,' 'The Battle of Trafalgar,' and 'Wreck off Hastings,' which appeared first in the 'Art Journal' and afterwards in the 'Turner Gallery;' views of 'Dryburgh Abbey,' 'Melrose,' 'Edinburgh,' 'Loch Katrine,' 'Loch Achray,' 'Skiddaw,' and 'Berwick upon Tweed,' for Sir Walter Scott's 'Poetical Works,' 1833–34; thirty-one plates for Scott's 'Miscellaneous Prose Works,' 1834–6; 'Nantes,' 'Between Clairmont and Mauves,' 'Château de Nantes,' 'Rouen' (two views), 'Pont Neuf, Paris,' and 'Melun,' for Turner's 'Annual Tour,' or 'Rivers of France,' 1833–1835; the 'Tower of London,' for the 'Literary Souvenir' of 1832; 'Marly' and 'The Palace of La Belle Gabrielle,' for the 'Keepsake' of 1832 and 1834; and four illustrations for Rogers's 'Poems,' 1834. Although highly successful in the execution of his larger plates after Turner, it was in the delicacy of touch and refinement of style with which he rendered the marvellous drawing of the skies, or suggested the magical charm of the mountain distances, in the smaller book illustrations that his full sympathy with the painter was shown to the greatest advantage.

Miller's larger plates after other masters were 'Edinburgh' (1826), after H. W. Williams; 'The Watering Place' (1836), after the picture by Gainsborough in the National Gallery; 'The Schule Scalin,' left unfinished by William Howison, and 'An Incident in the Life of Napoleon,' after Sir George Harvey, P.R.S.A.; 'The Battle of Trafalgar' (1839), after Clarkson Stanfield, R.A., and 'A Sunset at Sea after a Storm' (1849), after F. Danby, A.R.A., both for Finden's 'Royal Gallery of British Art.' He also engraved for the Royal Association for the Promotion of the Fine Arts in Scotland, 'Loch an Eilan,' after Horatio MacCulloch, R.S.A.; 'Italian Goatherds,' after R. Scott Lauder, R.S.A.; 'Kilchurn Castle,' after Turner; 'Dunluce Castle,' after the Rev. John Thomson of Duddingston, and six smaller plates. There are likewise six plates by him in the Vernon Gallery and Royal Gallery of Art, which were issued first in the 'Art Journal.' His book plates after artists other than Turner comprise three for Stanfield's 'Coast Scenery of the English Channel,' 1836, thirty-four after Stanfield and others for the Abbotsford edition of the 'Waverley Novels,' 1842–7, five after Stanfield for the 'Picturesque Annual,' 1832–4, and others for the 'Winter's Wreath,' 1828–32, 'Landscape Annual,' 1830–2, 'Keepsake,' 1831, 'Literary Souvenir,' 1833, Hall's 'Book of Gems,' 1836–8, Lockhart's 'Life of Scott,' 1839, 'The Land of Burns,' 1840, Kitto's 'Daily Bible Illustrations,' 1850–4, Alaric Watts's 'Lyrics of the Heart,' 1851, and an exquisite vignette of 'Rab's Grave,' for Dr. John Brown's 'Rab and his Friends,' 1862. His latest works were forty-four plates for 'Hood's Poems illustrated by Birket Foster,' 1871, and 'Hood's Poems again illustrated by Birket Foster,' 1872.

Miller was an honorary member of the Royal Scottish Academy and occasionally contributed water-colour drawings to its exhibitions. During the last ten years of his life he retired from the active work of his profession, but found congenial occupation in water-colour painting and in philanthropic work.

He resided throughout his life at Millerfield House, Edinburgh, but died at Sheffield, while on a visit to his daughter, on 20 Jan. 1882. He was interred in the burial-ground attached to the meeting-house of the Society of Friends in Pleasance, Edinburgh.

[Scotsman, 21 Jan. 1882; Annual Report of the Royal Scottish Academy, 1882; Catalogue of Engravings by William Miller, H.R.S.A., by W. F. M[iller], 1866, with portrait, privately printed]. R. E. G.

MILLER, WILLIAM ALLEN (1817–1870), chemist, was born at Ipswich on 17 Dec. 1817. His father, William Miller, having acted, during nearly twenty years, as secretary to the General Hospital, Birmingham, became a brewer in the Borough, London, and married Frances Bowyer, whose strong, sagacious character her son inherited. After a year at Merchant Taylors' School, Miller was transferred to a quakers' seminary at Ackworth in Yorkshire. There he met William Allen (1770–1843) [q. v.], whose name he bore, and had his scientific tastes stimulated by chemical lectures and the occasional use of a telescope. At the age of fifteen he was apprenticed to his uncle, Bowyer Vaux, a surgeon in the Birmingham General Hospital, and five years later entered the medical department of King's College, London. Having obtained in 1839 the Warneford prize in theology, he worked for some months of 1840 in Liebig's laboratory at Giessen, was appointed on his return to England demonstrator of chemistry in King's College, and in 1841–2 took degrees of M.B. and M.D. in the university of London. John Frederic Daniell [q. v.] warmly patronised him. Miller was his assistant lecturer from 1841, co-operated in all his investigations, and joined with him in communicating to the Royal Society on 25 Feb. 1844 'Additional Researches on the Electrolysis of Secondary Compounds' (*Phil. Trans.* cxxxiv. 1). On Daniell's death in 1845, he succeeded to the chair of chemistry in King's College, and was elected a fellow of the Royal Society. His lecture-notes furnished the materials for his 'Elements of Chemistry, Theoretical and Practical,' of which the first part, on 'Chemical Physics,' was published in 1855; the second and third parts, on 'Inorganic' and 'Organic Chemistry,' appearing successively in 1856 and 1857. A sixth edition of the first and second parts was issued in 1877–8, a fifth edition of the third, mostly rewritten by Dr. Armstrong and Mr. C. E. Groves in 1880. The work was also several times reprinted in the United States, and by its sound and useful character deserved the popularity it attained.

Miller's first experiments in spectrum analysis were made in a lumber-room underneath the lecture theatre at King's College. They applied both to absorption and flame-spectra, and their results, including some observations of the 'rain-band,' were made known at the Cambridge meeting of the British Association in 1845, and printed in the 'Philosophical Magazine' (xxvii. 81). Diagrams of flame-spectra were here for the first time given. At the Manchester meeting of the British Association in 1861 Miller delivered a lecture on spectrum analysis of considerable historical value, which he repeated on 15 Jan. 1862 before the Pharmaceutical Society of London (*Pharmaceutical Journal*, iii. 399, 2nd ser.) Six months later he communicated to the Royal Society a paper 'On the Photographic Transparency of various Bodies, and on the Photographic Effects of Metallic and other Spectra obtained by means of the Electric Spark' (*Phil. Trans.* clii. 861). The use of quartz-prisms had enabled him to get collodion-negatives of the spectra of twenty-five metals, showing great and characteristic differences. A 'Note on the Spectrum of Thallium' followed (*Proc. of the Royal Society*, xii. 407).

In 1862 Miller entered, with Dr. Huggins, his neighbour at Tulse Hill, upon a memorable series of investigations into the spectra of the heavenly bodies. Having constructed a special apparatus, they analysed with till then unapproached accuracy the light of the moon, Jupiter, Mars, and many of the fixed stars; and through their original method of direct comparison with terrestrial spectra, procured the first detailed and trustworthy information regarding stellar chemistry. Their results, in a preliminary form, were laid before the Royal Society on 19 Feb. 1863, and more fully on 26 May 1864 (*ib.* xii. 444; *Phil. Trans.* cliv. 413). The gold medal of the Royal Astronomical Society was conferred upon them jointly in 1867 for these 'discoveries in astronomical physics.' A photograph of the spectrum of Sirius, the earliest specimen of its class, taken by himself and Dr. Huggins, was exhibited by Miller in the course of a lecture at the Royal Institution on 6 March 1863 (*Proc. of the Royal Institution*, iv. 42). He was soon, indeed, obliged to desist from adding night-work to his arduous daily duties, yet he assisted Dr. Huggins in spectroscopic observations in 1866 of *a* Orionis (*Monthly Notices*, xxvi. 215), and of the temporary star in Corona Borealis (*Proc. of the Royal Society*, xv. 146). In

May 1867 he gave a course of four lectures on spectrum analysis at the Royal Institution (*Chemical News*, vol. xv.), and explained the bearing of the method on astronomy to the working men of Exeter during the meeting there of the British Association in 1869 (*Popular Science Review*, viii. 335).

Miller prepared in 1851, at the request of the government, with Professors Graham and Hofmann, a 'Report on the Metropolitan Water Supply' (*Quarterly Journal of the Chemical Society*, iv. 376), investigated the combined action of water and air upon lead, and lectured before the Chemical Society in 1865 on the analysis of drinking water. He reported to the British Association in 1857 on the 'Recent Progress of Electro-chemical Research' (*Report*, p. 158), and served on the several committees appointed by the same body to superintend the working of Kew Observatory, to provide for uniformity in weights and measures, and to determine standards of electrical resistance. He moreover presided over the chemical section at the Birmingham meeting in 1865. His useful invention of a 'self-registering thermometer adapted to deep-sea soundings' (*Proc. of the Royal Society*, xvii. 483) resulted from his attendance at the committee of scientific preparation for the voyage of the Porcupine, and he served from 1866 on the committee for organising meteorological observations under the board of trade. He became a member of the senate of the university of London in 1865, sat on the royal commission on scientific instruction in 1870, aided in the chemical testing of the stone employed in building the houses of parliament, and was assayer to the mint and the Bank of England. His services to the Royal Society as member of council, 1848–1850 and 1855–7, and as treasurer from 1861 until his death, were of great value. He took a prominent part in the foundation of the Chemical Society in 1841, and was twice its president. A degree of LL.D. was conferred upon him by the university of Edinburgh in 1860; he was made D.C.L. of Oxford in 1868, and LL.D. of Cambridge in 1869, when he was Rede's lecturer, 'Coal-tar Colours' forming the subject of his discourse.

Travelling to Liverpool for the meeting of the British Association, Miller was struck with illness resulting from brain fatigue, and died of apoplexy at Liverpool on 30 Sept. 1870. He was buried in Norwood cemetery beside his wife, who had died a year previously. He had married in 1842 Eliza, eldest daughter of Edward Forrest of Birmingham, by whom he had two daughters and one son.

Miller was a man of sound and penetrating judgment. His ideas were slowly formed, but tenaciously held, and unswerving integrity was united in him with a refined and sensitive nature. On one occasion, when under cross-examination as a scientific witness in a patent case, he fainted on the judge throwing momentary doubt upon his veracity. The religious convictions, which were the mainspring of his life, obtained partial expression in an address on 'The Bible and Science' to the Church Congress at Wolverhampton on 3 Oct. 1867, and in an introductory lecture at King's College on 1 Oct. 1859. Miller edited Daniell's 'Meteorological Essays' in 1845, and his 'Introduction to the Study of Inorganic Chemistry' appeared posthumously in Goodeve's 'Text-Books of Science,' 1871.

[Proc. of the Royal Soc. vol. xix. p. xix; Quarterly Journal of the Chemical Soc. ix. 617; Nature, ii. 517; Robinson's Reg. of Merchant Taylors' School; Ward's Men of the Reign; Poggendorff's Biog. Lit. Handwörterbuch; Royal Society's Cat. of Scientific Papers.] A. M. C.

MILLER, WILLIAM HALLOWES (1801–1880), mineralogist, born 6 April 1801, at Velindre, near Llandovery, was son of Captain Miller by a second marriage. The father had served in the American war, and the associations of the family were military. The son, after receiving his earlier education at private schools, proceeded to St. John's College, Cambridge, and graduated as fifth wrangler in 1826. He was elected to a college fellowship in 1829, and to the professorship of mineralogy in 1832. In accordance with the statutes he proceeded in 1841 to the degree of M.D. in order to retain his fellowship, which, however, he vacated by marriage with Harriet Susan Minty in 1844. They had two sons and four daughters, but one of the former and two of the latter died before their father.

An occasional visit to the continent, often more or less on scientific business, but sometimes extended to a holiday trip in the Eastern Alps, alone interrupted the round of Miller's daily work in his university. A diligent student and lover of science, with a memory singularly accurate and retentive, he possessed an exceptionally wide knowledge of natural philosophy; but it was in crystallography, a branch of his special science, that his great reputation was won. Starting from the groundwork already laid by Whewell and Neumann, Miller developed a system of crystallography which was far more simple, symmetrical, and adapted to mathematical calculations than any which had yet been devised. His system 'gave expressions adapted for working all the problems that a crystal can present, and it gave them in a form that appealed at once to the sense of symmetry and appropriateness of the mathematician . . . he thus placed the keystone into the arch of the science of crystallography' (Professor MASKELYNE). Miller's system was published in 1838; it quickly obtained favour, and has more than maintained its ground with mineralogists.

Another important work in which Miller had a large share was the reconstruction of the standards of length and weight which had been destroyed in 1834 when the houses of parliament were burnt. He took part in more than one royal commission for this purpose, and gave an account of the operations for restoring the value of the old standard of weight in the 'Philosophical Transactions' for 1856. He was also of great service on the Commission Internationale du Mètre, to which he was appointed in 1870. He received the honorary degrees of LL.D. from Dublin in 1865, of D.C.L. from Oxford in 1876, and was re-elected a fellow of his old college in 1874. He was admitted into the Royal Society in 1838, was foreign secretary from 1856 to 1873, and was awarded a royal medal in 1870. He was a knight of the order of St. Maurice and St. Lazare in Italy, of the order of Leopold in Belgium, and a corresponding member of many foreign societies, including the French Academy. In 1876 his health began to fail; he had a slight stroke of paralysis in the autumn, and after a slow decline of the vital powers he died on 20 May 1880.

Before the work on crystallography mentioned above Miller had published brief but valuable text-books on hydrostatics and hydrodynamics. He contributed largely to scientific publications, no less than 45 papers appearing in the 'Royal Society's Catalogue.' He also contributed very largely to a new edition of William Phillips's 'Elementary Introduction to Mineralogy'—'a monument to Miller's name, though he almost expunged that name from it' (MASKELYNE).

Miller was a short, rather square-set man, with a roundish face, placid expression, and well-developed forehead. Though of retiring habits, and caring little for society, he was not only respected, but even beloved, by those who enjoyed his friendship. His knowledge, his vigour and grasp of mind, and his inventiveness were all remarkable, and he accomplished much with very simple means, some of his laboratory fittings being of the homeliest kind.

[Obituary notices in Proc. Royal Society, No. 206, 1880, by the present writer; and by Professor Maskelyne in Nature, xxii. 247; Memorial by Mrs. Miller (privately printed).]

T. G. B.

MILLER, WILLIAM HENRY (1789–1848), book collector, the only child of William Miller of Craigentinny, Midlothian, was born in 1789. He received a liberal education, and throughout life retained a taste for classical literature. In 1830 he entered parliament as one of the members for the borough of Newcastle-under-Lyme, defeating John Evelyn Denison, afterwards speaker. He was re-elected in 1831, 1832, 1835, and 1837, each time after a contest, and on two occasions at the head of the poll. In 1841, however, he was defeated, and he was again unsuccessful as a candidate for Berwick at the general election of 1847. He died, unmarried, at Craigentinny House, near Edinburgh, on 31 Oct. 1848, in his sixtieth year, and was by his own desire buried on his estate in a mausoleum erected after his decease, and decorated with sculptured friezes by Alfred Gatley.

As a book collector, Miller was regarded as the successor of Richard Heber, and many of the rarest works from the collections of the latter passed into the library which he formed at Britwell Court, near Burnham, Buckinghamshire. He was extremely particular in his choice of copies, and from his habit of carrying about with him a foot rule in order to measure the exact size of a 'tall' copy of a book which he wished to buy, he became known at sales and among collectors as 'Measure Miller.'

The Britwell Library, formed chiefly at the time of the dispersal of the Heber and other important collections of half a century ago, and since added to by acquisitions from the Corser, Laing, and other sales of more recent years, is unrivalled among private libraries for the number, rarity, and condition of its examples of early English and Scottish literature. It contains six works from Caxton's press, many printed by Wynkyn de Worde and Pynson, and the greater part of the Heber collection of ballads and broadsides. It is especially rich in early English poetry, and possesses also the finest and most complete series in existence of De Bry's collections of voyages to the East and West Indies, both in Latin and in German.

Britwell Court and its library were bequeathed by Miller to his cousin Miss Marsh, from whom they passed to Samuel Christie-Miller, M.P. for Newcastle-under-Lyme from 1847 to 1859, and on his death, on 5 April 1889, to Wakefield Christie-Miller (*d.* 1898), whose sons inherited them.

A portrait of William Henry Miller, by Sir Thomas Lawrence, has been engraved.

[Gent. Mag. 1849, i. 98; private information.]

R. E. G.

MILLES, ISAAC (1638–1720), divine, born on 19 Sept. 1638, was youngest son of Thomas Milles, esq., of Cockfield, near Bury, Suffolk. Of his elder brothers, Samuel, of Queens' College, Cambridge, was vicar of Royston, Hertfordshire, and John 'a very considerable tradesman' at Dedham, Essex. After spending seven years at King Edward VI's School, Bury, where Lord-keeper North was among his schoolfellows, Isaac was admitted at St. John's College, Cambridge, in 1656, and graduated M.A. in 1663. His tutor at Cambridge was Francis Turner, afterwards the nonjuring bishop of Ely, who was his lifelong friend. On leaving the university Milles took holy orders, and became curate in sole charge of Barley, Hertfordshire, the rector, Dr. Joseph Beaumont [q. v.], master of Peterhouse, being non-resident. In 1674, by the influence of his friend, Chief Baron Atkins, he obtained the vicarage of Chipping Wycombe, Buckinghamshire. Here he made the acquaintance of Dodwell, and became intimate with Dr. Martin Lluelyn [q. v.], whose epitaph in Wycombe Church he wrote.

While at Cambridge he had met Edward Coleman [q. v.], Oates's victim, and seems to have read Coleman's letters to Père la Chaise before they were printed. He came to the conclusion that no popish plot existed, and gave offence by expressing his conviction to that effect in his sermons. It was only the reputation which his high character had won for him which saved him from prosecution.

In 1680 he was presented by Sir Robert Sawyer to the living of Highclere, Hampshire, where he remained till his death. Milles took pupils there, including the sons of Thomas Herbert, eighth earl of Pembroke [q. v.], the new proprietor of Highclere. Chief among his friends at this period were Dr. George Hooper, incumbent of East Woodhay and Ashmansworth, afterwards bishop of St. Asaph and Bath and Wells, and his successor at Woodhay, John Herne, canon of Windsor. For some time he had scruples about taking the oath of allegiance after the revolution. Turner the nonjuror appears to have persuaded him to do so.

Milles, a strong tory and high churchman, was a model parish priest. The parish register of Highclere describes him as 'for 39 years 2 months and 7 days the constant resident rector and pastor of this parish,' and records his 'primitive integrity and piety' and his charity to the poor. 'He never refused any of his neighbours that desired to borrow any money of him, leaving it to them to take their own time to repay it, without usury.' He laid out between 400*l.* and 500*l.* on the parsonage house and outhouses, but 'never exacted the utmost of his tithes.' He died of paralysis on 6 July 1720, and was buried on 9 July in the chancel of Highclere Church, where a black marble slab with a Latin inscription was put up to his memory by his children. A white marble monument with inscription was also placed by his eldest son on the north wall of the chancel. Bromley mentions a rare engraved portrait of him, signed by Vertue.

Milles married in 1670 Elizabeth Luckin of Springfield, Essex, who died of smallpox on 4 Jan. 1708. His eldest son, Thomas, bishop of Waterford, is separately noticed. Of his younger sons, Jeremiah Milles (1675–1746), fellow and tutor at Balliol College, Oxford, from 1696 to 1705, became rector of Riseholm, Lincolnshire, in 1704, and was rector of Duloe, Cornwall, from 1704 till his death; his son Jeremiah [q. v.] was dean of Exeter.

Another son, Isaac Milles the younger (*fl.* 1701–1727), B.A. of Balliol College 1696, graduated M.A. from Sidney Sussex, Cambridge, in 1701, was treasurer of the diocese of Waterford 21 May 1714, and prebendary of Lismore 6 Sept. 1716, but was non-resident, and carried on his father's school at Highclere. In 1727 he resigned his Irish benefices to become rector of Ludshelfe or Litchfield, Hampshire.

[The quaint Life of Isaac Milles, published in 1721, was written by or under the influence of Bishop Thomas Milles. With it is printed a funeral sermon by J. W., a neighbouring clergyman. In 1842 a duodecimo edition of the Life, summarised, and containing preface and some additional matter, with three illustrations, was published. See also Cotton's Fasti Eccles. Hibern. i. 23, 27, 56, 74; Grad. Cant.; and Foster's Alumni Oxon.] G. Le G. N.

MILLES, JEREMIAH (1714–1784), antiquary, said to have been born at Duloe, Cornwall, in 1714, was son of the Rev. Jeremiah Milles, forty-two years vicar of Duloe [see under Milles, Isaac], but the entry of Milles's baptism does not appear in Duloe parish registers. He was educated at the expense of his uncle, Dr. Thomas Milles [q. v.], bishop of Waterford and Lismore, first as an oppidan at Eton, and then at Corpus Christi College, Oxford, where he matriculated on 9 July 1729 as a gentleman-commoner (B.A. 1733, M.A. 1735, and B.D. and D.D. 1747). The greater part of the years 1733–7 was spent by Milles and his cousin, Richard Pococke [q. v.], afterwards bishop of Meath, in travelling through Europe. Numerous manuscripts descriptive of these and of his later expeditions and a register of letters written by him from abroad are among the British Museum Addit. MSS. He was ordained in the English church, and at once received from his uncle, Bishop Milles, preferment in Ireland. From 1735 to 1745 he held the treasurership of Lismore Cathedral, he was precentor of Waterford Cathedral from 31 Dec. 1737 to 12 Nov. 1744, and for a short time he had a living near Waterford; but on the death of his uncle in 1740 he inherited a considerable fortune, and he preferred to live in England. While in Ireland he gave 50*l.* for the adornment of Waterford Cathedral (POCOCKE, *Irish Tour*, 1752, p. 132).

Milles was from early life interested in archæology. He was elected F.S.A. in 1741, F.R.S. in 1742, and about that date he became a member of the Egyptian Club 'to inquire into Egyptian antiquities.' Through his marriage, on 29 May 1745, to Edith, daughter of Archbishop Potter, ample preferments came to him. From 1744 to 1746 he was rector of Saltwood with Hythe in Kent, he enjoyed the sinecure rectory of West Tarring in Sussex for many years to 1779, when he resigned in favour of his son; from 1745 to his death he filled the benefice of Merstham in Surrey, and from 1746 until he died he held the valuable rectory of St. Edmund the King with St. Nicholas Acons, Lombard Street, in the city of London. At West Tarring Milles repaired the old parsonage hall, and adapted it for a charity school (*Topographical Miscellanies*, 1792, sub 'Terring'), and the rectory house at Merstham was rebuilt by him in 1768, but some of the stained glass in the church windows is said to have 'vanished' during his incumbency. On the presentation of his father-in-law, 'patron for that turn by reason of a grant made by the Bishop of Exeter to him,' he was admitted on 11 May 1747 to the precentorship of Exeter Cathedral and to a prebendal stall, with the emoluments of a canon residentiary. He repainted the stately mantelpiece in the great hall of the precentor's house, and surmounted it with the arms of his family and those of Archbishop Potter. The stall was retained by Milles until his death, but he vacated the precentorship on 28 April 1762, through his election by the chapter to succeed Bishop Lyttelton as their dean. An interesting letter from him to George Grenville on the deanery house at Exeter is in the 'Grenville Papers,' iv. 20–3. Milles, on Lyttleton's death at the close of 1768, also succeeded him as president of the Society of Antiquaries, a position which he retained as long as he lived. As prolocutor of the lower house of convocation he was presented to the upper house by Bishop John Butler on 23 Jan. 1775, and the 'Oratiuncula' then delivered by Butler is printed in his 'Concio ad clerum Cant. Provinciæ, 1775.' Milles died at Harley Street, London, on 13 Feb. 1784, and on 19 Feb. was buried by the side of his wife (who had died on 9 June 1761, aged 35) in the church of St. Edmund the King. A monument by Bacon was placed there to their memory. Their issue was three sons, Jeremiah, Richard, and Thomas, and two daughters, one of whom married Captain Blake (COTTLE, *Early Recollections*, i. 34). Many references to the sons are in the 'Early Diary of Frances Burney' (i. 234–51), where they are praised as 'very agreeable and amiable,' appearing 'to regard their father only as an elder brother.' Richard Gough speaks of the dean's 'domestic happiness,' but thought that he did not maintain sufficient control over the proceedings of the Antiquaries.

Unfortunately for his reputation Milles rushed into the Chatterton dispute with an extravagant edition of 'Poems supposed to have been written at Bristol in the Fifteenth Century by Thomas Rowley, Priest. With a Commentary,' 1782, copies of which, with numerous manuscript notes by Haslewood, Dr. Sherwen, and Horace Walpole, are in the British Museum. In this work he maintained the antiquity of the poems, and committed himself to the assertion, when writing on the poem of the death of 'Syr Charles Bawdin,' that 'a greater variety of internal proofs may be produced for its authenticity than for that of any other piece in the whole collection.' His ingenuous comments provoked replies from Edmund Malone, Thomas Tyrwhitt, and Thomas Warton, and a very severe 'Archæological Epistle to Dean Milles,' 1782, which, though long attributed to the poet Mason, was written by John Baynes [q. v.] On the dean's part in this controversy S. T. Coleridge wrote that he 'foully calumniated Chatterton, an owl mangling a poor dead nightingale,' and that 'though only a dean, he was in dulness and malignity most episcopally eminent' (JOSEPH COTTLE, *Early Recollections*, i. 36).

Milles also wrote: 1. 'Inscriptionum Antiquarum liber alter à Jeremia Milles et Richardo Pococke editus,' 1752, printed as an appendix, pp. 100–127 of Pococke's work on the same subject. 2. 'Observations on the Wardrobe Account for 1483, the Coronation of Richard III,' 1770. This originally appeared in the 'Archæologia,' i. 361–83, and it produced from Horace Walpole 'A Reply to the Observations of Dean Milles on the Ward Robe Account,' 24 pages, of which six copies only, dated 28 Aug. 1770, were printed at Strawberry Hill. 3. 'A Speech delivered to the Society of Antiquaries, 11 Jan. 1781, on their Removal to Somerset House,' 1781. He also contributed numerous papers to the 'Philosophical Transactions' and the 'Archæologia.'

Milles's library was sold by Leigh Sotheby on 10 April 1843 and four following days, when several of his manuscripts were acquired for the British Museum (cf. *Bibl. Corn.* and Boase, *Collectanea Cornub.*) Milles was the medium, on 9 May 1766, of the presentation of Pococke's Irish collections to the British Museum. His 'Topographical Notes on Bath, Wells,' &c. were printed from the original manuscript by J. G. Bell in 1851, in a series of tracts on British topography. In early life he made large collections for a history of Devonshire, and for illustrating the Domesday survey and the Danish coinage. Letters to and from him are in Nichols's 'Literary Anecdotes,' iii. 295, vi. 297–9, viii. 10, and in the 'Gentleman's Magazine,' 1823, pt. ii. pp. 327–8; he is frequently mentioned with keen dislike in Walpole's 'Correspondence,' and he was lashed, with his brother antiquaries, by Foote in the comedy of the 'Nabob.'

A bust portrait of him, life size, with face seen in three quarters, is in the possession of the Society of Antiquaries. It was copied by Miss Black, by direction of the Earl of Leicester, from the original belonging to the family. A comical sketch by George Steevens of his wig is in the 'Gentleman's Magazine,' 1782, p. 288.

[Gent. Mag. 1745 p. 276, 1784 pt. i. pp. 153, 234, 1786 pt. i. p. 480, 1823 pt. i. pp. 516–17; Foster's Alumni Oxon.; Fowler's Corpus Christi Coll. (Oxford Hist. Soc.), pp. 282–3; Scharf's Cat. of Pictures of Soc. of Antiquaries, p. 41; Polwhele's Biog. Sketches, ii. 6–13; Le Neve's Fasti, i. 388, 413, 429, 431; Cotton's Fasti Eccl. Hib. i. 23, 56; Boase and Courtney's Bibl. Cornub. vols. i. and iii.; Hasted's Kent, iii. 410; Nichols's Lit. Anecd. ii. 657, iv. 471–3, v. 334, vi. 620–626; Nichols's Illustr. of Lit. i. 707–8, vii. 460; Oliver's Bishops of Exeter, pp. 263–4; Manning and Bray's Surrey, ii. 261–4; Biog. of Bishop Richard Pococke in Tours in Scotland (Scottish Hist. Soc.), pp. xxxvi, lx–lxvi; information from Mr. Arthur Burch, Diocesan Registry, Exeter.]

W. P. C.

MILLES, THOMAS (*d.* 1627?), customer of Sandwich, son of Richard Milles of Ashford, by his first wife Joan, daughter of Thomas Glover of Ashford, and sister of Robert Glover, Somerset herald, was born in Kent about 1550. Educated at a 'free school' (*Customer's Alphabet, MS. Bodl.* 913, manuscript note by Milles), he entered the public service about 1570, and during the next sixteen years he was frequently employed in France, Flanders, and Scotland. He is said to have received a chapeau winged as an augmentation to his armorial bearings for his 'great fidelity and incredible celerity' on a mission to Henry IV of France (Noble, *College of Arms*, p. 181). In 1579 he was appointed bailiff of Sandwich. He was employed by Walsingham as an agent between England and Scotland in 1585, and in the following year he accompanied Randolph to Edinburgh, where he rendered great service during the negotiations on the treaty of Berwick. On the conclusion of the treaty, 'desirous to betake himself to some staid course of life,' he obtained the lucrative post of customer of Sandwich. This position gave him great facilities for the interception of foreign agents and correspondence, and the government employed him in unravelling the numerous plots of the period. In 1591 he was recommended to be sent to Brittany to view and report on the forces there, and after the expedition to Cadiz (1596) he was appointed a prize commissioner at Plymouth. In 1598 he acted as secretary to Lord Cobham, lord warden of the Cinque ports, and in the same year (15 June) he obtained, in reversion after Sir Ralph Bourchier, the keepership of Rochester Castle. On the death of George Gilpin in 1602 he applied, without success, for the post of councillor to the council of estate in the Low Countries. He devoted the rest of his life to the defence of the staple system. On his resignation in 1623 of the post of bailiff of Sandwich, he was succeeded (10 July) by John Philipot. His will was proved in 1627.

Milles married, about 1614, Anne, daughter of John Polhill of Otford, Kent, and widow of William Nutt of Canterbury, counsellor-at-law, by whom he had two daughters: Anne, born in 1615; and a daughter born in 1618, who died young. His wife died in 1624 at Davington Hall, and was buried by the side of her younger daughter in St. George's Church, Canterbury, where a monument was erected to her memory. His daughter Anne inherited Norton, purchased by him in the reign of Elizabeth, and Davington, purchased early in the reign of James I, and married in 1627 John Milles, afterwards knighted.

Milles's economical works show the relation of the doctrines of the mercantilist writers to those of the later canonists. An uncompromising advocate of the staple system on the ground that, while it made possible exchange without usury, it was favourable to freedom of enterprise and the development of commerce, he denounced the usurious practices of the new school, and argued that the monopoly of the Merchant Adventurers led to the growth of London at the expense of the outports, deprived merchants of 'their generall inheritance' of free traffic, and diminished the revenue. Two years' experience as customer of Sandwich convinced him of the desirability of reviving the staple system, and after consultation with Thomas Fanshawe, remembrancer of the exchequer, he prepared a statement of his views, which was brought to the notice of Burghley. Failing in this attempt to influence the government, he published 'The Custumers Apology: that is to say, A generall Answere to Informers of all Sortes,' &c. [London, 1601], fol. Only fifty copies of this work were printed, and they were circulated among the members of the privy council. The Bodleian copy has many valuable manuscript notes by the author. There is no copy in the British Museum, which, however, contains three abridgments published in [1602], [1609], and 1619, with manuscript notes and additions. To meet the attacks made upon the 'Apology' by Wheeler, secretary to the Merchant Adventurers' Company (*Treatise of Commerce*, 1601, pp. 61, 62), Milles published 'The Customers Replie, or Second Apologie: that is to say, An Aunswer to a confused Treatise of Publicke Commerce . . . in favour of the . . . Merchants Adventurers,' &c., London, 1604, fol. With the exception of the epistle dedicatory, the preface, and the conclusion, this work consists of 'A Treatise of Exchange in Merchandise and Merchandising Exchange,' written about the time of the conference at Bruges (1564–5), by a merchant adventurer, who, 'out of conscience and duty, bewrayed the practises and advantages of the Company by usury.' Of two other of Milles's books, 'A Caution against Extreamity by Farmers,' &c. [1606], and 'The True Vse of Port-Bandes' [1606], there is apparently no copy in existence. The 'Caution' was directed against the practice of farming out the customs, and Milles was 'gratiously chidden and shent' by the lords of the council 'for foretelling . . . the mischiefes wherein traffick now stickes' (*Customers Accompt*, manuscript note). About 1608 Milles prepared an 'Answere' to the critics of the 'True Use of Port-Bandes,' but its publication was 'stayed by a supersedeas from the Exchequer' (*Customers Alphabet*, manuscript note). Later publications on cognate topics were: 1. 'The Customers Alphabet and Primer. Conteining theire Creede . . . theire Ten Commandements . . . and Forme of Prayers . . .,' &c. [London], 1608, fol. This work, the 'Apologie,' and the 'Replie,' bound together in one volume (MS. Bodl. 913), with manuscript notes and additions, were presented by the author to the Bodleian Library. 2. 'Acroamata [for Bullion and Staples]: that is to say, Private Lessons speld out of a Customers late Alphabet and Primer' [London, 1608], fol. There is no copy of this work in the British Museum. The Bodleian copy is without its own title-page, and that of the 'Mistery of Iniquity' has been pasted in. 3. 'The Mistery of Iniquity. Discovered in these Acroamaticall Lessons, shewing, by way of Antitheses, the ascention or discention of Summum Bonum and Summa Miseria' [London, 1609], fol. This work 'grew first from the king's own commandment by Sir Alexander Hay upon his reading the preface' to the 'Acroamata' (*ib.*) In it Christian exchange is contrasted with Jewish usury, and 'staple cities fit for open commerce' with 'obscure places apt for privy shifts.' 4. 'An out-Port-Customers Accompt . . . wherein he plainely sets downe, as well the motives and occasions, as the Method and Style of all his former writings,' &c. (manuscript notes by the author in the Bodleian copy), [London, 1610, fol.]

Milles also published: 5. 'Nobilitas Politica et Civilis,' &c. (edited from the manuscripts of Robert Glover, with copious notes and additions by Milles), London, 1608, fol. 6. 'The Catalogue of Honor, or Treasury of True Nobility, Peculiar and Proper to the Isle of Great Britaine, &c. . . . Translated out of Latyne,' &c., London, 1610, fol. This work was begun by Glover and left with Milles 'to foster' (Ep. Ded.) Milles was assisted in its preparation by Lord William Howard, Sir Robert Cotton, William Camden, Nicholas Charles, and others. The original manuscript, with a note to that effect by Peter le Neve on the title-page, and the printed lists, with manuscript notes and additions to 1634, are in the Bodleian Library (Rawl. MSS. 65 B, 113 B). 7. 'The Treasurie of Auncient and Moderne Times. Conteining . . . Collections . . . Readings . . . and . . . Observations . . . translated out of . . . P. Mexia, . . . F. Sansovino, . . . A. du Verdier,' &c., London, 1613–19, 2 vols. fol. There is also in the Bodleian Library (Ashm. MS. 1119 x.) a manuscript catalogue by Milles of the knights of the Garter, in chronological order, with notes and additions (1607–25) by Ashmole.

[Ashmolean MSS. (Bibl. Bodl.) vol. 840, ff. 585, 715–16, 717; Philipot's Villare Cantianum, pp. 130, 256; Boys's Collections for a History of Sandwich, p. 424; Berry's Kent Genealogies, pp. 309, 335; Hasted's Hist. of Kent, ii. 728, iii. 262, iv. 469; Thomas's Historical Notes, i.

444; Gray Papers (Bannatyne Club), pp. 65, 66, 71, 74, 105; Archæologia Cantiana, x. lxxxvii, lxxxix; Hamilton Papers, ii. 662, 669, 676, 694, 703, 705; Cal. State Papers, Dom. Eliz., cxlix. 10, ccxxiv. 3, ccxxxix. 123, 135, 142, 150, ccxl. 52, ccxlii. 45, ccxliii. 34, cclvii. 3, 5, cclix. 88, cclxiv. 167, cclxvii. 49, 116, cclxxxii. 53, cclxxxiv. 84, cclxxxv. 48, *ib.* (Jac. I), i. 109, cxlviii. 73, *ib.* (Car. I) xiv. 68; Calendar of Hatfield MSS. iii. 99, 225, 231, 353, 376; Hist. MSS. Comm. 12th Rep. App. iv. pp. 191, 192.] W. A. S. H.

MILLES, THOMAS (1671–1740), bishop of Waterford, eldest son of Isaac Milles the elder [q. v.], was born at Barley, Hertfordshire, on 19 June 1671. He matriculated at Wadham College, Oxford, on 12 March 1689, was exhibitioner of the college in 1691–2, and graduated B.A. in 1692, M.A. in 1695, and B.D. in 1704.

Having been ordained by Bishop Hough, he became chaplain of Christ Church, Oxford, in 1694, and was from 1695 to 1707 vice-principal of St. Edmund Hall. According to Wood (*Antiq. Oxon.*, ed. Gutch, vol. ii. pt. ii. p. 855) he was appointed regius professor of Greek in 1705; but Le Neve (*Fasti Eccles.* iii. 516) gives the date of his nomination as 8 Feb. 1706–7. In April 1707 he accompanied to Ireland as chaplain the new lord-lieutenant, Thomas Herbert, earl of Pembroke, and on 11 March 1708 was appointed bishop of Waterford and Lismore. He was consecrated in St. Patrick's, Dublin, on 18 April.

Milles's appointment was unpopular in Ireland. On 28 Feb. 1708 Archbishop King wrote to Swift: 'You will not expect from me any account of how it [the appointment] is relished here. Some say if General Laureston had been primate it would not have been so.' On 7 Jan. 1720 Swift wrote to Dr. Charlet: 'I do not wonder at the Bishop of Waterford appearing among the Sorbonne doctors. I do not hear that he showed his crucifix that he wears continually at his breast. He is one you sent us, and you must answer for him' (Mant, *History of the Irish Church*, ii. 98).

Archbishop King, in a letter of 29 Dec. 1725, charged Milles with not only giving 'all livings of value in his gift to brothers and relations, but likewise his vicar-generalship and registry, tho' none of them reside in the kingdom' (*ib.* ii. 445, cf. art. Isaac Milles). As bishop, Milles is said to have taken great pains in restoring decayed churches and to have contributed liberally from his own purse to the work.

After an episcopate of more than forty years he died of the stone at Waterford on 13 May 1740, and was buried in the cathedral. He was unmarried, and left his property to his nephew Jeremiah [q. v.], afterwards dean of Exeter.

Milles was a man of considerable learning. In 1703 he published while at Oxford a valuable folio edition of the works of St. Cyril of Jerusalem, with Greek and Latin notes; and in addition to some controversial tracts and sermons (see Harris's edition of Ware's *History of Ireland*) he was author of: 1. 'The Natural Immortality of the Soul asserted and proved from Scripture and the first Fathers, in answer to Mr. Dodwell,' Oxford, 1707, 8vo; 2nd ed. 1726. 2. 'De Officio eorum qui de Fide certant; concio coram Acad. Oxon.' 1707, 4to. An 'Account of the Life and Conversation of Isaac Milles of Highcleer [his father],' London, 1721, 8vo, is also attributed to him (Halkett and Laing, *Dict. of Anonymous and Pseudon. Lit.* col. 22).

[The Life of Isaac Milles is the only authority which states accurately Thomas Milles's parentage. Besides the works mentioned above, see Cotton's Fasti Eccles. Hibern. i. 13, 14, v. 20; Foster's Alumni Oxon. 1500–1714; Chalmers's Biog. Dict. art. 'Jeremiah Milles;' Gent. Mag. 1740, p. 262; Brit. Mus. Cat.] G. Le G. N.

MILLHOUSE, ROBERT (1788–1839), weaver and poet, second son of John and Mary Millhouse, was born on 14 (or 17?) Oct. 1788, at Nottingham. His only education was obtained at a Sunday-school. At the age of ten he worked at a stocking-loom and sang in the choir of St. Peter's Church. During 1804 he read with his elder brother John much poetry, including the works of Shakespeare, Milton, Pope, and Gray. In 1810, at the age of twenty-two, he joined the Nottinghamshire militia, and it was while with his regiment at Plymouth that his first verses were written and sent to the 'Nottingham Review.' When the regiment was disbanded in 1814, Millhouse resumed his weaving, employing his leisure in writing verses. His poems attracted favourable notice (vide Appendix to *Songs of the Patriot*), and he found friends who in 1822 obtained for him a grant from the Royal Literary Fund. Ten years afterwards he became assistant at a savings bank, and was thus able to devote more of his time to literary pursuits. His friends Thomas Wakefield, Colonel Gardiner, and Mrs. Howitt Watts, daughter of William and Mary Howitt, were of great assistance in his later years, and among those who helped him in his last illness was Ebenezer Elliott. He died on 13 April 1839, and was buried on the eastern side of the Nottingham cemetery, some lines being inscribed on the tomb a few years later by his friend Dr. Spencer T. Hall [q. v.] An oak in Sherwood Forest, under which Millhouse and Spencer Hall took refuge during a storm, bears the name of the poet.

Millhouse married first, in 1818, Eliza Morley, by whom he had eight children; and secondly, in 1836, Marion Moore, by whom he had two children. He is described as steady, sober, and honest, but in his later years he looked upon any but literary work as derogatory to his talent. His poems show facility in versification and true feeling for nature. He handles the sonnet courageously, but his defective education and narrow experiences deprived him of largeness of view or 'sustained strength.'

Millhouse's published works are: 1. 'Blossoms,' a selection of sonnets, with prefatory remarks by L. Booker, LL.D.; 2nd edit. 1823. 2 'Vicissitude,' a poem in four books; 'Nottingham Park' and other pieces, with preface, by J. Millhouse, Nottingham, 1821. 3. 'The Song of the Patriot,' sonnets and songs, with brief memoir of the author by J. Millhouse, 1826. 4. 'Sherwood Forest, and other Poems,' London, 1827. 5. 'The Destinies of Man,' London, 1832, printed at Nottingham. The 'Sonnets and Songs of Robert Millhouse,' a selection from his works with a biographical sketch, edited by J. P. Briscoe, was published at Nottingham in 1881. Some of his best pieces appear in 'Sketches of Obscure Poets,' London, 1833.

[Memoirs by J. Millhouse, Dr. Booker, and J. P. Briscoe, prefixed to works in above list; Ann. Reg. vol. lxxxi., Appendix to Chronicle, p. 333; Gent. Mag. 1839, i. 662–3, from Lit. Gazette, 27 April 1839; In the Footsteps of Robert Millhouse, 1908.] G. Le G. N.

MILLIKEN or MILLIKIN, RICHARD ALFRED (1767–1815), poet, was born at Castlemartyr, co. Cork, on 8 Sept. 1767. His father, Robert Milliken, was of Scottish origin, and before coming to Cork, where he joined the established church, was a quaker. Richard was apprenticed to an attorney, and after being admitted and sworn he began business for himself in Cork. He was not much employed in his profession, and most of his time was devoted to painting, poetry, and music. In 1795 he contributed poetical pieces to the Cork 'Monthly Miscellany,' and in April 1797 started, jointly with his sister, who wrote some historical novels, a magazine entitled 'The Casket,' which appeared monthly till February 1798. On the breaking out of the rebellion he joined the Royal Cork volunteers, and became notorious for his 'zeal and efficiency.' In 1807 he published at Cork 'The Riverside,' a blank-verse poem and in 1810 a short tale, 'The Slave of Surinam.' In 1815 he laid the foundation of a society for the promotion of the fine arts in Cork, which followed an exhibition of his own and other local artists' drawings. He died 16 Dec. 1815, and was buried with a public funeral at Douglas, near Cork.

Milliken is now remembered chiefly as the author of the song 'The Groves of Blarney, they look so charming,' a burlesque of a doggerel ballad, 'Castle Hyde,' written by an itinerant poet named Barrett about 1790. There are various readings of the song, the rebellion having given rise to some scurrilous additions to the original, and a version is printed in 'The Reliques of Father Prout.' The song was frequently sung on the stage by the elder Charles Mathews. Other of Milliken's lyrics, which figure in Irish anthologies, are the 'Groves of de Pool' and 'Had I the Tun which Bacchus used.' Of several dramas and farces apparently never published, 'Dugourney in Egypt, an afterpiece,' was played with success at Sadler's Wells in 1805–6.

In 1823 a volume of 'Poetical Fragments of the late Richard Alfred Milliken,' with memoir and portrait, was published in London by subscription. Neither the 'Groves of Blarney' nor the 'Groves of de Pool' is included.

[Memoir in Poetical Fragments, as above; Crofton Croker's Popular Songs of Ireland, 1839, pp. 89, 141; O'Donoghue's Poets of Ireland, p. 163; H. Halliday Sparling's Irish Minstrelsy; Notes and Queries, 2nd ser. xi. 452.] J. C. H.

MILLINGEN, JAMES (1774–1845), archæologist, brother of John Gideon Millingen [q. v.], was second son of Michael Millingen, a Dutch merchant who had emigrated from Rotterdam to Batavia, and had married there Elizabeth Westflaten Coole, daughter of the Dutch governor of the island. The family sprang from the small town named Millingen in the north-west of Holland. Leaving Batavia, the elder Millingen settled in Queen's Square, Westminster, where James was born on 18 Jan. 1774. An elder brother died at the age of fourteen and was buried in the abbey cloisters. The epitaph was written by the poet Cowper, who was friendly with the family. James was educated at Westminster School, and soon attracted the attention of his father's friend and neighbour, Clayton Mordaunt Cracherode [q. v.], who encouraged him to study numismatics. Millingen also studied the science of war, but his health prevented him from pursuing a design of entering the engineer corps. The father's business seriously decreased while James was still a youth, and when the family in 1790 migrated to Paris, in a vague hope of benefiting under the régime initiated by the French revolution, James reluctantly became a clerk in the banking house of M. Van de Nyver, a connection of his mother. After the events of 10 Aug. 1792, Mrs. Millingen with her two sons escaped to Calais, but the elder Millingen soon brought them again to Paris.

James obtained a post in the French mint. There he became acquainted with Monger, the director, a well-known mineralogist, while he made the acquaintance at the Royal (or National) Library of the director, the Abbé Courcy Barthélemy, and of the geographer Barbié du Bocage, and also came to know Walckenaer, De Non, D'Aumont, and other archæologists.

Late in 1792 Millingen was arrested as a British subject by a decree of the National Convention, and confined first in the prison of the Madelonettes, then in that of the Luxembourg, and finally in the Collège des Écossais, where he remained till the events of 9 Thermidor (27 July 1794). At the Collège des Écossais he became acquainted with two fellow-prisoners, Charles Este, son of the Rev. Charles Este (1753–1829), and Sir Robert Smith of Beerchurch Hall, Essex.

On obtaining his liberty Millingen settled in Calais, but subsequently became a partner in the banking house of Sir Robert Smith & Co. in the Rue Céruti, Paris. The concern failed, and Millingen was thrown on his own resources. A martyr to asthma, he resided in Italy, where he compiled valuable works on coins, medals, Etruscan vases, and kindred subjects. He wrote admirably in French and Italian. He bought antiquities with rare judgment, and supplied most of the great museums of Europe with their choicest specimens of ancient art. He frequently offered his purchases to the trustees of the British Museum. For some time he lived at Rome and at Naples, where he made the acquaintance of Lady Blessington, but latterly settled at Florence, paying occasional visits to Paris and London. A civil list pension of 100*l.* a year was granted him, and he was royal associate and later honorary member of the Royal Society of Literature, fellow of the Societies of Antiquaries of London and of France, correspondent of the Institute of France (18 Jan. 1833), and member of many other learned academies of Europe.

Millingen, when on the eve of removing from Florence to London, died of a severe catarrhal affection on 1 Oct. 1845. He married, at Calais about 1797, Elizabeth Penny, daughter of Christopher White of Calais, and had three sons: Horace, a captain in the Madras army (invalided in 1830); Julius Michael [q. v.]; and Augustus, assistant surgeon in the East India Company's service at Madras (retired in 1831); and a daughter. He was a staunch churchman, and when his wife and daughter became Roman catholics a separation between him and them followed. In his later years he was much distressed by a detention, owing to his wife's machinations, of his son Julius in a school of the inquisition.

His works are: 1. 'Recueil de quelques Médailles Grecques inédites,' 4to, Rome, 1812. 2. 'Peintures antiques et inédites de Vases Grecs; avec des explications,' fol. Rome, 1813; from a collection formerly in the possession of Caroline Murat, queen of Naples. Included in vol. ii. of S. Reinach's 'Bibliothèque des Monuments figurés,' 4to, 1891. 3. 'Peintures antiques de Vases Grecs de la collection de Sir J. Coghill,' fol. Rome, 1817. 4. 'Ancient Unedited Monuments, Painted Greek Vases, Statues, Busts, Bas-Reliefs, and other Remains of Grecian Art, from Collections in various Countries, illustrated and explained,' three pts. 4to, London, 1822–6, discontinued for want of public patronage. 5. 'Ancient Coins of Greek Cities and Kings, from various collections . . . illustrated and explained,' 4to, London, 1831. 6. 'Some Remarks on the State of Learning and Fine Arts in Great Britain; on the Deficiency of Public Institutions,' etc., 8vo, London, 1831. 7. 'Sylloge of Ancient Unedited Coins of Greek Cities and Kings, from various Collections,' 4to, London, 1837. 8. 'Considérations sur la Numismatique de l'Ancienne Italie, principalement sous le rapport de monumens historiques et philologiques (avec Supplément),' 8vo, Florence 1841–4. He left in manuscript another work on unedited and obscure Greek coins.

Millingen translated from the French of A. L. Millin de Grandmaison, and edited, with a supplement, 'Medallic History of Napoleon,' &c., 2 vols. 4to, London, 1819–21. To the 'Archæologia' (xix. 70–4), he contributed in 1818 'Some Observations on an Antique Bas-Relief, on which the Evil Eye, or Fascinum, is represented,' which was reissued in a separate form. He likewise contributed some excellent papers to the 'Transactions' of the Royal Society of Literature, the 'Revue de la Numismatique Française,' and to the 'Annali' and 'Bullettini' of the Instituto Archeologico di Roma. His valuable library was sold in London on 25–9 June 1849.

[Information kindly supplied by T. Bailey Saunders, esq.; Gent. Mag. 1846 pt. i. pp. 98–9; Classical Museum, iv. 91–5; Biographie Universelle (Michaud), xxviii. 306–7; Nouvelle Biographie Générale, xxxv. 541–3; Athenæum,

1 Nov. 1845, p. 1058; Addit. MS. 22891, f. 339; East India Register; Moore's Life of Byron (1847); J. Gideon Millingen's Recollections of Republican France; Literary Life and Correspondence of the Countess of Blessington, ii. 144.] G. G.

MILLINGEN, JOHN GIDEON (1782–1862), physician and writer, born at 9 Queen's Square, Westminster, on 8 Sept. 1782, was younger brother of James Millingen [q. v.] At the age of eight he was taken by his father to Paris, and lived through the horrors of the revolution. During the imprisonment of his brother, whose liberation he claims to have tried to effect, he, according to his own story, repeatedly met Robespierre, Danton, Barère, and other Jacobin leaders, although he was only ten or eleven years old at the time (cf. his *Recollections of Republican France*). He matriculated at the École de Médecine, and after studying under Sue and Boyer obtained a medical degree. On 26 Jan. 1802 he joined the British army as assistant-surgeon in the 97th foot (Queen's Own), and was ordered to Egypt. On 16 Nov. 1809 he was appointed surgeon in the 31st (Huntingdonshire) foot, and full surgeon to the forces on 26 May 1814. He served in all the Peninsular campaigns under Wellington and Lord Hill, and he was present at Waterloo as principal surgeon of cavalry and at the surrender of Paris. He was afterwards sent to the West Indies, but loss of health compelled him to retire on half-pay in 1823, with the Waterloo and other medals. After leaving the army he lived for some time in Boulogne, where he brought out in 1826 his 'Sketches of Ancient and Modern Boulogne.' He was connected in a medical capacity with the Military Lunatic Asylum at Chatham, and in 1837 was appointed, on the resignation of Sir William Ellis, resident physician to the Middlesex Pauper Lunatic Asylum at Hanwell. On resigning this post early in 1839, he is said to have opened a private lunatic asylum in Kensington. He died in London in 1862.

Millingen's first literary work seems to have been the libretto of a musical farce by Horn, entitled 'The Bee-Hive,' which was produced at the Lyceum by the Drury Lane Company 19 Jan. 1811, and published in the same year. His other dramatic writings are: 'Who'll Lend me a Wife?' a farce in two acts and in prose; 'Borrowed Feathers,' a farce in one act and in prose (both these were published in Duncombe's edition of the 'British Theatre,' London, 1825, &c.); 'The Miser's Daughter,' a drama in two acts, London, 1835; 'The Illustrious Stranger, or Married and Single,' a farce in one act and in prose, in collaboration with James Kenney [q. v.], published in 'Home Plays,' pt. i., London, 1862; 'Ladies at Home, or Gentlemen, we can do without you,' a female interlude, in one act and in prose, published in Lacy's 'Acting Edition of Plays,' London, 1850.

He also published: 1. 'Adventures of an Irish Gentleman,' a novel, London, 1830. 2. 'Curiosities of Medical Experience,' a laborious compilation, similar in design to Disraeli's 'Curiosities of Literature,' London, 1837. 3. 'Popular View of the Homœopathic Doctrine,' London, 1837. 4. 'Stories of Torres Vedras,' 3 vols., London, 1839. 5. 'Aphorisms on the Treatment and Management of the Insane, with Considerations on Public and Private Lunatic Asylums, pointing out the Errors in the present System,' London, 1840. 6. 'The History of Duelling, including Narratives of the most Remarkable Personal Encounters, &c.,' 2 vols., London, 1841 (cf. *Edinburgh Review*, July 1842. 7. 'Jack Hornet, or the March of Intellect,' London, 1845. 8. 'Mind and Matter, illustrated by Considerations on Hereditary Insanity,' London, 1847. 9. 'Recollections of Republican France from 1790 to 1801,' a somewhat highly coloured narrative of juvenile experience, vol. i., London, 1848, with portrait.

[Millingen's Recollections of Republican France; Notes and Queries, 7th ser. x. 384; information from descendants; Brit. Mus. Cat.; Army Lists, 1803, 1815, 1824.] T. B. S.

MILLINGEN, JULIUS MICHAEL (1800–1878), physician and writer, born in London on 19 July 1800, was son of James Millingen [q. v.], archæologist. Millingen spent his early years between Calais and Paris, and was sent to school in Rome. In his holidays he took walking tours in Germany, on one of which he is said to have visited Goethe in Weimar. In 1817 he entered the university of Edinburgh, and attended medical classes there every winter until 1821, when he received a diploma from the Royal College of Surgeons of Edinburgh.

On the Greek committee being formed, Millingen, who seems to have been then living in London, was recommended to its notice by William Smith, M.P. for Norwich, and on 27 Aug. 1823 he left England for Corfu, with letters of introduction to the Greek government and to Lord Byron. Arriving at Asso in Cephalonia in November of that year, he found Byron at Metaxata, and spent some time with him there. He afterwards accompanied him to Missolonghi, and attended him in his last illness, which, at the autopsy, Millingen pronounced to be purulent meningitis (see MOORE, *Life*, edit. of 1832, vi. 209

et seq., where much of the account of Byron's last hours is taken from Millingen's 'Memoirs'). He was charged by Bruno, another of Byron's doctors, in an article in the 'Westminster Review,' with having caused the poet's death by delaying phlebotomy. Millingen replied at length in his 'Memoirs.'

Soon after Byron's death in 1824 Millingen had a severe attack of typhoid fever, and his life was saved by the friendly aid of Lord Charles Murray, son of the Duke of Athole. On recovering he was appointed surgeon in the Greek army, in which he served until its surrender to the Turks. He was taken prisoner by Ibrahim Pasha, and released only upon the urgent representations of Stratford Canning, then British ambassador to the Porte. In November 1826 Millingen went to Smyrna, and after a short stay in Kutaya and Broussa, settled in 1827 in Constantinople. There he attained considerable reputation as a physician, being attached in that capacity to the Dutch legation, and becoming Dutch delegate to the International Board of Health sitting at Galata. Millingen was also court physician to five successive sultans, Mahmud, Abdul Medjid, Abdul Aziz, Murad, and Abdul Hamid. He was one of a commission appointed to inquire into the death of Abdul Aziz (see Sir Henry Elliot's article in the *Nineteenth Century*, February 1888). He was also a member of the International Medical Congress on Cholera held in Constantinople in 1866, and an original member and afterwards president of the General Society of Medicine. He did something to introduce the use of the Turkish bath in England in 1860; it was apparently at Millingen's persuasion that David Urquhart [q. v.] then established one in London.

Like his father, Millingen was an archæologist. For many years he was president of the Greek Syllogos or Literary Society of Constantinople, where he lectured in Greek on archæological subjects. He discovered the ruins of Aczani in Phrygia, an account of which was published by Keppel, and excavated the site of the temple of Jupiter Urius on the Bosphorus. Several of his manuscripts, including a life of Byron, were destroyed in the great fire at Pera in 1870, in which he lost nearly all his personal effects. Millingen died in Constantinople on 30 Nov. 1878. There is a portrait of him in Mavrogény's pamphlet mentioned below.

He was married three times, having separated from his first wife, a Roman catholic who thereupon embraced Islamism and entered a harem. Her son, Frederick Millingen, became Osman Bey in the Turkish army, and afterwards turned Greek under the name Alexis Andrejevitch. Millingen had two other sons, one of whom was an oculist well known in the east of Europe.

Millingen published: 1. 'Memoirs of the Affairs of Greece, with Anecdotes relating to Lord Byron,' London, 1831, vol. i. (vol. ii. remaining in manuscript). 2. 'Arbitrary Detention by the Inquisition at Rome of three Protestant Children in Defiance of the Will of their Father,' London, 1842. He also contributed an article in French on 'Oriental Baths' to the 'Gazette Médicale d'Orient,' 1 Jan. 1858.

[Information from Millingen's sons, supplementing the Memoirs; Les Bains Orientaux, avec une notice biographique de Jules van Millingen, par le docteur S. S. Mavrogény, Strasburg, 1891; information from the registrar of Edinburgh University; Times, 17 Dec. 1878 (slightly inaccurate); Brit. Mus. Cat.] T. B. S.

MILLINGTON, GILBERT (*d.* 1666), regicide, was eldest son of Anthony Millington of Felley Abbey, Nottinghamshire, by Prudence, daughter of William Gilbert, proctor of the arches, of Colchester (*Visitation of Essex*, Harl. Soc., xiii. 405). On 19 Oct. 1614 he was admitted a member of Lincoln's Inn (*Register*). By 1635 he was acting as J.P. for Nottinghamshire, in which county he possessed considerable influence (*Cal. State Papers*, Dom. 1635–6, p. 137). He was a man of some talent, fond of public business, but weak and shifty. In May 1639 George, viscount Chaworth, asked leave, on account of bad health, to nominate Millington as his deputy in the sheriffdom of Nottinghamshire (*ib.* 1639, p. 151). In the Long parliament and subsequently Millington represented Nottingham, and took an active part against the king. On 1 July 1642 he was appointed deputy-lieutenant for Nottingham (*Commons' Journal*, ii. 647), and on all occasions appears to have acted as attorney for the town. He was, in fact, the principal agent of communication between Colonel John Hutchinson (1615–1664) [q.v.], the governor, and the parliament. On 25 Dec. 1643 he was ordered to write to Hutchinson a letter of thanks for his fidelity to religion and the parliament, and to see that the garrison at Nottingham was supplied with all necessaries (*ib.* iii. 352–3). In reply to an urgent appeal from Hutchinson on behalf of the 'poor neglected garrison,' the house ordered, on 15 Jan. 1644, a thousand pounds to be sent to its relief. Through Millington's 'negligent prosecution of the business,' says Mrs. Hutchinson, the money was lost (*Life of Colonel Hutchinson*, ed. Firth, i. 305,

379–81). According to the same authority, Millington frequently abused his position for his personal advantage. He would appear, however, to have retained the confidence of the town and corporation, as well as the garrison. Several sums of money, accompanied by votes of thanks, are recorded in the hall books of the borough about this time as having been paid to him for his services as burgess in parliament (Bailey, *Annals of Nottinghamshire*, ii. 708–9). In July 1644 he was sent by the committee of both kingdoms to Nottingham, with the view of composing the differences between the garrisons of the castle and town and between members of the committees there. He was made at the same time a member of the Nottingham committees and a member of the committee of both kingdoms at the leaguer before York (*Cal. State Papers*, Dom. 1644, pp. 350, 368). Mrs. Hutchinson unsparingly denounces Millington's conduct at Nottingham. Colonel Hutchinson, it seems, was unpopular with a 'faction,' and to this faction Millington lent his countenance, professing all the while to be the colonel's staunch friend. The discontented committee-men 'hired him with a subscription for losses, for which they gave him public credit double to what he really had lost,' and they offered him a share of the governor's spoils if he would help to 'make him a prey' (Mrs. Hutchinson, ii. 9–76). Walker declares that Millington received in this manner, in March 1647–8, 2,000*l.* (*Hist. of Independency*, ed. 1661, pt. i. p. 81). Parliament showed appreciation of his services by voting him an allowance of 4*l.* a week from 3 June 1645 until 20 Aug. 1646 (*Commons' Journals*, iv. 161, 649). By November 1645 he was acting, without, it was said, much sense of justice, as clerk of the committee for plundered ministers (*Cal. of Comm. for Compounding*, passim; cf. *Mystery of the Good Old Cause*; *Cal. State Papers*, Dom. 1649–50 p. 373, 1654 p. 358). In July 1646 he was appointed one of the English commissioners for preserving the peace between England and Scotland (Thurloe, *State Papers*, i. 79). On the ensuing 5 Dec. he petitioned parliament to award him compensation for losses incurred during the civil war (*Commons' Journals*, v. 1). He was chosen one of the king's judges, attended every day of the trial, and signed the death-warrant (Nalson, *Trial of Charles I*, ed. 1684). During 1649 he acted as clerk to the parliamentary committee for the appointment of ministers (*Addit. MS.* 25302, f. 145). On 8 May 1651 parliament ordered that 1,700*l.* be allowed him; he was also offered the preemption of Ansley Woodhouse and Kirkby Woodhouse, Nottinghamshire, part of the lands of the Earl of Newcastle (*Commons' Journals*, vi. 565, 567, 571).

At the Restoration Millington was excepted out of the bill as to pains and penalties. When arraigned, on 16 Oct. 1660, he abjectly 'confessed himself guilty every way.' He excused his signing the warrant because 'he was awed by the power then in being' (*Trials of the Regicides*, p. 246). Sentence of death was pronounced on the following day, but it was commuted into imprisonment for life, his name having been inserted in the clause for suspending execution in case of attainder (*Commons' Journals*, viii. 61, 139). Millington died at Jersey in September or October 1666, and was buried 'in common ground' (*Cal. State Papers*, Dom. 1666–67, p. 192). His property was seized by the crown. Some letters from Millington are among the Tanner MSS. in the Bodleian Library.

In 1644 immediately after burying his first wife, 'a religious, matronly gentlewoman,' at Greasley, he married a 'flirtish girl of sixteen' from an alehouse (Mrs. Hutchinson, ii. 46). The scandal brought him into temporary disfavour.

[Cal. State Papers, Dom. 1623–9 (letters from his brother John); Hist. MSS. Comm. 7th Rep. pp. ix, 157; Brown's Worthies of Nottinghamshire; Bailey's Annals of Nottinghamshire, iii. 882–3; Coxe's Cat. Cod. MSS. Bibl. Bodl. pt. iv. p. 1026.] G. G.

MILLINGTON, JAMES HEATH (*d.* 1873), painter, was born at Cork, though not of Irish parentage. In 1826 he entered the schools of the Royal Academy in London, and gained many prizes there, though he was not successful in winning the gold medal for painting. He first exhibited at the Royal Academy in 1831, sending 'A Portrait of J. C. Bishop, esq.,' and 'Vulcan's Cave.' He continued to be a frequent exhibitor of subject pictures, portraits, and miniatures there and also at the British Institution and Suffolk Street Galleries up to 1870. Millington, who was for a short time curator of the School of Painting at the Royal Academy, died in 1873.

[Redgrave's Dict. of Artists; Graves's Dict. of Artists, 1760–1880; Royal Academy Catalogues.] L. C.

MILLINGTON, JOHN (1779–1868), engineer, scientific writer, and lecturer, was born in London on 11 May 1779, and is said to have studied medicine and to have gained the degree of M.D. He commenced lecturing at the Royal Institution, London, in 1815, and was appointed professor of mechanics there 7 July 1817. He gave annual courses of lectures on natural philosophy, mechanics, and astronomy until 1829. He was one of the original fellows of the Astronomical Society of London, and he held the office of secretary from 14 Feb. 1823 to 10 Feb. 1826. He was also on the teaching staff of Guy's Hospital, and vice-president of Dr. Birkbeck's London Mechanics' Institution. He appears to have left this country for America about 1829 or 1830, to become chief engineer of silver mines and chief superintendent of a mint in Mexico. The preface to the revised edition of his 'Elementary Principles of Natural Philosophy' was dated 'Guanaxuato, August 1830.' The book was affectionately dedicated to Dr. Birkbeck and the officers and members of the London Mechanics' Institution. In 1834–5 Millington was residing at Philadelphia, and a paper of his 'On the Rappahannock Gold Mines in Virginia' appears in the 'Transactions of the Pennsylvania Geological Society,' 1835, i. 147. Two years later he became professor of chemistry and natural philosophy at the William and Mary College, Williamsburg, Virginia, and was subsequently state geologist of Mississippi. He died 10 July 1868, and was buried in Bruton parish churchyard, Williamsburg, where there is a monument with a long inscription to his memory.

Millington's published works are: 'Epitome of the Elementary Principles of Natural and Experimental Philosophy,' London, 1823; 2nd edit. 1830. 'Elements of Civil Engineering,' Philadelphia, 1839. He also contributed a paper on the hydraulic ram to the 'Quarterly Journal of Science,' 1816, i. 211, and one on street illumination to the same periodical, 1818, v. 177. In 1816 he obtained a patent (No. 3977) for a ship's propeller, and he gave evidence in 1817 before a select committee of the House of Commons on Hill and Bundy's patent. He was also examined in May 1829 before the select committee on the patent laws. It appears from his evidence that he had for many years carried on a considerable practice as a patent agent.

[Millington's Works; information kindly supplied by Mr. C. W. Coleman, librarian to the William and Mary College, Virginia.] R. B. P.

MILLINGTON, Sir THOMAS (1628–1704), physician, son of Thomas Millington, esq., of Newbury, Berkshire, was born at Newbury in 1628. He was sent to Westminster School, whence he was elected to Trinity College, Cambridge, in 1645, graduating A.B. in 1649 and M.A. in 1657. He then removed to Oxford, where he graduated M.D. in 1659 and became fellow of All Souls' College. Here he took part with Wilkins, Boyle, Wallis, Wren, and Willis in those scientific meetings in which originated the Royal Society, of which he was an original member. In 1672 he became a fellow of the College of Physicians; in 1678 he was chosen censor; in 1679 Harveian orator; from 1686 to 1689 treasurer; and from 1696 till his death, president. In 1675 he was appointed Sedleian professor of natural philosophy at Oxford. His inaugural lecture on 12 April 1676 was, according to Wood, 'much commended' (Wood, *Life and Times*, ed. Clark, ii. 343). He retained the post till his death, but generally performed the duties of the office by deputy. He became physician to William and Mary; was knighted in 1680; and occupied the same office under Queen Anne. In 1701, by an advance of 2,000*l.* he freed the College of Physicians of a debt of nearly 7,000*l.* Millington died of asthma in London, 5 Jan. 1704, and was buried on the 28th in the Wentworth Chapel of Gosfield Church, Essex, where there was a fine monumental brass to his memory, which, with the exception of some coats of arms, was stolen from its Purbeck-marble slab at the beginning of the nineteenth century.

Millington is spoken of in laudatory terms as a physician by Sydenham, and under the name of 'Machaon' in Garth's 'Dispensary,' but is now chiefly remembered as the alleged discoverer of sexuality in plants. Nehemiah Grew [q. v.], in a lecture on the anatomy of flowers, read to the Royal Society on 6 Nov. 1676, says: 'In discourse hereof with our learned Savilian [an error] professor, Sir Thomas Millington, he told me, that he conceived that the attire [stamens] doth serve as the male for the generation of the seed. I immediately replied, that I was of the same opinion . . .' As Pulteney points out (*Sketches of the Progress of Botany*, i. 336), the credit probably belongs rather to Grew himself, Millington being, as Sachs says (*History of Botany*, p. 382, English translation), 'a botanist otherwise unknown to history;' but the date of this lecture is six years earlier than Grew's 'Anatomy of Plants.'

There is a fine portrait of Millington at the Royal College of Physicians, and the younger Linnæus commemorated him in the genus *Millingtonia* among Bignoniaceæ.

[Munk's Coll. of Phys. 1878, i. 363; Patrick's Autobiography, passim.] G. S. B.

MILLINGTON, WILLIAM, D.D. (*d.* 1466?), the first provost of King's College, Cambridge, was a native of Pocklington, Yorkshire. He was probably educated at Clare Hall, Cambridge. He was ordained deacon and priest in Lent 1420, receiving his title from the priory of Ellerton in the county of his birth (*Baker MSS.* xxxi. 238). He rose to eminence in his university. Capgrave from personal knowledge speaks of him as 'surpassing many of his predecessors in scholastic questions, literary depth, and ripeness of character' (*De Illustr. Henricis*, p. 133), and Harrison, in his 'Chronographia,' describes him as 'laudabilis et famosus Theologiæ doctor.' His learning and general worth led to his selection by Henry VI to preside over his new foundation at Cambridge. In the charter of the original foundation, 12 Feb. 1440, he appears under the title of 'rector,' which on the enlargement of the scheme in 1443 was exchanged for that of 'provost.' He seems to have had no hand in framing the statutes of King's College. During his tenure of the provostship he was one of the contracting parties in the 'Amicabilis Concordia,' with the provost of Eton and the wardens of New College and Winchester, in which they bound themselves to render each other mutual support in maintaining the common interests of their foundations. In 1446 he refused to acquiesce in the sweeping changes proposed in the constitution of the college, by which it was to be made altogether independent not only of the bishop of the diocese, but also of the university authorities, and its benefits limited to scholars from Eton. He regarded compliance as 'involving perjury,' since he had already sworn to the observance of the original code. Alnwick, bishop of Lincoln, vainly endeavoured to induce him to resign, and finally sentence of deprivation was reluctantly passed on him by royal commissioners. In a curious correspondence with Bishop Beckington of Bath and Wells [q. v.] (the letters bear no date, but internal evidence places them after 1452) he attacked the bishop in violent and unscrupulous language for the part he had taken as one of the royal commissioners in his deprivation, and threatens him with vengeance. The statement of Fuller and others that he was deprived for a 'factious endeavour to prefer his countrymen of Yorkshire' to the scholarships of his college may be safely rejected.

On his deprivation he retired to Clare Hall, and appears in the college records as a benefactor to that house and a donor of books and vestments. John Millington became master there in 1455, and William has been at times confused with him. In 1448 William was appointed with others to draw up the statutes for Queens' College, founded by Henry's consort, Margaret of Anjou, an appointment twice renewed, and according to Parker (*Hist. Univ. Cambr.* p. 85) he was vice-chancellor of the university in 1457. He was also one of the most distinguished of the antagonists of Bishop Reginald Pecock [q. v.], 'Egregie determinans contra R. Pecock' (*Gascoigne MSS.* 524, 542, quoted by WILLIAMS, p. 302), replying to his famous sermon preached at Paul's Cross in 1447 from the same place, and declaring that 'England would never suffer those who patronised Pecock to prosper' (BABINGTON'S preface to PECOCK'S *Repressor*, p. xvii; LEWIS, *Life of R. Pecock*, p. 142, ed. 1820; WOOD, *Hist. et Antiq. Univ. Oxon.* bk. i. p. 221 *a*). Millington probably died about 1466. He was buried in St. Edward's Church, the south chancel aisle of which was used as a chapel by Clare Hall.

[Mullinger's Hist. of Univ. of Cambridge, i. 295, 306, 309; Fuller's Hist. of Cambridge, pp. 85, 152; the Rev. G. Williams's Notices of William Millington, first provost of King's College, published in communications to the Cambr. Antiq. Soc. i. 287–328.] E. V.

MILLNER. [See also MILNER.]

MILLNER, JOHN (*fl.* 1712), was captain in the Scots royal (1st royal Scots foot) during the time that regiment was commanded by George Hamilton, earl of Orkney [q. v.] A captain 'Milner' was wounded with the 2nd battalion of the regiment at Blenheim (see Blenheim Roll in *Treasury Papers*, vol. xciii.) Millner appears to have served through Marlborough's campaigns with Orkney's regiment, but in what rank is not clear. By some he is said to have been what would now be called orderly-room sergeant. He was the author of a 'Compendious Journal of all the Marches, Battles, Sieges . . . and other Actions of the Allies in their War against France in Holland, Germany, and Flanders, under the Duke of Marlborough,' London, 8vo, which was published in 1733, and is chiefly noticeable for its very precise itinerary of all the marches of the army from 1702 to 1712. The exact date of his death has not been discovered, but his name does not appear in the lists of officers, serving and reduced, published a few years later.

[Home Office Papers; Military Records; Millner's book.] H. M. C.

MILLS, ALFRED (1776–1833), draughtsman, was a skilful designer of illustrations to small books of juvenile instruction, such as 'Pictures of Roman History in Miniature,' 1809, 'Pictures of English History,' 1811, 'Portraits of the Sovereigns of England,' 1817. He worked in this line for about forty years. He also frequently drew designs on blocks for the leading wood-engravers. In

1807 he exhibited three figure-drawings at the Royal Academy. After an industrious life he died at Walworth on 7 Dec. 1833, aged 57, leaving a wife and six children.

[Gent. Mag. 1834, pt. i. p. 116; Brit. Mus. Cat.] L. C.

MILLS, CHARLES (1788–1826), historical writer, born on 29 July 1788 at Croom's Hill, Greenwich, was youngest son of Samuel Gillam Mills, surgeon. He was educated privately, and, after a brief experience in a merchant's counting-house, was articled in 1804 to a firm of solicitors. In 1810 he placed himself for a year's study in conveyancing under James Humphreys. From boyhood he had always been a hard reader, and he now permanently injured his health by studying through the night. An attack of lung disease compelled him to winter in Nice in 1814–15. He had no liking for the law, and, on inheriting a moderate fortune, abandoned it for literature. Neglecting the directions of his doctors, he died of a recurrence of his old complaint at Southampton on 9 Oct. 1826. He was a bachelor. A few months before his death he was elected one of the knights of Malta, in recognition of his allusions to that fraternity in his 'History of the Crusades.'

Mills was a man of learning, but as an historian was a very humble follower of Gibbon. His first work, 'An History of Muhammedanism,' 8vo, London, 1817 (2nd edit. 1818), had been accidentally seen in manuscript by Sir John Malcolm [q. v.], who not only warmly recommended its publication, but aided in the revision by the loan of many valuable Oriental treatises from his own library. It was translated into French by G. Buisson, 8vo, Guernsey, 1826. His next book 'The History of the Crusades,' 2 vols. 8vo, London, 1820 (4th edit. 1828), bears fewer traces of the influence of Gibbon, and was praised by Sir Walter Scott, who assisted him with notes from the Scottish chronicles (letter of Scott to Mills in *Book Circular* of William Downing of Birmingham, No. 254, p. 9). An ambitious imitation of the 'Travels of Anacharsis' entitled 'The Travels of Theodore Ducas of Candia in Various Countries in Europe at the Revival of Letters and Art,' 2 vols. 8vo, London, 1822, followed. It proved unsuccessful, and only the first part, comprising 'Italy,' appeared. A design of writing a history of Rome came to nothing. Mills soon afterwards became absorbed in his last and most popular book, 'The History of Chivalry, or Knighthood and its Times,' 2 vols. 8vo, London, 1825 (2nd edit. 1826). Scott was delighted with it, and, through the medium of Constable, sent the author a letter full of generous praise. Mills's collective works were translated into French by P. Tiby (7 vols. 8vo, Paris, 1825).

A bust of Mills was executed about 1824 by Sievier, from which a portrait was engraved.

[Memoir (by A. Skottowe), 1828; Gent. Mag. 1826 pt. ii. pp. 559–60.] G. G.

MILLS, GEORGE (1792?–1824), medallist, was born in 1792 or before 28 Jan. 1793. He gained three gold medals from the Society of Arts, and exhibited at the Royal Academy from 1816 to 1823 (Redgrave, *Dict. of Artists*). His first patron was Benjamin West, P.R.A., who pronounced him the first medallist in England, and to whose memory Mills dedicated a portrait-medal. He was never employed at the Royal Mint, but engraved for James Mudie a silver pattern-crown of George III (Crowther, *Engl. Pattern Coins*, p. 38), and a pattern-crown (in gold and silver) of George IV, published by Whiteave (*ib.* p. 41). These patterns show little decorative taste, but he obtained three gold medals from the Society of Arts, presented as the reward of merit. Among Mills's medals which display moderate ability the following may be mentioned: 1. Admiral Sir J. T. Duckworth [1817?] (*Num. Chron.* 1890, p. 96, pl. iv. 15). 2. James Watt, rev. Watt's steam-engine [1819?] (Cochran-Patrick, *Catal. of Scott. Medals*, p. 117; pl. xxiv. 2). 3. Benjamin West [1820?] (Wroth, *English Personal Medals*, p. 21). 4. Medals for J. Mudie's series of 'National Medals' issued about 1820, including battle of Talavera (Grueber, *Brit. Mus. Guide to Engl. Medals*, No. 545), Sir John Moore, Lord Hill, Sir Thomas Picton, and Lord Lynedoch (*ib.* Nos. 554–7). 5. Visit of George IV to Ireland [1821], (reverse only; obv. by B. Wyon). 6. Medal of the Astronomical Society, first awarded in 1822, obv. bust of Newton, rev. Herschel's telescope (Hawkins, *Med. Illustr.* ii. 472, No. 88). 7. Lismore School medal (W. Frazer, *Medallists of Ireland*). Mills died at Birmingham on 28 Jan. 1824, aged 31 (*Gent. Mag.* 1824, pt. i. p. 186). His works are usually signed MILLS, sometimes G. MILLS.

[Authorities cited above.] W. W.

MILLS, GEORGE (1808–1881), shipbuilder, journalist, and novelist, born in 1808, was son of William Mills, lord provost of Glasgow 1833–6. He was educated at the university of Glasgow, and from 1827 to 1833 was manager for the company then started by his father to run steamers from Leith to London. From 1835, in partnership with Charles Wood, he carried on the business of shipbuilding at Bowling-on-the-Clyde, under the style of Wood & Mills. In 1838 the firm, the first, it is said, on the Clyde, began building iron steamers; they built also a large number of iron canal boats, many of which are still (1894) existent. In 1844, in consequence of the depression in the trade, Mills withdrew from the concern, and from 1845 to 1850 was a stockbroker; he was at the same time manager of the Bowling and Balloch Railway and of the Loch Lomond Steamboat Company. In 1857 he started the 'Glasgow Advertiser and Shipping Gazette,' a weekly penny paper, the first penny paper published in Glasgow. When in the following year the daily papers reduced their price to a penny, the 'Gazette' was beaten out of the field. After that Mills designed and had built, by Messrs. Tod & McGregor, a double-bodied steamer with central wheel, named the Alliance. She was the first steamer on the Clyde which had a saloon on deck, but she had not sufficient speed. She was sold, and afterwards, it is said, proved very successful as a blockade-runner, a service for which, with her slow speed and small carrying capacity, she does not seem to have been well adapted. She was lost in or about 1867. In 1869 Mills started a halfpenny paper, called 'The Northern Star,' in Aberdeen. It was given up in 1871. He was also for many years the literary critic of the 'Glasgow Mail.' In 1866 he started the Milton Chemical Works, which he carried on till his death. He was also the author of 'Craigclutha: a Tale of Old Glasgow and the West of Scotland,' 1857, 'I remember,' 1858, and 'The Beggar's Benison, or a Hero without a Name, but with an Aim: a Clydesdale Story,' 1866, 2 vols. post 8vo. They were all published anonymously; only the last is in the British Museum. Mills died at Glasgow in May 1881. He was married, and left issue one son.

[Information from the family.] J. K. L.

MILLS, JOHN (*d.* 1736), actor, said by Downes in his 'Roscius Anglicanus' to 'excel in Tragedy,' appears to have joined the company at Drury Lane and Dorset Garden after the secession in 1695 of Betterton, Mrs. Barry, and other actors to Lincoln's Inn Fields. Judging by the parts then assigned him, he must have had some previous experience. He was the original Lawyer in Cibber's 'Love's Last Shift,' January 1695-6, and in the same year the original Jack Stanmore in Southerne's 'Oronooko;' Nennius in an alteration of 'Bonduca;' Mustapha in 'Ibrahim XIII [should be XII], Emperour of the Turks,' by Mrs. Pix; Peregrine in the 'Cornish Comedy,' and Castillio in 'Neglected Virtue, or the Unhappy Conqueror,' founded on the 'Pilgrim.' During his first season at Drury Lane his wife played Margaret, a subordinate part, in the 'Cornish Comedy.' At Drury Lane, with one or two migrations to the Haymarket, Mills remained forty years. His early assumptions were principally comic. He played in 1697, among other parts, the first Sir John Friendly in Vanbrugh's 'Relapse, or Virtue in Danger,' and Ned Stanmore in Settle's 'World in the Moon,' and undertook Leontius in the 'Humorous Lieutenant.' In 1698 he was Merope, king of Egypt, in Gildon's 'Phaeton, or the Fatal Divorce,' Colonel Dorange in D'Urfey's 'Campaigners,' Winlove in 'Sawny the Scot' (Lacy's alteration of the 'Taming of the Shrew'), Artan (a devil) in Powell's 'Imposture Defeated, or a Trick to Cheat the Devil;' in 1699 Lovewell in Farquhar's 'Love and a Bottle,' in which Mrs. Mills was Trudge, and Sir Harry Wildair in Farquhar's 'Constant Couple, or a Trip to the Jubilee.' He also played, among other parts, Agamemnon in 'Achilles, or Iphigenia in Aulis,' extracted by Boyer from Racine. Following years saw him as the original Ned in Burnaby's 'Reformed Wife' (the cast of which is not in Genest); Arcadius in Oldmixon's 'Grove, or Love's Paradise;' Count Bassino in Mrs. Centlivre's 'Perjured Husband;' Don Duart in Cibber's 'Love makes a Man, or the Fop's Fortune;' Colonel Standard in Farquhar's 'Sir Harry Wildair;' Dugard in Farquhar's 'Inconstant, or the Way to win him;' Campley in Steele's 'Funeral;' Octavio in Cibber's 'She would and she would not,' 26 Nov. 1702; Trueman in Farquhar's 'Twin Rivals,' 14 Dec. 1702; Octavio in Mrs. Carroll's 'Love's Contrivance, or Le Medecin malgre Lui' (*sic*), 4 June 1703; Clerimont Senior in Steele's 'Tender Husband,' 23 April 1705, and many similar parts. In the autumn of 1706 a contingent of actors from Drury Lane appeared, under the direction of Swiney, at the Haymarket. Among them was Mills, who played, 26 Oct. 1706, Douglas in the 'First Part of King Henry IV,' and on 30 Oct. Edmund in 'King Lear.' He also enacted the King in the 'Maid's Tragedy,' Lord Morelove in the 'Careless Husband,' Bertram in the 'Spanish Fryar,' Leon in 'Rule a Wife and have a Wife,' the Ghost in 'Hamlet, Volpone, Timon of Athens, Petruchio in 'Sawny the Scot,' Bosola in the 'Duchess of Malfi,' Pierre in 'Venice Preserved,' Octavius in 'Julius Cæsar,' and many other serious parts, and was the original Aimwell in Farquhar's 'Beaux' Stratagem.'

On 15 Jan. 1708 Mills rejoined, as Horatio

in 'Hamlet,' Drury Lane, where he remained until his death. A list of his parts, of those even which were original, would occupy columns. The chief are Prospero, 1708; Melantius in the 'Maid's Tragedy;' Antonio; Macbeth; Pylades, an original part, in Philips's 'Distressed Mother,' 17 March 1712; Julius Cæsar; Sempronius; Buckingham in 'King Richard III;' Falstaff; Bajazet; Titus Andronicus; Cassius; Lear; Othello; Cato; Orestes; Hamlet; and Wolsey. He was the original Belmour in 'Jane Shore,' 2 Feb. 1714; Fantôme in the 'Drummer,' 10 March 1716; Zanga in the 'Revenge,' 18 April 1721; Sir John Bevil in Steele's 'Conscious Lovers,' 7 Nov. 1722; and Manly in Vanbrugh and Cibber's 'Provoked Husband,' 10 Jan. 1728. At the close of the season of 1734–5 Mills was selected as one of a committee of management at Drury Lane, but this arrangement was not carried out. His last performance (4 Dec. 1736) was as the King in the 'Second Part of King Henry IV.' He was afterwards announced for Macbeth, and was seen by Davies hurrying to the theatre to play it, but was taken ill, and resigned the rôle to Quin. He died on the 17th, after an illness of twelve days, at his residence in Martlet's Court, Bow Street, and was interred in the parish church of St. Martin's-in-the-Fields on the 20th, his pall-bearers being Charles Fletewood (*sic*), Colley Cibber, Johnson, Quin, Griffin, and Theophilus Cibber.

The 'London Evening Post,' 18 Dec. 1736, says that 'he deservedly acquir'd a very great reputation; not only for his capacity, but also for his application and diligence in his profession,' and for his conduct in public and private life. It adds: 'He liv'd so generally and deservedly beloved that his loss is not only a great misfortune to the stage and his brethren there, but to the public in general, he being in all respects a very worthy and good man.' This testimony is borne out from other sources. Victor calls him 'the most useful actor that ever served a theatre,' speaks in high praise of his Bajazet, and describes his person as 'nearly approaching to the graceful; and his voice a full deep melodious tenor, which suited the characters of rage.' His features appear, however, to have been large rather than expressive. Colley Cibber says that he owed his advancement to Wilks, to whose friendship his qualities as an 'honest, quiet, careful man, of as few faults as excellences, commended him,' and adds that he was advanced to a salary larger than any man actor had enjoyed during his (Cibber's) time on the stage. Mills's salary, 4*l.* a week, with 1*l.* for his wife, was in fact the same as Betterton's. Rich, in an advertisement provoked by a quarrel with his players, says that 'the salary was paid for little or nothing.' Steele in the 'Tatler,' No. 201, taxes Mills with want of sentiment, and suggests that 'making gesture too much his study, he neglected the higher attributes of his art.' Pierre, in which 'he is charged with wearing a white hat,' was his best part, in the opinion of the actors and of the public. As Corvino in 'Volpone' he was held to surpass Colley Cibber.

His wife played few important parts. William Mills, his son, known as 'the younger Mills,' died of dropsy 18 Aug. 1750, his benefit being announced for the 21st. Davies praises his Julius Cæsar, and says 'he was in general a snip-snap speaker,' whose eccentricities Garrick mimicked very happily in the 'Rehearsal.' He was an indifferent actor.

[Genest's Account of the English Stage; Cibber's Apology, ed. Lowe; Downes's Roscius Anglicanus; Davies's Dramatic Miscellanies; Victor's History of the Theatres; Notes and Queries, 8th ser. i. 25, 78.] J. K.

MILLS, JOHN (*d.* 1784?), writer on agriculture, was in Paris in 1743 for the purpose of bringing out, in concert with Sellius, a German historian, a French edition of Ephraim Chambers's 'Cyclopædia;' but Lebreton, the printer commissioned by him to manage the undertaking, cheated him out of the subscription money, assaulted him, and ultimately obtained a license in his own name. This was the origin of the famous 'Encyclopédie.' Mills, unable to obtain redress, returned to England, and Sellius died at Charenton Lunatic Asylum in 1787. In 1763 Mills continued, completed, and dedicated to the Earl of Bute 'Memoirs of the Court of Augustus,' by Thomas Blackwell the younger [q. v.] Finding his true vocation as a writer on agriculture, he translated in 1762 Duhamel du Monceau's 'Practical Treatise of Husbandry.' In 1766 he published an 'Essay on the Management of Bees;' in 1770 a translation from the Latin of G. A. Gyllenberg's 'Natural and Chemical Elements of Agriculture;' in 1772 an 'Essay on the Weather' (translated into Dutch in 1772), and 'Essays, Moral, Philosophical, and Political' (anonymous, but advertised under his name); and in 1776 a 'Treatise on Cattle.' His chief work, 'A New System of Practical Husbandry,' in 5 vols., appeared in 1767. It was the earliest complete treatise on all branches of agriculture, and contains the first mention of the potato as grown in fields. It combines the results of the experience and observations of such writers as Evelyn, Duhamel, John Worlidge, and Jethro Tull, and is highly commended by Donaldson, who gives an abstract of its contents. Mills was a warm advocate of small farms. In 1766 he was elected a F.R.S., and he was the first foreign associate of the French Agricultural Society, on whose list his name, with London as his residence, appears from 1767 to 1784, in which year he probably died. One John Mills died at Glanton, Northumberland, 8 Nov. 1786 (*Gent. Mag.* 1786, pt. ii. p. 1002).

[J. Donaldson's Agricultural Biography, 1854, p. 51 *; Mémoires Secrets de la République de Lettres, v. 340; Brit. Mus. Cat.] J. G. A.

MILLS, JOHN (1812–1873), author and Calvinistic methodist minister, born 19 Dec. 1812 at Llanidloes, Montgomeryshire, was son of Edward Mills, by his wife Mary. Devoting himself to music, he travelled through the country, establishing musical societies in various places, and thus greatly extended musical culture in Wales. In 1846 he went to London to act as a missionary to the Jews on behalf of the Welsh Calvinistic methodists. In 1855 and 1859 he visited the Holy Land in order to better equip himself for this work. He was a member of many learned societies connected with biblical and oriental studies. He died in London, 28 July 1873.

His chief works are: 1. 'Grammadeg Cerddoriaeth,' a grammar of music (Llanidloes, 1838), the first complete musical handbook published in the Welsh language. 2. 'British Jews,' London, 1853. 3. 'Palestina,' in Welsh only, Llanidloes, 1858. 4. 'Three Months' Residence in Nablûs, and an Account of the Modern Samaritans,' London, 1864.

[Biography of the Rev. John Mills, by Mr. Richard Mills and the Rev. N. C. Jones, D.D. (in Welsh), Aberdare, 1881.] J. A. J.

MILLS, RICHARD (1809–1844), Welsh musician, was the son of Henry Mills, and was born at Ty Newydd, Llanidloes, in March 1809. He showed musical talent at an early age, and competed successfully at eisteddfodau upon musical and literary subjects. In 1838 he published some of his literary compositions; better known, however, are his musical publications, 'Caniadau Seion' (1840), a collection of congregational tunes, and 'Yr Arweinydd Cerddorol,' published in three parts (1840–5), and consisting chiefly of musical instruction. Richard Mills and his nephews, John and Richard, who carried on his work, did much to improve the character of Welsh ecclesiastical music, and to popularise musical knowledge in Wales. They were the pioneers of the modern musical movement in that country. Mills died on 24 Dec. 1844. His brother James (*d.* 1844) was also a musician of talent.

[Montgomeryshire Worthies in Montgomeryshire Collections, xv. 49]. J. E. L.

MILLWARD. [See Milward.]

MILLYNG, THOMAS (*d.* 1492), bishop of Hereford, became about 1447, when quite a youth, a monk at Westminster, and thence proceeded to the Benedictine College, Gloucester Hall (now Worcester College), Oxford, where he remained till he graduated D.D. He then returned to Westminster, and in 1465 succeeded the chronicler John Flete [q. v.] as prior. The abbot George Norwych had wasted the revenues and incurred large debts, and he was now forced to retire to another Benedictine house, with an annual pension of a hundred marks. Although he retained the nominal title of abbot, Millyng, aided by two senior monks, one of whom, John Esteney, was afterwards (1474) abbot, governed the house, and on Norwych's death in 1469 was 'unanimously' elected in his place. The wars of the roses were then raging, and when in October 1470 Edward IV fled abroad, his queen, Elizabeth Woodville [q. v.], took sanctuary at Westminster. The abbot received her in his lodgings, where her elder son, afterwards Edward V [q. v.], was born on 2 or 3 Nov., and christened without pomp by the sub-prior on 4 Nov., the abbot and prior (Esteney) standing godfathers. The royal family remained in sanctuary, receiving 'half a loafe and two muttons daily' from the abbot till Edward's return in April 1471. The king rewarded Millyng by making him a privy councillor, and three years later advanced him to the bishopric of Hereford, to which see he was consecrated in the lady chapel at Westminster 21 Aug. 1474. The temporalities were restored on 15 Aug. Millyng died at Hereford before 11 March 1492, and was buried in the centre of St. John the Baptist's Chapel; the stone coffin, with the Hereford badge (a cross fleury), resting on Fascet's tomb, is most probably his. It was removed to make room in the vaults for other interments in the seventeenth century. Millyng was noted for his learning, especially for his knowledge of Greek, a rare accomplishment for monks in those days. He was also a good preacher. Leland (*De Script. Brit.* p. 483) speaks of his works, but had never seen any, and none are known to be extant.

[Godwin's Catalogue of Bishops, p. 380; Pits, de Rebus Angl. p. 916; Fabyan and Holinshed's Chronicles; Camden's Reges . . . in Eccles. . . . West. p. 60; Keepe's Monumenta Westm. p. 122; Syllabus of Rymer's Fœdera, ii. 705, 725–7; Dart, Widmore, Neale, and Brayley's Histories of the Abbey; Stanley's Memorials, pp. 221, 357.] E. T. S.

MILMAN, Sir FRANCIS, M.D. (1746–1821), physician, was born on 31 Aug. 1746 at East Ogwell, Devonshire. His father, Francis Milman, was rector of that parish, and vicar of Abbots Kerswell, in the same county. His grandfather, also Francis Milman, was rector of Marldon and vicar of Paignton, Devonshire. On 30 June 1760 he matriculated at Exeter College, Oxford, whence he graduated B.A. 9 May 1764, M.A. 14 Jan. 1767, M.B. 7 July 1770, M.D. 23 Nov. 1776. In 1765 he was elected to a college fellowship, and in May 1771 a Radcliffe travelling fellow. He was elected physician to the Middlesex Hospital (1777–1779), and a fellow of the College of Physicians of London 30 Sept. 1778. He had made the acquaintance of the Duke of Gloucester at Rome, and by his influence obtained practice in London. In 1785 he was made physician extraordinary to the king's household, and in 1806 became physician in ordinary to the king. At the College of Physicians he delivered the Gulstonian lectures on scurvy in 1780, was five times censor between 1779 and 1799, delivered the Croonian lectures in 1781, and the Harveian oration, which was not printed, in 1782. He was elected president in 1811 and 1812, and resigned 6 Oct. 1813. In 1800 he was created a baronet. His published works are only two, and appeared respectively in 1782 and 1799. The former, 'Animadversiones de Natura Hydropis ejusque curatione,' is dedicated to the Radcliffe trustees, and is in part based upon observations made during his travels abroad. It never rises above the level of a moderately good graduation thesis, and shows that its author did not distinguish between dropsies due to cirrhosis of the liver, to malignant growth of the peritoneum, and to renal disease. He recommends purgatives and tonics, and thinks that the patient's fluid food need not be restricted. His other book, 'An Enquiry into the Source from whence the Symptoms of the Scurvy and of Putrid Fevers arise,' is dedicated to Lord Southampton, and is a compilation showing little practical acquaintance with the disease. He agrees in general with James Lind [q.v.], whom he quotes, and almost the only original passage in the 230 octavo pages is one in which he comments on a passage of Strabo, bk. xvi., and shows that the disease from which the army of Ælius Gallus suffered in Arabia in the reign of Augustus was a form of scurvy. He died at Pinner Grove, Middlesex, 24 June 1821, and was buried in the church of St. Luke at Chelsea. He was a courtly person, of no great medical attainments.

Milman married, 20 July 1779, Frances, daughter of William Hart of Stapleton, Gloucestershire; she died in 1836, at the age of eighty-one, having borne three sons. His eldest son, William George, born on 19 April 1781 and died on 21 Aug. 1857, succeeded him in the baronetcy, and was father of Robert Milman, D.D., bishop of Calcutta [q. v.]; his youngest son, Henry Hart Milman [q. v.], was dean of St. Paul's.

The second son, Francis Miles Milman (1783–1856), an officer in the army, born on 22 Aug. 1783, served in the Peninsular War, was present at the battles of Roriça and Vimiero (August 1808), at the retreat of Corunna, at the passage of the Douro and the capture of Oporto (May 1809), and at the battle of Talavera (27–28 July 1809). In the last engagement he was severely wounded, and was taken prisoner. Detained in France until 1814, he was on his release awarded the war-medal and four clasps. He was afterwards in command of the Coldstream Guards, and colonel of the eighty-second regiment, being promoted major-general on 23 Nov. 1841, and lieutenant-general on 11 Nov. 1851. He died on 9 Dec. 1856. He married, on 8 March 1817, Maria Margaretta, eldest daughter of Sir Charles (Gould) Morgan, bart., of Tredegar, co. Monmouth, sister of the first Baron Tredegar; she died on 15 May 1875. Five of their sons entered the army. The eldest son, Egerton Charles William Miles Milman (born on 6 Feb. 1819 and died on 23 Oct. 1869), became major-general on 9 Nov. 1862. The third son, Lieutenant-general Sir George Bryan Milman, K.C.B. (born on 30 Dec. 1832), served through the Indian Mutiny, and became major of the Tower of London in 1870. The fourth son, Gustavus Hamilton Lockwood Milman, served in the royal artillery at Sebastopol, 1855 (major-general 8 Sept. 1875). Everard Stepney Milman, sixth son, lieutenant-colonel R.A., was governor of Holloway Prison, and the seventh and youngest son, Wilbraham Digby Milman, captain R.A., died at Calcutta 20 Dec. 1860.

[Works; Munk's Coll. of Phys. ii. 316; Gent. Mag. 1821; Annual Reg. 1821; Foster's Alumni Oxon.; Boase's Reg. Coll. Exon. xxiv. 107; information from Dr. J. B. Nias.] N. M.

MILMAN, HENRY HART (1791–1868), dean of St. Paul's, born in London 10 Feb. 1791, was the third son of Sir Francis Milman, bart. [q. v.], physician to George III. He was educated under Dr. Burney at Greenwich, and subsequently at Eton and Brasenose College, Oxford, where his career was remarkably brilliant. He matriculated 25 May 1810, and graduated B.A. 1814, M.A. 1816, B.D. and D.D. 1849. In 1812 he won the Newdigate prize with an English poem on the 'Apollo Belvidere,' which was considered by Dean Stanley the most perfect of Oxford prize poems. In 1814 Milman was elected fellow of Brasenose, and in 1816 was awarded the chancellor's prize for an English essay on 'A Comparative Estimate of Sculpture and Painting.' He was an early and intimate friend of Reginald Heber, for whose 'Hymnal' he wrote 'By thy birth and early years,' 'Brother, thou art gone before us,' 'When our heads are bowed with woe,' and other hymns, which have acquired and retain high popularity. In 1821 he was elected professor of poetry at Oxford, but did not make the mark of Keble, who succeeded him in 1831. He had meanwhile taken orders (1816), and was in 1818 presented to the important living of St. Mary's, Reading.

Though attentive to his clerical duties, Milman continued for some time to be known principally as a poet. It was the day of Scott, Byron, and Moore, who irresistibly attracted all talent of the imitative order, to which Milman's poetical gift certainly belonged. His first poetical publication was a drama, 'Fazio,' composed at Oxford, and described by the author as 'an attempt at reviving the old national drama with greater simplicity of plot.' Though 'written with some view to the stage,' it was published in book form in 1815 (2nd edit. 1816). It was first acted at the Surrey Theatre, without the author's knowledge, under the title of 'The Italian Wife.' Having succeeded there and at Bath, it was appropriated by the managers of Covent Garden, who astonished Milman by the request that Charles Kemble might be allowed to read the part of Fazio to him. The imperfection of the law of copyright would have frustrated any objections that he might have entertained, but, though protesting, he was flattered by the compliment, and the play was performed for the first time in London on 5 Feb. 1818, with triumphant effect, mainly owing to the acting of Miss O'Neill, who had seen the piece before publication and had then discouraged Milman from anticipating for it any success on the stage. Fanny Kemble subsequently played the part of Bianca with great effect, both in England and America, while Madame Ristori, when at the height of her fame in 1856, had it translated into Italian and appeared with much success as Bianca both in London and abroad. The plot, indeed, which is taken from a story in 'Varieties of Literature,' reprinted in 1795 by the 'Annual Register,' where Milman saw it, is powerful, and much the most effective element in the play. The diction is florid, and full of the false taste which had come in by perhaps inevitable reaction from the inanimate style of the eighteenth century. Milman's next publication, 'Samor, the Lord of the Bright City' (1818; 2nd edit. same year), an epic of the class of Southey's 'Madoc' and Landor's 'Gebir,' though not recalling the manner of either of these poets, had been begun at Eton, and nearly finished at Oxford. The subject is the Saxon invasion of Britain in Vortigern's days. The 'bright city' is Gloucester. The poem contains much fine writing in both senses of the term, and the author in after life subjected it to a severe revision. Southey, in criticising the poem, suggested that Milman's powers were 'better fitted for the drama than for narration' (SOUTHEY, *Corresp.* chap. xii.), and he told Scott that 'Samor' was 'too full' of power and beauty. Milman's next works were more mature in thought and independent in style, and the vital interest of their subjects almost raised him to the rank of an original poet. In 'The Fall of Jerusalem,' a dramatic poem (1820), the conflict between Jewish conservatism and new truth is forcibly depicted (*Corresp. of John Jebb and Alex. Knox*, ii. 434–44). In 'The Martyr of Antioch,' another dramatic poem (1822), a no less effective contrast is delineated in the struggle between human affections and fidelity to conviction. The description of Jerusalem put into the mouth of Titus has been greatly admired, and with reason, but is unfortunately too fair a sample of the entire work. 'Belshazzar,' also a dramatic poem (1822), is chiefly remarkable for its lyrics; and 'Anne Boleyn' (1826), a poor performance, terminated Milman's career as a dramatist.

But he was still to render an important and an unprecedented service to English poetry by his translations from the Sanscrit. These he was led to make by having exhausted the subjects which he had prescribed to himself for his lectures as Oxford professor of poetry. Having gained some acquaintance with Indian poetry from the works of foreign scholars, he taught himself to a certain extent Sanscrit, whose resemblance to Greek delighted him, and, with the assistance of Professor H. H. Wilson [q. v.], produced some very creditable versions of passages from the Indian epics, especially the pathetic story of Nala and Damayanti. These were published in 1835. They have been long superseded, but the achievement was none the less memorable. At a later period (1849) he published an elegant edition of 'Horace,' and in 1865 excellent translations of the 'Agamemnon' and the 'Bacchæ.'

In 1827 Milman was selected to deliver the Bampton lectures, and took as his subject the evidence for Christianity derived from the conduct and character of the apostles. The treatment was no more original than the theme. Three years afterwards, however, a book appeared from his pen, to which, though not in itself of extraordinary merit, the epithet 'epoch-making' might be applied with perfect propriety. It is his 'History of the Jews' (1830), written for Murray's 'Family Library.' In this unpretending book for the first time 'an English clergyman treated the Jews as an oriental tribe, recognised sheiks and emirs in the Old Testament, sifted and classified documentary evidence, and evaded or minimised the miraculous.' Consternation, which the author had not anticipated, spread among the orthodox; the sale of the book was not only stopped, but the publication of the series in which it appeared ceased. Bishop Mant and Dr. Faussett were among the more conspicuous of his assailants, and a greater man, John Henry Newman, who reviewed it in the 'British Critic' so late as January 1841, has recorded in his 'Apologia' the unfavourable impression it produced upon him at the time. It was, however, well reviewed in the 'Gentleman's Magazine' (1830, i. 134–7) as an 'excellent work,' 'written upon those enlightened principles which alone will be regarded in modern times,' while some representative Jews presented Milman with a piece of plate in recognition of his liberal treatment of their history. The book was republished in 1863 and again in 1867, with great improvements, and an able introduction, in which Milman clearly defined his own position. This he further illustrated in his university sermon on Hebrew prophecy, preached in 1865.

Milman's preferment seemed likely to be long impeded, but in 1835 Sir Robert Peel took advantage of his brief tenure of office to make him canon of Westminster and rector of St. Margaret's, Westminster, dignities invariably conferred on men of special eminence. He was still, nevertheless, regarded with distrust and dislike, and when his 'History of Christianity under the Empire' appeared in 1840, it was, said Lord Melbourne, as completely ignored as if the clergy had taken a universal oath never to mention it to any one. In 1849, however, Lord John Russell advanced Milman to the deanery of St. Paul's. No position in the church could have better become him than the charge of a great historical cathedral, and he speedily obtained the general recognition which his talents and accomplishments had always merited.

The historical character of Milman's mind was shown by the principal literary labours of his later years. In 1838 he had edited Gibbon, a task which hardly admits of satisfactory performance. So vast is the theme, so enormous the amount of illustration supplied by recent research, that either the editor's labours must appear inadequate, or the text must disappear beneath the commentary. Milman chose the former alternative, but his edition, with the reinforcement of Guizot's notes, remained the standard one until it was superseded by that of Prof. J. B. Bury (1896–1900). In 1839 Milman published the 'Life of E. Gibbon, Esq., with Selections from his Correspondence and Illustrations.' There followed in 1855 his own great historical work, 'The History of Latin Christianity down to the Death of Pope Nicholas V.' Milman here selected a subject on which libraries might be written, but the necessity for a comparatively brief general survey will always exist, and Milman's book, while meeting this want, is at the same time executed on a scale and in a style answerable to the dignity of history. Macaulay deemed the substance 'excellent,' although the style was, in his opinion, 'very much otherwise.' The call for a second edition in 1856 was described by Macaulay as 'creditable to the age' (*Life*, p. 626). The task was one for which the cast of Milman's mind and the tenor of his studies fully qualified him. The shortcomings and minor inaccuracies are amply compensated by qualities till then rare in ecclesiastical historians—liberality, candour, sympathy, and catholic appreciation of every estimable quality in every person or party—which not only contributed an especial charm to the work, but may be said to have permanently raised the standard of ecclesiastical history. Milman also possessed the fine sense of historical continuity, and the power of endowing institutions with personality, so necessary to the historian of an august corporation like the Latin church. The fundamental distinctions between Latin and Greek or oriental Christianity and the parallelisms between Latin and Teutonic Christianity are admirably worked out. His great defect is the one visible in his dramas—the lack of creative imagination, which prevented him from drawing striking portraits of the great company of illustrious men who passed under his review.

The remainder of Milman's life was principally occupied in the discharge of the duties of his office, where his intellectual superiority acquired for him the designation of 'the great dean.' To him were due several innovations calculated to make the services at St. Paul's popular and accessible. On Advent Sunday, 28 Nov. 1858, he inaugurated evening services under the dome. He bequeathed, moreover, such a memorial to his cathedral as few deans would have been able to bequeath, in his delightful history of the edifice, completed and published by his son after his death in 1868. In 1859 he had written, for the 'Transactions of the Royal Society,' a memoir of his friend Macaulay, which was prefixed to later editions of the historian's works. Some of his articles in the 'Quarterly Review,' to which in his early days he was a constant, and in later years an occasional contributor, including essays on 'Erasmus' and 'Savonarola,' were collected and published by his son in 1870. Milman died on 24 Sept. 1868 at a house near Ascot which he had taken for the summer. He was buried in St. Paul's Cathedral, and a monument was erected by public subscription in the south aisle of the choir. On 11 March 1824 he had married Mary Ann, daughter of Lieutenant-general William Cockell, by whom he had four sons and two daughters.

Milman was highly esteemed in society, and his intimate friends included Macaulay, Hallam, Sydney Smith, Lockhart, and his publisher, John Murray. Mr. Lecky has eulogised him unstintedly, and has described the harmony and symmetry of his mind and its freedom from eccentricity or habits of exaggeration. Although he was far from contemptible as a poet, his reputation must rest on his historical work. 'That such a writer,' writes Mr. Lecky, 'should have devoted himself to the department of history, which, more than any other, has been distorted by ignorance, puerility, and dishonesty, I conceive to be one of the happiest facts of English literature' (*European Morals*, Pref. p. x). His intellect may have lacked originality, but he was a pioneer in the study of Sanscrit poetry and in the application of criticism to Jewish history.

A portrait by G. F. Watts was presented to the National Portrait Gallery by his sons An engraving by W. Holl is prefixed to the 'History of Latin Christianity' (4th edit.)

[Annual Register, 1868; Encycl. Brit. 9th edit.; North British Review, vol. l.; Blackwood's Mag. vol. civ.; Fraser's Mag. vol. lxxviii.; Dean Stanley in Macmillan's Mag. vol. xix.; Quarterly Review, January 1854; Smiles's Memoir of John Murray, vol. ii.; Arthur Milman's Sketch of the Life of Dean Milman, 1900.] R. G.

MILMAN, ROBERT (1816–1876), bishop of Calcutta, third son of Sir William George Milman, bart., of Levaton in Devonshire, by his wife Elizabeth Hurry, daughter of Robert Alderson, recorder of Norwich, and nephew of Henry Hart Milman [q. v.], dean of St. Paul's, was born at Easton in Gordano, Somerset, on 25 Jan. 1816. He was sent when young as a day-scholar to Westminster School, where in 1833 he obtained one of the Ireland prizes (Welch, pp. 520, 541). In the May of that year he matriculated at Exeter College, Oxford, where he obtained a scholarship in 1834, and having taken a second class in 1837, graduated B.A. in 1838, and proceeded M.A. in 1867, in which year he was created D.D. (Foster, *Alumni Oxonienses*, iii. 960). He was a good linguist, and found the acquisition of languages easy. In 1839 he was ordained to the curacy of Winwick, Northamptonshire, and in 1840 was presented to the vicarage of Chaddleworth, Berkshire, by the dean and chapter of Westminster, on the nomination of his uncle, then canon of Westminster. There he had daily service, and, while working conscientiously as a clergyman, found time for much study, and wrote a 'Life of Tasso' and some smaller books. In 1851 he exchanged Chaddleworth for the larger living of Lambourn, also in Berkshire, at that time a wild and neglected place (*Memoir*, p. 4). He worked hard there, building a church and schools in the hamlet of Eastbury, and restoring the chancel of Lambourn church, chiefly out of his own pocket, holding daily service and weekly celebrations, and doing all in his power for the welfare of his parishioners. In 1858 his sister, Maria Frances Milman, went to live with him, and remained his companion during the rest of his life. At the request of the Bishop of Oxford (Wilberforce), who esteemed him highly, he accepted in 1862 the living of Great Marlow, Buckinghamshire, though the change was in every respect an act of self-sacrifice. While there he lectured frequently at Cuddesdon Theological College, being well versed in patristic learning and the history of the primitive church, and also conducted several clerical 'retreats.' His preaching was eloquent and his sermons full of matter.

Being appointed bishop of Calcutta in January 1867, he was consecrated at Canterbury on 2 Feb., and landed at Calcutta with his sister on 31 March. His diocese, which at that date included the Central Provinces, the Punjaub on the west, and British Burmah on the east, extended over nearly a million square miles. Milman performed the duties of his office with extraordinary energy, and during a large part of every year was travelling on visitation tours, visiting in the year of his arrival Burmah and the North-west Provinces. A dispute among the Lutheran missionaries in Chota Nagpore having led the Kôl converts to desire to join the English church, Milman received them in 1869, ordaining three German pastors and a catechist, and administering the sacrament to 650 persons at Ranchi. In matters of order he desired that the church at Ranchi should retain all its former customs and observances that were not inconsistent with the English prayer-book. Though his conduct was not universally approved, the Chota Nagpore Church grew and flourished; he took great delight in it, and visited the district seven times during his episcopate (*ib.* pp. 95–104, 322). In 1870 he again visited Burmah, where the king was patronising a school at Mandalay under missionary superintendence, but he declined an interview with the king because he could not be received except with formalities that would have implied an inferiority to a Buddhist religious teacher. Thence he proceeded on a metropolitical visitation to Madras, Ceylon, and Bombay. He was anxious for an extension of the episcopate in India, and in 1872 vainly pressed the government to found a bishopric of Lahore, but was not pleased at hearing, in 1873, that the Archbishop of Canterbury had sanctioned a proposal for ordaining bishops to be sent out from England to act as commissary-bishops in India; the Bishop of Madras nominated two for Tinnivelly. The two great English church missionary societies proposed that each of them should have its own missionary bishop, which Milman saw would be highly objectionable. Having refused his consent to the archbishop's proposal and taken counsel with the viceroy and others, he held a meeting with the Bishops of Bombay and Madras in November, and the Bishop of Madras was induced to withdraw his nomination. Milman did not cease to urge a legal and canonical division of the Indian dioceses, but failing that, would have welcomed the appointment of suffragan bishops (*ib.* pp. 263–73, 375). He established a lay-diaconate and sub-diaconate in his diocese, and was anxious to see brotherhoods and sisterhoods formed in India. While desirous of unity between Christians, he would sanction nothing that might impair the position of his own church, insisting on a formal act of renunciation and profession from converts from Roman catholicism, and refusing to allow his clergy to minister in dissenting chapels. Though he refused in 1872 to join in a memorial against ritualistic practices, holding that it was vague and likely to engender disputes, he warned his clergy against practices that might offend others, and disapproved of the use of eucharistic vestments and incense. He did much for the benefit of the English artisans in his diocese, and for the soldiers of the British army. With the natives of all classes he was extremely popular, and the extraordinary facility with which, though landing in India after his fiftieth year, he learnt to speak in Bengali, Hindustani, Hindi, and various cognate dialects, increased his influence over them. Holding that the bishops in India should be 'a link between Europeans and natives' (*ib.* p. 299), he gave parties to which both were invited, and tried in every way to make the natives feel at ease in European society. While travelling on his duty from Calcutta to Peshawur in February 1876 he took a chill, was laid up at the house of Sir Richard Pollock at Peshawur, but getting better on 7 March was moved to Rawul Pindi, where he died on the 15th. He was buried the next day. The viceroy, Lord Northbrook, immediately published a 'Gazette' containing a warm acknowledgment of the excellence of his character and work, and the government of India erected a monument to him in the cathedral at Calcutta. He was at once zealous and wise, an indefatigable worker and a consistent churchman. While staunch in his principles he was conciliatory in his conduct, and large-hearted and liberal both in his acts and sympathies. He was never married.

Milman published: 'Meditations on Confirmation,' 12mo, and some other small books or tracts in 1849 and 1850; 'Life of Torquato Tasso,' 2 vols. 1850, a careful biography, but lacking references, exhibiting no great acquaintance with literary history, and avoiding any attempt at criticism; it is in places too rhetorical, in others rather slovenly in expression; the versified translations from poems of biographical interest are literal but not particularly graceful; 'Love of the Atonement,' 1853, 8vo; 'Mitslav, or the Conversion of Pomerania,' 1854, 8vo, also in 'Home Library,' 1882, 8vo; 'Inkermann,' a poem, 1855, 12mo; 'Convalescence,' 1865, 8vo; some sermons and an article in the 'Calcutta Review,' reprinted in the 'Memoir' (see below).

[Memoir, 1879, by the Bishop's sister and companion, Frances Maria; Welch's Alumni Westmon. pp. 520, 541; Burke's Peerage and Baronetage, art. 'Milman;' Foster's Alumni Oxon. iii. 960; Honours Reg. of Oxford, 1883, p. 229; Times, 20 March 1876, p. 5; Guardian, 22 March 1876, p. 369; for reviews of Life of Tasso, Edinb. Rev. 1850, xcii. 533 sq., and Athenæum, 1850, 26 Jan. p. 95 sq.] W. H.

MILN, JAMES (1819–1881), archæologist, born in 1819, was the son of James Maud Miln of Woodhill, Barry, Forfarshire. He entered the navy, serving in the China war of 1842, and was afterwards a merchant in China and India. Returning to Scotland, where he inherited Murie, Perthshire, from his father, and Woodhill from his brother, he interested himself in small arms, astronomy, archæology, and photography, designed rifles, and made telescopic lenses. In order to compare Scottish with Breton antiquities, he went in 1873 to Carnac, intending to stay only a few days, but remained, with short intermissions, for seven years. In 1874-6 he excavated the hillocks of the Bossenno, bringing to light a Gallo-Roman villa of eleven rooms, the upper story of which had evidently been destroyed by fire, probably in the third century. He also found traces of a villa on the flank of the adjoining Mont St.-Michel. Of these discoveries he published an account, 'Excavations at Carnac, Brittany,' in French and English versions, published respectively at Paris and Edinburgh, 1877. He next explored three circular sepultures at Kermario, finding pre-Roman buildings and defences. In November 1880 he left for Paris and Edinburgh, to arrange for the publication of a second volume, but was attacked at Edinburgh by typhoid fever and died there 28 Jan. 1881. The volume was issued, also in English and French, by his brother, Mr. Robert Miln. The Miln Museum at Carnac contains his collections of antiquities. He was a F.S.A. Scotland, vice-president of the Morbihan Philomathic and French Archæological Societies, and a member of other learned bodies, British and foreign. His manuscripts were handed by his brother Robert to the Abbé Luco of Vannes.

[Information from Mr. George Hay, Arbroath; Luco's J. Miln et les trois sépultures circulaires, Tours, 1881; Proceedings of Soc. of Antiquaries of Scotland, xvi. 7; Notes and Queries, 8th ser. ii. 232.] J. G. A.

MILN, WALTER (*d.* 1558), Scottish protestant martyr. [See MYLNE.]

MILNE, COLIN (1743?-1815), divine and botanist, was born at Aberdeen about 1743. He was educated at the Marischal College under his uncle, Dr. Campbell, and afterwards received the degree of LL.D. from the university. He removed to Edinburgh, and became tutor to Lord Algernon Percy, second son of Hugh Smithson, afterwards Percy, duke of Northumberland. He took Anglican orders, and soon made his mark as a preacher. He was appointed evening preacher to the City of London Lying-in Hospital, lecturer to both the Old and the New Church at Deptford, and subsequently rector of North Chapel, near Petworth, Sussex. He continued, however, to reside at Deptford (*Cottage Gardener*, viii. 185; NICHOLS, *Anecdotes*, iii. 760), where in 1783 he founded the Kent Dispensary, now the Miller Hospital, Greenwich. He was a prominent promoter of the Royal Humane Society, and several times preached the anniversary sermon for the society (NICHOLS, *Literary Illustrations*, i. 165). As a botanist he was chosen to preach the Fairchild sermon, and sermons which he delivered before the Grand Lodge of Freemasons and at the Maidstone assizes were also printed (cf. NICHOLS, *Literary Anecdotes*, iii. 760). He died at Deptford on 2 Oct. 1815.

He published: 1. 'A Botanical Dictionary, or Elements of Systematic and Philosophical Botany,' 1770, 8vo, dedicated to the Duke of Northumberland, 2nd ed. 1778, 3rd ed. 1805. 2. 'Institutes of Botany, a Translation of the Genera Plantarum of Linnæus,' pt. i. 1771, 4to, pt. ii. 1772, not completed. 3. 'Sermons,' 1780, 8vo. 4. In conjunction with Alexander Gordon (M.D. of Aberdeen, 'reader in botany in London,' son of James Gordon, the nurseryman of Mile End, who corresponded with Linnæus), 'Indigenous Botany . . . the result of several Botanical Excursions chiefly in Kent, Middlesex, and the adjacent Counties in 1790, 1791, and 1793,' vol. i. (all issued), 1793, 8vo.

[Hist. of English Gardening, by G. W. Johnson, 1829, p. 232; Records of the Miller Hospital, Greenwich, by John Poland, F.R.C.S. (in the press); Biog. Index of . . . Botanists, by J. Britten and G. S. Boulger, 1893.] G. S. B.

MILNE, SIR DAVID (1763-1845), admiral, son of David Milne, merchant of Edinburgh, and of Susan, daughter of Mr. Vernor of Musselburgh, was born in Edinburgh on 25 May 1763. He entered the navy in May 1779, on board the Canada, with Captain Hugh Dalrymple, and continuing in the same ship with Sir George Collier [q. v.] and Captain William Cornwallis [q. v.], was present at the second relief of Gibraltar, at the capture of the Spanish frigate Leocadia, at the operations at St. Kitts in January 1782, in the actions off Dominica on 9 and 12 April 1782, and in the disastrous hurricane of 16-17 Sept. 1782. On arriving in England he was appointed to the Elizabeth of 74 guns; but she was paid off at the peace; and Milne, having no prospect of further employment, entered the merchant service, apparently in the East India trade, and continued in it until the outbreak of the war in 1793, when he joined the Boyne, going out to the West Indies with the flag of Sir John Jervis. On 13 Jan. 1794 Jervis promoted him to be lieutenant of the Blanche, in which, under the command of Captain Robert Faulknor [q. v.], he repeatedly distinguished himself, and more especially in the celebrated capture of the Pique (5 Jan. 1795). When, after a very severe action, the Pique struck, neither ship had a boat that could float, and the prize was taken possession of by Milne and ten seamen swimming to her. For his gallantry he was promoted to be commander of the Inspector sloop, 26 April 1795; and on 2 Oct. 1795 he was posted to the Matilda frigate in reward for his service as superintendent of transports, an office he continued to hold while the Matilda cruised under the command of her first lieutenant.

In January 1796 he was appointed, at his own request, to the Pique, 'the frigate he had so materially contributed to capture' (O'Byrne), and being stationed at Demerara for the protection of trade, the governor forwarded to him on 16 July a memorial from the resident merchants, to the effect that the admiral had promised them a convoy to St. Kitts by 15 July; that if their ships waited longer, they would miss the convoy to England; and that if they sailed without convoy they would forfeit their insurance. Under these circumstances, Milne consented to take them to St. Kitts; and arriving there too late for the convoy to England, on the further representation of the masters of the vessels, he took charge of them for the voyage home, anchoring at Spithead on 10 Oct. On the 11th he wrote to the admiralty, explaining his reasons, and enclosing copies of the correspondence with the governor and merchants of Demerara (*Captains' Letters*, M. 1796). His conduct, under the exceptional circumstances, was approved, and the Pique was attached to the Channel fleet. She was thus involved in the mutinies at Spithead in 1797, and when these were happily suppressed, was actively employed on the coast of France. On 29 June 1798, in company with the Jason and Mermaid frigates, she fell in, near the Penmarks, on the south coast of Brittany, with the French 40-gun frigate Seine, and brought her to action suffering severely before the Jason could come up. The three all got aground, and after an obstinate fight the Seine surrendered as the Mermaid also drew near. The Jason and Seine were afterwards floated off, but the Pique, being bilged, was abandoned and burnt. Milne, with her other officers and men, brought the Seine to England, and was appointed to command her, on her being bought into the English navy (James, ii. 247; Troude, iii. 137).

In October 1799 he went on the west coast of Africa, whence, some months later, he convoyed the trade to the West Indies. In August 1800 he was cruising in the Mona passage, and on the morning of the 20th sighted the French frigate Vengeance, a ship of the same size and force as the Seine. The Vengeance was under orders to make the best of her way to France, and endeavoured to avoid her enemy. It was thus close on midnight before Milne succeeded in bringing her to action. Twice the combatants separated to repair damages; twice the fight was renewed; and it was not till near eleven o'clock the next forenoon, 21 Aug., that the Vengeance—dismasted and sinking—hailed to say that she surrendered. It was one of the very few frigate actions fought fairly to an end without any interruption from outside; and from the equality of the parties, is aptly pronounced by James to have been 'as pretty a frigate match as any fought during the war' (James, iii. 23; Troude, iii. 215; Chevalier, iii. 25). But Milne received no reward. He continued to command the Seine in the West Indies and Gulf of Mexico till the peace, when he took her to England and paid her off, April 1802. He was reappointed to her in April 1803; but three months later, 21 July, she was wrecked on a sandbank near the Texel, owing to the ignorance of the pilots, who were cashiered by sentence of the court martial, which honourably acquitted Milne. He was then for several years in charge of the Forth district of Sea Fencibles. In 1811–12 he commanded the Impétueux off Cherbourg and on the Lisbon station. He was then appointed to the Dublin, from which he was moved into the Venerable. This ship was reported to be one of the dullest sailers in the service, but by a readjustment of her stowage she became, under his command, one of the fastest. Milne afterwards commanded the Bulwark on the coast of North America, returning to England as a passenger on board the Loire frigate in November, on the news of his promotion to flag-rank on 4 June 1814.

In May 1816 he was appointed commander-in-chief on the North American station, with his flag in the Leander, but his sailing was delayed to permit of his going as second in command under Lord Exmouth in the expedition against Algiers [see Pellew, Edward, Viscount Exmouth]. For this purpose, he hoisted his flag in the Impregnable of 98 guns, and in her took a very prominent part in the action of 27 Aug. 1816 in which the Impregnable received 233 shot in her hull, many of them between wind and water, and sustained a loss in men of fifty killed and 160 wounded. It was a curious coincidence that the ship which, after the Impregnable, suffered most severely was the Leander, commanded by Captain Chetham, Milne's old first lieutenant in the Seine. The loss of the two together in killed was more than half of the total loss sustained by the English fleet. For his services on this occasion Milne was nominated a K.C.B.

19 Sept. 1816, and was permitted to accept and wear the orders of Wilhelm of the Netherlands and Saint Januarius of Naples. The city of London presented him with its freedom and a sword; and as a personal acknowledgment Lord Exmouth gave him a gold snuff-box.

In the following year Milne went out to his command in North American waters, returning to England in the summer of 1819. In 1820 he was elected member of parliament for Berwick. He was made vice-admiral on 27 May 1825, G.C.B. 4 July 1840, admiral 23 Nov. 1841. From April 1842 to April 1845 he was commander-in-chief at Plymouth, with his flag in the Caledonia. On his way to Scotland after completing this service, he died on board the Clarence, packet-steamer from London to Granton, 5 May 1845. A portrait by Sir Henry Raeburn, in the uniform of a rear-admiral, painted in 1819, is in the possession of the family; a copy, by G. F. Clarke, is in the Painted Hall at Greenwich, to which it was presented by Milne's sons.

Milne was twice married: first, in 1804, to Grace, daughter of Sir Alexander Purves, bart.; and secondly, in 1819, to Agnes, daughter of George Stephen of the island of Grenada. By the first marriage he had two sons. The younger son, admiral of the fleet Sir Alexander Milne, bart., is noticed in the SUPPLEMENT. The elder, DAVID MILNE-HOME (1805–1890), was one of the founders, and for many years chairman of the council of the Scottish Meteorological Society. It was he who, in 1877, first urged 'the singular advantages of Ben Nevis for a high-level observatory,' and it was largely through his energy and influence that the proposal was carried into effect in 1883 (*Report of the Council of the Scottish Met. Soc.*, 25 March 1891).

[Information from Sir Alexander Milne; O'Byrne's Nav. Biog. Dict.; Marshall's Roy. Nav. Biog. ii. (vol. i. pt. ii.) 681; Naval Chronicle, xxxvi. 353; James's Naval History (edit. of 1860); Troude's Batailles navales de la France; Chevalier's Hist. de la Marine française; Foster's Baronetage.] J. K. L.

MILNE, JOSHUA (1776–1851), actuary, born in 1776, was appointed actuary to the Sun Life Assurance Society on 15 June 1810. His great knowledge of mathematics well qualified him for the reconstruction of the life tables then in use, which were based upon the table deduced by Dr. Richard Price from the burial registers (1735–80) of All Saints' Church, Northampton. Milne took as the basis of his calculations the Carlisle bills of mortality, which had been prepared by Dr. John Heysham, and after a long correspondence (12 Sept. 1812—14 June 1814) with Heysham he published his famous work, 'A Treatise on the Valuation of Annuities and Assurances on Lives and Survivorships; on the Construction of Tables of Mortality; and on the Probabilities and Expectations of Life,' &c., London, 1815, 2 vols. 8vo. The result was a revolution in actuarial science. Milne's table, which, considering the narrow data from which he had to work, was remarkably accurate, was very generally adopted by insurance societies, and subsequent writers have been greatly indebted to his investigations.

Milne was the first to compute with accuracy, though with unnecessary complexity, the value of fines, and his notation for the expression of life contingencies suggested that afterwards adopted by Augustus De Morgan in his 'Essay on Probabilities.' His book may still be read with profit. Milne could never be induced to revise his algebraical calculations, although they to some extent marred by their complexity the usefulness of his work. He gave evidence before the select committee on the laws respecting friendly societies (1825 and 1827), but long before his death he appears to have abandoned the subject with which his name is identified. 'I am far from taking an interest now,' he wrote to Augustus De Morgan (May 1839), 'in investigations of the values of life contingencies. I have long since had too much of that, and been desirous of prosecuting inquiries into the phenomena of nature, which I have always regarded with intense interest.' He had an 'unusually minute' knowledge of natural history, and is said to have possessed one of the best botanical libraries in London. He resigned his position in the Sun Life Office, owing to growing weakness, on 19 Dec. 1843, and died at Upper Clapton on 4 Jan. 1851.

In addition to the work mentioned above he contributed to the 'Encyclopædia Britannica,' 4th edit., articles on 'Annuities,' 'Bills of Mortality,' and 'Law of Mortality.' The last was reprinted in 1827 (*Report from the Select Committee on the Laws respecting Friendly Societies*, 1827, App. G 3), together with a valuable statement on the Carlisle and Northampton tables of mortality (*ib.* App. B). The Carlisle table was largely superseded by that published by the Institute of Actuaries in 1870.

[Gent. Mag. 1851, i. 215; Engl. Cycl. 1856, iv. 251; Assurance Mag. xiv. 69; Report . . . respecting Friendly Societies, 1825, p. 56, and 1827, pp. 22, 24; De Morgan's Essay on Probabilities, x, xi, 197, Appendix, ii, xv; information kindly given by Harris C. L. Saunders, esq., of the Sun Life Office; Milne's correspondence with Heysham in H. Lonsdale's Life of John

Heysham, London, 1870. Numerous comments, &c., on his work will be found in the Assurance Mag. and Statistical Journal.] W. A. S. H.

MILNE, WILLIAM (1785–1822), missionary, was born in 1785, in the parish of Kinnethmont, Aberdeenshire, and employed in his early years as a shepherd. At the age of twenty he resolved to become a missionary, and passing through the regular course of studies at the college of the London Missionary Society at Gosport, he was ordained there in 1812. In September he sailed for the east, arriving at Macao in July 1813. An order from the Portuguese governor compelled him to leave the settlement, and Milne proceeded in a small boat to Canton, where he was joined by his colleague, Robert Morrison [q. v.] Shortly afterwards Milne made a year's tour through the Malay Archipelago. Settling down at Malacca he mastered the Chinese language, opened a school for Chinese converts, and set up a printing-press, from which was issued the 'Chinese Gleaner.' He also translated portions of the Old Testament into Chinese, and became principal of an Anglo-Chinese College, which he was mainly instrumental in founding at Malacca. In 1818 he received the degree of D.D. from Glasgow University, and in 1822 his health failed, and he went on a visit to Singapore and Penang, but died on 27 May, four days after his return to Malacca. Milne married in 1812 a daughter of Charles Gowrie of Aberdeen, who predeceased him in 1819.

Milne was author of: 1. 'The Sacred Edict,' London, 1817, 8vo. 2. 'A Retrospect of the First Ten Years of the Protestant Mission to China,' Malacca, 1820, 8vo. 3. 'Some Account of a Secret Association,' a paper read before the Royal Asiatic Society by the Rev. Robert Morrison, 5 Feb. 1825.

One of his sons, William Charles Milne (1815–1863), missionary to China, ordained 19 July, and appointed to Canton, sailed on 28 July 1837, arriving on 18 Dec. at Macao, where he assisted until 1842 in the Morrison Education Society's House. Proceeding *via* Chusan, Tinghae, Ningpo, and Canton, he arrived at Hongkong in August 1843, and was nominated with Dr. Medhurst [q. v.] to commence a station at Shanghai. In 1844 Milne visited England, but, returning to China in 1846, he served on the Translation Committee, part of whose work he subsequently attacked. In 1852 he again visited England, and terminated his connection with the London Missionary Society. He afterwards went back to China as an interpreter under the British government, became assistant Chinese secretary to the legation at Pekin, and died there on 15 May 1863. Milne married Frances Williamina, daughter of the Rev. Dr. Beaumont. He was author of: 1. 'Life in China,' 1858. 2. 'Critical Remarks on Dr. Medhurst's Version of the First Chapter of St. John,' and contributed to the 'Edinburgh Review,' of October 1855, an 'Account of the Political Disturbances in China.'

[Works in Brit. Museum Library; Memoir by the Rev. Robert Morrison, D.D.; Life and Opinions of Rev. William Milne, by Robert Phillip; Memoir in the Christian Library, vol. i.; Gent. Mag. 1822, ii. 649, 1863, ii. 381; Irving's Eminent Scotsmen; information supplied by the Rev. G. Cousins.] A. F. P.

MILNER. [See also Millner.]

MILNER, ISAAC (1750–1820), mathematician and divine, was born at Leeds on 11 Jan. 1750. His education began at the grammar school, but on the sudden death of his father, who had been unsuccessful in business, he was taken away when only ten years old, and set to earn his livelihood as a weaver. He followed this trade until his eldest brother, Joseph [q. v.], who had been sent to Cambridge by the kindness of friends, had taken his degree, and obtained the mastership of the grammar school at Hull. As soon as he was established there he appointed Isaac his usher (1768). It is said that the friend whom he sent to make inquiries as to his brother's fitness for the post found him at his loom with Tacitus and a Greek author by his side. It seems certain that he had obtained considerable knowledge of Latin, Greek, and mathematics before he went to Hull, and that while there he became, as he said himself, 'a tolerably good classic, and acquainted with six books of Euclid' (*Life*, p. 523). In 1770 Joseph Milner found means to enter him as a sizar at Queens' College, Cambridge. The brothers came up together on foot, with occasional lifts in a wagon (*ib.* p. 128).

Milner found the menial duties then incumbent on sizars so distasteful, that when reproved for upsetting a tureen of soup, he exclaimed, 'When I get into power I will abolish this nuisance' (which he did). He refused to sign a petition against subscription to the Thirty-nine Articles; and, when keeping the 'opponency,' then required of all candidates for the B.A. degree, he used an argument so ingenious as to puzzle even the moderator, who said, 'Domine opponens, argumentum sane novum et difficile, nec pudet fateri meipsum nodum solvere non posse' (*ib.* p. 8). Hard reading combined with his natural talents secured for him the first place in the mathematical tripos of 1774, and enabled him to outstrip his competitors so completely that the moderators wrote the word *Incomparabilis* after his name. Like many men who have taken high degrees, he was so dissatisfied with his own performance that he thought he had completely failed (*ib.* p. 707). He also obtained the first Smith's prize. He was ordained deacon in 1775; became fellow of his college in 1776; and tutor and priest in 1777. In 1778 he was presented by his college to the rectory of St. Botolph, Cambridge, which he held till 1792. In 1780 and 1783 he was moderator. His reputation as an examiner stood very high in the university, and for many years he was constantly appealed to to settle disputed questions about brackets. His method of examination was peculiar. His keen sense of humour led him to joke over failures, especially those of stupid men, whom he called 'sooty fellows,' and when he had such to examine he would shout to the moderator in a voice which could be heard from one end of the senate house to the other, 'In rebus fuliginosis versatus sum' (GUNNING, *Reminiscences*, i. 83). When he examined *viva voce* he interspersed his questions with anecdotes and irrelevant remarks. In spite of this habit, however, he had a wonderful instinct for discovering the best men.

In 1776, while still B.A., Milner was elected fellow of the Royal Society, and subsequently contributed four papers to the 'Philosophical Transactions.' But before long he gave up mathematics, and turned his attention to other subjects. He had a strong natural taste for practical mechanics, and is said to have constructed a sundial when only eight years old. After taking his degree he studied chemistry in Professor Watson's lecture room, and in 1782 lectured on it as deputy for Professor Pennington. In the following year, upon the university's acceptance of the professorship of natural philosophy founded by Richard Jackson [q. v.], he became the first professor. He took great pains with his lectures, working indeed so hard at the preparation of them as to injure his health, and those on chemistry are said to have been excellent. He corresponded with several scientific men, but his name is not associated with any important discovery. His lectures on natural philosophy, which he delivered alternately with those on chemistry, are described as amusing rather than instructive (*ib.* i. 236). It would seem that he could not divest himself of his love of burlesque, even in the lecture-room. Notwithstanding these defects Professor William Smyth [q. v.] thought him 'a very capital lecturer,' adding that 'what with him and his German assistant, Hoffmann, the audience was always in a high state of interest and entertainment' (*Life*, p. 32).

The close friendship with William Wilberforce [q. v.], which lasted during Milner's whole life, began at Scarborough in 1784, when Wilberforce asked him to be his companion in an expedition to the south of France. They left England in October 1784, and were absent for about a year, with the exception of a few months in the spring of 1785. Wilberforce says of Milner, at the beginning of their residence at Nice, that his 'religious principles were in theory much the same as in later life, yet they had at this time little practical effect on his conduct. He was free from any taint of vice, but not more attentive than others to religion; he appeared in all respects like an ordinary man of the world, mixing like myself in all companies, and joining as readily as others in the prevalent Sunday parties' (*Life of Wilberforce*, i. 75). In the latter part of their tour, however, Wilberforce and Milner read the New Testament together in the original Greek, and debated on the doctrines which it teaches. In those conversations the foundation was undoubtedly laid of the great change which about this time took place in Wilberforce's convictions.

In 1786 Milner proceeded to the degree of bachelor in divinity. His 'act' excited the greatest interest, on account not of his talents only, but of those of his opponent, William Coulthurst, of Sidney Sussex College, who had been specially selected to ensure an effective contest. Professor Watson, who presided as regius professor of divinity, paid them the compliment of saying, 'non necesse est descendere in arenam, arcades enim ambo estis.' The subject, St. Paul's teaching on faith and works, is said to have been handled by the disputants with a wonderful combination of knowledge, eloquence, and ingenuity, long remembered in the university, and referred to as a type of what a divinity 'act' ought to be.

In 1788, on the death of Dr. Plumptre, Milner was elected president of Queens' College. He set to work at once, with characteristic energy, to change the tone of the college, to increase its importance as a place of education, and at the same time to make it a centre for the spread of those evangelical opinions of which he was recognised as one of the principal promoters in the university. The tutorship was, by custom, in the gift of the president, and Milner, in order to effect the latter object, deliberately rejected, as he himself admits (*Life*, p. 243), several fellows who were intellectually well fitted for the office, because he thought them 'Jacobites and infidels,' and sought elsewhere for men whose opinions were identical with his own.

Those he forced the society to elect to fellowships. His proceedings excited considerable opposition at first, but gradually the society submitted, and to the last he ruled over the college with a despotism that was rarely called in question. Nor was he unpopular. The numbers steadily increased, and though sneered at as 'a nursery of evangelical neophytes,' Queens' College stood fourth on the list of Cambridge colleges in 1814.

In December 1791 Milner was presented to the deanery of Carlisle. He owed this preferment to the active friendship of Dr. Thomas Pretyman, afterwards Tomline [q. v.], bishop of Lincoln, who had been Pitt's tutor. In consequence of his university duties he was installed by proxy—a beginning which might have been regarded as typical of his whole career as dean, for during his twenty-nine years of office he never, except once towards the close of his life, resided at Carlisle for more than three or four months in each year. He made a point of presiding at the annual chapter. He preached frequently in the cathedral, and energetically supported all measures for moral and material improvement, but this was all (*Life*, p. 101).

Milner resigned the Jacksonian professorship in 1792, and thenceforward gave up chemistry, and science in general, except as an amusement. To the end of his life he was, however, continually inventing something—as for instance a lamp or a water-clock—in the workshop fitted up for his private use in Queens' Lodge. He was also a member of the board of longitude. But after his election to the headship of his college he became daily more and more immersed in, and devoted to, university affairs. In November 1792 he was elected vice-chancellor. His year of office was rendered memorable by the trial in the vice-chancellor's court of the Rev. William Frend [q. v.] for publishing 'Peace and Union,' a tract recommending both political and religious reforms. Frend announced himself a unitarian, and objected to various parts of the liturgy. But the prosecution was political rather than religious. Mr. Gunning, who was present at the trial, says that 'it was apparent from the first that the vice-chancellor was determined to convict' (*Reminiscences*, i. 272). Milner hated what he called 'Jacobinical and heterodox principles,' and had, moreover, personal reasons for exhibiting himself as the assertor of law and order at this particular time. He was ambitious, and the piece of preferment that he most ardently coveted was the mastership of Trinity College. This is evident from a remarkable letter to Wilberforce, dated 13 May 1798 (*Life*, p. 161), in which he admits that he 'should not have been sorry to have been their master' in 1789, when Dr. Postlethwaite was appointed. In 1798 the office was again vacant, and the letter was written in the hope of influencing Pitt in the choice of a successor. In the course of it this sentence occurs: 'I don't believe Pitt was ever aware of how much consequence the expulsion of Frend was. It was the ruin of the Jacobinical party as a university thing, so that that party is almost entirely confined to Trinity College.' Then, after discussing various claimants, he adds: 'When I say that in all I have said, I have, on this occasion, whatever I might have had formerly, no respect to myself, I am sure you will believe me.' Wilberforce may have believed his correspondent, but it is difficult for posterity to be equally credulous.

In November 1797 Milner lost his elder brother, Joseph. The grateful affection with which he had always regarded him is one of the most pleasing traits in his character. During the rest of his life his best efforts were directed to preserve his brother's memory. He edited, with additions, the volumes of his 'History of the Church of Christ' which had already appeared, and continued it to 1530. He prided himself greatly on the importance assigned to Luther, and on his character as there set forth; but the writer's ignorance of German, and his religious prejudices, must throw doubt on the accuracy of his statements. In connection with this work he was led into a controversy with Dr. Thomas Haweis [q. v.]

In 1798 Milner was elected Lucasian professor of mathematics, a post which he held till his death. He delivered no lectures, but performed the other duties, such as examining for the Smith's prizes, very efficiently.

The remainder of Milner's life was apportioned, with undeviating regularity, between Cambridge and Carlisle. In 1809–10 he was again vice-chancellor, and in 1813 he had a brisk controversy with Dr. Herbert Marsh [q. v.] on the Bible Society. Marsh had addressed the senate on the impropriety of circulating the Bible without the prayer-book, and of allowing an auxiliary branch of the society to establish itself at Cambridge. Milner had spoken (12 Dec. 1811), at the meeting called to establish the auxiliary branch; and subsequently elaborated a volume of 'Strictures on some of the Publications of the Rev. Herbert Marsh,' in which he traversed almost the whole of his life and writings. Marsh replied, and his antagonist did not venture to enter the lists with him again.

Milner was fond of describing himself

as an invalid, and towards the end of his life rarely quitted his lodge. In the spring of 1820, while on a visit to Wilberforce at Kensington Gore, he had a more than usually severe attack. No danger was at first apprehended, but he grew gradually weaker, and passed away peacefully 1 April 1820. He was buried in Queens' College Chapel.

In person Milner was tall, with a frame that indicated great bodily strength, and regular features. In old age he became excessively corpulent. He was constitutionally gay; and his religious views, though they made him disapprove of amusements of various kinds, did not impose upon him gravity in society. He was 'the life of the party' (*Life*, p. 329), and if the official dinners which, as vice-chancellor, he gave on Sunday before the afternoon service at St. Mary's were very merry, his private parties were uproarious (GUNNING, *Reminiscences*, i. 246). Sir James Stephen, who knew him well, says of his conversation: 'He had looked into innumerable books, had dipped into most subjects, whether of vulgar or of learned inquiry, and talked with shrewdness, animation, and intrepidity on them all. Whatever the company or whatever the theme, his sonorous voice predominated over all other voices, even as his lofty stature, vast girth, and superincumbent wig, defied all competitors.' He was a popular and effective preacher, and when he occupied the pulpit at Carlisle, 'you might walk on the heads of the people' (*Life*, p. 116). His thirst for knowledge prompted him to discourse affably with anybody from whom he could extract information or amusement. In charity he was profusely generous, and contributed annually to the distressed poor of Leeds. He delighted in the society of young people, and spared no pains to make their time with him amusing. In politics he was a staunch tory, and an equally staunch supporter of the established church as a state institution. His friendship with Wilberforce made him an abolitionist, but he nearly quarrelled with him over catholic emancipation. There is a portrait in oils of Milner by Opie, in the dining-room of Queens' College Lodge, and a second, by an unknown artist, in the combination-room. He was also drawn in chalk by the Rev. Thomas Kerrich [q. v.] in 1810.

He wrote: 1. 'Reflections on the Communication of Motion by Impact and Gravity,' 26 Feb. 1778, 'Phil. Trans.' lxviii. 344. 2. 'Observations on the Limits of Algebraical Equations,' 26 Feb. 1777, *ib.* p. 380. 3. 'On the Precession of the Equinoxes produced by the Sun's Attraction,' 24 June 1779, *ib.* lxix. 505. 4. 'A Plan of a Course of Chemical Lectures,' 8vo, Cambridge, 1784. 5. 'A Plan of a Course of Experimental Lectures Introductory to the Study of Chemistry and other Branches of Natural Philosophy,' 8vo, Cambridge, n.d. 6. 'A Plan of a Course of Chemical Lectures,' 8vo, Cambridge, 1788. 7. 'On the Production of Nitrous Acid and Nitrous Air,' 2 July 1789, 'Phil. Trans.' lxxix. 300. 8. 'Animadversions on Dr. Haweis's Impartial and Succinct History of the Church of Christ; being the Preface to the 2nd edition of vol. i. of the late Rev. Jos. Milner's History of the Church of Christ,' 8vo, Cambridge, 1800. 9. 'Further Animadversions on Dr. Haweis's Misquotations and Misrepresentations of the Rev. Mr. Milner's History of the Church of Christ,' 8vo, Cambridge, 1801. 10. 'An Account of the Life and Character of the late Rev. Joseph Milner,' 8vo, Cambridge, 1801. 11. The same, enlarged and corrected, 2nd edit. 8vo, Cambridge, 1802. 12. 'Strictures on some of the Publications of the Rev. Herbert Marsh,' 8vo, London, 1813. 13. 'The History of the Church of Christ, by the late Rev. Jos. Milner, A.M., with Additions and Corrections by the Rev. I. Milner, D.D.,' 8vo, London, 1816. 14. 'Sermons by the late Jos. Milner. Edited by I. Milner,' 2 vols. 8vo, London, 1820. 15. 'An Essay on Human Liberty, by the late I. Milner,' 8vo, London, 1824.

[Life of Isaac Milner, D.D., by his niece Mary Milner, 8vo, London, 1842; Essays in Ecclesiastical Biography, by Sir James Stephen, 1849, ii. 358–67; Life of Wilberforce, passim, see index; Gunning's Reminiscences, 1855, i. 83–5, 234–51, 255–84; the Missionary Secretariat of Henry Venn, by W. Knight, 1880, p. 10.] J. W. C-K.

MILNER, JAMES (*d.* 1721), merchant of London, was extensively engaged in the trade with Portugal, and his commercial transactions with that country enabled him to render great service to the government in the remittance of money abroad. During the controversy on the eighth and ninth clauses of the commercial treaty with France (1713) he contributed to the 'British Merchant' several articles on the 'Methuen Treaty and the Trade with Portugal,' in which he combated the arguments advanced by Defoe in the 'Mercator.' He was returned to parliament for the borough of Minehead on 11 April 1717, and he voted for the repeal of the acts to prevent occasional conformity in January 1718–19. He died on 24 Nov. 1721.

Milner's articles on the trade with Portugal, which had first appeared in 1713–14, were republished, under the editorship of Charles King [q. v.], in the 'British Merchant,' London, 1721, 8vo (i. 206–22, iii. 3–92), but there is no evidence to show to what extent he was aided by other writers in the same work. He also published 'Three Letters relating to the South Sea Company and the Bank,' &c., London, 1720, 8vo, in which he foretold the disastrous results of the South Sea scheme.

[The British Merchant, 1721, I. xiv; Boyer's Political State of Great Britain, xx. 411, xxii. 548; Guide to the Electors of Great Britain, 1722, p. 12; Return of Members of Parliament, pt. ii. p. 43; Calendar of Treasury Papers, c. 104, cxii. 40, cxxi 12, cxxx. 17, cxl. 16, cxlii. 23, clvi. 3, 9, clxx. 3.] W. A. S. H.

MILNER, JOHN (1628–1702), nonjuring minister, second son of John Milner and Mary, daughter of Gilbert Ramsden, was born at Skircoat, in the parish of Halifax, and was baptised 10 Feb. 1627–8. He was educated at the Halifax grammar school and entered at Christ's College, Cambridge, 21 June 1642. He probably left without a degree before the parliamentary visitation of the university. Returning to Halifax he made the acquaintance of John Lake [q. v.], subsequently bishop of Chichester, whose sister he seems to have married. Milner was probably with Lake at Oldham in 1651. He is stated to have been curate of Middleton, but the Middleton registers contain no mention of him. In the accounts of the quarrel between Lake and the presbyterian classis of the neighbourhood, a John Milner is styled 'of Chadderton,' near Oldham, where a schoolmaster of that name is known to have been appointed in August 1641. Lake's friend was preaching at Oldham as late as 1654. Milner is said to have subsequently returned to Halifax, and at the Restoration was given the curacy of Beeston in the parish of Halifax by Lake, who had then become vicar of Leeds. In 1662 he obtained the degree of B.D. at Cambridge by royal letters. His petition for his degree states that he had been deprived of a good benefice during the rebellion. In the same year he was made minister of St. John's, Leeds, was inducted vicar of Leeds 4 Aug. 1673, and elected prebendary of Ripon 29 March 1681.

On the revolution of 1688 he joined the nonjurors, was deprived of all his preferments, and retired to St. John's College, Cambridge, where he lived in comparative ease and much respected. He died 16 Feb. 1702, and was buried in the college chapel on 19 Feb. with great state. He had a good reputation for skill in Eastern languages, but was exceedingly modest. His only son, Thomas, vicar of Bexhill, Sussex, proved a great benefactor to Magdalene College, Cambridge, under his will dated 5 Sept. 1721.

Milner published: 1. 'Conjectanea in Isaiam ix. 1, item in Parallela quædam Veteris ac Novi Testamenti in quibus Versionis LXX Interpretum . . . cum Textu Hebræo conciliationem meditatur Author,' a work of considerable learning, dedicated to D. Duport, master of Magdalene College, Cambridge, and Dr. Costel, professor of Arabic there, London, 1673. 2. 'A Collection of the Church History of Palestine from the Birth of Christ to the Beginning of the Empire of Diocletian,' London, 1688, 4to. 3. 'A Short Dissertation concerning the Four Last Kings of Judah,' London, 1687 or 1689, 4to, occasioned by Joseph Scaliger's 'Judicium de Thesi Chronologica.' 4. 'De Nethinim sive Nethinæis et de eis qui se Corban Deo nominabant disputatiuncula adversus Eugabinum, Card. Baronium,' Cambridge, 1690, 4to. 5. 'A Defence of Archbishop Usher against Dr. Cary and Dr. Isaac Vossius, . . . with an Introduction concerning the Uncertainty of Chronology,' Cambridge, 1694, 8vo. 6. 'A Discourse of Conscience,' &c., London, 1697 or 1699, 8vo. 7. 'A View of the Dissertation upon the Epistles of Phalaris, Themistocles, &c., lately published by the Rev. Dr. Bentley, also of the Examination of that Dissertation by the Honourable Mr. Boyle,' London, 1698, 8vo. 8. 'A Brief Examination of Some Passages to the Chronological Fact of a Letter written to Dr. Sherlock in his Vindication, in a letter to a friend,' with 'A Further Examination [of the above] in a second letter.' 9. 'An Account of Mr. Locke's Religion out of his own Writings,' &c. (charging Locke with Socinianism), London, 1700, 8vo. 10. 'Animadversiones upon M. Le Clerc's Reflexions upon our Saviour and His Apostles,' Cambridge, 1702, 8vo. Two anonymous pamphlets on Bishop John Lake's 'Dying Profession,' sometimes assigned to Milner, seem to be by Robert Jenkin [q. v.] They were published at London in 1690.

Milner left in manuscript a translation in Latin of the Targum on the First and Second Book of Chronicles, and other works on Scriptural chronology and current ecclesiastical controversies.

[Watson's Halifax; Thoresby's Vicaria Leodiensis; State Papers, October and November 1661; Appendix iii. to Minutes of Manchester Classis (Chetham Soc.); Oldham Local Notes and Queries; Lists of the Probators of 1641–2 (House of Lords' MSS.); Raines MSS. xxxii. 20 seq. (Chetham Library, Manchester); Wilford's Memorials; Watt's Bibl. Brit.; Graduati

Cantabrigienses; information from Dr. John Peile, master of Christ's College, Cambridge, and rector of Middleton.] W. A. S.

MILNER, JOHN, D.D. (1752–1826), bishop of Castabala and vicar-apostolic of the western district of England, was born in London on 14 Oct. 1752. His father was a tailor, and the proper name of the family, which came originally from Lancashire, was Miller. He received his early education at Edgbaston, Birmingham, but was transferred in his thirteenth year to the school at Sedgley Park, Staffordshire. He left there in April 1766 for the English College at Douay, where he was entered in August, on the recommendation of Bishop Challoner. In 1777 he was ordained priest and returned to England, where he laboured on the mission, first in London, without any separate charge, and afterwards at Winchester, where he was appointed pastor of the catholic congregation in 1779. In 1781 he preached the funeral sermon of Bishop Challoner, and about the same time he took lessons in elocution of the rhetorician and lexicographer, John Walker. He established at Winchester the Benedictine nuns who had fled from Brussels at the time of the French revolution. The handsome chapel erected at Winchester in 1792, through his exertions, was the first example in England of an ecclesiastical edifice built in the Gothic style since the Reformation. He himself sketched the design, which was carried out by John Carter (1748–1817) [q. v.] While at Winchester he ardently pursued antiquarian studies, and on the recommendation of Richard Gough he was elected a fellow of the Society of Antiquaries in 1790.

Between 1782 and 1791 various committees of English catholics (chiefly laymen) were formed for the purpose of promoting catholic emancipation [see under BUTLER, CHARLES, 1750–1832], but their members also wished to substitute a regular hierarchy in lieu of vicars-apostolic. At the same time they showed an impatience of the pretensions of their ecclesiastical leaders, and their attitude seemed to touch the authority of the papal see itself. To all claims on the part of laymen to interference in matters of religion Milner energetically opposed himself. When the Catholic Committee in 1791 pushed forward a proposed Bill for Catholic Relief, which embodied a form of the oath of allegiance already condemned by the three vicars-apostolic, Walmesley, Gibson, and Douglass, Milner acted as agent for the latter in their opposition to the measure, and visited Burke, Fox, Windham, Dundas, Pitt, Wilberforce, and other members of parliament, to urge the prelates' objections. His exertions were successful. The oath of the committee was rejected, and the Catholic Relief Act, which was passed on 7 June 1791, contained the Irish oath of 1788. But the 'Catholic Committee,' reorganised as the 'Cisalpine Club' in 1792, still carried on the old agitation, and was attacked by Milner. He thus grew to be regarded by his coreligionists as the champion of catholic orthodoxy. In his work entitled 'Democracy Detected,' he openly proclaimed his belief in the inerrancy of the holy see, and he frequently declared that he could not endure Gallican doctrines.

On the death of Dr. Gregory Stapleton, Pope Pius VII, by brief dated 1 March 1803, appointed Milner bishop of Castabala *in partibus*, and vicar-apostolic of the Midland district. He was consecrated at St. Peter's Chapel, Winchester, on 22 May 1803. After his consecration he went to Long Birch, a mansion on the Chillington estate that had been occupied by his episcopal predecessors, but in September 1804 he took up his residence permanently in the town of Wolverhampton.

Much work which was political as well as ecclesiastical fell to Milner's lot in those eventful times. The question whether the English government should have a 'veto' on the appointment of catholic bishops in the United Kingdom was then in agitation. In May 1808 the 'Catholic Board' was formed in England to carry on the agitation for catholic emancipation on the lines adopted by the Catholic Committee. Milner, who at first had been disposed to think that a royal veto might be accepted by catholics, afterwards became its uncompromising opponent. His attitude led to his expulsion from the Catholic Board and to his exclusion from a meeting of vicars-apostolic held at Durham in October 1813. Milner meanwhile enjoyed the full confidence of the Irish prelates, and acted as their agent in London, where he was permitted to reside when necessary under a papal dispensation, dated 11 April 1808. Milner twice visited Ireland in 1807–8. With the majority of the Irish prelates Milner now joined the party of catholics who were steadfastly opposed to any plan for Roman catholic emancipation which should recognise a right of veto in the English government. After the rejection of a bill introduced in 1813 for the settlement of the catholic question on the lines obnoxious to Milner and his friends, Sir John Coxe Hippisley [q. v.] procured from Monsignor Quarantotti, secretary of the propaganda, a rescript declaring 'that the catholics ought to receive and embrace with content and gratitude the law proposed for their emancipation.' This document, when published in England, caused alarm among the opponents of the veto, and the Irish bishops, at a meeting held at Maynooth on 25 May 1814, deputed Dr. Daniel Murray [q. v.], coadjutor bishop of Dublin, and Milner to be their agents at Rome for procuring its recall. At Rome Milner remained for nearly nine months, and to Cardinal Litta he gave a written memorial of his controversies with the 'veto' party, led by Dr. Poynter and the Catholic Board. He offered to resign his vicariate if he were deemed unworthy of the confidence of the holy see. At the same time Dr. Poynter defended himself in an 'Apologetical Epistle,' but it was signified to Milner that his conduct was in the main approved by the pope and cardinals, though he was recommended to be more cautious and moderate. The opposition of Milner and the Irish prelates to the veto was ultimately successful, and it was finally abandoned by Peel when he introduced the Catholic Relief Act of 1829.

Milner's literary contributions to the 'Orthodox Journal' gave offence to some of his episcopal brethren, and the prefect of propaganda on 29 April 1820 directed him to discontinue his letters to that periodical, but Milner continued to defend, in various books and pamphlets, the principles which he believed to be essential to the welfare of the Roman catholic church. In particular he warmly opposed two bills introduced into the House of Commons by William Conyngham, afterwards lord Plunket [q. v.], one of which was for the removal of the disqualifications of catholics, and the other for regulating the intercourse of the catholic clergy with Rome.

Milner's health began to break after he had attained the age of seventy. In 1824 he had two serious attacks of paralysis, and in 1825 he received a coadjutor in the person of Dr. Thomas Walsh, who was consecrated at Wolverhampton on 1 May, when Milner was thoroughly reconciled to his former controversial opponents, Bishops Poynter and Collingridge, who assisted at the ceremony. Milner died at Wolverhampton on 19 April 1826, and was buried in the church of St. Peter and St. Paul, where a memorial brass was placed, with a full-size figure of the bishop in his episcopal robes. His fiftieth anniversary was celebrated 27 Aug. 1876 at Wolverhampton, on which occasion two sermons were preached by the Rev. Thomas Harper, S.J.

Milner was of middle stature, and was stoutly built. His complexion was florid; he had hazel eyes, a well-formed nose, and dark expressive eyebrows (Husenbeth, *Life*, p. 231). His figure was dignified and imposing. By his coreligionists he is generally regarded as the most illustrious of the vicars-apostolic; and his successful efforts to prevent the Roman catholic church in the United Kingdom from becoming subject to state control by means of the veto have been fully acknowledged. By Dr. (afterwards Cardinal) Newman he was styled the 'English Athanasius.' He was a divine of the ultramontane type, and detested all Gallican teaching. In discipline the rigidity of his theological training overcame the indulgent kindness of his nature. In devotional matters he was the first to object to the cold and argumentative tone of the old-fashioned prayer-books, and in their place he introduced devotions to the Sacred Heart and the Meditations of St. Teresa. His influence was shown by the conversions which in 1825 had become frequent in this country. After his death the devotional and liturgical changes introduced by him were carried out to their full development, and were made instrumental to the introduction of an Italian and Roman standard of tone and spirit among English catholics.

Milner was a good archæologist. His chief archæological publication was: 'The History, Civil and Ecclesiastical, and Survey of the Antiquities of Winchester,' 2 vols. Winchester, 1798–1801, 4to; 2nd edit. enlarged, 2 vols. Winchester, 1809, 4to; 3rd edit., with supplement and memoir of the author, by F. C. Husenbeth, D.D., 2 vols. Winchester, 1839, 8vo. Notwithstanding the Roman catholic bias of the author, this performance 'will always keep its place among the few standard works in English topography' (Lowndes, *Bibl. Man.* ed. Bohn, vi. 1554). The first edition must claim the preference as regards quality of paper and typography. In connection with this work Milner issued 'Letters to a Prebendary: being an Answer to Reflexions on Popery by the Rev. J. Sturges, LL.D., with Remarks on the Opposition of Hoadlyism to the Doctrines of the Church of England, and on various Publications occasioned by the late Civil and Ecclesiastical History of Winchester,' Winchester, 1800, 4to; 2nd edit. enlarged, Cork, 1802, 8vo; 7th edit. London, 1822, 8vo: another edition, Derby, 1843, 16mo. The Rev. Robert Hoadly Ashe published in 1799 'A Letter to the Rev. J. Milner, occasioned by his Aspersions [in his History of Winchester] on the Memory and Writings of Bishop Hoadly.' Milner also published a 'Treatise on the Ecclesiastical Architecture of England during the Middle Ages,' London, 1811, 8vo; 3rd edit. London, 1835, 8vo. The article on 'Gothic Architecture' in Rees's 'Cyclopædia' is by him, and he wrote papers in the 'Archæologia' (enumerated in the 'Gentleman's Magazine,' 1826, ii. 180).

Milner's chief theological publication was: 'The End of Religious Controversy, in a friendly Correspondence between a Religious Society of Protestants and a Roman Catholic Divine. Addressed to . . . Dr. Burgess, in Answer to his Lordship's Protestant Catechism,' London, 1818, 8vo; 2nd edit. 1819; 5th edit. 'with considerable emendations by the author,' 1824; 8th edit. 'in which is introduced a Vindication of the Objections raised by R. Grier' [1836?]; other editions, Derby, 1842, 12mo; London, 1853, 12mo; Dublin, 1859, 12mo. This work was composed in 1801–2, but its publication was deferred for sixteen years at the request of Dr. Horsley, bishop of St. Asaph, who had defended Milner in the House of Lords at the period of his dispute with Dr. Sturges. Dr. Husenbeth says 'that multitudes of converts have been made by that work — probably more than by all our other controversial works put together.' It drew forth replies from Blakeney, Collette, Fossey, Garbett, Grier, Hearn, Hopkins, Jackson, Lowe, afterwards dean of Exeter, MacGavin, Ouseley, and Phillpotts, afterwards bishop of Exeter.

His other works are: 1. 'A Sermon [on Deut. xxxii. 39] preached at Winchester, 23 April 1789, being the General Thanksgiving Day for His Majesty's Happy Recovery. . . . With Notes, Historical, Explanatory,' &c., London, 1789, 4to. In reply to this, J. Williamson, B.D., published 'A Defence of the Doctrines . . . of the Church of England from the Charges of the Rev. J. Milner,' 1790. 2. 'The Divine Right of Episcopacy,' 1791, 8vo. 3. 'Ecclesiastical Democracy detected,' 1792, 8vo. 4. 'An Historical and Critical Enquiry into the Existence and Character of St. George, patron of England, of the Order of the Garter, and of the Antiquarian Society; in which the Assertions of Edward Gibbon, esq., History of Decline and Fall, cap. 23; and of certain other Modern Writers, concerning this Saint, are discussed,' London, 1792, 8vo. 5. 'The Funeral Oration of . . . Louis XVI, pronounced at the Funeral Service performed by the French Clergy of the King's House, Winchester, at St. Peter's Chapel in the said City, 12 April 1793.' 6. 'Account of the Communities of British Subjects, Sufferers by the French Revolution;' in the 'Laity's Directory' for 1795, 1796, and 1797. 7. 'A Serious Expostulation with the Rev. Joseph Berington, upon his Theological Errors concerning Miracles and other Subjects,' 1797. 8. 'Dissertation on the Modern Style of altering Antient Cathedrals, as exemplified in the Cathedral of Salisbury,' London, 1798, 4to; 2nd edit. 1811. 9. 'Life of Bishop Challoner,' prefixed to that prelate's 'Grounds of the Old Religion,' London, 1798, 12mo. 10. 'The Case of Conscience solved, in Answer to Mr. Reeves on the Coronation Oath,' 1801. This elicited replies from T. Le Mesurier and Dr. Phillpotts, bishop of Exeter. 11. 'Authentic Documents relative to the Miraculous Cure of Winefrid White, of the Town of Wolverhampton, at Holywell, in Flintshire,' London, 1805, 12mo; 3rd edit. London, 1806, 8vo. Peter Roberts published 'Animadversions' on this work in 1814. 12. 'An Inquiry into certain Vulgar Opinions concerning the Catholic Inhabitants and the Antiquities of Ireland, in a series of Letters,' London, 1808, 8vo; 3rd edit. 'with copious additions, including the account of a second tour through Ireland, by the author, and answers to Sir R. Musgrave, Dr. Ryan, Dr. Elrington,' &c., London, 1810, 8vo. 13. 'A Pastoral Letter [dated 10 Aug. 1808] addressed to the Roman Catholic Clergy of his District in England. Shewing the dangerous tendency of various Pamphlets lately published in the French Language by certain Emigrants, and more particularly cautioning the faithful against two publications by the Abbé Blanchard and Mons. Gaschet,' London, 1808, 8vo; another edition, Dublin, 1808, 8vo. This pastoral gave rise to an embittered controversy. 14. 'Dr. Milner's Appeal to the Catholics of Ireland,' deprecating attacks made upon him by Sir R. Musgrave, T. Le Mesurier, &c., Dublin, 1809, 8vo. 15. 'An Elucidation of the Veto,' London, 1810, 8vo. 16. 'Instructions addressed to the Catholics of the Midland Counties of England on the State and Dangers of their Religion,' Wolverhampton, 1811, 8vo. 17. 'Letters to a Roman Catholic Prelate of Ireland in refutation of Counsellor Charles Butler's Letter to an Irish Catholic Gentleman; to which is added a Postscript containing a Review of Doctor O'Connor's Works entitled Columbanus ad Hibernos on the Liberty of the Irish Church,' Dublin, 1811, 8vo. 18. 'A Brief Summary of the History and Doctrine of the Holy Scriptures,' London, 1819, 8vo. 19. 'Supplementary Memoirs of English Catholics, addressed to Charles Butler, esq., author of Historical Memoirs of the English Catholics,' London, 1820, 8vo. Additional notes to this valuable historical work were printed in 1821. 20. 'The Catholic Scriptural Catechism,' 1820, reprinted in vol. i. of the tracts issued by the Catholic Institute, 1838. 21. 'On Devotion to the Sacred Heart of Jesus,' 1821, reprinted, London, 1867, 32mo. 22. 'A Vindication of "The End of Religious Controversy" from the exceptions of Dr. Thomas Burgess, bishop of St. Davids, and the Rev. Richard Grier,' London, 1822, 8vo. 23. 'A Letter to the Catholic Clergy of the Midland District' [on 'a certain new Creed or Formulary published in this District, called Roman Catholic Principles in reference to God and the Country'], London, 1823, 8vo. The treatise referred to was written by the Benedictine father, James Corker [q. v.] 25. 'Strictures on the Poet Laureate's [i.e. Robert Southey's] Book of the Church,' London, 1824, 8vo. 24. 'A Parting Word to the Rev. Richard Grier, D.D. . . . With a Brief Notice of Dr. Samuel Parr's posthumous Letter to Dr. Milner,' London, 1825.

Some papers by him are in the 'Catholic Gentleman's Magazine,' and the 'Catholicon;' and many in the 'Orthodox Journal.'

His portrait has been engraved by Radclyffe, from a portrait at St. Mary's College, Oscott.

[Life by F. C. Husenbeth, D.D., Dublin, 1862, 8vo; Memoir by Husenbeth, prefixed to 3rd edit. of Hist. of Winchester; Amherst's Hist. of Catholic Emancipation; Biog. Dict. of Living Authors, p. 235; Bodleian Cat.; Brady's Episcopal Succession, iii. 221; Catholic Miscellany, 1826, v. 376–93, new ser. 1828, i. 21; Catholicon, 1816, ii. 75, vi. 61, 396; Flanagan's Hist. of the Church in England, ii. 537; Gent. Mag. 1826 ii. 175, 303, 392; Home and Foreign Review, ii. 531; Laity's Directory, 1827, portrait; Nichols's Lit. Anecd. ix. 215; Oscotian, new ser. iv. 118, with portrait vi. 64, also jubilee vol. 1888, p. 28; Smith's Brewood, 2nd edit. 1874, p. 49; Tablet, 4 Oct. 1862, 8 Oct. 1870, p. 454; 29 Aug. 1874, p. 271.] T. C.

MILNER, JOSEPH (1744–1797), divine, was born at Quarry Hill, then in the neighbourhood, now in the midst of Leeds, on 2 Jan. 1744, and was baptised in Leeds parish church. He was educated at Leeds grammar school. An attack of the measles when he was three years old left him permanently delicate; but he early developed great precocity and a wonderfully retentive memory. His father was poor, but through the pecuniary help of friends he was sent to Catharine Hall, Cambridge, where he was appointed chapel clerk. He had little taste for mathematics, and the classical tripos was not then founded. But he achieved the respectable position of third senior optime, and thus qualified himself to compete for the chancellor's medals for classical proficiency, the second of which he won in 1766 in an unusually strong competition. He then went to Thorp Arch, near Tadcaster, Yorkshire, as assistant in a school kept by Christopher Atkinson, the vicar of the parish, received holy orders, and became Atkinson's curate. At Thorp Arch he contracted a lifelong friendship with the son of the vicar, Myles Atkinson, who subsequently became a leader of the evangelical party and vicar of St. Paul's, Leeds. While yet in deacon's orders he left Thorp Arch to become head-master of the grammar school at Hull, which greatly improved under his direction, and he was in 1768 elected afternoon lecturer at Holy Trinity, or the High Church, in that town. He was now in a position to assist his family, and he paid for the education of his brother Isaac [q. v.] In 1770 he became an ardent disciple of the rising evangelical school, and incurred the disfavour which then attached to those who were suspected of 'methodism.' He lost most of the rich members of his congregation at the High Church, but the poor flocked to hear him. He also undertook the charge of North Ferriby, a village on the Humber, about nine miles from Hull, where he officiated first as curate and then as vicar for seventeen years. At North Ferriby many Hull merchants had country seats, and among them he was long unpopular. But after seven or eight years opposition ceased both at Hull and Ferriby, and for the last twenty years of his life he was a great moral power in both places. Largely owing to him Hull became a centre of evangelicalism. His chief friends were the Rev. James Stillingfleet of Hotham, at whose rectory he wrote a great part of his 'Church History,' and the Rev. William Richardson of York, who both shared his own religious views. In 1792 he had a severe attack of fever, from the effects of which he never fully recovered. In 1797 the mayor and corporation offered him the living of Holy Trinity, mainly through the efforts of William Wilberforce, M.P. for Yorkshire. The corporation also voted him 40*l.* a year to keep a second usher at his school. On his journey to York for institution he caught a cold, which ended his life in a few weeks (15 Nov. 1797). He was buried in Holy Trinity Church, and a monument to his memory was erected in it.

As a writer Milner is chiefly known in connection with 'The History of the Church of Christ' which bears his name, though the literary history of that work is a curious medley. The excellent and somewhat novel idea of the book is no doubt exclusively his. He was painfully struck by the fact that most church histories were in reality little more than records of the errors and disputes of Christians, and thus too often played into the hands of unbelievers. Perhaps the recent publication of Gibbon's 'Decline and Fall' (first volume, 1776) strengthened this feeling.

At any rate his object was to bring out into greater prominence the bright side of church history. 'The terms "church" and "Christian,"' he says, 'in their natural sense respect only good men. Such a succession of pious men in all ages existed, and it will be no contemptible use of such a history as this if it prove that in every age there have been *real* followers of Christ.' With this end in view he brought out the first three volumes—vol. i. in 1794, vol. ii. in 1795, and vol. iii. in 1797. Then death cut short his labours; but even in these first three volumes the hand of Isaac as well as of Joseph may be found, and after Joseph's death Isaac published in 1800 a new and greatly revised edition of vol. i. Vols. ii. and iii. did not require so much revision, because they had been corrected by Isaac in manuscript. In 1803 appeared vol. iv., and in 1809 vol. v., both edited by Isaac, but still containing much of Joseph's work. In 1810 the five volumes were re-edited by Isaac, and John Scott published a new continuation of Milner's 'Church History' in three volumes (1826, 1829, and 1831). Both Joseph and Isaac Milner were amateur rather than professional historians, for Joseph's forte was classics, Isaac's mathematics, and both were very busy men also in other departments. When Samuel Roffey Maitland [q. v.] brought his unrivalled knowledge of 'the dark ages' to bear upon that part of Joseph Milner's history which related to the Waldenses (1832), he was able to find many flaws in it. Joseph Milner's fellow-townsman, the Rev. John King, ably defended him, but Maitland remained master of the field. His 'Strictures on Milner's Church History' (1834) appeared at the time when the high church party was reviving. A controversy ensued, and fresh attention was called to the Milners' work, a new and greatly improved edition of which was published by the Rev. F. Grantham in 1847.

The other works published by Milner in his lifetime were: 1. 'Gibbon's Account of Christianity considered, with some Strictures on Hume's Dialogues on Natural Religion,' 1781. 2. 'Some Remarkable Passages in the Life of William Howard, who died at North Ferriby on 2 March 1784,' 1785, a tract which passed through several editions. 3. 'Essays on several Religious Subjects, chiefly tending to illustrate the Scripture Doctrine of the Influence of the Holy Spirit,' 1789. He also edited, with the Rev. W. Richardson, 'Thomas Adam's Posthumous Works,' 1786. After Joseph Milner's death a vast number of his sermons were found, and these were published in four volumes under the title of 'Practical Sermons,' the first (1800) with a brief but touching memoir by the editor, Isaac Milner; the second (1809), edited by the Rev. W. Richardson. These two were afterwards republished together. A third volume (1823) was edited by the Rev. John Fawcett, and a fourth (1830), 'On the Epistles to the Seven Churches, the Millennium, the Church Triumphant, and the 130th Psalm,' by Edward Bickersteth. In 1855 Milner's 'Essentials of Christianity, theoretically and practically considered,' which had been left by the author in a complete state for publication, and had been revised by his brother, was edited for the Religious Tract Society by Mary Milner, the orphan niece of whom Joseph Milner had taken charge, and writer of her uncle Isaac's 'Life.'

[Joseph Milner's Works, passim; Dean Isaac Milner's Life of Joseph Milner, prefixed to the first volume of Joseph Milner's Practical Sermons; Mrs. Mary Milner's Life of Dean Milner.]

J. H. O.

MILNER, THOMAS, M.D. (1719–1797), physician, son of John Milner, a presbyterian minister, was born at Peckham, near London, where his father preached and kept a school famous in literature from the fact that Goldsmith was in 1757 one of its ushers (Forster, *Life of Goldsmith*). He graduated M.D. at St. Andrews 20 June 1740, and in 1759 was elected physician to St. Thomas's Hospital. He became a licentiate of the College of Physicians 30 Sept. 1760, but in 1762 resigned his physiciancy at St. Thomas's, and settled in Maidstone, where he attained to large practice and used to walk to the parish church every Sunday bearing a gold-headed cane, and followed in linear succession by the three unmarried sisters who lived with him. In 1783 he published in London 'Experiments and Observations on Electricity,' a work in which he described some of the effects which an electrical power is capable of producing on conducting substances, similar effects of the same power on electric bodies themselves, and observations on the air, electric repulsion, the electrified cup, and the analogy between electricity and magnetism. He died at Maidstone 13 Sept. 1797, and is buried in All Saints' Church there.

[Munk's Coll. of Phys. ii. 229; Works.]

N. M.

MILNER-GIBSON, THOMAS (1806–1884), statesman. [See Gibson, Thomas Milner-.]

MILNES, RICHARD MONCKTON, first Baron Houghton (1809–1885), born on 19 June 1809 in Bolton Street, Mayfair, London, was only son of Robert Pember-

TON MILNES (1784–1858) of Fryston Hall, near Wakefield, by the Hon. Henrietta Maria Monckton, second daughter of the fourth Viscount Galway. The family, originally from Derbyshire, was in the eighteenth century largely interested in the cloth trade. The father achieved some distinction. Born in 1784, eldest son of Richard Slater Milnes, M.P. for York, by Rachel, daughter of Hans Busk of Leeds, he was educated at a private school in Liverpool and at Trinity College, Cambridge, where he had a brilliant career, proceeding B.A. in 1804. In 1806, at the age of twenty-two, he became M.P. for Pontefract, and on 15 April 1807 he defended the Duke of Portland's administration in a remarkable speech, which was long remembered. In October 1809 he declined the offer of a seat in Mr. Perceval's administration, and retiring to Yorkshire as a country gentleman led the politics of the county, supporting catholic emancipation and opposing the repeal of the corn laws. After paying a brother's debts he found himself forced to reside abroad, chiefly at Milan and Rome, for several years from 1829. In 1831 he travelled in southern Italy, and afterwards printed the journal of his tour for private circulation. He was highly popular in society, but of a fastidious nature, and he refused a peerage offered by Lord Palmerston in 1856. He died on 9 Nov. 1858.

Monckton Milnes, who was delicate as a child, was educated at Hundhill Hall school, near Doncaster, and then privately, until in October 1827 he was entered as a fellow-commoner at Trinity College, Cambridge. There he owed much to the influence of his tutor, Connop Thirlwall [q. v.], afterwards bishop of St. Davids, and without great academic success he won notice. A conspicuous member of the association known as the 'Apostles,' he was intimate with Tennyson, Hallam, Thackeray, and other promising men of his time; he spoke often and well at the Union Debating Society, and was a fair amateur actor. He also contributed occasional reviews and poems to the 'Athenæum.' In December 1829, on the invitation of F. H. Doyle and W. E. Gladstone, he went with Hallam and Thomas Sunderland as a deputation from the Cambridge to the Oxford Union Society, to argue the superiority of Shelley as a poet to Byron.

On leaving Cambridge, where he proceeded M.A. in 1831, Milnes went to London, and attended classes at the recently founded University College, Gower Street, and associated with Thomas Campbell, F. D. Maurice, John Sterling, and others. After travelling in Germany, where he spent some time at the university of Bonn, he went to Italy, and became popular in Italian society. He visited Landor at Florence. With Christopher Wordsworth he made a tour in Greece, and afterwards described it in a volume of poetical 'Memorials' (London, 1834), which drew praise from Christopher North. Returning to England in 1835, he began his life in London society in the following year. In spite of certain foreign manners which at first made him enemies, his social and literary qualities, the number and variety of his friendships, and a kind of bland audacity, obtained him an entrance into the best circles, in particular to Lansdowne, Holland, and Gore Houses, then recognised salons. He was a constant guest at Samuel Rogers's breakfast-parties in St. James's Place, and he began himself to give parties of a similar but more comprehensive nature in the rooms he took at 26 Pall Mall in the spring of 1837. Both then and afterwards it was notoriously Milnes's pleasure to bring together men of widely different pursuits, opinions, and social position, and no one was unwelcome who had any celebrity, or was likely to attain it.

In the general election in June 1837 Milnes became conservative M.P. for Pontefract, and in the following December made a successful maiden speech. But he afterwards adopted a serious and at times pompous vein which was not appreciated; and although he was a warm advocate of several useful measures, he failed to make any mark as a politician. In 1839 he published a speech he had delivered on the question of the ballot, and a pamphlet on 'Purity of Election.' He often visited the continent, and increased his acquaintance with men of note, meeting in 1840 King Louis-Philippe, De Tocqueville, Lamartine, and others. With Guizot he kept up a correspondence on English politics. His interest in foreign affairs led him to expect office, and he was disappointed at not receiving a place in Peel's ministry in 1841. He did much to secure the passing of the Copyright Act, and he introduced a bill for establishing reformatories for juvenile offenders. In Irish questions he urged a scheme for endowing catholic concurrently with Anglican clergy, as likely to aid in averting a repeal of the union. On Peel's conversion to free trade, Milnes, who had hitherto supported him, unlike the other Peelites who formed a separate party, joined the liberals. In 1848 he went to Paris to see something of the revolution, and to fraternise with both sides. On his return he wrote, as a 'Letter to Lord Lansdowne,' 1848, a pamphlet on the events of that year, in which he offended the conservatives by his sympathy with continental liberalism, and in particular with the struggle of Italy against Austria. The pamphlet excited some controversy and much hostile criticism, which came to a head in a leading article in the 'Morning Chronicle,' written by George Smythe, afterwards Lord Strangford, whom, in December 1845, Peel had preferred to Milnes for the under-secretaryship for foreign affairs. Milnes, who was coarsely handled in the article, at once challenged the writer; but Smythe made an apology, and it was accepted.

Milnes had meanwhile continued his efforts as a writer. In December 1836 he had assisted Lord Northampton to prepare 'The Tribute,' a Christmas annual, for which he obtained contributions from his friends, in particular from Tennyson. After some hesitation, the latter sent Milnes the stanzas which afterwards formed the germ of 'Maud.' He published two volumes of verse in 1838, and a third in 1840. His poems excited some public interest, and a few of them became popular, especially when set to music. In the 'Westminster Review' he wrote a notice of the works of Emerson, who sent him a friendly acknowledgment. In the controversy over the anglo-catholic revival he supported the movement in his 'One Tract More, by a layman' (1841), a pamphlet which was favourably noticed by Newman (*Apologia*, ch. ii. note ad fin.) In the winter of 1842–3 he visited Egypt and the Levant, where he was commonly supposed to have had numerous adventures, and in 1844 he published his poetical impressions of the tour in a volume entitled 'Palm Leaves.' Milnes, who was always ready to assist any one connected with literature, at this time exerted himself to obtain a civil list pension for Tennyson, and he helped Hood in his last days, and on his death befriended his family. In 1848 he collected and arranged various papers relating to Keats, and published them as the 'Life and Letters' of the poet. Much of the material was presented to him by Keats's friend, Charles Armitage Brown [q. v.] The memoir, greatly abbreviated, was afterwards prefixed to an edition of Keats's poems, which Milnes issued in 1854. He also contributed several articles to the 'Edinburgh Review,' and took an interest in the management of the Royal Literary Fund.

On 30 July 1851 Milnes married the Hon. Annabel Crewe, younger daughter of the second Baron Crewe. They went to Vienna for the honeymoon, and proposed to visit Hungary; but the Austrian government refused the author of the pamphlet on the events of 1848 entrance into that kingdom. On his return Milnes resumed his literary work, and partly from disappointed expectations, partly from disagreement with either party, relinquished his practical interest in politics; he refused a lordship of the treasury offered him by Lord Palmerston, whom he now followed. He revised Gladstone's translation of Farini's 'History of the Roman State;' and in 1853 he and M. Van de Weyer, Belgian minister in London, established the Philobiblon Society, a small circle of eminent men at home and abroad, interested in rare books and manuscripts. Milnes edited its 'Transactions.' During the Crimean war he addressed meetings on behalf of Miss Nightingale's fund, and in September 1855 published in the 'Times' a poem on the English graves at Scutari. In 1857 he attended and spoke at the recently established Social Science Congress, over which he presided later on (1873) when it met at Norwich; and he warmly advocated the formation of mechanics' institutes and penny banks.

In July 1863 Milnes was at Palmerston's instance created Baron Houghton of Great Houghton, in the West Riding of Yorkshire. Differences of opinion respecting the pronunciation of his new name were commemorated in J. R. Planché's poem in 'Punch' (Locker-Lampson, *Lyra Elegantiarum*, 1891, p. 376). In the House of Lords Houghton spoke against the condemnation by convocation of 'Essays and Reviews,' and in aid of the movement for legalising marriage with a deceased wife's sister. He was one of the few peers who eagerly supported the reform of the franchise, which he advocated at a meeting at Leeds, and, with John Bright, at a banquet at Manchester. To a volume of 'Essays on Reform' (1867) he contributed an article on 'The Admission of the Working Classes as a part of the Social System.'

In 1866 he delivered the inaugural address at the opening of new rooms for the Cambridge Union Society. He was president of the group of liberal arts at the French Exhibition of 1867, when he spent some months in Paris, and met most of the leading statesmen of Europe. In 1869 he represented the Royal Geographical Society at the opening of the Suez Canal, and presented a report on his return. In 1873 he published, under the title 'Monographs,' interesting recollections of some friends, the Miss Berrys, Landor, Sydney Smith, Wiseman, and others; and in 1875 an edition of Peacock's novels, with a preface.

In his later years Houghton's social qualities were given the fullest play. Both at Fryston and in London, at 16 Upper Brook Street, he was constantly entertaining his distinguished friends; and he continued to relieve genius in distress. In 1860 he befriended David Gray [q. v.], and in 1862 wrote a preface to his poem 'The Luggie.' Milnes was also instrumental in making Mr. A. C. Swinburne known to the public, and he drew attention to 'Atalanta in Calydon' in the 'Edinburgh Review.' He knew every one of note, and was present at almost every great social gathering. In 1875 he visited Canada and the United States, where he met Longfellow, Emerson, Lowell, and was everywhere widely received by leading men, partly for the sympathy he had shown with the north during the civil war. Towards the close of his life, Houghton, already a fellow of the Royal Society, honorary D.C.L. of Oxford, and LL.D. of Edinburgh, became an honorary fellow of Trinity College, Cambridge, secretary for foreign correspondence in the Royal Academy, and a trustee of the British Museum. He succeeded Carlyle, who had been his lifelong friend, as president of the London Library in 1882. In May 1885 he took part in unveiling a bust of Coleridge in Westminster Abbey, and of Gray at Cambridge. His last speech was at a meeting of the short-lived Wordsworth Society in July. He died at Vichy on 11 Aug. 1885, and was buried at Fryston (20 Aug.) His wife predeceased him (Feb. 1874). He left two daughters and a son (created Earl of Crewe in 1895), who filled from 1892 high office in successive Liberal ministries.

Houghton abounded in friendliness, but his sympathies were broad rather than deep. Naturally generous and always ready to offer his help, he found a romantic pleasure of his own in giving it. His poetry is of the meditative kind, cultured and graceful; but it lacks fire. In society, where he found his chief occupation and success, especially as an after-dinner speaker, he was always amusing, and many stories were told of his humorous originality. But he was eminently a dilettante; while his interests were wide, he shirked the trouble necessary for judgments other than superficial. He had many fine tastes and some coarse ones.

Houghton's poetical works are: 1. 'Memorials of a Tour in some parts of Greece, chiefly Poetical,' London, 1834. 2. 'Memorials of a Residence on the Continent, and Historical Poems,' London, 1838, of which an enlarged edition appeared in 1844. 3. 'Poems of many Years,' London, 1838. 4. 'Poetry for the People, and other Poems,' London, 1840. 5. 'Poems, Legendary and Historical,' London, 1844, which included pieces previously published. 6. 'Palm Leaves,' London, 1844. He also issued several songs in single sheets. A collected edition in two volumes, with a preface and portrait, appeared in London in 1876.

His prose writings include, besides those noticed, pamphlets and articles in newspapers and reviews: 1. 'A Speech on the Ballot, delivered in the House of Commons,' London, 1839. 2. 'Thoughts on Purity of Election,' London, 1842. 3. 'Answer to R. Baxter on the South Yorkshire Isle of Axholme Bill,' Pontefract, 1852. 4. Preface to 'Another Version of Keats's "Hyperion,"' London, 1856. 5. 'Address on Social Economy' at the Social Science Congress, London, 1862. 6. 'On the present Social Results of Classical Education,' in F. W. Farrar's 'Essays on a Liberal Education,' London, 1867. He also edited various papers in the publications of the Philobiblon Society and the Grampian Club; and he wrote a preface to the 'History of Grillion's Club, from its Origin in 1812 to its 50th Anniversary,' London, 1880.

[The Life, Letters, and Friendships of Richard Monckton Milnes, first Lord Houghton, by T. Wemyss Reid, London, 1890, is a generous account of its subject. See also the Times, 12 Aug. 1885; and the Athenæum, Academy, and Saturday Review (art. by G. S. Venables) for 15 Aug. 1885; Sir F. H. Doyle's Reminiscences and Opinions, pp. 109 et seq., and the Correspondence of Carlyle and Emerson, London, 1883, i. 263.] T. B. S.

MILO OF GLOUCESTER. [See GLOUCESTER, MILES DE, EARL OF HEREFORD, *d.* 1143.]

MILRED or **MILRET** (*d.* 775), bishop of Worcester, was perhaps coadjutor bishop to Wilfrith, bishop of the Hwiccas, the people of the present Worcestershire and Gloucestershire (GREEN, *Making of England*, pp. 129, 130). His name appears as bishop along with that of Wilfrith in the attestation of a charter (*Codex Diplomaticus*, No. 95) of Ethelbald or Æthelbald (*d.* 757) [q. v.], king of the Mercians, and on the death of Wilfrith he succeeded to the see in 743 (FLORENCE, sub an.; 744 *A.-S. Chronicle*; 745 SYMEON, *Historia Regum*, c. 40, and HOVEDEN, i. 6). William of Malmesbury (*Gesta Pontificum*, p. 9) records his presence at the council of Clovesho held in 747. In 754, or early in 755, he visited Boniface, archbishop of Mentz, and Bishop Lullus in Germany, and on hearing less than a year afterwards of the martyrdom of Boniface (5 June 755), wrote to Lullus expressing his grief, and sending some small presents, but not sending a book ('librum pyrpyri metri'), for which Lullus had apparently asked, because Archbishop Cuthbert (*d.* 758) [q. v.] had delayed to return it (*Monumenta Moguntina*, pp. 267, 268). During the reign of Offa of Mercia Milred received many grants, some of which are historically important, as evidence of the absorption of small monasteries by episcopal churches, and of the growth alongside St. Peter's, the old cathedral church of Worcester, of the newer monastic foundation of St. Mary's, which afterwards became the church of the see (GREEN, *History and Antiquities of Worcester*, i. 24, 25; *Monasticon*, i. 567, and specially BISHOP STUBBS sub 'Milred,' ap. *Dictionary of Christian Biography*). Some of the following charters are marked as spurious by Kemble, but Bishop Stubbs considers that they represent actual grants. From Offa Milred received for himself as hereditary property land at Wick, 'to the west of the Severn' (*Codex Diplomaticus*, No. 126), and at 'Pirigtun' (*ib.* No. 129), and from Eanbert and his brothers, under-kings of the Hwiccas, lands for the church of St. Peter's (*ib.* No. 102); he attests a grant of Uhtred, one of these under-kings, in 770, giving Stoke in Worcestershire to the monastery of St. Mary's at Worcester (*ib.* No. 118), and another by which Uhtred gave lands on the Stour 'at the ford called Scepesuuasce (Sheepwash),' now Shipston in Worcestershire, to the same monastery (*ib.* No. 128). He also attests a grant by Abbot Ceolfrith, who had inherited his abbey or abbeys from his father Cynebert, of the monasteries of Heanburh or Hanbury, and Sture in Usmorn, now Kidderminster, in Worcestershire, to St. Peter's (*ib.* No. 127). A monastery had been founded at Withington in Gloucestershire by Oshere [q. v.] (comp. *ib.* No. 36), and had been left to his daughter, the abbess Hrothwara, who had made it over to Mildred. In 774 Milred made over this monastery to Æthelburga, an abbess who appears to have inherited from her father Alfred a monastery at Worcester, on condition that at her death these monasteries at Withington and Worcester should pass to the church of St. Peter (*ib.* No. 124). Milred died in 775 (FLORENCE; 772, *A.-S. Chronicle*), and was succeeded by Weremund.

[Kemble's Codex Dipl. i. 114, 123, 145, 152–155 (Engl. Hist. Soc.); A.-S. Chron. ann. 744, 772; Flor. Wig. ann. 743, 774 (Engl. Hist. Soc.); Will. of Malmesbury's Gesta Pontiff. p. 9 (Rolls Ser.); Mon. Moguntina, pp. 267, 268, ed. Jaffé; Symeon of Durham's Hist. Reg. ap. Op. ii. 39 (Rolls Ser.); Hoveden, i. 6 (Rolls Ser.); Green's Hist. and Antiq. of Worcester, i. 24, 25; Dugdale's Monasticon, i. 567; Bishop Stubbs's art. 'Milred' ap. Dict. Chr. Biog. iii. 915.]

W. H.

MILROY, GAVIN (1805–1886), medical writer and founder of the 'Milroy lectureship' at the Royal College of Physicians, was born in Edinburgh, where his father was in business, in 1805. He received his general education at the high school, and conducted his professional studies at the university. He became M.R.C.S. Edin. in June 1824, and M.D. Edin. in July 1828. He was one of the founders and active members of the Hunterian Society of Edinburgh, but soon settled as a general practitioner in London. He made a voyage as medical officer in the government packet service to the West Indies and the Mediterranean, and thenceforth chiefly devoted himself to writing for medical papers. From 1844 he was co-editor of Johnson's 'Medico-Chirurgical Review' till it was amalgamated with Forbes's 'British and Foreign Medical Review' in 1847. In October 1846 (iv. 285) he wrote in it an elaborate review on a French report on 'Plague and Quarantine,' by Dr. Prus (2 vols. 8vo, Paris, 1846), and published an abridged translation, with preface and notes, as 'Quarantine and the Plague,' 8vo, London, 1846. He recommended the mitigation or total abolition of quarantine, and at the same time the dependence on sanitary measures alone for preservation from foreign pestilences. He at once became an authority on all questions of epidemiology, and was employed in several government commissions of inspection and inquiry. In 1849–50 he was a superintendent medical inspector of the general board of health; in 1852 he was sent by the colonial office to Jamaica 'to inspect and report on the sanitary condition of that island,' and gave the results in an official report. During the Crimean war in 1855–6 he was a member of the sanitary commission sent out to the army in the east; and when the commission was recalled at the end of the war, Milroy joined Dr. John Sutherland [q. v.] in drawing up the report of its transactions. In 1858 he was honorary secretary of the committee appointed by the Social Science Association to inquire into the practice and results of quarantine, and the results of the inquiries were printed in three parliamentary papers. Milroy belonged to the Medical and Chirurgical Society, and took a very active part in the establishment and management of the Epidemiological Society. He was admitted a licentiate of the College of Physicians on 22 Dec. 1847, and was elected a fellow in 1853. In 1862 he was a member of a committee appointed by the college at the request of the colonial office for the purpose of collecting information on the subject of leprosy. The report was printed in 1867, and in the appendix (p. 230) are some brief and sensible 'Notes respecting the Leprosy of Scripture' by Milroy. He never received from government any permanent medical appointment, but a civil list pension of 100*l.* a year was granted him. In later life he lived at Richmond in Surrey, where he died 11 Jan. 1886, at the age of eighty-one. He was buried in Kensal Green cemetery. He survived his wife (Miss Sophia Chapman) about three years, and had no children. He was a modest, unassuming man, of sound judgment, and considerable intellectual powers. He was brought up as a member of the Scottish kirk, but in later years attended the services of the Anglican church. He left a legacy of 2,000*l.* to the London College of Physicians for the endowment of a lectureship on 'state medicine and public health, and subjects connected therewith,' with a memorandum of 'suggestions,' dated 14 Feb. 1879. At the present time (1893) the lectures are four in number, and the lecturer's honorarium is sixty-six guineas.

Milroy also wrote some articles on 'Sydenham' in the 'Lancet,' 1846–7; the article on 'Plague' in Reynolds's 'System of Medicine,' vol. i., and many other anonymous articles in the medical journals.

[Lancet, 27 Feb. 1886; Brit. Med. Journ. same date; family information; personal knowledge.]
W. A. G.

MILTON, Lord. [See Fletcher, Andrew, 1692–1766, lord justice clerk.]

MILTON, Sir CHRISTOPHER (1615–1693), judge, brother of the poet John Milton, being the younger son of John Milton, scrivener [q. v.], by Sarah Jeffrey, his wife, was born in Bread Street, London, November 1615, and educated at St. Paul's School and Christ's College, Cambridge, where he was admitted a pensioner on 15 Feb. 1630–1631. The same year he entered the Inner Temple, where, having left the university without a degree, he was called to the bar in 1639. At the outbreak of the civil war he resided at Reading, and by virtue of a commission under the great seal sequestered the estates of parliamentarians in three counties. After the surrender of Reading to the parliament (April 1643), he 'steered his course according to the motion of the king's army,' and was in Exeter during Fairfax's siege of that place. On its surrender in the spring of 1646, his town house, the Cross Keys, Ludgate, was sequestered, and he compounded for 80*l.*, a tenth of its value. Only a moiety of the composition, however, was paid by him, and inquiries, apparently ineffectual, were made for estates supposed to belong to him in Suffolk and Berkshire. During the Commonwealth his practice consisted chiefly of composition cases, among them that of his brother's mother-in-law, Mrs. Anne Powell. In November 1660 he was elected a bencher of the Inner Temple, where he was reader in the autumn of 1667. At the date of his brother's death, whose nuncupative will he attested (5 Dec. 1674), he was deputy-recorder of Ipswich. In later life he was, or professed to be, a Roman catholic, and accordingly, though no great lawyer, was raised by James II to the exchequer bench, 26 April 1686, being first invested with the coif (21 April), and knighted (25 April). His tenure of office was equally brief and undistinguished. On 16 April 1687 he was transferred to the common pleas, being dispensed from taking the oaths, and on 6 July 1688 he was discharged as superannuated, retaining his salary. He died in March 1692–3, and was buried (22 March) in the church of St. Nicholas, Ipswich. Besides his house at Ipswich he had a villa at Rushmere, about two miles from the town. He married, probably in 1638, Thomasine, daughter of William Webber of London, by whom he had issue a son, who died in infancy in March 1639; another, Thomas, sometime deputy-clerk of the crown in chancery; and three daughters, Sarah, Mary, and Catherine.

[John Milton's note on the flyleaf of his Bible, Addit. MS. 32310; Addit. MS. 24501, ff. 12, 23; Gardiner's Reg. of St. Paul's School; Phillips's Life of Milton prefixed to Letters of State written by Mr. John Milton, London, 1694, 12mo; Papers relating to Milton (Camd. Soc.); Chetham Miscellanies (Chetham Soc.), vol. i. (Milton Papers), p. 38; Le Neve's Pedigrees of Knights (Harl. Soc.); Inner Temple Books; Dugdale's Orig. p. 169; London Gazette, April 1686 and 1687; Sir John Bramston's Autobiog. (Camd. Soc.); Skinner's Reports, pp. 251–2; Luttrell's Relation of State Affairs, i. 375, 449; Evelyn's Diary, 2 June 1686; Todd's Milton, i. 257–9; Masson's Life of Milton, vi. 727, 761–2; Foss's Lives of the Judges.] J. M. R.

MILTON, JOHN, the elder (1563?–1647), musician, father of the poet, born about 1563, was son of Richard Milton of Stanton St. John, near Oxford (Masson). The Miltons were catholics of the yeoman class, and according to one account Richard was an 'under-ranger' of Shotover Forest (Wood); he was a staunch catholic, and was fined as a recusant in 1601. John was educated at Christ Church, Oxford, where he was perhaps a chorister (*Notes and Queries*, 6th ser. i. 115, 259), and while there embraced protestantism, to the annoyance of his father, who promptly disinherited him. Milton, on leaving Oxford, went to London 'to seek in a manner his fortune' (Wood). After trying various means of gaining a livelihood, he adopted, in 1595, the profession of a scrivener, and on 27 Feb. 1599–1600 was admitted to the Company of Scriveners. About 1600 he started business for himself in Bread Street, Cheapside, at the sign of the Spread Eagle, the family arms; and about the same time married Sarah, daughter of Paul Jeffrey, merchant taylor of St. Swithin's, London; she was about nine years his junior (Masson). Aubrey's statement that her maiden name was Bradshaw, and her grandson Edward Phillips's remark that she was 'of the family of the Castons,' were disproved by Colonel Chester the genealogist (cf. Stern, *Milton und seine Zeit*, i. 345–8). Milton's business prospered rapidly, and in the end he had a 'plentiful estate' (Aubrey). He died in March 1647, and was buried 15 March at St. Giles's, Cripplegate. Of six children, three survived infancy, viz. Anne—by whose first husband, Edward Phillips, she was mother of Edward Phillips (1630–1698) [q. v.] and of John Phillips (*fl.* 1700) [q. v.]—John the poet [q. v.], and Christopher [q. v.] the judge. The poet says that his mother was well known in her neighbourhood for her charities (*Defensio secunda*); she died on 3 April 1637.

Milton, who was a man of high character and a fair scholar, had a special faculty for music, to the practice of which he devoted his leisure. He had an organ and other instruments in his house. His musical abilities are celebrated by his son in a Latin poem, 'Ad Patrem.' To Morley's 'Triumphes of Oriana,' London, 1601 (reprinted by William Hawes 1815), he contributed a six-part madrigal (No. 18), 'Fayre Oriana in the Morne;' and to Leighton's 'Teares or Lamentacions of a Sorrowfull Soule,' London, 1614, four motets, specimens of which are printed by Hawkins and Burney. Ravenscroft's 'Whole Booke of Psalmes,' London, 1621, contains, among other melodies ascribed to him, the commonmetre tune 'York,' once immensely popular (see Hawkins) and still widely used. The melody is, however, probably not his own invention. The tunes in Ravenscroft are described as being 'composed into four parts'—i.e. harmonised—and as 'York' was so treated by one Simon Stubbs, as well as by Milton, the former might share the authorship (cf. Love). He is said (Phillips) to have composed an 'In nomine' in forty parts, for which he received a gold chain and medal from a Polish prince, to whom he presented it. A sonnet in his honour, written by John Lane [q. v.] (Harl. MS. 5243), is printed by Masson and others.

[Masson's Life of Milton and generally the other biographical works cited under Milton, John, poet; Wood's Athenæ Oxonienses; Godwin's Lives of Edward and John Phillips, with Aubrey's Sketch; Milton Papers, edited by John Fitchett Marsh (Chetham Soc.); Athenæum and Notes and Queries, 19 March 1859; Grove's Dict. of Music; Hawkins's and Burney's Histories of Music; Parr's Church of England Psalmody; Love's Scottish Church Music, p. 250.]

J. C. H.

MILTON, JOHN (1608–1674), poet, born 9 Dec. 1608 at the house of his father, John Milton [see under Milton, John, the elder], scrivener, in Bread Street, Cheapside. The child was christened at Allhallows Church, destroyed in the fire of 1666. A tablet to commemorate the fact, erected in the nineteenth century in the new church, was removed, upon the demolition of that church in 1876, to Bow Church, Cheapside. Milton was a beautiful boy, as appears from a portrait taken when he was ten years old, and soon showed remarkable literary promise. His father (who himself instructed him in music, and, according to Aubrey, made him a skilful organist) had him taught by a private tutor, Thomas Young [q. v.], a Scottish clergyman, afterwards a well-known presbyterian divine, who became in 1644 master of Jesus College, Cambridge. Milton was also sent to St. Paul's School, not later than 1620. Alexander Gill the elder [q. v.] was head-master, and his son, Alexander Gill the younger [q. v.], became assistant-master in 1621. Milton took to study passionately. He seldom left his lessons for bed till midnight, a practice which produced frequent headaches, and, as he thought, was the first cause of injury to his eyes. Besides Latin and Greek, he appears to have learnt French, Italian, and some Hebrew (see his *Ad Patrem*), and had read much English literature. He was a poet, says Aubrey, from the age of ten. Spenser's 'Faery Queen' and Sylvester's translation of Du Bartas were among his favourites. Two paraphrases of Psalms were written when he was fifteen. He became intimate with the younger Gill, and made a closer friendship with Charles Diodati, a schoolfellow of his own age, son of a physician of Italian origin, and a nephew of John Diodati, a famous theologian at Geneva. With Charles Diodati, who entered Trinity College, Oxford, in February 1622–3, Milton kept up an affectionate correspondence.

Milton was admitted as a pensioner of Christ's College, Cambridge, on 12 Feb. 1624–5, and was matriculated on 9 April following. His tutor was William Chappell [q. v.], famous for his skill in disputation, who was afterwards promoted by Laud's favour to the bishopric of Cork. Milton's rooms at Christ's College are still pointed out on the first floor of the western staircase on the north side of the great court. Wordsworth paid his respects to the place, drinking, for once, till he was 'dizzy' (see the *Prelude*, bk. iii.) Milton kept every term at Cambridge until he graduated as M.A. 3 July 1632. He took his B.A. degree 26 March 1629. Rumours of some disgrace in his university career were spread by some of his opponents in later years. Aubrey says that Chappell showed him 'some unkindness,' above which in the original manuscript is the interlineation 'whipt him.' This 'whipping' was accepted by Johnson, and the practice of flogging, though declining, was not yet obsolete. In a Latin epistle to Diodati, probably (see Masson, i. 161) of the spring of 1626, Milton speaks of the harsh threats of a master:—

Cæteraque ingenio non subeunda meo.

Milton clearly had some quarrel with Chappell, and had to leave Cambridge for a time, though without losing his term. He was then transferred from the tutorship of Chappell to that of Nathaniel Tovey.

In replying to the attacks upon him Milton was able to assert that he had been esteemed above his equals by the fellows of the college, and that they had been anxious that he should continue in residence after he had taken his M.A. degree. His biographers, Aubrey and Wood, speak of the respect paid to his abilities. Milton while at college corresponded with Diodati, Gill, and his old preceptor, Young, in Latin prose and verse. He wrote some Latin poems upon events at the university and on the Gunpowder plot, and seven 'Prolusiones Oratoriæ' (published in 1674) were originally pronounced as exercises in the schools and in college. One of them, given in the college hall in 1628, was originally concluded by the address to his native language in English. Milton wrote the copy of Latin verses distributed, according to custom, at the commencement of 1628. He had also written some English poems, the sonnet to Shakespeare (1630, first published in the second folio, 1632, of Shakespeare), that 'On having arrived at the Age of Twenty-three' (1631), the clumsy attempt at humour upon the death of the carrier Thomas Hobson [q. v.], and the noble 'Ode on the Nativity' (Christmas, 1629), in which his characteristic majesty of style first appears, although marred by occasional conceits. Milton (*Apology for Smectymnuus*) speaks with great contempt of dramatic performances which he had heard at the university, and (letter to Gill, 2 July 1628) expresses his scorn for the narrow theological studies of his companions, and their ignorance of philosophy.

Milton was nicknamed the 'lady' at college, from his delicate complexion and slight make. He was, however, a good fencer, and thought himself a 'match for any one.' Although respected by the authorities, his proud and austere character probably kept him aloof from much of the coarser society of the place. He shared the growing aversion to the scholasticism against which one of his exercises is directed. Like Henry More, who entered Christ's in Milton's last year, he was strongly attracted by Plato, although he was never so much a philosopher as a poet. He already considered himself as dedicated to the utterance of great thoughts, and to the strictest chastity and self-respect, on the ground that he who would 'write well hereafter in laudable things ought himself to be a true poem' (*Apology for Smectymnuus*). Milton's father had retired by 1632 from an active share in his business. He had handed this over to a partner, John Bower, and retired to a house at Horton, Buckinghamshire, a village near Colnbrook. Milton had been educated with a view to taking orders, and a letter (now in Trinity College Library), ending with the sonnet upon completing his twenty-third year, gives reasons for postponing but not for abandoning his intention. He was, however, alienated by the church policy which became dominant under Laud, and says, in 1641 (*Reasons of Church Government*), that he was unwilling to take the necessary oaths, and was (in this sense) 'church-outed by the prelates.' There are slight indications that he thought of studying law (Masson, i. 327), but he soon abandoned this and resolved to devote himself exclusively to literature. His style, 'by certain vital signs it had, was likely to live,' he says, and in the Latin epistle 'Ad Patrem,' probably written about this time, he thanks his father for consenting to his plans. Milton therefore settled with his father at Horton for nearly six years—July 1632 to April 1638. The house is said by Todd to have been pulled down about 1795. Tradition says that it was on the site of Byrken manor-house, near the church. Milton frequently visited London, eighteen miles distant, to take lessons in mathematics and music. He read the classical writers, and studied Greek and Italian history (to C. Diodati, 23 Sept. 1637), and he wrote poems already displaying his full powers. The 'Allegro' and 'Penseroso,' the most perfect record in the language of the impression made by natural scenery upon a thorough scholar, were probably (Masson, i. 589) written in 1632. The Countess-dowager of Derby, who had been the wife of Ferdinando, fifth earl of Derby, and afterwards of Thomas Egerton, lord Ellesmere [q. v.], was living at Harefield, near Uxbridge. Her family presented a masque before her in 1633, or possibly in 1634, for which Lawes composed the music and Milton the words, afterwards published as 'Arcades.' Milton's acquaintance with Henry Lawes [q. v.] was probably the cause of his employment, as no other connection with the Egerton family is known. John Egerton, first earl of Bridgewater [q. v.], the stepson, and also son-in-law of the Dowager-countess of Derby, had been appointed in 1631 president of the council of Wales. He went to his official residence at Ludlow Castle in 1633, and in Sept. 1634 his family performed the masque of 'Comus' in the hall of the castle, Milton and Lawes being again the composers (cf. SIR FREDERICK BRIDGE'S *Comus: the original music*, 1908). This noble poem was appreciated at the time. Lawes received so many applications for copies that he published it (without Milton's name) in 1634. The last of the great poems of his youthful period, 'Lycidas,' was written in Nov. 1637, on the death of Edward King (1612–1637) [q. v.], for the collection of poems published by King's friends at Cambridge in 1638. The poetry already written by Milton would by itself entitle him to the front rank in our literature, and has a charm of sweetness which is absent from the sublimer and sterner works of his later years. The famous apostrophe of St. Peter in 'Lycidas' shows his growing interest in theological controversy.

Milton's mother died on 3 April 1637, and was buried in the chancel of Horton Church. The elder Milton was at the same time charged by a client with misconduct in respect of funds trusted to him for investment. A lawsuit ended on 1 Feb. 1637–8 by an order of court completely exonerating him from all charges (MASSON, i. 627–38, 661). Milton now obtained his father's consent to a journey abroad. His brother Christopher, who had followed him to St. Paul's School and Christ's College, was now a law student; he married about this time, and was probably resident at Horton during the elder brother's absence. Milton took a servant, and the expense of a year abroad, as calculated by Howell at the time, would be not under 300*l.* for a well-to-do traveller and 50*l.* for his servant. As Milton had no means of his own, his father must have been both able and willing to be liberal. Milton started in April 1638; he made a short stay in Paris, where, according to Wood, he disliked 'the manners and genius' of the place; he travelled to Nice; went by sea to Genoa and to Leghorn, and thence by Pisa to Florence, where he stayed two months, probably August and September. About the end of September he went to Rome and spent two months there. He then went to Naples and heard news of the Scottish troubles, which determined him to return, lest, as he said, he should be travelling abroad while his countrymen were fighting for liberty. He made a second stay at Rome, spent two more months in Florence (where he was present in March 1639), and thence went to Venice by Bologna and Ferrara. From Venice he sent home a collection of books and music. He left Italy by Verona, Milan, and the Pennine Alps, probably the Simplon. He spent some time at Geneva, where he was present (as appears from an autograph in an album) on 10 July 1639; and thence returned by Paris, reaching England about the end of July 1639, after fifteen months' absence. (The dates are fixed by the short account of his travels in the 'Defensio Secunda' and references in his 'Occasional Poems and Epistles.')

Milton declares his freedom from all vice during his foreign journey. His statement is confirmed by a letter of Nicholas Heinsius written from Venice 27 Feb. 1652–3, on occasion of Milton's controversy with Salmasius. Heinsius says that Milton had offended the Italians by his strict morality and by his outspoken attacks on popery (in P. BURMANN'S *Sylloge Epistolarum*). His reception by distinguished persons indicates the impression made upon his contemporaries by his lofty character, prepossessing appearance, and literary culture. Lawes had obtained a passport for him. Sir Henry Wotton, then provost of Eton, and his neighbour at Horton, sent him a friendly letter on his departure, thanking him for a gift of 'Comus,' and giving his favourite piece of advice, 'I pensieri stretti ed il viso sciolto.' Wotton added a letter of introduction; and by others he was introduced to Lord Scudamore, the English ambassador in Paris. Scudamore introduced him to Grotius, then Queen Christina's ambassador, who, according to Phillips, received him kindly. At Florence Milton was received with singular warmth. He was welcomed by the members of all the popular academies, of which he speaks with the enthusiasm of gratitude. The chief among them were Jacopo Gaddi, Carlo Date, Agostino Colsellino, Benedetto Bonmattei, and Antonio Malatesti (see extracts from the 'pastorals' of the Academy of the Svogliati in STERN, bk. ii. p. 499). A reference in the 'Areopagitica' tells how they complained to him of the tyranny over freedom of speech exercised by the Inquisition. He read Latin poems at their meetings, and was repaid by complimentary effusions given in his subsequent collections of poems (for the history of a manuscript given by Malatesti to Milton, containing some equivocal sonnets, which was afterwards in possession of Thomas Hollis, see MASSON, i. 786–7 *n.*) At Florence Milton, as he states in the 'Areopagitica,' saw Galileo. References in 'Paradise Lost' (i. 287–91, v. 262) also indicate the impression made upon Milton by this interview; and the noble lines upon Vallombrosa commemorate a visit of which there was said to be some tradition at the convent (WORDSWORTH's poem, *At Vallombrosa*, 1837; works by KNIGHT, vi. 82). Two Latin letters written by Milton to the convent had been shown at Vallombrosa a 'few years ago' in 1877 (*Notes and Queries*, 5th ser. viii. 117). At Rome Milton's chief association was apparently with Lucas Holsten or Holstenius, librarian of the Vatican, who had lived at Oxford, and afterwards became a convert to catholicism. Holstenius showed him collections of books and manuscripts, and introduced him to his patron, Cardinal Barberini. Milton attended a concert at Barberini's palace, and there probably heard the great singer, Leonora Baroni, to whom he addressed three Latin epigrams. At Naples Milton was introduced by 'a certain eremite,' with whom he had travelled from Rome, to the aged Manso, formerly the patron of Tasso and Marini. To Manso he addressed an epistle in Latin hexameters, and received in acknowledgment two richly worked cups (described in his 'Epitaphium Damonis'). Manso, says Milton, excused himself for not showing more attentions on account of his guest's freedom in conversations upon religion. Milton was afterwards told that the English jesuits at Rome intended to lay snares for him upon the same ground. He determined, however, to speak freely if he should be attacked, and, though carrying out his resolution, was not molested. Milton wrote five Italian sonnets and a canzone, professing love to a beautiful Italian lady of Bologna, which from the allusions to the scenery are supposed to have been written during his visit to that place in the spring of 1639. One of them, however, is addressed to Charles Diodati, who died in August 1638, but it is possible that Milton may not have heard of his loss. Nothing further is known of the lady, whom Warton arbitrarily identified with the singer Leonora; and they are chiefly remarkable as proofs of Milton's facility in writing Italian, although not without occasional slips of grammar and idiom (MASSON, i. 826–7 *n.*)

Milton soon after his return to England took lodgings at a tailor's house in St. Bride's Churchyard. His sister, Mrs. Phillips, had lost her husband in 1631, and afterwards married Thomas Agar, who had succeeded her first husband as secondary in the crown office. She had two sons by her first marriage: Edward, aged about nine, and John, a year younger, who now became pupils of their uncle, the youngest being 'wholly committed to his charge.' After a short stay in lodgings, where he had no room for his books, he took a 'pretty garden-house' in Aldersgate Street, then, says Phillips, one of the quietest streets in London. Professor Masson (ii. 207) thinks that it was near Golden Lion Court. The elder nephew now came to board with him also, and the household became an example of 'hard study and spare diet.' Once a month or so he allowed himself a 'gaudy day,' with some 'beaux of these times,' but otherwise he devoted himself to carrying out the system of education described in his treatise on that subject (letter to Hartlib, published in June 1644). He gives a portentous list of books to be read; and his pupils are to be trained in athletic and military sports, and in poetry and philosophy, besides obtaining a vast amount of useful knowledge so far as such knowledge is accessible through classical authors. Phillips gives some account of his practice. In 1643 he began to take more pupils. Meanwhile he was busy with literary projects. The 'Epitaphium Damonis,' written soon after his return, commemorates, in the form of a pastoral idyll in Latin hexameters, his grief for the loss of Diodati, and incidentally states the resolution, to which he adhered, of henceforth writing in the vernacular. He sketches the plan of an heroic poem upon Arthur. A notebook, now in the library of Trinity College, Cambridge, gives a list of ninety-nine subjects for poems extracted from scripture and English history. Four drafts show that he was already contemplating a poem on 'Paradise Lost,' which was, however, to be in the form of the Greek tragedy. The other subjects are more briefly noticed, and probably few of them occupied his attention for more than the moment. A passage in his 'Reason of Church-Government' (1641) describes his meditations upon some great moral and religious poem, the poem and topic being still undecided (for the reasons for assigning the date of about 1640 to these jottings see MASSON, ii. 121).

Milton's attention was soon diverted from poetry to ecclesiastical disputes. The meeting of the Long parliament in November 1640 was the signal for urgent attacks upon the episcopacy. Numerously signed petitions were followed by proceedings in parliament, and accompanied by a shower of books and pamphlets. The chief champion of episcopacy was Joseph Hall [q. v.], bishop of Exeter, who had published in the previous February a defence of the 'Divine Right of Episcopacy,' and now (January 1640–1) brought out a 'Humble Remonstrance' to parliament. He was opposed by the five ministers whose united initials formed the name Smectymnuus. Their book appeared in March. Hall replied in April by a 'Defence' of the 'Remonstrance,' and also persuaded Archbishop Ussher to publish (in May) a short tract entitled 'The Judgment of Doctor Rainoldes,' supporting a qualified version of the episcopal theory. Smectymnuus rejoined in June by a 'Vindication' of the previous book. Professor Masson thinks, on rather slight grounds, that Milton had some hand in this 'Vindication' (Masson, ii. 260).

One of the Smectymnuan divines was Thomas Young, Milton's old teacher. Milton now supported Smectymnuus in three pamphlets. The first, 'Of Reformation touching Church Discipline in England' (May – June 1641), vehemently attacked episcopacy upon historical grounds. The second, on 'Prelatical Episcopacy' (June–July), was a reply to Ussher. The third, 'Animadversions upon the Remonstrance Defence' (July), was a fierce attack upon Hall's last book, from which a series of passages were cited, with a bitter comment appended to each. These writings were all anonymous, though no secret was made of the authorship. In February 1641–2 Milton published, under his own name, a pamphlet called 'The Reason of Church-Government urged against Prelacy,' containing an elaborate argument upon general grounds, and including, after his custom, a remarkable autobiographical statement (at the beginning of the second book). The argument refers partly to a collection of seven tracts upon the episcopal side, published in 1641 as 'Certaine Briefe Treatises.' Meanwhile Hall, after a 'Short Answer' to the Smectymnuus in the autumn of 1641, left Milton's animadversions unnoticed till in the beginning of 1642 he issued a 'Modest Confutation of a Slanderous and Scurrilous Libel.' This pamphlet seems to have been the joint work of Hall and his son Robert, a canon of Exeter and a Cambridge man, two years older than Milton. They had made inquiries as to Milton's character, and the result appeared in much personal abuse. To this Milton replied by an 'Apology' (about April 1642), defending himself, attacking the bishops, and savagely reviling Hall, with frequent references to his enemy's early satires and other questionable writings. This ended Milton's share in the discussion. The pamphlets are characteristic, though not now easily readable. They breathe throughout a vehemence of passion which distorts the style, perplexes the argument, and disfigures his invective with unworthy personalities. His characteristic self-assertion, however, acquires dignity from his genuine conviction that he is dedicated to the loftiest purposes; and in his autobiographical and some other passages he rises to an eloquence rarely approached, and shows the poet of 'Paradise Lost' struggling against the trammels of prose. The ecclesiastical doctrine shows that he was at this time inclined to presbyterianism (see Masson, ii. 229, 239, 249, 361, 398, for dates of his pamphlets).

The outbreak of the civil war at the end of 1642 did not induce Milton to enter the army. He says himself (*Defensio Secunda*) that as his mind had always been stronger than his body, he did not court camps in which any common person would have been as useful as himself. Professor Masson thinks, but upon apparently very inadequate grounds, that he had practised himself in military exercises (Masson, ii. 402, 473–81), and Phillips gives an obviously incredible report that there was a design for making him adjutant-general in Waller's army. The expected assault on the city when the king's army was at Brentford in 1642 occasioned Milton's sonnet, which decidedly claims a peaceful character. Meanwhile his father and his brother Christopher had removed to Reading, which was taken by the Earl of Essex in April 1643. About Whitsuntide (21 May 1643) Milton took a journey into the country, assigning no reason, and came back with a wife (Phillips). She was Mary, eldest daughter of Richard Powell of Forest Hill, near Shotover, Oxfordshire. Powell had bought an estate at Forest Hill about 1621. He had also a small estate at Wheatley, valued at 40*l*. a year. Altogether he had about 300*l*. a year, but with many encumbrances. Mary (baptised 24 Jan. 1625) was the third of eleven children, and Powell appears to have been a jovial and free-living cavalier. Forest Hill was in the neighbourhood in which Milton's ancestors had lived, and with which the descendants possibly kept up some connection. For some unknown reason Powell had in 1627 acknowledged a debt of 312*l*. to Milton, who was then an undergraduate, and this debt, among others, was still undischarged. There are no other traces of previous familiarity to explain Milton's sudden journey into a royalist district and his return with a bride of seventeen. Milton's father, dislodged from Reading, came to live with him at the time of his marriage, and some of his wife's family paid him a visit, when there were 'feastings for some days.' The wife soon found the house dull after the gaiety of her father's home; there was no society; the nephews (says Aubrey) were often beaten and crying, and Milton discovered that his bride was stupid. She returned to her father's house after trying 'a philosophical life' for a month, with the understanding, however, that she was to return at Michaelmas. Phillips says that as Mrs. Milton did not come back at the appointed time Milton sent a messenger to her home. The family, who disliked the connection with a puritan and were encouraged by the prosperity of the royalist cause, sent back the messenger 'with some sort of contempt' ('evilly entreated' him, as Aubrey thinks). Milton was so indignant that he resolved never to take her back, and proceeded to write his book upon divorce. Professor Masson, however, has pointed out that Thomason, the collector of the king's pamphlets in the British Museum, has marked a copy of this with the date 'Aug. 1st,' that is, 1 Aug. 1643. Unless, therefore, there is some mistake, Milton must have written and published the pamphlet within less than three months of his marriage, and, since his wife came to London (by Phillips's account) in June and stayed there a month, almost by the time of her departure. It is impossible to reconcile this with the circumstantial and apparently authentic story about the messenger; but, on the other hand, there is no reason for suspecting Thomason's date. Milton's pamphlet is sufficient to show that the ground of quarrel was some profound sense of personal incompatibility, and not any external quarrel. Such a piece of literary work during a honeymoon, however, is so strange that some very serious cause must be supposed. Pattison sanctions the conjecture, supported by a passage in the pamphlet, that the bride may have refused to Milton the rights of a husband.

However this may be, Milton's indignation took the form, usual to him, of seeing in his particular case the illustration of a general principle to be enunciated in the most unqualified terms. His 'doctrine and discipline of divorce' supports the thesis that 'indisposition, unfitness, or contrariety of mind arising from a cause in nature unchangeable . . . is a greater reason of divorce than natural frigidity, especially if there be no children or that there be mutual consent.' He asserts this doctrine in his usual passionate style, and appeals to the highest moral principles in its support. He looks at the matter entirely from the husband's point of view, is supremely indifferent to all practical difficulties, and proposes, by a sweeping reform of the marriage law, to 'wipe away ten thousand tears out of the life of men.' The pamphlet attracted notice. Howell calls its author a 'shallow-pated puppy' (*Familiar Letters*, bk. iv. letter 7). Hall was amazed to find that so able an author was serious in so monstrous a scheme; and the clergy began to attack him. He thereupon brought out a second edition with his name to it (2 Feb. 1643-4). It contained many additions, including the striking passage of the myth of Anteros.

Milton's views upon divorce made him notorious, and he is mentioned by the various writers against the sects, whose multiplication was a significant sign of the times, as in Ephraim Paget's 'Heresiography' and Thomas Edwards's 'Gangræna.' Edwards tells the story of a Mrs. Attaway who left her 'unsanctified' husband to take up with a preacher, and justified her conduct by Milton's book. On 15 July 1644 Milton published a second pamphlet, 'The Judgment of Martin Bucer on Divorce,' justifying himself by the authority of the reformer, and appealing for parliamentary support. Soon afterwards Herbert Palmer, a divine of the Westminster Assembly, declared, in a sermon preached before parliament on a solemn fast-day (13 Aug. 1644), that Milton's book ought to be burnt. The presbyterians were denouncing toleration and demanding a general suppression of sects. Their demands were universally supported by the Stationers' Company. The licensing system had broken down in the confusion of the civil troubles and under the pressure of all kinds of publications. The Stationers' Company complained, not only on account of the character of many of the pamphlets, but because their copyrights were frequently disregarded. They petitioned the House of Commons, which (26 Aug. 1644) directed that 'an ordinance' should be prepared, and meanwhile directed a search for the authors and printers of Milton's pamphlet 'concerning divorce.' An ordinance had already been passed a year before (June 1643), and Milton had disregarded its regulations and published the divorce pamphlets, like their predecessors, without license. Although the new ordinance was passed (1 Oct. 1644), no further notice was taken of Milton in the commons. Milton, however, was led by these attacks to write his 'Areopagitica,' which appeared on 24 Nov. 1644. The book is directly devoted to the question of unlicensed prints, and though in favour of such toleration as was then practicable, he makes some reserves in his application of the principle. The right of the 'Areopagitica' to rank as the best, as it is clearly the most popular, of Milton's prose works, has been disputed by the jealous admirers of others. The popularity, no doubt due in part to the subject, is also to be ascribed to the greater equability and clearness of the style. If he does not soar to quite such heights, there are fewer descents and contortions, and it remains at a high level of lofty eloquence. In the following December the House of Lords, in the course of some proceedings about an alleged libel, were invited by the wardens of the Stationers' Company to examine Milton. An examination was ordered accordingly, but nothing more is said of it. Milton ended his writings upon divorce by two more pamphlets, both published 4 March 1644–5—the 'Tetrachordon,' a 'proof' that the four chief passages in the Bible which relate to divorce confirm his views; and the 'Colasterion,' intended as a castigation of Joseph Caryl [q. v.], who had licensed an anonymous answer, with an expression of approval of the anonymous answerer himself, and (briefly) of Prynne, who had attacked him in 'twelve considerable serious queries.'

A third edition of the treatise on divorce appeared in 1645. Milton, according to Phillips, was proposing to apply his principles by marrying the daughter of a Dr. Davis, who was handsome and witty, but 'averse to this motion.' After the separation Milton, as Phillips says, had frequented the house of Lady Margaret Ley, now married to a Colonel Hobson. His fine sonnet to Lady Margaret commemorates this friendship, and that addressed to a 'virtuous' (and unmarried) 'young lady' shows that he saw some female society.

Meanwhile the ruin of the royal cause had brought the Powells into distress, and they desired to restore his real wife to Milton. They introduced her to the house of a Mr. Blackborough, a relative and neighbour of Milton, and when he paid his usual visit his wife was suddenly brought to him. She begged pardon on her knees, and, after some struggle, he consented to receive her again. Passages in 'Samson Agonistes' (725–47) and 'Paradise Lost' (bk. x. 937–46) may be accepted as autobiographical reminiscences of his resentment and relenting. She came to him in a new house in the Barbican (now destroyed by a railway), which was larger than that in Aldersgate Street, and therefore more convenient for an increased number of pupils, who were now being pressed upon him. His first child, Anne, was born on 29 July 1646; his second, Mary, on 25 Oct. 1648; his third, John (died in infancy), on 16 March 1650–1; and his last daughter, Deborah, on 2 May 1652. His wife died in the same year, probably from the effects of her last confinement.

The surrender of Oxford on 24 June 1646 completed the ruin of the Powells. Powell, already deeply in debt, had surrendered his estate to Sir Robert Pye, to whom it had been mortgaged. The moveable property had been sold under a sequestration, and the timber granted to the parishioners by the House of Commons (Masson, iii. 473 seq., 487). It seems probable that the transaction with Pye involved some friendly understanding, as the Powells subsequently regained the estate. Powell, with his wife and some of his children, came to live with Milton and arrange for a composition. He had hardly completed the arrangement when he died, 1 Jan. 1646–7, leaving a will which proves that his affairs were hopelessly confused, though there were hopes of saving something. Mrs. Powell, who administered to the will, her eldest son declining, left Milton's house soon afterwards (*ib.* pp. 632–40). She continued to prosecute her claims, which were finally settled in February 1650–1. In the result Milton, in consideration of the old debt from Powell, and 1,000*l.* which had been promised with his wife, had an 'extent' upon the Wheatley estate, valued after the war at 80*l.* a year, but had to pay Powell's composition, fixed at 130*l.*, and also paid Mrs. Powell's jointure of 26*l.* 13*s.* 4*d.* a year (*ib.* iv. 81, 236–46). Disputes arose upon this, in the course of which Mrs. Powell said that Milton was a 'harsh, choleric man,' and referred to his turning her daughter out of doors. She found the allowance insufficient for eight children. Milton was apparently willing to pay, but differed as to the way in which it was to be charged to the estate (see *ib.* iii. 632–40, iv. 145–6, 236–46, 336–41, and Hamilton's *Original Papers*). Milton's father died on 15 March 1646–7, and was buried in the chancel of St. Giles's, Cripplegate. His brother Christopher, who had also taken the royalist side, had to compound, and was in difficulties for some years (Masson, iii. 633). A sonnet addressed to Lawes, dated 9 Feb. 1645–6, and a later correspondence with one of his Italian friends, Carlo Dati, suggest some literary occupation at this time (for the Dati correspondence see the *Milton Papers* printed for the Chetham Society in 1851 by Mr. J. F. Marsh of Warrington, from manuscripts in his possession). The first edition of his collected poems was published in 1645, the English and Latin being separately paged. An ugly portrait by William Marshall is prefixed, under which Milton, with ingenious malice, got the artist to engrave some Greek verses ridiculing it as a caricature. Sonnets written just after this express the antipathy with which he now regarded the presbyterians.

In 1647 the number of Milton's pupils had slightly increased, according to Phillips. Phillips, however, is anxious to explain that he was not a professional schoolmaster. He was only persuaded to impart learning to the sons of some intimate friends. Among his pupils were Cyriac Skinner, grandson by his mother of Sir Edward Coke, and the second Earl of Barrymore, son of Lady Ranelagh, the elder and attached sister of Robert Boyle, well known to literary circles in London, and afterwards a friend of Milton. She also sent to him her nephew, Richard Jones, afterwards first earl Ranelagh [q. v.] In the autumn of 1647, however, Milton moved to a small house in High Holborn, opening at the back into Lincoln's Inn Fields. He gave up teaching, and as, in spite of the many claims upon him, he was able to dispense with this source of income, it may be inferred that he had inherited a competence from his father.

Milton fully sympathised with the army in their triumph over the parliamentary and presbyterian party. His feelings are expressed in the sonnet to Fairfax upon the siege of Colchester (August 1648). About the same time he was composing his doggerel version of the Psalms, of which he turned eight into rhyme in 1648, adding nine more in 1653. He also employed himself upon compiling the 'History of Britain,' of which he had written four books (*Defensio Secunda*). He was recalled to public affairs by the events which led to the execution of Charles I. Immediately after the king's death appeared his 'Tenure of Kings and Magistrates' (13 Feb. 1648-9), an argument in favour of the right of the people to judge their rulers. The newly formed council of state invited Milton directly afterwards to become their Latin secretary. He accepted the offer at once, and was sworn in on 15 March 1648-9. His salary was 15*s.* 10½*d.* a day (or 289*l.* 14*s.* 4½*d.* a year). The chief secretary received about 730*l.* a year. Milton's chief duty was to translate foreign despatches into dignified Latin. He was employed, however, upon a number of other tasks, which are fully indicated by the extract from the 'Proceedings of the Council' given in Professor Masson's book. He was concerned in the various dealings of the government with the press; he had to examine papers seized upon suspected persons; to arrange for the publication of answers to various attacks, and to write answers himself. He also appears as licensing the official 'Mercurius Politicus,' of which Marchmont Needham [q. v.] was the regular writer. Needham became 'a crony' according to Wood, and during 1651 Milton superintended the paper, and may probably have inspired some articles. Stern (bk. iii. 287-297) gives a previously unpublished correspondence of Milton in his official capacity with Mylius, envoy from Oldenburg. By order of the House of Commons he appended 'Observations' to the 'Articles of Peace' between Ormonde and the Irish, published 16 May 1649. He was directed also to answer the 'Eikon Basilike,' written, as is now known, by John Gauden [q. v.], and published 9 Feb. 1648-9. Milton's 'Eikonoklastes,' the answer in question, appeared 6 Oct. 1649, a work as tiresome as the original, and, like Milton's controversial works in general, proceeding by begging the question. By the council's order a French translation of the 'Eikonoklastes' by John Durie (1596-1680) [q. v.] was published in 1652. Milton hints a suspicion that Charles was not the real author of the 'Eikon.' He attacks with special severity the insertion of a prayer plagiarised from Sidney's 'Arcadia,' and enlarged this attack in a second edition published in 1650. The prayer had only been appended to a few copies of the 'Eikon.' This led to the absurd story, unfortunately sanctioned in Johnson's 'Life,' that Milton had compelled William Dugard [q. v.], then in prison, to insert the prayer in order to give ground for the attack. The impossibility of the story is shown by Professor Masson (iv. 249-50 *n.*, 252). Dugard was concerned in printing the 'Eikon,' was imprisoned upon that ground in February 1649-50, a year after the publication, and, on being released at Milton's intervention, published Milton's book against Salmasius. Salmasius (Claude de Saumaise, 1588-1653), a 'man of enormous reading and no judgment' (Pattison), was now a professor at Leyden. He had been invited by the Scottish presbyterians to write in their behalf. Charles II, who was at the Hague, induced him to write the 'Defensio Regia pro Carolo I,' published in November 1649. Milton was ordered to reply by the council on 8 Jan. 1650, and his 'Pro Populo Anglicano Defensio' appeared in March 1650. Hobbes, in his 'Behemoth' (*English Works*, vi. 368), says that it is hardly to be judged which is the best Latin or which is the worst reasoning, and compares them to two declamations made by the same man in a rhetoric school. Milton did not, as has been said, receive '1,000*l.*' for his defence. A hundred pounds was voted to him by the council of state;

but the order was cancelled, Milton having no doubt refused to accept it. He had taunted Salmasius (in error apparently) for having received one hundred jacobuses from Charles II, and could not condescend to take a reward for himself. He finally lost his eyesight by the work. It had been failing for some years, and he persisted, in spite of a physician's warnings, in finishing his book (*Def. Secunda*) at the expense of his eyes. In a famous sonnet he congratulates himself on his resolution. His eyes, he says, were not injured to 'outward view.' The disease was by himself attributed either to cataract or amaurosis (*Paradise Lost*, iii. 25), but is said to have been more probably glaucoma (the fullest account is given in Milton's letter to Leonard Philaras or Villeré, 28 Sept. 1654). Salmasius replied in a 'Responsio,' but he died at Spa on 6 Sept. 1653, and his book was not published till 1660. Meanwhile other attacks had been made upon Milton. An anonymous pamphlet by John Rowland (Phillips erroneously ascribed it to Bramhall), 'Pro Rege et Populo Anglicano' (1651), was answered by Milton's nephew, John Phillips, and the answer—which, according to Edward Phillips, was corrected by their uncle—has been published in Milton's works. Peter du Moulin the younger [q. v.], son of a famous French Calvinist, attacked Milton with gross personal abuse in his 'Regii Sanguinis Clamor ad cœlum' (March 1652) (Masson, v. 217–224. For Du Moulin's account see *Gent. Mag.* 1773, pp. 369–70, and his *Parerga*, 1670; also Wood, *Fasti*, ii. 195). This was edited and provided with a dedicatory epistle by Alexander Morus (or More), son of a Scottish principal of a French protestant college. Milton supposed the true author to be the nominal editor, whom he had perhaps met at Geneva, where More was professor of Greek. He had now become a professor at Middleburg. There were scandals as to More's relations to women, especially to a maid of Salmasius. Milton was ordered by the council to reply to the 'Clamor,' and his answer, the 'Defensio Secunda,' appeared in May 1654. It was full of savage abuse of Morus, whom Milton declared to be the author, and to be guilty of all the immorality imputed to him. It fortunately contains also one of the most interesting of Milton's autobiographical passages, and an apostrophe to Cromwell and other leaders of the Commonwealth, which illustrates his political sentiments. The 'Defensio Secunda' was republished by Ulac, the publisher of the 'Clamor,' in October 1654, with 'Fides Publica,' a reply by Morus, which was afterwards completed by a 'Supplementum' in 1655. Morus denied the authorship, and Milton in his final reply, 'Pro se Defensio' (August 1655), to which is subjoined a 'Responsio' to Morus's 'Supplementum,' reduces his charge to the statement that, in any case, Morus was responsible for editing the book. He had received sufficient testimony from various quarters to convince him that Morus was not really the author, had he been convincible (Masson, iv. 627–34). He continued to maintain his other charges, but happily this was the end of a controversy which had degenerated into mere personalities.

Milton, upon becoming Latin secretary to the council, had been allowed chambers in Whitehall. At the end of 1651 they had been given to others, and he had moved to another 'pretty garden-house' in Petty France, Westminster. It afterwards became No. 19 York Street, belonged to Bentham, was occupied successively by James Mill and Hazlitt, and finally demolished in 1877. Here he lived until the Restoration. Milton was helped in his duties, made difficult on account of his blindness, successively by a Mr. Weckherlin, by Philip Meadows [q. v.], and finally by Andrew Marvell. He continued to serve throughout the Protectorate, though in later years, after Thurloe became secretary and kept the minutes in a less explicit form, his services are less traceable. His inability to discharge his duties fully was probably taken into account in an order made in 1655, by which (among other reductions, however) his salary is reduced to 150*l.* a year, though this sum was to be paid for his life. The amount appears to have been finally fixed at 200*l.* *ib.* v. 177, 180–3). He could not regularly attend the council, but despatches requiring dignified language were sent to him for translation. The most famous of these were the letters (dated chiefly 25 May 1655) which Cromwell wrote to various powers to protest against the atrocious persecution of the Vaudois. The letters were restrained in language by diplomatic necessities; but Milton expressed his own feeling in the famous sonnet.

On 12 Nov. 1656 he married Catharine Woodcock, of whom nothing more is known than can be inferred from his sonnet after her death. She gave birth to a daughter 19 Oct. 1657. The mother and child both died in the following February (*ib.* v. 376, 382). A memorial window to her, erected at the cost of Mr. G. W. Childs of Philadelphia, in St. Margaret's, Westminster, was unveiled on 13 Feb. 1888, when Matthew Arnold gave an address, published in his 'Essays on Criticism' (2nd ser. 1888, pp. 56–69). Milton had a small circle of friends. Lady Ranelagh is mentioned by Phillips, and there are two letters to her son at Oxford, showing that Milton disapproved even of the reformed university. He also saw Hartlib, Marchmont Needham, and Henry Oldenburg [q. v.], who was tutor to Lady Ranelagh's son at Oxford. His old pupil, Cyriac Skinner, and Henry Lawrence, son of the president of Cromwell's council, were also friends. But his most famous acquaintance was Andrew Marvell, who succeeded Meadows in 1657, though Milton had recommended him as early as 1652 as his assistant in the secretary's office. There are no traces of acquaintance with other famous men of the time. His religious prejudices separated him from all but a small party, and the lofty severity of his character probably emphasised such separation. It has been vaguely suggested that Milton procured an offer of help from the council for Brian Walton's Polyglott Bible. Foreigners, however, frequently came to see Milton (Phillips), and, according to Aubrey, visited England expressly to see Milton and Cromwell. His writings upon the regicide were received with interest by learned men on the continent, who were surprised that a fanatic could write Latin as well as Salmasius. It is said that Milton had an allowance from parliament, and afterwards from Cromwell, to keep a 'weekly table' for the entertainment of distinguished foreigners (Mitford, *Life of Milton*, App. p. cxlvi).

Milton retained his secretaryship during the protectorate of Richard Cromwell and through the distracted period which intervened before the Restoration. Some brief pamphlets written at this time are a despairing appeal on behalf of a policy which all practical men could perceive to be hopeless. Two of them, published in 1659, are arguments in favour of a purely voluntary ecclesiastical system. In another, published early in 1660, he proposes that parliament should simply make itself perpetual. A second edition was apparently quashed by the speedy establishment of the monarchy. Finally, as late as April 1660, he wrote 'Brief Notes,' attacking a royalist sermon. These writings show that Milton was now inclined to the old republican party. His republicanism was anything but democratic. He desired the permanent rule of the chiefs of the army and the council, with a complete separation between church and state, and abstention from arbitrary measures of government.

At the Restoration Milton concealed himself in a friend's house in Bartholomew Close. He remained there during the long debates as to the list of regicides to be excepted from pardon. On 16 June 1660 it was ordered by the House of Commons that Milton's 'Defensio' and John Goodwin's 'Obstructors of Justice' should be burnt by the common hangman, and that Milton and Goodwin should be indicted by the attorney-general, and taken into custody by the serjeant-at-arms. A proclamation was issued on 13 Aug. ordering the surrender of all copies of the books named. It states that both the authors have hitherto concealed themselves. Milton was arrested in the course of the summer, but in the next session it was ordered that he should be released on paying his fees. Milton protested, through Marvell, against the excessive amount of the fees (150*l.*), and his complaint was referred to the committee on privileges. The Indemnity Act freed him from all legal consequences of his actions.

Pattison thinks that Milton owed his escape to his 'insignificance and harmlessness.' Burnet, however, says that his escape caused general surprise. Pattison's sense of the unpractical nature of Milton's political writings probably led him to underestimate the reputation which they enjoyed at the time. A new edition of the 'Defensio' had appeared in 1658, and Salmasius's posthumous 'Responsio' was published in September 1660. Cominges, the French ambassador in London, writing to his master on 2 April 1663 of the condition of English literature, declared that in recent times there was only one man of letters—'un nommé Miltonius qui s'est rendu plus infâme par ses dangereux écrits que ces bourreaux et les assassins de leur roi' (Jusserand, *French Ambassador at the Court of Charles II*, p. 205). Milton clearly had enemies who might have sought to make him an example. Professor Masson has endeavoured to construct a history of the negotiations by which such attempts, if made, may have been frustrated (vi. 162–95). The only direct statements are by Phillips and Richardson. Phillips says that Marvell 'made a considerable party' for Milton in the House of Commons, and, with the help of other friends, obtained immunity for him. He adds incorrectly that Milton was disqualified for holding office. Richardson, writing in 1734 (*Explanatory Notes*, p. lxxxix), mentions a report that Secretary William Morice [q. v.] and Sir Thomas Clarges [q. v.] 'managed matters artfully in his favour.' He gives, however, as the real secret that Milton had entreated for the life of Sir William D'Avenant [q. v.], and that D'Avenant now returned the favour. Richardson heard this from Pope, Pope heard it from Betterton, and Betterton from his steady patron, D'Avenant. The objection to the anecdote is its neatness.

No good story is quite true. Clarges, as Monck's brother-in-law, and Marvell, as Monck's intimate friend, had both influence at the time, and, as Professor Masson also notes, Arthur Annesley, afterwards first Earl of Anglesey [q. v.], was a close friend of Milton in later years, and was at this time a chief manager of the Restoration and in favour of lenity. It cannot be now decided how far any of these stories represents the facts. An incredible story of a mock funeral, carried out by his friends, was given in Cunningham's 'History of Great Britain,' 1787, i. 14. On regaining his liberty, Milton took a house in Holborn, near Red Lion Fields (PHILLIPS), and soon afterwards moved to Jewin Street. He lost much in money. He had, according to Phillips, put 2,000*l.* into the excise office, and could never get it out. He lost another sum invested somewhere injudiciously. He had to give up property valued at 60*l.*, which he had bought out of the estates of Westminster. Professor Masson calculates that before the catastrophe he had about 4,000*l.* variously invested, and some house property in London, which, with his official income and some other investments, would bring him in some 500*l.* a year. This may have been reduced to 200*l.* Milton was frugal and temperate, and Phillips thinks that, 'all things considered,' he had still a 'considerable estate' (MASSON, vi. 444–5). Mrs. Powell renewed her attempts to recover the property after the Restoration. Her eldest son finally regained Forest Hill, and Milton apparently made over the Wheatley estate to the Powells, though it does not appear what he received for the old debt, or for his promised marriage portion of 1,000*l.* (*ib.* vi. 449–51).

Milton soon found it desirable to take a third wife who could look after his affairs. His eldest daughter was in her seventeenth year, and the household apparently much mismanaged, when on 24 Feb. 1662–3 he married Elizabeth Minshull. She was born on 30 Dec. 1638, and was a cousin of Milton's friend, Dr. Nathan Paget, by whom the match was arranged. The marriage, though not romantic, was successful. Shortly afterwards Milton moved to a house in Artillery Walk, Bunhill Fields. It was small, but, like all Milton's houses, had a garden. He lived there for the rest of his life, except that, according to Richardson, he lodged for a time (about 1670) with the bookseller Millington. During the plague of 1665 Milton retired to Chalfont St. Giles, Buckinghamshire, where a 'pretty box' was taken for him by the quaker Thomas Ellwood [q. v.] Ellwood had been introduced to Milton in 1662 by Paget; in order to improve his scholarship he had offered to read Latin books to the blind man, who became interested in him and encouraged his studies. Ellwood afterwards became a tutor in the family of the Penningtons at Chalfont. The cottage in which Milton stayed at Chalfont is now preserved, having been bought by public subscription in 1887, and is the only house connected with Milton which still exists. Ellwood visited Milton there one day, and received from him the complete manuscript of 'Paradise Lost.' 'Thou hast said much here of "Paradise Lost,"' he observed, 'but what hast thou to say of Paradise Found?'

Blind, infirm, and poor, depressed by the triumph of the principles which he most detested, Milton had determined to achieve the great purpose to which from early youth he had been self-devoted. His sonnet upon completing his twenty-third year, and the letter with which it was accompanied (MASSON, i. 324, first published in BIRCH's *Life*), show that he was then looking forward to some great work. He had resolved to write a poem which should be national in character, and set forth his conception of the providential order of the world. At the time of his foreign journey he had contemplated a poem upon the Arthurian legend, to which he refers in the 'Epistle to Manso' and the 'Epitaphium Damonis,' 1638–9. At the time of his jottings, however, about 1641, his chief interest had come to be in a dramatic treatment of the fall of man, although in the 'Reasons of Church-Government,' 1641–2, he declares his resolution to take full time for meditation on a fit subject. Phillips reports that the opening passage of this, composed about 1642, was the speech of Satan, which is now at the beginning of the fourth book of 'Paradise Lost.' Milton's controversies and business distracted his mind from poetry, and he produced little except the few noble sonnets which commemorate his political emotions. In 1658 he settled down to the composition of 'Paradise Lost.' It is said by Aubrey to have been finished in 1663. Among earlier poems from which Milton may have taken hints are especially noticeable: the Anglo-Saxon poem attributed to Cædmon [q. v.], and published in 1655 by Francis Junius; the 'Adamo' of Andreini, which was translated by Cowper for Hayley's edition of Milton, and is in Cowper's 'Works' by Southey (1837, vol. x.); and the 'Lucifer' of Joost van Vondel, published in 1654. The coincidences with the last are the most remarkable (cf. GOSSE's *Literature of Northern Europe*, 1883, pp. 278-312; and EDMUNDSON's *Milton and Vondel*, 1885). At an uncertain date Milton obtained a license for 'Paradise Lost' from Thomas Tomkyns, chaplain to the Archbishop of Canterbury. Tomkyns, according to Toland (*Life*, 1709, p. 130), hesitated for a time, on account of the lines in the first book about fear of change perplexing monarchs. The fire of 1666 destroyed the house in Bread Street which Milton had inherited from his father, and diminished his income. Many booksellers were ruined by the loss of their stock. On 27 April 1667, however, Milton signed an agreement with Samuel Simmons or Symons for the copyright. Simmons's copy of the agreement passed to the Tonsons, who became proprietors of the copyright, and was presented to the British Museum by Samuel Rogers in 1852. Milton was to receive 5*l.* down, and 5*l.* more upon the sale of each of three editions. The editions were to be accounted as ended when thirteen hundred copies of each were sold 'to particular reading customers,' and were not to exceed fifteen hundred copies apiece. Milton received the second 5*l.* in April 1669, that is 10*l.* in all. His widow in 1680 settled for 8*l.* all claims upon Simmons, who became perpetual proprietor of the copyright. The scrivener's original manuscript of the first book of the poem, which was submitted for license and sent to press, descended through the Tonsons to H. C. Baker (of Bayfordbury, Herts), who sold it in March 1904 to J. Pierpont Morgan, of New York.

The reception of 'Paradise Lost' has been the subject of some controversy. No poet ever put more of himself into his work, and Milton's singular loftiness of character and contemptuous tone of superiority to the dominant political and religious parties of his day might be expected to keep readers at a distance. The degree to which the poetry is saturated with the reading of a fine classical scholar might also alienate the unlearned. Milton rather conquers than attracts unless his readers be men of highly cultivated taste. On the other hand, little merit of other kinds is generally required for the popularity of a religious poem. Although 'Paradise Lost' has been mentioned as an instance of popular neglect, it would seem on the whole that the sale of thirteen hundred copies in eighteen months and some 4,500 by 1688 marks, as Johnson maintained, a fair degree of success. Richardson (*Explanatory Notes*, p. cxix) preserved a tradition that Sir John Denham had, upon reading a sheet 'wet from the press,' pronounced 'Paradise Lost' to be the noblest poem ever written. He adds that it was unknown for two years, when Buckhurst, afterwards Lord Dorset, found it on an old stall, that it was given to him as waste paper, and that Dryden, to whom he showed it, declared that 'this man cuts us all out, and the ancients too.' Dryden's phrase may be accepted, and is characteristic of his generosity in criticism; but the anecdotes, which involve various inaccuracies, are obviously so distorted, if at all founded on fact, as to prove nothing. Phillips tells us that Milton in his later years was much visited by foreigners and by men of rank, especially Arthur Annesley, earl of Anglesey; and Toland says that Sir Robert Howard, Dryden's brother-in-law, was a 'particular acquaintance.' Edward Phillips says in his edition of the 'Thesaurus' of Buchler (1675) that many persons thought Milton to have reached the perfection of epic poetry. The commendatory poems by Samuel Barrow and Marvell, prefixed to the second edition of 'Paradise Lost' (1674), imply that Milton's position was already regarded as established. Marvell's poem contains a reference to a well-known anecdote of Dryden. Dryden, according to Aubrey, asked Milton's leave to put 'Paradise Lost' into a drama in rhyme. Milton told Dryden that he might 'tag his verses.' The result was Dryden's 'Heroick Opera,' 'The Fall of Angels and Man in Innocence' (licensed 17 April 1674). The performance is a contemptible travesty; but in the preface to it, as published in 1675, Dryden speaks emphatically of the sublimity of the original. He told Dennis twenty years afterwards that he knew not at this time 'half the extent of Milton's excellence.' Wentworth Dillon, fourth earl of Roscommon [q. v.], inserts a passage from 'Paradise Lost' into his 'Essay on Translated Verse' (2nd edit. 1685), which is generally mentioned as the first public recognition of Milton's merits. A few other notices are collected by Professor Masson (vi. 781–5). In 1688 Tonson published by subscription a sumptuous edition in folio. Among the subscribers were Somers, who is said to have exerted himself greatly for its success, and Atterbury, who was always an enthusiastic admirer. Dryden's well-known flashy epigram is placed under the portrait. In 1708, when a monument was erected to John Philips (1676–1708) [q. v.] in Westminster Abbey, the dean (Sprat) suppressed the words 'soli Miltono secundus,' as that name was too detestable to be used in a sacred building. Atterbury withdrew the prohibition. A monument was erected to Milton himself by William Benson [q. v.] in 1737 (Stanley, *Memorials*, pp. 306–8; Johnson, *Lives of Milton* and *Philips*). Milton's fame was now established, and the triumph of the whigs removed one external obstacle. Addison's papers in the 'Spectator' (1712) only ratified the then orthodox opinion. A German translation had been published by E. G. von Berge at Zerbst in 1682, while Latin translations and an annotated edition had already shown the growing reputation of the poem.

Milton's last poems, 'Paradise Regained' and 'Samson Agonistes,' appeared together in 1671. Ellwood says that Milton acknowledged that the 'Paradise Regained' was due to his hint at Chalfont. Philips says that Milton could not bear to hear it mentioned as inferior to its predecessor. Its studied severity of style has hindered its popularity, though such critics as Coleridge and Wordsworth have spoken of it as perfect. Although dramatically feeble, the 'Samson Agonistes' is to some readers among the most interesting of all Milton's poems from the singular intensity of the scarcely concealed autobiographic utterance.

Milton wrote no more poetry, but in 1673 produced a new edition of the early poems. He published in 1669 his Latin grammar and his 'History of Britain,' written long before, and only noticeable as an indication that his name was now exciting interest. His compendium of Ramus's 'Logic' came out in 1672. A tract upon 'True Religion' of 1673, suggested by Charles II's declaration of 15 March 1672, is a slight performance, giving reasons against tolerating the open exercise of popery. His 'Familiar Epistles' and 'College Exercises' were published in 1674, though the intended publication at the same time of his official letters was forbidden.

Milton was declining in health and suffered much from gout. His domestic life had been troubled. His eldest daughter, Anne, was deformed and had a defect of speech. None of the children were sent to school, but they were taught, according to the youngest, Deborah, by a mistress at home. Phillips states that the two youngest were brought up to read to him in various languages, including Hebrew, perhaps Syriac, Greek, and Latin, without knowing the meaning. Though, as Professor Masson remarks, this more probably represents the result than the intention—for Ellwood speaks of Milton's annoyance at hearing words read when the meaning was not understood—the practice was doubtless unpleasant. Their grandmother, Mrs. Powell, would probably not make things pleasanter. It was declared by a servant (see below) that Milton had told her, on the authority of a previous servant, that about 1662 the children combined to cheat their father in household affairs and wished to sell his books. His third marriage annoyed them, and Mary is reported, on the same authority, to have said that a wedding was no news, but that 'if she could hear of his death that were something.' The daughters remained with their father till about 1670. The trial of their patience in reading had become 'almost beyond endurance' (Phillips), and they were all sent out to learn such 'curious and ingenious sorts of manufacture' as are 'proper for women,' especially embroidery in gold and silver.

Milton died on 8 Nov. 1674 of 'gout struck in,' so peacefully that the time of death was not perceived. He was buried in St. Giles's, Cripplegate, beside his father, with the Anglican service. Many friends and a 'concourse of the vulgar' were present, according to Phillips and Toland (for accounts of an alleged exhumation in 1790 see *Notes and Queries*, 7th ser. ix. 361–4). A statue was placed in St. Giles' churchyard in 1904. Upon Milton's death his wife produced a nuncupative will. The daughters objected, and the widow became administratrix. She settled matters by paying the daughters 100*l*. apiece, and had about 600*l*. for herself. The will had been declared to Milton's brother Christopher on 20 July 1674. Milton had then said that he wished to leave to his 'undutiful children' what was due to him from the Powells. He intended 'all the rest to go to his loving wife.' Evidence of a maid-servant and her sister was produced to prove this to have been his intention; and he also stated that he had spent 'the greatest part of his estate' in providing for his daughters. The servant might probably be prejudiced in Mrs. Milton's favour; but the general impression is no doubt correct that Milton's relations to his daughters were, from whatever cause, unfortunate. (The evidence, from the records of the court, was first printed in the second edition of the 'Minor Poems' by Warton, 1791, and is also given in Todd's 'Life of Milton' and in the 'Chetham Miscellanies,' vol. xxiv.)

Milton's appearance and manners are described with little difference by Aubrey, Phillips, and Richardson. He was rather below the middle height, but well made, with light brown or auburn hair and delicate complexion. He was stately and courteous, though he could be satirical. He would sit at his house-door in a grey coarse cloth coat in fine weather to receive visitors; indoors he is described as neatly dressed in black, pale but not cadaverous; with his 'fingers gouty and with chalk-stones' (Ri-

CHARDSON). Aubrey and Toland tell us that he rose as early as four in summer and five in winter. Before breakfast the Bible was read to him in Hebrew. He afterwards read or dictated till midday, when he dined very temperately. He took some exercise, walking when possible, and in bad weather swinging. He always had music in the afternoon. He then retired for a time, but again saw his friends after six o'clock, had a supper of 'olives or some light thing' at eight, and after a pipe and a glass of water went to bed. According to Phillips, Milton composed freely only from 'the autumnal equinoctial to the vernal;' the account was confirmed by Mrs. Milton (NEWTON, p. lxxx), though Toland fancies that Phillips has inverted the period, because in his early 'In Adventum Veris' (1629) he welcomes the revival of his genius in spring. He frequently dictated from ten to thirty lines to any one who happened to be at the house, leaning in his easy chair, adds Richardson, with a leg thrown over the elbow. At times he would compose during sleepless nights, and would call up and dictate to his daughter. He would dictate forty lines in a breath, and then reduce them to twenty. The sonnet to Lawrence gives an impression of Milton in his sociable hours. Milton had come to stand apart from all sects, though apparently finding the quakers most congenial. He never went to any religious services in his later years. When a servant brought back accounts of sermons from nonconformist meetings, Milton became so sarcastic that the man at last gave up his place (RICHARDSON).

Portraits of Milton, known to be authentic, are: (1) A portrait at the age of ten, ascribed to Cornelius Janssen (engraved as frontispiece to Masson's 'Life,' vol. i.; see pp. 66 *n.*, 308 *n.*), is in the possession of Passmore Edwards. (2) A portrait taken at Cambridge at the age of twenty, engraved by Vertue in 1731 and 1756, and by other artists. The later portrait belonged to Speaker Onslow, and is generally known as the 'Onslow' portrait. It has disappeared since a sale of Lord Onslow's pictures in 1828. Both these belonged to Milton's widow. (3) The portrait engraved by Faithorne for the 'History of Britain;' the original crayon-drawing was in possession of the Tonsons in 1760, and an etching from it is given in the 'Memoirs of Thomas Hollis,' p. 529. Another crayon-drawing, now at Bayfordbury, belonged to Richardson, and resembles the preceding so clearly, that its independence is doubtful. This was the portrait recognised by Milton's daughter Deborah when the engraver Vertue saw her about 1725 (HOLLIS, *Memoirs*, p. 625). The 'Onslow' portrait is the original of the caricature by Marshall, prefixed to the 1645 poems. A mezzotint by J. Simon is inscribed 'R. White ad vivum delin.,' but there are no traces of the original. A bust in Christ's College, left to it by John Disney (1746–1816) [q. v.], is said to be a 'plaster cast from the original mould,' taken by 'one Pierce' who executed the bust of Wren now in the Bodleian Library. A mis-identified miniature by Samuel Cooper once belonged to Reynolds, who had a controversy about it with Lord Hailes (see *Gent. Mag.* 1791; MASSON, i. 66 *n.*, 308–10 *n.*, vi. 754–7 *n.*; SOTHEBY, *Ramblings*, pp. xvii–xxv; J. FITCHETT MARSH in Lancashire and Cheshire Hist. Soc. 1855; Dr. G. C. WILLIAMSON'S *Cat. of Portraits of Milton* exhibited at Christ's College, Cambridge, on the occasion of the Milton Tercentenary 1908).

Milton's widow retired to Nantwich, Cheshire, where her family lived, and died in the autumn of 1727. Some stories derived from her are given by Newton. She said that her husband had been asked to write for the court, but would not write against his conscience (NEWTON, p. lxxx). Richardson's report that he was asked to resume the Latin secretaryship (an incredible statement), and told his wife that she wanted to ride in her coach, but that he would live and die an honest man, is probably an elaboration of this very doubtful statement. Anne Milton married a 'master-builder,' and died in childbed before 26 Oct. 1678, when her grandmother, Mrs. Powell (who died in 1682), made a bequest of 10*l.* apiece to the other daughters. Mary died unmarried by 1694. Deborah had gone to Dublin as companion to a lady before her father's death, and soon after it married a weaver, Abraham Clarke. The Clarkes settled in Spitalfields, and had ten children. She died 24 Sept. 1727, being then a widow; her only surviving son was Urban Clarke, a weaver in Spitalfields, who died unmarried. Her only surviving daughter, Elizabeth, had married Thomas Foster, another weaver. Her eldest son, Caleb Clarke, had emigrated to Madras, where he was married in 1703, had children, and died in 1719. The last trace of descendants was the birth of Mary, daughter of Caleb's son Abraham, at Madras in 1727. Deborah Clarke received some notice before her death. Addison visited her, gave her some money, and proposed to get her a pension, but died (1719) before doing so. She was seen by Professor Ward of Gresham College, confirmed the stories about reading unknown languages to her father, and is said to have repeated verses from Homer, Ovid, and

Euripides. She spoke, however, with affection (RICHARDSON, *Explanatory Notes*, p. xxxvi) of her father, though not of her stepmother. Queen Caroline is said to have given her fifty guineas, and Voltaire says that when her existence was known she 'became rich in a quarter of an hour.' Her daughter, Elizabeth Foster, had seven children, all of whom died before her without issue. Mrs. Foster was visited by Newton and Birch, and 'Comus' was performed for her benefit at Drury Lane 5 April 1750. Johnson wrote the prologue, and about 130*l.* was raised [cf. art. LAUDER, WILLIAM]. She died at Islington, 9 May 1754, probably the last of Milton's descendants. The tercentenary of Milton's birth was celebrated with much ceremony in London in December 1908.

Milton's works are: 1. 'A Masque presented at Ludlow Castle, 1634, on Michaelmasse Night, before the Right Honourable the Earle of Bridgwater, Viscount Brackly, Lord President of Wales, and one of his Majesties Most Honourable Privie Counsell,' London, 1637 (with Dedicatory Letter by H. Lawes; the name 'Comus' is not in this or in Milton's 'Poems' of 1645 or 1673; a manuscript in the Bridgewater Library was printed by Todd in his edition of 'Comus' in 1798). 2. 'Obsequies to the Memorie of Mr. Edward King, Anno Dom. 1638,' thirteen English poems, of which Milton's 'Lycidas' is the last; published and sometimes bound with twenty-three Latin and Greek poems, 'Justa Edovardo King Naufrago ab amicis mœrentibus amoris et μνείας χάριν.' 3. 'Of Reformation touching Church Discipline in England, and the Causes that hitherto have hindered it: Two Books written to a Friend,' 1641. 4. 'Of Prelatical Episcopacy, and whether it may be deduced from the Apostolical Times by vertue of those Testimonies which are alledg'd to that purpose in some late Treatises; one whereof goes under the Name of James, Archbishop of Armagh,' 1641. 5. 'Animadversions upon the Remonstrant's Defence against Smectymnuus,' 1641. 6. 'The Reason of Church Government urged against Prelaty, by Mr. John Milton,' 1641 (early in 1641–2). 7. 'An Apology against a Pamphlet called "A Modest Confutation of the Animadversions . . .,"' 1642 (March and April 1642). 8. 'The Doctrine and Discipline of Divorce, Restor'd, to the good of both sexes, from the Bondage of Canon Law and other Mistakes, to Christian Freedom, guided by the Rule of Charity; wherein also many places of Scripture have recovered their long-lost Meaning; reasonable to be now thought of in the Reformation intended,' 1643 (1 Aug.? see above); 2nd enlarged edition, 2 Feb. 1643–4, 'the author J. M.' 9. 'Of Education: to Mr. Samuel Hartlib,' 5 June 1644 (a facsimile of the edition of this, appended to the 'Poems' of 1673, was edited by Oscar Browning in 1883). 10. 'The Judgement of Martin Bucer concerning Divorce. Writt'n to King Edward the Sixt, in his Second Book of the Kingdom of Christ. And now Englisht. Wherein a late Book restoring the Doctrine and Discipline of Divorce is heer confirm'd and justify'd by the Authoritie of Martin Bucer. To the Parlament of England,' 1644. 11. 'Areopagitica. A Speech of Mr. John Milton for the Liberty of Unlicensed Printing, to the Parlament of England,' 1644 (November). 12. 'Tetrachordon: Expositions upon the foure chief Places in Scripture which treat of Marriage, or Nullities in Marriage. . . . By the former Author, J. M.,' 1645 (14 March 1644–5). 13. 'Colasterion: A Reply to a Nameles Answer against "The Doctrine and Discipline of Divorce." Wherein the trivial Author of that Answer is discover'd, the License conferred with, and the opinion which they traduce defended. By the former Author, J. M.,' 1645 (4 March 1644–5). 14. 'Poems of Mr. John Milton, both English and Latin, compos'd at several times. Printed by his true copies. The songs were set in Musick by Mr. Henry Lawes, Gentleman of the King's Chappel, and one of His Majesties Private Musick,' 1645. An address by the stationer, Humphrey Moseley, to the reader is prefixed; Sir H. Wotton's letter to Milton and verses by his Italian friends are also given, and a portrait by W. Marshall. A second edition, called 'Poems, &c., upon several Occasions,' with 'A small Tractate of Education to Mr. Hartlib,' appeared in 1673. It included the poems written since the first publication, excepting the sonnets to Cromwell, Fairfax, Vane, and the second to Cyriac Skinner, which first appeared with the 'Letters of State' in 1694. Some youthful poems are added; and the dedication of 'Comus' to Bridgewater and Wotton's letter are omitted. T. Warton published an edition in 1785; a second, enlarged, appeared in 1791. 15. 'The Tenure of Kings and Magistrates, proving that it is lawful . . . for any who have the power to call to account a Tyrant or wicked King, and after due Conviction, to depose and put him to Death, if the ordinary Magistrate have neglected or denied to do it,' 1648–9; 2nd edition in 1650. 16. 'Observations on the Articles of Peace' (between Ormonde and the Irish), 1649. 17. 'Εἰκονοκλαστης in Answer to a Book entitled "Εἰκων βασιλικη,"' 1649;

October, 2nd edition, 1650; French translation, 1652. 18. 'Joannis Miltoni Angli pro Populo Anglicano Defensio contra Claudii anonymi, alias Salmasii Defensionem Regiam,' 1650–1. A folio, a quarto, and several 12mo editions were published in 1651, another in 1652, and one in 1658. 19. 'Joannis Miltoni Angli pro Populo Anglicano Defensio Secunda contra infamem Libellum anonymum cui titulus Regis Sanguinis Clamor . . .,' 1654. 20. 'Joannis Miltoni pro se Defensio contra Alexandrum Morum Ecclesiasten, Libelli famosi cui titulus Regis Sanguinis Clamor . . . Authorem recte dictum,' 1655 (August). To this was appended 21. 'Joannis Miltoni ad Alexandri Mori Supplementum Responsio,' 1655. 22. 'Scriptum Domini Protectoris . . . contra Hispanos . . .,' 1655 (a translation, with James Thomson's 'Britannia,' was published in 1738). 23. 'A Treatise of Civil Power in Ecclesiastical Causes, showing that it is not lawfull to compell in Matters of Religion,' 1658–9. 24. 'Considerations touching the likeliest Means to remove Hirelings out of the Church, wherein is also discoursed of Tithes, Church-Fees, and Church Revenues . . .,' 1659. 25. 'A Letter to a Friend concerning the Ruptures of the Commonwealth,' dated 20 Oct. 1659 (this and No. 27 published in 'Prose Works' of 1698, 'from the manuscript'). 26. 'The Ready and Easy Way to establish a Free Commonwealth and the Excellencies thereof compared with the Inconveniences and Dangers of readmitting Kingship in this Nation,' 1659–60; 2nd edition, April 1660. 27. 'The Present Means and Brief Delineation of a Free Commonwealth, easy to be put in Practice and without Delay, in a Letter to General Monk,' 1660. 28. 'Brief Notes upon a late Sermon . . . by Matthew Griffith, D.D.,' 1660. 29. 'Paradise Lost: A Poem written in Ten Books, by John Milton.' Nine different title-pages were prefixed to successive issues of the first edition. In the fifth were added fourteen pages, containing a prose 'Argument' and the paragraph headed the 'Verse,' defending the absence of rhyme (see MASSON, vi. 622–8, and his preface to the facsimile published by Elliot Stock in 1877, for an account of these variations). The 2nd edition ('revised and augmented,' in which the poem was first divided into twelve books) appeared in 1674, the 3rd in 1678, and the 4th in 1688. Latin translations of the first book were published in 1686 and 1691; of the whole, as also of 'Paradise Regained' and 'Samson Agonistes,' by W. Hog, in 1690; of the whole, by M. B[old], in 1702; by Joseph Trapp in 1740–4. 2 vols.; and by W. Dobson, in 1750–3, 2 vols. The British Museum contains translations into Armenian, Danish, Dutch (1728, &c.), French (1729, &c.), German (1682, &c.), Greek, Hungarian, Icelandic, Italian (1735, &c.), Manx (1796), Polish (1791), Portuguese, Russian, Spanish, Swedish, and Welsh. 30. 'Accidence commenc't Grammar . . .,' 1669. 31. 'The History of Britain, that Part especially now called England. From the first traditional Beginning continued to the Norman Conquest, collected out of the antientest and best Authours thereof by John Milton,' 1670. 32. 'Artis Logicæ Plenior Institutio ad P. Remi Methodum concinnata,' 1670, also 1672 and 1673. 33. 'Paradise Regained, a Poem in IV Books; To which is added "Samson Agonistes." The author John Milton,' 1671, also 1680, 1688, and 1793. Editions of these, often with 'Paradise Lost,' as 'Poetical Works.' 34. 'Of True Religion, Heresy, Schism, Toleration, and what best Means may be us'd against the Growth of Popery,' 1673. 35. 'Joannis Miltoni Angli Epistolarum Familiarium Liber unus; quibus accesserunt ejusdem (jam olim in Collegio adolescentis) Prolusiones quædam Oratoriæ,' 1674. 36. 'A Declaration or Letters Patent of the Election of this present King of Poland, John II,' translated 1674 (anonymous translation, but published as Milton's in the 'Prose Works,' 1698). 37. 'Literæ Pseudo-Senatus Anglicani, necnon Cromwell reliquorumque Perduellium nomine ac jussu conscriptæ a Joanne Miltono,' 1676 (this was a surreptitious publication of Milton's despatches. It was reprinted at Leipzig in 1690; and an English translation, 'Letters of State,' by Phillips, with a life of Milton prefixed, in 1694). 38. 'Mr. John Milton's Character of the Long Parliament and Assembly of Divines. In MDCXLI.,' 1681 (professes to be a passage omitted from the 'History of Britain,' in later editions of which it is now inserted. The authenticity is doubtful, see MASSON, vi. 807–12). 39. 'A Brief History of Moscovia . . . Gather'd from the Writings of several Eye-witnesses . . .,' 1682 (said by the publisher to have been written by Milton's own hand before he lost his sight). 40. 'J. Miltoni Angli de doctrina Christiana Libri duo posthumi,' 1825. Edited by Sumner, afterwards bishop of Winchester, from a manuscript in the State Paper Office. This manuscript, together with a copy of the 'Literæ Pseudo-Senatus,' had been entrusted by Milton to Daniel Skinner, who after Milton's death had offered them for publication to Elzevir at Amsterdam. Skinner was compelled to surrender them to government, and both manuscripts were discovered in the State Paper Office by Robert Lemon in 1823. Such of the state letters as had not been already published were edited by W. D. Hamilton for the Camden Society in 'Original Papers' (1859). The 'Christian Doctrine' gives Milton's theological views. Accepting absolutely the divine authority of the Bible, he works out a scheme of semi-Arianism, and defends the doctrine of free-will against the Calvinist view. He shows little knowledge of ecclesiastical authorities. Sumner published a translation of the 'Christian Doctrine,' reprinted in Bohn's edition of the 'Prose Works.' In 1658 Milton published Raleigh's 'Cabinet Council' from a manuscript in his possession. 'Original Letters and Papers of State addressed to Oliver Cromwell . . . found among the Political Collections of Mr. John Milton,' 1743. contains papers stated to have been given by Milton to Ellwood (see MASSON, vi. 814).

Milton's 'Collections for a Latin Dictionary' were used by E. Phillips in his 'Enchiridion' and 'Speculum' in 1684 (WOOD), and 'three large folios' of Milton's collections for the 'Cambridge Dictionary' of 1693.

An 'Argument on the great Question concerning the Militia, by J. M.,' 1642, which, according to Todd (i. 223), is ascribed to Milton in a copy in the Bridgewater Library, was by John March (1612–1657) [q. v.] Two of Milton's commonplace books were edited by Alfred J. Horwood, one from a copy belonging to Sir F. W. Graham in 1876 (privately printed), and another for the Camden Society (1876, revised 1877). They contain nothing original. A manuscript poem, dated 1647, discovered by Henry Morley [q. v.] in a blank page of the 1673 volume, was attributed by him to Milton, and became the subject of a warm newspaper controversy in 1868. The weight of authority seems to be against it; if Milton's, he suppressed it judiciously. It has been claimed for Jasper Mayne [q. v.] The Milton MSS. in the library of Trinity College, Cambridge, apparently formed part of a donation to the college by Sir Henry Newton (afterwards Puckering) [q. v.] in 1691. They contain 'Comus' and 'Lycidas,' the 'jottings' mentioned above, early poems, sonnets in Milton's hand, besides copies of a few in other hands. They were issued in facsimile under the direction of W. Aldis Wright in 1899. The Trustees of the British Museum issued in Dec. 1908 a useful catalogue of autograph MSS. and early editions of Milton's works, which were exhibited at the Museum during the Tercentenary celebration (Dec. 1908).

The first annotated edition of Milton's poems appeared in 1695 by P[atrick] H[ume] [q. v.] John Callander [q. v.] was accused of appropriating the notes unfairly in his edition of the first book of 'Paradise Lost' in 1750. Bentley's famous edition appeared in 1732, and was attacked by Zachary Pearce [q. v.] in that year. The edition by Newton of 'Paradise Lost' appeared in 1749, 2 vols. 4to, and of the other poems, 1 vol. 4to, in 1750, and has been frequently reprinted. Baskerville's quarto edition of 1758, from Newton's text, is handsome but 'full of misprints.' Another of Baskerville's followed in 1759. Boydell's sumptuous edition, with plates, after Westall, and a life by Hayley, appeared in 1794. Cowper's translations of the Latin and Italian poems were published separately by Hayley in 1808, and are in the tenth volume of Cowper's 'Works' by Southey (1837). Todd's 'Variorum' edition appeared in 6 vols. 8vo in 1801, 7 vols. 8vo in 1808, and in 1826. The 'Aldine' edition of 1826 contains the life by Phillips, Cowper's translations of Latin and Italian poems, and an introduction by J[oseph] P[arkes]; that of 1832, a life by J. Mitford. Sir Egerton Brydges edited an edition (6 vols. 8vo) in 1835, and James Montgomery an edition (2 vols. 8vo) in 1843. Professor Masson edited the 'Cambridge' Milton, 3 vols. 8vo, in 1877, and again in 1890, and also an edition in the 'Golden Treasury' series in 1874, and the 'Globe' Milton in 1877. Canon Beeching edited the 'Poetical Works' after the original texts (Oxford, 1900). There is an edition of the English 'Prose Works,' in 1 vol. folio, 1697, without the name of printer or place of publication (Brit. Museum). The 'Prose Works' were collected by Toland in 1698 in 3 vols. folio, Amsterdam (really London). They were republished by Birch in 1738, 2 vols. folio, and again in 1753 (when Richard Baron [q. v.] restored the later editions of tracts printed by Toland from earlier copies). They were edited by Charles Symmons, D.D., in 7 vols. 8vo, in 1806. A selection appeared in 1809. A one-volume edition was edited by J. Fletcher in 1833, and has been reprinted. They are also contained, together with the 'Christian Doctrine,' in Bohn's edition, 5 vols. 8vo, edited by J. A. St. John, 1848–53. The 'Works in Prose and Verse,' in 8 vols. 8vo, were edited by John Mitford in 1851, but without the 'Christian Doctrine.'

[Everything knowable about Milton has been given, with careful references to original sources, in Professor Masson's Life of John Milton, narrated in connection with the Political, Ecclesiastical, and Literary History of his Time, 6 vols. 8vo, 1859–80. A new and revised edition of vol. i. (cited above) appeared in 1881. The original sources are: Life in Wood's Fasti (Bliss), i. 480–6 (first published in 1691–2). Wood's information came chiefly from Aubrey, whose memoir was published in the Lives (1813). A copy from the original manuscripts is appended to Godwin's Lives of E. and J. Phillips (1815), and another in Stern (i. 337–44). The life by Edward Phillips, which is the most valuable, was originally prefixed to the Letters of State, 1694, and is reprinted in Godwin's Lives of the Phillipses, and in the Poems, 1826. Toland's sketch was originally prefixed to the Prose Works of 1698, and appeared separately in 1699 and 1761. A brief life by Elijah Fenton [q.v.] was prefixed to an edition of the Poems in 1725, and to many later editions. The Explanatory Notes on Paradise Lost, by Jonathan Richardson, Father and Son, 1734, contain a life of Milton by the father, who collected a few original facts. A life by Thomas Birch was prefixed to the Prose Works of 1738 and 1753. Peck's New Memoirs of the Life . . . of Mr. John Milton, 1740, is a 'silly medley of odds and ends' (Masson). The life by Newton, prefixed to Works in 1749, adds a fact or two from Milton's widow and granddaughter. The famous life by Johnson first appeared in 1779 in the collection of English Poets. An edition, edited by Mr. C. H. Firth, was published in 1891. The evidence taken upon the will was first published in the second edition of the Minor Poems by T. Warton in 1791. H. J. Todd's life was first prefixed to the 'Variorum' edition of 1801. In a third edition (1826) Todd first made use of the records of Milton's official career, preserved in the State Paper Office. The notes to the 'Variorum' edition contain most of the accessible information. A life by Charles Symmons forms the seventh volume of the Prose Works of 1806. Other lives are by Sir Egerton Brydges (Poems of 1835), by James Montgomery (Poems, 1843), by C. R. Edmonds (1851), specially referring to Milton's ecclesiastical principles, and by Thomas Keightley (Life, Opinions, and Writings of Milton, 1855). The standard life previous to Professor Masson was that by J. Mitford, prefixed to Works, 1851. Milton und seine Zeit, in 2 pts. 1877–9, by Alfred Stern, is an independent and well-written, though less comprehensive, work on the same lines. See also the short but admirable lives by Pattison in the Men of Letters series, and by Dr. Garnett in the Great Writers series. Among special publications are Ramblings in Elucidation of the Autograph of Milton, by Samuel Leigh Sotheby, F.S.A., imperial 4to, 1861; Papers connected with Milton and his Family, by John Fitchett Marsh, in Chetham Society Miscellanies (vol. xxiv. of Publications), 1851; A Sheaf of Gleanings, by Joseph Hunter, 1850; and Original Papers illustrative of the Life and Writings of John Milton, with an Appendix of Papers relating to his connection with the Powell Family, by W. Douglas Hamilton (Camd. Soc.), 1859.] L. S.

MILTON, JOHN (*fl.* 1770), painter, was a descendant of Sir Christopher Milton [q. v.], brother of the poet. He worked in the neighbourhood of London, first at Charlton, and later at Peckham, exhibiting with the Free Society from 1768 to 1774, and with the Society of Artists in 1773 and 1774. Milton chiefly painted sea-pieces, with an occasional landscape, and some animal subjects; he excelled in the representation of dogs. His 'Strong Gale' was finely mezzotinted by R. Laurie, and his 'English Setter' was engraved by J. Cook and S. Smith as a companion plate to Woollett's 'Spanish Pointer,' after Stubbs. He was the father of Thomas Milton, the landscape engraver, who is noticed in a separate article.

[Nagler's Allgemeines Kunstler-Lexicon; Redgrave's Dict. of Artists; Graves's Dict. of Artists.] F. M. O'D.

MILTON, JOHN (*d.* 1805), medallist, worked from about 1760 to 1802. He was an assistant engraver at the Royal Mint from 1789 to 1798, and was also medallist to the Prince of Wales (George IV). He exhibited at the Royal Academy from 1785 to 1802. At the close of the eighteenth century he executed the dies of the following provincial tokens, all of which are creditable works of their kind: Anglesey penny (Pye, *Provincial Copper Coins*, pl. 28, 3); Hackney penny, 1795, with a view of Hackney Church, made for Mr. D. A. Rebello, a coin collector (*ib.* pl. 34, 1); Richardson's lottery tokens, London (Sharp, *Chetwynd Coll.* p. 68); Ipswich penny (*ib.* p. 89); Wroxham (Norfolk) 3*d.* token, 1797 (*ib.* p. 3). He also made the Isle of Man penny, 1786 (*ib.* p. 240); the Barbados penny and halfpenny (Pye, pl. 19, 2, 4; Sharp, p. 242), and the set of Scottish patterns, with the head of Prince George (IV), executed for Colonel Fullerton in 1799 (Crowther, *Engl. Pattern Coins*, p. 46). Milton's medals are not numerous or important. The following may be mentioned: Matthew Prior (bust only), probably an early work (Hawkins, *Med. Illustr.* ii. 456); Winchester College prize medal (*ib.* i. 11); John Hunter and George Fordyce (Cochran-Patrick, *Catal. of Scott. Med.* p. 110, pl. xxi. 3; cp. p. 115, No. 46); medal of university of Glasgow (*ib.* p. 151).

Milton, who was elected a fellow of the Society of Antiquaries 24 May 1792, died on 10 Feb. 1805, leaving one son and two daughters. His coins and medals were sold by Leigh & Sotheby 30 May 1805 (cf. *Sale Cat.*)

His usual signature is J. MILTON. George Valentin Bauert of Altona was his pupil, and made a medal of Walpole in conjunction with him (HAWKINS, op. cit. ii. 585–6).

[Works cited above; Redgrave's Dict. of Artists; James Conder's Arrangement of Provincial Coins, Tokens, and Medalets; J. Atkins's Coins and Tokens.] W. W.

MILTON, THOMAS (1743–1827), engraver, born in 1743, was a son of John Milton (*fl.* 1770) [q. v.], marine painter. From the character of his plates it seems probable that Milton was a pupil of Woollett, and he is said to have practised for some time in London, but nothing is known of the work of his early life. He was living in Dublin in 1783, in which year appeared the first number of his 'Views of Seats in Ireland,' a series of twenty-four plates of singular beauty from drawings by Ashford, Barralet, Wheatley, and others; this work, upon which Milton's reputation entirely rests, was completed in 1793, he having returned to London in 1786. His only other important plate was 'The Deluge,' engraved for Macklin's Bible from a picture by De Loutherbourg, now in the South Kensington Museum; but specimens of his work occur in Boydell's, Kearsley's, and Steevens's editions of Shakespeare, and Ottley's 'Stafford Gallery,' 1818. In 1801 appeared 'Views in Egypt, from the original Drawings in the possession of Sir Robert Ainslie, taken during his Embassy to Constantinople by Luigi Mayer, engraved by and under the direction of Thomas Milton,' a series of coloured aquatints. Milton was a governor of the short-lived Society of Engravers founded in 1803. He died at Bristol on 27 Feb. 1827. W. Bell Scott, in his 'Autobiographical Notes,' 1892, observes of Milton: 'He had a unique power of distinguishing the foliage of trees and the texture of all bodies, especially water, as it never had been done before, and never will be done again.'

[Redgrave's Dict. of Artists; Dodd's manuscript Hist. of English Engravers (Brit. Mus. Add. MS. 33403); Universal Cat. of Books on Art; Pye's Patronage of British Art, 1845, p. 312; Gent. Mag. 1827, i. 379.] F. M. O'D.

MILTON, WILLIAM OF (*d.* 1261), Franciscan. [See MELITON.]

MILVERLEY, WILLIAM (*fl.* 1350), schoolman, was an Oxford student, who flourished in the middle of the fourteenth century. In Latin he is called Milverlegus. He wrote: 1. 'Compendium de quinque universalibus,' incipit 'Pro superficiali noticia.' Of this there are numerous manuscripts at Oxford, Bodley MS. O. C. 2593, New College 289, ff. 58–63, Oriel College 35, ff. 1–4, Magdalen College 162, ff. 1–4, and 47, ff. 34–7, where it is entitled 'Universalia abbreviata,' and Corpus Christi College 103, ff. 32–40, from which it appears that it is a commentary on the work of Porphyrius. 2. 'Commentarii in sex principia Gilberti Porretani,' MS. Oriel College 35, ff. 134–152, Magdalen College 47, ff. 67–86, and Lambeth 393, ff. 143 *b*–184. 3. 'Sophismata. De incipere, differre et scire.' In MS. New College 289 we have 'Materia bona et utilis de inceptione secundum Mag. W. Mylverlye' on f. 71, 'Materia . . . de Differt' on f. 81, and 'Materia . . . de scientia' on f. 90. In Corpus Christi College MS. 116, f. 5, there is 'Materia de incipit Mirwirley.' Tanner attributes to Milverley the anonymous tract 'De qualitate' in MS. C.C.C. Oxon. 103, which is perhaps more probably assigned to John Chilmark [q. v.]

[Bale, v. 85; Tanner's Bibl. Brit.-Hib. 528; Coxe's Catalogus . . . MSS. in Coll. Aulisque Oxon.] C. L. K.

MILVERTON, JOHN (*d.* 1487), Carmelite, was a native of Milverton, Somerset, and became a Carmelite friar at Bristol. Afterwards he studied at Oxford, where he became prior of the house of his order (WOOD, *City of Oxford*, ii. 440, Oxf. Hist. Soc.), and disputed as doctor of divinity in January or February 1451–2 (BOASE, *Reg. Univ. Oxon.* i. 16, Oxf. Hist. Soc.) He was chosen English provincial of the order in a general chapter at Paris in 1456, and held the office until 1465, but was restored in 1469, and retained the post till 1482 (*Harley MS.* 3838, f. 39). Milverton wrote against the doctrines of Reginald Pecock [q. v.] When the Carmelites Henry Parker and Thomas Holden were censured by the Bishop of London for preaching the doctrine of evangelical poverty Milverton took up their defence. He was opposed by William Ive or Ivy [q. v.], and in October 1464 was excommunicated and imprisoned by his bishop. Afterwards he was summoned, or went, to Rome, where, his explanations not being satisfactory, he was for three years imprisoned by Paul II in the castle of St. Angelo. Eventually his case was remitted to the consideration of seven cardinals, who acquitted him of heresy. The pope is stated to have then offered to make him a cardinal, an honour which Milverton declined. Previously to his imprisonment Milverton is alleged to have been chosen bishop of St. Davids, but owing to the accusations against him never consecrated; it is, however, to be noticed that the last vacancy was in 1460. In Lambeth MS. 580 ff. 213–7 there is a bull of Paul II as to Milverton's controversy, and a letter from some English theologians on the matter, both dated 1464, and a later bull dated 1468, as to the recantation and restitution of John Milverton, who is styled provincial. Milverton died in London 30 Jan. 1486–7, and was buried in Whitefriars; Weever quotes his epitaph (*Funerall Monuments*, p. 439). Bale (*Harley MS.* 3838, f. 105) gives another epitaph beginning:

Mylvertonus erat doctrine firmus amator.

Elsewhere (*Harley* 1819, f. 67 *b*) he quotes some other lines, of which the first two are:

Deditus hic studio totus miranda reliquit
Scripta, nec insignior ipse loquendo fuit,

and states that he was called 'doctor probatus.'

Milverton wrote: 1. 'Ad papam Pium II super articulis, examinatione, disputatione, ac tandem revocatione R. Pecock.' 2. 'De paupertate Christi.' 3. 'Symbolum sue fidei.' 4. 'Epistolæ lxiv ad amicos.' He is also credited with lectures, determinations, sermons, and commentaries on scripture, together with various letters to the cardinals, to whom his case was referred, and to others, besides some other works, the distinct identity of which seems doubtful. None of Milverton's writings appear to have survived. His controversies are alleged to have damaged the position of his order in England, a statement which De Villiers repudiates.

[Bale's Heliades in Harley MSS. 1819 ff. 38–9, 67 *b*, 107, 216, and 3838 f. 105; Tanner's Bibl. Brit.-Hib. pp. 528–9; C. De Villiers's Bibl. Carmel. ii. 56–9; Todd's Catalogue of Lambeth MSS.; Gregory's Chronicle (Camden Soc.); Wood's Hist. and Antiq. Univ. Oxford, i. 605, 626.] C. L. K.

MILWARD, EDWARD (1712?–1757), physician, was born about 1712, probably at Lindridge, Worcestershire, where his family resided. He was entered at Trinity College, Cambridge, but left without graduating, and acquired the degree of doctor of medicine from some foreign university, possibly Leyden, though his name does not appear in the 'Album Studiosorum' of that university. We find from the date of his first book that he was in 1733 a doctor of medicine, living in London at Queen's Square, Ormond Street, whence he removed to Portugal Row, Lincoln's Inn Fields. On 7 July 1741 he was created by royal mandate M.D. of Cambridge as a member of Trinity College. He was admitted licentiate of the College of Physicians 30 Sept. 1747, and fellow 30 Sept. 1748; was censor 1752, and in the same year delivered the Harveian oration. He became fellow of the Royal Society 21 Jan. 1741–2. Subsequently removing to Worcester, he died there 26 Aug. 1757 (*Gent. Mag.* 1757, p. 435), and was buried in the Knighton Chapel, Lindridge, among other members of his family. His epitaph, given in Nash's 'Worcestershire' (ii. 98), states that he died at the age of forty-five.

Milward was a man of considerable learning, and a diligent student of the classical medical writers. His only important work was his essay on Alexander Trallianus, a Greek physician of the sixth century, whom he sought to rescue from unmerited obscurity. It shows wide reading and an originality remarkable in a young man of twenty-one. It is spoken of with respect by the latest editor of Alexander (PUSCHMANN, *Alexander von Tralles*, Vienna, 1878, i. 100). Milward intended this essay to be the prelude to a new edition of the text of Alexander, for which he had made, he says, elaborate preparations, but this never appeared. Another ambitious scheme was that which occasioned his 'Letter to Learned Men,' namely, the plan of a complete history of British writers on medicine and surgery, for which he desired to obtain the assistance of other scholars, and had himself made large collections. Among these were the papers of William Becket [q. v.] the surgeon, who had for thirty years been collecting materials for such a purpose, but died without carrying out his intention. The acquisition of these papers from Curll the bookseller was the starting-point of Milward's scheme; he again refers to it in the preface to Drake's 'Orationes,' but the projected work was never published. Another projected but unpublished work is advertised at the close of the 'Circular Letter' as preparing for the press, viz., 'Gangrænologia, sive de Gangræna et sphacelo liber,' intended to be an elaborate treatise on gangrene. The important materials collected by the author with a view to these works seem to have unfortunately disappeared.

Of his published works, 1., 'The Essay on Trallianus,' appears with two different title-pages, though the text in each case is identical. (a) 'A Letter to Sir Hans Sloane in Vindication of the Character of those Greek Writers on Physic that flourished after Galen, but particularly of Alexander Trallian, etc. By E. Milward, M.D., formerly of Trinity College, Cambridge,' London, 1733, 8vo. (b) 'Trallianus Reviviscens, or an Account of Alexander Trallian, &c., being a Supplement to Dr. Freind's "History of Physick," in a Letter to Sir Hans Sloane,' London, 1734, 8vo. 2. 'A Circular Invitatory Letter to all Orders of Learned Men . . . concerning an Attempt towards an History of the Lives, etc., of the most celebrated

British Physical and Chirurgical Writers,' London, 1740, 8vo, 63 pp. 3. 'Oratio Harvæana,' 1752, London, 1753, 4to. He also edited 'Jacobi Drakei Orationes tres de febre intermittente,' &c., London, 1742, 4to. In the British Museum Library (Sloane MS. 4435, f. 281) are reports of three medical cases by Milward, presented to the Royal Society in 1739 but not published.

[Milward's Works; Munk's Coll. of Phys. 1878, ii. 166.] J. F. P.

MILWARD, JOHN (1556–1609), divine, born in 1556, was a member of the Cambridgeshire family of that name. He was admitted a scholar of St. John's College, Cambridge, 5 Nov. 1579, graduated B.A., and then appears to have matriculated from Christ Church, Oxford, 23 Nov. 1581, aged 25, proceeding B.A. on 19 Jan. 1582, and M.A. and D.D. in 1584 (*Oxf. Univ. Reg.*, Oxf. Hist. Soc. vol. ii. pt. i. p. 17, pt. ii. p. 105, pt. iii. p. 100). He may have been the John Milward presented on 17 Jan. 1590–1 to the vicarage of Dullingham, Cambridgeshire (Gibbons, *Ely Episcopal Records*, p. 447), and, 28 Dec. 1596, by Lord North to the vicarage of Bovey Tracey, Devonshire. About 1605 he became rector of Passenham, Northamptonshire (Bridges, *Northamptonshire*, i. 307). On 8 Nov. 1608 he was presented by the mayor, commonalty, and citizens of London to the rectory of St. Margaret Pattens, Billingsgate ward. About 1605 he was defeated in a contest for the office of lecturer at Christ Church, Newgate Street, by William Bradshaw [q. v.]; he was, however, subsequently appointed (see his will, and cf. Clarke, *Lives*, 1677, ii. 45).

Soon after the accession of James I Milward was appointed one of his chaplains, and on 5 Aug. 1607 he was commanded to preach a thanksgiving sermon at St. Paul's for the deliverance of his majesty from the Gowrie conspiracy [see Ruthven]. Milward's sermon, which was printed, under the title of 'Jacob's Great Day of Trouble and Deliverance,' with a preface by Matthias Milward (see below), London, 1610, is an ingenious parody of the life of Jacob, full of witty and classical allusions.

In April 1609 Milward was ordered to visit Scotland, in company with Dr. William Goodwin [q. v.], in order to aid in the re-establishment of episcopacy. The Earl of Dunfermline, writing to the king on 5 July 1609, testifies to the great contentment and satisfaction 'your highnes twa chaplaynes, Doctor Goodwin and Doctor Milwaird, hes given to all in this cuntrie in their doctrine, boithe in learning, eloquence, and godliness' (*Letters and State Papers of James VI*, Abbotsford Club, Edinburgh, 1838, p. 169). An annuity of a hundred marks was granted him on 15 April 1609, in recognition of his services (*Warrant Book*, James I).

Milward died in the house of the lord chancellor, the Earl of Dunfermline, Edinburgh, on 1 Aug. 1609. He married Agnes How the younger, and left a son, James, and two daughters, Mary and Margaret. He owned at the time of his death houses in Warwick Lane, in the city of London, and at Hertford, as well as land at Sutton, Cambridgeshire.

Milward, Matthias (*fl.* 1603–1641), younger brother of the preceding, scholar of St. John's College, Cambridge, and curate of Wentworth, Cambridgeshire, in 1600 (*Ely Episc. Rec.* p. 371), was presented by James I to the rectory of East Barnet, Hertfordshire, on 18 May 1603. A successor was appointed in 1639 (Newcourt, i. 806). He was admitted a member of Gray's Inn on 1 Nov. 1624 (Foster, *Admissions*, p. 174). He was afterwards rector of St. Helen's, Bishopsgate, London. On 31 Aug. 1641 he preached at St. Michael's, Cornhill, to the Company of Artillery, Thomas Soame, colonel, a sermon which was printed under the title of 'The Souldiers Triumph and the Preachers Glory,' 1641, and was dedicated to Prince Charles. He died before 1648. He married, on 28 March 1605, Anne Evans of Cripplegate (Chester, *Marr. Licenses*, p. 927). A son Joseph, born at Barnet in 1621, was a scholar of Gonville and Caius College, Cambridge (Venn, *Admissions*, p. 198).

Another John Milward (1619–1683), nonconformist divine, son of George Milward, gentleman, of Shepton Mallet, Somerset, was born there in 1619. He matriculated at New Inn Hall, Oxford, on 16 March 1637–8, graduated B.A. on 1 July 1641, was elected a fellow of Corpus Christi College, and was created M.A. on 14 April 1648. He was appointed a delegate of visitors in 1649, and soon afterwards was made rector of the first mediety of the living of Darfield in the West Riding of Yorkshire, but was ejected about 1660. His successor, Robert Rogers, was instituted on 9 Nov. 1661. Milward then settled in London, and occasionally preached at the morning exercises in Cripplegate. Two of his sermons, entitled 'How ought we to love our neighbours as ourselves?' 'How ought we to do our duty towards others, though they do not do theirs towards us?' were published by Samuel Annesley [q. v.] in 'The Morning Exercises,' &c., 1676 and 1683 (cf. 5th edit. ed. Nicholls, 6 vols. 1844). Milward died unmarried at Islington, London, in 1683. By his will he left sums for books to the Bodleian and the library of

Corpus Christi, also to ten ejected ministers, or their wives or families, five of Yorkshire and five of Somerset. He directed that his funeral expenses should not exceed 30*l.*, and divided the remainder between his brother, Daniel Milward, merchant, of London, and his sisters Katherine Stephens and Anne Burnell.

[For the elder Milward see Wood's Fasti, i. 217, 226; Newcourt's Repert. Eccl. i. 409; State Papers, Dom. James I, 1603–10, pp. 116, 119, 504; Nichols's Progresses of James I, p. 289; Cooper's Athen. Cantab. ii. 522; Preface to Jacob's Great Day of Trouble (an extract from this sermon is to be found in a collection of commonplaces against popery, Add. MS. 12515); will at Somerset House, P. C. C., 84 Dorset. For the second John Milward see Wood's Fasti, ii. 111; Calamy and Palmer's Nonconf. Mem. i. 228; Calamy's Account, ii. 66; Hunter's Deanery of Doncaster, ii. 116; Foster's Alumni Oxon. 1500–1714; Dunn's Seventy-five Divines, p. 76; Burrows's Register of the Visitors of the Univ. of Oxford, 1881, p. 498; will at Somerset House, P. C. C., 115 Drax.] C. F. S.

MILWARD, RICHARD (1609–1680), editor of Selden's 'Table Talk,' a son of Richard Milward, was born at Flitton in Bedfordshire, and baptised there on 25 April 1609 (parish reg.) He matriculated as a sizar from Trinity College, Cambridge, on 7 July 1625, was elected scholar of his college on 13 April 1627, proceeded B.A. in 1628, M.A. in 1632, and D.D. by royal mandate in 1662. He became rector of Great Braxted in Essex on 12 Dec. 1643, and held the living for the rest of his life. He was appointed canon of Windsor 31 May, and installed 30 June 1666, and was vicar of Isleworth, Middlesex, from 3 July 1678 till his death on 20 Dec. 1680; he was buried at Great Braxted on 24 Dec., and a black marble slab erected to his memory is now on the north side of the church. At the time of his death he was possessed of lands at Flitton and Higham Gobion in Bedfordshire, which he left to his widow, Mary, daughter of Sir Anthony Thomas of Cobham, Surrey, and after her death to his only daughter and heiress, Mary, wife of Sir Anthony Abdy of Kelvedon, Essex.

Milward long acted as amanuensis to John Selden [q. v.], and 'had the opportunity to hear his discourse twenty years together.' The notes that he made from time to time of 'those excellent things that usually fell from him' were afterwards sorted and arranged by him for publication, though the first edition of the 'Table Talk' did not appear till 1689, nine years after Milward's death. Discredit has been thrown upon the authenticity of the compilation, on the ground that it contains many things unworthy of Selden, and at variance with his principles and practice. David Wilkins [q. v.], Selden's editor and biographer, strongly held this view (cf. *Acta Eruditorum*, Leipzig, Suppl. i. 1692, p. 426). There are three manuscript copies of the work in the British Museum (*Harl. MSS.* 690, 1315, and *Sloane MS.* 2513), but none of them original. The second edition of the 'Table Talk' (1696), printed for Jacob Tonson, and Awnsham, and John Churchill, was probably based on the Harleian MS. 1315. It was reprinted in 1716. In the Advocates' Library, Edinburgh, is also a manuscript copy, which differs in some details from the first edition.

[Newcourt's Repertorium, i. 676, ii. 92; Kennett's Reg. p. 685; Cal. State Papers, Dom. Ser. 1661–2, p. 371; Le Neve's Fasti (Hardy), iii. 403; P. C. C. (North, 60); Visitation of Essex (Harl. Soc. Publ.), xiv. 628; Wright's Essex, ii. 411; Milward's dedication of Table Talk, 1689; Aikin's Lives of Selden and Usher, pp. 167–8; Singer's Preface to Table Talk, edit. 1856, and Irving's Notes, edit. 1854; for relative value of the various manuscripts and printed editions, Reynolds's Introduction to Table Talk, Oxford, 1892, pp. xi–xiii; Trin. Coll. Camb. Admission Registers; information from J. W. Clark, esq., Cambridge, and the Rev. W. H. Rowlandson, Great Braxted.] B. P.

MIMPRISS, ROBERT (1797–1875), Sunday-school worker, was born at Deptford, Kent, 14 Jan. 1797. His father was an official in Deptford dockyard, and had nine sons, of whom Robert and Thomas, afterwards a surgeon, alone survived infancy. After education at a Blackheath boarding school Robert, at the age of sixteen, went to sea as purser on a foreign merchantman. But after the first voyage he abandoned the occupation, and after a brief trial of a clerkship in a London merchant's office, and subsequently of a desultory study of art, he married a lady of fortune in 1821, and thenceforth devoted himself to the development of Sunday schools. He devised what was known as the 'Mimpriss System of Graduated Simultaneous Instruction,' based on Greswell's 'Harmony of the Gospels' [see GRESWELL, EDWARD]. He moulded the gospel history into a continuous narrative, and divided it into one hundred lessons. The course was illustrated by pictorial maps, charts, and tables, in the preparation of which he was assisted by John Wilson, author of 'Lectures on the Israelitish Origin of the English Nation.' From 1830 to 1850 Mimpriss was chiefly engaged in writing books in connection with his system, but he repeatedly travelled round the country setting forth its merits or advocating millenarian and teetotal principles.

In 1860 the illness of his wife and pecuniary losses, due to the partial failure of his publications, led him to relax his efforts. He died at Clapham, 20 Dec. 1875. His widow and his brother Thomas survived him. A portrait is prefixed to the memoir of 1876.

His works, apart from elementary manuals for the use of schools, were: 1. 'A Pictorial, Geographical, Chronological, and Historical Chart, delineating the Rise and Progress of the Evangelical or Christian Dispensation to the Ascension of our Lord,' London, 1832 (with a key, 8vo). 2. 'A Harmony of the Four Gospels in the English Authorised Version, arranged according to Greswell's "Harmonia Evangelica," in Greek . . .' intended principally as an accompaniment to No. 1, London, 1833, 8vo. 3. 'Gospel Recreations for Sabbath Evenings,' London, 1836, 8vo (with a set of card-pictures); 2nd edit. 1839, revised and much enlarged, under the title of 'Conversations for Sabbath Evenings on our Lord's Life and Ministry.' 4. 'The Acts of the Apostles and Epistles historically and geographically delineated according to Greswell's arrangement,' Lond. 1837, 8vo (with a chart). 5. 'The Treasury Harmony of the Four Evangelists, in the words of the Authorised Version, according to Greswell's "Harmonia Evangelica," &c.,' 2 vols. London, 1849–51, 12mo; republished as the 'Gospel Treasury,' new edit., London, 1884, 4to. 6. A Full Development of Mimpriss's System of Graduated Simultaneous Instruction,' London [1855], 8vo. 7. 'The Mimpriss System. The Amalgamated Manual for Superintendents,' London [1855], 8vo.

[Robert Mimpriss: a Memoir of his Life and Work, London [1876], 8vo; Record and Rock for December 1875; the author's works; private information.] E. G. H.

MINIFIE, SUSANNAH (1740?–1800), novelist. [See GUNNING.]

MINNAN, SAINT (*d.* 875?). [See MONAN.]

MINNES, SIR JOHN (1599–1671), admiral. [See MENNES.]

MINNS or **MINGH, SIR CHRISTOPHER** (1625–1666), vice-admiral. [See MYNGS.]

MINOT, LAURENCE (1300?–1352?), lyric poet, was probably born and bred in the north-east midlands of England. The evidence of this, however, is solely the character of his dialect, coupled with the frequency of his allusions to Yorkshire personages (cf. HALL, p. x). Of his life nothing is known on external authority. Even his name is attested only by his own mention of it in two passages of his poems (v. 1, and vii. 20: 'Now *Laurence Minot* will bigin'). The family of Minot (Miniot, Minyot, Mynyot) was, however, widely dispersed in the fourteenth century, especially in Yorkshire and Norfolk (cf. HALL, Introd. pp. x–xii). It included knights, wealthy London merchants, and, in particular, a Thomas Mynot, the king's notary, who is known to have been officially employed in Flanders at the date of the capture of Guisnes (1352), which Minot in his last poem describes with an air of exceptional knowledge. Minot's status and occupation cannot be certainly determined. The view that he was a monk (RITSON) or a priest (BIERBAUM) may be dismissed as baseless. The religious allusions are, indeed, not rare, but they are such as formed the common stock of middle-English romance, and their piety is that of the soldier, not of the cleric. A contemptuous allusion to being 'polled like a frere' (vii. 131) is also significant. Far more probable is the view that Minot was a soldierly minstrel, who wrote and sang mainly for the army, but was also favoured by the court. His songs appear, by their varying use of homelier and more cultivated metres, to be designed for audiences of varying rank. The alliterative long-line was in particular characteristic of the camp-song, as in the lines sung before Bannockburn (BRANDL, *Thomas of Erceldoune*, p. 16). He expresses throughout a personal devotion to Edward III, whom he celebrates (vi. vii. xi.), according to the current interpretation of Merlin's prophecy, as the boar of Windsor, and may have moved in his circle; it is clear, however, that he was not always present on Edward's campaigns, since he describes (iii. 86 foll.) the king as taking part in the fight off Southampton, which the other evidence shows that he did not. Even his testimony to Edward's personal valour at Sluys (v. 78), which none of the English chroniclers mention, but which is attested by Le Bel, does not imply his presence at the fight. It is probable, however, that his songs are not founded solely upon hearsay. Though he has no set descriptions, he occasionally lets fall a detail which suggests the eye-witness. There are many signs that he wrote while the events were still fresh, in some cases while their final issue was still pending. The triumphant poem (vi.) on the siege of Tournay (which opened 23 July 1340) was evidently written originally between that date and 25 Sept. following, when Edward unexpectedly raised the siege. Slight changes have, however, been made in some of the poems (esp. in vi.) at a later date, doubtless by Minot himself. No inference can be drawn from the abrupt termination of the series at 1352. Since the series of stirring events by no means ceased then, it is likely that Minot either died or produced songs which have been lost. The absence of any development of style in the series makes it probable that he was not very young at the outset (1333).

Minot neither founded nor belonged to a school. In metrical form he presents, in various combinations, the accentual, alliterative verse of the west and north; and the syllabic, rhymed verse of the east and south; rhyme and some degree of alliteration being constant features. His most frequent measure is the popular six-line strophe (ii. v. ix. x. xi.), while the remaining five songs have each a distinct stanza of more artificial structure, or the rhymed couplet. The alliterative measure seems therefore to have grown upon him. He tends also to multiply the alliterating words without need, at times using double alliteration in the same line (e.g. x. 1). He also uses the refrain (ii.), and is fond of repeating the last words of a stanza in the opening of the next (i. vi. vii.) While thus profuse in metrical ornament, Minot cannot, however, be said to show any further care for literary art. He writes in impetuous haste, but without true lyric inspiration; and his energy often confuses his narrative instead of driving it home. But while Minot has no great literary value, and gives almost no new information, he embodies in a most vivid way the militant England of his day. He has but one subject, the triumph of England and the English king over French and Scots. The class divisions among Englishmen are for him wholly merged in the unity of England; himself probably of Norman origin, his habitual language is the strongest and homeliest Saxon. His verse is throughout inspired by savage triumph in the national successes. He has no elegiac or tender note. If he alludes to Bannockburn (ii. 1) it is in order to proclaim the vengeance of Halidon Hill. His account of the capitulation of Calais ignores the intervention of the queen (viii. 57 f.) Even the brilliant pageantry of fourteenth century warfare is only casually reproduced (vii. 46). He does not approach his Scottish rival, Barbour, either in humanity or in poetic power.

Minot's poems exist only in a manuscript in the Cotton Library of the British Museum (Galba, E. ix. fol. 52 foll.), written by a single hand in the early years of the fifteenth century. The scribe was unquestionably northern, but the evidence of the rhymes shows that the originals contained both northern and midland forms (e.g. pres. part. in *-and*; plur. pres. in *-in*, vii. 135).

The following is a list of Minot's extant poems. None of them has a title; but all (except iv.) are headed by a couplet in which the subject is announced: 1. 'Lithes and I sall tell ȝow tyll | þe bataile of Halidon Hyll.' 2. 'Now for to tell ȝow will I turn | Of þe batayl of Banocburn.' In reality, however, a continuation of 1. 3. 'How Edward þe king come in Braband | And toke homage of all þe land.' 4. The first invasion of France, 1339. 5. 'Lithes and þe batail I sal bigyn | Of Inglisch men and Normandes in þe Swyn.' 6. 'Herkins how King Edward lay | With his men bifor Tournay.' 7. 'How Edward at Hogges unto land wan | And rade thurgh France or ever he blan.' The battle of Crécy. 8. 'How Edward als þe romance sais | Held his sege bifor Calais.' 9. 'Sir David had of his men grete loss | With Sir Edward at þe Nevil Cross.' 10. 'How King Edward and his menȝe | Met with þe Spaniardes in þe see.' 11. 'How gentill Sir Edward with his grete engines | Wan with his wight men þe castell of Gynes.'

Hall is inclined to attribute to Minot also the 'Hymn to Jesus Christ and the Virgin' (Early English Text Society, No. 26, p. 75) on grounds of style and language.

Minot's poems, discovered by Tyrwhitt, were first printed by Ritson, under the title, 'Poems on Interesting Events in the Reign of King Edward III, written in the year MCCCLII. by Laurence Minot,' 1795 and 1825. They were reissued by T. Wright in 'Political Poems,' i. 58 sq. (1859). Two good recent editions exist: 'Laurence Minot's Lieder,' von Wilhelm Scholle (*Quellen und Forschungen*, No. 52), 1884, with a valuable study of the grammar and metre; and 'The Poems of Laurence Minot,' by Joseph Hall, with admirable introduction and illustrative notes (Clarendon Press, 1887). Mätzner (*Sprachproben*) has also printed i–iv.; Wülcker, 'Altenglisches Lesebuch,' ii. and ix.; Morris and Skeat, 'Specimens,' iii. iv. and part of vii.

[Scholle's and Hall's Introductions and the Poems themselves; Ten Brink's Englische Litteraturgeschichte, i. 404 f.; Bierbaum's Ueber Laurence Minot und seine Lieder, 1876; Brandl's Mittelenglische Literatur in Paul's Grundriss der german. Philologie, p. 648.] C. H. H.

MINSHEU, JOHN (*fl.* 1617), lexicographer, lived chiefly in London, and made his living as a teacher of languages. He was poor, was married, and had children. Often, as may be gathered from his works, his lexicographical works were at a standstill for want of money, but generous friends, such as Sir Henry Spelman, helped him, and he managed to carry out his expensive undertakings. To finish his Spanish dictionary he went down to Cambridge, where, as may be seen from the subscription list prefixed to the 'Guide into the Tongues,' he made many friends. At Oxford he passed some months, with 'his company of strangers and scholars,' revising his 'Guide,' but although the vice-chancellor gave him in 1610 a certificate signed by himself and several heads of houses to the effect that the 'Dictionary' or 'Guide' was worthy of publication, Oxford did not furnish any subscribers. He seems to have been a laborious student, lighting the candle, as he says, for others and burning out himself. Ben Jonson describes him as a 'rogue' (*Conversations with Drummond*, ed. Laing, p. 4).

Minsheu wrote: 1. 'A Dictionarie in Spanish and English,' London, 1599, fol. 2. 'A Spanish Grammar,' London, 1599, fol. Minsheu's 'Dictionary' and 'Grammar' were both founded on the works of Richard Percival [q. v.] He also about this time seems to have published another shorter Spanish dictionary, more in the nature of an encyclopædia (cf. Arber, *Stationers' Registers*, iii. 145-6). 3. 'Vocabularium Hispanico-Latinum et Anglicum copiosissimum. . . . A most copious Spanish Dictionarie with Latine and English (and sometime other Languages),' London, 1617 (?) fol. 4. 'Ἡγεμὼν εἰς τὰς γλώσσας, id est Ductor in Linguas, the Guide into Tongues,' London, 1617, fol., containing equivalents in eleven languages (2nd edit. 1626, in nine languages and much altered). This great lexicon is of great value as a dictionary of Elizabethan English; it is also in all probability the first English book printed by subscription, or at all events the first which contains a list of the subscribers. Minsheu obtained a license (granted to John Minshon) for the sole printing of the 'Glosson' for twenty-one years on 20 Feb. 1611. It seems that Bishop Wren had annotated a copy of the second edition with a view to republishing it himself.

[Works; Gent. Mag. 1786 ii. 1073, 1787 i. 16, 121; H. B. Wheatley's Chron. Notices of the Dictionaries of the English Language in Proc. of Philol. Soc. 1865, p. 230; Notes and Queries, 2nd ser. viii. 269, ix. 447, xi. 422; Cal. State Papers, Dom. 1611-18, p. 10.] W. A. J. A.

MINSHULL or MYNSHUL, GEFFRAY (1594?-1668), author, son of Edward Minshull of Nantwich, Cheshire, and his wife Margaret, daughter of Thomas Mainwaring, was born about 1594, and admitted at Gray's Inn on 11 March 1611-12. In 1617 he was imprisoned for debt in the King's Bench prison, and while there occupied himself by writing a series of 'characters,' which he sent to his uncle Matthew Mainwaring [q. v.], who generously helped him out of his difficulties. These experiences of prison life were published in 1618, with the title of 'Essayes and Characters of a Prison and Prisoners. Written by G. M. of Grayes-Inn, Gent.' (small quarto). The volume was reissued without alteration in 1638; the title-page bears the inscription 'with some new additions,' but the contents are precisely the same as those of the 1618 edition; it was reprinted at Edinburgh in 1821. To this last edition, of which only 150 copies were printed, an introductory notice was prefixed by the anonymous editor. All these editions are in the British Museum Library. Minshull died in 1668 at Nantwich, where he was buried on 1 Nov.

[Brit. Mus. Cat.; Hall's Hist. of Nantwich, 1883, pp. 469, 471; Gray's Inn Admission Register (Foster), p. 129.] C. W. S.

MINTO, Earls of. [See Elliot, Sir Gilbert, 1751-1814, first Earl; Elliot, Gilbert, 1782-1859, second Earl.]

MINTO, Lords. [See Elliot, Sir Gilbert, 1651-1718; Elliot, Sir Gilbert, 1693-1766.]

MINTO, WILLIAM (1845-1893), critic, born 10 Oct. 1845, near Alford, Aberdeenshire, was son of James Minto, by his wife Barbara Copland. Gaining a bursary, he entered Aberdeen University in 1861. Here he steadily outdistanced competitors, until on graduating M.A. in 1865 he carried off the leading money prizes and took honours in three departments—classics, mathematics, and philosophy—a feat unprecedented and still unique. In 1866 he went to Merton College, Oxford, but left next year without taking a degree. Returning to Aberdeen he became assistant to the professor of logic and English literature, Dr. Alexander Bain. It was while thus engaged that he turned his mind towards the study of English literature, and planned his 'Manual of English Prose Literature, Biographical and Critical,' which he published in 1872.

In 1873 he moved to London and engaged in literary work, contributing to the now extinct 'Examiner,' of which paper he was editor for four years, 1874-8. Subsequently he was on the leader-writing staff of the 'Daily News' and 'Pall Mall Gazette.' In 1874 he published his 'Characteristics of English Poets from Chaucer to Shirley,' and in 1879 a monograph on Defoe for the 'English Men of Letters' series. Besides contributing to the leading reviews he wrote for the 'Encyclopædia Britannica' a number of important articles on literary subjects.

On 8 Jan. 1880 he married Cornelia, daughter of the Rev. Lewis Griffiths, rector of Swindon, Gloucestershire. In the same year, on the retirement of Professor Bain, he was elected to the chair of logic and English in Aberdeen University. During his professoriate he wrote three novels—'The Crack of Doom,' 1886, 'The Mediation of Ralph Hardelot,' 1888, and 'Was she good or bad?' 1889. He edited Scott's 'Lay,' Oxford, 1886, and 'Lady of the Lake,' 1891, Scott's poetical works, 1887, and 'Autobiographical Notes of the Life of William Bell Scott,' 1892 (cf. correspondence in *Academy*, 1892).

His health began to decline in 1891, and although a voyage to Greece served temporarily to brace his system, he succumbed to a complication of ailments on 1 March 1893, just when the separation of logic from English in his dual chair appeared to open up fresh opportunities of pursuing his favourite subject. After his death appeared 'University Extension Manual on Logic' and 'Plain Principles of Prose Composition,' both in 1893, and a third volume, 'English Literature under the Georges' (1894).

Minto was a versatile writer. He advocated advanced liberal opinions in politics, and during Lord Beaconsfield's Afghan war reviewed the government policy from day to day in the 'Daily News' with conspicuous ability. He claimed that he gave currency to the word 'jingoism.' His novels, though clever and ingenious, do not retain permanent interest. As an editor he discovered and encouraged many young authors, since famous, and as a professor he exercised a stimulating influence on his students through the contagion of his enthusiasm.

But his chief work was done in criticism. Laying an admirable foundation of scholarship in the wide reading involved in preparing his first two volumes, the one an exhaustive and systematic survey of English literature, and the other a minutely analytic and detailed comparison of styles and characteristics, he judged for himself with penetration, originality, and sanity. He therefore often struck out a novel line, as when he argued that Burns was not merely a genius, but a disciplined student of literature, and that the poet owed his recognition not to the public but to the critics of his time. Coming with an open mind to controverted subjects, he often offered a new hypothesis. He identified Chapman with the 'rival poet' of Shakespeare's sonnets, and added a new sonnet to the recognised number—'Phaeton to his friend Florio,' prefixed to Florio's 'Second Fruits' (1591).

[Personal knowledge.] A. M.

MINTON, HERBERT (1793–1858), manufacturer of pottery and porcelain, second son of Thomas Minton, potter, was born at Stoke-on-Trent, 4 Feb. 1793. His father was a native of Shropshire, and was brought up as an engraver at the Caughley pottery works, near Broseley, under John Turner, who is stated to have discovered the art of printing in blue on china. He afterwards went to London and worked for Spode at his London house of business in Lincoln's Inn Fields. In 1788 he settled at Stoke and founded the concern which has since become celebrated.

Herbert Minton was educated at Audlem school, Cheshire, and in 1817 he and his elder brother were taken into partnership. The father died in 1836, and the brother entered the church. Herbert was thus left alone in the business. 'Neither a man of profound research nor an educated artist,' wrote Mr. Digby Wyatt, in a paper read before the Society of Arts, 'neither an economist nor an inventor, by courage and ceaseless energy he brought to bear upon the creation of his ultimately colossal business such a combination of science, art, organisation, and invention as can be paralleled only' in the case of 'his great predecessor Josiah Wedgwood.' Like Wedgwood, Minton surrounded himself with talented artists and ingenious inventors. Down to about 1830 nothing but earthenware and ordinary soft porcelain were made by the firm, but by the efforts of Minton and his partners the manufacture of hard porcelain, parian, encaustic tiles, azulejos or coloured enamel tiles, mosaics, Della Robbia ware, majolica, and Palissy ware was gradually introduced. The firm was fortunate in obtaining the patronage of the Duke of Sutherland, who lived at Trentham. Minton contributed a remarkable collection to the exhibition held in Birmingham in 1849 in connection with the meeting of the British Association. He was awarded a council medal at the Great Exhibition of 1851, and his specimens of majolica ware at the Paris exhibition of 1855 created great interest. About 1800 some fifty hands were employed at the works, but when Minton died the number reached fifteen hundred. The business was divided between his two nephews in 1868, Mr. C. Minton Campbell retaining the china and earthenware business, while Mr. M. D. Hollins took the encaustic tile manufactory. He lived for many years at Hartshill, near Stoke, where in 1842 he built and endowed a church and schools. The church is one of Sir George Gilbert Scott's early works. He died at Torquay, 1 April 1858, and was buried at Hartshill. The School of Art at Stoke was erected by public subscription as a memorial to Minton. It was opened in 1860.

[L. Arnoux's Lecture on Ceramic Manufactures at the Exhibition of 1851, delivered at the Society of Arts 2 June 1852; Digby Wyatt's paper on the Influence exercised on Ceramic Manufactures by the late Herbert Minton, read before the Society of Arts 26 May 1858; Account of a Visit to the Works of Mintons (Lim.), Stoke-upon-Trent, 1884; Spon's Encycl. of the Industrial Arts, p. 1590; Account of Minton's china works in Staffordshire Times, 30 Oct. 1875; Gent Mag. 1859, ii. 432.] R. B. P.

MIRFELD, JOHN (*fl.* 1393), writer on medicine, whose name is written Marifeldus by Leland (*Commentarii de Scriptt. Brit.* c. 582), was a canon regular of St. Austin in the priory of St. Bartholomew in West Smithfield, London. He studied at Oxford, and there attended the medical lectures of Nicholas Tyngewich. He received medical instruction from a London practitioner, whom he calls 'my master,' but does not name, and who was a bold operator. He witnessed tapping of the brain and the healing of an incised wound of the stomach, as well as the partial cure of a paralysis due to cerebral hæmorrhage caused by a fall from a horse. John Helme, one of the brethren of the neighbouring foundation of St. Bartholomew's Hospital, taught him how to treat the plague. About 1387 he wrote a great treatise on medicine, entitled 'Breviarium Bartholomæi,' of which there is a fine manuscript copy, written in that year for the hospital of St. John the Baptist attached to the Abbey of Abingdon, in the library of Pembroke College, Oxford, and two imperfect ones in the British Museum, which both belonged to Dr. John Dee [q.v.] The 'Breviarium' is divided into fifteen parts, viz.: 1, fevers; 2, affections of the whole body; 3, of the head, neck, and throat; 4, of the chest; 5, of the abdomen; 6, of the pelvic organs; 7, of the legs; 8, of boils; 9, of wounds and bruises; 10, of fractures and dislocations; 11, of dislocations of joints; 12, of simple medicines; 13, of compound medicines; 14, of purgatives; 15, of the preservation and recovery of health. It contains many interesting cases and original remarks. He had read Gaddesden, the Arabians, and the 'Regimen Sanitatis Salerni.' He tells how to make gingerbread, and gives the English names of many diseases, among them 'smalpockes,' one of the earliest citations of this term. He is an excellent teller of stories, and his accounts of the Augustinian canon thrown from his horse, of the fraudulent innkeeper's tricks, and of the doings of a mad dog are superior in detail and liveliness to the best narratives of Gaddesden. He also wrote 'Parvus Tractatus de Signis Prognosticis Mortis' (Lambeth Library MS. 444). In 1393 he appeared in a court of law to represent the convent of St. Bartholomew in West Smithfield.

[Breviarium Bartholomæi, manuscript in library of Pembroke College, Oxford, and that in the Harleian Collection, No. 3; Anecdota Oxoniensa, Sinonima Bartholomei, edited by J. L. G. Mowat (this is a part of the Pembroke copy of the Breviarium); Norman Moore's Progress of Medicine at St. Bartholomew's Hospital, 1889, an Introductory Lecture on the Principles and Practice of Medicine, Lancet, No. 3659, containing several extracts from the Pembroke MS.] N. M.

MIRK, JOHN (*fl.* 1403?), prior of Lilleshall in Shropshire, is chiefly known by his 'Liber ffestialis,' written in English. The manuscript, in Cott. Claud. A. II. f. 123, has the colophon: 'Explicit tractus qui dicitur ffestial. Per fratrem Johannem Mirkus compositus, canonicum regularem Monasterii de Lulshull.' The 'Festival' begins with a preface in which the writer speaks of himself as of one who has charge of souls, and must teach his parishioners about the principal feasts, information respecting which he has partly drawn from the 'Legenda Aurea.' Each sermon begins with moral reflections and ends with a 'narracio,' the source of which is often named. The Cott. MS. contains a story about a man of Lilleshall (f. 116), and sermons for the feasts of the local saints, St. Wenefreda and St. Alkemund of Shrewsbury. The Cambridge University Library MS. Dd. 10. 50 omits the local legends and the colophon (Ee. II. 15 and Nn. III. 10 are mutilated). The Harl. MSS. 2371 and 2391 supply the sermons, without the local legends and preface, and are arranged 'de tempore' and 'de sanctis.' The Lansdowne MS. 392 (1), which resembles Cott. Claud. A. II., omits twelve sermons between St. Margaret's day and the Ember days, and ends at All Saints' day. The conclusion of the manuscript is imperfect. No common origin has yet been assigned to the numerous manuscripts of the 'Liber Festialis.' The printed editions of the 'Festial' by Caxton (1483) and Wynkyn De Worde (1493) have Mirk's preface, but are arranged like the Harl. MSS., with various omissions.

Mirk wrote also the 'Manuale Sacerdotum,' found in Harl. 5306, Bodl. Cod. Digb. 75(26), f. 162, imperfect, Jesus Coll. Oxon. I., and Cambridge University Library, Ff. 1, 14. The title of Harl. 5306, in a later hand, states that the author was John Miræus. The Jesus Coll. MS. removes any uncertainty by the colophon, 'Explicit libellus dictus ... secundum Johannem Marcus, priorem abathie de Lilyshel.' Both this manuscript and Harl. 5306 begin with a letter: 'Amico suo Karissimo domino iohanni de S. uicario de A. frater iohannis dictus prior de l. salutem.' The writer humbly asks for corrections, and hopes J. de S. may not long delay to turn the work into English. In Harl. MS. 5306 the last eight chapters of the fifth part are missing. The Cambridge MS. does not contain the letter, but is entitled 'Manuale Sacerdotis' (Johannis Lilleshullensis); it is complete, and the transcriber's name, Robert Wasselyn, chaplain, is recorded. Mr. Bradshaw noted that the subject and treatment of the 'Manual' are much like that of Mirk's 'Instructions to Parish Priests,' an English poem in rhyming couplets, printed for the Early English Text Society from the Cott. MS. Claud. A. II. ff. 127, 152. This poem, which Mirk says he translated from the Latin called 'Pars Oculi,' is neither a versified translation of John de Burgh's 'Pupilla Oculi' (a dictionary of theological subjects alphabetically arranged), nor of Mirk's 'Manual,' as has been suggested, but of the 'Pupilla Oculi' by William de Pagula [q. v.] Of this Mirk has used both the 'dextra' and the 'sinistra pars,' but chiefly the 'dextra.'

No list of the priors of the canons regular of Lilleshull is known, and Mirk's date cannot be ascertained. Pits gives it as 1403.

[Manuscripts quoted in the text (Early English Text Soc.); Instructions to Parish Priests, ed. Perry, with note by H. Bradshaw. On the early editions of the Liber Festialis see Lowndes's Bibliog. Manual, s.v. 'Festival.'] M. B.

MISAUBIN, JOHN, M.D. (*d.* 1734), was born in France, and graduated M.D. at the university of Cahors on 7 July 1687. He settled in London, and became a licentiate of the College of Physicians on 25 June 1719. His foreign manner and accent sometimes excited ridicule, and though he was a regular licentiate his arrogance and method of practice caused him to be described and caricatured as a quack. In one print of the time he is represented as saying 'Prenez des pilules, prenez des pilules,' and Fielding relates (*Tom Jones*, bk. xiii. chap. ii.) that he 'used to say that the proper direction to him was to Dr. Misaubin "in the world," intimating that there were few people in it to whom his great reputation was not known.' He has left no writings, and his chief claim to recollection is that he is one of the four medical practitioners mentioned in 'Tom Jones,' the others being Dr. Sydenham [q. v.] and the surgeons John Freke [q. v.] and John Ranby [q. v.] He lived near Covent Garden, and died on 20 April 1734.

[Munk's Coll. of Phys. ii. 67; Fielding's Tom Jones, ed. 1749, v. 8; William Wadd's Nugæ Chirurgicæ, London, 1824.] N. M.

MISSELDEN, EDWARD (*fl.* 1608–1654), merchant and economic writer, was deputy-governor of the Merchant Adventurers' Company at Delft from 1623 until 1633. Upon his departure from England (October 1623) the East India Company invited him to act as one of their commissioners at Amsterdam to negotiate a private treaty with the Dutch. He appears to have been well qualified for the position. He was 'reputed a proper merchant and a good civilian' (*Court Minutes*, 17–21 Oct. 1623; *State Papers*, East Indies), and had probably been employed by the Merchant Adventurers' Company in 1616 in a similar capacity (*Carleton Letters*, 1615–16–1620, pp. 63, 64). His fellow-commissioner was Robert Barlow, East India merchant. The negotiations, however, were fruitless, owing chiefly to the unreasonable attitude of the Dutch. Upon the report of the outrages at Amboyna new difficulties arose, and Misselden himself suffered from ill-health. He returned to England, and presented to the company an account of the negotiations (3 Nov. 1624). The court acknowledged that 'he had failed in no point of sufficiency or integrity, and so, in respect he was sickly, wished him to take his ease.' He received 100*l.* as 'a token of the well-acceptance of his services.' He returned to Delft at the end of November 1624, and during the next four years he was again employed by the East India Company in their attempts to obtain satisfaction for the outrages at Amboyna. He was also entrusted with the negotiations on behalf of the Merchant Adventurers' Company for a reduction of the duties on English cloth (*Court Minutes*, 3 Feb. 1626; *Ashmolean MS.* 831, f. 251). Carleton, the English ambassador at the Hague, believed that he had been bribed by the Dutch to secretly undermine the influence of the two companies in Holland, but there is no evidence of the truth of this accusation, and the East India Company rewarded him (27 June 1628) for 'his great pains about the business of Amboyna.' The States-General, on the other hand, suspected him of compromising their interests by sending secret information to England, and confronted him (October 1628) with some of his letters. 'But when he had given his answers they had not much to say' (Misselden to Lord Dorchester, 18 Oct. 1628, *State Papers*, East Indies). He was so aggrieved at his treatment that he declined to have anything further to do with the East India Company's affairs. His case, however, was taken up by the privy council, and reparation was made (*Court Minutes*, 24 and 26 Nov. 1628).

Misselden threw himself heartily into Laud's schemes for bringing the practice of the English congregations abroad into conformity with that of the church of England. The merchant adventurers at Delft were strongly presbyterian, and John Forbes, their preacher, exercised great influence. Misselden's attempts to thrust the prayer-book upon them were met by plots to eject him from his position, and he and Forbes were 'irreconcilably at variance' (William Boswell to the council, 18 March 1633, *State Papers*, Dom. Ser.) He was ultimately turned out, and the company chose in his place Samuel Avery, an ardent presbyterian. Two years later (1635) abortive attempts were made to obtain his election as deputy-governor at Rotterdam, and the king addressed a letter to the Merchant Adventurers' Company vainly recommending them to deprive Robert Edwards, whom they had recently chosen for that post (the king to the merchant adventurers, 19 May 1635, *ib.*) His aid in thrusting the prayer-book on the merchant adventurers did not constitute Misselden's sole claim to recognition; he had furnished Philip Burlamachi with large sums for the king's service, of which, in May 1633, 13,000*l.* remained unpaid. He was to be satisfied out of Burlamachi's estate 'as soon as possible.'

Misselden was subsequently employed by the Merchant Adventurers' Company on various missions. A rumour at the end of 1649 that he was to be appointed deputy at Hamburg gave some dissatisfaction, for he was 'reported to be not only a royal malignant but a scandalous man in his life and conversation' (Walter Strickland to the council of state, 23-13 Dec. 1649; Cary, *Memorials of the Civil War*, ii. 207). He was at Hamburg in the following year on some business of the merchant adventurers. He was well-accepted' and likely to 'prove very serviceable to the company' (Richard Bradshaw to my Lord President, 3 Sept. 1650, *Hist. MSS. Comm.* 6th Rep. p. 430). It is probable that he was at this time trying to find favour with the parliament. Four years later he addressed a letter to Cromwell, pointing out his previous services (Thurloe, iii. 13). He had furnished the council of state with maps of Holland and Brabant, particulars relative to the navigation of the Scheldt, and a narrative of the Amboyna negotiations. But he 'never received an answere, nor soe much as his charges for lawyers' fees, and length of time, study, and labour.'

Misselden's economic writings were primarily called forth by the appointment of the standing commission on trade (1622). In his 'Free Trade, or the Means to make Trade flourish,' London, 1622, he discussed the causes of the alleged decay of trade, which he attributed to the excessive consumption of foreign commodities, the exportation of bullion by the East India Company, and defective searching in the cloth trade. His object appears to have been to disarm the opposition to the regulated companies, especially the Merchant Adventurers', and turn it against the joint-stock associations. The views which he put forth on the East India trade are inconsistent with those which he advocated in the following year. Gerard Malynes [q. v.] immediately attacked his pamphlet, urging in opposition the principles of foreign exchange with which his name is identified. In reply Misselden published 'The Circle of Commerce, or the Ballance of Trade, in Defence of Free Trade, opposed to Malynes' "Little Fish and his Great Whale," and poized against them in the Scale,' London, 1623, 4to. After refuting Malynes's views, and stating a substantially accurate theory of exchange, he discussed the balance of trade. He defended the exportation of bullion on the ground that by the re-exportation of the commodities which the country was thus enabled to purchase the treasure of the nation was augmented. His theory of the balance of trade differs in no important respect from that which was afterwards elaborated by Thomas Mun [q. v.] Like Mun, Misselden lived at one time at Hackney; the two writers must have been brought into close relations with each other during the Amboyna negotiations.

[The authorities quoted; Gardiner's History, vii. 315; Clarendon State Papers, 1621, p. 184; Cal. State Papers, East Indies, 1621-9 passim; State Papers, Dom. Ser. 1611-43; Hist. MSS. Comm. 3rd Rep. p. 174, 12th Rep. i. 465, 467. For Misselden's economic views vide authorities quoted under Gerard Malynes and Thomas Mun.] W. A. S. H.

MISSON, FRANCIS MAXIMILIAN (1650?-1722), traveller and author, was born in France about 1650, and was one of the protestant judges in the 'chamber of the edict' in the parlement of Paris. On the revocation in 1685 he found refuge in England, and was chosen by James, first duke of Ormonde [q. v.], to be tutor to his younger grandson, Charles Butler, afterwards Earl of Arran. Misson made the grand tour with his pupil during 1687 and 1688, travelling to Italy through Rotterdam, Cologne, Nuremberg, Munich, and Innspruck, over the Brenner, and thence by Verona to Venice. He visited the Santa Casa at Loretto and the places of interest round about Naples, made a long sojourn in Rome, and returned by leisurely stages through Bologna, Modena, Parma, Milan, Pavia, Genoa, Turin, Chambéry, Geneva, Strasburg, and Brussels. A product of the journey was a work which remained the standard 'Handbook' for Italy for at least fifty years after its publication, the much-quoted 'Nouveau Voyage d'Italie, avec un Memoire contenant des avis utiles à ceux qui voudront faire le mesme voyage,' 2 vols. 12mo, the Hague, 1691. The dedication to Charles Butler is dated London, 1 Jan. 1691 (2nd ed. 'beaucoup augmentée,' 1694, 12mo; 4th edit. 1698, 12mo; 5th ed. 'contenant les remarques que M. Addisson a faites dans son Voyage d'Italie,' Utrecht, 1722, 12mo; 6th ed. the Hague, 1731, 8vo. The first English translation appeared in 1695, London, 8vo; a second in 1699; the fourth in 1714: it formed part, together with the European travels of Dr. Edward Brown and John Ray, of the second volume of John Harris's 'Navigantium atque Itinerantium Bibliotheca,' 1705, and occupies vols. xviii. and xix. of 'The World Displayed,' 1774).

Addison, in the preface to his 'Travels,' remarked with justice of Misson that 'his account of Italy in general is more correct than that of any writer before him, as he particularly excels in the plan of the country which he has given in true and lively colours.' The work is not, as has often been stated, aggressively protestant; it nevertheless provoked in 1705 'Remarques historiques et critiques faites dans un Voyage d'Italie,' by P. Freschot, a Benedictine of Franche-Comté, Cologne, 1705, 8vo. Misson replied with unnecessary acrimony in the preface to his edition of the voyages of François Leguat [q. v.], and Freschot replied in 'Nouvelle Relation de la Voyage de Venise.' A few historical errors on Misson's part are pointed out by Francis Pegge in his 'Anonymiana' (1809, pp. 210–13).

Misson's second work, which has proved itself almost if not quite as quotable as his first, was 'Mémoires et Observations faites par un voyageur en Angleterre . . . avec une description particulière de ce qu'il y a de plus curieux dans Londres,' the Hague, 1698. The plates of the original edition are curious, notably one entitled 'Coacres et Coacresses dans leurs assemblées.' A translation by J. Ozell [q. v.] appeared at London in 1719, 8vo. The observations, which are disposed in alphabetical order, forming a descriptive dictionary of London, are both humorous and original; among the most entertaining are those on 'Beaux,' 'Benefit of clergy,' 'Boats,' 'Coals,' 'Funerals,' 'Hanging,' 'Jacobites,' 'King's Evil,' 'Penny Post,' 'Quakers,' 'Sports,' 'Wales, Prince of' (containing a racy supplement to the warming-pan legend), and 'Weddings.' The best part of the material is embodied in Mr. Ashton's valuable 'Social Life in the Reign of Queen Anne.'

From 1698 Misson appears to have lived in London and to have participated largely in the dissensions of the resident French colony. In his 'Théâtre Sacré des Cevennes, ou Recit des prodiges arrivés dans cette partie du Languedoc' (London, 1707), he espoused the cause of the 'French prophets' with a pathetic credulity, and his championship of Elias Marion and his confederates might well have brought him to the pillory (BOYER, *Queen Anne*, 1735, p. 317). For an English version of Misson's 'Théâtre,' entitled 'A Cry from the Desart: or Testimonials of the Miraculous Things lately come to pass in the Cevennes, verified upon oath and by other proofs' (1707), John Lacy [q. v.], the pseudo-prophet, appears to have been responsible. The work evoked several critical and satirical pamphlets (see 'Lettre d'un Particulier à Mr. Misson, l'honnête homme, touchant les Miracles, burlesques,' &c., 1707, and 'Meslanges de Literature historique et critique sur ce qui regarde l'état extraordinaire des Cévennois, appelez Camisards.' See also authorities under LACY, JOHN). Misson died in London on 12 Jan. 1722 (*Hist. Reg. Chron. Diary*, p. 7). Hearne calls him, truly, 'vir navus et industrius, summaque humanitate præditus' (*Collect.*, ed. Doble, ii. 226).

[Moreri's Dict. Historique; Chalmers's Biog. Dict. xxii. 200; Biog. Univ. xxviii. 400; McClintock and Strong's Cyclopædia, vi. 382; Aikin's General Biog. vii. 120; Agnew's Protestant Exiles, p. 303; Smiles's Huguenot Refugees, p. 415; Weiss's Protestant Refugees, p. 266; Lowndes's Bibl. Man. (Bohn); Southey's Commonplace Book, ii. 50; Hudibras, ed. Zach. Grey, 1819, iii. 92 *n.*; Halkett and Laing's Dict. of Anon. and Pseudon. Lit. col. 546; Brit. Mus. Cat.] T. S.

MIST, NATHANIEL (*d.* 1737), printer, may have been the son of James Mist of Easton, Wiltshire, and Martha Stagg of Kensington, to whom a license for marriage was granted by the vicar-general in October 1666. In early life, he tells us, he served in the navy, especially in the Spanish seas (MIST'S *Weekly Journal*, 25 Oct. 1718), probably as a common sailor (*Hist. MSS. Comm.* 10th Rep. pt. i., 'Manuscripts of C. F. W. Underwood, esq.,' p. 495). On 15 Dec. 1716 he was a printer in Great Carter Lane, and commenced a folio newspaper of six pages, the 'Weekly Journal, or Saturday's Post,' which became the organ of the Jacobites and 'High-flyers.' In April 1717 Mist was arrested on suspicion of printing libels against the government, but was released after examination (Mist's *Journal*, 26 April 1717). Next week he was tried for printing 'The Case of Mr. Francis Francia, the Reputed Jew,' but was at once discharged (*ib.* 4 May 1717). The 'Journal' for 3 Aug. contained an editorial manifesto, protesting against charges of disloyalty, and promising that every effort should be used to obtain early news, especially direct news from abroad, 'translated by the ablest hands.' This address to the reader is, there can be little doubt, the first contribution to the paper by Daniel Defoe [q. v.], who, acting as an agent of the whig government, introduced himself 'in the disguise of a translator of the foreign news' into the office of the 'Journal' with the object of thus rendering its contents harmless without exciting the suspicion of the proprietor. Defoe's connection with the paper was soon well known; it was referred to in Read's whig 'Weekly Journal' for 14 Dec., and in the same paper for 28 Dec. it was alleged that messengers sent to search Mist's house had found the originals of seditious articles, which the publisher swore were in Defoe's handwriting. In Mist's 'Journal' for 21 Dec. a correspondent complained that the paper seemed to be turning whig, and a paragraph in reply to Read declared that Defoe was 'no way at all concerned' in it; yet in the next number appeared an able article against the imprisonment of honest but disabled debtors, bearing Defoe's own initials, 'D. D. F.'

Between April and June 1718 Defoe placed on record, in a series of letters to Mr. Charles Delafaye (to be found in Mr. William Lee's 'Life of Defoe'), an account of his connection with Mist's 'Journal' and other tory papers. Sometimes he sent to the secretary of state's office objectionable articles which he had stopped; sometimes he apologised for having overlooked certain paragraphs, and said he had warned Mist to be more wary. At last he thought he had Mist 'absolutely resigned to proper measures, which would make his paper even serviceable to the government.' On 4 June he spoke of an attempt made by Edmund Curll [q. v.] to trepan Mist into words against the government, with a view of informing against him. On 5 and 12 April Defoe had published in Mist's 'Journal' attacks on Curll's indecent publications, and Curll replied in 'Curlicism display'd . . . in a Letter to Mr. Mist.' Mist seems to have challenged Curll, and he concluded a letter on the subject in the 'Journal' for 14 June with the words, 'O Cur— thou liest.' According to Read's 'Journal' of the same date, Mist was the coward, as he did not keep the engagement. In his 'Journal' for 21 and 28 June and 26 July Mist replied to scandalous tales in Ridpath's 'Flying Post,' and each party threatened the other with an action for libel. On 20 and 27 Sept. Defoe printed letters in the 'Journal' warning Mist not to give the government an opportunity of prosecuting him. In October Read's 'Journal' spoke of Defoe and Mist as 'Daniel Foe and his printer;' and in the same month Mist's life was threatened by two men because of a letter he had published charging some ladies with irreverence in church (*Journal*, 4 and 11 Oct.) On 17 Oct. Mist was seized by a messenger, and on the following day was examined before Mr. Delafaye respecting a manuscript, 'Mr. Kerr's Secret Memoirs' [see Ker, John, of Kersland], which had been found upon him. He was told that he might be bailed when he pleased, but he did not furnish sureties till the following Saturday. Most of the time, however, he spent at his own house, on parole (*State Papers*, Dom., George I, Bundle 15, Nos. 14, 29). On that Saturday (25 Oct.) an article appeared in the 'Journal,' signed 'Sir Andrew Politick,' attacking the war with Spain; but Defoe appended a note qualifying the writer's statements. The number was seized, and an official memorandum says: 'It is scarce credible what numbers of these papers are distributed both in town and country, where they do more mischief than any other libel, being wrote *ad captum* of the common people' (*ib.* No. 29). On 1 Nov. Mist was examined before Lord Stanhope and Craggs, when he said that it was Defoe who had written the objectionable letter, together with the answer; and this statement was to some extent corroborated by Thomas Warner, printer of the 'Journal' (*ib.* Nos. 30, 33). In the 'Whitehall Evening Post' (1 Nov.) Defoe described the searching of Mist's premises, the finding of a seditious libel in the ceiling, and the committal of Mist, who, however, was soon discharged through Defoe's intervention. Read's 'Journal' alleged that Defoe had a security of 500*l.* from Mist not to discover him. This Mist denied on 8 Nov., boldly saying that Defoe never had any share in the 'Journal,' save that he sometimes translated foreign letters in the absence of the person usually employed. Defoe now ceased for a short time to have any connection with Mist, whose 'Journal' for 8 Nov. was presented by the grand jury for Middlesex on 28 Nov. as a false, seditious, scandalous, and profane libel. In January 1719 Defoe again began to write for the paper on the condition that its tone was to be very moderate (Lee, i. 289).

Early in 1719 Mist published 'The History of the Reign of King George, from the Death of her late Majesty Queen Anne to the First of August 1718; to be continued yearly.' James Crossley [q. v.] was of opinion that Defoe compiled this volume. No subsequent issues seem to have appeared.

In June 1720 Mist published news articles reflecting on the aid rendered to the protestants in the Palatinate by the interposition of the English government; and Dr. Willis, bishop of Gloucester, having brought the matter before the House of Lords, Mist was ordered to be prosecuted by the attorney-general. He was accordingly arrested, and committed to the King's Bench prison. Defoe, who was ill at the time, found it necessary to protest his innocence of any share in Mist's present excesses. On 3 Dec. Mist was tried before Lord Chief-justice Pratt, at the Guildhall, and was found guilty of scandalously reflecting on the king's interposition in favour of the protestants abroad. On 13 Feb. 1721 he was brought up upon his recognisance for judgment, and sentenced to stand in the pillory at Charing Cross and the Royal Exchange, to pay a fine of 50*l.*, to suffer three months' imprisonment in the King's Bench, and to give security for good behaviour for seven years. Both at the Royal Exchange, on the 20th, and at Charing Cross, on the 23rd, Mist was very well treated by the mob (Read's *Journal*, 25 Feb.; Boyer, *Political State*; *Notes and Queries*, 4th ser. v. 2). Unable to pay the fine, Mist remained in prison, and in May, owing to the publication in his 'Journal' of articles which reflected upon the king and the Duke of Marlborough, he was placed at the bar of the House of Commons, and, as he would not give up the names of the writers of the letters, committed to Newgate, together with several persons who sold the paper. Defoe, writing in 'Applebee's Journal,' urged the government to show clemency towards the offenders, visited Mist in prison, and helped him to prepare a selection, in two volumes, of the letters that had appeared in the 'Journal.' Illness, brought on by anxiety and the unhealthy conditions of prison life, made it necessary to postpone Mist's trial from 9 Oct. to 9 Dec., when, no evidence being brought against him, he was discharged.

The 'Collection of Miscellany Letters, selected out of Mist's Weekly Journal,' appeared on 9 Jan. 1722, in two volumes, with dedications dated from the King's Bench prison, 29 Sept. and 10 Nov. 1721 respectively, in which Mist explained the cause of the delay in the publication of the book, and said that his troubles had cost him more than 1,000*l.* From 16 Dec. 1721 to 29 Sept. 1722 the 'Journal' was 'printed by Dr. Gayland for N. Mist.'

On 8 June 1723 Mist again printed a libel upon the government, and was again in trouble at the end of the month (*Journal*, 6 July), but he was liberated on a recognisance of 1,400*l.* On 24 Feb. 1724 he was tried at the King's Bench and found guilty. The recognisance was estreated (*ib.* 29 Feb.) He was brought up for judgment on 18 May, and was sentenced to pay a fine of 100*l.*, to suffer a year's imprisonment, and to find sureties for good behaviour during life. Mr. Abel Kettelby of the Middle Temple was counsel both for Mist and for Payne of the 'True Briton,' but though he pleaded eloquently, the court 'thought their offences too great to allow of any mitigation' (*Parker's London News*, 20 May 1724). One number of the 'Journal' (20 June) was 'printed by W. Wilkins, at the Dolphin in Little Britain, and sold by J. Peele, Paternoster Row.' The new Stamp Act of 1725 brought the original series to an end (24 April), but a new series was begun on 1 May, with the title 'Mist's Weekly Journal.' The price was raised from three halfpence to twopence, and the paper reduced to a quarto sheet of four pages. The size of the page was enlarged on 30 April 1726. On 25 March 1727 Mist brought out third and fourth volumes of 'Miscellany Letters,' taken from the 'Journal.' From 2 Dec. 1727 to 31 Aug. 1728 the 'Journal' was printed by John Wolfe, Great Carter Lane.

In 1727 Mist was again tried at the court of king's bench for a libel on George I, and was sentenced to pay a fine of 100*l.*, to give security for good behaviour during life, and to be imprisoned till the sentence was fulfilled. The sentence remained in abeyance till 15 Sept., when an escape warrant was issued for seizing Mist at the King's Arms Tavern on Ludgate Hill. Mist's friends are said to have turned out the lights and thrust him out in the confusion that ensued (*Citizen*, 25 Sept.); but he surrendered on the following day. Mist afterwards, however, denied this story (*Journal*, 30 Sept.), saying that when the messenger appeared he went with him into another room, and, after examining the warrant (the force of which he at first disputed, because it was signed in the reign of the late King George I), surrendered himself, and was, he added, still in custody.

In March 1728 the 'Journal' contained several articles directed against Pope, which Fenton noticed in writing to William Broome [q. v.] on 3 April (POPE, *Works*, ed. Elwin and Courthope, viii. 143); and afterwards various letters from Lewis Theobald, hero of the 'Dunciad,' were printed. In that poem (i. 208) Pope spoke incidentally of Mist himself: 'To Dulness Ridpath is as dear as Mist;' and among the 'Testimonies of Authors' Pope included many passages from the 'Journal.'

In January 1728 Mist had found it prudent to retire to France, where he joined the banished Duke of Wharton (READ'S *Journal*, 20 Jan.) In March James Watson, who was in custody for printing matter directed against the government, said that Mist had left a certain Mr. Bingley in chief charge of his affairs, and that Bingley might properly be called the author of the 'Journal,' except the political essay at the beginning, which he knew to be written by another. An unsuccessful attempt was then made to arrest Bingley (*State Papers*, Dom. George II, Bundle 7, Nos. 42–5, 106). On 27 July the 'Journal' had a paragraph stating that the Duke of Wharton had set up a school in Rouen, and had taken Bingley, formerly a prisoner in Newgate, to be his usher; and that at the same place Mist was driving a hackney coach. All were, it was said, in a fair way of getting a decent livelihood.

On 24 Aug. a letter signed 'Amos Drudge,' and directed against Walpole and the government, was printed in the 'Journal.' Active steps were at once taken against those who were responsible, but Mist was in safety at Rouen (cf. READ, *Journal*, 31 Aug.) The king was of opinion that the author, printers, and publishers of the paper should be punished with the utmost severity of the law (*State Papers*, Dom. George II, Bundle 6, No. 105). The manuscript of the letter signed 'Amos Drudge' was seized by the king's messengers, and more than twenty persons were arrested (*ib.* Bundle 5, Nos. 71, 74) and examined at Hampton Court on 29 and 30 Aug. Among those arrested then or in the following month were James Wolfe, printer, Elizabeth Nutt, widow of Nutt the bookseller, and her daughter Catherine, William Burton, printer, Mist's maid and nephew, Dr. Gayland, and Farley, who had reprinted the letter in a paper he published at Exeter. On 31 Aug. the grand jury for the county of Middlesex expressed their abhorrence at the article, and other grand juries followed the example (BOYER, *Political State*, August and October 1728). The 'Journals' for 7 and 14 Sept. appeared as one number, and the 'Journal' for 21 Sept. was the last that appeared. These were printed by J. Wilford, and a warrant was issued against him on account of an attack in the paper for 7 and 14 Sept. upon the action of the legislature against the South Sea Company. Wilford surrendered himself, and was admitted to bail (READ'S *Journal*, 28 Sept.) Wolfe, who had supervised the press for Mist, retired to join his master, then at Boulogne (BUDGELL'S *Bee*, February 1733); but other friends continued the 'Journal' under the new name of 'Fog's Weekly Journal,' of which the first number, containing a letter signed 'N. Mist,' appeared on 28 Sept. Various persons had been arrested when 'Mist's Journal' for 7 and 14 Sept. was seized, and the press was destroyed. There are several petitions from these persons among the 'State Papers' (Bundle 5, Nos. 70, 80–6; Bundle 6, Nos. 54, 55, 74–80).

About the end of 1724 Defoe, writing anonymously in 'Applebee's Journal,' said that he had been abused and insulted by one whom he had fetched three times out of prison; and that this person had at length drawn a sword upon him, but that, being disarmed, he had been forgiven, and the wound inflicted in self-defence attended to. But, said Defoe, this kindness was followed only by more ingratitude. In 1730, when Defoe was ill and was living in concealment near Greenwich, he spoke of having received a blow 'from a wicked, perjured, and contemptible enemy, that has broken in upon my spirit.' Mr. Lee has argued, very plausibly, that this enemy was Mist, who, it is suggested, had represented to the English government the share Defoe had taken in various tory journals, perhaps supporting his statements by the production of objectionable articles, with alterations in Defoe's writing. The discovery by Mist of Defoe's secret understanding with the whigs when working for tory papers probably accounts for his active hostility.

In 1734 the titular Earl of Dunbar had a clandestine correspondence with Mist. In it he requested Mist's aid in bringing out some 'Observations,' in answer to a libel which had been issued against him by Charles Hamilton [q. v.] Mist seems to have complied. Dunbar thereupon assured his Jacobite friends and the pretender himself that the paper had been printed without his knowledge. But his letter to Mist was discovered in 1737 and forwarded to the pretender as a demonstrative proof that Dunbar 'is and has been of a long time a hired spy to the Elector of Hanover' (*Hist. MSS. Comm.* 10th Rep. pt. i. pp. 490–1, 493–5, 503, 518).

Mist died of asthma on 20 Sept. 1737. He

was 'well esteemed in private life' (*Gent. Mag.* p. 574; *Hist. Reg. Chron.* p. 22; *London Mag.* p. 517). Letters of administration were granted on 3 Nov. to Anne, widow of Nathaniel Mist, 'late of St Clement Danes, but at Boulogne in France deceased.'

[Authorities cited; Lee's Life and Newly Discovered Writings of Daniel Defoe, 1869; Cat. of the Hope Colln. of Newspapers in Bodleian Lib.; Pope's Works, ed. Elwin and Courthope, vols. iii. iv. viii. x.; Curll Papers; Boyer's Political State; Hist. Reg.; House of Commons' Journal, xix. 562; Hallam's Constit. Hist. chap. xvi.; Andrews's Hist. of Brit. Journalism, i. 121–2.] G. A. A.

MISYN, RICHARD (*d.* 1462?), Carmelite, and probably bishop of Dromore, translated Hampole's 'De Emendatione Vitæ' and 'Incendium Amoris' into English. Both are found in the MS. Corp. Christi Oxon. ccxxxvi., written on vellum in a clear fifteenth-century hand; but their claim to be in Misyn's autograph and dialect has been abandoned. The 'Emendation' begins on f. 45 and has at the end: 'Thus endys the xii chapetyrs of Richarde Hampole, in to Englys translate be Frere Richard Misyn to informacioun of Cristyn sauls, 1434.' The 'Incendium,' in two books, begins on f. 1 with a preface, 'to ye askynge of thi desyre Systre Margarete;' at the end of book i. is the statement that the translator is Richard Misyn, hermit, and of the Carmelite order, bachelor of sacred theology, 1435. The end of book ii. further adds that he was then prior of the Lincoln house of Carmelites, and wrote and corrected the above (though this cannot be taken literally) on 12 July, the feast of the translation of St. Martin, 1435 (*Guild of Corpus Christi, York*, Surtees Soc. 1872, pp. 62, 240, 291). Misyn's 'Fire of Love' and 'Mending of Life' were issued by the Early English Text Society in 1896.

In MS. Vernon and in Addit. MS. 22283, f. 147 *b* (later version), is the 'fourme of parfyt living,' by Richard Rolle of Hampole [q. v.], and there is no warrant for ascribing it to Misyn (Warton, ed. Hazlitt, ii. 243; cf. *Cat. MSS. Univ. Cambr. Corrigenda*, v. 596).

The translator is probably identical with a Richard Mysyn, suffragan and Carmelite, who in 1461 was admitted a member of the Corpus Christi guild of York, and also with the 'Beschope Musin' whose name is engraved on a cup that belonged to that guild. His see was probably Dromore, for Richard Mesin or Mesyn, bishop of Dromore, according to Bale (Carmelite Collections, *Harl. MS.* 3838, f. 38), died in 1462 and was buried in York monastery. Pits (*Illustr. Angl. Script.* p. 897), writing of one Richard Mesin as the author of several works, the names of which are not given, observes that he is said to have been buried among the Carmelites of York. Villiers de St.-Etienne (*Bibl. Carmel.* ii. 683–4) quotes from the consistorial acts of Calixtus III to prove that Richard Messin, Myssin, or Mesin was made bishop of Dromore on the death of Nicholas, 29 July 1457; and he was buried among the Carmelites of York. Stubbs (*Registr. Angl.* p. 148) gives Richard Mesin as one of the Irish bishops who was suffragan to the diocese of York in 1460.

Another Richard was bishop of Dromore in 1409 (*Cal. Rot. Canc. Hibern.* i. 190), and he has generally, but without sufficient authority, been called Richard Messing (Reeves, *Eccles. Antiq. of Down*, p. 308; Ware, *Hibernia Sacra*, p. 92; Cotton, *Fasti Eccles. Hib.* iii. 277; *Notes and Queries*, 2nd ser. No. 27, p. 1). This so-called Richard Messing is said to have made profession of obedience in 1408 to John Colton [q. v.], archbishop of Armagh, but Colton died in 1404.

[H. O. Coxe's Cat. Cod. in Coll. Oxon. vol. ii. Corpus Christi, No. ccxxxvi.; Tanner's Bibl. Brit.; Brady's Episcopal Succession, St.-Etienne's Bibl. Carmel. vol. ii.] M. B.

MITAN, JAMES (1776–1822), engraver, was born in London on 13 Feb. 1776, and educated at an academy in Soho. In 1790 he was articled to a writing engraver named Vincent; but, desiring to qualify himself for higher work, he obtained instruction from J. S. Agar, studied in the schools of the Royal Academy, and made copies of Bartolozzi's tickets. Mitan became an able engraver in the line-manner, chiefly of book illustrations; but as he worked largely for other engravers, the plates bearing his name are not numerous. Of these the best were done for Mrs. Inchbald's 'British Theatre,' 1806–9, Sharpe's 'Poets' and 'Classics,' Bannatyne's edition of Shakespeare, T. Moore's 'Irish National Airs' (after Stothard), 1818, Dibdin's 'Bibliographical Tour through France and Germany,' 1821, and 'Ædes Althorpianæ,' 1822, and Jarvis's translation of 'Don Quixote' (after Smirke), 1825. A set of fifty-six small plates of natural history engraved by Mitan, apparently from his own designs, was published in 1822. Between 1802 and 1805 he exhibited at the Royal Academy a series of compositions illustrating George Moore's 'Theodosius de Zulvin,' and in 1818 a design for a national memorial of the victory of Waterloo. In the latter year he also made a design, eighteen feet long, for a chain bridge over the Mersey. Mitan did much work for the admiralty and the Freemasons. He died of paralysis in Warren Street, Fitzroy Square, on 16 Aug.

1822, leaving a wife and family. A plate of C. R. Leslie's 'Anne Page and Slender,' which Mitan left unfinished, was completed by Engleheart and published in 1823.

MITAN, SAMUEL (1786–1843), brother and pupil of James Mitan, practised in the same style. He engraved many of the plates in Captain Batty's 'French Scenery,' 1822, and was employed upon Ackermann's various publications. He became a member of the Artists' Annuity Fund in 1810, and died at the Polygon, Somers Town, 3 June 1843.

[Gent. Mag. 1823 ii. 86, 1843 ii. 104; Redgrave's Dict. of Artists; Royal Academy Catalogues.] F. M. O'D.

MITAND, LOUIS HUGUENIN DU (*fl.* 1816), educational writer, born in Paris in 1748, was son of Huguenin du Mitand. His father at one time possessed an ample fortune, but ultimately lost it. Louis, however, received an excellent education, and on coming to London about 1777 obtained a livelihood by teaching Greek, Latin, French, and Italian, according to principles laid down in his 'Plan of a New Method for Teaching Languages,' 12mo, London, 1778. In the introduction of this work he has given a humorous account of himself. He undertook a work in fourteen languages, to comprise an abstract of the best books written in each of them, accompanied by grammars, but did not complete it. His Greek and French grammars and other school-books had a considerable sale. To the 'Morning Chronicle' he contributed from time to time Latin verses on various public events, which he printed in 1780, 4to. He also edited the eighth edition of John Palairet's 'Abrégé sur les Sciences et sur les Arts,' 12mo, London, 1778, and published a greatly improved edition of Boyer's 'French Dictionary,' 2 vols. 4to, London, 1816.

[Dict. of Living Authors under Du Mitand.] G. G.

MITCH, RICHARD (*fl.* 1557), lawyer, of an Essex family, was educated at Cambridge (B.A. 1542, M.A. 1544). He was admitted a fellow of St. John's College 14 March 1542–3, but subsequently removed to Trinity Hall. Mitch was an active opponent at Cambridge of the growth of the reformed religion. On 27 Jan. 1547 he was constituted one of Gardiner's proctors to produce evidence on the examination and trial of that bishop. On the accession of Queen Mary he organised a curious attack in the regent house on Dr. Sandys, the vice-chancellor, who had exhibited sympathy for Lady Jane Grey (FOXE, *Acts and Monuments*, viii. 592). In 1556 Mitch was one of the examiners of John Hullier, preacher, of Lynn, on the charge of heresy, for which the latter was subsequently burnt, and the same year he gave active assistance to Cardinal Pole's delegates during the visitation of the university of Cambridge. He was among the lawyers and heads of houses who, in January 1556–7, were called and sworn to give evidence against the heresies of Bucer and Fagius before the exhumation and burning of the bodies of those reformers.

Mitch commenced LL.D. 1557, and was admitted an advocate at Doctors' Commons 26 April 1559, and an advocate of the court of arches about the same date (STRYPE, *Life of Parker*, i. 87). Subsequently, owing doubtless to his religious opinions, he left the country, and his name occurs in a list of recusants from Essex, who were fugitives over seas (STRYPE, *Annals*, vol. ii. pt. ii. p. 596).

[Lamb's Coll. of Doc. from Corpus Christi Coll.; Strype's Annals; Baker's History of St. John's Coll.; Cooper's Annals of Cambridge; Cooper's Athenæ Cantabrigienses; Coote's Civilians; Foxe's Acts and Monuments; Fuller's Hist. of Univ. of Cambridge.] W. C-R.

MITCHEL. [See also MICHELL and MITCHELL.]

MITCHEL, JOHN (1815–1875), Irish nationalist, the third son of the Rev. John Mitchel of Dromalane, Newry, a presbyterian minister, by his wife Mary Haslett, was born at Camnish, near Dungiven, co. Londonderry, on 3 Nov. 1815. He was educated at Dr. Henderson's school at Newry, where he became acquainted with his lifelong friend John Martin (1812–1875) [q. v.], and in 1830 matriculated at Trinity College, Dublin. According to his biographer, Mitchel took his degree in 1834 (DILLON, i. 15), but his name does not appear in the 'Catalogue of Graduates.' Though intended by his father for the ministry, Mitchel began life as a bank clerk at Londonderry, and subsequently entered the office of John Quinn, a solicitor at Newry. At the close of 1836 he eloped with Jane, only daughter of Captain James Verner of Newry, a schoolgirl of sixteen. The fugitives were captured at Chester, and Mitchel was taken back in custody to Ireland, where he was kept a few days in prison before being released on bail. Their second attempt was, however, more successful, and on 3 Feb. 1837 they were married at Drumcree. Mitchel was admitted a solicitor in 1840, and commenced practice at Banbridge, some ten miles from Newry. In 1842 he became acquainted with Thomas Osborne Davis [q. v.], the friend who, in Mitchel's own words, 'first filled his soul with the passion of a great ambition and a lofty purpose' (*ib.* i. 70). In the following year Mitchel joined the Repeal Association, and in the autumn of 1845 abandoned his profession and accepted a place on the staff of the 'Nation' under Charles Gavan Duffy. In June 1846 Duffy was prosecuted for publishing in the 'Nation' for 22 Nov. 1845 Mitchel's 'Railway Article,' which was described as a seditious libel. Mitchel acted as Duffy's attorney, and the jury was ultimately discharged without coming to an agreement. Mitchel took a leading part in the discussions on the 'moral force' resolutions in Conciliation Hall, Dublin, and seceded from the Repeal Association with the rest of the Young Ireland party on 28 July 1846. Under the influence of James Finton Lalor [q. v.], Mitchel's political views became still more advanced; and at length, finding himself unable any longer to agree with Duffy's more cautious policy, he retired from the 'Nation' in December 1847. As the Irish Confederation failed to concur with his views, Mitchel shortly afterwards withdrew from any active part in its proceedings, and after the Limerick riot resigned his membership.

On 12 Feb. 1848 Mitchel issued the first number of the 'United Irishman,' a weekly newspaper published in Dublin, in which he wrote his well-known letters to Lord Clarendon, and openly incited his fellow-countrymen to rebellion. On 20 March following he was called upon to give bail to stand his trial in the queen's bench for sedition. The charge, however, was never proceeded with, as the juries could not be relied on to convict, and on 13 May Mitchel was arrested under the new Treason Felony Act, which had received the royal assent in the previous month. He was tried at the commission court in Green Street, Dublin, before Baron Lefroy and Justice Moore, on 25 and 26 May 1848, and was sentenced on the following day to transportation for fourteen years. The sixteenth and last number of the 'United Irishman' appeared on 27 May 1848. In June Mitchel was conveyed in the Scourge to Bermuda, where he was confined to the hulks. In consequence of the bad state of his health he was subsequently removed in the Neptune to the Cape of Good Hope. Owing to the refusal of the colonists to permit the convicts to land, the Neptune remained at anchor in Simon's Bay from 19 Sept. 1849 to 19 Feb. 1850. In the following April Mitchel was landed in Van Diemen's Land, where he was allowed to reside in one of the police districts on a ticket of leave. Here he lived with his old friend John Martin, and in June 1851 was joined by his wife and family. In the summer of 1853 Mitchel, having previously resigned his ticket of leave, escaped from Van Diemen's Land with the aid of P. J. Smyth, and in October landed at San Francisco, where he met with an enthusiastic welcome. On 7 Jan. 1854 he started a newspaper at New York called 'The Citizen,' which was mainly distinguished while under his editorship for its strenuous opposition to the abolition movement. With the close of the year Mitchel ended his connection with the 'Citizen,' and took to farming and lecturing. From October 1857 to August 1859 he conducted the 'Southern Citizen,' a weekly journal in the interests of the slaveholders, which was first published at Knoxville, and subsequently at Washington. In August 1859 Mitchel visited Paris, where he went to reside in the following year. He returned to New York in September 1862, and managed after much difficulty to get through the Federal lines to Richmond. Finding that he was disqualified for military service by reason of his eyesight, he accepted the editorship of the 'Enquirer,' the semi-official organ of President Davis. Owing to the divergence of their views Mitchel subsequently resigned this post, and wrote the leading articles for the 'Examiner.' On the conclusion of the war Mitchel went to New York, where he became editor of the 'Daily News.' In consequence of his articles in defence of the southern cause Mitchel was arrested by the military authorities on 14 June 1865, and confined in Fortress Monroe for nearly five months. Shortly after his release Mitchel went to Paris as the financial agent of the Fenian Brotherhood in that city, but resigning that office in the following year he returned to America in October 1866. In February 1867 he refused the post of chief executive officer of the Fenian Brotherhood in America, and on 19 Oct. following published at New York the first number of the 'Irish Citizen.' In this paper, which was strongly democratic in American politics, he managed to offend both the Fenians and the home rulers, and owing to his health giving way it was discontinued on 27 July 1872. In the summer of 1872 Mitchel paid a short visit to Ireland, but was unmolested by the government. At the general election in February 1874 he was nominated as a candidate for the representation of Tipperary, while in America, but was unsuccessful. He was, however, elected unopposed for that constituency on 16 Feb. 1875, and landed at Queenstown on the following day. On 18 Feb. Disraeli's motion declaring Mitchel 'incapable of being elected or returned as a member' on the ground of his being a convicted felon was carried, and a new writ ordered (*Parl. Debates*, 3rd ser. ccxxii. 493–539). Mitchel was again returned by a majority of 2,368 votes over his conservative opponent, Mr. Stephen Moore, and in his address of thanks to the electors he once more declared his intention of 'discrediting and exploding the fraudulent pretence of Irish representation by declining to attend the sittings of parliament.' Before the petition was presented against his return Mitchel died at Dromalane on 20 March 1875, aged 59. He was buried on the 23rd of the same month in the unitarian cemetery in High Street, Newry, where a monument was erected to his memory by his widow. On 26 May 1875 the Irish court of common pleas decided that Mitchel, being both an alien and a convicted felon, was not duly elected, and that Mr. Stephen Moore was duly returned (O'MALLEY and HARDCASTLE, iii. 19–49).

Mitchel was an honest, but hopelessly unpractical man. Though possessing considerable force of character he was deficient in judgment, and his whole mind was warped by his implacable hatred of England. In appearance Mitchel 'was tall and gaunt, his eyes were gray and piercing, his expression of countenance self-contained, if not saturnine, his features bony and sallow, with an inclining to the tawny tint, high cheeks and determined chin' (O'SHEA, i. 12). Mitchel was a ready and incisive speaker as well as a forcible writer. In his domestic life he is said to have been one of the gentlest of men. Carlyle, who met Mitchel in Ireland in September 1846, refers to him as 'a fine elastic-spirited young fellow, whom I grieved to see rushing on destruction palpable, by attack of windmills, but on whom all my persuasions were thrown away.' He appears also to have told Mitchel that he would most likely be hanged, but 'they could not hang the immortal part of him' (FROUDE, *Carlyle*, 1834–1881, i. 399). Mitchel had a family of six children. His three sons all fought on the confederate side in the American civil war. The eldest was killed at Fort Sumter, and the youngest at Gettysburg, while the second lost his right arm in one of the battles round Richmond.

Mitchel edited the poems of Thomas Osborne Davis (New York, 1846) and of James Clarence Mangan [q. v.] (New York, 1859, 8vo). The lecture which he delivered at New York on 20 Dec. 1872, on 'Froude from the standpoint of an Irish Protestant,' will be found in 'Froude's Crusade—Both Sides' (New York, 1873, 8vo). He was also the author of the following works: 1. 'The Life and Times of Aodh O'Neill, Prince of Ulster; called by the English, Hugh, Earl, of Tyrone. With some Account of his Predecessors, Con, Shane, and Tirlough,' Dublin, 1846, 12mo, in 'Duffy's Library of Ireland;' as 'Life of Hugh O'Neill, Earl of Tyrone,' New York, 12mo, 1868. 2. 'Jail Journal, or Five Years in British Prisons,' &c., New York, 1854, 12mo; author's edition, Glasgow [1856], 8vo; new edition, New York, 1868, 12mo. The 'Journal' was afterwards continued by Mitchel in the 'Irish Citizen,' and brought down to 1866. 3. 'The Last Conquest of Ireland (perhaps),' New York, 1860, Dublin and Glasgow, 1861, 8vo. Reprinted in 'The Crusade of the Period,' &c., see infra; 'author's edition,' Glasgow [1876], 8vo. 4. 'An Apology for the British Government in Ireland,' Dublin, 1860; another edition, 1882. 5. 'The History of Ireland, from the Treaty of Limerick to the Present Time; being a Continuation of the History of the Abbé Macgeoghegan,' New York, 1868, 8vo; other editions, Dublin, 1869, 8vo, 2 vols., Glasgow, 1869, 8vo. The latter portion was reprinted in 1871 as 'Ireland since '98,' &c., Glasgow, 8vo. 6. 'The Crusade of the Period: and Last Conquest of Ireland (perhaps),' New York, 1873, 12mo, in the Irish-American Library, vol. iv.; a reply to Mr. Froude's 'English in Ireland.'

[Mitchel's Jail Journal, and other works; W. Dillon's John Mitchel, 1888, with portrait; Duffy's Four Years of Irish History, 1845–9, 1883; Sullivan's Speeches from the Dock, 1887, pp. 74–96; O'Shea's Leaves from the Life of a Special Correspondent, 1885, i. 9–24; Hodges's Report of the Trial of John Mitchel, 1848; May's Parliamentary Practice, 1883, pp. 39, 724–5; Webb's Compendium of Irish Biography, 1878, pp. 340–2; Wills's Irish Nation, 1875, iv. 695–7; Read's Cabinet of Irish Literature, 1880, iii. 329–36; Life of Mitchel, by P. A. Sillard (Duffy's National Library), 1889; Appleton's Cyclop. of American Biog. 1878, iv. 341; Gent. Mag. 1875, new ser. xiv. 593–608; Annual Register, 1875, pt. i. pp. 8–11, pt. ii. p. 137; Dublin Univ. Mag. lxxxv. 481–92; Democratic Review, xxiii. 149, xxx. 97–128, with portrait; Times, 22, 24, 29 March 1875; Freeman's Journal, 22 and 24 March 1875; Nation, 20 and 27 March 1875, with portrait; Allibone's Dict. of Engl. Lit. Suppl. ii. 1119; Brit. Mus. Cat.]

G. F. R. B.

MITCHEL, JONATHAN (1624?–1668), New England divine, born in Halifax, Yorkshire, about 1624, was son of Matthew Mitchel (SAVAGE, *Genealog. Dict.* iii. 220). He accompanied his parents to America in 1635, graduated at Harvard in 1647, and on 24 June 1649 preached at Hartford, Connecticut, with such acceptance that he was invited to succeed Thomas Hooker (1586–1647) [q. v.] This offer he declined. In May 1650 he was elected fellow of Harvard, and appears to have acted as tutor. He did much towards promoting the prosperity of the college. After being ordained at Cambridge, Massachusetts, on 21 Aug. 1650, he succeeded Thomas Shepard as pastor of that town. When his old preceptor, Henry Dunster [q. v.], president of Harvard, openly announced his conversion to the doctrines of the baptists, Mitchel opposed him, although retaining his friendship. Dunster died in 1659, and Mitchel wrote some wretched lines in his memory, printed in Cotton Mather's 'Ecclesiastes' (p. 70), and in the same author's 'Magnalia' (bk. iv. sect. 175). Mitchel hospitably entertained the regicides Whalley and Goffe when they sought refuge in Cambridge in July 1660. In June 1661 he was one of the committee appointed to defend the privileges of the colony, then menaced by the English government. In 1662 he was a member of the synod that met at Boston to discuss questions of church membership and discipline. Its report was chiefly written by him, and he was mainly responsible for the adoption of the so-called 'half-way covenant.' On 8 Oct. 1662 he and Captain Daniel Gookin [q. v.] were appointed the first licensers of the press in Massachusetts. With Francis Willoughby and Major-general John Leverett, Mitchel was entrusted with the task of drawing up a petition to Charles II respecting the colony's charter on 3 Aug. 1664, and he wrote it entirely himself. In ecclesiastical councils, to which he was frequently called, and in weighty cases in which the general court often consulted the clergy, 'the sense and hand of no man was relied more upon than his for the exact result of all.' Overwork at length told on him, and he died of fever at Cambridge on 9 July 1668.

His union with Sarah, daughter of the Rev. John Cotton (*d.* 1652) [q. v.], having been prevented by her death in January 1650, he married on 19 Nov. following Margaret Boradale, widow of his predecessor, Thomas Shepard, by whom he left issue (Savage, iv. 76).

Mitchel wrote several sermons and treatises, among which were: 1. 'Letter to his brother' David 'concerning your spiritual condition,' dated 19 May 1649; many editions. 2. Propositions concerning the subject of Baptism and Consociation of Churches, collected and confirmed out of the Word of God by a Synod of Elders . . . assembled at Boston in 1662,' 4to, Cambridge, Massachusetts, 1662; chiefly written by Mitchel. 3. 'A Defence of the Answer and Arguments of the Synod met at Boston in 1662 . . . against the reply made thereto by the Rev. Mr. John Davenport. . . By some of the Elders,' 4to, Cambridge, Massachusetts, 1664. Of this work the first 46 pages, designated 'Answer' on the title-page, were by Mitchel. 4. 'A Discourse of the Glory to which God hath called Believers by Jesus Christ delivered in some sermons . . . together with an annexed letter' [to his brother], edited by J. Collins, 8vo, London, 1677; 2nd edition, with a preface by Increase Mather, 12mo, Boston, Massachusetts, 1721. 5. 'A Letter concerning the subject of Baptisme,' dated 26 Dec. 1667; printed in the 'Postscript' of Increase Mather's 'First Principles of New-England,' 4to, Cambridge, Massachusetts, 1675. 6. 'The Great End and Interest of New England stated by the memorable Mr. J. Mitchel, extracted from an instrument of his which bears date 31 Dec. 1662.' This tract constitutes pp. 1–5 of Increase Mather's 'Elijah's Mantle,' 8vo, Boston, Massachusetts, 1722. Mitchel also edited Thomas Shepard's 'Parable of the Ten Virgins,' fol. 1660.

[Sibley's Biog. Sketches of Graduates of Harvard University, i. 141–57; Cotton Mather's Ecclesiastes: the Life of J. Mitchel, 1697; Cotton Mather's Magnalia Christi Americana, bk. iv. sects. 158, 166; Walker's Hist. of the First Church in Hartford.] G. G.

MITCHEL, WILLIAM (1672–1740?), pamphleteer, known as the 'Tinklarian Doctor,' seems to have gone to Edinburgh about 1696 to earn a poor livelihood as a tinsmith at the head of the West-Bow. For twelve years he superintended the lighting of the town-lamps. A disastrous fire at the Bowhead (1706?), by which he lost thirteen hundred merks, and his dismissal from his post in 1707 reduced him to penury. He continued his tinkering, but found time to issue a large number of 'books,' or rather broad-sheets, which he sold at his shop 'at very reasonable rates.' In 1712 he was restored to his former post. He survived the Porteous riots (about which he is stated to have written a pamphlet) in 1736. Chambers states that he died in 1740.

His tracts deal chiefly with religion and church politics, and especially with the shortcomings of the professional ministry. 'Give the clergy,' says his petition to Queen Anne, 'less wages, and lay more dutie upon gouf [golf] clubs, and then fewer of them and others would go to the gouf.' His claim was 'to give light,' a metaphor which he proudly borrowed from his experience in lamps. His writings are extremely illiterate, and show, even in their titles, the audacity and incoherence of a madman. They are badly printed on shabby paper, most of them on single sheets.

The following are known: 1. 'Dr. Mitchel's Strange and Wonderful Discourse concerning the Witches and Warlocks in West Calder.' 2. 'The Tinklar's Testament' (in several parts, including 'The Tincklar's Reformation Sermon' and a 'Speech in commendation of the Scriptures'), 1711. 3. Petitions to Queen Anne (ten in number), 1711, &c. 4. 'The Advantagious Way of Gaming, or Game to be rich. In a letter to Collonel Charters,' 1711 (?). 5. 'The Tinklar's Speech to . . . the laird of Carnwath,' 1712. 6. 'The Great Tincklarian Doctor Mitchel his fearful book, to the condemnation of all swearers. Dedicated to the Devil's captains,' 1712. 7. 'Speech concerning Lawful and Unlawful Oaths,' 1712. 8. 'Proposals for the better reformation of Edinburgh.' 9. 'The Tinclarian Doctor Mitchel's description of the Divisions of the Church of Scotland.' 10. 'A new and wonderful Way of electing Magistrates.' 11. 'A Seasonable Warning to beware of the Lutherians, writen by the Tinclarian Doctor,' 1713. 12. 'Great News! Strange Alteration concerning the Tinckler, who wrote his Testament long before his Death, and no Man knows his Heir.' 13. 'The Tinclarian Doctor Mitchel's Letter to the King of France,' 1713 (?). 14. 'Letter to the Pope.' 15. 'The Tinclarian Doctor Mitchel's Letter to Her Majesty Queen Ann'—'to make me your Majesty's Advocat.' 16. 'The Tinclarian Doctor Mitchel's Lamentation, dedicated to James Stewart, one of the Royal Family.' 17. Letter to George I. 18. 'Inward and Outward Light to be Sold,' 1731. 19. 'Second Day's Journey of the Tinclarian Doctor,' 1733. 20. 'Short History to the Commendation of the Royal Archers,' &c., with 'One Man's Meat is another Man's Poison' (in verse), 1734. 21. 'The Voice of the Tinklarian Doctor's last Trumpet, sounding for the Downfall of Babylon, and his last Arrow shot at her,' 1737. 22. 'Prophecy of an Old Prophet concerning Kings, and Judges, and Rulers, and of the Magistrates of Edinburgh, and also of the Downfall of Babylon, which is Locusts, who is King of the Bottomless Pit. Dedicated to all Members of Parliament,' 1737. 23. 'Revelation of the Voice of the Fifth Angel's Trumpet,' 1737. 24. 'The Tinklarian Doctor's Four Catechisms,' published separately 1736-7-8. 25. 'Tinklarian Doctor's Dream concerning those Locusts, who hath come out of the Smoke of the Pit and hath Power to hurt all Nations,' 1739. A number of these broadsheets are found bound together with the following title: 'The whole Works of that Eminent Divine and Historian Doctor William Mitchel. Professor of Tincklarianism in the University of the Bow-head; being Essays of Divinity, Humanity, History, and Philosophy; composed at various occasions for his own satisfaction, Reader's Edification, and the World's Illumination.' In one of his publications of 1713 Mitchel incidentally remarks that he had then issued twenty-one 'books.'

[Tracts (*a*) in the Advocates' Library, (*b*) in the possession of William Cowan, esq., Edinburgh; Chambers's Domestic Annals, iii. 361, and Traditions of Edinburgh, pp. 53-5; Irving's Dict. of Eminent Scotsmen; Maidment's Pasquils, p. 74.] G. G. S.

MITCHELBURN. [See Michelborne.]

MITCHELL. [See also Michell and Mitchel.]

MITCHELL, ALEXANDER (1780-1868), civil engineer, born in Dublin on 13 April 1780, was son of William Mitchell, inspector-general of barracks in Ireland. At school he showed a marked taste for mathematics. In 1802 his eyesight, always defective in consequence of an attack of small-pox, almost totally failed him. He soon carried on, in Belfast, the joint business of brickmaking and building, from which he retired in 1832, having previously invented several machines employed in those trades. In 1842 he became known as the inventor and patentee of the Mitchell screw-pile and mooring, a simple yet effective means of constructing durable lighthouses in deep water, on mudbanks and shifting sands, of fixing beacons, and of mooring ships. For this invention he was chosen an associate of the Institution of Civil Engineers, and in 1848 was elected a member, receiving the Telford silver medal for a paper on his own invention. His system was generally approved of by engineers of eminence (*Proc. of Inst. of Civ. Eng.* ii. 150, vii. 108). He established himself at Belfast, and at 17 Great George Street, Westminster, as 'Mitchell's Screw-Pile and Mooring Company.' At the expiration of his patent in 1847 the privy council, in consideration of its merit, granted a renewal for fourteen years.

Mitchell's screw-pile was first used for the foundation of the Maplin Sand Lighthouse at the mouth of the Thames in 1838 (*ib.* vii. 146). In 1839 he designed and constructed, with the aid of his son, the Fleetwood-on-Wyre Lighthouse, Morecambe Bay. In the summer of 1844 a screw-pile lighthouse, serving also as a pilot station, was successfully placed by him in Belfast Lough, Carrickfergus Bay; but his attempt to construct a lighthouse on the Kish Bank, between Dublin Bay and Waterford, proved a failure. He also constructed, in the summer of 1847, a screw-pile jetty at Courtown on the coast of Wexford. After the success of screw-piles had been established, they were applied to more extensive undertakings. The great government breakwater at Portland, the long viaduct and bridges on the Bombay and Baroda railway, the whole system of Indian telegraphs, and the Madras pier, were among the works executed with this invention.

His improved method of mooring ships was likewise generally adopted. The corporation of Newcastle-upon-Tyne purchased, for 2,500*l.*, the right of putting down screw moorings in the Tyne.

Mitchell, who retired from the Engineers' Institution in 1857 (*ib.* xvii. 85), settled first at Farm Hill, but latterly at Glen Devis, near Belfast, where he died on 25 June 1868. He had a family of two sons and three daughters, of whom only one, the wife of Professor Burden of Queen's College, Belfast, survived him.

He published: **1.** 'Description of a Patent Screw-pile Battery and Lighthouse,' 8vo, Belfast, 1843. 2. 'On Submarine Foundations, particularly the Screw-pile and Moorings,' 8vo, London, 1848, a description of his invention, read before the Institution of Civil Engineers on 22 Feb. 1848.

[Belfast News-Letter, 29 June 1868; Men of the Time, 1868 p. 586, 1872 p. 1001; Denham's Mersey and Dee Navigation; Hugh M'Call's Ireland and her Staple Manufactures.] G. G.

MITCHELL, Sir ANDREW (1708–1771), diplomatist, born at Edinburgh on 15 April 1708, was the only surviving son of William Mitchell, of an Aberdeenshire family, minister of St. Giles's, Edinburgh, and one of the king's chaplains for Scotland. Mitchell received part of his education at the university of Edinburgh. Before he was twenty-one he married his cousin, Barbara Mitchell, an only daughter, and heiress of the lands of Thainston in Aberdeenshire. She died about 1729, having given birth to an only daughter, who did not survive infancy. At the time Mitchell was studying for the Scottish bar, but the event affected him so deeply that he never afterwards resided in Scotland for any length of time. After several years spent in foreign travel, he was entered at Leyden University 5 Oct. 1730, and having formed at Paris an intimacy with Montesquieu, he settled in London in 1735 and studied for the English bar. He was elected a member of the Royal Society in March 1735, and was called to the bar at the Middle Temple on 12 May 1738. In 1741 he was served, in right of his wife, heir to the Thainston estates. In the following year the Marquis of Tweeddale [see Hay, John, fourth Marquis], on becoming secretary of state for Scotland, appointed him under-secretary. Quin the actor, in conversation with Mitchell, hinted that his official employment was simply that of Will helping Jack to do nothing (Walpole, v. 235), but with the breaking out of the rebellion of 1745 Mitchell's office became no sinecure. His functions ceased in 1747 with the abolition of the Scottish secretaryship of state. But he was afterwards consulted by the government respecting the affairs of Scotland, and the Duke of Newcastle aided him in what proved to be his successful candidature for Aberdeenshire. He was elected as a staunch whig in 1747. He was an intimate friend of James Thomson, the poet of the 'Seasons,' who, dying in 1748, left Mitchell one of his executors. He spoke occasionally in the House of Commons, and in 1751–2 he was at Brussels as one of the British commissioners appointed to negotiate a commercial treaty with Austria and the Netherlands. From 1755 to 1761 he was M.P. for the Elgin burghs, but during most of the period he was absent from England, having been appointed in 1756 British envoy to Frederick the Great.

Mitchell reached Berlin just before the breaking out of the seven years' war and the formation of an Anglo-Prussian alliance. Frederick and he became strongly attracted to each other. Mitchell was admitted to confidential intercourse with the king, whose appeals for a strict fulfilment of the engagements which England had entered into with Prussia were warmly supported by Mitchell in his correspondence with his government. Frederick willingly acceded to Mitchell's application, made in pursuance of instructions from home, to be allowed to accompany him in his campaigns, and he was often by the king's side in the battle-field and under fire. The clear and instructive narratives of military operations sent home by Mitchell interested George II, and their value has been recognised by Carlyle. Mitchell's reports of Frederick's frank and lively conversations with him abound in striking traits and anecdotes of the great king. Some remarks in one of his despatches appear to have given offence to the elder Pitt, and he was recalled, General Yorke being sent to supersede him. But Frederick insisted that Mitchell should remain, and without quitting Berlin he resumed his functions as envoy. This was in 1758, and in 1759 he was raised to the rank of plenipotentiary. While attached to Frederick and approving of his policy, Mitchell did not hesitate to speak his mind freely to him in regard both to politics and to religion. They had more than once discussions on the providential government of the world, in which Frederick did not believe, while Mitchell advocated the orthodox view. In the intervals of campaigning Mitchell learnt German, one of his earliest teachers being Gottsched, whose attack on Shakespeare for neglecting the unities he repelled with considerable wit (Carlyle, vii. 317). Mitchell's acquaintance with the rising German literature of the time was much greater than that of Frederick, on whom he urged its claims to royal recognition (*ib.* ix. 154).

Lord Bute, on becoming prime minister in 1762, aimed at bringing the seven years' war to an end, and discontinued the subsidies to Frederick, who wrote in that year to one of his correspondents: 'Messieurs the English continue to betray. Poor M. Mitchell has had a stroke of apoplexy on hearing of it.' There was now a diminution of the king's confidential intercourse with Mitchell, who had become the envoy of a government unfriendly to Frederick. In 1764, peace having been restored to Europe, Mitchell revisited England. He had been re-elected for the Elgin burghs in 1761, and continued to represent them, at least nominally, until his death. In 1765 he was invested, but not installed, a knight of the Bath (Foster, p. 252). In the following year he returned as envoy to Berlin. But as Frederick rejected Chatham's proposal of a triple alliance between England, Prussia, and Russia, which Mitchell was instructed to urge on him, the old intimacy of the king and Mitchell remained in abeyance. Mitchell's later despatches contain severe animadversions on Frederick's debasement of the coinage and general fiscal policy.

Mitchell died at Berlin on 28 Jan. 1771, and Frederick is said to have shed tears as he witnessed from a balcony the funeral procession. He was buried in a Berlin church, in which a year or so afterwards a bust of him was placed at the instance of Prince Henry, Frederick's brother. Mitchell is described as strongly built, and rather above the middle height. His portrait at Thainston is that of a bold, straightforward, and most sagacious man. He is said to have been taking in his manner, but rather blunt. Carlyle speaks of him as 'an Aberdeen Scotchman creditable to his country; hard-headed, sagacious, sceptical of shows, but capable of recognising substances withal and of standing loyal to them, stubbornly if needful . . . whose Letters are among the perennially valuable Documents on Friedrich's History.' The anecdotes of Mitchell, given by Thiébault, some of which are often quoted, are not to be relied on when Thiébault is repeating the gossip of others. Mitchell himself, however, told him, he asserts, that when Frederick was least satisfied with England, Mitchell was reproached by the government at home with not reporting Frederick's bitter sarcasms on their policy, and that in reply he declared his determination to resign rather than play the part of tale-bearer.

[Mitchell's Diplomatic and Private Correspondence, in sixty-nine volumes, is in the British Museum, Addit. MSS. 6804–72. Copious and interesting extracts from them form the basis of Mr. Andrew Bisset's Memoirs and Papers of Sir Andrew Mitchell (2 vols. 1850), which is the chief printed authority for Mitchell's biography. Mr. Bisset has also made use of a considerable number of Mitchell's letters in the possession of his heirs, and not included in the Museum collection. Lord Glenbervie began for publication a selection from the Mitchell Papers in the Museum, but was stopped by order of George III. Those which he did select constitute the volumes of Addit. MSS. 11260–2. There are a number of Mitchell's letters printed in the Culloden Papers (1815), and several in the Chatham Correspondence (1838–40), and in Von Raumer's Beiträge zur neueren Geschichte aus dem Britischen Museum und Reichsarchive (1836–7, English translation 1837). The references in the preceding article are to Carlyle's History of Friedrich II, library ed. 1870; Horace Walpole's Letters (1857–9); Foster's Members of Parliament, Scotland (2nd edit. 1882); Thiébault's Mes Souvenirs de Vingt Ans de Séjour à Berlin (2nd edit. 1805), tom. iii., 'Les Ministres Etrangers à la Cour de Berlin: Légation d'Angleterre.'] F. E.

MITCHELL, Sir ANDREW (1757–1806), admiral, second son of Charles Mitchell of Baldridge, near Dunfermline in Fife, born in 1757, was educated at the high school, Edinburgh. He entered the navy in 1771 on board the Deal Castle. After serving in different ships on the home station, in 1776 he went out to the East Indies in the Ripon with Sir Edward Vernon [q.v.], by whom he was promoted to be lieutenant of the Coventry frigate, 11 Oct. 1777, and to be captain, also of the Coventry, after the skirmish off Pondicherry on 10 Aug. 1778. His post rank was confirmed by the admiralty to 25 Oct. 1778. Mitchell continued in the Coventry after Sir Edward Hughes [q.v.] took command of the station; and on 12 Aug. 1782 fought a severe but indecisive action with the French 40-gun frigate Bellona off Friar's Hood in Ceylon. In September Hughes appointed him to the Sultan, in which he took part in the fight off Cuddalore on 20 June 1783. After the peace Mitchell remained on the station as commodore of a small squadron (Beatson, *Naval and Mil. Memoirs*, vi. 360), with his broad pennant in the Defence. He returned to England in 1786, having acquired in ten years' service a very considerable sum, which was lost by the bankruptcy of his agent. In the armament of 1790 he commanded the Asia, which was paid off on the settlement of the dispute; and in February 1795 he was appointed to the Impregnable in the Channel fleet. From her on 1 June 1795 he was promoted to the rank of rear-admiral.

On 14 Feb. 1799 he was advanced to be vice-admiral, and in April was appointed to a command in the North Sea under Lord Duncan. In August he had charge of the transports for the expedition to Holland; and though Duncan himself convoyed them across and superintended the disembarkation of the troops, he left the further operations to Mitchell, who on 30 Aug. received the surrender of the Dutch ships, consequent on the mutiny of the Dutch seamen, who refused to fight against the allies of the Prince of Orange. Their brethren on shore took a different view of the position, and in conjunction with the French repulsed the English and Russian army; so that the Duke of York, who was in command, was compelled to ask for an armistice, on the basis of an immediate evacuation of Holland. Mitchell, who, with a squadron of small vessels, had made himself master of the Zuyder Zee, was bound by the same treaty, and withdrew his ships; but neither he nor Sir Ralph Abercromby, who had commanded the army at its first landing, was blamed for the ignominious termination of the campaign; the thanks of parliament were given to both, as well as to the officers and men; and Mitchell was nominated a K.B., 9 Jan. 1800. The city of London, too, presented him with a sword of the value of one hundred guineas.

During 1800 and 1801 he commanded in the Channel fleet, under Lord St. Vincent and Admiral Cornwallis, and in November 1801 was detached with a squadron to the coast of Ireland and to Bantry Bay. In December, on some of the ships being ordered to sail for the West Indies, a mutiny broke out, especially on board the Téméraire, the flagship of Rear-admiral George Campbell. The mutiny was suppressed, and some twenty of the ringleaders, having been made prisoners, were brought round to Spithead, where they were tried by a court-martial, of which Mitchell was president. The greater number of them were found guilty and were executed (the minutes of the court-martial were published, 8vo, 1802). In the spring of 1802 Mitchell was appointed commander-in-chief on the North American station. On 9 Nov. 1805 he was promoted to be admiral; after a short illness he died at Bermuda on 26 Feb. 1806, and was buried there with military honours. He was twice married, having by his first wife three sons, Charles, Nathaniel, and Andrew (Marshall, *Roy. Nav. Biog.* vii. 325, viii. 380, and ix. 215), who all died captains in the navy. By his second wife he had a daughter. His portrait by Bowyer has been engraved (*Catalogue of the Naval Exhibition*, 1891).

[Ralfe's Nav. Biog. ii. 91; Naval Chronicle, with portrait after Bowyer, xvi. 89; James's Nav. Hist. 1860, ii. 343.] J. K. L.

MITCHELL, CORNELIUS (*d.* 1749?), captain in the navy, entered the navy in 1709 on board the Ranelagh, then carrying the flag of Sir John Norris in the Channel. On 22 Dec. 1720 he was promoted by Commodore Charles Stewart, in the Mediterranean, to be lieutenant of the Dover. In 1726 he was a lieutenant of the Weymouth, and in June 1729 he was appointed to the Lion going out to the West Indies with the flag of his old patron Stewart, at this time a rear-admiral. By Stewart he was promoted, on 14 June 1731, to be captain of the Lark, which he took to England and paid off in the following February. From that time he had no service till August 1739, when he was appointed to the Rochester. In the following year he was moved into the Torbay, and afterwards into the Buckingham, in which he sailed for the West Indies in the fleet under Sir Chaloner Ogle (*d.* 1751) [q. v.] On the way out, however, the Buckingham was disabled in a storm and was sent home (Beatson, iii. 27), and Mitchell, appointed to the Kent, went out later. In December 1743 he was moved by Ogle into the Adventure; and again by Davers in July 1745 into the Strafford. In the following December, with the Plymouth and Lyme frigate in company, he was convoying a fleet of merchant ships through the Windward Passage, when on the 15th he fell in with three French ships of war off Cape Nicolas. A slight engagement ensued, and, content with having beaten off the enemy, Mitchell pursued his voyage. A court-martial afterwards decided that he was justified in so doing, as the French force was superior, and the safety of the convoy was the first consideration.

In August 1746 Mitchell was again in command of a squadron, and again met a French squadron off Cape Nicolas, but the circumstances were reversed. The French had the convoy; Mitchell had the superior force. He had four ships of the line, one of 44 guns, and a small frigate, against three ships of the line, and one of 44 guns (*ib.* iii. 65–6). Mitchell, although his duty to attack was plain, hesitated; and when the French, encouraged by his apparent timidity, chased, he fled under a press of sail. At night he gave orders to show no lights; but he did not part company with the enemy, and day after day the experience was repeated. Once only did the squadrons engage, and after a few broadsides Mitchell drew off. On the tenth day, 13 Aug., the French entered the harbour of Cape François, where 'they fired guns very merrily, and in the dusk of the evening had great illuminations in the town.'

Mitchell's conduct was severely commented on; but the admiral was sick and incapable. Mitchell, next to him, was the senior officer on the station; and it was only when the affair was reported to the admiralty that special orders were sent out to try him by court-martial. Even then there was some difficulty about forming a court, and it was thus 27 Oct. 1747 before he was put on his trial. The evidence against him was very positive; the hearing lasted nearly three months; the minutes of it fill about a thousand closely written foolscap pages; and on 28 Jan. 1747–8 the court determined that Mitchell 'fell under part of the 12th and 14th articles of war,' and sentenced him 'to be cashiered and rendered incapable of ever being employed in his Majesty's service' (cf. MAHAN, *Influence of Sea Power upon History*, p. 267 *n.*) There was a strong feeling that the punishment was inadequate; so that when in 1749 parliament undertook to revise the code of naval discipline the discretionary power of courts-martial in cases such as Mitchell's was abolished, and under the altered regulations Admiral Byng suffered death in 1757.

Charnock incorrectly says that Mitchell was even restored to his half-pay of ten shillings a day. His name does not appear on the half-pay lists; and though it is possible that an equivalent pension was given him in some irregular manner, no minutes of such can be found. There is no official record of his death, which is said to have taken place in 1749.

[Charnock's Biog. Nav. iv. 230; Beatson's Nav. and Mil. Mem. i. 320; Campbell's Lives of the Admirals, iv. 62; minutes of the courts-martial, commission and warrant books, and half-pay lists in Public Record Office.] J. K. L.

MITCHELL, SIR DAVID (1650?–1710), vice-admiral, was bound apprentice to the master of a Leith trading vessel. Afterwards he was mate of a ship in the Baltic trade, and in 1672 was pressed into the navy. His conduct and appearance attracted attention; he was placed on the quarter-deck, and on 16 Jan. 1677–8 was promoted to be lieutenant of the Defiance in the Mediterranean with Captain Edward Russell, afterwards Earl of Orford [q. v.], whom in March he followed to the Swiftsure, and again in August 1680 to the Newcastle. In May 1682 he was appointed lieutenant of the Tiger, and on 1 Oct. 1683 promoted to the command of the Ruby. Whether in compliment to his patron Russell, who retired from the service on the execution of his cousin William, or finding that he no longer had any interest, he also seems to have retired. He may have commanded ships in the merchant service, or followed the fortunes of Russell, and acted as his agent in his political intrigues at home and in Holland. After the revolution he was appointed to the Elizabeth of 70 guns, and in her took part in the battle of Beachy Head, 30 June 1690. In 1691, when Russell was appointed to the command of the fleet, Mitchell was appointed first captain of the Britannia, his flagship, an office now known as captain of the fleet. He was still first captain of the Britannia at the battle of Barfleur, 19 May 1692, and in the subsequent operations, culminating in the burning of the French ships in the bay of La Hogue, 23–4 May.

For his conduct on this occasion Mitchell was appointed by the king one of the grooms of the bedchamber, and on 8 Feb. 1692–3 was promoted to be rear-admiral of the blue. In March, with his flag in the Essex, he commanded the squadron which convoyed the king to Holland. During the year he served with the main fleet under the command of the joint admirals, and in October escorted the king back from Holland. In February 1693–4 he had command of a squadron to the westward, for the guard of the Channel and the protection of trade; and on his return from this service he was knighted. In May he joined the grand fleet, now again under the command of Russell, whom he accompanied to the Mediterranean. When Russell returned home in the autumn of 1695, Mitchell was left commander-in-chief, till superseded by Sir George Rooke [q. v.], who brought out his commission as vice-admiral of the blue, and with whom he returned to England in the spring of 1696. During the rest of the year he was second in command of the fleet in the Channel, under Rooke; and in 1697 commanded a detached squadron cruising on the Soundings till the conclusion of the peace. In January 1697–8 he was sent with a small squadron of ships of war and yachts to bring the czar Peter to England. He was afterwards, at the czar's request, appointed to attend on him during his stay in this country, and to command the squadron which convoyed him back to Holland. In this connection several anecdotes of doubtful authenticity are related (CAMPBELL, iii. 426). It is also said that the czar invited him to Russia, with the offer of a very lucrative post, which Mitchell declined.

In June 1699 he was appointed one of the lords commissioners of the admiralty, in which post he remained till April 1701, when the Earl of Pembroke was made lord high admiral. He was afterwards usher of the black rod; and on the accession of Queen Anne, when Prince George became lord high admiral, Mitchell was appointed one of his council, in which office he continued till April 1708. It was apparently in 1709 that he was sent to Holland 'to negotiate matters relating to the sea with the States-General.' He died at his seat, Popes in Hertfordshire, on 1 June 1710, 'about the 60th year of his age' (inscription on his tombstone). He was buried in the church at Hatfield beneath a slab, on which a lengthy inscription summarises his services. It also bears the arms of Mitchell of Tillygreig, Aberdeen (1672). Le Neve (*Pedigrees of the Knights*, p. 461), says, 'He bears arms but hath no right,' and tells an absurd story how, as 'a poor boy from Scotland,' he was pressed from a Newcastle collier, and was pulled out from under the coals, where he had hidden himself. The arms on an escutcheon of pretence which he assumed were by right of his wife Mary, daughter and coheiress of Robert Dod of Chorley in Shropshire, by whom he had one son, died an infant. Dame Mary died 30 Sept. 1722, aged 62, and was also buried in the church at Hatfield; but the slab, bearing the inscription, 'Heare lyes the body,' &c., is now in the churchyard (information from the sexton of Hatfield; cf. BURKE, *Hist. of Commoners*, i. 298).

[Boyer's Hist. of Queen Anne (App. ii.), p. 53; Campbell's Lives of the Admirals, iii. 423; Charnock's Biog. Nav. ii. 105; inscriptions on the tombstones at Hatfield; that on Mitchell's is printed in John Le Neve's Monumenta Anglicana, 1700-15, p. 188.] J. K. L.

MITCHELL, HUGH HENRY (1770-1817), colonel, born on 9 June 1770, was appointed ensign in the 101st regiment in January 1782, and lieutenant in June 1783. He served with that regiment in India and until it was disbanded in 1784. In May 1786 he was gazetted to the 26th, and served with it in the latter part of the campaign of 1801 in Egypt. He rose in the 26th to the rank of lieutenant-colonel in December 1805. In June 1811 he exchanged to the 51st light infantry, and commanded that regiment in the Peninsula War till its conclusion in 1814. He obtained the rank of colonel in June 1813, and the order of companion of the Bath on 4 June 1815. In the Waterloo campaign Mitchell commanded a brigade consisting of the 3rd battalion of the 14th, the 23rd fusiliers, and the 51st light infantry.

Wellington was sparing—almost niggardly—in his expressions of praise, and never mentioned an officer in his despatches merely because he commanded a brigade or division, or was on the staff. Mitchell was the only commander of a brigade at Waterloo under the rank of general officer who was thus honoured. For his services in the campaign he received from the Emperor of Russia the order of St. Vladimir of the third class, and also the Russian order of St. Ann.

Mitchell died 20 April 1817, in Queen Anne Street, London.

[Gent. Mag. 1817, pt. i. p. 473; Wellington's Despatches; Gazettes; Army Lists, &c.] E. O'C.

MITCHELL or MITCHEL, JAMES (*d.* 1678), fanatic, was the son of obscure parents in Midlothian. He graduated at Edinburgh University on 9 July 1656, and at the same time signed the national covenant and the solemn league and covenant. He attached himself to the party of remonstrator presbyterians, and studied popular divinity under David Dickson (1583?-1663) [q. v.] He was refused by the presbytery of Dalkeith on the grounds of insufficiency, and appears to have become 'a preacher, but no actual minister,' in or near Edinburgh. In 1661 he was recommended to some ministers in Galloway by Trail, a minister in Edinburgh, as suitable for teaching in a school or as private tutor. He entered the house of the Laird of Dundas as domestic chaplain and tutor to his children, but was dismissed for immoral conduct. Returning to Edinburgh he made the acquaintance of Major John Weir [q. v.], who procured for him the post of chaplain in a 'fanatical family, the lady whereof was niece to Sir Archibald Johnston' of Warriston. He quitted this post in November 1666 to join the rising of the covenanters in the west at Ayr. He was in Edinburgh on 28 Nov., when the rebels were defeated at Pentland, but was pronounced guilty of treason in a proclamation of 4 Dec. 1666, and on 1 Oct. 1667 was excluded from the pardon granted to those engaged in the rising. Mitchell effected his escape to Holland, where he joined a cousin, a factor in Rotterdam. After wandering in England and Ireland he returned to Edinburgh in 1668. There he married, and opened a shop for the sale of tobacco and spirits.

Mitchell resolved to revenge himself on James Sharp, archbishop of St. Andrews, for his desertion of the presbyterian cause, and on 11 July 1668 he fired a pistol at him as he sat in his coach in Blackfriars Wynd in Edinburgh. The shot missed the archbishop, but entered the hand of his companion, Andrew Honeyman, bishop of Orkney. Mitchell passed down Niddry's Wynd without opposition, and, despite the reward of five thousand marks offered for his apprehension, quitted the country. He returned to Scotland towards the end of 1673. Early in 1674 he was recognised in the street by the archbishop, whose brother, Sir William Sharp, obtained a confession from him, after the archbishop had pledged himself that no harm should come to him. But he was imprisoned, and at the instigation of Sharp brought before the council on 10 Feb. 1674. He again made a full confession on 12 Feb. on receiving a promise of his life. After further imprisonment in the Tolbooth he was brought before the justiciary court on 2 March 1674 to receive sentence, but he denied that he was guilty, though he was told that he would lose the benefit of the assurance of life if he persisted in his denial. On 6 March the council framed an act in which they declared themselves free of any promise made. On 25 March Mitchell was again brought before the court, but there being no evidence against him beyond the confession, since retracted, the lords of justiciary deserted the diet, with the consent of the lord advocate, Sir John Nisbet [q. v.] Mitchell was returned to the Tolbooth and afterwards removed to the Bass Rock. On 18 Jan. 1677 he again, in the presence of a committee of justices, of which Linlithgow [see LIVINGSTONE, GEORGE, third EARL OF] was chairman, denied his confession. A further attempt was made on 22 Jan. with the same result, despite a threat of the 'boots.' On 24 Jan., in the Parliament House, he was examined under torture as to his connection with the rebellion of 1666. This accusation he also denied, and reminded those present that there were two other James Mitchells in Midlothian. The torture and questioning continued till the prisoner fainted, when he was carried back to the Tolbooth.

In December 1677 the council ordered criminal proceedings against him for the attempted assassination of the archbishop. On 7 Jan. the trial commenced; he was ably defended by Sir George Lockhart [q. v.] and John Elies. His former confession was the sole evidence against him. Rothes swore to having seen Mitchell sign his confession, which was countersigned by himself. But both he and the archbishop denied that the promise of life had been given. Mitchell's counsel produced a copy of the Act of Council of 12 March 1674, in which his confession under promise of life was recorded, but a request that the books of the council might be produced was refused. The trial was remarkable for the number of witnesses of high station, and the perjury of Rothes, Halton, and Lauderdale has rarely been paralleled. The following day, 10 Jan., sentence of death was passed, and Mitchell was executed in the Grassmarket of Edinburgh on Friday, 18 Jan. 1678.

Halton was indicted for the perjury on 28 July 1681, the evidence against him being two letters that he had written on 10 and 12 Feb. 1674 to the Earl of Kincardine [see BRUCE, ALEXANDER, second EARL], in which he gave an account of Mitchell's confession, 'upon assurance of his life.' The letters are printed in Wodrow, ii. 248–9.

Mitchell is described as 'a lean, hollow-cheeked man, of a truculent countenance' (*Ravillac Redivivus*, p. 11). He himself attributed his attempt on Sharp as 'ane impulse of the spirit of God' (KIRKTON, *History of the Church of Scotland*, p. 387). His son James, who graduated at the university of Edinburgh on 11 Nov. 1698, was licensed by the presbytery there on 26 July 1704, ordained on 5 April 1710, and became minister of Dunnotar in the same year. He was summoned to appear before the justices of the peace on 24 March 1713 to answer for the exercise of church discipline in the session. He died on 26 June 1734.

[The fullest account of Mitchell's attempt at assassination and trials is given in Wodrow's History of the Sufferings of the Church of Scotland, ed. Burns, ii. 115–17, 248–52, 454–73. A prejudiced account, entitled Ravillac Redivivus, being a Narrative of the late Tryal, was published anonymously in 1678, 4to. It was the work of George Hickes [q. v.], who, as chaplain to Lauderdale, accompanied him to Scotland in May 1677, and was in Edinburgh at the time of Mitchell's trial. Somers's Tracts, viii., contains a reprint of the work with notes (pp. 510–53). A pamphlet entitled 'The Spirit of Fanaticism exemplified' is an amplified version of the work, published by Curll in 1710. Stephen's Life of Sharp, pp. 383, 458–61; Omond's Lord Advocates of Scotland, i. 192, 214–15; Sir James Turner's Memoirs (Bannatyne Club), pp. 166, 180; Kirkton's Church of Scotland, pp. 383–8; Burnet's Hist of his own Time, ii. 125–32, 298–9; Cobbett's State Trials, vol. vi. cols. 1207–66; Mackenzie's Memoirs, pp. 326–7; Edinburgh Graduates, pp. 77, 161; Scott's Fasti Eccles. Scot. vol. iii. pt. ii. pp. 861–2.]

B. P.

MITCHELL, JAMES (1786?–1844), scientific writer, was born in or near Aberdeen about 1786. He was educated at the university of that town, graduated M.A. at University and King's college in 1804, and was subsequently created LL.D. His whole fortune when he came to London in 1805 was 10*l.*, and he supported himself by teaching until he became secretary, first to the Star Insurance Company, then to the British Annuity Company. He was employed as actuary to the parliamentary commission on factories, and as sub-commissioner on those relating to handloom-weaving and the condition of women and children in collieries. Overtasked by these labours, he was struck with paralysis in June 1843, and died of apoplexy on 3 Sept. 1844, in the house of his nephew, Mr. Templeton, at Exeter, aged 58. He was a fellow of the Geological Society of London, to which he made numerous communications, and from 1823 a corresponding member of the Society of Scottish Antiquaries.

His works include: 1. 'On the Plurality of Worlds,' London, 1813. 2. 'An Easy System of Shorthand,' 1815. 3. 'A Tour through Belgium, Holland, &c., in the Summer of 1816,' 1816. 4. 'The Elements of Natural Philosophy,' 1819. 5. 'The Elements of Astronomy,' 1820. 6. 'A Dictionary of the Mathematical and Physical Sciences,' 1823. 7. 'A Dictionary of Chemistry, Mineralogy, and Geology,' 1823. 8. 'The Scotsman's Library,' Edinburgh, 1825, &c. He left besides many folio volumes in manuscript descriptive of the geology of London and its neighbourhood; and he made at great expense collections relative to Scottish antiquities, some of which he presented to the Society of Scottish Antiquaries, while the remainder were bequeathed by him to the university of Aberdeen.

[Gent. Mag. 1844, ii. 432; Ann. Reg. 1844, p. 267; Allibone's Dict. of English Literature; Ward's Men of the Reign; Poggendorff's Biog. Lit. Handwörterbuch; Roy. Soc. Cat. of Scientific Papers; Brit. Mus. Cat.] A. M. C.

MITCHELL, JAMES (1791–1852), line-engraver, was born in 1791. His most important works were 'Alfred in the Neatherd's Cottage,' 1829, and 'Rat Hunters,' 1830, both after Sir David Wilkie, R.A. He engraved also 'The Contadina,' after Sir Charles L. Eastlake, P.R.A., and 'Lady Jane Grey,' after James Northcote, R.A., for the 'Literary Souvenir' of 1827 and 1832; 'The Farewell,' after Abraham Cooper, R.A.; 'Saturday Night' and 'The Dorty Bairn,' after Sir David Wilkie, and 'The Corsair,' after H. P. Briggs, R.A., for the 'Gem' of 1829, 1830, and 1832; and 'The Secret,' after Robert Smirke, R.A., for 'The Keepsake' of 1831. Besides these he produced 'Edie Ochiltree,' after Sir Edwin Landseer, and five other illustrations, after Kidd, Stanfield, J. W. Wright, and Alexander Fraser, for the author's edition of the 'Waverley Novels,' 1829–33. He died in London on 29 Nov. 1852, aged 61.

Robert Mitchell (1820–1873), his son, born on 19 May 1820, engraved in mezzotint 'Tapageur, a fashionable Member of the Canine Society,' after Sir Edwin Landseer, 1852, and 'The Parish Beauty' and 'The Pastor's Pet,' a pair after Alfred Rankley, 1853 and 1854; and in the mixed style 'The Happy Mothers' and 'The Startled Twins,' a pair after Richard Ansdell, R.A., 1850, and 'Christ walking on the Sea,' after Robert Scott Lauder, R.S.A., 1854. He also etched several plates, which were completed in mezzotint by other engravers. He died at Bromley, Kent, on 16 May 1873.

[Private information.] R. E. G.

MITCHELL or MYCHELL, JOHN (*fl.* 1556), printer, pursued his trade in St. Paul, Canterbury. From 'A Cronicle of Yeres' (1543 and 1544) he compiled, with large additions, 'A breviat Cronicle contaynynge all the Kinges from Brut to this daye, and manye notable actes gathered oute of diuers Cronicles from Willyam Conquerour vnto the yere of Christ a. M. V. c. l. ii.,' 8vo, Canterbury, 1551; another edit. 1553. In a quaint dedication to Sir Anthony Aucher, master of the king's jewel-house, whom he asks to aid him in improving the next issue of the book, he implores his friends and brother-printers to suffer him quietly to enjoy the benefit of his labours. His request was apparently disregarded, as his book was reissued at other presses at London in 1555, 1556, 1559, and about 1561.

Mitchell printed at Canterbury: 1. 'The Psalter . . . after the translacion of the great Bible,' 4to, 1549 and 1550. 2. 'A Treatise of Predestination,' by John Lambert, 8vo, 1550. 3. 'Two Dyaloges wrytten in laten by Desiderius Erasmus, translated in to Englyshe by Edmund Becke,' 8vo (1550). 4. 'Articles to be enquired in thordinary Visitacion of . . . the Lord Cardinall Poole's Grace, Archebyshop of Canterburie within hys Dioces of Canterbury, 1556,' 4to, 1556. 5. 'A shorte Epistle to all such as do contempne the Marriage of us poor Preestes,' 16mo, undated. 6. 'The spirituall Matrimonye betwene Chryste and the Soul,' 24mo, undated. 7. 'An Exposytion upon the Epistyll of Saynt Paul to the Phillipians,' by Lancelot Ridley, 8vo, undated. 8. 'The Confession of Fayth, writtyn in Latyn by Ph. Melanchton . . . translated . . . by Robert Syngylton,' 8vo, undated. 9. 'Newes from Rome concerning the blasphemous sacrifice of the papisticall Masse,' by Randall Hurlestone, 8vo, undated, but about 1560.

[Tanner's Bibl. Brit.; Watt's Bibl. Brit.; Cat. of Books in Brit. Mus. to 1640.] G. G.

MITCHELL, JOHN (*d.* 1768), botanist, born and educated in England, graduated M.D., although at what university is uncertain. There were several John Mitchells at Oxford at the beginning of the eighteenth century, more than one at Cambridge, and one who entered Leyden on 12 Feb. 1712, but none of these can be certainly identified with the botanist. Mitchell is said to have emigrated to America about 1700, and resided in Virginia, at Urbanna, on the Rappahannock river, about seventy-three miles from Richmond. He devoted himself to botanical and other scientific studies, and discovered several new species of plants, one of which was called after him, 'Mitchella repens,' by Linnæus. In 1738 he wrote a 'Dissertatio brevis de principiis botanicorum,' dedicated to Sir Hans Sloane, and in 1741 'Nova Plantarum genera,' dedicated to Peter Collinson [q. v.], both of which were subsequently printed at Nuremberg, 1769. In 1743 Mitchell prepared an 'Essay upon the Causes of the different Colours of People in different Climates,' which was read before the Royal Society by Peter Collinson at various meetings between 3 May and 14 June 1744, and published in the 'Philosophical Transactions' (xliii. 102, &c.) It was designed as a solution of a prize problem set by the academy of Bordeaux. Mitchell maintains that the influence of climate and mode of life is sufficient to account for differences in colour.

Either in 1747 or 1748 Mitchell returned to England. On 17 and 24 Nov. 1748 his essay 'Of the Preparation and Use of various kinds of Potash' was read before the Royal Society (*Phil. Trans.* xlv. 541, &c.), and on 15 Dec. of the same year Mitchell himself became F.R.S. In December 1759 he contributed to the 'Philosophical Transactions a 'Letter concerning the Force of Electrical Cohesion,' dated from Kew. Mitchell died in March 1768. He must be carefully distinguished from John Michell (*d.* 1793) [q. v.], astronomer.

Besides the works already mentioned Mitchell published: 1. 'A Map of the British and French Dominions in North America,' London, 1755, which is said to 'mark an era in the geography' of North America, and was often quoted in boundary negotiations; a French version was published at Paris in 1756, and a second edition appeared in 1757, which was reprinted in 1782. There are copies of all in the British Museum Library. 2. 'The Contest in America between Great Britain and France, by an Impartial Hand,' London, 1757, 8vo. 3. 'The Present State of Great Britain and North America,' 1767, 8vo. He also left in manuscript 'An Account of the Yellow Fever which prevailed in Virginia in 1737, 1741, and 1742,' in letters to Cadwallader Colden and Benjamin Franklin, which were published, together with Colden's and Franklin's replies, by Professor Rush in the 'American Medical and Philosophical Register' (iv. 181 *sqq.*)

[Works in Brit. Mus. Library; Lists of Fellows of the Royal Society, 1748–67; Phil. Trans. passim; Pulteney's Progress of Botany (with manuscript notes), ii. 278–81; Gent. Mag. 1768, p. 142; Miller's Retrospect of the Eighteenth Century, i. 318, ii. 367; Ramsay's Eulogy on Dr. Rush, pp. 84–5; Thacher's American Medical Biog. i. 392–3; Rich's Bibl. Amer. Nova, i. 36, &c.; American Medical and Phil. Register, vol. iv.] A. F. P.

MITCHELL, JOHN (1785–1859), major-general, born 11 June 1785 in Stirlingshire, was the son of John Mitchell of the diplomatic service, sometime consul-general for Norway, and afterwards engaged on missions to the court of Stockholm and Copenhagen. In 1797 Mitchell went to Berlin with his father, who was despatched on a mission to the court of the new king, Frederick William III. He was placed at the Ritter academy at Lüneburg, where he acquired a knowledge of languages and a love of literature. In 1801 he was sent to a mathematical school in London taught by a Mr. Nicholson, and on 9 July 1803 was commissioned as ensign in the 57th regiment. On 5 Dec. 1804 he was promoted to a lieutenancy in the 1st royals, and went with the 1st battalion of his regiment to the West Indies. On 1 Oct. 1807 he was promoted captain in the 1st royals. In 1809 he joined the 3rd battalion of his regiment at Walcheren, and was present at the siege of Flushing. He served with the same battalion in the Peninsula from 1810 to 1812, and was present at the battles of Busaco and Fuentes d'Onoro, in the action of Sabugal, and in those of the retreat of Masséna. He accompanied the 4th battalion on the expedition under Major-general Gibbs to Stralsund in 1813, but served on the staff as a deputy assistant quartermaster-general. He also served in a similar capacity in the campaign of 1814 in Holland and Flanders, and with the head-quarters of the army of occupation in Paris. His knowledge of languages made him of use to Wellington in correspondence and negotiations with the allied powers. He was promoted major on 19 July 1821, and placed on the unattached half-pay list on 1 June 1826. His father died in Edinburgh on 17 Oct. the same year.

Mitchell did not return to military duty, but devoted himself to literature, passing a considerable portion of each year on the continent up to 1848, after which he spent the remainder of his life with his sisters in Edinburgh. In 1833–4 he contributed a series of articles to 'Fraser's Magazine,' under the name of 'Bombardino,' or 'Captain Orlando Sabretache.' In 1837 he published a life of Wallenstein, making himself thoroughly acquainted with the scenes of his life by visiting all the localities. Between 1841 and 1855 he contributed to the 'United Service Journal,' and in 1841–2 he wrote seven letters to the 'Times' newspaper dealing with defects in the British army. In 1845 he published 'The Fall of Napoleon,' and soon after received a diamond brooch from King Augustus of Hanover as a token of his majesty's appreciation of the light he had thrown on the history of the emperor. He also received a complimentary letter from Sir Robert Peel. In 1846 he contributed to 'Fraser's Magazine' a series of articles on Napoleon's early campaigns. He was promoted lieutenant-colonel unattached on 10 Jan. 1837, colonel 11 Nov. 1851, and major-general on 31 Aug. 1855. Mitchell was a man of handsome exterior and pleasing manners and address. He died in Edinburgh on 9 July 1859, and was buried in the family vault in the Canongate churchyard.

The following are his principal works: 1. 'The Life of Wallenstein, Duke of Friedland,' 8vo, London, 1837; 2nd edit. 1853. 2. 'Thoughts on Tactics and Military Organisation, together with an Enquiry into the Power and Position of Russia,' 8vo, London, 1838. 3. 'The Art of Conversation, with Remarks on Fashion and Address, by Captain Orlando Sabretache,' 8vo, London, 1842. 4. 'The Fall of Napoleon: an Historical Memoir,' 3 vols. 8vo, London, 1845. 5. 'Biographies of Eminent Soldiers of the Last Four Centuries: edited, with a Memoir of the Author, by Leonhard Schmitz,' Edinburgh and London, 8vo, 1865.

[Cates's Biog. Dict.; Chambers's Biog. Dict. of Eminent Scotsmen; Military Records; Allibone's Dict. of English Lit.] R. H. V.

MITCHELL, JOHN (1806–1874), theatre and music agent and manager, was born on 21 April 1806. Early in life he was employed by William Sams of St. James's Street, London, who started the modern system of theatrical agency. In 1834 Mitchell opened a library in Old Bond Street, the headquarters of his extensive business for forty years. He made a practice of engaging a large number of the best seats in every theatre and public hall.

In 1836 and the two following seasons Mitchell opened the Lyceum Theatre for Italian comic opera, giving to it the name of 'Opera Buffa.' 'L'Elisir d'Amore,' on 10 Dec. 1836, was the first of a series of light operas, which, as well as Rossini's 'Stabat Mater' in 1842, were thus introduced to England. In 1842 Mitchell brought over French plays and players, who for a number of years performed at St. James's Theatre. For the same theatre he engaged a French comic opera company, which opened with 'Le Domino Noir' on 15 Jan. 1849. In 1853 he brought the Cologne Choir to London.

Mitchell was held in great esteem and friendship by the leaders of the stage and concert-room. He died in London on 11 Dec. 1874, in his sixty-eighth year, leaving a son and daughter.

[The Choir, xxiii. 400; Grove's Dictionary, ii. 338; Times and Daily Telegraph, quoted by Musical World, 1874, p. 842; Era, 20 Dec. 1874; Athenæum theatrical notices, 1836 et seq.] L. M. M.

MITCHELL, RIGHT HON. SIR JOHN (1804–1886), field-marshal. [See MICHEL.]

MITCHELL, JOHN MITCHELL (1789–1865), antiquary, was the second son of John Mitchell of Falkirk, where he was born in 1789. Sir Thomas Livingstone Mitchell [q. v.] was his brother. He was educated at the Polmont school in Falkirk, and subsequently at the university of Edinburgh. For nearly half a century he was engaged in business as a merchant at Leith, and for some time acted as consul-general for Belgium. Nevertheless Mitchell found time for the study of archæology, natural history, and mineralogy, and was a student of Scandinavian languages and literature. He was fellow (and joint secretary for its foreign correspondence) of the Society of Antiquaries of Scotland, of the Royal Physical Society, and the Royal Society of Northern Antiquaries of Denmark, contributing to the 'Transactions' of each many valuable papers. He lived on terms of friendly intercourse with the king of Denmark and the king of the Belgians, and received from the latter the gold medal of the order of Leopold. Mitchell died at his residence, Mayville, Trinity, near Edinburgh, on 24 April 1865. He was unmarried.

Mitchell's chief works were: 1. 'Mesehowe: Illustrations of the Runic Literature of Scandinavia,' Edinburgh, 1863, 4to, including translations in Danish and English of inscriptions found in the mound of Mesehowe in Orkney, opened in 1861. 2. 'The Herring, its Natural History and National Importance,' Edinburgh, 1864, 8vo, an elaborate work, embodying the study and research of many years, and constituting an authority on the subject to which it relates; it is an expansion of a paper which gained the medal offered by the Royal Scottish Society of Arts. He was also author of a pamphlet 'On British Commercial Legislation in reference to the Tariff on Import Duties, and the injustice of interfering with the Navigation Laws,' Edinburgh, 1849, 8vo; 2nd edition, 1852.

[Works in Brit. Mus. Libr.; Cat. Advocates' Libr.; Proc. Soc. of Antiquaries of Scotland, passim; Gent. Mag. 1865, pt. i. pp. 796–7.]
W. C. S.

MITCHELL, JOSEPH (1684–1738), dramatist, son of a Scottish stonemason, was born in 1684. After receiving (according to Cibber) a university education in Scotland, he settled in London, where he secured the patronage of the Earl of Stair and Sir Robert Walpole, and by his steady dependence earned the title of 'Sir Robert Walpole's Poet.' Constantly improvident, he speedily squandered 1,000*l.* received at his wife's death. Literary friends as well as noblemen helped him, and once in his distress Aaron Hill presented to him a one-act drama, 'The Fatal Extravagance,' which was performed at Lincoln's Inn Fields 21 April 1721, repeated at Dublin the same year, and printed in Mitchell's name in 1726 (Genest, iii. 63). Ultimately, however, Mitchell disclosed the transaction, which is something to set against Cibber's estimate of him as 'vicious and dishonest,' 'governed by every gust of irregular appetite.' Discourtesy seems to have been among his characteristics, for he returned to Thomson a copy of 'Winter,' together with the couplet,

Beauties and faults so thick lie scattered here,
Those I could read if these were not so near.

Thomson winced under his criticism, and writing to Mallet in 1726 called him a 'planet-blasted fool' (Appendix to Sir Harris Nicolas's 'Life of Thompson' in *Aldine Poets*). Cibber mentions that Thomson pinned Mitchell in an epigram as a critic with a 'blasted eye,' but on learning that his victim was really *captus altero oculo* he wrote—

Why all not faults, injurious Mitchell! why
Appears one beauty to thy *blasting* eye?

Pope is said, at Mitchell's own request, to have erased his name from the first draft of the 'Dunciad.' Mitchell died 6 Feb. 1738.

Mitchell's 'Poems on Several Occasions,' in 2 vols. 8vo, were published in 1729, and his opera, 'The Highland Fair, or the Union of the Clans,' was performed at Drury Lane 20 March 1731, and is described by Genest as 'a very pleasing piece' (iii. 290). Among his occasional verse a poem called 'The Shoeheel' was 'much read on account of the low humour it contains;' another, on the subject of Jonah in the whale's belly (1720), was ironically dedicated to Dr. Watts on the ground that it 'was written to raise an emulation among our young poets to attempt divine composures.' His 'Sick-bed Soliloquy to an Empty Purse' appeared both in Latin and English, London (1735), 4to. A tragedy entitled 'The Fate of King James I,' upon which he was said by Mallet to have been engaged in 1721, was apparently never completed. He is represented by two songs in Ramsay's 'Tea Table Miscellany,' 1724; by one in Watts's 'Musical Miscellany,' 1731; by his 'Charms of Indolence,' in Southey's 'Later English Poets,' i. 361, and by several lyrics in Johnson's 'Musical Museum.' As a lyrist Mitchell is fluent, if not always melodious, and his heroic couplets are of average merit. His dramatic sense was not strong.

[Theophilus Cibber's Lives of the Poets, 1753, iv. 347 sq., v. 197; Baker's Biog. Dram. i. 520; Chalmers's Biog. Dict. vol. xxii.; Johnson's Scots Musical Museum, vol. iv. ed. Laing.] T. B.

MITCHELL, ROBERT (*fl.* 1800), architect, resided in London, first in Upper Marylebone Street, and afterwards in Newman Street. In the Royal Academy Exhibitions of 1782 and 1798 he exhibited designs for ecclesiastical edifices. He designed Silwood Park, near Staines (drawing of west front in Royal Academy Exhibition, 1796, and of staircase 1797, view in Neale, *Seats*, i. 1818); Heath Lane Lodge, Twickenham; Cottisbroke Hall, Northamptonshire (view in Bridges, *Northamptonshire* (Whalley), i. 554); Moore Place, near Hertford; Preston Hall, Midlothian (elevation in Royal Academy Exhibition, 1794); and, 1793–4, the Rotunda, Leicester Square, for Robert Barker (1737–1806) [q. v.], who exhibited there his panoramas. The building is now the Roman catholic school of Notre Dame de France.

He published: 'Plans and Views in Perspective, with Descriptions of Buildings erected in England and Scotland; and also an Essay to elucidate the Grecian, Roman, and Gothic Architecture, accompanied with

Designs,' London, 1801, in English and French. The work contains views of the buildings mentioned above.

[Dict. of Architecture; Redgrave's Dict. of Artists; Royal Academy Catalogues; Gent. Mag. 1801, pp. 639–41.] B. P.

MITCHELL, THOMAS (*fl.* 1735–1790), marine-painter and naval official, was a shipwright by profession who also practised with some success as a painter of marine subjects. He first exhibited at the Free Society of Artists in 1763, when he was residing on Tower Hill. He exhibited there again in 1768 and the following years, when he was employed as assistant shipbuilder at Chatham dockyard. In 1774 he appears as builder's assistant at Deptford dockyard, and was afterwards employed in the navy office, becoming eventually assistant surveyor of the navy. He exhibited at the Royal Academy from 1774 to 1789. A number of drawings by Mitchell are in the print room at the British Museum, the earliest dated being a view of Westminster Bridge in 1735. Some of his drawings were engraved.

[Redgrave's Dict. of Artists; Graves's Dict. of Artists, 1760–1880; Catalogues of the Free Society of Artists and the Royal Academy.] L. C.

MITCHELL, THOMAS (1783–1845), classical scholar, born on 30 May 1783, was son of Alexander Mitchell, riding master, successively of Hamilton Place and Grosvenor Place, London. In June 1790 he was admitted to Christ's Hospital, and in October 1802 went to Pembroke College, Cambridge, with one of the hospital exhibitions (*List of University Exhibitioners*, ed. Lockhart, 2nd edit.) In 1806 he graduated B.A. as eighth senior optime and was first chancellor's medallist. By reason of a novel regulation, which enacted that not more than two students educated at the same school should be fellows of the college at one time, he was refused a fellowship at Pembroke, greatly to his disappointment, as he could have held it without taking orders. In 1809 he proceeded M.A. and was elected to an open fellowship at Sidney Sussex, which he had to vacate in 1812 on account of his refusal to be ordained. He supported himself by private tuition and literary work. From 1806 to 1816 he was tutor successively in the families of Sir George Henry Rose, Robert Smith (whose son, afterwards the Right Hon. Vernon Smith, was his favourite pupil), and Thomas Hope. In 1810 he was introduced to William Gifford [q. v.], and in 1813 he commenced a series of articles in the 'Quarterly Review' on Aristophanes and Athenian manners (Nos. xvii. xlii. xliii. xlv. xlviii. liv. lviii. lxvi. lxxxviii.), the success of which subsequently induced him to undertake his spirited and accurate verse translation of Aristophanes's comedies of the 'Acharnians,' 'Knights,' 'Clouds,' and 'Wasps,' (2 vols. 1820–2). He declined soon afterwards a vacant Greek chair in Scotland, on account of his objection to sign the confession of the Scotch kirk. In June 1813 Leigh Hunt invited him to dinner in Horsemonger Lane gaol, along with Byron and Moore (Moore, *Life of Byron*, 1847, p. 183). Byron afterwards spoke of his translation of Aristophanes as 'excellent' (*ib.* p. 455).

For the last twenty years of his life Mitchell resided with his relatives in Oxfordshire, occasionally superintending the publication of the Greek authors by the Clarendon Press. During 1834–8 he edited in separate volumes for John Murray the 'Acharnians' (1835), 'Wasps' (1835), 'Knights' (1836), 'Clouds (1838), and 'Frogs' (1839) of Aristophanes, with English notes. This edition was adversely criticised by the Rev. George John Kennedy, fellow of St. John's College, Cambridge, and Mitchell published a reply to Kennedy in 1841. His 'Preliminary Discourse' was republished in vol. xiii. of Philippus Invernizi's edition of 'Aristophanes,' 1826. In 1839 he entered into an engagement with John Henry Parker [q.v.], publisher, of Oxford, to edit 'Sophocles,' but after the publication of three plays in 1842, Parker suspended the edition on the ground that schoolmasters objected to the diffuseness of English notes. Mitchell, left without regular employment, fell into straitened circumstances, but was granted by Sir Robert Peel 150*l.* from the royal bounty. In 1843 Parker resumed his publication of 'Sophocles,' and Mitchell edited the remaining four plays, with shorter notes than before, and in 1844 he began a school edition of a 'Pentalogia Aristophanica,' with brief Latin notes. He had nearly completed this task when he died suddenly of apoplexy, on 4 May 1845, at his house at Steeple Aston, near Woodstock. He was unmarried.

Mitchell also published useful indexes to Reiske's edition of the 'Oratores Attici' (2 vols. 8vo, Oxford, 1828), 'Isocrates' (8vo, Oxford, 1828), and 'Plato' (2 vols. 8vo, Oxford, 1832).

In the British Museum Library are Mitchell's copiously annotated copies of 'Æschylus,' 'Euripides,' 'Aristophanes,' and Bekker's edition of the 'Oratores Attici.'

[Classical Museum, iii. 213–16; Gent. Mag. 1845 pt. ii. pp. 202–4; Trollope's History of Christ's Hospital, pp. 141, 306; Brit. Mus. Cat.; Cambridge University Calendars.] G. G.

MITCHELL, Sir THOMAS LIVINGSTONE (1792–1855), Australian explorer, born 16 June 1792, was son of John Mitchell of Craigend, Stirlingshire, by the daughter of Alexander Miln of Carron Works. At the age of sixteen he joined the army in the Peninsula as a volunteer, and three years later he received a commission in the 95th regiment or rifle brigade. He was employed for a long time on the quartermaster-general's staff, thus obtaining much experience in military sketching, and he was present at Ciudad Rodrigo, Badajoz, Salamanca, the Pyrenees, and St. Sebastian, for which he received a silver medal with five clasps. After the war was over he was sent back to Spain and Portugal on a special mission, to survey the battlefields and the positions of the armies. He was promoted to the rank of lieutenant on 16 Sept. 1813, placed on half-pay in 1818, came on full pay again in 1821, and served in the 2nd, 54th, and 97th regiments of foot until 1826, when his active career in the army ended. He was promoted to the rank of captain on 3 Oct. 1822, and to that of major on 29 Aug. 1826.

In 1827 Mitchell published his 'Outlines of a System of Surveying for Geographical and Military Purposes,' a useful little work at the time. During 1827 he was appointed deputy surveyor-general to the colony of New South Wales, and in the following year he succeeded to the surveyor-generalship, an appointment he held until his death. During his tenure of office his work was of the greatest possible use to the colony, especially in connection with laying out new roads. In 1830 he completed his survey of the great road to the Western Plains and Bathurst, and although this route was not accepted at the time, the soundness of his judgment is proved by the fact that both the road and railway now follow the track then laid down by him. His survey of the colony was published in three sheets in 1835, a work remarkable for the accuracy with which the natural features are delineated.

Mitchell will, however, be chiefly remembered on account of his four explorations into the then unknown interior of Australia, expeditions which place him in the first rank of the pioneers of that continent. The first exploration was due to the interest aroused in the colony by the fabulous tale of a convict, who pretended that he had discovered a wide and navigable river to the northward of the Liverpool range, and that he had followed it to the north coast. As a search for the mythical stream must in any case settle many important geographical problems, the government accepted Mitchell's offer to lead an exploring party in the direction indicated. He left Sydney in November 1831, and entered *terra incognita* near where Tamworth and its railway station now stand. Continuing his northward journey, he crossed the Gwydir, and struck the Barwan near the present boundary of Queensland. This was the furthest point he reached, for the murder of two of his party by natives, as they were bringing up a reserve supply of provisions, made a return to the colony a necessity. But during his three months' absence he had proved that no great river flowing northward existed in that part of the country, and he rendered it almost certain that all the rivers he had crossed flowed into the Darling.

Mitchell's second exploration was undertaken in consequence of representations from the government at home that a survey of the course of the Darling would be very desirable. Leaving Sydney in 1835, he descended the valley of the Bogan river, the course of which was only partially known, and he reached Bourke on the Darling. During this advance Richard Cunningham, the botanist to the expedition, lost his way and was killed by the natives, although every effort was made to find him. Bourke had previously been reached by Sturt, and that traveller had also discovered the existence of a large river entering the Murray, but the true identity of this stream with the Darling was only conjectural. Mitchell succeeded in tracing the Darling to within a hundred miles of its junction with the Murray, but beyond this point it was not possible to proceed, on account of the threatening attitude of the natives, which had already resulted in a conflict and loss of life on their side. He traced his way back along the bank of this weary river, which at this arid season was not joined by a single tributary for over three hundred miles, and which flowed through a country quite uninhabitable by man or beast, according to our explorer, but for this solitary stream.

Mitchell's third, and perhaps most important, journey was undertaken with the view of definitely connecting the Murray with the Darling. He left Sydney in 1836, descended the valleys of the Lachlan and the Murrumbidgee to the Murray, and then passed along the banks of this latter stream to the mouth of the Darling. He ascended the Darling valley sufficiently far to render it certain that it was in fact the same watercourse that he had descended on his last expedition, and then faced about and retraced his steps up the Murray river. During this advance he had a somewhat serious encounter with his old enemies, the Darling tribe, in which several of the natives were killed. From this point his discoveries became of the first importance. After ascending the Murray to near its junction with the Goulburn, he turned off to the south-west, drawn in that direction by the fine quality of the country. The region he thus opened up was called by him Australia Felix, and it no doubt forms one of the richest tracts in Australia. Continuing his journey in this direction, he struck the Glenelg, as he named it, after the colonial secretary, Charles Grant, lord Glenelg [q. v.], and followed it to the sea. At Portland Bay he found one solitary settler, Edward Henty [q. v.] He returned to Sydney by a route parallel to that of his advance from the Murray, but nearer to the sea. Here he soon came into country more or less known through the travels of Hovell and Hume, and near where Albury now stands. He found the country on the eve of being taken up by colonists. This journey, which lasted over seven months, thus added greatly to the knowledge of a very fertile region of Australia.

Mitchell went on leave to England in 1839, and the value of his services was recognised by his being knighted, and he received the honorary degree of D.C.L. at Oxford. He returned to Australia in 1840, and was promoted to the rank of lieutenant-colonel on 23 Nov. 1841. In 1844 he was elected as a member of council to represent Melbourne, but on its being indicated to him that his vote as government officer was required by the government, he resigned his seat.

The dangers attendant on the navigation of the Torres Straits made it appear very desirable to open an overland route to the gulf of Carpentaria, especially with the view of facilitating the trade in horses with India. Mitchell's fourth expedition was undertaken with the object of ascertaining if a practical road could be found. He left Sydney in November 1845, accompanied by E. B. Kennedy as second in command, and by W. Stephenson as naturalist. He first ascended the valley of the Narran, a river which had quite recently been discovered by his own son; then, entering quite unknown land, he traced the Maranoa up to close to its source, and thence struck across more difficult country to the head waters of the Belyando. After tracing this river for some two hundred miles towards the sea, and after coming to the conclusion that it must join the Suttor river of Leichhardt [q. v.], he retraced his steps to the Belyando. Hence he struck out again in a north-westerly direction, and discovered the sources of the Barcoo. He felt certain—but in this he was in error—that this must be the great river flowing into the gulf of Carpentaria, along the banks of which the great road to the north would be found. He traced the Barcoo to within a few miles of the point where it turns in a south-westerly direction, and he thus found nothing to shake the confidence of his belief. This was his furthest point, and he returned to civilisation in January 1847, after an absence of over a year.

Despite Mitchell's mistaken supposition, this last journey only served to confirm his high reputation as an explorer. On all his expeditions, which made great additions to Australian botany, he was accompanied by a comparatively large number of followers (twenty-nine men on the last occasion), and all the details were carefully thought out beforehand. The rank and file of his expeditions always consisted of convicts, who almost invariably did good service in the hope of a free pardon as a reward; but that such men should have been led for so many months without any serious disturbance must be attributed to the personal qualities of their chief. A man of great personal courage, he had a somewhat imperious manner and temper, and spoke out so fearlessly that he made many enemies. He was evidently impressed with a strong sense of justice towards the natives and hated cruelty to animals. In 1851 he was sent to report on the Bathurst goldfields. He again visited England in 1853, and patented a new screw-propeller for steam-vessels called the 'Boomerang,' respecting which he published a lecture delivered at the United Institution. He died at his house, Carthona, Darling Point, 5 Oct. 1855. The cause of his death was variously attributed to worry concerning an inquiry that was being held on the department under his charge, or to exposure while on his last expedition. He married in 1818 a daughter of Lieutenant-colonel Blunt. His son Roderick (1824–1852) was engaged in surveying to the north of New England (New South Wales), and was appointed to the command of the expedition in search of Leichhardt, but was drowned on the passage from Newcastle.

Mitchell, a fellow of the Royal and Geographical Societies, was a man of much literary culture. He published a technical work, 'Outlines of a System for Geographical and Military Purposes,' 1827, besides two volumes recounting his explorations, which, though accurate and painstaking, somewhat reflect the monotonous character of the country and of the methods of travel described. Their titles ran: 'Three Expeditions into the Interior of Eastern Australia, with Description of the recently explored Region of Australia Felix, and of the present Colony of New South Wales,' London, 1839; 'Journal of an Expedition into Tropical Australia in search of a Route from Sydney to the gulf of Carpentaria,' London, 1848. Other of Mitchell's published works were: 1. 'Notes on the Cultivation of the Vine and the Olive and on the Method of Making Oil and Wine in the Southern parts of Europe,' 4to, Sydney, 1849. 2. 'A Trigonometrical Survey of Port Jackson.' 3. 'Australian Geography, with the Shores of the Pacific and those of the Indian Ocean,' Sydney, 1850. 4. 'The Lusiad of Camoens closely translated,' London, 1854; written in a small clipper during his last voyage to England round Cape Horn.

[Journal of the Royal Geographical Society, vol. vii. 1837; Annual Register, 1855; Mitchell's Works; Gent. Mag. 1856, i. 301; Heaton's Australian Dict. of Dates.] L. D.

MITCHELL, Sir WILLIAM (1811–1878), maritime writer, son of John Mitchell of Modbury in Devon, was born at Modbury in 1811. At an early age he came to London as a journalist, was for some time on the 'True Sun,' and from 1836 was chief proprietor and editor of the 'Shipping and Mercantile Gazette,' a daily paper which he established, and which at once took the high position it has since maintained. In 1840 he began to urge the importance, and indeed the necessity, of compulsory examinations for officers of merchant ships; and it was mainly in consequence of his action that the Mercantile Marine Act of 1850 was passed (13 & 14 Vict. cap. 93). In 1857 he was called on to advise with the registrar-general of seamen in the preparation of the measure for the royal naval reserve, which eventually took form in the act of 1859 'for the Establishment of a Reserve Volunteer Force of Seamen, and for the Government of the same' (22 & 23 Vict. cap. 40). He succeeded in introducing an international code of signals, which was gradually adopted by every maritime country, and in establishing signal stations for reporting the movements of all ships using the international code. In reward for his public services he was knighted in 1867, and in 1869 was nominated by the king of Sweden a knight commander of the order of St. Olaf. He edited 'A Review of the Merchant Shipping Bill, being a Series of Leading Articles . . . from the "Shipping and Mercantile Gazette,"' 1869, 8vo, and 'Maritime Notes and Queries, a Record of Shipping Law and Usage,' 1873–6, 4to. He died at Strode, near Ivybridge, Devonshire, on 1 May 1878. He married in 1835 Caroline, eldest daughter of Richard Andrews of Modbury.

[Men of the Reign; Times, 4 May 1878.] J. K. L.

MITCHELL, Sir WILLIAM HENRY FANCOURT (1811–1884), Australian politician, born in England in 1811, was son of George Berkley Mitchell, vicar of St. Mary's from 1813, and of All Saints' from 1820, both parishes of the town of Leicester. At an early age William was sent out to Tasmania, where on 2 April 1833 he was appointed writer in the colonial secretary's office, becoming on 1 Aug. 1839 assistant colonial secretary. In 1840 he went over to Port Phillip district (afterwards Victoria), and entered on an active squatter's life near Kyneton and Mount Macedon. On 1 Jan. 1853, when the discovery of gold in Port Phillip threw the whole district into disorder, he was specially invited by the lieutenant-governor to take the supreme command of the police. In this capacity, receiving almost unlimited powers, he reorganised the force on a new basis, restored order in the gold districts, and stamped out bush-ranging. In 1855 private affairs took him back to England.

On his return to Victoria in September 1856 he was elected to the legislative council as one of the five original members for the North-Western Province, and joined the Haines ministry—the first under responsible government—representing it for six months in the upper chamber without portfolio. In Haines's next administration he was postmaster-general from April 1857 to March 1858, and is credited with a complete reform of the post-office. In 1858 he was defeated at the polls and was out of parliament for a short time, but in 1860 he was again elected to the council for the North-Western Province, and in December 1861 became commissioner of railways in O'Shanassy's administration, which lasted till June 1863. Throughout the sessions of 1866–8 he devoted special attention to the bill respecting the constitution of the legislative council, which became law September 1868. In 1869 he was elected chairman of committees in the legislative council, and in 1870 the president of the council. In this capacity he served till his death, through a period of considerable anxiety, leading the opposition of the council to the assembly in the disputes with the government of Sir James McCulloch [q. v.] as to the protective tariff and the Darling grant, and again respecting payment of members. As president he distinguished himself by the vigour of his ruling.

In 1875 Mitchell was knighted. During his last years he used crutches. He died at his residence, Barfold, near Kyneton, on 24 Nov. 1884. The house of assembly as well as the council adjourned as a mark of respect—the first time that it had ever adjourned in consequence of the death of a member of the other chamber.

He was at the time of his death a large landed proprietor near Kyneton and the chairman of R. Goldsborough & Co.

[Melbourne Argus, 25 Nov. 1884; Mennell's Dict. Austral. Biog.; Victorian Parliamentary Debates.] C. A. H.

MITFORD, JOHN (1782–1831), miscellaneous writer, was born at Newton Red House and baptised in the parish church of Mitford, on 22 Jan. 1782. He was a member of the elder branch of the family of Mitford of Mitford Castle in Northumberland, was third cousin of the Rev. John Mitford [q. v.], and second cousin three times removed of William Mitford [q. v.] and of John Freeman-Mitford, lord Redesdale [q. v.] In April 1795, by Lord Redesdale's interest, he entered the navy as midshipman of the Victory, in which he went out to the Mediterranean, and was present in the battle off Toulon on 13 July 1795. In the following year he was moved into the Zealous with Captain (afterwards Sir Samuel) Hood [q. v.], and in her was present in the disastrous attack on Santa Cruz in July 1797, and at the battle of the Nile 1–2 Aug. 1798, where, according to his own statement, he was sent in a four-oared boat from the Zealous to the Vanguard, and from the Vanguard to the Leander, then engaged with the Tonnant. The latter, he says, presently struck to the Leander, when he was sent back with the news to the admiral. The story affords a measure of Mitford's credibility: the Tonnant did not surrender till the forenoon of 3 Aug.; she surrendered to the Theseus, and, as it was broad daylight and no other fighting was going on, it could not be necessary to report it on board the flagship by a casual boat from another ship. Mitford was afterwards with Hood in the Courageux. According to his own account, after drinking freely on Christmas day 1800, he insulted his captain and left the service, that is to say, deserted; but as he was with Hood in 1801 in the Venerable the desertion may have been only imagined. From 1804 to 1806 he commanded a revenue cutter on the coast of Ireland, and from 1809 to 1811 was acting master of the Philomel brig in the Mediterranean.

Mitford states that he received a letter from his wife in September 1811 while at Port Mahon, acquainting him with an offer made by Viscountess Perceval, a connection of Lady Redesdale, to secure him a lucrative appointment in the civil service. Accordingly, though not without difficulty, he obtained his transfer to the Canopus for a passage to England. But Lady Perceval's promises proved delusive. She received him on a footing of intimacy, but merely employed him to write in the 'Star,' edited by John Mayne, or the 'News,' edited by T. A. Phipps, articles in support of the Princess of Wales, to whose cause she was enthusiastically devoted. While thus employed, Mitford's brain gave way, and he was removed to Mr. Warburton's private lunatic asylum at Whitmore House, Hoxton. Warburton, calling on Phipps on 8 April 1813, 'stated, in the presence of two witnesses, that Mitford had been under confinement at his house from May 1812 to March 1813' (*The Important Trial*, &c., p. 121). In March he was liberated at the desire of Lady Perceval, but afterwards, finding that her writings in the papers were likely to get her into serious trouble, she induced Mitford and his wife to destroy her letters to him, and then brought an action against him for having falsely sworn that the articles were by her. The case was tried before Lord Ellenborough on 24 Feb. 1814, when Phipps produced some of Lady Perceval's letters which had not been destroyed. The evidence was conclusive against her, and Mitford was acquitted.

At the same time Mitford was discharged from the navy as insane, and he took to journalism and strong drink. His wife and family were provided for by Lord Redesdale, but he refused all assistance for himself, and sank to the lowest depths of poverty. He is said to have edited the 'Scourge, or Monthly Expositor of Imposture and Folly,' which, after running for five years, died in December 1815; but though he contributed to the last four volumes, it does not appear that he was the editor. After this he wrote 'The Adventures of Johnny Newcome in the Navy, a Poem in four Cantos,' 1st edit., published under the pseudonym of Alfred Burton, 1818, 8vo; 2nd edit. 1819. The publisher who employed him found that the only way to make him work was to keep him without money. He therefore limited him to a shilling a day, which Mitford expended on two pennyworth of bread and cheese and an onion, and the balance on gin. With this, and his day's supply of paper and ink, he repaired to an old gravel-pit in Battersea Fields, and there wrote and slept till it was time to take in his work and get his next shilling. For forty-three days he is said to have lived in this manner, and, the weather continuing fine, without being conscious of discomfort. The poem is in octosyllabic verse, reeled off with the most careless ease, but the lines scan, the rhymes are good, and the 'yarns' such as might have been heard any day in the midshipman's berth. 'The Poems of a British Sailor,' 1818, 8vo, if more reputable is more stupid: it consists of occasional verses written during his life at sea.

His other literary work was anonymous. He is said to have written 'a libellous life of Sir John Sylvester,' recorder of the city of London; to have edited 'The Bon Ton Magazine,' and to have been kept the while by his publisher in a cellar, with a candle, a bottle of gin, and a rag of old carpet for a coverlet. In 1827 he contributed a memoir of William Mitford the historian to the 'Literary Gazette' (p. 187), which called forth a remonstrance from the family, contradicting every detailed statement (p. 220), and an apologetic note from the editor to the effect that the writer had represented himself as a namesake and near relative of the deceased, and 'we could not be aware that he was imposing on us for his wages.' But Mitford had lost the power of distinguishing truth from falsehood. Ragged and filthy in his person, he was no doubt the John Mitford described by Captain Brenton as 'lodging over a coal-shed in some obscure street near Leicester Square' (NICOLAS, *Despatches and Letters of Lord Nelson*, iii. 521). All attempts made by his friends to reclaim him failed. He was editing a paper called the 'Quizzical Gazette' at the time of his death, which took place in St. Giles's workhouse on 24 Dec. 1831. He was buried in the graveyard of St. Dunstan's, Fleet Street. He had married in 1808 Emily, daughter of Charles Street of Dullintabor, N.B., and left issue.

[Gent. Mag. 1831, pt. ii. p. 647; Sketches of Obscure Poets, with Specimens of their Writings, 1833, p. 91; Quizzical Gazette, No. 20; Scourge, vol. vii. freq.; A Description of the Crimes and Horrors in the Interior of Warburton's Private Madhouse at Hoxton, by John Mitford; The Important Trial of John Mitford, Esq., on the Prosecution of Lady Viscountess Perceval for Perjury; Foster's Peerage, s.n. 'Redesdale;' private information.] J. K. L.

MITFORD, JOHN (1781–1859), miscellaneous writer, descended from the Mitfords of Mitford Castle, Northumberland, and nearly related to John Freeman Mitford, lord Redesdale [q. v.], who patronised him, and to William Mitford [q. v.], the historian of Greece, was born at Richmond, Surrey, on 13 Aug. 1781. He was the elder son of John Mitford (*d.* 18 May 1806), commander of a vessel engaged in the China trade of the East India Company, by his second wife, Mary, eldest daughter of J. Allen of Clifton, Bristol. Early in life he went to school at Richmond, and for a time he was at Tunbridge grammar school, under Vicesimus Knox [q. v.], but most of his younger days were passed in the diocese of Winchester, where the Rev. John Baynes of Exton, near Droxford, Hampshire, was his friend and tutor. After a brief experience as clerk in the army pay office, he on 6 March 1801 matriculated at Oriel College, Oxford, under the tutorship of Copleston, with Reginald Heber as his 'intimate associate,' and graduated B.A. on 17 Dec. 1804. When Heber won the English verse prize with his poem of 'Palestine,' his most prominent competitor was Mitford. In the autumn of 1809 he was ordained in the English church, being licensed to the curacy of Kelsale in Suffolk, but he had little aptitude for clerical work. Charles Lamb speaks of him as 'a pleasant layman spoiled,' and Mrs. Houstoun in graver terms condemns some of his errors in conduct. Within three months he obtained through Lord Redesdale's interest the vicarage of Benhall, near Saxmundham, Suffolk, to which he was instituted on 17 Feb. 1810, and in August 1815 he became domestic chaplain to that peer. In the same month he was appointed to the rectory of Weston St. Mary, and a few years later he was nominated to the rectory of Stratford St. Andrew, both in Suffolk, and then in crown patronage. The whole of these livings were united, during his incumbency, in 1824, when he was reinstituted, and he retained them all until his death. At Benhall he built a handsome parsonage, consolidated the glebe, and gratified his love of shrubs and books by planting 'a great variety of ornamental and foreign trees,' and by forming an extensive library, mainly of English poetry. Lamb, in a letter to Bernard Barton, writes: 'Your description of Mr. Mitford's place makes me long for a pippin, some caraways, and a cup of sack in his orchard, when the sweets of the night come in.' The care of his livings did not hinder him from renting for many years permanent lodgings in Sloane Street, London, where he enjoyed 'the most perfect intimacy with Samuel Rogers for more than twenty years.' In order to indulge his love of paintings and landscape gardening he travelled all over England, and in search of the picturesque he explored the scenery on all the chief rivers of Europe.

In 1833 he began to contribute to the 'Gentleman's Magazine' a series of articles on the old English poets and on sacred poetry, paying particular attention to the works of Prudentius. During that year William Pickering [q. v.], the publisher, purchased a share in the magazine, and a new series was started in January 1834, when Mitford became editor. For seventeen years Mitford's contributions never failed for a single month, and he edited the magazine 'assiduously and successfully' until the close of 1850. During these years, the palmy years of that periodical, he varied this drudgery with the composition of numerous poems signed J. M. His communications after 1850 were few. One of the last of his articles was a letter respecting Samuel Rogers, in the volume for 1856, pt. i. pp. 147–8.

After a long life spent in his favourite pursuits Mitford was afflicted by a slight attack of paralysis, fell down in a London street, and never recovered from the shock. For some time he was imprisoned in his rooms in Sloane Street, but at last he was removed to his living, and died at Benhall vicarage on 27 April 1859, being buried at Stratford St. Andrew. He married at St. George's, Hanover Square, London, on 21 Oct. 1814, Augusta, second daughter of Edward Boodle, of Brook Street, Grosvenor Square, London, who died at her son's house, Weston Lodge, Hampstead, on 25 Dec. 1886, aged 92, and was buried at Hampstead cemetery on 29 Dec. The marriage was not attended with happiness. Their only child, Robert Henry Mitford, was born on 24 July 1815, and married at Wellow, Somerset, on 12 Aug. 1847, Anne, youngest daughter of Lieutenant-colonel William Henry Wilby, their eldest son being Robert Sidney Mitford of the home office.

Mitford is praised by Mrs. Houstoun for his 'brilliant conversation, totally unmarred by any desire to shine.' He was an indefatigable student of the Greek and Roman classics, and was well acquainted with the principal French, German, and Italian authors. In English literature he was deeply read, and he was an ardent lover of painting, especially of the works of the Italian school. Country life had many charms for him, and his knowledge of the ways of birds and the shapes of trees is evidenced in many of his writings.

As early in his life as 1811 Mitford contemplated an edition of Gray's 'Works' (cf. Southey, *Letters*, ed. Warter, ii. 244). In 1814 he edited the first accurate edition of 'The Poems of Thomas Gray, with Critical Notes, a Life of the Author, and an Essay on his Poetry,' and in 1816 he embodied this matter in two quarto volumes of 'The Works of Thomas Gray,' which contained very large additions to the published letters of the poet, and for which the publisher paid him the sum of 500*l.* Much of his work reappeared in the Aldine edition of Gray's 'Works,' in 5 vols. (2 vols. in 1835, 2 vols. in 1836, 1 vol. in 1843). The last volume, however, consisted mainly of the poet's correspondence with the Rev. Norton Nicholls, and this was also issued in a separate volume, with a distinct title-page. The first volume of this edition, comprising the poems, was reprinted in 1853, and reissued at Boston in 1857, and in the reprint of the Aldine Poets in 1866. The Eton edition in 1847 of the poems contained 'An Original Life of Gray' by Mitford, which was inserted in the subsequent impressions of 1852 and 1863. In 1853 he edited the 'Correspondence of Gray and Mason, with some Letters addressed by Gray to the Rev. James Brown, D.D.,' and some pages of 'Additional Notes thereto' were printed in 1855. Many of Mitford's comments are reproduced in Mr. Gosse's edition of Gray, while from his manuscripts at the British Museum, which were intended 'to supplement his long labours' on his favourite writer, is drawn much of the information in Tovey's 'Gray and his Friends.'

When Pickering set on foot the Aldine edition of the British poets he enlisted the services of Mitford. For it he edited, with memoirs, in addition to the poems of Gray, those of Cowper, 1830, 3 vols. (memoir written by John Bruce in 1865 edit.); Goldsmith, 1831; Milton, 1832, 3 vols., with sonnet to Charles Sumner, bishop of Winchester; Dryden, 1832–3, 5 vols. (life rewritten by the Rev. Richard Hooper in the 1865 and 1866 editions); Parnell, 1833 and 1866 (with epistle in verse to Alexander Dyce); Swift, 1833–4, 3 vols., and 1866; Young, 1834, 2 vols. (with sonnet), 1858 and 1866; Prior, 1835, 2 vols., 1866; Butler, 1835, 2 vols. (with verses to W. L. Bowles), 1866; Falconer, 1836, 1866 (with sonnet); Spenser, 1839, 5 vols. (with four sonnets, re-edited by J. P. Collier in 1866). The text and lives by Mitford in the original Aldine edition were reprinted at Boston, United States, in 1854–6, and his notes to 'Milton's Poems' were reprinted, after considerable correction, in an edition of the 'Poetical Works of Milton and Marvell,' Boston, in 1878. In 1851 he edited 'The Works of Milton in Verse and Prose,' 8 vols., and wrote for it a memoir, expanded from that in the 1832 edition of the 'Poems.'

Among Mitford's other works were: 1. 'Agnes, the Indian Captive,' a poem, in four cantos. With other poems, 1811. 2. 'A Letter to Richard Heber on Mr. Weber's late edition of Ford's Dramatic Works,' 1812, a severe criticism. The letter to J. P. Kemble (1811) on the same subject, which is said by Halkett and Laing (ii. 1382) to have been 'written chiefly by Mitford,' is assigned in the British Museum Catalogue to G. D. Whittington of Cambridge. 3. 'Sacred Specimens selected from the Early English Poets, with Prefatory Remarks,' 1827. Charles Lamb called this a 'thankful addition' to his shelves, but regretted the errors in printing. 4. 'Poemata Latine partim reddita partim scripta a V. Bourne,' 1840; with life by Mitford. 5. 'Correspondence of Horace Walpole and Rev. W. Mason,' ed., with notes, by Mitford, 1851, 2 vols. This, like all Mitford's works, shows much knowledge of the last century, but great laxity of supervision. Some of his annotations are reproduced by Peter Cunningham in his edition of Walpole's 'Letters.' 6. 'Lines suggested by a fatal Shipwreck near Aldborough, 3 Nov. 1855,' n.p. 1855, 12mo; 2nd edit., Woodbridge, 1856. 7. 'Cursory Notes on various Passages in the Text of Beaumont and Fletcher, as edited by Rev. Alexander Dyce,' 1856; complimentary to Dyce. 8. 'Miscellaneous Poems,' 1858; a selection from his fugitive pieces. At the end was announced a volume, hitherto unpublished, of 'Passages of Scripture, illustrated by Specimens from the Works of the Old Masters of Painting.' Raw's 'Pocket-book' for 1830 and later years contained poems by him; his impromptu lines 'On the Aldine Anchor,' printed in the 'Gentleman's Magazine' for 1836, pt. i. p. 501, and in 'Notes and Queries,' 3rd ser. x. 327, and 5th ser. xii. 44, were struck off for separate circulation. Further poems of his composition are inserted in the last periodical, 3rd ser. ix. 58, in Mrs. Houstoun's 'A Woman's Memories' and her 'Sylvanus Redivivus,' and in Glyde's 'New Suffolk Garland,' 1866, p. 375, and some 'Remarks by him on the Mustard Tree of Scripture' are at the Dyce Library, South Kensington Museum.

Mitford's collections were dispersed after his death by Sotheby & Wilkinson. His fine art collection of silver Greek coins, cameos, and miniatures was sold on 30 June 1859, the engravings and drawings on 23 July 1859 and two following days, his Greek and Latin classics on 17 Dec. 1859 and six following days. This sale produced 1,029*l.* 19*s.* The library of English history, plays, and poetry was sold on 24 April 1860 and eleven following days, producing 2,999*l.* 2*s.*; and his manuscripts on 9 July 1860, producing 817*l.* 3*s.* The manuscripts contained three volumes of autograph letters, papers relating to Gray, his own recollections in fifty-five volumes, the correspondence of Toup. Many of the books, with his notes, are now in the libraries of the Rev. Alexander Dyce and John Forster at the South Kensington Museum, or in the library of the British Museum. His commonplace-books are Addit. MSS. 32559–32575 at the British Museum, and from them were printed 'Some Conversations with the Duke of Wellington' (*Temple Bar*, April 1888, pp. 507–13). Mitford was in early life a great cricketer, and from the conversation of William Fennex, a cricket veteran whom he supported by charitable work in his garden at Benhall, he wrote many newspaper articles and compiled a manuscript volume, which he gave to the Rev. James Pycroft in 1836, and on it Pycroft laid the structure of his work on the 'Cricket Field,' 1851 (Pycroft, *Oxford Memories*, ii. 120–1). On his letters was based a volume of 'Sylvanus Redivivus (the Rev. John Mitford). With a short Memoir of Edward Jesse. By M. Houstoun,' 1889, reissued in 1891, with new title-page and slip of errata as 'Letters and Reminiscences of the Rev. John Mitford. With a Sketch of Edward Jesse. By C. M.' He wrote many letters to Bernard Barton (one of which is printed in 'Selections from Poems and Letters of Barton,' 1849, p. xxiii, and in 'Poems and Letters of Barton,' 1853, p. xxiv), and Charles Lamb frequently refers to him in his correspondence with Barton (*ib.* pp. 126–39, and Lamb, *Letters*, ed. Ainger, ii. passim). Many of his letters afterwards passed to Edward FitzGerald, who collected and bound together Mitford's papers in the 'Gentleman's Magazine;' the volume is now the property of Dr. W. Aldis Wright. A letter from him on his notice of the early works of Mary Russell Mitford [q. v.] in the 'Quarterly Review,' which was much mutilated by Gifford, is in 'Friendships of Miss Mitford,' i. 53-4, and a communication on an ancient garden at Chelsea is in L'Estrange's 'Village of Palaces,' ii. 288–91. He recommended to J. B. Nichols the publication of 'Bishop Percy's Correspondence,' which forms the staple of the seventh and eighth volumes of the 'Illustrations of the Literary History of the Eighteenth Century;' the seventh volume was dedicated to him.

[Gent. Mag. 1847 pt. ii. p. 534, 1859 pt. i. p. 652, pt. ii. pp. 84–6, 206; Foster's Alumni Oxon.; Foster's Index Ecclesiasticus; Foster's Peerage, sub 'Redesdale;' Mrs. Houstoun's Woman's Memories, i. 122–5, 178–204; Mrs. Houstoun's Sylvanus Redivivus; information from Dr. W. Aldis Wright and Mr. R. H. Mitford; Mitford's Works, passim.] W. P. C.

MITFORD, JOHN FREEMAN-, first Baron Redesdale (1748-1830), younger son of John Mitford of Newton House, Kent, and Exbury, Hampshire, by his wife Philadelphia, daughter of William Reveley of Newby Wiske, Yorkshire, was born in the parish of St. Andrew, Holborn, on 18 Aug. 1748, and was educated with his brother William [q. v.] at Cheam, under the Rev. William Gilpin [q. v.] At an early age he entered the Six Clerks' office, but afterwards determined to be a barrister, and in 1772 was admitted a student of the Inner Temple. He was called to the bar on 9 May 1777, and in 1780 published 'A Treatise on the Pleadings in Suits in the Court of Chancery by English Bill,' London, 8vo, anon. Lord Eldon subsequently characterised this treatise as 'a wonderful effort to collect what is to be deduced from authorities speaking so little what is clear' (Preface to the fifth edition by J. W. Smith, 1847), while Sir Thomas Plumer declared that it reduced 'the whole subject to a system with such universally acknowledged learning, accuracy, and discrimination, as to have been ever since received by the whole profession as an authoritative standard and guide' (Jacob and Walker, *Reports*, ii. 151–2). Owing to the success of his book (which has passed through several English and American editions), Mitford rapidly acquired a large practice at the chancery bar. Through the influence of his cousin, the Duke of Northumberland, he was returned to parliament for the borough of Beeralston, Devonshire, in December 1788, and in July 1789 became a king's counsel, and was appointed a Welsh judge. In 1791 he introduced a bill for 'the relief of persons calling themselves protesting dissenting Catholics, under certain conditions and restrictions' (*Parl. Hist.* xxviii. 1262–4, 1364–5), which after some amendment was passed through both houses and became law (31 Geo. III, c. 32). Mitford, however, opposed Fox's motion for the repeal of the penal statutes respecting religious opinions in the following year (*ib.* xxix. 1398). In January 1793 he supported the Alien Bill in a vigorous speech (*ib.* xxx. 217–19), and on 13 Feb. following he was appointed solicitor-general in the place of Sir John Scott (afterwards Lord Eldon), receiving the honour of knighthood two days afterwards. As counsel for the crown, Mitford took part in the prosecutions of Daniel Isaac Eaton, Thomas Hardy, John Horne Tooke, William Stone, Robert Thomas Crossfield, John Reeves, and James O'Coigley (see Howell, *State Trials*, vols. xxii. xxiv–xxvii.) He succeeded Scott as attorney-general on 17 July 1799, and, resigning his seat at Beeralston, was returned for the borough of East Looe, Cornwall. On 11 Feb. 1801, after a futile attempt at opposition on the part of Sheridan, he was elected speaker of the House of Commons in the place of Addington (*Parl. Hist.* xxxv. 948–55), and was admitted to the privy council on the 18th of the same month. On Lord Clare's death Mitford was appointed lord chancellor of Ireland (9 Feb. 1802), and was created a peer of the United Kingdom, with the title of Baron Redesdale of Redesdale in the county of Northumberland, on 15 Feb. 1802. He was sworn a member of the Irish privy council on 9 March, and took his seat in the Irish court of chancery for the first time on 5 May 1802. Though his conduct on the bench was beyond suspicion, Redesdale was unpopular with the majority of the Irish people, owing to his bitter opposition to catholic emancipation and his openly expressed distrust of the catholic priesthood. His letters to the Earl of Fingal, in which he wantonly attacked the Roman catholics, were severely criticised in the House of Commons by Canning and Fox (*Parl. Debates*, 1st ser. i. 760–2, 787–8). In May 1804 Cobbett was convicted of libelling Redesdale and Hardwicke (the lord-lieutenant) in certain letters on the affairs of Ireland, signed 'Inverna,' which appeared in the 'Political Register.' After his conviction it was discovered that the letters had been written by Robert Johnson, one of the justices of the common pleas in Ireland, who was tried at bar in the king's bench at Westminster on 23 Nov. 1805, and found guilty. Redesdale made an elaborate speech against Lord Grenville's motion for a committee on the Roman catholic petition on 10 May 1805, and declared that the abolition of the Roman catholic 'hierarchy was in his opinion the first step to that conciliation which he believed could alone produce peace to Ireland' (*ib.* iv. 1061–1082). At the beginning of 1806 he involved himself in an injudicious controversy with Valentine, lord Cloncurry, who was desirous of being placed upon the commission of the peace (*Personal Recollections of Lord Cloncurry*, 1849, pp. 221–30). On the formation of the ministry of All the Talents, Redesdale was promptly dismissed from the chancellorship, and took leave of the Irish bar on 4 March 1806. He accepted a seat at the board of trade and foreign plantations on 30 March 1808, but refused the offer of his old office in Ireland, which his brother-in-law, Perceval, is said to have made to him on becoming premier. He took an active part in the parliamentary debates and in the hearing of appeals and peerage claims. He introduced the bill for the creation of the office of the vice-chancellor for England (53 Geo. III, c. 24), and, in spite of the opposition of Eldon and Ellenborough, his bills for the relief of insolvent debtors (53 Geo. III, c. 102, and 54 Geo. III, c. 23) passed into law (see *Parl. Debates*, 1st ser.

xxiv. 182; *Memoirs of Sir Samuel Romilly*, 1840, iii. 107–13, 118, 120–4). He opposed to the last the repeal of the Test and Corporation Acts and the emancipation of the Roman catholics, and continued to support the restrictions on the importation of corn. He spoke for the last time in the House of Lords on 21 May 1829 (*Parl. Debates*, 2nd ser. xxi. 1507). He died at Batsford Park, near Moreton-in-the-Marsh, Gloucestershire, on 16 Jan. 1830, aged 81, and was buried in Batsford Church, which he had rebuilt in 1822.

Redesdale was 'a sallow man, with round face and blunt features, of a middle height, thickly and heavily built, and had a heavy, drawling, tedious manner of speech' (Sir E. Brydges, *Autobiography*, i. 159). Sheil says that he introduced a reformation in Irish practice by substituting 'great learning, unwearied diligence, and a spirit of scientific discussion for the flippant apothegms and irritable self-sufficiency of Lord Clare' [see Fitzgibbon, John] (*Sketches of the Irish Bar*, 1854, i. 228), and Story has pronounced him to be 'one of the ablest judges that ever sat in equity' (*Commentaries on Equity Jurisprudence*, 1884, i. 14). His integrity was unimpeachable, his manners were stiff, and his sense of humour was deficient. An amusing anecdote of his encounter with the wits of the Irish bar will be found in Sir Jonah Barrington's 'Personal Sketches of his own Times,' 1869, i. 185–7. Redesdale married, on 6 June 1803, Lady Frances Perceval, seventh daughter of John, second earl of Egmont, by whom he had an only son, John Thomas Freeman-Mitford, earl of Redesdale [q. v.], and three daughters, viz. Frances Elizabeth, who died at Batsford Park on 7 Nov. 1866, aged 62, and Catherine and Elizabeth, both of whom died young. His wife died in Harley Street, London, on 22 Aug. 1817, aged 49. Redesdale was elected a bencher of the Inner Temple on 13 Nov. 1789, and acted as treasurer of the society in 1796. He was elected F.S.A. on 9 Jan. 1794, and F.R.S. on 6 March 1794. He succeeded Eldon as chancellor of Durham, and was a member of the first, second, and third commissions on public records, and also of the commission of inquiry into the practice of the court of chancery. On the death of Thomas Edwards Freeman (whose ancestor, Richard Freeman, held the post of lord chancellor of Ireland from 1707 to 1710) in February 1808, Redesdale came into the possession of the Batsford property, and assumed the additional surname of Freeman by royal icense of 28 Jan. 1809 (*London Gazettes*, 1809, pt. i. p. 131). There is an engraved portrait of Redesdale by G. Clint, after Sir Thomas Lawrence. Redesdale's Irish judgments will be found in Schoales and Lefroy's 'Reports of Cases argued and determined in the High Court of Chancery in Ireland,' &c., Dublin, 1806–10, 8vo, 2 vols. His letter to Lord Hardwicke upon the state of the public records of Ireland is printed in the appendix to the 'First General Report from the Commissioners on Public Records' (pp. 309–10). He drew up the 'Report from the Lords' Committees appointed to search the Journals of the House . . . for all Matters touching the Dignity of a Peer,' &c. (*Parl. Papers*, 1821, xi. 181 et seq.), and wrote 'a short account' of his brother, William Mitford, which was prefixed to William King's edition of the 'History of Greece,' London, 1822, 8vo. A number of Redesdale's letters are published in Lord Colchester's 'Diary and Correspondence,' 1861.

He was also the author of: 1. 'The Catholic Question. Correspondence between . . . Lord Redesdale . . . and . . . the Earl of Fingall . . . [on the appointment of the latter as a justice of the peace for the county of Meath] from 28 Aug. to 26 Sept. 1803,' Dublin, 1804, 8vo. 2. 'Observations occasioned by a Pamphlet entitled "Objections to the Project of creating a Vice-chancellor of England,"' London, 1813, 8vo. 3. 'Considerations suggested by the Report made to his Majesty . . . respecting the Court of Chancery,' London, 1826, 8vo. 4. 'An Address to the Protestants of the United Kingdom . . . and to those Roman Catholics whose Religious Opinions do not wholly overcome a just regard to the free Constitution of the British Government,' &c., London, 1829, 8vo. 5. 'Nine Letters to Lord Colchester on the Catholic Question,' London, 1829, 8vo. 6. 'A Political View of the Roman Catholic Question, especially regarding the Supremacy usurped by the Church of Rome,' &c., London, 1829, 8vo.

[O'Flanagan's Lives of the Lord Chancellors of Ireland, 1870, ii. 284–322; Burke's Hist. of the Lord Chancellors of Ireland, 1879, pp. 181–192; Townsend's Lives of Twelve Eminent Judges, 1846, ii. 145–90; Sir E. Brydges's Autobiography, 1834, i. 157–9, 250–1, 260–5, 268–9, 298–9, 306–9, 357–60; Walpole's Hist. of England, 1st edit. i. 318, 509, ii. 77, 217–18, 221, 245, 474, iii. 46, 60; Manning's Speakers of the House of Commons, 1851, pp. 473–9; Law Mag. (1830), iii. 297–9; Gent. Mag. 1830, pt. i. p. 267; Ann. Reg. 1830, pt. ii. pp. 473–9; Doyle's Official Baronage, 1886, iii. 103–4; Burke's Peerage, 1890, pp. 1509–10; Masters of the Bench of the Inner Temple, 1883, p. 85; Official Return of Lists of Members of Parliament, ii. 177, 189, 201, 202; Dict. of Living Authors, 1816, p. 283; Advocates' Libr. Cat.; Brit. Mus. Cat.] G. F. R. B.

MITFORD, JOHN THOMAS FREEMAN-, EARL OF REDESDALE (1805–1886), son of John Freeman-Mitford, first baron Redesdale [q. v.], was born in Dublin 9 Sept. 1805. He was educated at Eton and New College, Oxford (B.A. 1825, M.A. 1828, D.C.L. 1853). On the death of his father in 1830 he succeeded as second baron, but took little part in the debates of the House of Lords until 1837, when he began to interest himself in the wording and detail of parliamentary bills. Wellington recommended him to study the private business of the house, so as to qualify himself for the chairmanship of committees, and on the resignation of the sixth Earl of Shaftesbury (Cropley-Ashley), 4 Feb. 1851, Redesdale was unanimously chosen his successor, with the approval of Lansdowne, Stanley, and Wellington (*Hansard*, 3rd ser. vol. cxiv. cols. 47–51). This appointment he held with general credit until his death, and though assiduous in presiding when bills were in committee, made his power chiefly felt over private bill legislation. His shrewdness and independence of judgment enabled him to detect the artifices of attorneys and agents, while his dictatorial manner was proverbial. Though he regarded all things, great and small, with a genuine conservatism, yet he never allowed his peculiar views to warp his decisions (Lord Granville and Lord Salisbury in the House of Lords, 6 May 1886, *ib.* vol. cccv. cols. 355–8). Redesdale was especially severe on the drafting of railway bills, and in 1867 threatened to hale a contractor named France to the bar of the house for expressions reflecting on him as chairman. The correspondence showed that he was acting under a misapprehension (*Lord Redesdale and the New Railways; Correspondence between his Lordship and Mr. France*, 1867). Nevertheless his firm and honest management increased the authority of the House of Lords in connection with private business.

Redesdale was also a frequent speaker on general topics, e.g. the Reform Bill of 1867, when he opposed Earl Grey's amendment for the disfranchisement of certain boroughs, on the ground that the matter was beyond the proper jurisdiction of the peers, and that it was a mistake to make the franchise a party question (*Hansard*, 3rd ser. vol. clxxxix. col. 935). On the Alabama affair he maintained in 1872 that the United States had no claims to compensation because the Southerners had reentered the Union at the close of the war (*ib.* vol. ccxi. col. 270). But his interests lay chiefly in religious topics, on which he assumed a pronouncedly protestant and orthodox attitude. He published in 1849 some 'Reflections on the Doctrine of Regeneration and its Connection with both Sacraments,' and in 1850 some 'Observations on the Gorham Judgment and its Consequences.' In 1853 he was one of the revivers of convocation. He refused to sign the report of the royal commission on the law of divorce, of which he was a member, on the ground that the dissolution of the marriage tie was contrary to Scripture, and besides vindicating his views in a pamphlet entitled 'The Law of Scripture against Divorce' (1856), offered vigorous opposition to the measure of the following year (*ib.* vol. ccxlv. esp. cols. 515–16). Equally outspoken was his resistance to the disestablishment of the Irish church, which he maintained to be a violation of the coronation oath. On 17 July 1868 he moved for a copy of the oath (*ib.* vol. cxciii. col. 1345), besides publishing two pamphlets, 'Some of the Arguments by which Mr. Gladstone's Resolutions are supported considered' (1868), and 'Lord Macaulay on the Coronation Oath' (1869). In 1874 appeared 'Reasoning on some Points of Doctrine,' and in 1875 Redesdale entered into a controversy with Cardinal Manning in the 'Daily Telegraph' on the subject of communion in both kinds (*Daily Telegraph*, 1 Oct.—14 Dec.) The correspondence was republished by the 'Press and St. James's Chronicle,' under the title of 'The Infallible Church and the Holy Communion.' Redesdale displayed considerable ingenuity in forcing the cardinal to base his arguments on authorities whose cogency he had denied, but, as might be expected from the predispositions of the dialecticians, the dispute led to no practical result. On 3 Jan. 1877 he was on Beaconsfield's recommendation created earl of Redesdale. On 14 June he called attention in the House of Lords to a manual entitled 'The Priest in Absolution,' published privately for the use of the clergy by the Society of the Holy Cross, and elicited a strong condemnation of its doctrines from Archbishop Tait (*Hansard*, 3rd ser. vol. ccxxxiv. cols. 1741–53, and DAVIDSON and BENHAM, *Life of Tait*, ii. 171 et seq., where the authorship of the work is ascribed to the Rev. C. F. Chambers). In the same year also appeared his 'Apostolic Doctrine of the Real Presence,' and in 1879 'On the Doctrine of the Real Presence; Correspondence between the Earl of Redesdale and the Hon. C. L. Wood,' a discussion evoked by a speech of the latter at a meeting of the university branch of the English Church Union.

Redesdale also published 'Thoughts on English Prosody and Translations from Horace,' and 'Further Thoughts on English Prosody' (1859), odd attempts, suggested by an article in the 'Quarterly Review,' vol. cxiv., on 'Horace and his Translators,' to formulate rules of quantity for the English language on Latin models. His last pamphlet was 'The Earldom of Mar: a Letter to the Lord Register of Scotland, the Earl of Glasgow,' a reply to the Earl of Crawford's criticisms on Glasgow's judgment. He died unmarried 2 May 1886, when the peerage became extinct, but Algernon Bertram Mitford, great-grandson of William Mitford, was created Baron Redesdale in 1902. To the end of his days the earl wore the old-fashioned tail-coat and brass buttons of the previous generation.

[Foster's Alumni Oxon, 1715–1886; Burke's Peerage for 1886; Times, 3 May 1886; Annual Register. 1886.] L. C. S.

MITFORD, MARY RUSSELL (1787–1855), novelist and dramatist, born at Alresford, Hampshire, on 16 Dec. 1787, was the only child of George Mitford or Midford, descended from an ancient Northumberlandshire family, and of Mary Russell, an heiress, the only surviving child of Dr. Richard Russell, a richly-beneficed clergyman, who held the livings of Overton and Ash, both in Hampshire, for more than sixty years. George Mitford, who was ten years his wife's junior, had been educated for the medical profession, and was a graduate of Edinburgh University. He was clever, selfish, unprincipled, and extravagant, with an unhappy love of speculation and whist. He squandered altogether in his life about 70,000*l.*, and finally became entirely dependent on his daughter's literary earnings. William Harness, who was Miss Mitford's lifelong friend, called him 'a detestable old humbug,' but his many failings never succeeded in alienating the affections of his wife and daughter.

Mary was a very precocious child, and could read before she was three years old. In 1797 she drew a prize in a lottery worth 20,000*l.* The child herself insisted on choosing the number, 2224, because its digits made up the sum of her age. On the strength of it Dr. Mitford built a house at Reading. Between 1798 and 1802 the girl was at a good school at 22 Hans Place, London, kept by Mrs. St. Quintin, a French refugee, where Lady Caroline Lamb [q. v.] had been an earlier pupil, and 'L. E. L.' was later educated. In 1802 Mary settled at home with her parents, and her literary taste began to develope. She read enormously. In 1806 she mastered fifty-five volumes in thirty-one days, and in 1810 appeared her first published work, 'Miscellaneous Poems.' The volume, dedicated to the Hon. William Herbert, is a collection of fugitive pieces, written at an earlier period. Some were in honour of her father's friends, others recorded her own tastes and pursuits, and illustrate her love of nature and the country. In the spring of the same year she made the acquaintance of Sir William Elford [q. v.], a dilettante painter, and in 1812 began a long correspondence with him. Through him she came to know Haydon, who subsequently painted her portrait. Meanwhile she continued publishing poetry. 'Christina, or the Maid of the South Seas,' appeared in 1811; 'Blanch of Castile,' which had been submitted in manuscript to Coleridge, in 1812; and 'Poems on the Female Character,' dedicated to the third Lord Holland, in 1813. Her poems were severely criticised in the 'Quarterly,' but the volume of 1810 passed into a second edition (1811), and all the volumes met with much success in America. At this period Miss Mitford paid frequent visits to London, and stayed at the house of James Perry, editor of the 'Morning Chronicle;' there she met, among others, Lord Erskine, Sir Samuel Romilly, Dr. Parr, Lord Brougham, and Moore.

By March 1820 Dr. Mitford's irregularities had reduced his family to the utmost poverty, and it was necessary for Mary to turn to literature for the means of livelihood. The household removed to Three Mile Cross, a village on the turnpike road between Reading and Basingstoke, and lived there in 'an insufficient and meanly furnished labourer's cottage' (Chorley, *Autob.*) The largest room was about 'eight feet square' (*Our Village*). Miss Mitford resided there for more than thirty years, allowing herself only one luxury—a flower garden. She wrote much for the magazines, but soon grew convinced that her talent lay in tragedy, a view in which Coleridge, on reading 'Blanch of Castile,' had encouraged her. Her earliest dramatic efforts were rejected, but Macready, to whom Talfourd gave her an introduction, accepted 'Julian,' and with the great actor in the title-rôle it was performed at Covent Garden, 15 March 1823. Acted eight times, it brought her 200*l.* Macready, in his 'Reminiscences' (i. 278), states that the performance made little impression, and was soon forgotten. Neither prologue nor epilogue was introduced into the performance, and that innovation, which soon became the rule, is ascribed to Miss Mitford's influence. A second piece by Miss Mitford, 'Foscari,' with Charles Kemble as the hero, was produced at Covent Garden, 4 Nov. 1826, and was played fifteen times. According to her own statement, it was completed and presented to Covent Garden Theatre before the publication in 1821 of Byron's drama on the same subject. The best of her plays was 'Rienzi,' a poetical tragedy of merit, which was produced at Drury Lane, 9 Oct. 1828. Young played the hero, and Stanfield painted the scenery. It was acted thirty-four times, and Miss Mitford received 400*l.* from the theatre, besides selling eight thousand copies of the printed play. Its success caused a temporary coolness between Miss Mitford and her friend Talfourd, who fancied that his 'Ion,' which was being performed at the same time, was unduly neglected through 'Rienzi's' popularity. The piece became popular in America, where Miss Charlotte Cushman assumed the part of Claudia. Another of Miss Mitford's tragedies, 'Charles I,' was rejected by Colman because the lord chamberlain refused it his license, but in 1834, when urgently in need of money, Miss Mitford disposed of it on liberal terms to the manager of the Victoria Theatre, on the Surrey side of the Thames, and beyond the lord chamberlain's jurisdiction. Miss Mitford also wrote 'Mary Queen of Scots,' a scena in English verse, 1831, and an opera libretto, 'Sadak and Kalascade,' produced in 1835, and she contributed several dramatic scenes to the 'London Magazine' and other periodicals. Genest (*Hist. of the Stage*, ix. 201–2, 384–5, 454–5) finds her plays meritorious, but dull. They met with the approval of Miss Edgeworth, Joanna Baillie, and Mrs. Hemans. After passing separately through several editions, they were published collectively in 1854 in two volumes, with a valuable autobiographical introduction describing the influences under which they were written, and their adventures among the theatrical managers.

Happily, the pressing necessity of earning money led Miss Mitford to turn, as she says herself, 'from the lofty steep of tragic poetry to the every-day path of village stories.' Her inimitable series of country sketches, drawn from her own experiences at Three Mile Cross, entitled 'Our Village,' began to appear in 1819 in the 'Lady's Magazine,' a little-known periodical, whose sale was thereby increased from 250 to 2,000. She had previously offered them to Thomas Campbell for the 'New Monthly Magazine,' but he rejected them as unsuited to the dignity of his pages. The sketches had an enormous success, and were collected in five volumes (1824, 1826, 1828, 1830 and 1832). New editions came out in 1843 and many later years, while of numerous selections which have appeared since 1870 that of 1893 was edited by Lady Richmond Ritchie, with illustrations by Hugh Thomson.

The book may be said to have laid the foundation of a branch of literature hitherto untried. The sketches resemble Dutch paintings in their fidelity of detail, and in the brightness and quaint humour of their style. Chorley (*Authors of England*) calls Mitford the Claude of English village life. The tales at once made Miss Mitford famous. Charles Lamb declared that nothing so fresh and characteristic had appeared for a long time; Christopher North spoke of their 'genuine rural spirit;' Mrs. Hemans was cheered by them in sickness; Mrs. S. C. Hall acknowledges that they suggested her own 'Sketches of Irish Character;' Mrs. Browning called Miss Mitford 'a sort of prose Crabbe in the sun;' while Harriet Martineau looked upon her as the originator of the new style of 'graphic description.' Distinguished visitors crowded to her cottage. Passing coachmen and post-boys pointed out to travellers the localities in the village described in the book, and children were named after Miss Mitford's village urchins and pet greyhounds. She was fêted on her visits to the metropolis. In 1836 Mr. Kenyon introduced her to Elizabeth Barrett, afterwards Mrs. Browning, and the acquaintance speedily ripened into friendship.

Miss Mitford's popularity enabled her to command high prices for her work. Writing to Miss Mitford in 1832, Mrs. Trollope says that 'Whittaker (the publisher) told me some time ago that your name would sell anything.' In 1835 Miss Mitford remarked: 'It is one of the signs of the times that a periodical selling for three halfpence ['Chambers's Edinburgh Journal'] should engage so high-priced a writer as myself.' But her mother died on 1 Jan. 1830, and her father's increasing extravagances kept her poor. She confessed to Miss Barrett that 'although want, actual want has not come, yet fear and anxiety have never been absent.' Miss Mitford still wrote with energy, but the strain injured her style. A novel, 'Belford Regis, or Sketches of a Country Town,' viz. Reading, appeared in 1835, and, although Mrs. Browning ranked it with Miss Mitford's best work, it plainly lacks the spontaneity and charm of 'Our Village.' A second and third edition appeared respectively in 1846 and 1849. In 1837 she received a civil list pension of 100*l.* a year, and on 11 Dec. 1842 her father died. His heavy liabilities were met by a public subscription, which left a surplus to be added to the daughter's narrow income. 'I have not bought a bonnet, a cloak, a gown, hardly a pair of gloves, for four years' (10 Jan. 1842). In 1851 Miss Mitford removed to her last residence, a little cottage at Swallowfield, near Reading, 'placed where three roads meet' (PAYN). Though her cheerfulness and industry were unabated, her health was broken by her earlier anxieties, and she was crippled with rheumatism. In 1852 she published 'Recollections of a Literary Life, or Books, Places, and People,' three volumes of delightful gossip, much of it autobiographical. Other editions came out in 1853, 1857, and 1859. Her last production, 'Atherton, and other Tales,' published in 1854, won high praise from Mr. Ruskin. Her death, hastened by a carriage accident, took place at Swallowfield on 10 Jan. 1855. On the 18th she was buried in the village churchyard. A few months before her death Walter Savage Landor addressed to her some eloquent verses in praise of her 'pleasant tales.' Nor could, he concluded, any tell

> The country's purer charms so well
> As Mary Mitford.

In childhood Mr. Harness remarks the 'sedateness and gravity of her face;' Miss Sedgwick describes her in 1839 as 'truly a little body. . . . She has a pale gray soul-lit eye, and hair as white as snow;' Mr. Hablot Browne spoke of 'that wonderful wall of forehead;' and both Mr. Horne and Miss Cushman mention the wonderful animation of her face. Charles Kingsley asserts that 'the glitter and depth' of her eyes gave a 'French or rather Gallic' character to her countenance. The best portrait of her was that painted by Lucas in 1852, now in the National Portrait Gallery. It was engraved by S. Freeman. There is a drawing in crayon also executed by Lucas in 1852. Haydon's portrait is exaggerated and unsatisfactory. Her figure appears in outline by D. Maclise in 'Fraser's Magazine,' May 1831, with a notice by Maginn.

Miss Mitford was an admirable talker; both Mrs. Browning and Mr. Horne preferred her conversation to her books. Mr. Fields called her voice 'a beautiful chime of silver bells.' About her friends she was always enthusiastic, and to the last respected her father's memory. She was very widely read in English literature, and was catholic and unconventional in her literary judgment. Her familiarity with French writers is traceable in her clear English style. She was an inveterate letter writer, and corresponded with scores of persons whom she never met. Her letters, scribbled on innumerable small scraps of paper, are fully as attractive as her books. The most interesting are those written to Sir William Elford and Miss Barrett. But her correspondents also included Macready, Mrs. Hemans, Mrs. Trollope, Dyce, Charles Boner, Allan Cunningham, Mr. and Mrs. S. C. Hall, Haydon, Douglas Jerrold, Mary Howitt, Harriet Martineau, Mrs. Jameson, and Barry Cornwall. Vexatious difficulties were placed by her servants, her residuary legatees, in the way of the publication of the letters, but they were finally overcome by Mr. L'Estrange, and her correspondence was issued in 1870.

In addition to the works already mentioned, Miss Mitford published: 1. 'Dramatic Scenes, Sonnets, and other Poems,' 1827. 2. 'Stories of American Life,' 1830. 3. 'American Stories for Children,' 1832. She contributed to Mrs. Johnstone's 'Edinburgh Tales,' the 'London Magazine,' the 'Reading Mercury,' Mr. S. C. Hall's 'Amulet,' a religious annual (1826–36), Mrs. S. C. Hall's 'Juvenile Forget-me-not,' and others. She edited 'Finden's Tableaux,' a fashionable annual, from 1838 to 1841, and a selection from Dumas for the young, 1846.

[Life of Mary Russell Mitford, ed. by the Rev. A. G. L'Estrange, 1870; Friendships of Mary Russell Mitford, ed. by same; Lit. Life of the Rev. William Harness, ed. by same; Letters of Mary Russell Mitford, 2nd ser. ed. H. Chorley; Chorley's Memorials of Mrs. Hemans, 1836; Letters of Elizabeth Barrett Browning to R. H. Horne; Chorley's Autob. 1873; Memoirs of Charles Boner, 1871; Chorley's Authors of Engl. 1861; S. C. Hall's Book of Memories, 1877; James Payn's Lit. Recollections, 1885, pp. 74–97.] E. L.

MITFORD, WILLIAM (1744–1827), historian, born in London on 10 Feb. 1744, was the elder of the two sons of John Mitford, barrister-at-law, of Exbury House, Hampshire, by his wife Philadelphia, daughter of W. Reveley of Newton Underwood and Throphill, Northumberland. John Freeman-Mitford, baron Redesdale [q. v.], lord chancellor of Ireland, was the younger son. William Mitford was educated at Cheam school, Surrey, under William Gilpin [q. v.], whom he afterwards presented, in 1777, to the vicarage of Boldre in the New Forest (Nichols, *Lit. Illustr.* i. 778; on Mitford's supposed education at Westminster School, cf. *Notes and Queries*, 7th ser. vii. 278, and Welch, *Alumni Westmonast.* p. 548). He matriculated at Queen's College, Oxford, 16 July 1761, but neglected the ordinary studies, and left without a degree. At Queen's, where he was distinguished by his good looks and his personal strength, he was of the same breakfast club as Jeremy Bentham, who 'thought his conversation commonplace' (Bowring, *Life of Bentham*, p. 40 *a*). In the vacations, however, he read some Greek and attended Blackstone's Vinerian lectures at Oxford with a view to the bar. He became a student of the Middle Temple in 1763, but never practised. On his father's death in 1761 he succeeded to the property at Exbury. In 1802 he acquired the Reveley estates in Yorkshire, through his mother's family, but continued till his death to live at Exbury, where he rebuilt the house about 1800. From 1761 Mitford lived for several years in comparative retirement at Exbury, and devoted himself to the study of Greek. He was verderer of the New Forest in 1778, and was colonel in the South Hampshire militia, in which Gibbon, the historian, was a brother-officer. While in the militia Mitford published a 'Treatise on the Military Force, and particularly the Militia (of England),' and on Gibbon's suggestion undertook his principal work, the 'History of Greece.' The first volume appeared in 1784, 4to, and vol. ii. in 1790, but the book was not completed till 1810. Other editions appeared (1789–1818, 4to; 1795–7, 8vo; 1818–20, 8vo; 1822, 8vo; 1829, 8vo; 1835, 12mo). Mitford's history for many years remained popular, and had the merit of supplying a laborious English work on a comparatively neglected subject. It was superior at most points to the Greek history by John Gillies (1747–1836) [q. v.], published in 1786. It was praised by Brougham in the 'Edinburgh Review,' and by Alison (*Hist. of Europe*, 1815–52, chap. v.); but the obscurity and oddity of the author's style have been severely commented on by Byron (*Don Juan*, canto xii. st. xix, note) and Macaulay. Clinton (*Fasti Hellenici*) has attacked the work for its chronological shortcomings, and Grote (*Hist. of Greece*, Preface) contrasts its tone unfavourably with 'the liberal spirit of criticism' displayed by Thirlwall. Alison considers that the author, writing at the time of the French revolution, intended chiefly to counteract visionary ideas as to the blessings of Athenian democracy. Dr. Arnold thought that Mitford's anti-Jacobin partialities at any rate saved his history from dulness (cf. BYRON, loc. cit.) Lord Redesdale, in the preface to the 1822 edition of the 'History of Greece,' attempts an ingenious defence of his brother's treatment of ancient Hellenic politics. It may be added that Mitford never visited Greece, never travelling beyond Naples.

Mitford was M.P. for Newport, Cornwall, 1785–90; for Beeralston, 1796–1806; New Romney, 1812–18. In parliament he upheld the militia system, in which he strongly deprecated any innovations, but seldom spoke. He was a fellow of the Society of Antiquaries and professor of ancient history at the Royal Academy. He died at his seat, Exbury, on 10 Feb. 1827. There is a monument to him in the church at Exbury. A portrait is prefixed to the last edition of his 'History' (1835). Mitford married, 18 May 1766, Frances, daughter of James Molloy of Dublin, by Anne, daughter of Henry Pye, M.P. for Faringdon, Berkshire, and had issue five sons and one daughter. Henry Mitford (1769–1803) the second son, was captain in the R.N. and grandfather of Algernon Bertram Mitford, first Baron Redesdale (of the second creation); another son, Bertram (1774–1844), was LLD. and a commissioner of bankrupts in Ireland. Mrs. Mitford died 27 April 1827.

Besides the works already mentioned, Mitford published: 1. 'An Essay on the Harmony of Language,' &c. (especially the English language), 1774, 8vo; 2nd edit. 1804. 2. 'Considerations, &c., on the Corn Laws' (contending that England could grow wheat enough for its own supply), London, 1791, 8vo. 3. 'Observations on the History . . . of Christianity, and . . . on the Primeval Religion, on the Judaic and on the Heathen, Public, Mystical and Philosophical, the latter . . . an Appendix to the . . . "History of Greece,"' London, 1823, 8vo. 4. 'Principles of Design in Architecture, traced in Observations on Buildings,' &c., 2nd edit. London, 1824, 8vo. A 'Review of the Early History of the Arabs,' in two chapters, which forms the introduction to Shakespear and Horne's 'History of the Mahometan Empire in Spain' (London, 1816), may be attributed to him.

[Burke's Landed Gentry, 'Mitford of Exbury;' Foster's Alumni Oxon. 1715–1886; Mitford's Hist. of Greece, with Lord Redesdale's Memoir; Lit. Memoirs of Living Authors, 1798, ii. 49; Allibone's Dict. Engl. Lit.; Gent. Mag. 1827, pt. i. pp. 368–9; Brit. Mus. Cat.; private information.] W. W.

MOBERLY, GEORGE (1803–1885), bishop of Salisbury, seventh son of Edward Moberly of St. Petersburg, a Russia merchant, by his wife Sarah, daughter of John Cayley, British consul-general in Russia, was born 10 Oct. 1803. He was educated first at Winchester College and then at Balliol College, Oxford, where he matriculated with a scholarship 13 March 1822. He graduated B.A. in 1825 with a first class in *literæ humaniores*, gained the chancellor's prize for the English essay in 1826, on the subject, 'Is a rude or a refined age more favourable to the production of works of fiction?' proceeded M.A. in 1828, and D.C.L. in 1836. He was select preacher before the university in 1833, 1858, and 1863, and Bampton lecturer in 1868. In 1826 he was elected to a fellowship at Balliol College, and was for some years one of the most brilliant and successful of the tutors who assisted Dr. Jenkyns to make Balliol the foremost college in Oxford. He was a public examiner in 1830, and again in 1833, 1834, and 1835. Manning was among his pupils, and also Tait, who succeeded him in his tutorship, and eventually consecrated him bishop of Salisbury. He vacated his fellowship on his marriage in 1834 with Mary, daughter of Thomas Crokat of Leghorn; but in 1835 he was appointed head-master of Winchester, a post which he held for thirty years. Leaving Oxford on the eve of the 'Oxford movement,' he took little, if any, active part in the various ecclesiastical controversies which were occasioned by it. His sympathies and opinions, however, were of the high-church school. Keble was his neighbour at Winchester and intimate friend, and he formally protested against the sentence of degradation pronounced upon W. G. Ward for the opinions expressed in his 'Ideal of a Christian Church considered.' This protest, contained in a letter to Richard Jenkyns [q. v.], master of Balliol, was published in 1845. As a schoolmaster he exerted much personal influence over his boys. When examining Rugby School along with Christopher Wordsworth he caught from Arnold much of his enthusiasm and some of his views. He approved the 'fagging' system (cf. his *Winchester College Sermons*, 2nd ser. Pref.), supported all the school traditions, and was conservative in his modes of teaching. Although beloved by many pupils, it cannot be said that he gave any impulse to the fame or progress of the school, and the numbers did not increase under his rule. In 1866 he resigned, and was presented to the rectory of Brighstone, Isle of Wight, and in 1868 became a canon of Chester Cathedral.

Moberly had been regarded as a possible bishop ever since 1850, and in 1857 an unsuccessful attempt had been made to induce the Duke of Newcastle to appoint him bishop of Sydney. But his promotion was delayed in consequence of his high-church leanings. At length in 1869 he was appointed by Mr. Gladstone to succeed Walter Kerr Hamilton [q. v.] as bishop of Salisbury, the first high-church appointment for many years, and he was consecrated 28 Oct.

In the administration of his diocese he followed the lines of his predecessor. He avoided dissensions; he founded a 'Diocesan Synod;' he escaped public attention. He was a diligent attendant in convocation and an infrequent one in the House of Lords, and, though a fairly impressive preacher, spoke rarely in either assembly. Though not unfavourable to the principle of the Public Worship Regulation Act of 1874, he voted for its withdrawal in deference to the public outcry which it occasioned, and refused to sign the bishops' pastoral, which was issued before the act came into operation. In 1872 he issued an appeal to churchmen, much to the indignation of the ritualists, to consent to the omission of the damnatory clauses from the Athanasian Creed; in 1873 he was a member of the committee appointed by convocation to consider the attitude of the church towards auricular confession, and assisted to draw its report; and in 1877 he spoke strongly in convocation against the use of the confessional, especially in schools (see *Chronicle of Convocation*, 6 July 1877, p. 331). The most concise indication of his general ecclesiastical position is to be found in the preface to the second edition of his university sermons on the 'Beatitudes' (1861). His publications were numerous, but consisted chiefly of single sermons and episcopal charges. The others are: 'Remarks on the proposed admission of Dissenters to the University of Oxford,' 1834; 'Practical Sermons,' 1838; 'Sermons at Winchester College,' 1844 (2nd series, 1848); 'The Sayings of the Great Forty Days,' 1844, frequently republished; 'The Law of the Love of God,' an essay on the commandments, 1854; sermons on the 'Beatitudes,' 1860 (2nd edition, with remarks on 'Essays and Reviews,' 1861); 'Letters to Sir W. Heathcote on Public Schools,' 1861; 'Brightstone Sermons,' 1867, frequently republished; 'The Administration of the Holy Spirit in the Body of Christ, being the Bampton Lectures for 1868,' 1868; and he also contributed to a revision of portions of the New Testament, published by 'Five Clergymen' in 1857, 1858, and 1861.

For some time before his death his faculties had been decaying, and his episcopal duties were discharged by J. B. K. Kelly, formerly bishop of Newfoundland. In 1884 his resignation was determined upon, but the papers had not received his signature when he died at Salisbury on 6 July 1885. Five sons and seven daughters survived him.

[Guardian, 8 July 1885; Times, 7 July 1885; Sat. Review, lx. 47; Davidson's Life of Archbishop Tait; Wilberforce's Life of Bishop Wilberforce; T. Mozley's Reminiscences of Oriel; Foster's Alumni Oxon.; Wilfrid Ward's Life of W. G. Ward; R. E. Prothero's Dean Stanley, 1894; Brit. Mus. Cat.]

J. A. H.

MOCHAEI (*d.* 497), saint and bishop of Aendruim, is also known as Cailan or Caelan, from *caol*, i.e. slender, according to Bishop Reeves. His mother is said to have been Bronach, daughter of Miliuc, son of Buan, king of North Dalaradia, co. Antrim. With Miliuc St. Patrick was at one time in captivity. One day when journeying from Saul to Derlas, south of Downpatrick Patrick met Mochaei, then 'a tender youth,' employed in herding swine. Observing his intelligence, Patrick instructed him in the holy scriptures, in due time baptised him, and eventually ordained him. This occurrence has been doubtfully dated in 433 by Bishop Reeves; it probably belongs to a later year. On his ordination St. Patrick presented Mochaei with a book of the gospels and *menistir*, apparently the case containing a chalice and paten. Another gift of the saint was the *Eitech Mochaei*, or Mochaei's winged crozier, which is said to have fallen from heaven while Mochaei and Patrick were conversing on sacred things. Mochaei seems to have been the first in Ireland to whom St. Patrick gave a gospel and a crozier. The gift appears to have been made on the occasion of the foundation of Mochaei's church of Aendruim. This church, called in the 'Acta Sanctorum' Nendrum, and in the 'Monasticon' Neddrum, was situate thirteen miles N.N.E. of Downpatrick, on an island in Strangford Lough—now known, after Mochaei's name, as Mahee Island. Mahee Island contains the remains of a round tower, about nine feet high, and the ruins of a church enclosed by three ramparts or cashels, evidently for the security of the community. The ruins are not those of the original church built by Mochaei, as that was of wattles plastered over. According to the 'Martyrology of Donegal,' Mochaei went into the forest with sevenscore young men to cut wattles, and a legend states that while thus engaged an angel in the shape of a bird sang so sweetly to him that 'three fifties' of years passed over like an hour. When the song ceased and he awoke from his trance, every one he knew was dead, and an oratory had been built to his memory. The 'Calendar of Oengus' says: 'Of the members of the saint's congregation, nothing remained but the skulls.' Bishop Reeves suggests that the legend may be explained by the fact that another Mochaei is recorded as having died in 664, a hundred and thirty-eight years later, with whom our saint has been confused. The elder Mochaei's monastery was also a school for the education of the clergy, and among the pupils received there were St. Finnian of Moville, and St. Colman of Dromore. 'A shaven pig' was annually presented by Mochaei's community, in commemoration of the saint's original occupation as a swineherd, to the church of Down, which was popularly associated with the name of St. Patrick. Mochaei died on 23 June 497.

[The Tripartite Life of St. Patrick, by Whitley Stokes, D.C.L., Rolls Ser. i. 40; Reeves's Antiquities of Down, Connor, and Dromore, pp. 144, 187–97; Martyrology of Donegal, p. 177; Calendar of Oengus, p. cvii.] T. O.

MOCHAEMOG or **Pulcherius, Saint** (*d.* 655), was the son of an artisan named Beoan, who left his native place, Conmaicne (now Connamara), in Connaught, and settled in Húi Conaill Gabhra in the south of the county of Limerick. Nessa, who lived with her sister Ita in the neighbourhood, at Cill-Ita (now Killeedy), became Beoan's wife. By Ita's intercession a son was born after long delay. Before his birth St. Fachtna [q. v.] of Ross Ailither is said to have been cured of an affection of the eyes by bathing them in the milk of Beoan's wife. Ita first named Nessa's son *Caem-ghin*, 'a fair offspring,' but afterwards substituted *og* for *ghin* and prefixed *mo*, thus forming Mochaemog, 'My-fair-youth' (in Latin, Pulcherius). On attaining the age of twenty Mochaemog proceeded to Bangor in Ulster, where he studied under St. Comgall, and was in due time sent forth as a missionary by St. Comgall, his companions being SS. Laichtín, Molua Mac Ochai, one of the Findbarrs, and Luchtigern. Arrived at southern Ely in co. Tipperary, he was granted by the chieftain a site for a monastery, in a retired part of a forest near the marsh of Lake Lurgan; it has since been known as Liathmochaemog or Leamokeavogue, and is in the parish of Twomile Borris, barony of Eliogarty, co. Tipperary. Subsequently, when Failbhe Fland, king of Munster (619–634), who lived at Cashel, sent his horses to pasture on the lands of the monastery, the saint drove them away, and the king straightway ordered the chieftain of Ely to expel Mochaemog. The saint went to King Failbhe to remonstrate, but the latter was obdurate, and taunted Mochaemog with baldness. Thereupon Mochaemog is said to have caused the king's sight to fail, while St. Patrick and all the saints of Ireland, male and female, threatened him in visions with immediate death unless he treated Mochaemog with respect.

Failbhe's successor, Ronan, son of Bledin, although hostile to Mochaemog, renewed the grant to him, and the saint commended his soul on his death to God, and defended this act of charity against the adverse criticism of a scribe. Many other stories prove Mochaemog's influence with local kings or chieftains. In the 'Calendar of Oengus' his name is associated with that of Cuangus, a student of science, who is termed 'the blind youth.' He himself, his mother, and aunt, are all credited with curing blindness. They doubtless possessed some knowledge of ophthalmic science. Among his friends were St. Colman of Doiremor, whose monastery was only four miles off, and St. Fursa [q. v.] of Peronne in France. He was the tutor of Dagan of Inverdaoile, who is mentioned as a violent opponent of the Roman Easter, in the letter written in 609 by the bishops Laurentius, Mellitus, and Justus (cf. BEDE, *Ecclesiastical History*). Another church bearing Mochaemog's name is in the barony of Ida, co. Kilkenny. His death took place on 13 March 655, at an advanced age. Lanigan suggests 106 years, but this is far exceeded by a poem quoted in the 'Four Masters' and the 'Martyrology of Donegal,' which prolongs his life to 413 years. O'Donovan, however, agrees with Colgan that this is due to a scribal error, and that the true reading is 'ar ċoem ċéd,' 'over one hundred,' instead of 'four hundred.'

[Vita S. Mochoemoci seu Pulcherii Abbatis, xiii. Martii, ii. 281 seq, ; Lanigan's Eccles. Hist. ii. 310, 358, iii. 23–8 ; Annals of the Four Masters, i. 267 ; Martyrology of Donegal, at 13 March ; Calendar of Oengus, pp. lvi, lxiii.] T. O.

MOCHUA or CRONÁN, SAINT (580?–637), was the son of Becan and descended from Lugaid (from whom were the Húi Luigdech) son of Dalann of Ulaid. His mother, Cumne, was daughter of Conamail of the Dal Buain, also of Ulaid. Their family consisted of three sons and three daughters, the least esteemed of the children being Mochua, the hair of whose head, owing to disease, fell out in patches. St. Comgall of Bangor happening to visit his father's house, and finding him neglected by the family, took him with him to Bangor to educate him. There a woman, who sought Mochua's intercession with the Lord that she might obtain offspring, found him absorbed in prayer and bathed in tears, but catching his tears in the hollow of her hand she drank them and obtained her desire. On the completion of his education at Bangor, Mochua collected a party of his friends, and guided, it is said, by a marvellous moving fountain, which recalls the 'Arabian Nights' Entertainment,' passed through the town of Gael, in the territory of the Fir Rois in the south of Oriel, a territory which included the present county of Armagh. There he visited Bishop Gabren, and then passed on to Fobar (Fore) in Westmeath, where St. Fechin [q. v.] received him enthusiastically. Mochua is said to have miraculously pierced a mountain which lay between Lough Leane and Fore, and thus to have brought water to Fore to work a mill erected there by Fechin, but hitherto without means of propulsion. Travelling from Fore by Tech Telle (now Tehelly), near Durrow in King's County, and over the Shannon into Connaught, Mochua was welcomed by the chiefs of Hy Many. Subsequently at Lough Cimè (now Lough Hackett in the barony of Clare, co. Galway), he is reported to have subdued a monster which dwelt in the lake. Crossing the river Robe to the barony of Ceara, he arrived at Ross Darbrech, where the miraculous fountain, which is said to have hitherto accompanied him, became stationary. It was at once surrounded by a wall of massive stones—a mention of stone buildings rare in the seventh century. The well thus obtained the name of Balla or 'The Wall.' The ruins of a church and round tower attest the ancient importance of the place. Mochua seems to have lived there as a hermit, for when Eochaidh Minnech, a chieftain of the Clan Fiachra, came to expel him, he was 'in a prison of stone,' that is, apparently walled up in a stone cell. Eventually this chieftain and his nobles conferred the site on him, with certain lands and revenues, describing him as 'Mochua of the narrow prison.' He then appointed three bishops to consecrate his graveyards and his great churches and to allot the land to his monks. When the great pestilence called the Yellow Plague raged in Connaught he effected many cures, and was believed to have transferred the yellow colour from his patients to his crozier, which was thenceforth known as the Bachall Buidhe or 'Yellow Crozier.' Among the wild heathen people of the neighbourhood were two amazons named Bec and Lithben, who usually stationed themselves by a long, narrow creek, with precipitous rocks on either side, and swung every passer-by in a basket over the awful precipice. Mochua reclaimed them from barbarism, and both they and their fathers received baptism. He is further said by the miraculous shaking of his crozier to have created a road connecting Inis Amalgaid (now Inishlee), an island in Lough Conn, with the mainland. This mention of a causeway, combined with the stories of his bringing water to Fore and of the fountain attending Mochua, doubtless indicates possession of some engineering skill. According to the 'Lebar Brecc' he also brought 'bags of water from Ulster.' Mochua was thirty-five years of age when he came to Balla and after labouring twenty-one years, or, as another reading has it, thirty-one, he died on 30 March 637.

[Vita S. Mochuæ sive Cronani Abbatis Ballensis, in Colgan's Act. Sanct. xxx. Mart. pp. 789 seq. ; Lives of Saints from the Book of Lismore, edited by Whitley Stokes, D.C.L. ; Anecdota Oxoniensia, 1890, pp. 281–9, and notes pp. 260, 261 ; O'Donovan's Annals of the Four Masters, A.D. 837, p. 1179 ; Calendar of Oengus, 30 March ; Petrie's Essay on the Origin and use of the Round Towers, pp. 349–51.] T. O.

MOCHUDA (*d.* 636), bishop of Lismore. [See CARTHACH, SAINT, the younger.]

MOCKET, MOKET, or MOQUET, RICHARD (1577–1618), warden of All Souls, was born at Dorchester in Dorset in 1577. He graduated B.A. from Brasenose College, Oxford, on 16 Feb. 1595, and was elected fellow of All Souls in 1599, proceeding M.A. on 5 April 1600, B.D. on 23 April 1607, and D.D. 26 June 1609. George Abbot [q. v.], then bishop of London, presented him to the rectory of St. Clement's, Eastcheap, on 29 Dec. 1610, and to that of St. Michael's, Crooked Lane, on 1 Oct. 1611. He resigned St. Clement's before 9 Dec. 1611, and St. Michael's before 17 June 1614. He held the rectories of Newington, Oxfordshire, and of West Tarring, Sussex, from 1614, and of Monks Risborough, Buckinghamshire, from 1615 till his death. He was for some time domestic chaplain to Abbot, and one of the king's commissioners concerning ecclesiastical affairs. From March 1610 to June 1614 he was actively employed in licensing books for entry at Stationers' Hall. On 12 April 1614 he was elected warden of All Souls' College, Oxford.

The authorship of a curious tract, upholding the obligation of the oath of allegiance, and entitled 'God and the King,' has been ascribed to Mocket. The work was 'Imprinted by his Majesties special privilege and command,' in London in 1615, in both Latin and English; London, 1616, in Latin only; Edinburgh, 1617, in one or both languages; London, 1663; Edinburgh, 1725; London, 1727 (published by Nathaniel Booth). The book was commanded to be taught in all schools and universities, and by all ministers of the church, and to be purchased by all householders in England and Scotland. This command was enjoined by the privy council of Scotland in June 1616, and by the general assembly at Aberdeen in August 1616, and the work had in consequence an enormous sale.

In 1616, in London, Mocket published a volume in Latin, containing (1) Bishop Jewel's 'Apology,' (2) The Church Catechism, (3) Nowell's Catechism, (4) The Thirty-Nine Articles, (5) The Liturgy of the Church of England, and (6) The Book of Ordination of Bishops, Priests, and Deacons. To these he added a work of his own entitled 'Doctrina et Politia Ecclesiæ Anglicanæ,' which was a general view of ecclesiastical jurisdiction in the English church, mainly prepared for the information of foreigners. The book offended the king, and by public edict was condemned and burnt in 1617. Fuller (*Church Hist.* ed. Brewer, v. 444–6) considered that Mocket suffered on account of his patron Abbot, 'against whom many bishops began then to combine.' Heylyn (*Cyprianus Anglicus*, pp. 75–6), while condemning the writer's 'little knowledge in the constitution of the church,' and his bias 'towards those of Calvin's platform,' was of opinion that the real offence was the omission of the first clause in the translation of the twentieth of the Thirty-Nine Articles, which runs: 'The Church hath power to decree rites or ceremonies, and authority in controversies of faith.' It is also said that Mocket's extracts from the homilies were made so as to support the views of Abbot, and that as a translator he had usurped the duties of a commentator, while James Montagu [q. v.], bishop of Winchester, resented the order in which the bishoprics were enumerated. The 1616 edition of the 'Doctrina et Politia Ecclesiæ Anglicanæ' was reprinted in 1617. Mocket's work, without the rest of the volume, was republished in London in 1683, under the title, 'Tractatus de Politia Ecclesiæ Anglicanæ,' and with it was printed Richard Zouch's 'Descriptio Juris et Judicii Ecclesiastici.' A third edition appeared in London in 1705.

Mocket died (it is said) from disappointment at the reception of his book on 6 July 1618, and was buried in the chapel of All Souls' College. A marble tablet with a Latin inscription was fixed to the south wall of the inner chapel (removed to the north wall of the outer chapel in 1664).

[Hutchins's Dorset, ii. 376; Wood's Athenæ, ed. Bliss, ii. cols. 232–4; Reg. Univ. Oxon. (Oxford Hist. Soc.), vol. ii. pt. iii. p. 195; Wood's Hist. and Antiq. of Colleges and Halls, ed. Gutch, pp. 271, 292; Newcourt's Repert. i. 327, 486; Foster's Alumni Oxon. 1500–1714; Heylyn's Examen Historicum, pp. 185–7; Arber's Stationers' Registers, vol. iii. passim; Notes and Queries, 2nd ser. iv. 141, x. 27, 295, 5th ser. ii. 9, 59, v. 236–7; Lee's Lectures on the Hist. of the Church of Scotland, ii. 364.] B. P.

MOCKET, THOMAS (1602–1670?), puritan divine, born in 1602, matriculated as a sizar of Queens' College, Cambridge, 4 July 1622, and graduated B.A. in 1625, and M.A. in 1631. He was incorporated in the latter degree at Oxford in July 1639 (WOOD, *Fasti Oxon.* ed. Bliss, i. 511). For some time he was chaplain to John Egerton, first earl of Bridgewater [q. v.], president of the marches in Wales, by whom he was favoured and promised preferment. He adopted puritan principles. In 1642 he was preacher at Holt, Denbighshire; and in or before 1648 he obtained the rectory of Gilston, Hertfordshire, on the sequestration of Christopher Webb, M.A., to whom he resigned the living on the Restoration in 1660 (CLUTTERBUCK, *Hertfordshire*, iii. 171, 173 *n.*) He appears to have died in 1670.

His works are: 1. 'The Churches Troubles and Deliverance, or certaine Sermons tending to shew the Reasons why the Lord doth sometimes bring his People into extremities,' London [12 Aug.], 1642. 2. 'The Nationall Covenant. Or a Discourse on the Covenant. Wherein also the severall parts of the late Protestation are proved to be grounded on Religion and Reason,' London [20 Aug. 1642], 4to. 3. 'A View of the Solemn League and Covenant for Reformation, Defence of Religion, the Honour and Happynesse of the King, and the Peace, Safety, and Union of the Three Kingdoms,' London, 1644, 4to. The copy in the British Museum is dated in manuscript, 21 Sept. 1643. 4. 'The Covenanters Looking-Glasse; discovering his duty and dignity, &c.; also an Epistle containing a relation of all the most principal things done in the Parliament of England, since their first sitting to the present day,' London, 1644, 4to. 5. 'A New Catechisme,' London, 1647, 8vo. 6. 'Gospel Duty and Dignity. A Discourse of the Duty of Christians, and their Priviledges by Christ,' London, 1648, 4to. 7. 'Christmas, the Christians grand Feast: its Original, Growth, and Observation, also of Easter, Whitsontide, and other Holydayes modestly discussed and determined, also the beginning of the year & other things observable,' London, 1651, 4to. 8. 'Christian Advice to Old and Young, Rich and Poor,' London, 1671, 8vo. Prefixed is a portrait of the author, engraved by Cross at the expense of Edward Brewster.

[Addit. MS. 5876, f. 90; Bodleian Cat.; Calamy's Life of Baxter, i. 368, ii. 531; Granger's Biog. Hist. of England, 5th edit. iii. 340; Palmer's Nonconformist's Memorial, 2nd ed. ii. 303; Cat. of Dr. Williams's Library, ii. 253; Watt's Bibl. Brit.] T. C.

MODESTUS, SAINT (*fl.* 777), missionary to the Carinthians and regionary bishop, was an Irishman by birth (*Ep.* vii. quoted by DEMPSTER, *Hist. Eccles. Gent. Scot.* xii. No. 920). He was a disciple of St. Fergil or Virgilius [q. v.], bishop of Salzburg, who sent him with a band of missionaries to preach among the Carinthians, then under the rule of Chetmar. Modestus received authority as a bishop, but probably, after the Irish custom, was without a definite see. It is only in the late anonymous life of Gebehard (*Mon. Germ. Scriptores*, xi. 38 l. 38), that he is called bishop of Liburnia. Modestus and his companions founded one church at S. Maria in Solio, now Maria-Saal, another at a place called Liburnia or Tiburnia, the site of which is probably now marked by a field called Lurnfeld, in Spital, Upper Carinthia, and a third at a place, Adandrinas or Undrimas, spelt by the manuscripts in a variety of ways, believed to be a valley situated between S. Vitus and Maria-Saal (*ib.* xi. p. 7 l. 30 and p. 87; EICHHORN, *Beiträge zur Gesch. Kärnthen*, ii. 95). Modestus is said to have baptised St. Domitian, a Carinthian prince, at Milstadt, which may, perhaps, be identical with Adandrinas (HANSITZ, *Ger. Sac.* ii. 92; *Acta SS.* 1 Feb. 700). According to the older manuscripts, Modestus stayed in Carinthia till his death; one late manuscript says he died in France (HANSITZ, *ib.*), but his tomb is shown at Maria-Saal (EICHHORN, p. 112, § 4). His feast is celebrated on 5 Dec. (DEMPSTER, *Menology*, in FORBES, *Kal. Scottish Saints*, p. 221). Dempster calls him a companion of St. Boniface [q. v.], and Ferrarius says he is mentioned in Boniface's life (*Cat. Gen. SS. qui in Martyrol. Rom. non sunt*, 1625, p. 468). It is probable that in both cases St. Fergil was meant.

A manuscript by him, 'ad ecclesiam suam,' was said to be at Salzburg, and a volume of his letters at Strasburg (DEMPSTER, *Hist. Gent. Scot.* loc. cit.) Neither manuscript can now be traced.

[Gesta Archiep. Salisburg.; the Life of St. Virgilius, by a disciple of Eberhard; the anonymous Life of St. Gebehard, all in Pertz's Mon. Germ. Scriptores, vol. xi.; Tanner's Bibliotheca Britannica.] M. B.

MODWENNA or **MONINNE, SAINT** (*d.* 518), was the daughter of Maucteus (Mochta), king of Iveagh in Uladh and of the territory round Armagh. He was of the race of Irial, son of Conal Cearnach, the original possessors of Iveagh. Modwenna's mother, Coman, was daughter of Dallbronach, ruler of a terriority in Magh-Breagh (Meath), whose fort, 'Fossa [i.e. Raith] Dallbronig,' is mentioned in the 'Tripartite Life of St. Patrick.' She is said to have been originally called Darerca, and Ussher doubtfully identifies her with a so-called sister of St. Patrick of that name. But St. Darerca's festival was held on 22 March, while that of Modwenna was dated 6 July. The name Moninne, by which the saint is generally known in Ireland, was believed to have some connection with that of Nine the poet, who was cured of dumbness through her prayers. When St. Patrick was in her neighbourhood she visited him, and he 'blessed her [which appears to mean that he baptised her] at the little fish-pond of a Hospitaller,' which was thenceforward credited with healing virtues. Taking up her abode at Fochart, now Faugher, in the county of Louth, she was joined by seven maidens and a widow with an infant son, who afterwards became a king.

Finding herself exposed to the depredations of robbers, and too much occupied with secular engagements, she removed to one of the remote Aran islands, where her kinsman, St. Ibar, was then settled. Subsequently she accompanied the saint to another of the islands, and finally to that of Beg Eire in Wexford harbour. Returning to Faugher with her maidens, now 150 in number, she was disturbed by the coarse language and boisterous singing at a wedding feast near, and moved away to the north, arriving at Slieve Cuillinn in the barony of Orior and county of Armagh. Here they were reduced to living on the bark of trees, while the king was considering whether to permit their settlement or no. Modwenna succeeded, however, in converting to Christianity a robber chief named Glunsalach, of the same race as herself, who infested a waste territory near, and plundered those who travelled by the great road from Tara to the north, known as the Slighe Midluachra. He and his nephew Aiffen left their companions and came to her church at Killevy. There they were baptised and she taught them the psalter, and they became holy bishops. St. Kevin or Coemgen [q. v.], whose place in heaven she is said to have conferred on the robber chief, at the latter's earnest entreaty, is represented as being instigated by the devil to destroy her monastery. But she disarmed St. Kevin's wrath, brought him with her to Killevy, and dedicated to him, under the title of St. Kevin's Bath, a pool on the mountain-side, to which she led the water miraculously with her crozier, and in which she used to stand up to her breasts all night chanting the psalter. 'The Martyrology of Donegal' gives a somewhat different account of the relations between St. Kevin and Modwenna's robber convert, who is represented merely as one of St. Kevin's disciples, and as having been buried at Glendalough.

According to Conchubran's early life of the saint, Alfred, son of a king of the Angli, who entered the service of Conall, an Irish king, was cured by Modwenna of a dangerous illness; but Conall, wishing to make him a present before his return to England, and not having the money, ordered the sack of Killevy, that he might bestow the proceeds on the English prince. In great trouble at the ruin of her monastery, Modwenna made her way to England in search of the English prince, taking with her SS. Brigit and Luga. She found him at Streneshalen, near the wood of Arden in Warwickshire, and on hearing her story he made restitution of all her goods, and she and Brigit then returned and rebuilt the monastery. She also set up one at Arden, in which she was joined by Ita and Ositha. But it is very uncertain if this story can apply to the Modwenna of the sixth century. The English prince referred to was doubtless Ailfrid, son of Oswy, king of Northumbria, who succeeded to his father's throne in 671, and had, according to St. Cuthbert's biographer, spent much time previously in Ireland in an endeavour to obtain the cure of an illness, but as another saint of the same name flourished in Ireland in 630, the relations with the English prince must be assigned to her.

The earlier Modwenna doubtless travelled to England and Scotland in the course of her missionary labours, and founded several churches there, among which were Chilnacase in Galloway, one on the summit of Mount Dundevenal in Laudonia, one on Dunbreten, another at Castle Strivelin, a fifth at Dunedin, now Edinburgh, one on Mount Dunpelder, and one at Lanfortin, near Dundee, where she died in 518. In Ireland she founded churches at Faugher, Killevy, Cheveglas, Surde (Swords), Armagh, and Meath. A contest is said to have taken place among the English, Irish, and Scots for the possession of her remains. She is believed to have been buried at Burton-on-Trent. Some ruins of her church, near which formerly stood a round tower, are still to be seen at Killevy.

[Vita Moduennæ seu Monynnæ ex codice MS. Bibliothecæ Cottonianæ; Bollandists' Acta Sanct. vol. ii. Julii 6; Ussher's Works, vi. 248, 347, 604, with extracts from Conchubran's life of the saint; Annals of the Four Masters, A.D. 518; Martyrology of Donegal, 3 June, 6 July; Calendar of Oengus, p. cxvi; Reeves's Columba, p. 182, note *l*.]

T. O.

MODYFORD, Sir JAMES (*d.* 1673), merchant, colonial agent, deputy-governor of Jamaica, younger brother of Sir Thomas Modyford [q. v.], was, as a youth, at Constantinople in the service of the Turkey Company (*Cal. State Papers*, Dom. 30 June 1666). Afterwards he appears to have been settled at Chelsea as a merchant, and under the Commonwealth was employed in Ireland, presumably through the interest of his cousin George Monck, first duke of Albemarle [q. v.] On 18 Oct. 1660 he was appointed 'clerk of the first-fruits in Ireland,' was knighted about the same time, and on 18 Feb. 1660–1 was created a baronet in consideration of his having 'liberally and generously provided and sustained thirty men for three years for the care and defence of Ireland' (*Patent Roll*,

13 Car. II, pt. i. No. 2). In 1663 he was named as one of the Royal African Company (10 Jan.; *Cal. State Papers*, America and West Indies, p. 121). In that year he was in Jamaica, and sent home a survey and description of the island (*ib.* p. 177). In 1664, on the appointment of his brother as governor of Jamaica, he returned to England, and for the next two or three years was employed as agent for the colony (*ib.* 13 Oct., 29 Nov. 1664, 20 Feb. 1665, 1 March, 21 Aug. 1666, &c.) On 30 June 1666 he was recommended by the Duke of Albemarle for the embassy at Constantinople, as one 'who was bred up in the country, knows the language, and was formerly desired by the Turkey Company for the employment' (*ib.* Dom.) The recommendation was unsuccessful, and on 10 Nov. following he was appointed lieutenant-governor of the island of Providence, or Santa Catalina, then newly recovered by a party of buccaneers (*ib.* America and West Indies; cf. Morgan, Sir Henry). Having been detained for eleven weeks at Barbados, 'through the ignorance rather than the malice of Lord Willoughby,' he did not reach Jamaica till 15 July 1667, when he found that Santa Catalina had been recaptured by the Spaniards (*ib.* 29, 30 July, 3 Aug.) He was then appointed by his brother lieutenant-general, deputy-governor, and chief judge of the admiralty court at Jamaica. His commissions appear to have lapsed with the supersession of Sir Thomas in June 1671, but he remained at Jamaica about his private business, and died there in January 1672–3 (*Addit. MS.* 27968, f. 30).

Modyford married Elizabeth, daughter and heiress of Sir Nicholas Stanning of Maristow, Devonshire, and by her had issue a son, Thomas, who succeeded to the baronetcy, but died a minor in 1678, when the title became extinct. He left also two daughters, Grace and Mary. Elizabeth, lady Modyford, died 30 March 1724 at the age of ninety-four, and was buried in the church of Bickleigh, Devonshire.

[Calendars of State Papers, Domestic and Colonial; Burke's Extinct Baronetcies; Chester's Westminster Registers, p. 194; Marshall's Genealogist, v. 149.] J. K. L.

MODYFORD, Sir THOMAS (1620?–1679), governor of Jamaica, son of John Modyford, mayor of Exeter in 1622, and of Maria, daughter of Thomas Walker, alderman of Exeter, was probably born about 1620. Sir James Modyford [q. v.] was his brother. He was a 'kinsman' or 'cousin' of George Monck, duke of Albemarle, though the exact relationship does not appear (*Addit. MS.* 27968, f. 164 *b*; *Cal. State Papers*, America and West Indies, 16 Feb. 1652, 25 Jan. 1661, 31 Aug. 1663, &c.) He was a barrister of Lincoln's Inn (*ib.* March 1661, No. 40; *ib.* Dom. 18 Feb. 1664), served in the king's army during the civil war, and in June 1647 sailed for Barbados. There he settled down as a planter, buying a half share of an estate for 7,000*l.* (Ligon, *A True and Exact History of the Island of Barbados*), and seems to have immediately taken a prominent place in the little community. When the island proclaimed Charles II and established the church of England, Colonel Modyford figured as a zealous royalist; and on 5 Nov. 1651, as a member of council, signed the royalist declaration in reply to the summons of Sir George Ayscue (*Cal. State Papers*, America and West Indies, 13 Nov. 1651). Afterwards, however, he personally made his peace with Ayscue, and won over his regiment to the side of the parliament, so that, mainly through his defection or treachery, Lord Willoughby, the royalist governor, was obliged to yield (*ib.* 7 Jan., 16 Feb. 1652, August? 1653, p. 416). Ayscue renewed Modyford's commission as colonel; but he was naturally looked on with suspicion by the zealous parliamentarians, and in the course of 1653 was deprived of his command by Governor Searle. On his petition to Cromwell, however, he was ordered to be restored, and to be put in the council (*ib.* 14 Jan. 1654). And so he continued till the Restoration. His name frequently occurs in the minutes of council. On 20 March 1654–5 he handed to General Venables [q.v.] a protestation 'that he utterly abhorred and abjured the interest of the Stuarts' (Macray, *Cal. of Clarendon State Papers*, iii. 26). On 16 July 1660 he had received a commission as governor of Barbados, dated 24 April 1660, on which Searle resigned without dispute and the king was proclaimed (*Cal. State Papers*, America and West Indies). Meantime, on 9 July the king had signed a commission appointing Lord Willoughby governor of Barbados and the adjacent islands. The announcement of this reached the island on 17 Dec., and though Modyford had an intimation that it would not be acted on, he judged it right to resign (*ib.*, Modyford to the Duke of Albemarle, 25 Jan. 1661, No. 6). He was then made speaker of the assembly; and though charges of treason were alleged against him, and letters written denouncing 'his treachery in betraying the island to the usurper, and his persecution of royalists ever since' (*ib.* 29 March 1661, No. 60), the interest of Albemarle bore down all opposition and maintained him in his post till, on 15 Feb. 1664, he was appointed governor of Jamaica, with very full powers and instructions to take as many settlers from Barbados as were willing to accompany him (*ib.* Nos. 656, 664, 687, &c.) At the same time, 18 Feb., he was created a baronet (*ib.* Dom.)

In June he arrived in Jamaica, and for the next seven years identified himself with the island. It was admitted that under his rule the colony made rapid advances in material prosperity; but it was alleged that he encouraged pirates, and that the wealth which flowed into the island was mainly the ill-gotten spoils of piracy, spent in filthy debauchery. Modyford's friends asserted, on the other hand, that while pirates were duly hanged, the buccaneers or privateers were honest fellows, who, though occasionally too convivial, rendered good service to the king and the colony, and their gains were not nearly so large as was reported. According to Modyford, the most 'intemperate' men on the island were the old army officers, 'who, from strict saints, were turned the most debauched devils.' 'The Spaniards,' he wrote, 'wondered much at the sickness of our people, until they knew of the strength of their drinks, but then wondered more that they were not all dead' (*ib.* America and West Indies, 16 Nov. 1665). It is quite certain that the deeds which rendered the name of buccaneer terrible and famous were performed under valid commissions from the governor in council, who, in the king's name, received a fifteenth of their prize-money (see MORGAN, SIR HENRY; *ib.* 28 June 1671). These commissions, Modyford argued, were rendered necessary by the aggressions of the Spaniards who had landed in Jamaica, had captured English vessels, and were preparing for hostilities on a grander scale. The king's instructions empowered him 'on extraordinary cases, by the council's advice, to use extraordinary remedies' (*ib.* June? 1671, No. 578; cf. also 1 March 1666, No. 1144, 14 Jan. 1667, No. 1383, 23 Aug. 1669, No. 103, &c.)

So long as the first Duke of Albemarle was living his great interest supported Modyford. But after Albemarle's death, in January 1669–70, in order to give effect to 'the treaty for establishing peace in America concluded at Madrid on 8 July 1670,' Modyford's commission was revoked in December, and Sir Thomas Lynch [q. v.], appointed to supersede him, was ordered to send him home under arrest (*ib.* Nos. 367, 405, 602), on the charge of 'making war and committing depredations and acts of hostility upon the subjects and territories of the King of Spain in America, contrary to his Majesty's express order and command.' In the middle of June Modyford received Lynch with 'abundance of civility,' but on 12 Aug. he was inveigled on board the Assistance frigate, and there told that he was to be sent home a prisoner. He was allowed to go to England in one of his own ships, though in charge of a guard (*ib.* Nos. 587–8, 604, 655). He arrived about the middle of November, and was committed to the Tower (*ib.* Nos. 653–4, 17 Nov. 1671). On 14 Aug. 1672 he was ordered to have the liberty of the Tower, but he seems to have been still a prisoner at the end of 1674. It is not improbable that he was released and went out to Jamaica with Sir Henry Morgan in 1675. He died at Jamaica, and was buried in the cathedral church at Spanish Town on 2 Sept. 1679.

Modyford married, about 1640, Elizabeth, daughter of Lewin Palmer of Devonshire. She died on 12 Nov. 1668—of, it is said, the plague, brought by Morgan from Portobello (*The Present State of Jamaica*, p. 40)—leaving a daughter, Elizabeth, and two sons, of whom Thomas, the elder, survived his father little more than a month. The younger, Charles, succeeded to the baronetcy, which became extinct, with the third generation, in 1703.

[Calendars of State Papers, North America and West Indies; Addit. MSS. 12408, 27968; New History of Jamaica, 1740; Present State of Jamaica, 1683; Long's Hist. of Jamaica, 1774; Archer's Monumental Inscriptions of the British West Indies; Davis's Cavaliers and Roundheads of Barbadoes; Hatton Correspondence (Camd. Soc.), i. 56, 108.] J. K. L.

MOELES, BALDWIN OF (*d.* 1100?). [See BALDWIN.]

MOELMUD, DYFNWAL (*fl.* 500), Northern British prince, appears in the tenth-century genealogies of Harleian MS. 3859 (*Cymmrodor*, ix. 174) as a grandson of Coel Odebog. This is the sole reference to him which can be called historical. In later Welsh literature he plays a purely mythical part. He becomes the primitive legislator of the Britons, the deviser of all early British institutions. In this capacity he appears in the narrative of Geoffrey of Monmouth, who makes him the son of Cloten, king of Cornwall, and says that the laws drawn up by him were still in use among the English. Geoffrey's account is accepted by the compiler of the 'Venedotian Code,' who flourished about 1220; according to this writer, Hywel the Good, while altering greatly the old laws of Dyfnwal, left untouched the primitive land measurements (*Ancient Laws of Wales*, 1841 edit. i. 184). Dyfnwal is not mentioned in the two earlier sets of 'Historical Triads,' but is prominent in the third, having a place assigned him among the Columns, the Mighty Binders, the Primitive Instructors, and the Benign Monarchs of the isle of Britain (*Myvyrian Archaiology*, 2nd edition, pp. 400, 404, 406, 407). About the time when this series of 'Triads' was composed, viz., in the sixteenth century, the legislator's fame stood so high as to induce a Welsh antiquary to give the name 'The Triads of Dyfnwal Moelmud' to the collection of legal maxims in which he had embodied his views as to ideal social relations in Wales. These 'Triads' form book xiii. in Mr. Aneurin Owen's edition of the Welsh laws. Attempts have been made to show that they contain remnants of ancient tradition (e.g. by Peter Roberts in an appendix to his translation of the 'Chronicle of the Kings of Britain,' 1811), but they are beyond doubt modern in form and substance. Professor Rhys treats even Dyfnwal himself as an entirely mythical person, classing him with the dark or Chthonian divinities of the Celtic pantheon (*Celtic Heathendom*, p. 449; *Arthurian Legend*, pp. 261, 394).

[Genealogies in Harleian MS. 3859; Ancient Welsh Laws, 1841 edit.; Geoffrey of Monmouth; Historical Triads in Myvyrian Archaiology, 2nd edit.] J. E. L.

MOELS or MOLIS, NICHOLAS DE (*fl.* 1250), seneschal of Gascony, was perhaps a native of Hampshire. His parentage is unknown; but a Roger de Molis occurs in the reign of Stephen. Nicholas de Moels is first mentioned as being in the royal service in September 1215, and again in March 1217 (*Cal. Rot. Claus.* i. 229, 301). In January 1224 he is said to be going abroad on the royal service, and in the following year he was sent as a royal messenger to Cologne, in connection with the mission of Walter Mauclerk [q. v.] (*ib.* ii. 11; SHIRLEY, i. 253, 259). In August 1226 Moels was despatched as messenger to the king's brother, Earl Richard, in Poitou, and in the following March is spoken of as being still in Gascony (*Cal. Rot. Claus.* ii. 133–4, 179 *b*). From 1228 to 1232 he was sheriff of Hampshire and custos of Winchester Castle. In May 1230 he was with the king in Brittany, and was sent by him on a mission to Hugh, count of Marche, and his wife, Queen Isabella, the king's mother. In 1234 Moels was again sheriff of Hampshire, and in the same year had charge of the Channel Islands. From 1239 to 1241 he was sheriff of Yorkshire, and in 1241 was guardian of the bishopric of Durham during a vacancy (*Cal. Documents relating to Scotland,* i. 1539). In 1242 Moels accompanied the king to Poitou, and was sent with Ralph FitzNicholas on an unsuccessful mission to Louis IX at Frontenay, for the purpose of arranging a truce. In the following year, about midsummer, Henry appointed Moels as seneschal of Gascony (MATT. PARIS, iv. 244, 254; *Fœdera*, i. 253). Moels was in this capacity employed at the siege of Gramont, near Bidache, in August. Trouble was already impending with Thibaut, king of Navarre, who in the following year threatened Bayonne. Eventually, in the autumn of 1244, Moels defeated the king (*ib.* i. 225; SHIRLEY, ii. 41; MATT. PARIS, iv. 396). The only other known incident of his seneschalship is a conflict with Amigot de Garro, a Gascon robber-lord, who had captured certain messengers whom Moels had sent to Thibaut. Amigot, whose castle was seized by Moels in punishment, was afterwards taken into favour by Simon de Montfort (BÉMONT, pp. 39, 305–6). Moels appears to have returned to England in the early part of 1245, and later in that year was employed in Wales as governor of Cardigan and Caermarthen Castles. On 22 Jan. 1251, on the complaint of the Gascons against Simon de Montfort, he was despatched with Drogo de Barentin to investigate the truth of the charges. The general tenor of their report was favourable to the earl (*ib.* pp. 45, 268–77). Moels was still in Gascony in June 1252, when he was appointed a conservator of the truce there in conjunction with Rocelin de Fos (SHIRLEY, ii. 391). In 1254, when warden of Oxford Castle, Moels gave to Henry de Hanna, the provincial of the Carmelites, a house in Oxford, which was the first establishment of that order in the university (WOOD, *City of Oxford*, ii. 415, Oxf. Hist. Soc.) In 1257 he was engaged in the Welsh war. In January 1258 he was made constable of Dover and warden of the Cinque ports, and in March sheriff of Kent, with the charge of the castles of Rochester and Canterbury. After the parliament of Oxford, Moels, as a supporter of the king, was removed from his office as warden, but retained the castles of Rochester and Canterbury (*Annales Monastici*, i. 453). In 1261 he had charge of Sherborne Castle, and in 1263 of Corfe Castle. Probably he died not much later. Matthew Paris (iv. 254) calls him 'miles strenuissimus et circumspectus.'

Moels married before 1231 Hawyse, daughter of James de Newmarch, in whose right he held Cadbury in Somerset, and Sapperton in Gloucestershire. He had two sons, Roger, and James who was educated with the king's son Edward. Roger de Moels fought in the Welsh wars of Edward I, and dying in 1285 was succeeded by his son John (1259–1310), who was summoned to parliament from 1293 to 1310. John was succeeded by three sons, Nicholas, Roger, and John, on the death of the last of whom, in 1338, the barony fell into abeyance between his two daughters.

[Matthew Paris; Shirley's Royal and Historical Letters of the Reign of Henry III (both in the Rolls Series); Cal. of Close Rolls (the Close Rolls include a number of references to Colinus as well as to Nicholas de Moels: it seems clear that the two are identical, cf. i. 599); Fœdera (Record edition); Bémont's Simon de Montfort; Dugdale's Baronage, i. 619–20; Coll. Top. et Gen. iv. 360–1; Balasque et Dulaurens' Études Historiques sur la ville de Bayonne, ii. 84–90.] C. L. K.

MOETHEU, THOMAS (1530–1620?), Welsh bard. [See Jones, Thomas.]

MOFFAT, ROBERT (1795–1883), missionary, was born at Ormiston, East Lothian, on 21 Dec. 1795. His father was a customhouse officer; the family of his mother, Ann Gardiner, had lived for several generations at Ormiston. In 1797 the Moffats moved to Portsay, near Banff, and in 1806 to Carronshore, near Falkirk. Robert went at an early age to the parish school, and when he was eleven was sent, with an elder brother, to Mr. Paton's school at Falkirk. In 1809 he was apprenticed to a gardener, John Robertson of Parkhill, Polmont. During his apprenticeship he attended evening classes, learned to play a little on the violin, and took some lessons at the anvil. In 1811 his father was transferred to Inverkeithing, and the following year, on the expiration of his apprenticeship, Robert obtained a situation at Donibristle, Lord Moray's seat near Aberdour, Fifeshire. At the end of 1813 he was engaged as under-gardener by Mr. Leigh of High Leigh, Cheshire. He had received much religious training at home, and while in Leigh's service he came under the influence of some earnest Wesleyan methodists, which determined him to devote his life to religious work. After attending a missionary meeting at Warrington, held by William Roby of Manchester, he decided, if possible, to be a missionary. On 23 Dec. 1815 he left Leigh's service for the nursery garden of James Smith, a pious nonconformist Scotsman from Perthshire, who had settled at Dukinfield, near Manchester. There Moffat contrived to study under the guidance of Roby, who interested himself on his behalf with the directors of the London Missionary Society. His master had married in 1792 Mary Gray of York, a member of the church of England, and two of their sons became missionaries. During his stay at Dukinfield Moffat became engaged to their only daughter, Mary, who, born in 1795 at New Windsor, now part of Salford, had been educated at the Moravian school at Fairfield, and had formed strong religious convictions. But her parents at this time objected to the match.

In the summer of 1816 Moffat was accepted by the society as a missionary, and on 30 Sept. was set apart for the ministry in the Surrey Chapel, London. On 18 Oct. he embarked in the ship Alacrity, Captain Findlay, for South Africa, and arrived at Cape Town on 13 Jan. 1817. Moffat was destined for Namaqualand, beyond the border of the colony, but permission to go thither was temporarily refused by the governor for political reasons, and Moffat went to Stellenbosch to learn Dutch. On 22 Sept. permission to cross the frontier was given, and Moffat started for the interior with some other missionaries. Moffat went to the chief Afrikaner's kraal at Vredeburg. He stayed in Namaqualand a little over a year, living like a native. A long expedition with Afrikaner to the north convinced Moffat that there was no hope of forming a missionary settlement in that quarter. He also made a journey to the eastward, across the great Kalahari desert, as far as Griquatown and Lattakoo. On his return he found himself the only European in Namaqualand, as Mr. Ebner, a missionary who had accompanied him to Vredeburg from Cape Town, and was the only other European north of the Orange river, was leaving the country.

At the beginning of 1819 Moffat determined to take Afrikaner, who had become a true convert, to Cape Town. A few years before a price had been set by the government on Afrikaner's head; his conversion brought home to the authorities that the mission had solved a political difficulty, and did something to enlist their sympathy. In December 1819 Mary Smith, who had overcome her parents' objection to her marriage with Moffat, arrived at Cape Town and married him on 27 Dec. 1819 in St. George's church, Cape Town. For fifty years Mary Moffat shared all her husband's hardships and trials, and her name must be associated with his among the pioneers of South African mission work.

A deputation from the London Missionary Society, consisting of Dr. Philip and John Campbell, arrived at Cape Town at the close of 1819. They appointed Moffat superintendent at Lattakoo, and he set out early in 1820 with his wife, arriving at Lattakoo, about one hundred miles from Griquatown, at the end of March. Shortly after their arrival they made an expedition to the westward, along the bed of the Kuruman river, among the villages of the Botswanas. On their return to Lattakoo they were informed by letter from Cape Town that permission had not been granted for them to remain there, and they went to Griquatown, then inhabited by a mixed multitude of Griquas, Korannas, Hottentots, Bakwanas, and Bushmen, to assist Mr. Helm in organising the mission there. On permission arriving from Cape Town the Moffats returned to Lattakoo 17 May 1821, and devoted themselves to mission work and to acquiring a knowledge of the language.

Troubles, however, soon began. The warlike Matabele tribe, under Mosilikatse, climbed the Kwathlamba range and drove out many of the Bapedi and Bakwana tribes, the fugitives pouring down on the western Bakwanas. Moffat, who had heard only vague rumours of what was going on, made a reconnaissance to the north-east. On arriving at Mosite, after some days of travel, he learnt that the Mantatees, as the fugitive tribes were called, were in actual possession of the Baralong towns close to the eastward of the mission, and were on their way to Lattakoo. Moffat hurried home, warned his own people, and hastened to Griquatown to seek the aid of the Griquas. By the time the government commissioner, Mr. Melville, and the Griqua chief Waterboer, with one hundred men, reached the station, the Mantatees had occupied Letakong, only thirty-six miles away. The two Europeans, Moffat and Melville, with Waterboer and his men, met them halfway at the Matlwaring river, and after vain attempts to get speech with them were driven back, and obliged in self-defence to fight. About five hundred Mantatees were killed and some thousands put to flight. The mission was saved, the invaders retiring never to return. Moffat had distinguished himself by his devotion to the wounded and the women and children, and he gained a personal ascendency which he never lost over the tribes that he had protected.

Circumstances, however, still appeared so threatening that Moffat sent his wife and children for a time to Griquatown, and towards the end of the year (1823) he took them a two months' journey to Cape Town, where he obtained supplies, and conferred with Dr. Philip about the removal of the mission from Lattakoo to Kuruman. They returned to their station in May (1824). Moffat went on 1 July on a long-promised visit to Makaba, the chief of the Bangwaketsi, at Kwakwe. During his absence his wife was in a position of great anxiety. A horde of evil characters, marauding runaways of mixed blood, from the Cape Colony, with Korannas, Bushmen, and Namaquas, had established themselves in the mountains to the westward of Griquatown, and had been joined by renegade Griquas, mounted and armed with guns, who resented the discipline of Waterboer and the other Griqua chiefs. So great was the disquiet and the fear of an attack on Lattakoo that a second time Moffat and his family took refuge at Griquatown.

Early in 1825, the western banditti having retired, the Moffats commenced to lay out the new station at Kuruman, to which they had been ordered to remove from Lattakoo. They raised three temporary dwellings, when again a band of armed and mounted marauders made their appearance. The natives at the old station gave way before them, losing nearly all their cattle, and could not be persuaded to return, but drifted away eastward to the Hart or Kolong river. With a dwindled population the work of the missionaries was less onerous, and Moffat commenced his first regular effort to lay the foundation of a Sechwana literature. A spelling-book was prepared and sent to Cape Town to be printed. In 1826 steady progress was made in the erection of the mission buildings, and Moffat devoted all his spare time to manual labour. In 1827 the station at Kuruman was sufficiently advanced to permit Moffat to perfect himself in the Sechwana language, by spending a couple of months in the encampment of Bogacho, a chief of the Baralongs, on the border of the Kalahari desert. On his return the marauders again appeared, and the missionaries had a third time to retire temporarily to Griquatown.

From the commencement stolid indifference to the work had reigned among the natives. But the missionaries worked on, mainly encouraged by the sanguine temper of Mary Moffat. In 1829 the desired awakening came. The services were crowded, the schools flourished, and gradually and with much caution some of the natives were admitted to baptism, and a permanent church and a schoolhouse were erected by the natives without cost to the society. Moffat at length enjoyed sufficient leisure to translate into Sechwana the Gospel of St. Luke and a selection of other scriptures. The same year Mosilikatse, chief of the Matabele, sent messengers to inquire into the manners and teaching of the white men at Kuruman. Moffat showed them every attention, and when difficulties arose as to their return through a country occupied by tribes who both feared and hated Mosilikatse, he escorted them home to the banks of the Oori, a long journey through a country which, although it had once contained a dense population, had been so ravaged that it had become the home of wild beasts and venomous reptiles. Moffat stayed eight days with Mosilikatse, by whom he was received with many tokens of friendship; he returned to Kuruman after an absence of two months.

In June 1830 the Moffats visited Grahamstown to put their elder children to school, and, leaving his wife to follow by sea, Moffat hurried to Cape Town, riding some four hundred miles in nine days, to start the printing of such parts of the New Testament as had been translated. At Cape Town he could find no printing office able to undertake the work. But the Government put at their disposal their own printing office, although unable to supply workmen, and Moffat and another missionary, Mr. Edwards, with such guidance as the man in charge could give them, performed the work themselves. The exertion, however, brought on an illness, and Moffat had to be carried on board ship on his return journey to Algoa Bay. He and his wife reached Kuruman at the end of June 1831, taking with them a printing press.

Early in 1835 a scientific expedition, headed by Dr. Andrew Smith, arrived from Cape Colony, and Moffat accompanied them in May to Mosilikatse's headquarters, to open a way for mission work among the chief's people, and to obtain timber to roof in the church at Kuruman. In 1836 Moffat, after seeing his wife across the Vaal river on her way to pay a visit in Cape Town, made a detour on his return to Kuruman to visit Mothibi, the old chief of the Batlaping. His journey was well timed, and he was cheered by the interest taken in his teaching. Some American missionaries arrived, who were sent to Mosilikatse, and a volume of 443 pages of translation of scripture lessons into Sechwana was completed before his wife's return in July.

In 1837 the emigration of Dutch farmers disaffected to British rule commenced, and a party of them came into collision with Mosilikatse and the Matabele. The American mission station was destroyed, and a great booty in cattle swept away. Mosilikatse and his people disappeared the following year into the unknown region south of the Zambesi, and missionary work was greatly retarded. Towards the end of 1838 Moffat went to Cape Town with his family, taking with him the complete translation of the New Testament into the Sechwana language, and, sailing for England, arrived in London in June 1839. While the translation was in the press, Moffat commenced a translation of the Psalms, and stayed in England to complete it. It was printed and bound up with the New Testament. He also revised the scripture lessons, of which an edition of six thousand was printed, and wrote 'Labours and Scenes in South Africa,' which was published in the spring of 1842, and met with a very favourable reception. In addition to his literary labours, Moffat was much engaged in preaching and lecturing all over the country on behalf of the London Missionary Society. In 1840 Moffat met David Livingstone in London, and was the means of securing his services for the Bakwana mission. On 30 Jan. 1843, after valedictory services, addresses, and presentations, the Moffats sailed again for South Africa. While waiting at Bethelsdorp in April for their heavy baggage, Moffat made a journey on horseback to Kaffraria, and visited all the eastern stations of the Missionary Society. The Moffats and their party were met by Livingstone at the Vaal river, and reached Kuruman in December.

The mission staff having been increased, the younger missionaries were sent some two or three hundred miles further inland, to various tribes of the Bakwanas. Livingstone, who went to Mabotsa, returned to Kuruman after an accident, was nursed by the Moffats, and married their eldest daughter Mary in 1844. The Livingstones then went to Chonwane, and to this and the other distant stations Kuruman was a centre of administration from which supplies and assistance were drawn. For several years subsequent to 1845 Moffat was hard at work translating into Sechwana the book of Isaiah, and other parts of the Old Testament, and the 'Pilgrim's Progress,' which were published in the colony. He also visited some of the Bakwana tribes. In May 1854, accompanied by two young Englishmen—James Chapman and Samuel Edwards—Moffat crossed the edge of the Kalahari desert, found Sechele and his people among the precipices of Lethubaruba, passed over 120 miles of desert to Shoshong, the residence of Sekhomi, chief of the Bamangwato tribe, then by compass over an unknown and uninhabited country in a north-easterly direction for eighteen days, until he reached Mosilikatse and the Matabele. The chief was almost helpless with dropsy, but accompanied Moffat in a further journey to the outposts of the tribe, in the hope of hearing news of Livingstone. The obstacles at last proved insuperable, and Moffat had to content himself with an undertaking from the chief, which he kept, that he would take charge of the supplies for Livingstone, and deliver them to the Makololo. Moffat made his return journey of seven hundred miles to Kuruman without incident.

In 1857 the translation of the Old Testament was finished, and the whole Bible in the Sechwana language was printed and distributed. In the same year, by order of the home authorities of the mission, Moffat returned to the Matabeles and obtained the chief's consent to establish a station among them. There followed a meeting with Livingstone at the Cape to define their spheres of labour, and after some delay at Kuruman, owing to quarrels between the Boers and the natives, during which Moffat printed a new hymn-book, he, with three companions, including his younger son, reached the headquarters of the Matabele chief Mosilikatse at the end of October 1859. The chief was at first far from cordial, having heard of the doings of the Transvaal Boers, who so often followed in the wake of the missionaries. Eventually, however, in December a station was formed at Inyati, and Moffat worked hard at the forge and the bench to help forward the necessary buildings, until in June the mission was sufficiently established for him to leave it to itself.

Failing health and domestic troubles led Moffat to finally leave Africa for England on 10 June 1870. He was most warmly received. His wife died at Brixton in January 1871, and Moffat subsequently until his death travelled about the United Kingdom preaching and advocating the cause of missions. He also revised the Sechwana translation of the Old Testament. In 1872 he was made a D.D. of Edinburgh. In 1873 he settled in Knowle Road, Brixton, South London, and was presented with upwards of 5,000*l.* by his friends. In 1874 he went to Southampton to meet and identify the remains of Livingstone, and was present at the funeral in Westminster Abbey. In August 1876 he was present at the unveiling of the statue of Livingstone in Edinburgh, when Queen Victoria, who was at Holyrood, sent for him and gave him a short interview. In April 1877, at the invitation of the French Missionary Society, he visited Paris, and through Theodore Monod addressed four thousand French children. In November 1879 he removed to Leigh, near Tunbridge. He was deeply interested in the Transvaal war, and, believing in the advantages of British rule for the natives, he was greatly shocked at the triumph of the Boers and the acquiescence of the English government in defeat. On 7 May 1881 he was entertained at the Mansion House, London, at a dinner given by the lord mayor in his honour, which the Archbishop of Canterbury, representatives of both houses of parliament, and all the leading men of the religious and philanthropic world attended. In 1882 he visited the Zulu chief Ketchwayo, then in England, and was able to converse with one of his attendants in the Sechwana language. Moffat died peacefully at Leigh on 8 Aug. 1883, and was buried at Norwood cemetery beside the remains of his wife. A monument was erected to his memory at Ormiston, his birthplace in East Lothian.

Moffat's eldest son Robert, and his daughter, Mrs. Livingstone, both died in 1862. Another daughter Bessie married in October 1861 the African missionary, Roger Price. His second daughter married Jean Frédoux, a French missionary, who was killed in 1866, leaving his widow and seven children unprovided for.

Tall and manly, with shaggy hair and beard, clear cut features and piercing eyes, Moffat's exterior was one to impress native races, while his childlike spirit and modest and unselfish nature insured a commanding influence. He was the father and pioneer of South African mission work, and will be remembered as a staunch friend of the natives, an industrious translator, a persevering teacher, and a skilful organiser.

Moffat was the author of: 1. 'Translation of the Gospel of St. Luke into Sechwana,' 12mo, 1830. 2. 'Translation into Sechwana of parts of the Old Testament,' 8vo, 1831. 3. 'A Book of Hymns in Sechwana, Schlapi dialect, 80 pages,' Mission Press, Kuruman, 2nd edition, 1838. 4. 'Africa, or Gospel Light shining in the midst of Heathen Darkness, a Sermon on Isaiah ix. 2, preached before the Directors of the London Missionary Society, &c., with Notes,' 8vo, London, 1840. 5. 'Missionary Labours and Scenes in Southern Africa,' 4th edition, London, 8vo, 1842; 11th thousand, with portrait, 8vo, London, 1846. 6. 'Mr. Moffat and the Bechwanas,' 32mo, 1842. 7. 'Visit to the Children of Manchester,' 32mo, 1842. 8. 'Hymns in the Sechwana Language,' Religious Tract Society, 12mo, London, 1843. 9. 'Rivers of Waters in Dry Places; an Account of the Introduction of Christianity into South Africa, and of Mr. Moffat's Missionary Labours,' 8vo, 1863; new edition, 1867; Philadelphia, 1869. 10. 'New Testament translated into Sechwana,' 8vo, 1872. 11. 'The Bible translated into Sechwana,' 8vo, 1872.

[The Lives of Robert and Mary Moffat, by their son, John Smith Moffat, with Portraits, Maps, and Illustrations, 8vo, London, 1885; new edition, 1886; popular edition, 1889; Heroes of the Desert; The Story of the Lives and Labours of Moffat and Livingstone, by Miss A. Manning, 8vo, 1875; new and enlarged edition, 1885; The Farewell Services of Robert Moffat,

&c., by Dr. John Campbell, 12mo, London, 1843; Life of Robert Moffat, by J. Marrat; Life by D. J. Deane; Life by E. F. Cherry; A Life's Labour in South Africa, the Story of the Life Work of Robert Moffat, with Portrait, London, Aylesbury, 8vo, printed 1871; Moffat the Missionary, &c., 8vo, London, 1846; Robert Moffat, an Example of Missionary Heroism, 8vo, London, 1878.] R. H. V.

MOFFATT, JOHN MARKS (*d.* 1802), antiquary, was minister of a congregation of protestant dissenters at the Forest Green, Avening, Gloucestershire, at Nailsworth in the same county, and lastly at Malmesbury, Wiltshire. He died at Malmesbury on 25 Dec. 1802 (*Gent. Mag.* 1803, pt. i. p. 193), leaving a widow and seven children.

His writings are: 1. 'The Duty and Interest of every private Person and the Kingdom at large at the present juncture,' 8vo, 1778. 2. 'The Protestant's Prayer-Book . . . to which are added Hymns,' &c., 8vo, Bristol, 1783. 3. 'The History of the Town of Malmesbury and of its ancient Abbey,' 8vo, Tetbury, 1805, published posthumously for the benefit of the author's family.

[Monthly Mag. 1803, pt. i. pp. 96, 197; Watt's Bibl. Brit.; Reuss's Alphabetical Register, 1790–1803.] G. G.

MOFFETT, MOUFET, or MUFFET, THOMAS (1553–1604), physician and author, born in 1553, probably in the parish of St. Leonard's, Shoreditch, was of Scottish descent, and the second son of Thomas Moffett, citizen and haberdasher of London, who was also free of the Girdlers' Company. His mother was Alice Ashley of Kent (*Ashmole MS.* 799, f. 130). Both the physician and his father should, it seems, be distinguished from a third Thomas Moffett, who in January 1575 was employed at Antwerp on political business, and endeavoured under the directions of Burghley and Leicester to win the confidence of the Earl of Westmorland and other English rebels in exile, in order to induce them to quit the Low Countries (*Cal. Hatfield MSS.* ii. 86–93). This man was reported to be too reckless a dice-player to satisfy his employers (*ib.*), and he is doubtless the 'Captain Thomas Moffett' who petitioned Elizabeth in March 1589 for a license to export four hundred tuns of beer, on the ground that he had served Edward VI and Queen Mary in many countries (*Cal. State Papers*, Dom. 1581–90, p. 586).

An elder brother of the physician resided at Aldham Hall, Essex. PETER MOFFETT (*d.* 1617), apparently a younger brother, was rector of Fobbing, Essex, from 1592 till his death in the autumn of 1617 (NEWCOURT, *Repertorium*, ii. 268), and seems to have been author of 'The Excellencie of the Mysterie of Christ Jesus,' London, 1590, 8vo (dedicated to Margaret, countess of Cumberland, and Anne, countess of Warwick), and of 'A Commentarie upon the whole Booke of the Proverbs of Solomon,' London, 1596, 12mo (dedicated to Edward Russell, earl of Bedford).

After spending, it is said, five years at Merchant Taylors' School (FOSTER, *Alumni Oxon.*), Thomas matriculated as a pensioner of Trinity College, Cambridge, in May 1569, but migrated, 6 Oct. 1572, to Caius College, where he graduated B.A. While becoming an efficient classic, he studied medicine under Thomas Lorkin [q.v.] and John Caius (1510–1573) [q.v.] His fellow-students and friends included Peter Turner [q.v.], Timothy Bright [q.v.], and Thomas Penny [q.v.], who all distinguished themselves in medical science. During his undergraduate days he was nearly poisoned by eating mussels (*Health's Improvement*, p. 250; *Theatrum Insectorum*, p. 283, in English, p. 1107). Choosing to proceed M.A. from Trinity in 1576, he was expelled from Caius by Thomas Legge, the master [q.v.] In 1581 the latter was charged, among other offences, with having expelled Moffett without the fellows' consent. Wood's suggestion that Moffett was educated at Oxford appears to be erroneous (*Athenæ Oxon.* ed. Bliss, i. 574–5).

On leaving Cambridge Moffett went abroad. At Basle he attended the medical lectures of Felix Plater and Zwinger, and after defending publicly many medical theses there in 1578, he received the degree of M.D. In the same year he published at Basle (1578, 4to) two collections of his theses: one entitled 'De Anodinis Medicamentis,' the other 'De Venis Mesaraicis Obstrvctis ipsarvmqve ita affectarum Curatione,' with a dedication to Penny. A copy of the latter in the Cambridge University Library has an affectionate inscription in Moffett's autograph addressed to his old tutor Lorkin. In 1579 Moffett visited Italy and Spain; there he studied the culture of the silkworm, which he made the subject of a poem, and became an acute observer of all forms of insect life. He was at Nuremberg in July 1580, and frequently at Frankfort between the following October and the spring of 1582. Four letters which he addressed between 1580 and 1582 to Petrus Monavius are printed in Laurentius Scholz's 'Epistolarum Philosophicarum Volumen,' Frankfort, 1598.

Moffett, while on the continent, adopted with enthusiasm the Paracelsian system of medicine, and when he settled again in England he shared with John Hester [q. v.] the chief burden of upholding its principles there. He returned to Cambridge in 1582, and was incorporated M.D. In July he accompanied Peregrine Bertie, lord Willoughby [q. v.], to Elsinore, to invest King Frederick of Denmark with the order of the Garter. He notes that the court dinners lasted from seven to eight hours (*Health's Improvement*, p. 294), and that he made the acquaintance of Tycho Brahe and Peter Severinus. At the end of 1583 he completed in London, with a dedication to Severinus, his most elaborate exposition of his medical principles, 'De Jure et Præstantia Chemicorum Medicamentorum Dialogus Apologeticus' (Frankfort, 1584, 12mo; new edit. Ursel in Nassau, 1602, 8vo). In style Moffett sought to imitate Erasmus's 'Colloquia.' With this essay he printed five letters dated from London between February and April 1584—four addressed to 'Philalethes Germanus' and one to 'Endymion Luddipolensis.' The work attracted attention abroad and figured in Lazarus Zetzner's 'Theatrum Chemicum,' Strasburg, 8vo, 1613 (i. 63–90). Moffett subsequently illustrated his sobriety as an investigator by publishing a digest of Hippocrates, whose merits were unduly disparaged by many of the newer school of medicine to which Moffett belonged. This book he entitled 'Nosomantica Hippocratea sive Hippocratis Prognostica cuncta ex omnibus ipsius scriptis methodice digesta' (Frankfort, 1588, 8vo).

By 1588 Moffett had secured a good practice, at first apparently in Ipswich and afterwards in London. On 22 Dec. 1585 he was admitted a candidate of the College of Physicians, and on 29 Feb. 1588 a fellow, becoming censor in the same year. Among his early patients were Lady Penruddock and Sir Thomas and Edmund Knyvet of Norfolk. In July 1586 he and Penny attended during her last illness at Hansworth Anne Seymour, duchess of Somerset, widow of the protector, and they attested her will. Moffett seems to have first made the lady's acquaintance in early youth (*Theatrum Insectorum*, pp. 14, 21). In 1590 he was in attendance on Sir Francis Walsingham at Barn Elms, Surrey. Next year he was appointed physician to the forces serving in Normandy under the Earl of Essex; and on 6 Jan. 1591–2 he sent a note to the earl from Dieppe advising him to return to England (*Cal. Hatfield MSS.* iv. 174). On settling again in London, Moffett appears to have spent much time at court. He came to know Sir Francis Drake, who first showed him a flying-fish, 'milvus marinus' (*Health's Improvement*, p. 245); interested himself in the eccentricities of Woolmer, 'the foul feeder' (*ib.* pp. 123, 376), and was much patronised by Henry Herbert, second earl of Pembroke [q. v.], and his family. Mary Herbert [q. v.], the earl's wife, attracted by his cultured tastes, ultimately induced him to leave London for her own home in Wiltshire, and the latter part of his life was spent at or near Wilton as a pensioner of her husband. By the earl's influence he was elected M.P. for Wilton on 24 Oct. 1597. Walter Sweeper, when dedicating to William, third earl of Pembroke, his 'Brief Treatise' in 1622, wrote that 'that godly and learned phisitian and skilful mathematician Mr. Doctor Moffet, my most worthy and kind friend,' resided in Wilton House, but according to Aubrey, his patron soon gave him the neighbouring manor-house of Bulbridge for his residence (*Nat. Hist.* p. 89). He died there on 5 June 1604, and was buried in Wilton Church.

Moffett combined with his interests in science real literary aptitude. An 'epitaphe or epigram or elegies, done by Mr. Morfet,' was entered in the books of the Stationers' Company, by Edmund Bollifant, 15 Jan. 1588–9, but of this effort nothing else is known. Ten years later he published pseudonymously an interesting poem, embodying some of his observations in Italy and Spain. It is entitled 'The Silkwormes and their Flies; Lively described in verse, by T. M. a Countrie Farmar, and an Apprentice in Physicke. For the great benefit and enriching of England. Printed at London by V. S. for Nicholas Ling, and are to be sold at his shop at the West ende of Paules,' 1599, 4to. It is dedicated to the Countess of Pembroke, whom he describes as 'the most renowned patroness and noble nurse of learning,' and he notices in detail her literary labours (Collier, *Bibl. Cat.* i. 539). A copy is in the British Museum. Chamberlain wrote to Carleton, 1 March 1598–9, 'The Silkworme is thought to be Dr. Muffetts, and in mine opinion is no bad piece of poetrie' (Chamberlain, *Letters*, Camd. Soc., p. 47). 'Moffatts Silkwormes and their Flies' is highly praised in Nicholas Baxter's 'Sir Philip Sydney's Ourania,' 1606.

Moffett has been hastily identified with the T. M. who wrote the prose tracts 'Father Hubbards Tales,' and 'The Blacke Booke,' both issued in 1604, but his claim may be safely rejected [see Middleton, Thomas, 1570?–1627].

Two professional works by Moffett appeared posthumously. He had completed in 1590 a valuable work on the natural history of insects, partly compiled from the writings of Edward Wotton and Conrad Gesner, and from papers left to him by his friend Penny. He obtained permission to print it at the Hague on 24 May 1590, and wrote an elaborate dedication to the queen, but delays followed. Laurence Scholz of Frankfort is said to have roughly edited the manuscript in 1598. When James I ascended the English throne, Moffett readdressed the dedication to him. At Moffett's death the manuscript, still unprinted, came into the hands of Darnell, his apothecary, who sold it to Sir Theodore Mayerne [q. v.], and in 1634 Mayerne published it, dedicating it to Sir William Paddy, and describing Moffett as 'an eminent ornament of the Society of Physicians, a man of the more polite and solid learning, and renowned in most branches of science.' The original manuscript, with the two dedications addressed respectively to Elizabeth and to James I, is now in Sloane MS. 4014. The title of the printed volume ran: 'Insectorum sive Minimorum Animalium Theatrum . . . ad vivum expressis Iconibus super quingentis illustratum,' London, 1634, fol. Translated into English by J. R. as 'The Theater of Insects, or lesser living Creatures,' it was appended with the plates to Edward Topsell's 'History of Four-footed Beasts and Serpents' (1658). Haller in his notes on Herman Boerhaave's 'Methodus Studii Medici' praises the copiousness of the species described and the character of the engravings, and while admitting that Moffett gave credence to too many fabulous reports, acknowledged him to be the prince of entomologists before John Swammerdam (1637–1680).

Moffett's second posthumously issued book was: 'Health's Improvement; or Rules comprising and discovering the Nature, Method, and Manner of Preparing all sorts of Food used in this Nation. Written by that ever Famous Thomas Mvffett, Doctor of Phisick; corrected and enlarged by Christopher Bennet, Doctor of Physick and Fellow of the Colledg of Physitians of London,' London, 4to, 1655. This is a gossipy collection of maxims respecting diet, which Moffett intended to supplement by a similar work on 'drinks' (p. 221). It was probably compiled about 1595. Another edition was published in 12mo, 1746, with a life of the author, by William Oldys, and an introduction by R. James, M.D.

In Sloane MS. 4014 ('Theatrum Insectorum') a frontispiece engraved by William Rogers supplies a portrait of Moffett, and at the foot of the dedication he is described as 'Scot-Anglus.' Gesner, Edward Wotton, and Penny are depicted on the same plate.

By license dated 23 Dec. 1580 Moffett married, at St. Mary Cole Church, London, his first wife Jane, daughter of Richard Wheeler of a Worcestershire family, though she was described at the time of her marriage as a spinster of St. Ethelburgh's parish (Chester, *Marriage Licences*, ed. Foster, p. 952). She was buried at Wilton 18 April 1600. Moffett's second wife was a widow named Catherine Brown. She survived him, and to her children by her first husband—two sons Richard and Benedict, and two daughters Susan and Martha—Moffett left, with other bequests, his musical instruments, including a pair of virginals. Of his will (proved 20 Nov. 1604 and printed by Oldys) his brothers William and Thomas were overseers, and mention is made in it of his own daughter Patience and his 'dear friend and father in Christe, Mr. Parker.' His widow appears to have died at Calne, Wiltshire, in 1626. By her will, proved 26 June in that year, she left a portrait of Moffett and a book in his writing, probably 'Health's Improvement,' to his daughter Patience. The William Moffett (1607–1679), M.A. of Sidney Sussex College, Cambridge, and vicar of Edmonton from 1631 till his death (Newcourt, *Repert.* i. 600), who has verses prefixed to William Hodgson's 'Divine Cosmographie,' 1640, was doubtless the physician's nephew; he married, as a widower, aged 56, on 24 Oct. 1663, Mary Borne of Edmonton (Chester, *Marriage Licences*, ed. Foster, p. 931).

[Life by Oldys in Moffett's Health's Improvement, 1746; Cooper's Athenæ Cantabr.; Hoefer's Hist. de la Chimie, ii. 26; Moffett's Works; Joannes Antonius Van der Linden's De Scriptis Medicis, Amsterdam, 1637, p. 454; Hunter's manuscript Chorus Vatum (Addit. MS. 24487, ff. 441 sq.); Brit. Mus. Cat. s. v. 'Moufet;' Hazlitt's Bibliographical Handbooks.] S. L.

MOGFORD, THOMAS (1809–1868), painter, born at Exeter on 1 May 1809, was son of a veterinary surgeon at Northlew, Devonshire. He showed an early talent for drawing, as well as mechanics and chemistry, but eventually decided on painting in preference to engineering. He studied in Exeter under John Gendall [q. v.], and was articled for some years to him and to Mr. Cole. At the end of his appenticeship he married Cole's eldest daughter, and settled in Northernhay Place, Exeter. He sent three pictures to the Royal Academy in 1838, and three in 1839, including a full-length portrait of Sir Thomas Lethbridge, bart., with his horse and dog. About 1843 he removed to London, and subsequently exhibited at the Royal Academy portraits of E. H. Baily, R.A. (now in the possession of the Royal Academy), Samuel

Cousins, the engraver, Professor J. C. Adams, the astronomer, for Cambridge University (engraved by S. Cousins), Colonel Napier, the historian, and others. He also painted and exhibited 'The Sacrifice of Noah' and 'The Loves of the Angels' (Royal Academy 1846), the latter a very original work. Subsequently he removed to Guernsey, and practised almost entirely as a landscape painter, occasionally revisiting England and Exeter to paint portraits. Though for some years crippled by palsy through the effects of lead poisoning, he continued to paint up to the day of his death, which took place at Guernsey in 1868. He founded a school of painting in Guernsey.

[Pycroft's Art in Devonshire; Redgrave's Dict. of Artists; Royal Acad. Catalogues.]

L. C.

MOGRIDGE, GEORGE (1787–1854), miscellaneous writer, was born on 17 Feb. 1787, at Ashted, near Birmingham. His father, Mathias, a canal agent, was grandson of the Rev. Anthony Mogridge (*fl.* 1750) of Martley, Worcestershire, who is said to have written a book called 'The Conscience's Recorder,' and was descended from a John Mogridge, who in 1530 founded an almshouse at Exeter. George, after attending a school at Boarcote, was apprenticed to a japanner in Birmingham, and spent his leisure in reading Chaucer, Spenser, and Ossian. He subsequently entered into partnership with his elder brother in the japan trade at Birmingham, and wrote in the provincial journals under the pseudonym 'Jeremy Jaunt,' articles urging structural improvements in the town of Birmingham and the abolition of the slave trade. Failing in business, Mogridge took to writing for a livelihood. He died on 2 Nov. 1854 at Hastings, and was buried there in the All Saints' burial-ground.

Mogridge married, first, Elizabeth Bloomer (*d.* 1822?), by whom he had two sons and a daughter; by his second wife, Mary, he had one son. A portrait, drawn by A. Stanesby and engraved by D. J. Pound, is prefixed to 'George Mogridge: his Life, Character, and Writings,' by the Rev. C. Williams; another to the 'Memoir' of him published by the Tract Society. Mogridge's publications amount to nearly two hundred, and consist principally of tales and religious books for children, religious tracts and ballads. Several appeared under the various pseudonyms: 'Uncle Adam,' 'Old Alan Gray,' 'Ephraim Holding,' 'Uncle Newbury,' and 'Aunt Newbury.' Forty-four appeared under his best-known pseudonym of 'Old Humphrey,' and a series of 'Tales' under that of 'Peter Parley.' The assumption of the last name by Mogridge was naturally objected to by the American writer, Samuel Griswold Goodrich, who was the first to adopt it (*Recollections*, ii. 553–4; cf. also MARTIN, WILLIAM, 1801–1867). Of his religious ballads 'Thomas Brown' was the most popular. Besides these works Mogridge published nearly fifty under his own name, the principal of which are: 1. 'The Juvenile Culprits,' 1829, 12mo. 2. 'The Juvenile Moralists,' 1829, 12mo. 3. 'The Churchyard Lyrist,' 1832, 12mo. 4. 'The Encourager,' 1835, 16mo. 5. 'A Ramble in the Woods,' 1840 (?), 16mo. 6. 'Soldiers and Sailors,' 1842, 8vo. 7. 'The Old Sea Captain,' 1842, 16mo. 8. 'Footprints of Popery,' 1843, 12mo. 9. 'The Indians of North America,' 1843, 16mo. 10. 'The Country,' 1844, 12mo. 11. 'Learning to Think,' 1844 (?), 12mo. 12. 'Old Anthony's Hints to Young People,' 1844 (?), 18mo. 13. 'Points and Pickings of Information about China,' 1844, 8vo. 14. 'Learning to Feel,' 1845 (?), 12mo. 15. 'Rural Pickings,' 1846, 8vo. 16. 'Learning to Act,' 1846 (?), 12mo. 17. 'Helps for Every Hour,' 1846, 12mo. 18. 'Calls of Usefulness,' 1846, 12mo. 19. 'Wanderings in the Isle of Wight,' 1846, 16mo. 20. 'Loiterings among the Lakes of Cumberland and Westmoreland,' 1849, 16mo. 21. 'Things that have Wings,' 1851, 16mo. 22. 'Peter and Patty,' 1852, 16mo. 23. 'Aunt Rose and her Nieces,' 1852, 16mo. 24. 'Learning to Converse,' 1854, 18mo. His second wife, Mary, wrote 'Domestic Addresses,' and edited several of her husband's works.

[Brit. Mus. Cat.; Allibone's Dict. of English Lit. s. v. 'Humphrey, Old;' Williams's George Mogridge, his Life, Character, and Writings; Memoir published by the Tract Society; Gent. Mag. 1854, ii. 645; Goodrich's Recollections, ii. 553–4.]

A. F. P.

MOHL, MADAME MARY, whose maiden name was CLARKE (1793–1883), conversationalist, was born at Millbank Row, Westminster, in 1793, her father, Charles Clarke, being the son of an Irish Jacobite, and her mother, Elizabeth Hay, the daughter of Captain David Hay of Hopes, Haddingtonshire. In 1801 her mother and maternal grandmother took her to Toulouse, where she was placed in a convent school. Her mother, on becoming a widow, removed with her to Paris, and from 1831 to 1838 they occupied apartments adjoining those of Madame Récamier at the Abbaye-aux-Bois. For eighteen years Mary Clarke was a daily visitor of Madame Récamier, helping to amuse Chateaubriand in his closing years. She became engaged to Auguste Sirey, but his early death prevented the marriage and led to litigation with his family. She seems to have been next in love with Claude Fauriel, who, however, twenty-one years her senior, was accustomed to merely platonic attachments. He joined the Clarkes in Switzerland in 1823, accompanied them to Milan, where he introduced them to Manzoni, and parted from them at Venice. He appointed Mary his literary executor (1844), and he had long previously introduced to her Julius Mohl (1800–1876), the accomplished orientalist, whose indications led Botta to the discovery of the ruins of Nineveh. In 1847, after her mother's death, and after making him wait eighteen years, she married Mohl and found him a home, for he had till then been living with Ampère. Not liking to be thought older than her husband, she made a mystery of her age, and at her marriage appears to have given it, or at least allowed it to be entered, as thirty-nine (*Le Curieux*, August 1885). Her receptions in the Rue du Bac for nearly forty years attracted a galaxy of talent. Ticknor in 1837 found her circle, with one exception, the most intellectual in Paris, and in 1857 he describes her as 'talking as amusingly as ever, full of good-natured kindness, with a little subacid as usual to give it a good flavour.' Ampère thought her 'a charming mixture of French vivacity and English originality,' and her old-fashioned English and sometimes peculiar French gave an additional zest to conversation quite devoid of pedantry, albeit she was a great reader and good art connoisseur. She was an ardent Orleanist, never referring to Napoleon III except as 'cet homme' or 'le monsieur,' and was so outspoken as sometimes to give offence. The Queen of Holland called on her in 1867, and her long list of friends included Quinet, one of her earliest admirers, De Tocqueville, Guizot, Thiers, Mignet, Thierry, the Duc de Broglie, Scherer, and Renan. Dean Stanley first met at her dinner-table his future wife, Lady Augusta Bruce, and among her English visitors were Thackeray, Nassau Senior, Lord Houghton, and Mrs. Gaskell, who wrote while staying with her the greater part of her 'Wives and Daughters.' Lord John and Lady Russell visited them in 1870. On her husband's death in 1876 Madame Mohl discontinued her receptions, and her memory was latterly impaired. She died in Paris 14 May 1883, and was buried at Père-Lachaise. Her only, and that an anonymous, attempt at authorship was an article on Madame Récamier, in the 'National Review, 1860, expanded into a volume entitled 'Madame Recamier, with a Sketch of the History of Society in France,' London, 1862. Her husband's nieces have carried out her intention of commemorating him by endowing a bed at the Hospitalité de Nuit, Paris.

[Mrs. Simpson's Letters of J. and M. Mohl, London, 1887; N. W. Senior's Conversations, London, 1868–78; Life of Ticknor, Boston, 1876; K. O'Meara's Madame Mohl, London, 1886 (often inaccurate); Contemp. Review, 1878; Macmillan's Mag. 1883; Journal des Débats, 4 and 5 July 1885; R. E. Prothero's Dean Stanley, 1894.] J. G. A.

MOHUN, CHARLES, fourth Baron Mohun (1675?–1712), duellist, born, it is believed, in 1675, was eldest son of Charles, third baron (*d.* 1677), by Philippa, fourth daughter of Arthur Annesley, first earl of Anglesey. His grandfather, Warwick, second lord Mohun, died in 1667, and in 1668 an order in council was issued that the widow, Catherine, lady Mohun, the natural guardian of the family, should as a Roman catholic give security 'to breed her children in the protestant religion.' His parents were not married before 1673, at the earliest. On 2 Dec. 1674 they were reconciled after an estrangement, by the lady's father, the Earl of Anglesey, who took his son-in-law's view of the difference, and regretted that he lacked power to beat his daughter for 'an impudent baggage' (*Hist. MSS. Comm.* 13th Rep. App. pt. vi. pp. 275–7). When he was only a year old his father was mortally wounded while acting as second in a duel between Lord Cavendish and Lord Power, and after lingering for many months died on 1 Oct. 1677, and was buried in St. Giles's-in-the-Fields (*ib.* 12th Rep. App. vii. 130). Thenceforth the young peer appears to have been subjected to no control. On 7 Dec. 1692 he quarrelled over the dice with Lord Kennedy, and was confined to his lodgings; he nevertheless broke out with the aid of his constant ally, Edward Rich, earl of Warwick, and fought his first recorded duel, in which both parties were disarmed. Two days later he played a sorry part in the death of William Mountfort [q. v.] He and Captain Richard Hill, who was jealous of Mrs. Bracegirdle's supposed partiality for Mountfort, paraded Howard Street in company, with their swords drawn, lying in wait for the actor. The latter, upon his arrival, was greeted with drunken cordiality by Mohun. Mountfort, however, thought fit to remonstrate with his lordship upon the company he was keeping, whereupon, after a brief scuffle, Hill ran the player through the body (Colley Cibber, *Apology*, ed. Lowe, ii. 243–245). Mohun, who, unlike Hill, made no attempt to evade justice, was arrested, and the grand jury of Middlesex found a true bill of murder against him. His trial before his peers in Westminster Hall, in January 1692–3, was the sensation of the hour. The king is said to have been constant in his attendance. After a protracted and impartial trial, the accused was on 4 Feb. acquitted by sixty-nine votes to fourteen. Mohun was consequently released from the Tower; he was but seventeen years of age at the time (a circumstance omitted by Macaulay), and a relative is stated to have suggested during the trial that he should 'be taken away and whipt' (Henry North to Archbishop Sancroft in *Tanner MSS.* xxv. 7, where there are other curious particulars; cf. *State Trials*, xii. 950–1050; Macaulay, *Hist. of England*, 1858, iv. 310–11). In October of this year Mohun was lying dangerously ill at Bath. His recovery was followed by a resumption of his riotous life in London. In October 1694 he was engaged in a duel with Francis Scobell, M.P. for Grampound, who had remonstrated with him in Pall Mall concerning a murderous assault which he was making upon an offending coachman. In this year also he volunteered for the Brest expedition, and was made a captain of horse in Lord Macclesfield's regiment. He served with distinction in Flanders during the next two years, but returned to England early in 1697 in as aggressive and turbulent a mood as ever. No later than April 1697 he was involved in a duel with Captain Bingham, in St. James's Park, but the combatants were separated by the sentinels before any serious damage was done. On 14 Sept. however, he was in at the death of Captain Hill, which occurred in a confused and discreditable brawl at the Rummer Tavern, and in November 1698 he was engaged with his old associates, Warwick and Docwra, in deep potations at Lockets', which were followed by an affray in Leicester Square, and a mortal wound inflicted upon a Captain Richard Coote. True bills of murder were brought in against both Warwick and Mohun, but the latter was not tried by his peers until 29 March 1699, when he was acquitted. It appeared in evidence that he had not fomented the quarrel, but rather the reverse; and before leaving the bar he uttered some expression of contrition for his past life, which seems to have been for the time sincere.

Thenceforward Mohun occasionally took a prominent part in the debates in the House of Lords, and was a staunch supporter of the whigs. On 13 March 1703 he stood proxy for the elector of Hanover when the latter was installed knight of the Garter. In the debate on the Occasional Conformity Bill he remarked bluntly that if the Bill passed they might as well tack the Pretender to it. When in the debate on the Act of Security (1704) Nottingham appeared to cast a slur upon William III, Mohun was with difficulty restrained from proposing to send him to the Tower. Finally, when in a debate in the House of Lords the Duke of Marlborough was grossly insulted by Earl Powlett, it was Mohun who was commissioned to bear Marlborough's invitation to the earl 'to take the air in the country.'

Meanwhile in June 1701 Mohun had been appointed to attend Charles Gerard, earl of Macclesfield [q. v.], who was sent as envoy-extraordinary to present the electress-dowager Sophia with a copy of the Act of Succession. Macclesfield died on 5 Nov. 1701, and by his will Mohun came in for the personal estate valued at 20,000*l.* With regard to the real property he entered upon a long, complicated, and fluctuating lawsuit both with the crown and James Douglas, fourth duke of Hamilton [q. v.] Mohun claimed through his first wife, Macclesfield's niece Charlotte, daughter of Thomas Manwaring; Hamilton through his second wife, also a niece of Macclesfield's, while the crown claimed the reversion on the ground that the reversal of Macclesfield's attainder had never been legally recorded. In the course of the proceedings the duke and Mohun met in the chambers of Mr. Orlebar, a master in chancery, on 13 Nov. 1712. On the duke remarking of a witness named Whitworth, 'There is no truth or justice in him,' Mohun rejoined, 'I know Mr. Whitworth, he is an honest man, and has as much truth as your grace.' A challenge ensued, not from the duke, but from Mohun. The duel took place in Hyde Park, between 6 and 7 A.M. on Sunday 15 Nov. Mohun spent the previous night at the Bagnio in Long Acre. On the parties arriving on the ground, Mohun said the seconds should have no share, but his friend, Colonel George Maccartney [q. v.], demurred, and the duke, turning to Colonel John Hamilton, remarked, 'There is my friend, he will take a share in my dance.' They fought until their principals fell, when Maccartney went to Mohun and turned him on his face 'that he might die the more easily.' Neither Mohun nor his adversary attempted to parry, but thrust without intermission, 'fighting,' says a contemporary, 'like enraged lyons.' Mohun was riddled with dreadful wounds (see the account of Le Sage, the surgeon), but it is said that he only inflicted the duke's death-wound with a shortened sword as Hamilton was bending over him. The duel was at once interpreted by the dominant party as a whig conspiracy, Swift in the 'Post Boy' (for 18 and 20 Nov.), and in the 'Examiner' (20 Nov.), suggesting that 'the faction, being weary of Mohun, resolved to employ him in some real service to the cause,' i.e. in the prevention of Hamilton's projected embassy to France, which it was dreaded would be favourable to the cause of the Pretender.

Mohun was buried in St. Martin's-in-the-Fields on 25 Nov.

By his will, which was proved on 6 March 1712–13, within four months of his death, Mohun left everything to his second wife, Elizabeth, daughter of Thomas Lawrence, state physician to the queen, on condition of her paying 100*l.* to 'Elizabeth, my pretended daughter by my first wife' (Crisp, *Somersetshire Wills*, 5th ser. p. 11). The peerage became extinct upon Mohun's tragic death.

Though perhaps excessively vilified by tory writers (who regarded him, not altogether without reason, as the bully of the whig party), there can hardly be two opinions as to Mohun's character. Hearne, mentioning his death, says with probable truth, 'he should have been hanged before . . . divers times.' Macky writes, 'In his youth a scandal to the peerage, he now rectifies as fast as he can his former slips.' By 1705 he certainly manifested a tendency to corpulency, hardly compatible with the wild excesses of his youth. Swift adds to Macky, 'He was little better than a conceited talker in company.'

The fatal duel with Hamilton, coming so soon after that of Sir Cholmondeley Dering, evoked much unfavourable comment, and a Bill was introduced into the Commons for the prevention of duelling, but was lost on a second reading. The duel also forms an incident in Thackeray's 'Esmond,' in which novel a Lord 'Harry' Mohun, who has little in common with the historical character, figures as villain.

A portrait was painted for the Kit-Cat Club, of which Mohun was a member, by Sir Godfrey Kneller in 1707, and was engraved by John Faber the younger in 1732.

[The whole Life and History of my Lord Mohun and the Earl of Warwick, with their comical frolicks that they played, London, 1711, sm. 4to; Lives and Characters of the most Illustrious Persons who died in 1712, pp. 402–10; Smith's Lives of the Highwaymen; Burke's Extinct Peerages; G. E. C.'s Peerage; Gent. Mag, 1852, i. 219; Luttrell's Brief Historical Relation of State Affairs, vols. ii.–vi. passim; Wyon's Queen Anne, i. 217, 316, ii. 270, 388; Swift's Journal to Stella and Four Last Years of Queen Anne; Evelyn's Diary; State Trials (Howell), xii. 950, xiii. 306; Roxburghe Ballads, iii. 390–1; Hatton Correspondence (Camd. Soc.), i. 142, ii. 187–9, 235; Macpherson's Original Papers, ii. 364; Boyer's Annals of Queen Anne, 1735, passim; Reliq. Hearnianæ, i. 208; Hearne's Collectanea, ed. Doble, iii. 483–6; Calamy's Hist. Account, i. 428, ii. 4, 255; Spence's Anecdotes (1858), p. 256; Elwin's Pope, v. 73, ix. 382; Macknight's Bolingbroke, p. 316; Thornbury's Haunted London, 1880, p. 50; Tom Brown's Works, iii. passim; Tyburn Chron. i. 139 (with fancy picture of the duel); Lysons's Environs of London, i. 781; Noble's Continuation of Granger's Biog. Hist. 1806, ii. 55; Chambers's Book of Days, ii. 583; Larwood's Story of the London Parks, i. 101, 103; Millingen's History of Duelling, ii. 29; Steinmetz's Romance of Duelling (1868), i. 233; Mackay's Popular Delusions, ii. 289-91; Knight Hunt's Fourth Estate, i. 165; Memoirs of the Kit-Cat Club, p. 120; Boase and Courtney's Bibl. Cornub. i. 312 (containing an account of all the chapbooks and pamphlets evoked by Mohun's trials for murder and more especially by his duel with Hamilton); Ashton's Social Life in the Reign of Queen Anne, p. 362; Notes and Queries, 2nd. ser. x. 481, 3rd ser. v. 135, 312, 6th ser. xii. passim; Add. MS. 33051 f. 223 (containing the order of Sir Christopher Wren to erect seats of 750 persons in Westminster Hall, preparatory to trial of Mohun and Warwick); Egerton MS. 2623 f. 53; Hist. MSS. Comm. 11th Rep. App. v. (Dartmouth MSS.) contains a full account of the evidence given on the subject of the duel before the privy council, pp. 311–14; see also articles Douglas, James, fourth Duke of Hamilton; Maccartney, George; and Mountfort, William.] T. S.

MOHUN, JOHN de (1270?–1330), baron, lord of Dunster in Somerset, son of John de Mohun, the grandson of Reginald de Mohun [q.v.] and Eleanor Fitzpiers, was about nine years old at his father's death in 1279, and was a ward of Edward I (Lyte, p. 16). He received many summonses to perform military service, as in 1297 to serve in Flanders, in 1299 to join the muster at Carlisle, which was afterwards put off and held at York on 12 Nov., and again in 1300 to serve against the Scots. At the parliament held at Lincoln in January 1301 he joined in the letter of the barons to the pope, and is therein described as 'dominus de Dunsterre' (*Fœdera*, i. ii. 926). He was summoned to the muster at Berwick on 24 June, and again to the muster to be held at Berwick on 25 May 1303. He was at Perth early in 1304, for he dined there with the Prince of Wales on Candlemas day. He was a conservator of the peace for the county of Somerset in 1307, and in 1308 and 1309 was summoned to do service against the Scots. In 1311 he held a commission as one of the king's justices. He joined the party of Thomas, earl of Lancaster, and was concerned in the execution of Gaveston, for which he received a pardon in 1313 (*ib.* ii. i. 231). Summonses were sent to him to serve against the Scots in 1315, 1316, and

1319. In 1321 he was warned to abstain from the parliament that the Earl of Lancaster designed to hold at Doncaster (*ib.* pp. 442, 459). He gave charters to the priories of Dunster and Bruton, and to the townsmen of Dunster (LYTE). Certain lands in Ireland [see under MOHUN, REGINALD DE] he exchanged with the king for the manor of Long Compton in Warwickshire (*ib.*; *Fœdera,* I. ii. 949). He died in 1330.

He married first Ada, daughter of Robert, or Payn, Tiptoft, by whom he had seven sons and a daughter, and secondly a wife named Sybilla (LYTE). From Sir Reginald, his fifth son, descended the Mohuns of Cornwall, of which house were the Mohuns, barons of Okehampton (*ib.* p. 37). His eldest son, John, was a knight-banneret, was present at the battle of Boroughbridge, and, dying in Scotland perhaps in 1322, was, it is said, buried in the church of the Grey Friars at York (*ib.*; *Parliamentary Writs,* II. iii. 1177); he married Christian, daughter of Sir John Segrave, by whom he had a son, John (1320–1376) [q.v.], who succeeded his grandfather (LYTE).

[Lyte's Dunster and its Lords, privately printed, and largely from papers in the Archæological Journal, contains full information, with references, concerning John and the house of Mohun generally; Dugdale's Baronage, ii. 498; Cal. of Docs., Scotland, ii. No. 1516 (Rolls Ser.); Prynne's Parliamentary Writs, I. 740, II. iii. 1176, 1177; Rymer's Fœdera, I. ii. II. i. passim.] W. H.

MOHUN, JOHN DE (1320–1375), baron, lord of Dunster, son and heir of Sir John de Mohun (*d.* 1322), the eldest son of John de Mohun (1270?–1330) [q. v.], lord of Dunster, was ten years old at his grandfather's death in 1330, and was made a ward of Henry Burghersh [q. v.], bishop of Lincoln, at whose instance he received livery of his lands in 1341, though still under age. About that time he married his guardian's niece Joan, daughter of Bartholomew, lord Burghersh, the elder (*d.* 1355) [q. v.] In the same year he received a summons to do service in Scotland, and in 1342 took part in the expedition into Brittany, marching under the command of his father-in-law. After serving as a commissioner of array for the county of Somerset in 1346, he joined in the invasion of France, where he also appears in later years as one of the retinue of the Prince of Wales. He was one of the original knights of the order of the Garter, and his name and arms are still in St. George's Chapel, Windsor. He served also in later expeditions against the French (DUGDALE, *Baronage*). He seems to have fallen into money difficulties, and in 1369 made over his chief estates, the castle and manor of Dunster, Minehead, and the hundred of Carhampton, to feoffees for the benefit of his wife (LYTE). He gave a charter to the monks of Dunster. He died on 15 Sept. 1375, leaving no sons, and was buried in Bruton priory (*ib.*) By his wife Joan he had three daughters, who all made grand marriages: Elizabeth married William de Montacute, earl of Salisbury (*d.* 1397), and died 1415; Philippa married (1) Walter, lord FitzWalter (*d.* 1386), (2) Sir John Golofre (*d.* 1396), and (3) Edward, duke of York (*d.* 1415), and died 1431; and Matilda married John, lord Strange (*d.* 1397) of Knockin in Shropshire, and died before 1376, leaving a son, Richard, in whom the barony of Mohun vested (COURTHOPE, *Historic Peerage,* pp. 324, 453). There is an idle legend that Joan, wife of John, lord Mohun, obtained from her husband as much common land for the poor of Dunster as she could walk round barefoot in a day (CAMDEN, *Britannia,* col. 58; FULLER, *Worthies,* ii. 289). No such gift can be traced (LYTE). After her husband's death she obtained from the feoffees a conveyance of the estates vested in them to herself for life with remainder to Lady Elizabeth, widow of Sir Andrew Luttrell of Chilton in Thorverton, Devonshire, who paid her for this purchase 3,333*l.* 6*s.* 8*d.* Lady Mohun lived much at court, where she and her daughter, the Countess of Salisbury, used to appear in the robes of the Garter (*ib.*; BELTZ). She built and endowed a chantry chapel in the undercroft of Christ Church, Canterbury, and, dying on 4 Oct. 1404, was there buried. The effigy on her tomb is given by Stothard (*Monumental Effigies*), and has been copied by Mr. Lyte (*Dunster and its Lords*). At her death Sir Hugh Luttrell, son of Sir Andrew and Lady Elizabeth, came into possession of Dunster as his mother's heir.

[Lyte's Dunster and its Lords, pp. 19–23, 34; Dugdale's Baronage, i. 498; Beltz's Order of the Garter, cxlix. and pp. 49–51, 248, 249, 255; Nicolas's Historic Peerage, pp. 324, 453, ed. Courthope; Froissart, i. 264, ed. Buchon, i. 218*n.*; Camden's Britannia, col. 58. ed. Gibson, 1695; Fuller's Worthies, ii. 289, ed. Nichols.] W. H.

MOHUN, JOHN, first BARON MOHUN (1592?–1641), royalist politician, was the only son of Sir Reginald Mohun, bart., who died 26 Dec. 1639, by his second wife, Philippa, daughter of John Heale. He matriculated from Exeter College, Oxford, on 15 Nov. 1605, aged 13, graduated B.A. on 7 July 1608, and in 1610 was entered as a student at the Middle Temple. In the parliaments of 1623–4 and 1625 he sat for the borough of Grampound, Cornwall, and was among the supporters of the Duke of Buckingham, through whose favour he was recommended in 1620 for the office of vice-warden of the Stannaries. During 1626 and 1627 he was a member of several commissions in the west of England, including one of inquiry into the acts of Sir John Eliot as vice-admiral of Devon. At the general election in 1627–8 Mohun was put forward by the court party for the county of Cornwall in opposition to Eliot and Coryton, but lost the election. Sir James Bagg, the duke's chief agent in the west, thereupon pressed for Mohun's elevation to the peerage, and on 15 April 1628 he was created Baron Mohun of Okehampton, Devonshire. The circumstances of this election came before a special committee, and Eliot obtained the appointment of a committee of the House of Commons to investigate Mohun's conduct as vice-warden of the Stannaries. A formal charge was brought against him, and a conference of the lords and commons followed, but in consequence of the death of Eliot's wife the matter was allowed to drop. In 1634 he charged Bagg with having 'cozened the king of 20,000*l.*,' and the case came on in the Star-chamber. The king sent a guarded letter to the lords of the council, and after the inquiry had lasted some years, Mohun seems to have been fined 500*l.* 'for undue inquiries into his majesty's debts.' A man of turbulent disposition, he quarrelled with another peer at the christening in 1633 of James, duke of York (STRAFFORD, *Letters and Despatches*, i. 166).

Mohun died on 28 March 1641 (*Inq. post mortem*, c. II. 607, no. 102). His wife was Cordelia, daughter of Sir John Stanhope, and relict of Sir Roger Aston, who was buried at St. Martin's-in-the-Fields, Middlesex, 2 Oct. 1639. She was sister to Anne Cokayne, mother of Sir Aston Cokayne [q. v.], who in his 'Small Poems of divers sorts,' 1658, included (pp. 80–2) a poetical letter to 'John, lord Mohun, my uncle-in-law,' and some lines (pp. 156–7) on his visit to Mohun's house in Cornwall. Letter xlii. of book i. sect. 5 of James Howell's 'Letters,' dated 30 Aug. 1632, and descriptive of the inquisition, is addressed to Mohun, and Massinger, to whom Sir Aston Cokayne introduced him, dedicated to him, as his 'especial good lord,' the play of the 'Emperor of the East.'

[Foster's Alumni Oxon. (1500–1714); Maxwell-Lyte's Dunster and its Lords, p. 37; State Papers, 1625 et seq.; Forster's Sir John Eliot, passim; Epistolæ Ho-Elianæ, ed. Jacobs, i. 290–292; Boase and Courtney's Bibl. Cornub. i. 364, iii. 1285.] W. P. C.

MOHUN, MICHAEL (1620?–1684), actor, was, according to Bellchambers, born about 1625, but 1620 is probably a nearer approximation. Before the civil war he performed under Beeston, at the Cockpit in Drury Lane, where, among other characters, he played Bellamente in Shirley's 'Love's Cruelty,' licensed 14 Nov. 1631, and published 1640. Subsequently he fought on the side of Charles I, attaining the rank of captain, and on the close of the wars went to Flanders, where he acquitted himself with credit, and received the style and pay of major.

Upon the Restoration Mohun returned with Charles II, and resumed his original occupation, joining Killigrew's company, with which he acted, 1660–3, at the theatre in Vere Street, Clare Market, erected on the site of Gibbon's Tennis Court. It seems probable that the company also played at the Cockpit in Drury Lane, and at the Red Bull Theatre in St. John Street. Pepys saw Mohun, or Moone, for the first time at the Vere Street Theatre on 20 Nov. 1660 in the 'Beggar's Bush' of Beaumont and Fletcher, and says that he is declared to be 'the best actor in the world.' Mohun was the original Mopus to the Scruple of Lacy in Wilson's comedy 'Cheats' (1662), and on the opening of the Theatre Royal, on the site now occupied by Drury Lane Theatre, 8 April 1663, with the 'Humourous Lieutenant' of Beaumont and Fletcher, he was Leontius (GENEST, i. 34, 44). He subsequently played Leon in 'Rule a Wife and have a Wife,' and Truewit in Jonson's 'Epicœne, or the Silent Woman.' Face in the 'Alchemist' and Volpone in the 'Fox' followed, and in 1665 he was the original Montezuma in Dryden's 'Indian Emperor, or the Conquest of Mexico.' Melantius in the 'Maid's Tragedy' became one of his great parts. Rymer praises Hart and Mohun in Amintor and Melantius, saying, 'There we have our Roscius and Æsopus both on the stage together.' Proof of the estimation in which Mohun was held by Charles is supplied in the fact that when the king, finding his court attacked to his face by Lacy in Howard's 'Change of Crownes,' forbade the players acting again, Mohun obtained a reversal of the decision, except so far as that special play was concerned. On 2 March 1667 Mohun was the original Philocles in Dryden's 'Secret Love, or the Maiden Queen;' on 5 Oct. Alberto in Rhodes's 'Flora's Vagaries,' and, 19 Oct., Edward III in Lord Orrery's 'Black Prince.' On 22 June 1668 Mohun was the first Bellamy (to Hart's Wildblood) in Dryden's 'Evening's Love, or the Mock Astrologer.' The same year he played Cethegus in 'Catiline,' and in 1669 was Iago, Ruy

Dias in Fletcher's 'Island Princess,' and on 9 Feb. the original Maximilian in Dryden's 'Tyrannick Love, or the Royal Martyr.' In 1670 he was the original Abdelmelech in the 'Conquest of Granada,' a play by Dryden in two parts, and in 1671 the original Valentius in Joyner's 'Roman Empress,' and Don Alvarez in Corey's 'Generous Enemies.' The Theatre Royal having been burnt in January 1671–2, the players opened in February at Lincoln's Inn Fields with 'Wit without Money,' in which Mohun was Valentine. He was the first Rhodophil in Dryden's 'Marriage à la Mode,' Dapperwit in Wycherley's 'Love in a Wood, or St. James's Park,' and Duke of Mantua in Dryden's 'Assignation, or Love in a Nunnery.'

At Lincoln's Inn Fields in 1673 he was the original Beamont in Dryden's 'Amboyna,' and Pinchwife in Wycherley's 'Country Wife.' On 26 March 1674 the new Theatre Royal, subsequently known as Drury Lane, was opened. In the following year Mohun was the original Britannicus in Lee's 'Nero,' Trivultio in Fane's 'Love in the Dark, or the Man of Business,' and Old Emperor in Dryden's 'Aurenge-Zebe, or the Great Mogul.' Augustus Cæsar in Lee's 'Gloriana, or the Court of Augustus Cæsar,' and Hannibal in the same author's 'Sophonisba, or Hannibal's Overthrow,' followed in 1676, and Clytus in Lee's 'Rival Queens,' Edgar in Ravenscroft's 'King Edgar and Alfreda,' and Matthias in the two parts of Crowne's 'Destruction of Jerusalem by Titus Vespasian' in 1677. In 1676 he was Mardonius in 'A King and No King,' a performance overlooked by Genest. In 1678 he was the original Ventidius in Dryden's 'All for Love, or the World well Lost,' Mithridates in Lee's 'Mithridates, King of Pontus,' Breakbond in the 'Man of Newmarket,' by the Hon. Edward Howard [q. v.], and Sir Wilding Frolick in D'Urfey's 'Trick for Trick, or the Debauched Hypocrite.' Mohun is then unheard of until, in 1682, he played Ismael in Southerne's 'Loyal Brother and the Persian Prince,' and he disappears with the part of Burleigh in Banks's 'Unhappy Favourite, or the Earl of Essex.' He is also known to have acted Cassius and Aubrey in 'Rollo,' and to have repeated his early character of Bellamente, which was assumed by Bellchambers to be a woman, and led him and some other stage chroniclers astray. Genest says that Mohun 'joined the Duke's company, but did not continue long on the stage after the union' of the two companies in 1682.

Pepys, 6 Feb. 1668–9, says of his Iago that it was inferior to that of Clun. Downes declares that he was eminent for Volpone, Face, Melantius, Mardonius, Cassius, Clytus, Mithridates, &c., and says: 'An eminent poet [Lee] seeing him act this last [Mithridates], vented suddenly this saying, O Mohun, Mohun! Thou little man of mettle, if I should write a hundred plays, I'd write [always] a part for thy mouth.' Mohun generally played second to Hart, but was scarcely held an inferior actor. Powell, in his dedication of the 'Treacherous Brothers,' speaks of Mohun and Hart by their good acting getting authors their 'third nights,' and being consequently more substantial patrons than the greatest name in the frontispiece of a dedication. In the Epilogue to 'Love in the Dark' Dryden says of Mohun that Nature 'bid him speak as she bid Shakespeare write,' and satirises the 'cripples in their art' who

> Mimick his foot but not his speaking part.
> Let them the Traytor or Volpone try!
> Could they . . .
> Rage like Cethegus, or like Cassius die?

From the allusion in the first line Genest supposes Mohun to have suffered from the gout. Rochester praises his dignity and elegance. Wright, in the 'Historia Histrionica,' 1699, speaks of Mohun, with Hart, Burt, and others, as much superior to the actors of subsequent days. In the Tatler (No. 99), 26 Nov. 1709, Steele says: 'My old friends, Hart and Mohun, the one by his natural and proper force, the other by his great skill and art, never failed to send me home full of such ideas as affected my behaviour, and made me insensibly more courteous and humane to my friends and acquaintances.' In 'A Comparison between two Stages' Gildon mentions that the plays were at this time so good and so well acted by Hart and Mohun that the audience would not be distracted to see the best dancing in Europe, and St. André, a French dancer brought over by the Duke of Monmouth, was consequently a failure.

Mohun lived in 1665 on the south side of Russell Street, Covent Garden, and was assessed at 10*s.*, the highest rate levied in the street, and from 1671 to 1676 in a house on the east side of Bow Street. He died in Brownlow Street (now Betterton Street), Drury Lane, in October 1684, and was buried in the church of St. Giles's-in-the-Fields. Mohun was small and well-built.

An original picture of Mohun, engraved in 1793, is now at Knowle Park. It shows a young, pleasing-faced boy grasping a sword.

[Genest's Account of the English Stage; Downes's Roscius Anglicanus; Historia Histrionica; A Comparison between two Stages; Cibber's Apology, ed. Lowe; Doran's Their Majesties' Servants, ed. Lowe; Pepys's Diary; Wheatley's London Past and Present.] J. K.

MOHUN, MOUN, or MOYUN, REGINALD DE (*d.* 1258), called by mistake Earl of Somerset, was son of Reginald de Mohun, lord of Dunster in Somerset, the great-grandson of William de Mohun (*fl.* 1141) [q. v.], earl of Somerset; his mother was Alice, fourth daughter of William Brewer or Briwere [q.v.], who brought a large inheritance to her husband's family (DUGDALE, *Baronage*, ii. 497), and married for her second husband William Paynell (*Excerpta e Rotulis Finium*, i. 169). Reginald was under age at the time of his father's death, which took place in or before 1213, and was a ward, first, of Henry Fitz-Count, son of the Earl of Cornwall, and afterwards of his own grandfather, William Brewer (*ib.* pp. 79, 242, 243). In 1234 he sat among the king's justices (Foss), in 1242 and 1252 he was chief justice of the forests south of Trent, and he received from Henry III rights of warren and of the chase and of a weekly market at Dunster. Among the lands that he inherited from his mother was Torre or Tor in Devonshire, where William Brewer had in 1196 founded a Premonstratensian abbey (*Monasticon*, vi. 923). There he often resided, having a court-house there, whence the place became called Torre Mohun or Tor-Moham. The Mohun arms are still to be seen on the ruins of the abbey, Reginald having confirmed the grants of his grandfather to the convent. His younger brother, William, having conveyed to him lands at Tor and Maryansleigh in Devonshire, at Endicombe, near Dunster, and at Clythorn, near Woodstock, in Oxfordshire, in order that he might build a Cistercian abbey in a suitable place, desiring that Reginald should be the founder and patron, he, with the advice of Alcius of Gisors, abbot of Beaulieu in Hampshire, founded in 1246 the abbey of Newenham at Axminster in Devonshire, and placed therein a colony of monks from Beaulieu, who took possession of their new house with much ceremony in the presence of Reginald and William on 6 Jan. 1247. In that year his foundation was confirmed by Pope Innocent IV, and a curious legend records that the pope, on his appearing at the papal court at Lyons, presented him with a rose, or other flower, of gold, and asked him of what degree he was. Reginald replied that he was a plain knight bachelor, on which the pope said that, as such a gift could be made only to kings, dukes, or earls, Reginald should be earl of 'Este,' or Somerset, and to maintain his title granted him two hundred marks a year, and created him a count apostolic, with power to appoint public notaries (FULLER, *Church History*, ii. 178–80). It is certain that he bore as his arms a dexter hand holding a fleur-de-lys and habited in a maunch (figured by LYTE, p. 24; the false statement that he styled himself Earl of Somerset rests on a forged charter). He and his brother William joined in laying foundation-stones of the church of Newenham in 1254. Reginald also made a grant to the convent of Bath for a mass to be said for ever for the souls of his son John, lately dead, and other members of his house, by a monk of Dunster priory [see under MOHUN, WILLIAM DE, *fl.* 1066], or a secular priest, in the chapel of Dunster Castle (LYTE). He was a benefactor to the canons of Bruton [see under MOHUN, WILLIAM DE, *fl.* 1141] and the abbey of Cleeve. He gave two charters to the townsmen of Dunster (LYTE). He died at Tor in Devonshire on 20 Jan. 1258 (OLIVER, *Monasticon Diocesis Exoniensis*, p. 358), and was buried on the left side of the high altar at Newenham. A long account of his holy death is extant, by a monk of Newenham (*ib.*), who says that thirty-five years after Reginald's death the writer saw and touched the founder's body, which was then uncorrupt.

Reginald's first wife was named Avice; her surname is not known (it was not Bohun, as Dugdale says, mistaking the M of her married name for B, LYTE, p. 14; *Somerset Archæological Society's Proceedings*, VI. i. 27, 28). It has been suggested that she may have been the heiress of the Flemyngs of Ottery (LYTE, u. s.) By her he had a son John, who married Joan, daughter of William Ferrers, earl of Derby, and died in Gascony in 1254, leaving a son named John (*d.* 1279), whose son John (1270?–1330) is separately noticed. Reginald's second wife was Isabel, widow of Gilbert Basset [q. v.], and daughter of William Ferrers, earl of Derby, by Sybilla, fourth daughter of William Marshal, earl of Pembroke (*d.* 1219) [q. v.], and so sister of her stepson's wife. By this marriage a part of the inheritance of the Earls Marshal fell to the Mohuns; this part included certain lands in Leinster about which Reginald and his wife appear to have been involved in some legal proceedings (*Calendar of Documents*, Ireland, i. Nos. 2949, 3080, ii. Nos. 29, 139, 184). By Isabel Reginald had a son named William, who, besides inheriting part of the Marshal estates, was in occupation of an estate that belonged to the Flemyngs, but he was merely associated with that estate as tenant under his elder half-brother. Reginald was succeeded by his grandson John.

His brother William died on 17 Sept. 1265, and was buried in Newenham Abbey.

[Lyte's Dunster and its Lords, pp. 9–15, 24, 34; Oliver's Monasticon Dioc. Exon. pp. 169, 185, 357–71; Oliver's Eccl. Antiq. of Devon, i. 205–8; Davidson's Hist. of Newenham Abbey, pp. 2–11, 210–14; Foss's Judges, ii. 409; Fuller's Ch. Hist. ii. 178–80, ed. Brewer; Dugdale's Monasticon, v. 690 sq., vi. ii. 926; Dugdale's Baronage, ii. 497; Savage's Hist. of Carhampton, p. 468; Excerpta e Rot. Fin. i. 79, 169, 242, 243, ed. Roberts (Record Publ.); Cal. Geneal. i. 94, 227, ed. Roberts (Record Publ.); Cal. of Docs., Ireland, i. Nos. 2949, 3080, ii. 29, 139, 184, ed. Sweetman (Rolls Ser.); Somerset Archæol. Soc.'s Proc. 1856, vi. ii. 27.] W. H.

MOHUN or **MOION, WILLIAM** de (*fl.* 1066), baron and sheriff of Somerset, took his designation from the lordship of Moyun, near St. Lo in Normandy, which remained in his family until 1204 (Lyte, *Dunster and its Lords*, p. 2; *Somerset Archæological Society's Proceedings*, xix. ii. 96). He followed Duke William when he invaded England in 1066 (Wace, *Roman de Rou*, l. 13620; by a curious error he is stated to have had in his following forty-seven or fifty-seven of the greatest lords in the army, Leland, *Collectanea*, i. 202; Dugdale, *Baronage*, i. 497; Collinson, *Hist. of Somerset*, ii. 7; for the correction of this misstatement, see Planché, *The Conqueror and his Companions*, ii. 120, and Lyte, u.s.) In calling him 'le viel,' Wace merely distinguishes him from his son; for as William de Moion the elder was alive in and perhaps after 1090 he can scarcely have been old in 1066. He received as many as sixty-eight manors in the west of England, one being in Devonshire, one in Wiltshire, eleven in Dorset, one of them Ham, which fell to a younger branch of his descendants, and was called Ham-Mohun, or as now Hammoon (Eyton, *Key to Domesday, Dorset*, p. 12), and fifty-five in Somerset. In the 'Domesday Survey' it is noted that he himself held 'Torre, and there is his castle.' Torre is Dunster, where on the conical hill, or tor as it is still called, William no doubt found a fortress of older days, which he probably to some extent remodelled, though no remains of Norman work have been found on the tor (Clark ap. Lyte, *Dunster*, u.s. p. xiv). His home estate consisted of the ancient hundreds of Cutcomb and Minehead, in the parishes of Minehead, Cutcomb, and Dunster, with some additions, being in all 19,726 acres. He evidently paid some attention to the breeding of horses; we learn that on his estate at Cutcomb, where he had a tenant, there were kept large numbers of unbroken brood-mares (Eyton, *Domesday Studies, Somerset*, i. 129, ii. 19, 25). Either in his lifetime or shortly afterwards his estates were formed into an 'honour,' Dunster being the 'caput honoris.' He was sheriff of Somerset, whence his estate at Brompton-Ralph is in a coeval index called 'Brunetone Vicecomitis' (*ib.* i. 110). William de Moion is usually spoken of as the founder of Dunster priory (*Monasticon*, iv. 200). What exactly he did in this matter was that at some date between 1090 and 1100 he granted the church of St. George, at Dunster, where some Norman work still remains (*Somerset Archæological Society's Proceedings*, vi. ii. 6), together with certain land and tithes and a tenth of his mares, to the abbey of St. Peter at Bath and John de Villula (*d.* 1122) [q. v.], the bishop, that they might 'build and exalt' the said church. The convent of Bath accordingly made at Dunster a cell of their own abbey under the rule of a prior (Lyte, u. s. pp. 4 and 27, where William's charter is given from a manuscript at Corpus Christi College, Cambridge). William in this charter declared his wish to be buried in Bath Abbey (he was therefore not buried at Dunster as Leland, u. s., records). His wife's name was Adelisa, and he had three sons, William de Mohun, earl of Somerset [q. v.], who succeeded him, Geoffrey, and Robert, all living at the date of his grant to Bath.

[Lyte's Dunster and its Lords, reprinted for the most part from the Archæological Journal of 1880, 1881, with an account of the castle, by G. T. Clark, pp. xiii, xiv, 1–5, 26, 27, contains nearly all that is known about W. de Moion. See also Wace's Roman de Rou, l. 13620, ed. Pluquet; Leland's Collectanea, i. 202; Dugdale's Baronage, i. 497, and Monasticon, iv. 200; Ellis's Introduction to Domesday, i. 214, ii. 355; Eyton's Domesday Studies, Somerset, i. 45, 110, 129, ii. 19, and passim; Eyton's Key to Domesday, Dorset, p. 12; Planché's Conqueror and his Companions, ii. 120 sq.; Somerset Archæol. Soc.'s Proc. 1856, vi. ii. 6, 1875, xix. ii. 96; Collinson's Hist. of Somerset, ii. 7; Hutchins's Hist. of Dorset, i. 273.] W. H.

MOHUN, MOION, or **MOYNE, WILLIAM** de, Earl of Somerset or Dorset (*fl.* 1141), eldest son of William de Mohun (*fl.* 1066) [q. v.], by his wife Adelisa, was possessed of forty-four knights' fees, and in 1131 was present at the council held by Henry I at Northampton, and one of the witnesses of the charter there granted by the king to the church of Salisbury. He rose against Stephen in 1138, and, relying on the strength of his castle of Dunster, committed many deeds of violence and cruelty in the west country. Stephen marched against him, but believing Dunster Castle to be impregnable, and being unwilling to remain long enough before it to compel its surrender by blockade, marched away, leaving Henry Tracy to carry on the war in those parts. This Tracy did with success, preventing William from continuing his expeditions from Dunster, and on one occasion taking 104 knights prisoners. William was humbled and compelled to remain quiet (*Gesta Stephani*, pp. 52, 53). He was with the empress at Westminster in June 1141, and marched with her to the siege of Winchester. There it is said (*ib.* p. 81) that the empress made him Earl of Dorset, but it appears that he was an earl when he was at Westminster in June (Round, *Geoffrey de Mandeville*, p. 93). He called himself Earl of Somerset (*Monasticon*, vi. 335), but the close connection then existing between the two shires renders this apparent discrepancy of no importance. In 1142 he founded a priory at Bruton for Augustinian canons. He also granted land to the monks of Dunster to pray for the soul of his son Ralph (Lyte, p. 28). By his wife Agnes he had six sons, of whom four were clerks, and another, Ralph, predeceased him. A son William succeeded him, without, as far as known, the title of earl, and was in turn succeeded by his son William, whose grandson was Reginald de Mohun (*d.* 1257) [q. v.]

[Lyte's Dunster and its Lords, pp. 5, 6, 28; Gesta Stephani, pp. 52, 53, 81 (Engl. Hist. Soc.); Ann. Wav. ap. Ann. Monastici, ii. 226 (Rolls Ser.); Sarum Charters, p. 7 (Rolls Ser.); Liber Niger Scacc. i. 91, ed. Hearne; Dugdale's Monasticon, vi. 335; Dugdale's Baronage, i. 497; Round's Geoffrey de Mandeville, pp. 93, 95, 125, 271, 277; Stubbs's Const. Hist. i. 362, 451; Somerset Archæol. Soc.'s Proc. 1857 vii. ii. 73–75, 1873 xix. ii. 96.] W. H.

MOINENNO, Saint (*d.* 570), suffragan bishop of Clonfert, was a disciple of St. Brendan of Clonfert [q. v.] His name also appears as Mon-nennio, Moinnend, Maoinenn, or Moenu, and in Latin as Moinennus. He must be distinguished from Mo-nennius [q. v.], bishop of Whithorn; but whether Moenna or Moena, a bishop and disciple of St. Brendan, has a separate identity is not so clear. The bishop of Clonfert's feast is celebrated on 1 March, Moenna's on 26 Feb. Colgan distinguishes the two by making Moenna identical with Moenus, Mainus, who lived near Dol in Brittany, but the Breton saint's feast is 15 June (Todd, *Book of Hymns*, fasc. i. 104). St. Moinenno died in 570. The feasts of St. Monan [q. v.] and Moinenno both fall on 1 March, and Skene suggests that the two were confused in the accounts which represent St. Monan as the companion of St. Adrian, afterwards bishop of St. Andrews, in his missionary efforts among the Picts of the ninth century. According to Skene, the monastery with which Moinenno was associated at Clonfert was broken up between 841 and 845, when St. Adrian's expedition was leaving Ireland for Fife, and St. Adrian possibly carried with him the relics of the dead St. Moinenno, and not the living St. Monan.

[Colgan's Acta SS. Hibern. 1 March; Skene's Celtic Scotland, ii. 314.] M. B.

MOIR, DAVID MACBETH (1798–1851), physician and author, known as Delta (Δ), son of Robert Moir and Elizabeth Macbeth, was born at Musselburgh on 5 Jan. 1798, and received his school education there. At the age of thirteen he was apprenticed for four years to Dr. Stewart, a physician in that town, and studied medicine in Edinburgh, obtaining his surgeon's diploma in his nineteenth year (1816). In 1817 he entered into partnership with Dr. Brown of Musselburgh, whose practice, he tells us, kept him so occupied that he did not spend a night out of the town between that year and 1828.

Moir began to write as early as 1812, about which year he sent two essays to 'The Cheap Magazine,' published at Haddington. In 1816 he wrote his first articles for the 'Scots Magazine,' and published anonymously 'The Bombardment of Algiers, and other Poems.' After entering on professional practice he contributed to 'Constable's Edinburgh Magazine' and to 'Blackwood's Magazine.' In the latter he became a regular writer of *jeux d'esprit*, which were at first ascribed to William Maginn [q. v.], as well as of essays and serious verse over the signature 'Δ.' His connection with 'Blackwood' was the means of introducing him to Christopher North, and in 1823 to Galt, the novelist, for whom Moir wrote the concluding chapters of 'The Last of the Lairds.' In the autumn of 1824 appeared 'The Legend of Genevieve, with other Tales and Poems,' in part a reprint of magazine pieces, and the first instalments in 'Blackwood' of 'The Autobiography of Mansie Wauch,' republished in book form, with additions, in 1828. He had the offer from Mr. Blackwood in 1829 of the editorship of the 'Quarterly Journal of Agriculture,' and was urged by him and other friends to settle in Edinburgh, but he refused both proposals (Letters quoted by Aird). He continued to write for the magazines, and soon included 'Fraser' and the 'Edinburgh Literary Gazette' among the periodicals to which he contributed.

Moir's first professional publication was 'Outlines of the Ancient History of Medicine' (1831), intended as the first instalment of a complete history. Pressure of medical duties, caused partly by the serious outbreak of cholera in Musselburgh in 1832, and partly by the retirement of Dr. Brown early in 1833, interfered with his design. He wrote a pamphlet entitled 'Practical Observations on Malignant Cholera' (1832), being a general answer to the inquiries which he received as secretary of the board of health of his heavily stricken town. Shortly afterwards he published 'Proofs of the Contagion of Malignant Cholera,' 1832. In the autumn of that year he attended the meeting of the British Association at Oxford, and visited Cheltenham and London, where his friend Galt was then living. In 1843 appeared 'Domestic Verses,' a volume of elegies prompted by the deaths of three of his children and of a number of the 'Blackwood' circle. In the following year he contracted a serious illness by sitting all night in damp clothes by the bed of a patient, and in 1846 his health was further broken by a carriage accident. His remaining years were devoted to social functions and to intercourse with literary friends. He had already edited Mrs. Hemans's works in seven volumes, and in 1848 prepared a single volume edition. In 1849 he made an excursion to the highlands with Christopher North. He was a member of several scientific societies, including the Medico-Chirurgical, Harveian, Antiquarian, and Highland Societies, and he was the author of the account of the 'Antiquities of the Parish of Inveresk,' published in the 'Statistical Account of Scotland' in 1845, and separately in 1860. In the spring of 1851 he delivered a course of six lectures at Edinburgh on 'The Poetical Literature of the past Half Century,' published in the same year. In 'Blackwood' of July 1851 appeared his last literary effort, 'The Lament of Selim.' On 22 June he received further injury when dismounting from his horse, and died at Dumfries on Sunday, 6 July. He was buried at Inveresk. A statue by Ritchie was erected in 1854 on the bank of the Esk, within his native town.

He married Catherine E. Bell of Leith on 8 June 1828, and had eleven children; a son Robert was house-surgeon of the Royal Infirmary of Edinburgh in 1851, afterwards in St. Andrews.

His literary works, other than those already noticed, are: 1. 'School Recollections' (published in 'Friendship's Offering' in 1829). 2. 'Memoir of Alexander Balfour' (as Preface to Balfour's 'Weeds and Wild Flowers,' 1830). 3. 'Memoir of Galt' (in the 'Literary Life'), 1834. 4. 'Life of Macnish' (in 'The Modern Pythagorean'), 1837 and 1844. 5. 'Memoirs of Rennie of Phantassie and Sir John Sinclair' (in the 'Journal of Agriculture'), and a sketch of Admiral Sir David Milne [q. v.] A list of his contributions to 'Blackwood,' nearly four hundred in number, will be found on p. 128 of the General Index to vols. i–l. 'The Poetical Works of David Macbeth Moir, Δ. Edited by Thomas Aird. With a Memoir of the Author,' appeared in 2 vols. at Edinburgh in 1852.

The eulogies of 'Delta' by the 'Blackwood' coterie will probably not be accepted by present-day critics. His verse will be commended for its study of nature and its pleasing rhythm. His humorous pieces, though sprightly, have, for the most part, a solely contemporary interest. His reputation now rests on his novel, 'Mansie Wauch,' written in the manner of Galt.

[Memoir by Aird (see above); Blackwood's Magazine, pp. lxx, 249, and passim; Fraser's Magazine, viii. 290, and passim; Noctes Ambrosianæ. This biography has been kindly revised by Dr. Robert Moir, St. Andrews, and Dr. Thomas Scott, Musselburgh.] G. G. S.

MOIR, GEORGE (1800–1870), advocate and author, son of George Moir, was born in 1800 at Aberdeen, and educated there. Migrating to Edinburgh, he entered a lawyer's office, but devoted considerable time to literary pursuits. In 1824, when engaged on an article on the ancient ballad poetry of Spain for the 'Edinburgh Review,' a common friend suggested to Moir that he might seek information from Sir William Hamilton [q. v.] They met in the Advocates' Library, and this was the commencement of 'a warm and lifelong friendship' (Veitch, *Memoir of Sir W. Hamilton*). On 2 July 1825 Moir was admitted advocate. In 1827 he published a verse translation of Schiller's 'Piccolomini' and 'Wallenstein;' it was dedicated to Hamilton, who revised the proof-sheets, and it met with a favourable reception. This was followed in 1828 by a translation of Schiller's 'Thirty Years' War,' with a short life of the author. Moir had been a whig, but now threw in his lot with the tories, and became a regular contributor to 'Blackwood's Magazine.' About the same time he made the acquaintance of Carlyle. 'Moir,' writes the latter from Edinburgh on 3 Feb. 1833, 'has been here, in all senses a *neat* man, in none a strong one;' and again on 10 Feb., 'George Moir has got a house in Northumberland Street, a wife, too, and infants; is become a conservative, settled everywhere into *dilettante*, not very happy, I think; dry, civil, and seems to feel *unheimlich* in my company' (Froude, *First*

Forty Years of Carlyle's Life, ii. 330, 332). From 1835 to 1840 he was professor of rhetoric and belles lettres in the university of Edinburgh. He enjoyed a fair practice at the Scottish bar, and in 1855 was appointed sheriff of Ross and Cromarty, an office which in 1859 he exchanged for the shrievalty of Stirlingshire. In 1864 the Faculty of Advocates chose Moir as professor of Scots law in the university of Edinburgh, but owing to ill-health he resigned in less than a year. His shrievalty he gave up in 1868, and died rather suddenly at his house in Charlotte Square, Edinburgh, on 19 Oct. 1870. His death was 'an incalculable loss to the legal literature of Scotland.'

Moir's works are: 1. 'Schiller's Piccolomini and Wallenstein,' translated, with a critical preface, Edinburgh, 1827. 2. 'Schiller's Thirty Years' War,' translated, with biographical notice, 2 vols. Edinburgh, 1828. 3. 'The Appellate Jurisdiction of Scotch Appeals,' Edinburgh, 1851. 4. 'Magic and Witchcraft,' London, 1852. Copious extracts from his manuscript lectures were incorporated by Guthrie in the fourteenth edition of Erskine's 'Principles of the Law of Scotland,' 1870. Moir also contributed articles on poetry and modern romance to the 'Encyclopædia Britannica,' which, with Spalding's article on rhetoric, were published in a separate volume; and wrote a 'Sonnet to Clara,' privately printed, and included in 'Poetic Tracts,' 1795–1834, in the British Museum, vol. ii.

[Works in Brit. Mus.; Scotsman, 21 Oct. 1870; Froude's First Forty Years of Carlyle's Life, ii. 330. 332; Veitch's Memoir of Sir W. Hamilton, bart., 1869, passim; Edinburgh Univ. Cal.; Annals of our Time; Allibone's Dict. of English and American Lit. vol. ii. and Suppl. vol. ii.; information kindly supplied by the keeper of the Advocates' Library.] A. F. P.

MOIRA, Earl of. [See Hastings, Francis Rawdon-, second Earl, 1754–1826.]

MOISES, HUGH (1722–1806), schoolmaster, son of Edward Moises, M.A., vicar of Wymeswold, Leicestershire, was born at that place on 9 April 1722, and was educated first at Wrexham School, Denbighshire, and afterwards at the grammar-school of Chesterfield, Derbyshire, under the Rev. Dr. Burroughs. In 1741 he removed to Trinity College, Cambridge, of which society his elder brother, Edward Moises, afterwards vicar of Masham, Yorkshire, was a fellow. He graduated B.A. in 1745, with a good reputation as a classical scholar, and was soon afterwards elected a fellow of Peterhouse. In the same year he became an assistant in the school of his old master at Chesterfield, where he continued till 1749. In that year he proceeded M.A., and was, on the recommendation of Bishop Keene, appointed headmaster of the grammar-school at Newcastle-upon-Tyne in succession to Richard Dawes [q. v.] The school at the time had scarcely any scholars, but Moises soon raised it to a high state of efficiency, 'not only,' as Brand observes, 'by his great learning and abilities, but by the sweetest manners and most uniform conduct' (*Hist. of Newcastle*, i. 390). His dignified demeanour during school-hours is said to have inspired his pupils with 'reverence and awe,' but unlike Busby, with whom his biographer compares him, he 'tempered necessary severity with affability and kindness.' Early in the year after his appointment the corporation of Newcastle raised his salary from 50*l.* to 120*l.* a year, and on 21 April 1761 they appointed him to the morning-lectureship of All Saints' in consideration of the continued success of the school. He was, on 14 June 1779, appointed master of St. Mary's Hospital, Newcastle. He lived to see many of his scholars occupying positions of high dignity and importance. The most distinguished of them were John Scott, afterwards Earl of Eldon and lord-chancellor; his brother, William Scott, afterwards Lord Stowell; and Cuthbert Collingwood, afterwards Lord Collingwood, the admiral.

In 1787 Moises was presented to the rectory of Greystoke, Cumberland, and resigned the mastership of the school, after holding it for nearly forty years, being succeeded by his nephew, the Rev. Edward Moises, M.A., vicar of Hart and Hartlepool from 1811. After residing at Greystoke for some years he resigned the rectory at the patron's request, and he spent the latter years of his life in Newcastle. In 1801 he was appointed one of the chaplains to his old pupil, Lord Eldon, who had just been raised to the woolsack, He died at his house in Northumberland Street, Newcastle, on 5 July 1806. In 1810 a fine mural monument, executed by Flaxman, with an elegant Latin inscription composed by Sir William Scott, afterwards Lord Stowell, was erected to his memory in St. Mary's porch, St. Nicholas's Church. The expenses, amounting to about 400*l.*, were defrayed by a subscription among his pupils, whose names are printed in Nichols's 'Illustrations of Literature' (v. 120).

[Memoirs by the Rev. John Brewster (privately printed), Newcastle, 1823, 8vo, reprinted in Nichols's Illustr. of Lit. v. 94–129; Campbell's Lives of the Chancellors, 1847, vii. 7–10, 15, 19, 66; Gent. Mag. July 1806 p. 684; Graduati Cantabr.; Martin's Privately Printed Books, 2nd edit. p. 310; Richardson's Table Book, iii. 55; Twiss's Life of Lord Eldon, i. 31.]

T. C.

MOIVRE, ABRAHAM DE (1667–1754), mathematician, was the son of a surgeon at Vitry in Champagne, where he was born on 26 May 1667. His education was begun by the Christian Brothers, but he was sent at the age of eleven to the protestant university of Sedan, and was there during four years trained by Du Rondel in Greek. A year's study of logic at Saumur followed; then, after a course of physics in 1684 at the Collège d'Harcourt in Paris, and a trip to Burgundy, he devoted himself to mathematics under Ozanam in Paris, where his parents were then settled. The revocation of the edict of Nantes in 1685, however, led to his temporary seclusion in the priory of St. Martin, and on his release, 27 April 1688, he repaired to London. A call at the Earl of Devonshire's, with a recommendatory letter, chanced to introduce him to Newton's 'Principia.' He procured the book, divided it into separate leaves for convenience of transport in his pocket, and eagerly studied it on the peregrinations intervening between the lessons and lectures by which he earned a subsistence. In 1692 he became known to Halley, and shortly afterwards to Newton and Nicolas Faccio [q. v.] His first communication to the Royal Society was in March 1695, on some points connected with the 'Method of Fluxions' (*Phil. Trans.* xix. 52), and he was elected a fellow in 1697. His 'Animadversiones in D. Georgii Cheynæi Tractatum de Fluxionum Methodo inversa,' published in 1704, procured him the notice of Bernoulli. The rejoinder of George Cheyne [q. v.] was purely personal, and De Moivre left it unnoticed.

De Moivre's essay, 'De Mensura Sortis,' presented to the Royal Society in 1711 (*ib.* xxvii. 213), originated in a suggestion by Francis Robartes, later earl of Radnor, that he should deal on broader principles with the problems treated by Montmort in his 'Essai d'Analyse sur les Jeux de Hasard,' Paris, 1708. The resulting controversy with this author terminated amicably. De Moivre pursued the investigation in his 'Doctrine of Chances,' published in 1718, in the preface to which he indicated the nature of 'recurring series.' He introduced besides the principle that the probability of a compound event is the product of the probabilities of the simple events composing it, and the whole subject, Todhunter remarks, 'owes more to him than to any other mathematician, with the single exception of Laplace' (*History of the Theory of Probability*, p. 193). The first edition of the work was dedicated to Sir Isaac Newton; subsequent enlarged editions, dedicated to Lord Carpenter [see CARPENTER, GEORGE, LORD CARPENTER], appeared in 1738 and 1756.

De Moivre came next to Halley as a founder of a science of life-contingencies. His 'Annuities upon Lives,' first published in 1725, with a dedication to the Earl of Macclesfield [see PARKER, THOMAS, EARL OF MACCLESFIELD], was reissued, corrected and improved, in 1743, 1750, 1752, and 1756, and in an Italian version by Fontana, at Milan, in 1776. The merit and usefulness of his celebrated hypothesis, that 'the decrements of life are in arithmetical progression,' were maintained by Francis Baily [q. v.] in chap. ix. of his 'Doctrine of Life-Annuities,' 1813, against the strictures of Price and De Morgan. The appearance of Simpson's 'Doctrine of Annuities' in 1742 gave occasion to a groundless imputation of plagiarism made by De Moivre in the second edition of his work; it was, however, successfully refuted, and silently omitted from subsequent editions. De Moivre's most important work, 'Miscellanea Analytica,' London, 1730, was his last. He demonstrated in it his method of recurring series, created 'imaginary trigonometry,' through the invention of the theorem known by his name, and generalised Cotes's 'Theorem on the Property of the Circle' (p. 17). Naudé's presentation of the book to the Berlin Academy of Sciences procured the election by acclamation of its author as a member of that body on 23 Aug. 1735.

Leibnitz, who made De Moivre's acquaintance in London, vainly endeavoured to secure for him a professorial position in Germany; and his foreign origin similarly barred the way to his promotion in England. So he continued all his life to support himself by teaching, and answering questions on the chances of play and the values of annuities. Bernoulli wrote of him to Leibnitz in 1710 as struggling with want and misery; yet he was one of the commissioners appointed by the Royal Society in 1712 to arbitrate on the claims of Newton and Leibnitz to the invention of the infinitesimal calculus. He was the intimate friend of Newton, who used to fetch him each evening, for philosophical discourse at his own house, from the coffee-house in St. Martin's Lane (probably Slaughter's), where he spent most of his time (BREWSTER, *Life of Newton*, i. 248); and Newton's favourite method in his old age of dealing with questioners about the 'Principia' was to refer them to

De Moivre. The Latin translation of Newton's 'Optics' was carefully revised by him in 1706.

De Moivre was described by Jordan in 1733 as 'un homme d'esprit, et d'un commerce très agréable' (*Voyage Littéraire*, p. 147). He was unmarried, and spent his closing years in peaceful study. Literature, ancient and modern, furnished his recreation; he once said that he would rather have been Molière than Newton; and he knew his works and those of Rabelais almost by heart. He continued all his life a steadfast Christian. After sight and hearing had successively failed, he was still capable of rapturous delight at his election as a foreign associate of the Paris Academy of Sciences, on 27 June 1754. He died at last by somnolence. Twenty hours' sleep daily became habitual with him; and he ceased to wake on 27 Nov. 1754, at the age of eighty-seven. His portrait, painted by Joseph Highmore [q. v.] in 1736, is in the possession of the Royal Society, and was engraved by Faber. Dassier executed a medal of him in 1741. His numerous contributions to the 'Philosophical Transactions,' no less than his other writings, show great analytical power, skill, and inventiveness.

[Haag's La France Protestante, 1860; Grand-Jean de Fouchy's Éloge, Mémoires de l'Acad. des Sciences, Paris, 1754, Histoire, p. 175; Maty's Mémoire sur la Vie de M. de Moivre, La Haye, 1760; Phil. Trans. Abridged, iv. 14; Gent. Mag. 1754, p. 530; Montucla's Hist. des Mathématiques, iii. 155; Marie's Hist. des Sciences, vii. 199; Hoefer's Hist. des Mathématiques, p. 519; Hutton's Mathematical Dict. 1815; Weld's Descriptive Cat. of Portraits in the possession of the Roy. Soc. p. 49; Bromley's Cat. of Engraved Portraits, p. 292; Suter's Geschichte der math. Wissenschaften, ii. 350; Poggendorff's Biog.-Lit. Handwörterbuch; Watt's Bibl. Brit.] A. M. C.

MOLAGA or **MOLACA** (*fl.* 650), Irish saint, of Leaba Molaga and Tigh Molaga, now Timoleage, co. Cork, was son of Duibligid, of the family of Ui Coscraidh, descendants of the Druid Mogh Ruith, who was of the race of Fergus MacRoigh, king of Ulster. The family occupied a territory in the present barony of Fermoy, their chief town being Liathmuine, now Cloghleafin, in the parish of Kilgullane. One day, while Duibligid was sowing flax-seed near Carncuille, now Aghacross, he is said to have been visited by SS. Cuimin fada and his brother Comdan on their way southward accompanied by a clerical party. On learning that he was still labouring, notwithstanding his advanced age, because he had no son, St. Cuimin foretold he should have one who should illuminate both the Scotias (Ireland and Scotland) with his holiness. Seven months later the child was born, and was baptised by St. Cuimin. Arrived at a suitable age, he studied the scriptures in his native place, and eventually built a monastery hard by at Tulach min, now Leaba Molaga. He subsequently had to leave it, and made his way to Connor in Ulster, from which, passing westward, he crossed the Bann at the ford of Camus, but having forgotten his bell it was, according to legend, divinely restored to him, and the place was thenceforth known as *Termon an cluig*, 'the sanctuary of the bell,' now Kilfoda or Senchill. Thence he proceeded to Scotland and on to Wales, where he and St. David formed a mutual friendship. There he was known as Lachín, the usual prefix *mo* being omitted, and the diminutive *in* added. When leaving, St. David gave him a bell, which was known as the Bobán Molaga. Warned by an angel to return to Ireland, he crossed over to the city called Dun Duiblinne, the fortress of Dublin, otherwise named *Ath-cliath*, or the ford of hurdles. At this time the king of Dublin was suffering from profuse perspirations, and Molaga, having been called in, is said to have cured him by transferring the perspiration to his bell. The grateful king bestowed on him a town in Fingal with a perpetual rent. There he erected a church and established a swarm of bees, which he obtained from St. Damongoc or Domnog of Tiprat Fachtna in Ossory, a pilgrim, who brought them from Wales (cf. *Calendar of Oengus*). The ruins of the monastery or church founded by him, and which was known as Lann-beachair (the Beeman's church), may still be seen to the north of Balbriggan, co. Dublin. It is now known as Lambechair. Returning thence to Tulach mín at the request of the people, he was appointed confessor to the king, and it was determined that his church should be constituted a termon or sanctuary. The four pillars which marked the boundaries of the sanctuary still remain. Some time afterwards Flann king of the Hy Fidgeinte, in the present baronies of Upper and Lower Connello, co. Limerick, came with a crowd of followers to visit Molaga's king, Cai gan mathair, and behaved so turbulently that Molaga, according to his biographers, summoned wild beasts from the forest, and produced an earthquake, in order to terrify the king, and thus induce him to protect the monastery. The king is said to have prostrated himself before the saint, who placed his foot on his neck seven times, and, moved by his penitence, declared that seven kings should spring from him.

At this time the pestilence called the *Buidhe Chonnail*, or yellow plague, was raging at Corcabascin, co. Clare, and Molaga successfully exerted himself to arrest its spread. He died on 20 Jan., but nothing is known of the year beyond the fact that he survived the great plague of 664. At Leaba Molaga in the barony of Condons and Clongibbons are to be seen the ruins of his oratory, with the cashel or enclosing wall and two crosses. To the south, at a distance of eighty yards, are the four pillar stones enclosing the termon or sanctuary. A square tomb beneath the south wall is supposed to be the grave of the saint.

[Vita Molaggæ seu Molaci Confessoris ex Hibernico versa; Colgan's Acta Sanct. pp. 145 sq.; Calendar of Oengus, p. xlii; Giraldus Cambrensis's Topographia, cap. v. (Rolls Ser.); Die Irische Kanonensammlung, von H. Wasserschleben, zweite Auflage, p. 175; Lord Dunraven's Notes on Irish Architecture, pp. 61, &c.; Lanigan's Eccl. Hist. iii. 83; D. J. O'Donovan's Martyrology of Donegal, 20 Jan.] T. O.

MOLAISSI (533–563), Irish saint, son of Nadfraech and Monua, was a descendant of Conall Cernach, and was born in 533. He founded a church on an island in Loch Erne known in Irish as Daimhinis, or Stag Island, and at the present day as Devinish. A round tower and a church, both of much later date than the saint, with some ancient tombs, are to be seen on the island. He lived there with a community of monks, subject to a rule instituted by him. It was not wanting in austerity, for throughout Lent it allowed only one handful of barley grain each twenty-four hours. He lived through the *Buidhe Chonnail*, or plague of the reign of Diarmait and Blathmac, in which both kings and St. Fechin of Fore [q. v.] perished. He is described as going about in a hood of badgers' skins, long afterwards preserved as a relic, and called the brocainech. Another was a little evangelistarium called the soiscela beg, which he used to carry about with him. He made a pilgrimage to Rome. The rest of his life presents a long series of miracles and of austerities. He died on 12 Sept. 563. Michael O'Clery mentions an ancient Irish life (*Felire na Naomh Nerennach*, p. 245), and quotes a poem on him by Cuimin of Coindeire, beginning 'Carais Molaisi an locha-Molaissi of the lake loves.' S. H. O'Grady has printed and translated another Irish life of him from a copy in a sixteenth-century Irish manuscript now in the British Museum (Addit. MS. 18205). He is sometimes called Laisren or Lasrianus, and his name is also spelt Molaise. A fragment of his ancient office has been preserved by Michael O'Clery. He is described as tall, and had three sisters: Muadhnat, Tallulla, abbess of Kildare, and Osnat.

He is to be distinguished from Molaissi of Leighlin, whose feast was 18 April; from Molaissi of Inis Muiredhaigh, who is venerated on Inishmurray to this day, and whose day is 12 Aug.; and from Molaissi of Cill-Molaissi, in South Munster.

[J. O'Donovan's Martyrology of Donegal, Dublin, 1864; S. H. O'Grady's Silva Gadelica, 1892; W. Stokes's Calendar of Oengus, 1871.] N. M.

MOLE, JOHN (1743–1827), mathematician, the son of an agricultural labourer, was born at Old Newton, near Stowmarket, Suffolk, 10 March 1743 (O.S.) His mother, whose maiden name was Sarah Martin, taught him to read, but he received no school education. He obtained employment as a farmer's servant, and at the age of twenty-seven displayed extraordinary powers of mental calculation, and subsequently acquired, without tuition, an intimate knowledge of algebra. In 1773 he opened a school at Nacton, near Ipswich. His 'Elements of Algebra, to which is prefixed a choice collection of Arithmetical Questions, with their Solutions, including some New Improvements worthy the attention of Mathematicians,' London, 1788, 8vo, was highly commended by the reviews. In April 1788 the author paid a visit to London, and was introduced to Dr. Tomline [q. v.], bishop of Lincoln, and Lord Walpole. He was an occasional contributor of pieces in prose and verse to the 'Ipswich Magazine' (1799–1800). In 1793 he relinquished his school at Nacton, and removed to Witnesham, a village on the other side of Ipswich, where he again commenced the drudgery of tuition. While there he published 'A Treatise on Algebra,' Ipswich, 1809, 8vo. In 1811 he returned to Nacton, where he died on 20 Sept. 1827. He was twice married, but left no issue.

[Addit. MSS. 19167 f. 162, 19170 f. 145; De Morgan's Arithmetical Books, p. 117; Gent. Mag. 1788 p. 410, February 1828 p. 185; Nichols's Illustr. of Lit. vi. 887–91.] T. C.

MOLE, JOHN HENRY (1814–1886), water-colour painter, was born at Alnwick, Northumberland, in 1814. His early years were passed in a solicitor's office in Newcastle-on-Tyne, but his leisure time was devoted to art, and at the age of twenty-one he began his professional career by painting miniatures. He first exhibited in London at the Royal Academy, where he had four miniatures in 1845 and six in 1846. He also painted landscapes and figure subjects in water-colours, and this led to his election in

1847 as an associate, and in 1848 as a full member, of the New Society of Painters in Water-Colours. He then gave up miniature painting, and about the same time removed to London; thenceforward he contributed regularly to the annual exhibitions of the New Society, afterwards the Royal Institute, of Painters in Water-Colours, of which he became vice-president in 1884. He occasionally painted in oil-colours, and sent a picture, entitled 'Carrying Peat,' to the Royal Academy in 1879. His water-colour drawings met with considerable success, and three of them, 'Tynemouth,' 'Coast of Devon, Gleaners Returning,' and 'Hellersdon Wood, Devonshire,' are in the South Kensington Museum.

Mole died at 7 Guilford Place, Russell Square, London, on 13 Dec. 1886, aged 72, and was buried in Brompton cemetery.

[Athenæum, 1886, ii. 833; Catalogue of the National Gallery of British Art at South Kensington, 1893; Royal Academy Exhibition Catalogues, 1845–79; Exhibition Catalogues of the New Society (afterwards Royal Institute) of Painters in Water-Colours, 1847–87.]

R. E. G.

MOLESWORTH, JOHN EDWARD NASSAU (1790–1877), vicar of Rochdale, only son of John Molesworth, by his wife Frances, daughter of Matthew Hill, esq., and great-grandson of Robert, first viscount Molesworth [q. v.], was born in London on 4 Feb. 1790, and educated under Dr. Alexander Crombie [q. v.] of Greenwich. Passing to Trinity College, Oxford, he graduated B.A. in 1812, M.A. in 1817, B.D. and D.D. in 1838. For sixteen years he was curate of Millbrook, Hampshire, and while there wrote, at the instigation of Dr. Rennell, dean of Winchester, a reply to Davison's 'Inquiry into the Origin and Intent of Primitive Sacrifice' (1826), a work which procured him the friendship of Dr. Howley, then bishop of London, afterwards archbishop of Canterbury [q. v.] Howley presented him in succession to the livings of Wirksworth, Derbyshire (1828), and St. Martin's, Canterbury (1829); appointed him one of the 'six preachers' at Canterbury; recommended him unsuccessfully for the vicarage of Leeds when Hook was elected, and in 1839 presented him to the vicarage of Minster-in-Thanet, and a few months later (3 March 1840) to Rochdale. The last preferment he held for thirty-eight years. At Canterbury, during the stormy period of the Reform Bill, his talents, which were allied with a combative temperament, found abundant occupation, and both by voice and pen he became recognised as the leader of the church party in the diocese. But he was no less a zealous parish priest, and to him is due the first venture in cheap church periodical literature. The 'Penny Sunday Reader,' which he edited and very largely wrote for five years, is said to have enjoyed an extraordinary popularity among the working men of many large towns. At Rochdale Molesworth had an ample field for all his activities. He succeeded an Erastian and absentee vicar, and found church life and work in the town at the last gasp. Dissenters at this time were agitating for abolition of church rates, and in Rochdale they had a doughty leader in the quaker John Bright, who fleshed his virgin sword in this controversy. Each party started a magazine, in which their case was defended and their opponents ridiculed. Molesworth fought in behalf of the rates, with a vigour and determination which, according to Bright (*Speeches*, ii. 517), was not 'surpassed in any other parish in the kingdom,' but his cause was a lost one, and defeat for his party inevitable.

The vicar was able to augment largely the value of the living by calling to account the leaseholders of its property, who had neglected to build upon the land according to their covenant; and with the increased means at his disposal he promoted church building, giving 1,000*l.* to each new church for which the parishioners raised an equal sum. Four churches so endowed were added to the original fourteen. He also rebuilt the grammar school founded by Archbishop Parker, and built parish schools, which were long celebrated for their efficiency. The value of the living, which was 1,800*l.* when Molesworth went to Rochdale, was meanwhile rapidly increasing with the spread of factories over the vicarage estate and the erection upon it of the railway station and canal terminus. In 1866, when his income had reached 5,000*l.*, Molesworth, following twenty years later Hook's example at Leeds, promoted the Rochdale Vicarage Act, by which the thirteen chapels of ease were converted into parish churches, and their endowments raised, some to 200*l.*, some to 300*l.*, and one to 500*l.* By this act his own income was limited to 4,000*l.*, while his successor was to receive 1,500*l.*

With very many persons and societies in his parish did the vicar continue to wage war with published letters and tracts. An unfortunate difference between him and his bishop, James Prince Lee [q. v.], was the subject of many pamphlets. Molesworth had protested against Lee's appointment in 1847, on the ground that a charge of drunkenness had been brought against him and remained unrebutted. But after a libel action had proved the falsity of the accusation, Molesworth and the bishop maintained for some two years very friendly relations. A dispute, however, subsequently arose over a church-building question, and the bishop was determinedly hostile to the vicar during the last twenty years of his episcopate.

The closing years of Molesworth's life were spent in comparative peace. He died on 21 April 1877, and was buried at St. Martin's, Castleton Moor, Lancashire. He was twice married, first, in 1815, to Harriet, daughter of W. Mackinnon, esq., of Newton Park, by whom he had six sons and three daughters, among whom were William Nassau Molesworth [q. v.], the historian, and Sir Guilford Molesworth, K.C.I.E., the distinguished engineer; secondly, in 1854, to Harriett Elizabeth, daughter of the Rev. Sir Robert Affleck, bart., and widow of J. T. Bridges, esq., of St. Nicholas Court, Thanet, and Walmer.

Molesworth was a high churchman before tractarianism and, like W. F. Hook, whom in many points of character and circumstance he resembled, found himself sometimes in agreement, sometimes in disagreement, with the leaders of the Oxford movement. He was a friend of Hugh James Rose [q. v.], and contributed to the 'British Magazine' and 'Encyclopædia Metropolitana,' of which Rose was editor. The courage and zeal with which he advocated unpopular opinions could not fail to arouse opposition and resentment, but his good temper and generosity disarmed many an adversary, and it was characteristic of him that he never allowed public quarrels to be carried into private life. Besides his sermons and pamphlets he published 'The Rick-burners,' a tale which enjoyed a large circulation at the time of the chartist riots. There is an engraved portrait by H. Cook.

[The Vicars of Rochdale, by the Rev. Canon Raines (Chetham Soc.); Foster's Peerage; private information.] H. C. B.

MOLESWORTH, Hon. MARY (*d.* 1715), poetess. [See Monck.]

MOLESWORTH, RICHARD, third Viscount Molesworth (1680–1758), field-marshal, born in 1680, was second son of Robert, first viscount Molesworth [q. v.] He was destined for the law and was entered at the Temple, but abandoning his studies set off with a servant to join the army in Holland, where he presented himself to his father's intimate friend Lord George Hamilton, earl of Orkney [q. v.] He served at first as a volunteer and was afterwards appointed captain in Orkney's regiment, the Scots Royal (1st foot), with which he was present at Blenheim ('Blenheim Roll' in *Treasury Papers*, vol. xciii.) He was one of Marlborough's aides-de-camp, and saved the duke's life at the battle of Ramillies, 23 May 1706. Different versions of the incident have been given, but the most authentic appears to be that Marlborough, seeing the allied left, on the open ground to the left of the village of Ramillies, was sore pressed, had ordered reinforcements to proceed thither from the right, and was himself personally leading up some squadrons of horse of the left wing which he had rallied with great difficulty, when he was unhorsed and ridden over by a body of Dutch cavalry retiring in disorder. His horse galloped away among the Dutch, and his aide-de-camp, Molesworth, seeing his chief in immediate danger of capture from the pursuing squadrons of French, put him on his own horse and persuaded him to ride away. In the ardour of the pursuit Molesworth was overlooked, and the French were presently brought up by the steady fire of Albemarle's Dutch-Swiss, under Colonel Constant. Molesworth recovered Marlborough's horse from a soldier, and found his chief in the village of Ramillies, issuing orders. Marlborough essayed to shift back to his own horse, when he was stunned by a round-shot, which took off the head of his principal aide-de-camp, Colonel Bringfield of Lumley's horse, who was holding his stirrup. The affair was carefully hushed up at the time.

Molesworth was appointed a captain and lieutenant-colonel in the Coldstream guards the year after, served in Flanders, and was blown up by a mine at the siege of Mons, but without receiving much injury. In 1710 he was appointed colonel of a regiment of foot, in succession to Colonel Moore, and went with it to Spain the year after. The regiment was disbanded at the peace of Utrecht. Molesworth was made lieutenant of the ordnance in Ireland, 11 Dec. 1714, and was returned as M.P. for Swords, co. Dublin. During the Jacobite rising of 1715 he raised a regiment of dragoons, with which he served, under General Carpenter, against the rebels in Lancashire. The regiment was disbanded, and on 19 March 1724 Molesworth was appointed colonel of the 27th Inniskilling foot. On 5 Oct. 1731 he succeeded to the title on the death of his elder brother, John, second viscount, ambassador in Tuscany and Sardinia [see under Molesworth, Robert, first Viscount]. On 31 May 1732 Molesworth succeeded General Crofts as colonel of the 9th dragoons (now lancers); on 26 Oct. 1733 was sworn of the Irish privy council; on 18 Dec. 1735 became a major-general; on 19 Dec. 1736 he was sworn one of the lords justices of Ireland;

succeeded General Wynne as colonel of the 5th royal Irish dragoons, 27 June 1737; became a lieutenant-general in Ireland in 1739, and master-general of the ordnance in Ireland in 1740; a lieutenant-general on the English establishment, 1 July 1742; a general of horse, 24 March 1746; commander-in-chief in Ireland in September 1751, and a field-marshal in 1757. He was governor of Kilmainham, and was admitted a member of the Royal Society 15 March 1721 (Thompson, App. iv. p. xxxv.) He died 12 Oct. 1758, aged 78. A portrait of Molesworth was painted by Lee and engraved by Brooks.

Molesworth married, first, Jane, daughter of Mr. Lucas of Dublin (she died 1 April 1742, having had a son, who died an infant, and three daughters, and was buried at Swords); secondly, Mary, daughter of the Rev. William Usher, archdeacon of Clonfert, by whom he had one son, Richard Nassau, fourth viscount, and seven daughters. At his death, Molesworth's widow received a pension of 500*l.* a year, and seven of his unmarried daughters pensions of 70*l.* a year each. The second Lady Molesworth met with a tragic fate. She, her brother, Captain Usher (royal navy), two of her daughters, their governess, and four servants were burned in their beds by a fire originating in the nursery of her house in Upper Brook Street, Grosvenor Square, London, early in the morning of 7 May 1763. Captain Usher's servant, who had in the first instance escaped, gallantly went back to save his master, and perished. George III directed 200*l.* a year to be added to the family pension in consideration of their misfortune (*Gent. Mag.* 1763, p. 255).

[Lodge's Peerage of Ireland, vol. iii. Burke's Peerage, under 'Molesworth;' 'Succession of Colonels,' in Cannon's Hist. Rec. 9th Lancers.]

H. M. C.

MOLESWORTH, ROBERT, first Viscount Molesworth (1656–1725), was the eldest son of Robert Molesworth (*d.* 3 Sept. 1656), who fought on the parliament side in the civil war, and at its conclusion obtained as an undertaker 2,500 acres of land in the county of Meath; he afterwards became a merchant in Dublin, accumulated great wealth, and was high in Cromwell's favour (cf. Gilbert, *History of Dublin*, i. 58–9). The Molesworth family, of Northamptonshire origin, was very ancient. An ancestor, Sir Walter de Molesworth, attended Edward I to the Holy Land and was appointed sheriff of Bedfordshire and Buckinghamshire for a period of ten years in 1304. One of Sir Walter's descendants, Anthony Molesworth, nearly ruined himself by his profuse hospitality to Queen Elizabeth at Fotheringay. The younger of this Anthony's sons, Nathaniel, accompanied Sir Walter Raleigh in his voyage to Guiana; the elder, William, who was the first viscount's grandfather, took part in Buckingham's expedition to Ré, and died about 1640, leaving issue a daughter, Elizabeth (1606–1661), who was married to Gervase Holles [q.v.], and three sons, of whom the youngest was the father of the subject of this memoir. His mother was Judith, daughter and coheiress of John Bysse, by Margaret, daughter of Sir Gerard Lowther.

Born in Fishamble Street, Dublin, on 7 Sept. 1656, four days after his father's death, Robert was educated at home and at Dublin University, where he 'had a high character for abilities and learning,' and is stated by Taylor (*Univ. of Dublin*, p. 385) to have graduated with distinction, though his name does not appear in the list of Dublin graduates. In the struggle that attended the revolution of 1688 in Ireland, he became prominent in support of the Prince of Orange; he was consequently attainted and his estate, valued at 2,285*l.* per annum, sequestered by James's parliament on 7 May 1689. After the Boyne he was restored to his possessions and summoned to William's privy council. He appears to have been sent on a private mission to Denmark during 1689–90 and in 1692 he was despatched as envoy extraordinary to that country. He managed, however, to give serious offence to the court of Copenhagen, and left the country abruptly and without the usual formality of an audience of leave in 1694. The only account of the circumstance is that published by Molesworth's adversary, Dr. William King (1663–1712) [q. v.], who stated, on the authority of Scheel, the Danish envoy, that Molesworth had most unwarrantably outraged the Danish sense of propriety by poaching in the king's private preserves and forcing the passage of a road exclusively reserved for the royal chariot. The charges are probably not devoid of truth, for Molesworth was an ardent admirer of Algernon Sidney, but the gravity of the offences may have been exaggerated by Dr. King. The aggrieved envoy withdrew to Flanders, where his resentment took shape in 'An Account of Denmark as it was in the year 1692' (London, 1694). There the Danish government was represented as arbitrary and tyrannical and held up as an object lesson to men of enlightenment. The book, which was half a political pamphlet in support of revolution principles, and was also strongly anti-clerical in tone, at once obtained popularity and distinction. It was highly approved by Shaftesbury and by Locke, to whom it introduced the author; as late as 1758 it was described by Lord Orford in his preface to Whitworth's 'Account of Russia' (p. iv), as 'one of our standard books.' The strictures on the Danish authorities incensed the Princess Anne, the wife of Prince George of Denmark, and interest was made with William to procure the punishment of the author. Scheel also protested on behalf of the Danish government, but in vain. Vindications appeared. One by Dr. King, already alluded to, entitled 'Animadversions on the Pretended Account of Denmark,' was inspired by Scheel. Two more, one entitled, 'The Commonwealth's man unmasqu'd, or a just rebuke to the author of the Account of Denmark' [see Rogers, Thomas (1660–1694)], were issued before the close of 1694, and a 'Deffense du Danemark,' at Cologne two years later.

Early in 1695 Molesworth returned to Ireland, and during the four following years sat in the Irish parliament as member for Dublin. He was made a privy councillor for Ireland in August 1697, and shortly afterwards prepared a bill 'for the encouragement of protestant strangers' in Ireland. He sat for Swords in the Irish parliament (1703–1705) and for Lostwithiel and East Retford in the English House of Commons (1705–1708). He continued a member of the Irish privy council until January 1712–13, when he was removed upon a complaint against him, presented on 2 Dec. by the prolocutor of convocation to the House of Lords, charging him with the utterance, 'They that have turned the world upside down are come hither also.' Steele vindicated him in his 'Englishman,' and a few weeks later in 'The Crisis;' Molesworth was nevertheless let off easily in 'The Public Spirit of the Whigs,' Swift's tory rejoinder. The political conjuncture occasioned the reprinting of Molesworth's 'Preface' to a translation of Francis Hotoman's 'Franco-Gallia, or an Account of the Ancient Free State of France and most other parts of Europe before the loss of their liberties,' which he had executed in 1711 (London, 8vo), 'with historical and political remarks, to which is added a true state of his case with respect to the Irish Convocation' (London [1713]; 2nd edit. 1721; and the work was reprinted for the London association in 1775, under the title 'The Principles of a Real Whig').

On the accession of George I Molesworth was restored to place and fame; he obtained a seat in the English parliament for St. Michaels, was on 9 Oct. 1714 named a privy councillor for Ireland, and in November a commissioner for trade and plantations. On 16 July 1719 he was created Baron Molesworth of Philipstown and Viscount Molesworth of Swords; in the spring of this year he had vigorously supported the Peerage Bill, writing in its defence 'A Letter from a Member of the House of Commons to a gentleman without doors relating to the Bill of Peerage.' In 1723 appeared his 'Considerations for promoting Agriculture' (Dublin, 8vo), described by Swift as 'an excellent discourse full of most useful hints, which I hope the honourable assembly will consider as they deserve.' 'I am no stranger to his lordship,' he adds, 'and excepting in what relates to the church there are few persons with whose opinions I am better pleased to agree' (cf. Brydges, *Censura Lit.* iv. 144). Swift subsequently dedicated to Molesworth, as an Irish patriot, the fifth of the 'Drapier's Letters' (3 Dec. 1724). The last four years of his life were spent by Molesworth in studious retirement at his seat at Brackenstown, near Dublin. He died there on 22 May 1725, and was buried at Swords. He had another seat in England at Edlington, near Tickhill, Yorkshire.

Molesworth had been an active fellow of the Royal Society, to which he was admitted 6 April 1698 (Thomson, *Royal Society*, App. iv. p. xxxi), and he is described by Locke as 'an ingenious and extraordinary man.' Among his closest friends were William Molyneux [q. v.] and John Toland [q. v.] in conjunction with whom he supplied many notes to William Martin's 'Western Islands of Scotland' (1716). He shared the sceptical views of Toland, but left by his will 50*l.* towards building a church at Philipstown.

Molesworth married Letitia (*d.* 18 March 1729), third daughter of Richard Coote, lord Coloony, and sister of the Earl of Bellamont. By her (she died 18 March 1729, and was buried at St. Audoen's, Dublin) he had seven sons and four daughters. His eldest son and successor, John Molesworth (1679–1726), was appointed a commissioner of the stamp office in May 1706 (Luttrell, vi. 50), a post in which he was succeeded in 1709 by Sir Richard Steele. Early in 1710 he was appointed envoy to the Duke of Tuscany, but returned during the summer. Swift met him frequently during September and October 1710, once at the house of William Pate [q. v.], the learned woollendraper. Charles Dartiquenave [q. v.], the epicure and humorist, was another common friend. He sailed again for Tuscany on 3 Nov. 1710, but was recalled from Genoa rather abruptly in the following February (*Hist. MSS. Comm.* 11th Rep. App. v. 305). In December 1715 he succeeded his father as a commissioner of trade and plantations, and undertook several diplomatic missions. At the time of his father's death he was at Turin in the capacity of plenipotentiary. He died a few months after his succession to the title and was succeeded by his brother Richard, who is separately noticed. Molesworth's second daughter, Mary, married George Monck [see MONCK, MARY]. Her father prefixed to her 'Marinda'(1716) a dedication to the Princess of Wales, afterwards Queen Caroline.

A portrait of Molesworth by Thomas Gibson (1680?–1751) [q. v.] was engraved by P. Pelham (1721) and E. Cooper.

[Biog. Brit.; Chalmers's Biog. Dict.; Walpole's Cat. of Royal and Noble Authors, ed. Park, v. 231–4, 239; Wills's Irish Nation, ii. 729; Cunningham's Eminent Englishmen, iv. 122; Familiar Letters between Mr. Locke and several of his friends, p. 260; Georgian Era, i. 350; Lodge's Irish Peerage, v. 134–6; The New Peerage, 2nd edit. 1778, iii. 209; G. E. C.'s Peerage, s.v. 'Molesworth;' Luttrell's Brief Historical Relation, passim; Swift's Works, ed. Scott, ii. iii. passim and viii. 299; Forster's Life of Swift; Granger's Biog. Hist. continued by Noble, iii. 63; Watt's Bibl. Brit.; Bromley's Cat. of Engraved Portraits, p. 210; Hist. Reg. 1716, p. 353, and 1725, Chron. Diary, p. 26.] T. S.

MOLESWORTH, SIR WILLIAM (1810–1855), politician, born in Upper Brook Street, London, on 23 May 1810, was son of Sir Arscott-Ourry Molesworth, by Mary, daughter of Patrick Brown of Edinburgh. The Molesworths had been settled at Pencarrow, near Bodmin, Cornwall, since the time of Elizabeth. Sir Arscott was the seventh baronet (created in 1688). William had a bad constitution and was disfigured in childhood by scrofula. He was sent very early to a boarding-school near London, where the boys teased him on account of his infirmity. His father died 30 Dec. 1823. His mother then bestowed more care upon him; his health improved. With his mother and two sisters he removed during 1824 to Edinburgh, and studied at the university till 1827. In that year he entered St. John's College, Cambridge, but soon migrated to Trinity. He gave promise of mathematical distinction, but a quarrel with his tutor led to his expulsion in April 1828. He sent his tutor a challenge, and both were bound over by the mayor of Cambridge to keep the peace for a year. Molesworth spent the next few months in the family of Dr. Bekker at Offenbach, near Frankfort, studying German and philosophy. At the end of a year he travelled by coach to Munich to fight the postponed duel with his Cambridge tutor. Lord Queensberry acted as his second. Shots were exchanged, but neither was hurt. Molesworth then broke away 'for the south of Europe,' and stayed at Rome and Naples, where he found some young Englishmen, with whom he indulged in 'some youthful follies.' His follies, however, did not prevent him from studying Arabic for several hours a day with a view to eastern travel. His treatment by his father and at Cambridge had made him dislike all authority; in Germany he had become democratic; in Scotland, sceptical; and he had found Cambridge at a period of remarkable intellectual 'activity' (*Philosophical Radicals*, pp. 50–3). The utilitarian propaganda had been actively carried on there by Charles Buller [q. v.] and others. Receiving news at Naples of the growing excitement about parliamentary reform, he thought it a duty to take part in the contest. He made his first public appearance at a reform meeting in Cornwall in 1831; and he was returned as member for East Cornwall (December 1832) in the first reformed parliament. His Cornish connection made him known to Charles Buller, who had also been his contemporary at Cambridge, and was returned at the same election for Liskeard. He made the acquaintance of Grote in the house of commons, and by Grote was introduced to James Mill. Mill thought highly of his abilities, and he was accepted as one of the faithful utilitarians. Grote was for some years his political and philosophical mentor. He was also a favourite of Mrs. Grote, to whom he confided more than one love affair at this period. Two young ladies, to whom he made offers, rejected him at the bidding of their guardians on account of his infidel and radical opinions. Molesworth was embittered by his disappointments; and for some years tried to console himself by study, and received many reproaches from Mrs. Grote for his unsocial habits. He declared that he preferred to be disliked.

Molesworth was again returned for East Cornwall at the general election at the end of 1835. He had meanwhile projected the 'London Review,' of which the first number appeared in April 1835 [see under MILL, JOHN STUART]. James Mill contributed to it his last articles, and J. S. Mill was practically editor; while it was supported by the 'philosophical radicals' generally. In 1836 Molesworth purchased the 'Westminster Review' and amalgamated the two. In 1837 he transferred the ownership to J. S. Mill.

Molesworth continued to follow Grote's lead in politics. He voted against the repeal of the malt-tax under Peel's short administration in 1835, because he could not bear to vote against Grote, though many radicals differed from him. He was also a staunch supporter of the ballot—Grote's favourite measure—but his especial province was colonial policy. He obtained a committee to inquire into the system of transportation in 1837, and wrote the report. He continued to attack the system, and contributed to its ultimate abandonment. In his colonial policy he accepted the theories of Edward Gibbon Wakefield [q. v.], then in much favour. He supported all measures for colonial self-government, and protested with his party against the coercive measures adopted by the whig ministry during the Canadian troubles, after championing Lord Durham's policy. The 'philosophical radicals,' however, gradually sank into insignificance. As early as 1836 Buller observed to Grote that their duties would soon be confined to 'telling' Molesworth. His Cornish constituency became dissatisfied with him, he was disliked by the country gentlemen for his extreme views, the whigs resolved to give him up, and he did not satisfy the agricultural interest. He wrote to his constituents (September 1836) that he should not stand again, and looked out for a metropolitan constituency. He took part in founding the Reform Club during the same year. He was finally accepted as a candidate for Leeds, and was elected with Edward Baines [q. v.] in July 1837. An attempt to form a 'radical brigade' in this parliament failed, owing to a proposal from O'Connell to join it. The radicals were afraid that they would be swamped, and the scheme fell through (*Phil. Radicals*, p. 32). On 2 March 1838 Molesworth moved a vote of censure upon the colonial secretary [see Grant, Charles, Baron Glenelg]. An amendment was proposed by Lord Sandon [see Ryder, Dudley, second Earl of Harrowby] condemning the Canadian policy, when the original motion was withdrawn. The government had a majority of 29, Molesworth and Grote not voting. During the next few years Molesworth was much occupied with his edition of 'Hobbes's Works.' It was published in sixteen volumes, from 1839 to 1845, with dedication in English and Latin to Grote. He engaged as literary assistant Mr. Edward Grubbe (*ib.* p. 67). The book is said to have cost 'many thousand pounds.' It is the standard edition; but unfortunately Molesworth never finished the life of Hobbes, which was to complete it, although at his death it was reported to be in manuscript (*Gent. Mag.* 1855, pt. ii. p. 647). Molesworth joined Grote in subsidising Comte in 1840.

At the general election of 1841 Molesworth did not stand. He had offended many of his constituents in 1840 by holding a peace meeting at Leeds during the French difficulties of 1840, when he strongly advocated an alliance with France and attacked Russia. He remained quietly at Pencarrow studying mathematics. Another love affair, of which Mrs. Grote gives full details, had occupied him in 1840 and 1841, which again failed from the objections of the family to his principles. In 1844, however, he met a lady, who was happily at her own disposal. He was married, on 4 July 1844, to Andalusia Grant, daughter of Bruce Carstairs, and widow of Temple West of Mathon Lodge, Worcestershire. His friends thought, according to Mrs. Grote, that the lady's social position was too humble to justify the step. Mrs. Grote says that she defended him to her friends, but Molesworth, hearing that she had made some 'ill-natured remarks about his marriage,' curtly signified to her husband his wish to hear no more from her. Although Charles Austin made some attempts to make up the quarrel, the intimacy with the Grotes was finally broken off.

Molesworth after his marriage gave up his recluse habits, being anxious, as Mrs. Grote surmises, to show that he could conquer the world, from which he had received many mortifications. It may also be guessed that his marriage had made him happier. In any case he again entered parliament, being returned for Southwark in September 1845, with 1,943 votes against 1,182 for a tory candidate, and 352 for the representative of the dissenters and radicals, Edward Miall [q. v.] His support of the Maynooth grant was the chief ground of opposition, and a cry was raised of 'No Hobbes!' Molesworth retained his seat at Southwark till his death. On 20 May 1851 he moved for the discontinuance of transportation to Van Diemen's Land, but the house was counted out. He gave a general support to the whigs in the following years, and upon the formation of Lord Aberdeen's government in January 1853 became first commissioner of the board of works, with a seat in the cabinet. Cobden regarded his accession to office as an apostasy, and on the approach of the Crimean war taunted him with inconsistency. Molesworth defended himself by referring to the Leeds speech of 1840, in which he had avowed the same foreign policy. He had, however, broken with his old allies. He has the credit of having opened Kew Gardens to the public on Sundays. Upon Lord John Russell's resignation in 1855, Molesworth became colonial secretary (2 July). It was a position for which he had specially qualified himself; but his strength had already failed. He died 22 Oct. following, and was buried at Kensal Green.

As Molesworth left no issue, and as his

brothers had died before him, his cousin, the Rev. Sir Hugh Henry Molesworth, succeeded to the baronetcy. He left Pencarrow to his widow for her life. She was a well-known member of London society till her death, 16 May 1888. His sister Mary became in 1851 the wife of Richard Ford [q. v.], author of the 'Handbook to Spain.' A bust of Molesworth by Behnes, executed in 1843, was presented by him to Mrs. Grote; on her death it passed to his sister, Mrs. Ford, who presented it to the parliament house at Ottawa. Another bust is in the library of the National Liberal Club. A drawing is in the 'Maclise Portrait Gallery,' p. 211. Mrs. Grote says of him at the age of twenty-three, he had 'a pleasant countenance, expressive blue eyes, florid complexion, and light brown hair; a slim and neatly made figure, about 5 ft. 10 in. in height, with small, well-shaped hands and feet.' His health was always weak, and caused him many forebodings. This, as well as his unlucky love affairs and the dispiriting position of his party, probably increased his dislike to society in early life. In late years he seems to have been much liked. He was no debater; his speeches in parliament were carefully prepared essays, but were received with respect.

Molesworth reprinted some of his speeches in parliament, and wrote articles in the 'London and Westminster Review.'

[Mrs. Fawcett's Life, 1903; The Philosophical Radicals of 1832, comprising the Life of Sir William Molesworth, and incidents connected with the Reform Movement 1832–1844, privately printed by Mrs. Grote, with letters from Molesworth and anecdotes, not very discreet nor very accurate (1866). The contemporary notices in the Times, 23 Oct. 1855; Gent. Mag. 1855, pp. 645–8; New Monthly, 1855, pp. 394–400; and other journals are collected in a privately printed volume, Notices of Sir W. Molesworth [by T. Woolcombe], 1885. See also Morley's Cobden, 1881, i. 137, ii. 127, 160; Boase and Courtney's Bibl. Cornub.; Burke's Peerage and Baronetage.] L. S.

MOLESWORTH, WILLIAM NASSAU (1816–1890), historian, eldest son of the Rev. John Edward Nassau Molesworth, [q. v.], vicar of Rochdale, Lancashire, by his first wife, was born 8 Nov. 1816, at Millbrook, near Southampton, where his father then held a curacy. He was educated at the King's School, Canterbury, and at St. John's and Pembroke Colleges, Cambridge, where, as a senior optime, he graduated B.A. in 1839. In 1842 he proceeded to the degree of M.A., and in 1883 the university of Glasgow bestowed on him its LL.D. degree. He was ordained in 1839, and became curate to his father at Rochdale, but in 1841 the wardens and fellows of the Manchester Collegiate Church presented him to the incumbency of St. Andrew's Church, Travis Street, Ancoats, in Manchester, and in 1844 his father presented him to the church of St. Clement, Spotland, near Rochdale, which living he held till his resignation through ill-health in 1889. Though a poor preacher, he was a zealous and earnest parish priest; and in 1881 his labours were rewarded by an honorary canonry in Manchester Cathedral, conferred on him by Bishop Fraser. Ecclesiastically he was a high churchman; politically a radical. He was the friend of Bright, who publicly praised one of his histories (*Speeches*, ii. 110), and of Cobden, and received information from Lord Brougham for his 'History of the Reform Bill.' He was among the first to support the co-operative movement, which he knew through the 'Rochdale Pioneers.' Though described as 'angular in manner,' he appears to have been agreeable and estimable in private life. After some years of ill-health, he died at Rochdale 19 Dec. 1890, and was buried at Spotland. He married, 3 Sept. 1844, Margaret, daughter of George Murray of Ancoats Hall, Manchester, by whom he had six sons and one daughter.

Molesworth wrote a number of political and historical works, 'rather annals than history,' but copious and accurate. His principal work was 'History of England from 1830' [to the date of publication], 1871–3, and incorporating an earlier work on the Reform Bill; it reached a fifth thousand in 1874, and an abridged edition was published in 1887. His other works were: 1. 'Essay on the Religious Importance of Secular Instruction,' 1857. 2. 'Essay on the French Alliance,' which in 1860 gained the Emerton prize adjudicated by Lords Brougham, Clarendon, and Shaftesbury. 3. 'Plain Lectures on Astronomy,' 1862. 4. 'History of the Reform Bill of 1832,' 1864. 5. 'History of the Church of England from 1660,' 1882. He also edited, with his father, 'Common Sense,' 1842–3.

[Times, 20 Dec. 1890; Manchester Guardian, 20 Dec. 1890; Brit. Mus. Cat.] J. A. H.

MOLEYNS, Baron. [See Hungerford, Robert, 1431–1464.]

MOLEYNS, ADAM (*d.* 1450), bishop of Chichester. [See Molyneux.]

MOLINES or MULLEN, ALLAN, M.D. (*d.* 1690), anatomist, born in the north of Ireland, was educated in Dublin University, where he graduated B.A. and M.B. in 1676, and M.D. in 1684 (*Cat. of Graduates*, ed. Todd, pp. 416, 417). In the latter year he was apparently elected fellow of the College of Physicians in Ireland (*Register*, 1865, p. 92). He attempted original research in anatomy, and became a prominent member of the Dublin Philosophical Society, to which he contributed valuable papers on human and comparative anatomy. The most important was that in which he described the vascularity of the lens of the eye, to the discovery of which he appears to have been led by the dissection of an elephant. On 18 July 1683 he was elected F.R.S. (Thomson, *Hist of Roy. Soc.* App. iv.) A discreditable love affair obliged him to remove to London in 1686, and thence he went with William O'Brien, second earl of Inchiquin [q. v.], in 1690 to the West Indies, hoping to improve his fortunes by the discovery of some mines there. He died soon after landing at Barbados from the effects of intoxication.

Mullen published 'An Anatomical Account of the Elephant accidentally burnt in Dublin on 17 June 1681; together with a Relation of new Anatomical Observations on the Eyes of Animals. By A. M.,' &c., 2 pts. 4to, London, 1682. His examination was made with such accuracy that his descriptions have been quoted by writers down to the present time. The 'Philosophical Transactions' for 1685 contain an account of his dissection of a 'monstrous double cat' (xv. 1135). In the volume for 1687 he gave a close estimate of the quantity of blood contained in the body (xvi. 433). His experiments 'On the Injection of Mercury into the Blood' (xvii. 486), 'On a Black shining Sand brought from Virginia' (xvii. 624), and 'Anatomical Observations on the Heads of Fowls' (xvii. 711) are also recorded. His discovery of several structures in the tunics of the eye is acknowledged by Albrecht Haller.

[Ware's Writers of Ireland (Harris), p. 206; Cameron's College of Surgeons in Ireland, pp. 9–11, 94; Mapother's Lessons from the Lives of Irish Surgeons.] G. G.

MOLINES, MOLEYNS, or MULLINS, JAMES (*d.* 1639), surgeon, was born in the latter part of the sixteenth century, and appears at least as early as 1607 a member of the Barber-Surgeons' Company, of which he became a warden in 1625, and master in 1632. He was elected, 20 Jan. 1622–3, surgeon 'for the cutting of the stone' to St. Bartholomew's and St. Thomas's Hospitals, and held this office till his death in 1639. He was a noted surgeon in his day.

His son, Edward Molines (*d.* 1663), was appointed surgeon to St. Thomas's Hospital in his father's lifetime, and surgeon for the cutting of the stone to St. Bartholomew's, 6 July 1639, in succession to his father. He appears to have been a man of violent temper, as on one occasion he defied the authority of the Barber-Surgeons' Company, to which he belonged, being fined in consequence, and never holding any office in the company. On the breaking out of the war between Charles I and the parliament he joined the royal army, and was taken in arms at Arundel Castle when it was surrendered to the parliamentary forces in 1643. In consequence, the House of Commons ordered the governors of St. Thomas's Hospital to dismiss Molines from his office, which was done 25 Jan. 1643–4. He is mentioned as having compounded for his estate, the matter being finally settled in 1653 (Green, *Cal. State Papers*, Dom. Ser.; *Proceedings of Committee for Compounding*, 1643–60, p. 2554). He was replaced in his hospital office after the Restoration, 20 July 1660, in compliance with a letter from Charles II, and died in 1663.

James Molines (1628–1686), the eldest son of Edward Molines, was elected, 8 Nov. 1663, in compliance with a recommendation—equivalent to a command—from Charles II, surgeon to St. Thomas's Hospital 'as to ordinary avocations,' and joint surgeon with Mr. Hollyer 'for the cutting of the stone.' He was afterwards appointed surgeon in ordinary to Charles II and James II, and received the degree of M.D. from the university of Oxford 28 Sept. 1681. He died 8 Feb. 1686, and was buried in St. Bride's Church, Fleet Street, where his memorial tablet still exists. His name appears as giving an *imprimatur* to certain surgical works, but he does not seem to have contributed to the literature of the profession.

William Molines (*fl.* 1680), who was possibly a younger son of Edward, is mentioned in the 'Records of the Barber-Surgeons' as engaged in the anatomical dissections at their hall in 1648. He was the author or editor of a modest little work on anatomy, entitled 'Myotomia, or the Anatomical Administration of all the Muscles of an Humane Body' (London, 1680, sm. 8vo), and intended as a manual of dissection.

A third James Molines (*fl.* 1675) appears as the author of a manuscript volume in the British Museum Library (Sloane, 3293), containing, among other things, interesting notes of the surgical practice at St. Thomas's Hospital in 1675. He speaks of James Molines (the second) as his cousin, and of his father as being also a surgeon, so that he may possibly have been a son of William Molines. He was a student when he wrote these notes, and nothing further is known of him.

[Archives of St. Thomas's and St. Bartholomew's Hospitals; Sidney Young's Annals of the Barber-Surgeons, London, 1890; Paget's Records of Harvey, 1846, p. 30.] J. F. P.

MOLINES, MOLYNS, or MOLEYNS, SIR JOHN DE (*d.* 1362?), soldier, son of Vincent de Molines, who was returned to parliament as knight of the shire for Southampton in 1301 (*Parl. Writs*, i. 471), and his wife, Isabella (DUGDALE, *Baronage*, ii. 147), is said to have been descended from a Robert de Molines of Molines in the Bourbonnais, who came into England in the time of Henry I, and was probably connected with the Molines or Molyneux of Sefton, Lancashire, who traced their origin to the same town [see MOLYNEUX, ADAM DE]. John de Molines appears to have been in the service of the chancellor in 1325 (RYMER, *Fœdera*, II. i. 164), and was perhaps a clerk in chancery. In 1329 he was sent abroad on some mission with William de Montacute [q. v.], afterwards first earl of Salisbury, in whose service he was. Both had returned in 1330, and in October were employed to penetrate Nottingham Castle and arrest Roger Mortimer, first earl of March [q. v.] (LINGARD, iii. 49; STUBBS, ii. 390; DUGDALE, ii. 145). Molines was formally pardoned for killing one of Mortimer's attendants, and during the next few years Molines received numerous grants from Edward III, chiefly of manors and seignorial rights (cf. *Cal. Inquisitionum post Mortem*; RYMER, *Fœdera*; DUGDALE, *Baronage*, passim; and especially *Cal. Rot. Pat. in Turri Londin.* i. 113–39, where nearly every page contains some grant to Molines). He had previously acquired Stoke Poges, Buckinghamshire, by his marriage with Egidia, cousin and heir of Margaret, daughter of Robert Poges of Stoke Poges, and her husband, John Mauduit of Somerford, Wiltshire, and his favour with the king enabled him to 'multiply his territorial possessions to an enormous and dangerous extent' (LIPSCOMB, *Buckinghamshire*, passim). In 1335 he received pardon for entertaining John Maltravers, lately banished, Thomas de Berkeley, and others. In the same year he is spoken of as 'valettus' to the king, and received lands in the manors of Datchet and Fulmer, Buckinghamshire, for services to the king and to Montacute (*Cal. Rot. Pat. in Turri Londin.* i. 123 *b*; *Abbreviatio Rot. Orig.* ii. 65), and the king granted him the manor of Ludgershall, forfeited by Hugh le Despenser the elder (1262–1326) [q. v.] During the next two years Molines was serving under Montacute in the Scottish wars, for which in 1338 he received 220*l.* 10*s.* 1*d.* as wages and compensation for the horses he had lost. In 1337 he is again spoken of as 'valettus' to the king, and was treasurer of the king's chamber, in which capacity, perhaps, he was commissioned to seize all the Lombard merchants in London 'exceptis illis qui sunt de societatibus Bardorum et Peruch' and hand them over to Montacute, governor of the Tower (*Abbreviatio*, ii. 116). On 1 July he was commissioned to seize the goods of the French king (RYMER, II. ii. 982); before the end of the year was sent on a mission to Flanders in connection with the negotiations with the Flemish princes and burghers, and was made overseer of certain royal castles and lands in the Isle of Wight, Hampshire, and Yorkshire (*Abbreviatio*, ii. 118). In 1338 he received the custody of the king's hawks and other birds and numerous other grants (*ib.* passim), was created a knight-banneret, and employed in negotiating an alliance with the Duke of Brabant. In November he was sent on a similar mission to the German nobles.

In 1340 he was one of those who undertook to raise wools for the king's aid; but the supplies which reached Edward were quite insufficient. The king was compelled to raise the siege of Tournay, returned suddenly to London on 30 Nov., and arresting Stratford, to whose party Molines may have belonged, and the chief treasury officials, including Molines, imprisoned them in the Tower (STUBBS, ii. 402; *Cal. Rot. Pat. in Turri Londin.* I. i. 139 *b*; *Rolls of Parl.* ii. 119 *a*; LE BAKER, *Chron.*, ed. Maunde Thompson, p. 72; *Year-books of Edward III*, Rolls Ser. 1341, pp. 138–46; DUGDALE, ii. 146). Molines was apprehended by Montacute, but escaped from the Tower, and apparently refused to appear before the king's justices. For this 'rebellion' his lands were forfeited. In 1345, however, he was pardoned, and his lands were gradually restored to him, with numerous additional grants. On 18 Sept. 1346 he was directed, with all the men-at-arms and archers he could muster, to proceed to the defence of Sandwich, then threatened by the French; and in 1347 he was summoned as a baron to attend a council or parliament. But this summons did not entitle him to an hereditary writ, and neither his son nor his grandson received it. In the same year he was summoned to serve in the war against France (RYMER, III. i. 120). In 1352 he became steward to Queen Philippa and overseer of her castles, and in 1353 the commons petitioned against the excessive fines he levied; he had previously, in 1347, been accused of causing waste in Bernwood forest, and the king promised redress to the victims (*Rolls of Parl.* ii. 253 *a*). An inquiry was instituted into these 'treasons' (*Cal. Rot. Parl. in Turri Londin.* 167 *b*), Molines was thrown into prison, and his lands were forfeited; in 1358, however, his son William was admitted to some of them, and his wife Egidia retained others. In 1359 Molines was removed from Nottingham Castle, the scene of Mortimer's arrest, to Cambridge Castle. In 1362 he was accused of falsely indicting Robert Lambard for breaking into the queen's park (*Rolls of Parl.* ii. 274 *b*). His death took place probably in this year in Cambridge Castle, and he was buried in Stoke Poges Church, where a monument without any inscription, close to the altar, is said to be his. He was a considerable benefactor to religious foundations, especially to the canons of St. Mary Overy, Southwark, who inscribed his name in their martyrology, and to St. Frideswide's, Oxford. His wife Egidia died in 1367, seised of most of Molines's lands, which passed to his eldest son, William, who in 1355 had been in the expedition to France, was in 1379 knight of the shire for Bucks, and died in 1381, having married Margery, daughter of Edmund Bacoun. His son Richard died in 1384, and his grandson, William, was killed at Orleans in 1429, leaving an only daughter, Alianore, who married Robert Hungerford, lord Moleyns and Hungerford [q. v.]

[Lansdowne MS. 229; Cal. Rot. Pat. in Turri Londinensi, passim; Rolls of Parl. passim; Cal. Inquisitionum post Mortem; Inquisit. Nonarum; Year-books of Edward III, passim; Rymer's Fœdera, vols. ii. iii. passim; Abbreviatio Rot. Originalium, ii. passim; Cal. Rot. Chartarum et Inquisit. Ad quod Damnum, passim; Geoffrey le Baker, p. 72; Stow's Annals, p. 238; Dugdale's Baronage, ii. 145–8; Monasticon, passim; White Kennett's Parochial Antiquities of Ambrosden, Burcester, &c., passim; Barnes's Edward III, pp. 47, 101, 104, 213; Sheahan's Hist. of Bucks; Lipscomb's Buckinghamshire, passim; A Brief Hist. of Stoke Poges; Burke's Extinct Peerage; G. E. C.'s Peerage.]

A. F. P.

MOLINEUX, THOMAS (1759–1850), stenographer, born at Manchester on 14 May 1759, received his education in the school kept at Salford by Henry Clarke [q. v.], who taught him Byrom's system of shorthand, and before he was seventeen he became a writing-master and teacher of accounts in King Edward VI's Grammar School at Macclesfield. He resigned that situation in 1802, and died at Macclesfield on 15 Nov. 1850, aged 91.

He published 'An Abridgement of Mr. Byrom's Universal English Short-hand,' London, 1796, 8vo, called the second edition, though it was really the first. It is mainly a simpler representation of the system with a few alterations. Molineux afterwards brought out other works on the same subject, with beautifully engraved copperplates. One of them is partly written in an epistolary form. They were very popular, and passed through about twelve editions. Some of these are entitled 'An Introduction to Byrom's Universal English Short-hand,' and others 'The Short-hand Instructor or Stenographical Copy Book.' To the editions of the 'Instructor' published in 1824 and 1838 the portrait of the author, engraved by Roffe from a painting by Scott, is prefixed. Molineux was also the author of a small treatise on arithmetic.

His letters to Robert Cabbell Roffe, an engraver of London, whom he taught shorthand by correspondence, and who became the author of another modification of the same system, were edited and printed privately (London, 1860, 4to), but the impression was limited to twenty copies. The volume bears the title of 'The Grand Master,' suggested by the appellation given to Byrom by his pupils. This quaint book contains many gossiping notes on shorthand authors, including Byrom, Palmer, Gawtress, Lewis (whose 'History' and works are alleged to have been written by Hewson Clark), Carstairs, Nightingale, Gurney, Kitchingman, and Shorter.

[Bailey's Memoir of Dr. Henry Clarke, p. xxxviii; Biog. Dict. of Living Authors, p. 237; Evans's Cat. of Engraved Portraits, No. 7276; Journalist, 15 July 1887, p. 223; Phonotypic Journal, 1847, p. 332 *n.*; Sutton's Lancashire Authors, p. 161; Watt's Bibl. Brit.] T. C.

MOLINS, LEWIS DU (1606–1680), nonconformist controversialist. [See MOULIN.]

MOLL, HERMAN (*d.* 1732), geographer, a Dutchman, came to London about 1698, and finally established himself 'overagainst Devereux Court, between Temple Bar and St. Clement's Church in the Strand,' where he acquired considerable reputation for the excellence of his maps and geographical compilations. He was an 'old acquaintance' of Dr. William Stukeley, to whom he dedicated his 'Geographia Antiqua,' 1721. They belonged to the same club (STUKELEY, *Diaries and Letters*, Surtees Soc. i. 98, 134), and Stukeley possessed a profile portrait of Moll dated 17 April 1723 (*ib.* iii. 486). Moll died on 22 Sept. 1732 in St. Clements Danes (*Gent. Mag.* 1732, p. 979), leaving all he possessed to his only daughter Henderina Amelia Moll (will registered in P. C. C. 251, Bedford).

Moll published: 1. 'A System of Geography . . . illustrated with history and topography, and maps of every country,' 2 pts. fol. London, 1701. 2. 'A History of the English Wars in France, Spain, Portugal, Netherlands, Germany, &c. . . . with a large map of the same countries,' fol. London, 1705. 3. 'A View of the Coasts, Countries, and Islands within the limits of the South Sea Company,' 8vo, London, 1711; 2nd edit. undated, but about 1720. 4. 'Atlas Geographus . . . Ancient and Modern, illustrated with about 100 maps,' 5 vols. 4to, London, 1711–17. 5. 'Geographia antiqua Latinorum & Græcorum tabulis xxxii . . . expressa,' Latin and English, 4to, London, 1721; 2nd edit. 1726; other edits. 1732 and 1739. 6. 'A new Description of England and Wales . . . to which is added a new . . . set of maps of each county,' fol. London, 1724.

Moll's maps are also found in: 1. 'The Compleat Geographer,' 3rd edit. 2 pts. fol. London, 1709; 4th edit. 1723-22. 2. 'The British Empire in America, by John Oldmixon,' 2 vols. 8vo, London, 1708; also in the German translation, 4to, 1776, &c. 3. 'Modern History, by Thomas Salmon,' 3rd edit. 3 vols. fol. London, 1744–6. 4. 'The Agreeable Historian, by Samuel Simpson,' 3 vols. 8vo, London, 1746.

Of maps of general geography Moll published: 1. 'A Modern Atlas,' without title, 4to, about 1700. 2. 'Athlas [sic] Royal,' fol. 1708–20. 3. 'Atlas Minor . . . (62 maps),' oblong 4to, about 1732. 4. 'New Map of ye Earth and Water, according to Wright's alias Mercator's projection,' 12 sheets and index map. 5. 'The Whole World,' 2 sheets, 1719; others about 1732 and 1735. Of Great Britain he published singly: 'A new Map,' 1710; 'The South Part' (England and Wales), 1710; 'Fifty Maps of England and Wales,' 1724; 'A Pocket Companion of ye Roads of ye South,' 1717; 'Survey of the Roads from London to Berwick (1718), and to Holy Head,' about 1718; 'The Towns round London,' about 1710; 'Lincolnshire,' about 1724; 'Scotland,' 1714; '36 . . . Maps of Scotland,' about 1725; 'Ireland,' 1714, and with P. Lea, 4 sheets; 'Gurnsey, Jersey, Alderney,' about 1710; 'A Chart of the Channel between England and France,' about 1730; 'Parts of the Sea-coast of England, Holland, and Flanders,' about 1710; 'A General Chart of the Northern Navigation from England to Russia,' about 1710.

His maps of Continental Europe include: 'Plans of several Roads in different parts of Europe,' oblong 4to, 1732; 'Europe,' 1708; 'Spain and Portugal,' 1711; 'Plan of Gibraltar,' about 1725; 'France,' about 1710; 'Italy,' 1714; 'The Upper Part of Italy,' about 1731; 'Sea-coast of Naples,' about 1710; 'The Turkish Empire in Europe, Asia, and Africa . . . as also the dominions of the Emperor of Morocco,' about 1710; 'Germany,' 1712; 'The Empire of Germany,' about 1740; 'The Electorate of Brunswick—Lunenberg (or Hannover),' about 1715; 'Les Provinces des Pays-Bas Catholiques, or . . . Map of Flanders or Austrian Netherlands,' about 1705; 'United Provinces or the Netherlands,' about 1715; 'Denmark and Sweden,' about 1712; 'The Baltick,' about 1713; 'The Caspian Sea,' copied from C. van Verden; 'The North Pole,' about 1732.

On Asia he issued: 'A General Map,' about 1710; 'Arabia, agreeable to Modern History,' about 1715; 'India Proper,' about 1710; 'East Indies and the adjacent Countries,' about 1710; 'China and Japan,' about 1720.

His maps of Africa comprise 'A Map,' about 1710; 'The West (— East) part of Barbary,' 1732; 'Negroland and Guinea,' about 1732; 'St. Helena,' about 1732; 'The South Part and . . . Madagascar,' about 1720; 'The Bay of Agoa de Saldhana,' about 1732.

Those of North America, the West Indies, and South America comprise: 'America,' about 1720; 'Map of North America,' about 1710; 'Nieuwe Kaart van Noord-Amerika,' about 1720; 'A . . . Map of the Dominions of the King of Great Britain on ye Continent of North America,' 1711 (another, 2 sheets, 1715); 'Dominia Anglorum in America Septentrionali,' about 1735; 'A New Map of the North Parts . . . claimed by France' (Louisiana, Mississippi), 1720; 'A Map of New England, New York, . . . New Jersey, and Pennsilvania,' 1730; 'New Caledonia,' 1699; 'Newfoundland, St. Laurence Bay, the Fishing Banks, Acadia, and part of New Scotland,' about 1700; 'Virginia and Maryland,' about 1732; 'Carolina,' about 1710 (another, about 1732); 'A Plan of Port Royal Harbour in Carolina,' about 1710; 'New Mexico and Florida,' about 1700; 'Florida,' about 1732; 'A Chart of the West Indies,' about 1710; 'A Map of the West Indies . . . (A Draught of St. Augustin and its harbour),' about 1710; 'Jamaica,' about 1732; 'St. Christophers alias Kitts,' about 1732; 'South America,' about 1712 (another, 2 sheets, about 1720; 'The Island of Antego' [Antigua], about 1700.

[Brit. Mus. Catalogues of Printed Books and Maps; Allibone's Dict.; Boase and Courtney's Bibl. Cornub.; Gough's Brit. Topography; Watt's Bibl. Brit.] G. G.

MOLLINEUX, HENRY (*d.* 1719), quaker, born at Lydiate, near Ormskirk, Lancashire, was in 1684 imprisoned in Lancaster Castle for attending quakers' meetings. While in gaol he met Mary Southworth of Warrington, who was imprisoned on the same ground. He married her at Penketh, near Warrington, on 10 Feb. 1685, she being then thirty-four years old. Mollineux was sent to Lancaster Castle again in December 1690, on this occasion for non-payment of tithes, and after being detained several months was liberated through his wife's personal appeal to Bishop Stratford. He died at Lydiate on 16 Nov. 1719. He wrote several books in defence of quaker principles: 1. 'Antichrist Unvailed by the Finger of God's Power . . .' 1695, 8vo. 2. 'An Invitation from the Spirit of Christ to all that are athirst to come and drink of the Waters of Life freely . . .' 1696, 12mo. 3. 'Popery exposed by its own Authors, and two Romish Champions checked . . . being an Answer . . . to James Wetmough and Matthew Hall,' 1718, 8vo.

His wife died at Liverpool on 3 Nov. 1695, aged 44, leaving children. She was a facile writer of pious verse, a collection of which was published in 1702, under the title of 'Fruits of Retirement, or Miscellaneous Poems, Moral and Divine, &c.' It passed through six editions, the last of which was printed in 1772.

[Joseph Smith's Cat. of Friends' Books, ii. 180; Besse's Sufferings of the Quakers, i. 327; Mary Mollineux's Poems; Roger Haydock's Writings, 1700; extracts from Lancashire Friends' Registers, kindly furnished by Mr. Jos. H. King, Manchester.] C. W. S.

MOLLING (*d.* 696), saint and bishop. [See Daircell or Taircell.]

MOLLOY, CHARLES (1646–1690), legal writer, a native of King's County, born in 1646, was probably a member of the family of Molloy of Clonbeale, which claims to be the representative of the O'Molloys of Farcale or O'Molloys' Country. He seems to have entered at Lincoln's Inn on the last day of Trinity term 1663, and Gray's Inn on 28 June 1669. In the books of Gray's Inn it is stated that in consequence of his previous standing at Lincoln's Inn his admission was to date from 7 Aug. 1667.

Molloy was the compiler of an extensive treatise on maritime law and commerce, entitled 'De Jure Maritimo et Navali,' which was the standard work on the subject till superseded by the publications of J. A. Park, S. Marshall, and Lord Tenterden. Molloy's work contained little that was not also to be found in the 'Consuetudo vel Lex Mercatoria' by Gerard Malynes [q. v.] The small portion of the book devoted to the law concerning bills of exchange is said by Kent (*Commercial and Maritime Law,* p. 122) to be inferior to the treatise of John Marius. 'De Jure Maritimo' was published in London in 1676, 1677, 1682, 1688, 1690, 1707, 1722, 1744, 1769, 1778. Molloy also published 'Holland's Ingratitude, or a Serious Expostulation with the Dutch,' London, 1666, in which he introduced laudatory verses on George Monck, duke of Albemarle, and Prince Rupert.

Molloy married, at East Barnet, on 17 Dec. 1670 (par. reg.), Elizabeth Day, by whom he had at least one son, Charles, who edited the 1722 edition of 'De Jure Maritimo.' Molloy died in Crane Lane Court, Fleet Street, in 1690, his wife having predeceased him. Administration was granted to his creditors in April 1692.

[Burke's Landed Gentry, 1886, vol. ii.; Webb's Compendium of Irish Biography; Ware's Writers, ed. Harris, p. 203; Marvin's Legal Bibliography; Reddie's Maritime Commerce, p. 431; Story's Miscellaneous Writings, pp. 265–6; Admon. P. C. C. April 1692; Catalogues of Library at Lincoln's Inn, Bodleian Library, Library of Incorporated Law Soc.; Admissions Reg. of Gray's Inn, per Dennis W. Douthwaite, esq.] B. P.

MOLLOY, CHARLES (*d.* 1767), journalist and dramatist, born probably at Bir in King's County, was educated in Dublin. The statements that he was a member of Trinity College, Dublin, and the Middle Temple are erroneous. On 23 May 1764, being then a resident of St. Anne, Soho, London, he became a student of Gray's Inn (*Register*, ed. Foster, p. 384).

Molloy was author of three dramas: 1. 'The Perplex'd Couple; or, Mistake upon Mistake,' 12mo, London, 1715, a comedy mostly borrowed from Molière's 'Cocu Imaginaire.' It was brought out at Lincoln's Inn Fields on 16 Feb. 1715, and acted three times, with little success (Genest, *Hist. of the Stage*, ii. 567). 2. 'The Coquet; or, the English Chevalier,' 8vo, London, 1718, a comedy acted with applause at Lincoln's Inn Fields on 19 April 1718 and two following nights, and revived at the Haymarket on 23 Nov. 1793 with alterations (*ib.* ii. 630). 3. 'The Half-pay Officers,' 12mo, London, 1720, a comedy founded in part on Sir William

Davenant's 'Love and Honour.' It was first performed at Lincoln's Inn Fields on 11 Jan. 1720, and ran seven nights (*ib.* iii. 35). Much of its success was due to the fact that Peg Fryer, an actress of Charles II's days, who was then eighty-five, and had not appeared upon the stage for fifty years, took the part of Widow Rich. She acted admirably, and at the close of the performance danced a jig with wonderful agility.

Molloy ultimately adopted whig journalism as his profession, and became the principal writer in 'Fog's Weekly Journal,' the successor of 'Mist's Journal,' the first number of which appeared in October 1728 (Fox Bourne, *English Newspapers*, i. 122). He was also almost the sole author of another periodical, entitled 'Common Sense; or, the Englishman's Journal,' a collection of letters, political, humorous, and moral, extending from 5 Feb. 1737 to 27 Jan. 1739, afterwards collected into 2 vols. 12mo, 1738–9. To this journal Dr. William King, Lord Chesterfield, and Lord Lyttelton were occasional contributors. His papers are remarkable for their bright style, knowledge of affairs, and closeness of reasoning.

He died in Soho Square on 16 July 1767 (*Probate Act Book, P. C. C.*, 1767), and was buried on the 20th at Edmonton, Middlesex. In July 1742 he had married Miss Sarah Duffkin (1702–1758) of Nuneaton, Warwickshire, who brought him an ample fortune. He had no issue (Robinson, *Hist. of Edmonton*, pp. 72, 105).

[Baker's Biog. Dramat. 1812; Lysons's Environs, ii. 262, 272; Will of Sarah Molloy, formerly Duffkin, in P. C. C. 47, Hutton; Will of Charles Molloy in P. C. C. 174, Legard.] G. G.

MOLLOY or **O'MAOLMHUAIDH, FRANCIS** (*fl.* 1660), theologian and grammarian, was a native of the county of Meath, Ireland. The family of which he was a member had extensive landed possessions in the district known as O'Molloys' Country, and some of them engaged actively in the Irish movements from 1641 to 1652.

Francis Molloy entered the order of St. Francis, became a priest, was appointed professor of theology at St. Isidore's College, Rome, and acted as agent for the Irish catholics at the papal court in the reign of Charles II. His first published work was entitled 'Tractatus de Incarnatione ad mentem Scoti,' 1645. This was followed in 1658 by 'Jubilatia genethliaca in honorem Prosperi Balthasaris Philippi, Hispani principis, carmine,' and by a Latin treatise on theology in 1666. A catechism of the doctrines of the catholic church in the Irish language was published by Molloy in 1676 with the title: 'Lucerna fidelium, seu fasciculus decerptus ab authoribus magis versatis qui tractarunt de doctrina Christiana.' It was printed at Rome at the press of the Congregation 'de propaganda fide,' from which, in 1677, issued another book by Molloy, entitled 'Grammatica Latino-Hibernica,' 12mo, the first printed grammar of the Irish language. It is in Latin, and consists of twenty-five chapters: nine on the letters of the alphabet, three on etymology, one on contractions and cryptic writings, and twelve on prosody and versification. At the end is an Irish poem by Molloy on the neglect of the ancient language of Ireland and the prospects of its resuscitation.

Edward Lhuyd [q. v.], in his 'Archæologia Britannica,' published at Oxford in 1707, mentioned that he had seen a manuscript grammar of the Irish language copied at Louvain in 1669 which partially corresponded with that of Molloy. He added that Molloy's grammar, although the most complete extant in his time, was deficient as to syntax and the variation of the nouns and verbs. The date of Molloy's death has not been ascertained.

[Manuscripts in the Library of the Royal Irish Academy, Dublin; Wadding's Scriptores Ordinis Minorum, ed. Sbaralæus, Rome, 1806; Transactions of Iberno-Celtic Society, 1820; Remarks on the Irish Language, by J. Scurry, 1827; Grammar of the Irish Language, by J. O'Donovan, 1845; Contemporary Hist. of Affairs in Ireland, 1641–1652, Dublin, 1879.] J. T. G.

MOLUA, Saint (554?–608?). [See Lugid.]

MOLYNEUX, MOLEYNS, or **MOLINS, ADAM de** (*d.* 1450), bishop of Chichester, and keeper of the privy seal, was second son of Sir Richard Molyneux of Sefton, Lancashire, by his wife Ellen, daughter of Sir T. Ursewick, and brother of Sir Richard Molyneux (*d.* 1439), whose son, Sir Richard (*d.* 1459), is separately noticed. The family traced its descent from William de Molines, one of the Norman invaders, whose name is derived from a town in the Bourbonnais, and stands eighteenth on the Battle Abbey Roll. William de Molines obtained from Roger of Poitiers the grant of Sefton, where the family have since been seated, its present representative being William Philip, fourth earl of Sefton. Adam's grandfather, William Molyneux, was made a knight-banneret after the battle of Navarret, in 1367, by the Black Prince, with whom he served in the French and Spanish wars. From 1436 to 1441 Adam was clerk of the council to Henry VI (*Proceedings of the Privy Council*, v. Pref. viii). Immediately before the election of Albert II as king of the Romans in 1438 he was ordered to go with a knight of Rhodes to Aix-la-Chapelle and Cologne to congratulate the new 'emperor' (*ib.* pp. 89, 91). In 1440 he was made archdeacon of Taunton (Le Neve, *Fasti*, i. 167), a prebendary of St. Paul's, London (*ib.* ii. 448), and archdeacon of Salisbury (*ib.* p. 624). He successfully petitioned the king in 1441 to confer on him the living of Cottingham, Yorkshire, and being then dean of St. Buryan's College, Cornwall, was elected dean of Salisbury (*ib.* p. 616). In that year he was sent on the king's business to Frankfort, whence he proceeded to Rome with letters from Henry to Pope Eugenius IV, requesting the canonisation of Osmund, bishop of Sarum, and King Alfred. In October he exhibited articles before the commissioners for the trial of Eleanor Cobham, duchess of Gloucester [see under Humphrey, Duke of Gloucester], for sorcery (*English Chronicle*, p. 59). By the spring of 1442 he had resigned his place as clerk, and become a member of the privy council (*Proceedings*, v. 157, 173). He attached himself to the Beaufort party, and to the leadership of William de la Pole (1397–1450) [q. v.], earl, and afterwards duke of Suffolk, and was in February 1443 sent to John Beaufort (*d.* 1444), earl, and in that year duke, of Somerset [q. v.], to whom he would be an acceptable messenger, with a flattering message from the king with reference to the earl's new command as captain-general of Guienne, and to inquire specially as to his intentions with respect to the war (*ib.* p. 226 *postea*). He received a present of a hundred marks from the king for his services, and was commissioned to treat with envoys from Holland and Zealand concerning the complaints of their merchants (*ib.* p. 307). On 11 Feb. 1444 Moleyns was appointed keeper of the privy seal, in succession to Thomas Beckington [q. v.], bishop of Bath and Wells, and on the same day was commissioned with Suffolk and Sir Robert Roos as ambassador to conclude a peace or a truce with France (*Fœdera*, xi. 53, 58, 60). In May the ambassadors succeeded in arranging a truce, and obtained the betrothal of Margaret of Anjou [q. v.] to King Henry (*ib.* pp. 61, 74). Moleyns was prominent at the reception of, and in the negotiations with, the French ambassadors who came to London in July 1445, when the truce was prolonged (Stevenson, *French Wars*, i. 101 sq.) He was rewarded with the see of Chichester, to which he was, after papal provision, consecrated on 6 Feb. 1446 (Le Neve, *Fasti*, i. 247). He received a grant of exemption of all the coast within his lands from the jurisdiction of the court of admiralty (Stephens), and he held the living of Harrietsham, Kent, *in commendam.* As Henry had not fulfilled his engagement to surrender Le Mans, Moleyns was sent to Charles VII of France to request an extension of time (*Fœdera*, xi. 138; *Proceedings of the Privy Council*, vi. 51).

As keeper of the privy seal Moleyns must in 1447 have sealed the warrant for the arrest of Suffolk's great rival, the Duke of Gloucester, who died a few days afterwards (Stubbs, *Constitutional History*, iii. 137, where it is remarked that there is nothing in the history of Moleyns to give probability to a charge of connivance at the murder of the duke). He received a patent from the king for the exportation of wool, which Henry bought back from him for 1,000*l.* (Ramsay, *Lancaster and York*, ii. 79), and also had license to 'impark' twelve thousand acres, and to fortify twelve manor-houses (Stephens). Le Mans being threatened by the French, Moleyns and Roos were commissioned in January 1448 to negotiate for peace or a truce, and went to France to do the best they could for the town and its garrison (Ramsay, ii. 84; *Fœdera*, xi. 196, 216). They obtained an extension of the truce, and made terms for the surrender of the town. Other difficulties having arisen between England and France, Edmund Beaufort, duke of Somerset (*d.* 1455) [q. v.], then lieutenant of France, requested Charles VII to lay the matters before Moleyns and Roos, as more acquainted than he was with the arrangements between the two courts. By the time that his letter arrived the English ambassadors had left the French court and gone into Brittany, where the duke had cause of complaint against the English (Ramsay, ii. 85, 86). Early in 1449 Moleyns was engaged in negotiations with the Scots. The surrender of Maine and Anjou and the failure of Suffolk's policy caused general dissatisfaction in England, which was increased by the loss of a great part of Normandy. Moleyns was regarded as, next to Suffolk, responsible for the surrender of Maine, and was accordingly the object of popular hatred. On 9 Dec. he resigned the privy seal, and received the king's permission to travel on either side of the Channel (*Fœdera*, xi. 255). He went down to Portsmouth, where a force was gathered for the relief of Normandy, to pay the men their wages, and lodged in the hospital called God's House. The men were out of control, and were committing all manner of excesses. A dispute arose about the payment of the sailors

Moleyns was accused of docking their wages, and is said to have spoken haughtily. The sailors cried out that he was a traitor, and had sold Normandy to the French, fell upon him, and ill-used him so severely that he died on 9 Jan. 1450. When attacked he is reported to have said something that was held to seriously reflect on Suffolk, who when on his trial laid the blame of the actual delivery of Le Mans on the murdered bishop (Ramsay, ii. 118; *Rolls of Parl.* v. 176, 180).

Some declared that Moleyns owed his death to his covetousness, others ascribed it, though without ground, to the procurement of the Duke of York (Gregory, p. 189; Stow, *Annals*, p. 387), and Æneas Sylvius believed that his head was cut off (Æneas Sylvius, *Opp.* p. 443). He bequeathed some handsome church ornaments to his cathedral (Stephens). Moleyns seems to have been a capable and diligent politician of the second rank, a useful agent for carrying out the designs of greater men. The charge that he in any way betrayed the interests of England is untrue. Suffolk's policy, of which after his elevation he was doubtless something more than the agent, proved unsuccessful, and its failure excited popular indignation against him. This indignation is recorded in a contemporary poem (*Political Songs*, ii. 234, where the editor wrongly attributes the reference to Robert, lord Molines, and Hungerford [q. v.]; cf. Sir F. Madden in *Archæologia*, vol. xxix.) He was greedy of gain, though probably to no greater degree than most other politicians of his time. He evidently had a share in the revival of letters, and was a man of learning and culture; for he was a friend of 'Vincent Clement' (Beckington, *Correspondence*, ii. 115), and corresponded with and was esteemed by Æneas Sylvius, who commended his literary style (Æneas Sylvius, *Epp.* 80, 186; *De Europa*, p. 443). An epitaph written for him commemorates his prudence in affairs and his desire for peace (*Chronicon Henrici VI*, p. 38).

[Proc. of Privy Council, vols. v. vi. passim, ed. Nicolas; Rymer's Fœdera, xi. 53, 58, 60, 61, 74, 138, 160, 196, 216, 255, ed. 1710; Rolls of Parliament, v. 176, 180; Le Neve's Fasti, i. 167, 247, ii. 448, 616, 624, ed. Hardy; Stevenson's Wars in France, with W. Worcester, i. 101–21, 204, 207, ii. 583, 717, 764, 766, 771 (Rolls Ser.); Engl. Chron. ed. Davies, pp. 59, 61, 64 (Camden Soc.); Chron. Hen. VI, pp. 37, 38, ed. Giles; Three Fifteenth-Cent. Chrons. pp. 64, 101, 151 (Camden Soc.); Collections of London Citizen (Gregory), pp. 187, 189 (Camden Soc.); Beckington's Correspondence, i. 115, 117, 119 (Rolls Ser.); Stow's Annals, p. 387; Polit. Poems, ii. 234 (Rolls Ser.); Archæologia, vol. xxix.; Æneas Sylvius (Pius II), Opp. pp. 443, 563, 755, ed. 1571; Stephens's South Saxon See, pp. 149, 150; Ramsay's Lanc. and York, ii. 59, 79, 84–6, 118; Stubbs's Const. Hist. iii. 137, 143, 146; Gisborne Molineux's Memoir of the Molineux Family. For the pedigree cf. authorities under Molyneux, Sir Richard (*d.* 1459).] W. H.

MOLYNEUX, Sir EDMUND (*d.* 1552), judge, was eldest son of Sir Thomas Molyneux of Haughton, Nottinghamshire, by his second wife, Catherine, daughter of John Cotton of Hamstall Ridware, Staffordshire, relict of Thomas Poutrell of Hallam, Derbyshire. He graduated B.A. at Oxford on 1 July 1510, and about the same time entered Gray's Inn, where he was made an ancient in 1528, and elected Lent reader in 1532 and 1536. On 20 Nov. 1542 he was called to the degree of serjeant-at-law, and on the coronation of Edward VI was made a knight of the Bath (20 Feb. 1546–7). He appears as one of the witnesses to the patent of 24 Dec. 1547, by which the powers of the protector Somerset were at once amplified and made terminable at the pleasure of the king, signified under the great seal. In 1549 he was placed on the council of the north, and on 22 Oct. 1550 was created a justice of the common pleas. He appears to have been a sound lawyer. He died in 1552.

Molyneux was lord of the manor of Thorpe, near Newark, and of lands adjoining which had belonged to the Knights Hospitallers of the Preceptory of Eagle. By his wife Jane, daughter of John Cheyney of Chesham Bois, Buckinghamshire, he had issue four sons—one of whom, Edmund, is noticed below—and four daughters.

[Burke's Extinct Baronetage; Wotton's Baronetage, i. 148–50; Reg. Univ. Oxon. (Oxford Hist. Soc.), i. 70; Dugdale's Orig. pp. 292, 293; Chron. Ser. p. 87; Nicolas's Orders of Knighthood, vol. iii. Chron. List, p. xiii; Thoroton's Nottinghamshire, pp. 13, 179; Cal. State Papers, Dom. 1601–3, Addenda, 1547–65, p. 399; Archæologia, xxx. 463 et seq.; Strype's Mem. fol. vol. i. pt. i. pp. 22–3, pt. ii. p. 458; Burnet's Reformation, vol. ii. pt. ii. p. 312; Visitation of Nottinghamshire (Harl. Soc.), iv. 72; Visitation of Huntingdonshire (Camden Soc.), p. 26; Plowden's Reports, p. 49; Foss's Lives of the Judges.] J. M. R.

MOLYNEUX, EDMUND (*fl.* 1587), biographer, was third son of Sir Edmund Molyneux [q. v.] by Jane, daughter of John Cheney of Chesham Bois, Buckinghamshire (Gisborne Molineux, *Memoir of the Molineux Family*, p. 30). Tanner, citing 'Cabala,' ed. 1663, p. 140, identifies him with 'one Moleneux,' who, after being in the employ of Sir William Cecil and 'misusing' him, sought in August 1567 the post of secretary to Sir Henry Norris, the French ambassador. An Edmund Molyneux was admitted of Gray's Inn in 1574 (*Harl. MS.* 1912, f. 53). Edmund Molyneux became secretary to Sir Henry Sidney, and accompanied him to Ireland, where he acted as clerk of the council (*Cal. State Papers,* Irish Ser. 1509–73, pp. 422, 443). Sidney did his best to advance his interests at court. On 20 Sept. 1576 he wrote a long letter in his favour to Burghley (*ib.* 1574–85, p. 99), and in November 1576 vainly asked the privy council to appoint Molyneux, along with another, supervisor of the attorneys, who had 'grown very crafty and corrupt' (COLLINS, *Sidney Letters and Memorials,* i. 145, 187–8, 194). In September 1578 he was sent by Sidney to London to report upon the state of Ireland. On 31 Dec. 1579 he petitioned the privy council for his 'despatch and payment after long suit' (*Cal. State Papers,* Irish Ser. 1574–85, pp. 142, 203).

Molyneux furnished an account of Sir Henry, Sir Philip, Sir Robert, and Thomas Sidney to Holinshed's 'Chronicles' (ed. 1587, iii. 1548–56), in which he complained that Sir Henry Sidney, however he might strive, never succeeded in obtaining for him a comfortable office or reward of any kind. The enmity of Burghley probably retarded his advancement.

[Cal. State Papers, Carew MSS. 1515–74, pp. 401, 402; Tanner's Bibl. Brit. p. 530; Holinshed's Chronicle, ed. 1587, iii. 1590; Cal. State Papers, Dom. 1547–80, p. 195; Collins's Sidney Letters and Memorials, i. 66, 210, 227, 239, 240, 296.] G. G.

MOLYNEUX, SIR RICHARD (*d.* 1459), soldier, was son of Sir Richard Molyneux (*d.* 1439), whose brother Adam Molyneux or Moleyns, bishop of Chichester, is separately noticed. The father served under Henry V in the French wars, and especially distinguished himself at Agincourt in 1415, after which he was knighted. He was lord of Haydike, Warrington, Burtonwood, and Newton-in-the-dale, all in Lancashire. In 3 Henry VI (1 Sept. 1424–31 August 1425) he had a feud with Thomas Stanley, and both were arrested for riot (GREGSON, *Portfolio of Fragments,* p. 163). This Sir Richard died in 1439 at Sefton, Lancashire, where there is a monument to his memory (BRIDGENS, *Church of Sefton*). He married, first, Helene, daughter of Sir W. Harrington of Hombie, Lancashire, by whom he had two daughters; and, secondly, Joan, daughter and heiress of Sir Gilbert Haydocke of Bradley, Lancashire, and widow of Sir Pyers Legh, by whom he had eight sons and three daughters (cf. pedigree in *Visitation of Lancashire,* 1567, Chetham Soc.) One of his sons, Sir Robert Molyneux, was in 1448 taken prisoner by the Turks (*Hist. of Chantries,* Chetham Soc., p. 110).

The eldest son, Richard, received, by patent dated 26 July 1446, the chief forestership of the royal forests and parks in the wapentake of West Derbyshire, the constableship of Liverpool, with which the family had long been connected, and stewardship of West Derbyshire and Salfordshire, a grant which was confirmed in 1459. He became a favourite of Henry VI, was usher of the privy chamber, and when, in 1458, a partial resumption of grants was made, a special clause exempted the lands of Molyneux. He sided with Henry in the wars of the Roses, and fell in 1459 at Bloore Heath (cf. DRAYTON, *Polyolbion,* song xxii). Some of the family sided with the Yorkists, and a confusion among them led to the statement that Sir Richard joined Salisbury on his march to Bloore Heath, and fought on the Yorkist side. Molyneux married Elizabeth, second daughter of Sir Thomas Stanley, and his son Sir Thomas fought against the Scots during Edward IV's reign, was knighted by Gloucester on 24 July 1482 at the siege of Berwick, and was one of the pall-bearers at Edward IV's funeral.

SIR WILLIAM MOLYNEUX (1483–1548), son of Sir Thomas, by his wife Anne, daughter and coheir of Sir Thomas Dutton, led a considerable force to serve in 1513 under his cousin Sir Edward Stanley at Flodden Field, where he took with his own hands two Scottish banners and the Earl of Huntly's arms; for this service he was personally thanked in a letter by Henry VIII. He joined Derby's Sallee expedition in 1536 (GAIRDNER, *Letters and Papers,* ii. 1251), and died in 1548, aged 65, being buried in Sefton Church, where there is a monument and eulogistic Latin inscription to his memory. He was twice married, and his son Richard by his first wife, Jane, only daughter and heir of Richard Rydge or Rugge of Ridge, Shropshire, was knighted at Mary's accession in 1553, served as sheriff of Lancashire in 1566, and died in 1569. He also was twice married, and by his first wife, Eleanor, daughter of Sir Alexander Radcliffe, was father of William, who predeceased him in 1567, and grandfather of Richard Molyneux, created baronet in 1611, who was father of Richard, first viscount Maryborough [q. v.] (*Visitations of Lancashire,* Chetham Soc.; BAINES, *Co. Lancaster,* iv. 216–17; cf. also *Letters and Papers,* ed. Brewer and ed. Gairdner, passim; *Ducatus Lancastriæ,* passim; HALL, *Chronicle,* p. 240; STOW, p. 405; STRYPE, *Index*; METCALFE, *Book of Knights*; WEBER, *Battle of Flodden,* and authorities quoted below.)

[The following of the Chetham Society's publications contain particulars of the Molyneux family: Correspondence of the third Earl of Derby, Lancashire Funeral Certificates, Visitations of Lancashire, 1533 and 1567, Wills and Inventories, Norris Papers, Hist. of Chantries; Proceedings of Historic Society of Lancashire and Cheshire, vols. iv. v. vi.; Rymer's Fœdera; Holinshed's Chronicle, p. 649; Ramsay's Lancaster and York, ii. 215; Baines's Lancashire and Cheshire Past and Present, i. 377; Baines's County of Lancaster, passim; Bridgens's Church of Sefton; Ashcroft's Description of the Church of Sefton, pp. 14–24; Britton's Lancashire; Gregson's Fragments, passim.] A. F. P.

MOLYNEUX, Sir RICHARD, first Viscount Maryborough (1593–1636), born in 1593, was eldest surviving son of Sir Richard Molyneux of Sefton in Lancashire, and Frances, eldest daughter of Sir Gilbert Gerard [q. v.], master of the rolls. Sir Richard Molyneux (*d.* 1459) [q. v.] was his ancestor. He succeeded his father as receiver-general of the duchy of Lancaster, and on 22 Dec. 1628 he was advanced to the peerage of Ireland as Viscount Molyneux of Maryborough, in consideration of his distinguished merit and ancient extraction. He died on 8 May 1636, and was buried at Sefton. He married Mary, daughter and coheiress of Sir Thomas Caryll of Bentons in Shipley, Sussex, by whom he had issue: Richard, second viscount Maryborough (see below); Caryll, third viscount; Frances, who died young; Charlotte, who married Sir William Stanley of Hooton in Cheshire; and Mary, who married Sir George Selby of Whitehouse in the diocese of Durham. Shortly after his death his widow married Raphael Tarterean, carver to the queen, and died in 1639, at her house in St. Martin's Lane in the Fields.

Molyneux, Sir Richard, second Viscount Maryborough (1617?–1654?), eldest son of the above, was born about 1617. On 20 June 1642 he attended the commission of array on Preston Moor, and assisted at the seizure of the magazine at Preston. On the outbreak of the civil war he raised two regiments, one of horse and the other of foot, composed chiefly of Roman catholics, for the service of the king, forming part of the Lancashire forces under the command of the Earl of Derby. He was present at the siege of Manchester in September 1642, and on 20 April 1643 was defeated by Captain Ashton at Whalley. After the surprise of Wakefield on 21 May 1643, the Earl of Derby being then with the queen at York, Molyneux was ordered to conduct the Lancashire forces thither. He was defeated on 20 Aug. 1644 by Major-general Sir John Meldrum [q. v.] at Ormskirk, and narrowly escaped capture by hiding in a field of corn. He was at Oxford on 24 June 1646, when the city surrendered to the parliament. On 30 June 1648 a warrant was signed by the committee of Derby House for his arrest, as having, contrary to an ordinance of parliament, approached within twenty miles of London. He was suspected of being concerned in the rising of the royalist gentry at Kingston on 5 July, but four days later an order was issued for his discharge. He joined Charles II on his march to Worcester, and escaped after the battle on 3 Sept. 1651, but died shortly afterwards, probably in 1654. He married the Lady Frances Seymour, eldest daughter of William, marquis of Hertford, but had no issue, and was succeeded by his brother, **Caryll Molyneux, third Viscount Maryborough** (1621–1699), who played an active part during the civil war on the royalist side. His estate was sequestrated by the Commonwealth, but after the Restoration he lived in great splendour at Croxteth, near Liverpool. In the reign of James II, by whom he was constituted lord-lieutenant and custos rotulorum of the county of Lancaster, and admiral of the Narrow Seas, he was the centre of a number of catholic intrigues, and in 1688 he appeared in arms against William. He was deprived by the revolution of his offices and the greater part of his influence. He was arrested on 17 July 1694, with other catholic gentlemen of Lancashire, on a charge of high treason, was tried by a special commission at Manchester, and acquitted. He died on 2 Feb. 1698–9 (or according to Luttrell 1699–1700), and was buried at Sefton. He had issue by his wife Mary, daughter of Sir Alexander Barlow of Barlow in Lancashire, Richard, who predeceased him; Caryll, who died young; William (1656–1717), fourth viscount Maryborough; Mary, wife of Sir Thomas Preston of Furness; Frances, wife of Sir Neil O'Neill of Killileagh, co. Antrim; Margaret, who married first Jenico, seventh viscount Gormanstown, second Robert Casey, esq., third James Butler of Killveloigher in co. Tipperary; Elizabeth, wife of Edward Widdrington of Horsley, Northumberland; and Anne, wife of William Widdrington of Cheeseburn Grange in the same county.

[Lodge's Peerage, ed. Archdall, iii. 254–5; Berry's County Genealogies, Sussex, p. 359; Dodd's Church Hist. iii. 51; Cal. State Papers, Dom. Ser. 1636 p. 413, 1637–8 pp. 183, 225, 1639 pp. 308, 359, 385, 1644 p. 443, 1648–9 pp. 148, 165, 178; Baines's Hist. of the County of Lancaster; Gregson's Portfolio of Fragments; Seacome's Hist. of the House of Stanley; St. George's Visitation of Lancaster, 1613 (Chetham

Soc.); Civil War Tracts of Lancashire (ib.); Lancashire Lieutenancy under the Stuarts (ib.); Norris Papers (ib.); Lancashire Funeral Certificates (ib.); Dugdale's Visitation of Lancaster (ib.); Trials at Manchester in 1694 (ib.); Hibbert's Hist. of the Collegiate Church, Manchester, i. 192; Luttrell's Relation of State Affairs; Kingston's True History of the Several Designs and Conspiracies against William III; Gisborne Molineux's Memoir of the Molineux Family; Hist. MSS. Comm. 3rd Rep. pp. 148, 150, 4th Rep. p. 409, 5th Rep. pp. 142, 278, 293, 7th Rep. pp. 18, 190, 502.] R. D.

MOLYNEUX, SAMUEL (1689–1728), astronomer and politician, born at Chester on 18 July 1689, was the only child of William Molyneux [q. v.] who survived infancy. His father zealously undertook his education on Locke's principles, but died in 1698, leaving him to the care of his uncle, Dr. (afterwards Sir) Thomas Molyneux (1661–1733) [q. v.] He had lost his mother in 1691. Matriculating in his sixteenth year at Trinity College, Dublin, he there formed a friendship with George Berkeley (1685–1753) [q. v.], who dedicated to him in 1707 his 'Miscellanea Mathematica.' Having graduated B.A. in 1708 and M.A. in 1710, Molyneux devoted two years to the improvement of his estate in co. Armagh, then quitted Ireland, and visited the universities of Oxford and Cambridge, and the seats of some of the English nobility. He met with much civility from the Duke and Duchess of Marlborough at Antwerp during the winter of 1712–13, and was sent by the former in 1714 on a political mission to the court of Hanover, where he witnessed, in the Herrenhausen Garden, the sudden death of the Electress Sophia on 8 June 1714 (Coxe, *Life of Marlborough*, iii. 360, Wade's edition). He accompanied the royal family to England after the death of Queen Anne, and was made secretary to the Prince of Wales, a post which he retained until the prince became George II.

Molyneux married in 1717 Lady Elizabeth Capel, eldest daughter of Algernon, second earl of Essex. Her fortune was 10,000*l.*, and she inherited 18,000*l.* with Kew House, on the death, in 1721, of Lady Capel of Tewkesbury, her great-uncle's widow. They had no children. The cultivation of astronomy and optics now engaged Molyneux's efforts. He made the acquaintance of James Bradley [q. v.], and experimented with his assistance, from 1723 to 1725, on the construction of reflecting telescopes of Newtonian design. Their first successful speculum, completed in May 1724, was of twenty-six inches focus. They afterwards turned out one of eight feet, and Molyneux presented to John V, king of Portugal, a reflector made by himself, described and figured in Smith's 'Optics,' ii. 363, plate liii. His communication of the perfected process to Scarlett, the king's optician, and Hearne, a mathematical instrument maker in Whitefriars, was the means of bringing reflecting telescopes into general use.

In 1725 Molyneux resolved to repeat Hooke's attempts to determine stellar annual parallax [see Hooke, Robert], and ordered from Graham a zenith-sector of twenty-four feet radius, with an arc of only 25′, showing single seconds by the aid of a vernier. It was mounted on 26 Nov. 1725 in his private observatory at Kew House, and the observations of γ Draconis made with it by him and Bradley from 3 Dec. 1725 to 29 Dec. 1727 led to the latter's discovery of the aberration of light. Molyneux assisted in setting up Bradley's sector at Wanstead on 19 Aug. 1727, but was unable to prosecute the inquiry much further, owing to the pressure of public business ensuing upon his appointment, on 29 July 1727, as one of the lords of the admiralty. He formed schemes for the improvement of the navy, which his colleagues actively opposed, and these contrarieties perhaps hastened the development of brain disease inherited from his mother. He was seized with a fit in the House of Commons, and, after lingering a few days in stupor, died on 13 April 1728, at the age of thirty-eight. He was a man of winning manners and, obliging temper, and united Irish wit to social accomplishments. His inflexible integrity seemed alone to stand in the way of his high advancement. He was a privy councillor both in England and Ireland, represented the boroughs of Bossiney and St. Mawes, and the city of Exeter in the English parliaments of 1715, 1726, and 1727 respectively, and was returned in 1727 to the parliament of Ireland as member for the university of Dublin. He was elected a fellow of the Royal Society in 1712. Some time before his death he gave his optical collections and papers to Dr. Robert Smith of Cambridge, inviting him to live in his house and complete his proposed investigations. The resulting work on 'Optics,' Cambridge, 1738, included a chapter by Molyneux on 'The Method of Grinding and Polishing Glasses for Telescopes,' and one begun by him but finished by John Hadley [q. v.] on 'The Casting and Polishing of Specula.' Molyneux's description of his zenith-sector and journal of the Kew observations were printed by Rigaud in 1832 among Bradley's 'Miscellaneous Works.' Subsequently to the remarriage of Molyneux's widow to Nathaniel St. André, on 17 May 1730, Kew House was leased by Frederick, prince of Wales. It was demolished in 1804, and a sundial, erected by William IV in 1834, now commemorates the observations made there. Nothing is known of the fate of the Kew sector.

[Sir Capel Molyneux's Account of the Family of Sir Thomas Molyneux, 1820; Nichol's Hogarth, i. 476; Biog. Brit.; Hutton's Mathemat. Dict. 1815; Bradley's Works, p. xxix; Delambre's Hist. de l'Astronomie au XVIIIe Siècle, p. 414; Wolf's Geschichte der Astronomie, p. 484; Manning and Bray's Hist. of Surrey, i. 446; R. H. Scott on Hist. of Kew Observatory, Proc. of Roy. Soc. xxxix. 37; Chron. Diary in Hist. Reg. for 1728, p. 23; Hist. MSS. Comm. 11th Rep. pt. iii. pp. 31–40.] A. M. C.

MOLYNEUX or **MOLINEL**, **Sir THOMAS** (1531–1597), chancellor of exchequer in Ireland, was born at Calais in 1531. His parents, of whom he was the only child, died while he was young, and he was brought up by John Brishin, an alderman of Calais. When that town was taken from the English by the Duke of Guise in 1558, Molyneux was made prisoner. Having ransomed himself by payment of five hundred crowns, he removed to Bruges, and there married Catherine Staboert, daughter of an opulent burgomaster, portraits of both of whom are in the possession of Molyneux's descendants. On account of Alva's persecutions Molyneux removed to London in 1568, and in 1576 settled in Dublin (extract from 'Memoranda,' *Roll of Excheq. of Ireland*, p. 4). In 1578 he received a grant in connection with the town of Swords near that city, and was employed as surveyor of victuals for the army in Ireland and as deputy to the collector of customs on wines there. He was appointed chancellor of the exchequer in Ireland in 1590, and in the succeeding year obtained the office of receiver of customs and imposts on wines. At this time he contributed 40*l.* towards the building of Trinity College, Dublin. In consequence of an impugnment of the legality of Molyneux's official employment under the queen, on the allegation that he was an alien, an inquiry was instituted in the court of exchequer at Dublin in 1594. Witnesses examined there, before the attorney-general, deposed that Molyneux was an Englishman, born in Calais, while that town was under the crown of England; that he was a true and loyal subject, 'of Christian religion, using sermons and other goodly exercises' (*ib.* p. 4). Molyneux died at Dublin on 24 Jan. 1596–7, and was buried there in the cathedral of Christ Church. He left two daughters and two sons, Samuel and Daniel, both of whom sat in the Irish parliament of 1613: Samuel became surveyor-general of buildings and works in Ireland, and Daniel (1568–1632) was Ulster king-of-arms, and by Jane, daughter of Sir William Usher, had eight children, of whom the third, Samuel, was father of William and Sir Thomas, who are noticed separately.

[Chancery and Exchequer Records, Dublin; Extract from the Memoranda Roll of the Exchequer of Ireland, privately printed at Evesham, 1850 (?), 4to; Account of Sir T. Molyneux, 1820; Carew MSS. 1589–1600, p. 255; Cal. State Papers, Ireland, 1592–6; Lascelles, Liber Munerum, vol. i. pt. ii. p. 48.] J. T. G.

MOLYNEUX, **Sir THOMAS** (1661–1733), physician, brother of William Molyneux [q. v.], was born in Dublin, 14 April 1661. He was educated at Dr. Henry Rider's school in Dublin, and entered Trinity College, Dublin, in 1676. He graduated M.A. and M.B. in 1683, and then started for Leyden in order to extend his medical knowledge before proceeding to the degree of M.D. He sailed from Dublin in the first week of May 1683, rested at Chester for five days, and was introduced to Bishop Pearson [q. v.], whom he at once recognised from the frontispiece of his 'Treatise on the Creed.' On 12 May he arrived in London and took lodgings at the Flower de Luce, near St. Dunstan's Church in Fleet Street. He called on Nehemiah Grew [q. v.], and there met Thomas Burnet [q.v.], author of 'Theoria Telluris,' and Robert Boyle [q. v.], at whose house he made the acquaintance of Sir William Petty [q. v.] Soon after he was introduced to Dr. Edward Browne [q. v.], and on 23 May attended a meeting of the Royal Society in Gresham College and saw Sir Isaac Newton, John Evelyn, and Dr. Edward Tyson [q. v.] He enjoyed the conversation of all these famous men as well as that of John Flamsteed [q. v.], the astronomer. Early in June he visited Eton and saw King William and Queen Mary at supper at Windsor, and later in the month met Dryden in London. He went to Cambridge, where he saw 'that extraordinary platonick philosopher,' Dr. Henry More, and was surprised at the purple gowns of the Trinity undergraduates. On 17 July he went to Oxford, attended a lecture of Dr. Luff, the professor of physic, on the first aphorism of Hippocrates, and made the acquaintance of several learned men. On 20 July he sailed from Billingsgate to Rotterdam, visited Amsterdam, Haarlem, and Utrecht, and finally entered at the university of Leyden. While there next year he met Locke, who afterwards wrote a letter to him from Utrecht on 22 Dec. 1684, thanking him for his kindness. In the 'Philosophical Transactions,' No. 168, he published an essay on a human frontal bone in the museum at Leyden, of extreme size and thickness, an example either of Parrot's disease or of the osteitis deformans of Paget. On 14 March 1685 he made a report to the Royal Society on the collections of Swammerdam and Hermann, and in the same year went to Paris, where he stayed till his return to London in March 1686. In April 1687 he returned to Dublin, there graduated M.D., and on 3 Nov. 1687 was elected F.R.S. The troubles of the times led him to move to Chester and begin practice there, but in 1690, after the battle of the Boyne, he came back to Dublin, lived in his father's house, and practised as a physician. He kept up his correspondence with Locke, who sometimes consulted him, and with other learned acquaintances, and in the new charter to the Irish College of Physicians, 15 Dec. 1692, he is named as a fellow. His practice was so successful that in 1693 he bought an estate of 100*l.* a year. In the same year (*Phil. Trans.* No. 202) he published an essay on calculus, and in 1698 a further paper on the same subject. He married in 1693 Catharine Howard, daughter of Dr. Robert Howard, a lady accomplished as a painter. In 1694 he published in the 'Philosophical Transactions' a medical essay 'On the late Coughs and Colds,' and shortly after 'Notes on the Giant's Causeway,' the first publication in which the opinion that it is a natural production and not a work of man is maintained. He had a drawing made of it, and in a second paper (*ib.* No. 241) describes the details of drawing. He was interested in all parts of natural science, and having found in the stomach of a codfish a specimen of *Aphrodite aculeata*, an annulate animal with iridescent hairs, he dissected it and sent an account of its anatomy in a letter to Locke, who forwarded it to the Royal Society. It is the earliest account of the structure of the sea mouse, and is printed in the 'Philosophical Transactions,' No. 225. In April 1696 he published the first scientific account of the Irish elk (*Cervus megaceros*), 'A Discourse concerning the large Horns frequently found underground in Ireland.' He also published a letter to Dr. Ashe, bishop of Clogher, 'On the Swarms of Insects of late years seen in the County Longford.' His brother William, to whom he was deeply attached, died in 1698, and Locke wrote him a consolatory letter on the occasion. In 1699 he again visited London and was painted by Kneller. The picture is preserved in Trinity College, Dublin. He next published (*Phil. Trans.* No. 261) an essay on giants, and in 1701 'Notes on an Epidemic of Eye-disease which occurred at Castletown Delvin, co. Westmeath,' followed in 1702 by a 'Letter on the Lyre of the Greeks and Romans.' On 19 Oct. 1702 he was elected president of the College of Physicians of Ireland, and held the same office in 1709, 1713, and 1720. In 1711 he built himself a large town house in Peter Street, Dublin, and in 1715 he was appointed state physician in Ireland, and in January 1717 professor of medicine in the university of Dublin. He was also physician-general to the army. He did not conclude his scientific writings, but published in 1715 an account of an elephant's jaw found in Cavan, and in 1725 'A Discourse on Danish Forts.' In 1727 he wrote, but did not print, 'Some Observations on the Taxes paid by Ireland to support the Government.' On 30 July 1730 he was created a baronet, and his successor in title is seated at Castle Dillon, co. Armagh. He had sixteen children. He died in 1733, and is buried in Armagh Cathedral, where there is a fine statue of him by Roubiliac (*Notes and Queries*, 3rd ser. xviii. 114). His published observations show him to have been an excellent physician. Several of his zoological papers are the first upon their subjects, and he took an active interest in every branch of learning, and delighted in the society of all learned men. He occupied a position in Ireland resembling that of Richard Mead [q. v.] in England, but in mental activity, as well as in the highest qualities included in the term 'good breeding,' he excelled Mead.

[Dublin University Magazine, vol. xviii., where many of his letters are printed in full; Locke's Works; Chalmers's Biog. Dict.; A. Webb's Compendium of Irish Biography; Sir C. A. Cameron's Hist. of the Royal College of Surgeons in Ireland; Works.] N. M.

MOLYNEUX, WILLIAM (1656–1698), philosopher, was born at his father's house in New Row, Dublin, on 17 April 1656. He was the eldest surviving son of Samuel Molyneux (1616–1693) by Margaret, daughter and coheiress of William Dowdall, esq., of Dublin. The family was descended from Sir Thomas Molyneux [q. v.], chancellor of the Irish exchequer in 1590. The father, a gentleman of property in several counties, had acquired considerable fame as a master-gunner during the rebellion, particularly at the battle of Ross in 1643 (Carte, *Life of Ormonde*, i. 405), and afterwards as an experimentalist in the science of gunnery, on which subject he published a treatise when seventy years of age; he died on 23 Jan. 1693. A younger son, Sir Thomas Molyneux (1661–1733), is separately noticed. After receiving a good elementary education, William entered Trinity College, Dublin, on 10 April 1671, and was placed under the tuition of Dr. William Palliser [q. v.], afterwards archbishop of Cashel (TAYLOR, *Dublin Univ.* p. 377). Having graduated B.A. he quitted the university with credit, and proceeding to London entered the Middle Temple as a student of law on 23 June 1675. The heir to an easy fortune, and having no particular predilection for law, he devoted himself chiefly to philosophy and applied mathematics. In June 1678 he returned to Dublin, and with his father's consent married, on 19 Sept., Lucy, youngest daughter of Sir William Domvile, attorney-general of Ireland. Mrs. Molyneux was a lady of remarkable beauty and of an amiable disposition, but unfortunately, only three months after her marriage, she was attacked by an illness which not only deprived her of sight, but until her death, thirteen years later, caused her intolerable pain. Molyneux himself suffered from an hereditary affection of the kidneys, which seriously interfered with his enjoyment of life, and was eventually the cause of his premature death.

After some time spent in England in the vain endeavour to obtain medical relief for his wife, Molyneux settled down in Dublin. He resumed his philosophical studies, and during the winter of 1679 he made an English version of Descartes's 'Meditations,' which was published in London in April 1680. His interest in optics and astronomy was stimulated by a correspondence which he opened with John Flamsteed [q. v.], astronomer royal, in 1681. This intercourse continued till 1692, when, according to Molyneux, Flamsteed broke off relations with him owing to some offence Molyneux had given him in his 'Dioptrica Nova.' In the summer of 1682 he was engaged in collecting materials for a 'Description of Ireland,' to form part of Moses Pitt's 'Atlas;' it was never published owing to Pitt's failure to carry out his project. Among others with whom he in this way became acquainted was Roderick O'Flaherty [q. v.], whom he assisted in the publication of his 'Ogygia,' and Peter Walsh [q. v.], to whom he owed an introduction to the Duke of Ormonde. His interest in science, and the example furnished by the Royal Society, led him to take an active part in the foundation in 1683 of the Dublin Philosophical Society, the precursor of the Royal Irish Academy, of which he was the first secretary, and Sir William Petty [q. v.], the first president.

By the influence of the Duke of Ormonde Molyneux was in 1684 appointed, jointly with (Sir) William Robinson, chief engineer and surveyor-general of the king's buildings and works, in which capacity he built that part of Dublin Castle which stands upon the Piazza, with the turrets to the south; but he was ejected from office in 1688 by Tyrconnel on account of his religion. In 1685 he was elected a fellow of the Royal Society; and it being his intention that summer to visit his brother, Thomas (afterwards Sir Thomas) Molyneux [q. v.], at Leyden, he received a concordatum of 100*l.* from the Irish government to enable him to view and make draughts of the principal fortresses in Flanders. He left Dublin on 13 May, and meeting at Calais Viscount Mountjoy he travelled with him through the Netherlands and parts of Germany and France, including Paris, where, by means of letters of recommendation from Flamsteed, he made the acquaintance of the astronomer Cassini and other eminent men of science.

He returned to Ireland at the end of September, and was almost immediately prostrated by a severe illness. Early in the following year (1686) he published his 'Sciothericum Telescopicum: or, A New Contrivance of adapting a Telescope to a Horizontal Dial,' with a dedication to the lord-lieutenant, the Earl of Clarendon, in which he raised the question 'whether the natural philosophy formerly professed in the schools or that which is at present prosecuted by the societies lately instituted in several of the most noted parts of Europe be the true philosophy or method of investigating nature?' The telescopic dial itself never came into general use, and was practically condemned by Flamsteed. On the appearance of Sir Isaac Newton's 'Principia' in 1687 Molyneux candidly admitted that his knowledge of mathematics was not sufficient to enable him to understand it. Becoming alarmed at the policy of proscription pursued by Tyrconnel, and dreading a repetition of the horrors of 1641, he retired on 31 Jan. 1689, with his wife, to Chester, where he resided in a little house outside the north gate for nearly two years. There he wrote the greater part of his 'Dioptrica Nova,' in which he was assisted by Flamsteed. The book, which was for a long time the standard work on optics, was published at London in 1692, the sheets being revised by Edmund Halley [q. v.] the astronomer, who, at Molyneux's request, allowed his celebrated theorem for finding the foci of optic glasses to be printed in the appendix. A passage in the Epistle Dedicatory in warm commendation of Locke's 'Essay on the Human Understanding' obtained grateful acknowledgment from that philosopher, and was the beginning of a long and friendly correspondence between them (see *Some Familiar Letters between*

Mr. Locke and several of his Friends, London, 1708).

Immediately after the battle of the Boyne (1 July 1690) Molyneux paid a hurried visit to his old father, who had persisted in remaining in Dublin. On his return through Wales he was mistaken by the Denbighshire militia for William Molyneux, eldest son of Lord Molyneux, for whose apprehension 500*l.* reward had been offered; but having proved his identity he was, after a brief detention, allowed to proceed on his journey. In December 1690 he was suddenly recalled to Dublin by the news that he had been placed on a commission for stating the accounts of the army. He was shortly afterwards rejoined by his wife and infant son, but recent events had proved too much for her delicate constitution, and on 9 May 1691 she died. A parliament, the first with the exception of Tyrconnel's convention that had met for twenty-six years, having been summoned for October 1692, Molyneux was returned as one of the representatives of Dublin University. In the discussion on the right of the commons to originate money bills Molyneux appears to have played a neutral part, for shortly before the dissolution he was nominated a commissioner of forfeited estates, with a salary of 400*l.* a year. But the ill reputation of the commissioners with whom he was to act induced him to decline the appointment, and his conduct, which was highly applauded, led to a reconstitution of the board. In July 1693 Trinity College conferred on him its honorary degree of LL.D., and in 1695 he was again chosen to represent the university in parliament. He was assiduous in his attention to his parliamentary duties, and during the absence of the lords justices Galway and Winchester in the winter of 1697–8 he shared the responsibility of government with the lord chancellor, John Methuen [q. v.], and the lord mayor, Mr. Van Homrigh.

From his correspondence with Locke it appears that Molyneux was at this time engaged in investigating the effect that the recent legislation of the English parliament was having on the linen and woollen industries of Ireland. His interest in the matter moved Molyneux to publish early in 1698 the work by which he is best known —viz. 'The Case of Ireland's being bound by Acts of Parliament in England stated.' It was, he admitted to Locke (*Familiar Letters*, p. 269), 'a nice subject,' but he thought he had treated it with discretion, and consequently had not hesitated to put his name to it and even to dedicate it to his majesty. None the less, he thought it prudent, till he saw how it was taken by the English parliament, not to cross the Channel, for though 'not apprehensive of any mischief from them, yet God only knows what resentments captious men may take on such occasions.' In substance the book is based on the treatise, 'A Declaration setting forth how and by what means the Laws and Statutes of England from time to time came to be in force in Ireland,' attributed by some to Patrick Darcy [q. v.] and by others to Sir Richard Bolton [q. v.] But Molyneux's effort has special value of its own as an attempt to prove the legislative independence of the Irish parliament. It made an immediate sensation, and two replies were at once forthcoming—viz. 'A Vindication of the Parliament of England,' &c., by John Cary [q. v.], London, 1698, and 'The History and Reasons of the Dependency of Ireland,' &c., by William Atwood [q. v.], London, 1698. The Irish government was supposed to have given some encouragement to its publication, and Methuen, as if to divert responsibility from the Irish ministry, himself introduced it to the notice of the English House of Commons on 21 May 1698 (Vernon, *Letters*, ii. 83). The business was referred to a committee. On 22 June the committee reported, and it was unanimously resolved 'that the said book was of dangerous consequence to the crown and parliament of England' (*Parl. Hist.* v. 1181). An address embodying the resolution was presented to the king (*Journals, House of Commons*, xii. 337); but there appears to be no ground for Macaulay's opinion (*Hist. of England*, v. 60) that Molyneux himself stood in any personal danger, or for the general belief that the book was condemned to be burnt by the common hangman.

About the beginning of July Molyneux went to England in fulfilment of a long-standing promise to visit Locke. 'I reckon it the happiest scene of my whole life,' he wrote (*Familiar Letters*, p. 272), in reference to his meeting with Locke and to the time he spent with him at Oates and in London. He reached Dublin again on 15 Sept., but shortly afterwards he was attacked with a severe fit of the stone. He died on 11 Oct. 1698, and was buried beside his wife, in the tomb of his great-grandfather, Sir William Ussher, in the north aisle of St. Audoen's Church, Dublin, where a monument with a long Latin inscription (cf. Gilbert, *Hist. of Dublin*, i. 283) was erected to his memory. The monument was removed by his grand-nephew, Sir Capel Molyneux, in order to be repaired, but owing to Sir Capel's death soon afterwards it was never replaced. In 1869 a tablet was fixed in the church on its site by a niece of Sir Capel's wife, the widow of the Hon. Henry Caulfeild (*Notes and Queries*, 4th ser. v. 291). The new inscription describes Molyneux as one 'whom Locke was proud to call his friend.' In appearance Molyneux was said somewhat to have resembled Locke (*Familiar Letters*, p. 172), to whom in his will, by a clause written with his own hand, he bequeathed 'the sum of five pounds to buy him a ring, in memory of the value and esteem I had for him' (*ib.* p. 292).

A portrait of Molyneux hangs in the examination hall, Trinity College, Dublin, beside that of Archbishop King. There is also an engraved portrait by Simms prefixed to 'The Case of Ireland,' Dublin, 1725.

Molyneux had two sons, of whom Samuel Molyneux [q. v.] survived him.

In addition to the works already mentioned, Molyneux contributed some papers to the Royal Society, which were printed in the 'Philosophical Transactions,' 1686–1689.

'A Journal of the Three Month's (*sic*) Royal Campaign of His Majesty in Ireland; with a Diary of the Siege of Lymerick,' London, 1690, is wrongly attributed to him.

[The chief authority for the life of Molyneux is a short account written by himself in 1694, at the request of his brother Thomas, edited and printed for private circulation at Evesham in 1820 by Sir Capel Molyneux. The best life, and that on which the life in the Biographia Britannica is based, was contributed by the Rev. John Madden in 1738 to Bayle's General Dictionary (English translation, with additions, London, 1734–41), where also is an interesting series of letters between Molyneux and Flamsteed, communicated by James Hodgson [q. v.], who married a niece of Flamsteed. The originals of these letters, with others of Samuel Molyneux, subsequently found their way into the possession of the corporation of the town of Southampton (Hist. MSS. Comm. 11th Rep. App. iii. p. 31). See also Molyneux's correspondence with Locke, now in the possession of Alfred Morrison, esq. (Hist. MSS. Comm. 9th Rep. App. p. 409), but printed in Some Familiar Letters between Mr. Locke and several of his Friends, London, 1708; Letters to Sir H. Sloane, in Sloane MS. 4053, ff. 175, 177, 181, 183; Molyneux's own works, particularly Dioptrica Nova; Birch's Hist. of the Royal Society, London, 1756–7, vol. iv.; Weld's History of the Royal Society; James Vernon's Letters, illustrative of the reign of William III; Notes and Queries, 1870.] R. D.

MOLYNS, JOHN (*d.* 1591), divine, born in Somerset, was made probationary fellow of Magdalen College, Oxford, 1541, and proceeded B.A. 1541, M.A. 1545, D.D. 1565–6. In Queen Mary's reign he left for Zurich, after Bishop Gardiner's visitation of his college, and at Frankfort was reader in Greek to the exiled English. He returned to England in Elizabeth's reign, and was appointed in 1559 canon of St. Paul's and archdeacon of London. In February 1561 he was collated to the rectory of Theydon Gernon, Essex, and in May 1577 to the rectory of Bocking, Essex. He was made dean of Bocking in October 1583, along with Dr. Still. He died in June 1591, and was buried in the north aisle of St. Paul's Cathedral. By his will he left 200*l.* to purchase lands to endow an exhibition for two scholars at Magdalen College. He is said to have published several books and sermons, but there is extant only 'Carmina Latina et Græca in Mortem duorum fratrum Suffolciensium, Henrici et Caroli Brandon,' 1552, 4to.

[Strype's Works, passim, vide Index, sub 'Mullings;' Wood's Athenæ Oxon. ed. Bliss, i. 581, ii. 8, 34; Tanner's Bibliotheca, p. 530; Register of the University of Oxford (Boase), i. 200; Newcourt's Repertorium, i. 63, 171, 309, 687, ii. 68–9, 584; Dugdale's Hist. of St. Paul's, p. 105.] R. B.

MOMPESSON, Sir GILES (1584–1651?), politician, born in 1584, was son of Thomas Mompesson of Bathampton, Wiltshire (*d.* 1587), by his second wife, Honor, daughter of Giles Estcourt of Salisbury (Hoare, *Wiltshire*, i. ii. 219—*Heytesbury Hundred*). He had two brothers, Thomas (1587–1640) and John (*d.* 1645), rector of Codford St. Mary (*ib.* p. 232; *Harl. MS.* 1443, fol. 161; Crisp, *Somersetshire Wills*, 4th ser. 28, 6th ser. 14). With a first cousin, Jasper Mompesson, two years his senior, Giles matriculated from Hart Hall, Oxford, on 24 Oct. 1600 (*Oxf. Univ. Reg.*, Oxf. Hist. Soc., ii. ii. 242; cf. *Cal. State Papers*, Dom. 1603–1610, p. 511). Neither seems to have taken a degree. About 1612 Mompesson married Catharine, a younger daughter of Sir John St. John of Lydiard Tregooze. The lady's elder sister, Barbara, was already the wife of Sir Edward Villiers, the half-brother of James I's powerful favourite, George Villiers, subsequently Duke of Buckingham. Through this connection George Villiers came to take some interest in Mompesson, and in 1614 he was elected to parliament for Great Bedwin as a subservient ally of the court (Spedding, *Bacon*, v. 65; *Return of Members of Parl.* App. x). In 1616 he suggested to the favourite Villiers the creation of a special commission for the purpose of granting licenses to keepers of inns and alehouses, whereby the pockets of the special commissioners and the king's impoverished exchequer might both benefit. Villiers adopted the suggestion. It was urged that the functions of the new commissioners would clash with those of the justices of the peace, but Bacon, then attorney-general, and three judges were consulted, and the referees were of opinion that the patent for the commission was perfectly legal. Accordingly, in October 1616, Mompesson and two others were nominated commissioners for the licensing of inns, and invested with the fullest powers, but the patent was not sealed by Lord-chancellor Egerton till March 1617, and then only under great pressure from the king (*Cal. State Papers*, 1611–18, p. 439). The fees which the commissioners were allowed to charge for the grant of licenses were practically left to their discretion, although it was stipulated that four-fifths of the sums received were to be paid into the exchequer (SPEDDING, *Bacon*, vi. 98–9; *Cal. State Papers*, 1611–18, p. 439). To increase his dignity in his new office, Mompesson was knighted by James I at Newmarket on 18 Nov. 1616 (NICHOLS, *Progresses*, iii. 227). Bacon wrote to Villiers that he was glad that the honour had been conferred on Mompesson: 'he may the better fight with the Bulls and the Bears, and the Saracens' Heads, and such fearful creatures' (SPEDDING, vi. 102). Mompesson performed his duties with reckless audacity. He charged exorbitant fees, exacted heavy fines from respectable innkeepers for trifling neglect of the licensing laws, and largely increased the number of inns by granting, on payment of heavy sums, new licenses to keepers of houses that had been closed on account of disorderly conduct.

Mompesson thus acquired a very evil reputation (cf. *Cal. State Papers*, 1611–18, p. 473), but his intimate relations remained unchanged with Buckingham and with Bacon, who became lord keeper 7 March 1616–17, and chancellor 7 Jan. 1617–18. At the end of 1619 Bacon frequently consulted him on matters affecting the public revenue, and on 12 Dec. invited him to Kew in order to confer with him the more quietly (SPEDDING, vii. 68–9).

Meanwhile, in 1618, Mompesson's functions were extended. Early in the year a commission had been issued for the purpose of imposing heavy penalties on all who engaged in the manufacture of gold and silver thread without a special license, which the commissioners were empowered to sell at a high price. On 20 Oct. 1618 the punitive powers of the commissioners were enlarged and their number increased by the addition of Mompesson. He at once set energetically to work, and threatened all goldsmiths and silkmen that they should 'rot in prison' unless they proved submissive. His activity satisfied the court. On 19 Feb. 1619 Sir Henry Savile wrote that Mompesson and Sir Albertus Morton were acting as clerks of the council (*Cal. State Papers*, 1619–23, p. 16), and on 9 Nov. 1619 James granted the former the office of surveyor of the profits of the New River Company, with an annual income of 200*l.* 'from the king's moieties of the profits of the said river' (*ib.* p. 91). On 25 April 1620 he received a license to convert coal and other fuel, excepting wood, into charcoal (*ib.* p. 139). But public feeling was running very high against him, and his re-election as M.P. for Great Bedwin in 1620 was quickly followed by retribution. On 19 Feb. 1620–1 the House of Commons considered Noy's proposal to inquire into the procedure of all commissions lately created to enforce such monopoly-patents as those affecting inns or gold and silver thread. Although that resolution was not adopted, a committee of the whole house opened, on 20 Feb., an investigation into the patent for licensing inns. Witnesses came forward to give convincing testimony of the infamous tyranny with which Mompesson or his agents had performed the duties of his office (GARDINER, iv. 42; *Archæologia*, vol. xli.) The patent was unanimously condemned. Mompesson at once admitted his fault, and, in a petition which was read in the house on 24 Feb., threw himself on the mercy of the house, but his appeal was heard in silence (SPEDDING, vii. 186). In a letter to Buckingham he promised to clear himself of all imputations if the king would direct the commons to specify the charges in greater detail (*Lords' Debates in* 1621, ed. Gardiner, Camd. Soc., p. 150). On 27 Feb. Coke, when reporting the committee's decision to the house, declared Mompesson to be the original projector of the scheme, to have prosecuted no less than 3,320 innkeepers for technical breaches of obsolete statutes, and to have licensed, in Hampshire alone, sixteen inns that had been previously closed by the justices as disorderly houses. Mompesson was summoned to the bar of the house and rigorously examined. He endeavoured to throw the responsibility on the lord chancellor and the judges who had declared the patent to be legal. Finally he was ordered to attend the house every forenoon, and to render his attendance the more certain he was committed to the care of the serjeant-at-arms (*Commons' Journals*, i. 532). The commons, at the same time, invited the lords to confer with them respecting his punishment. New charges against him accumulated daily, and his fears grew proportionately. On 3 March he managed to elude the vigilance of his gaolers, and before the alarm was raised was on his way to France. Notice was sent to all the ports to stay his flight; a proclamation was issued for his apprehension, and he was expelled from his seat in parliament (*ib.* i. 536). On 15 March the commons sent up to the lords a full account of his offences, and on the 27th the lord chief justice pronounced sentence upon him in the House of Lords, to which the commons were specially invited for the occasion (*Lords' Journals*, i. 72 *b*). He was to be degraded from the order of knighthood, to be conducted along the Strand with his face to the horse's tail, to pay a fine of ten thousand pounds, to be imprisoned for life, and to be for ever held an infamous person (Rushworth, *Hist. Coll.* i. 27; D'Ewes, *Diary*, i. 176). On 30 March a printed proclamation added, not quite logically, perpetual banishment to his punishment.

A rare illustrated tract, entitled 'The Description of Giles Mompesson, late Knight, censured by Parliament the 17th [i.e. the 27th] of March A° 1620[–1],' compared him to Sir Richard Empson [q. v.], the extortionate minister of Henry VII, and credited him with having filled his coffers with his ill-gotten gains. The indictment against Empson had been examined by the lords when they were proceeding against him, and a popular anagram on his name was 'No Empsons' (*Cal. State Papers*, 1619–23, p. 238). It is probable that Sir Giles Overreach ('a cruel extortioner'), the leading character in Massinger's 'New Way to Pay Old Debts,' was intended as a portrait of Mompesson. The play was written soon after his flight.

Lady Mompesson remained in England, and her friends made every effort to secure provision for her out of her husband's estate. On 7 July 1621 the fine of 10,000*l.* due from Mompesson was assigned to his father-in-law, Sir John St. John, and Edward Hungerford, together with all his goods and chattels, saving the annuity of 200*l.* allowed him by the New River Company. That asset was reserved for Lady Mompesson and her child (*ib.* p. 273). In the same year Mompesson petitioned Charles I to recall him so that he might answer the charges alleged against him, and he bitterly complained of the comparison made between him and Dudley or Empson (*Clarendon State Papers Cal.* i. 25). On 17 Feb. 1622–3 Lady Mompesson presented a similar petition, on the ground that his presence in England was necessary to settle his estate, most of which was illegally detained by his brother Thomas (*Cal. State Papers*, 1619–23, p. 419). Next day this application was granted for a term of three months, on the understanding that Mompesson should not appear at court and should confine himself to his private business (*ib.*) Later in the year (1623) Mompesson was not only in England, but was, according to Chamberlain, putting his patent for alehouses into execution on the ground that it had not been technically abrogated by parliament (*ib.* 1623–5, p. 13). On 10 Aug. 1623 a new warrant gave him permission to remain in England three months longer on the old understanding that he should solely devote himself to his private affairs (*ib.* p. 52). On 8 Feb. 1623–4 he was ordered to quit the country within five days (*ib.* p. 165). If he did so, he was soon back again. He lived till his death in retirement among his kinsfolk in Wiltshire. On 4 Feb. 1629–30 he acted with his brother Thomas as overseer of the will of his maternal cousin, Edward Estcourt of New Sarum (Crisp, *Somersetshire Wills*, 6th ser. p. 7), and he is mentioned in his brother Thomas's will, which was proved in 1640 (*ib.* 4th ser. p. 28). With Sir Edward Hyde, afterwards the great Earl of Clarendon, he seems to have been long on friendly terms. He employed Hyde in a lawsuit in 1640, and lent him 104*l.* in September 1643 (*Clarendon State Papers Cal.* i. 209, 211, 217, 244). Although a non-combatant he was a royalist, and in April 1647 went to the king's quarters at Hereford. His property was sequestrated by the parliament, and on 1 May 1647 he was fined 561*l.* 9*s.* (*Cal. of Proc. for Compounding*, pp. 77, 1738). The parliamentary committee for the advance of money assessed him at 800*l.* on 26 Dec. 1645 (*ib.* p. 666) and at 200*l.* on 2 Sept. 1651 (*ib.* p. 1388).

He is not heard of at a later date. He bequeathed 1*l.* 6*s.* 8*d.* to Tisbury parish wherewith to buy canvas for the poor (Hoare, *Wiltshire—Parish of Dunworth*—iv. 152).

[Gardiner's Hist. of England, vol. iv.; Spedding's Life of Bacon, vol. vii.; Wilson's Hist. of James I; Lords' Debates, 1621 (Camd. Soc.); Cat. of Satiric Prints in Brit. Mus. i. 55; Journals of Lords, i. 72 sq. and Commons, i. 530–75; Nichols's Progresses of James I, iii. 660.] S. L.

MOMPESSON, WILLIAM (1639–1709), hero of the 'plague at Eyam,' may be identified with the William Mompesson who in 1662 graduated M.A. from Peterhouse, Cambridge (*Cat. Cambr. Grad.*); the son and grandson mentioned below were educated at the same college. Becoming chaplain to Sir George Savile, lord Halifax, he was presented by his patron in 1664 to the rectory of Eyam, Derbyshire, then a flourishing centre of the lead-mining industry. To this village the infection of the great plague was conveyed in a box of cloths. The epidemic broke out on 7 Sept. 1665, and between that date and 11 Oct. 1666, 259 persons were carried off (so Mompesson's letters; the register gives 267 deaths) out of a population of about 350. Mompesson and his wife Catherine, daughter of Ralph Carr of Cocken, Durham (SURTEES, *Durham*, vol. iv. pt. ii. p. 208), remained at Eyam and did everything that could be done for the parishioners. When the plague was at its worst, June–August 1666, Mompesson, with the assistance of Thomas Stanley, a former rector of Eyam, who had been ejected in 1662 (W. BAGSHAW, *De Spiritualibus Pecci*, 1702), induced the people to confine themselves entirely to the parish, receiving necessaries from the Earl of Devonshire and from neighbouring villages in exchange for money placed in troughs of running water ('Mompesson's Well'). He read prayers on Sundays in a small valley known as The Delf, and preached from a perforated rock, still called Cucklet Church (figured in *Gent. Mag.* 1801, pt. ii. p. 785). Dr. Charles Creighton (*Hist. of Epidemics*, pp. 682–7) describes this visitation medically, and pronounces Mompesson's measures well meant, but wholly unnecessary and unsound. Mompesson escaped the disease himself, but his wife died on 25 Aug. 1666; and after her death, while not expecting to survive, he wrote farewell letters to his infant children and to his patron. Together with a third letter, written 20 Nov. 1666, to John Beilby of York, these were first printed by William Seward (*Anecdotes of some Distinguished Persons*, 1795, ii. 27–44) from what were described as the originals, in the possession of a gentleman of Eyam (possibly the Rev. Thomas Seward). They appear to be genuine; but though pathetic, are rather stilted, and were probably intended to be copied and preserved as formal records of the events.

In 1669 Mompesson was presented by Savile to the rectory of Eakring, near Ollerton, Nottinghamshire; the people, for fear of the plague, refused to admit him, and for some time he was forced to live in a hut in Rufford Park (note in *The Desolation of Eyam*, p. 46). He was subsequently made prebendary of Southwell (1676) and York, and is said to have declined the deanery of Lincoln in favour of Dr. Samuel Fuller (not Dr. Thomas Fuller as is frequently stated) in 1695. Mompesson died 7 March 1708–9 at Eakring, where there is a brass plate with three modern windows in the chancel to his memory (note from the Rev. W. L. B. Cator, rector of Eakring).

By a second wife, the widow of Charles Newby, Mompesson had two daughters. His only son, George, was rector of Barnburgh, Yorkshire, and had two sons: John (*d.* 1722), rector of Hassingham, Norfolk, and William, vicar of Mansfield, Nottinghamshire, one of whose daughters died in 1798, unmarried, while another was represented in 1865 by G. Mompesson Heathcote of Newbold, near Chesterfield.

[The best and most accurate account is that by William Wood in the History and Antiquities of Eyam, 4th ed. 1865, and the Reliquary, vol. iv. No. 13, 1863. The original authorities are (1) the letters mentioned above, (2) a Juvenile Letter by Anna Seward (whose father was rector of Eyam 1739–90), written in 1765 and printed in Gent. Mag. 1801, pt. ii. p. 300), based on the letters, local traditions, and (possibly) family information from Miss Mompesson. The story of the plague at Eyam was popularised mainly by William and Mary Howitt in The Desolation of Eyam and other Poems, 1827, noticed in Hone's Table Book, ii. cols. 481–96, 629. It is the subject of a considerable number of poems, on which the later popular versions appear to be based; they state as facts various details due to poetic imagination. Among the latest references see C. M. Yonge's Book of Golden Deeds, pp. 290–5, and Lantern Reading: the Story of Eyam, Sheffield (? 1881). See also Le Neve's Fasti (Hardy). A few facts are in Dr. R. Mead's History of the Plague, 1721 (Works, i. 290 or ed. 1775 pp. 216–17). Miss Seward's story of the reappearance of the plague in 1757 cannot be substantiated from the parish registers, but seventeen deaths from a 'putrid fever' are recorded in 1779.] H. E. D. B.

MONAHAN, JAMES HENRY (1804–1878), Irish judge, eldest son of Michael Monahan of Heathlawn, near Portumna, in Galway, by his marriage with Mary, daughter of Stephen Bloomfield of Eyrecourt in the same county, was born at Portumna in 1804. He was educated at the endowed school of Banagher in the King's County, and at Trinity College, Dublin, where he graduated in 1823, being first in science, and taking the gold medal. Entering the King's Inns, Dublin, in Easter term 1823, and Gray's Inn in Hilary term 1826, he was called to the Irish bar in Easter term 1828, and joined the Connaught circuit. In Dublin Monahan's success was at first slow, and his practice mainly on the chancery side, but on circuit he rapidly came to the front, and soon acquired the principal business there. In 1840 he was appointed Q.C., and from that time until he became a judge was one of the recognised leaders in the court of chancery. He practised also on the common law side, and was one of the counsel for the defendants in the trial of Daniel O'Connell ('the Liberator') and others for conspiracy in 1844.

On the formation of Lord John Russell's government, in 1846, Monahan was appointed solicitor-general for Ireland, and in the following year was elected a bencher of the King's Inns. At a by-election, in February 1847, he was returned for Galway Borough, after a severe contest, by a majority of four votes, but at the general election in August of that year the opposition of the Young Ireland party to the government prevented his re-election. In December 1847 he became attorney-general for Ireland, and in 1848 he was sworn of the Irish privy council. As attorney-general he conducted in 1848 the prosecutions arising out of the revolutionary movement of that year, including those of Smith O'Brien, Meagher and McManus at Clonmel, and of Gavan Duffy, Martin, and Mitchel in Dublin. He was accused of jury-packing by excluding catholics from the jury-box. In his speech in Mitchel's trial he warmly repudiated the charge, referred to the fact that he was himself a catholic, and stated that his instructions to the crown solicitor were to exclude no one on account of his religion, but only those, whatever their religion, who he believed would not give an impartial verdict (*Report of Trial of John Mitchel*, pp. 32–3, Dublin, 1848). In October 1850 Monahan was appointed chief justice of the common pleas in succession to Doherty. He held that office till January 1876, when he resigned owing to failing health. In 1867 he presided at the special commission for the trial of the Fenian prisoners at Cork and Limerick. He was an able and conscientious judge, uniting a comprehensive knowledge of law with strong, practical common-sense. He possessed the confidence alike of the bar and the public. The university of Dublin conferred upon him the degree of LL.D. in 1860, and placed him upon the senate. In 1861 he was appointed a commissioner of national education. He died on 8 Dec. 1878 at his residence, 5 Fitzwilliam Square, Dublin. In 1833 he married Fanny, daughter of Nicholas Harrington of Dublin; two sons (James Henry, called to the Irish bar 1856, Q.C. 1868; Henry, registrar of the consolidated nisi prius court) and four daughters survived him.

[Ann. Reg. 1878; Times, 13 Jan. 1876; Irish Times, 10 Dec. 1878; Report of Trial of William Smith O'Brien, Dublin, 1849; Report of Proceedings under the Treason Felony Act, Dublin, 1848; Four Years of Irish History, by Sir Charles Gavan Duffy; information from family.]
J. D. F.

MONAMY, PETER (1670?–1749), marine painter, born of poor parents about 1670, was a native of Jersey. He was sent to London when a boy, and apprenticed to an ordinary house-painter on London Bridge, but having a real aptitude for painting he devoted himself to drawing the shipping and other similar subjects on the Thames. He based his manner on those of the two William Van de Veldes, and soon became known to the seafaring community. His pictures were marked not only by good execution, but by close and accurate acquaintance with all the minor details of shipping. His colour was, however, somewhat tame and ineffective. There are two pictures by him at Hampton Court, and a large sea-piece by him is in the hall of the Painter-Stainers' Company, to which it was presented by the painter in 1726. Monamy painted parts of the decorative paintings at Vauxhall, including some representing Admiral Vernon's victories. He also decorated a carriage for the ill-fated Admiral Byng. He resided during the latter part of his life on the riverside in Westminster, where he died early in February 1749 in poor circumstances, as most of his work was done for dealers. His portrait, painted by H. Stubly, was engraved in mezzotint by J. Faber, junior, in 1731, another, engraved by Bretherton, is in Walpole's 'Painters.' An interesting picture of Monamy showing a picture to a patron, Thomas Walker, is in the possession of the Earl of Derby, and was formerly at Strawberry Hill; the figures were painted by William Hogarth, and the sea-piece by Monamy. Monamy also executed a few etchings.

[Walpole's Anecdotes of Painting, ed. Wornum; Vertue's MSS. (Brit. Mus. Add. MSS. 23074 f. 1, 23076 f. 13; Redgrave's Dict. of Artists; Catalogue of a Century of British Art (Grosvenor Gallery, 1887–8).]
L. C.

MONAN, Saint (*d.* 875?), missionary in Fifeshire, is called in the Scottish calendars (Forbes, *Kal. Scottish Saints*, passim) archdeacon, confessor or abbot, and his name is variously spelt as Mynnanus, Minnan, or Monon. According to the legend in the Aberdeen Breviary (*Pars Hyem.* f. lix.), he was born in Pannonia, and came over to preach among the Picts with a troop of Hungarians, numbering 6,606, led by St. Adrian, afterwards bishop of St. Andrews. This legend was accepted by many of the chroniclers (Skene, *Celtic Scotland*, ii. 312); but Hector Boece or Boethius [q. v.], probably using materials now lost (Forbes, loc. cit. p. 413), states that, though some call these men Hungarians, others say they were Scots from Ireland and Angles (*Scottish Hist.* vol. x. p. ccvi), and this is far more probable, for the Hungarians were not christianised in the ninth century (Bollandists' *Acta SS.* 1 March, p. 86). Scottish clergy, moreover, were leaving Ireland in large numbers at that time, and may have joined in Kenneth MacAlpine's invasion of the Picts, which accounts for the christianising of Fifeshire in the middle of the ninth century (*Celtic Scotland*, i. 320). The saint's name with its prefix, 'Mo,' also suggests an Irish origin.

Boethius was the first to call him 'Archdeacon of St. Andrews,' and in all probability had no historical warrant for so doing. According to the Breviary, Monan, after preaching on the mainland of Fife, at a place called Invere, passed over to the Isle of May, in the Firth of Forth, and was there martyred with many others by the Danes on 4 March 874–5. The Pictish chronicle refers to a great fight between the Danes and the Scots in 875, and this may be the occasion alluded to (Skene in *Proceedings Roy. Soc. of Antiquaries of Scotland*, iv. 316).

At the church of Abercromby St. Monance the saint's relics are said to have worked miracles in favour of David I [q. v.], and in the same village a cell is shown which St. Monan is said to have occupied when he withdrew from the neighbouring monastery of Pittenweem in the sixth century (*New Statistical Account*, p. 338), but the legend has probably no historical foundation. The name of a burn, Inweary, on the west of this parish, recalls the 'Invere' mentioned as the saint's temporary home in the Breviary. There is a chapelry of St. Monon in Kiltearn, Ross (*Orig. Par.* ii. 478), and a Kilminning farm and rock in the parish of Crail (*New Statistical Account*, 'Fife,' p. 966). St. Minnan's fair is held on 2 March at an old chapel at Freswick in Caithness (Forbes, p. 413). St. Monan's feast is 1 March. Dempster states, without authority, that St. Monan wrote a book of epistles and of hymns.

Colgan improbably suggests that an Irish saint, named Mannanus, of whom nothing is known save that he and his companion, named Tiaanus, were probably martyrs, and that their feast was celebrated on 23 Feb., is identical with the subject of this article (*Acta SS. Hib.* p. 392). Dempster speaks of St. Minnan, an archdeacon, living in 878, whose feast is celebrated on 1 March, as an independent personality. He says that a church, Kilminnan in Galloway, is dedicated to St. Minnan, and that he wrote several books. This account cannot be trusted, and Minnan is doubtless a variant of Monan (Bollandists' *Acta SS.* 1 March, p. 87).

[Bollandists' Acta SS. 1 March, pp. 86 sqq., 324–6; O'Hanlon's Irish Saints, iii. 63; Dempster's Hist. Eccles. Gent. Scot. xii. No. 834; Dict. Christ. Biog; see also article Moinenno.]

M. B.

MONBODDO, Lord. [See Burnett, James, 1714–1799, Scottish judge.]

MONCK. [See also Monk.]

MONCK, CHRISTOPHER, second Duke of Albemarle (1653–1688), born in 1653, only surviving son of George Monck, duke of Albemarle [q. v.], was known as Earl of Torrington from 1660 to 1670. He succeeded his father as second duke on his death, 3 Jan. 1670. Charles II had designed to bestow the first duke's vacant garter on his friend and kinsman, John Grenville, earl of Bath [q. v.], in accordance with a promise under the king's sign-manual made to the first duke that the Earl of Bath should be made Duke of Albemarle, in case his own son died without issue. The Earl of Bath, however, generously refused the garter, and warmly solicited it for the son of his friend. Accordingly when the young duke went to Windsor to deliver to the king his father's ensigns of the order, Charles returned them to him, and declared his election as knight of the Garter (*Biog. Brit.*)

In 1673 Monck was made colonel of a regiment of foot, and on 15 Oct. 1675 privy councillor. In the same year he became lord-lieutenant of Devonshire (except Plymouth), and joint lord-lieutenant of Essex. In 1678 he was made colonel of the 'Queen's' regiment of horse, and was again sworn privy councillor in April of the next year. In the following November he became captain and colonel of the 1st (King's Own) troop of horse guards, in place of Monmouth, with whom he shortly afterwards quarrelled, and captain of all the king's guards of horse; in 1681 joint lord-lieutenant of Wiltshire; in 1682 chancellor of the university of Cambridge, in place of the Duke of Monmouth, and a lord of trade and foreign plantations. He was also recorder of Colchester, and at the coronation of James II (25 April 1685) bearer of the sceptre with the dove. In 1685 he raised the militia of Devonshire and Cornwall against the Duke of Monmouth, when he landed at Lyme in Dorset, but retired on the approach of Monmouth, who wrote to Monck commanding him to lay down his arms and repair to his camp, where he 'should not fail of receiving a very kind reception,' on pain of being denounced as a rebel and traitor. Monck replied that he 'never was nor never will be a rebell to my lawful king, who is James the Second.' On 23 June 1685, a fortnight before the battle of Sedgemoor, Albemarle sent from Taunton to the Earl of Sunderland for his 'diversion' 'severall proclamations' issued in the city by Monmouth. In May 1686 he gave sumptuous entertainment to the king at his seat of New Hall in Essex. In 1687 he subscribed largely to a plan started by one Captain Phipps for fishing on a Spanish wreck off Hispaniola. The adventure was successful, and he received 40,000*l.* as his share of the profits. On 26 Nov. 1687 Monck was made governor-general of Jamaica, an honour he did not long enjoy, as he died there early in the autumn of the next year. He left no issue.

Sir Hans Sloane, who accompanied him to Jamaica as his physician, gives a detailed account of his last illness, which commenced before he left England, and appears to have been aggravated, if not caused, by his intemperate habits. Sloane describes the duke as 'of a sanguine complexion, his face reddish and eyes yellow, as also his skin, and accustomed by being at court to sitting up late and often being merry' (Collection of Sir Hans Sloane's loose papers). He married, at the age of sixteen, Elizabeth, eldest daughter of Henry Cavendish, second duke of Newcastle, and after his death she married Ralph Montagu, first duke of Montagu [q. v.], but left no family by either husband.

[Biographia Britannica; Doyle's Official Baronage of England; Minutes of the Council of Jamaica, 1687–8; Burke's Extinct Peerage; Reresby's Memoirs, passim; Hatton Correspondence (Camden Soc.), i. 207, ii. 12, 67, 69; Egerton MS. 2395; Add. MS. 5852; Sloane MS. 3984; Notes and Queries, 3rd ser. i. 77, 137.]

L. M. M. S.

MONCK or **MONK**, GEORGE, first Duke of Albemarle (1608–1670), born 6 Dec. 1608 at Potheridge, near Torrington in Devonshire, was the second son of Sir Thomas Monck, knt., by Elizabeth, daughter of Sir George Smith of Maydford in the same county (Gumble, *Life of Monck*, 8vo, 1671, p. 1; *Visitation of Devonshire*, 1620, ed. Colby, pp. 188–91). In 1625 the under-sheriff of Devonshire perfidiously arrested Sir Thomas Monck as he went to pay his respects to the king, and George Monck avenged his father's wrongs by thrashing the under-sheriff. To avoid legal proceedings he took service as a volunteer in the expedition to Cadiz, under his kinsman, Sir Richard Grenville, who was then major to the regiment of Sir John Borough. In 1627 he distinguished himself by bringing a letter from the king to the Duke of Buckingham in the Isle of Ré, 'passing the army, which lay before Rochelle, with great hazard of his life.' It was probably as a reward for this service that he now obtained an ensign's commission in Borough's regiment (Gumble, p. 4; *Works of George Granville, Lord Lansdowne*, ed. 1736, iii. 253). About 1629 Monck entered the Dutch service, serving in the regiment of the Earl of Oxford, which after Oxford's death became the regiment of George Goring. At the siege of Breda, in 1637, Monck led the forlorn hope in the assault on one of the outworks of the town. He distinguished himself also as a strict disciplinarian, and earned a reputation as a good officer. A quarrel with the magistrates of Dort on the question of their jurisdiction over the soldiers under Monck's command finally led to his quitting the Dutch service. A scheme was at this time on foot in England for the colonisation of Madagascar by a joint-stock company, and Monck thought of becoming one of the adventurers in that enterprise. But the outbreak of the Scottish troubles provided him employment in England (Gumble, pp. 5–11; Hexham, *Brief Relation of the Siege of Breda*, 4to, 1637, p. 27). In the list of the army under the command of the Earl of Northumberland, in 1640, Monck appears as lieutenant-colonel of the foot regiment of the Earl of Newport (Peacock, *Army Lists*, 2nd edit. p. 75). Gumble attributes to Monck's good conduct the saving of the English guns in the rout at Newburn (p. 10; cf. Skinner, *Life of Monck*, 1724, p. 18).

At the outbreak of the Irish rebellion the Earl of Leicester—a relative of Monck's—was lord-lieutenant of Ireland, and at once offered Monck the command of his own regiment of foot. The regiment, consisting of twelve hundred men, landed at Dublin on 21 Feb. 1642 (Gumble, p. 15; Nalson, *Historical Collections*, ii. 919). Monck gained much honour at the battle of Kilrush, and by defeating the Irish in a number of skirmishes and forays (Borlase, *Irish Rebellion*, ed. 1743, p. 100). In June 1642 he 'took Castleknock, and killed eighty rebels, besides some that he hanged; and a while after he took the castles of Rathroffy and Clongoweswood in the county of Kildare, and did good execution upon the enemy' (Coxe, *Hibernia Anglicana*, ii. 107). In December 1642 he relieved Ballinakill, besieged by General Preston, and defeated at Tymachoe an attempt of the Irish to intercept his return to Dublin (Carte, *Ormonde*, ed. 1851, ii. 386; Bellings, *Hist. of the Irish Catholic Confederation*, i. 91, ii. 177). In the summer of 1643 he conducted an expedition for the relief of Castle-Jordan in King's County, captured various places in Wicklow, and took part in an unsuccessful campaign against Owen O'Neill (*ib.* i. 161, ii. 271, 363; Carte, ii. 500). On 7 June 1643 the Earl of Leicester commissioned Monck as governor of Dublin, with a salary of 40*s.* a day, but the king, at the request of the lords justices, appointed Lord Lambert instead (*ib.* ii. 347; BELLINGS, ii. 44). Though he failed to obtain this public recognition of his services, he had gained the confidence of his men, and was 'the most beloved by the soldiers of any officer in the army' (CARTE, iii. 43).

Even before the cessation of September 1643 Monck had obtained leave to return to England, possibly on account of the death of his father. His refusal to take the oath which Ormonde imposed on the Irish army before it was transported to England to serve Charles I proceeded, according to Carte, from a desire to consult his patron, the Earl of Leicester, or to obtain his arrears from the parliament before again entering the king's service, nor did it prevent Ormonde granting him a pass. But some loose talk of Lord Lisle's about the possibility of gaining over Monck to the parliamentary cause, and a message which Pym had sent to Monck with that object, drew suspicion upon him. Ormonde consequently sent him under safe custody to Bristol till the king's pleasure should be known, at the same time telling the governor that Monck was a person 'that hath very well deserved in the service of this kingdom,' and that 'no unworthy thing' was laid to his charge. The governor allowed him to go to Oxford to justify himself, which he succeeded in doing without difficulty. In his interview with Charles I he frankly criticised the conduct of the war in Ireland, and asserted that ten thousand men properly disciplined and equipped, and commanded by officers of experience, could bring it to a conclusion (*ib.* iii. 37, v. 504, 525; GUMBLE, p. 17).

His old regiment had been given to his second in command, but he obtained a commission to raise a new one. He rejoined the army just before its defeat by Fairfax at Nantwich (25 Jan. 1644), fought as a volunteer at the head of his old regiment, and was taken prisoner. On 8 July he was brought to the bar of the House of Commons, charged with high treason, and committed to the Tower, where he remained for two years, finding it very difficult even to subsist (SKINNER, p. 23; CARTE, *Original Letters*, i. 38, 41; *Commons' Journals*, iii. 554). His elder brother, Thomas, who was not rich, and was actively engaged in the king's cause, sent him 50*l.* In a letter begging for another 50*l.*, on the score of his great necessities, Monck adds: 'I shall entreat you to be mindful of me concerning my exchange; for I doubt all my friends have forgotten me.' Prince Rupert made an attempt to get him exchanged for Sir Robert Pye [q. v.], and the king sent him 100*l.*, a gift which he often mentioned with gratitude in later days (GUMBLE, p. 20; SKINNER, p. xix; *Hist. MSS. Comm.* 6th Rep. p. 63; *Cal. of Compounders*, p. 1366; *Notes and Queries*, 8th ser. iv. 241).

In September 1646, when Ormonde was negotiating with the parliament, one of his requests was that Monck and some other imprisoned officers might be released and sent over to Ireland, 'being men that knew the country and were experienced in the service, and therefore fitter to be employed than others' (CARTE, iii. 270). For the same reason, when the parliament took the Irish war into its own hands, it decided to employ Monck. On 1 July he obtained leave to go beyond seas, on condition of taking the 'negative oath.' But Lord Lisle, who was chosen by parliament lord-lieutenant of Ireland, persuaded Monck to offer to serve there. On 12 Nov. 1646 Lisle reported to the lords from the Derby House committee that Monck had engaged his honour that he would faithfully serve the parliament if he were employed in Ireland; and, moreover, that he had taken the negative oath, was willing to take the covenant, and was ready to start at a moment's notice (*Commons' Journals*, iv. 595, 720; *Lords' Journals*, viii. 562). The offer was accepted, and there can be little doubt that Monck actually did take the covenant, though the fact has been much disputed (GARDINER, *Great Civil War*, iii. 352; GUIZOT, *Life of Monck*, ed. Wortley, p. 39). A royalist tradition represents Monck before he left the Tower as solemnly begging the blessing of his fellow-prisoner, Dr. Wren, and pledging himself never to be an enemy to the king. Whether the story is true or not, Monck, like Lord Broghill and others, certainly drew a distinction between bearing arms against the Irish rebels and bearing arms against the king. But once embarked in the service of the parliament, military honour led him to be unswervingly faithful to the government whose pay he took (BARWICK, *Life of John Barwick*, p. 267). In February 1647 Monck set out with Lord Lisle for Munster, with the rank of adjutant-general, returning in April, when Lisle's commission expired. Parliament now determined to divide the command, assigning the government of Leinster to Michael Jones [q. v.], and that of Ulster to Monck (CARTE, iii. 324, 331; GUMBLE, p. 25; *Lords' Journals*, ix. 336).

During the next two years Monck's ability was chiefly shown by the skill with which he contrived to maintain his position and to provide for his men in a ravaged and barren country. In October 1647, and again in August 1648 he joined Jones, and the two made brief campaigns together and captured a few small fortresses (*Cal. State Papers*, Dom. 1645–7, p. 593; *Hist. MSS. Comm.* 6th Rep. p. 205; *Hist. of the War in Ireland, by an Officer of Sir John Clotworthy's Regiment*, Dublin, 1873, pp. 58–62; *Portland MSS.* p. 493). In 1648 the defection of the Scottish army in Ulster made his position extremely precarious; but by a skilfully arranged plot he surprised their headquarters at Carrickfergus (16 Sept.) and Belfast, and sent their general, Robert Monro [q. v.], a prisoner to England (*Hist. MSS. Comm.* 7th Rep. p. 52; Borlase, p. 255).

On 28 Sept. parliament appointed Monck governor of Carrickfergus, and voted him a gratuity of 500*l.* The king's execution led to further divisions among the adherents of the parliament, and the 'old Scots'—the colony established in Ulster by the plantation of James I—now declared against the parliament, and summoned Monck to join them in support of Charles II (*The Declaration of the British in the North of Ireland, with some Queries of Colonel Monck*, &c., 1648, 4to; Hill, *The Montgomery MSS.*, i. 177–90). Belfast and Carrickfergus fell into their hands, and Monck was obliged to retire to Dundalk (April 1649). In this extremity, finding Jones unable to give him any help, he concluded a cessation of arms for three months with Owen Roe O'Neill [q. v.] (8 May 1649). Monck was well aware that the peace propositions put forward by O'Neill were not likely to be accepted by the parliament. He succeeded in persuading O'Neill to modify them, but even when amended considered them 'wonderful high,' and believed that O'Neill would be satisfied with much less than he demanded. As an excuse for his action in concluding the armistice he pleaded simply military necessity, the ill condition in which he was between the forces of O'Neill and the Scots, and the paramount importance of preventing O'Neill from joining Ormonde in an attempt to drive the English out of Ireland. In forwarding the convention and O'Neill's propositions to Cromwell personally, instead of to the council of state, he wrote: 'Since there was great necessity for me to do it I hope it will beget no ill construction, when the advantage gained to the service, by dividing Ormonde and MacArt, is fully weighed' (25 May 1649). From a military point of view the arrangement with O'Neill did produce some of the results anticipated by Monck. On the other hand, as soon as it became known, the fidelity of Monck's own men was shattered. Inchiquin, whom Ormonde sent against him, took Drogheda, induced nearly all its garrison to join his army, and intercepted the convoy of ammunition which Monck forwarded to O'Neill, with a request for help (15 July). Two days afterwards Inchiquin invested Dundalk, and Monck's own soldiers forced him to surrender (17 July). Monck then proceeded to England, landed at Chester on 26 July, and appeared before the parliament on 10 Aug. The house passed a vote in which they 'utterly disapproved' of his proceedings in the treaty with O'Neill, but declared their belief in his good faith, and promised not to question his conduct further. Monck asserted that he had acted solely on his own responsibility (*Commons' Journals*, vi. 277; cf. *Aphorismical Discovery*, ii. vii. 216; Carte, *Original Letters*, ii. 388; Walker, *History of Independency*, ed. 1661, ii. 230; *The True State of the Transactions of Col. Geo. Monck with Owen Roe MacArt, O'Neill*, &c., 1649, 4to).

In July 1650 Cromwell invaded Scotland, and took Monck with him. There was some difficulty, however, in finding him a command. Bright's regiment, which had fought against Monck at Nantwich, was indignant at the suggestion that he should become their colonel. Cromwell formed a new regiment for him, by taking five companies from Fenwick's and five from Hesilrige's. On 13 Aug. parliament ordered the regiment thus made to be placed on the establishment, and it became at the Restoration the Coldstream guards (*Memoirs of Capt. John Hodgson*, ed. 1806, p. 139; Mackinnon, *The Coldstream Guards*, 1833, i. 4). At Dunbar Monck led the brigade of foot, and did good service, though Gumble probably exaggerates when he represents him as teaching Cromwell and the other officers the art of war, and gives him the whole credit of the victory (Carlyle, *Cromwell*, Letter cxl.; Gumble, pp. 34–8). He was subsequently engaged during November 1650 in the siege of Dirleton Castle and other small places, and in the spring of 1651 in the capture of the more important fortresses of Tantallon and Blackness. 'Thereby,' says Gumble, 'he increased in reputation and credit with the general, and seemed to bear the greatest sway in the councils of war, which drew upon him the envy of all the old officers.'

In May 1651 Monck was appointed lieutenant-general of the ordnance, and when Cromwell marched into England in pursuit of Charles II he left Monck as commander-in-chief in Scotland (Mackinnon, i. 32–6; *Mercurius Politicus*, 29 May–5 June 1651). They parted on 4 Aug. 1651, and the forces left with Monck amounted, according to Cromwell's estimate, to five or six thousand men.

On 6 Aug. he summoned Stirling, which capitulated on the 14th. On the 28th a party of horse, under Colonel Alured, captured the Earl of Leven and the Scottish committee of estates at Alyth in Perthshire. On 1 Sept. Dundee was taken by storm, after it had been besieged for about ten days. About five hundred of the garrison were killed, and for the rest of the day and the following night the soldiers were allowed to plunder at will. 'The stubbornness of the people,' apologised Monck to Cromwell, 'enforced the soldiers to plunder the town.' Ludlow accused Monck of ordering Lumsden, the governor of Dundee, to be put to death in cold blood, but the statement is contradicted by other authorities, and is improbable. There is no ground for charging him with exceptional barbarity, and his despatch shows that the garrison were not indiscriminately put to the sword (Cary, *Memorials of the Civil War*, ii. 327, 345; *Old Parliamentary History*, xx. 18; Guizot, p. 61).

In his answer to the thanks of the parliament, and in previous letters Monck complained that he was in urgent need of reinforcements (Cary, ii. 365; *Cal. State Papers*, Dom. 1651, p. 399). He himself was taken ill with gout or rheumatism soon after the capture of Dundee. Hence, though Montrose, Aberdeen, and other places submitted, and the Marquis of Huntly and other leaders laid down their arms, the conquest of Scotland was not completed till the following year. Lambert was sent to Scotland in November 1651, and eight commissioners, of whom Monck was one, were appointed to effect the civil settlement of the country (25 Oct., *Commons' Journals*, vii. 30). Monck left Scotland in February 1652, and proceeded to Bath to recruit his health (Gumble, p. 46; *Mercurius Politicus*, 6–13 Nov. 1650). In June the council of state contemplated ordering him back to his command, but on second thoughts they retained him in England, to supervise the fortifications of Yarmouth (*Cal. State Papers*, Dom. 1652–3, pp. 329, 624).

With Monck's appointment as one of the three generals of the fleet on 26 Nov. 1652, a new period in his career begins. Unlike his two colleagues, Blake and Deane, he had no naval experience, but parliament regarded energy, resolution, and the habit of command as sufficient qualifications. The fleet put to sea on 8 Feb., and a three days' battle with the Dutch began off Portland, 18 Feb. 1653. In the first day's battle, 'General Monck, in the Vanguard, then admiral of the white, and all his division, being at least four miles to leeward of the other generals when the fight began ... the main stress of the fight lay upon the red and blue divisions' (*Memorials of Sir William Penn*, p. 478). But the white division came into action later, and Mildmay, the captain of the Vanguard, was among the slain. Of the merchantmen Tromp was convoying twenty-four were taken, while four Dutch men-of-war were captured and five sunk (*ib.* pp. 475, 477; *Life of Cornelius Tromp*, 1697, pp. 89–104). A second battle took place on 2 and 3 June, off the coast of the Netherlands. Blake's squadron did not arrive till after the first day's fight was over, and Deane was killed early on the first day, so that Monck was in sole command during great part of the battle. Tromp admitted the loss of eight ships, and the Dutch fleet retired behind the shoals known as the Wielings, between Ostend and Sluys. The command of the sea fell into the hands of the English fleet, many rich merchantmen were captured, and the English 'held the coast of Holland as 'twere besieged' (*ib.* p. 129; Penn, i. 491–8). Blake having fallen ill, the council of state on 9 July 1652 sent Monck a commission authorising him to exercise all the powers which had been granted to the three admirals jointly (*ib.* p. 500). Tromp sailed out from his anchorage on 27 July, and a still bloodier battle took place on 29 and 31 July, in which Tromp was killed, and the Dutch lost twenty-six men-of-war.

The success of the English fleet was partly due to the restoration of discipline among the officers, and to improved organisation. A letter from Deane and Monck to the council of state shows with what vigour they urged their advice, and insisted upon extended powers when the good of the service required it (*Life of Deane*, pp. 601, 604, 631). As much, or more, was due to improved tactics. 'Our fleet,' says a description of the second battle, 'did work together in better order than before, and seconded one another' (*ib.* p. 648). The third battle, an officer who took part in it terms 'a very orderly battle,' and a French eye-witness describes the English fleet as 'drawn up in a line extending above four leagues' (Gumble, p. 67; *Life of Penn*, i. 510). Both the biographers of Penn and Deane claim the adoption of this system of tactics as due to those admirals, but all the arguments by which Deane's claim is supported apply with equal force to Monck's. The essence of the system was the attempt to introduce into naval warfare something of the order which distinguished scientifically fought land-battles. In technical matters Monck undoubtedly owed much to his subordinates, and his special recommendation of Penn to succeed Deane shows that he recognised the necessity of professional assistance (*ib.* i. 492). He held regular councils of war, and one of his officers describes him as telling his assembled flag-officers, in a meeting held after Deane's death, that their joint advice should be as binding to him as an act of parliament (Gumble, p. 64).

These three great battles practically ended the Dutch war, though peace was not concluded till the following year. The parliament voted Monck a gold chain of the value of 300*l.*, and a medal commemorating his victories (*Commons' Journals*, vii. 296; cf. Mackinnon, i. 58). On 1 Oct. 1653 he received the formal thanks of the house on taking his seat there as one of the members for Devonshire (*Commons' Journals*, vii. 328).

During Monck's absence at sea Cromwell forcibly dissolved the Long parliament (20 April 1653). In the 'Declaration of the generals at sea, and captains under their command' (23 April 1653), Monck and his colleague Deane accepted the change, and replied simply that it was 'set upon their hearts' that they were called and entrusted by the nation to defend it against its enemies at sea, whether Dutchmen or others, and were resolved unanimously to prosecute that end (Deane, *Memoirs of General Deane*, p. 618; *Cal. State Papers*, Dom. 1652–3, p. 289). It is evident that Monck did not share the enthusiastic hopes with which many of his fellow-soldiers regarded this revolution. In 1659, when he was taunted with his acquiescence in 1653, he explained that 'the variety of times doth much vary the nature of affairs, and what might then patiently be submitted unto, we being engaged with a foreign enemy in a bloody war, cannot be drawn into a precedent at this time, after our repentance' (Letter to Vice-admiral Goodson, 4 Nov. 1659). According to Gumble, Cromwell did not venture to act till he had sounded Monck, and discovered that he had no concern for the Long parliament, nor any obligation to them (p. 73). But this is improbable, for Monck had hitherto taken no part at all in political matters.

In the spring of 1654 Monck again took the command of the army in Scotland. A royalist insurrection with which his successor, Robert Lilburne, was unable to cope had broken out in the preceding summer, and was at its height when Monck arrived (Monck's commission, dated 8 April 1654, is printed in Thurloe, ii. 222). His first act was to issue a proclamation offering an amnesty to all persons who laid down their arms within twenty days, and promising a reward of 200*l.* for Middleton [see Middleton, John, first Earl of Middleton], and four other leaders of the insurrection, dead or alive (4 May 1654, Thurloe, ii. 261). As he received considerable reinforcements from England, and was assisted by an expedition from the north of Ireland, he was able to undertake a skilfully combined campaign in the highlands. His plan was to burn the corn, to destroy the strongholds of the enemy, and to establish garrisons at strategic points. So closely were the royalists pressed that Middleton's army rapidly diminished, and on 19 July Colonel Morgan overtook him at Lochgarry (*Mercurius Politicus*, 27 July–3 Aug., and 10–17 Aug. 1654; Baillie, iii. 255). He followed up his victory by 'destroying,' as he terms it, 'those parts of the country where the enemy usually harboured in winter.' 'By this means,' he reported, 'and by the sending some of them to the Barbadoes, their spirits do begin to fail them' (Thurloe, ii. 526, 555). Before the summer ended the submission of the royalists made rapid progress. The Earl of Glencairn made terms on 29 Aug., Lord Kenmure on 14 Sept., and Middleton escaped to the continent about February 1655 (Nickolls, *Letters and Papers addressed to Cromwell*, 1743, p. 130).

In December 1654 the success of Monck's work was threatened by widespread dissatisfaction among the English troops in Scotland. A portion of the officers were in close communication with the parliamentary opposition to Cromwell, and were spreading seditious pamphlets in the army. Some of the non-commissioned officers were conspiring with the Levellers in England, and a plot had been formed to seize Monck and march into England to overthrow the Protector. Overton, Monck's second in command, who was believed to sympathise with the movement, was to be placed at its head. What made the danger greater was that the pay of the soldiers was many months in arrear. Monck, with his usual promptitude, suppressed the incendiary pamphlets, arrested the conspirators, cashiered the minor offenders, and shipped off the leaders to England. 'My opinion is,' he wrote, 'that unless his highness be very severe with those that are disturbers of the peace, we shall never have any certain settlement' (Thurloe, iii. 45, 76, 179). During the later years of his government he carefully purged his army of anabaptists and quakers.

From July 1655 Monck was assisted in the civil government of Scotland by a council, to which very extended powers were granted. Its most important member was Lord Broghill [see Boyle, Roger, Baron Broghill and first Earl of Orrery], and it contained two Scots, John Swinton and

William Lockhart (*Cal. State Papers*, Dom. 1655, pp. 108, 152, 255). But Monck's influence alone inspired the government, and little difference of policy can be detected. Justice was administered without distinction of persons, caterans and moss-troopers transported to the sugar plantations, and order rigidly maintained. 'A man,' boasted one of the council, 'may ride all Scotland over with a switch in his hand and 100*l*. in his pocket, which he could not have done these 500 years' (BURTON, *Diary*, iv. 168). The taxes levied on Scotland were extremely heavy, and Monck urgently pressed their reduction (THURLOE, vi. 330). In ecclesiastical matters he favoured the 'protesters,' whom he termed 'the honest party,' as against the 'resolutionists,' but strongly opposed a proposal to interfere with the autonomy of the Scottish burghs in favour of the former party (*ib.* iii. 117, vi. 529). His courtesy to the Scottish nobility is highly praised by Gumble, and by the end of his rule he had gained considerable popularity. 'That worthy person, General Monck,' said a Scottish member in Richard Cromwell's parliament, 'and those worthy officers amongst us, have won our affections' (BURTON, *Diary*, iii. 138; GUMBLE, p. 89).

On the intrigues of the royalists Monck kept a very vigilant eye. In December 1654 there was a rumour that Charles II was about to land in Scotland. 'If he comes,' wrote Monck, 'I doubt not we shall (through the blessing of God) keep him back in such a country where he cannot ride or travell but in "trowses" and a plaid' (THURLOE, iii. 3; cf. v. 348). In spite of this Charles II, in 1655, sent a letter to Monck, expressing the belief that he still retained his old affection for his sovereign, and bidding him reserve himself for the opportunity of future service. Monck duly forwarded a copy of the letter to Cromwell, and abated nothing of his activity in arresting the king's agents (GUIZOT, *Life of Monck*, ed. Wortley, p. 85).

Between Monck and Cromwell cordial and unbroken confidence throughout existed. 'Your honest general, George Monck, who is a simple-hearted man,' was the Protector's description of him to one of the officers under his command. In 1657 the Protector summoned Monck to a seat in his new House of Lords, but he begged to be excused, on the ground that his presence was indispensable in Scotland. The royalists eagerly spread unfounded reports that he had refused to obey the Protector's orders. Cromwell made a jest of these stories, and is said to have written to Monck: 'There be that tell me there is a certain cunning fellow in Scotland called George Monck, who is said to lie in wait there to introduce Charles Stuart; I pray, use your diligence to apprehend him, and send him up to me' (THURLOE, vi. 741, 863; PRICE, ed. Maseres, p. 712). On Cromwell's death Monck wrote to Henry Cromwell, promising his support to the new protector (*Lansdowne MS.* 822, f. 243). He procured an address of recognition from the army in Scotland, and exerted himself to return supporters of the government to parliament (THURLOE, vii. 404, 411, 574, 613).

A few days after Richard's accession Monck sent him, through his brother-in-law, Thomas Clarges [q. v.], a paper of advice, specially valuable for the light which it throws on its author's political views. In ecclesiastical matters he advised the protector to favour the moderate presbyterians, and to call an assembly of divines to endeavour to find some way of union among the different sects, hinting, in conclusion, that to his mind toleration had gone a little too far. In civil affairs he bade him rely upon St. John, Broghill, Thurloe, and similar councillors, and to endeavour to engage to himself 'those of power and interest amongst the people, for which he has a better opportunity than his father, having not the same obligations to so many disquiet spirits.' Monck's distrust of the leaders of the English army is very noticeable. He urged Richard to reduce its expense by putting two regiments into one, which would give him an opportunity to get rid of 'some insolent spirits' among the commanders. 'There is not,' he added, 'an officer in the army upon any discontent that has power to draw two men after him *if he be out of place*' (*ib.* vii. 37).

Of his own power to suppress either a royalist rising or a military revolt, Monck wrote with easy confidence (*ib.* vii. 545, 616). Richard made Monck keeper of Holyrood House, and invited him to sit in his House of Lords, but, as before, Monck represented that he could not be spared from Scotland (*ib.* vii. 526, 579). When the protector quarrelled with the army some of his friends urged Monck to march into England to his support, and he would doubtless have done so had not Richard been induced to dissolve his parliament. A royalist represents Monck as saying: 'Richard Cromwell forsook himself, else I had never failed my promise to his father or regard to his memory,' and the phrase truthfully sums up his conduct (LUDLOW, *Memoirs*, ed. 1698, p. 643; GUMBLE, p. 97; *Clarendon State Papers*, iii. 628). All parties watched Monck's action with great interest, but he took the restoration of the Long parliament with composure, and put his name to the fervid address of congratulation forwarded by his army to the parliament. In a private letter he simply expressed his pleasure that so great a change had been effected without bloodshed, and his hope that the men in power would 'enter upon something to keep us in peace and quietness' (*ib.* iii. 475, 480; THURLOE, vii. 667, 669). But when the newly appointed commissioners for the nomination of officers began to remove and to change the officers of the regiments under his command, Monck at once signified his dissatisfaction (BAKER, *Chronicle*, ed. Phillips, pp. 670, 675; *Old Parliamentary History*, xxi. 427). His discontent was well known, and in the summer of 1659 overtures were made to him from the royalists.

Immediately on receiving the news of Cromwell's death Lord Colepepper had pointed Monck out to Hyde as the instrument best able to effect the king's restoration. He 'commandeth,' Colepepper wrote, 'absolutely at his devotion . . . a better army than that in England is, and in the king's quarrel can bring with him the strength of Scotland. . . . I need not give you his character; you know he is a sullen man that values him enough, and much believes that his knowledge and reputation in arms fits him for the title of Highness and the office of Protector better than Mr. Richard Cromwell's skill in horse-racing and husbandry doth. You know, besides, that the only ties that have hitherto kept him from grumbling have been the vanity of constancy to his professions, and his affection to Cromwell's person. . . . Nothing of either of them can now stick with him. The way to deal with him is, by some fit person to shew him plainly, and to give him all imaginable security for it, that he shall better find all his ends (those of honour, power, profit, and safety) with the king than in any other way he can take' (*Clarendon State Papers*, iii. 413). It was accordingly resolved to approach Monck through his cousin, Sir John Grenville, and his brother, Nicholas Monck [q. v.] Charles, on 21 July 1659, gave Grenville full powers to treat with Monck, and undertook to make good any engagements he might make to Monck or his officers. At the same time he drew up a letter to the general himself. 'I cannot think,' he wrote, 'you wish me ill, for you have no reason to do so; and the good I expect from you will bring so great benefit to your country and yourself, that I cannot think you will decline my interest. . . . If you once resolve to take my interest to heart, I will leave the way and manner of declaring it entirely to your own judgment, and will comply with the advice you shall give me' (BAKER, *Chronicle*, ed. Phillips, p. 672; *Clarendon State Papers*, iii. 417, 421, 516). Nicholas Monck arrived at Dalkeith at the beginning of August 1659, on the ostensible pretext of arranging a match for his daughter. He communicated the contents of the king's letter to his brother. The general allowed him to talk freely and listened favourably, but would not promise to receive the letter (*ib.* iii. 543, 618). Monck's chaplains, Gumble and Price, have both left accounts of this incident, but Price was at the time more trusted. He goes too far, however, when he represents Monck as henceforth resolved to restore the king, and has to admit that neither then nor much later durst he venture to mention his name to the general. Both agree, however, in stating that Monck resolved to co-operate with, or take advantage of the royalist-presbyterian rising then on foot in England, and that he concerted some of the necessary military preparations for that step. Price himself was charged to draw up a letter from the army in Scotland to the parliament, declaring for a full and free parliament and for the known laws and liberties of the nation. But Monck postponed action till the arrival of the next post from England, and it brought the news of Lambert's defeat of Sir George Booth [q. v.] The plan was immediately abandoned, the letter burnt, and the conspirators sworn to secrecy.

Disheartened by this check, and finding the independence of his command greatly limited by the action of parliament in displacing many of his officers, Monck wrote to Lenthall begging leave to retire (3 Sept.) His intention was to go to Ireland and live on the estate which he had purchased with his arrears of pay. But Clarges, Monck's agent in London, and Speaker Lenthall, contrived to keep back the letter for ten days, till Monck changed his mind (BAKER, p. 675). One of the reasons for this course was the prospect of an immediate breach between the parliament and the army. 'I see now,' said Monck, 'that I shall have a better game to play than I had before. I know Lambert so well that I am sure he will not let those people at Westminster sit till Christmas-day' (PRICE, p. 726). Through Clarges, Monck promised support to the parliamentary leaders, and a letter which parliament received from him on 5 Oct. emboldened them to deal severely with Lambert and his followers. When they revoked Fleetwood's commission as commander-in-chief, Monck was one of the persons in whose hands they vested the command of the army (BAKER, p. 682; *Commons' Journals*, vii. 792; cf. *A Letter from*

General Monck to the Speaker, 13 Oct. 4to, 1659).

The army leaders had not anticipated Monck's opposition. They invited him to sign their petition to parliament, to which he returned an emphatic refusal, and sent Colonel Cobbet to him to explain the causes of their conduct. Monck received the news of the expulsion of the parliament on 17 Oct., concerted his measures the same night, and in the next two days secured Edinburgh, Leith, Berwick, and other fortresses, placed officers whom he could trust in command of his regiments, and arrested those whose defection he feared. On 20 Oct. he despatched a letter to Lenthall announcing his resolve 'to assert the liberty and authority of parliament,' and with it expostulations addressed to Lambert and Fleetwood, telling the one that England would not endure any arbitrary power, and the other not to be deluded by the specious pretences of ambitious persons (*Old Parliamentary History*, xxii. 4; BAKER, p. 685). These were followed by a series of declarations to the army, the churches, and the nation (*True Narrative of the Proceedings in Parliament, Council of State, General Council of the Army, etc., from Sept.* 22 *to this present*, 4to, 1659). All were conciliatory in tone, and as would-be mediators were many, Monck agreed to send three commissioners to negotiate with the leaders of the English army. The commissioners came to an agreement on 15 Nov., but he refused to ratify it, on the ground that they had gone beyond their instructions (BAKER, pp. 693–5). Further negotiations to take place at Newcastle were accordingly agreed to. Delay strengthened Monck's position, for he had 70,000*l.* in hand, while the troops opposed to him under the leadership of Lambert were ill-paid and afterwards unpaid. He was also enabled thereby to complete his communications with the opponents of military rule in England and Ireland, and to give them time to come to his aid. Nine of the old council of state met together in London, and sent him a letter of thanks (19 Nov.), followed by a commission constituting him absolute commander-in-chief of all the forces in England and Scotland (24 Nov.; BAKER, p. 695). At their instigation the garrison of Portsmouth declared for the restoration of the parliament (3 Dec.); then the fleet in the Downs followed Portsmouth's example (13 Dec.), and finally a revolution in the Irish army, headed by Sir Charles Coote and Lord Broghill, placed the government of that country in the hands of Monck's supporters (14 Dec.) The troops in London abandoned the struggle and submitted to the parliament, which again resumed its place at Westminster on 26 Dec.

Monck was now able to advance into England. His forces were inferior in number to Lambert's, and he was especially weak in horse. To remedy this he had increased the number of pikemen in each regiment, and turned his dragoons into regular cavalry. His determination to maintain English authority in Scotland obliged him to leave four regiments of foot to hold the Scottish fortresses and to reject suggestions that he should summon the Scots to his assistance. A certain number of Scotsmen were enlisted to fill the vacancies in his foot regiments. Monck also persuaded the Convention of Estates to facilitate his march by guaranteeing the early payment of the assessments due from the country. More than a benevolent neutrality he knew he could not expect, unless he were to declare openly for the king.

Monck had established his headquarters at Coldstream on the Tweed, about nine miles from Berwick, a position which would enable him either to bar Lambert's advance if he marched by the east coast, or to march directly on London if Lambert invaded Scotland by way of Carlisle (8 Dec.) On 24 Dec. he broke off the negotiations with Lambert, and on 2 Jan. 1660 crossed the Tweed into England. His forces amounted to about five thousand foot and two thousand horse. Lambert's army broke up as Monck's advanced. Monck marched slowly towards London, disbanding or purging the rebellious regiments of Lambert's army on his way. An opportune riot among some of the soldiers in London supplied him with a plausible reason for requiring that Fleetwood's forces should leave London to make room for the troops which he brought with him. He felt strong enough to send part of his forces back to Scotland, and entered London on 3 Feb. with four thousand foot and eighteen hundred horse.

Throughout this journey Monck was besieged by addresses from all parts of England, asking for the readmission of the excluded members of parliament. The city, with which he had long been in correspondence, sent messengers to demand a full and free parliament (*Old Parliamentary History*, xxii. 46). Parliament itself had sent two commissioners to congratulate Monck, and to watch his movements. He frequently left them the task of answering the petitioners, his own return 'consisting in a nod, a frown, or the rubbing of his forehead if the speech were long' (PRICE, p. 755). In a letter answering the petition of the gentlemen of Devonshire, he urged submission to the existing parliament, and argued that the readmission of the excluded members or the restoration of monarchy would be contrary to the interests of the nation. But to the demands of some of his officers that he should solemnly engage his army to be 'obedient to the parliament in all things, except the bringing of Charles Stuart,' he answered that they must not seem to dictate to parliament, or they would fall into the same error as the English army (*ib.* p. 754; KENNETT, p. 32). And though publicly discountenancing the demands of the city he gave private encouragement to its leaders through his chaplain Gumble (GUMBLE, pp. 209–20; *Clarendon State Papers*, iii. 649). The ambiguity of his utterances and the contradiction between his words and his actions puzzled the shrewdest observers. Neither Hyde nor the royalist agents in England could guess whether he meant to serve the king or to maintain the Rump in power.

Parliament had been profusely grateful to Monck for Lambert's overthrow. On 2 Jan. they elected him one of the council of state, on the 12th they ordered a bill to be brought in to justify and approve all his actions, on the 16th they voted him 1,000*l.* a year, and on 2 Feb. appointed him ranger of St. James's Park. The commission as commander-in-chief, granted him by the old council of state, had been confirmed on 26 Jan. Nevertheless, the parliamentary leaders regarded him with suspicion.

Monck entered London on 3 Feb., and on 6 Feb. was solemnly thanked by Speaker Lenthall on behalf of parliament. In reply he summarised his answers to the addresses he had received, and set forth the policy he desired parliament to follow. They were to reconcile the 'sober gentry' to the government and to protect the 'sober interest,' allowing neither cavaliers nor fanatics any share of power. Two points in his speech were more alarming. He plainly hinted that he had pledged himself that the parliament should be filled up, and its sittings speedily determined. At the same time he warned them against the proposed imposition of an oath abjuring the house of Stuart, and it was known that he himself, on taking his place in the council of state, had refused to take the oath (GUMBLE, p. 229).

Immediately after Monck's arrival the quarrel between the parliament and the city came to a head, and the latter refused to pay taxes. On the morning of 9 Feb. Monck marched into the city with orders to arrest eleven leading citizens, take away the posts and chains in the streets, and make the gates indefensible. Having carried out the greater part of his task, he wrote to the house that he had forborne taking down the gates and portcullises in order not to exasperate the city, and begged that tenderness might be used towards it. But the parliamentary leaders were too exalted by his obedience to listen to his remonstrances. 'All is our own,' said Heselrige, 'he will be honest;' or, according to another story, 'Now, George, we have thee, body and soul' (LUDLOW, ii. 825). They commanded him to execute his orders to the letter, and on the following day he completed his task (*Old Parliamentary History*, xxii. 93). The result of the two days' work was to change the temper of Monck's soldiers, and rouse their indignation against the parliament. No doubt Monck foresaw this result, and counted on it. When Price soon after asked him how he was engaged to undertake this detestable piece of service, he answered: 'This was a trick you knew not of, and I assure you that I could not have done my business so soon without it, and possibly not at all' (PRICE, p. 763). He now drew up a letter to parliament peremptorily demanding the issue of writs for a new parliament within the next week, and the fixing of a date for the dissolution of the present assembly (*Old Parliamentary History*, xxii. 98). The letter was presented to the house on the morning of 11 Feb., and on the afternoon of the same day Monck met the corporation in the Guildhall, told them what he had done, and apologised for his late ungrateful duty. His declaration was received with general joy, and celebrated by bonfires, in which the Rump was burnt in effigy all over London. The parliament received Monck's letter with feigned thanks, but showed its real distrust by vesting the control of the army in five commissioners, of whom Monck was one, while three were of their own faction (LUDLOW, ii. 830). The council of state humbly pressed him to return to Whitehall, but Monck turned a deaf ear to their appeals. He was now bent on procuring the readmission of the members expelled in 1648, and with that object obtained a conference between the 'secluded' and the sitting members. But the conference led to no result, and he solved the difficulty by ordering the guards to admit the secluded members to the house (21 Feb.) Before they took their seats he pledged them to settle the government of the army, call a new parliament for 20 April, dissolve the present one within a month, and appoint a new council of state to govern in the interval (BAKER, p. 710; *Old Parliamentary History*, xxii. 140). They kept their word, elected a new council with Monck at the head of the list (21 Feb.), appointed him general-in-chief of all the land forces in the three kingdoms (25 Feb.) and joint-commander of the navy (2 March). On 16 March parliament was dissolved, but not till it had annulled the engagement to be faithful to a commonwealth previously required from all persons in office.

Hitherto Monck had lulled the suspicions of the republicans by public and private protestations of his fidelity to the republic. 'As for a Commonwealth,' he wrote to Heselrige on 13 Feb., 'believe me, Sir, for I speak it in the presence of God, it is the desire of my soul, and shall (the Lord assisting) be witnessed by the actions of my life, that these nations be so settled in a free state, without a king, single person, or House of Peers, that they may be governed by their representatives in parliament successively' (*Clarendon State Papers*, iii. 678). In his speeches and manifestoes he was equally vehement (Kennett, p. 63; Baker, p. 711). Hitherto the republicans had hoped that 'Monck could not be such a devil to betray a trust so freely reposed in him' (Ludlow, ii. 816). Now convinced that the restoration of the Stuarts was imminent, Heselrige and others offered the supreme power to Monck, and Bordeaux, the French ambassador, assured him of the support of Mazarin, if he chose to accept the offer (Baker, pp. 715, 717; Guizot, *Richard Cromwell*, ii. 293). But Monck refused to listen to these suggestions, and ordered Bordeaux not to interfere in matters of government.

More serious was the danger of a military revolt. Monck had prepared to deal with it by removing Fleetwood's troops from London, quartering the regiments in small sections, and replacing inflexible republicans by colonels whom he could trust. On 15 March a meeting of officers demanded that he should send to the parliament to re-enact the engagement against a monarchy, but he told them 'that he brought them not out of Scotland for his nor the parliament's council; that for his part he should obey the parliament, and expected they should do the same' (*Clarendon State Papers*, iii. 696; Baker, p. 716). He then ordered them to their regiments and forbade them to assemble again, and finally obtained from the whole army an engagement to submit to whatsoever the Lord should bring forth from the consultations of the coming parliament (9 April; Baker, p. 719). So effectual were these measures, that when Lambert escaped from the Tower, he was only joined by seven or eight troops of horse and a few cashiered officers, and his recapture put an end to the insurrection (22 April).

Before this time Monck had entered into direct communication with Charles II. The precise date at which he resolved to restore the king has been much disputed. Speaking of Nicholas Monck's visit to his brother in July 1659, Clarendon says: 'At that time there is no question the general had not the least thought or purpose to contribute to the king's restoration, the hope whereof he believed to be desperate; and the disposition that did grow in him afterwards did arise from those accidents which fell out, and even obliged him to undertake that which proved so much to his profit and glory ...' 'It was the king's great happiness that he never had it in his power to serve him till it fell to be in his power, and, indeed, till he had nothing else in his power to do' (*Rebellion*, xvi. 100, 115). On the other hand, Price represents Monck as first conceiving the idea of a restoration in July 1659, and covertly avowing his intention before he entered England (Price, ed. Maseres, pp. 721, 746). As early as November 1659 Monck told Clarges that he intended to readmit the 'secluded members,' and every politician knew that this meant the restoration of the monarchy (Baker, p. 688). His conduct when he declared against the army in October 1659, the foresight with which he provided for every possibility, and the decision with which he acted, all render it difficult to suppose that he had no clear conception of his ultimate object.

Much of Monck's success was due to his judicious selection of his instruments. In dealing with the republicans he had made Gumble his mouthpiece, Sharpe was his agent with the presbyterians, and Clarges with the officers. To negotiate with royalists a new personage was required, and for that purpose he had made choice of his relative William Morice [q. v.], one of the secluded members, whom he summoned from Devonshire and made governor of Plymouth (Clarendon, *Rebellion*, xvi. 162; Baker, p. 712). Through Morice he arranged an interview with Sir John Grenville (19 March), and at last received from his hands the letter the king had sent him in the previous summer. 'My heart,' he told Grenville, 'was ever faithful to the king, but I was never able to do him service till the present time.' He refused to give Grenville a letter for the king, but made him commit his instructions to memory, and despatched him at once to Brussels. Monck's recommendations were that the king should remove at once to Breda, and thence offer a general pardon and indemnity, guarantee all sales of land effected by the late authorities, and promise religious toleration. In the Declaration of Breda (4 April) the king practically adopted Monck's suggestions, but by Hyde's advice referred to the ultimate decision of parliament the interpretation and execution of his general promises. With the declaration, Charles sent Monck a commission as captain-general, authority to appoint a secretary of state, and letters for the city, the council of state, and the parliament (PRICE, pp. 783–91; CLARENDON, xvi. 166–74). Monck silently laid them aside until the meeting of parliament. His negotiation with the king meant, as Charles told Grenville, 'the king's restoration without conditions.' Monck's apology for thus anticipating the action of parliament lay in the belief that he could not guarantee the peace of the nation during the time that a treaty would require (BURNET, *Own Time*, i. 161, ed. 1833). Parliament met on 25 April, and the next day Monck was solemnly thanked by both houses. The king's letters were presented on 1 May, and the restoration of the monarchy was voted the same day.

On 25 May the king landed at Dover. Monck met him on the shore with expressions of humility and devotion. Charles 'embraced and kissed him' (cf. GUMBLE, p. 383). Next day at Canterbury Monck was knighted, invested with the order of the Garter and made master of the horse (*Cal. State Papers*, Dom. 1659–60, p. 447). On 7 July he was raised to the peerage by the titles Baron Monck of Potheridge, Beauchamp, and Teyes, Earl of Torrington, and Duke of Albemarle, granted a pension of 700*l.* a year, and given the estate of New Hall in Essex. The selection of these titles was an implicit admission of the claims set forth in the pedigree which his panegyrists had lately published, representing him as descended from Richard Beauchamp, earl of Warwick, and from Arthur Plantagenet, a natural son of Edward IV (*Complete Peerage*, by G. E. C., i. 58). But his paramount merit was that set forth in Sir Richard Fanshawe's Latin preamble to his patent, whose recital of his services closes with the words, 'hæc omnia, prudentia ac felicitate summa, *victor sine sanguine*, perfecit' (PECK, *Desiderata Curiosa*, ii. 514). For the moment the king's obligations made Monck's influence enormous, but he used it with moderation. He presented Charles with a list of about seventy persons recommended for office, but greatly to the king's relief explained that it was a mere formality. Of his kinsmen, Morice became secretary of state, Nicholas Monck bishop of Hereford, and Clarges was knighted and made commissary-general of the musters. He never wearied of advancing the interests of Grenville and his family, and Ashley Cooper owed to Monck's special recommendation his immediate admission to the privy council (CLARENDON, *Continuation*, § 13; *Cal. State Papers*, Dom. 1664–5, p. 436).

Monck's influence was naturally greatest in military affairs. His position as captain-general was confirmed by a patent for life (3 Aug. 1660). While the rest of the army was disbanded, his own regiment of foot was continued as the king's guards, and a large part of his horse regiment was re-enlisted in the horse guards. Their necessity had been shown by Venner's insurrection (7 Jan. 1661).

In purely political questions Monck's influence was far less powerful. His views as to the details of the restoration settlement are contained in a paper sent to the king about 9 May 1660 (LISTER, *Life of Clarendon*, iii. 500). He proposed that five persons only should be excepted from the Act of Oblivion; that the sales of church lands and crown lands by the late authorities should be confirmed as leases for a term of years; and that those who had bought lands belonging to private persons should have the usufruct of them until the purchase-money was repaid. The solution which the royalist zeal of the convention preferred was far more sweeping. Monck himself sat among the judges of the regicides, but cannot fairly be blamed. He was not, like some of his colleagues, partly responsible for the policy which prepared the way for the king's execution; he had endeavoured to limit the number of victims, and he faithfully observed his personal pledges to Heselrige and others, whose lives he had promised to save (*Hist. MSS. Comm.* 8th Rep. p. 212).

In ecclesiastical matters also the policy adopted was not that which he advocated. All the evidence tends to prove that Monck was at heart a moderate presbyterian, just as his wife was a violent one. 'Moderate, not rigid, presbyterian government, with a sufficient liberty for consciences truly tender,' was his definition of the settlement he desired the 'secluded members' to establish. It was with great difficulty that Price induced him to promise not to engage himself against bishops (*Old Parliamentary History*, xxii. 142; PRICE, p. 774; WODROW, *Church History*, ed. 1828, i. 5–19). The compromise Monck proposed to the king was that an assembly of divines should be called to settle, in conjunction with parliament, the future government of the church. As an advocate of comprehension he was present at the Worcester House conference (22 Oct. 1660), and two years later intervened in support of the attempt to suspend the enforcement of the Act of Uniformity (CLARENDON, *Continuation*, §§ 335–8; PEPYS, *Diary*, 3 Sept. 1662).

In the settlement of Scotland Monck's advice naturally had considerable weight. He appears, however, to have been opposed to the withdrawal of the English garrisons and to the destruction of the forts erected there during the English conquest (WODROW, *Church History*, ed. R. Burns, 1827, i. 44). But he had promised the Scots nobility before going into England that 'he would befriend them in all their just liberties,' and this was one of the points they had most at heart. To the Scottish clergy, with whose leaders he had been in communication through James Sharpe, he was pledged for the maintenance of presbyterianism, and therefore opposed the immediate introduction of episcopacy (CLARENDON, *Continuation*, § 105). He had recommended Sharpe to Hyde and to the king as likely to prove useful in the settlement of church matters (*Clarendon State Papers*, iii. 741). Clarendon also attributes Glencairne's employment to Monck's recommendation (*Continuation*, § 95). The part which Monck took in procuring Argyll's condemnation has been much controverted. One of the charges against Argyll was his active support of the English government of Scotland against the Scottish royalists, and when there was a difficulty about proving it Monck forwarded a selection from Argyll's letters to himself and other English governors. This fact, asserted by Baillie and Burnet, but denied by later writers, is now conclusively proved (BURNET, i. 225; BAILLIE, ed. Laing, iii. 465; *Hist. MSS. Comm.* 6th Rep. p. 617; for the controversy, see GUIZOT, *Monk*, ed. Wortley, p. 293). Burnet terms this an act of 'inexcusable baseness;' on the other hand, the letters were not of the private nature which he asserts, but a part of the official correspondence of the English government in Scotland which had, according to custom, remained in Monck's possession (*Own Time*, i. 225).

At the Restoration Monck had been appointed lord-lieutenant of Ireland, but was unwilling either to quit England or to resign his post. His Irish estate, according to Clarendon, amounted to 4,000*l.* a year, 'which he thought he could best preserve in the supreme government, though he was willing to have it believed in the city and the army that he retained it only for the good of the adventurers, and that the soldiers might be justly dealt with for their arrears' (*Continuation*, § 124). In the Act of Settlement provisos were inserted in favour of Monck's rights, and his influence was undoubtedly used on behalf of the English colony. At first the king appointed Lord Roberts to act as Monck's deputy, but as that arrangement proved unsatisfactory three lords justices were appointed instead (December 1660). The death of one of these caused a new difficulty, which Monck solved by resigning his commission and begging the king to make Ormonde lord-lieutenant (November 1661; *ib.* §§ 198, 234).

Monck's part in the foreign policy pursued during the early years of the reign is obscure. Burnet, on the doubtful authority of Sir Robert Southwell, attributes to him the suggestion of the Portuguese match. It is clear that Monck was a strong supporter of the scheme, if not actually its originator (*Own Time*, i. 300; KENNETT, *Register*, p. 394; CARTE, *Ormonde*, iv. 102). Burnet represents him as the chief adviser of the sale of Dunkirk, but, according to the letters of d'Estrades, Clarendon told him that Monck was one of its chief opponents. Nevertheless, his position as lord-general naturally led to his appointment as one of the commissioners to arrange the details of the sale (*Own Time*, i. 312; *Clarendon State Papers*, iii. Appendix, p. xxv; LANSDOWNE, *Works*, 1732, i. 459). Public opinion regarded Monck as one of the instigators of the Dutch war. 'Some,' says Gumble, 'did report him the chief councillor, but they are mistaken, for he scarce declared himself in it till the parliament had voted to adhere with their lives and fortunes' (p. 410). Foreign observers, however, shared the popular view, and the Dutch ambassador reported to his masters a conversation in which Monck announced that at any cost England must have her proper share in the trade of the world (PONTALIS, *Jean de Witt*, i. 325; CHRISTIE, *Life of Shaftesbury*, i. 278). Throughout the war, whether Monck was at home or at sea, the burden of its management rested largely on his shoulders. When the Duke of York took command of the fleet he deputed his authority as lord high admiral to Monck instead of entrusting it to commissioners (22 March 1665; *Memoirs of Naval Affairs*, 1729, p. 124). 'It is a thing that do cheer my heart,' wrote Pepys; 'for the other would have vexed us with attendance, and never done the business' (*Diary*, 17 March 1665). All through the plague-year Monck remained in London, executing the duties of his office, maintaining order in the city, and, with the assistance of William Craven, earl of Craven (1606–1697) [q. v.], superintending the measures taken to check the plague. His example and his presence were of the greatest value (CLARENDON, *Con-*

tinuation, §§ 662; GUMBLE, *Life of Monk*, p. 419).

In November 1665 the king decided to employ Monck at sea. At first he hesitated to accept, on the ground that he was more necessary in London, 'as he thought he had done the king better service by staying in London than he could have done in any other place' (CLARENDON). Finally he consented, but begged that his acceptance might remain a secret for the present; 'for if his wife should come to know it, before he had by degrees prepared her for it, she would break out into such passions as would be very uneasy to him.' Her 'cursed words' when she did learn it are recorded by Pepys (*Diary*, 9 Dec. 1665).

With Rupert as his colleague in command Monck put to sea on 23 April 1666. Rupert with twenty ships was detached in May to prevent the junction of the French squadron with the Dutch. This resolution was taken, according to Sir William Coventry, 'with the full consent and advice' of Monck (*ib.* 24 June 1666; CLARENDON, *Continuation*, § 868). During Rupert's absence the Dutch fleet appeared off the North Foreland (1 June), and though Monck had but fifty-four ships to their eighty he at once attacked. The English fleet had the weather gauge, but could not use their lower deck guns. Monck's tactics have been highly praised by a modern critic, but when the day closed the English fleet, especially the white squadron, had lost heavily (MAHAN, *The Influence of Sea Power upon History*, p. 121). The Swiftsure, which carried the flag of Vice-admiral Sir William Berkeley, had been taken, and Rear-admiral Sir John Harman's ship, the Henry, completely disabled. The next day the battle was renewed, the Dutch, according to English accounts, receiving a reinforcement of sixteen ships. By night the English fleet, reduced to thirty-four fighting ships, was in full retreat. On the third day the retreat continued. 'My Lord-general's conduct,' wrote Sir Thomas Clifford, 'was here well seen to be very good, for he chose out sixteen of the greatest ships of these thirty-four to be a bulwark to the rest, and to bring up the rear in a breast, and so shoved on the others in a line before him, and in this way we maintained an orderly and good retreat all Sunday' (*Cal. State Papers*, Dom. 1665–6, p. xx). At three in the afternoon Prince Rupert's squadron was sighted, but the junction of the two fleets was attended by the loss of the Royal Prince, Sir George Ayscue's flagship, which struck on the Galloper Sands, and was burnt by the Dutch. Monck's own ship, the Royal Charles, also grounded but was got off, and his evident determination to blow her up rather than surrender greatly alarmed the gentlemen volunteers on board (GUMBLE, p. 436; *Works of Sheffield, Duke of Buckingham*, ii. 6). On the fourth day the English fleet again attacked and was worsted, but the Dutch were in no condition to keep the seas, and both navies returned to their ports to refit. The lowest estimate of the English loss was eight hundred killed and fifteen hundred wounded. The Dutch claimed to have taken twenty-three men of war and lost but four.

Monck's conduct in engaging at once instead of waiting for Rupert to join him was severely criticised. It was said that his success in beating the Dutch in the earlier war had made him over-confident and foolhardy (EVELYN, *Diary*, 6 June; PEPYS, *Diary*, 4 July). On the other hand Monck had good reason to believe that Rupert would have joined him before the fleet was shattered by two days' hard fighting. He also complained bitterly of the conduct of his captains. 'I assure you,' he wrote to Coventry, 'I never fought with worse officers than now in my life, for not above twenty of them behaved like men' (PEPYS, *Correspondence*, ed. Smith, i. 110). The sailors, however, never fought better (cf. TEMPLE, *Works*, ed. 1754, i. 144).

Monck and Rupert put to sea again on 17 July, and on the 25th and 26th engaged the Dutch. The jealousy which existed between Tromp and De Ruyter facilitated victory for the English. The Dutch lost two ships only, but three admirals and a great number of men, and were driven to take shelter in their ports (*Life of Cornelius Tromp*, pp. 374–89; *Cal. State Papers*, Dom. 1665–6, p. 579). A fortnight later (8, 9 Aug.) a detached squadron of small ships from the English fleet landed one thousand men on the islands of Vlie and Schelling, and burnt 160 Dutch merchantmen in harbour, whose cargoes were valued at a million sterling.

Monck was summoned from sea by the news of the great fire of London. He was back by 8 Sept., and his influence in the city was of the greatest use in restoring order (PEPYS, *Diary*, 8 Sept.) He could not be spared to resume his command of the fleet during 1666, and for 1667 the government, at its wits' end for money, took the fatal resolution of laying up the great ships in harbour. The lighter ships were to be sent out to prey on Dutch commerce, and the English coast was to be protected by fortifications at Sheerness, Portsmouth, and Harwich. Sir William Coventry was credited with the suggestion, but the council in general shares the blame of its adoption, and popular rumour represented Monck as unsuccessfully opposing it (*Cal. State Papers*, Dom. 1667, pp. xxiv, xxvii; PEPYS, *Diary*, 14 June 1667). When the Dutch fleet appeared in the Thames, he was, as usual, despatched to the point of danger (cf. MARVELL, *Last Instructions to a Painter*, l. 510). By sinking ships and raising batteries he endeavoured to protect the men-of-war laid up at Chatham, and wrote hopefully that he had made them safe (PEPYS, *Diary*, 12 June, 20 Oct. 1667). But the negligence with which his orders were executed rendered all his exertions fruitless, for on 12 June the Dutch broke the chain across the Medway, burnt eight great ships, and captured Monck's old flagship, the Royal Charles. The narrative which Monck laid before the House of Commons proved that he did all a commander so badly seconded could do, and the house thanked him for his eminent merit in the late war (*Commons' Journals*, ix. 6, 11). 'The blockhead Albemarle,' comments Pepys, 'hath strange luck to be loved, though he be the heaviest man in the world, but stout and honest to his country' (*Diary*, 23 Oct. 1667).

This was Monck's last public service. He had been appointed first lord of the treasury when it was put into commission (24 May 1667); but he took little part in the business of the board. When Clarendon fell into disgrace, Monck at first tried to reconcile him with the king, but finally used his influence in parliament against him (CLARENDON, *Continuation*, §§ 1136, 1177). Towards the end of 1668 his increasing infirmities obliged him to retire permanently to New Hall. Ever since his recovery from a dangerous fever (August 1661) he had been liable to asthma, and to swellings which finally developed into dropsy. He was suffering from these complaints when he entertained Cosmo III of Tuscany (12 June 1669), grew rapidly worse in the following December, and died on the morning of 3 Jan. 1670. He died, wrote an eye-witness, 'like a Roman general and soldier, standing almost up in his chair, his chamber like a tent open, and all his officers about him' (*Monckton Papers*, ed. Peacock, 1885, p. 94).

His old friend, Seth Ward, who was with him in his last moments, preached his funeral sermon ('The Christian's Victory over Death,' 4to, 1670). The grateful king took the charge of funeral and monument out of Christopher Monck's hands, and announced that he would bear the cost of both himself. Monck's funeral was consequently long delayed. 'It is almost three months,' wrote Marvell on 21 March, 'and he yet lies in the dark unburied, and no talk of him' (*Works*, ed. Grosart, ii. 317). The funeral, celebrated with great pomp, took place in Westminster Abbey on 30 April 1670 (SANDFORD, *The Order used at the Solemn Interment of George, Duke of Albemarle*, fol. 1670; MACKINNON, i. 132). The monument Charles never erected, but one was at last put up in 1720, in pursuance of the will of Christopher, second duke of Albemarle. Monck's effigy, dressed in armour, was long one of the sights of the abbey, and the contributions of the curious were usually collected in his cap. The effigy is still preserved, but for a time was only shown to visitors by the dean's order; it can, however, now be seen, but is in a very decayed condition (STANLEY, *Memorials of Westminster*, ed. 1868, pp. 228, 343; DART, *Westmonasterium*, i. 153).

A portrait of Monck, by Walker, is in the possession of the Earl of Sandwich, and one by Lely is in the Painted Hall at Greenwich; a third, by an unknown painter, was No. 815 in the National Portrait Exhibition of 1866; and a fourth was painted by Dr. Logan, an engraving of which and two others are in the possession of James Falconer, esq. The Sutherland Collection in the Bodleian Library contains about twenty engraved portraits.

Monck's appearance is thus described by Gumble: 'He was of a very comely personage, his countenance very manly and majestic, the whole fabric of his body very strong.' A French traveller who saw him in 1663 is more explicit: 'Il est petit et gros; mais il a la physionomie de l'esprit le plus solide, et de la conscience la plus tranquille du monde, et avec cela une froideur sans affectation, et sans orgueil, ni dédain; il a enfin tout l'air d'un homme fort moderé et fort prudent' (*Voyages de B. de Monconys*, ed. 1695, II. ii. 167). An Italian, writing of six years later, describes him as 'of the middle size, of a stout and square-built make, of a complexion partly sanguine and partly phlegmatic, as indeed is generally the case with the English; his face is fair, but somewhat wrinkled with age; his hair is grey, and his features not particularly fine or noble' (MAGALOTTI, *Travels of the Grand Duke Cosmo III*, 1821, p. 469). Of Monck's habits Gumble gives a minute account (pp. 465–75). He was very temperate, and before his sickness 'was never known to desire meat or drink till called to it, which was but once a day, and seldom drank but at his meals.' But if occasion arose he could drink deep, and when some young lords forced him to take part in a drinking bout, he saw them all under the table, and withdrew sober to the privy council (JUSSERAND, *A French Ambassador at the*

Court of Charles II, 1892, p. 96). Throughout he retained much of the puritan in his manners, was 'never heard to swear an oath,' and never gambled till his physicians advised it as a distraction. In religion Monck was careful in all observances, at heart 'inclined much to the rigidest points of predestination,' and he sometimes inserted religious reflections in his despatches. His courage, which was always conspicuous, was 'a settled habit of mind,' and 'as great in suffering as in doing.' But the virtue which his biographer praises as 'paramount in him and mistress of all the rest' was his prudence, including under that term the practical dexterity with which he made use of all men and all means to bring about the Restoration. The perjuries which it cost him to effect it never troubled his conscience. He regarded them as legitimate stratagems sanctified by the end in view. His natural reserve had made dissimulation easy to him, and his character for honesty and simplicity made him readily believed.

Monck was an indefatigable official, rising early, sleeping little, and despatching an enormous amount of business. He had very little education, spelt badly, and expressed himself awkwardly, and often tautologically, but his letters are always clear and to the point. As a general he was remarkable for his care of his men, and for a knowledge of military science rare among the self-taught commanders of the Commonwealth. He occupies a place in Walpole's 'Royal and Noble Authors' by virtue of 'Observations upon Military and Political Affairs,' written when he was a prisoner in the Tower, and published by John Heath in 1671.

Anne, duchess of Albemarle, born 25 March 1619 (*Sloane MS.* 1708, f. 117), was the daughter of John Clarges, a farrier in the Savoy, by his wife, Anne Leaver. She married, on 28 Feb. 1632-3, Thomas Radford, also a farrier, and afterwards a servant to Prince Charles, 'from whom she was separated in 1649, but of whose death before her second marriage no evidence appears to have been obtained.' Her remarriage to Monck took place on 23 Jan. 1652-3 at St. George's, Southwark (Chester, *Westminster Abbey Registers*, p. 171). Aubrey asserts that she was Monck's seamstress when he was prisoner in the Tower, and hints that she was also his mistress. A letter written in September 1653, mentioning the marriage, describes her character in the harshest terms, but these scandalous stories contain inaccuracies which destroy their credit (*Letters from the Bodleian*, ii. 452; Thurloe, i. 470). By her Monck had two sons: first, Christopher, born in 1653, second duke of Albemarle [q. v.]; secondly, George, who died an infant, and was buried in the chapel at Dalkeith House (Skinner, p. 70).

In 1659 all Mrs. Monck's influence with her husband was exercised on behalf of the restoration of the monarchy. Price dwells on the freedom she was wont to use in her evening conversations with the general after his day's work was over. At night too he was sometimes 'quickened with a curtain lecture of damnation—a text that his lady often preached upon to him' (Price, ed. Maseres, pp. 712, 716). This zeal gained her the praise of Hyde's correspondents, who speak of her as 'an extreme good woman,' and 'a happy instrument in this glorious work' (*Clarendon State Papers*, iii. 739, 741, 749). After the Restoration her defects became more obvious, and Clarendon terms her 'a woman of the lowest extraction, the least wit, and less beauty;' 'nihil muliebre præter corpus gerens' (*Rebellion*, xvi. 98). To Pepys she seemed 'a plain, homely dowdy,' and he complains that when he dined at the duke's he found him with 'dirty dishes, and a nasty wife at table and bad meat' (*Diary*, 4 April 1667). Her worst fault, however, was avarice, and she was commonly accused of selling offices in her husband's department, and of even worse methods of extortion (*ib.* 22 June 1660; 16 May 1667). She died on 29 Jan. 1670, aged nearly 51, and was buried in Westminster Abbey on 28 Feb. (Chester, p. 171).

[Of separately published lives of Monck the most important is The Life of General Monck, Duke of Albemarle, with Remarks upon his Actions, by Thomas Gumble, D.D., 8vo, 1671. Gumble was Monck's chaplain during 1659 and part of 1660, and derived much of his information from Monck and his officers. The Life by Thomas Skinner is for the most part a mere compilation, though Skinner was promised the use of original papers by Lord Bath and the second Duke of Albemarle (*Notes and Queries*, 1st ser. i. 377, 8th ser. iv. 421). It was first published in 1723 by William Webster, curate of St. Dunstan's-in-the-West, London, who added a preface containing some original documents. Of modern lives the most important is that by Guizot, originally published in 1837. Of this there are two translations, the first, published in 1838, with valuable annotations by J. Stuart Wortley, the second, published in 1851, by A. R. Scoble, from Guizot's revised edition of his work (1850), with an appendix of diplomatic correspondence. A life, by Julian Corbett, 1889, is included in the series of English Men of Action. Lives of Monck are also in Winstanley's Worthies, 1684; Biographia Britannica, v. 3134; Campbell's British Admirals, 1744; Prince's Worthies of Devon, 1701. A pedigree is given in the Visitations of Devon, ed. by Colby. In 1660 a pamphlet was printed, entitled The Pedigree and Descent of his Excellency, General George Monk, setting forth how he is descended from King Edward III, by a Branch and Slip of the White Rose, the House of York; and likewise his Extraction from Richard, King of the Romans.

For particular portions of Monck's career the following are the chief authorities: 1. For his service in Ireland: Carte's Life of Ormonde; Carte's MSS. in the Bodleian Library; Gilbert's Aphorismical Discovery of Treasonable Faction. 2. For his services at sea: Granville Penn's Memorials of Sir William Penn, 1833; J. B. Deane's Life of Richard Deane; The Life of Cornelius Van Tromp, translated 1697; the parliamentary newspapers for 1653, and the Calendar of Domestic State Papers. 3. For his government of Scotland: The Thurloe State Papers, 1742; MSS. of Sir William Clarke at Worcester College, Oxford (published by Camden Soc.); Mackinnon's Hist. of the Coldstream Guards, 1833; Masson's Life of Milton, vol. v. 4. For the Restoration: The Mystery and Method of his Majesty's happy Restoration, by John Price, one of Monk's chaplains, 8vo, 1680; reprinted by Maseres in Select Tracts relating to the Civil Wars in England, 1815; The Continuation of Sir Richard Baker's Chronicle of the Kings of England, by Edward Phillips, printed in the edition of 1661 and subsequent editions, in what relates to Monck is based on the papers of his brother-in-law, Sir Thomas Clarges; the papers of Monck's secretary, Sir William Clarke, throw much light on the history of this part of Monck's life (published by Camden Soc. from MSS. at Worcester College, Oxford, or in the possession of F. Leyborne Popham, esq., of Littlecote); Ludlow's Memoirs, 1698; the Clarendon State Papers, vol. iii.; Guizot's Hist. of Richard Cromwell and the Restoration of Charles II, translated by A. R. Scoble, 1856. Letters and declarations by Monck during this period, reprinted from contemporary pamphlets, are to be found in the Old Parliamentary History. Shortly after the Restoration A Collection of Letters and Declarations, &c., sent by General Monk, 4to, 1660, was published, which was reprinted in 1714 in 8vo. This was meant to expose his perfidy, and his protestations in favour of a republic were all printed in italics. It contained a letter to the king on 30 Dec. 1659, which is a forgery. 5. For the post-Restoration period of Monck's life: Burnet's Hist. of his own Time; the Continuation of Clarendon's Life, and the Diary of Samuel Pepys. A Vindication of General Monck from some Calumnies of Dr. Burnet and some Mistakes of Dr. Echard, in relation to the sale of Dunkirk and the Portuguese match, was published by George Granville. It called forth an answer, to which Granville replied in A Letter to the Author of Reflections Historical and Political, occasioned by a Treatise in Vindication of General Monk. Both are reprinted in the Genuine Works of Lord Lansdowne, 2 vols. 1736. On Monck's death the university of Oxford published a collection of Latin verses, Epicedia Universitatis Oxoniensis in Obitum Georgii ducis Albemarliæ, fol., 1670; and Cambridge added Musarum Cantabrigiensium Threnodia, 1670, 4to. Payne Fisher wrote an Elogium Sepulchrale, and Thomas Flatman a Pindarique Ode. Robert Wild, Iter Boreale, 1660, 4to, celebrates Monck's march from Scotland, and Dryden's Annus Mirabilis, 1667, his four days' sea-fight.] C. H. F.

MONCK, MARY (*d.* 1715), poetess, was the second daughter of Robert Molesworth, first viscount Molesworth [q. v.], by Letitia, third daughter of Richard, lord Colooney, and sister of Richard, earl of Bellamont. She became the first wife of George Monck of St. Stephen's Green, Dublin, and died at Bath in 1715.

By her own application she acquired a knowledge of the Latin, Italian, and Spanish languages, and read much English literature. Some poems by her appeared shortly after her death under the title of 'Marinda. Poems and Translations upon several occasions,' London, 1716, 8vo. A long and fulsome dedication to Carolina, princess of Wales, was prefixed by her father, Lord Molesworth. On her deathbed she wrote some very affecting verses to her husband, which are not included in her works, but which were printed in Barber's collection of 'Poems by Eminent Ladies' (London, 1755, 12mo), ii. 195.

[Ballard's Memoirs of Ladies, 1775, p. 288; Cibber's Lives of the Poets, iii. 201; Hist. Reg. 1726, Chronology, p. 31; Jacob's Lives of the Poets, 1720, ii. 106; Lodge's Peerage of Ireland (Archdall), iii. 138, 140 *n.*; Ware's Writers of Ireland (Harris), p. 287.] T. C.

MONCK or **MONK, NICHOLAS** (1610–1661), provost of Eton and bishop of Hereford, was the third son of Sir Thomas Monck, knt., of Potheridge, Devonshire, and younger brother to George [q. v.], the famous general. He was born at Potheridge in 1610, and in 1629 matriculated at Wadham College, Oxford. He graduated B.A. 3 March 1630–1, and M.A. 30 Oct. 1633. Instead of entering the army like his brothers, he took holy orders. The small living of Plymtree in Devonshire, which he obtained after 1646 through his marriage in 1642 with the daughter of the then rector, whose family had the presentation, was confirmed to him by General Monck's influence with Cromwell; but his sympathies certainly leaned to the royalist side, and he was in 1653 presented by his kinsman, Sir John Grenville [q. v.], to the valuable living of Kilhampton, Cornwall, worth about 260*l.* a year. After Cromwell's death Grenville sent 'the honest clergyman' up to London, where he received through George Monck's brother-in-law, Thomas Clarges [q. v.], instructions to go to Scotland and ascertain his brother's intentions. Nicholas therefore sailed for Edinburgh (August 1659) on the ostensible errand of arranging a marriage for one of his daughters. He found the general engaged with a council of officers, but confided his mission to the general's chaplain, John Price, who was in the confidence of the royalist party. From Price Monck received every encouragement. The next day the brothers met, and various accounts are given of their interview, but all agree that the general refused to commit himself as to his future conduct (cf. KENNETT, iii. 215–16, and art. MONCK, GEORGE).

After the Restoration Nicholas was made provost of Eton on the recommendation of Grenville. There was no pretence of election on the part of the fellows, who, much incensed by Charles's arbitrary proceeding, refused to make an entry of the appointment in the college register. A copy of the royal letter, dated 7 July 1660, nominating Monck is extant in the Eton Library. Most of the puritan fellows resigned or were ejected, and new regulations were drawn up by the new provost and fellows, the former's stipend being fixed at 500*l.* a year, besides 'wood, capons, 20 dozen of candles, and 20 loads of hay.' On 1 Aug. 1660 Nicholas was created D.D. at Oxford *per litt. reg.*, and on 1 Dec. he was appointed bishop of Hereford, a see which had been vacant fourteen years. He was to hold his provostship in addition for two years. Consecrated on 6 Jan. 1660–1 in Westminster Abbey by the Archbishop of York, he lived to enjoy his new dignity only for eleven months. He died on 17 Dec. 1661, aged 51, at his lodgings in Old Palace Yard, and was buried on the 20th in Westminster Abbey, his brother George attending the funeral as chief mourner.

By his wife Susannah, daughter of Thomas Payne, rector of Plymtree, Devonshire, and widow of Christopher Trosse, whom he married in 1642, Nicholas had two daughters, Mary, married to Arthur Fairwell of Westminster, and Elizabeth, married to Curwen Rawlinson of Carke Hall, Cartmell, Lancashire. A son Nicholas died young. On the daughter Elizabeth's monument, put up by her son Christopher Rawlinson at St. Mary's Church, Cartmell, Nicholas is described as 'a great assistant in the Restoration to his brother.' In 1723 Christopher Rawlinson erected a pyramidical monument of black and white marble to the bishop in St. Edmund's Chapel, Westminster Abbey. Upon it is an elaborate Latin inscription.

A portrait of Monck in the print of the Rawlinson family of Carke Hall, Lancashire, is mentioned by Bromley.

[Wood's Athenæ Oxon. iv. 815; Wood's Fasti, i. 454, 469, ii. 236; Walker's Sufferings of the Clergy, ii. 306; Clarendon's History, Clar. Press edit., 1826, vii. 383; Price's Mystery and Method of his Majesty's Happy Restoration, London, 1680, p. 5 &c.; Maxwell Lyte's Hist. of Eton College, p. 240; Chester's Register of Westminster Abbey, p. 155; information supplied by Mrs. Frances Troup, Rockbeare House, near Exeter, Devonshire.] E. T. S.

MONCKTON, MARY, afterwards COUNTESS OF CORK AND ORRERY (1746–1840), born on 21 May 1746, was the youngest child and only surviving daughter of John Monckton, first viscount Galway (1695–1751), by his second wife, Jane, fourth daughter of Henry Warner Westenra, esq., of Rathleagh, Queen's County, Ireland. From an early age she interested herself in literature and learning, and as a young woman became known as a 'blue-stocking.' During the whole of her long life she was renowned for her vivacity, sparkling wit, and great conversational powers. While young she made her mother's house in Charles Street, Berkeley Square, London, the rendezvous of persons of genius and talent. Dr. Johnson was often her guest, and Boswell describes her in 1781 as 'the lively Miss Monckton who used to have the finest *bit of blue*' at her house. 'Her vivacity,' he goes on, 'enchanted the sage, and they used to talk together with all imaginable ease.' On one occasion when Johnson denied that Sterne's writings were pathetic, Miss Monckton declared that they certainly affected her. 'That is,' said Johnson, 'because, dearest, you're a dunce.' When she reminded him of this some time afterwards, Johnson said, 'Madam, if I had thought so I certainly should not have said it' (BOSWELL, *Life*, ed. Hill, iv. 108, passim). After Johnson became too ill to go into society Miss Monckton visited him at his house. Hannah More, writing to her sister in April 1784, says: 'Did I tell you I went to see Dr. Johnson? Miss Monckton carried me, and we paid him a very long visit.' Frances Burney describes Miss Monckton in 1782 as 'one of those who stand foremost in collecting all extraordinary or curious people to her London conversaziones, which like those of Mrs. Vesey mix the rank and the literature, and exclude all besides. . . . She is between thirty and forty, very short, very fat, but handsome, splendidly and fantastically dressed, rouged not unbecomingly, yet evidently and palpably desirous of gaining notice and admiration. She has an easy levity in her air, manner, voice, and discourse.' According to Miss Burney the guests at Miss Monckton's parties were not announced, and the hostess received them seated.

They were never allowed to sit in a circle, since such an arrangement impeded conversation, which was as a rule the only amusement (*Diary of Mme. d'Arblay*, ii. 179, passim). Miss Monckton, like Mrs. Elizabeth Montagu [q. v.], deprecated card-playing at private parties. Among her guests when Miss Burney knew her were, besides Johnson, Burke, Reynolds, Sheridan (then only regarded as the beautiful Miss Linley's 'drag of a husband'), Horace Walpole, Mrs. Thrale, and Mrs. Siddons, who was Miss Monckton's intimate friend.

In June 1786 Miss Monckton married Edmund Boyle, seventh earl of Cork and Orrery, who died in 1798. She was his second wife. There were no children of the marriage.

As Lady Cork her passion for entertaining persons of note increased. Lady Charleville, writing to Mrs. Opie in 1809, says: 'Lady Cork's activity in pursuit of amusement is a pleasant proof of vivacity and spirit surviving youth' (Brightwell, *Memorials of Mrs. Opie*, p. 139). In her journal for 1811 Miss Mary Berry [q. v.] describes one party as 'curious,' and another as 'a great assembly. The prince was there and all the world.' Mrs. Opie, whose friendship with Lady Cork was of long standing, mentions a reception at Lady Cork's at which she was present in 1814, when General Blücher was expected, but did not come (*ib.* p. 101). Mrs. Opie gives also an amusing account of Lady Cork's patronage of James Hogg [q. v.], the Ettrick shepherd (*ib.* pp. 349–52). The advance of age did not diminish Lady Cork's love of society. C. R. Leslie, writing in 1834, says: 'Lady Cork is very old, infirm, and diminutive . . . her features are delicate and her skin fair, and notwithstanding her great age she is very animated. . . . The old lady, who was a lion hunter in her youth, is as much one now as ever' (*Autobiography*, i. 136, 243). To her dinners and receptions in her last years came, among others, the prince regent, Canning, Castlereagh, Lord Byron, Sir Walter Scott, Sheridan, Lord John Russell, Sir Robert Peel, Theodore Hook, Samuel Rogers, and Sydney Smith. Her bias was whig, but ability and distinction insured a welcome to members of all parties.

Of her many peculiarities and eccentricities in her old age numerous anecdotes are told. It is said that she suffered from kleptomania, and that when she dined out her host would leave a pewter fork or spoon in the hall for her to carry off in her muff. On one occasion when leaving a breakfast party, she coolly took a friend's carriage without permission, and kept it out the whole afternoon. On meeting the owner Lady Cork merely complained that the high steps of the carriage did not suit her short legs. Her memory was extraordinary. One evening, when past eighty, she recited, at a friend's house, half a book of Pope's 'Iliad' while waiting for her carriage. Until a few days before her death she rose at six in the morning, and dined out when she had not company at home. When out of London she spent much time at Fineshade Abbey, Northamptonshire, with her brother, Colonel the Hon. John Monckton. She died in London at her house in New Burlington Street on 30 May 1840, at the age of ninety-four, and was buried at Brewood, Staffordshire. In the church is a tablet to her memory.

Lord Beaconsfield knew Lady Cork well, and is said to have described her accurately as 'Lady Bellair' in 'Henrietta Temple,' and it is thought that Dickens drew on her for some of the features of 'Mrs. Leo Hunter' in 'Pickwick.'

In 1779 Miss Monckton sat to Sir Joshua Reynolds (Leslie, *Life of Reynolds*, ii. 278). The portrait, a full-length seated, is in the possession of Mr. Edward P. Monckton of Fineshade Abbey, Northamptonshire. It is a very fine picture, and was engraved in mezzotint by John Jacobé in 1779. A painting by H. P. Briggs, R.A., a three-quarter length, seated, is in the possession of Viscount Galway of Serlby Hall, Nottinghamshire. Miss Anna Maria Monckton of Somerford, a niece of Lady Cork, made a sketch of her which still exists, and there is written beneath it,

Look at me,
I'm 93,
And all my faculties I keep;
Eat, drink, and laugh, and soundly sleep.

[A Genealogical Hist. of the Family of Moncton by David Henry Moncton, M.D., pp. 135, 136, 139–47; Annual Register, 1840, p. 166; Bentley's Miscellany, xix. 293; information supplied by Mr. Edward P. Moncton.] E. L.

MONCKTON, Sir **PHILIP** (1620?–1679), royalist, was son of Sir Francis Monckton, knight, by Margaret, daughter of Thomas Savile of Northgate Head, Wakefield. Both his father, who was knighted by Charles I on 25 June 1642, and his grandfather, Sir Philip Monckton of Cavil Hall, near Howden in Yorkshire, adopted the cause of Charles I, and were fined by the parliament as delinquents (*Calendar of Compounders*, p. 1074). Philip Monckton the younger was captain of Sir Thomas Metham's regiment of foot when the king attacked Hull in July 1642, distinguished himself at the battle of Atherton Moor, and in Newcastle's campaign against the Scots in the spring of 1644. He had a horse killed under him at Marston Moor, and three at Naseby, and was wounded at the battle of Rowton Heath. He was knighted at Newcastle, probably in 1644 (*Monckton Papers*, pp. 1–21). In the second civil war Monckton had (in the absence of Sir Marmaduke Langdale) the chief command of the Yorkshire cavaliers, which he shared with Major-general Gilbert Byron and Colonel Robert Portington. He was defeated by Colonel Edward Rossiter at Willoughby Field, on the borders of Nottinghamshire (5 July 1648), and taken prisoner (*ib.* pp. 22, 44; Zachary Grey, *Examination of Neal's Hist. of the Puritans*, iii. 24; Rushworth, vii. 1183). After five months' imprisonment in Lincoln Castle he was given a pass for the continent by Lord Fairfax (December 1648), and was allowed by parliament to compound for his estate on payment of 220*l.* 14*s.* 6*d.* He returned to England about 1650, engaged in plots for Charles II, and in 1655 was for some months imprisoned in Lambeth House (*Cal. Clarendon Papers*, ii. 400, 440; *Cal. State Papers*, Dom. 1655, p. 215; *Monckton Papers*, pp. 86, 100). Again, in August 1659, he concerted the surprise of York, and in January 1660, when the gates of York were opened to Lord Fairfax, Monckton claims that he was mainly instrumental in procuring the submission of the garrison (*ib.* pp. 24–42; Kennett, *Register*, p. 6). He greatly exaggerated his own services, and asserted in 1673 that he was 'more instrumental in his majesty's restoration than any man alive.' In a petition which he presented to Charles in 1667, he reminded the king of a promise made in 1653, that if it pleased God to restore him, Monckton should share with him (*Monckton Papers*, pp. 86, 102). All he received, however, was the post of controller of the excise and customs at Dunkirk (August 1661; *Cal. State Papers*, Dom. 1661–2, p. 78). On 3 Dec. 1673 he was granted the profits of the seigniory of Howdenshire belonging to the bishopric of Durham (*Monckton Papers*, p. 105). The meagreness of these rewards he attributed to the malign influence of Clarendon, who 'said he was mad and not fit for any employment.' Consequently he accused Clarendon of duplicity, and of favouring the king's enemies, and complained that he disregarded a dangerous nonconformist plot which Monckton's exertions had discovered (Lister, *Life of Clarendon*, iii. 532). He also threatened to accuse Lord Belasyse of betraying the king's adherents to Cromwell unless Belasyse [see Belasyse, John, Baron Belasyse, 1614–1689] did something for him (*Monckton Papers*, p. 100). It is not surprising that in July 1676 Monckton was committed to the Tower 'for writing into the country scandalous letters to defame the government and privy councillors' (*Hist. MSS. Comm.* 12th Rep. pt. vii. p. 128). Monckton was sheriff of Yorkshire in 1675, and was returned to parliament for Scarborough in November 1670. He also held various military appointments. On 16 July 1660 Monck commissioned him as captain in the foot regiment of Lord Belasyse; on 2 July 1666 he received a commission as lieutenant of Sir George Savile's troop of horse, and on 26 March 1668 he was given a company in Colonel John Russell's regiment of guards. His will, dated 7 Feb. 1678, was proved at York on 12 April 1679.

Monckton married Anne, daughter of Robert Eyre of High Low, Derbyshire. His grandson, John Monckton, was in 1727 created Viscount Galway in the peerage of Ireland. A portrait of Sir Philip and other relics are in the possession of the present Viscount Galway. The portrait was No. 770 in the Exhibition of National Portraits of 1866.

[The main authority for Monckton's life is his own memoir, printed, with letters and other documents, from the originals in the possession of Lord Galway, by Mr. Edward Peacock, for the Philobiblon Society in 1884. Part of this memoir is printed in the Annual Register, 1805, p. 883, and some extracts are in Kennett's Register, 1728, p. 6, and in Lister's Life of Clarendon, 1837, iii. 532–5; see Lansdowne MS. 988, f. 320. The defeat at Willoughby Field is the subject of a pamphlet, 'An important and true Relation of the great Victory obtained . . . by the conjoined Forces of Lincoln, Nottingham, &c., under the Command of Colonel Edward Rossiter,' 4to, 1648, reprinted in the Monckton Papers, App., and in the Life of Col. Hutchinson, ed. 1885, ii. 380.]

C. H. F.

MONCKTON, ROBERT (1726–1782), lieutenant-general, born on 24 June 1726, was second son of John Monckton of Cavil and Hodroyd in Yorkshire, who was created Viscount Galway in 1727. Lady Elizabeth, daughter of John Manners, second duke of Rutland, was his mother. Monckton received a commission in the 3rd (Earl of Dunmore's) regiment of guards in 1741, and on 17 May 1742 sailed with that regiment for Flanders to co-operate with the Dutch in the cause of Maria Theresa. He remained at Ghent until 1743, when the army advanced into Germany. At Dettingen he is stated to have served on the king's guard (note in manuscript order book at Fineshade Abbey, and Aikin, *Nova Scotia*, p. 391 *n.*) On 27 June 1744 he received a captain's commission in Cholmondeley's (34th) regiment of foot (*Mil. Entry Book*, vol. xviii., in Record Office). Through the campaign of 1745 in Flanders he served with the Duke of Cumberland, was present at Fontenoy (11 May 1745), and on 19 May was appointed one of the aides-de-camp to Lord Dunmore, who had command of the foot. His regiment was recalled to aid in the suppression of the rebellion in Scotland in 1745, but Monckton remained in Flanders some months longer, and it is doubtful whether he took part in the war in the north. On 15 Feb. 1747 he became a major in the 34th, and on 28 Feb. 1751 lieutenant-colonel of the 47th, Lascelles's regiment of foot (*Ledger of Comm.* 1742–8, and *Mil. Entry Book*, vol. xxii. f. 181, in Record Office).

In November 1751 Monckton was elected M.P. for Pontefract on the death of his father. In 1752 he was sent to Nova Scotia, and was nominated a member of the council at Halifax on 28 Aug. 1753 (*Underwood Papers*; *Minutes of Council* in Record Office, p. 44). Soon afterwards he, with two hundred men, quelled an insurrection of the German settlers in the province at Lunenberg, and on 21 Aug. 1754 he was appointed lieutenant-governor of Annapolis Royal, in the place of Charles Lawrence [q. v.], who became lieutenant-governor of Nova Scotia (*Minutes of Council*; manuscript at Serlby Hall; *Mil. Entry Book*, vol. xxiii.)

Lawrence soon decided to attack the French, who occupied the isthmus connecting Nova Scotia with the mainland, and Monckton was sent to Shirley, the governor of Massachusetts, in order to raise two thousand auxiliaries. Meanwhile an attack on the French in Nova Scotia was included in the plan of campaign for 1755, which Braddock arrived from England to carry out (cf. Parkman, *Montcalm and Wolfe*; Bancroft, *Hist.*; Wilson, *Diary*, in Coll. Nova Scotia Hist. Soc. i. 119–40). On 22 May Monckton set sail from Boston with a force of about three hundred regular troops and fifteen hundred provincials. He reached Annapolis 25 May; on 1 June sailed up the Bay of Fundy, and, landing on the 2nd, opened fire (14 June) on the French fort of Beauséjour, which was garrisoned by 160 regulars and some three hundred Acadians. On the 16th the fort capitulated (Parkman, *Montcalm and Wolfe*, i. 249; Beatson, *Nav. and Mil. Memoirs*, vol. ii. App. p. 7; *Letters from Lawrence*, Record Office; Wilson, *Journal*). A small fort named Gaspereau, on the Baye Verte, surrendered on the 18th, and was renamed Fort Monckton. Beauséjour was renamed Fort Cumberland. Another of the enemy's forts at the mouth of the St. John's River was at the same time abandoned. Thus the whole of Nova Scotia was in the possession of the British, and Monckton was ordered by Lawrence to expel all French settlers from the province (manuscripts at Fineshade Abbey). In December, when Lawrence was appointed governor, Monckton took his place as lieutenant-governor. Both were at Halifax during the greater part of 1756–7, and had no small trouble in protecting the outlying settlements from French and Indians. On 20 Dec. 1757 Monckton was appointed fourth colonel-commandant of the 60th royal American regiment. Monckton reluctantly remained at Halifax in 1758, while Lawrence was engaged with General Amherst in capturing Louisbourg. In September Monckton, acting under orders from Amherst, destroyed some French settlements up the St. John's River, and early in 1759 he was summoned to New York to take command in the south in the event of General Forbes's death. Forbes died on 11 March, but Pitt had in the meantime appointed Monckton second in command of the famous expedition under General Wolfe destined for Quebec. On 4 June Wolfe sailed from Louisbourg, and by the 25th all the transports had surmounted the difficulties of the St. Lawrence, and disembarked off the Isle of Orleans.

On 29 June Monckton was sent with four battalions to drive the enemy from Point Levi on the south shore of the St. Lawrence, and immediately opposite Quebec, and by 1 July he had erected batteries, which played with terrible effect on the lower part of the town of Quebec (Wright, *Wolfe*, p. 527). The French made futile attempts to dislodge Monckton (Parkman, ii. 215). On 31 July Wolfe made an unsuccessful attack on the French who were established between Quebec and the River Montmorenci. Monckton's boats grounded on a ledge, and thirteen companies of grenadiers, who, together with two hundred of the Royal Americans, were first on shore, rushed on the French lines without waiting for Monckton's men, and were repulsed with great loss. Eventually Monckton's men landed in good order; Wolfe recalled the grenadiers, and the troops were drawn off unmolested. Next day Wolfe wrote to Monckton: 'This check must not dishearten us; prepare for another and better attempt' (manuscript at Serlby Hall).

Early in August Brigadier Murray with 1,260 men was sent up the river, and established himself above Quebec. Wolfe's illness caused delay in the further movements of the troops, but the position became so serious that on 29 Aug. he gave written instructions to the three brigadier-generals, Monckton, Townshend, and Murray, to consider plans for an engagement. They met at

Monckton's quarters, and advised an attack on the town from the west. Wolfe adopted their advice. On the 13th the attack took place, and the victory was decisive. Wolfe died on the field. Monckton was wounded while leading Lascelles's regiment, and the command therefore devolved on Brigadier Townshend, but Monckton was well enough on the 15th to write a short note to Pitt, and another to Lord Galway (manuscript at Serlby Hall, Record Office).

On 18 Sept. Quebec capitulated. The terms were drawn up and signed by Townshend and Admiral Saunders. Monckton to his deep annoyance was not consulted, and Townshend subsequently apologised for the omission. On 24 Oct. Monckton was appointed colonel of the 17th foot. After putting things in order at Quebec for the winter, and leaving Murray in command, Monckton reached New York by 16 Dec. Early in 1760 he was appointed to succeed General Stanwix in the command of the troops at Philadelphia. Later in the year he was engaged in a conference with Indians, who appeared more favourable to the British than formerly, although a great outbreak followed in 1761. He also sought to induce the governments of Pennsylvania, Virginia, and Maryland to raise troops. On 20 Feb. (or 21) 1761 he was given the rank of major-general, and on 20 March 1761 he was appointed governor of New York, and commander-in-chief of the province.

At the end of 1761 he was placed in command of a force destined for the conquest of Martinique, and on 19 Nov. he sailed with 6,667 men from New York. The naval force was under Rodney, and the total land force under Monckton numbered nearly twelve thousand men. They landed on 16 Jan. 1762. On 4 Feb., after some sharp fighting, Fort Royal capitulated, and this success was followed by the surrender not only of Martinique, but also of Grenada, St. Lucia, and St. Vincent. Monckton and Rodney received the thanks of the House of Commons, and on 12 June the former was back again in New York.

On 28 June 1763 he left for England, and on 14 June 1765, when Sir Henry Moore succeeded him in New York, he was appointed governor of Berwick-on-Tweed and Holy Island; on 30 April 1770 he was promoted to the rank of lieutenant-general, and on 31 Feb. 1771 he received the freedom of the city of Edinburgh. He was recommended without result as commander-in-chief for India in 1773. In 1778 he became governor of Portsmouth, and he represented that town in parliament from 1779 till his death on 3 May 1782. He was buried on 26 May at Kensington parish church. He was unmarried. Fort Monckton, near Gosport, was named after him.

His portrait, by Benjamin West, belonging to Viscount Galway, was engraved by J. Watson; a medallion by James Tassie is in the National Portrait Gallery, Edinburgh; and two other portraits are mentioned by Bromley.

[Dr. Monckton's Hist. of the Family of Monckton (privately printed), and the authorities cited.]

H. W. M.

MONCREIFF, Sir HENRY, D.D., bart., afterwards Sir Henry Moncreiff Wellwood of Tulliebole (1750–1827), Scottish divine, born at Blackford, Perthshire, on 6 Feb. 1750, was eldest son of Sir William Moncreiff (*d.* 1767), minister of the parish of Blackford, who by the death of Sir Hugh succeeded to the baronetcy in 1744. His mother, Catharine, was eldest daughter of Robert Wellwood of Garvock. He received his early education at Blackford parish school, and in 1763, when only thirteen years old, matriculated in Glasgow University, where he continued to study till the death of his father in 1767. He then removed to Edinburgh University, where he finished his course in 1771. Such was the respect entertained in Blackford for the family that, with the sanction of the presbytery, the parish was kept vacant from the time of Sir William's death until 1771, when Henry received the presentation, and on 15 Aug. was ordained its minister, being the third Moncreiff who had held the living in succession. He proved himself a very diligent and efficient clergyman, and when one of the charges of St. Cuthbert's, Edinburgh, fell vacant, he was, on the recommendation of the heritors, appointed to it by the crown, as colleague to the Rev. John Gibson. Inducted on 26 Oct. 1775, he quickly became one of the most influential ministers of the city. A very eloquent and vigorous preacher, he also took a leading part in the business of the church courts, especially the general assembly, where he rose to be the leader of the evangelical party (vide Lockhart's *Peter's Letters to his Kinsfolk*, iii. 45 and 74, for graphic sketches of his appearances in the pulpit and general assembly). In 1785 he was elected moderator of the assembly, and in the same year received the degree of D.D. from the university of Glasgow, and was appointed chaplain to the Prince of Wales. He took an active part in the foundation of the Society for the Benefit of the Sons of the Clergy and in the management of the ministers' widows' fund (of which he was collector for many years) and of other benevolent schemes. In 1793 he was appointed chaplain to

George III. In 1825 he lost the sight of an eye through illness, and on 9 Aug. 1827 he died in Edinburgh. He was buried in the West Church burying-ground there; and a monument in the vestibule of St. Cuthbert's hard by tells of the high place which he occupied in the regard of his parishioners and of the citizens of Edinburgh generally. For over half a century Moncreiff was one of the leading figures in the church of Scotland, and perhaps its most influential clergyman (cf. Lord Brougham in *Edinb. Review*, xlvii. 242).

In 1773 Moncreiff married his cousin, Susan Robertson, eldest daughter of James Robertson Barclay, writer to the signet, of Keavil, Fifeshire, by whom he had five sons and two daughters. The eldest son, William Wellwood, became judge-advocate of Malta, and died in 1813; his second son, Sir James Wellwood, afterwards Lord Moncreiff, is separately noticed. The eldest daughter married Sir John Stoddart, afterwards chief justice of Malta.

He added Wellwood to his name at the desire of his grand-uncle, Henry Wellwood of Garvock, on having the estate of Tulliebole in Kinross-shire, which had previously belonged to the Wellwood family, settled on him. Moncreiff published, in addition to many pamphlets and tracts: 1. Four volumes of 'Sermons' in 1805, 1806, 1822, 1831. 2. 'Discourses on the Evidence of the Jewish and Christian Revelations,' 1815. 3. 'Account of the Life and Writings of John Erskine, D.D.,' 1818. 4. 'Life of Dr. Henry,' prefixed to vol. vi. of his 'History of England,' which Moncreiff edited, 1793.

[Preface by Sir James W. Moncreiff to posthumous volume of sermons, 1831, pp. ix-xxv; Peter's Letters to his Kinsfolk, iii. 45, 74; Edinburgh Review, xlvii. 242; Chambers's Biog. Dict. of Eminent Scotsmen, iv. 434; Scott's Fasti, i. 122; Cockburn's Memorials; information supplied by Lord Moncreiff.] T. H.

MONCREIFF, Sir HENRY WELLWOOD (1809–1883), Scottish divine, born at Edinburgh 21 May 1809, was eldest son of Sir James Wellwood Moncreiff, afterwards Lord Moncreiff [q. v.] He was educated at the Edinburgh High School and University, but (5 April 1827) matriculated at New College, Oxford, whence he graduated B.A. in 1831. While at Oxford he was on intimate terms with Mr. Gladstone. Returning to Scotland he studied divinity under Dr. Chalmers, and after completing his course was ordained minister of the parish of Baldernock in Stirlingshire in 1836. In the following year he obtained the more important charge of East Kilbride in Lanarkshire. Moncreiff took part in the controversy which ended in the disruption of the church of Scotland. He joined the free church in June 1843, and from that date till 1852 he was the minister of Free East Kilbride. He succeeded to the baronetcy and assumed the name Wellwood on the death of his father in 1851. In 1852 he became minister of Free St. Cuthbert's in Edinburgh, where his grandfather, Sir Henry Moncreiff (1750–1827) [q.v.], passed fifty-two years of his ministry. He was appointed joint principal clerk to the free general assembly in 1855, was created D.D. by Glasgow University in 1860, and appointed moderator of the free church assembly in 1869. In 1862 he was appointed secretary of the Bible Board, and held that office at his death, which took place 4 Nov. 1883.

Moncreiff was twice married, first, on 8 Feb. 1838, to Alexandrina Mary, daughter of George Bell, a surgeon in Edinburgh; and secondly in 1875 to Lucretia, daughter of Andrew Murray of Murrayshall in Perthshire. There was no issue by either marriage.

His social position, knowledge of church law, and readiness to place his knowledge and experience at the disposal of his fellow-ministers, rendered Moncreiff one of the most influential supporters of the free church. His published writings included 'A Vindication of the Free Church Claim of Right' (1877) and 'The Free Church Principle, its Character and History,' being the first series of the Chalmers Lectures (1883).

[Irving's Book of Eminent Scotsmen; Hew Scott's Fasti, ii. 291; some autobiographical information is contained in The Free Church Principle, its Character and History, publ. 1883, pp. 330–3; Memorials of R. S. Candlish, by Dr. W. Wilson, pp. 225–59.] A. J. M. M.

MONCREIFF, Sir JAMES WELLWOOD, Lord Moncreiff (1776–1851), Scottish judge, was the second son of the Rev. Sir Henry Moncreiff Wellwood [q. v.] of Tulliebole in Kinross-shire, baronet, a well-known minister of the established church of Scotland, in which five of his ancestors had served. Born 13 Sept. 1776, James was educated at school in Edinburgh and at Glasgow University, and held an exhibition at Balliol College, Oxford, whence he graduated B.C.L. in 1800. He was called to the Scottish bar on 26 Jan. 1799. His family was strongly presbyterian, whiggish, and patriotic, and he adopted their principles from conviction as well as hereditary association. In 1795, when a youth of sixteen, he attracted attention by carrying a lighted tallow candle to allow the face of Henry Erskine to be seen at the meeting to protest against the continuation of the war; for his share in the meeting Erskine was deposed by a large majority from the deanship of the Faculty of Advocates. He returned from Oxford as strong a presbyterian and whig as when he went there, and throughout life took a leading part in support of the whig party both in civil and ecclesiastical politics. In the assembly of the established church he was one of the lay leaders of the popular party which opposed private patronage. In 1806 he stood for the office of procurator or legal adviser of the church, but was defeated by Sir John Connell.

On 7 Feb. 1807 he was appointed sheriff of Clackmannan and Kinross, and soon acquired a considerable practice at the bar, of which he became one of the leaders. On 19 Dec. 1820 he presided at the Pantheon meeting, which passed resolutions in favour of a petition to the crown for the dismissal of the tory ministry of Lord Liverpool. On 22 Nov. 1826 he was elected dean of the Faculty of Advocates, Jeffrey, though his senior, gracefully ceding his claim in favour of his friend. In 1828, following a custom of the bar that no criminal however poor should be undefended, and if necessary might receive the services even of its professional head, he defended the 'resurrectionist' Burke. In March 1829 he spoke at a great meeting in Edinburgh in favour of catholic emancipation. On 24 June of the same year he was made a judge of the court of session by Sir Robert Peel, in succession to Lord Alloway, and was succeeded as dean of faculty by Jeffrey. After becoming a judge he still acted as a member of the general assembly, and carried in 1834 a motion in favour of a popular veto on patronage. According to Lord Cockburn, who drew his character with the feelings of a friend and the fidelity of an artist, 'while grounded in the knowledge necessary for the profession of a liberal lawyer, he was not a well-read man. Without his father's dignified manner, his outward appearance was rather insignificant, but his countenance was marked by a pair of fine compressed lips, denoting great vigour. Always simple, direct, and practical, he had little need of imagination. . . . He added to these negative qualities great power of reasoning, unconquerable energy, and the habitual and conscientious practice of all the respectable and all the amiable virtues. His reasoning power and great legal knowledge made him the best working counsel in court. Everything was a matter of duty with him, and he gave his whole soul to it. Jeffrey called him the whole duty of man!'

Such qualities rendered him one of the best judges of his time. At the disruption in 1843 he joined the free church, whose secession was the logical outcome of the views he had supported in the assembly. He died on 30 March 1851. By his marriage in 1808 with Ann, daughter of Captain J. Robertson, R.N., he had five sons and three daughters. His eldest son was the Rev. Sir Henry Wellwood Moncreiff [q. v.] His second son, James, who followed his father's profession, became lord advocate, dean of faculty, and lord justice clerk, an office which he resigned in 1889.

There is an excellent engraving of Moncreiff by Charles Holl in Chambers's 'Eminent Scotsmen' (vol. iii.), from a portrait by Raeburn, and a bust by Samuel Joseph is in the National Portrait Gallery, Edinburgh.

[Foster's Alumni Oxon. 1715–1886; Brunton and Haig's Senators of the College of Justice; Cockburn's Memorials.] Æ. M.

MONCRIEFF, ALEXANDER (1695–1761), presbyterian minister, born in 1695, was the eldest son of the laird of Culfargie in the parish of Abernethy, Perthshire, and, as his father died when Alexander was a boy, became heir to that estate. His grandfather, Alexander Moncrieff of Scoonie, Fifeshire, was the companion of the martyr James Guthrie [q. v.], whose history and character deeply influenced Moncrieff. After passing through the grammar school at Perth he attended the university of St. Andrews, where he took his degree, and then entered the Divinity Hall of the same university. At the conclusion of his curriculum, in 1716 he went to Leyden, where he pursued his studies for a year. He was licensed by the presbytery of Perth as a preacher in 1718, and in September 1720 he was ordained in his native parish of Abernethy. Keen controversies were agitating the church of Scotland. The Marrow controversy, in which Thomas Boston [q. v.] of Ettrick was a conspicuous leader, began shortly after Moncrieff's ordination, and he joined the little band who were contending for purity of doctrine in the church. The agitation regarding patronage, or the power of patrons to present to vacant churches, apart from the co-operation or even against the wish of the people, followed. Moncrieff joined the Erskines in denouncing attempts to invade the people's rights. He was one of the four ministers whom the assembly suspended, and who, having formally separated themselves from the judicatories of the church of Scotland, formed on 6 Dec. 1733, at Gairney Bridge, Kinross-shire, the secession church of Scotland [see Erskine, Ebenezer]. The new denomination met with much sympathy and success, and was soon able not only to supply ordinances in different parts of the country, but even to organise a theological hall for the training of its future ministers In February 1742 Moncrieff was unanimously chosen professor of divinity, a position which he filled with great ability and zeal. He was also an active and influential member of the associate presbytery and synod. In 1749 his son was ordained as his colleague and successor in the charge of the congregation at Abernethy. Moncrieff published in 1750 a vindication of the secession church, and in 1756 'England's Alarm, which is also directed to Scotland and Ireland, in several Discourses, which contains a warning against the great Wickedness of these lands.' A little devotional work by him, entitled 'A Drop of Honey from the Rock of Christ,' was published posthumously at Glasgow (1778). He died on 7 Oct. 1761, in the sixty-seventh year of his age and the forty-second of his ministry.

He appears to have been a man of resolution and daring. He was jocularly called 'the lion of the secession church' by his colleagues. With Erskine, William Wilson, and James Fisher he was joint author of the 'judicial testimony' against the church of Scotland, issued in December 1736. His church, since its union with the relief church, forms the united presbyterian church.

[Young's Memorials of the Rev. Alex. Moncrieff of Abernethy, with a Selection from his Works, 1849; McKerrow's Hist. of the Secession Church, 1848; Landreth's United Presbyterian Divinity Hall, 1876.] T. B. J.

MONCRIEFF, JAMES (1744–1793), colonel, military engineer, son of James Moncrieff, esq., of Sauchop in Fifeshire, was born in 1744. He entered the Royal Military Academy at Woolwich on 11 March 1759, and was appointed practitioner engineer and ensign on 28 Jan. 1762. He joined the expedition under the Earl of Albemarle to capture the Havannah, and disembarked on 7 June 1762. He was appointed ensign in the 100th foot on 10 July. The siege was a long and a difficult one, and the brunt fell upon the engineers. The Moro Castle was captured on 30 July after a struggle of forty-four days, but it was not until 14 Aug. that the Havannah fell into the hands of the British. Moncrieff was severely wounded. He continued to serve in the West Indies, East Florida, and other parts of North America for many years. On the disbandment of his regiment on 18 Nov. 1763 he resigned the ensigncy, and was promoted sub-engineer and lieutenant on 4 Dec. 1770, and engineer extraordinary and captain-lieutenant on 10 June 1776. On 11 Sept. 1776 he was present at the battle of Brandywine and guided the 4th regiment across a ford of the river. In 1777 he constructed a bridge over the river Rariton, near New York, for the passage of the troops: a model of this bridge is in the Royal Military Repository at Woolwich. During 1777 and the following year Moncrieff was actively employed in the American campaign.

In 1779 General Prevost [q. v.] carried the war into Carolina, and Moncrieff distinguished himself in the operations. At the pass of Stono Ferry Colonel Maitland and Moncrieff were strongly posted with the 71st regiment, the Hessians, and some militia, numbering in all some eight hundred men, when they were attacked by five thousand men under Major-general Lincoln, but after a stubborn fight won the day. Moncrieff joined in the pursuit of the flying enemy, and captured an ammunition wagon with his own hand. After the action Prevost was able to establish himself securely in the harbour of Port Royal, which gave him a firm footing in South Carolina, while he covered Georgia and kept open communication with Savannah.

When, on 9 Sept. 1779, Admiral D'Estaing anchored his fleet off the bar of Tybee at the mouth of the Savannah River, the British force was still at Port Royal, but General Prevost and Moncrieff were in Savannah, where only some ten guns were mounted in position. The troops were at once summoned from Port Royal, and by the extraordinary zeal and exertions of Moncrieff guns were landed from ships and taken from store until, in an incredibly short space of time, nearly a hundred pieces of cannon were mounted and a garrison of three thousand men concentrated at Savannah. D'Estaing sent a summons to the towns to surrender on the 9th, but two days later, after Generals Lincoln and Pulawski had joined D'Estaing's camp, Prevost, having determined to hold out, defied the enemy. Moncrieff lost no time in completing his line of intrenchments with redoubt and batteries. He sank two vessels in the channel, and constructed above the town a boom, which was covered by the guns of the Germaine. He threw up earthworks with a celerity that led the French to declare that the English engineer made his batteries spring up like mushrooms in a night. The forces opposed to the British were much superior in number, the assailants being seven thousand strong; while the garrison, including sailors and every sort of man, did not exceed three thousand. The enemy opened their trenches about the middle of September, and by the 24th had pushed their sap to within three hundred yards of the intrenchments. On that day a sortie was made which created great havoc in the besieger's works, but the advance was continued until the night of 3 Oct., when a violent bombardment was opened upon the town from both fleet and army, and on 9 Oct. a general assault was delivered. The assault was successfully resisted, and the enemy was forced to retire with a very heavy loss. Admiral D'Estaing was among the wounded. This failure so disheartened the besiegers that on 18 Oct. the operations were abandoned. General Prevost, in his despatch to the secretary of state, observed in reference to Moncrieff's services: 'There is not an officer or soldier of this little army, capable of reflecting and judging, who will not regard as personal to himself any mark of royal favour graciously conferred, through your lordship, on Captain Moncrieff.' Moncrieff was promoted for his services to be brevet-major on 27 Dec. 1779, and the promotion was dated, to give it more distinction, from the day on which the despatches relating the triumph at Savannah were presented to the king.

The troops remained in Savannah during the winter of 1779-80, expecting a force from New York to enable them to besiege Charlestown. This force, under Sir Henry Clinton the elder [q. v.], arrived in February 1780, and Charlestown was invested. Moncrieff was chief engineer. The batteries were opened on 10 April, and the siege was prosecuted with vigour and assiduity. On the capitulation of the place on 9 May, six thousand Americans with seven generals and a commodore became prisoners, and four hundred pieces of artillery were captured. The French ships lying in the harbour, with a thousand seamen, fell into the hands of the British. The loss to the British was 76 killed and 189 wounded. Clinton, in his despatch to Lord George Germaine, on 13 May, credited Moncrieff with the success of the operations. The only reward which Moncrieff received was promotion to be a brevet lieutenant-colonel on 27 Sept. 1780.

At the close of the war Moncrieff returned to England and was employed in the southern district, chiefly at Gosport. He was promoted to be engineer in ordinary and regimental captain on 1 Oct. 1784 and brevet-colonel on 18 Nov. 1790. On 14 July 1790 he had been appointed deputy quartermaster-general of the forces. In 1792-3 he reported to the Duke of Richmond on the defences of the coast of Kent, and was a member of a committee on the defences of Chatham.

When the French national convention declared war against Great Britain on 1 Feb. 1793, Moncrieff was appointed quartermaster-general to the force sent to Holland, under the Duke of York, to operate with the allies against the French. At the siege of Valenciennes Moncrieff, although on the staff, acted as chief engineer for the British force. The first parallel was traced on 13 June, and the batteries opened fire on the 18th, on which day Moncrieff received his promotion as regimental lieutenant-colonel of royal engineers. The trenches were pushed forward steadily until on the 28th the third parallel was formed by flying sap. From this point mining commenced, and the greater part of July was spent in subterranean warfare. The assault was delivered on 25 July, and the allies established themselves in the outworks. The town surrendered on 28 July.

On 23 Aug. the Duke of York laid siege to Dunkirk, but owing to delay in the arrival of the siege train from England, Moncrieff was unable to trace the first parallel until the 29th, and the forces were not in position until some days later. In the meantime the French were making active preparations to raise the siege. On 5 Sept., as Moncrieff was arming the batteries, an alarm was given of a sortie from the town at midday, and although the sortie was repulsed by the guard of the trenches, the besiegers' position was endangered. On the afternoon of the next day the garrison of Dunkirk attacked the right wing of the Duke of York's besieging army, and although they were driven back before sunset the 14th regiment suffered severely, and Moncrieff received a mortal wound. He died the next day, 7 Sept. 1793, and was buried at Ostend on 10 Sept. with military honours, the prince, General Ainslie, and all the officers available attending the funeral.

Moncrieff was unmarried and left to his sisters the estate of Airdrie in Scotland, which he had purchased from Sir John Anstruther, together with considerable property in the West Indies.

[Despatches; War Office Records; Royal Engineers' Records; Cust's Annals of the Wars of the Eighteenth Century, vols. iii. and iv.; Scots Magazine, 1779 and 1780; Gent. Mag. 1762, 1779, 1787, 1793; Dodsley's Annual Register, 1779; Beatson's Naval and Military Memoirs, vol. iv.; Stewart's Sketches of the Highlanders; Hist. of the Civil War in America, 1780; European Mag. 1790, vol. xviii.; Journal and Correspondence of General Sir Harry Calvert, by Sir Harry Verney, 1853.] R. H. V.

MONCRIEFF, WILLIAM THOMAS (1794-1857), dramatist, son of a tradesman in Newcastle Street, Strand, was born in London on 24 Aug. 1794. About 1804 he became a clerk in a solicitor's office, and afterwards entered the service of Moses Hooper, solicitor, Great Marlborough Street. At this early period he wrote songs, among them 'Pretty star of the night all others outshining,' which became popular. He soon became manager of the Regency Theatre (afterwards known as the Queen's Theatre, and then as the Prince of Wales's), for which, in 1810, under the name of William George Thomas Moncrieff, he wrote 'Moscow, or the Cossack's Daughter,' to which succeeded several other original dramas. When the theatre closed he wrote articles in magazines, and the theatrical criticisms for the 'Satirist' [cf. MANNERS, GEORGE] and the 'Scourge.' After gaining a livelihood as a working law stationer, he was introduced to Robert William Elliston [q. v.], lessee of the Olympic, and wrote and produced at that house 'All at Coventry,' a musical farce, 20 Oct. 1815; 'The Diamond Arrow,' a comedy, 18 Dec. 1815; 'Giovanni in London, or the Libertine Reclaimed,' an extravaganza, 26 Dec. 1817; and 'Rochester, or King Charles the Second's Merry Days,' a musical comedy, 16 Nov. 1818. Becoming manager at Astley's, he put on the stage an equestrian drama, 'The Dandy Family,' which ran nearly one hundred nights. From Astley's he removed to the Coburg Theatre, which he managed for Joseph Glossop, where he brought out in rapid succession the 'Vampire,' 'Gipsey Jack,' 'Reform, or John Bull,' the 'Ravens of Orleans,' the 'Shipwreck of the Medusa,' and, in 1820, the 'Lear of Private Life,' a drama founded on Mrs. Opie's 'Father and Daughter,' in which Junius Brutus Booth [q. v.] played the hero with brilliant success for fifty-three nights. In 1820 he joined Elliston at Drury Lane, and wrote for him 'Wanted a Wife,' 3 May 1819 (reproduced under the title of 'A Cheque on my Banker,' 13 Aug. 1821); 'Monsieur Tonson,' a successful farce, 20 Sept. 1821; 'The Spectre Bridegroom,' 2 July 1821; 'The Cataract of the Ganges,' a romantic drama, 27 Oct. 1823, which, owing to the introduction of a real waterfall, then a great novelty, drew large audiences; and 'Zoroaster,' a melodrama, 19 April 1824. During the same period he became connected with William Oxberry [q. v.], comedian and printer, and with him published in 1818 and the following years Pierce Egan's 'Boxiana.' He afterwards dramatised Egan's 'Life in London,' under the title of 'Tom and Jerry, or Life in London,' and produced it at the Adelphi Theatre on 26 Nov. 1821. The piece met with a success only second to that of the 'Beggar's Opera;' it ran consecutively for nearly two seasons, introduced slang into the drawing-room, and was equally popular in town and country (C. HINDLEY, *The True History of Tom and Jerry*, 1890; H. B. BAKER, *London Stage*, 1889, ii. 77–82; see also EGAN, PIERCE, 1772–1849). At the Adelphi he also brought out his 'Secret,' 29 Feb. 1823; 'Bringing Home the Bride,' March 1825; 'Monsieur Mallet,' 22 Jan. 1829; and the 'Hearts of London,' February 1830. At Easter 1822 he brought Monsieur N. M. Alexandre the ventriloquist to London, and wrote for him an entertainment entitled 'Rogueries of Nicholas,' which well paid both author and actor. For his friend Charles Mathews the elder [q. v.] he wrote 'The Bashful Man,' a comic drama, produced at the English Opera House (now the Lyceum), 1826, besides furnishing him with many entertainments. In 1827 he undertook the management of Vauxhall Gardens, when his 'Actors al Fresco, or the Play in the Pleasure Ground,' a vaudeville, 4 June, and 'The Kiss and the Rose,' an operetta, 29 June, were first seen. In 1828, in conjunction with John Barnett, he opened a music shop in Regent Street. On 17 Feb. in the same year 'The Somnambulist, or the Phantom of the Village,' a dramatic entertainment, was produced at Covent Garden, and 'One Fault' on 7 Jan. 1833.

At the Surrey also many of his pieces were put on the stage, among others, 'Old Heads and Young Shoulders,' 8 Jan. 1828; 'The Irresistibles,' a comic drama, 11 Aug. 1828; 'Shakespeare's Festival, or a New Comedy of Errors,' a drama, April 1830, and 'Tobit's Dog,' 30 April 1838. At the Haymarket 'The Peer and the Peasant' was acted 11 Sept. 1832. He became lessee of the City Theatre, Milton Street, in 1833, for which he wrote two pieces, both acted on 4 Nov., 'How to take up a Bill' and 'The Birthday Dinner.' His next successful plays were 'Lestocq, or the Conspirators of St. Petersburg,' 2 March 1835; 'The Jewess, or the Council of Constance,' 30 Nov. 1835; and 'The Parson's Nose,' a comedietta, 1837, all acted at the Victoria Theatre. His sight now began to fail him, but he accepted an engagement with W. J. Hammond at the Strand Theatre, for whom he wrote 'My Aunt the Dowager,' 5 June 1837; 'Sam Weller, or the Pickwickians,' 10 July 1837; and 'Tarnation Strange, or More Jonathans,' 3 Aug. 1838. At Sadler's Wells he produced 'Giselle, or the Phantom Night Dancers,' 23 Aug. 1841; 'Perourou, the Bellows Mender, and the Beauty of Lyons,' 7 Feb. 1842; 'The Scamps of London,' 13 Nov. 1843; and 'The Mistress of the Mill,' a comedietta, 17 Oct. 1849. In

1843 he had become totally blind, but he wrote a series of articles entitled 'Ellistoniana' in the 'New Monthly Magazine.' In 1844, on the presentation of the queen, he became a brother of the Charterhouse. His theatrical reminiscences, under the title of 'Dramatic Feuilletons,' he contributed to the 'Sunday Times' in 1851. He died in the Charterhouse, London, on 3 Dec. 1857.

In addition to writing upwards of 170 dramatic pieces, he was the author of 'Prison Thoughts; Elegy written in the King's Bench in imitation of Gray, by a Collegian,' 1821; 'A New Guide to the Spa of Leamington Priors, to which is added "Historical Notices of Warwick and its Castle,"' 1822, 3rd edition, 1824; 'Excursions to Stratford-upon-Avon, with a Compendious Life of Shakespeare, Account of the Jubilee, and Catalogue of the Shakespeare Relics,' 1824; 'Poems,' 1829; 'Old Booty, a Serio-Comic Sailors' Tale,' 1830; 'The Triumph of Reform, a Comic Poem,' 1832; 'Selections from Dramatic Works,' 3 vols. 1850, containing twenty-four of his own pieces. He likewise edited Richardson's 'New Minor Drama, with Remarks Biographical and Critical,' 4 vols. 1828–30.

[Reynolds's Miscellany, 1853, ix. 28–9, with portrait; Era, 13 Dec. 1857, p. 11; Genest, 1832, viii. 688 et seq.; British Drama, vol. iii. et seq.; Cumberland's Minor Theatre, vol. vii. et seq.; Cumberland's British Theatre, vol. xvi. et seq.; Lacy's Acting Edition of Plays, vol. xxi. et seq.; Notes and Queries, 1876, 5th ser. vi. 160.] G. C. B.

MO-NENNIUS (*fl.* 500), bishop of Whithorn, and teacher of many Irish saints, was of Irish birth, but lived at Whithorn, Wigtownshire (Whitaern, Alba or Candida Casa), where St. Ninian was bishop early in the fifth century. He was apparently a *protégé* of that saint, and it is suggested that his name, which appears in many forms, was derived from Nennio, a variant of Ninian, combined with the Irish prefix Mo-, denoting affection. Mo-nennius was a coarb or successor of St. Ninian as bishop of Whithorn, probably before 497, when he visited the island of Nendrum, now Mahee, on Strangford Lough, and was described as a bishop (*Tighernach Annals*). At Whithorn was a celebrated school sometimes called Monasterium Rosnatense, or by Irish writers Futerna, which has occasionally been awkwardly confused with St. David's Magnum Monasterium or 'Rosina Vallis' in Wales. Of the establishment at Whithorn Monennius, who is otherwise known as Mansennus or Mugint, appears to have been master or abbat. While the school was under his direction Colman, bishop of Dromore, sent thither Finian of Moville to complete his education. Saints Eugenius, Enna, and Tigernach also seem to have been Monennius's pupils, as well as Rioc, Talmach, and a lady, Drusticc, daughter of a British king, Drustic. The lady Drusticc fell in love with her fellow-pupil Rioc, and begged Finian to assist her union with Rioc, promising in return to get all their teacher's books for him to copy. Finian made himself in some measure a party to her plot, and when it was discovered, Mo-nennius, or Mugint as he is called in connection with this story, determined to kill him. In the belief that Finian would be the first to visit the church, he gave orders that the first to arrive there should be slain. The blow Mugint destined for Finian was, however, received by himself. In the lives of Finian the story of the plot is told in an altered form. The cause of their hostility is here said to have been the superior popularity of Finian's lectures. Mo-nennius was author of a hymn modelled on the penitential psalms, which is extant under the title of the 'Hymn of Mugint.' It is in Irish prose, and parts of it are embodied in the Anglican church service.

MEIGANT, MAUGANTIUS, MEUGAN, MEUGANT (*fl.* 6th cent.), a Welsh saint or druid, ought probably to be distinguished from the foregoing. His father was Gwynd af Hên, the son of Emyr Llydaw, and his mother was Gwenonwy, daughter of Meirig, king of Morganwg, the son of Tewdrig. Meigant was president of the college of St. Illtyd [q. v.] at Llantwit, called also the White House. He seems subsequently to have removed to the establishment of St. Dubricius [q. v.], who died in 612. He is doubtless identical with Mancennus or Mancan, who is mentioned as the head of a monastery, and as having received a present from St. David's father to be kept for his unborn son. From that time Mancan's house was called the 'house of the deposit.'

[In Dr. Todd's Irish Hymns, fascic. i., is printed Mugint's hymn with the Scholiast's Preface (Dr. Todd considers it a document of great antiquity, not far removed from Mugint's own period). See also Colgan's Acta SS. Hibern. p. 438; Lanigan's Eccles. Hist. Ireland, i. 437; Dict. Christian Biog.; Rees's Welsh Saints, p. 219; Iolo MSS. printed for Welsh MSS. Soc., p. 132; Life of St. David in Capgrave's Nova Legenda, and in W. J. Rees's Cambro-British Saints.] M. B.

MONEY, JOHN (1752–1817), aeronaut and general, born in 1752, began his military career in the Norfolk militia, but entering the army became cornet in the 6th Inniskilling dragoons 11 March 1762, captain in the 9th foot 10 Feb. 1770, major 28 Sept. 1781. He went on half-pay in 1784, and never rejoined the active list, but was made lieutenant-colonel by brevet 18 Nov. 1790, colonel 21 Aug. 1795, major-general 18 June 1798, lieutenant-general 30 Oct. 1805, and general 4 June 1814. Money saw a good deal of active service. He was present at the battle of Fellinghausen in 1761 and in various skirmishes with Elliot's light dragoons. He served in Canada in 1777 in General Burgoyne's disastrous descent on Albany from the north, and was present at several engagements. He was taken prisoner in September, and does not appear to have been released till the end of the war.

Money was one of the earliest English aeronauts, making two ascents in 1785, that is, within two years of Montgolfier's first aerial voyage [cf. LUNARDI, VINCENZO]. On 22 July in that year he made an ascent from Norwich; an 'improper current' took him out to sea, and then, dipping into the water, he 'remained for seven hours struggling with his fate,' till rescued in a small boat. In 'A Treatise on the Use of Balloons and Field Observators' (1803) he advocated the use of balloons for military purposes (*Royal Engineer Corps Papers*, 1863).

Money offered his services to the rebel party in the Austrian Netherlands in 1790, when, after experiencing some successes, their prospects were growing critical. After a first refusal his offer was accepted. He was given a commission as major-general, and was placed in command of a force of about four or five thousand men at Tirlemont. His troops were half-hearted, and in the end, after one sharp engagement, he had to join in the general retreat on Brussels, a retreat which ended the rebellion. He utilised his knowledge of the country in his 'History of the Campaign of 1792,' 1794, 8vo. He died at Trowse Hall, Norfolk, 26 March 1817.

[Philippart's Royal Military Calendar, 1815; Monk Mason's Aeronautica, London, 1838; 9th Regiment Historical Records.] L. D.

MONGRÉDIEN, AUGUSTUS (1807–1888), political economist and miscellaneous writer, born in London in 1807, was son of a French officer who fled to England after Bonaparte's *coup d'état* in 1798. He was educated in the Roman catholic college at Penn, Buckinghamshire, and continued his studies long after leaving that institution. He entered commercial life at an early age, and was the owner of the first screw steamers to the Levant. In 1859 he became a member of the firm of H. J. Johnston & Co., and when it was broken up in 1864 he began as a cornbroker on his own account. In 1862 he purchased Heatherside, Surrey.

Gradually he withdrew from business and devoted most of his attention to literary pursuits. He had joined the National Political Union in 1831, and in 1872 he was elected a member of the Cobden Club, under the auspices of which society several of his treatises were published. He thoroughly grasped the free-trade question, and expounded his views on the most difficult problems of political economy with great lucidity. He was a good musician and an excellent botanist, and was elected president of the Chess Club in 1839; he had a colloquial knowledge of seven languages, could recite many pages of the Koran, and spoke modern Greek like a native. Mr. Gladstone, in recognition of his merits, placed his name on the Civil Pension List. Mongrédien died at Forest Hill, London, on 30 March 1888.

His principal works are: 1. 'Trees and Shrubs for English Plantations; a selection and description of the most Ornamental Trees and Shrubs, Native and Foreign, which will flourish in the Open Air in our Climate . . . . with Illustrations,' London, 1870, 8vo. 2. 'England's Foreign Policy; an Enquiry as to whether we should continue a Policy of Intervention,' London, 1871, 8vo. 3. 'The Heatherside Manual of Hardy Trees and Shrubs,' London, 1874–5, 8vo. 4. 'Frank Allerton. An Autobiography,' 3 vols. London, 1878, 8vo. 5. 'Free Trade and English Commerce,' 2nd edit. London [1879], 8vo; answered by F. J. B. Hooper, 1880; and in 'Half-a-pair of Scissors; or what is our (so-called) Free Trade?' (anon.), Manchester, 1885. 6. 'The Western Farmer of America,' London, 1880, 8vo, reprinted 1886; replied to by T. H. Dudley and J. W. Hinton. 7. 'History of the Free-Trade Movement in England,' London, 1881, 8vo, translated into French by H. Gravez, Paris, 1885, 8vo. 8. 'Pleas for Protection examined,' London, 1882, 8vo; reprinted 1888. 9. 'Wealth-Creation,' London, 1882, 8vo. 10. 'The Suez Canal Question,' 1883, 8vo. 11. 'Trade Depression, recent and present' [1885], 8vo. 12. 'On the Displacement of Labour and Capital,' 1886, 8vo.

[Private information; Times, 4 April 1888, p. 10; Athenæum, 7 April 1888, p. 437; Annual Register, 1888, Chron. p. 141; Appleton's Annual Cycl. 1888, p. 665.] T. C.

MONK. [See also MONCK.]

MONK, JAMES HENRY (1784–1856), bishop of Gloucester and Bristol, born early in 1784 at Buntingford, Hertfordshire, was the only son of Charles Monk, an officer of the 40th regiment, and nephew of Sir James Monk, chief justice of Montreal; his mother was the daughter of Joshua Waddington, vicar of Harworth, Nottinghamshire. He was first taught at Norwich by Dr. Foster, and in 1798 entered the Charterhouse, where, under Dr. Raine, he laid the foundation of his accurate classical scholarship. He entered Trinity College, Cambridge, in October 1800, and was elected scholar in 1801. He graduated B.A. as seventh wrangler in 1804, in which year he was also second chancellor's medallist, M.A. 1807, B.D. 1818, D.D. *per Lit. Reg.* 1822. On 1 Oct. 1805 he was elected fellow of Trinity. In October 1807 he became assistant-tutor of his college, and during the fifteen years of his tutorship his pupils carried off the greater part of the higher classical honours at Cambridge. In January 1809, being then only twenty-five, he was elected to the regius professorship of Greek, in succession to Porson. In this position he published several tracts advocating the establishment of a classical tripos, with public examinations and honours open only to those who had obtained a place in the mathematical tripos. His first edition of the classics, the 'Hippolytus' of Euripides, appeared in 1811, and was favourably noticed in the 'Quarterly Review' by his friend C. J. Blomfield [q. v.], afterwards bishop of London. In conjunction with Blomfield he edited Porson's 'Adversaria' in 1812, and in 1813–14 was joint editor with Blomfield of the 'Museum Criticum,' a publication to which several scholars of repute contributed, though only eight numbers were issued. Monk resigned his Greek professorship in June 1823.

Monk had been ordained deacon in 1809 and priest in 1810. In 1812 he was Whitehall preacher, and attracted the attention of the premier, Lord Liverpool, who afterwards bestowed on him the deanery of Peterborough, 7 March 1822. In right of his deanery Monk nominated himself to the rectory of Fiskerton, Lincolnshire, 12 July 1822, afterwards holding the rectory of Peakirk-cum-Glinton, Northamptonshire, 27 March 1829. As dean he collected 6,000*l.* for the restoration of Peterborough Cathedral, himself contributing liberally. In 1830 he was given a canonry at Westminster, and in the same year he published his 'Life of Richard Bentley,' a work which was praised in the 'Quarterly Review' for November 1831, and in 'Blackwood's Magazine' by Professor Wilson.

On 11 July 1830 Monk was consecrated bishop of Gloucester. In 1836 the see was amalgamated with that of Bristol, in accordance with the recommendation of the ecclesiastical commission, of which Monk was an original member. Monk was not a good speaker, and in the House of Lords seldom did more than record his vote in the conservative interest. He had a severe skirmish with Sydney Smith, who ridiculed his toryism in his 'Third Letter to Archdeacon Singleton' on the ecclesiastical commission (S. SMITH, *Works*, 1854, pp. 642–3). On religious questions Monk observed 'a safe and cautious line, as his easy and open nature probably inclined him.' His favour, however, was generally shown to the high-church rather than to the evangelical party, whose influence at Bristol, Clifton, and elsewhere in the diocese occasionally proved a source of trouble to him. He expressed a qualified approval of the Bristol Church Union, and supported its demand for the revival of convocation. In 1841 he severely censured Isaac Williams's 'Tract for the Times' on 'Reserve in communicating Religious Knowledge' (cp. MOZLEY, *Reminiscences of Oriel*, i. 436), and was one of the bishops who in 1848 protested against the appointment of Dr. Hampden to the see of Hereford. Monk gave largely to charities, and for many years devoted part of his income to the augmentation of small livings in his diocese. For some years before his death he suffered from partial blindness, and during the last six months of his life was physically almost prostrate. He died at the Palace, Stapleton, near Bristol, on 6 June 1856, aged 72. His wife Jane, only daughter of H. Hughes of Nuneaton, rector of Hardwick, Northamptonshire, survived him. By this marriage, which took place in 1823, he had three daughters and one son, Charles James (born in 1824), who graduated at Trinity College, Cambridge, became chancellor of Bristol (1855) and M.P. for Gloucester.

Monk's principal publications are: 1. Euripides, 'Hippolytus,' with notes, 1811, 8vo; 1813, 1821, 1823, 1840. 2. 'R. Porsoni Adversaria,' edited by Monk and C. J. Blomfield, 1812, 8vo. 3. 'Museum Criticum, or Cambridge Classical Researches,' edited by Monk and C. J. Blomfield, 1814, 8vo. 4. Euripides, 'Alcestis,' Greek with Latin notes, 1816, 8vo; 1818, 1823, 1826, 1837. 5. 'A Vindication of the University of Cambridge from the Reflections of Sir J. E. Smith,' &c., London, 1818, 8vo. 6. 'A Letter . . . respecting an additional Examination of Students in the University of Cambridge,' by 'Philograntus' (i.e. Monk), London, 1822, 8vo. 7. 'Cambridge Classical Examinations,' edited by Monk, &c., 1824, 8vo. 8. 'The Life of R. Bentley,' London, 1830, 4to; 2nd edit. 1833, 8vo. 9. Euripides, 'Iphigenia in Aulis,' 1840, 8vo. 10. 'Correspondence between [Monk] and H. Hallam,' 1844, 8vo. Privately printed (as to a note respecting Le Clerc in Hallam's 'Literature of Europe'). 11. Euripides, 'Iphigenia in Tauris,' 1845, 8vo. 12. Various publications relating to Horfield Manor, 1848, 1852, &c. 13. Various sermons and charges published from 1832 to 1854. 14. 'Euripidis Fabulæ quatuor scilicet Hippolytus Coronifer, Alcestis, Iphigenia in Aulide, Iphigenia in Tauris,' 1857, 8vo (posthumous).

[Memoir in Gent. Mag. 1856, pt. ii. pp. 115–117; J. Foster's Index Ecclesiasticus, 'Monk;' Luard's Graduati Cant.; Life of Bishop S. Wilberforce; Brit. Mus. Cat.] W. W.

MONK, RICHARD (*fl.* 1434), chronologer, described as an English chaplain, compiled at Oxford in 1434 certain chronological tables, which are preserved in Laud. MS. Misc. 594 in the Bodleian Library. They are (1) 'Tabulæ de veris litteris dominicalibus et primacionibus ab origine mundi,' f. 14*b*; (2) 'Kalendarium verum anni mundi,' ff. 15–20; (3) 'Tabulæ Solis veræ atque perpetuæ,' f. 21.

[Tanner's Bibl. Brit.-Hib. p. 530; Cat. of Laudian MSS.] C. L. K.

MONK, WILLIAM HENRY (1823–1889), composer, son of William Monk, of an old Oxford family, was born in Brompton, London, on 16 March 1823. After studying music under Thomas Adams, J. A. Hamilton, and G. A. Griesbach, he was organist and choir-master successively of Eaton Chapel, Pimlico (1841–3), St. George's Chapel, Albemarle Street (1843–5), and Portman Chapel, Marylebone (1845–7). In 1847 he was appointed choirmaster, in 1849 organist, and in 1874 (in succession to John Hullah, with whose work of 'Popular Musical Education' he was early associated) professor of vocal music at King's College, London. In 1851 he became professor of music at the School for the Indigent Blind, and in 1853 was appointed to his last post of organist at St. Matthias', Stoke Newington, where he established a daily choral service, with a voluntary choir. He was also professor in the National Training School for Music (1876), and in Bedford College, London (1878). From 1850 to 1854 he gave lectures on music at the London Institution, and at other times lectured at the Philosophical Institution, Edinburgh, and the Royal Institution, Manchester. In 1882 he received the honorary degree of Mus.Doc. from Durham University. He died in London on 1 March 1889, and was buried in Highgate cemetery, where a memorial cross, erected by public subscription, marks his grave.

Monk was best known as the musical editor of 'Hymns Ancient and Modern,' which has passed through several editions since its first issue in 1861, and has had a sale of about thirty million copies. He had no share in the profits of the work. He was sole musical editor of the first edition (the statement in Grove that he was 'one of the editors' is calculated to mislead), and only when an enlarged edition was called for did he have assistance. He had just sent to press the edition of 1889 when he died. His best hymn tunes, by which he will be remembered, were written for 'Hymns Ancient and Modern,' but many appear in other collections. A few are sung everywhere, and 'Abide with me' and 'Sweet Saviour, bless us ere we go' (the words of which are by Lyte and Faber respectively) are not likely to be superseded. He was musical editor of the 'Parish Choir' from the fortieth number (not the tenth, as stated in Grove) to its close in 1851. He also edited for the church of Scotland their Psalter, Hymnal, and Anthem Book, the tunes to Bishop Wordsworth's 'Hymns for the Holy Year,' 1865, an edition of Dr. Allon's 'Congregational Psalmist,' and 'The Book of Common Prayer, with Plain Song and Appropriate Music,' as well as editions of Handel's 'Acis and Galatea,' fol., and 'L'Allegro,' 8vo.

Monk composed a good deal of miscellaneous church music, mostly of an intentionally simple nature, such as anthems, chants, Te Deums, &c., some of which is widely used. He was essentially a church musician, and used the organ more for devotion than for display.

[Grove's Dict. of Music, ii. 353; Musical Herald, April 1889, where his portrait is given; Brown's Dict. of Musicians; Love's Scottish Church Music, where date of his death has to be corrected; St. Matthias's Mag., April 1889, December 1891; Funeral Sermon preached at St. Matthias's Church; Church Times, 6 Nov. 1891; private information from his widow.] J. C. H.

MONKSWELL, first Baron. [See Collier, Sir Robert Porrett, 1817–1886.]

MONMOUTH, Duke of. [See Scott, James, 1649–1685.]

MONMOUTH, Earls of. [See Carey, Robert, first Earl, 1560?–1639; Carey, Henry, second Earl, 1596–1661; Mordaunt, Charles, first Earl of the second creation, 1658–1735.]

MONMOUTH, titular Earl of. [See Middleton, Charles, 1640?–1719.]

MONMOUTH, GEOFFREY of (1100?–1154), bishop of St. Asaph. [See Geoffrey.]

MONMOUTH or **MONEMUE, JOHN** de (1182?–1247?), lord marcher, born about 1182, was son of Gilbert de Monmouth, and great-great-grandson of William FitzBalderon, who is recorded in Domesday Book as the possessor of many lands and lordships in Gloucestershire, Herefordshire, and Monmouthshire; Rose or Roysya de Monemue, wife of Hugh de Lacy, fifth baron Lacy [q.v.], was probably his aunt (cf. *Reg. Abbey of St. Thomas, Dublin*, passim), and her son Walter de Lacy married Margaret, the daughter of Monmouth's guardian, William de Braose [q. v.] In 1201–2 Monmouth was a minor in the wardship of De Braose, and the latter in 1206 was placed in possession of Grosmont, Llantilio, and Skenfrith castles, probably belonging to the Monmouth family. Monmouth came of age before 1205, when he held fifteen knights' fees, and in 1208 his two infant sons, John and Philip, were demanded by King John as hostages for his good behaviour, probably as a precaution against Monmouth's joining William de Braose in his rebellion (*Rot. Pat. in Turri Londin.* i. 87; Foss, i. 410); he paid a large fine for restoration to royal favour, and his children were liberated. In 1213 another son William appears to have been held as a hostage by John (*Rot. Pat.* i. 103), but Monmouth remained to the end an active and faithful partisan of the king. In 1214 he was ordered to attend John at Cirencester, and received a completely equipped horse for his prompt obedience. On 10 Feb. 1215 he was appointed one of the custodians of William de Lacy, half-brother of Monmouth's cousin Walter, sixth baron Lacy [q. v.] (Sweetman, *Cal. Doc.* 1171–1251, No. 536), and was commissioned to negotiate with the barons of Herefordshire, and in April to raise a loan in Gloucestershire (*Rot. Claus.* i. 197 *b*). On 21 Aug. he was made governor of St. Briavel's Castle, Gloucestershire, and later in that year and in 1216 he was granted custody of the castles of Elmley in Worcestershire, Bramber in Sussex, which had belonged to William de Braose, Grosmont, Llantilio, and Skenfrith in Wales, the Forest of Dean, and lands in Bedford and Cambridge shires forfeited by Hugh Malebysse (Dugdale, *Baronage*, i. 442; Foss, i. 410; *Rot. Pat.* i. 153, 160), besides those of his sister-in-law, Albreda de Boterel, who had sided with the barons, and of Walbar de Stokes (cf. *Close and Patent Rolls*; Eyton, *Antiquities of Shropshire*, vi. 153). During 1216 Monmouth owned a ship in John's service, and was made one of the executors of his will (*Close Rolls*, vol. i. passim; Rymer, *Fœdera*, I. i. 144).

After the accession of Henry III Monmouth received further promotion. In 1221 he was justice itinerant in Gloucestershire; in January 1224 he was directed again to take over St. Briavel's, but was prevented by illness; on 8 Aug. he was present at Bedford, where Falkes de Breauté [q. v.] was besieged (Shirley, *Royal and Historical Letters*, Rolls Ser. i. 511; Rymer, i. 175). Next year he was witness to the reissue of the Great Charter (Luard, *Annal. Mon.* i. 232). In 1226 he built for the Cistercian order the abbey of Grace Dieu in Wales (*ib.* ii. 302); and in May became security for his cousin Walter de Lacy (Sweetman, 1171–1251, No. 1372–3); on 2 Sept. he was appointed to attend the meeting of Llywelyn, William Marshal, and other barons at Shrewsbury, and to report on the result (cf. Llywelyn ab Iorwerth, *d.* 1240, and Marshal, William, *d.* 1231). In 1228 he was made sheriff of Shropshire and Staffordshire, but this appointment was soon revoked (Blakeway, *Sheriffs of Shropshire*, p. 5); in the same year, apparently by right of his wife, he was keeper of New, Clarendon, Pancet, and Bocholte forests, offices held by his father-in-law, Walter de Waleron (Dugdale; Foss; *Cal. Rot. Pat.* ii. 146). In 1229 he mediated between the town and abbey of Dunstable, and witnessed a grant from Henry to David, son of Llywelyn, and other charters (Giraldus Cambrensis, ed. Dimock, vii. 231). The castles and honours of Striguil and Hereford were committed to his custody, on the death of William Marshal, in 1231, and in December he negotiated the truce that was patched up with Llywelyn. In the same year he granted to some monks the hospital of St. John at Monmouth.

On the revolt of Richard Marshal in 1233 Monmouth bore the brunt of his attack. He was justiciar, and commanded the king's Poitevin mercenaries in South Wales, and on 26 Dec. collected a large force, intending to make a secret attack on Marshal. The earl, however, learning his design, set an ambush for Monmouth in a wood near Grosmont, and completely routed his forces, Monmouth himself escaping only by a hasty flight. Marshal proceeded to destroy Monmouth's lands and buildings, including, at the instigation of his Welsh allies, the abbey of Grace Dieu (Matthew Paris, *Chron. Majora*, ii. 254; *Hist. Angl.* ii. 364, iii. 269; Roger Wendover, iii. 60; *Annal. Mon.* ii. 312, iii. 136). On 28 March 1234 Henry informed him that he had concluded a truce with Marshal and Llywelyn, and in July Monmouth was ordered to besiege the castles in the hands of Peter des Rivaulx, should he refuse to give them up. At the marriage of Eleanor and Henry III on 14 Jan. 1236 Monmouth claimed the right as a lord marcher to carry the canopy (DUGDALE). In the same year he witnessed the confirmation of Magna Charta, and rebuilt the abbey of Grace Dieu. At Easter 1238 he was summoned to parliament at Oxford to advise Henry on the probable outbreak of war with Llywelyn. In 1240 he was appointed one of the arbiters to decide on the disputed points between Davydd II [q. v.] and the king. On 2 Jan. 1241–2 he witnessed at Westminster the grant of liberties and franchises to the citizens of Cork (SWEETMAN, 1171–1251, No. 2552). In 1242 he was ordered to provide five hundred Welsh soldiers for the expected war with France, and in the same year was appointed chief bailiff of Cardigan, Caermarthen, and South Wales (*Cal. Rot. Pat.* ii. 19 *b*). With the Earl of Clare he resisted Davydd's invasion in 1244, receiving a grant of three hundred marks on 3 June for that purpose, and inflicted a severe defeat on the Welsh; in January next year he was directed to summon the Welsh barons to answer for the depredations they had committed. He died probably in 1247.

Monmouth married Cecilia, daughter and heiress of Walter de Waleron, and by her had apparently three sons, John, Philip, and William. Of these John alone survived, and had livery of his father's lands in 32 Hen. III (28 Oct. 1247, 27 Oct. 1248). He had two daughters, but no male issue, and died in 1257, leaving the castle and honour to Prince Edward. Another JOHN DE MONMOUTH (*fl.* 1320) is frequently mentioned in the 'Parliamentary Writs,' especially cap. II. iii. 1182, and was apparently a partisan of Roger Mortimer, first earl of March [q. v.] (cf. BARNES, *Edward III*); a third was in 1297 appointed bishop of Llandaff, and died on 8 April 1323 (LE NEVE, ii. 245-6).

[Dugdale's Baronage, i. 442-3; Monasticon, passim; Foss's Judges of England, i. 410; Close and Patent Rolls, vols. i. and ii. passim; Cal. Inquisit. post Mortem, i. 15; Cal. Rotulorum Chartarum et Inquisit. ad quod Damnum; Parl. Writs; Rymer's Fœdera, passim; Annales Monastici, Royal and Historical Letters, Hist. et Cartul. Mon. S. Petri, Matthew Paris's Chron. Majora and Hist. Angl., Roger Wendover, Flores Historiarum, Giraldus Cambrensis and Walsingham's Hist. Angl. and Ypodigma, and Memoranda de Parliamento (all in the Rolls Ser. passim); Williams's Monmouthshire, pp. 190–1, App. p. xxxiv; Eyton's Antiquities of Shropshire; Sweetman's Cal. of Documents relating to Ireland, 1171–1251; Wright's Hist. of Ludlow.] A. F. P.

MONNOYER, JEAN BAPTISTE, better known by the surname of BAPTISTE (1634–1699), flower-painter, was born at Lille on 19 July 1634. He went when very young to Paris, and his admirable pictures of flowers and fruit, which he painted almost always from nature, soon gained him a great reputation. His works became the fashion among the wealthy, and he was received into the Royal Academy of Painting on 14 April 1663. His admission was afterwards annulled on account of some informality, and he was received anew on 3 Oct. 1665. His *pièce de réception*, representing flowers and fruit, is now in the Musée at Montpellier. He exhibited at the Salon only in 1673, when he sent four flower-pieces under the name of Baptiste. Although much engaged in the decoration of the royal palaces of Versailles, Marly, Vincennes, and Meudon, and of the Hôtel de Bretonvilliers, he was induced by Ralph Montagu, afterwards Duke of Montagu [q. v.], then British ambassador to France, to accompany him on his return to England in 1678, and to assist in the decoration of Montagu House, Bloomsbury, which in 1754 became the British Museum. He subsequently painted numerous flower-pieces and panels at Hampton Court, Kensington Palace, Burlington House, Kedleston Hall, and other royal and noble residences, and often painted the flowers in Sir Godfrey Kneller's portraits. His works have not the high finish and velvety softness of those of Van Huysum and some other flower-painters of the Dutch school, but they possess greater freshness of touch and vigour in composition. The Louvre has eight of his undoubted works, and three more are attributed to him. Many others are in the provincial museums of France and in the private collections of England. About eighty of them have been engraved by John Smith, Poilly, Vauquer, Avril the elder, and others. He etched thirty-four of his own compositions, consisting of bouquets, garlands, and vases and baskets of flowers, which are for the most part executed on a white ground. The 'Livre de toutes sortes de fleurs d'après nature,' often attributed to him, was engraved by Vauquer from his designs.

Monnoyer died in London on 16 Feb. 1699, and was buried in St. James's Church, Piccadilly. Sir Godfrey Kneller painted his portrait, which was engraved in mezzotint by George Smith and by Edward Fisher.

ANTOINE MONNOYER (*d.* 1747), called 'Young Baptiste,' one of his sons, was his pupil, and also a painter of flowers, but his works are much inferior to his father's. He also came to London, but was in Paris in 1704, when he was received at the Academy, and again in 1715. He returned to England at the beginning of 1717, and remained here until 1734. He died at St. Germain-en-Laye in 1747. Another of his sons, known as 'Frère Baptiste,' who went to Rome and became a Dominican monk, was likewise a painter. He was a pupil of his father and of Jean Baptiste Corneille the younger, and painted some large pictures of scenes in the life of St. Dominic for the schools of his convent. Belin de Fontenay (1653–1715) the flower-painter was also a pupil of Monnoyer, and married his daughter Marie in 1687.

[Walpole's Anecdotes of Painting in England, ed. Wornum, 1849, ii. 599; Mariette's Abecedario, 1851–60, iv. 7; Bellier de la Chavignerie's Dictionnaire général des Artistes de l'École Française, 1868–85, ii. 110; Jal's Dictionnaire critique de Biographie et d'Histoire, 1872, p. 880; Villot's Notice des Tableaux du Musée National du Louvre (École Française), 1880, pp. 230–3; Robert-Dumesnil's Peintre-Graveur Français, 1835–71, iii. 229–38.] R. E. G.

MONRO. [See also MUNRO.]

MONRO, ALEXANDER (*d.* 1715?), principal of Edinburgh University, was the son of Hugh Monro of Fyresh, a branch of the house of Foulis. He appears to have been educated at St. Andrews (BOWER). In 1673 he was appointed minister of the second charge of Dunfermline, and was translated to Kinglassie in 1676, and to Wemyss in 1678. In 1682 he was created D.D. by the university of St. Andrews, and in the same year became professor of divinity in St. Mary's College there. In December 1685 he was appointed principal of Edinburgh University and minister of the high church, succeeding Andrew Cant in both offices. Said to have been originally a Roman catholic (WODROW, *Analecta*, ii. 49), Monro, though professedly presbyterian, had strong leanings towards episcopacy, and was strongly attached to the cause of James II. Consequently, when the presbyterians came into power at the revolution, he resigned his ministerial charge, and was forced to demit his office of principal. In 1688 he was nominated bishop of Argyle by the influence of Viscount Dundee, but he was neither elected nor consecrated. The commission appointed to see the Privy Council Act of 1690 carried out in the Scottish universities made many charges against Monro, and his replies, given in his anonymously published 'Presbyterian Inquisition' (London, 1691), throw much light on the internal condition of Edinburgh University. It was one of the singular circumstances of the case that the declaration of the Prince of Orange was conveyed to the Edinburgh magistrates by Monro, instead of being sent directly to them by the government (*Council Reg.* xxxii. 297). His career subsequently to September 1690 cannot be definitely ascertained. According to Bower, after his expulsion from the university he 'acted as an Episcopal clergyman in Edinburgh, and died in 1715,' but there are doubts as to the correctness of the date (see SCOTT, *Fasti*). In 1673 he married Anna Logan, by whom he had two daughters and a son James [q. v.] As principal he proved himself a weak disciplinarian, or else he 'sacrificed discipline to ecclesiastical partiality' (GRANT). His published writings, several of which are anonymous, include 'An Apology for the Church of Scotland,' London, 1693; 'Spirit of Calumny,' &c., London, 1693; 'Sermons preached on Several Occasions,' London, 1693; and 'Letter to Sir Robert Howard occasioned by his Twofold Vindication of Bishop Tillotson,' London, 1696.

[Bower's History of the University of Edinburgh, i. 309; Sir Alexander Grant's Story of the University of Edinburgh, ii. 254, 478; Grub's Eccl. Hist. of Scotland, iii. 291, 319; Apology for the Clergy of Scotland; Lawson's Hist. of the Scottish Episcopal Church from the Revolution to the Present Time; Keith's Catalogue of Bishops; Hew Scott's Fasti Ecclesiæ Scoticanæ, ii. 547, 562, 571; Fountainhall's Historical Notices (Bannatyne Club); Fernie's and Chalmers's Histories of Dunfermline; Wodrow's Analecta (Maitland Club); Wodrow's Correspondence (Wodrow Soc.).] J. C. H.

MONRO, ALEXANDER, primus (1697–1767), physician, was son of John Monro, a surgeon in William III's army, whose father, Sir Alexander Monro, fought in the battle of Worcester on the royalist side. His mother was a Miss Forbes of the family of Culloden. His father, while the army was in winter quarters, annually obtained leave to reside in London, where his son Alexander was born 8 Sept. 1697. John Monro afterwards settled in Edinburgh as a surgeon, and his son studied at the university and there graduated M.D. He then went to London and attended lectures by Hawksbee and Whiston on experimental philosophy and dissected under Cheselden. He sent home many anatomical specimens prepared by himself, and thus began to establish an anatomical reputation in Edinburgh. After some months in Paris he went in 1718 to Leyden and studied under Boerhaave. In the autumn of 1719 he returned to Edinburgh, where he was appointed professor of anatomy and surgery to the Surgeons' Company, and began to lecture in the winter of 1720. Up to that time there had been no professors of anatomy or of medicine in the university of Edinburgh, and in 1720 Monro was appointed the first university professor of anatomy, but was not formally inducted till 1725. Thenceforward he gave a course of lectures every year from October to May for thirty-nine years, beginning always with the history of the subject, then treating of osteology, then of the soft parts, then of the relation of the anatomy of animals to that of man, then of surgical operations, and finally of general physiology. In 1725 he married Isabella, second daughter of Sir Donald MacDonald of the Isle of Skye. In 1726 he published 'Osteology, a Treatise on the Anatomy of the Human Bones,' which went through several editions, to the sixth of which, 1758, is added an account of the nerves. He begins with an account of the periosteum, thence proceeds to the structure of bone and of joints, and then to the detailed description of the several bones. A medico-chirurgical society was formed in Edinburgh of which he was secretary, and he edited in 1732 its first volume of 'Transactions,' and subsequently five other volumes, writing in them many original papers, all of which are reprinted in the collected edition of his 'Works,' published in Edinburgh in 1781. After the battle of Prestonpans in 1745 he attended the wounded on the field, and while firmly attached to the house of Hanover did all in his power to obtain a pardon for Dr. Cameron the Jacobite. In 1764 he resigned his professorship, but continued to give clinical lectures at the hospital, and in that year he published 'An Account of the Inoculation of Small-pox in Scotland.' His separate papers, fifty-three in number, are on a great variety of medical subjects. He had observed the results of the falling of solid bodies into the appendix vermiformis, and shows much sagacity in an argument establishing the modern view that jaundice is very rarely, if ever, due to any cause but obstruction of the common bile duct. He knew a great deal of comparative anatomy and was well read in authors, especially admiring Wiseman among the older surgeons. He was a muscular man of middle stature, and was in the habit of being bled twice a year. In 1762 he had influenza with severe vesical catarrh, and he once fractured his heel tendon, and has written (*Collected Works*, p. 661) an account of his own case and cure. He died of a pelvic cancer 10 July 1767, after a long and painful illness, the chief symptoms of which are described in a letter to his son, Dr. Donald Monro [q. v.], dated 11 June 1766. A portrait of Monro, painted by Allan Ramsay, is in the National Portrait Gallery, Edinburgh. It was engraved by Basire and prefixed to the collected edition of his 'Works,' published by his son Dr. Alexander Monro secundus [q. v.], Edinburgh, 1781.

[Memoir by Dr. Donald Monro prefixed to Works, 1781; Works.] N. M.

MONRO, ALEXANDER, secundus, M.D. (1733–1817), anatomist, younger son of Alexander Monro primus [q. v.], by Isabella, second daughter of Sir Donald MacDonald, bart., of the Isle of Skye, was born at Edinburgh 20 May 1733. He was sent with his elder brother Donald [q. v.] to the school of Mr. Mundell, and in 1752 entered the university of Edinburgh. He occasionally lectured for his father from 1753, and on 12 July 1755 was formally appointed professor of anatomy and surgery as coadjutor to his father. He took the degree of M.D. 17 Oct. 1755, the subject of his inaugural dissertation being 'De Testibus et Semine in variis Animalibus.' It is dedicated to his father, and shows that he had worked diligently at minute anatomy. Soon after graduation he went to London, where he attended William Hunter's lectures, and afterwards to Paris, Leyden, and Berlin. At Leyden University he matriculated 17 Sept. 1757 (Peacock, *Index*, p. 70). He resided at Berlin in the house of Professor Meckel (Johann Friedrich, the elder), and worked under that distinguished anatomist, his obligations to whom he used to acknowledge in nearly every course of lectures which he delivered. In 1758 he returned to Edinburgh, was admitted a licentiate of the College of Physicians of Edinburgh, and 1 May 1759 was elected a fellow. He became secretary of the Philosophical Society of Edinburgh in succession to his father. This society published three volumes of essays. The first, which appeared in 1754, contains 'a description of the vesiculæ seminales' and 'observations on gravid uteri' by him; the second, issued in 1756, 'a description of a monster without head, arms, heart, or legs,' and 'the history of a genuine volvulus;' while in the last, in 1771, he wrote a paper on the effect of drugs on the nervous system. He published two controversial 'observations' on the lymphatics in 1758, maintaining that he, in a short essay printed at Berlin in 1758, and reprinted in 1761 and 1770, 'De Venis Lymphaticis Valvulosis,' and not William Hunter, had first correctly described the general communications of the lymphatic system. Frederick Hoffman had, however, preceded both Monro and Hunter in the description. In 1783 he published in Edinburgh 'Observations on the Structure and Functions of the

Nervous System,' dedicated to the Right Hon. Henry Dundas [q. v.], and it is in consequence of the description in this book of the communication between the lateral ventricles of the brain that his name is known to every student of medicine at the present day. The opening now always spoken of as the 'foramen of Monro' is very small in the healthy brain, but when water on the brain is present may be as large as a sixpence. It was this morbid condition that drew Monro's attention to the foramen, and he first described it in a paper read before the Philosophical Society of Edinburgh in 1764, but gives a fuller account in this work on the nervous system (*Nervous System*, tab. iii. and iv.)

He had always paid much attention to comparative anatomy, and published in 1785 'The Structure and Physiology of Fishes explained and compared with those of Man and other Animals.' In 1788 he published an account of seventy pairs of bursæ under the title, 'Description of all the Bursæ Mucosæ of the Human Body, their Structure, Accidents, and Diseases, and Operations for their Cure,' which is stated by several anatomical writers to be the first full description of the bursæ. In 1793 he published 'Experiments on the Nervous System with Opium and Metalline Substances, to determine the Nature and Effects of Animal Electricity.' These experiments led him to the conclusion that nerve force was not identical with electricity. His last book, 'Three Treatises on the Brain, the Eye, and the Ear,' was published at Edinburgh in 1797. Manuscript copies of notes of his lectures on anatomy delivered in 1774 and 1775 are preserved in the library of the Royal Medical and Chirurgical Society of London, and some 'Essays and Heads of Lectures on Anatomy, Physiology, Pathology, Surgery,' very imperfectly arranged, were printed by his son Alexander [q. v.] in 1840.

Monro, who in 1777 successfully resisted the appointment of a separate professor of surgery, gave a full course of lectures every year from 1759 to 1800. From 1800 to 1807 he delivered part of the course, his son Alexander completing it, and in 1808 gave the introductory lecture only. This was his last lecture, and after it his faculties gradually decayed. He became drowsy after dinner, and his nose used to bleed from time to time. In 1813 he had an apoplectic attack, and he died 2 Oct. 1817. He attained extensive practice as a physician, but never allowed his practice to interrupt the regularity of his lectures. He was fond of gardening, and bought the estate of Craiglockhart on the Leith water, where he had a cottage, and cultivated many kinds of fruit. He would have no bedroom in the cottage, as he thought that a physician in practice should always spend the night in his town-house. He enjoyed the theatre, was a warm admirer of Mrs. Siddons, and was proud of having been consulted by her about her health. He was a popular member of the Harveian Society of Edinburgh, a convivial as well as learned society, and at its meetings, according to Dr. Duncan, the father of the Royal College of Physicians of Edinburgh, 'without transgressing the bounds of the most strict sobriety, he afforded us demonstrative evidence of the exhilarating power of wine.' He was certainly the ablest of the three professors of his family. His portrait was painted by Kay, by Seton, and by Sir H. Raeburn, and an engraving of his head from the picture of the last is prefixed to his son's memoir of his life; a bust by an unknown sculptor is in the National Portrait Gallery, Edinburgh.

[A. Monro's (tertius) Memoir, Edinburgh, 1840; Dr. Andrew Duncan's Account of the Life, Writings, and Character of the late Dr. Alexander Monro secundus, Edinb. 1818; Works.] N. M.

MONRO, ALEXANDER, tertius, M.D. (1773–1859), anatomist, son of Alexander Monro secundus, was born at Edinburgh 5 Nov. 1773. He was sent to the high school there, and afterwards to the university, where he graduated M.D. in 1797, writing a thesis, 'De Dysphagia.' In 1798 he was appointed to assist his father in his lectures, but the appointment was nominal, as he went to London, and there worked at anatomy under Wilson. After also visiting Paris, he returned to Edinburgh in 1800, and was appointed conjoint professor (with his father) of medicine, surgery, and anatomy. From 1808 he delivered the whole course, and from 1817 to 1846 was sole professor. His lectures were less popular than those of his father and grandfather (*An Answer to several Attacks which have appeared against the University of Edinburgh*, 1819, p. 65), but among his pupils were Christison, Syme, Liston, Edward Forbes, Abercrombie, Bright, Marshall Hall, Sir Henry Holland, and Sir Humphry Davy. He published in 1803 'Observations on Crural Hernia;' in 1811, 'Morbid Anatomy of the Human Gullet, Stomach, and Intestines;' in 1813, 'Outlines of the Anatomy of the Human Body;' in 1814, 'Engravings of the Thoracic and Abdominal Viscera;' in 1818, 'Observations on the different kinds of Small-pox;' in 1827, 'Morbid Anatomy of the Brain,' vol. i., 'Hydrocephalus' and 'Anatomy of the Pelvis of the Male;' in 1831, 'The Anatomy of the Brain;' in 1840, 'Essays and Heads of Lectures of A. Munro secundus, with Memoir;' and in 1842, 'Anatomy of the Urinary Bladder and Perinæum in the Male.' None of his works are of permanent value, and those written when he was in the prime of life are as confused, prolix, and illogical as his senile productions. A basis of notes made by his more industrious father and grandfather is to be detected throughout, and to this he has added only imperfect observations and superficial reading. Thus in his account of lead colic he shows no acquaintance with the recent and admirable discoveries of Sir George Baker [q. v.] He died at Craiglockhart, near Edinburgh, 10 March 1859. He married first, in 1800, the daughter of Dr. Carmichael Smyth, by whom he had twelve children, one of whom, Sir David Monro, is separately noticed; and secondly, in 1836, the daughter of David Hunter, who survived him. A portrait by Kenneth Macleay is in the National Portrait Gallery, Edinburgh.

[Lancet, 1859, i. 331; Works.] N. M.

MONRO, Sir DAVID (1813–1877), colonial politician, son of Dr. Alexander Monro tertius [q. v.], was born in 1813. At a very early age he settled in New Zealand. When the first general assembly was convened, 24 May 1854, he was returned as a member of it, and was chosen to second the address to the governor. He was speaker of the House of Representatives in 1861 and 1862, and was knighted. At the general election in 1866 he was elected member for Cheviot, and was again speaker until 1870, when he retired from this post. He was then much incensed at the failure of William Fox, leader of the house, to propose any vote of thanks for his services; and in order to attack him he obtained a seat, but lost it on petition. Thereupon the House of Representatives adopted an address praying that some mark of favour might be shown him for his long services; but Fox still refused to recommend so outspoken an opponent for a seat in the Legislative Council. Monro was then elected to the house for Waikonati, and opposed Fox's government. He died at Newstead, near Nelson, in 1877. His wife was a daughter of J. Secker of Widford, Gloucestershire.

[Times, 2 May 1877; G. W. Rusden's Hist. of New Zealand.] J. A. H.

MONRO, DONALD (*fl.* 1550), known as 'High Dean of the Isles,' first appears on record as parson of Kiltearn, in the presbytery of Dingwall, Ross-shire. On 26 June 1563 he was appointed by the general assembly of the kirk commissioner 'within the bounds of Ross, to assist the Bishop of Caithness in preaching of the Gospell and planting of kirkis' (Calderwood, ii. 224), at a salary of four hundred merks for one year. On 27 Dec. following a complaint was made in the assembly that he 'was not so apt to teache as his charge required' (*ib.* p. 245). Six members of the assembly were appointed 'to trie his gifts,' and to report. His ignorance of Gaelic seems to have been his chief fault, for on 5 July 1570 it was objected that 'he was not prompt in the Scottish tongue.' His commission was, however, renewed in August 1573 (*ib.* p. 275). Tradition says that when at Kiltearn he lived in Castle Craig, and crossed the Firth to his duties. About 1574 he was translated to the neighbouring parish of Lymlair, with a stipend of 66*l.* 13*s.* 4*d.* Scots, and kirk-land. His title, 'High Dean of the Isles,' may have had some pre-reformation significance, but was more probably one of those titles of courtesy satirised by Sir David Lyndsay in his 'Monarchie' (bk. iii. 1290, &c.)

He made a systematic tour through the western islands of Scotland in 1549, of which he has left an interesting account. George Buchanan made use of it for the geographical portion of his 'History of Scotland,' and acknowledged his indebtedness (*Works*, folio edit. 1715, pp. 13, 18). Monro also wrote a small book, entitled 'The Genealogies of the Cheiff Clans of the Isles.' Both works were printed at Edinburgh, 1773–4, with the common title, 'Description of the Western Isles of Scotland, called Hybrides. With his Genealogies of the Chief Clans of the Isles. Now first published from the Manuscript.' Another edition appeared at Edinburgh in 1805, and in 1818 the account was included in the second volume of 'Miscellanea Scotica.' Two manuscript copies of his works are preserved in the Advocates' Library.

[Calderwood's History of the Kirk (Wodrow Soc. edit.); Miscellany of the Wodrow Society; i. 335; Hew Scott's Fasti Ecclesiæ Scoticanæ, pt. v. pp. 299, 302, 455.] G. G. S.

MONRO, DONALD, M.D. (1727–1802), medical writer, born in 1727, was second surviving son of Alexander Monro primus [q.v.], by Isabella, second daughter of Sir Donald MacDonald of the Isle of Skye. He was educated at Edinburgh under the care of his father, and graduated M.D. on 8 June 1753, the subject of his inaugural dissertation being 'De Hydrope.' Soon afterwards he was appointed physician to the army. On 12 April 1756 he was admitted a licentiate of the College of Physicians, London, and on 3 Nov. 1758 was elected physician to St. George's Hospital. During his absence abroad as army physician, from December 1760 until March 1763, Dr. (afterwards Sir) Richard Jebb [q. v.] was chosen to fill his place at the hospital. He was admitted a fellow of the College of Physicians, by a special grace, on 30 Sept. 1771; was censor in 1772, 1781, 1785, and 1789; and was named an elect on 10 July 1788. He delivered the Croonian lectures in 1774 and 1775, and the Harveian oration in 1775. Ill-health obliged him to resign his office at St. George's Hospital in 1786. At the same time he withdrew himself altogether from practice, and in great measure from society. He died in Argyll Street on 9 June 1802 (*Gent. Mag.* 1802, pt. ii. p. 687).

Monro, who is represented as a man of 'varied attainments, of considerable skill in his profession,' and in high esteem with his contemporaries, was admitted a fellow of the Royal Society on 1 May 1766. He published: 1. 'Dissertatio . . . de hydrope,' &c., 8vo, Edinburgh, 1753; reprinted in vol. ii. of the Edinburgh 'Thesaurus Medicus,' 1785. The second edition was published in English as 'An Essay on the Dropsy and its Different Species,' 8vo, London, 1756; 3rd edit. 1765. 2. 'An Account of the Diseases which were most frequent in the British Military Hospitals in Germany from January 1761 to . . . March 1763,' &c., 8vo, London, 1764. Appended is an essay on the means of preserving the health of soldiers, and conducting military hospitals. 3. 'A Treatise on Mineral Waters,' 2 vols. 8vo, London, 1770. 4. 'Prælectiones Medicæ,' 8vo, London, 1776, being his Croonian lectures and Harveian oration. 5. 'Observations on the Means of Preserving the Health of Soldiers, and of conducting Military Hospitals, and on the Diseases incident to Soldiers,' 2 vols. 8vo, London, 1780, a greatly enlarged edition of the 'Essay' appended to his 'Account.' John Millar, M.D. (1733-1805) [q. v.], published in 1784 a reply to Monro's arguments in 'Observations,' &c. 6. 'A Treatise on Medical and Pharmaceutical Chymistry and the Materia Medica,' 3 vols. 8vo, London, 1788, with a translation of the 'Pharmacopœia.' He likewise contributed various papers to 'Essays, Physical and Literary,' and to the 'Transactions' of various medical societies, and wrote the memoir prefixed to the quarto edition of his father's collected works, published at Edinburgh in 1781.

[Munk's Coll. of Phys. 1878, ii. 293–5; Life of Dr. A. Monro, prefixed to his Works, 1781; Watt's Bibl. Brit.; Cat. of Libr. of Med. and Chirurg. Soc.] G. G.

MONRO, EDWARD (1815–1866), divine and author, eldest son of Edward Thomas Monro, M.D. (1790–1856), physician to Bethlehem Hospital, grandson of Dr. Thomas Monro [q. v.], and brother of Henry Monro (1817–1891) [q. v.], was born at London in 1815. Educated at Harrow, he graduated at Oriel College, Oxford, with third-class honours in 1836, and was ordained shortly afterwards. From 1842 to 1860 he was perpetual curate of Harrow Weald, and from 1860 till his death vicar of St. John's, Leeds. Monro quickly attained a wide reputation as a preacher, and was select preacher at Oxford in 1862. Originally trained in the evangelical school, he was much influenced by the tractarian movement, which during his college life was in full tide, but the fervour of his religious zeal and his singular affection for the poor neutralised all party bias. Devoted to the welfare of boys in humble life, he established a college for them, called the 'College of St. Andrews,' at Harrow Weald, by the help of friends, such as Lords Selborne and Nelson, Bishop Blomfield, and others. The boys were boarded and received the education of gentlemen free of charge, and did credit to their training in after life, but the great expense of the college led the enthusiastic founder into pecuniary embarrassments, from which he was extricated with difficulty by friends and admirers. Monro had the rare talent of the Italian improvisatore, and most of the stories and allegories for which he became famous were delivered impromptu to village lads. The institution was without endowment, and the handsome and commodious buildings disappeared after Monro left Harrow Weald. At Leeds Monro put into effect on a larger scale the noble ideal of parochial work described in his books. The candidates for confirmation and communicants in his parish reached exceptional numbers. But his incessant labours affected his health, and he died at Leeds 13 Dec. 1866, after two years of illness. He was buried at Harrow Weald.

Monro's remarkable influence was extended by his writings far beyond the scene of his personal labours. Several of his stories and allegories passed through many editions, and are still in request. His chief publications are: 1. 'The Combatants,' 1848. 2. 'The Revellers,' 1850. 3. 'The Dark River,' 1850. 4. 'True Stories of Cottagers,' 1850. 5. 'Sermons on the Responsibility of the Ministerial Office.' 6. 'View of Parochial Life,' 1851. 7. 'The Parish,' a poem, 1853. 8. 'Walter the Schoolmaster,' 1854. 9. 'The Journey Home,' 1855. 10. 'Daily Studies during Lent,' 1856. 11. 'Leonard and Dennis,' 1856. 12. 'The

Dark Mountains,' 1858. 13. 'Characters of the Old Testament,' 1858. 14. 'Parochial Papers,' 1858. 15. 'Parochial Lectures on English Poetry,' 1860. 16. 'Pastoral Life,' 1862. 17. 'Harry and Archie,' 1862.

Monro married in 1838 Emma, daughter of Dr. Hay of Madras. He had no children.

[Personal knowledge; John Bull and Churchman newspapers.] M. B-s.

MONRO or MUNRO, Sir GEORGE (*d.* 1693), of Culrain and Newmore, royalist general, was the third son of Colonel John Monro of Obisdale, by Catherine, daughter of John Gordon of Embo. He served in the wars of Gustavus Adolphus under his uncle, Robert Monro of Foulis (*d.* 1633) [q. v.], styled the 'Black Baron,' and was present at the battle of Lützen, 16 Nov. 1632. Afterwards he held a command in Ireland under his uncle Colonel Robert Munro (*d.* 1680?) [q. v.], who on 21 Jan. 1644–5 sent him to represent the grievances of the Scottish army in Ireland to both houses of parliament (*Hist. MSS. Comm.* 6th Rep. p. 48), and on 28 Jan. he received a commission to command the troops sent to reinforce the Scottish army there (*Cal. State Papers*, Dom. Ser. 1644–5, p. 277). When Robert Munro was defeated by Owen Roe O'Neill at Benburb on 5 June 1646, George Monro, who, with the rank of colonel, was in command of three troops of horse and 240 musqueteers, occupied an isolated position in dangerous proximity to the enemy, but after the battle with 'his party miraculously retreated home from the enemy' 'without the loss of a man' (Rushworth, *Historical Collections*, pt. iv. vol. i. p. 400).

In 1648 the Scottish parliament recalled Monro from Ireland to join the expedition into England under Hamilton for the relief of the king (Guthry, *Memoirs*, p. 260). He left Ireland in opposition to the orders of Monck (*Thurloe State Papers*, ii. 427), with a contingent of two hundred foot and one thousand horse. Hamilton had begun his march before his arrival, but he followed hard after him (Guthry, p. 279). He was not, however, suffered to come up with Hamilton, being kept behind to bring up the Scottish cannon (*ib.* p. 283). Consequently he was about thirty miles in the rear at the time of the battle of Preston, and when Sir Thomas Tildesley (who was then besieging Lancaster) heard of the disaster, he, with his own forces and others he had collected from the rout at Preston, retired north to Monro, and asked him to put his forces under his command and 'follow Cromwell in the rear as he harassed the Scots' (Clarendon, *History of the Rebellion*, iii. 242). This, however, Monro declined to do, and after lingering for some time in Westmoreland, Cumberland, and Northumberland, he also declined an offer of the northern royalists to assist him in maintaining the cause of the king in Scotland, and resolved to march thither and await further orders (*ib.* p. 243). In Scotland he was joined by the Earl of Lanark [see Hamilton, William, second Duke of Hamilton], whom he acknowledged as general (Guthry, p. 208). On 11 Sept. he appeared before Edinburgh, but finding it occupied by the whigamores, who pointed the cannon of the castle against him, he marched westwards with the view of cutting off Argyll at Stirling. According to a letter from the headquarters of Cromwell, he seized the bridge of Stirling while in treaty with Argyll (Rushworth, pt. iv. vol. ii. p. 1276). Taking up his position at Stirling, he endeavoured to make it a rendezvous for reinforcements, but not succeeding in this, he finally agreed, before 1 Oct., to the articles (*ib.* pp. 1288–9) providing for the disbandment of his forces, on condition that he should not be challenged for being accessory to the 'Engagement.' After the disbandment he came to Edinburgh, but a proclamation being made that all 'malignants' should depart the city, and not remain within six miles of it (*ib.* p. 1296), he took ship for Holland (Guthry, p. 296).

Monro was included in the act passed by the Scottish estates on 17 May 1650 excluding divers persons 'from beyond seas with his majesty from entering the kingdom until they had given satisfaction to church and state' (Balfour, iv. 14), and he was included in a similar act passed on 4 June (*ib.* p. 42). He, however, returned to Scotland after the arrival of Charles II, and on 22 Nov. 1650, in answer to a request to the 'king's majesty and estates' for a 'convenient time to transport himself out of the country,' the committee of estates gave him till 1 Jan. (*ib.* p. 169). When an attempt was made in 1654 to promote a rising on behalf of Charles in the highlands, Monro was appointed lieutenant-general under Middleton, but his unpopularity prevented many of the clans from joining it (*Clarendon State Papers*, ii. 441). Its success was further endangered by a quarrel between him and the Earl of Glencairn, whom he challenged to a duel, but was defeated (*ib.* ii. 371; Baillie, iii. 255). This led to strained relations between him and Middleton, and in December he deserted him and came to terms with the government (Thurloe, iii. 42; *Hist. MSS. Comm.* 11th Rep. pt. vi. p. 137).

After the Restoration Monro represented

Ross-shire in parliament 1661–3, Sutherland 1669–74, and Ross-shire 1680–6 and 1689–1693. In August 1665 he was suspected of designs against the government and imprisoned (*Cal. State Papers*, Dom. Ser. 1664–1665, p. 514). According to Wodrow, the only reason for his imprisonment was his bantering the Bishop of Ross for his ignorance of Latin (*Analecta*, iv. 4). When he received his liberty is uncertain. Lauder of Fountainhall mentions that in 1680 Monro, while in the streets of Edinburgh, had a vision of a man calling on him to tell the Duke of York to request his brother the king to extirpate papists (*Hist. Observes*, p. 11).

Monro was made a knight of the Bath by Charles II, but the date or place is not recorded. He subsequently supported the revolution, and, although old and infirm, was appointed by the convention in Edinburgh to the command of the militia raised to protect it against Dundee and the royalists. He died 11 Jan. 1693. By his wife Margaret, daughter of Sir Frederick Hamilton and sister of Gustavus, first viscount Boyne, he left issue. The present Sir Hector Munro, eleventh baronet of Foulis, is a direct descendant. Sir George's elder brother, Sir Robert, third baronet (*d.* 1688), was grandfather of Robert Munro, sixth baronet [q. v.]

[Guthry's Memoirs; Robert Baillie's Letters and Journals (Bannatyne Club); Clarendon's History of the Rebellion; Rushworth's Historical Collections; Thurloe State Papers; Cal. State Papers, Dom. Ser.; Carlyle's Cromwell; Foster's Members of Scottish Parl.; Foster's Baronetage and Knightage.] T. F. H.

MONRO, MONROE, or MUNRO, HENRY (1768–1798), United Irishman, born in 1768, was the only son of a presbyterian tradesman of Scottish descent settled at Lisburn. The father died in 1793, leaving a widow, whose maiden name had been Gorman. She brought up Henry and her two daughters according to the principles of the church of England, and died at Lisburn about 1832.

Henry received a good mercantile education in his native town, and having gone through an apprenticeship entered the linen business about 1788. He afterwards paid frequent visits to England to buy silks and cloth and sell linen. While still a youth he joined the volunteers, and is said to have been adjutant of the Lisburn corps. He is described as rather under the middle height, but strong and agile, with deep blue eyes and an intelligent expression; honourable in his dealings and prosperous in trade, a good speaker, romantic in his views, without decided intellectual tastes. In 1795 he joined the United Irishmen with the view of forwarding the cause of catholic emancipation and parliamentary reform.

On the outbreak of the rebellion in co. Down in the early summer of 1798, Monroe, after the arrest of Dickson, was chosen by the committee of leaders at Belfast to take the command. On 11 June, while at the head of a force of rebels seven thousand strong at Saintfield, he sent a detachment to seize the town of Ballinahinch, halfway between Lisburn and Downpatrick. The town was occupied without opposition; but it was evacuated on the evening of the 12th, when General Nugent advanced from Belfast with a force inferior in numbers to the rebels, but much superior to them in artillery. During the night, word was brought to Monroe, who had taken up a position outside the town, that the victorious troops within were in a state of disorder, drinking, burning, and plundering, but he declined to direct a night attack, on the ground that it was unfair. The result was that several hundred of his best men immediately deserted. About two o'clock on the morning of 13 June the rebels succeeded in effecting an entrance into the town, and had apparently gained the day when the bugle sounded for the retreat of the royal troops, and the rebels, mistaking the signal for the *pas de charge*, fled in disorder from the south, while Nugent's men were evacuating Ballinahinch by the north. The latter soon rallied and cut off the retreat of the Irish in all directions but one. Through this loophole Monroe led about 150 men after the rest had been hopelessly routed. In the pursuit no quarter was given. Monroe fled alone to the mountains. He was taken early in the morning of 15 June about six miles from Ballinahinch. He was immediately removed with one Kane, or Keane, who was captured at the same time, to Hillsborough, whence he was taken to Lisburn, tried by court-martial, and hanged opposite his own door, and in sight, it was said, of his wife and sisters. He behaved with marvellous coolness to the last. He settled a money account with Captain Stewart, a yeomanry officer, at the foot of the gallows, then said a short prayer and mounted the ladder. A rung gave way, and he was thrown to the ground. On reascending it, he gave the signal for his execution, after uttering the words, 'Tell my country I deserved better of it.' His head was afterwards fixed on a pike and placed upon the market-house of Lisburn. His house and property were destroyed by the royal troops. The green and white plume which he wore at Ballinahinch was afterwards given to Bishop Percy, 27 Oct. 1798.

A proclamation put in at the court-martial advising the soldiers and inhabitants of co. Down to pay no rent to 'the disaffected landlords, as such rent is confiscated to the use of the National Liberty War,' Madden thinks a fabrication.

Monroe married in 1795 Margaret Johnston, fourth daughter of Robert Johnston of Seymour Hill in Antrim. His widow died at Belfast in February 1840. His daughter married one Hanson, an independent minister.

[Madden's United Irishmen, 3rd ser. i. 378–401; Teeling's Personal Narrative of the Rebellion, Glasgow ed. vol. i. ch. xix.; Sir R. Musgrave's Rebellions in Ireland, 3rd ed. ii. 103–7; W. H. Maxwell's Hist. of the Irish Rebellion, ch. xx.; A. Webb's Compendium of Irish Biography; Lecky's England in 18th Cent. viii. 131–5.] G. Le G. N.

MONRO, HENRY (1791–1814), portrait and subject painter, the son of Dr. Thomas Monro [q. v.], was born 30 Aug. 1791. After two years at Harrow he entered the navy, but quitted it from distaste, after a few days on board the frigate Amelia. His inclinations then wavered between the army and art, but he finally chose the latter, and was admitted a student of the Royal Academy in 1806. Here and at the colour school of the British Institution he studied with great diligence and distinction. In 1811 he exhibited 'A Laughing Boy,' 'Boys at Marbles,' a portrait of his father, and two other portraits, and in the following year a 'Boy Grinding Colours,' a 'Lace-maker,' and four portraits, including one of Thomas Hearne and another of himself. In 1813 he sent a 'Head,' some studies from nature in pen and ink, and 'Othello, Desdemona, and Iago' to the Royal Academy, and 'The Disgrace of Wolsey' to the British Institution; for the latter he was awarded a premium of a hundred guineas. In 1811 he had visited Scotland, and sustained serious injuries by a fall from his horse, and in January 1814 he was seized with a cold, which affected his lungs, and cut short his promising career at the age of twenty-three. A portrait by him of his father (in coloured chalks) is in the College of Physicians. He died on 5 March 1814, and was buried at Bushey, where a monument was erected to his memory.

[Redgrave's Dict.; Bryan's Dict.; Munk's Coll. of Phys. (under 'Dr. Thomas Monro'); Royal Academy Catalogues; Annals of the Fine Arts, 1816, pp. 342–6; Clutterbuck's History of Hertfordshire.] C. M.

MONRO, HENRY (1817–1891), physician and philanthropist, second son of Edward Thomas Monro, grandson of Dr. Thomas Monro [q. v.], and brother of Edward Monro [q. v.], was born in 1817, and was educated at Harrow and at Oriel College, Oxford (B.A. 1839, B. Med. 1844, and D. Med. 1863). He studied medicine at St. Bartholomew's Hospital; became a fellow of the College of Physicians in 1848, and, devoting himself to the study of insanity, was appointed physician to Bethlehem Hospital in the same year. 'He was the last of a long line of physicians who from father to son followed the same speciality, four being in direct succession physicians to Bethlehem Hospital' [see Monro, John; and Monro, Thomas, 1759–1833]. In 1864 he became president of the Medical Psychological Society. In the midst of the engrossing duties of his profession Monro found time to establish, like his brother Edward, institutions for the benefit of the poor. Assisted by many friends, he was the founder in 1846 of the House of Charity in Rose Street, Soho, which 'still flourishes, with a larger development in Soho Square. It is a home for the destitute and friendless, chiefly those who, by no fault of their own, have been plunged into extreme distress and helplessness.' To this he gave unremitting attention for forty-five years, and also, in a less degree, to the Walton Convalescent Home, which his younger brother, Theodore Monro, founded at about the same time. Monro died in 1891. He married in 1842 Jane, daughter of Sir William Russell, bart., and left several children. He published in 1850 a treatise on 'Stammering,' and in the following year his 'Remarks on Insanity,' the principles of which were accepted by Dr. D. H. Tuke and by Dr. Hughlings Jackson. Monro was no mean artist, a gift which was hereditary in his family. He painted his own portrait and that of his father, for presentation to the College of Physicians, where they hang beside portraits of three earlier members of the family, Alexander, John, and Thomas, who were distinguished as physicians.

[Journal of Mental Science, July 1891, notice by Dr. G. F. Blandford; Memoir privately printed by the Rev. Canon W. Foxley Norris, M.A.; personal knowledge.] M. B-s.

MONRO, JAMES (1680–1752), physician, born in Scotland 2 Sept. 1680, was son of Alexander Monro (*d.* 1715?) [q. v.] He came to London with his father in 1691, and matriculated at Balliol College, Oxford, 8 July 1699, graduating B.A. 15 June 1703, M.A. 3 June 1708, M.B. 25 May 1709. He does not appear to have practised medicine, at least in London, till middle life, since it was not till 9 July 1722 that he took the degree of M.D., and six years later, 23 Dec. 1728, was admitted candidate of the College of Physicians of London, succeeding to the fellowship 22 Dec. 1729. He was elected physician to Bethlehem Hospital for lunatics 9 Oct. 1728, which appointment he held till his death. For the rest of his life he devoted himself to the treatment of insanity. He is said to have been a skilful and honourable physician. His policy in not admitting students or physicians to the practice of his hospital was the subject of hostile criticism in Dr. Battie's treatise on 'Madness' (London, 1758, 4to), and was defended in a pamphlet by his son John Monro, who is separately noticed. James Monro's only literary production was the Harveian oration at the College of Physicians in 1737. He died 4 Nov. 1752, at Sunninghill, Berkshire, and is buried there. A portrait of him is in the College of Physicians.

[Foster's Alumni Oxon. (1500–1714), Munk's Coll. of Phys. 1878, ii. 115; information supplied by the family.] J. F. P.

MONRO, JOHN (1715–1791), physician, eldest son of James Monro, M.D. [q. v.], was born at Greenwich 16 Nov. 1715. He was educated at Merchant Taylors' School, and passed in 1733 to St. John's College, Oxford, where he ultimately succeeded to a fellowship. He graduated B.A. 31 May 1737, M.A. 11 July 1740, and in April 1741 was elected Radcliffe travelling fellow, an appointment then tenable for ten years, and carrying with it the obligation of studying medicine on the continent. He studied first at Edinburgh, afterwards at Leyden, and took his degree as M.B. at Oxford, 10 Dec. 1743. Subsequently he spent some years in travelling through France, Holland, Italy, and Germany, returning to England in 1751. He had the degree of M.D. conferred on him in his absence by diploma, 27 June 1747. In 1751 (24 July) he was appointed joint physician to Bethlehem Hospital with his father, whose health had begun to decline, and on his death, in the next year, John Monro became sole physician to the hospital.

He was admitted candidate of the College of Physicians 25 June 1752, fellow on the same date of the next year, was censor on several occasions, and delivered the Harveian oration in 1757. In 1787, in consideration of his failing health, his son Thomas was appointed his assistant at Bethlehem Hospital. He then gradually retired from practice, and died at Hadley, Barnet, 27 Dec. 1791.

Monro, like his father, devoted himself to the study and treatment of insanity, and is said to have attained eminence and success. He wrote nothing except 'Remarks on Dr. Battie's Treatise on Madness,' London, 1758, 8vo. Dr. Battie had alluded to certain physicians (meaning the physicians to Bethlehem Hospital) who kept their knowledge and methods of treatment to themselves, not communicating them to the profession by writing or teaching. This touched John Monro, as well as his father, and his answer was, in effect, that a knowledge of the subject could be obtained only by observation, and in retaliation he criticised very severely other parts of Dr. Battie's work. The appointment of physician to Bethlehem and a great reputation in the treatment of insanity were transmitted in the Monro family for several generations.

Monro had acquired (probably on his travels) a taste for the fine arts, especially engravings, and assisted Strutt in the preparation of his 'History of Engravers.' He is also said to have communicated notes to Steevens for his edition of Shakespeare. A portrait of him is in the College of Physicians. His son Thomas (1759–1833) is separately noticed.

[Munk's Coll. of Phys.; Brit. Med. Journal, 1851, i. 1262.] J. F. P.

MONRO or MUNRO, ROBERT (*d.* 1633), styled the 'Black Baron,' eighteenth chief of Foulis, was the eldest son of Hector Monro of Foulis, by Anne, daughter of Hugh, sixth lord Fraser of Lovat. His father died on 14 Nov. 1603, and while a minor he received a dispensation and special license from the king, dated 8 Jan. 1608, upon which by a precept from chancery he was infeft in all the lands possessed by his father on 26, 27, 28 and 29 April. On account of expensive living during his travels abroad he greatly embarrassed his estate; but having engaged his revenues for ten years to pay his creditors, he in 1626 joined as a volunteer the Scottish corps raised by Sir Donald Mackay, first lord Reay [q. v.], for the German wars. At first he was captain of a company of Scots soldiers raised by himself. Subsequently he was advanced to be colonel of a Dutch regiment of horse and foot under Gustavus Adolphus, and specially distinguished himself in various actions. He died at Ulm in 1633, after six weeks' illness from a wound by a musket-ball in the foot. Although a spendthrift in his earlier years, he latterly became exemplarily pious, being, according to his relative, General Robert Monro [q.v.], 'a true Christian and a right traveller' (*Monro his Expedition with the Worthy Scots Regiment*, pt. ii. p. 49). By his first wife, Margaret, daughter of William Sutherland, seventh baron of Duffus, he had one daughter, Margaret, married to Kenneth Mackenzie of Scotwell, and by his second wife, Mary Haynes, an English lady, he had a daughter Elizabeth. As he left no male issue, he was succeeded in the barony of Foulis by his brother Hector, who also obtained the rank of colonel in the service of Gustavus Adolphus, and on his return to Scotland was on 7 June 1634 created by Charles I a baronet of Nova Scotia.

[Monro his Expedition with the Worthy Scots Regiment, called Mackay's, 1637; particulars concerning the Munros in Doddridge's Life of Colonel Gardiner; Douglas's Baronage of Scotland, pp. 83–4.] T. F. H.

MONRO or **MUNRO**, **ROBERT** (*d.* 1680?), general, was of the family of Foulis Castle in Ross-shire, and followed his cousin, Robert Monro of Foulis, the 'Black Baron' [q. v.], the then head of the house, to the continental war. Thither also went his nephew, Sir George Monro [q. v.] The nature of his service there may be gathered from the title-page of the narrative which he published in London in 1637: 'Expedition with the worthy Scots Regiment called Mackey's Regiment, levied in August 1626 . . . for His Majesty's service of Denmark and reduced after the Battle of Nerling [Nordlingen] to one company in September 1634 at Worms . . . afterwards under the invincible King of Sweden . . . and since under the Director-general, the Rex-chancellor Oxenstiern and his Generals.' Munro served thus for seven years, beginning as lieutenant and ending as colonel. His first service was in Holstein, in 1627, and he notices that 'the Danish king was of absolute authority in his kingdom, as all Christian kings ought to be.' Denmark made a separate peace in 1627, and Munro, with his fourteen hundred Scottish comrades, transferred his allegiance to Gustavus Adolphus, whom, like Dugald Dalgetty, he is fond of calling 'the lion of the North.' In the Swedish king's service there were at one time, it is said, not less than three generals, eight colonels, five lieutenant-colonels, eleven majors, and above thirty captains, all of the name of Munro, besides a great number of subalterns (cf. ANDERSON, *Scottish Nation*, iii. 215). He visited Sweden in 1630, missed the battle of Lützen (16 Nov. 1632), and continued in the service after that fatal day. He was in Scotland recruiting in 1634, but returned to the continent. From a letter preserved at Dunrobin it appears that he was at Hamburg in October 1636 (*Hist. MSS. Comm.* 2nd Rep. p. 178).

When the troubles began between Charles I and the Scots, Munro sided with his own countrymen, and was soon employed. In June 1639 he commanded a division of the army which repulsed Holland from Kelso (BAILLIE, i. 210). At the end of May 1640 he was sent with about eight hundred men to Aberdeen, where he acted with severity. Spalding, who is full of lamentations, particularly mentions that 'he caused set up between the crosses ane timber mare, whereupon runagate knaves and runaway soldiers should ride. Uncouth to see sic discipline in Aberdeen, and more painful to the trespasser to suffer.' His troops were ill-paid, but he maintained order, and even killed a mutineer with his own hand. In September, much to Spalding's disgust, he and his officers were made burgesses of Aberdeen, and soon afterwards they marched to Edinburgh. On the breaking out of the Irish rebellion the Scots estates offered ten thousand men with three thousand stand of arms to the English parliament. The offer was accepted, and the command given to Alexander Leslie [q. v.], with Munro as his second, but only about four thousand really landed in Ireland. Leslie did not go over until some time after his vanguard, and then only for a short visit, so that the leadership of the new Scotch, as they were called, really devolved upon Munro, who was called major-general.

Munro was wind-bound for a month on the Ayrshire coast and in Arran, but reached Carrickfergus on 15 April 1642 with about 2,500 men. Lord Conway and Colonel Chichester retired to Belfast, but acknowledged him as their general, and he was soon in command of 3,500 men. On 30 April, having dispersed Lord Iveagh's forces near Moira, he attacked Newry, plundered the town, and put all in the castle to the sword. Several women were killed by the soldiers, some of whom were punished by the general, but little quarter was given anywhere during the war (PIKE; TURNER). A week later Munro tried to surprise Sir Phelim O'Neill [q. v.] near Armagh, but the latter burned the town and retired to Charlemont. Munro withdrew to Carrickfergus, where he lay inactive for some time, losing many men by Irish ague, and complaining that he could not get provisions (Letter to Leslie in *Contemp. History*, i. 419). No help could be given to the garrison of Londonderry, who were threatened by Sir Phelim, but early in June Munro was strong enough to capture Randal Macdonnell, second earl of Antrim [q. v.] at Dunluce. The earl attempted to stand neuter, with the usual result, but there were eight hundred MacDonnells in arms on the Irish side, and Munro was probably justified in making him a prisoner. He escaped by a stratagem some months later (*War of*

Ireland, p. 25; BAILLIE, ii. 73), but his castles were garrisoned by Argyll's regiment, which might be trusted to keep MacDonnell strongholds safely. Munro failed to take Charlemont, and the Irish were strengthened by the arrival of Owen Roe O'Neill [q. v.], who landed in Lough Swilly at the end of July. During the autumn and winter Munro was inactive, but in the early spring of 1643 he relieved Sir John Clotworthy's men, who were hard pressed at Mountjoy on Lough Neagh. In May Munro took the field with about two thousand men, and gained some rather dubious advantage over Owen Roe at Loughgall, near Charlemont. Turner, who was present, adversely criticises his arrangements, and Colonel O'Neill says his horse were broken, and that he had to alight, crying 'Fay, fay, run away from a wheen rebels' (*Des. Cur.* p. 490). A less doubtful success was the recapture of Antrim, who had just landed with important letters. Ormonde's cessation [see BUTLER, JAMES] of arms with the Irish confederates was not acknowledged by Munro, for his masters in Scotland were no parties to it, but the want of supplies prevented him from doing anything. The answer to this cessation was the solemn league and covenant, and in November Owen O'Connolly was chosen by the English parliament as their emissary to Ulster, while Lord Leven was made commander over the English as well as the Scottish forces there, and authorised to name Munro as his substitute. This new commission arrived in April 1644, but many officers would have preferred to remain under Ormonde's orders, and among them was Colonel Chichester at Belfast. On 14 May Munro surprised that town. Between Scottish, English, and Ulster protestants he could now take the field with six thousand or seven thousand effective men (*War of Ireland*, p. 38). Dundalk and Newry were held for Ormonde, and Munro was repulsed from the latter place. He was then on his return from a raid into the Pale, and his movements from 27 June to 15 July are detailed in a contemporary pamphlet (London, 27 Aug. 1644). In August and September he had to defend his own province against Castlehaven, who was baffled in the end by disease and famine, and perhaps by Owen Roe's jealousy (*ib.* p. 41; CASTLEHAVEN, p. 53). During 1645 there was no fighting, but much plundering and burning by Munro's orders. His plots to obtain possession of Drogheda and Dundalk were unsuccessful (CARTE). His force was weakened by the withdrawal of troops to face Montrose in Scotland, but he managed to avoid going himself. Rinuccini reached Ireland in October, and added a fresh element to the general confusion. Owen Roe got a substantial part of the papal subsidy, and with its help raised his force to its greatest strength. On 5 June 1646 he routed Munro at Benburb, the latter flying to Lisburn without coat or wig. Five contemporary accounts of this battle are printed by Mr. Gilbert (*Contemp. Hist.* i. 676). A covenanter confesses that this disaster was something of a judgment on the Scottish army, many of the soldiers being 'prodigiously profane and wicked in their lives,' and pitiless plunderers of the poor country (REID, ii. 30). O'Neill marched southward at Rinuccini's call, thus losing the fruits of his victory, and Munro was left unmolested at Carrickfergus.

It soon appeared that Ormonde had no alternative but to leave the protestants of Ireland at the mercy of O'Neill and the nuncio, or to place them under the protection of the English parliament. After long negotiations Dublin was occupied by the parliamentary forces in June 1647. On 16 March an ordinance had been passed that the Scottish army should be paid and should leave Ireland; but they never received their arrears, and in the meantime refused to surrender Carrickfergus or Belfast. Munro thought it prudent to write to the neighbouring clergy disclaiming any sympathy with the English sectaries (Letter in REID, ii. 56). The British regiments, as they were called —that is, the English and Ulster protestants —were placed under Monck's command, and Munro's importance was thus greatly diminished. The Scots had not been recruited since Benburb, and were reduced to a 'remnant of six regiments' (*War of Ireland*, p. 65). In May 1648 the Hamilton party in Scotland invited Munro to join their engagement against 'the sectaries and their adherents in England' (Documents in REID, ii. 544), and he lent a favouring ear to their proposals. Monck thereupon received positive orders from the parliament to seize Belfast and to let no one land from Scotland (Letter in BENN, p. 122). He straightway came to an understanding with some discontented officers, and on the night of 12 Sept. the north gate of Carrickfergus was thrown open to him (REID, ii. 76). Munro was seized in his bed and shipped for England, and Belfast surrendered immediately afterwards (BENN, p. 123). The vessel which took away Munro had lain for a fortnight in the lough, which made many think that he connived at his own arrest and that he was well paid; but his long imprisonment seems to refute this. 500*l.* was voted to Monck, and Munro, on his arrival, was committed to the Fleet 'for joining with the enemy in Scotland and perfidiously breaking the trust reposed in him' (WHITELOCKE, 2 Oct. 1648).

Munro was transferred to the Tower, where he remained about five years, during which he is said to have been often consulted by Cromwell. While in Ireland he had married Lady Jean Alexander, daughter of the first Earl of Stirling and widow of the second Viscount Montgomery of Ardes. He acquired lands through his wife, and there was every disposition to deal harshly with him until Cromwell interfered in his favour in 1654. He was allowed to return to Ireland, lived on the Montgomery estate near Comber, co. Down (BENN, p. 138), and was pall-bearer at the funeral of his wife's son, Hugh Montgomery, earl of Mount Alexander, at Newtownards in October 1663 (HILL, p. 252; see art. MONTGOMERY, HUGH, *d.* 1672). Henry Cromwell had allowed the earl, although a royalist, to live in peace along with his mother, grandmother, brother, and sister, and 'honest, kind Major-general Munro, fitter than the other four to converse with his melancholy' (*ib.* p. 213). Lady Montgomery died in 1670, but Munro survived her for ten years or more, and continued to live in co. Down. Munro shares with Sir James Turner, who accuses him of wanting military forethought and of despising his enemy, the honour of furnishing a model for the immortal picture of Dugald Dalgetty in 'The Legend of Montrose.'

[Montgomery MSS. ed. Hill; Roger Pike's Relation in Ulster Journals of Archæology, viii. 7; John Spalding's Memorials of the Troubles in Scotland and England (Spalding Club ed.); Scott's Preface to his Legend of Montrose; Sir James Turner's Memoirs; Burton's Hist. of Scotland, chap. lxxiii., and his Scot Abroad, vol. ii. chap. ii.; Contemp. Hist. of Affairs in Ireland, ed. Gilbert; Reid's Hist. of Presbyterian Church in Ireland, ed. Killen; Hist. of War in Ireland, by a British officer in Sir John Clotworthy's Regiment; Benn's Hist. of Belfast; Rinuccini's Embassy in Ireland, English transl.; Robert Baillie's Letters; Carte's Ormonde; Colonel O'Neill's narrative in Desiderata Curiosa Hibernica, vol. ii.; Whitelocke's Memorials; Castlehaven's Memoirs, ed. 1815.] R. B-L.

MONRO or **MUNRO**, SIR **ROBERT**, twenty-seventh BARON and sixth BARONET OF FOULIS (*d.* 1746), was the eldest son of Sir Robert, fifth baronet, high sheriff of Ross, by his wife Jean, daughter of John Forbes [q. v.] of Culloden. Sir George Monro [q. v.] was his granduncle. He entered the army at an early age and served with distinction in Flanders, obtaining, before the cessation of the war in 1712, the rank of captain in the Royal Scots. During the war he made the acquaintance of Colonel James Gardiner [q. v.], with whose subsequent religious views his own closely coincided. He entered parliament for Wick in 1710, and suffered a reduction of military rank for his lack of subservience to the tory ministers. He continued to represent the same burgh until 1741. On the outbreak of the rebellion in 1715, Munro, with three hundred of his clan, assisted the Earl of Sutherland in detaining the Earl of Seaforth, with three thousand men, in Caithness, and preventing him from reinforcing the rebels under Mar at Perth until sufficient forces had been gathered under the Duke of Argyll to check Mar's progress southwards by Stirling. The rendezvous of Sutherland's men was at Alves, in the country of the Munros, and Seaforth resolved to attack him there; but Sutherland retired slowly northwards into his own country, whereupon Seaforth ravaged all the country of the Munros (Lord Lovat's 'Account of the Taking of Inverness' in PATTEN, *Hist. of the Rebellion*, 2nd ed. pt. ii. p. 144). On the capture of Inverness (13 Nov.), Munro, with his clan, was left to garrison it (*ib.* p. 154). On the retreat of Seaforth northwards, after the flight of the Pretender and the dispersal of his forces, Munro joined the Earl of Sutherland at Beauly in order to give him battle, being specially desirous to avenge the devastation of his lands; but Seaforth deemed it advisable to capitulate (*ib.* p. 157).

In 1716 Munro was appointed one of the commission of inquiry into the forfeited estates of the highland chiefs, and it was chiefly at his instance that various new parishes were erected and endowed through the highlands out of the proceeds of the sale of confiscated lands. From the termination of the commission in 1724 Munro, with the exception of representing Wick in parliament, held no office of public trust until in 1739 he was appointed lieutenant-colonel of the new highland regiment, then known as the 43rd, or Black Watch, afterwards famed as the 42nd, formed out of the independent highland companies. The colonel of the regiment was the Earl of Crawford, but as he was abroad, the organisation and training of the regiment were deputed to Munro, who devoted sixteen months to this object, the regiment being quartered on the banks of the Tay and Lyon. The regiment remained in Scotland until March 1743, when it proceeded south to London, on the way to Flanders. A rumour reached the men that they were about to be sent to the plantations, and a large number, after the regiment arrived in London, endeavoured to make their way back to the highlands. After they had been brought back and three of them shot as deserters, the regiment embarked for Flanders towards the end of May, but was not engaged in active service till the arrival of the Duke of Cumberland in April 1745, when an attempt was made to raise the siege of Tournay. The regiment greatly distinguished itself in various skirmishes previous to the battle of Fontenoy on 11 May. On the day of the battle, Munro 'obtained leave of the Duke of Cumberland to allow them to fight in their own way.' Accordingly they were ordered to 'clap to the ground' on receiving the French fire, and instantly after it they sprang up, before the enemy could reload, and, rushing in upon them, poured in their shot with such effect as to drive them into confusion. This manœuvre was repeated by them on several occasions with similar effect (account by PHILIP DODDRIDGE in Appendix to the *Life of Colonel Gardiner*). Munro himself, being old and corpulent, was unable to 'clap to the ground' with his men, but although he alone of the regiment remained erect, with the colours behind him, he escaped scatheless. In the charges he showed equal activity with his men, and when in the trenches was pulled out by them by the legs and arms (*ib.*) The regiment's peculiar mode of fighting attracted the special notice of the French. 'The highland fiends,' wrote a French eyewitness, 'rushed in upon us with more violence than ever did a sea driven by a tempest' (account of the battle, published at Paris, 26 May 1745, in STEWART, *Highlanders*, i. 283). The valour and determination shown by the regiment led the Duke of Cumberland to choose it, along with the 19th, to cover the retreat, which was done with perfect steadiness. In acknowledgment of his services Munro was in June promoted to the command of the 37th regiment, previously held by General Ponsonby, who was slain at Fontenoy.

On the outbreak of the rebellion in 1745, Munro's regiment was ordered to Scotland, and at the battle of Falkirk, 17 Jan. 1746, formed part of the left wing. When the regiment gave way before the charging clans, Munro alone held his ground. Although simultaneously attacked by six men of Lochiel's clan, he gallantly defended himself, killing two of them, but a seventh coming up shot him in the groin with a pistol, whereupon he fell forward, and was at once struck to the ground and killed on the spot. His brother, Dr. Robert Munro, who had come to his assistance, was killed about the same time. Next day their bodies were discovered by some of the Macdonalds, and buried in the churchyard of Falkirk, all the chiefs of the rebel clans attending the funeral. The right hand of Munro after death still clutched the pommel of the sword, from which the blade was broken off. By his wife Mary, daughter of Henry Seymour of Woodlands, he had three sons: Robert, who died young; Harry, who succeeded him; and George, an officer in the royal navy, who died in 1743.

[Account of the Munros of Foulis in Appendix to Doddridge's Life of Colonel Gardiner; Stewart's Highlanders of Scotland; Cannon's Records of the British Army; Patten's History of the Rebellion; Culloden Papers; Douglas's Baronage of Scotland; Foster's Baronetage.] T. F. H.

MONRO, THOMAS (1764–1815), miscellaneous writer, son of the Rev. Thomas Monro of Wargrave, Berkshire, was born 9 Oct. 1764. He was nephew of Dr. Alexander Monro primus [q. v.], and first cousin of Dr. Alexander Monro secundus [q. v.] He was educated in the free schools of Colchester and Norwich under Dr. Samuel Parr [q.v.], who always held him in high regard. On 11 July 1782 he matriculated at St. Mary Hall, Oxford, and in 1783 he was elected to a demyship at Magdalen College, which he resigned on his marriage, 7 June 1797. He graduated B.A. in 1787, and M.A. in 1791. He was curate of Selborne, Hampshire, from 1798 till 1800, when he was presented by Lord Maynard to the rectory of Little Easton, Essex, where he died on 25 Sept. 1815.

His works are: 1. 'Olla Podrida, a Periodical Work,' comprising forty-eight weekly numbers, Oxford, 1787, fol.; 2nd edit. London, 1788, 8vo; reprinted in Lynam's edition of the 'British Essayists,' vol. xxviii. (London, 1827, 12mo). In conducting this periodical, of which he was the projector and editor, he was assisted by Bishop Horne, then president of Magdalen College, Messrs. Headley, Kett, Gower, and other Oxford men. 2. 'Essays on various Subjects,' London, 1790, 8vo. 3. 'Alciphron's Epistles; in which are described the Domestic Manners, the Courtesans, and Parasites of Greece. Now first translated from the Greek,' London, 1791, 8vo, by Monro and William Beloe [q. v.] 4. 'Modern Britons, and Spring in London,' London, 1792. 5. 'Philoctetes in Lemnos. A Drama in three acts. To which is prefixed A Greenroom Scene, exhibiting a Sketch of the present Theatrical Taste: inscribed with due Deference to the Managers of Covent Garden and Drury Lane Theatres by their humble servant, Oxoniensis,' London, 1795, 8vo (cf. BAKER, *Biog. Dram.* ed. Reed and Jones, iii. 144).

[Biog. Dict. of Living Authors, 1816, p. 238; Bloxam's Magd. Coll. Registers, vii. 77, 81; Foster's Alumni Oxon., later ser. iii. 970; Gent. Mag. October 1815, p. 378; Johnstone's Life of Parr, i. 163, 211, 558, vii. 441; Lowndes's Bibl. Man. (Bohn), p. 26; Nichols's Illustr. of Lit. vii. 340; Nichols's Lit. Anecd. ix. 40, 77, 91, 95, 124, 158, x. 630; Notes and Queries, 7th ser. ii. 407, 449.] T. C.

MONRO, THOMAS (1759-1833), doctor of medicine and connoisseur, youngest son of Dr. John Monro [q. v.] and grandson of James Monro [q. v.], was born in London in 1759. He was educated under Dr. Parr, at Stanmore, Middlesex, and at Oriel College, Oxford, whence he graduated B.A. 1780, M.A. 1783, and M.D. 1787. He became a candidate of the College of Physicians in 1790, and a fellow in 1791. He was censor in 1792, 1799, and 1812; Harveian orator in 1799; and was named an elect in 1811. He assisted his father in his profession, and succeeded him as physician to Bridewell and Bethlehem Hospital in 1792. This post he held till 1816, when he in turn was succeeded by his son, Dr. Edward Thomas Monro (1790–1856), who was also educated at Oriel, graduating M.D. in 1814 and becoming F.R.C.P. in 1806. He attended George III during his illness in 1811–12, and is said to have prescribed a hop pillow for his royal patient. Some charges which had been made against the treatment of patients at Bethlehem caused him to issue a pamphlet entitled 'Observations,' &c., on the subject in 1816.

Dr. John Monro was a man of culture, as well as a distinguished physician, and had made a considerable collection of engravings and other works of art, and Thomas Monro inherited his taste, and became not only one of the best-known connoisseurs of the day, but an amateur artist, a teacher, and a patron, who specially devoted himself to assisting and training young artists in the practice of landscape-painting in water-colour, which was then in its infancy. About 1793 he removed from Bedford Square, where his father lived, to the house in Adelphi Terrace (No. 8), which has become famous in the annals of water-colour painting. He encouraged (perhaps in Bedford Square, certainly in Adelphi Terrace) the younger 'draftsmen' to make a studio of his house in winter evenings. They sat at desks opposite to one another, with one candle serving for a *vis-à-vis*. He had been a pupil of John Laporte [q. v.], and was himself an ardent sketcher, and he gave his pupils outlines to fill with colour, and drawings to copy, watching them and assisting them with advice. He retained their work, and gave them 2*s*. or 2*s*. 6*d*. an evening and a good supper. His house was full of pictures and drawings, many of them by Gainsborough and Cozens, and he allowed them to be freely copied by his *protégés*. He had also a country house, first at Fetcham, Surrey, and afterwards (from about 1805) at Bushey, Hertfordshire. A drawing by Girtin of his house at Fetcham is in the South Kensington Museum. To these houses he would invite his favourites, and employ them in making sketches from nature. By these means he stimulated, perhaps more than any other man, the growth of the art of water-colour, which resulted in the formation of a distinct school and of the Society of Painters in Water-colours.

Chief among those who profited by his kind patronage were J. M. W. Turner [q.v.], Thomas Girtin [q. v.], John Varley [q. v.], Joshua Cristall [q. v.], Peter De Wint [q. v.], William Henry Hunt [q. v.], and John Linnell [q. v.] He attended John Robert Cozens [q. v.] with the greatest kindness, and with little or no charge, after Cozens lost his reason until his death. He buried and raised monuments to Thomas Hearne [q. v.] (the artist) and Henry Edridge [q. v.] in the churchyard at Bushey. He died at Bushey on 14 May 1833, in his seventy-fourth year, having many years previously retired from the practice of his profession. He was buried in Bushey churchyard beside his father and other members of his family, whose memory is honoured by a stained-glass window in the church. His extensive collection of water-colour drawings was sold at Christie's in June 1833, and contained a large number of early drawings by Turner, as well as some fine later ones.

Monro's second son was Henry (1791–1814) [q. v.]; his eldest son, Edward Thomas, was father of Edward and Henry (1817–1891), who are also separately noticed.

[Munk's Coll. of Phys. ii. 414; Gent. Mag. 1833, pt. i. p. 477; Roget's 'Old' Water-colour Society; Thornbury's Life of Turner; Somerset House Gazette, ii. 9; Notes and Queries, 7th ser. i. 475, 514, ii. 59.] C. M.

MONSELL, JOHN SAMUEL BEWLEY (1811–1875), hymn-writer, son of Thomas Bewley Monsell, archdeacon of Derry and precentor of Christ Church Cathedral, was born at St. Columb's, Derry, on 2 March 1811. He entered Trinity College, Dublin, and graduated B.A. in 1832, and LL.B. and LL.D. in 1856. He was ordained deacon in 1834, and priest in 1835, and was successively chaplain to Bishop Mant [q. v.], chancellor of the diocese of Connor, rector of Ramoan, co. Antrim, vicar of Egham, Surrey, and rector of St. Nicholas, Guildford. He died on 9 April 1875, at Guildford, from injuries received in a fall from the roof of his church, then in course of reconstruction.

Monsell was a popular hymn-writer, and not a few of his books ran through several editions. Julian's 'Dictionary of Hymnology' (p. 762) gives a list of seventy-two of his better-known hymns. He has a place in nearly all anthologies of religious verse, eight of his pieces being included in M'Ilwaine's 'Lyra Hibernica Sacra,' 1869. Besides leaflets and occasional sermons, he published: 1. 'Hymns and Miscellaneous Poems,' 12mo, Dublin, 1837. 2. 'Cottage Controversy, or Dialogues between Thomas and Andrew on the Errors of the Church of Rome,' 8vo, Limerick, 1839. 3. 'Parish Musings, or Devotional Poems,' 12mo, London, 1850; 7th edition, 12mo, 1863. 4. 'Daughter of Christian England,' a poem on Miss Nightingale's mission to Scutari, 12mo, London, 1854. 5. 'His Presence, not his Memory,' poems, 1855; 2nd edition, 1858; 3rd edition, 8vo, London, 1860; 8th edition, London, 1881. 6. 'Spiritual Songs for the Sundays and Holidays throughout the Year,' 8vo, London, 1857; 2nd edition, 1859. 7. 'Hymns of Love and Praise for the Church's Year,' 8vo, London, 1863; 2nd edition, London, 1866. 8. 'The Passing Bell, and other Poems,' 1867; 2nd edition, 16mo, London, 1869. 9. 'Our New Vicar, or Plain Words on Ritual and Parish Work,' 8vo, London, 1867. 10. 'Lights and Shadows,' 'by the Old Vicar,' 16mo, 1868. 11. 'Litany Hymns,' 1869. 12. 'Teachings of the Epiphany,' 8vo, London, 1871. 13. 'The Winton Church Catechist,' in 4 parts, 16mo, London, 1871. 14. 'Nursery Carols,' 8vo, London, 1873. 15. 'The Parish Hymnal,' a collection edited by him, 16mo, London, 1873. 16. 'Simon the Cyrenian, and other Poems,' 16mo, London, 1876. 17. 'Near Home at Last,' verse, 16mo, London, 1876.

[Wilson's Singers and Songs of the Church, 1869, p. 515; Julian's Dict. of Hymnology, p. 762; Brit. Mus. Cat.; Todd's List of Dublin Graduates; O'Donoghue's Poets of Ireland, p. 164.] D. J. O'D.

MONSEY, MESSENGER (1693–1788), physician, born in 1693, was eldest son of Robert Monsey, some time rector of Bawdeswell, Norfolk, but ejected as a nonjuror, and his wife Mary, daughter of the Rev. Roger Clopton. (The family of Monsey or Mounsey is supposed to be derived from the Norman house of De Monceaux.) Monsey was educated at home, and afterwards at Pembroke College, Cambridge, where he graduated B.A. in 1714. He studied medicine at Norwich under Sir Benjamin Wrench, and was admitted extra licentiate of the College of Physicians on 30 Sept. 1723. He then settled in practice at Bury St. Edmund's, where he married. While at Bury Monsey had the good fortune to be called in to attend the Earl of Godolphin, who was taken ill on a journey, and recommended himself so well by his skill or by his wit that Godolphin induced him to come to London, and ultimately obtained for him the appointment of physician to Chelsea Hospital, at first without the obligation of residence. This post he held till his death.

Through Godolphin's influence Monsey was introduced to Sir Robert Walpole, Lord Chesterfield, and other members of the whig party, whose principles he warmly espoused. Among them he became so popular as to be considered the chief medical adviser of the politicians of that school. Always eccentric and rough in his manners, he treated his noble patrons with ostentatious familiarity. Walpole once asked how it was that no one but Monsey ever contradicted him. He also acquired connections of a literary kind with such people as Mrs. Elizabeth Montagu [q. v.] and Garrick. For many years he and the Earl of Bath were accounted rivals in a prolonged flirtation with Mrs. Montagu. Monsey's friendship with Garrick was broken off by an unfortunate quarrel, and he was never in favour with Dr. Johnson, who disapproved of his loose style of conversation. A specimen of his rhymed letters to Mrs. Montagu, in the manner of Swift, has been preserved, and shows him to have been a lively correspondent (J. Cordy Jeaffreson, *A Book about Doctors*; cf. Doran, *Lady of the Last Century*, pp. 70, 73, 132, 370).

In religion Monsey was a freethinker. Late in life his peculiarities became accentuated, till his coarse ribaldry and bearish demeanour made him the subject of innumerable anecdotes. It is reported that he was wont to receive with savage delight, in his old age, the expectants who were waiting for the reversion of his appointment at Chelsea Hospital, and came to inspect the place. The terrible old man used to prophesy to each that he would die before him, and in most cases his prediction proved true. He quarrelled with his colleagues, and lived the life of a lettered but morose hermit in Chelsea College. He had given directions that his body was to be dissected after death and the remnants thrown away. On 12 May 1787, when seriously ill, and thinking himself about to die, he wrote to W. C. Cruikshank, the anatomist, begging him to dissect his body after death, as he feared his own surgeon, Mr. Forster, who was then at Norwich and had undertaken the duty, might return too late. He died at Chelsea College 26 Dec. 1788. The post-mortem examination was, it is said, actually made by Mr. Forster before the students of Guy's Hospital.

Monsey was buried at Chelsea; but in 1868 a tablet was erected to his memory by his descendants, John Collyer and John Monsey Collyer, in the church of Whitwell, now Hackford, Norfolk, a small manor which he had inherited from his father, whom he commemorated in a similar manner.

He left an only daughter, who married William Alexander, elder brother of the first Earl of Caledon, and was grandmother of Robert Monsey Rolfe, the first lord Cranworth, lord chancellor.

The College of Physicians possesses a fine portrait in oils of Monsey, painted by Mary Black in 1764. A singular drawing of him in extreme old age, by Forster, was engraved by Bromley. A caricature portrait in colours, entitled 'Ornaments of Chelsea Hospital,' was published 19 Jan. 1789, without any artist's name, but with some irreverent verses by Peter Pindar, which have been wrongly attributed to Monsey himself. Some manuscript letters and verses by Monsey are in the library of the Royal College of Surgeons of England.

[Sketch of the Life and Character of the late Dr. Monsey, London, 1789, 8vo (anon.); J. Cordy Jeaffreson's Book about Doctors, partly from original documents; Munk's Coll. of Phys. 1878, ii. 84; information kindly supplied by J. B. Bailey, esq.] J. F. P.

MONSON, GEORGE (1730–1776), Indian officer and opponent of Warren Hastings, born 18 April 1730, in Arlington Street, London, was third and youngest son of John, first lord Monson (1693–1748) [q. v.], and his wife, Lady Margaret Watson, youngest daughter of Lewis, first earl of Rockingham. At the age of nine he was sent to Westminster School, then under the mastership of Dr. Nicholls. He went to the continent in 1747, remained abroad a year or two, and was at Geneva 8 Nov. 1748. He received his commission of ensign in the 1st foot-guards 24 Nov. 1750. On 5 Jan. 1754 he received a lieutenant's commission, with rank of captain in the army. He was elected one of the members for the city of Lincoln in 1754, and re-elected in 1761, retaining his seat till 1768. In 1756 he was appointed one of the grooms of the bedchamber in the household of the young Prince of Wales; and he retained the post when the prince became king, 25 Nov. 1760. He exchanged from the guards into Draper's regiment (first the 64th and afterwards made the 79th), which was raised in 1757, and his major's commission in it bore date 18 Aug. 1757. He sailed for India with his regiment 5 March 1758, and reached Bombay 14 Nov. and Madras in February 1759. He was second in command at the siege of Pondicherry, 1760, and Colonel Eyre Coote was superseded in his favour by an order from the directors of the East India Company. But before Coote sailed from Bengal Monson was seriously wounded, and the conduct of affairs fell again into Coote's hands. The town surrendered on 14 Jan. 1761. Monson especially distinguished himself at the capture of Manilla, 1762. He became lieutenant-colonel in September 1760, and was on 20 Jan. 1761 given command of the 96th foot. He received the rank of brigadier-general in India 7 July 1763. At the peace of Paris he returned to England, was presented to the king 23 Dec. 1764, and assiduously supported Lord North in parliament. On 30 Nov. 1769 he became full colonel and aide-de-camp to the king, who said that 'though not a strong man he had excellent brains' (MERIVALE, *Life of Francis*, i. 326).

In the Regulating Act of 1773 he was named one of the supreme council of Bengal. He arrived at Calcutta, with his wife, on 19 Oct. 1774, and took his seat in the council on 25 Oct. His wife had been previously acquainted with Warren Hastings, and the governor-general welcomed him in a specially courteous and cordial letter (GLEIG, *Life of Warren Hastings*, i. 452–3). From the first he united with General (Sir John) Clavering [q. v.] and (Sir Philip) Francis [q. v.] in opposition to the policy of the governor-general. Hastings at first spoke well of him as 'a sensible man,' but before long he began to consider him even more dangerous than his colleagues. 'Colonel Monson, with a more guarded temper and a more regular conduct, now appears to be the most determined of the three. The rudeness of General Clavering and the petulancy of Francis are more provoking, but it is from the former only that I apprehend any effectual injury' (*ib.* p. 517). Monson was especially active in the affair of Nanda-Kumár (Nuncomar)—'he receives, and I have been assured even condescends to solicit, accusations' (*ib.* p. 516)—and himself moved that the rájá be called before the board to substantiate his charges against Hastings (FORREST, *Selections from State Papers, &c.*,

p. 305, 13 March 1775). He refused, however, to take any part in saving his life after he was convicted of forgery (SIR JAMES STEPHEN, *Nuncomar and Impey*, i. 232–3; see art. IMPEY, SIR ELIJAH).

Monson engaged also in the conflict with the supreme court, severely condemning the conduct of the judges in a minute of 11 April 1775 (*ib.* ii. 133). Throughout he appears to have been almost entirely under the influence of Francis, 'who ruled him by making him believe that he was ruled by him,' but who found him very difficult to manage. He was, says Impey, 'a proud, rash, self-willed man, though easily misled and very greedy for patronage and power' (MERIVALE, i. 326).

Accusations of corruption were made against him (GLEIG, i. 511), but doubtless without foundation. He repeatedly expressed aversion even to the customary presents (FORREST, p. 130). Possibly his opposition to Hastings was embittered by illness, for he suffered almost from the day of his arrival in India. He was soon 'obliged to go to sea to save his life' (BUSTEED, *Echoes of Old Calcutta*, from Francis's *Diary*, p. 154); he recovered for a time, and resigned his position in September 1776 with the intention of returning to England, but he died on the 25th of the same month. He was made colonel of the 50th foot 1 Sept. 1775, and before news of his death reached England he had been promoted to the rank of lieutenant-general.

He married in 1757 Lady Anne Vane, daughter of Henry, earl of Darlington, and widow of the Hon. Charles Hope Weir, who was four years his senior. Her mother was Lady Grace Fitzroy, and she was thus a great-granddaughter of Charles II. There was some scandal about her early life; she was a prominent figure in Calcutta society and 'a very superior whist-player' (MACRABIE, *Diary*). She died on 18 Feb. 1776. They had no children.

[Information kindly supplied by Viscount Oxenbridge; The Selections from the Letters, Despatches, and other State Papers preserved in the Foreign Department of the Government of India, ed. G. W. Forrest, Calcutta, 1890, the primary authority for the most important part of Monson's life; Gleig's Life of Warren Hastings; Mill's History of British India, ed. H. H. Wilson, vol. iii.; Sir J. F. Stephen's Nuncomar and Impey; Collins's Peerage, 5th edit. 1779, vii. 289; Busteed's Echoes of Old Calcutta; Parker and Merivale's Life of Philip Francis.] W. H. H.

MONSON, SIR JOHN (1600–1683), second baronet, royalist, eldest son of Sir Thomas Monson [q. v.] of Carlton in Lincolnshire, and of his wife Margaret, daughter of Sir Edmund Anderson [q. v.], lord chief justice of the common pleas, was born in the parish of St. Sepulchre, London, in 1600. Sir William Monson (1569–1643) [q. v.], naval commander, was his uncle, and care must be taken to distinguish him from his uncle's son, also Sir John Monson. Sir William Monson (*d.* 1672?) [q. v.] was his brother. John, who was not entered at either of the universities, studied law in London, represented the city of Lincoln in the first parliament of Charles I (elected 25 April 1625), and the county of Lincoln in the second parliament, and was made knight of the Bath by Charles at his coronation, 2 Feb. 1625–6.

In 1635, in view of the necessity of reclaiming and draining the low-lying lands by the banks of the river Ancholme in Lincolnshire, the commissioners for the Fens endeavoured to negotiate with 'some foreign undertakers' for the carrying out of the works, but failed to come to terms. Thereupon Monson offered himself as undertaker, 'out of a noble desire to serve his country,' and his services were accepted (DUGDALE, *Imbanking and Draining*, p. 151). The drainage was completed to the satisfaction of the commissioners on 19 Feb. 1638–9, and 5,827 acres of the reclaimed land were allotted to Monson on 4 March following, in accordance with previous arrangement. Complaints and dissatisfaction, however, arose among the neighbouring landlords. An order made in 1635 by Monson as justice of the peace for Lincolnshire condemned the moral character of John Pregion, registrar of Lincoln. When the Bishop of Lincoln [see WILLIAMS, JOHN, archbishop of York] was brought before the Star-chamber in 1637, on a charge of revealing counsels of state, Pregion was one of the bishop's leading witnesses, and Williams endeavoured to obtain a reversal of Monson's judgment. But Monson's decision was upheld, and he was awarded a thousand marks compensation out of the bishop's fine (cf. Monson's letters to Laud, of 11 Dec. 1635 and 9 Aug. 1606, and his petition to the king in *Lambeth MSS.*)

In 1641 Monson succeeded to his father's baronetcy. His legal acumen had been noticed by the king, and he offered Charles much useful advice during his disagreements with the parliament (1640–2). On the departure of Charles from London, Monson retired to Oxford, where, on 1 (or 2) Nov. 1642, he was created D.C.L. In 1643, when the proximity of the armies threatened the safety of Oxford, Monson sent his wife to London, while he remained behind to take part in the negotiations. In May 1646 Fairfax demanded the surrender of the town, and Monson and Philip Warwick were sent (11 May) to confer with him. Monson was one of the fourteen commissioners for Oxford who met the parliamentary commissioners at 'Mr. Crooke's house at Marston' on 18 May, and for a month was actively occupied in framing the articles for the surrender of the town (agreed to on 22 June). His conduct throughout gained for him the respect of both parties. Subsequently he applied for and was granted permission to compound for his estates on the terms granted by the Oxford articles, according to which the fine should not exceed two years of the revenue. But he failed to pay the composition, and the estate was ordered to be sequestered on 8 March 1648. Sir Thomas Fairfax and Cromwell both deemed his usage needlessly severe, but it was not until July 1651 that parliament removed the sequestration. In December 1652 Monson signed the engagement to the Commonwealth. He was again in difficulties at the end of 1655, when he refused to pay the decimation tax, levied to meet insurrection, and was imprisoned in his own house, but he was discharged from further proceedings on 22 Jan. 1656-7.

During the civil wars Monson's drainage works were injured and neglected. On his petition (15 Dec. 1654) the business was referred to the committee for the Fens, without result, but he petitioned again on 14 May 1661, and, despite the opposition of two of the Fen towns—Winterton and Bishop Norton—a bill confirming Monson's former privileges was passed by parliament early in 1662. As guardian and trustee for John Sheffield, third earl of Mulgrave and duke of Buckinghamshire (1649-1720), Monson undertook in December 1663 to farm the earl's alum mines at Mulgrave in Yorkshire, allowing the king almost half the profits. He died on 29 Dec. 1683, and was buried at South Carlton. He built and endowed a free school in South Carlton and a hospital in Burton, and left money to the towns in Lincolnshire of which he was lord.

Monson married Ursula, daughter of Sir Robert Oxenbridge of Hurstbourne in Hampshire. Through his wife he became possessed in 1645 of the manor of Broxbourne in Hertfordshire, which was the seat of the family for many years. His widow died in December 1692. His only son, John (1628-1674), M.P. for Lincoln from 1660 till his death, and made K.B. 20 April 1660, was father of both Henry (1653-1718), third baronet, who was M.P. for Lincoln from 1675 to 1689, and high sheriff for the county in 1685 and 1688; and of William (1654-1727), fourth baronet, who was M.P. for Lincoln and high sheriff of the county in 1695. The fourth baronet's nephew and successor, John Monson, first baron Monson, is separately noticed.

Monson published: 1. 'A Short Essay of Afflictions. Or, Balm to Comfort if not Cure those that Sinke or Languish under present Misfortunes,' London, 1647 (anon.) Monson's name can be spelt out from a curious monogram on the title-page. It was written as advice to his son while he was in the garrison at Oxford. After the Restoration it was reprinted. 2. 'An Antidote against the Errors and Opinions of many in their days, concerning some of the Highest and Chiefest Duties of Religion' (anon.), London, 1647, 1661-2. 3. 'A Short Answer to several Questions proposed to a Gentleman of Quality by a great Minister of State' (anon.), London, 1678. 4. 'A Discourse concerning Supreme Power and Common Right. By a Person of Quality,' London, 1680.

[Jacob's Peerage, ii. 531; Visitation of Lincolnshire, Harl. MS. No. 1550, f. 69; Cal. State Papers, Dom. Ser. 1611-66; Metcalfe's Knights, p. 186; Official Returns of Members of Parliament, pt. i. pp. 464, 470, 525, 536, 542, 543, 560, pt. ii. pp. 46, 53, 64; Dugdale's Imbanking and Draining, pp. 151-3; Wood's Fasti (Bliss), vol. ii. cols. 40-1; Foster's Alumni Oxon. 1500-1714; Lords' Journals, iv. 254, vi. 806, x. 222-5, xi. 395, 397, 398, 399, 406, 473; Commons' Journals, vi. 610-11, vii. 402, viii. 186, 248, 252, 257, 296, 374; Rushworth's Hist. Collections, ii. 416 et seq.; Hacket's Life of Williams, pt. ii. pp. 123, 128; Rossingham's News Letter; State Papers, Car. I, 1637, vol. ccclxiii. f. 119; Lambeth MS. 1030, ff. 39, 40, 41, 42, 48; The Passage of the Treaty for the Surrender of Oxford, pp. 1-3 (E. 337 [30]); The Kingdom's Weekly Intelligencer, 12-19 May 1646; Notes and Queries, 2nd ser. x. 64-5, 95-6, 136; Cal. of the Committee for the Advance of Money, pp. 745, 1047; Cal. of the Committee for Compounding, pp. 623, 1431-3, 2047-8; contemporary sheet respecting Monson's bill (816, m. 8 [20]); Foster's Peerage; Hist. MSS. Comm. 11th Rep. pt. ii. pp. 74-5; Clutterbuck's Hertfordshire, ii. 55; Chauncey's Antiquities of Hertfordshire, pp. 289-90; Kennett's Reg. p. 410; Tables of the High Sheriffs of the County of Lincoln, p. 38; Harl. Soc. Publications, x. 12, xxiv. 132, 189, xxxi. 134, 254; P. C. C. 6 Hare, 81 Tenison, 68 Farrant, 247 Straham, Admon. Act Book, 1674; information from the Rev. John Salwey of Broxbourne.] B. P.

MONSON, SIR JOHN, first BARON MONSON (1693-1748), son of George Monson of Broxbourne, Hertfordshire, by Anne, daughter of Charles Wren of the Isle of Ely, was born in 1693. He matriculated from Christ Church, Oxford, on 26 Jan. 1708. On 4 April

1722 he was returned to parliament for the city of Lincoln, and was re-elected on 30 Aug. 1727. Created a knight of the Bath (17 June 1725), when that order was reconstituted by George I, he succeeded to the family baronetcy, in March 1727, on the death of his uncle Sir William. On 28 May of the following year he was created a peer, with the title of Baron Monson of Burton, Lincolnshire. Lord Hervey in mentioning him among the new creations calls him wrongly Sir William (*Mem.* i. 89). In June 1733 Monson was named captain of the band of gentlemen pensioners, and in June 1737 was appointed first commissioner of trade and plantations. In this office he was confirmed when the board was reconstituted in 1745, and he continued to hold it till his death. He was also, on 31 July 1737, made a privy councillor.

Monson died on 20 July 1748, and the Duke of Newcastle, in a letter to the Duke of Bedford, dated 12 Aug. 1748, condoles with him upon 'the loss of so valuable a man and so amiable a friend,' and Bedford in reply uses similar expressions of regret (*Bedford Corr.* i. 440–1). By his wife, Lady Margaret Watson, youngest daughter of Lewis, first earl of Rockingham, whom he married on 8 April 1725, he had three sons, viz. John, second baron Monson (see below); Lewis Thomas, who assumed the name of Watson, and was created Baron Sondes in 1760; and George Monson [q. v.]

John Monson, second baron (1727–1774), born 23 July 1727, was created LL.D. of Cambridge University in 1749. On 5 Nov. 1765 he was appointed warden and chief justice in eyre of the forests south of Trent (*Gent. Mag.* 1765, p. 539). On the fall of the first Rockingham ministry he was offered an earldom on the condition that he would relinquish the place; he declined the proposal (Rockingham, *Mem.* ii. 17, 18; and Walpole, *Mem. George III*, ii. 368). He ultimately resigned with Portland and other whigs on 27 Nov. (Rockingham, *Mem.* ii. 25); but is mentioned by Walpole (*Mem. of George III*, ii. 454) as subsequently voting with the court on Bedford's motion that the privy council should take notice of the action of the Massachusetts assembly in pardoning the late insurrection. In 1768 he signed a protest against the bill to limit the dividends of the East India Company (*Protests of the Lords*, ii. 98). Monson died at his house in Albemarle Street on 23 July 1774 (*Gent. Mag.* p. 334). He married, 23 June 1752, Theodosia, daughter of John Maddison, esq., of Harpswell, Lincolnshire, by whom he had five sons and two daughters. His fourth son, William (1760–1807), is separately noticed.

[Lodge's Genealogy of the Peerage; Foster's Peerage and Alumni Oxon. 1500–1714; Hist. Reg. 1725 p. 25, 1728 p. 30, 1733 p. 30, 1737 p. 8; Gent. Mag. 1733, p. 328; Return of Members of Parl.; authorities cited above.] G. Le G. N.

MONSON, ROBERT (*d.* 1583), judge, was the second son of William Monson of South Carlton, Lincolnshire, by Elizabeth, daughter of Sir Robert Tyrwhitt of Kettelby in the same county, of which he was a native. The Monsons, Mounsons, or Munsons, as the name was variously spelt, belonged to an old Lincolnshire family, tracing their descent from one John Monson, living in 1378 at East Reson. Robert studied at Cambridge and entered, 23 Jan. 1545–6, Lincoln's Inn, where he was called to the bar 2 Feb. 1549–1550, elected reader in the autumn of 1565—his reading 'On the Act for the True Payment of Tithes' is extant in Harl. MS. 5265—and again in Lent 1570. In the first parliament of Queen Mary (5 Oct.–5 Dec. 1553) he sat for Dunheved, Cornwall, in the second (2 April–5 May 1554) for Looe in the same county, and in the third (12 Nov. 1554–16 Jan. 1554–5) for Newport-juxta-Launceston. In the parliament of 1557–8 he again represented Dunheved. In the first two parliaments of Elizabeth (1558–9–1566–7) he sat for Lincoln, in the fourth, which met in 1572, for Totnes, Devonshire. In the house he acted with Robert Bell [q. v.], sat on many important committees, and distinguished himself by boldness of speech, particularly in the autumn of 1566, when he offended the queen by the persistence with which he pressed for a direct answer to a petition of both houses praying her to marry and nominate her successor in the event of her death without issue. This, however, did not prevent his being placed on the high court of ecclesiastical commission on its renewal in 1570, and in Michaelmas term 1572 he was called to the degree of serjeant-at-law by special mandate of the queen, and immediately afterwards raised to the bench of the common pleas (31 Oct.)

Monson was a member of a special commission, appointed 11 May 1575, for the examination of suspected anabaptists. Most of the heretics recanted, but two Dutchmen, John Peters and Henry Turnwert, stood firm, and on 22 July were burned at West Smithfield. In December 1577 Monson gave an extra-judicial opinion in favour of the legality of punishing non-attendance at church by fine. For questioning the legality of the sentence passed on John Stubbs [q. v.] for his pamphlet against the French match he was committed to the Fleet in November 1579. He was released in the following

February, and had leave to go down into Lincolnshire; nor did he ever resume his seat on the bench, though fines continue to be recorded as levied before him until the middle of Easter term, when he formally resigned. His successor, William Peryam, however, was not appointed until February 1580–1.

Monson spent the rest of his days on his estate in Lincolnshire, where he died on 23 Sept. 1583. He was buried in Lincoln Cathedral, his tomb being marked by a brass with a quaint Latin inscription (see Collins, *Peerage*, ed. Bridges, vii. 230. Other versions, given in Peck's 'Desiderata Curiosa,' lib. viii. No. viii. § iii., Cooper's 'Athenæ Cantabr.,' and Foss's 'Lives of the Judges,' are in various ways corrupt). Monson married Elizabeth, daughter of Sir John Dyson, by whom he had no issue. She survived him.

Monson's decisions are reported by Dyer, Coke, and Plowden. Two letters relating to a lawsuit in which he was engaged, both dated in November 1576, and addressed to Walsingham and Burghley respectively, are preserved in Lansd. MS. 23, art. 85, and the State Paper Office (see *Cal. State Papers*, Dom. 1547–80, p. 530).

[Lincoln's Inn Reg.; Dugdale's Orig. pp. 48, 253, and Chron. Ser. pp. 92, 93; Lists of Members of Parliament (Official); Willis's Not. Parl. vol. iii.; Sir Simonds D'Ewes's Journal of the Parliaments of Elizabeth, ed. 1682, pp. 103, 159, 164, 176–90, 207, 220–2; Hist. MSS. Comm. 9th Rep. App. (Cal. Cecil MSS.), p. 341; Parker Corresp. (Parker Soc.), pp. 370, 383, 390; Strype's Parker (fol.), ii. 327; Strype's Grindal (fol.), p. 233; Strype's Annals (fol.), i. 530; Cal. State Papers, Dom. 1547–80, p. 530; Rymer's Fœdera, xv. 740; Fuller's Church Hist. bk. iv. p. 104; Harl. MS. 6992, art. 59; Lodge's Illustr. (4to), ii. 224; Dyer's Reports, p. 310; authorities cited in the text.] J. M. R.

MONSON, Sir THOMAS (1564–1641), master of the armoury at the Tower, eldest surviving son of Sir John Monson, knight, by Jane, daughter of Robert Dighton of Little Sturton, Lincolnshire, and elder brother of Admiral Sir William Monson [q. v.], was born in 1564 at his father's manor at South Carlton, Lincolnshire. Robert Monson [q. v.] was his granduncle. Thomas matriculated, aged fifteen, 9 Dec. 1579, from Magdalen College, Oxford, but left the university without a degree. He was created M.A. on 30 Aug. 1605, when he accompanied James I on a visit to Oxford. He was knighted the year of the Armada (1588), and in 1593 succeeded to all his father's estates in Lincolnshire and to Dunham Manor in Nottinghamshire. He first entered parliament on 10 Oct. 1597 as member for Lincoln county, sat for Castle Rising in 1603–4, and Cricklade in 1614 (*Official Returns*).

He became a favourite with James I, who made him his master falconer early in his reign, 'such a faulconer,' says Weldon, 'as no prince in Christendom ever had, for what flights other princes had he would excell them for his master, in which one was at the kite.' Weldon adds an account of a trial of skill between Monson and some French falconers (*Secret History of James I*, pp. 412 sq.) One preferment rapidly followed another. He was at first appointed chancellor to Anne of Denmark, then keeper of the armoury at Greenwich, and in June 1611 master of the armoury at the Tower. On 29 June 1611 a baronetcy was granted to him, and the next year he was made keeper of the naval and other warlike instruments at the Tower.

But his posts at the Tower proved his temporary ruin, for he was accused of complicity in the Overbury poisoning case in October 1615, and imprisoned [see Overbury, Sir Thomas]. The chief indictments were that he recommended Weston as Overbury's keeper by the Countess of Somerset's desire; that he was a friend of Northampton, and concerned in the correspondence between Overbury and Somerset; but beyond the fact that Sir Gervase Helwys [q. v.] died openly accusing Northampton and Monson of complicity, there is no circumstantial evidence against him, and he 'stedfastly affirmed his innocency.'

The case, however, proved more complicated than at first appeared. On 30 Nov. Monson appeared at the bar in the Guildhall, but was remanded till 4 Dec., when the indictment was read, and he pleaded not guilty. Coke abused him as a papist, and hinted that he was accused of worse crimes, alluding mysteriously to Prince Henry's sudden death. The trial was stopped and Monson remanded to the Tower 20 Dec. 1615. Weldon's story that James had interrupted the trial for fear of disagreeable revelations is refuted by the fact that the king was then at Newmarket, too far off to interpose. Coke certainly had a personal spite against Monson, and finding the evidence insufficient to condemn him probably hurried him back to the Tower for fear of a favourable verdict. The story that he made him walk on foot in the rain is denied by an eye-witness who saw him in Sir George More's [q. v.] coach. The acquittal might also have been unfavourable to the prosecution of Somerset. Though the king is reported to have seen 'nothing worthy of death or bonds' in Monson's case, he remained some months in prison, 'evermore discoursing of his innocency.' He had the liberty of the Tower in August 1616, and in October was let out on bail for a year. Coke's fall operated in his favour. On 12 Feb. 1617 Bacon and Yelverton both agreed that a fresh trial was unadvisable, since the evidence was purely conjectural, and to 'rip up those matters now' would be a mistake on the king's part. They therefore advised that Monson should plead his innocence again publicly and receive pardon. Accordingly, Monson was brought to the bar of the king's bench; his pardon was read; he affirmed his innocence, and reflected on Coke's treatment of him (22 Feb. 1617).

Although released, he was not restored to royal favour till 1620, when he was allowed to kiss hands. His posts had all been taken from him in 1615, and his affairs seem to have become embarrassed. In 1620 he had to lease his lands in Lincolnshire to pay his debts, and there are various petitions about his money matters in the state paper office. In 1625 he received the small office of clerk for the king's letters, bills, and declarations before the council of the north; about 1618 he and his son John had a grant of the stewardship of the duchy of Lancaster.

Monson spent his old age in retirement. He amused himself by writing a book of advice for his grandson: 'An Essay on Afflictions,' printed 1661–2, and another on 'Fasting, Adoration, and Prayer.' He was an accomplished man, 'a great lover of music.' He seems to have educated young musicians 'as good as England had,' especially singers, in his household, and 'was at infinite charge in breeding some [singers] in Italy.' His enemies called him 'proud and odious.' He died at South Carlton in May 1641, aged 77, and was buried 29 May in the church there. By his wife Margaret (*d.* 1630), daughter of Sir Edmund Anderson [q. v.], lord chief justice of the common pleas, he had four sons, three of whom lived to maturity, and four daughters. His eldest son, Sir John (1600–1683), and the second, Sir William (*d.* 1672?), are separately noticed.

[Collins's Peerage, 1779, vii. 284; Carew's Letters, pp. 17, 20, 363; State Trials, ii. 949; Amos's Great Oyer of Poisoning, p. 213, &c.; Wilson's Truth brought to Light; Nichols's Progresses of James I, i. 164, 555, ii. 24 *n.*, 452; Oxf. Univ. Registers, i. 237, ii. 89; State Papers, James I, 1603–36; Gardiner's History, ii. 180, 334, 345, 363; Lives of Bacon and Coke, &c.] E. T. S.

MONSON, Sir WILLIAM (1569–1643), admiral, was the third son of Sir John Monson of South Carlton in Lincolnshire, where his family had been settled for many generations. On 2 May 1581 he matriculated from Balliol College, Oxford, being registered as then fourteen (Foster, *Alumni Oxon.*); but he himself has recorded that in 1585, being then sixteen, he went off to sea without the knowledge of his mother or father, and entered on board a ship with letters of reprisal. After a long cruise, they fell in with a Biscay ship one September evening. A very severe fight followed. The English boarded the Spaniard; but the sea got up and their ship was obliged to cast off, leaving her men to their fate. The struggle went on all night; and the next morning, most of the English and nearly all the Spaniards being killed or wounded, the ship was surrendered. She was the first Spanish prize, Monson says, that ever saw the English shore. The success confirmed him in his adventurous career, and, having been reconciled to his father, he was put in command of a private ship of war, in which he cruised as far as the Canaries. The voyage lasted longer than was expected; their provisions ran short, and with great difficulty, in storm and fog, they made Dingle Bay in Ireland, just as they were reduced to their last biscuit.

In 1588 Monson was lieutenant of the Charles, a small queen's ship, one of the fleet against the Armada; and in 1589 he commanded the Margaret, one of the ships with the Earl of Cumberland in his voyage to the Azores and the Canaries [see Clifford, George, third Earl of Cumberland]. The Margaret was sent home with some of the prizes, while Monson, moving into the Victory, remained with the earl. They were unable to water at the Canaries, and were reduced to very terrible straits on the homeward voyage. 'The extremity we endured,' says Monson, 'was more terrible than befel any ship in the eighteen years' war;' but when he adds 'for sixteen days together we never tasted drop of drink, either beer, wine, or water' (*Naval Tracts*, 461), it is quite certain that his memory was guilty of some exaggeration. Privation and suffering brought on a severe illness, and for the next year Monson remained on shore. In 1591 he commanded the Garland in Cumberland's expedition to the coast of Spain, and was left in charge of a Dutch ship with a Portuguese cargo. She was recaptured by the Spaniards, and Monson became a prisoner. For two years he was detained, part of the time on board the galleys at Cascaes or in the Tagus, and part of the time in the castle of Lisbon. Although not actually ill-used, the treatment of a prisoner was severe, the confinement was close, and the daily allowance for food was equivalent to threepence. One day he saw a 'sumptuous galeon,' named the St. Andrew, sailing up the river, and laid a wager of one to ten that if he lived he would be at the taking of her, which he actually was, at Cadiz, in 1596.

In 1593, Monson, having been released, joined Cumberland in the Golden Lion, a queen's ship. They captured a fleet of Spanish ships laden with powder, and Monson was left to examine half of them, while Cumberland took the rest out to sea. Towards night he released them, without taking any precautions; they accordingly returned to attack Monson, who, having no adequate force with him, jumped into his boat on one side as they boarded on the other, receiving a hurt in the leg which he felt all the rest of his life. Cumberland afterwards fell sick; he longed for milk, and Monson, going on shore at Corvo, in the Azores, brought off a cow, and then, with the earl, returned to England. In 1594 Monson took his M.A. degree at Oxford, and in 1595 he married. He had previously engaged to go to sea with Cumberland, and very shortly after his marriage took command of the Allsides, 'a goodly ship of the merchants,' Cumberland himself being in the Malice Scourge. They sailed from Plymouth; but when they had got some eight or nine leagues to sea, Cumberland went back, leaving the Malice Scourge in command of another captain, without holding any communication with Monson, which, he says, 'did so much disconcert me for the present, that I abandoned the company of his ship at sea, and betook myself to my own adventure. This bred an after quarrel betwixt my lord and me, and it was a long time before we were reconciled' (*ib.* p. 462). His solitary cruise had no success, and after being nearly lost in a violent storm, he arrived at Plymouth just in time to go out with Drake and look for some Spanish ships which had sacked Penzance. The Spaniards had, however, departed, with 'the poor spoil they found in the town, not worth their labour.' In the following year Monson commanded the Repulse in the expedition against Cadiz [see Devereux, Robert, second Earl of Essex; Howard, Charles, Earl of Nottingham]. He landed with Essex, and with him, in some sharp fighting, won his way to the market-place. He had one or two narrow escapes, one shot smashing the hilt of his sword as it hung by his side, 'without any further hurt.' This, he says, was the second time his sword had preserved his life; the first was in 1589, at the island of St. Mary's. For his conduct on this occasion he was knighted by Essex.

In the Islands' voyage, the next year, Monson commanded the Rainbow; and in 1599 commanded the Defiance in the Downs, under Lord Thomas Howard. During the two following years he was continuously in the Downs and Narrow Seas, in command of the Garland, Nonpareil, Swiftsure, Mary Rose, and Mer Honour; but nothing called for any active service. 'Never,' wrote Monson, 'was greater expectation of war with less performance.' Early in 1602 a squadron of nine ships was ordered to sea, under the command of Sir Richard Leveson [q. v.], to intercept the Spanish treasure fleet. Monson, as vice-admiral of the squadron, was left to wait for the arrival of the Dutch contingent, but on further orders from the queen, he sailed without it to join Leveson. The delay was fatal to the intended blow, for Leveson, having met the treasure fleet before he was joined by Monson, was unable to effect anything against them; and the sole result of the cruise was the capture of eleven galleys and a richly laden carrack at Cezimbra, after a stubborn fight on 3 June, with, to Monson, the special gratification of finding among the prizes the galley on board which he had been a prisoner eleven years before. Leveson then returned to England, leaving Monson in the Nonpareil, to command on the coast of Portugal, and in daily expectation of being joined by the Dutch ships and other reinforcements. A succession of bad weather obliged him to bear for England; but on intelligence that the Spaniards were meditating another attempt on Ireland, he was at once ordered back to keep watch off Corunna. There he learned that the fleet, which had been suspected of a design against Ireland, had gone to Lisbon. Thither Monson followed. But his squadron was scattered in a storm; he had with him, besides his own ship, the Swiftsure, only two others, one of which was but a pinnace, when, on the night of 26 Sept., he fell in among the Spanish fleet, and on the morning of the 27th was seen and chased. The enemy were fast coming up with the pinnace, which sailed badly and was of no force, when Monson, 'resolving not to see a pinnace of her majesty's so lost if he could rescue her with the loss of his life,' shortened sail and waited for her; on which the leading Spaniards also shortened sail to wait for the rest of their ships. After this, Monson cruised for some time off Cape St. Vincent, and on 21 Oct. attempted to capture a galeon which took refuge under the guns of the castle. He was beaten off, and on 24 Nov. returned to England. It was the last squadron against the Spaniards in the time of Elizabeth, and Monson prided himself on having been engaged in the capture of the first Spanish prize that was taken to England, and on now being in command of the last fleet in the reign of Elizabeth.

Two other fleets were, indeed, ordered for the following spring, but the death of the queen changed the plans, and one fleet under Leveson and Monson was stationed to keep watch on the coast of France and Flanders, against any attempt to interfere with the succession. Monson at this time had his flag in the Mer Honour, while Leveson was ordered to hoist his on board the Repulse, a smaller ship. Monson's explanation of this is that the lords of the council feared Leveson's ambition, and though they would not take the extreme step of deposing him from the command, they appointed Monson as his second, in a larger ship, with the understanding that if any opposition was offered to the accession of James, Lord Thomas Howard, afterwards Earl of Suffolk, was to take command of the fleet on board the Mer Honour, and send Monson to the Repulse to supersede Leveson. The precaution, however, proved needless, and on the king's arrival in London the ships were ordered to Chatham.

In July 1604 Monson was appointed admiral of the narrow seas. He accepted the office with some misgiving, pointing out to Cecil (afterwards Earl of Salisbury) that he might be called on to prevent the Dutch and Spaniards from fighting in English waters; after the long alliance with Holland, after the long war with Spain, the Dutch had come to consider it their right and in the natural course of things to attack the Spaniards wherever they met them. This forecast was soon verified. During the war the right of the flag had been waived in favour of the Dutch, and they were unwilling now again to recognise it; they enforced the blockade of the coast of Flanders and seized any English vessels that attempted to break it; their ships came into the Downs and made no secret of their intention to seize any Spaniard that might be there. At Monson's request a proclamation prohibited 'all nations from offering violence one to another, within the compass of a line drawn from headland to headland.' On 10 May 1605, when Monson anchored in the Downs, he found there six Dutch ships which had come in, with the evident intention of seizing a Dunkirker, then lying in the harbour of Sandwich. Monson made the Dutch captains acquainted with the proclamation; and on their refusing to obey it, he angrily answered that if one shot was fired at the Dunkirker, he would sink them. In the end they permitted the ship to escape (*ib.* p. 213). Such incidents were constantly recurring, and obtained for Monson the cordial hatred of the Dutch.

An important part of his duty at this time was the carrying ambassadors or princely visitors backwards and forwards across the Channel or to Spain. These, with their retinue, numbering sometimes as many as three hundred persons, were on board perhaps a day, or it might be a month. During this time their maintenance was at the admiral's cost, amounting, he says, between 1604 and 1616 to not less than 1,500*l.*, which was never repaid him. Another extremely important service which he was called on to perform was the suppression of the pirates, who had established themselves in the creeks, lochs, and firths of the west of Scotland, among the Hebrides, and still more on the west coast of Ireland. In 1614, after searching along the coast of Scotland and through the islands, Monson arrived in the end of June at Broad Haven, in co. Mayo, 'the well-head of all pirates.' Here he found that the most friendly relations existed between the pirates and the natives; and when he led the latter to believe that he too was a pirate, he and his people were entertained with the utmost cordiality. The men, and still more the women, received them with open arms; and in feasting, drinking, dancing, and love-making the days passed merrily, till Monson, having tracked out the whole organisation, suddenly seized all the principal persons of the neighbourhood, and for four-and-twenty hours kept them prisoners in the expectation of being hanged. He then released them with a caution; one only, an Englishman, who had fraudulently obtained a pass from the sheriff, being sent out of the country. The Irish were, however, so frightened that a few days later they betrayed to Monson a large pirate vessel which incautiously ran into a neighbouring river. The pirates were brought prisoners to Broad Haven, and there the chief of them were hanged—scoundrels 'who had tasted twice before of his majesty's gracious pardon.' The executions struck such terror into the community that 'the pirates ever after became strangers to that harbour of Broad Haven, and in a little time wholly abandoned Ireland' (*ib.* p. 221).

In June 1611 Monson arrested the unfortunate Lady Arabella Seymour as she was escaping to France (*ib.* p. 210). Monson believed that he incurred the hatred of many for his share in the business; but he also believed that his being 'too forward in complaining, and wishing a reformation' of the navy had 'purchased him much envy,' and especially the ill-will of the Earl of Nottingham. That in later years Nottingham was no friend of his appears from his confining John, Monson's son, in the Gatehouse as 'a most dangerous papist' (*Cal. State Papers*, Dom. 20, 30 May 1623); but if his feelings towards Monson were all along as bitter as Monson loved to fancy, he would not have continued him for twelve years in the command of the narrow seas. In 1615 Monson's elder brother, Sir Thomas [q.v.], fell under suspicion of being mixed up with the murder of Overbury; Monson was involved in the same suspicion, and on 12 Jan. 1615–16 he was sent to the Tower (*Hist. MSS. Comm.* 12th Rep. i. 91). There was, however, no evidence against him, and in July he was released (Gardiner, ii. 346, 363, iii. 186). He was not, however, restored to his command, nor had he any employment at sea for nearly twenty years. He claims, indeed, to have been frequently consulted by the admiralty, and to have given his opinion freely on the several expeditions that were fitted out. It may, however, be doubted whether the very frank criticisms which he penned were communicated to any except a few trusted friends (*Naval Tracts*, pp. 223, 228, 244). The papers which we know to have been delivered are of a very different sort, such as a proposal for a lighthouse on the Lizard, or suggestions for the establishment of fishing stations in Orkney and Shetland, and of schools for the children of the islanders (*Cal. State Papers*, Dom. 4 Feb. 1624, November 1629).

Of the king's action in the matter of ship-money he approved. He was one of the few who could see the necessity of increasing the strength of the navy, who understood that the attitude of France and Holland was really dangerous; and for the constitutional question raised by Hampden he cared nothing. He was likewise eager to see a severe lesson given to the Dutch, whom he considered as personal enemies; and he distinctly approved of the policy which, in 1635, appointed him to be vice-admiral of the fleet, under the command of the Earl of Lindsey. The French and Dutch had formed a combined fleet off Portland, 'in the bragging pretence of questioning his majesty's prerogative on the narrow seas;' but on learning that the English fleet was at sea, they drew back to their own shores. Lindsey, however, remained out till October; during which time, says Monson, 'we made good our seas and shores, gave laws to our neighbour nations, and restored the ancient sovereignty of the narrow seas to our gracious king, as was ever due to his Majesty's progenitors' (*Naval Tracts*, p. 257).

This was Monson's last service. He retired to his seat at Kinnersley in Surrey, where during his remaining years he occupied himself in writing or arranging his 'Naval Tracts,' a work of greater interest and value for its pictures of the state of our own and other navies than for its historical narratives, which, written apparently from memory long years after the events recorded—events, too, which he had known only by hearsay—are not to be implicitly accepted. He died at Kinnersley in February 1642–3, and was buried at St. Martin's-in-the-Fields in London. He married in 1595 the daughter of one Goodwin, who was the widow of one Smith, and by her had a large family (Collins, vii. 241). One of his daughters, Jane, married Sir Francis, second son of Sir William Howard of Lingfield, and nephew of the great Earl of Nottingham (*ib.* p. 126). Of the sons, John, the younger, was the 'pestilent papist.' The elder, William, was put forward by Lord Suffolk in 1618 as a rival to Buckingham in the king's favour, though whether with his father's approval is doubtful.

[The principal authority for the Life of Monson is the Naval Tracts, to a large extent autobiographical, which form part of Churchill's Collection of Voyages, first issued in 1704. A few copies of Monson's Tracts were bound separately (with unaltered pagination) but with title-page variously dated 1703 and 1704. The edition of Churchill here referred to is that of 1732. The original manuscript, corrected for the press by the author, and dated 1624, is in Sloane MS. 2496, ff. 113–188. Another manuscript is in the possession of Lord Leconfield at Petworth. An excerpt was published in 1682 under the title of 'A True and Exact Account of the Wars with Spain in the Reign of Queen Elizabeth.' See also Cal. State Papers, Domestic; Gardiner's Hist. of England.] J. K. L.

MONSON, Sir WILLIAM, Viscount Monson of Castlemaine (*d.* 1672?), regicide, second son of Sir Thomas Monson [q. v.], by Margaret (*d.* 1630), daughter of Sir Edmund Anderson [q. v.], lord chief justice of common pleas, was raised to the peerage of Ireland as Viscount Monson of Castlemaine, co. Kerry, by letters patent dated 23 Aug. 1628 (Burke, *Extinct Peerage*, 1883, p. 371), and was knighted on 13 Aug. 1633 (Metcalfe, *Book of Knights*, p. 201). On the same day he became a member of Gray's Inn (*Register*, ed. Foster, p. 201). By his first marriage he acquired an estate at Reigate, Surrey (Brayley and Britton, *Surrey*, iv. 219–23), but owing to his dissolute habits he was soon in debt. He refused to pay ship-money (*Cal. State Papers*, Dom. 1637–8, p. 198), and when elected M.P. for Reigate, 21 Oct. 1640, he opposed the court, and subsequently acted as a committee-man for Surrey. On being nominated one of the king's judges, he attended on 20, 22, and 23 Jan. 1649, but refused to take part in the ultimate proceedings (NALSON, *Trial of Charles I*, ed. 1684). He was, however, placed by the parliament on the committee appointed to receive and take note of the dissent of any member from the vote of 5 Dec. 1648 (*Cal. State Papers*, Dom. 1649–50, p. 1). On 19 July 1649 he tried to persuade the house into the belief that the sum of 4,500*l.* was owing him as arrears of the pension due to his late wife the Countess of Nottingham (*Commons' Journals*, vi. 264), but he lost his motion by two votes. The Long parliament, when restored in May 1659, was obliged, in order to form a quorum, to send for Monson and Henry Marten [q.v.] from the Fleet prison, where they were both confined for debt (*England's Confusion*, 1659, p. 10).

At the Restoration he was excepted out of the bill of pardon as to pains and penalties, and upon surrendering himself on 21 June 1660 was recommitted to the Fleet. On 1 July 1661 he was brought up to the bar of the House of Commons, and, after being made to confess his crime, was degraded from all his honours and titles and deprived of his property. He was also sentenced to be drawn from the Tower through the city of London to Tyburn, and so back again, with a halter about his neck, and to be imprisoned for life (*Commons' Journals*, viii. 60, 70, 285–6). In petitioning the House of Lords on 25 July 1661 to remit what was most ignominious in his sentence, Monson declared that his design in sitting at the king's trial was, if possible, to prevent 'that horrid murder' (*Hist. MSS. Comm.* 7th Rep. pp. ix, 150). The ignominious part of the sentence was duly carried out each year on the anniversary of the king's sentence (27 Jan.; *Cal. State Papers*, Dom. 1661–2, p. 225; PEPYS, *Diary*, ed. Bright, i. 407, 528–9). Monson appears to have died in the Fleet prison about 1672. His estate at Reigate was granted to the Duke of York.

Monson married, first, Margaret (*d.* 1639), daughter of James Stewart, earl of Murray, and widow of Charles Howard, earl of Nottingham (1536–1624) [q. v.]; secondly, Frances, daughter of Thomas Alston of Polstead, Suffolk, by whom he left a son Alston (*d.* 1674 without issue); and thirdly, Elizabeth (*d.* 1695), second daughter of Sir George Reresby, knt., of Thrybergh, Yorkshire, widow of Sir Francis Foljambe, bart., of Aldwark in the same county, and of Edward, younger son of Sir John Horner of Mells, Somerset. By his last wife (who married, fourthly, Adam, eldest son of Sir Henry Felton, bart., of Playford, Suffolk) he had an only daughter, Elizabeth, married, first, to Sir Philip Hungate, bart., of Saxton, Yorkshire; and, secondly, to Lewis Smith of Wotton, Warwickshire (NICHOLS, *Collectanea*, ii. 82). At the intercession of her nephew, Sir John Reresby, Lady Monson was restored to her title of Viscountess Castlemaine (RERESBY, *Memoirs*, ed. Cartwright, p. 13).

[Noble's Lives of the English Regicides; Collins's Peerage, 1812, vii. 239–40; Commons' Journals, ii. 200, 549, 556, 955; The Traytor's Pilgrimage from the Tower to Tyburn.]

G. G.

MONSON, WILLIAM (1760–1807), Indian officer, fourth son of John, second baron Monson [see under MONSON, SIR JOHN, first baron], by his wife Theodosia, daughter of John Maddison of Harpswell, Lincolnshire, was born 15 Dec. 1760. In 1780 he received a commission in the 52nd regiment of infantry, with which he proceeded to India. By 5 Aug. 1785 he had risen to the rank of captain. Taking part in the war carried on by the English against Tippoo, sultan of Mysore, during the administration of Charles, lord Cornwallis [q. v.], he commanded a light company of the 52nd regiment, which successfully attacked the southern entrenchment of Seringapatam, Tippoo's capital, on 22 Feb. 1792. Monson continued in India after the peace, and had by September 1795 reached the rank of major. In 1797 he exchanged into the 76th English regiment, which had recently come out to India, and received the grade of lieutenant-colonel. On the outbreak of the Mahratta war in 1803 Monson was appointed by Lord Lake [see LAKE, GERARD] to the command of the first infantry brigade of the army destined for the invasion of the Mahratta dependencies in Northern India, and he led the storming party which took Allyghur on 4 Sept. 1803, receiving a severe wound, which incapacitated him from field duty for six months. In April 1804 Monson, now restored to health, and in high favour with Lord Lake, was sent, with a force of about four thousand men, all natives except the artillerymen, to keep watch on the large army of Jeswunt Rao Holkar, who was threatening our ally the rajah of Jeypore. Monson reached Jeypore on 21 April. Two days later Holkar broke up his camp and retreated southwards, Monson steadily following till the Mahratta chief crossed the Chumbul, when he was directed by Lord Lake to take up a position at Kotah, so as to guard against any attempt of Holkar to return north. He, however, persisted in advancing, on his own responsibility, due south, along the line of the Chumbul, thinking that a continued pursuit would cause Holkar to disband his army. But he had no sooner reached the village of Peeplah than Holkar, with an overwhelming force, estimated at seventy thousand strong, retraced his steps and took up a strong position at Rampoorah, on the banks of the Chumbul. Monson advanced up to the Mahratta camp in battle array. But Holkar gave no sign of alarm, and the English commander, losing his presence of mind, determined to retreat. The Mahrattas, flushed with triumph, started in pursuit. They annihilated his cavalry detachment, under Lieutenant Lucan, near Peeplah, but Monson, with the infantry, managed to escape. He marched by Mokundra and Tonk Rampura to Hindown, which was reached on 27 Aug. Monson's little force had been hotly pursued the whole way by Holkar's numerous cavalry, and owing to the bad state of the roads they had been compelled to abandon all their guns and baggage. A final and determined attempt was made by Holkar to bar Monson's path outside Hindown, but Monson's sepoys held firm, and the Mahrattas drew off. The remnant of Monson's corps straggled into Agra on 29 Aug. Only a few hundred out of the original force seem to have survived.

Monson's retreat inflicted a severe blow on English prestige. He himself was to blame, first for the advance beyond Kotah, and secondly for the movement up to the Mahratta camp, followed by a sudden retreat, which had the natural result of drawing the Mahrattas after him. On the other hand, Lake has been censured for sending Monson out with so small a force, and for not coming to his assistance the moment the retreat began. In spite of his defeat Monson was again employed by Lake in the final operations against Holkar in Northern India. At the battle of Deeg, 14 Nov. 1805, he acted as second in command to General Fraser, and on his superior being wounded Monson obtained the chief command, and the privilege of writing a report of the victory to Lord Wellesley. On 21 Feb. 1806 Monson was chosen by Lord Lake to head the last of the four unsuccessful assaults on Bhurtpoor. Monson now returned to England. In December 1806 he entered parliament as member for Lincoln. He died at Bath in December 1807.

Monson married at Calcutta, 10 Jan. 1786, Anne, youngest daughter of John Debonnaire. She died 26 Feb. 1841. Their only son, William John (1796–1862), became sixth Baron Monson in 1841, and the sixth baron's son and successor, William John, was created Viscount Oxenbridge in 1886, and was master of the horse in Mr. Gladstone's fourth ministry.

[Collins's Peerage, ed. 1812; Gent. Mag. 1807, pt. ii. p. 1235; Philippart's East India Military Calendar; Thorn's Last War in India against the Mahrattas; Grant Duff's Hist. of the Mahrattas; Cornwallis Corresp.; Wellesley Despatches (Owen's selections); Army Lists; Mill's Hist. of India; Malleson's Essay on Lord Lake, Calcutta Review, May 1866.] G. P. M-y.

MONT, MOUNT, MUNDT, or MONTABORINUS, CHRISTOPHER (*d.* 1572), English agent in Germany, was a native of Cologne. He seems from a passage in a letter of Melanchthon to have been brought up as a lawyer, and to have received the degree of D.C.L. He was made a denizen of England on 4 Oct. 1531, and entered Cromwell's service. Cromwell employed him, according to Chapuys, as a German servant, doubtless as an interpreter, and he spent his spare time in translating German chronicles into Latin, for which on one occasion he received 6*l.* 13*s.* 4*d.* (cf. *Letters and Papers Henry VIII*, ed. Gairdner, vi. 717 and 1448).

In July 1533 Mont and Vaughan, another of Cromwell's men, were sent by Henry VIII to Germany to report on the political situation there. They arrived at Nuremberg on 22 Aug., and thence Mont went to Augsburg to confer with the heads of the Suabian League or their deputies. Vaughan wished to go home, remarking that Mont could do as well as both. From this time onwards Mont was constantly employed in Germany, and only returned to England for short periods. He gave satisfaction to his masters from the outset (cf. *ib.* iv. 1374), and his salary was for some time more punctually paid than that of Henry's other servants. In January 1534 Nicholas Heath [q. v.] was sent out to join him (*ib.* vii. 166), and their instructions, which have been preserved, are obviously Henry's own composition. Their mission was to the German princes, to whom, the king said, they had to declare the whole progress of his great cause of matrimony, the intolerable injuries done him by the pope, and the means by which he intended to maintain his just cause (cf. FROUDE, ii. 199). As an advanced Lutheran Mont found the work congenial. On 26 June 1534 he was granted an annuity of 20*l.* for life. In July 1535 he was instructed with Dr. Simon Heynes [q. v.] to go unofficially into France, and there to counteract the influence which the French were bringing to bear on Germany; above all to invite Melanchthon to England. Contrary to expectation, Melanchthon was still in Germany, whither Mont went to find him, and though he could not induce Melanchthon to come to England, he induced him to abstain from visiting France. They became friends, and Melanchthon wrote of Mont later that he was a cultivated man (*Letters and Papers*, ix. 540, 593). During his residence in Germany he found the friendship of the leading reformers of very great service to him. Mont seems to have been skilful in answering unpleasant questions, and managed to reassure the Germans when in 1539 they were disturbed by Henry's refusal to allow the priests to marry. He had a still more difficult task in explaining Henry's conduct in regard to Anne of Cleves.

Early in Edward VI's reign he was living at Strasbourg, and he continued to act as agent, going on one occasion as ambassador to the senate of Zurich; his pension was also paid regularly. Under Mary he was recalled (*Acts of the Privy Council*, 1552–4, p. 346). But he regained his position when Elizabeth became queen, and kept it, though strongly opposed to the queen on the question of vestments. He lived as before chiefly at Strasbourg, where he died between 8 July and 15 Sept. 1572.

Many of his letters will be found in 'Zurich Letters,' 'Calendar of MSS. at Hatfield,' 'State Papers,' 'Letters and Papers of Henry VIII,' manuscripts at the Record Office, and the Cotton MSS. An interesting account by him of the progress of Lutheranism, written from Strasburg on 10 Oct. 1549 to the Duke of Somerset, was printed in 'Troubles connected with the Prayer Book of 1549' (Camd. Soc.), 110–11.

[Froude's Hist. of Engl., ii. 199, iv. 380 sq.; Dixon's Hist. of the Church of Engl. i. 509, ii. 105 &c., iii. 98; Thomas's Hist. Notes (with details of Mont's missions under Henry VIII); Letters and Papers Hen. VIII, passim; Cal. of State Papers (Engl. and Spain), IV. ii. 877, 996, V. ii. 3, 25, 511, 1558–67 pp. 203, &c.; Cal. of State Papers, For. Ser. 1547–72, passim (many letters); Strype's Memorials, I. i. 355 &c., II. i. 167 &c., ii. 18, 87, Life of Sir Thomas Smith, p. 75, Annals, II. i. 163, &c.; Ascham's Letters, ed. Oxf. 1703 (where he is called Montius); Cranmer's Works, ii. 377 *n.*; Zurich Letters (Parker Soc.); Trevelyan Papers (Camden Soc.), ii. 19.] W. A. J. A.

MONT, WILLIAM DU (*d.* 1213), theologian. [See William.]

MONTACUTE, Baron (1492?–1535). [See Pole, Henry.]

MONTACUTE or **MONTAGU, JOHN DE**, third Earl of Salisbury (1350?–1400), son of Sir John de Montacute, younger brother of William de Montacute, second earl [q. v.], a distinguished warrior, who was summoned to parliament as John de Montacute (1357–1389), and died in 1390, by Margaret, granddaughter and heiress of Ralph de Monthermer [q. v.], by his son Thomas, was born about 1350. While serving in France in 1369 he received knighthood from the Earl of Cambridge before Bourdeille, and highly distinguished himself at the taking of that town (Froissart, i. 582). Having on his father's death received livery of his lands, he obtained license in 1391 to go on a crusade into Prussia with ten horses and ten servants, apparently on the same expedition as that joined by the Earl of Derby [see under Henry IV], and in November was summoned to parliament as Baron de Montagu. He held a command in Ireland during the visit of Richard II to that country in 1394 and 1395. For some years he had been known as one of the most prominent supporters of the lollards; he and others of his party attended their meetings armed, he kept a lollard priest as his chaplain, it was reported, though as it seems falsely, that he had dishonoured the host, and he had caused all the images in the chapel of his manor of Shenley, Hertfordshire, which had come to him by his wife, to be pulled down, only allowing the image of St. Catherine to be set up in his mill, on account of the popular reverence for it (Walsingham, *Historia*, ii. 159; *Ypodigma Neustriæ*, pp. 368, 390; Capgrave, *Chronicle*, p. 245). Before Richard's return from Ireland he and other lords presented a bill in parliament containing a lollard attack on the church, and affixed the same to the doors of St. Paul's, London, and of Westminster Abbey. When the king came back he summoned John and the rest before him, and rated and threatened them (Walsingham, *Historia*, ii. 217; Fox ap. *English Chronicle*, p. 112). By the death of his mother he inherited the barony and estates of Monthermer, and received livery of her lands in this year, when he appears as a member of the king's council (*Proceedings of the Privy Council*, i. 59). He advocated a peace with France and the king's marriage with Isabella of France [q. v.], daughter of Charles VI, and was in France in 1396 when the king went over to marry that princess, and possibly earlier. While there he met with Christine de Pisan, gave her much encouragement, and took back with him to England a collection of her poems. The next year Christine sent her son to be educated in his household (Boivin).

On the death of his uncle, Earl William, in 1397, he succeeded to his lands and dignity as Earl of Salisbury. The part that he took with reference to the peace and the king's marriage secured him Richard's confidence, and he was a favourite with him and a prominent member of the court party. With the people at large, and specially with the Londoners, who were displeased at the peace and at the king's doings generally, he was unpopular. On one occasion he is represented as replying on behalf of the king to a deputation of London citizens, who had been stirred up by the Duke of Gloucester to inquire of the king concerning a rumour that he was about to surrender Calais (Froissart, iii. 289). In common with other lords, he advised the arrest of Gloucester and the Earl of Warwick, and at a conference of the court party at Nottingham on 5 Aug. 1397 agreed to be one of eight lords who were to appeal them and others of treason in the coming parliament (*Annales Ricardi*, p. 207; *Chronique de la Traïson*, pp. 6–9). The appeal was made on 21 Sept. (*Rolls of Parliament*, iii. 357), but Salisbury prevailed on the king to spare the life of Warwick, his former companion in arms (Froissart, iii. 310). He received a part of Warwick's estates, and was made a knight of the Garter, having a grant of robes made him for the feast of the order on 23 April 1399 (Beltz). By the parliament of Shrewsbury, which in January 1398 made the king virtually absolute, Salisbury was appointed one of the committee for discharging the functions of parliament. In September he was made deputy-marshal of England for three years in the absence of the Duke of Surrey [see Holland, Thomas, Duke of Surrey]. In December he was appointed joint ambassador to France, and, much against his will, received special orders to urge the king of France to prevent the marriage of Henry of Derby, duke of Hereford [see under Henry IV], to the daughter of the Duke of Berry. In this he was successful, and avoided seeing Henry, who was highly displeased at his conduct. He was much blamed for carrying the king's message. The Londoners, with whom Henry was popular, were specially incensed against him, and men said that he would rue the day when he consented to thwart Henry's wishes (Froissart, iii. 334, 336). On his return he with other lords assented to the repeal of the patent allowing Hereford to have control of his estates (*Rolls of Parliament*, iii. 372). In March 1399 he was appointed a commissioner to treat with the Scots (*Fœdera*, viii. 69).

Salisbury accompanied the king to Ireland in May, and on the news of the landing and success of the Duke of Lancaster (Henry IV) reaching the king, was sent across to Wales to raise a force to oppose him. He landed at Conway, and sent messengers to call the forces of Wales and Chester to the king's help. The troops that he collected and those that the king brought over deserted, and Salisbury is said to have advised Richard to flee to Bordeaux. At Conway he was present at the interview between the king and the Earl of Northumberland. He accompanied Richard to Flint, and Henry, who met Richard there, refused to speak to Salisbury. He took leave of Richard at Chester, received a summons to attend parliament on 6 Oct., and was probably present at the proceedings connected with the accession of Henry IV. On the 16th the commons petitioned that Richard's evil counsellors might be arrested. Lord Morley accused Salisbury of complicity in Gloucester's death, and challenged him to combat. Salisbury accepted the challenge, and was committed to the Tower. In common with the other surviving appellants of 1397, he was called upon to answer for his conduct, and pleaded that he had acted through fear. He was not included in the sentence pronounced on the rest on 3 Nov., but was left to prove his innocence by combat with Morley at Newcastle. The Londoners clamoured for his execution, but he was released from prison on the intercession of Henry's sister, Elizabeth, countess of Huntingdon, and the Earl of Kent became surety for him. On 17 Dec. he met the Earls of Huntingdon, Kent, and Rutland at the abbot's house at Westminster, and entered into a conspiracy to surprise Henry at the jousts that were to be held at Windsor on Twelfth-day, and to restore Richard. According to arrangement he met his fellow-conspirators at Kingston on 4 Jan. 1400, but on reaching Windsor with Kent he found that the king, who had been warned of the plot, had gone to London. He and Kent, seeing that their plan had failed, rode to Reading, visited Queen Isabella at Sonning, and tried to raise the people. The rebel leaders decided to retreat to the Welsh marches, and Salisbury led a body of their forces to Woodstock, where he was joined by Kent, and pressing on reached Cirencester on the night of the 6th, with greatly diminished numbers. In the night the townsmen attacked the house where the rebel leaders lay; they were compelled to surrender on the following morning, and were lodged in the abbey. In the afternoon some houses in the town were set on fire, and a rescue was attempted. The mob rushed to the abbey and demanded the prisoners. Lord Berkeley, who had charge of them, was forced to give them up, and in the evening Salisbury, Kent, and Lumley were beheaded by the mob; Salisbury, 'the supporter of lollards, the despiser of images, and the mocker at the sacraments,' refusing, it is said, the rites of the church at his death (*Annales*, p. 326; the stories, in the *Traïson*, p. 88, that he fell fighting, and in Froissart, iii. 363, that he was beheaded by knights and esquires sent against the rebels by the king, are merely attempts to provide him with a more honourable end). His head was sent to the king at Oxford, and was set on London Bridge; his body was buried at Cirencester Abbey, but his widow was allowed by Henry V to remove it to Bisham Priory, Berkshire, of which he was the hereditary patron.

Salisbury's lollardism and his attachment to Richard II account for the bitterness with which the English clerical chroniclers speak of him. He was brave, courteous, and loyal, a munificent patron of poets, and a poet himself, being the author of many 'beautiful ballads, songs, roundels, and lays.' None of his poems, which were doubtless written in French, are now known to be extant. They are noticed by Christine de Pisan and by Creton, who was a member of his household, and who writes of him in terms of the highest praise (Boivin, *Vie de Christine de Pisan; Metrical History* ap. *Archæologia*, vol. xx.) It is evident that he loved French culture and manners, and his French sympathies made him one of Richard's most trusted counsellors during the latter part of that king's reign, led him to abet the king's attempt to establish an absolute sovereignty, and exposed him to the hatred of his own countrymen. He is represented in Shakespeare's play of 'Richard II.' His portrait is engraved in Doyle's 'Official Baronage,' from Harl. MS. 1719.

Salisbury married Maud, daughter of Sir Adam Francis, a citizen of London, and already widow successively of John Aubrey, a citizen of London, and of Sir Alan Buxhull, K.G. (*d.* 1372). After Salisbury's death, his lands being forfeited by reason of attainder in 1400, his widow received from the crown a grant for life of the manors of Stokenham and Polehampton, Devonshire, for her maintenance. By her Salisbury had two sons—Thomas de Montacute, fourth earl of Salisbury of his house (1388–1428) [q. v.], and Richard, who left no issue—and three daughters: Anne, married, first Sir Richard Hankford, secondly Sir John Fitzlewes, and thirdly John Holland, duke of Exeter and earl of Huntingdon (1395–1447) [q. v.], and died in 1457; Margaret, married William, lord Ferrers of Groby (*d.* 1445); and Elizabeth, married Robert, lord Willoughby of Eresby (*d.* 1452) (Dugdale, *Baronage*, p. 651). Salisbury's attainder was reversed on the accession of Edward IV in 1461 (*Rolls of Parliament*, v. 484).

[Ann. Ricard. II et Hen. IV ap. Trokelowe, &c. pp. 174, 207, 250, 303, 313, 325, 326 (Rolls Ser.); Walsingham's Historia, ii. 159, 160, 216, and Ypodigma Neustriæ, pp. 368, 390 (Rolls Ser.); Froissart, i. 582, iii. 280, 310, 334, 336, 363, ed. Buchon (Panthéon Litt.); Traïson et Mort, ed. Williams, passim (Engl. Hist. Soc.); Metrical Hist. ed. Webb ap. Archæologia, xx. 56, 59, 70–4; English Chron. ed. Davies, pp. 21, 112 (Camden Soc.); Vita Ric. II, pp. 150, 155, ed. Hearne; Chron. Angliæ, p. 377 (Rolls Ser.); Eulogium, iii. 373, 385, 386 (Rolls Ser.); Capgrave's Chron. pp. 245, 260, 276; J. de Wavrin, vol. iv. bk. v. (Rolls Ser.); Rolls of Parliament, iii. 348, 350, 357, 368, 372, 451; Rymer's Fœdera, viii. 16, 69, 79, ed. 1709; Dugdale's Baronage, i. 650; Doyle's Official Baronage, iii. 240; Beltz's Order of the Garter, p. 362; Dugdale's Monasticon, vi. 528; Boivin's Vie de Christine de Pisan ap. Collection des meilleurs ouvrages françois, ii. 118, ed. Kéralio; Stubbs's Const. Hist. ii. 488, 494, 498, iii. 21, 25, ed. 1878; Wylie's Hen. IV, i. 75, 92–100; Ramsay's Lancaster and York, i. 20.] W. H.

MONTACUTE, NICHOLAS (*fl.* 1466), historian, had, according to Bale, a great reputation for learning. He was not eloquent, says Bale, but lucid, and less credulous than his contemporaries. From the fact that his writings were in the sixteenth century preserved in the library of Eton College, Pits rashly conjectured that he had been a teacher in the school. His works, which seem to have disappeared from the Eton library by Tanner's time, are: 1. 'De Romanis pontificibus a S. Petro ad Eugenium III.' Pits and Tanner mention a manuscript of this book in the Lumley library, which does not appear with the rest of the collection incorporated with the Royal Library in the British Museum; a copy in the Cottonian Library bears the title 'Nicolai Manuacutii versus ad incorrupta nomina pontificum conservanda in quibus series illorum continetur,' Domit. A. xiii. f. 96 *b*. 2. 'De regibus Anglorum.' 3. 'De episcopis Anglorum,' also in the Lumley library. 4. 'Scala temporum a Christo nato.' 5. 'Epigrammata.' These appear to have been all written in verse, but Bale says that he wrote other works, both in prose and verse, whose titles he could not learn.

[Bale's Catalogus Scriptorum illustrium Brytanniæ, i. 596; Pits, De illustr. Angliæ Scriptoribus, p. 656; Tanner's Bibl. Brit.-Hib. p. 531.] J. T-t.

MONTACUTE, SIMON de, first Baron Montacute (*d.* 1317), descended from Drogo de Montacute, who came across with the Conqueror, and received grants in Somerset, was son of William de Montacute (*fl.* 1257) and Bertha, his wife. William had constantly served in the Welsh wars, and Simon first appears during Edward's great campaign in 1277 against Llywelyn ab Gruffydd (*d.* 1282) [q. v.] (*Parl. Writs.* i. 742); in 1282 he served in a similar campaign, when Edward finally crushed that prince (*ib.*; DUGDALE, *Baronage*, i. 644; RYMER, *Fœdera*, I. ii. 619), and during the autumn attended the king at Rhuddlan. Next year he was summoned to the parliament which met on 30 Sept. at Shrewsbury for the trial of Llywelyn's brother, Davydd III [q. v.] In 1290 he was apparently confirmed in the possession of Shipton Montacute, Somerset, and received additional grants in Dorset, Devonshire, Buckinghamshire, and Oxfordshire (cf. DUGDALE). On 14 June 1294 he was summoned to meet the king at Portsmouth on 1 Sept. and accompany him to Gascony (RYMER, I. ii. 801), but his services were apparently for the time dispensed with (*Parl. Writs*, i. 742). In 1296, however, he was in command of a vessel, and by his bravery broke through the French fleet blockading Bordeaux, re-victualled the town, and caused the siege to be raised (WALSINGHAM, *Hist. Anglicana*, Rolls Ser., i. 55; LELAND, *Collectanea*, i. 180); he appears to have remained in Gascony until 1297. In March 1298 a truce was made with France, and in May Montacute was summoned as a baron to an assembly of the lay estates at York; on 26 Sept. he was summoned to serve in the war with Scotland, and again in August and December 1299. In the latter year he was made governor of Corfe Castle. The next two years he attended parliament, and served in the Scottish war, and in 1301 signed, as 'Simon dominus de Monte Acuto,' the famous letter of the barons to the pope (*Chronicles of Edward I and Edward II*, i. 123; RYMER; *Parl. Writs*, i. 742; DUGDALE). In 1306, for his services in Scotland and elsewhere, he was pardoned a debt of 120*l.* which his father had owed to the exchequer (cf. *Memoranda de Parliamento*, ed. Maitland, Rolls Ser. pp. 112, 280, 283); on 5 April he was asked for an aid on the occasion of the knighting of Prince Edward, at which he was present, and was serving in the Scottish wars until Edward's death on 7 July 1307. He was summoned to attend parliament at the coronation of Edward II, and in 1308 was made governor of Beaumaris Castle, Anglesey; during this and the next year he was serving against the Scots, and was also appointed justice to try persons guilty of forestalling in London. In 1310 he was constituted admiral of the fleet employed against the Scots; and from 1313 was in constant attendance in parliament and in the Scottish war. He was stationed in the north to watch the frontier during the winter campaign of 1315–16, and was summoned to the parliament of Lincoln in January 1316. He died in 1317 (*Continuatio Nicholas Trivet*, ed. 1722, p. 24; *Parl. Writs*). Montacute married Aufricia, daughter of Fergus, and sister of Orray, king of Man, by whom he had two sons, William, who succeeded him, and is separately noticed, and Simon.

[Rolls of Parliament, vol. i.; Parliamentary Writs; Rymer's Fœdera, passim; Chronicles of Edward I and Edward II, i. 123; Walsingham's Historia Anglicana, i. 55; Cal. Rot. Pat. 76; Memoranda de Parliamento, ed. Maitland (Rolls Ser.); Dugdale's Baronage, i. 643–5; Peerage, ed. G. E. C.; Burke's Extinct Peerage; Collinson's Somerset, iii. 45–9; A Compleat History of Somerset, 1742, fol., p. 87.] A. F. P.

MONTACUTE or **MONTAGU, THOMAS DE**, fourth EARL OF SALISBURY (1388–1428), elder son of John de Montacute, third earl [q.v.], by his wife Maud, was born in 1388. His father's lands being forfeited for his treason, he received a portion of them from the king, and further increased his possessions by marrying Eleanor, fourth daughter of Thomas Holland, second earl of Kent [q. v.], and coheiress of her brother, Edmund Holland, fourth earl (1384–1408). He was summoned to parliament as Earl of Salisbury in October 1409, but was not restored to the dignity held by his father until 1421 (NICOLAS, *Historic Peerage*). He was made a knight of the Garter in 1414, was in May appointed joint commissioner to treat with France concerning the rights of Henry V and a marriage between him and Catherine, daughter of Charles VI, and was in France on this business from July to October (*Fœdera*, ix. 130, 190, 204). War being decided upon he engaged in June 1415 to serve the king with his retinue for one year in France, being paid 12*d.* a day for his own services (*ib.* p. 256), and in July was one of the seven peers appointed to try the Earl of Cambridge and other conspirators, and joined in pronouncing sentence on them on 5 Aug. (*Rolls of Parliament*, iv. 65). On the 11th he sailed from Portsmouth with the king, and took part in the siege of Harfleur and the battle of Agincourt, where his retinue consisted of three knights, thirty-six esquires, forty men-at-arms, and eighty mounted archers (NICOLAS, *Agincourt*, p. 373). The next year, having again engaged to serve the king, he sailed in August with John, duke of Bedford [q. v.], who was sent with reinforcements to Harfleur, and took part in the naval engagement with the French at the mouth of the Seine (*Fœdera*, ix. 355; NICOLAS, *Royal Navy*, ii. 418–25). In February 1417 he attended the privy council, and in July sailed with the king for Normandy. He took part in the siege of Caen and in other operations during that year, being in command of the rear division of the king's army (WALSINGHAM, ii. 322; ELMHAM, p. 99; DES URSINS, p. 534), and received from the king the lordship of Auvilliers. After assisting at the siege of Falaise he accompanied the Duke of Clarence in the spring of 1418 on a successful expedition against Harcourt, Courtonne, La Rivière-Thibouville, and Chambrais (*Gesta Henrici V*, p. 119), and on 1 June received from the king at Bernay the grant of Neubourg and two other lordships, to be held by the service of presenting the iron head of a lance every Christmas at the castle of Caen (*Norman Rolls*, i. 34). During the siege of Rouen, begun 1 Aug., he highly distinguished himself, being posted in front of the strongly fortified abbey of St. Catherine, used as a detached fort, which yielded on 1 Sept. (TITUS LIVIUS, p. 61; *Chronique de Normandie*, pp. 188, 190). He was made warden of the New Forest, lieutenant and warden of Evreux and Alençon (DOYLE), and in October was appointed a joint-commissioner to treat with the dauphin (*Fœdera*, ix. 626). The negotiations which were carried on at Alençon were fruitless. Early in 1419 Salisbury took Fécamp, Monteville, Gournay, Eu, and Honfleur, which he besieged from 4 Jan. to 12 March.

In April he was appointed lieutenant-general of Normandy, and was created Earl of Perche by the service of rendering to the king each year at the castle of Caen a sheathed sword. He was engaged at Rouen in negotiations with the ambassadors of John, duke of Burgundy, and in May accompanied the king to the conference which Henry held near Mantes with the queen of France and the Duke of Burgundy (HALL, p. 91). The king sent him in the autumn to lay siege to Meulan, joined him there, and received the surrender of the town on 6 Nov. In May 1420 he was besieging Frénay with a large force when a French army advanced to its relief, and was defeated by John Holland, earl of Huntingdon, afterwards Duke of Exeter (1395–1447) [q.v.], and in July he was present at the siege of Melun, which was not surrendered until November (ELMHAM, p. 244; *Gesta Henrici V*, p. 144). He attended Henry and his queen, Catherine of France, on their entry into Paris with King Charles and Duke Philip of Burgundy on 1 Dec. (WAVRIN, v. ii. 325). In January 1421 he was at the parliament held by Henry at Rouen, and there did homage for the earldom of Perche. When the king returned to England shortly afterwards, Salisbury remained in France to support the Duke of Clarence (CHASTELLAIN, p. 204).

Soon after the king's departure he marched with Clarence and a large force into Maine and Anjou. On 21 March Clarence insisted on attacking the allied army of the French and Scots at Baugé with his cavalry without waiting for the rear division under Salisbury. He was defeated and slain, and when Salisbury came on the field of battle it was too late to retrieve the disaster. Nevertheless, he and the archers under him pressed so vigorously on the French that he was able to bring off the duke's body (WAVRIN, v. ii. 338). He made an attempt to relieve Alençon, but was intercepted and retreated, not without loss, to Bec. When, however, the besiegers drew off, he again took the field and advanced as far west as the immediate neighbourhood of Angers (*Fœdera*, x. 131). Henry V having died in France in August 1422, and Charles VI having died shortly afterwards, Bedford, the regent of France, marched with Salisbury to recover Meulan from the French. The siege lasted until 1 March, when Salisbury was appointed to arrange terms for the surrender of the place. In June he was at Paris with the regent, then newly married, who sent him to besiege the castle of Orsay; he took it after about three weeks, and led the defenders, bare-headed and with ropes about their necks, into Paris (WAVRIN, v. iii. 23; *Journal d'un Bourgeois* ap. *Mémoires*, iii. 238). Bedford appointed him governor of Champagne and Brie, and he went to Champagne and laid siege to Montaguillon, a fortress near Provins. The place was well defended, and he had to employ a large siege-train and much ordnance. Charles intended to relieve it, but was forced to send his army to Crevant-sur-Yonne, which had fallen into the hands of the Burgundians. Salisbury was ordered by the regent to go to the relief of Crevant, and received reinforcements under the earl-marshal and Lord Willoughby. On 30 July he appeared before Crevant, made, it is said, eighty knights, and attacked the French and the Scots under the walls of the town. He commanded the left wing of his army, and crying 'St. George! Avant banner!' dashed into the river, while Willoughby with the right wing forced his way across the bridge. Salisbury gained the bank; the garrison sallied and attacked the besiegers in the rear, and his victory was complete. The chief loss fell on the Scots. The English and Burgundians entered the town in triumph, and returned thanks for their victory (WAVRIN, v. iii. 45; RAMSAY, *Lancaster and York*,

i. 334; BARANTE, v. 147–53). Salisbury was joyfully received by the regent and then went back to Champagne, where he carried on the war with success, resuming the siege of Montaguillon, taking Sézanne by assault, and holding the country so vigorously that the French could do nothing against him, specially as north of him Suffolk and John of Luxemburg forced their army to retreat beyond the Meuse (*Mémoires concernant la Pucelle* ap. *Mémoires*, iii. 70). In 1424 Salisbury's success continued, and early in the spring Montaguillon at last surrendered. The French having seized Verneuil in August, he went to the help of the regent, who sent him with Suffolk to Breteuil to watch the movements of the enemy. On the 17th he took part in the battle of Verneuil; the division under his command was attacked by the Vicomte de Narbonne, who was slain; he bore the brunt of the battle, and the victory of the English is attributed by a warm admirer to his ability and valour. Verneuil surrendered upon terms, and Salisbury was forced to slay two or three of his men with his own hand, in order to prevent the rest from violating the conditions. He was present in November at the festivities given in Paris by Philip of Burgundy to celebrate the marriage of John de la Trémoille. His wife—probably his second wife—was with him. She was a very handsome woman, and the duke courted her. Salisbury was deeply offended, and is said to have repaid the duke by taking part with the Duke of Gloucester against him (FÉNIN, ap. *Mémoires*, ii. 624). He completed the subjugation of Champagne, receiving the submission of Montaimé in June 1625, he took Étampes, Rambouillet, and other places in the same district, and then made a campaign in the west, taking Beaumont le Vicomte, overrunning Maine, and receiving the submission of Le Mans, Mayenne, St. Suzanne, and other places. He lost some men by surprise near Seez in the course of these successful operations, and met with a stubborn resistance at La Ferté Bernard, which was not surrendered until after a siege of three months (RAMSAY, i. 363). When Bedford left France in the winter, Salisbury remained in charge of Upper Normandy and Maine (STEVENSON, *Wars*, vol. i. p. lx; RAMSAY, i. 364), and in 1426 took Mondoubleau, and also acted with John of Luxemburg in the recovery of Moynier in the county of Virtus in Champagne (*Journal d'un Bourgeois*, p. 246).

In 1427 Salisbury went to England to obtain reinforcements, and took his seat at the council on 15 July. He upheld Gloucester, who was then preparing to send an expedition to Holland [see under HUMPHREY, DUKE OF GLOUCESTER], and declared himself ready to take the command, but the scheme was stopped by Bedford. The wages of his retinue in the campaign of 1415 had not yet been paid, and he presented a petition in parliament for payment (*Rolls of Parliament*, iv. 320). In March 1428 parliament allowed securities for 24,000*l.* to be given to him and others who advanced money for the war (*ib.* p. 317). He was busy gathering a force which he mustered at Sandwich in July, and sailed with 450 spears and 2,250 archers (STEVENSON, *Wars*, i. 403–20). It was decided that he should lay siege to Angers, and accordingly, having been appointed 'lieutenant-general for the field,' he marched south-west from Paris, and took Rambouillet, Nogent-le-Roi, and other places. Then he changed the plan of the campaign, turned towards Orleans, and decided, against the will of Bedford, to undertake the siege of that city. He took Puiset by storm and hanged the garrison, battered Janville with his artillery, and, though it was bravely defended, compelled it to capitulate on 29 Aug., by which date he had gained thirty-eight places 'of one sort or another' (RAMSAY, i. 381; DELPIT, *Documents Français*, p. 237). From Janville he sent an expedition to plunder the rich church of Cléry, and on 8 Sept. marched to Meung, which had already surrendered to him, passing by Orleans, and skirmishing with the Bastard of Orleans, La Hire, and others who sallied from the city to interrupt his march. On the 25th he compelled the surrender of the castle and abbey of Beaugency, and received the submission of La Ferté-Hubert. He sent Sir John de la Pole against Jargeau, which surrendered on 5 Oct., and Pole also received the surrender of Chateauneuf. Salisbury began the siege of Orleans on the 12th, and on the 23rd, in spite of a repulse on the 21st, compelled the French to evacuate a position which defended Tourelles, the fortification at the southern end of the bridge. On the 24th he stormed Tourelles, and ordered Glasdale to fortify and occupy it. While he was surveying the city from a window of Tourelles on the 27th, a stone ball from a cannon shattered the stone and iron work of the window. One of his eyes was destroyed and his face otherwise grievously wounded. He was carried to Meung, and died there on 3 Nov. (*Pucelle*, pp. 84–6). As he lay dying he exhorted the English captains by no means to give up the siege. His body was conveyed to England and buried with much pomp with his fathers in his priory at Bisham in Berkshire (HALL, p. 145).

Salisbury was the most famous and skilful captain on the English side; well skilled in war, and specially, it would seem from the records of his sieges, in the use of artillery. His support of Gloucester was the result of his anger at a personal grievance; but this, combined with his apparently headstrong determination to besiege Orleans, seems to suggest that he was less great as a politician than as a commander. Courteous, liberal, and brave, he was beloved by his followers, and was, it seems, generally popular with his countrymen. Though French writers charge him with cruelty, he seems not to have acted otherwise than in accordance with the usages of war, or than other leaders on both sides. His death was held to be an event of supreme importance in the course of the war, the French regarding it as a divine judgment on their most puissant and cruel enemy, the English, as a mark of God's anger, and the presage of many calamities (*Pucelle*, p. 86; WAVRIN, v. iii. 246; POLYDORE VERGIL, p. 598). He married (1) Eleanor, daughter of Thomas, earl of Kent, by whom he had a daughter Alice, who married Richard Neville, afterwards Earl of Salisbury [q. v.], and (2) Alice, daughter of Thomas Chaucer [q. v.], by whom he had no issue. He left a natural son named John (DUGDALE, *Baronage*, i. 652, which see for his will). A portrait of him is given in Harl. MS. 4826, and is engraved in Strutt's 'Regal Antiquities' and Doyle's 'Official Baronage.'

[Gesta Henrici V, with Chronique de Normandie, pp. 119, 188, 190, 204 (Engl. Hist. Soc.); Elmham's Vita Henrici V, pp. 99, 244, ed. Hearne; T. Livii Vita Hen. V, pp. 32, 34, 61, 70, ed. Hearne; Redman's Vita Hen. V, ap. Memorials of Hen. V, p. 56; Walsingham's Hist. Angl. ii. 322; Wavrin's Recueil des Chroniques, vols. ii. iii. (ii. 325, 338, iii. 8, 23, 41, 45, 68, 88, 125, 133, 230, 246) (Rolls Ser.); J. des Ursins, ap. Mém. ii. 534, 565 (Michaud); P. de Fénin, ap. Mémoires, ii. 624, 627 (Michaud); Journal d'un Bourgeois, ap. Mém. iii. 238, 246, 251 (Michaud); Mémoires concernant La Pucelle, ap. Mém. iii. 70, 74–6, 84–6 (Michaud); Stevenson's Wars of the English in France, I. lx, ii. 43, 80, 88 (Rolls Ser.); Monstrelet's Chron. i. cc. 238, 239, ii. cc. 9, 49, 52, ap. vol. i. 459, 498, 543, 545 (Johnes's transl.); Polydore Vergil, pp. 588, 598, ed. 1651; Hall's Chron. pp. 91, 145, ed. Ellis; Hardyng's Chron. p. 393, ed. Ellis; Delpit's Documents Français, ap. Doc. Inédits, p. 327; Norman Rolls, i. 34, 157, 283 (Hardy); Rymer's Fœdera, ix. 150, 190, 204, 256, x. 131, ed. 1709; Rot. Parl. iv. 65, 320; Acts of P. C. iii. 213, 274, 279, (Nicolas); Ramsay's Lancaster and York, i. 334, 363, 364, 376–84; Barante's Ducs de Bourgogne, v. 147–52, 155, 180, 249, 250, 256–8; Nicolas's Hist. Peerage, p. 438 (Courthope); Nicolas's Agincourt, pp. 127, 373; Nicolas's Royal Navy, ii. 418–25; Dugdale's Baronage, i. 652; Doyle's Official Baronage, iii. 241.] W. H.

MONTACUTE, WILLIAM DE, second BARON MONTACUTE (*d.* 1319), son of Simon de Montacute, first baron Montacute [q. v.], and his wife, Aufricia, was summoned to serve against the Scots in 1301 and in 1304. In the latter year he was imprisoned in the Tower for treason. On 22 May 1306 he was knighted at Westminster at the same time as Prince Edward, whom he accompanied into Scotland, where he remained till next year. In 1311 he was again in Scotland, and in 1313 was placed in command of the fleet at Sandwich, and accompanied the king and queen to France to be present at the coronation of Louis X. Next year he was again in Scotland, and in 1316 was a commander in the expedition against Llywelyn ab Rhys (*d.* 1317) [q. v.], and shortly afterwards negotiated peace (RYMER, ii. 283, 288; *Chronicles of Edward I and Edward II*, ii. 217; *Parl. Writs*, II. iii. 1182; *Cal. Rot. Pat.*); the same year he was sent to negotiate peace with Scotland, and in 1317 succeeded his father as second Baron Montacute. Edward also made him steward of his household, and the Lancastrian chronicler calls him 'fautor mendacii ipso Petro [i.e. Gaveston] nequior.' The next two years he attended parliament as one of the 'barones majores,' and served in the Scottish wars. On 20 Nov. 1318 he was made seneschal of Aquitaine and Gascony, and governor of the island of Oleron; Edward commended him to the king of France on his departure for Gascony, where he remained until his death at the end of October 1319 (RYMER, ii. 377–8, 380, 406). He married Elizabeth, daughter of Peter de Montfort, who afterwards married Sir Thomas de Furnivall; his eldest son, William (1301–1344), is separately noticed. His second son, SIMON DE MONTACUTE, studied at Oxford, and was on 29 Nov. 1318 recommended by Edward II to the pope's favour on the plea of poverty through being a younger son (*ib.* ii. 380); he became successively archdeacon of Canterbury, bishop of Worcester in 1334, and bishop of Ely in 1337, and died on 20 June 1345 (*Rolls of Parl.*; MURIMUTH, passim; GODWIN, *De Præsulibus Angliæ*, pp. 261, 443; LELAND, *Collectanea*, i. 606, iii. 24; LE NEVE, iii. 56, i. 334). A third son, Sir Edward Montacute, was actively engaged in the Scottish wars under Edward III.

[Dugdale's Baronage and Monasticon; Rolls of Parliament; Chronicles of Edward I and Edward II; Collinson's Somerset; Peerages by Burke and G. E. C.] A. F. P.

MONTACUTE or **MONTAGU, WILLIAM DE**, third BARON MONTACUTE and first EARL OF SALISBURY (1301–1344), born in 1301, was eldest son of William de Montacute, second baron Montacute (*d.* 1319) [q. v.], and succeeded his father as third baron on 6 Nov. 1319, being granted wardship of his own lands, though yet a minor. In 1322 he came of age, and received livery of his lands, together with the grant of Lundy Isle. In 1325 he was knighted, and received letters of protection on his departure for France (RYMER, II. i. 606). In 1327 he went with Edward III to repel the Scottish invasion, when the latter nearly missed capture. In 1329 he accompanied the king abroad and was sent in June to treat for a marriage between the eldest son of the king of France and Edward's sister Alianore (*ib.* II. ii. 764, 766). In September he was despatched with Bartholomew de Burghersh (*d.* 1355) [q. v.] on an embassy to the pope at Avignon, returning before the end of the year, when, in his capacity as executor of Blanche, queen of Navarre, he lent the king two thousand marks that had belonged to her, and were deposited at Whitefriars.

Next year the young king took him into his confidence about his plans for the arrest of Mortimer. During the parliament held at Nottingham in October 1330, Montacute, with a band of retainers, including Sir John de Molines [q. v.], penetrated by a secret passage into the castle, where they found Mortimer in the queen-mother's apartments (MURIMUTH, p. 61). After a struggle, in which two of Mortimer's attendants were killed, his arrest was effected, and he was sent to London for trial [see MORTIMER, ROGER IV DE, first EARL OF MARCH; and BARNES, *Edward III*, pp. 47–8]. Edward obtained from parliament indemnity on Montacute's behalf for all consequences of the death of Mortimer's attendants, and rewarded him with various grants of land forfeited by Mortimer in Hampshire, Berkshire, Buckinghamshire, Kent, and Wales, including Sherborne, Corfe Castle, and Purbeck Chase in Dorset, and the lordship of Denbigh (*Rolls of Parl.* ii. 60*b*; GALFRIDI LE BAKER, *Chron.* ed. Maunde Thompson, pp. 46, 226–8; WALSINGHAM, *Ypodigma Neustriæ*, p. 270; MURIMUTH, pp. 62, 285; DUGDALE; STOW, *Annals*, p. 229; STUBBS, ii. 390; LONGMAN, *Edward III*, i. 35). On 4 April 1331 Montacute accompanied Edward III when, disguised as a merchant and attended by a handful of men-at-arms, the king paid a secret visit to France; he was present when Edward repeated his homage to the French king at Amiens on 13 April, and returned with him to Dover on 20 April (FROISSART, ed. Lettenhove, ii. 232; RYMER, II. ii. 818). In September Montacute held a tournament in Cheapside, entertaining his guests in the Bishop of London's palace.

Next year he attended the king in Scotland, and in 1333 was present at the siege of Berwick and the battle of Halidon Hill (BARNES, p. 80); in the same year Edward made over to him all his rights to the Isle of Man. He appears to have accompanied Balliol to Scotland, and in February 1334 was deputed by him to excuse his absence from the parliament held at York. On 30 March Montacute was appointed envoy to France with the Archbishop of Canterbury and two others (RYMER; BARNES, p. 92); but in June was again in Scotland, where in 1335 he was left in command of the army with Arundel. In the same year he was granted the forests of Selkirk and Ettrick and town of Peebles, made governor of the Channel Islands and constable of the Tower. In November he was given power to treat with Andrew Murray, constable of Scotland; on 27 Jan. 1336 he commenced the siege of Dunbar Castle, but after nineteen weeks the blockade was raised by Alexander Ramsay, and Montacute gave it up in despair, making a truce that was strongly disapproved of in England (WALSINGHAM, *Ypodigma*, p. 275; *Hist. Angl.* p. 200; STOW, p. 231; LONGMAN, p. 189; LETTENHOVE, xxiii. 93–7; BARNES, pp. 101 sqq.) In the same year he was appointed admiral of the fleet from the mouth of the Thames westward.

On 16 March 1337, at the parliament held in London, Montacute was created Earl of Salisbury. In the following April he was sent to Philip to declare Edward's claim to the French crown, and thence on an embassy to the emperor Lewis, Rupert, Count Palatine, the Duke of Bavaria, and other princes of Germany and the Netherlands, to organise a league against France (LETTENHOVE, xxiii. 97; RYMER, II. ii. 969, 992, 995). In October he was commissioned to treat with Scotland, but in July 1338 commanded a successful raid into Scotland from Carlisle. Later on in the year he sailed with Edward from the Orwell to Flanders, and by a patent, dated Antwerp 20 Sept. 1338 (RYMER), was appointed marshal of England, an office then vacant by the death of Thomas, earl of Norfolk. He remained in Flanders, where he was one of the captains of the Engl.sh forces, for the next two years, during part of which he was in garrison at Ypres (LETTENHOVE, passim). In November 1338 he was one of those appointed to treat with Philip of Valois at the desire of the pope; shortly after he made an inroad into the territories of the Bishop of Liège, and in February 1339 negotiated an agreement with the Archbishop of Trèves and the Duke of Brabant, and was subsequently employed in various other negotiations. In 1340, induced, perhaps, by treachery within the walls, Salisbury and Suffolk with a small force made an attempt on Lille; the attack failed, and both were taken prisoners and conveyed to Paris, when Salisbury, it is said, owed his life to the intervention of the king of Bohemia (MURIMUTH, p. 104; *Chronicon Angliæ*, ed. Maunde Thompson, p. 10; WALSINGHAM, *Ypodigma*, p. 278; *Hist. Angl.* i. 226; FROISSART, *Chron.* ed. Lettenhove, ii. 5; GALF. LE BAKER, *Chron.* pp. 67, 241–2; BARNES, pp. 168–9, and STOW, p. 369, who gives a very different account from FROISSART). On 18 Oct. Edward demanded a levy of wools to secure his liberation. He was set free, on condition of never serving against Philip in France, at the peace negotiated after the siege of Tournay, in exchange for the Earl of Moray, who had been captured in the Scottish wars (RYMER, passim; *Cal. Rot. Parl.* p. 138 *b*).

He returned to England in November, and took part in Edward's arrest of the treasury officials and others [see MOLINES, JOHN DE]; in May 1341 he was commissioned to examine into the charges against Stratford (MURIMUTH, p. 120). Perhaps it was at this time that he conquered the Isle of Man from the Scots and was crowned king there; but the event has also been assigned to 1340 and 1342 (cf. *Annals of England*, p. 193; LETTENHOVE, GALF. LE BAKER, STOW, and LONGMAN). In May 1343 Salisbury embarked with Robert d'Artois for Brittany (LETTENHOVE), captured Vannes, and proceeded to besiege Rennes (LONGMAN, *Edward III*, i. 212; BARNES, pp. 281–5). After the death of Artois and some months' ineffectual fighting a truce was signed, and in August Salisbury was sent on an embassy to the court of Castile, and took part in the siege of Algeçiras, which Alfonso XI was then prosecuting against the Moors (LETTENHOVE; RYMER, II. ii. 1232; DUGDALE antedates this occurrence by two years). He was soon recalled to England, and sent against the Scots. He died on 30 Jan. 1344 from bruises, it is said, received during a tournament held at Windsor, and was buried at Whitefriars, London. Montacute was a liberal benefactor of the church, his principal foundation being Bustleham, or Bisham, Berkshire. Walsingham says of him 'de elegantia, strenuitate, sapientia, et animositate, scribere, speciales actus requirit.' He married Catharine, daughter of William de Grandison, first baron Grandison, by whom he had two sons, William, second earl of Salisbury [q. v.], and John, and four daughters, one of whom, Philippa, married Roger Mortimer, second earl of March [q. v.]

The Countess of Salisbury in 1341, with her brother-in-law, Sir Edward Montacute, defended for some months the castle of Wark, Northumberland, against the Scots; the siege was raised by Edward III, who is said on this occasion to have fallen in love with her. A similar story attributes to her a share in the origin of the order of the Garter. She is said to have dropped her garter at a court ball; Edward, who was in love with her, picked it up, and overhearing a courtier's jest, bound it on his own knee with the remark 'Honi soit qui mal y pense,' which became the motto of the order he then resolved to establish. Both these stories confuse the countess with Joan, the 'Fair Maid of Kent' [q. v.], daughter of Edmund, earl of Kent [q. v.], who was betrothed, but never married, to William, second earl of Salisbury, and attribute Joan's youth and beauty to the Countess of Salisbury. Polydore Vergil, who visited England a hundred and fifty years later, is said to be the earliest authority for the story, which is palpably fictitious. Edward had already determined on the establishment of the order, and it is possible that some such incident, quite unconnected with the Countess of Salisbury, may have given the name to the order (cf. FROISSART, ed. Lettenhove, xxiii. 105–9; JEHAN LE BEL, *Chronique*; ASHMOLE, *Order of the Garter*; NICOLAS, *Orders of Knighthood*, i. 18; BARNES, *Edward III*; and LONGMAN, i. 295–8). She died in 1349 or 1354, and was interred in her husband's foundation at Bisham, which became the family burial-place.

[The best connected accounts of Montacute are in Lettenhove's Froissart, xxiii. 93–109, and Dugdale's Baronage and Monasticon, passim; Cal. Rotulorum Patent.; Rolls of Parliament; Parliamentary Writs; Rymer, II. i. ii. passim; Murimuth and Robert of Avesbury, Chronicles of Edward I and Edward II, Capgrave's Chronicle of England, pp. 203–4, Flores Historiarum, ii. 178, Chronicon Angliæ, ed. Maunde Thompson, pp. 5, 8, 10, Walsingham's Hist. Anglicana and Ypodigma Neustriæ, Knighton's Chronicon Leycestrensis, p. 478, &c., all in Rolls Series; Galfridi le Baker's Chronicon, ed. Maunde Thompson, passim; Chronique de Jehan Le Bel, passim; Stow's Annals, passim; Holinshed's Chronicles, iii. 348, 366; Barnes's History of Reign of Edward III, passim; Weever's Funerall Monuments, p. 437; Ashmole's Order of the Garter, pp. 647–50; Collinson's Somerset, passim; Lingard, vol. iii.; Stubbs, vol. ii.; Annals of England; Longman's Edward III, passim; Peerages by Burke and G. E. C.] A. F. P.

MONTACUTE or **MONTAGU, WILLIAM DE**, second EARL OF SALISBURY (1328–1397), elder son of William de Montacute, first earl [q. v.], by his countess Catharine, was born 25 June 1328, and succeeding to his father's honours while yet a minor in 1344, was a ward of John de Somerton and Thomas Waryn. He accompanied the king in his expedition against France in 1346; on landing at La Hogue on 13 July he was knighted by the Prince of Wales, and served in the ensuing campaign. A contract of marriage was made between him and Joan (1328–1385), the 'Fair Maid of Kent' [q. v.], daughter of Edmund of Woodstock, earl of Kent [q. v.], but the lady was claimed by Sir Thomas Holland, first earl of Kent of the Holland family [q. v.], and her contract with Salisbury was annulled by a papal bull, dated 13 Nov. 1349. In that year he obtained livery of his lands. In 1350 he was one of the original knights of the order of the Garter, and in August shared in the king's victory over the Spaniards off Winchelsea. He did homage in 1353 for the lordship of Denbigh in North Wales, which he inherited from his father, and being the following year appointed constable of the king's army in France, he sailed for Bordeaux with the Prince of Wales on 30 June 1355, having received a protection for two years in respect of any debts for which he might be liable in Gascony. The rear-guard of the prince's army was under his command, and he bore his part in the ravage of the south of France (AVESBURY). On 17 Sept. 1356 he held the command of the rear of the prince's army, with the Earl of Suffolk, at the battle of Poitiers, defending the gap in the hedge that covered the English position with dismounted men-at-arms and archers, and, fighting 'like a lion,' routed the attack of the marshal, Jean de Clermont. He served in France in 1357, in 1359, and again in 1360, in which last year he received a commission to treat with the enemy, and assisted to make the treaty of Bretigni (*Fœdera*, III. i. 483, 493). By the death of Joanna, dowager-countess of Surrey, in 1361, he came into possession of the castle of Trowbridge, Wiltshire, together with lands in that county and in Somerset and Dorset, of which his father had obtained the reversion from the crown (*ib.* p. 638). In 1364 he received commission to treat with the Count of Flanders for a marriage between the king's son Edmund, earl of Cambridge [see under LANGLEY, EDMUND DE, first DUKE OF YORK], and the count's daughter Margaret. He was at this time a member of the king's council, and as such joined in sending letters to the Prince of Wales in 1366 assenting to his expedition in aid of Pedro of Castile. In August 1369 he served under the Duke of Lancaster [see JOHN OF GAUNT] in the north of France. On the defeat of the Earl of Pembroke in 1372 the king designed to send him to the relief of Rochelle, but the plan came to nought and Rochelle was lost. He took part in the abortive attempt that the king made in September to relieve Thouars. On 16 Feb. 1373 he was appointed commander of an expedition to guard the coast, and contracted to serve himself for six months with twenty knights, 279 esquires, and as many bowmen. Being joined by the admirals of the western and northern fleets, he sailed from Cornwall in March, and burnt seven Spanish ships in the port of St. Malo. He thence sailed to Brest, and having received reinforcements from England, cruised about off the coasts of Normandy and Brittany. He was called to the relief of Brest, the garrison having given hostages to Du Guesclin, and promised to surrender to him on a certain day unless they were relieved by a force sufficient to meet him in the field. Salisbury landed his troops and sent a message to Du Guesclin bidding him either meet him or give up the hostages. The constable would not accept his challenge, and after the day fixed for the surrender had passed without his doing so, Salisbury reinforced and revictualled the place, and left it to return to his work of guarding the coasts. At the opening of parliament in November, the chancellor, Sir John Knyvet [q. v.], spoke in strong terms of the success of this expedition (*Rolls of Parliament*, ii. 316).

In February 1375 Salisbury was appointed joint-ambassador to attend the congress at Bruges, and in the following September was a joint-commissioner to treat of peace with France. He was made admiral of the western fleet in July 1376, but was relieved of that office in November. In the course of that year he was sent by the king to summon the king of Navarre to a conference (*Continuatio Eulogii*, iii. 340). A French invasion being expected, he was ordered in March 1377 to go down to his estate in the Isle of Wight with all his household and such force as he could muster for the defence of the island (*Fœdera*, III. ii. 1073). In April he was appointed joint-commissioner to treat with France, crossed the Channel and entered into negotiations, but was unable to obtain more than a month's truce (*ib.* p. 1076; *Chronicon Angliæ*, p. 140). He returned to England in June about the time of the king's death (FROISSART, i. 709), and in July received charge of the defence of the coasts of Hampshire and Dorset, and bore a royal vestment at the coronation of Richard II. Having entered into an engagement to serve abroad, he embarked with the Earl of Arundel [see FITZALAN, RICHARD III, EARL OF ARUNDEL], and having reconnoitred, persuaded the inhabitants of Cherbourg to place their town in the hands of the English king. He was lying with his ships at Plymouth in June waiting for a wind to go to the relief of Brest and Hennebon, when Lancaster took command. He sailed with the duke as admiral. The expedition did not accomplish anything [see under JOHN OF GAUNT]. Having been made captain of Calais in February 1379, an office which he held until the following January, he went thither and made forays, bringing much cattle into the town. In September he was appointed chief commissioner to treat with France. When the revolt of the villeins broke out in June 1381, he was with the king in the Tower of London; he counselled Richard to speak gently to the insurgents, and accompaned him from the Wardrobe to Smithfield, where he is said, after the death of Wat Tyler, to have commended the king's resolution not to take instant vengeance upon the rebels (FROISSART, ii. 154–63). He was in July appointed captain against the rebels in Somerset and Dorset. In common with other lords he tried to make peace between Lancaster and Northumberland, who quarrelled violently in the presence of the council at Berkhampstead [see under JOHN OF GAUNT]. In December he met the king's bride, Anne of Bohemia [q. v.], at Gravelines, and escorted her to Calais. In 1385 he was made captain of the Isle of Wight for life, accompanied the king in his invasion of Scotland, and was the next year also summoned to serve against the Scots. He shared in the anger with which the lords generally regarded the elevation of Robert de Vere as Duke of Ireland, and in their dissatisfaction with the king's misgovernment, and is said to have joined the king's uncles in their resistance to the duke (*ib.* pp. 606, 609, 622). In 1389 and 1392 he was appointed commissioner to treat with France, and in 1390 was employed in the march of Calais. Having no son living, he sold the lordship of Man to William le Scrope of Bolton, afterwards Earl of Wiltshire, in 1393, together with the crown thereof; for it was the right of the island that the chief lord of it should be called king and should be crowned with a gold crown (*Annales Ricardi II*, p. 157). Nevertheless he retained the title of Lord of Man until his death, using it in his will, dated 20 April 1397, by which he bequeathed five hundred marks to complete the buildings of Bisham priory, where he desired to be buried, and to make a tomb there for his father and mother, and another for himself and his son (DUGDALE). He died on 3 June following, and was succeeded by his nephew John Montacute, third earl of Salisbury [q. v.]

He was an active, valiant, and prudent man, and was skilled in war from his youth. After the declaration of the nullity of his contract of marriage with Joan of Kent, he married Elizabeth, daughter of John de Mohun, ninth lord Mohun of Dunster [q. v.], who survived him, and had by her Sir William Montacute and two daughters. Sir William, who married Elizabeth, daughter of Richard, earl of Arundel, was killed at a tilting at Windsor in 1383, by, it is said, his father; he left no issue.

[Geoffrey le Baker, ed. Thompson; Froissart, ed. Buchon; Chandos Herald, ed. Michel; Rymer's Fœdera (Record ed.); Chron. Angliæ, a Mon. S. Albani, 1328–88 (Rolls Ser.); Walsingham (*ib.*); Eulogii Cont. ap. Eulogium, vol. iii. (*ib.*); Annales Ric. II, ap. Trokelowe et Annales (*ib.*); Vita Ric. II, ed. Hearne; Stow's Annals; Dugdale's Baronage; Doyle's Official Baronage; Nicolas's Royal Navy; Nicolas's Orders of Knighthood; Beltz's Order of the Garter.]

W. H.

MONTAGU, MARQUIS OF. [See NEVILL, JOHN, *d.* 1471.]

MONTAGU or MONTAGUE, VISCOUNT. [See BROWNE, ANTHONY, first VISCOUNT, 1526–1592.]

MONTAGU, BASIL (1770–1851), legal and miscellaneous writer and philanthropist, second (natural) son of John Montagu, fourth earl of Sandwich, by Martha Ray [see HACKMAN, JAMES], born on 24 April 1770, was acknowledged by his father, brought up at Hinchinbrook, Huntingdonshire, and educated at the Charterhouse and Christ's College, Cambridge, where he matriculated in 1786, graduated B.A. (fifth wrangler) in 1790, and proceeded M.A. in 1793. On 30 Jan. 1789 he was admitted a member of Gray's Inn, but continued to reside at Cambridge until 1795, when, having by a technical flaw lost the portion intended for him by his father, he came to London to read for the bar. He was on intimate terms with Coleridge and Wordsworth, whose juvenile enthusiasm for the ideas of 1789 he shared. In the autumn of 1797 he made a tour in the midland counties with William Godwin the elder [q. v.] He was called to the bar on

19 May 1798. By Sir James Mackintosh, whose acquaintance he soon afterwards made, and with whom he went the Norfolk circuit, he was converted to political common sense and the study of Bacon. Montagu was also a friend of Dr. Parr, whom he visited at Hatton (cf. a funny story in De la Pryme, *Autobiography*, p. 261, of his falling asleep in church while Parr was officiating, and being roused by the doctor himself in time for the repetition of the creed with the peremptory command, 'Basil, stand up'). Montagu never became eminent as a pleader, but he gradually acquired an extensive practice in chancery and bankruptcy; his leisure time he devoted to legal and miscellaneous literary work.

In 1801 he published 'A Summary of the Law of Set Off, with an Appendix of Cases argued and determined in the Courts of Law and Equity upon that subject,' London, 8vo, a valuable treatise on an obscure and intricate branch of the law; and between 1805 and 1807 compiled 'A Digest of the Bankrupt Laws, with a Collection of the Cases argued and determined in the Courts of Law and Equity upon that subject,' London, 4 vols. 8vo. Appointed by Lord Erskine, 1806–7, to a commissionership in bankruptcy, he at once set himself to reform the bankruptcy law. In 1809 he published 'An Enquiry respecting the Expediency of Limiting the Creditor's power to refuse a Bankrupt's Certificate,' London, 8vo; in 1810 an 'Enquiry respecting the Mode of Issuing Commissions in Bankruptcy,' London, 8vo, a protest against the bad practice then in vogue of initiating bankruptcy proceedings by means of secret commissions; and in 1811 'Enquiries respecting the Administration of Bankrupts' Estates by Assignees,' London, 8vo. He also founded in 1809 the Society for the Diffusion of Knowledge upon the Punishment of Death; published the same year a volume of selections entitled 'The Opinions of different Authors upon the Punishment of Death,' London, 8vo; and in subsequent years a variety of pamphlets on the same topic, for which see bibliographical note *infra*. In 1813 appeared his 'Enquiries respecting the Proposed Alteration of the Law of Copyright as it affects Authors and Universities,' London, 8vo; in 1815 'A Digest of the Law of Partnership, with a Collection of Cases decided in the Courts of Law and Equity,' London, 2 vols. 8vo; and in 1816 'Enquiries respecting the Insolvent Debtors' Bill, with the Opinions of Dr. Paley, Mr. Burke, and Dr. Johnson upon Imprisonment for Debt,' London, 8vo. 'A Summary of the Law of Lien' followed, and 'Suggestions respecting the Improvement of the Bankrupt Laws' in 1821, London, 8vo; 'Some Observations upon the Bill for the Improvement of the Bankrupt Laws' in 1822, London, 8vo; 'A Summary of the Law of Composition with Creditors' in 1823, London, 8vo; and 'A Digest of Pleading in Equity, with Notes of the Cases decided in different Courts of Equity upon that subject,' in 1824, London, 2 vols. 8vo.

In 1825 he exposed (against his own interest) the ruinous delay and expense involved in the existing bankruptcy procedure in 'Inquiries respecting the Courts of Commissioners of Bankrupts and Lord Chancellor's Court,' London, 8vo; and in July of the same year gave evidence before the chancery commission, and suggested a radical reform. In 1826 he edited 'The Evidence in Bankruptcy before the Chancery Commission, with the Report,' London, 8vo; and in 1826–7 published two 'Letters on the Report of the Chancery Commissioners to the Right Honourable Robert Peel,' London, 8vo. He also published in 1827 'Observations upon the Act for Consolidating the Bankrupt Laws,' London, 8vo; 'Reform,' London, 8vo (a tract chiefly relating to bankruptcy); and in conjunction with Francis Gregg 'A Digest of the Bankrupt Laws as altered by the New Statutes,' London, 2 vols. 8vo. 'Letters on the Bankrupt Laws to Edward Burtenshaw Sugden, Esq.' (afterwards Lord St. Leonards), followed in 1829, London, 8vo; and in 1831 'The New Bankrupt Court Act, arranged with a copious Index and Observations upon the Erroneous Principle on which it is Founded,' London, 1831, 8vo.

In Trinity term 1835 Montagu was made K.C., and soon afterwards accountant-general in bankruptcy. His tenure of this office, which lasted until 1846, he made memorable by establishing the liability of the Bank of England to pay interest on bankruptcy deposits. In 1837 he published, in conjunction with Scrope Ayrton, 'The Law and Practice in Bankruptcy as altered by the New Statutes, Orders, and Decisions,' London, 2 vols. 8vo; 2nd edit. 1844. Montagu also published several excellent series of bankruptcy reports, viz.: in conjunction with John Macarthur, London, 1830, 8vo, 1832, 8vo; in conjunction with Scrope Ayrton, 1834–9, 3 vols. 8vo; in conjunction with Richard Bligh, 1835, 8vo; in conjunction with Edward Chitty, 1840, 8vo; in conjunction with Edward E. Deacon and John De Gex, 1842–5, 3 vols. 8vo.

To the 'Retrospective Review' Montagu contributed in 1821 two articles on the 'Novum Organum' of Lord Bacon, whose

'Works' he edited, in 16 vols. 8vo, between 1825 and 1837. His qualifications for the task were by no means of the highest order. His knowledge of the history of philosophy was far too slight and superficial to enable him to form a just appreciation of Bacon's contribution to scientific method, while he exhausted the resources of special pleading in the attempt to rehabilitate his character as a man. His perverse ingenuity provoked the trenchant censures of Macaulay's celebrated 'Essay' originally published in the 'Edinburgh Review' for July 1837. In 1841 Montagu began the publication of a series of 'Letters to the Right Hon. T. B. Macaulay upon the Review of the Life of Lord Bacon.' Only the first, however, dealing with Bacon's conduct in Peacham's case, seems to have appeared. His reputation suffered unduly by Macaulay's strictures, for with all its faults his edition, by its approximate completeness, was of indubitable value, although it was practically superseded by Mr. Spedding's labours in 1860 and following years. He was assisted in it by Francis Wrangham [q. v.] and William Page Wood, afterwards Lord Hatherley [q. v.], who were responsible for the translations of the Latin treatises.

Montagu also published a volume of 'Essays,' chiefly reprints, with 'An Outline of a Course of Lectures upon the Conduct of the Understanding,' London, 1824, 8vo; 'Thoughts on Laughter,' London, 1830, 12mo; 'Thoughts of Divines and Philosophers,' London, 1832, 24mo (a volume of selections); 'Lectures delivered at the Mechanics' Institution upon the connexion between Knowledge and Happiness,' London, 1832, 8vo; 'Essays and Selections,' London, 1837, 8vo; and 'Thoughts on the Conduct of the Understanding,' a fragment of a *magnum opus* which he had on hand for thirty years, printed for private circulation, probably in 1847, 8vo. He was a member of the Athenæum Club, and his town house, 25 Bedford Square, was for many years a centre of reunion for London literary society. He was one of the most attentive listeners to Coleridge's monologues at Highgate. He died at Boulogne-sur-Mer on 27 Nov. 1851.

Montagu married thrice: (1) On 4 Sept. 1790, Caroline Matilda Want of Brampton, Huntingdonshire; (2) at Glasgow, in 1801, Laura, eldest daughter of Sir William Beaumaris Rush of Roydon, Suffolk, and Wimbledon, Surrey; (3) the widow of Thomas Skepper, lawyer, of York. He had by his first wife a son Edward, mentioned in Wordsworth's lines 'To my Sister' and 'Anecdotes for Fathers' (see *Poems referring to the Period of Childhood*, No. xii.; and *Poems of Sentiment and Reflection*, No. v.) By his second wife he had three sons; and two sons and a daughter by his third wife. All his children but two (his daughter and one of his sons by his third wife) died in his lifetime, and none now survive. His third wife, whose maiden name was Benson, was the daughter of a wine merchant of York, and in her youth had known Burns (cf. his complimentary letter to her dated Dumfries, 21 March 1793, in his *Correspondence*). She was a fine woman, and in her middle age fascinated Edward Irving, who gave her the sobriquet of 'the noble lady.' Carlyle, introduced to her by Irving in 1824, corresponded with her in a somewhat stilted and adulatory style, and during the earlier years of his residence in London was a frequent visitor at 25 Bedford Square. His pride was wounded by an offer of a clerkship at 200*l.* a year which her husband made him in 1837, and he vented his spleen in his 'Reminiscences.' His portrait of 'the noble lady' is, however, by no means unfavourable. His early letters to her were printed for private circulation by her daughter by her first husband, Mrs. Procter, soon after the publication of the 'Reminiscences' [see PROCTER, BRYAN WALLER].

A portrait of Montagu by Opie was lent by Bryan Waller Procter ('Barry Cornwall') to the third Loan Exhibition (No. 183).

Besides the works above mentioned, and a long series of pamphlets denouncing the punishment of death (1811–30), and two on the emancipation of the Jews (1833–4), Montagu published: 'Enquiries and Observations respecting the University Library,' Cambridge, 1805, 8vo; 'Selections from the Works of Taylor, Hooker, Hall, and Lord Bacon, with an Analysis of the Advancement of Learning,' London, 1805, 8vo; 'An Examination of some Observations upon a passage in Dr. Paley's Moral Philosophy on the Punishment of Death,' London, 1810, 8vo; 'Some Enquiries into the Effects of Fermented Liquors,' London, 1814, 8vo; 'Some Thoughts upon Liberty, and the Rights of Englishmen,' London, 1819, 8vo; 'The Private Tutor, or Thoughts upon the Love of Excelling and the Love of Excellence,' London, 1820, 8vo; 'A Letter to the Right Hon. Charles, Lord Cottenham, Lord High Chancellor of Great Britain, on the Separation of the Judicial and Political Functions of the Lord Chancellor,' London, 1836, 8vo; 'Knowledge, Error, Prejudice, and Reform,' London, 1836, 8vo; 'Rules for the Construction of Statutes, Deeds, and Wills,' London, 1836, 8vo; 'Adam in Paradise, or a View of Man in his first State,' London, 1837, 16mo (a reprint of

South's sermon on Gen. i. 27); 'A Letter addressed to Charles Purton Cooper, Esq., Secretary to the Commissioners on the Public Records upon the Report of the recent Record Committee,' London, 1837, 8vo; 'The Law of Parliamentary Elections' (in conjunction with W. Johnson Neale), London, 1839, 8vo; 'The Funerals of the Quakers,' London, 1840, 12mo; 'The Law and Practice upon Election Petitions before Committees of the House of Commons,' London, 1840, 8vo; 'Three Lectures on the Works of Lord Bacon' (of uncertain date).

[Gent. Mag. 1790 pt. ii. p. 858, 1806 pt. i. p. 590, 1824 pt. ii. p. 560, 1852 pt. i. p. 410; Athenæum, 1851, p. 1282; Law Times, xliii. 237; Gunning's Reminiscences, i. 155 et seq.; Cambridge Triposes, 1754–1807; Grad. Cant.; Foster's Gray's Inn Reg.; Law List, 1799, 1836, and 1847; Knight's English Cyclopædia; Knight's Life of Wordsworth, i. 103, ii. 169–73, 278, iii. 214; Sir James Mackintosh's Memoirs, 2nd ed. pp. 147–66; Kegan Paul's William Godwin, his Friends and Contemporaries; Crabb Robinson's Diary, i. 371, 488, ii. 37, 129, 252, 254; Sir Samuel Romilly's Memoirs, ii. 410; An Account of the Origin and Object of the Society for the Diffusion of Knowledge upon the Punishment of Death and the Improvement of Prison Discipline, London, 1812, 8vo; Allsop's Letters, Conversations, and Recollections of S. T. Coleridge, i. 102, ii. 69, 211; Stephens's Memoir of the Right Hon. William Page Wood, Baron Hatherley, i. 51, 57, 160, 175, ii. 120; Fitzgerald's Life and Letters of C. Lamb, iii. 22; Carlyle's Reminiscences (under Edward Irving); Froude's Thomas Carlyle, 1795–1835 and 1830–1881; Bryan Waller Procter's Autobiography, p. 56; Mrs. Oliphant's Life of Edward Irving, 4th ed. pp. 91, 103, 111, and Literary History of England in the end of the 18th and the beginning of the 19th Century, ii. 316; Letters addressed to Mrs. Basil Montagu and B. W. Procter by Mr. Thomas Carlyle, with prefatory note by Anne Benson Procter, 1881; Visitations of Essex (Harl. Soc.), pt. ii. p. 704; Add. MS. 24811, ff. 308–11.] J. M. R.

MONTAGU, CHARLES, Earl of Halifax (1661–1715), said to have been born at Horton, Northamptonshire, on 16 April 1661, was fourth son of George Montagu of Horton, by his wife Elizabeth, daughter of Sir Anthony Irby, knight, of Boston, Lincolnshire. His father was son of Sir Henry Montagu, first earl of Manchester [q. v.], by his third wife, and Sir James Montagu [q. v.] was his brother. Charles was baptised at St. Margaret's, Westminster, on 12 May 1661, and in 1675 entered Westminster School, where in 1677 he was admitted on the foundation as the captain of his election. At Westminster he distinguished himself by his 'extempore epigrams made upon theses appointed for the king's scholars at the time of election, and had more presents made him, according to custom, on that account than any one of his contemporaries' (*Life*, p. 4). Leaving school before he was entitled to compete for the scholarships, he was admitted to Trinity College, Cambridge, in 1679 as a fellow-commoner. Here he commenced his lifelong friendship with Isaac Newton, whom he assisted in an unsuccessful attempt to establish a philosophical society at Cambridge in 1685. Montagu's ingenious and fulsome verses on the death of Charles II, which were published in 'Mœstissimæ ac Lætissimæ Academiæ Cantabrigiensis affectus,' &c. (Cambridge, 1684–1685, 4to), attracted the attention of the Earl of Dorset, by whom he was invited to London and introduced to the wits of the town. Previously to the publication of this book Montagu had been created a Master of Arts and elected a fellow of Trinity. In 1687 he wrote in conjunction with Matthew Prior [q. v.] 'The Hind and the Panther transvers'd to the Story of the Country Mouse and the City Mouse' (London, 4to), a clever burlesque of Dryden's poem, which was received with great applause. In the following year he signed the letter of invitation to William, prince of Orange, and joined the rising in Northamptonshire in the prince's favour (*Hatton Correspondence*, Camd. Soc. Publ., 1878, ii. 116). He now abandoned his original intention of taking orders, and in January 1689 was returned to the Convention parliament for the borough of Maldon, which he continued to represent until October 1695. In February 1689 he became one of the clerks of the privy council, a post which he purchased for 1,500*l.* Shortly after William's coronation Dorset is said to have introduced Montagu to the king, with the remark that he had 'brought a Mouse to have the honour of kissing his hand,' to which the king replied, 'You will do well to put me in the way of making a man of him,' and thereupon ordered him a pension of 500*l.* a year until the opportunity should arise (*Life*, p. 17, but see Johnson, *Works*, x. 44–5). In December 1691 Montagu was elected chairman of the committee of the House of Commons appointed to confer with a committee of the House of Lords on the amendments to the bill for regulating trials in the cases of high treason.

In consequence of the great ability which he displayed as a debater on this occasion, Montagu was appointed a lord of the treasury on 21 March 1692. His proposal to raise a million by way of loan was approved by the House of Commons in committee on 15 Dec. 1692, and a bill was ordered to be brought in. By this bill new duties were imposed on beer and other liquors, on the credit of which a million was to be raised by life annuities. As the annuitants died their annuities were to be divided among the survivors until their number was reduced to seven, when the remaining annuities as they fell in were to lapse to the government. The bill was rapidly passed through both houses (4 William and Mary, c. iii.), and the loan which it authorised was the origin of our national debt (MACAULAY, *Hist. of England*, iv. 325–326). Adopting Patterson's scheme for a national bank, Montagu in the spring of 1694 introduced the Tonnage Bill, by which a loan was to be raised to meet the expenses of the French war. In order to induce the capitalists to advance the 1,200,000*l.* required, the subscribers were to be formed into a corporation, known as the Governor and Company of the Bank of England, and were to be allowed to treat the loan to the government as part of their capital, the interest on which, at 8*l.* per cent., was to be secured by taxes. In spite of considerable opposition in both houses, and a furious paper warfare outside, Montagu's bill, by which the Bank of England was established, became law (5 William and Mary, c. xx.) So eagerly was the new investment taken up in the city that in ten days after the books were opened it was announced that the whole of the money had been subscribed (LUTTRELL, iii. 331–2, 333, 338). As a reward for his brilliant services Montagu was promoted to the office of chancellor of the exchequer on 30 April 1694, and was sworn a member of the privy council on 10 May following. On 20 Feb. 1695 he was appointed a commissioner of Greenwich Hospital. At the general election in October 1695 Montagu was returned to parliament for the city of Westminster. While supporting the bill for regulating trials in cases of high treason, which had been reintroduced early in the first session of the new parliament, Montagu suddenly 'seem'd to be so surpriz'd that for a while he could not go on; but having recovered himself, took occasion from his very surprize to enforce the necessity of allowing Council to Prisoners, who were to appear before their Judges, since he who was not only innocent and unaccus'd, but one of their own members, was so dash'd when he was to speak before that wise and illustrious Assembly' (*Life*, p. 30). The use of this oratorical device is, however, attributed to Anthony, third earl of Shaftesbury, by Horace Walpole and others (*Cat. of Royal and Noble Authors*, iv. 56; see also *Parl. Hist.* v. 966, and MACAULAY, *Hist. of England*, iv. 644).

Aided by Somers, Locke, Newton, and Halley, Montagu determined to remedy the alarming depreciation of the currency. To such an extent had the nefarious practices of clipping and counterfeiting been carried, that the current coinage throughout the country was on an average but little more than half its proper weight. After much controversy, Montagu, on 10 Dec. 1695, carried eleven resolutions, by which it was agreed that the new coinage should be 'according to the established standard of the mint both as to weight and fineness,' that the loss on the clipped silver should be borne by the public, that all crowns and half-crowns should be in future milled, and that a day should be fixed after which no clipped money should pass (*Journals of the House of Commons*, xi. 358). Owing to the amendments made in the House of Lords to the Re-coinage Bill, which had been framed in conformity with these resolutions, Montagu was obliged to bring in a fresh bill in a slightly modified form, which he succeeded in passing through both houses (7 & 8 William III, c. i.) To provide for the expense of the re-coinage, which occupied four years, and was not completed until 1699, Montagu instituted the window tax (7 & 8 William III, c. xviii.) While the provisions for the new currency were being carried out the credit of the government reached its lowest ebb. Most of the old silver had been withdrawn, and but little of the new had got into circulation. At this crisis Montagu availed himself of the clauses which he had succeeded in grafting on Harley's National Land Bank Bill (7 & 8 William III, c. xxxi.), empowering the government to issue negotiable paper bearing interest at the rate of threepence a day on a hundred pounds, and he issued the first exchequer bills. They were drawn for various small amounts varying from five to one hundred pounds, were rapidly distributed over the kingdom by post, and were everywhere welcome. By this ingenious scheme credit was revived, and ever since 'the issue of Exchequer bills has been the form in which Government gets its first credit from the House of Commons' (THOROLD ROGERS, *Historical Gleanings*, 1st ser. p. 33, and *First Nine Years of the Bank of England*, p. 67; cf. art. LOWNDES, WILLIAM). In the autumn of 1696 Montagu warmly supported the bill of attainder against Sir John Fenwick, and still further increased his reputation in the House of Commons as a consummate debater. In the same session he carried his scheme popularly known as the General Mortgage, whereby a consolidated fund was formed for the purpose of meeting the interest on the various government loans (8 & 9 William III, c. xx.) By the same act the capital stock of the Bank of England was enlarged by a new subscription, which was immediately taken up by the public, and afforded a further proof of Montagu's commercial sagacity.

Sir Stephen Fox having withdrawn his claim to the post, Montagu was appointed first lord of the treasury on 1 May 1697 in the place of Godolphin, whose resignation had been accepted in the previous October. With the object of damaging Montagu, Charles Duncombe [q. v.] accused the treasury board of tampering with exchequer bills. An inquiry was instituted and the board acquitted; while Duncombe, who confessed under cross-examination to being a party to an infamous fraud when receiver of excise, was committed to the Tower (*Journals of the House of Commons*, xii. 63). On 16 Feb. 1698 Colonel Granville charged Montagu in the House of Commons with having obtained for himself a grant, in the name of one Thomas Railton, of certain securities forfeited to the king in Ireland of the value of about 10,000*l.* A warm debate ensued, during which Montagu avowed the truth of the charge and defended his conduct. The question that he should withdraw from the house after his speech was defeated by 209 to 97, and it was resolved that 'the Honourable Charles Mountague, Esquire, Chancellor of the Exchequer, for his good services to this Government does deserve his Majesty's Favour' (*ib.* xii. 116). In the same year Montagu's bill for the promotion of the General Society, to which the monopoly of the Indian trade was to be given, and by which a loan of 2,000,000*l.*, bearing interest at 8*l.* per cent. was to be advanced to the government, was carried through both houses (9 & 10 William III, c. xliv.) In spite of the forebodings of his opponents, who predicted the immediate failure of the scheme, the whole sum was subscribed in a few days. At the general election in July 1698 Montagu was again returned for Westminster, and the petition which was lodged against his return was dismissed as 'frivolous, vexatious, and scandalous' in the following December (*ib.* xii. 365–6). On the death of Sir Robert Howard, Montagu secured the auditorship of the exchequer, and placed his brother in the post until he should want it himself (5 Sept. 1698). The reversion of this place, worth some 4,000*l.* a year, had been granted by Charles II to the Marquis of Carmarthen (afterwards second Duke of Leeds), who, however, failed ultimately to establish his title to it (Luttrell, iv. 423, v. 185, 190–1, 290, 308–9, 314). Montagu was a lord justice in the king's absence in 1698–9.

Hitherto Montagu's career had been one of uninterrupted success, though his overbearing conduct and his extreme vanity had made him many enemies. Fortune now rapidly began to desert him. He was assailed on all sides by a crowd of libellers, who accused him of boundless corruption, gave him the nickname of 'Filcher,' and invented fabulous stories of his extravagant mode of life. Even in the House of Commons, where he 'had gained such a visible ascendant over all that were zealous for the king's service that he gave the law to the rest' (Burnet, *Hist. of my own Time*, iii. 397–398), Montagu now found himself thwarted and opposed at every turn. Having lost his position as leader of the house, he resigned the office of chancellor of the exchequer in May, and that of first lord of the treasury in November 1699. He took his seat as auditor of the exchequer on 18 Nov. 1699 (Luttrell, iv. 583), and was created Baron Halifax of Halifax in the county of York on 13 Dec. 1700 with remainder on failure of male issue to his nephew George, the son and heir of his elder brother, Edward Montagu. Halifax took his seat in the House of Lords on 11 Feb. 1701 (*Journals of the House of Lords*, xvi. 593). On 14 April 1701 a motion declaring Halifax to be 'guilty of a high crime and misdemeanor' on account of his share in the Partition Treaty was carried in the House of Commons by 186 votes to 136, and a unanimous resolution that he should be impeached was subsequently passed (*Journals of the House of Commons*, xiii. 490). A few days afterwards an address was presented to the king from the House of Commons praying him to dismiss Halifax, Somers, Orford, and Portland from his 'Council and Presence for ever' (*ib.* p. 497), while a counter-address was presented from the House of Lords beseeching him not to pass any censure upon the four lords until judgment had been given on the impeachment (*Journals of the House of Lords*, xvi. 655). On 14 June six articles of impeachment against Halifax were brought up from the House of Commons. The first five articles mainly related to the grants which Halifax had obtained from the king in the names of Thomas Railton, Henry Seager, and Christopher Montagu in trust for himself, while the sixth charged him with advising and promoting the conclusion of the Partition Treaty. In his answer Halifax acknowledged obtaining these grants, but denied that he had ever advised, or had even been consulted about the treaty (*ib.* pp. 750–2), and on 24 June the House of Lords dismissed the impeachment for want of prosecution (*ib.* p. 769). During the debate on the third reading of the Occasional Conformity Bill in December 1702, Halifax carried a resolution declaring that 'the annexing any clause or clauses to a bill of aid or supply, the matter of which is foreign to and different from the matter of the said bill of aid or supply, is unparliamentary and tends to the destruction of the constitution of this Government' (*ib.* xvii. 185), and as one of the managers of the subsequent conferences he successfully resisted the passing of the bill.

Halifax had now been struck off the list of privy councillors, but this was not considered enough by the more violent tories who regarded him with abhorrence. In January 1703 a resolution was passed in the House of Commons charging Halifax with neglect of his duty as auditor of the exchequer (*Journals of the House of Commons*, xiv. 140, 143). A committee of the House of Lords was appointed to consider this charge, which arose out of a recently delivered report of the commissioners of the public accounts. Halifax was examined before the committee, and on 5 Feb. a unanimous resolution was passed approving of his conduct as auditor (*Journals of the House of Lords*, xvii. 270–1). This led to an interminable wrangle between the two houses, and an address was presented by the House of Commons to the queen repeating the charge against Halifax, and requesting her to order the attorney-general 'effectually to prosecute at law the said Auditor of Receipt' (*Journals of the House of Commons*, xiv. 188–91). After much delay the case against Halifax was heard on 23 June 1704, and a *nolle prosequi* entered, 'so no verdict was given' (Luttrell, v. 438–9, 443; see also 483, 487, 488, 518). On 14 Dec. 1703 Halifax successfully moved the rejection of the Occasional Conformity Bill, and in the following year wrote 'an answer' to Bromley's speech in favour of tacking the Occasional Conformity Bill to the Land Tax Bill (*Life*, pp. 113–30). In March 1705 Halifax served as one of the managers on the part of the lords in their conference with the commons on the Aylesbury case. He continued out of office during the whole of Anne's reign, but on 10 April 1706 he was appointed one of the commissioners for negotiating the union with Scotland, and in the same month was selected to carry the insignia of the order of the Garter to the electoral prince. On 3 June 1709 he was made keeper of Bushey Park and Hampton Court. In 1710 he published 'Seasonable Questions concerning a New Parliament' (*ib.* pp. 157–9). He was appointed joint plenipotentiary to the Hague in July 1710, a post from which he had hitherto been excluded by Marlborough (see Coxe, *Memoirs of the Duke of Marlborough*, ii. 253–5, iii. 7–8, 268–70). On 15 Feb. 1712 Halifax carried, in the House of Lords, an address to the queen against the French project of treaty. In May 1713 he declared himself in favour of dissolving the union with Scotland, provided the Hanoverian succession could be secured (*Parl. Hist.* vi. 1219). He unsuccessfully opposed the passing of the Schism Bill in the following year and drew up an elaborate protest against it (Rogers, *Complete Collection of the Protests of the House of Lords*, 1875, i. 218–21). The 'queries,' which he handed in to the House during this debate, for 'the serious consideration' of the bishops, were written by Edmund Calamy, and not by Halifax as the author of Halifax's 'Life' would seem to imply (*Life*, pp. 236–9, and Calamy, *Hist. Account of his own Life*, ii. 284, 543–6). On the death of Anne, Halifax acted as one of the lords justices of Great Britain until the arrival of George I. On 11 Oct. 1714 he was appointed first lord of the treasury, and on the 16th of the same month was invested with the order of the Garter. By letters patent dated 19 Oct. 1714 he was raised to the dignities of Viscount Sunbury and Earl of Halifax, and as such took his seat in the House of Lords on 21 March 1715 (*Journals of the House of Lords*, xx. 26). On 13 Dec. 1714 he became lord-lieutenant of Surrey. Disappointed at not being made lord high treasurer, Halifax is said to have commenced negotiations with the tories (see Coxe, *Life of Sir Robert Walpole*, i. 81, and Lord Mahon, *History of England*, 1858, i. 133), but of this there seems to be little or no evidence. Halifax was taken suddenly ill on 15 May 1715 at the house of Mynheer Duvenvoord, one of the Dutch ambassadors, and died of inflammation of the lungs on the 19th. He was buried on the 26th of the same month in the Duke of Albemarle's vault on the north side of Henry VII's Chapel in Westminster Abbey, where a monument was erected to his memory (Neale, *Westminster Abbey*, vol. i. pt. ii. pp. 63–4).

Halifax possessed great administrative ability and keen business faculties. As a finance minister he achieved a series of brilliant successes. As a parliamentary orator his only rival was Somers. His ambition was great, his vanity excessive, and his arrogance unbounded. He was president of the Royal Society from 30 Nov. 1695 to 30 Nov. 1698, and he was a munificent patron of literature. Addison, Congreve, Newton, Prior, Stepney, were all indebted to him for preferment. Pope, however, holds up Halifax's patronage of men of letters to the bitterest scorn in the 'Epistle to Dr. Arbuthnot' (lines 231–248)—

Proud as Apollo on his forked hill
Sat full-blown Bufo, puff'd by every quill, &c.,

and Swift declares that the only encouragements which Halifax ever gave to learned men were 'good words and good dinners' (SWIFT, *Works*, x. 303). Halifax seems, however, to have made some effort to retain Swift's services on the whig side in 1710. 'He was,' says Swift, 'continually teasing me to go to his house.' He went to see him at Hampton Court in October 1710 (Halifax was then ranger of Bushey Park), and the statesman proposed as a toast 'the resurrection of the whigs,' 'which,' Swift remarks, 'I refused, unless he would add their reformation too; and I told him he was the only whig in England I loved or had any good opinion of' (*Journal to Stella*). He was the last of Swift's friends among the prominent whigs. The Duchess of Marlborough, in a most unflattering account of his character, spitefully declares 'he was so great a manager' that when he dined alone 'he eat upon pewter for fear of lessening the value of his plate by cleaning it often,' that 'he was a frightful figure, and yet pretended to be a lover, and followed several beauties, who laughed at him for it,' and that 'he was as renowned for ill-breeding as Sir Robert Walpole is' (*Private Corr. of the Duchess of Marlborough*, ii. 147–8).

He married, in February 1688 (LUTTRELL, i. 432), Anne, daughter of Sir Christopher Yelverton, bart., of Easton Maudit, Northamptonshire, and widow of Robert, third earl of Manchester [see under MONTAGU, EDWARD, second EARL], by whom he had no issue. His wife died in July 1698. After her death Halifax formed an extraordinary intimacy with Isaac Newton's niece, 'the gay and witty' Catherine Barton. She was the second daughter of Robert Barton of Brigstock, Northamptonshire, by his second wife, Hannah, daughter of the Rev. Barnabas Smith, rector of North Witham, Lincolnshire. Whether the attachment was purely platonic or not it is now impossible to say. The scandal of the day stigmatised her as his mistress. Professor De Morgan, who minutely investigated the subject in 'Newton, his Friend, and his Niece' (1885), came to the conclusion that she was privately married to Halifax. Colonel Chester gives some cogent reasons to show that she was not his wife (*Westminster Abbey Registers*, p. 354). That she was his mistress it is difficult to believe, seeing that her uncle, whose character is above reproach, must have connived at such an intimacy had it existed. The earldom and viscounty became extinct upon Halifax's death, but the barony of Halifax devolved upon his nephew, George Montagu, who was created Viscount Sunbury and Earl of Halifax on 14 June 1715, died in 1739, and was father of George Montagu Dunk, second earl of Halifax of the second creation [q. v.]

Halifax acted as chairman of the committees of the House of Lords appointed from time to time to inquire into the state of the records, and is said to have suggested the purchase of the Cotton. MSS. with a view to the formation of a public library. He appears also to have been one of the principal promoters of Rymer's 'Fœdera,' the origin of which has been erroneously attributed to Harley (HARDY, *Syllabus of Rymer's Fœdera*, 1869, i. vii–xiv). His collection of prints, medals, and coins was sold in 1740, and his collection of manuscripts relating to public affairs in 1760. His poems, which have little merit (in spite of Addison's description of their author as 'the greatest of English poets'), were published in a collected form, under the title of 'The Works and Life of the Right Hon. Charles, late Earl of Halifax, including the History of his Lordship's Times,' London, 1715, 8vo; second edition (with a slightly altered title), London, 1716, 8vo. They are to be found in Chalmers's 'English Poets' and similar collections.

There is a half-length portrait of Halifax by Sir Godfrey Kneller at Trinity College, Cambridge. It has been engraved by Smith (1693), G. Vertue (1710), Vandergucht (1715), T. Faber (1782), Pierre Drevet, and others.

[The Works and Life of the Right Hon. Charles, late Earl of Halifax, 1715; Burnet's History of his own Time, 1883, vols. iv. v. vi.; Luttrell's Brief Relation, vols. iii. iv. v. vi.; Swift's Works, 1814; Coxe's Memoirs of the Duke of Marlborough, 1818–19; Coxe's Shrewsbury Correspondence, 1821; Private Corr. of Sarah, Duchess of Marlborough, 1838; Diary of Mary, Countess Cowper, 1864; Calamy's Historical Account, 1830; Sir David Brewster's Memoirs of Isaac Newton, 1855; Lord Macaulay's History of England, 1st edit. vols. ii. iv. v.; Lord Stanhope's Reign of Queen Anne, 1872; Ranke's History of England, 1875, vol. v.; Rogers's Historical Gleanings, 1869, 1st ser. pp. 3–45; Macky's Memoirs, 1733, pp. 51–4; Biographia Brit. 1760, v. 3149–57; Chalmers's Biog. Dict. 1815, xxii. 256–60; Johnson's Works, 1810, x. 43–8; Park's edition of Walpole's Catalogue of Royal and Noble Authors, 1806, iv.

62–70; Pope's Works, ed. Elwin and Courthope; Howell's State Trials, 1812, xiv. 233–50; Weld's History of the Royal Society, 1848, i. 305–6, 331–7, 399; Ruding's Annals of the Coinage of Great Britain, 1840, ii. 36–59; Rogers's First Nine Years of the Bank of England, 1887; Noble's Continuation of Granger's Biog. Hist. 1806, i. 250–3; Alumni Westmon. 1852; Chester's Westminster Abbey Registers, 1876, pp. 283, 354; Doyle's Official Baronage, 1886, ii. 95–6; Burke's Extinct Peerage, 1866, p. 373; Official Return of Lists of Members of Parliament, pt. i. pp. 559, 566, 574, 581; Haydn's Book of Dignities, 1890; Notes and Queries, 1st ser. viii. 429, 543, 590, ix. 18, 2nd ser. ii. 161, 265, 390, iii. 41, 250, ix. 420, x. 188, 521, xi. 443, 3rd ser. ii. 404, 4th ser. ii. 413, 517, 8th ser. ii. 166, 167, 189; Brit. Mus. Cat.]

G. F. R. B.

MONTAGU, CHARLES, first Duke of Manchester (1660?–1722), diplomatist, third and eldest surviving son of Robert, third earl of Manchester [see under Montagu, Edward, second Earl], by Anne, daughter of Sir Christopher Yelverton of Easton Maudit, Northamptonshire, born about 1660, was educated at Trinity College, Cambridge, and abroad. In 1680 he was created M.A. at Cambridge. He succeeded as Earl of Manchester and Viscount Mandeville on the death of his father, 14 March 1682. Of handsome appearance, he was chosen to serve the office of lord carver to the queen at the coronation of James II, 23 April 1685. On 12 May following he took his seat in the House of Lords, but soon afterwards went abroad in disgust at the revival of arbitrary power, had an audience of the Prince of Orange, and was made a party to his designs. Returning to England, he raised a troop of horse in Nottinghamshire, and joined the prince on his landing. At his coronation, 11 April 1689, he carried St. Edward's staff, and the same year was made captain of the yeomen of the guard and lord-lieutenant of Huntingdonshire. He attended the king to Ireland in June 1690, and fought at the Boyne and before Limerick. In the winter of 1697–8 he was at Venice on an extraordinary mission to obtain the release of certain English seamen detained in the galleys of the republic. The doge and signory received and entertained him with great ceremony, but returned evasive answers to his representations, and the prisoners had not been released when, in the spring of 1698, he was recalled.

On his return to England, Manchester was sworn of the privy council (8 June), and in the following year succeeded Lord Jersey as ambassador extraordinary at the court of France. He arrived in Paris on 5 Aug. 1699, and had his first audience of Louis XIV on 15 Nov. His principal function was to watch and, as far as possible, counteract the intrigues of the court of St. Germains, and accordingly, on the death of James II and the recognition of the Pretender by Louis, he was recalled without leave-taking (September 1701). From 4 Jan. 1701–2 to 15 May following, Manchester held the seal of secretary of state for the northern department. In 1707 he was again ambassador extraordinary at Venice, to negotiate the adhesion of the republic to the grand alliance. Travelling by Vienna, where he had an audience of the emperor (27 April), he reached Venice on 30 June. The signory, as on a former occasion, treated him with marked distinction, and returned evasive answers to his proposals, and in September 1708 he was recalled. On the accession of George I he was resworn of the privy council, to which he was first admitted 9 June 1698, and was appointed lord of the bedchamber, and on 30 April 1719 was created Duke of Manchester. He died on 20 Jan. 1721–2, and was buried at Kimbolton.

Manchester married, on 26 Feb. 1690–1, Dodington, second daughter and coheiress of Robert Greville, fourth lord Brooke, by whom he had two sons, William (1700–1739) and Robert (*d.* 1762), who in turn succeeded to the title, and four daughters.

In person, Manchester was of the middle height, with an elegant figure and fine features. As a public man he was of the highest integrity, but had 'more application than capacity.' The portrait of him by Kneller as a member of the Kit-Cat Club was engraved by J. Faber.

[Cole's Hist. and Polit. Memoirs from the Courts in Europe from 1697 to 1708; Granger's Biog. Hist. ed. Noble, 1806, iii. 28; Hist. Reg. Chron. Diary, 1722, p. 8; Duke of Manchester's Court and Society from Elizabeth to Anne, ii. 90; Sandford's Hist. of the Coronation of James II; Form of the Proceeding to the Coronation of King William and Queen Mary; Clarendon and Rochester Corresp.; Luttrell's Relation of State Affairs; Chamberlayne's Angliæ Notitia, 1691; Story's Continuation of the Hist. of the Wars of Ireland, 1693, pp. 18 et seq.; Beatson's Polit. Index, i. 448; Hist. MSS. Comm. 1st Rep. App. p. 193, 3rd Rep. App. p. 193, 7th Rep. App. p. 418, 8th Rep. App. pp. 35, 47, 10th Rep. App. pt. v. p. 130; Grimblot's Letters of William III, 1848, ii. 449, 450, 479; Collins's Peerage, ed. Brydges, iii. 83; Doyle's Official Baronage.]

J. M. R.

MONTAGU, Sir EDWARD (*d.* 1557), judge, second son of Thomas Montagu, lord of the manors of Hanging Houghton and Hemington, Northamptonshire, by Agnes, daughter of William Dudley of Clopton, near Oundle, in the same county, born in the royal manor-house of Brigstock towards the close of the fifteenth century, studied at Cambridge, and was called to the bar at the Middle Temple, where he was autumn reader in 1524 and 1531. His family claimed descent from the Earls of Salisbury. His father died on 5 Sept. 1517, and on the subsequent death of his elder brother without issue Montagu succeeded to the family estates. In 1524 he was in the commission of the peace for the counties of Northampton, Huntingdon, and Rutland. A tradition that he was speaker of the House of Commons in 1523, and was then bidden by the king to procure the passing of the Subsidy Bill on pain of death if he should fail, is inauthentic, Sir Thomas More having been speaker in that year; nor is there evidence that Montagu was ever in parliament.

In 1524 he was one of the subsidy commissioners for the county, and in 1525 in the commission of gaol delivery for the castle of Northampton. He was also commissioner under the Vagrant Act and the acts against forestalling and regrating for the town of Northampton in 1527, and in 1530 commissioner for ascertaining the extent of Wolsey's possessions within the county. In 1531 he was in the commission of sewers for Huntingdon and some neighbouring counties, and the same year was called to the degree of serjeant-at-law (12 Nov.) The event was celebrated at Ely House in a feast of unusual extravagance, which lasted five days. Among the guests were the king and queen.

On the outbreak of the insurrection known as the 'Pilgrimage of Grace' Montagu acted as commissariat commissioner to the royal forces in Northamptonshire (October 1536), and in the following year was made king's serjeant. He profited largely by the dissolution of religious houses, receiving as his share of the spoil the numerous estates held in Northamptonshire by the abbey of Bury St. Edmunds, and other church lands in that and adjacent counties. He was knighted at the creation of the Earl of Hertford and Southampton, 18 Oct. 1537, and was advanced to the chief justiceship of the king's bench, 21 Jan. 1538–9. In December 1541 he assisted the privy council in the examination of the Duchess of Norfolk, and other proceedings preliminary to the bill of attainder against Catherine Howard. From the king's bench he was transferred to the less dignified, but also less onerous, post of chief justice of the common pleas, 6 Nov. 1545. He was a member of the commission which extorted a confession from the Duke of Norfolk, 12 Jan. 1546–7 [see Howard, Thomas II, Earl of Surrey, and third Duke of Norfolk of the Howard house, 1473–1554], and of the council of regency appointed by Henry VIII's will to carry on the government during the minority of Edward VI. In the council he acted with the party adverse to Somerset, whose patent of protector he refused to attest (12 March 1546–7). On the other hand, he attested the patent of 24 Dec. 1547, by which the protector's authority was made terminable at the pleasure of the king, and in October 1549 he concurred in his deposition.

Montagu was a member of the commission of heresy which tried Nicholas Shaxton, 18 June 1546, and of that which confirmed Bonner's deprivation, 7 Feb. 1549–50. An important case of peculation, that of Sir William Sherington, treasurer of the mint at Bristol, came before him at Guildhall on 14 Feb. 1548–9, and ended in the condemnation of the accused to a traitor's death. On the resumption by the crown of the privileges of the merchants of the Steelyard he was appointed, 2 March 1551–2, commissioner for adjusting their equitable claims. Summoned to council at Greenwich 11 June 1553, he attended next day, was apprised of the Duke of Northumberland's scheme for altering the succession in favour of Lady Jane Grey, and required to draft the necessary clauses for insertion in the king's will. He objected that they would be void as contravening the Act of Settlement, and obtained leave to consult his colleagues. They met at Ely House, and after a day spent in conference resolved that the project was treasonable. This resolution Montagu communicated to the council on the 14th, but was answered that the sanction of parliament would be obtained and peremptorily ordered to draft the clauses. He still hesitated, but his scruples were removed by a commission under the great seal and the promise of a general pardon, and he not only drafted the clauses, but appended his signature to the will as one of its guarantors. On the accession of Mary he was committed to the Tower, 26 July, but was discharged on 6 Sept. with a fine of 1,000*l.* and the forfeiture of some of his estates. He was superseded on the bench by Sir Richard Morgan [q. v.]

Montagu retired to the manor of Boughton, Northamptonshire, which he had bought in 1528, where he died on 10 Feb. 1556–7. He was buried on 5 March with much pomp (including a 'hearse of wax') in the neighbouring church of St. Mary, Weekley, where an altar-tomb with his effigy and the legend 'pour unge pleasoir mille dolours' is still to be seen.

His will is printed in Sir Nicholas Harris Nicolas's 'Testamenta Vetusta,' p. 743. An apology for his part in the attempted settlement of the crown upon Lady Jane Grey, found among his papers and printed by Fuller (*Church History*, vol. viii. § 1), is aptly described by Coke as 'a simple and sinewless defence' (*Hist. MSS. Comm.* 9th Rep. pt. ii. App. p. 366).

Montagu married thrice: (1) Cicily or Elizabeth, daughter of William Lane of Orlingbury, Northamptonshire; (2) Agnes, daughter of George Kirkham of Warmington in the same county; (3) Ellen, daughter of John Roper [q. v.], attorney-general to Henry VIII, relict of John Moreton, and after Montagu's death wife of Sir John Digby. Montagu left male issue by his third wife alone—viz. five sons and six daughters. Edward, the eldest son, was father of Edward Montagu, first baron Montagu [q. v.], of James Montagu, bishop of Winchester [q. v.], and of Sir Henry Montagu, first earl of Manchester [q. v.] His widow died in May 1563.

Two portraits of the lord chief justice are preserved at Boughton.

[Wise's Montagus of Boughton and their Northamptonshire Homes, 1888; Fuller's Worthies (Northamptonshire); Bridges's Northamptonshire, i. 565, ii. 19, 31, 38, 117, 125, 211, 231, 284, 309, 347, 349, 367, 400, 403, 420, 565; Collins's Peerage (Brydges), ii. 42; Dugdale's Orig. pp. 127, 216; Chron. Ser. pp. 83–5; Stow's London, 6th edit. i. 723; Letters and Papers, Foreign and Domestic, Henry VIII; State Papers, Henry VIII, 1830, i. 702 et seq.; Metcalfe's Book of Knights; Camden Miscellany, Camden Soc. (London Chronicle), iv. 18; Wriothesley's Chronicle (Camden Soc.), i. 161, 167–8, ii. 7–8, 91, 103; Hayward's Life of Edward VI, ad fin.; Trevelyan Papers (Camden Soc.), i. 199, 205, ii. 26, 34; Archæologia, xxx. 463, 474–6; Strype's Mem. (fol.) vol. ii. pt. i. pp. 11, 15, 296, pt. ii. pp. 457, 480, vol. iii. pt. i. pp. 15, 22, 25, 313; Rymer's Fœdera, 2nd edit. xiv. 402, xv. 110, 217; Strype's Cranmer (fol.), i. 293, ii. 163; Lord Herbert of Cherbury's Life of Henry VIII (ed. 1683), p. 630; Cobbett's State Trials, i. 458; Burnet's Reformation, ed. Pocock; Troubles connected with the Prayer Book of 1549 (Camden Soc.); Foxe's Martyrs, ed. 1689, book ix. p. 46; Ellis's Letters, ii. 169 et seq.; The Chronicle of Queen Jane (Camden Soc.); Machyn's Diary (Camden Soc.); Burghley State Papers (Haynes), p. 174; 10th Rep. Dep.-Keeper Publ. Rec. App. ii. p. 240; Hist. MSS. Comm. 4th Rep. App. p. 12; Froude's Hist. of England; Foss's Lives of the Judges; Lord Campbell's Lives of the Chief Justices; Cooper's Athenæ Cantabr.; Lingard's Hist. of England, 2nd edit. vii. 138.] J. M. R.

MONTAGU, EDWARD, first Baron Montagu of Boughton (1562–1644), born in 1562, was the second son of Sir Edward Montagu, knt. (1532–1602), of Boughton Castle, Northamptonshire, high sheriff for the county in 1567, by his wife Elizabeth (*d.* 1618), daughter of Sir James Harington of Exton, Rutland. His grandfather was Sir Edward Montagu (*d.* 1557) [q.v.], chief justice of the king's bench. James Montagu, [q. v.], bishop of Winchester, Sir Henry Montagu, first earl of Manchester [q. v.], and Sir Sidney Montagu, master of requests, who was the ancestor of the Earls of Sandwich, were his brothers. Montagu matriculated from Christ Church, Oxford, about 1574, graduated B.A. 14 March 1578–9, and was a student of the Middle Temple in 1580. He represented Brackley, Northamptonshire, in the parliament of 1601, and Northamptonshire in those of 1603–4—1611, 1614, and 1620–1–2. He was made K.B. by James I at his coronation, 25 July 1603, and created Baron Montagu of Boughton on 29 June 1621.

On 9 Feb. 1604–5, with other gentlemen of Northamptonshire, he presented a petition to the king in favour of those ministers in the county who refused subscription. The petitioners were warned that their combination 'in a cause against which the king had shewed his mislike . . . was little less than treason.' Montagu was for the time deprived of his lieutenancy and justiceship of the peace in the county (Winwood, *Memorials*, ii. 48–9).

From 1635 to 1637 he was occupied with the ship-money assessment of the county. In February 1638–9, when summoned to attend the king at York, he obeyed, though then seventy-six years of age, and with 'some great infirmities' upon him. As lord-lieutenant of Northamptonshire he put in execution the commission of array, but he voted against the king on the question of precedency of supply on 24 April 1640 (*Cal. State Papers*, 1640, p. 66). On 11 Sept. 1640 he wrote to his nephew, Edward Montagu (afterwards second earl of Manchester) [q. v.], in support of the petition to the king for summoning a new parliament (*Duke of Manchester's MSS.*), and on 21 March 1641–2 complained in a second letter to his nephew that the parliament had been guilty of the grave sin of usury (*ib.*) His popularity and influence in Northamptonshire, combined with his known loyalty, led to an order of parliament (24 Aug. 1642) for bringing Montagu as a prisoner to London. On his way thither he encountered at Barnet the Earl of Essex, who was marching north with the parliamentary army. The earl stopped to salute the aged lord, but Montagu peremptorily ordered his coachman to drive on. Having refused the parliament's offer of residence in the house of his own daughter, the Countess of Rutland, he was committed to the Tower on 10 Sept., but on account of his health was afterwards moved to his house in the Savoy, where he died a prisoner on 15 June 1644. He was buried at Weekley, Northamptonshire, on 26 June (par. reg.)

A strict upholder of the church and its ceremonies, and of the Book of Common Prayer, Montagu led so severe and regular a life that he was frequently reckoned among the puritans. He was a hospitable neighbour, a good landlord, and a firm administrator of justice. He was no courtier, and, though regular in his attendance in parliament, was rarely at Whitehall. In 1613 he built and endowed a hospital for aged men at Weekley, and was also a benefactor to Sidney Sussex College, Cambridge, and to the town of Northampton. A portrait of Montagu belongs to the Earl of Sandwich.

Montagu married Elizabeth (*d.* 6 Dec. 1611), daughter of John Jeffrey [q. v.] of Chiddingly in Sussex, chief baron of the exchequer, by whom he had an only daughter, Elizabeth (*d.* 30 Nov. 1654), who married Robert, lord Willoughby of Eresby, afterwards first Earl of Lindsey, who fell at the battle of Edgehill. He married secondly Frances, daughter of Thomas Cotton of Connington in Huntingdonshire, and half-sister of Sir Robert Bruce Cotton [q. v.], by whom he had three sons and one daughter: Edward, who succeeded him, and is noticed below; Christopher, born 1618, admitted to Sidney Sussex College, Cambridge, 20 March 1633, and died 1641; Sir William (1619–1706) [q. v.], chief baron of the exchequer; and Frances (*d.* 19 May 1671), who married in 1628 John Manners, eighth earl of Rutland [q. v.] His second wife dying in May 1620 (buried 16 May, par. reg.), Montagu married thirdly, on 16 Feb. 1624–5, at St. Michael's, Cornhill, Anne, daughter of John Crouch of Cornbury in Hertfordshire, and widow of Sir Ralph Hare of Stow in Norfolk. She died on 11 June 1648, aged 75.

Edward Montagu, second Baron Montagu of Boughton (1616–1684), was born at Weekley on 11 July 1616 (par. reg.), and entered Sidney Sussex College, Cambridge, on 2 March 1631. He represented the borough of Huntingdon in the Long parliament (elected 23 Oct. 1640) until called to the upper house on the death of his father in 1644. He took the engagement to the Commonwealth in October 1644, and was constantly in the House of Lords during the proceedings against Archbishop Laud. On 18 July 1645 he was nominated by both houses of parliament one of the commissioners to reside with the Scottish army in England, and in that capacity treated for the surrender of Newark in May 1646. His letter to the House of Lords on sending a copy of the articles of the surrender of Newark (6 May 1646) is among the Tanner MSS. in the Bodleian Library (lix. f. 135). With the Earls of Pembroke and Denbigh he received the king's person from the Scots, and conducted him to Holdenby or Holmby. His report, read in the House of Lords on 10 June 1647, appeared in pamphlet form in London, 1647 (Brit. Mus., E. 392 (10)). He afterwards attended Charles till his escape in 1647. He took no part in the trial of the king, was summoned to sit as one of Cromwell's lords in December 1657, and eagerly welcomed the return of Charles II. After the Restoration he resided chiefly at Boughton, died on 10 Jan. 1683–4, and was buried at Weekley. He married Anne, daughter, and eventually heir, of Sir Ralph Winwood [q. v.] of Ditton Park, Buckinghamshire, by whom he had two sons and one daughter: Edward, noticed below, whom he survived; Ralph, who succeeded him [see Montagu, Ralph, first Duke of Montagu]; and Elizabeth, who married Sir Daniel Harvey, ambassador at Constantinople. Several letters of his to Lord and Lady Hatton, mostly on family matters, are in the British Museum (Addit. MSS. 29550 ff. 166, 175, 177, 186, 188, 196, 29551 ff. 5, 18, 29553 f. 349, 29557 ff. 91, 93, 29558 ff. 25, 26, 28).

Edward Montagu (1635–1665), eldest son of the second Baron Montagu, was educated at Westminster School, matriculated from Christ Church, Oxford, on 5 June 1651, and was admitted at Sidney Sussex College, Cambridge, on 25 Sept. 1651. He was created M.A. of Oxford on 9 Sept. 1661. In 1659 he joined his cousin, Admiral Montagu [see Montagu, Edward, Earl of Sandwich], with a view to influencing him in favour of the Restoration, and was acting as a medium of communication between Charles and the admiral in April 1660 (Pepys, *Diary*, 1848, i. 57). He represented Sandwich in parliament from 1661 to 1665, and was master of the horse to Queen Catharine. He was killed at Bergen in Norway in August 1665, in an attack on the Dutch East India fleet.

[Burke's Extinct Peerage; Jacob's Peerage, i. 273–4 (pedigree opposite p. 386); Foster's Alumni Oxon. 1500–1714; Wise's Montagus of Boughton, pp. 24–37, 54–56, 73; Winwood's Memorials, ii. 48–9; Cal. State Papers, Dom. Ser. 1603–47; Ellis's Original Letters, 2nd ser. iii. 216; Warwick's Memoires, pp. 221–6; Bridges's Northamptonshire, ii. 347–8, 350–1; Carter's Cambridge, p. 375; Blomefield's Norfolk, vii. 442; Clarendon's Hist. of the Rebellion, ed. Macray, bk. vi. par. 35, xvi. par. 153–6; Lords' Journals, vols. iii. v. vi. ix. x.; Harl. MSS. 7038 f. 356, 2224 ff. 32–7, 47, 49; Yorkshire Diaries (Surtees Soc. vol. lxv.), i. 142; Official List of Members of Parliament, pt. i. pp. 439, 445, 452, 490, 532; monument in Chiddingly Church; Parl. Hist. iii. col. 1518; admission registers of Sidney Sussex College, per the master; P. C. C. Twisse, 99.] B. P.

MONTAGU, EDWARD, second Earl of Manchester (1602–1671), born in 1602, was the eldest son of Sir Henry Montagu, first earl of Manchester [q. v.], by Catherine, second daughter of Sir William Spencer of Yarnton in Oxfordshire, who was the third son of Sir John Spencer of Althorp, Lincolnshire. After a desultory education, he entered Sidney Sussex College, Cambridge, on 27 Jan. 1618 (*Admission Registers*). He represented the county of Huntingdon in the parliaments of 1623–4, 1625, and 1625–6. In 1623 he attended Prince Charles in Spain, and was by him created a knight of the Bath at his coronation on 1 Feb. 1625–6. On 22 May 1626, through the influence of the Duke of Buckingham, he was raised to the upper house with the title of Baron Montagu of Kimbolton. In the same year he became known by the courtesy title of Viscount Mandeville, on his father being created Earl of Manchester. Being allowed but a small income from his father, Mandeville resided little in London, and mixed much with the relations of his second wife, the daughter of Robert Rich, second earl of Warwick. By them he was led to lean towards the puritan party, and to detach himself from the court.

On 24 April 1640, during the sitting of the Short parliament, he voted with the minority against the king on the question of the precedency of supply (*Cal. State Papers*, 1640, p. 66). In June 1640 he signed the hesitating reply sent by some of the peers to Lord Warriston's curious appeal to them to aid the Scots in an invasion of England [see Johnston, Archibald] (Gardiner, *Fall of Charles I*, p. 402; Mandeville, MS. Memoirs in *Addit. MS.* 15567, ff. 7–8). Mandeville signed the petition of the twelve peers (28 Aug. 1640) urging the king to call a parliament, and with Lord Howard of Escrick presented it to Charles on 5 Sept. In the same month he obeyed the king's summons to the grand council of peers at York, and was one of those chosen to treat with the Scottish commissioners at Ripon on 1 Oct. In the negotiations he took an active part, passing frequently to and fro between Ripon and York, urging an accommodation (*Harl. MS.* 456, ff. 38–40), and drawing up the articles (Borough, *Treaty of Ripon*, pp. 44, 55).

Mandeville was during the early sittings of the Long parliament an acknowledged leader of the popular and puritan party in the lords. He was in complete accord with Pym, Hampden, Fiennes, and St. John, and he held constant meetings with them in his house at Chelsea (Evelyn, *Diary of Correspondence*, iv. 75–6). On the discovery of the 'first army plot,' in May 1641, he was despatched by the lords to Portsmouth with a warrant to examine the governor [see Goring, George, Lord Goring], and to send him up to London to appear before parliament (*Lords' Journals*, iv. 238). He was one of the sixteen peers chosen as a committee to transact business during the adjournment from 9 Sept. to 20 Oct. 1641. On 24 Dec. he protested against the adjournment of the debate on the removal of Sir Thomas Lunsford [q. v.] from the command of the Tower.

His position was very clearly defined when his name was joined with those of the five members who were impeached by the king of high treason on 3 Jan. 1642, although his inclusion appears to have been an afterthought (*Nicholas Papers*, Camden Soc., i. 62). When the articles of impeachment were read, Mandeville at once offered, 'with a great deal of cheerfulness,' to obey the commands of the house, and demanded that, 'as he had a public charge, so he might have a public clearing' (*Lords' Journals*, iv. 501). This demand he reiterated in the house on 11 Jan., and again on 13 Jan., notwithstanding the message from the king waiving the proceedings (*ib.* pp. 505, 511). A bill was finally passed by both houses in March 1642 (*ib.* p. 649), clearing him from the accusation (cf. v. 564).

Having thus identified himself with the popular party, he was among the few peers who remained with the parliament in August 1642, and in the following month he took command of a regiment of foot in Essex's army. When the king retired to Oxford, Mandeville (who had succeeded his father as Earl of Manchester in November) returned to London and occupied himself in raising money for the army (*Comm. for the Advance of Money*, p. 1), and in the negotiations for the cessation of arms. He was made lord-lieutenant of Huntingdonshire and Northamptonshire by the parliament in 1642. On the first suspicion of the Tomkins and Challoner plot [see Waller, Edmund], Manchester, with Viscount Saye and Sele and others, managed (on Sunday, 28 May 1643) to elicit from Roe, a clerk of Tomkins, so many important secrets, that the whole conspiracy was speedily discovered. He afterwards acted as president in the resulting court-martial in June and July (SANFORD, *Studies*, p. 561, quoting from D'Ewes). Manchester was one of the ten peers nominated to sit as lay members in the Westminster Assembly of Divines in July of the same year.

The fortunes of the parliamentary forces in the eastern counties had in the early summer been seriously imperilled by local quarrels. Cromwell recognised the danger, and appealed to parliament to appoint a commander of high position and authority. On 9 Aug. accordingly the commons resolved to make Manchester major-general of the associated counties in the place of Lord Grey of Wark. The choice was confirmed by the lords on the following day, and Essex at once complied with the request to give him the commission (GARDINER, *Civil War*, i. 224–6). Cromwell and Manchester were thus brought into close connection. They were already well acquainted with each other. Each belonged to a leading family of Huntingdonshire, had been educated at Sidney Sussex, Cambridge (SANFORD, *Studies*, pp. 202–5), and had been concerned in a dispute relating to the enclosing of common lands in the eastern counties, which had been before a committee of the House of Commons (CLARENDON, *Life*, 1857, i. 73–4; CARLYLE, *Cromwell's Letters and Speeches*, 1866, i. 90).

By 28 Aug. Manchester, in his new capacity, was besieging Lynn-Regis in Norfolk; the town capitulated 16 Sept., and the governorship was bestowed upon him (21 Sept.) On 9 Oct. he joined Cromwell and Fairfax, then besieging Bolingbroke Castle, and the three commanders won Winceby or Horncastle fight on 11 Oct. (see Manchester's letter of 12 Oct. in *Lords' Journals*, vi. 255–6). On 20 Oct. the town of Lincoln surrendered to Manchester. On Cromwell's motion (22 Jan. 1644), Lord Willoughby of Parham, who had been commanding in Lincolnshire as serjeant-major-general of the county, was ordered to place himself under Manchester's orders. Charges of misconduct had been brought against Willoughby, who resented the position now forced on him, and challenged Manchester as he was on his way to the House of Lords. Both houses treated Willoughby's conduct as a breach of privilege, but after Manchester had defended himself against Willoughby's complaints, the subject dropped (*Harl. MS.* 2224, ff. 12–16), and Willoughby returned to his duties under him.

On 22 Jan. 1644 (HUSBAND, p. 415), Manchester was directed to 'regulate' the university of Cambridge, and to remove scandalous ministers in the associated counties. On 24 Feb. he accordingly issued his warrants to the heads of colleges, and began the work of reformation. About the same time (19 Dec. 1643) he authorised William Dowsing [q. v.] to destroy 'superstitious pictures and ornaments.' In February 1644 Manchester became a member of the new committee of both kingdoms, meeting at Derby House. In April he was again with his army watching the movements of Prince Rupert. The town of Lincoln had been retaken by the royalists in March, but Manchester successfully stormed the close on 6 May, and thus secured the county for the parliament (*True Relation*, E. 47 [2], Manchester's letter read in the House of Commons on 9 May). A bridge was thrown over the Trent at Gainsborough, and Manchester marched to the aid of Lord Fairfax and the Scots, who were besieging York. This junction was effected on 3 June. On the same day the committee of both kingdoms sent Vane to York, ostensibly to urge the generals to send a force into Lancashire to arrest Prince Rupert's progress, but in reality to propose the formation of a government from which Charles was to be excluded. Manchester and his colleagues rejected the suggestion, but Cromwell, Manchester's lieutenant-general, probably accepted Vane's proposals, and to this difference of view may be traced the subsequent breach between the two (GARDINER, *Civil War*, i. 431–3). Cromwell at the battle of Marston Moor (1 July) commanded Manchester's horse, while the earl himself exercised a general control as a field officer. Though carried away in the flight, he soon returned to the field, and successfully rallied some of the fugitives. After the surrender of the city of York on 16 July, the armies divided, and Manchester marched to Doncaster, which he reached on 23 July. While there Tickhill Castle surrendered (26 July) to John Lilburne [q. v.], who had summoned it contrary to Manchester's orders, Sheffield Castle surrendered (10 Aug.) to Major-general Lawrence Crawford [q. v.], and Welbeck House to Manchester himself (11 Aug.) But Pontefract Castle had been passed by, and Manchester paid no attention to the entreaty of the officers to blockade Newark (Pickering's Deposition, *Cal. State Papers*, 1644, p. 151). Proceeding leisurely to Lincoln, he subsided into inaction. The committee of both kingdoms (3 Aug.) directed him to march against Prince Rupert, but he (10 Aug.) shrank from 'so large a commission, and a worke so difficult,' in the unsatisfactory condition of his men, and the lateness of the season (*Quarrel of Manchester and Cromwell*, p. 9), and though constantly urged to make his way westward, the earl made no movement till the beginning of September (*ib.* pp. 20–4). By 22 Sept. he was at Watford, on his way to the general rendezvous at Abingdon, and reached Reading on 29 Sept. Here he remained till the middle of October, notwithstanding the urgent desire of the committee in London that he should move forwards. He had reached Basingstoke by 17 Oct., was joined by Waller on the 19th, and by Essex on 21 Oct. For the command of the three armies thus united, a council of war, consisting of the three generals, with Johnston of Warriston and Crewe, had been appointed by the committee of both kingdoms.

At the second battle of Newbury, on 28 Oct., Manchester's lethargy became fatally conspicuous. Delaying to make the attack assigned to him till too late in the day, he failed in his attempt on Shaw House, and the royalist army under cover of the darkness made its escape westward, within 'little more than musket-shot' of the earl's position (Watson's Deposition, *Cal. State Papers*, 1644–5, p. 150). At the council held the following day Manchester opposed Waller's and Cromwell's advice to pursue the enemy, and preferred to summon Donnington Castle. Failing in his attempt to storm it on 1 Nov. he leisurely withdrew, and the castle thus abandoned was relieved by the king on the 9th. At a council of war at Shaw Field on 10 Nov. Manchester plainly declared his horror of prosecution of the war. 'If we beat the king 99 times,' he said, 'he is king still, and so will his posterity be after him; but if the king beat us once, we shall be all hanged, and our posterity be made slaves.' On 17 Nov. he left Newbury for the purpose of protecting the besiegers of Basing House. But Basing was never reached. His starving men were deserting him, and with the remains of his army he made his way to Reading. The siege of Basing House was necessarily abandoned (Gardiner, *Civil War*, i. 518).

Manchester's religious views, though sincere, were not very deep. He inclined to presbyterianism from circumstances rather than from conviction, and had not attempted to curtail Cromwell's efforts to 'seduce' the army 'to independency' (Baillie, *Letters and Journals*, ii. 185). Discords among his officers were growing, and in September he had paid a hurried and fruitless visit to London in the hope of healing them [see Cromwell, Oliver, and Crawford, Lawrence]. But the breach between him and Cromwell was soon irreparable. On 25 Nov. Cromwell laid before the House of Commons a narrative, charging Manchester with neglect and incompetency in the prosecution of the war (*Quarrel of Manchester and Cromwell*, Camden Soc., pp. 78–95). He called attention to 'his Lordshipe's continued backwardness to all action, his aversenes to engagement or what tendes thereto, his neglecting of opportunityes and declineing to take or pursue advantages upon the enemy, and this (in many particulars) contrary to advice given him, contrary to commands received, and when there had been noe impediment or other employment for his army' (Cromwell's Narrative in *Quarrel*, p. 79). Cromwell's charges were probably not exaggerated. Manchester, a civilian at heart, was always of opinion 'that this war would not be ended by the sword, for if it were so concluded, it would be an occasion of rising again or of a future quarrel, but it would be better for the kingdom if it were ended by an accommodation' (Pickering's Deposition, *Cal. State Papers*, 1644–5, p. 152). Manchester defended himself in the House of Lords on 27 Nov., when a committee of inquiry was appointed (*Lords' Journals*, vii. 76), and made a vigorous attack on Cromwell (*Camden Miscellany*, vol. viii.) But the presentation of the bill for new modelling the army turned the course of public debate from the shortcomings of individuals to more general principles. The commons (26 Dec., 30 Dec., and 1 Jan.), although urged by the lords to deliver their reports respecting Manchester, centred all their energies on the struggle for the passing of the self-denying ordinance, and on 2 April 1645 (the day before the ordinance passed the lords) Manchester, like Essex and Denbigh, resigned his commission in the army. Forty of his officers in January 1645 signed a petition for his continuance in the service, fearing that his removal would 'breed a great confusion amongst them by reason of the differences between the Presbyterians and Independents' (Whitacre, *Diary*, Addit. MS. 31116, f. 185).

Manchester, although relieved of military duty, still (4 April) retained his powers for regulating the university of Cambridge, was a constant attendant on the committee of both kingdoms, and frequently acted as speaker of the House of Lords. In the propositions for peace at the end of 1645 it was recommended that he should be made a marquis. He was one of those to whom Charles on 26 Dec. 1645 expressed himself willing to entrust the militia, in accordance with the Uxbridge proposals, and was a commissioner for framing the articles of peace between the kingdoms of England and Scotland in July 1646 (Thurloe, *State Papers*, i. 77–9). With William Lenthall [q. v.] he was entrusted with the charge of the great seal from 30 Oct. 1646 to 15 March 1648. Early in 1647 he was busy with other leading presbyterian peers in sketching out a pacification more likely to meet with the royal approval. When the houses of parliament were attacked by the London mob in July 1647, Manchester, notwithstanding his presbyterian leanings, fled to the army on Hounslow Heath with the independent members, and signed the engagement of 4 Aug. to stand by the army for the freedom of parliament (Rushworth, vii. 754). On 6 Aug. he returned to London escorted by Fairfax and resumed his duties as speaker of the upper chamber.

Manchester stoutly opposed the ordinance for the king's trial in the House of Lords on 2 Jan. 1649, and retired from public life when the formation of a commonwealth grew inevitable. After the death of the Earl of Holland he was, on 15 March 1649, made chancellor of the university of Cambridge, a post of which he was deprived in November 1651 for refusing to take the engagement (see letters in *Hist. MSS. Comm.* 8th Rep. pt. ii. p. 64). Cromwell summoned him to sit in his upper house in December 1657 (*Parl. Hist.* iii. col. 1518), but the summons was not obeyed. Manchester took an active part in bringing about the restoration, and as speaker of the lords welcomed the king on his arrival (29 May). He was speedily invested with many honours. On 27 April 1660 he was appointed one of the commissioners of the great seal, on 22 May was restored to his lord-lieutenancy of the counties of Northampton and Huntingdon (*Hist. MSS. Comm.* 8th Rep. pt. ii. p. 65), and on the 26th to the chancellorship of Cambridge. He was made lord chamberlain of the household on 30 May, privy councillor on 1 June, and was also chamberlain of South Wales.

From 9 to 19 Oct. he was engaged on the trial of the regicides, and appears to have inclined to leniency (*Exact and most impartial Account*, E. 1047 [3], p. 53 *b*). At the coronation of Charles II on 23 April 1661 he bore the sword of state, and was made a knight of the Garter. He became joint commissioner for the office of earl-marshal on 26 May 1662, and was incorporated M.A. in the university of Oxford on 8 Sept. 1665. When, in 1667, the Dutch appeared in the Channel, Manchester was made a general, and a regiment was raised under his command (15 June). He was a fellow of the Royal Society from 1667 till his death. He died on 5 May 1671, and was buried in Kimbolton Church, Huntingdonshire.

Manchester was of a generous and gentle disposition. Burnet (*Own Time*, i. 98) speaks of him as 'of a soft and obliging temper, of no great depth, but universally beloved, being both a virtuous and a generous man,' and this view is corroborated even by Clarendon (*Hist. of the Rebellion*, ed. Macray, i. 242, ii. 545). Sir Philip Warwick (*Memoirs*, p. 246) describes him as 'of a debonnair nature, but very facile and changeable,' while Baillie (*Letters and Journals*, ii. 229) calls him 'a sweet, meek man.' Peace, a constitutional monarchy, and puritanism were the objects at which he aimed, and his inactivity in the army dated from the time when protracted war, the rule of the people, and independency seemed to be the inevitable outcome of the struggle. It was easy to begin a war, he was in the habit of saying, but no man knew when it would end, and a war was not the way to advance religion (*Cal. State Papers*, 1644–5, Pickering's Deposition, p. 152). When actually in the field, his sense of duty and his humanity prompted him to activity. To encourage his men he marched among them for many a weary mile (Ashe, *Particular Relation*), or spent the night after an engagement in riding from regiment to regiment, thanking the soldiers and endeavouring to supply their wants (Sanford, *Studies*, p. 608). The same longing for peace and accommodation is exemplified in his religious connections. A presbyterian member of the assembly of divines, he used his influence to have Philip Nye, the independent, appointed to the vicarage of Kimbolton, and in the hearing of Baxter pleaded for moderate episcopacy and a liturgy (Sylvester, *Reliq. Baxterianæ*, p. 278). Baxter, while designating him 'a good man,' complains that he would have drawn the presbyterians to yield more than they did, and was earnest in urging the suppression of passages that were 'too vehement' (*ib.* p. 365).

A portrait by Vandyck belongs to the Duke of Manchester. Engraved portraits of him have been published in Vicars's 'England's Worthies,' 1647, p. 16, by Hollar in 1644; in Ricraft's 'England's Champions,' London, 1647, p. 17, reproduced in an edition of the work entitled 'Portraits of the Parliamentary Officers,' London, 1873, p. 20; in Clarendon's 'History,' Oxford, 1721, vol. i. pt. i. p. 54, by M. Vandergucht; in Birch's 'Heads,' London, 1751, p. 31, by Houbraken; in Smollett's 'History of England,' 1759, vii. 209, by Benoist; in Lodge's 'Portraits,' vol. iii., by Dean, from a painting at Woburn

Abbey. Many of Manchester's letters on army business are in the British Museum (Egerton MSS. 2643 ff. 9, 23, 2647 ff. 136, 229, 241, 319; Addit. MS. 18979, f. 158; Harl. MS. 7001, ff. 170, 172, 174, 202) and in the Bodleian Library (Tanner MSS. lxiii. f. 130, lxiv. f. 91, lxii. ff. 431, 471, lvii. f. 194).

Manchester married five times. His first wife was Susanna, daughter of John Hill of Honiley in Warwickshire, and of his wife Dorothy Beaumont, sister to the Duke of Buckingham's mother. Pecuniary arrangements between the duke and Manchester's father were amicably concluded by means of the match. The marriage ceremony, which took place early in February 1623, was performed in the king's bedchamber, where James was confined to his bed. He was not, however, incapable of throwing his shoe after the bridal party as they left the room. Susanna Montagu died in January 1625. As Lord Mandeville, Manchester married at Newington Church, on 1 July 1626, Anne, daughter of Robert Rich, second earl of Warwick, lord admiral of the Long parliament, by whom he had three children: Robert, his successor, noticed below; Frances, who married Henry, son of Dr. Robert Sanderson, bishop of Lincoln; and Anne, who married Robert Rich, second earl of Holland and fifth earl of Warwick. Anne, lady Mandeville, died on 14 or 19 Feb. 1641–2, and was buried at Kimbolton. There is a portrait of her at Kimbolton Castle. His third wife was Essex (*d.* 28 Sept. 1658), daughter of Sir Thomas Cheke of Pirgo in Essex, by his wife Essex Rich, daughter of Robert, first earl of Warwick, and widow of Sir Robert Bevil (*d.* 1640) of Chesterton in Huntingdonshire, by whom he had six sons and two daughters. Of the daughters, Essex (born 1644) married, in June 1661, Henry Ingram, viscount Irwin. Of the six sons, Edward, Henry, Charles, and Thomas were members of Corpus Christi College, Cambridge. Manchester married a fourth wife in July 1659; she was Ellinor, daughter of Sir Richard Wortley of Wortley in Yorkshire, and he was her fourth husband. She had previously married Sir Henry Lee, first baronet (*d.* 1631), of Ditchley in Oxfordshire; Edward Radcliffe, sixth earl of Sussex (*d.* 1641); and Robert Rich, second earl of Warwick (*d.* 1658) (the father of Manchester's second wife). She died in January 1666–7. In August 1667, at St. Martin's-in-the-Fields, Manchester married his fifth wife, Margaret, daughter of Francis Russell, fourth earl of Bedford, a widow of James Hay, second earl of Carlisle (*d.* 1660). She died in November 1676, and was buried at Chenies, Buckinghamshire.

Robert Montagu, third Earl of Manchester (1634–1683), was born in the parish of St. Margaret's, Westminster, and baptised there on 25 April 1634. He represented Huntingdonshire in the Convention parliament of 25 April 1660, and in the following month was one of the members who waited upon the king at the Hague. He was again elected for Huntingdonshire in the parliament of 1661. In 1663 he was sent on a mission to the French king; on 8 Sept. 1665 he was created M.A. by the university of Oxford, and in February 1666 he succeeded the Earl of Newport as gentleman of the bedchamber to the king. In 1666 and 1667 he commanded a troop of horse in the eastern counties while the Dutch were on the coast. He died at Montpellier on 14 March 1683, and was buried at Kimbolton. He married, on 27 June 1655, at St. Giles's-in-the-Fields, Anne, daughter of Sir Christopher Yelverton of Easton Maudit in Northamptonshire, by whom he had five sons and four daughters. His two eldest sons, Edward and Henry, dying young, he was succeeded by his third son, Charles, who became first duke of Manchester, and is separately noticed. His widow afterwards married Charles Montagu, earl of Halifax [q. v.]

[Burke's Peerage; Harl. MS. 7038, f. 355; Official List of M.P.s, i. 458, 464, 469; Forster's Grand Remonstrance, pp. 251–2 *n.*; Manchester's Memoirs (Addit. MS. 15567); Borough's Notes of the Treaty of Ripon, ed. Bruce (Camden Soc.), pp. 2, 29, 47, 54; Borough's Minutes of the Treaty with the Scotch Commissioners, 1640–1 (Harl. MSS. 456, 457, passim); Cal. of State Papers, Dom. Ser. 1619–67. Much information as to Manchester's military movements is in the Calendar for 1644; the Calendar for 1644–5, pp. 146–61, contains an epitome of the Depositions against Manchester in his quarrel with Cromwell; Rushworth's Historical Collections; Nalson's Affairs of State, i. 447 et seq., 456, ii. 272–275, 815, 835; Hardwicke State Papers, ii. 257, 279, 290, 293, 298; Clarendon's Hist. of the Rebellion, ed. Macray; Forster's Arrest of the Five Members, passim; List of the Army raised under the Earl of Essex (E. 117 [3]); Sanford's Studies of the Great Rebellion; Lords' Journals, iii. iv. v. vi. vii. xi. passim; Commons' Journals, ii. iii. iv. vii. passim; Lightfoot's Journal of the Proceedings of the Assembly of Divines (Works, 1824, vol. xiii.); Hetherington's Hist. of the Westminster Assembly, p. 123; Richards's Hist. of Lynn, ii. 755–6; Bell's Memorials of the Civil War, i. 62–3; Walker's Sufferings of the Clergy, pt. i. pp. 111–14; Querela Cantabrigiensis, Preface; Dowsing's Journal, passim; Good's Continuation of True Intelligence (E. 6. 17), pp. 4–7; Husband's Ordinances, pp. 275, 360; Hunter's Hallamshire, p. 141; Quarrel of Manchester and Cromwell (Camden Soc.), passim;

Gardiner's Hist. of the Great Civil War; Harl. Misc. iii. 247–8; Holles's Memoirs, pp. 146–7; Addit. MS. 5850, f. 192; Gumble's Life of Monk, pp. 260–1; Wood's Fasti (Bliss), ii. 283–4; Lists of the Royal Society; Le Neve's Monumenta Anglicana, 1650–79, pp. 63–147; Lysons's Environs, iii. 297, 590; Collins's Peerage (Brydges), ii. 81–3; Nichols's Herald and Genealogist, v. 444–5; G. E. C[okayne's] Peerage; Harl. Soc. Publ. xxvi. 283; Lady Verney's The Verneys in the Civil War, i. 242, 268, 272–3, 275; Chester's Marriage Licenses; Hist. MSS. Comm. 1st Rep. pt. i. p. 26, 5th Rep. p. 146, 7th Rep. p. 461, 8th Rep. pt. ii. p. 64; Manchester's Court and Society from Elizabeth to Anne, i. 312–14, 375, 377, 381–2; Masters's Hist. of Corpus Christi Coll. Cambr. ed. Lamb, pp. 368–9, 480; Foss's Lives of the Judges, vi. 457; P. C. C. 80, Duke; Admissions Registers of Sidney Sussex and Corpus Christi Colleges, Cambr., per the masters; Cambr. Univ. Reg.; Notes and Queries, 3rd ser. xii. 324.] B. P.

MONTAGU, or more properly **MOUNTAGU, EDWARD**, first Earl of Sandwich (1625–1672), admiral and general at sea, only surviving son of Sir Sidney Montagu or Mountagu (*d.* 1644) (younger brother of Edward, first lord Montagu of Boughton [q. v.], and of Sir Henry Montagu, first earl of Manchester [q. v.]), by Paulina, daughter of John Pepys of Cottenham, Cambridgeshire, was born on 27 July 1625. His father was member for Huntingdonshire in the Long parliament, and in 1642 was expelled as a royalist. Edward, on the other hand, while still a mere lad, threw in his lot with the parliament, probably influenced by his cousin, the Earl of Manchester, or by his father-in-law, John Crew, afterwards Lord Crew of Stene [q. v.], whose eldest daughter Jemimah he married in November 1642. In 1643 he raised a regiment of foot in Cambridgeshire, and joined Manchester's army in November; took part in the storming of Lincoln, 6 May, and in the battle of Marston Moor on 2 July 1644. He was on 10 Jan. 1645, although not yet twenty, appointed by Manchester governor of Henley. In the following April he was given a regiment in the New Model, fought at Naseby (14 June), and distinguished himself at the storming of Bristol on 10 Sept. About this time he was returned to parliament for Huntingdonshire, but it does not appear that he took any part in their proceedings. Neither was he serving with the army for the next three years; he had no share in the second civil war in 1648, or in the king's trial and execution. He had no scruples, however, about co-operating with the council of state, of which he was nominated a member in July 1653. Notwithstanding the difference in their age, he appears to have been bound to Cromwell by ties of personal friendship and the early connection between the families [cf. Cromwell, Oliver]. This friendship seems to have been the determining factor of his conduct during the next few years. He was appointed one of the commissioners of the treasury (3 Aug. 1654); and when Blake desired to have a colleague in the command of the fleet [cf. Blake, Robert], Mountagu was appointed as conjoint general at sea (2 Jan. 1656). He had no previous experience at sea, if indeed he had ever even seen the sea; and the statement that he was appointed at the particular request of Blake (Lediard, p. 566) is quite unsupported. It is very probable that Cromwell desired to strengthen his own influence in the fleet, but if it was true, as Pepys heard (*Diary*, 23 June 1662), that Mountagu was deeply in debt, there was a very obvious reason for his wishing to take part in the war against Spain.

His command, however, proved uneventful. The Barbary pirates had been brought to terms by Blake the year before; active operations against Spanish territory were forbidden; and though the West India treasure fleet was engaged and captured outside Cadiz on 8 Sept. [see Stayner, Sir Richard], Mountagu, who at the time was with Blake at Alveiro, had no part in the achievement further than reporting the success to his government (Thurloe, *State Papers*, v. 509), and afterwards carrying the treasure to England. The bullion, to the amount, it was said, of 600,000*l.*, was carried through London in a triumphal procession, and Mountagu received the formal thanks of the parliament for his good service (4 Nov. 1656) (Whitelocke, *Memorials*, p. 653). The victory was celebrated by Edmund Waller in his poem 'Of a War with Spain and Fight at Sea by General Montagu in the year 1656.'

In 1657–8 Mountagu had command of the fleet stationed in the Downs, and covering, though not directly participating in, the operations against Dunkirk [see Goodsonn, William]. During this time he was also in frequent attendance on Cromwell; is said to have been one of those who strongly urged him to take the title of 'king' (Clarendon, *Hist.* xvi. 153); and was present with a drawn sword at his second installation as Protector on 26 June 1657 (Whitelocke, *Memorials*, p. 662). In December 1657 he was nominated one of Cromwell's House of Lords, and was given the command of a regiment of horse. After Cromwell's death Mountagu loyally supported the new protector, and in March 1659 assumed command of the fleet ordered to the Sound to arrange, or, if necessary, to enforce, a peace between Sweden and Denmark [see MEADOWS, SIR PHILIP]. On the fall of Richard Cromwell [q. v.], Mountagu felt no obligation to the new and unsettled government, which showed its want of confidence in him by depriving him of the command of his regiment of horse, and by associating with him in his mission three colleagues whom he looked on rather as spies or supervisors, and who in fact had secret instructions to depose him from the command and send him home under arrest if they had reason to mistrust his intentions (*Cal. State Papers*, Dom. 1 July 1659; CLARENDON, *Hist.* xvi. 157).

In this state of difficulty and discontent Mountagu was not unwilling to listen to overtures from the king. His young cousin, Edward Montagu, son of the first Lord Montagu of Boughton [q. v.], and an active agent of Charles, had embarked with him in, it was said, the special object of sounding the admiral, and now succeeded in representing to him the king's wish that he should take the fleet back to England so as to be ready to co-operate with Sir George Booth (1622–1684) [q. v.], already in command of a royalist army in Cheshire. Mountagu, discontented, discouraged, possibly foreseeing the coming anarchy, and honestly considering the restoration of the monarchy the best solution of the difficulty, but certainly judging that it might be most to his own interest (cf. PEPYS, 15 May 1660), assented to his cousin's proposals, and was from this time actually engaged in the king's interest (*Clarendon State Papers*, iii. 493, 565, 580). Taking advantage of the absence of diplomatic colleagues at Copenhagen, Mountagu summoned a council of war, which resolved that, as their present stay was useless and their provisions were running short, it was expedient to sail for England at once. This resolution Mountagu carried into effect, leaving the other plenipotentiaries behind him. On his return Mountagu reported what had been done to the council of state and the parliament (*Cal. State Papers*, Dom. 10, 16 Sept. 1659), but as the premature attempt in favour of the king had been overthrown, and Booth was a prisoner in the Tower, he judged it prudent to resign the command of the fleet, which for the next few months was held by Lawson, though only with the rank of vice-admiral [see LAWSON, SIR JOHN].

During the autumn and winter Mountagu lived in retirement, apparently at Hinchinbroke, his country seat near Huntingdon; but on 23 Feb. 1659–60 he was reappointed general of the fleet, jointly with George Monck, afterwards Duke of Albemarle [q. v.], and with the sanction of the king, with whom he had been in frequent correspondence (CLARENDON, *Hist.* xvi. 152; PEPYS, 3 May 1660). The mutual jealousies between Monck and Mountagu seem to have been at this time the principal barrier to the Restoration, while the king felt quite sure of neither. When Mountagu took command of the fleet he found that there was a practical unanimity as to the necessity of bringing in the king, although there might be some who would have wished it otherwise (cf. PEPYS, 29 March, 11, 17 April 1660), and on 3 May he called a council of war, and read the king's letter of 4 April to the officers assembled. Mountagu's resolution in favour of the king was agreed to without dissent; after which, going on deck with the others, he read the king's letter and the resolution of the council of war to the ship's company, who cried out 'God bless King Charles' 'with the greatest joy imaginable' (*ib.* 3 May; the text of the king's letter to the generals and the fleet is in CLARENDON, *History*, xvi. 199, 200). Pepys, Mountagu's secretary, afterwards went to all the ships in the fleet, and read the king's letter and the resolution of the council of war to their several crews with like result. 'My Lord was much pleased,' he wrote, 'to hear how all the fleet took it in a transport of joy, showed me a private letter of the king's to him, and another from the Duke of York, in such familiar style as to their common friend, with all kindness imaginable. . . . In the evening the general began to fire his guns, which he did all that he had in the ship, and so did all the rest of the commanders' (*Diary*, 3 May).

After this there was no disguise; preparations for going to Holland were openly made; official persons came on board for a passage; young Edward Montagu was sent in advance to acquaint the king with the progress of affairs (*ib.* 4 May; CLARENDON, *History*, xvi. 227; LISTER, *Life of Clarendon*, iii. 404). The general appeared, wrote Pepys, to be 'willing to do all the honour in the world to Monck, and to let him have all the honour of doing the business, though he will many times express his thoughts of him to be but a thick-sculled fool.' On 8 May the king was proclaimed, and on the 10th Mountagu received an order from the parliament 'to set sail presently for the king' (PEPYS, 10 May; cf. CLARENDON, *History*, xvi. 237); on the 11th, likewise in obedience to the order of parliament, the state's arms were taken down and painters brought from Dover to set up the king's arms; and on the 12th the fleet sailed from the Downs. On the 14th it anchored at Scheveling; on the

23rd the king embarked on board Mountagu's flagship, the Naseby (Mountagu to Monck, *Eg. MS.* 2618, f. 77), whose name was thenceforth changed to Royal Charles, and on the 25th he landed at Dover. During the nine days' stay of the fleet at Scheveling, and the attendant festivities, Mountagu never went on shore, nor did he leave the ship till the king was on the point of embarking, when he went in the boat to the landing-place and in her received the king, who 'did, with a great deal of affection, kiss him upon his first meeting' (PEPYS, 23 May).

For his services at this critical juncture Mountagu was nominated a knight of the Garter, garter king-at-arms coming on board the Royal Charles at Dover on 27 May, and investing him with the insignia of the order; on 19 June and again on 24 July he was thanked by the House of Commons 'for his late service to his king and country;' and on 29 June a warrant was issued to create him Viscount Hinchinbroke and Earl of Portsmouth, but the last title was changed on 12 July to Earl of Sandwich. He was also appointed master of the wardrobe, admiral of the narrow seas, and lieutenant-admiral to the Duke of York. As admiral of the narrow seas he had to provide for the escort and care of all the persons of rank and distinction passing to and fro; in September he brought the princess royal from Holland, in October the queen-dowager from France, and in the following January took them both to France. On the king's coronation, 23 April 1661, he carried the sceptre, wearing a dress, made in France, very rich with embroidery, which cost him 200*l.* (*ib.* 22 April 1661). In June he was elected master of the Trinity House, and on the 19th sailed from the Downs in command of the fleet for the Mediterranean, having also in charge to bring home the young queen, Catherine of Braganza.

After being laid up for some days at Alicante, sick with a fever, he went to Algiers and tried to negotiate. The Algerines answered they would have no peace without liberty to search English ships, whereupon on 31 July Sandwich attempted to bring them to terms by force. An easterly wind and a rolling sea rendered the attempt ineffectual; and, as the weather continued bad, he left the fleet under the command of Sir John Lawson, while he himself with a few ships went to Lisbon. After some little stay there he took his squadron to Tangier, where he anchored on 10 Oct. By the marriage treaty Tangier was ceded to the English as part of the queen's dowry; but among the Portuguese there was a great deal of popular feeling against the marriage of the infanta to a heretic, and the surrender of Tangier or any other place to the commercial rival of Portugal in the far east (CLARENDON, *Continuation*, p. 353). At Bombay the governor refused to carry out the cession [cf. LEY, JAMES, third EARL OF MARLBOROUGH], and at Tangier the governor had a similar intention. There was thus a considerable delay, which was brought to an end after three months by the garrison sustaining a signal defeat from the Moors and being reduced to ask Sandwich for assistance (12–14 Jan. 1661–2; KENNETT, *Register and Chronicle*, p. 617; CLARENDON, *Continuation*, p. 354). After this there was no further reluctance on the part of the Portuguese, and Sandwich, on establishing an English garrison and leaving the Earl of Peterborough as governor, returned to Lisbon.

His official reception was all that he could wish, and the opportunity of assisting in the repulse of a Spanish attack won for him the favour of the populace (*ib.* p. 355). There was, however, a difficulty about the payment of the dowry. The Portuguese were not only unable to pay the whole amount, 300,000*l.*, but when, contrary to his instructions, Sandwich consented to receive the half, it appeared that even that could not be paid in cash. Merchandise he agreed to take, but bills of exchange he refused, and some six weeks passed before the matter could be settled. The queen embarked on 13 April, and on 14 May the squadron anchored at Spithead. Sandwich's conduct of the whole business was approved, and for some time he was in high favour at court; but afterwards, when quarrels began between king and queen, he found himself blamed by each: by the king for bringing only half the money, and by the queen for having drawn too favourable a picture of the king's 'virtue and good-nature.' According to Clarendon, 'the tempest of so much injustice and the extreme affliction of mind' threw him into 'such a fever as brought him to the brink of his grave' (*ib.* p. 362); but Pepys, in constant attendance on Sandwich, though he speaks of his serious illness (19 Jan.–6 April 1663), describes it as a feverish cold of the nature of influenza, and refers to him, a few days before he was taken ill, as in the king's intimate confidence (12 Jan. 1662–3).

In November 1664, when the fleet was got together under the command of the Duke of York, with Prince Rupert as vice-admiral and admiral of the white, Sandwich, with his flag in the Prince, was rear-admiral of the fleet and admiral of the blue squadron (*Cal. State Papers*, Dom. 13 Nov.) He continued in that capacity during the winter and spring of 1665; and in the action off Lowestoft on 3 June succeeded, after an obstinate struggle, in breaking through the Dutch line, separating their fleet into two parts, and throwing the whole into confusion, in the midst of which the Dutch flagship Eendracht was brought to close action by the Royal Charles and accidentally blown up [see JAMES II]. Other terrible losses following in close succession struck panic into the Dutch, and they fled, leaving the victory with the English.

On the return of the fleet and the retirement of the Duke of York, Sandwich was appointed commander-in-chief (*Cal. State Papers*, Dom. 2 July 1665; CLARENDON, *Continuation*, pp. 659–61), and, sailing from Solebay on 5 July, went towards Bergen, where, according to his intelligence, the Dutch East India ships had arrived and were waiting for an escort of men-of-war. At the same time he had an intimation that the king of Denmark was not unwilling that retribution should fall on the Dutch, who had drawn him into a war with Sweden for their selfish ends; and, though he could get no writing to that effect, the assurances he received appeared to warrant him in attempting to seize the Dutch ships in the neutral port. Accordingly, on 1 Aug. Sir Thomas Teddeman [q. v.] was sent in with a squadron of some twenty-four ships; but on the 2nd, the Danish governor making common cause with the Dutch, who had also thrown up some heavy batteries on shore, the English, in an engagement of two hours and a half, were beaten off and driven out of the harbour (*Cal. State Papers*, Dom., James Coleman to Pepys, 21 Aug.) The governor of Bergen and the Danish viceroy afterwards endeavoured to reopen negotiations; but Sandwich, indignant at their two-faced conduct, and fearing lest he might be caught by De Ruyter on that dangerous coast, returned south and anchored in Solebay (CLARENDON, *Continuation*, pp. 685–9; Sandwich to Duke of Albemarle, 25 Aug. in *Cal. State Papers*, Dom.) After refitting, he put to sea again on the 30th (*ib.*, Sandwich to Lord Arlington, 30 Aug.), and on 3 Sept. fell in with three Dutch East Indiamen under the convoy of four ships of war. They were all captured, as on the next day were six more merchant-men; the fleet thereupon returned to the river (*ib.*, Sandwich to the king, 5 Sept., Sandwich to Lord Arlington, 5 Sept., Coventry to Lord Arlington, 8 Sept.)

The prizes, especially the Indiamen, were extremely valuable, and Sandwich, through carelessness or ignorance, or, as his enemies alleged, through greed, permitted the hatches to be taken off and a part of the cargo to be assigned to the several flag officers. It was stated that they each received to the value of 1,000*l.*, and that Sandwich himself received to the value of 2,000*l.*; but it was afterwards admitted that Sandwich had received to the value of nearly 5,000*l.*, and we may suppose that the other shares were of proportionate magnitude. The action, illegal and ill-judged, raised a great storm. The prizes, it was alleged with some appearance of truth, had been indiscriminately plundered by the seamen (*ib.* 22 Nov., 2 Dec. 1665, January 1666, p. 218); the East India Company were alarmed at the idea of vast quantities of Indian wares being thrown on the market at reduced prices; the king was angry because Sandwich, having written to him for leave to make this distribution to the flag officers, had anticipated his consent before he received the king's reply; the Duke of York was angry because he considered that Sandwich had infringed the prerogative of the lord high admiral, and was endeavouring to curry favour with the officers of the fleet. All this indignation, it was said, was fanned and kept alive by Sir William Coventry [q. v.] and the Duke of Albemarle, both of whom were jealous of Sandwich's influence at court (CLARENDON, *Continuation*, pp. 746–749). Albemarle sent orders to the ports to seize all goods which were attempted to be landed from the fleet, and accordingly not only Sandwich's share of the plunder, but his own furniture and plate, were stopped at Lynn, where the boats came on their way to Huntingdon (*ib.* pp. 751–2; *Cal. State Papers*, Dom. 14 Dec. 1665). They were soon allowed to pass; but the ill-feeling between Albemarle and Sandwich was much embittered. Coventry, too, continued to incense the Duke of York, not only with reports of excessive plundering, but with charges of misconduct of the fleet, to which the miscarriage at Bergen was attributed. There was some talk of bringing the matter before parliament, if not of impeaching the admiral (CLARENDON, *Continuation*, p. 758), rather, it would seem, to frighten the king and the duke into taking summary notice of the offence, so as to avoid a public inquiry. The king and the duke had both accepted Sandwich's explanations; but the virulence of his enemies seemed to render it impossible to continue him in the command of the fleet. The matter was referred to Clarendon, who arranged that he should quit the command on appointment as ambassador extraordinary to Madrid, 'to correct and amend the mistakes and errors in the late treaty, as further to mediate the peace with Portugal' (*ib.* pp. 760–9).

On 3 March Sandwich accordingly sailed from Portsmouth, and arrived at Madrid on 26 May 1666. In September 1668 he returned to England, having satisfactorily accomplished the objects of his mission, and concluded a treaty with Spain which Pepys heard 'was acknowledged by the merchants to be the best peace that ever England had with them' (27 Sept. 1667). In August 1670 he was appointed president of the council of trade and plantations, and on the outbreak of the Dutch war in 1672 was second in command of the English fleet under the Duke of York. When the French contingent, under the Count d'Estrées, had joined, it formed the white squadron, and Sandwich was admiral of the blue. So organised, the fleet numbered some eighty-one capital ships besides small craft, fireships, &c., bringing the total up to about 118. On 22 May they anchored in Solebay, in line parallel to the coast, the blue squadron being to the north. The story is told on weak evidence, although in its general outlines it is not improbable, that on the 27th Sandwich pointed out to the duke that with the wind easterly, as it then was, the fleet would be in great danger if the Dutch came suddenly on them, and advised either that they should put to sea, or—an absurd alternative not likely to have been suggested—that they should move nearer in shore; but that the duke slighted his advice, with some 'indecent reflection' that it was dictated by a fear for his own safety (Burnet, *Hist. of own Time*, i. 562; *Columna Rostrata*, p. 217; Campbell, ii. 234). The fleet did not move, and the danger which Sandwich is said to have anticipated actually occurred the next day, 28 May. The wind was north-easterly, and at daybreak the Dutch fleet was seen coming down before it. Fortunately, the breeze died away; and when it had freshened again, it had shifted to the southward of east. This gave the English time to prepare hurriedly for action, and to stand out to meet the enemy, Sandwich, with the blue squadron, leading. D'Estrées, with the French squadron, not understanding, or not choosing to follow, when, as vice-admiral, it was his privilege to lead, went off on the other tack to the southward. There he was kept in check all day by a squadron of the enemy, while between their main fleet and the English the fight raged with exceeding fury. The English were outnumbered and surprised, and nothing but their obstinate valour—especially that of Sandwich and the blue squadron—prevented their being overpowered. Sir Joseph Jordan [q. v.], who, as vice-admiral of the blue squadron, commanded the van, beat back his immediate assailants and was able to go to the assistance of the duke, who was hard pressed. Sandwich, in the Royal James, was at the time holding his own. He had beaten off repeated attacks and had sunk several fireships. Later on, in the heat of the action, while the captain was below in the hands of the surgeon [see Haddock, Sir Richard], the Royal James was successfully grappled by a fireship. Almost immediately she was wrapped in flames, and presently blew up, with the loss of Sandwich and nearly all on board. It was said that Sandwich was urged to leave the ship, but refused, in consequence of the insulting remark of the duke the day before; it is more probable that the catastrophe followed so quickly that time was not permitted him. On 10 June a man-of-war ketch found the body floating on the sea near Harwich. It was recognised by the star on his coat, and brought into Harwich. The face was slightly burnt, otherwise the body was unblemished. It was embalmed and taken to London, where, in a public funeral, it was buried in the Chapel of Henry VII in Westminster Abbey, 3 July 1672.

The accidents of fortune and the sensational manner of his death have perhaps given Sandwich a greater reputation than he deserved. His birth, his marriage, and the friendship of Cromwell had raised him, without any proof of remarkable ability, to the command of the fleet under the Commonwealth. On the resignation of Richard Cromwell, bound by no ties to the parliamentary government, he was easily persuaded that patriotism agreed with interest, and that it would be advantageous to the country and to himself to support the king. He then raised himself to a position of honour and authority. His daily gossip and behaviour, as recorded by Pepys, often in minute detail, show him as a man of easy, comfort-loving temper, with notions of morality not too strait-laced for the times, and broad views about religion which, in that age, might seem atheistical (*e.g.* 7 Oct. 1660, 12 Jan., 9 Sept. 1663). On the other hand, amid almost universal corruption and greed, no special charge was laid against him save that of 'breaking bulk' in the case of the prizes, which, though a grave indiscretion, was certainly not the gross abuse it was represented to be. Except off Bergen, he never commanded in chief; and though the decisive movement off Lowestoft on 3 June 1665 was made by him, and the credit of snatching the victory from De Ruyter at

Solebay was his, they speak rather to tenacious courage than to any particular brilliance of conception. His scientific studies were probably vicarious, though he claimed to have personally taken the soundings at Tangier in order to determine 'the most convenient place for making a mole' (6 Feb. 1661–2; KENNETT, p. 634). He contributed to the 'Philosophical Transactions' (No. 21, p. 390) 'Observations of an Eclipse of the Sun at Madrid on 22 June 1666 and of other phenomena.' He was also credited with the translation from the Spanish of Barba's 'Art of Metals.' The first edition (2 vols. 12mo, 1670) is anonymous; the second edition, published after his death (1674), bears his name on the title-page. One portrait by Lely belongs to the Earl of Sandwich, and another is in the Painted Hall at Greenwich. A third portrait is in Hampton Court Palace.

By his wife, Jemimah Crew, whom he married at the age of seventeen, Sandwich had four daughters and six sons, of whom the eldest, Edward, the 'child' of Pepys's 'Diary,' succeeded to the title. The fourth son, John, dean of Durham, is separately noticed.

The spelling of the name Mountagu is that of his signature.

[Memoirs of Sandwich are in Campbell's Lives of the Admirals, ii. 216; Collins's Peerage (ed. of 1768, iii. 287); Charnock's Biographia Navalis, i. 29; Southey's Lives of the Admirals, v. 222. The original source of much of their information is Clarendon's History of the Rebellion and its Continuation. Other references are given by Campbell. An abstract of Sandwich's Journal during his voyage to Lisbon and the Mediterranean in 1661–2 is printed in Kennett's Register and Chronicle, p. 471, &c.; and many of his letters to Arlington during his mission in Spain in 1667 are in Hispania Illustrata, 1703, catalogued in the British Museum under 'Spain,' 596, e. 17. Four volumes of Sandwich's papers are in the Carte Collection in the Bodleian Library. Others are in the possession of the present Earl of Sandwich. The Calendars of State Papers, Domestic, elucidate many obscure passages in his career; but by far the most important addition to our knowledge since the days of Charnock is Pepys's Diary, of which Sandwich may be called the hero, but which Southey practically ignored. See also Lediard's Nav. Hist.; Columna Rostrata; Orig. letters . . . of Sir Richard Fanshaw, Earl of Sandwich, and others, Lond. 1724; C. R. Markham's Great Lord Fairfax; Doyle's Baronage; Brandt's Vie de Ruiter; Basnage's Annales des Provinces-Unies; Jal's Abraham Du Quesne, ii. 66 et seq.; Add. MS. 27990, ff. 48 et seq.; Harl. MS. 1625, ff. 1 et seq.] J. K. L.

MONTAGU, EDWARD (1755–1799), Indian officer, born in 1755, was youngest son of Admiral John Montagu, and brother to Admiral Sir George Montagu and Captain James Montagu, all of whom are separately noticed. Educated at the Royal Academy of Woolwich, he went out to Bengal as an East India cadet in 1770. There being no commission vacant on his arrival, he was first placed in the 'select picket,' a military body composed of the cadets then present at Calcutta. On 16 May 1772 he was admitted into the Bengal artillery as lieutenant-fireworker, and by 24 Sept 1777 he had risen to the rank of first-lieutenant of artillery. He was attached to Brigadier-general Goddard's [q. v.] army during the Mahratta campaign of 1781, and was successfully employed against certain Mahratta forts on the Rohilcund border, on one occasion being severely wounded in the face by an arrow. In 1782 he accompanied Colonel Pearce's detachment, sent to join Sir Eyre Coote (1726–1783) [q. v.], then engaged against Hyder Ali and his French allies in the Carnatic, and in 1783 he commanded the English artillery in the siege unsuccessfully attempted by General Stuart of Cuddalore, a strong Carnatic fortress then held by the French. On the conclusion of the war in the Carnatic (1784), Montagu returned to Bengal. He was promoted to a captaincy on 13 Oct. 1784. He took a prominent part in the invasion of Mysore, conducted by Lord Cornwallis [see CORNWALLIS, CHARLES] in 1791. He superintended the artillery employed in the sieges of Nandidrúg (captured 19 Oct. 1791) and Savandrúg (captured 21 Dec. 1791). For his skill and vigour Montagu received special commendation from Lord Cornwallis. The war concluded in favour of the English in 1792. On 1 March 1794 Montagu was made lieutenant-colonel, being now third on the list of Bengal artillery officers.

In the final war against Tippoo, sultan of Mysore (1799), Montagu, as commander of the Bengal artillery, accompanied the army under General Harris which was directed to invade Mysore from Madras. On 9 April 1799 Seringapatam, the Mysore capital, was formally invested. On 2 May Montagu, while directing his battery, was struck in the shoulder by a cannon-shot from the enemy's lines. He died from the effects of the wound on 8 May 1799.

[Philippart's East India Military Calendar; Beatson's View of the Origin and Conduct of the War with Tippoo Sultaun; Dodwell and Miles's Alphabetical List of Officers in the Indian Army; Cornwallis Corresp.] G. P. M-Y.

MONTAGU, EDWARD WORTLEY (1713–1776), author and traveller, son of Edward Wortley Montagu by Lady Mary [see

MONTAGU, LADY MARY WORTLEY], daughter of Evelyn Pierrepont, first duke of Kingston, was born in the summer of 1713. In 1716 he was taken by his parents to Constantinople, and at Pera in March 1716–17 was inoculated for the small-pox, being the first native of the United Kingdom to undergo the operation. On the return of his parents to England in 1718 he was placed at Westminster School, from which he ran away more than once. On the first occasion, July 1726, he was traced to Oxford, and was with difficulty 'reduced to the humble condition of a schoolboy.' He decamped again in August 1727, and was not recovered for some months. Two similar escapades are mentioned by his tutor, Forster, chaplain to the Duchess of Kingston, but without dates. The first ended in his discovery, after a year's absence, crying fish in Blackwall; on the second occasion he worked his passage out to Oporto, deserted, went up country, and found employment in the vineyards, but returning to Oporto in charge of some asses, was arrested at the instance of the British consul, brought back to his ship, identified and restored to his parents by the master. After some time spent with a tutor in the West Indies, Montagu came home about 1733, and in a freak married a woman much his senior, and of no social position. His parents now treated him as deranged, induced the wife by a small pension to forego her rights, and packed him off to Holland in charge of a keeper, in time to prevent the birth of a child. At first the keeper's office was no sinecure, and Montagu was several times put in confinement. Nevertheless he studied Arabic to purpose under Schultens of Leyden, and became proficient in French and other European languages. On 6 Sept. 1741 his name was entered as a student on the register of Leyden University. His allowance was small (300*l.* a year), and his gambling and other debts exorbitant. His mother, who saw him from time to time on the continent, describes him as an excellent linguist, a thorough liar, and so weak-minded as to be capable of turning 'monk one day, and a Turk three days after.' Nevertheless Montagu held for a time a commission in the army of the allies, served without discredit at the battle of Fontenoy on 11 May (N.S.) 1745, was returned to parliament for the borough of Huntingdon in 1747, and in July 1748 was appointed one of the commissioners to execute the office of secretary at the congress of Aix-la-Chapelle. He returned to London in January 1750–1, and astonished the town by the height of his play and the extravagance of his dress. With his diamond shoe-buckles and snuff-boxes, and a wig of iron wire marvellously contrived to look like hair, he was 'computed to walk 2,500*l.*,' and was forthwith elected fellow of the Royal Society. In the autumn of 1751 he made a jaunt to Paris in company with a certain Miss Ashe (a lady of doubtful reputation, commonly known as 'The Pollard Ashe,' with whom he had previously gone through the ceremony of marriage), Theobald Taaffe, M.P. for Arundel, and Lord Southwell, and on 31 Oct. was committed to the Châtelet prison on a charge of cheating a Jew at faro and extorting payment by force. Taaffe and Lord Southwell were also incriminated, but were not arrested. Montagu pleaded not guilty, and by the interest of the British ambassador, Lord Albemarle, obtained his liberty after eleven days' incarceration. He then brought an action of false imprisonment against his accuser, and obtained judgment on 25 Jan. 1751–2, which, however, was reversed on appeal. He published the same year his own version of this episode in both French and English (see infra).

From 1754 to 1762 Montagu sat in parliament, a silent member, for the borough of Bossiney, Cornwall. In 1759 he published a sort of historico-didactical essay, entitled 'Reflections on the Rise and Fall of the Antient Republics. Adapted to the Present State of Great Britain,' London, 8vo; later editions in 1769 and 1778. The composition of this work has been attributed, on insufficient grounds, to his former tutor, Forster. On his father's death, 22 Jan. 1761, Montagu found himself cut off with an annuity of 1,000*l.*, to be raised to 2,000*l.* on the death of his mother. Leaving England soon afterwards he re-entered himself (19 Feb. 1761) at Leyden, being described in the university register as 'Linguarum Orientalium Cultor.' He started early in 1762 for the East, and was in Italy when Lady Mary died, having bequeathed him a guinea. The family estates went to his sister, Lady Bute, but provision was made for his son, if he should leave one. At Turin Montagu inspected the recently discovered bust upon which John Turberville Needham [q. v.] had founded his fantastic theory of the Egyptian origin of the Chinese, which he examined in a letter to the Earl of Macclesfield, read before the Royal Society on 25 Nov. 1762. The letter does not appear in the 'Philosophical Transactions,' but, with a rejoinder to Needham's reply, was published in pamphlet form in 1763, under the title 'Observations upon a supposed Antique Bust at Turin,' London, 4to.

At Rome Montagu became intimate with Winckelmann, whom he at first dazzled by his various accomplishments. He left Italy in the autumn of 1762, and wintered in Egypt, where he went through the ceremony of marriage with Caroline Dormer, the Irish Roman catholic wife of one Feroe, a protestant merchant of Danish nationality, settled at Alexandria. In Feroe's absence he induced her to believe him dead. He then took her with him to Cairo, and on her discovering the ruse quieted her scruples of conscience by the assurance that her marriage with the Dane, which had been solemnised in Italy, was null and void by reason of the difference of faith, and promising to get it so declared. Pursued by the Dane, the pair travelled by the supposed route of the Exodus to Sinai, and thence to Jerusalem, where on 26 Nov. 1764 Montagu was received into the church of Rome. He then parted with the lady, leaving her in a convent on Mount Lebanon, while he visited Armenia and returned to Italy. He reached Venice in September 1765, and passed the winter at Pisa, whence he communicated to the Royal Society a narrative of his journey from Cairo to Sinai (*Phil. Trans.* lvi. 40 et seq. and cf. *Gent. Mag.* 1767, pp. 374, 401). He afterwards visited Leghorn, and having instituted the process for obtaining the decree of nullity, returned to the Levant, and rejoined the lady. From Zante in 1767 he communicated to the Royal Society 'New Observations on what is called Pompey's Pillar in Egypt,' the date of which he assigned to a period subsequent to the reign of Vespasian (*Phil. Trans.* lvii. 438). He was at Smyrna with his mistress in 1769 when the decree was pronounced. The pair afterwards lived at Rosetta in Egypt, but separated in 1772, Montagu having become enamoured of a fair Nubian. While in the East he conformed to the Turkish regimen, religion, and costume. In 1775 he was at Venice, where he continued to live like a Turk, and received visitors squatting on the floor. Among them was the painter, George Romney, who painted a half-length portrait of him in his oriental costume, now in the possession of Lord Wharncliffe. A crayon sketch of his head by the same artist appears to be lost (see frontispieces to Moy Thomas's edition of the *Letters and Works of Lady Mary Wortley Montagu*, 1861, vol. ii. and *Europ. Mag.* 1793; and cf. HORNE'S *Catalogue of Engraved Portraits, &c., by Gainsborough and Romney*, 1891).

While at Venice Montagu heard of the death of his wife, and was on his way home with the intention of marrying, when he died at Padua on 29 April 1776. His death is said to have been due to the swallowing of a fish-bone. He was buried in the cloister of the Eremetani, Padua. An obscene advertisement for a wife, which appeared in the 'Public Advertiser' of 16 April 1776, was supposed to have been inserted by him. He left several illegitimate children, for whom he provided by his will. Montagu had a handsome person and lively parts. His linguistic faculty was extraordinary and his conversational powers great. He is said to have possessed, and perhaps did pretend to possess, the power of divination. His loose and roving life made him the hero of much vulgar and indecent romance. There is little doubt that he was more or less insane. A portrait by Romney is in the possession of the Earl of Wharncliffe; another by Peters was engraved by J. R. Smith in 1776.

Montagu's narrative of the affair with the Jew at Paris appeared in French as 'Mémoire pour Edouard Wortley Montagu, Membre du Parlement d'Angleterre, contre Abraham Payba, se disant Jacques Roberts,' Paris, 1752, 4to. An English translation appeared the same year, with the title 'Memorial of Edward Wortley Montagu, Esq. Written by himself in French, and published lately at Paris against Abraham Payba, a Jew by birth, who assumed the name of James Roberts,' London, 8vo. In connection with this affair there also appeared 'The Sentence of the Lieutenant Criminal at Paris in the Extraordinary Cause between Abraham Payba, *alias* James Roberts, Plaintiff, and Edward Wortley Montagu and Theobald Taaffe, Esqrs., Members of the Hon. House of Commons, Defendants,' London, 1752, 8vo; and 'A Memorial or Humble Petition presented to the Judges in the High Court of the Tournelle in Paris by the Honourable Edward Wortley Montagu, Esq., Member of Parliament for the County of Huntingdon, and Theobald Taaffe, Esq., Member of Parliament for Arundel, against Abraham Payba, *alias* James Roberts, and Louis Pierre, Jeweller, appealing from the Sentence given in favour of the said Roberts and Pierre the 14th June, 1752.' Translated from the original, printed at Paris, London (no date), 8vo. Some of Montagu's letters are printed in Seward's 'Anecdotes,' 1804, ii. 404–18, in Nichols's 'Literary Anecdotes,' iv. 64 et seq., and ix. 792 et seq., and Winckelmann's 'Briefe,' ed. Förster, iii. 122; others are preserved in Add. MSS. 32703 f. 483, 32718 f. 3, 32805 f. 23, 32831 ff. 121, 123, 32832 f. 215, 32833 f. 163. (See also Add. MS. 21416, ff. 52, 60, and Eg. MS. 2002, ff. 134, 136, 145–55, 191.) During a tour in Epirus and Thessaly he 'took exact plans of Actium and Pharsalia,' now lost. While at Rosetta he translated Veneroni's 'Dialogues' into Arabic. He is said to have written an 'Explication of the

Causes of Earthquakes,' which, if it ever existed, has disappeared. His manuscripts were sold in 1787.

[Letters and Works of Lady Mary Wortley Montagu (Bohn's Standard Library), ed. Moy Thomas, 1887; Nichols's Lit. Anecd. i. 619 *n*., ii. 243–4 *n*., iii. 623, iv. 64 et seq., viii. 247, ix. 792 et seq.; Seward's Anecd. ii. 404 et seq.; Gent. Mag. 1748 p. 333, 1777 p. 376, 1778 p. 221; List of Fellows of the Royal Soc. (official), 1752; Europ. Mag. 1793, pp. 1–5, 129–31, 164–6, 250–254; Collins's Peerage (Brydges), ii, 577, iii. 461–462; Horace Walpole's Letters, ed. Cunningham, ii. 99, 241, 273, iii. 376; Notes and Queries, 2nd ser. x. 507, 3rd ser. x. 290, xi. 373, 4th ser. v. 245, 601, xi. 7; Hist. MSS. Comm. 9th Rep. App. pt. ii. p. 402, 10th Rep. App. p. 383; Letters of Mrs. Montagu, 1813, iii. 174; Life and Correspondence of Mrs. Delany, 2nd ser. ii. 198, 220; Sharpe's Letters from Italy, 1766, p. 9; Moore's Soc. and Manners in Italy, i. 31; Doran's Mann and Manners at the Court of Florence, ii. 97, and Lady of the Last Century (Mrs. Elizabeth Montagu), illustrated in her Unpublished Letters (1873), p. 130; Carsten Niebuhr's Reisebeschreibung nach Arabien, 1837, iii. 30 et seq.; Peacock's Index to English-speaking Students at Leyden, p. 106; Winckelmann's Briefe, ed. Förster, ii. 126, 128, 322, 405, iii. 11, 16, 28, 122; Lamberg's Memorial d'un Mondain, 1774, p. 10; Rede's Anecd. p. 298; Temple Bar, xxxvii. 500 et seq.; Mrs. Piozzi's Observations and Reflections made in the course of a Journey through France, Italy, and Germany, 1789, i. 161; Hayley's Life of Romney, p. 59; Rev. John Romney's Life of Romney, 1830, p. 123; Ann. Reg. 1776, Characters, p. 34; Lord Teignmouth's Life of Sir William Jones, p. 125; Memoirs of the late Edw. W——ly M——tague, Esq., with Remarks on the Manners and Customs of the Oriental World, 1779, are inauthentic, as also are Coates's The British Don Juan, being a Narrative of the singular Amours, entertaining Adventures, remarkable Travels, &c., of the Hon. Edward W. Montagu, 1823, and Edward Wortley Montagu, an Autobiography, 1869, a three-volume novel by 'Y.,' i.e. E. V. H. Kenealy.]

J. M. R.

MONTAGU, Mrs. ELIZABETH (1720–1800), authoress and leader of society, born at York 2 Oct. 1720, was elder daughter of Matthew Robinson (1694–1778) of West Layton, Yorkshire, by Elizabeth, daughter of Robert Drake, recorder of Cambridge. Both the father and mother were rich and well connected. In 1777 Richard Robinson, her father's cousin (of an elder branch of the family), was created Baron Rokeby of Armagh in the Irish peerage, with remainder to her father and her brothers. Her eldest brother, Matthew (1713–1800), accordingly succeeded to the title in 1794. Meanwhile her mother had inherited, on the death of her only brother, Morris Drake Morris [q. v.], the large property of her maternal grandfather, Thomas Morris of Mount Morris in the parish of Horton, near Hythe, Kent. Elizabeth's only sister, Sarah (*d.* 1795), was wife of George Lewis Scott [q. v.], and Zachary Grey [q. v.] claimed relationship with her.

Elizabeth's earliest youth was spent with her family at Coveney, Cambridgeshire, an estate belonging to her mother. She was a frequent visitor in Cambridge at the house of Dr. Conyers Middleton [q. v.], who was second husband of her grandmother (Mrs. Drake). Under Dr. Middleton's influence, she developed a precocious interest in literature, and before she was eight had copied out the whole of Addison's 'Spectator.' From her twelfth year she corresponded with a girl five years her senior, Lady Margaret Cavendish Harley, daughter of the last Earl of Oxford—Prior's 'lovely little Peggy'—who married in 1734 William Bentinck, second duke of Portland. The correspondence continued for nearly half a century—till the duchess's death in 1785. High-spirited, restless, and fond of dancing, Elizabeth acquired in youth the sobriquet of 'Fidget,' but was always 'a most entertaining creature,' 'handsome, fat, and merry' (Delany, *Autob.* ii. 95, 134). When in London in 1738 she delighted in visits to Marylebone Gardens or Vauxhall, and George, first lord Lyttelton [q. v.], whom she met at court, then showed her attentions, which led to a long friendship. On 5 Aug. 1742 she married Edward Montagu, second son by a second wife of Charles Montagu, fifth son of the first Earl of Sandwich. His wife's senior by many years, Montagu was a serious-minded man of wealth, with coal mines at Denton, Northumberland, and estates in Yorkshire and Berkshire. He interested himself in agriculture and mathematics, and from 1734 till his retirement in 1768 sat in parliament as member for Huntingdon in the whig interest. In 1748 he acquired new wealth on succeeding to the property of his elder brother James at Newbold Verdon, Leicestershire (Nichols, *Lit. Anecdotes*, iv. 645 sq. ix. 593–4).

The early months of their married life were spent at Montagu's country houses at Allerthorpe, Yorkshire, or at Sandleford, Berkshire. Mrs. Montagu's vivacity charmed her husband's relatives, and his cousin, Edward Wortley Montagu [q. v.], declared she was 'the most accomplished lady he ever saw' and an 'honour to her sex, country, and family.' Early in 1744 she gave birth to a son, her only child, who died in September following. This bereavement was followed by the death of her mother in 1746 and of her second brother, Thomas, barrister-at-law, in 1747. In search of distraction, she paid long visits to Bath (always a favourite resort of hers) and to Tunbridge Wells. She drank the waters assiduously, made the acquaintance of the poet Young at Bath, discussed religion with Gilbert West [q. v.], and humorously described in a voluminous correspondence the many books she read, and the valetudinarian eccentricities of her neighbours.

Conscious of great social gifts, she soon found that permanent residence in London could alone supply adequate scope for their development. From 1750 onwards she sought to make her husband's house in Hill Street, Mayfair, 'the central point of union' for all the intellect and fashion of the metropolis, but she invariably gave intellect the precedence of rank. 'I never invite idiots to my house,' she wrote to Garrick in 1770 (Mr. Alfred Morrison's manuscripts, *Hist. MSS. Comm.* 9th Rep. pt. ii. p. 480 *a*). In the early days of her London career she mainly confined her efforts as a hostess to literary breakfast parties, of which Madame Bocage, a French visitor to London in 1750, gave a very flattering description (*Letters*, 1770, i. 7). But Mrs. Montagu soon added to this modest form of hospitality more elaborate evening assemblies, which were known as 'conversation parties;' and their resemblance to similar meetings in the Rue St. Honoré in Paris gave her a right to the title, according to Wraxall, of 'the Madame du Deffand of the English capital.' Card-playing was not permitted, and the guests were only encouraged to discuss literary topics. But occasionally Garrick or a distinguished French actor was invited to recite.

Other ladies—Mrs. Montagu's friend the Duchess of Portland, Mrs. Ord, Mrs. Vesey, wife of Agmondesham Vesey, Mrs. Boscawen, wife of the admiral, and Mrs. Greville, wife of Fulke Greville—endeavoured to rival Mrs. Montagu's entertainments; but for nearly fifty years she maintained a practically undisputed supremacy as hostess in the intellectual society of London, and to her assemblies was, apparently for the first time, applied the now accepted epithet of 'blue-stocking.' Two explanations of the term have been suggested. According to the ordinary account, which was adopted by Sir William Forbes in his 'Life of Beattie,' in 1806 (i. 210), full dress was not insisted on at Mrs. Montagu's assemblies, and Benjamin Stillingfleet [q. v.], who regularly attended them, as well as the rival assemblies presided over by Mrs. Vesey or Mrs. Boscawen, habitually infringed social conventions by appearing in blue worsted instead of black silk stockings; consequently, Admiral Boscawen, a scoffer at his wife's social ambitions, is stated to have applied the epithet 'blue-stocking' to all ladies' conversaziones. On the other hand, Lady Crewe, daughter of Mrs. Greville, who was one of Mrs. Montagu's rival hostesses, stated that the ladies themselves at Mrs. Montagu's parties wore 'blue stockings as a distinction,' in imitation of a fashionable French visitor, Madame de Polignac (Hayward, *Life of Mrs. Piozzi*, 1861).

Despite ridicule, Mrs. Montagu helped to refine contemporary London society. Hannah More, in her poem 'Bas Bleu,' written in 1781, divides among Mrs. Montagu, Mrs. Vesey, and Mrs. Boscawen the credit of having, by the invention of 'blue-stocking' assemblies, rescued fashionable life from the tyranny of whist and quadrille. Among Mrs. Montagu's regular visitors between 1750 and 1780 were Lord Lyttelton, Horace Walpole, Dr. Johnson, Burke, Garrick, and Sir Joshua Reynolds. She undoubtedly had a rare faculty of exciting enthusiasm among her distinguished friends. William Pulteney, earl of Bath, who, like another frequent guest, Dr. Messenger Monsey [q. v.], was currently reported to have fallen madly in love with her, declared that he did not believe a more perfect human being was ever created; and when Reynolds repeated the remark to Burke, the latter, who often invited her to Beaconsfield, replied, 'And I do not think that he said a word too much.' Dr. Johnson thoroughly enjoyed a conversation with her. 'She diffuses more knowledge,' he told Mrs. Thrale, 'than any woman I know, or, indeed, almost any man.' 'Conversing with her,' he said on another occasion, 'you may find variety in one' (cf. Boswell, iv. 275). She patronised Beattie when he came to London in 1771, and sent a copy of his 'Minstrel' to Lord Chatham as soon as it was issued. Beattie dedicated to her the first collected edition of his poems (cf. Delany, *Autob.* v. 165), named a son Montagu after her (Forbes, *Beattie*, iii. 163), and was for twenty years a 'very punctual correspondent.' Another of her protégés, Richard Price, the philosopher, she introduced to Lord Shelburne. She delighted in the society of Mrs. Elizabeth Carter [q. v.], whose acquaintance she made in 1758, and of Mrs. Hester Chapone [q. v.], and she came to know Mrs. Thrale, who openly endeavoured to outshine her in conversation whenever they chanced to meet (D'Arblay; Hayward, *Mrs. Piozzi*, i. 22).

In later life the two ladies quarrelled, but Mrs. Piozzi (as Mrs. Thrale became in 1782) admitted after Mrs. Montagu's death that 'she had a great deal of ready wit' (manuscript note in her copy of FORBES's *Life of Beattie*, iii. 163, in Brit. Mus.) Mrs. Montagu's younger associates included Hannah More and Fanny Burney. Miss Burney, whom she first met at Mrs. Thrale's, found her 'brilliant in diamonds, solid in judgment, and critical in talk' (D'ARBLAY, *Memoirs*, ii. 8), but deemed her a person 'to respect rather than to love' (*ib.* p. 9). Miss More, who first dined with her in Hill Street early in 1775 (along with Mrs. Carter, Dr. Johnson, Solander, Paul Henry Maty, Mrs. Boscawen, Sir Joshua and Miss Reynolds), was dazzled by the magnificence of the entertainment and the youthful sprightliness of the hostess (cf. LESLIE and TAYLOR, *Reynolds*, ii. 108-9).

In 1760 Mrs. Montagu gave practical proof of her literary capacity by anonymously contributing three dialogues (Nos. xxvi. xxvii. and xxviii.) to her friend Lyttelton's 'Dialogues of the Dead.' In No. xxviii., in which Plutarch, Charon, and a modern bookseller were the speakers, she complimented Richardson on his 'Clarissa' (p. 318). She visited Paris after the peace of 1763, 'when she displayed to the astonished *literati* of that metropolis the extent of her pecuniary as well as of her mental resources' (WRAXALL), and with her husband in the same year accompanied the Earl and Countess of Bath and Mrs. Carter on a tour through Germany and Holland (cf. *European Magazine*, 1800, pt. ii. p. 244). In 1766 she visited Scotland, staying some weeks at Blair Drummond, the seat of Henry Home, lord Kames [q. v.], and meeting Dr. John Gregory (1724–1773) [q. v.] and other celebrities at Edinburgh (HOME, *Memoirs*, ii. 44, iii. 279). Offended by Voltaire's contemptuous references to Shakespeare, she undertook on her return to London to refute him, and in 1769 published anonymously 'An Essay on the Writings and Genius of Shakespear compared with the Greek and French Dramatic Poets, with some Remarks upon the Misrepresentations of Mons. de Voltaire,' London, 1769, 8vo. A second edition appeared in 1770, and a third edition in 1772, while it was translated into both French (Paris, 1777) and Italian (Florence, 1828). The chapters deal with 'Dramatic Poetry,' 'Historical Drama,' 'Henry IV, pts. 1 and 2,' 'Preternatural Beings,' 'Macbeth,' Corneille's 'Cinna,' and the 'Death of Julius Cæsar.' Sensible and sympathetic, the book fulfilled its purpose. This Johnson admitted according to Seward, but Boswell credits the doctor with the assertion that there was not one sentence of true criticism in the essay, an opinion echoed by Boswell and Mrs. Thrale (cf. BOSWELL, ii. 88, iv. 16, v. 245). It had unequivocal admirers in Reynolds, Lyttelton, and Lord Grenville, whose praises made the authoress 'very happy' (*Grenville Correspondence*, iv. 4, 425). On 27 May 1788 Cowper, a later acquaintance, wrote of the work to Lady Hesketh: 'I no longer wonder that Mrs. Montagu stands at the head of all that is called learned, and that every critic veils his bonnet to her superior judgment. . . . The learning, the good sense, the sound judgment, and the wit displayed in it [*i.e.* the 'Essay'] fully justify not only my compliment, but all compliments that either have been already paid to her talent or shall be paid hereafter' (HAYLEY, *Life of Cowper*, 1824, ii. 340).

On 12 May 1775 Mrs. Montagu's husband died after a tedious illness. He left her 7,000*l.* a year, all his fortune except 3,000*l.* (DELANY, v. 126; WALPOLE, vi. 217). She was fully equal to her increased responsibilities. The large estates, with the collieries at Denton, which were now her property, she frequently visited, and generously entertained her tenants and colliers. According to Boswell and Jenyns, she was generous 'from vanity,' but Johnson argued that, whatever her motive, no one did so much good from benevolence as she, even if her methods were in a few cases mistaken (HAYWARD, i. 154). At the same time her increasing years did not diminish her love of pleasure. In the autumn of 1775 she hired a house for a few months at Montauban (FORBES, *Beattie*, i. 114). In the summer of 1776 she went to Paris and heard 'an invective against Shakespeare' by Voltaire read at the French Academy. On settling again in England, she devoted herself to house-building. At Sandleford she erected in 1781 a noble mansion after plans by Wyatt. In the same year she began to build Montagu House, at the north-west corner of Portman Square, by Upper Berkeley Street, now No. 22 Portman Square. Designed by James ('Athenian') Stuart, it was sumptuously decorated, and, although 'grand,' was not 'tawdry' (WALPOLE, viii. 156). The walls of one room —'the room of cupidons'—were painted with roses and jessamine intertwined with 'little cupids' (DELANY, iv. 508). Another room, 'the feather room,' was ornamented by hangings made by herself from the plumage of almost every kind of bird; of this feature of the building the poet Cowper wrote in enthusiastic verse. Some paintings by Angelica Kauffmann still remain on the walls. On

Easter day 1782, when the 'palace' was completed, Mrs. Montagu invited her friends to a house-warming, and for more than ten years, with even greater zeal than of old, she organised breakfast and dinner parties and evening receptions—all inconveniently crowded. She still adhered to some of her 'blue-stocking' proclivities, but in 1781 a depreciatory remark on the 'Dialogues of the Dead' in Johnson's 'Life of Lyttelton' caused a breach between Mrs. Montagu and the doctor (BOSWELL, iv. 64). 'Mrs. Montagu and her Mænades intend,' wrote Walpole, 'to tear him limb from limb.' But Mrs. Montagu still asked him to dinner, although she took little notice of him, and he regretfully confessed that she had dropped him. Among her friends of a newer generation, William Wilberforce [q. v.] spent a whole day with her in 1789, and admired 'her many and great amiable qualities' (WILBERFORCE, *Life of Wilberforce*, 1839, i. 236). Early in June 1791 she entertained the king and queen (WALPOLE, ix. 325), and on 13 June she accommodated as many as seven hundred guests at breakfast in 'the feather room' (cf. D'ARBLAY, *Memoirs*, v. 302). But mindful of her poorer neighbours, she invited the youthful chimney-sweepers of London to eat roast beef and plum pudding on the lawn before her house every May-day morning. She is 'the kind-hearted lady' commemorated in William Lisle Bowles's poem on the 'Little Sweep' (cf. JAMES MONTGOMERY, *Chimney Sweep Album*; BOWLES, *Poems*, ed. Gilfillan, ii. 263).

To the world at large Mrs. Montagu's devotion to society in extreme old age excited much sarcasm. Her love of finery, which Johnson had excused as a pardonable foible, did not diminish. Samuel Rogers, who came to know her in her latest years, regarded her as 'a composition of art,' and as 'long attached to the trick and show of life' (CLAYDEN, *Early Life of Rogers*, p. 173). Cumberland, in a paper called 'The Feast of Reason,' in his periodical 'The Observer,' No. 25, ridiculed her under the name of Vanessa (D'ARBLAY, ii. 208), and in February 1785, when she fell downstairs at a drawing-room, Jerningham penned some amusing verses (DELANY, vi. 251). Her friend Hannah More, on the other hand, described her in her last days as an affectionate, zealous, and constant friend, and an instructive and pleasant companion. Beattie wrote of her on receiving a false report of her death in March 1799 as 'a faithful and affectionate friend, especially in seasons of distress and difficulty' (FORBES, iii. 163). With members of her own family she was always on affectionate terms. A nephew, Matthew—son of her brother, Morris Robinson, of the six clerks' office, who died in 1777—she brought up and amply provided for. He was her constant companion after her husband's death, taking her own surname of Montagu 3 June 1776 (cf. WILBERFORCE, *Life of Wilberforce*, i. 236). In 1798, though she still entertained a few 'blue-stockings,' she was almost blind and very feeble (D'ARBLAY, vi. 211). She died at Montagu House on 25 Aug. 1800, within six weeks of her eightieth birthday. Her epitaph (she suggested) should record that she had done neither harm nor good, and only asked oblivion.

All her property, which was said to amount to 10,000*l*. a year, went to her nephew, Matthew Montagu. Born on 23 Nov. 1762, he entered parliament as M.P. for Bossiney in 1786, seconded the address in 1787, was elected for Tregony in 1790, and for St. Germains in 1806 and 1807 (cf. WRAXALL, iv. 377 sq.) He succeeded his brother, Morris Robinson, as fourth Lord Rokeby in 1829, and died 1 Sept. 1831. By his wife Elizabeth, daughter of Francis Charlton (*d.* 1817), he was father of Edward Montagu, fifth lord Rokeby (1787–1847), and of Henry Robinson Montagu, K.C.B. (1798–1883), a general in the army, who was the sixth and last lord Rokeby.

A miniature portrait of Mrs. Montagu, then Miss Robinson, in the character of Anne Boleyn, was painted by Zinke, and was engraved by R. Cooper. The engraving appears in Wraxall's 'Memoirs,' vol. i. A portrait by Sir Joshua Reynolds belonged to the last lord Rokeby; an engraving by Bartolozzi and a mezzotint by J. R. Smith are both valuable. A medallion portrait was engraved by Thomas Holloway for the 'European Magazine' (1800, pt. ii. p. 243).

Mrs. Montagu was a voluminous correspondent, writing with vivacity, but with too much prolixity to be altogether readable. William Windham, the statesman, commended the easy and natural yet sparkling style of her letters (*Diary*, 1866, p. 498). In 1809 Matthew Montagu, her nephew and executor, published two volumes of them. Two more volumes followed in 1813. The latest letter in this collection is one addressed to Mrs. Carter in September 1761. Her correspondence in later years, chiefly with her sister-in-law, Mary, wife of William Robinson, rector of Burghfield, Berkshire, and of Denton, Kent, was published in 1873 by Dr. Doran from the originals in the possession of Richard Bentley, the publisher. Of other extant letters by her, two to Lord Lyttelton, dated 1769, appear in the 'Grenville Correspondence' (iv. 425, 496); one to Mrs.

M. Hartley on Euripides, dated 28 Feb. 1787, in R. Warner's 'Original Letters,' 1817, p. 232; eleven, dated between 1771 and 1779, to Beattie, in Forbes's 'Life of Beattie' (1806); and several in the 'Memoirs of Henry Home of Kames' (1814), iii. 279 sq.

Another contemporary Mrs. Montagu 'of Hanover Square,' also known in society, was mother of Frederick Montagu [q. v.]

[A Lady of the Last Century (Mrs. Elizabeth Montagu), illustrated by her unpublished letters, by Dr. Doran, 1873; Elizabeth Montagu, the queen of the blue-stockings: her correspondence 1720–61, by E. J. Climenson, 1906, 2 vols.; R. Huchon's Mrs. Montagu and her friends, London, 1907; Mrs. Montagu's Correspondence; Gent. Mag. 1800, pt. ii. p. 904; European Mag. 1800, pt. ii. p. 243; Nichols's Lit. Illustr. iv. 244; Boswell's Life of Johnson, ed. Hill; Johnson's Letters, ed. Hill; Hayward's Life of Mrs. Piozzi; Mrs. Delany's Autobiography; Wraxall's Memoirs; Memoirs of Madame d'Arblay; W. Roberts's Life of Hannah More, 1834; Forbes's Life of Beattie, 1806; Pennington's Mrs. Carter, 1808; Walpole's Letters; Foster's and Burke's Peerages, s.v. 'Rokeby.'] S. L.

MONTAGU, FREDERICK (1733–1800), politician, born in July 1733, was son of Charles Montagu (*d.* 1759) of Papplewick, Nottinghamshire, a nephew of George Montagu, earl of Halifax (of the second creation) (cf. *Hist. Reg., Chron. Diary*, 1730, p. 64). The father was auditor-general of the duchy of Cornwall while Frederick was Prince of Wales; was M.P. for Westminster in 1722, for St. Germans in 1734, for Camelford in 1741, and for Northampton in 1754, and died on 29 May 1759 (cf. W. P. Courtney, *Parliamentary Representation of Cornwall*, 1889, pp. 290, 349). Frederick's mother, well known in society after her husband's death, was an intimate friend of Mary, dowager-countess of Gower (the widow of John Leveson-Gower, first earl Gower), and of Mrs. Delany, in whose published 'Correspondence' she frequently figures as '*my* Mrs. Montague' (cf. v. 476, 502, 505), in order to distinguish her from the better known Mrs. Elizabeth Montagu [q. v.] Her London residence was in Hanover Square. She died 31 May 1780 (*Gent. Mag.* 1780, p. 299). Frederick, after being educated at Eton, became a fellow-commoner of Trinity College, Cambridge, 8 Feb. 1750. He seems to have won Dr. Paris's college declamation prize, and his oration was published at the request of the master and fellows as 'Oratio in laudes Baconi,' Cambridge, 1755, 4to. He graduated M.A. *per lit. reg.* in 1757. At Cambridge Montagu made the acquaintance of the poets Gray and Mason, which he sedulously cultivated afterwards (cf. Gray, *Works*, ed. Gosse, ii. 284, 557). To his influence Mason owed his appointment to a canonry at York in 1762 (*ib.* p. 82). Admitted a barrister of Lincoln's Inn in 1757, Montagu became a bencher in 1782 (Foster, *Alumni Oxon.*) He was M.P. for Northampton from 1759 to 1767, in succession to his father, and for Higham Ferrers from 1768 to 1790. In 1763 his cousin, George Montagu Dunk, second earl of Halifax (of the second creation) [q. v.], pressed Lord Grenville to obtain a post for him in the board of trade (*Grenville Correspondence*, ii. 221), and he was subsequently 'a devoted adherent to the Cavendish and Rockingham interest' (Wraxall, *Memoirs*, ii. 348). In 1772 he moved in vain to abolish the fast of 30 Jan., the date of Charles I's execution; the fast was not abolished till 1859 (Boswell, *Johnson*, ed. Hill, ii. 152). In 1780 he was generally expected to succeed Sir Fletcher Norton [q. v.] as speaker of the House of Commons (Walpole, *Letters*, ix. 354; *Hist. MSS. Comm.* 10th Rep. vi. 38, cf. 29). He became a lord of the treasury in 1782 under the Marquis of Rockingham, and again in 1783 in the Duke of Portland's coalition ministry. In 1787 he was a member of the committee that prepared the articles of Warren Hastings's impeachment (Wraxall, iv. 446). He was popular in society, and had literary tastes. Wraxall describes him as 'a man of distinguished probity' (ii. 348). On retiring from the House of Commons in 1790, he was made a privy councillor, and lived mainly at his house at Papplewick, which he had rebuilt in 1787 (cf. Thoroton, *Nottinghamshire*, ed. Throsby, ii. 288). He was created D.C.L. at Oxford on 3 July 1793. He died at Papplewick on 30 July 1800 (*Gent. Mag.* 1800, pt. ii. p. 801). Thirteen of his letters to Mrs. Delany are printed in that lady's 'Correspondence,' vols. v. and vi., and two are among the Duke of Manchester's manuscripts (*Hist. MSS. Comm.* 8th Rep. ii. 128, 136). A sister Ann, who died on 10 Sept. 1786, was wife of John Fountayne [q. v.], dean of York, to whose grandson, Richard Fountayne Wilson, the estate of Papplewick passed, together with the name of Montagu.

[Information kindly supplied by Dr. W. Aldis Wright of Trinity College, Cambridge; Burke's Landed Gentry, s.v. 'Montagu of Papplewick;' authorities cited.] S. L.

MONTAGU, GEORGE, second Earl of Halifax (1716–1771). [See Dunk.]

MONTAGU, GEORGE, fourth Duke of Manchester (1737–1788), son of Robert, third duke, vice-chamberlain to Queen Caroline and Queen Charlotte, by Harriet, daughter and coheiress of Edmund Dunch, esq., of Little Wittenham, Berkshire, was born on 6 April 1737. As Viscount Mandeville he was granted an ensign's commission, 13 July 1757, and supported George III's train at his coronation. On 28 March 1761 he was elected M.P. for Huntingdonshire in the whig interest. Soon after succeeding to the dukedom, 10 May 1762, he was appointed lord-lieutenant of the county and high steward of Godmanchester, as well as collector of the subsidies of tonnage and poundage outwards in the port of London. He was colonel of the Huntingdonshire regiment of militia from 1758 (cf. *Home Office Papers*, 1760–5, p. 22). In 1763 he succeeded Rockingham as a lord of the bedchamber, and held the appointment till 17 Jan. 1770. After the fall of the Grafton ministry he went into opposition, acting usually with the whigs of the Rockingham section. He signed their protests, and took a prominent part in the debates of the House of Lords. On 10 Dec. 1770 he moved an address to the crown, praying for the immediate despatch of forces to protect Gibraltar, Minorca, and Jamaica, and is said to have spoken 'with an uncommon degree of eloquence,' although his speech was interrupted by a motion to 'clear the house,' and a scene of great confusion followed (*Parl. Hist.* xvi. 1317). The motion was rejected on the following day by 40 to 14 (*ib.* pp. 1319–1320). He subsequently made vain efforts to improve the arrangements for the admission of members of the lower house and other strangers to the lords' debates. On 30 March 1771 he went with Rockingham, Portland, Burke, and other members of the opposition to the Tower to see Crosby, the lord mayor, and Alderman Oliver, who were confined there.

Throughout the struggle with America he sided with the colonies. On 20 April 1774 he wrote to Rockingham that he was 'convinced that the northern governments of America do call loudly for reformation.' On 1 Feb. 1775 he spoke in favour of Chatham's bill for a provisional settlement with America, and 'drew the attention of every side of the House' (*ib.* xviii. 215). In the same session, on 16 March, he vehemently condemned the bill restraining the trade of the New England colonies (*ib.* p. 433); and on 21 March spoke against treating the southern colonies with greater favour than the northern (*ib.* pp. 455–6). On 18 May he presented a memorial from the New York assembly, part of which he read (*ib.* pp. 666, 684). On 1 Nov. he moved 'that the bringing into any part of the dominions of the crown of Great Britain the electoral troops of his majesty or any other foreign power is dangerous and unconstitutional.' The motion was lost by 75 to 32 (*ib.* pp. 798 et seq.)

During 1776 he was equally active. In supporting a motion by the Duke of Richmond on 5 March to suspend hostilities with the colonists, he declared that it was too late to treat them as rebels—they were 'a powerful nation, a formidable enemy.' The Americans, he believed, dreaded to be forced into independency (*ib.* pp. 1202–6). At the opening of the next session (October) Manchester, in supporting Rockingham's amendment to the address, gave particulars of the preparations that France was making to help America (*ib.* pp. 1370–2). Despite his connection with the Rockingham whigs, Manchester admired Chatham, and supported him on the last two great occasions on which he spoke, viz. 30 May and 5 Dec. 1777 (*ib.* xix. 503). On 17 March, when moving an amendment to the address, he declared that the incapacity of ministers had brought us 'to the melancholy dilemma of not being in a state to make peace or to prosecute war' (*ib.* pp. 915 et seq.) On 23 March he supported the Duke of Richmond's motion for an address to the crown requesting the withdrawal of troops from America. In 1779 he foretold that Ireland was likely to assume the same attitude as America, and that the claims to independence of parliament put forward on behalf of the king might end in a civil war in England.

Manchester differed with most of his political friends in deprecating the relief of the Roman catholics. He was one of a minority of three who voted against a bill prohibiting the holding of debates and selling of provisions on Sunday (*ib.* xxiii. 284). In January 1781 he wrote to Rockingham that it was hopeless for the opposition to make any further attacks upon ministers until his party could show 'at least a little unanimity.'

When in April 1782 Rockingham became once more premier, Manchester was appointed lord chamberlain, and also became a privy councillor (*ib.* p. 65). On 9 April 1783 he was named ambassador to France, to treat for peace, and his action was generally approved; but he resisted Pitt's commercial treaty of 1786.

He caught a chill after attending the trial of Warren Hastings, and some days later took cold at a cricket match. He died at Brighton on 2 Sept. 1788, and was buried at Kimbolton, Huntingdonshire, on 14 Sept. A portrait by Peters, engraved by Leney, represents him in his robes as grand master of masons, holding a compass. Another portrait, depicting him as lord chamberlain, with his wand of office, was painted by C. G. Stuart and engraved by John Jones. Wraxall thus characterises him: 'His figure, which was noble, his manners affable and corresponding with his high rank, prepossessed in his favour, but his fortune bore no proportion to his dignity. Though a man of very dissipated habits, and unaccustomed to diplomatic business, he did not want talents.'

Manchester married, on 22 Oct. 1762, Elizabeth, eldest daughter of Sir Francis Dashwood, bart. She died on 26 June 1832, having had four sons and two daughters. The second son, William, fifth duke of Manchester, is separately noticed.

[Burke's Peerage; Lodge's Genealogy of the Peerage; Doyle's Baronage; Playfair's British Families of Antiquity; Brayley's Beauties of England, vii. 563; Gent. Mag. 1788, p. 839; European Mag. p. 231; Walpole's Mem. George III (Le Marchant), i. 205, iv. 216-19, 226, and Last Journals (Doran), ii. 237, 517, ii. 594, 616; Rockingham Memoirs, i. passim; Thackeray's Chatham, ii. 235, 317, 351, 388; Trevelyan's Early Hist. of Charles J. Fox, p. 322; Wraxall's Hist. Memoirs, iii. 388; Haydn's Book of Dignities; Evans's and Bromley's Cat. of Engraved Portraits; Rogers's Protests of the Lords, vol. ii. passim; Parl. Hist. vols. xvi-xxvi. passim.]

G. Le G. N.

MONTAGU, GEORGE (1751-1815), writer on natural history, born at Lackham in 1751, was son of James Montagu (*d.* 1790) of Lackham, Wiltshire, by his wife Elizabeth, daughter and heiress of William Hedges of Alderton Hall, Wiltshire, a granddaughter of Sir Charles Hedges [q. v.], Queen Anne's secretary. A brother James was high sheriff of Wiltshire in 1795. Montagu's father was fourth in descent from James Montagu, third son of Sir Henry Montagu, first earl of Manchester [q. v.] (Foster, *Peerage*, s. v. 'Manchester'). At an early age George entered the army, and served as a captain in the 15th regiment of foot during the war with the American colonies. Subsequently settling at Easton Grey, near Tedbury, he acted as lieutenant-colonel of the militia of Wiltshire for many years. But he mainly devoted himself to scientific study, and was always an indefatigable and very careful worker in natural history. Two extant letters from him to Gilbert White illustrate his devotion to science. In one, dated 29 June 1789, he writes: 'I have delighted in being an ornithologist from infancy, and, was I not bound by conjugal attachment, should like to ride my hobby to distant parts.' Montagu was among the earliest members of the Linnean Society (instituted 1788), and wrote for it many dissertations and memoirs on the birds and shells of the south of England. Late in life he removed to Knowle House, near Kingsbridge, Devonshire, where he died, 28 Aug. 1815, aged 64, of lockjaw, owing to a wound in his foot caused by a rusty nail. He had married, at the early age of eighteen, Anne, daughter of William Courtenay, by Jane, sister of John Stuart, marquis of Bute. She died at Bristol Hotwells 10 Feb. 1816. By her Montagu was father of George Conway Courtenay Montagu (1776-1847), his heir, who succeeded to the estates of Lackham and Alderton; of Frederick, an officer in the army, killed at Albuera, and of two daughters.

Montagu was an active collector of books and coins, birds and other animals. Leigh & Sotheby sold his library in 1798, and his coins in the same year, and after his death his Greek coins and English medals were also disposed of, along with more than three hundred letters of John, duke of Marlborough, a few of Queen Anne, and other papers descending to him through his wife's grandfather, Sir Charles Hedges (6 Aug. 1816). His collection of birds and other animals was purchased by the British Museum.

Montagu's chief works are: 1. 'The Sportsman's Directory,' London, 1792, dedicated to Lord Porchester. This treats with much detail on the penetration of gunpowder, on shooting flying, and the like. It condemns rifled barrels, and gives curious directions to duellists on the best position in which to stand when receiving an adversary's fire. 2. 'Ornithological Dictionary or Alphabetical Synopsis of British Birds,' 2 vols. London, 1802, followed by a 'Supplement' (Exeter, 1813), with twenty-four plates. In this book Montagu's industry and caution are seen at their best. It is an admirable compendium for the time at which it was written. Thus he gives the great black woodpecker a place in his list, 'with considerable doubt;' he 'cannot speak of it from his own knowledge.' Modern ornithologists entirely bear him out. His account of the great bustard is very valuable, now that the bird is extinct in Great Britain, while his characteristic reticence in the presence of a paucity of facts is apparent in his account of the great auk: 'it is said to breed in the isle of St. Kilda.' Montagu's dictionary was reprinted with additions by Rennie in 1831; by E. Newman, also with additions, in 1866; and again (n.d.) by Sonnenschein and Allen. 3. 'Testacea Britannica, a History of British Marine, Land, and Fresh-water Shells,' in two parts, 1803 (Romsey). A 'Supplement' was published at Exeter in 1808. Montagu here follows in the researches of Lister and Da

Costa, the coloured plates of shells are of considerable beauty, and the book is a monument of careful study and enthusiasm.

The following are Montagu's minor contributions to science. For the Linnean Society he wrote: 'Observations on British Quadrupeds, Birds, and Fishes' (vii. 274); 'On the Horseshoe Bats and the Barbastelle' (ix. 162); 'On three rare Species of British Birds' (iv. 35); 'On Falco cyaneus and pygargus' (ix. 182); 'On some rare Marine British Shells' (xi. 2, 179); 'On the Black Stork' (xiii. 19); 'On remarkable Marine Animals discovered on the South Coast of Devon' (vii. 61, ix. 81, xi. 1); and 'On Five British Species of Terebella' (xii. 2, 340). For the Wernerian Society he wrote: 'On some rare British Fishes' (i. 79); 'On the Gannet' (i. 176); 'On Fasciola in Poultry' (i. 194); 'On British Sponges' (ii. 67); 'On Fishes taken in South Devon' (ii. 413); 'On a supposed new Species of Dolphin' (iii. 75).

[Gent. Mag. 1815, pt. ii. p. 281; Agassiz's Catalogue of Books on Zoology, by Strickland, 1852, iii. 614; two letters to Gilbert White in Bell's History of Selborne, ii. 236; Memoir by Mr. Cunnington in the Wiltshire Mag. 1857, iii. 87; Nichols's Lit. Illustrations, vi. 718–20, 725, 896.] M. G. W.

MONTAGU, Sir **GEORGE** (1750–1829), admiral, second son of Admiral John Montagu [q. v.], and brother of Captain James Montagu [q. v.], and of Edward Montagu (1755–1799) [q. v.], was born on 12 Dec. 1750. In 1763 he entered the Royal Academy at Portsmouth, and was thence appointed to the Preston with Captain Alan (afterwards lord) Gardner [q. v.], going out to the Jamaica station with the flag of Rear-admiral William Parry. In the Preston he continued for three years, was afterwards in the Levant with Captain Gardner, and returned to England in 1770. He passed his examination on 2 Oct. 1770, and on 14 Jan. 1771 was promoted to be lieutenant of the Marlborough. In February he was moved into the Captain, going out to North America as the flagship of his father. The latter on 9 April 1773 made him commander in the Kingfisher sloop, and on 15 April 1774 (*Pay-book of the Fowey*) he was posted to the Fowey. In her he continued on the North-American station during the early years of the war of independence, actively co-operating with the army in the embarkation at Boston in March, and in the reduction of New York in October 1776. Shortly after he returned to England in bad health. From 1777 to 1779 he commanded the Romney, as flag-captain to his father at Newfoundland. On his return he was appointed to the 32-gun frigate Pearl, in which, cruising near the Azores, he captured the Spanish frigate Santa Monica, of equal force, on 14 Sept. 1779. In December the Pearl sailed with the fleet under Sir George Rodney [q. v.], and assisted in the capture of the Caracas convoy; but having sprung her foremast, was ordered home with the prizes. She was afterwards sent out to North America, and on 30 Sept. 1780, while on a cruise off the Bermudas, captured the Espérance, a frigate-built privateer of 32 guns. In the action off Cape Henry, on 16 March 1781 [see Arbuthnot, Marriot], she acted as repeating frigate. She was not with the fleet on 5 Sept. [see Graves, Thomas, Lord], but joined it, still off Cape Henry, on the 14th, and was left to keep watch on the movements of the French till the 25th, when she sailed for New York. On 19 Oct. she sailed again with the fleet, and on the 23rd was stationed ahead as a look-out (*Pearl's Log*). She returned to England in 1782.

In the armament of 1790 Montagu was appointed to the Hector of 74 guns, and, continuing to command her, went out to the Leeward Islands in 1793 with Rear-admiral Gardner, and thence to Jamaica, to convoy the homeward-bound trade. He was afterwards with the squadron in the Downs, under the orders of Rear-admiral Macbride, till 12 April 1794, when he was promoted to the rank of rear-admiral, and, hoisting his flag in the Hector, joined the grand fleet under Lord Howe [see Howe, Richard, Earl]. On 4 May he was detached, with a squadron of six sail of the line, to convoy a large fleet of merchant ships as far as Cape Finisterre. His further orders were to cruise to the westward till 20 May, in the hope of meeting the French provision convoy daily expected from America. The convoy, however, did not arrive at that time, and Montagu, after making several important captures, returned to Plymouth on 30 May. He had extended his cruise for several days beyond the prescribed limit, but had not been able to communicate with Howe. On 2 June he received orders from the admiralty to put to sea again with every available ship, and to cruise off Brest in order to intercept the French provision fleet. On the 3rd the Audacious came in with news of the partial action of 28 May; but Montagu, having no other orders, put to sea on 4 June with nine sail of the line. On the evening of the 8th he chased a French squadron of eight ships into Brest, and at daybreak on the 9th found a French fleet of nineteen ships of the line a few miles to the westward of him. Though several of these were under jurymasts, or in tow of others, they all appeared capable of defending themselves, and fourteen of them seemed to be ordinarily effective. Of Howe's success Montagu had no information. All he could hope was that by stretching to the southward, with a northerly wind, he might tempt the French so far to leeward of their port that Howe, if following them up, might be able to secure them. The French commander, Villaret, however, was not inclined to run such a risk, and, after a slight demonstration of chasing him, resumed his course and steered for Brest, while Montagu, after looking for Howe to the north-west, and failing to find him, bore away for the Channel, and on the 12th anchored in Cawsand Bay.

In 1823 Captain Brenton, in relating these events in the first volume of his 'Naval History,' pp. 296–300, attacked Montagu's conduct in not bringing on a general action, and said that 'Lord Chatham and the board of admiralty expressed some displeasure at the conduct of the rear-admiral, and he was ordered or permitted to strike his flag.' Montagu published 'A Refutation of the Incorrect Statements and Unjust Insinuations contained in Captain Brenton's "Naval History of Great Britain," as far as the same refers to the Conduct of Admiral Sir George Montagu; in a Letter addressed to the Author.' Montagu was perhaps too old, too angry, and too little practised in literary fence to punish Brenton as he deserved; but he had no difficulty in showing that Brenton's facts were untrue [see BRENTON, EDWARD PELHAM].

Howe and the admiralty fully approved of Montagu's conduct; and when, in bad health, rendered worse by the shock of his brother's death on 1 June, he applied for permission to resign his command, they both expressed their regret and a hope that his absence might be short (MARSHALL, i. 41–2). On 1 June 1795 he was promoted to be vice-admiral, and in March 1799 he was offered the command at the Nore, which he declined, as beneath his rank. In April 1800 Lord St. Vincent offered him the post of second in command in the Channel; but other officers were appointed by the admiralty, and there was no vacancy (*Addit. MS.* 31158, ff. 113, 117). On 1 Jan. 1801 he was made admiral; but when shortly afterwards he applied for a command, St. Vincent, who had become first lord of the admiralty, replied that he had learned there was 'an insuperable bar' to his 'being employed in any way.' He refused to say what the bar was; but it would appear to have been some misunderstanding of his conduct in 1794, as it gave way on a perusal of the official letters which Montagu had received at the time, and in 1803 he was appointed commander-in-chief at Portsmouth. He held this post for five years and a half, and in August 1810 was presented with 'a superb piece of plate' as 'a tribute of respect and esteem' by the captains who had fitted out at Portsmouth during his command. On 2 Jan. 1815 he was nominated a G.C.B., but had no service after the peace. He died on 24 Dec. 1829.

Montagu married in 1783 his first cousin, Charlotte, daughter and coheiress of George Wroughton of Wilcot, Wiltshire, and had issue a daughter and four sons, of whom the eldest, George Wroughton, assumed the name of Wroughton in 1826, and died a lieutenant-colonel in the army in 1871. The second, John William, died an admiral on the retired list in 1882; the third, James, was also a retired admiral at his death in 1868; the fourth, Edward (*d.* 1820), was in holy orders. The daughter, Georgiana (*d.* 1836), married Sir John Gore [q. v.]

[Ralfe's Naval Biog. ii. 6; Marshall's Roy. Nav. Biog. i. 39; O'Byrne's Nav. Biog. Dict. s.n. 'Montagu, John William;' lists, log-books, &c., in the Public Record Office.] J. K. L.

MONTAGU (formerly BRUDENELL), GEORGE BRUDENELL, DUKE OF MONTAGU of a new creation, and fourth EARL OF CARDIGAN (1712–1790), eldest son of George Brudenell, third earl of Cardigan, and his wife Lady Elizabeth Bruce, eldest daughter of Thomas, second earl of Ailesbury, was born on 26 July 1712, and on the death of his father, 5 July 1732, succeeded as fourth earl of Cardigan. He married in 1730 the Lady Mary Montagu, third daughter and coheiress of John, second duke of Montagu, and last of that creation [see MONTAGU, JOHN, second DUKE OF MONTAGU], and on the death of that nobleman in 1749 took the name and arms of Montagu. On 13 March 1762 he was made K.G. while beyond seas, this being the first investiture of a subject *in absentia.* In 1766 dukedoms were offered to Cardigan and Sir Hugh Smithson, both being husbands of daughters of dukes whose ducal honours had become extinct at their death. But George III proposed to limit the titles in entail to the issue in each case of the ladies whose ducal parentage suggested the new titles. Smithson accepted, and was at once made Duke of Northumberland, but Cardigan objected to the restriction, and soon after (6 Nov. 1766) received the dukedom of Montagu without the limitation (WALPOLE, *Letters,* vi. 209). In 1776 Montagu was appointed governor to the youthful Prince of Wales [see GEORGE IV] and his brother, the

Bishop of Osnaburg [see Frederick Augustus, Duke of York and Albany]. At the time of his death the duke was master of the horse, governor and captain of Windsor Castle, a privy councillor, lord-lieutenant of Huntingdon, president of the London Hospital and of the Society of Arts. He died at his residence in Privy Gardens, London, on 23 May 1790, when the dukedom and marquisate became extinct, and the earldom of Cardigan devolved on his next brother, James Brudenell, fifth earl.

By his marriage the duke had four children, viz. a son, who was called to the upper house as Baron Montagu of Boughton, and died unmarried in 1775, and three daughters, one of whom, Lady Elizabeth, married in 1767 Henry, second duke of Buccleuch, while two died unmarried. The entailed estates (12,000*l.* a year) went with the earldom; but the personal estate (100,000*l.*), the family jewels (valued at 50,000*l.*), the plate, and various residences passed to the Duchess of Buccleuch. The duke directed in his will that his town house should be kept up, and their full wages paid to all his servants as long as they lived.

[Collins's Peerage, 1812 ed. iii. 498–9; Burke's Extinct Peerage; Gent. Mag. 1790, pt. i. pp. 482, 568.] H. M. C.

MONTAGU, Sir HENRY, first Earl of Manchester (1563?–1642), judge and statesman, fourth son of Sir Edward Montagu, by Elizabeth, daughter of Sir James Harington of Exton, Rutland, and grandson of Chief-justice Sir Edward Montagu [q. v.], was born at Boughton, Northamptonshire, about 1563. He entered Christ's College, Cambridge, in 1583, and was called to the bar at the Middle Temple, where he was elected autumn reader in 1606. In the autumn of 1601 he entered parliament as member for Higham Ferrers. At first he took the popular side so far as to protest against the doctrine that the king could impose taxes at will. Nevertheless, by the recommendation of King James, he was elected recorder of London 26 May 1603, and on 23 July following he was knighted at Whitehall. He displayed his gratitude in a courtly speech on occasion of James's visit to the city, 15 March 1603–4, nor did he fail to turn to account several other opportunities which his office afforded of ingratiating himself with the king. He was appointed king's counsel 11 Sept. 1607, called to the degree of serjeant-at-law 4 Feb. 1610–11, and made king's serjeant a few days later (11 Feb.), retaining the recordership by express leave of the king. In 1612 he distinguished himself by the zeal and ability with which, in conjunction with Bacon, then solicitor-general, he investigated the frauds committed by the farmers of the customs. In the parliaments of 1604–11 and 1614 he sat for London, and was one of the managers of the conferences with the lords on commutation of tenures (1610) and impositions (1614). He was one of the examiners, 18 Jan. 1614–15, and afterwards one of the judges (7 Aug.) of the puritan, Edmund Peacham [q. v.], and opened the case against Lord and Lady Somerset [see Carr, Robert, Earl of Somerset] on their trial for the murder of Sir Thomas Overbury [q. v.], May 1616. On 16 Nov. following he resigned the recordership, to succeed Coke as chief justice of the king's bench. On the 18th he rode in great state, attended by 'earls, lords, and others of great quality, to the number of fifty horse,' to Westminster Hall, where he was installed by Lord-chancellor Ellesmere [see Egerton, Sir Thomas, Baron Ellesmere and Viscount Brackley] in a speech full of bitter reflections on Coke and commendations of subserviency, to which Montagu replied in a tone of due humility.

Montagu's tenure of this office was brief, and the only case of great public interest which came before him was that of Sir Walter Raleigh, against whom, in a speech not unworthy of the occasion, he made award of execution on 28 Oct. 1618. He was one of Bacon's colleagues in the commission for the protection of the gold and silver thread monopoly appointed 22 April 1618, but whether by accident or design did not sign the general search-warrant, the issue of which was one of the first, and not the least arbitrary acts of the commissioners. In 1620 he exchanged Westminster Hall for the council table, being made lord high treasurer of England, by delivery of the white staff of office, at Newmarket on 3 Dec., and as he paid 20,000*l.* for the place, which was tenable only during the royal pleasure, the *bon mot* was current that wood was very dear at Newmarket. The transaction was afterwards made the subject of the tenth article of the impeachment of Buckingham, who admitted the receipt of the money, but represented it as a mere loan to the king. The value of the place varied with the conscience of the holder. Montagu himself estimated it at 'some thousands of pounds to him who, after death, would go instantly to salvation, twice as much to him who would go to purgatory, and a *nemo scit* to him who would adventure to a worse place.' It carried, however, a peerage with it, and after taking the oaths (16 Dec.) Montagu, who had recently bought Kimbolton Castle, the ancient seat of the Mandevilles, was created Baron Montagu of Kimbolton, Huntingdonshire, and Viscount Mandeville (19 Dec.)

Mandeville was a member of the committee of lords and commons which sat in the Painted Chamber to confer on Bacon's case (19 March 1620–1), and one of the commissioners of the great seal in the interval (1 May–10 July) between the disgrace of the chancellor and its delivery to his successor, Lord-keeper Williams. At Buckingham's instance he resigned the lord-treasurership, to make way for Lord Cranfield, in the following September [see CRANFIELD, LIONEL, EARL OF MIDDLESEX], and was sworn president of the council, upon which Bacon punningly remarked that, as the king had made a strange example of him, so he had made a strange precedent (president) of Mandeville.

In 1624 Mandeville was appointed master of the court of wards (21 May), and placed at the head of the Virginia commission (15 June). By Charles I he was continued in office as lord president, and created Earl of Manchester 5 Feb. 1625–6. He so far sympathised with those who refused to subscribe the forced loan of 1626–7, though himself one of the commissioners for raising it, as to procure their enlargement from the Gatehouse during the summer. In 1628 he sat on two commissions nominated the same day (29 Feb.)—one to treat with the Dutch ambassadors, the other to devise ways and means of raising money, known as the commission of excise, and soon afterwards dissolved in deference to the remonstrances of the commons. On 30 June he was made lord privy seal. As lord-lieutenant of Huntingdonshire he was commissioned to take compositions in lieu of compulsory knighthood within the county, and among others took in 1631 that of Oliver Cromwell, whose quarrel with the newly elected mayor and recorder of Huntingdon he had composed the preceding year.

Manchester was one of the most assiduous members of the court of Star-chamber, and equally resolute in enforcing the law against puritan and papist. In 1634 he was placed on the legislative council for the colonies (28 April). In 1635 he was made a commissioner of the treasury (15 March), and on 6 April placed on the committee for trade.

Manchester was one of Charles's most trusted advisers and loyal adherents. Though far from wealthy for his station, he subscribed, in 1639, 4,000*l.* for the public service, and in the following year exhausted all his eloquence in endeavouring to raise a loan of 200,000*l.* in the city of London. The aldermen, however, were very shy, and he only succeeded in obtaining a fourth of the amount. The same year he sat on a special commission, appointed 20 May, to collect arrears of ship-money, and on the commission of peace and safety, in which the executive was vested on the king's departure for the north (12 Sept.) On 9 Aug. 1641 he was appointed one of the guardians of the realm during the king's absence in Scotland, and one of the commissioners for giving the royal assent to bills. During part of May 1642 he acted as speaker of the House of Lords. He died on 7 Nov. following, and was buried at Kimbolton. Besides Kimbolton, Manchester held, by royal grant of 1631, the adjacent estate of Naybridge Park in fee farm. He had also a villa at Totteridge, Hertfordshire. His town house was in Aldersgate Street. Though hardly in the front rank, either as a lawyer or as a statesman, Manchester was a man of high and various ability and untarnished honour. Clarendon justly praises his great 'industry and sagacity,' his 'integrity and zeal to the protestant religion as it was established by law,' and his 'unquestionable loyalty.' He is the subject of a somewhat ponderous elegy in Glapthorne's 'Whitehall,' 1643. He married thrice: first, Catherine, daughter of Sir William Spencer of Yarnton, Oxfordshire; secondly, in 1613, Anne, daughter of William Wincot of Langham, Suffolk, and relict of Sir Leonard Haliday, lord mayor of London in 1606; thirdly, on 26 April 1620, Margaret, daughter of John Crouch of Cornbury, Hertfordshire, and relict of John Hare, clerk of the court of wards, who survived him, and died in 1653. By his first wife he had four sons—Edward [q.v.], who succeeded him; Walter [q.v.]; James of Lackham, ancestor of the Montagus of Wiltshire [see MONTAGU, JOHN, 1719–1795]; and Henry, master of St. Catherine's Hospital, near the Tower, London—and three daughters. By his second wife he had no issue. By his third he had two sons, George, father of Sir James [q.v.] and of Charles Montagu, earl of Halifax [q.v.], and Sidney (who, admitted fellow-commoner at Christ's College, Cambridge, 20 May 1641, graduated M.A. in that year, entered the Middle Temple 2 Aug. 1642, and died early), also two daughters, the second, Susannah, marrying, 14 Dec. 1637, George Brydges, sixth lord Chandos.

Manchester is the author of 'Contemplatio Mortis et Immortalitatis,' published anonymously in 1631, London, 12mo; reprinted under the title 'Manchester al Mondo. Contemplatio Mortis et Immortalitatis,' 1633, 12mo; 3rd edit., much enlarged, 1635, 12mo; other editions, 1639, 1642, 1676, 1688, 1690,

12mo. It exhibits much learning, patristic and philosophical, and considerable command of dignified English. A copy of Manchester's letter to his son Walter Montagu [q. v.], on his conversion to the church of Rome, is preserved in Harl. MS. 1506, No. 8. Some of Manchester's letters are printed in the late Duke of Manchester's 'Court and Society from Elizabeth to Anne,' and 'Hist. MSS. Comm.,' 8th Rep. App. pt. ii. pp. 10, 50–9; others are preserved in the State Paper Office, and a few are at Hatfield (see *Hist. MSS. Comm.* 3rd Rep. App.) His judgments while lord chief justice are reported by Croke; see also Jardine's 'Criminal Trials,' i. 499, Cobbett's 'State Trials,' ii. 1078, 'Cases in the Courts of Star Chamber and High Commission' (Camden Soc.), and 'Documents relating to the Proceedings against William Prynne' (Camden Soc.) Two of his speeches while recorder are printed in Nichols's 'Progresses' (James I), i. 360, ii. 155, and his speech on his installation as lord chief justice in Moore's 'Reports,' pp. 829 et seq.; see also 'Hist. MSS. Comm.,' 11th Rep. App. pt. vii. p. 289. A portrait of Manchester is in the possession of the Duke of Manchester.

[Fuller's Worthies of Engl. (Northamptonshire); Bridges's Northamptonshire, ii. 347; Collins's Peerage, ed. Brydges, ii. 51 et seq.; Clarendon's Rebellion, ed. 1849, bk. i. §§ 101 and 116–117; Court and Times of James I, i. 370, 440, ii. 87, 241, 270–1, 297, 362, 396, 497, 506; Sir Simonds D'Ewes's Autobiog. i. 160; Dugdale's Orig. pp. 98, 219, Chron. Ser. p. 104; Parl. Hist. i. 921; Nichols's Progr. James I, i. 332–3, iii. 629; Metcalfe's Book of Knights, p. 145; Parl. Debates in 1610 (Camden Soc.); Wynne's Serjeant-at-Law; Archæologia, x. 144, xli. 251; Analytical Index to Remembrancia, pp. 23, 288, 300; Spedding's Letters and Life of Bacon, iv. 48, 337, v. 93–4, vi. 84, vii. 149 *n.*; Diary of Walter Yonge (Camden Soc.), p. 28; Letters of George, Lord Carew, to Sir Thomas Roe (Camden Soc.), p. 56; Debates in the House of Lords in 1621 (Camden Soc.), p. 149; Hutton's Reports, p. 21; Croke's Reports (Jac.), pp. 407, 495; Whitelocke's Lib. Famel. (Camden Soc.), p. 51; Jardine on Torture, p. 106; Cobbett's State Trials, ii. 966 et seq.; Hardy's Cat. Chanc. iii. 764; Court and Times of Charles I, i. 162, 241, 375, ii. 106, 145, 152; Cal. State Papers, Dom. 1603–40, passim; Cal. State Papers, Colon. 1574–1660, pp. 64, 177; Rushworth's Hist. Coll. i. 334, 387, 614, 628, iii. 1180; Hist. MSS. Comm. 10th Rep. App. p. 23; Lords' Journals, iii. 53, iv. 32, v. 64 et seq.; Nicholas Papers (Camden Soc.), i. 3; Lloyd's State Worthies, ii. 351; Rymer's Fœdera (Sanderson), xviii. 975, xix. 766, xx. 439, 481–2; Obituary of Richard Smyth (Camden Soc.), p. 20; Notes and Queries, 5th ser. viii. 153; Campbell's Lives of the Chief Justices; Gardiner's Hist. of England; Foss's Lives of the Judges; Manchester's Court and Society from Elizabeth to Anne; Wood's Fasti Oxon. (Bliss), ii. 284; Walpole's Royal and Noble Authors; Lowndes's Bibl. Man.] J. M. R.

MONTAGU or **MOUNTAGUE, JAMES** (1568?–1618), bishop of Winchester, fifth son of Sir Edward Montagu of Boughton, Northamptonshire, by Elizabeth, daughter of Sir James Harington of Exton, Rutlandshire, was born about 1568, his eldest brother being Edward [q.v.], created Lord Montagu of Boughton in 1621, and his third brother being Henry Montagu, first earl of Manchester [q. v.] He was a fellow-commoner of Christ's College, Cambridge, and was appointed first master of Sidney Sussex College (Le Neve, *Fasti*, iii. 703), signing in 1596 a letter from the vice-chancellor and other heads to Lord Burghley, complaining of the teaching of Peter Baro [q. v.] He beautified the interior of his college chapel, and expended 100*l.* of his own money in purifying the King's Ditch in Cambridge (Willis and Clark). In 1603 he was installed dean of Lichfield, but resigned that office the next year on being appointed dean of Worcester (Le Neve, i. 56). Being already dean of the chapel to James, he was in 1608 elected to the bishopric of Bath and Wells, and, resigning his mastership, was consecrated on 17 April. He repaired the episcopal palace at Wells and the manor-house at Banwell, and vigorously took in hand the restoration of the nave of the abbey-church at Bath, spending, it is said, 1,000*l.* upon it. There is a story that Sir John Harington [q. v.] of Kelston, walking with him one day in the rain, took him into the abbey, then roofless, under pretence of seeking shelter, and, by this means impressing upon Montagu the neglected state of the building, stirred him to exert himself to repair it. On 4 Oct. 1616 he was translated to the see of Winchester. He died of jaundice and dropsy at Greenwich on 20 July 1618, at the age of fifty, and was buried in Bath Abbey, where a tomb with his effigy is on the north side of the nave. Over the west door of the church are the arms of the see impaling Montagu. He edited and translated the works of King James I [q. v.], published in English in one vol. fol. in 1616, and in Latin in the same form, 1619. Montagu's portrait is in the bishop's palace at Wells, and has been engraved by Renold Elstracke [q. v.] and Pass, and an engraving is also in the 'Herωologia Anglica' of Henry Holland [q. v.]

[Cassan's Bishops of Bath and Wells, pt. i. p. 69, ii. 22; Cassan's Bishops of Winchester, pt. ii. p. 78; Le Neve's Fasti, i. 145, 563, iii. 703, ed. Hardy; Willis and Clark's Architectural Hist.

of Cambridge, ii. 739; Fuller's Worthies (Northamptonshire), ii. 164; Strype's Annals, III. i. 719, iv. 322, and Whitgift, ii. 437; Collinson's Somerset, iii. 388; Warner's Hist. of Bath, p. 159; Dugdale's Monasticon, ii. 261, 282; Somerset Archæol. and Nat. Hist. Society's Proc. 1876, XXII. i. 33, 34.] W. H.

MONTAGU, Sir JAMES (1666–1723), judge, sixth son of George Montagu of Horton in Northamptonshire, by his wife Elizabeth, daughter of Sir Anthony Irby, was born on 2 Feb. 1665-6. His father was son of Sir Henry Montagu, first earl of Manchester [q. v.], by his third wife, and his brother was Charles Montagu, earl of Halifax [q. v.] James was entered at the Middle Temple, and called to the bar. In 1695 Montagu became member of parliament for Tregony, and for Beeralston in 1698, when he was also made chief justice of Ely. In 1704 he successfully defended John Tutchin [q. v.], indicted for a libel published in his periodical, 'The Observator,' and two years later he was leading counsel in the prosecution of Beau Feilding for bigamy in marrying the Duchess of Cleveland [see Feilding, Robert]. In 1705 he was committed by the House of Commons to the custody of the serjeant-at-arms for having in 1704 demanded a habeas corpus on behalf of the Aylesbury men, whom the house had committed to Newgate for bringing actions against the returning officer; Montagu pleaded strongly against the privilege claimed by the commons. He remained in custody from 26 Feb. to 14 March, when parliament was prorogued and afterwards dissolved. In April 1705 he was knighted at Cambridge, and made one of her majesty's counsel in November of the same year.

In the second parliament of Queen Anne Montagu was returned for Carlisle; he became solicitor-general in 1707, and was attorney-general from 1708 to 1710, when the queen granted him a pension of 1,000*l.* This pension was made the subject of a motion brought before the house in 1711, in which Colonel Gledhill represented it as intended to defray the expenses of Montagu's election at Carlisle; the charge was, however, disproved. As attorney-general Montagu opened the case in the House of Lords against Dr. Sacheverell. He received the degree of the coif on 26 Oct. 1714, was made baron of the exchequer on 22 Nov. 1714, and was lord commissioner of the great seal (on the resignation of Lord Cowper) from 18 April to 12 May 1718, when Lord Parker became lord chancellor. Montagu succeeded Sir Thomas Bury as chief baron of the exchequer in May 1722. He died on 1 Oct. 1723.

He married in 1694 Tufton Wray, daughter of Sir William Wray of Ashby, bart.; she died in 1712, and he married as his second wife his cousin Elizabeth, daughter of Robert, third earl of Manchester, by whom he had a son Charles, afterwards M.P. for St. Albans.

[Foss's Judges of England; parish register of Horton.] L. M. M. S.

MONTAGU, JAMES (1752–1794), captain in the navy, third son of Admiral John Montagu [q. v.], and brother of Admiral George Montagu [q. v.] and of Edward Montagu (1755–1799) [q. v.], was born on 12 Aug. 1752. On 18 Aug. 1771 he was promoted by his father to the rank of lieutenant, and on 11 Sept. 1773 to be commander of the Tamar sloop. In her, and afterwards in the Kingfisher, he continued on the North American station, and on 14 Nov. 1775 he was posted to the Mercury. In December 1776 he was sent to England with the despatches announcing the capture of Rhode Island by Sir Peter Parker and General Clinton. He then returned to North America; but on 24 Dec. 1777, coming down the North (or Hudson's) River, the Mercury struck on a hulk which the enemy had sunk in the fairway, and became a total wreck. Montagu was tried by court-martial at New York, but acquitted of all blame, and in July 1778 he was appointed to the Medea frigate, which for the next two years he commanded on the home station, cruising in the North Sea, in the Channel, or occasionally as far south as Lisbon. In October 1780 he was moved into the Juno, and, after a year of similar service in the Channel, in February 1782 sailed with Sir Richard Bickerton [q. v.] for the East Indies. The Juno arrived at Bombay in August 1782, and on 20 June 1783 was present at the action off Cuddalore, the last between Sir Edward Hughes [q. v.] and the Bailli de Suffren. Montagu returned to England in the beginning of 1785, and being then unable to obtain employment afloat he went, in October 1786, to France on a twelvemonths' leave. In October 1787 he was back in England, but had no employment till the outbreak of the revolutionary war, when at his own special request—apparently on account of the name—he was appointed to the 74-gun ship Montagu, one of the grand fleet under Lord Howe during the campaigns of 1793 and 1794 [see Howe, Richard, Earl]. In the battle off Ushant, on 1 June 1794, Montagu was killed. A monumental statue, by Flaxman, is in Westminster Abbey.

[Official letters and other documents in the Public Record Office; James's Naval Hist. ed. of 1860, i. 185.] J. K. L.

MONTAGU, JOHN (1655?–1728), divine, fourth son of Edward Montagu, first earl of Sandwich [q. v.], was admitted a fellow-commoner at Trinity College, Cambridge, on 12 April 1672, and was elected fellow in 1674. He proceeded M.A. *jure natalium*, 1673, and D.D. (by royal mandate) on 27 Sept. 1686. In 1680 he was made master of Sherburn Hospital, Durham, by his relative, Bishop Crewe, and in 1683 he became prebendary of Durham Cathedral. In the same year (12 May) he was made master of Trinity College, Cambridge, by the crown. In 1687–8 he was vice-chancellor. In 1699 he resigned the mastership on being made dean of Durham. Montagu was admitted a member of the Gentlemen's Society at Spalding on 22 Aug. 1723. He died unmarried, at his house in Bedford Row, Holborn, London, on 23 Feb. 1728, aged 73, and was interred at Barnwell, Northamptonshire, the burying-place of his family (NICHOLS, *Lit. Anecd.* vi. 99).

Trinity College is said to have declined in numbers or reputation during Montagu's mastership, on account of the relaxation of discipline which his easy temper encouraged. He was a liberal benefactor to the college, subscribing 228*l.* towards the cost of the new library, and allowing 170*l.*, due to him as master when he resigned, to be expended in purchasing furniture for the master's lodge. This sum had been claimed by his successor, Dr. Bentley, and the above compromise was not effected till 1702, when the thanks of the society were given to Montagu, and his name inscribed in the register of benefactors by the master. In 1720, when Bentley was projecting an edition of the New Testament, Montagu lent him some manuscripts from the Chapter Library at Durham.

[Collins's Peerage, iii. 464; Surtees's Durham, i. 142; Hutchinson's Durham, ii. 169, 185, 213; Le Neve, iii. 300; Monk's Bentley, i. 143, 147, ii. 120; Alumni Westmon. p. 28.]

J. W. C–K.

MONTAGU, JOHN, second DUKE OF MONTAGU (1688?–1749), courtier, born in 1688 or 1689, was eldest surviving son of Ralph, first duke of Montagu [q. v.], by his first wife, the Lady Elizabeth, daughter of Thomas Wriothesley, earl of Southampton, and widow of Joceline Percy, eleventh earl of Northumberland. In 1709 he succeeded his father as second duke, and visited Marlborough's headquarters in Flanders (*Marlborough Despatches*, vol. iv.), but he does not appear to have then held any military rank. He officiated as high constable at the coronation of George I, who appointed him colonel of the 1st troop of horse guards and gold stick. On 23 Oct. 1717 he was admitted a fellow of the Royal College of Physicians, London, at his own request. He often attended the delivery of the Harveian orations, and not unfrequently the annual dinners. By letters patent of 22 June 1722 George I granted him the islands of St. Lucia and St. Vincent's in the West Indies, and appointed him governor and captain-general thereof. Montagu appointed a Captain Uring deputy-governor, and sent him out with seven ships containing settlers and their families. The British men-of-war on the station would not directly support the enterprise, and when the French landed a body of troops from Martinique to oppose him, Uring was compelled to conclude a treaty agreeing to quit St. Lucia within seven days. A similar attempt to obtain a footing in St. Vincent's was opposed by the inhabitants, and also ended in failure. Montagu is said to have lost 40,000*l.* over the undertaking.

The duke carried the sceptre and cross at the coronation of George II. In 1737 he was reappointed colonel of the 1st troop of horse guards, but was removed the same year. He was appointed master-general of the ordnance in 1740, was succeeded by John, duke of Argyll and Greenwich, the year after, and on the death of the latter nobleman in October 1743 was reappointed, and held the office until his death. In 1745 he raised a regiment of horse, called 'Montagu's Carabineers,' and a regiment of 'ordnance foot,' both of which, after brief service in the south of England, were disbanded after Culloden. The duke, who was K.G. (1719), grand master of the order of the Bath (1725), master of the Great Wardrobe, colonel of the queen's regiment of horse (now 2nd dragoon guards or queen's bays), and F.R.S., died of a violent fever on 6 July 1749, when, in default of surviving male issue, the dukedom became extinct.

The duke appears to have been a man of some talent, but with much of the buffoon about him. He was the originator of the famous hoax at the Haymarket Theatre of a man squeezing himself into a quart bottle. Sarah, duchess of Marlborough, wrote of him to Lord Stair: 'All my son-in-law's talents lie in things natural to boys of fifteen, and he is about two and fifty. To get people into his gardens and wet them with squirts, to invite people to his country house and put things in their beds to make them itch, and twenty other such pretty fancies' (WALPOLE, *Letters*, i. 339). As patron of the living of St. Andrew's, Holborn, he was a party to the proceedings taken by Dr. Henry Sacheverell, the rector, against persons who had built a chapel in the parish. A statement of the case was published. The duke's correspondence with Holles, duke of Newcastle, and some other letters are among the Additional MSS. in the British Museum. Some sprightly letters from the duke to Dr. Stukeley are printed in Nichols's 'Literary Illustrations,' ii. 786, &c. A portrait of Montagu by Kneller is in the possession of W. R. Barker, esq.; and two others, by T. Hudson and M. Dahl, have been engraved (BROMLEY).

The duke's country place, Boughton, Northamptonshire, now belonging to the Buccleuch family, was laid out by him as a miniature Versailles. After his death his town residence, Montagu House, Bloomsbury, on the present site of the British Museum, received and for many years held the national collections, which under the name of the British Museum were first opened to the public in 1759. The name Montagu survives in the topography of the district.

Montagu married the Lady Mary Churchill, youngest daughter of the great Duke of Marlborough, and had two sons and three daughters. The youngest of the daughters, Lady Mary Montagu, married in 1730 George Brudenell, fourth earl of Cardigan [see MONTAGU, GEORGE BRUDENELL, DUKE OF MONTAGU].

[Stukeley's Family Memoirs. i. 115; Burke's Extinct Peerage; Munk's Coll. of Phys. ii. 58; Walpole's Correspondence, ed. Cunningham, vols. i. ii. and iv.; Gent. Mag. 1749, pp. 223, 531; Relation of the Intended Settlement at St. Lucia and St. Vincent's, in America, in right of the Duke of Montagu, London, 1725.] H. M. C.

MONTAGU, JOHN, fourth EARL OF SANDWICH (1718–1792), born on 3 Nov. 1718, was eldest son of Edward Richard Montagu, viscount Hinchinbroke (*d.* 1722), by Elizabeth, daughter of Alexander Popham of Littlecote in Wiltshire, and was grandson of Edward, third earl of Sandwich (*d.* 1729), whom he succeeded in the peerage at the age of eleven. His younger brother, William (1720?–1757), is separately noticed. After some years at Eton John entered Trinity College, Cambridge, in April 1735. He remained there for two years, but left without a degree, and went to the continent. He appears to have remained in France for a twelvemonth, and in July 1738 he started on a prolonged tour, which included Leghorn, Palermo, several of the Greek islands, Athens, Constantinople, Smyrna, Egypt, Malta, Lisbon, Gibraltar, Malaga, Minorca, and Genoa. Seven years after his death a book purporting to be his journal at this time was published under the title of 'A Voyage performed by the late Earl of Sandwich round the Mediterranean in the years 1738 and 1739' (1799, 4to). From its character, style, and numerous classical quotations, we may judge it to have been either written or corrected by his tutor, whose name does not appear. Even at that early age, however, Sandwich seems to have had some wish to pose as a patron of art, and brought home a collection of coins and archæological remains, as well as a large marble tablet, now in the library of Trinity College. An account of the tablet by Dr. John Taylor was published in 1743, under the title of 'Marmor Sandvicense.' On 20 March 1739–40 Sandwich was elected a fellow of the Royal Society.

On returning to England in 1739 and taking his seat in the House of Lords, Sandwich at once plunged into party politics, and attached himself to the Duke of Bedford, under whom, in December 1744, he was appointed a lord commissioner of the admiralty. In August 1745 he was sent on a mission to Holland, and was shortly afterwards appointed, in quick succession, captain in the Duke of Bedford's regiment of foot, 27 Sept., aide-de-camp to the Duke of Bedford, colonel in the army, 4 Oct., and second colonel of the Duke of Montagu's ordnance regiment of foot, 22 Nov. 1745. His frequent absences from England and his duties at the admiralty must have rendered his military service purely nominal, but he rose to the highest ranks in regular gradation, and at his death was the senior general on the list. During the early part of 1746 he was in London, taking an intelligent interest in the business of the admiralty, of which, in the absence of the Duke of Bedford, he was the nominal head. Several of his letters to Bedford and to Anson at this time show his anxiety to render the department efficient, despite the strong partisan feeling with which he conducted business (cf. BARROW, *Life of Anson*, p. 167). In July 1746 he was nominated plenipotentiary at the conferences at Breda, and he continued to represent the interests of this country in the tangled negotiations of 1747, and at the conclusion of the treaty at Aix-la-Chapelle in 1748. His youth led the French plenipotentiary, the Count de Saint-Séverin, to suppose that some advantage might be won from his inexperience, and he assured Sandwich that he had certain proofs that Austria and Spain had agreed on a separate treaty. This statement, which had not a word of truth in it, necessarily puzzled Sandwich, though it does not seem to have materially affected his conduct, and the terms on which he agreed with Saint-Séverin were essentially those which had been proposed at the beginning (cf. DE

Broglie, *La Paix d'Aix-la-Chapelle*, pp. 143 et seq.)

Sandwich was still a member of the admiralty board, and in February 1747–8, on the Duke of Bedford's appointment as secretary of state, he became first lord, delegating the duties of the office to Anson, notwithstanding the seniority of Lord Vere Beauclerk on the patent [see Anson, George, Lord]. On his return to England he was elected, 8 April 1749, an elder brother, and a few weeks later, 22 May, master of the Trinity House. He is said by Barrow to have originated and carried through an exact visitation of the dockyards and naval establishments, which led to the detection of many gross abuses and the introduction of stringent reforms (*Life of Anson*, pp. 214–16). The credit of the measure is more probably Anson's, Sandwich's share in it being little more than supporting Anson with his name and influence. Similarly, the act of 1749, for regulating the discipline of the navy, was essentially Anson's, though introduced under the sanction and authority of Sandwich. In 1751 the jealousy between Bedford and the Duke of Newcastle became very acute, and with the view of driving Bedford from office Newcastle succeeded in dismissing Sandwich from the admiralty [see Russell, John, fourth Duke of Bedford]. On 12 June he received the king's orders to acquaint Sandwich 'that his majesty had no further occasion for his service,' and Bedford at once resigned the seals (*Bedford Correspondence*, ii. 89–90).

For the next few years Sandwich had no public employment, till in December 1755 he was appointed, with two others, joint vice-treasurer and receiver of the revenues of Ireland. He held this office till February 1763, when he was appointed ambassador extraordinary to the court of Madrid. In April, however, before he could go out, he was nominated first lord of the admiralty, and in August one of the principal secretaries of state, in which office he continued till July 1765.

It was during this time that, by the part which he took in the prosecution of John Wilkes [q. v.], he laid the foundation of the mass of opprobrium which still clings to his name. For some years previously, Sandwich, with the Earl of March, Sir Francis Dashwood, Potter, and others, had been associated with Wilkes in the 'brotherhood of Medmenham.' As far as companionship in vicious pleasures, uncleanness, and blasphemy constituted friendship, they were friends, though it may well be that a practical joke of Wilkes was sullenly resented by his more aristocratic associates (*Chrysal*, 1768, iii. 232). It is certain that, when Wilkes's papers were seized, Sandwich and Dashwood, then Lord Le Despencer, took an active part in collecting proofs against Wilkes (Sandwich to Lord Le Despencer, 1 Nov. 1763; *Egerton MS.* 2136, f. 85); March's chaplain, the infamous John Kidgell [q. v.], suborned some of the men in Wilkes's employ and fraudulently obtained a copy of the 'Essay on Woman,' and Sandwich brought it before the House of Lords, pretending that the fact that it was addressed to him constituted a breach of his privilege as a peer, and insisted on reading aloud the filthy verses. Sandwich was believed to have been of the select company to whom the poem (which is also stated, though probably erroneously, to have commenced 'Awake, my Sandwich') was read over after its composition. Public opinion rightly condemned the men who for mere party ends thus sacrificed the ties of friendship, and at a performance of the 'Beggar's Opera' the house rose to the words of Macheath in the last scene, 'That Jemmy Twitcher should peach me, I own surprised me,' and from that day Sandwich was known as Jemmy Twitcher. A still severer castigation was administered by Wilkes's more faithful ally, Charles Churchill [q. v.], who described him as

> Too infamous to have a friend,
> Too bad for bad men to commend
> (*The Duellist*, iii. 401),

and as one who

> Wrought sin with greediness, and sought for shame
> With greater zeal than good men seek for fame'
> (*The Candidate*, ll. 315–16).

Denunciation, however, does not seem to have disturbed Sandwich's temper any more than it affected his conduct.

In the Rockingham administration he had no part, but in January 1768 he accepted office as postmaster-general under the Duke of Grafton. In December 1770 he was nominated one of the secretaries of state under Lord North, and on 12 Jan. 1771 became again first lord of the admiralty under the same minister. He now held this office for eleven years, during which time his conduct was as great a scandal to public as it had all along been to private morality. Throughout his long administration he rendered the business of the admiralty subservient to the interests of his party, and employed the vast patronage of the office as an engine for bribery and political jobbery. Other and more shady motives were also attributed to him. Early in 1773 it was currently reported that a vacancy at the navy board had been offered to Captain Luttrell of the navy for 2,000*l.* The statement was published, as a matter of common notoriety, in the 'Evening Post' of 30 Jan.–2 Feb., and repeated in the issue of 13–16 Feb., to say that it remained uncontradicted. On this second attack, Sandwich indicted Miller, the printer of the 'Evening Post,' for libel. The case was tried before Lord Mansfield on 8 July 1773, when Captain Luttrell gave evidence that he had been asked if he would give the 2,000*l.* for the vacant commissionership. It was supposed that the offer came virtually from Miss Ray, Sandwich's mistress; but evidence of agency was wanting, and Miller was cast in heavy damages (*The Evidence in the Trial*, 1773; *Gent. Mag.* 1773, p. 346).

Five years later, Captain Thomas Baillie [q. v.], after vainly trying to get the abuses at Greenwich remedied, published a very uncompromising account of them. Baillie was tried for libelling Sandwich's tools and mercenary place-holders, and was fully acquitted, though deprived by Sandwich of his office and refused all employment in the navy. On the other hand a committee of the House of Lords appointed to examine into the state of the hospital reported, on 7 June 1779, that the book contained 'a groundless and malicious misrepresentation of the conduct of the Earl of Sandwich and others, the commissioners, &c. of Greenwich Hospital.'

In 1783, when attention was called to abuses in the public offices, Mr. Pitt stated in the House of Commons that though it had been officially declared that no fees were received by the navy office, it appeared that very considerable sums were received by the officers under the name of 'gifts' (17 June, *Parl. Hist.* xxiii. 949). Exact inquiry disclosed wholesale robbery rather than peculation. The accounts showed a deficit of about three hundred thousand pounds of bread in 1780, besides beef, pork, and other provisions. It was shown that the contract price of bread was more than 4*s.* per cwt. above the market price, and that the bread actually supplied was 4*s.* per cwt. inferior to the contract; that the men in charge of the storehouses kept hogs in them, and fed them on serviceable biscuit; that stores of different kinds and in large quantities had been taken out of the yards not for the private use of the officers, but for sale, and that everywhere intimidation or guilty complicity had kept the knowledge of these abominations secret (*Parliamentary Report*, 1783–4). The dockyards had been sinks of iniquity before that time, and were so after it [cf. Jervis, John, Earl of St. Vincent], but at no time were they so utterly bad as during the war of American independence.

It is not to be supposed that Sandwich had any knowledge of, still less any direct part in, these evil transactions; but they were the direct outcome of his procedure, and of his assigning the charge of departments and of stores to men without a single qualification beyond their votes or their command of votes. It is not therefore to be wondered at that when war with France broke out in 1778 the number of ships in the navy was inadequate, and that of what there were many were not seaworthy; that the naval storehouses were empty; that the ships sent to America under Admiral John Byron [q. v.] were rigged with twice-laid rope; that it was only with the greatest difficulty and after most vexatious delay that Keppel got to sea with a fleet still numerically inferior to that under D'Orvilliers, and that on his return to Plymouth after the indecisive action of 27 July there were neither masts, nor spars, nor rope for the necessary refitting [see Keppel, Augustus, Viscount]. This was at the very beginning of the war, but the same want of ships and of stores continued throughout. In 1779, when Spain became the ally of France, the English were everywhere outnumbered. At home, when the allied fleet invaded the Channel, the English fleet, of barely half the numbers of the enemy, could only draw back to Spithead; while in the West Indies, Barrington at St. Lucia in December 1778, and Byron at Granada or St. Kitts in July 1779, were opposed by vastly superior forces. Captain Mahan has rightly spoken of 'the military difficulty of England's position in this great and unequal war,' and has criticised her policy in 'awaiting attacks, which the enemies, superior in every case, could make at their own choice and their own time' (*Influence of Sea Power upon History*, pp. 392–3). He has perhaps not allowed sufficient weight to the degradation of the navy under such a chief. In the terrible deficiency of numbers any rotten hulk that could float was made to do duty as a ship of war. The worn-out 70-gun ship Northumberland, converted into the Leviathan store-ship, had guns put on board her, and formed part of Howe's line of defence at Sandy Hook in 1778. She foundered in the West Indies in 1780 [see James, Bartholomew]. The Terrible sank after the battle off the Chesapeake, 5 Sept. 1781, not so much from the actual damage she had received, as from her decayed condition, and the Royal George went down in still water at Spithead in consequence of a great piece of her bottom falling out. Several of the ships which were engaged on the Doggerbank on 5 Aug. 1781 were in a similar category [see PARKER, SIR HYDE, 1714–1782].

In other respects, also, Sandwich's administration proved disastrous. Rightly or wrongly the heads of the whig party believed that his appointment of Keppel to the command in 1778 was a trick to put the disgrace which might accrue from the inadequacy of the fleet on a political opponent; and the way in which he ordered and pushed the court-martial on Keppel was denounced as scandalous not only by the navy, but by public opinion. On Keppel's acquittal the mob, drunk with joy and strong waters, made a savage attack on Sandwich's official residence at the admiralty. The navy more sternly resented his conduct, and many officers of character and ability—Harland, Howe, and Barrington among others—refused to accept a command while he remained at the admiralty, not scrupling to say that under such a chief their honour was not safe. One man alone, of real ability, forced by pecuniary embarrassment, was willing to serve. This was Sir George Brydges Rodney, afterwards Lord Rodney, who went out to the West Indies as commander-in-chief early in 1780. Rodney had formerly been on friendly terms with Sandwich, but the whole tenor of his correspondence from the West Indies betrays the irritation, if not exasperation, which he felt at the conduct of the first lord. It should be observed, however, that Sandwich interested himself in getting Captain Cook's two vessels fitted out in an adequate manner in 1778, and it was after the first lord that Cook named the Sandwich Islands.

Shortly after the acquittal of Keppel, while Sandwich's unpopularity was at its highest, the town was shocked by the murder of Sandwich's mistress, Margaret or Martha Ray, on 7 April 1779, by a young clergyman who had unsuccessfully sought her hand in marriage [see HACKMAN, JAMES]. With the murder Sandwich had absolutely nothing to do; he seems to have been much attached to the woman, who had lived with him for sixteen years, and to have sincerely mourned her death. But the revelation that he, a man of over sixty, had a mistress permanently residing in his house led to an outburst of indignation on the part of the public who hated him. On the fall of the North administration in March 1782 Sandwich retired in great measure from public life, and though he accepted the office of ranger of St. James's and Hyde Parks under the coalition, it was but for a few months. During the following years he resided for the most part at Hinchinbroke, and died in London on 30 April 1792.

No public man of the last century was the mark of such bitter, such violent invective. On the other hand he was esteemed and loved by the subordinates at the admiralty, men who were content to serve him to the best of their ability, and to receive in thankfulness such gifts as he could bestow. That their adulation was not entirely mercenary appears from the posthumous notices of his life, such as that by the Rev. J. Cooke, printed as an introduction to the 'Voyage round the Mediterranean,' or that in the 'Gentleman's Magazine,' 1792, pt. i. p. 482. That Sandwich was assiduous and punctual in the despatch of business is attested not only by many witnesses, but by his own letters (e.g. to Mr., afterwards Sir George Jackson; *Add. MS.* 9344; CRADOCK, iv. 164; BUTLER, i. 72); but his industry was frittered away over details which seemed to increase his personal consequence, while matters of the first importance were left in the hands of incompetent and dishonest subordinates.

In society he is described as having a singular charm of manner. 'Few houses were more pleasant than his; it was filled with rank, beauty, and talent, and every one was at ease.' The musical entertainments at Hinchinbroke had a distinct reputation, and Miss Ray, whose natural talent had been cultivated under the best masters, was the admired prima donna; 'he was the soul of the Catch Club, and one of the directors of the Concert of Ancient Music, but he had not the least real ear for music, and was equally insensible of harmony and melody' (BUTLER, i. 72). His gait is described as awkward and shambling. Seeing him at a distance, a gentleman said, 'I am sure it is Lord Sandwich; for, if you observe, he is walking down both sides of the street at once;' and Sandwich himself used to tell how, on taking leave of his dancing-master in Paris, and offering him any service in London, the man answered, 'I should take it as a particular favour if your Lordship would never tell any one of whom you learned to dance' (CRADOCK, iv. 166). Churchill of course refers to this uncouthness, and adds that his visage is that of one 'half hanged,' with the inference that he had been 'cut down by mistake' (*The Duellist*, iii. 360). This unflattering description is to some extent supported by the portrait by Gainsborough in the Painted Hall at Greenwich, which has a ghastly effect, chiefly due perhaps to the fading of the flesh tints. Other portraits by Zoffany—one belonging to the family, one in the National Portrait Gallery, and one in the Trinity House—though not prepossessing, are less repulsive. Sandwich married in 1741 Judith, third daughter of Charles Fane, first viscount Fane, and had by her, besides other children who predeceased him, one son, John, who succeeded as fifth earl. By Miss Ray he also had children, of whom one son, Basil, is separately noticed; another, Robert, died an admiral in 1830.

[The very adulatory Memoir by the Rev. J. Cooke, prefixed to the Voyage round the Mediterranean, is the only one of any length that has been published. Another, not adulatory, said to have been printed in 1770, is Life, Adventures, Intrigues, and Amours of the celebrated Jemmy Twitcher, exhibiting many striking proofs to what baseness the human heart is capable of descending. It is extremely rare. The public life of Sandwich is to be traced in the history, and especially the naval history, of his time; in Parliamentary History, more especially 1770–82; Coxe's Memoirs of the Pelham Administration; Walpole's Letters and Memoirs of George III; Correspondence of John, fourth Duke of Bedford; Correspondence of the Earl of Chatham; Barrow's Life of Anson; Keppel's Life of Keppel; Jesse's George Selwyn and his Contemporaries; Dilke's Papers of a Critic; Chesterfield's Letters; Trevelyan's Early Life of C. J. Fox. There are numerous references to the diplomatic correspondence, 1745–8, in the Brit. Mus. Catalogues of Add. MSS. 1854–75 and 1882–7. Cf. Cradock's Literary and Miscellaneous Memoirs, especially i. 117–19, 139–54, and iv. 163–76, and Charles Butler's Reminiscences, i. 70–2. Skits, squibs, and abusive pamphlets are numerous, among which may be named The Duenna, London, 1776. The copy in the Brit. Mus. [643, i. 17 (4)] has 'by Mr. Sheridan' written on the title-page; but the statement seems extremely doubtful. See also Doyle's Baronage; Gent. Mag. 1792, i. 482; and Collins's Peerage, 1812, iii. 470.] J. K. L.

MONTAGU, JOHN (1719–1795), admiral, born in 1719, son of James Montagu of Lackham in Wiltshire (*d.* 1747), and great-grandson of James Montagu of Lackham (1602–1665), third son of Henry Montagu, first earl of Manchester [q. v.], entered the Royal Academy at Portsmouth on 14 Aug. 1733. He afterwards served in the Yarmouth, in the Dreadnought with Captain Medley, in the Shoreham, in the Dragon with Curtis Barnett, in the Dauphin with Lord Aubrey Beauclerk—all on the home or Mediterranean station. He passed his examination on 5 June 1740, was promoted to be lieutenant on 22 Dec., and on 2 Feb. 1740–1 was appointed to the Buckingham. In her he was present at the battle off Toulon on 11 Feb. 1743–4, though not engaged, the Buckingham being in the rear with Vice-admiral Richard Lestock [q. v.] At the court-martial on Lestock his deposition was adverse to the prisoner, who in cross-examining suggested that Montagu's evidence was dictated by Towry, captain of the Buckingham. 'I never ask any man's opinion,' answered Montagu, 'but go by my own. I always judged Mr. Lestock's conduct on that day unlike an officer, and always said so' (*Minutes of the Court-martial*).

Shortly afterwards Montagu was moved into the Namur, the flagship of Admiral Mathews, and on 2 March 1744–5 he was promoted to command the Hinchinbroke. In the following January he was posted to the Ambuscade of 40 guns, which in the spring of 1747 was attached to the squadron under Anson, and was present in the action off Cape Finisterre on 3 May. After commanding for short periods various frigates, in one of which, the Kent, he was succeeded by Rodney in January 1753, he was in January 1757 appointed to the Monarque at Portsmouth, and on 14 March had the painful duty of superintending the execution of Admiral Byng, who was shot on the Monarque's quarter-deck. Two months later the Monarque went out to the Mediterranean with Admiral Henry Osborn [q. v.], and on 28 Feb. 1758 assisted in the scattering and destruction of De la Clue's squadron off Cartagena. In February 1759 he was appointed to the Raisonnable, and in her joined Commodore John Moore [q. v.] in the West Indies. He was there moved into the Panther, which he brought home, and, again in rapid succession, into the Terrible, the Newark, and the Princess Amelia, one of the fleet with Hawke in the Bay of Biscay in 1760–1. On 22 June 1762 he was moved into the Magnanime [cf. Howe, Richard, Earl], and in May 1763 to the Dragon, which he commanded as guardship at Chatham till 1766. In July 1769 he was appointed to the Bellona, and on 18 Oct. 1770 was promoted to the rank of rear-admiral. From March 1771 to 1774 he was commander-in-chief on the North American station, defined as 'from the River St. Lawrence to Cape Florida and the Bahama Islands.' On 3 Feb. 1776 he was promoted to be vice-admiral, and shortly afterwards appointed commander-in-chief at Newfoundland, where, during the next three years, he was chiefly occupied in maintaining a system of active cruising against the enemy's privateers, and, on the outbreak of the war with France, in detaching a squadron to take possession of the islands Saint Pierre and Miquelon. He returned to Portsmouth just in time to sit on the court-martial on Admiral Keppel. On 8 April 1782 he was promoted to be admiral of the blue, and from 1783 to 1786 was commander-in-chief at

Portsmouth. On 24 Sept. 1787 he became admiral of the white squadron. During his later years he settled at Fareham in Hampshire, where he died in August 1795.

He married in 1748 Sophia, daughter of James Wroughton of Wilcot, Wiltshire, and by her had issue a daughter and four sons. Of these the eldest, John, D.D., fellow of All Souls, Oxford, died unmarried in 1818. The second, George (1750–1829), the third, James (1752–1794), and the youngest, Edward, lieutenant-colonel R.A., slain at the siege of Seringapatam in May 1799, are separately noticed. Until 1749 Montagu wrote his name Mountagu; he then adopted the spelling here followed for the rest of his life.

[Charnock's Biog. Nav. v. 480; commission and warrant books and official letters in the Public Record Office.] J. K. L.

MONTAGU, Lady MARY WORTLEY (1689–1762), writer of 'Letters,' baptised at Covent Garden, 26 May 1689, was the eldest daughter of Evelyn Pierrepont, who in 1690 became fifth Earl of Kingston (created Marquis of Dorchester in 1706, and Duke of Kingston in 1715), by Mary, daughter of William Feilding, earl of Denbigh. Her mother died in 1694, leaving three other children: William, Frances (afterwards Countess of Mar), and Evelyn (afterwards Countess of Gower). Mary showed early abilities, and, according to one account, her father had her taught Greek and Latin by her brother's tutor. The Greek, however, is doubtful, and it seems probable that she taught herself Latin (Spence, *Anecdotes*, p. 232). Lord Kingston, though a man of pleasure and generally a careless father, was proud of his daughter, and it is said that 'before she was eight' he nominated her as a 'toast' at the Kit-Cat Club (generally said, however, to have been founded in 1702; see under Cat, Christopher). As she was not known to the members, he sent for her to the club, when she was elected by acclamation. She always declared afterwards that this was the happiest day of her life. She became an eager reader, devouring the old romances and the old dramatists, besides more solid literature. She was encouraged by an uncle, William Feilding, and by Bishop Burnet. She submitted to Burnet in 1710 a translation of the 'Encheiridion' of Epictetus from the Latin version (printed in Lord Wharncliffe's edition of her 'Works,' i. 225). She became a friend of Mary Astell [q. v.], the defender of woman's rights in her day, who in 1724 wrote a preface to Lady Mary's 'Letters from the East' (first published with the 'Letters' in 1763). Another friend was Anne, daughter of Sidney Wortley Montagu, second son of Edward, first earl of Sandwich [q. v.], who had taken the name of Wortley on his marriage to Anne, daughter of Sir Francis Wortley. Lady Mary was writing enthusiastically about her studies and state of mind to her friend in 1709. Edward Wortley Montagu, brother of Anne, was a man of ability, a good scholar, well known to the whig leaders, and especially attached to Addison. The second volume of the 'Tatler' is dedicated to him. He represented Huntingdon in the House of Commons from 1705 to 1713. He met Lady Mary in his sister's company, was delighted with her knowledge of Latin, as well as with her wit and beauty, sent her at once a copy of verses, wrote letters of warm compliment to be copied and sent to her in his sister's name, and soon became an avowed suitor. His sister died soon after the acquaintance had been formed. A long correspondence followed. Lady Mary's 'Letters' are remarkably well written, and show masculine sense rather than tenderness. She says that she can be a friend, but does not know whether she can love. She probably felt a real passion, although she makes it a point of honour to state fairly every objection to the match. Montagu applied to Lady Mary's father, then Lord Dorchester, but he was finally rejected, upon his refusal to entail his estates upon his eldest son, or to promise his wife a fixed establishment in London. Montagu (see Moy Thomas) gave notes for No. 223 of the 'Tatler' (12 Sept. 1710), which attacks the practice of marriage settlements. The father hereupon ordered Lady Mary to marry another man. Settlements were drawn, and the wedding-day fixed, when Lady Mary left the house and married Montagu privately by special license, dated 12 Aug. 1712. She lived for the next few years in different houses, generally in Yorkshire, her husband's father still occupying Wharncliffe Lodge, near Sheffield. Her husband was often separated from her by his parliamentary duties, and her 'Letters' show occasional discords. Her son, Edward Wortley Montagu (who is separately noticed), was born in 1713. In the same year her sister Frances married John Erskine, sixth or eleventh earl of Mar [q. v.] Her brother, Lord Kingston, died soon afterwards, leaving a son, who became the second and last duke. Upon the formation of the first ministry of George I (October 1714), Montagu became one of the commissioners of the treasury, his cousin Charles, lord Halifax [q. v.], being first lord. Montagu, it is said, was the only man at the board who could talk French, and who could therefore converse with the king. When after the death of Halifax in 1715 Walpole became first lord, Montagu lost his place, and his remarks on the 'state of party' (published in Lady Mary's 'Works') show that he had a strong dislike to Walpole. Lady Mary was often at court, and was in favour with the Princess of Wales, afterwards Queen Caroline. 'Dolly' Walpole, Sir Robert's sister, afterwards Lady Townshend, had been an early friend, but Sir Robert's wife was her decided enemy. She became well known to all the wits, and among others to Pope, who professed especial admiration for her. Upon the surreptitious publication of her 'Court Poems' (afterwards called 'Town Eclogues') in 1716, Pope revenged her or himself by administering an emetic to Curll [see under CURLL, EDMUND]. On 5 June 1716 Montagu was appointed ambassador to the Porte, then at war with Austria. The embassy was intended to reconcile the Turks and the emperor. Montagu left London with his wife and their child at the end of July. They reached Vienna at the beginning of September, and, after visiting other German courts, left Vienna on 17 Jan. 1717, and travelled to Adrianople, where they stayed for two months, reaching Constantinople at the end of May. On 28 Oct. following Montagu received letters of recall, with a private letter from Addison, who had now become secretary of state. Addison's endeavours to assign complimentary reasons for the recall imply a consciousness that Montagu would scarcely see the measure in that light. Montagu was not, as Addison suggested, anxious to return to England, for he remained at Constantinople till 6 June 1718. His daughter Mary (afterwards Lady Bute) was born in February 1718. The Montagus returned by sea to Genoa, and reached England at the end of October. Montagu collected some oriental manuscripts, and presented an inscribed marble to Trinity College, Cambridge. Lady Mary's interest in the manners of the country is shown by her 'Letters,' and she learnt a little Turkish. At Adrianople she had noticed the practice of inoculation for the small-pox (see letter of 1 April 1717). She had her son inoculated, and took much pains to introduce the practice upon her return to England. The physician of the embassy, a Mr. Maitland, inoculated in London under her patronage, and in 1724 Steele celebrated her merits in a paper in the 'Plain Dealer,' 3 July (*Gent. Mag.* xxvii. 409; *Phil. Trans.* 1757, No. lxxi.), and congratulated her upon her 'godlike delight' of saving 'many thousand British lives' every year.

For many years after her return to England Lady Mary was a leader in London society. Her 'Letters' show that she was not without a keen appetite for the scandal of the times, and she was one of the greatest sufferers by the same propensity in her neighbours. Her husband again represented Huntingdon in the parliaments elected in 1722 and 1727. He afterwards sat for Peterborough from 1734 to 1747, and from 1754 till 1761. He never took any conspicuous part in politics, and devoted himself chiefly to saving money.

Upon returning to England Lady Mary had resumed intercourse with Pope. Pope had celebrated her in the 'Epistle to Jervas' (published 1717), and more than one copy of occasional verses (POPE, *Works,* ed. Elwin and Courthope, iv. 491–3). The thought of her inspired the 'Epistle of Eloisa to Abelard,' and to her during her journey were addressed letters of the most stilted and fine-spun gallantry. She replied, checking his ecstasies with calm good breeding and sense. On 1 Sept. 1718 Pope wrote to her the well-known letter upon the romantic death of two rustic lovers struck by lightning, to which she replied from Dover (1 Nov.), on her way home, by a bit of cynicism, too true to be pleasant. He continued his adoration, and persuaded her and her husband to take a cottage at Twickenham, in order to be his neighbours. The close relation between the keen woman of the world and the querulous and morbidly sensitive poet was dangerous. The friendship continued for a time. Sir Godfrey Kneller painted her picture for the poet in 1719; his last letter, in September 1721, is in the old style; and in the spring of 1722 she says in a letter to her sister that she seldom sees him, but encloses some of his verses containing a compliment to her. A quarrel followed, the causes of which have been much discussed. Various stories are given: Miss Hawkins (*Anecdotes*, p. 75) reported that the quarrel was due to a pair of sheets lent by Pope to the Montagus and returned unwashed. This was confirmed by Worsdale the painter (*Life of Malone*, p. 150). Lady Mary herself told Spence (*Anecdotes*, 1820, p. 233) that Pope told Arbuthnot that he had refused to write a satire upon somebody when requested to do so by Lady Mary and Lord Hervey; Lady Mary implies that this story was false, but speaks as though she did not know the true cause. Mr. Moy Thomas and Dilke think that the quarrel arose out of her ridicule of his story of the lovers killed by lightning. This assumes that the letter to him was not really sent at the date assigned to it, which is possible, but is a mere guess. Mr. Courthope thinks, and with apparent justice, that there is no reason for doubting the account given, according to Lady Louisa

Stuart, by Lady Mary herself, that Pope was betrayed into a declaration of love, which Lady Mary received with a fit of laughter. This story is in harmony with all that we know of their relations; and if, as is probable, the declaration was meant to be taken in a poetic sense, the laughter was painfully sincere. The more serious the cause the greater is the excuse for Pope's subsequent malignity, though no excuse can be more than a slight palliation. A coarse lampoon upon Lady Mary by Swift, 'The Capon's Tale,' first published in the 'Miscellany' of 1727, implies that the quarrel had begun, and hints at previous lampoons attributed to her. Pope's references to 'Sappho' are in the 'Dunciad,' bk. ii. l. 136 (1728, and note added in 1729); the 'Epistle to Lord Bathurst' (1732), ll. 121–2; the 'Imitation of the 1st Satire of the 2nd Book of Horace' (1732–3), ll. 83–4; the 'Epistle to Martha Blount' (1734–5), ll. 25–6; the 'Epistle to Arbuthnot' (1734–5), ll. 368–9; 'Versification of Donne' (1735), i. 6; and the 'Epilogue to the Satires' (1738), i. 113, ii. 19. Pope was apparently the aggressor in this warfare, although it seems that he suspected Lady Mary of being concerned in a previous libel called 'A Pop upon Pope' (1728), a story of his being whipped in revenge for the 'Dunciad' (see Carruthers, *Pope*, 1857, pp. 258–9, and *Pope's Works*, x. 119). When the atrocious allusion in the 'Imitations of Horace' appeared, Lady Mary asked Peterborough to remonstrate with Pope. Pope made the obvious reply that he wondered that Lady Mary should suppose the lines to apply to any but some notoriously abandoned woman. It is of course impossible to prove who was in Pope's head when he wrote, but he certainly endeavoured to confirm the application to Lady Mary when it was made by the town (see Mr. Courthope's remarks in *Pope's Works*, iii. 279–84). The 'Verses addressed to an Imitator of Horace by a Lady,' published in 1733, are generally attributed to Lady Mary, in co-operation with her friend and fellow-victim to Pope's satire, Lord Hervey (see Courthope in *Pope's Works* as above, and v. 259–61). They insult Pope's family and person with a brutality only exceeded by his own. His base insinuations probably injured Lady Mary's reputation in her time. Two of the points to which he refers, that she 'starved a sister' and 'denied a debt' (Epilogue to *Satires*), were of importance in her history.

A Frenchman named Rémond (who is described in *St.-Simon's Memoirs*, 1829, xvii. 306) made love to her; and, though she did not encourage his passion, she seems to have written some imprudent letters to him. She thought that she would get rid of him handsomely by making some money for him in the South Sea speculation. He gained something by selling out on her advice, but left the money in her hands to be again invested. In one of his last letters (22 Aug. 1720) Pope had advised her to buy at a time when the stock was rapidly declining in value. Whether she lost on her own account does not appear; but the 900*l.* which she invested for Rémond soon sank in value to 400*l.* He then claimed the repayment of the original sum as a debt, and threatened to publish her letters. She was certainly alarmed, and especially anxious to keep the matter from her husband, who was severe in all questions of money. Our knowledge of the affair is derived from her letters upon the subject to Lady Mar. Horace Walpole, who saw them, gave a distorted version of their purport to Sir Horace Mann. But in fact, although they show her to have been imprudent, they refute any worse imputation upon her character or her honesty. Rémond appears to have spread reports which must have reached Pope, who knew something of the South Sea speculation.

The story about her sister refers to Lady Mar, who was for a time disordered in mind. Her brother-in-law, James Erskine, lord Grange [q. v.], famous for the violent imprisonment of his wife, tried also to get hold of Lady Mar. Lady Mary obtained a warrant from the king's bench in 1731, and was for some time her sister's guardian. There does not appear to be any ground for a charge of harsh treatment.

Lady Mary was on very friendly terms with Lord Hervey, and on hostile terms with his wife. Her favour was courted by Young, of the 'Night Thoughts,' who in 1726 consulted her about his tragedy, 'The Brothers,' and by her second cousin, Fielding, who dedicated his first comedy to her in 1727, and asked her to read his 'Modern Husband.' She managed to be on good terms with the redoubtable Sarah, duchess of Marlborough; but she seems to have made enemies by her satirical wit.

In 1739 she went abroad, for reasons which have not been explained. Her letters to her husband imply that they still remained on friendly terms, and she speaks of him to their daughter with apparent affection. She told a correspondent that he had been detained by business till she was tired of waiting, and went abroad, expecting him to follow in six weeks (to Lady Pomfret, from Venice, n.d., probably in 1740). In any case, they did not again meet. She left England in July 1739, and travelled to Venice. In the autumn of 1740 she went to Florence, where she met Horace Walpole, who gives a disgusting account of her slovenly appearance, her 'impudence,' avarice, and absurdity (WALPOLE, *Letters*, ed. Cunningham, i. 55, 57). She visited Rome and Naples, and at the end of 1741 crossed the Alps to Geneva and Chambéry. In 1742 she settled at Avignon, where the town gave her a piece of land with an old mill, which she patched up for a house. The 'increase of Scottish and Irish rebels' (to the Countess of Oxford, 29 Nov. 1747) in 1746 made the place unpleasant to her, and she moved to Brescia, where she bought the shell of an old palace, fitted it up, and stayed for some years, spending her summers at Lovere, on the Lago d'Iseo. She thought Lovere 'the most beautifully romantic place' she ever saw, and compares it to Tunbridge Wells (to Lady Bute, 21 July 1747). She made occasional excursions elsewhere, and in 1758 settled at Venice. She corresponded with her daughter, Lady Bute, reporting her impressions of Italian society and of the books which she read. She admired Fielding and Smollett, but despised Richardson, though she could not help crying over him. She wished her granddaughters to acquire some learning, but hoped that they would not marry, and that their mother would 'moderate her fondness' for them. In the last years of her stay she became intimate with Sir James Denham Steuart [q. v.], who dedicated to her the first two books of his 'Inquiry into the Principles of Political Economy.'

Lady Mary's husband died in January 1761, aged 83. Horace Walpole describes him living at Wharncliffe, the seat of the Wortleys, in 1756, in the most miserly fashion, his only indulgence being tokay (WALPOLE, *Letters*, iii. 29). He was reported to have left 1,350,000*l.* (*ib.* iii. 377; and Gray to Wharton, 31 Jan. 1761). Pope (*Horace*, bk. ii. sat. ii. ll. 49–60) satirised the pair as 'Avidien and his wife,' and Montagu appears to have done little beyond saving money in later years. Walpole rightly prophesied that Lady Mary would return to England.

Her daughter's husband was now in power (secretary of state 25 March 1761), and Lady Bute begged her mother to come to her. Lady Mary's health was breaking, but she left Venice in the autumn, and reached England in the beginning of 1762. She died on 21 Aug. following. A cenotaph was erected to her memory in Lichfield Cathedral, commemorating her introduction of inoculation.

Lady Mary had herself suffered from smallpox, which 'deprived her of very fine eyelashes' and impaired her beauty. The portrait painted by Kneller in 1719, apparently for Pope, came into the possession of Lord Bute. A portrait painted by Charles della Rusca in 1739, and presented by her to the Countess of Oxford, is at Wortley Hall. A third portrait, by Jonathan Richardson, belongs to the Earl of Wharncliffe, and another of Lady Mary by Highmore is in the possession of T. Humphry Ward, esq. An enamel by Zincke (1738), engraved by Vertue, is at Welbeck. A miniature in possession of Lord Harrington is engraved in the editions of her 'Works' by Wharncliffe and Thomas.

Lady Mary's 'Town Eclogues' were first published piratically as 'Court Poems' in 1716 (misdated 1706 on title-page). They were republished, with others, by Dodsley in 1747, and again in his 'Miscellany.' They were edited by Isaac Reed in 1768, and are included in his 'Works.' Lady Mary's letters from the East were given by her when at Rotterdam in 1761 to a Mr. Sowden, minister of the English church there, with a note by herself, stating that she authorised him to use them as he pleased. He is said to have sold them to her daughter for 500*l.* Another copy, given by Lady Mary to Mr. Molesworth, also came into possession of Lord Bute. An edition appeared in 1763, in 3 vols. 12mo, as 'Letters of Lady M—y W——y M——,' said to have been edited by the disreputable John Cleland [q. v.] A fourth volume appeared in 1767, of doubtful authority, and probably forged by Cleland, though reprinted by later editors. A story is told by Dallaway of a device by which the manuscript of the letters was surreptitiously copied while in Sowden's possession; but Mr. Moy Thomas says that this edition follows the Molesworth MS., which differs considerably from the other. It is doubtful how far the letters were sent as they now appear, or made out of a diary kept at the time; they were, previous to 1763, handed about in manuscript.

In 1803 an edition of the 'Works,' including the above, with other letters and poems, was published by James Dallaway [q. v.], with materials supplied by Lord Bute, and a memoir. A second edition, with letters to Mrs. Hewitt, appeared in 1817. A new edition, in 3 vols. 8vo, edited by Lady Mary's great-grandson, Lord Wharncliffe, was published in 1837. To this were added the very interesting 'Introductory Anecdotes' by Lady Louisa Stuart, Lady Bute's daughter. The last edition, by Mr. Moy Thomas, in 2 vols. 8vo, with a new life, appeared in 1861. The correspondence with Pope is in Pope's 'Works' (Courthope and Elwin, ix. 339–415).

[Lives, as above, prefixed to Works, by Dallaway and Moy Thomas, and Introductory Anecdotes; Spence's Anecdotes, 1820, pp. 224, 230, &c., 292, 371. Pope's Works (Courthope and Elwin) give full discussions of all the disputed points. See also Dilke's Papers of a Critic, i. 343–60.] L. S.

MONTAGU, RALPH, Duke of Montagu (1638?–1709), born about 1638, was the second son of Edward Montagu, second lord Montagu of Boughton [see under Montagu, Edward, first Baron Montagu of Boughton], by Anne, daughter of Sir Ralph Winwood, knight (Doyle, *Official Baronage*, ii. 521). Montagu began his career as master of the horse to the Duchess of York, and on the death of his elder brother Edward succeeded him as master of the horse to Queen Catherine (28 Dec. 1665; *Cal. State Papers*, Dom. 1665–6, p. 120; *Hist. MSS. Comm.* 8th Rep. p. 279). In the court of Charles II he speedily distinguished himself by his successes in gallantry, and Grammont describes him as the favoured lover of the beautiful Mrs. Myddelton [q. v.] As a rival, says Grammont, he was 'peu dangereux pour sa figure, mais fort à craindre par son assiduité, par l'addresse de son esprit, et par d'autres talens' (*Mémoires de la Vie du Comte de Grammont*, ed. 1716, p. 98). Dartmouth, in one of his notes on Burnet, attributes Montagu's rapid rise to female influence (*Own Time*, ed. 1833, i. 616). On 1 Jan. 1669 Montagu was appointed ambassador extraordinary to Louis XIV (for his instructions see *Hist. MSS. Comm.* 5th Rep. p. 316, and Bebington, *Arlington's Letters to Temple*, p. 393). It is evident, however, that Montagu was not yet initiated in the secrets of his master's foreign policy, and he first learnt from the mouth of the Duchess of Orleans that Charles II intended to make a secret alliance with Louis XIV against the Dutch (Mignet, *Négociations relatives à la succession d'Espagne*, iii. 88, 91; Bebington, p. 440). He was present in June 1670 at the deathbed of the duchess, received her last messages to her brother, and diligently inquired into the rumour that she was poisoned (*ib.* pp. 438–47; Lafayette, *Henriette d'Angleterre*, ed. Anatole France, 1882, p. 142). Charles II was so satisfied with his conduct that at his return Montagu was admitted to the privy council (2 Jan. 1672), and backed by the king in a quarrel with the Duke of Buckingham (Dalrymple, *Memoirs of Great Britain and Ireland*, ed. 1790, i. 127). On 12 Aug. 1671 Montagu purchased from his cousin, the Earl of Sandwich, for 14,000*l.*, the mastership of the great wardrobe (Doyle, ii. 522; Boyer, *Annals*, viii. 369).

A lucky marriage now crowned Montagu's fortunes. The great match of the day was Elizabeth Wriothesley, daughter of Thomas, earl of Southampton, and widow of Joceline Percy, eleventh earl of Northumberland, who was reputed to be worth 6,000*l.* a year. She was unsuccessfully wooed by Harry Savile and others, and was reported to be reserving herself for the widowed Duke of York (*Hatton Correspondence*, i. 68; *Savile Correspondence*, pp. 32, 38). Tradition represents her as flying to France to avoid the designs of Charles II against her honour, and marrying Ralph Montagu during this enforced exile. But the marriage really took place at Titchfield, Hampshire, on 24 Aug. 1673, and was forwarded by the king in spite of the opposition of the lady's relatives (*Letters to Sir Joseph Williamson*, Camd. Soc., i. 164, 176, 179, 184). Two months later the countess and her husband began to quarrel, she alleging that he spread a report that he had 'bought her of her maid for 500*l.* per annum,' and a separation was talked of (*ib.* ii. 35, 63, 71). In December Montagu was sent to the Tower for challenging the Duke of Buckingham in the king's drawing-room, but released a few days later (*ib.* ii. 89).

On 1 Sept. 1676, and again in the following year, Montagu was appointed ambassador extraordinary to Louis XIV, and took a very active part in the bargains about the price of England's neutrality during the war between France and Holland (Dalrymple, i. 153; Mignet, iii. 529, 572). He aimed, however, higher than an embassy, and in the spring of 1678 was negotiating for the post of secretary of state, and had agreed with Henry Coventry to give him 10,000*l.* for his place. But Danby, whose assent was necessary, held himself pre-engaged to Sir William Temple, and refused to sanction the bargain. In the end Coventry was succeeded by Sir Leoline Jenkins [q. v.] (*Letters written to and from the Earl of Danby*, 1710, 8vo, pp. 83, 88). While his ambition was thus checked; Montagu's diplomatic career was brought to a close by a quarrel with the Duchess of Cleveland. She had left England, and had established herself at Paris with her daughter, the Countess of Sussex. During the mother's temporary absence Montagu, apparently at the instigation of Charles II, persuaded the daughter to leave the convent where she had been placed and to take up her residence at the English embassy. Eager for revenge for this and other wrongs, the duchess wrote to Charles II denouncing Montagu, and revealing his political intrigues, with which their previous intimacy had made her acquainted. Montagu had told her, she declared, that he meant to make the secretaryship merely a stepping-stone to the treasurership; then he would easily supply Charles with money for his pocket and his women, and lead him by the nose. A French astrologer in whom the king believed had been corrupted by Montagu that he might mould the king to his designs. 'He has neither conscience nor honour, and has several times told me that in his heart he despised you and your brother, and that for his part he wished with all his heart that the parliament would send you both to travel, for you were a dull, governable fool, and the duke a wilful fool. So that it were yet better to have you than him, but that you always chose a greater beast than yourself to govern you' (HARRIS, *Lives*, ed. 1814, v. 372; *Life of the Duchess of Cleveland*, by G. Steinman-Steinman, p. 154; cf. BURNET, ii. 143). Montagu hurried back to defend himself without waiting for leave to quit his post, and found himself struck out of the privy council (12 July 1678) and superseded as ambassador by the Earl of Sunderland. To secure immunity from further punishment and to retaliate on Danby, Montagu now entered into a negotiation with Barillon, the French ambassador, offering to cause Danby's fall within six months, on promise of a pension of forty thousand livres a year, or one hundred thousand crowns in hand (DALRYMPLE, i. 249). The proposal was accepted, and he then stood for the borough of Northampton, beat the government candidate, and prepared to accuse Danby in the House of Commons (GREY, *Debates*, vi. 186). Danby resolved to be beforehand with his accuser, and on 19 Dec. 1678 the chancellor of the exchequer informed the house 'that his majesty having received information that his late ambassador in France, Mr. Montagu, had held several private conferences with the pope's nuncio there, has, to the end that he may discover the truth of the matter, given order for the seizing Mr. Montagu's papers.' But the house took up the cause of its member, and ordered the sequestered papers to be brought to Westminster and examined there. Montagu selected from them two letters in which Danby demanded six million livres from Louis XIV as the price of peace with France and the prorogation of parliament. Before the sitting closed it was voted by 179 to 116 votes that there was sufficient ground for the impeachment of the lord treasurer. And though Danby's defenders produced letters of Montagu's proving that he was equally guilty, parliament refused to pay any attention to the countercharge (*ib.* pp. 337–87; RERESBY, *Memoirs*, ed. Cartwright, p. 155; *Hist. MSS. Comm.* 6th Rep. p. 389).

The dissolution of parliament (30 Dec. 1678) was a momentary check to Montagu's triumph. He was greatly afraid of being sent to the Tower, and 'swore he had no mind to eat meat of others dressing, where he must either eat poison or starve.' After lying concealed in London for three weeks, he endeavoured to escape to France in disguise, but was arrested at Dover, and obliged to give security not to leave the kingdom (DANBY, *Letters*, pp. 116–22; *Hatton Correspondence*, i. 170). According to Barillon this attempted flight to France was also part of a new intrigue. Montagu had taken up the cause of Monmouth, and hoped to induce Louis XIV to get him declared Prince of Wales by his father, urging that a disputed succession in England would be an advantage to France. Montagu was also Barillon's chief agent in his dealing with the English opposition. In these negotiations he was greatly aided by his sister, Anne Montagu, the wife of Sir Daniel Harvey. 'She is a woman of a bold and enterprising spirit,' wrote Barillon, 'and has interest and connections with a great number of persons of the court and parliament' (DALRYMPLE, i. 312, 341, 355). As deep in the political intrigues of the day as her brother, she was equally famous for her gallantries, and both were at this time members of the cabal which met at the Duchess of Mazarin's (FORNERON, *Louise de Kéroualle*, 1886, pp. 94, 138; MANCHESTER, *Court and Society from Elizabeth to Anne*, i. 275). But in spite of his skill and unscrupulousness Montagu's schemes were far from successful. Barillon and his master refused to support the plan for Monmouth's elevation, though encouraging Montagu just enough to prevent Monmouth from losing altogether the hope of French protection (DALRYMPLE, i. 349). Shaftesbury repudiated the alliance offered him, saying that he had never had anything to do with Mr. Montagu, and never would (SIDNEY, *Diary*, ii. 13). He found great difficulty in obtaining the money which Barillon had promised him, and received in the end only fifty thousand out of the one hundred thousand crowns for which he had sold his services (DALRYMPLE, i. 334, 384). The ambassador reported in December 1680 that Montagu would willingly be reconciled with the court, 'and have a great place if it were possible,' but the court showed no willingness to accept his terms (*ib.* p. 355; SIDNEY, *Diary*, ii. 11). Accordingly, when the exclusion movement failed, he thought it best to consult his own safety and retired to the continent.

In 1683 he was at Paris, where he vainly sought a private audience with Louis XIV and further payments for his past services

(*Hist. MSS. Comm.* 7th Rep. p. 202). On 10 Jan. 1683–4 he succeeded his father as third Lord Montagu of Boughton. At the accession of James II he lost the post of master of the robes, which was given to Lord Preston. Nevertheless he still hoped for employment, and boldly announced to Lord Rochester his intention of attending the coronation. 'I know not how unfortunate I may be as to be under his majesty's displeasure, but I know the generosity of his nature to be such, that, as Louis, duke of Orleans, when he came to the crown of France, said it was not for a king of France to remember the quarrels and grudges of a duke of Orleans, so I hope his majesty will be pleased to think the king is not to remember anything that has passed in relation to the Duke of York, for whatever my opinions were when I delivered them, being trusted by the public, they are altered now I am become his subject, knowing myself obliged, by the laws of God and man, to hazard life and fortune in the defence of his sacred person, crown, and dignity' (Singer, *Correspondence of Henry Hyde, Earl of Clarendon*, i. 114). Montagu was allowed to return to England, and was very well received by James. It was even reported that he was to be made secretary of state, or again employed as ambassador to France (*ib.* i. 522; *Ellis Corresp.* i. 154–9).

At the revolution Montagu was one of the first to embrace the cause of William III. He was made one of the privy council (14 Feb. 1689), and William created him Viscount Monthermer and Earl of Montagu (9 April 1689). But Montagu, who had taken an active part in the debates on the deposition of James II, did not regard this as sufficient reward. On 18 May 1694 he wrote to William, setting forth his claims to a dukedom at length. He represented the oldest branch of one of the oldest English families; he had been one of the first, and had held out to the last, in that cause which had brought William to the crown. Lastly, he had won over three wavering peers to vote against the proposed regency, and thus decided the question whether William should be king (Dalrymple, ii. 256). This request was refused, but a suit at law restored to Montagu his lucrative mastership of the wardrobe (Luttrell, *Diary*, ii. 48). He increased his wealth still further by a second marriage. The Countess of Northumberland died in September 1690, and on 8 Sept. 1692 Montagu married Elizabeth Cavendish, eldest daughter of Henry Cavendish, second duke of Newcastle, and widow of Christopher Monck, second duke of Albemarle [q. v.] She was very rich and very mad, and was said to have declared that she would give her hand to nobody but a crowned head. Montagu wooed and won her in the character of Emperor of China (Granger, *Biographical Hist.* ed. 1804, iv. 158; Walpole, *Letters*, ed. 1880, viii. 514; Luttrell, *Diary*, ii. 563). The mad duchess lived till 1734, and was kept in such close seclusion that it was rumoured she was dead, and that her husband concealed her death in order to retain the enjoyment of her 7,000*l.* a year (Chester, *Westminster Abbey Registers*, p. 341; Cartwright, *Strafford Papers*, p. 79). The marriage resulted in several lawsuits concerning the Albemarle property, one of which, between Montagu and the Earl of Bath, lasted for seven years, and cost the two litigants 20,000*l.* between them. It was finally settled in October 1698 by a compromise, but not until four or more of Montagu's witnesses had been convicted of perjury, suborned, as it was asserted, by one of his chaplains (James, *Vernon's Letters to the Duke of Shrewsbury*, i. 240, 287, 303; Luttrell, iii. 140, iv. 78, 355, 443).

On 2 March 1705 Montagu's son John (1688?–1749) [q. v.], who succeeded him in the dukedom, was married to Lady Mary Churchill, the youngest daughter of the Duke of Marlborough (Boyer, *Annals of the Reign of Anne*, viii. 373; Luttrell, *Diary*, v. 537). The marriage was a political alliance, dictated by Marlborough's desire of making his political position secure against a possible combination of whigs and tories (Thompson, *Memoirs of Sarah, Duchess of Marlborough*, ii. 9–16). As a consequence Montagu at length attained the goal of his ambition, and was raised to the dignity of Marquis of Monthermer and Duke of Montagu (12 April 1705). He survived his promotion four years only, dying at the age of seventy-one on 9 March 1708–9 (Doyle, p. 522).

Montagu left, besides his son John, a daughter, Anne, who married Alexander Popham of Littlecote, Wiltshire. An elder son, Ralph Winwood, died in May 1702 (Collins, *Peerage*, iii. 469; Luttrell, v. 170). Two engraved portraits of Montagu are among the Sutherland collection in the Bodleian Library (*Catalogue*, i. 648). Macky describes him as 'of a middle stature, inclining to fat, of a coarse, dark complexion.' Swift adds the very just comment, 'as arrant a knave as any in his time' (Macky, *Secret Services*, &c., 1733, p. 44; Swift, *Works*, ed. 1824, xii. 237). If Montagu was perfectly unscrupulous in obtaining money, he at least knew how to spend his wealth with dignity. His public entry into Paris as ambassador in 1669 'was so magnificent that it has scarce ever been since equalled' (BOYER, viii. 366). He built two great houses, 'which remain still as the best patterns of building we have in England, and show the genius of the great contriver' (*ib.* p. 371). One of these was Boughton House in Northamptonshire, 'contrived after the model of Versailles.' The other was Montagu House in Bloomsbury, 'without comparison the finest building in the whole city of London or county of Middlesex, Hampton Court alone excepted' (*ib.*) Evelyn, who describes it at length in his 'Diary,' under 10 Oct. 1683, terms it 'a fine palace, built after the French pavilion way, by Mr. Hooke' [see HOOKE, ROBERT]. It was burnt down on the night of 19 Jan. 1686, owing to the negligence of a servant; but Montagu, after an unsuccessful lawsuit with his tenant, the Earl of Devonshire, rebuilt the house with very little alteration. The second Montagu House was purchased by the government in 1753 to establish the British Museum, and was demolished between 1840 and 1849, and replaced by the present museum building (EVELYN, *Diary*, ed. 1879, ii. 319, 421, iii. 16; ELLIS, *Correspondence*, i. 25; WHEATLEY, *London Past and Present*, i. 251, ii. 555).

[Lives of Montagu are contained in Boyer's Annals of Queen Anne, viii. 363–74, and in Memoirs for the Curious, February and March 1709. Montagu's correspondence with Lord Arlington and Sir H. Coventry is in the possession of the Marquis of Bath; Hist. MSS. Comm. 4th Rep. p. 245. His correspondence with Danby between 1676 and 1678 was printed by Danby in his own vindication: Copies and Extracts of some Letters written to and from the Earl of Danby, now Duke of Leeds, in 1676, 1677, and 1678, with particular Remarks upon some of them. Published by his Grace's direction, 8vo, 1710. The original letters are now in the possession of Mr. Alfred Morrison, and are reprinted in the catalogue of his autographs. Other authorities are cited in the article.] C. H. F.

MONTAGU or MOUNTAGUE, RICHARD (1577–1641), controversialist and bishop, was born during Christmastide 1577 (cf. *MS. Reg. King's College, Cambridge*) at Dorney, Buckinghamshire, of which parish his father, Laurence Mountague, was vicar (LIPSCOMB, *Buckinghamshire*, iii. 275; HARWOOD, *Alumni Etonenses*, pp. 63–4). He was elected from Eton to a scholarship at King's College, Cambridge, and admitted on 24 Aug. 1594. His name occurs in the list of junior fellows for the quarter Midsummer to Michaelmas 1597. He graduated B.A. before Lady Day 1598, M.A. 1602, B.D. 1609. He assisted Sir Henry Savile [q. v.] in the literary work which he carried on at Eton, and the second book issued from the Eton press was his edition of 'The two Invectives of Gregory Nazianzen against Julian,' 1610. He was also to have edited St. Basil the Great, but the work was never completed. In 1610 he received the living of Wootton Courtney, Somerset; on 29 April 1613 he was admitted fellow of Eton, and in the same year received the rectory of Stanford Rivers, Essex. On 9 Dec. 1616 he was installed dean of Hereford, a post which he exchanged with Dr. Oliver Lloyd for a canonry of Windsor, in which he was installed on 6 Sept. 1617. He was admitted archdeacon of Hereford on 15 Sept. 1617. He held also the rectory of Petworth, Sussex, where he rebuilt the parsonage, and was chaplain to the king. He held these preferments with his fellowship at Eton by dispensation from James I (*Cal. of State Papers*, 1619–28, p. 546).

On the death, in 1614, of Isaac Casaubon [q. v.], with whom he had previously corresponded (*Epp. Casaubon*, ed. 1709, ep. 698, not 693, as in Pattison's 'Casaubon') about the 'Exercitationes ad Baronii Annales,' Montagu was directed by the king to publish that work. It appeared the same year, and in 1615 James requested him to prepare an answer to Baronius on similar lines. This work was at first apparently suppressed at Archbishop Abbot's command (MARK PATTISON, *Casaubon*, p. 375), but it was issued in 1622 under the title of 'Analecta Ecclesiasticarum Exercitationum.' In the epistle dedicatory addressed to the king the author pays tribute to the memory of the great scholar, 'magnum illud Galliæ et literarum monumentum' (see Introduction to vol. ii. of *The Critical History of England*, pp. 23, 24, for charge of plagiarism), and states his object to be to trace the *origines* of Christian faith and doctrine, and show that the Anglican position was derived from the 'ancient founts.' The work displays great knowledge of classical and patristic antiquity.

Through life Montagu's aim was to support the church of England against its enemies on both sides—'to stand in the gapp against puritanisme and popery, the Scilla and Charybdis of Ancient Piety' (Montagu to Cosin, *Cosin Correspondence*, i. 21). He would not recognise the foreign reformed bodies as lawful branches of the church, 'non est sacerdotium nisi in ecclesia, non est ecclesia sine sacerdotio' (*Orig. Eccl.* p. 464). His theses in fact were similar to those of the Caroline and tractarian divines; but he never completed the task which he had set himself: he only 'began his ecclesiastical history,' says Fuller, 'which had he finished might be balanced with that of Baronius, and which could have swayed with it for learning and weighed it down for truth.'

So far Montagu's work was almost entirely scholastic. In his 'Diatribæ upon the first part of the late History of Tithes,' 1621, 4to, he entered directly into one of the most popular controversies of the day. This work, dedicated to the king, was an attempt to beat Selden with his own weapons of philological and classical learning. 'Tithes are due by divine right' (p. 210), and he traces their history through the Jewish records from patriarchal to rabbinical times. He finds them in secular as well as sacred writers, and finally declares that no nation or country can be discovered that did not pay tithes to their deities, and that the custom is thus universal, as well as divinely originated. This book attracted considerable attention, but by his next work he sprang at once into popular fame. About 1619 he found that certain 'Romish rangers' had visited his parish and endeavoured to convert his flock. He invited them to meet him and discuss, but they did not come. He then drew up three propositions, promising to become a Roman catholic if any of them were successfully oppugned: 1, That the present Roman church is neither the catholic church nor a sound branch of the catholic church; 2, That the present English church is a sound member of the catholic church; and 3, That none of the points which the former maintains against the latter was the perpetual doctrine of the catholic church. He was answered in a pamphlet called 'A Gag for the New Gospel,' by Matthew Kellison [q. v.] To this he immediately replied by a trenchant rejoinder, 'A Gagg for the New Gospell? No. A New Gagg for an old Goose,' 1624. The 'Gagg' had contained forty-seven propositions which it attributed to the church of England. Of these Montagu only allows eight to be her true doctrine. The work, considered as a whole, was 'a temperate exposition of the reasons which were leading an increasing body of scholars to reject the doctrines of Rome and of Geneva alike' (GARDINER, *History of England*, v. 352).

Almost simultaneously with the publication of the 'New Gagg' Montagu issued his 'Immediate Addresse unto God alone, first delivered in a Sermon before his Majestie at Windsore, since reuised and inlarged to a just treatise of Invocation of Saints,' 1624, 4to. Three years ago, he explained, he had preached before the king on Psalm l. verse 15. There was present Marco Antonio de Dominis [q. v.], archbishop of Spalatro, who charged Montagu with supporting 'that ridiculous Roman doctrine and practice of praying unto saints and angels in time of need.' To meet the accusation Montagu now published the brief original draft of the sermon. The puritans were irritated by Montagu's attitude. Answer after answer poured forth from the press, and the House of Commons, on the complaint of two Ipswich ministers, Yates and Ward, referred the book to Abbot. Abbot applied for authority to the king, and remonstrated with Montagu. But James himself saw the pamphleteer, and approved of his work. 'If that is to be a Papist,' he said, 'so am I a Papist.' The matter did not rest with the king's death. The bishops of Rochester (Buckeridge), Oxford (Howson), and St. David's (Laud) wrote to Buckingham (LAUD, *Works*, vi. 244–6) in support of Montagu, and he published his most famous work, 'Appello Cæsarem: a just Appeale from two unjust Informers,' early in 1625. With an imprimatur from Dr. White, dean of Carlisle, in spite of Abbot's refusal to license it, it was issued from the press. It was a vindication of his teaching from the charge of Arminianism and popery. 'I am none of that fraternity—no Calvinist, no Lutheran, but a Christian' (p. 45). The House of Commons took up the matter at once, and accused the author of 'dishonouring the late king, of disturbing Church and State, and of treating the rights and privileges of Parliament with contempt.' A hot debate on the matter (see GARDINER, *History of England*, v. 362) was followed by Montagu's committal to the custody of the serjeant-at-arms. He was, however, allowed to return to Stanford Rivers on giving a bond of 2,000*l.* to the serjeant to return on the reassembling of parliament (see Montagu's Letter to Buckingham, *Cabala*, ed. 1663, p. 116, and Joseph Mead [q. v.] to Sir M. Stuteville, *Court and Times of Charles I*, i. 96). Charles thereupon made Montagu one of his chaplains, and intimated to the commons on 9 July that 'what had been spoken in the House and informed against Mr. Mountague was displeasing to him. He hoped one of his chaplains might have as much protection as the servant of an ordinary burgess' (RUSHWORTH, i. 174; cf. LAUD, *Diary*, 9 July 1625; and GARDINER, *History of England*, v. 372–3). On the 11th parliament was prorogued. On 2 Aug., when the parliament was sitting at Oxford, Montagu was too ill to attend (cf. COSIN, *Correspondence*, i. 76 sqq.), and after a hot discussion, in which Coke and Heath took part, the matter was allowed to drop. But the question was far too serious to rest for long. On 16 and 17 Jan. 1625–6 a conference was held by Charles's command, as the result of which the bishops of London (Montaigne), Durham (Neile), Winchester (Andrewes), Rochester (Buckeridge), and St. David's (Laud) reported to Buckingham that Montagu 'hath not affirmed anything to be the doctrine of the Church of England, but that which in our opinions is the doctrine of the Church of England, or agreeable thereunto' (LAUD, *Works*, vi. 249). This was followed on 11 Feb. by a conference, held 'at the desire of the Earl of Warwick' in Buckingham's house, between the Bishop of Lichfield (Morton) and the master of Emmanuel College, Cambridge (Dr. Preston), representing the opposition to Montagu and Dr. White, dean of Carlisle, as his defender. It lasted for two days, 'many of the nobility being present' (LAUD, *Works*, iii. 178–9). The result of the conference can hardly be expressed better than in the words of the Earl of Pembroke, 'that none returned Arminians thence save such as repaired thither with the same opinions' (FULLER, *Church History*, XI. i. 35). The committee of religion renewed their censure of the 'Appeal,' and the House of Commons voted a petition to the king that the author might be fitly punished and his book burned (RUSHWORTH, i. 212). The king issued a proclamation (14 June 1626) commanding silence on points of controversy. In March 1628 the House of Commons again appointed a committee of religion to inquire into the cases of Montague, Mainwaring, and Cosin.

It was only in appearance that the king had ceased to protect Montagu, for Montagu had the strongest supporters at court in Laud and Buckingham himself (cf. LAUD, *Works*, iv. 273); and on the death of Carleton, bishop of Chichester, who had not long before hotly controverted the tenets of the 'Appeal,' he was appointed to the vacant see. He was elected on 14 July 1628 (LE NEVE, *Dignitaries*, ed. 1716, p. 114), received dispensation to hold Petworth with his bishopric (*Cal. State Papers*, 18 July 1628), did homage (*ib.* 24 July ?), and on 22 Aug. was confirmed in Bow Church. During the ceremony one Jones, a stationer, made objection to the confirmation (full details in FULLER, *Church History*, xi. 67–9; and cf. Sir Francis Nethersole to Elizabeth, queen of Bohemia, *Cal. State Papers*, 14 Feb. 1629, &c.), but the objection was overruled as informal; and on 24 Aug. (St. Bartholomew's Day) he was consecrated at Croydon, on the same day that news came of Buckingham's assassination (LAUD, *Diary* in *Works*, iii. 208). He was installed on 22 Sept. (*Cal. State Papers*). The appointment was a rash one; more magnanimous, as Heylyn says, than safe (*Cyprianus Anglicus*, p. 185). A bitter pamphlet, called 'Anti-Montacutum, an Appeale or Remonstrance of the Orthodox Ministers of the Church of England against Richard Mountague,' was published in 1629 (at Edinburgh, thus throwing light upon its presbyterian origin) and addressed to parliament. To this was added 'the character of an Arminian or mere Montaguist,' in which the bishop is thus described: 'He is an animal scarce rational, whose study is to read and applaud Peter Lambard and John Duns before Peter Martyr and John Calvin, and for more modern polemics he prefers Bellarmine before Chamierus.' The House of Commons at once took up the matter, and great alarm was felt among the king's advisers (cf. Letter of Heath to Montagu, quoted in GARDINER, vii. 19–20). Attempts were made at conciliation, by the issue of the declaration prefixed to the Thirty-nine Articles and still printed in the Book of Common Prayer, by a letter from Montagu to Abbot disclaiming Arminianism, by the grant of a special pardon to Montagu, and by the issue of a proclamation suppressing the 'Appello Cæsarem' (*Cal. State Papers*, 17 Jan. 1629). But the commons were in no mood to surrender their position. A vain attempt was made to show that Jones's objection to his confirmation was illegally disallowed.

Montagu set himself at once, and diligently, to the work of his diocese. He lived chiefly, 'without state or retinue,' at Aldingbourne, the summer residence of the bishops of Chichester, which he repaired (cf. Letter to Windebanke, *Cal. State Papers*, 26 June 1632), but we still find letters from him dated Petworth. His first endeavour was to recover the alienated estates of the see (*ib.* 1629–34, passim; and his own case in manuscript, Harleian MS. No. 7381). He was not wholly successful; his process to recover the estate and manor of Selsey, Sussex, for instance, being decided against him by Heath, chief justice, in the common pleas, in 1635. His primary visitation was held in 1635, and the articles which he then issued were afterwards reprinted (PRYNNE, *Canterburie's Doome*, p. 94). He was diligent in procuring obedience to church discipline in his diocese (e.g. Letter to Laud, 16 Jan. 1632). He pressed on the general collections for St. Paul's Cathedral (*Cal. State Papers*, 18 June 1635, 12 Feb. 1636, 2 May 1637, &c.) He was also engaged in his researches into ecclesiastical history, and published several learned treatises. In 1638 he was at work on a book on the Eucharistic Sacrifice, which he submitted to the approval of Laud (*ib.* 29 March 1638; PRYNNE, *Canterburie's*

Doome, p. 351). He was also apparently at this time much mixed up in the tortuous negotiations with the papacy which were conducted through Panzani. Panzani recorded that in an interview on 3 Nov. 1635 Montagu spoke slightingly of the obstacles to reunion, admitted the authority of the pope, suggested a conference in France, 'said freely that he believed all that I believed except transubstantiation,' adding that Laud was 'pauroso e circonspetto.' At a later interview he seemed, according to Panzani, to think reunion quite easy (see *Memoirs of Gregorio Panzani*, by Joseph Berington, 1793, pp. 237, 241, 246; and Mr. S. R. GARDINER's transcripts from the Record Office quoted in his *History*, viii. 138-9, 143). These statements must be received with considerable distrust (cf. a Roman catholic writer, C. Plowden [q. v.], *Remarks on Panzani's Memoirs*, Liège, 1794), as Panzani was notoriously ignorant of English opinion, and Montagu's writings maintain throughout an unflinchingly Anglican and anti-Roman position. But at the same time Montagu was asking license for his son to visit Rome (see letter to Windebanke, *Cal. State Papers*, 26 Jan. 1634-5), and the matter became in the hands of Prynne a plausible accusation of romanising (see *Hidden Workes of Darkenesse brought to Publike Light*, 1645, pp. 146-7).

On the translation of Wren, bishop of Norwich, to Ely, Montagu was appointed to the vacant see. He was elected on 4 May 1638, and the election received the royal assent on 9 May (LE NEVE, *Dignitaries*, p. 212, and *Cal. State Papers*). The temporalities were restored to him on 19 May (*ib.*) In Laud's annual accounts of his province to the king we find that in 1638 the bishop complained much of the impoverishing of the see by his predecessors' long leases and exchanges of land (LAUD, *Works*, v. 359. His report for 1638 is Lambeth MS. No. 943). The next year he declared his diocese 'as quiet, uniform, and comformable as any in the kingdom if not more' (LAUD, *Works*, v. 364). He had long been suffering from a quartan ague, as well as gout and stone (*ib.* p. 353, and *Cosin Correspondence*, vol. i. passim). But he was not to die without further public criticism. He was again attacked in the House of Commons on 23 Feb. 1641 on account of a petition from the inhabitants of St. Peter Mancroft, Norwich, against an inhibition directed by the bishop against Mr. Carter, parson of that parish, and a commission was appointed to consider his offences. Before any further steps were taken he died on 13 April 1641, and was buried in his cathedral, with a simple monument and epitaph written by himself—'Depositum Montacutii Episcopi.'

Selden and Savile both bore testimony to his great learning, and Laud described him as 'a very good scholar and a right honest man.' His works show him to have been a man of erudition, with a considerable gift of sarcasm, which he expressed in somewhat cumbrous Latin, but in clear and trenchant English. Both in Latin and in English he shows himself a writer of great power. Fuller says of him that 'his great parts were attended with a tartness of writing, very sharp the nip of his pen, and much gall mingled in his ink against such as opposed him. However such the equability of the sharpness of his style, he was impartial therein; be he ancient or modern writer, papist or protestant, that stood in his way, they shuld all equally taste thereof' (*Church History*, bk. xi. c. 7). His humorous, familiar letters to his intimate friend, Cosin (*Cosin Correspondence*, vol. i., Surtees Soc., 1869, No. 52), afford interesting details as to the composition of his different books. A scholar and theologian rather than a politician or man of the world, he was an enthusiast for his leading idea, the catholicity of the English church. In theological literature he was probably at least as powerful an influence as Andrewes or Jeremy Taylor. The 'Appello Cæsarem' was certainly one of the most famous pamphlets in an age of controversial activity.

Besides the works already mentioned, Montagu wrote: 1. 'Antidiatribæ ad priorem partem diatribæ J. Cæsaris Bulengeri,' Cambridge, 1625. 2. 'Eusebii de Demonstratione Evangelicâ libri decem . . . omnia studio R. M. Latine facta, notis illustrata,' 1628. 3. 'Apparatus ad Origines Ecclesiasticas,' Oxford, 1635. 4. 'De Originibus Ecclesiasticis,' first part, London, 1636; second part, London, 1640. 5. 'Articles of Inquiry put forth at his Primary Visitation as Bishop of Norwich' (unauthorised), Cambridge, 1638; (corrected by the bishop), London, 1638; new edition, Cambridge, 1841. 6. 'Acts and Monuments of the Church,' London, 1642. 7. 'Versio et Notæ in Photii Epistolas,' London, 1651.

[Le Neve's Dignitaries, ed. 1716; Calendar of State Papers; T. Harwood's Alumni Etonienses, 1797; Catalogue of Provosts, Fellows, and Scholars of King's College, Cambridge, by Anthony Allen, circa 1750 (King's College MSS.); Maxwell Lyte's History of Eton College; Isaac Casaubon's Epistolæ, ed. 1709; Mark Pattison's Life of Casaubon; Cosin Correspondence, vol. i. (Surtees Society, vol. lii.); Godwin's Bishops, ed. 1615, with manuscript notes in continuation, by Mr. Godwyn of Balliol College, in Bodleian Library; William Prynne's Hidden Workes of Darkenesse, 1645, and Canterburie's Doome, 1646; Heylyn's Cyprianus Anglicus; Fuller's Church History; Laud's Works; S. R. Gardiner's History of England, 1603–42; Perry's History of the Church of England; Lipscomb's History of Buckinghamshire; Wood's Athenæ Oxonienses. The controversies in which Montagu was engaged provoked a mass of fugitive literature.]

W. H. H.

MONTAGU, WALTER (1603?–1677), abbot of St. Martin's, near Pontoise, was the second son of Sir Henry Montagu, first earl of Manchester [q. v.], by his first wife, Catherine, second daughter of Sir William Spencer of Yarnton, Oxfordshire. Edward Montagu, second earl of Manchester [q. v.], was his brother. Born in the parish of St. Botolph without Aldgate, London, in or about 1603, Walter was admitted on 27 Jan. 1617–18 a fellow-commoner of Sidney Sussex College, Cambridge. On leaving the university he went abroad to improve himself in modern languages 'and other qualifications proper for a nobleman.' On his return he was well received at court, and was employed by the Duke of Buckingham, who sent him on a secret mission to France in 1624, when the marriage with the Princess Henrietta Maria was first in contemplation (Hardwicke, *State Papers*, i. 465). In March 1624–5 Buckingham was 'preparing for France,' as 'Wat Montagu brings word that all is forward, and the lady shall be delivered in thirty days.' Montagu, who was rewarded with 200*l.* for this 'special service,' thus formed a friendship with Henrietta Maria, which ended only with his life. In 1625 he was again despatched to France on business connected with her arbitrary seizure of some English vessels, and on his return in January 1625–6 he brought with him a promise of restitution of our ships, and an assurance that peace was about to be concluded by the French government with the protestants.

In 1627 he graduated M.A. at Cambridge as a nobleman's son (Wood, *Fasti Oxon.* ii. 284 *n.*); and in the same year he was sent to Lorraine and Italy to stir up discontent against France, but he met with little encouragement. In October he reported to Charles I that in case of a continental war he would have no allies. Shortly afterwards an officer commissioned by Richelieu suddenly arrested him as he was passing through Lorraine, and, in spite of the protection of neutral territory, carried him and his despatches to Paris, where he was lodged in the Bastille. He soon regained his liberty, however, as he was present at the assassination of the Duke of Buckingham at Portsmouth in August 1628. Later in that year he went abroad to negotiate with Richelieu an exchange of prisoners. In March 1631 the sum of 1,100*l.* was paid to him 'for his Majesty's secret service in France,' with an additional 400*l.* 'for his charges in his journey.' He did not return permanently to England till 1633.

Subsequently he was residing in Paris as attaché to the British embassy, when out of curiosity he went to Loudun to witness the exorcisms of the Ursuline nuns, which were then the talk of all France. What he witnessed led him to become a catholic, and in July 1635 he arrived in London to announce his departure for Rome and his intention to join the fathers of the Oratory. It appears that he finally made his abjuration in the hands of the pope himself (Foley, *Records*, v. 606). His conversion became a matter of gossip at the court, and the letter in which he announced it to his father, the Earl of Manchester, passed from hand to hand (Gardiner, *Hist. of England*, viii. 139).

Afterwards he was allowed to return to England, though he was received more warmly at Somerset House, the queen's residence, than at Whitehall, and he zealously seconded Father Con's efforts to induce the queen to take an active part in the propagation of the Roman catholic religion. He also acted in April 1639 with Sir Kenelm Digby [q. v.] as her majesty's agent in collecting a contribution from the catholics towards defraying the expense of the royal army. In 1641 the House of Commons ordered him, Sir John Winter, the queen's secretary, Sir Kenelm Digby, and two other catholic gentlemen, to give an account of their part in the collection of this contribution. Various entries in the 'Journals' of the two houses indicate his activity in the support of the royal cause. He was obliged to retire to France, taking with him a strong recommendatory letter from the queen (Green, *Letters of Henrietta Maria*, p. 38). In March 1642–3 a letter in cipher from the king to Montagu was intercepted in Bedfordshire, and in October 1643 Montagu was apprehended at Rochester, brought up to London, and ordered by the House of Commons to be detained as a close prisoner in the Tower (*Commons' Journals*, ii. 1005, 1007, iii. 260; Green, *Letters of Henrietta Maria*, p. 228). It appears that he had upon him letters sealed with the arms of France, and directed to both their majesties of England. On 9 Feb. 1643–4 it was resolved by the commons that all his goods should be seized and sold for the use of the forces under Lord Fairfax. During his imprisonment he engaged in a disputation with Dr. John Bastwick [q. v.], who published an account of the controversy, under the title of 'The Church of England a true Church,' 1645.

He remained a prisoner in the Tower until July 1647, when he was allowed to go 'on good bail' to Tunbridge to drink the waters for two months, and he obtained from time to time further extensions of this privilege. Finally, on 31 Aug. 1649, the House of Commons resolved that he, Sir John Winter, and Sir Kenelm Digby should depart this nation within ten days, and should not return upon pain of death and the confiscation of their estates.

Soon afterwards Montagu, by the interest of the queen-dowager of France, was made abbot of the Benedictine monastery of Nanteuil in the diocese of Metz, and subsequently obtained the rich abbey of St. Martin, near Pontoise. He was frequently consulted on affairs of state, and was for a time on friendly terms with Cardinal Mazarin, but a quarrel between them followed. Montagu had, says Dodd, the ear of three great princesses—the queen-mother of France, Mary de Medicis, Henrietta Maria, queen of England, who had retired to France in 1644, and Henrietta's daughter, the Duchess of Orleans, being almoner to the two last. In 1654 Charles I's son, Henry, duke of Gloucester, was committed by Henrietta Maria to Montagu's care at Pontoise, and Montagu, at the queen's instigation, pressed upon the young prince, with the utmost assiduity although without success, the claims of the catholic religion [see under Henry, Duke of Gloucester, 1639-1660]. Towards the close of 1660 he came secretly to England on a visit to his brother, Edward, earl of Manchester.

Queen Henrietta Maria died in 1669, and in the following year Montagu was requested by the French government to resign his office of abbot of St. Martin in favour of the young Cardinal Bouillon. He was, however, allowed to remove his furniture, and continued to enjoy the revenues of the abbey. His income as commendatory abbot amounted to 5,000*l.* sterling, and this sum, augmented by the charities of well-disposed persons which passed through his hands, enabled him to give pecuniary aid to many of his poor countrymen, both catholics and protestants, whom the civil war had forced into exile (cf. Wood). He passed his latter years in Paris, where he died, in the Hospital of Incurables, on 5 Feb. 1676-7 (Foley, *Records*, v. 604). He was buried at Pontoise.

Montagu had literary tastes, and verses by him are prefixed to 'Theophila, or Love's Sacrifice,' by Edward Benlowes, 1652. He also published 'The Accomplish'd Woman,' translated from the French, London, 1656, 12mo, and dedicated to the Duchess of Buckingham; and was author of 'The Shepheard's Paradise, a Comedy [in five acts and in prose]. Privately acted before the late King Charls by the Queens Majesty, and Ladies of Honour,' London, 1659, 8vo. Of this piece there is a copy in the British Museum, with a new title-page, bearing the date 1629, probably a misprint for 1659, as 'the late King Charls' is mentioned in the title. It is not entered in the books of the Stationers' Company for 1629. This comedy is ridiculed by Sir John Suckling in his 'Session of the Poets' (cf. *Addit. MS.* 24491, v. 234).

His other works—political or theological—are: 1. 'The Coppy of a Letter sent from France by Mr. Walter Montagu to his Father, the Lord Privie Seale [giving his Reasons for embracing the Roman Catholic Religion], with his Answere thereunto. Also a Second Answere to the same Letter by the Lord Falkland' [London], 1641, 4to; another edition, printed with Lucius Cary, viscount Falkland's 'Discourse of Infallibility,' 1651; 3rd edit. 1660. 2. 'The Letter sent by Sir Kenelme Digby and Mr. Mountague concerning the Contribution.' Printed with 'A Coppy of the Letter sent by the Queenes Majestie [Henrietta Maria] concerning the Collection of the Recusants Mony for the Scottish Warre,' London, 1641, 4to. 3. 'Miscellanea Spiritualia: or Devovt Essaies,' London, 1648, 4to; second part, 1654, dedicated to Queen Henrietta Maria. 4. 'An Exposition of the Doctrine of the Catholique Church,' translated from the French of Bossuet, Paris, 1672, 12mo.

His portrait has been engraved by Marshall.

[Add. MSS. 5821 ff. 75 *b*, 140, 5835 ff. 48, 91, 92, 5876 ff. 14, 212; Hunter's Chorus Vatum, Add. MS. 24491, v. 234-5; Baker's Biog. Dram. i. 35; Baker's MSS. No. 2; Birch's Hist. of Royal Soc. 1757, ii. 81; Butler's Lives of the Saints, ii. 58; Clarendon's Hist. of the Rebellion, iii. 401, vi. 391, 392, 546, 547, 690, 691; Clarendon's Life, 1760, i. 187, 267, ii. 425, 435, 436, 442, 504; Pref. to William Clifford's Little Manual of the Poor Man's Daily Devotion, 1705; Collins's Peerage, i. 316; Commons' Journals, ii. 1005, 1007, iii. 260, 266, 363, 394, 396, 560, v. 239, 289, 296, 378, 590, vi. 82, 162, 288; Dalrymple's Memoirs of Great Britain and Ireland, i. 169; Dodd's Church Hist. iii. 93, 181, 184, 350; Félibien's Hist. de l'Abbaye de St. Denys, pp. 509, 510; Foley's Records, v. 604,

606, vi. 609; Gardiner's Hist. of England, x. 330; Granger's Biog. Hist. of England, 5th edit. iii. 144; Hardwicke State Papers, i. 465; Harl. MS. 6987, art. 99, f. 115; Heylyn's Life of Laud, pp. 337, 338, 370, 386, 424; Kennett's Register, pp. 598, 652; La Fayette's Hist. de Henriette, Duchesse d'Orléans, pp. 54, 210–213; Legenda Lignea, pp. 137–41; Lloyd's Memoires, 1677, p. 159; Lowndes's Bibl. Man. (Bohn), p. 1588; Macpherson's Original Papers, i. 21; Duke of Manchester's Court and Society, 1864, i. 308, ii. 1–20; Madame de Motteville's Memoirs of Anne of Austria, i. 113, 119, 123, v. 23, 95, 97, 143, 151, 165, 225, 252, 261–267, 273, 276, 280, 291, 292, 293, 331, 332; Nalson's Collections, i. 738, 741, 792, ii. 311, 316; Panzani's Memoirs, pp. 190–2, 194, 211, sq.; Mémoires de Monsieur de la Porte, pp. 37 sq., 45, 235; Prynne's Hidden Workes of Darkenesse; Prynne's Canterburie's Doome; Mémoires du Card. de Retz, ii. 325, 362; Wadsworth's Spanish Pilgrim, p. 13; Walpole's Anecd. of Painting, 2nd edit. ii. 141; Wharton's Troubles and Tryal of Archbishop Laud, p. 55; Wood's Fasti (Bliss), ii. 284; Wren's Parentalia, p. 8.]
T. C.

MONTAGU, Sir WILLIAM (1619?–1706), judge, second son of Edward, first baron Montagu [q. v.], of Boughton, Northamptonshire, by his second wife, Frances, daughter of Thomas Cotton of Connington, Huntingdonshire, and half-sister of Sir Robert Bruce Cotton [q. v.], born about 1619, entered Sidney Sussex College, Cambridge, in 1632, but left without a degree, and was admitted in 1635 a member of the Middle Temple, where he was called to the bar in 1641. He represented Huntingdon in the Short parliament of 1640, but did not again sit in parliament until the Restoration. He was then returned for the university of Cambridge, 22 June 1660; and he afterwards sat for Stamford in the Pensionary parliament. He was appointed attorney-general to the queen, 10 June 1662, and was the same year elected a bencher of his inn, of which he was treasurer in 1663, and autumn reader in 1664. He was called to the degree of serjeant-at-law and created lord chief baron of the exchequer, 12 April 1676. He sat with Sir William Scroggs at the Old Bailey to try William Ireland [q. v.], Pickering, and others of the supposed popish plotters, on 17 Dec. 1678, but took little part in the proceedings, and he subsequently, when called as a witness to Oates's character on his trial in 1685, avowed that he 'had never any great faith in him.' He also sat as assessor to the House of Lords on the occasion of the impeachment of William Howard, viscount Stafford, November 1680, and was a member of the court which tried Lord William Russell, 13 July 1683. On the western circuit in March 1684 he sentenced to death Alicia Welland, almost the last person executed for witchcraft in England. Consulted by James II as to the validity of a grant of the excise made by the late king shortly before his death, he gave offence by advising that it determined by that event, and it was expected that his 'quietus' would immediately follow. It was deferred, however, until after 'the bloody assizes,' in which he was one of Jeffreys's colleagues, and was occasioned by his refusal in April 1686 to give an unqualified opinion in favour of the prerogative of dispensation, upon which he was removed (21 April) to make way for a more subservient judge. He returned to the bar, practised as a serjeant, and on the second flight of the king was nominated, 22 Jan. 1688–9, assessor to the Convention, but took little part in its proceedings. He died on 26 Aug. 1706.

Montagu married (1) Elizabeth, eldest daughter of Ralph Freeman of Aspeden, Hertfordshire, by whom he had a son, Christopher; (2) Mary, daughter of Sir John Aubrey, bart. His second wife was much admired by Pepys (*Diary*, 2 Jan. 1661–2, and 30 Dec. 1667). She bore him a son and a daughter, and died on 10 March 1699–1700. The son, William, married, 29 May 1670, Mary Anne, daughter of Richard Evelyn of Woodcote, Surrey, brother of the diarist (Evelyn, *Diary*, 29 May 1670), and died without issue in 1690; the daughter, Elizabeth, married Sir William Drake of Shardeloes, Buckinghamshire. Montagu has also been credited with a son Charles, apparently in error (cf. *Hist. Reg.* 1730, p. 65).

[Bridges's Northamptonshire, ii. 348, 352; Visitation of Huntingdonshire (Camden Soc.), p. 28; Dugdale's Orig. pp. 220, 222, Chron. Ser. p. 118; Cal. State Papers, Dom. 1661–2, p. 404; Hist. MSS. Comm. 7th Rep. App. p. 493; Wynne's Miscellany, p. 303; Cobbett's State Trials, vii. 120, 1168, 1527, ix. 591; Parl. Hist. p. 693; Lists of Members of Parl. (Official); Bramston's Autobiog. (Camden Soc.), pp. 193, 207, 223; Reresby's Mem., ed. Cartwright, p. 361; Clarendon and Rochester Corresp. ii. 252; Hatton Corresp. (Camden. Soc.), ii. 131; Luttrell's Relation of State Affairs, i. 375, 547, vi. 81; North's Life of Lord-Keeper Guilford, i. 96; Lord Russell's Life of Lord John Russell, ii. 39; Le Neve's Pedigrees of Knights (Harl. Soc.), p. 219; Chauncy's Antiq. Hertfordshire, p. 125; Dugdale's Baronage, ii. 444; Wotton's Baronetage, vol. iii. pt. i. p. 112; Burke's Extinct Peerage; Misc. Gen. et Herald. 2nd ser. iii. 270; Duke of Manchester's Court and Society from Elizabeth to Anne, i. 272; Inderwick's Side Lights on the Stuarts; Addit. MSS. 5520 art. 64 *b*, 27447 ff.

374, 419, 29551 ff. 481–90, 29558 f. 28 *b*; Macaulay's Hist. of England, ii. 83; Foss's Lives of the Judges; Haydn's Book of Dignities, ed. Ockerby.] J. M. R.

MONTAGU, WILLIAM (1720?–1757), captain in the navy, son of Edward Richard Montagu, viscount Hinchinbroke (*d.* 1722), by Elizabeth, daughter of Alexander Popham of Littlecote, Wiltshire, and younger brother of John Montagu, fourth earl of Sandwich [q. v.], was on 20 Sept. 1740 promoted to be lieutenant of the Defiance, one of the ships going out to the West Indies with Sir Chaloner Ogle (*d.* 1750) [q. v.], and in her was present at the unsuccessful attack on Cartagena in March–April 1741. He was afterwards moved into the Launceston, one of the squadron with Commodore Warren [see Warren, Sir Peter] at the Leeward Islands, and by Warren he was promoted, on 23 May 1744, to the command of the Mercury sloop. On the night of 20 Oct. 1744, as the ship was lying at Antigua, a boat prowling round would not answer when hailed. Montagu ordered the sentry to fire at her, and the boat then came alongside with a negro in her, shot through the calf of the leg, who, through the incompetence of the surgeon of the Mercury, bled to death. The surgeon was dismissed the service by sentence of court-martial, but Commodore Knowles, apparently believing that Montagu was to blame for the man's death, suspended him from his command, and sent him under arrest on board the Eltham for a passage to England. Despite Montagu's appeal, Knowles refused either to try him by court-martial or to hand him over to the civil power at Antigua, and Montagu in the Eltham was carried to New England, where, after he had been seven months under arrest, he was promoted by Warren to the post-ship Mermaid on 23 May 1745 (Montagu's petition to the first lord of the admiralty, not dated, read 14 Aug. 1745 in *Captain's Letters*, M. 11). On arriving in England in August, he vainly petitioned the first lord of the admiralty to try Knowles, who had just returned to England, for his tyrannical conduct. In a civil suit (25 June 1752), however, Montagu was successful. Heavy damages, it is said, would have been awarded, but his counsel only demanded a nominal penalty of ten guineas and the costs of the suit.

Meantime he was appointed to the Prince Edward on 20 Aug. 1745, and in July 1746 to the Bristol of 50 guns, one of the ships in the squadron under Anson in the following spring. In the action of 3 May [see Anson, George, Lord] Montagu's conduct was described as extremely brilliant. He closely engaged the 74-gun ship Invincible; Captain Fincher of the Pembroke, thinking Montagu's little ship was overmatched, tried to push in between her and the Frenchman, but, finding there was not sufficient room, hailed the Bristol to put her helm a starboard or the Pembroke would run foul of her. To which Montagu hailed back, 'Run foul of me and be damned; neither you nor any man in the world shall come between me and my enemy.' And he stuck to the Invincible till, with the assistance of the Devonshire, her guns were silenced, when, exclaiming 'Come, my boys, we must have another of them,' he ran his ship alongside the Diamant of 66 guns, which, after a sharp contest, struck to the Bristol (*Gent. Mag.* 1747, p. 272). The story is told in a letter from Portsmouth, dated 30 May 1747; but neither in his official letter to the admiralty, nor in his private letter to the Duke of Bedford, does Anson say anything about it or about Montagu (Barrow, *Life of Anson*, pp. 162–165; *Correspondence of John, fourth Duke of Bedford*, i. 213–15). As the Invincible finally struck to the Prince George, Anson may very well have preferred not describing her as a beaten ship when the Prince George closed her. The writer in the 'Gentleman's Magazine' attributes his silence to jealousy.

During the rest of the year the Bristol was employed on detached service and independent cruising. On 12 Dec. Montagu fell in with Rear-admiral Boscawen in the Namur off Madeira, and anchored there with him. Boscawen, who had charge of a large convoy of East Indiamen, wrote to Anson on the 21st that he had been obliged to confine Montagu, at the desire of the governor, for threatening the life of one of the captains of the Indiaman (Barrow, p. 160; *Addit. MS.* 15955). The Bristol, he added, was in great want of stores, and was going to Lisbon to refit. It was found necessary for her to go to England, and to be paid off. In September 1748, however, Montagu was appointed to her again; and in January 1749–50 he was moved into the Cumberland, guardship at Chatham. In November 1745 he was returned to parliament for the county of Huntingdon, and in February 1752 for the borough of Bossiney in Cornwall. He died in the early part of 1757.

Montagu is said to have been known in the navy of his time as 'Mad Montagu,' and several anecdotes are related of his eccentricities. But though Charnock, who tells them, presumably received them from Locker [see Locker, William] and from Forbes, it is not altogether improbable that they had been told, before their time, of men of the older navy. Montagu married Charlotte.

daughter of Francis Nailour of Offord Darcy in Huntingdonshire, but died without issue (Collins, *Peerage*, iii. 302).

[Charnock's Biog. Nav. v. 400; commission and warrant books and other documents in the Public Record Office.] J. K. L.

MONTAGU, WILLIAM, fifth Duke of Manchester (1768–1843), governor of Jamaica, second son of George, fourth duke [q. v.], was born 21 Oct. 1768, and succeeded to the title in September 1788. His elder brother, George, had died 24 Feb. 1772. After having been educated at Harrow, he was gazetted ensign in the 35th foot on 27 Oct. 1787, and lieutenant in the 76th on 25 Dec. of the same year. He also held a commission in the 50th foot from January 1788 to May 1790, and exchanged into the 73rd regiment on 29 Feb. 1792. He attained the rank of colonel in the army on 14 March 1794, having been gazetted colonel of the Hunts Militia on 8 March of the preceding year. His youth and early manhood seem to have been passed in travel and field sports. He specially excelled as a rower, and is said to have pulled a wherry from London to Gravesend without a rest. In May 1791 he travelled continuously for a fortnight on his way from Rome to Potsdam in order to witness a great review of Prussian troops, but fatigue prevented him from attending the manœuvres.

Manchester was elected, on 4 Jan. 1792, high steward of Godmanchester, and on 1 March 1793 was appointed lord-lieutenant and custos rotulorum for the county of Huntingdon. On 6 Jan. 1808 he was made governor of Jamaica. He sailed in the Guerrier on 23 Jan., and arrived in Kingston on 26 March. The nineteen years of his government of the colony were times of great distress and anxiety. Two months after his arrival, on 30 May 1808, a mutiny of the 2nd West India regiment, a negro corps, led to a quarrel between Carmichael, the commander-in-chief, and the colonial assembly. Manchester applied to the home authorities, and prorogued the assembly when it ordered Carmichael into custody. Five months later the general, under orders from the crown, apologised to the assembly, and Manchester's discretion was generally commended.

In 1811 Manchester paid a visit to England, returning to Jamaica in 1813. During the following year attempts were made to effect further reforms in the law courts and post-office by fixing the amount of all fees; and a law was passed allowing free people of colour to give evidence, but precluding them from holding offices. In 1815 Manchester sought to alleviate the distress caused by the destruction of Port Royal by fire on 13 July, and by the hurricanes and floods which destroyed the sugar and coffee plantations of the island on 18 and 19 Oct. He showed great administrative ability during the panic which prevailed in the colony owing to the insurrection of slaves in Barbados, and by his personal influence pacified the Jamaica slaves. The colony gratefully voted him an addition to his personal establishment. In 1816 he risked his popularity with the planters by vigorously supporting a bill for the registry of slaves, in accordance with the recommendation of the imperial government.

In 1820 Manchester was thrown from his carriage and fractured his skull. The assembly voted five hundred guineas to the surgeons who attended him. After recruiting his health in Europe, he returned in 1822, and the last years of his administration were marked by the introduction of measures preparatory to the emancipation of the slaves. Much resistance was offered by the planters. The Jamaica government was called upon by the colonial office to abolish Sunday markets, to forbid the carrying of whips, and to exempt women from flogging. All these reforms were carried out with great difficulty. In 1824 the negroes rose in the west of the island, and a plot was discovered for the massacre of the whites in the north and east. In 1825 the assembly rejected a bill allowing slaves to give evidence; but in the following year Manchester succeeded in securing a temporary measure to be in operation for five years. In this form, however, the law was vetoed by the home government, but before the imperial decision was known a conviction for murder was obtained by the evidence of slaves given under the temporary law. In the midst of the consequent confusion Manchester finally left Port Royal on 2 July 1827 (*Royal Gazette of Jamaica*, 7 July 1827).

Soon after his return to England, on 27 Sept. 1827, Manchester was appointed postmaster-general in the Duke of Wellington's ministry, and held office till the accession of the whigs to power at the end of 1830. He voted against the Reform Bill in the House of Lords on 7 Oct. 1831, and was in the minority when the second reading was carried on 13 April 1832 (Hansard, 3rd ser. viii. 339, xii. 456). He also voted for Lord Lyndhurst's motion to postpone the disfranchisement clauses (*ib.* xii. 723). In the autumn of 1841 he resigned his lord-lieutenancy owing to failing health, which had never recovered from the accident of 1820, and he died at Rome on 18 March 1843.

Manchester married, on 7 Oct. 1793, Lady Susan Gordon, third daughter of Alexander, fourth duke of Gordon, and had by her two sons and five daughters. The marriage was unhappy; and before he went to Jamaica, Manchester separated from his wife, who died on 26 Aug. 1828. When young he is said to have been 'one of the finest and handsomest men of his time.' A portrait of him when a child, as Cupid, with his mother as Diana, was painted by Reynolds and engraved by Watson, and another by Saunders is in the possession of the Duke of Manchester.

[Lodge's Genealogy of the Peerage; Burke's and Foster's Peerage and Doyle's Baronage (the two latter give wrong date of birth); Playfair's Brit. Fam. Antiq. i. 137 (where christian name is given wrongly); Fox's Hist. of Godmanchester, pp. 162–3; Bridges's Annals of Jamaica, chaps. xvii. xviii.; T. Southey's Chron. Hist. of West Indies, iii. 407, 468; Handbook of Jamaica, 1892, pp. 43, 44; Raikes's Journal, new edition, ii. 349; Public Characters, 1823, ii. 272; Haydn's Book of Dignities; Ann. Reg. Appendix to Chron., p. 242 (from Times, 13 March 1843.)]

G. Le G. N.

MONTAGUE. [See also Montagu.]

MONTAGUE, Baron (1492?–1539). [See Pole, Henry.]

MONTAGUE, HENRY JAMES (1843?–1878), actor, whose real name was Mann, held an appointment in the Sun Fire Office. After playing as an amateur he appeared at Astley's Theatre under Dion Boucicault, enacting on 26 Jan. 1863 the Junior Counsel for the Defence in the 'Trial of Effie Deans,' extracted by Boucicault from the 'Heart of Midlothian.' At the St. James's on 11 Jan. 1864 he appeared with Charles Mathews in the 'Adventures of a Love Letter,' an adaptation by Mathews of M. Sardou's 'Pattes de Mouche,' was Faust in Mr. Burnand's burlesque 'Faust and Marguerite,' 9 July, and 1 Oct. Christopher Larkins in 'Woodcock's Little Game.' On 29 June 1865 he was the original Launcelot Darrell, a murderer, in 'Eleanor's Victory,' adapted from Miss Braddon by John Oxenford; at the Olympic, 9 Dec., the original Clement Austin in 'Henry Dunbar, or the Outcast,' adapted by Tom Taylor from 'L'Ouvrière de Londres,' itself founded by M. Hostein on Miss Braddon's novel; on 25 April 1866 was the first Sir Charles Ormond in Leicester Buckingham's 'Love's Martyrdom;' and on 27 Sept. 1866 the first Captain Trevor in Tom Taylor's 'Whiteboy.' On the production of Wilkie Collins's 'Frozen Deep,' 27 Oct. 1866, he was Frank Aldersley, and he played Mars in Mr. Burnand's burlesque 'Olympic Games' on 25 May 1867. Montague's first appearance at the Prince of Wales's under the Bancroft management took place as Dick Heartley, an original part, in Boucicault's 'How she loves him,' 21 Dec. 1867, and Frank Price in Robertson's 'Play' followed, 15 Feb. 1868. At the Princess's, 12 Aug. 1868, he was the original Sir George Medhurst in 'After Dark,' an adaptation by Boucicault of 'Les Oiseaux de Proie' of D'Ennery and Grangé. Back at the Prince of Wales's he was, 12 Dec. 1868, the original Waverham in Mr. Edmund Yates's 'Tame Cats,' and on 16 Jan. 1869 made his first distinct mark as Lord Beaufoy in Robertson's 'School.' In partnership with David James (*d.* 1893) and Mr. Thomas Thorne he opened the Vaudeville Theatre on 16 April 1870, speaking an address by Shirley Brooks, and playing George Anderson in Andrew Halliday's comedy 'For Love or Money.' In Albery's 'Two Roses,' 4 June 1870, he made a hit as Jack Wyatt to the Digby Grant of Mr. Henry Irving. In 1871 he seceded from the management, and became sole lessee of the Globe, opening 7 Oct. 1871 with Byron's 'Partners for Life,' in which he played Tom Gilroy, a young barrister. Here he remained till 1874, playing numerous original parts, among which were: Claude Redruth in Albery's 'Forgiven,' 9 March 1872; Walker in Byron's 'Spur of the Moment,' founded on Hooke's 'Gilbert Gurney,' 4 May 1872; Lord Chilton in Frank Marshall's 'False Shame,' 4 Nov. 1872; Wilfrid Cumberledge in 'Tears, Idle Tears,' adapted by Mr. Clement Scott from the 'Marcel' of Jules Sandeau, 4 Dec. 1872; King Raymond in Albery's 'Oriana,' 5 Feb. 1873; Sir Henry Gaisford in Byron's 'Fine Feathers,' 26 April 1873; Toots in 'Heart's Delight,' adapted by Halliday from 'Dombey and Son,' 17 Dec. 1873; and Alfred Trimble in 'Committed for Trial,' Mr. Gilbert's adaptation of 'Le Réveillon,' 24 Jan. 1874. This was the last original character he played in England. He had also been seen in the 'Liar,' had played Max Harkaway in 'London Assurance,' Cyril in Byron's 'Cyril's Success,' Felix in Jerrold's 'Time works Wonders,' John Hawksley in 'Still Waters run deep,' and Claude Melnotte in the 'Lady of Lyons.' He also gave dramatic readings at Hanover Square Rooms. In 1874 he started for the United States, was in London in 1876, and assumed for a benefit, 27 July 1876, his original part of Jack Wyatt in 'Two Roses;' then returned to America, dying in San Francisco on 11 Aug. 1878, while on tour with a company playing 'Diplomacy.' A bright, versatile man, with a pleasant face and good figure and sociable manners, Montague was a favourite on and off the stage, founding convivial clubs in both London and New York. He had some earnestness and force, but was seen to most advantage in juvenile parts. His Claude Melnotte was poor, and in other serious parts he was not very successful.

[Personal reminiscences; Sunday Times newspaper, 1863–74; Era newspaper, 18 Oct. 1878; Era Almanack, 1879; Scott and Howard's Life and Reminiscences of E. L. Blanchard; Mr. and Mrs. Bancroft on and off the Stage.] J. K.

MONTAIGNE or **MOUNTAIN, GEORGE** (1569–1628), archbishop of York, was born in 1569 at Cawood, Yorkshire, of humble parents. The statement that he belonged to the Montaignes of Weston is incorrect. According to local tradition he was the son of a small farmer at Cawood, the site of whose homestead was long pointed out (Erskine Neale, *Chancellor's Chaplain*, p. 80), and determined in his youth to become archbishop of York and to occupy the palace at Cawood. Another less trustworthy story (*Notes and Queries*, 7th ser. xii. 38) says his mother was a beggar-woman in the neighbourhood of Lincoln, and that, fearing punishment for some fault, he ran away from her and entered the household of a Lincoln gentleman, who educated him with his son. When bishop of Lincoln he is said to have discovered his mother in a beggar who opened a gate for him, and to have handsomely provided for her. He entered Queens' College, Cambridge, as a sizar 24 Oct. 1586, and matriculated 10 Dec. (his name is written 'Moonta' in the register). He graduated B.A. 1589–90, M.A. 1593, and was admitted fellow of his college 8 July 1592 (elected in 1591). In January 1594–5 he was ordained by Howland, bishop of Peterborough, and graduated B.A. Becoming chaplain to Robert Devereux, second earl of Essex, he attended the earl, according to Fuller, on the expedition to Cadiz in 1596, and showed 'such personall valour that out of his gown he would turn his back to no man' (Fuller, *Worthies*, 'Yorkshire,' p. 199). After Essex's disgrace he returned to Cambridge, and was appointed proctor in 1600. On 27 May 1602 he became rector of Great Cressingham, Norfolk, and obtained a dispensation to enjoy his fellowship for seven years, with any living within thirty miles of Cambridge (*Cal. State Papers*, James I, 1603–10, p. 142). On 4 March 1607 he was appointed professor of divinity at Gresham College, London, and proceeded D.D. at Cambridge in the same year. For some time he acted as chaplain to Sir Robert Cecil, afterwards earl of Salisbury, and probably thus first came under the notice of James I. His conversational facility and ready wit pleased the king, and promotion followed rapidly. On 22 Oct. 1608 the king granted him the mastership of the Savoy for life, made him one of his chaplains, and presented him in 1609 to the living of Cheam, Surrey. On 28 Nov. 1610 he was appointed dean of Westminster. But Montaigne's chief desire—to become provost of his own college (Queens')—was not realised. He had given a piece of plate, afterwards called 'poculum caritatis,' to the college, with the inscription 'incipio,' which, on his failure to obtain the vacant provostship in 1614, he wished to change into 'sic desino.' He founded, however, two scholarships at the college. On 22 June 1614 he was made one of the first governors of the new Charterhouse hospital. During his residence at Westminster two royal persons, Prince Henry [q. v.] and Arabella Stuart [q. v.], were buried in the abbey, and Mary Queen of Scots' coffin brought thither from Peterborough (1612). On 18 Oct. 1615 Robert Carr, earl of Somerset [q. v.], for complicity in the Overbury murder, was committed to the dean's custody till 2 Nov., when he was sent to the Tower.

From Westminster Montaigne was promoted in October 1617 to the bishopric of Lincoln, to which see he was consecrated 14 Dec. in Lambeth Chapel. His friend, Marco Antonio de Dominis [q. v.], archbishop of Spalatro, assisted in the ceremony, but five years later Montaigne took part in sentencing the archbishop to banishment from the realm for holding intercourse with the pope (*Cal. State Papers*, James I, 1619–23, pp. 366, 370). In June 1619 Montaigne succeeded the Bishop of Winchester as lord high almoner, and in October entertained the king at his episcopal palace of Buckden, Huntingdonshire. In March 1621 he and Bishop Andrewes of Winchester, in the name of the other prelates, presented a grant of subsidies passed by the clergy of the province of Canterbury to the king at Hampton Court. In June Montaigne was promoted to the bishopric of London and enthroned on 10 Sept. His first official act was the consecration of Williams, dean of Westminster, to the bishopric of Lincoln, in Westminster Abbey, 11 Nov. 1621. Montaigne belonged to the high church party, and sided with Laud in successfully contesting the right of Archbishop George Abbot [q. v.], who had accidentally shot a gamekeeper, to perform the ceremony. He soon proved himself an ardent ally of Laud; preached the doctrine of passive obedience from the pulpit, and was commended by the king for permitting the erection and adoration of images in churches, and for suppressing popular lay lecturers. When Abbot refused to license sermons by Sibthorp and Roger Manwaring for the press, Montaigne asserted that they were 'fit to be printed' (LAUD, *Works*, vii. 7), and gave his license for their publication. But he afterwards declared from his place in the House of Lords that he had not read the sermons himself, and had licensed them only on the express command of the king (FORSTER, *Eliot*, ii. 308).

In 1623 he consecrated the new chapel at Lincoln's Inn, where an inscription recording the fact was placed beneath the arms of the see. Montaigne's ambition was still unsatisfied, and he 'would often pleasantly say that of him the proverb would be verified, "Lincoln was, and London is, and York shall be."' It was therefore a bitter blow when, late in 1627, Charles appointed him bishop of Durham, to make room for Laud in the London see. Charles, less attached to Montaigne than his father, looked upon him as 'a man unactive,' and 'one that loved his own ease too well to disturb himself in the concernments of the church' (HEYLYN, *Cyp. Angl.* p. 174). This opinion seemed justified by the earnestness with which the bishop now protested that Durham was 'the worst kind of banishment, next neighbour to a civil death.' By his perseverance he obtained permission to remain 'in the warm air of the court,' only removing from London House in the city to Durham House in the Strand. He was elected to Durham 15 Feb. 1627-8, but in April the see of York was vacated by the death of Tobie Matthew [q. v.] Montaigne strained every nerve to obtain this prize, and, according to a well-known anecdote, when Charles was discussing the question of the vacant see in his presence, he remarked: '"Hadst thou faith as a grain of mustard seed, thou wouldst say unto this mountain (at the same time laying his hand upon his breast), be removed into that sea."' The king laughed, and at once wrote to the dean and chapter of York (4 June 1628) to elect the witty prelate to the archbishopric.

The election took place on 1 July, but the primate was 'scarce warm in his church yet cold in his coffin' (FULLER), for he died in London, aged 59, on 24 Oct., the very day he was enthroned by commission at York. He was buried by his own desire in Cawood Church, where his brother Isaac put up a monument to him (now much dilapidated), with a Latin inscription and verses by Hugh Holland [q. v.] the poet. His benevolence left him poor. He bequeathed the bulk of his property to his brother, and 100*l.* to the poor at Cawood, besides rings to four little girls, whom he was wont pleasantly to call his wives. John Ward, author of 'Gresham Professors,' declares that he knew a Lincolnshire clergyman, one Farmery, who called himself great-grandson to the archbishop, his great-grandfather having, he said, married Montaigne's daughter, but there is no mention of either wife or daughter in the archbishop's will, dated 12 Feb. 1627.

Besides his benefactions to Queens' College, Cambridge, Montaigne, while bishop of London, zealously promoted the building of St. Paul's, preaching on the subject at St. Paul's Cross, and giving a large sum of money towards the purchase of Portland stone.

[Authorities quoted in text; Le Neve's Lives of the Protestant Bishops, i. 117; Syllabus of Rymer's Fœdera, ii. 840; Heylyn's Life of Laud, p. 166; Yonge's Diary, pp. 44, 50, 109; Newcourt's Repertorium, i. 29, 30, 719; Neale and Brayley's History of Westminster Abbey, i. 129-31; Calendars of State Papers, Dom. James I, 1610-30; Notes and Queries, 7th ser. xi. 487.] E. T. S.

MONTALBA, HENRIETTA SKERRETT (1856-1893), sculptor, born in London in 1856, was the youngest of the four daughters of Anthony Rubens and Emeline Montalba, all of whom, especially the eldest, Miss Clara Montalba, attained high repute as artists. Miss Montalba, who adopted sculpture for her branch of art, studied first at South Kensington, and then in the school of the Belle Arti at Venice. Later she became a pupil of M. Jules Dalou, the eminent French sculptor, during his residence in London. Miss Montalba first exhibited at the Royal Academy in 1876, and her work was often seen at the Grosvenor Gallery, the New Gallery, and elsewhere. She mainly devoted herself to portrait or fancy busts; some executed in marble, like those of Doctor Mezger of Amsterdam (Grosvenor Gallery, 1886), and Dr. Schollander, the Scandinavian artist; others in bronze, like that of the Marquis of Lorne; but the greater part of her work was executed in terra-cotta, as in the case of her bust of Robert Browning (Grosvenor Gallery, 1883). Other works worthy of note were 'A Dalecarlian Peasant Woman' and 'The Raven,' representing a raven seated on a bust of Pallas, from the poem by E. A. Poe. Her last work was of a more ambitious nature, being a life-size figure of 'A Venetian Boy catching a Crab,' executed in bronze, which was exhibited at the Royal Academy in 1893, and at the International Exhibition, Chicago, in the same year. Miss Montalba was never separated from her family, residing in later days chiefly at Venice, and making frequent visits with them in Italy, Sweden, and elsewhere. Her pleasing and attractive personality gained her numerous friends. Besides her artistic gifts she possessed great linguistic talent. In 1892 her health began to fail her, and after a lingering illness she died at the Palazzo Trevisan, Zattere, Venice, on 14 Sept. 1893, and was buried near her father in the neighbouring cemetery of S. Michele. Miss Montalba was on terms of friendship with the Princess Louise (Duchess of Argyll), who painted a portrait of her and presented it to the Academy of Ottawa in Canada (see *The Queen*, 7 Oct. 1893). Other portraits of her, by her sisters, Hilda and Ellen Montalba, remain in the possession of her family.

[The Queen, 7 Oct. 1893; private information; personal knowledge.] L. C.

MONTE, ROBERT DE (1110?–1186), chronicler. [See Robert.]

MONTEAGE, STEPHEN (1623?–1687), merchant and accountant, born about 1623, was son of Stephen Monteage of Buckingham and of his wife Jane (*d.* 1670), daughter of Edward Deane of Pinnock in Gloucestershire. He was apprenticed to James Houblon, merchant, of London (*Addit. MS.* 29559, f. 175), with whose family he remained on terms of friendship all his life [see Houblon, Sir John]. Monteage did much towards bringing into general use the method of keeping accounts by double entry. In 1670 he was residing in Broad Street, London (*ib.* 29552, f. 406), and in 1677 in Winchester Street. He was agent to Christopher Hatton, first viscount Hatton (1632–1706) [q. v.], and his letters in that capacity are now in the British Museum. Monteage was as zealous in small matters as large; his letters are as precise in detail whether they refer to the extra yard or two of velvet which he saved by personally superintending the cutting-out of Lord Hatton's robe for the coronation of James II (*ib.* 29561, ff. 91–132), or to the large sums required for the payment of the troops in Guernsey. Monteage died on 21 Oct. 1687, and was buried in the church of All Hallows-on-the-Wall (parish register). He left several children. His eldest son, Dean Monteage, succeeded him as agent to Lord Hatton, and was accomptant-general to the commissioners of excise. Another son, John, who had been 'very chargeable in his education and travels abroad,' was in business as a merchant in January 1687, and was residing in Bond's Court, Walbrook, in 1694. Monteage also left two daughters. His grandson, Stephen Monteage (born 5 July 1681, son of Dean Monteage), was in 1735 stock accomptant to the York Buildings Company, of which company he was also a 'proprietor.' He was in 1738 employed on the accounts of the South Sea Company, and later on in the customs.

Monteage published: 1. 'Debtor and Creditor,' London, 1675, to which his portrait, engraved by E. le Davis, is prefixed. 2. 'Instructions for Rent-gatherers' Accompts, &c., made easie,' London, 1683.

[Granger's Biographical History of England, iv. 101; London Directory, 1677 (reprint of 1878); Browne Willis's Hist. of Buckingham, pp. 68, 72; P. C. C., 140, Foot; Political State, March 1735, p. 223; List of the Corporation of the York Buildings Company, 1735; Addit. MSS. 29555–64, passim; Diary of Stephen Monteage the younger, MS. 205 in the Guildhall Library.] B. P.

MONTEAGLE, Barons. [See Stanley, Edward, first Baron, 1460?–1523; Parker, William, fourth Baron, 1575–1622.]

MONTEAGLE of Brandon, first Baron (1790–1866). [See Spring-Rice, Thomas.]

MONTEATH, GEORGE CUNNINGHAM (1788–1828), physician and oculist, son of John Monteath, minister of the parish of Neilston, was born there on 4 Dec. 1788. He attended the medical classes in Glasgow, and afterwards studied under Sir Astley Cooper in London, where he was licensed as a practitioner by the Royal College of Surgeons. From 1809 to 1813 he acted as surgeon to the Northumberland regiment of militia, and then established himself in Glasgow as a physician and oculist. His practice increased rapidly. He was the first specialist in cases of eye disease to practise in Glasgow, and every case of difficulty in the west of Scotland came under his treatment. In 1821 he published a 'Manual of the Diseases of the Human Eye,' 2 vols. 8vo, which was long a standard book. Monteath died from a chill in Glasgow on 25 Jan. 1828.

[Chambers's Biog. Dict. of Eminent Scotsmen; Anderson's Popular Scottish Biography.] G. S-h.

MONTEATH, Sir THOMAS (1787–1868), general. [See Douglas, Sir Thomas Monteath.]

MONTEFIORE, Sir MOSES HAIM (1784–1885), philanthropist and centenarian, eldest son of Joseph Eliahu Montefiore, Italian merchant, of London, by Rachel, daughter of Abraham Lumbroso de Mattos Mocatta, was born in the Via Reale, Leghorn, on 24 Oct. 1784. His paternal ancestors were Jewish merchants settled in the seventeenth century at Ancona and Leghorn, his grandfather and namesake having emigrated from the latter place to London in 1758. His mother's family was of the most ancient among the Spanish Jews.

Montefiore received an ordinary commercial education in London, and, after spending some time in a mercantile house, acquired for 1,200*l.* the right to act as a broker on the London Stock Exchange, where the number of Jewish brokers was then limited to twelve. He rapidly amassed a fortune, and in 1824 retired from business. Thenceforth he gave himself up almost entirely to the service of the Jewish race at home and abroad. In 1827, on his way to Jerusalem, he paid a first visit to Egypt, where he had a private audience of Mehemet Ali. On his return to England he became a member of the United Deputies of British Jews, and threw himself with energy into the struggle for emancipation. In 1837 he was chosen sheriff of London, and knighted on the occasion of the queen's visit to Guildhall (9 Nov.) Full of a scheme for planting Jewish colonies in Syria, he returned to the Levant in 1839, and submitted it to Mehemet Ali, who promised to give it favourable consideration, and suffered it to fall through. In the following summer he intervened on behalf of some unfortunate Jews who had been arrested and tortured at Damascus on a charge of 'ritual murder.' At the head of a deputation from the Jewish communities of England and France, he pleaded the cause of the prisoners before Mehemet Ali, convinced him of their innocence, and obtained their release (September 1840). He then proceeded to Constantinople, and obtained from the sultan a firman, placing Jews on the same footing as other aliens throughout the Ottoman empire (November). On his return to England Montefiore was presented to the queen, who testified her sympathy with his self-denying exertions on behalf of his race by granting him the privilege of bearing supporters to his arms, with the inscription 'Jerusalem' in Hebrew characters. His own people recognised his services by the appointment of a day of thanksgiving, and the presentation to him of a silver pyramid ornamented with allegorical figures.

On 20 April 1844 (O.S.) Tsar Nicholas of Russia issued a ukase for the removal into the interior of all Jews domiciled within fifty versts of the German and Austrian frontiers. When the news of this unjust act reached England, Montefiore made strong representations to the Russian ambassador, Count Brunnow, which resulted in a suspension of the ukase. Its threatened reissue brought Montefiore to St. Petersburg in the spring of 1846. He was admitted by the tsar to a private audience, and obtained the abrogation of the obnoxious ukase. At the tsar's suggestion he made a tour in Eastern Russia, in the course of which he made careful notes of the condition of the Jewish population, which he afterwards communicated to the Russian ministry. On his return to England a baronetcy was conferred upon him (23 July 1846).

In consequence of a revival of strong anti-Semitic feeling in Syria in 1847, Montefiore obtained through Guizot (9 Aug.) a private audience of Louis-Philippe, whom he besought, as protector of the Christians in that country, to repress the agitation. The king received him with marked respect, and gave and kept the desired promise.

Montefiore took a principal part in the collection and distribution of the fund for the relief of the sufferers by the Syrian famine of 1855, in the summer of which year he founded at Jerusalem a girls' school and hospital; some almshouses were erected at a later date. In 1858 Montefiore's attention was engrossed by the celebrated Mortara case. Edgar Mortara, a child of Jewish parents resident at Bologna, had been secretly baptised by his catholic nurse, who disclosed the fact in the confessional; and on 23 June 1858 the papal police, acting under the instructions of the holy office, removed the child from the custody of his parents and placed him in a Dominican convent to be educated as a Christian. The child's father applied in vain both to the holy office and to the pope for his restitution, and his mother died of grief. The affair created a panic among the Jewish population of Italy, and aroused the utmost indignation throughout Europe, and remonstrances were addressed to the papal government by the great powers, but without effect. As a last resource Montefiore undertook the almost hopeless enterprise of personal appeal to Pope Pius IX, and in April 1859 went to Rome for the purpose. The audience was refused; the pope consented, through Cardinal Antonelli, to receive Montefiore's petition, but remained inflexible. Mortara was educated as a catholic, and eventually entered the priesthood.

In 1860 Montefiore's impartial philanthropy was exercised in raising funds for the relief both of Jewish refugees, whom the apprehension of war between Spain and Morocco had brought to Gibraltar, and of the Christian survivors of the massacre of the Lebanon. In the spring of 1863 he visited Constantinople, and obtained the confirmation by the new Sultan, Abdul-Aziz, of all firmans granted by his predecessor in favour of the Jews. An outbreak of anti-Semitic fanaticism in Tangier in the following autumn led the veteran philanthropist, now in his eighty-first year, to undertake a mission to Morocco. H.M.S. Magicienne carried him from Gibraltar to Mogador, whence, under an escort provided by the sultan, he crossed the Atlas desert, arriving at Morocco on 26 Jan. 1864. He was well received by the sultan, who issued an edict placing the Jews upon a footing of perfect equality with his other subjects. In 1866 he was once more in Syria, distributing alms to the sufferers by a recent plague of locusts and epidemic of cholera. In the following year he visited Bucharest, and interceded with Prince Charles on behalf of the persecuted Jews of Moldavia (August 1867). By the prince he was well received, but the excited populace surrounded his hotel and threatened his life. Though in ill-health, he maintained perfect self-possession, quieted the mob by addressing them from an open window, and afterwards drove through the streets without escort in an open carriage. In 1872, on the occasion of the bicentenary of the birth of Peter the Great, Montefiore carried to St. Petersburg an address from the British Jewish community felicitating Tsar Alexander II upon the event. He was then in his eighty-eighth year, and the tsar, to mark his respect for his aged visitor, left his troops, whose summer manœuvres he was then directing, and returned to St. Petersburg to receive him at the Winter Palace (24 July). A seventh and final pilgrimage to Jerusalem, which Montefiore made in the summer of 1875, is described in his 'Narrative of a Forty Days' Sojourn in the Holy Land,' printed for private circulation on his return.

He passed the rest of his days in comparative seclusion at his seat, East Cliff Lodge, Ramsgate, where he died on 28 July 1885, within three months of completing his hundred and first year. His remains were interred in a private mausoleum on his estate. Montefiore was one of the strictest of Jews, rigidly orthodox in his religious opinions, and scrupulously exact in his observance of the precepts of the Mosaic law. On his death without issue the baronetcy became extinct, but a similar honour was conferred, on 16 Feb. 1886, on Montefiore's grandnephew, Francis Abraham Montefiore (*b.* 1860). Montefiore was brought into close relationship with the Rothschild family by his marriage, 10 June 1812, with Judith, second daughter of Levi Barent Cohen, whose sister Hannah was wife of Baron Nathan Mayer de Rothschild (1777–1836). Lady Montefiore was a woman no less remarkable for vigour and refinement of mind than for beauty, piety, and benevolence. She died on 24 Sept. 1862, and was buried in the mausoleum at Ramsgate.

Lady Montefiore was her husband's inseparable companion in his wanderings, which not unfrequently involved great personal risk and hardship. Their first expedition to the East is described in her entertaining 'Private Journal of a Visit to Egypt and Palestine by way of Italy and the Mediterranean,' printed for private circulation, London, 1836, 8vo. A portrait of Montefiore by H. Weigall was lent by him to the Victorian Exhibition.

[Diaries of Sir Moses and Lady Montefiore, ed. Dr. L. Loewe, 1890 (portrait); Wolf's Sir Moses Montefiore, 1884; Bailey's Modern Methuselahs, 1888; An Open Letter addressed to Sir Moses Montefiore, bart., &c., 1875.] J. M. R.

MONTEITH, ROBERT (*fl.* 1621–1660), historian. [See Menteith.]

MONTEITH, WILLIAM (1790–1864), lieutenant-general Indian army, diplomatist and historian, son of William Monteith and his wife Janet Goodwin, was born in the Abbey parish, Paisley, Renfrewshire, on 22 June 1790. On 18 March 1809 he was appointed a lieutenant in the Madras engineers, and became captain in that corps on 2 May 1817, lieutenant-colonel on 4 Nov. 1824, colonel on 13 May 1839 (brevet on 18 June 1831). Monteith accompanied Sir John Malcolm's embassy to Persia, and when at Tabriz, in February 1810, was sent to reconnoitre the Russian frontier-posts on the Arras, near Megeri, at the request of Abbas Mirza, the prince royal of Persia. When Malcolm's embassy quitted Persia, Monteith was one of the officers left behind. He went with Abbas Mirza to Erivan, and accompanied an expedition into Georgia, in which the Persians were unsuccessful. During the four succeeding campaigns against the Russians in 1810–13 Monteith was in command of a frontier force of cavalry with six guns, and of the garrison of Erivan. He was engaged in many skirmishes, and once was wounded. The war against Russia was supported by the British minister, Sir Harford Jones Brydges [q. v.]; but the Moscow retreat brought about a reversal of British policy. When Henry Ellis [see Ellis, Sir Henry, 1777–1855] and David Richard Morier [q. v.] concluded the treaty of Teheran between Great Britain and Persia, which was signed on 25 Nov. 1814, and remained in force until the war of 1857, Monteith acted as secretary to Morier. He was still in Persia in 1819, and acted as aide-de-camp to Sir William Grant Keir, afterwards Keir Grant [q. v.], commanding the Bombay force sent against the Wahabee pirates of the Persian Gulf, which destroyed their stronghold of Ras-el-Khymeh. He was present with the Persians during the war with Turkey, which was ended by the visitation of Asiatic cholera in 1821. He was then employed to ascertain the boundary between Persia and Turkey.

In 1826 the threatened storm from the north broke, and in the unsuccessful operations of the Persians against the Russians Monteith was present at the Persian headquarters. Peace was signed between Russia and Persia on 21 Feb. 1828, and Monteith was appointed commissioner for the payment of the indemnity of 400,000*l.* exacted from Persia by Russia, part of which was conveyed by him personally into the Russian camp. He was thus brought into contact with the Russian commander, Prince Paskiewitch, which led to his presence at the Russian headquarters at Tiflis during the war between the Russians and Turks in 1828. He was ordered to remain in Persia until the settlement of the Russo-Persian boundary. He left Persia in October 1829, and on his way home was present with the French army at the capture of Algiers in July 1830. Monteith married on 23 March 1831. He returned to India in July 1832, and was appointed chief engineer at Madras, but in January 1834 was superseded by the arrival of Colonel Gurnard, who was ten years his senior. Monteith then became superintending engineer at the presidency, but on Gurnard's death, 2 Sept. 1836, he again became chief engineer, and, *ex officio*, a member of the military board, a position he held to 18 July 1842. He became a major-general on 23 Nov. 1841, retired from the service in 1847, and attained the honorary rank of lieutenant-general in 1854. He died at his residence, Upper Wigmore Street, London, on 18 April 1864, aged 73.

Monteith wrote: 'Kars and Erzeroum, with the Campaign of Prince Paskiewitch,' London, 1856, 8vo; translated 'The Diplomatists of Europe' from the French of Capefigue, London, 1845, 8vo; and edited 'Narrative of the Conquest of Finland by the Russians in 1808–9,' London, 1854, 8vo. He was also author of the following geographical works: 1. 'Mémoire pour servir à la Descript. Géogr. de la Perse,' in 'Soc. Géogr. Bulletin,' 1826, vi. 35–41. 2. 'Account of the Ragery Hills, near Madras,' 'Geogr. Soc. Journal,' 1835, p. 404. 3. 'Account of the Operations for widening the Pamban Passage in the Gulf of Manaar,' 'Madras Journal,' 1836, vi. 111–36. 4. 'Journal of a Tour through Azerdbijan and the Shores of the Caspian,' 'Geogr. Soc. Journal,' 1838, iii. 1–58. 5. 'Notes on the Routes from Bushire to Shiraz,' 'Geogr. Soc. Journal,' 1857, xxvii. 108–19. Monteith was F.R.S. and F.R.G.S. London, a member of various foreign learned societies, and a knight of the Persian order of the Lion and Sun.

[Information supplied by the India Office; Vibart's Hist. of the Madras Sappers and Miners, London, 1884, ii. 113–31; Brit. Museum Catalogues, and Cat. of Scient. Papers; Gent. Mag. 1864, i. 378.] H. M. C.

MONTEZ, LOLA (1818–1861), dancer and adventuress. [See Gilbert, Marie Dolores Eliza Rosanna.]

MONTFICHET, RICHARD de (*d.* 1268), justiciar, was son of Richard de Montfichet, whom Henry II made forester of Essex. Richard the elder was son of Gilbert and grandson of William de Montfichet, founder of the abbey of Stratford-Langton Essex; he was with Richard I in Normandy in 1195, was sheriff of Essex and Hertfordshire in 1202, and died next year, leaving one son by his wife Milisent. The young Richard was then about ten years old, and was at first a ward of Roger de Lacy [q. v.] He appears as witnessing several charters in 1214, and on 21 June 1215 received charge of the forests of Essex as his by hereditary right. He had nevertheless acted previously with the baronial party, and been present at the meeting at Stamford in March. He was one of the twenty-five barons appointed to enforce the observance of Magna Charta, and as a prominent member of the party was excommunicated by the pope in 1216. He supported Louis of France both before and after John's death, and fighting at Lincoln against William Marshal on 20 May 1217 was then taken prisoner. He returned to loyalty, and recovered his lands in the following October (*Cal. Rot. Claus.* i. 327). In 1223 his lands were again for a time seized by the king in consequence of his presence at a prohibited tournament at Blythe. In 1225 he was a justice-itinerant for Essex and Hertfordshire (*ib.* ii. 76), and in the same year was a witness to the confirmation of Magna Charta. In 1234 he was admitted to sit as a baron of the exchequer, and in 1236 again witnessed the confirmation of the charter. He was justice of the forest for nineteen counties in 1237, and from 1242 to 1246 sheriff of Essex and Hertfordshire, the counties in which his estates lay. Montfichet was one of the baronial representatives on the committee to consider the king's demand for a subsidy in 1244, and probably therefore had a share in drafting the remarkable scheme of reform of that year (Matt. Paris, iv. 362–8). He died in 1268 without issue, and his estates passed to the children of his three sisters. Montfichet is of chief note for his share in the struggle for the charter. He was the last survivor of the twenty-five; his age probably prevented his taking any part in the later barons' war, which he outlived.

[Matthew Paris; Annales Monastici; Calendars of Close and Patent Rolls; Dugdale's Baronage, i. 438–9; Foss's Judges of England, pp. 412–14; Stubbs's Constitutional History, §175.] C. L. K.

MONTFORT, ALMERIC OF (*d.* 1292?), was a son of Simon of Montfort, earl of Leicester [q. v.], and his wife Eleanor, daughter of King John. Almeric seems to have been their fourth child, and must have been born between 1244 and 1250. Destined for holy orders, he was appointed canon and treasurer of York Minster in February 1265 (BLAAUW, *Barons' War*, p. 333, *n.* 3). After his father's fall these preferments were withdrawn, 7 Aug. 1265 (BOTFIELD, App. p. 87). One chronicle says that he stole from the minster-treasury part of the eleven thousand marks which he and his brother Richard carried with them to Gravelines on 18 Sept. (cf. BOTFIELD, p. 74; *ib.* App. p. 88; GREEN, *Princesses*, ii. 147). On 4 Dec. 1267 the Archbishop of Rouen granted him a license to receive ordination from any continental bishop (BÉMONT, p. 255, *n.* 10). In 1268 he went to Italy, and for the next three years studied at the university of Padua; he was also made one of the pope's chaplains. In April 1271 he was charged with complicity in the murder of Henry of Cornwall [q. v.] at Viterbo, but the bishop and chapter of Padua, the doctors and scholars of the university, and the whole body of friars in the city, cleared him by joining in a written declaration that he had never been out of Padua since October, and that at the time of the murder, 13 March, he was at death's door with fever. On 19 April 1272 he was at Rome, whence he returned to the abbot of Monte Cassino three books on medicine which he had borrowed, probably for his studies at Padua. He still called himself treasurer of York, and his only surviving brother, Guy [q. v.], being now an outlaw, he had also assumed the title of Earl of Leicester (BÉMONT, App. pp. 365–7). Next year he attempted to return to England in the company of his father's old friend, Stephen Berksted [q. v.], bishop of Chichester, but Edward I refused to let either Stephen or Almeric set foot in the country (*Chron. Maj. Lond.* p. 159). In October 1274 Almeric was suing Edmund Mortimer, who had been made treasurer of York in his place, before the official of Paris, and he seems to have induced the pope to threaten Edmund with excommunication (BÉMONT, p. 256, *n.* 3). A year later he appears to have been striving for a revocation of the papal censures which still rested on his father's memory (*Hist. MSS. Comm.* 4th Rep. p. 396). Late in 1275, or early in 1276, when escorting his sister [see MONTFORT, ELEANOR OF] into Wales, he was captured at Bristol; Edward I, who still suspected him of murder and treason, kept him in prison for six years, first at Corfe, and afterwards at Sherborne (*Ann. Osney*, p. 267; RISHANGER, p. 87; GREEN, *Princesses*, ii. 163; *Cont.* WILL. TYR. l. ii. c. 22). Liberated on 21 April 1282, on condition of abjuring the realm (*Fœdera*, vol. i. pt. ii. p. 605), he wrote to the king from Arras on 22 May, thanking him for his grace, promising fidelity, and asking for liberty to 'recover his rights' by process of law in England (CHAMPOLLION, *Lettres de Rois*, i. 301). The demand being refused or ignored, in December 1284 he began a suit in the court of Rome against Edmund of Lancaster, the king's brother, for restitution of his inheritance (*Fœdera*, vol. i. pt. ii. p. 651). He was in Paris again on 18 June 1286 (BÉMONT, App. pp. 369–70). It was reported that on his brother Guy's death in 1287–8 Almeric renounced his orders and became a knight (*Flores Hist.* iii. 67). He is said to have lived till 1292 (BÉMONT, p. 258). He was in any case the last male survivor of his family; for the fifth brother, Richard, who had accompanied him into exile in 1265, died in France shortly afterwards (*Ann. Dunst.* p. 259).

[Documents in Rymer's Fœdera, vol. i. pt. i.; Bémont's Simon de Montfort; Botfield and Turner's Manners and Household Expenses in Thirteenth Century (Roxburghe Club); Mrs. Everett Green's Princesses of England, vol. ii.; Rishanger's Chronicle, ed. Riley, Flores Historiarum ('Matt. Westminster,' ed. Luard), Annals of Osney (Annales Monastici, vol. iv.) and of Dunstable (*ib.* vol. iii.), all in Rolls Ser.; Chronica Majorum Londoniarum, ed. Stapleton (Liber de Antiquis Legibus, Camden Soc.)] K. N.

MONTFORT, ELEANOR OF (1252–1282), only daughter of Simon of Montfort, earl of Leicester [q. v.], and Eleanor his wife, seems to have been their youngest child, born at Kenilworth in October 1252 (ADAM MARSH, *Epp.* p. 262; cf. GREEN, *Princesses*, ii. 104). She went into exile in France with her mother about November 1265 (cf. *Ann. Monast.* iii. 259, and GREEN, ii. 149–51). In 1275 she was married by proxy to Llywelyn ab Gruffydd [q. v.], prince of Wales, to whom she had been betrothed before her father's death, and at the close of the year she set out with her brother Almeric [q. v.] for Wales, but their ship was captured in the Bristol Channel on behalf of the English king (*Ann. Monast.* ii. 121, iii. 259, 266, iv. 266–7; *Cont.* GERV. CANT. ii. 283; *Cont.* WILL. TYR. l. ii. c. 22). Eleanor was imprisoned for a week at Bristol, and afterwards at Windsor (GREEN, *Princesses*, ii. 163–4) till 1278, when Llywelyn submitted to Edward I, and was married to her in Edward's presence at Worcester on 13 Oct. (*Cont.* FLOR. WORC. ii. 219). In January 1281 Eleanor was at Windsor again, on a visit to the English court (GREEN, ii. 168); on 19 June 1282 she died, at the birth of a daughter, Gwenllian (*Cont.* FLOR. WORC. ii. 226). The child, whose father was killed in battle shortly after, was brought to England 'in her cradle,' passed her whole life as a nun at Sempringham, and died there on 7 June 1337 (BRUNNE, *Langtoft*, ii. 243).

[Letters of Adam Marsh (Monumenta Franciscana, vol. i.), Continuation of Gervase of Canterbury, Annales Monastici, vols. ii. iii. iv., all in Rolls Ser.; Continuation of Florence of Worcester (Engl. Hist. Soc.); Robert of Brunne's translation of Peter of Langtoft, ed. Hearne; Mrs. Everett Green's Princesses of England, vol. ii. Three letters from Eleanor to Edward I are in Rymer's Fœdera, vol. i. pt. ii.] K. N.

MONTFORT, GUY OF (1243?–1288?), son of Simon of Montfort, earl of Leicester [q. v.], and Eleanor his wife, seems to have been their third child, and was probably born about 1243. He shared with his eldest brother [see MONTFORT, HENRY OF] the command of the van of the barons' army at Lewes on 14 May 1264. At the battle of Evesham, 4 Aug. 1265, he was wounded and taken prisoner. Confined first at Windsor, and afterwards in Dover Castle, he escaped on 23 April (*Cont.* GERV. CANT. ii. 245), or in Whitsun week, 16–23 May 1266 (T. WYKES, p. 190), to France. Two or three years later he went to Italy, was made in 1268 governor of Tuscany for Charles of Anjou (*Flores Hist.* iii. 17; VILLANI, col. 260), and on 10 Aug. 1270 married the only child of Count Aldobrandino Rosso dell' Anguillara (*Cont.* FLOR. WORC. ii. 205–6). On 13 March 1271 he and his brother Simon [see MONTFORT, SIMON OF, the younger] murdered their cousin, Henry of Cornwall [q. v.] in a church at Viterbo, Guy taking the most prominent and brutal part in the crime, which he called vengeance for his father's death (RISHANGER, p. 67; VILLANI, col. 261). Sheltered by Rosso, Guy for two years eluded the justice of the king of Naples; at last, in March 1273, Edward I stirred up Pope Gregory X to call the sacrilegious criminal to account. Guy failed to obey the pope's citation, and was excommunicated and outlawed on 1 April. Some months later, as Gregory was passing through Florence, Guy appeared, barefooted, in his shirt, with a rope round his neck, and thus followed the pope for two miles along the road, begging for mercy. Gregory put him as a prisoner of the church into the custody of the king of Sicily. In May 1274 he seems to have bought his freedom by a payment of a thousand ounces of gold, furnished by his kinsfolk in France and by the Guelf cities of Italy. In the spring of 1279 the Prince of Salerno vainly interceded for him with Edward I; in January 1280 he was believed to be in Norway, and the Norwegian barons apologised to Edward for having failed to arrest his enemy, and promised to track him and catch him if they could; later in the year he was reported captured (RYMER, vol. i. pt. ii. pp. 501–2, 507, 512–13, 568, 577, 587). Either, however, they caught the wrong man, or he escaped again, for he was at large when in 1283 a new pope, Martin IV, not only pardoned him and allowed him to reclaim his wife's estates in Romagna, but on 11 May appointed him captain-general of the papal forces in Romagna (DUCHESNE, *Hist. Franc. Scriptt.* v. 886; cf. RISHANGER, p. 105, and W. NANGIS, p. 524). He was again in the service of Charles of Anjou when on 23 June 1287, while endeavouring to succour the French garrison at Catania, he was captured by the Aragonese admiral, Roger de Loria (*Chron. Rotom. Contin.* p. 345; cf. *Ann. Dunst.* p. 340); he died shortly afterwards in a Sicilian prison (PTOL. LUCCA, col. 1164; W. NANGIS, p. 572). He is said to have had two daughters, both of whom married and left descendants in Italy (CAMPANILE, *Armi dei Nobili*, p. 46).

[Continuation of Gervase of Canterbury, Annals of Dunstable (Annales Monastici, vol. iii.), Wykes (*ib.* vol. iv.), Flores Historiarum ('Matthew of Westminster'), Rishanger's Chronicle, ed. Riley, all in Rolls Ser.; Continuation of Florence of Worcester (Engl. Hist. Soc.); Rymer's Fœdera, vol. i. pt. ii.; Villani (Muratori's Rerum Italicarum Scriptores, vol. xiii.); Ptolemy of Lucca (*ib.* vol. xi.); William of Nangis (Rerum Gallicarum Scriptores, vol. xx.); Chronicon Rotomagense (*ib.* vol. xxiii.) See also Blaauw's Barons' War and Bémont's Simon de Montfort.] K. N.

MONTFORT, HENRY OF (1238–1265), eldest son of Simon of Montfort, earl of Leicester [q. v.], and his wife Eleanor of England, was born in Kenilworth Castle in December 1238 (MATT. PARIS, *Chron. Majora*, iii. 518). Henry III was his godfather (*ib.* p. 498). He was partly brought up in the household of Bishop Grosseteste (ADAM

MARSH, *Epp.* pp. 110, 129, 163). In June 1252 he accompanied his father to Gascony (*ib.* p. 129). When the king's half-brothers were expelled from England in 1258, Henry of Montfort secretly followed them to Boulogne and stirred up his father's friends to besiege them there (MATT. PARIS, *Chron. Majora*, v. 703). On 1 Jan. 1259 he was in France with his father, and with his own hand wrote his father's will (BÉMONT, *Simon de Montfort*, App. p. 330). On 13 Oct. 1260 he and his brother Simon [see MONTFORT, SIMON, the younger] were knighted by their cousin, the king's son Edward [see EDWARD I, king of England], and afterwards went with him to a tournament in France (*Flores Hist.* ii. 456). In January 1264 Henry was one of the deputies sent to represent the barons at the Mise of Amiens (HALLIWELL, Notes to RISHANGER, p. 122). When the Mise was set aside he commanded a body of troops despatched to secure the Welsh border. On 28 Feb. he stormed and sacked Worcester (*Ann. Worc.* p. 448), and soon afterwards took Gloucester, but on Edward's approach he made a truce with him and retired to Kenilworth (*Ann. Dunstable*, pp. 227–8; cf. RISHANGER, p. 21). With his brother Guy [q. v.] he led the van at the battle of Lewes, 14 May 1264 (HEMINGFORD, i. 315). After the victory, on 28 May, he was made constable of Dover Castle, governor of the Cinque ports, and treasurer of Sandwich (*Fœdera*, I. i. 441). In this capacity he gained the nickname of 'the wool-merchant,' by enforcing the prohibition laid by the new government on the export of wool so strictly that he was accused of seizing the wool for his own profit (*Ann. Wykes*, pp. 158–9). As constable of Dover he had for some time the custody of his captive cousin Edward (*ib.* p. 153). He fought and fell at Evesham, 4 Aug. 1265, by his father's side, and was buried with him in the neighbouring abbey.

[Letters of Adam Marsh (Monumenta Franciscana, vol. i.); Matt. Paris, Chronica Majora; Flores Historiarum ('Matt. Westminster'), Ann. Dunstaple (Annales Monastici, vol. iii.), Ann. Worcester and Wykes (*ib.* vol. iv.), all in Rolls Series; Rishanger's Chronicle, ed. Halliwell (Camden Soc.); Walter of Hemingford (Engl. Hist. Soc.)]
K. N.

MONTFORT, SIMON OF, EARL OF LEICESTER (1208?–1265), was son of Simon IV of Montfort l'Amaury (Normandy) and his wife Alice of Montmorency. The first lord of Montfort had owned nothing but a little castle on a 'strong mount,' halfway between Paris and Chartres, whence the family took its name. His son, Simon I, married the heiress of Evreux; their grandson, Simon III, married Amicia, daughter of Robert of Beaumont, third earl of Leicester. The fourth Earl of Leicester died childless in 1204 or 1205. In the partition of his inheritance between his two sisters the honour of Leicester fell to Amicia's share, and, her husband and her eldest son being dead, devolved upon her second son, Simon IV of Montfort. John recognised him as 'Earl of Leicester' in August 1206, but it does not appear that he was ever formally invested with the earldom, and in February 1207 John seized all the English estates of 'Count Simon of Montfort,' nominally for a debt which Simon owed him. They were restored a month later, but confiscated again before the end of the year. The Count of Montfort had been content to enter upon his patrimony, and also upon the Norman heritage of the Beaumonts, under the overlordship of Philip of France, and he had to pay the penalty laid upon all Norman barons having claims on both sides of the sea who took this course, the loss of his English inheritance. He now threw in his lot wholly with France and with the party of ecclesiastical orthodoxy against which, in the person of Pope Innocent III, John was setting himself in opposition. In 1208 Simon became captain-general of the French forces in the crusade against the Albigensians, who were supported by John's brother-in-law, Raymond of Toulouse. Simon's skill, courage, energy, and ruthlessness carried all before him, and speedily made him master of all southern Gaul. He continued to style himself Earl of Leicester, and he seems to have kept up his communications with England and to have been an object of deep interest and admiration to his fellow-barons there, for in 1210 John was scared by a rumour that they were plotting to set up Simon of Montfort as king in his stead. One of the conditions required by the pope for reconciliation with John in 1213 was that Simon should be restored to his rights. This John at first refused, but in July 1215 he yielded so far as to give the honour of Leicester into the charge of Simon's nephew Ralf, earl of Chester, 'for the benefit of the said Simon.' In May 1216 Simon, having gone to Paris to collect fresh troops for his war with the Aragonese, and to settle the questions as to the disposal of the family heritage which had arisen owing to his mother's death, joined with the legate Gualo in endeavouring to dissuade Louis of France from his designs upon England (ROBERT OF AUXERRE, *Rer. Gall. Scriptt.* xviii. 283–4). The Leicester estates seem to have been still in the hands of Ralf when Simon was killed at the siege of Toulouse, 25 June 1218. After some changes of custody, they were put under Ralf's charge again in 1220, and it seems that Henry III afterwards actually granted them to him and his heirs in fee. In vain did Simon's eldest son, Almeric, appeal against this exclusion from the heritage of his English grandmother. At last he proposed to transfer his claim upon it to his only surviving brother Simon, in exchange for Simon's share in their continental patrimony.

Simon V of Montfort seems to have been the third son of Simon IV (*Bibl. de l'École des Chartes,* xxxiv. 49). He was probably born about 1208. He is first named in a charter of his father's in 1217. In 1229, having somehow incurred the wrath of the queen-regent of France (W. Nangis, *Rer. Gall. Scriptt.* xx. 584; N. Trivet, Engl. Hist. Soc., p. 226), he was glad to accept his brother's suggestion of trying his fortune beyond the sea. 'Hereupon,' he says himself, 'I went to England, and besought my lord the king that he would restore my father's heritage unto me.' He carried a letter from Almeric, entreating the king to restore the lands either to the writer or to the bearer. 'But he answered that he could not do so, because he had given them to the Earl of Chester and his heirs by a charter. So I returned without finding grace.' Henry, however, held out hopes of ultimate restitution, and offered the claimant a yearly pension of four hundred marks meanwhile, on condition of entering his service in England or elsewhere. This proposal was accepted by Simon after his return to Normandy, and ratified by the king on 8 April 1230. In that year 'the king,' continues Simon, 'crossed into Brittany, and the Earl of Chester with him; and I went to the Earl, and begged him to help me to get back my heritage. He consented, and next August took me with him to England, and besought the king to receive my homage for my patrimony, to which, as he said, I had more right than he; and he quit-claimed to the king all that the king had given him therein; and the king received my homage, and gave me back my lands.' On 13 Aug. 1231 Henry ordered that seisin should be given to Simon of all the lands which his father had held, 'and which belong to him by hereditary right.'

The one extant portrait of Simon of Montfort dates from the year of his adoption as an Englishman. In a window of Chartres Cathedral he is painted as a young knight, on horseback, with banner and shield, while from beneath the raised vizor a face with marked features and large prominent eyes looks out with an expression which makes one feel that the likeness, though rude, must be genuine. Several years passed before his position in England was secured. Even after a second renunciation from Almeric, Simon neither assumed the title of Earl of Leicester, nor was it given to him in official documents. Not only had a large share of the Leicester property passed away to Amicia's younger sister, the Countess of Winchester, but what remained of it had, as Simon declared, suffered so much 'destruction of wood and other great damages done by divers people to whom the king had given it in charge,' that it was quite inadequate to support the rank and dignity of an earl. A license granted by Henry III in June 1232 to 'our trusty and well-beloved Simon of Montfort,' to 'keep in his own hands or bestow at his will any escheats of land held by Normans of his fee in England, which may hereafter fall in, until our lands of England and Normandy shall be one again,' may have helped him a little. In April 1234 he seems to have contemplated buying back from his brother his share of the Montfort patrimony. In a list of nobles present at a parliament at Westminster, 12 Oct. 1234, 'Simon of Montfort' appears not among the earls, but next after them (Appendix to Bracton, ed. Twiss, ii. 608). On 20 Jan. 1236 he officiated as grand seneschal at the queen's coronation, despite a protest from the Earl of Norfolk, Roger Bigod, the office of seneschal having long been in dispute between the Earls of Norfolk and of Leicester. On 28 Jan. 1237, at Westminster, 'Simon of Montfort' again appears, immediately after the earls, as witness to the king's promise to observe the charters. He was still with the king at Westminster on 24 March (*Munimenta Gildhallæ,* ii. 669), and again on 3 Aug. (Champollion, *Lettres de Rois,* i. 52). In September he witnessed the treaty at York between Henry and the king of Scots. This time his name, though still without a title, precedes that of the Earl of Pembroke, who stands last among the English earls. Simon was now seeking the hand of the widowed Countess of Flanders, but this project, like an earlier one for his marriage with another middle-aged widow, the Countess of Boulogne, was frustrated by the king of France, who looked upon it as part of a dangerous political scheme (Alberic of Trois-Fontaines, *Rer. Gall. Scriptt.* xxi. 619; cf. *Layettes du Trésor des Chartes,* ii. 336–7). A far higher match was in store for Simon. Henry III had now taken him into his closest confidence. Suspected in France on account of his relations with England, Simon was no less suspected and disliked by the English barons, as being one of the three counsellors who were believed to be instigating Henry's subservience to the pope and his legate, and whose encouragement of the king's unpatriotic policy was the more resented because —as Matthew Paris observes in words which strikingly witness to Simon's early adoption as an Englishman—'they drew their origin from the realm itself' (*Chron. Maj.* iii. 412). There seems to be no evidence for the charge against Simon beyond the fact that he was one of the nobles who acted as bodyguard to the legate on his way to and from a council at St. Paul's in November 1237, a precaution which, as his enemies were reported to be lying in wait to kill him, was hardly more than the honour of king and kingdom required. It was, however, only natural that the barons should greet with a burst of indignation the discovery that on 7 Jan. 1238 Simon had been privately married in the royal chapel at Westminster to the king's sister Eleanor, the king himself giving away the bride.

Eighteen months later, when the brothers-in-law quarrelled, Henry declared that he had but yielded to the necessity of covering his sister's shame; but it is impossible to believe that he spoke truth. Eleanor's marriage was, however, an offence against ecclesiastical discipline, for on the death of her first husband, William Marshal, second earl of Pembroke [q. v.], in 1231, she had taken, in the presence of Archbishop Edmund, a vow of perpetual widowhood. It seems, indeed, that Edmund, before he left England in December 1237 [see Edmund, Saint, archbishop of Canterbury], knew of the king's project and protested against it. When the marriage became known, the king's brother, Earl Richard of Cornwall [see Richard, king of the Romans], in his own name and that of the other barons, vehemently reproached Henry for having disposed of the hand of a royal ward without their consent or knowledge. An actual revolt was threatening, but on 23 Feb. Simon 'humbled himself to Earl Richard, and by means of many intercessors and certain gifts obtained from him the kiss of peace.' On 27 March Henry commended to the pope 'our trusty and well-beloved brother Simon of Montfort, whom we are sending to Rome on business touching the honour and welfare of ourself and our realm.' The business was to get a dispensation for Eleanor's marriage; this was granted 10 May. In England, however, the marriage was not yet wholly forgiven, and Simon gave time for the storm to die down by lingering on the continent throughout the summer. It was probably now, rather than, as Matthew Paris says, on his way to Rome, that he engaged for a while in military service under the emperor. He was well received on his return to England, 14 Oct. His first child, born in Advent, was joyfully hailed as a possible heir to the crown; and on 2 Feb. 1239 he was at last formally invested with the earldom of Leicester.

On 20 June 1239 Simon stood godfather to the king's eldest son [see Edward I]. In August he and his wife were invited to the queen's churching at Westminster; on the night before the ceremony, however, they met with a most insulting reception from the king. A debt which Simon owed to Count Peter of Brittany, and for non-payment of which, due in the summer of 1237, he had been threatened with excommunication, had been somehow transferred to the queen's uncle, Thomas of Savoy. Thomas had apparently set the king to enforce its payment. Henry chose to mix up this story with a wholly different one, and to accuse Simon of having led Eleanor into sin before their marriage, gained a dispensation by promising large sums to Rome, then incurred excommunication by failing to pay them, and finally used the king's own name as security without his permission or knowledge. Simon answered that he was willing to fulfil his legal obligations, but desired leave to defend himself according to law. Henry, according to Simon's account, ordered out 'the commons of London' to seize him that night and carry him to the Tower, but this was prevented by Richard of Cornwall. Next evening the earl and countess escaped down the Thames. They withdrew 'first beyond the sea, and then beyond the Alps.' Simon appears to have taken the cross immediately after his marriage, but postponed the fulfilment of his vow at the pope's express desire. He now renewed it, and, thus protected against the royal wrath, came back to England on 1 April 1240. The quarrel was compromised, Henry taking on himself a part of the debt, and Simon selling some of his woods to pay the rest. He then proceeded with the other English crusaders to Marseilles, and thence overland through Italy to embark at Brindisi for the Holy Land. His cousin Philip de Montfort, lord of Toron, was one of the leaders of a party among the nobles of Palestine who were struggling against the control of Richard Filangieri, the bailiff set over them by the Emperor Frederic II, whose young son Conrad was heir to the crown of Jerusalem. On 7 June 1241 this party proposed to Frederic that he should end the strife by appointing, in Filangieri's stead, Earl Simon of Leicester to be bailiff and viceroy of Palestine until Conrad should attain his majority

(*Archives de l'Orient Latin*, i. 402–3; Botfield, p. xix note). Their request was not granted; but that they should have ever seriously made it to the emperor is a striking proof of the high repute in which Simon already stood alike in east and west. Next spring, however, Simon was back in Europe. In Burgundy he received a command to join the English king in Poitou, where Henry, having just landed with an army of invasion, wanted his help, and was glad to purchase it by a very insufficient indemnity for the forced sale of the Leicester woods. Simon did good service at the battle of Saintes, 22 July, and was one of the few barons who stayed with the king, 'to the great damage of their own fortunes and interests,' when the rest went back to England in the autumn. A year later king and earl alike went home, and the royal appreciation of Simon's services was shown by liberal grants to him and his wife.

In 1244 Simon appears for the first time as taking part in English politics. Matthew Paris states that the parliament of that year appointed twelve commissioners to answer the king's demand for money; that of these twelve Simon was one; and that their answer took the form of a remonstrance against the king's wastefulness and his non-observance of the charters, and a demand for the appointment of responsible ministers of state. He inserts under the same year a draft scheme of administrative reform which he says 'the magnates devised with the king's consent,' and which in a remarkable way 'anticipates several of the later points of the programme of Simon de Montfort' (Stubbs, ii. 63). Yet he also says that when Henry refused all concession, and sought to treat with the different orders singly, Simon was one of the bearers of the royal appeal to the clergy. From these obscure notices no theory can be formed as to Simon's actual position or policy. In May 1246 his name follows that of the Earl of Cornwall at the head of a remonstrance against the demands of the pope. In 1247 he went to France 'on secret business' for the king, returning 13 Oct. At the close of the year he again took the cross. It seems to have been contemplated that he should lead the English contingent in the crusade about to set forth under Louis of France; the pope desired the English clergy to supply the earl with funds, and in August 1248 the Bishops of Lincoln and Worcester promised him four thousand marks from their dioceses whenever he should start for the Holy Land. By that time, however, his crusade was indefinitely postponed. In the spring Henry III had asked him to undertake the government of Gascony, which nobody else had ever been able to manage. Simon, 'not wishing,' as he says, 'that the king should suffer for lack of aught that I could do for him,' accepted the task on condition that he should be secured in the office of governor for seven years, should have absolute control over the revenues and feudal services of the land during that time, and should be entitled to claim the obedience of the people as if he were the king himself. For the government and internal pacification of the country he took the whole responsibility on himself; only in case of attack from the neighbouring sovereigns did he stipulate for aid from Henry. A commission on these terms was issued to him on 1 May 1248, the king undertaking to give him two thousand marks, and to supply him with fifty knights for a year.

In the autumn he set out. On 20 Sept. he was at Lorris, making a truce for two months with the queen-regent of France. At Epiphany 1249 he reappeared at Westminster to report the success of his first three months' work in the south. Two of the worst troublers of the land were in prison; a third, Gaston of Béarn, had been forced to make a truce; a fourth, the king of Navarre, had in a personal interview been persuaded to submit to arbitration all his disputes with the English king; the turbulent robber-knights, the stubborn burghers of the Gascon towns, had all been made to feel the strength of their new ruler's hand. He was back again by the end of June, when he suppressed a faction fight at Bordeaux, and threw the heads of one of the rival factions into prison; he put down by sheer force a similar tumult at Bazas; he razed the castle of Fronsac, and seized the estates of its lord, who was accused of traitorous dealings with France; he captured Gaston of Béarn and sent him over sea to beg pardon of the king. By the end of the year the whole country appeared subdued; so 'manfully and faithfully,' as Matthew Paris says, had the earl laboured at his task, 'striving in all things to follow his father's steps, or even to outgo them.'

Simon was in truth imitating but too well his father's high-handed severity and repression of independence among a people whom the ordinary machinery of civil government was powerless to control, and who were above all others quick to resent any interference with the local franchises and the unbridled license which for ages they had regarded as their birthright. The mutterings of a coming storm reached his ears early in 1250. In March he went to Paris to negotiate a five years' truce between Henry and the queen-regent. Thence, on Easter eve (27 March), was written to King Henry the sole extant letter of Simon of Montfort. He has heard, he says, that certain Gascon knights whose lands he has seized for the king, and who know that they have no chance of recovering them by process of Gascon law, are resolved to regain them by force, and intend to begin the enterprise directly after Whitsuntide. 'And forasmuch as the great folk of the land look upon me with evil eyes, because I uphold against them your rights and those of the poor people, it would be peril and shame to me, and great damage to you, if I went back to the country without having seen you and received your instructions. For when I am there, and they stir up war against me, I shall have to return to you, because I cannot get a penny of your revenue—the king of France holds it all—and I cannot trust the people of the land; nor can they be checked by an army as in a regular war, for they will only rob and burn, and take prisoners and ransom them, and ride about at night like thieves in companies. Therefore, so please you, I must by all means speak with you first, for those who have hinted to you many sinister things about me would all tell you that it is I who have given occasion for the war.' He went over to England accordingly, early in May. By the end of the month he was back again, making good use of some money which had been furnished him, buying here the custody of a castle, there a plot of land on which to build a new one, here the friendship of one baron, there the homage of another, and at last, on 27 Nov., dictating to the citizens of Bordeaux terms which left them wholly at his mercy.

Suddenly, on 6 Jan. 1251, he reappeared in England, weary and downcast, with a train of only three squres, mounted on horses almost worn out with the haste of their journey. He went straight to the king with a passionate appeal for money and men to 'repress the insolence of rebellious Gascony.' His funds, public and private, were exhausted; he could not, he declared, carry on single-handed such a costly struggle. Henry, while despatching two commissioners to 'inquire into, report upon, and appease the discord' between governor and subjects, gave him three thousand marks; Simon collected what he could from his own estates, hired two hundred soldiers and a few crossbowmen from the Duke of Brabant, and once more returned to his post. This time all Gascony was up in arms. The chiefs of the malcontents were assembled at Castillon; there Simon besieged them in April; they proposed to submit the quarrel to arbitration; he refused, and took the place. On 25 May they accepted his terms: submission of all matters in dispute to the judgment of a tribunal to consist of the king's two commissioners and four other judges chosen by them. This tribunal seems never to have sat, but one by one the rebel leaders made their peace with the crown; and in November Simon could leave Gascony to the care of his lieutenants, go to England, report that his work was done, and ask the king to accept his resignation and indemnify him for the expenses incurred in his service. Henry, however, refused to pay for the maintenance of the castles, and required Simon to maintain them at his own cost for the rest of his term of office. The queen arranged a compromise; on 4 Jan. 1252 Henry appointed arbiters to determine the amount due to the Earl of Leicester according to the terms of his commission, and on the understanding that this amount should be paid him, Simon agreed to resume the government.

At that very moment Simon—now at York with the king—received news of a fresh rising in Gascony. He would have set out at once to suppress it, but Henry refused to let him go, saying he had been given to understand that it was caused by the misdoings of the earl himself. Simon instantly demanded to be confronted with his accusers in the king's presence in London. On 6 Jan. Henry despatched two envoys into Gascony, with instructions to the civic communities, the Archbishop of Bordeaux, the Bishop of Bayonne, and the malcontent barons, to present their grievances in person or by deputy at Westminster within a week after Easter. Citizens, prelates, and barons at first declared that they dared not leave the country to the mercy of Simon's constables; in the end, however, they obeyed the royal summons. On 23 March Henry notified to Simon their impending arrival, and forbade his return to Gascony meanwhile. Simon went nevertheless, gathered troops in France, and set to work 'to exterminate his enemies.' On reaching Bordeaux, however, he learned that the Gascon deputies were actually on their way to England, and hurried back thither to meet them. The Gascons arrived first; according to one account, Henry felt so doubtful of their truthfulness that he sent another pair of commissioners—the same whom he had sent in 1251 —to make further inquiries, and they returned with a report that Simon 'had treated some people rather inhumanly, but they seemed to have deserved it.' By that time, however, the Gascons had got the king's ear; he gave Simon the cold shoulder on his return, and lost no opportunity of slighting him in public, while showing all possible favour to his opponents, and delaying the trial for nearly two months. Simon kept his temper admirably; he knew, indeed, that the English barons were on his side—'they would by no means suffer so noble a man, and natural subject of the crown, to be imprisoned as a traitor at the pleasure of these aliens.' At last he obtained a day for the public hearing of the case. The Gascons had put their complaints in writing; he answered them in the same way, point by point. He was charged with stirring up factions in the towns by siding unduly with one party for his own interest; ordering arbitrary arrests and punishments, and extorting arbitrary fines and ransoms; refusing trial to prisoners, even when ordered by the king; seizing and destroying castles, lands, and goods without reason and without compensation, or on false pretences, and committing sundry acts of violence, both in person and by his deputies; interfering with the law and administration of the land, by drawing to his own cognisance as viceroy suits which ought to have been left to the local courts of towns or barons, and overawing the courts in general, all over Gascony; appointing bailiffs, vicars, provosts, &c., on lands which were lawfully exempt from such interference; exacting tallages from lands which of old right owed no such impost; overriding the privileges of certain towns as touching the swearing of fealty to the king or his lieutenant, the amount of military service due to him, and of purveyance due to his bailiffs, &c.; selling the office of bailiff to men who oppressed the people to such a degree that they were driven to leave the country; appointing to posts of authority persons who were, or had been, in treasonable correspondence with France. Some of the individual charges Simon utterly denied; in the majority of cases he acknowledged the fact, but gave it a wholly different colour. For some of his arbitrary acts he alleged provocations which, if his allegations were true, went far to justify them; others he asserted to have been not arbitrary at all, but done after due sentence from the local courts of justice; and he further pointed out, with perfect truth, that he had accepted the government not as a mere seneschal, but on the express understanding that he was to be in all things as the king himself, without appeal. His prohibition of the forcible seizure of goods for pledge, and of the maintenance of armed 'companies,' and his strict punishment of its infringement, he defended on the grounds that the former practice was 'the beginning of all strife,' that the 'companies' were 'nothing but packs of thieves,' and that both regulations had been duly passed in a parliament at Dax. Against the other charges his defence practically came to this: that no system short of 'thorough' was of any avail with these contemptuous cities and lawless robber-nobles, and that the chastisements which he had inflicted on them were less than they deserved. Orally, indeed, he summed it all up in one burst of scorn: 'Your testimony against me is worthless, for you are all liars and traitors.' Nevertheless, he offered either to settle the matter at once by ordeal of battle between some of the accusers and the witnesses whom he had brought over on his side, or to give security for submitting to its settlement by any method that might be agreed upon either in England or Gascony. The accusers, however, would agree to nothing; 'if the king would not believe what they told him, he had only to send them safe home again.' So to answer was virtually to throw up their own case, and the unanimous verdict of the council forced the king to declare Simon acquitted. The very next day, however, Henry picked a quarrel with Simon in open council. Simon reproached him for his ingratitude, and urged the fulfilment of the terms on which he had undertaken the Gascon viceroyalty; Henry retorted that he would keep no covenant with a traitor. 'That word is a lie,' burst out Simon, 'and were you not my sovereign, an ill hour would it be for you in which you dared to utter it.' Henry would have arrested him, but the magnates all took Simon's part, and separated them after a bitter altercation. A few days later Simon offered the king three alternatives: peace between himself and his accusers to be made at the king's discretion, and the earl then to return to Gascony and hold it for the king according to the terms of that pacification; if peace were refused by the other party, the king to furnish the earl with troops and arms, and the earl to return to Gascony and go on as before, fighting down rebellion and holding the land for the king by force; or the earl to resign his commission as viceroy, provided that the king indemnified him for his expenses and secured his honour from reproach, and the persons and lands of his adherents from the vengeance of the Gascons; and provided also 'that the prelates, nobles, and counsellors gave their consent.' Henry rejected all three propositions; instead, he proposed to reopen the case in Gascony as soon as he could go thither himself, and meanwhile to prolong the truce which had been arranged there till that period should arrive. The king's parting sarcasm, 'Go back to Gascony, thou lover and maker of strife, and reap its reward like thy father before thee,' was met by the quiet reply: 'Gladly will I go; nor do I think to return till I have made thine enemies thy footstool, ungrateful though thou be.' Ten years later Henry asserted that he had ordered Simon to follow him to Windsor, and that Simon had disobeyed the order and gone straight to France without his knowledge; Simon, however, declared that he had set out 'from Windsor.' Landing at Boulogne on 13 June, he learned that Gaston of Béarn, despite the truce, was besieging the citadel of La Réole; he collected troops in France and hurried to the rescue. Meanwhile his accusers had hastened home and gathered forces to meet him; in the first battle he was victorious; soon afterwards he was blockaded in Montauban, and escaped with some difficulty. While revictualling La Réole he was overtaken by two royal commissioners with letters from the king bidding him respect the truce; he retorted that he could not keep a truce which the other party had broken. The commissioners then handed him another letter whereby he was removed from his office. He answered that the king was acting 'wilfully, not in reason,' and that the office which had been entrusted to him 'by the counsel of the wise men' he would not give up till the seven years were expired; and therewith he went off to besiege another rebel castle. The English parliament in October utterly refused to sanction his deposition; Henry next offered to buy him out with seven thousand marks down and a promise to pay all his Gascon debts. Simon yielded, made a formal resignation of his office, 29 Sept. 1252, and withdrew into France. There the nobles, 'knowing his constancy and strength of character,' pressed him to accept the office of seneschal of the kingdom, and with it a foremost place in the council of regency, left headless by the death of the queen-mother. Simon refused; 'he would not seem a deserter.'

Gascony had risen more madly than ever as soon as his back was turned, and when Henry arrived there in August 1253 the first thing he did was to call Simon to his aid. Simon at first took no notice; but a second appeal in October brought him back, sick though he was, at the head of his picked band of knights, ready to forgive and help his brother-in-law once again. The result was a gradual subsidence of the revolt; Simon spent Christmas with the king, and at Easter 1254 was back in London, enlightening the English parliament as to the state of things in Gascony and the meaning of the royal demands for money.

On 25 Aug. Henry sent Earl Simon into Scotland, 'entrusting him with a secret to reveal to the Scottish king.' On 18 May 1255 Simon was coupled with Peter of Savoy on a mission to France for a renewal of the truce, which was obtained in June. On 16 Aug. 1256 he was with the king at Woodstock; and in the same year he was one of four noble laymen whom the king appointed as being 'learned and skilful in the laws of the land, and mighty men, whom neither fear nor favour could corrupt,' to inquire into a charge against the sheriff of Northampton which had baffled the sagacity of the itinerant judges. In February 1257 Henry proposed to send Simon, with another envoy, to treat for peace with France. Simon seems to have been there when ordered off in June on a further errand, to expedite arrangements with the pope for Edmund's establishment as king of Sicily [see under Richard, Earl of Cornwall]. Of the four envoys originally named for this mission, however, only one went, and that one was not the Earl of Leicester. He remained in France, but met with no success in his negotiations, and returned in February 1258.

Some time in 1257 hot words had passed between Simon and the king's half-brother, William of Valence. William had encroached on Simon's land; Simon remonstrated before the council; William met the remonstrance by calling him traitor; and the strife would have passed from words to blows had not the king thrown himself between them. The quarrel broke out again in the Hoketide parliament of 1258. William repeated his insult; Simon retorted, 'No, no, William! I am neither traitor nor traitor's son; my father was not like yours;' and again Henry had to separate them. Their quarrel was only a part of the great national quarrel which occupied the whole session (9 April–5 May 1258), the quarrel of the English people, who were soon to recognise Simon as their champion against the king and his Poitevin favourites, of whom William was the chief. On 12 April Simon and six other nobles banded themselves together in a sworn league 'to help one another, ourselves, and our men against all folk, doing right and obtaining right, as much as we can, without wronging any man, and saving our faith to the king.' On 2 May Henry sanctioned the appointment of twenty-four commissioners—twelve of his own council and twelve chosen by the barons—to draw up a scheme of administrative reform. One of the latter was Simon of Montfort. On 8 May five nobles, of whom Simon was one, were appointed to prolong the truce with France, that the work of reform might proceed without external hindrance. There was a further project, strongly supported if not originated by Simon, for turning the truce into a definite peace, and on 28 May its terms were virtually agreed upon. Simon was still in France on 1 June. He was back on 11 June, when the parliament reassembled, and the commissioners' scheme was elaborated into the 'Provisions of Oxford.' Besides the redress of a number of administrative grievances, these included the appointment of a permanent council of fifteen, who were, 'in fact, not only to act as the king's private council, but to have a constraining power over all his public acts' (STUBBS, ii. 76), and the election by the barons of twenty-four commissioners to treat of the aid demanded by the king. Of both these bodies Simon was a member, as well as of the original committee of twenty-four which was now to undertake the reform of the church. As soon as the 'Provisions' were ratified, Simon, in accordance with a clause requiring all warders of royal castles to surrender them to the king, resigned the custody of Odiham and Kenilworth. 'Your castles or your head' was the alternative he offered to William of Valence, who refused to follow his example. Simon headed the deputation of barons who obtained the adhesion of the London citizens to the 'Provisions,' 22 July. He was also one of those who drew up a letter to the pope giving an account of the proceedings at Oxford, and protesting against the appointment of Aymer of Valence to the see of Winchester. About the same time Henry was overtaken by a thunderstorm one day when in a boat on the Thames. Driven to seek shelter in the house which Simon then occupied, he answered the earl's welcome by declaring that he feared his host 'more than all the thunder and lightning in the world.' 'Fear your enemies, my lord king—those who flatter you to your ruin—not me, your constant and faithful friend,' was the earl's reply. On 25 Aug. he was accredited on a mission to Scotland; on 18 Oct. 'Sim' of Muntfort, Eorl on Leirchestr',' witnessed, as one of the king's fifteen 'sworn redesmen,' Henry's English proclamation of the 'Provisions.' In November the barons chose him, with two bishops and the earl-marshal, to represent England at a conference which was to be held at Cambray between the kings of France and Germany, and in which Henry had been invited to take part. The conference, however, never came to pass.

At the end of January 1259 Simon was still in France, and his absence was causing great anxiety to the English people, 'who did not know what had become of him over sea.' He returned for the meeting of parliament in London, 9 Feb. On 16 March he was sent back again, with the Earl of Gloucester and four others, to resume negotiations for peace with France on the basis of a resignation of the English claims on the heritage of the Angevin house. The French king, however, required the Countess of Leicester and her sons to join in her brother's renunciation; and this she and her husband alike refused without adequate security for at least a certain portion of the many debts for which Henry was answerable to them both. The negotiation therefore failed, and the ambassadors went home, not before Gloucester had flung insulting words at Leicester as the cause of its failure, and Leicester had retorted with a vehemence that almost led to bloodshed. At the close of a second meeting of parliament a quarrel arose between them on higher grounds. Gloucester, who outwardly ranked with Simon as leader of the reforming party, was showing signs of lukewarmness in the cause. Simon upbraided him severely, and at last exclaiming 'I care not to live and act with men so fickle and so false,' withdrew over sea. There, however, he worked on at the treaty. It was proclaimed in the October meeting of the parliament, where also an amended set of ordinances, the 'Provisions of Westminster,' was issued. Simon was absent in the body, but present in the spirit. The barons had implored him not to withdraw from their councils, and he had sent them back a solemn assurance that he would keep his word, no matter what came of it (PRIMAT, *Rer. Gall. Scriptt.* xxiii. 17).

On 4 Dec. 1259 the treaty was ratified in Paris by the two kings in person, Simon and Eleanor making at the same time a complete renunciation of their claims. On 16 Jan. 1260 Henry forbade the parliament to assemble in his absence. This step threatened a violation of the 'Provisions,' which enacted that parliament should always meet thrice a year—at Candlemas (2 Feb.), in June, and October. Simon waited for the king till the eleventh hour, and then, 'to save his oath,' hurried to England just in time to meet the rest of the royal council in London on Candlemas-day. Hearing from the justiciar that the king was expected in three weeks, they adjourned the parliament from day to day during that time. Henry, however, did not come till 30 April; then he shut Simon out of London, and laid before the council a string of written charges against him. Some were connected with the eternal matter of money which always lay between them—the dowry of Eleanor. Then Henry accused Simon of quitting Paris without taking leave of him; coming to the parliament in defiance of his prohibition, and with horses and arms, which was also forbidden; procuring the removal of a member of the council without the king's knowledge; 'drawing people to him and making new alliances,' thus disturbing the country and obliging the king to bring over a costly force of mercenaries; threatening that these mercenaries 'should be so lodged that no others would ever care to follow them;' bidding the justiciar tell the king that the mercenaries should be shut out of the realm, and undertaking to uphold the justiciar in this defiance; forbidding the justiciar to send money to the king, and declaring that if it were sent the justiciar should be forced to refund it. The more frivolous of these charges Simon passed over with a scornful word—'It might be so;' to the rest he answered that he had done and spoken nothing save for the public good and the royal honour, and with the knowledge and in the presence of the whole council. So 'by God's grace,' as the Dunstable annalist says, the attack ended in failure.

Simon was one of the tenants-in-chief summoned to meet the king at Chester on 8 Sept. for an expedition into Wales. One chronicler says that, as 'the wisest and stoutest warrior in England,' he was put in command of the host (*Flores Histor.* ii. 454); but this statement seems to have arisen out of a confusion between Simon and Peter. He was, however, absent from the wedding of the king's daughter Beatrice on 13 Oct., when he appointed his wife's nephew, Henry of Cornwall [q. v.], to act as seneschal in his stead. On 14 March 1261 he and Eleanor were in London, and joined with the king in submitting the money matters in dispute between them to the arbitration of the king and queen of France. On 18 July Simon, with five other barons, appealed to St. Louis for help in coming to terms with Henry. A month later Henry proclaimed his intention of appointing his own ministers, recalling his foreign favourites, and governing once more as he pleased. Simon, in conjunction with Gloucester and a few other barons who remained faithful to the 'Provisions,' answered the royal challenge by summoning three knights from every shire south of Trent to meet them at St. Albans on 21 Sept., 'to treat of the common affairs of the realm.' Henry issued a countersummons, bidding the knights come not to St. Albans, but to Windsor, where he purposed to hold, on the same day, a meeting with the barons to treat for peace. Before the day came Gloucester had 'apostatized,' and Simon, thinking the cause lost, had again withdrawn over sea, declaring he would rather die in exile than live in faithlessness. In his despair he talked of going to the Holy Land, but he only went to France; and in December his consent was asked to a new scheme of arbitration between the barons and the king. His reply is unknown; but when asked to join in ratifying the agreement drawn up by the arbitrators at Whitsuntide 1262 he refused, and it fell through in consequence. Later in the year king and earl met at the French court, and Henry took occasion to mix up with the money question, on which alone Queen Margaret had to arbitrate, a variety of complaints about Simon's 'ingratitude,' and a recapitulation of the charges as to his proceedings in Gascony and in England, on which he had been tried and acquitted in 1252 and 1260. Simon briefly repeated his former defence, and nothing came of the affair.

In December Henry went home; Simon followed at the end of April (1263). Gloucester was dead, and the barons had secretly recalled their true leader. At the Whitsuntide parliament, having vainly petitioned for a new confirmation of the charters, they denounced the king as false to his oath, and proclaimed war upon all violators of the 'Provisions.' Simon was at once recognised as their captain, and took the command of a force which marched upon Hereford, and soon mastered the foreign interlopers in the west. At midsummer the Londoners were called upon, by a writ sealed with Simon's seal, to choose a side in the struggle. They chose that of the earl. About the same time the scholars whom Henry had recently expelled from Oxford were brought back under Simon's protection. On 16 June Henry had given the earl a safe-conduct for the purpose of negotiation; on 29–30 June Simon was at Reading, whence the king of the Romans invited him to a conference at Lodden Bridge; but he declined it, and went on to Guildford and thence to Dover. In July the king accepted his terms, and on the 15th Simon and the barons entered London. Simon went straight to the king and made him ratify his concessions, and the first step in their fulfilment, the appointment of a new treasurer, was taken 'in Earl Simon's presence' at Westminster on 19 July.

On 26 Sept. king and earl met at Boulogne, by the invitation and in the presence of St. Louis. Once again the old charges were flung in Simon's face; once again he answered them, to the French king's entire satisfaction. He was home again for the meeting of parliament on 13 Oct. It broke up in confusion, the king's party flew to arms, and Simon, lodging at Southwark with a very small train, would have been surrounded and captured had not the Londoners rushed out to rescue him. Four wealthy citizens who had been in the plot with the king were punished by imprisonment and by a fine, of which Simon applied the proceeds to strengthen the defences of the city. Fearing a similar trap, he disregarded the royal summons to another parliament at Reading. On 13 Dec. he joined with the other barons in an agreement to refer to the arbitration of St. Louis 'all contentions and discords' between themselves and their sovereign respecting the 'Provisions,' and swore to abide by the French king's decision. That decision—the Mise of Amiens—was given on 23 Jan. 1264. It quashed the 'Provisions' altogether, and restored to the king the privileges which he claimed; but it reserved 'the rights which the English people had acquired' before the passing of the 'Provisions.' That reservation saved everything. It justified the barons in setting aside the award; for 'it was easy for Simon to prove that the arbitrary power it gave to the crown was as contrary to the Charter as to the Provisions themselves' (Green, *Hist. Engl. People*, i. 297–8). Before the Mise was agreed upon he had said: 'Though all should forsake me I will stand firm, with my four sons, in the just cause to which my faith is pledged; nor will I fear to risk the fortune of war.' But he was not forsaken; the whole English people was with him now. A broken leg, caused by a fall from his horse, had prevented him from attending the Mise of Amiens. He now despatched his eldest son to the western border, where he had secured the alliance of Llywelyn of Wales; he himself, as soon as he could move, went to secure London, and thence marched northward to relieve Northampton, where his second son was besieged by the king; but on hearing of its capture (5 April) he turned southward again, and in Holy Week laid siege to Rochester. On Henry's approach he again withdrew to London (26 April). He was, in fact, recalled by tidings of a plot for the betrayal of the city to Edward. After taking measures for its security he again set forth on the track of the royalists. On 12 May he encamped at Fletching, Sussex; the king was ten miles off at Lewes. One last appeal to Henry, signed by Simon and his young colleague, the new Earl of Gloucester, was answered by a formal defiance of 'Simon of Montfort, Gilbert of Clare, and their fellows.' On 14 May the decisive battle took place, and Simon's anxious night of thought and prayer, his stirring appeal to his followers, his daring and skilful plan of attack, were rewarded by the total defeat of the royalists and the capture of the king himself.

A convention drawn up that night, and known as the Mise of Lewes, 'furnished the basis of the new constitution which Simon proposed to create, and forms the link between it and the earlier one devised in 1258' (Stubbs, ii. 90). That new constitution, set up at the midsummer parliament, empowered the Earls of Leicester and Gloucester and the Bishop of Chichester to elect a council of nine, by whose advice the king was to govern, while the three electors were to remain as a court of appeal in case of disagreement among the nine, and were themselves to be removable at the will of the parliament. From that moment Simon was virtually governor of king and kingdom. His exceptional importance, and the exceptional danger to which it exposed him, were marked by his solitary exemption from a decree forbidding all persons to wear arms (16 July), and by a warning written to the barons by 'a faithful Englishman,' to bethink them of another leader in case he should die. Dangers indeed were thickening round him. In September he and his partisans were excommunicated by a papal legate. In November the lawless doings of the royalists on the Welsh border forced him to march against them. Llywelyn's help enabled him to subdue them for the moment, but Gloucester protected them, the great lords of the north were hostile, and 'it was the weakness of his party among the baronage at this great crisis which drove Earl Simon to a constitutional change of mighty issue in our history' (Green, i. 300). By writs issued in the king's name on 14 and 24 Dec. he summoned to a parliament in London on 30 Jan. 1265, not only 120 churchmen, twenty-three lay barons, and two knights from every shire, but also two citizens from every borough in England. The only recorded event of the session was a quarrel between the Earls of Leicester and Gloucester. Gilbert accused Simon of illegally keeping foreign garrisons in the castles of which he had custody. The question was dropped for a while, but on Shrove Tuesday (17 Feb.) Simon forcibly prevented a tournament between his sons and Gloucester at Dunstable, and on 11 April he had to do the like again at Northampton. Gloucester hereupon joined the marcher lords, who were still in revolt, and openly welcomed back some of the foreign exiles. Simon, with the king in his train, followed him to Hereford, where another reconciliation was patched up on

12 May; but on the 28th Gloucester was joined by Edward, and hostilities began at once. While the new allies secured the eastern side of the Severn valley, Simon hurried into Glamorgan, made in the king's name a treaty with Llywelyn (19 June), marched to Monmouth (28 June), and thence to Newport, intending to cross over to Bristol; but his transports were intercepted, and he was forced to return to Hereford. On Sunday, 2 Aug., he set out again, crossed the Severn, and late on the Monday night, or early on Tuesday morning, reached Evesham, where he hoped that his son would meet him. His godson, Edward, met him instead, with a force so overwhelming that Simon at once exclaimed, 'Let us commend our souls to God, for our bodies are theirs.' At the close of a three hours' massacre—'for battle none it was,' as a chronicler says—he fell, almost the last of his little band, crying 'God's grace!' as he passed away.

In the eyes of the king's party Simon was a 'traitor.' Setting that charge aside, the only faults of which he could be accused were ambition, avarice, pride, and a fierce and overbearing temper. Ambitious he undoubtedly was, especially in his youth. His perpetual wranglings with the king over money matters seem at times to indicate a grasping disposition; but Henry's slipperiness in such matters was incalculable; Simon's expenditure in the royal service must have been enormous; and, moreover, a considerable part of the claims which he pressed so persistently were not his own claims, but those of his wife, Henry's sister, whom he had married without any dowry at all, whose dowry on her first marriage Henry had never reclaimed for her from the Marshals, and who was anything but a thrifty housekeeper. The heavy expenses of Simon's visit to Rome in 1238 were defrayed by forced contributions from the tenants of the honour of Leicester, claimed apparently as arrears of dues unpaid since his recognition as their lord; but on his return, moved by a remonstrance from his friend Robert Grosseteste [see Grosseteste, Robert, bishop of Lincoln], he made restitution to them all. His will, made on 1 Jan. 1259, begins with an anxious injunction that his debts shall be paid, and that all claims made against him shall be satisfied without question and without delay; 'where there is any doubt let it not rest on my side, cost what it may, so that I be free of it, for I would not remain in debt or under suspicion of debt to any one.' He was certainly often in debt during his lifetime; probably the earl was as bad a manager as the countess; but it was not on self-indulgence that he spent; he was noted for his temperance, sobriety, and simplicity of life. His private life was in fact that of a saint; his closest friends were the holiest men of the day—Grosseteste, Walter Cantelupe [q. v.], Adam Marsh [see Adam de Marisco]; and Adam, at least, lectured him about his temper with a frankness which shows that his pride was of the kind that does not turn away from deserved rebuke. Though his wife was nearly as fiery as himself, he, at least, seems to have found her 'good woman through all.' They were seldom long apart without necessity; he appointed her sole executrix of his testamentary dispositions, and bade his sons be guided by her counsels; he left her in command of Kenilworth during his last campaign; and she spent her nine years of widowhood at Montargis, in a convent founded by his sister. For their children see Montfort, Almeric, Eleanor, Guy, Henry, and Simon the younger.

Piety and culture were the characteristics of Simon's home. He knew all the morning and night offices of the church by heart, and went through them almost as regularly as a priest, spending more of the night in devotion than in sleep. He was a fair Latin scholar, a lover of books, a pleasant and cheerful talker. Chroniclers and poets called him 'the flower of all chivalry.' Like his father, he was counted the finest soldier of his generation. At the siege of Rochester in 1264 it was remarked that he 'showed the English the right way to assault a town, a matter about which they were at that time wholly ignorant;' while at Lewes his plan of attack was 'laid with a care and foresight, and executed with a combination of resource and decision, which would be sufficient, even if we knew nothing more of his military prowess, to support his reputation as the first general of his day' (Prothero, p. 273). As a statesman he has been in modern times not so much overrated as misunderstood. He was not the inventor of the representative system, nor the 'creator of the House of Commons.' We have no means of ascertaining how much or how little of the complicated executive machinery set up by the 'Provisions of Oxford' was of his devising, nor do we know how far he himself was conscious that he had 'created a new force in English politics' when he issued the writ 'that first summoned the merchant and the trader to sit beside the knight of the shire, the baron and the bishop, in the parliament of the realm' (Green, i. 301). What Englishmen of his own day saw in him was not so much a reformer of government as a champion of righteousness, not so much a statesman as a hero. 'While other men wavered and faltered and fell away, the enthusiastic love of the people clung to the grave, stern soldier, who stood like a pillar, unshaken by promise or threat or fear of death, by the oath he had sworn.' The excommunication issued against him in 1264 avowedly rested on political grounds alone; one chronicler indeed says that in 1268 Clement IV absolved the dead earl and all his adherents, declaring that the sentence against them had been won on false pretences from his predecessor (*Cont.* GERV. CANT. ii. 247), but this can hardly be, for in 1275 we find Edward I trying to prevent Simon's son, Almeric, from getting the excommunication revoked at Rome (*Hist. MSS. Comm.* 4th Rep. p. 396). It had, however, never been published in England, and was never recognised there. The tomb which covered the shockingly mutilated corpse in the abbey church of Evesham at once became a shrine where miracles were wrought. The Franciscans, in whose schemes of religious revival Simon had shared heart and soul, drew up in his honour immediately after his death an office in which he was invoked as the 'guardian of the English people.' In popular song the martyr of Evesham was coupled with the martyr of Canterbury. The tomb and the church which contained it have perished; but under a window in the north aisle of the nave of Westminster Abbey there still remains a monument to Simon of Montfort: his shield of arms, sculptured there when he stood high in the favour of Henry III, and left untouched after his fall. The cause which seemed to have fallen with him gained in fact more from his death than from his life. In October 1267 'a series of demands, strangely neglected by historians, but constituting a solemn assertion of English liberty' (J. R. GREEN, *Archæol. Journ.* xxi. 297), were embodied in the Ban of Kenilworth, to which Henry and Edward gave their assent. In November 1269 king and parliament passed the statute of Marlborough, 'where the very spirit of the great earl and of freedom is alive again' (*ib.* p. 277). Nor was the final acceptance of Simon's greatest constitutional innovation long delayed; 'in the parliament of 1295 that of 1265 found itself at last reproduced' (GREEN, *Hist. Engl. People*, i. 356). 'The victor of Evesham was the true pupil of the vanquished; the statesmanship of De Montfort is interwoven, warp and woof, into the government of Edward I' (SHIRLEY, *Quarterly Review*, cxix. 57).

[Matthew Paris's Chronica Majora, vols. iii–v., and Historia Anglorum, vols. ii. iii.; Annales Monastici, vols. i–iv.; Robert of Gloucester, vol. ii.; John of Oxenedes; Royal Letters, vols. i. ii.; Letters of Adam Marsh (Monumenta Franciscana, vol. i.) and of Robert Grosseteste (all in Rolls Ser.); Chronicles of Melrose and of Lanercost (Bannatyne Club); Rishanger's Chronicle, ed. Halliwell, Political Songs, ed. Wright, and Chronica Majorum Londoniarum, published with Liber de Antiquis Legibus (Camden Soc.); documents in Patent and Close Rolls of John and Henry III; Rymer's Fœdera, vol. i. pt. i.; Nichols's Hist. of Leicester, vol. i.; Manners and Household Expenses in XIII Cent., ed. Botfield and Turner (Roxburghe Club); Layettes du Trésor des Chartes, vols. ii. and iii., ed. Teulet and Laborde. A short account of Simon which occurs in the so-called Chronicle of the Templar of Tyre (Gestes des Chiprois, ed. G. Raynaud, Soc. de l'Orient Latin, série historique, v. 172–176) is interesting as the work of a writer who had once been page to the wife of John de Montfort, lord of Tyre, whose father (Philip) was first cousin to the earl, and is also curious as showing how fully and, on the whole, how accurately the main principles and features of the struggle in England were known and appreciated in so distant a land. Simon's first modern biographer was the Rev. Sambrook Russell, who contributed a fair sketch of his life to Nichols's History of Leicester. Dr. Pauli's work on Simon of Montfort, Creator of the House of Commons, may be best consulted in the English translation by Miss Una M. Goodwin, the text having been so revised as to be virtually a new edition. As its title implies, it deals with Simon almost exclusively from the point of view of English constitutional history. Mr. G. W. Prothero's Simon de Montfort is a more elaborate study of the earl's character and career as a whole; but no complete biography of him was possible till the store of documents bearing upon his government in Gascony, his diplomatic relations with France, and his personal relations with Henry III, which are preserved in the national archives of France and among the Additional MSS. in the British Museum, were unearthed, some by MM. Balasque and Dulaurens (Etudes sur Bayonne, vol. ii., appendices), more by M. Charles Bémont, whose Simon de Montfort has virtually superseded all the earlier lives. M. Bémont has also dealt with the Gascon affair in Revue Historique, iv. 241–77. For Simon's place among English statesmen see Bishop Stubbs's Constitutional History, vol. ii. ch. xiv., and the remarkable contemporary Song of Lewes, edited by T. Wright among the Political Songs (Camden Soc.), and separately by Mr. C. L. Kingsford in 1890. See also Blaauw's Barons' War, ed. Mr. C. H. Pearson; art. by Dr. Shirley in Quarterly Review, cxix. 26–57; Stubbs's Early Plantagenets; and J. R. Green's Hist. of the English People.] K. N.

MONTFORT, SIMON OF, the younger (1240–1271), second child of Simon of Montfort, earl of Leicester [q. v.], and Eleanor his wife, was born near Brindisi in the summer of 1240 (cf. *Flores Histor.* iii. 264, and

MATT. PARIS, *Chron. Maj.* iv. 7 and 44 note). On 13 Oct. 1260 he was knighted, with his brother Henry [q. v.], by the king's son Edward. At the opening of the barons' war (1264) he defended Northampton against the king, but was captured after a gallant fight on 5 April, and imprisoned at Windsor. Released by his father's victory at Lewes, 14 May 1264, he was made 'custos pacis' in Surrey and Sussex (June) and constable of Porchester (24 Dec.) In September–November 1264 he unsuccessfully blockaded an alien garrison in Pevensey Castle; he was at the same task again in June 1265 when called away to help his father in the west. After wasting a month in collecting fresh troops in London, plundering Winchester, and making a triumphal progress to Oxford and Northampton, he reached Kenilworth on 31 July, only to be surprised and routed by Edward next morning. On 3 Aug. he set out again to join his father, but, owing to an unlucky halt at Alcester, he only reached Evesham in time to see from afar his father's head borne off on a spear-point as a trophy of the royalists' victory (4 Aug.) He withdrew again to Kenilworth; there the garrison, in their thirst to avenge the earl, were for slaughtering the king's brother Richard [see RICHARD, EARL OF CORNWALL], who was a prisoner in Simon's custody; Simon, however, withstood their demand, and on 6 Sept. set Richard at liberty. On 23 Nov., having fortified and victualled Kenilworth for a long siege, he went to join some of his father's friends who were entrenched in the Isle of Axholme. There, at Christmas, he was forced to accept Edward's terms, and submit himself to the judgment of king and council at Northampton. They pardoned him on condition that he would surrender Kenilworth and quit England for life, with a yearly pension of 400*l.* He was taken in the king's train to Kenilworth, but when he called upon the garrison to surrender, they refused, clearly with his connivance; he was led back to London, and thence, on the night of 10 Feb. 1266, escaped to Winchelsea. After acting for a time as leader of the Cinque Port pirates, he went over sea. On 18 May a proclamation was issued against his expected attempt to re-enter England by force, and he kept up a correspondence with Kenilworth till the eve of its surrender in December. In September 1267 King Louis of France was negotiating with Henry III for Simon's return to England, but he was still in France on 26 March 1268 (BÉMONT, *Simon de Montfort*, p. 251, note 4). Bartholomew Cotton (p. 146, Rolls ed.) says that Simon came over in 1271 to visit the graves of his father and eldest brother; the visit, if it took place, must have been a hasty and stolen one. On 13 March of that year he was at Viterbo, taking part with his brother Guy [q. v.] in the murder of Henry of Cornwall [q. v.], and was only saved from justice by his death in the same year, at a castle near Siena.

[Annales Monastici, vols. ii. iii. iv.; Flores Historiarum ('Matt. Westminster'), vol. iii.; Robert of Gloucester, vol. ii.; Royal Letters, vol. ii. (all in Rolls Series); Chronica Majorum Londoniarum, ed. Stapleton (with Liber de Antiquis Legibus), and Rishanger's Chronicle, ed. Halliwell (Camden Soc.); Rymer's Fœdera, vol. i. pt. i.; Patent Rolls 48 & 49 Hen. III; see also J. R. Green's article on the Ban of Kenilworth in Archæol. Journ. xxi. 277 et seq.] K. N.

MONTGOMERIE, SIR ALEXANDER DE, of Ardrossan, first BARON MONTGOMERIE (*d.* 1470?), was the eldest son of Sir John Montgomerie of Eaglesham, Eglinton, and Ardrossan, by his wife Agnes, daughter of Alexander, earl of Ross, lord of the Isles. His grandfather, Sir John Montgomerie (*d.* 1398?), is separately noticed. The father was a hostage for the Earl of Douglas in 1408, a hostage for James I in 1423, and one of the jury on the trial of Murdac, duke of Albany, in 1425. In 1425 the son was chosen a member of the privy council of James I. He succeeded his father some time before 22 Nov. 1429, and in August 1430 he was, jointly with his brother-in-law, Sir Robert Cunningham of Kilmaurs, appointed governor of Cantyre and Knapdale. On 30 Nov. 1436 he was appointed a commissioner to conclude a treaty with England (*Cal. Documents relating to Scotland*, iv. 1103), and he was one of the conservators of the truce concluded on 31 March for nine years (*ib.* p. 1111). With the other Scottish commissioners he received the present of a silver cup from Henry VI (*ib.* p. 1109). On 5 Feb. 1444 he had a safe-conduct to go to Durham to treat for the extension of the truce and the return of the Scottish hostages (*ib.* p. 1162).

In 1444 Montgomerie was appointed keeper of Brodick Castle in the Isle of Arran (*Exchequer Rolls of Scotland*, v. 163). He was one of those who set their seals to instruments passed by the parliament held at Perth on 9 June 1445 against those lords who had rebelled against James II. He was created a lord of parliament by the title of Lord Montgomerie some time before 3 July 1445 (*Acta Parl. Scot.* ii. 59; *Hist. MSS. Comm.* 11th Rep. pt. vi. p. 16). On 31 Jan. 1448–9 he had a grant of the office of bailiary of Cunningham. On 14 Aug. 1451 he was a conservator for a truce with England (*Cal.*

Documents relating to Scotland, iv. 1239), and in subsequent years he was sent to England on various other important embassies. He died about 1470. By his wife Margaret, second daughter of Sir Thomas Boyd of Kilmarnock, father of the first Lord Boyd, he had three, or possibly four sons and three daughters: Alexander, master of Montgomerie, who died in 1452, leaving by his wife Elizabeth, eldest daughter of Sir Adam Hepburn of Hales, a son, Alexander, second lord Montgomerie, father of Hugh, first earl of Eglinton [q. v.]; George, ancestor of the Montgomeries of Skelmorlie; Thomas, parson of Eaglesham, and rector of the university of Glasgow; John of Giffen (doubtful); Margaret, married to Sir John Stewart of Darnley, who was created Lord Darnley, and for a time was titular Earl of Lennox; Elizabeth, to John, lord Kennedy, seventh earl of Cassillis; and Agnes, to William Cunningham of Glengarnock.

[Cal. Documents relating to Scotland, vol. iv.; Exchequer Rolls of Scotland, vol. ii.; Reg. Mag. Sig. Scot. vol. i.; Sir William Fraser's Earls of Eglinton; Douglas's Scottish Peerage (Wood), i. 495–6.] T. F. H.

MONTGOMERIE, ALEXANDER (1556?–1610?), Scottish poet, second son of Hugh Montgomerie of Hessilhead Castle, Ayrshire (Timothy Pont, *Topography of Cunningham*, Maitland Club, p. 19), was, according to one of his poems, born 'on Eister day at morne,' probably in 1556. His father was a kinsman of the Eglinton family (G. S. Montgomery, *Hist. of Montgomery of Ballyleck*, p. 115). His mother was a daughter of Houston of Houston. A sister Elizabeth became the wife of Sir William Mure of Rowallan, father of Sir William Mure [q. v.] The eldest brother John succeeded to Hessilhead. A younger brother, Robert (*d.* 1609), is separately noticed.

Montgomerie's poems show that he received a scholarly training in youth. If one can trust a statement by Sir Patrick Hume [q. v.] of Polwarth, his antagonist in the 'Flyting,' he must have been sent to Argyleshire for a part of his education (*Flyting*, ll. 183, 184). The circumstance may account for his being called by Dempster *Eques Montanus*, an expression probably equivalent to 'highland trooper.' Montgomerie was never knighted.

On his return from Argyleshire he appears to have resided for a time at Compston Castle, a little way above Kirkcudbright, near the junction of the Dee and the Tarff. Andrew Symson, in his 'Large Description of Galloway' (*MS. Adv. Lib.*), drawn up in 1684 and enlarged in 1692, mentions a report current in his day to the effect that Montgomerie's fancy had been quickened by the romantic scenery of the Dee when he composed 'The Cherrie and the Slae.' Symson's statement is supported by Robert Sempill, Montgomerie's contemporary, who, in 'The Legend of the Bischop of St. Androis Lyfe,' calls him Captain Kirkburne, in obvious allusion to his residence in the stewartry.

Montgomerie soon obtained an introduction to the Scottish court. In 1577 he was in the suite of the Regent Morton, on whose compulsory resignation in the following year he was retained in the king's service. His official duties apparently entitled him to the style of captain, and he also became the laureate of the court. The king, in his 'Revlis and Cavtelis of Scottis Poesie,' recognised his abilities by quoting passages from his poems as examples of different kinds of verse. But he somehow fell into disgrace, although his services were rewarded with a pension of five hundred marks, payable from certain rents of the archbishopric of Glasgow. The date of this grant is not known, but it was confirmed in 1583, when payment was to be computed from the previous year.

In 1586 he obtained a royal license to leave the kingdom for five years, and to visit France, Flanders, Spain, and other countries. During his travels he was confined in a foreign prison, and his pension was withheld, an act which led to a protracted lawsuit in the court of session. Eventually the grant was renewed and confirmed by a writ of privy seal dated at Holyrood House 21 March 1588–9. Dempster says he died in 1591, bewailed by his sovereign, who was charmed with the effusions of his mirthful muse. But at least two pieces by Montgomerie refer to events that took place in 1592, and we have no reason to doubt that he was alive in 1605, when his 'Mindes Melodie' was printed by Robert Charteris. His death occurred, however, before 1615, as on the title-page of the edition of 'The Cherrie and the Slae,' printed by Andro Hart in that year, the poem is said to have undergone careful revision by the author not long before his death. He married and had issue Alexander and Margaret. The latter in March 1622 was tried for witchcraft (Montgomery, p. 117).

Montgomerie occupies a conspicuous place in the poetical literature of Scotland during a period almost barren of poetic genius. 'The Cherrie and the Slae,' which has long been popular with his countrymen, is written in a fourteen-line stanza, of which, if Montgomerie was not the inventor, he is certainly the greatest master. It is wanting in design, and bears unmistakable traces of having been written at considerable intervals. The first portion is a love-piece, obviously written at an earlier date than the rest of the poem; the remainder, which in the first and second editions ended in the middle of the 77th stanza, and was afterwards extended to 114 stanzas, is a moral allegory, in which Virtue is represented by the cherry and Vice by the sloe. The poem contains many passages of singular freshness and beauty, and bristles with homely proverbs pithily and tersely put. The first edition was printed by Robert Walde-graue in 1597 (no copy extant); 2nd edit. same year (copy in the Advocates' Library, Edinb.); by Andro Hart, 1615 (no copy extant); in Allan Ramsay's 'Evergreen,' 1724; Foulis, Glasgow, 1746 and 1751; Urie, Glasgow, 1754. A spirited Latin version by Dempster—'Cerasum et Silvestre Prunum'—appeared in 1631.

'The Flyting betwixt Montgomery and Polwart' was first published by Andro Hart in 1621 (the only known copy was in the Harleian Library at its dispersion, but all trace of it has been lost); another edit., by 'The Heires of Andro Hart,' was dated 1629. 'The Flyting' belongs to a species of composition scurrilous and vituperative in the extreme, but much relished by the Scots of the sixteenth century. It is an imitation of 'The Flyting' of Dunbar and Kennedie, and quite as coarse and abusive. A portion of it was quoted in King James's 'Revlis and Cavtelis of Scottis Poesie' in 1584. 'The Mindes Melodie' (Edinburgh, by Robert Charteris, 1605)—a version of fifteen of the psalms, Simeon's song, and 'Gloria Patri'—was among his last works.

Other poems are found in the following manuscripts:—The Drummond MS. in the university of Edinburgh has seventy sonnets and many miscellaneous and devotional poems; the Bannatyne MS. in the Advocates' Library, Edinburgh, has seven smaller poems. The sonnets are valuable for the light they throw on the poet's life and character. Those in praise of the king are marred by flattery and cringing servility; a few that owe their origin to his vexatious lawsuit are unspeakably bitter; others, addressed to friends, are models of good taste and feeling. The miscellaneous poems are cast in a great variety of measures, and are largely amatory. Two pieces, 'The Navigatioun' and 'A Cartell of thre ventrous Knichts,' are noteworthy as pageants written in Montgomerie's capacity of court poet. They were evidently composed on the occasion of the king's 'first and magnificent entry' into Edinburgh in 1579, when he assumed the reins of government. The Maitland MS. in the Pepysian Library, Magdalene College, Cambridge, has poems on Lady Margaret Montgomerie and 'The Bankis of Helicon,' which have been doubtfully attributed to Montgomerie.

The first complete collection of Montgomerie's works, with a biographical sketch by Dr. Irving, was issued under Dr. Laing's supervision in 1821. The latest edition, with introduction, bibliography, notes, and glossary, by the present writer, was published by the Scottish Text Society, 1887.

[James Melville's Diary; Dempster's Ecclesiastical History of the Scottish Nation; Pont's Topography of Cunningham (Maitland Club), pp. 19, 89–91; Pinkerton's Ancient Scotish Poems; Lyle's Ancient Ballads and Songs; Biographical Notice in Laing's edition; Montgomerie's Poems, ed. Scottish Text Society.] J. C-N.

MONTGOMERIE or SETON, ALEXANDER, sixth Earl of Eglinton (1588–1661), born in 1588, was third son of Robert Seton, first earl of Wintoun, by Margaret, eldest daughter of Hugh Montgomerie, third earl of Eglinton [q. v.] Hugh, fifth earl of Eglinton, the third earl's grandson, was thus his first cousin. He is first known as Sir Alexander Seton of Foulstruther. On 2 July 1606 he and his brother George, master of Wintoun, were summoned to appear before the privy council to answer for an attack on the Earl of Glencairn at Perth (*Reg. P. C. Scotl.* vii. 222). Having failed to appear, they were on 10 July denounced as rebels (*ib.* p. 224). On 30 July they, however, gave sureties to answer before the council on the 14th of the following October (*ib.* p. 646); and the matter was finally settled by an order on 23 Dec. to the master of Wintoun and the Earl of Glencairn to subscribe an assurance (*ib.* p. 288).

The fifth Earl of Eglinton having no issue made a resignation and settlement of the earldom and entail on his cousin and heirs male of his body, he and they taking the name and arms of Montgomerie. This settlement was confirmed by charter under the great seal, dated 28 Nov. 1611, and after the death of the earl in 1612, Seton was infeft in the earldom on 30 Oct. King James, however, challenged the transference of the title as having been done without his authority, and on 28 April 1613 the privy council decided that Seton should be charged to appear before it on 18 May, to 'hear and see him discharged of all assuming unto himself the style, title, and name of earl' (*ib.* x. 32). This he declined to do, but ultimately on 15 March 1615 he appeared before the council, apologised for having used the title without the king's authority, and resigned it into the king's hands. Thereupon the king, in accordance with a previous arrangement, was graciously pleased to confer it on him (*ib.* pp. 310–11), and on 13 April following he was infeft in the earldom, under the designation of Alexander Montgomerie, Earl of Eglinton, Lord Montgomerie and Kilwinning. According to tradition the king was finally induced to this decision through the interposition of his favourite, Robert Car, earl of Somerset, after Eglinton had explained to him that, though ignorant of the intricacies of law, he knew the use of the sword, and had intimated that he would challenge the favourite to a duel unless the opposition to his assumption of the title were withdrawn. From the incident Eglinton, who was a very skilful swordsman, obtained the surname of 'Graysteel.' In 1617 James when in Scotland paid a visit to Eglinton. The latter was one of the Scots nobles who on 7 May 1625 attended the funeral of King James in Westminster Abbey (Balfour, *Annals*, ii. 118). He formed one of the procession at the state entry of Charles into Edinburgh on 15 June 1633 (*ib.* iv. 354); at the coronation on 18 June he carried the spurs (*ib.* p. 357); and at the rising of the parliament on 24 June he carried the sword (*ib.* p. 364).

From an early period Eglinton was a staunch presbyterian, chiefly owing to the influence of David Dickson or Dick [q. v.], minister of Irvine, who he affirmed was 'the instrument to reclaim him from popery,' the traditional faith of the Montgomeries. He was one of the commissioners who at the parliament of 1621 voted against the five articles of Perth (Calderwood, vii. 498). After Dickson was deprived of his ministry at Irvine for publicly protesting against the five articles, the earl obtained for him liberty 'to come to Eglinton and to visit now and then his family at Irvine, but not to preach there' (*ib.* p. 541). On his arrival Eglinton arranged that he should preach in the hall of the castle, and afterwards in the close, when the multitudes who thronged to hear him became too great for the hall; but after two months he was ordered to proceed to ward (*ib.*) Eglinton was, however, ultimately successful in obtaining consent to his return to Irvine (*ib.* p. 568).

Eglinton was no doubt further confirmed in his presbyterianism by intercourse with Robert Baillie [q. v.], minister of Kilwinning. He was one of the noblemen who after the tumult in St. Giles's Church, Edinburgh, on account of the introduction of the prayer-book, presented a petition against it (Guthry, *Memoirs*, p. 25). He also took an active part in the movement for the preparation of the national covenant (*ib.* p. 137), and was a witness of the oaths of the people to it (Robert Baillie, *Letters and Journals*, i. 88). He attended the general assembly of 1638 as commissioner from the presbytery of Glasgow, and was one of the committee appointed by the assembly for taking in complaints against the bishops (Gordon, *Scots Affairs*, ii. 29). When in 1639 it was resolved to withstand by force of arms the attempt of Charles to concuss the covenanters, Eglinton 'came away with the whole country at his back' (Robert Baillie, *Letters and Journals*, i. 201), and joined the force which under Leslie encamped at Dunse Law to bar the northward march of the king. In April 1640 he was along with Argyll deputed by the convention of estates to watch the western parts of Scotland against the landing of forces from Ireland, the portion assigned to him being that south of the Firth of Clyde (Gordon, iii. 163). After Charles had come to a temporary agreement with the Scots, Eglinton was on 17 Sept. 1641 nominated one of the privy council (Balfour, *Annals*, iii. 67), and the choice was confirmed by parliament on 13 Nov. (*ib.* p. 149). He was also one of the committee appointed to inquire into the 'Incident' or supposed plot against Argyll (*ib.* p. 127).

In 1643 Eglinton was appointed to the command of a regiment of horse in the army sent by the Scots to the assistance of the English parliament against the king (Spalding, *Memoriall of the Trubles*, ii. 294). He was present at the siege of York in April–June 1644, and on one occasion, with four thousand Scots, entered some of the gates and made a passage to the manor-house, a strong party who sallied out of the city being beaten back with loss (Whitelocke, *Memorials*, p. 90). At the battle of Marston Moor, 2 July 1644, he rendered signal service by keeping his ground with his regiment when the charge of Prince Rupert swept the remainder of the left wing into confusion (Baillie, ii. 204; also *Full and True Relation of the Victory obtained by the Forces under command of General Lesley, Lord Fairfax, and the Earl of Manchester*, 1644). Shortly afterwards he returned to Scotland, and was present at the meeting of parliament on 28 July (Balfour, *Annals*, iii. 240). He was one of the committee of estates appointed in 1645 to consider the petition of General Baillie for a trial regarding his conduct at the battle of Kilsyth, and on 30 Jan. 1646 was named one of the committee of estates during the interval between the sessions of parliament.

Eglinton disapproved of the 'Engagement' of 1648 to march into England for the relief of the king, and after the defeat of Hamilton at Preston headed the raid of the western whigamores, who took possession of Edinburgh, and afterwards entered into communication with Cromwell. On the execution of Charles I he supported the proposal for the recall of Charles II as a 'covenanted king.' Charles after his arrival appointed him on 22 July 1650 colonel of the cavalry regiment of life-guards (Balfour, iv. 85); and at his instigation the king came on the 29th from Stirling to the army at Leith (*ib.* p. 86). He was present at Dunfermline on 13 Aug., at the first council held by the king since his coming to Scotland (*ib.* p. 90). After the king joined the northern loyalists Eglinton assembled with those nobles who met at Perth, and sent him a discreet letter asking him to return (*ib.* p. 115). Eglinton supported the policy of Argyll, in opposition to the extreme covenanters of the west, and even proposed that the western remonstrance should be declared scandalous and treasonable, and be publicly burnt by the hangman (*ib.* p. 172). Afterwards he was appointed with Argyll and the lord chancellor to speak privately with some of the western gentlemen regarding an agreement for a union of the forces (*ib.* p. 186). In 1651 he raised a regiment for the service of the king (*ib.* p. 272); but while in Dumbartonshire he and his sons were betrayed to the soldiers of Cromwell, and captured in their beds. For betraying them one Archibald Hamilton was hanged at Stirling in April 1651 (Nicoll, *Diary*, p. 52). After being detained for some time in the castle of Edinburgh, Eglinton was sent a prisoner to Hull, and afterwards to Berwick-on-Tweed. The statement made by most authorities that he was detained a prisoner there till the Restoration is, however, without foundation. On 15 Oct. 1652 he was allowed the liberty of the town of Berwick (*Cal. State Papers*, Dom. Ser. 1651–2, p. 440), and subsequently his liberty was further extended, for on 18 July 1654 the governor of Berwick was ordered to secure him and Lord Montgomerie till they procure Colonel Robert Montgomerie and give him in charge to the constable, or till they give security that he will depart the Commonwealth (*ib.* 1654, p. 258). Although his son, Hugh, lord Montgomerie, afterwards seventh earl, was also excluded from Cromwell's Act of Grace, the sixth earl was included in it, and his estates returned to him after two years' sequestration (*ib.* 1657–8, p. 284). On Montgomerie's marriage in 1631, Eglinton had settled the estates on him, reserving for himself only a life-rent, but in 1635 Montgomerie bound himself not to interfere with the estates during his father's lifetime (*ib.* pp. 284–5), and not being forfeited, they were in 1655 settled by Eglinton on Montgomerie's eldest son (*ib.*) In August 1659 Eglinton was secured and put in prison by General Monck, lest he should take up arms in favour of Charles (Nicoll, *Diary*). He lived to see the Restoration, but died at Eglinton Castle on 7 Jan. 1661. There is an engraving of the sixth earl in Sir William Fraser's 'Earls of Eglinton.' By his first wife, Anna (*d.* 1632), eldest daughter of Alexander Livingstone, first earl of Linlithgow [q. v.], he had five sons and three daughters: Hugh, seventh earl [q. v.], Sir Henry of Giffen, Alexander, Colonel James of Coilsfield, ancestor of the twelfth and succeeding earls of Eglinton; General Robert Montgomerie [q. v.]; Margaret, married first to John, first earl of Tweeddale, and secondly to William, ninth earl of Glencairn; Helenor died young, and Anna died unmarried. By his second wife, Margaret (*d.* 1651), eldest daughter of Walter, first lord Scott of Buccleugh, and relict of James, first lord Ross, he had no issue.

[Histories of Calderwood and Spotiswood; Robert Baillie's Letters and Journals (Bannatyne Club); Balfour's Annals; Guthry's Memoirs; Nicoll's Diary (Bannatyne Club); Lamont's Diary; Rothes's Short Relation (Bannatyne Club); Spalding's Memoriall of the Trubles (Spalding Club); Gordon's Scots Affairs (Spalding Club); Reg. P. C. Scotl.; Cal. State Papers, Dom. Ser.; Patterson's Hist. of Ayr; Sir William Fraser's Earls of Eglinton; Douglas's Scottish Peerage (Wood), i. 502–3.] T. F. H.

MONTGOMERIE, ALEXANDER, ninth Earl of Eglinton (1660?–1729), eldest son of Alexander, eighth earl of Eglinton, by his first wife, Lady Elizabeth Crichton, eldest daughter of William, second earl of Dumfries, was born about 1660. From the time of the death of his grandfather, Hugh [q. v.], in 1669, he was boarded with Matthew Fleming, the minister of Culross, Perthshire, who superintended his education at the school of Culross until 1673, when he was sent to the university of St. Andrews, where he remained till Lammas 1676. A few months after leaving the university he married Lady Margaret Cochrane, eldest daughter of Lord Cochrane, the son of the first Earl of Dundonald, on which occasion his father made over to him the Eglinton estates. After the revolution he was chosen a privy councillor by King William, and also a lord of the treasury. In 1700 he obtained a letter from the king to sit and vote in the Scots parliament in place of the lord high treasurer. He succeeded to the earldom on the death of his father in 1701. On Queen Anne's accession in 1702 Eglinton was chosen a privy councillor, and in 1711 he was named one of the commissioners of the chamberlain's court. In 1710, and again in 1713, he was elected one of the Scottish representative peers. Lockhart, who was his son-in-law, states that when he himself proposed to bring in a bill for resuming the bishops' revenues in Scotland, and applying them to the episcopal clergy there, Eglinton gave his support to the measure, and assured Queen Anne that the presbyterians would not actively oppose it (*Papers*, i. 450). This is corroborated by Wodrow, who asserts that Lockhart, either in the House of Peers or in the privy council, proposed 'that as we are one in civil we should be one in church matters' (*Analecta*, i. 318). Wodrow also states that his speech on patronage and toleration was 'so very good' that it was supposed 'it was done by somebody for him' (*ib.* p. 320). In June 1712 he also proposed a bill for prolonging the time for taking the oath of abjuration till 1 Nov. (*ib.* ii. 54).

Lockhart affirms that Eglinton at last professed himself a Jacobite, and promised him three thousand guineas 'to help the Pretender in his restoration' (*Papers*, ii. 9). Wodrow also relates that shortly before the rebellion in 1715 Eglinton 'was at a meeting of the Jacobites where the rebellion, as to the manner of carrying out, was concerted, and heard all their proposals' (*Analecta*, ii. 359). Nevertheless, during the crisis he raised and disciplined the Ayrshire fencibles, with which on 22 Aug. he joined the Earls of Kilmarnock and Glasgow and Lord Semple at Irvine in support of the government (Rae, *History of the Rebellion*, 2nd edit. p. 203). He died suddenly at Eglinton on 18 Feb. 1729. Between nine hundred and a thousand beggars are stated to have attended his funeral, 50*l.* being divided among them.

Eglinton was thrice married. By his first wife, Margaret Cochrane, he had three sons and six daughters: Hugh, lord Montgomerie, died in 1696; Alexander, died young; John, died young; Catherine, married to James, fifth earl of Galloway; Elizabeth, died young; Jean, died young; Euphemia, married to George Lockhart of Carnwath [q. v.]; Grace, to Robert, sixth earl of Carnwath; and Jean, to Sir Alexander Maxwell of Monreith, Wigtownshire. By his second wife, Lady Anne Gordon, daughter of George, first earl of Aberdeen, lord high chancellor of Scotland, he had one daughter, Mary—married to Sir David Cuningham of Milncraig, Ayrshire—a celebrated beauty, whose charms are sung by Hamilton of Bangour. By his third wife, Susannah, daughter of Sir Archibald Kennedy of Culzean, Ayrshire, he had three sons and seven daughters: James, lord Montgomerie; Alexander, tenth earl of Eglinton [q. v.], and Archibald, eleventh earl [q. v.]; Helen, married to the Hon. Francis Stuart of Pittendriech, third son of James, eighth earl of Moray; Mary, to Sir Alexander Macleod of Macleod; Frances, unmarried; Christian, married to James Moray of Abercairney; Grace, to Charles Byrne, a cornet in Bland's dragoons; Charlotte, died young; and Susannah (*d.* 1754) married to John Renton of Lamerton in Berwickshire.

The third Countess of Eglinton (1689–1780) and her daughters were celebrated for a characteristic gracefulness of feature and bearing known as the 'Eglinton air.' The personal attractiveness of the countess was also enhanced by her wit and her intellectual accomplishments. To her Allan Ramsay dedicated his 'Gentle Shepherd,' and to the dedication Hamilton of Bangour added a poetical address to the countess in heroic couplets. Subsequently Allan Ramsay presented to her the original manuscript of the poem, and it was given by her to James Boswell. The countess entertained Dr. Johnson in 1773 at Auchans, Ayrshire, on his return from the Hebrides. Although then in her eighty-fifth year, she retained much of her personal charm and her intellectual vivacity. Johnson told her she 'was married the year before he was born,' upon which she said 'she might have been his mother and would adopt him,' and at parting embraced him as her son. She died 18 March 1780, at the age of ninety-one. Two engravings of the Countess Susannah, from family portraits, are in Sir William Fraser's 'Earls of Eglinton.' One by Gavin Hamilton [q. v.] belonged to the Rev. W. K. R. Bedford of Sutton Coldfield.

[Lockhart Papers; Wodrow's Analecta (Spalding Club); Rae's Hist. of Rebellion; Johnson's Tour to the Hebrides; Sir William Fraser's Earls of Eglinton; Douglas's Scottish Peerage (Wood), i 506–7.] T. F. H.

MONTGOMERIE, ALEXANDER, tenth Earl of Eglinton (1723–1769), fourth son of Alexander, ninth earl [q. v.], and second son by his third wife, Susannah, daughter of Sir Archibald Kennedy of Culzean, was born 10 Feb. 1723, and succeeded his father 18 Feb. 1729. He received his early education at the grammar school of Irvine, after which he was, in May 1737, transferred to Haddington, and thence, in October 1738, to Winchester, where he remained, somewhat to his dissatisfaction, beyond the usual school age. In 1742 he went to Paris, and became specially proficient in dancing, fencing, and riding.

In 1748 Eglinton, under the act for abolishing heritable jurisdictions, obtained 7,500*l.* for the redeemable sheriffship of Renfrew, the bailiary of the regality of Kilwinning and the regality of Cunningham, which had since 1498 been in dispute between the Earls of Eglinton and Glencairn [see under Hugh, first Earl of Eglinton]. In 1759 he was promised the governorship of Dumbarton Castle (cf. *MSS. Addit.* 32903 f. 273). From the accession of George III he was a lord of the bedchamber for six years. It was owing chiefly to the exertions of Eglinton that the optional clause was abolished in the Scottish Bank Act which enabled the banks to delay payment of their notes for six months after demand. He was also strongly opposed to the accumulation of public debt, and under the signature 'A. M.' published in 1754 a pamphlet on the subject, entitled 'Inquiry into the Origin and Consequences of the Public Debt, by a Person of Distinction.' Deeming that he might as a commoner find a more useful and important sphere for his ambition, he at one time cherished the purpose of dispeering himself, and took the advice of counsel on the subject, but their opinion being unfavourable he gave up the project. In 1761, and again in 1768, he was chosen a representative peer for Scotland. While taking an active interest in matters of public and political interest, he also devoted much attention to the management of his estate, and was one of the chief pioneers of agricultural improvement in Ayrshire.

The earl was mortally wounded on 24 Oct. 1769 by a gun fired by Mungo Campbell, an officer of excise at Salcoats, and died on the following morning at Eglinton Castle. Campbell, who had formerly been detected shooting a hare on Eglinton's estate, was seen by some servants on the grounds of the earl near Ardrossan, gun in hand. The earl, who was passing at the time in his carriage, was informed of the circumstance, and alighting, demanded that Campbell should give up his gun. This Campbell, who affirmed that he was merely walking through the earl's grounds for a short cut, and had no intention of poaching, declined to do. The earl determined to compel him, whereupon Campbell, keeping the gun pointed at him, warned him that 'he would give it up to no man.' As the earl advanced, Campbell stepped backwards, until he stumbled over a stone and fell; immediately after the earl was shot he was put into his coach and carried to Eglinton Castle, where he died at two o'clock the next morning, having employed the interval in giving orders and making provision for his servants. According to the dying declaration of the earl and the statements of his servants, Campbell shot him deliberately, but Campbell himself persisted in asserting that the gun went off accidentally. He was tried before the high court of justiciary of Edinburgh, and condemned to death, but avoided execution by hanging himself in prison on the morning after the trial. The body was delivered to his friends, who buried it near Salisbury Crags, but the rabble of Edinburgh having discovered the grave disentombed it, and treated it with brutal contumely, and ultimately it was taken by the friends and sunk in the sea. Eglinton at the time of his death was engaged to be married to Jane, daughter of Sir John Maxwell of Pollok, Renfrewshire, and widow of James Montgomerie of Lainshaw, Ayrshire. As he left no children, he was succeeded in the estates and titles by his brother Archibald (1726–1796) [q. v.]

It was to Eglinton that Boswell was indebted for introduction to what he terms 'the circle of the great, the gay, and the ingenious.' Boswell also states that the earl, 'who loved wit more than wine, and men of genius more than sycophants, had a great admiration of Johnson, but from the remarkable elegance of his own manners was perhaps too delicately sensible of the roughness which sometimes appeared in Johnson's behaviour.'

[Trial of Mungo Campbell, 1770; Information for Mungo Campbell, 1770; Sermon preached on the occasion of the Death of the late Alex., Earl of Eglinton, by Alex. Cuningham, minister of Symington, 1769; A Dialogue of the Dead between Lord Eglinton and Mungo Campbell, 1770; Boswell's Life of Johnson; Paterson's Hist. of Ayr; Sir William Fraser's Earls of Eglinton; Douglas's Scottish Peerage (Wood), i. 506–7.]

T. F. H.

MONTGOMERIE, ARCHIBALD, eleventh Earl of Eglinton in the peerage of Scotland (1726–1796), born 18 May 1726, was third son (by his third wife, Susannah, daughter of Sir Archibald Kennedy, bart., of Culzean, Ayrshire) of Alexander, ninth earl [q. v.] When Pitt decided to form regiments of highlanders at the beginning of the seven years' war, Montgomerie was a young major in the 36th foot, a high-spirited young fellow, with a strong dash of romantic enthusiasm about him, and very popular in the highlands, where he had two sisters married to influential lairds. He accordingly raised in a short time a very fine regiment of highlanders of thirteen companies of 105 rank and file each. It at first appeared in the 'Army List' as the 2nd highland regiment, but immediately afterwards was numbered as the 77th foot, being the first of the three regiments that have successively borne that number. Montgomerie was appointed lieutenant-colonel commandant 4 Jan. 1757. He took the regiment out to America, where it formed the advance in the second expedition to Fort Duquesne, under Brigadier-general Forbes, in 1758, and afterwards went through much adventurous service in the remote wilds of the neighbouring country. Montgomerie was sent with twelve hundred men against the Cherokees; he destroyed Estatoe and other Indian villages, and defeated the Indians in a pitched battle at Etchocy in 1760, and again at War-Woman's Creek in 1761. He was put on half-pay when his regiment was disbanded in 1764. In 1769 he was appointed colonel 51st foot, and succeeded his elder brother, Alexander, tenth earl [q. v.], in the earldom the same year. He became a major-general in 1772, lieutenant-general in 1777, and governor of Edinburgh Castle in 1782. He died a full general and colonel of the Scots greys 30 Oct. 1796. Eglinton married, first, in 1772, Lady Jean Lindsay, eldest daughter of George, eighteenth earl of Crawford, who died childless; secondly, in 1783, Frances, only daughter of Sir William Twysden, bart., of Roydon Hall, Kent, by whom he had two daughters. The elder, Mary, married Archibald, lord Montgomerie, eldest son of Hugh, twelfth earl [q. v.], a kinsman who succeeded to the title, while most of the family estates passed to Lady Mary. The eleventh earl's widow remarried Francis, brother of General Sir John Moore [q. v.]

[Foster's Peerage, under 'Eglinton' and 'Winton;' Army Lists; Stewart's Scottish Highlanders, ii. 59 et seq.; Parkman's Montcalm and Wolfe, ii. 158, and Conspiracy of Pontiac, vol. ii.] H. M. C.

MONTGOMERIE, ARCHIBALD WILLIAM, thirteenth Earl of Eglinton, and first Earl of Winton in the peerage of the United Kingdom (1812–1861), born at Palermo in Sicily on 29 Sept. 1812, was the elder son of Major-general the Hon. Archibald Montgomerie, lord Montgomerie, by his wife, Lady Mary Montgomerie, the elder daughter of Archibald, eleventh earl of Eglinton [q. v.] His father died at Alicante on 4 Jan. 1814, and on 30 Jan. 1815 his mother became the wife of Sir Charles Montolieu Lamb, bart. He was educated at Eton, and succeeded to the peerage on the death of his grandfather, Hugh, twelfth earl of Eglinton [q. v.], in December 1819. Eglinton took his seat in the House of Lords as Baron Ardrossan on 1 May 1834 (*Journals of the House of Lords*, lxvi. 193), and in December 1840 was served heir male general of George, fourth earl of Winton, the fifth earl, who was attainted in 1716, having left no issue. Eglinton was appointed lord-lieutenant and sheriff principal of Ayrshire on 17 Aug. 1842, and at the opening of parliament in February 1843 he seconded the address in the House of Lords (*Parl. Debates*, 3rd ser. lxvi. 15–19). He was chosen one of the whips of the protection party in the House of Lords in 1846, and spoke against the second reading of the Corn Importation Bill on 28 May in that year (*ib.* lxxxvi. 1355–9). In April 1847 he obtained the appointment of a select committee to inquire into the regulations relating to the elections of the Scottish representative peers (*ib.* xcii. 201–3), and in the same session carried through the house a bill for the correction of the abuses which prevailed at those elections (10 & 11 Vict. cap. 52). In May 1848 he opposed the second reading of the Jewish Disabilities Bill (*ib.* xcviii. 1384–6). Upon the formation of Lord Derby's first administration [see Stanley, Edward Geoffrey, fourteenth Earl of Derby] Eglinton was appointed lord-lieutenant of Ireland, and was sworn a member of the privy council (27 Feb. 1852). His open-handed hospitality made him an exceedingly popular viceroy among the upper classes in Ireland, and upon his retirement from office in December 1852 it was asserted that no lord-lieutenant since the Duke of Northumberland in 1829–30 [see Percy Hugh, third Duke of Northumberland] had kept up the viceregal court in such a princely style. He was invested with the order of the Thistle at Buckingham Palace on 18 June 1853. In February 1854 a select committee was appointed by the House of Lords at Eglinton's instance to inquire into the practical working of the system of national education in Ireland (*ib.* cxxx. 783–790). On Lord Derby's return to power Eglinton was again appointed lord-lieutenant of Ireland (26 Feb. 1858). He resigned office with the rest of his colleagues in June 1859, and was created Earl of Winton in the peerage of the United Kingdom on the 25th of the same month. Eglinton spoke for the last time in the House of Lords on 11 July 1861 (*ib.* clxiv. 690). He died of apoplexy at Mount Melville House, near St. Andrews, the residence of J. Whyte Melville, on 4 Oct. 1861, aged 49, and was buried in the family vault at Kilwinning, Ayrshire, on the 11th of the same month.

Eglinton was a high-minded nobleman and a thorough sportsman, with frank and genial manners, and no particular ability. In August 1839 he held the famous tournament at Eglinton Castle, described by Disraeli in 'Endymion' (vol. ii. chap. xxiii.), and presided over by Lady Seymour (afterwards the Duchess of Somerset) as the queen of beauty. This remarkable entertainment, which created an immense sensation at the time, is said to have cost him between 30,000*l.* and 40,000*l.*, and to have made him the most popular nobleman in Scotland. He was a great supporter of the turf for a number of years, and at one time had one of the largest and best racing studs in the country. He won the St. Leger with Blue Bonnet in 1842, with Van Tromp in 1847, and the Derby and the St. Leger with the Flying Dutchman in 1849. The match between the Flying Dutchman and Lord Zetland's Voltigeur at the York Spring Meeting of 1851, in which Lord Eglinton's horse was victorious, has taken its place as one of the classic events of the turf. He unsuccessfully contested the rectorship of Glasgow against Fox Maule [see Maule, Fox, second Baron Panmure and eleventh Earl of Dalhousie] in November 1843, and against Rutherford in November 1844, but was elected lord rector both of Marischal College, Aberdeen, and of the university of Glasgow in 1852. He presided at the commemoration of Burns at Ayr on 6 Aug. 1844, and was created a D.C.L. of Oxford University on 7 June 1853.

Eglinton married first, on 17 Feb. 1841, Theresa, daughter of Charles Newcomen of Clonahard, co. Longford, and widow of Richard Howe Cockerell, commander in the royal navy, by whom he had three sons and one daughter. His wife died on 16 Dec. 1853, and on 2 Nov. 1858 he married secondly Lady Adela Caroline Harriet Capel, only daughter of Arthur, sixth earl of Essex, by whom he had two daughters. This lady died on 31 Dec. 1860. He was succeeded by his eldest son, Archibald William, lord Montgomerie, the fourteenth earl of Eglinton, who died on 30 Aug. 1892, aged 50. There are two portraits of Eglinton in Sir William Fraser's 'Memorials of the Montgomeries' (i. 396–7), and there is an engraving by Hodgetts after Steevens.

[Sir William Fraser's Memorials of the Montgomeries, Earls of Eglinton, 1859, i. 138–41, 152–3, 396–7; Lord Lamington's In the Days of the Dandies, 1890, pp. 50–5, 63; Journal of Henry Cockburn, 1874, i. 239–41, ii. 53, 87, 97, 275–6, 291; Lord Malmesbury's Memoirs of an ex-Minister, 1884, i. 169, 278, ii. 71, 170, 260–1; Duke of Buckingham's Memoirs of the Courts and Cabinets of William IV and Victoria, 1861, ii. 396–7; Dublin University Mag. lviii. 629–31; Blackwood's Mag. xc. 642–4; Anderson's Scottish Nation, 1863, ii. 125; Nixon and Richardson's Eglinton Tournament, 1843; Bulkeley's Righte Faithfull Chronique, &c., 1840; Notes and Queries, 3rd ser. x. 223, 276, 322, 404, xi. 21, 66, 162; Rice's History of the British Turf, 1879, i. 195–6, 242–7, 281–4, ii. 374, 378; Sporting Magazine, June 1858 pp. 452–5, November 1861 pp. 320–3; Times, 5 Oct. 1861; Scotsman, 5, 11, 14 Oct. 1861; Illustrated London News, 19 Oct. 1861 (portrait); Sporting Times, 28 March 1885; Gent. Mag. 1839 pt. ii. pp. 414–16, 1861 pt. ii. pp. 563–5; Doyle's Official Baronage, 1886, iii. 711–12; Foster's Alumni Oxon. 1888, iii. 971; Stapylton's Eton School Lists, 1864, p. 125; Haydn's Book of Dignities, 1890.] G. F. R. B.

MONTGOMERIE, HUGH, third Baron Montgomerie and first Earl of Eglinton (1460?–1545), eldest son of Alexander, second lord Montgomerie, by his wife Catherine, daughter of Gilbert, lord Kennedy, was born about 1460. His grandfather was Alexander, first lord Montgomerie [q. v.] He succeeded his father before 29 Aug. 1483. He was infeft in the lands of Ardrossan and other estates of the family 5 June 1484, and on 11 Oct. he executed a revocation of all acts made during his minority. He was one of the commissioners appointed by the treaty of Nottingham on 22 Sept. of the same year to settle disputes on the marches. Having supported the cause of the nobles against James III at the battle of Sauchieburn, 1 June 1488, he, on the accession of James IV, obtained a remission for throwing down the house of Turnelaw (Kerrielaw), and for all other offences committed by him up to 29 Aug. He had also a commission to repress crime in the districts of Carrick, Kyle, Ayr, and Cunningham. In the following year he was chosen a privy councillor, and appointed constable of the royal castle of Rothesay. On 4 July 1498 he obtained a grant of the bailiary of Cunningham, and was made chamberlain of the town of Irvine. The former grant gave rise to a long chronic feud between the Montgomeries and the Cunninghams, earls of Glencairn.

Montgomerie was created Earl of Eglinton between the 3rd and 20th Jan. 1506. He was one of those peers who after the battle of Flodden, 9 Sept. 1513, at which James IV was slain, met at Perth to arrange for the coronation of the infant prince, James V, and was nominated one of the guardians of the prince. On 28 Oct. 1515 he was made keeper of the isle of Little Cumbrae, for the preservation of the game, until the king came of age. On 2 Feb. 1526–7 he was appointed justice-general of the northern parts of Scotland. He was one of the lords who attended the council of the king at Stirling in June 1528, after his escape from the Douglases. In November of the same year his house of Eglinton was burnt down by William Cunningham, master of Glencairn, and the charters of his lands having been all destroyed, the king granted him a new charter dated 23 Jan. 1528–9. On 18 Aug. 1533 Patrick, earl of Bothwell, great admiral of Scotland, appointed him admiral-depute within the bounds of Cunningham. During the absence of the king in France in 1536, to bring home his bride, the Princess Magdalen, he acted as one of the council of regency. He died in June 1545, and was succeeded in the earldom by his grandson Hugh (*d.* 1546). By his wife Helen, third daughter of Colin, first earl of Argyll, he had six sons and eight daughters: Alexander, master of Montgomerie, who died young; John, lord Montgomerie, killed in the skirmish in the High Street of Edinburgh called 'Cleanse the Causeway,' 2 May 1520, and father of Hugh, second earl; Sir Neil of Langshaw; William of Greenfield; Hugh, killed at the battle of Pinkie in 1547; Robert, first rector of Kirkmichael, and afterwards bishop of Argyll; Margaret, married to William, second lord Semple; Marjory, to William, second lord Somerville; Maud, to Colin Campbell of Ardkinglass; Isobel, to John Mure of Caldwell; Elizabeth, to John Blair of that ilk; Agnes, to John Ker of Kersland; Janet, to Campbell of Cessnock; and Catherine, to George Montgomerie of Skelmorlie.

[Reg. Mag. Sig. Scot.; Exchequer Rolls of Scotl.; Pitscottie's Chron.; Balfour's Annals; Sir William Fraser's Earls of Eglinton; Paterson's Hist. of Ayr; Douglas's Scottish Peerage (Wood), i. 496–8.] T. F. H.

MONTGOMERIE, HUGH, third Earl of Eglinton (1531?–1585), eldest son of Hugh, second earl, by his wife Mariot, daughter of George, third lord Seton, was born about 1531. He succeeded to the estates on the death of his father, 3 Sept. 1546. Hugh Montgomerie, first earl [q. v.], was his great-grandfather. With his brother William he was incorporated a student of St. Mary's College, St. Andrews, in 1552. Having married Lady Janet Hamilton, daughter of the regent Arran, he for some time acted, although a catholic, in concert with Arran in political matters. He assembled his forces with Arran in October 1559 in Edinburgh in support of the congregation (*Cal. State Papers*, For. Ser. 1559–60, entry 130), and in December he was stated to have declared openly against the French (*ib.* entry 392). Yet in the February following he was reported to be wholly addicted to the queen's cause (Crofts to Cecil, 23 Feb., *ib.* entry 762); and he was one of those who after the death of Francis II, husband of Mary Stuart, attended a convention at Dunbar on 10 Dec. 1560, when a bond was signed on behalf of the queen (*ib.* 1560, entry 818). In February following he set out to visit Mary in France (*ib.* entry 968), and remaining there till her return to Scotland in August, set sail in one of the vessels of her train, which was captured and for a short time detained by the English.

Eglinton was one of the most constant and persistent supporters of Mary Stuart in her catholic policy, and especially in her efforts to establish the mass. On 3 June 1562 Randolph reports that he and the Bishop of St. Andrews hear daily masses (*ib.* 1562, entry 145), and Knox mentions him as present with other papists at the mass in the chapel of Holyrood when Darnley, in February 1565–6, received the order of the Cockle from the king of France (*Works*, ii. 519). At the marriage banquet of Mary and Darnley, 29 July 1565, he was one of the nobles who waited on Darnley. With other lords and barons of the west he also, on 5 Sept., signed a bond for the king and queen (*Reg. P. C. Scotl.* i. 363); and in the 'roundabout raid' against Moray his forces formed part of the van (*ib.* p. 379). He was one of the lords who, 17 Dec. 1566, assisted at the baptism of the young prince James, at Stirling, according to the rites of the Romish church (Knox, ii. 536).

Eglinton had no connection with the murder of Darnley, and with other catholic lords was opposed to the marriage with Bothwell, although at first he maintained a position of neutrality. He attended the supper given by Bothwell in Ainslie's tavern, 19 April 1567, but, alone of those present, managed to slip out without signing the bond for the marriage. He joined the lords who met at Stirling to take measures for the deliverance of the queen from Bothwell, but did not support their action after her confinement in Lochleven, and held aloof from the parliament convened by the regent's party in the following December (Calderwood, ii. 550). He joined the Hamiltons and other supporters of the queen after her escape from Lochleven (*Cal. State Papers*, For. Ser. 1566–8, entry 2172), and fought for her at Langside, 15 May 1568. After the battle he made his escape by hiding himself till nightfall in the straw of an outhouse. On the 24th he was charged to deliver up the castles and fortalices of Eglinton and Ardrossan (*Reg. P. C. Scotl.* i. 626). This he failed to do; and having, with the Hamiltons and others, held a convention on behalf of the queen at Ayr on 29 July (*Cal. State Papers*, For. Ser. 1566–8, entry 2397), he was at a parliament held on 19 Aug. declared guilty of treason. For some time he adhered to the party of the queen, but in May 1571 gave sureties to the regent (*ib.* 1569–71, entry 1620; CALDERWOOD, iii. 33). He was, notwithstanding, sent to ward to the castle of Doune, Perthshire, but obtained his release in July, and on 12 Aug. subscribed at Stirling his obedience to the regent (*ib.* p. 135). He was present with the nobles of the regent's party at Stirling on 3 Sept., when the town was entered by the Hamiltons and others, and the regent Lennox slain. During the raid he was shut up by them as a prisoner in his lodgings under a guard. On the accession of Mar to the regency an order was granted on 7 Sept. discharging Eglinton and his sureties from all pains and penalties (*Reg. P. C. Scotl.* ii. 79). After the election of Morton to the regency, Eglinton at the parliament held in February 1573 endeavoured with Lord Lindsay to secure toleration for the catholics (*Cal. State Papers*, Scott. Ser. i. 368), but he also supported the league with England, and took care to express special detestation of the St. Bartholomew massacres.

After the fall of Morton in 1578 Eglinton attended the meeting of the lords in the Tolbooth on 9 April, when measures were taken for the safety of the king's person and the peace of the country (MOYSIE, *Memoirs*, p. 6). On the reconciliation with Morton he was chosen a lord of the articles and a member of the new privy council. On 17 June a complaint was made against him by Alexander Cunningham, commendator of Kilwinning, for occupying the steeple of Kilwinning, when both parties were commanded to cease from using the steeple as 'ane house of war' in time coming (*Reg. P. C. Scotl.* iii. 2), but the arrangement by no means ended the dispute (*ib.* passim).

Eglinton subscribed the order of 30 April 1579 for the prosecution of the Hamiltons for the murder of the regents Moray and Lennox (*ib.* p. 147), and having been appointed one of the commission of lieutenancy to carry the order into effect, received on 22 May the thanks and exoneration of the council for the discharge of his duties (*ib.* p. 165). He was one of the assize for the trial of Morton in 1581; but though not directly connected with the raid of Ruthven, was present at the convention, 18 Oct. 1582, in Holyrood, which formally approved of the raid (MOYSIE, p. 40). He was also one of the privy council which on 4 Feb. 1582–1583 offered a reward of 500*l.* for the name of the author of the pasquil against the raid (*Reg. P. C. Scotl.* iii. 549). He died 3 June 1585.

In April 1562 Eglinton raised a process of divorce against his first wife, Janet Hamilton, on the ground of consanguinity (FRASER, *Earls of Eglinton*, ii. 163–81). The marriage on this ground was dissolved by the pope, but at the instance of the countess Eglinton was divorced from her by the kirk on the ground of adultery (*ib.* ii. 183–5). By this marriage he had no issue. The first countess died in December 1596, and was buried in Holyrood Abbey. Shortly after the divorce Eglinton married Margaret, daughter of Sir John Drummond of Innerpeffrey, and widow of Sir Hugh Campbell of Loudoun, by whom he had two sons and two daughters: Hugh, fourth earl, slain by the Cunninghams on 18 April 1586; Robert of Giffen; Margaret, celebrated by the poet Alexander Montgomerie [q. v.], married to Robert Seton, first earl of Wintoun, by whom she had, among other issue, Alexander, sixth earl of Eglinton [q. v.]; and Agnes, married to Robert, first lord Semple. The second countess remarried in 1588 Patrick, third lord Drummond.

[Histories of Knox, Calderwood, and Keith; Moysie's Memoirs (Bannatyne Club); Cal. State Papers, For. Ser. and Scott. Ser.; Reg. P. C. Scotl. vols. i–iii.; Paterson's Hist. of Ayr; Sir William Fraser's Earls of Eglinton; Douglas's Scottish Peerage (Wood), i. 499–500.] T. F. H.

MONTGOMERIE, HUGH, seventh EARL OF EGLINTON (1613–1669), eldest son of Alexander, sixth earl [q. v.], by his first wife, Lady Anna Livingstone, daughter of Alexander, first earl of Linlithgow [q. v.], was born 30 May 1613. Robert Baillie (1599–1662) [q. v.], whom he afterwards got appointed to the church of Kilwinning, had for some years the superintendence of his education (ROBERT BAILLIE, *Letters and Journals*, iii. 446). Until he succeeded to the earldom he was known as Lord Montgomerie. On 29 Feb. 1628 he was enrolled a student of Glasgow University. In 1633 he went to Paris, where he spent over a year in the prosecution of his studies, especially in the art of fortification.

Like his father, Montgomerie took a prominent part in opposing the ecclesiastical policy of Charles I in the assembly of 1638, strongly supporting the proposals against the bishops (*ib.* i. 125, 137, 147). When the covenanters in 1639 determined to resist the march of Charles northwards, he was chosen colonel of the men of Renfrewshire (*ib.* p. 201). He also joined the army which under Leslie marched into England in April 1640, and commanded a brigade of eighteen hundred men at the battle of Newburn. When the Scots came before Newcastle, he made an attempt to seize Gateshead, but was unsuccessful (*Thurloe State Papers*, i. 41). On 15 Sept. 1640 he was sent to occupy the castle of Tynemouth. He remained with his brigade in England until the return of the Scottish army after the ratification of Ripon in August 1641. Some time afterwards he was suspected by the covenanters of lukewarmness, and it was greatly feared that he would definitely join Montrose (BAILLIE, ii. 11, 35–7). The statement sometimes made, that he and his father actually fought on opposite sides at Marston Moor, 2 July 1644, is, however, without foundation. He does not appear to have fought on either side at that battle, but on 11 Oct. he joined the rendezvous at Glasgow against Montrose (*ib.* ii. 234). Along with other Scots lords in Leven's army, Montgomerie, after the battle of Naseby, made vain attempts on 21 July to open communications with Charles.

In 1646 Montgomerie was engaged in the northern campaign under Middleton, and on 27 April entered Aberdeen with four troops of horse (*Burgh Records of Aberdeen*, 1643–1747, p. 63). In addition to his horse he had under his command two regiments of foot, and he was entrusted with the duty of holding the city; but on 14 May it was entered by a large force under the Marquis of Huntly, who defeated Montgomerie and took above three hundred of his men prisoners (*ib.* p. 68). Nevertheless a council of war declared on 8 June that Montgomerie had conducted himself in the affair 'with as much prudence and gallantry as could have been expected' (*ib.* p. 64).

Montgomerie did not, as is sometimes stated, join the 'Engagement' under his brother-in-law, the Duke of Hamilton, for the rescue of the king. By the act of classes he was disqualified for all public service as having been accessory to it; but while admitting that he had been appointed colonel, and had consented to nominate officers, he declared that he declined to go into England on finding that the 'malignants' had been invited to join in the scheme (*Hist. MSS. Comm.* 11th Rep. pt. i. p. 37). He also denied that he had given any support to William Hamilton, second earl of Lanark [q. v.], or Monro on their retreat from England (*ib.*) On this account he petitioned the states to be reponed, producing a recommendation from the commission of the kirk in his favour (BALFOUR, *Annals*, iv. 127), and he was finally, on 17 Dec. 1650, declared by the parliament capable of public employment (*ib.* p. 206). In 1651 he defended himself in his house of Cumbrae against Cromwell, Robert Baillie taking shelter with him (*ib.* p. 244; BAILLIE, iii. 119). He was taken prisoner (*ib.* p. 317). Subsequently he received his liberty, but on 18 July 1654 the governor of Berwick was ordered to secure him and his father till they procured Colonel Robert Montgomerie (*d.* 1684) [q. v.], or gave security that he should leave the kingdom (*Cal. State Papers*, Dom. Ser. 1654, p. 258). As Robert Montgomerie was captured, Lord Montgomerie was no doubt soon afterwards set at liberty. He was excepted from Cromwell's Act of Grace in 1654. The yearly value of his estate was then stated at 271*l.* 3*s.* 11*d.*, and the charges on it 5,236*l.* 18*s.* In addition to the fine on his own estates he was also fined 1,400*l.* for his interest in the estate of his father, but petitioned to be relieved (*ib.* 1657–8, p. 128), and the petition was granted on 1 June 1658 (*ib.* 1658–9, p. 41).

Montgomerie succeeded his father in the earldom, 7 Jan. 1661. On 1 Jan. 1662 he obtained from Charles the citadel of Ayr. He died towards the close of February 1669. By his first wife, Anne, eldest daughter of James, second marquis of Hamilton, he had one daughter, Anne. By his second wife, Lady Mary Leslie, daughter of John, fifth earl of Rothes, he had two sons and five daughters: Alexander, eighth earl (*d.* 1701), a staunch supporter of the covenanters, and afterwards a privy councillor of William III, and father of Alexander, ninth earl [q. v.]; Francis, a commissioner of the treasury under William, and one of the commissioners of the union with England; Mary, married to George, fourth earl of Wintoun; Margaret, to James, second earl of Loudoun; Eleonora, to Sir David Dunbar of Baldoon, Wigtownshire; Christian, to John, fourth lord Balmerino; and Anne, to Sir Andrew Ramsay of Abbotshall. There is an engraving of the earl in Sir William Fraser's 'Earls of Eglinton,' from a portrait in the family collection.

[Robert Baillie's Letters and Journals (Bannatyne Club); Sir James Balfour's Annals; Burgh Records of Aberdeen; Guthry's Memoirs; Thurloe State Papers; Cal. State Papers, Dom. Ser., during the Commonwealth; Hist. MSS. Comm. 11th Rep. pt. i.; Paterson's Hist. of Ayr; Sir William Fraser's Earls of Eglinton; Douglas's Scottish Peerage (Wood), i. 503–504.]

T. F. H.

MONTGOMERIE, HUGH, twelfth EARL OF EGLINTON (1739–1819), son of Alexander Montgomerie of Coilsfield, Ayrshire—the 'Castle of Montgomerie' celebrated by Burns—descended from Colonel James Montgomerie, fourth son of Alexander, sixth earl of Eglinton [q. v.], was born on 29 Nov. 1739. His mother was Lillias (*d.* 1783), daughter of Sir Robert Montgomery, eleventh baronet of Skelmorlie [q. v.] Entering the army in 1756, he served in the American war as captain in the 78th foot, and afterwards as captain in the first royals. On the outbreak of the French war in 1788 he was appointed major in the Argyll or Western fencibles, raised jointly by the Argyll and Eglinton families, with Lord Frederick Campbell as colonel. In 1780, and again in 1784, he was elected to parliament as member for Ayrshire. If we may trust the testimony of Burns, in his 'Earnest Cry and Prayer,' Montgomerie's oratorical power was less conspicuous than his courage:—

I ken, if that your sword were wanted,
Ye'd lend a hand;
But when there's ought to say anent it,
Ye're at a stand.

In 1783 Montgomerie succeeded his brother in the estate of Skelmorlie, and his father in that of Coilsfield. In 1789 he resigned his seat in the commons on being appointed inspector of military roads in Scotland. During his term of office he was instrumental in greatly extending and improving the roads in the highlands. On the declaration of war by France in 1793 he was appointed colonel of the West Lowland fencibles, raised by the eleventh Earl of Eglinton in Ayrshire. Soon afterwards he himself raised the regiment of the line called the Glasgow regiment, which was disbanded in 1795. During the crisis he was also appointed governor of Edinburgh in room of Lord Livingstone. In 1796 he was again returned member for Ayr, but on 30 Oct. he succeeded to the earldom of Eglinton on the death of Archibald, eleventh earl [q. v.] Part of the estates devolved on the eleventh earl's eldest and only surviving daughter, Lady Mary Montgomerie; but as she married Archibald, lord Montgomerie, eldest son of the twelfth earl, the lineal and male branches were ultimately united, and the whole estates were again joined with the earldom.

In 1798 Eglinton was elected a representative peer of Scotland, and he was re-elected in 1802. On 15 Feb. 1806 he was created a peer of the United Kingdom, by the title of Baron Ardrossan of Ardrossan, Ayrshire. He was also made a knight of the Thistle, and appointed lord-lieutenant of Ayrshire, and one of the state councillors to the prince regent. He died 15 Dec. 1819.

By his cousin Eleonora, daughter of Robert Hamilton of Bourtreehill, Ayrshire, he had three sons and three daughters: Archibald, lord Montgomerie, who became a major-general, and died on 4 Jan. 1814 at Alicante in Spain; Roger, who was a lieutenant in the royal navy, and died at Port Royal in Jamaica in January 1799; Alexander; Jane, married to Edward Archibald Hamilton of Blackhouse; Lillias, married first to Robert Dundas Macqueen of Braxfield, and secondly to Richard Alexander Oswald of Auchincruive—the 'wealthy young Richard' of Burns's 'Election Day;' and Mary, who died young. He was succeeded in the earldom by his grandson, Archibald William Montgomerie [q. v.]

Soon after his accession to the earldom, Eglinton began to rebuild, as the principal residence of the family, the castle of Eglinton, one of the finest examples of modern castellated architecture. Besides continuing the agricultural improvements on his estates begun by his predecessors, he also, in July 1806, commenced on a great scale a harbour for Ardrossan, with the view of making this town the port of Glasgow, with which it was to be connected by the Glasgow, Paisley, and Johnstone Canal. After 100,000*l.* had been expended on the harbour and canal, the work was suspended, on account of the great excess of expenditure over the estimates; it was found that to complete it would require an additional 300,000*l.* The canal was only completed between Glasgow and Johnstone, but the harbour of Ardrossan, on a greatly reduced scale, though amply sufficient for the wants of the port, was ultimately finished by the thirteenth earl at a cost in all of about 200,000*l.*

Eglinton possessed many of the characteristics of the ancient feudal baron; and if both in his private life and his schemes for the welfare of the community he manifested an excessive bias towards magnificence, his enterprise and public spirit deserve the highest praise. He had also cultivated tastes, being specially fond of music, and, besides performing on the violoncello, was the composer of a number of popular airs, including 'Lady Montgomerie's Lament' and 'Ayrshire Lasses.' His portrait, by Raeburn, in the costume of the west lowland fencibles, is in the County Buildings, Ayr.

[Works of Burns; Paterson's Hist. of Ayr; Sir William Fraser's Earls of Eglinton; Douglas's Scottish Peerage (Wood), i. 509–10.]

T. F. H.

MONTGOMERIE, Sir **JOHN**, ninth of Eaglesham and first of Eglinton and Ardrossan (*d.* 1398?), was the only son of Sir Alexander de Montgomerie, eighth of Eaglesham and first of Eglinton and Ardrossan, by a daughter of William, first earl of Douglas. The Montgomeries of Scotland trace their descent from Robert de Montgomerie (*d.* 1177), a supposed descendant of Roger of Montgomery (*d.* 1094) [q. v.], who was created Earl of Shrewsbury, and was father of Hugh, earl of Shrewsbury (*d.* 1098) [q. v.] Robert de Montgomerie accompanied Walter, son of Alan, first high steward of Scotland, from Wales to Scotland, and received from him the manor of Eaglesham, Renfrewshire.

Sir John Montgomerie, ninth of Eaglesham, succeeded his father about 1380, and by his marriage with Elizabeth de Eglinton, sole heiress of Sir Hugh de Eglinton of Eglinton, justiciary of Lothian in 1361, obtained the baronies of Eglinton and Ardrossan. In 1388 he accompanied his brother-in-law, Sir James Douglas, second earl of Douglas [q. v.], in an expedition to England. At the battle of Otterburn, where Douglas was slain, Montgomerie, according to the Scots version of the ballad on the battle, worsted Sir Henry Percy, surnamed Hotspur, the commander of the English, in single combat and took him prisoner. With the ransom of Percy he built at Eaglesham the castle of Polnoon, now in ruins, but long the chief seat of the Eglinton family. In 1391 Montgomerie, for service to the king and the Duke of Rothesay, received an annuity from the customs of Edinburgh and Linlithgow (*Exchequer Rolls of Scotland*, iii. 280 et seq.) He died about 1398, leaving three sons—Sir John, who succeeded him, and was father of Sir Alexander, first lord Montgomerie [q. v.]; Alexander of Bonnington, and Hugh, shot with an arrow through the heart at Otterburn.

[Froissart's Chronicles; ancient ballad on the battle of Otterburn; Exchequer Rolls of Scotland, vol. iii.; Sir William Fraser's Earls of Eglinton; Douglas's Scottish Peerage (Wood), i. 494.] T. F. H.

MONTGOMERIE, ROBERT (*d.* 1609), titular archbishop of Glasgow, was the third son of Hugh Montgomerie of Hessilhead, Ayrshire, by a daughter of Houston of Houston, and a younger brother of Alexander Montgomerie [q. v.] the poet (pedigree in General G. S. Montgomery's *History of the Montgomerys*). He is mentioned by the first general assembly of the reformed kirk, 20 Dec. 1560, as one of those thought able to minister (Calderwood, ii. 46), and was appointed to the charge of Cupar Fife about 1562. In 1567 he was translated to Dunblane, and in 1572 to Stirling. He was one of a commission who in 1572 met in the house of Knox to arrange certain articles to be propounded to the regent and council (*ib.* iii. 210); in 1580 he received a commission to warn the bishops of Argyll and the Isles to appear before the assembly to answer such things as might be laid to their charge (*ib.* p. 465); and in 1581 he was named a commissioner for the establishment of a presbytery in Stirling and Linlithgow (*ib.* p. 524).

After the death in 1581 of James Boyd, titular archbishop of Glasgow, James VI, on the recommendation of Esmé Stewart, duke of Lennox, presented Montgomerie with the bishopric, Montgomerie, on the payment of 1,000*l.* Scots, giving a bond to Lennox to dispone to him and his heirs all the income of his see. The general assembly censured Montgomerie for agreeing to accept a bishopric, and interdicted him from undertaking the office. Montgomerie was supported by the king and council, who denied the illegality of episcopacy, but the kirk met this by articles against Montgomerie, declaring him unfit for any high office, and commanding him to remain at Stirling under pain of the highest censures of the kirk (*ib.* p. 580). Montgomerie thereupon set them at defiance, and on 8 March entered the church of Glasgow accompanied by a band of the royal guard, and in the king's name commanded the officiating minister to come down from the pulpit (*ib.* p. 595). This he declined, and through the interference of the laird of Minto, Montgomerie was induced to desist (*ib.*) The students of Glasgow University also took the part of the kirk against Montgomerie, and on 22 April were summoned to answer before the council on 10 Sept. for riots in opposition to him (*Reg. P. C. Scotl.* iii. 490). On 12 April an order was also made by the council forbidding the presbyteries, synods, and general assemblies of the kirk from proceeding against Montgomerie (*ib.* p. 476). Nevertheless the kirk resolved to proceed to excommunication, unless he desisted from his purpose (Calderwood, iii. 596–7), and summoned him to appear before the next general assembly. He appeared, and, after protesting against their proceedings as illegal, declined their jurisdiction in the matter in dispute. They were proceeding to his excommunication when a messenger from the king appeared charging them to desist under pain of rebellion and horning, and although this did not prevent them passing a resolution for his excommunication, they resolved to delay sentence till they had held further conference with him. The result was that he 'granted, as appeared with all submission, his offences in every point, to the great admiration and contentment of the assembly,' and promised to 'attempt nothing further concerning the bishopric' (*ib.* pp. 599–607). Finding afterwards, however, that he had the strong support of the king and council, he resiled from his promise, and consequently on 10 June was excommunicated by the presbytery of

Edinburgh (*ib.* p. 621). As excommunication by the kirk then meant expulsion from all human society, the Earl of Gowrie was on 26 June summoned before the presbytery of Edinburgh for having received Montgomerie into his house (*ib.* p. 622). Notwithstanding also that on 25 July proclamation was made at the cross of Edinburgh in the king's name declaring the excommunication null and void, he was expelled from the town of Edinburgh, where he had shown himself publicly in the streets. As he was removed out of the town the people waited for him, 'craftsmen with batons, wives and boys with stones and rotten eggs. If he had not been conveyed by the provost down the Kirk Wynd, he had barely escaped danger of his life' (*ib.* p. 634). The incident so tickled the fancy of the king that 'he lay down on the Inch of Perth not able to contain himself for laughter.' Soon afterwards occurred the raid of Ruthven, which was followed on 12 Sept. by a proclamation by the king virtually resiling from all further opposition to the assembly. Montgomerie consequently on 13 Nov. presented a supplication to the presbytery of Edinburgh containing a confession of his offences and a suit to be restored, but was directed to make his suit to the general assembly (*ib.* p. 691). On 22 May 1584 his excommunication was declared by parliament to be null and void, but on 7 Dec. 1585 the king promised that he should be produced for trial before the first general assembly he should appoint (the king's interpretation of his acts of parliament set forth in May 1584, *ib.* iv. 459-63). Finally in 1587 Montgomerie, finding the bishopric to be of no pecuniary value to him, resigned it, and the assembly on certain conditions agreed to 'dispense with' him 'in some ceremonies used in repentance' (*ib.* p. 631). On his supplication the assembly in 1588 further decided that he might be admitted pastor over a flock, provided he was 'found qualified in life and doctrine' (*ib.* p. 670). He was accordingly in the same year settled at Symington, Ayrshire, whence in 1589 he was transferred to Ayr. He died after 25 March 1609. By his wife Beatrice Jameson he had a son Robert, who after the appointment of his father to the bishopric of Glasgow obtained from the king the stipend of the kirk of Stirling until the grant was revoked on 1 Nov. 1583 (*Reg. P. C. Scotl.* iii. 606).

[Histories of Calderwood and Spotiswood; James Melville's Diary; Reg. P. C. Scotl. vols. iii-iv.; Keith's Scottish Bishops; Hew Scott's Fasti, ii. 144, 188, 459, 671, 715; General Montgomery's Hist. of the Montgomerys.] T. F. H.

MONTGOMERIE, ROBERT (*d.* 1684), parliamentary and afterwards royalist officer, was the fifth son of Alexander, sixth earl of Eglinton [q. v.], by Lady Anna Livingstone, daughter of Alexander, first earl of Linlithgow [q.v.] He was educated at the university of Glasgow, where he was enrolled a student 1 March 1637. He fought under his father at the battle of Marston Moor, 2 July 1644, and was severely wounded in the arm (Robert Baillie, *Letters and Journals*, ii. 204). In 1646 he held, under Middleton, the command of a regiment of dragoons in the north of Scotland, with which on 3 Jan. 1646 he entered the city of Aberdeen (*Burgh Records of Aberdeen*, 1643-1747, p. 60). He was opposed to the expedition under the Duke of Hamilton in 1648 for the relief of the king, and after the defeat of Hamilton at Preston on 17 Aug. became known he gathered a body of western covenanters, with which he routed a number of horse under the Earl of Lanark, quartered in Ayrshire. This procedure led the committee of estates to call out the fencible men; but their action was anticipated by the march to Edinburgh of the western whigamores under Montgomerie's father, the Earl of Eglinton [see Montgomerie or Seton, Alexander, sixth Earl of Eglinton]. After the arrival of Cromwell in Edinburgh, Montgomerie, in 1648, set out for London, carrying a letter from Cromwell (No. lxxviii. in Carlyle's *Cromwell*), recommending him, 'as one of the most active against the late invaders of England,' to have an order for two thousand of the Scottish prisoners taken at Preston. Montgomerie's purpose was to sell them to the king of Spain for service in the Low Countries; but negotiations, both with Spain and France, proved abortive.

After the recall of Charles II Montgomerie took a prominent part in the contest against Cromwell. On 29 July 1650 (Letter by Cromwell, No. lxxxv., *ib.*) he attacked Cromwell's forces in the early morning near Musselburgh, beat in his guards, and 'put a regiment of horse in some disorder,' but failed in his attempt to surprise them, and was forced to retreat towards Edinburgh. Cromwell asserted that, so far as he had heard, his own loss was 'only a cornet and four men;' but Sir James Balfour represents the Cromwellian loss as very severe (*Annals*, iv. 87). Montgomerie fought at the battle of Dunbar on 3 Sept. After the battle he retired with the other troops under Leslie beyond the Forth. When Charles, in October, suddenly left Perth to join the northern loyalists, Montgomerie was in the neighbourhood of Forfar, in command of two regiments of horse, and being informed of his escape marched towards Atholl, where two of his officers discovered him in a poor cottage belonging to the laird of Clova. On the appearance of Montgomerie with his troops, Charles consented to accompany him back to Huntly Castle, in the Carse of Gowrie (Balfour, *Annals*, iv. 114; Robert Baillie, *Letters and Journals*, iii. 117).

On 14 Oct. Montgomerie was ordered by the committee of estates to join the Lord-general Leslie, who was to employ him in any way he thought most advantageous to the country and hurtful to the enemy (*ib.* p. 123), and on 25 Oct. he was ordered to take certain dragoon regiments under his command and remove to the west (Wodrow, *Sufferings of the Kirk of Scotland*, i. 166). On 28 Nov. it was agreed that there should be a union of the forces in the west under his command (Balfour, iv. 187), and on 2 Dec. it was ordered by parliament that the western forces, with the three regiments of Kirkcudbright, Galloway, and Dumfries, be joined to his (*ib.* p. 193). Montgomerie was at this time in Stirling, whence he was proceeding with four or five regiments of horse to carry out the commission entrusted to him, when, according to Cromwell, 'he was put to a stand' by the news of the defeat of Colonel Ker at Hamilton (letter, 4 Dec. 1650, No. cliii. in Carlyle's *Cromwell*). Nevertheless, he shortly afterwards forced his way by Kilsyth, killing seven of the enemy and taking four prisoners (Balfour, iv. 195).

With the rank of major-general Montgomerie was appointed to the command of the second brigade in the army which in the autumn of 1651 marched under David Leslie and Charles II into England (*ib.* p. 300). At the battle of Worcester on 3 Sept. his brigade was posted opposite Powick Bridge; and although furiously attacked by Fleetwood he maintained his post with great determination until his ammunition was expended, when he retreated towards the city (*Boscobel Tracts*, ed. 1857, pp. 37–9). He was taken prisoner either at or after the battle (Nicoll, *Diary*, p. 59; Lamont, *Diary*, p. 43), and sent to the Tower, from which in July 1654 he made his escape (Nicoll, p. 135). On it becoming known that he had returned to Scotland orders were given to arrest the Earl of Eglinton, his father, and Lord Montgomerie, his brother, and detain them until they either delivered him up or gave security that he should leave the country (*Cal. State Papers*, Dom. Ser. 1654, p. 258). Shortly afterwards Montgomerie was arrested in Renfrewshire, and confined in the castle of Edinburgh, but on 29 Feb. 1656–1657 made his escape (*Thurloe State Papers*, ii. 81) in coalmen's clothes (Nicoll, *Diary*, p. 192). In October 1657 he went to Leghorn to offer his services to the king of Sweden (*Thurloe State Papers*, ii. 564); and he subsequently obtained employment in Denmark, but through the interposition of Cromwell he was dismissed (*Clarendon State Papers*, iii. 397). In October 1658 he was at Tours in France. After the Restoration he was made by Charles II a lord of the bedchamber, but his strong presbyterian sympathies subsequently lost him the king's favour. In August 1665 an order was on this account made for his imprisonment (*Cal. State Papers*, Dom. Ser. 1664–5, p. 514), and it was not till 22 Jan. 1668 that he obtained his liberty (Wodrow, *Sufferings of the Kirk of Scotland*, ii. 99). He died in December 1684. By his wife Elizabeth Livingstone, daughter of James, viscount Kilsyth, he had a daughter and two sons, all of whom died with issue.

[Robert Baillie's Letters and Journals (Bannatyne Club); Nicoll's Diary (Bannatyne Club); Sir James Balfour's Annals; Wodrow's Sufferings of the Kirk of Scotland; Thurloe State Papers; Clarendon State Papers; Cal. State Papers, Dom. Ser. during the Commonwealth and reign of Charles II; Boscobel Tracts; Carlyle's Cromwell; Gardiner's Great Civil War; Paterson's History of Ayr; Sir William Fraser's Earls of Eglinton; Douglas's Scottish Peerage (Wood), i. 503.]

T. F. H.

MONTGOMERIE, THOMAS GEORGE (1830–1878), colonel royal engineers and geographer, fourth son of Colonel W. E. Montgomerie of the Ayrshire yeomanry and of Annick Lodge, Ayrshire, was born on 23 April 1830. He was educated at Addiscombe for the East India Company's army, and passed out first of his term, winning the Pollock medal as the most distinguished cadet. He was gazetted a second lieutenant in the Bengal engineers on 9 June 1849, and went through the usual course of training at Chatham. He went to India in 1851, arriving in June, and, after serving for a year at Roorkee with the headquarters of the corps of Bengal sappers and miners, was posted to the great trigonometrical survey, then under Colonel (afterwards Sir) Andrew Scott-Waugh. Among his earlier duties on the survey he assisted in the measurement of the bases of verification on the plain of Chach (near Attok on the Indus) in 1853, and at Karachi in 1854–5. He was promoted first lieutenant on 1 Aug. 1854.

On the conclusion of the Karachi measurement he was given the charge of the trigo-topographical survey of the whole dominions of the maharajahs of Janin and Kashmir, including the Tibetan regions of Ladakh and Balti, an area of about seventy thousand square miles. This survey constituted a network of geometry, thrown with much labour over an unknown country, embracing one of the most stupendous mountain tracts in the world. Many of the stations of observation exceeded fifteen thousand feet in height, while some ranged from eighteen to twenty thousand. Success attended the whole of the prolonged operations.

Besides the triangulation of the particular country in hand, peaks were fixed rising out of distant and inaccessible regions, such as those on the west of the Indus, towards Upper Swaton, in the ranges beyond Gilghit, which were either unknown or known only in inaccurate generalities. But a greater difficulty than either the physical character of the country or the constant toil of training fresh hands, arose from the work being carried on in the territory of a quasi-independent prince. The tact and ability which Montgomerie exercised in maintaining amicable relations with the court, and in preserving discipline among his own large and mixed establishment, earned just praise from the government. The old maharajah, Goolab Singh, regarded Montgomerie as a friend, and after the maharajah's death the same kindly relations were maintained by his successor.

At the time of the Indian mutiny, Sir John Lawrence, for political reasons, considered it inexpedient to stop the survey, and Montgomerie carried it on during that critical time. He was promoted captain on 27 Aug. 1858. A degree sheet of the survey was sent home in August 1859 by Lord Canning, who wrote to Sir Roderick Murchison from Calcutta in the highest terms of praise of both the map and its author. The survey was completed without a single casualty or serious failure in 1863–4, and Montgomerie, whose health had broken down, went to Europe on medical certificate. In May 1865 he received, at the hands of Sir Roderick Murchison, the founder's medal of the Royal Geographical Society.

Montgomerie returned to India early in 1867, and in May was appointed to the charge of the Himalayan survey in Kumaon and Gurhwal. Long before the completion of the Kashmir survey Montgomerie had considered the means of extending accurate reconnaissance in the country beyond the Indian frontier. It was not possible to extend the survey itself, or any work of European officers, without the risk of political complications, but there was no reason why properly trained natives, equipped as traders, should not pass freely to and fro and bring back good geographical results. A letter which Montgomerie wrote to the Asiatic Society of Bengal (21 July 1862) contained the germ of such a scheme. It was supported by the society, and eventually by the government. A beginning was made in 1863 by the despatch of a Mohammedan munshi, Abdul Hamid, to survey the route to Yarkand. The journey was successfully accomplished, but unfortunately the munshi died on the return journey, within a few days' journey of Ladak. Montgomerie contributed an account of this journey to the Royal Geographical Society in 1868, and mentioned another expedition of like kind, but of still greater interest, that he had started just before leaving India in 1864. This was the journey of the (long anonymous) 'Pundit,' from Nipal to Lhása, and along the upper valley of the Brahmaputra to the source of that river, a journey of great importance to geography, and which for the first time determined the position on secure grounds of the capital of the pope of northern Buddhism. The names of Montgomerie's emissaries were, for obvious reasons of precaution, kept secret till death or retirement, and it was not till long after that the most eminent of them, Nain Singh, was known by name. The word 'pundit' acquired a new significance, and in a manner became a name for a trained explorer. After 1868 Montgomerie's reports of such explorations were as eagerly looked for by foreign geographers as by his own countrymen. Till he finally left India, whatever were his other duties, he continued to supervise the reduction of the observations of the emissaries beyond our frontier, and to combine their results.

In 1870–71–73, during the absence of Colonel Walker, Montgomerie officiated as superintendent of the great trigonometrical survey of India. He was promoted major on 5 July 1872. In 1873 he was compelled by ill-health to return to England. The foundation of serious disease had been laid during his prolonged and arduous toil on the Kashmir survey.

Montgomerie was in 1872 elected a fellow of the Royal Society. He was an honorary member of the Italian and other foreign geographical societies. In 1875 he was the representative of the British and Indian governments, and agent of the Royal Geographical Society at the Geographical Congress held in Paris, when he was decorated by the French government as 'Officer of the University of Paris, and of Public Instruction.' He was promoted lieutenant-colonel on 1 April 1874, and retired from the service with the rank of colonel in 1876. His last public appearance was at the meeting of the British Association at Bristol in 1875, when he read an interesting paper on the Himalayan glaciers. Montgomerie died at Bath on 31 Jan. 1878. He married in 1864 Jane Farrington, by whom he left three children.

The following is a list of papers contributed by Montgomerie to geographical or scientific periodicals: 1. 'The Nanga Parbat, and other Snowy Mountains of the Himalaya Range adjacent to Kashmir' (*Journ. Asiat. Soc. Bengal*, xxvi. 1857). 2. 'The Great Flood of the River Indus, which reached Attok on 10 Aug. 1858' (*ib.* xxix. 1860): corroborating conclusions already arrived at by Colonel R. Strachey and others, that the flood in question, by which the Attok was raised ninety feet in seven hours, had nothing to do with the subsidence of a glacier in the Shayok branch of the Upper Indus, as had been alleged, nor probably had the similar great flood of 1841, which had been ascribed to a catastrophe in the same locality. 3. 'Memorandum drawn up by order of Colonel A. Scott-Waugh on the Progress of the Kashmir Series of the Great Trigonometrical Survey of India, with Map, and Observations on the late Conquest of Gilgit, and other incidental matters' (*ib.* xxx. 1861). 4. 'On the Geographical Position of Yarkund and some other places in Central Asia' (*Journ. R. Geogr. Soc.* xxxvi. 1866). 5. 'Report of a Route Survey made by Pundit —— from Nipal to Lhasa and thence through the Upper Valley of the Brahmaputra to its Source' (*ib.* xxxviii. 1868; cf. *Proc. R. Geogr. Soc.* xii. 146). 6. 'Report of the Trans-Himalayan Explorations during 1867' (*Journ. R. Geogr. Soc.* xxxix. 1869; cf. *Proc.* xiii. 183). 7. 'Report of the Mirza's Exploration from Kabul to Kashghar' (*Journ. R. Geogr. Soc.* xli. 1871; cf. *Proc.* xv. 181). 8. 'A Havildar's Journey through Chitral to Faizabad in 1870' (*Journ. R. Geogr. Soc.* xlii. 1872; cf. *Proc.* xvi. 253). 9. 'Narrative of an Exploration of the Namcho, or Tengri Nur Lake in Great Tibet, made by a Native Explorer in 1871–2,' with memorandum on the results of the above explorations (*Journ. R. Geogr. Soc.* xlv. 1875). 10. 'Journey to Shigatze in Tibet, and Return by Tengri Maidan in Nipal in 1871 by the Native Explorer' (*ib.* xlvii.) 11. 'Extracts from an Explorer's Narrative of his Journey from Petoraghar in Kumaon, viâ Jumla to Tadum, and back by the Kali Gandak to British Territory' (*ib.*) 12. 'Account of the Pundit's Journey in Great Tibet from Leh in Ladakh to Lhasa, and of his Return Journey to India viâ Assam' (*ib.*) 13. 'Meteorological Observations taken at Lé by W. H. Johnson, with Remarks by Major T. G. Montgomerie' (*Proc. R. Geogr. Soc.* xvii.) 14. Remarks in regard to Trans-Himalayan problems and explorations (*ib.* xix. and xx.) 15. Note on Himalayan glaciers (*Brit. Assoc. Rep.* 1875).

[Records of the Corps of Royal Engineers; Memoir in vol. viii. Royal Engineers' Journal by Colonel Henry Yule; obituary notice in vol. xlviii. Journal of the Royal Geographical Society.] R. H. V.

MONTGOMERY, Earls of. [See Herbert, Philip, first Earl, 1584–1650; Herbert, Henry, sixth Earl, 1693–1751; Herbert, Henry, seventh Earl, 1734–1794; Herbert, George Augustus, eighth Earl, 1759–1827.]

MONTGOMERY, Countess of. [See Clifford, Anne, 1590–1676.]

MONTGOMERY, HENRY, LL.D. (1788–1865), founder of the remonstrant synod of Ulster, fifth son and youngest child of Archibald Montgomery, was born at Boltnaconnel House, in the parish of Killead, co. Antrim, on 16 Jan. 1788. His father had held a commission in the Irish volunteers of 1778 and was usually styled lieutenant. His mother was Sarah, daughter of William Campbell of Killealy, in the same parish. His brothers, William and John, being 'United Irishmen,' were engaged in the battle of Antrim, 7 June 1798. On 9 June a body of yeomanry, in search of the fugitives, plundered and burned his father's house. Henry received his schooling in 1799 from Alexander Greer, at Lyle Hill, co. Antrim, and in 1802 from Nathaniel Alexander (*d.* 7 April 1837), presbyterian minister of Crumlin, co. Antrim. In November 1804 he entered Glasgow College as a student for the ministry. He graduated M.A. in 1807, and after acting for a few months as tutor in the family of Thomas Stewart of Seapark, Carrickfergus, returned to Glasgow for a year's study of divinity. He preached his first sermon at Killead on 8 Jan. 1809, and on 5 Feb. was licensed by Templepatrick presbytery. In May he preached as candidate at Donegore, co. Antrim, but was rejected on his refusal to subscribe the Westminster confession. His lifelong antagonist, Henry Cooke, D.D. [q.v.], was ultimately the successful candidate. On 11 June he preached for the first time at Dunmurry, co. Antrim, within four miles of Belfast, received a call on 9 July, and was ordained by Bangor presbytery on 24 Sept. as successor to Andrew George Malcom, D.D. [q. v.] In this pastoral charge he remained till his death.

From the beginning of his settlement at Dunmurry, Montgomery engaged in tuition, and from 1815 boarded pupils in his house. On 3 Oct. 1817 he was elected head-master, in succession to James Knowles [q. v.] of the English school in the Belfast Academical Institution, his congregation agreeing that he should reside there. He had just declined an invitation, made through Archibald Hamilton Rowan [q. v.], to preach on trial at Killeleagh, co. Down, the charge to which Cooke was subsequently elected. He held the mastership till June 1839, and exercised much influence on the literary education of Ulster. Children of all presbyterian ministers he taught without fee. His connection with the institution naturally led him to vehemently repel the attacks made upon it as a 'seminary of Arianism' by Cooke from 1822.

Montgomery's first appearance as a debater in the general synod of Ulster was in June 1813, when he espoused the cause of William Steel Dickson, D.D. [q. v.], and helped to break the power of Robert Black, D.D. [q. v.], who, though a liberal in theology, had hitherto swayed the synod in the interests of political conservatism. In 1816 Montgomery was a candidate for the clerkship of synod, but withdrew in favour of William Porter (1774–1843), minister of Newtownlimavady, co. Derry. On 30 June 1818, at an unusually early age, he was elected moderator of the general synod.

Since 1783, owing to the action of William Campbell, D.D. [q. v.], subscription had ceased to be in full force. Ten of the fourteen presbyteries composing the synod treated subscription as optional. The result was a considerable amount of undemonstrative heterodoxy. A code of discipline, which had been contemplated since 1810, was adopted by the general synod at Moneymore, co. Derry, in 1824. It provided that presbyteries should ascertain 'soundness in the faith,' either by subscription or by examination. This compromise, suggested by Samuel Hanna, D.D. [q. v.], was accepted by all parties. But Cooke persistently sought to render the discipline more stringent. To defeat Cooke's policy was the object to which Montgomery devoted the marvellous resources of his commanding eloquence. The resulting struggle is described by Classon Porter as 'almost entirely a duel' between the two leaders, who were exactly matched in age; though, if Latimer be right in affirming that Cooke was the son of John McCooke, and born about 1783, he was some years the senior.

At Strabane in 1827 Cooke carried a proposal that members of synod should declare whether or no they believed the doctrine of the Trinity. Only two voted 'Not.' Montgomery, who proclaimed himself an Arian, withdrew with others before the roll-call. His speech on this occasion, in favour of religious liberty, made a deep impression; it was circulated over Ireland, and a service of plate was presented to him (18 June 1828) by members of various denominations, including Roman catholics. He had advocated catholic emancipation from 1813.

At Cookstown in 1828 James Morell, minister of Ballybay, co. Monaghan, carried a resolution for the appointment of a committee for the theological examination of all candidates for the ministry. This was meant to defeat the action of liberal presbyteries, and cut off the supply of Arian clergy. On 16 Oct. 1828 Montgomery and his friends adopted a 'remonstrance' at a presbyterian meeting in Belfast, attended by Cooke. The last of Montgomery's brilliant speeches in the general synod was delivered at Lurgan on 3 July 1829. The remonstrance was presented at a special meeting of synod, held at Cookstown on 18 Aug., and terms of separation were arranged at a conference on 8 Sept. The first meeting of the remonstrant synod was held on 25 May 1830; it consisted of three presbyteries containing seventeen congregations; it retained the 1824 code of discipline, and its ministers were secured in the possession of *regium donum*.

Meanwhile Montgomery had visited the English unitarians, and advocated catholic emancipation at public dinners in Manchester (December 1828) and London (January 1829). On his return he spoke in the same strain from the altar of St. Patrick's, Belfast, at a meeting (27 Jan. 1829) presided over by William Crolly, D.D. [q. v.], then Roman catholic bishop of Down and Connor. To O'Connell's agitation for repeal of the union he was strongly opposed; his letter to O'Connell (1 Feb. 1831) was among the most powerful attacks upon the Liberator's position, and did much to alienate Irish liberals from his cause. He was in favour of Irish disestablishment, and gave evidence in this sense before parliamentary committees in 1832. He warmly supported the national system of education (established in 1831), which Cooke as warmly opposed. In 1833 he received the degree of LL.D. from Glasgow University. His last great personal encounter with Cooke was in connection with the management (1838–41) of the Belfast academical institution; his speech of 13 April 1841 was followed by the defeat of Cooke's endeavour to exclude Arian professors of theology from chairs in the faculty. In the struggle for the tenure of meeting-house properties and endowments by unitarians, resulting in the Dissenters' Chapels Act of 1844 [see FIELD, EDWIN WILKINS], Montgomery took a very important and laborious part. His exertions brought on an illness in London (1844), when Peel, whose support of the measure Montgomery had secured, showed him much personal attention.

In 1835 was founded the association of Irish non-subscribing presbyterians, a union, though not an amalgamation, of the remonstrant synod with the Antrim presbytery and the Munster synod. Montgomery, who had since 1832 given regular courses of lectures to non-subscribing divinity students, was on 10 July 1838 appointed the association's professor of ecclesiastical history and pastoral theology. The office was without salary, till in 1847 the government endowed the chair with 150*l.* per annum out of *regium donum.* Many of the students became ministers to the English unitarians. A controversy on the efficiency of the system of ministerial training arose in 1847. Montgomery founded in his synod in 1857 a revised code of discipline, which restricted the wide range already given to presbyteries in the matter of ministerial examination; but the new questions were withdrawn in 1863 in consequence of a legal decision in the Ballyclare case.

Montgomery, who had suffered from calculus, died at the Glebe, Dunmurry, on 18 Dec. 1865, and was buried in the ground attached to his meeting-house on 20 Dec. His funeral was attended by all ranks and classes, including his old opponent Cooke, with whom in later years he had been on terms of friendship, and the Bishop of Down, Connor, and Dromore. The funeral sermon was preached (24 Dec.) by Charles James McAlester (1810–1891) of Holywood, co. Down. Montgomery married, on 6 April 1812, Elizabeth (*d.* 16 Jan. 1872, aged 78), fourth daughter of Hugh Swan of Summerhill, co. Antrim, by whom he had ten children, of whom four died under age.

In person Montgomery was of commanding stature and handsome presence, with a voice of great sweetness, and fascinating manners. His portrait, painted in 1835 by John Prescott Knight [q. v.], has been several times engraved. Classon Porter describes him as 'a born diplomatist;' his political influence with successive governments was undoubted. His politics in later life became more conservative. It has been alleged that his religious sentiments likewise underwent a change, but his theology neither advanced nor receded. He was much in controversy with later developments of unitarian thought, which he viewed as equivalent to deism. On his deathbed he recommended to his successor, Thomas Hugh Marshall Scott, his 'Creed of an Arian' (1830), as containing his lifelong opinions. Having a remarkable memory, he rarely wrote either sermons or speeches. His first publication seems to have been an anonymous catechism (1811, 12mo); his best printed sermon is an anniversary discourse, 'We persuade men,' 1843, 8vo. His oratory was more polished than that of Cooke; in pathos and in sarcasm he was Cooke's equal, but he had not Cooke's mastery of the passions of a crowd. Some of his best speeches are reprinted in his 'Life,' others are to be sought in separate pamphlets and in the 'Northern Whig.' In 1830 he was one of the original editors of the 'Bible Christian,' with Fletcher Blakely [q. v.] and William Bruce (1790–1868) [q. v.] In 1846–7 he contributed to the 'Irish Unitarian Magazine' a valuable series of 'Outlines of the History of Presbyterianism in Ireland.'

[Funeral sermon by McAlester, 1866; Life, by John A. Crozier (his son-in-law), 1875, vol. i. (portrait, no more published, extends to 1831); Henry Montgomery, 1888 (short life, by the same); Unitarian Herald, 29 Dec. 1865; Christian Unitarian, January 1866; J. L. Porter's Life and Times of Henry Cooke, 1875; Classon Porter's Irish Presbyterian Biog. Sketches, 1883, pp. 34 sq.; Latimer's Hist. of the Irish Presbyterians, 1893, pp. 192 sq.; Minutes of General Synod and of Remonstrant Synod; information from the Revs. J. A. Crozier and T. H. M. Scott.]

A. G.

MONTGOMERY, HUGH OF, EARL OF SHREWSBURY (*d.* 1098). [See HUGH.]

MONTGOMERY, HUGH, third VISCOUNT MONTGOMERY of the Ards, and first EARL OF MOUNT ALEXANDER (1623?–1663), born about 1623, was eldest son of Hugh, second viscount Montgomery, and his wife, Jean Alexander, eldest daughter of Sir William Alexander, first earl of Stirling [q. v.] In his childhood his left side was severely injured by a fall, and an extensive abscess was formed, which on healing left a large cavity through which the action of the heart could be plainly discerned (HARVEY, *Works*, Sydenham Society, pp. 382–4). He wore a metal plate over the opening. Notwithstanding, he had a fairly good constitution, and before reaching his twentieth year travelled through

France and Italy. On his return he was brought to Charles I at Oxford, who was curious to see the strange phenomenon presented in Montgomery's case. He remained some days with the king, and went home, after receiving tokens of the royal favour, and giving assurances of his own loyalty.

By this time the Irish rebellion had broken out, and Montgomery's father had raised troops in maintenance of the royal authority, but he died suddenly on 15 Nov. 1642. Montgomery succeeded as third viscount, and was appointed to the command of his father's regiment. Under Major-general Robert Monro or Munro (*d.* 1680?) [q. v.], who married his mother, Montgomery fought at Benburb in June 1646. The king's troops were defeated, and the viscount, when heading a charge of cavalry, was made prisoner. He was sent to Clochwater Castle, where he remained until October 1647, when he was exchanged for the Earl of Westmeath. He took a leading part in proclaiming Charles II at Newtown in February 1649. At the same time the solemn league and covenant was renewed, and General Monck, refusing either to take the covenant or declare for the king, was forced out of Ulster. Montgomery was thereupon commissioned by the king as commander-in-chief of the royal army in Ulster (14 May 1649), with instructions to co-operate with the Marquis of Ormonde (*State Papers*, Dom. Ser. 1649–50, p. 140); and in the warlike operations which followed, he successively seized Belfast, Antrim, and Carrickfergus, and, passing through Coleraine, laid siege to Londonderry. After four months' investiture, however, he was compelled to retire, but joined Ormonde, and aided him in his final efforts against the Commonwealth. Forced at last to surrender to Cromwell, he was, after appearing before parliament in London, banished to Holland, under strict prohibition from corresponding with Charles II. In 1652 he solicited and received permission to return to London, and after much delay was allowed subsistence for himself and his family out of his confiscated estates (*ib.* 1651–2, pp. 99–364, passim). He was afterwards permitted to return to Ireland, and lived there under strict surveillance, and for a time was imprisoned in Kilkenny Castle.

On the restoration of the monarchy in 1660 Montgomery visited the king at Whitehall. He was appointed for life master of ordnance in Ireland (12 Sept. 1660), was placed on the commission for the settlement of Irish affairs (19 Feb. 1661), and was created Earl of Mount Alexander 20 June 1661. He died suddenly at Dromore on 15 Sept 1663, while engaged in tracking out Major Blood's plot. He was buried in the chancel of the church at Newtown.

In personal appearance Montgomery is described as of medium height, ruddy complexioned, with curly reddish hair and a quick grey eye. He was twice married: first, in December 1648, to Mary, eldest daughter of Charles, second viscount Moore, by whom he had two sons—Hugh and Henry, who were successively second and third earls of Mount Alexander—and a daughter, Jean, who died unmarried in 1673; secondly, in 1660, to Catherine Jones, daughter of Arthur, second viscount Ranelagh, and widow of Sir William Parsons of Bellamont.

[Montgomery MSS., by the Rev. George Hill, 1869, i. 151–259.] H. P.

MONTGOMERY or **MONTGOMERIE**, **Sir JAMES**, tenth **Baronet of Skelmorlie** (*d.* 1694), politician, was eldest son of Sir Robert Montgomery, ninth baronet, by his wife, Anna or Antonia, second daughter and coheiress of Sir John Scott, knight, of Rossie, Fifeshire. His father died on 7 Feb. 1684, and he was served heir to him on 3 Feb. 1685. In April 1684 his widowed mother made a strong appeal to him to make suitable provision for her and her fatherless children, but to this he replied that, for the sake of peace, he had already conceded more than legal obligations required (letter quoted in Sir William Fraser's *Earls of Eglinton*, i. 164). On 2 Oct. 1684 Montgomery was imprisoned and fined for harbouring rebels, that is covenanters (Lauder of Fountainhall, *Hist. Notices*, p. 563), and on 7 May 1685 he and his mother were pursued on account of conventicles held in his father's lifetime, but both pleaded that they were not responsible (*ib.* p. 699). Montgomery visited Holland in connection with the invitation to William, prince of Orange, to invade England on behalf of protestantism; but Balcarres scouts the notion that Montgomery had any commission to do so, since he possessed no influence, 'except with some few of the most bigoted fanatics' (*Memoirs*, p. 8). He was chosen member for the county of Ayr in the Convention parliament of 1689, when he distinguished himself by his eloquent advocacy of the resolution proposed by Sir John Dalrymple, that King James had forfeited his throne and kingdom. The resolution being carried, Montgomery was named one of three commissioners—that for the shires—to offer the Scottish crown to William and Mary. His ambition had already selected the office of secretary of state for Scotland, as that alone commensurate with his services and abilities; and when George, first earl of

Melville [q. v.], chiefly on account of his moderate opinions, was preferred, Montgomery, although offered the office of lord justice clerk, so deeply resented the supposed slight that he determined at all hazards to have revenge, and immediately set himself to organise a political society called The Club, the main purpose of which was to concert measures against the government. In parliament he led with great ability and eloquence the opposition against Sir John Dalrymple, the two, according to Balcarres, frequently scolding each other 'like watermen' (*ib.* p. 59). Towards the close of the session he went to London with his closest confederates, the Earl of Annandale and Lord Ross, to present a declaration of Scottish grievances to the king, but the king declined to listen to their complaints. Thereupon Montgomery entered into communication with the Jacobite agent, Neville Payne [q. v.], and they concerted together a plot for the restoration of King James, known as the Montgomery Plot, each being, according to Balcarres, more or less the dupe of the other (*ib.* p. 57). Montgomery's coalition with the Jacobites proved to him rather a hindrance than a help in parliament, and as soon as his influence began to wane the Jacobites revolted against him. A quarrel ensued, and soon afterwards Lord Ross made confession of his connection with the plot to a presbyterian minister, who informed Melville. On learning this Montgomery went to Melville, and on promise of an indemnity confessed all he knew, making it, however, a condition that he should not be obliged to be 'an evidence or legal witness' (*Leven and Melville Papers*, pp. 457, 479, 520). Melville sent him, with a recommendation in his favour, to Queen Mary, to whom he pleaded for 'some place which might enable him to subsist with decency' (Macaulay, *History*, ed. 1883, ii. 224). She wrote on his behalf to King William, but the king had conceived such an antipathy to him that he declined to utilise his services on any consideration (Balcarres, *Memoirs*, p. 66). According to Burnet, Montgomery's 'art in managing such a design, and his firmness in not discovering his accomplices raised his character as much as it ruined his fortunes' (*Own Time*, ed. 1838, p, 561). After lying for some time in concealment in London, he passed over to Paris, where he was well received by the Jacobites (Balcarres, *Memoirs*, p. 66). Some time afterwards he returned to London, and on 11 Jan. 1693–4 was taken into custody, on the accusation of being the author of several virulent papers against the government (Luttrell, *Short Relation*, iii. 252); but on the 18th he made his escape from the house of the messenger where he was confined, the two sentinels who guarded the door leaving their arms and going with him (*ib.* p. 255). He escaped to the continent, reaching Paris by 15 Feb. (*ib.* p. 269), and he died at St. Germains before 6 Oct. 1694 (*ib.* p. 380). By Lady Margaret Johnstone, second daughter of James, earl of Annandale, he had two sons, Robert (1680–1731) [q. v.] and William.

Montgomery was the author of 'The People of England's Grievances to be enquired into and redressed by their Representatives in Parliament,' reprinted in 'Somers Tracts,' x. 542–6. The authorship of other political pamphlets attributed to him has been claimed by Robert Ferguson [q. v.] the Plotter, and in some instances there may have been a joint authorship. A portrait of Montgomerie in armour has been engraved.

[Balcarres's Memoirs, Lauder of Fountainhall's Historical Notices, and Leven and Melville Papers, all in the Bannatyne Club; Burnet's Own Time; Luttrell's Short Relation; Carstares State Papers; Macaulay's Hist. of England; Ferguson's Robert Ferguson the Plotter; Noble's Continuation of Granger, i. 219–20; Douglas's Scottish Peerage (Wood), i. 509; Sir William Fraser's Montgomeries, Earls of Eglinton, i. 162–5.] T. F. H.

MONTGOMERY, JAMES (1771–1854), poet, was born at Irvine in Ayrshire, 4 Nov. 1771. His family, originally Scottish, had for several generations been settled in Ulster, where his great-grandfather is said to have possessed and dissipated a landed estate. His father, John Montgomery, had at all events been born in the condition of a labourer at Ballykennedy, co. Antrim, in 1733. Having embraced the tenets of the Moravians, who had founded a settlement in the neighbourhood, to which they had given the name of Grace Hill, the elder Montgomery became a minister; married a member of the Moravian community in 1768, and at the time of his son's birth had just arrived at Irvine to take charge of the Moravian congregation, at that time the only one in Scotland. He returned to Ireland in 1775, and in 1777 James was sent to school at the Moravian establishment at Fulneck, near Leeds. His parents proceeded in 1783 as missionaries to Barbados, and there his father died of yellow fever in 1791. His mother, Mary Montgomery, had died at Tobago in the previous year.

Meanwhile James had met with some adventures. Neglecting the studies considered essential at Fulneck, he employed himself in the composition of two epic poems, one on Alfred, the other entitled 'The World,' in the manner of Milton. The principal incident in the latter was the Archangel Michael taking Satan by surprise and lopping off one of his wings. The Moravians for a time clipped Montgomery's own wings by placing him with a baker; but the employment proved intolerable, and in 1787 Montgomery ran away with three and sixpence in his pocket and a bundle of verses, which proved more valuable than might have been expected, for a poem, written out fairly and presented to Earl Fitzwilliam, brought him a guinea. He was, nevertheless, soon obliged to apply for a character to his old instructors and to his master, who treated him with much kindness, and he obtained a situation in a general store in the little town of Wath. After a year he quitted this and made his way with his manuscripts to London, but, finding no encouragement from the publishers, returned to Wath, and remained there till April 1792, when, by answering an advertisement in the 'Sheffield Register,' he obtained a situation as clerk and bookkeeper in the office of that newspaper. This change brought Montgomery into intellectual society; his literary talent began to be appreciated; he gradually became an extensive contributor to the paper; and an unexpected circumstance opened up the path to independence. This was the prosecution and flight of Mr. Gales, the proprietor and editor of the 'Register,' and an ardent reformer, on account of a letter found on the person of Thomas Hardy on his apprehension, and attributed to Gales, who was in fact cognisant of its having been sent, though he was not the actual writer. Gales escaped to America; money to carry on the paper was found by a wealthy townsman named Naylor, and Montgomery became the working editor of the journal, which endeavoured to disarm the hostility of the government by changing its title to the 'Sheffield Iris,' and adopting a more moderate line in politics. In 1795 Naylor retired from the paper on account of his marriage, and it became the property of Montgomery, who also entered into business as a general printer. Within a few years he was enabled to pay off the purchase-money of the journal, and to obtain a highly respectable competence. Before this was achieved, however, he had to bear the brunt of two prosecutions for libel, each of which resulted in his conviction and imprisonment for a term in York Castle, though neither could affix the least stigma to his character. The first prosecution (January 1795) was on account of a ballad in commemoration of the Fall of the Bastille, a few copies of which had been sold to a travelling hawker; it had been printed by Montgomery's predecessor, and had in fact no reference to the events of the day. It was subsequently shown by official correspondence that the prosecution was instituted as a means of intimidating the Sheffield political clubs. The second prosecution (January 1796) Montgomery undoubtedly brought upon himself by statements respecting the behaviour of a magistrate, Colonel Athorpe, in dispersing a riotous assemblage, which could not be fully justified, although the explanations he was ready to have offered would probably have been accepted but for the embittered state of political feeling at the time. After his release in July he published the 'Prison Amusements' which had enlivened his confinement, and in 1798 a volume of essays entitled 'The Whisperer,' under the pseudonym of 'Gabriel Silvertongue.' He subsequently destroyed every copy he could lay his hands on; while a novel, in four volumes, completed during his second imprisonment, was destroyed in manuscript.

For some time the 'Iris' was the only newspaper in Sheffield; but beyond the ability to produce fairly creditable articles from week to week, Montgomery was entirely devoid of the journalistic faculties which would have enabled him to take advantage of his position. Other newspapers arose to fill the place which his might have occupied, and in 1825 the journal passed into other hands. During the greater part of this period he had given more attention to poetry than to journalism. 'The Ocean' (1805) attracted little attention, but 'The Wanderer of Switzerland' (1806), founded upon the French conquest of Switzerland, took the public ear at once, probably on account of the subject, and from the merit of some of the miscellaneous pieces accompanying it, especially the really fine and still popular lyric, 'The Grave.' The principal poem is as a whole very feeble, though a happy thought or vigorous expression may be found here and there. The volume nevertheless speedily went through three editions, and its sale was not materially checked by a caustic review from the pen of Jeffrey (*Edinb. Rev.* January 1807), which indeed gained Montgomery many friends. He himself became a reviewer, taking an important part in the newly established 'Eclectic Review,' in which he afterwards declared that he had noticed every contemporary of note except Byron. His criticism evinces little insight; he is a tolerably safe guide where no guidance is needed, but is slow, though by no means through unwillingness to appreciate the merits of contemporaries. A more thoroughly impartial critic never wrote. The success of 'The Wanderer' brought him in 1807 a commission from the printer Bowyer to write a poem on the abolition of the slave trade, to be published along with other poems on the subject in a handsome illustrated volume. The subject was well adapted to Montgomery's powers, appealing at once to the philanthropic enthusiasm in which his strength lay, and to his own touching associations with the West Indies. His poem entitled 'The West Indies' accordingly appeared in Bowyer's illustrated publication in 1809. It is a great improvement on 'The Wanderer,' and, although rather rhetoric than poetry, is in general well conceived and well expressed, and skilful as well as sincere in its appeals to public sentiment. On its first appearance in Bowyer's volume it proved a failure, but when published separately (London, 1810, 12mo) it obtained great popularity. 'The World before the Flood' (1812), also in heroic verse, is a more ambitious attempt, and displays more poetic fire and spirit than any of Montgomery's previous performances; nor is it so deficient in human interest as might have been expected in an epic on the wars of the giants and the patriarchs. The descriptive passages frequently possess great merit, which is even exceeded in Montgomery's next considerable effort, 'Greenland' (1819), a poem founded on the Moravian missions to Greenland. Montgomery's last important poem, 'The Pelican Island' (1826), also contains very fine descriptive passages, but with more preaching has less human interest than 'Greenland,' and is marred by being written in blank verse, of which the author was by no means a master. A considerable part of his reputation with the public at large rests upon his numerous hymns, which were collected in 1853. The finest were those written in his earlier years, including 'Go to dark Gethsemane,' 'Songs of praise the Angels sang,' and 'For ever with the Lord.' Over a hundred of his other hymns are still in use (JULIAN, *Dict. of Hymnology*, p. 764).

After retiring from the 'Iris,' Montgomery continued to reside at Sheffield, where he had come to be accounted a local hero, and grew more and more in the respect of his fellow-townsmen by his exemplary life and activity in furthering every good work, whether philanthropic or religious. In 1830 and 1831 he delivered lectures on poetry at the Royal Institution, which were published in 1833. They are, perhaps, of all his writings those which it is easiest to praise unreservedly, the opinions being almost invariably just, and conveyed with a force and sometimes even a poetry of diction which nothing in his previous criticisms had seemed to promise. In 1831 he also compiled from the original documents the journals of D. Tyerman and G. Bennet, who had been deputed by the London Missionary Society to visit their stations in the South Sea Islands, China, and India. In 1835 he received a pension of 150*l.* on the recommendation of Sir Robert Peel, and about the same time contributed fairly adequate accounts of Dante, Ariosto, and Tasso to Lardner's 'Cabinet Cyclopædia.' The remainder of his life was devoted to religious and philanthropic undertakings. He died rather suddenly on 30 April 1854. He was honoured by a public funeral, and a monument designed by John Bell was erected over his grave in the Sheffield cemetery. He was unmarried.

Montgomery was emphatically a good man; greatness, whether intellectual or poetical, cannot be claimed for him. He had sound plain sense; his conversation, judging from the copious specimens recorded by his biographers, was instructive and entertaining, but neither brilliant nor profound; his letters, though expressive of his admirable character, are in general grievously verbose. As a poet he is only eminent in descriptive passages, for which he is usually indebted to books rather than his own observation of nature. There are some indications of creative power in 'The World before the Flood,' and the character of Javan is well drawn; but, as Mrs. Hofland remarked, he drew from himself. The minor pieces which have obtained a wide circulation usually deserve it, but they are buried in his works among masses of commonplace which should never have been printed. He is largely indebted for his fame to the approbation of religious circles, better judges of his sentiments than of his poetry: this has, on the other hand, occasioned unreasonable prejudice against him in other quarters. On the whole he may be characterised as something less than a genius and something more than a mediocrity.

The best portraits of Montgomery are those respectively painted by the sculptor Chantrey in 1805, and by John Jackson in 1827. A full-length by Barber is in the Sheffield Literary and Philosophical Institute.

The first collective edition of Montgomery's poems, edited by himself, appeared in four volumes, London, 1841, 8vo. This passed through several editions, the most recent being that of 1881. His poems form volumes in the 'Lansdowne Poets,' the 'Chandos Poets,' and the 'Chandos Classics.'

[The life of Montgomery has been written with the most formidable prolixity by his friends, Dr. John Holland and the Rev. James Everett, in seven volumes, London, 1854–6. The compendious biography by J. W. King, 1858, is easier to consult, but is full of affectations and irrelevancies. Carruthers's Memoir, prefixed to the American works, is, on the other hand, too meagre. There are numerous references to Montgomery in Southey's Correspondence and similar contemporary collections. Cf. S. C. Hall's Book of Memories, 1883, pp. 81–93; and two essays by Mr. G. W. Tallent-Bateman —an estimate and a valuable bibliography—in the Papers of the Manchester Literary Club, 1889, pp. 385–92, 435–40.] R. G.

MONTGOMERY, Sir JAMES WILLIAM (1721–1803), Scottish judge, second son of William Montgomery, advocate, of Coldcoat or Magbie Hill, Peeblesshire, was born at Magbie Hill in October 1721. His mother was Barbara, daughter of Robert Rutherford of Bowland, Midlothian. After some schooling at the parish school at Linton, he studied law in Edinburgh, and was called to the Scottish bar on 19 Feb. 1743. In 1748, after heritable jurisdictions had been abolished, he was appointed the first sheriff of Peeblesshire under the new system, and on 30 April 1760, thanks to the influence of his friend Robert Dundas, then newly appointed lord president, he succeeded Sir Thomas Miller (1717–1789) [q. v.] as solicitor-general jointly with Francis Garden (1721–1793) [q. v.] In 1764 he became sole solicitor-general, and in 1766 lord advocate in succession to Miller, to whose parliamentary seat for the Dumfries Burghs he succeeded also. But at the general election of 1768 he was returned for Peeblesshire, a seat which he retained till he was raised to the bench. A learned lawyer and an improving landlord, he was peculiarly fitted to deal with the question of entails, which had now become pressing, owing to the extent to which entails fettered the practical management of land. The existing statute was Sir George Mackenzie's Act of 1685, and since it passed 485 deeds of entail had been registered under it. The public demanded a reform; the Faculty of Advocates had passed resolutions approving it. Montgomery accordingly introduced a measure in March 1770, which passed into law (10 Geo. III, c. 51) and considerably enlarged the powers of the heir of an entail in respect of leasing and improving the entailed lands, and even provided for the exchange of land in spite of an entail.

Though he remained in parliament, Montgomery took little further interest in its proceedings after the passage of his bill. In June 1775 he was created lord chief baron of the Scottish exchequer, and in 1781 he was elected fellow of the Society of Antiquaries of Scotland; he resigned his judgeship in April 1801, and in July was made a baronet.

Montgomery was, like his father, skilled in farming, and in 1763 bought a half-reclaimed estate of Lord Islay's in Peeblesshire, originally called Blair Bog, but afterwards 'The Whim,' which eventually became his favourite residence. In 1767 he bought for 40,000*l.* Stanhope and Stobo in Peeblesshire, part of the estates of Sir David Murray, confiscated 1745. He thenceforward chiefly resided in the country, where his good methods of farming and the improvements which he promoted, notably the Peebles and Edinburgh road in 1770, gained for him the title of 'The Father of the County.' He died on 2 April 1803. He married Margaret, daughter and heiress of Robert Scott of Killearn, Stirlingshire, and was succeeded in the title by Sir James, his second son, afterwards lord advocate, his eldest son, William, a lieutenant-colonel in the 43rd foot, having predeceased him. Cockburn (*Memorials of his own Time*, p. 183), speaks of him as an 'excellent and venerable man,' and says that he was exceedingly benevolent. Two portraits of Montgomery were painted by Raeburn; another by John Brown is engraved in Chambers's 'Peeblesshire,' p. 437.

[Omond's Lord Advocates; Omond's Arniston Memoirs; Scots Magazine, 1803; Chambers's Peeblesshire; Kay's Portraits, i. 136–8; Anderson's Scottish Nation, iii. 182.] J. A. H.

MONTGOMERY, JEMIMA (1807–1893), novelist. [See Tautphœus, Baroness von.]

MONTGOMERY, PHILIP of (*d.* 1099), called Grammaticus. [See under Roger de Montgomery, Earl of Shrewsbury (*d.* 1093).]

MONTGOMERY, RICHARD (1736–1775), major-general, born in Swords, near Feltrim, co. Dublin, on 2 Dec. 1736, was third son of Thomas Montgomery, M.P. for Lifford, by Mary Franklin, and younger brother of Captain Alexander Montgomery ('Black Montgomery'), M.P. for Drogheda. Educated at St. Andrews and Trinity College, Dublin, he was, on 21 Sept. 1756, appointed ensign in the 17th foot, in which he became lieutenant on 10 July 1759, and captain on 6 May 1762. He served with his regiment at the siege of Louisburg, Cape Breton, in 1757, and in the expedition against the French posts on Lake Champlain in 1759, and was regimental adjutant in the force under General (then Colonel) William Haviland [q. v.], sent from Crown Point to join the forces under Murray and Amherst converging on Montreal. After the fall of Montreal he was present with his regiment at the capture of

Martinique, and at the siege and capture of the Havana. At the peace of 1763 he went with his regiment from Cuba to New York, and in 1765 returned home with it. While at home he appears to have made the acquaintance of Colonel Isaac Barré [q. v.], Edmund Burke [q. v.], Charles James Fox [q. v.], and other men of liberal views. Seeing no prospects of professional advancement he sold out of the army in 1772, and bought a farm of sixty-seven acres at King's Bridge, now a part of the city of New York, and soon after married. He then purchased a handsome estate on the river Hudson, but spent the few years of his married life at his wife's residence, Grassmere, near Rheinbeck.

In 1775 Montgomery was sent as a delegate to the first provincial congress at New York, and in June of the same year 'sadly and reluctantly' consented to be made a brigadier-general in the continental (i.e. American) army, ranking second among the eight appointed, and being the only one not a native of New England. He consoled himself with the reflection that 'the will of an oppressed people, compelled to choose between liberty and slavery, must be respected.' He parted from his young wife at Saratoga, and started as second in command of the expedition under Major-general Philip Schuyler, which was instructed 'to take possession of St. John's, Montreal, and pursue any other measures in Canada to promote the furtherance and safety of the American cause.' The expedition aroused great resentment in Canada, as congress a short time before had expressly disavowed any intention of invading Canada, and had caused the disavowal to be widely circulated there. The Americans took Isle aux Noix, but failed at St. John's. Schuyler then fell sick, and the change in the command was soon apparent. The troops (chiefly New England men) were of the worst character, 'every man a general, and not one of them a soldier,' Montgomery wrote. Supplies were bad and desertion rife. Nevertheless, Montgomery took Fort Chamblai, where was a stock of ammunition, of which the Americans were much in need, and afterwards captured St. John's, a more important conquest, where were taken, among other captures, the colours of the British royal fusiliers (7th fusiliers), the first British regimental colours taken in the war. 'Till Quebec is taken, Canada remains unconquered,' Montgomery wrote to congress. In December 1775 he effected a junction with Benedict Arnold [q. v.], at Point aux Trembles, and laid siege to Quebec. The American effectives are said to have numbered about eight hundred. Small-pox was in the camp; the men's engagements were coming to an end. It was decided to try an assault. On 31 Dec. 1775, Montgomery, starting from Wolfe's Cove, in a blinding snowstorm, led an attack on the southern part of the lower town, while Arnold attacked the upper town. Calling on the 'men of New York' to follow, Montgomery dashed on, but, with two officers by his side, was struck down by the first discharge of artillery. Both attempts failed, and Arnold drew off to the Plains of Abraham, where he kept up a desultory sort of blockade until the spring of 1776, when the Americans withdrew from Canada. Montgomery's body was recognised and buried with full military honours, the governor and the officers of the garrison of Quebec attending. Congress, 'desiring to transmit to future ages' the 'patriotic conduct, enterprise, and prowess' of Montgomery, desired a memorial in marble to be erected to him in the graveyard of St. Paul's Episcopal Church, New York. The memorial was ordered in Paris by Benjamin Franklin. In 1818 congress passed an 'Act of Honour,' by which permission of the Canadian government was obtained for the removal of Montgomery's remains, which were then laid in St. Paul's Church, New York. An inscription on the rocks at Cape Diamond shows the spot where he fell.

Parkman states that some writers have confused him, ignorantly and most unjustly, with Captain Alexander Montgomery, 43rd regiment (his elder brother?), who incurred the censure of his brother officers for inhumanity to some prisoners that fell into his hands when serving under Wolfe before Quebec (see *Montcalm and Wolfe*, vol. ii.)

Montgomery married Jane, daughter of Judge R. R. Livingstone of New York, but left no issue. His widow survived 'her soldier,' as she called him, fifty-three years, dying in 1828.

[Burke's Landed Gentry, 1886 ed., under 'Montgomery of Beaulieu;' English Annual Army Lists; Jesse's Life and Times of George III, vol. ii.; Bancroft's Hist. United States; Appleton's Encycl. American Biog., with portrait.]

H. M. C.

MONTGOMERY, Sir ROBERT, eleventh Baronet of Skelmorlie (1680–1731), the projector of a scheme for colonisation in America, born at Skelmorlie Castle, Ayrshire, in 1680, was son of Sir James Montgomery or Montgomerie, tenth baronet (*d.* 1694) [q. v.], by his wife Lady Margaret, second daughter of James Johnstone, second earl of Annandale (Douglas, ed. Wood, i. 74). Robert entered the English army and saw service in the war of the Spanish succession

(1702–13). Like his father he early interested himself in practical schemes of colonisation, and after the peace he set about a project which the war had deferred. On 19 June 1717 he received from the lords proprietors of Carolina a grant of land between the rivers Allatamaha and Savanna, and published a full prospectus of the method by which he proposed to settle the territory, which he called the Margravate of Azilia. His tract was entitled 'A Discourse concerning the designed Establishment of a New Colony to the South of Carolina,' 1717. On 20 Feb. 1718 the lords proprietors recommended him to the council as life governor of the southern part of Carolina; on attendance before the council he stated that he had raised 30,000*l.* among his friends, and needed no money from the crown. On 24 July the scheme was approved. But it seems never to have taken practical shape. It is doubtful whether he even went out to Carolina himself. Doubtless the assumption of the government by the crown a little later put an end to the project, for on 15 Sept. 1720 an application was made to the council to restrain action 'upon some advertisement now published by Sir Robert Montgomery,' which suggested that he was sending persons 'to the Golden Islands, one of which islands lies in the mouth of the River Allatamaha, which has been proposed to be secured.' In August 1731 he died in Ireland, and in the following year a new undertaker made the first effort to plant, under the name of Georgia, the territory which had belonged to Montgomery. He married Frances, eldest daughter of Colonel Francis Stirling; she died at Skelmorlie on 9 June 1759, leaving three daughters, one of whom, Lillias, inherited Coilsfield; she married Alexander Montgomerie, by whom she was mother of Hugh, twelfth earl of Eglinton [q. v.], and died at Coilsfield on 18 Nov. 1783. On Sir Robert's death his title devolved on his uncle, Sir Hugh Montgomery, M.P. for Glasgow, and became extinct on Sir Hugh's death, 14 Jan. 1735.

[Douglas's Peerage of Scotland, ed. Wood, i. 508–9; Appleton's Cycl. of American Biog.; reprint of Montgomery's Discourse in Peter Force's Selection of Tracts and Papers on North America, Washington, 1836–46; State Papers in Record Office.] C. A. H.

MONTGOMERY, ROBERT (1807–1855), poetaster, born at Bath in 1807, was the natural son of Robert Gomery—'a most gentlemanly and well-informed man,' and for many years clown at the Bath Theatre—by 'a lady who kept a school at Bath, and who subsequently removed from that city and married a respectable schoolmaster.' Gomery afterwards married a Mrs. Power (whom he survived), and died at Walcot Buildings, Bath, on 14 June 1853. His last appearance on the Bath stage, as recorded by Genest (viii. 439, ix. 215), was as Master Heriot in the 'Fortunes of Nigel,' 7 Dec. 1822. The son was fairly well educated, at Dr. Arnot's school in his native town, became well known among his father's friends as a future Byron, and assumed the aristocratic prefix Mont. When about seventeen he founded a weekly paper at Bath called 'The Inspector,' which had a brief existence. His first considerable poem, 'The Stage Coach,' was written in 1827; it was followed in the same year by 'The Age Reviewed,' a satire upon contemporary mankind, in two parts. In 1828, with a dedication to Bishop Howley, appeared 'The Omnipresence of the Deity,' a poem which proved so acceptable to the religious sentiment of the day that it passed through eight editions in as many months. Prefixed to the later editions was a portrait of the youthful author (who is admitted by his detractors to have 'looked like a poet'), with open collar and upward gaze so arranged as to resemble as nearly as possible the well-known features of Byron. In the same year appeared another volume of blank verse, dedicated to Sharon Turner, and entitled 'A Universal Prayer; Death; a Vision of Heaven; and a Vision of Hell.' Inflated eulogies of these productions appeared in the chief London and provincial papers. Edward Clarkson, who reviewed them in the 'Sunday Times' and the 'British Traveller,' compared Montgomery with Milton. Southey, Bowles, Crabbe, and other men of letters hailed him as a rising poet of much promise; Southey afterwards wrote of him to Caroline Bowles (1832) as 'a fine young man who has been wickedly puffed and wickedly abused.'

There followed from his pen in rapid succession 'The Puffiad,' a satire (1830), and 'Satan, or Intellect without God,' a poem (1830). The last work commended itself strongly to the evangelical party (see *Evangel. Mag.* February 1830), and seemed likely to surpass in popularity all the poet's previous effusions. It ran through more editions, and suddenly elicited more contemporary fame than the publication of any poet since the death of Byron. Severe criticism was, however, by no means withheld. Montgomery was smartly denounced in the first volume of 'Fraser,' and he received a tolerably candid admonition from Wilson in 'Blackwood' (cf. *London Monthly Review*, cxvii. 30). But a sterner Nemesis was in store for him. In March 1830 Macaulay wrote to Macvey

Napier: 'There is a wretched poetaster of the name of Robert Montgomery, who has written some volumes of detestable verses on religious subjects, which by mere puffing in magazines and newspapers have had an immense sale, and some of which are now in their 11th or 12th editions. . . . I really think we ought to try what effect satire will have upon this nuisance, and I doubt whether we can ever find a better opportunity' (NAPIER, *Corresp.* p. 80). The classic castigation which has perpetuated the memory of its victim followed in the 'Edinburgh Review' for April 1830. Though its severity was, doubtless, well intentioned, the article is conspicuous neither for good taste nor fairness. Montgomery made a contemptuous rejoinder. 'The reviewer,' he concludes, 'is, we believe, still alive, and from time to time employs himself in making mouths at distinguished men. Most heartily do we wish him a nobler office than that of being the hired assassin of a bigoted review.' He seems to have for some time meditated a libel action (cf. TREVELYAN, *Life of Macaulay*, 1889, pp. 538, 599). The immediate sale of the poems was by no means arrested. 'The Omnipresence of the Deity' progressed steadily to its twenty-eighth edition in 1858, and 'Satan' traversed eight editions between the appearance of the article and 1842. Selections from his poems, including 'The Omnipresence,' 'Woman,' 'Satan,' and a number of minor pieces, were published in 3 vols. Glasgow, 1839. The work had a large sale, and a chorus of praise went up from the provincial press. Two collective editions in 6 vols. appeared in 1840 and 1841 respectively. A fourth edition, in one large 8vo volume, appeared in 1853, with a doctrinal and analytical index by the Rev. J. Twycross.

Encouraged by the advice and assistance of Bowles and Sharon Turner, Montgomery had meanwhile matriculated from Lincoln College, Oxford, on 18 Feb. 1830, 'aged 22,' graduating B.A. in fourth-class honours in 1833, and M.A. in 1838. In 1831 appeared 'Oxford,' a poem, which seems to have elicited much ridicule at Oxford, but not elsewhere (3rd edit. 1843); in 1832 'The Messiah, in six Books' (8th edit. 1842), dedicated to Queen Adelaide, who acknowledged the compliment by presenting the author with a medal, and in 1833 'Woman, the Angel of Life, and other Poems' (5th edit. 1841). The most ambitious of his later works was 'Luther: a Poem' (1842, 8vo; 6th edit. 1851). Of immense length, comprising thirty-one cantos, a copious introduction, and notes, this is also noteworthy as containing Montgomery's one memorable line—'The solitary monk that shook the world' (p. 25), which in the later editions was adopted as a motto.

On 3 May 1835 Montgomery was ordained at St. Asaph, and for the next year served a curacy at Whittington, Shropshire, which he left amid universal regret in 1836 for the charge of the episcopal church of St. Jude in Glasgow. He proved a successful preacher, and wrote copiously on theological subjects. In October 1843 he became minister of Percy Chapel, in the parish of St. Pancras in London, and retained this charge until his death at Brighton in December 1855. In 1843 he had married Rachel, youngest daughter of A. Mackenzie of Bursledon, Hampshire, and left one child.

With an unfortunate facility in florid versification Montgomery combined no genuinely poetic gift. Macaulay, in trying to anticipate the office of time, only succeeded in rescuing him from the oblivion to which he was properly destined. His style of preaching is said to have resembled that of his poetical effusions. His manners, in spite of his vanity, are said to have been engaging; he was generous, and his congregations were much attached to him. He did a great deal to promote the welfare of the Brompton Consumption Hospital, and devoted much of his later life to similar causes.

Portraits by Hobday, Macnee, and C. Grant were engraved by Thomson, Finden, and T. Romney respectively.

[Foster's Alumni Oxon. 1715–1886; Annual Register, 1855, p. 322; Notes and Queries, 2nd ser. vols. i. ii. passim; Fraser's Magazine, i. 95, 721 (two capital articles, humorous, and quite as conclusive as the famous essay of Macaulay), and iv. 672 (with portrait); Blackwood, xxiii. 751, xxvi. 242, xxxi. 592 (a burlesque on 'Satan'); London Monthly Review, 1831 to 1833, passim; Athenæum, 1832 p. 348, 1833 p. 772; Westminster Review, xii. 355; Southey's Correspondence with Caroline Bowles, ed. Dowden, passim; Southey's Life and Correspondence, passim; R. H. Horne's New Spirit of the Age, 1844, ii. 233; S. C. Hall's Retrospect of a Long Life, 1883, ii. 191–2; Allibone's Dict. of English Lit. (containing lists of his minor works; Gent. Mag. 1856, i. 312 (with full bibliography); British Museum Catalogue.] T. S.

MONTGOMERY, SIR ROBERT (1809–1887), Indian administrator, born in 1809, was son of Samuel Law Montgomery, rector of Lower Moville, co. Donegal. He was educated at Foyle College, Londonderry, and at Wraxall Hall School, North Wiltshire, and was appointed to the Bengal civil service in 1827. After filling various subordinate posts in the North-West Provinces, among others in 1838 that of magistrate and collector at Allahabad, he was, on the recommendation of Sir Henry Montgomery Lawrence [q. v.], his old friend and schoolfellow, transferred by Lord Dalhousie to the Punjáb, where he took a large part in organising that newly annexed province, and occupied successively the arduous and responsible posts of commissioner of the Lahore division in 1849, member of the board of administration, on which he succeeded Charles Grenville Mansel [q. v.] in 1850, and eventually, on the dissolution of the board in 1853, judicial commissioner, his duties being not merely legal, but including the superintendence of education, roads, police, and municipalities. It was in the early days of the mutiny that he performed his greatest and most signal service, the disarmament of the sepoys at Lahore on 13 May 1857. On 12 May, when the telegraph brought to Lahore the news of the capture of Delhi by the mutineers, Lawrence was at Rawal Pindi, beyond reach of telegrams, and Montgomery was the chief civil officer in Lahore. Montgomery, who had news that the four native regiments cantoned at Mean Meer, five miles off, were ready to rise as soon as they heard that the Delhi troops had risen, summoned his chief civil officers, who all agreed that the troops ought to be disarmed. In the course of the day Montgomery brought General Corbett, who commanded at Mean Meer, to the same view. To avoid any suspicion of what was intended, a great ball, which was fixed for that night, was allowed to take place. A general parade was ordered for the following morning, the 13th, and it was then, if at all, that the disarmament was to be effected. The only European forces at command were five companies of the 81st and twelve guns, and the sepoys were three regiments of foot, the 16th, 26th, and 49th, and one of horse, the 8th. The hazard was great, for a mutiny in Lahore would, for the time being, have lost the Punjáb, and it was from the Punjáb that Lower India was at first reconquered; but under orders from the brigadier and under the muzzles of the guns of the white troops the sepoys, taken unawares, piled their arms. Simultaneously Montgomery caused three white companies to disarm the sepoys in the Lahore fort, and despatched a company of the 81st, later in the day, to make Umritsur and Govindghur safe. He also sent timely warning to Ferozepore, Mooltan, and Kangra, and called on his local officials to place their treasure in charge of the nearest white troops, and to be on their guard. This wise temerity was of inestimable service to the English cause in India at that juncture. Accordingly Lord Canning appointed him to succeed Sir James Outram as chief commissioner of Oudh in June 1858, and there it became his duty to enforce the confiscation proclamation. Thanks to his great administrative skill, rare knowledge of and command over the temper of the natives, and genuine benevolence mixed with equal firmness, he effected that object quietly, until he was supported by Sir Hope Grant and his force. In 1859 he was appointed lieutenant-governor of the Punjáb, and held that post till 1865, when he resigned and returned to England on pension. He had been made a civil K.C.B. on 19 May 1859. On 20 Feb. 1866 he was made a G.C.S.I., and in 1868 was appointed a member of the council of the secretary of state for India. This office he held until his death on 28 Dec. 1887 in London of bronchitis; he was buried in the vault of his family at Londonderry 3 Jan. 1888. He married Frances, a sister of James Thomason [q. v.], the Indian administrator; she died of small-pox at Allahabad in 1842. His chief characteristics were insatiable industry, cool decision, kindness of heart, and personal modesty. His benevolence was recognised in the service in India by the nickname of 'Pickwick.' He was author of one work, 'Abstract Principles of Law for the use of Civil Administrative Officers,' published at Bangalore, 1864.

[Times, 29, 30, and 31 Dec. 1887; Dodwell and Miles's Bengal Civil Servants; Bosworth Smith's Life of Lord Lawrence, i. 369, ii. 6; Edwardes and Merivale's Life of Henry Lawrence, 3rd edit. p. 113; Kaye's Sepoy War, ii. 425; Malleson's Sepoy War, iii. 262; Temple's Life of Thomason, 1893.] J. A. H.

MONTGOMERY, ROGER of, Earl of Shrewsbury (*d.* 1093). [See Roger.]

MONTGOMERY, WALTER (1827–1871), actor, whose real name was Richard Tomlinson, is said to have been a descendant of an old Norfolk family. He was born 25 Aug. 1827, at Gawennis, Long Island, United States, America, but soon settled in England. While occupied in business in Cheapside with a shawl manufacturer named Warwick he took part in amateur entertainments, appearing at the Soho Theatre, subsequently known as the Royalty, in 'Othello.' Engaged by Chute, the manager of the Bath stage, he played at that house and in Bristol, Birmingham, Norwich, and Yarmouth. In Nottingham, where he became a favourite, he entered on management. His first appearance in London took place at the Princess's, 20 June 1863, as Othello, and inspired little interest. On the 24th he played Romeo to the Juliet of Stella Colas. Under his own management he appeared as Shylock, 22 Aug. In the following March he gave, at the St. James's Hall, readings from Shakespeare, Hood, Tennyson, Macaulay, and the 'Ingoldsby Legends.' At Drury Lane he replaced Phelps 6 March 1865 as Leonatus Posthumus to the Imogen of Miss Helen Faucit, and in April, for the benefit of James Anderson, who enacted Mark Antony, he played Cassius in 'Julius Cæsar.' In July he undertook a temporary management of the Haymarket, at which house, with Miss Madge Robertson (now Mrs. Kendal) as Ophelia, he appeared on the 29th as Hamlet, obtaining a moderate success. He also played Claude Melnotte in the 'Lady of Lyons,' King John, Shylock, and Iago to the Othello of Ira Aldridge, and was the original Lorenzo in 'Fra Angelo,' a tragedy in blank verse, by Mr. William Clark Russell. A not very successful experiment closed on 9 Nov. In November 1866 Miss Faucit began a twelve nights' engagement at Drury Lane, and Montgomery was Orlando to her Rosalind, and Sir Thomas Clifford in the 'Hunchback' to her Julia. He made soon afterwards some reputation in America and Australia, being well received as Louis XI and Sir Giles Overreach. On 31 July 1871 he began with 'Hamlet' a short and unprosperous season at the Gaiety, in the course of which he played, besides other characters, Sir Giles Overreach, Louis XI, and Meg Merrilies. He married on 30 Aug. Miss Laleah Burpee Bigelow, an American. On 1 Sept., at 2 Stafford Street, Bond Street, he shot himself, while, according to the verdict given at an inquest, of unsound mind. He was buried in Brompton cemetery. His acting was pleasing if not very subtle. His appearance was good and his voice powerful.

[Personal recollection; Scott and Howard's E. L. Blanchard; Times, 4 Sept. 1871; Era, 10 Sept. 1871.] J. K.

MONTGOMERY, WILLIAM (1633–1707), historian, son of Sir James Montgomery, second son of Hugh, first Viscount Montgomery of the Great Ards, by Katharine, daughter of Sir William Stewart, was born on 27 Oct. 1633 at Aughaintain, co. Tyrone. He was a delicate child, and was of small stature in a tall family, but used to exercise with a real pike and musket made for his size. He was drilling with a company of foot commanded by his grandfather, Sir William Stewart, at four in the afternoon, on 23 Oct. 1641, when a fugitive brought news of the Irish rising. The next day he was sent by Strabane to Derry, and thence to Glasgow, where he went for a year to the high school, and was well grounded in Despautère's grammar. In 1642 he returned to Derry, where he studied heraldry and painted coats of arms. In May 1644 he went to his father's seat of Rosemount, co. Down, for the first time. His education was there continued by Alexander Boyd till, in June 1646, the Irish victory of Benburb caused him to be sent to Carrickfergus for safety. He went to Glasgow University in 1649, learnt Greek, and did so well that he began to hope he might gain an estate by his book. War for the third time interfered with his education, and after the battle of Dunbar he sailed from Inverness to Leyden, and there studied philosophy, dancing, French, and Dutch. His chamber-fellow was a Frenchman, and they conversed in Latin, and were both instructed by a Dr. Adam Stewart, to whom he dedicated his graduation thesis, his first published work, in 1652. In June 1652 he heard of his father's death in a sea-fight, and went to London and thence, in 1653, to Dublin. Soon after, with some difficulty, he obtained possession of Rosemount, which became thenceforward his principal residence. He heard Richard Cromwell proclaimed in Dublin in 1658, and having been a consistent royalist was delighted at the Restoration. In June 1660 he married Elizabeth Montgomery, his cousin, daughter of Hugh, second viscount Montgomery of the Ards, and at his wedding was attended by the heads of six branches of the Montgomery family in Ulster. He was returned member of parliament for Newtownards 18 April 1661; lived on his estate, and from 1667 began to write historical books, of which the chief are: 'Incidentall Remembrances of the Two Ancient Families of the Savadges,' 'The Narrative of Gransheogh,' 'Some few Memoires of the Montgomeries of Ireland,' 'Some Memoires of William Montgomery of Rosemount,' 'An Historical Narrative of the Montgomerys in England and Scotland.' The first was printed in 1830; the last four were printed in full at Belfast in 1869, with notes by the Rev. George Hill, and parts of them had been printed in the 'Belfast Newsletter' in 1785 and 1786, and in 1822, and in a duodecimo volume edited by Dr. James Macknight of Londonderry in 1830 under the title of 'The Montgomery Manuscripts.' He also wrote in 1683 a treatise on the duties of the office of custos rotulorum, which is not extant, and a 'Description of the Ards,' published at Dublin in 1683. He speaks of his 'Treatise on Funeralls,' but it is not now known. His writings are interesting, resembling those of Sir William Mure of Rowallan [q. v.] in style, but containing more of their author's personal experience. His conversation was sought after in his own time; he enjoyed the friendship of James Butler, first duke of Ormonde [q. v.], and dined with Jeremy Taylor, who found him a warm supporter of episcopacy. He visited his kinsmen in Ulster and in Dublin, and took an active part in all local affairs, being high sheriff of Down in 1670. He died 7 Jan. 1707, and was buried at Grey Abbey, co. Down, where his monument was restored in 1839. He left one son, James, who married in 1687 Elizabeth, daughter of Archibald Edmonstone of Duntreath, and had several children, but the male line of his descendants became extinct in the next generation.

[Montgomery Manuscripts, Belfast, 1830 (this contains, p. 325, a catalogue of his works made by himself in 1701); Montgomery Manuscripts, ed. by the Rev. George Hill, Belfast, 1869 (this contains an account of the actual custody of the several manuscripts); T. K. Lowry's Hamilton Manuscripts, Belfast, 1867; Burke's Extinct Peerages, p. 378; Lodge's Peerage of Ireland, Dublin, 1754.] N. M.

MONTHERMER, RALPH de, Earl of Gloucester and Hertford (*d.* 1325?), is obscurely mentioned in the 'Annales Londonienses' as 'Comes Gloucestriæ, J. Bastard qui dicitur, Radulfus Heanmer' (*Chron. Edward I and II*, i. 132). Before 1296 he was a squire in the service of Gilbert de Clare, earl of Gloucester (1243–1295) [q. v.] Earl Gilbert's widow, Joanna of Acre [q. v.], daughter of Edward I, fell in love with him, and, after inducing her father to knight him, married him privately early in 1297 (Hemingburgh, ii. 70). When in April Joanna was forced to reveal the marriage, the king had Monthermer imprisoned at Bristol. The 'Song of Caerlaverock' says that Monthermer 'acquired, after great doubts and fears, the love of the Countess of Gloucester, for whom he a long time endured great sufferings.' Eventually Edward's wrath was appeased and Monthermer released. He did homage at Eltham on 2 Aug. 1297, when he is styled 'miles.' On 8 Sept. he was summoned to appear with horse and arms at Rochester. After this time he is styled Earl of Gloucester and Hertford, in right of his wife. Under this title he was present with his wife at the parliament held at York on 14 Jan. 1298 (Hemingburgh, ii. 156), and took part in the subsequent invasion of Scotland under the Earl of Warenne, when Berwick and Roxburgh were captured. On 10 April he was summoned to attend at York in June. When the Earls of Norfolk and Hereford demanded the reconfirmation of the charters, Gloucester was one of those nominated to swear on the king's behalf. Gloucester was with Edward in Scotland in June (*Cal. Documents relating to Scotland*, ii. 988), and was presumably present at Falkirk on 22 July. In December he was serving in Scotland with a hundred horse (*ib.* ii. 1044). In June 1300 he fought at the siege of Caerlaverock. In February 1301 he was present at the parliament of Lincoln, and joined in the letter of the English barons to the pope. On 24 June he was summoned to attend the Prince of Wales at Carlisle for the Scottish war (*ib.* ii. 1191), and again served in Scotland in 1303, 1304, and 1306. In the last year, on 12 Oct., he received the earldom of Athol in Scotland, together with the lands of Annandale. During the winter he was one of the three wardens in Scotland, and was besieged by Robert Bruce in the castle of Ayr. On 23 April 1307 Joanna of Acre died; after this time Monthermer seems to have been no longer styled Earl of Gloucester, and in March 1308 his stepson was summoned under that title. In June 1307, just before the death of Edward I, Monthermer also surrendered his Scottish earldom of Athol in return for ten thousand marks, wherewith to buy one thousand marks of land by the year for the support of himself and his children (*ib.* ii. 1945). On 24 June of the same year he was appointed keeper of Cardiff and other castles in Wales. On 4 March 1309 he was again summoned to parliament as Baron Monthermer, and on 16 Sept. 1309 and 24 Dec. 1310 received grants of land at Warblington and Westenden for himself and his sons (*Fœdera*, ii. 92, 124). In 1311 and 1312 Monthermer served as warden and lieutenant for the king in Scotland (*Cal. Doc. Scotl.* ii. 393–403), and received three hundred marks in reward for his services. In 1314 he once more served in Scotland, was taken prisoner at Bannockburn, and owed his release without ransom to his former acquaintance with Bruce. On 19 Feb. 1315 he was appointed warden of the royal forests south of the Trent, an office which he held till 18 May 1320. On 30 Dec. 1315 he had leave to appoint a deputy while on a pilgrimage to St. James of Compostella (*Fœdera*, ii. 282). Earlier in this year he had held an inquest on the claim of John, earl of Richmond, to the towns of Great Yarmouth and Gorleston (*Rolls of Parliament*, i. 301). After this there is no mention of Monthermer in public affairs, though he was summoned to parliament as a baron down to 30 Oct. 1324; he probably died not long after this last date. Monthermer had married as his second wife Isabella, widow of John Hastings (1262–1313) [q. v.], and sister and coheiress of Aymer de Valence, earl of Pembroke. He had pardon for this marriage on 12 Aug. 1319 (*Fœdera*, ii. 403). Isabella survived him, and died in 1326.

By Joanna Monthermer had two sons, Thomas and Edward, and a daughter Mary, who married Duncan, twelfth earl of Fife. Thomas de Monthermer was never summoned to parliament. During the early troubles of the reign of Edward III he supported Henry of Lancaster, for which he received pardon 30 July 1330 (*Cal. Patent Rolls, Edward III*, i. 547). He served in Scotland in 1333, 1335, and 1337, and was killed in the sea-fight off Sluys 24 June 1340 (MURIMUTH, p. 109). By his wife Margaret he left a daughter, Margaret de Monthermer, who married Sir John de Montacute, second son of William, first earl of Salisbury. Montacute was summoned to parliament in 1357, apparently in the right of his wife. This barony was afterwards merged in the earldom of Salisbury, and was finally forfeited at the death of Richard Neville, earl of Warwick [q. v.], in 1471. The titles of Viscount and Marquis of Monthermer were borne in the last century by the Dukes of Montagu, who claimed descent from Thomas de Monthermer. Edward de Monthermer served in Scotland in 1334, and, though the second son, was summoned to parliament in 1337; nothing further is known of him, and he does not seem to have left any heirs; he was buried by his mother at Stoke Clare (WEEVER, *Funerall Monuments*, p. 740).

[Walter de Hemingburgh (Engl. Hist. Soc.); Bartholomew Cotton; Chronicles of Edward I and Edward II; Rishanger; Trokelowe, Blaneforde, &c. (all in the Rolls Ser.); Cal. of Documents relating to Scotland; Fœdera (Record edit.); Nicolas's Song of Caerlaverock, pp. 277–279; Dugdale's Baronage, i. 217; Doyle's Official Baronage, ii. 16.] C. L. K.

MONTJOY. [See MOUNTJOY.]

MONTMORENCY, HERVEY DE (*fl.* 1169), invader of Ireland. [See MOUNT-MAURICE.]

MONTRESOR, JAMES GABRIEL (1702–1776), director and colonel royal engineers, son and heir of James Gabriel Le Trésor, esq., of Thurland Hall, Nottinghamshire, and Nanon, daughter of Colonel de Hauteville of Normandy, but in the English service, was born at Fort William, Scotland, 19 Nov. 1702. His father, descended from William Le Trésor, Viscompte de Condé sur Mogleaux, was born at Caen, Normandy, and naturalised in England during the reign of William III. He was major of the 21st foot, and lieutenant-governor of Fort William, Scotland, where he died 29 Jan. 1724, aged 56.

Montresor was a matross at Mahon, Minorca, in 1727, with pay at 1*s.* per diem. The following year he was at Gibraltar, where he was a bombardier at 1*s.* 8*d.* per diem, and distinguished himself at the siege. He was given a commission as practitioner-engineer on 2 Oct. 1731, and on 5 April 1732 was gazetted an ensign in the 14th foot. In August he went to England on four months' leave of absence, but returned to Gibraltar, where his skill as a draughtsman and ability in the execution of works won him some distinction. On 23 July 1737 he was promoted lieutenant in the 14th foot, on 7 Feb. 1739 sub-engineer, and on 3 July 1742 engineer extraordinary. The following year he was sent to Port Mahon as engineer in ordinary, his commission dating from 5 Oct. 1743. He carried out his new charge with credit until 1747, when he was appointed on 2 Jan. chief engineer at Gibraltar, with pay of 20*s.* per diem, in succession to Skinner, required for duty in Scotland. As chief engineer he greatly improved the defences, and some thirty drawings in the war office testify to the numerous services he carried out between 1747 and 1754. On 17 Dec. 1752 he was promoted sub-director. In June 1754 he returned to England, and on 9 Nov. was appointed chief engineer of the expedition to North America under Major-general Braddock. He preceded the army in June 1755 to prepare roads for Braddock's advance from Alexandria in Virginia, over the Alleghany mountains, through a difficult and unexplored country. He was present on 9 July at the disastrous battle of Du Quesne, where he was wounded and lost all his baggage and the engineer stores. He made his way with the retreating army to Fort Cumberland, and thence on 2 Aug. to Philadelphia, and finally, under orders from General Shirley, Braddock's successor, he went to Albany, where he remained for seven months, preparing plans and projects for the ensuing campaign.

In 1756 Montresor surveyed Lake Champlain and the military positions in its vicinity, and produced a map of part of the lake, showing the forts of Edward and William and other defences. He designed in 1756 a typical field redoubt for use against the Indians, which was ordered to be generally adopted. By General Shirley's directions he went to Lake George, and he reported so unfavourably on a fort recently constructed that he was ordered to reconstruct it. Montresor was much consulted by Shirley, and attended all his councils of war at Albany.

On 14 May 1757 he was gazetted major in the army, and on 4 Jan. 1758 he was promoted director and lieutenant-colonel.

In 1758 Montresor was sent to Annapolis, Nova Scotia, to report on the defences, but when the campaign opened he rejoined the army for service in the lake country. In 1759 he accompanied the army of General Amherst, and as chief engineer distinguished himself by his fertility of resource and by the work he accomplished with insufficient means and materials collected in the emergency. In June he went to Lake George, put the field-fort there in repair, and in concert with the general selected a site for a permanent fort. He traced out the defence works, and remained on the spot to superintend its erection. The work was well advanced in 1760, with accommodation for six hundred men, and called Fort George. While constructing the fort Montresor was in command of the troops and outposts of the line of communications between Albany and Lake George, a command he held till his return to England in the spring of 1760.

The fatigues of the campaigns had told upon his health, and although appointed on 1 Oct. 1760 chief engineer of the expedition against Belle Isle, he was too ill to go. He was on the sick list for the next two years, travelling about in search of health. On 3 Feb. 1762 he resigned his commission in the 14th foot. From 1763 to 1765 he was employed in designing and superintending the erection of the new powder magazines at Purfleet in place of those at Greenwich, which, by an act of parliament of 1761, were ordered to be destroyed. In 1769 he was chief engineer at Chatham. On 25 May 1772 he was promoted colonel. He died on 6 Jan. 1776 at New Gardens, Teynham, Kent. He was buried at Teynham, and there is a tablet on the north wall of the chancel of the church to his memory and to that of his third wife and her first husband. The epitaph gives Montresor's age at his death as sixty-six; it should be seventy-three.

Montresor married, first, at Gibraltar, on 11 June 1735, Mary, daughter of Robert Haswell, esq. (she died 5 March 1761); secondly, on 25 Aug. 1766, Henrietta, daughter of Henry Fielding, esq.; and thirdly, Frances, daughter of H. Nicholls, esq., and relict of William Kemp, esq., of New Gardens, Teynham. By his first marriage he had several sons: John [q. v.], who became chief engineer in America; James, a lieutenant in the navy, lost in the frigate Aurora; and Henry, who died of wounds received at the siege of Trichinopoly.

The following plans drawn by Montresor are in the British Museum: (1) A drawn plan of the city and peninsula of Gibraltar with the Spanish lines, in five sheets, 1742; (2) A drawn plan of the isthmus, city, and fortifications of Gibraltar, with elevation and sections of the principal public buildings, profiles through the two extremities of the rock and fort built by the Spaniards, with several additional designs for better defending and securing the place, eight sheets, 1753. The following plans, lately in the war office, are now in the archives of the Dominion of Canada: (1) Plan of part of river of St. Lawrence from Montreal to Isle of Quesny; (2) Part of Lake Champlain, showing Forts Edward, William, &c., 1756.

The following plans are in the war office: (1) Description and map of Gibraltar, coast of Spain and Barbary, 1748; (2) Particular survey of the city of Gibraltar, showing government property, 1753. Also twenty-six plans of various parts of the works of defence, with sections of the fortress of Gibraltar, and of the barracks and also of the Spanish lines and forts, dating from 1747 to 1752.

[Royal Engineers' Corps Records; War Office and Board of Ordnance Records; Burke's Landed Gentry.]
R. H. V.

MONTRESOR, JOHN (1736–1788?), major, royal engineers, eldest son of Colonel James Gabriel Montresor [q. v.], was born at Gibraltar on 6 April 1736. When in 1754 his father was appointed chief engineer of the expedition to North America, he accompanied him and joined the 48th foot. He obtained a commission as lieutenant in that regiment on 4 July 1755. He served with the regiment in Braddock's expedition, to which his father was chief engineer. He was wounded at the disastrous battle of Du Quesne on 14 July 1755. On 19 May 1758 he obtained a commission in the engineers as practitioner engineer, and on 17 March 1759 he was promoted sub-engineer. He was at the siege of Quebec in 1759, and at great personal risk carried despatches from the governor to General Amherst. He took an active part in the reduction of Canada. In 1764 he constructed a chain of redoubts near Niagara, and built a fort on the shore of Lake Erie. He was promoted engineer extraordinary and captain lieutenant on 20 Dec. 1765. He continued to serve in America for many years, but there is no special record until 1775, when he was at Bunker's Hill. He made a survey of the position and plans of the works. He was appointed chief engineer in America on 18 Dec. 1775, and was promoted captain and engineer in ordinary on 10 Jan. 1776. He was present at the attack and capture of

Long Island on 27 Aug. 1776 and the action of Quibbletown on 26 June 1777. Montresor Island, in the vicinity of Hell Gate at New York, was named after him. He constructed the lines of defence of Philadelphia, and was present on 18 June 1778, when the British troops marched out to join the army in New Jersey, which Montresor accompanied to New York. He also organised the extravagant farewell entertainment given by his officers to Sir William (afterwards fifth viscount) Howe [q. v.] before his departure for England.

Montresor retired from the service on 26 March 1779. On his arrival in England he was one of the five officers called upon to give evidence before a committee of the House of Commons appointed to inquire into the conduct of the war. His evidence tended to vindicate the general and to throw discredit on the ministers concerned. On his retirement he purchased the estate and house of Belmont in Throwley parish, Faversham, Kent, and resided there for some time. In 1781 he presented a peal of six bells to St. Michael's Church, Throwley. The same year he bought Syndal in the parish of Ospringe, and several other properties in the neighbourhood of Faversham. In 1782 he was examined before the commissioner of public accounts with respect to expenditure for the army in America. In 1787 he purchased Huntingfield, Faversham. He had also a house in Portland Place, London. He died about 1788.

He married, on 1 March 1764, Frances, only child of Thomas Tucker of Bermuda, and had five children: (1) Henry Tucker; (2) John, who was colonel of the 80th foot, and died on passage from Madras to Penang in 1805; (3) Thomas Gage, who married Mary, daughter of Major-general F. G. Mulcaster, and was a general and K.C.H.; (4) William Robert; (5) Mary Lucy, who married Lieutenant-general Sir F. W. Mulcaster, K.C.H., R.E.

The following plans were engraved and published by A. Dury of Duke's Court, London: (1) 'Plan of Boston, its Environs and Harbours, with the Rebel Works raised against the Town in 1775, from the Observations of Lieutenant Page, and from the Plans of Captain Montresor;' (2) 'Plan of the Action of Bunker's Hill on 17 June 1775, from an actual Survey by Captain Montresor;' (3) 'Plan of the City of New York and its Environs to Greenwich, on the North of Hudson's River, and to Crown Point on the East or Sound River, surveyed in the Winter of 1775, dedicated to Major-general Gage, by John Montresor.'

The following plans drawn by Montresor are in the British Museum: (1) A drawn elevation of part of the north front of Albany; (2) A drawn plan of Port Erie, built under the direction of John Montresor, 1764; (3) A drawn plan of Fort Niagara, with a design for constructing the same, 1768; (4) Map of Nova Scotia or Acadia, with the Islands of Cape Breton and St. John's, four sheets, 1768; (5) A drawn project for taking post at Crown Point, 13 May 1774; (6) A map of the province of New York, with part of Pennsylvania and New England, four sheets, 1775; (7) A drawn survey of the city of Philadelphia and its environs, four small sheets, 1777.

[Royal Engineers' Corps Records; War Office and Board of Ordnance Records; Burke's Landed Gentry; private manuscripts.] R. H. V.

MONTROSE, Dukes of. [See Lindsay, David, first Duke, 1440?–1495; Graham, James, first Duke of the second creation, *d.* 1742; Graham, James, third Duke, 1755–1836; Graham, James, fourth Duke, 1799–1874.]

MONTROSE, Marquises of. [See Graham, James, first Marquis, 1612–1650; Graham, James, second Marquis, 1631?–1669; Graham, James, fourth Marquis, *d.* 1742.]

MONTROSE, Earls of. [See Graham, John, third Earl, 1547?–1608; Graham, James, fifth Earl, 1612–1650.]

MOODIE, DONALD (*d.* 1861), commander royal navy and colonial secretary in Natal, was son of Major James Moodie of Melsetter, Orkney, and great-grandson of Captain James Moodie, royal navy, who received an 'honourable augmentation' to his arms for the relief of Denia in Spain during the war of the Spanish succession, and at the age of eighty was murdered by Jacobites in the streets of Kirkwall on 26 Oct. 1725.

Donald entered the navy in 1808 as a first-class volunteer in the Ardent of 64 guns, flagship at Leith. In 1809 he served in the Spitfire sloop of war in the North Sea, at Quebec, and on the coast of Spain. In 1811 he was rated midshipman in the America of 74 guns, Captain Josias Rowley, and served in the Mediterranean, including the attack on Leghorn in 1814, and at the capture of Genoa. At Leghorn, his elder brother, who was first lieutenant of the ship, was killed. He afterwards served in the Glasgow of 50 guns off Ushant and Madeira, and in the Impregnable of 104 guns in the Mediterranean. He was made lieutenant on 8 Dec. 1816, and placed on half-pay.

Thereupon he emigrated to the Cape Colony, and afterwards entered the civil service there. In 1825 he was specially commended by the royal commissioners of colonial inquiry for the attention he had given to the question of land appropriation, and was appointed resident magistrate at Port Francis. In 1828 he was resident magistrate at Graham's Town, and in 1830-4 protector of slaves in the eastern district. In 1838 he brought out his 'Cape Record,' a work now very scarce, consisting of translations from the colonial archives illustrative of the condition and treatment of the native tribes in the early days of the settlement. The work commences with the 'remonstrance' of Janz and Proot, dated 26 July 1649, in which they set forth the advantages and profit that will accrue to the Dutch East India Company by making a fort and garden at the Cabo de Esperance. In 1840 Moodie was appointed superintendent of the Government Bank, Cape Town, then heavily in debt, and afterwards was sent as acting commissioner to George, to extricate that district from the disorder into which it had fallen. His various services met with the approval of successive governors. On 29 Aug. 1845 Moodie was appointed secretary to the government of Natal, to exercise therewith the functions of colonial treasurer, receiver-general, and registrar of deeds in the new colony, at a salary of 500*l.* a year. He held the post until 1851. He became unpopular in the colony through his advocacy of the claims of the Kafirs to lands of which they had been dispossessed. He died at Pietermaritzburg in 1861. Of the two elder sons, W. J. Dunbar Moodie, sometime resident magistrate at the Umkomas, Natal, compiled and issued the 'Natal Ordinances;' and D. C. F. Moodie is the author of 'History of the Battles, Adventures, &c., in Southern Africa,' Adelaide, 1879, Cape Town, 1888.

Besides the 'Cape Record' (Cape Town, 1838-41) Moodie published: 1. 'Specimens from the authentic Records of the Colony of the Cape of Good Hope, being extracts from the "Cape Record,"' London and Cape Town, 4 pts. 1841. 2. 'A Voice from the Kahlamba: a Lecture on Intercourse with Natal in the Eighteenth Century, and early Relations between the Dutch and Kafirs,' Pietermaritzburg, 1857. 3. 'South African Annals, 1652-1792' (chap. i. only), Pietermaritzburg, 1860.

MOODIE, JOHN WEDDERBURN DUNBAR (1797-1869), a brother of Donald Moodie, born in 1797, was appointed second lieutenant 21st Royal North British fusiliers on 24 Feb. 1813, became first lieutenant in 1814, and was placed on half-pay on 25 March 1816. He was severely wounded in the left wrist in the night attack on Bergen-op-Zoom, 8 March 1814. He emigrated to South Africa to join his elder brothers, James and Donald, and spent ten adventurous years there. After his return to England he married Miss Susannah Strickland, youngest sister of Agnes Strickland [q. v.], authoress of the 'Queens of England.' With his wife he emigrated to Upper Canada, and acquired land at Belleville. He served as a captain of militia on the Niagara frontier during the insurrection of 1837, and was afterwards paymaster of militia detachments distributed along the shores of Lake Ontario and the bay of Quinte. In 1839 he was appointed sheriff of Vittoria, now Hastings County, Ontario. Through some technical irregularity in the appointment of a deputy sheriff he was subjected to a long and vexatious prosecution. By advice of the solicitor-general he resigned his post before the long-deferred judgment was given in 1863. Moodie, who besides his other adversities had in 1861 a severe attack of paralysis, from which he never wholly recovered, died in 1869.

He was author of: 1. 'The Campaigns in Holland in 1814,' in 'Memoirs of the late War,' London, 1831, 12mo. 2. 'Ten Years in South Africa, including a Particular Description of the Wild Sports,' London, 1835, 2 vols. 3. 'Roughing it in the Bush,' London, 1852.

MOODIE, MRS. SUSANNAH (1803-1885), authoress, wife of John Wedderburn Dunbar Moodie [see above], born in 1803, was youngest daughter of Thomas Strickland of Reydon Hall, Suffolk, and, like her sisters, appears to have acquired literary tastes, despite her surroundings (cf. *Life of Agnes Strickland*). Her first published work was a little volume entitled 'Enthusiasm, and other Poems' (London and Bungay, 1831). In 1832 she emigrated with her husband to Canada. During the family troubles of later years she resumed her pen, and in 1852-68 published numerous minor works of fiction. Her last was 'The World before them,' London, 1868, which was described by a reviewer as the 'handiwork of a sensible, amiable, refined, and very religious lady . . . innocent and negative' (*Athenæum*, 1868, i. 16). She died in 1885.

[For Donald Moodie: Information from private sources; O'Byrne's Naval Biog.; Colonial Services of Donald Moodie, Pietermaritzburg, 1862, 8vo. For John Wedderburn Dunbar Moodie: Manuscript autobiographical notes; Brit. Mus. Cat. of Printed Books. For Mrs. Susannah Moodie: Strickland's Life of Agnes Strickland; Moodie's Roughing it in the Bush; Mrs. Moodie's writings.] H. M. C.

MOODY, JOHN (1727?–1812), actor, son of a hairdresser named Cochran, was born in Cork, and followed his father's occupation. He himself stated that he was born in Stanhope Street, Clare Market, London. After incurring, as is said, some danger of being forced into the rising of 1745, he went to Jamaica, and acted with some reputation in Kingston as Lear, Hamlet, Romeo, &c. Returning to England with a property of consequence, which he subsequently augmented, he went on the Norwich circuit, where he took the lead in tragedy and comedy, and was Claudio in 'Measure for Measure' on the occasion when Petersen, an actor in the company, playing the king, expired while uttering the speech, 'Reason thus with life.' Tate Wilkinson claims to have been, 20 June 1759, at Portsmouth, Lord Townly in the 'Provoked Husband' to Moody's Manly, and speaks of Moody as having just arrived from Jamaica. He adds that Garrick saw Moody as Locket in the 'Beggar's Opera,' and engaged him for London at thirty shillings a week, Moody stipulating that he should first appear as King Henry VIII (*Memoirs*, ii. 95 et seq.) This date is not reconcilable with the statements in the lives of Moody in the 'Dramatic Mirror' and elsewhere, according to which Moody played at Drury Lane Thyreus in Capell's alteration of 'Antony and Cleopatra,' vacated through illness by Holland, 12 Jan. 1759, receiving for his performance five guineas from Garrick, and on 22 May appeared as King Henry VIII. Genest first mentions Moody's Henry VIII 22 Oct. 1759, and says that he acted previously Mopsus in 'Damon and Phillida,' presumably on 12 Oct. On 31 Oct. he was the original Kingston in 'High Life below Stairs,' and on 12 Feb. 1760 created his great character of Sir Callaghan O'Brallaghan in Macklin's 'Love à la Mode.' During this season he was the first clown in Garrick's pantomime, 'Harlequin's Invasion,' played an original part in 'Every Woman in her Humour,' assigned to Mrs. Clive, and was Sable in the 'Funeral.'

Moody soon made himself useful to Garrick, and, with one season at the Haymarket and occasional visits to the country, remained at Drury Lane until the end of his theatrical career. In the disgraceful riot against Garrick, led by an Irishman named Fitzpatrick in 1763, Moody had thrust upon him an undesirable publicity. He seized and extinguished, on 25 Jan., a torch with which a maniac in the audience was seeking to set fire to the house. An apology for this was demanded on the following night. Thinking to appease the mob, Moody said, in Irish tones such as he was accustomed to employ, that 'he was very sorry he had displeased them by saving their lives in putting out the fire.' This was held an aggravation of his offence, and the audience insisted that he should go on his knees. He exclaimed, 'I will not, by heaven,' and left the stage, to be embraced by Garrick, who declared that while he had a guinea he would pay Moody his salary. Garrick was compelled to promise that Moody should not appear again on the stage while under the displeasure of the audience. Moody, however, bearded Fitzpatrick, who found himself compelled to withdraw the prohibition, and to promise on behalf of himself and his friends support to the actor on his reappearance.

In the season of 1760–1, among other parts, he essayed Teague in the 'Committee,' one of his great parts, Foigard in the 'Stratagem,' Obediah Prim in 'A Bold Stroke for a Wife,' Robin in 'Contrivances,' Vulture in 'Woman's a Riddle,' and was the original Captain O'Cutter in Colman's 'Jealous Wife,' and Irishman in Reed's 'Register Office.' Among characters assigned him in years immediately following were Henry VI, Richard III, the Miller of Mansfield, Peachum in the 'Beggar's Opera,' Bullock in the 'Recruiting Officer,' Stephano in the 'Tempest,' John Moody in the 'Provoked Husband,' Adam in 'As you like it,' Ben in 'Love for Love,' Teague in the 'Twin Rivals,' Simon Burly in the 'Anatomist,' Vamp in the 'Author,' and innumerable others. He was the original Cratander in Delap's rendering of 'Hecuba,' the Irishman in the 'Jubilee,' and on 19 Jan. 1771 Major O'Flaherty in Cumberland's 'West Indian.' In the last two parts he strengthened his reputation as a comic Irishman, a part which was now ordinarily written for him or assigned to him. He played a Scottish servant, Colin MacLeod, in Cumberland's 'Fashionable Lover,' 20 Jan. 1772, but he resumed his Irish 'creation' as Sir Patrick O'Neale in the 'Irish Widow,' 23 Oct. 1772, an adaptation by Garrick from Molière, and O'Flam in Foote's 'Bankrupt,' in which, 21 July 1773, he appeared at the Haymarket. Back at Drury Lane he was, 9 Nov. 1773, the original Commodore Flip in the 'Fair Quaker,' an alteration, attributed to Captain Thompson, of the 'Fair Quaker of Deal;' Conolly, an Irish clerk, in Kelly's 'School for Wives,' 11 Dec. 1773; and McCormuck, 9 Feb. 1774, in 'Note of Hand, or a Trip to Newmarket,' written expressly for him by Cumberland. At Drury Lane he played in following years Cacafogo in 'Rule a Wife and have a Wife,' Second Witch in 'Macbeth,' Major Oldfox in the 'Plain Dealer,' Captain Bluff, Sir Sampson Legend, Sir Lucius O'Trigger, Sir Toby Belch, Roger in 'Æsop,' Gripe in the 'Confederacy,' Sir Wilful Witwou'd, Dr. Cantwell, Dogberry, &c. On 21 Sept. 1776 he was the original Phelim in Colman's 'New Brooms;' 24 Feb. 1777 the original Sir Tunbelly Clumsey in the 'Trip to Scarborough,' altered from Vanbrugh by Sheridan; 15 Oct. 1778 the original O'Daub in the 'Camp,' erroneously assigned to Sheridan; and, 29 Oct. 1779, Lord Burleigh in the 'Critic.' His other original parts of any importance were Dennis Dogherty in Jackman's 'Divorce,' 10 Nov. 1781; Major O'Flaherty in Cumberland's 'Natural Son,' 22 Dec. 1784; and Hugo in Cobb's 'Haunted Tower,' 24 Nov. 1789. In Liverpool, where he acted during the summer, and in other country towns, he tried more ambitious parts, as King in 'First Part of King Henry IV,' Iago, and Shylock.

After the season of 1795–6 the management, in answer to constant complaints of his heaviness, did not engage him, and he went into compulsory retirement, from which he emerged to play at Covent Garden, for the benefit of the Bayswater Hospital, 26 June 1804, Jobson in the 'Devil to Pay.' This was announced as 'his first appearance these ten years, and positively his last on any stage.' He retired to Barnes Common, where he lived in comfort, adding to his income by growing vegetables for the London market, sometimes himself driving his produce into town. Here, at Shepherd's Bush according to the 'Gentleman's Magazine,' or in Leicester Square according to the 'European Magazine,' he died 26 Dec. 1812. He requested that he might be buried in St. Clement's burial-ground, Portugal Street, Lincoln's Inn Fields, and that the head-stone should bear the words, 'A native of this parish, and an old member of Drury Lane Theatre.' The cemetery was full, however, and his remains were interred in the churchyard at Barnes, near those of his first wife, who died 12 May 1805, aged 88. His widow, Kitty Ann Moody, died 29 Oct. 1846, aged 83 (see *Notes and Queries*, 8th ser. ii. 292).

In his early career Moody was much praised, being declared the best Teague that the stage had produced. His Captain O'Cutter was highly popular, and secured him the praise of Churchill, who devotes ten lines to him in the 'Rosciad.' He was held a principal support of the 'Jubilee,' and played in the 'West Indian' with such judgment and masterly execution as to divide applause with the author. Tate Wilkinson praises highly his comic characters and his wisdom and sagacity, professing a great friendship for him. In his later days he incurred much condemnation, going through his parts in a state of 'torpor, bordering upon sleep.' Mrs. Mathews says that Moody, 'afraid of o'erstepping Nature, occasionally came short of her.' Thomas Dibdin relates a racy interview which he had with 'the venerable Hibernian' when he was over eighty, but still full of 'excellent humour' (*Reminiscences*, i. 258).

Portraits of Moody as Teague in the 'Committee,' with Parsons as Obadiah, by Vandergutch; by Drummond, R.A., as Jobson in the 'Devil to Pay;' and as one of a club of twelve persons called the 'School of Garrick,' are in the Garrick Club, and two engravings, one by J. Marchi from a painting by Zoffany, and the other by T. Hardy from one of his own paintings, are in the National Portrait Gallery, Dublin. Prints of Garrick as Foigard and as the Irishman in the 'Register Office' are in existence.

[Some confusion as to Moody's early life is due to the fact that he wished to be accepted as an Englishman, and to hide his humble origin. Lives of him are given in Theatrical Biography, 1772, the Georgian Era, the Thespian Dictionary, the Dramatic Mirror, the Secret History of the Green Room, the Monthly Mirror, vol. iii., and the European Magazine, vol. xviii. See also Genest's Account of the English Stage, Tate Wilkinson's Memoirs, the Garrick Correspondence, the Dramatic Censor, Cumberland's Memoirs, O'Keeffe's Recollections, Boaden's Life of John Philip Kemble, Clark Russell's Representative Actors, Dibdin's History of the Stage.]

J. K.

MOODY, RICHARD CLEMENT (1813–1887), major-general royal engineers, colonial governor, second son of Colonel Thomas Moody, royal engineers, by his wife, whose maiden name was Clement, was born in St. Ann's garrison at Barbados, West Indies, on 13 Feb. 1813. His brothers were Colonel Hampden Moody of the royal engineers, who died when commanding royal engineer at Belfast in 1869, and the Rev. J. L. Moody, army chaplain. After being educated at private schools and by a tutor at home, he entered the Royal Military Academy at Woolwich in February 1827 and left in December 1829, as the custom then was, to receive instruction in the ordnance survey. He was gazetted a second lieutenant in the royal engineers 5 Nov. 1830, and was posted to the ordnance survey in Ireland on 30 May 1832; but early in 1833 he fell ill, and on his recovery was stationed at Woolwich; in October he embarked for the West Indies, and was for some years at St. Vincent. He was promoted first lieutenant on 25 June 1835. In

September 1837 he was invalided home after an attack of yellow fever, and, being granted sick leave, accompanied Sir Charles Felix Smith on a tour in the United States. On his return he was stationed at Devonport for a short time. He was appointed on 3 July 1838 professor of fortification at the Royal Military Academy at Woolwich, and shortly after was selected as the first governor of the Falkland Islands. He embarked on 1 Oct. 1841. The colony was at the time almost in a state of anarchy, and the young governor was given exceptional powers, which he used with great wisdom and moderation. During his term of office he introduced the tussac-grass into Great Britain, of which he gave an account in the 'Journal of the Royal Agricultural Society,' iv. 17, v. 50, vii. 73; for this service he received the society's gold medal. On 6 March 1844 Moody was promoted second captain, and on 19 Aug. 1847 first captain. He returned to England in February 1849, and was employed under the colonial office on special duty until November. He went to Chatham for a year, and was then appointed commanding royal engineer at Newcastle-on-Tyne. While in the northern district a great reservoir at Holmfirth, Yorkshire, burst on 5 Feb. 1852, destroying life and property, and Moody was employed to report on the accident and to inspect other large reservoirs in the district. In 1854 he was sent to Malta. On 13 Jan. 1855 he was promoted lieutenant-colonel. In May he was attacked by a local fever and was invalided home. He spent his leave in Germany. On 8 Nov. 1855 he was appointed commanding royal engineer in North Britain.

Moody was a skilled draughtsman, and delighted in architecture. While in Scotland he drew up plans for the restoration of Edinburgh Castle, with which Lord Panmure, then secretary of state for war, was so pleased that Moody was commanded to proceed to Windsor and submit them to the queen and the prince consort. On 28 April 1858 Moody was promoted brevet-colonel, and in the autumn he was appointed lieutenant-governor and chief commissioner of lands and works in the colony of British Colombia. The colony was a new one. Moody founded the capital New Westminster, and drew the original plan for this town when the site was a dense forest of Douglas pine. He designed various settlements, arranged the tracks of roads through the country, which were executed by a company of royal engineers under Captain J. M. Grant, and during an uphill period earned the goodwill of the colonists and the approbation of the authorities at home. The Pacific terminus of the Canadian and Pacific Railway was at first at the head of Burrard's Inlet, at Port Moody, so named in the governor's honour. The railway has since been carried to the mouth of the inlet, and now terminates at Vancouver. On 8 Dec. 1863 Moody became a regimental colonel, and returned home the same month. In March 1864 he was appointed commanding royal engineer of the Chatham district. He was promoted major-general on 25 Jan. 1866, and retired from the service on full pay. After his retirement he lived quietly at Lyme Regis, and was in 1868 commissioner for the extension of municipal boundaries. He died on 31 March 1887 of apoplexy during a visit to Bournemouth. Moody married at Newcastle-on-Tyne, on 6 July 1852, Mary Susanna, daughter of Joseph Hawks, esq., J.P., D.L., of that town. He left eleven children.

[Royal Engineers' Corps Records; War Office and Colonial Office Records; Royal Engineers' Journal, vol. xvii.; Royal Agricultural Society's Journal, passim.] R. H. V.

MOON, Sir FRANCIS GRAHAM (1796–1871), printseller and publisher, born on 28 Oct. 1796 in St. Andrew, Holborn, was youngest son of Christopher Moon, gold and silver smith, by Ann, daughter of T. Withry (Burke, *Peerage*, 1890, p. 979). Placed with Mr. Tugwell, book and print seller of Threadneedle Street, he made many friends, by whose assistance he was enabled on Tugwell's death to take over the business. Subsequently he devoted himself to print-publishing upon a large scale. For this business, as a man of remarkable taste and judgment, he was admirably qualified, and he gradually rose to be the acknowledged head of his trade. In 1825 Messrs. Hurst, Robinson, & Co., the immediate successors of John Boydell [q. v.], became bankrupt, and Moon purchased the greater part of their stock. At the same time he joined the firm of Moon, Boys, & Graves in Pall Mall, but still carried on his own business at the corner of Finch Lane, Threadneedle Street. Moon was liberal in his dealings with artists, and popular with them. Sir David Wilkie once presented him with the copyright of one of his paintings. Others, especially C. R. Leslie, R.A., gave him drawings and the original sketches for their great pictures. He reproduced some of the finest works of Wilkie, Sir Charles Eastlake, Sir Edwin Landseer, David Roberts, Samuel Prout, C. R. Leslie, Clarkson Stanfield, and George Cattermole. One of his most celebrated publications was David Roberts's 'Sketches in the Holy Land,' &c., which cost 50,000*l.* to bring out. Moon's taste and persuasive manners were humorously noticed in some verses by Hood (cited in *City Press*, 28 Oct. 1871, p. 2, col. 6). He received the patronage of the English and many European courts, and was invited by Louis-Philippe as a private guest to St. Cloud.

In 1830 Moon was elected a common councilman; in 1843 he acted as sheriff of London and Middlesex; in 1844 he was chosen alderman of Portsoken Ward; and in 1854 he became lord mayor. On 28 April 1855 he received at Guildhall the emperor and empress of the French, and was created a baronet on 4 May following. Moon in turn visited Paris, where the emperor made him a chevalier of the Legion of Honour. In the spring of 1871 he resigned his aldermanic gown, accepting that of Bridge Without. He died at Brighton on 13 Oct. 1871, and was buried on the 20th in Fetcham Churchyard, Surrey. By his marriage, on 28 Oct. 1818, to Anne, eldest daughter of John Chancellor, carriage builder, of Kensington, he had four sons and four daughters. Of the former the eldest, the Rev. Sir Edward Graham Moon (1825–1904), was rector and patron of Fetcham. Lady Moon died on 24 May 1870.

[City Press, 21 and 28 Oct. 1871; Illustrated London News, 21 and 28 Oct. 1871 (with portrait); Men of the Time, 1868, p. 594; Foster's Alumni Oxon. 1715-1886, iii. 972; Walford's County Families, 1893.] G. G.

MOONE, PETER (*fl.* 1548), poet, was author of 'A Short Treatise of certayne Thinges abused in the Popysh Church, long used, but now abolyshed, to our consolation, and God's Word avaunced, the Lyght of our Salvation.' This is a poem in thirty-seven eight-line stanzas, rhyming *a b a b b c b c*, the last line being a refrain used in all the stanzas. After the poem follows, 'To God onely gyve the glory, quod Peter Moone. Imprinted at Ippyswyche by me, Jhon Oswen.' The work is excessively rare. The date 1548 is added in writing in the copy in the British Museum. There is an allusion to 'my Lorde Protector' [Somerset] in the poem. Hunter suggests that 'Mrs. Amy Moon of Norfolk,' second wife of Thomas Tusser [q. v.], was a relative, 'perhaps sister,' of the poet (*Chorus Vatum*, Add. MS. 24488–506).

[Tanner's Bibliotheca, p. 531; British Museum Cat.] R. B.

MOOR. [See also MOORE and MORE.]

MOOR, EDWARD (1771–1848), writer on Hindoo mythology, born in 1771, was appointed a cadet on the Bombay establishment of the Hon. East India Company in May 1782, and sailed for India in the September following, being then under twelve years of age. In consequence of adverse winds the fleet in which he sailed put into Madras in April 1783, and Moor was transferred to the Madras establishment. He was promoted lieutenant in September 1788, and three months later adjutant and quartermaster of the 9th battalion native infantry. Though then but seventeen, his 'very great proficiency' in the native tongue was noticed in the certificate of the examining committee. On the outbreak of war in 1790 Moor resigned his adjutancy, and proceeded in command of a grenadier company of the 9th battalion to join the brigade under Captain John Little, then serving with the Mahratta army at the siege of Dharwar. He was of the storming party on the assault of that stronghold on 7 Feb. 1791, and on 13 June he was shot in the shoulder while heading the leading company in an assault of the hill fort Doridroog, near Bangalore. He rejoined his corps within four months, and on 29 Dec. 1791 led the two flank companies of the 9th battalion at the battle of Gadjmoor, where the enemy, though vastly superior in numbers, were totally routed, and Moor was specially complimented on his gallantry in renewing the British attack on the right. In this engagement Moor received two wounds, and was eventually compelled to return home on sick leave. During his consequent leisure he wrote 'A Narrative of the Operations of Captain Little's Detachment and of the Mahratta Army commanded by Purseram Bhow during the late Confederacy in India against the Nawab Tippoo Sultan Bahadur' (London, 1794, 4to). Moor re-embarked for Bombay in April 1796, with the brevet rank of captain, and in July 1799 he was appointed garrison storekeeper (commissary-general) at Bombay, a post which he held with credit until his departure from India in February 1805. In 1800, at the request of Governor Duncan, he made a 'Digest of the Military Orders and Regulations of the Bombay Army,' which was printed at the expense of the government. The latter, on 14 Sept. 1800, awarded the compiler ten thousand rupees for the original work, and two thousand more for the additions subsequently made to it. The state of his health precluding his return to India, Moor retired from the company's service in 1806, receiving a special pension for his distinguished service in addition to his half-pay.

In 1810 Moor published his 'Hindu Pantheon' (London, roy. 4to), a work of considerable value, which for more than fifty years remained the only book of authority in English upon its subject. A collection of pictures and engravings of Hindu deities formed the nucleus of the book. Round these the author accumulated a mass of information, partly gathered by himself, but largely derived from correspondents, and supplemented from the works of Sir William Jones and other orientalists. Though prolix and heavy in style and overweighted with classical parallels and irrelevancies, its intrinsic value carried the book through several editions. A beautiful series of illustrative plates (engraved by J. Dadley after drawings by M. Houghton) was edited by the Rev. A. P. Moore in 1861, London, 4to, and another edition with fresh plates appeared at Madras in 1864. Moor's other works on Indian subjects were 'Hindu Infanticide; an Account of the Measures adopted for suppressing the Practice' (London, 1811, 4to), and 'Oriental Fragments' (1834), comprising descriptions of gems and inscriptions and general reflections upon Hindu mythology and religion. During his retirement at Great Bealings in Suffolk he also wrote 'The Gentle Sponge' (1829, 8vo), a proposal for reducing the interest on the national debt, and a collection of 'Suffolk Words and Phrases' (1823, 12mo), containing many elaborate articles (e.g. cantle and sibrit) of some interest, but little etymological value, besides several pamphlets. He also contributed Indian articles to Rees's 'Cyclopædia.'

Moor died at the house of his son-in-law in Great George Street, Westminster, on 26 Feb. 1848. He married, on 10 July 1794, Elizabeth, daughter of James Lynn of Woodbridge, surgeon. By her (she died on 13 Dec. 1835) he had issue a son, Edward J. Moor, who became rector of Great Bealings, and a daughter, Charlotte, who married William Page Wood, afterwards Baron Hatterley and lord chancellor [q. v.].

Moor was elected a member of the Asiatic Society of Calcutta in 1796, of the Royal Society in 1806, and of the Society of Antiquaries in 1818. He was member of other learned societies in India, England and France.

[Gent. Mag. 1848, i. 549, 550; East India Military Calendar, 1823, pp. 339, 349; J. Grant Duff's History of the Mahrattas, 1873, p. 492; Allibone's Dictionary of English Literature; Moor's Works in British Museum Library.]

T. S.

MOOR, JAMES (1712–1779), professor of Greek, was the son of Robert Moor, a schoolmaster in Glasgow, where he was born on 22 June 1712. In 1725 he entered Glasgow University, and distinguished himself especially in classics and mathematics. After graduating M.A., he was engaged for some time as teacher in a school in his native city, and subsequently travelled abroad as tutor to the Earls of Selkirk and Errol. He was afterwards tutor to William Boyd, fourth earl of Kilmarnock [q. v.], till 1742, when he became librarian of the university of Glasgow. In 1746 he was elected to the chair of Greek there, promotion which he owed to the assistance of Dunbar (Hamilton) Douglas, fourth earl of Selkirk. In 1745 Moor made a journey to London in an endeavour to obtain a pardon for his patron the Earl of Kilmarnock, who had been condemned for his share in the Jacobite rebellion. His efforts were unsuccessful.

At the request of the university, Moor, in conjunction with Muirhead, professor of humanity, superintended the production, in four folio volumes, of a magnificent edition of Homer, published by the Foulises of Glasgow. To insure the utmost accuracy of text every sheet was read six times before it was sent to press, twice by the ordinary corrector, once by Andrew Foulis [q. v.], once by each of the editors separately, and finally by both conjunctly. Copies of this edition (1747) are now very rare. For the Foulis press Moor also edited Herodotus and other classics. In 1761 he was appointed vice-rector of the university, and he received in 1763 the degree of Doctor of Laws. Owing to bad health Moor resigned his chair in 1774, and died in Glasgow on 17 Sept. 1779. During the period of his retirement Moor amused himself by writing Hudibrastic verses and epigrams, of which a number have appeared in 'Notes and Queries.' His valuable library and cabinet of medals were purchased by the university authorities.

Besides editing Homer, Herodotus, Tyrtæus, and other classical authors for the Foulises, Moor wrote several learned treatises, including: 1. 'Essays read to a Literary Society at their Weekly Meetings,' Glasgow, 1759. 2. 'On the End of Tragedy, according to Aristotle,' Glasgow, 1763. 3. 'Addison's Cato, done into Latin Verse, without the Love Scenes,' Glasgow, 1764. 4. 'On the Prepositions of the Greek Language,' Glasgow, 1766 (reprinted at Richmond, 1830). 5. 'A Vindication of Virgil from the Charge of Puerility imputed to him by Dr. Pearce,' Glasgow, 1766. 6. 'Elementa Linguæ Græcæ Pars Prima,' Glasgow, 1766; a favourite school-book in Scotland; it passed through many editions in Latin, and an English version by J. C. Rowlatt appeared in 1836.

[Chambers's Biog. Dict. of Eminent Scotsmen; Catalogue of the Advocates' Library; the Library, i. 93; Notes and Queries, 2nd ser. iii. 21, 121, iv. 104, vii. 453; Scots Mag. 1779.]

G. S-h.

MOOR, MICHAEL (1640–1726), provost of Trinity College, Dublin, born in Bridge Street, Dublin, in 1640, was son of Patrick Moor, a Roman catholic merchant, in whose house Roger O'More, the leader of the rebellion of 1641, had lodged just before the outbreak. His mother was Mary Dowdal of Mountown. 'Having laid in a competent stock of grammar learning at home,' Michael was sent to France, and studied philosophy and divinity first at Nantes under the Oratorians, and afterwards at Paris. After teaching for some years at Grassin he returned to Ireland, and reluctantly took priest's orders, being ordained in 1684 by Luke Wadding [q. v.], Roman catholic bishop of Ferns. In 1685 he was made prebendary of Tymothan in St. Patrick's, and as vicar-general of Patrick Russell, titular archbishop of Dublin, had complete charge of that diocese. He also became chaplain to Richard Talbot, earl of Tyrconnel, and was by him introduced to the notice of James II. Moor persuaded the king not to confer Trinity College, Dublin, upon the jesuits, and was himself made provost in 1689, 'on the unanimous recommendation of the then prevailing Roman catholic bishops.' While holding this position he exercised his influence to mitigate the sufferings of the protestant prisoners in Dublin; and during the military occupation of Trinity College he, together with M'Carthy, the librarian, also a catholic, succeeded in saving the library from being burnt by the soldiery. The jesuits, however, had not forgiven him, and took advantage of a sermon preached by Moor before James, from Matthew xv. 14 ('Let them alone, they be blind leaders of the blind; and if the blind lead the blind both of them shall fall into the ditch'), to procure his deposition. It was said that the king and Father Petre, who had a defect in his eyesight, were especially pointed at.

Moor was not only dismissed but ordered to leave the kingdom. He betook himself to Paris, where he was 'highly caressed on the score of his learning and integrity;' but on the arrival of James in France after the battle of the Boyne, he proceeded to Italy. He was made censor of books at Rome, and became rector of Barbarigo's newly established college of Montefiascone. He was in great favour with Pope Clement XI, who was prevented only by the representations of the jesuits from placing his nephew under his charge.

Soon after the death of James II Moor again settled in Paris, and was in 1702 selected to deliver the annual *éloge* on Louis XIV, which had been founded by the city of Paris. He is described as then rector of the university of Paris (MORERI, *Le Grand Dictionnaire Historique*, 1759, vii. 808), an elevation for which he was doubtless largely indebted to the good offices of his friend Cardinal de Noailles. He is said to have twice held the rectorship, and was also principal of the Collège de Navarre, and professor of Greek and Latin philosophy at the Collège de France. He helped to remodel the university for Louis XIV, who founded for him the college of Cambray. Moor also 'joined with one Dr. John Farrely (or Fealy) in purchasing a house contiguous to the Irish College for the reception of such poor young men of Ireland who came there to study' (WARE, ed. Harris). To the Irish College he left what survived of his fine library from the depredations of an amanuensis, whom Moor, being blind in his later years, employed to read to him. His plate went to the Leinster provisor. Moor died, 22 Aug. 1726, in his rooms at the Collège de Navarre, and was buried, in accordance with his expressed wishes, in the vault under the chapel of the Irish College.

Moor seems to have been a learned divine and philosopher of the old school, and his 'critical knowledge' of Greek is especially spoken of. He published: 1. 'De Existentia Dei et Humanæ Mentis Immortalitate, secundum Cartesii et Aristotelis Doctrinam, Disputatio, in duobus libris divisa,' Paris, 1692, 8vo. Ware speaks of an English translation of this 'by Mr. Blackmore,' but this is not to be found. 2. 'Hortatio ad Studium Linguæ Græcæ et Hebraicæ recitata coram eminenti M. Antonio Barbarigo, Card. Archiep. de Montefaliscone,' Montefiascone, 1700, 12mo. 3. 'Vera Sciendi Methodus,' Paris, 1716, 8vo; a dialogue written against the Cartesian philosophy.

[Sir J. Ware's Hist. of Ireland, ed. W. Harris, ii. 288–90; Moreri's Le Grand Dictionnaire Historique, 1740, vi. 467 (art. 'Morus, Michel'); Brechillet-Jourdain's Hist. de l'Université de Paris, p. 285; W. B. S. Taylor's Hist. of University of Dublin, pp. 54–5, 245–6; J. T. Gilbert's Hist. of Dublin, i. 329–30; Webb's Compendium of Irish Biog.] G. LE G. N.

MOOR, ROBERT (1568–1640), chronographer, was born in 1568 at Holyard in Hampshire, and elected a scholar at Winchester in 1579 (KIRBY, *Winchester Scholars*, s. v. 'More,' p. 148). Proceeding to New College, Oxford, he matriculated 12 July 1588, and graduated B.A. 5 April 1591, M.A. 15 Jan. 1595, B.D. and D.D. (by accumulation) 5 July 1614. He was made perpetual fellow of his college in 1589, but left it in 1597 for the rectory of West Meon and the vicarage of East Meon, which he held conjointly. On

4 June 1613 he was installed prebendary of Winchester on the death of Dr. George Ryves (Hyde and Gale, *Hist. and Antiq. of Winchester Cathedral*). Here he was frequently involved in controversies with Bishop Neile on account of certain ceremonies which he had introduced into the cathedral. He is said to have been adorned in his youth with variety of learning, and in his later life to have been celebrated as an eloquent preacher and learned divine. He died 20 Feb. 1639-1640, and was buried in the chancel of West Meon Church.

He published a poem of great length written in Latin hexameters, intended as a universal chronology, and entitled: 'Diarium Historico-poeticum, in quo præter Constellationum utriusque Hemisphærii, et Zodiaci Ortus et Occasus . . . declarantur cujusque Mensis Dies fere singuli . . . sic ut nihil pæne desiderari possit, ad perfectam rerum gestarum Chronologiam . . ., Oxonii,' 1595, 4to.

[Wood's Athenæ Oxon. ed. Bliss, ii. 654; Fasti Oxon. ed. Bliss, i. 254, 267, 357-8; Reg. Univ. Oxon. pt. ii. p. 165.] G. T. D.

MOOR, THOMAS de la (*fl.* 1327-1347), alleged chronicler. [See More.]

MOORCROFT, WILLIAM (1765?-1825), veterinary surgeon and traveller in Central Asia, a native of Lancashire, was educated at Liverpool for the medical profession. While he was a pupil under Dr. Lyon at the Liverpool Infirmary, the attention of the local medical authorities was directed to the outbreak of a serious epidemic among cattle in the district (presumably the Derbyshire cattle-plague of 1783). It was agreed to depute a student to investigate the disease. The choice fell on Moorcroft, who carried out his task in conjunction with a Mr. Wilson, described by him as 'the ablest farmer of his time.' Encouraged by a reported remark of the anatomist John Hunter, that but for his age he would address himself to the study of animal pathology the next day (Moorcroft, *Travels*, vol. i. Preface), Moorcroft spent some years in France studying veterinary science. He afterwards settled in London, at first in partnership with Mr. Field, and for some years had a very lucrative veterinary practice. In Kelly's 'Directory' for 1800 his name appears at 224 Oxford Street. He seems to have realised an ample fortune; but he lost largely over patents which he took out in 1796 and in 1800 (Patents No. 2104, 16 April 1796, No. 2398, 3 May 1800) for the manufacture of horseshoes by machinery (Fleming, *Horse Shoes*, p. 516). He therefore readily accepted the offer in 1808 of an appointment as veterinary surgeon to the Bengal army and superintendent of the East India Company's stud at Púsá, near Cawnpore. He advocated the improvement of the native cavalry horse by the introduction of English or Turcoman bone and muscle.

His preference for the Turcoman over the Arab horse appears to have directed his attention to the possibilities of commercial intercourse between British India and the countries behind the Himalaya. In 1811-12, accompanied by Captain (afterwards Major) Hyder Young Hearsey, he crossed the Himalaya by the Niti Pass and made his way to the great plain between it and the Kuen-Lun chain; he examined the sources and upper courses of the Sutlej and the eastern branch of the Indus, and found the positions of Lakes Ravan and Manaforavara. He was the first British traveller to cross the Himalaya. An account of his journey appeared in 'Asiatic Researches,' xii. (1816) 375-534. Seven years afterwards, in the latter part of 1819, Moorcroft again set out on an exploring expedition, taking much merchandise with him. He visited Runjeet Singh at Lahore, and thence made his way into Ladakh and resided some time at the capital, Lé. When asked what the British desired, Moorcroft replied: 1. Liberty to trade with Ladakh. 2. Moderate duties. 3. A permanent footing in Ladakh. 4. The good offices of the government with that of Gordakh to induce the latter to open the Niti Ghât to British commerce. He had previously made proposals to Runjeet Singh at Lahore for increased facilities of commercial intercourse. The important political arrangements which Moorcroft proposed to the independent states adjoining British India were wholly unauthorised by the government. Disapproving his long sojourn at Lé, the Bengal government suspended his pay and allowances during absence. Moorcroft spared no effort to obtain permission to enter Chinese Tartary, but in this he was unsuccessful. From Lé he proceeded to Cashmere, entering that city on 3 Nov. 1822. His zealous inquiries into the management of the shawl-wool goat and the various processes of the Cashmere shawl manufacture, together with the specimens he sent home, are allowed to have contributed much to the improvement of the shawl industry at home. He finally quitted Cashmere by the Pir Punjáb mountains, descending into the Punjáb by a route new to Europeans, and proceeding by way of Attock and Peshawur to Cabul, on the line of route previously pursued by the embassy under Mountstuart Elphinstone [q. v.] He asked the Indian government for a letter to the king of Bokhara, which was refused. He nevertheless made his way from Cabul to Bokhara, and 'met with as much kindness from the king as could be expected from a selfish, narrow-minded bigot.' He got rid of all his merchandise, and bought some valuable horns to take back to India. The route from Cabul to Bokhara was then new to Europeans. Moorcroft wrote: 'Before I leave Turkestan I mean to penetrate into that tract that contains perhaps the finest horses in the world, but with which all intercourse has been suspended during the last five years. The expedition is full of hazard, but "le jeu vaut bien la chandelle."' He started from Bokhara on his return on 4–5 Aug. 1825. With a few servants he separated from his party to visit Maimama. But he was taken by robbers, and he died, by some accounts of fever, by others of poison, at Andekhui, after a few days' illness. His body was brought on a camel to Balkh, and was buried outside the walls. George Trebeck, a young Englishman who had accompanied Moorcroft from Calcutta, was too ill when Moorcroft's body arrived at Balkh to investigate the case. Trebeck died of fever shortly afterwards at Mazar.

As Moorcroft's pay had been suspended, there was a question as to the ownership of his papers. This was settled, and the papers became the property of the Indian government, by whom they were made over to the Asiatic Society of Bengal. A summary of those in the India House, arranged by the Hon. Mountstuart Elphinstone, appeared in vol. i. of the 'Journal of the Royal Geographical Society of London.' The narrative of Moorcroft's 'Travels in the Himalayan Provinces of Hindustan and the Panjab . . . from 1819 to 1825,' ending with his arrival at Bokhara, was published in 1841 under the editorship of Professor H. H. Wilson. In a review of the work the 'Athenæum' observed with much truth: 'When we take into account the difficulties experienced by those who followed in his [Moorcroft's] track, we hardly know how to express sufficiently our admiration of his hardihood and address, and to do him justice we must remind our readers that not only did death overtake him at a time when he had triumphed over the chief difficulties of his undertaking, but that his papers remained unnoticed until those who followed his example had carried off the honours that were justly his due.'

Moorcroft was author of: 1. An English translation of Valli's 'Experiments in Animal Electricity,' London, 1793. 2. 'Directions for Using the Portable Horse-Medicine Chest adopted for Service in India,' London, 1795. 3. 'Cursory Account of the Various Methods of Shoeing Horses hitherto in Use,' London, 1800.

The following papers were published, the first excepted, after his death: 1. 'Journey to Lake Mánafóravara in Little Tibet' (*sic*), 'Asiatic Researches,' xii. 375–534. 2. 'On the Pūrik Goat of Ladakh,' 'Asiatic Society's Transactions,' vol. i. 1827; 'Froriep Notizen,' xxviii. (1830) 275–6. 3. 'Notice on Khoten,' 'Geographical Society's Journal,' i. (1832) 233–46. 4. 'Notices of the Native Productions of Cashmere,' *ib.* ii. 253–68.

[East India Registers and Army Lists, 1809–1825; Moorcroft's writings; Journ. Roy. Geogr. Soc., London, vol. i. and notices in vols. xii. xxi. xxiii.; Sir Alexander Burne's Travels, i. 243; Moorcroft and Trebeck's Travels, ed. H. H. Wilson, London, 1841, with biographical notice in Preface, pp. xlix et seq.; review of the work in the Athenæum, 20 Feb. 1841.] H. M. C.

MOORE. [See also MOOR and MORE.]

MOORE, ALBERT JOSEPH (1841–1893), painter, born at York on 4 Sept. 1841, was thirteenth son and fourteenth child of William Moore [q. v.], portrait-painter, and Sarah Collingham, his wife. Several of his numerous brothers were educated as artists, including Henry Moore, the sea painter [see SUPPLEMENT]. Albert Moore was educated at Archbishop Holgate's School, and also at St. Peter's School at York, receiving at the same time instruction in drawing and painting from his father. He made such progress that he gained a medal from the Department of Science and Art at Kensington in May 1853, before completing his twelfth year. After his father's death in 1851 Moore owed much to the care and tuition of his brother, John Collingham Moore [see under MOORE, WILLIAM]. In 1855 he came to London and attended the Kensington grammar school till 1858, when he became a student in the art school of the Royal Academy. He had already exhibited there in 1857, when he sent 'A Goldfinch' and 'A Woodcock.' In the two following years he sent more natural history studies, but in 1861 he made a new venture with two sacred subjects, 'The Mother of Sisera looked out of a Window,' and 'Elijah running to Jezreel before Ahab's Chariot.' He exhibited other sacred pictures in 1862 and 1865. Meanwhile Moore had given signs elsewhere of the remarkable skill which he afterwards displayed as a decorative artist. After designing pictorial figures for architects in ceilings, altar-pieces, &c., he about 1860 painted a ceiling at Shipley, followed by another at Croxteth Park, Lancashire. He spent the winter of 1862–3 in Rome, and in the latter year executed a wall painting in the kitchen of Combe Abbey for the Earl of Craven. In 1864 he exhibited at the Royal Academy a group in fresco, entitled 'The Seasons,' which attracted notice from the graceful pose of the limbs in the figures, and the delicate folds of the draperies. In 1865 Moore exhibited at the Royal Academy 'The Marble Seat,' the first of a long series of purely decorative pictures, with which his name will always be associated. Henceforth he devoted himself entirely to this class of painting, and every picture was the result of a carefully thought out and elaborated harmony in pose and colour, having as its basis the human form, studied in the true Hellenic spirit. The chief charm of Moore's pictures lay in the delicate low tones of the diaphanous, tissue-like garments in which the figures were draped. The names attached to the pictures were generally suggested by the completed work, and rarely represented any preconceived idea in the artist's mind. Among them were such titles as 'A Painter's Tribute to Music,' 'Shells,' 'The Reader,' 'Dreamers,' 'Battledore,' 'Shuttlecock,' 'Azaleas,' &c. In so limited a sphere of art Moore found his admirers among the few true connoisseurs of art rather than among the general public. His pictures were frequently sold off the easel before completion, but it was not till late in his life that he obtained what may be called direct patronage. He executed other important decorative works, like 'The Last Supper' and some paintings for a church at Rochdale, the hall at Claremont, the proscenium of the Queen's Theatre, Long Acre, and a frieze of peacocks for Mr. Lehmann. Moore was of an independent disposition, and relied solely on his own judgment in matters both social and artistic. His somewhat outspoken views proved a bar to his admission into the ranks of the Royal Academy, for which he was many years a candidate, and where his works were long a chief source of attraction. Though suffering from a painful and incurable illness Moore worked up to the last, completing by sheer courage and determination an important picture just before his death, which occurred on 25 Sept. 1893, at 2 Spenser Street, Victoria Street, Westminster. He was buried at Highgate cemetery. His last picture, 'The Loves of the Seasons and the Winds,' is one of his most elaborate and painstaking works; it was painted for Mr. McCulloch, and Moore wrote three stanzas of verse to explain the title. His work is now represented in many important public collections, such as those of Birmingham, Liverpool, Manchester, and elsewhere. An exhibition of his works was held at the Grafton Gallery, London, in 1894.

[Obituary notices: Athenæum and Pall Mall Gazette, 30 Sept. 1893, Westminster Gazette, 4 Oct. 1893, &c.; The Portfolio, i. 5; Champlin and Perkins's Cyclopædia of Painters and Painting; Scribner's Magazine, December 1891; private information.] L. C.

MOORE, ANN (*fl.* 1813), 'the fasting-woman of Tutbury,' born on 31 Oct. 1761 at Rosliston, Derbyshire, was the daughter of a day-labourer named Pegg. In 1788 she inveigled into marriage a farm servant, James Moore, who soon deserted her, but while her good looks lasted Ann found no difficulty in obtaining occupation, and became the mother of a large family. About 1800 she made her way to Tutbury, and endeavoured to find honest employment. Reduced to dire poverty, she subsisted on the minimum amount of food necessary to support a human being, and the astonishment created locally by her long fasts doubtless encouraged her to undertake the imposture which made her notorious. It was given out that she had lost all desire for food from November 1806. Six months later the interest taken in her in the neighbourhood was sufficient to warrant her in taking permanently to her bed. On 20 May 1807 it was reported that she attempted to swallow a piece of biscuit, but the effort was followed by great pain and vomiting of blood. 'The last food she ever took was a few black currants, on 17 July 1807,' and in August 'she gradually diminished her liquids.' Details were multiplied in the pamphlets which narrated her case. One learned writer proved that she lived on air, another that the phenomenon was due to disease of the œsophagus, while a third was convinced that her condition was a manifestation of the supernatural power of God. Joanna Southcott declared that the advent of the fasting-woman presaged a three years' famine in France. In the meantime the local doctors had taken the matter up. By two of these, Robert Taylor and John Allen (both of whom made communications on the subject of the case to the 'Medical Journal,' November and December 1808), an investigation was set on foot in September 1808, and a succession of four hours' watches, undertaken by the chief inhabitants of the district, was arranged to cover a period of sixteen days. Bulletins were posted from time to time in Tutbury, to record progress, and a list of the watchers was published. At the commencement of the ordeal Mrs. Moore was described as terribly worn and emaciated, but as it progressed she sensibly improved in health and spirits. The report of the committee was generally held to be conclusive evidence of Ann's veracity. For the next four years she continued to attract crowds of visitors from all parts of the country, who, in commiseration of her sufferings, or to reward her devoutness, which was attested by the Rev. Mr. Hutchinson, seldom left her without making a substantial offering. In 1812 she deposited 400*l.* in the funds. But in the summer of that year Alexander Henderson (1780–1863) [q. v.], physician to the Westminster General Dispensary, wrote an able 'Examination' of the imposture, showing the inconsistencies and absurdities of the woman's statements, and the curious parallel between the case and that of Anna M. Kinker, a girl of Osnaburg, who practised a similar imposture in Germany in 1800. It was in answer to this publication that, greatly to the fasting-lady's disgust, a second watch was insisted upon by her supporters. At her own request, none but ministers of the church of England, medical men, and magistrates were eligible, and a committee was formed, under Sir Oswald Mosley, bart. It met on 20 April 1813, and a period of one month was fixed upon. At the end of seven days the public were informed that Ann Moore had taken no food whatever. On the ninth day the watchers were alarmed by her loss of weight and extreme prostration. Two physicians present were of opinion that she could not live two hours. Thereupon, at the earnest request of her daughter, Mary Moore, the watch reluctantly broke up, and a few hours afterwards the woman confessed to her imposture. It is supposed that during the previous watch nourishment was conveyed to her in liquid form by her daughter when she kissed her night and morning. An engraving by Lines represented Mrs. Moore in bed in her garret. Another portrait was drawn by Linsell, and engraved by Cardon. Her face is not unpleasing, and her eyes are thoughtful and penetrating. She was evidently a woman of great resolution and cunning. Nothing is known of her subsequent career beyond the fact that she was in Macclesfield and Knutsford gaols for robbing her lodgings.

[Monthly Mag. October 1811; Edinburgh Med. Journal, v. 321; Medical and Physical Journal, xx. 529; Gent. Mag. 1813, i. 479; Chambers's Book of Days, ii.; Faithful Relation of Ann Moore of Tutbury, who for nearly 4 years has, and still continues to live, without any kind of Food, 4th edit. 1811; The Life of Ann Moore, with Observations and Reflections, by Edward Anderson, n.d.; An Account of the extraordinary Abstinence of Ann Moor of Tutbury, Uttoxeter, 1809, numerous editions; An Examination of the Imposture of Ann Moore, the Fasting-woman of Tutbury, 1813; A full Exposure of Ann Moore, the pretended Fasting-woman of Tutbury, 3rd edit. 1813; Leisure Hour, 1869, 1870, passim; Mosley's Hist. of Tutbury; Medical Observer, v. 163; Simm's Staffordshire Bibl. p. 314.] T. S.

MOORE, ARTHUR (1666?–1730), economist and politician, said to have been born in Monaghan, Ireland, about 1666, was either the son of the gaoler or of the publican at the prison gate. He was brought up, according to some authorities, as a groom, but Burnet says that he rose 'from being a footman without any education.' He studied trade questions, made money rapidly, and in 1695 was returned to parliament for the borough of Grimsby, Lincolnshire. At the election of February 1700–1 general bribery prevailed in that constituency, and although Moore petitioned against the members that were returned he did not claim the seat, and bribery was proved in his interest. With the exception of that short parliament he represented the borough from 1695 to 1715, and he was again elected on a by-vacancy in February 1720–1. In October 1722 he petitioned for the seat, but withdrew his claim next month. He had a house in Grimsby, and was high steward of the borough from 1714 to 1730 (George Oliver, *Great Grimsby*, 1825, p. 121).

Moore's name appears in 1702 among the managers of the 'united trade to the East Indies.' He was a director of the South Sea Company, and was appointed comptroller of the army accounts in 1704. It was reported on 15 April 1704 that he was about to be added to the Prince of Denmark's council on admiralty affairs. On 30 Sept. 1710, 'to the great surprise of many wealthy citizens,' he was made one of the lords commissioners of trade and plantations (Boyer, p. 476); he held this post during the remainder of the reign. During the last years of Queen Anne he showed great ability in parliament, and was deemed 'capable of the highest parts of business.' In January 1712, on the Earl of Strafford objecting to Prior as third British plenipotentiary in charge of commercial affairs, the lord privy seal was appointed, who, 'not being versed in those matters, was obliged to direct himself by the lights he received from Mr. Arthur Moore' (*ib.* p. 556). His brother Thomas Moore was made paymaster of the land forces abroad in August 1713. Moore mediated between Harley and St. John in their quarrels, but at last threw in his lot with the latter, and would have filled the office of chancellor of exchequer in the administration which

Bolingbroke contemplated. In after years he supported Walpole.

The articles of the treaties with France and Spain (1712) which related to commerce were mainly drawn up by Moore. He was wholly responsible for the eighth and ninth clauses of the 'Treaty of Commerce,' which stipulated for a reciprocal tariff between England and France, and he was the most frequent speaker throughout the debates (TINDAL, *Rapin*, iv. 320; CHANDLER, *Debates*, v. 4, 11; *Wentworth Papers*, passim). The treaty, which was the most important approach to free trade before that of Pitt in 1786, raised a storm of angry criticism. St. John wrote to the Duke of Shrewsbury on 25 Jan. 1712–13: 'Never poor proposition was so bandied about as this of using each other reciprocally, *ut amicissima gens*, has been. The French were in the right to perplex it, because they had a mind to evade it; but surely we from the first should have stuck to that plain article, which is contained in the papers drawn by Mr. Moore' (*Correspondence*, ii. 207–9). The articles were eventually cancelled, but Moore's vigorous defence of the principles involved in them marked him out for subsequent attack by the irate whigs of the city.

In 1714 it was alleged that Moore, among others, was an interested party in the Assiento contract. His views on the articles of the treaty were certainly very unpalatable to the merchant class, and especially to the South Sea Company, and they had to be largely modified before they won acceptance. On 10 June a committee was appointed by the directors of the South Sea Company to investigate certain charges made against Moore, the most specific being that he had superseded a certain Captain Johnson for conscientiously refusing to take on board his ship sixty tons of goods, to be sent to the West Indies on a private account. The practice of clandestine private trading was by no means unusual at the time. Moore insisted on his complete innocence; but apprehensive that, should a breach of trust be made out against him, he would forfeit all the South Sea stock in his possession, he with great prudence transferred it on the following day (11 June), a proceeding which was generally looked upon as a plain indication that he was not altogether innocent (cf. BOYER, *Queen Anne*, p. 666). Speaker Onslow, his neighbour in Surrey, who knew him well, goes so far as to apply to him the words, 'Vendidit hic auro patriam.' In July 1714 he was censured by the South Sea Company, of which he had been a director, for being privy to a clandestine trade to the prejudice of the corporation; and he was declared incapable of further employment by the company, to the great wrath of Bolingbroke (*ib.* pp. 710, 712). The charges against Moore, however, must be carefully discounted in view of the great hostility with which he was regarded, on account of his advanced views, by the bulk of the trading classes (see *Treasury Papers*, clxxviii. 19).

Moore bought much property in Surrey, including the chief mansion at Fetcham and the advowson of that benefice, the estate of Randalls in Leatherhead, and the farm of Polesden in Great Bookham, but 'his profusion consumed all.' He died on 4 May 1730, 'broken in all respects but in his parts and spirit,' and was buried at Fetcham. A description of his house, which was designed by Tallmen and ornamented by Laguerre, is given in 'Notes and Queries,' 4th ser. ix. 307.

Moore married at St. Bride's, London, on 17 March 1691–2, Susanna, eldest daughter of Dr. Edward Browne (1644–1708) [q. v.], and granddaughter of Sir Thomas Browne [q. v.], by whom he had two daughters, who died in early infancy. His wife was baptised at St. Bride's 4 Sept. 1673, died 23 Feb. 1694–5, and was buried at St. Bride's on 2 March, but the body appears to have been removed to Northfleet in Kent, where a monument was erected to her memory. He married at Westminster Abbey, on 4 Nov. 1696, his second wife, Theophila Smythe of Epsom, daughter and heiress of William Smythe of the Inner Temple, paymaster of the band of pensioners, by Lady Elizabeth, eldest daughter of George, first earl of Berkeley. She was then aged about 20, and she lived until 1739. By this union there were three sons and three daughters. The best known was the third son, James Moore, who assumed the name of Smythe [see SMYTHE, JAMES MOORE].

Moore's figure was disadvantageous, but his manner was 'equal almost to any rank.' His talk was 'a history of the age,' for he was of great experience in business as well as in current affairs, and he knew everybody. The satires and pamphlets of the day often allude to his varied career. He appears to have been on familiar terms with Davenant and with Gregory King. Pope refers to him in the 'Prologue to the Satires,' and Gay, in the lines on Pope's return from Troy, speaks of his 'gravity.'

[Burnet's Hist. of his own Time, ed. 1823, vi. 137, 151–2; Notes and Queries, 1st ser. xi. 157, 177, 197, 2nd ser. v. 8, vi. 13; Chester's Westminster Abbey, p. 34; Sir Thomas Browne's Works, 1836, i. p. cx, pedigree No. 3; Harrop's Bolingbroke, pp. 149, 204–6, 245; Wentworth Papers, pp. 394–405; Luttrell's Brief Hist. Relation, v. 414, 434, vi. 617; Hist. MSS. Comm.

11th Rep. App. v. p. 315, 12th Rep. App. ii. p. 410; Rawlinson MS. A. 289 ff. 134, 202, 207, C. 367 f. 96; Add. MS. 22851, ff. 56, 58; Oldfield's Representative Hist. iv. 149–53; Manning and Bray's Surrey, i. 482–3, ii. 671, 689–91; Somerville's Hist. of Great Britain under Queen Anne, pp. 562–3; information most kindly supplied by W. A. S. Hewins, esq., of Oxford.]

W. P. C.

MOORE, AUBREY LACKINGTON (1848–1890), writer on theology and philosophy, born in 1848, was second son of Daniel Moore, vicar of Holy Trinity, Paddington, and prebendary of St. Paul's. He was educated at St. Paul's School (1860–7), which he left with an exhibition, matriculating as a commoner of Exeter College, Oxford, 1867, whence, after obtaining first class honours in classical moderations and *literæ humaniores*, he graduated B.A. in 1871 (M.A. 1874). He was fellow of St. John's College, Oxford, 1872–1876; became a lecturer and tutor (1874); was assistant tutor at Magdalen College (1875); and was rector of Frenchay, near Bristol, from 1876 to 1881, when he was appointed a tutor of Keble College. He became examining chaplain to Bishops Mackarness and Stubbs of Oxford, select preacher at Oxford 1885–6, Whitehall preacher 1887–8, and hon. canon of Christ Church 1887. A few weeks before his death he accepted an official fellowship as dean of divinity at Magdalen, and when nominated simultaneously to examine in the final honour schools of theology and *literæ humaniores*, accepted the latter post. He died after a very brief illness on 17 Jan. 1890, and was buried in Holywell cemetery. At Oxford Moore had a unique position as at once a theologian and a philosopher of recognised attainments in natural science, dealing fearlessly with the metaphysical and scientific questions affecting theology. He lectured mainly on philosophy and on the history of the Reformation. Though rendered constitutionally weak by physical deformity, he had great powers of endurance and hard work, was a brilliant talker and preacher, and distinguished as a botanist.

He married in 1876 Catharine, daughter of Frank Hurt, esq., by whom he left three daughters. A fund of nearly 1,000*l.* was subscribed to his memory by friends, from which an 'Aubrey Moore' studentship (for theological research), open to graduates of Oxford, was founded in 1890, and a posthumous portrait of him by C. W. Furse was placed in Keble College Hall in 1892 (cf. *Report of Committee*, June 1892).

He published, besides a few scattered sermons, a valuable essay on 'The Christian Doctrine of God' in 'Lux Mundi' (1889); 'Holy Week Addresses' on the 'Appeal and Claim of Christ' (1888); 'Science and the Faith,' 1889 (a series of essays on apologetic subjects contributed mainly to the 'Guardian,' in which he had written constantly since 1883). His executors published a further selection of 'Essays Scientific and Philosophical' and 'Lectures on the History of the Reformation' in 1890, a volume of sermons on 'Some Aspects of Sin' in 1891, 'The Message of the Gospel' (ordination addresses) and 'From Advent to Advent' (sermons) in 1892.

[Memoirs in the Guardian, 29 Jan. 1890, by E. S. Talbot, D.D., and in the Oxford Mag. 22 Jan. 1890, by the Rev. W. Lock, both reprinted in Essays Scient. and Phil.; Gardiner's St. Paul's School Register, p. 340; Foster's Alumni Oxon.; Crockford; information from the Rev. W. Lock of Keble College.] H. E. D. B.

MOORE, SIR CHARLES, second Viscount Moore of Drogheda (1603–1643), third and eldest surviving son of Sir Garret Moore, viscount Drogheda [q. v.], was born in 1603. He succeeded his father in 1627, and on 18 Aug. 1628 he was appointed a commissioner for regranting escheated lands in Ulster. He was present at the opening of parliament on 14 July 1634, and was a member of the lords' committee of grievances. When the news of the outbreak of the rebellion of 1641 reached him, he was living quietly with his family at Mellifont. He acted with great promptitude, and on the night of 26 Oct. threw himself with his troop of sixty-six horse into Drogheda, but failing to stimulate the mayor and aldermen to take immediate measures for the defence of the town, and 'conceiving his continued presence might be prevalent,' he removed his family thither, and energetically set about repairing the fortifications of the town. Having done all he could in this respect, he posted to Dublin in order to procure assistance from the government. But in this he was at first not very successful, obtaining merely a commission to raise a company of the townsmen, together with some arms and ammunition. Meanwhile the governor of Drogheda, Sir Faithful Fortescue [q. v.], either out of sheer cowardice or disgust at the conduct of the lords justices, threw up his commission, and Sir Henry Tichborne [q. v.], having been appointed governor in his place, entered Drogheda with one thousand foot and one hundred horse on 4 Nov.

His arrival relieved Moore of further responsibility, but did not cause him to relax his exertions to place the town in a posture of defence, and fearing that the force at the governor's disposal would be insufficient to resist the attack of the enemy, he took advantage of the reassembling of parliament on 16 Nov. to make a fresh appeal to the government at Dublin. His offer to raise six hundred men at his own expense on condition that the four independent companies in Drogheda were embodied in one regiment and placed under his command for the defence of the county, though approved by the Earl of Ormonde, was not accepted by the lords justices. But by an ordinance of the two houses he was appointed a commissioner 'to confer with the rebels in Ulster and other parts, touching the causes of their taking arms.' The Irish, influenced no doubt by the well-known friendship that had existed between the Earl of Tyrone and Moore's father and grandfather, made several ineffectual efforts to win him over to their side. On 21 Nov. Mellifont was attacked, and, after a short but brave defence, captured and looted. Towards the end of the month Drogheda was invested on all sides.

The siege lasted several months, and, though the rebels on 12 Jan. 1642 narrowly missed capturing the place, they were by the vigilance of the governor and Moore finally compelled to desist from the attempt. In a sally on 5 March, which caused them to raise the siege on the north side, 'my lord Moore, by the acclamation of all men, behaved himself very valiantly, to the greater hazard of his person than his captaines were pleased with' (Bernard, *Whole Proceedings of the Siege of Drogheda*, p. 69). A few days later, the Earl of Ormonde arriving at Drogheda, it was determined to pursue the rebels as far as Newry, but peremptory orders coming from the lords justices forbidding him to cross the Boyne, 'my lord Moore and our governor (who in all things have proceeded very unanimously) . . . resolved to adventure the same design.' In this they were successful, and on 26 March, after some sharp fighting, recaptured Dundalk. But Sir Henry Tichburne deeming it necessary to remain there himself, the government of Drogheda devolved upon Moore.

During the summer he displayed great activity in suppressing the rebellion in co. Meath. On 25 April he attacked a body of them in the neighbourhood of Navan, and burnt their quarters, and in August he captured the strong castle of Siddan. By letters dated York, 30 June, and Stoneleigh Abbey, 20 Aug., he was constituted governor of co. Louth and barony of Slane by the king, but being a staunch royalist the lords justices, who inclined to the side of the parliament, found means to frustrate the king's intention in this respect (Carte, *Ormonde*, i. 362). In consequence of a petition addressed to the king by the confederate catholics in October 1642, Moore was on 11 Jan. 1643 appointed a commissioner to hear their grievances, and accordingly on 17 March he went with the other commissioners to Trim in order to meet the agents of the confederates, and to receive from them their 'Remonstrance.' In April he conducted a foraging expedition into the counties of Louth and Cavan for the relief of the forces about Dublin, but was compelled from want of provisions himself, after capturing Ballisloe, to return into garrison. In September he advanced against Owen O'Neill [q. v.] at Portlester on the Blackwater, but during the engagement on the 11th he was knocked off his horse and killed by a cannon-ball, fired, it is said, by O'Neill. He was taken next day to Mellifont, and subsequently interred in St. Peter's Church, Drogheda. 'He was,' says Clogy (*Life of Bedell*, p. 177), 'a most noble and worthy person, valiant for the truth, and exceeding bountiful to the soldiers for their encouragement.'

Moore married Alice, younger daughter of Sir Adam Loftus, first viscount Loftus of Ely [q. v.], by whom he had five sons and four daughters, viz. Henry, his successor, who was created Earl of Drogheda on 14 June 1661, and died on 11 Jan. 1675; John, who died young; Garret, who died without issue in 1665; Randal and Adam; Mary, who married Hugh, viscount Montgomery; Sarah, who married William, viscount Charlemont; Anne, who married Thomas Caulfeild, esq.; and Lettice, born after her father's death on 15 Jan. 1643-4, and who married Hercules Davis, son and heir of John Davis of Carrickfergus.

Shortly after her husband's death Lady Moore was involved in a plot to betray Drogheda into the hands of Robert Monro [q. v.] and the Scots. She was committed with her accomplices to Dublin Castle, and it is apparent from her deposition that her object was to break off the peace between Charles and the Irish, because she had been told that her husband 'by declaring himself so much against the Irish in the war had contracted a general hatred for himself and all his relations.' She was liberated after a short detention. According to Lodge she broke her leg by a fall from her horse on 10 June 1649, in a sudden outburst of grief at the first sight of St. Peter's Church in Drogheda, where her husband lay buried. She died three days afterwards of a gangrene, and was buried the same night by her husband's side.

[Lodge's Peerage, ed. Archdall, vol. ii.; Collins's Peerage, vol. ix.; Strafford's Letters; Journals of the House of Lords (Ireland), vol. i.; D'Alton's Hist. of Drogheda; Dean Bernard's The Whole Proceedings of the Siege of Drogheda in Ireland; An Exact Relation of a Battell fought by the Lord Moore against the Rebels in Ireland, 1641; Gilbert's Hist. of the Confederation and Contemporary Hist. of Affairs; Whitelocke's Memorials; Clogy's Life of Bishop Bedell; Nalson's Affairs of State; Carte's Life of Ormonde; Mellifont Abbey, Dublin, 1885.] R. D.

MOORE, CHARLES, sixth Earl and first Marquis of Drogheda (1730–1822), born on 29 June 1730, was eldest son of Edward, fifth earl of Drogheda, and Sarah, eldest daughter of Brabazon Ponsonby, first earl of Bessborough. He entered the army on 18 Nov. 1755, and represented St. Canice (*alias* Irishtown) in the Irish parliament in 1756–8. He succeeded his father on 28 Oct. 1758, taking his seat in the House of Lords on 16 Oct. 1759. On 12 Jan. 1759 he was made governor of co. Meath, and on 7 Dec. was appointed lieutenant-colonel commandant of the 19th, afterwards the 18th regiment of light dragoons, of which he was colonel from 3 Aug. 1762 till its disbandment in September 1821, and was very active during 1762–4 in repressing Whiteboy outrages. He succeeded 'Single-speech Hamilton' [see Hamilton, William Gerard] as secretary to the lord-lieutenant on the appointment of the Earl of Northumberland as viceroy in 1763, and in April 1766, during the absence of the Marquis of Hertford, he was appointed a lord justice. In general he was a consistent supporter of government, but in 1769, during the viceroyalty of Lord Townshend, being disappointed in his expectation of a marquisate, he threw his parliamentary influence on to the side of the opposition. He was, nevertheless, in the same year made governor and *custos rotulorum* of Queen's County. He was promoted major-general on 30 Aug. 1770, lieutenant-general 29 Aug. 1777, general 12 Oct. 1793, and finally rose to be field-marshal on 19 July 1821, but apparently never saw active service. From September 1776 to July 1780 he represented Horsham in the English parliament. He was created a knight of the order of St. Patrick on 17 March 1783, being one of the fifteen original knights, and on 5 July 1791 he was created Marquis of Drogheda. He was joint postmaster-general from 1797 to 1806, and, in consequence of the support given by him in parliament to the union, he was, on 17 Jan. 1801, created Baron Moore of Moore Place in Kent. The honour was reluctantly conceded to him by the Duke of Portland, and only in order to facilitate the arrangements made by Lord Cornwallis in regard to the representative peers. 'He is,' wrote Cornwallis to Major Ross on 3 July 1800, 'perfectly insignificant in respect to weight and interest in the country, and I only recommended him as being the oldest marquis in order to assist me in providing room for friends in the representative peerage' (Cornwallis, *Corresp.* iii. 269). He died in Dublin on 22 Dec. 1822, and was buried in St. Peter's Church, Drogheda, with great pomp as being the oldest freeman of the city.

He married, on 15 Feb. 1766, Anne, daughter of Francis Seymour-Conway, first marquis of Hertford, and by her, who died on 4 Nov. 1784, had issue: Charles, seventh earl and second marquis, an imbecile, born 23 Aug. 1770 and died unmarried in 1837; Henry Seymour, who married, on 28 Sept. 1824, Mary Letitia, second daughter of Sir Henry Brooke Parnell [q. v.], afterwards Lord Congleton, and died in 1825; Isabella, who died in 1787; Elizabeth Emily, who married George Frederick, seventh earl of Westmeath; Mary, who married Alexander Stuart, esq., of Ards, brother to Robert, first marquis of Londonderry, and died in 1842; Gertrude; Alice, who died in 1789; Anne, who died in 1788; and Frances, who married in 1800 the Right Hon. John Ormsby Vandeleur, and died on 28 Nov. 1828.

[Lodge's Peerage, ed. Archdall; Collins's Peerage; Burke's Peerage; Official Returns of Members of Parliament; Cornwallis's Corresp.; Froude's English in Ireland; Lecky's England in the Eighteenth Century; Charlemont's Corresp. in Hist. MSS. Comm. 12th Rep. App. pt. x.; D'Alton's Hist. of Drogheda; Gent. Mag. 1823, p. 83; Army Lists, 1762–1821.] R. D.

MOORE, CHARLES (1815–1881), geologist, the second son, but third child, of John Moore, by his wife Sophia (*née* Eames), was born at Ilminster, Somerset, on 8 June 1815. He attended the commercial school of that town from an early age till 1827, when he was removed to the free grammar school for one year. He then assisted his father in carrying on the business of printer and bookseller, and his uncle, Samuel Moore, who conducted a like business at Castle Cary.

About 1837 Moore appears to have first gone to Bath, where he was connected with Mr. Meyler, bookseller, in the Abbey churchyard, adjoining the Grand Pump Room. On the death of his father in 1844 he returned to Ilminster, and continued the business, with his eldest sister for a partner, till 1853, when he went back to Bath, and relinquishing business, devoted himself to his favourite pursuit, geology, and to municipal affairs. He was elected a councillor for the Syncombe and Widcombe ward on 1 Sept. 1868, and alderman on 11 Nov. 1874. He died at Bath on 8 Dec. 1881. His wife Eliza, whom he married in 1853, was only daughter of Mr. Deare of Widcombe.

Moore's attention was first directed to geology by the accidental discovery, when a boy, of a fossil fish in a nodule; from that time he became an ardent collector, and before his second removal to Bath had laid the foundation of the collection which, arranged by his own hands, now forms the 'Geological Museum' of the Bath Royal Literary and Scientific Institute. He was elected a fellow of the Geological Society in 1854. In 1864 he announced at the meeting of the British Association in Bath his important discovery of the existence in England of the Rhætic Beds, which had previously been overlooked. From these beds Moore obtained at the same time twenty-nine teeth of one of the oldest known mammals (*Microlestes Moorei*, Owen).

Moore was the author of some thirty papers on geological subjects contributed to the 'Quarterly Journal of the Geological Society,' the 'Geological Magazine,' the 'Reports of the British Association,' the 'Transactions of the Bath Royal Literary and Scientific Association,' &c.

[Charles Moore, by the Rev. H. H. Winwood, in Proc. Bath Nat. Hist. Soc. (1892) vii. 232–269; information kindly supplied by the same authority; Geol. Mag. 1882, p. 94.] B. B. W.

MOORE, DAVID (1807–1879), botanist, born at Dundee in 1807, was brought up as a gardener. In 1828 he migrated to Ireland and became assistant to Dr. James Townsend Mackay [q. v.] in the Dublin University botanic garden. He thenceforward spelt his name Moore instead of Muir, thinking that his Scottish origin might thus be less noticed in Dublin, where Moore is a common native surname. All his publications appear under this name, and his original designation is only known from his own verbal statement. He worked hard at botany, and in 1838 was appointed director of the botanic garden at Glasnevin, co. Dublin, a post which he held till his death. He kept the garden in a high state of efficiency and gave all the help in his power to students. He published numerous papers in the 'Phytologist' (1845, 1852, 1854, 1857), in the 'Natural History Review' (vols. vi. and vii.), in the 'Dublin University Zoological and Botanical Proceedings' (1863), in 'Leeman's Journal of Botany' (1864, 1865), in the 'Proceedings of the Royal Irish Academy,' and in other scientific periodical publications. He worked chiefly at mosses and hepaticæ, and published in 1873 a 'Synopsis of Mosses,' and in 1876 a 'Report on Hepaticæ' (*Proceedings of Royal Irish Academy*). In 1866 he published, with Mr. Alexander Goodman More, an English botanist settled in Ireland, 'Contributions towards a Cybele Hibernica, being Outlines of the Geographical Distribution of Plants in Ireland,' a laborious work of great value, which was begun in 1836, when he thoroughly investigated in the field the flora of the counties of Derry and Antrim for the ordnance survey. His last work was a description of a new species of Isoetes, which he called after his friend More (*Journal of Botany*, 1878, p. 353). He died at Glasnevin 9 June 1879.

[Memoir in Journal of Botany, 1879; Ordnance Survey of the County of Londonderry, vol. i. 1837; information supplied in 1867 by Mr. A. G. More; personal knowledge.] N. M.

MOORE, DUGALD (1805–1841), Scottish poet, son of a private soldier who died young, was born in Stockwell Street, Glasgow, 12 Aug. 1805. After receiving some rudimentary education from his mother he was apprenticed to a tobacco manufacturer, and then entered the copper-printing branch in the business of Messrs. James Lumsden & Sons, booksellers, &c., Glasgow. He had early begun to write verses, and Lumsden helped him to secure subscribers for his first volume, 'The African, a Tale, and other Poems,' 1829. A second edition appeared in 1830. Two years later, on the strength of profits accruing from this and subsequent publications, Moore started business in Glasgow as a bookseller, and was largely patronised. In the midst of his success he died, after a short illness, 2 Jan. 1841, leaving a competence to his mother. A stately monument marks his burial-place in the Glasgow necropolis.

Moore's other publications were: 1. 'Scenes from the Flood, the Tenth Plague, and other Poems,' 1830. 2. 'The Bridal Night and other Poems,' 1831. 3. 'The Bard of the North, a series of Poetical Tales, illustrative of Highland Scenery and Character,' 1833. 4. 'The Hour of Retribution and other Poems,' 1835. 5. 'The Devoted One and other Poems,' 1839. Moore has a genuine gift of lyrical expression. Professor Wilson considered his 'African' and 'Bard of the North' 'full of uncommon power.'

[Rogers's Modern Scottish Minstrel; Grant Wilson's Poets and Poetry of Scotland; Men of the Reign, p. 640.] T. B.

MOORE, Sir EDWARD (1530?–1602), constable of Philipstown, second son of John Moore of Benenden in Kent, and Margaret, daughter and heiress of John Brent, and widow of John Dering of Surrenden in Pluckley, was born apparently about 1530. Sir Henry Sidney speaks of him (Collins, *Sidney Papers*, i. 282) as his kinsman and the Earl of Warwick's man; but it is uncertain what the relationship exactly was. He came to Ireland about the beginning of Elizabeth's reign with his brothers Owen, the eldest, who became clerk of the check, and died in 1585; George, who was killed at Glenmalure in August 1580; and Thomas, the youngest, afterwards Sir Thomas of Croghan in the King's County, who was ancestor of the extinct house of Charleville, and died in December 1598. Moore is described (*Cal. Fiants*, Eliz. 641) in May 1564 as Edward Moore of Mellifont, esq., from which it would appear that he had already, at that time, obtained a lease of the dissolved abbey of Mellifont, which, from its position on the northern confines of the Pale, was a post of considerable strategic importance, and as such had not escaped the notice of Shane O'Neill (*State Papers*, Ireland, Eliz. ix. 65). Moore, though not actually in the queen's service, frequently furnished information to the government of the movements of the Irish in the north, and on more than one occasion rendered valuable assistance to the marshal of the army, Sir Nicholas Bagenal, in holding them in check (*ib.* xxix. 34, 36, 54, 70). He was warmly commended by Sir William Fitzwilliam (1526–1599) [q.v.], and his services were recognised by leases of lands in the neighbourhood of Mellifont (*ib.* xxxiv. 31; *Cal. Fiants*, 1723).

In 1571 he appears as sheriff of the county of Louth, and in the same year he extended his influence by a prudent marriage into the Brabazon family (*Cal. Fiants*, 1832; *State Papers*, Ireland, Eliz. xxxiv. 31). He rendered what assistance he could to the ill-starred colonisation scheme of Walter Devereux, first earl of Essex; but in May 1574 he was appointed governor of Offaly, in place of Henry Colley, and on 2 June he was reported to have entered on his charge, and to have made a likely beginning against the O'Conors (*ib.* xlii. 58, xlv. 71, xlvi. 41, 54; *Cal. Fiants*, 2391, 2403). He was absent in England during the greater part of 1575, but on 24 May 1576 he obtained a grant during pleasure of the office of constable of Philipstown. On 22 Oct. he was made a commissioner for concealed lands, and for ecclesiastical causes in May 1577 (*State Papers*, Ireland, Eliz. l. 85, 73, 74; *Cal. Fiants*, 2810, 2906, 3047). He was knighted by Sir William Drury in 1579, and in the same year obtained additional leases of lands in the counties of Louth, Meath, Kildare, and Queen's County (*ib.* 3559, 3564–5, 3593–6, 3599, 3615). During 1579–80 he was 'a very good instrument' in effecting an arrangement with the Baron of Dungannon for the preservation of the Pale from the depredations of Turlough Luineach O'Neill, MacMahon, and others (*Cal. Carew MSS.* ii. 177, 232, 304).

In March 1587 he visited England 'for divers causes, much importing himself,' connected probably with some property he inherited from his cousin, Nicholas Moore of Cranbrooke and Wigmore. 'He is,' said Sir John Perrot [q. v.] in commending him to the attention of Walsingham, 'a valiant gentleman, and hath served her majesty long here, and very chargeably in all journeys with me since my coming over, having no charge of horsemen or footmen, or other certain entertainment from her majesty during my time, saving the constableship of the fort in Offaly' (*Cal. State Papers*, Ireland, Eliz. iii. 281). Shortly after his return to Ireland he was, on 28 Sept. 1589, created a privy councillor (*ib.* iv. 241). In the examination of the witnesses against Perrot he was regarded as leaning unduly in his favour, and at the instance of Sir William Fitzwilliam, who looked askance at him, as being 'grown to be a man of party in his quarters,' and a friend to the Earl of Tyrone, he was placed upon his bond to appear when required (*ib.* iv. 322, 357, 399, 451). He did not return to Ireland till September 1594, when he was at once, as always having lived on friendly terms with the Earl of Tyrone, despatched north in order, if possible, to effect a settlement between him and the state (*Cal. Carew MSS.* iii. 223). Though unsuccessful, he displayed great prudence in his management of the business, and took a principal part in subsequent similar negotiations in 1595–6 (*ib.* iii. 181; *Cal. State Papers*, Ireland, Eliz. v. 529, 534). In May 1599, during the absence of the Earl of Essex in the 'remote parts of the kingdom,' and again in May 1601, during the absence of Lord Mountjoy, he acted as a commissioner for the preservation of the peace of Leinster (*Cal. Fiants*, 6293, 6326, 6527). He died early in 1602 (*ib.* 6590), and was probably buried in St. Peter's Church, Drogheda.

According to Lodge (*Peerage*, ed. Archdall, vol. ii.), Moore married, first, Mildred, daughter and heiress of Nicholas Clifford of Chart in Kent, widow of Sir George Harpur of Sutton Valence, who died without bearing him children; secondly, Margaret, daughter of William, fourth son of John Brabazon of Eastwell in Leicestershire, and widow of Warren and Blount, by whom he had (1) Henry, who married Mary, daughter of Francis Agard of Fawston in Staffordshire, and died without issue during his father's lifetime, about 1590; (2) Sir Garret [q. v.], who succeeded him; (3) Sir John, who died without issue; and (4) William of Barmeath in co. Louth. But according to Hasted (*Kent*, ii. 412), Sir Garret Moore, the ancestor of the earls of Drogheda, was son of Moore's first wife, Mildred Clifford. It is certain that in 1571 Moore married 'the Lady Brabazon,' and as Garret, according to Lodge, was born about 1560, it is evident that Hasted is correct (cf. *Archæologia Cantiana*, x. 327). According to another account (Irish genealogies in Harl. MS. 1425), Moore is said to have been married three times. The name of his first wife is not given. His second is said to have been the widow of a gentleman of the name of Wentworth in Essex, and his third, the mother of Garret, and ancestress of the earls of Drogheda, is confusedly stated to have been the daughter of Clifford of Kent, widow to Sir William Brabazon, Humphrey Warren, and Mr. Blunt.

[Authorities quoted above.] R. D.

MOORE, EDWARD (1712–1757), fabulist and dramatist, born at Abingdon, Berkshire, on 22 March 1711–12, was third son of Thomas Moore, M.A., dissenting minister, of Abingdon, by Mary, daughter of Thomas Alder of Drayton in the same county, and grandson of the Rev. John Moore, curate of Holnest, Dorset, one of 'the ejected.' Having lost his father when he was about ten years old, he was brought up by his uncle, John Moore, a schoolmaster at Bridgwater, Somerset. He also spent some time at a school in East Orchard, Dorset, and was then apprenticed to a linendraper in London, where (after some years spent in Ireland as a factor) he eventually set up in business on his own account, and, not succeeding, turned to literature as a last resource. His 'Fables for the Female Sex' (London, 1744, 8vo) have an excellent moral turn, but are somewhat deficient in the sprightliness which is especially demanded in that species of composition. The three last and best were contributed by Henry Brooke [cf. Brooke, Henry, 1703?–1783]. Brooke also wrote the prologue to Moore's first comedy, 'The Foundling,' produced at the Theatre Royal, Drury Lane, on 13 Feb. 1747–8, and damned with faint praise. At Drury Lane also on 2 Feb. 1751 was produced his second play, 'Gil Blas,' founded on the story of Aurora in Le Sage's romance, which, though ill received, was kept on the boards for nine nights. His domestic tragedy, 'The Gamester,' produced at the same theatre on 7 Feb. 1753, though it set tradition at nought by being written in prose, was on the whole a success. The prologue and some of the most admired passages, including the greater part of the scene between Lewson and Stukely in the fourth act, were written by Garrick, who played the principal part. The piece ran with applause for eleven nights, and has since kept the stage. Moore found patrons in George, first lord Lyttelton of Frankley [q. v.], and Henry Pelham [q. v.] His ingenious poem, 'The Trial of Selim the Persian,' published in 1748, is a covert panegyric upon the former. A fine ode on the death of the latter (1754), which in six weeks went through four editions, has been ascribed to Moore (cf. *Brit. Mus. Cat.*), but was written by Garrick. Another ode, in praise of Pelham, which holds the place of honour in the collective edition of Moore's 'Poems, Fables, and Plays,' London, 1756, 4to, is in the same stanza, and probably by the same hand.

Through Lyttelton's influence Moore was appointed in 1753 editor of 'The World,' a weekly periodical started in that year, and devoted to satirising the vices and follies of fashionable society. With the exception of Moore, who under the *nom de guerre* of Adam FitzAdam wrote sixty-one out of 210 numbers, the contributors were men of fashion (they included Lords Lyttelton, Bath, and Chesterfield, Soame Jenyns, Horace Walpole, and Edward Lovibond [q. v.]), and Moore was permitted to take the entire profits of the venture. The circulation averaged from two thousand to three thousand copies. After a course of four years 'The World' was brought to a close with an announcement of the dangerous illness of the editor, and by a curious coincidence Moore, who was then in good health, barely survived the revision of the collective edition, dying at his house in South Lambeth on 1 March 1757. He died, as he had lived, in poverty, and was buried in the South Lambeth parish graveyard, near High Street, without even a stone to mark the spot. Moore married, on 10 Aug. 1749, Jenny, daughter of Hamilton, table-decker to the princesses, who survived him. By her he had an only son, Edward, who was educated and pensioned by Lord Chesterfield, entered the naval service, and died at sea in 1773.

Besides the collective edition of Moore's 'Poems, Fables, and Plays' mentioned above, a separate edition of his 'Dramatic Works' was published at London in 1788, 8vo, and the latter have since been reprinted from time to time in the principal collections of English dramatic literature. 'The Foundling' has been translated into French, and 'The Gamester' into French, German, and Dutch. The 'Fables and Poems' are included in the collections of English poetry edited by Anderson, 1793–1807; Park, 1808; Chalmers, 1810; and Davenport, 1822. Separate reprints of the 'Fables' appeared at London in 1768, 8vo; 1770, 12mo; 1771, 12mo; 1783, 8vo; 1786, 12mo; 1795, 24mo; 1799, 8vo; 1806, 12mo. A joint edition of 'Fables by John Gay and Edward Moore' appeared at Paris in 1802, 12mo. The 'Fables' have also been translated into German. 'The World' appeared in collective form at London in 1757, 2 vols. fol. and 6 vols. 12mo, and in 1761 4 vols. 8vo; reprinted in 1772, 8vo, 1793, 8vo, and in 1794, 24mo. It is also included in the series of 'British Essayists' edited by Ferguson and Chalmers in 1823, and by Robert Lynam [q. v.] in 1827. A portrait of Moore by T. Worlidge belongs to Dr. Edward Hamilton. It was engraved by Neagle, and prefixed to the 1788 edition of his 'Dramatic Works.'

[Lives by Anderson and Chalmers; Calamy's Continuation, 1727, p. 412; Boswell's Johnson, ed. Birkbeck Hill, i. 202 *n.*, 257, 269, iii. 424 *n.*; Notes and Queries, 1st ser. p. 428; Davies's Memoirs of David Garrick, i. 176; Fitzgerald's Life of Garrick, 1868; Murphy's Life of Garrick, 1801; Chesterfield's Letters, ed. Lord Mahon, v. 241; Phillimore's Life of George, Lord Lyttelton, i. 260, 326, 328; Genest's English Stage, iv. 237, 321, 359; Gent. Mag. 1748 pp. 114–15, 1749 p. 380, 1751 pp. 74–8, 1753 pp. 59–61; Scots Mag. 1757, p. 111; Horace Walpole's Letters, ed. Cunningham, i. p. lxvii; Nichols's Lit. Anecd. ii. 320, vi. 458, ix. 497; Coxe's Pelham, ii. 305; Bromley's Engraved Portraits, p. 292; Gifford's Baviad and Mæviad; Rose's Biog. Dict.; Baker's Biog. Dram.] J. M. R.

MOORE, ELEANORA, otherwise **NELLY** (*d.* 1869), actress, played in Manchester and made her first appearance in London at the St. James's Theatre, 29 Oct. 1859, as the original Winifred in Leicester Buckingham's 'Cupid's Ladder,' a part in which she displayed much promise. On 29 Oct. 1860 she was at the same house, under Alfred Wigan [q. v.], the first Margaret Lovell in Tom Taylor's 'Up at the Hills.' She was seen for the first time at the Haymarket, 29 March 1864, as Venus in Mr. Burnand's 'Venus and Adonis.' On 30 April she was the original Ada Ingot in T. W. Robertson's 'David Garrick,' Sothern being Garrick. She played in the 'Castle of Andalusia,' and was once more Venus, this time in Planché's 'Orpheus in the Haymarket,' December 1865. She was the original Lucy Lorrington in Westland Marston's 'Favourite of Fortune,' 2 April 1866; was Cicely Homespun in the 'Heir-at-Law,' Celia in 'As you like it,' Mary in Tom Taylor's 'Lesson for Life,' and was the original Maud in 'Diamonds and Hearts,' an adaptation by the younger Gilbert à Becket of Sardou's 'Nos bons Villageois,' 4 March 1867. At the Princess's she played, 15 June 1867, Mabel in a revival of 'True to the Core,' by A. Slous; made, 11 April 1868, her first appearance at the Queen's as Nancy in 'Oliver Twist,' to the Bill Sikes of (Sir) Henry Irving and the Artful Dodger of John Laurence Toole; was, on 29 June, the original Marian Beck in 'Time and the Hour,' by J. Palgrave Simpson and Felix Dale (Herman Merivale), and 24 July 1868 was Ruth Kirby in Byron's 'Lancashire Lass.' This was her last performance. She died on 22 Jan. 1869. Miss Moore played at various houses, but her chief success was obtained at the Haymarket with Sothern. She was fair, with bright yellow hair, well-proportioned, a pleasant and sympathetic actress, and a woman of unblemished reputation. Her sister Louisa was also an actress, and others of her family were more or less intimately connected with the stage.

[Personal recollections; Scott and Howard's Life and Reminiscences of E. L. Blanchard; Era newspaper, 31 Jan. 1869; Era Almanack, various years; Sunday Times, various years.] J. K.

MOORE, SIR FRANCIS (1558–1621), law reporter, born in 1558, was son of Edward Moore of East Tildesley, near Wantage, Berkshire, by Elizabeth Hall of Tilehurst in the same county (BURKE, *Extinct Baronetage*, p. 365). After attending Reading grammar school he entered St. John's College, Oxford, as a commoner in 1574, but did not graduate (FOSTER, *Alumni Oxon.* 1500–1714, iii. 1022). He subsequently became a member of New Inn, and entered himself of the Middle Temple on 6 Aug. 1580, being chosen autumn reader in 1607. One of the ablest lawyers of his day, Moore was appointed counsel and under-steward to Oxford University, of which he was created M.A. on 30 Oct. 1612. At Michaelmas 1614 he became serjeant-at-law, and on 17 March 1616 was knighted at Theobalds. He was M.P. for Boroughbridge, Yorkshire, in 1588–9, and for Reading in 1597–8, 1601, 1604–11, and 1614. In parliament he was a frequent speaker, and is supposed to have drawn the well-known statute of Charitable Uses which was passed in 1601. The conveyance known as lease and release was his invention.

Moore died on 20 Nov. 1621, and was buried at Great Fawley, Berkshire, where he resided. By his marriage to Anne, daughter of William Twitty of Boreham, Essex, he had three sons and four daughters. His eldest surviving son, Henry, was created a baronet on 21 May 1627.

Moore's reports, 'Cases collect & report . . . per Sir F. Moore,' fol. London, 1663 (2nd edit. with portrait, 1688), extend from 1512 to 1621, and have always enjoyed a reputation for accuracy. They had the advantage of being edited by Sir Geoffrey Palmer [q. v.], a son-in-law of Moore, and commended in a 'prefatory certificate' by Sir Matthew Hale [q. v.], who married one of Moore's granddaughters. There is an abridgment of them in English by William Hughes (8vo, London, 1665). Four manuscripts of these reports are in the British Museum, being Harleian MS. 4585, Lansdowne MS. 1059, and Additional MSS. 25191–2.

Besides his reports, Moore was the author of readings made before the Temple on the statute of charitable uses, which were abridged by himself, and printed by George Duke in his commentary on that statute in 1676, and again by R. W. Bridgman in 1805.

There are two engravings of Moore, one by Faithorne, the other by 'F. V. W.;' neither possesses much interest.

[Wood's Athenæ Oxon. (Bliss), ii. 304; Cal. State Papers, Dom. 1610–20; Wallace's Reporters, 3rd edit. p. 85; Granger's Biog. Hist. of Engl., 2nd edit. i. 392; Addit. MS. 28676A, f. 245 (portrait); Will in P. C. C. 98, Dale.]

G. G.

MOORE, FRANCIS (1657–1715 ?), astrologer and almanac-maker, born at Bridgnorth, Shropshire, on 29 Jan. 1656–7, is said to have acted for some time as assistant to John Partridge (1644–1715) [q. v.] (*Gent. Mag.* 1785, pt. i. p. 268), and to have then lived at the north corner of Calcot's Alley in Lambeth High Street. On obtaining a license to practise physic, he established himself in 1698 at the sign of 'Dr. Lilly's Head,' in Crown Court, near Cupid's Bridge, Lambeth, in the threefold capacity of physician, astrologer, and schoolmaster. To promote the sale of some wonderful pills of his own compounding, he published in 1699 an almanac entitled 'Kalendarium Ecclesiasticum: . . . a new Two-fold Kalendar,' 12mo, London. In this compilation the prophecies are confined to the weather. By 6 July 1700 Moore had completed the first of his famous 'Vox Stellarum; being an Almanack for . . . 1701,' 12mo, London, 1701, of which the 'Astrological Observations' form a prominent feature. Moore dedicated it to Sir Edward Acton, recorder of and M.P. for Bridgnorth. The almanac has been published ever since as 'Old Moore's Almanac,' and even now has a large sale. Its success gave rise to many imitations. In 1702 Moore was living 'near the Old Barge House,' in the parish of Christchurch, Southwark, where he probably died between July 1714 and July 1715; at any rate he was not responsible for the 'Vox Stellarum' issued in 1716. His almanac was continued respectively by Tycho Wing and Henry Andrews [q. v.]

Moore's portrait was engraved 'ad vivum' by John Drapentier. It represents Moore as a fat-faced man, in a wig and large neckcloth, and is now very rare.

[Notes and Queries, 1st ser. vols. iii. iv., 2nd ser. vols. iii. viii., 5th ser. vols. ix. x. xi., 6th ser. vol. i., 7th ser. vol. iii.; Noble's Continuation of Granger's Biog. Hist. of Engl. i. 235–6; Knight's London, iii. 246 (with an imaginary portrait); Bromley's Cat. of Engraved Portraits; Allen's Hist. of Lambeth, pp. 343, 345 *n.*]

G. G.

MOORE, FRANCIS (*fl.* 1744), traveller, born in Worcester, was appointed in 1730 by the Royal African Company of England a writer at James Fort on James Island in the river Gambia. In January 1732 he was promoted to be factor at Joar in conjunction with William Roberts. He had much trouble with his colleague, who was a slave to drink and whose jealousy was extreme. Roberts finally betook himself to a town called Cower, about three miles away, along with all the servants of the factory, except the cook. He incited the natives to molest and threaten Moore, and was at length cashiered. Soon afterwards Moore went up five hundred miles inland, making careful observations and drawings. He left Africa in May 1735. In the ensuing October he was engaged by the trustees for establishing the colony of Georgia in America as storekeeper, and accompanied James Oglethorpe thither, staying there until July 1736. He made another voyage to Georgia in 1738, and remained until 1743, having witnessed the siege of Saint Augustine in 1740 and the Spanish invasion of Georgia in 1742.

Moore kept journals of his travels and published: 1. 'Travels into the Inland Parts of Africa, containing a description of the several nations for the space of six hundred miles up the river Gambia . . . to which is added Capt. Stibbs's Voyage up the Gambia in . . . 1723 . . . also extracts from . . .

authors concerning the Niger Nile, or Gambia,' &c., with map and plates after drawings by the author, 2 pts. 8vo, London, 1738; 2nd edit. about 1740, a valuable work, included in 'A New General Collection of Voyages and Travels,' 1745 (vol. ii.), in J. J. Schwabe's 'Allgemeine Historie der Reisen,' 1747 (vol. iii.), and in 'The World Displayed,' 1774 (vol. xvii.) 2. 'A Voyage to Georgia begun in . . . 2735, containing an account of the settling the town of Frederica . . . also a description of . . . Savannah,' 8vo, London, 1744. He would have published his journal of his second visit to Georgia had he received sufficient encouragement.

[Moore's Works; Stevenson's Hist. Sketch, p. 600, in vol. xviii. of Kerr's Collection of Voyages and Travels, 1824.] G. G.

MOORE, Sir GARRET, Baron Moore of Mellifont, **Viscount Moore** of Drogheda (1560?–1627), second and eldest surviving son of Sir Edward Moore [q. v.], was born about 1560. He was associated, in March 1594, with commissioners Loftus and Gardiner, and again in January 1596 with commissioners Wallop and Gardiner, in trying to arrange matters between the English government and the Earl of Tyrone (*Cal. State Papers*, Eliz. Ireland, v. 222, 454). On 8 Sept. 1595 he was appointed register and scribe of the supreme commissioners for ecclesiastical causes and clerk of recognisances (Morrin, *Cal. Pat. Rolls*, ii. 350), and on 1 May 1598 he was placed on the commission for the execution of martial law in the counties of Meath and Louth (*Cal. Fiants*, Eliz. 6223). He succeeded on the death of his father, in 1602, to the office of constable of the castle of Philipstown (*ib.* 6590), and on 12 April 1604 he obtained a confirmation of all the leases he inherited from his father (Erck, *Repertory*, pp. 173–81; *Cal. State Papers*, James I, Ireland, i. 157). Being a man of considerable standing, 'paying the greatest rent to the king of any man in the kingdom,' he was, in October 1604, sworn a privy councillor (*ib.* i. 208, iii. 423). He resided chiefly at Mellifont, and was the terror of the idle swordsmen of the district (Shirley, *Monaghan*, p. 111).

Like his father, he had always lived on terms of friendly intercourse with the Earl of Tyrone, and the fact that the earl visited him at Mellifont on the eve of his flight from Ireland (September 1607) furnished his enemies with a plausible pretext to reflect on his loyalty. Lord Howth, whom Moore had personally offended, carried his malice so far as openly to charge him with complicity in Tyrone's schemes. So persistently did he urge his accusation that Chichester, who had at first scouted it as ridiculous, was obliged to place Moore under bonds to the extent of 9,000*l.* (*State Papers*, James I, Ireland, ii. 463, 496, 515, 534–7). But when called upon to substantiate his charge, Howth flatly declined to produce his evidence before the council at Dublin, on the ground of its partiality to Moore. The case accordingly was transferred to England, and after a patient hearing of all that could be alleged against him, Moore was, in April 1609, fully acquitted and his bonds cancelled (*ib.* iii. 25, 41, 48, 113, 115, 134, 150, 162, 164–8, 201).

Unabashed, however, by his failure, Howth shortly afterwards preferred a new charge against Moore, of conspiring with Chichester to take his life. This time the charge was made so apparently recklessly that the lords of the council, after sharply reprimanding Howth and ordering him 'to retire himself to his own house and the parts adjoining, that the world may take notice that his majesty disliketh his proud carriage towards the supreme officers of the kingdom,' assured Moore that the king did not question his loyalty (*ib.* iii. 380, 387, 427). As an undertaker in the Ulster plantation, Moore obtained a thousand acres in the precinct of Orier, co. Armagh, and according to the inquisition of 1622 he had built a good bawn with two flankers, in one of which was a good strong house, where an Englishman, Townly, with his family resided (*Addit. MS.* 4756). In 1613 he represented the borough of Dungannon in parliament. He was created Baron Moore of Mellifont on 15 Feb. 1615, and on 7 Feb. 1621 Viscount Moore of Drogheda. He died, aged 67, on 9 Nov. 1627, at Drogheda, and was buried in St. Peter's Church in that town.

Moore married Mary, daughter of Sir Henry Colley of Castle Carbery, co. Kildare, by whom he had seven sons and five daughters, viz. Sir Edward, who was M.P. for Charlemont in 1613, but predeceased his father; Sir Thomas, who died aged 30 on 1 Dec. 1623; Sir Charles [q. v.], who succeeded as second Viscount Moore of Drogheda; Sir James of Ardee, who married Jane, daughter of Edward, first lord Blayney, and died 27 Feb. 1639; Arthur of Dunmoghan, co. Louth; Lieutenant-colonel Francis, who died unmarried in 1662; and John; Ursula, who married Sir Nicholas White of Leixlip, co. Kildare; Frances, who married Sir Roger Jones of Dollardstown, co. Meath; Anne, who married Sir Faithful Fortescue [q. v.]; Eleanor, who married Sir John Denham, chief justice of the king's bench in Ireland, and second baron of the exchequer in England; and Jane, who married Henry, second lord Blayney, died 22 Oct. 1686, and was buried in St. Michan's Church, Oxmantown, Dublin. Lady Moore subsequently married Sir Charles Wilmot [q. v.], lord president of Connaught.

[Lodge's Peerage, ed. Archdall, vol. ii.; Cal. Fiants, Eliz.; Morrin's Cal. Patent Rolls; Cal. State Papers, Ireland, ed. Hamilton, and Russell and Prendergast; Erck's Repertory; E. Shirley's Hist. of Monaghan; Pynnar's Survey in Harris's Hibernica; Sloane MS. 4756; E. Rowley-Morris's Family of Blayney; D'Alton's Hist. of Drogheda; Lord Clermont's Hist. of the Family of Fortescue.] R. D.

MOORE, GEORGE (1806–1876), philanthropist, son of John Moore and Peggy Lowes his wife, was born at Mealsgate, Cumberland, on 9 April 1806. His ancestors were 'statesmen,' who for more than three centuries had lived upon their own land at Overgates. After receiving some education at village schools, Moore, at thirteen, determined to begin life for himself. It was against family precedent, but at last his father agreed that the boy should be bound apprentice to a draper at Wigton, Cumberland, and the self-reliance which would not allow him to remain a labourer in the country ultimately drove him to London, where he arrived in 1825. His first success was won upon the day after his arrival, when he came off victorious in some wrestling at Chelsea. It was less easy to succeed in business. Work of any kind was for a time sought in vain, and it was to the clannish goodwill of a Cumberland man that he at last owed a modest place with Flint, Ray, & Co., drapers. He made little progress, but, with characteristic resolution, determined to marry Ray's daughter. In 1826 he entered the service of Fisher, Stroud, & Robinson, then deemed the first lace-house in the city, with whom he wore down prejudice by steady industry.

The turning-point in Moore's life came when in 1827 he was made town traveller. He prospered at once. At twenty-one he was sent to the north, and worked with such extraordinary success as to be called 'The Napoleon of Watling Street.' At twenty-three a rival firm of lacemen, which began in a small room over a trunk shop in Cheapside, and became one of the largest in London, offered Moore a partnership, and the firm became Groucock, Copestake, & Moore. By his own capacity and toil Moore contributed much to its success, and in 1840, after suffering one refusal, he was able to marry Eliza Flint Ray.

In 1841 Moore gave up the active life of a traveller. City work at once told upon him. He tried hunting; and in 1844 went to America for three months. In the retirement occasioned by ill-health his religious opinions became pronounced, and on his return from America he plunged into philanthropy with the same zest that he gave to business. A list of the institutions for which he worked shows that he distributed his charity impartially. The first charitable institution in which he interested himself was the Cumberland Benevolent Society. Then he threw himself into the cause of the Commercial Travellers' Schools, for which he secured the interest of Charles Dickens. An article in 'Household Words' for August 1850 moved him to help in establishing the British Home for Incurables. He was the chief promoter of a reformatory for young men at Brixton, the only work, Moore used to say, he had 'begun and given up.' The Warehousemen and Clerks' Schools virtually had their origin on the premises of Moore's firm in Bow Churchyard. The Porters' Benevolent Association also owed its existence to his encouragement. For the Royal Free Hospital, over the general committee of which Moore presided, he collected large sums of money. He was a governor of Christ's Hospital, a warm friend of such societies as the London City Mission, the Reformatory and Refuge Union, the County Towns' Mission, Field Lane Ragged School, and the Little Boys' Homes, and a liberal donor to Cumberland charities. Much of such work was necessarily public; much was only known after his death. When Paris was opened after the siege (January 1871), he started at a few hours' notice to carry food and money from the Mansion House Committee. Moore was indifferent to honours. When elected sheriff of London, he escaped by paying the fine. Six times he refused to stand for parliament, although invitations came from the city of London, from Middlesex, from Nottingham, and elsewhere. The devotion to philanthropy to which Moore at first gave himself as a relief from the cares of business continued to the end of his life. On his way to speak at a meeting of the Nurses' Institution at Carlisle he was knocked down by a runaway horse, and died on the following day, 21 Nov. 1876, in the inn where he had slept on his way to London in 1825.

Inexhaustible energy was the dominant quality in Moore's character, and marked all that he did in business or in philanthropy, in the hunting-field or in his religious life. He was intolerant of the lazy or the careless. His benefactions were princely; yet he threw his counting-house into a ferment because no voucher could be found for an omnibus fare.

Some critics called him a fanatic; but few men had broader sympathies, or more wisely directed a vast expenditure in the interests of good works.

Moore's first wife, Eliza Flint Ray, died on 4 Dec. 1858; on 28 Nov. 1861 he married Agnes, second daughter of Richard Breeks, who survived him. There were no children of either union.

[Smiles's George Moore, Lond. 1878; O'Brien's Two Sermons, Lond. 1876.] A. R. B.

MOORE, GEORGE (1803–1880), physician and author, was born 11 March 1803 at Plymouth, where his father was dispenser at the infirmary. After attending Abernethy's lectures and surgical practice at St. Bartholomew's Hospital, London, he studied anatomy in Paris in company with Erasmus Wilson [q. v.], and attended Dupuytren's practice. In 1829 he became M.R.C.S. England, in 1830 L.S.A., in 1841 M.D. St. Andrews, in 1843 ext. L.R.C.P., and in 1859 M.R.C.P. He settled first at Camberwell, near London, where he practised successfully for eight years. In March 1835 he obtained the Fothergillian gold medal for his essay on 'Puerperal Fever,' which was favourably reviewed in the 'British and Foreign Medical Review' (ii. 481). In 1838 his health broke down, and he removed to Hastings, where he remained for ten years. During part of this time he was physician to the Hastings Dispensary, with his friend Dr. James Mackness [q. v.] as a colleague. In 1845 he published the most popular of his books, 'The Power of the Soul over the Body,' which reached a sixth edition in 1868. In 1848 his health obliged him to seek comparative retirement at Tunbridge Wells, but he returned in 1857 to Hastings. Here he passed the rest of his life, engaged in literary work, and, till within a few years of his death, in medical practice. He died there 30 Oct. 1880. He was married three times (his first wife having died very shortly after marriage), and by his second wife, who died in 1850, he had several children, who survived him. He was a man of very high moral and religious character, and of considerable learning. In 1840 he published a work on 'Infant Baptism Reconsidered,' being a baptist by conviction, but in his latter years he attended congregational or church of England services.

His principal work was 'The Lost Tribes and the Saxons of the East and of the West, with New Views of Buddhism, and Translations of Rock-Records in India,' with fourteen illustrations, 8vo, London, 1861, in which he endeavours to demonstrate the connection of the Buddhists with the Israelites, and of both with the *Sacæ* (or *Sakai*), and of the Sacæ with the Saxons.

Some of his other works are: 1. 'The Use of the Body in relation to the Mind,' 1846; 3rd edition, 1852. 2. 'Man and his Motives,' 1848; 3rd edition, 1852. 3. 'Health, Disease, and Remedy,' 1850. 4. 'Ancient Pillar Stones of Scotland,' 1865. 5. 'The First Man and his Place in Creation,' 1866. 6. 'The Training of Young Children on Christian and Natural Principles,' 1872. He also published in 1826 'The Minstrel's Tale, and other Poems,' and in later life composed many hymns and short religious poems, some of which appeared in the 'Hastings and St. Leonards News.'

[Medical Directory; Hastings and St. Leonards News, 5 and 12 Nov. 1880; personal knowledge and recollection; information from the family.] W. A. G.

MOORE, GEORGE BELTON (1806–1875), painter and drawing-master, born in 1806, exhibited landscapes at the Royal Academy and other exhibitions from 1830 until his death. He was drawing-master at the Royal Military Academy, Woolwich, and at University College, London. In 1851 he published 'Perspective, its Principles and Practice,' and 'The Principles of Colour applied to Decorative Art.' Moore died in November 1875, in his seventieth year.

[Redgrave's Dict. of Artists; Graves's Dict. of Artists, 1760–1880; Royal Academy Catalogues.] L. C.

MOORE, GEORGE HENRY (1811–1870), Irish politician, son of George Moore of Moore Hall, co. Mayo, by his wife, granddaughter of John Browne, first earl of Altamont, was born at Moore Hall in 1811. The family was catholic, and had been long settled in Mayo. He entered Oscott College, Birmingham, about 1817, and became one of the editors of the 'Oscotian,' a magazine published at the college, contributing in 1826 poems of much promise to it and to the 'Dublin and London Magazine.' In 1827 he entered Christ's College, Cambridge, but does not appear to have graduated. In 1847 he was elected M.P. for his native county. His brilliant oratorical gifts soon brought him to the front, and he became one of the leaders of the tenant-right movement, initiated by Frederick Lucas [q. v.] and Charles (now Sir Charles) Gavan Duffy. He was acknowledged to be the best orator of his party. In 1852 he was again returned for Mayo. The 'great betrayal' by Sadleir and Keogh, the departure of Gavan Duffy for Australia in 1855, and the death of Frederick Lucas, left him at the head of the tenant-right movement in parliament, and, according to A. M. Sullivan, 'assuredly if genius, courage, and devotion could have repaired what perfidy had destroyed, that gifted son of Mayo had retrieved all' (*New Ireland*, 1878, p. 248). In 1857 he was again elected, but was unseated on the ground of clerical intimidation. He was offered other constituencies, but, soured by disappointment and disheartened at the state of Irish representation, he remained out of parliament till 1868, when he was once more elected for Mayo without opposition. He died suddenly on 19 April 1870 at Moore Hall, and was buried in the mausoleum attached to his mansion. He married in 1851 Mary, daughter of Maurice Blake, J.P., of Ballinafad, co. Mayo, by whom he left a family. George Moore, novelist and art critic, is his son.

Moore was highly esteemed personally. Sir C. Gavan Duffy says he possessed 'a fine intellect, which was highly cultivated, and rhetorical gifts little inferior to those which had made Sheil a parliamentary personage. . . . Among men whom he esteemed and who were his intellectual peers he was a charming companion, frank, cordial, and winning. . . . With a powerful party behind him he would have uttered speeches almost as full of high passion and as glittering with brilliant conceits as Grattan's' (*League of North and South*, 1886, pp. 135, 227–8). It was proposed after his death to collect and publish his letters and speeches, and the work was announced as in preparation, but it was never published. His writings and speeches have a distinct literary flavour. A portrait of him appeared in the 'Nation' of 8 Aug. 1868.

[Freeman's Journal, 21 April 1870; Nation, 23 April 1870; other authorities cited in text.]

D. J. O'D.

MOORE, Sir GRAHAM (1764–1843), admiral, third surviving son of Dr. John Moore (1729–1802) [q. v.], was younger brother of Lieutenant-general Sir John Moore [q. v.] and of James Carrick Moore [q. v.] He entered the navy in 1777, and served in the West Indies, on the North American station, and in the Channel. On 8 March 1782 he was promoted to be lieutenant of the Crown, one of the fleet with Lord Howe at the relief of Gibraltar, and in the rencounter with the allied fleet off Cape Spartel in October 1782. After the peace he went to France to perfect himself in the language, but was recalled by an appointment to the Perseus, in which, in the Dido, and in the Adamant, flagship of Sir Richard Hughes at Halifax, he served continuously till promoted, 22 Nov. 1790, to be commander of the Bonetta sloop; in her he returned to England in 1793. On 2 April 1794 he was posted to the Syren frigate, employed during the year in the North Sea, and afterwards on the coast of France, as one of the squadron under the orders of Sir Richard John Strachan [q. v.] In September 1795 he was moved into the Melampus of 42 guns, and, remaining on the same station, cruised with distinguished success against the French privateers and coasting trade. In the summer of 1798 he was attached to the squadron on the coast of Ireland, under Sir John Borlase Warren [q. v.], assisted in the defeat of the French squadron on 12 Oct., and on the 14th captured the Resolve of 40 guns, with five hundred men, including soldiers, on board. In February 1800 he went out to the West Indies; but after eighteen months he broke down under the trial of a summer in the Gulf of Mexico, and in August 1801 was compelled to invalid.

On the renewal of the war in 1803 he refused to stay on shore, and was appointed to the Indefatigable, a 46-gun frigate, attached to the fleet off Brest under Admiral Cornwallis. In September 1804, in consequence of the threatening attitude of Spain, and the intelligence that a large quantity of treasure expected at Cadiz was intended for the service of France, Moore, in command of a small frigate squadron, four in all, was sent to watch off Cadiz and intercept the treasure ships. On 4 Oct. they were sighted, four frigates under the command of a rear-admiral. The two squadrons approached each other in line of battle. On a shot being fired across his bows the Spanish admiral brought to, and Moore sent an officer on board to say that he had orders to detain the ships and carry them to England, that he wished to execute his orders without bloodshed, but the admiral's determination must be made at once. The Spanish admiral refused to yield to a nominally equal force. A sharp action took place, three of the Spanish frigates were captured, the fourth was blown up, with the loss of nearly all on board. The treasure taken amounted to upwards of three and a half million dollars, and was condemned as the prize of the captors, although war was not declared till 24 Jan. 1805, more than three months afterwards.

In August 1807 Moore was appointed to the 74-gun ship Marlborough, on the coast of Portugal. In November he was ordered to hoist a broad pennant and escort the royal family of Portugal to the Brazils. With a squadron of four English and five Portuguese ships of the line, besides frigates, smaller vessels, and a large number of merchantmen, he sailed from the Tagus on 27 Nov., and arrived at Rio de Janeiro on 7 March 1808. Before leaving again for Europe he was invested by the prince regent with the order of the Tower and Sword. In the autumn of 1809 the Marlborough formed part of the force under Sir Richard Strachan in the Walcheren expedition; and when the island had to be evacuated, Moore was charged with the destruction of the basin, arsenal, and sea defences of Flushing. In August 1811 he was offered the command of the Royal Sovereign yacht; he declined it, preferring active service, and in January 1812 he was appointed to the Chatham of 74 guns. On 12 Aug. 1812 he was promoted to the rank of rear-admiral, after which for a short time he commanded in the Baltic, with his flag in the Fame. In 1814 he was captain of the fleet to Lord Keith in the Channel [see Elphinstone, George Keith, Viscount Keith]. On 2 Jan. 1815 he was nominated a K.C.B., and on the escape of Napoleon from Elba was ordered out to the Mediterranean as second in command. The appointment was cancelled on the abrupt termination of the war, and in the following spring Moore was appointed one of the lords of the admiralty. In this post he remained for four years.

On 12 April 1819 he was promoted to be vice-admiral, and in 1820 went out as commander-in-chief in the Mediterranean, with his flag in the Rochefort. Shortly after his arrival on the station he took the king of Naples to Leghorn, on his way to attend the congress at Laybach. On the king's return to Naples he wished to confer on Moore the grand cross of the order of St. Ferdinand and Merit, 'for the important services rendered to the king and the royal family by the British squadron during the revolution.' Moore, however, declined it as contrary to the regulations of the English service. He was nominated a G.C.M.G. on 28 Sept. 1820. He returned to England in 1823; was made a G.C.B. on 11 March 1836, and admiral 10 Jan. 1837. From 1839 to 1842 he was commander-in-chief at Plymouth. During the latter part of the time his health was very much broken. He died at Cobham in Surrey on 25 Nov. 1843, and was buried there in the churchyard, where there is a plain monument to his memory. Moore married in 1812 Dora, daughter of Thomas Eden, deputy-auditor of Greenwich Hospital, brother of William, first lord Auckland. By her he had issue one son, John, who was promoted to the rank of commander in the navy three days before his father's death, and died a captain in 1866. Moore's portrait was painted by Sir T. Lawrence, P.R.A.

[Memoir of Sir Graham Moore, by Sir Robert Gardiner; Marshall's Roy. Nav. Biog. ii. (vol. i. pt. ii.) 533; Ralfe's Naval Biog. iii. 206; James's Naval Hist.; information from the vicar of Cobham.]

J. K. L.

MOORE, Sir HENRY (1713–1769), colonial governor, born in Vere, Jamaica, on 7 Feb. 1713, was son of Samuel Moore, a planter, by his wife Elizabeth, daughter of Samuel Lowe of Goadby, Leicestershire. His grandfather, John Moore, settled at Barbados in Charles II's reign, and subsequently migrated to Jamaica. Described as 'Jamaica Britannus,' Henry matriculated in Leyden University on 21 March 1731 (Peacock, *Index*, p. 70). After receiving a training in the militia and taking a part in local Jamaica politics, he was appointed lieutenant-governor of Jamaica, under a dormant commission, apparently in 1755 (Southey). He then took up his residence at Spanish Town. When the governor, Admiral Knowles, was recalled, he assumed the administration of the government, and displayed tact and firmness in attempting to remove local rivalries. He twice judiciously allayed quarrels between the two houses of the legislature; yet when martial law was proclaimed in 1759, and the council attempted to obstruct the administration, he suspended the ringleaders in that body, and procured compliance with his instructions. His own example was good, 'his system of administration was accurate,' in marked contrast with his predecessor's, and his personal superintendence was active. Thus, as a pledge that the trouble over the removal of the seat of government was at an end, he actively prosecuted the erection of the government buildings which still grace Spanish Town, and form the most striking façade in Jamaica. For a few weeks in 1759 he was superseded by a full governor, Haldane, whose death again placed Moore in command, and left him to cope with the serious slave-rising which broke out at Easter 1760. This rising developed into a war which lingered on more than a year and taxed Moore's energies to the utmost. He proclaimed martial law, and placed himself at the head of the British regiments quartered in the island. The guerilla warfare adopted by the negroes was very harassing to the regular troops, and it was only through Moore's personal resource and rapidity of execution that the rising was finally suppressed; not before he had twice fallen into ambuscade and barely escaped with his life, and on another occasion, when reconnoitring alone, had only been saved by his skill as a pistol-shot. His administration came to an end in February 1762, upon which he was made a baronet for his services.

In July 1765 he was appointed governor of New York, where he arrived in November 1765, just at the beginning of the troubles over the Stamp Act. His first proposal to his council was to insist on putting the act in force; but perceiving the bent of public feeling he forthwith adopted a strong popular line, suspending the execution of the act and dismantling the fort, to the great annoyance of Colden, the lieutenant-governor. In 1766 he provoked unnecessary opposition to the Billeting Act of the imperial government by attempting to establish a playhouse, and thus alienating the presbyterians. In October 1767 he tried unsuccessfully to settle the question of boundary with Massachusetts. His administration was terminated by his death on 11 Sept. 1769. 'Well-meaning but indolent' is Bancroft's description of his character as governor of New York; but he was personally liked by all parties.

Moore married Catharina Maria, eldest daughter of Samuel Long, esq., of Longville, Jamaica, and sister of Edward Long [q. v.], the historian of Jamaica. Their only son, John Henry, second baronet, is noticed separately.

[Burke's Extinct Baronetage; Appleton's Cyclop. Amer. Biog.; Bridge's Annals of Jamaica, vol. ii.; Gardner's History of Jamaica; Bancroft's History of the American Revolution, vol. i.] C. A. H.

MOORE, HENRY (1732-1802), unitarian minister and hymn-writer, son of Henry Moore, minister of Treville Street presbyterian congregation, Plymouth, was born at Plymouth on 30 March 1732. His mother was the daughter of William Bellew, of Stockleigh Court, Devonshire. His schoolmaster was Bedford, afterwards vicar of St. Charles the Martyr's, Plymouth. In 1749 he entered Doddridge's academy at Northampton, and, after Doddridge's death, removed on 9 Nov. 1752 to the Daventry academy, under Caleb Ashworth [q. v.] Here he was a fellow-student with Priestley. In 1755 or 1756 he became minister of a small presbyterian congregation at Dulverton, Somerset, but removed in 1757 to the presbyterian congregation at Modbury, Devonshire. He was at this time an Arian. It was not until 6 July 1768 that he was ordained at Plymouth. His congregation at Modbury went over to methodism. About the end of 1787 he removed to the presbyterian congregation at Liskeard, Cornwall.

Moore was a man of considerable learning and some humour, as his critique on Madan shows. His disposition was very retiring. Priestley, who thought highly of his exegetical powers, secured him as a contributor to his 'Commentaries and Essays,' 1785-99, 8vo, 2 vols.; the second volume is chiefly occupied with Moore's interpretations of passages in the Old Testament, which won the commendation of Alexander Geddes [q. v.] In 1789 Priestley applied to him, through Michael Dodson [q. v.], to take part in a projected version of the scriptures. He wrote much devotional verse, some of it of great beauty. He seems to have retired from active duty before 1792, when Thomas Morgan, one of the founders of the Western Unitarian Society, is described as minister at Liskeard. Shortly before his death he became paralysed, when an edition of his poems by subscription was projected by John Aikin (1747-1822), but not published till some years after his death. He died unmarried at Liskeard on 2 Nov. 1802.

He published: 1. 'An Essay on Fundamentals,' &c., 1759, 8vo (allows but two: that Christ is a king, and that his kingdom is not of this world). 2. 'A Word to Mr. Madan,' &c., 1781, 8vo (anon.); two editions same year: in reply to the 'Thelyphthora' of Martin Madan [q. v.] 3. 'Private Life: A Moral Rhapsody,' &c., Plymouth, 1795, 12mo. Posthumous was: 4. 'Lyrical and Miscellaneous Poems,' &c., 1803, 4to, 1806, 12mo (edited by Aikin). One of his pieces is in Lord Selborne's 'Book of Praise,' 1863; others are in most of the older unitarian collections; they are purely devotional, without specific doctrinal suggestion. A beautiful hymn, 'Amidst a world of hopes and fears,' which appears with the initials 'H. M.,' is often ascribed to him, but is by Hannah Merivale. A collection of his poems, in autograph, was in the possession (1878) of the late Rev. W. J. Odgers, Bath.

[Aikin's biographical preface, 1806; Monthly Repository, 1815 p. 688, 1822 p. 163; Rutt's Memoir of Priestley, 1831-2, i. 395, ii. 24; Murch's Hist. Presb. and Gen. Bapt. Congr. in West of England, 1835, pp. 503, 511 sq.; Christian Reformer, 1857, pp. 170 sq.; Julian's Dictionary of Hymnology, 1892, p. 1196.] A. G.

MOORE, HENRY (1751-1844), Wesleyan minister and biographer, only surviving son of Richard Moore (*d.* 1763, aged 46), a farmer and grazier, was born at Drumcondra, a suburb of Dublin, on 21 Dec. 1751. Having received a good education under Williamson, a clergyman at St. Paul's, Oxmantown, he was apprenticed to a wood-carver. This calling he followed in London in 1771 and

1773–6. When very young he had heard John Wesley preach in Dublin, but was disappointed at finding him no orator. He nevertheless frequented methodist services, and dates his conversion in February 1777, soon after which he was admitted a member of the methodist society in Dublin. He began to preach, gave up his handicraft, and started a classical school, which promised well. Fearing that success would make him worldly, he left Dublin for Liverpool, where he received an appointment (May 1779) as itinerant preacher in the Londonderry circuit. Here he acquired the friendship of Alexander Knox [q. v.], whose parents were methodists. After fulfilling other Irish appointments he was sent to London, and acted (1784–6) as John Wesley's assistant, travelling companion, and amanuensis. His knowledge of French, which Wesley 'had very much forgotten,' made him especially useful. He was next stationed in Dublin, where, on the advice of a physician, he began to study medicine, but soon abandoned it as incompatible with his preaching engagements. In 1788–90 he was again in the closest association with Wesley. He could hold his own on occasion against Wesley, who said, 'No man in England has contradicted me so much as you have done, and yet, Henry, I love you still.' He had resisted the suggestion of Charles Wesley that he should take Anglican orders, but on 27 Feb. 1789 he was ordained a presbyter by John Wesley, with the concurrence of James Creighton and Peard Dickenson, both Anglican clergymen. At the time of Wesley's last illness he was stationed at Bristol, but came up to London the day before Wesley's death (2 March 1791), and was with him at the last.

By his last will (dated 5 Oct. 1789) Wesley had made Moore one of his literary executors, in conjunction with Thomas Coke, D.C.L. [q. v.], and John Whitehead, M.D., and had named him as one of twelve preachers (four of them Anglican clergymen) who during their lives were to regulate the services at City Road Chapel in independence of the conference. Both these charges brought much anxiety and trouble to Moore.

It was agreed by the executors that a life of Wesley should be brought out, after the appearance of memoirs announced by John Hampson [q. v.], and published in June 1791. Whitehead was to write the life, and was entrusted with all Wesley's papers. He declined to obey an order of the conference directing the executors to sift the papers. The dispute led to the issue (1792), 8vo, under the authority of conference, of a life by Coke and Moore, chiefly written by Moore, and without access to the papers. Whitehead's life was issued in 1793–6. Ultimately Moore obtained access to the bulk of the papers, some having been destroyed (1797) by John Pawson as 'worthless lumber;' he accordingly brought out a new life of Wesley in 1824–5. This is a work of the first importance; though written with reverence, it displays intimate and discriminating knowledge. A large number of Wesley's papers, including his original memorandum books, some of them in Byrom's shorthand, passed on Moore's death to his executor, William Gandy (*d.* 28 Aug. 1882); they were in the possession of J. J. Colman, esq., formerly M.P.

Moore, although he had independent power (ultimately sole power) of appointment to City Road Chapel, was throughout life loyal to the principle of the authority of the conference (of which he was president in 1804 and 1823), even when differing from the conference policy. He was a man of no ambition, and refused every engagement which could interfere with his work as a 'travelling preacher.' Thus he declined (1789) the editorship of the 'Arminian Magazine.' He remained in the active duties of the itinerant ministry till his eighty-third year, when he became (1833) a supernumerary preacher. Of Wesley's methods he was extremely conservative. He strongly opposed (1834) the establishment of a theological institution for the training of ministers, and on the formation of the 'centenary fund' (1839) he expressed his objections to the acquirement of funded property by the methodist body. He had opposed Coke's Lichfield scheme (1794) for the creation of a methodist hierarchy, thinking the desire should have first been expressed by the conference; but when (1837) the conference itself resolved to ordain ministers by imposition of hands, he remonstrated on the irregularity, regarding himself as the only surviving person to whom Wesley had committed a power of ordination.

Personally he was a man of deep and even mystical piety, and to extreme old age exhibited a characteristic example of the devout simplicity of early methodism. He had good conversational powers and some humour. From 1832 his right side was more or less disabled by paralytic attacks. He died at his residence, Brunswick Place, City Road, on 27 April 1844, and was buried in the ground attached to City Road Chapel. He married, first, in 1779, Anne Young (*b.* 1756, *d.* 26 March 1813) of Coleraine; secondly, in August 1814, Miss Hind (*d.* 18 Aug. 1834), but had no issue by either marriage.

He published: 1. 'The Life of the Rev.

John Wesley,' 1792, 8vo. 2. 'A Reply to . . . Considerations on a Separation of the Methodists from the Established Church,' 1794, 8vo. 3. 'Thoughts on the Eternal Sonship,' 1816, 8vo (in reply to Adam Clarke [q.v.]) 4. 'The Life of Mrs. Mary Fletcher . . . of Madeley,' 1817, 12mo, 2 vols. 5. 'The Life of the Rev. John Wesley . . . including the Life of his Brother . . . Charles . . . and Memoirs of their Family,' 1824–5, 8vo, 2 vols. 6. 'Sermons,' 1830, 12mo (with autobiography to 1791, and portrait).

[Life, by Mrs. Richard Smith, 1844 (with autobiography); private information.] A. G.

MOORE, JAMES (1702–1734), playwright. [See SMYTHE, JAMES MOORE.]

MOORE, afterwards CARRICK-MOORE, JAMES (1762–1860), surgeon, second son of Dr. John Moore (1729–1802) [q. v.], was born at Glasgow 21 Dec. 1762, and studied medicine in Edinburgh and London. He published in 1784 'A Method of Preventing or Diminishing Pain in several Operations of Surgery,' in 1789 'A Dissertation on the Processes of Nature in filling up of Cavities,' and in 1793 'An Essay on the Materia Medica, in which the Theories of the late Dr. Cullen are considered.' In 1792 he became a member of the Corporation of Surgeons of London, and resided in Great Pulteney Street. From 1793 to 1802 he lived in Lower Grosvenor Street, and from 1803 to 1824 in Conduit Street. He was a friend of Edward Jenner [q. v.], and in 1806 wrote two pamphlets in support of vaccination, 'A Reply to the Antivaccinists,' and 'Remarks on Mr. Birch's serious Reasons for uniformly objecting to the Practice of Vaccination.' In 1808 Jenner appointed him assistant director of the national vaccine establishment, and in 1809, when Jenner resigned, he became director. In that year, after the death of his brother, Sir John Moore [q. v.], at the battle of Corunna, he published 'A Narrative of the Campaign of the British Army in Spain, commanded by his Excellency Lieutenant-General Sir John Moore, K.B.,' which gives a plain account of the campaign and of his brother's death, with full extracts from the despatches and other official documents. The book is dedicated to his mother. In 1821 he assumed the name of Carrick-Moore on succeeding to the property of a relative named Carrick. He published in 1834 a fuller account of his brother, 'The Life of Lieutenant-General Sir John Moore' (3 vols.) He describes in it his own visit to the general when on service in Ireland against the rebels in 1798. He became surgeon to the second regiment of life guards, and continued his direction of the vaccine establishment. In 1811 he published 'Two Letters to Dr. Jones on the Composition of the Eau Médicinale d'Husson,' a quack medicine which he had discovered to consist of a spirituous solution of hellebore and opium. He published in 1815 'A History of the Smallpox,' dedicated to Edward Jenner, and in 1817 'The History and Practice of Vaccination.' He had in 1809 communicated to the Medical and Chirurgical Society a paper 'On Gouty Concretions or Chalk Stones' (*Transactions*, i. 112), and seems to have paid much attention to chemistry. In 1825 he retired from practice, but he lived on till June 1860, having reached his 98th year. A daughter survived till July 1904, when she died at the age of 100 years and seven months.

[R. Anderson's Life of John Moore, M.D., Edinburgh, 1820; Lists of the Corporation and College of Surgeons, 1792–1834; E. M. Crookshank's Hist. and Pathology of Vaccination, London, 1889, vol. i.; Baron's Life of Jenner; Moore's Works.] N. M.

MOORE, JOHN (*d.* 1619), divine, descended from the Moores of Moorehays, Cullompton, Devonshire, entered University College, Oxford, as a commoner in or before 1572. According to Wood he left the university without a degree (*Athenæ Oxon.* ed. Bliss, ii. 193). He may, however, be identical with John Moore who graduated B.A. on 16 Dec. 1573, and M.A. on 2 July 1576 (FOSTER, *Alumni Oxon.* 1500–1714, p. 1023). He was engaged in 'some petite employments' until 1586, when he became rector of Knaptoft, Leicestershire. About 1610 he removed to Shearsby, Leicestershire. The enclosures in that county at the beginning of the seventeenth century aroused his sympathy with the customary tenants and the labourers, and he denounced the greed and extravagance of the landlords, to which he attributed the substitution of pasture for arable land. He published: 1. 'A Target for Tillage, briefely containing the most necessary, pretious, and profitable use thereof, both for King and State,' London, 1612, 8vo; reprinted in 1613. 2. 'A Mappe of Man's Mortalitie. Clearly manifesting the Originall of Death, with the Nature, Fruits, and Effects thereof, both to the Vnregenerate and Elect Children of God,' &c., London, 1617, 8vo. He died in 1619.

His son, JOHN MOORE (1595?–1657), born at Knaptoft, is probably the John Moore who matriculated from Exeter College, Oxford, on 9 May 1617, aged 22 (*ib.* p. 1024). He was living at Knaptoft in 1619, and he succeeded William Fallowes as rector of that parish in 1638. In 1647 the parliamentary sequestrators appointed him rector of Lutterworth. Moore was buried at Knaptoft on 29 Aug.

1657. Like his father, he was opposed to enclosures, and his attempts to prevent them in his own neighbourhood cost him upwards of 100*l*. He published: 1. 'The Crying Sin of England, of not caring for the Poor, wherein Inclosure, viz. such as doth Unpeople Townes and Uncorn Fields, is Arraigned, Convicted, and Condemned by the Word of God,' &c., London, 1653, 8vo. This pamphlet, which consists of two sermons preached by Moore at Lutterworth in May 1653, directed mainly against the enclosures at Catthorpe, Leicestershire, provoked a reply, 'Considerations concerning Common Fields and Inclosures, Dialoguewise, Digested into a Deliberative Discourse between two supposed friends, Philopeustus and Parrhesiastes,' &c. [by the Rev. Joseph Lee, rector of Cottesbach, Leicestershire], London, 1654 [1653], 8vo, in which the author ably refuted Moore's arguments. 2. 'A Reply to a Pamphlet intituled Considerations,' &c., London, 1653. Lee continued the controversy in 'A Vindication of the Considerations,' &c. This pamphlet, though dated 7 March 1653–4, was not published till 1656, when it was accompanied by 'Εὐταξία τοῦ 'Αγροῦ; or a Vindication of a Regulated Enclosure, &c., by Joseph Lee, Minister of the Gospel,' London, 1656, 8vo. He married Eleanor, daughter of Kirk of Northampton, by whom he had issue (1) John, baptised 30 Jan. 1619–20, settled at Stamford, Lincolnshire, and died in 1698; (2) Thomas (1621–1686) became an ironmonger at Market Harborough, Leicestershire, and married Elizabeth, daughter of Edward Wright of Sutton, in the parish of Broughton, Leicestershire, by whom he was the father of John Moore [q. v.], bishop of Norwich.

[Authorities quoted; Nichols's Hist. of Leicestershire, vol. iv. pt. i. pp. 83–99, 222–9, 265; Blomefield's Norfolk, ii. 42.] W. A. S. H.

MOORE, Sir JOHN (1620–1702), lord mayor of London, second son of Charles Moore of Stretton, Derbyshire, afterwards lord of the manor of Appleby Parva, Leicestershire, and Cicely Yates, was born at Norton, near Twycross in Leicestershire, and baptised there on 11 June 1620. His father, who had five other children, was lineally descended from the Moores of Moor Hall and Bank Hall, Lancashire. Moore came to London, entered the East India trade, carrying on business in Mincing Lane (*Little London Directory*, 1677), and soon realised an ample fortune. He was a member, and became master, of the Grocers' Company. He was in due time elected to the offices of alderman and sheriff, but was discharged on payment of the usual fines, on account of his religious scruples as a nonconformist. These scruples were overcome in 1671, when he was elected alderman for Walbrook ward and conformed to the sacramental test. On the death of Sir Jonathan Dawes, one of the sheriffs, who was buried on 16 May 1672, Moore was elected sheriff in his place. He had been knighted by Charles II at Whitehall three days before. In 1681 Moore was next in seniority for the mayoralty, but, being known to be favourably disposed to the court, a determined though vain attempt was made to set him aside. Moore carried the election after a poll, and the day ended 'with shouts, ringing of bells, and bon-fires in some places' (Luttrell, *Relation of State Affairs*, i. 128–30). On 29 Oct. Charles and his queen came to the city to see the show, and afterwards dined at the Guildhall. The pageant was prepared, at the cost of the Grocers' Company, by Thomas Jordan [q. v.], the city poet. The book of sixteen pages describing the 'triumph' is entitled 'London's Joy, or the Lord Mayor's Show,' London, 1681. In the British Museum are two ballads celebrating Moore's election as lord mayor, 'Vive le Roy, or London's Joy,' and 'A Congratulatory Poem to Sir John Moor, Knight;' the former is reprinted by Heath in his 'History of the Grocers' Company' (pp. 293–6). During his mayoralty (30 May) he was appointed colonel of the yellow regiment of London militia (Luttrell, i. 191). A trial of strength between the court and popular parties again took place on 15 June on the election of an alderman for Aldersgate ward, when Moore was one of the four candidates of the court party who were returned by the ward to the court of aldermen, but he declined to change his ward, and Sir Richard Howe was elected (*ib.* p. 194). The whig party being in the ascendency in the city, the tories rallied under the lord mayor in an attempt to secure the election of sheriffs in their favour on Midsummer day.

Moore was induced by court influence to use the lord mayor's privilege of nominating one of the sheriffs (though the custom had long been in abeyance) by drinking to a citizen at the bridgemaster's feast. Dudley North, brother to the lord chief justice, was thus nominated; the other court candidate was Ralph Box. The whigs brought forward Thomas Papillon [q. v.] and Dubois. Although Moore declared North and Box duly elected at the common hall, the sheriffs then in office, who belonged to the popular party, opened a poll, and, after two adjournments, declared the result on 5 July, when it appeared that Papillon and Dubois had a majority of nearly two to one over the court candidates. At the close of the proceedings the lord mayor was jostled and had his hat knocked off, and the sheriffs were accused before the king of having occasioned a riot, and were sent to the Tower. The lord mayor ordered another poll, and the court party eventually gained the day, North and Peter Rich (Box having declined to take office) being sworn in as sheriffs on 28 Sept. (LUTTRELL, passim; A. F. W. PAPILLON, *Memoirs of Thomas Papillon*, 1887, pp. 205 et seq.)

Moore's action in connection with the shrievalty election was prompted throughout by the king and his ministers, and during the struggle the Duke of Ormonde dined with him twice or thrice a week (CARTE, *Ormonde*, 1736, ii. 522–4). The episode called forth many controversial tracts. Burnet says that Moore was originally a nonconformist till he grew rich and aspired to the dignities of the city, and that though he conformed to the church he was still looked on as one who favoured the sectaries. The influence of secretary Jenkins brought him over to the court, and the opposition to his election determined him in his new resolve (BURNET, *History of his own Time*, 1823, vii. 324–5). Roger North in his 'Examen' gives a more flattering picture of Moore and his motives (1740, pp. 596 et seq.) Dryden, in his 'Absalom and Achitophel,' celebrates Moore as Ziloah (*Works*, ed. Scott, 1808, ix. 402–4). Moore was elected one of the city representatives in the parliament which met in 1685, and one of James II's last acts as king was to grant him a general pardon under the great seal, 22 Oct. 1688 (now belonging to J. G. Moore, esq., J.P., D.L., of Appleby Hall, near Atherstone).

On 20 March 1688–9, on the death of Sir John Chapman, Moore and Sir Jonathan Raymond were put forward by the tory party for election as lord mayor, by way of protest against the vote of a committee of the House of Commons, which declared Moore a betrayer of the liberties of the city of London in 1682. Alderman Pilkington, who was one of the whig sheriffs during his mayoralty, was, however, elected by a majority of two to one (LUTTRELL, i. 513–14). Moore in 1682 defrayed nearly the entire cost of rebuilding the Grocers' Company's Hall, the company then being on the verge of financial ruin; in acknowledgment they ordered his portrait to be painted and preserved in their hall (HEATH, *Grocers' Company*, 1854, pp. 287–8).

Moore died 2 June 1702, aged nearly 82, and was buried in the church of St. Dunstan's-in-the-East. In the church, on the south side, is a marble monument, the inscription on which states that Moore 'for his great and exemplary loyalty to the crown was impower'd by King Charles the 2nd to bear on a canton gules one of the lions of England as an augmentation to his arms' (HATTON, *New View of London*, 1708, pp. 216–17). The king's grant was dated 25 Aug. 1683, and was conferred upon his father's descendants also. A manuscript ode on Moore's death by Elkanah Settle, finely bound, belongs to Mr. Moore of Appleby Hall.

Moore was married in 1652 to Mary Maddox, who died on 16 May 1690 in her fifty-eighth year, and was buried beneath a sumptuous monument in the church of St. Dunstan's-in-the-East (*ib.* p. 216). He had no children and left the principal part of his estates, amounting to about 80,000*l.* in value, to his nephews, John Moore, son of his brother Charles, and John Moore, son of his brother George, the latter being appointed his executor and residuary legatee. His will, dated 25 May 1702, was proved in the P.C.C. on 3 June 1702 (Hern, 101).

Moore was a liberal benefactor to the charitable institutions of the city. He gave 500*l.* to the hospitals of Bridewell and Bethlehem, and in 1694 built, at an expense of 10,000*l.*, the writing and mathematical schools in Christ's Hospital, of which he was president in 1681. A statue was erected there to his memory, and a portrait is in the court-room of the hospital. At his home-town of Appleby, Leicestershire, he founded and endowed a grammar school in 1697 for the education of boys in Appleby and the neighbouring parishes, which was, under the statutes of 1706, made free for all England. The building was erected by Sir Christopher Wren, and at the upper end of the hall is a statue of Moore with an inscription. There is a good mezzotint of Moore sitting in a chair in his lord mayor's robes, engraved by McArdell from a portrait by Lely, and another print by Clamp, in 1796, from a portrait by Harding.

[Granger's Biographical History of England, 5th ed. v. 171; Roger North's Examen, 1740, pp. 596 et seq.; Guillim's Display of Heraldry, 1724, p. 194; Nichols's History of Leicestershire, iv. 440, 851*; Le Neve's Pedigrees of Knights, pp. 277–8; Maitland's History of London, 1739, i. 473–6; City Records; Records of the Grocers' Company; authorities above cited.] C. W-H.

MOORE, JOHN (1646–1714), bishop successively of Norwich and Ely, born at Sutton-juxta-Broughton, Leicestershire, in 1646, was the eldest son of Thomas Moore by his wife Elizabeth, daughter of Edward Wright of Sutton-juxta-Broughton. His father, an ironmonger at Market Harborough, born in 1621, was son of John Moore (1595?-

1657) [see under MOORE, JOHN, *d.* 1619]; he died in 1686, and was buried under an altar-tomb at St. Mary-in-Arden. John was educated at the free school, Market Harborough, and at Clare College, Cambridge, where he was admitted as 'sizer and pupil to Mr. Mowsse' on 28 June 1662. He graduated at Cambridge B.A. 1665–6, M.A. 1669, D.D. 1681, and he was incorporated D.D. at Oxford on 15 July 1673 (WOOD, *Fasti Oxon.* pt. ii. p. 337). The satires of the period often refer to his delight in medicine, and a few months before his death he promised to prescribe for Thoresby's son; from this love of physic he has been sometimes credited with the degree of M.D. On 17 Sept. 1667 Moore was elected a fellow of Clare College on the Freeman foundation, which he retained until the latter part of 1677. His fortune was made when he became chaplain to Heneage Finch, first earl of Nottingham [q. v.], who was lord keeper in 1673, and lord chancellor in 1675. On 23 Oct. 1676 he was collated to the rectory of Blaby in Leicestershire, and he held it until the close of 1687. Through his patron's interest he was nominated canon of the first stall in Ely Cathedral in September 1677, but the bishop of the diocese claimed the preferment, and he was not installed until 28 June 1679. Moore's services as a popular preacher were often employed in the London pulpits, and when the new church of St. Anne's, Soho, was consecrated in 1686 he officiated as its minister. He was drawn permanently to London by his appointment to the rectory of St. Augustine, or Austin-at-the-Gate, London, on 31 Dec. 1687, and on 26 Oct. 1689 he was advanced to the rich rectory of St. Andrew's, Holborn, holding it with his canonry at Ely until 1691. As chaplain to William and Mary he often preached before them, and when the see of Norwich became vacant by the deprivation of William Lloyd (1637–1710) [q. v.], Moore was appointed to the bishopric. He was consecrated at St. Mary-le-Bow, London, on 5 July 1691, and remained in that see until 1707, when he was translated (31 July) to the wealthier bishopric of Ely. This appointment was distasteful to Queen Anne, for Moore was a whig in politics, and strenuously supported the religious views of the low church party. Immediately after his confirmation he began to rebuild and repair the episcopal house in Ely Place, Holborn, and he was never happier than when he could show a visitor to London the treasures of his library (THORESBY, *Diary*, i. 334–5, 342, ii. 116, 220). His books and manuscripts were liberally placed at the disposal of the chief divines in England, such as Bentley, Burnet, and Strype, and he aided the principal scholars abroad. Among those to whom he gave preferment were Samuel Clarke, William Whiston, and Samuel Knight, and Whiston as an undergraduate at Cambridge received from him a substantial sum of money. When it was proposed that Bentley should be appointed to the see of Chichester (1709), the support of Moore was enlisted on his behalf. As visitor of Trinity College, Cambridge, he presided at the trial of Bentley, and a draft sentence of deprivation was found among his papers. During the long sittings at Ely House, London, which the trial demanded, he caught cold and died on 31 July 1714. On 5 Aug. he was buried in Ely Cathedral, at the north side of the choir, near the remains of Symon Patrick [q. v.], bishop of Ely, who died in 1707. A monument, with an epitaph by Clarke, was placed in the south aisle of the choir.

Moore married, on 22 May 1679, Rose, fifth daughter of Nevill Thomas Butler of Barnwell Priory, Cambridge, by Mary, daughter of Sir Gilbert Dethick [q. v.] She died 18 Aug. 1689, and was buried in the chancel of St. Giles-in-the-Fields, London. They had issue three sons and three daughters, the eldest of whom, Rose, married Bishop Tanner. The bishop married as his second wife Dorothy, daughter of William Barnes of Darlington, relict (1) of Michael Blackett of Morton Palms, Durham, (2) of Sir Richard Browne. She bore him three sons.

Moore was the author of many sermons, one of which, preached before the queen on 6 March 1691–2 and treating of religious melancholy, reached a seventh edition in 1708. All his printed sermons, twelve in number, were collected together after his death by Samuel Clarke, and published in one volume in 1715. A second issue in two volumes appeared under the same editorship in 1724, the first volume being a reprint of the previous set, and the second consisting of sixteen discourses, none of which had been printed before. His sermons are said to have been translated into Dutch and printed at Delft in 1700. He edited in 1704 'A Form of Prayer used by K. William III when he received the Holy Sacrament,' which was reprinted at Dublin in 1839, and he is asserted to have written the preface to 'An Introduction to a Breviary of the History of England. Written by Sir Walter Raleigh,' 1693, and to have 'committed the work to the press.' A reply to his sermon 'before their Majesties at Hampton Court, 14 July 1689, wherein he charges the Protestant Dissenters with Schism,' came out in that year, and about 1740 there was published a pamphlet commending his views on justification by faith only to the followers of George Whitefield.

The address presented to him by his college in 1708 on his first visitation of Cambridge as bishop of Ely refers to his munificent gifts to Clare library, and to the help which he had given in the rebuilding of the college. The library which Moore collected and retained was famous throughout Europe. At his death he had accumulated nearly 29,000 books and 1,790 manuscripts, and Dibdin did not exaggerate in calling him 'the father of black-letter collectors in this country.' The scandalous stories repeated by one gossiping antiquary after another as to the means by which he formed his collection may be dismissed from consideration. Bagford was the chief assistant in its formation, and in return the bishop obtained for him at the close of his life a place in the Charterhouse. The library was offered to Lord Oxford in 1714 for 8,000*l.*, and on his refusal was sold for six thousand guineas to George I, who gave it, on the instigation of Lord Townshend, to the university of Cambridge. The letter of thanks for this service is in the Townshend MSS. ('Historical Manuscripts Commission,' 11th Rep. App. pt. iv. p. 341), and the gift occasioned the two well-known epigrams referred to under SIR WILLIAM BROWNE. Some particulars of this famous library are in Bernard's 'Catalogus Lib. MSS. Angliæ et Hiberniæ,' 1697, vol. ii. pt. ii. pp. 361–84, 390, 393–9, and from the insertions in the copy of that work in the Cambridge University Library the additions to 1714 may be ascertained. [See also the notes of Oldys and Bagford on London libraries, which appeared in 'Notes and Queries' for May and June 1861, Hartshorne's 'Book Rarities at Cambridge,' pp. 18–24, Cambridge University Library MSS. Nos. 3236 and 3247, and Additional MSS. British Museum 5827, 6261–2.] The rarest volumes in the collection are frequently mentioned by T. F. Dibdin in his edition of Ames's 'Typographical Antiquities.' The bishop's unpublished diaries, numerous letters to him, and his private accounts are also preserved in the library at Cambridge.

A half-length portrait of Moore when bishop of Norwich was painted and engraved by R. White, and a reproduction by T. Hodgetts of the same print was prefixed to the second volume of Dibdin's Ames. A second portrait by Sir Godfrey Kneller was engraved by W. Faithorne, and sold by E. Cooper at the 'Three Pidgeons' in Bedford Street. This picture is at Lambeth Palace, and copies are in the Cambridge University Library, in the lodge at Clare College, and in Ely Palace. In the combination room at Clare College is another portrait of him when bishop of Ely and advanced in years, which may have been painted by Kersseboom. His arms are given in Bentham's 'Ely' (ed. 1812), App. p. *47.

[A life of the bishop by the Rev. Cecil Moore appeared in the Bibliographer in 1884, and was published separately, with the date of 1885. A supplement from the same pen appeared in Book-Lore, i. 75–82, and the writer designed a larger volume with letters and fuller particulars. Consult also Foster's Alumni Oxon.; Nichols's Leicestershire, vol. ii. pt. ii. pp. 483, 502–3, vol. iv. pt. i. pp. 53, 63, 222; Newcourt's Repertorium Lond. i. 275, 288; Bentham's Ely, ed. 1812, pp. 207–208, 242–3, 287; Le Neve's Fasti, i. 345, 355, ii. 473; Blomefield's Norfolk, 1806, iii. 589–92; Luttrell's Brief Hist. Relation, ii. 259–60, vi. 178, 200; Whiston's Memoirs, pp. 25–6, 41, 123, 150; Dibdin's Bibliomania, ed. 1876, pp. 318–319; Hearne's Collections (Oxf. Hist. Soc.), vols. i. and ii. passim; Willis and Clark's Cambridge, iii. 29–34, 75–7; Nichols's Lit. Anecd. i. 542–7, ii. 465, viii. 360–1, ix. 611; Monk's Bentley, vol. i. passim; Western Antiquary, v. 247; information from the Rev. Dr. Atkinson of Clare College, Cambridge.] W. P. C.

MOORE, JOHN (1642?–1717), dissenting minister, was born about 1642 at Musbury, Devonshire, and was educated at Colyton. In July 1660 he entered Brasenose College, Oxford, where John Prince [q. v.], author of the 'Worthies of Devon,' was a friend and fellow-student. He received episcopal ordination and became curate of Long Burton, Dorset, with the chapelry of Holnest, in 1662. His daughter Margaret was baptised at Long Burton on 2 Aug. 1667. Making the acquaintance of certain dissenting ministers, among them 'T. Crane of Rampesham,' he declared himself of their number, and was in consequence silenced in 1667 under the Act of Uniformity. He retired to a small paternal estate at Ottery St. Mary, and there preached occasionally to the people, but a second persecution obliged him to move again into Dorset. In 1676 he became pastor to a large dissenting congregation at Christ Church Chapel, Bridgwater, Somerset, and remained in charge there for thirty-six years. The union of the Somerset, followed by that of the Devonshire, dissenting ministers, in imitation of the work already begun among the London ministers, was initiated by Moore, 'Mr. Weeks of Bristol, and a Mr. Sinclair.' In his later years, from 1688, he also kept an academy at Bridgwater, which enjoyed some repute. Moore died on 23 Aug. 1717, leaving two sons, of whom the elder, John (1673–1747), graduated B.A. from Brasenose, 1695, succeeded his father at

Bridgwater and in the superintendence of the academy, and published 'A Piece called Propositions, or Natural and Revealed Religion.'

Another JOHN MOORE (*fl.* 1721) also kept a seminary at Bridgwater. He entered the ministry at Wattisfield in Suffolk, but about 1687 removed to Tiverton in Devonshire. He published 'A calm Defence of the Deity of Jesus Christ, in Remarks on a Letter to a Dissenter at Exeter, 1721.'

A third JOHN MOORE (*fl.* 1696), a stout episcopalian, born at Worcester in 1621, was in 1696 curate of Brislington and Queen Charlton (diocese of Bath and Wells), and published 'The Banner of Corah, Dathan, and Abiram displayed and their Sin discovered,' 1696 (with portrait of the author), being the substance of several sermons preached at Bristol, and probably also (1) 'Protection proclaimed,' London, &c., 1656; (2) 'A Leaf pulled from the Tree of Life, medicinal for the healing of England's Division, or a Glimpse at the Excellency of a Kingly Government,' London, 1660; (3) 'Of Patience and Submission to Authority,' 1684.

A fourth JOHN MOORE (*fl.* 1669), of West Cowes, Isle of Wight, published at London in 1669, 'Moses revived, or a Vindication of an ancient and righteous Law of God [against the eating of blood], and 176 sacred Observations upon the several Verses of the . . . 119th Psalm.'

[Hole's Correct Copy of some Letters written to J. M., a Nonconformist Teacher, concerning the Gift and Forms of Prayer, London, 1698; Calamy's Account and Continuation; Murch's Presbyterian and General Baptist Churches in West of England; Bogue and Bennett, iii. 289; Hutchins's Dorset, iv. 139; R. N. Worth's Puritanism in Devon, in the Transactions of the Devonshire Association, 1877, containing the early Minutes of the Exeter Assembly; a loose sheet of ordinations pasted in the minute-book of the Exeter Assembly in possession of Mr. Hill of Moreton Hampstead, Devonshire; Granger's Biog. Hist.; Foster's Alumni Oxon. 1500–1714; P. C. C. (175, Whitfield); information from the Revs. C. H. Mayo, vicar of Long Burton, A. W. Milroy of West Cowes, Howard McCririck of Wiveliscombe, and J. H. Green of Mowsley.] W. A. S.

MOORE, SIR JOHN (1718–1779), admiral, grandson of Henry, third earl of Drogheda, and third son of Henry Moore, D.D., rector of Malpas in Cheshire, by Catherine, daughter of Sir Thomas Knatchbull, bart., and widow of Sir George Rooke [q. v.], was born on 24 March 1718. He received his early education at the grammar school of Whitchurch in Shropshire, and in 1729 was entered on the books of the Lion, going out to the West Indies with the flag of his kinsman, Rear-admiral Charles Stewart [q. v.] It may be doubted whether his service in the Lion was more than nominal. Before the ship sailed he was transferred to the Rupert, and afterwards to the Diamond, commanded in 1731 by George (afterwards Lord) Anson [q. v.] It was probably at this time that Moore's actual service began. After twelve months in the Diamond he was for a short time in the Princess Amelia, with Captain Edward Reddish, and then for three years and a half in the Squirrel, with Anson, on the coast of Carolina. He was afterwards for some months in the Edinburgh, carrying Vice-admiral Stewart's flag in the Channel, and then in the Torrington, with Captain William Parry. He passed his examination on 6 April 1738, and was promoted to be lieutenant of the Lancaster, one of the fleet off Cadiz or in the Mediterranean, with Rear-admiral Nicholas Haddock [q. v.] When Vice-admiral Mathews [q. v.] succeeded to the command, he moved Moore into the Namur, his flagship, but presently sent him to England in the Lennox, to be promoted by his kinsman, the Earl of Winchelsea, then first lord of the admiralty. On 24 Dec. 1743 Moore was accordingly posted to the Diamond frigate, one of the squadron which sailed for the East Indies in May 1744, with Commodore Curtis Barnett [q. v.] On leaving Madagascar the Diamond, with the Medway, under the command of Captain Edward Peyton [q. v.], was detached to the Straits of Malacca, where they captured a rich French ship from Manila, and a large privateer, which had been fitted out from Pondicherry, and was now brought into the English service as the Medway prize. In March 1745 Moore was moved into the Deptford, Barnett's flagship, in which, after Barnett's death, he was sent to England.

In 1747 he was appointed to the Devonshire, the ship in which Rear-admiral Hawke hoisted his flag for his autumn cruise in the Bay of Biscay, and in the action with L'Etenduère on 14 Oct. [see HAWKE, EDWARD, LORD], after which he was sent home with the despatches. 'I have sent this express,' Hawke wrote, 'by Captain Moore of the Devonshire . . . It would be doing great injustice to merit not to say that he signalized himself greatly in the action.' During the peace Moore commanded the William and Mary yacht, and in April 1756 was again appointed to the Devonshire. In the following January he was a member of the court-martial on Admiral Byng, and was afterwards one of those who petitioned to be released from the oath of secrecy. It is said that he was 'on intimate terms with Byng's family' (KEPPEL, *Life of Viscount Keppel*, i. 248). He was shortly afterwards moved into the Cambridge, and appointed commodore and commander-in-chief on the Leeward Islands station.

In January 1759, with a force of eleven ships of the line, besides frigates and small craft, he convoyed the expeditionary army under General Hopson, from Barbados to Martinique, reduced Fort Negro, and covered the landing of the troops in Fort Royal Bay. Hopson, however, worn with age and infirmities, seems to have been unequal to the exigencies of his position; and on intelligence from a deserter that the ground in front of the town was mined, he promptly abandoned the undertaking (*Gent. Mag.* 1759, 286–7). He proposed to attack St. Pierre, but on Moore's pointing out that after taking St. Pierre it would still be necessary to take Fort Royal before they could be masters of the island, it was resolved rather to attempt the reduction of Guadeloupe. On 22 Jan. the fleet was off Basseterre. During the early morning of the 23rd the ships took up their assigned positions, and at seven o'clock opened fire on the sea defences. Moore hoisted his broad pennant on board the Woolwich frigate, the better to see what was going on, and to consult with Hopson, who was also on board the Woolwich. For several hours the fire was extremely heavy on both sides, but before night the batteries were silenced, and the town, with its warehouses of rum and sugar, was in flames. The next day the troops were landed, and occupied the ruins. The French maintained their ground in the hill country, where they were secretly supplied with provisions by the Dutch. On 11 March, on intelligence that a strong French fleet had arrived at Martinique, Moore took up his post in Prince Rupert's Bay in Dominica, the better to flank any attempt that might be made to relieve Guadeloupe, and also for the health of his men, who were falling sick. On 1 May Guadeloupe capitulated, and with it the small islands adjacent, the Saintes and Deseada. In the following year Moore returned to England.

On 21 Oct. 1762 he was promoted to be rear-admiral, and for the rest of the war was commander-in-chief in the Downs. He was afterwards commander-in-chief at Portsmouth for three years. On 4 March 1766 he was created a baronet, was made vice-admiral on 18 Oct. 1770, K.B. in 1772, and admiral on 29 Jan. 1778. His health had for some time been failing; during 1777 he had suffered from violent attacks of gout. His last public duty was, in December 1778, to sign the protest against the holding a court-martial on Admiral Keppel, his signature coming second, immediately below Hawke's. He died on 2 Feb. 1779.

Moore married, about 1756, Penelope, daughter of General Matthews, and by her had issue a son, who died young, and four daughters, of whom the eldest, Catherine, married Sir Charles Warwick Bamfylde, bart., and the second, Penelope, married the Rev. Ralph Sneyd (see BURKE, *Peerage*, s.n. 'Poltimore'). His portrait, by Gainsborough, is at Poltimore Park (information from Lord Poltimore).

[Charnock's Biog. Navalis, v. 250; Naval Chronicle, iii. 421; Gardiner's Account of the Expedition to the West Indies; Beatson's Naval and Military Memoirs; official letters and other documents in the Public Record Office.]

J. K. L.

MOORE, JOHN, M.D. (1729–1802), physician and man of letters, was the second child and eldest son of Charles Moore of the family of Rowallan (letter in the *Caldwell Papers*), a presbyterian minister, and his wife Marion, daughter of John Anderson of Glasgow. He was born at Stirling in 1729, and was there baptised on 7 Dec. On her husband's death in 1737, his mother went to live in Glasgow, where, after education at the grammar school, he matriculated at the university. He was at the same time apprenticed to John Gordon, a surgeon in large practice, the surgical instructor of Smollett. Besides attending the medical courses, Moore devoted himself to literature, history, and philosophy. In 1747, having concluded his apprenticeship, he was made surgeon's mate in the Duke of Argyll's regiment, and his first service was at Maestricht, where the hospitals were filled with the wounded of the battle of Laffeldt. Mr. Middleton, the director-general of military hospitals, recommended him to George Keppel, third earl of Albemarle [q. v.], colonel of the Coldstream guards, and he became assistant to the surgeon of that regiment, attended its numerous sick at Flushing, and went into winter quarters at Breda in 1748 under General Braddock, with whom he returned to England when peace was made in the spring. He attended the lectures of Dr. William Hunter and then went to Paris with William Fordyce [q. v.] to continue his studies. He called on the Earl of Albemarle, then British ambassador, and was appointed surgeon to his household. This office introduced him to interesting society at the embassy, but with Fordyce he worked hard at the hospitals. In the summer of 1750 when

Smollett came to Paris they visited St. Cloud and Versailles together. In 1751 Gordon, his former teacher, invited him to become his partner in Glasgow. He agreed, but on his way back attended another course of Dr. William Hunter's lectures in London, and a course on midwifery by Dr. William Smellie [q.v.] For two years he practised in Glasgow with Gordon and then with Hamilton, the professor of anatomy. He married in 1757 Miss Simson, daughter of the professor of divinity in the university. In 1769 he attended James George, seventh duke of Hamilton, who died of phthisis in his fifteenth year. Moore wrote his epitaph in English verse, and the duchess placed her other son, Douglas, the eighth duke, under his care. In 1770 he graduated M.D. in the university of Glasgow, and in 1772 gave up practice and started with the duke for five years' travel on the continent. They returned to England in 1778 and remained friends for life. Moore took a house in Clarges Street, London, and had some medical practice. He published in 1779 'A View of Society and Manners in France, Switzerland, and Germany,' and in 1781 'A View of Society and Manners in Italy,' each in two volumes. A Dublin edition, in the usual Irish small octavo of that period, was published immediately after each, with the difference that the work on Italy was in three volumes. Several other editions followed. The contents of the volumes are arranged in a series of letters, and relate in a pleasant style the observations of his travels with the Duke of Hamilton. After seventeen letters from Paris, he describes Switzerland and then Germany, Bohemia, and Austria. He visited Voltaire at Ferney, and heard him talk on the Scots in France, on the ancient earls of Douglas, and on Robertson and Hume. At Berlin he had a share in a conversation with Frederick the Great (*View*, 4th ed. p. 166), who asked him about the American war and made a sarcastic remark on the retreat from Boston, when Moore explained that it was strategic. The travellers are starting for Venice at the end of the first work. The second begins with twenty-two letters on Venice, and then describes Padua, Ferrara, Bologna, and other cities on the way to Rome. After several letters from Naples, their return journey is described. At Florence he often saw Prince Charles Edward Stuart.

These volumes obtained Moore considerable reputation. On 30 May 1784 he met Dr. Johnson, and has recorded the conversation in his preface to an edition of Smollett's works. He moved to Clifford Street, and in 1786 published 'Medical Sketches,' in two parts. The first part is physiological, and its most original remarks are on the reflection and impressions from one nerve to another, illustrated by the fact that eating ice-creams gives a pain in the root of the nose. The effects of temporary pressure on the surface of a brain exposed by trephining are described from actual observation on a Parisian mendicant. The second part treats with no great clearness of several varieties of fever.

In 1786 Moore published his first novel, 'Zeluco: various Views of Human Nature, taken from Life and Manners, Foreign and Domestic,' in two volumes. The hero is a Sicilian, brought up without restraint, who begins by squeezing a pet sparrow to death, and who, after a selfish career, dies of a wound received in a duel. 'Tracing the windings of vice and delineating the disgusting features of villany are unpleasant tasks, and some people cannot bear to contemplate such a picture. It is fair, therefore, to warn readers of this turn of mind not to peruse the story of Zeluco.' The author's warning was disregarded, and several editions appeared in England and in Ireland, as well as a French translation (Paris, 1796, 4 vols. 12mo). The best passages are those describing the convivial meetings and the quarrels of Buchanan, a lowlander, and Targe, a highlander. In the preface to 'Childe Harold' Byron says that he meant to make his hero 'perhaps a poetical Zeluco.' A visit to Glasgow in 1786 followed the publication of 'Zeluco.' Moore stayed at Hamilton Palace, and wrote a poetical epistle on the scenery of the Clyde. Burns wrote to him, and he replied, 23 Jan. 1787, from Clifford Street, London (ANDERSON, *Life of Moore*, pp. xvii–xix). They corresponded for some time, and he sent Burns his 'View of Society and Manners,' and expressed warm admiration of 'Halloween.' He associated a good deal with the new whigs. William Smith [q.v.] entertained him at Parndon, Essex, where he talked with enthusiasm of his soldier son (letter in the possession of the late Miss Julia Smith). In 1792 he went to France with the Earl of Lauderdale, and saw in Paris the disturbances of 10 Aug. and the massacres of 29 Sept. He then left Paris, but returned thither from Calais on 10 Oct. and stayed till 5 Dec., when he left for England. In 1793 he published the first volume of an account of this journey, entitled 'A Journal during a Residence in France from the beginning of August to the middle of December 1792,' and the second volume in 1794. The narrative is a simple and obviously exact account of what he saw, and is often quoted by Carlyle in his 'French Revolution.' In 1795 he published 'A View of the Causes and Progress of the French Revolution,' in two volumes, dedicated to the Duke of Devonshire. His second novel, 'Edward; various Views of Human Nature, taken from Life and Manners, chiefly in England,' in two volumes, appeared in 1796, and is intended to illustrate the admirable side of human nature, the reverse of 'Zeluco.' It is a book altogether wanting in life, but Burns was pleased to be quoted in it (letter to Mrs. Dunlop, 12 Jan. 1796). In 1797 he wrote an interesting biography of Smollett, who had been both a friend and a patient of his, in 'The Works of Tobias Smollett with Memoirs of his Life, to which is prefixed a View of the Commencement and Progress of Romance.' In 1800 he published a third novel, 'Mordaunt: Sketches of Life, Character, and Manners in various Countries, including the Memoirs of a French Lady of Quality,' in three volumes, which is as dull as 'Edward.' His health was broken, and he went to live at Richmond, Surrey, for country air, and there died on 21 Jan. 1802. His wife survived him and died in London on 25 March 1820. He had one daughter and five sons: John (1761-1809) [q.v.], the general; James [q.v.], a surgeon; Graham [q.v.], an admiral; Francis, who was in the war office; and Charles, a barrister.

Moore was sagacious as a physician, and throughout life had intense enjoyment in general observation, and in every kind of good literature and good society. He was universally liked, and most of all in his own house. He had a well-built frame and regular features. Sir Thomas Lawrence painted his portrait; and there was another portrait of him with the eighth Duke of Hamilton and Sir John Moore, by Gavin Hamilton, at Hamilton Palace (cf. *Cat. Scottish National Portrait Gallery*), an engraving from which is the frontispiece of Dr. Anderson's 'Life.' An engraving from an original drawing of his head, by W. Lock, is the frontispiece of 'Mooriana; or Selections from the Moral, Philosophical, and Miscellaneous Works of Dr. John Moore, by Rev. F. Prevost and F. Blagdon,' London, 1803. This sketch has also been separately engraved. Lawrence's portrait has been engraved in mezzotint.

[Dr. Robert Anderson's Life of John Moore, M.D., Edinburgh, 1820; William Mure's Selections from the Family Papers at Caldwell, Glasgow, 1854; Biography prefixed to Mooriana, 1803; Gent. Mag. 1802, i. 277; Chalmers's Biog. Dict. xxii. 315-318; Works of Robert Burns, with his Life by Allan Cunningham, London, 1834, vii. 119, 294, 306; Works.]

N. M.

MOORE, JOHN (1730-1805), archbishop of Canterbury, son of Thomas Moore, was baptised in St. Michael's Church, Gloucester, on 13 Jan. 1729-30. His father is described as 'Mr.' in the parish register, and as 'gent.' in Gloucester municipal records in 1761, when John's name was entered on the freeman's roll. It is hence unlikely that the father was (as has been alleged) a butcher of the town, although he may have been a grazier of the neighbourhood. John was educated at the free grammar school of St. Mary de Crypt, Gloucester, and at Pembroke College, Oxford, where he entered with a Townsend close scholarship on 25 March 1744-5, graduated B.A. on 11 Oct. 1748, and proceeded M.A. on 28 June 1751. Having taken holy orders, he was for some years tutor to Lords Charles and Robert Spencer, younger sons of the second Duke of Marlborough. On 21 Sept. 1761 he was preferred to the fifth prebendal stall in the church of Durham, and in April 1763 to a canonry at Christ Church, Oxford. On 1 July following he took the degrees of B.D. and D.D. On 19 Sept. 1771 he was made dean of Canterbury, and on 10 Feb. 1775 bishop of Bangor. On the death of Archbishop Cornwallis he was translated to the see of Canterbury, 26 April 1783, on the joint recommendation of Bishops Lowth and Hurd, both of whom had declined the primacy. Though not a great ecclesiastic, Moore was an amiable and worthy prelate, a competent administrator, and a promoter of the Sunday-school movement and of missionary enterprise. He appears to have dispensed his patronage with somewhat more than due regard to the interests of his own family. He died at Lambeth Palace on 18 Jan. 1805, and was buried in Lambeth Church. Portraits of him (one by Romney) are at Lambeth and at the Deanery, Canterbury. Moore married twice, viz. first, a daughter of Robert Wright, chief justice of South Carolina; secondly, on 23 Jan. 1770, Catherine, daughter of Sir Robert Eden, bart., of West Auckland. He left issue.

[Foster's Alumni Oxon. 1715-1886; Public Characters of 1798-9, London, 1801, p. 276; Gent. Mag. 1763 p. 258, 1770 p. 46, 1805 pt. i. p. 94; Ann. Reg. 1805, Chron. pp. 80-2; Nichols's Lit. Anecd. iii. 219, v. 630, viii. 94-6; Illustr. Lit. viii. 380; Dr. Parr's Works, ed. Johnstone, vii. 380; Life and Letters of Sir Gilbert Eliot, first Earl of Minto, i. 130; Wraxall's Hist. and Posth. Mem. ed. Wheatley, iii. 33-5; Colchester Corresp. i. 483; Auckland Corresp. i. 434; Hurd's Autobiography; Hasted's Kent, iv. 663, 760; Le Neve's Fasti Eccl. Angl.; Hutchinson's Durham, iii. 338-9; Lodge's Genealogy of the

Peerage and Baronetage, 1859, p. 868; Burke's Peerage, 'Eden;' Church Times, 26 June, 3 and 17 July 1891; Abbey's English Church and its Bishops; Gloucestershire Notes and Queries, iv. 128, &c.; information kindly supplied by Canon Scott Robertson.] J. M. R.

MOORE, Sir JOHN (1761–1809), lieutenant-general, born in Glasgow 13 Nov. 1761, was third, but eldest surviving, son of Dr. John Moore (1729–1802) [q. v.], author of 'Zeluco.' Sir Graham Moore and James Carrick Moore, both noticed separately, were his younger brothers. John was sent to the high school, Glasgow, where Thomas (afterwards Sir Thomas) Munro [q. v.] was his schoolfellow. At the age of ten he was taken abroad by his father, who was medical attendant to Douglas Hamilton, eighth duke of Hamilton, a weakly youth travelling for health. He spent the next five years on the continent, partly at school at Geneva, partly travelling with his father in France, Germany, and Italy. 'He really is a pretty youth,' his father wrote from Geneva in September 1774; 'he dances, rides, and fences with unusual address; he draws tolerably, speaks and writes French admirably, and has a very good notion of geography, arithmetic, and practical geometry. He is always operating in the field, and showing me how Geneva can be taken' (*Life*, vol. i.) Later, he was with his father at Brunswick, learning the Prussian exercise from a drill-sergeant, who taught him 'to load and charge thirty times in the hour' (*ib.*) At the age of fifteen he obtained an ensigncy in the 51st foot, on 2 March 1776, and joined that corps at Minorca. On the formation of the old 82nd or Hamilton regiment (a lowland corps, wearing black facings, raised at the private cost of the Duke of Hamilton), Moore was appointed captain-lieutenant in it, 10 Jan. 1778. He served with the headquarters of the regiment in Nova Scotia, under Brigadier-general Francis Maclean, throughout the American war [see under Maclean, Allan, colonel]. Moore was with a party of two hundred of his regiment and the old 74th highlanders, which established a post on the Penobscot river. They were attacked in August 1779 by an American force from Boston, when Moore, who was on picket, was cut off with his party and nearly taken. The American force was beaten and destroyed by Admiral Sir George Collier [q. v.]

The Hamilton regiment was disbanded at the peace of 1783, and Moore, who had succeeded to a company, was placed on half-pay. In 1784, through the Hamilton interest, he was returned to parliament for the Linlithgow, Selkirk, Lanark, and Peebles group of burghs, which he represented till the dissolution of 1790, voting quite independently of party, but generally supporting Pitt. He appears to have paid great attention to his parliamentary duties as well as his military studies. On 23 Nov. 1785 he was brought on full pay into the old 100th foot, and purchased a majority the same day in the old 102nd foot, which was disbanded immediately afterwards. In September 1787 two additional battalions were added to the 60th royal Americans (since the 60th royal rifles), and on 16 Jan. 1788 Moore was brought into the new 4th battalion at Chatham, from which he exchanged immediately afterwards to his old corps, the 51st, in Ireland. The 51st is said to have been in a very bad state. Moore was too good a soldier to set himself in opposition to the commanding officer when he found his suggestions were unwelcome, but on succeeding to the lieutenant-colonelcy, 30 Nov. 1790, at the time of the Spanish armament, he set to work hard to bring the corps into shape (Wheaton). He spoke with pride of the conduct of the regiment, which consisted of about four hundred young soldiers, when embarking at Cork for Gibraltar, 8 March 1792. The men were not confined to barracks, but were told to be present and sober in the morning. Most of them returned to quarters at 9 p.m., and every man was present and sober when parading for embarkation at seven the next morning (*ib.*) The regiment remained at Gibraltar until December 1793, when it embarked, together with the 50th, as a reinforcement for Toulon, where Major-general David Dundas [q. v.] had just succeeded to the command. On arrival they found the English army had been withdrawn, and was with Lord Hood's fleet off Hyères.

Gilbert Elliot, afterwards first Earl of Minto [q. v.], Moore, and Major George Frederick Kœhler [q. v.] were despatched to Corsica to interview General Paoli and report on the practicability of reducing the French garrisons in the island. Lord Minto has left a lively account of the visit (*Life and Letters*, vol. ii.) A descent was decided on. Moore was engaged in the attack on Martello Bay, and commanded the troops that stormed Convention redoubt on Fornelli Heights, which he entered at the head of the grenadiers of the Royals. The garrison, old French troops of the line, fought stubbornly, and the affair is said to have been one of those rare occasions on which bayonets were fairly crossed. In May 1794 Lieutenant-general the Hon. Sir Charles Stuart, K.B., brother of the Marquis of Bute, succeeded to the command in Corsica, and placed Moore at the head of the reserve of grenadiers. Bastia capitulated on honourable terms, after a long siege, on 22 May. The siege of Calvi followed, in which Moore took a prominent part. He stormed the Mozzello fort, a regular casemated work, at the head of the grenadiers, and received his first wound from a fragment of shell. Calvi, which was the only remaining French stronghold in the island, fell on 10 Aug. 1794, after fifty-one days' siege. Stuart had by this time learned Moore's character, and appointed him adjutant-general.

Although Stuart was an admirable officer, there appears to have been much want of harmony between the military and naval forces. Nelson, who thought his services at Calvi, as senior sea-officer on shore, had been slighted by the military authorities, seems to have had a special prejudice against Moore. Writing to Lord Hood, during the siege of Calvi, he expressed the hope that 'the general, who seems to be a good officer and an amiable man, will not be led wrong, but Colonel Moore is his great friend' (NELSON, *Desp.* i. 445). Elliot, the new viceroy, quarrelled with Stuart and Paoli, and through the latter with Moore. Elliot professed that he only wished Moore to be promoted out of the island, as he thought he was meddling too much in politics, which appears to have been a groundless charge. The result of his representations to the Duke of Portland [see BENTINCK, WILLIAM HENRY CAVENDISH, third DUKE OF PORTLAND] was that Moore received orders from home to quit the island within forty-eight hours. Moore's letter to Paoli, dated Corte, 6 Oct. 1795, in which he avows his consciousness of having done nothing deserving reproach, is in the British Museum (Add. MS. 22688, ff. 114–15). He arrived in England at the end of November. He was well received by Pitt and the Duke of York, who assured him that his military character was in no wise affected. His reception appears to have caused Elliot much annoyance (see *Life and Letters of the 1st Earl of Minto*, vol. ii.)

Moore had become a brevet-colonel 21 Aug. 1795. On 9 Sept. following he had been appointed, with the local rank of brigadier-general in the West Indies, to command a brigade, consisting of the Choiseul hussars and of two other French emigrant regiments, which had been preparing in the Isle of Wight for San Domingo. While awaiting embarkation he was ordered, on 25 Feb. 1796, to take charge of Major-general Perryn's brigade, forming part of the armament proceeding to the West Indies under Sir Ralph Abercromby. Through some mistake Perryn had sailed without his brigade; Moore sailed with it at a few hours' notice, and arrived on 13 April at Barbados, where he had his first interview with Sir Ralph Abercromby. He commanded a brigade under Abercromby at the attack on St. Lucia, and with the 27th Inniskillings formed the lodgment at La Vigie on 24 May 1796, which led to the immediate surrender of the fortress of Morne Fortunée. Abercromby left Moore in command of the island, where he was engaged for some time, under difficulties of every description, in warring with the negro brigands, who swarmed in the woods. He re-established order and security. An officer who was present describes him as indefatigable in his exertions, visiting every post in the island, living on salt pork and biscuit like the men, and sleeping in the open (STEWART, *Scottish Highlanders*, i. 419). The second of two attacks of yellow fever sent him home in the summer of 1797. In November Abercromby was appointed to the chief command in Ireland and asked for the services of Moore, who arrived with him in Dublin on 2 Dec. On 1 Jan. 1798 he became a major-general and was made colonel of the 9th West India regiment. His command consisted of a force of three thousand men, regulars and militia, including several battalions of light companies, which had its headquarters at Bandon, and was regarded as the advanced corps of the army in the south. He was present with Sir Henry Johnson [q. v.] at the battle of New Ross (5 June 1798), after which he marched on Wexford, defeating seven thousand rebels, led by Father Roche, who attacked him on the way at Taghmone. He arrived at Wexford on 21 June in time to prevent a continuation of the outrages of the previous day (see LECKY, viii. 163). Lake, with the main body of the army, reached Wexford next morning. Moore continued on the staff in Ireland until June 1799, when he was ordered to England to command a brigade in the force proceeding to the Helder under Sir Ralph Abercromby. These troops, forming the advance of the Duke of York's army, left the Downs on 13 Aug., and landed near the Helder fort on 27 Aug. 1799. Abercromby, moving southwards, defeated the French and Dutch on 9 Sept., when Moore's brigade formed the advance, and was hotly engaged. Moore was wounded in the right hand, his spy-glass preventing the bullet from entering his body. The force was augmented by the arrival of more British troops and a Russian contingent, and the Duke of York assumed the command-in-chief. In the battle of 2 Oct. 1799 between Egmont and Bergen, known officially as the battle of Egmont-op-Zee, Moore's brigade had several hours' fighting among the sand-dunes, and had forty-four officers and six hundred men killed and wounded. Moore was shot in the thigh, but remained in the field. In a subsequent mêlée, when the French were repulsed by the 92nd highlanders, he was again wounded severely in the face. He was carried off the field in an insensible condition by two soldiers of the 92nd, whose names he never could discover, although he offered a reward of 20*l.* (cf. CANNON, *Hist. Rec. 92nd Foot*). Much interesting information respecting the campaign in Holland is given by Bunbury (see *Narrative*, pp. 37–56). When he was able to be moved, Moore was sent home. His very temperate habits aided his recovery, and on 24 Dec. 1799 he resumed command of his brigade at Chelmsford. On 25 Nov. he had been appointed colonel-commandant of a second battalion added to the 52nd foot, the regiment afterwards so closely associated with him.

When Abercromby was appointed to the Mediterranean command, Moore went out with him, arriving at Minorca on 22 June 1800. He commanded a division of the troops sent to relieve the Austrian garrison of Genoa, and after the failure returned to Minorca, where Abercromby made a strict investigation into the discipline and interior economy of the regiments under his command. Moore commanded a division of the army in the demonstration against Cadiz in October 1800, and afterwards accompanied Abercromby to Malta with the troops for Egypt. Abercromby despatched Moore to Jaffa to report on the state of the Turkish army there under the grand vizier. Moore arrived at Jaffa on 9 Jan. 1801, and was met by news of the death from plague of the British commissioner, Brigadier-general George Frederic Kœhler. He found the Turks an undisciplined mob, with their ranks never wholly free from the plague. On 20 Jan. he returned to Malta.

In the expedition to Egypt he commanded the reserves, consisting of the flank companies of the 40th, under Brent Spencer, the 23rd fusiliers, 28th foot, under Edward Paget, 42nd highlanders, and the Corsican rangers under Hudson Lowe, with the 11th dragoons and Hompesch hussars attached. Hildebrand Oakes [q. v.] was his second in command. Moore's reserves were the first troops to land at Aboukir on 8 March 1801, and in the battle of 21 March before Alexandria, where Abercromby fell, were on the British left, and bore the brunt of the fight. The 28th greatly distinguished themselves, as did the 42nd, who captured the standard of Bonaparte's 'invincibles' (cf. BUNBURY, pp. 57–155). Moore was severely wounded, and was sent on board the Diadem frigate. He recovered sufficiently to proceed up the Nile in a djerm, and resumed command of the reserve, before Cairo, on 29 June 1801. After the surrender of the French army in Cairo, Moore with his division escorted them to the coast to embark for France, marching and encamping nightly between the French troops and flotilla and the attendant horde of Turks under the capitan pacha. He remained in Egypt until the fall of Alexandria (2 Sept. 1801). On returning home, he received the thanks of parliament and the Turkish order of the Crescent.

Moore, while unemployed, spent most of his time in London with his family. On 18 Jan. 1803 the 52nd regiment, of which he had become colonel on 8 May 1801, at the death of General Cyrus Trapaud, was ordered to be formed into a light corps. On the renewal of the war with France, Moore was nominated to a brigade, first at Brighton, and afterwards at Canterbury. On 9 July 1803 he was appointed to a brigade, consisting at first of the 4th king's own, 52nd, 59th, 70th, and 95th rifles, which encamped on Shorncliffe, above Sandgate; the brigade was part of the division commanded by General David Dundas [q. v.], with Lord Chatham and Sir James Murray Pulteney as lieutenant-generals, the headquarters being at Chatham, and afterwards at Canterbury. The French armies intended for the invasion of England then lay encamped at Boulogne. Some of the regiments in Moore's brigade were shifted, and the 43rd, which had been in an unsatisfactory state, was put under him, and ordered to be trained as a light corps.

While at Minorca in 1800 Moore's attention had been directed by Abercromby to the need in the British army of a light infantry corps whose training should correspond with that of the French voltigeurs. A few battalions so trained under sensible officers might, it was suggested, serve as a model for the rest of the army (autograph letter from Abercromby in Edinburgh Naval and Military Exhibition, 1889). He had moreover noticed the system adopted by Major Kenneth Mackenzie, afterwards Sir Kenneth Douglas [q. v.], then in temporary command of the 90th foot at Minorca. This consisted in breaking up the battalion into skirmishers, supports, and reserve, on the plan afterwards adopted for light movements throughout the army. 'He was struck with its excellence, and with his usual openness and candour expressed his surprise that it had never before suggested itself to his mind' (STEWART, *Scottish Highlanders*, i. 433–4, footnote; MOORSOM). At Shorncliffe he now introduced not only the system of drill and manœuvre based upon these principles, but the admirable system of discipline and interior economy which laid the foundation of the famous Peninsular light division, and has been maintained ever since in the regiments trained under him (cf. *ib.* pp. 61–72). On 14 Nov. 1804 Moore was made K.B. He chose as supporters of his arms 'a light infantry soldier, as being colonel of the first light infantry regiment, and a 92nd highlander, in gratitude and acknowledgment of two soldiers of that regiment who saved my life in Holland, 2 Oct. 1799' (*ib.* p. 439). Moore's officers presented him with a diamond star of the Bath, worth 350 guineas. He became lieutenant-general on 2 Nov. 1805, but still had his headquarters at Shorncliffe. Moore commanded in Kent, and Lieutenant-general Charles Lennox, afterwards Duke of Richmond [q. v.], in Sussex, under David Dundas, who was still at Canterbury. Moore's reputation now stood very high. Pitt often went over from Walmer to Shorncliffe to consult him, and when, in 1806, it was proposed to send Moore as commander-in-chief to India, Charles James Fox protested against sending so skilled a general far away in the existing position of European affairs. In June 1806 Moore was ordered to Sicily to serve as second in command under General Henry Edward Fox [q. v.], who was appointed to the Mediterranean command, and accredited as ambassador to the court of Palermo. When Fox returned home in ill-health, Moore held the Mediterranean command. Bunbury gives many interesting particulars of the period, of the intrigues of the Neapolitan court, and of the luckless expedition to Egypt under command of Major-general Alexander Mackenzie Fraser [q. v.] (*Narrative*, pp. 267–330). In September 1807 Moore received orders from home to leave the command in Sicily to John Coape Sherbrooke, and to proceed to Gibraltar with seven thousand troops for the assistance of Portugal against the French invasion under Junot. The Portuguese royal family declined assistance and withdrew to Brazil, and Moore, in accordance with his instructions, brought the troops home to England without landing them.

In May 1808 Moore was sent to Sweden to assist the king, Gustavus IV, who was menaced by France, Russia, and Denmark. He arrived at Gothenburg on 17 May. He was not allowed to land his troops, but was summoned to Stockholm to confer with Gustavus, whom he found crazily bent on schemes of conquest. The king proposed that the British, with some Swedish troops, should seize Zealand, and afterwards that the British should go to Finland to fight the Russians. Moore objected that his force was insufficient for such projects, on which Gustavus ordered him not to leave the capital. He made his escape to Gothenburg in the guise of a peasant, and returned with the troops to England. Moore appeared to think that he had been sent on a wild-goose chase for some party purpose, and in a private letter referred to the service as the most painful on which he had been employed (*Life of Moore*, ii. 93). On arrival he was summoned to London, and told that he was to go out to Portugal to serve under Sir Hew Dalrymple and Sir Harry Burrard. He expressed himself very strongly to Lord Castlereagh at this treatment—that, after holding chief commands in Sicily and Sweden, he should be sent to serve without option under other officers, one of whom had never been employed as a general in the field (*ib.* ii. 104). But handing over the troops to Burrard, he sailed with him, as second in command, at the end of July 1808. From a frigate met off Finisterre they learned that Sir Arthur Wellesley had landed in Mondego Bay. Burrard pushed on to Oporto, leaving Moore with the troops off Vigo, whence he moved down to Mondego Bay and prepared to land.

Moore did not join the army until the convention of Cintra had been signed. He had an interview with Sir Arthur Wellesley, who was going home. Sir Hew Dalrymple resigned soon afterwards, and Sir Harry Burrard was recalled, leaving Moore, then at Lisbon, as commander-in-chief. A letter from Lord Castlereagh, dated 25 Sept. 1808, informed Moore that an army of not less than thirty-five thousand men was to be employed under his orders in the north of Spain, assisting the Spanish government; fifteen thousand men would be sent out to join him by way of Corunna. It was left to his judgment whether he should fix some point of rendezvous on the frontier of Leon or Galicia, or transport his troops by sea from Lisbon to Corunna. He chose the land route. He was faced by administrative difficulties of every kind, and appears to have had from the outset a melancholy foreboding of the end. He received a letter from Sir Arthur Wellesley, who appears to have taken on himself the part of a peacemaker, dated London, 8 Oct. 1808, saying: 'I told Lord Castlereagh that you thought that the government had not treated you well, and that you felt it incumbent on you to express your sentiments on that treatment, but that after you had done so you thought no more of the matter, and that it would be found that you would serve as cordially and zealously in any situation in which you might be employed as if nothing had ever passed. Lord Castlereagh said that he never entertained the slightest doubt of it, and his only object respecting you had been to employ you in the manner in which your services were most likely to be useful to the country' (WELLINGTON, *Suppl. Desp.* vol. v.) Moore left Lisbon on 27 Oct. 1808, most of the troops being already on their way to Burgos. He was assured that he would receive the support of sixty to seventy thousand Spanish troops, under Blake and Romana. George Canning told the Marquis Wellesley that Moore was actually offered the chief command of the Spanish armies, but declined it (*ib.* vi. 350). Almeida was reached on 8 Nov.; on 11 Nov. the British entered Spain; at Ciudad Rodrigo they were greeted with the greatest enthusiasm; on 13 Nov. they reached Salamanca.

Moore's services, great and varied as they had been, had not apparently given him the experience in dealing with administrative difficulties in the field that Wellington gained in his Indian campaigns; while John Hookham Frere, then British plenipotentiary in Spain, was injudicious and meddlesome (cf. FRERE, *Works*, with memoir by Bartle Frere, i. 89–122). At the end of November Moore found that the promises of support from the Spaniards were worthless. The Spanish armies were everywhere beaten in detail. His own difficulties, especially as regarded money, were accumulating daily. He decided to retreat into Portugal, ordering Hope, who had moved into Spain by a different route from Lisbon, to join him at once, and Baird, who was advancing, to return to Corunna. He did not propose to abandon the Spaniards altogether, but thought they could be aided by action elsewhere. On 1 Dec. he wrote to Sir Charles Stuart at Madrid that money must be had for the troops, even if it cost a hundred per cent. In reply he received an answer softening down the news of the latest Spanish defeat, and accompanied by a request from the whole junta that he would move to the defence of Madrid, which was prepared to make an energetic defence. The very next day, unknown to Moore and Frere, the Prince of Castelfranco and Don Thomas Morla were negotiating with the French to give up the city. Moore countermanded the retreat, believing that the altered circumstances justified his making a diversion in favour of the Spaniards by attacking Soult on the Carrion. He effected a junction with Baird at Majorga on 20 Dec. On 21 Dec. the British army, twenty-nine thousand strong—admirable troops, as the historian Napier describes them, robust, well-disciplined, needing but a campaign or two to make them perfect—was at Toro. On 23 Dec. Moore advanced with his whole force. The infantry was within two hours' march of the enemy when an intercepted letter brought the news that Napoleon in person had entered Madrid three weeks before, and that the French, who altogether had three hundred thousand men in Spain, had already cut off Moore's line of retreat into Portugal. It was resolved to retire at once on Vigo or Corunna. Thereupon commenced the historic retreat, over 250 miles of difficult country in midwinter, ending with the arrival of the dispirited army at Corunna on 13 Jan. 1809. A vivid description is given by the historian Napier. On 16 Jan. the transports had arrived, the embarkation had begun, when the French were seen descending the heights in three columns, the brunt of the attack falling on Lord William Bentinck's brigade in the British right wing. Moore, who had just been applauding a gallant charge of the 50th, under Majors Charles James Napier and Stanhope, was close to the 42nd highlanders, when a grape-shot struck him from his horse, shattering his left shoulder. A staff-officer, Henry Hardinge, afterwards Lord Hardinge [q. v.], went to his assistance, and a sergeant and two men of the 42nd carried him in a blanket to his quarters in the town, where he was laid on a mattress, and the news was presently brought that the French were beaten and in full retreat. His thoughtfulness for others rather than himself continued to the last; but in his latest moments of consciousness he expressed a hope that England would consider that he had done his duty; that his country would do him justice. At evening he died. A question arose whether his remains should be brought home, but it was decided to bury him in the citadel, beside his friend Robert Anstruther [q. v.], who had died the day the army reached Corunna. At midnight the officers of his staff carried his body to the quarters of his friend Colonel Thomas Graham, afterwards Lord Lynedoch [q. v.], in the citadel. Some soldiers of the 9th foot dug his grave; and as the dark January morning broke, and the French guns on the heights reopened fire on the harbour, he was hastily laid to rest 'with his martial cloak around him.' The burial service was read by the Rev. J. H. Symons, then chaplain of the brigade of guards, and afterwards vicar of St. Martin's, Hereford (see Mr. Symons's note in *Notes and Queries*, 1st ser. vi. 274). An authenticated account of the burial is given in James Carrick Moore's 'Narrative of the Campaign in Spain in 1809.' The army sailed for England the same day.

The historian Napier writes: 'The guns of

the enemy paid his funeral honours, and Soult, with a noble feeling of regard for his valour, raised a monument to his memory' (*Hist. Peninsular War*, rev. edit. i. 333). Soult bore generous witness to his opponent's skill, but the statement as to the monument requires correction. Howard Douglas [q. v.] has shown that it was erected by the Spanish commander the Marquis de la Romana. Romana returned to Corunna with his army, when the French abandoned Galicia on entering Portugal. Seeing the unmarked grave, Romana had a memorial, in the form of a broken shaft of a column, of wood, painted to resemble stone, raised over it upon a pediment of real guns and shells. On its completion he attended in state, and, in presence of the civic authorities of the place and the whole garrison, unveiled the column, and wrote on it in black chalk, with his own hand:—

A la Gloria del Excelentísimo Señor Don
Juan Moore,
General en Gefe del Exércitos Británicos,
Y á sus Valientes Soldados,
La España Agradecida,
Batalla de Elvinas, 16 Enero 1809.

Howard Douglas (see *Life of Sir H. Douglas*, by FULLOM) brought the matter under the notice of the prince regent, and on his return to Spain, late in 1811, was ordered to convert the memorial into a permanent one, with the aid of slabs of marble, to receive a Latin inscription by Dr. Samuel Parr. This was done (for the inscription see *Life of Moore*, ii. Appendix, pp. 238-9). It was restored by Consul Bartlett in 1834, and the oval enclosure was laid out as a pleasure-ground, chiefly through the exertions of General Mazaredo. 'The railing round the plain granite urn that now marks the site of the grave makes it difficult to read the inscriptions in Latin, English, and Spanish on the sides of the tomb' (FORD, *Handbook of Spain*, 5th edit.; BORROW, *Bible in Spain*, 1849 edit. p. 155).

Much crude and ungenerous criticism was evoked by the news of Moore's failure, but popular feeling soon accepted the view that his life was sacrificed in an enterprise which, under the circumstances, was impracticable (cf. MARQUIS WELLESLEY, *Despatches in Spain*; *Grenville Papers*; *Buckingham Papers*, iv. 311). Parliament passed a vote of thanks to his troops, and ordered a public monument to be erected to him in St. Paul's Cathedral. A motion on 19 Feb. for a parliamentary inquiry into the conduct of the campaign was defeated by 220 votes to 127 (*Parl. Debates*, pp. 1057-1119). A horse-guards order recorded his many services to his country (*Life*, ii. 235). His native city, Glasgow, erected a monument to him, in the shape of a bronze statue in George Square, at a cost of over 3,000*l.*; and the Rev. Charles Wolfe published his 'Funeral of Sir John Moore,' which has remained one of the most popular poems in the language.

Moore died unmarried. Bruce, the son-in-law and biographer of the historian Napier, states that when Moore was in Sicily he contemplated making an offer of marriage to Miss Caroline Fox, daughter of General Henry Edward Fox [q. v.], but was deterred by a chivalrous feeling of doubt that the disparity of age and his high position might influence her decision unwisely for her contentment in after life. The offer was never made, and in 1811 Miss Fox became the wife of the future Sir William Napier (BRUCE, *Life of Sir William Napier*, i. 61).

Moore, who possessed a very winning address, was in person tall and graceful, and his features, even when worn with service, were eminently handsome. A portrait by Sir Thomas Lawrence, P.R.A., is in possession of the family; it has been often and very badly engraved. The photograph from it in Moorsom's 'Historical Records 52nd Light Infantry' was taken by Claudet. Another portrait of Moore with his father and the eighth Duke of Hamilton, by Gavin Hamilton, is in the National Portrait Gallery, Edinburgh. With some of Moore's friends it was the fashion to call him an 'unlucky man,' chiefly because he was so often wounded in action. The epithet was once applied to him by Wellington. Bunbury says: 'Everything in Moore was real, solid, and unbending. He was penetrating and reflective. His manner was singularly agreeable to those whom he liked, but to those he did not esteem his bearing was severe' (*Narrative*, p. 271). No British commander was ever more popular with his officers, none have left a more lasting impress on the troops trained under them. In the Peninsular epoch, and long after, to have been 'one of Sir John Moore's men' carried with it a prestige quite *sui generis*. Napoleon said of him: 'His talents and firmness alone saved the British army [in Spain] from destruction; he was a brave soldier, an excellent officer, and a man of talent. He made a few mistakes, which were probably inseparable from the difficulties with which he was surrounded, and caused perhaps by his information having misled him.'

[James Carrick Moore's Life of Sir John Moore, 2 vols. London, 1835, and Narrative of the Campaign in Spain in 1809; Annual Registers under dates; Life and Letters of first Earl of Minto, vol. ii.; Wilson's Campaign in Egypt in

1801; Sir H. E. Bunbury's Narrative of Passages in the War with France—Holland pp. 37–56, Egypt pp. 57–155, Sicily pp. 267–330; Sir Bartle Frere's Works, J. Hookham Frere, vol. i. Memoir; Napier's Hist. Peninsular War, rev. edit., and Life and Opinions of Sir Charles James Napier; Gurwood's Wellington Desp. vol. iii.; Wellington's Suppl. Desp. vols. v. and vi., and for returns of British troops in the Peninsula, 1808–9, vol. xiii.; Brit. Military Panorama, vol. iii.; Wheaton's Hist. Records 51st Light Infantry; Moorsom's Hist. Records 52nd Light Infantry; Passages in the Military Life of Sir George Thomas Napier, London, 1888; Moore's Letters to Sir Hudson Lowe in Brit. Mus. Add. MSS.; official correspondence under Corsica, West Indies, Egypt, Mediterranean, &c., in Public Record Office.] H. M. C.

MOORE, JOHN (1742–1821), biblical scholar, son of John Moore, rector of St. Bartholomew the Great, London, by his wife Susanna, daughter of Peter Surel of Westminster, was born on 19 Dec. 1742, and educated at Merchant Taylors' School, where he became head scholar in 1756. He matriculated from St. John's College, Oxford, on 28 June 1759, graduated B.A. 15 April 1763, and subsequently took the degree of LL.B. During his residence at the university he was singularly serviceable to Kennicott in the arduous task of collating the Hebrew manuscripts of the Old Testament. On 11 Nov. 1766 he became sixth minor prebendary in the cathedral of St. Paul, London, and he was transferred to the twelfth minor prebend and appointed sacrist in 1783. He became priest of the chapel royal; lecturer of St. Sepulchre's; rector of St. Michael Bassishaw, London, 19 Oct. 1781; rector of Langdon Hill, Essex, 1798; and president of Sion College, London, in 1800. He died at Langdon Hill on 16 June 1821.

He married Sarah Lilley, and had a daughter, Mary Anne, wife of Harry Bristow Wilson, B.D., under-master of Merchant Taylors', and mother of Henry Bristow Wilson, the historian of the school.

His works are: 1. 'An Attempt to Recover the original reading of 1 Sam. xiii. 1, to which is added an Enquiry into the Duration of Solomon's Reign,' London, 1797, 8vo. 2. 'Prophetiæ de septuaginta hebdomadis apud Danielem explicatio; concio ad clerum habita in æde D. Alphægii; adjiciuntur ad calcem notæ, in quibus fusius tractantur quædam et illustrantur,' London, 1802, 8vo. 3. 'Case respecting the Maintenance of the London Clergy, briefly stated, and supported by Reference to Authentic Documents,' London, 1802, 8vo; 2nd edit. 1803; 3rd edit. 'altered to meet the Report made by a Special Committee of the Court of Common Council,' London, 1812, 8vo. 4. 'An attempt to throw further Light on the Prophecy of Isaiah, chap. vii. 14, 15, 16,' London, 1809, 8vo.

He vainly endeavoured to publish by subscription Brian Walton's very rare and curious work on the ecclesiastical history of London (Todd, *Life of Walton*, i. 7).

[Biog. Dict. of Living Authors, 1816; Bodleian Cat. ii. 783; Darling's Cycl. Bibl. ii. 2096; Foster's Alumni Oxon. 1715–1886, iii. 975; Gent. Mag. 1821, i. 574; Malcolm's Londinium Redivivum, i. 38, 39, iii. 29, 148, iv. 495; Nichols's Lit. Anecd. i. 344; Robinson's Register of Merchant Taylors' School, ii. 105; Watt's Bibl. Brit.; Wilson's Merchant Taylors' School, pp. 453, 454, 525, 1142, 1143, 1211, 1220.] T. C.

MOORE, JOHN FRANCIS (*d.* 1809), sculptor, a native of Hanover, resided in London for many years in Berners Street, Oxford Street. He obtained a premium from the Society of Arts in 1766 for an allegorical bas-relief. He was a member of the Free Society of Artists, and a frequent contributor to their exhibitions from 1766 to 1775, sending statues and busts in marble, models in clay, medallions, and bas-reliefs, the latter including one of the 'Aldobrandini Marriage.' When the corporation of London resolved to erect a monument to Lord Mayor William Beckford [q. v.], Moore was successful in the competition, and the monument now existing in the Guildhall was erected from his design at a cost of 1,300*l.* He exhibited the design in 1772, and an engraving of it by C. Grignion was published. Moore also executed monuments to Earl Ligonier and Robert, earl Ferrers. He executed for Dr. Thomas Wilson, in St. Stephen's, Walbrook, a statue of Mrs. Catherine Macaulay [q.v.], and a monument to Mrs. Wilson. He died in York Buildings, New Road, London, on 21 Jan. 1809. He had three sons, who practised as artists, and exhibited with the Free Society of Artists: John Moore, jun., who also practised as a sculptor; Charles Moore, who was a painter; and James Moore, also a painter. The last is possibly identical with James Moore who executed some mezzotint engravings after Amiconi, Vanloo, and others.

[Redgrave's Dict. of Artists; Catalogues of the Free Soc. of Artists; Chaloner Smith's Brit. Mezzotinto Portraits; Gent. Mag. 1809, p. 94.] L. C.

MOORE, Sir JOHN HENRY (1756–1780), poet, only son of Sir Henry Moore, bart. [q. v.], was born in Jamaica in 1756. His mother was Catharina Maria, eldest daughter of Samuel Long of Longville, Jamaica, and sister of Edward Long [q. v.], author of the 'History of Jamaica'(NICHOLS, *Lit. Anecdotes*, viii. 434). John succeeded to the baronetcy while still at Eton, in 1769, and proceeded to Cambridge, where he graduated from Emmanuel College, B.A. in 1773 and M.A. in 1776. In 1777 he issued, anonymously, through Almon, a volume of poems entitled 'The New Paradise of Dainty Devices,' which provoked a not unmerited sneer from the 'Critical Review' (xliii. 233). It contains, however, some fair occasional verses. The best of these, including an early parody of Gray's poem, entitled 'Elegy written in a College Library,' together with a few new pieces, and an excruciating 'palinode' deprecating the vigour of Langhorne and Kenrick, and beseeching them to 'untwist their bowels,' were issued again in 1778 as 'Poetical Trifles' (Bath, 1778, 12mo). Some lines 'To Melancholy' evidently inspired Rogers's 'Go, you may call it madness, folly.' Moore frequently resided at Bath, deposited verses in Lady Miller's urn at Bath Easton [see MILLER, ANNA, LADY], and took part in the other harmless fooleries of her coterie. He died unmarried, at Taplow, on 16 Jan. 1780, when the baronetcy became extinct. A third edition of his 'Trifles' appeared posthumously in 1783, edited by his friend Edward Jerningham [q. v.] His poems appear between those of Hoyland and Headley in vol. lxxiii. of 'The British Poets,' 1822, and in similar company in vol. xli. of Park's 'British Poets,' 1808.

[Kimber and Johnson's Baronetage of England, iii. 201; Burke's Extinct Baronetage; Chambers's Encycl. of English Literature, i. 707; Brydges's Censura, vii. 223; Moore's Works in the British Museum Library; Halkett and Laing's Dict. of Anon. and Pseud. Lit. col. 1958.]

T. S.

MOORE, SIR JONAS (1617–1679), mathematician, was born at Whittle in Lancashire on 8 Feb. 1617. He became clerk to Dr. Burghill, chancellor of Durham, and in 1640 was encouraged by the Rev. William Milbourne to undertake mathematical study, for his progress in which he acknowledged great obligations to William Oughtred [q.v.] Charles I, when at Durham in 1646, sent for him, and in the following year directed his employment as mathematical tutor to the Duke of York, then at St. James's. Ousted speedily from the post by what he called 'the malicious and cunning subtlety' of Anthony Ascham [q. v.], he set up as a teacher, and published in 1650 a book on 'Arithmetick,' to which was prefixed a portrait of the author by Stone, showing an impressive and intellectual countenance. He failed, however, to get pupils, and was in deep distress, when Colonel Giles Strangways, although himself a prisoner in the Tower, came to his assistance with money and recommendations. These last procured for him the appointment of surveyor in the work of draining the great level of the Fens, entered upon in 1649 by the first Duke of Bedford and his associates. He subsequently published an account of this undertaking, entitled 'The History of the Great Level of the Fennes . . . with a Map of the Level as drained by Sir T. M.,' 1685, 8vo. He gained reputation by his success in keeping the sea out of Norfolk, surveyed the coasts (SELLER, *English Pilot*, 1671), and constructed a map of Cambridgeshire, published in Philips's supplement to Speed's 'Maps,' 1676. Cromwell procured from him a model of a citadel 'to bridle the city of London,' and Pepys was said to possess a copy of his survey of the entire course of the Thames.

On the Restoration Moore republished his 'Arithmetick,' with a dedication to the Duke of York, in which he boasted that his 'name could not be found in the black list.' Appended were 'A New Contemplation General upon the Ellipsis' and 'Conical Sections,' taken from Mydorgius. A third edition appeared in 1688, with a portrait dated 1660. Moore was sent to Tangier in 1663 to inspect the place with a view to its fortification, and on his return was knighted, and appointed surveyor-general of the ordnance. He resided thenceforward in the Tower, and enjoyed high royal favour, which he turned to account for rescuing scientific merit from neglect. He invited John Flamsteed [q. v.] to London in 1674, with the design of installing him in a small observatory of his own in Chelsea College, but procured from the king instead the foundation of the Royal Observatory. He furnished him, moreover, at his private expense, with a seven-foot sextant, employed in Flamsteed's observations until 1688, as well as with two clocks by Tompion, and acted as his assiduous patron while he lived. The establishment of a mathematical school in Christ's Hospital, of which he was governor, was due to Moore's influence with the king. He entered the Royal Society in 1674. While travelling from Portsmouth to London he died suddenly, at Godalming, on 25 Aug. 1679, at the age of sixty-two, and was buried in the Tower chapel, with a salute of as many guns as he had counted years of life. The Luttrell collection of broadsides in the British Museum includes a poetical tribute to his memory. He had designed to bequeath his library, a splendid collection of scientific works in many languages, to the Royal Society, but died intestate, and it was sold by public auction in 1684.

Moore, by Aubrey's account, 'was a good mathematician, and a good fellow.' 'He was tall and very fat, thin skin, fair, clear grey eyes' (*Lives of Eminent Men*, p. 459). Moore left one son, Jonas, to whom he had secured the reversion of his place, and who was knighted at Whitehall on 9 Aug. 1680. He died early and was interred with his father in the Tower chapel, where a memorial tablet to both was erected by his sister, Mrs. Hanway. Some anonymous verses to his memory, entitled 'To the Memory of my most honoured Friend, Sir J. M.,' were published in the year of his death. Captain Jonas Moore [q. v.], military engineer, is believed to have been a grandson.

Moore's principal work, 'A New System of the Mathematicks,' appeared posthumously in 1681, under the supervision of his sons-in-law, William Hanway and John Potenger. It had been intended by him for use in the mathematical school of Christ's Hospital, and was dedicated to the king. The sections on arithmetic, practical geometry, trigonometry, and cosmography were written by Moore himself; those on algebra, Euclid, and navigation by Perkins, master of the said school; while Flamsteed communicated the astronomical tables. Among Moore's other works were: 1. 'Modern Fortification, or Elements of Military Architecture,' London, 1673; 2nd edit. 1689. 2. 'A Mathematical Compendium,' collected out of the notes and papers of Sir Jonas Moore by Nicholas Stephenson, London, 1674; 4th edit. 1705. 3. 'England's Interest, or the Gentleman and Farmer's Friend,' 2nd edit. 1703; 4th edit. 1721. His translation from the Italian of Moretti's 'Treatise of Artillery' was published in 1683.

[Phil. Trans. Abridged, ii. 80; Birch's Hist. of the Royal Society, iv. 106; Hutton's Mathematical Dict. 1815; Notes and Queries, 2nd ser. ix. 363, 391; Gent. Mag. 1817, ii. 3; Martin's Biog. Phil. p. 299; Rigaud's Correspondence of Scientific Men, passim; Baily's Account of the Rev. J. Flamsteed, pp. 34–44; Pepys's Diary, i. 235, 3rd edit.; Granger's Biog. Hist. of England, iii. 120; Gough's British Topography, p. 92; Wolf's Geschichte der Astronomie, p. 455; Poggendorff's Biog. Lit. Handwörterbuch; Watt's Bibl. Brit.; Ashmole's Diary, 25 Aug., 2 Sept. 1679; Bromley's Cat. of Engraved Portraits, p. 147; Sherburne's Sphere of Manilius, 1675, p. 93.] A. M. C.

MOORE, JONAS (1691?–1741), military engineer, probably grandson of Sir Jonas Moore [q. v.] the mathematician, received his commission as probationer engineer in October 1709. On 1 Jan. 1711 he was appointed sub-engineer at Gibraltar and attached to David Colyear, first earl of Portmore [q. v.], the governor, for special service. Later he was sent to Port Mahon, Minorca, where he remained for some years, returning to Gibraltar in August 1720. On 18 Nov. he was appointed chief engineer and commissioned as commander-in-chief of the train of artillery at Gibraltar. He was promoted sub-director of engineers and major on 1 Oct. 1722. He received several letters from the board of ordnance conveying their good opinion of his ability and economy, and in one, dated 22 Jan. 1727, he was informed that his care not to exceed the estimates has been noticed by the master-general and board, and 'gains much their esteem.'

Moore was chief engineer at Gibraltar during the siege by the Spaniards in 1727. The trenches were opened on 11 Feb., and the siege was not raised until 23 June. The Spaniards lost many men, but owing to the excellent cover provided by Moore, who went over to Morocco and visited Tetuan to secure supplies of fascines and brushwood, the British loss was comparatively small. On 19 March 1728 he was given the local rank of director of engineers. He remained at Gibraltar until 1740, and in October of that year was appointed chief engineer with the joint expedition which sailed from Spithead under Rear-admiral Sir Chaloner Ogle and General Lord Cathcart for Spanish America. On arrival at Dominica Lord Cathcart died, and was succeeded by General Wentworth, an incompetent officer. Ogle proceeded to Jamaica, where he joined Vice-admiral Vernon. After many conflicting schemes it was resolved to attack Carthagena, a strongly fortified place, well garrisoned and ably commanded.

Moore erected his batteries on the shore on 9 March 1741, and soon made a breach in Fort St. Louis, a work which mounted eighty-two guns and defended the mouth of the harbour. Moore was, however, struck on the 22nd by a fragment of a shell, and died the following day. His death was a serious blow to the enterprise. The incompetence of the general led to disaster which might have been avoided had the chief engineer survived. As it was, the land forces were re-embarked, and the expedition sailed back to Jamaica. Moore carried a dormant commission by order of the Duke of Montagu, dated 24 July 1740, to command the artillery in the event of the death of the two senior officers of that corps.

There are in the war office twenty plans and sections of Gibraltar and various works of defence in that fortress skilfully drawn by Moore.

[Despatches; War Office Records; Royal Engineers' Records; Beatson's Naval and Military Memoirs, 1804, vol. i.; Cust's Annals of the Wars of the Eighteenth Century, 1860.]

R. H. V.

MOORE, JOSEPH (1766–1851), Birmingham benefactor, born in 1766 at Shelsley-Beauchamp or Shelsley-Walsh, Worcestershire, was educated at Worcester. In 1781 he was sent to Birmingham to learn die-sinking, and afterwards entered into a partnership in the button trade. Acquiring an independent position he devoted his leisure to works of charity. In conjunction with Thomas Hawkes and others he founded a dispensary for the sick poor. He came to know Matthew Boulton [q. v.], of the Soho works, who introduced him to James Watt. At Boulton's instigation Moore formed a society for the performance of private concerts, the first of which took place in 1799 at Dee's Hotel. This society existed for several years, and developed a taste for high-class music. The festival committee now sought Moore's aid, and he planned the festival of 1799. From 1802 he virtually took the chief direction of the festivals, the profits of which went to support the General Hospital. In recognition of his services to the hospital he was presented, on 6 April 1812, with a service of plate (Langford, *Modern Birmingham*, i. 394), and his portrait by Wyatt was also purchased for the hospital.

In 1808 Moore established the Birmingham Oratorio Choral Society, with the view of bringing together for practice the local singers engaged at the triennial festivals (*ib.* ii. 124). In order to provide the town with a building sufficiently large to do justice to the festivals, Moore successfully agitated for the erection of the town-hall (1832–4). A public subscription was raised to pay for the organ. At the festival of 1834 both hall and organ were used for the first time. To enhance the fame of the festivals Moore went to Berlin, and induced Mendelssohn to compose, first, 'St. Paul,' which was given at the festival of 1837, and then 'Elijah,' performed in 1846. The net profits arising from the festivals while under Moore's management (1802–49) amounted to 51,756*l.*

Moore died at his house, Crescent, Birmingham, on 19 April 1851, and was buried in the church of England cemetery there. A monument was erected to his memory by subscription.

[The Birmingham General Hospital and the Triennial Festivals, by J. Thackray Bunce, pp. 106–9, 2nd edit. pp. 77, 91–4; Times cited in Gent. Mag. 1851, pt. i. pp. 670–1; Langford's Century of Birmingham Life, ii. 321; Dent's Old and New Birmingham, sect. iii. p. 437; Mendelssohn's Letters to Moscheles, 1888, p. 268.]

G. G.

MOORE, JOSEPH (1817–1892), medallist and die-sinker, born at Eastbourne, Sussex, in 1817, was the son of Edwin Moore, a builder of hothouses, who temporarily left his business during the Peninsular war and in a fit of enthusiasm joined the 10th hussars, with which he saw active service. A few weeks after Joseph Moore's birth his parents removed to Birmingham, where he continued to live all his life. He showed an early aptitude for drawing, and was apprenticed to Thomas Halliday, die-sinker, of Newhall Street, Birmingham. He also attended the drawing classes of Samuel Lines of Temple Row, Birmingham. For many years Moore was engaged in the production of dies for commercial uses, chiefly for buttons. In 1844 he entered into partnership with John Allen, a fellow-apprentice. The partners carried on business as Allen & Moore in Great Hampton Row, Birmingham, and manufactured articles of papier-mâché, and also metal vases, cups, and boxes. These metal wares, produced by machines invented by Allen, were 'engine-cut on bodies coated with colour, and portions being cut away by the lathe, the patterns, chiefly designed by Moore, were left in colour in low relief.' Partly owing to changes of fashion the works had to be closed, and Moore, after having lost all he had, began business for himself in 1856 as a die-sinker, first in Summer Lane and afterwards, and till his death, in Pitsford Street, Birmingham.

Moore's first medal, produced in 1846, was a large piece, nearly four inches in diameter, bearing the 'Salvator Mundi' of Da Vinci as the obverse, and the 'Christus Consolator' of Ary Scheffer as the reverse. Only a few copies of this medal, which was highly praised by Scheffer, were produced. From this time Moore had a large number of commissions for die-sinking and designing, and executed numerous prize and commemorative medals. Many of these, made for English and colonial trading firms, do not bear Moore's name. He employed his son and other assistants in his business, but the best of his works were cut by his own hand. A selection of his medals was presented by Moore to the Corporation Art Gallery of Birmingham.

Moore was an honourable and kind-hearted man, fond of music and art, and intensely devoted to his work. He was the first president of the Midland Art Club. In March

1892 he had a serious illness, and died, in his seventy-sixth year, on 7 Sept., in his house, which adjoined his workshops.

Moore married, on 27 Aug. 1839, at Aston, Warwickshire, Miss Mary Ann Hodgkins, and had issue.

[Birmingham Weekly Post, 10 Sept. 1892; information kindly given by Miss Moore, Mr. Whitworth Wallis, F.S.A., and Mr. R. B. Prosser.]

W. W.

MOORE, PETER (1753–1828), politician, born at Sedbergh in Yorkshire on 12 Feb. 1753, was youngest son, by Mary his wife, of Edward Moore, LL.B., vicar of Over in Cheshire, who claimed descent by a junior branch from Sir Thomas More, whose quartered arms he bore. His father dying when he was quite young, he was educated by his eldest brother, Edward, a barrister, who was eighteen years his senior. The influence of the latter with Lord Holland and the whig party obtained for him an appointment in the East India Company's service, in which he amassed a handsome fortune. On his return to England his knowledge of Indian affairs enabled him to supply important material to Burke and Sheridan for their attack on Warren Hastings, and he became a sort of whip for the radical section of the whig party, while his manor-house at Hadleigh served as a rendezvous for many of its leading members. Sheridan was a frequent visitor, and rooms in Moore's house were always at his disposal. In 1796 Moore himself stood as parliamentary candidate for Tewkesbury, in company with Sir Philip Francis, and they obtained a majority of the householders in their favour, but were unseated on the House of Commons resolving that the freemen and freeholders alone had a right to vote. In 1802, in conjunction with Wilberforce Bird, he contested Coventry without success. One of the members, however, was unseated on petition, and Moore, after another contest, was returned on 30 March 1803. The prime cost of his seat was 25,000*l.*, but he was reelected for Coventry in subsequent parliaments (29 Oct. 1806, 11 May 1807, 5 Oct. 1812, 25 June 1818, and 8 March 1820) at comparatively little expense. He took a prominent part in the Westminster election of 1804, as the proposer of Charles James Fox, and many scurrilities were levelled against him. In 1806, when Fox was endeavouring to form a ministry, Moore was selected as second on the Indian council, and was actually proposing to return to India when the king dissolved parliament. Had the whigs returned again to power after the dissolution, it was rumoured that a peerage dormant in his wife's family was to be conferred on Moore. As it was, he continued in the cold shade of opposition, but frequently spoke in the house, supported Romilly and other advanced whigs, and in 1807 voted in a minority of ten against the Duke of Wellington's Irish Insurrection Bill.

Moore was a member of the Beefsteak Club, and maintained intimate relations with all the leading men of his party. When it was decided that Sheridan should be buried in Westminster Abbey, his remains were deposited in Moore's house in Great George Street (July 1816), and it was Moore who had the memorial tablet placed above Sheridan's grave (Romilly, *Memoirs*, iii. 262). He was also distinguished as the most active promoter of a number of public works. Among these were the rebuilding of Drury Lane Theatre (in which he co-operated with Sheridan, and served for some time upon the committee of management), the Highgate tunnel, and the floating of the Imperial Gas Light Company. He became known as the most adroit and successful manager of private bills of his time, and the loss of his seat for Coventry in 1824 did not prevent the keenest competition for his services among projectors and company promoters of every kind. The freedom with which he lent his name as chairman or director eventually proved disastrous, and in 1825 he had to fly to Dieppe to escape arrest. He gave up all his property (except a small maintenance) for the benefit of persons who had lost money in companies with which he was associated, and spent the remainder of his days in the compilation of memoirs of his time, which did not, however, see the light. He died at Abbeville in France on 5 May 1828. He is stated to have been the last wearer of a pigtail in London society.

Moore married, in India, Sarah, one of the coheiresses of Colonel Richmond, *alias* Webb (the other became the wife of W. M. Thackeray, the grandfather of the novelist). Of Moore's children George Peter Moore was returned for Queenborough in 1806, but vacated his seat at Fox's request, to make way for Romilly. The only son who survived his father was Macartney Moore, who died in 1831, shortly after returning from India, leaving two sons, Captain Richard Moore, R.N., and the Rev. Peter Halhed Moore, present vicar of Chadkirk, Cheshire, and a daughter, who married Captain Gorle.

A portrait of Moore as a young man, by Gainsborough, is in the possession of Colonel Moore, C.B., of Frampton Hall, Lincolnshire, and a later portrait belongs to Colonel Marsden of Farnborough. A third portrait is in the possession of the Windus family, into which a sister of Moore married.

[Materials kindly furnished by Colonel Moore, C.B., F.S.A.; Gent. Mag. 1828, i. 568; Annual Register, 1828, p. 232; Pantheon of the Age (1825), p. 828; Notes and Queries, 7th ser. iv. 365; Romilly's Memoirs, passim; Moore's Byron, p. 288; Moore's Lives of the Sheridans; Clayden's Samuel Rogers and his Contemporaries, i. 217; Hansard's Parliamentary Debates, passim; Walter Arnold's Life and Death of the Sublime Society of Beefsteaks; Official Returns of Members of Parliament.] T. S.

MOORE, PHILIP (*fl.* 1573), medical writer, practised physic and chirurgery at Halesworth, Suffolk. He wrote 'The Hope of Health, wherein is conteined a goodlie regiment of life: as medicine, good diet, and the goodly vertues of sondrie herbes,' &c., with 'A Table for xxx. yeres to come,' 12mo, London, November 1565 (Brit. Mus.), which he dedicated on 1 May 1564 to Sir Owen Hopton. Prefixed to the book are a Latin epistle and some verses in mixed Latin and English by William Bullein [q. v.], who calls Moore his 'well-beloved friend.' Moore's object was to disseminate the knowledge of medicinal herbs among the poor, and to encourage their cultivation. Moore also published 'An Almanack and Prognostication for xxxiiii. yeares,' &c., 12mo, London, 1573.

[Work in the Brit. Mus. Libr.; Watt's Bibl. Brit.] G. G.

MOORE, PHILIP (1705–1783), Manx scholar, was born at Douglas in the Isle of Man on 22 Jan. 1705, and completed his studies under the care of Dr. Thomas Wilson (1663–1755) [q. v.], bishop of Sodor and Man, whose friend and companion he was for many years. After taking orders he became rector of Kirk Bride and officiating minister of the chapel of Douglas. He was also master of Douglas school for above forty years. At the funeral of Bishop Wilson in March 1755, he was appointed to preach the sermon, which is printed with that prelate's works. Under the auspices of Bishop Hildesley, and at the request of the Society for Promoting Christian Knowledge, he undertook the revision of a translation into Manx of the Holy Scriptures, the Book of Common Prayer, Bishop Wilson on the sacrament, and other religious pieces presented for the use of the diocese of Sodor and Man. During the execution of the first of these works he received advice from the two greatest hebraists of the age, Dr. Robert Lowth [q. v.], bishop of London, and Dr. Benjamin Kennicott [q.v.] He died at Douglas on 22 Jan. 1783, and was interred with great solemnity in the parish church of Kirk Braddan, where there is a tomb with an English inscription recording his merits. In 1785 a handsome marble monument was erected to his memory in the chapel of Douglas.

[Butler's Life of Bishop Hildesley, pp. 53, 55, 186, 223, 255; Nichols's Illustr. of Lit. iv. 687, 691.] T. C.

MOORE, RICHARD (1619–1683), nonconformist divine, son of William Moore, was born at Alvechurch in Worcestershire, and baptised there on 8 Aug. 1619 (par. reg.) He belonged to an ancient Worcestershire family who were settled in Alvechurch in the time of Edward II. Matriculating at Oxford from Magdalen Hall on 30 June 1637, he graduated B.A. 12 Nov. 1640. In 1647 he was possessed of property in Alvechurch and Weatheroak Hill. During the Commonwealth he was 'a preacher of God's word' in Worcester, sometimes at the cathedral, along with Simon Moore, who was ejected thence in 1662. In 1650 Richard Moore was occupying a house in Worcester 'next to the lead-house,' and was probably preaching. He 'intruded into the living' of Alvechurch, and was present at a parish meeting there on 12 Aug. 1658. After the Restoration he gave up the rectory, and obtained a license to preach in what he represented as his house and room adjoining at Withall, near Alvechurch. The house was really the curate's chamber over part of Withall Chapel, and the 'room adjoining,' the chapel itself, into which he had made an opening from the chamber (*State Papers*, Dom. Ser. 1662, vol. lxvi. f. 34). In 1662 the license was revoked. In April 1672 he was restored to the chapel, and remained there for two years. He afterwards preached privately in his house at the foot of Weatheroak Hill, near to the top of which stands Withall Chapel. The house, a farmhouse within the parish of Alvechurch, is still standing. Moore died in September 1683, and was buried at King's Norton on the 27th (par. reg.)

Moore was probably a presbyterian. He was author of 'Pearl in an Oyster-Shel, or Pretious Treasure put in Perishing Vessels,' London, 1675, the first part of which contains two sermons preached in Withall Chapel in 1674. The second part of the work, called 'Abel Redivivus, or the Dead Speaker,' supplies another sermon, the life of Thomas Hall (1610–1665) [q. v.] of King's Norton, with whom Moore was closely associated, and verses on Hall, John Ley, and other ministers. Calamy mentions another work, entitled 'Paul's Prayer for Israel,' but gives no date.

[Walker's Sufferings of the Clergy, pt. ii. p. 277; Palmer's Nonconformist's Memorial, iii.

383; Nash's Worcestershire, i. 26; Noake's Rambler in Worcestershire, p. 215, and Monastery and Cathedral of Worcester, p. 371; Moore's Pearl, passim; information from W. Salt-Brassington, esq., F.S.A.] B. P.

MOORE, RICHARD (1810–1878), politician, was born in London 16 Oct. 1810. He was a wood-carver of no mean skill, and eventually employed a considerable staff. While still very young he began to take a part in radical politics. He became in 1831 a member of the council of Sir Francis Burdett's National Political Union, and assisted Robert Owen in his efforts to amuse and instruct the working classes in Gray's Inn Lane. In 1834 he was the principal member of a deputation to Lord Melbourne on the question of the social condition of the people. He was a member of the committee for which Lovett drew up the People's Charter in 1837, being one of the representatives on it of the London Working-men's Association. In 1839 he was a member of the National Convention which met to promote the passing of the charter, was secretary of the testimonial committee which greeted Lovett and Collins on their release from gaol in 1840, and joined Lovett in the Working-men's Association in 1842. He took an active part in its meetings in the National Hall (now the Royal Music Hall), Holborn, and was also busy in the chartist cause, though he never approved of the physical force party, or professed to believe that the charter could remedy all the grievances of the working classes. When the People's Charter Union was formed on 10 April 1848, he was appointed its treasurer, and conducted its affairs with moderation and discretion at a time when few chartists showed those qualities. In 1849 he took up the reform with which he was most practically connected, the abolition of newspaper stamps, and urged Cobden to adopt it in order to keep the working classes and the middle classes in touch on the subject of financial reforms. The Charter Union appointed a committee on the question, which met at his house, and of which he became permanent chairman. This committee was afterwards absorbed in the Association for Promoting the Repeal of Taxes on Knowledge, and he was one of its most active members. Between 7 March 1849, when the first committee was formed, and the repeal of the paper duty in June 1861, Moore attended 390 meetings on the subject. During the same period he took part in almost every advanced radical movement, and was the constant colleague of Lovett, Henry Hetherington [q. v.], and James Watson. He was a member of the Society of the Friends of Italy, the Jamaica Committee, and of numberless other committees and societies, both on domestic and foreign questions. He worked hard to promote electoral purity in Finsbury, where he had lived from 1832, and assisted to manage the Regent's Park Sunday band. He died on 7 Dec. 1878. He had married, on 9 Dec. 1836, Mary Sharp of Malton, Yorkshire, a niece of James Watson, the publisher and chartist, who with four children survived him. A man of a singularly disinterested and modest disposition, he was temperate in speech and act, but zealous for the social and political reforms which were the aims of the radicals in his day, but which have for the most part been adopted in the programmes of all parties since.

[Pamphlet Life of Richard Moore by C. Dobson Collet, 1879; Annual Register, 1878; W. J. Linton in Century Mag. January 1882, with portrait; information from Mrs. M. E. Hatch, a daughter of Richard Moore.] J. A. H.

MOORE, ROBERT ROSS ROWAN (1811–1864), political economist, born in Dublin on 23 Dec. 1811, was eldest son of William Moore, the head of a branch of the family of Rowallan [see MURE, SIR WILLIAM] which had settled on a small estate in Ulster in 1610. His mother, Anne Rowan, who was her husband's first cousin, was daughter of Robert Ross Rowan of Mullaghmore, co. Down, a lieutenant in the 104th foot. Moore was sent in 1828 to the Luxemburg School, near Dublin, one of those established by Gregor Von Feinagle [q. v.] He obtained many prizes, and in 1831 entered Trinity College, Dublin, where he graduated B.A. in 1835. He spoke regularly at the Dublin University Debating Society, and was one of the chief opponents of his friend Thomas Osborne Davis [q. v.], maintaining that Ireland's prosperity would be better secured by general toleration, free trade, and closer relations with Great Britain, than by political independence. Their friendship was uninterrupted till the death of Davis (SIR C. GAVAN DUFFY, *Life of Davis*, p. 149). After taking pupils at Carlow he read law, and was called to the bar as a member of Gray's Inn 28 April 1837 (J. FOSTER, *Gray's Inn Register*, p. 455); but political economy was the subject to which he gave most of his time, and he took part in movements for popular improvement. On 15 Aug. 1839 he gave a lecture in Dublin 'On the Advantages of Mechanics' Institutions,' which was afterwards published. He became a member of an Irish anti-slavery society, and in 1841 visited Limerick, and successfully opposed a scheme for exporting apprentices to the West Indies.

Moore's economical studies led him to

take interest in the agitation then beginning for the repeal of the corn laws. George Thompson [q. v.] introduced him to John Bright, with whom and with Cobden he soon became intimate, and he joined the Anti-Cornlaw League. Bright in after years stated on several occasions that a large share of the success of the agitation was due to Moore's lucid exposition of economical principles, and to the illustrations of them by which he convinced masses of people in all parts of Great Britain that free trade would lead to national prosperity, and protection to continued arrest of trade. Bright and George Thompson visited Ireland in December 1841, and Moore's first important public speech on free trade was at a meeting held at the Mansion House, Dublin, on 23 Dec., when he moved a resolution in favour of the total and immediate repeal of the corn laws. From this date till the repeal in May 1846 he devoted his whole time and energy to the cause, speaking repeatedly as the representative of the league at meetings held in the chief towns of England and Scotland. With both Bright and Cobden he spoke several times at Salisbury, and often supped there with the father of Henry Fawcett (Stephen, *Life of Fawcett*, p. 4). At Cupar in January 1844 the freedom of the burgh was conferred upon Cobden and Moore after they had addressed a meeting in the town (Prentice, ii. 152). A month later Moore spoke at the great series of meetings in Covent Garden Theatre, and was invited to be a candidate for the representation of Hastings. In March 1844 he contested that borough at a by-election, but was defeated, receiving 174 votes (Acland, *Imperial Poll Book*). He was presented with a silver inkstand by his supporters, and an enthusiastic elector, Benjamin Smith, M.P. for Norwich, had a list of the 174 free-trade electors printed in letters of gold, and distributed as a record of the contest. The working men of Exeter in 1845 presented him with a piece of plate, with an inscription commemorating their admiration for his speeches in favour of free trade.

On 1 Jan. 1845 Moore married Rebecca, daughter of B. C. Fisher, and soon after took a house near Manchester, as the most convenient centre for his work in relation to the league. He gave much aid to J. L. Ricardo [q. v.] in the preparation of a book published in 1847, 'The Anatomy of the Navigation Laws' (Preface). When the corn laws were repealed he found it difficult to resume the work of his profession, in which his prospects of success in Ireland were secure. He remained in England, visiting Ireland occasionally, and withdrew altogether from public life. The constant exertion of oratory, and of travelling in the league agitation, had broken down a not very robust constitution. In the latter years of his life he wrote a volume of fables in rhyme for children, but they were not published. He went to Bath, and there died 6 Aug. 1864, of angina faucium. He was buried with his father in Mount Jerome cemetery, Dublin, and left an only son, the author of this biography. His portrait by C. A. Duval, to whom many of the supporters of the league sat, is in the possession of his son, and medallions of his head in relief were sold at the Anti-Cornlaw League bazaar held in Covent Garden Theatre in May 1845. He had inherited from his father a taste for literature, and had, besides a love of every kind of learning, an excellent memory. In speaking he excelled in lucid exposition, and in illustrations which came home to his hearers. He never drank wine, and was with difficulty persuaded to swallow some in his last illness. He gave his whole abilities and the flower of his life, without any prospect of personal advantage, to the spread of doctrines which he firmly believed would relieve misery and extend happiness.

[Archibald Prentice's Hist. of the Anti Cornlaw League, London, 1853; John Morley's Life of Richard Cobden, 1881, i. 275, 287; Henry Ashworth's Recollections of Richard Cobden, M.P., and the Anti-Cornlaw League, London, 1876; Henry Jephson's The Platform, its Rise and Progress, London, 1892, ii. 320; Holyoake's (with notes by John Bright) Sixty Years of an Agitator's Life, London, 1891, vol. i.; Anti-bread Tax Circular, 1841–3; The League, 1843–6; family papers; reports of speeches in numerous local newspapers.] N. M.

MOORE, SAMUEL (*fl.* 1680–1720), draughtsman and engraver, appears to have held some post in the custom-house, London. He is known by some engravings of historical interest, done from his own drawings. Among these were two of the plates to Sandford's 'History of the Coronation of James II, 1685,' and the plates in the 'Coronation Procession of William and Mary.' According to Vertue he drew medleys of various things, one of which he presented to Sir Robert Harley when speaker of the House of Commons (1701–4). He also engraved some costume plates.

[Redgrave's Dict. of Artists; Walpole's Anecdotes of Painting; Dodd's manuscript Hist. of English Engravers (British Museum Add. MS. 33403).] L. C.

MOORE, Sir THOMAS (*d.* 1735), playwright, said to have been a native of Surrey, is probably the Thomas, son of Adrian Moore of Milton Place, Egham, who matriculated from Corpus Christi College, Oxford, on 19 June 1674, aged 22, having previously, on 13 May 1670, been admitted a student of Gray's Inn (FOSTER, *Register*, p. 309, and *Alumni Oxon.* 1500–1714). He was knighted by George I in 1716, 'on what account we know not, but believe it could hardly be for his poetry.' He wrote 'Mangora, King of the Timbusians, or the Faithful Couple,' 1718, 4to, a tragedy in blank verse, which was played at Lincoln's Inn Fields Theatre, 14 Dec. 1717. The scene is laid in Paraguay, and the action being full of battle, murder, and sudden death, Rich probably thought that the bustle of the piece would carry it prosperously through five acts of absurdities. Moore, it is said, stimulated the actors during rehearsals by inviting them to supper, and the audience proved too hilarious to hiss. Genest asserts that there is no particular fault to be found with the plot of the play, which, nevertheless, provoked ferocious 'Reflections on Mangora' (1718). A reply, probably by Moore, was entitled 'The Muzze Muzzled, in answer to Reflections on Mangora' (1719, 4to). All these pieces are rare. Moore died at Leatherhead on 16 April 1735.

[Lowe's English Theatrical Lit. p. 243; Lit. of all the English Dramatic Poets to the year 1747, p. 262; Genest's Hist. of the Stage, ii. 628; Baker's Biog. Dram. i. 524; Doran's Annals of the Stage; Victor's Hist. of the Theatre, ii. 144; Notes and Queries, 1st ser, ii. 297; Brit. Mus. Cat.]

T. S.

MOORE, THOMAS (*d.* 1792), teacher of psalmody, was teaching music in Manchester in 1750. In 1755 the town council of Glasgow appointed him precentor of 'the new church in Bell's Yard' (Blackfriars) and teacher of psalmody in the town's hospital. In 1756 he was elected a burgess, and subsequently taught free music classes, by order of the magistrates, in the Tron Kirk, and kept a bookseller's shop, first in Princes Street and afterwards in Stockwell Street. He demitted his offices of precentor and psalmody teacher in 1787; and, from an advertisement in the 'Glasgow Courier' of 17 Nov. 1792, he appears to have died at Glasgow in that year. Moore edited several collections of psalmody, notably 'The Psalm Singer's Compleat Tutor and Divine Companion,' 2 vols. Manchester, *circa* 1750; 'The Psalm Singer's Pocket Companion,' Glasgow, 1756; and 'The Psalm Singer's Delightful Pocket Companion,' Glasgow, n.d. [1762]. In the 1756 collection appear, probably for the first time in Scotland, several church melodies, which were subsequently popular.

[Parr's Church of England Psalmody; Love's Scottish Church Music, Edinburgh, 1891; Brown's Biog. Dict. of Musicians; Glasgow, Past and Present, edited by Pagan, iii. 238.]

J. C. H.

MOORE, THOMAS (1779–1852), poet, was born at No. 12 Aungier Street, Dublin, 28 May 1779. His father, John Moore, a native of Kerry, was a grocer and wine merchant; his mother, Anastasia, was the eldest daughter of Thomas Codd, a provision dealer at Wexford. Both were Roman catholics. After receiving some education from an eccentric schoolmaster named Malone, Thomas was placed at the grammar school kept by Samuel Whyte. Whyte had been R. B. Sheridan's schoolmaster as long ago as 1758, and his school was considered the best in Dublin. The instruction given in Latin was very defective, but by the help of extra lessons from an usher named Donovan, Moore, who was a remarkably clever and forward boy, contrived to acquire sufficient Latin to justify his entrance at Trinity College, Dublin, in 1794, the partial removal of the Roman catholic disabilities in 1793 having enabled his mother to realise her wish of educating him for the bar. In 1793 also, Moore, who had already lisped in numbers, made his first appearance as a poet by contributing 'Lines to Zelia' and 'A Pastoral Ballad' to the 'Anthologia Hibernica,' one of the most respectable attempts at periodical literature, he says, that had ever been ventured upon in Ireland, but which ceased after two years, 'for the Irish never either fight or write well on their own soil.' In 1795 he commenced his college course, in which he obtained a considerable reputation for wit and literature, but few of even such university honours as were then open to Roman catholics. He formed an intimate friendship with Robert Emmet [q. v.], and narrowly escaped being drawn into the plots of the United Irishmen. His principal performance while at the college was a metrical translation of Anacreon, which the provost, Dr. Kearney, would willingly have recommended for a special reward, but doubted if the university could properly countenance anything 'so amatory and convivial.' Moore took it with him to London on going thither in 1799 to enter himself at the Middle Temple, and succeeded in arranging for its publication. It appeared in the following year, with the addition of copious notes. The publication was by subscription, and Moore was greatly annoyed to find only the provost and one fellow of Trinity among the subscribers. He found, however, a more distinguished patron in the Prince of Wales, to whom he was destined to become so inimical, but who then accepted the dedication of the book. Moore was personally introduced to him on 4 Aug. 1800, probably through the instrumentality of Lord Moira, and had a most gracious reception. The secret of his social success was less his promise as a poet than his remarkable musical gifts. His playing and singing had already created a furore in Dublin, and speedily opened the mansions of the English aristocracy to him. He was a welcome guest at Donington, Lord Moira's seat, and soon became virtually domiciled in England, though always maintaining an affectionate correspondence with his family, especially his mother, his devotion to whom is one of the most amiable features of his character.

In 1801 Moore's original amorous poetry, exceptionable on the ground of morality, and with no conspicuous literary recommendation except its sprightliness, appeared under the title of 'Poems by the late Thomas Little.' In August 1803 he received the appointment of admiralty registrar at Bermuda, and proceeded thither in the following month in a vessel bound to Norfolk in Virginia, where he was detained for a long time before he could reach his ultimate destination. He soon determined that it was not worth his while to remain, and, leaving his office to a deputy, he made his way to New York in April 1804. After a short stay he set out on a tour through the States, visiting Washington, Baltimore, Philadelphia, and Boston. He then went to Canada, where he was enraptured by the Falls of Niagara, and arrived in England in November. He again took up his residence in London, and followed his former course of life, generally admired and caressed, but pursuing no profession, writing the 'Canadian Boat Song' and other pieces, and endeavouring to procure a better appointment for himself, or one for his father. In 1806 his 'Odes and Epistles' were published, the latter containing some severe attacks upon America. Jeffrey, making this comparatively innocent book pay for the sins of the late Thomas Little, indited a savage review in the 'Edinburgh,' which led, in July of that year, to a hostile meeting between author and critic. Great ridicule was brought upon both by the seasonable interruption of Bow Street officers before a shot had been fired, and the circumstance that no bullet was found in Jeffrey's pistol. An explanation ensued, and the combatants were firm friends for the remainder of their lives; Moore became a frequent contributor to the 'Edinburgh,' and lived to refuse the editorship.

In the following year (1807) Moore entered upon the path in which he found his truest title to remembrance, and which at the same time procured him for many years a considerable income, by the publication of his 'Irish Melodies,' with music by Sir John Stevenson [q.v.] They were issued at irregular intervals in ten numbers, each containing twelve songs, except the last, which contained fourteen; and the publication did not cease until 1834. For each of these songs Moore received a hundred guineas, 12,810*l.* in all, or at the rate of 500*l.* a year, and the undertaking was as satisfactory to the publisher as to himself. What was of still more importance, it provided him with a solid basis for his reputation by making him the national lyrist of Ireland, a character which, notwithstanding the numerous charges which may justly be brought against his 'Irish Melodies,' on the ground both of false poetry and false patriotism, he must retain until some one arises to deprive him of it. Better isolated pieces have no doubt been written by some of his successors, but he, and he alone, has produced an imposing body of national song; nor have his fancy, melody, and pathos, on the whole, been yet equalled by any competitor. It is remarkable that while beginning to produce this airy music he should at the same time have been writing three heavy and ineffective satires—'Corruption' and 'Intolerance' (1808), and 'The Sceptic' (1809)—which fell very flat. He had not yet discovered the proper vehicle for his satiric power, but he was soon to do so. In 1811 the Prince of Wales became regent, and it speedily appeared that he had no intention of fulfilling the hopes which his constant support of the opposition during his father's government had excited among the supporters of catholic emancipation. Moore himself was too deeply committed to the cause of Irish patriotism to accept anything from a reactionary court, but his virtue was exposed to no trial, for Lord Moira, the only one of his patrons who had not utterly broken with the regent, accepted the governor-generalship of India, whither Moore could not accompany him. The hopes which had so long buoyed him up thus ended in his Bermuda sinecure and the post of barrack-master which Lord Moira had procured for his father; and private disappointment conspired with public spirit to animate the little metrical lampoons on the regent and his favourites which began to buzz about society at the time, and which, when collected in 1813 into a volume under the title of 'The Twopenny Post Bag,' obtained an unmeasured success. Nor was this unmerited; the best are the perfection of stinging satire, the very impersonation of gay, witty, airy malice. Form and matter are equally admirable, and they are not likely to be surpassed. Moore had struck an enduring vein, and so long as his powers remained unimpaired he was continually producing the like brilliant trifles, for which at one time he received a handsome annual salary from the 'Times.' His later performances in this style, however, are inferior to 'The Twopenny Post Bag;' detached strokes are as telling as ever, but there is less concentration and unity.

In the interim Moore had married, on 25 March 1811, Bessie Dyke, a young actress of no claims to birth, but who proved the best of wives, and who, as Earl Russell says, 'received from him the homage of a lover from the hour of their nuptials to that of his dissolution.' Accustomed though he was to the most brilliant society, he resolved to live mainly in the country, and settled for a time at Kegworth in Leicestershire, to be near Lord Moira's seat. After Lord Moira's departure for India he removed to Mayfield Cottage, near Ashbourne. In the same year he formed another intimacy which had much influence on his life—his friendship with Lord Byron, which, like his connection with Jeffrey, grew out of a misunderstanding. Moore's demand for an explanation of a passage and note in 'English Bards and Scotch Reviewers,' which he considered to convey an imputation upon the veracity of his account of his duel with Jeffrey, led ultimately to a meeting of the two beneath Rogers's roof, and the establishment of as close a friendship as the infinite dissimilarity of the parties would allow. Byron's regard for Moore hardly amounted to attachment, but was at least cordial and disinterested; and though Moore evidently felt more awe than love for his formidable ally, he was exemplary in the discharge of the ordinary duties of friendship. Another acquaintance, contracted a little later, that with Leigh Hunt (united with Moore in hostility to the regent), promised well, but soon grew cold under the influence of political estrangement, and was converted into bitter animosity on Moore's part by Leigh Hunt's posthumous attack on Byron.

With a young family rising around him, and disappointed in his hopes of provision from the public revenue, Moore found the necessity of increasing his means, and determined upon a great poetic effort. So high was his ability rated that his friend Perry, of the 'Morning Chronicle,' found no difficulty in enforcing on Longmans the stipulation that Moore should receive not less than the highest sum ever given for a poem. That, Longmans said, was 3,000*l.*, which they agreed to pay without having seen a line of the projected work. Moore chose an Eastern subject, wisely, for Byron had made the East the fashion. After many unsuccessful experiments, he hit upon the idea of 'Lalla Rookh,' shut himself up at Mayfield with a library of books upon the East, and by 1815 had produced enough to induce him to offer the publishers a sight of the manuscript. They declined, saying that they felt unbounded confidence in him. When at last the poem was completed in the commercially disastrous year 1816, Moore, with equal magnanimity, offered to rescind the contract if the publishers' affairs rendered this course expedient. They remained firm; 'Lalla Rookh' was published in 1817, and at once gained a success rivalling Scott and Byron. Moore's fame speedily became European; perhaps no English poem of that age has been so frequently translated. The style to which it belongs is now completely out of fashion; and were it to revive it may be doubted whether there would be any resurrection for a work of prodigious talent, but uninformed by creative or even true lyrical inspiration. Its most remarkable characteristic is perhaps the poet's extreme dexterity in cloaking Irish patriotic aspirations under the garb of oriental romance. Where he is thinking of Ireland he expresses himself with real emotion; and much praise is due to the graceful conception and elegant execution of 'Paradise and the Peri;' otherwise the poem is but the ware of a very accomplished purveyor of the literary market.

Shortly before its publication Moore had displayed more genuine inspiration in his 'National Airs' (1815) and 'Sacred Song' (1816). The words here adapted to music vied with the popularity of the 'Irish Melodies,' and included pieces so universally known as 'Oft in the Stilly Night' and 'Sound the Loud Timbrel.' 'The Fudge Family in Paris,' published under the name of Thomas Brown the younger, consists of humorous skits in the style of 'The Twopenny Post Bag,' inspired by a visit to Paris paid in Rogers's company in the autumn of 1817. 'The Fudges in England,' 'Rhymes on the Road,' and 'Fables for the Holy Alliance' were later attempts in the same manner, published under the same pseudonym, the last named appearing in 1823.

Moore now seemed at the summit of fame and fortune. On his return from Paris in 1817 he had found a delightful country retreat at Sloperton Cottage in Wiltshire, which he chose for the sake of being near

Lord Lansdowne. Scarcely was he established there when a sudden and entirely unforeseen calamity fell upon him by the defalcation of his deputy at Bermuda, which rendered him liable for 6,000*l.* In 1819 he took refuge in Paris, and almost immediately proceeded with Lord John Russell on a tour to Italy, where he met Byron at Venice, and received from him the gift of the 'Memoirs,' destined to give rise to so much discussion. He was unable to return to England until April 1822, when the debt to the admiralty, reduced by arrangement to 1,000*l.*, was paid by the help of Lord Lansdowne, whom Moore, with his constant spirit of independence, insisted on repaying almost immediately. He returned to Paris for a time, and finally took up his abode in England in November. While in Paris he had written 'The Loves of the Angels,' a poem on the same subject as Lamartine's 'Chute d'un Ange,' and with affinities to Byron's far more striking 'Heaven and Earth;' for the rest much in the style of 'Lalla Rookh,' but inferior. The scriptural relations of the piece excited considerable reprehension, unreasonable from any point of view, and utterly unforeseen by Moore, who had conceived himself to be atoning for the sins of his youth by a poem full of sound morality. After selling four editions he bent to the storm, and 'turned his angels from Jews into Turks,' not much to the advantage of his poem. He had also while in Paris commenced a new poem, 'Alciphron,' which, not answering his wish, he rewrote as a prose fiction, 'The Epicurean,' which was published in 1827; 'Alciphron' being added as an appendix in 1839. The tale is striking and picturesque, but its utter infidelity to ancient manners, and ignorance of the system of philosophy which the hero is supposed to represent, brought upon Moore a severe and humorous castigation from T. L. Peacock in the 'Westminster Review' for 1827. In April 1824 appeared his first serious prose work, though the machinery is humorous, 'The Memoirs of Captain Rock.' It is an indictment of the Irish church, principally on the ground of tithe exactions, clever and not unjust, though necessarily one-sided. In October 1825 appeared 'The Life of Sheridan,' his early schoolfellow, which he had meditated for many years. It is a fairly adequate piece of work. Moore narrates agreeably, but has little gift for the delineation of character.

Byron meanwhile had died (April 1824), and the disposition to be made of his memoirs had become an urgent question [see under BYRON]. It is difficult to believe that they might not have been published with some omissions, when we find Moore continually speaking in his diary of having read them with no expression of consternation or disgust. It is impossible, however, to judge positively of the weight of the objections in the absence of the document. Scott thought there was only one reason, but a sufficient one—'premat nox alta,' he adds. The perfect disinterestedness of Moore's conduct is unquestionable.

In November 1821 Moore had sold the 'Memoirs' to Murray, but on 17 May 1824 he induced Murray to return them to him, and at once burned them. But 'he repaid to Mr. Murray the sum (2,000 guineas) he had received for the "Memoirs," with interest' (*Memoirs of John Murray*, i. 444). To effect this, however, he had had to borrow from Longmans, and the desire to escape from debt led him ultimately, at the intercession of Hobhouse, to agree to write the life of Byron for Murray, the latter repaying the two thousand guineas, and adding 2,000*l.* more for the literary labour. It was indeed impossible that a tolerable biography should be written without the alliance of Moore and Murray, one having the best qualifications, and the other the best materials. The book appeared in 1830, and has ever since enjoyed a vigorous vitality as the indispensable companion of Byron's own writings. If Goethe's saying be true, that he who has done enough for his own time has done enough for all times, its reputation will long survive its circulation. It was exactly the biography which that age required: by no means complete or entirely authentic, nor claiming to be so, but presenting Byron in the light in which contemporaries desired to regard him, and in every respect a model of tact and propriety. The fearless criticism and the deep insight which are certainly missing were not at that time required, and until they are supplied elsewhere the work will rank as a classic, even though its interest be less due to the efforts of Moore's own pen than to the charm of the letters which he was the first to give to the world. The first edition was nevertheless published at a loss; but the book soon established itself, and Murray engaged Moore to edit Byron's works, a task of which he acquitted himself ably. At the same time he produced the biography of a very different person, Lord Edward Fitzgerald, in which he evinced some signs of dissatisfaction with his old friends, the whigs. Another book, which might be regarded as patriotic in some of its aspects, appeared in 1834, 'Travels of an Irish Gentleman in search of a Religion.' Though little more than a nominal catholic, Moore took considerable interest in theological questions, and this lively book displays not only humour but learning, for which he was partly indebted to his freethinking neighbour in Wiltshire, Dr. Brabant.

Moore's next and last work brought him money, but little else save trouble and mortification. It reflects credit upon his patriotism that he should have undertaken 'The History of Ireland' for Lardner's 'Cabinet Cyclopædia;' but the task was not only beyond his powers, but entirely out of his line. Moore depended even more than most writers upon subject; he was absolutely nothing without a theme to attract and dazzle, and no entertainment can be extracted from the confused annals of Ireland prior to the sixteenth century. He had himself sorely misconceived the conditions of his undertaking. The book, which was to have been completed in one volume, required four, the last of which did not appear until 1846, and the exhausted author fairly broke down under the effort to write the preface, which he was compelled to leave to the publisher (see Bates, *Maclise Portrait Gallery*, p. 123). The intervening years, though barren of any but domestic events, had been in this respect most unhappy, and only cheered by the bestowal in 1835 of a literary pension of 300*l.* through the interest of Lord John Russell, to which a civil list pension of 100*l.* was added in 1850. Most fortunate in his wife, Moore was most unfortunate in his children. He lost two daughters in infancy; in 1829 his most beloved child, Anastasia, died of consumption; his second son, John Russell, who had obtained a cadetship in the East India Company's service, died in 1842 of disease contracted from the climate of India; the eldest, Thomas Lansdowne Parr, a wild but gifted youth, after causing his parents great trouble and expense by his extravagance, disposed of the army commission which had been obtained for him, and eventually died in Algeria as an officer of the French foreign legion, March 1846. Moore had not only previously lost his parents, but also his sisters, and was absolutely bereaved of all his kindred. These trials, most terrible to his affectionate nature, combined with the crushing weight of his Irish history and the general consciousness of failing powers to reduce him to a condition little better than imbecility, though occasionally relieved by flashes which showed that, though the exercise of the mental powers was impeded, the powers themselves were not destroyed. In December 1849 he talked not only freely, but most agreeably, to Lord John Russell and Lord Lansdowne; but the same evening he was seized with a fit, after which his memory almost entirely failed him. He died 25 Feb. 1852, and was interred at Bromham, a neighbouring village about four miles from Devizes. A window in his honour was placed in the church there by public subscription. His civil list pension was continued to his widow, and for her benefit the 3,000*l.* paid by Longmans for the copyright of his 'Memoirs, Journals, and Correspondence' was invested in the purchase of an annuity; she died at Sloperton Cottage on 4 Sept. 1865 (*Gent. Mag.* 1865, ii. 531).

Moore's position as a poet cannot be considered high in comparison with that of his great contemporaries. Nevertheless, alone among modern poets, he united the arts of poetry and music in the same person, and revived the traditions of the minstrel and the troubadour of the middle ages. This affords a sufficient answer to most of the objections which have been urged against his 'Irish Melodies' and similar pieces, except those of occasional false taste and false glitter, against which no defence is possible. They have been said to be of little value divorced from their music; but, replies Professor Minto, they were never intended to be divorced from their music. On the same ground, deep thought would have been out of place. Moore's position as the national lyrist of Ireland is in some respects anomalous: endowed with the Celtic temperament in a high degree, he was entirely devoid of the peculiar magic, as Matthew Arnold describes it, which is the most infallible characteristic of Celtic genius. Apart from the conceits of his early lyrics, his is in an eminent degree the poetry of good sense; his highest flights are carefully calculated, he makes the best use of his material, and never surprises by any incommunicable beauty, or anything savouring in the remotest degree of preternatural inspiration. After the song, his most congenial sphere is the satiric epigram, where his supremacy is unquestionable. Everywhere else he appears as the poet of his day, adapting consummate talents to the description of composition most in vogue, as he might with equal success have adapted them to almost any other. He would have been a conspicuous figure in almost any age of poetry except a dramatic age, and many who have since depreciated him would find, were he their contemporary, that he greatly surpassed them in their own styles. Such ability is, of course, essentially secondrate.

As a man, Moore is entitled to very high praise. He was not only amiable, generous, and affectionate, but high-minded and independent to a very unusual degree. His history abounds with disinterested actions, and refusals of flattering offers which he feared might compromise his dignity or the dignity of letters. He has been unjustly blamed for neglecting his wife for London society. There can be no doubt that his principal motive for settling in the country was to exempt his wife from the mortification of vicinity to a society which would not have received her. This involved a great sacrifice on his part; to have renounced society himself would have been destructive of her interests as well as his. In truth, there seems little to censure or regret in Moore, except his disproportionate estimate of his own importance in comparison with some of his great contemporaries, in which, however, he merely concurred with the general opinion of the time.

A portrait of Moore (aged 40), engraved by Holl after Thomas Phillips, is prefixed to vol. i. of the 'Memoirs,' and another portrait of him (aged 58), after Maclise, to vol. viii. of the same work. The author of 'Lalla Rookh' also forms one of the sketches in the 'Maclise Portrait Gallery' (ed. Bates, pp. 22–30), and there are other portraits by Shee and Sir Thomas Lawrence.

[The principal authority for Moore's life is his Memoirs, Journals, and Correspondence in eight volumes, published in 1853–6 by Earl Russell, and consisting of an unfinished autobiography, extending to 1799, journals from 1818 to 1847, and about four hundred letters filling up the gap. The correspondence might easily have been made more copious, and the diary would have gained by abridgment. The want of an accompanying narrative is much felt. Earl Russell, it is to be regretted, failed to perform any of the duties of an editor as he should have done. The work is nevertheless the indispensable foundation of many short biographies which include that by H. R. Montgomery, the excellent memoir prefixed by Mr. Charles Kent to his edition of the poems, and the monograph by Stephen L. Gwynn in English Men of Letters series, 1905. The best criticisms on Moore will be found in Hazlitt's Spirit of the Age, allowing for the political hostility with which this is coloured; Professor Minto's article in the Encyclopædia Britannica, and an able paper in vol. iii. of the National Review. See also Moore's autobiographic notices in the prefaces to his poems in the collected edition of 1840–2. Contemporary literary biographies abound with references to him, especially his own Life of Byron.] R. G.

MOORE, THOMAS (1821–1887), gardener and botanist, was born at Stoke, near Guildford, Surrey, on 21 May 1821. He was brought up as a gardener, and was employed at Fraser's Lee Bridge Nursery, and subsequently, under Robert Marnock [q. v.], in the laying out of the Regent's Park gardens. In 1848, by the influence of Dr. John Lindley [q. v.], he was appointed curator of the Apothecaries' Company's Garden at Chelsea, in succession to Robert Fortune [q. v.], an appointment which gave him leisure for other work. He acted as an editor of the 'Gardeners' Magazine of Botany' from 1850 to 1851, of the 'Garden Companion and Florists' Guide' in 1852, of the 'Floral Magazine' in 1860 and 1861, of the 'Gardeners' Chronicle' from 1866 to 1882, of the 'Florist and Pomologist' from 1868 to 1874, and of the 'Orchid Album' from 1881 to 1887. He made a special study of ferns, most of his independent works being devoted to that group of plants; but he also acquired a knowledge of garden plants and florists' flowers generally, which was probably greater than that of any of his contemporaries. He acted as one of the secretaries of the International Flower-show in 1866, and was for many years secretary to the floral committee and floral director of the Royal Horticultural Society. Moore was elected a fellow of the Linnean Society in 1851, and was also a member ot the Pelargonium, Carnation, Auricula, and Dahlia Societies. He was constantly called upon to act as judge at horticultural shows, and only a short time before his death was engaged in classifying the Narcissi for the Daffodil Congress. After three or four years of infirm health he died at the Chelsea Botanical Garden on 1 Jan. 1887, and was buried in Brompton cemetery. His collection of ferns was purchased for the Kew herbarium. A somewhat roughly engraved portrait appears with an obituary notice in the 'Gardeners' Chronicle' for 1887 (i. 48).

Besides papers on ferns in various botanical journals (*Royal Society Cat. of Papers*, iv. 458, viii. 432), Moore's chief publications were: 1. 'Handbook of British Ferns,' 16mo, 1848. 2. 'Popular History of British Ferns,' 8vo, 1851, 2nd edit. 1855, abridged as 'British Ferns and their Allies,' 8vo, 1859, and also issued, with coloured illustrations by W. S. Coleman in 1861. 3. 'Ferns of Great Britain and Ireland,' edited by J. Lindley, and nature-printed by H. Bradbury, fol., 1855, and in 2 vols. 8vo, 1859. 4. 'Index Filicum,' 8vo, twenty parts, ending at the letter G, 1857–63. 5. 'Illustrations of Orchidaceous Plants,' 8vo, 1857. 6. 'The Field Botanist's Companion,' 8vo, 1862, of which a new edition appeared in 1867 as 'British Wild Flowers.' 7. 'The Elements of Botany for Families and Schools, 10th edit. 1865, 11th edit. 1875. 8. 'The Treasury of Botany,' with John Lindley, 2 vols. 8vo, 1866, 2nd edit. 1874. 9. 'The

Clematis as a Garden Flower,' with George Jackman, 8vo, 1872. 10. 'Thompson's Gardener's Assistant,' 2nd ed. 8vo, 1876. Moore also wrote the article 'Horticulture' in the ninth edition of the 'Encyclopædia Britannica,' in conjunction with Dr. Maxwell Masters, afterwards published in an expanded form as 'The Epitome of Gardening,' 8vo, 1881.

[Gardeners' Chron. 1887, i. 48; Annals of Botany, 1888, p. 409; Journal of Botany, 1887, p. 63.] G. S. B.

MOORE, WILLIAM (1590–1659), librarian, was son of William Moore of Gissing, Norfolk, where he was born in 1590. He was sent to the school of Moulton, a few miles from his father's house, and then kept by Mr. Matchet. He was admitted at Gonville and Caius College, Cambridge, as a scholar 22 June 1606, graduated M.A. in 1613, and on 17 Nov. in that year was admitted a fellow. He spent most of his life within the university, and became well known to all the literary men of his time (H. Bradshaw, *The University Library*). In 1638 he wrote a poem in the 'Obsequies to the Memorie of Mr. Edward King' (pp. 10, 11), in which Milton's 'Lycidas' was first printed. His name is spelt More in this publication, as well as in Dd. iv. 36, a manuscript in the Cambridge University Library containing a list of his books, but everywhere else it appears as Moore. The poem, which is signed at the end, begins,

I do not come like one affrighted from
The shades infernal or some troubled tomb,

and consists of forty lines of heroic verse. He was elected university librarian in 1653, and held office till his death in 1659. A small notebook of his containing receipts and a list of medicines with prices, dated 1657, is preserved in the Cambridge University Library. He received from Sir Samuel Morland [q. v.] the fine collection of Waldensian books now in the Cambridge Library, and was an assiduous librarian. In his own college he continued the 'Annales Collegii' begun by Dr. John Caius [q. v.], and bequeathed to it the whole of his own library. In spite of his learning and his benefactions, as Henry Bradshaw remarks, 'his fellowship, his college, and even his degree, are all ignored in the list of librarians in the printed Graduati, where he appears simply as Gul. Moore. In the list of the large collection of manuscripts given to his own college, printed in the Oxford catalogue of 1697, he is misnamed John Moore, while in the modern catalogue of the Caius manuscripts, compiled by one who ought to have known better, his name is most unaccountably passed over altogether in silence' (*The University Library*).

[J. Venn's Admissions to Gonville and Caius College, 1857; Justa Edwardo King and Obsequies to the Memorie of Mr. Edward King, Cambridge, 1638; Collected Papers of Henry Bradshaw, Cambridge, 1889; Catalogue of the Manuscripts preserved in the Library of the University of Cambridge, 1856, i. 237, 316.] N. M.

MOORE, WILLIAM (1790–1851), portrait-painter, born at Birmingham on 30 March 1790, studied under Richard Mills in that city, but after some employment as a designer for commercial purposes, he turned his hand to portrait-painting. In this line he achieved some success and some repute in London. Eventually he settled at York, where he obtained considerable patronage in that city and its neighbourhood. Moore worked in oil, water-colours, and pastel. The deleterious ingredients used in the last method brought on an illness, and hastened his death, which took place at York on 9 Oct. 1851. Moore was twice married: first, on 12 March 1812, to Martha Jackson of Birmingham; secondly, in 1828, at Gainsborough, to Sarah, daughter of Joseph Collingham of Newark. By them he was the father of fourteen children, including thirteen sons; several of the latter, besides Albert Joseph Moore, who is separately noticed, and the well-known painter, Henry Moore, R.A., he brought up to the artist's profession.

Moore, Edwin (1813–1893), painter, the eldest son by his first wife, was born on 29 Jan. 1813 at Birmingham. He studied water-colour painting under David Cox the elder, and also under Samuel Prout. He was employed for many years as a teacher of painting in water-colours at York, especially by the Society of Friends in their schools there, from whom he received a pension after fifty-seven years' work for them. Moore was an occasional exhibitor at the Royal Academy, and died at York on 27 July 1893.

Moore, John Collingham (1829–1880), painter, the eldest son of William Moore by his second wife, was born at Gainsborough on 12 March 1829. He practised early as a painter, studying under his father, and later, in 1851, in the schools of the Royal Academy. He was a constant exhibitor at the Royal Academy from 1853 to the year of his death. Moore was best known by his work in water-colour, and especially by his portraits of children and landscape views in or near Rome and Florence. He married in 1865 Miss Emily Simonds of Reading, and died in London on 12 July 1880.

[Private information.] L. C.

MOOREHEAD, JOHN (*d.* 1804), violinist and composer, was born in Ireland, where he received some musical instruction. After playing among the principals in the orchestra of the Three Choirs Festival at Worcester in 1794, he was brought to London by Thomas Dibdin, and engaged at Sadler's Wells Theatre as viola-player in the band and occasional composer. From 1796 to 1800 Moorehead set to music many of the entertainments performed at this theatre, among them 'Alonzo and Imogene,' 'Birds of a Feather,' 'Sadak and Kalasrade,' 'Old Fools,' and 'Blankenberg.'

About 1798 Moorehead entered the band of Covent Garden Theatre, and wrote the music of such pieces as 'The Naval Pillar,' produced on 7 Oct. 1799; 'The Volcano,' pantomime, 23 Dec. 1799; with Thomas Attwood [q. v.] he composed 'The Dominion of Fancy' and 'Il Bondocani,' musical farce, 15 Nov. 1800; with Davy, 'La Perouse,' historical pantomime, 28 Feb. 1801; with Reeve, Davy, Corri, and Braham, 'The Cabinet,' 9 Jan. 1802; with Braham and Reeve, 'Family Quarrels,' 18 Dec. 1802, all published. Besides the popular dance in 'Speed the Plough,' 8 Feb. 1800, songs in farces, several ballads, and a duo concertante for violins, he was also author of the 'favourite' overture to 'Harlequin Habeas,' 27 Dec. 1802. Many of these compositions possess exceptional originality.

After undertaking to compose music for the 'Cabinet,' Moorehead was attacked by a nervous malady, and was unable to produce more than four numbers. He grew rapidly worse, developed symptoms of insanity, and was confined in Northampton House, Clerkenwell, London, which he quitted for Richmond. Here, as T. Dibdin relates, 'a relapse led Moorehead into an extraordinary series of eccentricities . . . and he was committed in a strait-waistcoat to Tothill Fields Prison.' He was released, and was next heard of in 1803 on board H.M.S. Monarch as sailor, and afterwards bandmaster. About March 1804, during a walk in the neighbourhood of Deal, he hanged himself with a handkerchief to the bar of a gate.

Moorehead's brother, Alexander, violinist, and leader of the Sadler's Wells orchestra, died in 1803 in a Liverpool lunatic asylum.

[Annals of the Three Choirs, p. 76; Thomas Dibdin's Reminiscences, i. 190, 261, 314; Collection relating to Sadler's Wells, vol. iii. passim; European Mag. 1799 to 1803; St. James's Chron. 5 April 1804; Thespian Dict.; Grove's Dict. of Music and Musicians, ii. 362.] L. M. M.

MOORSOM, CONSTANTINE RICHARD (1792–1861), vice-admiral, born 22 Sept. 1792, was the son of Admiral Sir Robert Moorsom, K.C.B., who, after being present as a midshipman in Keppel's action off Ushant in 1778, and as a lieutenant at the relief of Gibraltar by Darby in 1781, and by Howe in 1782, commanded the Revenge at Trafalgar in 1805, was master-general of the ordnance in 1809, and died an admiral on 14 May 1835. His mother was Eleanor, daughter of Thomas Scarth of Stakesby, near Whitby, and William Scarth Moorsom [q. v.] was his brother (*Gent. Mag.* 1835, ii. 321). At the date of the battle of Trafalgar Constantine was nominally with his father on board the Revenge; actually he was at school, and in July 1807 entered the Royal Naval College at Portsmouth, then newly organised under the care of Dr. James Inman [q. v.] From the college he carried off the first medal and three mathematical prizes, and was appointed in November 1809 to the Revenge, employed on the coast of Portugal and at the defence of Cadiz. In May 1812 he returned to England in the Warspite, and on 6 June was promoted to the rank of lieutenant. He was afterwards in the Superb on the Cadiz station, in the Bay of Biscay, and on the coast of North America, till 19 July 1814, when he was promoted to the command of the Goree sloop at Bermuda. In June 1815 he was moved into the Terror bomb, which he took to England, and in July 1816 he was appointed to the Fury bomb for service in the expedition against Algiers, under Lord Exmouth [see Pellew, Edward, Viscount Exmouth]. In the bombardment of that stronghold of piracy, on 27 Aug. 1816, the Fury in nine hours threw 318 shells, or double the number thrown by any other bomb. This difference gave rise to an admiralty inquiry, when it was found to be due to the fitting of the mortars on a plan which Moorsom had himself devised. It was forthwith adopted for general service, but Moorsom did not receive post rank till 7 Dec. 1818, after he had commanded the Prometheus on the home station.

In April 1822 he was appointed to the Ariadne, and during the summer carried out a series of experimental cruises, with the Racehorse and Helicon under his orders. The Ariadne was originally built as a corvette, but had been converted into a frigate by the addition of a quarter-deck and six guns, thus increasing her draught of water, and most seriously affecting her sailing qualities. She appeared a hopeless failure, but Moorsom, by a readjustment of her stowage and ballast, 'succeeded in making her sail as fast, work as well, and prove as good a sea-boat as could possibly be expected.' He afterwards went out in her to the Cape of Good Hope, was for some time senior officer at the Mauritius, and on the death of Commodore Nourse, the commander-in-chief, in December 1824, he moved into the Andromache and hoisted a broad pennant, which he continued to fly till relieved by Commodore Christian. From December 1825 to the summer of 1827 he was captain of the Prince Regent, carrying the flag of his father as commander-in-chief at Chatham. He had no further service at sea, though advanced in due course to be rear-admiral on 17 Aug. 1851, and vice-admiral on 10 Sept. 1857. During his later years he was a director and afterwards chairman of the London and North-Western Railway. He had thus also the direction of the steam-packets from Holyhead to Dublin, and was led to consider the question of steam navigation. He was chairman of a committee on steamship performance appointed by the British Association, to which he presented reports in 1859 and 1860. He was also the author of an essay 'On the Principles of Naval Tactics,' privately printed in 1843, and published, with additions, in 1846. He died suddenly in Montagu Place, Russell Square, London, on 26 May 1861. He married in 1822 Mary, daughter of Jacob Maude of Silaby Hall, Durham, and by her had a large family.

His first cousin, William Moorsom (1817–1860), born in 1817, was a lieutenant of the Cornwallis in the first China war, was captain of the Firebrand in the Black Sea, and served with the naval brigade in the Crimea during the Russian war; was a C.B., an officer of the Legion of Honour, and had the Medjidié third class. In 1857 he was appointed to the Diadem frigate, in which, when just recovering from a severe attack of small-pox, he was sent to the West Indies and to Vera Cruz. There he contracted a low fever, which, on his return to England in October 1859, compelled him to resign his command. He died on 4 Feb. 1860. Moorsom was the inventor of the shell with the percussion fuze which bore his name. This shell, though long since superseded by the advance of rifled ordnance, was the first in which the difficulties inherent in the problem were satisfactorily overcome. He also invented the 'director,' an instrument for directing the concentration of a ship's broadside. In an improved form, and in combination with the system of electric firing, it is still used in our navy, and is believed to be the origin of the celebrated Watkin position-finder. Moorsom was the author of 'Suggestions for the Organisation and Manœuvres of Steam Fleets,' 1854, 4to, and of 'Remarks on the Construction of Ships of War and the Composition of War Fleets,' Portsea, 1857, 8vo.

[O'Byrne's Nav. Biog. Dict.; Gent. Mag. 1860, pt. i. p. 309, 1861, pt. ii. p. 88; information from the family; Memoir of Captain William Moorsom (privately printed, 1860).] J. K. L.

MOORSOM, WILLIAM SCARTH (1804–1863), captain, civil engineer, son of Admiral Sir Robert Moorsom, K.C.B. (*d.* 1835). William was born at his father's residence, Upper Stakesby, near Whitby, Yorkshire, in 1804. Constantine Richard Moorsom [q. v.] was his brother. He was educated at the Royal Military College, Sandhurst, where he took a very high position in fortification and military surveying, and was presented by his brother cadets with a sword in token of their general esteem. On 22 March 1821 he was appointed ensign in the 79th highlanders in Ireland. In Dublin he employed his leisure in making a trigonometrical survey of the city, which was used by the quartermaster-general's department until the introduction of the ordnance-map, and gained him a lieutenancy in the 7th royal fusiliers on 12 Feb. 1825. He was adjutant of the 'reserve companies,' or depôt of that regiment, until promoted to an unattached company on 26 Jan. 1826. He passed through half-pay of the 69th regiment to the 52nd light infantry in Nova Scotia.

In Nova Scotia he was an active explorer, and published a small volume of letters on the colony and its prospects. His survey of Halifax and its environs was for a long time, probably is still, the best extant. Sir Peregrine Maitland [q. v.] appointed him deputy quartermaster-general, and he collected valuable statistics of the military resources of Nova Scotia and New Brunswick. He sold out of the army on 2 March 1832, married, and resided chiefly with his father, until the death of the latter.

During this period he assisted in the establishment of the London and Birmingham Railway Company, of which his elder brother, Captain (afterwards Admiral) Constantine Richard Moorsom [q. v.], was director. His survey of a very difficult section of country, crossing the valley of the Ouse, attracted the notice of Robert Stephenson. In 1835–6 Moorsom visited and studied every railway and canal working or in progress of construction in England. He was employed by Messrs. Sturge of Birmingham to execute the surveys for a proposed line of railway from Birmingham to Gloucester. Moorsom proposed to approach the high table-lands of Staffordshire from the Severn valley by an incline of 1 in 37. Stephenson and Brunel advocated more circuitous routes to avoid the incline, but Moorsom's plan was preferred by the parliamentary committee. He completed the line from Birmingham to Gloucester at the same cost per mile as the Grand Junction railway was completed by Joseph Locke, F.R.S. [q. v.], a proof of his close attention to details. During the railway mania of 1844–8 Moorsom was employed in laying out many railway systems in England and Ireland, including the Shropshire system connecting Birmingham with Wolverhampton, Chester, &c., the Irish Great Western, and others, some of which were never carried out. In 1845 he received a Telford medal for the first practical application, in the construction of the cast-iron viaduct over the Avon at Tewkesbury, of the method of sinking iron caissons by their own weight in a river-bed, pumping out the interiors, and filling with concrete to form the piers (*Proc. Inst. Civ. Eng.* 1844, p. 60). In 1850 the Prussian government advertised for designs from engineers and architects of all nations for a great iron railway bridge over the Rhine at Cologne. Moorsom's plans (*ib.* xiv. 487) provided spans of six hundred feet of wrought iron, the piers, together with the abutments, forming casemate-batteries for the defence of the bridge against an advance upstream. They were adopted out of sixty-one competitors.

The cessation of railway enterprise in 1852–1856 told seriously on Moorsom's business prospects, and caused him to turn his attention to the extraction of gold in Great Britain. His reports to the Britannia and Poltimore Mining Companies in 1852 first placed the subject before the public in a practical light, but the yield was too small to cover the outlay, and the enterprise was perhaps too hastily abandoned. In the winter of 1856 Moorsom was sent by the government to Ceylon to report on the feasibility of a line of railway from Colombo to the highlands of Kandy. His report appears in 'Professional Papers of the Corps of Royal Engineers,' new ser. vol. vii.

Moorsom was elected an associate of the Institute of Civil Engineers, London, on 24 March 1835, and was transferred to the list of members on 20 Feb. 1849. He became a member of the Society of Arts in 1843, and was a frequent speaker at scientific meetings, and an indefatigable contributor to the proceedings of societies. He died at his residence in Great George Street, Westminster, after a long and painful illness, on 3 June 1863, at the age of fifty-nine. He left a large family.

Moorsom published: 1. 'Letters from Nova Scotia,' London, 1830, 12mo. 2. 'On Reorganising the Administration of India,' London, 1858, 8vo. 3. 'Historical Records 52nd Oxfordshire Light Infantry,' London, 1860, two editions. His papers include, in addition to those above mentioned, those on 'Locomotive Engines' (*Proc. Inst. Civil Engineers*, vols. i. ii. viii. xv. and xviii.); on 'Bridges' (*ib.* vol. iii.); 'Fireproof Buildings' (*ib.* vol. viii.); 'Junction of the Atlantic and Pacific Oceans across the Isthmus of Panama' (*ib.* vol. ix.); 'Horse Power' (*ib.* vol. x.); 'Buoys, Beacons, and Sea-lights' (*ib.* vol. xv.); 'Artillery,' 'Bore of Rifled Small Arms,' &c. (*ib.* vol. xix.); 'General System of National Defence, and what Civil Engineers have done and may do' (*ib.* vol. xx.); papers on surveying and levelling, measuring distances by telescope, determining the speed of the Great Eastern by telescope (*ib.* vol. xxii.), and many others. Moorsom was the author of a paper on the aneroid barometer as an orometer (*Proc. Royal Society*, 1857–9, ix. 143–4).

Moorsom's eldest son, William Robert Moorsom (1834–1858), captain in the 13th light infantry, was appointed ensign 52nd light infantry on 17 Aug. 1852, and lieutenant on 10 June 1853, purchasing both commissions. In 1857, when the tidings of the mutiny reached him, he was on leave from his regiment and employed on the railway survey in Ceylon. He at once started for Calcutta, and was sent to repair the telegraph line between Benares and Allahabad, which had been cut by the mutineers. On the approach of the Cawnpore mutineers Havelock [see Havelock, Sir Henry] appointed Moorsom his aide-de-camp and deputy-assistant adjutant and quartermaster-general of his division, with which he served at the relief of Lucknow. In the first action, at Futtehpore, he was present in plain clothes armed only with a stick. As deputy-assistant quartermaster-general he acted as quartermaster-general of Outram's division at the subsequent siege of Lucknow. Although young, he proved a most valuable officer. Malleson says that 'he united with the finest qualities of a fighting soldier the skill of an accomplished draughtsman; it was to his skill, indeed, that Outram and Havelock were indebted for the plans that enabled them so skilfully to penetrate into the residency' (*Hist. Indian Mutiny*, cab. edit. iv. 252). Moorsom was promoted to captain in the 13th light infantry on 2 March 1858, and was killed shortly afterwards, on 24 March 1858, during an attack on the iron bridge at Lucknow. A monument, erected to his memory by his regiment, is in Rochester Cathedral, and his name is inscribed below one of the seven lancet-shaped windows in the west aisle of the north transept in Westminster Abbey. Moorsom's sketch-maps of the march to Lucknow and of the city are now at the British Museum.

[Army Lists; Leake's Lord Seaton's Regiment at Waterloo, the account of the 52nd in Nova Scotia in vol. ii.; obit. notice of the father in Proc. Inst. of Civil Engineers, vol. xxiii.; Moorsom's Works; Malleson's Hist. Indian Mutiny, cab. edit. vol. iv.; Moorsom's Hist. Rec. 52nd Light Infantry, 2nd ed. pp. 410–17; Guide to Westminster Abbey; Gent. Mag. 1863, ii. 112, 245.] H. M. C.

MORANT, PHILIP (1700–1770), historian of Essex, born in St. Saviour's parish, Jersey, on 6 Oct. 1700, was second son of Steven Morant, by his wife Mary Filleul (Payne, *Armorial of Jersey*, pt. v. pp. 294–5). After attending Abingdon school he matriculated at Oxford from Pembroke College as 'Mourant' on 17 Dec. 1717, and graduated B.A. in 1721 (Foster, *Alumni Oxon.* 1715–1886, iii. 994). At midsummer 1722 he declined the office of preacher of the English church at Amsterdam. In 1724 he was licensed to the curacy of Great Waltham, Essex, and assisted the vicar, Nicholas Tindal [q. v.], in the preparation of a new edition of Rapin's 'History of England.' Tindal made some acknowledgment of Morant's help in the preface to the first volume. Morant also translated the notes to De Beausobre and Lenfant's 'Commentary on St. Matthew's Gospel,' the text of which had been translated by Tindal (1727). As a member of Sidney Sussex College, Cambridge, Morant proceeded M.A. in 1729. In 1724 he presented to Edmund Gibson, bishop of London, a manuscript 'Answer to the First Part of the Discourse of the Grounds and Reasons of the Christian Religion, in a Letter to a Friend.' The Bishop of London, impressed by Morant's argumentative power and antiquarian learning, conferred much patronage on him. On Gibson's recommendation he was, on 16 Aug. 1732, nominated by Queen Caroline to the chaplaincy of the English episcopal church at Amsterdam, which he retained until 29 Sept. 1734. He was presented to the rectory of Shellow Bowells on 20 April 1733, to the vicarage of Broomfield on 17 Jan. 1733–4, to the rectory of Chignal Smealey on 19 Sept. 1735, to that of St. Mary at the Walls, Colchester, on 9 March 1737, to that of Wickham Bishops on 21 Jan. 1742–3, and to that of Aldham on 14 Sept. 1745, all being in Essex. He held the Colchester and Aldham cures conjointly. At Colchester he did much towards rescuing Archbishop Harsnett's library from destruction, and prepared a catalogue. On 20 Nov. 1755 he was elected F.S.A. On the recommendation of his son-in-law, Thomas Astle [q. v.], Morant was entrusted by a committee of the House of Lords with the preparation for the press of the ancient records of parliament. His knowledge of Norman French and skill as a palæographer qualified him for the work. He was responsible for the text and notes of the edition of the 'Rotuli Parliamentorum' during the period 1278–1413. He died at South Lambeth on 25 Nov. 1770, and was buried in Aldham Church. The east window of the chancel of the new church at Aldham was filled with stained glass by subscription in 1854, 'In memoriam Phil. Morant, A.M.' By Anne, daughter and coheiress of Solomon Stebbing of the Brook House, Great Tey, Essex, he had an only daughter, Anna Maria, who was married, on 18 Dec. 1765, to Thomas Astle, keeper of the records in the Tower of London (*Transactions of Essex Archæolog. Soc.* iv. 43–4). His library of books and manuscripts came into the possession of Astle. Many of the books are now in the Royal Institution; the manuscripts (excepting the Holman volumes, which were presented to the corporation of Colchester by Robert Hills of Colne Park, Essex) form part of the Stowe collection in the British Museum.

In 1748 Morant published his 'History and Antiquities of Colchester,' fol. (2nd edit. 1768), of which only two hundred copies were printed, at the joint expense of William Bowyer [q. v.] and himself. It is painstaking and accurate, but was burlesqued as diffuse by John Clubbe [q. v.] in 'The History and Antiquities of the ancient Village of Wheatfield' (1758). His great work, 'The History and the Antiquities of the County of Essex,' 2 vols. fol. 1760–8, with which the 'History of Colchester' was incorporated, is based chiefly on the collections of Thomas Jekyll [q. v.] and William Holman [q. v.] On Holman's death in 1730 his manuscript history was placed in the hands of Nicholas Tindal, but he abandoned the project of editing it after two numbers had appeared. In 1739 Dr. Nathaniel Salmon purchased the manuscript with a view to publication. He, however, died in 1742, and the manuscript passed eventually into the hands of John Booth, F.S.A., of Barnard's Inn, under-sheriff of Essex, from whom it was acquired about 1750 by Morant (cf. Gough, *Anecd. of Brit. Topography*, i. 370). As an editor Morant was more competent than either of his predecessors. As a manorial history his work is most useful, but the genealogies are often defective and inaccurate: no monumental inscriptions or extracts from parish registers are given, while the lists of incumbents mostly commence with the eighteenth century only. A comparison of the history with the portion of the Holman manuscripts in the Colchester Museum (where the original manuscript of Morant's 'History' is also preserved) makes it apparent that Morant frequently neglected to make the best use of his materials. A third volume, containing additions and corrections, with arms and inscriptions, was promised, but never appeared. The book was reprinted in 1816 by Meggy & Chalk of Chelmsford.

Morant's other works are: 1. 'An Introduction to the Reading of the New Testament,' being a translation of that of MM. de Beausobre and Lenfant, prefixed to their edition of the New Testament, 2 vols. 4to, London, 1725–6. 2. 'The Cruelties and Persecutions of the Romish Church displayed,' 8vo, London, 1728 (translated into Welsh by Thomas Richards, 4to, Caer-Fyrddin, 1746). 3. 'Remarks on the 19th Chapter of the II[d] Book of Mr. Selden's "Mare Clausum,"' printed at the end of Falle's 'Cæsarea,' 8vo, 1734 and 1797. 4. Translation of the Notes in the second part of the 'Othoman History,' by Demetrius Cantimir, fol., London, 1735. 5. 'The History of England by way of Question and Answer,' revised and corrected for Thomas Astley, 12mo, London, 1737. 6. 'Account of the Spanish Invasion in 1588, by Way of Illustration to the Tapestry Hangings in the House of Lords and in the King's Wardrobe,' engraved and published by John Pine, fol. London, 1739; 2nd edit. 1753. 7. 'Geographia Antiqua & Nova,' with Cellarius's maps, 4to, London, 1742 (another edit. 1768), translated with additions from Du Fresnoy's 'Méthode pour étudier la Géographie.'

Under the signature 'C.' he wrote several articles for the first edition of the 'Biographia Britannica,' as well as that on Bishop Stillingfleet, which is unsigned. He revised, with numerous additions, Hearne's 'Ductor Historicus' (1723), and left in manuscript a 'Life of King Edward the Confessor.'

In the British Museum are Morant's letters to Dr. Thomas Birch [q. v.], 1748–62 (Addit. MS. 4314), and copies of his letters to Browne Willis, 1745–59 (*ib.* 5841), and of a letter to Dr. William Richardson, 1740 (*ib.* 5860).

[Nichols's Lit. Anecd. ii. 201 *n.*, 705, and elsewhere; Nichols's Illustr. of Lit.; Transactions of Essex Archæolog. Soc. ii. 148; Historians of Essex, III, 'Philip Morant' (a valuable article by Mr. C. F. D. Sperling in the Essex Review, January 1894); Ayscough's Cat. of MSS. in Brit. Mus. p. 719; Egerton MS. 2382, f. 179; Addit. MS. 23990, f. 62; Addit. (Cole) MS. vol. xxxiii. f. 104; Watt's Bibl. Brit.] G. G.

MORAY. [See Murray.]

MORAY or **MURRAY**, Earls of. [See Randolph, Sir Thomas, first Earl of the Randolph family, *d.* 1332; Randolph, John, third Earl, *d.* 1346; Stewart, James, first Earl of the Stewart family, 1499?–1544; Stewart, James, first Earl of a new creation, 1531?–1570; Stewart, James, second Earl, *d.* 1592; Stewart, Alexander, fifth Earl, *d.* 1701.]

MORAY, GILBERT of (*d.* 1245), bishop of Caithness. [See Gilbert.]

MORCAR or **MORKERE** (*fl.* 1066), earl of the Northumbrians, son of Ælfgar [q. v.], earl of the Mercians, was probably, along with his elder brother, Edwin or Eadwine, earl of the Mercians, concerned in stirring up the Northumbrians in 1065 to revolt against their earl, Tostig, the son of Earl Godwin [q. v.], and was chosen earl by the rebels at York in October. He at once satisfied the people of the Bernician district by making over the government of the country beyond the Tyne to Oswulf, the eldest son of Eadwulf, the Bernician earl, who had been slain by Siward in 1041. Marching southwards with the rebels he was joined by the men of Nottingham, Derby, and Lincoln, members of the old Danish confederacy of towns, and met Edwin, who was at the head of a force of Mercians and Welshmen, at Northampton. There the brothers and their army considered proposals for peace from Earl Harold [see Harold, 1022?–1066]. Negotiations were continued at Oxford, where, under pressure of the Northumbrians, Harold yielded (28 Oct.), and Morcar's election was legalised. On the death of Edward the Confessor Morcar professedly supported Harold, but the people of his earldom were dissatisfied, and Harold visited York, the seat of Morcar's government, in the spring of 1066, and overcame their disaffection by peaceful means. In the summer Morcar joined his brother Edwin in repulsing Tostig, who was ravaging the Mercian coast. When, however, Tostig and his ally Harold Hardrada invaded Northumbria in September, Morcar evidently was not ready to meet them; and it was not until York was threatened that, having then been joined by Edwin, he went out against them with a large army. The two earls were defeated at Fulford Gate, near York, in a fierce battle, in which, according to a Norse authority, Morcar seems to have been prominent (*Heimskringla*, ap. Laing, iii. 84). York was surrendered, and Harold had to march in haste to save the north by the battle of Stamford Bridge. Ungrateful for this deliverance, Morcar and his brother held back the forces of the north from joining Harold in the defence of the kingdom against the Normans.

After the battle of Hastings Morcar and his brother arrived at London, sent their sister Aldgyth [q. v.], Harold's widow, to Chester, and urged the citizens to raise one or other of them to the throne (WILLIAM OF MALMESBURY, *Gesta Regum*, iii. 247). They concurred in the election of Edgar or Eadgar the Ætheling [q. v.] (ORDERIC, p. 502), but disappointed of their hope left the city with their forces and returned to the north, believing that the Conqueror would not advance so far. Before long, however, they met William either at Berkhamstead (*A.-S. Chronicle*, an. 1066, Worcester; at 'Beorcham,' FLORENCE, an. 1066; SYMEON, *Historia Regum*, c. 150), or more probably at Barking, after his coronation (WILLIAM OF POITIERS, pp. 147, 148, see FREEMAN, *Norman Conquest*, iii. 794; PARKER, *Early History of Oxford*, pp. 186–190). William accepted their submission, received from them gifts and hostages, and they were reinstated. The Conqueror carried Morcar and his brother with him into Normandy in 1067, and after his return kept them at his court. In 1068 they withdrew from the court, reached their earldoms, and rebelled against William. They were supported by a large number both of English and Welsh; the clergy, the monks, and the poor were strongly on their side, and messages were sent to every part of the kingdom to stir up resistance. Morcar's activity may perhaps be inferred from the prominent part taken in the movement by York (ORDERIC, p. 511). It seems probable, however, that Eadgar was nominally the head of the rebellion, and that he was specially upheld by the Bernician district under Gospatric [q. v.] Morcar and his brother were not inclined to risk too much; they advanced with their men to Warwick, and there made submission to the Conqueror, were pardoned, and again kept at court, the king treating them with an appearance of favour. On their defection the rebellion came to nothing. In 1071 some mischief was made between them and the king, and William, it is said, was about to send them to prison, but they escaped secretly from the court. After wandering about for a while, keeping to wild country, they separated, and Morcar joined the insurgents in the isle of Ely, and remained with them until the surrender of the island. Morcar, it is said, surrendered himself on the assurance that the king would pardon him and receive him as a loyal friend (*ib.* p. 521; nothing is said about this by the chronicle-writers or Florence). William, however, committed him to the custody of Roger de Beaumont [see under BEAUMONT, ROBERT DE, *d.* 1118], who kept him closely imprisoned in Normandy. When the king was on his deathbed in 1087 he ordered that Morcar should be released, in common with others whom he had kept in prison in England and Normandy, on condition that they took an oath not to disturb the peace in either land. He was not long out of prison, for William Rufus took him to England with him, and on arriving at Winchester put him in prison there. Nothing further is known about him, and it is therefore probable that he died in prison. Little can be gathered about Morcar's character, for until the death of Edwin, who was slain by his own men, shortly after the brothers parted in 1071, he almost invariably appears as acting in conjunction with his elder brother, and apparently playing a secondary part. The actions of the brothers show that they were ambitious, selfish, and untrustworthy. Edwin was personally attractive and lovable; his death was universally mourned both in England and Normandy, and the Conqueror wept when he heard of it. The terms in which the brothers are spoken of (ORDERIC, p. 521; WILLIAM OF MALMESBURY, *Gesta Regum*, iii. 252; *Liber Eliensis*, pp. 230, 243, 245) indicate that Morcar had some share in his brother's more pleasing qualities.

[Freeman's Norman Conquest, vols. ii. iii. iv., and William Rufus, i. 13, 14, contain a full account of Morcar, whose name is there given as Morkere, according to the old English spelling. See also Parker's Early Hist. of Oxford, pp. 180, 184, 186, 187, 199 (Oxford Hist. Soc.); Lappenberg's England under Anglo-Norman Kings, pp. 102, 105, 108, 124, 159, ed. Thorpe; Green's Conquest of England, pp. 567, 584; A.-S. Chron. ann. 1065, 1066, 1071, 1072 (Rolls Ser.); Flor. Wig. ann. 1065, 1066, 1067, 1087 (Engl. Hist. Soc.); Vita Edw. ap. Lives of Edward the Confessor, p. 421 (Rolls Ser.); Symeon of Durham's Hist. Regum ap. Opp. ii. 198 (Rolls Ser.); Henry of Huntingdon's Hist. Angl. vi. 33 (Rolls Ser. p. 205); Will. of Malmesbury's Gesta Regum, ii. 200, 228, iii. 247, 248, 252 (Rolls Ser. pp. 246, 281, 307, 310, 311); Snorri's Heimskringla, iii. 84, ed. Laing; Orderic, pp. 511, 521 (Duchesne); Will. of Poitiers, pp. 148, 150 (Giles's SS. Rerum Gest. Will. Conq.). The notices in the stories about the defence of the isle of Ely in Gesta Herewardi (Chron. Anglo-Norm. ii. 56), Liber Eliensis, pp. 230, 243, 245 (Anglia Chr. Soc.), and the so-called Ingulf, pp. 900–2 (Savile), are untrustworthy, except so far as they may be confirmed by sufficient authority.]

W. H.

MORDAF HAEL (i.e. the GENEROUS) (*fl.* 550 ?), North British prince, figures in the 'Historical Triads' (*Myvyrian Archaiology*, 2nd edition, pp. 389, 397, 404) as one of the three lavish (princes) of the isle of Britain.

According to the tradition recorded in manuscript A of the 'Venedotian Code' (*Ancient Laws of Wales*, 1841 edition, i. 104), he was contemporary with the other two, viz., Rhydderch Hael (*fl.* 580) (see NENNIUS and ADAMNAN'S *Life of St. Columba*) and Nudd Hael, and joined them in the expedition undertaken by the northern princes in the time of Rhun ap Maelgwn Gwynedd (*fl.* 560) to avenge upon Arfon (the southern coast of the Menai) the death of Elidyr Mwynfawr. His father's name (Serguan, in mediæval Welsh Serfan) appears in the Nennian genealogies (*Cymmrodor*, ix. 175), but not in such a connection as to enable the date of Mordaf to be fixed with any certainty. Mordaf ap Serfan appears in two of the lists of saints printed in the Iolo MSS. (Liverpool edition, pp. 106, 138).

[Authorities cited.] J. E. L.

MORDAUNT, CHARLES, third EARL OF PETERBOROUGH (1658–1735), admiral, general, and diplomatist, was the eldest son of John Mordaunt, viscount Mordaunt (1627–1675) [q. v.], nephew of Henry Mordaunt, second earl of Peterborough [q. v.], and, through his grandmother Elizabeth, first countess of Peterborough, directly descended from Charles Howard, earl of Nottingham [q. v.] His mother, Elizabeth, daughter of Thomas Carey, was granddaughter of Robert Carey, first earl of Monmouth [q. v.], and niece of Henry Carey, second earl of Monmouth [q. v.] It is supposed that he received his early education at Eton. He matriculated at Christ Church, Oxford, on 11 April 1674, then 'aged 16' (FOSTER, *Alumni Oxon.*) His university career was short. In the following November he entered as a volunteer on board the Cambridge, commanded by his mother's stepbrother, Arthur Herbert, afterwards Earl of Torrington [q. v.], and went out to the Mediterranean in the squadron under Sir John Narbrough [q. v.] The Cambridge went home in the following year, but Mordaunt, moving into the Henrietta with Narbrough, did not return till 1677. By the death of his father on 5 June 1675 he had become Viscount Mordaunt, and now, when barely twenty, he married Carey, or Carry, daughter of Sir Alexander Fraser of Durris in Kincardineshire. In October 1678, however, he again sailed for the Mediterranean as a volunteer in the Bristol, when he was shipmate with the diarist Henry Teonge [q. v.], who amusingly recounts how, on 3 Nov., on the occasion of his not being very well, Mordaunt obtained the captain's leave to preach, and how he, Teonge, took measures to prevent him. Three weeks later, on the arrival of the squadron at Cadiz, Mordaunt moved into the Rupert, then carrying the flag of his uncle Herbert as vice-admiral and afterwards as commander-in-chief on the Barbary coast. He returned to England in the autumn of 1679, but again went out in June 1680, as a volunteer for service on shore at Tangier, then besieged by the Moors. It was only for a few months, and on his return he settled down at Fulham, in a house which, like most of his property, he had inherited from his mother; the bulk of his father's estate reverted to his uncle, the Earl of Peterborough. He at once busied himself in politics, took his seat in the House of Lords, and attached himself to Shaftesbury. He was one of the sixteen peers who, in January 1680–1, signed the petition against the meeting of the parliament at Oxford, and one of the twenty who, in March, protested against the refusal of the lords to proceed with the impeachment of Fitzharris [see COOPER, ANTHONY ASHLEY, first EARL OF SHAFTESBURY]. In November 1681 he declined the offer of an appointment as captain of a ship of war, which was possibly made with the idea of getting rid of him. In 1682 he was intimately associated with Essex, Russell, and Sidney, and in 1683 he was believed by many to be implicated in their alleged plot. On the accession of James II he delivered a speech, full of 'eloquence, sprightliness, and audacity,' against the increase of the standing army and the appointment of catholic officers (MACAULAY, ii. 287). When the parliament was prorogued, believing that further opposition at home was useless, and not improbably dangerous, he went to Holland. He is said to have been the first to press the Prince of Orange 'to undertake the business of England' (BURNET, *Hist. of his own Time*, iii. 262).

During the next three years he was active in intriguing against King James, and made several journeys between Holland and England. Towards the end of 1687 he had command of a small Dutch squadron in the West Indies. The object of this commission has not been explained, though it has been suggested that it was 'to try the temper of the English colonies and their attachment to the reigning sovereign.' It is probable also that Mordaunt was instructed to sound Narbrough, who was in command of an English squadron, at that time engaged in an attempt to recover treasure from a Spanish wreck. The actual pretext was an intention also to 'fish' for the treasure; but 'they were wholly unprovided to work the wreck,' and after a few days, during which the two commanders met on friendly terms, Mordaunt's Dutch squadron took its departure, and returned to Europe (CHARNOCK, iii. 316–17; *Hist. MSS. Comm.* 11th Rep. pt. v. p. 136). While in Holland Mordaunt cultivated a close friendship with John Locke [q. v.] the philosopher, but his most intimate associate was one Wildman, a violent upholder of revolutionary principles. Wildman objected to the first draft of the prince's declaration, as laying too much stress on 'what had been done to the bishops,' and Mordaunt induced the prince to modify it in this and some other respects (BURNET, iii. 295). In matters of religion Mordaunt was a freethinker, and he was especially hostile to the political principles with which the English church was at that time identified.

When 'the business of England' was finally resolved on, Mordaunt, with Herbert and Edward Russell (afterwards Earl of Orford) [q. v.], was in immediate attendance on the Prince of Orange. On landing in Torbay he was sent in advance, to levy a regiment of horse. He occupied Exeter on 8 Nov.; and, still in advance of the main army, raised Dorset and Wiltshire in the prince's favour. At this time William placed much confidence in him, and during the early months of 1689 appointed him a privy councillor (14 Feb.), gentleman of the bedchamber (1 March), colonel of a regiment of foot (1 April), first lord of the treasury (8 April), Earl of Monmouth (9 April), lord-lieutenant of Northamptonshire (29 April), colonel of horse (15 June), and water-bailiff of the Severn (9 Aug.) It was supposed by many that the title Monmouth was selected as an indication that William did not intend to revive it in favour of the late Duke of Monmouth's son. It seems more probable that it was chosen by Mordaunt himself as reviving the title of his mother's family. His appointment as first lord of the treasury was strange, for he had no experience of business, but the administration of the office virtually rested on Lord Godolphin [see SIDNEY, first EARL GODOLPHIN], whom, as a partisan of James to the last, it did not seem politic to place at the head of the board (MACAULAY, iv. 21). Monmouth's work was mainly limited to the distribution of patronage, and he is said to have managed it in a liberal spirit and with clean hands. He offered Locke the embassy to Berlin; and when Locke declined it, on the ground of ill-health, he nominated him to be a commissioner of appeals (KING, *Life of Locke*, Bohn, p. 172). He wished also to find some post for Isaac Newton; but before it could be arranged he quitted office (18 March 1689–90), accepting in lieu of it a pension and a promise of the manor of Reigate (MACAULAY, v. 168). There was, however, no coolness between him and the king, who, on going to Ireland in June, invited Monmouth to accompany him. Monmouth declined, preferring, apparently, to remain in England as one of the queen's 'council of nine.' The 'nine' were all jealous and mistrustful of each other; but Monmouth by his self-assertion and ability excited more jealousy among his colleagues than any other. When the French fleet was reported to be in the Channel, when Nottingham and Russell were accusing Torrington of neglect or of treason in not at once bringing Tourville to action, Monmouth proposed that he, with another—apparently Sir Richard Haddock—should go to the fleet as volunteers, with a secret commission to take the command if Torrington should be killed (the Queen to the King, 20 June 1690). But although Nottingham, who wished to get Monmouth out of London, supported this proposal, on the grounds that the king had thoughts of appointing Monmouth to command the fleet, Mary refused to give the commission. After the battle of Beachy Head was fought, the council agreed to send two of their body to the fleet as a commission of inquiry. Monmouth begged to be excused on account of his relationship to Torrington, 'especially as they were not to command the fleet;' but—he told the queen—as the king had previously thought of entrusting him with the command, he had reason to expect it now. 'As for that,' wrote Mary to her husband, 'I never heard you say it; and if you knew what I shall tell you, if ever I live to see you, you will wonder' (*ib.* 3 July).

The queen's secret was, no doubt, the story of certain anonymous letters addressed to a French agent at Antwerp. These had been intercepted. They were written in lemon-juice, but, on being held before the fire, were found to be detailed reports of the deliberations of the council. Some one of the nine was manifestly the traitor. Several of them believed that it was Monmouth, and were confirmed in that belief by the fact that the letters, which had been regularly despatched after every council meeting, stopped during Monmouth's absence. Carmarthen, Nottingham, Marlborough, and Russell gave the queen their opinion that the letters were written by Wildman on information from Monmouth. Monmouth, on the other hand, told the queen that they were written by some one in Nottingham's office in the service of France. The queen herself believed that, directly or indirectly, the letters were part of an attack by Monmouth on Nottingham (*ib.* 7 July).

William did not share the queen's dislike and mistrust, though, probably in deference to her opinion, he took Monmouth with him to Holland in the following January. He was again in Holland with the king in 1692, but whether he continued with him during the campaign is doubtful. The statement that he commanded the royal horse guards (the blues) at the battle of Steinkirk (RUSSELL, i. 96) is erroneous; at that date Monmouth was not an officer of the regiment, and the regiment itself was in England (PACKE, *Historical Record of the Royal Regiment of Horse Guards*, pp. 71–3). Monmouth had meantime conceived some pique against the king, and in December strongly supported the motion for an inquiry into the conduct of the war; on its rejection he was one of the eighteen peers, 'the bitterest whigs and the bitterest tories,' who signed the protest (MACAULAY, vi. 310). This ended his confidential friendship with the king; and in February 1693–4, consequent, it was said, on his advocacy of the bill for triennial parliaments, he was suspended from his post of gentleman of the bedchamber, his regiment of foot was given to his brother Henry, and he ceased to be summoned to the meetings of the privy council. All this increased his bitterness against the king's ministers. In January 1694–5 he supported Nottingham's motion for the consideration of the state of the nation; and a few weeks later was one of the joint committee appointed to consider the charges of receiving bribes which had been made against the Duke of Leeds, lord president of the council (*ib.* vii. 182 et seq.) The court now tried to appease him. In April he was again gentleman of the bedchamber, and continued in attendance on the king during the year. But he had not forgiven his enemies, and on the arrest of Sir John Fenwick (1645?–1697) [q. v.] in November 1696, he encouraged him in vain efforts to charge the ministers, Marlborough, Russell, Shrewsbury, and others with complicity in the plot, and suggested ways of emphasising or confirming the accusations, especially against Shrewsbury and Marlborough. The Earl of Carlisle, Lady Mary Fenwick's brother, brought Monmouth's conduct to the notice of the lords. By a very large majority they resolved that he had devised some papers found in Fenwick's possession, which had been concocted so as to incriminate the ministers, and that he 'had spoken undutiful words of the king.' He was ordered to the Tower; 'was turned out of all his places, and his name was struck out of the council-book' (*ib.* vii. 399). The persons charged by Fenwick were, undoubtedly, in treasonable correspondence with King James, and Monmouth had suggested new witnesses and incriminating interrogations. It does not appear that he himself, or even his enemies, considered that he was dishonoured by the resolutions of the house, and after an imprisonment of three months he was released, 30 March 1697. By the death of his uncle on 19 June 1697 he became Earl of Peterborough, and made up his quarrel with Marlborough and Godolphin. But he continued to wage war against Russell, now Earl of Orford; and took an active part in the motion for the impeachment of Lord Somers, which was managed in the House of Commons by his eldest son, John, lord Mordaunt, now just of age and member for Chippenham. His quarrel with Somers, however, was short-lived; and in 1702 he was, it is said, collaborating with him in an English version of the 'Olynthiacs' and 'Philippics' of Demosthenes, for which he translated the first of the three 'Olynthiacs.'

On the accession of Anne, Peterborough, through the influence of the Duchess of Marlborough, was again in favour at court. He was reappointed lord-lieutenant of Northamptonshire, and in December 1702 was appointed 'Captain-general and Governor of Jamaica and Admiral and Commander-in-chief of the ships of war employed on that station,' with the immediate prospect of active service against the Spanish settlements in the West Indies. It was intended that the expedition should consist of a combined English and Dutch force; but when the Dutch found that they could not spare the requisite number of men, Peterborough declined Godolphin's proposal to go alone. The English force was of inadequate strength. He was no worker of miracles, he said; and he had no wish to go to the other world loaded with empty titles (KING, *Life of Locke*, p. 242). His commission was therefore cancelled; and except that he vehemently opposed and assisted in rejecting the Bill for preventing Occasional Conformity, in December 1703, he led a comparatively private life till, in the beginning of 1705, he was offered the command of the expeditionary army to Spain. On 31 March he was appointed general and commander-in-chief of the forces in the fleet, and on 1 May was granted a further commission as admiral and commander-in-chief of the fleet, jointly with Sir Clowdisley Shovell [q. v.] The two were named 'joint admirals and chief-commanders of the fleet,' 'and in case of death, or in the absence or inability of either of you, the other of you' was to act as 'admiral and chief-commander.' Peterborough was entrusted with exactly the same powers as Shovell, and each was authorised 'to wear the union flag at the main-topmast-head aboard such ship of her Majesty's fleet where you shall happen at any time to be' (*Commission and Warrant Book*, vol. vi.) From the time of the Commonwealth such joint commissions had not been uncommon, and had twice been given in the preceding reign. But it was exceptional to give such a commission to one who, like Peterborough, had not regularly served in the subordinate grades. Since the Restoration this rule had been only broken in the case of the Duke of York.

The expedition sailed from St. Helens on 24 May 1705, and arrived at Lisbon on 9 June. There they were met by the Archduke Charles, styled the king of Spain by the English and their allies. They were joined also by the Earl of Galway, the commander-in-chief of the English forces already in the Peninsula; and after several councils of war and much discussion, it was agreed, in deference to the opinion of Charles, to attempt the capture of Barcelona, where the people were said to be favourable to his pretensions. Prince George of Hesse-Darmstadt, then commanding at Gibraltar, had proposed rather a landing in Valencia and a dash at Madrid (Prince George to King Charles, 21 May–1 June 1705, in Kunzel, *Leben und Briefwechsel des Landgrafen Georg von Hessen-Darmstadt*, pp. 571–2; Paul Methuen to his father, 13 Sept. (N. S). in *Addit. MS.* 28056, f. 324 *b*; Richards, *Diary*, xxv. 3 *b*); and Peterborough from the first advised operations in Italy, in concert with the Duke of Savoy. Both, however, gave way to the king's decision, and the expedition left the Tagus on 17 July. On 11 Aug. it anchored a few miles east of Barcelona. On the next day preparations were made for besieging the town.

It was only then that the military officers appear to have realised the difficulties of the task. The garrison, they understood, was nearly as numerous as the allied army; the Catalan levies were worthless; the fortifications were strong, and the ground over which they had to make their approaches was marshy and impracticable. Several councils of war were held, only to arrive at the same conclusion: the troops ought to be re-embarked and carried elsewhere. Shovell and Prince George dissented. Peterborough's lack of technical knowledge rendered him incapable of guiding their deliberations. When he attempted to press his colleagues' decision on the king it was ill received (*ib.* xxv. 6 *b*). Peterborough wished to take his little army to Italy, perhaps to the direct support of the Duke of Savoy, perhaps to make a diversion in Naples which he believed to be denuded of troops for service in Spain (Peterborough to Duke of Savoy, 4–15 Sept., 26 Oct.–6 Nov.; Parnell, p. 122 *n.*; *Addit. MS.* 28056, ff. 309, 351). Finally a compromise was arrived at, and on 30 Aug. the Archduke Charles, Prince George, and Peterborough concluded a formal agreement to break up the camp on 4 Sept., to march against Tarragona and so on to Valencia (Paul Methuen to his father, 13 Sept., 10 Oct. (N.S.) in *Addit. MS.* 28056, ff. 323, 337). But on 1 Sept. Peterborough received information respecting the unfinished and unprepared state of the defences of Montjuich, a hill fort about two-thirds of a mile south-west of Barcelona, and he sent Major-general Richards to Prince George to appoint a time of conference (Richards, xxv. 7, where the dates, wrongly written, are fixed by the days of the week). It was generally believed that an attack on Montjuich had previously been proposed by Prince George and refused (Boyer, *Annals*, iv. 146; *History*, pp. 203–4; Targe, iv. 46). But at this conference, between Peterborough and Prince George alone, without any council of war it was resolved, despite the recent agreement, to attack that fort.

About 6 p.m. on 2 Sept. a body of one thousand men marched out of camp. About ten o'clock Peterborough and Prince George joined them, and after some delay, caused by a mistake of the guides, the little force found itself, at daybreak on the 3rd, at the foot of Montjuich. The outer works were carried without difficulty, but the scaling ladders were too short, and, after some loss, the storming party was compelled to draw back. The Neapolitan defenders made a sally, and Prince George was killed. The English were retiring in disorder, when Peterborough, coming up, restored confidence, and the outworks were held. The next day Richards got up a couple of small mortars; on the 6th the garrison surrendered at discretion, after the governor had been killed by a shell. The attack was then turned on Barcelona On the 7th some three thousand men and several heavy guns were landed from the fleet, by the 22nd a large breach had been made in the walls, and on the 28th the governor signed the capitulation. On the next day the mob broke out into furious riot. The English were hastily called in, and by great personal exertions, and at personal risk, Peterborough restored order (Burnet, v. 214; Boyer, *Annals*, iv. 152). On 12 Oct. Charles made a formal entry into Barcelona and was proclaimed king of Spain. In England, parliament presented addresses to the queen on the glorious successes of her arms, and the sole credit was given to Peterborough.

At Barcelona he was nominally the governor, and for some months was engaged in bitter quarrels with everybody near him; with the Spanish king and the king's German ministers more especially. To remedy the defects of his associates, Peterborough requested to be made commander-in-chief of all the forces in Spain, with the sole command of the fleet, and the rank of vice-admiral of England. Under any other conditions he 'desired positively to come home' (Peterborough to Stanhope, 18 Nov. 1705). No notice seems to have been taken of these applications.

Meantime the province and city of Valencia had been won for Charles by native forces. On 24 Jan. Peterborough entered Valencia in triumph amid 'extraordinary demonstrations of joy.' For four nights the streets were illuminated, and the monks and the ladies are represented as being particularly enthusiastic in their welcome (Stebbing, p. 86). Charles had already given him a commission as captain-general in the Spanish service, and now sent him full powers for the civil administration of the province, for the efficient defence of which he drew a great part of the troops from Catalonia, so that by the middle of March the garrison of Barcelona was reduced to something less than fourteen hundred regulars, and this when a French army of twenty-five or thirty thousand men, under the Marshal de Tessé, was advancing to attempt its recapture. Charles was in dismay. The outlying garrisons were hastily called in, and expresses sent off to Peterborough and Sir John Leake [q. v.], calling for their immediate assistance. On 23 March Tessé sat down before the town, but he had not made himself master of the country as he advanced. Without lines of communication, he was dependent for his supplies on the French fleet which, under the command of the Count of Toulouse, arrived from Toulon and blockaded the town by sea.

Peterborough was still enjoying the gaieties of Valencia. On 10 March his commission as commander-in-chief of the fleet, jointly with Shovell, had been renewed (*Commission and Warrant Book*, vol. vi.; cf. Carleton, p. 146), but despite the position of affairs he showed no sign of leaving his quarters. On 10 March he ordered Leake, who in the absence of Shovell was left in command of the fleet, to land the troops which were on board the fleet, at or near Valencia. At the same time King Charles wrote urgently desiring Leake to hasten to the relief of Barcelona. Peterborough repeated his original orders, but Leake quietly put them on one side and prepared to do as the king requested. Peterborough himself did not leave Valencia till 27 March, and on his arrival near Barcelona, joined Cifuentes, who commanded the Catalan levies. Meanwhile, the town was very hard pressed. Montjuich had been taken, a practicable breach had been made in the walls; adverse winds delayed Leake; it was not till the evening of 26 April that he was known to be drawing near. The news reached the French fleet at the same time, and it departed at once, and so far the siege was raised by the mere threat of Leake's approach. On the morning of the 27th Peterborough went off to the fleet in a country boat, went on board the Prince George, hoisted the union flag as commander-in-chief, and thus, as the fleet anchored off Barcelona in the afternoon, claimed to have relieved the town. But in reality the town was saved by Leake, and by Leake alone, in direct disobedience of the orders he received from Peterborough. The later and contradictory orders which he received on 26 April, bidding him land the troops at Barcelona without a moment's loss of time, had no influence on his conduct (Parnell, p. 167; *Addit. MS.* 5438).

It may, indeed, be doubted whether Peterborough's delay at Valencia, and the delays which he so persistently urged on Leake, were not part of a scheme for ruining the cause of Charles. Writing to the Duke of Savoy on 30 March, Peterborough, after referring to Charles as hard pressed in Barcelona, had continued: 'In case of his death I shall give Spain to him who ought to have it [presumably to the Duke of Savoy]. . . . The game will be difficult and delicate; I can only say that I will do my best, for your interests will always be [dear] to me, and you cannot desire a more devoted or more faithful servant' (Parnell, p. 166; *Addit. MS.* 28057, f. 94*b*).

On the night of the third day, 30 April, the French secretly quitted their camp outside Barcelona. For eight days their retreat was harassed by the Spanish horse under Cifuentes, but none of the troops belonging to Peterborough's command took part in the pursuit. At home the news of the relief was received with much joy, and it was coupled with Marlborough's victory at Ramillies, in ordering a day of general thanksgiving. On 7 May, Charles, at Barcelona, held a grand council of all the ministers, generals, and admirals. It was proposed that he should march through Aragon to Madrid, there to join hands with Galway, who was advancing from Portugal, but Peterborough successfully urged the route by Valencia (*Minutes of the Council, Spain*, p. 135; Richards, xxv. 38). It was resolved that the cavalry should march to Valencia; the fleet could carry the foot soldiers; Charles should stay at Barcelona till the requisite preparations had been made. The troops, whom Peterborough accompanied, were landed at the Grao on 24 May, but Peterborough's statements at the council that there would be no difficulty about transport proved misleading; there was no money, and without money there was no transport (*ib.* xxv. 40–1). Peterborough, for the time, gave up the plan of a march on Madrid, engaged the troops in scattered expeditions, and wrote to the king 'that he had received such instructions and limitations about the public money, that he could no longer subsist the troops which he had with him in Valencia, much less could he supply him with any money for his journey to Madrid; that his troops were very sickly; that baggage mules and carts were not to be had . . . and therefore, seeing that his majesty had heretofore shown an inclination to go to Aragon, he now advised him to do so' (*ib.*; *Impartial Enquiry*, p. 181).

This letter reached Charles when already on the way to Valencia, the route almost forced upon him by Peterborough. Although naturally indignant, he turned aside towards Aragon, but he declined to retrace his steps, when, in consequence of a sharp letter from Stanhope, Peterborough again wrote to him bidding him make for Valencia (Richards, xxv. 45). Peterborough meanwhile wrote 'volumes' to the ministers at home, and afterwards published his complaints of the laziness and arrogance of the king.

While the king and the commander-in-chief were on these terms, the Castilians revolted against Galway and the Portuguese. Charles and his council, perceiving the situation to be extremely critical, wrote to Peterborough desiring him to hurry forward with every available man. There were in Valencia some five or six thousand regulars, but without organised transport they were useless. Peterborough started at once with four hundred dragoons, with which he joined the king on 24 July at Pastrana, and two days later escorted him into the camp of the allies at Guadalajara. The army, then some fifteen thousand strong, was opposed to the Duke of Berwick with nearly double the number. Peterborough's arrival, from which much had been expected, brought no increase of strength, and was, in itself, the signal for discord. There was 'a superfluity of generals' (Russell, ii. 46), and though Galway, still suffering from the loss of his arm, expressed his willingness, or indeed his wish, to resign in favour of Peterborough, his Portuguese colleague, Las Minas, would not agree, and the Dutch general preferred to be independent. Both Galway and Las Minas had reason to be dissatisfied with Peterborough, who, on learning, it seems clear, that they were at Madrid, had remained at Valencia, idly indulging his love of pleasure (*Impartial Enquiry*, p. 209; *Parl. Hist.* vi. 987).

Amid these personal recriminations Peterborough, at a council of war on 29 July, announced 'that he had orders from the queen to go to Italy,' and his colleagues were 'as well content to be rid of him as he was to go' (Godolphin to Marlborough, 30 Sept. in Coxe, *Life of Marlborough*, i. 471). Two days afterwards he started for Valencia with an escort of eighty dragoons. At Huete he learned that all his baggage, horses, and equipage, on their way up to the camp, had been taken by the enemy, leaving him, he wrote to Stanhope, with only one suit of clothes and six shirts. The value of the loss, which included 'eight waggons of good eatables and drink,' he estimated at 6,000*l.*, but his accounts, whether public or private, were always largely imaginary. Towards the middle of August he went to Alicante, presumably to confer with Leake. The town had been taken by storm on 28 July, and with the reduction of the castle, which did not surrender till 17 Sept., Peterborough had nothing immediately to do.

The remainder of July was occupied in forwarding to Stanhope spiteful accusations against Leake and others, charging them with irregularities, which, if they took place, must have been connived at by Peterborough himself. Simultaneously he resolved on an expedition to reduce the Balearic islands, but on receiving orders from England to despatch a squadron of nine ships of the line to the West Indies, he abandoned the expedition, judging that the fleet so reduced would be insufficient for the task, and failing in his efforts to induce Leake or a council of war to undertake the responsibility of disobeying the order from home. On 10 Sept. he sailed in the Resolution for Genoa, in order—according to his own account—to arrange with the Duke of Savoy for a combined attack on Toulon. The subject was, indeed, spoken of during Peterborough's visit to Turin; but he had no instructions about it, and the claim which he seems to have made to be the originator of the scheme, which was carried out next year, is without foundation. Both the inception and the maturing of the project were Marlborough's (*Impartial Enquiry*, p. 238).

The only real business which Peterborough engaged in was the negotiation of a loan of 100,000*l.* from the Jews of Genoa—a loan which he had no authority to contract, and for which he agreed to pay an exorbitant interest. His visit seems to have been principally one of pleasure, and partly in pique at the conduct of the king of Spain and of his own colleagues. By the end of December he rejoined the king at Valencia, where, on 11 Feb. 1706–7, he received orders recalling him to England to give an account of his conduct. Galway was at the same time appointed commander-in-chief of the forces in Spain.

On 13 March Peterborough again sailed for Genoa in the Resolution [see Mordaunt, Henry, 1681?–1710], and after narrowly escaping capture on the way, was put on shore at Oneglia. At Turin he was met by peremptory orders to return to England immediately. Nothing was further from his intentions than obedience; and finding that the Duke of Savoy, who had been duly informed that his commission was revoked, declined to discuss the operations of the coming campaign with him, he made a circular tour through Europe. At Vienna he was well received, and is said to have inspired the emperor with the idea of an expedition against Naples. Almanza had been fought and lost a few weeks before; and as Peterborough, after his quarrel with Galway, had prophesied misfortune, it was supposed that he had foreseen the course of the war. Accordingly Count Wratislaw, the emperor's minister, wrote to Marlborough on 21 June–2 July: 'When you have spoken to him you will probably be more satisfied with him than you imagine; for Prince Eugene has written to me that his lordship thinks like a general, though he does not always express himself with propriety' (Coxe, ii. 79). From Vienna Peterborough went to Leipzig, charged, it would appear, with some irregular mission from the Austrian court to the king of Sweden. At Leipzig Charles XII sought to avoid him, but Peterborough managed to point out to him that with an army such as his—nearly eighty thousand men of the best troops in the world—he might be the arbiter of the fate of Europe. Charles, however, had other designs, and Peterborough went on to Hanover, paid his court to the Electress Sophia, inspired her son, the future king of England, with antipathy, and early in August arrived at Soignies on a visit to Marlborough.

For some time back Marlborough had conceived a poor idea of Peterborough's conduct, and on 13 Sept. 1706 had written privately to the duchess that 'he did not think much ceremony ought to be used in removing him from a place where he has hazarded the loss of the whole country' (*ib.* i. 471). He was, however, quite sensible that Peterborough might be a dangerous man to offend, and now received him with civility but apparently with little confidence. 'By what he tells me,' he wrote to Godolphin on 18 Aug., 'he thinks he has demonstration to convince you that he has been injured in everything that has been reported to his disadvantage.' 'I have endeavoured,' he added four days later, 'to let him see that, for his own sake, he ought to clear up the objections against him, and he has promised me that he will acquaint you and Lord Sunderland with all he has to say' (*ib.* ii. 132).

By 20 Aug. Peterborough was in England. A proposal had been made by Harley, and endorsed by others of the cabinet, to arrest him and bring him to trial, but it was not acted on (*ib.* ii. 137). On 3 Sept. he applied for an audience. It was refused, on the ground that he could not be admitted to the queen's presence until he had explained 'why he did not in the preceding campaign march to Madrid with the army under his command; why he did not fulfil his instructions in advancing to the King of Spain the supplies entrusted to his disposition; and why he retired to Italy without orders, and borrowed large sums of money on disadvantageous terms' (*ib.* ii. 178). Peterborough made no attempt to clear himself officially, but he commissioned his friend, Dr. Freind, to publish an account of what had been done, and supplied him with such documents as he judged suitable. These documents were correctly reproduced, but Freind's 'Account of the Earl of Peterborough's Conduct in Spain' must be considered, as was said at the time, as 'the Earl of Monmouth's vindication of the Earl of Peterborough.' It is Peterborough's own story, and, except where extraneously supported, has no authority. Neither has the answer, under the title of 'Remarks upon Dr. Friend's Account,' any independent authority; it merely supplied glosses, pro or con, on such evidence as it suited Peterborough to produce. But Freind had also challenged an official inquiry, and an investigation began before the House of Lords in January 1707–8. It speedily became a trial of strength between the factions of the day; the tories upheld Peterborough, although he was the most radical of whigs, against the whig government, whose supporters had denounced him. After an examination extending over several weeks, the House of Lords refused to adopt the charges against him; but it also refused to pass a vote of thanks.

The government was loth to accept this ambiguous decision as an acquittal. Peterborough was, indeed, on 30 July, admitted to kiss the queen's hand; but he was also ordered to render an account of the money which he had received and expended during his command; and as he had kept no accounts (RICHARDS, xxv. 36–7), his property was attached till he should have cleared up his pay-lists. For the next two years he was occupied with 'the compilation of ledgers,' the trouble of which was broken only by his domestic sorrows. In March 1709 his wife, to whom, notwithstanding his reputation for gallantry, he seems to have been soberly attached, died of a quinsy; and in the early months of 1710 his two sons, first the younger and then the elder, died of small-pox. But the change of ministry came as a relief to his distress, personal and financial. Within a week it was rumoured that he was to be general of marines and first lord of the admiralty. On 2 Nov. he was actually appointed captain-general of marines with the pay of 5*l.* a day. In December he was nominated ambassador extraordinary to Vienna, and was on the point of starting when, at the request of the House of Lords, he was stayed, pending a renewed inquiry into the conduct of the war in Spain. Peterborough and Galway both gave their account of what had taken place, and after a warm debate, extending over several days, Peterborough's account was approved, and in an address to the queen the lords expressed their admiration for the many great and eminent services he had performed 'during the time he had the honour of commanding the army in Spain.' 'The votes of the peers proved literally nothing,' except that sixty-eight of them were tories and only forty-eight were whigs (STEBBING, p. 178). The majority voted panegyrics on Peterborough as implying censure on Marlborough. The mob, with whom Marlborough was out of favour, took the same view, and Peterborough was the idol of the hour. On one occasion, it is said, the mob mistook Peterborough for Marlborough, and were on the point of dragging him through the kennel, when Peterborough convinced them of their error by saying, 'In the first place, I have only five guineas in my pocket; and in the second, they are very much at your service.'

On 11 Feb. 1710–11, the day after the vote of thanks, Peterborough started for Vienna. The primary object of the mission was to get the ambassador out of London; the nominal end proposed was to bring about more cordial relations between the emperor and the Duke of Savoy. Peterborough's diplomacy seems to have been conducted with the same irregularity as his campaigning. Before his work at Vienna was half finished he went to Turin, and while there the death of the emperor Joseph I (6 April 1711) led him to recur to his former project of putting the Duke of Savoy on the throne of Spain. Returning to Vienna, he received despatches censuring his conduct. He started for England at once, and, travelling post, without stopping, landed at Yarmouth attended by only one servant. According to Swift (*Works*, xv. 455), he had scattered the rest of his suite in several parts of Germany. 'He sent expresses and got here before them.' The next day he had an audience of the queen, who received him graciously. The ministers did not conceal their dissatisfaction; but, troublesome colleague as he was, they recognised that he might be still more troublesome as an adversary, and hastened to get him out of the country by appointing him ambassador extraordinary to the diet about to assemble at Frankfort for the election of the emperor. At Frankfort he plunged into a sea of intrigue about matters outside his instructions. He is said to have suggested that, in default of male heirs to the new emperor, Charles VI, the Elector of Saxony ought to be king of the Romans. His idea, for the moment, was to have 'a levée of suppliant kings expecting their destinies from England.' He soon tired of the situation—everybody mistrusted him; and was glad to go to Italy on a nominal mission, the true object of which was to keep him out of the way.

During 1712 he was, for the most part, at Venice, busy over some make-believe political intrigue for his government, or engaged in some more real love intrigue for himself, possibly paying his court to Anastasia Robinson [q. v.], who was then living at Venice with her family. In January 1712–13 he returned to England, eager to be at work. Swift, who saw him on the afternoon of his arrival, wrote of him: 'He left England with a bruise by his coach overturning that made him spit blood, and was so ill, we expected every post to hear of his death; but he outrode it, or outdrank it, or something, and is come home lustier than ever. He is at least sixty, and has more spirits than any young fellow I know of in England' (*ib.* iii. 94). During the session he occasionally spoke in the House of Lords, and especially on 28 May, against the Earl of Findlater's motion for the repeal of the union with Scotland (*Parl. Hist.* vi. 1217). In his brief periods of leisure about London he made famous his hospitality at Parson's Green, where his conversation and his cookery, his music and his wall-fruit delighted the artistic and literary society of Queen Anne. The ministers, however, were anxious to keep him well-disposed. He was appointed colonel of the royal horse guards, and on 4 Aug. was nominated a K.G. In November he was sent as ambassador extraordinary to the Duke of Savoy (now become king of Sicily), and to the other Italian princes. It was a mere mission of compliment, and very positive instructions minimised his talent for mischief. In March 1714 he was appointed governor of Minorca, but before he could go thither the queen died, King George ascended the throne, and, on the return of the whigs to power, Peterborough was summarily recalled. On his way home through Paris he was entertained at dinner by the Marquis de Torcy, and Louis XIV 'ordered the fountains at Marly to be set working in his honour, keeping him by his side as he walked, and treating him "avec beaucoup de distinction"' (STEBBING, p. 191).

But in England he was 'a fallen star.' The day after his return he presented himself at court; he was coldly received, and an order was sent to him forbidding his reappearance. It was the end of his official career, though he continued to attend in the House of Lords as late as 1731, and frequently spoke with much wit and vehemence. In June 1715 he was deprived of his colonelcy of the blues (PACKE, p. 76). In 1717 he went to Italy in search of health. At Bologna he was arrested on suspicion of being concerned in a conspiracy against the Pretender, and was detained for a month till he made his identity clear to his captors. The excitement restored his health. He hastened back to England to clamour for revenge; but the story that the English fleet was sent off Civita Vecchia to exact compensation is not true. The papal government, however, expressed regret, laying the blame on the cardinal-legate at Bologna. In 1719 Peterborough again went to Italy on a self-constituted mission to the Duke of Parma, and is said to have brought about the downfall of Alberoni, who, on his part, had described him as 'a most pretentious fool and consummate blackguard' (ARMSTRONG, *Elisabeth Farnese*, p. 122). He was again in France in 1720, when Dubois wrote of him as likely to injure the Anglo-French alliance by his pernicious habit of belittling the resources of England. It was afterwards said that in 1722 he married Anastasia Robinson, the singer. At the time, however, the marriage—if there was one—was kept strictly secret; it was believed by many that she was Peterborough's mistress—a belief that gained ground when, apparently in January 1723–4, Peterborough publicly caned Senesino, the leading tenor of the opera company, for insolence to her, and compelled him to ask her pardon on his knees. Lord Stanhope, afterwards earl of Chesterfield, jestingly spoke of Peterborough as 'an old Don Quixote,' and in consequence received a challenge: the duel, however, was prevented by the civil power (*Letters of Lady Mary Wortley Montagu*, ed. Bohn, i. 352–3). After this, Miss Robinson, as she was to the world, quitted the stage and settled down in a house taken for her by Peterborough near Parson's Green, Fulham.

About the same time began a correspondence with Mrs. Howard, the mistress of the Prince of Wales, afterwards George II [see HOWARD, HENRIETTA, COUNTESS OF SUFFOLK]. A set of verses addressed to her, beginning 'I said to my heart between sleeping and waking,' are not without merit, and led Walpole to include Peterborough in his list of 'noble poets;' but the letters themselves, written by a man of seventy to a deaf woman of forty, are 'the silliest of superannuated philandering' (STEBBING). They may perhaps be counted as one of his literary amusements, in which, and in the society of literary men, more especially Swift and Pope, with Arbuthnot and Gay, much of his time was passed. Tours in France or other parts of the continent filled up the rest. Mr. Stebbing speaks too of his military duties. In May 1722 his commission as general of marines, originally given in 1710, was enlarged to 'General of all the Marine Forces of Great Britain;' but there were no marine forces at the time, and the only duty Peterborough could be called on to perform was to receive his pay.

He was always needy and in debt. He asserted that he had impoverished his estate by maintaining the army in Spain at his own cost; but he had no accounts to show in support of this statement, and no government could accept it. By reckless expenditure and by confusion between his own and the public money he unquestionably lavished a great deal, but not necessarily on the army. He had never been wealthy, and on the death of his uncle in 1697 the family estates, separated from the title, had gone to his cousin, Lady Mary, daughter of Henry Mordaunt, second earl of Petreborough [q. v.], in her own right Baroness Beauchamp and Mordaunt, and wife of Henry Howard, seventh duke of Norfolk [q. v.], from whom she was divorced in 1700. On the duke's death in 1701 she married Sir John Germain [q. v.], and though Peterborough endeavoured to recover the estates from her, the House of Lords, decided against him. At her death, in November 1705, Peterborough succeeded to the baronies, but she left the property to her husband. Peterborough contested Germain's right, but the House of Lords again decided against him. He found ways, however, of raising fresh actions, which were still pending when Germain died in 1718. The litigation then came to an end, Peterborough having already declared that he would withdraw his claim if Germain left the property to his second wife, Lady Elizabeth Germain [q. v.]

During his later years Peterborough resided for the most part near Southampton, in a pleasant cottage with a large garden, known as Bevis Mount, the site of the present Bevois town, but then 'beautiful beyond imagination,' as Pope wrote to Mrs. Knight (*Works*, ix. 451). He suffered from stone. For some years his death, at frequent intervals, had seemed imminent, and in the spring of 1735 he was advised that an operation offered the only chance of life. His wife, still unacknowledged, but latterly, in deference to her scruples, allowed to wear her wedding ring, was his constant attendant, 'the sunshine' of his home. Before undergoing the operation he assembled a party of his relations in the rooms of his nephew, Stephen Pointz, in St. James's Palace, and formally introduced her as the Countess of Peterborough (Burney, *Hist. of Music*, iv. 247–9). Shortly afterwards he publicly married her (Pope, *Works*, ix. 318).

In July he was at Bevis Mount, conscious of his approaching end, and writing to Lady Suffolk that the example of the Emperor Julian showed him 'how a soldier, how a philosopher, how a friend of Lady Suffolk's ought to die. I want,' he continued, 'to make an appointment with you, Mr. Pope, and a few friends more to meet upon the summit of my Bevis hill, and thence, after a speech and a tender farewell, I shall take my leap towards the clouds (as Julian expresses it) to mix amongst the stars.' Pope visited him towards the end of August, and was much struck by the extreme contrast between the vivacity and sprightliness of his mind and the attenuation of his body (*ib.* ix. 319–20). Peterborough was afterwards in London for a few days, alternating between bed and dinner parties. He had been meditating a journey to the south of France, but he ultimately went with his wife to Lisbon. He died there on 25 Oct. 1735, six days after his arrival. The body was brought back to England by his widow, and buried in the family vault in Turvey Church, Bedfordshire. His second son Henry is separately noticed.

For some years Peterborough had amused himself in writing his memoirs in three manuscript volumes. The countess, in looking over them, was so shocked that she burnt them. A lady who had also seen them told Dr. Burney that Peterborough boasted of having committed three capital crimes before he was twenty. But the memoirs were in all probability wholly or in great part fictitious. In Peterborough's mind there was a strange confusion between imagination and fact, and his unsupported assertions cannot be accepted as trustworthy contributions to his biography. In matters of history, where his character, his reputation, and his interest were at stake, statements emanating from him and known to be false must be held as substantiating the graver charge. He was of untiring energy, restless in mind and body. His parliamentary speeches and letters show him to have been clever, witty, incisive in thought and word. He was a generous and judicious patron of men of letters and science, who gratefully acknowledged his benefactions, and gave him a higher reputation than he otherwise deserved. Swift, however, who had a certain affection for him, calls him with friendly insight 'the ramblingest lying rogue on earth,' and to Macky's unflattering portrait in the 'Memoirs' Swift gave the rare distinction of his approval. He was as foolishly careless of his own as he was culpably careless of the public money; and the common idea that he was a distinguished commander of fleets or armies rests only on his own statements; while the official documents and the reports of the men who were with him in Spain testify to his incompetence. He is described as a little spare man, 'a skeleton in outward figure,' according to Swift's familiar lines, of pleasing appearance and winning manners. His portrait, by Dahl, is in the possession of the Earl of Carlisle; another, by Kneller, belonging to Mr. W. B. Stopford, was engraved by Houbraken. A third portrait belongs to Viscount Boyne.

[Of the biographies of Peterborough, that in the Men of Action Series, by Mr. William Stebbing, is the best. All the other memoirs—those by Colonel F. S. Russell (1887), by G. Warburton (1853), by Charnock (Biog. Nav. iii. 314), by Sir Walter Scott (Preface to the Memoirs of Captain George Carleton, 1809), or by Lord Ribblesdale (Fortnightly Review, August 1885), depend on the Memoirs of Captain Carleton, which Mr. Stebbing rightly treats as apocryphal, or on Peterborough's own imaginings. Colonel A. Parnell, in his History of the War of the Succession in Spain (1888), is the only recent historian who has shaken himself clear of Carleton's Memoirs, which he proves to be fictitious, and has based his history of the campaigns of 1705–1706 solely on official and contemporary accounts, which in their estimate of Peterborough's conduct differ considerably from that previously received. In a later article on Carleton in the English Historical Rev. (January 1891) Colonel Parnell reaches the conclusion that the part of the Memoirs relating to Peterborough was, directly or indirectly, supplied by Peterborough himself, and inclines to the belief that Swift was the author. One of Carleton's stories, quoted by every subsequent writer—that of Peterborough starting off in the night to the fleet, going on board Captain Price's ship (the Somerset, p. 148), or the Leopard (STANHOPE, *Reign of Queen Anne*, cabinet edit. i. 257), and sending off a pinnace in the dark with orders to the admiral—is contradicted by the logs of the Somerset and Leopard (in the Public Record Office), which are both unusually full. Of Freind's Account of the Earl of Peterborough's Conduct in Spain (1707) and Remarks on Dr. Freind's Account mention has been made in the text. In the Impartial Enquiry into the Management of the War in Spain . . . (1712), the anonymous author either printed, or referred to as printed in Freind's Account or elsewhere, all available papers bearing on his subject. His conclusion is adverse to Peterborough. The letters from Queen Mary to William in Ireland are in Dalrymple's Memoirs of Great Britain and Ireland (8vo, 1790), vol. iii. The letters of Marlborough and Godolphin, printed in Coxe's Life of Marlborough (Bohn's edition) are important; but Coxe's own narrative is based on Carleton and on Freind. References to the printed and manuscript material relating to the war in Spain and to Peterborough's conduct therein are given by Colonel Parnell. It is only necessary here to refer more particularly to Foreign Office Records, Spain, vols. 132–5; Richards's Journals in the British Museum (Stowe MS. 367, xxv); Peterborough's letters to Leake in Addit. MS. 5438; Boyer's Annals of the Reign of Queen Anne and his History of the Reign; Targe's Hist. de l'Avénement de la Maison de Bourbon au Trône d'Espagne; Parl. Hist. vols. v. and vi., and Lords' Journals, vol. xviii. Peterborough's letters to General Stanhope were privately printed by Lord Mahon (afterwards Stanhope) in 1834. There are some interesting notices of Peterborough in G. F. W. Munby and Thomas Wright's Turvey and the Mordaunts (1893), in Earl Cowper's Private Diary (p. 27), and the Duke of Manchester's Court and Society from Elizabeth to Anne (ii. 244–5, 269, 277), and very many in the letters of Pope, ed. Elwin and Courthope, and of Swift, ed. Scott. The letters to Mrs. Howard, printed in Croker's Letters to and from the Countess of Suffolk, are in Addit. MS. 22625. See also Collins's Peerage (1768), iii. 209, and Doyle's Baronage.]

J. K. L.

MORDAUNT, HENRY, second EARL OF PETERBOROUGH (1624?–1697), cavalier, eldest son of John, first earl of Peterborough, by Elizabeth, only daughter and heir of William, lord Howard of Effingham, was born about 1624. His grandfather, Henry, fourth lord Mordaunt, a strict Roman catholic, lay for a year in the Tower on suspicion of complicity in the Gunpowder plot, and died in 1608. His grandfather's widow, Lady Margaret, daughter of Henry, lord Compton, being also a staunch adherent of the ancient faith, was deprived by James I of the custody of her eldest child, JOHN, afterwards first EARL OF PETERBOROUGH (*d.* 1642), who was made a ward of Archbishop Abbot, and educated in protestant principles at Oxford. Removed to court by the king, who was struck by his beauty and intelligence, the first earl was made a K.B. on the occasion of Prince Charles being created Prince of Wales, 3 Nov. 1616, and was remitted a fine of 10,000*l.* which had been imposed upon and left unpaid by his father. By Charles I he was created Earl of Peterborough, by letters patent of 9 March 1627–8. On the outbreak of the civil war he adhered to the parliament, and held the commission of general of the ordnance under the Earl of Essex, but he died of consumption, 18 June 1642. He left, besides his heir, Henry, the second earl, a son John, afterwards Lord Mordaunt of Reigate and Viscount Mordaunt of Avalon [q. v.]; and a daughter, Elizabeth, who married Thomas, son and heir to Edward Howard, first lord Howard of Escrick [q. v.]

Henry, the second earl, was educated at Eton, under Sir Henry Wotton, and shortly before the outbreak of the civil war was sent to France to be out of harm's way. He returned to England in 1642, and served for a little while in the parliamentary army, but in April 1643 deserted to the king at Oxford. He fought gallantly at Newbury (20 Sept. 1643), being wounded in the arm and thigh, and having his horse shot under him. In command of a regiment raised at his own expense he served in the west during the following summer and winter, but was in France during the later phases of the struggle. In 1646 he returned to England and compounded for his estates. A private interview with Charles as he passed through Ampthill to Hampton Court, in the summer of 1647, prompted him to make a last effort on the king's behalf, and in July of the following year he united with the Duke of Buckingham and the Earl of Holland in raising the royal standard at Dorking. The design was to seize Reigate, but foiled in this, the insurgents were driven back upon Kingston, and eventually dispersed in the neighbourhood of Harrow by the parliamentary forces (7 July) [cf. RICH, HENRY, EARL OF HOLLAND, 1589?–1649, and VILLIERS, GEORGE, second DUKE OF BUCKINGHAM]. Mordaunt was severely wounded, but escaped to Antwerp, and in the following year returned to England and recompounded for his estates (May 1649). On the Restoration, Peterborough was appointed (6 Sept. 1661) governor of Tangier, of which he took possession on 30 Jan. 1661-2, but being inadequately provided with men and money for the defence and development of the place, and harassed by intrigues on the part of his subordinates, he resigned his command for a life pension of 1,000*l.* in the course of a few months. On his return to England he served in the Dutch war, at first as a volunteer in the fleet of the Earl of Sandwich, afterwards in command of a ship under the Duke of York (1664–5). In 1670 he was appointed groom of the stole to the Duke of York, and on 24 Feb. 1672–3 ambassador extraordinary to arrange the terms of his proposed marriage with the Archduchess Claudia Felicitas of Innsbruck. He had hardly crossed the Channel, however, when the news of the emperor's determination to marry the archduchess himself put an end to the project. He was then commissioned to ascertain the respective personal and other attractions of the Princess Mary of Modena [q. v.], and several other ladies between whom the duke's choice lay, and Mary having been fixed upon, proceeded to Modena in the following August as ambassador extraordinary to arrange the match. After some demur on the score of religion, the pope refusing a dispensation for the marriage of the princess with a prince who was not a declared catholic, the scruples of the family were overcome, Peterborough being proxy for the duke (30 Sept. 1673). Peterborough then escorted the princess to England, landing at Dover on 21 Nov.

On 10 July 1674 Peterborough was sworn of the privy council, and in 1676 was appointed deputy earl-marshal. In 1680 he was deprived of that office and his pension, and excluded from the council, on suspicion of complicity in the so-called Popish plot. Nevertheless, though suffering from fever, he had himself carried down to Westminster Hall, in order to vote against the condemnation of Lord Stafford (7 Dec.) In October 1681 he was summoned to Scotland by the Duke of York, whom he attended on his return to England in the following March. On 28 Feb. 1682–3 he was restored to his place in the council. He bore St. Edward's sceptre at the coronation of James II, by whom on 19 April 1685 he was appointed groom of the stole. On 18 June following he was made K.G., and soon afterwards colonel of the 3rd regiment of horse. In March 1686–7 he was received into the Roman church. At the revolution he attempted to make his escape from the country, but was taken near Ramsgate and committed to the Tower (24 Dec. 1688). On 26 Oct. 1689 he was impeached of high treason 'in departing from his allegiance, and being reconciled to the church of Rome.' The proceedings, however, abated by the subsequent dissolution, and on 9 Oct. 1690 he was released on bail. In February 1695–6 he again fell under suspicion of treasonable practices, and was confined to his own house, but was enlarged in the following May. Peterborough was lord of the manors of Turvey in Bedfordshire and Drayton in Northamptonshire, and was for many years lord-lieutenant of the latter county. He died on 19 June 1697, and was buried in the parish church of Turvey.

Peterborough married, in 1644, Lady Penelope O'Brien, daughter of Barnabas, sixth earl of Thomond, by whom he had two daughters: Elizabeth, who died unmarried, and Mary, who married Henry Howard, seventh duke of Norfolk [q. v.], from whom she was divorced in 1700. The Countess of Peterborough was groom of the stole to Mary of Modena, and survived till April 1702.

In his later years Peterborough gratified his pride and amused his leisure by compiling, with the assistance of his chaplain, 'Succinct Genealogies of the Noble and Ancient Houses of Alno or De Alneto, Latimer of Duntish, Drayton of Drayton, Mauduit of Werminster, Greene of Drayton, Vere of Addington, Fitz-Lewes of Westhornedon, Howard of Effingham, and Mordaunt of Turvey. Justified by Publick Records, Ancient and Extant Charters, Histories, and other Authentic Proofs, and enriched with divers Sculptures of Tombs, Images, Seals, and other Curiosities,' London, 1685, fol. The work is of extreme rarity, only a very few copies, probably not more than twenty-five in all, having been printed. It bears the pseudonym Robert Halstead on the title-page, and is dedicated to Peterborough, whose life is narrated at length, while his brother is barely mentioned (cf. DIBDIN, *Ædes Althorpianæ*, p. 186; *Notes and Queries*, 1st ser. vi. 553, 4th ser. iii. 481, 541, iv. 18; LOWNDES, *Bibl. Man.*)

[The principal authority is the Succinct Genealogies above mentioned. Subsidiary authorities are: Nichols's Progresses of James I, i. 221, ii. 333, iii. 215; Nicolas's Hist. of British Knighthood, vol. ii. Chron. List, p. lxviii, vol. iii. Chron. List, p. xv; Hist. MSS. Comm. 3rd Rep. App. p. 272, 5th Rep. App. p. 151, 7th Rep. App. pp. 467, 485, 490, 496, 744, 8th Rep. App. p. 280, 9th Rep. App. pp. 83, 112, 10th Rep. App. pt. iv. p. 64, 11th Rep. App. pt. v. pp. 228, 281, pt. vii. p. 30; Cal. State Papers, Dom. 1645–7 p. 571, 1648–9 p. 173, 1649–50 p. 529, 1650 p. 561, 1655 p. 220, 1664–5 pp. 56, 275, 537; Cal. Committee for Compounding, &c., 1665–6, p. 500; A Letter from Hampton Court, 1648, 4to; The Declaration of the Right Hon. the Duke of Buckingham and the Earles of Holland and Peterborough, &c., 1648, 4to; A Perfect Diurnal, 3–10 July 1648, and Perfect Occurrences, 7–14 July 1648 (King's Pamphlets E. 451 and 525); Whitelocke's Mem. p. 317; Bulstrode's Mem., 1721, p. 169; Evelyn's Diary, 1 Dec. 1661, 9 July 1677, 7 Feb. 1685; Pepys's Diary, ed. Lord Braybrooke; Chamberlayne's Angliæ Notitia, 1670 and 1677; Clarendon's Rebellion, book xi. §§ 5–7; Life, 1827, ii. 356; Burnet's Own Time, fol. i. 353, 360, 477, 591, 606; Reresby's Mem. ed. Cartwright, pp. 334, 424; Hatton Corresp. (Camden Soc.), i. 109–10, 201–202, 214; Luttrell's Relation of State Affairs, i. 17, 60, 336, 339, 355; Cobbett's State Trials, vii. 1553; Howell's State Trials, xii. 1234, 1238; Clarendon and Rochester Corresp.; Macpherson's Hist. of Great Britain, i. 187, 301; Clarendon State Papers, ii. 480; Collins's Peerage, ed. Brydges, iii. 319 et seq.; Burke's Extinct Peerage; Archdall's Peerage of Ireland, ii. 38; Klopp's Fall des Hauses Stuart, i. 354 et seq.; Strickland's Lives of the Queens of England, Mary of Modena, chap. i.; Notes and Queries, 2nd ser. vii. 93; Bridges's Northamptonshire, ii. 239, 250, 380; Baker's Northamptonshire; Lysons's Mag. Brit. i. 147; Reilly's Hist. Anecdotes of the Families of the Boleynes, Careys, Mordaunts, &c., 1839; Russell's Earl of Peterborough and Monmouth, 1887.] J. M. R.

MORDAUNT, HENRY (1681?–1710), captain in the navy, was the second son of Charles Mordaunt, third earl of Peterborough [q. v.], and nephew of Henry Mordaunt, member of parliament for Brackley from 1692 to 1701, with whom he has been strangely confused (Foster, *Alumni Oxonienses*; Collins, *Peerage*, pp. 207, 213; Charnock, iii. 274). On 9 April 1703 he was promoted to be captain of the Mary galley. In 1705 he was returned to parliament for Malmesbury, and in 1706 was captain of the Resolution of 70 guns in the Mediterranean. On 13 March 1706–7, with the Enterprise and Milford frigates in company, he sailed from Barcelona for Genoa, carrying as passengers his father, the Earl of Peterborough, and an ambassador from the titular king of Spain to the Duke of Savoy. On the 19th he fell in with a French squadron of six ships of the line, newly out of Toulon, and which, with clean bottoms, came up fast with the English. The Earl of Peterborough and the ambassador went on board the Enterprise, which, with the Milford, effected her escape. By daybreak of the 20th the enemy's ships were well up with and engaged the Resolution, which defended herself stoutly. In the afternoon, when she was much shattered, Mordaunt ran her ashore near Ventimiglia. The French then sent in their boats to burn her, but these were beaten off. During the night an 80-gun ship succeeded in getting within gunshot, and as the Resolution was by this time full of water, and her magazine drowned, it was resolved to set her on fire and abandon her. This was done during the morning of the 21st; her men were all landed, and by eleven o'clock the ship was burnt to the water. Mordaunt was severely wounded in the leg, and obliged to return to England, which he did overland, through France, on a passport readily given on his father's request. On 25 Nov. 1709 he was tried by court-martial for the loss of his ship, and acquitted, the court resolving that he had behaved with 'great courage and conduct' (*Minutes of the Court-martial*). Three months later, 24 Feb. 1709–10, he died at Bath, of small-pox. He was not married. His portrait, by Sir Godfrey Kneller, belongs to Sir Frederick Milner, bart.

[Charnock's Biog. Nav. iii. 274.] J. K. L.

MORDAUNT, Sir JOHN (*d.* 1504), speaker of the House of Commons, son and heir of William Mordaunt of Turvey, Bedfordshire, and his wife Margaret, daughter of John Peeke of Cople in that county, had succeeded to his paternal inheritance in 1481, at which time his mother was living. He was one of the commanders at the battle of Stoke, 20 June 1487, and was chosen speaker of the House of Commons in the parliament which assembled at Westminster on 3 Nov. the same year, being representative of the county of Bedford. He was called to the degree of serjeant-at-law 10 Sept. 1495, was constituted one of the king's serjeants on 25 Nov. following, and became chief justice of Chester in or about 1499. He received the honour of knighthood at the creation of Henry, prince of Wales, 18 Feb. 1502–3, and on 6 April 1504 was appointed high steward of the university of Cambridge (Cooper, *Athenæ Cantabr.* i. 9). He became chancellor of the duchy of Lancaster 24 June 1504, and on 28 Aug. following he had a grant from Pope Julius II of special liberties and privileges. For many years he was a member of the privy council. He died between 5 Sept. and 6 Dec. 1504, and was buried in the church of Turvey, where there is a handsome altar-tomb, with his effigy in armour, and a Latin inscription.

He married Edith, daughter and heiress of Sir Nicholas Latimer, knight of Duntish, Dorset, and by this lady, who survived him, left John, his son and heir (afterwards Lord Mordaunt of Turvey) [q. v.], William, and Joan, wife of Giles Strangeways.

By his will he gave legacies to the churches of Turvey, Mulso, and Stachedon, the monasteries of Newnham and Wardon, and for the establishment of a perpetual chantry in the church of Turvey, for two secular chaplains, one of whom was to teach grammar freely (NICOLAS, *Testamenta Vetusta*, p. 461).

[Cambridge Antiquarian Communications, i. 275; Churton's Lives of Smyth and Sutton, pp. 100–3, 247, 453, 490; Dugdale's Baronage; Halstead's Genealogies; Lysons's Bedfordshire, p. 147; Manning's Speakers, p. 129; Expenses of Elizabeth of York, pp. 101, 210; Sharpe's Peerage (1833), sig. 3 G 6.] T. C.

MORDAUNT, JOHN, first BARON MORDAUNT OF TURVEY (1490?–1562), born about 1490, was son of Sir John Mordaunt (*d.* 1504) [q. v.] He became a courtier of Henry VIII, was sheriff of Bedfordshire and Buckinghamshire in 1509, was knighted in 1520, and attended the meeting of Henry and Charles V at Gravelines, and the Field of the Cloth of Gold in the same year; in 1522 he met Charles again at Canterbury. In 1526 he became a privy councillor, received the office of general surveyor of the king's woods, and was a commissioner to report on some of the king's manors. In 1530 he helped to conduct the inquiry into the extent of Wolsey's property.

Mordaunt supported the reformation and watched for a chance of enriching himself; he was a personal friend of Cromwell. On 4 May 1532 he was made Baron Mordaunt of Turvey, and twelve days later was present when the submission of the clergy was made to the king. He went to Calais the same year with the king with twelve men in his train. On 31 May 1533 he received Anne Boleyn at the Tower when she came to be crowned. In 1534 he was one of the peers engaged in the trial of Lord Dacre. In conjunction with his son John, a strong catholic, he attempted to secure for himself the priory of Harwolde, by making the prioress sign a deed of the nature of which she was ignorant; but this scheme was duly reported by the watchful Richard Layton [q. v.] in 1535. In May 1536 he took part in Anne Boleyn's trial; he went against the northern rebels and assisted to bring them to justice. In 1537 he carried the banner at Jane Seymour's funeral. Henry wished to get Drayton Manor, Northamptonshire, from him, but died before the matter could be arranged. Mordaunt, now old, acquiesced in the changes under Edward VI, but took no part in them, supported the government under Mary, and died in 1562. He married Elizabeth, daughter of Henry Vere of Addington Magna, Northamptonshire, and by her left three sons and several daughters, one of whom, Etheldred, became a nun of Barking. His eldest son, Sir John Mordaunt, was knighted 31 May 1533 at the coronation of Anne Boleyn. He was one of the first who declared for Queen Mary, was of her privy council (*Acts Privy Council*, 1552–4, passim), and died in 1570, having married Ela, daughter of Richard Fitzlewis of Thornton, Essex. His great-grandson was John, first earl of Peterborough [see under MORDAUNT, HENRY, third EARL].

[Letters and Papers Henry VIII, ed. Brewer and Gairdner, passim; Collins's Peerage, ed. Brydges, iii. 314 sqq.; Visitations of Bedfordshire (Harl. Soc.), pp. 42, 125; Acts of the Privy Council, 1550–4; Reilly's Historical Anecdotes of the Families of the Boleynes, Careys, &c., pp. 45 sq.; Halstead's Succinct Genealogies, pp. 525 sq.; Strype's Annals, I. ii. 230, Memorials, II. i. 494, ii. 206, III. ii. 160 sq.] W. A. J. A.

MORDAUNT, JOHN, BARON MORDAUNT of Reigate in Surrey and VISCOUNT MORDAUNT of Avalon in Somerset (1627–1675), cavalier and conspirator, born in 1627, second son of John, first earl of Peterborough [see under MORDAUNT, HENRY, second EARL], and brother of Henry, second earl [q. v.], was educated in France and Italy. On his return to England he took part with his elder brother Henry in the insurrection of July 1648. During the interregnum he married Elizabeth Carey, second daughter of Thomas Carey, youngest son of Robert Carey, first earl of Monmouth [q. v.] She is described by Clarendon as 'a young, beautiful lady, of a very loyal spirit and notable vivacity of wit and humour, who concurred with him in all honourable dedication of himself' (*Rebellion*, book xv. § 93); and in the hazardous intrigues which preceded the Restoration she appears on more than one occasion to have rendered material service both to her husband and the royal cause. In these intrigues Mordaunt was the prime mover. Long before Ormonde's adventurous visit to England in January 1657–8 Mordaunt had opened communications with him from London, and placed himself unreservedly at the disposal of the king. A plot was thereupon laid for an insurrection in Sussex, and Mordaunt received commissions from Charles for the levy of troops. One of the commissions, however, came through the treachery of a subordinate into the Protector's hands, and Mordaunt was arrested and committed to the Tower (15 April 1658). He was tried for high treason with Dr. John Hewit [q. v.] and Sir Henry Slingsby in the Painted Chamber, Westminster, on 2 June following. The court, including the president, Lord-commissioner Lisle, consisted of forty members, who combined the functions of judge and jury. Mordaunt at first disputed their jurisdiction, while his wife was busy bribing them. This work accomplished, she contrived to convey to Mordaunt a scrap of paper on which was written, 'For God's sake plead, plead for my sake, and stand disputing it no longer.' He thereupon pleaded not guilty, and succeeded in partially breaking down the evidence against him. One of the judges, the celebrated Colonel Pride, was taken ill and left the court; of the rest nineteen acquitted and nineteen condemned Mordaunt; the president gave his casting vote in his favour.

No sooner was Mordaunt at large than he recommenced his intrigues on behalf of the king, who by commission dated 11 March 1658-9 gave him full powers to treat with his subjects for his restoration. By the end of June 1659 a plot was laid for a general and simultaneous insurrection on 10 July following. On the day appointed Mordaunt, who by patent of the same date was raised to the peerage in anticipation of the event by the title of Baron Mordaunt of Ryegate in Surrey and Viscount Mordaunt of Avalon in Somerset, appeared in the neighbourhood of Guildford, accompanied by Charles Stuart, earl of Lichfield, afterwards third duke of Richmond, and a few others of the more devoted adherents of the king. They failed, however, to raise the country, and were promptly dispersed by the forces of the Commonwealth. Mordaunt escaped to London, where he lay in hiding until the miscarriage of Sir George Booth's rising completed the discomfiture of the royalists. He then withdrew to Calais, whence he closely observed the course of events in England, and kept up a regular correspondence with the king, whom he joined at Brussels in March 1659-60. With Sir John Grenville he acted as Charles's messenger in the following April, bearing his letter and declaration to the mayor and corporation of London (*Cal. State Papers*, Dom. 1659-60, p. 430). At the head of 'a troop of Spanish merchants all in black velvet coats' he received the king on Barham Down on his landing at Dover on 25 May. On 30 June following he was appointed constable of Windsor Castle and lord-lieutenant of Surrey. For alleged arbitrary acts done in the former capacity articles of impeachment were exhibited against him in the winter of 1666-7. A timely dissolution, however, put an end to the proceedings, and before they could be renewed he had received a full pardon from the king. Nevertheless, he resigned his office. On the death of his mother, the Dowager Countess of Peterborough (1671), Mordaunt became entangled in litigation with his brother Henry about the manor of Reigate, part of the family estates which she had held under the will of the late earl, and had endeavoured to settle on Mordaunt. The dispute ended in a compromise.

Mordaunt died at his house at Parson's Green, Fulham, on 5 June 1675, and was buried in the south aisle of the neighbouring church of All Saints, where an elaborate marble monument, by Bushnell and Bird, perpetuates his memory.

By Lady Mordaunt, who survived until April 1679, he left issue five sons and four daughters. Of the sons, all but the youngest, who took holy orders, entered the army; the eldest and most distinguished being the celebrated Charles Mordaunt, third earl of Peterborough [q. v.] Mordaunt's youngest daughter, Anne, married James Hamilton of Tollymore, co. Down, father of the first Earl of Clanbrassill of the second creation.

Mordaunt was unquestionably one of the most loyal, active, and enterprising of King Charles's friends in adversity. The very grave charge which led to his dismissal from the command of Windsor Castle and his subsequent neglect are attributed by Clarendon to the malice of his enemies. An excellent engraving of his head and shoulders by Faithorne, probably from a picture by Vandyck, is prefixed to an account of his trial, published in 1661 (fol.)

Lady Mordaunt was an intimate friend of Mrs. Margaret Godolphin [q. v.] and of Evelyn, who calls her 'the most virtuous lady in the world.' Her journal, consisting largely of her prayers, edited for private circulation by Lord Roden in 1856, shows her in the light of a devout high churchwoman. Prefixed is a copy of her portrait, painted in 1665 by Louise, princess Palatine, daughter of the queen of Bohemia.

[Clarendon's Rebellion and Life; Halstead's Succinct Genealogies, p. 405; Collins's Peerage, ed. Brydges, iii. 319 et seq.; Burke's Extinct Peerage; Granger's Biog. Hist. ed. 1775, iii. 24; The Trial of Mr. Mordaunt, second son of John, Earl of Peterborough, at the pretended High Court of Justice in Westminster Hall, the first and second of June 1658, London, 1661, fol.; Thurloe State Papers, vii. 80 et seq.; Mercur. Polit. 27 May to 3 June 1658; Cobbett's State Trials, v. 907, vi. 786; Reilly's Historical Anecdotes of the Families of the Boleynes, Careys, Mordaunts, &c., 1839; Anecdotes, &c., of Elizabeth, Viscountess Mordaunt, commencing 1656, 1810; Russell's Earl of Peterborough and Monmouth, 1887; Manning and Bray's Surrey, i. 303-4; Whitelocke's Mem. pp. 683, 700; Baker's Chron. pp. 651 et seq.; Clarendon State Papers, iii. 423 et seq.; Carte's Ormonde Papers, ii. 173, 184, 214 et seq.; Cal.

State Papers, Dom. 1648–9 p. 178, 1658–9 p. 16, 1659–60, 1660–1 p. 241, 1661–2 p. 196, 1667 pp. 246, 277; Lords' Journ. xii. 60–2, 77–79; Harl. Misc. iii. 373; Hist. MSS. Comm. 5th Rep. App. pp. 145, 150–2, 171, 207, 300, 7th Rep. App. pp. 103, 679, 10th Rep. App. pt. vi. pp. 188–216; Pepys's Diary, ed. Lord Braybrooke; Evelyn's Diary, 23 Oct. 1666; Evelyn's Life of Mrs. Godolphin, 1888, p. 137; Hatton Corresp. (Camd. Soc.), i. 73; Lysons's Environs of London, ii. 380; The Priuate Diarie of Elizabeth, Viscountess Mordaunt, ed. Earl of Roden, Duncairn, 1856, 8vo; Fagan's Descr. Cat. Engr. Works of Wm. Faithorne, 1888; Complete Peerage, ed. G. E. C., 1889, ii. 250.] J. M. R.

MORDAUNT, Sir JOHN (1697–1780), general, born in 1697, was eldest son by his first wife of Lieutenant-general Hon. Henry Mordaunt, M.P., treasurer of the ordnance and colonel of a marine regiment, and nephew of Charles Mordaunt, third earl of Peterborough [q. v.] He entered the army in 1721, and rose to be captain and lieutenant-colonel in the 3rd foot-guards (Scots guards). He is not to be confused with a contemporary, Colonel Hon. John Mordaunt, who in 1735 married the widowed Countess of Pembroke. On 15 Jan. 1741 Mordaunt was appointed colonel 58th foot, afterwards 47th (Lancashire) foot, and now 1st North Lancashire regiment, which was then being raised in Scotland. In June 1745 he was made brigadier-general. He commanded a brigade of infantry at the battle of Falkirk, and was sent by the Duke of Cumberland, with two regiments of dragoons and the Campbell highlanders, in pursuit of the rebels from Stirling. He commanded a brigade at Culloden. Horace Walpole says that after the battle the Duke of Cumberland presented Mordaunt with the Pretender's coach, on condition that he drove up to London in it. 'That I will, sir,' he replied, 'and drive on till it stops at the Cocoa Tree,' a famous tory coffee-house (*Letters*, i. 32). Mordaunt afterwards served in Flanders, and commanded a brigade at the battle of Val or Laffeldt. Some of his letters at this period to Counts Bentinck and Van Serooskerken are in Egerton MSS. Nos. 1721 and 1739. After his return home Mordaunt was appointed one of the inspecting generals. James Wolfe, then a young field-officer in the 20th foot, appears to have formed an attachment to a Miss Lawson, one of the maids of honour, and a niece of Mordaunt's, who was much at her uncle's place, and his letters at this period contain frequent notices of Mordaunt. The attachment was broken off in 1753. Writing from Mordaunt's seat, Freefolk, near Whitchurch, Hampshire, in July 1754, Wolfe remarks that Mordaunt's 'civility, good-breeding, and good humour make his house very easy and pleasant to his guests, and the country round has a variety of charms to those who love sport' (Wright, p. 290).

When invasion threatened in 1756, Mordaunt, a lieutenant-general, was appointed to command the great camp formed near Blandford in Dorset, and in the following year, immediately on Pitt succeeding to the premiership, was entrusted with the command of an expedition against Rochefort. Intelligence had reached Sir John Ligonier [see Ligonier, John, Earl Ligonier], through one Robert Clark, a sub-engineer (lieutenant), who had visited Rochefort in 1753, that, despite its importance as a great naval arsenal, the defences were incomplete and the garrison weak. The object of the expedition was therefore to attempt a surprise. The naval portion was entrusted to Admiral Hawke. Mordaunt's force consisted of ten regiments of foot and two of marines, with a detachment of light horse and a train of field artillery—there were no siege guns—with Henry Seymour Conway [q. v.] and Edward Cornwallis as brigadier-generals, James Wolfe as quartermaster-general, and Robert Clark, promoted at a step from lieutenant to lieutenant-colonel, as commanding engineer (Porter, vol. i.) Owing to the delays in taking up transport, Mordaunt did not start until 10 Sept., a fortnight before the equinox. Mordaunt, who had been a very active, energetic man, appears to have been in broken health. His instructions were 'to make a descent on the French coast at or near Rochelle, and by a vigorous impression to force that place and destroy all magazines, arsenals, shipping, &c.' After the 'success or failure' of this he was to make like attempts on L'Orient or Bordeaux, or any places he might think suitable from Bordeaux homewards to Havre (*Proceedings of a General Court-martial*, &c.) Mordaunt asked what he should do if the ships were detained by contrary winds in sight of coast long enough to enable the French to mass troops on the menaced points, and was told that the practicability or otherwise of the descent must be left to his discretion (*ib.*) The islands of Rhé and Oleron were not sighted until 20 Sept. 1757. Three days elapsed before the ships could get into Basque Roads. Once in the roads the further initiative rested with the land officers. A week was passed in holding indecisive councils of war, while rumours came that the defences had been improved since Clark's visit, that the garrison had been largely reinforced, and that they had the power of flooding the ditches. At last it was decided not to run the risk of an attack, and at the beginning of October the expedition, which had cost the country over a million sterling, returned ignominiously home. Wolfe wrote to one of his friends: 'The whole affair turned on the practicability of escalading Rochefort, and the two evidences brought to prove that the ditch was wet (in opposition to the assertions of the chief engineer, who had been in the place) are persons to whom, in my mind, very little credit should be given. Without this evidence we should have landed, and must have marched to Rochefort, when, in my opinion, the place would have been taken or surrendered in forty-eight hours' (Wright, p. 397).

Pitt was furious at the failure, and declared from his place in the House of Commons that he 'believed there was a determined resolution, both in the naval and military commanders, against any vigorous exertion of the national power.' A court of inquiry was ordered, composed of Charles Spencer, duke of Marlborough, Lord George Sackville, and Major-general Waldegrave. They met on 9 Nov. 1757, and on 21 Nov. made a report unfavourable to Mordaunt. A general court-martial, of which Lord Tyrawley was president, the members including Charles, earl Cadogan [see under Cadogan, William, first Earl Cadogan], Sir Charles Howard [q. v.], Lord Delaware, and George Keppel, earl of Albemarle [q. v.], was assembled at Whitehall to try Mordaunt on the charge of disobeying his majesty's 'orders and instructions.' The court assembled on 14 Dec. 1757, and met, by successive adjournments, until 20 Dec., when it 'unanimously' found Mordaunt not guilty. After a week's consideration the king confirmed the finding.

Mordaunt, who was a K.B., and governor of Berwick, and was M.P. for Cockermouth from 1754 to 1767, became a major-general and colonel 12th dragoons (now lancers) in 1747, was transferred to the colonelcy of the 4th Irish horse (now 7th dragoon guards) in 1749, and to that of the 10th dragoons (now hussars) the same year; became a lieutenant-general in 1754 and general in 1770. He died a widower at Bevis Mount, Southampton, on 23 Oct. 1780, aged 83.

[Collins's Peerage, 5th edit. 1779, under 'Peterborough;' Home Office (War Office) Military Entry Books and London Gazettes under dates; Porter's Hist. Royal Engineers, vol. i.; Burrows's Life of Lord Hawke; H. Walpole's Letters; Wright's Life of Wolfe; Walpole's Hist. of George II, vol. iii.; Proceedings of the General Court-martial, of which there are numerous copies in the Brit. Mus.; also Egerton MSS. ut supra, and Add. MSS. in Nos. 23827-9, 32814, 32854, and 32876.]

H. M. C.

MORDEN, Sir JOHN (1623–1708), founder of Morden's College, Blackheath, son of George Morden (*d.* 1624), and grandson of Robert Morden of Thurlow in Suffolk, was born in the parish of St. Bride's, London, in the summer of 1623. As a 'Turkey' or Levantine merchant he, after some extraordinary vicissitudes, amassed a large fortune, returned to England 'from Aleppo' about the end of Charles II's reign, bought property in Charlton and Greenwich—his most considerable purchase being the manor of Wricklemarsh—and was on 20 Sept. 1688 made a baronet by James II. Morden was one of the twenty-four 'committees of the East India Company' to whom Robert Knox dedicated his 'Historical Relation of the Island of Ceylon' in 1681. He represented Colchester in parliament from 1695 to 1698, and was apparently a commissioner of excise in 1691. In 1695 he founded the excellent 'college' at Blackheath for the reception of 'poor, honest, sober, and discreet merchants who shall have lost their estates by accidents, dangers, and perils of the seas, or by any other accidents, ways, or means, in their honest endeavour to get their living by way of merchandising.' The pensioners were to be upwards of fifty years of age, bachelors or widowers, and members of the church of England. The first admission of members took place on 24 June 1700. The college, which is beautifully situated, is a quaint and spacious structure of richly coloured brick, with stone coigns and cornices, forming a quadrangle surrounded by piazzas. The building was designed by Sir Christopher Wren, and the chapel, consecrated by Bishop Spratt in 1705, contains some oak carving by Grinling Gibbons. Over the front are statues of Morden and his wife Susan, daughter of Sir Joseph Brand (*d.* 1674) of Edwardstone in Suffolk, and in the hall are their portraits, together with one of Queen Anne. An anagram and acrostic on John Morden ('I Honor Mend'), dated 1695, is also preserved in the college. In the chapel are the founder's arms, and a list of the benefactions made to the college since his death (given in Lysons, *Environs of London*, iii. 338). There is a cemetery (now disused) attached to the college.

Morden died on 6 Sept. 1708, and was buried on 20 Sept. in the chapel of his foundation. By his will, dated 15 Oct. 1702, and a codicil dated 9 March 1703, he endowed the college after his wife's death with a considerable real copyhold and personal property valued at about 1,300*l.* per annum. He placed in the college twelve 'decayed Turkey merchants,' each of whom wore a gown with his badge, and had 'a convenient apartment, with a cellar.' Their number was reduced by Lady Morden, but increased upon her death, on 27 June 1721, when the whole estate came to the charity. The college is administered by a treasurer, appointed by seven trustees, and Morden also bequeathed 30*l*. per annum for a chaplain, whose stipend was increased by Lady Morden to 60*l*. Among the past chaplains of the college was Moses Browne [q. v.], who is buried in the cemetery. The college now affords rooms, attendance, and an annual income of 113*l*., to about forty pensioners. There are in addition about one hundred out-pensioners, with allowances varying from 80*l*. downwards.

[Hasted's Kent, i. cv, 16, 36, and Hundred of Blackheath, ed. Drake, p. 126*n*.; Burke's Extinct Baronetages, p. 367; Le Neve's Pedigrees of the Knights, 1873, p. 331; Elmes's Life and Time of Sir Christopher Wren, 1852; Official Return of Members of Parl.; Roget's 'Old Water-Colour' Society, i. 180; Lysons's Collectanea, iii. passim; Stow's Survey, ed. Strype, bk. i. p. 220; Luttrell's Brief Hist. Relation, vi. 347; Hist. Register, 1721, Chron. Diary, p. 28; Notes and Queries, 7th ser. x. 56; Hist. MSS. Comm. 13th Rep. App. v. 412; E. C. Lefroy's Echoes from Theocritus, &c., 1885, containing two sonnets (xxv and xxvi) on 'A College for Decayed Merchants;' information kindly supplied by Horatio Elphinstone Rivers, esq., treasurer of the college from 1872, who possesses a volume of notes, papers, portraits, and poetical effusions relating to the college.] T. S.

MORDEN, ROBERT (*d.* 1703), geographer, commenced business in London as a map and globe maker about 1668. In 1688 he was in partnership with Thomas Cockerill at the Atlas in Cornhill. Though industrious he was always in pecuniary difficulties. His maps do not bear a high reputation. He died in St. Christopher-le-Stocks, London, in 1703, his estate being administered to on 13 Sept. of that year by his son Edward (*Administration Act Book, P. C. C.*, 1703, f. 176). His wife predeceased him.

Morden published: 1. 'Description . . . of a large Quadrant, contrived . . . by H. Sutton . . . with a description of a geodetical scheme and gnomonical instrument,' 8vo, London, 1669. 2. 'Geography rectified; or a description of the world in all its kingdoms, provinces, countries . . . their . . . names . . . customs . . . illustrated with seventy-six maps,' 4to, London, 1680 (2nd edit. 1688, 3rd edit. 1693, 4th edit. 1700). 3. 'A Book of the Prospects of the most remarkable places in and about the City of London. By R. Morden and P. Lea,' 4to, London [1700?]. 4. 'An Introduction to Astronomy, Geography, Navigation, etc., made easie by the description and uses of the cœlestial and terrestrial globes,' in seven parts, 8vo, London, 1702. 5. 'The new Description and State of England, containing the Maps of the Counties of England and Wales in fifty-three copper-plates,' 2nd edit., 4to, London, 1704. His maps were also used for the translation of Camden's 'Britannia,' edited by Bishop Gibson in 1695, 2 vols. folio, London, and for the Rev. Thomas Cox's 'Magna Britannia, antiqua et nova,' 6 vols. 4to, London, 1720–33.

Of Morden's maps issued separately the following are the most important: 1. An atlas of modern geography, without a title, about 1690. 2. 'Sea Atlas, drawn according to Mr. Wright's *alias* Mercator's projection,' 1699. 3. 'Atlas Terrestris,' 4to, London, about 1700. 4. 'Map of the World, drawn according to Mercator's projection,' about 1700. 5. 'A new Terrestrial Globe, made . . . by R. Morden and W. Berry,' about 1720.

His maps relating to Great Britain include: 1. 'Pocket-Book Maps of all the Counties of England and Wales,' 12mo, London, undated. 2. 'Cumberland,' about 1680. 3. 'A new Map of Ireland. By R. Morden and J. Overton,' about 1680. 4. 'The smaller Islands in the British Ocean,' about 1700. 5. 'Suffolk,' about 1700. 6. 'Actuall Survey of London, Westminster, and Southwark,' two sheets, 1700. 7. 'A Map containing the towns, villages, gentlemen's houses, roads, rivers . . . for twenty miles round London,' about 1700. 8. 'A Mapp of Scotland made by R. Gordon . . . corrected . . . by R. Morden,' about 1700. 9. 'Leicestershire,' about 1705. 10. 'Lincolnshire,' about 1705. 11. 'Middlesex and part of Hertfordshire, with the Roads,' 1730. 12. 'London, etc., accurately surveyed. By R. Morden and P. Lea,' 1732.

Of continental Europe his maps are: 1. 'France.' 2. 'Lorraine and Alsace. By R. Morden and W. Berry. With an alphabetical index in two sheets,' 1677. 3. 'A Map of the Seat of War in Germany and the Spanish Provinces. By R. Morden and W. Berry,' 1677. 4. 'Germany,' about 1680. 5. 'Parallela Græciæ veteris et novæ,' about 1700. 6. 'Sicily,' about 1700. 7. 'A new Mapp of the Estates of the Crown of Poland,' about 1700. 8. 'A new Draft of the Harbours of Vigo and Bayonna, shewing the late action of the English Fleet . . . with the forts and intrenchments,' about 1702. He likewise executed maps of 'Tartary,' about 1700, and the 'West Indies,' not published until 1740.

[Brit. Mus. Catalogues of Printed Books and Maps; Watt's Bibl. Brit.; Gough's Brit. Topography; Notes and Queries, 4th ser. ix. 64, 6th ser. xii. 227, 374, 7th ser. iv. 188; Boase and Courtney's Bibl. Cornub.] G. G.

MORDINGTON, Baron. [See Douglas, George, fourth Baron, *d.* 1741.]

MORE, ALEXANDER (1616–1670), protestant divine and Milton's antagonist, was born on 25 Sept. 1616 at Castres in Languedoc, where his father, a Scotsman, was rector of the protestant college. He was educated at Castres and Geneva, where in 1639 he was elected to the chair of Greek over the head of Stephen Le Clerc, and in 1642 succeeded Frederic Spanheim in the chair of theology. Grave charges of heresy and immorality, which he was unable to repel, led in 1648 to his resignation. He was, however, in the following year elected, through the influence of Salmasius, to the chair of theology at Middelburg, which he resigned in 1652 for that of ecclesiastical history at Amsterdam. On the appearance of the anonymous 'Regii Sanguinis Clamor ad Cœlum adversus Parricidas Anglicanos' (1652), it was generally, though falsely, ascribed to More, who was merely its editor, and Milton, who believed the common report, made a violent attack upon the supposed author's personal character in his 'Pro Populo Anglicano Defensio Secunda' [cf. Moulin, Peter du].

More published a spirited defence of his life entitled 'Alexandri Mori Ecclesiastæ et Sacrarum Litterarum Professoris Fides Publica contra Calumnias Joannis Miltoni' (the Hague, 1654, 4to), but suffered Milton to have the last word. In 1655 he visited Italy, returned to Holland in May 1656 to find his reputation fatally damaged, and in 1659 he was compelled to resign his professorship. Nevertheless, the church at Charenton, near Paris, welcomed him as its pastor; and there, except for a brief sojourn in England in the winter of 1661–2, he remained till his death on 28 Sept. 1670. He was interred in the Charenton cemetery. He did not marry.

More was a fine scholar and an eloquent preacher; in theology he leaned towards Arminianism; unless grossly calumniated throughout his public career, his morals must have been far less strict than his theology. Besides the 'Fides Publica' More's remains comprise some volumes of sermons and theological treatises, a few Latin poems, a 'Panegyric' on Calvin, and some other miscellanea. A portrait of More by Vaillant, and four engravings, two by Pass and Visscher, are mentioned by Bromley.

[The Fides Publica, above referred to; Senebier's Hist. Litt. de Genève, 1790, i. 195 et seq.; Haag's La France Protestante; Bruce's Critical Account of the Life, Character, and Discourses of Mr. Alexander Morus, 1813; Biographisch Woordenboek der Nederlanden, 1869; Masson's Life of Milton, 1871, iv. 586, 627; Bayle's Hist. and Crit. Dict. 2nd edit. (1737); Chalmers's Biog. Dict.; see art. Milton, John, poet.] J. M. R.

MORE, Sir ANTHONY, who is also known as Antonio Moro, but whose name was properly Anthonis Mor (1512?–1576?), portrait-painter, was born at Utrecht about 1512. His family was known as Mor van Dashorst, a small property near Utrecht, to distinguish them from a neighbouring family of Mor van Amersfoort; the names of his parents have not with certainty been ascertained. Mor was a pupil of the painter Jan Scorel, and his earlier works show that master's influence. A portrait of Scorel by Mor, painted in 1560, is in the collection of the Society of Antiquaries in London; this portrait is perhaps identical with that once forming part of Scorel's epitaph in St. Mary's Church at Utrecht. A portrait of a Utrecht canon in the Dresden Gallery by Mor has also been conjectured to represent Scorel. The earliest dated work of Mor is the double portrait, painted in 1544, of Cornelis van Horn and Antonis Taets, canons of Utrecht, which is now in the Berlin picture gallery. In 1547 Mor was admitted into the guild of St. Luke at Antwerp, and he spent 1550 and 1551 in Italy. Mor owed his advancement principally to Cardinal Granvelle, of whom he painted in 1549 a fine portrait, which is now in the Vienna picture gallery. Granvelle introduced Mor to the notice of the emperor Charles V and his son Philip of Spain. He was summoned to Madrid in 1552 and employed extensively at court, and was also sent on a commission to the court of Portugal, where he was treated with similar honour. Among the portraits still preserved at Madrid are those of Philip II, his sisters Joanna, princess of Brazil, and Mary, archduchess of Austria, and the latter's husband, afterwards the emperor Maximilian II. In 1553, when negotiations were commenced for a marriage between Philip and Queen Mary of England, Mor was sent to England to paint for Philip the well-known portrait of the queen which is now in the Prado Gallery at Madrid. Other portraits of the queen at this date are attributed to him, notably those in the collection of the Duke of Bedford at Woburn Abbey, of the dean and chapter at Durham Cathedral (Tudor Exhibition, 1890, No. 204), and in the picture gallery at Pesth. He appears to have received the honour of knighthood for his services, but the exact date is not known. It seems uncertain whether Mor returned to Madrid and then came back to England in the train of Philip, or whether he remained in England until Philip's arrival. He appears to have accompanied him to the Netherlands in 1555, when he was back at his home in Utrecht. He remained there or at Brussels for the next four years, but in 1559 was again in Madrid. Mor was on terms of great friendship with Philip. During a visit of Philip to his studio Mor excited the jealousy of the courtiers by the easy familiarity with which he treated the king. The authority of the inquisition was invoked, but on a hint from the king Mor secretly left Spain and returned to the Netherlands. Two versions of this incident are recorded, one by Carel van Mander (*Vie des Peintres*), and another by Palomino de Castro y Velasco (*Vidas de los Pintores*, quoted by Stirling-Maxwell in *Annals of the Artists of Spain*). Shortly afterwards Philip desired Mor to return to Spain, but the painter was retained at Brussels in the service of the Duke of Alva, and did not, or could not, comply with the king's request. Mor was residing at Utrecht again in 1564, but about 1568 he appears to have removed to Antwerp, where he remained for the rest of his life. The exact date of his death is uncertain, but he was employed on a picture of the 'Circumcision' for the cathedral at Antwerp in 1576, which he did not live to finish, and he was already dead in 1578, so that it appears probable that he died some time in the former year. By his wife Metge, Mor had several children, of whom Philips Mor van Dashorst was both a painter and a canon of Utrecht; a daughter, Catharina, the widow of one Casetta, died in 1589, and another daughter, Elisabeth, married Hendrik van der Horst, advocate, of Utrecht.

Mor ranks among the first portrait-painters of the world, but his religious or historical pictures merit little attention. His earlier pictures are fresher in colour and lighter in touch than those of his later years. His portraits are straightforward likenesses, set forth in a fine, picturesque, and essentially masculine style. They are to be seen in many collections on the continent, and there are also fine specimens in England, at Hampton Court and elsewhere. At Holyrood there is a fine portrait of Mary of Hungary, regent of the Netherlands, signed and dated 1554 (erroneously called Margaret, countess of Lenox). Among those in foreign galleries not already mentioned may be noticed the portraits of Hubert Goltzius (1576) at Brussels; the 'man with the gloves' (perhaps a portrait of Scorel) at Brunswick; the anonymous goldsmith (1564) in the Mauritshuis at the Hague; an anonymous portrait of a man (1565) in the Louvre at Paris; and those of Johann Gallus (1559) and his wife at Cassel. Another very fine portrait by Mor at the Hague, signed and dated 1561, probably represents William the Silent, prince of Orange, who in that year married Anna of Saxony, a portrait of whom by Mor was engraved by J. Houbraken (see *Oud Holland*, vii. 281).

Mor was so short a time in England that it would not be possible for him to have painted all the portraits of English patrons that are ascribed to him. It is doubtful whether any can be authenticated save those of Sir Thomas Gresham [q. v.] and Sir Henry Lee [q. v.], and both of them were probably painted by Mor at Antwerp. The fine portrait stated to represent the latter, in the collection of Viscount Dillon at Ditchley Park, Oxfordshire, is signed and dated 1568 (Tudor Exhibition, 1890, No. 268). Of Gresham several portraits exist, attributed with good reason to Mor; one, formerly in the Houghton collection, is now in the Hermitage Gallery at St. Petersburg (a replica, belonging to the Earl of Stamford, was in the Manchester Exhibition of 1857); a second is in the collection of Mr. G. W. G. Leveson Gower at Titsey, Surrey; a third in that of Sir John Neeld, bart. (engraved as frontispiece to Burgon's 'Life of Gresham'); a fourth at Mercers' Hall, and a fifth in the National Portrait Gallery—these two being replicas.

Mor painted several portraits of himself; one with a dog is in the collection of Earl Spencer at Althorp; another is in the Gallery of Painters at Florence, and another in the museum at Basle. In the collection of Sir Peter Lely there was a portrait of Mor with his wife, and in that of George Villiers, duke of Buckingham, were companion portraits of William Key the painter by Mor, and of Mor by Key. A portrait of Mor by himself was sold in Mr. Motteux's collection on 5 Feb. 1719. An engraved portrait of Mor drawing the portrait of Philip II is in the series published by H. Hondius, and, according to Carel van Mander, a medal was struck in Italy in his honour.

[Carel van Mander's Vie des Peintres, ed. H. Hymans; Van den Branden's Geschiedenis des Antwerpsche Schilder-School; Immerzeel's (and Kramm's) De Levens en Werken der Hollandsche en Vlaamsche Kunstschilders; Walpole's Anecdotes of Painting, ed. Wornum; Stirling-Maxwell's Annals of the Artists of Spain; Seguier's Dict. of Painters; Michiels's Histoire de la

Peinture Flamande; information from Dr. C. Hofstede de Groot and George Scharf, esq., C.B.] L. C.

MORE, EDWARD (1479–1541), divine, described as of Havant, was born in 1479, and was elected a scholar of Winchester College in 1492. He seems to have afterwards proceeded to New College, Oxford, and supplicated for the degree of B.D. in 1518. From 1498 to 1502 he held a fellowship at Winchester, and was head-master from 1508 to 1517. He was at a later date appointed canon of Chichester, was instituted vicar of Isleworth on 3 March 1514–15, and on resigning that living in August 1521 became rector of Cranford (Newcourt, *Repertorium*, i. 595, 675). On 29 Oct. 1526 he was admitted the eighth warden of Winchester College, and held that office, together with the rectory of Cranford, till his death. From 1528 to 1531 he was also archdeacon of Lewes (Le Neve, i. 263). As a schoolmaster he was reckoned a stern disciplinarian. In the Latin poem descriptive of the wardens of Winchester (in Willes's 'Poemata,' 1573), Christopher Johnson [q. v.], the author, writes:

Qui legit hic Morum, qui non et sensit eundem,
Gaudeat, et secum molliter esse putet.

More died in 1541, and was buried in the choir of Winchester College Chapel.

Another Edward More (1537?–1620), born about 1537, was third son (by his wife Anne Cresacre) of John More, the only son of Sir Thomas More [q. v.] He wrote a poem in rhyming ballad metre, entitled 'A lytle and bryefe treatyse called the Defence of Women, and especially of Englyshe women, made agaynst "The Schole House" [i.e. a published denunciation of women by Edward Gosynhyll, q. v.],' London, by John Kynge, 1560, 4to. More's book was licensed for publication in 1557–8. Copies are in the Bodleian and British Museum libraries. The dedication, dated 20 July 1557, from Hambledon, Buckinghamshire, is addressed to Sir Philip Hoby [q. v.] Hambledon was the seat of John Scrope, whose daughter married Edward More's eldest brother, Thomas. More describes himself at the time as twenty years old. Wood states that he wrote 'several little things' besides (*Athenæ Oxon.* ed. Bliss, i. 249–52). More's work was again licensed for publication to John Tisdale in 1563. Cresacre More, a nephew of Edward More, wrote of his uncle about 1600 that he was 'endowed with excellent gifts of nature, has a ready wit, tongue at will, and his pen glib, yet God knows he hath drowned all his talents in self-conceit in no worthy qualities.' He was buried at Barnborough, Yorkshire, on 2 May 1620. His sons Henry and Thomas, the jesuits, are noticed under Henry More, 1586–1661.

[Kirby's Winchester Scholars; Wood's Fasti Oxon.; H. C. Adams's Wykehamica, p. 75; Hazlitt's Bibliographical Collections; Ritson's Bibl. Poetica; Cresacre More's Life of Sir Thomas More, ed. Hunter, p. xlviii; cf. Foley's Records of Jesuits, xii. 702 sq.] S. L.

MORE or **MOORE**, Sir **GEORGE** (1553–1632), lieutenant of the Tower of London, eldest son of Sir William More, sheriff and vice-admiral of Surrey, was born on 28 Nov. 1553 at Loseley, near Guildford. A letter to his father from William Cole [q. v.], the president of Corpus Christi College, Oxford, proves that he was sent to study there in the summer of 1570 (1578 is an evident misprint), and was placed under the president's personal supervision (*Loseley MSS.* ed. Kempe). He was created M.A. on James's visit to Oxford on 30 Aug. 1605. Another George More matriculated at Exeter College, Oxford, on 3 Dec. 1575, aged 20, and took no degree (Wood, *Athenæ Oxon.* ii. 354). And yet another graduated B.A. 20 Feb. 1571–2 and M.A. 21 Jan. 1572–3. In 1574 the future lieutenant became a student at the Inner Temple (*ib.*) In 1604 he presented to the Bodleian some manuscripts and 40*l.* to buy books. More first entered parliament as member for Guildford in 1584–5, and represented that place in four parliaments of Elizabeth (1586–7, 1588–9, and 1593), and three of James I (1604–11, 1624–5). But he sat for Surrey in 1597–8, in 1614, and 1621–1622, and in the first two parliaments of Charles I's reign (1625 and 1626) (cf. Foster, *Alumni Oxon.* loc. cit.; *Official Returns of Members of Parliament*, passim). He is spoken of in Elizabeth's time as a frequent speaker, 'much esteemed for his excellent parts,' and his name constantly recurs in the debates under James I and Charles I, though he took no very prominent share in them. Wood says he was beloved of Elizabeth for his many services to the commonwealth. She knighted him in 1597, and at the same time he was made sheriff of Surrey and Sussex for the next year. About this time More obtained the wardship of young Edward Herbert, afterwards first Lord Herbert of Cherbury [q. v.], by the payment of 800*l.* to his guardian, Sir Francis Newport.

On his father's death in 1600 More succeeded to the Loseley estate, where the queen had previously paid the family four visits; on 3 Nov. 1601 he received a grant of the lordship and hundred of Godalming, and in 1602–3, shortly before the queen's death, was made one of the chamberlains of receipt of the exchequer. Elizabeth's favours were continued by James I, who with his queen twice visited More at Loseley, in August 1603 and in 1606. More was appointed receiver-general or treasurer to Prince Henry soon after the accession, and probably held this post till the prince's death in November 1612 (cf. BIRCH, *Life of Prince Henry*, p. 228). On 9 July 1611 More was made chancellor of the order of the Garter. After the arrest of Sir Gervase Helwys [q. v.] (1 Oct. 1615) More received the important and dangerous post of lieutenant of the Tower. The first state prisoner committed to his care was Robert Carr, earl of Somerset [q. v.], on 2 Nov. 1615. On Somerset's refusal to appear for trial More is said to have gone to Greenwich at midnight, and roused James, who was in bed. James, with tears in his eyes, besought his advice, and More subsequently persuaded the prisoner to give way, by the assurance that his trial was only a matter of form. James afterwards rewarded him by a gift of 1,000*l.*, of half of which he was said to have been cheated by Annandale (WELDON, *Secret History of James I*, ii. 233). The details of the story are not absolutely correct. James was at Newmarket at the time. It seems that some protest was made by Somerset before the trial, and that the king directed More in May 1616 to induce him to submit; if he still refused he was to be forced; but that if he seemed 'distracted in his wits' the trial must be adjourned (see letters printed in Kempe's edition of *Loseley MSS.*; SPEDDING, *Life of Bacon*, ii. 103–5, 131). In January 1617 More, 'wearye of that troublesome and dangerous office,' was trying to sell his post at the Tower, and in March Sir Allen Apsley (1569?–1630) [q. v.] (sworn lieutenant in his place on 3 April) bought it for 2,400*l.* More retired to Loseley, where in August he entertained Prince Charles. In 1621 he was granted a lease of crown lands at 60*l.* a year, in lieu of his pension as chancellor of the Garter, and in 1629 received a grant of 1,200*l.* for the surrender of this office. Although in 1624 'his long and faithful service to the king' is spoken of, James seems to have henceforth neglected him, and there are extant at Loseley many unanswered memorials of his to the king. He is spoken of as infirm and weak of body at James's funeral, but in spite of advancing age and infirmities kept his seat in parliament, and continued to speak (cf. the debate on Wentworth's election for Yorkshire). In August 1625 he opposed, as unconstitutional, Whistler's proposal to apply to the lords on the question of supply. That he supported Charles's early policy, however, is shown by the remark in March 1626 that he had 'lately shown leanings to the court,' and he voted for supply (FORSTER, *Eliot*, i. 277, 311, 315; FAWSLEY, *Debates*, Camd. Soc.) In 1625 he was one of the collectors of loans in Surrey. He died at Loseley on 16 Oct. 1632, aged 78, and was buried in the chapel there.

He published 'A Demonstration of God in his Workes,' London, 1597, 4to. 'Principles for Young Princes,' London, 1611 and 1629, is very doubtfully assigned to him (*Notes and Queries*, 3rd ser. vii. 57).

By his wife Anne (*d.* 1590), daughter of Sir Adrian Poynings, widow of a Hampshire gentleman, More had four sons and five daughters. The eldest, Robert, born 1581, was knighted by James, and died seven years before his father, to whose estates his eldest son, Poynings More, succeeded. More's third daughter, Ann, born in 1584, was secretly married in 1600 to John Donne [q. v.] A portrait of Sir George More is at Loseley.

[Manning's Surrey, i. 95, &c.; Carew's Letters (Camd. Soc.), p. 19; Nichols's Progresses of James I, i. 250, 556, ii. 374, iii. 119; State Papers from 1601 to 1630; Gardiner's History, ii. 351, 353, iv. 66, 120; Foster's Alumni Oxon. 1500–1714; Loseley MSS. ed. Kempe, 1836.]

E. T. S.

MORE, HANNAH (1745–1833), religious writer, born 2 Feb. 1745, at Stapleton, Gloucestershire, near Bristol, was fourth of the five daughters of Jacob More. Jacob More (*d.* 1783), born at Thorpe Hall, Harleston, Norfolk, had been educated at Norwich grammar school, with a view to taking orders. His prospects of an estate at Wenteaston, Suffolk, having been ruined by a lawsuit, he took a place in the excise, and afterwards obtained from Lord Bottetourt the mastership of the free school of Fishponds, Stapleton, where he married Mary, the daughter of John Grace, a farmer. His relatives had been generally presbyterians, and two of his great-uncles Cromwellian captains. He was himself a tory and high churchman. He and his wife were intelligent and sensible, and desired that their daughters should be so brought up as to be able to make their own living.

Hannah was a delicate and precocious child. Before she was four she had learnt to read by listening to her sisters' lessons, and could say the catechism so well as to astonish the clergyman of the parish. Her nurse had attended Dryden in his last illness, and Hannah was eager for stories about the poet. When she was eight she was fond of listening to stories of classical history and anecdotes from Plutarch related by her father. He then began to teach her Latin and mathematics, and was 'frightened at his own success,' though the entreaties of Hannah and her mother induced him to persevere. Her eldest sister was sent to take lessons at a French school at Bristol, and communicated her knowledge to Hannah, who further improved herself by talking to some French officers living on parole in the neighbourhood. She began to scribble childish essays. About 1757 her eldest sister, who was not quite twenty-one, set up a boarding-school in Trinity Street, Bristol, in which she was joined by the other sisters. The school flourished so well that the sisters built a new house in Park Street after a few years, and another for their father at Stony Hill, Bristol. Hannah took lessons from masters at the school, and acquired Italian, Spanish, and Latin. She made various translations, which she afterwards destroyed, except one from Metastasio's 'Regulus,' which she published in 1774 as 'The Inflexible Captive.' It was acted in 1775 at Exeter and Bath. In 1762 she published a 'pastoral drama' called 'The Search after Happiness,' intended to be learnt by heart by the school-children instead of less edifying dramas. She saw such literary and scientific people as were to be found at Bristol, and during a visit to Weston-super-Mare, caused by ill-health, made friends with the poet John Langhorne [q.v.], who wrote letters and addressed verses to her. At Bristol she was on friendly terms with Dean Tucker and Sir James Stonehouse, a clergyman who had previously been a physician. When she was about twenty-two she received an offer of marriage from a Mr. Turner, who had a fine house at Belmont, six miles from Bristol. He was an accomplished and honourable man, but was twenty years her senior and had a queer temper. She accepted him, and the wedding-day was more than once fixed. When it arrived, however, Turner did not feel himself equal to the occasion, and kept on putting off the marriage for six years. Stonehouse was at last asked to intervene. The engagement was broken off, and as Miss More had given up her share in the school in view of the marriage, Turner wished to make compensation. He offered 200*l.* a year, which Miss More declined positively to accept. Stonehouse, however, agreed to become trustee for the fund without the lady's knowledge. She was afterwards induced to take the money. Turner continued to admire her, visited her at Cowslip Green, and left her 1,000*l.* She resolved never to listen to another offer, and, it is added, had an opportunity soon afterwards of showing that she adhered to her decision. In 1773 or 1774 Hannah More paid a visit to London with two of her sisters, Sarah and Martha ('Patty'). She had written a letter describing the effect produced upon her mind by Garrick's Lear. Her correspondent knew Garrick and showed him the letter. He met his admirer a week after her arrival in town. She soon became intimate with Garrick and his wife, and in 1776 spent some months with them at the Adelphi and Hampton. She had been introduced in 1774 to Burke and Reynolds, and at Reynolds's house first met Dr. Johnson. She was soon afterwards thrilled by seeing the great doctor in his own house. Miss More became one of his favourites, and at a meeting at Reynolds's house the two tried, according to Sarah More, which could 'pepper the highest' (ROBERTS, i. 54). The exchange of flattery became, indeed, too strong for Johnson's taste. It was to Hannah More that he remarked, according to Mrs. Piozzi's version (*Anecdotes*, p. 183), that she should 'consider what her flattery was worth before she choked him with it.' Boswell, on the authority of Malone, softens the phrase, which is also repeated by Mme. d'Arblay (*Diary*, i. 103). Johnson afterwards asked Miss Reynolds to advise Miss More to flatter him less (BOSWELL, *Johnson*, ed. Hill, iii. 293, iv. 341–2). The lady staying at Bath in April 1776 of whom Johnson said that she was 'empty-headed' was certainly not Hannah More, who was then in London with the Garricks. Johnson called Miss More 'little fool,' 'love,' and 'dearest' (ROBERTS, i. 66), declared to Beattie that she was the most 'powerful versificatrix in the English language' (FORBES, *Beattie*, 1824, p. 320), and said that 'there was no name in poetry that might not be glad to own her "Bas Bleu"' (ROBERTS, i. 319). The flattery was certainly not one-sided.

The 'Bas Bleu' was circulated in manuscript in 1784, when Johnson saw it. It describes the 'blue-stocking clubs,' then popular among the literary ladies (BOSWELL, ed. Hill, iii. 109; and art. MONTAGU, MRS. ELIZABETH). Hannah More had long been a popular member. She had been introduced by Garrick on their first acquaintance to Mrs. Montagu, 'the wisest where all are wise' (ROBERTS, i. 57). She knew the venerable Mrs. Delany, and the respectable Mrs. Carter, and the admirable Mrs. Chapone, and the excellent Mrs. Boscawen, and all the good ladies who read the 'Spectator,' the 'Rambler,' and admired Mrs. Montagu's triumph over Voltaire. She resolved to put her merits to a better test by publishing an original poem. 'Sir Eldred of the Bower' was accordingly published in 1776. Cadell offered her a good price, and said that he would make it up to whatever Goldsmith had received for 'The Deserted Village.' The sum paid seems to have been forty guineas (THOMPSON, p. 29). Mrs. Montagu declared that her muse had done equal justice to Roman magnanimity and Gothic spirit. Garrick called her 'Nine,' as an embodiment of all the muses, and encouraged her to write for the stage, besides advising her in the course of her work. Her tragedy of 'Percy,' for which he wrote prologue and epilogue, was accordingly produced at Covent Garden, 10 Dec. 1777, and had a run of twenty-one nights. Four thousand copies of the first edition were sold in a fortnight. A charge of plagiarism made against her by Hannah Cowley [q. v.] appears to have been quite groundless. Miss More declared that she had never seen the manuscript from which she was supposed to have stolen. She began another tragedy, 'The Fatal Falsehood,' under Garrick's superintendence, which was produced on 6 May 1779 with less success at the same theatre soon after his death.

Garrick's death (20 Jan. 1779) formed, it is said, an era in Hannah More's life. She gradually retired from the gaieties to which he had introduced her. She came to think playgoing wrong, and first showed her resolution by refusing to attend the performance of 'Percy' in 1787, when it was revived, with Mrs. Siddons as the heroine (ROBERTS, iv. 374). Upon Garrick's death she was summoned by Mrs. Garrick, with whom she stayed for some time. The intimacy continued for a long time, and upon Mrs. Garrick's death in 1822 Hannah More speaks of having spent 'twenty winters' in her friend's house (*ib.* iv. 168). Although circumstances separated them in later years, there was no avowed coolness. Hannah More kept up her relations with London society for a time, and in 1781 made acquaintance with Horace Walpole. He printed a little poem of hers, 'Bonner's Ghost,' at the Strawberry Hill press in 1781, and wrote many letters to her in later years, which, in spite of his affectations, seem to indicate a genuine liking and admiration. He avoids offending her by too worldly a tone. Her biographer apologises for her friendly intercourse with the old courtier, but apology is hardly required.

In 1782 she published her 'Sacred Dramas,' intended chiefly for 'young persons.' Tate Wilkinson (*Wandering Patentee*, iv. 75, 80) proposed to bring these upon the stage at Hull in November 1793, as prepared by Mr. 'A. M.,' 'a gentleman of strong abilities,' but was deterred by a general outcry of profanity. One of them, 'Moses in the Bullrushes,' with other works of hers, was afterwards translated into Cingalese (ROBERTS, iv. 46).

In 1784 she found that a poor milkwoman at Bristol, a Mrs. Anne Yearsley [q. v.], had been writing poetry. Hannah More took her for a genius, edited a collection of her poems, and raised 500*l.* or 600*l.* for her benefit. She was greatly occupied in this benevolent task for more than a year. Mrs. Montagu, who thought that a study of the Bible had enabled Mrs. Yearsley to soar above Pindar and Æschylus (*ib.* i. 364), became trustee with Hannah More for the money. Unluckily the milkwoman wished to have the capital sum, which her trustees apparently feared would be spent upon drink. She became angry, accused them of theft, and declared that Hannah More was envious of her talents. The money was handed over by the trustees to a merchant at Bristol, and ultimately, it seems, to Mrs. Yearsley. She published a novel called 'The Man in the Iron Mask,' by which she made 200*l.*, produced a tragedy, 'Earl Goodwin,' and set up a circulating library. Cottle says that he helped her out of some difficulties. She lost her husband and two sons, and retired to Melksham in Wiltshire, where she died in 1806, in a state of almost 'total seclusion' (COTTLE, *Early Recollections*, i. 69–77; THOMPSON, p. 55).

Meanwhile Hannah More had been making more serious friendships, especially with Dr. Kennicott, Dr. (afterwards Bishop) Horne, Bishop Porteus, and other dignitaries. Her religious impressions became deeper. In 1780 she was much impressed by the 'Cardiphonia' of John Newton (1725–1807) [q. v.] In 1787 she heard a sermon from him, sat with him for an hour, and came home 'with two pockets full of sermons' (ROBERTS, ii. 54). He soon became a regular correspondent and adviser on religious topics. In 1787 she also saw much of Wilberforce, who was beginning the agitation against the slave-trade, and who was ever afterwards her close friend. She spent the summer at Cowslip Green, in the parish of Blagdon, ten miles from Bristol on the Exeter road, where she had built a cottage two years before. It is close to Wrington, where Locke was born. Mrs. Montagu presented her with an urn in memory of the philosopher, which was placed in her garden, and afterwards moved to Barley Wood, opposite Locke's birthplace. She amused herself with gardening, of which she was very fond, and seldom moved except to pay her annual visits to Mrs. Garrick and visit her friends about London. In 1788 appeared the first result of her more serious reflections: 'Thoughts on the Importance of the Manners of the Great to General Society.' It was anonymous, and at first attributed to Wilberforce. Several editions were sold with great rapidity, and it was afterwards followed by writings in the same vein of religious and moral reflections (see list below), which were among the most widely read books of the day. A poem upon 'Slavery,' published in the same year, was also well received. At the end of 1789 her sisters retired from their school in 'affluent circumstances' (*ib.* iv. 116). They built a house in Great Pulteney Street, Bath, and proposed to divide their time between Bath and Cowslip Green. In the summer of 1789 Martha (or Patty) More spent a long time with her sister at Cowslip Green, and made various excursions. They visited Cheddar with Wilberforce in August (*Life of Wilberforce*, i. 237–8), when he was shocked by the general ignorance and distress, and suggested that they should do something for the place. Thirteen adjoining parishes in the neighbourhood had not a single resident curate (Roberts, ii. 213). The incumbent of one was generally drunk six times a week, and often prevented from preaching by a couple of black eyes 'honestly earned' by fighting (*ib.* ii. 209, 216). The squire in one place was a shrewd atheist, the chief farmer preferred workmen to saints, and the farmer's wife held that the labourers were predestined to be 'poor, ignorant, and wicked.' In one parish there was only one bible, which served to prop a flower-pot (*ib.* p. 296). Hannah More and her sisters therefore met with considerable opposition when they resolved to set up Sunday schools in the districts. They made some impression by arguing that schools would teach children not to rob orchards. The plan is generally said to have been started by Robert Raikes [q. v.] of Gloucester in 1781. Mrs. Trimmer [q. v.] had started Sunday schools at Brentford in 1786. There was already one in their own parish (Blagdon) and in a neighbouring village. The Mores, in spite of many jealousies, went to work energetically, took a small house at Cheddar for six and a half guineas a year, hired a schoolmistress for 30*l.* a year, and by the end of the year had five hundred children in training in Cheddar and the neighbouring parish. They held evening readings of sermons, prayers, and hymns for the parents. They also promoted friendly societies among the women, had weekly schools in which the girls learnt reading and sewing, distributed prizes for good behaviour, and held annual school-feasts, which were largely attended. On Sundays the sisters drove round to the various villages to superintend the schools and other institutions.

Hannah More's views of education were not quite of the modern type. She taught the Bible and the catechism, and the pupils learnt on week-days 'such coarse works as may fit them for servants. I allow of no writing for the poor' (see letters to Wilberforce, Roberts, ii. 295–301, and to the Bishop of Bath and Wells, *ib.* iii. 122–39, for her own account). In 1823 she was rather scandalised by the advance of the scheme which she had done much to encourage, and protested against the doctrine that the poor were to be made 'scholars and philosophers' (*ib.* iv. 215). In 1800 she became involved in the 'Blagdon controversy.' The curate of Blagdon, Thomas Bere, had asked her to set up a school there in 1795. He afterwards complained that Young, the master, was holding a kind of conventicle, when Miss More at once stopped Young's irregularities. In March 1800 Bere again complained, and after an investigation, in which the chancellor of the diocese and the rector of Blagdon took part, Miss More dissolved the school in November 1800. Soon afterwards, however, the rector, thinking that Bere had behaved badly, gave him notice to resign the curacy, and the school was again started in January 1801. Bere refused to resign, and finally maintained his position, when Miss More again dissolved the school in September 1801. Upon the appointment of Richard Beadon [q. v.] to the bishopric of Bath and Wells in 1802, Miss More appealed to him for directions. He assured her of his support and approval, and this appears to have been regarded by her friends as a final triumph. The dispute involved all manner of minor issues and a general raking up of village scandals. Pamphlets were written (see a list in *Notes and Queries*, 3rd ser. viii. 168); the 'Anti-Jacobin Review,' the 'British Critic,' and the 'Christian Observer' wrote articles; and the characters of Miss More, Bere, and other clergymen more or less attacked. The real cause apparently was the suspicion that the schools had a methodist tendency, although Hannah More says that the methodists were opposed to her. She said in 1808 (Roberts, iii. 259) that 'two Jacobin and infidel curates' had tried to make themselves known by a virulent attack upon her. She was accused of being a 'hireling of Pitt,' and also of being a Jacobin. In 1802 she complains that she has been 'battered, hacked, scalped, tomahawked for three years' (*ib.* iii. 160). In fact her bad health and the contrast between the rough handling of pamphlets and the unctuous eulogies to which she was accustomed sufficiently explain her irritation. The whole disturbance was absurd to outsiders. After 1802 she met no further trouble of the kind. Only four of her schools, those at Cheddar, Nailsea, Shipham, and Wedmore, continued and the first three were still flourishing in 1825 (for an account of the schools see THOMPSON, pp. 95-122).

During the excitement caused by the French revolution Hannah More had been entrusted to provide an antidote for the poison. She wrote in 1792 a tract called 'Village Politics, by Will Chip,' which was published anonymously. It gained notice at once; many thousand copies were sent by government to Scotland and Ireland, and patriotic people printed large editions at their own expense. At the beginning of 1793 she published some 'Remarks on the Speech of M. Dupont,' who had avowed atheism in the convention, and sent the profits, amounting to 240*l.*, to the fund for the relief of the French emigrant clergy (ROBERTS, ii. 356). Encouraged by the success of 'Village Politics,' she resolved to publish a series of cheap tracts. With some help from her sisters and friends she produced three tracts a month (a tale, a ballad, and a tract for Sunday reading) for three years, which were sold for a penny, and afterwards collected in three volumes. They were called the 'Cheap Repository Tracts.' Some of them were illustrated by John Bewick [q. v.] Those signed 'Z.' were by Hannah, and those signed 'S.' by Sarah More. In almost every tract there was 'an exemplary parish priest' (THOMPSON, p. 210), as she boasted. The typical character was the 'Shepherd of Salisbury Plain' (said to have been meant for one Saunders of Cherrill Down), who lived on a shilling a day, rejoiced that only three of his children were under five years of age, and never complained of hunger, because he 'lived upon the promises.' Cobbett, then an anti-Jacobin, expressed his delight in them, and helped to circulate them in America (THOMPSON, p. 159; *Letters to Z. Macaulay*, p. 17). The circulation is said to have amounted to two millions in the first year (ROBERTS, iii. 423-4). The venture was, however, supported by committees formed in every part of the kingdom, and the circulation therefore represents the approval of the classes whose cause she supported as much as the taste of the persons to be converted. Her health suffered from the labour, and her income was not improved. They appear to have been partly suggested by Mrs. Trimmer's 'Family Magazine.' The organisation for circulating them seems to have led to the foundation of the Religious Tract Society in 1799 (for a discussion of the bibliography of these tracts see *Notes and Queries*, 3rd ser. ii. 241, by De Morgan, and p. 291, by W. Lee).

In 1802 Hannah More moved to Barley Wood, in Wrington parish, a mile from Cowslip Green, where she had built a comfortable house and laid out a garden. The sisters soon afterwards made it their sole residence, giving up the house at Bath. Hannah More lived there quietly for many years, writing industriously when her health permitted, and receiving visits from Wilberforce, Zachary Macaulay, and many well-known leaders of the 'Clapham sect.' Macaulay's wife had been a pupil at the Bristol school, and the correspondence with him begins in 1796, before his marriage. Hannah More made a pet of his son, Thomas Babington, who was often at Barley Wood in his childhood; she gave him his first books, and after her death he showed his affection by refusing to write about her in the 'Edinburgh Review' (letter to M. Napier, 15 June 1837). She had destined her library to him, but dissatisfaction with his religious views led her to bestow it elsewhere. In December 1809 she published the most popular of her works, 'Cœlebs in Search of a Wife.' Although anonymous it succeeded so rapidly that nine months later, when she had gone for rest to Dawlish, she was followed by the eleventh edition. Thirty editions were sold in America. She says in 1810 that she had spent 5,000*l.* in publishing it, besides the bookseller's profits; but had cleared 2,000*l.* and still had the copyright. Scott's 'Rokeby,' published in 1810, had gained for him the same sum; but 'Cœlebs' was sold for twelve shillings and 'Rokeby' for 2*l.* 2*s.* (ROBERTS, iii. 327). Sydney Smith's gibes in the 'Edinburgh' had not injured her circulation, though perhaps his judgment anticipates that of most modern readers. Her success shows the advantage from a worldly point of view of writing orthodox didactic works.

On 18 April 1813 Mary, the eldest of the sisters, died at Barley Wood, aged 75; Elizabeth More died 14 June 1816, aged 76; Sarah, 17 May 1817, aged 74; and Martha, 14 Sept. 1819, aged 60 (?) (see inscription on monument given in THOMPSON).

During the critical period which followed the peace Hannah More again wrote a series of tracts in prose and verse, which, as before, were circulated with the help of a committee formed in London, and are said by her biographer to have produced a 'very visible effect.' Upon the abolition of slavery in Ceylon she wrote a poetical dialogue called 'The Feast of Freedom,' which was translated into Cingalese by two Buddhist priests, and performed at a public ceremonial on the anniversary of the measure. It was set to music by Charles Wesley. Sir Alexander Johnstone, the governor of Ceylon, saw her in 1819, introduced the priests to her, and ordered her 'sacred dramas' to be translated, and begged her to write more (ROBERTS, iv. 45–57). She continued her series of moral and religious treatises, the last of which, her 'Moral Sketches,' appeared in 1819. Her health had been weak through life, and she was especially subject to inflammatory attacks of the lungs. She had dangerous illnesses in 1820, 1822, and 1824, during the last of which she compiled her 'Spirit of Prayer.' In later years she became infirm, though with fewer illnesses. After the death of her last sister she found the management of her household difficult, and her servants were spoilt by injudicious indulgence. Cottle gives a ludicrous account of the detection of their vagaries by an old friend. They all left the house at midnight to attend a village ball. Twelve gentlemen went to Barley Wood to protect Hannah More, when she called the servants up, solemnly gave them all warning, and explained that they had forced her to seek a refuge among strangers (a slightly different version in THOMPSON, pp. 318–19). She sold her carriage and horses, and exchanged 'eight pampered minions' for four sober servants (COTTLE, i. 94). She also sold Barley Wood to Mr. Harford, and parted with the copyright of her last books. She moved to 4 Windsor Terrace, Clifton, in 1828. She was surrounded by many affectionate and admiring friends, and so much overpowered by visits that she found it necessary to have two public days a week and pass the others in retirement. Her memory was beginning to fail, and she died peacefully 7 Sept. 1833. She left about 30,000*l.*, chiefly in legacies to charitable institutions and religious societies (see list in THOMPSON, i. 324). The residue of the estate was to go to the new church of St. Philip and St. Jacob in Bristol. Patty More had also left 10,000*l.* or 12,000*l.* in legacies. All the sisters were buried at Wrington.

Hannah More was one of the last of the group of learned ladies who had known Johnson, though Madame d'Arblay survived her for some years. Her writings have the old-fashioned flavour of the eighteenth century; while they now represent the teaching of the evangelical school, which looked up to Newton and Cecil, and of which William Wilberforce and his friends were the recognised political and social leaders. Though now out of fashion, they show not only high moral and religious purpose, but strong sense, as well as considerable intellectual vivacity. If their author showed a little self-complacency, the wonder is that her strong sense kept her from being spoilt by the uniform flattery poured upon her by her contemporaries. Her services to education at a time of general indifference deserve the highest praise, though her decided desire to keep the poor in their place is now out of fashion. In private life she seems to have been thoroughly amiable, kind to children, and as playful as her conscience would allow.

An engraving from a drawing by Miss Reynolds (sister of Sir Joshua) in 1780 is prefixed to Thompson's 'Memoir.' An engraving from a portrait by Opie, painted in 1786, is prefixed to Roberts's 'Memoir.' She was also painted by Pickersgill in 1822 for Sir Thomas Acland.

Hannah More's works are: 1. 'The Search after Happiness,' 1773; 11th edition, 1796. 2. 'The Inflexible Captive,' 1774. 3. 'Sir Eldred of the Bower, and the Bleeding Rock,' 1776. 4. 'Percy,' 1777. 5. 'Essays on Various Subjects, principally designed for Young Ladies,' 1778 (used in other works, and not reprinted in collected edition). 6. 'The Fatal Falsehood,' 1779. 7. 'Sacred Dramas,' with 'Sensibility, a Poem,' 1782; 24th edition, 1850. 8. 'Slavery, a Poem,' 1788. 9. 'Thoughts on the Importance of the Manners of the Great to General Society,' 1788; 8th edition, 1792. 10. 'An Estimate of the Religion of the Fashionable World,' 1790; 5th edition, 1793. 11. 'Remarks on the Speech of M. Dupont . . . on Religion and Public Education,' 1793. 12. 'Village Politics, by Will Chip,' 1793. 13. 'Cheap Repository Tracts,' 1795–8 (see above). 14. 'Strictures on the Modern System of Female Education, with a View of the Principles and Conduct prevalent among Women of Rank and Fortune,' 2 vols. 8vo, 1799; 13th edition, 1826. 15. 'Hints towards forming the Character of a Young Princess,' 2 vols. 8vo, 1805. 16. 'Cœlebs in Search of a Wife,' 1809 (name of author to 4th edition), 2 vols.; 16th edition, 1826. 17. 'Practical Piety, or the Influence of the Religion of the Heart on the Life and Manners,' 2 vols. 1811; 19th edition, 1850. 18. 'Christian Morals,' 2 vols. 8vo, 1813; 9th edition, 1826. 19. 'Essay on the Character and Practical Writings of St. Paul,' 1815; 7th edition, 1837. 20. 'Stories for the Middle Ranks of Society, and Tales for the Common People,' 1819 (reprints of 'Cheap Repository Tracts' and of the tracts written in 1817). 21. 'Moral Sketches of prevailing Opinions of Manners, Foreign and Domestic, with Reflections on Prayer,' 1819; 10th edition, 1830. 22. 'Bible Rhymes on the Names of all the Books of the Old and New Testaments, with Allusions to some of the Principal Characters and Incidents,'

1821. 23. 'The Spirit of Prayer,' 1825; 12th edition, 1849 (compiled by herself from previous writings). 24. 'The Feast of Freedom, on the Abolition of Domestic Slavery in Ceylon' (set to music by Charles Wesley, with a few trifles; and published in aid of protestant education in Ireland), 1827. Her 'Works' were collected in 8 vols. in 1801, in 19 vols. in 1818–19, and in 11 vols. in 1830, and later. Her 'Poems' were collected in 1816 and 1829.

[Memoir . . . of Hannah More, by William Roberts, 3rd edit. 4 vols. 8vo, 1838 (letters connected by a meagre and dateless narrative); Life of Hannah More, with Notices of her sisters, by the Rev. Henry Thompson, 1838 (the best); Cottle's Early Recollections, i. 77–97; Boswell's Life of Johnson; Horace Walpole's Correspondence (Cunningham), vols. viii. and ix.; Life of William Wilberforce, 5 vols. 1838 (contains many letters to her); Letters of Hannah More to Zachary Macaulay, edited by Arthur Roberts, 1860; T. S. Whalley's Journals, ed. Hill Wickham, 1863, passim; Dr. Doran's A Lady of the last Century (Mrs. Elizabeth Montagu); Mrs. Delany's Memoirs, vols. v. and vi. passim; Genest's Hist. of the Stage, vi. 16, 100, x. 189. A Life of Hannah More, with a Critical Review of her Writings, by the Rev. Archibald Macsarcasm, 1802, is an abusive pamphlet written by one of her antagonists in the Blagdon controversy, the Rev. William Shaw, rector of Chelvey, Somerset. Lowndes erroneously gives one life by Shaw and another by 'Macsarcasm.']
L. S.

MORE, HENRY (1586–1661), jesuit, was son of Edward More [see under MORE, EDWARD, 1479–1541], and great-grandson of Sir Thomas More [q. v.], lord chancellor of England. He must not be confused with his cousin, Henry More (*b.* 1567), who was son of Thomas More and Mary Scrope (cf. HUNTER's Preface to CRESACRE MORE's *Life of Sir T. More*). More was born in 1586 in Essex, according to the majority of the provincial catalogues, though a few of them give Cambridgeshire as the county of his birth. He made his humanity studies in the college of the English jesuits at St. Omer, and entered the novitiate of St. John's, Louvain, 19 Nov. 1607. His higher studies were probably made in Spain. In 1614 he filled the office of minister in the English college of St. Alban at Valladolid; he held the same office in the college at St. Omer in 1621; and he was professed of the four vows 12 May 1622. From the latter year till 1632 he was a missioner in the London district, and he was one of the jesuits arrested at the Clerkenwell residence by the officers of the privy council in March 1628. In 1632 he was in confinement in the New Prison, London, and was released in December 1633. He then became chaplain to Lord Petre at Ingatestone and Thorndon Hall, Essex. In 1635 he was declared provincial of his order. Again imprisoned, he was set free in July 1640. In 1642 he was vice-provincial of the order, residing in London, and acting for Father Matthew Wilson, *alias* Edward Knott [q. v.], the provincial, who was absent in Belgium. In 1645 he was rector of the college of St. Ignatius, which comprised the London district. He became rector of the college at St. Omer, and in 1655 he was again residing in Essex. In 1657 he was for the second time rector of the college at St. Omer, and he died at Watten, near that city, on 8 Dec. 1661.

His works are: 1. 'A Manual of Devout Meditations and Exercises, instructing how to pray mentally, translated from the Latin of Thomas Villa-Castin,' St. Omer, 1618 and 1624, 16mo. 2. 'The Happiness of a Religious State,' from the Latin of Father Jerome Platus, a Milanese jesuit, Rouen, 1632, 4to. 3. 'Vita et Doctrina Christi Domini notationibus, quæ quotidianam divina meditantibus materiam suggerere possunt, explicata; juxta quatuor partes anni Ecclesiastici in capita distributa,' Antwerp, 1649, 12mo. This work appeared also in English, Ghent, 1656, 8vo; reprinted London, 1880, 8vo, ed. Charles Henry Bowden. 4. 'Historia Missionis Anglicanæ Societatis Jesu ab anno salutis MDLXXX. ad DC.LIX. et vice-provinciæ primum, tum provinciæ ad ejusdem sæculi annum XXXV,' St. Omer, 1660, fol. pp. 518, a valuable historical work. 5. 'Dix-huit Sermons de M. Morus sur le huitième chapitre de l'Épitre de Saint Paul aux Romains,' Lausanne, 1691, 8vo.

His brother, THOMAS MORE, also a jesuit (1587–1623?), entered the Society of Jesus in 1611, and laboured many years among the English poor until he was arrested, tried, and condemned to banishment, probably in 1618; he retired to Flanders, and died at Ghent on 2 Jan. 1623. He published: 1. 'Guilielmi Watfordi Institutio Brevis,' St. Omer, 1617. 2. 'Joannis Floydi Dialogus inscriptus Deus et Rex,' Cologne, 1620. Both are translations from the English (FOLEY, *Records*, xii. 702–3).

[De Backer's Bibl. de la Compagnie de Jésus, ii. 1376; Dodd's Church Hist. iii. 120; Foley's Records, ii. 416–28, v. 702, vii. 518; Cresacre More's Life of Sir T. More, ed. Hunter, 1828, Pref. p. liii; Oliver's Jesuit Collections, p. 143; Southwell's Bibl. Scriptorum Soc. Jesu, p. 329; Alegambe's Bibliotheca Scriptt. Soc. Jesu, pp. 329–30, 764. Wood's notices of the More family in the Athenæ are very inaccurate.] T. C.

MORE, HENRY (1614–1687), theologian, born at Grantham in 1614, was son of 'Alexander More, esq., a gentleman of fair estate and fortune.' Both his parents were strong Calvinists, and from his childhood he took a deep interest in questions of theology, but could never accept the Calvinistic system. He appears to have been committed by his father to the care of his uncle, who threatened to flog him 'for his immature forwardness in philosophising concerning the mysteries of necessity and freewill.' At fourteen he was sent to 'Eton School . . . for the perfecting of the Greek and Latin tongue.' He made great progress in his studies, and in 1631 was admitted at Christ's College, Cambridge, about the time when John Milton was leaving it. In 1635 he graduated B.A., and for three or four years was still unsettled in regard to religion. But in 1639 he proceeded M.A., and was elected fellow of his college; and about the same time he received holy orders. Thenceforth he lived almost entirely within the walls of Christ's College, except when he went to stay with his 'heroine pupil' (as his biographer terms her), Anne, viscountess Conway [q. v.], at her country seat of Ragley in Warwickshire, where his great pleasure was to wander among the woods and glades. He won a high reputation both for saintliness and for intellectual power; but he refused all preferment, successively declining the mastership of his college (1654), the deanery of Christ Church, Oxford, the provostship of Trinity College, Dublin, with the deanery of St. Patrick's, and two bishoprics. Intensely loyal to the king, both during the civil wars and after the Restoration, he was once persuaded to make a journey to Whitehall to kiss his majesty's hands; but when he heard by the way that this would be the prelude to a bishopric he at once turned back. In 1676 he was persuaded by the lord chancellor, the Earl of Nottingham, to accept a prebend at Gloucester, but he resigned it immediately in favour of his friend Dr. Fowler, afterwards bishop of the diocese. He declined advancement simply 'from a pure love of contemplation and solitude, and because he thought he could do the church of God greater service in a private than in a public station.' He had many pupils at Christ's; he loved music, and used to play on the theorbo; he enjoyed a game at bowls, and still more a conversation with intimate friends, who listened to him as to an oracle; and he was so kind to the poor that it is said 'his very chamber-door was a hospital for the needy.' He shrank from bitter theological and political disputes; but he had the courage of his opinions, which were very definite. He made no secret of his attachment to the church of England at a time when it was dangerous to avow such sentiments; and he did not hesitate to use the church liturgy both in public and private when it was a crime to do so.

On 1 Sept. 1687 he died at Cambridge, and was buried in the chapel of his college. His life was published in 1710 by the Rev. R. Ward, rector of Ingoldsby, a living which was in More's gift; but he has himself given us a far more vivid and interesting picture of himself in the 'Præfatio generalissima' to the 1679 edition of his 'Opera Omnia.' An engraving of More by Faithorne is prefixed to his 'Opera Theologica,' 1675, and another by Loggan to his 'Works,' 1679 (BROMLEY).

More belonged to that little band of Christian Platonists which was formed at Cambridge in the middle of the seventeenth century, and the distinctive traits of their school of thought are perhaps best brought out in his writings. The 'occult science,' of which such men as Van Helmont and Greatrakes were in More's time the apostles, had a singular fascination for him; but he was saved from its extravagances by the firmly implanted conviction which tinges all his life and all his writings that holiness was the way to knowledge, 'being well advised,' he says, 'both by the dictates of my own conscience and the clear information of those holy oracles which we all deservedly reverence, that God reserves his choicest secrets for the purest minds.' He was a voluminous writer. Like many others he began as a poet and ended as a prose writer. His first work, published in 1642, but written two years earlier, was entitled 'Psychozoia Platonica: or, a Platonicall Song of the Soul, consisting of foure severall Poems.' This was followed in 1647 by his full collection of 'Philosophicall Poems,' which includes 'The Song of the Soul,' much enlarged, and is dedicated 'to his dear father.' A second edition was published in the same year, and it was included by Dr. A. B. Grosart in his Chertsey Worthies Library (1878).

His prose works are: 1. 'Observations upon Anthroposophia Theogmagica and Anima Magica Abscondita by Alazonomastix Philalethes,' 1650; in answer to Thomas Vaughan (brother of the poet), who replied in 'The Man-mouse taken in a Trape.' 2. 'The Second Lash of Alazonomastix,' a rejoinder to Vaughan, 1651. 3. 'An Anti-dote against Atheism, or an Appeal to the Naturall Faculties of the Minde of Man, whether there be not a God,' 1653; 2nd edit. 'corrected and enlarged: With an Appendix thereunto annexed,' 1655. 4. 'Conjectura Cabbalistica . . . or a Conjectural Essay of Interpreting the Minde of Moses, according to a Threefold Cabbala: viz. Literal, Philosophical, Mystical, or Divinely Moral,' 1653; dedicated to his brother Platonist, Dr. Cudworth. 5. 'Enthusiasmus Triumphatus, or a Discourse of the Nature, Causes, Kinds, and Cure of Enthusiasme; written by Philophilus Parrasiastes, and prefixed to Alazonomastix his Observations and Reply,' &c., 1656. 6. 'The Immortality of the Soul, so farre forth as it is demonstrable from the Knowledge of Nature and the Light of Reason,' 1659; dedicated to Viscount Conway, the husband of his 'heroine pupil.' 7. 'An Explanation of the Grand Mystery of Godliness; or a True and Faithful Representation of the Everlasting Gospel of our Lord and Saviour Jesus Christ,' 1660. 8. 'A Modest Enquiry into the Mystery of Iniquity,' and an 'Apologie,' &c., 1664. 9. 'Enchiridion Ethicum, præcipua Moralis Philosophiæ Rudimenta complectens, illustrata ut plurimum Veterum Monumentis, et ad Probitatem Vitæ perpetuo accommodata,' 1667, 1668, 1669, 1695, 1696, and 1711. 10. 'Divine Dialogues, containing sundry Disquisitions and Instructions concerning the Attributes of God and His Providence in the World,' 1668, More's best-known work. The most authentic edition appeared in 1713. 11. 'An Exposition of the Seven Epistles to the Seven Churches; Together with a Brief Discourse of Idolatry, with application to the Church of Rome.' The title of the latter in the volume itself is 'An Antidote against Idolatry,' and it elicited from More in reply to attacks 'A brief Reply to a late Answer to Dr. Henry More his antidote against Idolatry,' 1672, and 'An Appendix to the late Antidote against Idolatry,' 1673. 12. 'Enchiridion Metaphysicum; sive, de rebus incorporeis succincta et luculenta dissertatio; pars prima,' 1671, an attack on the Cartesian philosophy, which he had in earlier life admired. 13. 'Remarks upon two late ingenious Discourses [by Sir Matthew Hale, q.v.]; the one, an Essay, touching the Gravitation and non-Gravitation of Fluid Bodies; the other, touching the Torricellian Experiment, so far forth as they may concern any passages in his "Enchiridion Metaphysicum,"' 1676. 14. 'Apocalypsis Apocalypseos; or the Revelation of St. John the Divine unveiled: an exposition from chapter to chapter and from verse to verse of the whole Book of the Apocalypse,' 1680. 15. 'A Plain and continued Exposition of the several Prophecies or Divine Visions of the Prophet Daniel, which have or may concern the People of God, whether Jew or Christian,' &c., 1681. 16. 'A Brief Discourse of the Real Presence of the Body and Blood of Christ in the Celebration of the Holy Eucharist; wherein the Witty Artifices of the Bishop of Meaux [Bossuet] and of Monsieur Maimbourg are obviated, whereby they would draw in the Protestants to imbrace the doctrine of Transubstantiation,' 1681.

More is also believed to have written 'Philosophiæ Teutonicæ Censura,' 1670, a criticism of the theosophy of Jacob Boehme; and to have edited Joseph Glanvill's 'Sadducismus Triumphatus,' 1681. He certainly contributed largely to the volume, and also wrote many of the annotations to the same writer's 'Lux Orientalis,' 1682. More thoroughly sympathised with Glanvill in his intense belief in witchcraft and apparitions. Several letters from More to Dr. Worthington are printed in Dr. Worthington's 'Diary,' and some 'Letters Philosophical and Moral' between John Norris and Henry More are added to Norris's 'Theory and Regulation of Love,' 1688.

'A Collection of several Philosophical Writings of Dr. Henry More' includes his 'Antidote against Atheism,' with the Appendix, 'Enthusiasmus Triumphatus,' 'Letters to Des Cartes,' &c., 'Immortality of the Soul,' and 'Conjectura Cabbalistica.' A fourth edition, 'corrected and much enlarged,' was put forth in 1712, and was 'enriched with all the *Scholia* or *Notes* that he added afterwards in his *Latin* edition of these works.'

Between 1672 and 1675 More was principally engaged in translating his English works into Latin. In 1675 appeared 'Henrici Mori Cantabrigiensis Opera Theologica, Anglice quidem primitius scripta, nunc verò per autorem Latine reddita. Hisce novus præfixus est De Synchronismis Apocalypticis Tractatulus.' This was followed in 1679 by a larger work in 2 vols., 'Henrici Mori Cantabrigiensis Opera Omnia, tum quæ Latinè tum quæ Anglicè scripta sunt; nunc verò Latinitate donata instigatu et impensis generosissimi juvenis Johannis Cockshutt nobilis Angli.' Mr. Cockshutt of the Inner Temple had left a legacy of 300*l.* to More to have three of his principal pieces translated into Latin, but More complied with the terms of the legacy by translating into Latin many more of his English works. In 1692 were published 'Discourses on Several Texts of Scripture. By the late Pious and Learned Henry More, D.D.,' with a preface signed 'John Worthington;' and in 1694 'Letters on Several Subjects,' published by the Rev. E. Elys. Abridgments of and extracts from the works of More were numerous; and in 1708 a volume was published, especially for the use of 'all such Reverend clergymen as shall be fix'd in the places where charitable libraries are erected,' entitled 'The Theological Works of the most Pious and Learned Henry More.' The work is in English, but 'according to the author's Improvements in his Latin edition.'

More's biographer tells us that 'though he [More] had not wanted particular and extraordinary respects from many persons, yet the world in general had either been in part averse to his writings, or not known well what to make of some things in them;' and again: ''Tis very certain that his writings are not generally (I will not say, read, but) so much as known; and many scholars themselves are in a great measure strangers to them' (Ward, p. 72). On the other hand we are told that 'his writings were so much in vogue, that Mr. Chishull, an eminent bookseller, declared that for twenty years together, after the return of King Charles the Second, the "Mystery of Godliness" and Dr. More's other Works ruled all the Booksellers in London' (*Biog. Brit.*); while the editor of the 1743 edition of the 'Divine Dialogues' asserts that 'his works continued in high reputation long after his decease.' The mere fact of the continued reproduction, in whole or in part, of More's works is a proof that they were not neglected; and, considering how utterly the refined, dreamy, and poetical spirit of More was out of sympathy with the practical and prosaic mind of the eighteenth century, it is wonderful that his fame should have been so great as it was during that period. John Wesley, for instance, a man of an entirely different type of mind, strongly recommended More's writings to his brother-clergy. William Law, though he called More 'a Babylonish philosopher,' and is particularly severe upon the 'Divine Dialogues,' was deeply impressed with the piety and general interest of his character; and the edition of 1708 was issued through the exertions, and partly at the expense, of a gentleman the description of whom points very distinctly to Dr. Bray, who, except in the matters of piety and goodness, seems to have had little in common with More. S. T. Coleridge, as might be expected, had a high opinion of More's theological writings, declaring that they 'contained more original, enlarged, and elevating views of the Christian dispensation than he had met with in any other single volume' (*Lit. Rem.*) Principal Tulloch, in his valuable sketch of the Cambridge Platonists, treats More as at once the most interesting and the most unreadable of the whole band.

[Henry More's Works, passim, especially the Præfatio Generalissima to his Opera Omnia, 1679; Ward's Life of Henry More; Tulloch's Rational Theology, ii. 303–409; and valuable private information, especially about the bibliography, from Rev. J. Ingle Dredge.] J. H. O.

MORE, JACOB (1740–1793), landscape-painter, known as 'More of Rome,' was born at Edinburgh in 1740. He received his artistic training at Runciman's School of Design, and in 1771 exhibited with the Incorporated Society of Artists a 'View of Corehouse Linn, on the River Clyde,' a 'View from Dunbar Castle,' and four other landscapes. In 1773 he went to Italy, and settled in Rome, where he gained a considerable reputation, and was employed by Prince Borghese in the decoration of his villa near the Porta Pinciana. From Rome he sent to the exhibition of the Society of Artists in 1775 a 'View of the Lake of Albano,' and three other Italian landscapes; and in 1777 a 'View of the Lake of Nemi.' In 1783 he first exhibited at the Royal Academy, sending a 'View of the Cascade at Terni' and a 'View of the Campagna from Tivoli.' In 1784 he sent 'The Great Eruption of Mount Vesuvius, in which the elder Pliny lost his life;' in 1785, and again in 1786, two landscapes; in 1788, 'The Deluge' and 'An Eruption of Mount Etna;' and in 1789, two landscapes. His style was founded chiefly on that of Claude, and his paintings are mentioned with praise in Goethe's 'Winkelmann und sein Jahrhundert,' 1805, but they are much overrated when placed in comparison with the works of that master. Some of his landscapes were engraved for him in Rome, and the plates were brought to London after his death, and sold with his remaining works by auction at Christie's in 1796. Examples of his work are in the Villa Borghese at Rome and in the Hope collection at Deepdene, Dorking. His portrait, painted by himself, is in the Uffizi Gallery at Florence.

More died at Rome, of a bilious fever, shortly before November 1793. His property passed to a Mr. Moore of New Street, Covent Garden.

[Gent. Mag. 1793, ii. 1055; Edwards's Anecdotes of Painters, 1808, p. 213; Nagler's Künstler-Lexikon, 1835–52, ix. 443; Bryan's Dictionary of Painters and Engravers, ed. Graves and Armstrong, 1886–9, ii. 170; Catalogues of the Exhibitions of the Royal Incorporated Society of Artists, 1771–7; Royal Academy Exhibition Catalogues, 1783–9.] R. E. G.

MORE, Sir JOHN (1453?–1530), judge, and father of Sir Thomas More [q. v.], was son of John More. The origin of the chancellor's family has been much discussed, but no satisfactory pedigree is known. Richard Croke [q. v.] describes the chancellor in 1516 as 'natalibus generosissimus' in the dedication of his Latin version of Theodore Gaza's Greek grammar, but the chancellor himself described his family as 'non celebris sed honesta.' About 1390 John More, a London mercer, held one knight's fee of Thomas, duke of Gloucester, in North Mimms, Hertfordshire—property that undoubtedly descended to the chancellor's father (Clutterbuck, *Hertfordshire*, i. 449 sq.) According to the Ashmole MS. F 7, the mother of the judge's father was Joan, daughter of John Leycester, a country gentleman, and 'Judge More' is said to have borne 'arms from his birth' (Cresacre More, p. 11). The judge's father was in 1464 butler to the society of Lincoln's Inn, and was afterwards promoted to the superior office of seneschal or steward. In 1470, in consideration of his services to the inn, he was admitted a member, was afterwards called to the bar, was elected a bencher, and was twice appointed reader. He is not identical with the John More who died 25 April 1493, leaving a son John, aged 24 (*Inquisitio post mortem* 8 *Hen. VII*, No. 11; *Notes and Queries*, 4th ser. vii. 401).

The judge, who had two brothers, Richard and Christopher, passed in youth through similar experiences to his father. He began life as butler of Lincoln's Inn, to be subsequently elected a member of the society, and to be called to the bar. In November 1503 he was made a serjeant-at-law. Owing to the unconciliatory attitude in parliament of his famous son Thomas, he seems to have been imprisoned in the Tower next year, until he paid a fine of 100*l.* (Roper). Although no patent of his appointment as judge is known, he is mentioned as a judge of the common pleas in the 'Accounts of Fines' levied between Hilary term 1518 and Hilary term 1520. On 28 Nov. 1523 he is described as a judge of the king's bench in a list of judges liable for the subsidy of that year. A similar title is accorded him in the will that he made in February 1526. There is no official record of his transference from the common pleas to the king's bench, but it may have taken place in April 1520, when a new judge, Richard Broke, was appointed to the common pleas, to fill a vacancy, apparently caused by the removal of More to the king's bench. He is not known to have distinguished himself in judicial office. Thomas always treated him with the utmost filial tenderness, and is said when chancellor to have invariably visited his father's court to ask his blessing before taking his seat in his own court. In the epitaph which he wrote on himself in 1532 Sir Thomas described his father as 'civilis, suavis, innocens, mitis, misericors, æquus, et integer,' epithets which suggest incorruptibility in his public life, accompanied by more gentleness than strength. His promotions have been accounted for as concessions to his son's influence, or endeavours on the part of the crown to conciliate the chancellor. In his later years he resided with his son's family at Chelsea, and fully shared the simple delights of that united household. Like his son, he seems to have loved a jest, and he is credited with the remark that a man seeking a wife is like one putting his hand into a bag of snakes with one eel among them: he may light on the eel, but it is a hundred chances to one that 'he shall be stung with a snake' (Camden, *Remains*, p. 251; Cresacre More, *Life of Sir T. More*, ed. 1828, p. 10; More, *English Works*, p. 165, cf. p. 233). More's will was proved on 5 Dec. 1530. He was buried in the church of St. Lawrence Jewry. He figures in Holbein's sketch for his picture of the More family preserved at Basle, which was drawn near the year of his death. The inscription in his son's autograph gives his age as seventy-six. A crayon sketch by Holbein is at Windsor. Three paintings on panel are also attributed to Holbein (cf. *Cat. First Nat. Portrait Exhibition*, 1866, No. 89; *Tudor Exhibition Cat.* Nos. 70 and 100). The third picture, belonging to the Earl of Pembroke, is assigned to 1526, and was engraved by Lodge. A fourth painting by Holbein of More and his son, dated 1530, belongs to Sir Henry Vane (*Tudor Exhibition Cat.* No. 150). In the later pictures of the More family at Nostell Priory and at Cockthorpe Park Sir John fills a prominent place.

His first wife, according to his great-grandson Cresacre More, was Johanna, daughter of one Hancombe of Holywell, Bedfordshire, but entries in a contemporary manuscript (O. 2. 21) in the Gale collection in Trinity College Library, Cambridge (*Notes and Queries*, 4th ser. ii. 365), show that John More married, on 24 April 1474, when he was twenty-one, at St. Giles's Church, Cripplegate, Agnes, daughter of Thomas Graunger. It is possible that the latter belonged to the family of Hancombe, but that his branch of it adopted an alternative surname. Thomas Graunger was elected sheriff of London on 11 Nov. 1503, and died two days later at the serjeants' feast held on the occasion when More was made a serjeant (Stow, *Chron.* ed.

1580, p. 877). More's second wife was Mrs. Bowes, a widow, whose maiden name was Burton; and his third was Alice Clarke, at one time widow of William Huntyngdon of Exeter, and daughter of John More of Loseley in Surrey (*Cal. State Papers*, Dom. 1509–14, p. 292). He had issue only by his first wife. Two children seem to have died in infancy. Two sons, Thomas, the chancellor, and John, with two daughters, reached maturity. The younger son is noticed in Erasmus's correspondence as living in 1511, and as acting in the capacity of clerk to his distinguished brother (cf. *Erasmi Epistolæ*, ed. Le Clerc, Nos. 128, 139); Jane, born 11 March 1474–1475, married Richard Staffreton or Staidton; and Elizabeth, born 22 Sept. 1482, married John Rastell [q. v.] the printer, and was mother of Sir William Rastell [q. v.] the judge. More owned the manor of Gobions in the parish of North Mimms in Hertfordshire, and left it to his wife for life, with remainder to his son. On Sir Thomas More's attainder in 1534 his stepmother was expelled from Gobions, and she died in 1544 at Northall in the same county. Gobions seems to have been restored by Queen Mary to Sir John More's grandson, William Rastell, who bequeathed it in 1565 to his sister's son, Eliseus Heywood [q. v.], who made it over in 1572 by deed of gift to Franciscus de Borgia, superior-general of the Jesuits.

[Foss's Lives of the Judges; Cresacre More's Life of Sir T. More, ed. 1828, pp. 1–14; Bridgett's Life of Sir T. More, 1891.] S. L.

MORE, JOHN (*d.* 1592), the 'Apostle of Norwich,' born in Yorkshire, was elected a scholar of Christ's College, Cambridge, graduated B.A. in 1562, and was shortly afterwards chosen fellow of his college. During his Cambridge career he appears to have been influenced by Thomas Cartwright [q. v.], in whose favour he and other divines signed a testimonial addressed to Cecil in 1570. On leaving the university he was appointed minister of St. Andrew's Church, Norwich, where he remained until his death, in spite of numerous offers of higher preferment. He preached three and sometimes four times every Sunday, and made numerous converts. In 1573 he refused to wear the surplice, on the ground that it gave offence to others, and he was convened before John Parkhurst [q. v.], bishop of Norwich, who said mildly that it was better to offend a few private persons than to offend God and disobey the prince. In a letter to Archbishop Parker Parkhurst says: 'I have not known that he has at any time spoken against her Majesty's book of Injunctions, nor can I find any manner of stubbornness in him. And surely he is a godly and learned man, and hath done much good in this city' (Strype, *Life of Parker*, ii. 340). In the same year (1573) More confuted a sermon preached by Andrew Perne [q. v.] of Cambridge in Norwich Cathedral. The controversy 'presently grew to some jars amongst the citizens, according as they stood affected' (Strype, *Annals*, II. i. 417, 418), and Dr. Gardiner, one of the prebendaries of the cathedral, asked the bishop to interpose. More accordingly was prevented from carrying out his intention of further confuting Perne.

On 25 Sept. 1576 More and other puritan clergy round Norwich presented to the council a humble supplication against the imposition of ceremonies, and he was shortly afterwards suspended by Bishop Freke. Two years afterwards (21 Aug. 1578) More and his friends signed a 'submission' to their diocesan, in which they 'humbly crave favour to be restored to their preaching, upon submission to all those articles which concern the confession of the true Christian faith and doctrine of the sacraments, according to the words of the statute. And concerning ceremonies, order, and government, they acknowledge that they are so far tolerable, that for the same, no man ought to withdraw himself from hearing the word of God and receiving the sacraments; nor, on the same account, ought any minister to preach the word of God, or to administer the sacraments.' It is not clear how long More remained under episcopal censure. In 1584, after the publication of Whitgift's three articles, More and upwards of sixty other ministers of Norfolk presented to the archbishop their reasons for refusing to subscribe.

More died at Norwich, and was buried in the churchyard of St. Andrew's on 16 Jan. 1592. He left a wife, afterwards married to Dr. Nicholas Bownde or Bound [q. v.], and two daughters. He is described as 'incessu decorus, vestitu modestus, victu vinoque parcus, comitate severus, severitate comis.' His wide learning included a knowledge of Hebrew and Greek (Holland, *Herωologia*, 1620, p. 209). So great was his reputation in Norwich that he was commonly called 'the apostle' of that city. Robert Greene [q. v.] is generally supposed to allude to More's preaching in his account of the manner in which he was influenced by a sermon he heard in St. Andrew's Church, Norwich (*The Repentance of Robert Greene*, 1592). Granger mentions three portraits of More (*Biog. Hist.* i. 217, 218, 228), of which that in Holland's 'Herωologia' is the best. He is said to have worn the longest and largest beard of his time, for which he gave as a reason 'that no act of his life might be unworthy of the gravity of his appearance.'

More's works, all published after his death, are: 1. 'A Table from the beginning of the World to this day. Wherein is declared in what yeere of the World everything was done, both in the Scriptures mentioned and also in prophane matters,' Cambridge, 8vo, 1593. Edited by Nicholas Bownd. In the dedication Bownd states that not only were More's works committed to him, but 'the whole care and disposition of them by a certaine hereditarie right did fall unto him,' and, after commending the table, expresses the hope that in time 'the rest may follow, if the paucitie of Hebrue and Greeke characters in this land do not hinder some, and the great cost and charges of Printing Maps be a stay and bane to others. For in both these kinds there are certaine of his labours finished, and have bene longe since readie for the presse.' 2. 'John More his three Sermons . . . Also a Treatise of a contented Minde, by Nich. Bownde,' Cambridge, 4to, 1594. 3. 'A Lively Anatomy of Death, wherein you may see from whence it came, what it is by Nature, and what by Christ,' &c. [With a prefatory Epistle by W. Barforde], London, 1596, 8vo. 4. 'A Map of Palestine,' at Christ's College, Cambridge, attributed to More by Fuller [Cambridge, ed. Prichett and Wright, 1840]. 5. 'Catechismus Parvus.'

[Authorities quoted; Cooper's Athenæ Cant. ii. 117, 118, 546; Wood's Athenæ Oxon. (Bliss), ii. 193; Blomefield's History of Norfolk, iv. 301; Brook's Lives of the Puritans, i. 449–52; Neal's Hist. of the Puritans, i. 233.]

W. A. S. H.

MORE, JOHN (1630–1689), Franciscan. [See Cross.]

MORE, RICHARD (*d.* 1643), puritan, sprung from an ancient family which took its name from the parish of More, near Bishop's Castle, Shropshire, was son of Robert More of Linley, who was buried at More on 20 March 1603–4. His cousin, Jasper, whose only son had already been killed in a duel in 1607, died in 1613, leaving three daughters. Richard accordingly succeeded Jasper in the family estates of Larden and More, but was always called of Linley, which he inherited from his father. In 1610 he was elected a burgess of Bishop's Castle 'in regarde of his neare neighbourhode to that place' ('Bishop's Castle MSS.' in *Hist. MSS. Comm.* 10th Rep. App. pt. iv. p. 406). More is often said, in error, to have been sheriff of Shropshire in 1619 (cf. Blakeway, *The Sheriffs of Shropshire*, p. 215). Before 1633 he was a justice of the peace, and in that capacity had to find the offenders who had taken down Enoch ap Evan's body from the gibbet. Evan was a puritan, and his murder of his mother and brother was the occasion of an attack upon the puritans in 'The Looking-glasse of Schism,' by Peter Studley, London, 1635. To this More replied in 'A True Relation of the Murders, etc.,' but license to print was refused; Studley, however, heard of the book, and retorted in 'An Answer to Certaine Invective Criminations.' More was elected to the Short parliament as member for Bishop's Castle on 12 March 1639–40, and to the Long parliament for the same constituency on 12 Oct. 1640. When in 1641 a committee of the house was appointed to inquire into the complaints about the refusal of licenses for printing books, More's 'True Relation' was brought before it, and was ordered to be printed. More added an appendix in reply to Studley's 'Answer.' Before 1641 More had prepared a translation of Mede's 'Clavis Apocalyptica.' The book was ordered to be printed on 18 April 1642. It appeared in 1643, under the title 'The Key of the Revelation,' with a preface by Dr. Twisse. Through the opening year of the civil war More actively supported the parliamentary cause in Shropshire (cf. *Commons' Journals*, 1643, iii. 47, 72). He died on 6 Dec. 1643. He married a sister of Sir Thomas Harris, bart., of Boreaton, sheriff of Shropshire, in 1619. His son Samuel is separately noticed.

More must be distinguished from several contemporaries of the same name, viz. Richard Moore (1619–1683) [q. v.], dissenting divine; Richard More (*fl.* 1612), who, with Sir George Somers, Sir Thomas Gates [q. v.], and Captain Newport, was in 1609 wrecked on the Bermudas, became deputy-governor of the islands, and was author of a 'Copie of Articles,' in which the colonists bound themselves to defend the church of England against 'all atheists, popists, Brownists, and all other heretiques and sectaries whatever' (cf. *A Plaine Description of the Barmudas, now called Sommer Islands*, London, 1613, 4to); Richard More, bookseller, of St. Dunstan's Churchyard, who prefixed verses to the 1614 edition of 'England's Helicon' (cf. Brydges, *Censura Literaria*, i. 420–1); and, lastly, Richard More, author of the 'Carpenter's Rule,' London, 1602, 4to (cf. *Cat. of Early Printed Books*, ii. 1110).

[Works in Brit. Mus. Library; Official Returns of Members of Parliament; Journals of House of Commons; Hist. MSS. Comm. 10th Rep.; Blakeway's Sheriffs of Shropshire, pp. 215–20; Visitations of Shropshire (Harl. Soc.); Kittermaster's Shropshire Arms, &c.; The Castles and Old Mansions of Shropshire, pp. 28–9; Hulbert's County of Salop, pp. 266–7; Owen and Blakeway's Hist. of Shrewsbury, p. 215 *n.*; Burke's Landed Gentry.] A. F. P.

MORE, ROBERT (1671–1727?), writing-master, born in 1671, was the son of a writing-master living in King Street, Westminster. Having been educated by his father in the same profession, he 'taught writing, arithmetic, merchants' accounts, and shorthand, at the sign of the Golden Pen in Castle Street, near the Queen's Mews, Leicester Fields,' where he also announced that 'youths were boarded, or taught abroad.' He succeeded Colonel John Ayres [q. v.] in his school at St. Paul's Churchyard before May 1704 (Massey). More died about 1727, either going to or returning from a visit to the north of England. He was married, and had a 'dutifull daughter, Elizabeth More,' who wrote one or more of the pages for his 'Writing Master's Assistant.' Sir Richard Steele had a high opinion of his artistic penmanship (cf. Noble, ii. p. 358 *n.*)

More published in 1696 (the dedication to his father was dated 4 Nov.) 'The Writing Master's Assistant.' A second edition was issued in 1704 with a preface by Ayres, who says he 'extorted it from him that strangers might judge how early he began to deserve well of all ingenious persons.' He also published (without a date) 'A Striking Copy-book' of English, French, and Italian capitals. It contains eleven plates, but no engraver's name, and is dedicated to Josiah Diston, merchant, London. About 1710 followed 'Specimens of Penmanship,' and in 1716 'The First Invention of Writing. An Essay Compendiously Treating of the Whole Art. More particularly; Of Letters, their Number, Order, and of how many Variations capable: Of their First Invention; by ancient Writers ascribed to Adam himself, and for what Reasons. Of Short-hand. Of Secret Writing, Decypherable by the Key. Of Arithmetick, &c. Interspers'd with diverting History and Poetical Entertainments on the Subject. Whereunto are added, Several Pieces of the Hands in Use, not before Published.' This work is dedicated to 'Mr. George Shelley, Writing-Master of Christ's Hospital in London,' 23 April 1716. A fine portrait drawn and engraved by William Sherwin [q. v.] is prefixed. The portrait was reproduced, with the addition of the words 'ætatis 54 domini 1725,' in 'The General Penman,' published by More in that year. It was also included in a group of six writing-masters engraved by George Bickham, senior [q. v.], above his 'Poem on Writing,' no date (print room, British Museum). More is the author of some lines in the 'British Apollo,' 2nd edit. i. 173, on the art of writing.

[Noble's Continuation of Granger's Biog. Hist. of England, ii. 357–9; Massey's Origin and Progress of Letters, 1763, pt. ii. pp. 103–8; Ames's Cat. of English Heads, 1748, p. 119.] C. F. S.

MORE, ROGER (*fl.* 1620–1652), Irish rebel. [See O'More, Rory.]

MORE, SAMUEL (1594–1662), parliamentarian, born in 1594, was eldest son of Richard More [q. v.] of Linley, Shropshire, whom he succeeded in December 1643. Like his father, More became a zealous parliamentarian, an active soldier, and member of the 'committee of parliament for Shropshire, whose business it was to raise money for the good cause,' and whose proceedings are said to have been satirised in the 'Committee,' a comedy, by Sir Robert Howard (1626–1698) [q. v.] Soon after his father's death, More was summoned in February 1643–4 to take command of Hopton Castle, one of the few parliamentary strongholds in Shropshire. With thirty-one men he defended the castle for more than a month against a force of upwards of five hundred foot and horse; the siege, of which he has left a circumstantial account (printed in Blakeway, *The Sheriffs of Shropshire*, pp. 217–20), ended in unconditional surrender, and the whole garrison, with the exception of More, was put to death. More was imprisoned in Ludlow Castle, and then (*Hist. MSS. Comm.* 4th Rep. p. 266) exchanged for Edward Cresset, one of the leading royalists in Shropshire (cf. *The Ingagement and Resolution of the principal Gentlemen of Salop*, Oxford, 1642, 4to). From 18 May 1645 to 25 March 1647 he had charge of Montgomery Castle, with a salary of 20*s.* a day (*Cal. State Papers*, Dom. 1648–9, p. 14). On 9 Aug. 1645 he was also governor of Monmouth, and on 26 Sept. was ordered to 'improve his forces,' so as to alarm the Welsh and prevent them sending relief to Chester, which was being besieged by the parliamentarians (*ib.* 1644–1645 p. 308, 1645–7 p. 163). In December he was governor of Ludlow Castle, and on 6 June 1646 his appointment was confirmed (*Hist. MSS. Comm.* 6th Rep. p. 120, 7th Rep. p. 113). On 17 June 1647 he became governor of Hereford Castle. On 8 Aug. 1648 he was ordered to repair to Montgomery Castle and report on the state of the garrison (*Cal. State Papers*, Dom. 1648–9, p. 235). On 25 Feb. 1653–4 More was placed on the committee for assessment in Shropshire, and took a leading part in the internal regulation of the county. He was accused of complicity in an attempt to depose Cromwell from the protectorate, and when elected member for the county in the parliament of 1656 he was excluded by Cromwell (Noble, *Regicides*, ii. 84). He was elected M.P. for Bishop's Castle in January 1658 (*Hist. MSS. Comm.* 10th Rep. pt. iv. p. 405). He survived the Restoration, and died in May 1662.

More married, first, a daughter of his kinsman, Jasper More, by whom he had three children; by a second wife he had three sons and four daughters.

His eldest son, Richard (1627–1698), born in 1627, was admitted of Gray's Inn on 26 May 1646 (*Reg.* ed. Foster), was in 1644 lieutenant in Lord St. John's regiment, was made commissioner for compounding in 1646, frequently serving in that capacity until 1659 (cf. *Cal. Proc. Committee for Compounding*, passim), became commissioner for advance of money (*Cal.* pp. 1045, 1648), serjeant of Gray's Inn (Luttrell, *Brief Relation*, ii. 428), and sat in parliament as member for Bishop's Castle from 1680 until his death in 1698. He married, first, Ann, daughter of Sir Isaac Pennington [q. v.], lord mayor of London, but had no issue by her, from whom he was subsequently divorced; and, secondly, Dorcas Owen, by whom he had two sons, Thomas (*d.* 1731) and Richard, slain in battle in 1709.

Robert More (1703–1780), son of Robert, third son of Samuel More, travelled widely in Europe; in Spain he became intimate with Benjamin Keene [q. v.] and the Spanish ministers, and was the means of introducing many reforms into the administration. He was an enthusiastic botanist, a friend of Linnæus, and F.R.S. (cf. Dillon, *Travels through Spain*, p. 107, &c).

More must be distinguished from several officers of that name in the parliamentary army, especially Colonel John More of Bank Hall, Lancashire, who was M.P. for Liverpool in 1640, took part in the siege of Lathom House and several other actions during the civil war, was one of the king's judges, served in Ireland in 1650, and commanded Cromwell's Guards (cf. *Discourse of the Warr*, Chetham Soc.; *Norris Papers*, Chetham Soc.; Gregson, *Portfolio of Fragments*; Baines, *Lancashire and Cheshire*; Whitelocke, *Memorials*, p. 93; *Cal. State Papers*, Dom. passim; Sprigge, *Anglia Rediviva*, p. 332; Noble, *Regicides*, ii. 84); and from Samuel Moore or More, born in 1617, who wrote a preface to Robert Dingley's 'Messiah's Splendor,' 1649, and a work entitled 'Θεοσπλαγχνισθεις, or the Yernings of Christ's Bowels towards his languishing Friends,' 1648, 1654. The latter has a portrait engraved by W. Marshall. There was also a Colonel William Moore, who served in Ireland in 1656 (Noble, ii. 84).

[Hist. MSS. Comm., passim, especially 10th Rep. Appendix, pt. iv., containing the Corporation of Bishop's Castle MSS.; Peacock's Army Lists; Cal. State Papers, 1641–59, passim; Official Returns of Members of Parliament; Blakeway's Sheriffs of Shropshire; Visitations of Shropshire (Harl. Soc.); Castles and Old Mansions of Shropshire, pp. 28–9; Garrisons of Shropshire, pp. 50–2; Mercurius Britannicus, 1–8 April 1644; Noble's Regicides, ii. 84–5; Webb's Memorials of the Civil War in Herefordshire, i. 388, ii. 12; Hulbert's County of Salop, pp. 266–7; Owen and Blakeway's Hist. of Shrewsbury, i. 458, 460; Burke's Landed Gentry; authorities quoted.] A. F. P.

MORE or MOORE, Sir THOMAS de la (*fl.* 1327–1347), alleged chronicler, passed for three centuries as the unquestioned author of a short chronicle entitled 'Vita et Mors Edwardi Secundi, Gallice conscripta a generosissimo milite Thoma de la Moore, et in Latinum reducta ab alio quodam ejus synchrono,' first printed by Camden in his 'Anglica, Normannica, Hibernica,' &c., in 1603, and re-edited for the Rolls Series by Bishop Stubbs in 1883 in the second volume of 'Chronicles of the Reigns of Edward I and Edward II.' This chronicle, from which historians have drawn some of the most graphic details of Edward II's last days, was regarded as a contemporary Latin translation of a supposed French work by More, whence Geoffrey Baker [q. v.] or Galfrid le Baker de Swynebroke was also credited with having drawn his chronicle extending from 1303 to 1356. But Bishop Stubbs has proved that the 'Vita et Mors' usually associated with More's name is nothing but an abstract and extract from Baker's chronicle (Pref. to his edition, p. lxxi). He still thought it possible, however, that the lost French original of the latter, written by Sir Thomas de la Moore, might some day be recovered. Mr. Maunde Thompson has, however, come to the conclusion that no such original ever existed. Its existence was inferred from the passage in Galfrid le Baker (ed. Thompson, p. 27), where, in speaking of the deputation which went to Kenilworth in January 1327, to receive the king's abdication, he adds: 'Quorum comitivam, aderens predicto episcopo Wintoniensi, tu generose miles qui hec vidisti et in Gallico scripsisti, cuius ego sum talis qualis interpres, te dico domine Thoma de la More, tua sapienti et inclita presencia decorasti.' But Mr. Thompson is almost certainly right in holding that Baker is obviously only acknowledging his indebtedness to Sir Thomas de la Moore's account of a scene in which Moore had himself played a part (Preface, pp. vii–viii).

The patron who has thus by a singular chance for so long been regarded as the real author of his *protégé's* work was said by Camden in his preface, with a vague reference to ancient records, to have belonged to a Gloucestershire family of knightly rank, and to have served in the Scottish wars of Edward I, who knighted him. On this hint Sir Robert Atkyns made him the eldest son of Richard de la More of Eldland, in the parish of Bitton, Gloucestershire, who was knight of the shire for that county in 1290, and died in 1292 (*Hist. of Gloucestershire*, p. 287). Tanner accepted Atkyns's statement without question (*Bibl. Brit. Hib.* p. 531). But Bishop Stubbs has shown that it is erroneous, and that Galfrid le Baker's patron, who was in Bishop Stratford's train, perhaps as a young man, in 1327, may be safely identified with a Sir Thomas de la More of Mora or Moor (now Northmoor), in southern Oxfordshire, only eleven miles south-east of Swinebrook, who sat as knight of the shire for Oxfordshire in the first two parliaments of 1340, and served on the great committee appointed in the second session to sit from day to day until the business was finished and the petitions turned into a statute (Stubbs, Preface, p. lxi; *Rot. Parl.* ii. 113). His position as a person of weight in his county was shown by his re-election in 1343 and 1351. It was at his instance, Galfrid le Baker tells us, that he wrote his shorter chronicle, finished in 1347, and in his larger chronicle, besides the passage already quoted, he once addresses him as 'miles reverende' (ed. Thompson, p. 30). It is quite likely, therefore, that he was still alive when Baker wrote the final lines of this chronicle in 1358. It is not, indeed, impossible that he may be the Sir Thomas de la More who in 1370 was constable or vice-warden of Porchester Castle under the Earl of Arundel (Devon, *Issue Roll*, 5, 243, 372, 424; *Fœdera*, iii. 880; Stubbs, p. lxiii). The family of de la More, which was long seated at Northmoor, may perhaps, Bishop Stubbs thinks, have been connected with the Berkshire family of de la More or de la Mare (*ib.*) A Sir Thomas de la More, who was apparently a member of this family, was sheriff of Oxfordshire in 1370.

The 'Vita et Mors' ascribed to de la More exists in three manuscripts of the second half of the sixteenth century: 1. MS. Cotton, Vitellius E. 5, ff. 261–70, copied, perhaps, by Samuel Daniel (1562–1619) [q. v.], the historian, from a transcript by Laurence Nowell, brother of Alexander Nowell, dean of St. Paul's, who himself died dean of Lichfield in 1576 (Stubbs, Preface, p. lxvi). 2. MS. Inner Temple, Petyt, A. 7, ff. 303–14, formerly belonging to John Foxe the martyrologist. 3. MS. Harleian, 310. That numbered 81 in the Jekyll MSS. is no longer forthcoming (*ib.*)

[Authorities in the text; Baker's Chronicle, edited by Dr. Giles for the Caxton Society, 1841, and by Dr. E. Maunde Thompson, at Oxford, 1889. See also art. Baker, Geoffrey.]

J. T-t.

MORE, Sir THOMAS (1478–1535), lord chancellor of England and author, was born between two and three in the morning of Saturday, 7 Feb. 1477–8 (*Notes and Queries*, 4th ser. ii. 365, by Dr. W. Aldis Wright). He was the only surviving son of Sir John More, then a barrister, living in Milk Street, Cheapside. His mother was his father's first wife, Agnes, daughter of Thomas Graunger [see under More, Sir John]. Thomas was sent at an early age to St. Anthony's school in Threadneedle Street. The head-master, Nicholas Holt, had already had under his care John Colet [q. v.], the future dean of St. Paul's, and William Latimer [q. v.], both of whom were subsequently among More's intimate friends. At the age of thirteen More was placed by his father in the household of Thomas Morton [q. v.], archbishop of Canterbury and lord chancellor. He was a merry boy, and his intellectual alertness attracted the attention of his master, who prophesied that he would prove 'a marvellous man.' 'At Christmas time he would suddenly, sometimes, step in among the players [in the archbishop's house], making up an extemporary part of his own.' Morton inspired the lad with lasting respect (cf. *Utopia*, ed. Arber, p. 36), and gave practical proof of his interest in his welfare by recommending that he should be sent to Oxford. About 1492 he seems to have entered Canterbury Hall, which was afterwards absorbed in Christ Church (More). His father gave him barely sufficient money to supply himself with necessaries, and he consequently had no opportunity of neglecting his studies for frivolous amusements. He made the acquaintance of Thomas Linacre [q. v.] and of William Grocyn [q. v.], both of whom had lately returned from Italy, and from the former he received his earliest instruction in Greek. He never became a minute scholar, but by intuition, or an 'instinct of genius,' he was soon able at a glance to detect the meaning of any Greek sentence put before him (cf. Pace, *De Fructu*, 1517, p. 82), and by steady practice he came to write an easy and harmonious Latin prose (Erasmus, *Epist.* 447). Besides the classics, he studied French, mathematics, and history, and learned to play on the viol and flute (Stapleton).

His father, who had designed him for the bar, deprecated, according to Erasmus, his devotion to Greek, and feared that his religious orthodoxy might suffer by his growing enthusiasm for the new learning. It is certain that after two years' residence in Oxford More was recalled to London, and about 1494 was entered as a law student at New Inn. In February 1496 he was removed to Lincoln's Inn, and rapidly acquired a good knowledge of law. He was called to the outer bar after a shorter period of probation than was customary, and was appointed reader or lecturer on law at Furnival's Inn, which was dependent on Lincoln's Inn. His lectures were so satisfactory that he was invited to repeat them in three successive years.

While assiduously studying law, More devoted much of his leisure to literature. He wrote 'for his pastime' very promising verse in both Latin and English, and, according to Erasmus, tried his hand at 'little comedies' (*comœdiolas*), while he spent much time over the works of Pico della Mirandola. He sedulously cultivated the acquaintance of men of literary tastes; saw much of his Oxford tutors, Grocyn and Linacre, after they settled in London, and through them came to know Colet and William Lily [q. v.], both scholars of high attainments. Colet, who exercised a powerful influence over him, became his confessor, or, in his own words, 'the director of his life' (Stapleton). With Lily he engaged in friendly rivalry while rendering epigrams from the Greek anthology into Latin, and their joint efforts ('pro-gymnasmata') were published in 1518. But of greater satisfaction to him was his introduction in 1497 to Erasmus, who was then on a first visit to England. It is possible that they first met at the house of Erasmus's pupil and patron, Lord Mountjoy. More's handsome face, ready wit, and wide culture at once fascinated the great scholar. A very close intimacy followed, and they regularly corresponded with each other until separated by death. In the spring of 1499 More and Erasmus, while at Mountjoy's country house, walked over to a neighbouring mansion, where Henry VII's children were in residence. Prince Henry (afterwards Henry VIII), a boy of nine, stood in the hall, between his two sisters, Margaret and Mary, and More presented him with a poem. This is the earliest evidence of a meeting between More and his future master.

When nearly of age (in 1499) More experienced severe spiritual questionings, and contemplated becoming a priest. He went to live near the Charterhouse, so that he might take part daily in the spiritual exercises of the Carthusians, and devoted himself to 'vigils, fasts, and prayers, and similar austerities' (Erasmus). He wore 'a sharp shirt of hair next his skin, which he never left off wholly' (More), often scourged himself, and gave only four or five hours a day to sleep. He even thought of taking the vows of a Franciscan. While in this frame of mind he seems to have lectured in the church of St. Lawrence Jewry on St. Augustine's 'De Civitate Dei,' probably at the invitation of his friend Grocyn, who was rector of the church. His audience included Grocyn and other men of learning and influence in the city, but none of his lectures are extant. They possibly contained the germs of the 'Utopia.'

At the end of four years thus spent in religious contemplation (1499–1503), More suddenly abandoned all thought of the priesthood, and flung himself with redoubled energy into secular affairs. The cause of this change of purpose has been variously estimated. The discovery of notable corruptions within the church; a newly awakened ambition to make a name for himself either in politics or in his profession where his chances of success seemed secure; an unwillingness to submit to the restraints of celibacy, have all been suggested—the first with especial warmth by protestant writers. There is probably an element of truth in each, but strong religious excitement is not uncommon as a merely temporary phase in young men of highly nervous temperament or precociously developed intellect. While relinquishing ascetic practices, he continued till death scrupulously regular in all the religious observances expected of a pious catholic. But his alertness of intellect rendered him intolerant of inefficiency or insincerity in the priesthood, whose defects inspired many of his witty Latin epigrams. Like Erasmus and Colet he trusted to the intelligence of the higher clergy and to the progress of education to uproot ignorance and superstition (cf. his letter denouncing the follies of a friar at Coventry in Lambeth MS. 575, pp. 7–9, printed in Nichols, *Bibl. Top. Brit.* iv. No. xvii., 1780).

More's work at the bar was brilliantly successful, and he soon began a study of politics. In 1503 he lamented in English verse the death of Queen Elizabeth (*English Works*). In the spring of 1504 he was elected a member of parliament, but the extant returns fail to mention his constituency. Edmund Dudley [q. v.] was speaker. The heavy exactions for which Henry VII, with Dudley's aid, had made himself notorious excited More's disgust, and had formed the subject of some scathing Latin verse. When, therefore, a bill was introduced demanding an aid of three-fifteenths on the plea of the recent marriage of the king's eldest daughter Margaret with the king of Scotland, More took part in the debate, and used 'such arguments and reasons thereagainst that the king's demands were thereby clean overthrown.' The king had to forego the 113,000*l.* demanded, and felt bound to surrender 10,000*l.* of the 40,000*l.* offered by the commons in substitution (*Stat. of Realm*, ii. 975). More had not attacked the king directly; otherwise, Dudley told him later, he would have lost his head. But when Henry learned 'that a beardless boy,' who had nothing to lose, had 'disappointed all his purpose,' he revenged himself by devising 'a causeless quarrel against More's father, keeping him in the Tower till he had made him pay to him a hundred pounds fine.'

Meanwhile More was resorting 'to the house of one Maister [John] Colte, a gentleman of [Newhall, near Chelmsford] Essex, that had oft invited him thither,' and had three daughters. According to one of his Latin epigrams he had fallen in love in his sixteenth year, but the passion was transient. Now 'the honest conversation and virtuous education' of Colte's daughters provoked More 'there specially to set his affection.' 'And, albeit,' writes his biographer Roper, 'his mind most served him to the second daughter, for that he thought her the fairest and best favoured, yet when he considered that it would be both great grief and some shame also to the eldest to see her younger sister preferred before her in marriage, he then, of a certain pity, framed his fancy towards' the eldest. More accordingly married Jane Colte in 1505 and settled in Bucklersbury. He proved a model husband, delighting in domesticity, and dividing his leisure between the care of his household and literary pursuits. Within a year he invited Erasmus to stay with him, and they amused themselves by translating some of Lucian's dialogues into Latin. In 1508 he went abroad and visited the universities of Louvain and Paris, in which he detected no superiority over Oxford or Cambridge. In the same year Erasmus paid him another visit, and wrote under his roof the 'Moriæ Encomium,' the title of which was intended as a pun on More's surname, and to More the book was dedicated. His first wife died about 1511, after bearing four children, and according to his confessor, John Bouge or Bonge, he obtained a dispensation to marry again within a month of the lady's death, and 'without any banns asking' (*English Historical Review*, 1892, vii. 712–15). The second wife was a widow, Alice Middleton, with an only daughter, afterwards wife of Sir Giles Alington. She was seven years More's senior, and neither beautiful nor well educated, but she was an active and vigilant housewife. Although she was seldom able to appreciate her husband's jests, the union seems to have proved satisfactory. Cresacre More's story that More was drawn into the match while pleading the suit of a friend with Mrs. Middleton is uncorroborated. After his second marriage More removed to Crosby Place, in Bishopsgate Street Without, and in 1523 he bought land at Chelsea on which he built a far-famed mansion.

More's professional work soon brought him 400*l.* a year—equivalent to 5,000*l.* now—but he developed with his success a notable independence of character. He gave his numerous clients perfectly disinterested advice, and deprecated their proceeding with suits that seemed to him unjust or frivolous. Soon after Henry VIII's accession in 1509 he was elected a bencher of Lincoln's Inn, and was reader there for the first time in 1511, and again in Lent 1516. On 3 Sept. 1510 he had been made under-sheriff of London—an officer who then acted as a judicial representative of the sheriff in cases now relegated to the sheriff's court. In 1514 quarrels arose between the London merchants and the foreign traders of the Steelyard, and it was necessary to send an embassy to Flanders to secure by treaty fuller protection of English commercial interests. Flattering reports of More had reached the king and Wolsey, and when the London merchants represented to the latter that More could best support their views in the negotiations, Wolsey readily nominated 'young More' one of the envoys. He had already attracted Henry's notice by presenting to him an elaborate epithalamium on his marriage to Catherine of Aragon in June 1509. On 8 May 1514 it was agreed by the common council 'that Thomas More, gentleman, one of the under-sheriffs of London, should occupy his office and chamber by a sufficient deputy during his absence as the king's ambassador in Flanders.' But the embassy, which was under the direction of Cuthbert Tunstall, did not leave England till 12 May 1515, when a similar concession was made More by the corporation. More was absent more than six months, and he received only 13*s.* 4*d.* a day—a sum insufficient (he told Erasmus) to maintain himself abroad, as well as his wife and children in London. He could not induce his family (he humorously regretted) to fast in his absence (BREWER, i. 150). His time was chiefly spent at Bruges, Brussels, and Antwerp. In the latter city he delighted in the society of Peter Giles or Ægidius, a friend of Erasmus, and found time to sketch his imaginary island of 'Utopia.' The work was completed and published the next year.

In 1515 More was included in the commission of the peace for Hampshire, an honour that was again conferred on him in 1528 (*Letters and Papers of Henry VIII*, ii. 170, 670, 3917). In 1516 he wrote to Erasmus: 'When I returned from my embassage of Flanders the king's majesty would have granted me a yearly pension, which surely, if I should respect honour and profit, was not to be contemned by me; yet have I as yet refused it.' But neither Wolsey nor the king was willing to accept a refusal. On 17 Feb. 1516 More was reported to be frequently in Wolsey's antechamber, and on 10 March Erasmus expressed a fear that he would be carried away by a whirlwind of court favour (*Epist.* 21). In the same year he accepted a pension of 100*l.* for life (*Letters and Papers*, vol. ii. pt. i. No. 2736). A riot in the city on May-day 1517, caused by a sudden outbreak of popular fury against foreign merchants, brought More again to the notice of the authorities. He undertook to address the rioters near St. Martin's Gate, and entreated them to disperse (HALL). He was afterwards appointed by the city to examine into the causes of the disturbance (*Apology*, ch. xlvii.) In the following August, while the sweating sickness, he tells us, raged in London, he was nominated, much against his will, a member of a new embassy to Calais which was to arrange disputes with envoys of France (BREWER, i. 188). 'Thus it is,' wrote Erasmus regretfully (*Epist.* 318), 'that kings beatify their friends; this it is to be beloved of cardinals.' The squabblings of the conference disappointed More, who played a very subordinate part, but he was not home again till November (BREWER, i. 197). After his return he argued successfully in the Star-chamber against the claim of the crown to seize a ship belonging to the pope which had put in at Southampton. The adroitness of his argument impressed Henry VIII with the necessity of making him at once an officer of the crown. In 1518 he was nominated master of requests, or examiner of petitions presented to the king on his progresses through the country—an office which required its holder to reside with the court, and to be in constant personal relations with Henry. Although More is called 'councillor' in the pension grant of 1516, his actual introduction to the privy council seems to have been delayed till the summer of 1518 (*Venetian State Papers*, ii. 1072). His absorption by the court was completed on 23 July 1519, when he resigned the office of under-sheriff.

Although More had already in his 'Utopia' offered as a philosopher many counsels of perfection to politicians, he held no exaggerated views of the practical power of statesmen to root out evil opinions and practices 'in the commonwealth and in the councils of princes.' He was an intelligent, peace-loving conservative, sprung from the people, who desired the welfare of all classes; but he never contemplated achieving reform in any department of the state or church by revolution. By his tact and discretion a politician might so order what was bad, he thought, 'that it be not very bad' (*Utopia*, p. 65). 'For it is not possible,' he wrote, 'for all things to be well unless all men were good, which I think will not be yet these many years.' The first words that Henry VIII addressed to him on entering the royal household—'willing him first to look unto God and after God unto him'—largely indicated the spirit in which he devoted himself to political life.

Throughout his attendance at court More was enthusiastic in his praises of Henry's affability and courtesy, while Henry on his side was charmed by More's witty conversation, and treated him with exceptional familiarity. Henry would often send for him into his private chamber to talk 'in matters of astronomy, geometry, divinity, and such other faculties,' or would invite him to sup in private with him and the queen, 'to be merry with them.' At times, too, the king would present himself as an unbidden guest at dinner-time at More's own house, and would walk with More about his garden at Chelsea, 'holding his arm about his [councillor's] neck.' But More was under no delusion respecting his tenure of the king's affection. 'If my head should win him a castle in France,' he told Roper in 1525, 'it should not fail to go.' His devotion to the new learning met with Henry's full approval. When he was with the king at Abingdon in the spring of 1518, an old-fashioned clergyman preached at court against the study of Greek and against 'the new interpreters,' and after the sermon More was deputed to confute his arguments in the royal presence. More brought his opponent to his knees, to the amusement of his audience (ERASMUS, *Epist.* 346). Similarly when More called the king's attention to the outcry of the 'barbarians' at Oxford against the incursion of Greek learning into the university, he drew from Henry a strong expression of opinion adverse to the brawlers (*ib.*), and at the same time wrote a powerful letter to the university urging the tutors to recognise the necessity of extending the topics of education beyond mediæval limits. In 1520 he defended in a like spirit Erasmus's Latin translation of the Greek Testament and his 'Moriæ Encomium,' both of which had been attacked by a Louvain professor, Martin Dorpion or Dorpius.

As master of requests meanwhile More seized many opportunities of helping poor petitioners, and in 1521 the council, doubtless at his suggestion, put in force the statutes against unauthorised enclosures.

With More's natural grace of manner went a cultivated power of speech, and he was often selected as the spokesman of the court at ceremonial functions. When the legate Campeggio arrived in London in July 1518, More welcomed him in a Latin oration as he went in procession through Cheapside (Brewer, i. 281). In June 1520 he was with the king at the Field of the Cloth of Gold, and met at Calais Erasmus, who introduced him to a new friend, William Budée or Budæus, the French king's secretary and the greatest Greek scholar of the age. Budée was already favourably known to More by his writings. With another French attendant on the French royal family More's relations were less agreeable. He had in 1518 published in his 'Epigrammata' some severe epigrams on Germain de Brie (Brixius), the French queen's secretary, who had written a poem, 'Chordigera,' in celebration of the destruction of an English ship by the French ship Cordelier in 1512. De Brie retaliated in 1520 in a scurrilous pamphlet entitled 'Anti-Morus,' Basle, 1520, and More wrote a virulent reply. He showed it at Calais to Erasmus, who deprecated its publication. But at the close of 1520 it appeared in print. More's controversial tone was unfortunately as coarse as was habitual to the scholars and theologians of his time. He declared, however, that, in accordance with Erasmus's advice, he had distributed only seven copies of the impression (Erasmus, *Epist.* 571).

In the spring of 1521 More was knighted, and was made sub-treasurer to the king (*ib.* 605; cf. *Letters and Papers*, iii. 1437–1527). A month later he accompanied Wolsey to Calais and Bruges to conduct further negotiations with French and imperial envoys. While he was staying at Bruges a vainglorious student offered to publicly dispute on any subject of human learning. More jestingly challenged him to discuss with him 'An averia capta in withernamia sunt irreplegiabilia,' i.e. 'whether cattle seized under the writ termed withernam were irrepleviable,' but the student wisely acknowledged himself baffled by the question. More was sent by Wolsey, with Sir William Fitzwilliam, to carry special messages from Calais to Henry VIII (in October 1521), and next June he took part in the elaborate entertainments held in honour of Charles V's visit, welcoming him to London in a Latin speech (Brewer, i. 452). In 1522 and 1525 he was granted by Henry large gifts of land in Oxfordshire and Kent.

Wolsey's opinion of More increased with their intimacy; they corresponded repeatedly on official topics, and More, when in attendance at court, very often communicated to the cardinal Henry's advice on current politics (cf. Ellis, *Orig. Letters*, 1st ser. i. 195–213, 2nd ser. i. 289–91). In April 1523 Wolsey recommended More's election as speaker of the House of Commons. More 'disabled himself both in wit, learning, and discretion,' but Wolsey declared Henry to be well satisfied with the appointment (Hall). According to Roper, More's son-in-law, More showed more independence than was agreeable to his patron in his new office. The house evinced reluctance to grant the subsidy demanded by the crown, and when the cardinal came with a long retinue to make a personal appeal to the commons, More (in Roper's narrative) declined on his knees to give any answer until Wolsey's speech had been fully debated. When Wolsey next met More he remarked, 'Would God you had been at Rome when I made you speaker!' and recommended that he should be appointed to the embassy at Madrid. More is said to have begged the king to confer the post on another. 'It is not our pleasure, Mr. More,' Henry replied, 'to do you hurt, but to do you good would we be glad' (Roper). But Roper's story is contradicted by contemporary accounts of the proceedings of the parliament of 1523. No sign of disagreement between Wolsey and More was at any time apparent there, and More while speaker is represented as joining, contrary to usage, in the debates in order to urge on an unwilling house the duty of granting the full subsidy applied for by the king (Brewer, i. 469–80; cf. Hall). The subsidy was obtained in due course, and Wolsey soon afterwards recommended More, 24 Aug. 1523, for a gratuity of 100*l.* in addition to the fee of the same amount usually bestowed on the speaker (*Letters and Papers*, iii. 3270). 'I am the rather moved,' Wolsey wrote, 'to put your highness in remembrance thereof because he is not the most ready to speak and solicit his own cause.' More thanked Wolsey effusively (*MS. Cott. Titus*, B. I. f. 323; *Letters and*

Papers, iii. 3274). But some divergence in their views sprang up soon afterwards. When the cardinal proposed in the council the creation of a new dignity, that of supreme constable of the kingdom, More declared himself opposed to the scheme. 'You show yourself a foolish councillor,' said Wolsey. More retorted with thanks to God that the king had only one fool in his council.

More was appointed a collector of the subsidy in Middlesex in August 1523. In 1525 he became high steward of Cambridge University (COOPER, and cf. *MS.* 318, No. 2, at Corpus Christi Coll. Oxf.); in June he played a prominent part in the elaborate pageants which attended the creation of the king's natural son Henry as Duke of Richmond (BREWER, ii. 102). He was promoted in July to the chancellorship of the duchy of Lancaster, to be held with his other offices. He received a license to export one thousand woollen cloths in 1526, and in the same year he joined a sub-committee of the council, consisting of three persons, two of whom were to wait on the king every day (*ib.* i. 54). Soon afterwards he once again took part in important negotiations—in Wolsey's company at Amiens in August 1527, and in Tunstall's company at Cambray in July 1528.

Although More in early life had, like Colet and Erasmus, looked forward to a reformation of the church from within, he had no sympathy with Luther's attempt to reform the church from without. But he showed at first no anxiety to enter into the controversy. Henry VIII subsequently asserted that More persuaded him to write his 'Defensio Septem Sacramentorum' (1521) in reply to Luther's 'Babylonish Captivity;' but More claimed to have done no more than supply the index (ROPER, p. 25; cf. *Archæologia*, xxiii. 73). When Luther, however, retaliated in a scurrilous attack on Henry VIII, conscience led More into the fray. Under the pseudonym of William Ross, an Englishman represented as on a visit to Rome, and doubtfully said to be the name of an early friend of More lately dead, More put forward a bantering rejoinder (London, 1523, 4to), which, despite frequent lapses into vulgarity, embodied his most sacred convictions (BREWER, i. 608–9). In it he seriously appealed to 'illustrious Germany' to reject the heresies which Luther and his allies were disseminating, and he impressively asserted his faith in the papacy. He acknowledged the vices of some of the popes, but declined to impute them to the office, believing that God would yet raise up 'such popes as befit the dignity of the apostolic office.' The flowing tide of Lutheranism was not affected by More's onslaught, and he soon flung himself without disguise into the struggle. In March 1527 he received permission from Bishop Tunstall to read heretical books (BURNET, I. ii. 13), and the Hanse merchants issued in the same month a printed circular announcing that Wolsey and More had forbidden the importation of Lutheran works into England (cf. copy in Brit. Mus. C. 18. e. 1, No. 94). In 1528 More completed his 'Dialogue,' his first controversial book in English, which was directed mainly against Tindal's writings. Thenceforth with Tindal and his allies, Frith and George Joye, he waged unceasing battle till his death.

On 19 Oct. 1529 Wolsey was deprived of his post of chancellor. Archbishop Warham was pressed to accept the honourable office, but he declined it on the score of age (ERASMUS, *Epist.* 1151, ii. 1348; FOXE, iv. 610–11). On 25 Oct. the seals were handed to More by the king at Greenwich, and next day he took the oaths in Westminster Hall, when the Duke of Norfolk delivered to him the king's admonition to administer justice impartially. The promotion was without precedent. For the first time the chancellor was a layman. Erasmus wrote on hearing the news: 'I do indeed congratulate England, for a better or holier judge could not have been appointed' (*Epist.* 1034). But Henry made it plain that More's political power was very limited; the general direction of affairs was mainly in the hands of the Duke of Norfolk, the president of the council. According to Cardinal Pole, More owed his elevation to the king's desire to win his support in the proceedings he had begun for his divorce from Queen Catherine. But More never wavered in his devotion to her, or to the papacy which had championed her cause. 'He is,' wrote Chapuys at the time of his promotion, 'an upright and learned man, and a good servant of the queen' (*Letters and Papers*, iv. 6026). In a later letter to Cromwell (5 March 1534) More admitted that on his return from France in September 1527 the king first spoke to him of his scruples respecting the legitimacy of his union with the queen, and that he offered no opinion on the subject. After his appointment as chancellor, however, at Henry's invitation he seriously considered the king's views, but he announced that he was unable to agree with them. Thenceforth he declares he was left 'free,' but he did not conceal from himself the possible dangers to which even a silent divergence of opinion exposed him.

His first duty as chancellor was to open the new parliament meeting on 3 Nov. 1529 in the presence of the king. It was summoned, he was charged to say, 'to reform such things as had been used or permitted by inadvertence or by changes of time had become inexpedient' (Hall); but of the sweeping ecclesiastical reforms which were to be accomplished before this parliament was dissolved More clearly had no knowledge. According to Hall, an unfriendly witness, More added to his opening speech an unfriendly description of Wolsey as 'a great wether' that 'had craftily juggled with the king,' but neither Roper nor the parliamentary history gives any hint of the remark (Brewer, ii. 390–1). He signed the articles of Wolsey's impeachment, and doubtless assented as a lawyer to the policy both of declaring Wolsey guilty of a breach of the Præmunire Act, and of fining the clergy for having acknowledged Wolsey's legatine authority. But he had no share in penning the king's proclamation, ordering the clergy while paying their fines to acknowledge Henry, 'as far as the law of Christ will allow, supreme head of the church' (11 Feb. 1530–1). According to Chapuys, More proffered his resignation as soon as he heard of the king's 'usurpation' of a title hitherto reserved to the pope (*Letters and Papers*, v. 112). But the king had hopes of More, and he remained in office. In March 1531 he announced to the House of Lords the opinions of the universities respecting the divorce. More was invited to declare his private opinion of the proceedings against Queen Catherine, but he cautiously remarked that he had already announced his views to the king many times (*ib.* v. 171). Next year parliament was induced to revoke all constitutions made by the clergy in convocation, and to prohibit the holding of convocations thenceforward without the royal license (23 Hen. VIII, c. 19). This was the first of the acts that were to disestablish the papacy in England. There followed a bill to suspend the payment of first-fruits to the papacy. Sir George Throckmorton spoke against the bill, and More sent for him privately and commended his attitude (Froude, i. 360–1), while he vigorously opposed the proposal in the council, 13 May 1532. Nor did he conceal his dislike of the king's suggestion that the laws against heresy should be relaxed (cf. *Spanish Calendar*, iv. i. 446). The king showed signs of anger, and three days later More, perceiving his position impossible, resigned his office of chancellor in the gardens of York Place. He had held it little more than two years and a half. 'Every one is concerned,' wrote Chapuys, 'for there never was a better man in office' (*ib.* v. 1046). Going home, he broke the news to his wife and daughters with every appearance of light-hearted indifference. He at once adapted his household arrangements to his suddenly diminished income. He sold his plate, and cheerfully determined to live on some 100*l.* a year, the rent of lands which he had purchased, but for a time he received in addition some emoluments from the state (cf. *Letters and Papers*, 7 March 1534). In announcing his change of fortune to Erasmus he ascribed it to his ill-health, but Erasmus expressed his satisfaction at his withdrawal from politics (cf. Erasmus, *Epist.* 1856). When the Duke of Norfolk was inducting the new lord chancellor (Sir Thomas Audley) into office, More was gratified by the complimentary reference made to him, and he hotly denied the rumour that he had been dismissed from office, or had incurred the king's displeasure. In Chelsea Church he at once set up a tomb with a long epitaph upon it, in which he declared that he intended, as he had desired to do from a child, to devote his last years to preparing himself 'for the life to come' (*ib.* 1441–2).

As a judge More rendered his tenure of the chancellorship memorable. His rapidity and despatch were without precedent, and the chancery was soon so empty of causes that on one occasion he returned to his house at Chelsea at ten o'clock in the morning, and, calling for wine, thanked God 'he had not one cause' (Goodman, *Court of James I*, ed. Brewer, i. 227). A current rhyme was long remembered:

When More some time had Chancellor been,
No more suits did remain;
The like will never more be seen
Till More be there again.

(*Notes and Queries*, 1st ser. vii. 85, x. 173, 393.) The poorest suitor obtained ready access to him and speedy trial, while the claims of kindred found no favour (Foss). His son-in-law, Giles Heron, relying on the chancellor's family affection, once refused to accept a reasonable arbitrament, but More at once gave 'a flat decree against him.' He encouraged suitors to resort to him at his own house, 'where he would sit in his open hall, in many instances bringing the parties to a friendly reconcilement of their disputes. He forbade any subpœna to be granted until the matter in issue had been laid before him, with the lawyer's name attached to it, when, if he found it sufficient, he would add his fiat, but if too trifling for discussion would refuse a writ.' He did not refrain from the common judicial practice of seasoning his judgments with an unpretending joke. When a frivolous application was made to him by one Tubbe, an attorney, he returned a paper handed to him with the words 'a tale of a' prefixed to the lawyer's signature, 'Tubbe.' The common-law judges complained that their judgments were too often suspended by injunctions out of chancery; but Sir Thomas caused a list of his judgments to be drawn up, and, inviting the judges to dinner, discussed with them the grounds of his decision in each case. On their acknowledging his action to be reasonable, he recommended them in future to qualify the rigour of the law by equitable considerations.

After his retirement from the chancellorship one charge of taking a present of a gilt cup from a suitor was brought against him in the council. He had undoubtedly exchanged occasional gifts with suitors, in accordance with the evil custom of the day; but he had more often declined presents, and rebuked those who offered them, and no proof was adduced that his judgments were influenced by what was regarded as conventional marks of courtesy (BACON, *Lit. Works*, ii. 128; SPEDDING, *Bacon*, vii. 266).

On the other hand, the treatment to which More, as chancellor, subjected persons charged with heresy caused severe attacks on his administration by protestants in his own day, and has been the subject of much subsequent controversy. In his 'Utopia' the most advanced principles of religious toleration held sway. Although all Utopians attended a public worship which was so simple as to be in conflict with no particular form of religious belief, every man was practically permitted to hold in private whatever religious opinions he chose. Only two restrictions were imposed: first, any one rejecting belief in God or in a future state was ineligible for civic office; and, in the second place, a citizen who attacked the religion of his neighbour was held to be guilty of sedition, and was punishable by banishment. But no theory of toleration influenced More's official conduct. He hated heretics, he wrote to Erasmus in the summer of 1533 (*Epist.* 466), but it was their vices, not their persons, he explained elsewhere, that excited his hatred (*Apology*, ch. xlix.) He boasted of his hostility to heretics in his epitaph, where he described himself as 'hereticis molestus;' and he allowed that when every effort had failed 'to pull malicious folly out of a poisoned, proud, obstinate heart,' the heretic's death was preferable to his continued sojourn on earth, with power to disseminate pernicious opinions, to the destruction of others (*ib.*; see *English Works*, pp. 351–2). The contemporary chronicler Hall describes him as 'a great persecutor of such as detested the supremacy of the bishop of Rome' (p. 817). Foxe represents him as 'blinded in the zeal of popery' to all humane considerations in the treatment of Lutherans (iv. 688), and Mr. Froude denounces him as 'a merciless bigot.' More undoubtedly viewed with equanimity the cruel incidents of persecution; and although Stokesley, bishop of London, shares with him much of the blame attaching to his proceedings, his personal responsibility for the barbarous usage of many protestants has not been satisfactorily disputed (cf. FROUDE, i. 550; BRIDGETT, 264 sq.) When all allowances are made for the rancour of his protestant critics, it must be admitted that he caused suspected heretics to be carried to his house at Chelsea on slender pretences, to be imprisoned in the porter's lodge, and, when they failed to recant, to be racked in the Tower. In a few instances the complaints against him were, he tells us, investigated by the council after he went out of office, and although his judges were not too well disposed towards him, he claimed to have been acquitted of undue severity. He admitted, however, that he had caused the officers of the Marshalsea and other prisons to use with severity persons guilty of what he deemed to be sacrilege, and that he had kept heretics in safe custody at Chelsea. But in only two cases did he admit that he had recommended corporal punishment: he had caused a boy in his service, who taught heresy to a fellow-servant, to be whipped; and a madman, who brawled in churches and had been committed to a madhouse, was tied to a tree and beaten into orthodoxy by his orders (cf. *English Works*, p. 901). It is clear, however, that he under-estimated his activity. He is known to have personally searched for heretical books the house of John Petit, a friend of his in the city, and committed him to prison, where he soon died, before any distinct charge had been formulated against him (NICHOLS, *Narratives of the Reformation*, Camd. Soc., pp. 26–7). Of John Tewkesbury, an inoffensive leatherseller of London, who was burnt on 20 Dec. 1531, More wrote, 'There was never a wretch, I wene, better worthy' (*English Works*, p. 348; FOXE, iv. 688 sq.; cf. *Letters and Papers*, vi. p. 448); and the enormities practised in the case of James Bainham [q. v.] must be largely laid to More's charge.

For the year and a half following his resignation More lived in complete retirement, mainly engaged in religious controversy with Tindal and Frith. The king's relations with Anne Boleyn troubled him, and he kept away from court. To no purpose did Bishops

Tunstall, Clerk, and Gardiner forward to him 20*l.* with an invitation to attend the coronation of the new queen (1 June 1533); but he avoided all open rupture with the authorities. At Christmas 1533 the council issued a proclamation attacking the pope, and justifying Henry VIII's action in divorcing Queen Catherine. A pamphlet issued by More's nephew, William Rastell, defended the pope, and More was suspected by Cromwell of the authorship. Rastell was summoned before the council. He flatly denied his uncle's responsibility, and More repeated the denial in a letter to Cromwell. He solemnly assured Cromwell that he was not capable of dealing with such lofty matters of politics, and knew his bounden duty to his prince too well to criticise, or encourage others to criticise, his policy (1 Feb. 1533-4). The matter went no further, but both Cromwell and his master resented More's neutrality, and Cromwell awaited an opportunity of extorting a direct expression of opinion.

Throughout 1533 the Holy Maid of Kent [see Barton, Elizabeth] was prophesying with growing vehemence the king's perdition as the penalty he should pay for the divorce. At the close of the year she and the priests who had supported her pretensions to divine inspiration were arrested, and their confessions showed that More was among her disciples. Cromwell invited an explanation. More readily explained that eight or nine years ago he had examined some messages sent by the Maid to the king, and had regarded them as frivolous impostures; but during 1533 several friars of his acquaintance had awakened his interest in her anew, and he had visited her when she was sojourning with the Carthusians at Sion House. Her spiritual fervour then impressed him favourably, but he advised her to devote herself to pious exercises, and both by word of mouth and subsequently by a letter, of which he sent Cromwell a copy, he specially warned her against discussing political topics (Burnet). More's story of his relations with the woman is corroborated by her own confessions and those of her accomplices. After learning of their arrest and of the evidence adduced against them, he freely admitted that he had been the dupe of a foolish imposture (cf. *Letters and Papers*, 1534, pp. 118 sq.)

But Henry was not easily satisfied, and More found that his name figured as guilty of misprision of treason in the bill of attainder aimed at the nun's friends, which was introduced on 21 Feb. 1533-4 into the House of Lords (cf. *ib.* No. 1468, p. 2). More applied for permission to address the house in his defence. By way of reply he received a summons to appear before four members of the council (Cranmer, Audley, Norfolk, and Cromwell). When in their presence he found he had to meet another issue. He was asked why he had declined to acknowledge the wisdom and necessity of Henry's recent attitude to the pope. He replied that he wished to do all that was acceptable to the king, and that he had from time to time explained his position without incurring the royal displeasure. His personal popularity proved so great, however, that Henry reluctantly agreed to strike his name out of the bill, but not until it had been read a third time (*Lords' Journals*, p. 72). For this concession More wrote in grateful terms to the king (Ellis, *Orig. Lett.* ii. 48-52; cf. *Letters and Papers*, vol. vii. No. 387). The incident roused More to a sense of his danger, but did not disturb his equanimity. When warned by the Duke of Norfolk that 'indignatio principis mors est,' he coolly answered, 'Is that all, my lord? Then in good faith between your grace and me is but this, that I shall die to-day and you to-morrow.'

On 30 March 1534 a bill imposing an oath of adherence to the new act of succession which vested the crown in Anne Boleyn's issue received the royal assent. The commissioners nominated to administer the oath added to it a formula abjuring 'any foreign potentate,' and, in the case of the clergy, demanded a full renunciation of the pope. More was in no yielding mood. On 13 April, after hearing mass and taking the holy communion, he appeared by summons at Lambeth before the commissioners (Cranmer, Audley, Cromwell, and Benson, abbot of Westminster). He explained that, while ready to swear fidelity to the new succession act, he could take no oath that should impugn the pope's authority or assume the justice of the divorce. The abbot of Westminster urged that he was setting up his private judgment against the wisdom of the nation, as expressed by the parliament and council. More replied that the council of one realm was setting itself 'against the general council of Christendom' (More to his daughter, *English Works*, p. 1428). He was committed to the custody of the abbot of Westminster. Four days later Cranmer suggested that the king might be well advised in accepting More's modified oath of fidelity (17 April). But Anne Boleyn was especially incensed against him, and the king and Cromwell declined to make an exception in his favour. On 17 April he was committed to the Tower, and he remained a prisoner till death. His friend John Fisher, bishop of Rochester, assumed a like attitude to the new oath, and he shared More's punishment.

More's contention that the recent act of succession did not justify the oath impugning the papal supremacy was acknowledged by some members of the council. Accordingly, when parliament met again on 3 Nov. 1534, it was voted that the double-barrelled oath as administered to More and Fisher was to be 'reputed the very oath intended by the act of succession.' At the same time More was attainted of misprision of treason; grants of land made to him in 1522 and 1525 were resumed; he was declared to be a sower of sedition and guilty of ingratitude to his royal benefactor.

As a knight, More paid, while in the Tower, fees of 10*s.* a week for himself and 5*s.* for his servant, and was treated with much leniency by his gaolers. Although his physical health was bad—he suffered from oppression on the chest, gravel, stone, and cramp—his spirits were always untameable, and he talked with his family and friends, on their occasional visits to him, with infectious gaiety. In the first days of his imprisonment he wrote many letters, performed punctually all pious observances, and prepared a 'Dialogue of Comfort against Tribulation' and treatises on Christ's passion. His resolution to adhere to his position was immovable. His wife, who did not appreciate his conscientious scruples, urged him in vain to yield to the king and gain his freedom. His cheerful reply, 'Is not this house as nigh heaven as mine own?' failed to convince her. His stepdaughter, Lady Alington, and his daughter Margaret also begged him to reconsider his action with greater tact, but with no greater success. At the end of 1534 Lady More and her children petitioned Henry for his pardon and release on the ground of his sickness and their poverty. 'His offence,' they asserted, 'is not of malice or obstinacy, but of such a long-continued and deep-rooted scruple as passeth his power to avoid and put away' (*Arundel MS.* 152, f. 300 *b*). In May 1535 the appeal was renewed. Lady More had been compelled to sell her clothes to pay her husband's fees for board in prison (Wood, *Letters*, ii. 178–80). But Henry was obdurate. In January 1535 he bestowed More's Oxfordshire property (Doglington, Fringford, and Barly Park) on Henry Norris, and in April his manor of South in Kent on Anne Boleyn's brother, George, viscount Rochford. The Duke of Suffolk made application for the Chelsea property, but it was not immediately disposed of.

The parliament that had met in November 1534 conferred, for the first time, on Henry the title of Supreme Head of the Church, and rendered it high treason to 'maliciously' deny any of the royal titles. In April 1535 Cromwell went to the Tower and asked More for his opinion of these new statutes: were they lawful in his eyes, or no? More declared himself a faithful subject to the king, and declined any further answer. On 7 May and 3 June the scene was repeated. Cromwell at the third meeting threatened that the king would compel More to give a precise reply. On 12 June Rich, the solicitor-general, held a conversation with him, which is variously reported by the interlocutors. Rich asserted that More denied the right of parliament to confer the ecclesiastical supremacy on the king. On 7 June the discovery that More had succeeded in interchanging letters with his fellow-prisoner, Fisher, had given the council a new opportunity of attack. An inquiry, more rigorous than before, was held on 14 June; More admitted that he had sent Fisher from time to time accounts of his examinations, and had made similar communications to his daughter. He had received replies, but they had conspired together in nothing. The old questions were put to him again, but with the old result. He was accordingly deprived of books and writing materials, although he occasionally succeeded in writing to his wife and daughter Margaret on scraps of paper with pieces of coal. Thenceforth he caused the shutters of his cell to be closed, and spent most of his time in the dark.

The end was now near. On 19 June the Carthusians were convicted and executed for refusing to accept the king's supremacy. Six days later Fisher suffered in the same cause, and royal orders were issued the same day bidding the preachers dwell on his treason and on More's conjointly. More learned the tidings with the utmost calmness. On 1 July he was himself indicted of high treason at Westminster Hall. A special commission of oyer and terminer for Middlesex had been issued for the purpose five days earlier to Lord-chancellor Audley, the Dukes of Norfolk and Suffolk, Cromwell, Anne Boleyn's father and brother, four other peers, and ten judges. The indictment rehearsed at great length that the prisoner had in divers ways infringed the Act of Supremacy (26 Hen. VIII, caps. 1 and 23); it relied for proof on his answers to the council while in the Tower, on the alleged correspondence with Fisher, and on the alleged conversation with Rich. More, owing to his infirmities, was allowed to be seated. With much dignity he denied the principal charges. He had never maliciously opposed the king's second marriage; he had not advised Fisher to disobey the act of supremacy, nor had he described that act as a two-edged sword, approval of which ruined the soul, and disapproval the body. Rich, the solicitor-general, he denounced as a perjurer. The jury at once returned a verdict of guilty, and he was sentenced to be hanged at Tyburn. Before leaving the court More denied that any approved doctor of the church had admitted that a temporal lord could or ought to be head of the spirituality; when the papal authority was first threatened he had devoted seven years to a study of its history, and had arrived at the conclusion that it was grounded on divine law and prescription; he confessed that he had never consented to the king's union with Queen Anne (cf. *3rd Rep. of Deputy-Keeper of Records*, pp. 240–1; *Mémoires de Michel de Castelnau*, ed. J. Le Laboureur (1731), i. 415–18; *Letters and Papers*, viii. 385 sq.; *Archæologia*, xxvii. 361–74). His favourite daughter, Margaret, met him on the Tower wharf as he came from Westminster, and he gave her his blessing and words of comfort. On 5 July he wrote her his last letter (in English), full of kindly remembrances to her and other members of his household, and at the same time he thanked in Latin an Italian friend, Antonio Bonvisi, for his sympathy. Later in the day the king commuted the sentence of hanging to that of beheading—a favour which More grimly expressed the hope that his friends might be spared—and before nine o'clock next morning he was executed on Tower Hill. His composure on the scaffold is probably without parallel. 'I pray thee see me safely up,' he said to the lieutenant on reaching the steps, 'and for my coming down let me shift for myself.' With a light-hearted jest he encouraged the headsman to perform his duty fearlessly (cf. ADDISON, *Spectator*, No. 449). He moved his beard from the block with the remark that 'it had never committed treason' (MORE), told the bystanders that he died 'in and for the faith of the catholic church,' and prayed God to send the king good counsel. The king gave permission to his wife and children to attend his funeral.

More's body was buried in the church of St. Peter in the Tower; and, according to a Latin life of Fisher written in Queen Mary's reign (*Arundel MS.* 152, f. 233), Fisher's body, after lying seven years in Allhallows' churchyard, was removed to More's grave. Cresacre More states that Fisher's body was re-interred beside that of More within a fortnight of the former's death. More had, in 1532, set up a tomb for himself in Chelsea Church (cf. ERAS. *Epist.* 426 in App.), and Weever and Fuller both assert that his headless corpse was ultimately conveyed thither by his daughter. Neither Stapleton nor Cresacre More gives any hint of this; and William Roper, in his will (4 Jan. 1577–8), speaks of the More vault at Chelsea as the spot where his father-in-law 'did mind to be buried,' but clearly implies that he was buried elsewhere. More's head, after being parboiled, as was customary, was affixed to a pole and exhibited on London Bridge. In November 1535 it was reported to have turned black and been thrown into the river (*Letters and Papers*, ix. 294). Sir Richard Morison [q. v.], in his answer to Cochlæus, written in 1536, speaks of it as being still on the bridge in that year. But, according to Stapleton, it was privately purchased by his daughter Margaret within a month of its exposure, and she preserved it in spices till her death in 1544. She was buried in Chelsea Church, and the head is doubtfully said to have been buried with her. On the other hand, her husband, who had property in the parish of St. Dunstan's, Canterbury, was buried in 1578 in what was known as the Roper chancel in the church there. An ancient leaden box discovered in the Roper vault was opened in June 1824, and contained a head, which was assumed to be More's (*Gent. Mag.* 1824, i. 626; BRIDGETT, pp. 436–7).

Catholic Europe was startled by the news of More's death. Cardinal Pole asserted in his 'Pro Ecclesiæ Unitatis Defensione,' f. xciii, which he forwarded to Henry soon afterwards, that utter strangers wept at hearing the news. Pope Paul III extolled him as 'excelling in sacred learning and courageous in the defence of truth,' and prepared a bull excommunicating Henry for the crime. Charles V declared that had he had such a councillor he would have preferred to lose his best city. In order to allay the threatening excitement, the English ambassadors at foreign courts were instructed to announce that More and Fisher were found traitors by due course of law (*Letters and Papers*, ix. 70; STRYPE, *Memorials*, I. i. 360). An illustrated 'Expositio fidelis de Morte Thomæ Mori et quorundam aliorum insignium Virorum in Anglia' appeared at Paris in 1535 and Antwerp in 1536, and described in detail the martyr's death. Versions were also issued in French, Spanish, and German (*Letters and Papers*, ix. 395–6). The Latin poets on the continent freely drew parallels between More and Socrates, Seneca, Aristides, Boethius, or Cato (cf. prefatory verses in *Opera Omnia*, 1689).

Gregory XIII, on succeeding to the papacy in 1572, bestowed on More the honour of public veneration in the English College at Rome. On 9 Dec. 1886 he was beatified by

Pope Leo XIII. Various relics of More are religiously preserved at Stonyhurst College. They include his hat, silver seal, George, gold cross, and other articles. His hair shirt is said to be the property of the Augustinian canonesses of Abbot's Leigh, near Newton Abbot; and a cup once used by him is stated to belong to Monsignor Eyston of East Hendred, Berkshire. A statue was placed in 1889 over a doorway of a corner house in Carey Street, Chancery Lane, by George Arnold, esq., of Milton Hall, Gravesend, and a passage leading from Carey Street to New Square was christened More's Passage at the same time.

With his stern devotion to principle, his overmastering religious fervour, and his invincible courage, More combined an imperturbable cheerfulness which enabled him to detect a humorous element in the most unpromising situations. According to his friend Erasmus (*Epist.* 447, to Ulrich von Hutten, 1519), he was a second Democritus, always full of gaiety, excelling in witty repartees, and conversing with ease with men in every rank of life. The chronicler Hall complains that he could never make the most ordinary communication without importing 'some mocke' into it, and condemns as 'absurd' his 'idle jests' on the scaffold. Cresacre More says that his witty sayings and merry jests would fill a volume. His indulgences were few. He drank little wine; neither expensive food nor dress attracted him, and he wore his gown so loosely on his shoulders as to give him at times an appearance of deformity. The careless habit was, according to Ascham, imitated by a foolish admirer (*Scholemaster*, ed. Mayor, p. 180). He disliked all ceremony or ostentatious luxury in private life (cf. *Supplication of Souls*), and abhorred games of tennis, dice, or cards. At Chelsea he lived in a homely patriarchal fashion (*ib.* p. 426), 'surrounded by his numerous family, including his wife, his son and his son's wife, his three daughters and their husbands, with eleven grandchildren.' There also resided with him a learned young kinswoman, Margaret Giggs, who married John Clements [q. v.]; and before he was chancellor he delighted in the society of his fool, Henry Pates or Pattenson, who, when he retired from office, obtained a place in the lord mayor's household. John Harris, his secretary, he also highly valued. 'There is not,' Erasmus asserted, 'any man living so affectionate to his children as he, and he loveth his old wife as if she were a girl of fifteen.' Very charitable to his poor neighbours and a kindly master to his servants, he was a charming host to congenial friends. Much of his leisure was devoted to the education of his household. 'Plato's academy was revived again; only whereas in the academy the discussions turned upon geometry and the power of number, the house at Chelsea is a veritable school of the Christian religion. In it is none, man or woman, but readeth or studieth the liberal arts. Yet is their chief care of piety. There is never any seen idle. The head of the house governs it, not by lofty carriage and frequent rebukes, but by gentleness and amiable manners. Every member is busy in his place, performing his duty with alacrity, nor is sober mirth wanting.' Elsewhere Erasmus relates that Livy was the chief author recommended by More to his children to read (*Epist.* 605).

More was fond of animals, even of foxes, weasels, and monkeys, and had an aviary at Chelsea (Erasmus). A chained monkey is represented as playing at the side of his wife in Holbein's authentic picture of the family; he gave his friend Budæus two valuable dogs, apparently greyhounds, and wrote Latin epigrams on a cat playing with a mouse, and a spider and a fly.

More built his house at Chelsea at the north end of what is now Beaufort Row. A spacious garden and orchard, to which he devoted much attention, were attached, and at some distance from the dwelling he set up 'The New Building,' which contained a chapel, library, and gallery, to be used 'for devotion, study, or retirement.' The property seems to have been granted by Henry VIII to Sir William Paulet on 4 April 1537 (*Pat. Rot.* 28 Hen. VIII), and was known as 'The Great More House.' It was successively the residence of John Paulet, second marquis of Winchester; of Margaret, baroness Dacres; of Henry, earl of Lincoln; of Sir Arthur Gorges; of Lionel, earl of Middlesex, in 1629; of the Duke of Buckingham; of William Plummer, a citizen of London; and of the Earl of Bristol, from whose heirs it ultimately passed to the Duke of Beaufort. The latter rechristened it Beaufort House. It was sold to Sir Hans Sloane in 1738, and pulled down in 1740 (Lysons, *Environs*). A print by L. Knyff, dated 1699, is reproduced in the 'Gentleman's Magazine,' 1829, i. 497, and in Faulkner's 'Chelsea.' Some fragments of walls and windows at the south end of the Moravian burial-ground are said to be parts of the original building (*Gent. Mag.* 1833, ii. 482). More's house has been at times wrongly identified with Danvers House, built by Sir John Danvers on the site of the present Danvers Street (Faulkner, *Chelsea*, 2nd ed. i. 118; *Notes and Queries*, 2nd ser. ii.

324, 516, iii. 317, 495–7; *Gent. Mag.* 1829, i. 497).

To the parish church of Chelsea More, probably in 1528, added a chapel, at the southern side of 'the lower chancel,' and it now forms part of the south aisle. The 'More Chapel' was apparently built for the accommodation of his large household during divine service, and the right to the pew there was sold with More House until 1629. In the tomb in the chancel, built in 1532, he deposited the remains of his first wife, intending that he himself and his second wife should be also buried there; but that intention was frustrated. The epitaph written by himself and the armorial bearings of himself and his wives were engraved on the tomb (*Notes and Queries*, 4th ser. iv. 611). It was restored before 1638, and again in 1833, when the slab containing the epitaph was removed to another site near at hand, and the words attesting his severity to heretics erased (*Gent. Mag.* 1833, ii. 481–6).

Strict in his religious observances, and always wearing a hair shirt next his skin, More encouraged in his parish church at Chelsea very simple forms of worship, and was once found by his friend the Duke of Norfolk, to the duke's disgust, wearing a surplice and singing in the choir.

But, like all the scholars of the new learning, More had strong artistic tastes. He filled his house with curious furniture and plate. He was fond of music, and, according to Richard Pace, he induced his wife, who had no claims to culture, to learn the flute with him (PACE, *De Fructu qui ex doctrinâ percipitur*, Basle, 1517).

Of painting, More was both a critic and a patron, and his relations with Holbein give him a place in the history of art. To the 1518 edition of the 'Utopia' Holbein contributed, at the request of Froben and Erasmus, besides the map, a genre picture of More and his friends listening to Raphael's narration, and he permitted engraved borders already issued in other books to reappear there. In 1526 Holbein first came to England on a visit to More, to whom Erasmus had introduced him, and it is said he stayed at Chelsea for three years. Holbein is not known to have undertaken any work for Henry VIII until 1536, but the king doubtless met him at More's house for the first time. Holbein returned More's hospitality by painting portraits of him and his family.

Erasmus described More in 1519 as of middle height, a complexion not very highly coloured, dark brown hair, and greyish blue eyes. While in the Tower he let his beard grow, but through life he was almost clean shaven. It is thus that Holbein painted him. His expression in the pictures is always serious and penetrating, but the eyes look capable of a humorous twinkle. The earliest of Holbein's portraits of More is doubtless that painted in 1527, and now belonging to Edward Huth, esq. Two studies for it are in the royal collection at Windsor, along with sketches of More's father, his son, and daughter-in-law, and his daughters, Cecilia and Elizabeth; these were reproduced by Bartolozzi in Chamberlain's 'Heads' (1792). Another portrait, dated 1532, belongs to T. L. Thurlow, esq. More and his father were also painted together by Holbein in a picture belonging to Sir Henry Vane. A portrait, said to be by a pupil of Holbein, from the Windsor sketch is in the National Portrait Gallery. A half-length of uncertain authorship belongs to Baroness Burdett-Coutts, and another is at Knole House, Sevenoaks. A genuine Holbein in the Louvre, usually said to represent More, is a portrait of Sir Henry Wyatt; and a spurious Holbein in the Brussels Gallery, which was engraved by Vorsterman, and is reproduced in Le Clerc's edition of Erasmus's correspondence as a portrait of More, is by the French artist Clouet, and does not tally with any authentic picture of More. The face is bearded, and a dog lies before the figure.

Holbein also painted a large group of More's household. The original sketch, which More sent to Erasmus, is now in the Basle Museum, and supplies the names and ages, in More's handwriting, of all the persons depicted, with some suggestions for alterations in Holbein's autograph. It was engraved by Mechel in 1787, with the added inscription, 'Johannes Holbein ad vivum delin. Londini, 1530'—a date probably three years too late (SEEBOHM, pp. 525–6). A second engraving, by Mechel, of More's family, 'Ex tabula Joh. Holbenii in Anglia adservata,' was a fanciful exercise of the engraver (WOLTMANN, *Holbein*, p. 321, note). The Basle sketch includes More, his father, his second wife, three daughters, his son John More and his son's future wife, Anne Cresacre, his ward Mrs. Clements, and Henry Pattenson, his jester, with two servants in a room behind. The finished picture is lost. In 1530 it was in the collection of Andreas de Loo in London, whence it passed to William Roper at Well Hall, Eltham, and soon after his death in 1578 to a grandson of the chancellor. An authentic sixteenth-century copy is now at Nostell Priory, the property of Lord St. Oswald, to whose ancestor it came through the Roper family. It differs in some details—notably, the introduction of John Harris, More's secretary

—from the Basle sketch. A somewhat similar family group, painted by Rowland Lockey [q. v.] in 1593, included many later descendants; it formerly belonged to the Lenthall family of Burford Priory, was sold after 1829, and is now at Cockthorpe Park, Ducklington, near Witney, the property of Mrs. Strickland. It has been engraved by Lodge. A third copy, resembling that at Nostell, belongs to C. J. Eyston, esq., of East Hendred, Berkshire, and was at one time at Barnborough, the seat of the chancellor's son, John More, and his descendants.

Quintin Matsys, the painter of Antwerp, was also known to More. At More's desire he painted a portrait of Ægidius, who bears in his hand a letter from More, in which the latter's handwriting is exactly reproduced. More described this picture in both prose and verse (Erasmus, *Epist.* 287, 384, 1615, 1631, 1634). It is at Longford Castle; a portrait of Erasmus, probably painted on the same panel, has been detached from it, and has disappeared. Engravings of More appear in the 1573 edition of the 'Dialogue of Comfort,' and in Stapleton's 'Tres Thomæ' (1588). One by Anton Wierx is reproduced in Holland's 'Herωologia;' another, attributed to P. Galle, resembles that in Boissard's 'Bibliotheca' (1597–1628). Elstracke and Marshall, in More's 'Epigrams' (1638) and Houbraken in Birch's 'Heads' (1741) have also engraved portraits after Holbein.

More was an omnivorous reader. All the chief classical authors were at his command. Plato, Lucian, and the Greek anthology specially appealed to him; and of Latin writers he most frequently quoted Plautus, Terence, Horace, and Seneca. St. Augustine's works were often in his hands, and he had studied deeply the canon law and the 'Magister Sententiarum;' but it is doubtful if he were well versed in either scholastic or patristic literature. Of the works of contemporaries he laughed over Sebastian Brandt's 'Narrenschiff' (epigram *in Brixium*), and had derived the fullest satisfaction from the writings of such champions of the new learning as Pico della Mirandola and his friends Erasmus and Budæus. Erasmus's Latin version of the New Testament he studied with unalloyed admiration. His own contributions to literature, apart from the 'Utopia,' are of greater historic than æsthetic value. His best English poem, 'A Pageant of Life,' written to illustrate some tapestry in his father's house, is serious in thought and forcible in expression, but is not informed by genuine poetic genius. His Latin verse and prose are scholarly and fluent, and, although in the epigrams a coarse jest often does duty for point, they embody much shrewd satire on the follies and vices of mankind. His English prose in his controversial tracts is simple and direct: he delights in well-contested argument thrown into the form of a dialogue, and he is fertile in unexpected illustration and witty anecdote. He quotes his opponent's views with great verbal accuracy, but repeatedly descends to personal abuse, which appears childish to the modern reader. His devotional works, although often rising to passages of fervid eloquence, are mainly noticeable for their sincerity and inordinate length. For two centuries More was regarded in catholic Europe as one of the glories of English literature. In 1663 Cominges, the French ambassador at Charles II's court, when invited by his master to enumerate eminent English authors, recognised only three as worthy of mention, More and two others—Bacon and Buchanan (Jusserand, *French Ambassador*, p. 205).

More's 'Utopia'—his greatest literary effort—was written in Latin, and, unlike his controversial tracts, which he wrote in English, was addressed to the learned world. It is in two books—the second composed while on his first embassy to the Low Countries in 1515, the first after his return to London in 1516. In the first book More relates that while at Antwerp he had been introduced by Erasmus's friend, Peter Giles, to a Portuguese mariner, Raphael Hythlodaye, who had made several voyages with Amerigo Vespucci to the New World. The man, who is a wholly fictitious personage, informs More that on the last voyage he was, at his own wish, left behind near Cape Frio, and had thence made his way to the island of Utopia, where he found in operation an ideal constitution. The word 'Utopia' is formed from οὐ and τόπος, and is rendered in More's and most of his friends' Latin correspondence by 'Nusquama,' i.e. nowhere, while Budæus playfully paraphrases it as 'Udepotia,' from οὐδέποτε, and Sir Walter Scott translated it by 'Kennaquhair.' The supposition that it is derived from εὖ τόπος—'a place of felicity'—has nothing to support it (cf. *Notes and Queries*, 7th ser. v. 101, 229, 371). To More's question whether Raphael had visited England, he replies that he had spent some time there, and reports at length a conversation which he had with Cardinal Morton respecting its social defects. He found, he declares, the labouring classes in the direst poverty, owing to the severity of the criminal law, the substitution of pasture for arable land, the prevalence of high prices, the readiness of princes to engage in war, and the licentiousness and greed of the rich. The labourers were reduced to beasts of burden so that a few rich men might live in idleness and luxury. Raphael suggests as remedies the abolition of capital punishment for theft and the development of agriculture, and urges that the law should be so contrived as to bestow on all men equal portions of riches and commodities. Such a dispensation was 'the one and only way to the wealth of a community.' In the second book the traveller describes, by way of contrast to the principles of government prevailing in contemporary Europe, the political and social constitution of the imaginary island of Utopia. The king is an officer elected for life, but removable if suspected of attempting to enslave his people. Communism is the law of the land. No one is idle, yet the hours of labour are limited to six a day, and all leisure is devoted to the pursuit of the arts, literature, and science, with an occasional game of chess; but each citizen is allowed the fullest freedom in selecting his subject of study. A national system of education is extended as fully to women as to men. Sanitation is practised to perfection. No house is without a garden or abundant supply of fresh water. Hospitals and slaughterhouses are placed outside the towns. All meals are taken in common halls, as in the constitutions of Lycurgus. The Utopians never make leagues or treaties, nor engage in war unless in self-defence. They have few laws and no lawyers. Lawbreakers are condemned to slavery until they give promise of amendment. Their philosophy is pure utilitarianism, and recognises the felicity of the body politic as the *summum bonum* to which the immediate pleasure of the individual citizen must be postponed. In matters of religion the freest toleration is invariably recognised.

More conducts the dialogue between his fictitious traveller, Raphael, and living personages, like Peter Giles, Morton, and himself, with admirable dramatic skill, and a reader may easily be puzzled to detect where the fact ends and the fiction begins. In elaborating the details of his imaginary republic he displays fertile powers of invention, while his satiric reflections on the practices of the diplomatists and statesmen of his own day, especially in Raphael's remarks on leagues and treaties, could not have been bettered by Swift (cf. BREWER, *Henry VIII*, i. 288–97). But unless the poor-law legislation of Elizabeth's reign can be ascribed to its influence, the 'Utopia' cannot be credited with more practical effect than Plato's 'Republic.' It doubtless suggested such speculative treatises as Campanella's 'Civitas Solis,' Bacon's fragmentary 'New Atlantis,' Hobbes's 'Leviathan,' Harrington's 'Oceana,' and Filmer's 'Patriarcha.' In many ways, too, the work anticipates the arguments of modern socialists, and some socialist reformers, despite the facts that monarchy and slavery are essential features of the Utopian commonwealth, have of late years adopted it as their text-book.

More, although an expounder, was no serious champion of a socialistic system. The 'Utopia' was mainly an exercise of the imagination, a playful satire on the world as it was (cf. ERASMUS, *Epist.* ii. 1155). To a large extent it was an adaptation of Plato's 'Republic' and of the recorded practices of the early Christians, with some reminiscence of St. Augustine's 'Civitas Dei' (cf. PLATO, *Republic*, transl. by Jowett, Oxford, 1891, Preface). More doubtless believed that classical ideals and the spirit of early mediæval monasticism might be both studied with advantage in an epoch which seemed to him dominated by the avarice of the rich and by too exclusively a mercantile spirit. But he distinctly disavowed any personal belief in the practicability of communism, the leading principle in his fanciful State. After Raphael had explained his communistic panacea for the poverty of the many, More interposes in his own person the remark, 'But I am of a contrary opinion' (p. 69), and argues that 'continued sedition and bloodshed' must be the outcome of the abolition of private property. Subsequently in his 'Supplication of Souls'—his reply to Fish's 'Supplication of Beggars'— he sought with much vehemence to confute the theory that 'hand labour' was alone profitable to a state, and denounced Fish's proposal to confiscate church property on the ground that it would prove a prelude to a disastrous plunder of the rich by the poor. His theological tracts and his personal practice in and out of office amply prove that he viewed religious toleration in workaday life as undermining the foundations of society, and in conflict with laws both human and divine. More's practical opinions on religion and politics must be sought elsewhere than in the 'Utopia.'

Completed in October 1516, the 'Utopia' seems to have been sent in manuscript to Peter Giles, Tunstall, and Erasmus, all of whom were enthusiastic in its praise. Erasmus, who described it as a revelation of the source of all political evils, arranged for its first publication at Thierry Martin's press at Louvain. It appeared in December 1516, with the title, 'Libellus vere aureus nec minus salutaris quam festivus de optimo reip. statu deque nova Insula Utopia.' After a rough chart of the island, a fanciful Utopian alphabet, and a Utopian 'hexastichon,' appear commendatory letters or poems, by Peter Giles, John Paludanus, Busleyden, Cornelius Graphæus, and Gerardus Noviomagus. The book at once became popular. 'A burgomaster at Antwerp,' wrote Erasmus (ii. 963), 'is so pleased with it that he knows it all by heart,' and Ulrich von Hutten applied to Erasmus in 1519 for an account of the author. William Budæus described its merits in a letter to Lupset, who caused a second edition to be printed in Paris at the press of Gilles de Gourmont in March 1517. A third and corrected edition—by far the finest of the early issues—appeared with illustrations by Holbein, under Erasmus's auspices, at Froben's press at Basle in 1518, some copies giving the month as March and others as December. The title ran: 'De Optimo Reipublicæ Statu, deque nova insula Utopia, libellus vere aureus, nec minus salutaris quàm festivus, clarissimi disertissimique viri Thomæ Mori inclytæ civitatis Londinensis civis et vicecomitis;' with it the Latin epigrams of More and Erasmus were bound up, preceded by 'Erasmi Querela Pacis undique gentium et alia opuscula.' Other reissues of the Latin original are dated Vienna, 1519, 4to; Basle, 1520, 4to, with Holbein's border round the title; Louvain, 1548 (Brit. Mus.); Basle, 1563, with Nucerinus's account of More's and Fisher's death; Wittenberg, 1591, 8vo; Frankfort, 1601, 12mo; Cologne, 1629, 12mo; Hanover, 1613, 12mo; Amsterdam, 1629 and 1631, 12mo; Oxford, 1663, 12mo; Glasgow, 1750, 12mo (by Foulis). The 'Utopia' was translated into French before it appeared in English. The first French translation, by Jehan Leblond, was issued at Paris by L'Angelier in 1550, and this, corrected by Barthélemy Anneau, reappeared at Lyons (by J. Sangram) in 1559. It has been rendered into French in later years: by Samuel Sorbière (Amsterdam, J. Blaew, 1643); by N. P. Guendeville (Amsterdam, F. L'Honoré, 1715?); and by M. T. Rousseau, Paris, 1780, 2nd edit. 1789).

The 'Utopia' has been thrice translated into English. The earliest version, that by Raphe Robinson [q.v.], appeared in 1551. The title ran: 'A fruteful and pleasaunt Worke of the beste State of a publyque Weale, and of the newe yle called Utopia; written in Latine by Syr Thomas More, knyght, and translated into Englyshe by Ralph Robynson, Citizen and Goldsmythe of London, at the procurement, and earnest request of George Tadlowe, Citezein and Haberdassher of the same Citie. Imprinted at London by Abraham Vele, dwelling in Paul's Churcheyarde at the Sygne of the Lambe. Anno 1551,' 8vo, bl. l. (Brit. Mus.) After the dedication to William Cecil is More's epistle to Peter Giles, which is wanting in later impressions. Robinson's version was reissued in 1556 (Brit. Mus.); 1597 (*ib.*); 1624 (*ib.*, dedicated to Cresacre More); 1639 (*ib.*); 1808 (elaborately edited by T. F. Dibdin); in 1869 in Professor Arber's 'Reprints;' in 1878, edited by R. Roberts of Boston, Lincolnshire; in 1880 in the Pitt Press Series, ed. Lumby; in 1886 in Cassell's National Library, ed. Morley; and in 1893 at the Kelmscott Press, edited by Mr. William Morris.

The second translator, Gilbert Burnet, published his version in 1684, and reissues are dated Dublin, 1737; Glasgow, 1743; Oxford, 1751 (edited by Thomas Williamson); Oxford, 1753 (edited by 'a gentleman of Oxford'); London, 1758 (in Warner's 'Memoirs of More'); London, 1795, in 'Political Classics,' vol. iii., with Rousseau's 'Social Compact;' London, 1838, in 'The Masterpieces of Prose Literature,' vol. iv. (edited by J. A. St. John); London, 1849; London, 1850 (in John Minter Morgan's Phœnix Library). The third translator, Arthur Cayley, published his rendering in his 'Memoirs of More,' London, 1808 (2 vols.), ii. 1-145. The 'History of Richard III' and More's Latin poems are here also reprinted.

A German translation appeared at Basle in 1524 and at Leipzig in 1753 and 1846. An Italian version, translated by Hortensio Lando, and edited by A. F. Doni, was issued at Venice in 1548; a Dutch version at Antwerp in 1553 and 1562; and a Spanish at Madrid in 1790.

I. MORE'S ENGLISH WORKS.—Two poetic tracts in English were published by More in his lifetime, viz. 'A mery jest how a sergeant would learne to playe the frere,' London, by Julian Notary (reissued in the 'Workes,' 1557, and commemorated in Laneham's 'Account of Captain Coxe's Library' in 1575); and 'The Boke of the fayre Gentylwoman that no man shoulde put his truste or confydence in: that is to say, Lady Fortune.' London, 8vo, n. d., by Robert Wyer (unique copy at Lambeth). A few verses are in French; extracts only appear in More's English works, 1557; the whole is reprinted in Huth's 'Fugitive Tracts,' 1875, 1st ser.

In 1510 More published his 'Life of John Picus, Earl of Mirandula, a great Lord of Italy, an excellent, cunning man in all sciences, and virtuous of living, with divers *Epistles* and other works of the said John Picus,' printed by Wynkyn de Worde in 1510 in a small black letter 4to (Brit. Mus.) It was translated from the Latin of Pico's nephew, Giovanni Francesco Pico (Venice, 1498). More's dedication was addressed to his 'sister in Christ, Joyeuce Leigh,' possibly a nun. At the close is a paraphrase in English verse, from Pico's Latin prose, of 'Twelve Rules of a Christian Life.' An admirable reprint, edited by J. M. Rigg, esq., appeared in Nutt's Tudor Library in 1890.

More's incomplete 'History of Richard III,' with the life of Edward V, is said by his nephew Rastell to have been completed in 1513 (*English Workes*). It first appeared in an incorrect version in Grafton's continuation of Hardyng's 'Chronicle' (1543), and was largely used in Hall's 'Chronicle' (1548). It was first printed by Rastell from an authentic copy in More's 'Workes' in 1557, where the narrative ceased with the murder of the princes by Richard III. A Latin version appeared in the collected edition of More's Latin works in 1566. Between the English and Latin renderings are important differences, and the Latin seems to be the original, of which the English is a paraphrase. The tone is strongly Lancastrian, and often implies that the writer was a contemporary witness of some of the events described. This More could not have been, and the theory that Cardinal Morton wrote the work in Latin, which is inferior in style to More's authentic Latin prose, and that More supplied the English version, deserves careful consideration. Sir John Harington, according to his 'Metamorphosis of Ajax' (1596), heard that Morton was the author; while Sir George Buc [q. v.], in his 'History of Richard III' (1646), says that Morton wrote 'a book in Latin against King Richard, which afterwards came into the hands of Mr. More, sometime his servant. . . . This book was lately in the hands of Mr. Roper of Eltham.' Sir Henry Ellis (1777–1869) [q. v.] believed, with less reason, the English version to be by Morton and the Latin by More. The English work was edited by William Sheares, completing the reign of Richard III, mainly from Hall's text, in 1641. Mr. Singer reprinted it from Rastell's text in 1821, with a continuation from Grafton and Hall, and it was edited by Dr. Lumby in 1883 for the Pitt Press Series. It also appears in Kennett's 'Complete History,' 1706, fol. vol. i. (*Notes and Queries*, 2nd ser. i. 105, by Mr. James Gairdner).

More's English controversial works—all of which were published by his brother-in-law, John Rastell, or his nephew, William Rastell —began with 'A dyaloge of Syr Thomas More, knt., one of the council of our sovereign lord the king, and chancellor of his duchy of Lancaster. Wherein be treatyd divers matters, as of the veneration and worshyp of Ymagys and relygues, prayyng to sayntys and goyng on pylgrymage, wyth many othere thyngys touchyng the pestylent sect of Luther and Tyndale, by the tone bygone in Saxony, and by the tother laboryd to be brought into England. Made in the year of our Lord 1528,' London, 1529, 4to (by John Rastell), and again, 1530 (Lambeth Libr. and Brit. Mus.), and 'newly oversene,' 1531 (by William Rastell). In form it was a report of a conversation taking place in More's library at Chelsea, between More and a young man studying at a university, who was attracted by Lutheran doctrine as set forth by Tindal. The youth had been sent by a friend to More, to be drawn to the right path. It is in four books. The first two defend the theory and practice of catholicism, the third denounces Tindal's translation of the New Testament as heretical, the fourth is a personal attack on Luther.

There followed 'Supplycacyon of Soulys,' London, by W. Rastell, n.d. fol. (1529? Lambeth Libr. and Brit. Mus.), a reply to the 'Supplycacyon of the Beggars' by Simon Fish [q. v.] The clergy had been represented by Fish as idle 'thieves' and responsible for the distress prevailing among the English labouring classes. The 'souls of the dead in purgatory' debate in More's treatise the law of mortmain, currency questions, the evil of a general confiscation of church property, and defend the doctrine of purgatory and prayers for the dead (cf. Foxe, iv. 664 sq.)

'The Confutacyon of Tyndale's Answere' [to More's 'Dyaloge'], London, by Wyllyam Rastell, 1532, fol. (Brit. Mus.), contains three books of More's reply to Tindal's 'Answere.' Six more followed in 'The second parte of the Confutacyon of Tyndal's Answere, in which is also confuted the Chyrche that Tyndale deuyseth and the Chyrche also that Frere Barns deuyseth,' London, by W. Rastell, 1533, fol. (Brit. Mus.) In the last book More dealt with the writings of Robert Barnes [q. v.]

In 'The Apologye of Syr Thomas More, Knyght, made by him Anno 1533 after he had geuen over the office of Lord Chancellour of Englande' (by W. Rastell), 1533, 16mo (Brit. Mus.), More defended himself against charges of undue length and personal abuse in his controversial writing; he renews the attack on Tindal and Barnes and on Christopher St. German [q. v.], the anonymous author of 'The Pacifier of the Division between the Spirituality and the Temporality,' and defends a rigorous treatment of heretics.

This was answered by St. German in 'Salem and Bizance,' to which More retorted within a month in the 'Debellacyon of Salem and Bizance' (London,

1533, 8vo, by W. Rastell), another vindication of the severe punishment of heresy (Lambeth Libr. and Brit. Mus.) 'A Letter impugnynge the erronyouse wrytyng of John Fryth against the blessed Sacrament of the Aultare,' London, 1533, by W. Rastell, 12mo, was answered by John Frith [q. v.] and by R. Crowley in the same year. 'The Answer to the first part of the poysoned Booke which a nameless Hereticke hath named "The Supper of the Lord, Anno 1533,"' London, by W. Rastell, 1534, 8vo (Brit. Mus.), was mainly an exposition of the sixth chapter of the Gospel of St. John. A promised second book was never written. 'The nameless Heretic' was probably George Joye [q. v.], and not Tindal, as More assumes. Joye replied to More in 'The Subuersion of More's False Foundacion,' Emden, 1534.

When in the Tower, More wrote an ascetic treatise, chiefly for the comfort of his own family, 'A Dyaloge of Comfort against Tribulation.' He represented it as 'made by an Hungarian in Latin, and translated out of Latin into French, and out of French into English.' A manuscript is in the library of Corpus Christi College, Oxford (No. 37). It was first printed by Richard Tottel in 1553; and again by John Fowler at Antwerp in 1573, with a dedication to Jane Dormer, duchess of Feria [q. v.] It reappeared in the English Catholic Library in 1847.

William Rastell, More's nephew, to whom many of his manuscripts seem to have passed, collected most of his English writings in 'The Workes of Sir Thomas More, Knyght, sometyme Lord Chancellour of England; wrytten by him in the Englysh tonge. Printed at London, at the costes of John Cawod, John Waly, and Richarde Tottel. Anno 1557,' fol. 1458 pp. It is dedicated to Queen Mary by Rastell. The table of contents precedes an index by Thomas Paynell [q. v.] After his English poems come the 'Pico,' 'Richard III,' 'The Dyaloge,' and all his controversial publications. The previously unpublished material includes an unfinished Treatise 'uppon these words of Holy Scripture, "Memorare novissima et in eternum non peccabis,"' dated in 1522, and dealing with reflections on death, and several devotional works written by More in the Tower, viz. 'Treatice to receaue the blessed Body of our Lorde, sacramentally and virtually both;' 'Upon the Passion' (unfinished); 'An Exposition of a Part of the Passion' (translated by More's granddaughter, Mary Bassett, from the Latin); 'Certein deuout and vertuouse Instruccions, Meditacions, and Prayers,' and some letters written just before his death to his family and friends, including his pathetic correspondence with his daughter Margaret, which is calendared in 'Letters and Papers of Henry VIII,' 1534, vi. 429 sq. In the copy of the volume in the Grenville Library at the British Museum is an unpaged leaf after p. 1138—at the close of the 'Answer to the Supper'—supplying More's apology 'to the Christen reader' for a few printer's blunders. Thirty-one apophthegms attributed to More appear in a collection of 'Witty Apophthegms by King James, King Charles, the Marquis of Worcester, Francis Lord Bacon, and Sir Thomas Moore,' London, 1658, 12mo (pp. 155-68). A selection from his English writings by Father Bridgett—'The Wit and Wisdom of Sir Thomas More'—was published in 1891.

II. Latin Works (other than the 'Utopia') 1. 'Luciani . . . compluria opuscula longe festiuissima ab Erasmo Roterodamo et Thoma Moro interpretibus optimis in Latinorum lingua traducta hac sequentur serie,' Paris, 'ex ædibus Ascensianis,' 1506, fol. (Brit. Mus.) More translated four dialogues, the Cynicus, Menippus or Necromantia, Philopseudes, and 'Pro tyrannicida;' to the last More appended a 'declamatio' on the other side. These he dedicated to Thomas Ruthal, secretary to Henry VIII (afterwards bishop of Durham), with much praise of Lucian's wit and wisdom. Another edition appeared at Paris in 1514; a third at Venice (by Aldus) in 1516; a fourth at Basle by Froben in 1521, and a fifth at Leyden in 1528. An English verse rendering of the 'Necromantia,' published by John Rastell about 1520, may be by More, as well as the prose version of the 'Philopseudes,' appended to J. Wagstaffe's 'Question of Witchcraft Debated,' 1669. 2. 'Epigrammata clarissimi disertissimique viri Thomæ Mori Britanni, pleraque e Græcis versa,' Basle, March 1518—an excerpt from the Basle edition of the 'Utopia;' a separate edition, 1520, 'ad emendatum exemplar ipsius autoris excusa.' It is preceded by 'Progymnasmata Thomæ Mori et Guilielmi Lilii sodalium,' renderings of the Greek anthology. The epigrams were collected by Erasmus from scattered manuscripts, and were printed by Froben under the supervision of a scholar known as Beatus Rhenanus. The latter inscribed the volume to Bilibald Pirckheimer, a senator of Nuremberg, whose position in the councils of the emperor is compared to that of More at the English court. The Latin verses by More presented to Henry VIII on his marriage to Queen Catherine, which are printed in the volume, are preserved in a small illuminated manuscript in Brit. Mus. MS. Cotton Titus D. IV. More's 'Epigrammata' were republished in

London in 1638, and forty are translated in Thomas Pecke's 'Parnassi Puerperium' (1659), pp. 135–48. 3. 'Thomæ Mori Epistola ad Germanum Brixium: qui quum Morvs in Libellum eius quo contumeliosis Mendacijs incesserat Angliam lusisset aliquot epigrammata, ædidit adversus Morum libellum qui . . . suum infamat authorem,' London, 1520, 4to (by R. Pynson), Brit. Mus. 4. 'Eruditissimi viri G. Rossei opus . . . quo refellit . . . Lutheri calumnias, quibus . . . Angliæ . . . regem Henricum . . . octavum scurra turpissimus insectatur: excusum denuo . . . adjunctis indicibus opera . . . J. Carcellij,' London, 1523, 4to. 5. 'Epistola contra Pomeranum,' Louvain, 1568, an attack on a German Lutheran, Johann Bugenhagen, written about 1526, and published by John Fowler, an English exile, from More's autograph, doubtless derived from his secretary, John Harris. 6. 'Thomæ Mori v.c. Dissertatio Epistolica de aliquot sui temporis Theologastrorum ineptijs deque correctione translationis vulgatæ N. Testamenti. Ad Martinum Dorpium Theologum Lovaniensem,' Leyden, 1625, 12mo, preceded by Erasmus's letter to More dated Louvain, 1520. 7. 'Epistola T. Mori ad Academiam Oxon. Cui adjecta sunt quædam poemata . . . in mortem . . . R. Cottoni et T. Alleni [by Richard James q. v.],' Oxford, 1633, 4to.

The first collected edition of More's Latin works appeared at Basle in 1563, 'apud Episcopum F.,' as 'Thomæ Mori . . . Lucubrationes ab innumeris mendis repurgatæ.' This includes the 'Utopia,' all the Latin poems, and the renderings of Lucian, with the epistle to Dorpius (No. 6, supra). A fuller collection, prefaced by the Latin epitaph, and including the Latin version of 'Richard III' and the 'Rossei opus,' was issued at Louvain in 1565, and again in 1566 in folio ('Omnia opera Latina quorum aliqua nunc primum in lucem prodeunt'). In 1689 at Frankfort-on-Maine and Leipzig appeared the completest collection, 'Opera omnia quotquot reperiri potuerant ex Basileensi anni 1563, et Lovaniensi anni 1566, editionibus depromta.' Stapleton's 'Life of More' forms the preface; an 'expositio' on the Passion, 'Precatio ex Psalmis collecta,' and letters to Bonvisi and others are included. The first collected edition of Erasmus's 'Epistolæ' (London, 1642) supplies much of More's correspondence with Erasmus, while an appended and separately paged 'Auctarium Epistolarum ex Thoma Moro' (70 pp.) contains More's letter to Erasmus 'de Brixio,' the letter to Dorpius entitled there 'Apologia pro Moria Erasmi,' and letters to Giles (Ægidius), Brixius, and Bonvisi. Le Clerc's great collection of Erasmus's correspondence (Leyden, 1706) gives nineteen of More's letters to Erasmus and twenty-four of Erasmus's letters to More.

By his first wife, Jane, eldest daughter of John Colte of Newhall, More left three daughters, Margaret, Elizabeth, and Cecilia, and a son, John (1510–1547), the youngest child. His second wife, Mrs. Alice Middleton, by whom he had no children, survived him, and received an annuity of 20*l.* for life on 16 March 1536 (*Pat. Rot.*) Of the son More is reported to have said that his wife had prayed so long for a boy that now she had one who would be a boy as long as he lived. Wood says that he was 'little better than an idiot' (cf. Roper, *Life*, ed. Hearne). But his father praised his elegance and wit as a correspondent in Latin; and just before his death he wrote 'His towardly carriage towards me pleased me very much.' Erasmus styles him a youth of great hopes, and dedicated 'Aristotle' to him in 1531 (*Epist.* 1059), while Grynæus paid him a like compliment in his edition of 'Plato' (Basle, 1534), when he credited him with the highest accomplishment. On his father's death he was committed to the Tower and was condemned for refusing the oath of supremacy, but was set free, and probably retired to Yorkshire. He had married in 1529 Ann (1511–1577), the wealthy heiress of Edward Cresacre of Barnborough, Yorkshire. A book of hours, on vellum and beautifully illuminated, formerly belonging to Baron August Edward von Druffel of Münster, Westphalia, supplies notes in his autograph of the births of his children (*Notes and Queries*, 8th ser. ii. 121–2). After his death in 1547 his widow received from Queen Mary a re-grant of his grandfather's confiscated property at North Mimms; she afterwards married (13 June 1559) a Yorkshire neighbour, George West, nephew of Sir William West, but he died in June 1572, when she conveyed her property to her son, Thomas More (1531–1606). He had married in 1553 Mary Scrope, daughter of John Scrope of Hambledon, Buckinghamshire, and niece of Henry, lord Scrope of Bolton. Thomas's will was proved in 1606. He seems to have been an ardent although concealed catholic. Of his three brothers, two, Edward [q. v.] and one also named Thomas (*b.* 1538), left children; but the latter's sons fell into poverty and have not been traced. Of the elder Thomas's thirteen children—eight daughters and five sons—the eldest, John, who figures in the

Cockthorpe picture, died young. The second, Thomas (1565–1625), took orders in the English College at Rome, was chaplain to Magdalene, lady Montacute (*d.* 1608), and laboured later at Rome and in Spain in behalf of the English catholic clergy (Dodd, *Church History*; Wood, *Athenæ*). To his fourth brother, Cresacre, Thomas the priest resigned the property both at Barnborough and North Mimms.

Cresacre More (1572–1649) resided at More-Place or Gobions, in the parish of North Mimms, Hertfordshire. He remained a layman, although a fervent catholic, and at Gobions he wrote his 'Life of Sir Thomas More,' dedicated to Queen Henrietta Maria, without date or place, probably printed at Louvain in 1631, 4to; it was long erroneously assigned to his brother Thomas, who died in 1625. It was reprinted in 1726, and again in 1828, with preface and notes by the Rev. Joseph Hunter. More died on 26 March 1649. He married a daughter of Thomas Gage, and a descendant of Sir John Gage [q. v.]; she died on 15 July 1618. Cresacre had a son Thomas (*d.* 1660), and two daughters, Helen and Bridget.

Helen, born at Lowe Luton, Essex, on 25 March 1606, resolving to take the veil, changed her name to Gertrude More (1606–1633), and with eight other ladies crossed in 1623 to Douay, proceeding thence to Cambray, where she spent the rest of her life as a nun 'of the holy order of S. Bennet and English congregation of our Ladies of Comfort in Cambray.' She died on 18 Aug. 1633. In 1658 appeared 'The Spiritual Exercises of the Most Virtuous and Religious D. Gertrude More,' Paris, collected and arranged from her manuscripts by her confessor, Father Baker; these were published in another form, London, 1873, 32mo, by Father Henry Collins. The latter also published a 'Life of Dame Gertrude More,' London, 1877, 12mo, professing to be from ancient manuscripts, concerning which, however, no information is vouchsafed. Gertrude's sister Bridget was prioress of the English Benedictine nuns at Paris, and died on 11 Oct. 1692, aged 83.

Cresacre's son Thomas, who married a daughter of Sir Basil Brooke, was a royalist, and lost much of his property. His son Basil sold Gobions, and lived at Barnborough till his death in 1702. Basil's son, Christopher Cresacre More, had a daughter, Mary, wife of Charles Waterton, esq., of Walton (grandmother of Charles Waterton [q. v.] the naturalist), and a son, Thomas (*d.* 1739), who married Catherine, daughter of Peter Giffard of White Ladies, and was father of the last descendant of the chancellor in the male line,

Thomas More (1722–1795), a jesuit from 1766, and a provincial of the order from 1769 till the suppression of the society in 1773. He died at Bath 20 May 1795, and was buried in St. Joseph's catholic chapel at Bristol, where there is a monument with a long Latin inscription in the entrance to the sacristy (*Notes and Queries*, 2nd ser. xii. 109, 199). One of the jesuit's sisters, Mary Augustina More (*d.* 1807), became in 1761 prioress of the English priory of canonesses of St. Augustine at Bruges, where she claimed to preserve as a sacred relic her martyred ancestor's hat; but in 1794 the French revolution compelled her and her nuns to retire to England. They found an asylum at Hengrave Hall, Suffolk, the seat of Sir Thomas Gage, till 1802, when they repurchased the convent at Bruges and returned to it. Bridget, another of the jesuit's sisters, married, first, Peter Metcalfe (*d.* 1757?), and her son, Thomas Peter Metcalfe, was father of Thomas Peter Metcalfe (1794–1838), who assumed the surname of More and died unmarried, while his sister, Maria Teresa, married Charles Eyston, esq. (*d.* 1857), of East Hendred, and left issue (cf., for full pedigree of descendants of the chancellor's son John, Foley, *Records of Jesuits*, xii. 702 sq.)

Of More's daughters, the eldest, Margaret Roper (1505–1544)—the 'Meg' of her father's correspondence—was remarkable for her learning, which her father proudly encouraged and Erasmus and Reginald Pole commended. She was of a charmingly sympathetic disposition, gentle and affectionate in all domestic relations. She is said to have 'disputed of phylosophy' before Henry VIII (Collier, *English Dramatic Poetry*, i. 113), and was reckoned the equal in culture of Anne Cooke, Bacon's mother, and of her friend Mrs. Margaret Clements [q. v.] (Coke, *Debate*, 1550; Collier, *Bibl. Cat.* i. 447). She married William Roper of Eltham and Canterbury, prothonotary in the court of Canterbury, when about twenty. Her husband's accounts of her interviews with her father when in the Tower are among the most pathetic passages in biography, and she is commemorated in Tennyson's 'Dream of Fair Women' as the woman 'who clasp'd in her last trance her murdered father's head.' Dying in 1544, she was buried at Chelsea, leaving many children. Her last male descendant, Edward, died unmarried at Almanza in 1708, and his sister Elizabeth was wife of Charles Henshaw, of whose daughters Susanna married Sir Rowland Winn of Nostell; Elizabeth was wife of Sir Edward Dering; and Catherine was wife of Sir William Strickland.

More's second daughter, Elizabeth, married William Daunce, son of Sir John Daunce, apparently about 1535 (cf. *Pat. Rot.* 12 June, 27 Henry VIII), and the third daughter, Cecilia, was wife of Giles Heron, and lived at Shacklewell, a hamlet of Hackney; she seems to have had a son Thomas (*Notes and Queries*, 7th ser. ii. 35).

[The earliest life of More, The Life Arraignement and death of that Mirrour of all true Honour and Vertue, Syr Thomas More, was first published at Paris, 1626, with a dedication to the Countess of Banbury. It is by William Roper, More's son-in-law, and was reprinted by Hearne in 1716. An edition from a better manuscript was issued by the Rev. John Lewis in 1729; other reissues of Lewis's editions are dated 1731, 1765 (Dublin), and 1817, carefully edited by Samuel Weller Singer. It is full of attractive anecdote, and is the original source of all information respecting More's personal history. Manuscript copies are in Harl. MSS. 6166, 6254, 6362, and 7030. In 1556 Ellis Heywood wrote Il Moro (Florence), dedicated to Cardinal Pole, a fanciful account of More's relations with his learned guests at Chelsea. In 1588 appeared at Antwerp Stapleton's Tres Thomæ (i.e. St. Thomas, Thomas à Beckett, and More). Stapleton interweaves the narrative of Roper with passages from More's correspondence and notices of him in contemporary works. Contemporary English translations exist in manuscript in the Bodleian and Lambeth Libraries; it was reissued at Cologne in 1612, and again in 1689, both in the collected edition of the Latin works, and in a separate volume at Gratz. A life written in Queen Mary's reign by Nicholas Harpsfield is in Harleian MS. 6253, and another, written in 1599, with a preface signed 'B. R.,' appears in Wordsworth's Ecclesiastical Biog. ii. 143–85. More's great-grandson, Cresacre More (noticed above), a strong catholic, first published, probably in Paris, a new life, largely dependent on Stapleton and Roper, but adding many details, about 1631. This was reissued in 1726, and by the Rev. Joseph Hunter in 1828. Hunter first showed that Cresacre, and not his brother Thomas, was the author. J. Hoddesdon's Tho. Mori Vita et Exitus, or the History of Sir Thomas More, London, 1652, 12mo, is a mere compilation. An Italian life by Dominico Regi, first published at Milan in 1675, was reissued at Bologna in 1681. Thomas Morus aus den Quellen bearbeitet, by Dr. T. G. Rudhart, Nuremberg, 1829, is of value. Sir James Mackintosh's useful Life (1830) in Lardner's Cabinet Cyclopædia was separately reissued in 1844. But by far the best modern life, although unsatisfactory in its treatment of More's attitude to Lutherans, is by Father T. E. Bridgett, Life of Blessed Thomas More, 1891. More's Controversial Tracts, and the replies to them by Tindal, Frith, and Joye, give many biographic hints; while the Erasmi Epistolæ—especially that to Ulrich von Hutten, 23 July 1519, No. 447—are invaluable; cf. Le Clerc's edition (Leyden, 1706). Nisard's Renaissance et Réforme, Paris, 1855, contains an admirable essay on More. Philomorus, a brief Examination of the Latin Poems of Sir Thomas More, by John Howard Marsden [q. v.], 1842, 2nd edit. 1878, gives a gossipy account of More without quoting authorities. See also biography by W. H. Hutton, 1895, and essay in the present writer's Great Englishmen of the Sixteenth Century, 1904 (new edition 1907); Foss's Judges of Engl. v. 203; Lord Campbell's Chancellors; Wood's Athenæ Oxon. ed. Bliss, i. 79 seq.; Cooper's Athenæ Cantabr. i. 54; Henry VIII's Letters and Papers, with Calendars of Venetian and Spanish State Papers; Seebohm's Oxford Reformers; Lupton's Colet; Faulkner's Chelsea, 1829, i. 92–126; Clutterbuck's Hertfordshire, i. 449 sqq.; Woltmann's Life of Holbein (1874); Strype's Works; Burnet's Reformation; Ellis's Original Letters; Brewer's Henry VIII; Friedmann's Anne Boleyn; Chauncey's Martyrs. Dibdin's edition of the Utopia, 1808, and Prof. Arber's, 1869, both supply bibliographical details; cf. also Lowndes's Bibl. Man. ed. Bohn, Maitland's Books at Lambeth, and Brit. Mus. Cat. William Morris's preface to his reprint of the Utopia is suggestive. Miss Anne Manning's Household of Sir Thomas More (1851) is a fanciful but attractive sketch. A play on More's career, written about 1590, was edited by Dyce for Shakespeare Soc. in 1844 from Harl. MS. 7368, and a tragedy by James Hurdis [q. v.] was issued in 1792. In Southey's Sir Thomas More, or Colloquies on the Progress and Prospects of Society, 1829, More's ghost is introduced as a sympathetic interlocutor in a discussion on the evils of modern progress.] S. L.

MORE, THOMAS (*d.* 1685), author, was son of John More of Paynes Farm in the parish of Teynton, near Burford, Oxfordshire. On 22 June 1632 he matriculated from Merton College, Oxford, of which he became postmaster, and is said to have graduated B.A. He afterwards emigrated to St. Alban Hall. In 1642 he was called to the bar from Gray's Inn (cf. *Reg.* ed. Foster, p. 213). He joined the parliamentary army, took the covenant, and became in succession a gentleman of the guard to the Earl of Essex, lieutenant to a troop of horse belonging to Captain Richard Aylworth under the command of Colonel Edward Massey [q. v.], and cornet to the life guard of Sir Thomas Fairfax. Habitual indulgence in drink aggravated an hereditary tendency to insanity, and he failed both as a lawyer and a soldier. Dr. Skinner, bishop of Worcester, in ignorance of his real character, conferred holy orders on him. In one of his mad fits More fell downstairs at Burford, and died from his injuries 'about Michaelmas' 1685. He was buried at Teynton.

More was author of: 1. 'The English Catholike Christian; or, the Saints' Utopia: a treatise consisting of four sections—i. Josuah's Resolution; ii. Of the Common

Law; iii. Of Physick; iv. Of Divinity,' 4to, London, 1649. This eccentric farrago was written in 1641 and dedicated in a grotesque epistle, dated in February 1646, to Charles I. In the title-page the author calls himself 'Thomas de Eschallers De la More,' as having been descended from the Eschallers of Whaddon, near Royston, Cambridgeshire. 2. 'True old News, as it may appeare by several papers and certificates,' 4to, London, 1649, a rambling pamphlet, partly autobiographical. He also translated, but did not publish, the 'Vita et Mors Edwardi II' of Thomas de la More [q. v.]

[Wood's Athenæ Oxon. (Bliss), iv. 179; Brit. Mus. Cat. under 'Delamore.'] G. G.

MORE, WILLIAM (*d.* 1540), suffragan bishop of Colchester, is said to have been educated at both Oxford and Cambridge. He first appears as rector of Bradwell in Essex, having been collated 25 April 1534. On 5 Oct. of the same year he was further collated to the rectory of West Tilbury in the same county, and then held the degree S.T.B. On 3 Jan. 1534–5 a William More was collated prebendary of Sutton-in-the Marsh, Lincolnshire (Browne Willis, ii. 249), and was installed 6 March (Le Neve, ii. 218). On 20 Oct. 1536 he was consecrated bishop of Colchester as suffragan to the bishop of Ely. He was a master in chancery at the time (Rymer, *Fœdera*, xiv. 577). He became abbot of Walden *in commendam* at an unknown date. As abbot he presented to the vicarage of Walden on 29 Sept. 1537 (Newcourt, p. 627), and was afterwards vicar there himself till his death. On 11 March 1537–8 he was collated to the prebend of Givendale in the church of York, which he resigned in the following year. On 22 March 1537–8 (Kennett, *Monasticon*, iv. 135, note *t*) he surrendered the abbey of Walden on receiving a promise from Lord Audley to buy the archdeaconry of Leicester for him for 80*l.* (Braybrooke, *Audley End*, pp. 13, 19). This was probably in lieu of the pension of 200*l.* which Audley, in a letter to Cromwell, proposed he should receive. He obtained the archdeaconry in 1539 (14 Sept. Wood, ed. Bliss; 24 Sept. Le Neve, ii. 62), and died in 1540.

Another William More (1472–1559 ?), prior of Worcester, son of Richard and Ann Peers or Peres, entered the Worcester priory in 1488 at the age of sixteen; was kitchener in 1504 (Noake, *Monastery and Cathedral of Worcester*, p. 261), sub-prior under John Wednesbury (1507–18), and was made prior 2 Oct. 1518 (*Mon. Angl.* i. 581). He spent large sums on repairs, on plate for the churches upon the monastery's estates, and on books, including printed books for the convent (Noake, pp. 414, 417). He was fond of comfort, amusement, and display. A letter from a monk, John Musard, written while in prison, which has been printed by Noake from the MS. Cotton Cleop. E. iv. f. 99, contains a list of complaints against a certain 'untrue master,' who is clearly identical with More, for one charge is that he made a new mitre, a needless extravagance, and the costs of this mitre are entered in More's diary. Musard complains, too, of the prior's gifts to his relations, of the sale of the monastery's plate, and of neglect of the buildings. Musard had been put in prison by More in 1531. In February 1532 More served in the commission of the peace for Worcestershire (*Letters and Papers*, v. 399). Foreseeing the dissolution, he resigned in 1535 on condition that he was allowed a well-furnished room in the monastery, with a supply of fuel, and exemption from a debt of 100*l.*; and that his house at Crowle should be repaired. More died after 1558, and was buried in Crowle Church (Dingley, *History from Marble*, Camden Soc., ii. 116, cccvi, where his arms and coffin-lid are given).

The dean and chapter of Worcester possess an English journal and account-book, written by More, from which selections have been published (Noake, pp. 133 sqq.)

Two principals of Hart Hall (afterwards Hertford College), Oxford, who held the office in 1416 and 1544 respectively, were also named William More.

[Athenæ Cantabr. vol. i.; Le Neve's Fasti, vols. ii. iii.; Newcourt's Repertorium, vol. ii.; Notes and Queries, 2nd ser. ii. 2.] M. B.

MOREHEAD, CHARLES (1807–1882), member of the Bombay medical service, second son of Robert Morehead, rector of Easington in the North Riding of Yorkshire, and brother of William Ambrose Morehead [q. v.], was born at Edinburgh in 1807, and proceeded M.D. there. At Edinburgh his zeal for clinical medicine attracted the attention of Professor William Pulteney Alison [q. v.], and he continued his medical studies in Paris under Pierre Louis. In 1829 he entered the Bombay medical service, and was afterwards on the personal staff of the governor, Sir Robert Grant [q. v.] Morehead was the founder of native medical education in Western India. After Grant's death in 1838 he was appointed to the European and native general hospitals of Bombay, and it was owing to his efforts that the Grant Medical College at Bombay was erected as a memorial of Grant in 1845.

Morehead was appointed the first principal of the Grant College, and the first professor of medicine. He was also the first physician of the Jamsetjee Jeejeebhoy Hospital, in which the students of the college receive their clinical instruction. (This hospital was founded in Bombay in 1843 by Sir Jamsetjee Jeejeebhoy [q. v.], the famous philanthropist.) He originated the Bombay Medical and Physical Society for the advancement of medical science and its collateral branches, and also the Grant College Medical Society, designed as a bond of union among former students of the college. He was the author of an elaborate work entitled 'Researches on the Diseases of India,' 1856, 2 vols. 8vo, which passed through two editions, and is a standard authority. He was elected a fellow of the College of Physicians. Morehead retired from the Bombay medical service in 1862. In 1881 he was created a companion of the order of the Indian Empire. He died at Wilton Castle, Yorkshire, the seat of his brother-in-law, Sir Charles Lowther, on 24 Aug. 1882. In 1844 he married Harriet Anne, daughter of George Barnes, first archdeacon of Bombay.

[This article is mainly based upon a notice of Dr. Morehead, published in 1882, Edinburgh. See also Times, 28 Aug. 1882, and Lancet, 1882, ii. 468.] A. J. A.

MOREHEAD, WILLIAM (1637–1692), divine, born in 1637 in Lombard Street, London, was a nephew of General Monck [q. v.] His surname is often found spelt as Moorhead. He entered Winchester School at the age of eleven, and proceeded to New College, Oxford, where he graduated B.A. on 3 May 1660, and M.A. on 14 Jan. 1663. He was elected a fellow in 1658, and resigned in 1672. He was presented to the college living of Bucknell, Oxfordshire, by the warden and fellows of New College (14 July 1670), and also held the living of Whitfield in Northamptonshire, to which he was presented by Sir Thomas Spencer of Yarnton, Oxfordshire, lord of the manor. He chiefly resided there, employing a curate at Bucknell—procedure which led to dissatisfaction among the parishioners, and a petition to the bishop in 1680 or 1681 for a resident minister. The petition seems to have produced some effect on Morehead, who died at Bucknell 18 Feb. 1691-2, and was buried there.

Morehead or Moorhead wrote a poetic tract on Monck's departure from Scotland for England in 1660. It is now very rare; one copy is in the library of Mrs. Christie-Miller, at Britwell Court, near Maidenhead. The full title runs: 'Lachrymæ sive valedictio Scotiæ sub discessum clarissimi, &c. Gubernatoris Domini Georgii Monachi in Angliam (*sic*) Revocati. Authore Gulielmo Moorhead Nov. Coll. Oxon. Soc. The Tears and Valediction of Scotland upon the departing of her Governor the Lord-General George Monck: and Londons welcome Reception of his Excellencie, In being instrumentall in the bringing home our Gracious Soveraigne Lord King Charles the Second. London, printed by H. Brugis, living at the Sign of Sir John Old-Castle in Pye-Corner, for the Author. 1660. 4to. 24 leaves.' The verse is in both Latin and English, the two renderings appearing on opposite pages. Engraved portraits of both Charles II and of General Monck are inserted, the latter being the work of Richard Gaywood [q. v.]

William Morehead is also said by bibliographers to be the author of an anonymous translation, which was published some time after his death, of a famous treatise by Giordano Bruno. Bruno's work bears the title 'Spaccio de la bestia trienfante,' which was first published in 1584, ostensibly at Paris, though it was doubtless printed in London. In its English garb the work bore the title 'Spaccio de la bestia trienfante; or the expulsion of the triumphant beast, translated from the Italian.' It was issued at London in 1713 in an octavo volume of 280 pages in a limited edition of only fifty copies. The deist, John Toland, seems to have been responsible for the publication, and the rendering itself has been attributed to him. According, however, to the testimony of the well-known bookseller, Samuel Paterson [q. v.], the name of the translator was undoubtedly William Morehead, though there can be very little doubt that the translator was not identical with the nephew and panegyrist of General Monck. Paterson, who was in business during the middle of the eighteenth century, stated after 1750 in a sale catalogue that he was warranted in saying 'upon the authority of the translator himself, namely, the late William Morehead, Esquire,' that his English version of Bruno 'was hastily made by him for the private use of Mr. Collins [i.e. Anthony Collins (1676–1729), the deist, q. v.], nor ever intended to be printed, though shortly after taken out of Mr. Collins' library by Toland, as [Paterson] believed, and sent to the press.' Morehead, the alleged translator of Bruno, clearly lived far into the eighteenth century, more than fifty years after the death of Monck's nephew. This English translation of Bruno's treatise is now rare.

[Dunkin's Oxfordshire, i. 188–9; Kirby's Winchester Scholars, p. 184; Wood's Athenæ Oxon. iv. 353; Rawlinson MSS. D. 384, fol. 10; papers belonging to the archdeaconry of Oxford in the Bodleian Library, per the Rev. W. D. Macray.] C. F. S.

MOREHEAD, WILLIAM AMBROSE (1805–1863), Indian official, born in 1805, was the eldest son of Robert Morehead, D.D., and brother of Dr. Charles Morehead [q. v.] He entered the Madras civil service in 1825, in 1828 became assistant to the principal collector of North Arcot, and was appointed later in the year registrar of the Zillah court at Chingleput. In 1832, while sub-collector and joint-magistrate at Cuddapah, Morehead gave evidence of administrative capacity and firmness on the occasion of a fanatical outbreak, in which the head assistant-collector, Mr. Macdonald, was murdered. It devolved upon Morehead to restore order and bring to justice the perpetrators of the crime. Subsequently, as civil and sessions judge at Chingleput, he manifested considerable efficiency in judicial work. Consequently in 1846 he was chosen to fill a vacancy on the bench of the court of Sadr Adálut, the highest of the courts of the East India Company, which eventually, in 1862, was amalgamated with the supreme court under the designation of the High Court of Judicature. Morehead speedily justified his selection. In 1850, at the request of the colonial office, two Indian judicial officers, of whom Morehead was one, were sent to investigate certain occurrences which had taken place in Ceylon during the government of Lord Torrington. Morehead conducted this delicate duty with singular tact and independence of judgment.

In 1857, the year of the Indian mutiny, Morehead was appointed a member of the council of the governor of Madras, and held that office until his retirement from the public service in October 1862. On two occasions he acted as governor of the presidency, first on the recall of Sir Charles Trevelyan, and subsequently during the interregnum which took place between the death of Sir Henry Ward and the arrival of Sir William Denison. Morehead's views on the scheme of taxation proposed by Sir James Wilson, and adopted by the government of Lord Canning, for the purpose of establishing a financial equilibrium, were mainly in accord with those held by the governor, Sir Charles Trevelyan. He objected to an income-tax as being specially unsuited to India, and advocated in its stead the retention of an old native tax called the muhtarafa, and an increase in the salt-tax, combined with the establishment of government salt depôts wherever facilities existed for the carriage of salt in large quantities. He also advocated an extension of the stamp duties by requiring bills of exchange, cheques, and receipts above a certain amount to be taxed. But while agreeing with the governor as to the impolicy of the new legislation, Morehead strongly disapproved of the step taken by Sir C. Trevelyan in publishing in the newspapers the minutes which had been recorded on the subject by the members of the local government, and he stated that had Sir Charles Trevelyan informed his colleagues of his intention to take this step, he should have withdrawn his minute and 'refused to accede to its being used in a manner different to that which I intended when I wrote it.' During the following months, when in charge of the government, he rendered to the government of India a thoroughly loyal support, and received the thanks of Lord Canning and his colleagues in the supreme government. On Lord Canning's recommendation he was offered by the secretary of state a seat in the governor-general's council, upon Sir Bartle Frere's appointment as governor of Bombay; but this advancement, owing to the impaired state of his health, he declined. It is understood that Lord Canning also recommended that some other special mark of the queen's favour should be conferred upon him for his loyal support of the government of India at a difficult crisis. Morehead held for two years the office of vice-chancellor of the university of Madras, of which he was one of the original fellows.

Morehead finally left India in October 1862, and died in Edinburgh on 1 Dec. 1863. His character was singularly attractive. His keen perception of humour, and the strong sound sense which characterised all he said and did, rendered him a most delightful and instructive companion. He was much beloved by the natives, to whom he was always accessible. His picture hangs in the Madras Banqueting Hall. In the Dean cemetery in Edinburgh, where he was buried, his memory is preserved by a runic cross of polished Peterhead granite, erected by a number of his friends.

[Personal knowledge; Scotsman, 9 Jan. 1866; Parliamentary Return, 24 July 1860, containing correspondence on proposed financial measures in India.] A. J. A.

MORELL, Sir CHARLES, pseudonym. [See Ridley, James, 1736–1765, author.]

MORELL, JOHN DANIEL (1816–1891), philosopher and inspector of schools, born at Little Baddow, Essex, on 18 June 1816, was the ninth child of Stephen Morell by Jemima Robinson, his wife. The family was of French origin, and settled in England on the revocation of the edict of Nantes. The father was a congregationalist minister at Little Baddow from 1799 to 1852. The ministerial calling was widely followed in the family, and Morell himself tells us that he chose it as his own 'destination even from a child.' At seventeen, therefore, he was entered as a probationer at Homerton College under Dr. Pye Smith. He travelled far outside the ordinary class-work, and Greek and Latin, French and German, were added to the study of theology. The theological course over, Morell's health was so impaired that he resolved to qualify himself for teaching, lest pastoral work should be found beyond his strength. From Homerton he accordingly went to Glasgow University, where he read with diligence, and gained the first prize for logic and moral philosophy. He graduated B.A. with honours in 1840, and proceeded M.A. in 1841. Leaving Glasgow, he went, in the summer of 1841, to Bonn, where he gave himself to theology and philosophy, studying under Fichte, whose influence he felt all his life. Returning to England, Morell began his ministry as an independent at Gosport in August 1842, and in October of the same year was fully 'ordained.' His creed was hardly of the type usually associated with the nonconformity of a place like Gosport, and his ministry there closed in 1845.

In 1846 he published his 'Historical and Critical View of the Speculative Philosophy of Europe in the Nineteenth Century.' Though the book came from a young and unknown author, it reached a second edition in the year after its appearance. Not the least of its praises was Mansel's confession, years after its appearance, that this was the book which 'more than any other gave me a taste for philosophical study.' Chalmers was so impressed that he tried to secure for Morell the chair of moral philosophy at Edinburgh. Laurence Oliphant was 'much affected' by it (*Life of Laurence Oliphant*, i. 217); while Lord Lansdowne, then president of the privy council, who wanted a nonconformist as inspector of schools, offered the post to Morell on reading his book. After some hesitation he accepted the office, and held it from 1848 until 1876. As an inspector Morell was thorough, conscientious, and searching, kindly and sympathetic alike to children and teachers. But the new duties did not arrest Morell's literary work. Four lectures on 'The Philosophical Tendencies of the Age,' delivered in Edinburgh and Glasgow, were followed in 1849 by a careful and suggestive inquiry into 'The Philosophy of Religion,' which was keenly discussed, more especially in Scotland. Profiting by his close acquaintance with elementary school life, Morell in 1852 published the first of his works dealing with English grammar, 'The Analysis of Sentences.' Then came, in 1855, 'The Essentials of English Grammar and Analysis' and the 'Handbook of Logic,' while the 'Grammar of the English Language' appeared in 1857. Few educational works of that period had a larger circulation, and he mainly devoted his leisure thenceforth to their compilation; but the issue of his 'Philosophical Fragments' in 1878 showed that his regard for philosophic inquiry was not diminished. For some years he edited the 'School Magazine,' the pages of which illustrate another side of his literary character by some verses of more than respectable merit. In 1881 Morell's health began to break; softening of the brain developed, and he died on 1 April 1891. He married Elizabeth Morell Wreford, but left no issue.

Morell's own position in metaphysical philosophy was that of an eclectic, with a decided leaning to idealism. His theological position showed the same independence. From the creed of Homerton he passed into a broader faith, which allowed him to worship for some years with protestant nonconformists, then with Anglican churchmen, and finally with unitarians.

Morell's works were: 1. 'The Catholic Church: a Sermon,' London 1843. 2. 'The Evangelical Alliance,' a tract, London, 1846. 3. 'An Historical and Critical View of the Speculative Philosophy of Europe in the Nineteenth Century,' 2 vols. London, 1846; 2nd edit. enlarged, London and Edinburgh, 1847. 4. 'On the Philosophical Tendencies of the Age,' four lectures, London and Edinburgh, 1848. 5. 'The Philosophy of Religion,' London, 1849. 6. 'The Analysis of Sentences,' London, 1852. 7. 'The Elements of Psychology,' pt. i., London, 1853. 8. 'The Essentials of English Grammar and Analysis,' London, 1855. 9. 'Handbook of Logic,' London, 1855. 10. 'Modern German Philosophy,' 1856. 11. 'Poetical Reading Books, with Aids for Grammatical Analysis, &c.' (with Dr. Ihne), London, 1857. 12. 'A Grammar of the English Language, together with an Exposition of the Analysis of Sentences,' London, 1857; another edition, with exercises, London, 1857. 13. 'A Series of Graduated Exercises, adapted to Morell's Grammar and Analysis,' London, 1857. 14. 'On the Progress of Society in England as affected by the Advancement of National Education,' 1859. 15. 'Fichte's Contributions to Moral Philosophy' (translation), London, 1860. 16. 'An Elementary Reading Book,' London, 1865. 17. 'First Steps in English Grammar,' London, 1871. 18. 'A Complete Manual of Spelling,' London, 1872. 19. 'English Echoes of German Song,' translated by Morell and others, London, 1877. 20. 'Philosophical Fragments,'

London, 1878. 21. 'Wosco's Compendium of Italian History,' translated and completed, London, 1881. 22. 'Guide to Employment in the Civil Service,' with introduction, 1882. 23. 'An Introduction to Mental Philosophy on the Inductive Method,' London, 1884. 24. 'Hausrath's Antinous' (translation), London, 1884. 25. 'Manual of the History of Philosophy,' London, 1884.

[Theobald's Memorials of J. D. Morell, London, 1891; Tennemann's Hist. Philos., ed. J. R. Morell (cousin of the above), 1854, p. 490.]

A. R. B.

MORELL, THOMAS (1703–1784), classical scholar, born at Eton, Buckinghamshire, on 18 March 1703, was son of Thomas Morell. On his father's death his mother supported herself by keeping a boarding-house at Eton, on the foundation of which Thomas was admitted in 1715. On 3 Aug. 1722 he was elected to King's College, Cambridge, where he graduated B.A. in 1726, M.A. in 1730, and D.D. in 1743. In July 1733 he was admitted M.A. 'ad eundem' at Oxford, and on 28 June 1759 was 're-incorporated' as D.D. at Cambridge (Foster, *Alumni Oxon*, 1715–1886, iii. 985). He was appointed curate of Kew, Surrey, in 1731, and for a short time acted as curate of Twickenham, Middlesex. On 20 March 1737 the college presented him to the rectory of Buckland, Hertfordshire, (Cussans, *Hertfordshire*, Edwinstree Hundred, p. 53). He was elected F.S.A. on 20 Oct. following (Gough, *List of Soc. Antiq.*, 1798), and in 1768 was assistant secretary to the society (Nichols, *Lit. Anecd.* v. 446). On 16 June 1768 he became F.R.S. (Thomson, *Hist. of Roy. Society*, Append. iv). In 1775 he was appointed chaplain to the garrison at Portsmouth, and for several years he preached the Fairchild botanical sermon on Whit-Tuesday at St. Leonard's, Shoreditch.

Morell resided chiefly at Turnham Green, Middlesex, where he had for neighbours Thomson, Hogarth, and Garrick. Handel was also his friend. He died at Turnham Green on 19 Feb. 1784, and was buried on 27 Feb. at Chiswick (Lysons, *Environs*, ii. 216). In 1738 he married Anne, daughter of Henry Barker of Chiswick, by whom he had no issue. His library was sold in 1785 (Nichols, iii. 646).

Morell was a warm friend and a cheerful companion, who loved a jest, told a good story, and sang a good song. He was careless of his own interests and dressed ill, and his improvidence kept him always poor and in debt. His knowledge of music was considerable, and he played the organ with some skill. He maintained that choral services should be generally adopted in parish churches (cf. note by William Cole cited in Nichols, ix. 789).

Morell's reputation as a classical scholar rests on his 'Thesaurus Græcæ Poeseωs; sive Lexicon Græco-Prosodiacum,' 2 pts. 4to, Eton, 1762, of which improved editions by Edward Maltby [q. v.], afterwards bishop of Durham, were published in 1815 and 1824. The introduction was reprinted in P. Moccia's 'Prosodia Græca,' 1767, 8vo. He also published revised editions of Hederich's 'Greek Lexicon' (1766 and 1778), Ainsworth's 'Latin Dictionary' (1773), and the 'Gradus ad Parnassum' (1782). For Eton school he revised the 'Exempla Minora' (many editions) and edited the 'Hecuba,' 'Orestes,' 'Phœnissæ,' and 'Alcestis' of Euripides (2 vols. 8vo, London, 1748). His blank verse translation of the 'Hecuba' (8vo, 1749) is very feeble. In 1767 he edited the 'Prometheus Vinctus' of Æschylus, with a blank verse translation (8vo), and reissued it in quarto in 1773, when Garrick did his best to get him subscribers (Boswell, *Life of Johnson*, ed. 1848, p. 386). For the preparation of this work he used a copy of the 'Æschylus' published by Henry Stephens in 1557, which, coming into the possession of the Rev. Richard Hooper, was by him presented to Cambridge University Library (*Notes and Queries*, 1st ser. v. 604, vi. 125, 322, 373). Morell likewise edited the 'Philoctetes' of Sophocles (8vo, 1777), and compiled an 'Index ad Sophoclem' (4to, 1787). He made a creditable translation of Seneca's 'Epistles,' which, though completed in 1753, was not published until after his death (2 vols. 4to, 1786); the manuscript is in the British Museum, Additional MS. 10604.

Morell supplied the libretti for Handel's oratorios of 'Judas Maccabæus,' 1746, 'Alexander Balas,' 1748, 'Joshua,' 1748, 'Solomon,' 1749, 'Theodora,' 1750, 'Jephtha,' 1752, 'Gideon,' 1754, and 'The Triumph of Time and Truth,' 1758, a translation from the Italian of Cardinal Pamfili. The well-known lines beginning 'See the Conquering Hero comes' in 'Joshua' were subsequently transferred to 'Judas Maccabæus.' They were introduced into Nathaniel Lee's tragedy 'The Rival Queens' in late acting versions (cf. ed. 1785, p. 21), and have been on that account erroneously ascribed to Lee [q. v.] His other poetical writings are: 1. 'Poems on Divine Subjects, original and translated from the Latin of Marcus Hieronymus Vida, bishop of Alba (and M. A. Flaminius),' 8vo, London, 1732 (2nd edit. 1736). 2. 'Congratulatory Verses on the Marriage of the Prince of Orange with the Princess Anne,'

1737. 3. 'The Christian's Epinikion, or Song of Triumph: a Paraphrase on Chap. xv. of St. Paul's 1st Epistle to the Corinthians,' 4to, London, 1743, in blank verse. 4. 'Hope: a Poetical Essay in Blank Verse. In three Books,' 4to, London, 1745. Book i. only appeared. 5. 'Nabal, an Oratorio,' 4to, London, 1764. It was performed at Covent Garden, the words being adapted to several compositions of Handel. Among the Additional MSS. in the British Museum (Nos. 5832 and 29766) are 'Verses' and 'Sacred Poems' by Morell. He also published the 'Canterbury Tales' of Chaucer 'in the original, and as they are turned into modern language by the most eminent hands,' 8vo, London, 1737, and in 1747 is said to have issued by subscription an edition of Spenser's 'Works.'

His miscellaneous writings are: 1. 'Philalethes and Theophanes; or a Summary View of the last Controversy occasioned by a book entitled "The Moral Philosopher," pt. i.' 8vo, London, 1739; 2nd edit. 1740. 2. 'Catalogue of the Books in the Osterley Park Library,' 4to, 1771, of which only twenty-five copies were printed (Nichols, v. 327). 3. A Latin letter addressed in 1774 to Daines Barrington on the Corbridge altar, now in the British Museum, printed in the 'Archæologia,' iii. 332. 4. 'Sacred Annals' (harmonies on the Gospels), 12mo, London, 1776. 5. 'Notes and Annotations on Locke on the Human Understanding,' 8vo, London, 1794, written at the request of Queen Caroline. He revised Hogarth's 'Analysis of Beauty.' His 'literary portrait' of William Hogarth and his wife may be found in John Nichols's 'Biographical Anecdotes of Hogarth,' ed. 1810, i. 127. To the third edition of 'Sermons' by Edward Littleton (*d.* 1733) [q. v.] he contributed a biographical introduction (1749). He has essays and verses in the 'Gentleman's Magazine,' to which he was one of the earliest contributors, and occasionally published single sermons, including one on the 'Use and Importance of Music in the Sacrifice of Thanksgiving,' preached at the meeting of the three choirs, Worcester, Hereford, and Gloucester, 8vo, 1747.

In the British Museum are copies of the New Testament in Greek, 1632, the New Testament in English, 1647, and Plutarch's 'Moralia,' 1542, all copiously annotated by Morell. There is also a letter from him to Sir Hans Sloane in Additional MS. 4053. His commonplace book is Additional MS. 28846.

In 1762 Morell's portrait was drawn by Hogarth 'in the character of a cynic philosopher, with an organ near him.' The portrait was afterwards engraved by James Basire, and prefixed to Morell's 'Thesaurus.'

[Nichols's Lit. Anecd. i. 651, and elsewhere; Harwood's Alumni Etonenses, p. 302; Baker's Biog. Dramat. 1812; Walpole's Letters (Cunningham), v. 420; Addit. MSS. 5151, f. 249, 6402, f. 142; Will in P.C.C. 151, Rockingham.]
G. G.

MOREMAN, JOHN (1490?–1554), divine, was born at South Hole, Hartland, Devonshire, about 1490. He was sent to Oxford University about 1504, and graduated B.A. 29 Jan. 1508–9, M.A. 31 Jan. 1512–13, B.D. 18 Jan. 1526–7, and D.D. 8 April 1530. On 29 June 1510 he was elected to a fellowship at Exeter College. From 1516 to 1528 he held the vicarage of Midsomer Norton, Somerset, but he probably remained in residence at Oxford, as he retained his fellowship until 6 Nov. 1522, and was principal of Hart Hall from 1522 to 1527, when he severed his connection with the university. He was instituted by Bishop Voysey to the rectory of Holy Trinity, Exeter, on 25 Sept. 1528, but vacated it within less than six months upon his appointment, 25 Feb. 1529, by Exeter College, to the valuable vicarage of Menheniot, Cornwall, which he enjoyed for the rest of his life. His school in this parish became famous throughout the west of England; among his pupils was John Hooker, *alias* Vowell (1526?–1601) [q. v.] Moreman was also prebendary of Glasney College, near Penryn, Cornwall, canon of Exeter Cathedral 19 June 1544, and vicar of Colebrooke, Devonshire, 25 Oct. 1546.

At the university Moreman had strenuously opposed the divorce of Henry VIII from Queen Catherine. On the accession of Edward VI he was thrown into prison, and the eleventh demand of the Cornish rebels in June 1549 was, 'That Dr. Moreman and Crispin should be sent to them and put in their livings.' The answer of the Archbishop of Canterbury to this stipulation ran, that 'those were ignorant, superstitious, and deceitful persons.' On the accession of Queen Mary he was released from restraint, and in the disputation between Roman catholics and protestants which took place in the Convocation House, London, October 1553, he answered, as one of the champions of catholicism, the arguments of Cheney, archdeacon of Hereford, afterwards bishop of Gloucester, Phillips, dean of Rochester, and Aylmer, chaplain to the Duke of Suffolk. During the commotion at Exeter in January 1553–4 [see Carew, Sir Peter] Moreman was in residence and active against the malcontents. He took a leading part in church affairs at Exeter, but the statement of Foxe that he 'was coadjutor to Voysey, the bishop of Exeter, and after his decease became bishop of that see,' must be an error. Hooker says that he was nominated to the deanery of Exeter, but that he died before presentation. He died at Menheniot, between May and October 1554, and was buried in the church.

While vicar of Menheniot he taught the Creed, Lord's Prayer, and Commandments in English, the Cornish language having been in use before. A discourse by him, on St. Paul's Epistle to the Romans, was transcribed by the Rev. Lawrence Travers, vicar of Quethiock, Cornwall. He gave to the library of Oriel College, Oxford, three works (SHADWELL, *Reg. Orielense*, i. 398).

[Oliver's Eccl. Antiquities, ed. 1840, ii. 184–188; Oliver's Monasticon, p. 206; Foster's Alumni Oxon.; Boase's Reg. Univ. Oxford (Oxf. Hist. Soc.), i. 63; Boase's Exeter College, pp. xvii–xviii, 29, 200–2; Weaver's Somerset Incumbents, p. 143; Wood's Fasti, ed. Bliss, i. 24, 35, 82–3, 104; Wood's Univ. of Oxford, ed. Gutch, vol. ii. pt. i. pp. 45–6; Wood's Oxford Colleges, ed. Gutch, p. 646; Prince's Devon Worthies, ed. 1810, pp. 600–2; Moore's Devon, ii. 235–6; Journ. Roy. Instit. of Cornwall, October 1864 pp. 76–7, April 1865 pp. 36–7; Burnet's Reformation, ed. Pococke, ii. 210–211, 424–6, v. 601; Foxe's Monuments, ed. Townsend, vi. 397–411, 536; Maclean's Sir Peter Carew, pp. v, 159–64; Journal of State Papers (Foreign and Domestic, vol. v.), 1531–2, p. 6.]

W. P. C.

MORES, EDWARD ROWE (1731–1778), antiquary, born on 13 Jan. 1730, was son of Edward Mores, rector of Tunstall, Kent, and author of 'The Pious Example, a discourse occasioned by the death of Mrs. Anne Mores,' London, 1725; he married Miss Windsor, the sister of an undertaker in Union Court, Broad Street, and died in 1740 (NICHOLS, *Bibliotheca Topographica Britannica*, I. xvii.–xx. 58). In the same year Edward Rowe entered Merchant Taylors' School (*Register*, ed. Robinson, ii. 96), and proceeded thence to Oxford, matriculating as a commoner of Queen's College on 25 June 1746 (FOSTER, *Alumni Oxon.*, 1715–1886, iii. 978), and graduating B.A. in 1750, and M.A. in 1753. At Oxford he attracted attention by the extraordinary range and depth of his knowledge and the eccentricities of his conduct. His father wished him to take orders, but whether he did so is uncertain. In 1752 he was elected F.S.A., being the first new member after the grant of a charter to the society in November 1751; and in 1754 he was one of a committee for examining the society's minute books, with a view to selecting papers worthy of publication. After travelling abroad for some time he took up his residence at the Heralds' College, intending to become a member of that society, but about 1760 he retired to an estate left him by his father at Low Leyton, Essex. There he built a whimsical house, called Etlow Place, on a plan of one which he had seen in France. He used to mystify his friends by declaring that he had been created D.D. at the Sorbonne, and attired himself in some academical costume which he called that of a Dominican friar. He considered Latin the only language adapted to devotion and for universal use, and composed a creed in it, with a kind of mass on the death of his wife, of which he printed a few copies in his own house, under the disguised title of 'Ordinale Quotidianum, 1685. Ordo Trigintalis.' Of his daughter's education he was particularly careful. From her earliest infancy he talked to her principally in Latin. She was sent to a convent at Rouen for further training, and was there converted to Romanism, at which he pretended to be very angry.

The Society for Equitable Assurances, which had been first suggested by James Dodson [q. v.], owes its existence to Mores. He applied for a charter in 1761, but, failing of success, he, with sixteen more of the original subscribers, resolved to establish their society by deed. It was arranged that Mores should be perpetual director, with an annuity of 100*l.* In order to float the society, he published in 1762 'A Short Account of the Society for Equitable Assurances, &c.,' 8vo (7th edit. 1767), in 1766 'The Statutes' and 'Precedents of sundry Instruments relating to the Constitution and Practice of the Society,' 8vo, and in 1768 the 'Deed of Settlement . . . with the Declaration of Trust,' 8vo, and a 'List of the Policies and other printed Instruments of the Society,' 8vo; but some disputes arising between him and the original members, he declined to act further (see *Papers relating to the Disputes with the Charter Fund Proprietors in the Equitable Society*, 1769).

Towards the close of his life Mores fell into negligent and dissipated habits. He died at Low Leyton on 28 Nov. 1778, and was buried by his wife in Walthamstow churchyard. By his marriage with Susannah Bridgman (1730–1767), daughter of a Whitechapel grocer, he had a son, Edward Rowe Mores, who married in 1779 a Miss Spence, and a daughter, Sarah, married in 1774 to John Davis, house decorator of Walthamstow. His large collections of books, manuscripts, engravings, and printing types were dispersed by sale in August 1779. The more valuable portion of his books and manuscripts was purchased by Richard Gough [q. v.], and is now in the Bodleian Library. The remainder was chiefly acquired by Thomas Astle [q. v.] and John Nichols [q. v.]

While at Oxford in 1746 Mores assisted in correcting an edition of Calasio's 'Concordance,' projected by Jacob Ilive [q. v.], the printer, and published in 1747, 4 vols. fol. In 1749 he printed in black letter 'Nomina et Insignia Gentilitia Nobilium Equitumque sub Edvardo Primo Rege militantium. Accedunt classes exercitus Edvardi Tertii Regis Caletem obsidentis,' 4to, Oxford. He also printed a few copies, sold after his death, of an edition of Dionysius of Halicarnassus's 'De claris Rhetoribus,' with vignettes engraved by Green; the preface and notes were not completed. He applied, without success, to several continental scholars for assistance in the notes. An imperfect reissue is dated 1781, 8vo.

Mores made a few collections for a history of Merchant Taylors' School. In 1752 he printed in half a quarto sheet some corrections made by Francis Junius [q. v.] in his own copy of his edition of Cædmon's 'Saxon Paraphrase of Genesis,' and other parts of the Old Testament (Amsterdam, 1655), and in 1754 he issued in quarto fifteen of the drawings from the manuscript of Cædmon in the Bodleian, the plates of which were purchased by Gough and deposited in that library. He is stated in Pegge's 'Anonymiana' (cent. vi. No. 14) to have commenced a transcript of Junius's dictionaries, with a design of publishing them. He formed considerable collections for a history of Oxford, and especially that of his own college, whose archives he arranged and calendared. He commissioned B. Green to execute many drawings of Oxford and the neighbourhood, which were included in Gough's bequest. His manuscripts relating to Queen's, with his collections about All Souls', fell into the hands of Astle, who presented the former to John Price of the Bodleian.

Mores assisted John Bilson in his burlesque on All Souls', a folio sheet printed in 1752, entitled 'Preparing for the Press . . . a complete History of the Mallardians,' to which he contributed the prints of a cat said to have been starved in the library, and of two grotesque busts carved on the south wall of the college.

In 1759 he circulated queries for a 'Parochial History of Berkshire,' but made little progress. His collections were printed in 1783 in Nichols's 'Bibliotheca Topographica Britannica,' vol. iv. No. xvi, together with his 'Account of Great Coxwell, Berkshire,' vol. iv. No. xiii, where his family had been originally seated, and his excellent 'History of Tunstall, Kent,' vol. i. No. 1, with a memoir of him by R. Gough.

In the latter part of his life Mores projected a new edition of Ames's 'Typographical Antiquities.' On the death of John James of Bartholomew Close, the last of the old race of letter-founders, in June 1772, Mores purchased all the old portions of his immense collection of punches, matrices, and types which had been accumulating from the days of Wynkyn de Worde. From these materials he composed his valuable 'Dissertation upon English Typographical Founders and Founderies,' of which he printed eighty copies. John Nichols, who purchased the whole impression, published it with a short appendix in 1778, 8vo. He also included Mores's 'Narrative of Block Printing' in his 'Biographical Memoirs of William Ged,' &c., 8vo, 1781.

His manuscript, 'Commentarius de Ælfrico Dorobernensi Archiepiscopo,' which Astle bought, was published under the editorship of G. J. Thorkelin in 1789, 4to, London. In the British Museum are the following manuscripts by Mores: 1. Epitome of Archbishop Peckham's 'Register,' 1755 (Addit. MSS. 6110, 6111, 6112, 6114). 2. Kentish Pedigrees by him and Edward Hasted (Addit. MS. 5528). 3. List of rectories and vicarages in Kent (Addit. MS. 6408). 4. Copies of his letters to John Strype, 1710 (Addit. MS. 5853), and to Browne Willis, 1749, 1751 (Addit. MS. 5833). 5. Monuments of the Rowe family (Addit. MS. 6239). 6. Letters to Edward Lye, 1749–61 (Addit. MS. 32325). He wrote also part of Addit. MS. 5526 (copy of John Philpott's 'Visitation of Kent,' 1619) and of Addit. MS. 5532 (copy of Robert Cook's 'Visitation of Kent,' 1574), and assisted Andrew Coltee Ducarel [q. v.] in his abstract of the archiepiscopal registers at Lambeth (Addit. MSS. 6062–109).

A whole-length portrait of Mores was engraved by J. Mynde after a picture by R. van Bleeck.

[Gough's Memoir referred to; Rawl. MS. J. fol. 18, pp. 115–16; Nichols's Lit. Anecd. v. 389–405, and elsewhere; Nichols's Illustr. of Lit.; Addit. MSS. 5841 f. 294, 6401 f. 10; Evans's Cat. of Engraved Portraits, vol. ii.; notes kindly furnished by the provost of Queen's College, Oxford.] G. G.

MORESBY, Sir FAIRFAX (1786–1877), admiral of the fleet, son of Fairfax Moresby of Lichfield, entered the navy in December 1799, on board the London, with Captain John Child Purvis, whom he followed in 1801 to the Royal George. In March 1802 he joined the Alarm, with Captain (afterwards Sir William) Parker (1781–1866) [q. v.], and in November went with him to the Amazon, in which he served in the Mediterranean, and in the chase of the French fleet to the West Indies. In December 1805 he was appointed to the Puissant at Portsmouth, and on 10 April 1806 he was promoted to be lieutenant of the Ville de Paris. A few months later he was appointed to the Kent, in which, and afterwards in the Repulse, in the Mediterranean, he was frequently engaged in boat service. After some weeks in acting command of the Éclair and Acorn he was promoted to be commander of the Wizard brig, 18 April 1811, and was sent to the Archipelago to repress the pirates who, as well as the French privateers fitted out in Turkey, were just then extremely active. Of these he captured several, and in acknowledgment of his services he was presented by the merchants of Malta with a sword. Towards the end of 1812 the Wizard was sent to England with despatches, but, returning to the Mediterranean, was through the summer of 1813 attached to the squadron in the Adriatic, under the command of Rear-admiral, (afterwards Sir) Thomas Fremantle [q. v.] On several occasions, and more especially at the siege of Trieste in October, Moresby's services were highly commended. With the other captains of the squadron he was permitted to accept the cross of the order of Maria Theresa, 23 May 1814. He was advanced to post rank 7 June 1814, and was nominated a C.B. 4 June 1815.

In April 1819 he was appointed to the Menai, a 24-gun frigate, in which he went out to the Cape of Good Hope. In 1820 he surveyed Algoa Bay and its neighbourhood, arranged the landing of the settlers, to the number of two thousand, and organised the infant colony. In 1821 he was senior officer at Mauritius, with orders to suppress the slave trade. He captured or destroyed several of the more notorious vessels engaged in that trade, prosecuted the owners, and concluded a treaty with the imaum of Muscat conferring on English men-of-war the right of searching and seizing native vessels. At the request of Wilberforce he was kept out an additional year, till June 1823. The Menai was paid off in September. The arduous service on the coast of Africa had broken Moresby's health. From 1837 to 1840 he commanded the Pembroke in the Mediterranean, and from 1845 to 1848 the Canopus on the home station. On 20 Dec. 1849 he was promoted to be rear-admiral, and from 1850 to 1853 he was commander-in-chief in the Pacific. In 1854 he was made a D.C.L. of Oxford. He was nominated vice-admiral 12 Nov 1856, admiral 12 April 1862, G.C.B. 28 March 1865, and admiral of the fleet 21 Jan. 1870. He died on 21 Jan. 1877, in his ninety-first year.

Moresby married at Malta in 1814 Eliza Louisa, youngest daughter of John Williams of Bakewell, Derbyshire, and by her had two daughters and three sons, the eldest of whom, Fairfax, a commander in the navy, was lost in the Sappho brig, which went down with all hands in Bass's Straits early in 1858 (*Times*, 30 May, 30 June 1859).

[O'Byrne's Nav. Biog. Dict.; Ann. Reg. 1877, cxix. 135; Navy Lists.] J. K. L.

MORESIN, THOMAS (1558?–1603?), physician. [See Morison.]

MORET, HUBERT (*fl.* 1530–1550), goldsmith and jeweller, was a Paris merchant (*Acts of Privy Council*, 1547–50, p. 461), but was in the habit of visiting London with jewels and plate. Henry VIII occasionally purchased jewels from him (*Brit. Mus. Add. MS.* 20030) to a considerable amount, for in 1531 he received 56*l.* 9*s.* 4*d.*, and in 1536 282*l.* 6*s.* 8*d.* for jewels bought by the king (*Letters and Papers*, ed. Gardner, v. 757). Moret was a friend of Hans Holbein, and is said to have carried out in goldsmith's work many of that artist's designs. His portrait was formerly supposed to have been painted by Holbein, but the Morett portrait in question (picture and drawing at Dresden) really represents Charles de Solier, seigneur de Morette, an ambassador in the French service, who flourished in 1534 (see art. Holbein, Hans).

[Acts of Privy Council, 1547–50; Hans Holbein, par Paul Mantz; Brit. Mus. Print Room; Granger's Biog. Dict.] W. C–r.

MORETON, HENRY GEORGE FRANCIS, second Earl of Ducie (1802–1853), born in Conduit Street, London, on 8 May 1802, was eldest son of Thomas, fourth baron Ducie of Tortworth and first earl of Ducie (1775–1840), by his wife Lady Frances Herbert, only daughter of Henry, first earl of Carnarvon. His father, a whig and a supporter of the Reform Bill, was son of Francis, third baron Ducie of Tortworth (*d.* 1808), and was grandson of Elizabeth, daughter of Matthew Ducie Moreton, first baron Ducie of Moreton (*d.* 1735), by her second husband, Francis Reynolds. The first baron's heir, Matthew, second baron Ducie of Moreton, was created Baron Ducie of Tortworth in 1763, and died in 1770, leaving no issue. He was succeeded in the barony of Tortworth successively by his nephews Thomas and Francis Reynolds, the sons of his sister Elizabeth by her second marriage, who assumed the surname of Moreton in 1771.

Henry George was educated at Eton. He

was returned in the whig interest for Gloucestershire at the general election in May 1831, and sat for East Gloucestershire from December 1832 to December 1834. He succeeded his father as the second earl of Ducie in June 1840, and took his seat in the House of Lords for the first time on 31 July following (*Journals of the House of Lords*, lxxii. 375). Ducie moved the address at the opening of parliament in January 1841 (*Parl. Debates*, 3rd ser. lvi. 4–8), but except on two other occasions he does not appear to have spoken again in the house (*ib.* lviii. 1115, lix. 723–6). On the formation of Lord John Russell's first administration Ducie was appointed a lord-in-waiting to the queen (24 July 1846), a post which he resigned in November 1847. He served on the charity commission which was appointed on 18 Sept. 1849 (*Parl. Papers*, 1850, vol. xx.) He died on 2 June 1853 at Tortworth Court, Gloucestershire, aged 51, and was buried in Tortworth Church on the 10th of the same month. Ducie was a staunch advocate of free trade, and the speech which he delivered in favour of the repeal of the corn laws at the Hall of Commerce, London, on 29 May 1843, attracted considerable attention. He was best known, however, as a breeder of shorthorns and as one of the leading agriculturists of the day. He was master of the Vale of White Horse hounds from 1832 to 1842, and was president of the Royal Agricultural Society 1851–2. During the last seven years of his life he was a prominent member of the Evangelical Alliance. The sale of his famous collection of shorthorns in August 1853 realised over 9,000*l.* The 'Ducie cultivator,' the invention of which is generally ascribed to him, appears to have been invented by the managers of his ironworks at Uley, Gloucestershire. He married, on 29 June 1826, Lady Elizabeth Dutton, elder daughter of John, second baron Sherborne, by whom he had eleven sons and four daughters. His widow died on 15 March 1865, aged 58. He was succeeded in the peerage by his eldest son, the Hon. Henry John Reynolds-Moreton, lord Moreton, the third earl.

An engraved portrait of Ducie by J. B. Hunt, after H. P. Briggs, R.A., will be found in the 'Sporting Review,' vol. xxviii. opp. p. 64.

[Journal of the Royal Agricultural Society, ii. 42, iii. 122, xix. 147, 360; Gloucester Journal, 4 June 1853; Times, 4 June 1853; Illustrated London News, 17 July 1852 (portrait), 11 June 1853, 17 Sept. 1853; Mark Lane Express, 5 June 1843; Cecil's Records of the Chase, 1877, pp. 199–201; Sporting Review, xxviii. 64–6, xxx. 140–1; Gent. Mag. 1853, pt. ii. p. 87; Ann. Reg. 1853, App. to Chron. pp. 231–2; Stapylton's Eton School Lists, 1864, p. 84; Doyle's Official Baronage, 1886, i. 642; Burke's Peerage, 1890, pp. 442–3, 1244; Official Return of Lists of Members of Parliament, pt. ii. pp. 330, 341.]

G. F. R. B.

MORETON, ROBERT DE, COUNT OF MORTAIN (*d.* 1091?). [See MORTAIN, ROBERT OF.]

MORETON, WILLIAM (1641–1715), bishop successively of Kildare and Meath, born in Chester in 1641, was eldest son of EDWARD MORETON (1599–1665), prebendary of Chester. The father, son of William Moreton of Moreton, was educated at Eton and King's College, Cambridge, was incorporated at Oxford M.A. 1626 and D.D. 1636; was appointed vicar of Grinton, Yorkshire (1634); rector of Tattenhall, Cheshire, chaplain to Sir Thomas Coventry, lord keeper, and prebendary of Chester, all in 1637; and vicar of Sefton, Lancashire, in 1639. It appears that his property was sequestrated in 1645 (EARWAKER, *East Cheshire*, ii. 24), and that he was nominated by Lord Byron a commissioner to superintend the capitulation of Chester to the parliamentary forces in January 1646 (RUSHWORTH, IV. i. 139). Restored to his benefices at the Restoration, he died at Chester on 28 Feb. 1664–5, and was buried in Sefton Church, where a Latin inscription commemorates his equanimity under misfortune (WOOD, *Fasti*, i. 495; HARWOOD, *Alumni Eton.*)

Matriculating at Christ Church, Oxford, on 5 Dec. 1660, William graduated B.A. 19 Feb. 1664, M.A. 21 March 1667, and B.D. 3 Nov. 1674. In 1669 he became rector of Churchill, Worcestershire, and was also for some time chaplain to Aubrey Vere, earl of Oxford. In 1677 he accompanied James, duke of Ormonde, lord-lieutenant, to Ireland, as his chaplain; and on 12 Dec. of that year was created D.D. of Oxford by special decree. A few days later (22 Dec.) he was appointed dean of Christ Church, Dublin, in which capacity Mant speaks of him as 'the vehement and pertinacious opponent of the Archbishop of Dublin's episcopal jurisdiction.' On 13 Feb. 1682 he was appointed to the see of Kildare with the preceptory of Tully, and was consecrated in Christ Church, Dublin, on the 19th by the Archbishop of Armagh. The sermon, preached by Foley, bishop of Down and Connor, was published. Moreton was made a privy councillor of Ireland on 5 April 1682, and was created D.D. of Dublin in 1688; but when Tyrconnel held Ireland for James II he 'fled to England and there continued till that nation [the Irish] was settled.' Some time after his return to Ireland

Moreton sent a petition to the Irish House of Commons, asking them to give power to the trustees of the Irish forfeitures, in accordance with the Irish Act of Settlement, to set out land forfeited in the rebellion in augmentation of his bishopric. In the preamble to this petition, it was stated that the revenue of the see of Kildare, though the second in Ireland, did not exceed 170*l.* per annum (v. *Case of William, Lord Bishop of Kildare,* undated). He was translated to the see of Meath on 18 Sept. 1705, and was made a commissioner of the great seal by Queen Anne.

He died at Dublin on 21 Nov. 1715, and was buried in Christ Church Cathedral on the 24th. By his wife, whom he married in the summer of 1682, he appears to have left no issue. There is a portrait of him in the hall of Christ Church, Oxford.

[Ware's Hist. of Ireland, ed. W. Harris, i. 162, 395; Wood's Athenæ Oxon, ed. Bliss, iv. 891, and Fasti Oxon. ii. 265, 290, 345, 347, 365; Cotton's Fasti Eccles. Hibern. ii. 45, 234, iii. 121; Mant's Hist. of Irish Church, i. 685, ii. 174; Foster's Alumni Oxon. 1500–1714.]

G. Le G. N.

MOREVILLE, HUGH de (*d.* 1204), assassin of Thomas à Becket. [See Morville.]

MORGAN (*fl.* 400?), heresiarch. [See Pelagius.]

MORGAN Mwynfawr (*d.* 665?), regulus of Glamorgan, was the son of Athrwys ap Meurig ap Tewdrig (genealogies from *Cymmrodor,* ix. 181, 182, viii. 85), and may be the Morcant whose death is recorded in 'Annales Cambriæ' under the year 665 (*ib.* ix. 159). The charters contained in the 'Book of Llandaff' include a number of grants which he is said to have made to the church of Llandaff in the time of Bishops Oudoceus and Berthguin (*Liber Landavensis,* ed. Evans and Rhys, 1893, pp. 145, 148, 149, 151, 155, 156, 174). Other charters in the book of the time of Berthguin are attested by him (pp. 176, 182, 191), and an account is also given (pp. 152–4) of ecclesiastical proceedings taken against him by Oudoceus in consequence of his murdering his uncle Ffriog. Though the 'Book of Llandaff' was compiled about the middle of the twelfth century (preface to the edition of 1893), at a time when the see was vigorously asserting disputed claims, it nevertheless embodies a quantity of valuable old material, and (details apart) is probably to be relied upon in the general view it gives of the position of Morgan. He appears as owner of lands in Gower (p. 145), Glamorgan (p. 155), and Gwent (p. 156), and, since the latter two districts were afterwards ruled over by his descendants, was probably sovereign of most of the region between the Towy and the Wye.

It has been very generally supposed that Morgannwg—a term of varying application, but usually denoting the country between the Wye and the Tawe (*Red Book,* Oxford edit. ii. 412; *Cymmrodor,* ix. 331)—takes its name from Morgan Mwynfawr (*Iolo MSS.* p. 11). Mr. Phillimore, in a note to the Cymmrodorion edition of Owen's 'Pembrokeshire' (p. 208), suggests, however, that it is merely a variant of Gwlad Forgan [cf. art. on Morgan Hen], and that previous to the eleventh century the country was always known as Glywysing.

Morgan Mwynfawr, in common with many of his contemporaries, is a figure in the legends of the bards. He is mentioned in the 'Historical Triads' as one of the three Reddeners (i.e. devastators) of the isle of Britain (*Myvyrian Archaiology,* 2nd edit. pp. 389, 397, 404); in the 'Iolo MSS.' (p. 11) he is said to have been a cousin of King Arthur and a knight of his court, while his car was reckoned one of the nine treasures of Britain, for 'whoever sat in it would be immediately wheresoever he wished' (Lady Charlotte Guest, *Mabinogion,* 1877 edit. p. 286).

[Liber Landavensis, ed. Rhys and Evans, 1893; Iolo MSS., Liverpool reprint.] J. E. L.

MORGAN Hen (i.e. the Aged) (*d.* 973), regulus of Glamorgan, was the son of Owain ap Hywel ap Rhys (*Cymmrodor,* viii. 85, 86), his father being no doubt the Owen, king of Gwent, mentioned in the 'Anglo-Saxon Chronicle' under the year 926, and his grandfather the 'Houil filius Ris,' of whom Asser speaks as 'rex Gleguising.' According to the 'Book of Llandaff' (edition of Evans and Rhys, pp. 241, 248), he was ruler of the seven cantreds of Morgannwg between Towy and Wye; other records in the book show, however, that there were contemporary kings in the Margam district (Cadwgan ab Owain, p. 224), and in Gwent (Cadell ab Arthfael, p. 223; Arthfael ab Noe, p. 244). No doubt he was the chief prince of the region, and in that capacity attended the English court, where, until the accession of Edgar, he frequently appears as a witness to royal grants of land. He was with Athelstan in 930, 931, and 932, with Edred in 946 and 949, and with Edwy in 956 (Kemble, *Codex Dipl.,* 1839, Nos. 352, 1103, 1107, 411, 424, 426, 451). During his reign a contention arose between him and the house of Hywel Dda as to the possession of the districts of Ewias and Ystrad Yw, a matter which we are told was settled in favour of Morgan by the overlord of the Welsh princes, King Edgar (*Liber Landavensis*, 1893 edition, p. 248; Gwentian 'Brut y Tywysogion' in *Myvyrian Archaiology*, 2nd edition, p. 690). Morgan's epithet implies that he lived to a great age, though the statement of the Gwentian Brut that he died in 1001, in his hundred and thirtieth year (p. 693), is of course to be rejected. He is probably the Morgan whose death is recorded in one manuscript of 'Annales Cambriæ' under the year 973.

Gwlad Forgan, the later Glamorgan, undoubtedly took its name from Morgan Hen. Even in the 'Book of Llandaff' the form does not appear until we reach eleventh-century grants, and, unlike Morgannwg, it always excludes Gwent, which was, it has been shown, no part of the realm of Morgan Hen.

[Liber Landavensis, 1893 edit.; Iolo MSS. Liverpool reprint; Gwentian Brut y Tywysogion in Myvyrian Archaiology; Annales Cambriæ, Rolls edit.] J. E. L.

MORGAN (*fl.* 1294–1295), leader of the men of Glamorgan, appears, like his fellow-conspirator, Madog [q. v.], only in connection with the Welsh revolt which came to a head on Michaelmas day, 1294. In the 'Iolo MSS.' (p. 26) he is identified with Morgan ap Hywel of Caerleon, who belongs, however, to a much earlier part of the century (see *Brut y Tywysogion*, Oxford edition, pp. 368, 370). His ancestors had been deprived of their domains by Gilbert de Clare, eighth earl of Gloucester [q. v.] Walter of Hemingburgh makes him, as well as Madog, a descendant of Llywelyn ap Gruffydd, but this is also a mistake. The movement led by Morgan resulted in the expulsion of Earl Gilbert, who then brought an army into Glamorgan, but failed to re-establish his power. About the middle of June 1295 the king appeared in the district, and soon restored order, receiving the homage of the tenants himself. Morgan submitted shortly afterwards, having been brought into Edward's power, according to Hemingburgh and the 'Iolo MSS.' (p. 26), by the northern leader Madog.

[Annals of Trivet (Engl. Hist. Soc.), 1845 edit.; Chronicle of Walter of Hemingburgh (Engl. Hist. Soc.), 1849 edit.; Annales Prioratus de Wigornia, Rolls edit. 1869; cf. arts. on Edward I and Madog.] J. E. L.

MORGAN, ABEL (1673–1722), baptist minister, was born in 1673 at Allt Goch, Llanwenog, Cardiganshire. At an early age he removed to Abergavenny or its neighbourhood, became member of the baptist church at Llanwenarth in that district, and when about nineteen began to preach. In 1697 he was called to the pastorate of the newly formed church of Blaenau Gwent (Aberystruth and Mynydd Islwyn), but did not accept the invitation until 1700. In 1711 he resolved to emigrate to America, having laboured in the interval with much success, if we may judge from the fact that four years after his departure his church numbered one thousand members. He bade farewell to his flock at a meeting held on 23 Aug.; on 28 Sept. he took ship at Bristol. The voyage was a long and stormy one, and in the course of it he lost his wife and son. Accompanied by his brother, Enoch Morgan, and his half-brother, Benjamin Griffith, he settled in Pennsylvania, where there was a numerous Welsh colony, and there exercised the office of baptist minister until his death in 1722. Crosby's 'History of the English Baptists' contains a letter from him, in which he describes the position of the sect in Pennsylvania in 1715 (i. 122–123).

Morgan is best known as the compiler of the first 'Concordance of the Welsh Bible.' This he left in manuscript at his death. It was not published until 1730, when Enoch Morgan and some other friends caused it to be printed at Philadelphia. The printers, as we learn from the title-page, were 'Samuel Keimer' [q. v.] and 'Dafydd Harry,' both well known from the 'Autobiography of Benjamin Franklin.' It is a mistake, however, to suppose that Franklin himself worked at the book; for by this time he had left Keimer's printing-house, and was printing on his own account. The book was probably one of the last turned out by Keimer before he removed to Barbados. Morgan's 'Concordance' was the basis of the one published in 1773 by the Rev. Peter Williams, and now commonly used in Wales.

[Rees's Hist. of Protestant Nonconformity in Wales, 2nd edit. 1883, pp. 300, 301; Rowlands's Cambrian Bibliography, p. 356; cf. art. on Samuel Keimer.] J. E. L.

MORGAN, Mrs. ALICE MARY (1850–1890), painter, whose maiden name was Havers, was born in 1850. She was third daughter of Thomas Havers, esq., of Thelton Hall, Norfolk, where the family had been seated for many generations. As her father held the appointment of manager of the Falkland Islands, Miss Havers was brought up with her family first in those islands, and later at Montevideo. On her father's death in 1870 she returned to England and entered the school of art at South Kensington, where she gained a free studentship in the first year. In

April 1872 Miss Havers married Mr. Frederick Morgan, an artist, but she always continued to be known professionally under her maiden name. She first exhibited at the Society of British Artists in Suffolk Street, and in 1873 for the first time at the Royal Academy. She quickly obtained success and popularity, and her pictures were always given good places at the various exhibitions to which she contributed. One of her early pictures, 'Ought and carry one,' was purchased by the queen, and has been engraved. In 1888 she removed to Paris with her children, in order to be under the influence of the modern French school of painting. In 1889 she exhibited at the Salon two pictures, one of which (exhibited at the Royal Academy in 1888), 'And Mary kept all these sayings in her heart,' attracted much attention and was honourably commended. Her career was, however, cut short by her sudden death, at her residence in Marlborough Road, St. John's Wood, London, on 26 Aug. 1890. She left two sons and one daughter. Miss Havers was an industrious worker, and executed many kinds of tasteful art-illustration. She illustrated some of the stories written by her sister, Mrs. Boulger, better known under her pseudonym of 'Theo. Gift.'

[Private information.] L. C.

MORGAN, Sir ANTHONY (1621–1668), soldier, born in 1621, was son of Anthony Morgan, D.D., rector of Cottesbrook, Northamptonshire, fellow of Magdalen College, and principal of 'Alban Hall 1614–1620 (Foster, *Alumni Oxon.* 1500–1714, iii. 1027). The elder branches of the family were seated in Monmouthshire, where they possessed considerable influence. Anthony matriculated at Oxford from Magdalen Hall on 4 Nov. 1636, was demy of Magdalen College from 1640 until 1646, and graduated B.A. on 6 July 1641 (Bloxam, *Reg. of Magd. Coll.* v. 172). Upon the outbreak of the civil war he at first bore arms for the king, and was made a captain. The prospect of having his estate sequestered proved, however, little to his liking. He therefore, in March 1645, sent up his wife to inform the committee of both kingdoms that he and Sir Trevor Williams undertook to deliver Monmouthshire and Glamorganshire into the parliament's power if they received adequate support. He also hinted that he ought to be rewarded by the command of a regiment of horse. Colonel (afterwards Sir Edward) Massey [q. v.] was instructed to give him all necessary aid (*Cal. State Papers*, Dom. 1644–1645, p. 356). By January 1646 he had performed his task with such conspicuous success that Fairfax was directed to give him a command in his army until a regiment could be found for him in Wales (*ib.* 1645–7, p. 313), and on 3 Nov. following the order from the lords for taking off his sequestration was agreed to by the commons (*Commons' Journals*, iv. 713). Morgan, an able, cultured man, soon won the friendship of Fairfax. By Fairfax's recommendation he was created M.D. at Oxford on 8 May 1647 (Wood, *Fasti*, ed. Bliss, ii. 106). On 8 Oct. 1648 Fairfax wrote to the speaker, Lenthall, asking the commons to pass the ordinance from the lords for indemnifying Morgan for anything done by him in relation to the war, and on 27 Oct. he wrote again, strongly recommending Morgan for service in Ireland (letters in *Tanner MS.* lvii. 341, 391). Both his requests were granted (*Commons' Journals*, v. 668), and Morgan became captain in Ireton's regiment of horse (Sprigge, *Anglia Rediviva*, ed. 1647, p. 325). Various grievances existed at the time in the regiment, and the officers, knowing that Morgan could rely on the favour of Fairfax, asked him to forward a petition to the general (his letter to Fairfax, dated from Farnham, Surrey, 16 Oct. 1648, together with the petition, is printed in 'The Moderate,' 17–24 Oct. 1648). He took up his command in Ireland about 1649 (*Cal. State Papers*, Dom. 1656–7, p. 103).

In 1651 parliament granted him leave to stay in London for a few weeks to prosecute some chancery suits upon presenting a certificate that he had taken the engagement in Ireland (*Commons' Journals*, vi. 606); and in 1652, upon his petition, they declared him capable of serving the Commonwealth, notwithstanding his former delinquency (*ib.* vii. 169). He was then major. From 1654 until 1658 he represented in parliament the counties of Kildare and Wicklow, and in 1659 those of Meath and Louth. He became a great favourite with lord-deputy Henry Cromwell, and when in town corresponded with him frequently. His letters from 1656 to 1659 are preserved in Lansdowne MS. 822. In July 1656 on being sent over specially to inform the Protector of the state of Ireland (Thurloe, *State Papers*, v. 213), he was knighted at Whitehall. The next year Henry Cromwell requested him to assist Sir Timothy Tyrrell in arranging for the purchase of Archbishop Ussher's library. At the Restoration Charles knighted him, 19 Nov. 1660 (Townsend, *Cat. of Knights*, p. 49), and appointed him commissioner of the English auxiliaries in the French army. When the Royal Society was instituted Morgan was elected an original fellow, 20 May 1663 (Thomson, *Hist. of Roy.*

Soc. Append. iv. p. ii), and often served on the council. Pepys, who dined with him at Lord Brouncker's [see BROUNCKER, WILLIAM, second VISCOUNT BROUNCKER] in March 1668, thought him a 'very wise man' (*Diary*, ed. Braybrooke, 1848, iv. 380). He died in France between 3 Sept. and 24 Nov. 1668, the dates of the making and probate of his will (registered in P. C. C. 143, Hene; cf. Probate Act Book, P. C. C., 1668). Owing to political differences he lived on bad terms with his wife Elizabeth, who, being a staunch republican, objected to her husband turning loyalist.

Contemporary with the above was ANTHONY MORGAN (*d.* 1665), royalist, son of Sir William Morgan, knt., of Tredegar, Monmouthshire, by Bridget, daughter and heiress of Anthony Morgan of Heyford, Northamptonshire (BAKER, *Northamptonshire*, i. 184). He seems identical with the Anthony Morgan who was appointed by the Spanish ambassador Cardeñas, on 9 June 1640, to levy and transport the residue of the two thousand soldiers afforded to him by the king (*Hist. MSS. Comm.* 11th Rep. pt. vii. p. 241). On 21 Oct. 1642 he was knighted by Charles at Southam, Warwickshire (*Lands. MS.* 870, f. 70), and two days later fought at the battle of Edgehill. By the death of his half-brother, Colonel Thomas Morgan, who was killed at the battle of Newbury 20 Sept. 1643, he became possessed of the manors of Heyford and Clasthorpe, Northamptonshire; and had other property in Momouthshire, Warwickshire, and Westmoreland. He subsequently went abroad, but returned in 1648, when, though his estates were sequestered by the parliament by an ordinance dated 5 Jan. 1645-6, he imprisoned several of his tenants in Banbury Castle for not paying their rent to him (*Cal. of Proc. of Comm. for Advance of Money*, ii. 893). He tried to compound for his property in May 1650, and took the covenant and negative oath, but being represented as a 'papist delinquent,' he was unable to make terms (*Cal. of Comm. for Compounding*, pt. iii. p. 1898). In August 1658 he obtained leave to pay a visit to France (*Cal. State Papers*, Dom. 1658-9, p. 579). One Anthony Morgan was ordered to be arrested and brought before Secretary Bennet on 5 June 1663, and his papers were seized (*ib.* 1663-4, p. 163). He died in St. Giles-in-the-Fields, London, about June 1665 (Probate Act Book, P. C. C., 1665), leaving by his wife Elizabeth (? Fromond) an only daughter, Mary. In his will (P. C. C., 64, Hyde) he describes himself as of Kilfigin, Monmouthshire.

A third ANTHONY MORGAN (*fl.* 1652), royalist, born in 1627, is described as of Marshfield and Casebuchan, Monmouthshire. In 1642 he entered the service of the Earl of Worcester, for which his estate was sequestered. He begged to have the third of his estate, on the plea of never having 'intermeddled in the wars' (*Cal. of Comm. for Compounding*, pt. iii. p. 2123, pt. iv. p. 2807), but his name was ordered by the parliament to be inserted in the bill for sale of delinquents' estates (*Commons' Journals*, vii. 153).

[Authorities cited in the text.] G. G.

MORGAN, AUGUSTUS DE (1806-1871), mathematician. [See DE MORGAN.]

MORGAN, SIR CHARLES (1575 ?-1642), soldier, son of Edward Morgan of Pencarn, was born in 1574 or 1575. In 1596 he was captain in Sir John Wingfield's regiment at Cadiz, and afterwards saw much service in the Netherlands under the Veres. Having distinguished himself he was knighted at Whitehall, before the coronation of James I, on 23 July 1603 (METCALFE, *Book of Knights*, p. 147). In 1622 he commanded the English troops at the siege of Bergen until it was raised by Spinola, and in 1625 was at Breda when it was captured by the same general. In 1627 he was appointed commander of the four regiments sent to serve under the king of Denmark in Lower Saxony. They were in reality skeletons of those despatched to defend the Netherlands in 1624. At the siege of Groenlo his able lieutenant-colonel, Sir John Prowde, was killed (cf. *Poems of William Browne*, ed. Goodwin, ii. 288). Though recruits were sent out from time to time, they proved, from lack of training, worse than useless. On 23 July Morgan reported from his post near Bremen that his men were mutinous from want of pay, and would probably refuse to fight if the enemy attacked them. Edward Clarke (*d.* 1630) [q. v.] arrived with bills of exchange for a month's pay just in time to prevent Morgan's regiment from breaking up, but the fourteen hundred recruits brought by Clarke soon deserted. The bills proving valueless, Morgan borrowed three thousand dollars on his own credit, and wrote to Secretary Carleton on 7 Sept. in despair. 'What service,' he asked, 'can the king expect or draw from these unwilling men ?' Soon afterwards the margrave of Baden was defeated at Heiligenhafen. Morgan effected a masterly retreat across the Elbe (*Cal. State Papers*, Dom. Ser. 1627-8, p. 389), and with his little force—four thousand men in all—was entrusted with the keeping of Stade, one of the fortresses by which the mouth of the river was guarded. Here he was left to shift for himself. With the help of Sir Robert Anstruther, the Danish ambassador, he raised sufficient money to procure a fresh supply of shoes and stockings. He continued to defend Stade bravely, and made some successful sallies (*ib.* p. 587), but with his garrison reduced by want and disease to sixteen hundred, he knew that surrender was inevitable unless reinforcements arrived from England. On 18 March 1628 he wrote to Buckingham complaining that 'he and his troops seem to be forgotten of all the world,' and praying for relief (*ib.* 1628–9, p. 25). At length, on 27 April, he was obliged to surrender Stade to Tilly, but was allowed to march out with all the honours of war.

In June 1628 Morgan, who had returned to England, was ordered to gather together the remains of the garrison of Stade, and to carry them back to the king of Denmark. His instructions are contained in Add. MS. 4474 and Egerton MS. 2553, f. 63 *b*. Before his departure he had an audience of the king at Southwick, near Portsmouth, and bluntly told him that soldiers could not be expected to do their duty unless properly paid, fed, and clothed (*ib.* pp. 237, 253). A warrant for 2,000*l.* for his regiment was issued (*Egerton MS.* 2553, f. 40), and promises of regular payment were made. After the surrender of Krempe to the imperialists in the autumn, Morgan was ordered to remain at Glückstadt till the winter was over, and reinforcements could be sent. In August 1637 he was helping to besiege Breda (*ib.* 1637, p. 388), and subsequently became governor of Bergen, where he died and was buried in 1642. He was sixty-seven years old.

Morgan married Eliza, daughter of Philip von Marnix, lord of Ste. Aldegonde; she was buried in the old church at Delft before May 1634. His daughter and heiress Ann married Sir Lewis Morgan of Rhiwperra, and was naturalised by Act of Parliament 18 Feb. 1650–1. She subsequently married Walter Strickland of Flamborough, and died a widow at Chelsea in 1688, having expressed a wish to be buried with her mother at Delft (Clark, *Limbus Patrum Morganiæ*, pp. 319, 327).

Morgan is celebrated by William Crosse [q. v.] in his poem called 'Belgiaes Troubles and Triumphs,' 1625 (p. 49).

[Gardiner's Hist. of Engl. vol. vi.; Clark's Limbus Patrum Morganiæ; authorities cited.] G. G.

MORGAN, Sir CHARLES (1726–1806), judge advocate-general. [See Gould.]

MORGAN, CHARLES OCTAVIUS SWINNERTON (1803–1888), antiquary, born on 15 Sept. 1803, was the fourth son of Sir Charles Morgan [see under Gould, afterwards Morgan, Sir Charles], second baronet, of Tredegar Park, Monmouthshire, by Mary Magdalen, daughter of Captain George Stoney, R.N. Sir Charles Morgan Robinson Morgan, baron Tredegar (1794–1890), was his elder brother. Educated at Westminster School and Christ Church, Oxford, he graduated B.A. in 1825 and M.A. in 1832. From 1841 to 1874 he sat in parliament in the conservative interest, for the county of Monmouth, of which he was a justice of the peace and deputy-lieutenant. Interested in archæology, he read numerous papers before the Caerleon Antiquarian Association, of which he was president, and they were subsequently printed. In 1849 he communicated to the Society of Antiquaries some 'Observations on the History and Progress of the Art of Watchmaking from the earliest Period to Modern Times.' In 1850 he published a 'Report on the Excavations prosecuted by the Caerleon Antiquarian Association within the Walls of Caerwent.' In No. 35 of the 'Archæological Journal' there appears his 'Observations on the Early Communion Plate used in the Church of England, with Illustrations of the Chalice and Paten of Christchurch.' In 1869 he published a valuable account of the monuments in the church at Abergavenny.

He died, unmarried, 5 Aug. 1888, and was interred in the family vault at Bassaleg churchyard, Monmouthshire.

[Morgan's Works; G. T. Clark's Limbus Patrum Morganiæ, p. 313; Old Welsh Chips, August 1888, Brecon.] J. A. J.

MORGAN, DANIEL (1828?–1865), Australian bushranger, whose real name is said to have been Samuel Moran, and otherwise 'Down-the-River Jack' or 'Bill the Native,' is believed to have been born about 1828 at Campbeltown, New South Wales, to have been put to school in that place, and eventually to have taken up work on sheep stations and as a stock-rider. For a time he lived on Peechalba station, Victoria, where he eventually met his death. According to his own account he was unjustly condemned at Castlemaine in 1854 to twelve years' imprisonment, and vowed vengeance on society. He is said to have been at this time stock-riding on the station of one Rand at Mohonga, and if the date is correct he must have received a remission of sentence; for in 1863 a series of highway robberies was attributed to him, and on 5 Jan. 1864 a reward of 500*l.* was offered for his apprehension by the government of New South Wales. In June 1864 he shot Police-sergeant McGinnerty, and a few days later at Round Hill he killed one John

McLean and wounded two others. The reward offered for his capture was now increased to 1,000*l.* In September 1864 he shot Police-sergeant Smith, and as his raids were not checked the reward was made 1,500*l.* on 8 March 1865.

The last week of his life was typical of his proceedings. On Sunday, 1 April 1865, he 'stuck up' Bowler's station and carried off a well-known racing mare; on Tuesday he robbed one Brody, a butcher; next day he 'stuck up' Bond's station, Upotipotpa, and left a message for Bond that he wanted to shoot him; then he detained the Albury mail and robbed the bags, remarking that he had ridden one hundred miles for the purpose; next day he visited Evans's station and fired the granaries; he spent the Friday in robbing carriers on the road to Victoria, and arrived at Peechalba station in that colony on Saturday. Having successfully mastered the McPhersons at Peechalba, he proceeded to spend the evening with them, inviting them to sit down with him to tea, requesting Miss McPherson to play the piano to him, and talking freely of his mode of life. A maid-servant found means to evade his vigilance, and gave the alarm to a neighbour; the house was soon surrounded by civilians and a few police, who waited for the morning, when Morgan came out of the house driving his hosts before him with a revolver in each hand. One Wendlan (or Quinlan), to whom the duty had been assigned, shot him at sixty paces from behind cover. Morgan lingered about six hours, and died without making any confession (8 April). Six loaded revolvers and 300*l.* were found upon him at death. The coroner's jury returned a verdict of justifiable homicide, adding a rider in praise of the conduct of the persons concerned. Morgan's head was cut off and sent to Melbourne; his body was buried at the Murray.

Morgan was one of the most bloodstained of the Australian bushrangers. He was described as having a 'villainously low forehead with no development,' and a peculiarly long nose; as being 5 feet 10 inches high, and of spare build, so emaciated when taken as not to weigh more than nine stone. Morgan is said to be the original of Patrick in Rolf Boldrewood's well-known novel 'Robbery under Arms' (1888).

[Accounts of his own conversations, &c., from the New South Wales Empire, 6–16 April 1865; Cassell's Picturesque Australia, iv. 99, 100; Heaton's Austral. Dict. of Dates.] C. A. H.

MORGAN, GEORGE CADOGAN (1754–1798), scientific writer, born in 1754 at Bridgend, Glamorganshire, was the second son of William Morgan, a surgeon practising in that town, by Sarah, sister of Dr. Richard Price [q. v.] William Morgan [q. v.] was his elder brother. George was educated at Cowbridge grammar school and, for a time, at Jesus College, Oxford, whence he matriculated 10 Oct. 1771 (Foster, *Alumni Oxon.*) An intention of taking holy orders was abandoned, owing to the death of his father and the poverty of his family. His religious views also changed, and he soon became, under the guidance of his uncle, Dr. Price, a student at the dissenting academy at Hoxton, where he remained for several years. In 1776 he settled as unitarian minister at Norwich, where it is said that his advanced opinions exposed him to much annoyance from the clergy of the town. He was subsequently minister at Yarmouth for 1785–6, but removed to Hackney early in 1787, and became associated with Dr. Price in starting Hackney College, where he acted as tutor until 1791. In 1789, accompanied by three friends, he set out on a tour through France, and his letters to his wife descriptive of the journey are still preserved (see extracts printed in *A Welsh Family*, &c.) He was in Paris at the storming of the Bastille, and is supposed to have been the first to communicate the news to England (*ib.* p. 88). He sympathised with the revolution in its earlier stages, and held very optimistic views as to human progress, believing that the mind could be so developed as to receive, by intuition, knowledge which is now attainable only through research. In 1791 he was disappointed of Dr. Price's post as preacher at the Gravel-pit meeting-house at Hackney, and retired to Southgate in Middlesex. There he undertook the education of private pupils, and met with much success.

Morgan gained a high reputation as a scientific writer, his best-known work being his 'Lectures on Electricity' (Norwich, 1794, 16mo, 2 vols.), which he had delivered to the students at Hackney. In these he foreshadowed several of the discoveries of subsequent scientific men (see extracts in *A Welsh Family*). In chemistry he was an advocate of the opinions of Stahl in opposition to those of Lavoisier, and was engaged upon a work on the subject at the time of his death. In 1785 he communicated to the Royal Society a paper containing 'Observations and Experiments on the Light of Bodies in a state of Combustion' (*Phil. Trans.* vol. lxxv.) He was also the author of 'Directions for the use of a Scientific Table in the Collection and Application of Knowledge, . . . with a Life of the Author' (reprinted from the 'Monthly Magazine' for 1798),

London, 1826, 4to. This contains an elaborate table for the systematisation of all knowledge. He also made considerable progress in writing the memoirs of Dr. Richard Price.

He died on 17 Nov. 1798 of a fever contracted, it was supposed, while making a chemical experiment in which he inhaled some poison. He was a handsome man, and his portrait was painted by Opie.

By his wife, Nancy Hurry of Yarmouth, he had seven sons and one daughter, Sarah, wife of Luke Ashburner of Bombay, who was a prominent figure in Bombay society (see Basil Hall, *Voyages and Travels*, 2nd ser. iii. 134, which contains a sketch by Mrs. Ashburner). Two of the sons, William Ashburner Morgan and Edward Morgan, successively became solicitors to the East India Company, while most of the others settled in America, where the eldest, Richard Price Morgan, was connected with railroad and other engineering works (*A Welsh Family*, p. 145).

[A Welsh Family from the Beginning of the Eighteenth Century (8vo, London, 1885, 2nd ed. 1893), by Miss Caroline E. Williams, for private circulation; Gent. Mag. 1798, ii. 1144; Monthly Mag. for 1798; Memoirs of the Rev. Richard Price, 1815, pp. vi, vii, 178–81; Williams's Eminent Welshmen, p. 338; Foulkes's Enwogion Cymru, pp. 732–3.] D. Ll. T.

MORGAN, HECTOR DAVIES (1785–1850), theological writer, born in 1785, was the only son of Hector Davies of London (*d.* 6 March 1785, æt. 27) and Sophia, daughter of John Blackstone [q. v.], first cousin of Sir William Blackstone [q. v.] Morgan's grandfather, the Rev. David Davies, master of the free school of St. Mary's Overy, Southwark, took the name and arms of Morgan on his second marriage with Christiana, one of the four nieces and heiresses of John Morgan of Cardigan. Upon her death in 1800 Morgan succeeded to the name. He matriculated from Trinity College, Oxford, on 24 Feb. 1803, and proceeded B.A. in 1806, M.A. in 1815 (Foster, *Alumni*, 1715–1886). About September 1809 he was presented by Lewis Majendie to the donative curacy of Castle Hedingham in Essex, where he remained for thirty-seven years. On 7 Oct. 1817, shortly after the passing of 57 George III, c. 130, one of the earliest savings-banks in Essex was opened by Morgan's exertions at Castle Hedingham for the Hinckford hundred. He was acting secretary until 28 Nov. 1833, and while serving in this capacity issued 'The Expedience and Method of providing Assurance for the Poor,' 1830, and an address, 'The Beneficial Operation of Banks for Savings,' London, 1834, with a brief memoir of Lewis Majendie. About the same time Morgan became chaplain to George, second lord Kenyon.

Morgan was appointed Bampton lecturer in 1819, and was collated by the Bishop of St. Davids, on 7 Aug. 1820, to the small prebend of Trallong, in the collegiate church of Brecon (*Reports of the Eccles. Commis.* xxii. 80). He resigned the cure of Castle Hedingham in July or August 1846, and removed to Cardigan, where his second son, Thomas, was living. He died there on 23 Dec. 1850.

Two essays by Morgan—'A Survey of the Platform of the Christian Church exhibited in the Scriptures applied to its actual circumstances and conditions, with Suggestions for its Consolidation and Enlargement,' &c., Oxford, 1816; and 'The Doctrine of Regeneration as identified with Baptism and distinct from Renovation, investigated, in an Essay on Baptism,' &c., Oxford, 1817—each gained for Morgan the prize of 50*l.* from the Society for Promoting Christian Knowledge and Church Union in the Diocese of St. Davids, established on 10 Oct. 1804 by Thomas Burgess [q. v.], bishop of St. Davids. But his principal work was 'The Doctrine and Law of Marriage, Adultery, and Divorce, exhibiting a theological and practical view of the Divine Institution of Marriage; the religious ratification of Marriage; the Impediments which preclude and vitiate the contract of Marriage; the reciprocal Duties of Husbands and Wives, the sinful and criminal character of Adultery, and the difficulties which embarrass the Principle and Practice of Divorce,' &c., Oxford, 1826, 2 vols. This work shows accurate and extensive reading and legal knowledge.

Morgan's eldest son, John Blackstone Morgan (*d.* 1832), was curate of Garsington, Oxfordshire (Foster, *Alumni*, 1715–1886, iii. 981). A third son, James Davies Morgan (1810–1846), was an architect. There were also two daughters.

[Gent. Mag. 1827 pt. ii. p. 224, 1851 pt. i. p. 562; Index Eccles. 1800–40, p. 125; Collectanea Topograph. and Geneal. v. 402; registers of Castle Hedingham, per the Rev. H. A. Lake.] C. F. S.

MORGAN, HENRY (*d.* 1559), bishop of St. Davids, was born 'in Dewisland,' Pembrokeshire, and became a student in the university of Oxford in 1515. He proceeded B.C.L. 10 July 1522, and D.C.L. 17 July 1525, and soon after became principal of St. Edward's Hall, which was then a hostel for civilians. He was admitted at Doctors' Commons 27 Oct. 1528, and for several years acted as moderator of those who performed exercises for their degrees in civil law at Oxford. Taking holy orders he obtained much clerical preferment. He became rector of Walwyn's Castle, Pembrokeshire, 12 Feb. 1529–30; prebendary of Spaldwick in the diocese of Lincoln, 13 Dec. 1532 (Willis, *Cathedrals*, p. 232); prebendary of St. Margaret's, Leicester, also in the diocese of Lincoln, 7 June 1536 (*ib.* p. 202); canon of Bristol, 4 June 1542 (*ib.* p. 791); prebendary of the collegiate church of Crantock in Cornwall, 1547; canon of Exeter, 1548; rector of Mawgan, Cornwall, 1549, and of St. Columb Major, Cornwall, 1550; prebendary of Hampton in Herefordshire, 1 March 1551 (*ib.* p. 574).

Upon the deprivation of Robert Ferrar [q. v.] he was appointed by Queen Mary bishop of St. David's in 1554, which see he held until he was deprived of it, on the accession of Elizabeth, about midsummer 1559. He then retired to Wolvercote, near Oxford, where some relatives, including the Owens of Godstow House, resided. He died at Wolvercote 23 Dec. 1559, and was buried in the church there.

John Foxe, in his 'Acts and Monuments of the Church' (sub anno 1558), like Thomas Beard in his 'Theatre of God's Judgments,' i. cap. 13, states that Morgan was 'stricken by God's hand' with a very strange malady, of which he gives some gruesome details; but Wood could find no tradition to that effect among the inhabitants of Wolvercote, though he made a careful inquiry into the matter. Wood mentions several legacies left by Morgan, proving 'that he did not die in a mean condition.'

[Wood's Athenæ Oxon. ii. 788, Fasti i. 67; Boase's Register of the Univ. of Oxford, p. 124; Foster's Alumni Oxon.; Owen's Pembrokeshire, 1892, p. 240; Coote's English Civilians; Freeman and Jones's History of St. Davids.]

D. Ll. T.

MORGAN, Sir HENRY (1635?–1688), buccaneer, lieutenant-governor of Jamaica, eldest son of Robert Morgan of Llanrhymny, Glamorganshire, was born about 1635 (Clark, *Limbus Patrum Morganiæ*, p. 315). While still a mere lad he is said to have been kidnapped at Bristol and sold as a servant at Barbados, whence, on the expiration of his time, he found his way to Jamaica and joined the buccaneers. His uncle, Colonel Edward Morgan, went out as lieutenant-governor of Jamaica in 1664 (*ib.* ff. 189–90), and died in the attack on St. Eustatius, in July 1665 (*Cal. State Papers*, America and West Indies, 10 May 1664, No. 739; 23 Aug., 16 Nov. 1665, Nos. 1042, 1085, 1088). But Henry Morgan had no command in this expedition; and although the presence of at least three Morgans in the West Indies at the time renders identification difficult, it is possible that he was the Captain Morgan who, having commanded a privateer from the beginning of 1663, was, in January 1665, associated with John Morris and Jackman in their expedition up the river Tabasco in the Bay of Campeachy, when they took and plundered Vildemos; after which, returning eastwards, they crossed the Bay of Honduras, took Truxillo, and further south, went up the San Juan river in canoes as far as Lake Nicaragua, landed near Granada, which they sacked, and came away after overturning the guns and sinking the boats (*ib.* 1 March 1666, No. 1142). This appears the more probable, as the later career of John Morris was closely connected with that of Henry Morgan (*ib.* 7 Sept. 1668, No. 1838; 12 Oct. 1670, No. 293).

After the death of Colonel Edward Morgan, the governor of Jamaica, Sir Thomas Modyford [q. v.], commissioned a noted buccaneer, Edward Mansfield, to undertake the capture of Curaçoa, early in 1666. In that expedition Henry Morgan is first mentioned as commanding a ship, and he was with Mansfield when he seized the island of Providence or Santa Catalina, which the Spaniards had taken from the English in 1641. Leaving a small garrison in the island, Mansfield returned to Jamaica on 12 June (*ib.* 16 June 1666, No. 1216), but shortly afterwards, falling into the hands of the Spaniards, he was put to death (*ib.* No. 1827), and the buccaneers elected Morgan to be their 'admiral.' Santa Catalina was retaken by the Spaniards in August 1666. In the beginning of 1668 Morgan was directed by Modyford to levy a sufficient force and take some Spanish prisoners, so as to find out their intentions respecting a rumoured plan for the invasion of Jamaica. Morgan accordingly got together some ten ships with about five hundred men, at a rendezvous on the south side of Cuba, near the mouth of the San Pedro river. There, finding that the people had fled, and had driven all the cattle away, they marched inland to Puerto Principe, which, owing to its distance from the coast, had hitherto escaped such visits. The people mustered for the defence, but were quickly overpowered. The town was taken and plundered, but was not burnt on payment of a ransom of a thousand beeves, and Morgan was able to send Modyford word that considerable forces had been levied for an expedition against Jamaica.

Morgan himself, with his little fleet, sailed towards the mainland and resolved to attempt Porto Bello, where not only were levies for the attack on Jamaica being made, but where, it was said, several Englishmen were confined in the dungeons of the castle, and among them, according to popular rumour, Prince Maurice. The French who were with him refused to join in the attack, which seemed too hazardous; but on 26 June Morgan, leaving his ships some distance to the westward, rowed along the coast with twenty-three canoes, and landed about three o'clock next morning. The place was defended by three forts, the first of which was carried at once by escalade, and the garrison put to the sword. The second, to which the Spanish governor had retreated, offered a more obstinate resistance; but Morgan had a dozen or more ladders hastily made, so broad that three or four men could mount abreast. These he compelled the priests and nuns whom he had captured to carry up and plant against the walls of the castle; and though the governor did not scruple to shoot down the bearers, Morgan found plenty more to supply the place of the killed. The castle was stormed, though the stubborn resistance continued till the governor, refusing quarter, was slain. Then the third fort surrendered, and the town was at the mercy of the buccaneers. It was utterly sacked. The most fiendish tortures were practised on the inhabitants to make them reveal where their treasure was hidden, and for fifteen days the place was given up to brutal riot and debauchery.

On the fifth day the president of Panama, at the head of three thousand men, attempted to drive the invaders out, but was rudely beaten back. A negotiation was then entered into, by the terms of which Morgan withdrew his men on the payment of a hundred thousand pieces of eight and three hundred negroes. According to the official report made at Jamaica by Morgan and his fellows—John Morris among the number—the town and castles were left 'in as good condition as they found them,' and the people were so well treated that 'several ladies of great quality and other prisoners who were offered their liberty to go to the president's camp refused, saying they were now prisoners to a person of quality, who was more tender of their honours than they doubted to find in the president's camp, and so voluntarily continued with them' till their departure (*ib.* 7 Sept. 1668, No. 1838). But the story as told by Exquemeling, himself one of the gang, and with no apparent reason for falsifying the facts, represents their conduct in a very different light (cf. *ib.* 9 Nov. 1668, No. 1867). Exquemeling adds that the president of Panama, expressing his surprise that four hundred men without ordnance should have taken so strong a place, asked Morgan to send 'some small pattern of those arms wherewith he had taken so great a city.' Morgan sent a pistol and a few bullets, desiring him to keep them for a twelvemonth, when he would come to Panama and fetch them away. To which the president replied with the gift of a gold ring and a request that he would 'not give himself the labour of coming to Panama.'

In August, when Morgan returned to Jamaica, Modyford received him somewhat doubtfully, not feeling quite sure how his achievement might be regarded in England. His commission, he told him, was only against ships. But in forwarding Morgan's narrative to the Duke of Albemarle, he insisted that the Spaniards fully intended to attack Jamaica, and urged the need of allowing the English there a free hand, until England's title to Jamaica was formally acknowledged by Spain (*ib.* 1 Oct. 1668, No. 1850)

The Porto Bello spoil was no sooner squandered than Modyford again gave Morgan a commission to carry on hostilities against the Spaniards. Morgan assembled a considerable force at Isle de la Vache (which in an English form is sometimes called Cow Island, and sometimes Isle of Ash), on the south side of Hispaniola, and seems to have ravaged the coast of Cuba. In January 1669 the largest of his ships, the Oxford frigate, was accidentally blown up during a drinking bout on board, Morgan and the officers, in the after part of the ship, alone escaping. It was afterwards resolved to attempt Maracaybo; but many of the captains, refusing to adopt the scheme, separated, leaving Morgan with barely five hundred men in eight ships, the largest of which carried only fourteen small guns.

With these, in March 1669, he forced the entrance into the lake, dismantled the fort which commanded it, sacked the town of Maracaybo which the inhabitants had deserted, scoured the woods, making many prisoners, who were cruelly tortured to make them show where their treasure was hid; and after three weeks it was determined to go on to Gibraltar, at the head of the lake. Here the scenes of cruelty and rapine, 'murders, robberies, rapes, and such-like insolencies,' were repeated for five weeks; when, gathering together their plunder, the privateers returned to Maracaybo. There they learned that three Spanish ships of war were off the entrance of the lake, and that they had manned and armed the fort, putting it 'into a very good posture of defence.' Morgan, apparently to gain time, entered into some futile negotiations with the Spanish admiral, Don Alonso del Campo y Espinosa; and meanwhile the privateers prepared a fireship, with which in company they went to look for the Spanish ships. At dawn on 1 May 1669 they found them within the entrance of the lake, in a position clear of the guns of the fort, and steered straight for them, as though to engage. The fireship, disguised as a ship of war, closed the admiral's ship—a ship of 40 guns—grappled and set her in a flame. She presently sank. The second, of 30 guns, in dismay ran herself on shore and was burnt by her own men. The third was captured. As no quarter was asked or given, the slaughter must have been very great, though several from the flagship, including Don Alonso, succeeded in reaching the shore. From a few who were made prisoners Morgan learned that the sunken ship had forty thousand pieces of eight on board, of which he managed to recover fifteen thousand, besides a quantity of melted silver. Then, having refitted the prize and taken command of her himself, he reopened negotiations with Don Alonso, and was actually paid twenty thousand pieces of eight and five hundred head of cattle as a ransom for Maracaybo, but a pass for his fleet was refused. By an ingenious stratagem, however, Morgan led the Spaniards to believe that he was landing his men for an attack on the fort on the land side. They therefore moved their guns to that side, leaving the sea face almost unarmed. So in the night, with the ebb tide, he let his ships drop gently down till they were abreast the castle, when they quickly made good their escape.

On his return to Jamaica, Morgan was again reproved by Modyford for having exceeded his commission. But the Spaniards, on their side, were waging war according to their ability, capturing English ships, and ravaging the north coast of Jamaica. Provoked by such aggressions and by the copy of a commission from the queen regent of Spain, dated 20 April 1669, commanding her governors in the Indies to make open war against the English, the council of Jamaica ordered, and Modyford granted, a commission to Morgan, as 'commander-in-chief of all the ships of war' of Jamaica, to draw these into one fleet, and to put to sea for the security of the coast of the island; he was to seize and destroy all the enemy's vessels that came within his reach; to destroy stores and magazines laid up for the war; to land in the enemy's country as many of his men as he should judge needful, and with them to march to such places as these stores were collected in. The commission concluded with an order that 'as there is no other pay for the encouragement of the fleet, they shall have all the goods and merchandizes that shall be gotten in this expedition, to be divided amongst them, according to their rules' (*ib.* 29 July, 2 July 1670, Nos. 209, 211, 212; *Present State of Jamaica*, pp. 57–69).

Morgan sailed from Port Royal on 14 Aug. 1670, having appointed the Isle de la Vache as a rendezvous, from which, during the next three months, detached squadrons ravaged the coast of Cuba and the mainland of America, bringing in, more especially, provisions and intelligence. On 2 Dec. it was unanimously agreed, in a general meeting of the captains, thirty-seven in number, 'that it stands most for the good of Jamaica and safety of us all to take Panama, the president thereof having granted several commissions against the English.' Six days later they put to sea; on the 15th captured once again the island of Santa Catalina, whence a detachment of 470 men, commanded by a Colonel Bradley, was sent in advance to take the castle of Chagre. This was done in a few hours, in an exceedingly dashing manner; and Morgan bringing over the rest of his force, and securing his conquest, started up the river on 9 Jan. 1670–1, with fourteen hundred men, in seven ships and thirty-six boats. The next day the navigation of the river became impossible; so, leaving two hundred men in charge of the boats, the little army proceeded on foot. As the route was difficult, they carried no provisions, trusting to what they could plunder on the way. The Spaniards had carefully removed everything; but after many skirmishes and excessive sufferings, on the ninth day they crossed the summit of the ridge, saw the South Sea, and found an abundance of cattle. On the morning of the tenth day they advanced towards Panama. The Spaniards met them in the plain, with a well-appointed force of infantry and cavalry, to the number of about three thousand, some guns, and a vast herd of wild bulls, intended to break the English ranks and make the work of the cavalry easy. But many of the bulls were shot, and the rest, in a panic, turned back and trampled down the Spaniards, who, after a fight of some two hours' duration, threw down their arms and fled, leaving about six hundred dead on the field. The buccaneers had also lost heavily; but they advanced at once on the city, and by three o'clock in the afternoon were in quiet possession of it. It was, however, on fire, and was almost entirely burnt, whether, as Morgan asserted, by the Spaniards themselves; or, according to Exquemeling, by Morgan's orders; or, as is most probable, by some drunken English stragglers.

As a feat of irregular warfare, the enterprise

has not been surpassed, though its brilliance is clouded by the cruelty of the victors—a force levied without pay or discipline, and unchecked, if not encouraged in brutality by Morgan. But if we may credit Exquemeling, the invaders, owing to their drunkenness and dissolute indulgences, neglected to prevent the escape of a Spanish galeon, which put to sea, as soon as the Spaniards saw their men were defeated, with all that was of value in the town, including money and church plate, as well as many nuns. Much of the spoil was thus lost, and on 14 Feb. the buccaneers began their backward march. On the 26th they arrived at Chagre, and there the plunder was divided, every man receiving his share, or rather, according to Exquemeling, 'what part thereof Captain Morgan pleased to give them.' This, he says, was no more than two hundred dollars per head. Much discontent followed, and the men believed themselves cheated. But Captain Morgan, deaf to all complaints, got secretly on board his own ship, and, followed by only three or four vessels of the fleet, returned to Jamaica. Several of those left behind, the French especially, 'had much ado to find sufficient provisions for their voyage to Jamaica.'

At Jamaica Morgan received the formal thanks of the governor and the council on 31 May. But meantime, on 8 July 1670, that is, after the signing of Morgan's commission, a treaty concerning America had been concluded at Madrid; and although the publication of this treaty was only ordered to be made in America within eight months from 10 Oct. (*Cal. State Papers*, A. and W.I., 31 Dec. 1670, p. 146), and though in May 1671 Modyford had as yet no official knowledge of it (*ib.* No. 531), he was sent home a prisoner in the summer of 1671, to answer for his support of the buccaneers; and in April 1672 Morgan was also sent to England in the Welcome frigate (*ib.* No. 794). His disgrace, however, was short. By the summer of 1674 he was reported as in high favour with the king (*ib.* p. 623), and a few months later he was granted a commission, with the style of Colonel Henry Morgan, to be lieutenant-governor of Jamaica, 'his Majesty,' so it ran, 'reposing particular confidence in his loyalty, prudence and courage, and long experience fo that colony' (*ib.* 6 Nov. 1674, No. 1379). He sailed from England, in company with Lord Vaughan, early in December, having previously, probably early in November, been knighted. His voyage out was unfortunate. 'In the Downs,' wrote Vaughan from Jamaica, on 23 May 1675, 'I gave him orders in writing to keep me company. . . . However, he, coveting to be here before me, wilfully lost me,' and sailed directly for Isle de la Vache, where, through his folly, his ship was wrecked, and the stores which he had on board were lost (Dartmouth MSS., *Hist. MSS. Comm.* 11th Rep. pt. v. p. 25; cf. Bridge, *Annals of Jamaica*, i. 273).

For the rest of his life Morgan appears to have remained in Jamaica, a man of wealth and position, taking an active part in the affairs of the colony as lieutenant-governor, senior member of the council, and commander-in-chief of the forces. When Lord Vaughan was recalled, pending the arrival of the Earl of Carlisle, Morgan was for a few months acting governor, and again on Carlisle's return in 1680, till in 1682 he was relieved by Sir Thomas Lynch [q. v.] 'His inclination,' said the speaker in a formal address to the assembly on 21 July 1688, 'carried him on vigorously to his Majesty's service and this island's interest. His study and care was that there might be no murmuring, no complaining in our streets, no man in his property injured, or of his liberty restrained' (*Journals of the Assembly of Jamaica*, i. 121). About a month later Morgan died; he was buried at Port Royal, in St. Catherine's Church, on 26 Aug. 1688 (*Add. MS.* 27968, f. 29).

With very inadequate means Morgan accomplished a task—the reduction of Panama—which the great armament in the West Indies in 1741 feared even to attempt (cf. Vernon, Edward). Both in that expedition, and still more in his defeat of Don Alonso and his escape from the Lake of Maracaybo, his conduct as a leader seems even more remarkable than the reckless bravery of himself and his followers. By his enemies he was called a pirate, and if he had fallen into the hands of the Spaniards he would undoubtedly have experienced the fate of one. But no charge of indiscriminate robbery, such as was afterwards meant by piracy, was made against him. He attacked only recognised enemies, possibly Dutch or French, during the war, and certainly the Spaniards, with whom, as was agreed on both sides, 'there was no peace beyond the line,' a state of things which came to an end in 1671, when the Spaniards recognised our right to Jamaica and the navigation of West Indian waters. Moreover, all Morgan's acts were legalised by the commissions he held from the governor and council of Jamaica.

The brutality and cruelty which he permitted, or was unable to restrain, have unfortunately left a stain on his reputation; as also has his dishonesty in the distribution of the spoil among his followers (*Cal. State Papers*, A. and W.I., No. 580); 60*l.* per man for the sack of Porto Bello, 30*l.* as the results of the Maracaybo expedition (*ib.* 23 Aug. 1669, p. 39), or two hundred dollars for Panama, bear an unjustly small ratio to what must have been the total amount of the plunder (cf. *ib.* 6 April 1672, No. 798). Two engravings of Morgan are mentioned by Bromley—one by F. H. van Hove, the other prefixed to the 'History of the Buccaneers,' 1685.

Morgan married, some time after 1665, his first cousin, Mary Elizabeth, second daughter and fourth child of Colonel Edward Morgan, who died at St. Eustatius (*ib.* 16 Nov. 1665, No. 1085; *Add. MS.* 27968, f. 45), but left no children. Lady Morgan died in 1696, and was buried, also in St. Catherine's, on 3 March (*ib.* f. 29). By his will (copy, *ib.* f. 14), dated 17 June 1688, sworn 14 Sept. 1688, Morgan left the bulk of his property to his 'very well and entirely beloved wife' for life, and after her death to Charles, son of Colonel Robert Byndlos or Bundless and of Anna Petronella, his wife's eldest sister, conditionally on his taking the name of Morgan.

[Exquemeling's Buccaneers of America (1684), translated, through the Spanish, from the Dutch, and often reprinted wholly or in part (Adventure Series, 1891), forms the basis of all the popular accounts of Morgan. Exquemeling, himself a buccaneer who served under Morgan, and took part in some, if not all, of the achievements he describes, seems to be a perfectly honest witness. His dates are, indeed, very confused; but his accounts of such transactions as fell within the scope of his knowledge agree very closely with the official narratives, which, with much other interesting matter, may be found in the Calendars of State Papers, America and West Indies. They differ, indeed, as to the atrocities practised by the buccaneers; on which Exquemeling's evidence, even with some Spanish colouring, appears preferable to the necessarily biassed and partial narratives handed in by Morgan. Addit. MS. 27968 contains the account of many researches into Morgan's antecedents, though without reaching any definite conclusion. Other works are: The Present State of Jamaica, 1683; New History of Jamaica, 1740; History of Jamaica, 1774; Bridge's Annals of Jamaica; Journals of the Assembly of Jamaica, vol. i.]

J. K. L.

MORGAN, J. (*fl.* 1739), historical compiler, projected and edited a periodical of great merit, entitled 'Phœnix Britannicus, being a miscellaneous Collection of scarce and curious Tracts . . . interspersed with choice pieces from original MSS.,' the first number of which appeared in January 1731–1732. Owing to want of encouragement it was discontinued after six numbers had been issued, but Morgan republished them in a quarto volume, together with an excellent index. Prefixed is a curiously slavish dedication to Charles, duke of Richmond, whom Morgan greets as a brother freemason. Three editions of the work are in the British Museum Library. In 1739 Morgan compiled, chiefly from what purported to be papers of George Sale the orientalist, an entertaining volume called 'The Lives and Memorable Actions of many Illustrious Persons of the Eastern Nations,' 12mo, London.

[Lowndes's Bibl. Man. ed. Bohn.] G. G.

MORGAN, JAMES, D.D. (1799–1873), Irish presbyterian divine, son of Thomas Morgan, a linen merchant, of Cookstown, co. Tyrone, and Maria Collins of the same town, was born there on 15 June 1799. After attending several schools in his native place, he entered Glasgow University in November 1814, before he was fifteen, to prepare for the ministry, but after one session there studied subsequently in the old Belfast college. In February 1820 he was ordained by the presbytery of Dublin as minister of the presbyterian congregation of Carlow, a very small charge, which, however, increased greatly under his care. In 1824 he accepted a call from Lisburn, co. Antrim, to be colleague to the Rev. Andrew Craig, and for four years laboured most successfully there. In 1827 a new church was opened in Fisherwick Place, Belfast, and he became its first minister in November 1828. The congregation soon became a model of wise organisation and active work. Morgan also became prominently associated with all benevolent and philanthropic schemes in the town. In 1829 he joined with a few others in founding the Ulster Temperance Society. He was also most active in promoting church extension in Belfast. In 1840, when the general assembly's foreign mission was established, he was appointed its honorary secretary, and continued to hold this position with great advantage to the mission until his death. In 1842 he helped to found the Belfast town mission, and became one of its honorary secretaries. He was appointed moderator of the general assembly in 1846, and next year received the degree of D.D. from the university of Glasgow. He took a foremost part in the establishment of the assembly's college, Belfast, which was opened in 1853. He died in Belfast on 5 Aug. 1873, and was buried in the city cemetery.

Morgan was a voluminous writer. For some time he was joint editor of 'The Orthodox Presbyterian.' His chief works, besides sermons, tracts, and other fugitive publications, were: 1. 'Essays on some of the principal Doctrines and Duties of the Gospel,' 1837. 2. 'Lessons for Parents and Sabbath School Teachers,' 1849. 3. 'The Lord's Supper,' 1849. 4. 'Rome and the Gospel,' 1853. 5. 'The Penitent; an Exposition of the Fifty-first Psalm,' 1854. 6. 'The Hidden Life,' 1856. 7. 'The Scripture Testimony to the Holy Spirit,' 1865. 8. 'An Exposition of the First Epistle of John,' 1865. An autobiography was posthumously published in 1874, with selections from his journals, edited by his son, the Rev. Thomas Morgan, Rostrevor.

He married in 1823 Charlotte, daughter of John Gayer, one of the clerks of the Irish parliament at the time of the union, and by her had three sons and three daughters.

[Life and Times of Dr. Morgan, 1874; information supplied by the eldest and only surviving son, the Rev. Thomas Morgan; personal knowledge.] T. H.

MORGAN or **Yong, JOHN** (*d.* 1504), bishop of St. Davids, was the son of Morgan ab Siancyn, a cadet of the Morgan family of Tredegar and Machen in Monmouthshire, There was at least one daughter, Margaret, who was married to Lord St. John of Bletsoe, and there were also four sons besides Morgan or Yong, namely Trahaiarn, who settled at Kidwelly in Carmarthenshire, John, Morgan, and Evan. The surname Yong or Young sometimes applied to the bishop was probably adopted in order to distinguish him from the brother, also named John. He was educated at Oxford and became a doctor of laws. In a life of Sir Rhys ap Thomas, printed in 'The Cambrian Register,' he is reckoned among the counsellors of young Sir Rhys, and is described as a 'learned, grave, and reverend prelate' (i. 75). His brother, Trahaiarn Morgan of Kidwelly, 'a man deeplie read in the common lawes of the realme,' was also one of Sir Rhys's counsellors, and both appear to have incited Sir Rhys to throw in his lot with the cause of Henry of Richmond. Their brother Evan had already shared Richmond's exile, and was probably with him when he landed at Milford (Gairdner, *Richard III*, pp. 274–280). Morgan is also said to have offered to absolve Sir Rhys of his oath of allegiance to Richard III, and his friendship with Sir Rhys continued into old age. A few weeks after his accession Henry VII presented Morgan to the parish church of Hanslap in the diocese of Lincoln, and made him dean of St. George's, Windsor. He held the vicarage of Aldham in Essex from 7 June 1490 to 27 April 1492, and the prebendal stall of Rugmere in St. Paul's Cathedral from 5 Feb. 1492 till 1496 (Newcourt, *Repertorium*, i. 208). He was also clerk of the king's hanaper, and from 1493 to 1496 archdeacon of Carmarthen. Several of these preferments he held until he was made bishop of St. David's in 1496, the temporalities being restored to him, according to Wood, on 23 Nov. 1496. He died in the priory at Carmarthen about the end of April or the beginning of May 1504, and was buried in his own cathedral of St. David's. In his will, dated 24 April 1504, and proved 19 May following, he instructed that a chapel should be erected over his grave, but his executors erected instead a tomb of freestone, with an effigy of Morgan at length *in pontificalibus*; this is now much mutilated.

[Wood's Athenæ Oxon. ii. 693–4; Dwnn's Heraldic Visitations, i. 218; Cambrian Register, i. 75, 88, 104–5, 142; Gairdner's Richard III, pp. 274–80; Williams's Eminent Welshmen, p. 339.] D. Ll. T.

MORGAN, JOHN MINTER (1782–1854), miscellaneous writer, was probably born in London in 1782. His father, John Morgan, a wholesale stationer at 39 Ludgate Hill, and a member of the court of assistants of the Stationers' Company, died at Clayton, Suffolk, on 1 March 1807, aged 66. The son, inheriting an ample fortune, devoted himself to philanthropy. His projects were akin to those of Robert Owen of Lanark [q. v.], but were avowedly Christian. His first book, published in 1819, entitled 'Remarks on the Practicability of Mr. Owen's Plan to improve the Condition of the Lower Classes,' was dedicated to William Wilberforce, but met with slight acknowledgment. His next publication was an anonymous work in 1826, 'The Revolt of the Bees,' which contained his views on education. 'Hampden in the Nineteenth Century' appeared in 1834, and in 1837 he added a supplement to the work, entitled 'Colloquies on Religion and Religious Education.' In 1830 he delivered a lecture at the London Mechanics' Institution in defence of the Sunday morning lectures then given there. This was printed together with 'A Letter to the Bishop of London suggested by that Prelate's Letter to the Inhabitants of London and Westminster on the Profanation of the Sabbath.' Morgan presented petitions to parliament in July 1842 asking for an investigation of his plan for an experimental establishment to be called the 'Church of England Agricultural Self-supporting Institution,' which he further made known at public meetings, and by the publication in English and French in 1845 of 'The Christian Commonwealth.' In aid of his benevolent schemes he printed Pestalozzi's 'Letters on Early Education, with a Memoir of the Author,' in 1827; Hannah More's 'Essay on St. Paul,' 2 vols. 1850; and 'Extracts for Schools and Families in Aid of Moral and Religious Training,' 1851. He also edited in 1849 a translation of an essay entitled 'Extinction du Paupérisme,' written by Napoleon III, and in 1851 'The Triumph, or the Coming of Age of Christianity; Selections on the Necessity of Early and Consistent Training no less than Teaching.' In 1850 he reprinted some of his own and other works in thirteen volumes under the title of 'The Phœnix Library, a Series of Original and Reprinted Works bearing on the Renovation and Progress of Society in Religion, Morality, and Science; selected by J. M. Morgan.' Near his own residence on Ham Common he founded in 1849 the National Orphan Home, to which he admitted children left destitute by the ravages of the cholera. In 1850 he endeavoured to raise a sum of 50,000*l.* to erect a 'church of England self-supporting village,' but the scheme met with little support. He died at 12 Stratton Street, Piccadilly, London, on 26 Dec. 1854, and was buried in the church on Ham Common on 3 Jan. 1855.

Besides the works already mentioned, he published: 1. 'The Reproof of Brutus, a Poem,' 1830. 2. 'Address to the Proprietors of the University of London [on a professorship of education and the establishment of an hospital],' 1833. 3. 'A Brief Account of the Stockport Sunday School and on Sunday Schools in Rural Districts,' 1838. 4. 'Letters to a Clergyman on Institutions for Ameliorating the Condition of the People,' 1846; 3rd edition, 1851. 5. 'A Tour through Switzerland, and Italy, in the years 1846–1847,' 1851; first printed in the Phœnix Library, 1850.

[Gent. Mag. April 1855, pp. 430–1; Illustr. London News, 24 Aug. 1850, pp. 177–8, with a view of the proposed self-supporting village.]

G. C. B.

MORGAN, MACNAMARA (*d.* 1762), dramatist, born in Dublin, was called to the bar, though not from Lincoln's Inn as has been wrongly stated, and practised at Dublin. Through the influence of his friend Spranger Barry the actor, Morgan's tragedy, entitled 'Philoclea,' founded on a part of Sir Philip Sidney's 'Arcadia,' was brought out at Covent Garden on 20 or 22 Jan. 1754, and by the exertions of Barry and Miss Nossiter ran for nine nights, though both plot and diction are full of absurdities (GENEST, *Hist. of the Stage*, iv. 395). It was published at London the same year in 8vo. From Shakespeare's 'Winter's Tale' Morgan constructed a foolish farce called 'Florizel and Perdita, or the Sheepshearing,' first performed in Dublin, but soon after (25 March 1754) at Covent Garden, for the benefit of Barry, and it was frequently represented with success (*ib.* iv. 398). It was printed at London in 1754, 8vo, and again at Dublin in 1767, 12mo, as a 'pastoral comedy,' with a transposition of title.

There is reason for crediting Morgan with 'The Causidicade,' a satire on the appointment of William Murray, afterwards earl of Mansfield [q. v.], to the solicitor-generalship in November 1742 (included in 'Poems on various Subjects,' 8vo, Glasgow, 1756), and of another attack on Murray, called 'The Processionade,' 1746 (*Notes and Queries*, 2nd ser. iv. 94). Both, according to the title-page, are included in 'Remarkable Satires by Porcupinus Pelagius,' 8vo, London, 1760, but neither appears there. Copies of this work in contemporary binding are frequently found with the lettering 'Morgan's Satires.' 'The Pasquinade,' which is given in it, was written by William Kenrick, LL.D. [q. v.]

Morgan died in 1762.

[Baker's Biog. Dram. 1812.] G. G.

MORGAN, MATTHEW (1652–1703), verse writer, was born in the parish of St. Nicholas in Bristol, of which city his father, Edward Morgan, was alderman and mayor. He entered as a commoner at St. John's College, Oxford, in 1667, under John Rainstrop, graduated B.A. 18 May 1671, M.A. 9 July 1674, and B. and D.C.L. 7 July 1685. In 1684 he was associated in a translation of Plutarch's 'Morals,' to the first volume of which he also contributed the preface. Some reflections therein upon 'Ashmole's rarities' displeased Dr. Robert Plot [q. v.], who carried his complaint to Dr. Lloyd, the vice-chancellor. Morgan was threatened with expulsion, but he disowned his work, the responsibility for which was assumed by John Gellebrand, the bookseller. He was presented in 1688 to the vicarage of Congresbury, Somerset, but forfeited it owing to his failure to read the articles within the stipulated time. He was vicar of Wear from 1693 till his death in 1703.

Besides his work on Plutarch Morgan contributed the life of Atticus to a translation of the 'Lives of Illustrious Men,' 1684, and the life of Augustus to a translation of Suetonius, 1692. He also wrote: 'An Elegy on Robert Boyle,' 1691; 'A Poem upon the Late Victory over the French Fleet at Sea,' 1692; 'A Poem to the Queen upon the King's Victory in Ireland and his Voyage to Holland,' 1692; 'Eugenia: or an

Elegy upon the Death of the Honourable Madam ——,' 1694.

[Wood's Fasti Oxon. ed. Bliss, ii. 327, 344, 397; Athenæ Oxon. ed. Bliss, iv. 711; Brit. Mus. and Bodleian Library Catalogues; Foster's Alumni Oxon. 1500–1714.] G. T. D.

MORGAN, PHILIP (*d.* 1435), bishop successively of Worcester and Ely (1426), was a Welshman from the diocese of St. David's, who at some date before 1413 had taken the degree of doctor of laws, probably at Oxford (GODWIN, *De Præsulibus*, p. 267, ed. Richardson; WOOD, *Antiq. Univ. Oxon.* i. 213; *Anglia Sacra*, i. 537). He first appears in public life as a witness to Archbishop Arundel's sentence upon Sir John Oldcastle on 25 Sept. 1413 (*Rot. Parl.* iv. 109; *Fasciculi Zizaniorum*, p. 442). If he was not already in the royal service, he had not long to wait for that promotion. In the first days of June 1414, when Henry V had just broached his claims upon the French crown, Morgan was included with another lawyer in the embassy appointed to go under Henry, lord Le Scrope of Masham, to conclude the alliance, secretly agreed upon at Leicester a few days before (23 May) with John the Fearless, duke of Burgundy (DUFRESNE DE BEAUCOURT, *Histoire de Charles VII*, i. 132; *Fœdera*, ix. 136–8). He was apparently sent on ahead with a mission to the count of Holland, brother-in-law of Duke John, but had rejoined the others before they met the duke at Ypres on Monday, 16 July (*ib.* ix. 141; E. PETIT, *Itinéraires de Philippe le Hardi et de Jean sans Peur*, p. 410). For over two months they remained in Flanders, and were entertained by the duke at Ypres, Lille, and St. Omer. The Leicester convention was converted into a treaty (7 Aug.) at Ypres, and supplemented by an additional convention (29 Sept.) at St. Omer (*ib.* pp. 410–12; BEAUCOURT, i. 134). On his return, Morgan was sent (5 Dec. 1414) to Paris with the Earl of Dorset's embassy charged to press Henry's claims, continue the negotiations for his marriage with Katherine, and treat for a final peace (*Fœdera*, ix. 186–7; DEVON, *Issues of the Exchequer*, p. 336). In the middle of April 1415 and again at the beginning of June he was ordered to Paris to secure a prolongation of the truce with France (*Fœdera*, ix. 221, 260; *Ordinances of the Privy Council*, ii. 153). The day before Henry sailed for France (10 Aug.) Morgan was despatched as his secret agent to the Duke of Burgundy, in whose dominions he remained until December (*Fœdera*, ix. 304; BEAUCOURT, i. 134; RAMSAY, *Lancaster and York*, i. 241). He was rewarded (2 Jan. 1416) with the prebend of Biggleswade in Lincoln Cathedral (LE NEVE, *Fasti*, ii. 111; *Rot. Parl.* iv. 194). In February he was consulted by the council upon foreign affairs, and he was the chief agent in securing (22 May) the renewal of the special truce with Flanders which the Duke of Burgundy had concluded with Henry IV in 1411 (*Fœdera*, ix. 331, 352; *Ord. Privy Council*, ii. 191, 193; BEAUCOURT, i. 138).

Sigismund, king of the Romans, having now come to England in the hope of mediating a peace between France and England in the interests of the council of Constance, Henry consented (28 June) to send ambassadors, of whom Morgan was one, to treat for a truce and for an interview in Picardy between the two kings (*ib.* i. 263; *Fœdera*, ix. 365–6; LENZ, *König Sigismund und Heinrich der Fünfte*, p. 113). A truce for four months was concluded at Calais in September in the presence of Henry and Sigismund by Morgan, together with Richard Beauchamp, earl of Warwick, and Sir John Tiptoft (*Fœdera*, ix. 384; BEAUCOURT, i. 267; RAMSAY, i. 241; cf. *Fœdera*, ix. 375; BEAUCOURT, i. 139–41). In December Morgan and others were sent to secure an alliance with Genoa, whose ships had been assisting the French (*Fœdera*, ix. 414–15). They were also commissioned to treat with Alfonso of Arragon, the princes of Germany, and the Hanse merchants (*ib.* ix. 410, 412–13). He went on a further mission to the last-named in February 1417 (*ib.* ix. 437). In November Morgan took part in the futile negotiations at Barneville, near Honfleur, in February 1418 was ordered to hold musters at Bayeux and Caen, and on 8 April was appointed chancellor of the duchy of Normandy (*ib.* ix. 543, 571, 594; BEAUCOURT, i. 276–7). He was the spokesman of the English envoys in November in the negotiations at Alençon, in which the dauphin was offered Henry's assistance against Burgundy at the price of great territorial concessions (*Fœdera*, ix. 632–645; BEAUCOURT, i. 284–92).

Morgan had fairly earned further advancement, and the see of Worcester falling vacant in March 1419, he was elected (24 April) by the monks. Pope Martin V thought good in the interests of the papacy to specially provide him to the see by bull, dated 19 June (LE NEVE, iii. 60). He made his profession of obedience to Archbishop Chicheley on 9 Sept., received the temporalities on 18 Oct., and on 3 Dec. was consecrated in the cathedral at Rouen along with John Kemp [q.v.] by the Bishops of Evreux and Arras (*ib.*; STUBBS, *Registrum Sacrum*, p. 64; *Fœdera*, ix. 808). Meanwhile the bishop-elect had been on a mission to the king's 'Cousin of France' in July, and in October informed the pope, on behalf of the king, that Henry could not alter anti-papal statutes without the consent of parliament (*ib.* ix. 806; Beaucourt, i. 153). In July 1420 he was engaged in the negotiations for the release of Arthur of Brittany, captured at Agincourt (*Fœdera*, x. 4; Cosneau, *Le Connétable de Richemont*, p. 56).

Morgan became a privy councillor on his elevation to the episcopal bench, and after the king's death his diplomatic experience secured his inclusion (9 Dec. 1422) in the small representative council to which the conduct of the government during the minority of Henry VI was committed (*Rot. Parl.* iv. 175, 201; *Ord. Privy Council,* ii. 300, iii. 16, 157, 203). He was unwearied in his attendance (*ib.*) In nearly every parliament of the first eleven years of the reign he acted as a trier of petitions (*Rot. Parl.* iv. 170, &c.; cf. *Ord. Privy Council*, iii. 42, 61, 66; Milman, *Latin Christianity*, viii. 330). During the second half of 1423 he was engaged in the negotiations which issued in the liberation of the captive King James of Scotland (*Fœdera*, x. 294, 298–9, 301–2; *Rot. Parl.* iv. 211).

At the death of Henry Bowet [q. v.], archbishop of York, on 20 Oct. 1423, Morgan was designated his successor. His unanimous election by the chapter was notified by the king to the pope on 25 Jan. 1424 (*Fœdera*, x. 316). But Pope Martin was bent upon breaking down Henry V's policy of free election to English sees, a policy of which Morgan had been the mouthpiece in 1419 (cf. Löher, *Jakobäa von Bayern*, ii. 145, 536), and, ignoring Morgan's election, translated Richard Fleming [q. v.], bishop of Lincoln, to York (Stubbs, *Constit. Hist.* iii. 316; Ramsay, *Lancaster and York*, i. 378; Le Neve, ii. 17, iii. 109).

The council refused to submit to so violent an assertion of the papal pretensions, and the pope (20 July 1425) retranslated Fleming from York to Lincoln, but he provided, not Morgan, but John Kemp, bishop of London, to the archbishopric (Drake, *Eboracum*, App. lxvi.) The council finally accepted (14 Jan. 1426) this solution, on condition that Morgan was translated either to Ely or to Norwich, two sees both of which were vacant (*Ord. Privy Council*, iii. 180). Martin accordingly translated Morgan to Ely (27 Feb.), and the temporalities of that see were granted to him on 22 April (*ib.* iii. 192). Morgan made his profession of obedience to Archbishop Chicheley on 26 April in the chapter-house of St. Paul's, but was not enthroned until nearly a year later (23 March 1427) (Le Neve, i. 338; *Historia Eliensis* in *Anglia Sacra*, i. 666).

While his fortunes thus hung in the balance, Morgan had continued one of the most active members of the council, and in March 1426 acted as an arbitrator between Gloucester and Beaufort (*Rot. Parl.* iv. 297). He can hardly have been a partisan of the duke, for his name was attached to the very unpalatable answer of the peers to Humphrey's request on 3 March 1428 for a definition of his powers as protector (*ib.* iv. 326–7; Stubbs, *Constit. Hist.* iii. 107). In the autumn parliament of 1429 a suit against the Abbot of Strata Florida (Ystrad Flûr or Stratflower, now Mynachlogfawr, Cardiganshire) was referred to him and others, and he assisted in framing new regulations for the council on the termination of the protectorate (*ib.* iii. 110; *Rot. Parl.* iv. 334, 344; *Ord. Privy Council*, iv. 66). Next year he went to France in May as one of the council of the young king (*ib.* iv. 38; *Fœdera*, x. 458). In this or the previous year he had come into conflict with the university of Cambridge, which claimed exemption from his episcopal authority. Martin V appointed a commission of inquiry, which reported (7 July 1430) in favour of the university, a decision confirmed after Martin's death by Eugenius IV on 18 Sept. 1433 (Caius, *De Antiquit. Cantab.* p. 81, ed. 1568; Godwin, p. 267; *Anglia Sacra*, i. 666).

In the last years of his life Morgan was seemingly not quite so regular in his attendance at the council board as he had been. At least he was one of those who on 21 Dec. 1433, 'after many notable individual excuses,' promised to attend as often as was in their power, provided their vacations were left free (*Rot. Parl.* iv. 446). He died at Bishops Hatfield, Hertfordshire, on 25 Oct. 1435, having made his will four days before, and was buried in the church of the Charterhouse in London (Le Neve, i. 338; *Anglia Sacra*, i. 666). There must be some mistake about the entry on the minutes of the privy council, which represents him as present in his place on 5 May 1436 (*Ord. Privy Council*, iv. 339). The Ely historian charges his executors—Grey, bishop of Lincoln, Lord Cromwell, and Sir John Tiptoft—with neglecting to have prayers said for his soul, and with embezzling his property (*Anglia Sacra*, i. 666). Grey, however, survived him only a few months.

Morgan had the name of a reforming bishop. So stern a critic as Gascoigne is loud in praise of his vigilance in defeating evasions of the rule against unlicensed pluralities and other clerical abuses (*Loci e libro veritatum*, p. 133, ed. Thorold Rogers).

[The short fifteenth-century life by a monk of Ely, printed in Anglia Sacra, has been expanded from many different sources, which are indicated in the text. Rymer's Fœdera is quoted in the original edition.] J. T-T.

MORGAN, PHILIP (*d.* 1577), Roman catholic divine. [See PHILIPPS, MORGAN.]

MORGAN, SIR RICHARD (*d.* 1556), judge, was admitted at Lincoln's Inn 31 July 1523, called to the bar in 1529, was twice reader, in 1542 and 1546, became a serjeant-at-law in the latter year, and was elected recorder of Gloucester; he was also member of parliament for Gloucester in 1545–7 and 1553. A Roman catholic in religion, he was committed to the Fleet prison on 24 March 1551 (BURNET, *Hist. of the Reformation*, Oxford edit. 1865, v. 33) for hearing mass in the Princess Mary's chapel, but was discharged by the privy council with a caution on 4 May (*Acts of the Privy Council*, new ser. iii. 270). Immediately after King Edward's death he joined the Princess Mary and her adherents at Kenninghall Castle, Norfolk, 1553. Though he does not seem to have been a well-known lawyer, he was at once promoted in his profession. He was a commissioner to hear Bishop Tunstall's appeal against his conviction in June, was created chief justice of the common pleas in September, and was knighted on 2 Oct. He was in the commission for the trial of Lady Jane Grey on 13 Nov. and passed sentence upon her, but two years later, says Foxe (*Martyrs*, iii. 30), he 'fell mad, and in his raving cried out continually to have the Lady Jane taken away from him.' Accordingly, he quitted the bench in October 1555, and died in the early summer of the next year, being buried on 2 June at St. Magnus Church, near London Bridge.

[Foss's Lives of the Judges; Lincoln's Inn books; Dugdale's Origines, pp. 118, 152; Strype's Eccl. Mem. i. 78, 493, ii. 181; Rymer, xv. 334; Holinshed, ed. 1808, iv. 23, 45; Machyn's Diary, pp. 106, 335; Fourth Report, Public Record Commission, App. ii. 238.] J. A. H.

MORGAN, ROBERT (1608–1673), bishop of Bangor, born at Bronfraith in the parish of Llandyssilio in Montgomeryshire, was third son of Richard Morgan, gent., M.P. for Montgomery in 1592–3, and of his wife, Margaret, daughter of Thomas Lloyd of Gwernbuarth, gent. He was educated near Bronfraith, under the father of Simon Lloyd, archdeacon of Merioneth, and proceeded to Jesus College, Cambridge, where he entered 6 July 1624, and graduated M.A. in 1630.

He was appointed chaplain to Dolben on the election of the latter to the bishopric of Bangor, and was by him nominated to the vicarage of Llanwnol in Montgomeryshire, 16 Sept. 1632, and afterwards to the rectory of Llangynhafal and Dyffryn Clwyd. On Dolben's death in 1633 he returned to Cambridge, presumably to Jesus College, but on 25 June 1634, 'at his own request and for his own benefit,' he was transferred to St. John's College. The certificate given to him by Richard Sterne, master of Jesus College, mentions his 'manye yeares' civill and studious life there' (see MAYOR, *Admissions to St. John's*, p. 18).

Upon the advancement of Dr. William Roberts to the bishopric of Bangor in 1637, he returned to Wales as his chaplain, and received from him the vicarage of Llanfair in the deanery of Dyffryn Clwyd, 1637, and the rectory of Efenechtyd in 1638. On 1 July 1642 he was collated prebendary of Chester on the resignation of David Lloyd, but he does not appear to have retained it or to have recovered it at the Restoration (see, however, WALKER, *Sufferings*, ii. 11).

Having resigned Llangynhafal, he was instituted to Trefdraeth in Anglesea on 16 July 1642, being then B.D. In the same year he resigned Llanfair, and was inducted to Llandyvnan (19 Nov. 1642), also in Anglesea. At his own expense (300*l.*) he bought from the Bulkeleys of Baron Hill the unexpired term of a ninety-nine years' lease of the tithes of Llandyvnan. In consequence his title to the living was not questioned during the wars, although he was ejected from his other preferments. By leaving this lease to the church he raised its annual value from 38*l.* to 200*l.*

During the Commonwealth he resided chiefly at Henblas in the parish of Llangristiolus in Anglesea. In the manuscripts of Lord Mostyn at Mostyn Hall there is a manuscript sermon of his preached in December 1656. In 1657, on the death of Robert White, he was nominated to the prebend of Penmynyd (Bangor diocese), but was not installed till after the Restoration, and relinquished it before April 1661.

At the Restoration he recovered his living of Trefdraeth, received the degree of D.D. (1660), became archdeacon of Merioneth, 24 July 1660, and in the same month 'comportioner' of Llandinam. On the death of Dr. Robert Price he was elected bishop of Bangor (8 June 1666), and consecrated 1 July at Lambeth. He held the archdeaconry of Merioneth *in commendam* from July 1660 to 1666, when (23 Oct.) he was succeeded by John Lloyd (see his petition of date 21 June

1666 to be allowed to hold it *in commendam*, *State Papers*, Dom. Car. II, clix. 58). The definite union of the archdeaconry with the bishopric was accomplished by Morgan's successor. He was long engaged in litigation with Thomas Jones (1622–1682) [q.v.], who held the living of Llandyrnog, which was usually held by the bishops of Bangor *in commendam* because of its convenience for residence. Jones brought a charge against the bishop and two others early in 1669 in the court of arches (*Elymas the Sorcerer*, p. 29).

Morgan died 1 Sept. 1673, and was buried on 6 Sept. in the grave of Bishop Robinson, on the south side of the altar (for two different inscriptions see *Lansdowne MS.* 986, fol. 168). He effected considerable restorations in Bangor Cathedral, and gave an excellent organ. A preacher in English and Welsh, he is said to have worn himself away by his pulpit exertions. He left 'several things' fit for the press, but forbad their publication.

Morgan married Anne, daughter and heiress of William Lloyd, rector of Llanelian, Anglesey, and left four sons: (1) Richard, died young; (2) Owen, of Jesus College and Gray's Inn (1676), and attendant on Sir Leoline Jenkins at the treaty of Nimeguen, died 11 April 1679; (3) William (*b.* 1664), LL.B. of Jesus College, Oxford (1685), later chancellor of the diocese of Bangor; (4) Robert D.D. (*b.* 1665), of Christ Church, Oxford, canon of Hereford 1702, and rector of Ross, Herefordshire. Of four daughters: (1) Margaret was wife of Edward Wyn; (2) Anna, wife of Thomas Lloyd of Kefn, registrar of St. Asaph; (3) Elizabetha, married Humphrey Humphreys, dean of Bangor; and (4) Katherine, who died unmarried, was buried with her father.

[The single authority for the main facts is Bishop Humphrey's letter to Wood, given in Athenæ Oxon. ii. 890, and repeated almost verbatim in Williams's Eminent Welshmen, and, with a few additions, in vol. lii. of Bishop Kennett's Collections, Lansdowne MS. 986. See also Official Return of Members of Parliament; Lords' Journals, xii. 401 seq.; Commons' Journals, ix. 201–13; Hist. MSS. Comm. 4th Rep. p. 359; State Papers, Dom.; Professor Mayor's Admissions to St. John's College, Cambridge; Welch's Alum. West.; Lloyd's Memoirs; Byegones relating to Wales and the Northern Counties; Wood's Fasti, i. 441; Le Neve; Stubbs's Registrum; Thomas Jones's Elymas the Sorcerer; Walker's Sufferings of the Clergy; Browne Willis's Survey of the Cathedrals; D. R. Thomas's Hist. of the Diocese of St. Asaph; Baker's Hist. of St. John's College; information kindly supplied by the master of Jesus College, Cambridge.] W. A. S.

MORGAN, SYDNEY, LADY MORGAN (1783?–1859), novelist, was the eldest child of Robert Owenson [q. v.], by his wife Jane Mill, daughter of a Shrewsbury tradesman, who was once mayor of that town, and was a distant relative of the Mills of Hawkesley, Shropshire. According to her own account—but she was constitutionally inexact, avowed a scorn for dates, and sedulously concealed her age—Lady Morgan was born in Dublin one Christmas day, about 1785. The year generally given for her birth is 1783. Croker maliciously alleged that she was born on board the Dublin packet in 1775. Mr. Fitzpatrick adopts Croker's date (W. J. FITZPATRICK, *Lady Morgan*, 1860, p. 111). To a considerable extent she was brought up in the precincts of theatres and in the company of players; but she was put to various schools near or in Dublin, and very soon proved herself a bright and amusing child. She went with her father into the mixed society which he frequented, at first in Sligo and afterwards in Dublin. His affairs becoming hopelessly involved, and for a time (1798–1800) she was governess in the family of Featherstone of Bracklin Castle, Westmeath, and elsewhere. She is said to have appeared on the stage, though this cannot be verified; but she attracted considerable notice wherever she went by her wit and spirits, and by her dancing, singing, and playing upon the harp. She soon began to write verse of a sentimental character, and published her first volume in March 1801. She also collected a number of Irish tunes, wrote English words to them, and subsequently published them, an example speedily followed by Moore, Stevenson, and others. Excited by the report of Fanny Burney's gains she then took to fiction, and wrote in 1804 'St. Clair, or the Heiress of Desmond,' a trashy imitation of the 'Sorrows of Werther;' it was translated into Dutch. In 1805 appeared her 'Novice of St. Dominick,' in four volumes, a work of slight merit, yet not unsuccessful. It was published in London, and was read several times by Pitt in his last illness. To her is attributed the 'Few Reflections' which was issued in the same year on Croker's anonymous 'Present State of the Irish Stage;' but her next avowed work was the one which made her famous, 'The Wild Irish Girl,' published in 1806. It was very rhapsodical and sentimental, but it contained descriptions of real power, and may almost be called a work of genius, though misguided genius. Philips, her former publisher, refused it on account of its too openly avowed 'national' sentiments; but when Johnson, Miss Edgeworth's publisher, offered her three hundred guineas for it, Philips claimed and secured the right of publishing it. In less than two years it ran through seven editions, and has been reprinted since. The book became the subject of considerable political controversy in Dublin, and the liberal and catholic party championed her, and, after her heroine's name, knew her as 'Glorvina.' She was encouraged, under whig patronage, to bring out an opera, 'The First Attempt,' at the Theatre Royal, Dublin, 4 March 1807, which ran several nights, and brought her 400*l.*, but she wrote no more for the stage. Later in the year she published two volumes of 'Patriotic Sketches.' In 1805 she wrote 'The Lay of an Irish Harp,' metrical fragments collected in, or suggested by, a visit to Connaught, and, in 1809, 'Woman, or Ida of Athens,' a romance in four volumes. Quitting patriotic Irish subjects, she wrote in 1811 a novel called 'The Missionary,' which sold for 400*l.* This was remodelled in 1859 under her directions, and renamed 'Luxima the Prophetess.'

Miss Owenson's popularity in Dublin led to her being invited to become a permanent member of the household of the Marquis of Abercorn. There she greatly extended her acquaintance with fashionable society, and her accomplishments were fully appreciated. Her patron's surgeon, Thomas Charles Morgan [q. v.], devoted himself to her, and, on a hint of hers, as she alleged—more probably at Lady Abercorn's request—the Duke of Richmond knighted him. Subsequently, on 20 Jan. 1812, Sydney Owenson, somewhat reluctantly, became his second wife, under pressure from Lady Abercorn. In 1808 her younger sister, Olivia, had married Sir Arthur Clarke, M.D., who had been knighted for curing the Duke of Richmond of a cutaneous disease. For some time after her marriage Lady Morgan published nothing, but in 1814 appeared 'O'Donnel, a National Tale,' in which she set herself to describe Irish life as she actually saw it, under the colour of Irish history as she heard it from her friends (for Sir W. Scott's favourable criticism of it see Lockhart, *Scott*, vi. 264). The book was written to furnish her new house in Kildare Street, Dublin. It brought her 550*l.*, and being very popular with the 'patriots' she was fiercely attacked by the 'Quarterly Review.' These attacks were carried on by Gifford and Croker for years with indecent violence and malignity (cf. *Blackwood's Magazine*, xi. 695). In 1816 she published another Irish novel, 'Florence M'Carthy,' for which she received 1,200*l.*, and caricatured Croker in it as 'Counsellor Con Crowley.' Despite savage reviews, her next work, 'France,' 1817, 4to, a book dealing with travel, politics, and society, as observed by her in France in 1815, became very popular, and reached a fourth edition in 1818. On the strength of its success Colburn offered her 2,000*l.* for a similar book on Italy, and she left Dublin in August 1818 to travel through that country. She visited London, where she saw much of Lady Caroline Lamb and Lady Cork and met with much social success (Moore, *Memoirs*, iii. 36). At Paris she met Humboldt, Talma, Cuvier, Constant, and others, and she paid Lafayette a visit at La Grange. Eventually she reached Italy, where she spent more than a year and was presented to the pope. Her book, which was published 20 June 1821, induced Byron, who was not prepossessed in her favour, to call it 'fearless and excellent' (Byron to Moore, 24 Aug. 1821); on the other hand it was proscribed by the king of Sardinia, the emperor of Austria, and the pope, and was fiercely assailed by the English ministerial press. The 'Quarterly' said of it: 'Notwithstanding the obstetric skill of Sir Charles Morgan (who we believe is a man-midwife), this book dropt all but stillborn from the press,' but it sold well in England, and editions also appeared in Paris and in Belgium. In October 1821 she retaliated upon the reviewers in 'Colburn's New Monthly Magazine.' In 1823 appeared her 'Life of Salvator Rosa,' republished in 1855, and in 1825 she collected, from 'Colburn's New Monthly,' her papers on 'Absenteeism.' In November 1827 appeared her novel 'The O'Briens and the O'Flaherties,' which expressed vigorous emancipation sentiments. It was a hostile review of this book in the 'Literary Gazette' that induced Henry Colburn [q. v.] to join the 'Athenæum' established by James Silk Buckingham [q. v.] She next issued, in 1829, the 'Book of the Boudoir,' a series of autobiographical sketches. She again visited France in the same year, and in July 1830 produced her second work under that title, most of the permanent value of which was due to her husband's assistance. Its sale to Saunders & Otley for 1,000*l.* so infuriated Colburn that he advertised that all her previous works had been a loss to him. In 1833 she published 'Dramatic Scenes,' and having visited Belgium in 1835, embodied her observations in a novel called 'The Princess' in that year.

Lord Melbourne, on Lord Morpeth's solicitation, bestowed on her a pension of 300*l.* a year in 1837, 'in acknowledgment of the services rendered by her to the world of letters.' This was the first pension of the kind given to a woman. Her husband was also appointed a commissioner of Irish fisheries. She wrote occasionally for the 'Athenæum' in 1837 and 1838. In 1839 she removed from Kildare Street, Dublin, to 11 William Street,

Albert Gate, London, and making a considerable social figure there ceased to write. 'Woman and her Master,' which is rather poor vapouring, appeared in 1840, but it had been written before she left Ireland. She assisted her husband in 'The Book without a Name' in 1841, but it was only a collection of fugitive magazine pieces. In 1843 he died. Lady Morgan continued to move assiduously in London society. Her early works were republished in popular form in 1846, and she wrote fresh prefaces to several of them. Her sight failed, but in 1851 she engaged in a pamphlet controversy with Cardinal Wiseman about the authenticity of St. Peter's chair. In 1859 her amanuensis, Miss Jewsbury, arranged for publication her 'Diary and Correspondence in France' from August 1818 to May 1819. She died 14 April 1859, and was buried in the old Brompton cemetery; a tomb by Westmacott was placed over her grave. She left between 15,000*l.* and 16,000*l.*, and bequeathed her papers to W. Hepworth Dixon. She had no children.

There is a bust of her by D'Angers dated 1830, and a portrait by Berthen is in the Irish National Gallery. Her portrait was also painted by Lawrence; three others belong to Sir Charles W. Dilke, bart., including a painting by Sidney Morgan and a plaster model by David. H. F. Chorley's 'Authors of England,' 1838, and 'Fraser's Magazine,' xi. 529, contain engravings of her. In old age she is described as 'a little humpbacked old woman, absurdly attired, rouged and wigged; vivacious and somewhat silly; vain, gossiping, and ostentatious: larding her talk with scraps of French, often questionable in their idiom, always dreadful in their accent, exhibiting her acquaintance with titled people so prodigally as to raise a smile.' Yet in her younger days she must have been highly attractive, very vivacious and off-handed, yet shrewd and hard at a bargain. Her writing, though slipshod and often inflated, contained much humorous observation, and when describing what she understood, the lower-class Irish, she was as good as Lever or Banin.

[W. J. Fitzpatrick's Lady Morgan, 1860; Memoirs of Lady Morgan by W. Hepworth Dixon, with engraving of her after Lawrence; Cyrus Redding's Fifty Years' Recollections, iii. 215, and articles in New Monthly Magazine, cxvi. 206, cxxvii. 300; Cornhill Magazine, vii. 132; The Croker Papers, i. 109; Torrens's Memoirs of Lord Melbourne, i. 174; a sketch of her, probably by her husband, in the London and Dublin Mag. 1826.] J. A. H.

MORGAN, SYLVANUS (1620–1693), arms-painter and author, born in London in 1620, was brought up to and practised the profession of an arms-painter. In 1642 he wrote 'A Treatise of Honor and Honorable Men,' which remained in manuscript (see Brydges's *Censura Literaria*, viii. 236). In 1648 he printed a poem entitled 'London, King Charles his Augusta, or City Royal of the Founders;' and in 1652 'Horologiographia Optica, Dialling universal and particular.' In 1661 he published a work on heraldry, entitled 'The Sphere of Gentry, deduced from the Principles of Nature: an Historical and Genealogical Work of Arms and Blazon, in Four Books.' Morgan says that this book had taken him years to compile and had been originally intended for dedication to Charles I, and that he had neglected his trade as arms-painter, suffered much illness, and had had his house burnt down. It contains a title-page with a portrait of Morgan, etched by R. Gaywood. The work was pedantic, and was discredited by Sir William Dugdale [q. v.] and other heralds; and it was alleged that it was really the work of Edward Waterhouse [q. v.], the author of 'A Discourse and Defence of Arms and Armory,' 1660. As the book contains much information concerning the Waterhouse family, it may be assumed that Waterhouse assisted Morgan in its compilation. In 1666 Morgan published a supplement, entitled 'Armilogia, sive Ars Chromocritica: the Language of Arms by the Colours and Metals.' Morgan lived near the Royal Exchange in London, and died on 27 March 1693. He was buried in the church of St. Bartholomew, behind the Exchange. He left a large collection of manuscripts, which came by marriage to Josiah Jones, heraldic painter and painter to Drury Lane Theatre, by whom they were sold by auction in 1759.

[Moule's Bibliotheca Heraldica Magnæ Britanniæ; Gent. Mag. 1796, pt. i. p. 366; Nichols's Anecdotes of Literature, ix. 801; Lowndes's Bibl. Man.; Wood's Fasti Oxon, ed. Bliss, ii. 164.] L. C.

MORGAN, Sir THOMAS (*d.* 1595), 'the warrior,' was the younger son of William Morgan of St. George's and Pencarn, Glamorganshire, and Anne, daughter of Robert Fortescue of Wood in the county of Devon. He was apparently about thirty years of age, and had probably seen active service in France or Scotland, when he was appointed in April 1572 captain of the first band of English volunteers that served in the Low Countries under William of Orange. He landed with his company, three hundred strong, at Flushing on 6 June, in time to take part in the defence of that town. His soldiers were chiefly raw recruits, and it was long before they learned to stand the enemy's fire without flinching; but their decent and orderly behaviour, and the modesty of their commander, so favourably impressed the townsmen that they actually proposed to appoint him governor in the place of Jerome de t Zereerts. But 'to say troth,' says Roger Williams [q. v.], 'this captain had never any great ambition in him, although fortune presented faire unto him often beside this time.' He loyally supported de t Zereerts, and it was at his own suggestion that Sir Humphrey Gilbert [q. v.] superseded him for a time as colonel of the English forces in Holland. He took part in the abortive attempt made by de t Zereerts to besiege Tergoes; and when, owing to the refusal of the inhabitants of Flushing to readmit them into the town on account of their cowardly behaviour before Tergoes, he was exposed to a night attack by the governor of Middelburgh, he displayed great bravery, and was wounded in charging the enemy at the head of his men. But after a second and equally futile attempt against Tergoes, he returned to England with Sir H. Gilbert and the rest.

But failure had not dispirited him, and in February 1573 he returned to Holland with ten English companies, and took part in the attempt to relieve Haarlem and in the fight before Middelburgh; but owing to a disagreement as to the payment of his regiment, he returned to England early in January 1574, and 'being mustered before her majesty near to St. James's, the colonel and some five hundred of his best men were sent into Ireland, which, in truth, were the first perfect harquebushiers that were of our nation, and the first troupes that taught our nation to like the musket' (R. Williams, *The Actions of the Lowe Countries*). He landed at Dundalk in March, and in July he was sent into Munster to keep an eye on the Earl of Desmond and his brother John. He was wounded at the attack on Derrinlaur Castle on 19 Aug., and, returning to England in January 1575, he was warmly commended for his bravery, both by Sir William Fitzwilliam and the Earl of Essex. He remained apparently for some time in Wales, but in 1578 he again volunteered for service in the Low Countries under Captain (afterwards Sir John) Norris [q. v.] He took part in the battle of Rijnemants on 1 Aug., and in the numerous small skirmishes that took place in Brabant and Holland in 1579 and 1580. He was present at the relief of Steenwyk in February 1581, and the battle of Northorne on 30 Sept.; and at the battle with Parma's forces under the walls of Ghent on 27 Aug. 1582 he was conspicuous for his bravery. But difficulties were constantly arising between him and the States in regard to the payment of his troops, and apparently early in 1584 he was compelled to return to England. The Dutch community in London, however, recognising the important services he had rendered, subscribed nine thousand florins, and with the regiment which he was thus enabled to raise he returned to the Netherlands at the latter end of August, in time to take part in the defence of Antwerp. His troops were lodged in the suburbs of Burgerhout; but they became infected with the general spirit of insubordination, and he was compelled, in order to restore discipline, to execute Captains Lee and Powell. The post assigned to him was the defence of the Lillo fortress under La Noue, but it was in the attack on the Kowenstyn Dyke on 26 May 1585 that he most signally distinguished himself.

After the capitulation of Antwerp he was appointed for a time governor of Flushing, and it was here on 27 Dec., that he had that remarkable conversation with St. Aldegonde to which Motley (*United Netherlands*, i. 276–9) has drawn special attention. He was shortly afterwards placed in command of the important fortress of Rheinberg, where he was besieged by Parma, but almost immediately relieved by the counter attack of Leicester on Doesburg in July 1586. He was greatly annoyed by the attempt of Lord Willoughby (Peregrine Bertie [q.v.]), Leicester's successor, to oust him from the government of Bergen-op-Zoom, to which he claimed to have been appointed by the States-General. But, finding it impossible to obtain any redress of his grievances from Willoughby, he went to England in the spring of 1587, and was so successful in urging his claim that he was not merely knighted by Elizabeth for his services (but cf. *Hist. MSS. Comm.* 7th Rep. p. 519), but also obtained her letters to Willoughby expressly authorising his appointment as governor of Bergen-op-Zoom, and lieutenant-colonel of the English forces in the Netherlands. He landed at Flushing on 10 June, and having presented his letters to Willoughby at Middelburgh, he found him as obstinately opposed as ever to admit his claim, alleging a simple *non possumus* on the ground that he had had nothing to do with either appointment. The States-General also interfered in Morgan's behalf, but without immediate success. 'So as in lieu of my accustomed service,' he wrote bitterly to Elizabeth in July, 'done to your majesty and these countries, I must now spend my time in gazing after new.' He found temporary employment in conducting over to England part of the forces drawn from the Netherlands in anticipation of the Spanish

Armada. After the defeat of the Armada he re-embarked with his regiment, and arrived at Bergen-op-Zoom on 18 Sept. with a commission from the States to assume the government of that place, which Willoughby grudgingly surrendered to him. He took part in the defence of the city and continued governor of Bergen-op-Zoom till 1593, when he was rather ungraciously deprived of the post by the council of state in Holland on the ground that a governor was unnecessary, and that the charge might be entrusted to the senior captain in the garrison (but cf. FAURE, *Hist. de Bergen-op-Zoom*, p. 333, where one is led to infer that he remained governor till his death). He returned to England, and died at New Fulham on 22 Dec. 1595.

Morgan married in 1589 Anna, fourth child of Jan, baron van Merode, by whom he had two sons, Edward, who died young, and Maurice, and two daughters, Anne and Catherine. He was a brave soldier and a modest man; 'a very sufficient gallant gentleman,' said Willoughby, who had no great love for him, but 'unfurnished of language.' By his will, dated 18 Dec. 1595, he left his best rapier and dagger to Robert, earl of Essex; his best petronel, key and flask and touch-box to Lord Herbert; his grey hobbie to Henry, lord Hunsdon, and his gilt armour to his nephew, Sir Matthew Morgan. In October 1596 his widow presented a petition for payment of two warrants given by the Earl of Leicester and Lord Willoughby to her late husband for 1,200*l.* and 3,000*l.*, sums due to him for his company of two hundred men from 12 Oct. 1586 till his death in December 1595. Lady Morgan subsequently married Justinus van Nassau, natural son of William, prince of Orange, and died on 1 Oct. 1634, aged 72.

[G. T. Clark's Limbus Patrum Morganiæ et Glamorganiæ, p. 327; Lord Clermont's Hist. of the Family of Fortescue, p. 44*; Roger Williams's The Actions of the Lowe Countries, and A Brief Discourse of Warre; A True Discourse Historicall of the succeeding Governours in the Netherlands, &c., translated and collected by T. C[hurchyard] and Ric. Ro[binson], out of the Rev. E. Meteren, his Fifteene Books, Historiæ Belgicæ, and other collections added, London, 1602; W. Blandy's The Castle, or Picture of Policy; Wright's Queen Elizabeth and her Times, ii. 213, 388, 389, 391; Cal. of State Papers, Dom. Eliz. 1581–90 pp. 474, 526, 528, 538, 1591–4 pp. 242, 315, 332, 339, 398, 570, 1595–7 p. 300; Cal. of State Papers, Foreign, Eliz. 1572–4 pp. 130, 181, 406, 417, 432, 437; Collins's Sidney Papers, Introd. p. 53, i. 138, 315, 356, 384, 385, Leycester Corresp. (Camden Soc.), pp. 302, 353, State Papers, Ireland, Eliz. xliv. 9, 50, xlvii. 8; xlviii. 58, xlix. 7, 8, 9, 44. In this connection it is to be noted that the Index to the Cal. of Irish State Papers, ed. Hamilton, vol. ii., confounds Sir Thomas Morgan with his kinsman, Sir William Morgan (*d.* 1584) [q. v.], of Pencoyd, as indeed do most of the histories of the time; Lady Georgina Bertie's Five Generations of a Loyal House; C. R. Markham's The Fighting Veres; Grimeston's Historie of the Netherlands, London, 1608, p. 861; Camden's Annals passim; Meteren's Historia Belgica, pp. 311–12; Egerton MSS. Brit. Mus. 1694 f. 51 1943, ff. 47, 49, 53, 55, 57, 65, 69, 73 (corresp. with Lord Willoughby); Cotton MSS. Nero B. vi. f. 361 Galba C. vii. f. 135, viii. f. 57, xi. ff. 258, 272, Galba D. iii. ff. 201, 204, viii. f. 94, Titus B. vii. f. 38; Harleian MS. 287, f. 211; Cal. Hatfield MSS. ii. 55, iii. 100. 134; Hist. MSS. Comm. 7th Rep. p. 519 10th Rep. App. ii. p. 30; Jean Faure's Histoire Abrégée de la Ville de Bergen-op-Zoom, p. 333; A. J. Van der Aa's Biographisch Woordenboek, xii. 662, 1055, xiii. 77; A. Ferwerda's Adelyken Aanzienelyk Wappenboek van de Zeven Provincien, vol. i. pt. ii. art. Merode 13 Generatie.]

R. D.

MORGAN, THOMAS (1543–1606?), catholic conspirator, born in 1543, was the son of a Welsh catholic. He claimed to belong to 'a right worshipful family of Monmouthshire,' doubtless that of Llantarnan. He mentions two brothers, Harry and Rowland (*Cal. Hatfield MSS.* iv. 7–9). One brother is said to have been educated at the catholic college at Rheims, and after returning to England to have accepted protestantism, but suffered so much remorse that he drowned himself (FOLEY, *Records*, vi. 14). When Thomas was eighteen he entered the household of William Allen [q. v.], bishop of Exeter, and afterwards became secretary to Thomas Young, archbishop of York, with whom he remained till the archbishop's death on 26 June 1568. Both prelates were Calvinists, but Morgan concealed his creed while in their service, and, though a layman, he received from them, according to his own account, church preferment worth four thousand crowns a year. His attachment to his own faith nevertheless grew firmer, and when Young died he resolved to devote himself to the service of Mary Queen of Scots. Ignorant of his designs, Lord Northumberland and the Earl of Pembroke recommended him in 1569 as secretary to Lord Shrewsbury, in whose house at Tutbury the Scottish queen was then imprisoned. Morgan was soon installed at Tutbury, and was able to be useful to the queen. He managed her correspondence, and read and communicated to her what passed between his master and the court. Whenever her rooms and boxes were to be searched, he had notice beforehand, and concealed her papers. But Shrewsbury's suspicions were gradually aroused. On 28 Feb. 1571–2 he reported to Burghley that Morgan was conveying letters to the queen from the Bishop of Ross, and on 15 March sent him to London to be examined by the council (*Scottish State Papers*, ed. Thorpe, pp. 909 sq., 937). He was committed to the Tower, at the suggestion, it is said, of Leicester, on a charge of having been acquainted with the Ridolfi conspiracy (cf. FOLEY, vi. 14), but after ten months' confinement he was dismissed unpunished. He denied that he purchased his release by treachery. Burghley, he said, had interceded for him, he knew not why. There is no doubt of his fidelity to the cause he had espoused, and he still retained the confidence of the Queen of Scots. As soon as he regained his freedom she directed him to take up his residence in Paris, and to join Charles Paget in the office of secretary to James Beaton (1517–1603), archbishop of Glasgow, who was her ambassador at the French court. He carried with him recommendations to the Duke of Guise as well as to Beaton. On his settling in Paris Queen Mary allowed him thirty crowns a month out of her dowry, and soon placed her most confidential correspondence under his control. He arranged for her the ciphers in which she wrote her letters, and contrived to communicate with her regularly, besides forwarding letters from her or her advisers to the pope, to the nuncio in France, and to the English catholics at home and abroad who were taking part in the conspiracies against Elizabeth. He is said to have constructed as many as forty different ciphers (*ib.* vi. 14). Elizabeth was soon anxious to secure his arrest, and in January 1577–8 Sir Amias Paulet [q. v.], her ambassador in Paris, was considering the suggestion of a spy, Mazzini Delbena, who offered to invite Morgan to Rome, in order to capture him on the road (POULET, p. xxiv). Sir Amias regarded Morgan as Mary's 'professed minister,' whose doings he was always 'careful and curious to observe.'

In the autumn of 1583 Morgan received a visit from his well-known fellow countryman, William Parry [q. v.], and persuaded him to join in a plot for Queen Elizabeth's assassination. When Parry was arrested next year he threw the blame in his confession on Morgan, and Elizabeth, through her ambassador, Lord Derby, applied in March 1583 to the French government for his extradition. She promised to spare his life, but desired to obtain from him 'the circumstances of the practice.' The French king declined to surrender him, but arrested him and sent him to the Bastille. He had time to burn most of his papers, but a note from Parry respecting the plot, and containing a compromising reference to the Queen of Scots, fell into Lord Derby's hands. The queen was still dissatisfied, and soon sent Sir William Wade to demand his surrender. The nuncio at the French court interested himself in protecting Morgan, and the pope was even petitioned to demand his release, on the ground that his services were needed by the church. Wade returned home in May, with the assurance that Morgan was to be kept some time longer in his French prison. Queen Mary (*Letters*, ed. Labanoff, vi. 300) asserted that Morgan's imprisonment was really due to Leicester, who suspected that he was responsible for the libel known as 'Leicester's Commonwealth.' On 18 May 1585 Queen Mary wrote to the Bishop of Ross, begging him to use his influence to obtain Morgan's release (*ib.* vi. 307). On 20 July Morgan wrote to Queen Mary from the Bastille lamenting his fate, and regretting his consequent difficulties in dealing with her correspondence (MURDIN, pp. 446–52, cf. p. 443).

In October 1585 Morgan was visited in the Bastille by Gilbert Gifford [q. v.] Deceived by his feigned ardour in Mary's cause, Morgan enlisted him in her service as messenger between the imprisoned queen and her friends (cf. *Cal. Hatfield MSS.* iii. 347–9). Gifford soon placed himself in communication with Walsingham, but Morgan does not seem to have suspected his double dealing. Gifford's devices enabled Morgan to communicate with Mary with increased regularity, but all Morgan's letters were now copied by the English government before they reached her. In January 1586 Morgan heard that Elizabeth had offered 10,000*l.* for his delivery (MURDIN, p. 470), and Mary directed that two hundred crowns should be paid him (*Lettres*, vi. 263). Although still in prison Morgan helped to organise the conspiracy of Anthony Babington [q. v.] and his associates, and in April he advised Mary to send Babington the fatal letter approving his efforts in her behalf (MURDIN, pp. 513–14). On 16 July he introduced Christopher Blount to her notice (*Cal. Hatfield MSS.* iii. 151), and on 16 Jan. 1586–7 both Mary and her secretary, Gilbert Curle, wrote, condoling with him on his long imprisonment (*ib.* p. 271).

But the catholics abroad were divided among themselves, and Morgan and Paget were growing irreconcileably hostile to the jesuits, who were under the leadership of Cardinal Allen and Parsons (*Cal. State Papers*, Dom. Addenda, 1580-1625, 11 Aug. 1585; cf. *Cal. Hatfield MSS.* iv. 6 sq.) After spending nearly five years in the Bastille Morgan was released early in 1590, and made his way to Flanders. There his enemies contrived his arrest and a three years' imprisonment, culminating in an order of banishment from the dominions of Spain. He seems to have subsequently visited Italy, and had an audience of the pope, while secretly carrying on war with Cardinal Allen, until the latter's death in 1594 (*Scottish State Papers*, ed. Thorpe, p. 587). Returning to France, he was expelled in May 1596, but before long he returned to Paris.

In January 1605 it was reported that Morgan was involved in a 'plot of the French king's mistress' (*Cal. State Papers*, Dom. 1603–10, p. 187). In August 1605 the king of France expressed an intention of paying him two thousand French livres, a legacy which Queen Mary was said to have destined for him (*ib.* p. 232). Guy Fawkes, in his confession respecting the gunpowder plot in 1606, argued that Morgan had proposed 'the very same thing in Queen Elizabeth's time' (*ib.* p. 314). It is probable that he died in 1606.

[Most of Morgan's letters to Queen Mary appear in Murdin's State Papers. Queen Mary's communications with him are in Labanoff's Lettres de Marie Stuart, vols. v. vi. and vii. A mass of his correspondence is calendared in Thorpe's Scottish State Papers. Many of the originals are at Hatfield (cf. Cal. of Hatfield MSS. pts. iii. and iv.); see also Foley's Records of the Jesuits, vi. 14 sq.; Froude's Hist.; Cardinal Allen's Letters and Papers; Sir Amias Paulet's Letter-Book, ed. Father John Morris.] S. L.

MORGAN, Sir THOMAS (*d.* 1679?), soldier, second son of Robert Morgan of Llanrhymny (Clark, *Limbus Patrum Morganiæ*, p. 315), early sought his fortune as a soldier, and served in the Low Countries, and under Bernard of Saxe-Weimar in the thirty years' war (Aubrey, *Lives of Eminent Men, Letters from the Bodleian*, 1813, ii. 465). At what time he returned to take part in the English civil war is uncertain. Fairfax, recommending Morgan for a command in Ireland in October 1648, states that 'ever since the beginning of the first distractions' he had had 'constant experience of Colonel Morgan's fidelity' to the parliament's service (Cary, *Memorials of the Civil War*, ii. 45). Major Morgan, described as expert in sieges, was in Fairfax's army in March 1644, and 'one Morgan, one of Sir Thomas his colonels, a little man, short and peremptory,' took part in the siege of Lathom House during that month (*Fairfax Correspondence*, iii. 83; Ormerod, *Lancashire Civil War Tracts*, p. 166). On 18 June 1645 Morgan, who is described as 'colonel of dragoons, late under the command of the Lord Fairfax,' was appointed by parliament governor of Gloucester, in succession to Sir Edward Massey [q. v.], made colonel of a regiment of foot (5 July), and commander-in-chief of the forces of the country (31 Oct.) (*Lords' Journals*, vii. 440, 478, 670). In October 1645 he took Chepstow Castle and Monmouth (Phillips, *Civil War in Wales*, ii. 279; *Two Letters from Colonell Morgan*, London, 1645). Next, in conjunction with Colonel Birch, he took part in the surprise of Hereford (18 Dec. 1645; cf. *Two Letters sent . . by Colonell Morgan*, London, 22 Dec. 1645). Though 'under great distemper' from an ague, he endured all the hardships of a winter campaign, and personally led the horse in the assault (*Lords' Journals*, viii. 59; *Military Memoir of Colonel Birch*, p. 26; *Report on the Duke of Portland's MSS.* i. 328). On 21 March 1646 the combined forces of Morgan, Birch, and Sir William Brereton defeated Sir Jacob Astley at Stow-in-the-Wold, thus routing the last army which the king had in the field (*Lords' Journals*, viii. 231; *Memoir of Colonel Birch*, p. 34; Vicars, *Burning Bush*, p. 398). In June and July 1646 Morgan was engaged in besieging Raglan Castle, which finally surrendered to Fairfax on 19 Aug. (Phillips, *Civil War in Wales*, ii. 314; Cary, *Memorials*, i. 84, 131, 147).

For the next few years Morgan's history is again obscure. On 17 June 1647 he was again recommended as governor of Gloucester, but seems to have been superseded in January 1648 by Sir William Constable (*Cal. State Papers*, Dom. 1645–7, p. 563; Rushworth, *Historical Collections*, vii. 979). His application for an Irish command in October 1648 was without result (Cary, *Memorials*, ii. 45). In 1651 Morgan was in Scotland, and on 28 Aug. Monck requested Cromwell to 'send down a commission for Colonel Morgan to be colonel of the dragoons' (*ib.* ii. 347). Cromwell sent the commission, and for the next six years Morgan was Monck's most trusted coadjutor in the subjugation of Scotland, holding, for the latter part of the period, the rank of major-general in the army in Scotland. On 26 May 1652 Dunottar Castle surrendered to him after a siege of three weeks (Mackinnon, *History of the Coldstream Guards*, i. 48). On 19 June 1654 he defeated General Middleton at Lough Garry, thus striking a fatal blow at the rising headed by Middleton in the highlands (*Mercurius Politicus*, 27 June–3 Aug. 1654, 10–17 Aug.)

On 23 April 1657 Cromwell summoned Morgan from Scotland to take part in the expedition sent to the assistance of the French in Flanders. He was second in command to Sir John Reynolds, governor of Mardyke after its capture from the Spaniards, and practically commanded the English contingent after the death of Reynolds, though Lockhart nominally succeeded to the generalship. The reason for thus passing over Morgan was no doubt that, though he was well qualified to lead an army in the field, the relations between the allied armies required a general who was also a diplomatist. The narrative attributed to Morgan (printed in vol. i. of the 'Phœnix Britannicus,' a collection of tracts made by Morgan in 1732) claims all the successes of the campaign as his; but his own letters are modest enough (Thurloe, vii. 217, 258). He was wounded in the storming of an outwork at the siege of St. Venant (Heath, *Chronicle*, p. 726).

At the battle of the Dunes (4 June 1658) Lockhart was present and commanded the English contingent, but more than one account represents Morgan as its real leader (Thurloe, vii. 155; Clarke, *Life of James II*, i. 347). After the capture of Dunkirk, Morgan with three English regiments continued to serve in Turenne's army, while the rest were left in garrison, and he was again slightly wounded at the taking of Ypres (*Mercurius Politicus*, 17–24 June, 19–26 Aug. 1658). At the close of the campaign he returned to England, and was knighted by the protector, Richard Cromwell, on 25 Nov. 1658. His command in Scotland had been kept vacant, but illness delayed his return to it. In October 1659, when Monck declared against Lambert's expulsion of the parliament, Morgan was at York, where the gout had obliged him to halt on his way north. Monck was anxious for his assistance, but the letter which he sent him was intercepted by Colonel Robert Lilburne. Morgan was afraid that he would be stopped, but persuaded Lilburne and Lambert that he disapproved of Monck's proceedings, and they accordingly commissioned him to induce Monck to lay down his arms. He delivered his message, but at the same time told Monck that he meant to share his fortunes. 'You know,' he said, 'I am no statesman; I am sure you are a lover of your country, and therefore I will join with you in all your actions, and submit to your prudence and judgment in the conduct of them.' Morgan's coming 'was a great accession to Monck's party, and a great encouragement to all the officers and soldiers; for he was esteemed by them to be, next the general, a person of the best conduct of any then in arms in the three nations, having been nearly forty years in arms, and present in the greatest battles and sieges of Christendom for a great part of that time.' He was specially useful in the reorganisation of Monck's cavalry, which was the weak part of his army (Baker, *Chronicle*, ed. Phillips, 1670, pp. 688–90; Gumble, *Life of Monck*, p. 144; Price, *Mystery of His Majesty's Restoration*, ed. Maseres, p. 738). Morgan accompanied Monck in his march into England, but after the occupation of York was sent back to take the command of the forces left in Scotland. He played a conspicuous part in the celebration of the king's restoration at Edinburgh (19 June 1660), building an enormous bonfire at his door, and firing off Mons Meg with his own hand (*Mercurius Publicus*, 28 June–3 July 1660). His command in Scotland ended in December 1660, when the English regiments there were disbanded, but his services were rewarded by a baronetcy (1 Feb. 1661) and by the reversion of some beneficial leases in Herefordshire (*Cal. State Papers*, Dom., 1661–2, pp. 204, 384).

In 1665, during the war with Holland, a French attack on Jersey was feared, and Morgan was made governor of the island (20 Dec. 1665; for Morgan's instructions see *Rawlinson MSS.* A. 255, 25; cf. *Cal. State Papers*, Dom. 1665–6, pp. 110–19; Dalton, *English Army Lists*, i. 57). Morgan repaired the forts and reorganised the local militia. Falle, the contemporary historian of Jersey, gives him high praise for his vigilance and care. He 'would sit whole days on the carriage of a cannon hastening and encouraging the workmen.' But the discussions of the estates he found insufferably tedious, and would retire to smoke and walk about till they had finished (*Account of Jersey*, ed. Durell, pp. xxii, 141, 283). His correspondence with Lord Hatton during his government is in the British Museum (Additional MSS. 29552–7).

According to Burke's 'Extinct Baronetage' (ed. 1844, p. 369) Morgan died on 13 Aug. 1670, but Aubrey states that he died in 1679, and his correspondence with Hatton ends in 1678. Burke adds that Morgan married De la Riviere, daughter and heiress of Richard Cholmondley of Brame Hall, Yorkshire, and was succeeded in the baronetcy by his eldest son, Sir John Morgan of Kinnersley Castle, Herefordshire. The dignity became extinct in 1767 with the death of the fourth baronet. Noble states that Morgan's commissions and other papers were in the possession of Thomas Clutton of Kinnersley, to whose family the estate had descended (*House of Cromwell*, ed. 1787, i. 448).

A portrait of Morgan, engraved by Guleston, is said by Bromley (*Catalogue of Engraved British Portraits*, p. 95) to be given in 'Phœnix Britannicus,' p. 532; but it is not in any of the three editions in the British Museum. After the taking of Dunkirk, Mazarin and others, says Aubrey, 'had a great mind to see this famous warrior. They gave him a visit, and whereas they thought to have found an Achillean or gigantic person, they saw a little man, not many degrees above a dwarf, sitting in a hut of turfs with his fellow soldiers, smoking a pipe about three inches, or neer so long, with a green hat-case on. He spake with a very exile tone, and cried out to the soldiers when angry with them, "Sirrah, I'll cleave your skull," as if the words had been prolated by an eunuch' (*Letters from the Bodleian*, ii. 465).

In 1699 a pamphlet of sixteen pages, quarto, was published as 'A True and Just Relation of Major-general Morgan's Progress in France and Flanders, with the 6,000 English in the years 1657 and 1658 . . . as it was delivered by the General himself.' It was written by Morgan in 1675 at the request of Dr. Samuel Barrow, but its historical value is very doubtful (Godwin, *History of the Commonwealth*, iv. 547; *Egerton MS.* 2618, f. 127). It is reprinted in the 'Harleian Miscellany,' ed. Park, iii. 341. Some letters of Morgan's are among the Tanner MSS. in the Bodleian Library, and several printed letters are among the collection of pamphlets in the British Museum Library (cf. *Catalogue*, s. v. 'Morgan').

[Authorities mentioned in the article.]

C. H. F.

MORGAN, THOMAS (*d.* 1743), deist, of Welsh origin, is said to have been a 'poor lad in a farmer's house' near Bridgwater, Somerset. He showed talents which induced a dissenting minister, John Moore (1642?–1717) [q. v.], to give him a free education, the cost of his living being provided by his friends. He became independent minister at Burton in Somerset, but was ordained by the presbyterian John Bowder [q. v.] at Frome in 1716, and was minister of a congregation at Marlborough, Wiltshire. He was decidedly orthodox at the time of his ordination, but was dismissed from the ministry soon after 1720 in consequence of his views. He took to the study of medicine, and describes himself as M.D. on the title-pages of his books in 1726 and afterwards. He first appeared as a writer during the controversy among the dissenters at the time of the Salters' Hall conference, on the anti-subscription side. He afterwards defended Boulay's theory as to the corruption of human nature against the early writings of Thomas Chubb [q. v.], and was much puzzled about freewill. He became a freethinker, contributed some books to the latter part of the deist controversy, and described himself as a 'Christian deist.' He was opposed by Samuel Chandler [q. v.], John Chapman [q. v.], Thomas Chubb, Samuel Fancourt (1704–1784) [q. v.], John Leland (1691–1766) [q. v.], and other writers, but never obtained much notice. He died 'with a true Christian resignation' 14 Jan. 1742–3. Morgan married Mary, eldest daughter of Nathaniel Merriman, a prominent dissenter of Marlborough. By his wife, who survived him, he left an only son.

Morgan's writings are: 1. 'Philosophical Principles of Medicine,' 1725; 2nd edit., corrected, 1730. 2. 'A Collection of Tracts . . . occasioned by the late Trinitarian Controversy,' 1726. This includes the following reprints (dates of original publication are added): 'The Nature and Consequences of Enthusiasm considered . . . in a letter to Mr. Tong, Mr. Robinson, Mr. Smith, and Mr. Reynolds' (four ministers who had supported the subscribing party at Salters' Hall), 1719; a defence of this against Samuel Fancourt's 'Certainty and Infallibility,' 1720; another defence against Fancourt's 'Enthusiasm Retorted,' 1722; 'The Absurdity of Opposing Faith to Reason,' against Thomas Bradbury [q.v.], another writer on the same controversy, whom he had also attacked in a postscript to his first tract, 1722; the 'Grounds and Principles of Christian Communion,' 1720; a 'Letter to Sir Richard Blackmore, in reply to his 'Modern Arians Unmasked,' 1721; a 'Refutation of . . . Mr. Joseph Pyke,' author of an 'Impartial View,' with further remarks on Blackmore, 1722; a 'Letter to Dr. Waterland, occasioned by his late writings in defence of the Athanasian hypotheses,' 1722 (?); 'Enthusiasm in Distress,' an examination of 'Reflections upon Reason,' in a letter to Phileleutherus Britannicus,' 1722, with two postscripts in 1723 and 1724. 3. 'A Letter to Mr. Thomas Chubb, occasioned by his "Vindication of Human Nature,"' 1727, followed by 'A Defence of Natural and Revealed Religion,' occasioned by Chubb's 'Scripture Evidence,' 1728 (in defence of the views of Robert Barclay [q. v.], the quaker apologist). 4. 'The Mechanical Practice of Physic,' 1735. 5. 'The Moral Philosopher, in a dialogue between Philalethes, a Christian Deist, and Theophanus, a Christian Jew' [anon.], 1737; 2nd edit. 1738. A second volume, in answer to Leland and Chapman, by Philalethes appeared in 1739, and a third, against Leland and Lowman, in 1740. A fourth volume, called 'Physico Theology,' appeared in 1741. 6. 'Letter to Dr. Cheyne in defence of the "Mechanical Practice,"' 1738. 7. 'Vindication of the "Moral Philosopher,"' against

S. Chandler, 1741. 8. 'The History of Joseph considered . . . by Philalethes,' in answer to S. Chandler, 1744.

[Protestant Dissenters' Mag. i. 258; Monthly Repository, 1818, p. 735; Gent. Mag. 1743, p. 51; Williams's Eminent Welshmen, p. 342; Sermon at the ordination of T. Morgan, by N. Billingsley, with Morgan's 'Confession of Faith,' 1717.]
L. S.

MORGAN, Sir THOMAS CHARLES, M.D. (1783–1843), philosophical and miscellaneous writer, son of John Morgan of Charlotte Street, Bloomsbury, London, born in 1783, was educated at Eton, the Charterhouse, and Peterhouse, Cambridge, whence he graduated M.B. in 1804 and proceeded M.D. in 1809. He practised at first as a surgeon in Charlotte Street, and on 13 April 1805 married Miss Hammond, daughter of William Hammond of Queen Square, Bloomsbury, and the Stock Exchange. She died in 1809, leaving issue one child, a daughter. Morgan was a friend and admirer of Jenner, the discoverer of vaccination, and published in 1808 'An Expostulatory Letter to Dr. Moseley on his Review of the Report of the London College of Physicians,' London, 8vo. On 30 Sept. 1809 he was admitted a candidate, and on 1 Oct. 1810 a fellow of the College of Physicians. As physician to the first Marquis of Abercorn he attended him to Ireland, and through his interest was knighted by the lord-lieutenant, Charles Lennox, fourth duke of Richmond [q. v.], at Dublin on 17 Sept. 1811. At Abercorn's seat, Baron's Court, co. Tyrone, Morgan met, and on 12 Jan. 1812 married, a protégée of the marchioness, Sydney Owenson [see Morgan, Sydney, Lady], then rising into repute as a popular authoress. After the marriage Morgan obtained the post of physician to the Marshalsea, Dublin, and took a house in that city, No. 35 Kildare Street, with the view of establishing a practice. Between 1815 and 1824, however, most part of his time was spent abroad with Lady Morgan, to whose works 'France' (1818) and 'Italy' (1821) he contributed appendices on law, medicine, and other matters. In 1818 he published 'Sketches of the Philosophy of Life,' and in 1822 'Sketches of the Philosophy of Morals' (both London, 8vo), in which he attempted to popularise the ideas of Bichat, Cabanis, and Destutt de Tracy. The former work was unsparingly attacked on the ground of its materialism by the Rev. Thomas Rennell [q. v.], and Morgan's professional reputation was so seriously damaged that he retired from practice. The latter book fell almost stillborn from the press.

Morgan was a strenuous advocate of catholic emancipation and other liberal measures, and on the return of the whigs to power was placed on the commission of inquiry into the state of Irish fisheries (1835). He took an active part in the investigation, and compiled an 'Historical Sketch of the British and Irish Fisheries' for the appendix to the First Report (*Parl. Papers*, House of Commons, 1837, vol. xxii.) From 1824 to 1837 the Morgans resided at 35 Kildare Street, Dublin, where their evening receptions became famous [see Morgan, Sydney, Lady]. In the latter year they removed to William Street, Lowndes Square, London, where Morgan died on 28 Aug. 1843. For many years Morgan contributed slight essays or causeries to the 'New Monthly Magazine,' the 'Metropolitan,' and other periodicals. Those in the 'New Monthly' are distinguished by the signature μ. The best of these trifles are collected in the 'Book without a Name,' to which Lady Morgan also contributed, London, 1841, 2 vols. 12mo.

Morgan was an extremely minute philosopher, or rather *philosophe*. His mental calibre is evinced by an anecdote recorded by Crabb Robinson. Robinson quoted Kant's well-known apophthegm about the 'starry heavens' and the 'moral law,' upon which Morgan exclaimed contemptuously 'German sentiment and nothing else,' adding, 'The starry heavens, philosophically considered, are no more objects of admiration than a basin of water.'

Besides the above mentioned publications Morgan is the author of a pasquinade in ottava rima entitled 'The Royal Progress. A Canto: with Notes. Written on occasion of His M——y's Visit to Ireland, August 1821,' London, 1821, 12mo.

[Munk's Coll. of Phys. ii. 93; Gent. Mag. 1805 pt. i. p. 485, 1812 pt. i. p. 37, 1843 pt. ii. p. 436; Lit. Gaz. 1818 p. 721, 1822 p. 691; Townsend's Calendar of Knights, 1828, p. 203; Lady Morgan's Autobiography and Correspondence, ed. W. Hepworth Dixon, 1862; Lady Morgan's Passages from my Autobiography, 1859; Fitzpatrick's Friends, Foes, and Adventures of Lady Morgan, 1859, and Lady Morgan, her Career, Literary and Personal, 1860; Crabb Robinson's Diary, ed. Sadler, 1872, i. 408; Quarterly Review, vol. xvii.; Examiner, 2 Sept. 1843; Notes and Queries, 2nd ser. ix. 307; Athenæum, 1843, p. 794.]
J. M. R.

MORGAN, Sir WILLIAM (*d.* 1584), soldier, was the eldest son of Sir Thomas Morgan of Pencoyd and Langstone, Glamorganshire, and Cecilia, daughter of Sir George Herbert of Swansea. He succeeded to Pencoyd and Langstone on the death of his father in June 1566; but, being of an adventurous disposition, he went to France in 1569, shortly after the battle of Jarnac, as a volunteer in the army of the Huguenots. He subsequently became acquainted at Paris with Count Louis of Nassau, in whose service he enlisted, and took part in the capture of Valenciennes on 24 May 1572, and of Mons on the day following. At Valenciennes he had, according to Thomas Churchyard (*Churchyard's Choise*), 'a goodly gentilmannes house given hym, stuffed with gooddes and furnished with Wines and victuall for a long yere,' but, being summoned to Mons by Count Louis, he did not long enjoy it. He was present at the defence of that city, and by the articles of capitulation 'was allowed to march away in the same order and liberty of mind that the Count de Lodwick and his Almains had obtained.' He accompanied the Prince of Orange into Holland, and was sent by him to Sir Humphrey Gilbert and the English volunteers 'with large offers to stay them for his service,' just as they were embarking for England after their discomfiture before Tergoes. He returned to England early in 1573, and took part as a volunteer adventurer in the enterprise of Walter Devereux, earl of Essex [q. v.], for colonising Clandeboye and the north-eastern corner of Ireland. Unlike the majority of gentlemen-adventurers, who, 'having not forgotten the delicacies of England, and wanting resolute minds to endure the travail of a year or two in this waste country,' feigned excuses and returned to England, Morgan took his share of the privations and hard blows which it was their lot to encounter. 'I have great cause,' wrote Essex on 2 Nov., 'to commend unto your Majesty the service of . . . Will. Morgan of Penycoid, now Marshal by the departure of Sir Peter Carew, surely a very worthy gentleman' (DEVEREUX, *Lives of the Earls of Essex*, i. 46).

In the plot of the plantation Glenarm was assigned to him, but in May 1574 he was sent to England as the bearer of letters of submission on the part of Sir Brian Mac Phelim O'Neill [q. v.] In consequence of Essex's commendation he was knighted that year by Elizabeth, but his expenses in connection with the enterprise, which ultimately failed, were so great that he was compelled in 1577 to sell Langstone. The property was purchased by John Simmings, a London doctor, from whom it passed to Morgan's kinsman, William Morgan of Llantarnam, in Monmouthshire, whose great-grandson, Sir Edward Morgan, sold it about 1666 to Sir Thomas Gore of Barrow Court, Somerset, in whose family it continued till quite recently.

Morgan was vice-admiral of Glamorganshire, but exercised his office, apparently, through his deputy, William Morgan of Llantarnam, who in 1577 was summoned before the admiralty court for refusing his assistance to capture a pirate (*State Papers*, Dom. Eliz. cx. 2–4, cxii. 28). On 11 July 1578 Morgan was surprised by the watch, under very suspicious circumstances, in company with the French ambassador and Sir Warham St. Leger [q. v.], in Paris Gardens, a very hotbed, according to Recorder William Fleetwood [q. v.], of conspiracy (*ib.* cxxv. 20–4). He seems to have explained matters satisfactorily, for in November 1579 he succeeded Sir Drue Drury [q. v.] as governor of Dungarvan, and being appointed to conduct over certain forces for the service in Ireland, he landed at Waterford after a boisterous passage, apparently in December 1579. He was stationed by Sir William Pelham [q. v.] at Youghal, with twenty horse and two hundred foot, as lieutenant of the counties of Cork and Waterford, in which capacity he displayed great activity against the rebels in south Munster, particularly the seneschal of Imokilly. But his health broke down under the hard service and constant exposure of Irish warfare, and in June 1580 he obtained permission to return for a short time to England. Before his departure he was instrumental, at considerable personal danger, in securing the submission of the Earl of Clancar. Both Sir William Pelham and Sir Warham St. Leger wrote home in warm commendation of his conduct. His absence, wrote the latter, 'may verie ill be spared hence: his dealing in execution of justice being here so well liked of by those y[t] bee good, and feared of thill, as the son[r] hee returneth the bett[r] it wilbe for this estate' (*ib.* Irel. Eliz. lxiii. 42). His absence was of short duration. He sailed from Bristol at the end of July 1580, with reinforcements, for Ireland; but, being driven back by stormy weather, it was the end of August before he reached his destination.

But his health became rapidly worse, and in February 1581 he earnestly requested Burghley to be allowed to return to England. His request was granted, but, owing to the situation of affairs in Munster, he was unable to take immediate advantage of it. 'I have,' he wrote to Walsingham from Dunvargan on 7 Dec. 1581, 'beyne very sickly, and had my leave to come over long since, but because you were not att home, and the Rebelles hath so solemnly vowed the burnynge of this towen, I could not fynd in my harth to depart' (*ib.* lxxxvii. 10), and it was actually May or June 1582 before he was able to carry out his intention in that respect.

He died shortly after his return in 1584. Morgan married Elizabeth, daughter of Sir Andrew Judde, alderman of London; and, having no issue by her, he was succeeded to a very much encumbered estate by his brother Henry. Another brother, Robert Morgan, is said to have come to Ireland in the reign of Charles I, and to have been the founder of the family of Morgan of Cottelstown in co. Sligo.

[G. T. Clark's Limbus Patrum Morganiæ et Glamorganiæ, p. 321; Burke's Commoners, iv. 13; Thomas Churchyard's Choise; Roger Williams's Actions of the Low Countries; Morgan and Wakeman's Notices of Pencoyd Castle and Langstone (Caerleon Antiq. Assoc.); Wright's Queen Elizabeth and her Times, ii. 87; Cal. of State Papers, Eliz., Domestic and Ireland; George Hill's Macdonnells of Antrim, p. 417; Collins's Sidney Papers, i. 213; Cal. Carew MSS. ii. 171, 209, 218.] R. D.

MORGAN, WILLIAM (1540?–1604), bishop of St. Asaph, son of John ap Morgan ap Llywelyn and Lowri, daughter of William ap John ap Madog, was born at Ty Mawr, Gwibernant, in the parish of Penmachno, Carnarvonshire, about 1540. His father, a copyhold tenant upon the great estate of Gwydir, was in no position to give his son a liberal education. But, according to a local tradition, William was carefully taught at home by a monk, who, on the dissolution of the monasteries, had found a secret asylum among his relatives at Ty Mawr. The lad's proficiency soon attracted the attention of John (or Maurice?) Wynn of Gwydir, who took him under his patronage and had him taught at his own house, though no doubt on a menial footing. In 1565 he entered St. John's College, Cambridge, matriculating in the university as a sub-sizar on 26 Feb., and becoming a full sizar on 9 June. Cambridge, and in particular St. John's College, were at this time active protestant centres, and Morgan rapidly lost the Romanist sympathies which he probably brought with him from Wales. Hebrew was taught by Emanuel Tremellius [q. v.], and afterwards by Anthony Rodolph Chevallier [q. v.], and he thus laid the foundations of his proficiency in that language. He graduated B.A. in 1568, M.A. in 1571, B.D. in 1578, and D.D. in 1583. On 8 Aug. 1575 he became vicar of Welshpool, and in 1578 he was appointed one of the university preachers. On 1 Oct. of that year he was promoted to the vicarage of Llanrhaiadr Mochnant, Denbighshire, to which appears to have been added in 1579 the rectory of Llanfyllin, Montgomeryshire. The two parishes are not far apart, and Morgan probably found no difficulty in supervising Llanfyllin while residing at Llanrhaiadr. In a document styled 'A Discoverie of the present Estate of the Byshoppricke of St. Asaphe,' and dated 24 Feb. 1587, he is particularly mentioned as one of the three 'preachers' in the diocese who kept 'ordinary residence and hospitality' upon their livings.

It was at Llanrhaiadr that Morgan carried out the great enterprise of his life, the translation of the Bible into Welsh. Parliament had in 1563 enacted that the bishops of Hereford, St. David's, Bangor, St. Asaph, and Llandaff should provide for the issue within three years of a Welsh version of the scriptures, but this had only resulted in the appearance of William Salesbury's translation of the New Testament in 1567. Morgan appears to have taken up spontaneously the idea of completing Salesbury's work; after some years' labour he resolved upon publishing the Pentateuch as an experiment. But influential neighbours who had private grudges against him interposed, and endeavoured to persuade the authorities that Morgan's character was not such as to fit him for his self-sought position as translator, and he was accordingly summoned before Archbishop Whitgift to justify his pretensions. It is probable that the aspersions upon him had reference to the position of his wife, whom he is said to have married secretly before he went up to Cambridge. Sir John Wynn of Gwydir afterwards took credit to himself for having cleared the good name of the two by the certificates he and his friends sent up to London. The effect of the attack undoubtedly was not only to vindicate Morgan's character, but also to convince Whitgift of his talents as a translator, and to interest the archbishop in the work. It was resolved that the whole of the Old Testament and the Apocrypha should appear, and that Morgan should also revise Salesbury's translation of the New Testament. Towards the end of 1587 the printing of the book began at London; it went on for a year, during which Morgan was enabled to exercise a close supervision over the work through the hospitality of Gabriel Goodman [q. v.], dean of Westminster. It appeared in 1588, after the defeat of the Armada (to which reference is made in the preface), and before 20 Nov., the date inscribed in the copy presented by Morgan to the Westminster Abbey Library. The Latin dedication to Queen Elizabeth tells something of the history of the translation, and powerfully states the case for it against those advisers of the crown who disapproved of any official countenance being given to the Welsh language. Among those who helped in the production of the book are mentioned Archbishop Whitgift, William Hughes [q. v.] (bishop of St. Asaph), Hugh Bellot [q. v.] (bishop of Bangor), Dean Goodman, Dr. David Powel (author of the 'Historie of Cambria'), Edmund Prys (author of the Welsh metrical version of the Psalms), and Dr. Richard Vaughan (afterwards successively bishop of Bangor, of Chester, and of London).

Shortly before the appearance of the translation Morgan seems to have resigned his position at Llanrhaiadr in favour of his son, Evan Morgan, who held the vicarage until 1612. He himself was provided for by means of the sinecure rectory of Pennant Melangell, Montgomeryshire, bestowed upon him on 10 July 1588. He still lived, it would seem, at Llanrhaiadr, which led Sir John Wynn, in a letter written in 1603, to refer to him as though he had been vicar of that place at the time of his being made bishop. In 1594 his income was further augmented by the sinecure rectory of Denbigh (cf. Letter from Earl of Essex, 29 Jan. 1594–5, in STRYPE's *Annals*, edit. 1824, iv. 342).

Morgan was elected bishop of Llandaff on 30 June 1595, was consecrated on 20 July, and received the temporalities of the see on 7 Aug. Sir John Wynn of Gwydir at a later period took to himself the whole credit of this promotion, but there is no reason to doubt that Elizabeth and Whitgift felt a personal interest in the appointment, and made it for the good of Wales. The see was a poor one; hence it is not surprising that he retained the rectory of Llanfyllin, but he gave up that of Pennant, and in the next year that of Denbigh.

On the death of Bishop Hughes, Morgan was on 21 July 1601 elected to the somewhat wealthier see of St. Asaph. He now resigned Llanfyllin, but followed his predecessor in the see in retaining the archdeaconry in his own hands. Both at Llandaff and at St. Asaph he showed the energy to be expected of him. His successor in the former see, Francis Godwin [q. v.], speaks of his 'industria' there. At St. Asaph he took measures for establishing regular courses of sermons at the cathedral, repaired the chancel, and exercised a careful supervision over the property of the church in his diocese. His vigilance in the latter respect brought him into conflict with the great men of the district. Soon after his settlement at St. Asaph he had a dispute with David Holland of Teirdan, which was only composed by the intervention of Sir John Wynn of Gwydir; and in 1603, a few months before his death, he mortally offended Sir John himself by refusing to confirm a lease for three lives of the living of Llanrwst, by which Sir John hoped to profit. A correspondence on this matter is printed in Yorke's 'Royal Tribes of Wales' (edit. 1887, pp. 134–141), and shows the bishop firm and incorruptible, though possibly a little haughty, on the one hand, while Sir John is indignant at the ingratitude, under a feigned plea of conscience, of one for whom he holds he has done so much.

Morgan died, as 'Y Cwtta Cyfarwydd' tells us, 'upon Monday morning, being the xth day of September, 1604.' He was twice married, first to Ellen Salesbury, whom he married before going to Cambridge; and secondly to Catherine, daughter of George ap Richard ap John. He left one son, Evan, who became vicar of Llanrhaiadr Mochnant. The tercentenary of the translation of the Bible into Welsh in 1888 was marked by the erection of a memorial to Morgan and his helpers in the precincts of St. Asaph Cathedral.

[The fullest and most accurate biography of Morgan is that of Mr. Charles Ashton ('Bywyd ac Amserau yr Esgob Morgan,' Treherbert, 1891), which sifts almost all the material available for an account of his life. Two parts of 'The Life and Times of Bishop William Morgan,' by Mr. T. Evan Jacob (London, n.d.), have appeared; also a short biography by the Rev. W. Hughes, published by the Society for Promoting Christian Knowledge. All three appeared in connection with the tercentenary of the translation of the Bible into Welsh in 1588. See also letters in Yorke's Royal Tribes of Wales; Edwards's edition (1801) of Browne Willis's Survey of St. Asaph; Account of the Welsh Versions of the Bible, by Dr. Thomas Llewelyn, 1793.] J. E. L.

MORGAN, WILLIAM (1623–1689), jesuit, second son of Henry Morgan, by his first wife, Winefrid Gwynne, was born in Flint in 1623, and educated at Westminster School, where he was elected king's scholar, and passed on in 1640 to Trinity College, Cambridge, from which, after two years' residence, he was expelled by the Earl of Manchester for taking up arms in the royal cause (WELCH, *Alumni Westmon.* ed. Phillimore, p. 115). He was taken prisoner at the battle of Naseby, and after six months' confinement in Winchester gaol, he was sent into banishment, and entered the Spanish service in Colonel Cobb's regiment. Having been converted to the catholic religion, he entered the English College at Rome in 1648. He was admitted into the Society of Jesus in 1651, and was professed of the four vows, 2 Feb. 1665–6. In 1661 he became a professor in the jesuit college at Liège, whence he was sent in 1670 to the mission of North Wales. He was declared superior of the residence of St. Winefred in 1672, and in 1675 he was chaplain at Powis Castle. He was specially noted in Titus Oates's list as an intended victim of the persecution, but in February 1678–9 he with difficulty effected his escape to the continent. In October 1679 he was appointed socius to Father Warner, the provincial, and subsequently, on visiting England, he was arrested and imprisoned. In May 1683 he was declared rector of the English College at Rome. He was appointed provincial of his order 22 Aug. 1689, and died a few weeks afterwards in the college at St. Omer on 28 Sept. 1689.

Dr. Oliver says Morgan wrote the beautiful account of the reign of James II beginning 'Anni Septuagesimi Octavi,' &c., but omits to state where this work is to be found.

[Foley's Records, v. 990, vii. 523; Oliver's Jesuit Collections, p. 144.] T. C.

MORGAN, WILLIAM (1750-1833), actuary, born in June 1750 at Bridgend, Glamorganshire, was the eldest son of William Morgan, a surgeon practising in that town, by Sarah, sister of Dr. Richard Price [q. v.] George Cadogan Morgan [q. v.] was his only brother. He was intended for the medical profession; but owing to his father's limited means he was apprenticed, 11 July 1769, to a London apothecary. Towards the end of 1771 he returned home to assist his father, but on his death, in 1772, Morgan returned to London, and through the influence of Dr. Price became in February 1774 an assistant-actuary, and in February 1775 chief actuary to the Equitable Assurance Society, a post which he held until his resignation on 2 Dec. 1830. During the earlier part of this time he lived at the offices of the society in Chatham Place, Blackfriars, and there witnessed, in June 1780, the Gordon riots, his house being for a time threatened by the mob. He subsequently lived at Stamford Hill, where his house became a meeting-place for many of the advanced reformers of the day, including Horne Tooke and Sir Francis Burdett. On 20 April 1792 Samuel Rogers met Tom Paine at dinner at Morgan's house (CLAYDEN, *Early Life of Rogers*, p. 246). Morgan appears to have been at one time suspected by the authorities, and his name is said to have been on the list of those threatened with prosecution, before the acquittal of Horne Tooke. Despite his advanced views, Bishop Watson of Llandaff was an intimate friend. Morgan died at Stamford Hill on 4 May 1833, and was buried at Hornsey.

In 1781 Morgan married Susan Woodhouse by whom he had several children. A daughter, Sarah, was married to Benjamin Travers, the surgeon: the eldest son, William Morgan, who married Maria Towgood, the beautiful niece of Samuel Rogers, was for a time assistant-actuary at his father's office, but after his early death was succeeded by another son, Arthur Morgan, who held the position of chief actuary from his father's resignation, 2 Dec. 1830, till 3 March 1870, when he resigned. He died seven days after. Thus father and son were actuaries for a period of ninety-six years.

Morgan takes high rank among the pioneers of life assurance in England. The phenomenal success of the Equitable Society in the midst of so many contemporary failures was mainly due to his careful administration and sound actuarial advice. The details which he published from time to time as to the mortality experience of that society furnished data for the amendment of the Northampton tables, and the construction of others by various actuaries [see MILNE, JOSHUA]. The first instalment of Morgan's statistics was published in his 'Doctrine of Annuities and Assurances on Lives and Survivorships Stated and Explained,' London, 1779, 8vo, with a preface by Dr. Price. From 1786 onwards he delivered to the court of governors a series of addresses reviewing the policy of the society. Nine of the most important of these addresses were published, along with the 'Deed of Settlement of the Equitable Society,' in one volume, in 1833, four of them having been previously published in 1811, and six in 1820. A new edition, containing three additional addresses by Arthur Morgan, was issued in 1854. Upon the basis of Morgan's statements new tables of mortality were constructed, most notably by Griffith Davies and by T. Gompertz in 1825, and by Charles Babbage in 1826. Morgan also published a table of his own in 'A View of the Rise and Progress of the Equitable Society, and the Causes which have contributed to its Success,' London, 1828, 8vo (cf. a review in *Westminster Rev.* April 1828; *Phil. Mag.* 1828, an unsigned article by Dr. Thomas Young; *Times* of 26 June and 1 July 1828, attacks by Francis Baily and George Farren; *John Bull*, 28 March, probably by W. Baldwin, who issued a pamphlet on the subject in the following year). Morgan's table of mortality was revised by his son Arthur Morgan, and reissued in 1834.

In 1783 Morgan sent a paper on 'Probability of Survivorship' to the 'Philosophical Transactions,' and was awarded the gold medal of the Royal Society, being admitted a fellow shortly afterwards. Other papers, which appeared in 'Philosophical Transactions' for 1791, 1794, and 1799, were embodied in the second edition of his 'Doctrine of Annuities,' 1821. In 1827 he was examined before a select committee of the House of Commons on friendly societies. He was also much consulted on questions relating to ecclesiastical property. Morgan was a unitarian of a presbyterian type, like his uncle, Dr. Price, whose views on finance and politics he also inherited. He vigorously denounced the accumulation of the National Debt, and 'the improvident alienation of that fund by which it might have been redeemed.'

The following were his writings on this subject: 1. 'A Review of Dr. Price's Writings on the Subject of the Finances of the Kingdom, to which are added the three plans communicated by him to Mr. Pitt in 1786 for redeeming the National Debt,' London, 1792, 8vo; 2nd edit., 'with a supplement stating the amount of the debt in 1795,' 1795. 2. 'Facts addressed to the serious attention of the People of Great Britain, respecting the Expense of the War and the State of the National Debt in 1796.' Four editions were published in 1796, London, 8vo. 3. Additional facts on the same subject, London, 8vo; four editions published in 1796. 4. 'An Appeal to the People of Great Britain on the Present Alarming State of the Public Finances and of Public Credit,' London, 8vo, 1797, four editions. 5. 'A Comparative View of the Public Finances from the Beginning to the Close of the Late Administration,' London, 1801, three editions. 6. 'A Supplement to the Comparative View,' 1803. He was the author of a scientific work entitled 'An Examination of Dr. Crawford's Theory of Heat and Combustion,' London, 1781, 8vo, and also edited the following: 'Observations on Reversionary Payments, by Richard Price, to which are added Algebraical Notes by W. M.;' 5th edit. 1792-80; 7th edit. 1812, and many subsequent editions. Morgan also edited the 'Works of Dr. Price, with Memoirs of his Life,' London, 1816, 8vo, and Dr. Price's Sermons, 1816.

[The fullest account of Morgan's actuarial work is to be found in Walford's Insurance Cyclopædia, ii. 596-622, iii. 1-23. For all other facts the best authority is A Welsh Family, from the Beginning of the Eighteenth Century (London, 1885, 8vo; 2nd edit. 1893), by Miss Caroline E. Williams, for private circulation. See also Gent. Mag. for 1833, pt. i. p. 569; Memoirs of Dr. Price, ut supra.] D. Ll. T.

MORGAN, Sir WILLIAM (1829-1883), South Australian statesman, son of an English farmer, was born in 1829 at Wilshampstead, near Bedford. In 1848 he emigrated with two brothers and a sister, and arrived in South Australia in February 1849. He took the first work that offered, but after a short experience of bush life became an assistant in the grocery store of Messrs. Boord Brothers. In 1851, at the time of the Victoria gold rush, he went with his brother Thomas to the Bendigo diggings, and, succeeding better than the majority, came back to Adelaide and rejoined the Boords, purchasing their business after a short time, and extending it till, under the title of Morgan & Co., it became one of the leading mercantile houses in the colony.

In August 1869 Morgan first entered political life, standing for election as member of the legislative council. In spite of the uncompromising independence of his views on the leases and other questions which were exciting popular attention, he was duly returned on 6 Aug. In the council his shrewdness and foresight rapidly brought him to the front. In 1871 he was chosen by the ministers to be one of the delegates of South Australia to the intercolonial conference, which opened at Melbourne on 18 Sept. On 3 June 1875 Mr. Boucaut was called on to form a ministry, and selected Morgan as chief secretary to represent the government in the legislative council. This was the government locally known as that 'of the broad and comprehensive policy.' Its schemes for the undertaking of new and large public works, and for the readjustment of taxation with a view to its fairer incidence on all classes, were the subject of fierce debate, and were rejected in two consecutive sessions by the council. In the midst of the fight (25 March 1876) Morgan had to retire from the ministry to attend to the extra pressure of business entailed by his purchase of a share in the Balade mines of New Caledonia. In February 1877, when his term in the council had expired, although his private affairs made him anxious to retire for a time from political life, he was returned to the legislative council at the head of the poll.

The new parliament met on 31 May 1877, and Morgan, after leading the attack on Sir Henry Ayers, the chief secretary in the Colton administration, was by a unanimous vote of the house required to assume the duties of its leader in the place of Ayers. The defeat of the Colton administration in the assembly also followed, and Boucaut formed a ministry in which Morgan was chief secretary (October 1877). In October 1878 Boucaut retired, and Morgan himself became premier, holding the office till June 1881, when he retired owing to pressure of private business. The chief measures which occupied his ministry related to taxation, the land laws, schemes for public works, and the settlement of the Northern Territory. In 1880 he attended the intercolonial conference at Melbourne. In May 1883 he left the colony on a short visit to England to recruit his health. On his arrival he was created K.C.M.G., but he died on 2 Nov. at Brighton. Both houses of parliament in South Australia adjourned on the receipt of the news. He was buried at his old home in Bedfordshire. He married in 1854 Harriett, daughter of T. H. Matthews of Coromandel, who, with five children, survived him.

Morgan's political career was stormy. He displayed much administrative capacity; was shrewd and honest, genial and loyal. He has been called the 'Cobden of South Australia.'

[South Australian Register, 10 Nov. 1883; South Australian Advertiser, 10 Nov. 1883.]

C. A. H.

MORGANENSIS (*fl.* 1210), epigrammatist. [See MAURICE.]

MORGANN, MAURICE (1726–1802), commentator on the character of Sir John Falstaff, born in London in 1726, was descended from an ancient Welsh family. He was under-secretary of state to William Fitzmaurice Petty, earl of Shelburne, and afterwards first marquis of Lansdowne [q. v.], during his administration of 1782, and was secretary to the embassy for ratifying the peace with America in 1783. He was also one of the commissioners of the hackney coach office. Morgann, a man of rare modesty and uncommon powers, was highly esteemed by Lord Lansdowne, at whose seat at Wickham he once entertained Dr. Johnson during his lordship's absence. He and Johnson sat up late talking, and the latter as usual provoked a verbal encounter, in which Morgann more than held his own. The next morning at breakfast Johnson greeted him with 'Sir, I have been thinking over our dispute last night —you were in the right.' Morgann wrote several pamphlets on the burning questions of his day, all of which are distinguished for their philosophic tone and distinctively literary style. They were issued anonymously, but the following have been identified as his: 'An Enquiry concerning the Nature and End of a National Militia' (London [1758], 8vo); 'A Letter to my Lords the Bishops, on Occasion of the Present Bill for the Preventing of Adultery' (London, 1779, 8vo); 'Remarks on the Present Internal and External Condition of France' (1794, 8vo); and 'Remarks on the Slave Trade.' He appears to have written solely for his own gratification, and on his death at Knightsbridge on 28 March 1802 he directed his executors to destroy all his papers. 'Thus,' says his friend Dr. Symmons, 'were lost various compositions in politics, metaphysics, and criticism which would have planted a permanent laurel on his grave' (*Life of Milton*, 1810, pp. 122–4).

The admirable 'Essay on the Dramatic Character of Sir John Falstaff' (London, 1777, 8vo) by which Morgann is remembered has been very generally praised. The vindication of Falstaff's courage is the ostensible object of the work, and evoked Johnson's criticism. 'Why, sir, we shall have the man come forth again; and as he proved Falstaff to be no coward, he may prove Iago to be a very good character,' but the special plea, entertaining as it is, is really subordinate to a consideration of the larger problem of the whole character and to 'the arts and genius of his poetic maker' (cf. *London Mag.* 1820, i. 194; *Fraser*, xlvi. 408; WHITE, *Falstaff's Letters*, admired of Charles Lamb, and the 'Essay on Falstaff' appended to Mr. Birrell's 'Obiter Dicta'). For style, intellectuality, knowledge of human nature, and consequent profound appreciation of Shakespeare, Morgann's essay has not been surpassed. The author was too fastidious to reissue his book during his lifetime; it was, however, republished in 1820 and 1825. William Cooke's poem 'Conversation' (1807) was dedicated to Morgann, and in a second edition Cooke testified in the most enthusiastic terms to his friend's wide knowledge, pervading humour, and personal charm.

[Gent. Mag. 1802 i. 470, 582, 1807 ii. 643; European Mag. xli. 334; Boswell's Johnson, ed. G. B. Hill, iv. 192; Lord Edmond Fitzmaurice's Life of Shelburne, ii. 50, iii. 16; Halkett and Laing's Anon. and Pseudon. Lit. cols. 487, 765, 804, 1386; Monthly Review, lx. 399; Lowndes's Bibl. Man. 1612–13; Mathias' Pursuits of Lit. 1801, p. 353.]

T. S.

MORGANWG, IOLO (1746–1826), Welsh bard. [See WILLIAMS, EDWARD.]

MORGANWG, LEWIS (*fl.* 1500–1540), poet. [See LEWIS.]

MORI, NICOLAS (1797–1839), violinist, was born in London on 24 Jan. 1797, according to the inscription on a portrait of him issued in 1805. He received his first instruction, on a miniature violin at the age of three, from the great Barthélemon in 1800, and at a concert for his benefit given at the King's Theatre on 14 March 1805 (see portrait above referred to), under the patronage of the Duke and Duchess of York and the Dukes of Sussex and Cambridge, he played

Barthélemon's difficult concerto known as 'The Emperor.' In 1808 he took part in the concerts promoted by Mr. Heaviside the musical surgeon, and became a pupil of Viotti, then in exile in London. He remained till 1814 under Viotti's tuition, and under his tutor's auspices took part in the first Philharmonic Society's concert in 1813. In 1814, while still in the Philharmonic orchestra, he acted as one of the society's directors, and also became a member of the opera band. In 1816 he was appointed leader of the Philharmonic orchestra.

In 1819 Mori married the widow of the music publisher Lavenu, whose business he carried on at 28 New Bond Street, in conjunction with his stepson, Henry Louis Lavenu. It was in this capacity that he published for a few years (in collaboration with W. Ball) the excellent annual 'The Musical Gem,' and later (in 1837), after a keen competition with Novello, he issued Mendelssohn's Concerto in D Minor. From 1819 to 1826 he was the teacher of Dando, afterwards the eminent violinist. In 1823, on the establishment of the (now Royal) Academy of Music, he was a member of the first board of professors, and thenceforward became one of the principal orchestral leaders of provincial festivals. Thus we find him in September and October 1824 leading the band at the Wakefield and Newcastle festivals, and in September 1825, in conjunction with Kieswetter and Loder, at the York festival. It was here that he had the bad taste to challenge comparison with Kieswetter, by playing Mayseder's Concerto No. 3 in D, which Kieswetter had chosen as his *pièce de résistance*. A contemporary critic says: 'The two artists are not comparable together. Mr. Mori excels in tone and vigour, Mr. Kieswetter in delicacy and feeling.' In 1826 he led the band at the Covent Garden oratorios, and in 1827 succeeded Venua as leader of the Covent Garden opera band. He then (in 1831) became a member of the orchestra of the 'Concerts of Antient Music' at the New Rooms, Hanover Square. From this time his public appearances were mainly restricted to his own concerts, which were generally held in May. At his concert in 1835 he cleared 800*l*., and a similar sum in 1836, in which year he instituted a series of chamber music concerts, in continuation of those conducted by Blagrove, whom he virtually challenged by playing the same compositions. He died on 18 June 1839 from the breaking of an aneurism, having been for some years the victim of a cerebral derangement which rendered him at times brusque, irritable, and violent. Immediately before his death he announced a concert whose programmes were headed by the grim device of a death's head and the legend *Memento Mori*.

As a performer 'Mori's attitude had the grace of manly confidence. His bow arm was bold, free, and commanding, and the tone he produced was eminently firm, full, and impressive. His execution was alike marked by abundant force and fire, by extraordinary precision and prodigious facility, but lacked niceties of finish and the graces and delicacies of expression' (*Quarterly Mag. Music*, iii. 323).

He left behind him a son, Francis Mori (1820–1873), the composer of a cantata, entitled 'Fridolin;' an operetta, with words by George Linley [q. v.], entitled 'The River Sprite,' which was performed at Covent Garden on 9 Feb. 1865; many songs, and a series of vocal exercises. He died at Chamant, near Senlis, in France, on 2 Aug. 1873.

Mori's sister was a celebrated contralto. She was singing in Paris in 1830, married the singer Gosselin, and virtually retired in 1836, although she reappeared in Siena, Vicenza, Mantua, Verona, &c., in 1844.

[An account of his life and death appeared in the Morning Post of 24 June 1839, which was followed by a pamphlet, written in signally bad taste, entitled Particulars of the Illness and Death of the late Mr. Mori the Violinist, by E. W. Duffin, Surgeon (London, 1839, pp. 20). The published biographies of Mori are fragmentary, and for the most part incorrect. Fétis's notice, where the Christian name appears as Francis, is notably so. The best account is in Dubourg's work on the violin (edit. 1878, pp. 214–17). In the Musical World (ii. 144) occurs a charming sonnet upon him, signed 'William J. Thoms,' which is cleverly parodied at p. 207 by another signed 'Thomas J. Bhills.' A notice in the Quarterly Magazine of Music, 1821, iii. 323, was transferred almost bodily to the Biog. Dict. of Musicians, 1827, 2nd edit. ii. 179, and is paraphrased in Musical Recollections of the Last Half Century, London, 1872, i. 108. See also A. Pougin's Viotti, Paris, 1888; G. Dubourg's The Violin, London, 1878; unpublished documents in possession of the writer.] E. H.-A.

MORIARTY, DAVID (1814–1877), bishop of Kerry, son of David Moriarty, esq., by his wife, Bridget Stokes, was born at Derryvrin, in the parish of Kilcarah, co. Kerry, on 18 Aug. 1814. He was educated at home by private tutors, at Boulogne-sur-Mer in the Institution Haffreingue, and at the Royal College of St. Patrick, Maynooth (1831–9). He was appointed vice-rector of, and professor of sacred scripture in, the Irish college at Paris in 1839; and became rector of the Foreign Missionary College of All-hallows, Drumcondra, Dublin, in 1845. He was nominated coadjutor bishop of Kerry in 1854, and succeeded to the see on 22 July 1856. Many pastoral letters and sermons published by him attracted the attention of the public. He uniformly discountenanced all treasonable movements in Ireland, vigorously denounced the Fenian brotherhood, and subsequently opposed the home rule party. At the Vatican council he spoke and voted against the opportuneness of defining the papal infallibility, but he accepted the definition in all its fulness when it had been decreed. He died on 1 Oct. 1877.

[Brady's Episcopal Succession, ii. 63, 375; Men of the Time, 1875, p. 739; Tablet, 6 Oct. 1877, pp. 419, 437.] T. C.

MORICE. [See also Morris.]

MORICE, HUMPHRY (1671?–1731), governor of the Bank of England, born about 1671, was son of Humphry Morice (1640?–1696) [see under Morice, Sir William]. As a Turkey merchant, he carried on an extensive business with the East. At the general election of September 1713 he was returned to parliament for the borough of Newport, Cornwall, which was in the patronage of his first cousin, Sir Nicholas Morice, bart., of Werrington, Devonshire, his colleague in the representation. In the House of Commons he steadily supported the policy of Walpole, voting in 1714 against the expulsion of Steele for his published attacks upon the Harley-Bolingbroke ministry; in 1716, in support of the Septennial Bill; and in 1719, against a measure to restrict the creation of peers. Sir Nicholas Morice, in such of these divisions as he voted, sided with the tories; and, therefore, at the dissolution of March 1722, Humphry had to leave Newport for Grampound, another Cornish borough, where he was chosen as colleague of William Cavendish, marquis of Hartington, afterwards third Duke of Devonshire [q. v.] For Grampound he sat till his death, supporting Walpole to the last. Having in 1716 been chosen a director of the Bank of England, he occupied the post of deputy-governor for the years 1725-6, and of governor for 1727-8; but within a very few days after his death, on 16 Nov. 1731, it was discovered by his co-directors, with whom he had had financial relations up to a day or two before, that his apparent wealth was fictitious, and even based upon fraudulent pretences. The bank had discounted for him a great number of notes and bills of exchange, Morice having been 'for many Years before, and until his Death, reputed to be a Person of great Wealth, and of undoubted Fairness and Integrity in his Dealings. But shortly after his decease they 'found, to their great Surprize, that several of the Bills of Exchange, which, on the Face thereof appear'd to be foreign Bills, and drawn at different Places beyond the Seas, were not real but fictitious Bills, and feigned Names set thereto, by the Order of the said Humphry Morice, to gain Credit with the Appellants.' His widow, indeed, whom he had left sole executrix, admitted in an affidavit that, upon his death, 'his Affairs were found very much involved with Debts, and in the greatest Disorder and Confusion, insomuch that she had not been able to settle, and reduce the same to any Certainty as to [his] Debts, and the several Natures and Kinds thereof.' But the worst feature of the transaction was not in the debts due to tradesmen for work done or 'for Gold and Elephants' Teeth,' or even the alleged frauds upon the Bank of England; it was the absorption of moneys left in trust for his motherless daughters by a maternal uncle, as well as other trust-moneys, by which the children were the heaviest losers. The result was a complicated series of lawsuits, which extended over five years, and ended, upon appeal in the House of Lords, in the virtual defeat of his widow, who had struggled hard to secure something from the wreck for her stepdaughters and the other children involved. Among the portraits at Hartwell, Buckinghamshire, formerly the seat of Sir Thomas Lee, bart., M.P. for Aylesbury (who married a sister of Morice's first wife, and whose son, Sir George Lee [q. v.], married one of Morice's daughters), was one by Sir Godfrey Kneller of Morice, who is described as having appeared therein as 'an intelligent-looking middle-aged gentleman.' He married, as his first wife, Judith, daughter of Thomas Sandys or Sandes, a London merchant, by whom he had five daughters, two of whom died young; and his second wife, to whom he was married in June 1722, was Catherine, daughter of Peter Paggen of Wandsworth, and widow of William Hale of Hertfordshire, by whom he had two sons, Humphry (see below) and Nicholas (*d.* November 1748). This lady died on 30 August 1743, and was buried in the Paggen family vault at Mount Nod, the burial-ground of the Huguenots at Wandsworth.

Morice, Humphry (1723–1785), politician, born in 1723, elder son of the preceding, succeeded upon the death of his second cousin, Sir William Morice, third baronet, in January 1750, to the entailed estate of Werrington, and to the representation of Launceston in parliament. At the dissolution in April 1754 he put forward his full electoral powers over the parliamentary representation both of

Launceston and Newport, pocket boroughs of the owners of Werrington, and secured the election, as his colleague for Launceston, of Sir George Lee [q. v.], the husband of his step-sister Judith. He secured for Newport, after a contest with the Duke of Bedford's nominees, the return of Sir George's brother, Colonel John Lee, and Edward Bacon, a connection of the Walpoles. Morice at once sought a reward for his electoral successes from his leader, the Duke of Newcastle, and asked, among other things, for a place on the board of green cloth (June 1755). For the moment it was withheld; but Newcastle—who, on 23 Oct. 1755, wrote to Morice desiring to see him in order to explain, before parliament met, 'the measures which have been taken for the support of the Rights and Possessions of His Majesty's crown in North America'—was reminded of the green cloth promise in the later days of April 1757, when he was trying to form a ministry without Pitt. On 5 May Morice kissed hands on his appointment as one of the clerks-comptrollers of the household of George II; and a fortnight later he was re-elected for Launceston without opposition. In the winter of 1758, on Sir George Lee's death, Morice declared himself unable to secure the return for Launceston, as Newcastle requested, of Dr. (afterwards Sir Edward) Simpson, Lee's successor as Dean of the Arches. He himself put forward John, second earl Tylney, an Irish peer, in order that he might arrange an accommodation with the Duke of Bedford, with whom Tylney was connected; but Tylney was withdrawn owing to the local unpopularity of the Duke of Bedford, and Morice chose Peter Burrell of Haslemere to represent the constituency. Sir John St. Aubyn, a nephew of Sir William Morice, who had sat for the borough in the previous parliament, was, however, declared by the mayor to be returned by a majority of a single vote—fifteen to fourteen. But a petition was immediately presented to the House of Commons, and, owing to Morice's influence with the administration, Burrell was declared duly elected.

Later in 1759 Morice received threatening letters in an endeavour to extort money under peril of being accused of a serious offence. He at once faced the accusers, two of whom were sentenced to be imprisoned for three years in Newgate, and to stand in the pillory in Cheapside and Fleet Street; another accuser fled and the fourth turned informer. The sympathy of the populace was entirely with Morice, but it is evident from his various communications at that time to Newcastle that his health suffered from the consequent worry. In the spring of 1760 he went abroad, and Horace Walpole, with whom Morice had many tastes in common, recommended to the attention of Sir Horace Mann 'Mr. Morrice, Clerk of the Green Cloth, heir of Sir William Morrice, and of vast wealth,' who 'will ere long be at Florence, in his way to Naples for his health.'

Morice was still abroad when, in October 1760, George II died; and, despite the urgent appeal of some friends, his household appointment was not renewed. The Duke of Newcastle was in vain reminded that Morice had spent 20,000*l.* in support of the administration which had 'turn'd him adrift on the first occasion that offer'd.' Morice took the humiliation quietly; and when his protégé, Colonel Lee, M.P. for Newport, was dying, in September 1761, he sent from Naples an offer to place the coming vacancy at the disposal of the government. William de Grey, solicitor-general to the queen, afterwards first Baron Walsingham, was accordingly returned. His accommodating disposition was recognised by Bute, who at once appointed Morice comptroller of the household. He was re-elected for Launceston on 3 Jan. 1763, and seven days later was sworn of the privy council.

Although Bute gave place to George Grenville in the first week of the ensuing April, Morice's tenure of the comptrollership was continued; and he was also appointed lord warden of the stannaries, high steward of the duchy of Cornwall, and rider and master of the forest of Dartmoor. The question was at once raised in the commons, at Morice's own suggestion, whether, by accepting these latter appointments, he vacated his seat; but a motion that the seat was vacant was negatived without a division (19 April 1763), although, owing to his own scruples, his appointment was not formally made out till 28 June. With the fall of the Grenville ministry, in July 1765, Morice's ministerial career approached its end. On 4 Feb. 1771 he was chosen recorder of Launceston, and was sworn on the following 9 Dec. In October 1774, at the general election, there was a struggle against his influence; although he himself was returned for both Launceston and Newport, his power in the former borough was shown to be waning, and in the next year he sold Werrington, and with it the electoral patronage, to Hugh, first duke of Northumberland of the present creation—'a noble purchase,' as was said at the time, 'near 100,000*l.*' In 1780 Morice retired from parliament; in 1782 he resigned the recordership; and on 20 Nov. 1783 the coalition ministry of North and Fox ousted him from the lord wardenship of the stannaries, whereupon Sir Francis Basset, M.P. for Penryn (subsequently Lord de Dunstanville), who was related to Morice by marriage, wrote an indignant letter of protest to the Duke of Portland, the nominal prime minister, declaring it impossible for him to support the administration any longer.

Morice in his last years was a confirmed valetudinarian, visiting various health resorts. He was lying ill in 1782 at Bath, when he was cheered, according to Walpole, by the bequest of an estate for life of 1,500*l.* a year from 'old Lady Brown,' the widow of Sir Robert Brown, who had been a merchant at Venice. On 24 July 1782, just before leaving England for the last time, and while at his favourite residence, The Grove, Chiswick, he made his will. Three months later, when arrived at Nice, he executed a codicil giving to his trustees 600*l.* yearly from the estates he still possessed in Devonshire and Cornwall, 'to pay for the maintenance of the horses and dogs I leave behind me, and for the expense of servants to look after them,' such portion as was not required as the animals died off to be paid to the lady—Mrs. Levina Luther—whom he had made his heiress. He was always a lover of animals. According to George Colman the younger, 'all the stray animals which happened to follow him in London he sent down to this villa [The Grove, Chiswick]. . . . The honours shown by Mr. Morrice to his beasts of burthen were only inferior to those which Caligula lavished on his charger.' A year later Horace Walpole wrote of Morice to Lady Ossory that, whether he was better in health or worse, he was always in good spirits. But he was steadily preparing for death. A second codicil, executed at Naples on 14 March 1784, was characteristic. 'I desire,' he wrote, 'to be buried at Naples if I die there, and in a leaden coffin, if such a thing is to be had. Just before it is soldered I request the surgeon in Lord Tylney's house, or some other surgeon, to take out my heart, or to perform some other operation, to ascertain my being really dead.' He died at Naples on 18 Oct. 1785. A portrait at Hartwell shows him 'in an easy, reclining attitude, resting from field sports, with his dogs and gun, in a fine landscape scene.'

[For the father: Cases in Parliament, Wills, &c., 1684–1737 (in British Museum), ff. 106–12; Lords' Journals, xxv. 26–129–30; W. H. Smyth's Ædes Hartwellianæ, p. 114; Western Antiquary, xi. 6; A. F. Robbins's Launceston Past and Present, pp. 244–8–51; J. T. Squire's Mount Nod, p. 44. For the son see British Museum Addit. MSS. (Newcastle Correspondence) 32856 ff. 17, 459, 32860 ff. 142, 199, 32870 f. 457, 32871 f. 23, 32876 f. 108, 32879 f. 348, 32886 ff. 397, 505, 539, 32887 ff. 99, 197, 408, 32905 f. 250, 32907 f. 70, 32914 f. 37, 32920 ff. 57, 62, 308, 315, 362, 32930 ff. 70, 72, 32935 f. 133, 33067 f. 161: 21553 f. 55; Annual Register, 1759, pp. 99-100; European Mag. viii. 395*; Gent. Mag. vol. lv. pt. ii. p. 919; The Pocket Mag. xiii. 171; Calendar of Home Office Papers, 1760–5, pp. 285, 288, 289, 360; Domestic State Papers, George III, parcel 79, Nos. 37, 39, 45; Commons' Journals, xxix. 646; Ockerby's Book of Dignities, pp. 201, 292; Boase and Courtney's Bibl. Cornubiensis, pp. 1052, 1362; W. H. Smyth's Ædes Hartwellianæ, p. 114, and Addenda, p. 137; George Colman's Random Records, i. 280; Thomas Faulkner's History and Antiquities of Brentford, Ealing, and Chiswick, pp. 484–5; Horace Walpole's Letters, vol. i. p. lxx, iii. 302, iv. 1, 50, vi. 359, 461, 510, vii. 214, 421, 440, 448, 449, 458, 475, viii. 52, 66, 75, 94, 167, 266, 285, 286, 297, 310, 386, 388, 407, 526; D. Lysons's Magna Britannia, vol. vi. pp. cxxvii, 114, 323, 552; R. and O. B. Peter's Histories of Launceston and Dunheved, p. 406; A. F. Robbins's Launceston Past and Present, pp. 259, 260, 261, 262, 265, 268, 270, 271, 276; Notes and Queries, 2nd ser. ix. 486; Western Antiquary, viii. 20, 53, 75, 146, ix. 61, 85, 111, xi. 6–9; J. T. Squire's Mount Nod, pp. 44, 45; W. P. Courtney's Parliamentary History of Cornwall, pp. 370, 384.] A. F. R.

MORICE, RALPH (*fl.* 1523–1570), secretary to Archbishop Cranmer, born about 1500, was presumably younger son of James Morice, clerk of the kitchen and master of the works to Margaret, countess of Richmond. His father, who was living in 1537, amassed a considerable estate and lived at Chipping Ongar, Essex. His principal duty consisted in supervising the buildings of the countess at Cambridge (Willis and Clark, *Arch. Hist. of the Univ. of Cambridge*, ii. 192, &c.) The eldest son, William Morice (*fl.* 1547), was gentleman-usher, first to Richard Pace [q. v.], and afterwards to Henry VIII, and towards the end of Henry's reign was in gaol and in peril of his life from a charge of heresy, through the envy which his estate excited in some of the courtiers. John Southe saw him when kept in Southwell's house near the Charterhouse. He had added to the family estates by judicious investments in confiscated lands (cf. *Trevelyan Papers*, Camd. Soc., ii. 4). On his release from prison at Henry's death, and his election as member of parliament, he procured an act to be passed uniting the parishes of Ongar and Greenstead, he being the patron. This was repealed by an act of 1 Mary, Morice's labour being declared to be 'sinister,' and he to have been 'inordinately seeking his private lucre and profitt.' He died some time in Edward VI's reign.

Ralph Morice was educated at Cambridge; he graduated B.A. in 1523, and commenced M.A. in 1526. He became secretary to Cranmer in 1528 before his elevation to the archbishopric, and continued in the office until after Edward VI's death. In 1532 he went with Latimer, his brother, and others to see James Bainham [q. v.] in Newgate before his execution. On 18 June 1537 he and his father received a grant of the office of bailiff for some crown lands, and in 1547 he was made registrar to the commissioners appointed to visit the dioceses of Rochester, Canterbury, Chichester, and Winchester. His duties while secretary to the archbishop were severe. In a memorial printed in the Appendix to Strype's 'Cranmer,' and addressed to Queen Elizabeth, he speaks of writing much in defence of the ecclesiastical changes, and as he mentions that he 'most painfullie was occupied in writing of no small volumes from tyme to tyme' much of his work must have been anonymous. He had the farm of the parsonage of Chartham in Kent—that is to say he put in a curate, keeping the rest of the revenues. The curate, one Richard Turner, got into trouble for protestant preaching in 1544, but Morice managed to clear him. Under Mary, Morice was in some danger. His house was twice searched, and he lost many of his papers and had to fly. He was imprisoned, but escaped. The close of his life he passed at Bekesborne in Kent (HASTED, *Kent*, iii. 715). There he fell into poverty, and stated in one of his petitions to Queen Elizabeth that he had four daughters whom he wanted means to marry. Three of these, however, Margaret, Mary, and Anne, were married in January and February 1570–1. Alyce Morice, who was buried 25 Feb. 1561–2, may have been his wife. The date of his own death is uncertain.

Morice, from his official position, was in possession of much information, and helped Foxe and others in their literary researches, chiefly by supplying them with his 'Anecdotes of Cranmer.' This compilation was used by Strype in his 'Memorials of Cranmer,' and was reprinted from the manuscript at Corpus Christi College, Cambridge, in 'Narratives of the Reformation' (Camd. Soc.) Morice gave other assistance to Foxe, and wrote an account of Latimer's conversion, which is printed in Strype's 'Memorials' and in Latimer's 'Works.' The original is in Harl. MS. 422, art. 12. Art. 26 in the same manuscript, an account of the visit to Bainham, appears in Strype, Latimer's 'Works,' and in Foxe. Harl. MS. 6148 consists of copies of letters written by Morice on the archbishop's business. Transcripts by Strype of some of these form Lansdowne MS. 1045. They have been published by Jenkyns and Cox in their editions of Cranmer's 'Works.'

[Cooper's Athenæ Cantabr. i. 294; Narratives of the Reformation, ed. Nichols (Camd. Soc.), passim; Letters and Papers Henry VIII; Dixon's Hist. of Church of Engl. ii. 347; Cranmer's Remains, ed. Jenkyns, vol. i. p. cxviii; Todd's Life of Cranmer.] W. A. J. A.

MORICE, SIR WILLIAM (1602–1676), secretary of state and theologian, born in St. Martin's parish, Exeter, 6 Nov. 1602, was the elder son of Dr. Evan Morice of Carnarvonshire, who was chancellor of Exeter diocese in 1594, and died in 1605. His mother was Mary, daughter of John Castle of Scobchester in Ashbury, Devonshire; she became in 1611 the third wife of Sir Nicholas Prideaux of Solden, Devonshire, and died on 2 Oct. 1647. His younger brother, Laurence, died young, and the whole property came into the possession of the elder boy. William was educated 'in grammar learning' at Exeter, and entered at Exeter College, Oxford, as a fellow-commoner about 1619, when he was placed under the care of the Rev. Nathanael Carpenter [q. v.] and was patronised by Dr. Prideaux, its rector, who prophesied his rise in life. He graduated B.A. on 27 June 1622, and gave his college a silver bowl weighing seventeen and three-quarter ounces. For some years his life was spent in his native county, first at West Putford and afterwards at Werrington, which he bought of Sir Francis Drake in 1651. He also made considerable purchases of landed property near Plymouth, including the manor of Stoke Damerel. In 1640 he was made a county justice, and in 1651 he was appointed high sheriff of Devonshire. On 15 Aug. 1648 Morice was returned to parliament for Devonshire, but never sat, and was excluded in 'Pride's Purge.' On 12 July 1654 he was re-elected, and he was again returned in 1656, but was not allowed to sit, as he had not received the approval of the Protector's council, whereupon he and many others in a similar position published a remonstrance (WHITELOCKE, *Memorials*, pp. 651–3, 698). The borough of Newport in Cornwall, where he enjoyed great interest, chose him in 1658 and again in April 1660, when he preferred to sit for Plymouth, for which he had been returned 'by the freemen,' and he continued to represent that seaport until his death.

Morice was related, through his wife, to General Monck, whose property in Devonshire was placed under his care. The general possessed 'a great opinion of his prudence and integrity,' and imposed implicit reliance in his assurance that the residents in the west of England desired the king's return. When he followed Monck to London in 1659 and became an inmate at Monck's house as 'his elbow-counsellor and a state-blind,' they were greatly pleased. It was the duty of Morice 'to keep the expiring session of parliament steady and clear from intermeddling,' a task which he executed with great judgment. He received, through Sir John Grenville, a letter from Charles, urging him to bring Monck over to the restoration, which he answered with warmth, and he arranged the meeting of Grenville and Monck, guarding the door of the chamber while they were settling the terms for the king's return. In February 1659–60 Charles bestowed on him, with the general's approbation, 'the seal and signet, as the badge of the secretary of state's office,' and in the next month he was created by Monck colonel of a regiment of foot, and made governor with his son of the fort and island of Plymouth. Morice was knighted by Charles on his landing, and at Canterbury, during the king's journey to London, was confirmed in the post of secretary and sworn a privy councillor (26 May 1660). Many favours were bestowed upon him. He and his son William received the offices of keeper of the port of Plymouth, with certain ports in Cornwall and of Avenor of the duchy, and on their surrendering the patent for the governorship of Plymouth, a pension of 200*l.* a year was settled on the son, who was made a baronet on 20 April 1661. The father obtained an extended grant of land in Old Spring Gardens, London, and a charter for two fairs yearly at Broad Clist, Devonshire. With the old court party his tenure of the secretaryship was not popular. They complained of his lack of familiarity with foreign languages and of his ignorance of external affairs. His friends endeavoured in 1666 to make out that he was principal secretary of state, above Lord Arlington, but failed in their attempt, and at Michaelmas 1668 Morice found his position so intolerable that he resigned his office and retired to his property, where he spent the rest of his days in collecting a fine library and in studying literature. A letter about him, expressing his deep disgust against Charles II for not keeping his promises and for debauching the nation, is in 'Notes and Queries' (1st ser. ix. 7–8). Morice died at Werrington on 12 Dec. 1676, and was buried in the family aisle of its church. His wife was Elizabeth, younger daughter of Humphry Prideaux (eldest son of Sir Nicholas Prideaux), by his wife, Honour, daughter of Edmund Fortescue of Fallapit, Devonshire. She predeceased him in December 1663, having borne four sons (William, John, Humphry [see below], and Nicholas) and four daughters. Morice founded an almshouse in Sutcombe, near Holsworthy, Devonshire, for six poor people, and endowed it with lands.

There is a portrait of him in Houbraken and Birch's 'Heads' (1747, ii. 35–6); another hangs in Exeter College Hall (Boase, *Exeter Coll.* 1893).

Morice's learning was undoubted. When young he wrote poetry, and Prince had seen some of his verses that were 'full of life and briskness.' But his chief preoccupation was theology, and he continued through life a scrupulous censor of orthodox divinity. On a visit to Oxford in November 1665 he and some others complained of a sermon at St. Mary's with such effect that the preacher was forced to recant, and when William Oliver was ejected in 1662 from the church of St. Mary Magdalene, Launceston, he received from Morice 'a yearly pension for the support of his family.' The independent party in religion made it a rule in parochial cures to admit to the communion none but those who were 'most peculiarly their own flock,' and in Morice's district the sacrament was administered in the church of Pyworthy only. His views on this point, composed in two days, were set before the ministers, and about two years later their official answer came to him. He then composed a ponderous treatise in refutation of their arguments which he issued in 1657, with the title of 'Cœna, quasi Κοινὴ. The new Inclosures broken down and the Lord's Supper laid forth in common for all Church-members.' A second edition, 'corrected and much enlarged,' was published in 1660, with a dedication to General Monck. Many theologians took part in this controversy, and among them John Beverley of Rothwell, John Humfrey, Humphrey Saunders of Holsworthy, Anthony Palmer of Bourton-on-the-Water, Roger Drake, M.D., and John Timson, 'a private Christian of Great Bowden in Leicestershire.' From the heading of an article (v. 215) of the 'Weekly Pacquet of Advice from Rome,' it would seem that Morice printed a letter to Peter du Moulin [q. v.] on the share of the jesuits in causing the civil war in England, and two political pamphlets (1) 'A Letter to General Monck in answer to his directed to Mr. Rolle for the Gentlemen of Devon. By one of the excluded Members of Parliament. Signed R. M., 1659;' and (2) 'Animadversions upon General Monck's Letter to the Gentry of Devon. By M. W., 1659,' are sometimes attributed to him (Halkett and Laing, *Dict. of Anon. Literature*, i. 98, ii. 1380). John Owen dedicated to him the first volume

(1668) of 'Exercitations on the Epistle to the Hebrews,' and Malachy Thruston, M.D., did him a like honour in his thesis 'De Respirationis Usu Primario' (1670). A letter to Morice from Sir Bevil Grenville (who made him his trustee), written at Newcastle, 15 May 1639, is in the 'Thurloe State Papers' (i. 2-3).

The third son, HUMPHRY MORICE (1640?–1696), was in March 1663 granted the reversion of one of the seven auditorships of the exchequer, and ultimately succeeded to the position. His youngest brother, Nicholas, sat in parliament for Newport, Cornwall, from 1667 to 1679, and one of the two went to the Hague early in 1667 as secretary to Lord Holles and Henry Coventry, the commissioners engaged in an abortive endeavour to arrange a treaty with the Dutch. Of the appointment Pepys wrote: 'That which troubles me most is that we have chosen a son of Secretary Morris, a boy never used to any business, to go secretary to the embassy.' Humphrey married on 8 Jan. 1670 Alice, daughter of Lady Mary Trollope of Stamford, Lincolnshire. In his later years he engaged in mercantile pursuits, chiefly with Hamburg. He died in the winter of 1696, and on 29 Dec., as 'Mag^r. Humphrey Morice,' was buried at Werrington, Devonshire, the family seat, then occupied by his nephew, Sir Nicholas Morice, bart. His son Humphry is separately noticed.

[For the father: Wood's Athenæ, ed. Bliss, iii. 1087–90; Boase's Exeter Coll. p. lix; Foster's Alumni Oxon.; Vivian's Devon Visitation, p. 621; Worth's Plymouth, pp. 163, 168, 191, 421; Robbins's Launceston, pp. 208–9, 214; Worthington's Diary (Chetham Soc.), vol. ii. pt. i. p. 152; Wood's Life (Oxf. Hist. Soc.), ii. 66; Price's King's Restoration, passim; London Christian Instructor, vii. 1–4, 57–60 (1824); State Papers, 1659–67; Lysons's Devonshire, pt. ii. pp. 74, 466, 552. An elaborate monument to the families of Morice and Prideaux is printed in W. H. H. Rogers's Sepulchral Effigies of Devon, pp. 292–3. Several extracts, by the Rev. Edward King, from Werrington parish registers relating to his descendants are printed in the Genealogist, iv. 61–3. For the son: information from A. F. Robbins, esq.; Collins's English Baronetage, vol. iii. pt. i. p. 269; Pepys's Diary, iii. 65; Calendar of Domestic State Papers, 1663–4, pp. 94, 538, 1666–7, pp. 523, 601; Calendar of Treasury Papers, 1702–7, p. 121; Brit. Mus. Add. MSS. 28052, f. 72; Chester's London Marriage Licences, 1521–1869, p. 944; Western Antiquary, viii. 53, xi. 6.] W. P. C.

MORIER, DAVID (1705?–1770), painter, was born at Berne in Switzerland about 1705. He came to England in 1743, and obtained the patronage of William, duke of Cumberland, who gave him a pension of 200*l.* a year. Morier excelled in painting animals, especially horses, and executed several battle pieces and equestrian portraits. Among the latter were portraits of George II, George III (engraved by François Simon Ravenet [q. v.]), and the Duke of Cumberland (engraved by Lempereur). Portraits by Morier of the Duke of Cumberland and John Pixley, the Ipswich smuggler, were engraved in mezzotint by John Faber, jun. Morier exhibited at the first exhibition of the Society of Artists in 1760, and again in 1762, 1765, and 1768, sending equestrian portraits, and in the last year 'An Old Horse and the Farmer.' He fell into pecuniary difficulties, and was in 1769 confined in the Fleet prison, where he died in January 1770. He was buried on 8 Jan. in the burial-ground at St. James's Church, Clerkenwell, London, at the expense of the Society of Artists.

[Redgrave's Dict. of Artists; Chaloner Smith's British Mezzotinto Portraits; Catalogues of the Soc. of Artists.] L. C.

MORIER, DAVID RICHARD (1784–1877), diplomatist, was the third son of Isaac Morier [q. v.], consul-general to the Turkey Company at Constantinople, and was born at Smyrna 8 Jan. 1784. He was educated at Harrow, and entered the diplomatic service. In January 1804, at the age of twenty, he was appointed secretary to the political mission sent by the British government to 'Alî Pasha of Janina and to the Turkish governors of the Morea and other provinces, with a view to counteracting the influence of France in south-east Europe. In May 1807 he was ordered to take entire charge of the mission, but as the continued rupture of diplomatic relations between England and the Porte defeated his negotiations with the Turkish governors, he was presently transferred to Sir Arthur Paget's mission at the Dardanelles, the object of which was to re-establish peace. While attached to this mission he was despatched on special service to Egypt, where he was instructed to negotiate for the release of the British prisoners captured by Mohammed 'Alî during General Fraser's fruitless expedition against Rosetta in 1807. In the summer of 1808 he was attached to Mr. (afterwards Sir) Robert Adair's embassy, and in conjunction with Stratford Canning [q. v.], afterwards Viscount Stratford de Redcliffe, assisted in the negotiations which resulted in the treaty of the Dardanelles of 5 Jan. 1809. He proceeded with Adair and Canning to Constantinople, where, with the exception of a mission on special service to Tabrîz (where the British legation in Persia was then established) from October 1809 to the following summer, he remained engaged in the business of the embassy, first under Adair, and then (1810–12) as secretary of legation under his successor, Stratford Canning. (Some letters written during the period of his employment at Tabrîz are published in Lane-Poole's 'Life of Stratford Canning.') On the termination of Canning's appointment, Morier accompanied him (July 1812) on his return to England. In 1813 he was attached to Lord Aberdeen's mission to Vienna, and during the years 1813–1815 was continually employed in the most important diplomatic transactions of the century—the negotiations which accompanied the 'settlement of Europe' after the fall of Napoleon. He was with Lord Castlereagh at the conferences at Châtillon-sur-Seine, and assisted in the preparation of the treaties of Paris of May 1814. In the same year he attended the foreign minister at the famous congress of Vienna, and, when the Duke of Wellington succeeded Castlereagh in his difficult mission, Morier remained as one of the secretaries. In July 1815, after the final overthrow of Napoleon, Morier accompanied Castlereagh to Paris, and was occupied till September in drafting the celebrated treaties of 1815. He had been appointed consul-general for France in November 1814, but he did not take over the post until September of the following year, when the work upon the treaties was completed; and in the meanwhile he had married. At the same time he was named a commissioner for the settlement of the claims of British subjects upon the French government. The consul-generalship was abolished, and Morier retired on a pension 5 April 1832, but was almost immediately (5 June) appointed minister plenipotentiary to the Swiss Confederated States, a post which had previously been held by his old chief and lifelong friend, Stratford Canning. The fifteen years of his residence at Berne endeared him to British travellers and all who came under his genial and sympathetic influence. On 19 June 1847, at the age of sixty-three, he finally retired from the diplomatic service, and spent the remaining thirty years of his life in retirement.

Morier was a man of warm sympathies and transparent simplicity and honesty of character, and his varied experience of life and mankind never succeeded in chilling his heart or in clouding his gracious benignity. He was a staunch friend, and his affection for Lord Stratford de Redcliffe, for example, lasted unchanged for seventy years. His deep sense of religion led him to publish two pamphlets, entitled 'What has Religion to do with Politics?' (London, 1848), and 'The Basis of Morality' (London, 1869). At the age of seventy-three he published his one novel, 'Photo, the Suliote, a Tale of Modern Greece,' London, 1857, in which 'imperfect sketch' or 'fragment,' as he calls it, a vivid picture of Greek and Albanian life in the first quarter of the century is presented, with something of the graphic power of his more literary brother, the author of 'Hajji Baba.' The materials for the story, beyond his personal recollections, were supplied by a Greek physician with whom Morier was compelled to spend a period of quarantine at Corfu. He died in London 13 July 1877 at the age of ninety-three, but in full possession of his natural vivacity, a model, as Dean Stanley said, of the 'piety and virtue of the antique mould.' His only son, and last male representative of the family, Sir Robert Burnett David Morier, is noticed separately.

[Foreign Office List, 1877; Times (Dean Stanley), 16 July 1877; Lane-Poole's Life of Stratford Canning, Viscount Stratford de Redcliffe; private information.] S. L.-P.

MORIER, ISAAC (1750–1817), consul-general of the Levant Company at Constantinople, belonged to a Huguenot family, which on the revocation of the edict of Nantes migrated to Château d'Oex, in the valley of the Sarine, east of Montreux in Switzerland, where the name is still preserved. Some of the Moriers engaged in commerce at Smyrna, where Isaac was born 12 Aug. 1750, and where he married, in 1775, Clara van Lennep, daughter of the Dutch consul-general and president of the Dutch Levant Company. One of her sisters was married to Admiral Waldegrave, afterwards first Baron Radstock [q. v.], and another to the Marquis de Chabannes de la Palice, whose sons became as distinguished in France as their Morier cousins in England. The three sisters were all celebrated for their beauty, and Romney painted portraits of each of them. Isaac Morier was naturalised in England, but, losing his fortune in 1803, was obliged to seek employment in the East, and in 1804 was appointed the first consul-general of the Levant Company at Constantinople, a post which, on the dissolution of the company in 1806, was converted into that of his Britannic majesty's consul. To this Isaac Morier joined the functions of agent to the East India Company, and held these appointments till his death, of the plague, at Constantinople, in 1817. Four of his sons—David Richard, James Justinian, John Philip, and William—are noticed separately.

[Private information.] S. L.-P.

MORIER, JAMES JUSTINIAN (1780?–1849), diplomatist, traveller, and novelist, was the second son of Isaac Morier [q. v.], consul-general of the Levant Company at Constantinople, and was born at Smyrna, about 1780. Educated at Harrow, he joined his father at Constantinople some time before 1807 (Preface to *Hajji Baba*), and entered the diplomatic service in that year, being attached to Sir Harford Jones's mission to the court of Persia in the capacity of private secretary. The mission sailed from Portsmouth in H.M.S. Sapphire 27 Oct. 1807, and reached Bombay in April 1808. Here, after waiting some months, the envoy received (6 Sept.) his orders to proceed to Tehrân, and Morier was promoted to the post of secretary of legation (Morier, *Journey through Persia, Armenia, and Asia Minor to Constantinople in the Years* 1808 *and* 1809, London, 1812, p. 1). The mission arrived at Tehrân in February 1809, but after three months Morier was sent home (7 May), probably with despatches, and made his well-known journey by way of Turkey in Asia, arriving at Plymouth in H.M.S. Formidable 25 Nov. 1809. At Constantinople, on his way home, he was among his own family, for his father was British consul there, and his younger brother David was a secretary in the British embassy, while his elder brother John was at the same time consul-general in Albania. The record of his journey, published in 1812, during his second absence in Persia, at once took rank as an important authority on a country then little known to Englishmen, and by its admirable style and accurate observation, its humour and graphic power, still holds a foremost place among early books of travel in Persia. It was at once translated into French (1813), and soon after into German (1815). Morier had returned but a few months when he was appointed secretary of embassy to Sir Gore Ouseley, ambassador extraordinary to the court of Tehrân, and sailed with the ambassador and his brother, Sir William Ouseley, from Spithead 18 July 1810, on board the old Lion, the same ship which had carried Lord Macartney's mission to China eighteen years before (Morier, *A Second Journey through Persia*, pp. 2, 3). The embassy proceeded to Tabrîz, where the prince royal of Persia had his government, and opened negotiations with a view to obtaining the support of Persia against the then subsisting Russo-French alliance. The work of the embassy, and the share taken by Morier in the treaty concluded in May 1812, are described in 'A Second Journey through Persia,' London, 1818. On Sir Gore Ouseley's return to England, in 1814, Morier was left in charge of the embassy at Tehrân (see his despatch to foreign office, 25 June 1814). He did not long remain in command, however, for his letter of recall was sent out on 12 July 1815, and he left Tehrân 6 Oct. following. As in his former journey he went by Tabrîz and Asia Minor, reaching Constantinople 17 Dec. 1816. In 1817 he was granted a retiring pension by the government, and, except for a special service in Mexico (where he was special commissioner from 1824 to 1826, and was one of the plenipotentiaries who signed the treaty with Mexico in London 26 Dec. 1826), he was never again in the employment of the foreign office.

The rest of his life was devoted to literature. After the publication of his second book of travels he began a series of tales and romances, chiefly laid in Eastern scenes, of which the first and best was 'The Adventures of Hajji Baba of Ispahan,' 1824. The humour and true insight into oriental life displayed in this oriental 'Gil Blas' immediately seized the popular fancy. The book went to several editions; and Morier acquired a high reputation as a novelist, which his later works do not appear to have injured, though they are of very unequal merit. The best are 'Zohrab the Hostage,' 1832, and 'Ayesha, the Maid of Kars,' 1834, for here Morier was on familiar ground, and, as was said of him, 'he was never at home but when he was abroad.' So accurate was his delineation of Persian life and character that the Persian minister at St. James's is said to have remonstrated on behalf of his government with the plain-speaking and satire of 'Hajji Baba.' His other romances (see below) are of slight merit; but his high reputation is attested, not only by the remarkable statement of Sir Walter Scott in the 'Quarterly Review' that he was the best novelist of the day, but by the fact that his name was used, 'like the royal stamp on silver,' to accredit unknown authors to the public, as in the case of 'St. Roche' and 'The Banished.' Several of his novels were translated into French and German, and one into Swedish; and one, 'Martin Toutrond,' was written originally in French. Morier was a well-known figure in the society of his day, as a collector and dilettante and an amateur artist of considerable merit. In his later years he lived at Brighton, where he died 19 March 1849. By his marriage with Harriet, daughter of William Fulke Greville, he had a son, Greville, a clerk in the foreign office, who predeceased him.

The following is the list of his works: 1. 'A Journey through Persia, Armenia, and Asia Minor to Constantinople in the Years 1808 and 1809,' 1812. 2. 'A Second Journey through Persia,' 1818. 3. 'The Adventures of Hajji Baba of Ispahan in England,' 1824. 4. 'Zohrab the Hostage,' 1832. 5. 'Ayesha, the Maid of Kars,' 1834. 6. 'Abel Allnutt, a novel,' 1837. 7. 'The Banished' [by W. Hauff]: prefatory note by Morier, 1839. 8. 'The Adventures of Tom Spicer,' a poem, printed 1840. 9. 'The Mirza,' 1842. 10. 'Missel-mah, a Persian tale,' 1847. 11. 'St. Roche,' a romance (from the German), merely edited by Morier, 'the practised author,' 1847. 12. 'Martin Toutrond, or a Frenchman in London in 1831,' originally written by Morier in French, and translated by himself, 1849.

[Authorities cited in the article; Bates's Maclise Portrait Gallery, where there is a portrait of Morier; information from Sir E. Hertslet, librarian to the foreign office; private information; Fraser's Magazine, vii. 159; Quarterly Review, vols. xxi. xxxvi. xxxix. James Justinian has been confounded with his elder brother, John Philip, in biographical dictionaries.]
S. L.-P.

MORIER, JOHN PHILIP (1776–1853), diplomatist, was the eldest of the four sons of Isaac Morier [q. v.], and was born at Smyrna 9 Nov. 1776. He was attached to the embassy at Constantinople 5 April 1799, where he acted as private secretary to the ambassador, the seventh Earl of Elgin, best known for his acquisition of the 'Elgin marbles.' Morier was despatched on 22 Dec. 1799 on special service of observation to Egypt, to accompany the grand vezîr in the Turkish expedition against General Kléber, whom Napoleon had left to hold the country. Morier joined the Turkish army at El-'Arish, on the Egyptian frontier, 31 Jan. 1800, and remained with it until July. He published an admirable account of the campaign, under the title of 'Memoir of a Campaign with the Ottoman Army in Egypt from February to July 1800' (London, 8vo, 1801). According to the 'Nouvelle Biographie' he was taken prisoner by the French, but in spite of his character as the representative of a hostile power, entrusted, moreover, with a secret mission to co-operate diplomatically with the Turks with a view to the expulsion of the French from Egypt, he was set at liberty, with a warning that should he again be found in Egypt he would meet the fate of a spy. No authority, however, is adduced for this story, which is unsupported by any public or private evidence. In December 1803 Morier was appointed consul-general in Albania, where the policy of 'Alî Pasha of Jannina, the most powerful of the semi-independent vassals of the Porte, was for many years a subject of solicitude both to English and French diplomacy (Lane-Poole, *Life of Stratford Canning*, i. 104). In April 1810 he was promoted to be secretary of legation at Washington, and in October 1811 was gazetted a commissioner in Spanish America. On his return to England he became for a while acting under-secretary of state for foreign affairs in August 1815. In the following year, 5 Feb., he was appointed envoy extraordinary to the court of Saxony at Dresden, which post he held till his retirement, on pension, 5 Jan. 1825. He died in London 20 Aug. 1853. He had married, 3 Dec. 1814, Horatia Maria Frances (who survived him only six days), eldest daughter of Lord Hugh Seymour, youngest son of the first Marquis of Hertford, by whom he had seven daughters, one of whom married the last Duke of Somerset.

[Foreign Office List, 1854; London Gazette, 1 Oct. 1811; Ann. Reg. 1853; information from Sir E. Hertslet; private information.] S. L.-P.

MORIER, Sir ROBERT BURNETT DAVID (1826–1893), diplomatist, only son of David Richard Morier [q. v.], was born at Paris 31 March 1826. He was educated at first privately at home, and then at Balliol College, Oxford, where he took a second class in *litteræ humaniores* in 1849. To his Oxford training he owed in part the scholarly style and analytical insight which afterwards characterised his despatches. In January 1851 he was appointed a clerk in the education department, a post which he resigned in October of the following year in order to enter the diplomatic service. On 5 Sept. 1853 he became unpaid attaché at Vienna, and the next twenty-three years of his life were spent almost entirely in German countries. He was appointed paid attaché at Berlin, 20 Feb. 1858; accompanied Sir H. Elliot on his special mission to Naples, June 1859; and was assistant private secretary to Lord John Russell during his attendance upon the queen at Coburg in September to October 1860. On 1 Oct. 1862 he was made second secretary, on 1 March 1865 British commissioner at Vienna for arrangement of tariff, and on 10 Sept. 1865 secretary of legation at Athens, whence he was soon transferred in the same capacity to Frankfort on 30 Dec. 1865. His services were recognised by the companionship of the Bath in the following January. From March to July 1866 he was again engaged on a commission at Vienna, for carrying out the treaty of commerce, and on returning to Frankfort acted as chargé d'affaires, and was appointed secretary of legation at Darmstadt in the same year. Here, with an interval of commission work at Vienna upon the Anglo-Austrian tariff (May to September 1867), he remained for five years, until his appointment as chargé d'affaires at Stuttgart, 18 July 1871. From Stuttgart he was transferred with the same rank to Munich on 30 Jan. 1872, and after four years' charge of the Bavarian legation, left Germany on his appointment as minister plenipotentiary to the king of Portugal on 1 March 1876.

During these twenty-three years of diplomatic activity in Germany, he acquired an intimate and an unrivalled familiarity with the politics of the 'fatherland.' He was a hard worker and a close observer, and his very disregard of conventionality and his habits of camaraderie, which sometimes startled his more stiffly starched superiors, enabled him 'to keep in touch with all sorts and conditions of men and to get a firm practical grip of important political questions. When any important question of home or foreign politics arose, he knew the views and wishes, not only of the official world, but also of all the other classes who contribute to form public opinion; and he did not always confine himself to playing the passive rôle of an indifferent spectator. His naturally impulsive temperament, joined to a certain recklessness which was checked but never completely extinguished by official restraints, sometimes induced him to meddle in local politics to an extent which irritated the ruling powers; and there is reason to believe—indeed Sir Robert believed it himself—that the enmity of Prince Bismarck was first excited by activity of this kind. . . . In complicated questions of German politics, even when they did not properly belong to the post which he held for the moment, he was often consulted privately by the Foreign Office authorities, and he was justly regarded as one of the first authorities on the Schleswig-Holstein question, though the advice which he gave to her majesty's government on that subject was not always followed' (*Times*, 17 Nov. 1893). During his residence at Darmstadt he was brought into relations with the Princess Alice and the crown princess, and probably from this time may be dated the high opinion in which he was held at court, and also the disfavour with which he was regarded by Prince Bismarck. The general ascription of some unsigned letters in the 'Times' in 1875 on continental affairs to Morier's trenchant pen did not tend to diminish a dislike which the minister's outspoken language and unconcealed liberalism had contributed to excite, and it is noteworthy that the epoch of Bismarck's greatest power was also the date when the man who knew more than any other Englishman of German politics and public opinion was finally removed from diplomatic employment in Germany.

For five years (1876–81) he was minister at Lisbon, and on 22 June 1881 he was transferred to Madrid, where he remained only three years, until his appointment as ambassador at St. Petersburg on 1 Dec. 1884. He had been created a K.C.B. in October 1882, and was called to the privy council in January 1885; he received the grand cross of St. Michael and St. George in February 1886, and the grand cross of the Bath in September 1887; he received the honorary degree of D.C.L. at Oxford in 1889, and was also hon. LL.D. of Edinburgh University. These honours were in just recognition of the exceptional ability he displayed in the conduct of British relations with Russia, especially after the Penj-deh incident, when his tact and firmness contributed in a very great degree to the maintenance of peace. It has often been asserted that, but for Morier, England would have been at war with Russia in 1885. In spite, or perhaps on account, of his vivacity of temperament, frankness of expression, and uncompromising independence of character, he was popular at St. Petersburg, both with the tsar and the ministers, and his popularity was notably enhanced when the German press, acting presumably with Prince Bismarck's authority, circulated the scandalous fiction that he had transmitted secret military information to the French from his post at Darmstadt during the war of 1870. When Count Herbert Bismarck made himself responsible for the accusation by declining to contradict it, the ambassador published the correspondence, including an absolutely conclusive letter from Marshal Bazaine. The result was a universal condemnation of the accusers by public opinion, and Morier was warmly congratulated in very high quarters at St. Petersburg, where the German chancellor was no favourite. He used to relate with amusement the obsequious politeness of a French stationmaster, when travelling in France soon afterwards, which was explained by the official's audible comment to a friend as the train moved off, 'C'est le grand ambassadeur qui a roulé Bismarck!'

In 1891 Sir Robert Morier was gazetted as Lord Dufferin's successor in the embassy at Rome. The climate of St. Petersburg, joined to very arduous work, often protracted late into the night, had undermined his constitution, and the appointment to Rome was made at his own request, solely on the ground of health. Matters of importance and delicacy, however, remained to be settled at St. Petersburg, and the tsar personally expressed a hope that the ambassador would not abandon his post at such a juncture. Sir Robert reluctantly consented to remain in Russia, though he knew it was at the risk of his life. The premature death, in 1892, of his only son, Victor Albert Louis, at the age of twenty-five, broke his once buoyant spirits, and his already weakened constitution was unable to repel a severe attack of influenza in the spring of 1893. He went to the Crimea, and then to Reichenhall in Bavaria, without permanent improvement, and died at Montreux, near the ancient seat of his family, on 16 Nov. 1893. He married in 1861 Alice, daughter of General Jonathan Peel [q. v.], but no male issue survived him. With his death a distinguished line of diplomatists became extinct.

[Foreign Office List, 1893; Times, 17 Nov. 1893; personal knowledge.] S. L.-P.

MORIER, WILLIAM (1790–1864), admiral, fourth son of Isaac Morier [q.v.], consul-general at Constantinople, was born at Smyrna 25 Sept. 1790. He spent two years at Harrow School, entered the navy in November 1803 as first-class volunteer, on board the Illustrious, 74, and became midshipman on the Ambuscade, with which he saw much service in the Mediterranean. From 1807 to 1810 he was employed on the Mediterranean and Lisbon stations, and became acting lieutenant of the Zealous, 74, and took part in the defence of Cadiz. In 1811, on H.M.S. Thames, 32, he contributed to the reduction of the island of Ponza, and displayed characteristic zeal in the destruction of ten armed feluccas on the beach near Cetraro; and other boat engagements on the Calabrian coast. He was also present at the bombardment of Stonington, in 1813, in the American war, and commanded the Harrier and Childers sloops successively on the North Sea station in 1828. Becoming post-captain in January 1830, he retired, attaining the rank of retired rear-admiral in 1855 and vice-admiral 1862. In 1841 he married Fanny, daughter of D. Bevan of Belmont, Hertfordshire. He died at Eastbourne 29 July 1864.

[Navy List; private information.] S. L.-P.

MORINS, RICHARD DE (*d.* 1242), historian, was a canon of Merton, who in 1202 was elected prior of Dunstable. At the time of his election he was only a deacon, but on 21 Sept. he was ordained priest. He studied at Bologna (*Gesta Abbat.* i. 307), and seems to have been a person of importance, and a lay namesake who held lands in Berkshire is several times mentioned in the Close and Patent Rolls as in John's service. In February 1203 Morins was sent by the king to Rome, in order to obtain the pope's aid in arranging peace with France (cf. *Cal. Rot. Pat.* p. 26), and returned in July with John, cardinal of S. Maria in Via Lata, as papal legate. In 1206 the cardinal constituted Morins visitor of the religious houses in the diocese of Lincoln. In 1212 Morins was employed on the inquiry into the losses of the church through the interdict. In the same year he also acted for the preachers of the crusade in the counties of Huntingdon, Bedford, and Hertford. In 1214–15 Morins was one of the three ecclesiastics appointed to investigate the election of Hugh de Northwold [q. v.] as abbot of St. Edmund's (*ib.* i. 124, 140, 140 *b*; *Memorials of St. Edmund's Abbey*, ii. 69–121). Later, in 1215, Morins was present at the Lateran council, and on his way home remained at Paris for a year to study in the theological schools. In 1222 he was employed in the settlement of the dispute between the Bishop of London and the Abbey of Westminster (Matt. Paris, iii. 37), and in the next year was visitor for his order in the province of York. In 1228 he was again visitor for his order in the dioceses of Lichfield and Lincoln. In 1239 Morins drew up the case for submission to the pope as to the Archbishop of Canterbury's right of visiting the monasteries in the sees of his suffragans. In 1241 he was one of those to whom letters of absolution for the Canterbury monks were addressed (*ib.* iv. 103). Morins died on 9 April 1242. The most notable event in Morins's government of the abbey was the dispute with the townspeople of Dunstable. Morins also records a number of minor events connected with himself. The lady-chapel in the canons' cemetery was built by him.

Morins was the compiler or author of the early portion of the 'Dunstable Annals,' from their beginning to the time of his death. Down to 1201 the 'Annals' consist of an abridgment from the works of Ralph de Diceto, but from this point onwards they are original. From a reference in the opening words Morins would appear to have commenced the compilation of his 'Annals' in 1210, and afterwards to have continued it from year to year. The 'Annals' are mainly occupied with details as to the affairs of the priory. Still, 'very few contemporary chroniclers throw so much light on the general history of the country, and, what would scarcely be expected, on foreign affairs as well as those of England. Many historical facts are known solely from this chronicle' (Luard, Preface, p. xv). The manuscript of the 'Annals' is contained in Cotton. MS. Tiberius A. x., which was much damaged in the fire of 1731. There is also a transcript made by Humphrey Wanley [q. v] in Harleian MS. 4886. From the latter Hearne printed his edition in 1733, which is now very rare. The 'Annals' were re-edited from the original manuscript by Dr. H. R. Luard for the Rolls Series in 1866, forming the greater part of vol. iii. of the 'Annales Monastici.' The portion of which Morins was author comprises pp. 3–158 of the latter edition. The authorship of the remainder of the 'Annals' is unknown.

[Almost all our knowledge of Morins is due to the Dunstable Annals, but there are a few references in the Patent Rolls and in Matthew Paris. See also Luard's Preface to Annales Monastici, vol. iii. pp. xi–xix; Hardy's Descriptive Cat. of Brit. Hist. iii. 252.] C. L. K.

MORISON. [See also MORRISON.]

MORISON, SIR ALEXANDER, M.D. (1779–1866), physician, was born 1 May 1779 at Anchorfield, near Edinburgh, and was educated at the high school and university of Edinburgh, where he graduated M.D. 12 Sept. 1799. His graduation thesis was 'De Hydrocephalo Phrenitico,' and he continued throughout life to take special interest in cerebral and mental diseases. He became a licentiate of the Edinburgh College of Physicians in 1800 and a fellow in 1801. He practised in Edinburgh for a time, but in 1808 removed to London, and on 11 April was admitted a licentiate of the College of Physicians of London, and 10 July 1841 was elected a fellow. He was made inspecting physician of lunatic asylums in Surrey in 1810, and 7 May 1835 physician to Bethlehem Hospital. He used to give an annual course of lectures on mental diseases, and became a recognised authority on the subject. He was physician to the Princess Charlotte, and in 1838 he was knighted. He published in 1826 'Outlines of Lectures on Mental Diseases,' in 1828 'Cases of Mental Disease, with Practical Observations on the Medical Treatment,' and in 1840 'The Physiognomy of Mental Diseases.' His remarks in these works are brief, but are illustrated by a large series of interesting portraits of lunatics, among which is a striking one of Jonathan Martin [q. v.], the man who set fire to York Minster. Morison died in Scotland, 14 March 1866, and was buried at Currie.

[Works; Munk's Coll. of Phys. iii. 61.] N. M.

MORISON, DOUGLAS (1814–1847), painter, born at Tottenham in Middlesex on 22 Aug. 1814, was the son of Dr. Richard Morison of Datchet, near Windsor. He studied drawing under Frederick Tayler [q. v.], and practised chiefly in water colours. His works were principally of an architectural nature, but he painted several views in Scotland. He was elected an associate of the Royal Institute or New Society of Painters in Water-colours in 1836, but resigned in 1838. On 12 Feb. 1844 he was elected an associate of the Royal (or 'Old') Society of Painters in Water-colours. He also practised in lithography, published some illustrations of 'The Eglinton Tournament,' in 1842 a set of views in lithography of 'Haddon Hall,' and in 1846 lithographic 'Views of the Ducal Palaces of Saxe-Coburg and Gotha,' from sketches made on the spot, with notes and suggestions from the prince consort. He made some sketches for the queen at Windsor Castle, and he received several medals in recognition of his art. Morison died at his residence at Datchet on 12 Feb. 1847. He exhibited occasionally at the Royal Academy from 1836 to 1841. His sister Letitia was the wife of Percival Leigh [q. v.]

[Roget's Hist. of the 'Old Water-Colour' Soc.; Graves's Dict. of Artists, 1760–1880; information from Mrs. Dixon Kemp and F. J. Furnivall, esq.] L. C.

MORISON, JAMES (1708–1786), of Elsick, provost of Aberdeen, born in 1708, fifth son of James Morison, merchant in Aberdeen, was elected provost of Aberdeen in 1744, and held office at the outbreak of the Jacobite rising in the autumn of 1745. Morison and the town council resolved to put the burgh in a state of defence on the ground that 'there is ane insurrection in the highlands,' but on the representation of Sir John Cope [q. v.] the guns of the fort at the harbour and the small arms were sent to Edinburgh (15 Sept.), and the burgh was left without means of defence. On 25 Sept. a new town council was elected; but before the new and old members could meet for the election of a successor to Morison and the other magistrates, John Hamilton, chamberlain to the Duke of Gordon, representing the Pretender, entered the town, and the councillors took to flight. Morison's term of office had just expired, but, no new provost having been elected, he was summoned to appear before Hamilton. He hesitated, and, after a second message had threatened that his house would be burnt if he refused to appear, he was carried prisoner to the town house. Two other magistrates were also brought from their hiding-places, and the three men were forced to ascend to the top of the Town Cross and hear the proclamation of King James VIII.

Morison declined to drink the health of the newly proclaimed king, and the wine was poured down his breast. Lord-president Forbes commended his conduct in the crisis. He died on 5 Jan. 1786, in the seventy-eighth year of his age.

Morison married in 1740 Isobell, eldest daughter of James Dyce of Disblair, merchant in Aberdeen, by whom he had a family of five sons and eleven daughters. Of his sons, two reached manhood: THOMAS MORISON (*d.* 1824), an army surgeon, is best known for the share he had in bringing into notice the medicinal springs of Strathpeffer, Ross-shire. His portrait was presented to him in recognition of these services, and now hangs in the pump-room hall there. The younger son, GEORGE MORISON (1757–1845), after graduating at Aberdeen, was licensed as a probationer of the church of Scotland in January 1782, and was in the following year ordained minister of Oyne, Aberdeenshire, from which he was translated to Banchory-Devenick in 1785. He continued there during a long ministry of sixty-one years, receiving the degree of D.D. from Aberdeen University in 1824, and succeeding his brother in the estates of Elsick and Disblair in the same year. His benefactions to his parish were large, chief among them being the suspension bridge across the Dee, which was built by him at a cost of 1,400*l.* and is still the means of communication between the north and south portions of the parish. He died, 'Father of the Church of Scotland,' on 13 July 1845. Besides two sermons (1831–2) and accounts of Banchory in Sinclair's 'Statistical Account,' he published 'A Brief Outline . . . of the Church of Scotland as by Law Established,' Aberdeen, 1840, 8vo; and 'State of the Church of Scotland in 1830 and 1840 Contrasted,' Aberdeen, 1840, 8vo. He married in 1786 Margaret Jeffray (*d.* 1837), but left no issue (HEW SCOTT, *Fasti Eccles. Scotic.* pt. vi. pp. 493, 597).

[Records of Burgh of Aberdeen; family knowledge.] R. M.

MORISON, JAMES (1762–1809), theologian, born at Perth on 13 Dec. 1762, was son of a bookseller and postmaster there. He likewise became a bookseller, first at Leith and afterwards at Perth. In religion he was for some time a member of the Society of Glassites, from whom he seceded and founded a distinct sect, of which he became the minister. He frequently preached and lectured, much to the neglect of his business. His oratorical gifts are said to have been considerable. He died at Perth on 20 Feb. 1809. On 13 Dec. 1778 he married a daughter (*d.* 1789) of Thomas Mitchel, writer, of Perth, and on 20 Dec. 1790 he married again. He left a large family.

Of Morison's writings may be mentioned: 1. 'New Theological Dictionary,' 8vo, Edinburgh, 1807. 2. 'An Introductory Key to the first four Books of Moses, being an Attempt to analyse these Books . . . and . . . to shew that the great Design of the Things recorded therein was the Sufferings of Christ and the following Glory,' 8vo, Perth, 1810, which had been previously circulated in numbers. He also published some controversial pamphlets and an appendix to Bishop Newton's 'Dissertations on the Prophecies,' 1795.

[Gent. Mag. 1809, pt. i. p. 379.] G. G.

MORISON, JAMES (1770–1840), self styled 'the Hygeist,' born at Bognie, Aberdeenshire, in 1770, was youngest son of Alexander Morison. After studying at Aberdeen University and Hanau in Germany, he established himself at Riga as a merchant, and subsequently in the West Indies, where he acquired property. Ill-health obliged him to return to Europe, and about 1814 he settled at Bordeaux. After 'thirty-five years' inexpressible suffering' and the trial of every imaginable course of medical treatment, he accomplished 'his own extraordinary cure' about 1822 by the simple expedient of swallowing a few vegetable pills of his own compounding at bed-time and a glass of lemonade in the morning. His success induced him to set up in 1825 as the vendor of what he called the 'vegetable universal medicines,' commonly known as 'Morison's Pills,' the principal ingredient of which is said to be gamboge. His medicines soon became highly popular, especially in the west of England, and in 1828 he formed an establishment for their sale in Hamilton Place, New Road, London, which he dignified with the title of 'The British College of Health.' He bought a pleasant residence at Finchley, Middlesex, called Strawberry Vale Farm, but latterly he lived at Paris, and it is said that the profits from the sale of his medicines in France alone were sufficient to cover his expenditure there. From 1830 to 1840 he paid 60,000*l.* to the English government for medicine stamps.

Morison died at Paris on 3 May 1840. He married twice, and left four sons and several daughters. The only surviving child of his second marriage (with Clara, only daughter of Captain Cotter, R.N.) was James Augustus Cotter Morison, who is separately noticed.

Morison's writings are simply puffs of his medicines. Among them may be mentioned: 1. 'Some important Advice to the World' (with supplement entitled 'More New Truths'), 2 pts. 12mo, London, 1825. 2. 'A Letter to . . . the United East India Company, proposing a . . . Remedy for . . . the Cholera Morbus of India,' 8vo, London, 1825. 3. 'The Hygeian Treatment of the . . . Diseases of India,' 8vo, London, 1836. His essays were collected together in a volume called 'Morisoniana, or Family Adviser of the British College of Health,' 2nd edit. 8vo, London, 1829 (3rd edit. 1831), which was translated into several European languages. Prefixed to the volume is a portrait of the author from a picture by Clint.

In Robert Wilkie's farce of the 'Yalla Gaiters' (1840) the hero is fascinated by the vocal powers of a countryman who is singing a cleverly written ballad in praise of Morison's 'Vegetable Pills;' the verses are printed in 'Notes and Queries,' 3rd ser. x. 477-8. Carlyle, in his 'Past and Present,' frequently made scornful reference to 'Morison's Pills.'

[Biog. Sketch of Mr. Morison (with portrait); Gent. Mag. 1840, pt. ii. p. 437.] G. G.

MORISON, JAMES (1816-1893), founder of the evangelical union, son of Robert Morison (*d.* 5 Aug. 1855, aged 74), minister of the 'united secession' church, was born at Bathgate, Linlithgowshire, on 14 Feb. 1816. He was educated at the Edinburgh University, where his intellectual power attracted the notice of John Wilson ('Christopher North'), and in 1834 he entered on his training for the ministry in Edinburgh at the divinity hall of the 'united secession' church, under John Brown, D.D. (1784-1858) [q. v.] After license (1839) he preached as a probationer at Cabrach, Banffshire, and other places in the north of Scotland. His interest in the current movement of evangelical revival led him to study the doctrine of atonement; he embraced the view (rare among Calvinists) that our Lord made atonement, not simply for the elect, but for all mankind. In Nairn, Tain, Forres, and at Lerwick in the Shetland Islands, he preached with great success, and embodied his views in a tract, published in 1840, and entitled 'The Question, "What must I do to be saved?" answered by Philanthropos.' In the same year he received a call to the 'united secession' church, Clerk's Lane, Kilmarnock. On 29 Sept., the day appointed for his ordination by Kilmarnock presbytery, proceedings were delayed by the objections of two of its members, but Morison was ordained after explaining that he did not hold 'universal salvation,' and promising to suppress his tract. He acquiesced, however, in its being reprinted by Thomas William Baxter Aveling [q. v.], a congregational minister in London, and, from the reprint, editions were issued (not by Morison) in Dunfermline and Kilmarnock. Hereupon he was cited before the Kilmarnock presbytery, and suspended from the ministry on 9 March 1841. He appealed to the synod, the supreme court of his church, and, though his cause was advocated by Brown, his tutor, the suspension was confirmed (11 June) on the motion of Hugh Heugh, D.D. [q. v.] Morison protested, and declined to recognise the decision; he was enthusiastically supported by his congregation, to which in two years he added 578 members. His father, who shared his views, was suspended in May 1842; and in May 1843 there were further suspensions of Alexander Cumming Rutherford of Falkirk, and John Guthrie of Kendal.

The four suspended ministers, in concert with nine laymen, at a meeting in Kilmarnock (16-18 May 1843), formed the 'evangelical union.' They issued a statement of principles, showing a growth of opinion, inasmuch as they had now abandoned the Calvinistic doctrine of election. Their movement was reinforced by the expulsion (1 May 1844) of nine students from the theological academy of the congregationalists at Glasgow, under Ralph Wardlaw, D.D. [q. v.]; and by the disownment (1845) of nine congregational churches holding similar views. From the 'relief church' in 1844 John Hamilton of Lauder joined the movement; as did William Scott in June 1845, on his expulsion from Free St. Mark's, Glasgow. Not all who thus came over to Morison's views, and were hence known as Morisonians, became members of the 'evangelical union;' but they co-operated with it, and aided in the maintenance of a theological academy, established in 1843 by Morison, who held the chair of exegetical theology, and remained principal till his death. It is remarkable that the 'evangelical union' adopted no uniform system of church government. The union was an advisory body, not a judicature, and it included congregations both of the presbyterian and the congregational order, thus reproducing the policy of the 'happy union' originated in London in 1690 [see Howe, John, 1630-1705], but improving on it by the admission of lay delegates.

In 1851 Morison left Kilmarnock for Glasgow, where, in 1853, North Dundas Street Church was built for him. In 1855 his health temporarily gave way; from 1858 he was assisted by a succession of colleagues. He received the degree of D.D. in 1862 from the Adrian University in Michigan, and in 1883 from Glasgow University. In 1884 he retired from the active duties of the pastorate. Public presentations were made to him in 1864, and in 1889 on the occasion of his ministerial jubilee. In April 1890 an ineffectual attempt was made in the Paisley presbytery of the united presbyterian church (into which the 'united secession' church was incorporated in 1847) to recall the sentence of 1841; but in July 1893 Morison received a complimentary address signed by over nineteen hundred laymen of the united presbyterian church.

He died on 13 Nov. 1893 at his residence, Florentine Bank, Hillhead, Glasgow, and was buried on 16 Nov. in the Glasgow necropolis. He married, first, in 1841, Margaret (*d.* 1875), daughter of Thomas Dick of Edinburgh, by whom he had three children, the eldest being Marjory, married to George Gladstone, his assistant (from 1876) and successor; his eldest son, Robert, died of congestion of the lungs in 1873 on his passage to Australia. He married, secondly, in 1877, Margaret Aughton of Preston, who survived him. His portrait, painted by R. Gibb, R.S.A., was presented to him in 1889.

Morison was a man of real intellectual power and great gentleness of character. Probably of all Scottish sect makers he was the least sectarian. His personal influence and that of his writings extended much beyond the community which he headed, and, in a way none the less effective because steady and quiet, did much to widen the outlook of Scottish theology. Always a hard student, he had especially mastered the expository literature of the New Testament; and his permanent reputation as a writer will rest on his own commentaries, which are admirable alike for their compact presentation of the fruits of ample learning, and for the discriminating judgment of his own exegesis. The 'evangelical union,' which has been termed 'a successful experiment in heresy,' now numbers between ninety and one hundred churches, adhering to the well-marked lines of evangelical opinion laid down by its founder. Morison's original church removed from Clerk's Lane to Winton Place, Kilmarnock, in 1860; the old building was sold to a dissentient minority which left the 'evangelical union' in 1885.

He published: 1. 'The Question, "What must I do?"' &c., 1840; later edition, with title 'The Way of Salvation,' 1843, and 'Safe for Eternity' [1868]. 2. 'Not quite a Christian,' &c., 1840, often reprinted. 3. 'The Nature of the Atonement,' &c., 1841, often reprinted. 4. 'The Extent of the Atonement,' &c., 1841, often reprinted. 5. 'Saving Faith,' &c., 1844, reprinted. 6. 'A Gospel Alphabet,' &c., 1845. 7. 'The Declaration, "I Pray not for the World,"' &c., 1845, reprinted. 8. 'A Gospel Catechism,' &c., 1846, reprinted. 9. 'The Followers of . . . Timothy,' &c., 1847 (?). 10. 'An Exposition of the Ninth Chapter of Paul's Epistle to the Romans,' &c., 1849; new edition, re-written, with addition of tenth chapter, 1888. 11. 'Wherein the Evangelical Unionists are not Wrong,' &c., 1849. 12. 'Vindication of the Universality of the Atonement,' &c., 1861 (a reply to 'The Atonement,' by Robert Smith Candlish, D.D. [q. v.]). 13. 'Biblical Help towards Holiness,' &c., 1861. 14. 'Apology for . . . Evangelical Doctrines,' &c., 1862. 15. 'Questions on the Shorter Catechism,' &c., 1862. 16. 'A Critical Exposition of the Third Chapter of Paul's Epistle to the Romans,' &c., 1866. 17. 'A Practical Commentary on . . . St. Matthew,' &c., 1870. 18. 'A Practical Commentary on . . . St. Mark,' &c., 1873. 19. 'Exposition and Homiletics on Ruth,' &c., 1880 (in 'The Pulpit Commentary.') 20. 'St. Paul's Teaching on Sanctification,' &c., 1886. 21. 'Sheaves of Ministry; Sermons and Expositions,' &c., 1890. From 1854 to 1867 he edited and contributed largely to 'The Evangelical Repository,' a quarterly magazine.

[Morisonianism, by Fergus Ferguson, in Religions of the World, 1877, pp. 275 sq.; Irving's Book of Scotsmen, 1881, pp. 367 sq.; Memorial Volume of the Ministerial Jubilee of Principal Morison, 1889; Evangelical Union Jubilee Conference Memorial Volume, 1892; Christian News, 18 and 25 Nov. and 2 Dec. 1893; North Dundas Street Evangelical Union Church Monthly, December 1893; information from his son, Thomas Dick Morison, esq., and from the Rev. George Cron.] A. G.

MORISON, JAMES AUGUSTUS COTTER (1832–1888), author, born in London 20 April 1832 (he generally dropped the 'Augustus'), was the only surviving child by a second marriage of James Morison (1770–1840) [q. v.] The father from about 1834 till his death resided in Paris, where he had many distinguished friends. His son thus learnt French in his infancy, and afterwards gained a very wide knowledge of French history, life, and literature. After his father's death in 1840 he lived with his mother near London. His health was delicate and his education desultory. After travelling in Germany, he in March 1850 entered Lincoln College, Oxford. He was popular in university society, a 'good oar,' fencer, and rider, and a wide reader, although not according to the regular course. His university career was interrupted by visits to his mother, whose health was failing. He graduated B.A. and M.A. in 1859, and left

Oxford, having acquired many friends, especially Mark Pattison [q. v.], Dr. Fowler, then fellow of Lincoln, now president of Corpus, and Mr. John Morley. He soon began to write in periodicals, and became one of the best known of the staff of the 'Saturday Review' while John Douglas Cook [q. v.] was editor. In 1861 he married Frances, daughter of George Virtue the publisher. In 1863 he published his interesting 'Life of St. Bernard,' a book which was praised by Mark Pattison, Matthew Arnold, and Cardinal Manning. It shows great historical knowledge, and a keen interest in the mediæval church. He afterwards contemplated a study of French history during the period of Louis XIV, which occupied him intermittently during the rest of his life. Unfortunately, Morison was never able to concentrate himself upon what should have been the great task of his life.

His wife died in 1878, and he moved to 10 Montague Place, in order to be near to the British Museum, and afterwards to Fitz-John's Avenue, Hampstead. He was elected a member of the Athenæum Club 'under Rule II,' and was a very active member of the London Library Committee. He was a member of the Positivist Society, occasionally lectured at Newton Hall, and left a legacy to the society. A few years before his death symptoms of a fatal disease showed themselves, and he was thus forced to abandon the completion of his French history. In 1887 he published his 'Service of Man, an essay towards the Religion of the Future.' Although he regarded this as his best work, and contemplated a second part, to be called 'A Guide to Conduct,' his friends generally thought it an excursion beyond his proper field. His other works were numerous articles in the chief periodicals, a pamphlet upon 'Irish Grievances' in 1868, 'Mme. de Maintenon, an Étude,' in 1885, and excellent monographs upon 'Gibbon' (1878) and 'Macaulay' (1882) in John Morley's 'Men of Letters' series. He died at his house in FitzJohn's Avenue 26 Feb. 1888. He left three children—Theodore, principal of the college of Aligarh, India, 1899–1905, and member of the council of India from 19 Dec. 1906; Helen Cotter, and Margaret.

Few men had warmer and more numerous friends. He was a man of great powers of enjoyment, of most versatile tastes, and of singular social charm. He was familiar with a very wide range of literature in many departments, and the multiplicity of his interests prevented him from ever doing justice to powers recognised by all his friends. He was an enthusiastic admirer of every new book which to him appeared to show genius, and eager to cultivate the acquaintance of its author. No man had wider and more generous sympathies. He had no scientific training, and took comparatively little interest in immediate politics, although he once thought of trying to enter parliament; but there was apparently no other subject in which he was not warmly interested. His recreation he mainly sought in travelling and yachting. Perhaps his closest friends were those of the positivist circle, especially Mr. Frederic Harrison, Professor Beesly, and Mr. Vernon Lushington, but he had also a great number of literary friends, one of the warmest being Mr. George Meredith, who dedicated to him a volume of poems, and wrote a touching epitaph upon his death.

[The information for this article has been supplied by Morison's intimate friend and executor, Mr. Stephen Hamilton; also obituary notice in Times of 28 Feb. 1888, and personal knowledge.] L. S.

MORISON, JOHN (1750–1798), Scottish divine and poet, was born at Cairnie, Aberdeenshire, in June 1750. Educated at King's College, Aberdeen, he spent some years as a private tutor, first at Dunnet, Caithness-shire, and afterwards at Banniskirk. Graduating M.A. in 1771, he was schoolmaster at Thurso about 1773, subsequently went to Edinburgh for further study, and in September 1780 was appointed minister of Canisbay, Caithness-shire, the most northerly church on the mainland. In 1792 he received the degree of D.D. from Edinburgh University. He died, after many years' seclusion, at Canisbay, 12 June 1798.

Morison's claim to remembrance rests on his contributions to the final edition of the 'Scottish Paraphrases,' 1781. When the collection was in preparation, he submitted twenty-four pieces to the committee, of which he was himself a member, but only seven (Nos. 19, 21, 27, 28, 29, 30, and 35) were accepted, and some of these were slightly altered, probably by his friend John Logan [q. v.] Most of the seven became 'household words' in the presbyterian churches, and one or two are freely used as hymns by other denominations. The thirty-fifth, ''Twas on that night when doom'd to know,' has long been the Scottish communion hymn, but it appears to be founded partly on Watts's ''Twas on that dark, that doleful night,' and partly on a Latin hymn by Andreas Ellinger (cf. *Private Prayers* cited below; Maclagan, p. 107; Bonar, *Notes*). From 1771 to 1775 Morison contributed verses, under the signature of 'Musæus,' to Ruddiman's 'Edinburgh Weekly Magazine,' but these are of no particular merit. He wrote the account of the parish of Canisbay for Sinclair's 'Statistical Account,' and collected the topographical history of Caithness for Chalmers's 'Caledonia.' A translation of Herodian's 'History' from the Greek remained in manuscript. He was an accomplished classical scholar and an able preacher.

[Scott's Fasti Ecclesiæ Scoticanæ, iii. 359; Calder's History of Caithness; Maclagan's History of the Scottish Paraphrases; Julian's Dictionary of Hymnology; Burns's Memoir of Dr. Macgill; Bonar's Notes in Free Church Hymnal; Free Church Magazine, May 1847; Life and Work Magazine, January 1888; Private Prayers put forth by Authority during the Reign of Queen Elizabeth (Parker Soc.), p. 405; Cairnie parish register.] J. C. H.

MORISON, JOHN, D.D. (1791–1859), congregationalist minister, born at Millseat of Craigston, in the parish of King Edward, Aberdeenshire, on 8 July 1791, was apprenticed to a watchmaker at Banff, but, resolving to devote himself to the ministry, he became a student at Hoxton Academy in 1811. He was ordained 17 Feb. 1815, and became pastor of a congregation at Union Chapel, Sloane Street, Chelsea. In 1816 a larger place of worship was provided for him in the same parish. At the close of that year Trevor Chapel was opened, where he continued to labour for more than forty years. From about 1827 till 1857 he was editor of the 'Evangelical Magazine.' The university of Glasgow conferred upon him the degree of D.D. in 1830, and at a later period he received from an American university the honorary degree of LL.D. He died in London on 13 June 1859, and was buried in Abney Park cemetery.

He married in 1815 Elizabeth, second daughter of James Murray of Banff, and had several children. His portrait has been engraved by Cochran.

In addition to numerous minor works and discourses, he wrote: 1. 'Lectures on the principal Obligations of Life, or a Practical Exposition of Domestic, Ecclesiastical, Patriotic, and Mercantile Duties,' London, 1822, 8vo. 2. 'Counsels to a Newly-wedded Pair, or Friendly Suggestions to Husbands and Wives,' London, 1830, 16mo. 3. 'An Exposition of the Book of Psalms, Explanatory, Critical, and Devotional,' 3 vols. London, 1832, 8vo. 4. 'A Tribute of Filial Sympathy . . . or Memories of John Morison of Millseat, Aberdeenshire,' London, 1833, 12mo. 5. 'Morning Meditations for every Day in the Year,' London [1835], 16mo. 6. 'Family Prayers for every Morning and Evening throughout the Year,' 2nd edit., London [1837], 4to. 7. 'A Commentary on the Acts of the Apostles, in the Catechetical Form,' London, 1839, 12mo. 8. 'The Founders and Fathers of the London Missionary Society, with a brief Sketch of Methodism and Historical Notices of several Protestant Missions from 1556 to 1839,' 2 vols. London [1840], 8vo; new edition, with twenty-one portraits, London [1844], 8vo. 9. 'The Protestant Reformation in all Countries, including Sketches of the State and Prospects of the Reformed Churches,' London, 1843, 8vo.

[Memoirs by the Rev. John Kennedy, 1860; Evangelical Mag. September 1859 (by the Rev. A. Tidman); Smith's Cat. of Engraved Portraits, 1883; Funeral Sermon by the Rev. William Mann Statham, 1859; Congregational Year-Book, 1860, p. 200; Darling's Cycl. Bibl. ii. 2109.] T. C.

MORISON, Sir RICHARD (*d.* 1556), ambassador, was son of Thomas Morison of Hertfordshire, by a daughter of Thomas Merry of Hatfield. He is said to have been at Eton, but his name does not occur in Harwood's 'Alumni.' He graduated B.A. at Oxford on 19 Jan. 1527–8, and at once entered the service of Wolsey. He probably noted the way things were going, as he soon quitted the cardinal, visited Latimer at Cambridge, and went to Italy to study Greek. He became a proficient scholar, and was always interested in literature, although he adopted Calvinistic religious views. He lived at Venice and Padua, and endured all manner of hardships, according to the accounts given to his friends at home, from whom, although he had a pension, he was continually begging. In August 1535 he wrote to Starkey: 'You cannot imagine in what misery I have been, but that is past, and how great it would have been in winter if the kindness of Signor Polo had not rescued me from hunger, cold, and poverty. My books, good as they were, are a prey to the cruel Jews, for very little truly. . . my clothes are all gone. I am wearing Mr. Michael Throgmorton's breeches and doublet.' But at this time, as throughout his life, he exhibited a gaiety of disposition which caused him to be called 'the merry Morison' (cf. *Letters and Papers of Henry VIII*, XII. i. 430). Writing in February 1535–6 to Cromwell, he said that he wished to do something else than be wretched in Italy. Cromwell, who respected Morison's abilities, summoned him home in May 1535, and gave him an official appointment. On 17 July 1537 he became prebendary of Yatminster in the cathedral of Salisbury. Henry in 1541 is said to have given him the library of the Carmelites in London. He received the mastership of the hospitals of St. James's, Northallerton, Yorkshire, and St. Wulstan, Worcester, with other monastic grants (cf. App. ii. 10*th Rep. Dep.-Keeper Public Records*, p. 241).

In 1546 Morison went as ambassador to the Hanse towns. On Henry's death he was furnished with credentials to the king of Denmark, and ordered by the council to announce Edward's accession. He had a pension of 20*l.* a year throughout the reign. On 8 May 1549 he was made a commissioner to visit the university of Oxford, and before June 1550 was knighted; in July he went as ambassador to Charles V, Roger Ascham going with him, and the two reading Greek every day together. His despatches to the council were usually very long, but Morison found time to travel about Germany with his secretary, Ascham, who published in 1553 an account of their experiences in 'A Report of the Affaires of Germany.' The emperor, who was frequently remonstrating through Morison about the treatment of the Princess Mary, did not altogether like him; he was in the habit, as he said, of 'reading Ochino's Sermons or Machiavelli' to his household 'for the sake of the language,' and his friendship with the leading reformers must have made negotiations difficult. On 5 Aug. 1553 he and Sir Philip Hoby [q. v.] were recalled (they had alluded to Guilford Dudley as king in a letter to the council), but the next year Morison withdrew to Strasburg with Sir John Cheke [q. v.] and Cook, and spent his time in study under Peter Martyr, whose patron he had been at Oxford (Churton, *Life of Nowell*, p. 23). He was at Brussels early in 1555, and is said also to have passed into Italy, but he died at Strasburg on 17 March 1555–6. He had married Bridget, daughter of John, lord Hussey, who remarried in 1561 Henry Manners, earl of Rutland [q. v.] By her he had a son Charles, afterwards Sir Charles, kt., and three daughters: Jane married to Edward, lord Russell, Elizabeth to William Norreys, and Mary to Bartholomew Hales. Morison died very rich, and had begun to build the mansion of Cashiobury in Hertfordshire, which his son completed, and which passed into the Capel family by the marriage of Sir Charles's daughter Elizabeth with Arthur, lord Capel of Hadham [q. v.], and is now the property of the Earl of Essex. According to Wood, Morison left illegitimate children.

Morison wrote: 1. 'Apomaxis Calumniarum,' London, 1537, 8vo, an attack on Cochlæus, who had written against Henry VIII, and who retorted in 'Scopa in Araneas Ricardi Morison Angli,' Leipzig, 1538. 2. A translation of the 'Epistle' of Sturmius, London, 1538, 8vo. 3. 'An Invective ayenste the great detestable vice, Treason,' London, 1539, 8vo. 4. 'The Strategemes, Sleyghtes, and Policies of Warre, gathered together by S. Julius Frontinus,' London, 1539, 8vo. 5. A translation of the 'Introduction to Wisdom' by Vives, London, 1540 and 1544, dedicated to Gregory Cromwell. He is also said to have written 'Comfortable Consolation for the Birth of Prince Edward, rather than Sorrow for the Death of Queen Jane,' after the death of Jane Seymour on 24 Oct. 1537. 'A Defence of Priests' Marriages' is sometimes assigned to him. It is dated by some 1562, but more probably appeared between 1549 and 1553. In manuscript are 'Maxims and Sayings,' Sloane MS. 1523; 'A Treatise of Faith and Justification,' Harl. MS. 423 (4); 'Account of Mary's Persecution under Edward VI,' Harl. MS. 353.

[Letters and Papers of Henry VIII, ed. Gairdner, vols. vi. and seq. passim; Cal. of State Papers, For. Ser. 1547–53; Rymer's Fœdera, xiv. 671, xv. 183; Acts of the Privy Council, 1547–56, passim; Katterfeld's Roger Ascham, sein Leben und seine Werke, note to pp. 91 and 92; Ascham's Epistles, Oxford, 1703, passim; Ascham's English Works, 1815, xvii. 383; Lloyd's State Worthies; Fuller's Worthies, p. 227; Tanner's Bibl. Brit. p. 532; Clutterbuck's Herts, i. 237; Wood's Athenæ Oxon. ed. Bliss, i. 239; Fasti Oxon. i. 29; Dixon's Hist. of the Church of England, vol. iii. passim; Narratives of the Reformation (Camd. Soc.), p. 146; Trevelyan Papers (Camd. Soc.), ii. 25; Chron. of Queen Jane and of two years of Queen Mary (Camd. Soc.), pp. 108–9; Troubles connected with the Prayer-book of 1549 (Camd. Soc.), p. 104; Strype's Memorials, I. i. 64, &c., ii. i. 576, &c., II. ii. 18, &c., III. i. vi., &c.; Grindal, p. 12; Parker, ii. 446; Cranmer, pp. 1009, 1015; Cheke, pp. 19, 48; Annals, II. ii. 498; Lodge's Illustrations of Brit. Hist. i. 196, &c.; Lansd. MS. 980, 137; Thomas's Historical Notes, i. 218, 219.]

W. A. J. A.

MORISON, ROBERT (1620–1683), botanist, son of John Morison by his wife Anna Gray, was born at Aberdeen in 1620. He was educated at the university of that city, and in 1638 graduated as M.A. and Ph.D. He devoted himself at first to mathematics, and studied Hebrew, being intended by his parents for the ministry; but his attachment to the royalist cause led him to bear arms, and at the battle at the Brigg of Dee, when Middleton, the covenanter, was victorious, he received a dangerous wound in the head. Upon his recovery he, like so many of his royalist countrymen, went to Paris, where he became tutor to the son of a counsellor, named Bizet. Meanwhile he applied himself to the study of anatomy, zoology, botany, mineralogy, and chemistry, studying Theophrastus, Dioscorides, and the best commentators, and in 1648 took the degree of M.D. at Angers. On the recommendation of Vespasian Robin, the French king's botanist, he was received into the household of Gaston, duke of Orleans, in 1649 or 1650, as one of his physicians, and as a colleague of Abel Bruyner and Nicholas Marchant, the keepers of the duke's garden at Blois. This appointment, with a handsome salary, he retained until the duke's death in 1660. He was sent by the duke to Montpellier, Fontainebleau, Burgundy, Poitou, Brittany, Languedoc, and Provence in search of new plants, and seems to have explained to his patron his views on classification. At Blois Morison became known to Charles II, nephew of Gaston, through his mother, and on the Restoration was invited to accompany the king to England. Charles II made him his senior physician, king's botanist and superintendent of all the royal gardens, at a salary of 200*l.* and a house. On 16 Dec. 1669, he was elected professor of botany at Oxford, being recommended for that post partly by his 'Præludia Botanica,' then just published, and partly, no doubt, by his politics. On the following day he was incorporated as doctor of medicine from University College, but he did not commence his lectures until the following 2 Sept. Subsequently he lectured to considerable audiences three times a week for five weeks, beginning each September and May, at a table covered with specimens in the middle of the physic garden. The rest of his life was occupied, as Anthony à Wood says (*Fasti*, ii. 315), in 'prosecuting his large design of publishing the universal knowledge of simples,' his 'Historia Plantarum Oxoniensis.' During a visit to London in connection with its publication, he was struck on the chest by the pole of a coach while crossing the Strand between Northumberland House and St. Martin's Lane. Falling to the ground, he fractured his skull on a stone and was carried to his house in Green Street, Leicester Fields, where he died the next day, 10 Nov. 1683, without regaining consciousness. He was buried in St. Martin's-in-the-Fields.

Morison was credited in his own day with a clear intellect, a love of science and the public interest, and a hatred of sordid gain (cf. *Life*, attributed to Hearne, in *Sloane MS.* 3198, printed in *Plantarum Hist.* vol. ii.) 'He was,' wrote one R. Gray, apparently a relative, 'communicative of his knowledge, a true friend, an honest countryman, true to his religion, whom neither the fair promises of the papists nor the threatenings of others would prevail upon to alter' (*Sloane MS.* 3198). Tournefort said of Morison (*Élémens de Botanique*, 1694, p. 19): 'One does not know how to praise this author sufficiently; but he seems to praise himself overmuch, since, not content with the glory of having carried out a part of the grandest scheme ever made in botanical science, he dares to compare his discoveries to those of Christopher Columbus; and, without mentioning Gesner, Cæsalpinus, or Columna, he states in several passages in his writings that he has taken nothing except direct from nature. One might, perhaps, believe this if he had not taken the trouble to copy whole pages from the two authors last named, showing that their works were familiar enough to him.' Though Ray was simultaneously engaged in the study of classification, Morison apparently deserves the eulogy bestowed on him by Franchet (*Flore de Loir-et-Cher*, p. xiv), who says that his works made an epoch in botanical literature; that he formed a clear notion of genus and species, and a conception of the family almost identical with that which we now hold; and that he seems to have been the first to make use of dichotomous keys to specific characters. At the same time, one cannot deny the want of modesty and urbanity, the vanity and boastfulness which Boreau (*Flore du Centre de la France*, 1840, i. 37) finds in his works.

An oil-painting of Morison is preserved at the Oxford Botanical Garden, and an engraved portrait by R. White, after Sunman, is prefixed to the second volume of the 'Historia Plantarum Oxoniensis.' His name is perpetuated in the West Indian genus *Morisonia*, among the caper family. Though stated by Wood and Pulteney to have been a member of the Royal College of Physicians, Morison does not appear in Dr. Munk's 'Roll,' so that this statement is probably unfounded.

Morison was doubtless concerned in the compilation of 'Hortus Regius Blesensis' (1653, 2nd edit. 1655), which Morison seemed to describe as the joint work of himself and his colleagues, Abel Brunyer and Nicholas Marchant (*ib.*; and cf. letter in *Præludia Bot.* pt. ii.); but to Brunyer alone was the work officially entrusted (Franchet). In 1669 Morison issued his 'Præludia Botanica' (sm. 8vo). Part i. consists of a third edition of the Blois 'Hortus,' dedicated to Charles II, and contains the rudiments of Morison's system of classification, and a list of 260 plants supposed by him to be new species. Part ii. is styled 'Hallucinationes in Caspari Bauhini Pinace . . . item Animadversiones . . . Historiæ Plantarum Johannis Bauhini.' This work, which Haller calls 'invidiosum opus,' is dedicated to James, duke of York, and concludes with a dialogue asserting that generic characters should be based on the fruit, and denying spontaneous generation.

As a specimen of the great work he meditated, Morison next issued 'Plantarum Umbelliferarum Distributio nova,' Oxford, 1672, fol. pp. 91, with 12 plates, dedicated to the Duke of Ormonde, the chancellor, and the university. In 1674 he issued 'Icones et Descriptiones rariorum Plantarum Siciliæ, Melitæ, Galliæ, et Italiæ . . . auctore Paulo Boccone,' Oxford, 4to, pp. 96, with 52 plates, having 119 figures, a work sent to him at the author's request, by Charles Hatton, second son of Lord Hatton, who, about 1658, had been Morison's pupil in botany at St. Germains. In 1680 he published 'Plantarum Historiæ Universalis Oxoniensis pars secunda; seu Herbarum distributio nova, per tabulas cognationis et affinitatis, ex libro Naturæ observata,' Oxford, fol. pp. 617. The preface is dated 'Ex Musæo nostro in Collegio dicto Universitatis.' In this work, leaving trees, as a smaller subject, for separate treatment, Morison divides herbaceous plants into sixteen classes, but deals only with the first five. He dealt with four more before his death, and the work was completed, at the request of the university, in 1699, by Jacob Bobart the younger [q. v.], who had learnt Morison's system from its author. This second volume (pp. 655) contains numerous copper-plates, representing some 3,384 plants, engraved at the expense of Bishop Fell, Dean Aldrich, and others, the illustrations of the two volumes of the work being almost the earliest copper-plates in England. Speaking of this volume, Wood says: 'After this is done there will come out another volume of trees by the same hand.' This never appeared, but Schelhammer wrote, in 1687, that, eleven years before, he had seen the whole work nearly complete, at the author's house (*Hermanni Conringii in universam artem medicam Introductio*, Helmestadt, pp. 350–1). In the Botanical Department of the British Museum there is a volume from Sir Hans Sloane's library containing 128 cancelled pages from the beginning of the second volume. These differ mainly in containing the 'annotations of the eastern names,' mentioned by Wood (*Fasti*, ii. 315) as the work of 'Dr. Tho. Hyde, chief keeper of the Bodleian Library.' The volume also contains manuscript notes by Bobart.

[Pulteney's Sketches of the Progress of Botany, i. 298–327; Morison's Works; and the works above cited.] G. S. B.

MORISON or MORESIN, THOMAS, (1558?–1603?), physician and diplomatist, was born about 1558 it is said, in Aberdeen, but the statement is only based on the epithet 'Aberdonanus' or 'Aberdonnus' which Morison applies to himself. He may have been educated at Aberdeen, and Tanner calls him 'medicinæ doctor in academia Aberdonensi,' but his name does not appear in the published records. Like many of his countrymen (cf. Preface to *Fasti Aberdonenses*, Spalding Club), Morison studied at Montpellier, whence he probably took his degree of M.D. It was possibly during Anthony Bacon's visit to Montpellier in 1582 that Morison made his acquaintance [cf. BACON, ANTHONY]. Morison was probably at Arras in December 1592, for in a letter to Bacon he gives a remarkably minute account of the death of Alexander Farnese, which occurred there on 2 Dec. From that date until Bacon's death in 1601 Morison seems to have frequently corresponded with him, but few of his letters are preserved (BIRCH, *Memoirs of the Reign of Queen Elizabeth*, i. 99). Early in 1593 Morison appears to have been at Frankfort, where he published his first book, 'Liber novus de Metallorum causis et Transubstantione,' 1593, 8vo (Brit. Mus.); it is dedicated to James VI, and directed against alchemists and astrologers. In the same year Morison returned to Scotland, and through Bacon's influence became one of Essex's 'earliest, as well as most considerable, intelligencers there' (BIRCH). During a visit to the north of Scotland he fell in with the Earl of Huntly [see GORDON, GEORGE, sixth EARL, and first MARQUIS OF HUNTLY], and secured considerable influence with him, which Morison thought might be of use to the queen's envoys. Elizabeth appears to have been quite satisfied with Morison's services, which were well rewarded with money. In August 1593 he received 30*l.* from Bacon; Essex sent him a hundred crowns in September, and another hundred in March 1593–4. On 5 Feb. 1593–4 Morison dedicated to James his second book, 'Papatus, seu depravatæ religionis Origo et Incrementum,' Edinb. 1594, 8vo (Brit. Mus.) In spite of its fanciful alphabetical arrangement, it is a learned work, compiled from more than two hundred authors, and tracing the history of the papacy from its origin to the Reformation. It is quoted in Ussher's 'Historia Dogmatica,' p. 271, and 'is now of rare occurrence, and highly prized by the learned for its singular erudition.'

In 1594 Morison appears to have visited London and had an interview with Essex. Next year he was back again in Scotland sending accounts to his patron of James's behaviour and views on domestic and foreign policy, and describing the movements of

Huntly, Erroll, Angus, and a jesuit, John Morton, who had been Morison's schoolfellow (BIRCH, i. 224). After Anthony's death, in 1601, Francis Bacon seems to have maintained a correspondence with Morison. In 1603 he wrote soliciting Morison's interest with James, who was then about to take possession of his English crown. Probably Morison's death occurred soon after. Dempster dates it 1601, but this is obviously a mistake.

[Birch's Memoirs of the Reign of Queen Elizabeth, passim; Remaines of Francis Bacon, p. 63, and Works, ed. Montagu, xiii. 61, ed. Spedding, iii. 66; Linden, De Scriptis Medicis, p. 454; Bruce's Eminent Men of Aberdeen, pp. 76–80; The Book of Bon-Accord, pp. 307–8; Buchan's Scriptores Scoti, p. 19; Dempster, p. 499; Tanner's Bibl. Brit. p. 531 and Brit. Mus. Cat. s.v. 'Moresinus;' Cat. Advocates' Library; Anderson's Scottish Nation, iii. 207; Irving's Book of Scotsmen, p. 367; Brand's Popular Antiquities, p. xviii.] A. F. P.

MORLAND, GEORGE (1763–1804), painter, born in London on 26 June 1763, was the son of Henry Robert Morland [q. v.], and grandson of George Henry Morland [q. v.] He is said by Cunningham to have been lineally descended from Sir Samuel Morland [q. v.], while other biographers go so far as to say that he had only to claim the baronetcy in order to get it. He began to draw at three years old, and at the age of ten (1773) his name appears as an honorary exhibitor at the Royal Academy. His talents were carefully cultivated by his father, who has been accused of stimulating them unduly with a view to his own profit, shutting the child up in a garret to make drawings from pictures and casts for which he found a ready sale. The boy, on the other hand, is said to have soon found a way to make money for himself by hiding some of his drawings, and lowering them at nightfall out of his window to young accomplices, with whom he used to spend the proceeds in frolic and self-indulgence. It has been also asserted that his father, discovering this trick, tried to conciliate him by indulgence, humouring his whims and encouraging his low tastes. The truth seems to be that his father, if severe, was neither mercenary nor unprincipled, but tried to do his duty towards his son, who was also his apprentice, and that the son, possessed of unusual carelessness of disposition and love of pleasure, rebelled against all restraint, and developed early a taste for dissipation and low society which became ungovernable.

He was set by his father to copy pictures of all kinds, but especially of the Dutch and Flemish masters. Among others he copied Fuseli's 'Nightmare' and Reynolds's 'Garrick between Tragedy and Comedy.' He was also introduced to Sir Joshua Reynolds, and obtained permission to copy his pictures, and all accounts agree that before he was seventeen he had obtained considerable reputation not only with his friends and the dealers, but among artists of repute. A convincing proof of the skill in original composition which he had then attained is the fine engraving by William Ward [q. v.] after his picture of 'The Angler's Repast,' which was published in November 1780 by John Raphael Smith [q. v.] It is said that before his apprenticeship to his father came to an end, in 1784, Romney offered to take him into his own house, with a salary of 300*l.*, on condition of his signing articles for three years. But Morland, we are told, had had enough of restraint, and after a rupture with his father he set up on his own account in 1784 or 1785 at the house of a picture dealer, and commenced that life which, in its combination of hard work and hard drinking, is almost without a parallel.

Morland soon became the mere slave of the dealer with whom he lived. His boon companions were 'ostlers, potboys, horse jockeys, moneylenders, pawnbrokers, punks, and pugilists.' In this company the handsome young artist swaggered, dressed in a green coat, with large yellow buttons, leather breeches, and top boots. 'He was in the very extreme of foppish puppeyism,' says Hassell; 'his head, when ornamented according to his own taste, resembled a snowball, after the model of Tippey Bob, of dramatic memory, to which was attached a short, thick tail, not unlike a painter's brush.' His youth and strong constitution enabled him to recover rapidly from his excesses, and he not only employed the intervals in painting, but at this time, or shortly afterwards, taught himself to play the violin. He made also an effort, and a successful one, to free himself from his task-master, and escaped to Margate, where he painted miniatures for a while. He then paid a short visit to France.

Returning to London, he lodged in a house at Kensal Green, on the road to Harrow, near William Ward, intercourse with whose family seems for a time to have had a steadying influence. It resulted in his marriage with Miss Anne Ward (Nancy), the sister of his friend, in July 1786, and the bond between the families was strengthened a month later by the marriage of William Ward and Morland's sister Maria. The two newly married couples set up house together in High Street, Marylebone, and Morland for a while appeared to have become a reformed character. He was now becoming known by such engravings from his pictures as the large 'Children Nutting' (1783), and several smaller and more sentimental subjects published in 1785, like the 'Lass of Livingston.' To 1786, the year of his marriage, is said to belong the series of 'Letitia or Seduction' (well known from the engravings published in 1789), in which with much of the narrative power of Hogarth, but with softer touches, the 'Progress' of Letitia is told in six scenes admirable in design, and painted with great skill, finish, and refinement. About this period he was fond of visiting the Isle of Wight, where he painted his best coast scenes, and studied life and character in a low public-house at Freshwater Gate, called the Cabin.

After three months the double household was broken up by dissensions between the ladies, and Morland took lodgings in Great Portland Street, and afterwards moved to Camden Town, where he lived in a small house in Pleasing Passage, at the back of the tavern known as Mother Black Cap. The attractions of the neighbouring inns, and of the Assembly Rooms at Kentish Town, now proved too strong for him, and he returned to all his bad habits. A long illness of his wife, following her confinement and death of the child, further weakened the influence of home, and he neglected and ultimately left his wife, though he seems to have made her an allowance as long as he lived. When he finally separated from her it is not easy to determine, and his course afterwards was so erratic that it is difficult to trace it with minuteness and order. He moved from Pleasing Passage to Warrens Lane, and seems for some time to have made his headquarters at Paddington. It was here probably that he painted the celebrated picture of 'The Inside of a Stable,' now in the National Gallery, which was exhibited at the Royal Academy in 1791. The stable is said to be that of the White Lion Inn at Paddington, opposite to which he lived. At this time he was at the plenitude of his power, and dissipation had not impaired the sureness of his touch, his unusually fine sense of colour, or the refinement of his artistic feeling. He exhibited again in 1793 and 1794, but though he still painted finely he had become completely the prey of the dealers, painting as it were from hand to mouth to supply himself with funds for his extravagances. His art was so popular that, comparatively small as was the price which he actually received for his labour, he might have easily lived for a week on the earnings of a day. He was besieged by dealers who came to him, as it is said, with a purse in one hand and a bottle in the other. The amount of work he got through was prodigious. He would paint one or two pictures a day, and once painted a large landscape with six figures in the course of six hours. Every demand that was made upon him, whether a tavern score or the renewal of a bill, was paid by a picture. And they were good pictures too, generally worth many times the value of the account to be settled, and always popular in engravings. From 1788 to 1792 inclusive over a hundred engravings after Morland were published. They included 'A Visit to the Child at Home' and 'A Visit to the Boarding School,' two compositions of remarkable refinement and elegance, and a number of charming scenes of children's sports, like 'Children Birdnesting,' 'Juvenile Navigation,' 'The Kite entangled,' 'Blind Man's Buff,' and 'Children playing at Soldiers.' Equalling if not exceeding these in popularity were scenes of moral contrast, like 'The Fruits of early Industry and Economy' (1789) and 'The Effects of Extravagance and Idleness' (1794), the 'Miseries of Idleness' and the 'Comforts of Industry,' both published in 1790, and subjects appealing to national sentiment, like 'The Slave Trade' (1791) and 'African Hospitality.' Five hundred copies of the engraving of 'Dancing Dogs' (1790) were sold in a few weeks, and one dealer gave an order for nine dozen sets of the four plates of 'The Deserter' (1791). Elegant and refined subjects gradually gave place exclusively to scenes from humble life in town and country, including the coast with fishermen and smugglers, sporting scenes, but more frequently, in a plain but seldom a coarse manner, the life of the cottage, the stable, and the inn-yard, with lively groups of natural men and women, and still more natural horses, donkeys, dogs, pigs, poultry, and other animals. About 250 separate engravings from his works appeared in his lifetime.

Although the publishers reaped the benefits of their large sale, Morland's credit and resources enabled him for some years to lead the rollicking life he loved without much pressure of care. At one time he kept eight saddle horses at the White Lion. As time went on debts increased and creditors became more pressing, and he lived a hunted life, only able to escape from the bailiffs by his knowledge of London and the assistance of friends and dealers. He flitted from one house to another, residing among other places at Lambeth, East Sheen, Queen Anne Street, the Minories, Kensington, and Hackney. At Hackney his seclusion aroused the suspicion that he was a forger of bank notes, and his premises were searched at the instance of the bank directors, who afterwards made him a present of 40*l*. for the inconvenience caused by their mistake.

Dealers and innkeepers also would keep rooms ready for him to paint in, supplied with the necessary materials, and there was generally some dealer at hand ready to carry off his pictures before they were dry, often before they were finished. Morland was not, however, much more scrupulous in his dealings than the dealers themselves, and a picture begun under contract with one would be parted with to another who had money in his hand, if the rightful owner was not there to claim it. In this way a number of pictures got into the market commenced by Morland, and finished by inferior hands, while hundreds of copies were made and sold as originals. 'I once saw,' says Hassell, 'twelve copies from a small picture of Morland's at one time in a dealer's shop, with the original in the centre.' Another dealer (according to Redgrave), in whose house he painted under contract in the morning for several years (commencing about 1794), had each morning's work regularly copied. Occasionally Morland managed to escape from both dealers and bailiffs. Once he paid a visit to Claude Lorraine Smith in Leicestershire. He was apprehended as a spy at Yarmouth. He painted the sign of an inn called the Black Bull, somewhere on the road between Deal and London.

In November 1799 Morland was at last arrested for debt, but was allowed to take lodgings 'within the rules,' and these became the rendezvous of his most discreditable friends. During this mitigated confinement he sank lower and lower. He is said to have often been drunk for days together, and to have generally slept on the floor in a helpless condition. It is probable that these stories are exaggerated, for he still produced an enormous quantity of good work. 'For his brother alone,' says Redgrave, 'he painted 192 pictures between 1800 and 1804, and he probably painted as many more for other dealers during the same period, his terms being four guineas a day and his drink.' Another account says that during his last eight years he painted 490 pictures for his brother, and probably three hundred more for others, besides making hundreds of drawings. His total production is estimated at no less than four thousand pictures. In 1802 he was released under the Insolvent Debtors Act, but his health was ruined and his habits irremediable. About this time he was seized with palsy and lost the use of his left hand, so that he could not hold his palette. Notwithstanding he seems to have gone on painting to the last, when he was arrested again for a publican's score, and died in a sponging-house in Eyre Street, Cold Bath Fields, on 27 Oct. 1804. His much wronged wife was so afflicted at the news of his death that she died three days afterwards, and both were buried together in the burial-ground attached to St. James's Chapel in the Hampstead Road.

Morland's own epitaph on himself was 'Here lies a drunken dog.' His propensities to drink and low pleasure appear to have been unusually strong, he had opportunities of indulging them at an unusually early age, and throughout life, except for a short interval of courtship and domesticity, he was surrounded by associates who encouraged his degradation. But, though he was vain and dissolute, he was generous, good-natured, and industrious, and appears to have been free from the meaner and more malicious forms of vice. It should also be placed to his credit that however degraded his mode of life, he did not degrade his art to the same level. His most characteristic pictures are faithful reflections of lowly life in England as he saw it, with scarcely a taint of grossness or impurity. He treated it without the poetical sentiment of Gainsborough or the pretty affectations of Wheatley, but he was more natural and simple than either. Wherever he went he sketched and painted from the objects around him, and this is perhaps one reason why, despite his dissipation, he managed to infuse some freshness into his pictures, even when his execution was most hurried and mannered. His drawing was graceful, his composition elegant, and his colour rich and pure. In a word he was a master of *genre* and animal painting, an artist worthy to be placed in the same rank as the best of those Dutch masters whom he studied as a boy.

Morland's work, after a period of neglect, is now rising greatly in public estimation. Not only his pictures, but the engravings from them, are eagerly sought for. An exhibition of 'upwards of three hundred mezzotint engravings after George Morland' was held by Messrs. Vokins in Great Portland Street (December 1893). These were all executed between 1780 and 1817 by numerous engravers, the most important of whom were John Raphael Smith, William Ward (his brother-in-law), and S. W. Reynolds. One, 'The Idle Laundress,' was engraved by William Blake. A large selection of these plates has of late years been reproduced in small by Messrs. Graves & Co., and Mr. Joseph Grego has been long engaged on an important work on the painter, to be illustrated by fresh engravings.

There are two pictures by Morland in the National Gallery, six at South Kensington Museum, and two in the Gallery at Glasgow. A portrait painted by himself at an early age is in the National Portrait Gallery, London.

[Memoirs of the Painter, by F. W. Blagdon and J. Hassell; Life by George Dawe; Morland, his Life and Works, by Dr. G. C. Williamson, 1904; Memoirs of a Picture, &c., by William Collins; Redgrave's Artists; Bryan's Painters and Engravers; Algernon Graves's Dict. of Artists; Cunningham's Eminent British Painters, ed. Heaton; Nollekens and his Times; Edwards's Anecdotes; Notes and Queries, 2nd ser. iii. 8, vii. 58, 4th ser. xii. 389, &c.; Catalogue of Engravings at Messrs. Vokins's, 1893.] C. M.

MORLAND, GEORGE HENRY (*d.* 1789?), genre painter, was born early in the eighteenth century. His art at one time was popular, and some of his works, as 'The Pretty Ballad Singer,' 'The Fair Nun Unmasked,' were engraved by Watson, and 'The Oyster Woman' by Philip Dawe. The last of these pictures is now in the Glasgow Gallery. In 1760 he was assisted by a grant from the Incorporated Society of Artists. He lived on the south side of St. James's Square, and died in 1789 or after. His son, Henry Robert Morland [q. v.], was father of George Morland [q. v.]

[Redgrave's Dict.; Bryan's Dict. (Graves and Armstrong).] C. M.

MORLAND, Sir HENRY (1837–1891), Indian official, born on 9 April 1837, was third son of John Morland, esq., barrister-at-law, descendant of the Morlands of Capplethwaite and Killington Halls, Westmoreland, by Elizabeth, daughter of James Thompson, esq., of Grayrigg Hall in the same county. He was educated at Heversham and Bromsgrove schools, and also privately by Dr. Webster, mathematical master at Christ's Hospital. He entered the Indian navy in 1852, being appointed to the Akbar on 5 June. In September of the same year he joined the steamer Queen as midshipman. Between 1853 and 1856 he served on the north-east coast of Africa. He was present at the engagement with the Arabs at Shugra in 1853, and was in charge of the barque Norma, by which an Arab bugla which broke the Berbera blockade was captured in 1855. He next served on the Arabian coast, commanding a schooner at the reoccupation of Perim on 12 Jan. 1857, and a division of boats at the bombardment of Jeddah in July 1858. On 21 Nov. 1857 he became mate of the Dalhousie, and in the same month of the next year was fourth lieutenant on the Assaye. In October 1859, as the first lieutenant of the Clive, he took part in the naval operations on the coast of Kathiawar, Bombay Presidency, by which the Wagheer rising was put down. His last active service was with the Semiramis, January 1863, in the expedition by which the murderers of the officers of H.M.S. Penguin were punished. On 30 April 1863, when the order abolishing the Indian navy came into operation, he was placed on the retired list, with the rank of honorary lieutenant, and received a pension of 150*l*. He was now attached to the Indian marine, and in the spring of 1864 commanded the Dalhousie when engaged in laying down the marine cable of the Indo-European telegraph. Later in the same year he accompanied the convoy of the mission to Abyssinia, and was detained for some months at Massowah. In 1865 he became transport officer at Bombay, as well as dockmaster and signal officer; and in the following year superintendent of floating batteries. In 1866 he was in command of the party which rescued the Dalhousie when stranded on the Malabar coast on the sunken wreck of the Di Vernon.

He superintended the equipment and despatch of the fleet of transports of the Abyssinian expedition in 1867, when, besides twenty-seven thousand men and two thousand horses, forty-five elephants, six thousand bullocks, and three thousand mules and ponies were shipped. Morland was transport officer at Bombay till 1879, and in 1873 became conservator of the port, president of the board of marine examiners, and registrar of shipping. From April 1875 he also acted for a few months as secretary to the Bombay port trust.

In 1872 he went to Madras as a member of the commission to inquire into the recent wrecks, and he organised the commissariat and transport of the Afghan war. Meanwhile he also began to take an active part in municipal affairs at Bombay. In 1868 he was appointed J.P., and became a member of the corporation. In 1877 he was appointed a member of the town council. On 23 June 1886 he was elected chairman of the corporation, and was re-elected on 5 April 1887. He was chairman of the committee which drew up the Bombay jubilee address, which he took to England and presented to the queen at Windsor on 30 June, when he was knighted. He died at his residence in Rampart Row, Bombay, on 28 July 1891. He was buried with military honours.

Morland married in 1870 Alice Mary, second daughter of A. W. Critchley, esq., of Manchester, who died in 1871, leaving a daughter; and in 1875, Fanny Helen Hannah, second daughter of Jeronimo Carandini, twelfth marquis de Sarzano, by whom he had five children, of whom two died before him.

He was highly esteemed by Anglo-Indians and natives, and was a most efficient administrator. He was an enthusiastic freemason. In 1870, after having served in several minor offices, he was appointed by the grand lodge of Scotland to be provincial grandmaster for western India, including Ceylon, and in 1874 grandmaster of all Scottish freemasonry in India, including Aden. The foundation of the Mahometan lodge, 'Islam,' was almost entirely due to his influence. He was for some years secretary of the Bombay Geographical Society, to which in 1875 he read a paper on Abyssinia, and was also a fellow of Bombay University and of the Astronomical Society, and an associate of the Indian College of Engineers.

[Debrett's Peerage, &c., 1891; Bombay Gazette (weekly), 5 July 1887, 31 July, and 7 Aug. 1891; Overland Times of India (weekly), 31 July and 7 Aug. 1891; Times, 4 Aug. 1891, which gives age wrongly; Low's Hist of Indian Navy, ii. 411, 421, 422 (note), 554 (note), 572, Appendix A.] G. Le G. N.

MORLAND, HENRY ROBERT (1730?–1797), portrait-painter, the son of George Henry Morland [q. v.], was born probably about 1730. He was a painter of portraits and domestic subjects in oil and crayons, and between 1760 and 1791 exhibited 118 works at the Society of Artists, the Free Society, and the Royal Academy. He also engraved in mezzotint, cleaned and dealt in pictures, and sold artists' materials, including excellent crayons of his own manufacture. In spite of all these means of livelihood and a good character—for he is said to have been respected by all who knew him—he was unsuccessful in life, and more than once bankrupt. He painted a portrait of George III, which was engraved by Houston, and a portrait of Garrick as Richard III, which is in the Garrick Club. Lord Mansfield has two carefully finished pictures by him of young ladies—one washing, the other ironing—which used to pass as portraits of the celebrated Misses Gunning, but more probably were drawn from his own daughters or other models. He was an artist of some merit but of no conspicuous ability, and after an unsettled life, marked by frequent changes of residence, died in Stephen Street, Rathbone Place, 30 Nov. 1797. His age, at his death, has been stated as eighty-five, but this must be an exaggeration if his father was born in the eighteenth century. He was the father of George Morland [q. v.] Maria Morland, his wife, was also an artist, and exhibited at the Royal Academy in 1785 and 1786, one work in each year.

[Redgrave's Dict.; Bryan's Dict. (Graves and Armstrong); Algernon Graves's Dict.; Cunningham's Lives of Painters (ed. Heaton, article 'George Morland'). Some account of him will also be found in the Lives of his son quoted at end of article on George Morland.] C. M.

MORLAND, Sir SAMUEL (1625–1695), diplomatist, mathematician, and inventor, born in 1625 at Sulhampstead-Bannister, Berkshire, was son of Thomas Morland, rector of that parish. He entered Winchester School in 1638 (Kirby, *Winchester Scholars*, p. 178); and in May 1644, at the age of nineteen, entered as a sizar at Magdalene College, Cambridge, where he became acquainted with Bishop Cumberland (Payne, *Life of Cumberland*, p. 5). He was elected a fellow of the society on 30 Nov. 1649, and his name figures as tutor on the entry of Samuel Pepys at the college on 1 Oct. 1650 (information kindly supplied by A. G. Peskett, esq., Pepys librarian at Magdalene College). In his manuscript autobiography, preserved in the library at Lambeth Palace (No. 931), he states that after passing nine or ten years at the university, where he took no degree, he was solicited by some friends to enter into holy orders, but, not deeming himself 'fitly qualified,' he devoted his time to mathematical studies, which were the leading pursuit of his life. His last signature in the college books is dated 1653.

He was a zealous supporter of the parliamentarian party, and from 1647 onwards took part in public affairs. In 1653 he was sent in Whitelocke's retinue on the embassy to the queen of Sweden for the purpose of concluding an offensive and a defensive alliance (Whitelocke, *Journal*, 1772). Whitelocke describes him as 'a very civil man and an excellent scholar; modest and respectful: perfect in the Latin tongue: an ingenious mechanist.' Morland, according to his own account, was recommended on his return in 1654 as an assistant to Secretary Thurloe, and in May 1655 he was sent by Cromwell to the Duke of Savoy to remonstrate with him on cruelties inflicted by him upon the sect of Waldenses or Vaudois, which had strongly excited the English public. Morland carried a message to the duke beseeching him to rescind his persecuting edicts. He remained for some time at Geneva as the English resident, and he assisted the Rev. Dr. John Pell, resident ambassador with the Swiss cantons, in distributing the remittances sent by the charitable in England for the relief of the Waldenses. In August 1655 Morland was authorised to announce that the duke, at the request of the king of France, had granted an amnesty to the Waldenses, and confirmed their ancient privileges; and that the natives of the valleys, protestant and catholic, had met, embraced one another with tears, and sworn to live in perpetual amity together. During his residence in Geneva, Morland, at Thurloe's suggestion, prepared minutes, and procured records, vouchers, and attestations from which he might compile a correct history of the Waldenses (Vaughan, *Protectorate of Oliver Cromwell*, ii. 507). He arrived at Whitehall 18 Dec. 1656, and shortly afterwards received the thanks of a select committee appointed by Cromwell to inquire into his proceedings.

Two years later he published 'The History of the Evangelical Churches of the Valleys of Piemont. Together with a most naked and punctual relation of the late Bloudy Massacre, 1655. And a narrative of all the following transactions to the year of our Lord 1658. All which are justified, partly by divers ancient manuscripts written many hundred years before Calvin or Luther, and partly by the most authentick attestations: the true originals of the greatest part whereof are to be seen in their proper languages, by all the curious, in the Publick Library of the famous University of Cambridge,' London, 1658, fol. This volume, which was illustrated with sensational prints of the supposed sufferings of the Waldenses, 'operated like Fox's Book of Martyrs' (cf. Thomas Warton's note on Milton's sonnet 'On the late Massacre in Piemont,' in Milton's *Poems*, 1785, p. 357). Prefixed to the book is a fine portrait of Morland, engraved by P. Lombart, from a painting by Sir P. Lely, and an epistle dedicatory to Cromwell, couched in a strain of extreme adulation. In Hollis's 'Memoirs' it is stated that Morland afterwards withdrew this dedication from all the copies he could lay hands on.

Most of the Waldensian manuscripts brought to England and partly published by Morland were said by him to exhibit the date 1120, and they have been often quoted to prove the fabulous antiquity of the sect, which was falsely alleged to have existed long before the time of Peter Waldensis. Morland's documents have since been proved, however, to be forgeries of moderate skill and ingenuity. Morland was probably misled by incorrect statements of the Waldensian minister, Jean Leger, master of an academy at Geneva, whose 'Histoire Generale des Eglises Evangeliques de Piemont,' published at Amsterdam in 1680, may be regarded as an enlarged edition of Morland's book. Six of the most important manuscript volumes brought over by Morland were long supposed to have mysteriously disappeared from the Cambridge University Library, and it was generally believed that they had been abstracted by the puritans; but they were all discovered by Mr. Henry Bradshaw in 1862, in their proper places, where they had probably remained undisturbed for centuries (*Cambridge Antiquarian Communications*, ii. 203; *Athenæum*, 20 May 1865, p. 684; Todd, *Books of the Vaudois*, 1865; Melia, *Origin . . . of the Waldenses*, 1870; *Cat. of MSS. in Univ. Libr. Cambr.* i. 81–9, 548–52, v. 589).

Morland now became intimately associated with the government of the Commonwealth, and he admits that he was an eye and ear witness of Dr. Hewitt's being 'trepanned to death' by Thurloe and his agents. The most remarkable intrigue, however, which came to his knowledge was that usually called Sir Richard Willis's plot. Its object was to induce Charles II and his brother to effect a landing on the Sussex coast, under pretence of meeting many adherents, and to put them both to death the moment they disembarked. This plot is said to have formed the subject of a conference between Cromwell, Thurloe, and Willis at Thurloe's office, and the conversation was overheard by Morland, who pretended to be asleep at his desk. Welwood relates that when Cromwell discovered Morland's presence he drew his poniard, and would have killed him on the spot but for Thurloe's solemn assurance that his secretary had sat up two nights in succession, and was certainly fast asleep (Welwood, *Memoirs*, ed. 1820, p. 98). From this time Morland endeavoured to promote the Restoration. In justifying to himself the abandonment of his former principles and associates, he observes that avarice could not be his object, as he was at this time living in greater plenty than he ever did after the Restoration, 'having a house well furnished, an establishment of servants, a coach, &c., and 1,000*l.* a year to support all this, with several hundred pounds of ready money, and a beautiful young woman to his wife for a companion.' In order to save the king's life and promote the Restoration, he eventually went to Breda, where he arrived on 6–16 May 1660, bringing with him letters and notes of importance. The king welcomed him graciously, and publicly acknowledged the services he had rendered for some years past (Lower, *Charles II's Voiage and Residence in Holland*, 1660, p. 12; Kennett, *Register and Chronicle*, p. 135).

Grave charges of various kinds were brought against him by Sir Richard Willis, when he was pleading for a full pardon in 1661, but they do not seem to have received much credit. Among other statements was one to the effect that Morland boasted that he had 'poisoned Cromwell in a posset, and that Thurloe had a lick of it, which laid him up for a great while' (*State Papers*, Dom. 1661, p. 232). Pepys originally conceived a low opinion of Morland from the adverse rumours that were circulated about him; but when he heard his own account of his transactions with Thurloe and Willis 'began to think he was not so much a fool' as he had taken him to be.

The king made him liberal promises of future preferment, but these were for the most part unfulfilled, in consequence, as Morland supposed, of the enmity of Lord-chancellor Hyde. However, he was on 18 July 1660 created a baronet, being described as of Sulhampstead-Bannister, although it does not appear very clearly whether he was in possession of the manor or of any considerable property in the parish (BURKE, *Extinct Baronetcies*, 1844, p. 371). He was also made a gentleman of the privy chamber; but this appointment, he says, was rather expensive than profitable, as he was obliged to spend 450*l.* in two days on the ceremonies attending the coronation. He obtained, indeed, a pension of 500*l.* on the post-office (*State Papers*, Dom. 1661–2, pp. 64, 69), but his embarrassments obliged him to sell it, and, returning to his mathematical studies, he endeavoured by various experiments and the construction of machines to earn a livelihood. On 13 Jan. 1666–7 he obtained, with Richard Wigmore, Robert Lindsey, and Thomas Culpeper, a probably remunerative patent 'for making metal fire-hearths' (*ib.* 1666, pp. 434, 588). From a correspondence between Morland and Dr. Pell it appears that about this same time (1666) the former had intended to publish a work 'On the Quadrature of Curvilinear Spaces,' and had actually proceeded to print part of it, but was happily persuaded by Pell to lay it aside (*Birch MS.* 4279; cf. *Lansd. MS.* 751, f. 399).

In carrying out his experiments in hydrostatics and hydraulics he encountered many difficulties in consequence of their expense. On 12 Dec. 1672 the king granted to him the sum of 250*l.* to defray the charges of about five hundred looking-glasses 'to be by him provided and sett up in Ollive wood frames for our special use and service,' as well as an annuity of 300*l.*, 'in considerac'on of his keepinge and mainteyneing in constant repaire a certain private printing presse . . . which by our Especial Order and Appointment he hath lately erected and sett up' (*Gent. Mag.* April 1850, p. 394).

In 1677 he took a lease for twenty-one years of a house at Vauxhall, on the site subsequently occupied by Vauxhall Gardens. On the top of this house was a Punchinello holding a dial (AUBREY, *Surrey*, i. 12). In 1681 he was appointed 'magister mechanicorum' to the king, who in recognition of his ingenuity presented him with a medallion portrait of himself, set in diamonds, together with a medal as 'an honorable badge of his signal loyalty' (EVELYN, *Numismata*, p. 141). In October 1684 the king advanced him 200*l.*, and a year later Morland received a similar sum by way of 'bounty' (ACKERMAN, *Secret Services of Charles II and James II*, Camd. Soc., pp. 91, 112). About 1684 he removed to a house near the waterside at Hammersmith, which was afterwards tenanted by Dr. Bathie, and was known in 1813 as Walbrough House. According to his own account, his mechanical experiments pleased the king's fancy; but when he had spent 500*l.* or 1,000*l.* upon them, he received sometimes only half, and sometimes only a third, of the cost.

In 1682 Charles II sent him to France 'about the king's waterworks,' but there also he seems to have lost more than he gained. On his return James II restored to him his pensions, which had been for some reason withdrawn, and likewise granted him part of the arrears, but Morland was never repaid the expenses of the engine which he had constructed for bringing water from Blackmore Park, near Winkfield, to the top of Windsor Castle. During 1686 Morland was corresponding with Pepys about the new naval gun-carriages. In 1687 his pension was paid down to Ladyday 1689 (*ib.* p. 178).

In 1689 he addressed a long letter to Archbishop Tenison, giving an account of his life, and concluding with a declaration that his only wish was to retire and spend his life 'in Christian solitude;' and he begs the primate's 'helping hand to have his condition truly represented to his Majesty.' Tenison probably did something for him, as there is a letter of thanks for 'favours and acts of charity,' dated 5 March 1695. The errors of his life were probably considerable, as he speaks of having been at one time excommunicated; but some of his writings show that he was a sincere penitent, particularly 'The Urim of Conscience,' London, 1695, 8vo, written, as the title says, 'in blindness and retirement.' He lost his sight about three years before his death. Evelyn, in his 'Diary' (25 Oct. 1695), gives an interesting glimpse of him: 'The archbishop and myself went to Hammersmith to visit Sir Samuel Morland, who was entirely blind; a very mortifying sight. He showed us his invention of writing, which was very ingenious; also his wooden calendar, which instructed him all by feeling, and other pretty and useful inventions of mills, pumps, &c., and the pump he had erected that serves water to his garden and to passengers, with an inscription, and brings from a filthy part of the Thames near it a most perfect and pure water. He had newly buried 200*l.* worth of music books, being, as he said, love songs and vanity. He plays himself psalms and religious hymns on the Theorbo' (cf. FAULKNER, *Fulham*, p. 161). He died on 30 Dec. 1695, and was buried in Hammersmith Chapel on 6 Jan. 1695-6. He must have been in an extremely weak condition, as he was unable to sign his will. By it he disinherited his only son, Samuel, who was the second and last baronet of the family, and bequeathed his property to Mrs. Zenobia Hough.

He married, first, in 1657, Susanne, daughter of Daniel de Milleville, baron of Boissay in Normandy, and of the Lady Catherine, his wife; secondly, on 26 Oct. 1670, in Westminster Abbey, Carola, daughter of Sir Roger Harsnett, knight (she died on 10 Oct. 1674, aged 22); thirdly, on 16 Nov. 1676, in Westminster Abbey, Anne, third daughter of George Feilding of Solihull, Warwickshire, by May, second daughter of Sir Thomas Shirley, knight, of Wiston, Sussex (she died on 20 Feb. 1679-80, aged 18); fourthly, at Knightsbridge Chapel, Middlesex, on 1 Feb. 1686-7, Mary Aylif, a woman of low origin and infamous character, from whom he obtained a divorce on 16 July following, and who subsequently became the second wife of Sir Gilbert-Cosins Gerard (CHESTER, *Registers of Westminster Abbey*, p. 593; cf. PEPYS, v. 323, 329).

Morland was one of the chief mechanicians of his time. Aubrey credits him with the invention of 'drum cap-stands for weighing heavy anchors.' It is admitted that he invented the speaking-trumpet—though Kircher disputed his claim—and two arithmetical machines, of which he published a description under the following title: 'The Description and Use of two Arithmetick Instruments, together with a short treatise explaining and demonstrating the ordinary operations of arithmetick; as likewise, a perpetual almanack and several useful tables,' 4 parts, London, 1673, 16mo. The perpetual almanack is reprinted in Playford's 'Vade Mecum,' 1679, and in Falgate's 'Interest in Epitome,' 1725. The arithmetical machines, originally presented to Charles II in 1662, were manufactured for sale by Humphry Adanson, who lived with Jonas Moore, esq., in the Tower of London. By means of them the four fundamental rules of arithmetic were readily worked 'without charging the memory, disturbing the mind, or exposing the operations to any uncertainty.' This calculating machine appears to have been a modification of one constructed by Blaise Pascal about 1642. (For the subsequent development of the instrument, the prototype of the arithmometer of M. Thomas of Colmar, which is at present in extensive use, see the article 'Calculating Machines' in Walford's 'Insurance Cyclopædia,' i. 413; see also articles JOHN NAPIER of Merchiston and CHARLES BABBAGE.) One of Morland's machines is now at South Kensington. Pepys characterised one that he saw as very pretty but not very useful. A similar instrument seems to be indicated by No. 84 of the Marquis of Worcester's 'Century of Inventions.' Morland's treatise on the speaking-trumpet is entitled: 'Tuba Stentoro-Phonica, an Instrument of excellent use, as well at Sea, as at Land. Invented, and variously experimented in . . . 1670,' London, 1671, fol.; 2nd edit. London, 1672, fol. An advertisement states that the instruments of all sizes and dimensions were made and sold by Simon Beal, one of his majesty's trumpeters, in Suffolk Street. The tubes are stated in a French edition of the treatise published in London (1671) to be on sale by Moses Pitt for 2*l.* 5*s.* each. One is still preserved at Cambridge (see an account of the instrument in *Phil. Trans. Abridged*, i. 670; cf. *Notes and Queries*, 6th ser. ix. 423).

Morland's most important discoveries were in connection with hydrostatics, although the statement that he invented the fire-engine is untrue; he was only an improver of that machine [see under LUCAR, CYPRIAN, and GREATOREX, RALPH]. The problems connected with raising water to a height by mechanical means were receiving a great amount of attention during the middle of the seventeenth century, and to the discoveries made in this field (in which Morland bore an important part) are largely attributable the subsequent rapid development of the steam-engine and the accelerated rate of evolution in mechanical science generally. Morland may have had his attention drawn more particularly to this subject by Pascal's researches, which were then attracting attention in France, though Pascal's celebrated treatise 'Sur l'Équilibre des Liqueurs' was not published until 1663. It is certain that from Morland's return to England in 1660 water-engines of various kinds occupied the bulk of his time and capital. On 11 Dec. 1661 a royal warrant was issued for a grant to Morland of the sole use during fourteen years of his invention for raising 'water out of pits to any reasonable height by the force of aire and powder conjointly' (*Publ. Rec. Office Warrant Book*, v. 85; *Cal. State Papers*, Dom. 1661–2, pp. 175, 199). The method employed seems to have been as follows. An air-tight box or cistern was fixed at a height above the level of the water to be raised. A charge of gunpowder was exploded within this cistern, and the air expelled by means of valves; a (partial) vacuum being thus formed, the water is driven up from the reservoir below by the atmospheric pressure. The simple apparatus used was subsequently developed by Jean de Hauteville and by Huyghens (1679). In February 1674 a bill to enable Morland 'to enjoy the sole benefit of certain pumps and water-engines by him invented' was read a second time in the House of Commons (*Commons' Journals*, ix. 300, 308, 314). The introduction of the bill elicited 'Reasons offered against the passing of Sir Samuel Morland's Bill touching Water-Engines,' in which it was urged that the inventor should have recourse to the ordinary letters patent for fourteen years. Morland published an 'Answer,' stating that he had expended twenty years' study and some thousands of pounds on his experiments. The measure, however, failed to pass, as did a similar bill in 1677 (*ib.* ix. 403, 412), and he had to be content with a patent (No. 175, dated 14 March 1674). The pump in question, referred to as 'raising great quantities of water with farre less proportion of strength than can be performed by an Chayne or other Pumpe,' was apparently what is known as the 'plunger-pump,' the most important new feature in which is the gland and stuffing-box. This important contrivance, with which James Watt has often been wrongly credited, was undoubtedly the invention of Morland (cf. Pole, *Treatise on the Cornish Pumping-Engine*, 1844; P. R. Björling, *Pumps, historically, theoretically, and practically considered*, 1890, p. 11). With a cast-iron perpendicular-action pump of this nature it is stated that Morland in 1675 raised water from the Thames sixty feet above the top of Windsor Castle at the rate of sixty barrels per hour by eight men (cf. *Philosoph. Trans.* 1674, ix. 25). Elsewhere Morland states he raised twelve barrels of water 140 feet high in one hour by the force of one man. An interesting schedule of his prices, with other papers concerning his inventions, is among the 'British Museum Tracts' (816, m. 10). For a brass force-pump suitable for raising water from a deep well he charged 60*l.*, and for an 'engine to quench fire or wet the sails of a ship' from 23*l.* upwards.

Another very interesting and important evidence of Morland's inventive genius is supplied by a manuscript in the Harleian collection at the British Museum (No. 5771). This manuscript is a thin book upon vellum, written in elegant and ornamental characters, and entitled 'Elevation des Eaux, par toute sorte de machines, reduite à la mesure, au poids, et à la balance,' 1683. At page 35 is an account of what seems to be one of the first steps made towards the art of working by steam. It has this separate title: 'Les principes de la nouvelle force de feu; inventée par le Chev. Morland l'an 1682, et presentée à sa majesté tres Chrestienne, 1683.' The author thus reasons on his principle: 'L'Eau estant evaporée par la force de Feu, ces vapeurs demandent incontinent une plus grand' espace (environ deux mille fois) que l'eau n'occupoiet [*sic*] auparavant, et plus tost que d'etre toujours emprisonnées, feroient crever un piece de Canon. Mais estant bien gouvernées selon les regles de la Statique, et par science reduites à la mesure, au poids et à la balance, alors elles portent paisiblement leurs fardeaux (comme des bons chevaux) et ainsi servient elles du grand usage au gendre humain, particulierement pour l'elevation des Eaux.' Then follows a table of weights to be thus raised by cylinders half full of water, according to their diameters. Subsequently Morland printed a book at Paris, with the same title, from 'Elevation des Eaux' to 'à la balance,' after which it runs thus: 'par le moyen d'un nouveau piston, et corps de pompe, et d'un nouveau mouvement cyclo-elliptique, en rejettant l'usage de toute sorte de Manivelles ordinaires: avec huit problemes de mechanique proposez aux plus habiles et aux plus sçavans du siecle, pour le bien public,' Paris, 1685, 4to. In the dedication to the king of France Morland says that as his majesty was pleased with the models and ocular demonstrations he had the honour to exhibit at Saint-Germain, he thought himself obliged to present his book as a tribute to so great a monarch. He states that it contains an abridged account of the best experiments he had made for the last thirty years respecting the raising of water, with figures in profile and perspective, calculated to throw light upon the mysteries of hydrostatics. It begins with a perpetual almanac, showing the day of the month or week for the time past, present, and to come, and it contains various mathematical problems and tables. This suggestion for the employment of high-pressed steam to raise water (probably by means of Morland's own force-pump) was doubtless brought forward in connection with the many schemes suggested for supplying Versailles with water from the Seine. There is no exact description of the engine proposed by Morland, but the project is of the highest interest as one of the first to demonstrate the practical utility of steam-power. Morland's experiments must have been conducted with great care and skill, his estimate that at the temperature of boiling water steam was about two thousand times more bulky than water being substantially confirmed by Watt after careful investigation some hundred years later (cf. paper by Mr. E. H. COOPER in *Transactions of the Institute of Civil Engineers*, January 1884; MUIRHEAD, *Life of Watt*, 2nd ed. p. 76; ELIJAH GALLOWAY, *History of the Steam Engine*, 1831, p. 26; R. L. GALLOWAY, *Steam Engine*, pp. 108, 141; and cf. art. SOMERSET, EDWARD, second MARQUIS OF WORCESTER). From one of the several medals that were struck in Morland's honour and are now preserved in the British Museum, it would appear that he had also seriously considered the possibility of employing steam as a prime mover in the propulsion of vessels. The medal in question represents a conical-shaped vessel on a square wooden base, floating upon the sea. In the side is inserted a long pipe or arm, and from the top issues steam. In the distance is a ship in full sail, and the legend is 'Concordes . ignibvs . undæ.' (HAWKINS, *Medallic Illust.* p. 596; and art. HULLS, JONATHAN).

Morland's other works are: 1. 'A New Method of Criptography,' 1666, fol. 2. 'Four Diagrams of Fortifications' [1670?], fol.; attributed to him in the British Museum Catalogue. 3. 'The Count of Pagan's Method of delineating all manner of Fortifications from the exterior Polygone, reduced to English measure, and converted into Hereotectonick Lines,' London, 1672. 4. 'A new and most useful Instrument for Addition and Subtraction, &c., with a perpetual Almanack,' London, 1672, 8vo. The perpetual Almanack is reprinted in John Playford's 'Vade Mecum,' 1717. 5. 'The Doctrine of Interest, both simple and compound, explained . . . discovering the errors of the ordinary Tables of Rebate for Annuities, at simple interest,' London, 1679, 8vo. 6. 'The Poor Man's Dyal, with an Instrument to set it. Made applicable to any place in England, Scotland, Ireland, &c.,' London, 1689, 4to, pp. 5. This tract, giving directions for the construction of a simple sun-dial, was reprinted in facsimile by Mr. Richard B. Prosser [London, 1886], 4to, from a copy, probably unique, in the library at Lambeth. 7. 'Hydrostatics, or Instructions concerning Waterworks,' London, 1697, 12mo; a posthumous work, edited by his son, Samuel Morland, and containing an account of various methods of raising water and tables of square and cube roots. It appears from the preface that a number of mathematical papers, left by Morland, were then in his son's possession.

Besides Lely's portrait mentioned above, there is a portrait prefixed to the 'Description and Use of two Arithmetical Instruments,' and another after a drawing in the Pepysian collection is reproduced in 'Pepys's Diary' (ed. Wheatley, iii.) A miniature of Morland belonged to Bennet Woodcroft of the Patent Office.

[Addit. MSS. 5825 f. 145 *b*, 5876 f. 43; Birch MS. 4279; Bradshaw's Essays; Chalmers's Biog. Dict.; Clarendon's Hist. of the Rebellion, vi. 667, 668, 670; Dircks's Life of the Second Marquis of Worcester, pp. 353, 365, 512; Manning and Bray's Surrey, iii. 489, 901, 991, and App. cv.; Leupold's Theatrum Machinarum Hydraulicorum, Leipzig, 1725; Faulkner's Fulham, pp. 161, 357; Gent. Mag. 1818, ii. 12; Granger's Biog. Hist. of Engl. 5th ed. iii. 357; Gwillim's Heraldry (1724), p. 200; J. O. Halliwell's Life of Morland, privately printed, Cambridge, 1838, 8vo; Histoire de l'Acad. Roy. des Sciences, Paris, 1733, i. 448; Hollis's Memoirs, i. 142, 428, ii. 586–8; North's Life of Lord Keeper North, 1808, ii 251; Hatton Correspondence (Camd. Soc.), ii. 70; Nalson's Heraclitus Ridens (1713), p. 41; Nichols's Illustr. Lit. vi. 621; Pote's Windsor Castle; Rees's Cyclopædia; Stuart's Anecdotes of Steam Engines, i. 71–6; Tighe and Davis's Annals of Windsor, iii. 388–91; Walpole's Anecd. of Painting, iii. 88; D'Israeli's Curiosities of Literature, 1841, p. 480; Welwood's Memoirs (1700), p. 111; Notes and Queries, 8th ser. vi. 142.] T. C.

MORLEY, EARLS OF. [See PARKER, JOHN, first EARL, 1772–1840; PARKER, EDMUND, second EARL, 1810–1864, under PARKER, JOHN, first EARL.]

MORLEY, BARONS. [See PARKER, HENRY, eighth BARON, 1476 – 1556; PARKER, HENRY, ninth BARON, *d.* 1577, under PARKER, HENRY, eighth BARON.]

MORLEY, CHRISTOPHER LOVE (*fl.* 1700), physician, was born in or about 1646, and from his name may probably have been related to Christopher Love [q. v.] the presbyterian. He was entered as a medical student at Leyden 18 Feb. 1676 (*English Students at Leyden*, Index Society, 1883), being then thirty years of age (MUNK), and graduated M.D. in 1679. According to a short account of Morley in the preface to his 'Collectanea Chymica,' he had travelled widely, and apparently practised medicine before coming to Holland. At Leyden he attended the medical practice of Schacht and Drelincourt, with the anatomical lectures of the latter, and also studied chemistry with Maëts and others. Morley was accustomed to take copious notes of lectures, cases, &c., which ultimately extended, it is said, to more than forty quarto volumes. Thirty-six of these survive, and are now in the British Museum (Sloane MSS. 1256-8, 1259-80, 1282-94, 1297-9). They are dated 1677 to 1679, and not only show Morley's diligence as a student, but give an interesting picture of the state of medical education in Leyden at the time. On his return to England he published a little volume on an epidemic fever then prevalent in England, Holland, and elsewhere, which he dedicated to the College of Physicians ('De Morbo Epidemico,' 1678-9, &c., London, 1680, 12mo). It contains an account of his personal experience of the disease, and a letter from Professor Schacht of Leyden on the same subject, besides remarks on the state of medical practice in England and Holland. This probably led to his election as an honorary fellow of the College of Physicians 30 Sept. 1680 (since, not being an English graduate, he was not eligible to become an ordinary fellow). He did not immediately settle down, for in 1683 we find him going on a voyage to the Indies, but in 1684 he was practising in London.

In the new charter granted to the college in 1686 by James II Morley was named as an actual fellow, and was admitted in the following year. This fact shows that he was a partisan of James II, and probably a Roman catholic, so that he found a difficulty in taking the oaths required by the government after the revolution, and finally, in 1700, his name was on that ground withdrawn, at his own request, from the college list. His subsequent career cannot be traced.

Morley was evidently a man of remarkably wide knowledge in medicine and other sciences, but he did nothing in later life to justify his early promise. Beside the work mentioned above he published 'Collectanea Chemica Leydensia' (Leyden, 1684, 4to), which is evidently extracted from the notebooks above referred to. It consists of a large number of chemical and pharmaceutical receipts taken from the lectures of three professors of chemistry at Leyden—Maëts, Marggraff, and Le Mort. It was translated into German (Jena, 1696), and appeared in a second Latin edition (Antwerp, 1702, 12mo).

[Morley s works; Munk's Coll. of Phys. 1878, i. 450.] J. F. P.

MORLEY, MERLAI, MERLAC, or MARLACH, DANIEL OF (*fl.* 1170-1190), astronomer, apparently came from Morley, Norfolk (cf. BLOMEFIELD, *Norfolk*, passim), and is said to have been educated at Oxford. Thence he proceeded to the university of Paris, and applied himself especially to the study of mathematics; but dissatisfied with the teaching there, he left for Toledo, then famous for its school of Arabian philosophy. At Toledo he remained for some time. The statements of Pits, Wood, and Blomefield that he visited Arabia are erroneous. Morley returned to England with a valuable collection of books. He was apparently disappointed at the neglect of science in England, and a passage in his book has been interpreted to mean that he was on the point of setting out again for foreign parts when he met John of Oxford (1175-1200), bishop of Norwich, who persuaded him to remain. The date of Morley's death is unknown.

Morley was author of a book called both 'Philosophia Magistri Danielis de Merlac,' and 'Liber de Naturis inferiorum et superiorum,' dedicated to John of Oxford; it is in Arundel MS. 377 ff. 88-103, and from the preface is derived all that is known of Morley's life. The Arundel MS. divides the work into two books, one, 'De superiori parte mundi,' the other, 'De inferiori parte mundi;' in it Morley quotes frequently from Arabian and Greek philosophers, and vaunts the superiority of the former; he is not free, however, from astrological superstitions. Another copy of the work is No. 95 in the Corpus Christi College, Oxford, MSS., and is erroneously catalogued under W. de Conchys (COXE, *Cat. Cod. MSS. in Coll. Oxon.*) This copy lacks the preface, and mentions a third book of the work beginning 'Seneca loquens ad Lucilium,' which is not in the Arundel MS. Pits also attributes to Morley a treatise in one book called 'De Principiis Mathematicis,' and 'alia quædam,' which he does not specify.

[Arundel MS. 377; Coxe's Cat. Cod. MSS.; Wright's Biographia Literaria, ii. 227-30; Hardy's Descr. Cat. ii. 550; Leland's Scriptt. Ill. ed. Hall, p. 244, and Collectanea, iv. 192; Bale, ed. 1557, pp. 229-30; Pits, p. 254; Wood's Hist. and Antiquities, ed. Gutch, i. 168; Arthur Duck's De Vsu et Authoritate, vol. ii. cap. viii. p. 141; Burrows's Collectanea (Oxford Hist. Soc.), ii. 146, 171, 172, 323; Blomefield's Norfolk, iii. 477.] A. F. P.

MORLEY, GEORGE (1597-1684), bishop of Winchester, son of Francis Morley, esq., and Sarah, sister to Sir John Denham [q. v.], judge, was born in Cheapside, London, on 27 Feb. 1597. Both his parents died by the time that he was twelve, and his father having before his death fallen into difficulties by becoming surety for others, left him unprovided for. When he was about fourteen he was admitted king's scholar at Westminster, and in 1615 was elected to Christ Church, Oxford

(WELCH, *Alumni Westmonasterienses*, p. 83). He graduated B.A. in 1618, and proceeded M.A. in 1621, and D.D. in 1642. Remaining at Oxford, he made many friends, among whom were Henry Hammond [q. v.], Robert Sanderson [q. v.], afterwards bishop of Lincoln, William Chillingworth [q. v.], Gilbert Sheldon [q. v.], afterwards archbishop of Canterbury, Lucius Cary, afterwards second viscount Falkland [q. v.], at whose house at Great Tew, Oxfordshire, he was a frequent guest, and, above all, of Edward Hyde, afterwards earl of Clarendon. His remarkably cultured mind, his witty conversation, and his high moral character won him the regard and admiration of men of taste and learning. It is related that Edmund Waller the poet, when one day sitting with Chillingworth, Falkland, and others, heard that some one was arrested in the street below, found that it was 'one of Jonson's sons,' George Morley, and at once paid the debt of 100*l.*, on condition that Morley would stay with him. Morley constantly visited him at his house in Buckinghamshire, and Waller used to declare that it was from him that he learned to love the ancient poets (*Life of Waller*, pp. 8, 9, prefixed to *Works*). Morley's arrest must probably have arisen out of the debts which his father had incurred. He was a Calvinist, though at the same time a thorough churchman. Being once asked, apparently about 1635, what the Arminians held, he answered that they held all the best bishoprics and deaneries in England. Neither his opinions nor his wit pleased Laud, who had a prejudice against him, and his friendship with John Hampden (1594–1643) [q. v.], Arthur Goodwin [q. v.], and others of the same views, made some suspect that he was no true friend to the church (CLARENDON, *Life*, i. 50). He was for a time chaplain to Robert Dormer, earl of Carnarvon [q. v.], and was in 1640 presented to the sinecure rectory of Hartfield, Sussex. His friend Hyde evidently forwarded his interests, and in 1641 [see under HYDE for significance of date] he was made a canon of Christ Church, having previously been appointed one of the king's chaplains, gave his first year's stipend to help the king in his war [see under CHARLES I], and exchanged his sinecure for the rectory, with cure, of Mildenhall, Wiltshire.

He was appointed in 1642 to preach before the House of Commons, but his sermon was so little to the members' liking that they refrained from paying him the usual compliment of requesting him to print it (WOOD). Nevertheless he was appointed by both houses one of the assembly of divines, but he never attended any of its meetings, and served the king by all means in his power. In obedience to the king's direction he took a prominent part in the resistance of the university of Oxford to the parliamentary visitation of 1647, and served on the delegacy appointed by convocation to manage the opposition (BURROWS, *Visitors' Register*, Pref. lxiii; WOOD). When in the autumn the second attempt at visitation was resisted, and the heads of houses were summoned to appear before the committee of the two houses, Morley was selected to instruct counsel on their behalf. He was deprived of his canonry and his rectory. He resisted, and was finally ejected in the spring of 1648. In a letter to Whitelocke, which appears in Whitelocke's 'Memorials' under May 1647, he speaks of his canonry as all his subsistence (*Memorials*, ii. 150). It is said that he might have avoided ejectment if he would have promised to abstain from opposition to the visitors, and that he suffered a short imprisonment on account of it (WOOD; WALKER). In the summer of 1647 he attended the king as one of his chaplains at Newmarket (CLARENDON, *History*, x. 93), and is said to have taken part in the Newport negotiations in the autumn of 1648 (WOOD). In March 1649 he attended his friend, Arthur Capel, lord Capel [q. v.], after his sentence, and accompanied him to the foot of the scaffold (*ib.* xi. 264).

Morley then left England, went to the court of Charles II at St. Germains, and while in Paris officiated in the chapel of Sir Richard Browne (1605–1683) [q. v.] (EVELYN, *Diary*, i. 254, 271 *n.*) Having accompanied the king to Breda, he preached before him on the eve of Charles's departure for Scotland in 1650. Hyde wrote to Lady Morton [see under DOUGLAS, WILLIAM, seventh or eighth EARL OF MORTON], speaking of the comfort that Morley would be to her (*Cal. of Clarendon Papers*, ii. 21). At first the royalists at the Hague, where he remained after the king's departure, seem to have looked upon him with some coldness, believing that he had presbyterian leanings, and Hyde wrote again to Lady Morton to correct this impression (*ib.* p. 65). Some of them, however, immediately recognised his value, Lady Elizabeth Thynne being one of 'his elect ladies;' he read prayers twice a day, and performed the other offices of the church for the English royalists in every place at which he stayed during his exile, and was soon regarded as their most prominent and useful clergyman, being referred to somewhat later in correspondence as 'the honest doctor' (*ib.* passim; *Nicholas Papers*, i. 208; WOOD). He gratuitously acted as chaplain to Elizabeth, queen of Bohemia, and also served Lady Frances Hyde in the same capacity at Antwerp, where he was entertained by Sir Charles Cotterell [q. v.] He was in Antwerp for some time in 1653, where he formed a high opinion of Henry, duke of Gloucester, and had much conversation with Colonel Joseph Bampfield [q. v.], about which he wrote to Sir Edward Nicholas (*Nicholas Papers*, ii. 21). He was at Düsseldorf in October 1654, when the Duke of Neuburg entertained the king there. A malicious story, afterwards proved to be false, was set abroad about his indiscreet behaviour at the duke's table (*ib.* pp. 154, 170). He also visited Breda, where 'he was gallantly entertained,' and did not return to the Hague until April 1655 (*ib.* pp. 244, 251; *Cal. of Clarendon Papers*, ii. 333). Shortly before the Restoration he was sent over to England by Hyde to prepare the presbyterians to forward the king's return, and specially to contradict the report that Charles was a Roman catholic. He had great success, for he let his Calvinistic opinions be known, and spoke of his hopes of peace and union (Wood; Calamy, *Abridgment*, p. 569). He proposed to meet the presbyterians' demands with reference to the negative power of the presbyters and the validity of their orders, either by silence, or in the case of the latter demand, by a hypothetical re-ordination (*Clarendon State Papers*, pp. 727, 738).

At the Restoration Morley regained his canonry, and in July was made dean of Christ Church. When his former pupil, Anne Hyde, duchess of York [q. v.], was delivered of a son on 22 Oct. 1660 he was sent for, and put questions to her establishing the legitimacy of the child (Clarendon, *Life*, i. 333). On the 28th he was consecrated to the see of Worcester. He preached the sermon at the coronation on 23 April 1661, being then dean of the chapel royal. At the Savoy conference in May he was 'prime manager,' and the chief speaker of the bishops (Calamy, *Abridgment*, pp. 154, 171). In September he visited Oxford with the Earl of Clarendon, the new chancellor of the university (Wood, *Life and Times*, i. 411). Having refused to allow Richard Baxter [q. v.] to resume his ministry at Kidderminster, he went thither himself, and preached against presbyterianism. Baxter replied by publishing his 'Mischief of Self-ignorance.' In 1662 he was translated to the see of Winchester. Rich as that bishopric was, Charles, who knew Morley's munificence, declared that he would never be the richer for it. Besides giving away large sums, he was extremely hospitable. Among his guests was Isaac Walton [q. v.], who appears to have been much under his roof. The king and the Duke of York rather abused his hospitality, for Farnham Castle was conveniently situated for their hunting, and for the king to overlook the progress of his building at Winchester, and the bishop is said once to have asked Charles whether he meant to make his house an inn (Prideaux, *Letters*, p. 141). At Winchester he was brought into close relations with Thomas Ken [q. v.], afterwards bishop of Bath and Wells. On the Christmas day following his translation he preached at Whitehall, and 'reprehending the common jollity of the court . . . particularized concerning their excess in plays and gaming.' Pepys thought he made but a poor sermon, and others laughed in the chapel at his rebuke (*Diary*, ii. 84, 85). He was appointed a governor of the Charterhouse in May 1663 (information received from the master of the Charterhouse). In 1664 he visited the five Oxford colleges of which he was *ex officio* visitor, finding apparently no trouble except at Corpus Christi, where he 'bound some to their behaviour,' and had to punish a gross case of contempt of his authority (Wood, *Life and Times*, ii. 16–19). When an impeachment was drawn up against Clarendon in November 1667, Morley was sent to him by the Duke of York to signify the king's wish that he should leave the country (Clarendon, *Life*, ii. 484). Clarendon's fall for a time brought Morley into disgrace at court. Pepys heard that both he and the Bishop of Rochester, John Dolben [q. v.], afterwards archbishop of York, and some other great prelates were 'suspended,' and noted that the business would be a heavy blow to the clergy (*Diary*, iv. 297). Morley certainly withdrew from court for a season. In common with some other bishops, he was consulted by the ministers in 1674 with reference to measures to be taken against popery (Burnet, *History*, ii. 53). Some reflections were made upon him in a letter published in the 'Histoire du Calvinisme' of a Roman catholic priest named Maimburg, with reference to the cause of the conversion to Roman catholicism of Anne, late duchess of York, whose spiritual adviser he had been. By way of vindicating himself, he published in 1681 a letter that he had written to the duchess in 1670 on her neglect of the sacrament (see under Anne, Duchess of York; Evelyn, *Correspondence*, iii. 255, 257; Burnet, *History*, i. 537, 538). Not long before his death he is said to have sent a message to the Duke of York (James II) that 'if ever he depended on the doctrine of non-resistance he would find himself deceived' (*ib.* ii. 428 *n.*) He died at Farnham Castle on 29 Oct. 1684, in his eighty-eighth year, and was buried in Winchester Cathedral.

He was, Clarendon says, a man 'of eminent parts in all polite learning, of great wit, readiness, and subtlety in disputation, and of remarkable temper and prudence in conversation' (*Life*, i. 46). According to Burnet he was too easily provoked, and when angry exercised too little restraint over himself. Pious and high-minded, he was in the eyes of Clarendon 'the best man alive' (*Cal. of Clarendon Papers*, ii. 271). He retained his Calvinistic opinions through life; but while he was always a good churchman, he seems to have been brought by persecution to hold stronger church views than in his earlier days. He was, however, always moderate, and was courteous towards dissenters. He was a loyal subject and a faithful friend, and both in word and deed utterly fearless. He was hospitable and extremely liberal, his benefactions while bishop of Winchester amounting, it is said, to 40,000*l.* He rebuilt the episcopal palace at Wolvesey, repaired Farnham Castle, and purchased for the see Winchester House, Chelsea, for 4,000*l.*; he was a large contributor to the rebuilding of St. Paul's, gave 2,200*l.* to Christ Church, Oxford, founded five scholarships at Pembroke College for natives of Jersey and Guernsey (now consolidated into one scholarship of 80*l.* a year), and built and endowed the 'college for matrons' on the north side of the churchyard of Winchester Cathedral for the widows of the clergy of the dioceses of Worcester and Winchester. Moreover by his will he left 500*l.* to the Military Hospital at Chelsea, and his books for the use of the clergy of his diocese (Bingham, *Christiun Antiq.* 1708). In his habits he was active and ascetic, rising at five A.M. all the year round, sitting on winter mornings without a fire, and only making one meal a day. He retained a large amount of bodily and mental vigour in old age.

Though Morley was studious, he wrote little. His works, mostly short and polemical, are, omitting sermons: 1. 'A Letter concerning the Death of Lord Capel,' 4to, 1654; 2. 'A Vindication of himself from . . . Reflexion by Mr. Richard Baxter,' 4to (see above), to which Baxter replied. 3. 'Epistola Apologetica ad theologium quendam,' 4to, written at Breda in 1659, published in London in 1663 as 'Epistola ad virum clarissimum D. Cornelium Triglandium, an Answer to those who suspected Charles II of Popery.' 4. A volume (4to, 1683) containing seven pieces, viz. 'Sum of a Short Conference between Father Darcey and Dr. Morley at Brussels,' 'An Argument against Transubstantiation,' 'Vindication of an Argument,' 'Answer to Father Creasy's Letter,' 'Answer to a Letter,' 'Letter to Anne, Duchess of York' (see above), 'Ad . . . Janum Ulilium epistolæ duæ'—the last was translated in 1707, probably by Hilkiah Bedford [q. v.], with a commendatory letter by Dr. George Hickes [q. v.] (Hearne, *Collections*, ii. 12). 'A Letter to the Earl of Anglesey,' concerning measures against popery, 4to, 1683, is at the end of 'Proceedings between the Duke of Ormonde and the Earl of Anglesey' [see under Butler, James, twelfth Earl and first Duke of Ormonde]; and an 'Epitaph for James I,' at end of Spotiswood's 'History of the Church of Scotland' (Bliss). He drew up 'Injunctions for Magdalen College, Oxford,' as visitor, and appears to have been dissatisfied with the 'restless and unquiet' spirit of the college (*Magdalen College and James II*, pp. 55, 186). Besides these there are assigned to him 'A Modest Advertisement concerning Church Government,' 4to, 1641, and a character of Charles II (Bliss).

Morley's portrait was painted by Lely. Clarendon had a portrait of him in his palace in London (Evelyn, *Correspondence*, iii. 301), and other portraits of him are at Farnham Castle, at Christ Church, at Oriel and Pembroke Colleges, Oxford, and the Charterhouse. In that at Pembroke College Morley wears the mantle of the order of the Garter, of which as bishop of Winchester he was *ex officio* prelate. The Oriel picture at one time belonged to Walton. According to the portraits Morley's face was oval, and his nose long and straight. He wore a slight moustache and closely cut beard. Engravings from the pictures have been executed by Vertue and Thompson (Cassan, *Bishops of Winchester*, ii. 185; Granger, *Biog. Hist.* iii. 235). A drawing in coloured chalks by E. Lutterel is in the National Portrait Gallery, London.

[Wood's Athenæ Oxon. iv. 149, ed. Bliss, has an excellent memoir, also in great part in Biog. Brit. v. 3177, and inserted in Cassan's Bishops of Winchester, ii. 170 sq.; Welch's Alumni Westmonast. pp. 83, 84; Clarendon's Life, i. 34, 41, 46–50, 333, ii. 484; Clarendon's Hist. x. 93, xi. 264, ed. Macray; Cal. of Clarendon Papers, i. 371, ii. 21, 50, 65, 186, 271, 333; Nicholas Papers, i. 203, ii. 21, 156, 170, 244 (Camden Soc.); Evelyn's Diary and Correspondence, i. 254, 271 *n.*, iii. 255, 256, iv. 205, 211, ed. Bray; Pepys's Diary, ii. 84, iv. 297, ed. Braybrooke; Whitelocke's Memorials, ii. 149, 150, 8vo edit.; Burnet's Hist. of own Time, i. 18, 24, 88, 170, 177, ii. 53, 428, 8vo edit.; Burrows's Visitors' Reg. at Oxford, Pref. lxiii, p. 71 (Camden Soc.); Waller's Life, Pref. to Works, pp. viii, ix, ed. 1712; Calamy's Abridgment of Baxter's Life, pp. 154, 171, 569, 572; Walton's Lives, pp. 351, 390, 392, 446; Walker's Sufferings of Clergy, ii. 106, ed. 1714; Willis's Cathedrals, i. 651, ii. 442, 553; Wood's Life and Times, i. 411, ii. 16, 17 (Oxf. Hist. Soc.); Plumptre's Bishop

Ken, i. 82–6, 126, 175, 2nd edit.; Magdalen Coll. and James II, p. 186 (Oxf. Hist. Soc.); Granger's Biog. Hist. iii. 235; Notes and Queries, 8th ser. vi. 142.] W. H.

MORLEY, HENRY (1822–1894), author, son of Henry Morley of Midhurst, Sussex, was born in Hatton Garden, London, on 15 Sept. 1822. He was sent early to a Moravian school at Neuwied on the Rhine, and from 1838 to 1843 he studied at King's College, London. His father was a member of the Apothecaries' Company, and Morley was destined for the medical profession. But, while zealously pursuing his medical studies, he gave evidence of literary propensities as joint editor of a college magazine, and he contributed a digest of a German book upon Greece to the 'Foreign Quarterly Review.' In 1843 he passed Apothecaries' Hall, and he immediately commenced practice as assistant to a country doctor in Somerset, but presently bought a partnership with another doctor at Madeley in Shropshire, whom he unfortunately found to be dishonest. Stripped of all he had, he changed his plan of life in 1848, and set up a school at Manchester on the principles that he had admired at Neuwied. How severe his struggles were at this period he has himself related in his 'Early Papers and Some Memories,' published in 1891. But his spirit was high and bore him through. Much impressed by the continental revolutions of 1848, he put forth a small volume of verse called 'Sunrise in Italy.' He soon removed the school to Liverpool, where he remained for two years. In 1849 he began a set of ironical papers, entitled 'How to make Home Unhealthy,' in the 'Journal of Public Health,' which were interrupted by the discontinuance of that periodical, but afterwards reappeared and were completed in the 'Examiner,' then edited by John Forster. The papers attracted much attention, and caught the eye of Dickens. The author was asked to write for 'Household Words,' but, busy with his school, he at first sent only his 'Adventures in Skitzland,' a freak of his imagination in college days. A few weeks later he was pressed to give up his school and come to London to take part in the management of 'Household Words.' He was thus connected both with that serial and with its successor, 'All the Year Round,' from about 1850 to 1865. During this period he was also associated with the 'Examiner,' first as sub-editor and afterwards as editor, and published three important biographies. These were 'Palissy the Potter,' 1852; 'Jerome Cardan,' 1854; and 'Cornelius Agrippa,' 1856; and they were followed at a longer interval by 'Clement Marot,' 1870. Meanwhile he had followed up his first ironical work with 'A Defence of Ignorance,' 1851, and in 1857 he published his 'Memoirs of Bartholomew Fair,' soon succeeded by two volumes of fairy tales, 1859 and 1860.

In 1857 he was appointed English lecturer to evening classes at King's College, London, and the idea of a great history of English literature gradually took form in his mind. In 1864, accordingly, appeared the first volume of his 'English Writers,' coming down only to Chaucer, and the first part of a second volume in 1867 carried the story down to William Dunbar. The publication had probably much to do with his appointment as professor of the English language and literature at University College in 1865, when he withdrew from King's College. After 1867 the great work was long suspended, but it was begun again in 1887 in a new form, in which ten volumes, bringing the narrative down to Shakespeare, were completed before his death. Meanwhile 'A First Sketch of English Literature,' which was first published in 1873, and has since reached its thirteenth edition (thirty-first thousand), covered, on a smaller scale, the same field. In 1878 Morley was appointed professor of the English language and literature at Queen's College, London. His teaching power was unique, not only from his mastery of the facts, but from his personal warmth and geniality. He appreciated all that was best in every man he met and in every author he discussed, a fact strongly recommending him to popular audiences, whom he repeatedly addressed on literary topics in various parts of the country. In 1879 he received the honorary degree of LL.D. from the university of Edinburgh. From 1882 to 1890 he was principal of University Hall, Gordon Square. He then resigned his professorships and retired to Carisbrooke in the Isle of Wight, where he died on 14 May 1894.

He had married in 1852 a daughter of Joseph Sayer of Newport in the Isle of Wight, who died two years before him, and by her he had several children.

Morley's later years were largely spent in preparing editions at a low price of 'English Classics,' and of translations from foreign classics. These he induced two publishing houses to bring out in two series, respectively entitled 'Morley's Universal Library' (63 vols. at 1*s*. each), 1883–8, and 'Cassell's National Library' (214 vols. at 3*d*. each), 1886–90. Each of the volumes had an introduction from his own pen. He also published a 'Library of English Literature,' 5 vols. (1875–81), with much original comment, and the 'Carisbrooke Library' (1889–91), 14 vols.—reprints of less familiar English classics, besides 'Companion Poets' 9 vols. (1891–2). Although much of his work in literary history has value, his critical insight was less marked than his faculty for collecting information. It is as a populariser of literature that he did his countrymen the highest service.

[Life, by Henry Shaen Solly, 1898; personal information.] J. G.

MORLEY, HERBERT (1616–1667), colonel, baptised on 2 April 1616, was eldest son of Robert Morley (*d.* 1632) of Glynde, Sussex, by Susan (1595–1667), daughter and heiress of Thomas Hodgson of Framfield in the same county (BERRY, *County Genealogies*, 'Sussex,' p. 175; *Sussex Archæological Collections*, xxiv. 102). He was educated at Lewes free school along with John Evelyn (1620–1706) [q. v.] In November 1634 he became a member of the Inner Temple. On 3 Nov. 1640 he was elected M.P. for Lewes, and subsequently became a colonel in the parliamentary army. When the members subscribed on 9 April 1642 for the speedy reduction of the Irish rebels, Morley contributed 600*l.* (RUSHWORTH, *Historical Collections*, pt. iii. vol. i. p. 565; cf. *Commons' Journals*. ii. 647). In November 1642, having been chosen by parliament with three other deputy-lieutenants, he undertook to put Sussex in a position of defence, provide men for that county, and gunpowder for the defence of Lewes, to pay for which contributions of money and plate were raised in the town. When Chichester was besieged by Waller's forces he held a principal command, and for his success received the thanks of the house on 16 Jan. 1643 (*ib.* ii. 929). The command of two troops of horse was given him on 15 Feb. He was appointed the chief agent for raising troops, levying money, and sequestrating estates in Sussex, and became notorious for his rough usage of the clergy. Having been charged on 16 March 1643 'to take care that no horse do pass beyond seas without special warrant,' he arrested William, son of Lord Strafford, at Rye on his passage to France, but parliament on 23 March ordered his discharge, with a letter of thanks to Morley 'for his care' (*ib.* iii. 15).

In April he seized a vessel for conveying abroad the 'delinquent' John Tufton, second earl of Thanet (*ib.* iii. 67). In May he was active in parliament in promoting severe measures of retaliation on royalist prisoners in consequence of some parliamentarians having been ill-used at Oxford; and in July he was prominent in urging the lords to proceed more diligently with the impeachment of the queen and the making a new great seal. In December 1643, although he was unable to prevent the surprisal of Arundel by Lord Hopton [see HOPTON, RALPH, first BARON HOPTON], he beat back that general in his advance on Lewes (WHITELOCKE, *Memorials*, ed. 1732, p. 78), and soon afterwards assisted at the recapture of Arundel, over which he was placed in authority in conjunction with Sir William Springett (TIERNEY, *Arundel*, i. 62–3). He was again thanked by parliament on 21 June 1644 for his services at the siege of Basing House (WHITELOCKE, pp. 78, 103). Although nominated one of the king's judges, he refused to act. On 20 Feb. 1650 he became a member of the council of state, and served on various committees (*Cal. State Papers*, Dom. 1650, p. 5). He vigorously opposed Cromwell as long as he could do so with safety. On a motion in the House of Commons for fixing a day for its dissolution, a critical division ensued, 14 Nov. 1651, and while Cromwell and St. John as tellers for the ayes reckoned forty-nine votes, Morley and Dennis Bond told off forty-seven in opposition. On 19 Nov., however, he was re-elected to the council of state, and again in November 1652 (*Commons' Journals*, vii. 220). After the expulsion of the Long parliament in April 1653, Morley withdrew into private life, and though elected both for Rye and Sussex in 1654, he declined to attend parliament. He was as active as ever in having the coast watched and vessels searched for suspicious persons and papers (THURLOE, *State Papers*, iii. 369), but refused to be appointed a commissioner for Sussex in November 1655 (*ib.* iv. 161). He gave, however, valuable advice to Thurloe on the best methods of raising seamen and for securing the coasts of Kent and Sussex from the French frigates (*ib.* iv. 549, 574). He was again returned for Sussex in 1656, but rather than submit to the indignity of being ranked among the 'excluded members,' he preferred to 'live quietly' at Glynde, and refused to aid Sir Arthur Hesilrige [q. v.] in promoting the so-called 'Declaration of the Excluded Members,' though, greatly to his annoyance, his name was affixed to it (*ib.* v. 456, 490–1).

In 1659 Morley was returned both for Sussex and for Lewes, but on taking his seat on 11 Feb. he elected to sit for Sussex (BURTON, *Diary*, iii. 202). For some time he bore a prominent part in the debates. He was anxious to impose restraints upon the revived House of Lords, was jealous of the army, and was active in excluding 'delinquents' from parliament (*ib.* iii. 241, 337, iv. 59). On 24 Feb. he accused the council of having made a 'dishonourable peace and a worse war' with Holland (*ib.* iii. 478, 588). On 28 March he obtained leave to go into the country for ten days, and remained there until the dissolution of parliament on 22 April.

Morley was again elected one of the council of state on 14 May 1659 (*Commons' Journals*, vii. 654), and on 9 July, being then an admiralty commissioner, was added to the committee for officers (*Cal. State Papers*, Dom. 1659-60, p. 15). On 25 July he was made colonel of a regiment of foot (*Commons' Journals*, vii. 707, 708, 731). In conjunction with Hesilrige and five others he was appointed a commissioner for the government of the army on 12 Oct., in order to guard against the danger of military violence from Lambert (*ib.* vii. 796). On the very next day Lambert marched at the head of his troops through London, and came to the Palace Yard. There Morley met him pistol in hand, and swore if he stirred a foot further he would shoot him. To this Lambert answered, 'Colonel Morley, I will go another way; though, if I please, I could pass this.' He then marched into the Old Palace Yard, and ultimately succeeded in driving away all but his own friends from the House of Commons, his force being superior to Morley's owing to the city's inactivity (Carte, *Original Letters*, 1739, ii. 246). With Walton, Hesilrige, and others of the old council of state, Morley wrote a joint letter to Monck, promising to stand by him in the attempt to restore the parliament (Baker, *Chronicle*, ed. 1670, p. 695). Morley also promoted what he called the 'Humble Representation of Colonel Morley and some other late Officers of the Army to General Fleetwood,' dated 1 Nov. 1659 (Thurloe, vii. 771-4). In company with Hesilrige and Walton, Morley then repaired to Portsmouth, gained over the governor (3 Dec. 1659), and proceeded to collect troops against Lambert. Their power so quickly increased that they soon marched into London at the head of a body of cavalry, and there, on 26 Dec., restored the parliament. Morley received the thanks of the house on 29 Dec. (*Commons' Journals*, vii. 799), became a member of the new council of state two days later (*ib.* vii. 800), and was appointed lieutenant of the Tower on 7 Jan. 1659-60 (*ib.* vii. 805). On 11 Feb. he was named one of the five commissioners for the government of the army, and on 23 Feb. one of the council of state (*ib.* vii. 841, 849). Evelyn, knowing that Morley had influence enough in Sussex to secure a good reception for the king in case he might land there, urged him to declare for the restoration of the monarchy, and thereby gain the honours which would otherwise fall to Monck. He refused, however, to believe that Monck intended to do the king any service. Even on Monck's arrival in London (3 Feb. 1659-60) Morley failed to penetrate his intentions, and broke off correspondence with Evelyn, though he had been bargaining for the king's pardon of himself and his relations (Evelyn, *Diary*, ed. 1850-2, i. 334-6, 422-5). The republicans were alarmed, and Ludlow, apparently assured of Morley's support in maintaining the Commonweath, proposed that two thousand soldiers should be marched to the Tower to join with Morley's regiment there; 'he having sent to me,' says Ludlow, 'to let me know that the Tower should be at my command whensoever I pleased to desire it' (*Memoirs*, ed. 1751, ii. 360). Halting thus between two opinions, Morley missed playing the triumphant part, which Monck undertook.

After the Restoration Morley purchased his pardon by payment of 1,000*l.* (Evelyn, i. 336). He appears to have been elected M.P. for Rye, but probably never took his seat (*Cal. State Papers*, Dom. 1667, p. 543). He died at Glynde on 29 Sept. 1667. By license dated 26 Oct. 1648 he married Mary (1626-1656), daughter of Sir John Trevor, kt. (Chester, *London Marriage Licenses*, ed. Foster, col. 942), by whom he had three sons, Robert (*b.* 1650), Herbert (*b.* 1652; died before his father), and William (*b.* 1653), and a daughter Anne (will registered in P. C. C. 141, Carr).

In Flatman's 'Don Juan Lamberto' (pt. i. ch. ix.) Morley is described under the sobriquet of the 'Baron of Sussex,' in allusion to the story of his scene with Lambert. Whatever opinions Morley adopted in church and state he maintained conscientiously, without the suspicion of a meanness or self-interest. His reports and orders as admiralty commissioner, 1659-60, are in the British Museum (Addit. MS. 22546, ff. 225, 229), and the corporation of Rye possesses many of his letters (*Hist. MSS. Comm.* 13th Rep. App. p. iv).

[Sussex Archæological Collections; Lower's Worthies of Sussex, p. 336; Noble's Lives of the English Regicides; Burton's Diary, iv. 40, 104, 192; Evelyn's Diary, 1850-2, i. xxvii-viii. 278, 308; Clarendon's Rebellion (Macray); Ludlow's Memoirs, 1751, ii. 191, 340, 357; Coxe's Cat. Codicum MSS. Bibl. Bodl. pars v. fasc. ii. p. 827.]

G. G.

MORLEY, JOHN (1656-1732), known as 'Merchant Morley,' agent and land jobber, born at Halstead in Essex on 8 Feb. 1655-6, was originally a butcher, but rose by sheer business capacity to be one of the largest land jobbers, or agents for the disposing of land, in the kingdom. It is commonly stated that in honour of his first trade he annually killed a pig in Halstead market, and received a groat for the job. When he applied for a grant of arms in 1722, he assumed for his crest the figure of a butcher holding a pole-axe bend-wise. He became a sort of business agent for the Harleys, and in 1713, to the great contentment of Robert Harley, he negotiated the marriage between Edward Harley, afterwards second earl of Oxford [q. v.], and Lady Henrietta Holles, only daughter and heiress of the fourth Duke of Newcastle. He received a two and half per cent. commission on the dowry, or, in other words, 10,000*l.* Swift formed a low estimate of him. Writing to Barber in 1738, he said: 'I remember a rascally butcher, one Morley, a great land jobber and knave, who was his lordship's manager, and has been the principal cause of my lord's wrong conduct.' A vivacious sketch of Morley's character forms the staple of Matt Prior's diverting ballad of 'Down Hall,' 1723. The jobber is probably the 'hearty Morley' of Gay's 'Welcome.' Pope, to whom he occasionally sent presents of oysters and eringo roots, was most friendly with him, and when he was seriously ill during 1725-6, sent him a sympathetic and caressing letter. Morley bought about 1700 the messuage and house of Munchensies, in his native parish of Halstead; he rebuilt the house in 1713, and he died there on 20 Jan. 1732. He was buried beneath an altar-tomb in Halstead church, the arms of the Butchers' Company being blazoned above. Though so long 'dry nurse to estates and minors,' he seems to have behaved generously to his native place; and possessing the patronage of Gestingthorpe in Essex, he shortly before his death united with the rector, Moses Cooke, to augment the living by adding 200*l.* to Queen Anne's Bounty. Prior was a frequent visitor at Munchensies, and at Morley's request commemorated in verse the rebuilding of Halstead steeple. Morley married Elizabeth, daughter of Matthew Baker (who has been wrongly identified with 'Thalestris' of the 'Rape of the Lock,' a sister of 'Sir Plume,' *i.e.* Sir George Brown of Berkshire). Both Morley's son and grandson were called John. The latter, owner of Munchensies in 1768, is separately noticed. A portrait of the 'land jobber,' painted by Kneller, was engraved by Simon.

[Elwin's Pope, v. 177, viii. 216, x. 247–9; Morant's Essex, ii. 257; Wright's Essex, i. 467; Hist. of Essex, by a Gentleman, Chelmsford, 1769, ii. 63; W. J. Evans's Old and New Halstead, p. 22; Prior's Miscellaneous Works; Prior's Selected Poems, 1889, p. 93; Noble's Continuation of Granger, 1806, iii. 261–4; Swift's Works, ed. Scott, xix. 258; Southey's Commonplace Book, iv. 288; information kindly given by Miss C. Fell Smith.] T. S.

MORLEY, JOHN (*d.* 1776?), medical writer, was grandson and eventual heir of John Morley (1656-1732) [q. v.] of Halstead, Essex (Wright, *Essex*, i. 466, 470). He died in either December 1776 or January 1777, and was buried with his grandfather in Halstead churchyard (*Gent. Mag.* 1777, p. 47). By his wife Elizabeth, who survived him, he had three sons: John Jacob, Hildebrand, and Allington; and a daughter, Dorothy, married to Bridges Harvey. To his eldest son he bequeathed as an heirloom the coronation cup and cover of George I. (will proved on 27 Jan. 1777, and registered in P. C. C. 30, Collier).

A method of treating scrofula and kindred diseases having been imparted to Morley, he published it for the public benefit in 'An Essay on the Nature and Cure of Scrophulous Disorders,' 8vo, London, 1767 (11th edit., 1774). The principal cure, it appears, was a preparation of vervain root. He gave advice to all who sought it, without fee.

[Authorities cited; Watt's Bibl. Brit.] G. G.

MORLEY, ROBERT DE, second Baron Morley (1296?–1360), born about 1296, was eldest son of William, first baron Morley, who served with distinction in the Scottish wars, and was summoned to parliament as baron from 29 Dec. 1299 to 3 Oct. 1306 (*Parl. Writs*). Robert was first summoned to parliament in 1317, when he probably came of age. He appears to have joined Lancaster in his opposition to the king (cf. Rymer, ii. i. passim). On 21 Dec. 1324 he was summoned to serve in Gascony, but probably never went. In October 1326 he was at Bristol, when Prince Edward was declared 'guardian of the realm' (cf. Stubbs, ii. 375; Rymer, i. ii. 646). In April 1327 he was summoned to serve in Scotland. In right of his wife, daughter of William, lord Marshal, of Hingham, Norfolk, Morley had claims to the hereditary marshalship of Ireland, whither he was sent on 15 Oct. 1331. In March 1332-3 he was ordered to oppose the Scottish invasion. In August 1336 he was summoned to consult about the negotiations with Bruce and the king of France. In December 1338 he was commissioned to guard Yarmouth, Norfolk, from the French ships, and soon after was appointed admiral of the fleet from the Thames to Berwick. In that capacity, after having attempted to dissuade Edward from crossing from Orwell on 22 June (Murimuth, p. 311), he commanded at the battle of Sluys on 24 June 1340, when, breaking the first, second, and third lines of the

French fleet, he won the greatest naval victory the English had yet achieved (Rymer; *Eulog. Historiarum*, iii. 205; *Chronicles of Edward I and Edward II*, ii. 293). Soon after he sailed to Normandy and burnt eighty of the French ships and two villages; on 10 April 1341 he was transferred to the command of the fleet from the Thames westward (Rymer, i. ii. 1156). In the same year he received various grants in reward for his services (*ib.*), and in November set out with Robert d'Artois and Sir Walter de Manny [q. v.] on the expedition to Brittany. In 1343 he held a tournament in Smithfield (Murimuth, p. 230); and on 25 Aug. 1346 was present at the battle of Crecy. On 31 March 1347 he was summoned to Calais, which Edward was then besieging, and dispersed the French victualling ships which attempted to enter the harbour. He was reappointed admiral of the fleet from the Thames westward in 1348 and again in 1354. In 1355 he received the constableship of the Tower, and in 1359 was again serving in the French wars. He died in March 1360.

Morley, who 'was one of the most famous warriors of the period,' married, first, Hawyse (*b.* 1301), daughter of William, lord Marshal, and sister and heiress of John, lord Marshal (*d.* 1317), of Hingham. She brought Morley estates in Norfolk, Essex, and elsewhere, besides the claim to the hereditary marshalship of Ireland. By her Morley had a son William, who succeeded him as third Baron Morley, being thirty, or according to another inquisition forty, years old at his father's death. He served in the French wars, was knighted in 1356, and died in 1379, having married Cicely, daughter of Thomas, lord Bardolf. His son and heir, Thomas (1354–1416), was in 1416 captain-general of all the English forces in France. The barony passed into the Parker family by the marriage of a descendant, Alice, baroness Morley, with Sir William Parker, grandfather of Henry Parker, lord Morley [q. v.], the poet.

Morley married, secondly, Joan, daughter of Sir Peter de Tyes; his son by her, Robert, served in the French wars, and his line became extinct with his son Thomas, whose daughter and heiress married Sir Geoffrey Ratcliffe.

[Rymer's Fœdera, passim; Dugdale's Baronage; Cal. Rotul. Parl.; Rolls of Parl. ii. 27 *a*, &c.; Eulogium Historiarum, ii. 205; Murimuth, passim; Chronicles of Edward I and Edward II, i. 353, ii. 293; Froissart, ed. Lettenhove, ii. 142, vi. 497, xxii. 244; Barnes's Hist. of Reign of Edward III, pp. 125, 181, 471; Burke's Extinct Peerage; G. E. C.'s Peerage; Blomefield's Norfolk, passim; Clutterbuck's Hertfordshire, passim.]

A. F. P.

MORLEY, SAMUEL (1809–1886), politician, born in Well Street, Hackney, 15 Oct. 1809, was youngest child of John Morley, a member of a Nottingham family of tradesmen, who started a hosiery business in Wood Street, London, at the end of the last century. His mother Sarah was daughter of R. Poulton of Maidenhead. At the age of seven he was sent to the school of a congregational minister named Carver at Melbourn in Cambridgeshire, and afterwards to Mr. Buller's school at Southampton. He was industrious and energetic, and when he went into the Wood Street business at sixteen was a fairly educated lad for his age. Thenceforward he had little time for book-learning. For seven years he remained in the counting-house, and proved himself very competent in the management of the accounts.

In 1840 his father retired from the business, and from 1842 it was carried on by himself and his brother John. In 1855, his brother John retired from the London business of J. & R. Morley and left him sole partner. He became sole partner also in the Nottingham business in 1860, and, while maintaining his connection with the old-fashioned framework-knitters, not only had two mills in that town, but he built others at Loughborough, Leicester, Heanor in Derbyshire, and Daybrook and Sutton-in-Ashfield in Nottinghamshire. To his thousands of workpeople he granted pensions on a liberal scale, and provided for old employés at a cost of over 2,000*l.* a year. His business was the largest in the textile industries of its class, and his wealth was soon exceeded by that of few contemporaries.

In May 1841 he had married and settled at Five Houses, Lower Clapton. From 1854 till 1870 he lived at Craven Lodge, Stamford Hill.

Morley was deeply religious from youth, and became in manhood active in religious and philanthropic affairs. He was zealous for complete religious freedom, and exerted himself against church rates with great vigour. His house at Stamford Hill became a rendezvous for dissenting ministers and radical politicians, but, although busily concerned in the internal affairs of the independent body, he declined all his life to hold the office of deacon. In 1847 he became chairman of the dissenters' parliamentary committee, formed for the purpose of opposing Lord John Russell's education scheme and of promoting the return of dissenting members of parliament. For thirty years from 1849 he held the office of treasurer of the 'Ancient Merchants' Lecture.' In May 1855 he organised the 'Administrative Reform Association' for the purpose of having the civil services thrown open and of abolishing promotion otherwise than by merit. But the association produced little result. Eager for more work, he became treasurer to the Home Missionary Society in 1858, and visited the society's stations throughout England and Wales. About this time he first interested himself in the temperance movement, and became a total abstainer. He subsequently promoted religious services in theatres, discussed currency questions, and became chairman in 1861 of the 'Bank Act and Currency Reform Committee.' He attacked 'The Drinking Usages of the Commercial Room' at a temperance conference in Exeter Hall, 6 Aug. 1862; supported the celebration of the bicentenary of nonconformity in the same year, and contributed 6,000*l.* to the erection of the Congregationalist Memorial Hall in Farringdon Street, London. He was a munificent builder of chapels, and spent on them alone 14,000*l.* between 1864 and 1870, and he also organised a system of colporteurs and local preachers for poor districts.

Cobden had urged him to seek a seat in parliament in 1857, but he decided, judiciously as it proved, to wait. At length, in 1865, he reluctantly consented to be put in nomination for the representation of Nottingham, where his local influence as an employer of labour was very great. Yet it was not without a bitter contest that he was returned at the head of the poll. His first speech in the House of Commons was on the Church Rates Abolition Bill, 7 March 1866, but in April he was unseated on petition for colourable employment. No personal charge of corruption was made against him. He at the time interested himself in the promotion of the liberal press, became a principal proprietor of the 'Daily News,' and caused its price to be reduced to a penny.

Although the liberal party at Nottingham had offered him their support at the next general election, he contested Bristol at a by-election in April 1868, and was defeated by 196 votes. His opponent at Bristol was then unseated on petition, and at the general election in November Morley was returned by a triumphant majority. He continued to represent Bristol till his retirement in 1885. In parliament he was an unswerving and almost unquestioning follower of Mr. Gladstone. He contributed large sums to the election funds of liberal candidates, and found the money to enable several labour candidates to go to the poll. He seconded the address in the House of Commons in 1871, when he described himself as belonging to the class of 'silent members.' But, though not influential as a speaker, he spoke often. While anxious to disestablish the Irish church, he abandoned in later life any desire for the disestablishment of the church of England. In the Irish church debates he took no share, but spoke on the Bankruptcy Bill of 1869, and moved in 1870 for an inquiry into the working of the commercial treaty with France. After half a lifetime devoted to opposing every project of state interference with education, he became a convert to a state system of teaching, but he was very desirous of safeguarding the interests of dissenters. He voted against Henry Richard's motion, 19 June 1870, which required all religious teaching to be voluntary, and expressed himself in favour of biblical teaching by board-school teachers, subject always to the protection afforded by the conscience clause. He sat from 1870 to 1876 on the London School Board, and was always a warm supporter of biblical unsectarian teaching in the schools. He also took a large part both in and out of parliament in the movements for the removal of tests in universities and of dissenters' grievances as to burials. He was on the consulting committee of the Agricultural Labourers' Union from its foundation in 1872, and in 1877 he became, and for some years remained, an active director of the Artisans', Labourers', and General Dwellings Company.

In 1880 he inadvertently gave his support to the candidature of Charles Bradlaugh at Northampton, whose religious and social opinions he viewed with 'intense repugnance.' Not only did he publicly confess the mistake, but separated himself from his party, and voted steadily against Bradlaugh's admission to the House of Commons. He was one of the first to bring before the parliament of 1880 the unsatisfactory working of the Bankruptcy Act of 1869, and he took charge in the lower house of Earl Stanhope's bill prohibiting payment of wages in public-houses. But his principal public efforts during his remaining years were exerted in support of the temperance or 'blue-ribbon' movement, and he was prepared to abandon purely voluntary efforts in favour of temperance and demand legislative assistance.

The strain of his threefold series of occupations, mercantile, political, and philanthropic, at length broke down his strength. He vacated his seat in parliament at the general election of 1885. A peerage was offered to him in June, but he refused it. He was in ill-health through the early part of 1886, and never recovered from a severe attack of pneumonia in the summer. He died on 5 Sept. at his house, Hall Place, near Tonbridge. He was buried at Abney Park cemetery, and deputations from ninety-seven associations and institutions with which he was connected followed him to his grave. He had by his wife—Rebekah Maria, daughter of Samuel Hope of Liverpool—five sons and three daughters, Samuel, Howard, Charles, Arnold (privy-councillor and postmaster-general 1892–5), and Henry, Rebekah, Augusta, and Mary. To his children he bequeathed a great fortune. A portrait by H. T. Wells, R.A., was painted in 1875, and is in the library of the Congregationalist Memorial Hall, Farringdon Street; there is also a bad statue of him in marble at Bristol.

Morley had all the business talents of a man of this world and all the warmth of heart and piety of a man of the next. Endlessly active, a hater of waste or sloth, keen in a bargain and shrewd in his trade, he applied himself laboriously to spending for the good of others the wealth which his commanding aptitude for business had enabled him to accumulate. He loved a good horse; otherwise he not only had no hobby and pursued no sport, but discountenanced some sports, such as gaming, in others. In old age his views broadened and his temper mellowed; in middle life he was apt to be irritable and austere; but in religious matters, though always a professed congregationalist, he was undogmatic and liberal. Like Lord Shaftesbury and George Peabody, he erected benevolence into a business, which he carried on upon a scale hardly less huge than that on which he made his money. His numberless public and private acts of charity made him undoubtedly one of the most signal benefactors of his generation.

[His Life and Letters, based on family materials and the assistance of all his relatives and intimate friends, was brought out by Edwin Hodder in 1889; the Congregationalist, xv. 711, a eulogistic estimate by J. Guinness Rogers; Contemporary Magazine, l. 649.] J. A. H.

MORLEY, THOMAS (1557–1604?), musician, was born in 1557. This date is determined by the title of a 'Domine non est' preserved in the Bodleian Library, which runs: 'Thomæ Morley, ætatis suæ 19. Anno Domini 1576' (Grove, App. p. 720). He was a pupil of William Byrd, and possibly a chorister of St. Paul's Cathedral. He graduated Mus. Bac. at Oxford on 6 July 1588, and about three years later was appointed organist to St. Paul's. This post he resigned on being elected, on 24 July 1592, gentleman of the Chapel Royal, by which title he always describes himself in his works. He was also appointed epistler to the Chapel Royal, and on 18 Nov. 1592 gospeller.

In 1598 he was granted a patent, dated 11 Sept., similar to that previously held by Byrd, by which he enjoyed the exclusive right of printing books of music and selling ruled paper. While this remained in force it was as his 'assignes' that William Bartley, Thomas Este, Peter Short, John Windet, and others printed and issued musical works.

On 7 Oct. 1602 Morley was succeeded at the Chapel Royal by George Woodson, having probably resigned his post on account of his ill-health, to which he makes reference in his 'Plaine and Easie Introduction to Practicall Musicke.' The date of his death is uncertain; Hawkins and Burney both state it to have taken place in 1604.

Morley's skill and grace in the composition of madrigals are undoubted, but he has been accused of wholesale thefts from such Italian sources as the works of Anerio and Gastoldi. His reputation mainly rests on his work entitled 'A Plaine and Easie Introduction to Practicall Musicke,' London, 1597, which, as the first satisfactory musical treatise published in England, enjoyed great popularity for nearly two centuries. Eleven years after its first appearance it was reissued with a new title-page, and as late as 1771 a second edition was published, with an appendix of motets, &c., in score. In the seventeenth century Johann Caspar Trost, organist of St. Martin's, Halberstadt, translated it into German, under the title of 'Musica Practica.'

Morley's published compositions include: 1. 'Canzonets, or Little Short Songs to Three Voyces,' London, 1593; other editions 1606 and 1631. German translations of this were published at Cassel in 1612, and at Rostock in 1624. 2. 'Madrigalls to Foure Voyces, the first Booke,' London, 1594; 2nd edit. 1600. 3. 'The First Booke of Ballets to Five Voyces,' London, 1595. An edition of this with Italian words was published in London in the same year, and another, with English words, in London in 1600. A German translation was published at Nuremberg in 1609. The original was reprinted for the Musical Antiquarian Society by E. F. Rimbault in 1842. 4. 'The first Booke of Canzonets to Two Voyces, containing also seven Fantasies for Instruments,' London, 1595; reprinted in 1619. 5. 'Canzonets, or Little Short Aers to Five and Sixe Voices,' London, 1597. 6. 'The First Booke of Aires, or Little Short Songs, to sing and play to the Lute with the Base Viol,' London, 1600. In this is a setting of the Page's song, 'It was a Lover and his Lass,' from 'As you like it,' which is interesting as one of the few pieces of original Shakespearean music which have survived. It is reprinted in Knight's 'Shakspeare,' and also in Chappell's 'Popular Music of the Olden Time.' His canzonets and madrigals for three and four voices were republished by W. W. Holland and W. Cooke, London [1808?], and six of his canzonets for two voices have been edited in score by Welcker.

Morley edited: 1. 'Canzonets, or Little Short Songs to Foure Voyces, selected out of the best approved Italian Authors,' London, 1597. To this he contributed two madrigals of his own. 2. 'Madrigals to Five Voyces, selected out of the best approved Italian Authors,' London, 1598. 3. 'The First Booke of Consort Lessons, made by divers exquisite Authors for sixe Instruments to play together, viz. the Treble Lute, the Pandora, the Citterne, the Base Violl, the Flute, and the Treble Violl,' London, 1599; another edition, enlarged, 1611. 4. 'Madrigales. The Triumphs of Oriana, to Five and Sixe Voyces, composed by divers several Authors,' London, 1601; it is dedicated to Charles Howard, earl of Nottingham (cf. *Notes and Queries*, 1st ser. iv. 185–8). To this collection of twenty-five madrigals in praise of Queen Elizabeth Morley contributed two of his own. It was reissued, 'now first published in score,' by W. Hawes, London, 1814. In this edition four madrigals were added.

'Seven pieces for the Virginal' by Morley are included in the manuscript collection known as 'Queen Elizabeth's Virginal Book,' preserved in the Fitzwilliam Museum, Cambridge, and three in 'Will. Forster's Virginal Book,' preserved at Buckingham Palace. He wrote a considerable amount of church music, none of which was printed in his lifetime. Services in D minor and G minor and an anthem were subsequently printed by John Barnard in his 'First Book of Selected Church Music,' 1641, and in the manuscript collection made by Barnard for this work (and preserved in the library of the Sacred Harmonic Society) are a preces, psalms and responses, and three anthems by Morley. A Burial Service by him, the first of the kind written to English words, was printed by Dr. Boyce in vol. i. of his 'Cathedral Music,' 1760, and in James Clifford's 'Divine Services and Anthems,' 1663, are the words of several anthems by him. Some of his choral works are included in the manuscript collection of cathedral music made by Thomas Tudway for Lord Harley about 1720 (*Harl. MSS.* 7337–42). Manuscripts of Morley's are preserved in the Music School and Christ Church Libraries at Oxford, and in the Fitzwilliam Museum and Peterhouse Library at Cambridge. The words of several of his compositions are quoted in Mr. A. H. Bullen's 'Lyrics from the Song-books of the Elizabethan Age' and 'More Lyrics.'

[Grove's Dict. of Music, ii. 367, iv. 720; Brown's Biog. Dict. of Music, p. 434; Fétis's Biog. Univ. des Musiciens, vi. 205; Alumni Oxonienses, p. 1034; State Papers, Dom. Ser. 1598; Hawkins's Hist. of Music, p. 494; Harmonicon for 1826, p. 209; Burney's General Hist. of Music, iii. 101; Notes and Queries, 2nd ser. iii. 10, 6th ser. viii. 408, 503; Catalogues of Music at Christ Church, Oxford Music School, Peterhouse Coll. Cambridge, and Fitzwilliam Museum; Brit. Mus. Catalogues.] R. F. S.

MORLEY, WILLIAM, (*fl.* 1340), meteorologist. [See Merle.]

MORNINGTON, Earls of. [See Wellesley, Garrett, first Earl, 1735–1781; Wellesley, Richard Colley, second Earl, 1760–1842; Wellesley-Pole, William, third Earl, 1763–1845; Wellesley, William Pole Tylney Long-, fourth Earl, 1788–1857, under Wellesley-Pole, William, third Earl.]

MORNINGTON, Barons. [See Wellesley, Richard Colley, first Baron, 1690?–1758; Wellesley, Garrett, second Baron, 1735–1781.]

MORPETH, Viscount. [See Howard, George, sixth Earl of Carlisle, 1773–1848.]

MORPHETT, Sir **JOHN** (1809–1892), pioneer and politician of South Australia, son of Nathaniel Morphett, solicitor, was born in London on 4 May 1809, and educated at private schools for a mercantile career. Becoming connected in business with the so-called Adelphi party who took the lead in settling South Australia, he purchased land in the future colony, went out in the Cygnet, a pioneer ship of the South Australian Company, landed at Kangaroo Island on 11 Sept. 1836, and was present at the proclamation of the colony. Having devoted himself to the acquisition of land for himself and others, and established himself as a general merchant, he took an active part with the surveyor, Colonel Light, in laying out the town of Adelaide, and aided in the inauguration of a regular government. The next year (1838) was full of public work; he made a trip to Rapid Bay, then almost unknown, and reported on the district to the government; on 6 March he was appointed a member of the committee for the protection of aborigines; he founded the Literary Association and Mechanics' Institute, promoted the formation of the South Australian Joint-Stock Assurance Company, and took the leading part in a public meeting (there was as yet no legislature) respecting the survey of the colony and taxation. In letters, which were published locally, he sent home at this time sound advice for future colonists.

On 5 Dec. 1840 Morphett was made treasurer of the corporation of Adelaide, and in April 1841 a justice of the peace. On 15 June 1843 he was nominated by the crown to the first legislature of the colony, and although he was prominent in pressing the reform of the council and in opposing transportation in 1851, he was again nominated as a member when the council was reconstituted in that year, holding office as speaker from 20 Aug. 1851 till 1855. When in 1857 an elective constitution was granted, he was among the first eighteen members elected to the legislative council. He was chief secretary in the Reynolds administration from 4 Feb. to 8 Oct. 1861, but on no other occasion was he a minister of the crown. He did not care for party politics, and in March 1865, after his re-election to the legislative council, was chosen for the office of president. He held this position till 1873, when his term of office expired, and he did not seek re-election. The remainder of his life he passed in comparative seclusion, though he still sat on the boards of certain companies, notably that of the Bank of South Australia. He was knighted on 16 Feb. 1870. He died at his residence, Cummins, Glenelg, on 7 Nov. 1892.

With an admirable capacity for business Morphett combined considerable culture and a love of sport. He presided in April 1844 at a meeting out of which arose the Royal Agricultural Society of South Australia. He was a great patron of the turf, and in the early days of the colony often rode his own horses. In 1837 there were but two horses in the whole colony, and one was Morphett's. On 12 Jan. 1838 he entered a horse for the first Adelaide races.

He married, on 15 Aug. 1838, the daughter of Sir J. Hurtle Fisher, who preceded him as president of the legislative council. She and nine children survived him. One of the three sons is clerk of the legislative council. A brother, who also went out for a time to South Australia, is now living in England.

Morphett Street in Adelaide, Morphett Street at Mount Barker, Morphettville, and Morphett Vale were named after him.

[South Australian Register, 8 Nov. 1892; Mennell's Dict. Austral. Biog.] C. A. H.

MORRELL, HUGH (*d.* 1664?), merchant, descended from a family well known for their 'designs for the improvement of cloth and all woollen manufactures,' was probably a native of Exeter. In 1623 he was engaged in the export trade to France, and about the same time he and Peter du Boys proposed to James I a scheme for the improvement of commerce, probably by the establishment in every town of corporations to regulate the woollen manufactures. For this purpose he obtained a patent for Hertfordshire in 1624, and for Devonshire in 1626. He and his 'predecessors' had already spent 'much labour and 3,000*l.*' in the promotion of a similar object at Worcester. His plans were commended by thirty-one London merchants to whom they were submitted.

Some time before this Morrell had been established at Rouen in partnership with Charles Snelling, merchant, of London. In 1627 their goods, to the value of 7,600*l.*, were confiscated by the French in reprisal for goods seized by English ships at Conquett. Their fortunes ruined, and even their lives threatened, Morrell and Snelling were obliged to escape from France. They petitioned the king (June 1627) for satisfaction out of the profits on the sale of the French prizes, or by abatement of customs duties in their favour. Their claims were referred to Sir Henry Martin and Philip Burlamachi, who reported that their losses ought to be made good. It was proposed shortly afterwards to reimburse them out of the produce of an additional duty of three farthings per chaldron on coal exported from Newcastle, and the attorney-general was instructed to prepare a warrant for this purpose. The scheme, however, does not appear to have been carried into effect, owing probably to the opposition of the farmers of the coal duties, and as late as 1641 Morrell and Snelling had not received satisfaction.

On 9 Oct. 1633 Morrell, as agent and representative of the 'merchants of Exeter trading to France,' presented to the council a petition on their behalf, in which they desired the removal of their trade from Rouen and Morlaix to Havre, and the appointment of an English consul. In the following month he was chosen, along with Spicer, their governor, to represent the company at a conference (19 Nov.) with the 'merchants of London trading to France,' when articles of agreement were drawn up between the two associations. On 5 Dec. 1642 he was appointed one of the surveyors of the customs at Dover and the western ports.

Meanwhile Morrell had not abandoned his scheme for the reorganisation of the woollen trade. A committee of merchants recommended it to parliament in 1638, and shortly afterwards Morrell 'presented an instrument to his Majestie under the Broad Seale of England, in which much labour, care, and pains was taken to settle a government in our manufactures' (Morrell to Lenthall, 11 Jan. 1646-7, *Portland MSS.* i. 405). Charles I referred the scheme to a commission of thirty of the most experienced merchants of London, who spent eighteen months in the examination of the principal clothiers of the kingdom, and agreed upon a report, presented to the commons (March 1640) by Matthew Cradock. No further progress was made for seven years. Morrell then suggested the appointment of a commission of merchants or 'councell for trade . . . to whome overtures will be more freely presented, tendinge to the publike good, then they dare to doe to the parliament' (*ib.*) Among the subjects he proposed for consideration by the commission were the means by which England might be made 'the magazine of Christendom;' the foundation of a bank similar to the Bank of Amsterdam; the removal of the greater part of the duties on manufactures and the customs on wool imported, and the establishment of a merchants' court.

In 1650 Morrell was employed by parliament in commercial negotiations with France, but he appears to have exceeded his powers, for on 9 Dec. he was requested 'not to presume . . . to offer anything to the crown of France on behalf of the Commonwealth, nor to intermeddle concerning affairs of state, but to keep himself to the solicitation of merchants' affairs' (*Cal. State Papers*, Dom. 1653, xi. 112). His services, however, were retained, and he lived in Paris until the Restoration. He died probably about 1664.

[Authorities quoted and Thurloe's State Papers, ii. 61, iii. 444, iv. 525, 670, 692, 693; Calendars of State Papers Dom. 1623–62 passim; Hist. MSS. Comm. 3rd Rep. p. 178, 4th Rep. p. 313, 11th Rep. pt. iv. pp. 25, 41, pt. vii. p. 291.]

W. A. S. H.

MORRELL, WILLIAM (*fl.* 1625), New England poet, was an Anglican clergyman who went to Massachusetts in 1623 with the company sent out by the Plymouth council, under the command of Captain Robert Gorges, son of Sir Ferdinando Gorges [q. v.] He bore a commission from the ecclesiastical court to exercise superintendence over the churches that were, or might be, established in the colony. The attempt by this company to form a settlement at Wessagussett (now Weymouth) was unsuccessful. After Gorges's departure Morrell remained a year at Plymouth out of curiosity to learn something of the country, but made no use of his commission, nor even mentioned it till just before he sailed for England. He wrought the result of his observations into some elegant Latin hexameters, which he translated into English heroic verse, and published under the title of 'New-England, or a briefe Enarration of the Ayre, Earth, Water, Fish, and Fowles of that Country. With a Description of the . . . Habits and Religion of the Natives, in Latine and English Verse,' 4to, London, 1625. The English version, which is frequently harsh and obscure, is preceded by a poetical address to the king. A copy of this rare tract, which is dedicated to the lords, knights, and gentlemen, adventurers for New England, is in the British Museum; it was reprinted in 1792 in the 'Collections' of the Massachusetts Historical Society, 1st ser. vol. i. pp. 125–39. In a postscript Morrell announced his intention of publishing another book on New England.

[Appleton's Cyclop. of Amer. Biog. s. v.]

G. G.

MORREN, NATHANIEL (1798–1847), Scottish divine, born in Aberdeen 3 Feb. 1798, was educated at the grammar school and at Marischal College, where he graduated M.A. in 1814. He became a tutor at Fort George; subsequently taught at Caen, France; studied theology in the universities of Aberdeen and Edinburgh; was licensed by the presbytery of Aberdeen in October 1822; appointed minister of Blackhall Street (afterwards North) Church, Greenock, in June 1823; translated to the first charge of Brechin September 1843; and died of apoplexy 28 March 1847. He was a devoted minister, and a good scholar. The work by which he is best known is his 'Annals of the General Assembly from 1739 to 1766,' 2 vols. Edinburgh, 1838–40, which has been much quoted by subsequent historians of the Scottish church. He was also the author of 'Biblical Theology,' Edinburgh, 1835; 'My Church Politics,' Greenock, 1842; 'Dialogues on the Church Question,' Greenock, 1843; and of various articles in Kitto's 'Biblical Encyclopædia' and Macphail's 'Ecclesiastical Journal.' He annotated a pocket edition of the Bible, 1845; translated from the German Rosenmuller's 'Biblical Geography of Central Asia;' and, along with others, edited the 'Imperial Family Bible.'

[Hew Scott's Fasti Ecclesiæ Scoticanæ, ii. 245; Sermons, with a Memoir, Edinburgh, 1848; Presbytery Records; New Statistical Account, vol. vii.]

J. C. H.

MORRES, HERVEY MONTMORENCY (1767–1839), United Irishman, eldest son of Matthew Montmorency Morres and Margaret, second daughter of Francis Magan of Emo, co. Westmeath, was born at Rathailean Castle, co. Tipperary, on 7 March 1767. At the age of fifteen he entered the Austrian service. He served as ensign under Field-marshal Lacy against the Turks, distinguishing himself at the siege of Belgrade in 1788, and was transferred with the rank of lieutenant into Count Kavanagh's regiment of cuirassiers. He subsequently served as a volunteer in the army of Prince Hohenlohe against the French republic, and commanded a company of skirmishers at the siege of Thionville. He fought with distinction in the army of the Rhine under Marshal Wurmser in 1793, and was afterwards aide-de-camp to Prince Charles of Fürstemberg. He quitted the Austrian service in 1795, and, having in September of that year married Louise de Helmstadt at Heidelberg, he returned to Ireland and took up his residence at Knockalton in co. Tipperary. Shortly after his arrival he addressed a memorial to the lord-lieutenant, the Earl of Camden, on the disturbed state of Ireland, advocating the formation of a strong military force, composed impartially of catholics and protestants. He was thanked for his suggestions, but informed that they were impracticable.

On the rumour of Hoche's expedition in 1796 he accepted a commission as aide-de-camp to General Dundas; but, becoming disgusted at the violent measures of government, he became in November of that year a United Irishman. He was chosen a county representative for Tipperary in May 1797, and nominated colonel of the regiment of Nenagh infantry. In February 1798 he was attached to the general military committee, and soon after appointed adjutant-general of Munster. He was very active in forwarding the organisation of his province, and, subsequent to the arrest of the Leinster Directory on 12 March, he was made a member of the new executive. He avoided an attempt that was made to arrest him on 28 April, and having been assigned the capture of the batteries and magazines in the Phœnix Park, he was busily engaged in working out his plans when the whole scheme of the insurrection was frustrated by the capture of Lord Edward Fitzgerald. Morres managed to escape from Dublin on 4 June, and lay concealed in co. Westmeath till the arrival of Humbert's expedition on 22 Aug. Thinking that Humbert would not immediately risk a decisive engagement, he endeavoured to restrain the ardour of the men of Westmeath; but after the passage of the Shannon, 'taking part in the right flank of Lord Cornwallis's army, with a body of from two to three thousand ill-armed peasants and several chiefs of the union, he made such dispositions as he judged might prove most favourable to the progress of the invading army' (*Castlereagh Corresp.* ii. 95).

After the capitulation of the French army at Ballinamuck he escaped to Dublin, and thence through England to Hamburg, where he arrived on 7 Oct. He was cordially welcomed, as an old friend of her husband, by Lady Fitzgerald; but, having been included by name in the Rebel Fugitives Act, he did not feel secure in Hamburg, and applied to the French resident, Marragon, for permission to proceed to France. His apprehensions were not unfounded. His secret correspondence with the French minister was revealed to the English cabinet by Samuel Turner [q. v.], and on 24 Nov. he was arrested, at the instance of the British agent, Sir James Crawford, at the American Arms, together with Tandy, Corbet, and Blackwell. This act was contrary to the law of nations and despite the protests of Marragon. After ten months' close confinement the senate of Hamburg consented to his extradition, and at midnight on 28 Sept. 1799 he was, with his three companions, conveyed on board an English frigate at Cuxhaven. The subserviency of the senate of Hamburg caused universal indignation, and drew down upon them Napoleon's wrath, which was only appeased by the payment of a fine of four millions and a half francs and a public apology. The arrival of Morres and his companions in England caused considerable excitement, but they were shortly afterwards removed for trial to Ireland. The prosecution against Morres and Tandy broke down on a point of law. Morres pleaded that he had been arrested eight days before the time assigned by the act for his voluntary surrender had expired, and, after a long argument, his objection was sustained by Lord Kilwarden. But it was not till 10 Dec. 1801, after more than three years' imprisonment, that he was released on bail. His wife having died at the age of twenty-six, on the very day of his arrest at Hamburg, Morres, after a brief visit to Paris, married, at Dublin, Helen, widow of Dr. John Esmonde, hanged as a traitor in 1798, and daughter of Bartholomew O'Neill-Callan of Osbertstown House, co. Kildare.

He continued to reside in Ireland for several years, but about 1811 he was persuaded by the French minister of war, the Duc de Feltre, himself of Irish descent, to enter the French service. On 19 May 1812 he was appointed adjutant-commandant with the rank of colonel, made a member of the Legion of Honour, and placed on the staff of General Augereau at Lyons. Some futile efforts were made by his family to induce him to return to Ireland, and his offer, after the abdication of Napoleon, to serve under the English flag not meeting with a cordial response from Wellington and Castlereagh, he retained his commission in the French army, and on 3 Nov. 1816 he obtained letters of naturalisation. At the restoration of the monarchy he entered into communication with the head of the family of Montmorency in France with a view to his recognition as a descendant of the Irish branch of the same house. His overtures were not favourably received, and in justification of his claim he compiled an exhaustive genealogical memoir of the family of Montmorency; but, though absolutely conclusive on the point, it failed to remove the objections of the Duc de Montmorency. He continued to reside in Paris, occupied chiefly in literary researches, receiving the half-pay of a staff-colonel till his death, which took place at St. Germain-en-Laye on 9 May 1839. According to Miles Byrne, who knew him personally, 'he was brave and honourable, and much liked by his countrymen in France.' He left children by both his wives. His eldest daughter, Louise, born at Knockalton on 20 Sept. 1795, was for a time maid of honour to Queen Caroline of Bavaria. Three of his sons, Hervé, Geoffroy, and Mathieu, became officers in the Austrian service. He was much interested in Irish topography, and was regarded as an authority on the subject.

He published: 1. 'Nomenclatura Hibernica,' Dublin, 1810. 2. 'Reflections on the Veto.' 3. 'A Historical Inquiry into the Origin and Primitive Use of the Irish Pillar Tower,' London, 1821. 4. 'A Genealogical Memoir of the Family of Montmorency, styled De Marisco or Morres,' Paris, 1817. 5. 'Les Montmorency de France et les Montmorency d'Irlande,' Paris, 1825. He assisted in a new edition of Archdall's 'Monasticum Hibernicum,' and in a 'Topographical Dictionary of Ireland,' neither of which apparently was published; and contributed much valuable information to Brewer's 'Beauties of Ireland.'

[Biographie Nouvelle des Contemporains; Biographie Universelle des Contemporains (a very complete article, probably furnished by Morres himself, glossing over his career as a United Irishman, of which he appears to have become ashamed); Castlereagh's Corresp. ii. 93–100, containing his intercepted memoir to the French government in 1798; Fitzpatrick's Secret Service under Pitt; Madden's United Irishmen, i. 212; Miles Byrne's Memoirs, iii. 95; K. W. Harder's Die Auslieferung der vier politischen Flüchtlinge . . . im Jahre 1799, Leipzig, 1857; Morres's Les Montmorency de France et les Montmorency d'Irlande, especially the Introduction.] R. D.

MORRES, HERVEY REDMOND, second Viscount Mountmorres (1746?–1797), eldest son of Hervey Morres, baron Mountmorres, of Castle Morres in co. Kilkenny, who was created viscount Mountmorres in 1763, and Letitia, his first wife, daughter of Brabazon Ponsonby, first earl of Bessborough, was born about 1746. He matriculated from Christ Church, Oxford, on 27 April 1763, graduated B.A. on 8 Feb. 1766, was created M.A. on 3 July 1766, and D.C.L. on 8 July 1773. At college he was regarded as a man of considerable ability, but of singular habits. On the death of his father in April 1766 he succeeded to a very small encumbered estate, but by his prudent and even parsimonious manner of life he not only succeeded before his death in creating an easy fortune of 5,000*l.* a year, but was able to make a liberal allowance to the children of his father's second wife. In Dublin he resided for some time in the same boarding-house in Frederick Street as Sir Jonah Barrington [q.v.], who regarded him as 'a very clever and well informed, but eccentric man,' and records one or two curious anecdotes about him (*Personal Sketches*, i. 118). He took a profound interest in all questions affecting the privileges of the Irish House of Lords. On one occasion he furnished some amusement by publishing in the Dublin newspapers—and, Barrington maliciously adds, 'with all the supposititious cheerings, &c. duly interspersed'—a speech on the appellant jurisdiction of the House of Lords which he intended to deliver, but the debate never took place. His opinions on these subjects were always worth listening to, and still possess a certain historical value. On the regency question in 1788 he dissented from the view generally taken in Ireland, and argued strongly in support of the course pursued by Pitt and the English parliament. Latterly he resided much in London. He was greatly distressed by the news that reached him of the disturbed state of Ireland, and his mind, never very strong, giving way finally under the strain, he shot himself in a fit of temporary insanity at his lodgings, 6 York Street, St. James's Square, on 18 Aug. 1797. He was buried in St. James's Chapel, Hampstead Road, and never having married, was succeeded by his half-brother, Francis Hervey Morres. By all accounts he was a man of amiable and gentle manners, extremely polite, upright, and generous, fond of talking, but less from vanity than from the prevalence of strong animal spirits.

His more important publications are: 1. 'A Speech intended to have been spoken . . . on the Appellant Jurisdiction of the House of Lords of Ireland,' 1782. 2. 'Impartial Reflections upon the question of Equalising the duties upon the Trade between Great Britain and Ireland,' 1785. 3. 'A Speech delivered, 19 Feb. 1789, in the House of Lords, Ireland, on the Address to the Prince of Wales,' 1790. 4. 'The Danger of the Political Balance of Europe,' 1790; 2nd edit., greatly improved, 1791. 5. 'The History of the Principal Transactions of the Irish Parliament from 1634 to 1666. . . . To which is prefixed a Preliminary Discourse on the Ancient Parliaments of that Kingdom,' 2 vols. 1792. 6. 'The Crisis; a Collection of Essays . . . on Toleration, Public Credit, the Election Franchise in Ireland, the Emancipation of the Irish Catholics,' &c., 1794. 7. 'The Prodigal . . . a Comedy,' 1794, anon. (see Horace Walpole's copy in British Museum). 8. 'The Letters of Themistocles,' 1795, from the 'Public Advertiser.' 9. 'An Historical Dissertation upon the . . . Judicature and Independency of the Irish Parliament,' 1795. 10. 'Impartial Reflections upon the present Crisis, comprised in four Essays upon . . . Corn, the Assize of Bread, Tithes, and a general System of Inclosures,' 1796.

[Les Montmorency de France et les Montmorency d'Irlande . . . avec la généalogie . . . de Montmorency d'Irlande, Paris, 1828; Barrington's Personal Sketches; Gent. Mag. 1797, ii. 717, 744, 885; Walker's Hibernian Mag. 1797; Brit. Mus. Cat.] R. D.

MORRICE. [See MORICE and MORRIS.]

MORRIS. [See also MORICE.]

MORRIS, CHARLES (1745–1838), song-writer, one of the four sons of Captain Thomas Morris, author of the popular song 'Kitty Crowder,' and a descendant of a good Welsh family, was born in 1745. Both his father and grandfather had served in the 17th foot, and the latter, after having received a severe wound in the French war under Marlborough, had settled on a small landed property at Bell Bridge, near Carlisle. His father dying in his infancy, Charles was educated by his mother, entered the 17th foot in 1764, and after serving in America returned to England, and exchanged into the royal Irish dragoons. He shone greatly in convivial society, and found life out of London intolerable. Consequently, when, through a friend, Captain Topham, adjutant of the 2nd life-guards, an opportunity presented itself of exchanging into that regiment, he was not slow to take advantage of it. He became the boon-companion of the wits and beaux of the town, and from 14 Feb. 1785 punch-maker and bard of the Beefsteak Society, which, founded in 1735, was limited to twenty-four members, and was then in the zenith of its fame. He sang many of his wittiest songs for the first time after the club dinners over the stage at Covent Garden Theatre. Politically he became an associate of Fox's party, but had subsequently to complain of the neglect of his whig friends, for whom he wrote such popular ballads as 'Billy's too young to drive us' and 'Billy Pitt and the Farmer.' His lament took the form of 'an ode to his political vest,' entitled 'The old Whig Poet to his old Buff Waistcoat.' His political songs were numerous, but he is better remembered for his celebration of 'the sweet shady side of Pall Mall' in 'The Town and the Country, or the Contrast,' and his 'A Reason fair to fill my Glass,' which is reproduced in Locker-Lampson's 'Lyra Elegantiarum.' For his song 'Ad Poculum' he received a gold medal from the Harmonic Society, and the well-known lyric, 'The Triumph of Venus, or The Tear that bedews sensibility's shrine,' is correctly attributed to him. On 4 April 1785 Windham records that he dined with the whigs at the London Tavern, and first heard to advantage Captain Morris (*Diary*, p. 47). Morris was not long in becoming intimate with the Prince of Wales, after the latter's admission among 'the steaks' in 1785. At Carlton House he was subsequently a frequent guest, and earned the title of 'The Sun of the Table.' His social triumphs left him impecunious, but the prince was not ungrateful, and settled upon him an annuity of 200*l.* a year. In Morris's declining years Kemble induced the Duke of Norfolk (the eleventh duke, 'Jockey of Norfolk,' who was supposed by not a few, though erroneously, to be Morris's brother), for many years president of the Beefsteak Club, to give him the villa of Brockham, near Dorking. At Brockham he died, at the ripe age of ninety-three, on 11 July 1838, and was buried in Betchworth churchyard (MURRAY, *Handbook to Surrey*, p. 53). He retained his vivacity and humour to the last, justifying the remark which Curran once addressed to him: 'Die when you will, Charles, you will die in your youth.'

Morris was a born song-writer, who dashed off at random careless but fluent and effective verse of the genre that Tom Moore subsequently made his own. His 'Friends all gone!' in the key of Thackeray's 'Ballad of Bouille-baisse,' shows that he was not deficient in pathos, and, as the years rolled on, of a tendency to piety. His effect as a humorist was heightened by the solemnity of his demeanour. It is related how, when the original of Thackeray's Captain Costigan died, and was buried under the windows of Offley's, Morris gravely read a mock funeral service from the windows above, and then poured a bowl of punch over the grave.

Morris married the widow of Sir William Stanhope, but he told Lord Stowell shortly before his death that he had been in love all his life with a Miss Molly Dacre, who became Lady Clarke.

After his death his songs, a number of which had appeared in 1786 as 'A Collection of Songs by the inimitable Captain Morris,' were published in two volumes, under the title of 'Lyra Urbanica, or the Social Effusions of Captain Morris, of the late (sic) Life Guards' (London, 8vo, 1840; 2nd edit. 1844). Prefixed is a portrait engraved by Greatbatch from a picture in the possession of the family. An oil portrait by J. Lonsdale was, at the Beefsteak sale in 1867, purchased by Earl Dalhousie, and the bard's chair, with the initials 'C. M.,' was at the same time purchased by Charles Hallett.

Charles's elder brother, Captain THOMAS MORRIS (*fl.* 1806), was also a song-writer of repute in his day. Born at Carlisle, where he was baptised on 22 April 1732, he entered Winchester College as a scholar in 1741, and joined the 17th foot in Ireland on its return from Minorca in 1748. (He did not proceed to Oxford, as has been stated.) After serving with distinction at the siege of the Havannah, and under General Bradstreet in America, he returned to England in 1767, and two years later married a Miss Chubb, daughter of a merchant at Bridgwater, by whom he had six children. Morris was one of the original subscribers to the literary fund, at whose annual meetings (1794–7) he recited his own verses. He is stated in 1806 to have been living in retirement at Hampstead, where he amused himself by suggesting emendations to the works of Pope, and 'regularly read both the "Iliad" and "Odyssey" every year' (*Public Characters of* 1806, p. 342). His published volumes were: 1. 'The Bee, a Collection of Songs,' London, 1790, 8vo. 2. 'Miscellanies in Prose and Verse,' 1791, 8vo. 3. 'A Life of the Rev. D. Williams,' 1792, 8vo. 4. 'Quashy, or the Coal-black Maid. A tale relative to the Slave-trade,' 1796, 8vo (cf. REUSS, *Register of Living Authors*, 1804, pt. ii. p. 114).

Both Charles and Thomas must of course be distinguished from another Captain Morris, a convivial member of the Owls' Club at the beginning of this century, whose odd personality is vividly described by the Rev. J. Richardson in his 'Recollections of the last Half-Century' (i. 268–89).

[Gent. Mag. 1838, ii. 453; Notes and Queries, 2nd ser. ii. 412, 4th ser. i. 244, 6th ser. ii. 369; Public Characters of 1806, pp. 322–51; Walter Arnold's Life and Death of the Sublime Society of Beefsteaks, passim; Timbs's Clubs and Club Life in London, pp. 127–35, and Anecdote Lives of the Later Wits and Humorists, pp. 69–75; Blackwood's Magazine, January 1841, pp. 47–55; Irish Quarterly Review, March 1853 pp. 140–4 and September pp. 649–53; Fitzgerald's Lives of the Sheridans, i. 234; Monthly Review, No. 158; T. Moore's Memoirs, i. 8, ii. 175, vi. 93–4; Lowndes's Bibl. Man. 1617–18; Watt's Bibl. Brit.; Allibone's Dict. of English Lit.; Williams's Claims of Lit. (1802), pp. 169, 171, 181, 192.] T. S.

MORRIS, MORES, or MORICE, SIR CHRISTOPHER (1490?–1544), master of ordnance, was probably born about 1490. On 4 Dec. 1513 he was made gunner in the Tower of London, with a salary of 12*d.* a day, and the appointment was confirmed on 14 Aug. 1514 (BREWER, *Letters and Papers of Henry VIII*, i. No. 4591, 5340). In the following March Morris was serving at Tournai, but soon returned to his post at the Tower, where he apparently remained until the summer of 1522 (*ib.* II. pt. ii. p. 1514, III. pt. ii. No. 3288, g. 2923, 2992). He was on board one of the vessels which, under Surrey's command [see HOWARD, THOMAS II, EARL OF SURREY and third DUKE OF NORFOLK], escorted Charles V to Biscay after his visit to England in 1522; in July a detachment with artillery was landed on the coast of France near Morlaix, which was captured, 'for the master gunner, Christopher Morris, having certain falcons, with the shot of one of them struck the lock of the wicket in the gate, so that it flew open,' and the town was taken. In August 1523 Morris was acting as lieutenant-gunner before Calais, and on the 23rd of that month he sailed with the vice-admiral, Sir William Fitzwilliam (afterwards Earl of Southampton) [q. v.], and landed near Tréport; after severe fighting they re-embarked, burning seven ships and capturing twenty-seven pieces of ordnance. In April 1524 Morris was at Valenciennes in charge of the ordnance; in the same year he was appointed 'overseer of ordnance,' and commissioned to search the isle of Thanet for the goods of a Portuguese vessel that had been beached there.

For some time afterwards Morris was employed mainly in diplomatic work; at the end of 1526 or beginning of 1527 he was sent with letters to the English envoys at Valladolid, and started back with their despatches on 1 Feb. 1526–7. In the same year he was appointed chief gunner of the Tower, and in September was bearer of instructions to Knight, the envoy at Compiègne (BREWER, *Henry VIII*, ii. 224). In 1530 he served in Ireland, and in January 1530–1 before Calais; in the same year he inspected the mines at Llantrysaint, Glamorganshire, as the king's commissioner, and appears as owner of a ship, the inventory of which is given in Cotton

MS. App. xxviii. 1. After serving on a commission to survey the land and fortifications of Calais and Guisnes, commanding a company of artillery at the former place, and inspecting the fortifications of Carlisle in 1532, Morris was in 1535 despatched on a mission to North Germany and Denmark, probably to enlist gunners and engineers in the English service. He visited Hamburg, Lübeck, Rostock, and all the principal towns in Denmark and Zealand, returning on 27 June. In August he was at Greenwich, engaged in enlisting men, and in September was ordered to proceed with three ships to Denmark; the order was, however, countermanded, and Morris was again sent to Calais. On 8 Feb. 1536–7, he was made master of ordnance, with a salary of 2*s.* a day for himself, 6*d.* for a clerk, and 6*d.* for a yeoman. Before October he was recalled, and was in London ready to march northwards to assist in suppressing the Pilgrimage of Grace. In 1537 Morris was again at Carlisle inspecting the fortifications, which had been declared unsound; was granted license to be 'overseer of the science of artillery;' appointed master gunner of England, and on 31 July landed at Calais, where in 1539 he was one of the commissioners appointed to receive Anne of Cleves; on 18 Oct. he was knighted at the creation of the Earl of Hertford and Southampton. In 1542 Morris was in England superintending the artillery, not always with success, for of the pieces despatched for the Scottish war in October 1542 all but one burst (*Hamilton Papers*, i. 263). In March 1543–4 he joined the Earl of Hertford's expedition to Scotland. Landing near Leith, which was immediately captured, Morris accompanied the army to Edinburgh, where on 7 May he blew in Canongate with a culverin; the next day he bombarded the castle, without effect, for two hours and was compelled to retreat (cf. Froude, iv. 34–6). In the autumn Morris, as chief director of the batteries, was at Boulogne, where on 3 Sept. he received a wound, which apparently proved fatal. He was buried in St. Peter's Church, Cornhill, London.

[Letters and Papers of Henry VIII, ed. Brewer vols. i–iv., passim, ed. Gairdner vols. v–ix., passim; Hamilton Papers, vols. i. and ii.; Acts of Privy Council, 1542–7; Cotton MSS. App. xxviii, 1; Chronicle of Calais, p. 173; Stow's Survey; Thomas's Historical Notes, i. 218, 219; Proceedings of Royal Artillery Institute, xix. 221–3; Metcalfe's Book of Knights; Brewer's Henry VIII, ii. 224.] A. F. P.

MORRIS, CORBYN (*d.* 1779), commissioner of customs, first attracted notice by the publication of 'A Letter from a Bystander to a Member of Parliament, wherein is examined what necessity there is for the maintenance of a large regular land-force in this island; what proportions the Revenues of the Crown have borne to those of the people at different periods from the Restoration to his present Majesty's Accession; and whether the weight of Power in the Royal or popular side now preponderates,' London, 1741–2, 8vo; 3rd edit. 1743. In this pamphlet he shows that the power of the crown depends upon economic conditions, and, after an elaborate discussion of the relative resources of the crown and the people, decides that 'our tendency at present, unless it be rightly moderated, lies much stronger to democracy than to absolute monarchy' (p. 58). His estimates of national income are based on the mercantilist theory, that 'the whole annual income at any period is greater or less according to the quantity of coin then circulating in the kingdom' (p. 107). He concludes with a eulogy of Walpole's administration, and an appeal for a 'reasonable candour' in the inquiry into his conduct. The 'Letter from a Bystander' was generally supposed to have been written by Walpole or by his direction. On this assumption the author was vehemently attacked in 'A Proper Answer to the Bystander,' &c. (attributed to William Pulteney), London, 1742, 8vo, and 'A Full Answer to the "Letter from a Bystander" . . . by R—— H——, esq. [Thomas Carte],' London, 1742, 8vo (*Rawlinson MS.* D. 89; cf. *Carte MSS.*, Bodleian Library, 10705, f. 3). Morris replied with 'A Letter to the Rev. Mr. Thomas Carte . . . by a Gentleman of Cambridge,' London, 1743, 8vo. The controversy terminated with the publication by Carte of 'A Full and Clear Vindication of the Full Answer,' &c., London, 1743, 8vo. (*ib.*)

During the administrations of Pelham and Newcastle, Morris was employed by them 'in conciliating opponents' (Morris to Charles Yorke, 30 Dec. 1759, *Addit. MS.* 32900, f. 431). On the suppression of the rebellion of 1745 he submitted to Newcastle (8 May 1746) several proposals for the regulation of the highlands. He suggested (1) the registration of all lands and deeds at London and Stirling, and the reversion to the crown of lands not so registered; (2) the abolition of entail and the vesting in the landowner of absolute property in the land; (3) the division of the land among the children on the death of the landowners; (4) the payment of rent only in case of a written agreement between landlord and tenant; (5) the settlement of all forfeited lands with new tenants; and (6) the universal abolition of the highland dress. He pointed out that, unless they were dispersed, the power of the old highland families would be increased by the encouragement of trade and manufactures (*ib.* 32707, f. 162). On 3 June 1747 he drew up 'Hints respecting a Treaty with Spain' (*ib.* 32711, f. 194), in which he suggested the adoption, in the case of Spain, of the principle of the Methuen treaty, the exchange of Gibraltar for Ceuta and St. Augustine, and the removal from Minorca of the Roman catholic inhabitants.

In 1751 Morris was appointed by Pelham secretary of the customs and salt duty in Scotland. His salary was 500*l.* per annum. He was sent to Scotland to inquire into the state of the customs and the practices of the smugglers. As an administrator he showed great ability. He regulated the method of weighing tobacco, thus augmenting the customs, and by suppressing the importation, under the Spanish duty, of French wines into Scotland removed a grievance of which English merchants had long complained. He claimed that during the first five years of his secretaryship more money had been remitted from the customs in Scotland to the receiver-general in England than in all the preceding years since the union (*ib.* 32872, f. 198). As a result of his experience he submitted to Newcastle in 1752 and 1758 several suggestions for the better regulation of the customs and salt duties.

Meanwhile Morris's efforts for economic reform had not been confined to the sphere of his official duties. He had collected much useful information on the vital statistics of London, and in 1753 he prepared a bill 'for a general registry of the total number of the people of Great Britain, and of their annual increase and diminution by births and deaths.' On this work he consulted Dr. Squire, who was 'master of the whole plan' (Morris to the Duke of Newcastle, 22 Jan. 1753, *ib.* 32731, f. 67). He explained the advantages of a census to the Duke of Newcastle, under whose 'immediate direction' the bill was introduced into the House of Lords (*ib.* 20 May 1753, *ib.* f. 480). He was elected F.R.S. on 19 May 1757, and admitted to the society a week later. Dissatisfied with his position in Scotland, and anxious to return to England, Morris made many attempts to obtain from Newcastle an official appointment in the English revenue department. On 15 March 1763 he was appointed commissioner of the customs. Morris died on 24 Dec. 1779, and was buried at Wimbledon on 1 Jan. 1780. He married on 15 Sept. 1758 a Mrs. Wright.

Though a strong supporter of the mercantile theory, Morris's economic works are valuable. He was an able statistician. According to his friend David Hume, he used to say that he wrote all his books for the sake of their dedications (Hume to Gilbert Elliot of Minto, 12 March 1763; BURTON, *Life of Hume*, ii. 147). He published, in addition to the two pamphlets mentioned above: 1. 'An Essay towards fixing the True Standards of Wit, Humour, Raillery, Satire, and Ridicule, &c. Inscribed to the Right Honourable Robert, Earl of Orford,' London, 1744, 8vo. Horace Walpole sent this essay to Sir Horace Mann as one of 'the only new books at all worth reading. . . . The dedication to my father is fine; pray mind the quotation from Milton' (Walpole to Sir Horace Mann, 18 June 1744, *Letters*, ed. Cunningham, i. 306). 2. 'An Essay towards illustrating the Science of Insurance, wherein it is attempted to fix, by precise Calculation, several important Maxims upon this subject,' &c., London, 1747, 8vo. 3. 'An Essay towards deciding the important Question, Whether it be a National Advantage to Britain to insure the Ships of her Enemies? Addressed to the Right Honourable H. Pelham,' London [1747], 8vo; 2nd edition, with amendments, 'To which are now added, further considerations upon our Insurance of the French Commerce in the present juncture,' 2 parts, London, 1758, 8vo. 4. 'Observations on the past Growth and present State of the City of London. To which are annexed a complete Table of the Christnings and Burials within this City from 1601 to 1750 . . . together with a Table of the Numbers which have annually died of each Disease from 1675 to the present time,' &c., London, 1751, fol.; 'reprinted, . . . with a continuation of the tables to the end of . . . 1757,' London, 1757 and 1759, 4to. 5. 'A Letter balancing the Causes of the Present Scarcity of our Silver Coin, and the Means of Immediate Remedy, &c. Addressed to the . . . Earl of Powis,' London, 1757, 8vo. In this pamphlet Morris attributes the scarcity to exportation, arising from the fact that, while in the coinage of England the ratio of gold to silver was $1 : 15\frac{2859}{13640}$, the ratio abroad was $1 : 14\frac{1}{2}$. He intended to write some additional observations on this subject, and asked Newcastle for his patronage (Morris to the Duke of Newcastle, 29 June 1757, *Addit. MS.* 32871, f. 452), but nothing further was published. 6. 'A Plan for Arranging and Balancing the Accounts of Landed Estates,' &c., London, 1759, fol. 7. 'Remarks upon Mr. Mill's Proposals for publishing a Survey of the Trade of Great Britain, Ireland, and the British Colonies,' London, 1771, fol. An 'Account of the

Duties and Customs to which Foreign Merchants are Subject. Sent with a Letter to Lord Shelburne, 22 Aug. 1768,' among the Additional MSS. in the British Museum, is in Morris's handwriting (*ib.* 30228, f. 192). Some lines by Morris 'On reading Dr. Goldsmith's poem "The Deserted Village"' are printed in 'The New Foundling Hospital for Wit' (1784, vi. 95).

[Authorities quoted and Addit. MSS. (Brit. Mus.) 32705 f. 41, 32726 f. 12, 32860 f. 46, 32864 f. 287, 32866 f. 247, 32877 ff. 150, 448, 32878 f. 96, 32895 f. 436, 32968 f. 373; Thomson's Hist. of Royal Society, Appendix iv. xlviii.; Nichols's Lit. Anecd. ii. 227, 504, 508; Boswell's Johnson, ed. Hill, iv. 107.] W. A. S. H.

MORRIS, EDWARD (*d.* 1689), Welsh poet, of Perthi Llwydion, near Cerryg y Drudion, Denbighshire, was one of the best known writers of carols, ballads, and 'englynion' during the second half of the seventeenth century. Twelve of his pieces are to be found in 'Llyfr Carolau a Dyriau duwiol' (3rd edit. Shrewsbury, 1720), and eleven in 'Blodeugerdd Cymru' (1759). They are variously dated from 1656 to 1688. He was an intimate friend of his more famous brother bard, Huw Morris or Morus [q. v.], whose published works contain complimentary 'englynion' exchanged by the two poets, and an elegy composed by Huw Morus upon hearing of the death of his friend (*Eos Ceiriog*, ii. 363, 405–10, i. 21). From the latter we learn that Edward died in 1689 while travelling in Essex, no doubt in the pursuit of his occupation as drover. It would appear he was a fair English and Welsh scholar, for shortly before his death he was entrusted by Mrs. Margaret Vychan of Llwydiarth, Montgomeryshire, with the task of translating into Welsh an English theological work, which was published in 1689 (at Mrs. Vychan's expense) under the title 'Y Rhybuddiwr Crist'nogawl' (*ib.* ii. 360–4; W. Rowlands, *Cambrian Bibliography*, p. 246).

[Eos Ceiriog, ed. W[alter] D[avies], 1823.] J. E. L.

MORRIS, FRANCIS ORPEN (1810–1893), naturalist, born at Cove, near Cork, on 25 March 1810, was the eldest son of Rear-admiral Henry Gage Morris of York and Beverley, who served in the American and French wars. His mother, Rebecca Newenham Millerd, was a daughter of the Rev. Francis Orpen. His grandfather was Colonel Roger Morris [q. v.] Francis was educated at Bromsgrove School and Worcester College, Oxford, where he graduated B.A., with honours in classics, in 1833. He astonished his examiners by choosing Pliny's 'Natural History' for his voluntary thesis. He was admitted *ad eundem* at Durham in 1844.

In 1834 Morris was ordained to the perpetual curacy of Hanging Heaton, near Dewsbury. He was ordained priest at York in 1835 and served successively as curate at Taxal, Cheshire (1836), Christ Church, Doncaster (1836), Ordsall, Nottinghamshire (1838), and Crambe, Yorkshire (1842). In 1844 he was presented to the vicarage of Nafferton, near Driffield, and appointed chaplain to the Duke of Cleveland. In 1854 he was presented by the Archbishop of York to the rectory of Nunburnholme, Yorkshire, and he held that living till his death on 10 Feb. 1893; a few years before his death he received a civil list pension of 100*l.* He married in 1835 Ann, second daughter of Mr. C. Sanders of Bromsgrove, Worcestershire.

Morris wrote much on religious subjects, but he is best known by his works on natural history, which, although 'popular' rather than scientific, had much literary value. He was never able to accept the theory of evolution, and was an extreme anti-vivisectionist.

His great work was 'A History of British Birds,' in 6 vols. 8vo, London, 1851–7, a third edition of which appeared in 1891.

His other natural history writings include: 1. 'A Guide to the Arrangement of British Birds,' 8vo, London [1834]. 2. 'An Essay on Scientific Nomenclature,' 8vo, London, 1850. 3. 'Book of Natural History,' 8vo, London, 1852. 4. 'A Natural History of the Nests and Eggs of British Birds,' 3 vols. 8vo, London, 1853–6; 3rd edit. 1892. 5. 'A History of British Butterflies,' 8vo, London, 1853; 3rd edit. 1893. 6. 'A Natural History of British Moths,' 4 vols. 8vo, London, 1859–1870. 7. '"Fact is Stranger than Fiction." Anecdotes in Natural History,' 8vo, London, 1860. 8. 'Records of Animal Sagacity,' 12mo, London, 1861. 9. 'The Gamekeeper's Museum,' 8vo, London, 1864. 10. 'Catalogue of British Insects in all the Orders,' 8vo, London, 1865. 11. 'Dogs and their Doings,' 8vo, London, 1870; 2nd edit. [1887]. 12. 'Anecdotes in Natural History,' 8vo, London [1872]; 2nd edit. [1889]. 13. 'Birds' contributed to 'Simple Lessons for Home Use,' 16mo, 1877. 14. 'Letters to the "Times" about Birds,' 8vo, London [1880]. He also edited vols. vi. to viii. of 'The Naturalist,' 8vo, 1856–8.

In connection with the Darwinian question he wrote: 15. 'Difficulties of Darwinism,' 8vo, London, 1869. 16. 'A Double Dilemma in Darwinism,' 8vo, London [1870]. 17. 'A Guard against "The Guardian,"' 8vo, London, 1877. 18. 'All the Articles of the Darwin

Faith,' 8vo, London, 1877; 2nd edit. [1882]. 19. 'The Demands of Darwinism on Credulity,' 8vo, London [1890].

As a zoophilist he wrote: 20. 'A Word for God's Dumb Creatures,' 8vo, London [1876]. 21. 'A Dialogue about Fox-hunting,' 8vo, London [1878]. 22. 'The Curse of Cruelty,' a sermon, 8vo, London, 1886. 23. 'The Sparrow Shooter,' 8vo, London, 1886. 24. 'The Sea Gull Shooter,' 8vo, London [1890]. 25. 'The Cowardly Cruelty of the Experimenters on Living Animals,' 8vo [London, 1890]. 26. 'The Humanity Series of School Books,' 6 pts. 8vo, London, 1890. 27. 'A Defence of our Dumb Companions,' 8vo, London [1892].

His religious and ecclesiastical writings include: 28. 'Extracts from the Works of . . . J. Wesley,' 8vo, 1840. 29. 'An Essay on Baptismal Regeneration,' 8vo, London, 1850. 30. 'An Essay on the Eternal Duration of the Earth,' 8vo, London, 1850. 31. 'The Maxims of the Bible,' 12mo, 1855. 32. 'The Precepts of the Bible,' 24mo, 1855. 33. 'The Yorkshire Hymn Book,' 16mo, London, 1860. 34. 'Plain Sermons for Plain People,' 210 nos. 8vo, London [1862–90]. 35. 'A Handbook of Hymns for the Sick Bedside,' 8vo, London [1875?]. 36. 'Short Sermons for the People,' 4 nos. 8vo, London [1879]. 37. 'The Ghost of Wesley,' 8vo [1882]. 38. 'A Handbook of the Church and Dissent,' 8vo, London [1882]. 39. 'A Dialogue about the Church,' 2 editions, 8vo, London [1889]. 40. 'Methodism' [anon.], 8vo, London, 1890.

His other writings include: 41. 'Penny Postage,' 8vo, London, 1840. 42. 'A Plan for the Detection of Thefts by Letter Carriers,' 8vo, London, 1850. 43. 'National Adult Education. Read before the British Association,' 8vo, London, 1853. 44. 'The Present System of Hiring Farm Servants in the East Riding of Yorkshire,' 8vo, Driffield, 1854. 45. 'Account of the Siege of Killowen,' 8vo, Driffield, 1854. 46. 'Account of the Battle of the Monongahela River,' 8vo, Driffield, 1854. 47. 'The Country Seats of Noblemen and Gentlemen of Great Britain and Ireland,' 5 vols. 4to, London [1866–80]. 48. 'The Ancestral Homes of Britain,' 4to, London, 1868. 49. 'The Rights and Wrongs o Women,' 8vo, London [1870]. 50. 'A Hundred Reasons against the Land Craze,' 8vo, London [1885]. He also wrote letters to the 'Times' on natural history; contributed 'A Thousand and One Anecdotes on Natural History' to the 'Fireside Magazine,' and wrote for the 'Leisure Hour.'

[Yorkshire Post, 13 Feb. 1893; Daily Graphic, 16 Feb. 1893; The Naturalist of Nunburnholme, by E. W. Abram, in Good Words, September 1893 (with portrait); Crockford's Clerical Directory; Brit. Mus. Cat.; information kindly supplied by Miss L. A. G. Morris.] B. B. W.

MORRIS or MORUS, HUW (1622–1709), Welsh poet, was born at Pont y Meibion, which, though lying in the valley of the Ceiriog, is within the parish of Llansilin, Denbighshire. Being a younger (the third) son, he was apprenticed to a tanner, who lived at Gwaliau, near Overton, Flintshire, but he did not complete his term of apprenticeship. For the rest of his life he lived at Pont y Meibion, helping on the farm his father, his eldest brother, and his nephew in succession, and gradually winning a great reputation as a composer of ballads, carols, and occasional verse. He wrote much in the 'strict' metres, but is better known as a writer in the free ballad metres of the English type, which became popular in Wales with the decline of the older poetry in the seventeenth century. Next to the love poems the most familiar are those on political subjects. Huw Morus, like most of his countrymen, was a staunch royalist and supporter of the church of England. He satirised freely the roundhead preachers and soldiers, sometimes in allegory, and sometimes without any disguise. In 1660 he wrote an ironical 'Elegy upon Oliver's Men,' and a 'Welcome to General Monk.' Under Charles II he was still attached to the same interest, and vigorously denounced the Rye House plot in 1683. But his churchmanship was deeply protestant, and the trial of the seven bishops, of whom William Lloyd of St. Asaph had expressed admiration of his poetry, forced him to transfer his allegiance from James II to William of Orange, whose cause he warmly supported from 1688 onwards.

In his old age Huw Morus was revered by the countryside as a kind of oracle, and tradition says that in the customary procession out of Llansilin parish church after service the first place was always yielded to him by the vicar. He died unmarried on 31 Aug. 1709, and was buried at Llansilin, where a slab to his memory bears 'englynion,' by the Rev. Robert Wynne, Gwyddelwern. In appearance he was tall, sallow, and marked with small-pox. 'Cadair Huw Morus' (Huw Morus's chair), with the initials H. M. B. (Huw Morus, Bardd) upon the back, is still shown near Pont y Meibion. It is a stone seat fixed in a wall, and forms the subject of an engraving prefixed to the 1823 edition of the poet's works.

Poems by Huw Morus appear in the collection of songs printed for Foulk Owens in 1686, and reprinted (as 'Carolau a Dyriau Duwiol') in 1696 and 1729. He is represented also in 'Blodeugerdd Cymru' (1759). But no collected edition of his verse appeared until 1823, when the Rev. Walter Davies (Gwallter Mechain) published 'Eos Ceiriog' in two volumes, the former containing a prefatory sketch of the poet's life and character. This edition contains 147 poems, besides some two hundred 'englynion,' or single stanzas. Of seventy other poems the titles only are given. The author of the life in the 'Cambrian Register' (i. 436) tells us that one manuscript collection of Huw Morus's poems contained as many as three hundred pieces, and this is rendered likely by the fact that in a manuscript volume of seventeenth-century poetry Richard Williams of Newtown found twenty-two poems not even mentioned by Gwallter Mechain (*Geninen*, xi. 303).

[Life in the Cambrian Register, vol. i. by David Samwell (*d.* 1798); Eos Ceiriog (1823); Rowlands's Cambrian Bibl.; Borrow's Wild Wales chaps. xx. and lxviii.; Williams's Eminent Welshmen, p. 347.] J. E. L.

MORRIS, Sir JAMES NICOLL (1763?–1830), vice-admiral, was the son of Captain John Morris, who, in command of the Bristol, was mortally wounded in the unsuccessful attack on Sullivan's Island on 28 June 1776 [see Parker, Sir Peter, 1721–1811], and died on 2 July (Beatson, *Nav. and Mil. Memoirs*, iv. 152; Ralfe, *Nav. Biog.* i. 116*n.*) James is said to have entered the navy under the immediate command of his father (Marshall, ii. 489; *Gent. Mag.* 1830, i. 467). This seems doubtful, and in any case he was not with his father in the Bristol (*Bristol's Pay-book*). In 1778 and 1779 he was in the Prince of Wales, the flagship of Rear-admiral Samuel Barrington [q. v.] in the West Indies, and in her was present at the battles of St. Lucia and Grenada. He was promoted to be lieutenant on 14 April 1780, and was serving on board the Namur in the action off Dominica on 12 April 1782. He was again with Barrington in the Royal George during the Spanish armament in 1790, and by his interest was promoted to the rank of commander on 21 Sept. In 1791 he was appointed to the Pluto sloop on the Newfoundland station, where, on 25 July 1793, he captured the French sloop Lutine. On 7 Oct. 1793 he was posted to the Boston frigate, which he took to England and commanded for the next four years in the Channel, the Bay of Biscay, and the Spanish coast, cruising with good success against the enemy's merchant ships and privateers. Towards the end of 1797 he was moved into the Lively frigate, which was lost on Rota Point, near Cadiz, in the early part of 1798. In 1799 he was appointed to the Phaëton, in which in the autumn he carried Lord Elgin to Constantinople [see Bruce, Thomas, seventh Earl of Elgin]. In the following May the Phaëton was with the fleet off Genoa, and being detached to cooperate with the Austrians, inflicted severe loss on the retreating French at Loano and Alassio (Allardyce, *Memoir of Viscount Keith*, p. 206). In October she was off Malaga, and on the 28th her boats, under the command of Mr. Beaufort, her first lieutenant, captured and brought off a heavily armed polacca, which, with a French privateer schooner, was lying under the protection of a 5-gun battery [see Beaufort, Sir Francis]. During 1801 the Phaëton continued actively employed on the coast of Spain, and in the winter returned to England.

On the renewal of the war Morris was appointed to the Leopard, but was shortly afterwards moved into the Colossus, a new 74-gun ship, which, after some eighteen months off Brest, under Admiral Cornwallis, was, in October 1805, with Nelson off Cadiz, and on the 21st took part in the battle of Trafalgar. She was the sixth ship in the lee line, following Collingwood, and by the fortune of war sustained greater damage and heavier loss of men than any other ship in the fleet. Morris himself was severely wounded in the thigh, but the bleeding being stopped by a tourniquet, remained on deck till the close of the action. For the next three years he continued in command of the Colossus, on the home station or in the Mediterranean, and in 1810 commanded the Formidable of 98 guns. On 1 Aug. 1811 he was promoted to the rank of rear-admiral, and in 1812, at the special request of Sir James Saumarez, afterwards Lord de Saumarez [q. v.], was appointed third in command in the Baltic. On 2 Jan. 1815 he was nominated a K.C.B. He became a vice-admiral on 12 Aug. 1819, and died at his house at Marlow on 15 April 1830. He married, in October 1802, Margaretta Sarah, daughter of Thomas Somers Cocks, the well-known banker (1737–1796), and niece of Charles Somers Cocks, first lord Somers [q. v.]

[Marshall's Roy. Nav. Biog. ii. (vol. i. pt. ii.), 488; Gent. Mag. 1830, pt. i. p. 467; James's Nav. Hist.; Nicolas's Despatches and Letters of Lord Nelson (see index).] J. K. L.

MORRIS, JOHN (1617?–1649), soldier, was eldest son of Matthias Morris of Esthagh, in Elmsall, near Pontefract, Yorkshire (Dugdale, *Visit. of Yorkshire*, Surtees Soc., p. 267). He was brought up in the house of Thomas Wentworth, earl of Strafford. When Strafford became lord deputy of Ireland, he was at sixteen made ensign to Strafford's own company of foot, and soon afterwards lieutenant of his guard. The earl detected in him much military capacity, and foretold that he would 'outdo many of our old commanders.' After Strafford's death, Morris became captain in Sir Henry Tichborne's regiment. During the Irish rebellion he was appointed sergeant-major in the regiment commanded by Sir Francis Willoughby, and major by commission from the Earl of Ormonde (2 June 1642). In Ireland he performed some important services, especially after the storming of Ross Castle, when, although badly wounded, he rallied some English troops that were flying before General Preston, and 'charging the enemy, in the very head of them, obtained a victory' (HUNTER, *South Yorkshire*, ii. 98). On returning to England he served for a while in Lord Byron's regiment, but after the surrender of Liverpool in 1644, he threw up his commission in a moment of caprice, and joined the parliamentary army (LLOYD, *Memoires*, ed. 1668, p. 563). His pleasant manners made him a general favourite, while his genius for strategy and skill in handling troops quickly gained for him a colonelcy. But when the new model was introduced, the puritan officers looked askance on his easy-going ways, while he in turn laughed at their affected behaviour. He was not entrusted with command, though many flattering promises of future employment and reward were held out to him. Dissembling his anger under a smiling exterior, Morris betook himself to his estate of Esthagh, there to concoct a scheme by which he might effectually serve the king and avenge himself on his former comrades.

While serving against the king at the siege of Sandal in 1645 he had become acquainted with Colonel Overton, who had since been made governor of Pontefract. Having 'some assurance of his good affections to his Ma'tie,' Morris entered into a conspiracy with him for a surprise of the castle. Overton promised that he would open a 'sally port' whenever the king considered it convenient. But in November 1647 Overton was transferred to the governorship of Hull, and Morris had little or no acquaintance with Cotterell, who succeeded him at Pontefract. To gain his ends he succeeded in establishing some intimacy with two of the garrison who had formerly served the king, and an unsuccessful attempt to seize the castle by means of a scaling ladder was made on 18 May 1648. It failed, owing to the drunkenness of Morris's confederate, corporal Floyd, who had undertaken to place a friendly sentinel on duty and neglected to do so. The attacking party escaped unhurt, and no suspicions were attached to Morris. Cotterell at once ordered those of his garrison who were sleeping in the town to take up residence in the castle, and issued warrants for beds for a hundred men. Disguised as countrymen, Morris and William Paulden [see PAULDEN, THOMAS], each with four men carrying beds and with three others bringing money as though to compound for theirs, gained admission to the castle on 3 June, and offering quarter to the guard, secured them in the dungeon. The only blood shed was that of Cotterell, who, lying on his bed at the time, resisted Paulden's seizure of him, and was wounded. Horse and foot, which had been waiting in the locality, quickly joined the successful party, and a force of three hundred was raised with which to garrison the castle. Colonel Bonivent, who had been governor of Sandal Castle in 1644–5, was at first credited with the exploit, and it was some time before the truth was known (*Packets of Letters from Scotland*, &c., 6 June 1648, p. 6; *Declaration of Sir Thomas Glenham*, &c., E. 446 [3 and 29]). As a matter of policy Morris allowed Sir John Digby, who soon afterwards arrived from Nottingham, to assume the nominal command.

Morris answered Cromwell's summons to surrender (9 Nov.) with cheery defiance, but desertions were frequent. He made two determined sallies in February 1649, but was compelled on 3 March to treat with the parliamentarians. General Lambert, who was in command, insisted upon having six persons, whom he refused to name, excepted from mercy. Of these Morris was one. On 17 March the treaty was concluded. The excepted officers having liberty to make their escape if they could, Morris boldly charged through the enemy's army, and with Cornet Michael Blackborne got clear away into Lancashire. Lambert had given assurance for his safety could he escape five miles from the castle. Nevertheless he was betrayed at Oreton in Furness Fells, Lancashire, about ten days afterwards, and committed prisoner to Lancaster Castle. On 16 Aug. he was brought to trial at York assizes, and indicted on the statute of 25 Edw. III 'for levying war against the late King Charles.' The judges (Puleston and Thorpe) ordered him to be put in irons. He defended himself with admirable skill, and when condemned to death as a traitor, declared that he 'should die for a good cause, and with a good conscience.' Vain efforts were made to save him, even by officers of the parliamentary army. On the night of 20 Aug. Morris and his fellow-prisoner Blackborne contrived to escape from prison in York Castle, but in getting over the wall Blackborne broke his leg, and Morris refused to leave him. They were retaken, and executed on 23 Aug. By his desire Morris was buried at Wentworth, Yorkshire, near the grave of Lord Strafford.

Morris married Margery (1627-1665), eldest daughter of Dr. Robert Dawson, bishop of Clonfert and Kilmacduag, by whom he had issue Robert (*b.* 1645) of Esthagh, Castilian (1648-1702), and Mary. His widow remarried Jonas, fourth son of Abel Bulkley, of Bulkley, Lancashire.

His second son, Castilian, so named by reason of his having been born during the siege of Pontefract Castle, was appointed town clerk of Leeds in 1684 at the instance of Lord Chief-justice Jeffreys, and left descendants (THORESBY, *Ducatus Leodiensis*, ed. Whitaker). Some extracts from his diary are printed in the 'Yorkshire Archæological and Topographical Journal' (x. 159).

Morris's exploits were celebrated by Thomas Vaughan in five brief Latin elegiac poems printed at the end of Henry Vaughan's 'Thalia Rediviva' (1678).

[Appendix to Nathan Drake's Journal of the first and second Sieges of Pontefract Castle, 1644-5, in Miscellanies of Surtees Soc., xxxvii. 85-115 (with authorities cited there); Holmes's Collections towards the History of Pontefract II. (The Sieges of Pontefract Castle), pp. 291-9; Cobbett's State Trials, iv. 1250; William Smith's Old Yorkshire, vol. i.; Clarendon's Rebellion (Macray); Whitelocke's Memorials; Yorkshire Archæolog. and Topograph. Journal. x. 529; Henry Vaughan's Works (Grosart), ii. 365.]
G. G.

MORRIS, JOHN (1810-1886), geologist, was born in 1810 at Homerton, London, and educated at private schools. He was engaged for some years as a pharmaceutical chemist at Kensington, but soon became interested in geology and other branches of science, and ultimately retired from business. His published papers speedily attracted notice, and his 'Catalogue of British Fossils,' published in 1845, a work involving much critical research, added greatly to his reputation. In 1854 he was elected to the professorship of geology at University College, London, an office which he retained till 1877, when he was appointed on retirement emeritus professor in acknowledgment of his services. He died, after an illness of some duration, on 7 Jan. 1886, and was buried at Kensal Green. One daughter survived him.

In addition to his 'Catalogue of British Fossils' (of which a second edition appeared in 1854, and a third was in preparation but was left incomplete at his death) and to a memoir on the 'Great Oolite Mollusca,' written in conjunction with John Lycett, and published by the Palæontographical Society, Morris wrote numerous papers and notes on scientific subjects, mostly geological. He was elected F.G.S. in 1845, and, in addition to other awards, received the Lyell medal in 1876. In 1870 he was presented with a handsome testimonial in appreciation of his services to geology. He was president of the Geologists' Association, held various lectureships and examinerships, and was an honorary member of several scientific societies. In 1878 he was admitted to the freedom of the Turners' Company, and received in 1878 the honorary degree of master of arts from the university of Cambridge.

Morris was a born teacher, for he was not only full of enthusiasm, but also united to a memory of extraordinary retentiveness a remarkable power of lucid exposition; yet he was so singularly modest that it was often difficult to induce him to address an audience other than his class. His knowledge of geology was encyclopædic, his critical acumen great, but he disliked the labour of composition. In imparting knowledge verbally he was the most generous of men.

[Short memoir (with portrait), Geological Magazine [2] v. 481, and further notice *id.* [3] iii. 95. See also obituary notice, Proc. Geol. Soc. 1886, p. 44.] T. G. B.

MORRIS, JOHN (1826-1893), jesuit, son of John Carnac Morris [q. v.], was born at Ootacamund, on the Neilgherry Hills, Southern India, on 4 July 1826. At eight years of age he was sent to a private school at East Sheen, Surrey. Thence, in 1838, he was transferred to Harrow, but he remained there only one year. He then went to India, and lived with his parents for two years on the Neilgherry Hills. Returning to England, he was prepared for Cambridge by Henry Alford [q. v.]; in October term 1845 he was admitted a pensioner of Trinity College. Before the end of his freshman's year he embraced the catholic religion, being received into the Roman communion on 20 May 1846. His secession caused some sensation, and led to the submission next year of F. A. Paley [q. v.], his private tutor (BROWNE, *Annals of the Tractarian Movement*, pp. 130, 131).

After three years' study at the English College in Rome he was ordained priest in September 1849 in the cathedral church of St. John Lateran, and sent back to the English mission. He was stationed first at Northampton, next at Great Marlow, Buckinghamshire, and in 1852 he was appointed a canon of the newly founded diocese of Northampton. From 1852 to 1855 he was vice-rector of the English College at Rome. Having obtained from the pope release from his missionary oath, Morris returned to England with the intention of entering the religious state in the Society of Jesus. On his arrival, however, he was intercepted by Cardinal Wiseman, who was anxious to secure his services for the diocese of Westminster. Soon afterwards he became private secretary to the cardinal, and he continued to hold the office during the first two years of the episcopate of his successor, Cardinal Manning. In 1861 he had been made canon-penitentiary of the metropolitan chapter. At last, in February 1867, he fulfilled his long-cherished design of entering the Society of Jesus. His noviceship was passed partly at Manresa House, Roehampton, partly at Tronchiennes in Belgium, and on 1 March 1869 he took his first vows at Louvain.

Returning to England, he became successively minister at Roehampton, socius to the provincial, Father Whitty, first superior of the Oxford mission, which, in 1871, had again been entrusted to the jesuit order, and professor of ecclesiastical history and canon law in the college of St. Beuno, North Wales. In 1877 he was professed of the four vows, and appointed first rector of St. Ignatius's College, Malta; but, the climate not agreeing with his health, he was recalled to this country, and resumed his professorship at St. Beuno's in 1878. In 1879 he was appointed vice-rector and master of novices at Roehampton, and in 1880 rector—an office which he held till 1886. He was an enthusiastic worker in the cause of the beatification of the English martyrs, and the result of his efforts was the beatification by Leo XIII, on 29 Dec. 1886, of More, Fisher, and other Englishmen. On 10 Jan. 1889 Morris was elected fellow of the Society of Antiquaries. In 1891 he became head, in succession to Father Henry Coleridge, of the staff of jesuit writers at Farm Street, Berkeley Square, to which he had previously been attached.

In 1893 he retired to Wimbledon, and there engaged in writing the biography of Cardinal Wiseman, He had collected the materials, but only a few chapters were actually composed when he died, with startling suddenness, while preaching in the church at Wimbledon on Sunday morning, 22 Oct. 1893.

His most important work was 'The Troubles of our Catholic Forefathers, related by themselves,' 3 vols. London, 1872–7. Other works were: 1. 'The Life and Martyrdom of Saint Thomas Becket, Archbishop of Canterbury,' London, 1859, 8vo; 2nd and enlarged edit. London, 1885, 8vo. 2. 'Formularium Sacerdotale, seu diversarum Benedictiones Religionum; quas in unum collegit Joannes Morris,' London [1859], 8vo. 3. 'The Last Illness of His Eminence Cardinal Wiseman,' 3rd edit. London, 1865, 8vo; translated into German, Münster, 1865, 8vo. 4. 'The English Martyrs: a lecture given at Stonyhurst College, illustrated from contemporary prints,' London, 1887, 8vo. 5. 'The Venerable Sir Adrian Fortescue, Martyr,' London, 1887, 8vo. 6. 'The Relics of St. Thomas of Canterbury,' Canterbury, 1888, 8vo. 7. 'Canterbury: our old Metropolis,' Canterbury, 1889, 8vo. He also edited, with other historical and devotional works, Father Gerard's 'Narrative of the Gunpowder Plot,' with a life and notes under the title 'The Condition of Catholics under James I,' London, 1871, 2nd edit. 1872, 3rd edit. rewritten and enlarged 1881; 'Sir Amias Poulet's Letter-books,' 1874, in which he pointed out many inaccuracies in Mr. Froude's account of Mary Queen of Scots. He was a frequent contributor to the 'Month,' the 'Dublin Review,' and the 'Tablet.'

[Private information; Catholic News, 28 Oct. 1893; Men of the Time, 1884; Speaker, 28 Oct. 1893; Tablet, 28 Oct. 1893, p. 685, and 4 Nov. (funeral sermon by the Rev. Edward Purbrick, S. J.); Times, 23 Oct. 1893, p. 6; Weekly Register, 28 Oct. 1893, pp. 549, 563.] T. C.

MORRIS, JOHN BRANDE (1812–1880), theological writer, born at New Brentford in Middlesex, 4 Sept. 1812, was son of the Rev. John Morris, D.D., who was formerly Michel fellow of Queen's College, Oxford, and afterwards kept a high-class boarding-school. His mother, Anna F. Brande, was sister of the chemist, William Thomas Brande [q. v.]. After being educated at home, Morris matriculated from Balliol College, Oxford, 17 Dec. 1830. He graduated B.A. with a second class in classics 20 Nov. 1834, proceeding M.A. on 8 July 1837. On 30 June of the same year he was elected fellow of Exeter College, where he acted as Hebrew lecturer, and devoted himself to oriental and patristic theology. Eccentric in appearance and manner, he was brimful of genuine and multifarious learning, but so credulous that he seriously believed in the existence of the Phœnix (see *Notes and Queries*, 1888, p. 48). At the time of the Oxford movement he joined the extreme section of the so-called Tractarian party. Though an Anglican priest, he was always fond of ridiculing and finding fault with the English church, so that no surprise was felt when on 16 Jan. 1846 he followed Newman's example and joined the church of Rome. He resigned his fellowship 24 Jan. 1846, and finally left Oxford a few days later (cf. NEWMAN, *Letters*, vol. ii.; T. MOZLEY, *Reminiscences*, chap. lxx.; CHURCH, *Oxford Movement*; MARK PATTISON, *Memoirs*, pp. 184, 222).

Ordained priest at St. Mary's College, Oscott, in 1849, Morris was for a short time one of the professors at Prior Park, near Bath, in 1851, and was nominated canon of Plymouth Cathedral by Bishop Errington on 6 Dec. 1853. He was domestic chaplain to Mr. Bastard of Kitley in Devonshire in 1852; to his former pupil, Sir John Acton, of Aldenham Hall, Shropshire, in 1855; and to Mr. Coventry Patmore, at Heron's Ghyll in Sussex, in 1868. For a time, too, he had charge of a small mission at Shortwood in Somerset. He was latterly chaplain to a convent of nursing-nuns at Hammersmith, where he died on 9 April 1880. He was buried at Mortlake. His health was always weak, and probably accounted for much of the peculiarity of his character.

During his residence at Oxford he published, 1843, an 'Essay towards the Conversion of Learned and Philosophical Hindus,' for which he obtained the prize of 200*l.*, offered through the Bishop of Calcutta. It displays both learning and ability, but was not successful in its object, as it had no circulation in India. For the 'Library of the Fathers' he translated St. Chrysostom's 'Homilies on the Romans,' 1841, and 'Select Homilies of St. Ephrem,' from the Syriac, 1846. He published, 1842, 'Nature a Parable,' a poem in seven books, mystical and obscure, but containing passages of much beauty (cf. MOZLEY, *Reminiscences*, vol. ii.)

He also wrote: 1. 'Jesus the Son of Mary, or the Doctrine of the Catholic Church upon the Incarnation of God the Son: considered in its Bearings upon the Reverence shown by Catholics to His Blessed Mother,' dedicated to Cardinal Wiseman, 2 vols. 1851. 2. 'Taleetha Koomee: or the Gospel Prophecy of our Blessed Lady's Assumption,' a drama in four acts, in verse, London, 1858. 3. 'Eucharist on Calvary: an Essay upon the Relation of our Blessed Lord's First Mass to His adorable Passion,' London, 1878.

[C. W. Boase's Registr. Coll. Exon.; George Oliver's Hist. of Catholic Religion, &c., London, 1857, p. 358; Times, 12 April 1880; Tablet, 17 April 1880; personal knowledge and recollection; information from family. In G. V. Cox's Recollections of Oxford, 2nd edit. p. 328, J. B. Morris is confounded with his younger brother, Thomas E. Morris.] W. A. G.

MORRIS, JOHN CARNAC (1798–1858), Telugu scholar, born 16 Oct. 1798, was second son of John Morris of the Bombay civil service, who was subsequently a director of the East India Company.

The son entered the royal navy as a midshipman, and saw active service during the last two years of the French war. On the conclusion of the war in 1814 his father sent the following laconic note to his captain, George (afterwards Sir George) Sartorius: 'Your trade is up for the next half-century. Send my son John home by the next coach.'

After a brief period of training he went to the East India Company's college at Haileybury, and afterwards entered the Madras civil service, reaching India in 1818. Five of his brothers obtained similar employment under the East India Company. Morris served for a time at Masulipatam (in 1821) and Coimbatore. In 1823 a stroke of paralysis deprived him of the use of his legs; but his energy was not impaired by the misfortune, and his industry in sedentary occupation was exceptional. Most of his time was thenceforth spent at Madras in the secretariat.

Morris was Telugu translator to the government in India from 1832, and finally, in 1839, became civil auditor, a post of responsibility. Among his most successful services at Madras was the establishment in 1834 of the Madras government bank, of which he was the first secretary and treasurer, and in 1835 superintendent. The bank was subsequently transferred by the government to private hands.

Morris devoted his leisure to the study of the Hindustani language, and became very proficient in it; but in Telugu he chiefly interested himself. He was compiler of the well-known text-book 'Telugu Selections, with Translations and Grammatical Analyses: to which is added a Glossary of Revenue Terms used in the Northern Circars,' Madras, 1823, fol. (new and enlarged edition, Madras, 1855); and he was author of an 'English-Telugu Dictionary,' based on Johnson's 'English Dictionary,' and the first undertaking of its kind. It was issued at Madras in two quarto volumes, 1834–5. It is still a standard work. Morris was also for several years from 1834 editor of the Madras 'Journal of Literature and Science.' While on furlough in England between 1829 and 1831 he was elected a fellow of the Royal Society. He was very popular in Madras society, and was an enthusiastic freemason there and in England. On leaving India in July 1846, he received a testimonial from the native population.

Settling in Mansfield Street, Portland

Place, London, in 1848, Morris spent much of his time thenceforth in commercial enterprises. He failed in his persistent efforts to become, as his father had been, a director of the East India Company, but he successfully established a company to run steamers between Milford Haven and Australia by way of Panama, which lasted only a few years; and he promoted and was managing director of the London and Eastern Banking Company. In 1855 he resigned the management of the latter company to become chairman; but his colleagues entered into rash speculations, and in 1858 the bank was wound up. Morris placed all his resources at the disposal of the official liquidator, and retired to Jersey, where he died on 2 Aug. 1858. He was buried at St. Heliers.

He married Rosanna Curtis, second daughter of Peter Cherry of the East India Company's Madras civil service, on 4 Feb. 1823, and was father of John Morris (1826–1893), jesuit [q. v.], and of other sons.

[Private information; C. C. Prinsep's Madras Civil Servants, pp. 101–2; Madras Athenæum, 30 June and 9 July 1846; Madras Spectator, 29 June and 2 July 1846.]

MORRIS, JOHN WEBSTER (1763–1836), baptist minister and author, born in 1763, became a member of the baptist church at Worsted, Norfolk, before 1785. At that date he was resident at Market Dereham, and seems to have followed the trade of a journeyman printer. On 12 June 1785 he accepted the pastorate of the baptist church at Clipstone, Northamptonshire, and filled the post for eighteen years. While at Clipstone he became acquainted with Andrew Fuller [q. v.], Robert Hall (1764–1831) [q. v.], and William Carey, D.D. [q.v.], founder of the baptist missions in India. With Carey, too, Morris was on terms of close intimacy (cf. Dr. George Smith's *Life of Carey*). Morris joined the committee of the Baptist Missionary Society at Leicester on 20 March 1793, and for some years acted as Andrew Fuller's 'amanuensis.' Under Fuller's superintendence he edited and printed the first three volumes of 'The Periodical Accounts' of the society. In March 1803 Morris left Clipstone to become minister of the baptist church at Dunstable, Bedfordshire. There also he continued his business as a printer, setting up in type the works of Sutcliffe, Fuller, Hall, and others. About the same time he was editor and proprietor of the 'Biblical Magazine.' In 1806 he, with a fellow-minister named Blundell, proceeded as a deputation on behalf of the Baptist Missionary Society to Ireland, and before returning presented the lord-lieutenant (John Russell, ninth duke of Bedford) with a copy of the Bengalee New Testament. In 1809 Morris left Dunstable, and devoted the remainder of his life to authorship, editorial work, and occasional preaching.

In 1816 he published his notable 'Memoirs of the Life and Writing of Andrew Fuller.' A second edition appeared in 1826, revised and enlarged. In that year also he issued a companion volume, 'Miscellaneous Pieces on Various Subjects, being the last Remains of the Rev. Andrew Fuller, with occasional notes;' and 'A Brief Descriptive History of Holland, in Letters from a Grandfather to Marianne during an Excursion in the Summer of 1819.' Morris also published a 'Biographical History of the Christian Church from the Apostolic Age to the Times of Wicliffe the Reformer,' in 2 vols. 8vo, in 1827; and he edited an abridgment of Gurnall's 'Spiritual Warfare' and 'The Complete Works of Robert Hall' in 1828. In 1833 he published his 'Biographical Recollections of the Rev. Robert Hall, A.M.,' a second edition of which appeared in 1846. Morris also wrote a 'Sacred Biography, forming a Connected History of the Old and New Testament,' 2 vols. London, n.d. Most of these works, with the exception of the first mentioned, which was printed at High Wycombe, Buckinghamshire, were printed at Bungay, Suffolk, by his son, Joseph M. Morris.

He spent much time before his death in editing a new edition of Joseph Sutcliffe's 'Commentary on the Holy Scriptures,' which was published in 1838–9. He also edited 'The Preacher,' 8 vols. 12mo, n.d., and 'The Domestic Preacher; or Short Discourses from the Original Manuscripts of some eminent Ministers,' 2 vols. 12mo, 1826. Morris died suddenly at Ditchingham, near Bungay, where the last years of his life had been spent, on 19 Jan. 1836.

[Clipstone Baptist Church Book; Periodical Accounts of Baptist Missionary Society, vols. i. ii. iii. 1800–6; Eclectic Review, 1816; Life of Dr. Carey, by Dr. George Smith; Baptist Magazine, 1836; New Baptist Magazine, 1825–6; New Baptist Miscellany, 1827–8; works mentioned.]

W. P–s.

MORRIS or MORYS, LEWIS (1700–1765), Welsh poet, philologist, and antiquary, was the son of Morys ap Richard Morys and Margaret, daughter of Morys Owen of Bodafon y Glyn. In the memoir printed in the 'Cambrian Register' (ii. 232) the date of his birth is given as 1 March 1702; in that prefixed to the second edition of the 'Diddanwch Teuluaidd' it appears as 12 March 1700. Both dates must, however, be wrong, for according to the parish register of Llanfihangel Tre'r Beirdd he was baptised on 2 March 1700. His parents at this time lived at Tyddyn Melus, in the parish of Llanfihangel. Not long afterwards they removed to Pentref Eiriannell, in the parish of Penrhos Llugwy, and it was there Lewis and his brothers were brought up. The family numbered five in all—Lewis, Richard [q. v.], William, John, and Margaret. William, a customs officer at Holyhead, was specially skilful in plant lore, but, like his two elder brothers, took a keen interest in Welsh poetry. His collection of Welsh poems, 'Y Delyn Ledr' (the Leathern harp), transcribed by himself, is now in the British Museum. He died in December 1763. John entered the navy, and was killed in 1741 in the unsuccessful attack upon Carthagena.

Morys ap Richard came of one of the Fifteen (Noble) Tribes of Gwynedd, that of Gweirydd ap Rhys Goch (*Cymmrodorion MSS.* in Brit. Mus. No. 14942), and was connected on his mother's side with William Jones the mathematician [q. v.], father of Sir William Jones [q. v.] But he began life as a cooper, and was afterwards a corn factor. He gave his children only an ordinary village education. 'My education,' says Lewis in the important autobiographical letter to Samuel Pegge of 11 Feb. 1761, 'as to language was not regular, and my masters were chiefly sycamore and ash trees [the kind used by coopers], or at best a kind of wooden masters. . . . The English tongue is as much a foreign language to me as the French is' (*Cambrian Register*, i. 368). But, in spite of these disadvantages, Lewis and his brothers appear to have accumulated much knowledge and to have acquired facility in the use of English at a comparatively early age. Lewis speaks in the letter to Pegge of his youthful interest in natural philosophy and mathematics, and already in 1728 we find him a facile poet, a student of grammar, and a lover of antiquities (cf. *Geninen*, iii. 231–2).

On starting in life Lewis took up the business of land surveying, which brought him into association with the men of property in his district, and gave him excellent opportunities of adding to his botanical and antiquarian knowledge. On 29 March 1729 he married, and within a few years settled at Holyhead, obtaining an appointment as collector of customs and salt tax. In these improved circumstances he was able in 1735 to expend a considerable sum upon a printing press, which he set up at Holyhead for the purpose of printing Welsh books and popularising Welsh literature. It was, as he points out in his 'Anogaeth i Argraphu Llyfrau Cymraeg,' the first press established in North Wales. He appealed with much earnestness for public support, since he had gone to considerable expense for a patriotic purpose, viz. 'to entice the Anglophil Welshmen into reading Welsh.' With this object he began to issue in parts 'Tlysau yr Hen Oesoedd,' but soon had to abandon the project for want of patronage.

In 1737 the admiralty resolved, in consequence of the numerous wrecks and casualties on the Welsh coast, to obtain a new survey of it, and the matter was placed in the hands of Lewis Morris. He commenced his task near Penmaen Mawr, and carried on operations for a year, after which he was brought to a standstill by the want of instruments. In 1742 the work was resumed. He had surveyed the whole of the west coast as far as the entrance to the Bristol Channel, when in 1744 there was a second and final interruption, due to the declaration of war between this country and France. Morris now handed in to the lords of the admiralty his report of the work so far as it had been carried out. This it was decided not to publish until it could be completed, but a number of plans which he had prepared for his own convenience during the progress of the survey were, at the suggestion of the admiralty, published separately, appearing in 1748 under the title 'Plans of Harbours, Bars, Bays, and Roads in St. George's Channel.'

Morris was next appointed superintendent of crown lands in Wales, collector of customs at Aberdovey, and in 1750 superintendent of the king's mines in the Principality. Business and family ties now drew him from Holyhead to Cardiganshire, and Gallt Fadog in that county became for several years his home.

Meanwhile his official duties were heavy, and necessitated frequent journeys to London. He was brought, moreover, as a zealous servant of the crown, into conflict with the Cardiganshire landowners, who involved him in perpetual lawsuits with regard to their mineral rights, and did not scruple to attack his character and credit. An interesting letter to his brother William, dated 'Galltvadog, 24 Dec. 1753,' shows that Lewis was obliged about this time to satisfy the treasury that the aspersions made upon him were groundless by means of sworn testimony from Anglesey (*Adgof uwch Anghof*, Penygroes, 1883, pp. 4–6). Ultimately the protracted struggle with his powerful neighbours proved too much for him, and he retired to a little property called Penbryn, which came to him through his second wife, where, as he says, 'my garden, orchard, and farm, [and] some small mine works take a good part of my time' (11 Feb. 1761).

In spite of the pressing character of his business affairs, he contrived to devote much of his time to his favourite Welsh studies. In his youth, he tells us, music and poetry were his chief amusements. He could, according to the 'Diddanwch Teuluaidd,' both make a harp and play it, and the poems of 'Llywelyn Ddu o Fon' (his bardic title) form a substantial part of that collection of Welsh verse. He wrote with equal ease in the 'strict' and the 'free' metres, though little of his work is remembered save the well-known 'Lay of the Cuckoo to Merioneth.' He was familiar with the classical authors and acquainted with modern languages. His English style is clear and good, while his manuscript books show no small knowledge of mechanics, mining, and metallurgy. As he grew older he turned from poetry to Welsh history and antiquities. It became his great ambition to compile a dictionary of Celtic mythology, history, and geography, such as had been planned by Edward Lhuyd (1660–1709) [q. v.], but never carried out. 'I am now,' he says in a letter of 14 July 1751, 'at my leisure hours collecting the names of these famous men and women, mentioned by our poets, with a short history of them, as we have in our common Latin dictionaries of those of the Romans and Grecians' (*Cambrian Register*, ii. 332). About 1760 this work, an historical, topographical, and etymological dictionary, to which he gave the title 'Celtic Remains,' was completed. It was not, however, printed until 1878, when it was issued as an extra volume in connection with 'Archæologia Cambrensis,' edited by Canon Silvan Evans. Morris himself calls it the labour of forty years, and it certainly shows him to have been a remarkably industrious and intelligent student of Celtic antiquity, and a proficient in the obsolete philology of that day.

Morris corresponded with his friends with zeal and vivacity. The three brothers wrote constantly to each other, not only on family matters, but also on literary and poetical topics. Lewis maintained a long correspondence on historical questions with Ambrose Phillips, Carte, Samuel Pegge of Whittington, Vaughan of Nannau, and other scholars; while Welsh poetry he discussed in letters to William Wynn, Evan Evans (Ieuan Brydydd Hir), Goronwy Owain, and Edward Richard of Ystrad Meurig. He was quick to recognise and encourage poetical talent in others. Goronwy Owain he may almost be said to have discovered, for it was the opening of a correspondence between them about Christmas 1751 that induced the bard to resume poetical composition after a long silence, during which Goronwy had become unknown in Wales. The friendship between the two and Morris's admiration of 'the chief bard of all Wales' lasted until 1756, when the patron lost all patience with the poet's irregular habits. Shortly afterwards Goronwy emigrated to Virginia, yet he retained enough recollection of Morris's kindness to send to this country ten years afterwards a poem in praise of his benefactor, of whose death he had just heard. The death of Morris's mother Goronwy also lamented in touching verses.

Morris's last years were spent in retirement at Penbryn, and were much broken by ill-health. He died on 11 April 1765, and was buried in the chancel of Llanbadarn Fawr, near Aberystwyth, where a tablet has been placed to his memory. The memoir in the 'Cambrian Register' (vol. ii.) is accompanied by a portrait, which is said to be taken 'from a mezzotinto print, of about the same size, after a drawing done by Mr. Morris of himself.' There is a good picture of him at the Welsh school at Ashford, Kent.

By his first wife, Elizabeth Griffiths of Ty Wrydyn, Holyhead, he had three children: Lewis (born 29 Dec. 1729), who died young; Margaret (1731–1761), and Eleanor.

On 20 Oct. 1749 he married his second wife, Ann Lloyd, heiress of Penbryn y Barcut, Cardiganshire. By her he had nine children, Lewis (*d.* 1779), John, Elizabeth, Jane (died young), a second Jane, William, Richard, Mary, and Pryse. William married Mary Anne Reynolds, heiress of a branch of the Williamses (formerly Boleyns) of Breconshire. Their eldest son, Lewis Morris (*d.* 1872), was the first registrar of county courts for Glamorganshire, Breconshire, and Radnorshire, and father of Sir Lewis Morris, of Penbryn, Carmarthenshire (1833–1907), poet and promoter of higher education in Wales.

Morris's works are: 1. 'Tlysau yr Hen Oesoedd,' Holyhead, 1735. 2. 'Anogaeth i Argraphu Llyfrau Cymraeg,' Holyhead, 1735. 3. 'Plans of Harbours, Bars, Bays, and Roads in St. George's Channel,' 1748; 2nd edit., with additional matter, issued by William Morris (Lewis's son), Shrewsbury, 1801. 4. 'A Short History of the Crown Manor of Creuthyn, in the county of Cardigan, South Wales,' 1756. 5. 'Diddanwch Teuluaidd' contains the bulk of Morris's verse, London, 1763; 2nd ed. Carnarvon, 1817. 6. 'Celtic Remains,' Cambrian Archæological Association, 1878. 7. Many manuscript volumes now in the British Museum.

[Life in Cambrian Register, vol. ii.; Diddanwch Teuluaidd, 1817 edit.; Rowlands's Cambrian Bibliography; Correspondence in Cambrian Register, vols. i. and ii.; Life of Goronwy Owain, by the Rev. Robert Jones, 1876; Adgof uwch Anghof, 1883; Geninen, vols. iii. 1885, and iv. 1886; information kindly supplied by Lewis Morris, esq. of Penbryn, Carmarthenshire.] J. E. L.

MORRIS, MORRIS DRAKE (*fl.* 1717), biographer, born in Cambridge, was son of a barrister of Cambridge named Drake, for some years recorder of Cambridge, by Sarah, daughter of Thomas Morris, merchant, of London, and of Mount Morris in Horton, otherwise Monks Horton, Kent. After his father's death his mother married Dr. Conyers Middleton [q. v.] He was for some time fellow-commoner of Trinity College, Cambridge. On the death of his grandfather in 1717 he assumed the additional surname of Morris as the condition of succeeding to Mount Morris (will of Thomas Morris, registered in P. C. C., 141, Whitfield). He died without issue, at Coveney in the Isle of Ely, where he possessed property, and was buried at Horton, his death being accelerated by intemperance. The estate of Mount Morris went by entail to his sister, Elizabeth Drake, wife of Matthew Robinson of West Layton in Yorkshire, and mother of Mrs. Elizabeth Montagu [q. v.]

Morris compiled in 1715 and 1716, from very obvious sources of information, 'Lives of Famous Men educated in the University of Cambridge,' which he entered in two large folio volumes, and illustrated with engraved portraits. He presented them to Lord Oxford, and they are now Harleian MSS. 7176 and 7177. In 1749 Dr. Conyers Middleton, his stepfather, presented William Cole with Morris's rough drafts, which Cole indexed, and included in his manuscripts presented to the British Museum, where they are numbered among the Additional MSS. 5856-8.

[Hasted's Kent, folio edit. iii. 317; Brydges's Restituta, iii. 73; Addit. MS. 5876, f. 215 (Cole's Athenæ Cantabrigienses); Cat. of Harleian MSS. in Brit. Mus.] G. G.

MORRIS or MORYS, RICHARD (*d.* 1779), Welsh scholar, was a brother of Lewis Morris [q. v.], and, like him, combined a love of Welsh poetry and history with much business capacity. While still young he left Anglesey for London, and there obtained a position in the navy office, where he ultimately became chief clerk of foreign accounts. After a long term of service he was superannuated, and died in the Tower in 1779. The chief service he rendered to Wales was his careful supervision of the editions of the Welsh Bible printed in 1746 and 1752. These were issued by the Society for Promoting Christian Knowledge, in answer to the appeal of Griffith Jones of Llanddowror, Carmarthenshire, for a supply of bibles for his travelling free schools. 'Rhisiart Morys' not only supervised the orthography, but added tables of Jewish weights and measures. He also issued an illustrated translation into Welsh of the Book of Common Prayer. He was a leading figure among London Welshmen, and on the establishment of the original Cymmrodorion Society in September 1751 became its president. Among other Welshmen of talent whom his position enabled him to befriend, Goronwy Owain [q. v.] received much assistance from him, being employed to translate the rules of the society into Welsh.

[Diddanwch Teuluaidd, edit. 1817; Rowlands's Cambrian Bibliography; Life of Goronwy Owain, by Rev. Robert Jones, 1876.] J. E. L.

MORRIS, ROBERT (*fl.* 1754), architect, is described as 'of Twickenham' on the title-page of his 'Essay in Defence of Ancient Architecture,' published in 1728. He received his instruction in architecture in the service of his 'kinsman,' Roger Morris, 'Carpenter and principal engineer to the Board of Ordnance,' who died on 31 Jan. 1749 (*London Magazine*, 1749, p. 96).

The earliest executed work ascribed to Morris is Inverary Castle (Gothic), begun in 1745, and after considerable delay completed in 1761. It seems probable that Roger Morris was concerned in the design, and that the building was erected after his death under the supervision of his pupil Robert. The central tower was destroyed by fire on 12 Oct. 1877, and restored in 1880. With S. Wright, Morris erected for George II the central portion of the lodge in Richmond Park, the design of which is sometimes attributed to Thomas Herbert, tenth earl of Pembroke [q. v.] The wings were added in later years. About 1750 he repaired and modernised for G. Bubb Dodington (afterwards Lord Melcombe) [q. v.] the house at Hammersmith afterwards known as Brandenburgh House. It was pulled down in 1822, and a house of the same name was afterwards built in the grounds, but not on the same site. Morris also erected Coomb Bank, Kent, and Wimbledon House, Surrey. In the design of the latter he was probably associated with the Earl of Burlington. The house was destroyed by fire in 1785; the offices were subsequently used as a residence until 1801, when the new house designed by Henry Holland (1746?-1806) [q. v.] was completed. With the Earl of Burlington

Morris designed, about 1750, Kirby Hall, Yorkshire, in the interior of which John Carr of York [q. v.] was employed. The plans are said to have been suggested by the owner, S. Thompson. In 1736 he erected a bridge (after a design of Palladio) in the grounds of Wilton in Wiltshire.

He published: 1. 'An Essay in Defence of Ancient Architecture,' London, 1728. 2. 'Lectures on Architecture,' London, 1734; 2nd pt. 1736; 2nd edit. of pt. i. 1759. The lectures were delivered between 22 Oct. 1730 and 13 Jan. 1734-5 before a 'Society for the Improvement of Knowledge in Arts and Sciences,' established by Morris himself. Part ii. is dedicated to Roger Morris, to whom he acknowledges obligations. 3. 'Rural Architecture,' London, 1750 (at which time Morris was residing in Hyde Park Street). 4. 'The Architectural Remembrancer,' London, 1751. 5. 'Architecture Improved,' London, 1755. 6. 'Select Architecture,' London, 1755, 1759. Morris was also part author of 'The Modern Builder's Assistant,' with T. Lightoler and John and William Halfpenny [q. v.], London, 1742, 1757. 'An Essay on Harmony,' London, 1739, ascribed (with a query) to Morris by Halkett and Laing (*Dict. Anon. and Pseudon. Lit.*), was more probably by John Gwynn [q. v.] It is included in a list of Gwynn's works in an advertisement at the end of his 'Qualifications and Duty of a Surveyor.' Morris drew the plates for several of his own works.

[Dict. of Architecture; Builder, 1875, pp. 881-2; Morris's Works (in Brit. Museum and Soane Museum); Thorne's Environs of London, p. 276; Bartlett's Wimbledon, p. 69. For plans, elevations, and views of executed works, see Adams's Vitruvius Scoticus, plates 71-4, and Neale's Seats, 1st ser. vol. vi. 1823, for Inverary Castle; Campbell's Vitruvius Britannicus (edit. Woolfe and Gandon), vol. iv. plates 1-3, for Lodge in Richmond Park; ib. vol. iv. plates 26-7, and Lysons's Environs, ii. p. 402, for Brandenburgh House; Campbell, vol. iv. plates 75-7, engravings by Woollett and W. Angus, 1787, for Coomb Bank; ib. vol. v. plates 20-2, for Wimbledon House; ib. vol. v. plates 70-1, and engraving by Basire for Kirby Hall; Campbell, ib. vol. v. plates 88-9, engraving by Fourdrinier (drawn by Morris), by R. White (drawn by J. Rocque), another by Rocque in 1754, Watts's Seats, lxxxii. (from a picture by R. Wilson), for bridge at Wilton.] B. P.

MORRIS, ROGER (1727-1794), lieutenant-colonel, American loyalist, born in England on 28 Jan. 1727, was third son of Roger Morris of Netherby, in the North Riding of Yorkshire, by his first wife, the fourth daughter of Sir Peter Jackson, kt. He was appointed captain in Francis Ligonier's regiment (48th foot), of which Henry Seymour Conway [q. v.] was lieutenant-colonel, 13 Sept. 1745. The regiment served at Falkirk and Culloden and in Flanders. Morris went with it to America in 1755, and was aide-de-camp to Major-general Edward Braddock [q. v.] in the unfortunate expedition against Fort Duquesne, where he was wounded. Had the enterprise proved successful, Braddock proposed to bring a provincial regiment, serving with the expedition, into the line, and make Morris lieutenant-colonel of it (Winthrop Sargent, in *Trans. Hist. Soc. Pennsylvania*). Morris served at the siege of Louisburg, and was employed against the Indians on the frontier of Novia Scotia. On 16 Feb. 1758 he was promoted to a majority in the 35th foot, and in the same year he married. He was with Wolfe at Quebec, where he was wounded; with James Murray (1729-1794) [q. v.] at Sillery; and commanded one of the columns of Murray's force in the advance on Montreal. On 19 May 1760 he was made lieutenant-colonel 147th foot. He served as aide-de-camp to Generals Thomas Gage [q. v.] and Jeffrey Amherst, lord Amherst [q. v.], at various times. He sold out of the army in 1764, and settled at New York city, where he was made a member of the executive council in December of the same year. He built a mansion on the Hudson, where he lived with his wife until their property was confiscated in 1776. The house was Washington's headquarters at one time. Morris's plate and furniture were sold by auction some weeks later. Morris returned to England, and died at York 13 Sept. 1794.

Morris married Mary Philipse, who was born in 1730 at the Manor House, Hudson's River, the daughter of Frederick Philipse, the second lord of the manor. She was a handsome, rather imperious brunette, whom Fenimore Cooper drew as his heroine in 'The Spy.' In 1756, when on a visit to her brother-in-law, Beverley Robinson, at New York, she captivated George Washington, who was a guest in the house. She is said to have rejected his suit. Any way, she married Morris in 1758. American writers have speculated what might have been the consequence to American independence had Washington become united to so uncompromising a loyalist. Mrs. Morris inherited a large estate, part of which was in Putnam county, New York, including Lake Mahopac. This she used to visit half-yearly, to instruct her tenants in household and religious duties, until 1776, when it was confiscated. She, her sister Mrs. Beverley Robinson, and Mrs. Charles Inglis are said to have been the only three women attainted by the American government. She returned to England with her husband, and died at York in 1825 at the age of ninety-five. A monument to her and her husband is in St. Saviour's Gate Church, York. There were two sons and two daughters by the marriage. The eldest son, Amherst Morris, entered the royal navy, and was first lieutenant of the Nymphe frigate, Captain Sir Edward Pellew, afterwards Viscount Exmouth [q. v.], in her famous action with the French frigate La Cléopâtre. He died in 1802. The other son, Henry Gage Morris, also saw much service in the navy (see O'BYRNE, *Nav. Biog.*), and rose to the rank of rear-admiral. He afterwards resided at York and at Beverley. He died at Beverley on 24 Nov. 1851, and was buried in the churchyard of Beverley Minster. He was father of Francis Orpen Morris [q. v.]

The English attorney-general having given his opinion that property inherited by children at the demise of their parents was not included in the aforesaid attainder, in law or equity, the surviving children of Roger and Mary Morris in 1809 sold their reversionary interests to John Jacob Astor of New York for a sum of 20,000*l.*, to which the British government added 17,000*l.*, in compensation for their parents' losses.

Roger Morris the loyalist is sometimes confused with his kinsman and namesake, Lieutenant-colonel Roger Morris, who entered the Coldstream guards in 1782, and was killed when serving with that regiment under the Duke of York in Holland, 19 Sept. 1799.

[Burke's Landed Gentry, ed. 1886, vol. ii., under 'Morris of Netherby;' Appleton's Enc. Amer. Biography; Winthrop Sargent in Trans. Hist. Soc. Pennsylvania, vol. v.; Parkman's Montcalm and Wolfe, London, 1884; Sabine's American Worthies.] H. M. C.

MORRIS, THOMAS (1660–1748), nonjuror, born in 1660, may possibly be the Thomas Morris who graduated from King's College, Cambridge, B.A. in 1683, M.A. in 1688; in the latter year he was minor canon of Worcester and vicar of Claines, Worcestershire. Refusing to take the oath of supremacy in 1689, he was deprived of his ecclesiastical preferments, and reduced to live on the generosity of affluent Jacobites; he is nevertheless described as 'very charitable to the poor, and much esteem'd.' He died on 15 June 1748, aged 88, and was buried at the west end of the north aisle of the cloisters of Worcester Cathedral under a flat gravestone, on which was inscribed, at his request, the word, 'Miserimus,' without name, date, or comment. This inscription was nearly obliterated in 1829, but was soon after renewed with the more correct spelling, 'Miserrimus.'

In 1828 Wordsworth wrote in the 'Keepsake' a sonnet on 'Miserrimus,' apparently without any knowledge of Morris's history. It begins '"Miserrimus!" and neither name nor date.' Another sonnet, with the same title, by Edwin Lees, was published in 1828, and a third, by Henry Martin, was included in his 'Sonnets and Miscellaneous Poems,' Birmingham, 1830, 8vo. In 1832 Frederic Mansell Reynolds [q. v.] published a novel, 'Miserrimus,' which reached a second edition in the next year, and was dedicated to William Godwin. In the advertisement to the second edition Reynolds says he 'would never have adopted this epitaph as the groundwork for a fiction had he been aware that the name and career of the individual who selected it were known.' The 'Gentleman's Magazine' (1833, i. 245) calls it 'a posthumous libel on an innocent and helpless person whose story is widely different from that here inflicted on his memory.'

[Gent. Mag. 1748, p. 428, s.v. 'Maurice;' The Worcestershire Miscellany, p. 140, Suppl. pp. 37–40; Bowles's Life of Ken, ii. 181; Green's Hist. and Antiquities of Worcester, App. p. xxvii; Mackenzie Walcott's Memorials, p. 28; Britton's Hist. and Antiquities of Worcester Cathedral, pp. 23–4; Chambers's Biog. Illustr. of Worcestershire, pp. 310–11; Rep. of Brit. Archæol. Assoc. at Worcester, August 1848, p. 130; Notes and Queries, 1st ser. v. 354, 5th ser. xi. 348, 392–3 (by Cuthbert Bede), 432; Brit. Mus. Cat.] A. F. P.

MORRIS, CAPTAIN THOMAS (*fl.* 1806), song writer. [See under MORRIS, CHARLES.]

MORRIS, THOMAS (*fl.* 1780–1800), engraver, born about 1750, was a pupil of Woollett. He worked in the line manner, and confined himself to landscape, the figures in his plates being frequently put in by others. Morris was employed by Boydell, and, in conjunction with Gilpin and Garrard, produced some good sporting prints. His most important plates are: A landscape after G. Smith of Chichester, 1774; 'Hawking,' after Gilpin, 1780; 'Fox Hunting,' after Gilpin and Barret (the figures by Bartolozzi), 1783; view of Skiddaw, after Loutherbourg, 1787; 'Horse, Mare, and Foals,' after Gilpin; 'Mare and Foals,' after Garrard, 1793; views of the ranger's house in Greenwich Park and Sir Gregory Turner's mansion on Blackheath, a pair, after Robertson; and views of Ludgate Street and Fish Street Hill, a pair, after Marlow, 1795. A series of Indian views, from drawings by Hodges and others, was engraved by Morris for the 'European Magazine.' He also executed a few original etchings, including two views on the Avon at

Bristol, 1802. This is the latest date to be found on his work.

[Redgrave's Dict. of Artists; Huber and Martini's Manuel des Curieux, &c., 1808; Dodd's manuscript Hist. of English Engravers in British Museum Add. MS. 33403.] F. M. O'D.

MORRIS, Sir WILLIAM (1602–1676), secretary of state. [See Morice.]

MORRISON, CHARLES (*fl.* 1753), first projector of the electric telegraph, was a surgeon of Greenock. He is said to have subsequently engaged in the Glasgow tobacco trade, and to have emigrated to Virginia, where he died.

Morrison was identified by Brewster and others with the writer of a letter in the 'Scots Magazine' for 1753 (xv. 73), dated 'Renfrew, Feb. 1. 1753,' and signed with the initials 'C. M.' This letter contains a suggestion for conveying messages by means of electricity. The author proposes to set up a number of wires corresponding to the letters of the alphabet, extending from one station to the other. 'Let a ball be suspended from every wire,' says the writer, 'and about a sixth or an eighth of an inch below the balls place the letters of the alphabet, marked on bits of paper, or any other substance that may be light enough to rise to the electrified ball, and at the same time let it be so contrived that each of them may reassume its proper place when dropt.' Signals were to be conveyed by bringing the wire belonging to each letter successively into connection with the prime conductor of an electrical machine, when a current passes and electrifies the ball at the receiving end. The project was alluded to by Sir David Brewster in 1855 in the course of an article on the electric telegraph in the 'North British Review,' xxii. 545. In 1859 Brewster was informed by a Mr. Forman of Port Glasgow that, according to a letter (not now known to exist) dated 1750 addressed by Forman's grandfather to a Miss Margaret Wingate, residing at Craigengelt, near Denny, Charles Morrison had actually transmitted messages along wires by means of electricity, and he is stated to have communicated the results of his experiments to Sir Hans Sloane.

[Home Life of Sir David Brewster, 1869, p. 206; Brewster's correspondence on the subject is preserved at the Watt Monument, Greenock. Morrison's alleged letter to Sir Hans Sloane is not included in the Sloane MSS. at the British Museum, nor does Morrison's name occur in the various publications of the Historical Society of Virginia.] R. B. P.

MORRISON, GEORGE (1704?–1799), general, military engineer and quartermaster-general to the forces, entered the train of artillery as a gunner on 1 Oct. 1722, and was quartered at Edinburgh Castle until 1729. He distinguished himself in suppressing the Jacobite rebellion of 1745, and was sent to the Royal Military Academy at Woolwich as a cadet gunner. After he had been instructed in the theory of a profession of which he had already learned the practice, he was sent to Flanders with the temporary rank of engineer extraordinary from 3 Feb. 1747, and served under Captain Heath, chief engineer of the Duke of Cumberland's army. He was present at the battles of Roucoux and Val (July) and at the siege of Bergen-op-Zoom (12 July–16 Sept.) With the assistance of Engineer Hall he made a survey of the river Merk and of the adjoining country from Breda to Stoutersgut. The drawing of this survey is in the British Museum.

On 2 April 1748 Morrison was appointed to the permanent list as practitioner engineer, and on his return home, on the conclusion of peace, he was sent to Scotland and employed in surveying the highlands and constructing roads on a plan laid down by Marshal Wade. Under Morrison's superintendence part of the trunk road from Stirling to Fort William was made, and also the road through the wilds of Glenbeg and Glenshee to Dalbriggan. His surveys of the former, dated 9 Jan. 1749, and of the latter, dated 22 Feb. 1750, are in the war office. Part of the road between Blairgowrie and Braemar was made by a detachment of Lord Bury's regiment under Morrison's orders. His drawing of this road is in the British Museum.

On 18 April 1750 he was promoted to be sub-engineer, and sent to Northallerton in Yorkshire for duty. Possessed of personal attractions and accomplishments, and having earned the good opinion of the Duke of Cumberland, he was about this time brought to the notice of the king, and in 1751 he was attached to the person of the Prince of Wales. He was promoted engineer extraordinary on 1 Jan. 1753, captain lieutenant on 14 May 1757, and captain and engineer in ordinary on 4 Jan. 1758. On 25 April 1758 he was appointed to the expedition assembled in the Isle of Wight for a descent on the French coast. He took part under the Duke of Marlborough in the landing in June in Cancale Bay, near St. Malo, and the destruction of St. Servan and Solidore. The troops were thence conveyed to Havre and to Cherbourg, and returned home again. On 23 July Morrison embarked under General Bligh at Portsmouth, and sailed on 1 Aug. for Cherbourg. Forts Tourlaville, Galet, Hommet, Esqueurdreville, St. Anines, and

Querqueville, with the basin, built at considerable expense, were all destroyed. Bligh sailed for England on 15 Aug. On 31 Aug. Morrison again sailed with General Bligh with troops for St. Malo, and took part in the action of 9 Sept., and in the battle of St. Cas on 11 Sept. At the termination of these expeditions Morrison returned to court.

On 22 Feb. 1761 he was promoted lieutenant-colonel in the army and appointed deputy quartermaster-general on the headquarters staff. On the death of General Bland in June 1763 he was appointed quartermaster-general to the forces, and was in frequent attendance on the king. He was appointed equerry to the Duke of York, and travelled with him in 1764. He accompanied the duke when he left England on 7 July 1767, and attended him assiduously during his illness at Monaco, and was present at his death in September of that year. Morrison was ill himself, and it was with much difficulty that the dying prince could be prevailed on to accept his services. 'Your life, Morrison,' he said, 'is of more importance than mine. You have a family. Be careful of your health for their sake, and shun this chamber.' Morrison was much attached to the prince. He accompanied his remains to England, and attended their interment on the night of 3 Nov. in Westminster Abbey.

In 1769 he was a member of a committee appointed to consider the defences of Gibraltar. On 22 Dec. 1772 Morrison was promoted colonel in the army, and on 2 Feb. 1775 he was promoted to be sub-director and major in the corps of royal engineers. He was made a major-general on 29 Aug. 1777. In 1779 he was appointed colonel of the 75th regiment. In 1781 he attended Lord Amherst, the commander-in-chief, on an inspection of the east coast defences on the outbreak of the war with Holland. On 29 May 1782 he was transferred from the colonelcy of the 75th foot to that of the 17th regiment, and on 20 Nov. was promoted to be lieutenant-general. On 8 Aug. 1792 he was transferred from the colonelcy of the 17th foot to that of the 4th king's own regiment of foot. But little more is recorded of the ancient quartermaster-general except the changes of his residence. In 1792 he resided at Sion Hill near Barnet. On 3 May 1796, when he was promoted general, he was living at Fairy Hall near Eltham. He died at his house in Seymour Street, London, on 26 Nov. 1799, at about the age of ninety-five. He was married and had six children.

[Cannon's Historical Records of the 17th Regiment of Foot, 8vo, 1848; Ann. Reg. 1767, vol. x.; Journal of the Campaign on the Coast of France, 1758; Gent. Mag. 1763, 1792, 1799, passim; Correspondence of Earl of Chatham, 1840, vol. iv.; European Mag. 1799, vol. xxxvi.; Hasted's History of Kent; Ordnance Muster Rolls (Add. MSS. Brit. Mus.); War Office and Board of Ordnance Records; Royal Engineers' Records; Connolly Papers, manuscript; Jesse's Memoirs of the Life and Reign of George III, vol. i.] R. H. V.

MORRISON, JAMES (1790–1857), merchant and politician, born of yeoman parentage in Hampshire in 1790, began his career in a very humble capacity in a London warehouse. His industry, sagacity, and integrity eventually secured him a partnership in the general drapery business in Fore Street of Joseph Todd, whose daughter he married. The firm latterly became known as Morrison, Dillon & Co. and was afterwards converted into the Fore Street Limited Liability Company. Morrison was one of the first English traders to depend for his success on the lowest remunerative scale of profit. He thus endeavoured to secure a very rapid circulation of capital, his motto being 'small profits and quick returns.' He made an immense fortune, a great part of which he expended in buying land in Berkshire, Buckinghamshire, Kent, Wiltshire, Yorkshire, and Islay, Argyllshire. Southey saw him at Keswick in September 1823. He was then worth some 150,000*l*., and was on his way to New Lanark on the Clyde with the intention of investing 5,000*l*. in Robert Owen's experiment, 'if he should find his expectations confirmed by what he sees there' (Southey, *Life and Correspondence*, v. 144–5).

From his earliest settlement in London Morrison was associated with the liberal party in the city. In 1830 he entered parliament as member for St. Ives, Cornwall, which he helped to partially disfranchise by voting for the Reform Bill. He did not return to his offended constituents, but in 1831 he secured a seat at Ipswich for which he was again elected in December 1832. He was, however, defeated there on the 'Peel Dissolution' in January 1835. On an election petition, Fitzroy Kelly and Robert Adam Dundas, the members, were unseated, and Morrison with Rigby Wason headed the poll in June 1835. At the succeeding dissolution, in July 1837, Morrison remained out of parliament, and in the following December on the occasion of a by-election for a vacancy at Ipswich, he was defeated in a contest with Joseph Bailey. In March 1840 he re-entered the House of Commons as member for the Inverness Burghs, and was again returned unopposed in the general election of 1841, but on the dissolution of 1847, his health being much impaired, he finally retired.

On 17 May 1836 Morrison made an able speech on moving a resolution urging the periodical revision of tolls and charges levied on railroads and other public works. In 1845 he moved similar resolutions, and again in March 1846, when he finally succeeded in obtaining a select committee for the better promoting and securing of the interests of the public in railway acts. His draft report, not altogether adopted, was drawn with great skill, and many of its principles have been adopted in subsequent legislation.

Though an entirely self-educated man, Morrison possessed considerable literary tastes, which were exercised in the formation of a large library. He was likewise a lover of art and made a large collection of pictures of the old masters, Italian and Dutch, together with many fine examples of the English school. Dr. Waagen, in his 'Treasures of Art in Great Britain' (supplement, pp. 105–113, 300–12), enumerates thirty pictures of Morrison in his house in Harley Street as of the highest value. The pictures at Morrison's seat at Basildon Park, Berkshire, Waagen also describes as a 'collection of a very high class.'

Morrison died at Basildon Park on 30 Oct. 1857, possessed of property in England valued at between three and four millions, besides large investments in the United States. By his marriage to Mary Anne, daughter of Joseph Todd, he had, with other issue, four sons, Charles (*b.* 1817), of Basildon Park and Islay; Alfred (1821-1897), of Fonthill, Hindon, Wiltshire; Frank (1823-1904), of Hole Park, Rolvenden, Kent, and Strathraich, Garve, Ross-shire; and Walter (*b.* 1836), formerly M.P., of Malham Tarn, Settle, Yorkshire (Walford, *County Fam.* 1909, p. 789). The second son, Alfred, was known as an enthusiastic collector of autograph letters and engraved portraits.

Morrison published: 1. 'Rail Roads. Speech in the House of Commons,' &c., 8vo, London, 1836. 2. 'Observations illustrative of the defects of the English System of Railway Legislation,' &c., 8vo, London, 1846. 3. 'The Influence of English Railway Legislation on Trade and Industry,' &c., 8vo, London, 1848.

[Times cited in Gent. Mag. 1857, pt. ii. pp. 681–3; Ward's Men of the Reign, p. 645; Names of Members of Parliament, Official Return, pt. ii.; MacCulloch's Lit. Pol. Econ. p. 205.] G. G.

MORRISON, Sir RICHARD (1767–1849), architect, born in 1767, was son of John Morrison of Middleton, co. Cork, an architect of scientific attainments. Originally intended for the church, he was eventually placed as pupil with James Gandon [q. v.] the architect, in Dublin. He obtained through his godfather, the Earl of Shannon, a post in the ordnance department at Dublin; but this he abandoned, when he entered into full practice as an architect. Having resided for some time at Clonmel, he removed about 1800 to Dublin and settled at Bray. Morrison had very extensive public and private practice in Ireland. Among his public works were alterations to the cathedral at Cashel, the court-house and gaol at Galway, court-houses at Carlow, Clonmel, Roscommon, Wexford, and elsewhere, and the Roman catholic cathedral at Dublin. He built or altered very many mansions of the nobility and gentry in Ireland, and was knighted by the lord-lieutenant, Earl de Grey, in 1841. He died at Bray on 31 Oct. 1849, and was buried in the Mount Jerome cemetery, Dublin. He was president of the Institute of Architects of Ireland. In 1793 he published a volume of 'Designs.'

Morrison, William Vitruvius (1794–1838), architect, son of the above, was born at Clonmel on 22 April 1794. In 1821 he made an extensive tour on the continent, and on his return assisted his father in many of his works. He also had a large public and private practice in Ireland. His health, however, broke down, and after a second visit to the continent he died in his father's house at Bray on 16 Oct. 1838, and was buried in the Mount Jerome cemetery. He was a member of the Royal Irish Academy.

[Papworth's Dict. of Architecture; Redgrave's Dict. of Artists; Annual Register, 1849; English Cyclopædia; Webb's Compendium of Irish Biog. p. 352.] L. C.

MORRISON, RICHARD JAMES (1795–1874), inventor and astrologer, known chiefly by his pseudonym of 'Zadkiel,' was born 15 June 1795, being son of Richard Caleb Morrison, who for twenty-seven years was a gentleman pensioner under George III. His grandfather, Richard Morrison, was a captain in the service of the East India Company. Richard James entered the royal navy in 1806 as a first-class volunteer on board the Spartan, and saw much boat service in the Adriatic. He also, on 3 May 1810, shared in a brilliant and single-handed victory, gained by the Spartan in the Bay of Naples over a Franco-Neapolitan squadron. He continued in the same ship till December 1810, and was subsequently, between August 1811 and July 1815, employed as master's mate in the Elizabeth and the Myrtle, on the North Sea,

Baltic, and Cork stations. In the Myrtle he appears to have likewise performed the duties of lieutenant and master, and he took up, on leaving her, a lieutenant's commission, dated 3 March 1815. His last appointment was to the coastguard, in which he served from April 1827 until October 1829, when he resigned, owing to ill-health, induced by the exposure he had suffered in rescuing four men and a boy from a wreck in February 1828. His exertions on the occasion were acknowledged by a medal from the Society for the Preservation of Life from Shipwreck.

In 1824 he presented to the admiralty a plan, subsequently adopted in principle, 'for registering merchant seamen.' In 1827 he proposed another plan, 'for propelling ships of war in a calm,' and on 6 March 1835 he further suggested to the board 'a plan for providing an ample supply of seamen for the fleet without impressment.' For this scheme he received the thanks of their lordships. His arguments were immediately employed in the House of Commons by Sir James Graham, first lord of the admiralty, and they were partially enforced by the addition of a thousand boys to the naval force of the country.

He was chiefly remarkable, however, for his devotion, during nearly half a century, to the pseudo science of astrology. In 1831 he brought out 'The Herald of Astrology,' which was continued as 'The Astrological Almanac' and 'Zadkiel's Almanac.' This sixpenny pamphlet, in which he published his predictions, under the signature of 'Zadkiel Tao-Sze,' became known far and wide among the credulous. It sold annually by tens of thousands, running up sometimes to an edition of two hundred thousand copies, and it secured him a moderate competence. Among other periodicals of a similar character edited by him were 'The Horoscope' and 'The Voice of the Stars.'

Morrison, who was considered by some to be a charlatan and by others a victim of a distinct hallucination, brought in 1863 an action for libel in the court of queen's bench against Admiral Sir Edward Belcher, who in a letter to the 'Daily Telegraph' had stated that 'the author of "Zadkiel" is the crystal globe seer who gulled many of our nobility about the year 1852.' At the trial, on 29 June 1863, it appeared that Morrison had pretended that through the medium of the crystal globe various persons saw visions, and held converse with spirits. Some persons of rank, however, who had been present at the séances, were called on behalf of the plaintiff, and testified that the crystal globe had been shown to them without money payment. The jury returned a verdict for the plaintiff, with 20*s.* damages, and the lord chief justice (Sir Alexander Cockburn) refused a certificate for costs (*Times*, 30 June 1863, p. 13, col. 1, and 1 July, p. 11, col. 4; IRVING, *Annals of our Times*, p. 653). It was said that the crystal globe was that formerly possessed by Dr. Dee (see DEE, JOHN, and KELLEY, EDWARD; *Notes and Queries*, 3rd ser. iv. 109, 155, 288). Morrison died on 5 April 1874. He married, on 23 Aug. 1827, Miss Sarah Mary Paul of Waterford, and had issue nine children.

His works are: 1. 'Narrative of the Loss of the Rothsay Castle Steam Packet in Beaumaris Bay,' 4th edit. with additions, London, 1831, 12mo. 2. 'Observations on Dr. Halley's great Comet, which will appear in 1835; with a History of the Phenomena attending its Return for six hundred years past,' 2nd edit. London, 1835, 12mo. 3. William Lilly's 'Introduction to Astrology,' with emendations, London, 1835 and 1852, 8vo, afterwards reprinted as 'The Grammar of Astrology.' T. H. Moody published 'A Complete Refutation of Astrology, consisting principally of a Series of Letters . . . in reply to the Arguments of . . . Morrison,' 1838, 8vo. 4. 'Zadkiel's Legacy, containing a Judgment of the great Conjunction of Saturn and Jupiter, on the 26th of January, 1842 . . . also Essays on Hindu Astrology and the Nativity of Albert Edward, Prince of Wales,' London, 1842, 12mo. 5. 'Zadkiel's Magazine,' London, 1849, 8vo. 6. 'An Essay on Love and Matrimony,' London, 1851, 24mo. 7. 'The Solar System as it is, and not as it is represented,' London, 1857, 8vo, where the whole Newtonian scheme of the heavens is openly defied. 8. 'Explanation of the Bell Buoy invented by Lieut. Morrison,' London [1858], 8vo. 9. 'Astronomy in a Nutshell, or the leading Problems of the Solar System solved by Simple Proportion only, on the Theory of Magnetic Attraction,' London [1860], 8vo. 10. 'The Comet, a large lithographic Map on the true Course of Encke's Comet, with a letter to the Members of the Royal Astronomical Society,' London [1860], 8vo. 11. 'The Hand-Book of Astrology,' 2 vols. London, 1861–2, 12mo. 12. 'On the Great First Cause, his Existence and Attributes,' London, 1867, 12mo. 13. 'The New Principia, or true system of Astronomy. In which the Earth is proved to be the stationary Centre of the Solar System,' London [1868], 8vo; 2nd edit. 1872. 14. 'King David Triumphant! A Letter to the Astronomers of Benares,' London, 1871, 8vo.

[Athenæum, 1874, i. 630, 666, 701; Cooke's Curiosities of Occult Literature; De Morgan's Budget of Paradoxes, pp. 195, 277, 472; O'Byrne's Naval Biog. 1849, p. 790; Times, 11 May 1874, p. 8, col. 5.] T. C.

MORRISON, ROBERT (1782–1834), missionary in China, son of James Morrison, was born 5 Jan. 1782 at Buller's Green, Morpeth, in Northumberland. When he was three years old his parents removed to Newcastle. There he was taught reading and writing by his maternal uncle, who was a schoolmaster, and at the proper age he was apprenticed to his father as a last and boot-tree maker. In 1798 he joined the presbyterian church, and three years later entered on a course of study of Latin, Greek, and Hebrew under the instruction of the Rev. W. Laidler. In 1802 his mother died, and his inclinations, which had for some time tended towards missionary work, now determined him to enter that field. He obtained admission to the Hoxton Academy (now Highbury College), and stayed there for a year from 7 Jan. 1803. He was then sent to the Missionary Academy at Gosport, which was under the superintendence of Dr. David Bogue [q. v.] In 1805 he was transferred to London to study medicine and astronomy, and to pick up any knowledge of the Chinese language which he could gain, it having been determined by the London Missionary Society to send him to China. By good fortune he met a Chinaman named Yong Samtak, who agreed to give him lessons in the language. Having made some acquaintance with the Chinese written character, he made a transcript of a Chinese manuscript at the British Museum, containing a harmony of the Gospels, the Acts, and most of the Pauline epistles; and copied a manuscript Latin and Chinese dictionary which was lent to him by the Royal Society. On 8 Jan. 1807 he was ordained at the Scots Church, Swallow Street, and at the end of the same month he embarked at Gravesend for Canton *via* America. After two years' labour in China, on 20 Feb. 1809 he married Miss Morton, at Macao, and on the same day was appointed translator to the East India Company. The fact that he had printed and published the New Testament and several religious tracts in Chinese came in 1815 to the knowledge of the East India Company's directors, who, fearing that it might influence the Chinese against the company, proposed to sever their connection with him. But their agents in China successfully urged them to retain his services. In 1817 he accompanied Lord Amherst as interpreter on his abortive mission to Peking, and in the same year he was made D.D. by the university of Glasgow. In 1818 he succeeded in establishing the Anglo-Chinese College at Malacca for the training of missionaries for the far East. Three years later his wife died, and in 1824 he returned to England, bringing with him a large Chinese library, which he ultimately bequeathed to University College. In November 1824 he married, secondly, a Miss Armstrong. About this time he interested himself in the establishment of the Language Institution in Bartlett's Buildings, London, and in 1826 he returned to Canton, where he resided until his death on 1 Aug. 1834. On 5 Aug. he was buried at Macao. He left seven children, two by his first wife and five by his second.

Morrison was a voluminous writer both in English and Chinese. His *magnum opus* was his 'Dictionary of the Chinese Language,' which appeared in three parts, between 1815 and 1823. At the time, and for many years afterwards, this work was, as Professor Julien said, 'without dispute the best Chinese dictionary composed in a European language.' After the conclusion of the work, in 1824, Morrison was elected F.R.S. He published also a Chinese grammar and several treatises on the language. His most important work in Chinese was a translation of the Bible, which, with the help of Dr. William Milne [q. v.], he published at Malacca in 21 vols. in 1823. He was the author also of translations of hymns and of the prayer-book, as well as of a number of tracts and serial publications.

The eldest son, JOHN ROBERT MORRISON (1814–1843), born at Macao in 1814, became in 1830 translator to the English merchants at Canton, and in 1833 he published 'The Chinese Commercial Guide,' supplying much valuable information respecting British commerce in Canton. On his father's death in 1834 he succeeded him as Chinese secretary and interpreter under the new system adopted by the British government after the withdrawal of the East India Company's charter. During the diplomatic troubles which led to war between England and China in 1839, all the official correspondence of the English government with the Chinese authorities passed through Morrison's hands. He was attached to the British forces during the campaigns of 1840–2. When peace was made and Hongkong ceded to England, Morrison became a member of the legislative and executive council, and officiating colonial secretary of the Hongkong government. He died of malarial fever at Hongkong in the autumn of 1843. The English plenipotentiary there, Sir Henry

Pottinger, described his death as 'a positive national calamity.'

[Memoirs of Life and Labours of R. Morrison, D.D., by his widow, London, 1839. For the son: Gent. Mag. 1844, i. 210; and information kindly sent by Mrs. Mary R. Hobson and Mr. J. M. Hobson.] R. K. D.

MORRISON, THOMAS (*d.* 1835?), medical writer, studied at Edinburgh in 1784, but subsequently removed to London, where he became a member of the Royal College of Surgeons. In 1798 he was in practice at Chelsea, but by 1806 appears to have settled in Dublin. In the 'List of Members of the Royal College of Surgeons' in 1825 his address is given as Vale Grove, Chelsea. His name disappears from the lists before 1829. He died apparently at Dublin in 1835 (*Post Office Directory of Dublin*, 1807 and 1835). He published: 1. 'Reflections upon Armed Associations in an Appeal to the Impartial Inhabitants of Chelsea,' &c., 8vo, London, 1798. 2. 'An Examination into the Principles of what is commonly called the Brunonian System,' 8vo, London [1806]. 3. 'The Pharmacopœia of the King and Queen's College of Physicians, Ireland, translated into English with observations,' 8vo, Dublin, 1807. He also contributed two papers to Duncan's 'Annals of Medicine,' 1797 (ii. 240 and 246).

[List of Members of the Royal College of Surgeons, 1825; Reuss's Register of Authors; Watt's Bibl. Brit.; Dict. of Living Authors, 1816.] G. G.

MORRITT, JOHN BACON SAWREY (1772?–1843), traveller and classical scholar, born about 1772, was son and heir of John Sawrey Morritt, who died at Rokeby Park, Yorkshire, on 3 Aug. 1791, by his wife Anne (*d.* 1809), daughter of Henry Peirse of Bedale, M.P. for Northallerton. Both parents were buried in a vault in Rokeby Church, where their son erected to their memory a monument with a poetic inscription. Morritt, who had previously been in Paris during 1789, was educated at St. John's College, Cambridge, graduating B.A. 1794 and M.A. 1798. Early in 1794 he proceeded to the East, and spent two years in travelling, mainly in Greece and Asia Minor. He arrived, with the Rev. James Dallaway [q. v.] and a few other Englishmen, from Lesbos on 6 Nov. 1794, landing about twenty miles below Lectum, in the Sinus Adramyttenus, and proceeded to make a careful survey of the scene of the 'Iliad.' When Jacob Bryant published some works with the desire of proving that no such city as Troy had existed, Morritt's knowledge of the country led him to undertake Homer's defence, and he published at York in 1798 'A Vindication of Homer and of the Ancient Poets and Historians who have recorded the Siege and Fall of Troy.' This produced from Bryant 'Some Observations' in 1799, and when Dean Vincent reviewed Morritt's work in the 'British Critic' for 1 Jan. and 1 March 1799, and issued the criticisms in a separate form, Bryant rushed into print with an angry 'Expostulation addressed to the "British Critic,"' 1799, whereupon Morritt retaliated with 'Additional Remarks on the Topography of Troy, in answer to Mr. Bryant's last Publications,' 1800. Some account of his expedition to Troy is given by Dallaway in 'Constantinople, with Excursions to the Shores and Islands of the Archipelago, and to the Troad,' 1797, and his opinions are corroborated in 'Remarks and Observations on the Plain of Troy, made during an Excursion in June 1799,' by William Francklin [q. v.]

Morritt inherited a large fortune, including the estate of Rokeby, which his father had purchased from the 'long' Sir Thomas Robinson [q. v.] in 1769, and in 1806 he served as high sheriff of Yorkshire. A conservative in politics, he was returned to parliament by the borough of Beverley at a by-election in 1799, but was defeated at the dissolution in 1802. In 1814 he was elected on a by-vacancy for the constituency of Northallerton in Yorkshire, which he represented until 1818, and he sat for Shaftesbury, Dorset, from 1818 to 1820. In 1810 he published a pamphlet on the state of parties, entitled 'Advice to the Whigs, by an Englishman,' and in 1826 he gave Sir Walter Scott a copy of a printed 'Letter to R. Bethell,' in favour of the claims of the catholics, whereupon Scott noted in his diary that twenty years previously Morritt had entertained other views on that subject. A reply to this letter was published by the Rev. W. Metcalfe, perpetual curate of Kirk Hammerton. In 1807 he made an 'excellent speech' at the nomination of Wilberforce for Yorkshire.

Morritt paid Scott a visit in the summer of 1808, and was again his guest in 1816 and January 1829. Their friendship was never broken. Scott, on his return from London in 1809, spent a fortnight at Rokeby, and described it as one of the most enviable places that he had ever seen. In December 1811 he communicated to Morritt his intention of making it the scene of a poem, and received in reply a very long communication on its history and beauties. A second stay was made in the autumn of 1812, with the result that his poem of 'Rokeby,' although falling short of complete success, was lauded for the 'admirable, perhaps the unique fidelity of the local descriptions.' It was dedicated to Morritt 'in token of sincere friendship,' and with the public intimation that the scene had been laid in his 'beautiful demesne.' A further proof of this friendship was shown when Morritt was entrusted with the secret of the authorship of 'Waverley.' Scott's visits were renewed in 1815, 1826, 1828, and in September 1831, on his last journey to London and Italy. Many letters which passed between them are included in Lockhart's 'Life of Scott,' which contained particulars by Morritt of his visit to Scott in 1808 and of the manner in which Scott was lionised by London society in 1809. Many more of their letters are contained in the 'Familiar Letters of Sir Walter Scott,' 1894. Morritt was also acquainted with Stewart Rose, Payne Knight, Sir Humphry Davy, and Southey, the latter of whom stopped at Rokeby in July 1812, and made a short call there in November 1829 (Southey, *Life and Correspondence*, iii. 345–8, iv. 8, vi. 77).

Morritt, on Scott's invitation, became an occasional contributor to the 'Quarterly Review,' and his poem on 'The Curse of Moy, a Highland Tale,' appeared in the 'Minstrelsy of the Scottish Border' (5th edit. iii. 451). He was elected a member of the Dilettanti Society on 2 June 1799, and his portrait as 'arch-master' of its ceremonies, in the long crimson taffety-tasselled robe of office, was painted by Sir Martin Archer Shee for the society in 1831–2. An essay by him on the 'History and Principles of Antient Sculpture' forms the introduction to the second volume of 'Specimens of Antient Sculpture preserved in Great Britain,' which was issued by the society in 1835. The minutes of the council on its selection and printing are inserted in the 'Historical Notices of the Society of Dilettanti,' pp. 56–9. A volume of 'Miscellaneous Translations and Imitations of the Minor Greek Poets' was published by him in 1802. He composed the poetical inscription on the monument in York Minster to William Burgh [q. v.], whose widow left him the fine miniature of Milton which had been painted by Cooper.

Morritt died at Rokeby Park, 12 July 1843, aged 71. He married, by special license, at the house of Colonel Stanley, M.P., in Pall Mall, on 19 Nov. 1803, Katharine (*d.* 1815), second daughter of the Rev. Thomas Stanley, rector of Winwick in Lancashire. He was buried by his wife's side in a vault under Rokeby Church, where a marble tablet, surmounted by a bust of him, was placed in their memory.

Morritt was one of the founders and a member of the first committee of the Travellers' Club in 1819. Scott calls him 'a man unequalled in the mixture of sound good sense, high literary cultivation, and the kindest and sweetest temper that ever graced a human bosom.' Wilberforce described him as 'full of anecdote,' and Sir William Fraser mentions him as a brilliant *raconteur*.

[Gent. Mag. 1791 pt. ii. pp. 780, 1156, 1803 pt. ii. p. 1085, 1815 pt. ii. p. 637, 1843 pt. ii. pp. 547–8; Annual Reg. 1843, p. 281; Burke's Landed Gentry, 4th ed., sub 'Peirse' and 'Stanley;' Foster's York Pedigrees, sub 'Peirse;' Whitaker's Richmondshire; Park's Parl. Rep. of Yorkshire, pp. 151, 246; Lockhart's Scott, passim; Scott's Journal, i. 270–2, ii. 162–4, 195–7, 215; Sir W. Fraser's Hic et Ubique, pp. 238–43; Smiles's John Murray, ii. 453; Davies's York Press, pp. 300–1; Wilberforce's Life, iii. 318, iv. 392, v. 241–3; Portraits of Dilettanti Soc. p. 7; Hist. Notices, Dilettanti Soc. pp. 77–8.]

W. P. C.

MORS, RODERICK (*d.* 1546), Franciscan. [See Brinkelow, Henry.]

MORSE, HENRY (1595–1645), jesuit, known also as Claxton (his mother's name) and Warde, was born in Norfolk in 1595, and studied law in one of the inns of court in London. Harbouring doubts concerning the protestant religion, he retired to the continent, and was reconciled to the Roman church at Douay. Afterwards he became an alumnus of the English College there. He entered the English College at Rome 27 Dec. 1618, and having completed his theological studies, and received holy orders, he was sent from Douay to the English mission 19 June 1624. He entered the Society of Jesus in the London novitiate in 1625, and was soon afterwards removed to the Durham district. Being apprehended, he was committed to York Castle, where he remained in confinement for three years. In 1632 he was at Watten, acting as prefect of health and consultor of the college. In 1633 he was minister and consultor at Liège College, and in the same year he became a missioner in the London district. He was again apprehended, committed to Newgate, tried and condemned to death in 1637, but the sentence was commuted to banishment at the intercession of Queen Henrietta Maria. In 1641–2 he was camp missioner to the English mission at Ghent. Two years later he had returned to England, and again appears as a missioner in the Durham district. He was arrested, carried in chains to London, tried, and, being condemned to death as a traitor on account of his sacerdotal character, was executed at Tyburn on 1 Feb. (N.S.) 1644–5.

In Father Ambrose Corbie's 'Certamen Triplex,' Antwerp, 1645, is an engraved portrait, which is photographed in Foley's 'Records' [see CORBIE, AMBROSE]; two other portraits are mentioned by Granger (*Biog. Hist.* ii. 207).

A copy of Morse's diary, entitled 'Papers relating to the English Jesuits,' is preserved in the British Museum (Addit. MS. 21203).

His elder brother, WILLIAM MORSE (*d.* 1649), born in Norfolk in 1591, was likewise a convert to the catholic faith, became a jesuit, and laboured on the English mission until his death on 1 Jan. 1648-9.

[An account of Morse's execution, entitled Narratio Gloriosæ Mortis quam pro Religione Catholica P. Henricvs Mors è Societate Iesv Sacerdos fortiter oppetijt Londini in Anglia. Anno Salutis, 1645. 1 Februarij stylo nouo Quem hic stylum deinceps sequemur, Ghent, 1645, 4to, pp. 21; a memoir appears in Ambrose Corbie's Certamen Triplex, Antwerp, 1645, 4to, pp. 95-144. See also Challoner's Missionary Priests, ii. 180; Dodd's Church Hist. iii. 120; Florus Anglo-Bavaricus, p. 82; Foley's Records, i. 566-610, vi. 288, vii. 527; Oliver's Jesuit Collections, p. 146; Tanner's Societas Jesu usque ad sanguinis et vitæ profusionem militans.]

T. C.

MORSE, ROBERT (1743-1818), general, colonel commandant royal engineers, inspector-general of fortifications, second son of Thomas Morse, rector of Langatt, Somerset, was born on 29 Feb. 1743. He entered the Royal Military Academy at Woolwich on 1 Feb. 1756, and while still a cadet received a commission as ensign in the 12th foot on 24 Sept. 1757. He was permitted to continue his studies at the Royal Military Academy, and on 8 Feb. 1758 was gazetted practitioner engineer. In May he joined the expedition under the Duke of Marlborough destined for the capture and destruction of St. Malo. The troops were landed at Cancale on 5 June, and the engineers covered the place with strong lines of trenches, but with the exception of the destruction of shipping and of some magazines nothing was done, and the troops re-embarked, and after demonstrations at Cherbourg and Havre returned home. Morse then joined the expedition under General Bligh directed against Cherbourg. The troops disembarked without resistance on 6 Aug., and, the French having abandoned the forts, the engineers demolished the defences and the wharves and docks. The expedition sailed for England again on 18 Aug. Morse again accompanied Bligh the following month, when another attempt was made on St. Malo. The troops landed in St. Lunaire Bay on 4 Sept., but were unable to make any impression on the place. Morse took part in the skirmishes at Plancoet on the 8th and Mantignon on the 9th. On the 11th the expedition hastily retreated to their ships, and embarked under heavy fire from the French, when over eight hundred were killed, drowned, or made prisoners. Morse was slightly wounded.

Soon after his return to England he was placed on the staff of the expedition, under General Hobson, for the reduction of the French islands of the Caribbean Sea. The expedition sailed for Barbados on 12 Nov., and disembarked without loss in Martinique on 14 Jan. 1759. Shortly after the troops were re-embarked and carried to Guadeloupe. Basseterre, the capital, was taken, and the whole island reduced, the French evacuating it by the capitulation of 1 May. Morse was promoted lieutenant and sub-engineer on 10 Sept. 1759, and on his return to England at the end of the year was employed on the coast defences of Sussex.

In 1761 Morse served in the expedition against Belleisle, off the coast of Brittany, under General Hodgson. The force, which was strong in engineers, arrived off the island on 7 April, but an attempted disembarkation failed, with a loss of five hundred men. Bad weather prevented another attempt until 21 April, when a landing was effected, and the enemy driven into the citadel of Palais, a work of considerable strength, requiring a regular siege. There is a journal of the siege in the royal artillery library at Woolwich, 'by an officer who was present at the siege.' A practicable breach was established in June, and on the 7th of that month the garrison capitulated, and the fort and island were occupied by the British. Morse was employed in repairing and restoring the fortifications, and returned to England with General Hodgson.

Morse served with the British forces in Germany, under John Manners, marquis of Granby [q. v.], in 1762 and 1763, and acted as aide-de-camp to Granby, in addition to carrying out his duties as engineer. He was also assistant quartermaster-general. He was present at the various actions of the Westphalian campaign, in which the British force took part. At the close of the war he was one of the officers sent to Holland to make a convention with the States-General for the passage of the British troops through their country, and he attended the embarkation of the army. He was promoted captain-lieutenant and engineer-extraordinary on 6 May 1763.

On his return to England, through the good offices of Colonel George Morrison [q.v.], quartermaster-general of the forces, Morse was appointed assistant quartermaster-general at headquarters, an office which he held simultaneously with the engineer charge of the Medway division until 1766, and afterwards with that of the Tilbury division until 1769. In 1773 he was appointed commanding royal engineer of the West India islands of Dominica, St. Vincent, Grenada, and Tobago, which had been ceded to Great Britain by France at the conclusion of the seven years' war. Morse was promoted captain and engineer in ordinary on 30 Oct. 1775. He returned to England in 1779, and on 20 Aug. was placed on the staff and employed first on the defences of the Sussex coast, and later at Plymouth and Falmouth.

In June 1782 Morse accompanied Sir Guy Carleton [q. v.] to New York as chief engineer in North America. On 1 Jan. 1783 he was promoted lieutenant-colonel. On his return home he was employed at headquarters in London. He was promoted colonel on 6 June 1788, and in the summer of 1791 was sent to Gibraltar as commanding royal engineer. He was promoted major-general on 20 Dec. 1793. He remained five years at Gibraltar, when he was brought home by the Duke of Richmond to assist in the duties of the board of ordnance. On 10 March 1797 Morse was temporarily appointed chief engineer of Great Britain during the absence on leave of Sir William Green. He was promoted lieutenant-general on 26 June 1799. On 21 April 1802 the title of inspector-general of fortifications was substituted for that of chief engineer of Great Britain, and on 1 May Morse became the first incumbent of the new office, and was made a colonel commandant of royal engineers.

Morse held the post of inspector-general of fortifications for nine years, during which considerable works of defence were constructed on the coasts of Kent and Sussex against the threatened invasion by the French. He was promoted general on 25 April 1808. Owing to ill-health he resigned his appointment on 22 July 1811, and was granted by the Prince Regent an extra pension of twenty-five shillings a day for his good services. He died on 28 Jan. 1818 at his house in Devonshire Place, London, and was buried in Marylebone Church, where there is a tablet to his memory. He married, on 20 April 1785, Sophia, youngest daughter of Stephen Godin, esq., and left an only daughter, Harriet, who was married to Major-general Sir James Carmichael-Smyth, bart.

Morse was the author of 'A General Description of the Province of Nova Scotia, and a Report of the Present State of the Defences, with Observations leading to the further Growth and Security of this Colony, done by Lieutenant-Colonel Morse, Chief Engineer in America, upon a Tour of the Province in the Autumn of the Year 1783 and the Summer of 1784, under the Orders and Instructions of H.E. Sir Guy Carleton, General and Commander-in-Chief of H.M. Forces in North America. Given at Headquarters at New York, 28 July 1783,' 1 vol. text, 1 vol. plans, MSS. fol. (Brit. Mus.)

The following plans drawn by Morse are in the war office: 1. Town and River of Annapolis, 1784. 2. Fort Annapolis, with Projects for its Reform, 1784. 3. Cumberland Fort, Nova Scotia, 1784. 4. Town of Shelbourne, with Harbour, and Roseneath Island, 1784. The following are in the archives of the government of the Dominion of Canada: 1. Town and Harbour of St. John, New Brunswick, 1784. 2. Quebec, Cape Diamond, Proposed Barracks.

[Royal Engineers' Corps Records; War Office and Ordnance Records; Despatches.]

R. H. V.

MORSHEAD, HENRY ANDERSON (1774?–1831), colonel royal engineers, born about 1774, was the son of Colonel Henry Anderson of Fox Hall, co. Limerick. He entered the Royal Military Academy at Woolwich on 29 May 1790, and received a commission as second lieutenant in the royal artillery on 18 Sept. 1792. He served in the campaigns on the continent under the Duke of York in 1793–4, and was present at the action of Famars 23 May 1793, at the siege of Valenciennes in June and July, the siege of Dunkirk in August and September, and the battle of Hondschoote 8 Sept. He gained the esteem of his commanding officers, and in acknowledgment of his services was transferred, at his own request, to the corps of royal engineers on 1 Jan. 1794. He took part in the siege of Landrecies in April 1794, affair near Tournay on 23 May, and siege of Nimeguen in November. On his return to England he was sent, in June 1795, to Plymouth. He was promoted first lieutenant on 19 Nov. 1796, and in May 1797 he embarked with two companies of royal military artificers for St. Domingo, West Indies. On the evacuation of that island in 1798 he was attached to the staff of Sir Thomas Maitland [q. v.], who was his warm friend through life. When he returned to England in November 1798 he was employed in the Thames division, and stationed at Gravesend. He was promoted captain-lieutenant 18 April 1801, and was sent to Portsmouth, and subsequently to Plymouth. He was promoted captain 1 March 1805, and in that year he assumed by royal license the surname of Morshead in addition to that of Anderson.

In July 1807 he was sent to Dublin, and three months later was appointed commanding royal engineer of the expedition, under Brigadier-general Beresford, which sailed from Cork early in 1808, and in February took possession of Madeira. He remained in Madeira until 1812, and on his return to England in November of that year was posted to the Plymouth division. He was promoted lieutenant-colonel 21 July 1813, and sent to Dublin; was appointed commanding royal engineer in North Britain (March 1814), and in July 1815 was transferred as commanding royal engineer of the western district to Plymouth, where he remained for many years, and carried out important works for the ordnance and naval services in consultation with the Duke of Wellington and Lord Melville. On 29 July 1825 he was promoted colonel.

In 1829 he was appointed commanding royal engineer at Malta, and died at Valetta on 11 Nov. 1831, while acting governor. He was honoured with a public funeral, and was buried in the old saluting battery overlooking the grand harbour. He married in 1800 Elizabeth, only daughter of P. Morshead, esq., of Widey Court, Plymouth, Devonshire, by whom he had eleven children. A man of frank and engaging manners, a good conversationalist, and a clear writer, he was fond of society, and exercised a genial hospitality. There is a bust in the royal engineers' office in Valetta, Malta.

The following plans by Morshead are in the war office: 1. Edinburgh Castle, two plans, 1814 and 1815. 2. Whiteforland Point and Defences, two plans, 1814. 3. Leith Fort and Breakwater, 1815. 4. Plymouth, Survey and Drawings of various parts of the Defences, Piers, and Ordnance and Naval Buildings, nineteen drawings, 1815–26. 5. Plan of Plymouth Sound, showing intended breakwater and the soundings, with an original pencil sketch by Mr. Rennie of the lighthouse, 1816. 6. Plymouth Citadel, 1820. 7. Devonport Lines, 1820. 8. Scilly Islands, St. Mary's, Plan of the Defences, 1820. 9. St. Nicholas Island, Plymouth, 1820. 10. Pendennis Castle, Falmouth, 1821. 11. Pendennis Castle, and Falmouth Harbour, two plans, 1828–9. 12. St. Mawes Castle, Falmouth, 1829.

[Royal Engineers' Records; War Office and Board of Ordnance Records; United Service Journal.] R. H. V.

MORT, THOMAS SUTCLIFFE (1816–1878), a pioneer of commerce in New South Wales, was born at Bolton, Lancashire, on 23 Dec. 1816. As a boy he entered the warehouse of Messrs. H. & S. Henry of Manchester, and in 1838 was recommended by them to their correspondents, Messrs. Aspinall & Brown, in Sydney. With this firm and their successors he remained five years as clerk and salesman. In 1841 he made his first step in colonial enterprise, and became an active promoter of the Hunter River Steam Navigation Company, which afterwards developed into the Australasian Steam Navigation Company. But shortly after the panic of 1843, which ruined some of the best houses in Australia, the failure of the firm which he served threw him on his own resources. He then started in business as an auctioneer, and laid the foundations of the great firm which bore his name. It was in connection with this business that he started the public wool sales of the colony. And it was at this time also that he began experiments in regard to freezing meat. Residing quietly in a cottage at Double Bay, he devoted himself with an exclusive vigour to his new calling, and his wealth and influence increased. In 1846 he bought some land, which is described as 'two or three sandhills,' at Darling Point. Here a love of gardening, which had always characterised him, and his skill in management, had full scope, and he turned an uninviting tract into the lovely estate of Greenoaks.

In 1849 he took an active part in promoting the first line of railway in New South Wales, between Sydney and Paramatta. When the gold rush came he formed (in 1851) the Great Nugget Vein Mining Company. In 1856 he turned to the encouragement of the pastoral development of the country, and laid at Bodalla the foundations of a rural settlement for the supply of dairy produce to the large towns, which eventually spread over thirty-eight thousand acres, and absorbed 100,000*l.* of his own capital. It was the favourite resort of his later years. From 1857 to 1859 he was in England, collecting those works of art which eventually adorned his house at Greenoaks.

In 1863, with the view of promoting the use of steamers in the colonial trade, he commenced excavations for the great dock at Port Jackson, where again he invested some 100,000*l.*, and finally constituted the Mort Dock and Engineering Company. The latter years of his life were chiefly devoted to the attempt to perfect the machinery by which meat could be transported in a frozen state for long distances over seas. He was the originator of the modern frozen meat trade. After giving the subject much consideration, he began about 1870, with the aid of Mr. E. D. Nicolle, a series of experiments in freezing and thawing meat and vegetables. In 1875 he erected great slaughter-houses and a freezing establishment at Lithgow, and chartered the first steamer for the new trade. On the eve of its departure he collected around him at a great banquet the public men of the country, and declared that he had solved the problem of the world's food supply. The steamer's machinery failed; the metal did not stand the constant strain of refrigeration, and for a time the transport of frozen meat was thought impossible. Mort, deeply disappointed, gave up his cherished idea, and turned the great freezing-house into an ice factory and a depôt for sending cooked dishes into Sydney. He himself retired to Bodalla, his rural settlement. There on 9 May 1878 he died, 'the greatest benefactor that the working men of this country ever had,' and 'the most unselfish man that ever entered the colony.' He was twice married. To him was erected, at Sydney, the first statue with which an Australian citizen was honoured.

Mort was a man of indomitable energy, characterised at once by an intensely practical capacity for business and a love of natural scenery and the arts. He was broad and liberal in his views. In 1873 he offered his workmen shares in his business, and all his foremen became shareholders.

A bust of Mort, by Birch, A.R.A., is in the possession of his brother, Mr. William Mort, in London.

[Heaton's Australian Dict. of Dates and Men of the Time; private information.] C. A. H.

MORTAIN, ROBERT OF, COUNT OF MORTAIN, in the diocese of Avranches (*d.* 1091?), was uterine brother of William the Conqueror. He was the second son of Herlwin of Conteville, by his wife Herleva. His elder brother was Odo [q. v.], bishop of Bayeux. William the Warling, a cousin of Duke William, was in 1048–9 deprived of the county of Mortain, which was handed over to Robert, an instance of William's desire 'to raise up the humble kindred of his mother' while 'he plucked down the proud kindred of his father' (WILL. OF JUMIÈGES, vii. 19). In 1066 Robert was present at the select council held at Lillebonne to discuss the invasion of England; he contributed 120 ships to the fleet, according to Wace, a fact of doubtful authenticity (STUBBS, *Const. Hist.* i. 279 note), and fought at Senlac (*Roman de Rou*, l. 13765). In 1069 he was left in England to protect Lindsey against the Danes, and at the same time his castle of Montacute (Eng. Lutgaresburg) in Somerset was besieged. When William I lay dying, Robert was present and pleaded the cause of his brother Odo with success. He joined with Odo in supporting Robert Curthose against William II, and held the castle of Pevensey against the king from April to June 1088 (ORDERICUS VITALIS, iv. 17), but he soon yielded and was reconciled to Rufus.

His possessions in England were larger than those of any other follower of William (FREEMAN, *Norman Conquest*, iv. 764), and have been estimated at 793 manors (BRADY, *Introd. to Domesday Book*, p. 13). Of these, 623 in the south-west counties returned him 400*l.* a year (MORGAN, *England under the Normans*, p. 8). He had 248 manors in Cornwall, 196 in Yorkshire, 99 in Northamptonshire, 75 in Devonshire, with a church and house in Exeter, 54 in Sussex and the borough of Pevensey, 49 in Dorset, 29 in Buckinghamshire, and one or more in ten other counties (ELLIS, i. 455). He was charged by the Domesday jurors with many 'usurpations,' particularly on the see of Exeter, the churches of Bodmin and St. German, Mount St. Michael, Cornwall, and Westminster. The charter which records his grant of Mount St. Michael as a cell to Mont S. Michel is spurious (FREEMAN, iv. 766). There is no ground for believing that he was Earl of Cornwall (*Third Report on the Dignity of a Peer*).

He married Matilda, daughter of Roger of Montgomery [q. v.] In 1082 they founded a collegiate church in their castle of Mortain, under the guidance of their chaplain Vitalis, abbot of Savigny. Robert also made grants to Fleury and Marmoutier (STAPLETON, *Rot. Scacc. Nor.* i. p. lxxv), and gave to Fécamp what he took from Westminster (*Domesday Book*, f. 129). He had a son William, who forfeited Mortain after the battle of Tinchebrai, and possibly a son Nigel (STAPLETON, i. p. lxvii). His daughter Agnes married Andrew of Vitré, another married Guy de la Val, and another the Earl of Toulouse.

Robert died in 1091 (KELHAM, *Domesday Book Illustrated*, p. 39, quoting HEYLIN and MILLS, *Catalogue of Honor*).

[Ordericus Vitalis, ed. Le Prévost, ii. 194–223, 412, iii. c. xi. and p. 449, iv. 17; Domesday Book; Freeman's Norman Conquest, vols. ii–v. passim, and William Rufus.] M. B.

MORTEN, THOMAS (1836–1866), painter and book-illustrator, was born at Uxbridge, Middlesex, in 1836. He came to London and studied at the painting school kept by J. Mathews Leigh in Newman Street. Morten was chiefly employed as an illustrator of books and serials, mostly of a humorous nature. The most successful were his illustrations to an edition of Swift's 'Gulliver's Travels,' published in 1864, which ran into several editions. Morten also practised as a painter of domestic subjects, and was an occasional exhibitor at the Royal Academy, sending in 1866 'Pleading for the Prisoner.' His affairs, however, became embarrassed, and he committed suicide on 23 Sept. 1866.

[Redgrave's Dict. of Artists; Graves's Dict. of Artists, 1760–1880.] L. C.

MORTIMER, CROMWELL (*d.* 1752), physician, born in Essex, was second son of John Mortimer [q. v.] by his third wife, Elizabeth, daughter of Samuel Sanders of Derbyshire. He was educated under Boerhaave at Leyden University, where he was admitted in the medical division on 7 Sept. 1719, and graduated M.D. on 9 Aug. 1724. He became a licentiate of the College of Physicians, London, on 25 June 1725, and a fellow on 30 Sept. 1729, and he was created M.D. of Cambridge, comitiis regiis, on 11 May 1728. He practised at first in Hanover Square, London, but removed in 1729, at the request of Sir Hans Sloane, to Bloomsbury Square, where he had the benefit of Sloane's collections and conversation, and assisted to 1740 in prescribing for his patients. For ten years Mortimer had the sole care, as physician, of a London infirmary, and in 1744, when resident in Dartmouth Street, Westminster, he issued a circular, describing the system of payment for his services which he had adopted. This step did not tend to make him more popular with his professional colleagues. Some of the apothecaries refused to attend patients when he was called in. A satirical print of him, designed by Hogarth and engraved by Rigou, with several lines from Pope appended to it, was published about 1745 (*Catalogue of Satirical Prints at British Museum*, vol. iii. pt. i. p. 541), and in the 'Gentleman's Magazine' for 1780, page 510, he is dubbed 'an impertinent, assuming empiric.'

Mortimer was elected F.S.A. on 21 March 1734, and F.R.S. on 4 July 1728, and, mainly through the interest of Sloane, was second or acting secretary to the latter body from 30 Nov. 1730 until his death. From 28 July 1737 he was a member and correspondent of the Gentlemen's Society at Spalding, and he was also a corresponding member of the Royal Academy of Sciences at Paris. About 1738 'his vanity prompted him to write the history of the learned societies of Great Britain and Ireland, to have been prefixed to a volume of the "Philosophical Transactions,"' whereupon Maurice Johnson [q. v.] furnished him with a history of the Spalding society, and with many curious particulars of the Society of Antiquaries, but these materials were never utilised, and a long complaint from Johnson on his neglect is in Nichols's 'Literary Anecdotes,' vi. 2–3. Mortimer was absorbed in new schemes. In 1747 he proposed to establish in the College of Arms a registry for dissenters, and articles of agreement, approved by all parties, were drawn up. It was opened on 20 Feb. 1747–8, but did not succeed, through a misunderstanding between the ministers and the deputies of the congregations. About 1750 he promoted the scheme for the incorporation of the Society of Antiquaries, and he was one of the first members of its council, November 1751. On the death of his elder brother, Samuel Mortimer, a lawyer, he inherited the family estate of Toppingo Hall, Hatfield Peverel, Essex. He died there on 7 Jan. 1752, was buried on 13 Jan., and a monument was erected to his memory. His library was on sale at Thomas Osborne's on 26 Nov. 1753. By his wife Mary he had an only son, Hans, of Lincoln's Inn and Cauldthorp, near Burton-on-Trent, who about 1765 sold the property in Essex to the Earl of Abercorn.

Mortimer's dissertation 'De Ingressu Humorum in Corpus Humanum' for his doctor's degree at Leyden was printed in 1724, and was dedicated to Sloane. It was also inserted in the collections of medical treatises by Baron A. von Haller and F. J. de Oberkamp. His 'Address to the Publick, containing Narratives of the Effects of certain Chemical Remedies in most Diseases' appeared in 1745. The circular letter on his system of remuneration was published as an appendix to it and inserted in the 'Gentleman's Magazine' for 1779, pp. 541–2, and in Nichols's 'Literary Anecdotes,' v. 424. An English translation of the 'Elements of the Art of Assaying Metals. By Johann Andreas Cramer, M.D.,' to which Mortimer contributed notes, observations, and an appendix of authors, appeared in 1741, and a second edition was published in 1764. As secretary of the Royal Society he edited vols. xxxvi. to xlvi. of the 'Philosophical Transactions,' and contributed to them numerous papers (Watt, *Bibl. Brit.*) The most important, dealing with the then distemper in horned cattle, were inserted in the 'Gentleman's Magazine' for 1746, pp. 650–1, and 1747, pp. 55–6 (cf. *Gent. Mag.* 1749, pp. 491–5). Joseph Rogers, M.D., addressed to Mortimer in 1733 'Some Observations on the Translation and Abridgment of Dr. Boerhaave's Chymistry,' and Boerhaave communicated to him in September 1738 the symptoms of his illness (BURTON, *Memoir of Boerhaave*, p. 69). Some account of the Roman remains found by him near Maldon in Essex is in the 'Archæologia,' xvi. 149, four letters from him, and numerous communications to him are in the possession of the Royal Society, and a letter sent by him to Dr. Waller on 28 July 1729 is printed in the 'Reliquiæ Galeanæ' (*Bibl. Topogr. Brit.*iii. 155–6). He drew up an index to the fishes for the 1743 edition of Willoughby's four books on the history of fish, and Dr. Munk assigns to him a volume on 'The Volatile Spirit of Sulphur,' 1744. When Kalm came to England, on his way to America to report on its natural products, he visited Mortimer, and at his house made the acquaintance of many scientific men.

[Gent. Mag. 1752 p. 44, 1777 p. 266, 1780 pp. 17, 510; Nichols's Lit. Anecd. v. 7, 27, 423–6, 433, vi. 2–3, 99, 144–5, ix. 615; Munk's Coll. of Phys. 2nd edit. ii. 11; Memoirs of Martyn, 1830, pp. 40–2; Morant's Essex, ii. 133; Stukeley's Memoirs (Surtees Soc.), i. 233–4, 235, ii. 10–11, 320, iii. 6–7, 468; Dobson's Hogarth, p. 324; Thomson's Royal Soc. pp. 8, 10–11; Noble's College of Arms, p. 409; Cat. of MSS. and Letters of Royal Soc. passim; Kalm's Travels (trans. Lucas, 1892), pp. 19, 40, 61, 114–15.]

W. P. C.

MORTIMER, EDMUND (II) DE, third EARL OF MARCH (1351–1381), was the son of Roger de Mortimer (V), second earl of March [q. v.], and his wife Philippa, daughter of William Montacute, first earl of Salisbury [q. v.], and was born at 'Langonith' (? Llangynwyd or Llangynog) on 1 Feb. 1351 (*Monasticon*, vi. 353). When still a child there was an abortive proposal in 1354 to marry him to Alice Fitzalan, daughter of Richard Fitzalan II, earl of Arundel [q. v.] On 26 Feb. 1360 the death of his father procured for the young Edmund the succession to the title and estates of his house when only in his tenth year. He became the ward of Edward III, but was ultimately assigned to the custody of William of Wykeham [q. v.], bishop of Winchester, and of the above-mentioned Richard, earl of Arundel (DUGDALE, *Baronage*, i. 148). Henceforth he was closely associated with the king's sons, and especially with Edward the Black Prince. Mortimer's political importance dates from his marriage with Philippa, only daughter of Lionel of Antwerp, duke of Clarence [q. v.], the second surviving son of Edward III, by his wife Elizabeth de Burgh, the heiress of Ulster. Philippa was born in 1355, and her wedding with Mortimer took place in the spring of 1368, just before the departure of Lionel for Italy (*Cont. Eulogium Hist.* iii. 333). Before the end of the year Lionel's death gave to his son-in-law the enjoyment of his great estates. When, on coming of age, Mortimer entered into public life, he represented not simply the Mortimer inheritance, but also the great possessions of his wife. Besides his Shropshire, Herefordshire, Welsh, and Meath estates, which came from the Mortimers and Genvilles, he was, in name at least, lord of Ulster and Connaught, and by far the most conspicuous representative of the Anglo-Norman lords of Ireland. He was now styled Earl of Ulster as well as Earl of March. But important as were the immediate results of Edmund's marriage, the ulterior results were even more far-reaching. The descendants of Philippa before long became the nearest representatives of the line of Edward III, and handed on to the house of York that claim to the throne which resulted in the Wars of the Roses. And not only the legitimist claim but the territorial strength of the house of York was almost entirely derived from the Mortimer inheritance.

In 1369 Mortimer became marshal of England, an office which he held until 1377. In the same year he served against the French. On 8 Jan. 1371 he received his first summons to parliament (*Lords' Report on Dignity of a Peer*, iv. 648). In 1373 he received final livery of his own estates. On 8 Jan. 1373 he was sent as joint ambassador to France, and in March of the same year he was chief guardian of the truce with Scotland (DOYLE, *Official Baronage*, ii. 468). The Wigmore family chronicler (*Monasticon*, vi. 353) boasts of the extraordinary success with which he discharged these commissions, and erroneously says that he was only eighteen at the time. In 1375 he served in the expedition sent to Brittany to help John of Montfort, and captured the castle of Saint-Mathieu (WALSINGHAM, *Hist. Angl.* i. 318–319; FROISSART, viii. 212, ed. Luce).

Mortimer's close association with the Prince of Wales and his old guardian, William of Wykeham, necessarily involved an attitude of hostility to John of Gaunt. Ancient feuds between the houses of March and Lancaster still had their effects, and Edmund's dislike of Gaunt was strengthened by a feeling that Lancaster was a possible rival to the claims of his wife and son to the succession. Accordingly he took up a strong line in favour of the constitutional as against the court party, and was conspicuous among the aristocratic patrons of the popular opposition in the Good parliament of 1376. He was, with Bishop Courtenay of London, the leader of the committee of twelve magnates appointed at the beginning of the session, on

28 April, to confer with the commons (*Rot. Parl.* ii. 322; *Chron. Angliæ*, 1328–88, p. 70; Stubbs, *Const. Hist.* ii. 428–9). The commons showed their confidence in him by electing as their speaker Sir Peter De la Mare, his steward, who, as knight of the shire for Herefordshire, was probably returned to parliament through his lord's influence [see De la Mare, Sir Peter]. A vigorous attack on the courtiers was now conducted by the commons under their speaker; but the death of the Black Prince on 8 June weakened the effect of their action. John of Gaunt now sought to obtain from parliament a settlement of the succession in the case of the death of the Black Prince's only son, Richard. He even urged that, as in France, the succession should descend through males only, thus openly setting up his own claims against those of the Countess of March (*Chron. Angl.* 1328–88, pp. 92–3). The commons prudently declined to discuss the subject. Yet even with the support of the knights, the Earl of March and the constitutional bishops were not strong enough of themselves to resist Gaunt and the courtiers. But they continued their work until the end of the session, on 6 July, their last care being to enforce the appointment of a permanent council, some members of which were always to be in attendance on the king. The Earl of March was among the nine additional persons appointed to this council (*ib.* pp. lxviii, 100). But as soon as the parliament was dissolved, Lancaster, in the king's name, repudiated all its acts. The new councillors were dismissed, and March was ordered to discharge his office as marshal by surveying the defences of Calais and other of the more remote royal castles (*ib.* p. 107), while his steward, De la Mare, was thrown into prison. But March, 'preferring to lose his staff rather than his life,' and believing that he would be waylaid and murdered on the narrow seas, resigned the office of marshal (*ib.* p. 108).

After the accession of Richard II (21 June 1377), power remained with Lancaster, though he now chose to be more conciliatory. March's position was moreover immensely improved. The king was a young child. The next heir by blood was March's own son. On 16 July 1377 March bore the second sword and the spurs at the coronation of the little king. He was not, however, in a position to claim any great share in the administration, and contented himself with a place on the new council of government, into whose hands power now fell (*Fœdera*, iv. 10; Stubbs, *Const. Hist.* ii. 442). But he was as strong as ever in parliament. He was among the lords whose advice, as in 1376, was requested by the parliament of October 1377, and had the satisfaction of seeing his steward again elected as the speaker of this assembly. It was a further triumph when the young king was forced by the commons to remodel his council, and when March was one of the nine members of the new and extremely limited body thus selected (*ib.* ii. 444; cf. *Chron. Angl.* p. 164). On 1 Jan. 1378 he was appointed chief member of a commission to redress infractions of the truce with Scotland (*Fœdera*, iv. 26; cf. *Chron. Angl.* p. 203), and on 20 Jan. was put first on a commission appointed to inspect and strengthen the fortifications of the border strongholds of Berwick, Carlisle, Roxburgh, and Bamburgh (Doyle, *Official Baronage*, ii. 468). On 14 Feb. 1379 he was sent with other magnates on a special embassy to Scotland.

On 22 Oct. 1379 March was appointed lieutenant of Ireland (*Fœdera*, iv. 72). It was convenient for the party of Lancaster to get him out of the way, and his great interests in Ireland gave him a special claim to the thankless office. Those parts of the island, Ulster, Connaught, and Meath, over which he bore nominal sway, had long been the most disorderly districts; and so far back as 1373 the English in Ireland had sent a special commission to Edward III representing that the only way of abating the evils that were rampant in those regions was for the king to force the Earl of March to dwell upon his Irish estates and adequately defend them. Partly then to enter upon the effectual possession of his own estates ('ad recuperandum comitatum suum de Holuestre,' Monk of Evesham, p. 19), and partly to set the king's rule on a better footing, March now accepted the government of Ireland for three years. He stipulated for good terms. He was to have twenty thousand marks paid over to him, from which he was to provide troops, but he was not to be held accountable to the crown for his expenditure of the money. He was also to have the disposal of the king's ordinary revenue in Ireland. Before he left his Welsh estates he made his will, dated 1 May 1380, at Denbigh, the contents of which are summarised in Dugdale's 'Baronage,' i. 149, and printed in Nichols's 'Royal Wills,' pp. 104–16. On 15 May 1380 March arrived in Ireland (*Cart., &c., of St. Mary's, Dublin*, ii. 284), having among his other attendants a herald of his own, called March herald. His first work was to establish himself in his wife's Ulster estates. In Eastern Ulster his arms were successful, the more so as some of the native chieftains threw themselves on his side, though these before long deserted him, on account of his treacherous seizure of an important Irish leader, Magennis, lord of Iveagh, in what is now co. Down. But the O'Neils ruled without a rival over Western Ulster, and March could not even draw a supply of timber from the forests of the land that was nominally his own. He had to bring the oak timber used to build a bridge over the Bann, near Coleraine, from his South Welsh lands on the Usk. This bridge was protected by fortifications at each end and by a tower in the middle; thus only was it prevented from being captured by the Irish. March also made some efforts to obtain possession of Connaught, and succeeded in capturing Athlone from the O'Connors, and thus secured the passage over the Shannon. But Kilkenny Castle was now assailed by the Hibernised Norman sept of the Tobyns, to revenge the imprisonment of their chief within its walls. This and other business drew the viceroy into Munster. There he caught cold in crossing a river in winter time, and on 27 Dec. 1381 he died at the Dominican friary at Cork (Gilbert, *Viceroys of Ireland*, pp. 234, 242–7, gives the best modern account of March's Irish government). The Anglo-Irish writers, who thoroughly knew the difficulties of his position, say that after great efforts he appeased most of the wars in Ireland (*Cart., &c., of St. Mary's, Dublin*, ii. 285). In England his government of Ireland was regarded as pre-eminently wise and successful ('multum de hoc quod amisit recuperavit,' Monk of Evesham, p. 19; *Chron. Angl.* p. 334; Adam of Usk, p. 21).

According to the directions in his will, March's body was interred on the left hand of the high altar of Wigmore Abbey (Nichols, p. 104). An Irish chronicle speaks of his being buried in the church of the Holy Trinity at Cork, but this probably only refers to the more perishable parts of his body (*Cart., &c., of St. Mary's, Dublin*, ii. 285). March had been an extremely liberal benefactor to Wigmore Abbey, the chief foundation of his ancestors. The old fabric of the abbey church had become decayed and ruinous, and March granted lands in Radnor and elsewhere to the value of two thousand marks a year for its reconstruction. He laid the foundation-stone of the new structure with his own hands, and by the time of his death the walls had been carried up to their appointed height, and were only wanting a roof. He also presented to the canons costly vestments and many relics, especially the body of St. Seiriol, and a large piece of the wood of the true cross. He further promised, when he took his departure from the canons of Wigmore as he went to Ireland, that on his safe return he would confer on them the advowson of three churches and the appropriation of Stoke Priory. Further benefactions were made by him in his will, including a rare and choice collection of relics. For all this liberality he is warmly commended by the Wigmore annalist (*Monasticon*, vi. 353), who quotes the eulogistic epitaph of the grateful canons, which celebrated his constancy, wisdom, popularity, and bounty. March supported Adam of Usk, his tenant's son, when the future chronicler was studying civil and canon law at Oxford (Adam of Usk, p. 21), and in return Adam loudly celebrates his praises. March was also highly eulogised by the St. Albans chronicler, who was a warm partisan of the constitutional opposition.

The Countess Philippa died before her husband, who celebrated her interment at Wigmore by almost regal pomp. Her epitaph speaks of her liberality, kindness, royal descent, and severity of morals. The children of Edmund and Philippa were: (1) Elizabeth, the eldest, born at Usk on 12 Feb. 1371, and married to the famous 'Hotspur,' Henry Percy, son of the Earl of Northumberland [see Percy, Henry]. (2) Roger, also born at Usk on 11 April 1374 [see Mortimer, Roger VI, fourth Earl of March]. (3) Philippa, born at Ludlow on 21 Nov. 1375, who became first the second wife of Richard Fitzalan III, earl of Arundel [q. v.], and afterwards married John of St. John; she died in 1400 (Adam of Usk, p. 53). (4) Edmund, born at Ludlow on 9 Nov. 1376, the future ally of Owen Glendower [see Mortimer, Sir Edmund III, 1376–1409?]. The above dates are from the Wigmore annalist (*Monasticon*, vi. 354), who now becomes contemporary and fairly trustworthy. (5) Sir John Mortimer, executed in 1423 for treason, and sometimes described as a son of Mortimer's, must, if a son at all, have been illegitimate (Sandford, *Genealogical Hist.* pp. 222–3). He is not mentioned in March's will.

[Dugdale's Monasticon, vi. 352–4; Dugdale's Baronage, i. 148–50; Doyle's Official Baronage, ii. 468–9; Rolls of Parliament; Rymer's Fœdera; Chron. Angl. 1328–88 (Rolls Ser.); Adam of Usk, ed. Thompson; Chartularies, &c., of St. Mary's Abbey, Dublin (Rolls Ser.); Froissart, ed. Luce; Monk of Evesham, ed. Hearne; Sandford's Genealogical Hist. of the Kings of England, pp. 221–223; Gilbert's Viceroys of Ireland; Wright's Hist. of Ludlow; Stubbs's Const. Hist. vol. ii.]

T. F. T.

MORTIMER, Sir EDMUND (III) de (1376–1409?), was the youngest child of Edmund de Mortimer (II), third earl of March [q. v.], and his wife Philippa, the daughter of Lionel, duke of Clarence, and heiress of Ulster.

He was born at Ludlow on Monday, 9 Nov. 1376. Portents attended his birth. At the very moment he came into the world it was believed that the horses in his father's stables were found standing up to their knees in blood (MONK OF EVESHAM, p. 179; *Ann. Hen. IV*, apud TROKELOWE, p. 349). These stories are very generally but erroneously transferred to Owen Glendower [q. v.] His baptism was put off on the expectation of the arrival of John Swaffham, bishop of Bangor, who had been asked to be his godfather, but took place on 18 Nov., despite the bishop's absence, the Abbots of Evesham and Wigmore and the Lady Audley acting as his sponsors. Next day, however, the bishop arrived and administered to him the rite of confirmation (*Monasticon*, vi. 354). His father died when he was only five years old, but left him well provided for, bequeathing him land of the yearly value of three hundred marks (NICHOLS, *Royal Wills*, p. 113). On the death of his eldest brother, Roger Mortimer VI, fourth earl of March [q. v.], on 15 Aug. 1398, Edmund became, by reason of the minority of his nephew, Edmund Mortimer IV [q. v.], the most prominent representative of the family interests in the Welsh marches. When Henry of Lancaster passed through the marches on his way to his final triumph over Richard II, in North Wales, Mortimer at once adhered to his rising fortunes, and on 2 Aug. 1399 went with the Bishop of Hereford to make his submission to Henry at Hereford (MONK OF EVESHAM, p. 153). This may account for his not being involved in the suspicions which Richard II's patronage of the Mortimer claims to the succession might reasonably have excited. He resided on his estates, and when the revolt of Owen Glendower [q. v.] broke out was closely associated with his brother-in-law, Henry Percy [q. v.], the famous Hotspur, in the measures taken for putting down the Welsh rebel. At last, in June 1402, Glendower made a vigorous attack on Melenydd, a Welsh marchland district, including much of the modern Radnorshire, an ancient possession of the house of Mortimer. He took up a position on a hill called Bryngdas, between Pilleth and Knighton, not very far from Ludlow ('juxta Pylale' MONK OF EVESHAM, p. 178; 'Knighton' ADAM OF USK, p. 75; *Monasticon*, vi. 354). Edmund Mortimer was at the time at 'his own town' of Ludlow, and at once raised the men of Herefordshire and marched against Glendower (DUGDALE, *Baronage*, i. 151, here confuses Edmund with his nephew the Earl of March). His Welsh tenants of Melenydd obeyed his summons and joined his forces. On 22 June Mortimer attacked Glendower on his hill. He gallantly climbed up the mountain-side, but his Welsh followers, no doubt from sympathy with Glendower, ran away after a poor show of resistance, while some of the Welsh archers actually turned their weapons against Mortimer and his faithful adherents (*Ann. Hen. IV*, p. 341). The English fought better, but after losing largely, two hundred men (MONK OF EVESHAM, pp. 178, 1100; *Ann. Hen. IV*, p. 341), the victory declared against them, and Edmund, with many others, fell into the hands of Owen. This disaster was looked upon as fulfilling the grim portent that had attended his birth.

Owen took his captive to the 'mountains and caves of Snowdon,' but he treated him not only kindly but considerately, hoping to get political profit from his prisoner, and professing to regard him as a possible future king of England. But his powerful kinsfolk, foremost among whom were the Percies, busied themselves about procuring his ransom. But sinister rumours were abroad that Mortimer had himself sought the captivity into which he had fallen (*Ann. Hen. IV*, p. 341), and Henry now forbade the Percies to seek for their kinsman's liberation (*Cont. Eulog. Hist.* iii. 396; HARDYNG, pp. 360–1, ed. 1812). On 19 Oct. the king took the decisive step of seizing Mortimer's plate and jewels and taking them to the treasury (DEVON, *Issues of the Exchequer*, p. 295). Mortimer's fidelity, already perhaps wavering, was altogether shaken by the king's vigorous action. The weariness of captivity, or fear of death, or some more recondite and unknown cause (*Ann. Hen. IV*. p. 349), now led him to make common cause with his captor. About 30 Nov. (MONK OF EVESHAM, p. 182) he married Glendower's daughter, with great pomp and solemnity (*ib.* p. 182; *Ann. Hen. IV*, p. 349: 'Nuptias satis humiles et suæ generositati impares,' cf. ADAM OF USK, p. 75). Early in December Mortimer was back in Melenydd as the ally of Owen, and on 13 Dec. he issued a circular to 'all the gentles and commons of Radnor and Presteign,' in which he declared that he had joined Owen in his efforts either to restore the crown to King Richard, should the king prove to be still alive, or should Richard be dead, to confer the throne on his honoured nephew (the Earl of March), 'who is the right heir to the said Crown' (ELLIS, *Original Letters*, 2nd ser. i. 24–6). Most of the Mortimer lands in Wales, Melenydd, Gwrthrenion, Rhaiadr, Cwmteuddwr, Arwystli, Cyveiliog, and Caereineon were already in his hands.

The revolt of the Percies rapidly followed these transactions, but not even the defeat at

Shrewsbury affected the position of Glendower and his English ally. The famous treaty of partition, which was perhaps signed in the house of the Archdeacon of Bangor on 28 Feb. 1405, was the work of Owen and his son-in-law (*ib.* II. i. 27–8). In the threefold division of the kingdom which it proposed, Mortimer (his nephew's claims are now put on one side) was to have the whole of the south of England, though an engagement in which he resigned the marchland districts, in which his family was supreme, to Owen clearly bore the marks of coercion. But the whole question of the triple partition is a difficult and doubtful one. It plainly stands in close connection with the attempted abduction of the Earl of March in the same month and Northumberland's second rising (RAMSAY, *Lancaster and York*, i. 86). But the failure of the general English attacks on Henry gradually reduced Glendower's revolt to its original character of a native Welsh rising against the English, and, from this point of view, Mortimer's help was much less necessary to him than from the standpoint of a general Ricardian attack on Henry of Lancaster. Mortimer therefore gradually sank into the background. After 1404 his father-in-law's cause began to lose ground, and Mortimer himself was soon reduced to great distress. He was finally besieged in Harlech Castle by the now victorious English, and perished miserably during the siege (ADAM OF USK, p. 75). This was probably in the summer of 1409 (TYLER, *Henry V*, i. 230). Some of his strange adventures were commemorated in songs (ADAM OF USK, p. 75). By Owen's daughter Mortimer had one son, named Lionel, and three daughters. She, with her family, was already in the hands of Henry V in June 1413, perhaps since the capture of Harlech, being kept in custody within the city of London (DEVON, *Issue Rolls of Exchequer*, p. 321; TYLER, *Henry V*, i. 245). But before the end of the same year Lady Mortimer and her daughters were dead. They were buried at the expense of one pound within the church of St. Swithin's, London (DEVON, p. 327).

[Ann. Hen. IV, apud Trokelowe (Rolls Ser.); Chron. Angl. ed. Giles; Monk of Evesham, ed. Hearne; Adam of Usk, ed. Thompson; Dugdale's Monasticon, vi. 355; Ellis's Original Letters, 2nd ser. vol. i.; Rymer's Fœdera; Ramsay's Lancaster and York; Wylie's Henry IV.] T. F. T.

MORTIMER, EDMUND (IV) DE, fifth EARL OF MARCH and third EARL ULSTER (1391–1425), son of Roger de Mortimer (VI), fourth earl of March and Ulster [q. v.], and his wife Eleanor Holland, was born in the New Forest on 6 Nov. 1391 (*Monasticon*, vi. 355). In his seventh year he succeeded, by the untimely death of his father in Ireland, to the titles and estates of the Mortimers. As Richard II had already recognised his father as heir-presumptive to the throne, the young earl himself was now looked upon by Richard's partisans as their future king. Next year (1399), however, the Lancastrian revolution and the fall of Richard entirely changed Edmund's position and prospects. He was now put under guard at Windsor on the pretext that he was the king's ward. His younger brother Roger also shared his captivity. The first parliament of Henry IV, by recognising the new king's son as heir-apparent, excluded March from all prospects of the throne. But though careful to prevent the enemies of Lancaster getting hold of his person, Henry showed proper regard both for the honour and interests of his ward. In 1401 March was recognised as a coheir of his great-aunt Philippa, countess of Pembroke, and in 1409 as one of the coheirs of his uncle Edmund Holland, earl of Kent (DUGDALE, *Baronage*, i. 151). He remained in the king's custody (ADAM OF USK, p. 61). On 5 July 1402 he was put under the care of Sir Hugh Waterton at Berkhampstead Castle, along with the king's children, John and Philippa, and his own brother, Roger (*Fœdera*, viii. 268). The fact that his aunt was the wife of Hotspur was in itself sufficient to secure for him honourable treatment during Henry IV's early years.

But the constant revolts of the Ricardian partisans, the defection of the Percies, and, above all, the association of his uncle, Sir Edmund Mortimer [q. v.], with Owen Glendower, made the safe custody of the Ricardian pretender essential to the security of the Lancastrian dynasty, especially after it became an avowed object of Glendower and his English associates to make the Earl of March king of England. Early in 1405 March and his brother were at Windsor, when on the early morning of 13 Feb. a bold attempt was made to carry them off to join Glendower and their uncle in Wales. A blacksmith was bribed to make false keys (WALSINGHAM, *Ypodigma Neustriæ*, p. 412), and the children were successfully removed from the castle. They were, however, very soon recaptured, and Lady le Despenser, the daughter of Edmund of Langley, and the mistress of Edmund, earl of Kent, uncle of the two boys, was on 17 Feb. brought before the council charged with the offence (*Ann. Hen. IV*, p. 398; cf. RAMSAY, *Lancaster and York*, i. 83–4). The question of the safe custody of the young Mortimers was brought before the council and measures taken that they should be henceforth guarded with even greater strictness, especially during the absence of the king (*Ord. Privy Council*, ii. 106, ed. Nicolas). In 1406 they were put under the charge of Richard de Grey (*Rolls of Parl.* iii. 590). In 1409 the custody of the earl (his brother Roger died about this time) was confided to Henry, prince of Wales, afterwards Henry V (TYLER, *Henry V*, i. 236-7; *Monasticon*, vi. 355). March still remained under restraint until Henry IV's death in 1413. At the time of the coronation of Henry V, revolts in favour of the Mortimer claims to the throne were still expected (*Religieux de Saint-Denys*, iv. 770, in 'Documents Inédits'). Nevertheless, Henry V felt his position so assured that he released March from confinement and restored him to his estates (*Lords' Report on the Dignity of a Peer*, v. 170). In the next parliament March performed homage and took his seat. The day before Henry's coronation he had been made a knight of the Bath (DOYLE).

March repaid Henry's generosity by fidelity that withstood the severest temptations. His friends urged him to claim his rights, and his confessors imposed penances upon him for his negligence in asserting them (ELLIS, *Original Letters*, 2nd ser. i. 44–9; NICOLAS, *Battle of Agincourt*, App. pp. 19–20). At last, in 1415, Richard, earl of Cambridge [q. v.], who had married Mortimer's sister Anne, formed a plot to take him to Wales and have him proclaimed king there (*ib.* p. 19). March's own relations to the plot are not easy to determine. It is clear that he was sounded carefully, and the confessions of the conspirators represent that he had entered to a considerable extent into their plans (ELLIS, *Original Letters*, 2nd. ser. i. 45, 'by his owne assent;' *Deputy-Keeper's Forty-Third Report*, pp. 582–94). It seems at least certain that a dependent of his, named Lucy, who acted as a go-between, was implicated. But March's own account was that he refused to join the conspirators. Anyhow, he divulged all that he knew to the king, whether under pressure or spontaneously is not quite clear (*Gesta Hen. V*, Engl. Hist. Soc.; MONSTRELET, ii. 81, ed. Douët d'Arcq). Henry fully accepted March's protestations, and continued to regard him with high favour, putting him on the commission which on 5 Aug. condemned Cambridge to immediate execution (*Rot. Parl.* iv. 64–6). Immediately afterwards March accompanied Henry V on his first invasion of France, appearing with a following of sixty men-at-arms and 160 horse archers (NICOLAS, p. 373). During the siege of Harfleur March suffered severely from the prevailing epidemic of dysentery (WALSINGHAM, *Hist. Angl.* ii. 309; CAPGRAVE, *Chron.* p. 311), and was allowed to return home, though he is often said to have been one of those present at Agincourt. In 1416 March again saw service, being appointed on 15 Aug. as one of the king's captains at sea over the expedition sent to relieve Harfleur, under the command of John, duke of Bedford, and Sir Walter Hungerford. He served again in 1417 and 1418 in the army which invaded and conquered Normandy. He was at the head of ninety-three lances and 302 archers (App. to *Gesta Hen. V*, p. 266). In the spring of 1418 he made an attack on the Côtentin, and besieged Saint-Lô, and was later joined by Gloucester, who took the town (*Chron. Norm.* in *Gesta. Hen. V*, pp. 231–2). After the capture of Cherbourg had completed the conquest of the Cotentin, March rejoined Henry V at Rouen at the end of November (*ib.* p. 241). On 12 June 1418 he was appointed at Louviers lieutenant in the marches of Normandy (DOYLE, ii. 470), and in October 1418 lieutenant of the baillages of Caen and Coutances. On 27 Aug. 1419 he was further nominated as captain of Mantes (*ib.*; cf. App. to *Gesta Hen. V*, p. 277). In July 1420 March was at the siege of Melun (*ib.* p. 144). He remained with Henry in France, until in February 1421 he returned with the king and his new wife, Catharine of France, to London, travelling from Rouen by way of Amiens and Calais (*Chron. Norm.* apud *Gesta Hen. V*, p. 257). On 21 Feb. he bore the first sceptre at the coronation of the queen at Westminster. In June 1421 March accompanied Henry on his third and last expedition to France. He took part in the siege of Meaux in January 1422, lodging at the house of the Cordeliers (*ib.* pp. 260–79). After Henry's death he returned to England and was nominated a member of the council of regency established on 9 Dec. 1422, and on 9 May 1423 was appointed, as his father and grandfather had been, lieutenant of Ireland, with power, however, to select a deputy (*Fœdera*, x. 282). That power he at once exercised in favour of Edward Dantsey, bishop of Meath, and remained in England. But troubles now beset him. His cousin (GRAFTON) or illegitimate uncle (SANDFORD), Sir John Mortimer, who had been arrested in 1421 as a suspected traitor, had escaped in 1422, but being recaptured in 1424 was attainted and executed. Even before this Humphrey, duke of Gloucester [q. v.], the protector, had become jealous of March for his keeping open house, and had violently quarrelled with him (*Chron.* ed. Giles, p. 6). The result was that March was now sent out of the way to Ireland. On

14 Feb. 1424 shipping was ordered for his journey. It was high time he went, for many of the Irish lords were questioning the authority of his deputy, and the chronic confusion there was getting worse than ever. So far back as 1407 great loss had been inflicted on his Irish estates by the invasion of Ulster by the Earl of Orkney (Adam of Usk, p. 61). After his arrival March busied himself in negotiating with the native septs, who held nearly all his nominal earldom of Ulster; but on 19 Jan. 1425 he was cut off suddenly by the plague.

By his wife Anne, daughter of Edmund de Stafford, earl of Stafford, Edmund left no family, and as his brother Roger had predeceased him, the male line of the earls of March became extinct, while the Mortimer estates went to Richard, duke of York, son of Richard of Cambridge and Anne Mortimer, who was now recognised as Earl of March and Ulster (*Rot. Parl.* iv. 397). Dugdale (*Baronage*, i. 151–2) gives a list of the places of which March was seized at the time of his death. His widow, who had some difficulty in getting her dower from Humphrey of Gloucester, the guardian of the Mortimer estates, married, before 1427, John Holland, earl of Huntingdon (afterwards duke of Exeter), and died a few years later. At her request John Lydgate [q. v.] wrote his 'Life of St. Margaret.'

The friendly Wigmore chronicler describes Edmund as 'severe in his morals, composed in his acts, circumspect in his talk, and wise and cautious during the days of his adversity. He was surnamed "the Good," by reason of his exceeding kindness' (*Monasticon*, vi. 355). A poem attributed to Lydgate describes him as 'gracious in all degree' (Nicolas, *Agincourt*, p. 306).

March was the founder of a college of secular canons at Stoke-by-Clare in Suffolk. In that village there had long been a small Benedictine priory, which was a cell of Bec in Normandy. Richard II had freed the house from the rule of Bec by making it 'indigenous.' But though thus technically saved, it seemed likely to be involved in the common destruction now impending on all the 'alien priories.' March got permission from Pope John XXII, in a bull dated 16 Nov. 1414, to 'secularize' the foundation. The royal assent was also given. In 1421 March augmented its revenues, and in 1423 drew up statutes for it. In its final form the college was for a dean and six prebendaries (*Monasticon*, vi. 1415–1423). A charter of March to his Welsh follower Maredudd ap Adda Moel is printed in the 'Montgomeryshire Collections,' x. 59–60, of the Powysland Club.

[Dugdale's Monasticon, vi. 355; Dugdale's Baronage, i. 150–2; Doyle's Official Baronage, i. 470; Nicolas's Battle of Agincourt; Rymer's Fœdera; Adam of Usk, ed. Thompson; Annales Henrici IV, apud Trokelowe, Rolls Ser.; Monk of Evesham, ed. Hearne; Gesta Henrici V, ed. Williams, Engl. Hist. Soc.; Ellis's Original Letters, 2nd ser. vol. i.; Ramsay's Lancaster and York, vol. i.; Wylie's Henry IV.; Stubbs's Const. Hist. vol. iii.; Gilbert's Viceroys of Ireland, pp. 319–20; Tyler's Henry V.] T. F. T.

MORTIMER, Mrs. FAVELL LEE (1802–1878), authoress, second daughter of David Bevan, of the banking firm of Barclay, Bevan, & Co., born in London in 1802, was religiously educated, and in 1827 passed through the experience of conversion. She at once threw herself with great zeal into educational work, founding parish schools on her father's estates, and taking an active and intelligent part in their management. Through her brother she made the acquaintance of his schoolfellow and college friend, Henry Edward Manning [q. v.], with whom she corresponded on religious topics, and on whom she exercised for a time a considerable influence. In after years at his instance she returned his letters, while she allowed her own to remain in his hands. In 1841 she married Thomas Mortimer, minister of the Episcopal Chapel, Gray's Inn Road, after whose death in 1850 she devoted herself to the care of the destitute and the afflicted. She died on 22 Aug. 1878, and was buried in the churchyard, Upper Sheringham, Norfolk.

She is best known as the author of educational works for the young. Of these the most popular, 'The Peep of Day, or a Series of the Earliest Religious Instruction the Infant Mind is capable of receiving,' was first published in 1836, and it has passed through a multitude of later editions, having been translated into French and several barbarous dialects. It was followed by little manuals of a similar kind, viz. 'Line upon Line,' London, 1837, 12mo; 'More about Jesus,' London, 1839, 12mo; 'Lines left out,' London, 1862, 12mo; 'Precept upon Precept,' London, 1867, 16mo, 2nd edit. 1869. Hardly less deservedly popular were Mrs. Mortimer's manuals of elementary secular instruction, viz. 'Near Home, or the Countries of Europe described,' London, 1849, 8vo; 'Far off, or Asia and Australia described,' London, 1852–1854, 16mo, latest edit. 1890, 8vo; 'Reading without Tears,' London, 1857, 12mo; 'Reading Disentangled,' London, 1862, 16mo; 'Latin without Tears, or One Word a Day,' London, 1877, 8vo.

Mrs. Mortimer also published the following miscellanea: 1. 'The History of a Young

Jew, or of Alfred Moritz Myers,' Chester, 1840, 12mo. 2. 'The History of Job,' London, 1841, 18mo. 3. 'The English Mother,' 3rd edit. 1849, 18mo. 4. 'The Night of Toil,' 4th edit. 1853, 12mo. 5. 'The Angel's Message, or the Saviour made known to the Cottager,' London, 1857, 12mo. 6. 'Light in the Dwelling, or a Harmony of the Four Gospels,' London, 1858, 8vo. 7. 'Streaks of Light, or Fifty-two Tracts from the Bible for the Fifty-two Sundays of the Year,' London, 1861, 8vo, last edit. 1890. 8. 'The Apostles preaching to Jews and Gentiles,' London, 1873, 18mo, new edit. 1875. 9. 'The Captivity of Judah,' London, 1875, 18mo, new edit. 1870.

[The Family Friend, 1878, p. 183; Reminiscences, by Lord Forester, in the Times, 20 Jan. 1892; private information; Supplement to Allibone's Dict.; Brit. Mus. Cat.] J. M. R.

MORTIMER, GEORGE FERRIS WHIDBORNE (1805–1871), schoolmaster and divine, born on 22 July 1805 at Bishopsteignton in Devonshire, was the eldest son of William Mortimer, a country gentleman of that place. He was educated at the Exeter grammar school and at Balliol College, Oxford, where he matriculated 18 March 1823, and obtained an exhibition. Thence he migrated to Queen's, where he secured a Michel exhibition, and was placed in the first class of the final classical school at Michaelmas 1826 with the present archdeacon of Taunton, George Anthony Denison, and another. After graduating B.A. in 1826 he engaged actively in tuition. He proceeded M.A. in 1829, and D.D. in 1841, having been ordained on 24 Feb. 1829. He was successively head-master of the Newcastle grammar school (1828) and of the Western proprietary school at Brompton, London (1833). In 1840 he was appointed, in succession to John Allen Giles [q. v.], to the scene of his longest and most important labours, the headship of the City of London School. The school had been opened in 1837 [see under Carpenter, John, 1370?–1441?], but its prosperity had been injured by the action of the first head-master. Mortimer's administrative ability and genial manner rendered the success of the school certain. He treated with conspicuous honesty and fairness the large proportion of boys, not members of the church of England, who from various causes were found there. In 1861 he had the unique distinction of seeing two of his scholars respectively senior wrangler and senior classic at Cambridge. Charles Kingsley read privately with him for ordination. Dr. Mortimer received in 1864 the honorary prebend of Consumpta per mare in St. Paul's, and for many years was evening lecturer at St. Matthew's, Friday Street. At Michaelmas 1865 he resigned his head-mastership, and for the next few years interested himself actively in the Society of Schoolmasters and other educational institutions. He died 7 Sept. 1871, at Rose Hill, Hampton Wick, and was buried in Hampton churchyard. He married in 1830 Jane, daughter of Alexander Gordon of Bishopsteignton; and by this lady, who died in 1901, he left a numerous family.

Besides two sermons, Mortimer published while at Newcastle a pamphlet entitled 'The Immediate Abolition of Slavery compatible with the Safety and Prosperity of the Colonies' (1833, 8vo).

[Information from the family; personal knowledge.] J. H. L.

MORTIMER, HUGH (I) de (*d.* 1181), lord of Wigmore and founder of Wigmore Priory, was, according to the common accounts, the son of Ralph I de Mortimer [q. v.], and in any case his father's name was Ralph (*Brut y Tywysogion*, ed. Evans, p. 312). The only direct authority that makes him the son of the Domesday baron seems, however, to be the late and half-mythical history of Wigmore Priory, printed in the 'Monasticon,' vi. 348 sq., which, besides many statements directly at variance with known facts, gives an altogether fabulous account of Hugh's marriage, maintaining that his father, in his lifetime, fetched for him as his wife, from Normandy, 'Matilda Longespey, filiam Willelmi Longespey ducis Normanniæ,' who died in 942! It is hard to dogmatise when there is so little direct evidence, and Mr. Eyton and other good modern authorities accept the statement of the Wigmore annalist; but it seems more likely that a generation has been omitted, and that Hugh was really grandson of Ralph I de Mortimer, than that the latter begot in extreme old age a son, who succeeded without question to the paternal estates (*Shropshire*, iv. 200–1).

The troubled reign of Stephen gave ample opportunities to a great baron who was powerful, ambitious, and capable to extend his power. Hugh took little part in general politics, and it is uncertain whether he was a partisan of Stephen or Matilda. His main object was to strengthen his local position as the chief potentate of the middle marches of Wales. Stephen from the first recognised his power. The patent by which the king strove to create Robert de Beaumont earl of Hereford in 1140 especially reserved the rights of Hugh, who seems to have had exceptional franchises and wide jurisdiction within his barony (Duncumb, *Herefordshire*, i. 232; Eyton, *Shropshire*, iv. 201; cf., however, art. Beaumont, Robert de, 1104–1168). A few years later there were severe feuds between Hugh and Miles, earl of Hereford, a foremost enemy of Stephen, and Hugh continued the quarrel with Miles's son Roger. Nor was this Mortimer's only local feud. He carried on a fierce warfare with Joce de Dinant, lord of Ludlow, a partisan of the Lacys, who had formerly held that town and castle. He blockaded Ludlow so straightly that Joce was unable to move in or out of his abode. Despairing of prevailing by strength, Joce had recourse to treachery. He laid an ambush, which waylaid and captured Mortimer as he was travelling alone. For some time Mortimer was kept in prison, and only obtained his release by the payment of an extortionate ransom (*Monasticon*, vi. 346). A tower in Ludlow Castle, now called Mortimer's Tower, is sometimes said to be the place of Hugh's imprisonment; but being in the Gothic style, it must be two generations later in date (Clark, *Mediæval Military Architecture*, ii. 275). In 1144 Hugh repaired the castle of Cemaron, and conquered Melenydd a second time (*Brut y Tywysogion*, p. 312, s.a. 1143). In 1144 or 1145 he captured and imprisoned the Welsh prince Rhys ab Howel, whom in 1148 he blinded in his prison (*Annales Cambriæ*, pp. 43–4; cf. *Brut y Tywysogion*, p. 312). Next year (1146) he slew another chieftain, Maredudd ab Howel (*Annales Cambriæ*, p. 43). He ruled Melenydd for the rest of his life (*Monasticon*, vi. 349), and built several strong castles therein. Moreover, he took advantage of the king's weakness to get possession of the royal castle of Bridgnorth, which thereupon became, with Cleobury and Wigmore, the chief centre of his power.

The accession of Henry II put an end to the overweening power of Mortimer, but he would not resign his castles and authority without a last desperate effort to hold his own. He made common cause with his rival and neighbour, Earl Roger of Hereford, and fortified his own castles of Cleobury and Wigmore, along with the royal stronghold of Bridgnorth, thus proposing to shut the king out of a royal castle. Earl Roger soon deserted him, and submitted to Henry on 13 March (Gervase of Canterbury, *Opera Historica*, i. 162). But Hugh resolved singlehanded to carry on his resistance. Henry's delay, through the important business which detained him most of April at his Easter court of Wallingford, gave Hugh plenty of time. On Henry marching westwards the three castles were all ready for defence. The king thereupon divided his army into three divisions, and directed each section to undertake, simultaneously, the siege of one of Mortimer's strongholds. In May 1155 Henry himself besieged Bridgnorth, and a great gathering of magnates, the whole military force of England, was mustered under its walls. Cleobury was easily captured and destroyed (Robert of Torigny in Howlett, *Chronicles of Stephen, Henry II, and Richard I*, iv. 184, Rolls Ser.) But Bridgnorth and Wigmore held out longer, and it was not until 7 July that Mortimer, driven to despair, was forced to make his submission to the king and surrender the two castles (*ib.* iv. 185; cf., however, William of Newburgh, ed. Howlett, i. 105, which says that Bridgnorth was taken after a few days). Hugh was too strong to be dealt with severely. While surrendering Bridgnorth, he was allowed to retain possession of his own two castles. Mr. Eyton (*Shropshire*, iv. 203–4) quotes evidence to show that the special immunities which Mortimer had inherited with his Shropshire barony were still continued under him and his successors. He owed no military service. He never, save on one occasion in each case, contributed towards aids and scutages, while his land was omitted in the general list of knights' fees contained in the Black Book of the Exchequer. But, however great his power continued as a landlord, Hugh ceased for the future to play any great part in English politics. His further proceedings can only be traced by a few entries in the Pipe Rolls, from which he appears to have been very slow in paying his debts to the exchequer.

The great work of piety enjoined upon Hugh by Ralph Mortimer gave increasing occupation for his declining years. A French history of the foundation of Wigmore Priory, printed in the 'Monasticon,' vi. 344–8, supplies a minute and circumstantial account of the steps taken by Hugh to carry out his predecessor's wishes, and seems to be more trustworthy than the Latin annals of the foundation printed in the same collection, which have so often led astray the biographers of the Mortimers. Oliver de Merlimond, Hugh's steward, had built a church on his own estate at Shobden, and invited three canons of Saint-Victor at Paris to occupy it; but soon afterwards he attached himself to his master's foe, Earl Miles of Hereford. Mortimer was induced by Robert of Bethune, bishop of Hereford, not only to spare Oliver's church at Shobden, but to promise to confer on its canons the three prebends in Wigmore Church which Ralph Mortimer had established. Mortimer proved long unmindful of his promise, but at length transferred the foundation to a superior site called Eye, near the river Lug, whence he again removed it to Wigmore town. Thenceforth it was known as Wigmore Priory. But the brethren complained that their new abode was inconvenient, and Mortimer offered them a free choice of any of his lands. They ultimately found a fitting site about a mile from Wigmore, and Hugh, returning from the continent, visited their humble abode and laid the foundation-stone of their church. As he grew older he made fresh grants of lands and advowsons to the canons. The church was at last consecrated by Robert Foliot, bishop of Hereford after 1174, and dedicated to St. James. This event is dated by the inaccurate family annalist in 1179. A few years later Hugh died at Cleobury, 'full of good works.' On his deathbed he was admitted as a canon professed, and received the canonical habit from the Abbot Randolph. He was buried in Wigmore Abbey before the high altar. The date of his death is given by the Wigmore annalist as 26 Feb. 1185 (*Monasticon*, vi. 349; cf. 'Ann. Wigorn.' in *Ann. Monastici*, iv. 385). But the fact that Hugh's son Roger was answerable at the exchequer for his father's debts in 1181 suggests that year as the real date (Eyton, *Shropshire*, iv. 204–205). The misdeeds of his son Roger against the Welsh, and especially his murder of the South Welsh prince, Cadwallon, which were visited on Roger by two years' imprisonment, seem to have involved the old baron in the king's displeasure, and at the time of his death his estates were in the king's hands.

Hugh Mortimer is described by Robert of Torigny as a man of extreme arrogance and presumption (Howlett, iv. 184); and William of Newburgh says that his pride and wrath were greater than his endurance (*ib.* i. 105). Giraldus Cambrensis, who speaks of him as an excellent knight, holds him up as a terrible example for his signal failure in 1155 ('De Princ. Instruct.' in *Opera*, viii. 215, Rolls Ser.) The French historian of the foundation of Wigmore Abbey is more detailed and complimentary. Hugh was of 'lofty stature, valiant in arms, and very noble in speech. If the deeds that he had wrought in England, Wales, and elsewhere were put in writing, they would amount to a great volume' (*Monasticon*, vi. 344).

The name of Hugh's wife was apparently Matilda la Meschine (*Journal of British Archæological Assoc.* xxiv. 29). His sons were Roger I, his successor, Hugh, lord of Chelmarsh, Robert, founder of the Richard's Castle branch of the Mortimers, and Philip. Roger Mortimer I married Isabella de Ferrers, lost his Norman estates in 1204, and died on 24 June 1214. He was the father of Hugh Mortimer II of Wigmore, who died in 1227 without issue, and of Ralph Mortimer II, who married Gwladys Ddu (the dark), the daughter of Llywelyn ab Iorwerth, prince of Wales [q. v.], and was father of Roger Mortimer II (*d.* 1282) [q. v.]

[Dugdale's Monasticon, vi. 344–9; Dugdale's Baronage, i. 138–9; Eyton's Shropshire, especially iv. 200–6; Eyton's Itinerary of Henry II, pp. 10, 11, 228; Stapleton's Rotuli Normanniæ; Duncumb's Herefordshire; Wright's Hist. of Ludlow; Brut y Tywysogion, ed. Rhys and Evans, and in Rolls Ser.; Annales Cambriæ (Rolls Ser.); Howlett's Chron. of Stephen, Henry II, and Richard I (Rolls Ser.); Annales Monastici (Rolls Ser.); Pipe Rolls of Henry II (Pipe Roll Soc.)]

T. F. T.

MORTIMER, JOHN (1656?–1736), writer on agriculture, only son and heir of Mark Mortimer, of the old Somerset family of that name, by his wife Abigail Walmesly, of Blackmore in Essex, was born in London about 1656. He received a commercial education, and became a prosperous merchant on Tower Hill. In November 1693 he bought the estate of Toppingo Hall, Hatfield Peverel, Essex, which he greatly improved; a number of fine cedar trees planted by him on the estate are still in existence. Mortimer was thrice married. His first wife, Dorothy, born at Hursley, near Winchester, on 1 Aug. 1660, was the ninth child of Richard Cromwell, and it is supposed that the ex-protector's return to England in 1680 was prompted by a desire to be present at the wedding. She died in childbirth (14 May 1681) within a year of the marriage. He married, secondly, Sarah, daughter of Sir John Tippets, knight, surveyor of the navy, by whom he had a son and a daughter; and thirdly, Elizabeth, daughter of Samuel Sanders of Derbyshire, by whom he had four sons and two daughters. The second son by his third wife was Dr. Cromwell Mortimer [q. v.]

Mortimer's claim to remembrance is based upon his work entitled 'The whole Art of Husbandry, in the way of Managing and Improving of Land' (London, 1707, 8vo), which forms a landmark in English agricultural literature, and largely influenced husbandry in the 19th century. The writer states that he had read the best books on ancient and modern agriculture, and inspected the practice of the most diligent husbandmen in most countries. After duly digesting these he had added his own experiences. The book, which treats not only of the usual branches of agriculture, but also of fish-ponds, orchards, and of the culture of silkworms, and the making of cider, is justly said by Donaldson to 'form a very large advancement in the progress of agriculture from the preceding authors on the subject. Trees and fruits do still occupy too much room, but the animals are more largely introduced and systematically treated.' The work was dedicated to the Royal Society, of which Mortimer had been admitted a member in December 1705 (THOMSON, *Royal Society*, App. p. xxxi). A second edition was issued in 1708, and a third in 1712, 'containing such additions as are proper for the husbandman and gardiner (*sic*) . . . to which is added a Kalendar, shewing what is to be done every month in the flower garden.' It was translated into Swedish by Serenius in 1727, and a sixth edition, with additions, and revised by Thomas Mortimer [q. v.], the writer's grandson, appeared in 2 vols. 8vo, 1761.

Mortimer also wrote 'Some Considerations concerning the present State of Religion, with some Essays towards our Love and Union,' London, 1702, a severe indictment of sectarian animosities, and a sensible pamphlet, 'Advice to Parents, or Rules for the Education of Children,' London, 1704.

[Donaldson's Agricultural Biography, p. 41 (containing an abstract of the contents of the Art of Husbandry); Waylen's House of Cromwell, 1891, p. 21; Morant's Essex, ii. 133; Wright's Essex, ii. 743; Stukeley's Diaries and Letters (Surtees Soc.), i. 233 *n.*; Watt's Bibl. Brit. p. 687; Brit. Mus. Cat.] T. S.

MORTIMER, JOHN HAMILTON (1741–1779), historical painter, was born in 1741 at Eastbourne, where his father owned a mill, and was some time collector of customs. His uncle was a painter of some ability, and the boy, showing a disposition towards art, was sent to London and placed under Thomas Hudson [q. v.], the master of Sir Joshua Reynolds, and Joseph Wright (of Derby). The latter was his fellow-pupil and friend in after life. Mortimer studied at the Duke of Richmond's sculpture gallery, at the Academy in St. Martin's Lane, and also under Cipriani, Robert Edge Pine [q. v.], and Reynolds. His youthful drawings showed much ability, and he carried off the first prize of the Society of Arts for a drawing from the antique in 1763, and in the following year, in competition with Romney, the premium of one hundred guineas for the best historical picture, the subject being 'St. Paul converting the Britons.' This picture was in 1770 presented by Dr. Bates to the church of High Wycombe in Buckinghamshire. He became a member of the Incorporated Society of Arts, with whom he exhibited occasionally for ten years ending 1773, when he was elected vice-president. He resided in the neighbourhood of Covent Garden, and for many years was noted for the freedom and extravagance of his life. He was fond of company and sports, and vain of his personal attractions. He is said to have shattered his health by his excesses. In 1775 he married Jane Hurrell, a farmer's daughter. He now became a reformed character, and retired to Aylesbury, where he painted a series called 'The Progress of Vice,' which was well received, but a subsequent series called 'The Progress of Virtue' was less successful. In 1778 he exhibited for the first time at the Royal Academy, contributing a small whole-length family group, a subject from Spenser, and some landscapes. He was elected an associate in November of the same year, when he also returned to London, taking up his residence in Norfolk Street, Strand. By special grant of George III he was created a royal academician, but before he could receive his diploma he was taken ill of fever, and, after an illness of twelve days, died 4 Feb. 1779. He was buried at High Wycombe, where his picture of the 'Conversion of the Britons' still exists, though it has been removed from the church to the town-hall, and has undergone restoration by H. Lovegrove.

Nine of Mortimer's works were exhibited at the Royal Academy in 1799 after his death, in accordance with his wishes. They comprised 'The Battle of Agincourt,' 'Vortigern and Rowena,' a small landscape, and some washed drawings. In the South Kensington Museum there is a picture by Mortimer of 'Hercules slaying the Hydra,' as well as two water-colours, but his pictures are now rarely met with, and he is best known by his etchings, which are executed in a bold, free style, and show a preference for subjects of terror and wild romance. They are picturesque and spirited, but have a strong tendency to the extravagant and theatrical. Some of them are studies of figures of banditti, &c., after Salvator Rosa and others, but the majority are original, and include twelve plates of characters from Shakespeare, and 'Nature and Genius introducing Garrick into the Temple of Shakespeare.' Among his other works may be mentioned a ceiling in Brocket Hall, Hertfordshire, executed for Lord Melbourne, the design of 'The Elevation of the Brazen Serpent' for the great window in Salisbury Cathedral, and some stained glass at Brasenose College, Oxford. He also designed some illustrations for 'Bell's Theatre' and 'Bell's Poets.'

Some of his best designs were etched by Blyth. His picture of 'The Battle of Agincourt' was engraved by W. W. Ryland, and his own portrait of himself was mezzotinted by Valentine Green, and etched by R. Blyth. The latter is now in the National Portrait Gallery. In the diploma gallery of the Royal Academy is a portrait of Mortimer by Richard Wilson.

[Redgrave's Dict.; Redgraves' Century of Painters; Bryan's Dict. ed. Graves and Armstrong; Algernon Graves's Dict.; Wine and Walnuts; Bemrose's Life of Wright of Derby; Notes and Queries, v. 108, &c., vi. 156, &c.; Cunningham's Lives, ed. Heaton; Pilkington's Dict.; Edwards's Anecdotes; Cunningham's Cabinet Gallery of Pictures.] C. M.

MORTIMER, RALPH (I) DE (*d.* 1104?), Norman baron, was the son of Roger de Mortimer and his wife Hawise. This Roger was also called Roger, 'filius episcopi.' His father was Hugh, afterwards bishop of Coutances; his mother was the daughter of some unknown Danish chieftain, and the sister of Gunnor, the wife of Duke Richard I of Normandy, and of Herfast the Dane, the grandfather of William FitzOsbern, earl of Hereford (Stapleton, *Rotuli Normanniæ*, II. cxix.; Eyton, *Shropshire*, iv. 195; cf. Le Prévost's note to Ordericus Vitalis, iii. 236; Planché's art. on the genealogy of the family in *Journal of British Archæological Association*, xxiv. 1–35). Roger's brother Ralph, also called 'filius episcopi,' was founder of the house of Warren. The house of Mortimer was thus connected both with the ducal Norman house and with the great family which attained later the earldom of Hereford, while its kinship with the lords of the house of Warren, earls of Surrey after the Norman conquest, was even more direct. Roger, the bishop's son, is assumed to have been born before 990, the date at which his father became bishop of Coutances, but if so he must have lived to a green old age. All the Mortimers of the period, when their history is uncertain, became, according to the traditional account, extraordinarily old men. In latter times, when the facts are well known, they lived extremely short lives. This Roger seems to have been the first to assume the name of Mortimer, which was taken from the village and castle of Mortemer-en-Brai (mortuum mare), in the Pays de Caux, situated at the source of the little river Eaulne. In 1054 he won the victory of Mortemer, fought under the walls of his castle, against the troops of Henry I, king of the French (Ordericus Vitalis, *Hist. Eccl.* i. 184, iii. 160, 236–7, ed. Le Prévost). But Roger gave offence to Duke William by releasing one of his captives, and was accordingly deprived of his castle of Mortemer, which was transferred to his nephew, William de Warren, son of his brother Ralph, and afterwards first Earl of Surrey (*ib.* iii. 237; Stapleton, ubi supra). In the result Mortemer remained with the earls of Warren until the loss of Normandy in 1204, and was never restored to the house that obtained its name from it. The Mortimers transferred their chief seat to Saint-Victor-en Caux, where the priory, a cell of Saint-Ouen at Rouen, was in 1074 erected into an abbey by Roger and his wife Hawise. This is Roger's last recorded act. He must have been too old to have been present at Hastings, but some of his sons, perhaps Hugh (Wace, *Roman de Rou*, ii. 373, 740, ed. Andresen), or possibly Ralph himself (*Monasticon*, vi. 348), appeared on his behalf.

Ralph became his father's eventual successor both in Normandy and in England. There are no particulars about the manner in which he acquired his English estates, but he seems to have served under his kinsman, William FitzOsbern, earl of Hereford, and, if the loose traditions preserved by the Wigmore annalist have any foundation, to have done good service against Edric the Wild (*ib.* vi. 349; cf. Freeman, *Norman Conquest*, iii. 737). The fact that Ralph held at the time of the Domesday inquest several estates that had once belonged to Edric may invest this statement with some authority (*Domesday*, f. 183 *b*). However this may have been, the fall of the traitorous Earl Roger, son of William FitzOsbern, in 1074, marks the first establishment of the Mortimers in a leading position in the middle marches of Wales. Many of Roger's forfeited estates in Shropshire and Herefordshire were now granted by William the Conqueror to Ralph Mortimer, including the township and the castle of Wigmore, which had been built on waste ground by William FitzOsbern (*Domesday*, f. 183 *b*), and henceforth became the chief centre of the power of the Mortimers. It was very likely at this time that the estates of Edith, wife of Edward the Confessor, including Cleobury Mortimer, near Shrewsbury, in later times the chief Shropshire residence of the Mortimers, and Stoke Edith in Herefordshire, passed from Earl Roger to Ralph (Eyton, *Shropshire*, vi. 350). Moreover, a fourteenth-century record speaks of Mortimer as the seneschal of the Earl of Shrewsbury, and as holding Cleobury by that title. Though the record is inaccurate in other particulars, Mr. Eyton (*ib.* iv. 199–200) is disposed to accept its statement respecting Mortimer's tenure of the office of seneschal. Ralph Mortimer held no less than nineteen of his fifty Shropshire manors as sub-tenant of the Earl of Shrewsbury. Besides this great western estate, he held at the time of the Domesday inquest large territories in Yorkshire, Lincolnshire, Hampshire, Wiltshire, and more scattered possessions in Worcestershire, Berkshire, Somerset, Oxfordshire, Warwickshire, and Leicestershire (Ellis, *Introduction to Domesday*, i. 455–6).

On the accession of William Rufus, Ralph, like the other border barons, joined in the great rising of April 1088, of which Roger of Montgomery, then Earl of Shrewsbury, was one of the main leaders. He was among those who attacked the city of Worcester and were repulsed through the action of Bishop Wulfstan (Flor. Wig. ii. 24). But the tide of war soon flowed from the Welsh march to Kent and Sussex, and when the Earl of Shrewsbury reconciled himself with the king, Mortimer probably followed the same course. Next year (1089), as a partisan of Rufus in Normandy, he joined with nearly all the other barons of Caux in fortifying their houses and levying troops to repel French invasion, and received for that purpose large sums of money from the king (Ord. Vit. iii. 319–20). He does not seem to have joined in the subsequent feudal rebellions, and was probably much occupied in extending his English possessions westwards, at the expense of the Welsh. The family historian makes him the conqueror of Melenydd, a Welsh lordship afterwards continually in the hands of the Mortimers (*Monasticon*, vi. 349). In 1102 the fall of Robert of Bellême [q. v.], the last Montgomery earl of Shrewsbury, by removing the mightiest of his rivals, indirectly increased Ralph's power, and fresh estates fell into his hands. In 1104 his name appears among a long list of barons who upheld the cause of Henry I in Normandy against his brother Robert (Ord. Vit. iv. 199). This is probably the last authentic reference to him, for little trust can be placed in the statement of the Wigmore annalist that in 1106 he took a conspicuous part in the battle of Tenchebrai. The same writer also puts his death on 4 Aug. 1100, six years before (*Monasticon*, vi. 349). More credence perhaps is due to the story of the same writer, that Ralph in his old age resolved on the foundation of a monastery, a scheme which, under his son Hugh, finally resulted in the foundation of Wigmore Priory. He is also said to have constituted three prebends for secular canons in the parish church of Wigmore, which finally swelled the priory endowments. A late writer, Adam of Usk (p. 21), who had special sources of knowledge, says that Ralph went back to Normandy, and died there, perhaps in 1104, leaving his son Hugh in possession of Wigmore.

Ralph's wife's name was Millicent, or Melisendis, who inherited the town of Mers, in Le Vimeu, in the diocese of Amiens. She died before her husband (Stapleton, *Rot. Norm.* ii. cxx). Ralph is generally regarded as the father of Hugh Mortimer I [q. v.] His other children were William Mortimer, lord of Chelmarsh and Sidbury, and Hawise, who married Stephen, earl of Albemarle or Aumâle, and received her mother's lands as her marriage portion.

[Ordericus Vitalis, ed. Le Prévost (Soc. de l'Histoire de France); Florence of Worcester (Engl. Hist. Soc.); Domesday Book; Dugdale's Monasticon, vi. 348–9; Dugdale's Baronage, i. 138–9; Eyton's Shropshire, especially iv. 194–200; Stapleton's Rotuli Scaccarii Normanniæ, especially ii. cxix. sq.; Stapleton in Archæological Journal, iii. 1–26; Journal of the British Archæological Association, vol. xxiv.; Wright's Hist. of Ludlow; Freeman's Norman Conquest, iv. 39, 737, v. 78, 84, 754; and William Rufus, i. 34, 231.] T. F. T.

MORTIMER, ROGER (II) de, sixth Baron of Wigmore (1231?–1282), was the eldest son of Ralph de Mortimer II, the fifth baron, and of his Welsh wife Gwladys Ddu, daughter of Llywelyn ab Iorwerth [q. v.] His parents were married in 1230 (*Worcester Annals* in *Ann. Mon.* iv. 421), and Roger was probably born in the following year. His father died on 6 Aug. 1246, and after his estates had remained in the king's hands for six months, Roger paid the heavy fine of two thousand marks, in return for which he received the livery of his lands on 26 Feb. 1247. This payment may also be regarded as a composition for the remaining rights of wardship vested in the crown, since Roger could not yet have attained his legal majority. Before the end of the same year, 1247, Roger contracted a rich marriage with Matilda de Braose, eldest daughter and coheiress of William de Braose, whom Llywelyn ab Iorwerth had hanged in 1230, on a suspicion of adultery with his wife Joan (*d.* 1237), princess of Wales [q. v.] Matilda, who must have been her husband's senior by several years, brought to Mortimer a third of the great marcher lordship of Brecon, and a share in the still greater inheritance of the Earls Marshal, which came to her through her mother. Roger thus acquired the lordship of Radnor, which, like Brecon, admirably rounded off his Welsh and marcher estates, as well as important land in South Wales, England, and Ireland (Eyton, *Shropshire*, iv. 217). 'At this point,' Mr. Eyton says very truly, 'the history of the house of Mortimer passes from the scope of a merely provincial record and becomes a feature in the annals of a nation.'

Mortimer was dubbed knight by Henry III in person, when that king was celebrating his Whitsuntide court of 1253 at Winchester (*Tewkesbury Annals* in *Ann. Mon.* i. 152). In August of the same year he accompanied the king to Gascony (Dugdale, *Baronage*, i. 141). He was much occupied during the next few years in withstanding the rising power of his kinsman, Llywelyn ab Gruffydd [q. v.], prince of Wales, who, however, in 1256 succeeded in depriving him of his Welsh lordship of Gwrthrynion (*Annales Cambriæ*, p. 91; *Brut y Tywysogion*). In January 1257 Mortimer had letters of protection while engaged in the king's service in Wales. In April 1258 King Henry promised him large financial aid to enable him to continue his struggle with Llywelyn. Next year his wife's share of the Braose estates was finally determined. On 11 June 1259 Mortimer was among the commissioners assigned to treat for peace with Llywelyn. On 25 June he joined in signing a truce for a year with the Welsh prince at Montgomery (*Fœdera*, i. 387). But on 17 July 1260 the Welsh attacked and captured Builth Castle, which Mortimer held as representative of Edward, the king's son. Edward did not altogether acquit him of blame (*ib.* i. 398; *Brut y Tywysogion*, s.a. 1259, here unduly minimises Llywelyn's success). But in August Mortimer was again appointed as negotiator of a truce with Llywelyn, though his name does not appear among the signatories of the truce signed on 22 Aug. (Eyton, *Shropshire*, iv. 217–19).

On the outbreak of the great struggle between Henry III and the barons in 1258 Mortimer at first arrayed himself on the baronial side. He was one of the twelve chosen by the barons to form with twelve nominees of the king a great council to reform the state. He was also appointed one of the permanent council of fifteen who were jointly to exercise the royal power. He was also one of the twenty-four commissioners chosen on behalf of the whole community to treat of the aid which the king required to carry on the Welsh war. Yet the occupation of Mortimer in Wales must have prevented him from taking a very active part in affairs at Westminster, though in the provisions of 1259 he was appointed with Philip Basset to be always with the justiciar (*Ann. Burton.* in *Ann. Mon.* i. 479). Moreover, the increasingly close relations between his great enemy, Llywelyn of Wales, and the party of Montfort, must have made it extremely difficult for Mortimer to remain long on the side of the barons. He had close connections with Richard of Clare, seventh earl of Gloucester, and lord of Glamorgan [q. v.], and with the Lord Edward, who, as holding the king's lands in Wales, was directly associated in interest with the marcher party, of which Mortimer was in a sense the head. But the quarrel of Gloucester and Montfort, and the ultimate breaking off of all ties between Edward and the Montfort party, must have relaxed the strongest ties that bound Mortimer to the party of opposition. In November 1261 the barons were forced to make a compromise with Henry, who on 7 Dec. formally pardoned some of his chief opponents. The names of Leicester and Mortimer were both included in this list; but what with Leicester was but a temporary device to gain time marks with Mortimer a definite change of policy. Henceforth Mortimer was always on the royal side. All the marcher lords emulated his example, and became the strongest of royalist partisans. The Tewkesbury chronicler makes the hatred felt by the barons for Edward and Mortimer the mainspring of the civil troubles that now again broke out (*Ann. Tewkesbury* in *Ann. Mon.* i. 179).

In June 1262 Mortimer was waging war against Llywelyn, who bitterly complained to the king of his violation of the truce (*Fœdera*, i. 420), and obtained the appointment of a commission to investigate his complaints. But Llywelyn soon took the law into his own hands. In November the Welsh tenants of Mortimer in Melenydd rose in revolt, and called on Llywelyn, who in December attacked Mortimer's three castles of Knucklas, Bleddva, and Cevnllys (*Worcester Annals*, p. 447; *Fœdera*, i. 423). All three castles were soon taken. Mortimer himself defended Cevnllys, but was forced to march out with all his followers, and Llywelyn did not venture to assail him (*ib.* i. 423). However, Roger soon recovered this castle (*Royal Letters*, ii. 229). On 18 Feb. 1263 Mortimer, with other border barons, received royal letters of protection to last until 24 June, or as long as the war should endure in Wales. They were renewed in November of the same year. He remained in Wales, and inflicted terrible slaughter on his Welsh enemies. But he could not undo his rival's successes. His Brecon tenants took oaths to Llywelyn, and next year his castle of Radnor also fell into the hands of the Welsh prince's partisans. Some conquests made by Edward were, however, put into his hands (Rishanger, *De Bello*, p. 20, Camden Soc.) His English enemies took advantage of his troubles with the Welsh to assail his English estates. The same December that witnessed the loss of the castles of Melenydd saw a fierce attack on his lands by John Giffard [q. v.] (*Tewkes-*

bury Annals, p. 179); yet he hesitated not to provoke still further the wrath of Leicester by receiving a royal grant of three marcher townships which belonged to the earl (*Dunstaple Ann.* in *Ann. Mon.* iii. 226).

Mortimer was a party to the agreement to submit the disputes of king and baron to the arbitration of St. Louis. But when Leicester repudiated St. Louis's decision, Mortimer took a most active part in sustaining the king's side. He was specially opposed by two of Leicester's sons, Henry and Simon de Montfort (*ib.* p. 227). But while Henry was entangled in an attack on Edward at Gloucester, Mortimer with his wild band of marauders pursued Simon to the midlands, where Mortimer took a leading part in the capture of Northampton on 5–6 April (RISHANGER, *Chron.* p. 21, Rolls Ser.; cf. LELAND, *Collectanea*, i. 174). At Lewes, Mortimer, with his marcher followers, succeeded in escaping the worst consequences of the defeat. They retired to Pevensey, and, on Edward and Henry of Almaine being surrendered as hostages for their good behaviour, they were allowed to march back in arms to the west (*Dunstaple Ann.* pp. 232–4). On reaching his own district Mortimer at once prepared for further resistance. But Llywelyn was now omnipotent in Wales, and the marchers could expect little help from England. Accordingly, in August they again entered into negotiations with the triumphant Montfort party and surrendered hostages (*Rot. Pat.* in BÉMONT, *Simon de Montfort*, p. 220). But in the autumn Mortimer refused to attend Montfort's council at Oxford, and he and the marchers again took arms. Montfort summoned the whole military force of England to assemble at Michaelmas at Northampton in order to complete their destruction. In the early winter Mortimer felt the full force of the assault. Leicester, taking the king with him, marched to the west, united with Llywelyn, ravaged Mortimer's estates, and penetrated as far as Montgomery (RISHANGER, *De Bello*, pp. 35–40). So hard pressed were the marchers that they were forced to sue for peace, which they only obtained on the hard condition that those of their leaders who, like Mortimer, had abandoned the baronial for the royal side should be exiled (*ib.* p. 41; cf. *Ann. Londin.* in STUBBS, *Chron. Edward I and II*). Mortimer was to betake himself to Ireland.

The hard terms of surrender were never carried out. The baronial party was now breaking up, and the quarrel between Leicester and Gilbert of Clare, eighth earl of Gloucester [q. v.], gave another chance to the lords of the Welsh marches. At first Gloucester contented himself with persuading Mortimer not to go into exile, but Gloucester soon retired to the west, where he concluded a fresh confederacy with Mortimer and his party and prepared again for war. Montfort was forced to follow him, and for security brought with him the captive Edward. On 28 May 1265 Edward escaped from his captors near Hereford. The plan of escape had been prepared by Mortimer, who provided the swift horse on which Edward rode away (HEMINGBURGH, i. 320–1, Eng. Hist. Soc.), and who waited with a little army of followers to receive Edward in Tillington Park. Mortimer conducted Edward to Wigmore, where he entertained him (*Flor. Hist.* iii. 2). It was largely through Mortimer's influence that the close alliance between Edward and Gloucester was made at Ludlow. Civil war rapidly followed. Mortimer took a part only less conspicuous than those of Edward and Gloucester in the campaign that terminated at Evesham (4 Aug.), where he commanded the rear-guard of the royalist forces (HEMINGBURGH, i. 323). The wild ferocity of the marchers was conspicuous in the shameful mutilation inflicted on Montfort's body, and in sending the head of the great earl as a present to Mortimer's wife at Wigmore (RISHANGER, *De Bello*, p. 46; *Liber de Antiquis Legibus*, p. 76; ROBERT OF GLOUCESTER).

Mortimer's share in the struggle was by no means ended at Evesham. Llywelyn was still very formidable, and in a battle fought on 15 May 1266 at Brecon Mortimer's force was annihilated, he alone escaping from the field (*Waverley Ann.* in *Ann. Mon.* ii. 370). But a little later in the year Mortimer took a conspicuous part in the siege of Kenilworth, commanding one of the three divisions into which the king's army was divided (*Dunstaple Ann.* p. 242). He now received abundant rewards for his valour. He had the custody of Hereford Castle and the sheriffdom of Herefordshire. He was made lord of Kerry and Cydowain. His chief Shropshire estate of Cleobury received franchises, which made it an independent and autonomous liberty of the marcher type (EYTON, *Shropshire*, iii. 40, iv. 221–2). But his greed was insatiable. The Shropshire towns began to complain of the aggressions of his court at Cleobury. Moreover, he urged that the hardest conditions should be imposed on the 'Disinherited,' and sought to upset the Kenilworth compromise, fearing that any general measure of pardon might jeopardise his newly won estates. This attitude led to a violent quarrel with Gilbert of Gloucester, who in 1267 strongly took up the cause of the 'Disinherited' (RISHANGER,

Rolls Ser., pp. 45–6, 50, *De Bello*, pp. 59–60; *Dunstaple Ann.* p. 245). But the ultimate triumph rested with Gloucester and not with Mortimer, who, moreover, was suspected of plotting Gloucester's death.

Mortimer remained for the rest of his life a close friend of Edward. When the king's son went on crusade, Mortimer was on 2 Aug. 1270 chosen with the king of the Romans, Walter, archbishop of York, and two others, as guardians of Edward's children, lands and interests, during his absence (*Fœdera*, i. 484). In 1271 he is found acting in that capacity with the archbishop, Philip Basset, and Robert Burnell (*Letters from Northern Registers*, p. 39; *Royal Letters*, ii. 346–9). Even during Henry's lifetime Edward's representatives had plenty of work to do (*Letters from Northern Registers*, p. 40). After Henry's death in November 1272 the three became in fact, if not in name, regents of the kingdom until Edward I's return in August 1274. Their rule was peaceful but uneventful. The turbulent lord marcher now strove with all his might to uphold the king's peace. He put down a threatened rising in the north of England (*Flor. Hist.* iii. 32). He succeeded in punishing Andrew, the former prior of Winchester, who violently strove to regain his position in the monastery. Mortimer did not scruple to disregard ecclesiastical privilege and imprison Andrew's abettor, the archdeacon of Rochester (*Winchester Ann.* in *Ann. Mon.* ii. 117).

Mortimer took a conspicuous part in Edward I's early struggles against Llywelyn of Wales. On 15 Nov. 1276 he was appointed Edward's captain for Shropshire, Staffordshire, Herefordshire, and the adjoining district against the Welsh (*Fœdera*, i. 537). He had some share in the campaign of 1277, being assigned to widen the roads in Wales and Bromfield to facilitate the march of the king's troops (*Rotulus Walliæ*, 6 Edward I, p. 10). He wrested many lands from the defeated Welsh (*Cal. Patent Rolls*, 1281–92, p. 171), and received from the king a grant of fifty librates of waste lands (*Rotulus Walliæ*, 8 Edward I, p. 17). He was still active as a justice under the king's commission (*ib.* pp. 9, 10, 36, 37). In 1279 Mortimer, who was now growing old, solemnly celebrated his retirement from martial exercises by giving a great feast and holding a 'round table' tournament at Kenilworth, at which a hundred knights and as many ladies participated, and on which he lavished vast sums of money (*Chron. Osney* and Wykes in *Ann. Mon.* iv. 281–2; Rishanger, pp. 94–5, Rolls Ser.) The queen of Navarre, wife of Edmund of Lancaster, lord of the castle, was treated with special honour by Mortimer, though the Wigmore chronicler curiously misunderstands his acts (*Monasticon*, vi. 350). Mortimer was smitten with his mortal illness at Kingsland, Herefordshire, in the midst of the final campaign of Edward against Llywelyn. He was tormented about his debts to the crown, and fearing difficulties in the way of the execution of his will, obtained from Archbishop Peckham the confirmation of its provisions (Peckham, *Letters*, ii. 499). He died on 26 Oct. 1282 (*Worcester Annals* in *Ann. Mon.* iv. 481; cf. *Osney* and Wykes in *Ann. Mon.* iv. 290–1). On the day after his death Edward I issued from Denbigh a patent which, as a special favour 'never granted to blood relation before,' declared that if Roger died of the illness from which he was suffering, his executors should not be impeded in carrying out his will by reason of his debts to the exchequer, for the payment of which the king would look to his heirs (*Cal. Patent Rolls*, 1281–92, pp. 38–9). Adam, abbot of Wigmore, was his chief executor. He was buried with his ancestors in the priory of Wigmore. His epitaph is given in 'Monasticon,' vi. 355.

Matilda de Braose survived Mortimer for nineteen years. By her he had a numerous family. His eldest son, Ralph, who was made sheriff of Shropshire and Staffordshire during the time that Mortimer was one of the co-regents, died in 1275. Edmund I, the second son, who had been destined to the church, succeeded to his father's estates, and within six weeks of his father's death managed to entice Llywelyn of Wales to his doom. He married Margaret 'de Fendles,' a kinswoman of Queen Eleanor of Castile, and generally described as a Spaniard; but she was doubtless the daughter of William de Fiennes, a Picard nobleman, who was second cousin to Eleanor through her mother, Joan, countess of Ponthieu (*Notes and Queries*, 4th ser., vii. 318, 437–8). This Edmund died in 1304. He was the father of Roger Mortimer, first earl of March (1287–1330) [q. v.] The other children of Roger Mortimer and Matilda de Braose include: Roger Mortimer of Chirk (*d.* 1326) [q. v.], Geoffry, William, and Isabella, who married John Fitzalan III, and was the mother of Richard Fitzalan I, earl of Arundel (1267–1302) [q. v.]

[Annales Monastici (Rolls Ser.); Rishanger's Chronicle (Rolls Ser.), and Chron. de Bello (Camden Soc.); Annales Cambriæ (Rolls Ser.); Brut y Tywysogion, ed. Rhys and J. G. Evans, and in Rolls Ser.; Flores Hist. vols. ii. and iii. (Rolls Ser.); Walter of Hemingburgh (Engl. Hist. Soc.); Rymer's Fœdera, vol. i., Record ed.; Shirley's Royal Letters, vol. ii. (Rolls Ser.); Rotulus

Walliæ, temp. Edward I, privately printed by Sir T. Phillips; Eyton's Shropshire, especially iv. 216–23; Dugdale's Baronage, i. 141–3; Dugdale's Monasticon, vi. 350–1; Wright's Hist. of Ludlow; Bémont's Simon de Montfort; Stubbs's Const. Hist. vol. ii.; Blaauw's Barons' Wars.]

T. F. T.

MORTIMER, ROGER (III) DE, LORD OF CHIRK (1256?–1326), was the third son of Roger Mortimer II, sixth baron of Wigmore [q. v.], and his wife Matilda de Braose, and was therefore the uncle of Roger Mortimer IV, eighth lord Wigmore and first earl of March [q.v.] Edmund, his elder brother, the seventh lord of Wigmore, was born in or before 1255 (EYTON, *Shropshire*, iv. 197), and it is probable that Roger was not born much later than 1256. Unlike his elder brother Edmund, who had been destined for the church, Roger was knighted in his father's lifetime. In 1281 he received license to hunt the fox and hare throughout Shropshire and Staffordshire, provided that he took none of the king's great game (*Cal. Patent Rolls*, 1281–92, p. 2). After his father's death in 1282, Mortimer joined with his brothers, Edmund, William, and Geoffrey, in a plot to lure Llywelyn of Wales into the family estates in mid Wales (*Osney Annals* in *Ann. Mon.* iv. 290–1; *Worcester Ann.* in *ib.* iv. 485). Llywelyn fell into the trap, and after his death at the hands of Edmund, Roger took his head to London as a grateful present to Edward I (KNIGHTON, c. 2463, apud TWYSDEN, *Decem Scriptores*). At the same time Roger was accused before Archbishop Peckham, who at the time was holding a visitation of the vacant diocese of Hereford, of adultery with Margaret, wife of Roger of Radnor, and other women. He aggravated his offence by putting into prison a chaplain who had the boldness to reprove him for his sins. Peckham, fearing lest on his leaving the district the culprit might get off scot-free, empowered the Bishop of Llandaff to act for him, and impose on Roger canonical penance (PECKHAM, *Letters*, ii. 497–8, Rolls Ser.)

Though a younger son, Roger had the good fortune to obtain early an independent position for himself. Since the death of Gruffydd ab Madog, lord of Bromfield and Powys Vadog [q. v.], in 1269, the territories of the once important house of Powys had been falling into various owners' hands. In 1277 Madog, Gruffydd's son, died, leaving two infant children, Llywelyn and Gruffydd, as his heirs. On 4 Dec. 1278 Mortimer was appointed by Edward I as guardian of the two boys. But in 1281 the two heirs were drowned in the Dee, late Welsh tradition accusing Mortimer of the deed. Thereupon Edward I took all their lands into his hands. At the time of the final settlement of Wales Edward made all the lands between Llywelyn's principality and his own earldom of Chester march-ground. On 2 June 1282 Edward granted to Mortimer all the lands that had belonged to Llywelyn Vychan. The effect of the grant was to set up in favour of Roger Mortimer the new marcher lordship of Chirk (PALMER, *Tenures of Land in the Marches of North Wales*, p. 92; LLOYD, *Hist. of Powys Fadog*, i. 180, iv. 1–9). Roger was henceforward known as 'of Chirk,' and he built there a strong castle, which became his chief residence.

Mortimer took an active share in the wars of Edward I. In 1287 he took a conspicuous part in putting down the rising of Rhys ab Maredudd of Ystrad Towy in Wales, and was ordered to remain in residence in his estates in that country until the revolt was suppressed. The Welsh annalist says that Rhys captured his old fortress of Newcastle and took Roger Mortimer, its warden, prisoner (*Ann. Cambriæ*, p. 110). He constantly did good service for the king by enrolling Welsh infantry from his estates. In 1294 he took part in the expedition to Gascony, and, on the recapture of Bourg and Blaye, was made joint governor of those towns (*Worcester Annals* in *Ann. Mon.* iv. 519; HEMINGBURGH, ii. 48, Engl. Hist. Soc.) He was again in Gascony three years later, and in 1300 and 1301 served in the campaigns against the Scots (DUGDALE, *Baronage*, i. 145). He was among the famous warriors present at the siege of Carlaverock in 1300, he and William of Leybourne being appointed as conductors and guardians of the king's son Edward, afterwards Edward II (NICOLAS, *Siege of Carlaverock*, pp. 46–7). He was ultimately attended by two knights and fourteen squires, and received as wages for himself and his following 42*l.* He had first been summoned to parliament as a baron in 1299, and was now present at the Lincoln parliament in 1301, where he signed the famous letter of the barons to the pope. He was again in Scotland in 1303. At the end of Edward I's reign he incurred the king's displeasure by quitting the army in Scotland without leave, on which account his lands and chattels were for a time seized (*Rot. Parl.* i. 216*b*).

The accession of Edward II restored Mortimer to favour. He was appointed lieutenant of the king and justice of Wales. All the royal castles in Wales were entrusted to his keeping, with directions to maintain them well garrisoned and in good repair. The relaxation of the central power under a weak king practically gave an official invested with such extensive powers every regalian right, and Mortimer ruled all Wales like a king from 1307 to 1321, except for the years 1315 and 1316, during which he was replaced by John de Grey as justice of North Wales, while William Martyn and Maurice de Berkeley superseded him in turn for a slightly longer period in the south (*Cal. Close Rolls*, 1313–1317). He was largely assisted in his work by his nephew, Roger Mortimer, eighth baron of Wigmore [see Mortimer, Roger IV], who now becomes closely identified with his uncle's policy and acts. Modern writers have often been led by the identity of the two names to attribute to the more famous nephew acts that really belong to the uncle. Among the more noteworthy incidents of the elder Mortimer's government of Wales was his raising the siege of Welshpool and rescuing John Charlton [q. v.] and his wife, Hawise, from the vigorous attack of her uncle, Gruffydd de la Pole. During these years he raised large numbers of Welsh troops for the Scottish wars. He himself served in the Bannockburn campaign, and again in 1319 and 1320. In 1317 he was further appointed justice of North Wales, and in 1321 his commission as justice of Wales was renewed.

In 1321 Mortimer of Chirk joined vigorously in the attack on the Despensers [see for details Mortimer, Roger IV]. After taking a leading part, both in the parliaments and in the campaigns in Glamorgan and on the Severn, he was forced with his nephew, Roger Mortimer of Wigmore, to surrender to Edward II at Shrewsbury on 22 Jan. 1322. He was, like his nephew, imprisoned in the Tower of London, but, less fortunate than the lord of Wigmore, he did not succeed in subsequently effecting his escape. He died there, after more than four years of severe captivity, on 3 Aug. 1326. The accounts vary as to the place of burial. The 'Annales Paulini' say that it was at Chirk (Stubbs, *Chron. Edward I and Edward II*, i. 312). Blaneforde (apud Trokelowe, p. 147) says that he was buried at Bristol. The Wigmore annalist (*Monasticon*, vi. 351) states circumstantially that he was buried at Wigmore among his ancestors by his partisan bishop, Adam of Orleton, on 14 Sept. This is probably right, as the other writers also say he was buried 'among his ancestors,' whose remains would certainly not be found at Chirk or Bristol. The statement of the Wigmore annalist (*ib.* vi. 351) that Mortimer died in 1336 is a mere mistake, though repeated blindly by Dugdale in his 'Baronage' (i. 155), and adopted by Sir Harris Nicolas (*Siege of Carlaverock*, p. 264). Mortimer married Lucy, daughter and heiress of Robert de Wafre, by whom he had a son named Roger, who succeeded to the whole inheritance of his mother's father, married Joan of Turberville (*Monasticon*, vi. 351), and had a son John. But the real successor to Roger's estates and influence was his nephew, the first Earl of March. In 1334 Chirk was given to Richard Fitzalan II, earl of Arundel [q. v.] The house of Arundel proved too powerful to dislodge, and at last John Mortimer, grandson of Roger, sold such rights as he had over Chirk to the earl. Neither son nor grandson was summoned as a baron to parliament, and the family either became extinct or insignificant.

[Annales Monastici, Chronicles of Edward I and II, Flores Historiarum, Peckham's Letters, Blaneforde (in Trokelowe), Knighton, all in Rolls Series; Galfridus le Baker, ed. Thompson; Parl. Writs; Rymer's Fœdera; Rolls of Parliament; Dugdale's Monasticon, vi. 351; Lords' Report on the Dignity of a Peer, vol. iii.; Cal. Close Rolls, 1307–13 and 1313–18; Lloyd's Hist. of Powys Fadog; Eyton's Shropshire; Wright's Hist. of Ludlow; Stubbs's Const. Hist. vol. ii.; Dugdale's Baronage, i. 155. Nicolas's Siege of Carlaverock, pp. 259–64, gives a useful, but not always very precise, biography.]

T. F. T.

MORTIMER, ROGER (IV) de, eighth Baron of Wigmore and first Earl of March (1287?–1330), was the eldest son of Edmund Mortimer, seventh lord of Wigmore, and his wife Margaret de Fendles or Fiennes, the kinswoman of Eleanor of Castile (*Monasticon*, vi. 351; *Notes and Queries*, 4th ser. vii. 437-8). The inquests recording the date of his birth differ, but he was probably born either on 3 May 1286 or on 25 April 1287 (*Calendarium Genealogicum*, p. 668; cf. Eyton, *Shropshire*, iv. 223, and Doyle, *Official Baronage*, ii. 466, which latter dates the birth 29 April 1286). Mortimer's uncle was Roger de Mortimer (III) [q. v.] of Chirk. His father, Edmund, died before 25 July 1304 (Eyton, iv. 225; cf. *Monasticon*, vi. 351; *Worcester Ann.* in *Ann. Mon.* iv. 557), whereupon Roger succeeded him as eighth lord of Wigmore. He was still under age, and Edward I put him under the wardship of Peter Gaveston, then in favour as a chief friend of Edward, prince of Wales. Mortimer redeemed himself from Gaveston by paying a fine of 2,500 marks, and thereby obtained the right of marrying freely whomsoever he would (*Monasticon*, vi. 351). On Whitsunday, 22 May 1306, he was one of the great band of young lords who were dubbed knights at Westminster along with

Edward, prince of Wales, by the old king, Edward I, in person (*Worcester Ann.* p. 558). Mortimer figured in the coronation of Edward II on 25 Feb. 1308 as a bearer of the royal robes (*Fœdera*, ii. 36).

Mortimer had inherited from his father a great position in the Welsh marches, besides the lordships of Dunmask and other estates in Ireland. His importance was further increased by his marriage, before October 1306, with Joan de Genville. This lady, who was born on 2 Feb. 1286 (*Calendarium Genealogicum*, p. 449), was the daughter and heiress of Peter de Genville (*d.* 1292), by Joan, daughter of Hugh XII of Lusignan and La Marche. One Genville was lord of the castle and town of Ludlow in Shropshire, the marcher liberty of Ewyas Lacy, more to the south, and, as one of the representatives of the Irish branch of the Lacys, lord of the liberty of Trim, which included the moiety of the great Lacy palatinate of Meath (*Worcester Ann.* p. 560; Doyle, ii. 467). Two of his daughters became nuns at Acornbury (Eyton, v. 240), so that their sister brought to Mortimer the whole of her father's estates. The acquisition of Ludlow, subsequently the chief seat of the Mortimers' power, enormously increased their influence on the Welsh border, while the acquisition of half of Meath gave the young Roger a place among the greatest territorial magnates of Ireland. But both his Welsh and Irish estates were in a disturbed condition, and their affairs occupied him so completely for the first few years of Edward II's reign that he had comparatively little leisure for general English politics.

Ireland was Mortimer's first concern. In 1308 he went to that country, and was warmly welcomed by his wife's uncle, Geoffry de Genville, who surrendered all his own estates to him, and entered a house of Dominican friars, where he died (*Worcester Ann.* p. 560). Yet Mortimer's task was still a very difficult one. Rival families assailed his wife's inheritance, her kinsfolk the Lacys being particularly hostile to the interloper (cf. *Cal. Close Rolls*, 1307–13, p. 188). Another difficulty arose from Mortimer's claim on Leix, the modern Queen's County, which he inherited from his grandmother, Matilda de Braose (Gilbert, *Viceroys of Ireland*, p. 136). But his vigour and martial skill at length secured for him the real enjoyment of his Irish possessions, when the Lacys in despair turned to Scotland, and were largely instrumental in inducing Edward Bruce, brother of King Robert, to invade Ireland. In 1316 Mortimer was defeated by Bruce at Kells and driven to Dublin, whence he returned to England. Edward Bruce seemed now likely to become a real king of Ireland, and, to meet the danger, Edward II appointed Mortimer, on 23 Nov. 1316, warden and lieutenant of Ireland, with the very extensive powers necessary to make a good stand against him (*Fœdera*, ii. 301). All English lords holding Irish lands were required to serve the new viceroy in person or to contribute a force of soldiers commensurate with the extent of their possessions. In February 1317 a fleet was collected at Haverfordwest to transport the 'great multitude of soldiers, both horse and foot,' that had been collected to accompany Mortimer to Ireland. On Easter Thursday Mortimer landed at Youghal with a force, it was believed, of fifteen thousand men (*Fœdera*, ii. 309; *Parl. Writs*, ii. i. 484). On his approach Edward Bruce abandoned the south and retreated to his stronghold of Carrickfergus, while his brother, King Robert, who had come over to his aid, went back to Scotland. Old feuds stood in the new viceroy's way, especially one with Edmund Butler, yet Mortimer showed great activity in wreaking his vengeance on the remnants of the Bruces' followers in Leinster and Connaught. He procured the liberation of Richard de Burgh, second earl of Ulster [q.v.], whom the citizens of Dublin had imprisoned on account of a private feud. On 3 June 1317 he defeated Walter de Lacy, the real cause of the Scottish invasion, and next day successfully withstood another attack of the beaten chieftain and his brothers. He then caused the Lacys to be outlawed as 'felons and enemies of the king,' and ordered their estates to be taken into the king's hands (Gilbert, *Viceroys*, pp. 531–2). This triumph over the rivals of his wife's family for the lordship of Meath was a personal success for Mortimer as well as a political victory. The Lacys fled into Connaught, whither the king's troops pursued them, winning fresh victories over the Leinster clans, and strengthening the king's party beyond the Shannon. In 1318 Mortimer was recalled to England. He left behind him at Dublin debts to the amount of 1,000*l.*, which he owed for provisions (*ib.* p. 143). Even before his Irish command he had been forced to borrow money from the society of the Frescobaldi (*Cal. Close Rolls*, 1307–13, p. 55). Mortimer continued to hold the viceroyalty, being represented during his absence first by William FitzJohn, archbishop of Cashel, and afterwards by Alexander Bicknor [q.v.], archbishop of Dublin. While Bicknor was deputy Edward Bruce was defeated and slain.

In March 1319 Mortimer returned to Ireland, with the additional offices of justiciar of Ireland, constable of the town and castle of Athlone, and constable of the castles of Roscommon and Rawdon (DOYLE, ii. 466). He instituted a searching examination as to who had abetted Edward Bruce, and rewarded those who had remained faithful to the English crown by grants of confiscated estates. But English politics now demanded Mortimer's full attention. In 1321 he lost his position in Ireland altogether, and his successor's displacement of the officials he had appointed, on the ground of their incompetence, suggests that his removal involved a change in the policy of the Irish government corresponding to the changes which were brought about in England at the same time.

The circumstances of Wales and Ireland were during this period very similar, and Mortimer was able to apply the experience gained in Ireland to the government of his possessions in Wales and its marches. His uncle, Roger Mortimer of Chirk (with whom he is often confused), was justice of Wales, and he seems to have helped his uncle to establish the independent position of the house of Mortimer on a solid and satisfactory basis. The result was that uncle and nephew ruled North Wales almost as independent princes, though the younger Roger had no official position therein apart from his constableship of the king's castle of Builth, conferred in 1310 (*ib.*), and not held by him later than 1315 (*Cal. Close Rolls*, 1313–18, p. 153). But in 1312 the younger Mortimer took a decisive part in protecting the marcher lord, John Charlton of Powys [q. v.], who was besieged with his Welsh wife Hawyse in Pool Castle by her uncle Gruffydd, and after a good deal of fighting secured Charlton's position as lord of Powys, though for many years Gruffydd continued to assail it. This alliance with one of the strongest neighbours of the Mortimers was further strengthened by the marriage of John, the son of Charlton, with Matilda, daughter of the lord of Wigmore. It was part of a general scheme of binding together the lords marchers in a solid confederacy and with a common policy, such as had in earlier crises of English history, and notably during the barons' wars, made those turbulent chieftains a real power in English politics. The full effect of Mortimer's family connections came out after his quarrel with Edward II in 1321. In 1315 Mortimer took a conspicuous part in repressing the revolt of Llywelyn Bren [q. v.] On 18 March 1316 Llywelyn surrendered to the king's authority in Mortimer's presence (*Flor. Hist.* iii. 340).

Shrewdly and ardently pursuing his self-interest in Ireland and Wales, Mortimer had had no great leisure to take a prominent part in the early troubles of the reign of Edward II. He was one of the barons who signed the letter denouncing papal abuses, addressed to Clement V, on 6 Aug. 1309, at Stanford (*Ann. Londin.* in STUBBS, *Chron. of Edw. I and Edw. II*, i. 162). He does not seem to have taken a definite side, though in some ways his sympathies were with the king against the lords ordainers, who were active enemies of his ally John Charlton. Early in 1313 Mortimer was sent to Gascony 'on the king's service,' and on 2 April the sheriffs of Shropshire and Herefordshire and the bailiff of Builth were ordered to pay sums amounting in all to 100*l.* to him for his expenses (*Cal. Close Rolls*, 1307–13, p. 522). In 1316 he joined the Earl of Pembroke in putting down the revolt of Bristol (MONK OF MALMESBURY, p. 222). In 1318 Mortimer began to stand out more prominently in English politics. He seems to have attached himself to the middle party, which, under the Earl of Pembroke, himself the greatest of the lords marchers, strove to hold the balance between the Despensers and the courtiers and the regular opposition under Thomas of Lancaster. In 1318, when Pembroke strove to mediate between Edward and Lancaster, Mortimer appears as one of the king's sureties who accepted the treaty of Leek on 9 Aug. A little later he was one of those nominated to sit on the new council of the king, some members of which were to be in perpetual attendance, and without whose consent Edward was suffered to do nothing. He was also put by parliament on the commission appointed to reform the royal household (COLE, *Records*, p. 12). This is the first clear evidence of his acting even indirectly against the king.

Local rivalries now complicated general politics, and the danger threatened to his Welsh position first made Mortimer a violent opponent of Edward and the Despensers. William de Braose, the lord of Gower, was in embarrassed circumstances, and about 1320 offered Gower for sale to the highest bidder (TROKELOWE, p. 107). Humphrey VIII de Bohun, fourth earl of Hereford [q. v.], agreed to purchase it, thinking that it would round off conveniently his neighbouring lordship of Brecon. William de Braose died, but his son-in-law, John de Mowbray, who succeeded to his possessions by right of his wife, was willing to complete the arrangement, and entered into possession of the Braose lands. But the younger Hugh le Despenser [q. v.], who with the hand of Eleanor de Clare, the elder of the coheiresses of the Gloucester inheritance, had acquired the adjacent lordship of Glamorgan, was alarmed at the extension of the Bohun influence, and, on the pretext that Mowbray had taken possession of Gower without royal license, attacked him both in the law courts and in the field. A regular war now broke out for the possession of Gower, and a confederacy of barons was formed to back up the claims of Mowbray and Hereford. The two Mortimers threw themselves eagerly on to Hereford's side. [TROKELOWE, p. 111, describes them as 'quasi totius discordiæ incentores præcipui.'] Hereditary feuds heightened personal animosities. Hugh le Despenser proposed to avenge on the Mortimers the death of his grandfather slain in the barons' wars (MONK OF MALMESBURY, p. 256). The younger Mortimer had a special grievance, inasmuch as a castle in South Wales, bestowed formerly on him through the royal favour, had been violently seized by the younger Hugh le Despenser (*ib.* p. 224).

By Lent 1321 the war spread to Despenser's palatinate of Glamorgan. Mortimer and his friends carried all before them. In April 1321 Edward summoned Hereford to appear before him; but Mortimer of Wigmore joined with the earl in refusing to attend. On 1 May the king ordered them not to attack the Despensers. But on 4 May Mortimer and his confederates took Newport. Four days later, Cardiff, with its castle, the head of the lordship of Glamorgan, also fell into their hands (*Flor. Hist.* iii. 345; MURIMUTH, p. 33; *Monasticon*, vi. 352; *Ann. Paul.*, p. 293, which also speaks of the capture of Caerphilly). On 28 June both Mortimers appeared at the great baronial convention at Sherburn in Elmet (*Flor. Hist.* iii. 197). The current ran strongly against the favourites. In July a parliament assembled in London, to which Mortimer came up with his followers, 'all clothed in green, with their right hands yellow,' and took up his quarters at the priory of St. John's in Clerkenwell (*Ann. Paul.* p. 294). The Despensers were now attacked in parliament and banished. Mortimer took a conspicuous part against them. On 20 Aug. he was formally pardoned, with many others, before the conclusion of the session (*Parl. Writs*, II. ii. 168). Mortimer now retired to his strongholds in the marches. But Edward, profiting by the unexpected forces which gathered round him for the siege of Leeds in Kent, annulled the proceedings against the Despensers, and marched to the west, at the head of a large army, to take vengeance on the marcher confederacy. Mortimer, with his uncle and Hereford, had marched as far as Kingston-on-Thames (*Ann. Paul.* pp. 299–310); but they made no serious effort to relieve Leeds, and were forced to retreat to the west, whither Edward followed them. The Mortimers still took a leading part in resisting the progress of the king. They captured the town and castle of Gloucester. But they failed to withstand Edward's advance at Worcester, and, though they made a better show at Bridgnorth, Edward captured the castle and burnt the town. The king failed to effect his passage over the Severn, but continued his victorious career northwards to Shrewsbury. But the marcher lords were bitterly disappointed that neither the Earl of Lancaster nor the other great English earls who had encouraged them to resistance had come to their help against Edward. The Mortimers refused to resist Edward any longer, and, on the mediation of the earls of Arundel and Richmond, negotiated the conditions of a compromise (MONK OF MALMESBURY, p. 264; *Ann. Paul.* p. 301). On 17 Jan. 1322 Mortimer received a safe-conduct to treat (*Fœdera*, ii. 472). Five days later both he and his uncle made their submission to Edward at Shrewsbury (*Parl. Writs*, II. ii. 176; MURIMUTH, p. 35). They were both sent forthwith to the Tower of London to await their trial (*ib.*), while Edward marched northwards to complete his triumph. Before the end of March Lancaster and Hereford had been slain, and Edward and the Despensers ruled the land without further opposition. The commons of Wales, who hated the severity of the Mortimers' rule, petitioned the king to show no grace either to uncle or nephew for their treasons (*Rot. Parl.* i. 400 *a*), and on 13 June a commission was issued for their trial (*Parl. Writs*, II. ii. 193). On 14 July justices were appointed to pass sentence upon them; but on 22 July the penalty of death was commuted for one of perpetual imprisonment (*ib.* pp. 213, 216). Both remained in the Tower for more than two years under strict custody in a lofty and narrow chamber ('minus civiliter quam decuit,' BLANEFORDE apud TROKELOWE, p. 145). But they still had powerful friends outside. Adam of Orleton [q. v.], bishop of Hereford, who took his name from one of Mortimer's manors, and had closely co-operated with him in the attack on the Despensers, made preparations for his escape. Gerard de Alspaye, the sub-lieutenant of the Tower, was won over to procure the escape of the younger Mortimer (KNIGHTON, p. v.; *Chron. de London.* pp. 45–46; *Flor. Hist.* iii. 217; BLANEFORDE, pp. 145–146, which gives the most circumstantial account. MURIMUTH, p. 40, puts the escape a year too early). The night chosen was that of the feast of St. Peter ad Vincula, 1 Aug 1324. The guards, who had celebrated the feast by prolonged revels, had their drink drugged, and were plunged in deep stupor. With the help of his friend a hole was cut in the wall of Mortimer's cell, through which he escaped into the kitchen of the king's palace, from the roof of which he reached one of the wards of the castle. Then a rope ladder enabled him to descend to an outer ward, and so at last to reach the banks of the Thames. The Bishop of Hereford had got ready the external means of escape. Mortimer found a little boat manned by two men awaiting him and his accomplice. In this they were ferried over the river. On the Surrey bank they found horses ready, upon which they fled rapidly through byways to the sea-coast, where a ship was ready which took them over to France, despite the vigorous efforts made by Edward to recapture him (*Fœdera*, p. v.)

Even in exile Mortimer remained a danger to Edward and the Despensers. He went to Paris, and ingratiated himself in the favour of Charles IV, who was now at open war with his brother-in-law in Guienne, and glad to establish relations with a powerful English nobleman. His partisan, Adam Orleton, though attacked by the king for treason, was so strongly backed up by the bishops that Edward was forced to patch up some sort of reconciliation with him, and allow him to return to the west. Mortimer's mother, Margaret, convoked suspicious assemblies of his friends until in 1326 Edward shut her up in a monastery (Pauli, *Geschichte von England*, iv. 281, from *Patent and Close Rolls*, 19 Edw. II.) But a more formidable danger arose after the arrival in Paris of Isabella of France [q. v.], the queen of Edward II, in the spring of 1325. Even before her departure from England Isabella had sought the advice of Orleton. In September she was joined by her son Edward, sent to perform homage to the French king for his duchy of Aquitaine. After the ceremony was performed Isabella and her son still lingered at the court of Charles of France, and in the course of the winter a close connection between her and Mortimer was established, which was notorious in England in the spring of 1326. Walter Stapledon, bishop of Exeter, who had accompanied the young Duke of Aquitaine to France, not only found himself powerless in the queen's counsels, but believed that Mortimer had formed plans to take his life. On his sudden flight to England the last restraint was removed which prevented Isabella from falling wholly into the hands of the little band of exiles who now directed her counsels. It was soon notorious that Mortimer was not only her chief adviser ('jam tunc secretissimus atque principalis de privata familia reginæ,' Galfridus le Baker, p. 21, ed. Thompson), but her lover as well. The chroniclers both then and later speak with much reserve on so delicate a subject, but none of them ventured to deny so patent a fact.

Charles IV soon grew ashamed of supporting Isabella and Mortimer, and Isabella left Paris for the Low Countries. Mortimer accompanied her on her journey to the north, where, by betrothing young Edward to Philippa of Hainault, men and money were provided, and the support of a powerful foreign prince obtained for the bold scheme of invading England which Isabella and Mortimer seem by this time to have formed. Mortimer shared with John, brother of the Count of Hainault, the command of the little force of adventurers hastily collected from Hainault and Germany (G. le Baker, p. 21). He crossed over with the queen and the son to Orwell, where they landed on 24 Sept. 1326. The most complete success at once attended the invaders. Not only were they joined by Mortimer's old partisans, such as Bishop Orleton, but the whole of the Lancastrian connection, headed by Henry of Leicester, the brother of Earl Thomas, joined their standard. Edward II fled to Wales, hoping to find protection and refuge amidst the Despensers' lands in Glamorgan; but Mortimer, who was a greater power in Wales than the king, followed quickly in his steps. At Bristol he sat in judgment on the elder Despenser. On 16 Nov. Edward was taken prisoner. Mortimer was then with the queen at Hereford, where on 17 Nov. the Earl of Arundel was beheaded by his express command, and where on 24 Nov. his great enemy, the younger Despenser, suffered the same fate, he himself being among the judges who condemned him (*Ann. Paul.* p. 319).

The proceedings of the parliament which met on 7 Jan. 1327, deposed Edward and elected his son as king, were entirely directed by Mortimer's astute and unscrupulous agent, Adam Orleton. Mortimer himself went on 13 Jan. with a great following to the Guildhall of London, and promised to maintain the liberties of the city (*Ann. Paul.* p. 322), which had shown its faithfulness to him by murdering Bishop Stapledon. On 6 March he attested a new charter of liberties granted to the Londoners (*ib.* p. 332). But Edward III was a mere boy, and for the next four years Mortimer really ruled the realm through his influence over his paramour, Queen Isabella. He was conspicuous at the coronation of the young king on 1 Feb. 1327, on which day three of his sons received the honour of knighthood (MURIMUTH, p. 51; G. LE BAKER, p. 35). On 21 Feb. 1327 he obtained a formal pardon for his escape from prison and other offences (*Cal. Patent Rolls*, 1327-30, p. 14). He also procured from parliament the complete revocation of the sentence passed against him and his uncle in 1322, one of the grounds of the reversal being that, contrary to Magna Carta, they had never been allowed trial by their peers (*ib.* pp. 141–3). The immediate effect of this was to restore him to all his old possessions, and also to the estates of his uncle Chirk, who had died in prison in 1326. But Mortimer was possessed of insatiable greed, and he at once plunged into a course of self-aggrandisement that never ceased for a moment until his fall. The Rolls are filled with grants of estates, offices, wardships, and all sorts of positions of power and emolument to the successful lord of Wigmore. On 15 Feb. 1327, he was granted the lucrative custody of the lands of Thomas Beauchamp, the earl of Warwick, during his minority (DOYLE, ii. 466). On 20 Feb. of the same year he was appointed justiciar of the diocese of Llandaff, an office formerly held by his uncle (Doyle gives the wrong date; cf. *Cal. Patent Rolls*, p. 311). On 22 Feb. his appointment to the great post of justice of Wales, which had been so long in his uncle's hands, gave him a power over marches and principality even more complete than that formerly possessed by the lord of Chirk. This power was extended to the English border shires by his appointment on 8 June as chief keeper of the peace in the counties of Hereford, Stafford, and Worcester, in accordance with the statute of Winchester (*Cal. Patent Rolls*, p. 152), to which Staffordshire was added on 26 Oct. (*ib.* p. 214). On 12 June he was granted the custody of the lands of Glamorgan and Morganwg during pleasure, thus obtaining control of the old estates of the younger Despenser (*ib.* p. 125). On 13 Sept. 1327 he had a grant of lands worth 1,000*l.* a year, including the castle of Denbigh, once the property of the elder Despenser, and the castle of Oswestry with all the forfeited manors of Edmund Fitzalan, earl of Arundel [q.v.] (*ib.* p. 328). On 22 Nov. the manor of Church Stretton, Shropshire, was granted him 'in consideration of his services to Queen Isabella and the king, here and beyond seas' (*ib.* p. 192). On 29 Sept. 1328 Mortimer's barony was raised to an earldom, bearing the title of March (DOYLE, ii. 466; 'Et talis comitatus nunquam prius fuit nominatus in regno Angliæ,' *Ann. Paul.* p. 343). On 4 Nov. of the same year the new Earl of March was regranted the justiceship of Wales for life (*Cal. Patent Rolls*, p. 327), and on the same day he was made justice in the bishopric of St. David's, and received power to remove all inefficient ministers and bailiffs of the king in Wales and appoint others in their place (*ib.* p. 327). In many of the patents he is described as 'the king's kinsman.' The grants go on unbrokenly to the end. On 27 May 1330 he was allowed five hundred marks a year from the issues of Wales in addition to his accustomed fees as justice, 'in consideration of his continued stay with the king' (*ib.* p. 535). On 16 April Isabella made over to him her interests in the castle of Montgomery and the hundred of Chirbury (*ib.* p. 506), and on 20 April all his debts and arrears to the exchequer were forgiven (*ib.* p. 511). The Irish interests of Mortimer and his wife Joan were not forgotten. He was invested with complete palatine jurisdiction not only in the liberty of Trim, but over all the counties of Meath and Uriel (Louth), (*ib.* pp. 372, 538). The custody of the lands of the infant Richard Fitzgerald, third earl of Kildare [see under FITZGERALD, THOMAS, second EARL OF KILDARE], was also placed in his hands, together with the disposal of his hand in marriage (*ib.* p. 484). Nor did he forget the interests of his friends, who obtained offices, prebends, and grants in the greatest profusion. So careful was he to safeguard his dependents' welfare, that the old cook of Edward I and II was secured his pension and leave of absence at his special request (*ib.* p. 231). But while Mortimer provided for his friends at the expense of the state, he disbursed a trifling proportion of his vast estates in small pious foundations. He had on 15 Dec. 1328 license to alienate land in mortmain worth one hundred marks a year to support nine chaplains to say mass daily in Leintwardine Church for the souls of the king, the queen, Queen Isabella, with whom were rather oddly assorted Joan, Mortimer's wife, and their ancestors and successors (*ib.* p. 343; cf. EYTON, xi. 324). Two chaplains were also endowed by him with ten marks sent to say mass for the same persons in a chapel built in the outer ward of Ludlow Castle (*Cal. Patent Rolls*, p. 343). This foundation was in honour of St. Peter, on whose feast day he had escaped from the Tower (*Monasticon*, vi. 352). By giving the Leintwardine chaplains the advowson of Church Stretton, funds were found to raise their number to ten (*ib.* p. 494).

Mortimer held no formal office in the administration of Edward III, but his dependent, Orleton, was treasurer; the scarcely less subservient Bishop Hotham of Ely was chancellor; and partisans of less exalted rank, such as Sir Oliver Ingham [q. v.], held posts on the royal council. His policy seems to have been to rule indirectly through Queen Isabella, while putting as much of the responsibility of power as he could on Earl Henry of Lancaster and his connections. He was accused afterwards of accroaching to himself every royal power, and even suspected of a wish to make himself king. But it is hard to see any very definite policy in the greedy self-seeking beyond which Mortimer's statecraft hardly extended. The government, under his influence, was as feeble and incompetent as that of Edward II, and the worst crimes which it committed were popularly ascribed to the paramour of the queen-mother. Mortimer and Isabella were regarded as specially responsible for the murder of Edward II at Berkeley, for the failure of the expedition against the Scots in 1327 (*Bermondsey Annals*, p. 472), and for the 'Shameful Peace' concluded in 1328 at Northampton, by which Robert Bruce was acknowledged as king of an independent Scotland (MURIMUTH, p. 57; AVESBURY, p. 283; *Chron. de Lanercost*, p. 261). It was even reported that Mortimer was now seeking to get himself made king with the help of the Scots (G. LE BAKER, p. 41).

Mortimer now lived in the greatest pomp and luxury. In 1328 he held a 'Round Table' tournament at Bedford (KNIGHTON, c. 2553). At the end of May in the same year, immediately after the treaty with the Scots, the young king and his mother went to Hereford, where they were present at the marriage of two of Mortimer's daughters, Joan and Beatrice, and at the elaborate tournaments that celebrated the occasion (G. LE BAKER, p. 42). They also visited Mortimer at Ludlow and Wigmore (*Monasticon*, vi. 352).

Mortimer's commanding position naturally excited the greatest ill-will. Henry of Lancaster was thoroughly disgusted with the ignominious position to which he had been reduced. He had not taken up arms to forward the designs of the ambitious marcher, but to revenge the death of his brother, Earl Thomas. Significant changes in the ministry diminished the influence of Mortimer's supporters, and at last Lancaster declared openly against him. In October 1328 Lancaster refused to attend the Salisbury parliament at which Mortimer was made an earl. Mortimer disregarded his opposition, and in December went to London with Isabella and Edward. As usual he was well received by the citizens (*Ann. Paul.* p. 343). But on his quitting the capital, Lancaster entered it, and on 2 Jan. 1329 formed a powerful confederacy there, pledged to overthrow the favourite, against whom was drawn up a formidable series of articles (BARNES, *Hist. of Edward III*, p. 31). But the favourite still showed his wonted energy and ruthlessness. He devastated the lands of his rival with an army largely composed of his Welsh followers, and on 4 Jan. took possession of Leicester. Lancaster marched as far north as Bedford, hoping to fight Mortimer (KNIGHTON, c. 2553), but his partisans deserted him, and he was glad to accept the mediation of the new archbishop of Canterbury, Simon Meopham [q. v.] The subordinate agents of Lancaster were exempted from the pardon at Mortimer's special instance. Flushed with his new triumph, Mortimer wove an elaborate plot which resulted on 19 March 1330 in the execution for treason of the king's uncle Edmund, earl of Kent [q. v.] But this was the last of Mortimer's triumphs.

Mortimer was, in his insolence and ostentation, surrounded with greater pomp than the king, and enjoyed far greater power. The wild bands of Welsh mercenaries who attended his progresses worked ruin and desolation wherever they went. Edward III was himself impatient at his humiliating subjection to his mother and her lover, and at last found a confidential agent in William de Montacute [q. v.], afterwards first Earl of Salisbury. A parliament was summoned to meet in October 1330 at Nottingham, where the king and Montacute resolved to strike their decisive blow. Great circumspection was necessary. Mortimer and Isabella took up their quarters in Nottingham Castle along with the king, and Mortimer's armed following of Welsh mercenaries held strict guard and blocked up every approach to the king. But the castellan, William Holland, was won over by Edward and Montacute, and showed to the latter an underground passage by which access to the castle could be obtained. But Mortimer had now got a hint of the conspiracy, and in a stormy scene on 19 Oct. Mortimer denounced Montacute as a traitor, and accused the young king of complicity with his designs. But Montacute was safe outside the castle with an armed following, and Mortimer knew nothing of the secret access to the castle. On the very same night the decisive blow was struck. Montacute and his companies entered the stronghold through the underground passage, and Edward joined them in the castle yard. Edward and Montacute, with their followers, ascended to Mortimer's chamber, suspiciously chosen next to that of the queen, and heard him conferring with the chancellor and other ministers within. The doors were broken open. Two knights who sought to bar the passage were struck down, and after a sharp tussle, during which Mortimer slew one of his assailants (KNIGHTON, c. 2556), the favourite was arrested, despite the intervention of Isabella, who burst into the room crying, 'Fair son, have pity on the gentle Mortimer.' (Murimuth, p. 61, says Mortimer was captured 'in camera reginæ matris,' *Ann. Paul.* p. 352, cf. KNIGHTON, c. 2555, and *ib.* c. 2553, 'semper simul in uno hospitio hospitati sunt, unde multa obloquia et murmura de eis suspectuosa oriuntur.') It was all to no purpose. The Earl of March, with his close friends, Sir Oliver Ingham and Sir Simon Bereford, were removed amidst popular rejoicings and under strict guard, by way of Loughborough and Leicester, to the Tower of London, which was reached on 27 Oct. (*Ann. Paul.* p. 352). Edward issued next day a proclamation to his people that henceforth he had taken the government into his own hands. The parliament was prorogued to Westminster, where it met on 26 Nov. Its first business was to deal with the charges brought against Mortimer. The chief accusations against him were the following. He had stirred up dissension between Edward II and his queen; he had usurped the powers of the council of regency; he had procured the murder of Edward II; he had taught the young king to regard Henry of Lancaster as his enemy; he had deluded Edmund, earl of Kent, into the belief that his brother was still alive, and had procured his execution, though he was guiltless of crime; he had appropriated to his own use 20,000*l.* paid by the Scots as the price of the peace of Northampton; he had acted as if he were king; and had done great cruelties in Ireland (*Rot. Parl.* ii. 52–3; cf. 255–6; summarised in STUBBS, *Const. Hist.* ii. 373; cf. KNIGHTON, cc. 2556–8). The peers, following Mortimer's own examples in the time of his power, at once condemned him to death without so much as giving him an opportunity of appearing before them, or answering the charges brought against him. He confessed, however, privately, that the Earl of Kent had been guilty of no crime (*Rot. Parl.* ii. 33). On 29 Nov. Mortimer, clad in black, was conveyed through the city from the Tower to Tyburn Elms, and there hanged, drawn, and quartered, like a common malefactor ('tractus et suspensus,' G. LE BAKER, p. 47; 'super communi furca latronum,' MURIMUTH, p. 62). It was believed that the details of the execution were based on Mortimer's own orders in the case of the younger Despenser. His body remained two days exposed, but the king's clemency soon allowed it honourable burial. The exact place of its deposit does not seem certain. It was buried at some Franciscan church (CANON OF BRIDLINGTON, p. 102), either at Newgate in London (BARNES, p. 51), at Shrewsbury (*Monasticon*, vi. 352), or, as seems most probable from an official record, at Coventry (*Fœdera*, ii. 828; cf. WRIGHT, *Hist. of Ludlow*, p. 225). In any case, however, the remains were transferred in November 1331 to the family burial place in the Austin priory at Wigmore.

Mortimer's wife, Joan, survived him, dying in 1356. In 1347 she had the liberty of Trim restored to her (*Rot. Parl.* ii. 223 *a*). By her Mortimer had a numerous family. Their firstborn son, Edmund, married Elizabeth, daughter of Lord Badlesmere, and died when still young at Stanton Lacy in 1331. The family annalist maintains that he was Earl of March, but this was not the case. This Edmund's son Roger, who is separately noticed, was restored to the earldom of March in 1355, and is known as second earl.

Mortimer's younger sons were Roger, a knight; Geoffrey 'comes Jubmensis et dominus de Cowyth;' and John, slain in a tournament at Shrewsbury. His seven daughters were all married into powerful families. They were: Catharine, who married her father's ward, Thomas de Beauchamp, and was mother of Thomas de Beauchamp, earl of Warwick (*d.* 1401) [q. v.]; Joan, married to James of Audley; Agnes (*d.* 1368), married to another of Mortimer's wards, Laurence, son of John Hastings, and afterwards first earl of Pembroke [q. v.]; Margaret, married to Thomas, the son of Maurice of Berkeley [see BERKELEY, family of]; Matilda or Maud, married to John, son and heir of John Charlton, first lord Charlton of Powys [q. v.]; Blanche, married to Peter of Grandison; and Beatrice, married firstly to Edward, son and heir of Thomas of Brotherton, earl of Norfolk and elder son of Edward I (by his second wife Margaret), and after his death to Thomas de Braose (DUGDALE, *Monasticon*, vi. 352, corrected by DOYLE and EYTON).

[Rymer's Fœdera, vol. ii. Record ed.; Parl. Writs; Rot. Parl. vols. i. ii.; Annales Monastici, ed. Luard; Chronicles Edward I and II, ed. Stubbs; Murimuth and Avesbury, ed. Thompson; Flores Historiarum and Trokelowe (all in Rolls Series); Chronicon Galfridi le Baker, with E. M. Thompson's valuable notes and extracts from other Chronicles; Knighton apud Twysden, Decem Scriptores; Dugdale's Monasticon, vi. 351–352, ed. Caley, Ellis, and Bandinel; Dugdale's

Baronage, i. 144–7; Doyle's Official Baronage, ii.; Eyton's Shropshire, 466–7; especially vols. iv. and v.; Wright's Hist. of Ludlow, pp. 217–25; Stubbs's Const. Hist. vol. ii.; Pauli's Geschichte von England, vol. iv.; Barnes's History of Edward III. Besides his famous presentation in Marlowe's Edward II, Mortimer is the hero of a fragment of a tragedy by Ben Jonson entitled 'Mortimer, his Falle.' He is also the subject of an anonymous play, published in 1691 with a preface by William Mountfort, and revived with additions in 1731, its title being 'King Edward III, with the Fall of Mortimer, Earl of March.' A meagre and valueless life of Mortimer was published in 1711 as a political satire on Robert Harley, earl of Oxford, and Mortimer. Among the attacks on Sir R. Walpole there was published in 1732 the 'Norfolk Sting, or the History of the Fall of Evil Ministers,' which included a life of Mortimer.] T. F. T.

MORTIMER, ROGER (V) DE, second EARL OF MARCH (1327?–1360), was the son of Edmund Mortimer (*d.* 1331), and of his wife Elizabeth Badlesmere, and was born about 1327 (DOYLE, *Official Baronage*, ii. 467). This was during the lifetime of his famous grandfather Roger Mortimer IV, first earl of March [q. v.] But the fall and execution of his grandfather, quickly followed by the death of his father, left the infant Roger to incur the penalties of the treason of which he himself was innocent. But he was from the first dealt with very leniently, and as he grew up he was gradually restored to the family estates and honours. About 1342 he was granted the castle of Radnor, with the lands of Gwrthvyrion, Presteign, Knighton, and Norton, in Wales, though Knucklas and other castles of his were put under the care of William de Bohun, earl of Northampton (*d.* 1360) [q. v.], who had married his mother (DUGDALE, *Baronage*, i. 147). Next year he received livery of Wigmore, the original centre of his race. On 12 Sept. 1344 he distinguished himself at the age of seventeen at a tournament at Hereford (MURIMUTH, p. 159, Rolls Ser.) He took a conspicuous part in the famous invasion of France in 1346 (FROISSART, iii. 130, ed. Luce). Immediately on the landing of the expedition at La Hogue on 12 July Edward III dubbed his son Edward, prince of Wales, a knight, and immediately afterwards the young prince knighted Roger Mortimer and others of his youthful companions (G. LE BAKER, p. 79; cf. MURIMUTH, p. 199, and *Eulogium Hist.* iii. 207). He fought in the third and rearmost line of battle at Crecy along with the king. For his services against the French he received the livery of the rest of his lands on 6 Sept. 1346. He was one of the original knights of the Garter (G. LE BAKER, p. 109, cf. Mr. Thompson's note on pp. 278–9; cf. BELTZ, *Memorials of the Order of the Garter*, pp. 40–1), and on 20 Nov. 1348 was first summoned to parliament, though only as Baron Roger de Mortimer (*Lords' Report on Dignity of a Peer*, iv. 579). He was conspicuous in 1349 by his co-operation with the Black Prince in resisting the plot of the French to win back Calais (G. LE BAKER, p. 104). In 1354 he obtained a reversal of the sentence passed against his grandfather, and received the restoration of the remaining portions of the Mortimer inheritance, which had been forfeited to the crown (*Rot. Parl.* ii. 255; KNIGHTON, c. 2607, apud TWYSDEN, *Decem Scriptores*; DUGDALE, i. 147). Unable to wrest the lordship of Chirk from Richard Fitzalan, earl of Arundel, he contracted with him that his son Edmund should marry Richard's daughter, Alice (*ib.*) This marriage, however, never took place. He was already popularly described as Earl of March. At last, on 20 Sept. 1355 (*Lords' Report*, iv. 604), he was formally summoned to parliament under that title. Various offices were conferred on him in 1355, including the wardenship of Clarendon, the stewardship of Roos and Hamlake, and the constableship of Dover Castle, with the lord wardenship of the Cinque ports (DOYLE, ii. 467). In 1355 he started on the expedition of the Duke of Lancaster to France, which was delayed on the English coast by contrary winds and ultimately abandoned (AVESBURY, p. 425–6, Rolls Ser.) Later in the same year he accompanied the expedition led by Edward III himself (*ib.* p. 428). His estates were now much increased by his inheriting the large property of his grandmother, Joan de Genville, the widow of the first earl, who died about this time. These included the castle of Ludlow, now finally and definitively annexed to the possessions of the house of Mortimer, and henceforth the chief seat of its power (DUGDALE, *Baronage*, i. 148). He became a member of the royal council. In 1359 he was made constable of Montgomery, Bridgnorth, and Corfe castles, and keeper of Purbeck Chase. He also accompanied Edward III on his great invasion of France, which began in October 1359. In this he acted as constable, riding in the van at the head of five hundred men at arms and a thousand archers (FROISSART, v. 199, ed. Luce. Froissart, with characteristic inaccuracy, always calls him 'John'). He took part in the abortive siege of Rheims. He was then sent on to besiege Saint-Florentin, near Auxerre. He captured the town and was joined by Edward (*ib.* v. 223, but cf. Luce's note, p. lxix). Mortimer then accompanied Edward on his invasion of Burgundy. But on 26 Feb. 1360 he died suddenly at Rouvray, near Avalon (*Monasticon*, vi. 353). His bones were taken to England and buried with those of his ancestors in Wigmore Abbey (*ib.*; cf. however 'Chronicon Brevius' in *Eulogium Hist.* iii. 312, which says that he was buried in France). His obsequies were also solemnly performed in the king's chapel at Windsor.

The family panegyrist describes Mortimer as 'stout and strenuous in war, provident in counsel, and praiseworthy in his morals' (*Monasticon*, vi. 352). He married Philippa daughter of William de Montacute, second earl of Salisbury [q. v.] Their only son was Edmund de Mortimer II, third earl of March [q. v.] Philippa survived her husband, and died on 5 Jan. 1382, and was buried in the Austin priory of Bisham, near Marlow. Her will is printed in Nichols's 'Royal Wills,' pp. 98–103.

[Galfridus le Baker, ed. Thompson; Murimuth and Avesbury (Rolls Ser.); Eulogium Historiarum (Rolls Ser.); Froissart's Chroniques, ed. Luce (Soc. de l'Histoire de France); Dugdale's Monasticon, vi. 352–3; Dugdale's Baronage, i. 147–8; Doyle's Official Baronage, ii. 469; Barnes's History of Edward III; Lords' Report on the Dignity of a Peer, vol. iv.] T. F. T.

MORTIMER, ROGER (VI) DE, fourth Earl of March and Ulster (1374–1398), was the eldest son and second child of Edmund Mortimer II, third earl of March [q. v.], and his wife, Philippa of Clarence. He was born at Usk on 11 April 1374, and baptised on the following Sunday by Roger Cradock, bishop of Llandaff, who, with the abbot of Gloucester and the prioress of Usk, acted as his sponsors (*Monasticon*, vi. 354). His mother died when he was quite a child, and his father on 27 Dec. 1381, so that he succeeded to title and estates when only seven years old. His hereditary influence and position caused him to be appointed to the lord-lieutenancy of Ireland on 24 Jan. 1382, within a few months of his accession to the earldom. His uncle, Sir Thomas Mortimer, acted as his deputy, and the guardians of his person and estates covenanted that, in return for his receiving the revenues of Ireland and two thousand marks of money, he should be provided with proper counsellors, and that the receipts of his estates, instead of being paid over by the farmers of his lands to the crown, should be appropriated to the government of Ireland. It was also stipulated that on attaining his majority Roger should have liberty to resign his office. But the experiment of an infant viceroy did not answer. When the Irish parliament met in 1382 the viceroy could not attend because of indisposition, and the magnates and commons protested against a parliament being held in his absence. Next year Roger was superseded by Philip de Courtenay (Gilbert, *Viceroys of Ireland*, pp. 248–51).

Mortimer was brought up as a royal ward, his person being entrusted to the care of Thomas Holland, earl of Kent (1350–1397) [q. v.], the half-brother of Richard II, while his estates were farmed by Richard Fitzalan III, earl of Arundel, and others. Richard II at one time sold to Arundel the right of marrying the young earl, but, as Arundel became more conspicuously opposed to his policy, Richard transferred his right to Lord Abergavenny, and ultimately, at his mother's request, to the Earl of Kent, her son. The result was that Roger was married, not later than the beginning of 1388, to Eleanor Holland, Kent's eldest daughter and the king's niece. Thus March in his early life was connected with both political parties, and one element of his later popularity may be based upon the fact that his complicated connections with both factions prevented him from taking a strong side. But as time went on he fell more decidedly under the influence of the king and courtiers, who showed a tendency to play him off against the house of Lancaster, which he in later times seems somewhat to have resented. He became a very important personage when in the October parliament of 1385 Richard II publicly proclaimed him as the presumptive heir to the throne (*Cont. Eulogium Historiarum*, iii. 361; cf. Wallon, *Richard II*, i. 489–90). On 23 April 1390 Richard himself dubbed him a knight.

In 1393 March did homage and received livery of all his lands. His guardians had managed his estates so well that he entered into full enjoyment of his immense resources, having, it was said, a sum of forty thousand marks accumulated in his treasury (*Monasticon*, vi. 354). Between 16 Feb. and 30 March 1394 he acted as ambassador to treat with the Scots on the borders. But Ireland was still his chief care. His power there had become nearly nominal, and in 1393 the English privy council had granted him a thousand pounds in consideration of the devastation of his Irish estates by the rebel natives. In September 1394 he accompanied Richard II on that king's first expedition to Ireland, being attended by a very numerous following (*Annales Ricardi II*, apud Trokelowe, p. 172). Among the chieftains who submitted to Richard was the O'Neil. the real ruler of most of March's nominal earldom of Ulster. On 28 April 1395, just before his return to England, Richard appointed March lieutenant of Ulster, Connaught, and Meath, thus adding the weight of the royal commission to the authority which, as lord of these three liberties, March already possessed over those districts. He remained some time in Ireland, waging vigorous war against the native septs, but without any notable results. On 24 April 1397 he was further nominated lieutenant of Ireland.

The young earl was rapidly winning a great reputation. He was conspicuously brave, brilliant in the tournament, sumptuous in his hospitality, liberal in his gifts, of a ready wit, affable and jocose in conversation. He was of remarkable personal beauty and extremely popular. But his panegyrists admit that his morals were loose, and that he was too negligent of divine things (*Monasticon*, vi. 354; ADAM OF USK, p. 19; MONK OF EVESHAM, p. 127). He was prudent enough not to connect himself too closely with Richard II's great attempt at despotism in 1397. In the great parliament of 1397 the Earl of Salisbury brought a suit against him on 25 Sept. for the possession of Denbigh (ADAM OF USK, pp. 15, 16). His uncle, Sir Thomas Mortimer (his grandfather's illegitimate son), was in fact closely associated with the lords appellant, and on 22 Sept. 1397 was summoned to appear for trial within six months under pain of banishment (*ib.* pp. 41, 120; MONK OF EVESHAM, pp. 139–40; *Rot. Parl.*) Richard's remarks on this occasion suggest that he was already suspicious of the Earl of March (MONK OF EVESHAM, p. 138), whom he accused of remissness in apprehending his uncle. A little later Sir Thomas, who had fled to Scotland, appeared in Ireland under the protection of his nephew the viceroy (ADAM OF USK, p. 19), though on 24 Sept. he had been ordered to proclaim throughout Ireland that Thomas must appear within three months to answer the charges against him (*Fœdera*, viii. 16). As Richard's suspicions grew, March's favour with the populace increased. He was specially summoned, despite his absence beyond sea, to attend the parliament at Shrewsbury (*ib.* viii. 21). On 28 Jan. 1398 March arrived from Ireland. The people went out to meet him in vast crowds, receiving him with joy and delight, and wearing hoods of his colours, red and white. Such a reception increased Richard's suspicions, but March behaved with great caution or duplicity, and, by professing his approval of those acts which finally gave Richard despotic power, deprived Richard of any opportunity of attacking him (ADAM OF USK, pp. 18–19). But secret plots were formed against him, and his reception of his uncle was made an excuse for them. The earl therefore returned to Ireland, and soon became plunged into petty campaigns against the native chieftains. Such desire did he show to identify himself with his Irish subjects that, in gross violation of his grandfather's statute of Kilkenny, he assumed the Irish dress and horse trappings. His brother-in-law, Thomas Holland [q. v.], duke of Surrey, who hated him bitterly, was now ordered to go to Ireland to carry out the designs of the courtiers against him. But there was no need for Surrey's intervention. On 15 Aug. 1398 (20 July, according to *Monasticon*, vi. 355, and ADAM OF USK, p. 19), March was slain at Kells while he was engaged in a rash attack on some of the Leinster clans. In the fight he rushed on the foe far in advance of his followers, and, unrecognised by them in his Irish dress, was immediately slain. His body was torn in pieces (MONK OF EVESHAM, p. 127), but the fragments were ultimately recovered and conveyed to England for burial in the family place of sepulture, Wigmore Abbey. The death of the heir to the throne at the hands of the Irish induced Richard II to undertake his last fatal expedition to Ireland (*Annales Ricardi II*, p. 229).

His widow Eleanor married, very soon after her husband's death, Edward Charlton, fifth lord Charlton of Powys [q. v.] The sons of Roger and Eleanor were: (1) Edmund (IV) de Mortimer, fifth earl of March [q. v.], who was born on 6 Nov. 1391; (2) Roger, born at Netherwood on 23 April 1393, who died young about 1409. Of Roger's two daughters, Anne, the elder, born on 27 Dec. 1388, was wife of Richard, earl of Cambridge [q. v.], mother of Richard, duke of York, and grandmother of Edward IV, to whom, after the death of her two brothers without issue, she transmitted the estates of the Mortimers and the representation of Lionel of Clarence, the eldest surviving son of Edward III. The second daughter, Eleanor, married Edward Courtenay, eleventh earl of Devonshire, and died without issue in 1418.

[Adam of Usk, ed. Thompson; Annales Ricardi II apud Trokelowe (Rolls Ser.); Monk of Evesham, ed. Hearne; Dugdale's Baronage, i. 150–1; Dugdale's Monasticon, vi. 354–5; Rymer's Fœdera, vol. viii. (original edition); Doyle's Official Baronage, ii. 469; Gilbert's Viceroys of Ireland, pp. 248–51, 273–8; Wallon's Richard II; Sandford's Genealogical History of the Kings of England, pp. 224–6.] T. F. T.

MORTIMER, THOMAS (1730–1810), author, son of Thomas Mortimer (1706–1741), principal secretary to Sir Joseph Jekyll, master of the rolls, and grandson of John Mortimer (1656?–1736) [q. v.], was born on 9 Dec. 1730 in Carey Street, Lincoln's Inn Fields (cf. *Student's Pocket Dict.*) His mother died in 1744, and he was left under the guardianship of John Baker of Spitalfields. He went first to school at Harrow, under the Rev. Dr. Cox, and then to a private academy in the north, but his knowledge was chiefly due to his own efforts. In 1750 he published 'An Oration on the much lamented death of H.R.H. Frederick, Prince of Wales,' and as it was much admired he began to study elocution to qualify himself as a teacher of belles-lettres. He also learnt French and Italian in order that he might better study his favourite subject, modern history. In 1751 he translated from the French M. Gautier's 'Life and Exploits of Pyrrhus.' In November 1762 he was made English vice-consul for the Austrian Netherlands, on the recommendation of John Montagu, fourth earl of Sandwich [q. v.], secretary of state, and went to Ostend, where he performed his duties in a most satisfactory manner. The reversion of the consulship was promised to him by two secretaries of state, Lord Sandwich and the Marquis of Rockingham, and he was strongly recommended by Sir J. Porter and his successor, Sir W. Gordon, English ministers at Brussels, but through an intrigue of Robert Wood, under-secretary to Lord Weymouth, he was suddenly dismissed from the vice-consulship in 1768, and the post given to Mr. Irvine (*The Remarkable Case of Thomas Mortimer*). It was said that he had been too intimate with Wilkes, and too warm an opponent of jesuits and Jacobites, and was dismissed because he did his duty as an Englishman, to be replaced by a Scotsman (*Whisperer*, No. 57, 16 March 1771). He returned to England and resumed his work in literature and private tuition (cf. *Elements of Commerce*, 1780).

Mortimer died on 31 March 1810 in Clarendon Square, Somers Town (*Gent. Mag.* 1810, i. 396). There is a print of him in the 'European Magazine,' vol. xxxv. He married twice, and had a large family. A son, George, captain in the marines, published in 1791 'Observations during a Voyage in the South Seas and elsewhere in the brig "Mercury," commanded by J. H. Cox, esq.' (cf. *Biog. Dict. of Living Authors*, 1816).

Mortimer was a voluminous writer, chiefly on economic subjects, and complained when near eighty, says D'Israeli in 'Calamities of Authors,' of the 'paucity of literary employment and the preference given to young adventurers.' His largest work was 'The British Plutarch' (6 vols. 8vo, 1762; 2nd ed., revised and enlarged, 1774; translated into French by Madame de Vasse, 1785–6, Paris, 12 vols. 8vo), which contains lives of eminent inhabitants of Great Britain from the time of Henry VIII to George II.

Besides some pamphlets, Mortimer's economic publications were: 1. 'Every Man his own Broker; or Guide to Exchange Alley,' Lond. 12mo, 1761; 13th ed. 1801; the materials were supplied by his own experience on the Stock Exchange, where he states that in 1756 he 'lost a genteel fortune.' 2. 'The Universal Director,' Lond. 8vo, 1763. 3. 'New History of England,' dedicated to Queen Charlotte, Lond. 3 vols. fol. 1764–6. 4. 'Dictionary of Trade and Commerce,' Lond. 2 vols. fol. 1766; 'a more commodious and better arranged, but not a more valuable, work than that of Postlethwayt' (McCulloch). It embraces geography, manufactures, architecture, the land-tax, and multifarious topics not strictly within its sphere. A similar but not identical 'General Commercial Dictionary' by Mortimer appeared in 1810, 3rd ed. 1823. 5. 'The National Debt no Grievance, by a Financier,' 1768 (cf. *Monthly Review*, 1769, p. 41). 6. 'Elements of Commerce,' Lond. 4to, 1772; 2nd edit. 1802; translated into German by J. A. Englebrecht, Leipzig, 1783. This is a suggestive book of considerable merit, showing great knowledge of the works of previous economists. The material had been used by Mortimer in a series of lectures given in London. The author claims that from his suggestion Lord North adopted taxes on menial servants, horses, machines, post-chaises, &c., and that Lord Beauchamp's proposal for preventing arrests for debts under 6*l.* was derived from the same source. 7. 'Student's Pocket Dictionary,' Lond. 12mo, 1777; 2nd. edit. 1789. 8. 'Lectures on the Elements of Commerce, Politics, and Finance,' Lond. 8vo, 1801. 9. 'Nefarious Practice of Stock Jobbing,' Lond. 8vo. 10. 'A Grammar illustrating the Principles of Trade and Commerce,' Lond. 12mo, published after his death in 1810. He published revised editions of his grandfather's 'Whole Art of Husbandry' in 1761, and of Beawes's 'Lex Mercatoria' in 1783, and translated Necker's 'Treatise on the Finances of France,' Lond. 3 vols. 8vo, 1785.

[Watt's Bibl. Brit.; Extraordinary Case of Thomas Mortimer; European Mag. vol. xxxv.; Reuss's Register of Authors; McCulloch's Lit. of Pol. Econ. pp. 52, 53; Notes and Queries, 5th ser. i. 268, 315, 456; notes kindly supplied by W. A. S. Hewins, esq.] C. O.

MORTON, Earls of. [See Douglas, James, fourth Earl, *d.* 1581; Douglas, Sir William, of Lochleven, sixth or seventh

Earl, *d.* 1606; Douglas, William, seventh or eighth Earl, 1582–1650; Douglas, James, fourteenth Earl, 1702–1768; and Maxwell, John, 1553–1593.]

MORTON, Sir ALBERTUS (1584?–1625), secretary of state, born about 1584, was youngest of the three sons of George Morton of Eshere in Chilham, Kent, by Mary, daughter of Robert Honywood of Charing in the same county. He was descended from the family of Morton of Mildred St. Andrew, Dorset, of which John Morton [q. v.], archbishop of Canterbury, was a member. His grandmother, when left a widow, remarried Sir Thomas Wotton, and became the mother of Sir Henry Wotton [q. v.], who always called himself Albertus Morton's uncle. He was educated at Eton, and was elected to King's College, Cambridge, in 1603, apparently by royal influence (cf. *Cal. State Papers*, Dom. 1603–10, p. 185), but he did not graduate there. In July 1604 Wotton was appointed ambassador to Venice, and his nephew accompanied him as secretary (cf. *Life of Bishop Bedell*, Camden Soc., p. 102). In 1609 Morton returned to England, and among other papers he brought a letter from Wotton to the Prince of Wales, which is printed in Birch's 'Life of Henry, Prince of Wales.' In August 1613 he was talked of as minister to Savoy, but he met with a serious carriage accident in the same year (*Reliquiæ Wottonianæ*, p. 413), and he did not start until 12 May 1614. Before 22 Dec. of the same year he was appointed clerk to the council, and had certainly set off on his return from Savoy to take up the duties of his office before 6 April 1615. In April 1616 he went to Heidelberg as secretary to the Princess Elizabeth, wife of the elector palatine, and while on this service was granted a pension of 200*l.* a year, with an allowance of 50*l.* for expenses. He was knighted on 23 Sept. 1617, and cannot have seen much of the electress, as his brother, writing in October 1618, says that he had returned at that time and was ill, and under the care of an Italian doctor (*Cal. State Papers*, Dom. 1611–1618, p. 585). He may have given up his clerkship while with the electress (*ib.* 1619–1623, p. 16), but on 6 April 1619 he had a formal grant of the office for life. He collected subscriptions for the elector in 1620 (*ib.* p. 183), and in December of the same year he took over 30,000*l.* to the protestant princes of Germany (*ib.* p. 198; cf. p. 201). He returned before 12 March in the following year. He resigned his place in 1623 in a fit of pique, on not being allowed to be present when the Spanish marriage was discussed (*ib.* p. 480).

It was rumoured in April 1624 that he was to succeed Sir Edward Herbert, afterwards Lord Herbert of Cherbury [q. v.], as ambassador to France, and later that he had refused the appointment, which, Carleton wrote, was as strange as that it was offered to him. It is clear that he was by this time under the patronage of Buckingham, and before 26 July he was formally appointed to Paris, though the patent was not made out till August. He was injured in November of the same year by a fall from his horse. Early in 1625 Sir George Calvert gave up the secretaryship of state for a substantial consideration, and Morton was sworn in at Newmarket in his place. He was elected member for the county of Kent and for the university of Cambridge (he had been seriously proposed for the provostship of King's College) in the parliament of 1625. Buckingham had written to the mayor of Rochester in his favour (*Gent. Mag.* 1798, i. 117), and he chose to sit for Kent, but he died in November 1625, and was buried at Southampton, where apparently he had a house. Wotton, who always speaks of him in terms of affection, wrote an elegy upon him. Morton married Elizabeth, daughter of Sir Edward Apsley, but left no issue. His widow died very soon after him, and Wotton wrote an epigram upon her death. Morton was succeeded as secretary by Sir John Coke [q. v.]

[Notes and Queries, 4th ser. iii. 219; Hasted's Kent, iii. 136; Wood's Athenæ Oxon.; Reliquiæ Wottonianæ, ed. 1685, pp. 322, 388, 417, 421, 425, 443, 552; Hannah's Wotton, pp. 40 et seq.; Cartwright's Rape of Bramber (in Cartwright and Dallaway's West Sussex), p. 243; Harwood's Alumni Eton. p. 206; Nichols's Progresses of King James I, iii. 438; Gent. Mag. 1797 p. 840, 1798 pp. 20, 115; Calendars of State Papers, Dom. 1603–25; Autobiography of Lord Herbert of Cherbury, ed. Lee, 1886, pp. 161 and 250*n.*]

W. A. J. A.

MORTON, ANDREW (1802–1845), portrait-painter, born at Newcastle-on-Tyne on 25 July 1802, was son of Joseph Morton, master mariner in that town, and was an elder brother of Thomas Morton (1813–1849) [q. v.], the surgeon. He came to London and studied at the Royal Academy, gaining a silver medal in 1821. He exhibited for the first time at the Royal Academy in 1821, and was a frequent exhibitor of portraits there and at the British Institution until his death. His art was entirely confined to portraiture, in which his style resembled that of Sir Thomas Lawrence. He had a large practice and numerous sitters of distinction. In the National Gallery there are portraits by him of Sir James Cockburn, bart., Marianna, lady Cockburn, and Marianna Augusta, lady Hamilton,

In Greenwich Hospital there is a portrait of William IV by him. Morton died on 1 Aug. 1845.

[Redgrave's Dict. of Artists; Graves's Dict. of Artists, 1760–1880.] L. C.

MORTON, CHARLES (1627–1698), puritan divine, born at Pendavy, Egloshayle, in Cornwall, and baptised at Egloshayle on 15 Feb. 1626–7, was the eldest son of Nicholas Morton, who married, on 11 May 1616, Frances, only daughter of Thomas Kestell of Pendavy. He was probably the Charles Morton, undergraduate of New Inn Hall, Oxford, who submitted on 4 May 1648 to the jurisdiction of the parliamentary visitors (Burrows, *Register of Visitors*, Camden Soc., 1881, p. 569). On 7 Sept. 1649 he was elected a scholar of Wadham College, Oxford, and he graduated B.A. 6 Nov. 1649, M.A. 24 June 1652, being also incorporated at Cambridge in 1653. His antiquarian tastes developed early, for about 1647 an urn of ancient coins found near Stanton St. John, Oxfordshire, was purchased by him and another student (Wood, *Life and Times*, Oxford Hist. Soc., i. 265). At Oxford he was conspicuous for knowledge of mathematics, and he was much esteemed by Dr. Wilkins, the head of his college. His sympathies were at first with the royalist views of his grandfather, but when he found that the laxest members of the university were attracted to that side he examined the question more seriously, and became a puritan. In 1655 Morton was appointed to the rectory of Blisland in his native county, but he was ejected by the Act of Uniformity in 1662, whereupon he retired to a small tenement, his own property, in St. Ive. He lost much property through the fire of London, and was driven to London to support himself.

Morton was probably the 'Charles Morton, presbyterian,' who in 1672 was licensed for 'a room in his dwelling-house, Kennington, Lambeth' (Waddington, *Surrey Congreg. Hist.* p. 70). A few years later he carried on at Stoke Newington, near London, the chief school of the dissenters. His object was to give an education not inferior to that afforded by the universities, and his labours proved very successful (cf. Calamy, *Continuation of Ejected Ministers*, 1727, i. 177–97). Defoe was a pupil, and spoke well of the school, and many of the principal dissenting ministers—John Shower, Samuel Lawrence, Thomas Reynolds, and William Hocker—were educated by him. The names of some of them are printed in Toulmin's 'Protestant Dissenters,' pp. 570–574. In 1703 Samuel Wesley attacked the dissenting academies in his 'Letter from a Country Divine,' and among them the establishment of Morton, in which he himself had been educated. They were thereupon defended by the Rev. Samuel Palmer in 'A Defence of the Dissenters' Education in their Private Academies,' to which Wesley replied in 'A Defence of a Letter on the Education of Dissenters,' 1704, and Palmer retorted with 'A Vindication of the Learning, Loyalty, Morals of the Dissenters. In answer to Mr. Wesley,' 1705 (Tyerman, *Life and Times of S. Wesley*, pp. 66–76, 270–94).

Morton was so harried by processes from the bishop's court that he determined upon leaving the country. He arrived at New England in July 1686 with his wife, his pupil, Samuel Penhallow [q. v.], and his nephew, Charles Morton, M.D. Another nephew had preceded them in 1685. It had been proposed that Morton should become the principal of Harvard College, but through fear of displeasing the authorities another was appointed before his arrival. He was, however, made a member of the corporation of the college and its first vice-president, and he drew up a system of logic and a compendium of physics, which were for many years two of its text-books. Some lectures on philosophy which he read in his own rooms were attended by several students from the college, and one or two discontented scholars desired to become inmates of his house, but these proceedings gave offence to the governing body. The letter of request to him to refrain from receiving these persons is printed in the 'Mather Papers' (*Massachusetts Hist. Soc. Collections*, 4th ser. viii. 111–12). Morton was solemnly inducted as minister of the first church in Charlestown, New England, on 5 Nov. 1686, and was the first clergyman of the town who solemnised marriages. He was prosecuted for 'several seditious expressions' in a sermon preached on 2 Sept. 1687, but was acquitted. His name is the second of the petitioners to the council on 2 Oct. 1693 for some encouragement to a system of propagating Christianity among the Indians, and his was the senior signature to an association for mutual assistance among the ministers of New England (*ib.* 3rd ser. i. 134, and *New England Hist. Reg.* iv. 186). Numerous extracts from the record books of his church are in the 'New England Historical Register,' vols. xxv. xxvii. and xxviii.

About 1694 Morton's health began to fail, but no assistant could be found for him. He died at Charlestown on 11 April 1698, and was buried on 14 April, his funeral being attended by the officers of Harvard College and its students. By his will, dated November 1697, he left 50*l.* for the benefit of the college, and gave his executors power to dispose of 'his philosophical writings, sermon notes, pamphlets, mathematical instruments, and other rarities.' His houses and lands at Charlestown and in Cornwall with the rest of his property passed to his two nephews, Charles and John Morton, and his niece in equal shares. An epitaph was written for him by the Rev. Simon Bradstreet, his successor in the ministry.

Morton held the Greek maxim that a great book was a great evil. He published many small volumes on social and theological questions (see *Bibl. Cornub.* and CALAMY's *Contin.* i. 210–211). A paper by him on 'The Improvement of Cornwall by Seasand' is in the 'Philosophical Transactions,' x. 293–6, and his 'Enquiry into the Physical and Literal Sense of Jeremiah viii. 7—the stork in the heaven knoweth her appointed times,' is reprinted in the 'Harleian Miscellany,' 1744 ii. 558–567, 1809 ii. 578–88. It is a blot on his character that he acted with those who urged the prosecutions for witchcraft at Salem. John Dunton, the bookseller, lauds him as 'the very soul of philosophy, the repository of all arts and sciences, and of the graces too,' and describes his discourses as 'not stale, or studied, but always new and occasional. His sermons were high, but not soaring; practical, but not low. His memory was as vast as his knowledge' (*Life and Errors*, i. 123–4).

[Drake's Dict. American Biog.; Allen's American Biog. Dict.; Foster's Alumni Oxon.; Calamy's Account of Ejected Ministers, ed. 1713, ii. 144–145; Lee's Memoir of Defoe, i. 7–10, 89; J. Browne's Congregationalism, Norfolk and Suffolk, p. 239; Maclean's Trigg Minor, i. 53, 461; Savage's Geneal. Register, iii. 243; Frothingham's Charlestown, pp. 193–240; Massachusetts Hist. Soc. 2nd ser. i. 158–62; Sprague's Annals American Pulpit, i. 211–13; Budington's First Church, Charlestown, pp. 99–113, 184–5, 221–6, 250; Quincy's Harvard Univ. i. 69–92, 495–7, 599–600; Toulmin's Protestant Dissenters, pp. 232–5.] W. P. C.

MORTON, CHARLES (1716–1799), principal librarian of the British Museum, a native of Westmoreland, was born in 1716. He entered as a medical student at Leyden on 18 Sept. 1736, and graduated there as M.D. on 28 Aug. 1748 (PEACOCK, *Index of English-speaking Students at Leyden*, p. 71). He is said to have meanwhile practised at Kendal 'with much reputation,' and in September 1748 was admitted an extra-licentiate of the College of Physicians. He practised in London for several years, and on 19 April 1750 he was elected physician to the Middlesex Hospital. He was admitted licentiate of the College of Physicians on 1 April 1751, and in 1754 also became physician to the Foundling Hospital. On the establishment of the British Museum in 1756 Morton was appointed under-librarian or keeper of the manuscript and medal departments, and in that capacity continued the cataloguing of the Harleian MSS. He also acted for some time as secretary to the trustees. In 1768 he was appointed with Mr. Farley to superintend the publication of the 'Domesday Book,' but though he received a considerable sum the work was not carried out. On the death of Dr. Matthew Maty [q.v.] in 1776, Morton was appointed principal librarian and held the office till his death. His term of office was not marked by any striking improvements, but he is said to have always treated students and visitors with courtesy.

He was elected F.R.S. on 16 Jan. 1752, and was secretary of the Royal Society from 1760 to 1774 (THOMSON, *Hist. Roy. Soc.* App. iv. and v.) He contributed to the 'Transactions' in 1751 'Observations and Experiments upon Animal Bodies . . . or Inquiry into the cause of voluntary Muscular Motion' (*Phil. Trans.* xlvii. 305); and in 1768 a paper on the supposed connection between the hieroglyphic writing of Egypt and the Modern Chinese character (*ib.* lix. 489). He was a fellow of the Society of Antiquaries, the Imperial Academy of St. Petersburg, and of the Royal Academy of Göttingen. He is said to have been 'a person of great uprightness and integrity, and much admired as a scholar.' He died at his residence in the British Museum on 10 Feb. 1799, aged 83, and was buried at Twickenham, in the cemetery near the London Road.

Morton was thrice married: first, in 1744, to Mary Berkeley, niece of Lady Elizabeth (Betty) Germaine, by whom he had an only daughter; secondly, in 1772, to Lady Savile, who died 10 Feb. 1791; and, lastly, at the end of 1791, to Elizabeth Pratt, a near relation of his second wife.

Morton published: 1. An improved edition of Dr. Bernard's 'Engraved Table of Alphabets,' 1759, fol. 2. Whitelocke's 'Notes upon the King's Writ for choosing Members of Parliament,' 13 Car. II, 1766, 4to. 3. Whitelocke's 'Account of the Swedish Embassy in 1653–4,' 2 vols., 1772, 4to, dedicated to Viscount Lumley. Dr. Burn, in the preface to his 'Justice of the Peace,' acknowledges obligations to Morton for assistance in the work; and in Nichols's 'Literary Illustrations' there are several letters concerning him. In one from E. M. Da Costa [q. v.], of the Royal Society, dated 1 July 1751, he is asked to collect fossils and make observations on them in Westmoreland and Lancashire, and is given directions as to the localities where they are to be found and directions for cataloguing them. Daniel Wray wrote to John Nichols, 29 Sept. 1771, that Morton had imported the 'League and Covenant of 1638, the original upon a giant skin of parchment, signed by a handsome number.'

[Munk's Coll. of Phys. 2nd edit. ii. 174–5; Edwards's Founders of the Brit. Mus., pp. 344, 516; Lysons's Environs of London, Suppl. vol. pp. 319, 322; Nichols's Lit. Illustr. i. 139, ii. 757–9; Allibone's Dict. of Engl. Lit. ii. 1375; Gent. Mag. 1799 pt. i. p. 250, and Europ. Mag. same year, p. 143; Chalmers's Biog. Dict.; authorities cited in text.] G. Le G. N.

MORTON, JOHN (1420?–1500), archbishop of Canterbury and cardinal, was born in Dorset, at either Bere Regis or Milborne St. Andrew, about 1420. He was the eldest son of Richard Morton, who belonged to a Nottinghamshire family which had migrated to Dorset (Hutchins, *Dorset*, ii. 594). His family has been traced back to Edward III's time. He was educated at Cerne Abbey, a house of Benedictines near his home, and, going to Oxford, joined Balliol College, and proceeded D.C.L. He had chosen the profession of law, which necessarily made him take orders, and he appears as commissary for the university in 1446 (*Munimenta Academica*, Rolls Ser., ii. 552). He removed to London, but kept up his connection with the university (*ib.* p. 584), practising chiefly as an ecclesiastical lawyer in the court of arches. Here he came under the notice of Bourchier, archbishop of Canterbury, who became his patron. Morton was at once admitted to the privy council, and was appointed chancellor of the duchy of Cornwall and a master in chancery. From this time he had much preferment, and was a great pluralist. In 1450 he became subdean of Lincoln, in 1453 he held the principalship of Peckwater Inn at Oxford and the living of Bloxworth in Dorset. In 1458 he became prebendary of Salisbury and Lincoln, resigning his subdeanery at Lincoln.

In the struggle between Lancaster and York, Morton followed the Lancastrian party, though for a short time accepting the inevitable ascendency of the Yorkists. He was probably with the Lancastrians on their march from the north early in 1461, and after the second battle of St. Albans, being chancellor to the young Prince Edward, he took part in the ceremony of making him a knight. After the accession of Edward IV he was at Towton in March 1461, and must have been in actual risk of his life. He was reported to be captured (*Paston Letters*, ed. Gairdner, ii. 7), but followed Margaret and Prince Edward for some time in their subsequent wanderings. He was naturally attainted, and lost all (Ramsay, *Lancaster and York*, ii. 283). When Margaret and De Brezé made their descent on England in the autumn of 1462, Morton met them, and he sailed with them from Bamborough to Sluys, when Margaret went to throw herself upon the Duke of Burgundy's mercy in July or August 1463 (*ib.* p. 296; William Wyrcester in *Wars of the English in France*, Rolls Ser., ii. ii. 781). He seems to have had no share in the outbreaks which resulted in the battles of Hedgeley Moor and Hexham. He lived, like Sir John Fortescue and other Lancastrians (cf. *Arch. Journal*, vii. 171), with Margaret at St. Mihiel in Bar. But when Warwick and Clarence decided to join the Lancastrians, Morton bore a large part in the reconciliation, and must have been well known to Louis XI. He left Angers on 4 Aug. 1470, and landed at Dartmouth with Warwick on 13 Sept. He was at once sent in advance, with Sir John Fortescue, to London, to prepare for Warwick's march thither, and this seems to confirm Campbell's statement that he was popular at this period, though he certainly was not so later. After the battle of Barnet (April 1471) he went to Weymouth, to meet the queen and Prince Edward, and with them passed to his old school at Cerne, and thence to Beaulieu.

When the battle of Tewkesbury seemed to have ended the wars of the Roses, Morton submitted. He petitioned (*Rot. Parl.* vi. 26), and his attainder was reversed. Bourchier was still his friend, and collated him in 1472 to the rectory of St. Dunstan's-in-the-East. In the same year he received the prebend of Isledon in St. Paul's Cathedral, which he resigned on receiving that of Chiswick in the following year. On 16 March 1472–3 he became master of the rolls, his patent being renewed in 1475. Edward, who was always wisely forgetful of the past history of his opponents, thoroughly trusted him, and sent him in 1474 on an embassy to the emperor and the king of Hungary, to secure their adhesion to the league which England had made with Burgundy against Louis XI of France. He seems to have returned very quickly (*Paston Letters*, iii. 123), and was made archdeacon of Winchester and Chester the same year. In 1475 he was one of the counsellors who arranged the treaty of Pecquigny, and was bribed like the rest (Gairdner, *Richard III*, p. 33). He performed a doubtful service to the Lancastrian cause at the same time by arranging for Queen Margaret's ransom. Morton continued to accumulate preferments, and on 31 Jan. 1478–9 became bishop of Ely, in succession to William Gray. He comforted Edward when dying in 1483, was an executor to his will, and assisted at his funeral (*Letters, &c., Richard III and Henry VII*, ed. Gairdner, Rolls Ser., i. 4). He was, of course, present at the meeting of the council on 13 June 1483, when Richard's plans were fully put into action. Richard came late, and joked with Morton about the strawberries he was growing in the gardens at Ely Place, Holborn (cf. SHAKESPEARE, *Richard III*, act iii. sc. 4); but, as a powerful adherent of the young prince, he was one of those who were arrested when the meeting broke up (GAIRDNER, *Richard III*, pp. 81 et seq.) The university of Oxford petitioned for his release, calling him her dearest son (WOOD, *Athenæ*, ed. Bliss). He was at first confined in the Tower, and then, at Buckingham's request, removed to his custody at Brecknock Castle [see STAFFORD, HENRY, 1454?–1483]. Here in 1483 Buckingham had a conversation with his prisoner which showed his own schemes against Richard to have been already formed, and at the same time suggested to Morton a way of using him against the king and in favour of the young Earl of Richmond (cf. GAIRDNER, *Henry VII*, p. 10, and *Richard III*, pp. 138, 149). Morton skilfully encouraged the duke in his opposition to Richard III, and brought him, through Reginald Bray, into close communication with the Countess of Richmond, and with Elizabeth, the queen-dowager. It has been said that this plot was due to the fact that Buckingham knew of the murder of the young princes, but it is more probable that that had not yet taken place, and that Buckingham chose to join the party of Richmond, as safer than following Richard's example. Morton, having directed the plot, urged that he ought to be in Ely to raise the men of his bishopric. Buckingham hesitated to allow him to leave Brecknock Castle, and Morton fled by night to Ely, and thence to Flanders (GAIRDNER, *Richard III*, pp. 138 et seq., *Henry VII*, pp. 11 et seq.; POLYDORE VERGIL, *English Hist.* ed. Ellis, Camden Soc., p. 198). He continued in constant correspondence with Lancastrians in England. When Richard in 1484 was plotting the capture of Henry of Richmond in Brittany, Morton heard of the scheme in time to send Christopher Urswick to warn Henry to escape into France, and thus saved Henry's life (*ib.* p. 206).

Morton remained in Flanders till after the settlement of the kingdom upon Henry VII in the parliament of November 1485, when Henry summoned him home. To his counsels the final victory of the Lancastrians was in a large degree attributed; and he doubtless was the great advocate for Henry's marriage with Elizabeth of York. His attainder was reversed, he was made a privy councillor, and for the rest of his life, as More makes Hythloday say in the 'Utopia,' 'The king depended much on his counsels, and the government seemed to be chiefly supported by him.' On 6 Oct. 1486 he succeeded Bourchier as archbishop of Canterbury, and on 6 March following he succeeded John Alcock, the founder of Jesus College, Cambridge, as lord chancellor. The chancellorship in his hands was the most important office in the government (cf. CAMPBELL, *Lives of the Lord Chancellors*, i. 417), and probably he was much more concerned with secular than with spiritual affairs. Practically nothing was done in convocation while he was archbishop, which may be regarded as the result of his master's policy, but he tried to reform both the regular and secular clergy, obtaining a bull in 1489, in contravention of the statutes of præmunire, enabling him to visit the monasteries in his province, and proceeding vigorously against St. Albans. As chancellor he opened parliament with speeches which, according to Campbell, more closely resemble the modern sovereign's speech than had been usual in similar compositions before his time (cf. CUNNINGHAM, *Hist. of Brit. Industry and Commerce*, i. 430). His duties included the delivery of the official answers to the foreign ambassadors (BERNARD ANDREA, *Hist. of Henry VII* in *Memor. of Henry VII*, Rolls Ser., p. 55). But it is difficult to detect in his actions anything beyond a very literal and faithful fulfilment of the policy devised by Henry VII. There was no originality in his political conduct, and Mr. Gairdner has suggested that he was at heart an ecclesiastic. He recommended to Henry, it is said, the plan of obtaining a bull against his enemies, and he obtained another which restrained the rights of sanctuary. His character suffered by his devotion to Henry (cf. *Cal. State Papers*, Venetian, 1202–1509, p. 743). He assisted in collecting the benevolences in 1491 for the French war (WILL. WYRC. p. 793), and has been traditionally known as the author of 'Morton's Fork' or 'Morton's Crutch,' but the truth seems rather to be that he and Richard Foxe [q. v.] did their best at the council to restrain Henry's avarice. In 1493 he had a dispute with the Bishop of London as to their respective rights over wills of personalty, in which he came out victor. In the same year Pope Alexander VI, at Henry's request, made him a cardinal, with the title of St. Anastasia (cf. *Cal. State Papers*, Venetian, 1202–1509, p. 537). At the magnificent ceremony by which Prince Henry was knighted and created Duke of York, on 1 Nov. 1494, Morton said mass at the feast, and afterwards he sat alone with the king at the high table. The university of Oxford early in 1495 made him its chancellor, in succession to Bishop Russell, though he gave fair warning that he could not attend to the duties. He also refused to take the customary oath, alleging that his graduation oath was sufficient. He must have been very old, but his strength was maintained, and he opened the parliament of 1496 with a long speech. He cannot have been sent in 1499 as ambassador to Maximilian, though a suggestion to that effect is found in the 'Venetian Calendar' (1202–1509, 796, 799). He died of a quartan ague on 15 Sept. 1500 at Knowle in Kent. He was buried in the crypt of Canterbury Cathedral. According to Wood (*Annals*, i. 642), the tomb became cracked, and the bones disappeared slowly till only the skull was left, and that Ralph Sheldon begged of his brother the archbishop in 1670.

Bacon says of Morton that 'he was a wise man and an eloquent, but in his nature harsh and haughty, much accepted by the king, but envied by the nobility, and hated of the people.' This unfavourable view of his character is not so trustworthy as the opinion of More, who knew him intimately, and gave a very sympathetic description of him in his 'Utopia' (ed. Arber, p. 36). According to More, 'his conversation was easy, but serious and grave. He spoke both gracefully and weightily. He was eminently skilled in the law, had a vast understanding and a prodigious memory; and those excellent talents with which nature had furnished him were improved by study and experience.'

Morton was a great builder. He received a patent on 26 July 1493 empowering him to impress workmen to repair the houses of his province in Kent, Surrey, and Sussex (*Letters*, &c., ii. 374; *Chronicles of the White Rose*, p. 198). At Ely his memory is preserved by Morton's Dyke, a great drainage trench which he cut through the fens from Peterborough to Wisbech. He repaired the episcopal palace at Hatfield and the castle at Wisbech; his arms are on the church tower of Wisbech. At Oxford he repaired the school of Canon Law and helped to rebuild St. Mary's Church. To literature he extended some patronage. Thomas More he took into his household, and foretold a great career for him.

The 'History of Richard III,' usually ascribed to Sir Thomas More [q. v.], and printed in the collected editions of More's English and Latin works, was probably originally written in Latin by Morton (cf. WALPOLE, *Historic Doubts* in *Works*, ii. 111; BRIDGETT, *Sir Thomas More*, p. 79). It is clearly the work of a Lancastrian and a contemporary of Edward IV, which More was not, and it is assigned to Morton by Sir John Harington and by Sir George Buc. More's connection with the work seems to have been confined to translating it into English and to amplifying it in the English version (cf. *Notes and Queries*, 2nd ser. i. 105). The 'Chronicle' of Hall probably owed something to Morton's suggestions.

[Authorities quoted; Chronicles of Hall and Fabyan; Hook's Lives of the Archbishops of Canterbury, v. 387 et seq.; Continuator of Croyland in 'Rerum Anglic. Script.' (Fell and Fulman), p. 566; Hutchins's Dorset, i. 104, 154, 158, ii. 594; Basin's Hist. des regnes de Charles VII et Louis XI, ed. Quicherat (Soc. de l'Hist. de France), iii. 137; Mémoires de Ph. de Commynes, ed. Dupont (Soc. de l'Hist. de France), i. 352, ii. 166; Paston Letters, ed. Gairdner; Clermont's Life of Fortescue; Bates's Border Strongholds of Northumberland, i. 254 et seq.; Campbell's Materials for the Hist. of Henry VII; Bentham's Ely, p. 179 et seq.; Hasted's Kent, ii. 19, 95, 99, 694; Baker's Chron. pp. 228–37; Newcome's St. Albans, p. 403; T. Mozley's Henry VII, Prince Arthur, and Cardinal Morton; R. I. Woodhouse's Memoir of Morton, 1895; arts. EDWARD, PRINCE OF WALES, 1453–1471, and MARGARET OF ANJOU.]

W. A. J. A.

MORTON, JOHN (1671?–1726), naturalist, was born between 18 July 1670 and 18 July 1671. He matriculated at Cambridge on 17 Dec. 1688, graduated B.A. from Emmanuel College in 1691; took an *ad eundem* degree at Oxford in 1694, and proceeded M.A. in 1695. As early as 1694 (*Sloane MS.* 4062) Morton was curate of Great Oxendon, Northamptonshire; in 1703 he was elected fellow of the Royal Society. His first letter to Sloane (*Sloane MS.* 4053, f. 329) is dated 7 Feb. 1703, and alludes to Captain Hatton, to his recent election into the Royal Society, and his 'Natural History of Northamptonshire, then in progress.' In a letter to Dr. Richard Richardson [q. v.] of North Bierley (*Richardson Correspondence*, p. 85), dated 9 Nov. 1704, he writes: 'My acquaintance with Mr. Ray initiated me early in the search and study of plants: from the reading of Dr. Lister's books, I became an inquirer after fossil shells; and my correspondence with Dr. Woodward, Dr. Sloane, and Mr. Lhwyd, has supported my curiosity.' Sloane appears to have visited him at Oxendon between May 1705 and April 1706; and in the latter year Morton was instituted as rector of that place. In the 'Philosophical Transactions' for 1706 (No. 305, xxv. 2210) appeared 'A Letter from the Rev. Mr. Morton, A.M. and S.R.S., to Dr. Hans Sloane, S.R. Secr., containing a Relation of river and other Shells digg'd up, together with various Vegetable Bodies, in a bituminous marshy earth, near Mears-Ashby, in Northamptonshire: with some Reflections thereupon: as also an Account of the Progress he has made in the Natural History of Northamptonshire.' In this, and in his later work, Morton adopted the views of Dr. John Woodward as to the deluge and the entombment of fossils according to their gravities. In 1710 he became rector of Great Oxendon. In 1712 he published 'The Natural History of Northamptonshire, with some account of the Antiquities; to which is annexed a transcript of Domesday Book, as far as it relates to that County,' London, folio. This book deals largely with 'figured fossils,' of which it contains several plates, and Pulteney praises the botanical part; but in Whalley's 'History of Northamptonshire' the transcript of Domesday is said to be very inaccurate. Writing to Richardson in 1713, Morton says: 'I frequently drank your health with my friend Mr. Buddle, and other of the London botanists.' He died on 18 July 1726, aged 55, and was buried at Great Oxendon, where a monument, with an inscription to his memory, was erected at the expense of Sir Hans Sloane.

[Sloane MS. 4053, ff. 329–54; Nichols's Illustrations of the Literary History of the Eighteenth Century, i. 326; Pulteney's Sketches of the Progress of Botany, i. 354; Notes and Queries, 1st ser. vi. 358.] G. S. B.

MORTON, JOHN (1781–1864), agriculturist, born on 17 July 1781 at Ceres, Fifeshire, was the second son of Robert Morton, by his wife Kate Pitcairn. He was educated at the parish school till the family removed to Flisk. His first farm was 'Wester,' or 'Little Kinnear,' at Kilmany, Fifeshire. While there Morton employed his 'leisure periods' in walking repeatedly over most of the counties of England, noting their geology and farm practice. His notes were afterwards published in his book 'On Soils.' In 1810 he removed to Dulverton, Somerset, where he remained till 1818, when he was appointed agent to Lord Ducie's Gloucestershire estates. Here he projected and conducted the 'Whitfield Example Farm,' and established the 'Uley Agricultural Machine Factory.' He invented the 'Uley cultivator' and other agricultural appliances. In 1852 he resigned his charge and retired to Nailsworth, Gloucestershire, where he died on 26 July 1864. He married, on 15 Jan. 1812, Jean, sister of Dr. Thomas Chalmers [q.v.]

His work 'On the Nature and Property of Soils,' 8vo, London, 1838, 3rd edit. 1842, 4th edit. 1843, was the first attempt to connect the character of the soil with the geological formation beneath, and thus to give a scientific basis to the work of the land valuer. Shortly after its publication he was elected a fellow of the Geological Society. In conjunction with his friend J. Trimmer, the geologist [q. v.], he wrote 'An Attempt to Estimate the Effects of Protecting Duties on the Profits of Agriculture,' 8vo, London, 1845, advocating the repeal of the corn laws from the agricultural point of view. He also published A 'Report on the . . . Whitfield Farm,' 12mo, London, 1840.

His son, John Chalmers Morton (1821–1888), born on 1 July 1821, was educated at the Merchistoun Castle School, Edinburgh, under his uncle, Charles Chalmers. He afterwards attended some of the university lectures, took the first prize for mathematics, and was a student in David Low's agricultural classes [see Low, David]. In 1838 he went to assist his father on the Whitfield Example Farm, and shortly after joined the newly formed Royal Agricultural Society. He accepted the offer of the editorship of the 'Agricultural Gazette' on its foundation in 1844; this connection brought him to London, and continued till his death. When Low retired in 1854 from his chair at Edinburgh, Morton conducted the classes till the appointment of Professor Wilson. He was inspector under the land commissioners, and also served for six years (1868–74) with Dr. Frankland and Sir W. Denison on the royal commission for inquiry into the pollution of rivers. Morton died at his Harrow residence on 3 May 1888. He married in 1854 Miss Clarence Cooper Hayward of Frocester Court, Gloucestershire. A son, Mr. E. J. C. Morton, was elected M.P. for Devonport in 1892.

Morton edited and brought out: 1. 'A Cyclopædia of Agriculture' in 1855. 2. 'Morton's New Farmer's Almanac,' 12mo and 8vo, London, 1856–70. Continued as 'Morton's Almanac for Farmers and Landowners,' 1871, &c. 3. 'Handbook of Dairy Husbandry,' 8vo, London, 1860. 4. 'Handbook of Farm Labour,' 8vo, London, 1861; new edit. 1868. 5. 'The Prince Consort's Farms,' 4to, London, 1863. 6. 'An Abstract of the Agricultural Holdings . . . Act, 1875,' for Bayldon's 'Art of Valuing Rents,' &c. 9th edit. 8vo, London, 1876. He also edited 'Arthur Young's Farmer's Calendar,' 21st edit. 8vo, London, 1861–2, which he reissued as the 'Farmer's Calendar' in 1870; 6th edit. 1884; and the 'Handbooks of the Farm' Series, 7 vols. 1881–4, contributing to the series 'Diary of the Farm,' 'Equipment of the Farm,' and 'Soil of the Farm.' For a time he helped to edit the 'Journal of the

Royal Agricultural Society,' and contributed largely to its pages, as well as to the 'Journal of the Society of Arts.'

[Information kindly supplied by J. Morton, Earl of Ducie's Office, Manchester; Gardeners' Chron. and Agricultural Gazette, 4 Oct. 1873, with portrait; Agricultural Gazette, 30 July 1864 and 7 May 1888, p. 428, with portrait; Journ. Royal Agricultural Soc. 2nd ser. xxiv. 691; Brit. Mus. Cat.] B. B. W.

MORTON, JOHN MADDISON (1811–1891), dramatist, second son of Thomas Morton (1764?–1838) [q. v.], was born 3 Jan. 1811 at the Thames-side village of Pangbourne. Between 1817 and 1820 he was educated in France and Germany, and, after being for a short time at school in Islington, went to the well-known school on Clapham Common of Charles Richardson [q. v.], the lexicographer. Here he remained 1820–7, meeting Charles James Mathews [q. v.], Julian Young, and many others connected with the stage. Lord John Russell gave him in 1832 a clerkship in Chelsea Hospital, which he resigned in 1840. His first farce, produced in April 1835 at the Queen's Theatre in Tottenham Street, then under the management of Miss Mordaunt, subsequently known as Mrs. Nisbett, was called 'My First Fit of the Gout.' It was supported by Mrs. Nisbett, Wrench, and Morris Barnett. Between that time and the close of his life Morton wrote enough plays, chiefly farces, to entitle him to rank among the most prolific of dramatists. With few exceptions these are taken from the French. He showed exceptional facility in suiting French dialogues to English tastes, and many of his pieces enjoyed a marvellous success, and contributed greatly to build up the reputation of actors such as Buckstone, Wright, Harley, the Keeleys, Compton, and others.

To Drury Lane Theatre Morton gave the 'Attic Story;' 'A Thumping Legacy;' 'My Wife 's come;' 'The Alabama,' and pantomimes on the subjects of William Tell, Valentine and Orson, Gulliver, and St. George and the Dragon. At Covent Garden appeared his 'Original;' 'Chaos is come again;' 'Brother Ben;' 'Cousin Lambkin;' 'Sayings and Doings;' and the pantomime of 'Guy, Earl of Warwick.' Among the pieces sent to the Haymarket were 'Grimshaw, Bagshaw, and Bradshaw;' the 'Two Bonnycastles;' the 'Woman I adore;' 'A Capital Match;' 'Your Life's in Danger;' 'To Paris and Back for Five Pounds;' the 'Rights and Wrongs of Women;' 'Lend me Five Shillings;' 'Take Care of Dowb;' the 'Irish Tiger;' 'Old Honesty;' the 'Milliner's Holiday;' the 'King and I;' the 'Three Cuckoos;' the 'Double-bedded Room;' 'Fitzsmyth of Fitzsmyth Hall;' the 'Trumpeter's Wedding;' the 'Garden Party' (13 Aug. 1877); and 'Sink or Swim,' a two-act comedy written in conjunction with his father. The Adelphi produced 'A most Unwarrantable Intrusion;' 'Who stole the Pocket Book?' 'Slasher and Crasher;' 'My Precious Betsy;' 'A Desperate Game;' 'Whitebait at Greenwich;' 'Waiting for an Omnibus;' 'Going to the Derby;' 'Aunt Charlotte's Maid;' 'Margery Daw;' 'Love and Hunger;' and the 'Steeple Chase.' At the Princess's, chiefly under Charles Kean's management, were produced 'Betsy Baker;' 'From Village to Court' (13 Nov. 1850); 'Away with Melancholy;' 'A Game of Romps;' the Muleteer of Toledo;' 'How Stout you're getting;' 'Don't judge by Appearances;' 'A Prince for an Hour;' 'Sent to the Tower;' 'Our Wife;' 'Dying for Love;' 'Thirty-three next Birthday;' 'My Wife's Second Floor;' 'Master Jones's Birthday;' and the pantomimes of 'Aladdin,' 'Blue Beard, 'Miller and his Men,' and 'White Cat.' The Olympic saw 'All that glitters is not Gold;' 'Ticklish Times;' 'A Husband to Order;' 'A Regular Fix;' 'Wooing One's Wife;' 'My Wife's Bonnet;' and the 'Miser's Treasure,' 29 April 1878.

Morton's most popular piece, 'Box and Cox,' afterwards altered by (Sir) F. C. Burnand, and set to music by Sir Arthur Sullivan as 'Cox and Box,' was produced at the Lyceum 1 Nov. 1847. It is adapted from two French vaudevilles, one entitled 'Une Chambre à deux lits;' it has been played many hundreds of times, and translated into German, Dutch, and Russian. The same house had already seen on 24 Feb. 1847, 'Done on both Sides,' and the 'Spitfire;' and subsequently saw 'Poor Pillicoddy.' At Punch's playhouse, afterwards the Strand, he gave 'A Hopeless Passion;' 'John Dobbs;' 'Where there's a Will there's a Way;' 'Friend Waggles;' 'Which of the Two;' 'A Little Savage;' 'Catch a Weazel.' The St. James's saw the 'Pacha of Pimlico;' 'He would and she wouldn't;' 'Pouter's Wedding;' 'Newington Butts;' and 'Woodcock's Little Game.' At the Marylebone was seen a drama entitled the 'Midnight Watch.' To the Court he gave, 27 Jan. 1875, 'Maggie's Situation;' a comedietta, and to Toole's (his latest production) 7 Dec. 1885, a three-act farce, called 'Going it.' The popularity of burlesque diminished the influence of farce, and the altered conditions of playgoing from about 1860 onwards practically took away Morton's earnings. In 1867 he was giving public readings. On 15 Aug. 1881 he was, on the nomination of the Queen, appointed a brother of the Charterhouse. A benefit at which very many actors assisted was given him at the Haymarket on 16 Oct. 1889. Though somewhat soured in later life, Morton was a worthy and a not unamiable man. He was in early life an assiduous fisherman. His dialogue is full of *double entente*, sometimes, after the fashion of his day, a little coarse. It was generally humorous and telling. He may claim to have fitted to a nicety the best comedians of his day, and to have caused during the productive portion of his career from 1835 to 1865, more laughter than any other dramatist of his epoch. He died at the Charterhouse 19 Dec. 1891, being buried on the 23rd at Kensal Green.

Many of Morton's plays are published in the collections, English and American, of English plays.

[The chief source of information for Morton's early career is the short Memoir in Plays for Home Performance, by the author of Box and Cox, with Biographical Introduction by Clement Scott, 1889, the particulars being supplied by Morton himself. Personal knowledge furnishes a few facts. The Times for 21 and 24 Dec. 1891; the Era for 26 Dec. 1891; the Era Almanack, various years; the Sunday Times, various years; Notes and Queries, 8th ser. iv. 432, v. 144; and Scott and Howard's Life of E. L. Blanchard have been consulted. While not aiming at completeness, the list of plays is longer and more accurate than any that has appeared. Inextricable confusion is apparent in previously published lists.] J. K.

MORTON, NICHOLAS, D.D. (*fl.* 1586), papal agent, was son of Charles Morton, esq., of Bawtry, Yorkshire, by Maud, daughter of William Dallyson, esq., of Lincolnshire, his race, as Strype observes, being 'universally papists, descended as well by the man as woman' (*Annals of the Reformation*, ii. 389, fol.) He was born at Bawtry, and received his academical education in the university of Cambridge, where he graduated B.A. in 1542–1543 and commenced M.A. in 1545 (Cooper, *Athenæ Cantabr.* ii. 10). He was constituted one of the original fellows of Trinity College by the charter of foundation dated 19 Dec. 1546 (Rymer, *Fœdera*, xv. 107), and he was B.D. in 1554. In 1556 he was appointed by Cardinal Pole one of the six preachers in the cathedral church of Canterbury (Strype, *Memorials*, iii. 290). He is stated to have been a prebendary of York, but this appears somewhat doubtful (Dodd, *Church Hist.* ii. 114).

Adhering to the Roman catholic religion, he, soon after the coronation of Queen Elizabeth, withdrew to Rome, and was there created D.D. and constituted apostolical penitentiary. He was examined as a witness at the papal court in the proceedings there taken to excommunicate Queen Elizabeth, and was despatched to England to impart to the catholic priests, as from the pope, those faculties and that jurisdiction which they could no longer receive in the regular manner from their bishops, and to apprise them and the catholic gentry that a bull of deposition of Queen Elizabeth was in preparation. He landed in Lincolnshire, and the result of his intrigues was the northern rebellion of 1569 under the Earls of Northumberland and Westmoreland (Cooper, *Athenæ Cantabr.* ii. 11). Morton was 'the most earnest mover of the rebellion,' and his first persuasion was to tell the Earl of Northumberland and many others of the excommunication which threatened them, and of the dangers touching their souls and the loss of their country (*Cal. State Papers*, Dom. Eliz., Addenda, 1566–1579, p. 390). When and how Morton effected his escape from England does not appear.

About 1571 he went from Rome to the English College at Louvain, carrying letters and money to its inmates from the pope. On 24 May 1580 he and Thomas Goldwell, formerly bishop of St. Asaph, arrived at the English College at Rheims from Rome, to which city they returned on 8 Aug. the same year, after having in the interim paid a visit to Paris (*Douay Diaries*, pp. 165, 167, 169). The indictment framed in 1589 against Philip, earl of Arundel, for high treason states that William Allen, D.D., Dr. Morton, Robert Parsons, Edmund Campion, John Hart, and other false traitors, on 31 March 1580, at Rheims, and on other days at Rome and Rheims, compassed and imagined to depose and kill the queen, to raise war against her, and to subvert the established church and government (*Baga de Secretis*, pouch 49). In a list of certain English catholics abroad, sent by a secret agent to the English government about 1580, mention is made of 'Nycolas Morton, prieste and doctor, who was penytensiary for the Englyshe nation; but nowe dealythe no more in that office, and yet hathe out of the same xii crones by monthe, and everye daye ii loaves of brede and ii chambells; besydes a benyfice in Piacenza, worth V[c] crownes by yeare, w[ch] y[e] cardynall off Alexandria gave hym' (*Cal. State Papers*, Dom. Eliz. vol. cxlvi. *n.* 18). On 5 May 1582 a correspondent of Walsingham announced the arrest of Dr. Wendon, Dr. Morton, and other English pensioners at Rome. Morton was still a resident in that city on 9 Dec. 1586 when he was in company with Robert Morton, his nephew. The latter was son of his brother, Robert Morton, by his second wife, Ann, daughter of John Norton, esq., and widow of Robert Plumpton, esq., of Plumpton or Plompton, Yorkshire. This unfortunate nephew was executed in Lincoln's Inn Fields, London, on account of his sacerdotal character, on 26 Aug. 1588.

[Harleian Miscellany (Malham), ii. 173, 203, 208; Hunter's South Yorkshire, i. 76; Nichols's Collect. Topog. et Geneal. v. 80, 86; Records of the English Catholics, i. 433, ii. 403; Sanderus, De Visibili Monarchia, p. 730; Sharp's Memorials of the Northern Rebellion, pp. 264, 280, 281; Soames's Elizabethan Religious History, pp. 107, 108; Cal. State Papers, Dom. Eliz. 1547–80 pp. 651, 694, 1581–90 p. 53; Wood's Athenæ Oxon. (Bliss), i. 471; Lingard's Hist. of England, vi. 205.] T. C.

MORTON, RICHARD (1637–1698), ejected minister and physician, was the son of Robert Morton, minister of Bewdley Chapel, Worcestershire, from 1635 to 1646. Baxter speaks of the father as 'my old friend.' Richard was baptised at Ribbesford, the parish to which Bewdley belonged, on 30 July 1637 (par. reg.) He matriculated at Oxford as a commoner of Magdalen Hall on 17 March 1653–4, migrated to New College, whence he proceeded B.A. 30 Jan. 1656–7, and soon after became chaplain to his college. On 8 July 1659 he proceeded M.A. At the time he was chaplain in the family of Philip Foley of Prestwood in Staffordshire, and was appointed by him to the vicarage of Kinver in Staffordshire. The parish registers of Kinver show a distinct handwriting from 1659 to 1662, which is doubtless that of Morton. Being unable to comply with the requirements of the Act of Uniformity, he was ejected from his living in August 1662, when he turned his attention to medicine. On the nomination of the Prince of Orange he was created M.D. of Oxford on 20 Dec. 1670, and afterwards settled in London. He was admitted a candidate of the College of Physicians on 20 March 1675–6, and a fellow on 23 Dec. 1679. In 1680 he was incorporated at Cambridge on his doctor's degree. Morton was one of four fellows of the College of Physicians, whose names were omitted in the charter of James II in 1686, but he was restored to his position in 1689. He was censor in 1690, 1691, 1697, and was one of the physicians in ordinary to the king. He resided in London in Grey Friars Court, Newgate Street. He died on 30 Aug. 1698, and was buried in the nave of Christ Church, Newgate Street, on 7 Sept.

Baxter says of him that he was 'a man of great gravity, calmness, sound principles, of no faction, an excellent preacher, of an upright life.'

Morton had at least three children, a son, Richard (noticed below), and two daughters, Sarah born in 1685, and Marcia in 1689.

He published two important medical works: 1. 'Phthisiologia: seu Exercitationes de Phthisi,' London, 1689; Frankfort, 1690; London, 1694 (in English); London, 1696; Ulm, 1714; London, 1720 (in English); Helmstadt, 1780. 2. 'Πυρετολογία: seu Exercitationes de Morbis Universalibus Acutis,' London, 1692; 1693; Berne, 1693. Second part, entitled 'Πυρετολογίας pars altera, sive exercitatio de Febribus Inflammatoriis Universalibus,' Bremen, 1693; London, 1694. The first part was reviewed in No. 199 of the 'Philosophical Transactions,' xvii. 717–22, 1694. Morton's works, with others by Harris, Cole, Lister, and Sydenham, were published as 'Opera Medica,' Geneva, 1696; Amsterdam, 1696; Leyden, 1697; Lyons, 1697; Amsterdam, 1699; Geneva, 1727; Venice, 1733, 1737; Lyons, 1739, 1754; Leyden, 1757.

Morton's 'Phthisiologia' is a treatise of the highest value. Following the method of Sydenham, it is based on his own clinical observations, with very little reference to books. All the conditions of wasting which he had observed are described without regard to the anatomical origin of the wasting. The word phthisis Morton uses in a very wide sense. He not only describes the wasting due to tubercle in the lungs, to which the term is now generally restricted, but also the wasting effects of prolonged jaundice, gout, continued and intermittent fever, and other ailments. His 'Pyretologia,' a general treatise on fevers, is less original, but contains many interesting cases, among them an account of his own illness in 1690. Among the Rawlinson MSS. in the Bodleian Library are several methods of preparing Peruvian bark, one of which is said to be by Morton (c. 406 [5]). In the same collection are printed prospectuses, dated London, February 1680, of a work never published, but which appears to have been the first form of 'Phthisiologia' and Πυρετολογία (c. 406 [7], and c. 419 [4]).

Morton's portrait, from a painting by B. Orchard, has been frequently engraved, and is prefixed to several editions of his works, as well as to the notice of him in 'Lives of Eminent and Remarkable Characters in Essex, Suffolk, and Norfolk,' and in Manget's 'Bibliotheca Scriptorum Medicorum' (1731).

Richard Morton (1669-1730), his only son, was born in 1669. He was entered at Exeter College, Oxford (as of Enwood, Surrey), on 16 March 1685-6, and matriculated on 19 March of the same year. Leaving Oxford on 17 Oct. 1688, he migrated to Catharine Hall, Cambridge, where he was admitted fellow commoner on 22 Nov. 1688. He proceeded B.A. in 1691, and M.D. *per literas regias* in 1695. He was admitted a candidate of the College of Physicians on 22 Dec. 1695, and fellow on 22 Dec. 1707. He was appointed physician to Greenwich Hospital in April 1716, and died at Greenwich on 1 Feb. 1730, and was buried at Plumstead. Some verses of his appear among several eulogies by Clopton Havers [q. v.] and others on his father, prefixed to the first edition of the second volume of the Πυρετολογία (London, 1694).

[Munk's Coll. of Phys. i. 398-9, ii. 20; Sylvester's Reliq. Baxterianæ, pt. iii. p. 96; Lives of Eminent and Remarkable Characters in Essex, Suffolk, and Norfolk; Burton's Hist. of Bewdley, pp. 26, xxix, App.; Wood's Fasti (Bliss), vol. ii. cols. 191, 220, 326; Locke's Letters, 1708, pp. 281-4; Garth's Dispensary, 1775, pp. 11, 84; Addit. MS. 19165, ff. 579, 581; Palmer's Nonconformist's Memorial, iii. 235; Post Boy, 1-3 Sept. 1698; Eloy's Dict. Historique de la Médecine; Watt's Bibl. Brit.; Catalogues of Libraries of Surg. Gen. (Washington); Trin. Coll. Dublin, Med. and Chir. Soc.; Macray's Cat. of Rawlinson MSS. in Bodleian Library; information from the Rev. E. H. Winnington Ingram of Ribbesford, the Rev. John Hodgson of Kinver, and from Norman Moore, esq., M.D.; Registers of Exeter College, per the Rev. C. W. Boase; Records of Greenwich Hospital, per G. T. Lambert, esq.] B. P.

MORTON, ROBERT (*d.* 1497), bishop of Worcester, was the nephew of Cardinal John Morton (1420-1500) [q. v.] His father was William Morton (Nichols, *Collectanea Topographica et Geneal.* iii. 170), not Sir Rowland, who did not die till 1554 (Burke, *Extinct Baronage*, p. 373). He became prebendary of Thorngate, Lincoln, 16 Aug. 1471, and succeeded his uncle as archdeacon of Winchester in 1478. He held the degree of LL.D. (Wharton, *Anglia Sacra*, i. 538). On 30 May 1477 his uncle had secured the reversion of the office of master of the rolls for him in the event of his own death or resignation. Robert obtained it by a new patent 9 Jan. 1479. He kept the office under Edward IV and Edward V, and lost it under Richard III, when his uncle was in disgrace. He was reinstated by Henry VII, and named as one of the commissioners to perform the office of steward on Henry's coronation. He said he required help as master of the rolls because of his activity in the king's service, and a coadjutor was given him 13 Nov. 1485.

In 1481 he was canon of Windsor, but he resigned the office 8 March 1486. On 15 March following he was granted, jointly with Margaret, countess of Richmond, the advowson of a prebend in the church of Windsor and the advowson of a canonry in Windsor (21 Dec. 1487 and 12 Jan. 1488). On 8 June 1482 he was collated archdeacon of Gloucester, and resigned when he became a bishop. On 16 Oct. 1486 he received a papal provision for the bishopric of Worcester, obtained a license of consecration from his uncle 24 Jan. 1486-7, was consecrated 28 Jan., and received his temporalities 10 Feb. He was enthroned by proxy 22 July 1487; he instituted to vacant benefices as early as 8 Jan. (Thomas, *Account of the Bishops of Worcester*, p. 200).

On 15 March 1497 he received a pardon from Henry VII, which was intended to secure his property against extortions. He died in the following April or May. His arms are given in Thomas and his epitaph in Browne Willis. He was buried in the nave of St. Paul's Cathedral, London. In his will he gave twenty marks to the cathedral of Worcester, and directed that he should be buried in the cemetery of the place where he should die (Browne Willis, *Survey*, i. 643). The same writer states that Morton received many other preferments, but these seem to have belonged to a person named Robert Moreton, whom Le Neve does not identify with the bishop.

[Foss's Judges of England, v. 67, &c.; Le Neve's Fasti Ecclesiæ Anglicanæ, ed. Hardy, ii. 223, iii. 26, 78, 389; Thomas's Account of Bishops of Worcester, p. 200.] M. B.

MORTON, THOMAS (*d.* 1646), author of 'New English Canaan,' was an attorney of Clifford's Inn, London, who appears to have practised chiefly in the west of England (Young, *Chronicles of Massachusetts*, p. 321). He was a man of good education and an able lawyer, but he bore an evil reputation, ill-used his wife, and was even suspected of having murdered his partner (*Mass. Hist. Coll.* 3rd ser. viii. 323). The allusions in his book show that he was passionately fond of field sports and travelled much. In June 1622 he landed at New England with Thomas Weston's company, and remained for about three months, taking a survey of the country, with which he was delighted. In 1625, having bought a partnership in Captain Wollaston's venture, he again sailed for Massachusetts Bay. His leader fixed the plantation at 'Mount Wollaston' (now Braintree), on the shores of the bay. Wollaston soon left for Virginia with most of the servants, and Morton established himself in the summer of 1626 in control over the remainder at 'Mare-Mount' (Merry Mount), as he called the place. In the spring of 1627 he erected the maypole, and on May day, in company with the Indians, held high revel, greatly to the disgust of the Plymouth elders. The business methods which he pursued were, however, a more serious matter. In trading for furs with the Indians, he not only sold them guns and ammunition, but instructed them in their use. He was thus acting in violation of the law. When in 1625 the Plymouth people found their way into Maine, and first opened a trade with the Indians there, Morton was not slow in following them. In 1628 the Plymouth settlers established a permanent station on the Kennebec; yet in 1627, if not in 1626, Morton had forestalled them there, and hindered them of a season's furs. The Plymouth community ultimately resolved to suppress Merry Mount, which was rapidly developing into a nest of pirates. After endeavouring to reason with Morton, they sent Captain Miles Standish [q. v.] to arrest him. He was taken at Wessagusset (now Weymouth), but managed to escape in the night to Mount Wollaston, where, after offering some resistance, he was recaptured. He was sent back to England in 1628, in charge of Captain John Oldham (1600?–1636) [q. v.], with letters from Governor William Bradford [q. v.], addressed respectively to the council for New England and Sir Ferdinando Gorges [q.v.], requesting that he might be brought 'to his answer' (*ib.* 1st ser. iii. 62). In the meantime John Endecott [q. v.], as governor of the chartered new Massachusetts Company, had jurisdiction over Morton's establishment. He ordered the maypole to be cut down, and changed the name of the place to 'Mount Dagon.'

Morton managed to ingratiate himself with both Oldham and Gorges. Bradford's complaints were accordingly ignored. He also made himself useful to Isaac Allerton in his efforts to obtain a charter for the Plymouth colony. Allerton, when he returned to New England in August 1629, scandalised Plymouth by bringing Morton back with him, lodging him in his house, and for a while employing him as his secretary. Morton subsequently returned to Mount Wollaston, and encouraged the 'old planters' in their resistance to the new Massachusetts Company. He refused to sign articles which Endecott had drawn up for the better government and trade of the colony, and set his authority at defiance. There is reason to suppose that he was employed by Gorges to act as a spy, and was anticipating the arrival of John Oldham at the head of an expedition to be despatched by Gorges. He continued to deal with the Indians as he saw fit, though not in firearms. In August or September 1630 he was arrested, and after being set in the stocks was again banished to England, and his house was burned down. He had a long and tempestuous passage, and was nearly starved. For some time he was imprisoned in Exeter gaol, but by 1631 was at liberty, and busily engaged in Gorges's intrigues for the overthrow of the Massachusetts charter. A petition was presented to the privy council on 19 Dec. 1632 asking the lords to inquire into the methods through which the charter had been procured, and into the abuses which had been practised under it. The various allegations were based on the affidavits of Morton and two other witnesses. On 1 May 1634 he wrote to William Jeffreys, an 'old planter' at Wessagusset, triumphantly informing him that as a result a committee, with Laud at its head, had been appointed, which was to make Gorges governor-general of the colony (*Mass. Hist. Coll.* 2nd ser. vi. 428–30). In May 1635 Morton was appointed solicitor to the new organisation, and successfully prosecuted a 'suit at law for the repealing of the patent belonging to the Massachusetts Company.' In March 1636, while against the company, he seems to have been in the pay of George Cleaves, a man subsequently prominent in the early history of Maine (*ib.* 4th ser. vi. 127). In August 1637 Gorges wrote to Winthrop that Morton was 'wholely casheered from intermedlinge with anie our affaires hereafter' (*ib.* 4th ser. vii. 331); but in 1641, when Gorges, as 'lord of the province of Maine,' granted a municipal charter to the town of Acomenticus (now York), Morton's name appears as first of the three witnesses. The whole scheme failed for want of funds.

In the summer of 1643 Morton, starved out of England, reappeared once more at Plymouth, and endeavoured to pass himself off as a Commonwealth man who was commissioned by Alexander Rigby, M.P., to act in his behalf for a claim of territory in Maine. Not succeeding, he is said to have gone to Maine in June 1644. A warrant for his arrest was at once despatched. In August he was in Rhode Island, promising grants of land to all who professed loyalty to the new governor-general (Palfrey, *Collections*, ii. 147 *n.*) By 9 Sept. he was a prisoner at Boston. In November 1644 he was charged before the general court with libelling the colony before the privy council and in his book, and with promoting a quo warranto against it. His letter to Jeffreys was produced in evidence. The proceedings failed for want of proof, and he was ordered to be imprisoned until fresh evidence was brought from England. In May 1645 he petitioned for his release. After enduring a cruel confinement for about a year, he was again called before the court, formally fined 100*l.*, and set at liberty. He retired to Acomenticus, where he died in poverty in 1646 (WINTHROP, *History of New England*, ed. Savage, ii. 192).

Morton is author of 'New English Canaan, or New Canaan containing an Abstract of New England. Composed in three Bookes,' 4to, Amsterdam, 1637. His description of the natural features of the country and his account of the Indians are of interest and value, and he throws an amusing side-light upon the social history of the pilgrim and puritan colonies. Though printed in Holland in 1637, the book was entered in the 'Stationers' Register' in London on 18 Nov. 1633, in the name of Charles Greene as publisher, and at least one copy is known bearing Greene's imprint, but without a date. It has been reprinted by Force in vol. ii. of his American tracts, and by the Prince Society, with an introduction and notes, by C. F. Adams, jun., 4to, Boston, 1883. Morton's career is the subject of John Lothrop Motley's novels, 'Morton's Hope,' 1839, and 'Merry Mount,' 1849, and of Nathaniel Hawthorne's short story, 'The Maypole of Merry Mount.'

[Adams's Introduction referred to; Savage's Genealogical Dict. iii. 245; Winsor's Hist. of America, vol. iii.; Nathaniel Morton's New England's Memorial; A Few Observations on the Prince Society's Edition of the New English Canaan, reprinted from the Churchman, New York, 1883.] G. G.

MORTON, THOMAS (1564–1659), bishop successively of Chester, of Lichfield, and of Durham, the sixth of the nineteen children of Richard Morton, mercer, of York, and alderman of that city, by his wife Elizabeth Leedale, was born in the parish of All Saints Pavement, York, on 20 March 1564. He received his early education at the grammar schools of York and Halifax; at the former the conspirator Guy Fawkes [q. v.] was his schoolfellow. He entered St. John's College, Cambridge, as a pensioner in 1582, and was admitted scholar in 1584. He graduated B.A. in 1586, and M.A. in 1590. He was chosen fellow under Dr. Whitaker, 'against eight competitors well recommended and better befriended, purely for his learning and work' (BAKER, *Hist. of St. John's College*, i. 184). Ordained deacon in 1592, and priest in 1594, he took the degree of B.D. in 1598, and that of D.D. 'with great distinction' in 1606. He was appointed university lecturer in logic, and continued his studies at Cambridge till 1598, when, through his father's influence, he was presented to the rectory of Long Marston, near York. Here he devoted himself assiduously to his spiritual duties, but was soon appointed chaplain to Lord Huntingdon, lord president of the north, and his parochial work was undertaken in his absence by 'a pious and learned assistant.' In 1602, when the plague was raging at York, he devoted himself to the inmates of the pest-house. To avoid spreading the infection he suffered no servants to attend him, and carried on the crupper of his saddle sacks containing the food and medicaments needed by the sufferers.

While in the north he acquired great reputation for the skill with which he conducted disputations with Roman catholics, who were numerous there; many of them, we are told, including 'some of considerable standing'—Dr. Herbert Croft [q. v.], afterwards bishop of Hereford, being one—he brought over to the church of England. In 1602 he was selected, with Richard Crakanthorpe [q. v.] as his colleague, to accompany Lord Eure when sent by Elizabeth as her ambassador extraordinary to the emperor of Germany and the king of Denmark. He took advantage of this opportunity to make the acquaintance of foreign scholars and theologians, including several learned Jesuits, and to collect books at Frankfort and elsewhere, thus laying in stores 'on which,' Fuller says, 'he built to his death.' Among others he fell in with the learned but hot-tempered Hugh Broughton [q. v.], then residing at Middleburg, to whom he proposed his scriptural difficulties (S. CLARKE, *Lives*, 1683, pp. 5, 6). On the queen's death Morton returned to England, and became chaplain to Roger Manners, earl of Rutland. He thus had leisure for study and the preparation of theological works, while residence at Belvoir enabled him to consult the libraries of London. In 1605 he published the first part of his 'Apologia Catholica' on 'the marks of a true church,' a defence of the church of England against the calumnies of the Romanists, with a refutation of the jesuits' doctrine of equivocation. This work, which evoked more than one reply, exhibits unusual familiarity with recent ultramontane polemics, and Morton is believed to have derived aid from his younger friend John Donne [q. v.], afterwards dean of St. Paul's (SANDERSON, *Works*, iv. 328). These 'primitiæ,' as he calls them, were dedicated to Archbishop Bancroft, who, with a just discernment of his merits, had become his steady friend. Through Bancroft's recommendation he was appointed one of the king's chaplains, and in 1606 became dean of Gloucester, and, on the nomination of his former patron, Lord Eure, the lord president, member of the council of the marches. On accepting the deanery he offered to resign the living of Long Marston in favour of Donne, then in great straits through his ill-advised marriage. He hoped thereby to induce Donne to take holy orders (WALTON, *Life of Donne*; WORDSWORTH, *Eccl. Biography*, iii. 634–6). The offer was gratefully declined; but Morton still pressed on his friend the desirability of his undertaking the ministerial office (*Life*, by J. N[ELSON], p. 100). In the same year he visited Oxford, where he was received with great honour, and admitted to an *ad eundem* degree on 12 July. On this occasion he made the acquaintance of some eminent theologians, such as Dr. John King [q. v.], afterwards bishop of London; Dr. Reynolds [q. v.], president of Corpus; Dr. Airey [q. v.], provost of Queen's; and Daniel Featley [q. v.] In 1609 James I transferred him to the deanery of Winchester. Here he was welcomed by Bishop Bilson [q. v.], who conferred on him the living of Alresford. At Winchester he became the intimate friend of Dr. Arthur Lake [q. v.], then master of St. Cross, afterwards bishop of Bath and Wells, and of Dr. John Harmar [q. v.], head-master of Winchester school, and other scholars and theologians of repute. In 1610 he preached the sermon *ad clerum* at the opening of Convocation. When in London he lodged at the deanery of St. Paul's, with Dr. John Overall [q. v.], in whose house he enjoyed the society of Isaac Casaubon [q. v.], who became his intimate friend; of Scultetus, Diodati, Du Moulin and foreign scholars (*cf. Casauboni Epistolæ*, ed. 1709, Nos. 735, 751, 787, 802, 1048, 1050). On Casaubon's death in 1614 Morton caused a monument to be erected to him in Westminster Abbey at his own cost. Among his associates at a later period were Frederick Spanheim of Leyden, and Marco Antonio De Dominis [q. v.], archbishop of Spalato, whose high-flown pretensions to be regarded as the restorer of the unity of the church he seems to have estimated at their real worth (BARWICK, *Life*, p. 87; GARDINER, *Hist. of England*, iv. 287).

By this time Morton's character for learning and piety, as well as for practical wisdom, was fully established. The king valued him highly, and in 1610 he was nominated for one of the seventeen fellowships in the abortive college proposed by Sutcliffe, dean of Exeter, to be established at Chelsea for the study of controversial divinity (FULLER, *Church Hist.* v. 390; *Life*, by J. N. p. 37). Preferments followed one another with inconvenient rapidity. In July of the same year he was collated by Archbishop Toby Matthew [q. v.] to the canonry of Husthwait in York Minster (BAKER, *Hist. of St. John's College*, i. 194). In 1615, on the death of Dr. George Lloyd [q. v.], the king nominated him to the see of Chester. He accepted the nomination with great reluctance. His consecration was delayed till 7 July 1616. The ceremony, which was one of unusual stateliness, was performed at Lambeth by Archbishop Abbot, assisted by the primate of Ireland, the Bishop of Caithness, and others. While the palace at Chester was getting ready he stayed with Sir Christopher Hatton at Clay Hall, Essex, where he had a dangerous fever. He had resigned Alresford, but during his episcopate he held the living of Stopford, given him by the king *in commendam* that he might be better able to 'keep hospitality in that hospitable county.'

Difficulties which Morton had anticipated were not slow in presenting themselves at Chester. Few of the English dioceses at that time were so large, or exhibited greater differences in religion. Morton's see embraced, as indeed it did till the first half of the present century, not only the county of Chester, but the whole of Lancashire, the north-western portion of Yorkshire, and large portions of Cumberland and Westmoreland. In Lancashire the chief landowners, together with a large portion of the population, adhered to the old unreformed faith; while the minority, who had embraced the reformation, had adopted the most extreme opinions of the foreign divines. The sanctity of the Lord's day was one of the points at issue. An attempt had been made by the magistrates to suppress the diversions customary on Sunday afternoons. Many resented this interference with their liberties, and the quarrel grew serious. James applied for advice to Morton, who cautiously recommended that nothing should be permitted which might disturb the worshippers when engaged in divine service, and that it should be left to each man's conscience whether he should take part in the accustomed sports when service was over. At the same time all parishioners were to attend their own parish church, and those who refused to do so were to be debarred from engaging in the subsequent diversions. With the exception of the last proviso, which, as Mr. Gardiner says, 'bribed men to worship God by the alluring prospect of a dance in the afternoon' (GARDINER, *Hist. of England*, iii. 251), the bishop's temperate recommendations, on which James based his subsequent declaration (WILKINS, *Concilia*, iv. 483), were calculated to promote a peace in the church. But the king's rash publication of the 'Book of Sports' in the following year led to new disturbances. Morton's dealings with his nonconformist clergy were marked by fatherly moderation, and in friendly conference he sought to meet by argument their objections to the ceremonies. In 1619 he published 'a relation of the conference' under the title of 'A Defence of the Innocence of the three Ceremonies of the Surplice, the Cross in Baptism, and Kneeling at the Blessed Sacrament,' dedicated to George Villiers, marquis of Buckingham. In 1618, on his friend Overall's translation to Norwich, he was removed to Lichfield and Coventry, on the recommendation of Bishop Andrewes [q. v.], 'who was never known to do the like for any other.' With the bishopric he held the living of Clifton Camville *in commendam*. Here he continued his endeavours to win over both nonconformists and recusants. In 1621 he served on the commission for granting a dispensation to Archbishop Abbot for the casual homicide of a keeper in Bramshill Park (COLLIER, *Eccl. Hist.* vii. 418). In 1623 a curious correspondence took place between him and Lord Conway about a horse named 'Captain,' which on Lord Gerard's death the bishop had taken as a heriot. Gerard had bequeathed his two choicest horses to Prince Charles, then absent in Spain. Conway requested Morton in the king's name to forego his right; this he declined to do, but he obtained permission to present 'Captain' to the prince on his return (*Cal. State Papers*, Dom. 1623). In February 1626 he took a leading part in the conference on Bishop Montague's incriminated books held at the Duke of Buckingham's house, and with Dr. Preston, the puritan master of Emmanuel, did his best to impugn the statements contained in them on predestination and freewill (BIRCH, *Court of Charles I*, i. 86; cf. *Church Hist.* v. 449; see also *Addit. MS.* Brit. Mus. 5724, pp. 57 ff.)

The high esteem felt for Morton by James was continued by Charles I, and in June 1632 Morton was translated to the rich and important palatinate see of Durham, which he held by canonical right until his death in 1659, although parliament claimed to deprive him of it in 1647. His administration of the diocese, with its large secular jurisdiction and its princely revenues, fully justified his reputation. No complaints were made against him to the House of Commons during the civil wars, except by his scurrilous and wrongheaded prebendary, Peter Smart [q. v.] He showed great forbearance in claiming the undoubted rights of the palatinate in wardships, wrecks, and forfeitures for suicide. He was systematic and liberal in almsgiving, and maintained many poor scholars at the universities. He did all in his power to augment the poor benefices of his diocese, and exhibited extreme conscientiousness both in admission to holy orders and in the exercise of his patronage. His hospitality was profuse. On his journey to Scotland in 1633 Charles I and his suite were received by Morton, both at Auckland and at Durham, in such princely style that one day's entertainment is reported to have cost 1,500*l.* On Sunday, 2 June, on the occasion of the king's attending service in the cathedral, the bishop preached on the cursing of the fig-tree. Six years later, in May 1639, he again entertained Charles at the beginning of 'the First Bishops' War.' The next year, in the month of August, the Scots crossed the Tweed, and pushed on to Durham. The cathedral clergy fled, Morton himself retiring into Yorkshire. It is probable that he never again permanently resided in his bishopric.

Early in 1641 he was in London attending to his parliamentary duties, and was nominated a member of the sub-committee to prepare matters for the consideration of the abortive committee of the lords appointed on 1 March—the day of Laud's committal to the Tower—to take cognisance of innovations in religion (FULLER, *Church Hist.* vi. 188). In the following December an unruly mob threatened to drag him out of his coach when on his way to the House of Lords (BARWICK, *Life*, p. 103). Morton never took his seat in the lords again. Two days later, 29 Dec., he joined in Williams's ill-advised protest against the legality of all acts done in the enforced absence of the spiritual lords. For this he and his eleven associates were next day impeached of high treason on Prynne's motion, and the same night they were all committed to the Tower, with the exception of Morton and Wright, bishop of Lichfield, who, on account of their advanced age, were allowed to remain in the house of the usher of the black rod—a doubtful privilege, for the charges were far greater. After four months' imprisonment Morton was released without a trial, and remained unmolested at Durham House, in the Strand, till April 1645, when he was again brought before the bar of the House of Commons on the double charge of baptising the infant daughter of the Earl of Rutland according to the rites of the church of England, and of refusing to surrender the seal of the county palatine of Durham. He was committed to the custody of the serjeant-at-arms for six months (WHITELOCKE, *Memorials*, 1732, p. 14). On the abolition of episcopacy in 1646 an annual income of 800*l.* was assigned to him out of the revenues of the see. This, however, he never received, the authorities by whom it was to be paid not being specified. All he obtained was a sum of 1,000*l.* from the committee at Goldsmiths' Hall 'towards the arrears,' which he employed in paying his debts and purchasing an annuity of 200*l.* for life. In 1648 he was driven from Durham House by the soldiery, who took forcible possession of it. He then resided with his friends, the Earl and Countess of Rutland, at Exeter House in the Strand; but, being unwilling to live permanently at the charge of others, he left them, and passed his time with various royalist lay friends. At last he resolved to return to London. On his way thither, on horseback, he fell in with Sir Christopher Yelverton. There had been some previous relations between them. Sir Christopher was the son and heir of Sir Henry Yelverton [q.v.], James I's attorney-general, in whose behalf, when brought before the bar of the house in 1621 for an attack on the all-powerful Buckingham, Morton had remonstrated against the injustice of condemning him unheard. Sir Henry had also, in 1629, sat as judge of assize at Durham in the case of Morton's enemy, Peter Smart, and had charged the jury in his favour, declaring that he 'hoped to live and die a puritan.' Sir Christopher inherited his father's puritanical bias. On their meeting the bishop recognised him, though Sir Christopher did not recognise the bishop. To his inquiry who he was, Morton replied, 'I am that old man, the Bishop of Durham, in spite of all your votes;' to the further inquiry whither he was going, his answer was, 'To London, to live there a little while, and then to die.' Ultimately Sir Christopher invited him to his house at Easton-Mauduit, ten miles from Northampton. His visit only ended with his death. He became a revered member of Sir Christopher's family, and tutor to Henry, his eldest son, then a lad of sixteen, receiving 'from the whole family all the tender respect and care which a father could expect from his children' (BARWICK, *Life*, p. 123). At Easton-Mauduit Morton endeavoured to maintain the ministerial succession of the church of England by holding secret ordinations. Sir Christopher died in 1654. The bishop died at Easton-Mauduit on 22 Sept. 1659, 'blessed,' writes his friend Walton (*Life of Donne*, u.s., p. 634), 'with perfect intellectuals, and a cheerful heart,' in the ninety-fifth year of his age, and the forty-fourth of his episcopate, and the twenty-fourth of his translation to Durham. He was buried in the Yelverton chapel of the parish church. His chaplain, Dr. John Barwick [q.v.], afterwards dean of St. Paul's, preached the funeral sermon. One of his latest acts before his death was to publish a denial, fully attested, of the slanderous statement that he had in a speech in the House of Lords acknowledged the fiction of the 'Nag's Head Consecration' of Archbishop Parker (BRAMHALL, *Works*, iii. 5–10; STRYPE, *Parker*, i. 119; NEAL, *Puritans*, iv. 179; BARWICK, *Life*, pp. 108–20). By his will he left 10*l.* to the poor of the parish in which he died, and his chalice to All Saints, York, the parish in which he was born. He also bequeathed a silver-gilt chalice and paten of large size for the use of the chapel recently added to his manor-house by Sir Henry Yelverton. Since the demolition of the house these have been transferred to the parish church. A codicil to his will contained a declaration of his faith and of his adhesion to the church of England, solemnly attested by witnesses, as 'a legacy to all pious and sober Christians, but especially those of his diocese of Durham' (*ib.* p. 127). He died unmarried, having early in life 'resolved to die a single man' (WALTON, *Life of Donne*, p. 636).

Morton is described as small of stature, upright in person, and sprightly in motion, preserving the vigour of youth in extreme old age, of a sweet and serious countenance, grave and sober in speech, manifesting a gentleness which won all hearts and disarmed enmity; 'in the fullest sense of the word, a good man' (GARDINER, u.s. iii. 249). His habits were ascetic. He slept on a straw bed, and rose at 4 A.M., never retiring to rest till 10 P.M., drank wine but seldom, and then sparingly, and only took one full meal in the day. In his attire he was 'always decent in his lowest ebb, and never excessive in his highest tide,' never discarding the episcopal habit, even when it was perilous to wear it. Portraits of Morton are at Christ Church, Oxford, at St. John's College, Cambridge, and at Auckland Castle, Durham. An engraved portrait is prefixed to Barwick's 'Life.'

Morton was a great patron of good and learned men. His house was ever open to scholars as a home and as a place of refuge in poverty or trouble. At the commencement of the parliamentary war, while it was still in his power to do so, he offered Fuller a home and maintenance (FULLER, *Worthies*, ii. 541). Isaac Basire [q.v.] was one of the many deserving scholars whom he brought forward. Ralph Brownrig [q.v.], bishop of Exeter, Henry Ferne [q.v.], bishop of Chester, and John Barwick, dean of St. Paul's, were among his chaplains. He was a patron of foreign scholars of the reformed faith, whom he received into his house and dismissed, on leaving, with gifts of money and books. He warmly favoured the endeavours of John Durie (1596–1680) [q. v.] for reconciling the differences between the various branches of the reformed churches in France and Germany (cf. *De Pace inter Evangelicos procuranda*, 1638). He numbered Hooker among his friends as well as Hooker's biographer Walton, who speaks very gratefully of the information he derives from the bishop concerning one 'whose very name he loved.' Laud was one of his correspondents (cf. LAUD, *Works*, vi. 549, 560, 571). In theology he belonged to the school of Ussher and Bedell, and had little sympathy with the high-church doctrines of Laud. Baxter speaks of him as 'belonging to that class of episcopal divines who differ in nothing considerable from the rest of the reformed churches except in church government,' and Clarendon classes him with 'the less formal and more popular prelates' (SANDERSON, *Works*, vol. ii. p. xli). He was a sincere but by no means bigoted episcopalian. He regarded ordination by presbyters valid in case of necessity, no such necessity however warranting it in the church of England. From the moderation of his ecclesiastical views he was at one time regarded with friendly eyes by Prynne (cf. *Canterburies Doome*, p. 230). He would now be reckoned a low churchman. If he was sure that any one was a really good man, anxious to fulfil the object of his ministry, he was not over strict in exacting conformity. Calamy records with praise his liberal treatment of puritans like John Hieron, Richard Mather, and John Shaw of Christ's College (CALAMY, *Memorial*, pp. 162, 824; CLARKE, *Lives*, p. 128). His attitude towards the church of Rome was one of uncompromising hostility. He was one of the only three bishops who, according to a statement made to Panzani, the papal envoy, by Bishop Montague, were 'counted violently bent against the Papists' (PANZANI, *Memoirs*, p. 246).

The larger portion of his writings were devoted to the exposure of the fallacy of Romish doctrines. They display great learning and an intimate acquaintance with the arguments of his antagonists. It is no small praise that they exhibit none of the bitterness and scurrility which too commonly disfigure the polemics of the age. Besides the 'Apologia Catholica,' a work of immense learning and calm reasoning, he published in 1609 his 'Catholick Appeal,' which, according to Barwick (u.s. p. 132), dealt 'such a deadly blow to his Romish adversaries' that none of them even attempted to answer it. Ten years later, at James's command, he entered the lists against Bellarmine in defence of the oath of allegiance to a protestant sovereign in his 'Causa Regia.'

Morton's chief works were: 1. 'Apologia Catholica, ex meris Jesuitarum contradictionibus conflata,' &c., part 1, London [1605–1606], 4to. 2. 'An Exact Discoverie of Romish Doctrine in the case of Conspiracie and Rebellion,' &c., 1605, 4to. 3. 'Apologiæ Catholicæ, in qua parodoxa, hæreses, blasphemiæ, scelera, quæ Jesuitæ et Pontificii alii Protestantibus impingunt, fere omnia, ex ipsorum Pontificiorum testimoniis apertis diluuntur, libri duo. De notis Ecclesiæ. Editio castigatior,' 2 pts. London, 1606, 8vo. and 4to. 4. 'A Full Satisfaction concerning a Double Romish Iniquitie, hainous Rebellion, and more than heathenish Æquivocation. Containing three parts,' London, 1606, 4to. 5. 'A Preamble unto an Incounter with P. R. [R. Parsons], the Author of the deceitfull Treatise of Mitigation: concerning the Romish Doctrine both in question of Rebellion and of Aequivocation,' London, 1608, 4to. 6. 'A Catholic Appeal for Protestants, out of the Confessions of the Romane Doctors; particularly answering the mis-named Catholike Apologie for the Romane Faith, out of the Protestants [by J. Brereley],' London, 1610, fol. 7. 'A Direct Answer unto the scandalous Exceptions which T. Higgons hath lately objected against D. Morton [i.e. against his "Apologia Catholica"]. In which there is principally discussed two of the most notorious Objections used by the Romanists, viz.: (1) Martin Luther's Conference with the Divell; and (2) The Sence of the Article of Christ, His Discension into Hell (Animadversions),' London, 1609, 4to. 8. 'A Defence of the Innocencie of the Three Ceremonies of the Church of England, viz., the Surplice, Crosse after Baptisme, and Kneeling at the Receiving of the Blessed Sacrament,' London, 1609, 4to. 9. 'The Encounter against M. Parsons, by a Review of his last Sober Reckoning and his Exceptions urged in the Treatise of his Mitigation . . .,' London 1610, 4to. 10. 'Causa Regia, sive De Authoritate et Dignitate principum Christianorum adversus R. Bellarminum,' 1620. 11. 'The Grand Imposture of the (now) Church of Rome manifested in this one Article of the new Romane Creede, viz., "The Holy Catholike and Apostolike Romane Church, Mother and Mistresse of all other Churches, without which there is no salvation." The second edition, revised . . . with . . . Additions,' London, 1628, 4to. 12. 'Of the Institution of the Sacrament of the Blessed Bodie and

Blood of Christ,' &c., 2 pts., London, 1631, fol.; 2nd edit. 'enlarged . . . with particular answers,' London, 1635, fol. 13. 'A Discharge of Five Imputations of Mis-Allegations falsely charged upon the Bishop of Duresme by an English Baron (Arundell of Wardour),' London, 1633, 8vo. 14. 'Sacris ordinibus non rite initiati tenentur ad eos ritus ineundos. Non datur purgatorium Pontificium aut Platonicum' (in verse), Cambridge, 1633, s. sh. fol. 15. 'Antidotum adversus Ecclesiæ Romanæ de merito proprie dicto ex condigno venenum,' Cantabr. 1637, 4to. 16. 'De Eucharistia Controversiæ Decisio,' Cantabr. 1640. 17. 'The Opinion of . . . T. Morton . . . concerning the peace of the Church,' 1641, 4to.; a Latin version appeared in 1688. 18. 'The Necessity of Christian Subjection demonstrated . . . Also a Tract intituled "Christus Dei,"' &c., 1643, 4to; posthumously printed. 19. 'Ezekiel's Wheels: a Treatise concerning Divine Providence,' London, 1653, 8vo. 20. ''Επίσκοπος 'Αποστολικὸς, or the Episcopacy of the Church of England justified to be Apostolical. . . . Before which is prefixed a preface . . . by Sir H. Yelverton,' London, 1670, 8vo.

The three following works, which have been repeatedly but erroneously ascribed to the bishop of Durham, were in reality the works of another Thomas Morton of Berwick and Christ's College, Cambridge (see the bishop's 'Catholic Appeal for Protestants'): viz. 1. 'A Treatise of the Threefolde State of Man, wherein is handled: (1) His Created Holinesse in his Innocencie; (2) His Sinfulnesse since the Fall of Adam; (3) His Renewed Holinesse in his Regeneration,' London, 1596, 8vo. 2. 'Salomon, or a Treatise declaring the State of the Kingdom of Israel as it was in the Daies of Salomon. Whereunto is annexed another Treatise of the Church, or more particularly of the Right Constitution of a Church,' 2 pts., London, 1596, 4to. 3. 'A Treatise of the Nature of God,' London, 1599, 8vo.

[Dean Barwick's Life and Death of Thomas, late Lord Bishop of Duresme; Life by J[oseph] N[elson]; Biog. Brit. v. 3180 ff.; Baker's Hist. of St. John's College, i. 260 ff.; Lloyd's Memoirs, pp. 436–46; Fuller's Worthies, ii. 540 ff., Church History, v. 390, 449; Mayor's Materials for the Life of Thomas Morton; communications of the Camb. Antiq. Soc. iii. 1–36; Walton's Life of Donne, and of Hooker; Wordsworth's Eccles. Biog. iii. 450, 634; Walker's Sufferings, pt. ii. p. 17; Nichols's Leicestershire, ii. 53, 382; Surtees's Durham, i. pp. xci ff.; Ormerod's Cheshire, i. 76, 146; Baker's MSS. xxvii. 276–8; Laud's Works (Anglo-Catholic Lib.) vi. 549, 560, 571; Notes and Queries, 8th ser. vi. 142.] E. V.

MORTON, THOMAS (1781–1832), inventor of the 'patent slip' for docking vessels, was the son of Hugh Morton, wright and builder, of Leith, where he was born 8 Oct. 1781. In early life Morton seems to have been engaged in his father's business at Leith. In 1819 he patented his great invention (No. 4352), the object of which was to provide a cheap substitute for a dry dock in places where such a dock is inexpedient or impracticable. It consists of an inclined railway with three lines of rail running into the deep water of the harbour or tideway. A strongly built carriage, supported by a number of small wheels, travels upon the railway, and is let down into the water by means of a chain in connection with a capstan or a small winding engine. The ship to be hauled up is then floated over the submerged carriage so that the keel is exactly over the centre of the carriage, the position of which is indicated by rods projecting above the surface of the water. The vessel is then towed until the stem grounds on the front end of the carriage, when the hauling gear is set to work. As the carriage is drawn up the inclined way the vessel gradually settles down upon it, and in this way vessels of very large tonnage may be readily hauled up out of the water. The vessel is supported in an upright position by a system of chocks mounted on transverse slides, which are drawn under the bilge as the vessel leaves the water. This was a very important part of the invention, as the idea of drawing ships out of the water up an inclined plane was not new. Such a method was in use in the royal dockyard at Brest in the early part of the eighteenth century (*Machines approuvées par l'Académie des Sciences*, ii. 55, 57). Morton started the manufacture of the patent slip, and eventually acquired a large business. The first slip was built at Bo'ness about 1822; but the inventor was obliged to do the work partly at his own expense, in order to remove the prejudice against the new invention. It was afterwards adopted at Irvine, Whitehaven, and Dumbarton. The patent was infringed by one Barclay, who erected a slip on the same principle at Stobcross, and Morton brought an action for infringement, which was tried at Edinburgh 15 March 1824, when evidence was given on Morton's behalf by John Farey, the Rev. W. Scoresby, Captain Basil Hall, and other eminent men. Judgment was given in Morton's favour. In 1832 a bill was brought into the House of Commons for an extension of the patent. The select committee to which the bill was referred reported against it, but expressed a hope 'that some other means may be adopted to obtain for Mr. Morton a more adequate pecuniary recompense for the great benefit his invention has conferred upon the public, and the shipping interest in particular, than he appears to have derived from his patent.' It was proved by evidence given before the committee that the operation of placing a particular ship in a position to be repaired, which formerly cost 170*l.*, could be effected by Morton's slip for 3*l.* In 1832 forty slips were in operation, and at the present time one is to be found in nearly every important harbour.

Morton died 24 Dec. 1832, and was buried in South Leith parish church. After his death the business was carried on by Messrs. S. & H. Morton, Leith, and the firm is still in existence.

[Report of the Trial, Morton *v.* Barclay, Edinburgh, 1824; Report of the Committee of the House of Commons on the Bill for prolonging Morton's patent, 1832; Edinburgh Encyclopædia, xviii. 255; Weale's Quarterly Papers on Engineering, iv. 9; Bramwell's Paper on Docks in Proceedings of the Institution of Civil Engineers, xxv. 315.] R. B. P.

MORTON, THOMAS (1764?–1838), dramatist, youngest son of John Morton of Whickham in the county of Durham, gentleman, was born in Durham about 1764. After the death of his father he was educated at Soho Square school at the charge of his uncle Maddison, a stockbroker. Here amateur acting was in vogue, and Morton, who played with Joseph George Holman [q. v.], acquired a taste for the theatre. He entered at Lincoln's Inn 2 July 1784, but was not called to the bar. His first drama, 'Columbus, or A World Discovered,' 8vo, 1792, an historical play in five acts, founded in part upon 'Les Incas' of Marmontel, was produced with success at Covent Garden, 1 Dec. 1792, Holman playing the part of Alonzo. 'Children in the Wood,' a two-act musical entertainment, Dublin, 12mo, 1794 (a pirated edition), followed at the Haymarket 1 Oct. 1793. It was well acted by Suett Bannister, jun., and Miss De Camp, and was more than once revived. Similar fortune attended 'Zorinski,' 8vo, 1795, a three-act play founded on the adventures of Stanislaus, re-christened Casimir, king of Poland, Haymarket, 20 June 1795. In the same year appeared an anonymous pamphlet, 'Mr. Morton's "Zorinski" and Brooke's "Gustavus Vasa" Compared.' 'The Way to get Married,' 8vo, 1796, a comedy in five acts, with serious situations, was produced at Covent Garden 23 Jan. 1796, acted forty-one times, and became a stock piece. It supplied Munden with his favourite character of Caustic. 'A Cure for the Heart-Ache,' a five-act comedy, 8vo, 1797, Covent Garden, 10 Jan. 1797, furnished two excellent characters in Old and Young Rapid, and became also, with few other claims on attention, a stock play. 'Secrets worth Knowing,' a five-act comedy, 8vo, 1798, Covent Garden 11 Jan. 1798, though a better play than the preceding, was less popular. 'Speed the Plough,' a five-act comedy, 8vo, 1798, Covent Garden, 8 Feb. 1798, was acted forty-one times, and often revived. 'The Blind Girl, or a Receipt for Beauty,' a comic opera in three acts (songs only printed), Covent Garden, 22 April 1801, was played eight times. 'Beggar my Neighbour, or a Rogue's a Fool,' a comedy in three acts (unprinted), Haymarket, 10 July 1802, was assigned to Morton but unclaimed by him, being damned the first night. It was afterwards converted into 'How to tease and how to please,' Covent Garden, 29 March 1810, experienced very little better fortune, and remained unprinted. Part of the plot of 'Beggar my Neighbour' is said to have been taken from Iffland. 'The School of Reform, or How to rule a Husband,' 8vo, 1805, a five-act comedy, was played with remarkable success at Covent Garden, 15 Jan. 1805, and was revived so late as 20 Nov. 1867 at the St. James's, with Mr. John S. Clarke as Tyke and Mr. Irving as Ferment. Tyke was the greatest part of John Emery [q. v.] 'Town and Country, or which is best?' 8vo, 1807, a comedy in five acts, was given at Covent Garden 10 March 1807, with John Kemble as Reuben Glenroy and Charles Kemble as Plastic. For this piece Harris is said to have paid 1,000*l.* whether it succeeded or failed. 'The Knight of Snowdoun,' London, 1811, a musical drama in three acts, founded on 'The Lady of the Lake,' saw the light at Covent Garden 5 Feb. 1811. 'Education,' 8vo, 1813, a five-act comedy, Covent Garden, 27 April 1813, is taken in part from Iffland. In 'The Slave,' 8vo, 1816, Covent Garden, 12 Nov. 1816, a musical drama in three acts, Macready played Gambia, the slave. 'A Roland for an Oliver,' 8vo, 1819, produced at Covent Garden 29 April 1819, was a two-act musical farce. In 'Henri Quatre, or Paris in the Olden Time,' 8vo, 1820, Covent Garden, 22 April 1820, a musical romance in three acts, Macready was Henri. At the same theatre appeared 'School for Grown Children' (8vo, 1827), on 9 Jan. 1827, and 'The Invincibles,' 28 Feb. 1828, a musical farce in two acts, included in Cumberland's collection. With his second son, John Maddison Morton [q. v.], he was associated in the 'Writing on the Wall,' a three-act melodrama, produced at the Haymarket, and it is said in 'All that Glitters is not Gold,' a two-act comic drama played at the Olympic. ‘Judith of Geneva,’ a three-act melodrama, is assigned him in Duncombe's collection, and ‘Sink or Swim,’ a two-act comedy, in that of Lacy. In addition to these works the following plays in one act are assigned Morton in various collections: ‘Angel of the Attic,’ a serio-comic drama; ‘Another Glass,’ a one-act drama; ‘Dance of the Shirt, or the Sempstress's Ball,’ comic drama; ‘Go to Bed, Tom,’ a farce; ‘Great Russian Bear, or Another Retreat from Moscow;’ ‘Pretty Piece of Business,’ comedy; and ‘Seeing Warren,’ a farce. Morton died on 28 March 1838, leaving a widow and three children, his second son being the farce writer, John Maddison Morton. He was a man of reputable life and regular habits, who enjoyed, two years before his death, the rarely accorded honour of being elected (8 May 1837) an honorary member of the Garrick Club; he was, however, frequently ridiculed by Gifford in the ‘Baviad.’ He was very fond of cricket, and became the senior member of Lord's. For many years he resided at Pangbourne, on the Thames.

His portrait, painted by Sir Martin Archer Shee, originally placed in the Vernon Gallery, has been engraved by T. W. Hunt.

[Lincoln's Inn Registers (unprinted); Gent. Mag. 1838, pt. i.; Notes and Queries, 8th ser. iv. 432; Baker, Reed, and Jones's Biographia Dramatica; Genest's Account of the English Stage; Georgian Era; Era Almanack, various years.]

J. K.

MORTON, THOMAS (1813-1849), surgeon, born 20 March 1813 in the parish of St. Andrew, Newcastle-on-Tyne, was youngest son of Joseph Morton, a master mariner, and brother of Andrew Morton [q. v.] the portrait painter. Thomas was apprenticed to James Church, house-surgeon to the Newcastle-on-Tyne Infirmary, and, on the completion of his preliminary education there in 1832, entered at University College, London, to finish his medical education. Admitted a member of the Royal College of Surgeons of England on 24 July 1835, he was appointed house-surgeon at the North London (now University College) Hospital under Samuel Cooper, whose only daughter he afterwards married. He enjoyed the singular honour of being reappointed when his year of office had expired. In 1836 he was made demonstrator of anatomy conjointly with Mr. Ellis, a post he held for nine years. In 1842 he became assistant surgeon to the hospital, and he was thus the first student of the college to be placed upon the staff of the newly founded hospital. In 1848 he was appointed full surgeon to the hospital upon the resignation of Syme. He was also surgeon to the Queen's Bench prison in succession to Cooper, his father-in-law. Morton was a candidate for the professorship of surgery at University College when Arnott was appointed. He died very unexpectedly, by his own hand, on 29 Oct. 1849, at his house in Woburn Place, London.

Morton was one of the ablest of the younger surgeons whose sound work raised the medical school attached to University College to the high position it now holds. His death was a great blow to the prestige of the college, coming as it did so soon after the deaths of Potter, Liston, and Cooper, and the resignation of Syme. Morton was an excellent teacher of anatomy, and a sound clinical surgeon. He was dark-complexioned and sallow, and of a retiring, shy, and sensitive nature, which betokened a melancholy disposition, leading him to take too gloomy a view of his prospects in life.

His works are: 1. ‘Surgical Anatomy of the Perinæum,’ London, 1838. 2. ‘Surgical Anatomy of the Groin,’ London, 1839. 3. ‘Surgical Anatomy of Inguinal Herniæ,’ London, 1841. 4. ‘Anatomical Engravings,’ London, 1845. 5. ‘Surgical Anatomy, with Introduction by Mr. W. Cadge,’ London, 1850. All these works are remarkable, because they are illustrated by his brother, Andrew Morton, and mark the revival of an artistic representation of anatomical details. A life-size portrait, three-quarter length, by Andrew Morton, executed in oils, is now in the secretary's office at the Royal College of Surgeons in Lincoln's Inn Fields, London.

[Obituary notices in the Lancet, vol. ii. 1849, Gent. Mag. 1849, pt. ii. p. 658, Times, 30 Oct. and 2 Nov. 1849, p. 5; additional facts kindly given to the writer by Mr. Eric Erichsen, Mr. Cadge, and Dr. Embleton.]

D'A. P.

MORTON, SIR WILLIAM (*d.* 1672), judge, was the son of James Morton of Clifton, Worcestershire, by his wife Jane, daughter of William Cook of Shillwood, Worcestershire, and great-grandson to Sir Rowland Morton of Massington, Herefordshire, a master of requests in the time of Henry VIII. He became a member of Sidney Sussex College, Cambridge, graduating B.A. in 1622 and M.A. in 1625; and, having been a student of the Inner Temple concurrently since 24 Oct. 1622, he was called to the bar on 28 Nov. 1630. His name first appears in the ‘Reports’ in 1639, and shortly after that he took arms on the royal side, fought and was wounded in several actions. He was knighted, served as lieutenant-colonel in Lord Chandos's horse, and was governor of Lord Chandos's castle at Sudeley, Gloucestershire, when it surrendered in June 1644 to General Waller. Clarendon describes the surrender as forced upon him by the treachery of a subordinate and by the mutiny of his men; but there is no mention of this in Waller's own official account of the surrender (see *Cal. State Papers*, Dom. Ser. 1644, p. 219). Morton was sent to the Tower, and was imprisoned for some years. After hostilities were concluded he returned to the bar, though his name does not figure in the 'Reports.' He became a bencher of the Inner Temple on 24 Nov. 1659, and after the Restoration his courage and fidelity were rewarded. He received the degree of serjeant-at-law in 1660, was a commissioner of assize for Carmarthenshire in 1661, was appointed recorder of Gloucester early in 1662, and counsel to the dean and chapter of Worcester. He was made a king's serjeant in July 1663, and on 23 Nov. 1665 succeeded Sir John Kelynge in the king's bench, and 'discharged his office with much gravity and learning.' He is said to have particularly set his face against highway robbery, and prevented the grant of a pardon to Claude Duval [q. v.] after his conviction by threatening to resign his judgeship if a pardon were granted. He died in the autumn of 1672, and was buried in the Temple Church. He married Anne, daughter and heiress of John Smyth of Kidlington in Oxfordshire, by whom he had several children, of whom one, Sir James, succeeded him. Besides his lodgings in Serjeants' Inn, Fleet Street, which were burnt in the great fire, he had, through his wife, a house at Kidlington, and also was lord of the manor (Anthony à Wood, *Fasti Oxon.* i. 63; cf. Burton, *Diary*, iv. 262). A portrait of Morton in his robes, by Vandyck, belonging to Mr. Bulkeley Owen, was No. 963 in the first Loan Exhibition of National Portraits.

[Foss's Lives of the Judges; Croke's Reports; Visitations of Worcestershire, 1634; Clarendon, iv. 489; Cal. State Papers, Dom. 1661; Pope's Memoirs of Duval; Macaulay's Hist. i. 187.]

J. A. H.

MORVILLE, HUGH de (*d.* 1204), one of the murderers of St. Thomas of Canterbury, was most probably the son of Hugh de Morville, who held the barony of Burgh-by-Sands, Cumberland, and several other estates in the northern shires, in succession to his mother, Ada, daughter of William de Engaine (William of Canterbury in *Materials for Life of Becket*, i. 128; Richard of Hexham, *Chron. Stephen*, &c., Rolls Ser. iii. 178). He must be distinguished from Hugh de Morville (*d.* 1162) [see under Morville, Richard de (*d.* 1189)] and from Hugh de Morville (*d.* 1200). Hugh's mother was licentious and treacherous (William of Canterbury, *ib.*; the story there given does not, as Stanley, *Memorials of Canterbury*, p. 70, stated, refer to Hugh's wife, but to his mother; *Materials*, i. xxxii. note 1). He 'was of a viper's brood.' From the beginning of the reign of Henry II he was attached to the court, and is constantly mentioned as witnessing charters. His name occurs also as a witness to the Constitutions of Clarendon. He married Helwis de Stuteville, and thus became possessor of the castle of Knaresborough. This is denied by a writer in the 'Gentleman's Magazine,' 1856, ii. 381, but his authority does not outweigh that of the contemporary biographers. He was forester of Cumberland, and itinerant justice for Cumberland and Northumberland in 1170, and he held the manor of Westmereland. He had been one of Becket's men when he was chancellor; but he had always been of the king's party, and he was easily stirred by the king's bitter words to avenge him on the archbishop. In the verbal contest which preceded the murder he asked St. Thomas 'why, if the king's men had in aught offended him or his, he did not complain to the king before he took the law into his own hands and excommunicated them' (Roger of Pontigny, *Materials*, iv. 73). While the others were smiting the saint he kept back with his sword the crowd which was pouring into the transept from the nave, 'and so it happened that with his own hand he did not strike him' (*ib.* p. 77). After all was over he fled with the other knights to Saltwood, thence to South Malling, later to Scotland; but he was finally forced to flee to his own castle of Knaresborough, where he sheltered his fellow-criminals (Benedict of Peterborough, Rolls Ser., i. 13). There they remained, though they were accounted vile by all men of that shire. All shunned converse with them, nor would any eat or drink with them (*ib.* p. 14). Finally a penance of service in the Holy Land was given by the pope, but the murderers soon regained the royal favour. In 1200 Hugh de Morville paid fifteen marks and three good horses to hold his court with the rights of tol and theam, infangenetheof, and the ordeal of iron and of water, so long as his wife, in whose right he held it, should retain the secular habit. He obtained also license to hold a market at Kirkoswald, Cumberland, on Thursdays, and a fair on the feast of St. Oswald (Lysons, *Cumberland*, p. 127). He died shortly afterwards (1204), leaving two daughters: Ada, married in 1200 to Richard de Lucy, son of Reginald of Egremont (*Rot.

de Oblatis, p. 68), and afterwards to Thomas de Multon (*Excerpta e Rot. Finium*, i. 17, 155), and Joan, married to Richard de Gernum, nephew of William Brewer [q. v.], who had been appointed her guardian (Foss, *Judges of England*, i. 280). Legends soon attached to his sword, as to the sword of Tracy. It was said to have been long preserved in Carlisle Cathedral, and a sword, with a much later inscription, now at Brayton Castle, is supposed to be the one which he wore on the day of the murder.

This is the most probable account of his last years. But it may be that he was the Morville who was Richard I's hostage in 1194, in which case he would be noteworthy as having lent Ulrich of Zatzikoven the Anglo-Norman poem which Ulrich made the basis of his 'Lanzelet.' Tradition also states that he died in the Holy Land, and was buried in the porch outside the church of the Templars (afterwards the Mosque el Aksa) at Jerusalem. The tomb is now inside the building.

[Materials for the Hist. of Becket (Rolls Ser.), vols. i–iv.; William of Newburgh, lib. ii. cap. 25 (Rolls Ser. Chronicles Stephen, Henry II, and Richard I, i. 161–5); Benedict of Peterborough, Rolls Ser. i. 13; Garnier, ed. Hippeau, pp. 178–200; Pipe Rolls (Pipe Roll Soc.), 5 Henry II p. 29, 6 Henry II p. 14, 7 Henry II p. 35, 8 Henry II p. 51, 9 Henry II p. 57, 10 Henry II p. 11, 11 Henry II p. 47, 12 Henry II p. 35, 13 Henry II, p. 78, 14 Henry II p. 79, 15 Henry II p. 31; Thómas Saga, ed. Magnússon, Rolls Ser. i. 514; Foss's Judges of England, i. 279, 280; Stanley's Memorials of Canterbury, 4th edit. pp. 70, 107, 196; Lysons's Cumberland, p. 127; Eyton's Itinerary of Henry II, pp. 33, 53, 68, 78, 145, 150, 152; Robertson's Life of Becket, pp. 266 sqq.; Morris's St. Thomas Becket, pp. 137, 407 sqq.; Norgate's Angevin Kings, ii. 78, 432 note *n*; Gent. Mag. 1856, i. 380–2.]

W. H. H.

MORVILLE, RICHARD DE (*d.* 1189), constable of Scotland, was son of Hugh de Morville, by Beatrice de Beauchamp. HUGH DE MORVILLE (*d.* 1162) was a member of a family settled at Burgh-by-Sands, Cumberland, who took service under David I [q. v.], king of Scots, and received grants of land in Lauderdale, the Lothians, and Cunninghame. He was made constable of Scotland by David. His name first occurs as witness to the 'Inquisitio Davidis' in 1116, and after this is of frequent occurrence as a witness to royal charters. In 1140 he assisted David in his attempt to procure the bishopric of Durham for William Cumin. Hugh de Morville founded Dryburgh Abbey in 1150 (*Chron. de Mailros*, p. 78; but in the charter of foundation King David is named), and he and his wife and children were liberal benefactors of the abbey (*Reg. Dryburgh*, pp. 3, 9, 10). He also founded Kilwinning Abbey in 1140. By his wife, Beatrice, daughter of Pagan de Beauchamp or Bello-Campo (*Coll. Top. et Gen.* vi. 86), he had three sons, Richard, Roger, and Malcolm (who was killed when young), and a daughter, Ada (*Reg. Dryburgh*, pp. 9, 10, 68–70, 102). He was of the same family as Hugh de Morville (*d.* 1204) [q. v.], the murderer of Thomas Becket; but the true relationship seems doubtful. Dugdale's account of the family is clearly confused; nor does there seem to be any sufficient ground for supposing that they were father and son.

Richard de Morville is perhaps the son of Hugh, who was given as a hostage for the peace between England and Scotland in 1139 (RICHARD OF HEXHAM, in *Chron. Steph., Hen. II*, &c., iii. 178, Rolls Ser.; but cf. HUGH DE MORVILLE, *d.* 1204). He succeeded his father as constable in 1162, and occurs frequently as witness to charters in the reign of Malcolm IV. He was one of the chief advisers of William the Lion, and during the invasion of England in 1174 commanded a part of the Scottish army before Alnwick. Under the treaty of Falaise, in August 1175, Morville was one of the hostages given by William for its fulfilment (HOVEDEN, ii. 60, 75). For his share in this war Morville was for a time disseized of his English lands at Bozeat, Northamptonshire (*Cal. Documents relating to Scotland*, i. 294). In 1181 John, bishop of Glasgow, excommunicated Morville for having stirred up strife between him and the king (HOVEDEN, ii. 263). Morville was present as royal constable at the decision of the dispute between the abbey of Melrose and the men of Wedhale on 18 Oct. 1184. He died in 1189, having been for a short time previous to his death an inmate of Melrose Abbey.

Richard de Morville married before 1170 Avice, daughter of William de Lancastria (*Cal. Documents relating to Scotland*, i. 124). She gave Newby to the monks of Furness (*ib.* i. 195), and, together with her husband, was a benefactor of Melrose (*Munimenta de Melros*, p. 160). Avice died on 1 Jan. 1191. By her Morville had a son William, who was constable of Scotland, and died in 1196, leaving no offspring by his wife Christiana. The office of constable then passed to Rolland de Galloway, who had married William's sister, Elena or Helena. Elena had two sons, Alan de Galloway, and Thomas, earl of Athol. Alan, who died in 1234, left by Margaret, daughter of David, earl of Huntingdon, three daughters: Helena, wife of Roger de Quincy; Christiana, wife of

William de Fortibus, son of the Earl of Albemarle; and Devorguila, wife of John Baliol (*d.* 1269) [q. v.]

[Roger Hoveden (Rolls Ser.); Melrose Chron., Registers of Dryburgh, Dunfermline, and Newbottle (all these are published by the Bannatyne Club); Chalmers's Caledonia, i. 503–5, ii. 336; Dugdale's Baronage, i. 612; Gent. Mag. 1856, i. 380–2.] C. L. K.

MORWEN, MORING, or MORVEN, JOHN (1518?–1561?), divine, born about 1518, was a Devonshire man of a good family (*Visitations of Devon*, Harl. Soc., p. 193). Going to Oxford, he was placed under a relative, Robert Morwen [q. v.], the president of Corpus Christi College, and under Morwen's influence he adopted reactionary religious views. He was scholar of the college 1535, fellow 1539, graduated B.A. 1538, proceeded M.A. 1543, and B.D. 1552. Becoming a noted Greek scholar, he was appointed reader in that language in his college. Among his pupils was Jewel. Seeing how things went in Edward VI's time, he is said to have studied physic, but this, though confirmed by an entry in the registers, seems at variance with the fact of his graduation in divinity. When Mary came to the throne Morwen became prominent. He was secretary to Bonner, and assisted in the trials of heretics (cf. Foxe, *Acts and Monuments*, vi. 721). On Good Friday 1557 he preached at St. Paul's Cross. In 1558 he became a prebendary of St. Paul's, and received the livings of St. Martin's Ludgate, Copford, Asheldam, and Whickam Bishops, all in London diocese. He lost all at Elizabeth's accession, and was put in the Fleet for preaching at Ludgate in favour of the mass. He was released on submission, and perhaps was protected by William Roper, son-in-law to More, whose daughter he taught; but he was again in trouble in 1561 for scattering a libel in Cheshire—that is to say a reply to Pilkington's sermon about the fire at St. Paul's, which Romanists considered as a portent. From this time he disappeared.

Morwen contributed epitaphs in Greek and Latin on Henry and Charles Brandon to the collection issued in 1551, and published a Latin epitaph on Gardiner in 1555 (London, 4to), which Hearne reprinted in his 'Curious Discourses.' Julines Palmer [q. v.], who was burnt in 1556, composed a reply—an 'epicedium'—to the epitaph on Gardiner, and it was found when his study was searched. Bodleian MS. 439 contains opuscula in Greek and Latin by Morwen. Translations from Greek into Latin of 'The Lives of Artemius and other Saints,' dedicated to Queen Mary, form MS. Reg. 13, B, x, in the British Museum.

[Wood's Athenæ, ed. Bliss, i. 195; Le Neve's Fasti, ii. 384, 560, iii. 565; Prince's Worthies of Devon, p. 454; Narratives of the Reformation (Camd. Soc.), p. 84; Churton's Life of Alexander Nowell, pp. 52, 61; Dixon's Hist. of Church of England, iv. 182, 348, 687; Strype's Memorials, III. ii. 2, 29; Annals, I. i. 60, 61, 253, 414; Casley's Cat. Royal MSS. 221.] W. A. J. A.

MORWEN, MORWENT, or MORWINGE, PETER (1530?–1573?), translator, graduated B.A. from Magdalen College, Oxford, in 1550, and was elected a fellow in 1552. In June next year he supplicated for the degree of M.A., but he was a rigid protestant, and when Bishop Gardiner made a visitation of the university in October 1553, he was expelled from his fellowship. He took refuge in Germany (Bloxam, *Reg. Magdalen College, Oxford*, ii. pp. liv, cvi; Strype, *Memorials*, III. i. 82). On the accession of Elizabeth he returned home, was ordained deacon by Grindal on 25 Jan. 1559–60 (Strype, *Grindal*, p. 54), and was granted his master's degree at Oxford on 16 Feb. following. He became rector of Langwith, Nottinghamshire, in 1560; of Norbury, Derbyshire, in 1564, and of Ryton, Warwickshire, in 1556. Thomas Bentham [q. v.], bishop of Lichfield, an old college friend, made him his chaplain, and afterwards collated him to the prebend of Pipa Minor in the cathedral of Lichfield on 27 Oct. 1567. A successor was appointed in the prebend on 6 March 1572–3 (Le Neve, *Fasti*, i. 618). Morwen probably died a month or two before.

Morwen was a fair scholar and translated into English, apparently from the Hebrew,' Joseph Ben Gorion's 'History of the Jews.' This task Morwen undertook at the entreaty of the printer, Richard Jugge [q. v.], and it must have been mainly accomplished while Morwen was an exile in Germany. The first edition, of which no copy is in the British Museum, was dated 1558, and bore the title 'A compendious and moste marveylous History of the latter Times of the Jewes Commune Weale' (London, b. l. 8vo). Other editions—'newly corrected and amended'—appeared in 1561, 1567, 1575, 1579, 1593, and 1615. All these are in the British Museum. Morwen also rendered into English from the Latin, Conrad Gesner's 'Treasure of Euonymus conteyninge the Wonderfull hid Secretes of Nature touchinge the most apte formes to prepare and destyl medicines,' London, b. l. by John Daye, 1559, 4to. The printer signs an address to the Christian reader, which is dated 2 May 1559, and a few engravings are scattered through the text. A new edition —'A new Booke of Distillation of Waters, called the Treasure of Euonymus'—is dated 1565, b. l. 4to; it was also published by Daye.

[Foster's Alumni Oxon.; Wood's Athenæ Oxon. ed. Bliss, i. 454; Brit. Mus. Cat. s. v. 'Morwing.'] S. L.

MORWEN, MORWENT, or MORWYN, ROBERT (1486?–1558), president of Corpus Christi College, Oxford, was born at Harpery, near Gloucester. He was admitted B.A. at Oxford 8 Feb. 1506–7, from which date we may infer that he was probably born about 1486. He incepted as Master of Arts 30 June 1511. In 1510 he had become fellow of Magdalen College, and there filled various college offices. Shortly after Bishop Richard Foxe [q. v.] had founded his new college of Corpus Christi, he constituted, by letter dated 22 June 1517, Morwent perpetual vice-president and *sociis compar.* Morwent could not be made a fellow, *eo nomine*, because on his admission to his fellowship at Magdalen he had taken an oath that he would not accept a fellowship at any other college. In the supplementary statutes of 1527 Bishop Foxe nominated Morwent, whose industry and zeal he highly commended, to be successor to the first president, John Claymond [q. v.], taking the precaution to provide that this act should not be drawn into a precedent. A few days after Claymond's death Morwent was sworn president, 26 Nov. 1537. His practical capacity seems to be placed beyond doubt, but he appears, as Laurence Humfrey points out in his 'Life of Jewel' (p. 22), to have been rather a patron of learned men than a learned man himself. In a sermon preached before the university, according to Wood (*Colleges and Halls*, p. 395), he was styled 'pater patriæ literatæ Oxoniensis.' Morwent must have possessed the gift of pliancy as well as prudence, for he retained the presidency through the troubled times that intervened between 1537 and 1558.

There can be no doubt that Morwent was one of the secret catholics who outwardly conformed during Edward VI's time, and in return were allowed to retain their preferments. But on 31 May 1552 he was summoned before the council, together with two of the fellows, Walshe and Allen, 'for using upon Corpus Christi day other service than was appointed by the "Book of Service."' On 15 June they were committed to the Fleet. 'And a letter was sent to the College, to appoint Jewel [see Jewel, John] to govern the College during the imprisonment of the President.' 'July 17, the Warden of the Fleet was ordered to release the President of Corpus Christi, upon his being bound in a bond of 200*l.* to appear next term before the Council. Allen, upon his conforming to the King's orders, was restored to his Fellowship' (Strype, *Memorials*, bk. ii. ch. xviii.) Shortly after the accession of Mary, when Bishop Gardiner's commission visited the college, the president and Walshe boasted that throughout the time of King Edward they had carefully secreted and preserved all the ornaments, vessels, copes, cushions, plate, candlesticks, &c., which in the reign of Henry VIII had been used for the catholic service. 'In what condition,' says Wood (*Annals*, sub 1553), 'they found that College was such as if no Reformation at all had been there.'

On 25 Jan. 1555–6 Morwent was appointed, in convocation, one of the delegacy for selling the shelves and seats in the university library. 'The books of the public library,' says Mr. Macray (*Annals of the Bodleian Library*, 2nd ed. p. 13), 'had all disappeared; what need then to retain the shelves and stalls, when no one thought of replacing their contents?' In 1556 Morwent was nominated on Pole's commission for visiting the university. It was this commission which disinterred Catherine, the wife of Peter Martyr, who had been buried in the cathedral, near the reliques of St. Frideswide.

Fulman quotes from the 'Hist. Exhumationis et Restitutionis Catherinæ Uxoris Pet. Mart.,' fol. 197 *b*, printed at the end of Conrad Hubert's 'Life of Bucer and Fagius,' the graphic character of Morwent: 'Fuit Morwennus satis annosus pater, et parcus senex, ad rem tuendam paterfamilias bonus: ad doctrinæ et religionis controversias vindicandas judex parum aptus, acerrimus tamen vetustatis suæ defensor.' Friendly feelings seem to have subsisted between the president and his undergraduates, and Jewel in his earlier days at Corpus wrote at the new year some kindly verses on Morwent's dog, to which the president was much attached. He is said to have subsequently regretted the share which he was afterwards instigated to take in bringing about Jewel's departure from the college at the beginning of the Marian persecutions. Morwent died 16 Aug. 1558, three months before Queen Mary's death.

[Humfrey's Life of Jewel; Strype's Memorials; Wood's Annals; Wood's Colleges and Halls; Conrad Hubert's Life of Bucer and Fagius; Macray's Annals of the Bodleian Library; C. C. C. Register, vol. i.; Fulman MSS. in C. C. C. Library, vol. ix.; C. C. C. Statutes; Fowler's Hist. of C. C. C. in Oxf. Hist. Soc. vol. xxv.] T. F.

MORYS or MORIZ, Sir JOHN (*fl.* 1340), deputy of Ireland, was probably a member of a Bedfordshire family, who represented that county in the parliaments of May 1322, December 1326, December 1332, March 1336, and March 1340. On some of these occasions he was associated with Thomas Studley, who was afterwards his attorney in England. There was also a John Morice or Moriz who represented the borough of Cambridge in the parliaments of December 1326, April 1328, September 1337, February 1338 (*Return of Members of Parliament*, i. 64–130). Morys was commissioner of array for Bedfordshire and Buckinghamshire in 1322 and 1324 (*Parliamentary Writs*, iv. 1195). On 6 March 1327 he was placed on the commission of oyer and terminer for Bedfordshire and Buckinghamshire to inquire into the taking of prises by members of the royal household, and on 8 March 1327 he was placed on the commission of peace for Bedfordshire. On 8 July 1328 he was going to Ireland, and had letters nominating attorneys to act for him during two years. On 13 March 1329 he had protection for one year again when going to Ireland on the royal service, and on 11 April 1329 had leave to nominate attorneys as before (*Cal. Pat. Rolls, Edward III*, 1327–30). In May 1341 (*Chart. St. Mary's, Dublin*, ii. 382), when he was styled knight, he was said to be acting as deputy in Ireland for Sir John D'Arcy. In this capacity he held a parliament at Dublin in October 1341, when he had to enforce ordinances annulling royal grants made in the king's reign, and acquittances from crown debts, unless granted under the English seal. These measures were unpopular with the Anglo-Irish nobles, who perhaps also despised Morys as a man of small political or social importance. An opposition parliament was accordingly held under the Earl of Desmond at Kilkenny in November 1341, and an appeal made to the king against the abuses of the Irish administration. Morys was soon after displaced by Ralph Ufford. But in April 1346 he procured his own reappointment, and on the news of Ufford's death a few days after was ordered to proceed to Ireland (Gilbert, *Viceroys*, p. 541). There he arrived on 15 May, and at once released the Earl of Kildare, whom Ufford had imprisoned; but on the great massacre of the English in Ulster during June, Morys was once more displaced, and seems to disappear from history.

[Chartulary of S. Mary's, Dublin (Rolls Ser.); Gilbert's Viceroys of Ireland; Leland's Hist. of Ireland; Book of Howth, pp. 161, 164, 456; authorities quoted.] C. L. K.

MORYSINE, Sir RICHARD (*d.* 1556), diplomatist. [See Morison.]

MORYSON, FYNES (1566–1630), traveller, born in 1566, was younger son of Thomas Moryson (*d.* 1591) of Cadeby, Lincolnshire, clerk of the pipe, and M.P. for Great Grimsby in 1572, 1584, 1586, and 1588–9 (*Harl. MS.* 1550, f. 50 *b*; cf. *Itinerary*, pt. i. p. 19). His mother, Elizabeth, daughter of Thomas Moigne of Willingham, Lincolnshire, died in 1587 (*ib.*) He matriculated at Peterhouse, Cambridge, 18 May 1580, and, graduating B.A. (M.A. 1587), obtained a fellowship about 1584. The college allowed him to study civil law; but, 'from his tender youth, he had a great desire to see foreign countries' (*ib.* p. 197), and in 1589 he obtained a license to travel. Two years he spent either in London or on visits to friends in the country, preparing himself for his expedition, and on 22 March 1590–1 he was incorporated M.A. at Oxford. On 1 May 1591 he took ship at Leigh, near Southend, and for the greater part of the six years following wandered about Europe.

At the end of 1591 he reached Prague, where he dreamt of his father's death on the day of the event (*ib.* p. 19). The news was confirmed at Nuremberg, and after a year's leisurely tour through Germany he retraced his steps to the Low Countries in order to dispose of his modest patrimony. On 7 Jan. 1593 he entered himself as a student at Leyden University (Peacock, *Index*, p. 65). He subsequently passed through Denmark and Poland to Vienna, and thence by way of Pontena and Chiusa into Italy in October 1593 (*Itinerary*, pt. i. p. 68). After visiting Naples, he thoroughly explored Rome, where he paid visits to Cardinals Allen (*ib.* p. 121) and Bellarmine (p. 142). The former gave him every facility for viewing the antiquities. The cities of North Italy occupied him from April 1594 to the beginning of 1595. In the early spring of 1595 he had an interview with Theodore Beza at Geneva, and journeying hurriedly through France, caught a glimpse of Henri IV at Fontainebleau (*ib.* p. 195), and landed at Dover 13 May 1595.

On 8 Dec. of the same year Moryson started on a second journey, setting sail for Flushing. A younger brother, Henry, bore him company. Passing through Germany to Venice, they went, at the end of April 1596, by sea to Joppa, spent the first fortnight of June at Jerusalem, and thence went by Tripoli and Aleppo to Antioch. At Beilan, a neighbouring village, Henry Moryson died on 4 July 1596 (*ib.* p. 249); he was in his twenty-seventh year. Fynes afterwards made for Constantinople, where the English ambassador, Edward Barton [q.v.], hospitably entertained him (*ib.* pp. 260, 265). He finally reached London by way of Venice and Stade on 10 July 1597.

In April 1598 Moryson visited Scotland, but soon came home, and spent some time in the autumn with his sisters, Faith Mussendyne and Jane, wife of George Allington, of the pipe office. The former lived at Healing near the south bank of the Humber. During the greater part of 1599 he remained with his kinsfolk in Lincolnshire. At the time his brother Richard [see below] was taking an active part in the government of Ireland, and strongly recommended him to seek employment in Ireland. Accordingly Moryson went to Cambridge in July 1600 in order to formally resign his fellowship at Peterhouse, and the college presented him with 40*l.*, the amount of two years' income. In November he set out for Dublin (*ib.* pt. ii. p. 84). On the 13th he reached Dundalk, where his brother was governor; on the same day George Cranmer, the chief secretary of Sir Charles Blount [q. v.], the lord-deputy, was killed at Carlingford, and Moryson was at once appointed to his place (*ib.* pt. ii. p. 84). He found his new master all that he could wish, aided him in his efforts to suppress Tyrone's rebellion, and remained through life a devoted admirer (*ib.* pp. 45–50). On 20 Feb. 1601 he was wounded in the thigh while riding with Blount about MacGahagan's castle in Westmeath (*ib.* pt. ii. p. 88). At the end of the year he took part in the siege of Kinsale (*ib.* pp. 165 sq.), and he seems to have accompanied Blount on his return to England in May 1603 (*ib.* p. 296). On 19 June 1604 he received a pension of 6*s.* a day (*Cal. State Papers*, 1603-1610, p. 121; but cf. *ib.* Dom. Add. 1580-1625, p. 445). He continued in the service of Blount, who was created Earl of Devonshire in 1604, until the earl's death in 1606.

Moryson was in London on 26 Feb. 1611–1612, when he carried the pennon at the funeral of his sister Jane, in St. Botolph's Church, Aldersgate. In 1613 he revisited Ireland at the invitation of his brother, Sir Richard, then vice-president of Munster. After a narrow escape from shipwreck, he landed at Youghal on 9 Sept. He judged the outward appearances of tranquillity in Ireland delusive, and anticipated further 'combustions' unless justice were severely administered (*Itinerary*, pt. ii. p. 300).

After Lord Devonshire's death in 1606, Moryson had spent three years in making an abstract of the history of the twelve countries which he had visited, but his manuscript proved so bulky that with a consideration rare in authors he destroyed it, and turned his attention to a briefer record of his experiences of travel. Even this work he designed on a generous scale. It was to be in five parts, written in Latin, and he made an apparently vain appeal to William Herbert, earl of Pembroke, to accept the dedication (*Hist. MSS. Comm.* 4th Rep. p. 372). In 1617 he had completed three parts—of the first part the Latin version is in Harl. MSS. 5133—and had translated them into English. He obtained full copyright for twenty-one years for this portion of his undertaking, as well as for 'one or two parts more thereof, not yet finished, but shortly to be perfected.' The book, which was entered on the 'Registers' of the Stationers' Company 4 April 1617 (ed. Arber, iii. 606), appeared under the title, 'An Itinerary [by Fynes Moryson, Gent.], containing his ten years Travels through the twelve Dominions of Germany, Bohmerland, Sweitzerland, Netherland, Denmark, Poland, England, Scotland, and Ireland. Divided in three parts,' London, 1617, fol. The first part supplies a journal of his travels through Europe, Scotland, and Ireland, with plans of the chief cities, 'the rates of hiring coaches and horses from place to place with each day's expences for diet, horse-meat, and the like.' The second part is a valuable history of Tyrone's rebellion, with documents of state (cf. Spedding, *Bacon*, vols. ii. and iii.) The third part consists of essays on travel, geography, and national costume, character, religion, and constitutional practice. A manuscript fourth part, in English, treating of similar topics, is in the library of Corpus Christi College, Oxford (No. xciv), and was licensed for the press, though not then published, on 14 June 1626 (*Ashmol. MS.* ccc. 94). A large portion was first printed by Charles Hughes under the title of 'Shakespeare's Europe' (1903). The second part, together with part iii. book iii. chapter v. ('of the geographical description of Ireland, the situation, fertility, trafficke, and diet') was reprinted as 'A History of Ireland from 1599 to 1603,' at Dublin in 1735, and 'the description of Ireland,' again in Professor Henry Morley's Carisbrooke Library, in 1890. The whole of the 1617 edition was reissued in 1907–8 (Glasgow, 4 vols.)

Moryson is a sober and truthful writer, without imagination or much literary skill. He delights in statistics respecting the mileage of his daily journeys and the varieties in the values of the coins he encountered. His descriptions of the inns in which he lodged, of the costume and the food of the countries visited, render his work invaluable to the social historian.

Moryson died 12 Feb. 1629–30, having made his will the previous 15 Sept.

His brother, Sir Richard Moryson (1571?–1628), born about 1571, served successively as lieutenant and captain with the English troops employed under Sir Roger Williams in France and the Low Countries between 1591 and 1593 (*Cal. Carew MSS.* 1603–24, p. 429). In the Islands' Voyage of 1597 he acted as lieutenant-colonel under Sir Charles Blount [q.v.], and went as a colonel with Essex's army to Ireland in 1599 (*ib.*) He was knighted at Dublin by Essex, 5 Aug. 1599 (Chamberlain, *Letters*, p. 63), was soon made governor of Dundalk, and was afterwards removed to a like post at Lecale, co. Down. He vigorously aided Blount in his efforts to suppress Tyrone's rebellion, and on Blount's return to England became governor of Waterford and Wexford in July 1604 (*Cal. State Papers*, Ireland, 1603–6, pp. 185, 257, cf. *ib.* 1615–25, p. 61). In 1607, on the death of Sir Henry Brouncker, president of Munster, Moryson and the Earl of Thomond performed the duties of the vacant office until Henry, lord Danvers [q. v.], was appointed to it. In 1609 Moryson became vice-president of Munster, and in August recommended that Irish pirates who infested the coast of Munster should be transported to Virginia. Four years later he is said to have paid Lord Danvers 3,000*l.* with a view to obtaining the presidency of Munster, which Danvers was vacating (*ib.* Dom. 1611–18, under date 14 Jan. 1613). He was elected M.P. for Bandon to the Irish parliament in April 1613. In 1614 Danvers made vain efforts to secure the Munster presidency for Moryson, but it was given to Lord Thomond (*ib.* Ireland, 1611–14, p. 532; *Cal. Carew MSS.* 1603–24, pp. 428 sq.) A year later Moryson left Ireland after fifteen years' honourable service, and on 1 Jan. 1615–16 was appointed lieutenant-general of the ordnance in England for his own life and for that of his brother-in-law, Sir William Harington (*Cal. State Papers*, Dom. 1611–18, p. 342). He also held from 1616 the office of cessor of composition money for the province of Munster, and in 1618 was granted the reversion of the Munster presidency, which, however, never fell to him. Settling at Tooley Park, Leicestershire, he was elected M.P. for Leicester on 8 Jan. 1620–1. He appears to have zealously performed his duties at the ordnance office till his death in 1628. His widow, Elizabeth, daughter of Sir Henry Harington (son of Sir James Harington of Exton), survived him. His eldest son Henry was knighted at Whitehall 8 Oct. 1627. A daughter, Letitia, whose character somewhat resembled that of her distinguished husband, was wife of Lucius Cary, second viscount Falkland (cf. *ib.* 1629–31, pp. 146, 393; *Letters of George, Lord Carew*, Camd. Soc. p. 22 note).

[Wood's Fasti Oxon., ed. Bliss, i. 253; Notes and Queries, 2nd ser. xi. 321–6; Hughes's Shakespeare's Europe, 1903, introd.; Retrospective Rev. xi. 308 sq.; Foster's Alumni Oxon.] S. L.

MOSELEY. [See also Mosley.]

MOSELEY, BENJAMIN, M.D. (1742–1819), physician, was born in Essex in 1742. He studied medicine in London, Paris, and Leyden, and settled in practice in Jamaica in 1768, where he was appointed to the office of surgeon-general. He performed many operations, and records that a large number of his patients died of tetanus. He visited other parts of the West Indies and Newfoundland, and, when he grew rich from fees, returned to England and obtained the degree of M.D. at St. Andrews 12 May 1784. Beginning in the autumn of 1785, he made a series of tours on the continent, commencing with Normandy, and in 1786 visiting Strasburg, Dijon, Montpellier, and Aix. He visited the hospitals in each city, and at Lausanne talked with the celebrated Tissot; he crossed to Venice by the Mont Cenis pass, 23 Oct. 1787, and went on to Rome. He was admitted a licentiate of the College of Physicians of London 2 April 1787, and in the following year was appointed physician to the Royal Hospital at Chelsea, an office which he held till his death at Southend on 25 Sept. 1819. He was buried at Chelsea.

His first publication was 'Observations on the Dysentery of the West Indies, with a new and successful Method of treating it,' printed in Jamaica, and reprinted in London (1781). The method consisted in giving James's powder or some other diaphoretic, and wrapping the patient in blankets till he sweated profusely. In 1775 he published 'A Treatise concerning the Properties and Effects of Coffee,' a work of which the only interesting contents are some particulars as to the use of coffee in the West Indies, and the incidental evidence that even as late as 1785, when the third edition appeared, coffee was little drunk in England. A fifth edition appeared in 1792. His most important work appeared in 1787, 'A Treatise on Tropical Diseases and on the Climate of the West Indies.' In 1790 it was translated into German, and a fourth edition appeared in 1803. It contains some valuable medical observations, curious accounts of the superstitions of the negroes about Obi and Obea, thrilling tales of sharks, and an interesting history of the disastrous expeditions of General Dalling in January 1780 and of General Garth in August 1780 against the Spaniards. In 1799 he published 'A Treatise on Sugar,' which contains no scientific information of value, but the exciting story of the death of Three-fingered Jack, a famous negro outlaw slain by three Maroons, who described their encounter in 1781 to Dr. Moseley. In 1800 he published a volume of medical tracts on sugar, cow-pox, the yaws, African witchcraft, the plague, yellow fever, hospitals, goitre, and prisons. A second edition appeared in 1804. In 1808 he published in quarto 'On Hydrophobia, its Prevention and Cure.' He claims to be the first to have observed that the scratches of a mad cat will produce hydrophobia. His method of treatment, which he declares was always successful, was to extirpate the wounded part and to administer a full course of mercury. He also published many controversial letters and pamphlets on cow-pox, in which he declares himself an opponent of vaccination. In the West Indies, where he was engaged in active practice and in observation of a series of phenomena with which he became familiar, he made some small additions to knowledge; but in England, where he was in an unfamiliar field, his observations were of less value, and his professional repute seems to have gradually diminished. The unscientific character of his mind is illustrated by the fact that he believes the phases of the moon to be a cause of hæmorrhage from the lungs, because a captain in the third regiment of guards coughed up blood six times at full moon and twice just after the new moon (*Tropical Diseases*, p. 548). He often wrote letters in the 'Morning Herald' and other newspapers.

[Munk's Coll. of Phys. ii. 368; Gent. Mag. lx. 9–11; Morning Herald, 14 Nov., 15 Dec. 1807, 25 Jan. 1808; Works.] N. M.

MOSELEY, HENRY (1801–1872), mathematician, the son of Dr. William Willis Moseley, who kept a large private school at Newcastle-under-Lyme, and his wife Margaret (*née* Jackson), was born on 9 July 1801. He was sent at an early age to the grammar school of the town, and when fifteen or sixteen to a school at Abbeville. Afterwards he attended for a short time a naval school at Portsmouth, and while there wrote his first paper 'On measuring the Depth of the Cavities seen on the Surface of the Moon' (*Tilloch's Phil. Mag.* lii. 1818). In 1819 Moseley went to St. John's College, Cambridge. He graduated B.A. in 1826, coming out seventh wrangler, and proceeded M.A. in 1836. In 1870 he was made LL.D. *hon. causa*.

Moseley was ordained deacon in 1827 and priest in 1828, and became curate at West Monkton, near Taunton. There, in the intervals of his clerical duties, he devoted himself to mathematics, and wrote his first book, 'A Treatise on Hydrostatics,' 8vo, Cambridge, 1830. On 20 Jan. 1831 he was appointed 'Professor of Natural and Experimental Philosophy and Astronomy' at King's College, London, and he held the post till 12 Jan. 1844, when he was appointed one of the first of H. M. inspectors of normal schools. He was also chaplain of King's College from 31 Oct. 1831 to 8 Nov. 1833. As one of the jurors of the International Exhibition of 1851 he came under the notice of the prince consort, and in 1853 he was presented to a residential canonry in Bristol Cathedral; in 1854 became vicar of Olveston, Gloucestershire, and was appointed chaplain in ordinary to her majesty in 1855. He died at Olveston 20 Jan. 1872. He was elected a fellow of the Royal Society in February 1839. He was also a corresponding member of the Institute of France, a member of the Council of Military Education, and vice-president of the Institution of Naval Architects.

Moseley married, on 23 April 1835, Harriet, daughter of William Nottidge, esq., of Wandsworth Common, Surrey, by whom he was father of Henry Nottidge Moseley [q. v.]

Moseley's more important works were: 'Lectures on Astronomy,' delivered when professor at King's College (8vo, London, 1839, 4th edit. 1854); the article on 'Definite Integrals' in the 'Encyclopædia Metropolitana,' 1837; and his well-known volume on 'The Mechanical Principles of Engineering and Architecture' (8vo, London, 1843, 2nd edit. 1855), which was reprinted in America with notes by Professor Mahan for the use of the Military School at West Point, and translated into German by Professor Schefler of Brunswick.

One of the most extensively useful results of Moseley's mathematical labours was the publication of the formulæ by which the dynamical stabilities of all ships of war have since been calculated. These formulæ first appeared in a memoir 'On the Dynamical Stability and on the Oscillations of Floating Bodies,' read before the Royal Society, and published in their 'Philosophical Transactions for 1850.' Later in life the observed motion of the lead on the roof of the Bristol Cathedral under changes of temperature caused him to advance the theory that the motion of glaciers might be similarly explained.

Besides the works already cited Moseley published: 1. 'Syllabus of a Course of Experimental Lectures on the Theory of Equilibrium,' 8vo, London, 1831. 2. 'A Treatise on Mechanics, applied to the Arts, including Statics and Hydrostatics,' 8vo, London, 1834; 3rd edit. 1847. 3. 'Illustrations of Mechanics,' 8vo, London, 1839. 4. 'Theoretical and Practical Papers on Bridges,' 8vo, London, 1843 (Weale's Series, 'Bridges,' vol. i.) 5. 'Astro-Theology . . . 2nd edit.' 8vo, London, 1851, 3rd edit. 1860; this first appeared in a series of articles in the 'Church of England Magazine' for 1838. Some thirty-five papers on natural philosophy were written by him, and appeared in the 'Philosophical Magazine,' the 'Transactions of the Cambridge Philosophical Society,' the 'Philosophical Transactions,' the 'British Association Reports,' and other journals.

[Information kindly supplied by Moseley's daughters, Mrs. Ludlow and Mrs. Hardy, and by the secretary, King's College, London; Memoir in Trans. Institution of Naval Architects, xiii. 328–30; Crockford's Clerical Directory, 1872; Brit. Mus. Cat.; Roy. Soc. Cat.]

B. B. W.

MOSELEY, HENRY NOTTIDGE (1844–1891), naturalist, born in Wandsworth, Surrey, in 1844, was son of Henry Moseley [q. v.] the mathematician. He was educated at Harrow, whence he went in 1864 to Exeter College, Oxford. It was at first intended that he should take a degree in either mathematics or classics, but these subjects proved so uncongenial to him that he was finally allowed to join Professor Rolleston's laboratory. In 1868 he came out with a first class in the natural science schools. Elected to the Radcliffe travelling fellowship in 1869, Moseley, with Prof. (afterwards Sir) Ray Lankester, went to Vienna and studied in Rokitanski's laboratory. On returning to England he entered as a medical student at University College, London. In 1871, again with Professor Lankester, he went to the continent and studied at Leipzig under Professor Ludwig. While there he published his first scientific memoir, 'Ein Verfahren um die Blutgefässe der Coleopteren auszuspritzen' (*Bericht k. sächs. Gesell.* (1871), xxiii. 276–8). Returning home in the autumn of the same year, Moseley was invited to join the government Eclipse expedition, then fitting out for Ceylon. He did good service as a member of it by making valuable spectroscopic observations in the neighbourhood of Trincomalee; he also formed a miscellaneous collection of natural history objects, including a quantity of land planarians. These last he carefully studied on his return to Oxford, and published the results of his investigation in the first of a series of important biological memoirs which were read before the Royal Society.

In 1872 Moseley was appointed one of the naturalists on the scientific staff of the Challenger, and accompanied that expedition in its voyage round the world, which lasted till May 1876. There being no botanist attached to the expedition, Moseley undertook the collection of plants, and wherever the expedition touched land his zeal as a collector led him always to remain on shore till the last moment, a habit which resulted in his nearly being left behind at Kerguelen's Land.

On his arrival in England in 1876 Moseley was elected to a fellowship at his old college (Exeter), and spent several years at Oxford working out the results of the expedition and preparing his reports, as well as writing important memoirs on the corals and their allies. In the summer of 1877 Moseley was commissioned by an English company to report on certain lands in California and Oregon, and took the opportunity of visiting Washington Territory, Puget Sound, and Vancouver Island, and of studying some of the native races of America. On his return he published a book on 'Oregon' (1878), for which he received a formal vote of thanks from the legislative assembly of that state.

In 1879 Moseley was elected a fellow of the Royal Society, and was also appointed assistant registrar to the university of London, which post he held till 1881, when he succeeded his friend and teacher, Professor Rolleston, in the Linacre professorship of human and comparative anatomy at Oxford. At the same time he became, ex officio, a fellow of Merton College.

In addition to his work in the lecture-room and laboratory at Oxford, Moseley served twice on the council of the Royal Society, and was on that of the Zoological Society, of which he had become a fellow in 1879, as well as on the council of the Anthropological Institute, which he joined in 1885. He was, besides, a fellow of the Linnean Society from 1880, and of the Royal Geographical Society from 1881. In 1884 he was president of 'section D' of the British Association at Montreal, and received the honorary degree of LL.D. from the McGill University. He was also a founder and member of council of the Marine Biological Association. Owing to overwork his health gave way in 1887, and his professorial labours were thenceforth performed by deputy. He finally succumbed to an attack of bronchitis on 10 Nov. 1891. In 1881 he married the youngest daughter of John Gwyn Jeffreys [q. v.] the conchologist.

Moseley's principal characteristic was an inborn aversion to accept any statement or recorded observation which he had not been able to verify for himself. He was an effective lecturer. Personally he was very genial, and a staunch friend.

Among his scientific achievements may be named his discovery of a system of tracheal vessels in 'Peripatus' that furnished a new clue to the origin of tracheæ, while the memoir on 'Peripatus' itself constituted an important contribution towards a knowledge of the phylogeny of arthropods. His investigations on living corals were the means of clearing up many doubtful points concerning the relationships between the members of that group, and led to the establishment of the group of hydrocorallin. Moseley also was the discoverer of the eyes on the shells of several species of chiton, to the minute structure of which his last publication was devoted. It was in recognition of such services to biological science that the Royal Society in 1887 awarded him their 'royal medal.'

Of all his writings Moseley's 'Notes by a Naturalist on the Challenger,' 8vo, London, 1879, 2nd ed. 1892, is the one that appeals to the widest circle of readers, and approaches Darwin's 'Journal of the Cruise of the Beagle' in interest and importance.

To the official reports of the results of the cruise he contributed a portion of the 'Narrative' and two independent zoological reports: one 'On certain . . . Corals,' and the other 'On the Structure of the peculiar Organs on the Head of Ipnops.'

In addition to the foregoing, Moseley wrote a treatise 'On the Structure of the Stylasteridæ—Croonian Lecture,' 4to, London, 1878, and contributed upwards of thirty papers to the 'Quarterly Journal of Microscopical Science,' to the 'Proceedings' and 'Transactions' of the Royal Society, to the 'Transactions of the Linnean Society' and other journals, besides writing the section on zoology for the 'Admiralty Manual of Scientific Enquiry,' 8vo, 1886. Moseley's manuscript 'Journal of Zoological Observations made during the Voyage of H.M.S. Challenger' is preserved in the library of the zoological department of the British Museum (natural history).

[G. C. Bourne's Memoir, with portrait, in 2nd ed. of Moseley's Notes by a Naturalist, 1892; Times, 13 Nov. 1891; Nature, 26 Nov. 1891; Foster's Alumni Oxon.; information supplied by the Hon. G. C. Brodrick, formerly warden of Merton College, Oxford, and by Prof. (afterwards Sir) Ray Lankester.] B. B. W.

MOSELEY, HUMPHREY (*d.* 1661), bookseller, conjectured to be a son of Samuel Moseley, a Staffordshire man, who was a stationer in London (Arber, *Transcripts*, ii. 249, iii. 683), was admitted a freeman of the Stationers' Company in 1627 (*ib.* iii. 686), when he probably began business. He was 'clothed' of the same company on 28 Oct. 1633, and in July 1659 was chosen one of its wardens. The first entry of a book licensed to him in the 'Stationers' Register' is on 29 May 1630. He became the chief publisher of the 'finer literature' of his age (Masson, *Milton*, vi. 400). He published the first collected edition of Milton's 'Poems,' 1645, and prefixed an address to the reader, in which he said: 'It is the love I have to our own language that hath made me diligent to collect and set forth such pieces, both in prose and verse, as may renew the wonted honour and esteem of our English tongue.' He published also early editions of Howell, Waller, Crashaw, Denham, D'Avenant, Cartwright, Donne, Fanshawe, Henry Vaughan, and many other authors, as well as translations of Spanish and Italian novels and contemporary French romances. His shop was in St. Paul's Churchyard. He died on 31 Jan. 1660–1, and was buried in St. Gregory's Church. By his will he appointed his wife Anne and his only daughter Anne his executrices, and left bequests to his brothers Thomas and Charles Moseley and Richard Frampton, and 10*l.* for a bowl or cup for the Stationers' Company.

[Masson's Life of Milton, vi. 400; Arber's Transcripts of Stationers' Registers; Arber's List of London Booksellers, 1890; Smyth's Obituary (Camden Soc.), p. 53.] C. W. S.

MOSER, GEORGE MICHAEL (1704–1783), chaser and enameller, son of Michael Moser, an eminent Swiss engineer and worker in metal, was born at Schaffhausen in 1704. He studied at Geneva, and, coming early to England, was first employed by a cabinet-maker in Soho, named Trotter, as a chaser of brass ornaments for furniture. He subsequently rose to be head of his profession as a gold-chaser, medallist, and enameller, and was particularly distinguished for the compositions in enamel with which he ornamented the backs of watches, bracelets, and other trinkets. A beautiful example of this work was a watch-case executed for Queen Charlotte, adorned with whole-length figures of her two eldest children, for which he received 'a hatful of guineas.' Moser was drawing-master to George III during his boyhood, and on his accession to the throne was employed to engrave his first great seal. When the art school afterwards known as the St. Martin's Lane Academy was established about 1736, in Greyhound Court, Strand, he became manager and treasurer, and continued in that position until the school was absorbed in the Royal Academy. Moser was an original member, and afterwards a director, of the Incorporated Society of Artists, whose seal he designed and executed, and was one of the twenty-one directors whose retirement, in 1767, led to the establishment of the Royal Academy. To Moser's zeal and energy the latter event was largely due. In association with Chambers, West, and Cotes he framed the constitution of the new body, and on 28 Nov. 1768 presented the memorial to the king asking for his patronage. He became a foundation member, and was elected the first keeper, having rooms assigned to him in Somerset House. For this position he was well qualified by his powers as a draughtsman and knowledge of the human figure, while his ability and devotion as a teacher gained for him the strong affection of the pupils. Moser was greatly esteemed in private life, and enjoyed the friendship of Dr. Johnson, Goldsmith, and other literary celebrities of his day. According to Prior, he once greatly mortified Goldsmith by stopping him in the middle of a vivacious harangue with the exclamation, 'Stay, stay! Toctor Shonson's going to say something' (*Life of Goldsmith*, ii. 459). He died at Somerset House on 24 Jan. 1783, and was buried in the churchyard of St. Paul's, Covent Garden, his funeral being attended by almost all his fellow-academicians and pupils. On the day after Moser's death a notice of him from the pen of Sir Joshua Reynolds was published, in which he was described as the first goldchaser in the kingdom, possessed of a universal knowledge of all branches of painting and sculpture, and 'in every sense the father of the present race of artists.' In early life he had known Hogarth, John Ellys, Rysbrach, Vanderbank, and Roubiliac. He left an only daughter, Mary, who is noticed separately. Moser appears arranging the model in Zoffany's picture at Windsor, 'The Life School of the Royal Academy,' engraved by Earlom. A good portrait of him, accompanied by his daughter, belongs to Lord Ashcombe.

[Edwards's Anecd. of Painting, 1806; J. T. Smith's Nollekens and his Times, 1828; W. Sandby's Hist. of the Royal Academy, 1862; Leslie and Taylor's Life of Sir J. Reynolds, 1865; Boswell's Johnson, ed. G. B. Hill, ii. 258*n.*; Chalmers's Biog. Dict.; European Mag. 1803, ii. 83; Gent. Mag. 1783, i. 94, 180.]

F. M. O'D.

MOSER, JOSEPH (1748–1819), artist, author, and magistrate, son of Hans Jacob Moser, a Swiss artist, and nephew of George Michael Moser [q. v.], was born in Greek Street, Soho, in June 1748. He was instructed in enamel painting by his uncle, and exhibited at the Royal Academy from 1774 to 1782, and again in 1787, but after his marriage to a daughter of Peter Liege, an eminent surgeon of Holles Street, Cavendish Square, he abandoned the profession, and retired into the country. After an absence of three years Moser returned to London and devoted himself to literary pursuits. He wrote upon the topics of the day in the 'European Magazine' and other periodicals, and published many political pamphlets, dramas, and works of fiction, which enjoyed but a temporary popularity. About 1794 he was appointed a deputy-lieutenant for Middlesex and a magistrate for Westminster, sitting first at the Queen's Square court and subsequently at Worship Street. This post, the duties of which he fulfilled with zeal and ability, he held until his death, which took place at Romney Terrace, Westminster, 22 May 1819. Moser's writings included: 1. 'Adventures of Timothy Twig, Esq., in a Series of Poetical Epistles,' 1794. 2. 'Turkish Tales,' 1794. 3. 'Anecdotes of Richard Brothers,' 1795, in which he exposed the pretensions of that enthusiast and his supporter, N. B. Halhed [q. v.] 4. 'Tales and Romances of Ancient and Modern Times,' 5 vols. 1808. He also wrote several slight dramatic pieces of little merit; they are enumerated in Baker's 'Biographia Dramatica.' Four seem to have been published, but none are in the British Museum Library. A memoir of Moser, with a portrait engraved by W. Ridley from a picture by S. Drummond, appeared in the 'European Magazine,' August 1803.

[European Mag. 1803, ii. 83; Gent. Mag. 1819, i. 653; Baker's Biog. Dram. i. 527; Royal Academy Catalogues; Lowndes's Bibl. Man.]

F. M. O'D.

MOSER, MARY (*d.* 1819), flower painter, was the only child of George Michael Moser [q. v.] She received premiums of five guineas from the Society of Arts in 1758 and 1759, and exhibited with the Society of Artists from 1760 to 1768. Though extremely near-sighted, Miss Moser became celebrated for her pictures of flowers, which were gracefully and harmoniously composed and highly finished. She was much patronised by Queen Charlotte, who employed her to decorate an entire room at Frogmore, paying her more than 900*l.* for the work, and throughout her life she was on terms of intimacy with the princesses. When the Royal Academy was established, Miss Moser was chosen a foundation member, and frequently contributed to its exhibitions up to 1802, sending chiefly flowers, but occasionally a classical or historical subject. She was a clever and agreeable woman, and some lively letters from her have been printed, one of them addressed to Fuseli, for whom she is believed to have formed an unrequited attachment. On 26 Oct. 1793 Miss Moser married, as his second wife, Captain Hugh Lloyd of Chelsea, and afterwards only practised as an amateur. In 1805, when West was re-elected president of the Royal Academy, the only dissentient voice was that of Fuseli, who gave his vote for Mrs. Lloyd, justifying himself with the characteristic remark that he thought 'one old woman as good as another.' Surviving her husband several years, Mrs. Lloyd died in Upper Thornhaugh Street, London, on 2 May 1819, and was buried at Kensington. Her will, of which she appointed Joseph Nollekens [q. v.] and her cousin Joseph Moser [q. v.] the executors, is printed at length in Smith's 'Nollekens and his Times.' Portraits of Mrs. Lloyd and Angelica Kauffmann, the only two ladies ever elected royal academicians, appear as pictures on the wall in Zoffany's 'Life School of the Royal Academy,' engraved by Earlom.

[W. Sandby's Hist. of the Royal Academy; J. T. Smith's Nollekens and his Times; Gent. Mag. 1793, ii. 957, 1819 i. 492; Knowles's Life of Fuseli; Royal Acad. Catalogues.] F. M. O'D.

MOSES, HENRY (1782?–1870), engraver, worked throughout the first half of the present century, enjoying a great reputation for his outline plates, which are distinguished for the purity and correctness of the drawing. His art was peculiarly suited to the representation of sculpture and antiquities, and he published many sets of plates of that class; he was one of the engravers employed upon the official publication 'Ancient Marbles in the British Museum,' 1812–1845. Of the works wholly executed by himself the most important are: 'The Gallery of Pictures painted by Benjamin West,' 12 plates, 1811; 'A Collection of Antique Vases, Altars, &c., from various Museums and Collections,' 170 plates, 1814; 'Select Greek and Roman Antiquities,' 36 plates, 1817; 'Vases from the Collection of Sir Henry Englefield,' 40 plates, 1819; 'Examples of Ornamental Sculpture in Architecture, drawn by L. Vulliamy,' 36 plates, 1823; illustrations to Goethe's 'Faust,' after Retzsch, 26 plates, 1821; illustrations to Schiller's 'Fridolin' and 'Fight with the Dragon,' 1824 and 1825; Noehden's 'Specimens of Ancient Coins of Magna Græcia and Sicily,' 24 stipple plates, 1826; 'Works of Canova,' with text by Countess Albrizzi, 3 vols. 1824–8; and 'Selections of Ornamental Sculpture from the Louvre,' 9 plates, 1828. Moses also contributed many of the illustrations to Hakewill's 'Tour of Italy,' 1820, and 'Woburn Abbey Marbles,' 1822; he etched from his own designs 'Picturesque Views of Ramsgate,' 23 plates, 1817; 'Sketches of Shipping' and 'Marine Sketch Book,' 1824 (reissued by Ackermann, 1837); and 'Visit of William IV, when Duke of Clarence, to Portsmouth in 1827,' 17 plates, 1830. Moses's latest work was a set of twenty-two illustrations to 'Pilgrim's Progress,' after H. C. Selous, executed for the Art Union of London, 1844. He died at Cowley, Middlesex, 28 Feb. 1870.

[Redgrave's Dict. of Artists; Dodd's Collections in British Museum, Add. MS. 33403; Universal Cat. of Books on Art.] F. M. O'D.

MOSES, WILLIAM (1623?–1688), serjeant-at-law, son of John Moses, merchant tailor, was born in the parish of St. Saviour, Southwark, about 1623. On 28 March 1632, being 'of nine years,' he was admitted to Christ's Hospital, and proceeded in 1639 as an exhibitioner to Pembroke Hall, now Pembroke College, Cambridge, whence he graduated M.A. Early in 1655 he was elected master of Pembroke by the unanimous vote of the fellows. Benjamin Laney [q. v.] had been ejected from the mastership in March 1644, and the post had been successively held by Richard Vines and Sydrach Simpson. Cromwell demurred to the appointment of Moses, having designed another for the post, but on representation made of the services of Moses to the college, he withdrew his previous mandate. Moses was an admirable administrator, securing for his college the possession of the benefactions of Sir Robert Hitcham [q. v.], and rebuilding much of the fabric. He 'outwitted' Cromwell by proceeding to the election to a vacant post, in advance of the expected arrival of Cromwell's nomination.

At the Restoration Laney was reinstated. Moses was not in orders, and was disinclined to enter the ministry of the established church, though he was averse from presbyterianism and in favour of moderate episcopacy. His deeply religious mind was cast in a puritan mould; he ascribes his lasting religious impressions to the 'Institutions' of William Bucanus, which he read at Christ's Hospital in the English version by Robert Hill (*d.* 1623) [q. v.] Baxter was very desirous to have him appointed as one of the commissioners (25 March 1661) to the Savoy conference, but 'could not prevail.' His own health had led Moses to have some practical acquaintance with medicine, and he was the friend of several leading physicians. But after hesitating as to his future vocation he turned to the law, and became counsel to the East India Company. He was 'a very quick and ready man.' Charles II took particular notice of him when he pleaded for the company before the privy council. The lord chancellor, Heneage Finch, first earl of Nottingham [q. v.], said that had he taken earlier to law he would easily have been at the head of his profession. He saved his college 'some hundred of pounds in a law affair.' He was made serjeant-at-law on 11 June 1688; died 'a rich batchellor' in the same year, and left considerable benefactions to his college. A short Latin poem by him is included in 'Academiæ Cantabrigiensis Σωστρα,' &c., Cambridge, 1660, 4to, a congratulatory collection on the restoration of Charles II.

[Calamy's Account, 1713, p. 83; Calamy's Continuation, 1727, i. 115; Reliquiæ Baxterianæ, 1696, ii. 337; Chronica Juridicalia, 1739, App. p. 3; extracts from the Christ's Hospital Register of Exhibitioners, and from a manuscript Latin life of Moses by William Sampson, kindly furnished by the master of Pembroke College, Cambridge.] A. G.

MOSES, WILLIAM STAINTON (1840–1892), spiritualist, born in 1840, was eldest son of William Stainton Moses of Dorrington, Lincolnshire. He was educated at Bedford and Exeter College, Oxford, where he matriculated on 25 May 1858, graduated B.A. in 1863, and proceeded M.A. in 1865. He took holy orders, and was curate of Maughold in the Isle of Man from 1863 to 1868, and assistant chaplain of St. George's, Douglas, from 1868 to 1872, when he became interested in spiritualism, and resigned his cure for the post of English master at University College School. This office he held until 1890, when ill-health compelled his resignation. During his residence in London he devoted his leisure almost entirely to the exploration of the mysteries of spiritualism, to which he became a convert. He was one of the founders of the London Spiritualist Alliance, an active member and one of the vice-presidents of the Society for Psychical Research, a frequent contributor to 'Human Nature' and to 'Light,' and for some years editor of the latter journal. He died on 5 Sept. 1892.

Moses was a 'medium,' and conceived himself to be the recipient of spiritual revelations, which he published under the title of 'Spirit Teachings,' London, 1883, 8vo. He also wrote, under the disguised name 'M.A. Oxon.,' the following: 1. 'Carpenterian Criticism, being a Reply to an Article by Dr. W. B. Carpenter,' London, 1877, 8vo. 2. 'Psychography, or a Treatise on the Objective Forms of Psychic or Spiritual Phenomena,' London, 1878, 8vo; 2nd edit. 1882. 3. 'Spirit Identity,' London, 1879, 8vo. 4. 'Higher Aspects of Spiritualism,' London, 1880, 8vo. 5. 'Spiritualism at the Church Congress,' London, 1881, 8vo. Moses also contributed introductions to 'Ghostly Visitors,' published under the pseudonym 'Spectre-Stricken,' London, 1882, 8vo, and William Gregory's 'Animal Magnetism,' London, 1884, 8vo.

[Light, 10 Sept. 1892; Foster's Alumni Oxon.; Clergy List, 1867; Univ. Coll. Cal. 1872–3, and 1889–90; Crockford's Clerical Directory, 1889; Kirk's Suppl. to Allibone's Dict. of Engl. Lit.; Proceedings of the Soc. of Psychical Research.] J. M. R.

MOSLEY. [See also MOSELEY.]

MOSLEY, CHARLES (*d.* 1770?), engraver, worked during the second quarter of the eighteenth century. He was much engaged upon book illustrations, and was employed by Hogarth, whom he assisted in his 'Gate of Calais,' 1749. Mosley's best plates are his portraits, which include Charles I on horseback, after Vandyck; Nicholas Saunderson, after Gravelot; George Whitefield, after J. Smith; Theodore, king of Corsica, after Paulicino, 1739; Marshal Belleisle on horseback, and Mrs. Clive as the Lady in 'Lethe,' 1750. He also engraved 'The Procession of the Flitch of Bacon at Dunmow,' 1752, after David Ogborne; 'The Shooting of Three Highlanders in the Tower,' 1743; and, from his own designs, some popular satirical prints, dated 1739 and 1740. Mosley is said to have died about 1770.

[Redgrave's Dict. of Artists; Huber and Martini's Manuel des Curieux, &c., 1808; Dodd's manuscript Hist. of English Engravers in British Museum, Add. MS. 33403.] F. M. O'D.

MOSLEY, NICHOLAS (1611–1672), author, son of Oswald Mosley and his wife Anne, daughter of Ralph Lowe, was born at Ancoats Hall, Manchester, in 1611 (baptised at the collegiate church 26 Dec.) On the outbreak of the civil war he took the royalist side, and his estates were in consequence confiscated in 1643, but on 18 Aug. 1646 they were restored on his paying a heavy fine. In 1653 he published a philosophical treatise entitled '*Ψυχοσοφια*, or Natural and Divine Contemplations of the

Passions and Faculties of the Soul of Man' (London, Humphrey Moseley, 1653, 8vo). In 1657–8 he, along with other of his townsmen, engaged in a controversial discussion with Richard Heyrick [q. v.] and other leaders of the Manchester presbyterian classis. At the Restoration he mustered the remains of an auxiliary band, with whom he headed an imposing procession to the Manchester collegiate church on the coronation day, 23 Aug. 1661. Among other local public offices held by him were those of justice of the peace, boroughreeve of Manchester (1661–2), and feoffee of Chetham's Hospital and Library. He married Jane, daughter of John Lever of Alkrington, and died at Ancoats in October 1672, leaving three sons.

[Sir O. Mosley's Family Memoirs, 1849, p. 36; Local Gleanings, 1st ser. i. 248, 254, ii. 194; Earwaker's Manchester Court Leet Records, iv. 282, v. 154 et passim; Manchester Constables Accounts, vol. iii.; Foster's Lancashire Pedigrees; Commons' Journals, 5 and 12 May 1643.]
C. W. S.

MOSLEY, SAMUEL (*fl.* 1675–1676), New England settler, was in 1675 living at Boston, Massachusetts, apparently a man of repute and substance. Through his marriage with a sister of Isaac Addington, afterwards secretary of the colony, he was connected with most of the principal families of the town.

On the outbreak of the war with 'King Philip,' the chief of the Narragansett tribes, in June 1675, two companies of militia were raised by order of the Boston council. Mosley supplemented this little force by a third company of volunteers, or, as they were then called, 'privateers,' a term misunderstood by later writers, who have denounced Mosley as 'a ruffianly old privateer from Jamaica' (Doyle, ii. 220). There is no evidence to connect him either with Jamaica or the sea. The 'Philip's war' came to an end with the death of Philip on 12 Aug. 1676 at the hands of Captain Benjamin Church, but during the year of its continuance many sharp and bloody skirmishes were fought, in most of which Mosley took a distinguished part, more especially in the capture and destruction, on 19 Dec. 1675, of Canonicut, a fortified encampment to the west of Rhode Island. The small army of about a thousand men had to march thither some fifteen miles through the snow. Mosley and Devonport, a near connection of his, led the storming party, and the victory was complete, though with the loss of Devonport and two hundred killed and wounded. But the huts were burnt, and when the fight was over there was no shelter for the victors. Another terrible march in the snow was fatal to a large proportion of the wounded.

Mosley was said by the clergy of the Indian missions to be brutal in his treatment of the Indians, and especially of the Christian Indians. He is said, for instance, to have made an unprovoked raid on a mission at Marlborough, to have plundered and beaten the disciples, and to have driven eleven of them, including six children, three women, and one old man, into Boston (Gookin, p. 501). But another clergyman, not connected with the mission, declared that Mosley merely arrested at Marlborough eleven Indians who were reasonably suspected of murdering a white man, his wife, and two children at Lancaster, some nine miles off. 'But upon trial [at Boston] the said prisoners were all of them quitted from the fact' (Hubbard, p. 30). Mosley is said to be the original hero of the story of the man who scared the Indians by taking off his wig and hanging it on the branch of a tree, in order that he might fight more coolly. From the Indian point of view a man who could thus play with his scalp was an enemy not lightly to be encountered. The spelling of his name is taken from a facsimile of his signature given by Winsor (i. 313).

[The Present State of New England, being a Narrative of the Troubles with the Indians, by W. Hubbard, minister of Ipswich, passim; Gookin's History of the Christian Indians in Archæologia Americana, ii. 495 et seq.; The Memorial History of Boston . . . edited by Justin Winsor, i. 311 et seq., ii. 542; J. A. Doyle's English in America, the Puritan Colonies, ii. 220.]
J. K. L.

MOSS, CHARLES (1711–1802), bishop successively of St. David's and of Bath and Wells, son of William Moss and Sarah his wife, was born in 1711, and baptised 3 Jan. of that year. The elder Moss farmed a 'pretty estate,' inherited from his father, at Postwick, Norfolk (Nichols, *Lit. Anecd.* iv. 223). Charles's paternal uncle was Dr. Robert Moss [q. v.], dean of Ely, who at his death in 1729 bequeathed to him, as 'a promising youth' (*ib.*), the bulk of his large property. He had already, in 1727, entered Caius College, Cambridge, as a pensioner, whence he graduated B.A. in 1731, and M.A. in 1735, and in the latter year was elected to a fellowship. He was brought under the notice of Bishop Sherlock, then bishop of Salisbury, whose 'favourite chaplain' he became (Newton, *Autobiography*, p. 178), and was by him placed on the ladder of preferment, which he climbed rapidly. In 1738 he was collated to the prebend of Warminster in Salisbury Cathedral, and in 1740 he exchanged it for that of

Hurstbourne and Burbage. On Sherlock's translation to London, in 1748, he accompanied his patron, by whom he was appointed archdeacon of Colchester in 1749. From Sherlock also he received in succession the valuable livings of St. Andrew Undershaft, St. James's, Piccadilly (1750), and St. George's, Hanover Square (1759). In 1744 he defended Sherlock's 'Tryal of the Witnesses' against the strictures of Thomas Chubb [q. v.], in a tract entitled 'The Evidence of the Resurrection cleared from the exceptions of a late Pamphlet,' which was reissued in 1749 under the new title, 'The Sequel of the Trial of the Witnesses,' but without other alteration. He delivered the Boyle lectures for four years in succession, 1759-62. The lectures were not published (Nichols, *Lit. Anecd.* vi. 455). He was consecrated Bishop of St. David's, in succession to Robert Lowth [q. v.], 30 Nov. 1766, and in 1774 was translated to Bath and Wells, which see he retained until his death in 1802. He was a good average prelate, and, we are told, was 'much esteemed through his diocese for his urbanity and simplicity of manners, and reverenced for his piety and learning.' He warmly supported Hannah More [q. v.] in the promotion of Christian education in the Cheddar Valley, her schools being always 'honoured with his full sanction' (Roberts, *Life of H. More,* iii. 40, 136). Almost in the last year of his life, when she was threatened with prosecution by the farmers, under an obsolete statute, for her 'unlicensed schoolmasters,' he invited her to dinner at the palace, and 'received her with affectionate cordiality' (*ib.* p. 102). He died at his house in Grosvenor Square, 13 April 1802, and was buried in Grosvenor Chapel, South Audley Street.

Moss was a fellow of the Royal Society. With the exception of the above-mentioned reply to Chubb, his only printed works consisted of one archidiaconal charge, 1764, and some occasional sermons. There is a portrait of him in the vestry of St. James's Church, Piccadilly.

Out of a fortune of 140,000*l.*, he bequeathed 20,000*l.* to his only daughter, wife of Dr. King, and the remaining 120,000*l.* to his only surviving son, Dr. Charles Moss (1763-1811), a graduate of Christ Church, Oxford (B.A. 1783 and D.D. 1797), and chaplain of the House of Commons in 1789, to whom (aged eleven) his father gave the sub-deanery of Wells on his translation in 1774, and the precentorship in 1799, and three prebendal stalls in succession; in 1807 he was made bishop of Oxford, and died on 16 Dec. 1811. Bishop Charles Moss must be distinguished from his first cousin Charles Moss, who entered Caius College, Cambridge, in 1755, became archdeacon of Carmarthen Jan. 1767, and of St. David's Dec. 1767.

[Cassan's Lives of the Bishops of Bath and Wells, pp. 175-8; Britton's Wells Cathedral, p. 82; Roberts's Life of Hannah More; Nichols's Lit. Anecd. iv. 223, vi. 453.] E. V.

MOSS, JOSEPH WILLIAM (1803-1862), bibliographer, was born at Dudley, Worcestershire, in 1803. He matriculated at Magdalen Hall, Oxford, 21 March 1820, and while an undergraduate developed an ardent interest in classical bibliography. He graduated B.A. 1825, M.A. 1827, M.B. 1829, and settled in practice at Dudley.

He was elected fellow of the Royal Society on 18 Feb. 1830, but published nothing of a scientific nature. In 1847 he removed from Dudley to Longdon, near Lichfield, and in 1848 to the Manor House, Upton Bishop, near Ross, Herefordshire. In 1853 he again removed, to Hill Grove House, Wells, Somerset, where he died 23 May 1862. Towards the end of his life he was regarded as an eccentric recluse.

His claim upon posterity rests entirely upon his 'Manual of Classical Bibliography,' which, he says, was put to press early in 1823. The work was published in 1825, in two volumes, containing upwards of 1250 closely printed pages; and, considering the extreme youth of the author—he was not quite one-and-twenty—it is a very remarkable production. The advertisements declare that the 'Manual' combines the advantages of the 'Introduction' of Thomas Dibdin [q. v.], the 'Catalogues Raisonnés' of De Bure, and the 'Manuel' of Brunet. The author claimed to have consulted upwards of three thousand volumes, exclusive of innumerable editions and commentaries, to have produced a work fuller and more critical than the similar works by Michael Maittaire [q. v.], Dr. Edward Harwood [q. v.], and Dibdin, and to have been the first to include notices of critical publications connected with each author, together with the literary history of the translations made into the principal languages of Europe. In spite of very serious omissions, both among the editions and the translations, of some gross blunders, and of a lack of critical insight, the book remains a standard work of reference, especially with those who study the subsequent depreciation in the market value of editions of the classics.

Favourable reviews of the 'Manual' appeared in the 'Literary Chronicle' (1825), in the 'News of Literature' (1825), and in the 'Gentleman's Magazine' (1825, Suppl.) On the other hand, the 'Literary Gazette' (1825), in three articles, severely attacked the book. A detailed reply from Moss was subsequently issued with the publishers' advertisement, and with the 'Gentleman's Magazine' for September' 1825. In it Moss admits that he had borrowed the plan of his work from Dibdin, and claims, like Adam Clarke [q. v.], to have included the whole of Harwood's opinions. The 'Literary Magazine' published a rejoinder.

The 'Manual' was reprinted, with a new title-page, but with no corrections, in 1837, by Bohn. A 'Supplement,' compiled by the publisher, brings down the lists to 1836, and claims to supply omissions. The 'Supplement' is an indifferent catalogue, in which editions already noticed by Moss are wrongly included, and opinions of their merits wholly at variance with those pronounced by the author are quoted.

Three new works by Moss are announced in the reprint, viz., a 'Lexicon Aristotelicum,' a 'Catalogue Raisonné of the Collection of an Amateur,' and an edition of 'Lucretius' on an elaborate scale. But, though the first two were said to be in the press, none of these books appeared.

[Moss's Manual of Classical Bibliography; Allibone's Dict. of English Lit.; Foster's Alumni Oxon.; Gent. Mag. 1850, 1862; advertisements of the Literary Chronicle, 1825; the reviews above mentioned; information communicated.]

E. C. M.

MOSS, ROBERT (1666–1729), dean of Ely, eldest son of Robert and Mary Moss, was born at Gillingham in Norfolk in 1666 (so Masters; the 'Life' prefixed to his collected sermons says 'about 1667'). His father was a country gentleman in good circumstances, living at Postwick in the same county. After being educated at Norwich school he was admitted a sizar of Corpus Christi College, Cambridge, 19 April 1682, at the age of sixteen. He graduated in due course B.A. 1685, M.A. 1688, B.D. 1696, D.D. 1705. Soon after his first degree he was elected to a fellowship at his college. He was ordained deacon in 1688, and priest in 1690. In 1693 he was appointed by the university to be one of their twelve preachers, and his sermons at St. Mary's are said to have been much frequented. After missing by a few votes an appointment to the office of public orator at Cambridge in 1698, he was chosen preacher of Gray's Inn on 11 July of that year, in succession to Dr. Richardson, master of Peterhouse. In December 1716 he was allowed to nominate Dr. Thomas Gooch, master of Caius College, as his deputy in this office. Early in 1699 he was elected assistant-preacher at St. James's, Westminster, and was successively chaplain in ordinary to William III, Anne, and George I. In 1708 the parishioners of St. Lawrence Jewry offered him their Tuesday lectureship, which he accepted, succeeding Dr. Stanhope, then made dean of Canterbury.

Moss's preferments were now so numerous that the master of his college, Dr. Greene, was of opinion that his fellowship was virtually rendered void. A long and somewhat undignified controversy followed between Moss and the master, in which it was alleged that the total value of the church preferments held by Moss, 240*l.* in all, was equivalent to six fellowships. The master, however, did not proceed to extremities, and Moss retained his fellowship till 1714 (the correspondence is in Addit. MS. 10125).

In 1708, or soon afterwards, he was collated to the rectory of Gedelstone or Gilston, Hertfordshire; and on 16 May 1713 was installed dean of Ely. After suffering much from gout, he died 26 March 1729, and was buried in his own cathedral, where a Latin inscription with his arms (ermine, a cross patée) marks his resting-place. He had married a Mrs. Hinton of Cambridge, who survived him, but he left no issue. The bulk of his fortune, after deducting a small endowment for a sizarship at Caius College, was bequeathed to one of his nephews, Charles Moss [q. v.], bishop of Bath and Wells.

Moss is described as an excellent preacher and a kind and loyal friend. His sermons were collected and published in 1736, in 8 vols. 8vo, with a biographical preface by Dr. Zachary Grey [q. v.], who had married one of his step-daughters. An engraved portrait of the author by Vertue is prefixed.

[Masters's Hist. of Corpus Christi College, Cambridge, 1753, pp. 347–9; Life, by Dr. Z. Grey; Le Neve's Fasti; Nichols's Lit. Anecd. iv. 152; Cole's MSS. vol. xxx. fol. 166, &c.; Addit. MS. 10125; Notes and Queries, 8th ser. vi. 142.]

J. H. L.

MOSS, THOMAS (*d.* 1808), poet, received his education at Emmanuel College, Cambridge, where he graduated B.A. in 1761 (*Graduati Cantabr.* 1823, p. 332). Taking holy orders he became minister of Trentham, Staffordshire, and he was afterwards for many years minister of Brinley Hill Chapel in Worcestershire, and perpetual curate of Brierley Hill Chapel in the parish of Kingswinford, Staffordshire. He died at Stourbridge, Worcestershire, on 6 Dec. 1808.

He published anonymously 'Poems on several Occasions,' Wolverhampton, 1769, 4to, pp. 61. In an 'advertisement' to this small volume it is stated that most of the poems were written when the author was about twenty. The first piece is the pathetic and popular 'Beggar's Petition,' beginning with the line 'Pity the sorrows of a poor old man.' A Latin translation of this poem, 'Mendici Supplicatio,' was published by William Humphries, 'in scholâ paternâ de Baldock, alumnus,' London, 1790, 8vo, together with a Latin version of Goldsmith's 'Deserted Village.' Moss also published some occasional sermons and 'The Imperfection of Human Enjoyments,' a poem in blank verse, London, 1783, 4to.

[Chambers's Worcestershire Biog. p. 541; Cooper's Memorials of Cambridge, ii. 379; Watt's Bibl. Brit.; Gent. Mag. November 1790, p. 972, September 1791, p. 852, December 1808, p. 1133; Lowndes's Bibl. Man. (Bohn), p. 1622.]
T. C.

MOSSE, BARTHOLOMEW (1712–1759), philanthropist, born in 1712, was son of Thomas Mosse, rector of Maryborough, Queen's County. He was apprenticed to John Stone, a Dublin surgeon, and received a license to practise on 12 July 1733. In 1738 he was employed by the government to take charge of the men drafted from Ireland to complete the regiments in Minorca. Wishing to perfect himself in surgery and midwifery by intercourse with the practitioners of other countries, he subsequently travelled through England, France, Holland, and other parts of Europe. At length he settled in Dublin, and, having obtained a license in midwifery, he quitted the practice of surgery.

Struck by the misery of the poor lying-in women of Dublin, Mosse determined to establish a hospital for their relief. With the assistance of a few friends he rented a large house in George's Lane, which he furnished with beds and other necessaries, and opened it on 15 March 1745. This institution is said to have been the first of its kind in Great Britain. Encouraged by its usefulness, Mosse, on his own responsibility, took a large plot of ground on the north side of Dublin, and, with only 500*l.* in hand, set about the erection of the present Rotunda Hospital on the plans of Richard Cassels [q. v.] The foundation-stone was laid by the lord mayor on 24 May (=4 June) 1751. By subscriptions, parliamentary grants, and the proceeds of concerts, dramatic performances, and lotteries, the work was pushed on; and the institution was opened for the reception of patients on 8 Dec. 1757, having been incorporated by charter dated 2 Dec. 1756. Parliament on 11 Nov. 1757 granted 6,000*l.* to the hospital and 2,000*l.* to Mosse as a reward for his exertions. The house in George's Lane was now closed.

Mosse also formed a scheme, which was partly executed, for nursing, clothing, and maintaining all the children born in the hospital, whose parents consented to entrust them to his care. A technical school was to be opened and provided with able protestant masters, and he intended to establish a hardware manufactory in connection with it.

Mosse's philanthropic schemes involved him in debt and subjected him to much malicious misrepresentation. Worn out by his exertions he died at the house of Alderman Peter Barré at Cullenswood, near Dublin, on 16 Feb. 1759, and was buried at Donnybrook. By his wife Jane, daughter of Charles Whittingham, archdeacon of Dublin, he left two children. After his death parliament granted at various times 9,000*l.* to the hospital, and 2,500*l.* to Mrs. Mosse for the maintenance of herself and her children.

Mosse's portrait was presented by William Monck Mason [q. v.] to the hospital in November 1833, and now hangs in the boardroom; it has been engraved by Duncan. A plaster bust of Mosse, probably by Van Nost, stands in the hall. Mosse has been erroneously styled 'M.D.'

[Dublin Quarterly Journal of Medical Science, ii. 565–96 (with portrait); Warburton, Whitelaw, and Walsh's Hist. of Dublin, vol. ii.; Webb's Compendium of Irish Biography.] G. G.

MOSSE or MOSES, MILES (*fl.* 1580–1614), divine, educated at Cambridge University, proceeded D.D. between 1595 and 1603. About 1580 he became a minister at Norwich, where John, earl of Mar, and other Scottish nobles were afterwards among his congregation. 'It was my hap,' he says, 'through their honourable favour often to be present with some of them while they lay in the city of Norwich. There they many times partaked my publique ministry and I their private exercises' (*Scotland's Welcome*, 1603, p. 64). He afterwards became pastor of Combes, Suffolk. He published 1. 'A Catechism,' 1590, which is now only known by an answer by Thomas Rogers [q. v.], entitled, 'Miles Christianus: a Defence . . . written against an Epistle prefixed to a Catechism made by Miles Moses,' London, 1590, 4to. 2. 'The Arraignment and Conviction of Vsury,' &c., London, 8vo, 1595: sermons, preached at St. Edmundsbury, and directed against the growth of usury. Mosse shows great familiarity with the Canonist writers, and well represents the views of the clergy on usury at the end of the sixteenth century. He appears to have been greatly influenced by the teaching of Calvin and his school. 3. 'Scotland's Welcome,' London, 1603, 8vo; a sermon preached at Needham, Suffolk, and dedicated to John, earl of Mar. 4. 'Justifying and Saving Faith distinguished from the Faith of the Devils in a Sermon preached at Pauls Crosse, in London, 9 May 1613,' contains an account of the death of Queen Elizabeth (p. 77).

[Strype's Life of Whitgift, ii. 468; Ashley's Economic History, vol. i. pt. ii. p. 469. Mosse's autograph is in the Tanner MSS. (Bodleian Library), cclxxxiii. 69; Davy's manuscript Athenæ Suffolc. in Brit. Mus. i. 279.] W. A. S. H.

MOSSES, ALEXANDER (1793–1837), artist, born in 1793, was the son of a Liverpool tradesman. At an early age he showed a talent for drawing, but he had no instruction in art. He became nevertheless a masterly draughtsman and colourist. In the exhibition of the Liverpool Academy for 1811 he is represented by a 'View of Birkenhead Priory,' and in the following years by landscapes and figure pictures. In the catalogue of 1827 his name appears as 'Master of the Drawing Academy,' and he is represented by twelve works, among them the portraits of Edward Rushton, now hanging in the magistrates' room at the police office, Dale Street; of George Lyon, of William Swainson, F.R.S., F.L.S., and of Thomas Stewart Trail, M.D., president of the Liverpool Royal Institution, now in the Liverpool Institute. In 1829 he exhibited 'Christ's Agony in the Garden,' and 'The Expulsion from Paradise.' In 1831 he exhibited five pictures, the chief of which was the full-length portrait of Thomas (afterwards Sir Thomas) Branker, mayor of Liverpool. This excellent work is in the town-hall, Liverpool. In 1836 he exhibited a fine portrait of Dr. Rutter, now in the Royal Institution, Liverpool. He also painted the portrait of the Rev. John Yates of Liverpool, which was engraved by F. Engleheart. His only exhibit at the Royal Academy was in 1820, 'Dhama Rama and Munhi Rathama, two Budhist Priests from the Island of Ceylon.'

Mosses also practised as a teacher of drawing, among other places, at the Liverpool Royal Institution. One of his pupils there, William Daniels, rose to some note as an artist in Liverpool. A picture by Mosses, of blind Howard, a well-known inmate of the Blind Asylum, and his children, was engraved; another of a butcher lad, showing the town of Liverpool in the distance, was engraved on steel by H. Robinson. He died at his house, 18 Pleasant Street, Liverpool, 14 July 1837, leaving a widow and two sons. A portrait by himself, and a bust of him by Lyon, were in possession of his grandson, his last surviving descendant. He is represented in the permanent collection in the Walker Art Gallery, Liverpool, by a fine portrait of William Ewart, father of William Ewart, M.P. for Liverpool. This was presented in 1873 by Mr. W. E. Gladstone, M.P.

[Liverpool Lantern, 15 Jan. 1881; Liverpool Mercury, 21 July 1837; Liverpool Exhibition Catalogues; information supplied by Mrs. Bridger and Mr. Thomas Formby.] A. N.

MOSSMAN, GEORGE, M.D. (*fl.* 1800), medical writer, practised as a physician at Bradford, Yorkshire. On 6 July 1792 he married there a Miss Ramsbotham (*Gent. Mag.* 1792, pt. ii. p. 672). A marriage of Dr. Mossman, physician of Bradford, to Mrs. Ramsbottom of Barwick-in-Elmet, Yorkshire, is also recorded in 1812 (*ib.* 1812, pt. ii. p. 586).

Mossman wrote: 1. 'Observations on the Brunonian Practice of Physic: including a Reply to an anonymous Publication reprobating the Use of Stimulants in Fevers,' 8vo, London, 1788. 2. 'An Essay to elucidate the Nature, Origin, and Connexion of Srophula [*sic*] and glandular Consumption; including a brief History of the Effects of Ilkley Spaw; with Observation on the Medicinal Powers of the Digitalis,' &c., 8vo, Bradford [1792?] (another edit., London, 1800). He contributed four papers to Duncan's 'Annals of Medicine,' 1797 and 1799 (ii. 298, 307, 413, iv. 432), a paper in the 'Medical Repository' (i. 577), and numerous papers on the effects of digitalis in consumption to the 'Medical and Physical Journal.'

[Reuss's Register of Authors; Watt's Bibl. Brit.] G. G.

MOSSMAN, THOMAS WIMBERLEY (1826–1885), divine, born in 1826, eldest son of Robert Hume Mossman of Skipton, Yorkshire, matriculated from St. Edmund Hall, Oxford, on 17 Dec. 1845, and while an undergraduate became an adherent of the Oxford movement. He graduated B.A. in 1849, was ordained deacon in that year, and took priest's orders in 1850. He became curate of Donington-on-Bain in 1849, curate of Panton in 1852, vicar of Ranby, Lincolnshire, in 1854, and rector of East Torrington and vicar of West Torrington, near Wragby, in the same county, in 1859. He received the honorary degree of D.D. from the University of the South, U.S.A., in 1881. Becoming prominent among the leaders of the extreme ritualistic party, he waged incessant war with protestant principles. He was a member of the Order of Corporate Reunion, and it is said that he was one of its prelates, assuming the title of bishop of Selby

(*Church Times*, 10 July 1885, p. 531). During his last illness he was received into the Roman catholic church by his old friend, Cardinal Manning. He died at his rectory on 6 July 1885. He had previously taken steps to resign his rectory, but the necessary legal formalities were not completed.

His works are: 1. 'A Glossary of the principal Words used in a Figurative, Typical, or Mystical Sense in the Holy Scriptures,' London, 1854, 18mo. 2. 'Sermons,' London, 1857, 12mo. 3. 'Ritualism in its Relation to Reunion,' in 'Essays on the Reunion of Christendom,' edited by F. G. Lee, D.D., 1867. 4. 'The Primacy of St. Peter. A Translation of Cornelius à Lapide upon St. Matthew, xvi. 17–19, and St. John xxi. 15–17,' London [1870], 8vo. 5. A translation of the 'Speculum Spirituale' by Blosius. 6. 'A History of the Catholic Church of Jesus Christ from the Death of St. John to the middle of the Second Century,' London, 1873, 8vo. 7. 'Epiphanius; the History of his Childhood and Youth, told by himself. A Tale of the Early Church,' London [1874], 8vo. 8. 'A Reply to Professor Tyndall's Lucretian,' London, 1875, 8vo. 9. 'Freedom for the Church of God; an . . . Appeal to my High Church Brethren,' London, 1876, 8vo. 10. 'The Great Commentary of Cornelius à Lapide, translated . . . with the assistance of various scholars,' vol. i. (Matt. i–ix) London, 1876, 8vo, vol. ii. (Matt. x–xxi) 1876, vol. iii. (Matt. xxii–xxviii, and St. Mark's Gospel complete), 1881, vol. iv. (John i–xi), 1886, vol. v (John xii–xxi, and Epistles i. ii. and iii.) 1886. 11. 'The Relations which at present exist between Church and State in England. A Letter to the Right Hon. W. E. Gladstone,' London [1883], 8vo. 12. 'A Latin Letter (with an English translation) to his Holiness Pope Leo XIII,' London, 1884, 8vo.

[Church Times, 17 July 1885, p. 555; Crockford's Clerical Directory, 1885, p. 855; Foster's Alumni Oxon. 1715–1886, iii. 992; Lincolnshire Chron. 10 July 1885, p. 5, col. 7; Tablet, 18 July 1885, p. 103.] T. C.

MOSSOM, ROBERT (*d.* 1679), bishop of Derry, a native of Lincolnshire, entered Magdalene College, Cambridge, on 2 June 1631, but two months later migrated to Peterhouse, where he was admitted a sizar on 9 Aug., and where he was a fellow student with Richard Crashaw and Joseph Beaumont, afterwards master of the college. He graduated B.A. in 1634 and M.A. in 1638. In 1642 he was officiating at York as an army chaplain under Sir Thomas Glemham, and about this time he married a Miss Eland of Bedale. Subsequently, for at least five years (1650–5), during the interregnum, he publicly preached at St. Peter's, Paul's Wharf, London, where, notwithstanding the prohibition of the law, he used the Book of Common Prayer, and administered the holy communion monthly. This brought a great concourse of nobility and gentry to the church. After he had been silenced Mossom maintained himself by keeping a school.

With the Restoration came honour and preferment. By his majesty's letters mandatory, dated 21 July 1660, Mossom was on the following 5 Sept created D.D. at Cambridge, and on 20 Sept. in the same year he was collated to the prebend of Knaresborough-cum-Bickhill in the church of York. The original letter of Charles II appointing him dean of Christ Church, Dublin, is dated 25 Sept. 1660, and he was installed 2 Feb. 1660–1. By patent dated 13 Nov. 1660 he was presented by the crown to the precentorship of St. Patrick's, and he was installed on 27 Dec. On 21 May 1661 Mossom was elected prolocutor of the Lower House of Convocation, Dublin. He graduated D.D. (*ad eundem*) in the university of Dublin, 26 Jan. 1661–2. As prolocutor he delivered a congratulatory speech before the Duke of Ormonde 29 July 1662, on his arrival in Ireland as lord-lieutenant. After the death of George Wild, bishop of Derry, 29 Dec. 1665, Mossom was promoted to the vacant see. His patent bears date 26 March 1666, and he was consecrated in Christ Church, Dublin, on 1 April. Harris and Cotton erroneously state that he held the deanery of Christ Church *in commendam* with the bishopric. He died at Derry on 21 Dec. 1679, and was buried in his cathedral. In 1853 there was a full-sized portrait of him at Mount Eland, co. Kilkenny, the seat of Charles Eland Mossom, esq.

Mossom, who was 'a consistent, uncompromising loyalist, warmly attached to the Church of England,' was also 'a good classic scholar and deeply versed in theological literature.' Sound judgment and clear intelligence are conspicuous in his writings.

His works, excluding separately published sermons, are: 1. 'Anti-Paræus, or a Treatise in the Defence of the Royall Right of Kings [by David Owen], . . . New Translated and Published to confirme Men in their Loyalty to their King,' York, 1642, 4to. 2. 'The King on his Throne: or a Discourse maintaining the Dignity of a King, the Duty of a Subject, and the unlawfulnesse of Rebellion,' two sermons preached in York Cathedral, York, 1643, 4to. 3. 'Sion's Prospect in its First View. Presented in a Summary of Divine

Truths, consenting with the Faith professed by the Church of England,' London, 1651, 4to; again, 1653 and 1711, dedicated to Henry, marquis of Dorchester. 4. 'The Preachers Tripartite, in Three Books,' London, 1657, fol.; said to have been reprinted in 1685, fol., and a privately printed edition issued in 1845, 8vo, from the Rev. Henry A. Simcoe's Penheale press, Cornwall (BOASE and COURTNEY, *Bibl. Cornub.* p. 651). 5. 'Variæ Colloquendi Formulæ in usum Condiscipulorum in Palæstra Literaria sub paterno moderamine vires Minervales exercentium, partim collectæ, partim compositæ, a Roberto Mossom,' London, 1659. 6. 'An Apology in the behalf of the Sequestred Clergy, Presented to the High Court of Parliament,' London, 1660, 4to. Reprinted in Lord Somers's 'Tracts,' ii. 158, third collection. An anonymous answer appeared under the title of 'A Plea for Ministers in Sequestrations: wherein Mr. Mossom's Apology for the Sequestered Clergy is duly considered and discussed,' London, 1660, 4to. 7. 'The Copy of a Speech delivered by Dr. Mossom, Dean of Christ Church, and Prolocutor of the Lower House of Convocation, before the Lord Lieutenant, the 29th of July 1662' (cf. KENNETT, *Register and Chron.* p. 733).

[Cotton's Fasti, iii. 11, 319, v. 90, 255; Davies's York Press, p. 63; Evelyn's Diary; Kennett's Register and Chronicle; Le Neve's Fasti, ed. Hardy, iii. 193; Newcourt's Repertorium, i. 527; Nichols's Lit. Anecd. i. 33, 34; Palatine Note-Book, i. 147, 203; ii. 12, 60; Pepys's Diary, ed. Bright, i. 49, 73, 143; Ware's Bishops, ed. Harris, p. 295; Wood's Athenæ Oxon. ed. Bliss, iii. 721, 1143, 1172, iv. 830, Fasti, i. 328, ii. 38, 88; Worthington's Diary, i. 307.]

T. C.

MOSSOP, HENRY (1729?–1774?), actor, was son of John Mossop, M.A., of Trinity College, Dublin, who was collated to the prebend of Kilmeen, Tuam, on 10 Aug. 1737, and died in 1759 (COTTON, *Fasti Eccles. Hib.* iv. 43). As a boy Mossop stayed in Dublin with his uncle, a bookseller, went to a grammar school in Digges Street, and, with a view to taking holy orders, proceeded to Trinity College. Refused, on a visit to London, engagements on the stage by Garrick, and by Rich of Covent Garden, who both discouraged him from attempting to become an actor, he went on the introduction of Francis Gentleman [q. v.], to Sheridan, by whom he was engaged for Smock Alley Theatre, Dublin, where he appeared, 28 Nov. 1749, as Zanga in the 'Revenge.' Though awkward in manner and unpicturesque in appearance, he displayed an 'astonishing degree of beautiful wildness,' which a pit crowded with his friends and fellow-students warmly recognised. During the season he played Cassius, Polydore in the 'Orphan,' Glo'ster in 'Jane Shore,' and Ribemont in the 'Black Prince,' and in the following season he appeared as Richard III, dressed in white satin, 'puckered.' Hearing that his manager had condemned the dress as coxcombical, he sought him in his dressing-room, and, with the curiously pedantic and staccato delivery he retained until the last, said, 'Mr. She-ri-dan, I hear you said that I dressed Richard like a cox-comb—that is an af-front. You wear a sword, pull it out of the scabbard—I'll draw mine and thrust it into your bo-dy.' Sheridan smiled, and the explosion had no result; but Mossop, turbulent, vain, and unmanageable, soon left the theatre for London, where, under Garrick's management, he appeared at Drury Lane as Richard III 26 Sept. 1751. His success in this part, in which he was held only inferior to Garrick, was great. Garrick, not altogether pleased with the reception, applauded the lines of Taswell, an actor, on Mossop and Ross, another *débutant*:—

The Templars they cry Mossop,
The ladies they cry Ross up,
But which is the best is a toss-up.

Garrick, after his wont, gave him every chance, and Mossop during this and the three following seasons played Bajazet, Horatio in the 'Fair Penitent,' Theseus in 'Phædra and Hippolitus,' Orestes, Macbeth, Othello, Wolsey, Pierre, Comus, Dumont, King John, Coriolanus, Duke in 'Measure for Measure,' and other leading parts. He was the original Lewson in the 'Gambler,' 7 Feb. 1753; Perseus in Young's 'Brothers,' 3 March 1753; Ænobarbus in Glover's 'Boadicea,' 1 Dec. 1753; Appius in Crisp's 'Virginius,' 25 Feb. 1754; Phorbas in Whitehead's 'Creusa,' 20 April 1754; and Barbarossa in Brown's 'Barbarossa,' 17 Dec. 1754. Coriolanus and Barbarossa were held his great parts. On revisiting Smock Alley Theatre in 1755–6, on very advantageous terms, he chose Achmet in 'Barbarossa,' for which he was unsuited. On 21 Sept. 1756 he reappeared at Drury Lane as Richard, and played also Maskwell in the 'Double Dealer,' Osmyn in the 'Mourning Bride,' and Cato. In the two following seasons he was seen, among many other parts, as Prospero, Hamlet, Hastings, and Æsop, and was the original Agis in Home's 'Agis,' 21 Feb. 1758, and Etan in Murphy's 'Orphan of China,' 21 April 1759. Mossop then, having accepted an engagement from Barry and Woodward for Crow Street Theatre, Dublin, quitted London permanently. His own vanity and ill-temper had been played on by Fitzpatrick, a bitter enemy of Garrick and a would-be arbiter of the stage [see Garrick, David], and Mossop came to look upon himself as oppressed and injured. His reception at Crow Street was enthusiastic, and he added to his repertory Ventidius, Iago, and Kitely. Mossop and Barry formed an eminently popular combination. A further engagement was offered, on terms beyond precedent. Mossop declined, however, and announced his intention to open on his own account Smock Alley Theatre, a resolution which he carried out to his own ruin and that of his rival in Crow Street. Backed up by aristocratic patronage Mossop opened his season (17 Nov. 1760), as soon as the period of mourning for the death of George II had passed, with 'Venice Preserved,' Mossop playing Pierre, West Digges Jaffier, and Mrs. Bellamy Belvidera. A wild antagonism was carried on between the two houses, at which the same pieces were frequently played on the same night. During this and the following season Mossop made a fairly successful struggle, engaging Mrs. Fitzhenry, Mrs. Abington, Reddish, King, and Tate Wilkinson, but he owed his temporary escape from ruin to his engagement of an Italian opera company. In 1762–3 the receipts at the two houses were inadequate to the expenses at one. So impoverished was the treasury that actors of both sexes with a nominal salary of 5*l.* per week only received 6*l.* in as many months, and were in want of bread. Such money as Mossop received he spent in litigation or lost at the gambling-table, while Barry was arrested for debt on the stage. Mossop held on in a fashion until 1770–1, adding to his characters Zamti in the 'Orphan of China,' Leon in 'Rule a Wife and have a Wife,' Carlos in 'Like Master like Man,' Archer in the 'Stratagem,' Belcour in the 'West Indian,' and very many more characters, including, presumably, Brutus, Timon of Athens, the Old Bachelor, Lord Townly, Chamont, Hotspur, Sempronius, and Marcian. Such successes as he obtained were principally musical, Ann Catley [q. v.] in especial proving a great attraction.

In 1767–8 the retirement of Barry left Mossop without a competitor. He took possession immediately of both theatres, appearing as Richard at Crow Street 7 Dec. 1767. In the summer of 1769 he visited Cork. A third theatre in Capel Street, Dublin, was opened in 1776 by Dawson, Mahon, and Wilkes. Under Mossop's management tragedy had been acted at Crow Street, and comedy, rope-dancing, &c., at Smock Alley. In 1770 Mossop resigned Crow Street. Large sums of money had been taken and lost, the company had received mere driblets of money, and Mossop, though the idol of Dublin, found himself at times playing with a strong company to less than 5*l.* Under the weight of troubles, vexations, and debt he broke down in health, and solicited public generosity for a benefit 17 April 1771, at which he was unable to appear. Proceeding to London in search of recruits, he was arrested for debt by one of his company, and lodged in the King's Bench, which he only quitted as a bankrupt. Benefit followed benefit at Smock Alley, and earnest appeals were made to the Dublin world to rescue one of the 'best theatrical performers now living.' No permanent relief was obtained. On recovering his liberty he, with customary churlishness and vanity, refused to apply to Garrick, saying that Garrick knew he was in London, thereby implying that application should come from him. All chance of help from Garrick was destroyed by the publication in 1772 of 'A Letter to David Garrick on his Conduct,' written by the Rev. David Williams for the purpose of forcing an engagement from that actor. Negotiations were opened with Covent Garden, but Mrs. Barry refused to act with Mossop. A year's tour on the continent was undertaken with a friend named Smith. From this Mossop returned emaciated and depressed, and with inadequate command of his faculties, and he died in the Strand 18 Nov. 1773, or, according to the 'Gentleman's Magazine,' on 27 Dec. 1774, at Chelsea, in great poverty (4½*d.* only being in his possession), and, as was said, of a broken heart. An offer by Garrick to pay for his funeral was refused by Mossop's maternal uncle, a bencher of the Inner Temple. While in management he had borrowed money from Garrick, who proved against his estate for 200*l.*

A portrait of Mossop as Bajazet is mentioned by Bromley; he was of middle size, fairly well formed, with an expressive face and an eye of much fire. He had a voice deep and loud, not very capable of tenderness, but useful in rhetorical passages. A born actor, he was unaware of his own limitations, and, though without a superior in a part such as the Duke in 'Measure for Measure,' thrust himself into parts, such as Archer and Belcour, for which he had very slight qualifications. In amenability to flattery Garrick even could not surpass him, and his most grievous errors were due to listening to interested advisers. Mossop wasted his time in fashionable society, and lost in gambling the money he should have paid to his company. The 'Dramatic Censor' pronounces his Sempronius and Marcian unsurpassed, Churchill taxes him with 'studied impropriety of speech.' His syllables are said to have 'fallen from him like minute-guns,' while the nickname of the 'teapot actor' referred to his favourite attitude, with one arm on his hip and the other extended. Hitchcock, a somewhat prejudiced judge, declares him admirable in many heroic characters—Macbeth, Hotspur, King John, Ventidius, Cato, &c. Victor (*Works*, i. 158) describes Mossop as an actor of some promise, but an imitator of Quin.

[The best account of Mossop's life is given in the Theatrical Recorder, Dublin, 1821, and following years. Hitchcock's Historical View of the Irish Stage supplies an elaborate account of his management, which is condensed in Genest's Account of the English Stage. The Garrick Correspondence; Davies's Life of Garrick; Fitzgerald's Life of Garrick; Victor's Works; Dibdin's Hist. of the Stage, v. 205; the Preface to the Modish Wife, by F. Gentleman; Theatrical Review; Churchill's Rosciad; Lee Lewes's Memoirs; O'Keeffe's Memoirs; Bernard's Retrospections; Doran's Annals of the Stage, ed. Lowe, ii. 353; and Tate Wilkinson's Memoirs supply anecdotes and references. The following pamphlets deal with Mossop: 'A Letter to David Garrick on opening the Theatre, 1769,' should be 1759; 'An Attack on Mossop by Edward Purdon,' for which a public apology had to be made; 'An Estimate of the Theatrical Merits of the Two Tragedians at Crow Street (Mossop and Barry),' 1760; 'Zanga Triumph,' by Charles McLoughlin, 1762.]

J. K.

MOSSOP, WILLIAM (1751 - 1804), medallist, was born in 1751 in Mary's Parish, Dublin. His father, a Roman catholic named Browne, died when he was young, and his mother, on her second marriage to W. Mossop, a relative of Henry Mossop [q. v.] the actor, changed his name to Mossop in order to procure him admission to the Dublin Bluecoat School, a protestant institution. On leaving this school about 1765 Mossop was apprenticed to Stone, a die-sinker, who made seal-dies for the Linen Board. On Stone's death through intemperance Mossop contributed to the support of the family, and continued to work for the Linen Board till 1781, when he lost his employment on a change of management. In 1784, and afterwards, he lived at 13 Essex Quay, Dublin, describing his occupation as that of 'letter-cutter and die-sinker.' A chance purchase of a collection of medals turned his attention to medallic work, and in 1782 he produced his first medal, that of Ryder the actor. He was encouraged by Henry Quin, M.D., of Dublin. In 1793 he was employed by the firm Camac, Kyan, & Camac to superintend their private mint, and in making the dies for the 'Camac' halfpenny tokens. The failure of the firm cost him his appointment and involved him in pecuniary losses, and in 1797 he returned to his business as a private die-sinker. Besides designing medals, Mossop prepared the dies of numerous seals of various public bodies in Ireland. He also engraved a few compositions in cornelian and ivory. He died in Dublin in 1804, after a few hours' illness, from paralysis and apoplexy, aged 53. Mossop married (about 1781?), and had a family. William Stephen Mossop [q. v.] the medallist was his son.

Before cutting the steel die for his medals Mossop made a large model in wax. Some of the dies passed into the possession of Mr. J. Woodhouse, medallist, of Dublin. The following are the chief medals produced by Mossop: Thomas Ryder, 1782, signed W. M.; Right Hon. John and Mrs. Beresford, 1788, signed W. MOSSOP; Henry Quin, signed W. MOSSOP; David La Touche, 1785 (?); William Alexander, 1785; William Deane, 1785 (?); Edmund Sexton, viscount Pery (Lord Pery paid forty guineas for this medal, Mossop having asked only twenty); Cunningham prize medal of Royal Irish Academy (with portrait of Lord Charlemont, who gave Mossop access to his library and collection of coins and medals); Down Corporation of Horse Breeders, about 1787; Primate Robinson, Lord Rokeby, about 1789; medals given at the commencements, Trinity College, Dublin, about 1793; medal of the Friendly Brothers of St. Patrick; Dr. Barrett's school medal; Tyrone regiment, 1797 (?); Bantry Bay medal; Order of Orange and Blue (badge); Orange Association, 1798; Hon. Henry St. George Cole; Dublin Masonic School medal; College Historical Society, Dublin University; Mossop's medal, about 1801; Dublin Society medal, about 1802; medals of the Farming Society of Ireland; Navan Farming Society, 1802 (?); Irish Ordnance medal. Mossop, like his son, was an able medallist. His works are usually signed MOSSOP.

[The best account of Mossop is that given in the Medallists of Ireland and their Work, by Dr. William Frazer, of Dublin.]

W. W.

MOSSOP, WILLIAM STEPHEN (1788-1827), medallist, born in Dublin in 1788, was the son of William Mossop [q. v.], medallist. He was educated at the academy of Samuel White in Dublin, and in 1802 entered the Art Schools of the Royal Dublin Society under Francis West, the master of the figure school, who also gave him instruction privately. His first medal, that of the Incorporated Society for Charter Schools, was made when he was about seventeen. In 1806 he made a medal for the Farming Society of Ireland, and in 1810 one to commemorate the fiftieth year of George III's reign. In 1813 he received the premium of the Society of Arts for the die of a school medal, and in 1814 gained its premium for a medal bearing the head of Vulcan. About 1820 he contemplated a series of forty portrait-medals of distinguished Irishmen. He completed the medal of Grattan, and nearly finished those of Ussher, Charlemont, Swift, and Sheridan. The dies of these were left unhardened, but were afterwards annealed by Mr. J. Woodhouse of Dublin, into whose possession they came. Mossop followed the method adopted by his father in designing the model for his steel dies. He used a preparation of beeswax melted and softened with turpentine, and coloured white or brown. 'He spread this tempered wax upon a piece of glass or slate, adding and working in successive portions until the design was completed.' Several of Mossop's wax models are in the possession of Dr. Frazer of Dublin, and some of his steel dies became the property of the Royal Irish Academy and of Mr. J. Woodhouse. Some designs cast in plaster also became the property of Mr. Woodhouse. In addition to his work on medals Mossop was engaged in preparing the seals of various public bodies, including the Waterford chamber of commerce, Cork Institution (1807), County of Sligo Infirmary (1813), Irish treasury, Derry corporation, Prussian consulate, and Waterford harbour commission. He also made a series of dies for the stamp office, Dublin. Mossop was secretary to the Royal Hibernian Academy from its foundation till his death, which took place in the early part of 1827, after an attack of mental aberration. Mossop wrote a short account of his father and himself, which was printed in Gilbert's 'History of Dublin,' ii. 121, ff. and Appendix. The following is a selection from Mossop's medals: Incorporated Society for Charter Schools in Ireland (unsigned); Farming Society of Ireland (signed W. S. MOSSOP); George III's Jubilee; Kildare Farming Society, 1813; Centenary of House of Hanover, 1814; Daniel O'Connell, 1816 (the first medallic portrait of O'Connell); Feinaglian Institution; Cork Institution, 1817; North of Ireland Society; Dublin Society medal; Sir Charles Giesecke; Colonel Talbot; Grattan (the head on this medal was copied by the French artist, Galle; FRAZER, p. 326, citing T. MOORE'S *Diary*); Archbishop Ussher; Dean Swift; R. B. Sheridan; Lord Charlemont; Visit of George IV to Ireland. The medals are usually signed MOSSOP.

[Frazer's Medallists of Ireland.] W. W.

MOSTYN, SIR ROGER (1625?–1690), first baronet, royalist, born about 1625, was the son of Sir Roger Mostyn, knight, of Mostyn Hall, near Holywell, Flintshire, by Mary, daughter of Sir John Wynne of Gwydir. Sir Roger the elder (1567–1642) matriculated at Brasenose College, Oxford, on 8 May 1584, entered as a student at Lincoln's Inn in 1588 (FOSTER, *Alumni Oxon.*), was knighted on 23 May 1606, served as M.P. for Flintshire in 1621–2, died on 18 Aug. 1642, and was buried at Whiteford.

During the earlier conflicts between Charles I and parliament, the sympathies of the Mostyn family were on the side of the king, and the loyal address of the people of Flintshire, presented to Charles at York on 4 Aug. 1642, was probably inspired by Sir Roger or his father. When the king formally declared war and visited Chester towards the end of September, young Roger Mostyn and Captain Salesbury arrived there with troops of Welshmen, who, after the king's departure, ransacked the houses of supposed parliamentarians (PHILLIPS, *Civil War in Wales and the Marches*, i. 112, ii. 15). In January 1642–3, Mostyn, described by this time as colonel, brought a large number of Welshmen into Chester, and once more they gave vent to their loyalty by sacking the town-house of Sir William Brereton (*ib.* i. 142). Being appointed governor of Flint Castle, he repaired it and put it in a state of defence at his own cost, but in the autumn of 1643 after a long siege, during which the garrison were reduced to eating their horses, it was surrendered to Brereton and Sir Thomas Myddelton [q. v.] on honourable terms, as were also both the town and castle of Mostyn (WHITELOCKE, *Memorials*, p. 78; *The Kingdom's Weekly Intelligencer*, No. 23, p. 257). Shortly afterwards, on 18 Nov., a troop of Irish soldiers landed at Mostyn, and the parliamentarians withdrew hastily from that district. Mostyn also raised some Welsh recruits, and combining with the Irish captured Hawarden Castle (WHITELOCKE, *loc. cit.*), after a fortnight's siege, and probably proceeded afterwards to Chester. Lord Byron, complaining of the defenceless state of Chester in a letter addressed to Lord Digby on 26 April 1645, stated that he was 'left in the towne only with a garryson of citizens, and my owne and Colonell Mostin's regiment, which both together made not up above 600 men, whereof the one halfe being Mostin's men, I was forced soone after to send out of towne,' owing to their undisciplined conduct (*Cal. State Papers*, Dom. Ser. 1645). Towards the end of the year Mostyn went over to Ireland to try and muster recruits for the relief of Chester, and returned in January 1645-6 with a 'piece of a regiment,' some hundred and sixty men, and was expected 'to make it up two hundred upon his own credit,' in his own county, where he was a commissioner of array and peace (*Letter from Archbishop Williams to Lord Astley*, dated Conway, 25 Jan. 1645-6, printed in PHILLIPS's *Civil War*, ii. 290-1). These troops, and other royalist forces collected in North Wales under Lord St. Paul, were, however, prevented from marching to Chester by Colonel Mytton, who was despatched by Brereton to intercept them, and caused them to retreat to Denbigh and Conway. Mostyn himself succeeded in evading his enemies at the time and for many years after, but in May 1658 was captured by Colonel Carter at Conway. Whitelocke, however, who had married a member of the Mostyn family, procured his immediate release, 'upon his parole to be at his own house at Mostyn' (*Memorials*, p. 673). At the Restoration he was created a baronet, 3 Aug. 1660.

Mostyn is described by Whitelocke (*ib.* p. 78) as 'a gentleman of good address, and mettle, of a very ancient family, large possessions, and great interest in the county, so that in twelve hours he raised fifteen hundred men for the king.' He is said to have spent some 60,000*l.* in the service of the king, and his house at Mostyn stripped of all its valuables, so that after his release on parole he was so impoverished that he had to lie for many years in strict seclusion at a farmhouse called Plasucha; but by 1684 his fortunes were so improved, probably by profits derived from lead and coal mines which he worked by means of large engines (a drawing is given by Dineley in his *Beaufort Progress*, 1888 ed. p. 95), that he provided on 23 July 1684 at Mostyn a 'very great and noble entertainment' for the Duke of Beaufort and his suite on their official progress through Wales. He was then in command of the Flintshire militia, one company of which was composed of his servants, miners, and other adherents, clothed and paid at his own expense, and he was complimented on their smart manœuvres (*ib.* pp. 91-2).

He died in 1690, having been thrice married; his second wife, of whom there is a portrait at Mostyn, being Mary, the eldest daughter of Thomas, Lord Bulkeley of Baron Hill, Beaumaris (PENNANT, *Hist. of Whiteford and Holywell*, pp. 60-3). Sir Roger Mostyn, third baronet (1675-1739) [q. v.], was a grandson.

A portrait of Sir Roger Mostyn, which, according to a recently deciphered inscription, was painted by Sir Peter Lely in 1652, when the sitter is said to have been 28 years of age, is preserved at Mostyn Hall, and a copy of it by Leonard Hughes was presented at Christmas 1887 by Lord Mostyn to the corporation of Flint (*Archæologia Cambrensis*, 5th ser. viii. 110-13). In this Sir Roger is represented at kit-cat length, in a strange flaxen wig, a breast plate, buff skirts, and antique Roman sleeves—a negro holding his helmet (TAYLOR, *Hist. Notices of Flint*, p. 139).

[For the pedigree of the Mostyn family see Dwnn's Heraldic Visitations, ii. 307-9; Phillips's Civil War in Wales and Marches; Historic Notices of Flint, passim.] D. LL. T.

MOSTYN, SIR ROGER (1675-1739), third baronet, politician, born in 1675, was the eldest son of Sir Thomas Mostyn of Mostyn, Flintshire, second baronet, by Bridget, daughter and heiress of Darcy Savage, esq., of Leighton, Cheshire. Sir Roger Mostyn (*d.* 1690) [q.v.] was his grandfather. On 10 Feb. 1689-90 he matriculated from Jesus College, Oxford. He was returned as M.P. for Flintshire in December 1701, and in the following August both for Cheshire and for the borough of Flint; he elected to sit for the former. In the next parliament (1705-8) he represented Flintshire, and sat for the same constituency till 1734 (except in 1713, when he served for Flint borough). He was a tory and a supporter of Daniel Finch, second earl of Nottingham [q. v.], whose daughter he married. In 1711 he was appointed paymaster of the marines (*Treasury Papers*, xci. 70), and was one of the four tellers of the exchequer from 30 Dec. 1714 till 22 June 1716. He voted for tacking on the Occasional Conformity Bill to the Land-tax Bill in 1705, and against the articles of commerce in 1713. He voted against the Peerage Bill in 1719, and Walpole's excise scheme in 1733, and having opposed the Septennial Bill, supported the motion for its repeal in 1734. In consideration of his services and the expenses he incurred as paymaster of the marines he was allowed a sum of 300*l.* for eight years (*ib.* ccxlvi. 68). There is also among the 'Treasury Papers' a dormant warrant in favour of Mostyn as controller of the fines for the counties of Chester, Flint, and Carnarvon, dated 31 July 1704. He died on 5 May 1739, at his seat in Carnarvonshire. Farquhar's 'Constant Couple' was dedicated to him.

Mostyn married, on 20 July 1703, Lady Essex, daughter of Daniel Finch, second earl of Nottingham; she was noted for her beauty, and her portrait, painted by Kneller in 1703, was engraved by J. Smith in 1705 (NOBLE, ii. 375–6). She died of small-pox on 23 May 1721, leaving issue six sons and six daughters.

The eldest son, Thomas (1704–1758), became fourth baronet, with the death of whose grandson Thomas in 1831 the baronetcy expired. Of Sir Roger's younger sons Roger (1721–1775) was canon of Windsor, and Savage, vice-admiral, is separately noticed. Another son, JOHN MOSTYN (1710–1779), general, was elected to Westminster School in 1723, and to Christ Church, Oxford, in 1728. He was made captain in the 2nd foot-guards in 1743, aide-de-camp to the king in 1747, colonel of the king's own royal fusiliers in 1751, of the 13th dragoons in 1754, of the 5th dragoons in 1758, and of the 1st dragoons in 1763; major-general in 1757, lieutenant-general in 1759, and general in 1772. He became governor and commander-in-chief of Minorca in 1768, and in 1773 was defendant in an action in London brought by one Anthony Fabrigas, whom he had banished from the island (cf. *The Proceedings at Large*, London, 1773, fol.) In the parliaments which met in 1747, 1754, and 1761 he sat for Malton, Yorkshire. He was gentleman of the bedchamber to George II and George III, and died in Dover Street, London, on 16 Feb. 1779 (cf. *Notes and Queries*, 8th ser. i. 362; WELCH, *Alumni Westmonast.* p. 297; WALPOLE, *Memoirs of George III*).

[Foster's Alumni Oxon. 1500–1714; Burke's Extinct Baronetage, ii. 120; Boyer's Political State of Great Britain, vi. viii. 530; Gent. Mag. 1739, p. 272; Returns of Members of Parliament; Parl. Hist.; State Papers cited in text.] G. LE G. N.

MOSTYN, SAVAGE (*d.* 1757), vice-admiral, a younger son of Sir Roger Mostyn, bart. (1675–1739) [q. v.], was on 2 March 1733–4 promoted to be lieutenant of the Pembroke. He afterwards served in the Britannia, flagship of Sir John Norris [q. v.], and on 3 July 1739 was promoted to be commander of the Duke, fireship attached to the fleet off Cadiz under Rear-admiral Nicholas Haddock [q. v.], by whom, on 17 Dec. 1739, he was posted to the Seaford. The rank was confirmed by the admiralty to 6 March 1739–40. In April he was appointed to the Winchelsea, and towards the end of the year to the 60-gun ship Deptford, one of the fleet which went out to the West Indies with Sir Chaloner Ogle (*d.* 1751) [q. v.], and, under Vice-admiral Edward Vernon [q. v.], took part in the operations against Cartagena in March and April 1741. In December 1743 he was appointed to the Suffolk, one of the fleet with Sir John Norris off Dungeness, on 24 Feb. 1743–4.

In April he was moved to the Hampton Court, one of four ships which, on 29 Dec. 1744, lost sight of the fleet in the Soundings, and while looking for it broad off Ushant, fell in with two French ships of the line on 6 Jan. 1744–5. Two of the English ships, the Captain [see GRIFFIN, THOMAS, *d.* 1771] and the Sunderland, parted company [see BRETT, JOHN]. The Hampton Court and Dreadnought continued the chase; but, although the Hampton Court came up with the French ships, Mostyn did not engage, as the Dreadnought was then four or five miles astern. During the night and the next day the ships continued near each other, but the Dreadnought could not come up with the enemy; Mostyn would not engage without her; and thus the two Frenchmen got safely into Brest (Mostyn to the Secretary of the Admiralty, 23 Jan.; *Voyages and Cruises of Commodore Walker*, pp. 27 et seq.; LAUGHTON, *Studies in Naval History*, p. 231). In England Mostyn's conduct evoked unfavourable comment, and at his request the admiralty ordered a court-martial, but without appointing a prosecutor. The evidence brought before the court was to the effect that in the fresh breeze that was blowing the Hampton Court lay along so much that her lower deck ports were under water, and that her main-deck guns, with extreme elevation, would not have carried more than fifty yards, while the French ships were remarkably stiff and all their guns were effective. There was no cross-examination, and the court decided that Mostyn had done 'his duty as an experienced good officer, and as a man of courage and conduct' (*Minutes of the Court-martial*, published 1745, 8vo). It was probably influenced by the fact that Daniel Finch, second earl of Winchilsea, Mostyn's maternal uncle, had only just gone out of office as first lord of the admiralty and might hold that office again. Afterwards, in letters to the admiralty, Mostyn persistently urged that the ship's spars and weights ought to be reduced; that, 'if their lordships will give me leave to say, we have too much top for our bottom' (*Captains' Letters*, M. 11). It may be that his judgment and seamanship were more at fault than his personal courage; but public opinion was far from accepting the court's decision, which was palpably absurd, and was severely criticised in a pamphlet attributed to Admiral Vernon (*An Enquiry into the Conduct of Captain Mostyn, being Remarks on the Minutes of the Court-martial and other Incidental Matters.* Humbly addressed to the Honourable House of Commons by a Sea Officer, 1745, 8vo). Nearly a year afterwards, in November, Mostyn, still in command of the Hampton Court, was hooted out of Portsmouth dockyard and harbour by workmen and sailors calling out, 'All's well! there's no Frenchman in the way!' (CHARNOCK, iv. 431).

In the early months of 1746 Mostyn, still in the Hampton Court, commanded a cruising squadron in the Bay of Biscay. In July 1747 he was returned to parliament as member for Weobley in Herefordshire, and continued to represent the constituency till his death. On 22 March 1749 he was appointed comptroller of the navy. This office he resigned to accept his promotion to flag rank, 4 Feb. 1755, and in the summer of that year was second in command of the fleet sent to North America under the command of Vice-admiral Boscawen [q. v.] During the following year he was second in command of the western squadron under the command, successively, of Hawke, Boscawen, and Knowles. In April 1757 he was appointed a junior lord in the short-lived administration of the admiralty by the Earl of Winchilsea, which terminated in June. He died 16 Sept. 1757. A portrait of Mostyn in early youth was engraved by T. Worlidge.

[Charnock's Biog. Nav. iv. 429; official letters and other documents in the Public Record Office; other authorities in the text.] J. K. L.

MOTHERBY, GEORGE, M.D. (1732–1793), medical writer, born in Yorkshire in 1732, practised as a physician at Highgate, Middlesex. He died at Beverley, Yorkshire, on 19 July 1793 (*Gent. Mag.* 1793, pt. ii. p. 771). He compiled 'A new Medical Dictionary,' fol. London, 1776 or 1778 (2nd edit. 1785). Other editions, carefully revised by George Wallis, M.D., appeared in 1791, 1795, and 1801; the two last issues were in two volumes.

[Reuss's Register of Authors; Watt's Bibl. Brit.] G. G.

MOTHERWELL, WILLIAM (1797–1835), poet, born in Glasgow 13 Oct. 1797, was the son of an ironmonger, descended from an old Stirlingshire family. In his childhood the home was changed to Edinburgh. Here he began his education, which he completed by further school training at Paisley (residing there with an uncle). After studying classics for a year at Glasgow University (1818–19), he was received into the office of the sheriff-clerk at Paisley, and from May 1819 to November 1829 was sheriff-clerk depute of Renfrewshire. As a youth he had very advanced political opinions, but unpleasant personal relations with the ardent reformers whom he encountered transformed him into a zealous tory. For a time he was a trooper in the Renfrewshire yeomanry cavalry, and he became a respectable boxer and swordsman.

Motherwell wrote verse from an early age. The ballad 'Jeanie Morrison' was sketched in his fourteenth year, and published in an Edinburgh periodical in 1832. In 1818 Motherwell wrote verses for the Greenock 'Visitor.' He edited, with a preface, in 1819, 'The Harp of Renfrewshire,' a collection of songs by local authors. In 1824, under the pseudonym of 'Isaac Brown, late manufacturer in the Plunkin of Paisley,' he published 'Renfrewshire Characters and Scenery,' a good-natured local sketch in Spenserian stanza. In 1827 appeared in small 4to 'Minstrelsy Ancient and Modern,' a judicious collection of ballads, with a learned and discriminating introduction. This brought him into friendly relations with Scott.

In 1828 Motherwell conducted the 'Paisley Magazine,' and he edited the 'Paisley Advertiser' from 1828 to 1830, when he left Paisley to be editor of the 'Glasgow Courier.' In both Paisley papers he inserted many lyrics by himself. At Glasgow he threw himself with ardour into his work at an exciting and exacting time, and under his supervision his journal was distinguished by freshness and vigour. While editing the 'Courier' he wrote pretty largely for the 'Day,' a Glasgow periodical begun in 1832. In that year, too, he contributed a discursive preface to Andrew Henderson's 'Scottish Proverbs,' and issued his own 'Poems, Narrative and Lyrical.' In 1835 Motherwell collaborated with Hogg in an edition of Burns, to which he supplied valuable notes. His recent biographers are astray in crediting him with the bulk of the accompanying biography of Burns, which, with an acknowledged exception, is clearly the work of Hogg. Having identified himself with Orangeism, he was summoned to London in 1835 to give information on the subject before a special committee. Under examination he completely broke down, showing strange mental unreadiness and confusion, and was promptly sent home. For a time he seemed likely to recover, but the disease developed, and he died at Glasgow of apoplexy on 1 Nov. 1835.

A restrained conversationalist, Motherwell could be eager and even vehement when deeply moved, and with kindred spirits—such as R. A. Smith, the musician, and others of the 'Whistle Binkie' circle—he was both easy and affable. His social instinct and public spirit are illustrated in his spirited cavalier lyrics. His essentially superstitious temperament, clinging to the Scottish mythology that amused Burns, specially qualified him for writing weird lyrics like his 'Demon Lady' and such a successful fairy ballad as 'Elfinland Wud.'

Motherwell's range and grasp are very considerable. His pathetic lyrics—notably 'Jeanie Morrison' and 'My Head is like to rend, Willie'—show genuine feeling. This class of his work drew special praise from Miss Mitford in her 'Literary Recollections.' He was the first after Gray strongly to appreciate and utilise Scandinavian mythology, and his three ballads from this source are energetic yet graceful. Professor Wilson said of Motherwell: 'All his perceptions are clear, for all his senses are sound; he has fine and strong sensibilities and a powerful intellect' (*Blackwood*, xxxiii. 670).

A revised and enlarged edition of his poems, with biography by James M'Conechy, appeared in 1846, and in 1848 it was further supplemented and re-edited by William Kennedy [q. v.] A reprint based on these was published in 1881. M'Conechy says that Motherwell was, when he died, preparing materials for a biography of Tannahill. A portrait of Motherwell by Andrew Henderson and two busts by Fillans are in the National Portrait Gallery, Edinburgh.

[M'Conechy's Life prefixed to Poems of 1846; Whistle Binkie, vol. i. ed. 1853; Rogers's Modern Scottish Minstrel; Robert Brown's Paisley Poets.]
T. B.

MOTTE, BENJAMIN (*d.* 1738), bookseller and publisher, appears to have been originally a printer. He set up a publishing business at Middle Temple Gate, London, and in 1713 was among the subscribers to make up William Bowyer's losses after the great fire on his premises. In 1721, with the aid of his brother Andrew (see below), he edited, in three volumes, an 'Abridgment of the Royal Society's Transactions, from 1700 to 1720,' London, 4to. This abridgment was very incorrect, and was severely handled by a rival editor, Henry Jones, fellow of King's College, Cambridge. Motte rejoined in 'A Reply to the Preface published by Mr. Henry Jones with his Abridgment of the Philosophical Transactions,' London, 1722 (see Nichols, *Lit. Anecd.* i. 482). He was early in the century described by Samuel Negus as a 'highflyer,' and he gradually obtained the succession to most of Benjamin Tooke's business with Pope and the leading men of letters on the tory side. In 1726 Swift sent the manuscript of 'Gulliver's Travels' to Motte from Twickenham, where he was staying with Pope. His intermediaries were Charles Ford, who left the book at Motte's office late one night in November, and Erasmus Lewis [q. v.], to whom, writing under the disguised name of Sympson, Swift asked Motte to deliver a bank-bill of 200*l.* on undertaking publication. Motte cautiously demurred to immediate payment, but agreed to pay the sum demanded in six months, 'if the success would allow it.' In April 1727 Swift sent Lewis to demand the money for his 'cousin Gulliver's book,' and it appears to have been promptly paid. An interesting letter from Swift to Motte suggesting the passages in 'Gulliver' best fitted for illustration is given in the 'Gentleman's Magazine' for February 1855. In March 1727 Motte agreed to pay 4*l.* a sheet for the 'Miscellanies in Prose and Verse,' by Swift, Pope, Arbuthnot, and Gay. One volume had already been undertaken by Tooke; he published the second and third, but before the appearance of the fourth had quarrelled with his authors. In spite, however, of some differences on the subject of Irish copyright, Swift seems to have constantly maintained friendly relations with Motte, and to have utilised him as a sort of London agent. In 1733 Motte was deceived by a counterfeit 'Life and Character of Dean Swift, written by himself,' in verse, probably the work of Pilkington, who sold it to him on the plausible pretext that he was Swift's agent in the matter. On the other hand he obtained almost all the profits resulting from 'Gulliver' and Swift's other publications.

At his death, on 12 March 1738, Motte was succeeded by Charles Bathurst (1709–1786), who had for a short while previous been his partner. Bathurst published in 1768 the first collective edition of Swift's 'Works,' edited in sixteen volumes by Dr. Hawkesworth. It appears that he and Motte had both married daughters of the Rev. Thomas Brian, head-master of Harrow School.

Motte's younger brother, Andrew Motte (*d.* 1730), a mathematician of some ability, was a member of the Spalding Club, and, for a brief period previous to 1727, lecturer in geometry at Gresham College. He issued in 1727 'A Treatise of the Mechanical Powers, wherein the Laws of Motion and the Properties of those Powers are explained and demonstrated in an easy and familiar Method' (2nd edit. 1733, London, 8vo), and two years later 'The Mathematical Principles of Natural Philosophy (the "Principia"), by Sir Isaac Newton, translated into English . . . to which are added the Laws of the Moon's Motion according to Gravity, by John Machin' (2 vols. 1729, 8vo; 2nd edit. 1732).

The work is handsomely printed (for Benjamin Motte), and contains numerous plates of figures and an index. It anticipated a similar project on the part of Dr. Henry Pemberton [q. v.], who was better qualified for the work; it is nevertheless a highly creditable production (cf. BREWSTER, *Sir Isaac Newton*, ii. 383). Andrew Motte died in 1730. It is uncertain whether it is the bookseller or his brother who is alluded to by Dunton as 'learned Motte' (*Life and Errors*).

[Nichols's Literary Anecdotes, i. 63, 213, 482, 506, ii. 11, 25, vi. 99, viii. 369; Notes and Queries, I. xii. 60, 198, 358, 490; Gent. Mag. 1855 i. 150, 258, ii. 35, 232, 363; Elwin's Pope, vi. 437, vii. 86, 110, 178, 286, 324, ix. 524; Brit. Mus. Cat.] T. S.

MOTTERSHEAD, JOSEPH (1688–1771), dissenting minister, son of Joseph Mottershead, yeoman, was born near Stockport, Cheshire, on 17 Aug. 1688. He was educated at Attercliffe Academy under Timothy Jollie [q. v.], and afterwards studied for a year under Matthew Henry [q. v.] at Chester. After license he preached (1710–12) at Kingsley, in the parish of Frodsham, Cheshire. On 5 Aug. 1712 he was ordained at Knutsford as successor to Samuel Lawrence [q. v.] at Nantwich. Matthew Henry visited him in 1713, and died at his house in 1714. In 1717 Mottershead became minister of Cross Street Chapel, Manchester, and held this post till his death. His colleagues were Joshua Jones [see under JONES, JEREMIAH], John Seddon (1719–1769) [q. v.], and Robert Gore (1748–1779). When the Young Pretender entered Manchester in November 1745, Mottershead was selected as hostage for a pecuniary fine, but he had timely warning and made his escape. During his protracted ministry at Manchester, Mottershead, whom Halley calls 'a very quiet peaceable man,' passed from Calvinism to a type of Arianism. About 1756 there was a secession from the congregation owing to the Socinian tenets of Seddon, his colleague and son-in-law. Mottershead died on 4 Nov. 1771, and was buried near the pulpit in his meeting-house. His portrait, by Pickering, was engraved by William Pether [q. v.] He married, first, at Kingsley, the eldest daughter of Bennett of Hapsford, Cheshire; she died in October 1718, leaving four children; his only son was educated at Edinburgh as a physician, but took Anglican orders, acted as curate in Manchester, and was lost at sea as chaplain of a man-of-war; his eldest daughter married (February 1743) Seddon, his colleague; his second daughter, Sarah, married John Jones, founder of the banking house of Jones, Loyd, & Co., whose grandson was Samuel Jones Loyd, first baron Overstone [q. v.] He married, secondly, in January 1721, Margaret (*d.* 31 Jan. 1740), widow of Nathaniel Gaskell of Manchester; he was her third husband. He married, thirdly, in June 1742, Abigail (*d.* 28 Dec. 1753), daughter of Chewning Blackmore [see under BLACKMORE, WILLIAM].

Mottershead published, besides two sermons (1719–1745), 'Religious Discourses,' &c., Glasgow, 1759, 8vo. Under the signature 'Theophilus' he contributed essays to Priestley's 'Theological Repository,' 1769, i. 173 sq., 225 sq., and 1771, iii. 112 sq. He also published a revised edition of Matthew Henry's 'Plain Catechism' (no date).

[Biographical notice in Toulmin's Memoirs of S. Bourn, 1808, pp. 251 sq.; Urwick's Nonconformity in Cheshire, 1864, pp. 129 sq.; Halley's Lancashire, 1869, ii. 364, 447; Wade's Rise of Nonconformity in Manchester, 1880, pp. 34 sq.; Turner's Nonconformist Register of Heywood and Dickenson, 1881, pp. 215, 231, 232, 276; Baker's Mem. of a Dissenting Chapel, 1884, pp. 27 sq., 141 sq.; Nightingale's Lancashire Nonconformity (1893), v. 97 sq.] A. G.

MOTTEUX, PETER ANTHONY (1660–1718), translator and dramatist, was born 18 Feb. 1660 at Rouen, Normandy, being probably the son of Antoine le Motteux, a merchant of that town. He came to England at the revocation of the edict of Nantes in 1685, living at first with his godfather and relative, Paul Dominique. Afterwards he went into business, and had an East India warehouse in Leadenhall Street. In 1692 and 1693 he edited the 'Gentleman's Journal, or the Monthly Miscellany,' which contained verses by Prior, Sedley, Mrs. Behn, Oldmixon, Dennis, D'Urfey, Brown, and the editor. The first volume was dedicated to William, earl of Devonshire; the second to Charles Montague. In 1693, when Gildon satirised Dunton in the 'History of the Athenian Society,' Motteux, Tate, and others wrote prefatory verses for the skit. In the same year appeared Boileau's 'Ode sur la Prise de Namur. Avec une Parodie de la mesme Ode par le Sieur P. Motteux.' In 1693-4 a translation of Rabelais (books i. to iii.) by Motteux, Sir Thomas Urquhart, and others was published in three volumes, with a long introduction by Motteux. The remainder of the work (books iv. and v.) appeared in 1708. This excellent translation has been frequently reprinted down to the present day, and shows how thoroughly Motteux had mastered the English language. In 1695 he published 'Maria, a Poem occasioned by the Death of Her Majesty,' addressed to Montague, Normanby, and Dorset; and translated St. Olon's 'Present State of the Empire of Morocco,' with a dedication to Sir William Trumball, in which he said he endeavoured to appear as much an Englishman as he could, even in his writings. In the same year Motteux published on a single sheet 'Words for a Musical Entertainment [by John Eccles] at the New Theatre in Little Lincoln's Inn Fields, on the Taking of Namur, and His Majesty's safe Return.'

Motteux's first play, 'Love's a Jest,' a comedy from the Italian, was produced in 1696, with a dedication to Lord Clifford of Lanesborough. It was followed in 1697 by 'The Novelty. Every Act a Play. Being a short Pastoral, Comedy, Masque, Tragedy, and Farce, after the Italian manner,' by Motteux and others, with a dedication to Charles Cæsar; and by 'The Loves of Mars and Venus,' a masque (dedicated to Colonel Codrington), which was acted and printed in connection with the 'Anatomist,' by Motteux's friend Ravenscroft. In June 1698 Motteux produced a tragedy, 'Beauty in Distress,' to which were prefixed a 'Discourse of the Lawfulness and Unlawfulness of Plays, lately written in French by Father Caffaro,' and complimentary lines by Dryden, 'to my friend Mr. Motteux,' with reference to Collier's recent attack on the stage. The fault of the play, as Dryden hinted, is that the plot is too complicated. In the dedication to the Hon. Henry Heveningham, Motteux says that it had been the happy occasion of recommending him to the bounty of the Princess Anne, her gift alone outweighing the benefit of a sixth representation; but he adds that his uninterrupted success had created enemies. It was alleged by a satirist that Heveningham himself wrote this dedication, offering to pay Motteux five guineas for the use of his name (*Poems on Affairs of State*, 1703, ii. 248–54; *Egerton MS.* 2623, f. 68). In 1699 Motteux turned Fletcher's 'Island Princess' into an opera, wrote words for an interlude, 'The Four Lessons, or Love in every Age,' and contributed an epilogue to Henry Smith's 'Princess of Parma.'

From a letter of 28 April 1700 from Dubois, afterwards cardinal, to 'Monsieur Pierre Motteux à la grande Poste, à Londres' (*Hist. MSS. Comm.* 9th Rep. pt. ii. p. 464), it would appear that Motteux had then already received what the old biographers call 'a very genteel place in the General Post Office relating to foreign letters, being master of several languages;' but official records only show that by 1703 he had 40*l.* as a clerk in the foreign office of the post-office, and that by 1711 the place had been given to another. A song by Motteux, given at a post-office feast on the queen's birthday, is printed in Oldmixon's 'Muses Mercury' for January 1708. There are other verses by Motteux in the same paper for March 1707.

'Acis and Galatea,' a masque, was produced in 1701, and 'Britain's Happiness,' a musical interlude, in 1704. On 16 Jan. 1705 'Arsinoe, Queen of Cyprus, an Opera after the Italian manner,' was brought out at Drury Lane Theatre, and was acted fifteen times. It was printed in 1707 (see Addison, *Spectator*, 21 March 1711). 'The Amorous Miser,' a farcical comedy, appeared at the same theatre on 18 Jan. 1705, and was acted about six times. Motteux wrote an epilogue for Vanbrugh's 'Mistake,' first acted on 27 Dec. 1705; and on 7 March 1706 the 'Temple of Love, a Pastoral Opera, Englished from the Italian,' was performed at the Haymarket with but little success. In the following year (1 April 1707) 'Thomyris, Queen of Scythia, an Opera,' was produced under Dr. Pepusch's direction, and it was followed by 'Farewell Folly, or the Younger the Wiser, a Comedy. With a Musical Interlude called "The Mountebank, or the Humours of the Fair."' 'Love's Triumph,' an opera, 1708, was dedicated to Thomas Falkland, son of the postmaster-general; the words had been written, Motteux said, 'very near you, at a place where my duty often calls me from other business; ... they were in a manner done in Post-haste.' Early in 1712, or at the close of 1711, Motteux published a good though free translation of Cervantes's 'Don Quixote,' in four volumes. He was assisted by Ozell and others, but revised the whole himself. This work has been frequently reprinted. In the 'Spectator' for 30 Jan. 1712 (No. 288) appeared a letter from Motteux, who spoke of himself as 'an author turned dealer,' and described the large variety of goods which ladies would find at his warehouse in Leadenhall Street, many of them bought by himself abroad. In July 1712 he published, in folio and duodecimo, 'A Poem in Praise of Tea,' with a dedication to the 'Spectator,' in which he again referred to the way he was engrossed in his 'China and India trade, and all the distracting variety of a Doyly.' In December Steele drew an attractive picture of his friend's 'spacious warehouses, filled and adorned with tea, China and Indian wares' (*Spectator*, No. 552). From a letter of 1714 to Sir Hans Sloane, in the British Museum, it appears that Motteux dealt also in pictures (*Sloane MS.* 4054, f. 12).

Motteux's death took place on his birthday, 18 Feb. 1718, in a house of ill-fame in Star Court, Butcher Row, near St. Clement's Church. He went to the house with a woman named Mary Roberts, after calling at White's chocolate-house, and soon after midnight an apothecary was called in, who found him dead. The woman Roberts said that Motteux had been ill in the coach, and never spoke after they reached the house. He was buried at St. Andrew Undershaft, 25 Feb., and an inquest was held. The keeper of the house, her daughter, and others were committed to Newgate, and a reward of ten guineas was offered by Mrs. Motteux, of the 'Two Fans,' Leadenhall Street, to the coachman who drove Motteux to Star Court if he would state what condition the gentleman was in when he set him down. The coachman was found, and on 22 March a pardon was offered to any one, not the actual murderer, who had been concerned in the matter, and 50*l.* reward to any one discovering the murderer. The persons in custody were tried at the Old Bailey on 23 April. The defence was that Motteux had had a fit, and the prisoners were all acquitted, 'to the great surprise of most people' (there is a long report in BOYER's *Political State*, 1718, pp. 254, 425–36; see, too, *Applebee's Original Weekly Journal*, 26 April to 3 May 1718; *Daily Courant*, March and April 1718; and *Mist's Journal*, 26 April 1718, where it is said that the jury brought in a special verdict against the women, which was to be decided by the twelve judges).

Motteux had sons baptised at St. Andrew Undershaft on 3 Oct. 1705 and 13 April 1710. By his will, dated 23 Feb. 1709, and proved 24 Feb. 1717–18 by his wife Priscilla, sole executrix, Motteux (grocer and freeman of London) left his property to be divided equally among his wife and children, Peter, Henrietta, and Anthony, and others who might afterwards be born; 10*l.* were left to the poor of St. Andrew Undershaft. The son Peter, a surgeon, of Charterhouse Square, married Miss West in 1750, and died a widower in November 1769, leaving a daughter, Ann Bosquain; the other son, John Anthony, died in December 1741, a very eminent Hamburg merchant, leaving a widow, Ann. Motteux had a brother Timothy, merchant and salter, who was naturalised in March 1676–7 (*Hist. MSS. Comm.* 9th Rep. pt. ii. p. 87), and died in 1746, leaving money to his nephews and to the Walloon and Dutch churches. He was a director of the French Hospital in London (*London Mag.*; *Gent. Mag.* 1741, 1746, 1750, 1769; wills at Prerogative Court of Canterbury).

According to Pope Motteux was loquacious; 'Talkers I've learned to bear; Motteux I knew' (*Satires of Dr. Donne*, iv. 50); 'Motteux himself unfinished left his tale' (*Dunciad*, ii. 412); and in the 'Art of Sinking in Poetry,' chap. vi., he speaks of Motteux and others as 'obscure authors, that wrap themselves up in their own mud, but are mighty nimble and pert.' Motteux's claims to be remembered now rest upon his racy versions of Rabelais and Cervantes.

[Van Laun's Short Hist. of the late Mr. Peter Anthony Motteux, prefixed to his edition of Don Quixote, 1880, and privately printed in pamphlet form; Genest's Account of the English Stage, ii. 86, 116–18, 153, 164, 318–19, 350, 484; Biog. Dram.; Whincop's List of English Dramatic Poets, 1747; Weiss's Protestant Refugees; Nichols's Lit. Anecd. iii. 308, ix. 773. The Hist. of Kent, by Dr. John Harris, 1719, has prefixed to it an Ode in Praise of Kent, by Motteux, 'e Normania Britannus.' The full score, with libretto, of the Island Princess is in the Brit. Mus. Addit. MS. 15318; Notes and Queries, 8th ser. vi. 142.] G. A. A.

MOTTLEY, JOHN (1692–1750), dramatist and biographer, was the son of Colonel Thomas Mottley, an adherent of James II in his exile, who entered the service of Louis XIV, and was killed at the battle of Turin in 1706; his mother was Dionisia, daughter of John Guise of Ablode Court, Gloucestershire. John was born in London in 1692, was educated at Archbishop Tenison's grammar school in the parish of St. Martin's-in-the-Fields, and obtained a clerkship in the excise office in 1708. Owing to an 'unhappy contract' he was compelled to resign his post in 1720, and thenceforth gained a precarious subsistence by his pen. He made his début as a dramatic author with a frigid tragedy in the pseudo-classic style, entitled 'The Imperial Captives,' the scene of which is laid at Carthage, in the time of Genseric, who with the Empress Eudoxia and her daughter plays a principal part. The play was produced at the Theatre Royal, Lincoln's Inn Fields, in February 1719–20. At the same theatre was produced in April 1721 Mottley's only other effort in tragedy, 'Antiochus,' an extremely dull play, founded on the story of the surrender by Seleucus Nicator of his wife Stratonice to his son Antiochus. Both tragedies were printed on their production. In comedy Mottley was more successful. His dramatic opera, 'Penelope,' in which he was assisted by Thomas Cooke (1703–1756) [q. v.], a satire on Pope's 'Odyssey,' and his farce 'The Craftsman, or Weekly Journalist' (both performed at the Haymarket, and printed in 1728 and 1729 respectively), are not without humour. His comedy, 'The Widow Bewitched,' produced at Goodman's Fields Theatre in 1730, and printed, was a successful play.

Mottley was joint author with Charles Coffey [q. v.] of the comic opera, 'The Devil to pay, or the Wives Metamorphosed,' produced at Drury Lane on 6 Aug. 1731, and frequently revived. Under the pseudonym of Robert Seymour he edited in 1734 (perhaps with the assistance of Thomas Cooke) Stow's 'Survey of the Cities of London and Westminster' (London, 2 vols. fol.) Under the pseudonym of Elijah Jenkins he published in 1739 the classic jest-book, 'Joe Miller's Jests, or the Wit's Vade Mecum' [see MILLER, JOSEPH or JOSIAS].

Mottley is also the author of two historical works: 'The History of the Life of Peter I, Emperor of Russia,' London, 1739, 2 vols. 8vo, and 'The History of the Life and Reign of the Empress Catharine, containing a short History of the Russian Empire from its first Foundation to the Time of the Death of that Princess,' London, 1744, 2 vols. 8vo. He is the reputed author of the 'Compleat List of all the English Dramatic Poets and of all the Plays ever printed in the English Language to the Present Year 1747,' appended to Whincop's 'Scanderbeg,' in which it is clear from internal evidence that he wrote the article on himself. He died in 1750, having for some years previously been almost bedridden with the gout. A portrait is mentioned by Bromley.

[Transactions of the Bristol and Gloucestershire Archæological Soc. 1878–9, iii. 73; Whincop's Scanderbeg, 1747, p. 264 (with engraved portrait); Baker's Biog. Dramat. 1812; Genest's Hist. of the Stage, iii. 40, 61, 228, 277; Chamberlayne's Mag. Brit. Not. 1716 p. 514, 1718 p. 70; Notes and Queries, 2nd ser. xi. 102, 8th ser. iv. 9; Upcott's English Topogr. p. 620; Gent. Mag. 1820 pt. ii. p. 327, 1821 pt. i. p. 124.]
J. M. R.

MOTTRAM, CHARLES (1807–1876), engraver, born on 9 April 1807, worked in line, in mezzotint, and in the mixed style. His principal plates in the line manner were 'The Rescue,' 'Uncle Tom and his Wife for Sale,' and 'The Challenge,' after Sir Edwin Landseer, R.A.; 'Bœufs Bretons,' after Rosa Bonheur; and 'Duck Hunting,' after Friedrich Wilhelm Keyl. Among his mezzotint plates were 'The Morning before the Battle' and 'The Evening after the Battle,' after Thomas Jones Barker; 'Les Longs Rochers de Fontainebleau,' after Rosa Bonheur; 'Pilgrim Exiles' and 'The Belated Traveller,' after George Henry Boughton, A.R.A.; 'The Shadow of the Cross,' after Philip Richard Morris, A.R.A.; 'Pride and Humility,' after George Cole; and 'The Ashdown Coursing Meeting,' after Stephen Pearce. His plates in the mixed style were the most numerous, and included 'The Scape Goat,' after William Holman Hunt; 'The Highland Shepherd's Home' and 'The Stag at Bay' (the smallest plate), after Sir Edwin Landseer; 'The Last Judgment,' 'The Plains of Heaven,' and 'The Great Day of Wrath,' after John Martin; 'Jerusalem in her Grandeur' and 'Jerusalem in her Fall,' after Henry C. Selous; 'The Straits of Ballachulish' and 'A Scottish Raid,' after Rosa Bonheur; 'The Two Farewells,' after George H. Boughton; 'Corn Thrashing in Hungary,' after Otto von Thoren; 'Crossing a Highland Loch,' after Jacob Thomson; 'Abandoned' and 'In Danger,' a pair after Adolf Schreyer; 'A Charming Incident,' after Charles W. Nicholls, R.H.A.; and 'Out all Night,' after J. H. Beard. He engraved also several plates after Sir Edwin Landseer for the series of 'Her Majesty's Pets,' and a few portraits, one of which was a whole-length in mezzotint of Lord Napier of Magdala, after Sir Francis Grant, P.R.A.

Mottram's works were exhibited occasionally at the Royal Academy between 1861 and 1877. He died at 92 High Street, Camden Town, London, on 30 Aug. 1876.

[Royal Academy Exhibition Catalogues, 1861–1877; private information.] R. E. G.

MOUFET, THOMAS (1553–1604), physician. [See MOFFETT.]

MOULE, HENRY (1801–1880), divine and inventor, sixth son of George Moule, solicitor and banker, was born at Melksham, Wiltshire, 27 Jan. 1801, and educated at Marlborough grammar school. He was elected a foundation scholar of St. John's College, Cambridge, and graduated B.A. 1821 and M.A. 1826. He was ordained to the curacy of Melksham in 1823, and took sole charge of Gillingham, Dorset, in 1825. He was made vicar of Fordington in the same county in 1829, and remained there the remainder of his life. For some years he undertook the duty of chaplain to the troops in Dorchester barracks, for whose use, as well as for a detached district of his own parish, he built in 1846, partly from the proceeds of his published 'Barrack Sermons,' 1845 (2nd edit. 1847), a church known as Christ Church, West Fordington. In 1833 his protests brought to an end the evils connected with the race meetings at Dorchester. During the cholera visitations of 1849 and 1854 his exertions were unwearied. Impressed by the insalubrity of the houses, he turned his attention to sanitary science, and invented what is called the dry earth system. In partnership with James Bannehr, he took out a patent for the process (No. 1316, dated 28 May 1860). Among his works bearing on the subject were: 'The Advantages of the Dry Earth System,' 1868; 'The Impossibility overcome: or the Inoffensive, Safe, and Economical Disposal of the Refuse of Towns and Villages,' 1870; 'The Dry Earth System,' 1871; 'Town Refuse, the Remedy for Local Taxation,' 1872, and 'National Health and Wealth promoted by the general adoption of the Dry Earth System,' 1873. His system has been adopted in private houses, in rural districts, in military camps, in many hospitals, and extensively in India. He also wrote an important work, entitled 'Eight Letters to Prince Albert, as President of the Council of the Duchy of Cornwall,' 1855, prompted by the condition of Fordington parish, belonging to the duchy. In two letters in the 'Times' of 24 Feb. and 2 April 1874 he advocated a plan for extracting gas from Kimmeridge shale. He died at Fordington vicarage, 3 Feb. 1880, having married in 1824 Mary Mullett Evans, who died 21 Aug. 1877.

In addition to the works already mentioned, and many single sermons and pamphlets, Moule wrote: 1. 'Two Conversations between a Clergyman and one of his Parishioners on the Public Baptism of Infants,' 1843. 2. 'Scraps of Sacred Verse,' 1846. 3. 'Scriptural Church Teaching,' 1848. 4. 'Christian Oratory during the first Five Centuries,' 1859. 5. 'My Kitchen-Garden: by a Country Parson,' 1860. 6. 'Manure for the Million. A Letter to the Cottage Gardeners of England,' 1861; 11th thousand, 1870. 7. 'Self-supporting Boarding Schools and Day Schools for the Children of the Industrial Classes,' 1862; 3rd edit. 1871. 8. 'Good out of Evil. A Series of Letters publicly addressed to Dr. Colenso,' 1863. 9. 'Pardon and Peace: illustrated by ministerial Memorials, to which are added some Pieces of Sacred Verse,' 1865. 10. 'Our Home Heathen, how can the Church of England get at them,' 1868. 11. '"These from the Land of Sinim." The Narrative of the Conversion of a Chinese Physician [Dzing, Seen Sang],' 1868. 12. 'Land for the Million to rent. Addressed to the Working Classes of England; by H. M.,' 1870. 13. 'On the Warming of Churches,' 1870. 14. 'The Science of Manure as the Food of Plants,' 1870. 15. 'The Potatoe Disease, its Cause and Remedy. Three Letters to the Times,' 1872. 16. 'Harvest Hymns,' 1877.

[Crockford's Clerical Directory, 1878, p. 672; Men of the Time, 1879, p. 727; Times, 5 Feb. 1880, p. 8; Dorset County Chronicle, 5 Feb. 1880, p. 3; H. C. G. Moule's Sermons on the Death of H. Moule, M.A. 1880, Memoir, pp. 5–13; Chambers's Encycl. 1874, vol. x. Suppl. pp. 731–3; Patents for Inventions, Abridgements of Specifications relating to Closets, 1873, Introd. pp. x–xii, and 125–6.] G. C. B.

MOULE, THOMAS (1784–1851), writer on heraldry and antiquities, born 14 Jan. 1784 in the parish of St. Marylebone, London, carried on business as a bookseller in Duke Street, Grosvenor Square, from about 1816 till about 1823, and he was subsequently a clerk in the General Post Office, where he was inspector of 'blind' letters, his principal duty being to decipher such addresses as were illegible to the ordinary clerks. He retired after forty-four years' service in consequence of failing health. He also held for many years the office of chamber-keeper in the lord chamberlain's department, and this gave him an official residence in the Stable Yard, St. James's Palace, where he died on 14 Jan. 1851, leaving a widow and an only daughter, who had materially assisted him in his literary pursuits.

Moule was a member of the Numismatic Society, and contributed some papers to the 'Numismatic Chronicle.' His principal works are: 1. 'A Table of Dates for the use of Genealogists and Antiquaries' (anon.), 1820. 2. 'Bibliotheca Heraldica Magnæ Britanniæ. An Analytical Catalogue of Books in Genealogy, Heraldry, Nobility, Knighthood, and Ceremonies; with a List of Provincial Visitations . . . and other Manuscripts; and a Supplement enumerating the principal Foreign Genealogical Works,' Lond. 1822, 4to, with portrait of William Camden. In the British Museum there is a copy of this accurate and valuable work, interleaved with copious manuscript corrections and additions, and an additional volume of further corrections, &c., 3 vols. 4to. 3. 'Antiquities in Westminster Abbey, illustrated by twelve plates, from drawings by G. P. Harding,' Lond. 1825, 4to. 4. 'An Essay on the Roman Villas of the Augustan Age, their architectural disposition and enrichments, and on the Remains of Roman Domestic Edifices discovered in Great Britain,' Lond. 1833, 8vo. 5. 'English Counties delineated; or a Topographical Description of England. Illustrated by a Map of London and a complete Series of County Maps,' 2 vols. Lond. 1837, 4to; new title 1839. Moule personally visited every county in England excepting Devon and Cornwall. 6. 'Heraldry of Fish, Notices of the principal families bearing Fish in their Arms,' Lond. 1842, 8vo, with beautiful woodcuts, from drawings made by his daughter. He had formed a similar collection on the heraldry of trees and birds, the manuscript of which was sold with Sir Thomas Phillipps's collection on 21 June 1893.

Moule also contributed the letter-press to the following illustrated books: 7. Hewetson's 'Views of Noble Mansions in Hampshire,' 1825. 8. Neale and Le Keux's 'Views of Collegiate and Parochial Churches in Great Britain,' 1826. 9. Westall's 'Great Britain Illustrated,' 1830. 10. 'The History of Hatfield' in Robinson's 'Vitruvius Britannicus,' 1833. 11. 'Illustrations of the Works of Sir Walter Scott,' 1834, the following essays being by him: (*a*) Hall at Branxholm; (*b*) Lord Marmion's Armour; (*c*) Ellen Douglas and Fitz-James; (*d*) The Knight of Snowdoun; (*e*) The Tomb of Rokeby; (*f*) The Bier of De Argentine; (*g*) Ancient Furniture. 12. Descriptions of seven of the principal cathedrals included in vol. i. of Winkles's 'Cathedral Churches of England and Wales,' 1836, and the descriptions of the cathedrals of Amiens, Paris, and Chartres in the 'Continental Cathedrals' of the same artist. 13. Shaw's 'Details of Elizabethan Architecture,' 1839. 14. Descriptions of the arms and inscriptions in Ludlow Castle, in 'Documents connected with the History of Ludlow and the Lords Marchers,' by Robert Henry Clive, 1840. 15. G. P. Harding's 'Ancient Historical Pictures,' in continuation of the series engraved by the Granger Society.

[Addit. MS. 22651, f. 94; Gent. Mag. August 1851, p. 210; Lowndes's Bibl. Man. (Bohn), p. 1624; Martin's Privately Printed Books, 2nd edit. pref. xxi. p. 209 *n.*, 235.] T. C.

MOULIN, LEWIS DU (1606–1680), nonconformist controversialist, son of Pierre du Moulin [q. v.] and brother of Peter du Moulin [q. v.], was born at Paris on 25 Oct. 1606. He studied medicine at Leyden, taking the degree of M.D., and graduating also at Cambridge in 1634 and at Oxford in 1649. Becoming licentiate in 1640 of the London College of Physicians, he probably practised at Oxford, where in September 1648, as 'a person of piety and learning,' he was appointed Camden professor of ancient history in the place of Robert Waring, ejected as a royalist. In 1652 he published his inaugural lecture. Ousted in his turn at the Restoration, Du Moulin retired to Westminster. Wood calls him 'a fiery, violent, and hotheaded independent, a cross and ill-natured man,' but on his deathbed, in the presence of Bishop Burnet, he retracted his virulent attacks on Anglican theologians. This retractation was published, under the title of 'Last Words,' after his death, which took place at Westminster, 20 Oct. 1680. He was buried at St. Paul's, Covent Garden. Between 1637 and his death he had published upwards of twenty works, the chief of which are: 1. 'The Power of the Christian Magistrate,' London, 1650, 16mo. 2. 'Proposals and Reasons . . . presented to the Parliament,' London, 1659, 4to. 3. 'L. Molinæi Morum Exemplar,' 1662, 12mo. 4. 'Les Démarches de l'Angleterre vers Rome,' 1679, 12mo. 5. 'Considerations et ouvertures sur l'estat présent des affaires de l'Angleterre,' 1679, 12mo. 6. 'An Appeal of all the Nonconformists in England,' 1681, 4to. The last work was attacked by Jean Daillé in 'A Lively Picture of Lewis du Moulin;' Moulin retorted in 'A Sober Reply,' and was also defended by Richard Baxter [q. v.] in 'A Second True Defence of Nonconformists,' 1681, 4to. Moulin also wrote under the pseudonyms 'Christianus Alethocritus,' 'Colvinus Ludiomæus,' and 'Irenæus Philadelphus.' One of his last works was 'Moral Reflections upon the Number of the Elect, proving plainly from Scripture evidence, &c., that not one in a hundred (nay, not probably one in a million), from Adam down to our time, shall be saved,' London, 1680, 16mo. In the Harleian MS. 3520, fol. 5, British Museum, is an unpublished manuscript by him entitled 'New Light for the Composition of Church History.'

[Album Studiosorum Lugdunæ, the Hague, 1875; Haag's La France Protestante; Wood's Athenæ Oxon.; Munk's Coll. of Phys., London, 1878; Agnew's Protestant Exiles from France, 1886; Reg. of Visitors of Oxford, p. 492 (Camd. Soc.), 1881; Brit. Mus. Cat.] J. G. A.

MOULIN, PETER DU (1601–1684), Anglican divine, son of Pierre du Moulin [q. v.], was born at Paris on 24 April 1601. After studying at Sedan and Leyden, he repaired to Cambridge, where he received the degree of D.D. About 1625, after an imprisonment at Dunkirk, he was appointed to the living (refused by his father) of St. John's, Chester, but there is no trace in the church books of his having resided there. In 1640, however, on becoming D.D. at Leyden, he described himself as holding that benefice. Wood could not ascertain whether he held any English preferment prior to the civil war, but he was rector of Witherley, Leicestershire, in 1633, and of Wheldrake, Yorkshire, in 1641. During the civil war he was first in Ireland as tutor in the Boyle family, and was next tutor at Oxford to Richard Boyle and Lord Dungarvan, frequently preaching at St. Peter-in-the-East. He was rector of Adisham, Kent, from 1646 (with a short intermission in 1660 on the reinstatement of Dr. Oliver) till his death. He sided, like his father, with the royalists, and wrote the scurrilous reply to Milton, 'Regii Sanguinis Clamor,' mistakenly attributed to Alexander More [q. v.] Du Moulin concealed his authorship, was consequently unmolested, and was even in 1656 made D.D. at Oxford, then under puritan sway. At the Restoration he was rewarded by a chaplaincy to Charles II and by succeeding to his father's prebend at Canterbury. He took up his residence there, died 10 Oct. 1684, and was buried in the cathedral. He published 'A Treatise of Peace and Contentment of the Soul,' London, 1657, and about twenty other works in English, French, and Latin. Wood styles him 'an honest, zealous Calvinist.' By his marriage in 1633 with Anne, daughter of Matthew Claver of Foscott, Buckinghamshire, he had a son Lewis, grandfather of Peter du Moulin, one of Frederick II's best generals. Peter's brother, Cyrus, was for a time French pastor at Canterbury.

[Life in Lansdowne MS. 987, fol. 44, Brit. Mus.; Wood's Athenæ Oxon.; Dart's Canterbury, 1726, p. 200; Album Studiosorum Lugdunæ, the Hague, 1875; Agnew's Protestant Exiles from France, 1886; Haag's La France Protestante; Foster's Alumni Oxon. and London Marriage Licences; Archæologia Cantiana, 1882-3.]

J. G. A.

MOULIN, PIERRE DU (1568–1658), French protestant divine, was the son of Joachim du Moulin, an eminent pastor at Orleans, by Françoise Gabet, widow of Jacques du Plessis. He was born 18 Oct. 1568 at Buhy, Vexin Français, where his father had temporarily taken refuge, and was acting as chaplain to Pierre de Buhy, brother of the so-called 'Huguenot pope,' Philippe de Mornay. When he was four years old his parents, compelled to flee to avoid the St. Bartholomew massacres, left their four little children in charge of an old nurse, a catholic, at Cœuvres, near Soissons. Pierre's cries, being concealed under a mattress, on the murderers' approach, would have attracted their attention had not the nurse rattled her pots and pans, pretending to be cleaning them, and had not his sister Esther, aged 7, put her hand over his mouth. Pierre was educated at Sedan. In 1588 his father, harassed by persecutions, dismissed him with twelve crowns, bidding him seek his fortune in England. There he was befriended by Menillet, who afterwards married his sister, and the Countess of Rutland sent him as tutor to her son to Cambridge, where he continued his own studies under Whitaker. In September 1592 he embarked for Holland on a visit to Professor Junius of Leyden, but was shipwrecked off Walcheren, losing all his books and other possessions, a disaster which inspired his Latin poem 'Votiva Tabella.' For two months teacher in a Leyden college, he was then appointed professor of philosophy at the university. He lodged with Scaliger, and Grotius was one of his pupils. In 1598 he went to see his father at Jargeau, and was induced to enter the ministry, for which he had undergone preparatory training while in London. After a farewell visit to Leyden he took temporary duty at Blois, and in March 1599 was appointed to Charenton, the suburb where the Paris protestants worshipped. He accompanied, as chaplain, Catherine de Bourbon, Henry IV's sister, on her periodical visits to her husband, the Duke of Bar, at his palace in Lorraine, preaching before her during the journey in Meaux Cathedral and other catholic churches. While he was standing by her deathbed in 1604, Cardinal du Perron, sent by Henry IV to convert her to catholicism, tried to push him out of the room, but he clung to the bedpost, and Catherine declining to change her religion the cardinal retired. Du Moulin's house in Paris was the resort of French and foreign protestants, Andrew Melville [q. v.] staying there in 1611. It was twice pillaged by mobs, and he himself had narrow escapes from violence. In 1615 his fellow-countryman, Sir Theodore Mayerne [q. v.], recommended him to James I, who required a French divine to assist him in his 'Regis Declaratio pro Jure Regio,' and fetched him over to London. James took him with him to Cambridge, where he was made D.D., and gave him a benefice in Wales and a prebend at Canterbury, each worth 200*l.* a year. After a three months' stay he returned to Paris, and being forbidden by the French government to attend the synod of Dort, to which he was one of the four elected French delegates, he sent a long memorial against Arminius, and he obtained the adoption of the decisions of the synod by French protestants. In 1619 James, who had consulted him on his scheme of protestant union, gave him a pension chargeable on the deanery of Salisbury. In 1620 Edward Herbert, first lord Herbert of Cherbury [q. v.], British ambassador at Paris, pressed him to write to James on behalf of the elector palatine. Du Moulin reluctantly complied, but the letter was intercepted, or, according to another version, was treacherously divulged by Buckingham; and its exhortations to James to justify the hopes placed in him by continental protestants were construed as incitements to a foreign sovereign to interfere in French affairs. Du Moulin, by Herbert's advice, fled to Sedan, where the Duke of

Bouillon appointed him tutor to his son, pastor of the church, and professor of theology at the academy. In 1623 he revisited England. In 1628 he was allowed to return to Charenton, which charge he occupied altogether for twenty-one years; but, finding his position again dangerous, he withdrew first to the Hague and then to Sedan. That principality was annexed to France in 1642, but he was not molested, and continued to preach and lecture, notwithstanding his great age, till within a fortnight of his death, which took place 10 March 1658. He married in 1599 Marie de Colignon, who died in 1622, and in the following year he married Sarah de Geslay. Two sons by his first wife, Lewis and Peter, are separately noticed.

Moulin's autobiography to 1644, apparently a family copy, is in the library of the History of French Protestantism Society at Paris, and was printed in its 'Bulletin' in 1858. Several of his letters are in the same library and in the Burnet MSS., Brit. Mus., vols. 367 and 371. Haag enumerates eighty-two works published by him in French and Latin, and Gory mentions ten others; nearly all are in the British Museum Library. Most are controversial, and Bayle points out that he was one of the first French protestants who ignored and evidently discredited the Pope Joan legend. His 'Elementa Logica,' 1596, went through many editions, and was translated into English in 1624.

[Du Moulin is spoken of frequently as Molinæus in a multitude of contemporary publications. The chief authorities on his life are his autobiography; Quick's Icones (manuscript in Dr. Williams's Library, London); Quick's Synodicon, ii. 105; Dernières Heures de Du Moulin, Sedan, 1658; Biog. Dict. of Foreigners resident in England, MS. 34283 in Brit. Mus.; Walker's Sufferings of the Clergy; Bates's Vitæ Selectorum Virorum, London, 1681; Freher's Theatrum Virorum, 1688; Sax's Onomasticon, 1775; Charles Read's Daniel Chamier, Paris, 1858; Haag's La France Protestante, 2nd edit. Paris, 1881; Agnew's Protestant Exiles from France, 1886 edit.; G. Gory's Thèse sur Du Moulin, Paris, 1888; Michel's Les Écossais en France, ii. 118; Brit. Mus. Cat.] J. G. A.

MOULTON, THOMAS (*fl.* 1540?), Dominican, calls himself 'Doctor of Divinity of the order of Friar Preachers.' He was author of a curious work partly dealing with medicine, partly with astrology, entitled 'This is the Myrour or Glasse of Helthe necessary and nedefull for every persone to loke in that wyll kepe body frome the Syckness of the Pestilence. And it sheweth howe the Planetts reygne in every houre of the daye and nyght with the natures and exposicions of the xii signes devyded by the xii monthes of the yere, and sheweth the remedyes for many divers infirmities and dyseases that hurteth the body of man.' After the prologue and table of contents the author gives four reasons for the production of his book, first, the prayers of his own brethren; secondly, the prayers of 'many worthy gentiles;' thirdly, his compassion 'for the pore people that was and is destroyed every daye thereby for default of helpe;' fourthly, the working of pure conscience (cf. Brydges, *Censura Literaria*, iv. 156–7). One of the copies in the British Museum Library has the title-page of Andrew Boorde's 'Regyment of Helth' prefixed to it (cf. Furnivall, *Boorde's Introduction and Dyetary*, p. 12).

The first edition of Moulton's work was printed and published by Robert Wyer in 1539 (?), and seems to have been in considerable request. At least nine editions were published in London between 1539 and 1565. Moulton's name carried weight even as late as 1656, when it appeared on the title-page of a book called the 'Compleat Bone-Setter,' which was alleged to have been originally written by him, but contained little of his work.

[Tanner's Bibl. Brit.-Hib.; Ames's Typogr. Antiq.; Brit. Mus. Cat.] W. C-r.

MOULTRIE, JOHN (1799–1874), poet, born in Great Portland Street, London, on 30 Dec. 1799, at the house of his maternal grandmother, Mrs. Fendall, a woman of remarkable memory and critical faculty, was the eldest son of George Moultrie, rector of Cleobury Mortimer, Shropshire, by his wife Harriet (*d.* 1867). His father was the son of John Moultrie of Charleston in South Carolina, who, as governor of East Florida, retained his allegiance to the British crown; while his better known brother, William, fought with much distinction on the side of independence (in an action which forms the subject of the last chapter in Thackeray's 'Virginians'), his memory being perpetuated by Fort Moultrie (cf. Appleton, *American Cycl.* iv. 446). The poet's great-grandfather, John, had emigrated from Scotland about 1733, up to which date the Moultries had owned and occupied Scafield Tower, on the coast of Fife, of which the ruins are still standing. After preliminary education at Ramsbury, Wiltshire, John was in 1811 sent to Eton on the foundation; Dr. Keate, whose wrath he once excited by a stolen visit to Gray's monument at Stoke Poges, being then headmaster. Shelley was seven years Moultrie's senior, but among his friends were W. Sidney Walker [q. v.] (whose literary remains he subsequently edited in 1852), Lord Morpeth, Richard Okes, J. L. Petit, Henry Nelson and Edward Coleridge, and W. M. Praed. He composed with great facility in Latin, but was indifferent to school studies, distinguishing himself rather as a cricketer, an actor, and a school-wit and poet. He wrote for the 'College Magazine,' edited the subsequent 'Horæ Otiosæ,' and after leaving Eton contributed his best verses to the 'Etonian' during 1820–1. A sentimental poem written in October 1820, and entitled 'My Brother's Grave,' won general approval; while the young poet's treatment of the trying subject of 'Godiva' elicited warm praise from two critics so different and so eclectic as Gifford and Wordsworth. Both in the 'Etonian' and in Knight's 'Quarterly Magazine' his verses appeared under the pseudonym 'Gerard Montgomery.'

In October 1819 Moultrie entered as a commoner Trinity College, Cambridge, where he became intimate with Macaulay, Charles Austin, and others of their set. Proceeding M.A. in 1822, he began 'eating dinners' at the Middle Temple, but after acting for some time as tutor to the three sons of Lord Craven, he abjured the law and decided to take orders, his decision being assisted by an offer of the living of Rugby by Lord Craven in 1825. In 1825 he was also ordained, and on 28 July in that year he married Harriet Margaret Fergusson, sister of James Fergusson [q. v.], the historian of architecture. He had the parsonage at Rugby rebuilt, and went to reside there in 1828. Taking up his duties as rector of the parish almost simultaneously with Thomas Arnold's acceptance of the head-mastership of Rugby School, Moultrie and Arnold were thrown a good deal together and became firm friends. In an interesting communication to Derwent Coleridge, Moultrie's intimate friend, Bonamy Price [q. v.], describes the reciprocal influence of these 'two foci of a very small society.' 'Moultrie,' he adds, 'was always, without intending it, suggesting the ideal, not by direct allusion, but by raising the sensation that for him the outward practical working life had beneath it something which transcended and ennobled it.' In 1837 Moultrie issued a collection of his poems, which were favourably reviewed both in the 'Quarterly' and the 'Edinburgh.' In 1843 he published 'The Dream of Life; Lays of the English Church and other Poems.' The 'Dream of Life' is an autobiographical meditation in verse, which contains some interesting and perspicuous estimates of a number of contemporaries, including Macaulay, Henry Nelson Coleridge, Charles Austin, Chauncey Hare Townshend, and Charles Taylor. In 1850 appeared 'The Black Fence, a Lay of Modern Rome,' a vigorous denunciation of the aggressions of the papacy, and 'St. Mary, the Virgin and Wife,' both of which passed several editions. Moultrie also wrote a number of hymns, which treat of special subjects, and are consequently not so well known as they deserve to be. Most of them are in Benjamin Hall Kennedy's 'Hymnologia Christiana,' 1863.

In 1854 appeared his last volume of verse, 'Altars, Hearths, and Graves.' Among its contents is the well-written 'Three Minstrels,' giving an account of Moultrie's meeting, on different occasions, Wordsworth, Coleridge, and Tennyson. He died at Rugby on 26 Dec. 1874, and was buried in the parish church, to which an aisle was added in his memory. His wife had died in 1864, leaving three sons—Gerard (see below), George William, and John Fergusson—and four daughters.

Had Moultrie died shortly after the production of 'Godiva' and 'My Brother's Grave,' speculation might well have been busy as to the great poems which English literature had lost through his death. The passage concluding with the description of Lady Godiva's hair veiling her limbs,

> As clouds in the still firmament of June
> Shade the pale splendours of the midnight moon,

is well worthy of the admiring attention which Tennyson evidently bestowed upon it. Unfortunately, in his later writing much of the ideality and also much of the humour and pathos that were blended in his earlier work vanished, and Moultrie became the writer of much blank verse of a conscientious order, labouring under explanatory parentheses, and bearing a strong general resemblance to the least inspired portions of Wordsworth's 'Excursion.' The best of his later poems is the rhymed 'Three Sons,' which greatly affected Dr. Arnold. To Arnold two of Moultrie's best sonnets are dedicated. Another is addressed to Macaulay, who was grateful for a feeling allusion to the loss of his sister.

A complete edition of Moultrie's poems, with an exhaustive 'Memoir' by the Rev. Prebendary (Derwent) Coleridge, appeared in 2 vols. London, 1876. No portrait of Moultrie has been engraved.

The eldest son, Gerard Moultrie (1829–1885), devotional writer, was educated at Rugby School and at Exeter College, Oxford, whence he graduated B.A. in 1851. Taking orders, he became a master at Shrewsbury School. In 1869 he obtained the vicarage of

Southleigh, and in 1873 became warden of St. James's College, Southleigh. There he died on 25 April 1885. His publications include: 1. 'The Primer set forth at large for the use of the Faithful in Family and Private Prayer,' 1864. 2. 'Hymns and Lyrics for the Seasons and Saints' Days of the Church,' 1867. 3. 'The Espousals of St. Dorothea and other Verses,' 1870. 4. 'Cantica Sanctorum, or Hymns for the Black Letter Saints' Days in the English and Scottish Calendars, to which are added a few Hymns for special occasions,' 1880. Gerard Moultrie's hymns are less spontaneous than those of his father, but are scholarly and carefully studied in form. His translation of the 'Rhythms of St. Bernard de Morlaix' is specially praised by John Mason Neale among other critics.

The poet's eldest daughter, Mary Dunlop Moultrie (1837–1866), contributed some hymns to her brother's 'Hymns and Lyrics.' The second daughter, Margaret Harriet, married in 1863 the Rev. Offley H. Cary, grandson of the translator of Dante.

[Memoir as above; article in Macmillan's Mag. 1887, lvii. 123; Monthly Review, clxi. 309; Annual Register, 1874, p. 180; Guardian, 6 Jan. 1875; Athenæum, 1875, i. 20; Times, 30 Dec. 1874; Maxwell Lyte's Eton; Stanley's Life of Arnold, 1881, ii. 288; Notes and Queries, 1st ser. ix. 334, 5th ser. i. 246; Chambers's Encycl. of English Literature; Julian's Dictionary of Hymnology, pp. 772–3; Moir's Sketches of the Literature of the past Half-century; information kindly supplied by G. W. Moultrie, esq., of Manchester.] T. S.

MOUNDEFORD, THOMAS, M.D. (1550–1630), physician, fourth son of Osbert Moundeford and his wife Bridget, daughter of Sir John Spilman of Narburgh, Norfolk, was born in 1550 at Feltwell, Norfolk, where his father's monument is still to be seen in the parish church. He was educated at Eton and admitted a scholar of King's College, Cambridge, on 16 Aug. 1568. On 17 Aug. 1571 he was admitted a fellow, and graduated B.A. 1572 and M.A. 1576. On 18 July 1580 he diverted to the study of medicine. From 1580 to 1583 he was bursar of King's College and left the college in August 1583. He married soon after Mary Hill, daughter of Richard Hill, mercer, of Milk Street, London, but continued to reside in Cambridge till he had graduated M.D. He then moved to London, and 9 April 1593 was a licentiate of the College of Physicians, and 29 Jan. 1594 a fellow. He lived in Milk Street in the city of London. He was seven times a censor of the College of Physicians, was treasurer in 1608, and president 1612, 1613, 1614, 1619, 1621, 1622, and 1623. He published in 1622 a small book entitled 'Vir Bonus,' dedicated to James I, to John, bishop of Lincoln, and to four judges, Sir James Lee, Sir Julius Cæsar, Sir Henry Hobart, and Sir Laurence Tanfield. This large legal acquaintance was due to the fact that his daughter Bridget had, in 1606, married Sir John Bramston, afterwards, in 1635, chief justice of the king's bench. The book is divided into four parts, 'Temperantia,' 'Prudentia,' 'Justicia,' and 'Fortitudo.' He praises the king, denounces smoking, alludes to the 'Basilicon Doron,' and shows that he was well read in Cicero, Tertullian, the Greek testament, and the Latin bible, and expresses admiration of Beza. The whole is a summary of what experience had taught him of the conduct of life. He became blind and died in 1630 in Sir John Bramston's house in Philip Lane, London. He was buried in the church of St. Mary Magdalen, Milk Street, which was burnt in the great fire. His wife died in her ninety-fourth year, in 1656, in the house in which they had lived together in Milk Street. He had two sons: Osbert, admitted a scholar of King's College, Cambridge, on 25 Aug. 1601, aged 16; and Richard, admitted a scholar of the same college on 25 Aug. 1603. Both died before their father, and their epitaph, in English verse, is given in Stow's 'London.' It was in the church of St. Mary Magdalen. He had also two daughters, Bridget, above mentioned, and Katharine, who married Christopher Rander of Burton in Lincolnshire.

[Munk's Coll. of Phys. i. 103; Blomefield's Essay towards a Topographical History of the County of Norfolk, 1805, ii. 187; Autobiography of Sir John Bramston (Camden Soc.), 1845; extracts from the original Protocollum Book of King's College, Cambridge, kindly made by A. Tilley, fellow of the college; Works.] N. M.

MOUNSEY, MESSENGER (1693–1788), physician. [See Monsey.]

MOUNSLOW, Baron Littleton of. [See Littleton, Sir Edward, 1589–1645.]

MOUNSTEVEN, JOHN (1644–1706), politician, baptised at St. Mabyn, Cornwall, in 1644, was son of John Mounstephen or Mounsteven (*d.* 1672), who married at St. Mabyn in 1640 Elizabeth Tamlyn (*d.* 1664). He matriculated from Christ Church, Oxford, as pauper puer on 7 Dec. 1666, and graduated B.A. in 1671. After this he repaired to London and became secretary to the Earl of Sunderland, who, on receiving the appointment of secretary of state to James II, made him the under-secretary. When Sunderland lost his office he discarded his secretary, an event to which Prior refers in his 'Epistle to Fleetwood Shepherd,' 1689, in the words,

Nor leave me now at six and seven
As Sunderland has left Mun Stephen.

In 1685 he purchased the estate of Lancarfe in Bodmin, Cornwall. He was one of the free burgesses of Bodmin in the charter of 27 March 1685; represented the Cornish burgh of Bossiney from 1685 to 1688, and that of West Looe from 1695 to 1701, 1705 to 1706. Afterwards he fell into a despondent state and cut his throat on 19 Dec. 1706, dying intestate and without issue. His name frequently occurs in the diary of Henry Sidney, afterwards Earl of Romney, and he was a friend of Thomas Cartwright, bishop of Chester (*Diary*, Camden Soc., 1843, pp. 62–74). There are letters by him in Blencowe's 'Diary, &c., of Henry Sidney,' i. 97–101, 252–5, 282–3, ii. 22–3, and in the British Museum Addit. MS. 28876.

[Maclean's Trigg Minor, i. 216, 262, 300; Foster's Alumni Oxon.; Luttrell's Brief. Hist. Relation, vi. 119; Courtney's Parl. Repr. of Cornwall, pp. 136–330.] W. P. C.

MOUNT, CHRISTOPHER (*d.* 1572), diplomatist. [See MONT.]

MOUNT, WILLIAM (1545–1602), master of the Savoy, born at Mortlake, Surrey, in 1545, was educated at Eton, whence he proceeded to King's College, Cambridge, of which he was admitted scholar on 3 Oct. 1563 and fellow on 4 Oct. 1566. He graduated B.A. in 1567, and resigned his fellowship between Christmas 1569 and Lady-day, 1570. Mount, who owed much to the patronage of Secretary Sir Thomas Smith and Lord Burghley (*Cal. State Papers*, Dom. 1547–80, pp. 294, 301), at first studied medicine, but subsequently took orders, and was appointed master of the Savoy in January 1593–4. He was also domestic chaplain to Lord Burghley. He proceeded D.D., but no record of the degree exists at Cambridge. He died in December 1602 (CHAMBERLAIN, *Letters*, Camd. Soc., p. 170).

Mount was author of: 1. 'Directions for making distilled Waters, Compound and Simple,' 1590, in Lansdowne MS. 65, art. 75 2. 'Description of the Ingredients of a certain Composition called Sage Water,' 1591, in Lansdowne MS. 68, art. 88. 3. 'Latin Verses prefixed to Matthias de L'Obel's "Balsami, Opobalsami, Carpobalsami, & Xylobalsami, cum suo Cortice, explanatio,"' 1598. L'Obel, who visited Mount in 1597, expresses his admiration of Mount's skill in making distilled waters (p. 20).

[Cooper's Athenæ Cantabr. ii. 271.] G. G.

MOUNTAGU. [See MONTAGU.]

MOUNTAGUE, WILLIAM (1773–1843), architect and surveyor, born in 1773, was pupil and for many years principal assistant to George Dance the younger [q. v.] On the resignation by the latter of the post of clerk of the works to the corporation of the city of London, Mountague was appointed to act in his place until 22 Feb. 1816, when he was definitely appointed to the post. He had in 1812 been made surveyor to the corporation improvement committee. During his surveyorship numerous improvements were made in the city, including new streets, additions to the Guildhall, Farringdon Market, &c. Mountague also had a large private practice as a surveyor. He died on 12 April 1843, aged 70, and was buried in the Bunhill Fields burial-ground.

MOUNTAGUE, FREDERICK WILLIAM (*d.* 1841), architect and surveyor, was only son and chief assistant to the above. He was engaged as surveyor on many metropolitan improvements, and also had a large private practice. While engaged on a survey on the estate of the Duke of Buckingham he was thrown from his gig and died on 2 Dec. 1841.

[Papworth's Dict. of Architecture; Redgrave's Dict. of Artists.] L. C.

MOUNTAIGNE or MOUNTAIN, GEORGE (1569–1628), archbishop of York. [See MONTAIGNE.]

MOUNTAIN, ARMINE SIMCOE HENRY (1797–1854), colonel, adjutant-general of the queen's forces in India, fifth son of Jacob Mountain [q. v.], first protestant bishop of Quebec, and Eliza Mildred Wale Kentish, of Little Bardfield Hall, Essex, was born at Quebec on 4 Feb. 1797. After five years under a tutor in England he returned to Canada in 1810, and studied under the direction of his eldest brother, George Jehoshaphat (afterwards bishop of Montreal and Quebec), until he received a commission as ensign in the 96th regiment on 20 July 1815. He joined his regiment in Ireland in November, and made friends of the Bishop of Meath (O'Beirne) and Maria Edgeworth. The latter wrote of him: 'If you were to cut Armine Mountain into a hundred pieces, every one of them would be a gentleman.' In the summer of 1817 he went to Brunswick and studied at the college there until, on 3 Dec. 1818, he was promoted lieutenant on half-pay. In 1819 he returned to England to see his parents, who were on a visit from Canada. During the next four years he travelled through Germany, France, Switzerland, and

Italy with his friend John Angerstein, becoming an accomplished linguist. On his return, through his interest with the Duke of York he was brought into the 52nd light infantry, and after spending a few months in England joined his regiment at Halifax, Nova Scotia, in the autumn of 1823. In 1824 he went on detachment duty to New Brunswick and Prince Edward Island, and in the spring of 1825 was hastily summoned to Quebec to see his father, but the bishop died some days before he arrived. Mountain brought his mother and sister to England in October. He purchased a company in the 76th regiment and was gazetted captain on 26 May 1825. Joining the regiment in Jersey in the spring of 1826, he won the friendship of the governor, Sir Colin Halkett, through whose influence and that of Sir Astley Cooper he obtained an unattached majority on 30 Dec. 1826.

For the next two years he was unemployed, and resided with his mother at Hemel Hempstead, Hertfordshire, amusing himself with translating some of Schiller's poems and in writing the life of the Emperor Adrian for the 'Encyclopædia Metropolitana.' In December 1828, through the influence of his friend Lord Dalhousie, he was brought into the 26th Cameronians, then stationed at Madras, as regimental major, and in the following May he sailed for India. He arrived at Fort George in September and remained in Madras until the autumn of 1830, when the regiment marched to Meerut, arriving in March 1831. In July Mountain visited Lord Dalhousie, then commander-in-chief in India, at Simla, and in October marched with him back to Meerut. While visiting Lord William Bentinck, the governor-general, at Delhi, Mountain accepted from his old friend Sir Colin Halkett, who had just been appointed commander-in-chief at Bombay, the appointment on his staff of military secretary, and arrived in Bombay on 21 March 1832. Owing to differences with the governor, Lord Clare, Sir Colin Halkett was recalled towards the end of the following year, and Lord William Bentinck, appreciating the discretion with which Mountain had acted, appointed him one of his aides-de-camp. In August 1834 he obtained leave to join a force assembled at Meerut to march to Shehkawattee under General Stevenson, and rejoined the governor-general at Calcutta at the end of December, after a journey of nearly four thousand miles. In March 1835 he left for England with Lord William, and spent the next two years at home. In July 1836 he declined the post of military secretary to Sir Samford Whittingham in the West Indies. In February 1838 he rejoined the Cameronians at Fort William, Calcutta.

In 1840 the China war broke out, and Mountain was appointed deputy adjutant-general to the land forces sent from India, first under the command of Colonel Burrell and afterwards under Sir Hugh Gough. He was present at all the chief engagements, including the capture of Tinghae on 5 July, and of the Bogue forts 26 Feb. 1841, at the attack on, and capitulation of, Canton 25 May, capture of Amoy 26 Aug., occupation of Chusan, 1 Oct., capture of Chin-hai 10 Oct, and of Ning Po 13 Oct., attack on Chapoo 18 May 1842, capture of Shanghai 19 June, of Chin Keang 21 July, and the demonstration before Nankin in August which led to the treaty of peace. At the attack on Chapoo Mountain was struck by three musket balls while making a gallant rush into a large building defended with great obstinacy by the enemy. He was made a C.B. for his services.

From China he returned to India early in 1843, took command of his regiment and brought it to England, arriving in June. For the next four years he commanded the regiment at various stations in the United Kingdom and Ireland. In June 1845 he received his promotion to colonel in the army on being appointed aide-de-camp to the queen for his services in China.

In August 1847 Lord Dalhousie, then governor-general of India, gave him the appointment of military secretary, and he arrived in India in January 1848, having exchanged into the 29th regiment. After the murder of Anderson and Vans Agnew at Mooltan, Mountain obtained leave to join his regiment to take part in the second Sikh war under his old chief, Lord Gough. He was made a brigadier-general, and his brigade was composed of his own regiment and the 13th and 30th native infantry. On the death of Colonel Cureton the post of adjutant-general was accepted by Mountain on the condition that he should retain his brigade until the approval of his nomination arrived from home. He took a prominent part in the battle of Chillianwalla on 13 Jan. 1849. Lord Gough in his despatch says: 'The left brigade, under Brigadier Mountain, advanced under a heavy fire upon the enemy's guns in a manner that did credit to the brigadier and his gallant brigade, which came first into action and suffered severely.' He also took part in the battle of Guzerat on 21 Feb., and was afterwards appointed to command the Bengal division of the force under Sir Walter Gilbert to pursue the

Sikhs. On the march, near Jelum, his left hand was seriously injured by a pistol in his holster, which accidentally went off as he was mounting his horse. The accident obliged him to give up his divisional command, and on the arrival of the confirmation of his appointment as adjutant-general he went to Simla in March 1849 to take up his duties.

In the winter of 1849–50 Mountain accompanied Sir Charles Napier, the commander-in-chief, to Peshawur. In November 1850 he met Sir William Gomm, the new commander-in-chief, at Agra, and although Mountain had been ailing since he had recovered from an attack of cholera he was able to go into camp with Gomm. During the summer of 1852 Mountain's health was bad. In November he again went into camp with the commander-in-chief, but at the end of January, after leaving Cawnpore, he became very ill and died at Futtyghur after a few days' illness, attended by his wife, on 8 Feb. 1854, in a house belonging to the Maharajah Duleep Singh, who, with the commander-in-chief, the headquarters' staff, and all the troops, attended the funeral. A monument to his memory was erected by the commander-in-chief and the headquarters' staff in the cemetery at Futtyghur. A memorial brass tablet was placed by his widow in Simla Church, and a memorial window in a church in Quebec.

Mountain was twice married—first, in June 1837, to Jane O'Beirne (*d.* 1838), granddaughter of the Bishop of Meath; secondly, in February 1845, to Charlotte Anna, eldest daughter of Colonel T. Dundas of Fingask, who survived him and married Sir John Henry Lefroy [q. v.] A coloured crayon, done in India in 1853, was in the possession of Lady Lefroy.

[War Office Records; Memoirs and Letters of the late Colonel Armine S. H. Mountain, C.B., edited by Mrs. A. S. H. Mountain, 8vo, London, 1857; Despatches.] R. H. V.

MOUNTAIN, DIDYMUS, alleged writer on gardening, was the pseudonym under which was published in 1577 a valuable treatise on ornamental gardening by Thomas Hill (*fl.* 1590) [q. v.] The work assigned to the pseudonymous Mountain was entitled 'The Gardener's Labyrinth. Containing a Discourse of the Gardener's Life in the yearly Travels to be bestowed on his Plot of Earth, for the Use of a Garden; with Instructions for the choise of Seedes, apt Times for Sowing, Setting, Planting, and Watering, and Vessels and Instruments serving to that Use and Purpose: wherein are set forth divers Herbes, Knots, and Mazes, cunningly handled for the beautifying of Gardens; also the Physicke Benefit of each Herb, Plant, and Flowre, with the Vertues of the distilled Waters of every of them, as by the Sequel may further appeare, gathered out of the best approved Writers of Gardening, Husbandrie, and Phisicke, by Didymus Mountain,' London, by Henry Bynneman, 1577, 4to (in 2 parts). A dedication addressed to Lord Burghley is signed by Henry Dethicke, who states there that the author had recently died. Edmund Southerne, in his 'Treatise concerning the right use and ordering of Bees,' 1593 (B_4), describes the book as the work of Thomas Hill. Woodcut illustrations of much practical interest diversify the text. On p. 53 appears a curious plate, entitled 'Maner of watering with a pumpe in a tubbe.' Other editions are dated 1578, 1586 (by John Wolfe), 1594 (by Adam Islip), 1608 (by Henry Ballard), 1652, and 1656.

Hill had already published in 1567 'The Profitable Art of Gardening;' 'The Gardener's Labyrinth,' although different in plan, deals in greater detail with some of the topics already discussed in the earlier treatise.

[Brit. Mus. Addit. MS. 24490, p. 410; Samuel Felton's Gardeners' Portraits; Brydges's Restituta, i. 129; Notes and Queries, 2nd ser. xii. 85; Brit. Mus. Cat.; and see art. Hill, Thomas.] S. L.

MOUNTAIN, GEORGE JEHOSHAPHAT (1789–1863), protestant bishop of Quebec, second son of Jacob Mountain [q. v.], was born in Norwich on 27 July 1789, and was brought up in Quebec. Returning to England at the age of sixteen, he studied under private tutors until he matriculated from Trinity College, Cambridge, graduating B.A. in 1810, and D.D. in 1819. He removed again to Canada in 1811, and, becoming secretary to his father, was ordained deacon in 1812 and priest in 1816, at the same time being appointed evening lecturer in Quebec Cathedral. He was rector of Fredericton, New Brunswick, from 1814 to 1817, when he returned to Quebec as rector of that parish and bishop's official. In 1821 he became archdeacon of Lower Canada. On 14 Feb. 1836 he was consecrated, at Lambeth, bishop of Montreal, as coadjutor to Dr. Charles James Stewart, bishop of Quebec. Dr. Stewart shortly afterwards proceeded to England, and the charge of the entire diocese was under Mountain's care until 1839, when Upper Canada was made a separate see. It was through his earnest exertions that Rupert's Land was also, in 1849, erected into an episcopal see. He continued to have the sole charge of Lower Canada until 1850, when he secured the constitution of the diocese of Montreal, he himself retaining the diocese of Quebec, by far the poorer and more laborious of the two. During the greater part of his ministerial career he had to perform long, tedious, and oftentimes dangerous journeys into the interior of a wild and unsettled country, paying frequent visits to the north-west territory, the eastern townships, the Magdalen Islands, and the shores of Labrador; also to Rupert's Land, some three thousand six hundred miles, in an Indian canoe. He came to England in 1853 to confer with Dr. William Grant Broughton [q. v.], the metropolitan of Australasia, on the subject of synodical action in colonial churches, and he received the degree of D.C.L. at Oxford. The greatest of his works was the establishment in 1845 of the Lower Canadian Church University, Bishop's College, Lennoxville, for the education of clergymen. Mountain was a learned theologian, an elegant scholar, and powerful preacher. He died at Bardfield, Quebec, on 6 Jan. 1863.

Besides many single sermons, charges, and pamphlets, Mountain wrote: 1. 'The Journal of the Bishop of Montreal during a Visit to the Church Missionary Society's North-West American Mission,' 1845; 2nd edit. 1849. 2. 'Songs of the Wilderness; being a Collection of Poems,' 1846. 3. 'Journal of a Visitation in a Portion of the Diocese, by the Lord Bishop of Montreal,' 1847. 4. 'Sermons published at the Request of the Synod of the Diocese,' 1865.

[Armine W. Mountain's Memoir of G. J. Mountain, late Bishop of Quebec, 1866, with portrait; Morgan's Bibliotheca Canadensis, 1867, pp. 284–7; Appleton's American Biography, 1888, iv. 447–8, with portrait; Illustr. London News, 1862, xli. 576, 587; Gent. Mag. March 1863, pp. 388–9; Roe's First Hundred Years of the Diocese of Quebec; Taylor's The Last Three Bishops appointed by the Crown for the Anglican Church of Canada, 1870, pp. 131–86, with portrait.] G. C. B.

MOUNTAIN, JACOB (1749–1825), protestant bishop of Quebec, third son of Jacob Mountain of Thwaite Hall, Norfolk, by Ann, daughter of Jehoshaphat Postle of Wymondham, was born at Thwaite Hall on 30 Dec. 1749, and educated at Caius College, Cambridge, where he graduated B.A. 1774, M.A. 1777, and D.D. 1793. In 1779 he was elected a fellow of his college, and, after holding the living of St. Andrew, Norwich, was presented to the vicarages of Holbeach, Lincolnshire, and Buckden, Huntingdonshire (which he held together), and on 1 June 1788 was installed Castor prebendary in Lincoln Cathedral. These preferments he owed to the friendship of William Pitt, who also, on Dr. Tomline's recommendation, procured for him the appointment of the first Anglican bishop of Quebec. He was consecrated at Lambeth Palace on 7 July 1793. At that time there were only nine clergymen of the church of England in Canada—at his death there were sixty-one. During the succeeding thirty years Mountain raised the church to a flourishing condition (cf. Dr. Henry Roe, *Story of the First Hundred Years of the Diocese of Quebec*). He promoted missions and the erection of churches in all populous places. These he visited regularly, even when suffering from age and infirmities. The cathedral church at Quebec, which contains a monument to his memory, was erected under his auspices. He died at Marchmont House, Quebec, 16 June 1825. He married a daughter of John Kentish of Bardfield Hall, Essex, and left, with two daughters, five sons, of whom George Jehoshaphat Mountain and Armine Simcoe Mountain are separately noticed.

Mountain published 'Poetical Reveries,' 1777, besides separate sermons and charges.

[Appleton's American Biog. 1888, iv. 447; Bibliotheca Canadensis, 1867, p. 287; Gent. Mag. August 1825, p. 177; Quebec Gazette, June 1825; Church Times, 1 Sept. 1893.] G. C. B.

MOUNTAIN, Mrs. ROSOMAN (1768?–1841), vocalist and actress, was born in London about 1768. Her parents, named Wilkinson, were circus performers, and they appear to have named their child after one of the proprietors of Sadler's Wells. A brother, and Isabella, another member of the Wilkinson family, besides wire-dancing, played the musical glasses, the latter at Sadler's Wells about 1762. Charles Dibdin prepared Rosoman for the stage, and she seems to have made a few unimportant appearances at the Haymarket in 1782. On 4 Nov. of that year she achieved some success at the Royal Circus (afterwards the Surrey Theatre) in a burletta, 'Mount Parnassus,' in which she acted with other of Dibdin's pupils. 'Miss Decamp, Mrs. Mountain, and Mrs. Bland,' writes Charles Dibdin, 'are deservedly favourites as singers, merely because I took care they should be taught nothing more than correctness, expression, and an unaffected pronunciation of the words; the infallible and only way to perfect a singer' (*Professional Life*). The performances were considered marvellous; they continued, under the generic title 'The Fairy World,' for several years, and little Miss Wilkinson had a prominent part with a good salary until January 1784. She then travelled with her parents, arriving before the end of the year at Hull, where she called upon Tate Wilkinson, who was no relative, and succeeded in obtaining a hearing in public on 19 Nov. 1784 as Patty in the 'Maid of the Mill,' and on 3 Dec. as Rosetta in 'Love in a Village.' Tate Wilkinson soon gave her a regular engagement. She played Stella in 'Robin Hood,' and, for her benefit on 31 Dec., Clarissa in 'Lionel and Clarissa,' when Tate Wilkinson played Oldboy, and Mrs. Jordan generously came forward to play Lionel. The popular 'Lecture on Heads' by G. A. Stevens was part of Miss Wilkinson's early repertory. Her performances at York, Leeds, Liverpool, and Doncaster gained for her fresh laurels; she improved nightly, and when she accepted a lucrative engagement at Covent Garden, the manager deplored her loss as irreparable.

On 4 Oct. 1786 Miss Wilkinson made her London début as Fidelia in the 'Foundling' and Leonora in the 'Padlock.' Her performance was widely praised. The pretty regularity of her features and the simplicity of their expression, with her neat figure (judged by Wilkinson to be too *petite* for characters of importance), won general approval, while her voice, her manifest musical ability, and her animation of manner lifted her above the rank of ordinary stage-singers. The critics recommended her for the parts once taken by Mrs. Stephen Kemble, but the Covent Garden managers employed her chiefly in musical pieces, where she was heard at her best, and otherwise kept her somewhat in the background. In 1787 she married John Mountain the violinist, whom she had first met at Liverpool. The son of a Dublin musician (KELLY), he played in the Anacreontic quartet, the Philharmonic Society's orchestra, and elsewhere; and led at the Fantoccini Theatre in Savile Row, 1791, at Covent Garden, 1794 (POHL), and at the Vauxhall Gardens. A son was born in 1791 (*Gent. Mag.*)

Mrs. Mountain still remained at Covent Garden, and her parts included Norah, 'Poor Soldier;' Maria, 'Love and War;' Aurelia, 'Such Things are,' in 1787; Luciana, 'Comedy of Errors;' Harriet, 'Miser;' Pastoral Nymph, 'Comus;' Louisa, 'Duenna;' Clorinda, also Annette, 'Robin Hood;' Selima, 'Nunnery;' Louisa, 'Deserter;' Peggy, 'Marian;' Lucinda, 'Love in a Village;' Dorinda, 'Beaux' Stratagem;' Rosa, 'Fontainebleau;' Grace, 'Poor Vulcan;' Semira, 'Artaxerxes;' Jessica, 'Merchant of Venice;' Narcissa, 'Inkle and Yarico;' Clarissa, 'All in the Wrong,' in 1788; Rose, 'Rose and Colin;' Maria, 'Maid of the Oaks;' Victoria, 'Castle of Andalusia;' Jenny, 'Highland Reel;' Huncamunca, 'Tom Thumb;' Theodosia, 'Maid of the Mill,' in 1789; Constantia, 'Man of the World;' Isabinda, 'Busybody;' Nelly, 'Magician no Conjuror,' from 1790 to 1792. In 1793 'she looked beautiful as Mary in [O'Keeffe's] "Sprigs of Laurel"' (O'KEEFFE, *Recollections*). Between that year and 1795 she played Maria, 'World in a Village;' Ellen Woodbine, 'Netley Abbey;' Clara Sedley, 'The Rage;' Louisa Bowers, 'Arrived at Portsmouth;' Constantia, 'Mysteries of the Castle.' Between 1795 and 1798 she appeared as Shelah, 'Lad of the Hills;' Venus, 'Olympus in an Uproar;' Isabel, 'Italian Villagers;' Miss Sidney, 'Secrets worth knowing;' and Clara, 'Devil of a Lover.'

In 1798 Mrs. Mountain finally severed her connection with Covent Garden Theatre, after a series of disagreements with the manager (cf. PARKE, *Musical Memoirs*, i. 109). For a year or two she retired from the London stage, studying under Rauzzini at Bath, and visiting Ireland and the provinces. Panormo, Mountain's pupil, accompanied her on the piano. During her provincial tours of a later date she performed alone a piece of recitations and songs, written by Cherry for her, and called 'The Lyric Novelist.'

A short summer engagement at the Haymarket in 1800 added little to her repertory (Quashee's wife in 'Obi,' Leonora in 'What a Blunder,' and Lucy in 'Review'); but on 6 Oct. of the same year Mrs. Mountain sang for the first time at Drury Lane as Polly in the 'Beggar's Opera,' 'bursting upon London like a new character, having made such wonderful advancement in her profession.... She had always been a very interesting singer, a good actress, and a pretty woman; but she now ranked among the first-rate on the stage when considered as a vocal performer, and had arrived almost at the very summit of her profession in . . . oratorio singing' (C. H. WILSON). Some of the later parts she undertook at Drury Lane between 1800 and 1809 were: Jennet, 'Virginia;' Cicely, the 'Veteran Tar;' Marianne, 'Deaf and Dumb;' Orilla, 'Adelmorn;' Antonia, 'Gipsy Prince;' Daphne, 'Midas;' Frederika, 'Hero of the North;' Eugenia, 'Wife of two Husbands;' Rosa, 'The Dart;' Belinda, 'Soldier's Return;' Clotilde, 'Youth, Love, and Folly;' Celinda, 'Travellers;' Lady Gayland, 'False Alarms;' Carline, 'Young Hussar;' Leila, 'Kaïs,' with Braham; Zelma, 'Jew of Mogadore;' Lady Northland, 'Fortune-teller;' and Rachel, 'Circassian Bride.' At the

Lyceum, between 1809 and 1811 she played Juliana, 'Up all Night;' Adelnai, 'Russian Impostor;' Annette, 'Safe and Sound;' Lauretta, Bishop's 'Maniac;' Emily, 'Beehive;' Lodina, 'Americans;' Miss Selwyn, 'M.P.' She reappeared at the new Drury Lane house in 1813 as Cecilia in 'Who's to have her?' but was greatly hampered by ill-health. For a few nights subsequently she appeared at the Surrey Theatre.

Mrs. Mountain took her farewell of the stage at the King's Theatre on 4 May 1815, when the 'Cabinet' (Mrs. Mountain as Orlando), the 'Review,' and a ballet, &c., were given, before a house crowded to excess. She died at Hammersmith on 3 July 1841, aged about 73. Her husband survived her.

Among portraits of Mrs. Mountain are: 1. A half-length, engraved by Ridley, published by T. Bellamy at the 'Monthly Mirror' office, September 1797. 2. As Fidelia, after De Wilde, by Trotter. 3. As Matilda, after De Wilde, by Schiavonetti, published August 1806 by J. Cawthorn. 4. Bust engraved by E. Makenzie, from original drawing by Deighton. 5. Half-length, with guitar, by Buck, engraved in tinted chalk and stipple by T. Cheesman, published by W. Holland, October 1804. 6. Half-length by Masquerier, mezzotint by C. Turner, published January 1804 by C. Turner.

[Percival's Collection in British Museum relating to Sadler's Wells, vols. i. iii.; Thespian Dict.; Public Advertiser, 1782–6, passim; Dibdin's Professional Life, p. 113; Miles's Life of Grimaldi, p. 16; Tate Wilkinson's Wandering Patentee, ii. 174 et seq.; Gent. Mag. 1841, pt. ii. p. 325; Morning Chron. 5 Oct. 1786; Kelly's Reminiscences, i. ff. 8, 179; Pohl's Haydn in London, passim; O'Keeffe's Recollections, ii. 234; P. C. C. Administration Grant, 1841.]

L. M. M.

MOUNTAIN, THOMAS (*d.* 1561?), divine, son of Richard Mountain, servant to Henry VIII and Edward VI, proceeded M.A. at Cambridge, was admitted on 29 Oct. 1545 to the rectory of Milton-next-Gravesend, and on 29 Dec. 1550 to that of St. Michael Tower Royal, or Whittington College, in Rio Lane. He was at Cambridge with Northumberland in 1553, an active partisan of the duke, and on 11 Oct. was summoned before Gardiner for celebrating communion in two kinds; he was also charged with treason as having been 'in the field with Northumberland against the queen' (*Harl. MS.* 425, ff. 106–117). The following March he was cited to appear at Bow Church before the vicar-general for being married. He was imprisoned in the Marshalsea, and removed thence to stand his trial for treason at Cambridge; but no one appeared against him, and Mountain returned to London. He subsequently fled to Colchester, and thence to Antwerp, where he taught a school, removing to Duisburg near the Rhine after a year and a half. On the accession of Elizabeth he returned to England, and died apparently in 1561, possessed of the rectory of St. Pancras, Soper Lane, London.

Mountain left a circumstantial account of his troubles extant in Harl. MS. 425, ff. 106–117; copious extracts from it are incorporated in Strype's 'Ecclesiastical Memorials,' Froude's 'History of England,' v. 277–8, and Wordsworth's 'Ecclesiastical Biography,' iii. 285–314.

[Harl. MS. 425, ff. 106–17; Strype's Eccles. Memorials, and Cranmer, passim; Foxe's Acts and Monuments; Newcourt's Repertorium, i. 494, 519; Cooper's Athenæ Cantabr. i. 213, 553.]

A. F. P.

MOUNT ALEXANDER, first Earl of. [See Montgomery, Hugh, 1623?–1663.]

MOUNTCASHEL, Viscount. [See MacCarthy, Justin, *d.* 1694.]

MOUNT-EDGCUMBE, Earls of. [See Edgcumbe, George, first Earl, 1721–1795; Edgcumbe, Richard, second Earl, 1764–1839.]

MOUNTENEY or **MOUNTNEY, RICHARD** (1707–1768), Irish judge and classical scholar, son of Richard Mounteney, an officer in the customs house, by Maria, daughter of John Carey, esq., was born at Putney, Surrey, in 1707, and educated at Eton School. He was elected in 1725 to King's College, Cambridge, proved himself a good classical scholar, and became a fellow. He graduated B.A. in 1729, and M.A. in 1735 (*Graduati Cantabr.* 1823, p. 333). Among his intimate friends at the university were Sneyd Davies [q. v.] and Sir Edward Walpole. He was called to the bar at the Inner Temple, and by the influence of Sir Robert Walpole, to whom he had dedicated his edition of some of the orations of Demosthenes, he was appointed in 1737 one of the barons of the exchequer in Ireland. He was one of the judges who presided at the famous trial between James Annesley [q. v.] and Richard, earl of Anglesey, in 1743, and 'made a most respectable figure.' He died on 3 March 1768 at Belturbet, co. Cavan, while on circuit.

His first wife Margaret was buried at Donnybrook, near Dublin, on 8 April 1756, and his second marriage with the Dowager-countess of Mount Alexander (i.e. Manoah, widow of Thomas Montgomery, fifth earl and daughter of one Delacherois of Lisburn) was announced in Sleater's 'Public Gazetteer' on 6 Oct. 1759.

His works are: 1. 'Demosthenis selectæ Orationes (Philippica I) et tres Olynthiacæ orationes. Ad codices MSS. recensuit, textum, scholiasten, et versionem plurimis in locis castigavit, notis insuper illustravit Ricardus Mounteney,' Cambridge (University Press), 1731, 8vo; 2nd edit. London, 1748, 8vo; 3rd edit. Eton, 1755, 8vo (very incorrectly printed); other editions, London and Eton, 1764 and 1771, London, 1778, 1785, 1791, 1806, 1811, 1826, 1827. With reference to the second edition there appeared 'Baron Mountenay's celebrated Dedication of the select Orations of Demosthenes to the late Sir Robert Walpole, Bart. of Ministerial Memory, done into plain English, and illustrated with Notes and Comments, and dedicated to Trinity College, Dublin. By Æschines the third,' Dublin printed, London reprinted 1748, 8vo. 2. 'Observations on the probable Issue of the Congress' [i. e. of Aix-la-Chapelle], London, 1748, 8vo.

A fine portrait of Mounteney by Hogarth was in 1864 in the possession of the Rev. John Mounteney Jephson, who was maternally descended from him.

[Addit. MS. 5876, f. 226*b*; Brüggemann's View of English Editions of Greek and Latin Authors, p. 161; Gent. Mag. 1768 p. 198, 1781 p. 404; Harwood's Alumni Eton. p. 315; Lowndes's Bibl. Man. (Bohn), p. 627; Nichols's Illustr. Lit. i. 514, 558; Nichols's Lit. Anecd. ii. 192, iii. 106, vii. 279, x. 633; Notes and Queries, 2nd ser. xii. 170, 254, 526, 3rd ser. vi. 89, 235; Scots Mag. 1768, p. 223; Watt's Bibl. Brit.] T. C.

MOUNTFORT, Mrs. **SUSANNA** (1667?–1703), actress. [See VERBRUGGEN.]

MOUNTFORT, WILLIAM (1664?–1692), actor and dramatist, the son of Captain Mountfort, a gentleman of good family in Staffordshire, joined while a youth the Dorset Garden company, carrying out as the boy an original character in Leonard's 'Counterfeits,' licensed 29 Aug. 1678. His name then and for some time subsequently appears as young Mumford. He is next heard of in 1680 as the original Jock the Barber's Boy in the 'Revenge, or a Match at Newgate,' an alteration of Marston's 'Dutch Courtezan,' ascribed to Mrs. Behn. After the union of the two companies in 1682, Mountfort, now, according to Downes, 'grown up to the maturity' of a good actor, was at the Theatre Royal the first Alphonso Corso in the 'Duke of Guise' of Dryden and Lee. In 1684 he played Nonsense in a revival of Brome's 'Northern Lass,' and Metellus Cimber in 'Julius Cæsar,' and was, at Dorset Garden, both houses being under the same management. Heartwell in the first production of Ravenscroft's 'Dame Dobson, or the Cunning Woman.' In 1685 he greatly augmented his reputation by his 'creation' of the part of Sir Courtly Nice in Crowne's play of the same name, and in 1686 seems to have played with much success Tallboy in Brome's 'Jovial Crew.' By license dated 2 July 1686, he married at St. Giles-in-the-Fields, at the age of twenty-two, Mrs. Susanna Peircivall or Perceval [see VERBRUGGEN, MRS.], the daughter of an actor who joined the company in 1673 (cf. CHESTER, *Marriage Licenses*, ed. Foster, p. 950).

In Mrs. Behn's 'Emperor of the Moon,' acted in 1687, Mountfort was the original Don Charmante, and he also played Pymero in a new adaptation by Tate of Fletcher's 'Island Princess.' To the same year may presumably be assigned the production of Mountfort's tragedy, 'The Injur'd Lovers, or the Ambitious Father,' 4to, 1688. Genest assigns it to 1688, and puts Mountfort's version of Faustus before it. The opening lines of the prologue, spoken by Mountfort, are:

Jo Haynes's Fate is now become my Share,
For I'm a Poet, Marry'd, and a Player,

and subsequently speaks of this play as his first-begotten. His marriage and his appearance as poet may accordingly be supposed to be equally recent. In this he took the part of Dorenalus, a son of the ambitious father, Ghinotto, and in love with the Princess Oryala. It is a turgid piece, in one or two scenes of which the author imitates Marlowe, and, in spite of Mountfort's protestation in his prologue, appears to have been damned. The 'Life and Death of Dr. Faustus, with the Humours of Harlequin and Scaramouch,' London, 1697, was given at Dorset Garden Theatre and Lincoln's Inn Fields Theatre by Lee and Jevon. The actor first named died in 1688, so that the time of production is 1688 or before, while the words contained in it, 'My ears are as deaf to good counsel as French dragoons are to mercy,' are held to prove it later than the revocation of the edict of Nantes. Two-thirds of the play are from Marlowe, the poetry and much of the tragedy disappear, while songs and dances are introduced, together with much broadly comic business between Scaramouch, who is a servant of Faust, and Harlequin. In 1688 Mountfort created the part of Young Belfond in Shadwell's 'Squire of Alsatia,' and Lyonel, described as a mad part with songs, in D'Urfey's 'Fool's Preferment, or the Three Dukes of Dunstable.' In 1689 he was the first Wildish in Shadwell's 'Bury Fair,' and Young Wealthy in Carlile's 'Fortune

Hunters,' in 1690 King Charles IX in Lee's 'Massacre of Paris,' Don Antonio in Dryden's 'Don Sebastian, King of Portugal,' Ricardo in Joseph Harris's 'Mistakes, or the False Report,' and Silvio in his own 'Successful Strangers,' announced as a tragicomedy, but in fact a comedy with serious interest, 4to, 1690, founded on a novel by Scarron. It is an improvement on his previous plays, and was well received. The preface to this is quasi-autobiographical, Mountfort saying that he is no scholar, and consequently incapable of stealing from Greek and Latin authors. He complained that the town was as unwilling to encourage a young author as the playhouse a young actor.

The year 1691, the busiest apparently of Mountfort's life, saw him as the original Menaphon in Powell's 'Treacherous Brothers,' Hormidas in Settle's 'Distressed Innocence,' Valentine in Southerne's 'Sir Anthony Love,' Sir William Rant in Shadwell's 'Scowrers,' Bussy d'Ambois in 'Bussy d'Ambois,' altered from Chapman by D'Urfey, Cesario in Powell's 'Alphonso, King of Naples,' and Jack Amorous in D'Urfey's 'Love for Money, or the Boarding School.' He was also the first Lord Montacute in his own 'King Edward the Third, with the Fall of Mortimer,' 4to, 1691, and Young Reveller in his 'Greenwich Park,' 4to, 1691. Both plays are included in his collected works. The latter, a clever and passably licentious comedy, obtained a great success. The former, revived in 1731, and republished by Wilkes in 1763, with a sarcastic dedication to Bute, is in part historical. Coxeter says that it was written by John Bancroft [q. v.], and given by him to Mountfort. Of this piece, and of 'Henry the Second, King of England, with the Death of Rosamond,' which also, though the dedication is signed William Mountfort, is assigned to Bancroft, the editor or publisher of 'Six Plays written by Mr. Mountfort,' London, 8vo, 1720, says that though 'not wholly composed by him, it is presumed he had at least a share in fitting them for the stage.' In 1692 Mountfort was the original Sir Philip Freewit in D'Urfey's 'Marriage-maker Hatcht,' Asdrubal in Crowne's 'Regulus,' Friendall in Southerne's 'Wives Excuse,' Cleanthes in Dryden's 'Cleomenes.' Mountfort was also seen as Raymond Mountchensey in the 'Merry Devil of Edmonton,' Macduff, Alexander, Castalio, Sparkish, and was excellent in Mrs. Behn's 'Rover.'

Mountfort was on intimate terms with Judge Jeffreys, with whom he was in the habit of staying. At an entertainment of the lord mayor and court of aldermen in 1685 Jeffreys called for Mountfort, an excellent mimic, to plead a feigned cause, in which he imitated well-known lawyers. Mountfort is said in the year previous to the fall of Jefreys to have abandoned the stage for a while to live with the judge. There is only one year, however, 1686, subsequent to 1684, in which he did not take some original character in London. On 9 Dec. 1692 Mountfort was stabbed in Howard Street, Strand, before his own door, in the back by Captain Richard Hill, a known ruffler and cutthroat, and died on the following day. Hill had pestered Mrs. Bracegirdle [q. v.], and had attributed her coldness to her affection for Mountfort. Attended by his friend Lord Mohun [see MOHUN, CHARLES, fourth BARON], he accordingly laid wait for the actor. A warning sent from Mrs. Bracegirdle through Mrs. Mountfort failed to reach Mountfort, who returning home was held in conversation by Mohun, while Hill, coming behind, struck him a heavy blow on the head with his left hand and, before time was given him to draw, ran him through with the right. Hill escaped, and Lord Mohun was tried, 31 Jan. 1692–3, and acquitted, fourteen lords finding him guilty and sixty-nine innocent. Mountfort was buried in St. Clement Danes. Bellchambers, in his edition of Colley Cibber's 'Apology,' maintains that Mountfort was slain in a fair duel with Hill.

Cibber bestows on Mountfort warm praise, says that he was tall, well-made, fair, and of agreeable aspect; that his voice was clear, full, and melodious, adding that in tragedy he was the most affecting lover within his (Cibber's) memory. Mountfort filled the stage by surpassing those near him in true masterly touches, had particular talent in the delivery of repartee, and was credited with remarkable variety, being, it is said, especially distinguished in fine gentlemen. Among the parts singled out for highest praise are Alexander, in which 'we saw the great, the tender, the penitent, the despairing, the transported, and the amiable in the highest perfection,' Sparkish, and Sir Courtly Nice. Of the last two parts, which descended to him, Cibber says: 'If I myself had any success in either of these characters, I must pay the debt I owe to his memory in confessing the advantages I received . . . from his acting them.' Wilks also owned to Chetwood that Mountfort was the only actor on whom he modelled himself. Mountfort wrote many prologues and epilogues (cf. *Poems on Affairs of State*, 1703, i. 238).

By his wife, subsequently Mrs. Verbruggen, he had two daughters, one of whom, Susanna, is first heard of, though she had acted before, at Lincoln's Inn Fields, 26 June 1704, playing, as Miss Mountfort, Damaris in Betterton's 'Amorous Widow.' On 16 Oct. 1704 Mrs. Mountfort, which name she subsequently bore, played Betty Frisque in Crowne's 'Country Wit,' and, 14 June 1705, made, as Betty in 'Sir Solomon Single,' her first appearance at Drury Lane, where she remained, playing, among other characters, Estifania, Ophelia, Aspatia in the 'Maid's Tragedy,' Florimel in 'Marriage à la Mode,' and Elvira in the 'Spanish Fryar.' She was the original Rose in Farquhar's 'Recruiting Officer,' and Flora in Johnson's 'Country Lasses.' She is not heard of subsequently to 1718, and is said, in the edition of her father's plays, to have lately quitted the stage. She lived with Barton Booth [q. v.], who quitted her on account, it is said, of her misconduct. After this, misfortune, including loss of intellect, befell her. She is said to have once eluded her attendants, gone to Drury Lane dressed as Ophelia on a night for which 'Hamlet' was announced, to have hidden herself until the mad scene, and then, rushing on the stage before the official representative of Ophelia, to have performed the scene to the amazement of performers and audience.

[Genest's Account of the English Stage; Colley Cibber's Apology, ed. Lowe; Biog. Dram.; Memoir prefixed to edition of Mountfort's plays; Life of Barton Booth by Theophilus Cibber. In Cibber's Lives of the Poets, iii. 40–7, appears the account generally received of Mountfort's death. Galt's Lives of the Players, Doran's Their Majesties' Servants, and Notes and Queries, 1st ser. ii. 516, 5th ser. viii. 231, have also been consulted.] J. K.

MOUNTGARRET, third Viscount. [See Butler, Richard, 1578–1651.]

MOUNTIER, THOMAS (*fl.* 1719–1733), vocalist, whose name may be of French origin, or a corruption of the English name Mouncher, was lay vicar, and from 1719 to 1732 preceptor of the choristers, of Chichester Cathedral (*Chapter Books*). Before finally exchanging the cathedral for the theatre Mountier was in correspondence with the dean and chapter of Chichester, who on 12 May 1732 declared Mountier's place as lay vicar vacant. It was not until August that he resigned the preceptorship of the choristers.

It appears that Mountier sang for the first time in London at J. C. Smith's concert in Lincoln's Inn Fields Theatre on 2 April 1731. An advertisement of a later date runs: 'At the request of great numbers of gentlemen and ladies, for the benefit of Thomas Mountier, the Chichester boy (who sang at Mr. Smith's concert at the theatre in L. I. F.), at the New Theatre in the Haymarket, on 6 May 1731, a concert. . . . To prevent the house being crowded, no persons will be admitted without tickets' (*Daily Journal*). Mountier was also announced to sing in Geminiani's winter series of weekly concerts at Hickford's (*Daily Post*, 15 Nov. 1731), and Smith's and Lowe's benefit concerts, on 22 and 27 March 1732, songs in Italian and English (*Daily Journal*).

On 17 May 1732, under Dr. Arne at the New Theatre in the Haymarket, Handel's 'Acis and Galatea' was first 'performed with all the grand choruses, machines, and other decorations . . . in a theatrical way' (*Daily Post*, 6 May), Mountier in the part of Acis, and Miss Arne as Galatea. The choruses had taken more than a year's practice (Fitzball). A second performance was announced for 19 May. Mountier was cast for the part of Phœbus, but sang that of Neptune, in Lampe's 'Britannia.' In 1733 he joined the Italian opera troupe, and sang as Adelberto in the revival of Handel's 'Ottone' (Grove).

[Information kindly supplied by Prebendary Bennett, Chichester; Fitzball's Thirty-five Years of a Dramatic Author's Life; Grove's Dict. ii. 377.] L. M. M.

MOUNTJOY, Viscount. [See Stewart, William, 1653–1692.]

MOUNTJOY, Barons. [See Blount, Walter, first Baron, *d.* 1474; Blount, William, fourth Baron, *d.* 1534; Blount, Charles, fifth Baron, *d.* 1545; Blount, Charles, eighth Baron, 1563–1606; Blount, Mountjoy, ninth Baron, 1597?–1665.]

MOUNT-MAURICE, HERVEY de (*fl.* 1169), invader of Ireland, whose name appears variously as Monte Mauricii, Monte Marisco, Monte Marecy, Montmarreis, Montmorenci, Mumoreci, and Momorci, may not unreasonably be held to have belonged to the same line as the Montmorencies of France (of this there is no conclusive proof, but see Du Chesne, *Histoire Généalogique de la Maison de Montmorency*, pp. 9, 53, 87, 92; Montmorency-Morrès, *Genealogical Memoir*, passim; *L'Art de Vérifier*, xii. 9, and other French genealogists; the forms of the name borne by Hervey and the French Montmorencies suggest a common stock, and Hervé was a christian name much used by the French house; in connection with this see

GIRALDUS CAMBRENSIS, *De rebus a se gestis*, ii. c. 2, where the canon, afterwards the dean, of Paris there mentioned, the son of the castellan 'de Monte Mauricii,' was Hervé, son of Matthieu 'de Montmorency;' compare DU CHESNE, u.s. pp. 97, 106, and *Preuves*, pp. 39, 55). Hervey is said by M. de Montmorency-Morrès to have been the son of a Robert FitzGeoffrey, lord of lands in Thorney and of Huntspill-Marreis, Somerset, by his wife Lucia, daughter of Alexander de Alneto, and to have been half-brother of Stephen, constable of Cardigan. This bit of genealogy has, however, been made up to fall in with the erroneous belief that Giraldus asserts that Hervey was the uncle of Robert FitzStephen, and may be dismissed at once. According to Du Chesne (u.s.), followed in 'L'Art de Vérifier les Dates' (u.s.), Hervey was the son of Bouchard IV de Montmorency, by Agnes, daughter of Raoul de Pontoise; he served Louis VI and Louis VII of France, and coming to England married Elizabeth, daughter of Robert de Beaumont (*d.* 1118) [q. v.], Count of Meulan, and widow of Gilbert de Clare (*d.* 1148), earl of Pembroke, which would make him stepfather of Earl Richard, called Strongbow [see CLARE, RICHARD DE, or RICHARD STRONGBOW, second EARL OF PEMBROKE AND STRIGUIL, *d.* 1176]. Hervey, however, was paternal uncle of Earl Richard (GIRALDUS, *Expugnatio Hibernica*, p. 230), and must therefore have been a son by a second marriage of Adeliza, daughter of Hugh, count of Clermont (WILLIAM OF JUMIÈGES, viii. 37), who married for her first husband Gilbert FitzRichard [see CLARE, GILBERT DE, *d.* 1115?], the father of Gilbert, earl of Pembroke (see a charter in *MS. Register of Thorney*, pt. iv. c. 35, f. 30, printed in *Monasticon*, ii. 601, where Hervey is described as brother of Gilbert and the other children of Adeliza and Gilbert FitzRichard, and pt. ix. c. 11, f. 9, where Adeliza is styled 'de Monte Moraci, domina de Deneford,' and is also styled 'domina de Deneford,' pt. iv. c. 10, f. 2 *b*; see also pt. iv. c. 8, f. 2). The father of Hervey was no doubt called 'de Monte Moraci,' or Mount Maurice, but nothing has been ascertained about him (it is impossible to accept M. de Montmorency-Morrès's Hervey, son of Geoffrey, lord of Thorney, as an historic person, while his theory that there were two Herveys, cousins-german, is a mere device to get out of the difficulty caused by his confusing together Earl Richard and Robert FitzStephen).

Hervey was in early life a gallant warrior ('olim Gallica militia strenuus,' *Expugnatio*, p. 328, translated by Hooker, he 'had good experience in the feats of war, after the manner used in France,' *Irish Historie*, p. 38. This passage was no doubt the ground of Du Chesne's assertion that he served Louis VI and Louis VII). He was a man of broken fortunes when he was sent by his nephew, Earl Richard, to Ireland with Robert FitzStephen in 1169 to report on affairs there to the earl. After the victory of these first invaders at Wexford their ally Dermot, king of Leinster, rewarded him with two cantreds of land on the coast between Wexford and Waterford, and he appears to have shared in Dermot's raids on Ossory and Offaly (*Song of Dermot and the Earl*, ll. 606, 749, 930). On the landing of Raymond FitzGerald [q.v.] at Dundunnolf, near Waterford, Hervey joined him, and shared in his victory over the people of Waterford and the chief, Donnell O'Phelan. Giraldus puts into his mouth a speech recommending the slaughter of seventy Waterford men who had been taken prisoners; but the Anglo-Norman poet of the Conquest gives a wholly different version of the event (*ib.* ll. 1474–89). He remained with Raymond in an entrenched position in Bannow Bay until they were reinforced on 23 Aug. by the arrival of Earl Richard, who was joined by Hervey. Raymond's mission to Henry II having failed [see under FITZGERALD, RAYMOND], Earl Richard sent Hervey to the king, probably in August 1171 (*Gesta Henrici II*, i. 24), to make his peace. On his return Hervey met the earl at Waterford, told him that Henry required his attendance, accompanied him to England, and at Newnham, Gloucestershire, was the means of arranging matters between him and the king. During Henry's visit to Ireland Hervey probably acted as the marshal of the royal army; for in his charter for the foundation of the convent of Dunbrothy, where his name is given as 'Hereveius de Monte Moricii,' he is described as 'marshal of the army of the king for Ireland, and seneschal of all the lands of Earl Richard' (*Chartularies of St. Mary's Abbey*, ii. 151). While Earl Richard was in Normandy in 1173 Hervey was left in command. On the earl's return he is said to have found the Irish ready to rebel, and the troops dissatisfied and clamouring that Raymond should command them; for Hervey is represented as having wasted the money that was due to them in action (*Expugnatio*, p. 308). The earl yielded to the demand of the soldiers, and gave Raymond the command, but shortly afterwards refused to appoint him constable of Leinster, and gave the office to Hervey. To the bad advice of Hervey Giraldus attributes the earl's disastrous expedition into Munster in 1174 (*ib.* p. 310; compare *Annals of the Four Masters*, sub an. iii. 15, 17). After the defeat at Thurles the earl was forced to shut himself up in Waterford; he sent for Raymond to come to his help, and appointed him constable in place of Hervey (the order of these events is uncertain; that adopted here, which is also followed in the article on Raymond Fitzgerald, is that of the 'Expugnatio;' the order followed in the 'Song of Dermot' is on the whole represented in the article on Richard de Clare, 'Strongbow;' see *Expugnatio*, p. 308 *n.* 2, and p. 310 *n.* 2). Hervey received from the earl a grant of O'Barthy, of which the present barony of Bargy, co. Wexford, forms a part, was outwardly reconciled to his rival Raymond, and married Nesta, daughter of Maurice Fitzgerald (*d.* 1176) [q. v.], and Raymond's first cousin. Nevertheless in 1175 he sent messages to the king, accusing Raymond of a design to make himself independent of the royal authority, and was evidently believed by Henry.

Hervey's power in Ireland was probably shaken by the death of his nephew, Earl Richard, in 1176, and we find him in England in 1177, when he witnessed a charter of Henry II at Oxford, at which date his lands between Wexford and Waterford were made to do service to Waterford, then held by William Fitz Aldhelm (*Gesta Henrici II*, i. 163, 164). In 1178 he made a grant of lands in present co. Wexford to the convent of Buildwas, Shropshire, for the foundation on them of a Cistercian house (the date is determined by the attestation of Felix, bishop of Ossory). These lands included Dunbrodiki, or Dunbrothy, in the barony of Shelburne, and there a few years later was founded the convent called 'de portu S. Mariæ.' In 1179 he became a monk of Christ Church, Canterbury (*Annals* ap. *Chartularies of St. Mary's Abbey*, ii. 304; Giraldus dates his retirement about 1183; see *Expugnatio*, p. 352), making a grant to that house of lands and churches in Ireland. Many of these have been identified (*Kilkenny Archæological Journal*, 1855, iii. 216); they were in 1245 transferred by the convent to the abbot of Tintern, co. Wexford, for 625 marks, and an annual rent of ten marks, with the obligation of maintaining a chaplain at St. Brendan's chapel at Bannow, to pray for the souls of Hervey and other benefactors (*Literæ Cantuar.* iii. Pref. xl. sq. 361, 362). Giraldus says that Hervey was not a better man after his retirement than he had been before. A Hervey, cellarer and chanter of Christ Church, was excommunicated by Archbishop Baldwin for his share in the great quarrel between the archbishop and the convent, and was alive in 1191 (*Epistolæ Cantuar.* ed. Stubbs, pp. 308, 312, 315, 333), but he could scarcely have been Hervey de Mount-Maurice, who is described as 'conversus et benefactor' in the records of his obit on 12 March (*MSS. Cott.* Nero C. ix. i. ff. 5, 6, Galba E. iii. 2, fol. 32). M. de Montmorency-Morrès asserts, apparently without any ground, that he died in 1205, and says that his nephews, Geoffrey [see under Marisco, Geoffrey de] and Richard, bishop of Leighlin, transported his body from Canterbury to Dunbrothy, where they erected a tomb of black Kilkenny marble to him in the conventual church. Of this tomb and the recumbent figure upon it he gives two engravings; it was overthrown in 1798, and has since perished (*Genealogical Memoir of Montmorency*, plates 1 and 2). Hervey left no legitimate children (*Expugnatio*, pp. 345, 409). He is described by Giraldus as a tall and handsome man, with blue and prominent eyes, and cheerful countenance; he was broad-chested, and had long hands and arms, and well-shaped legs and feet. Morally, Giraldus says he belied his appearance; he was extremely lustful, envious, and deceitful, a slanderer, untrustworthy, and changeable, more given to spite than to gallant deeds, and fonder of pleasure than of profitable enterprise (*ib.* pp. 327, 328). From this estimate and from other evil things that Giraldus says of Hervey large deductions should be made, for Giraldus wrote in the interest of his relatives, the Geraldines, and speaks violently of all who opposed them. As, then, Hervey was the rival and enemy of Raymond Fitzgerald, he and his doings are represented in the 'Expugnatio' in a most unfavourable light. Even Giraldus, however, allows that Hervey was one of the four principal conquerors of the Irish (*ib.* p. 409).

[The manuscript register of Thorney, lately acquired by the Cambridge Univ. Library, has been examined for the purposes of this article by Miss Mary Bateson, who has also rendered other valuable help. See Dugdale's Monasticon, ii. 601, 603, v. 362; Will. of Jumièges, viii. c. 37, ed. Duchesne; H. R. de Montmorency-Morrès's (Viscount Mountmorres) Genealogical Memoir of Montmorency, 1817, and Les Montmorency de France et d'Irlande, 1828, were written to advance a claim to honours, and are full of assumptions not apparently borne out by the proofs adduced in their support; Du Chesne's Histoire Généalogique de la Maison de Montmorency, pp. 9, 10, 87, 92, 93, 97, 106, Preuves, 39, 55 (1624); L'Art de Vérifier, xii. 9; the Montmorency pedigrees by Anselme and Desormeaux may be disregarded as far as they concern Hervey; Giraldus Cambr. Expug. Hibern. ap. Opp. v. 207–411; Song of Dermot and the Earl, Pref. and ll. 457, 606, 749, 1140, 1475–89, 1496, 3071, ed. Orpen, also to be found quoted as 'Regan' from earlier and less perfect editions of Michel and Wright; Gesta Hen. II, i. 24, 164 (Rolls Ser.); Gervase of Cant. i. 234 (Rolls Ser.); Chartularies of St. Mary's Abbey, Dublin, i. 79, ii. Pref. and pp. 98, 141, 143, 151, 158, 223 (Rolls Ser.); Literæ Cantuar. iii. Pref. and pp. 361, 362 (Rolls Ser.); Epp. Cantuar. ap. Memorials of Richard I, ii. 308, 312, 315, 333 (Rolls Ser.); Reg. Abbey St. Thomas, Dublin (Rolls Ser.), p. 370; MSS. Cott. Nero C. ix. i. ff. 5, 6, Galba E. iii. 2, fol. 32; Kilkenny Archæol. Society's Journal, 1855–6, iii. 216; Ware's Antiqq. pp. 68, 81, Annals, pp. 2, 4, 6, 14, 24; Gilbert's Viceroys of Ireland, pp. 15, 37, 44–5; Norgate's Angevin Kings, ii. 101, 112.] W. H.

MOUNTMORRES, second VISCOUNT. [See MORRES, HERVEY REDMOND, 1746?–1797.]

MOUNTNEY, RICHARD (1707–1768), Irish judge. [See MOUNTENEY.]

MOUNTNORRIS, first BARON. [See ANNESLEY, SIR FRANCIS, 1585–1660.]

MOUNTRATH, first EARL OF. [See COOTE, SIR CHARLES, *d.* 1661.]

MOUTRAY, JOHN (*d.* 1785), captain in the navy, was on 12 May 1744 promoted by Sir Chaloner Ogle in the West Indies to be lieutenant of the Orford. After serving in several different ships, mostly on the home station, without any opportunity of distinction, he was promoted on 16 Feb. 1757 to the command of the Thetis hospital ship attached to the fleet, which, in the latter part of the year, sailed for the Basque Roads under Sir Edward Hawke. She was afterwards attached to the fleet in the Mediterranean, and on 28 Dec. 1758 Moutray was advanced to post rank by Rear-admiral Brodrick, though he remained in command of the Thetis during the war. This irregular promotion was confirmed by the admiralty on 24 Jan. 1763. In 1769 Moutray commanded the Emerald for a short time, and in 1774 the Thames in the Mediterranean (cf. PLAYFAIR, *Scourge of Christendom*, p. 211). In the Warwick, in 1778, he convoyed the East India trade to St. Helena. He was then appointed for a few months to the Britannia, and in March 1779 to the Ramillies. In July 1780, with the Thetis and Southampton frigates in company, he sailed in convoy of a large fleet of merchant ships and transports for the East and West Indies and for North America. In view of the exceptional importance and value of this fleet, two other line-of-battle ships and a frigate were ordered to accompany it a hundred leagues westward from the Scilly Islands. On the way it fell in with the Channel fleet under Admiral Geary, who also kept it company with his whole force, till 112 leagues to the westward; from that point the Ramillies, with the Thetis and Southampton, was considered sufficient protection.

The miscalculation was extraordinary, for the combined Franco-Spanish fleet was enforcing the blockade of Gibraltar, and might be met with anywhere off Cape St. Vincent. At sunset on 8 Aug. some distant sail in the south were reported. Moutray thought it a matter of no importance, and ran on with a fresh northerly breeze. At midnight lights were seen ahead, and not till then did it occur to Moutray that it would be prudent to alter his course. He made the night signal to steer to the westward, but the merchant ships, never quick at attending to signals, on this occasion paid no attention at all. By daylight they were right in among the enemy's fleet and were almost all captured. A few only, with the men-of-war, managed to escape. The loss was extremely heavy. To the underwriters it was estimated at upwards of a million and a half sterling, exclusive of the stores and reinforcements for the West Indian fleet. Diplomatically, too, the results were serious; the court of Spain, which was already listening to secret negotiations at Madrid, conceived new hopes and would hear of no terms which did not include the surrender of Gibraltar (R. CUMBERLAND, *Memoirs*, ii. 44, 112). Moutray meantime pursued his way to Jamaica, where, by order of the admiralty, he was tried by court-martial on 13 Feb. 1781; he was pronounced to be 'reprehensible in his conduct for the loss of the convoy,' and sentenced to be dismissed from the command of the Ramillies. In deference to the widespread personal interest in the case, the publication of the minutes was specially sanctioned by a resolution of the court, and it was ordered 'that they be sent to England by the first conveyance and published accordingly.' Moutray had certainly not taken proper precautions, and the finding of the court was perfectly just, but much of the blame properly rested with the admiralty, who had neglected the warning of the similar disaster which was sustained in the same locality ninety years before [see ROOKE, SIR GEORGE].

It has been incorrectly stated that Moutray had no further employment under Lord Sandwich's administration (CHARNOCK, vi. 333). He was appointed to the Edgar on 2 March 1782, nearly three weeks before the fall of the ministry. In May he was moved into the Vengeance, one of the fleet under Lord Howe at the relief of Gibraltar and the rencounter off Cape Spartel in October. It was Moutray's solitary experience of a battle. In February 1783 (just before the peace) he was appointed, in place of Sir John Laforey [q. v.], resident commissioner of the navy at Antigua, a civil appointment held on half-pay and giving the holder no executive rank or authority. Notwithstanding this, on 29 Dec. 1784, Sir Richard Hughes [q. v.] directed Moutray to hoist a broad pennant in the absence of the flag and to exercise the functions of senior officer. Nelson, coming to Antigua shortly afterwards, refused to acknowledge Moutray's authority, which Moutray, on his part, did not insist on. The matter was referred to the admiralty, who replied that the appointment was abolished, and it was therefore unnecessary to lay down any rule (Nicolas, *Despatches and Letters of Lord Nelson*, i. 118 et seq.; Laughton, *Letters and Despatches of Lord Nelson*, pp. 29–31). Moutray was accordingly recalled; he died at Bath a few months later, 22 Nov. 1785, and was buried in the Abbey Church (*Gent. Mag.* 1785, ii. 1008, 1788, i. 189). His wife, who appears to have been many years younger than himself, was with him at Antigua, where she won the affectionate friendship of Nelson and Collingwood, both young captains on the station. This friendship continued through Nelson's life, and after Trafalgar Collingwood sent her an account of Nelson's death (Nicolas, vii. 238). She had one son, James, a lieutenant in the navy, who died of fever at the siege of Calvi in 1794 (*ib.* i. 486).

[Charnock's Biog. Nav. vi. 331; commission and warrant books and other documents in the Public Record Office.] J. K. L.

MOWBRAY, JOHN (I) de, eighth Baron Mowbray (1286–1322), was great-grandson of William de Mowbray, fourth baron [q. v.], and son of Roger (III) de Mowbray, seventh baron (1266–1298). The latter in 1282 had entailed his lordships of Thirsk, Kirkby-Malzeard, Burton-in-Lonsdale, Hovingham, Melton Mowbray, and Epworth, with the whole Isle of Axholme, upon the heirs of his body, with remainder to Henry de Lacy, earl of Lincoln, and his heirs; he was summoned to the Shrewsbury 'parliament' of 1283 which condemned David of Wales, and to the parliaments of 1294–6, and died at Ghent in 1297 (Dugdale, *Baronage*, i. 126; *Monast. Angl.* vi. 320; *Rep. on Dignity of a Peer*, App. pp. 54, 65, 71, 76–7; cf. Grainge, *Vale of Mowbray*, pp. 360–3). He was buried at Fountains Abbey, where his effigy is still preserved. John's mother was Roysia, sister of Gilbert, earl of Gloucester and Clare, who is strangely identified by Dugdale with the Earl Gilbert who died in 1230 (*Baronage*, i. 209; cf. *Monast. Angl.* vi. 320). The inclusion of the Lacys in the Mowbray entail lends some probability to the conjecture that she was a daughter of Richard, earl of Gloucester (*d.* 1262), and Maud, aunt of Henry de Lacy, earl of Lincoln.

John de Mowbray, who was born on 2 Nov. 1286, was a boy of eleven at his father's death, and Edward immediately granted his marriage to William de Brewes (Braose or Brewose), lord of Bramber and Gower, who married him in 1298 at Swansea to Alicia (or Alina), the elder of his two daughters (Dugdale, *Baronage*, i. 126, 421; *Calendarium Genealogicum*, p. 555; *Hist. MSS. Comm.* 4th Rep. p. 358). With the uneasy inheritance of Gower went Bramber and other Sussex manors.

He was very early called upon to perform the duties of a northern baron in the Scottish wars. In June 1301 he received a summons to attend Edward, prince of Wales, to Carlisle (*Rep. on Dignity of a Peer*, App. p. 138). Five years later he served throughout the last Scottish expedition of the old king, Edward I, who before starting gave him livery of his lands, though he was not yet of age, and dubbed him knight, with the Prince of Wales and some three hundred other young men of noble families, at Westminster on Whitsunday 22 May 1306 (Dugdale, *Baronage*, i. 126).

Returning after the king's death, Mowbray was summoned to Edward II's first parliament at Northampton in October 1307, and henceforward received a summons to all the parliaments of the reign down to that of July 1321 (*Rep. on Dignity of a Peer*, App. pp. 174, 308). After attending the king's coronation in the February following he was ordered to Scotland in August, a summons repeated every summer for the next three years (*ib.* pp. 177, 181, 192–3, 202, 207). In 1311 he came into possession of the lands of his grandmother, Maud, who had inherited the best part of the lands of her father, William de Beauchamp of Bedford, including Bedford Castle (Dugdale, *Baronage*, i. 126, 224).

In the first great crisis of the reign Mowbray was faithful to the king, possibly through jealousy of his neighbour, Henry de Percy, who had disputed his custody of the Forest of Galtres outside York (*Cal. of Close Rolls*, 1307–13, p. 514). As keeper of the county and city of York he was ordered on 31 July

1312 to arrest Percy for permitting the death of Gaveston, and, on 15 Aug., in conjunction with the sheriff, to take the city into the king's hands if necessary (*ib.* pp. 468, 477; *Fœdera*, iii. 173, Record ed.)

From 1314 the Scottish war again absorbed Mowbray's attention. There was not a summer from that year to 1319 that he was not called out to do service against the Scots (*Rep. on Dignity of a Peer*). It is not quite certain, however, that he was the John de Mowbray who was a warden of the Scottish marches in the year of Bannockburn, and one of four 'capitanei et custodes partium ultra Trentam' appointed in January 1315, on the recommendation of a meeting of northern barons at York (Dugdale, i. 126; *Letters from Northern Registers*, pp. 237, 247–8; *Registrum Palatinum Dunelmense*, ii. 1034). This may have been the Scottish John de Mowbray who was also lord of Bolton in Cumberland, and fought and negotiated against Bruce, meeting his death at last in the defeat of Balliol at Annan in December 1332 (*Rot. Parl.* i. 160, 163; *Chron. de Lanercost*, pp. 204, 270; *Chron. de Melsa*, ii. 367; *Fœdera*, ii. 474; cf. Walsingham, *Hist. Angl.* ii. 194–7).

In this year, 1315, Mowbray was reimbursed for the expense to which he had been put for the defence of Yorkshire when he was sheriff by a charge of five hundred marks on the revenues of Penrith and Sowerby-in-Tyndale (Dugdale, *Baronage*, i. 126). Next year he was ordered to array the commons of five Yorkshire wapentakes for the Scottish war, and in 1317 was appointed governor of Malton and Scarborough (*ib.*) But three years after this the *damnosa hæreditas* of his wife in Gower involved him in a dispute with the king's powerful favourites, the Despensers, which proved fatal to him and to many active sympathisers of greater political prominence. It appears that his father-in-law, William de Brewes, had at some date, of which we are not precisely informed, made a special grant of his lordship of Gower in the marches of Wales to Mowbray and his wife, who was his only child, and their heirs, with remainder to Humphrey de Bohun, earl of Hereford and lord of Brecon, the grandson of one of the coheiresses of an earlier William de Brewes (*ib.* pp. 182, 420; cf. *Cal. of Pat. Rolls*, 1327–30, p. 248). But the king's greedy favourite, Hugh le Despenser the younger, was desirous of adding Gower to his neighbouring lordship of Glamorgan, and when Mowbray entered into possession without the formality of a royal license, he insisted that the fief was thereby forfeited to the crown, and induced the king to order legal proceedings against Mowbray (Monk of Malmesbury in *Chronicles of Edward I and Edward II*, ii. 254–5). Hereford and the other great lords-marcher whose interests were threatened by Despenser upheld Mowbray's contention that the king's license had never been necessary in the marches. Despenser scoffed at the law and customs of the marches, and more than hinted that those who appealed to them were guilty of treason (*ib.*) The situation, which was strained in the October parliament of 1320, became acutely critical in the early months of 1321. The discontented barons withdrew to the marches, and on 30 Jan. the king issued writs to twenty-nine lords, including Mowbray, forbidding them to assemble together for political purposes (*Rep. on Dignity of a Peer*, App. p. 302). In March they entered and harried Glamorgan. The writer of the 'Annales Paulini' (*Chronicles of Edward I and Edward II*, i. 293) adds that before the final breach the Earl of Hereford persuaded the king to allow him to enter into a contract with De Brewes to take possession of the fief in dispute, for the benefit, as he said, of his nephew, the Prince of Wales. A later and less trustworthy version of these events makes De Brewes, who, though 'perdives a parentela,' was 'dissipator substantiæ sibi relictæ,' sell Gower three times over—to Hereford, to Roger Mortimer of Chirk, jointly with his nephew, Roger Mortimer of Wigmore and to Hugh le Despenser (Trokelowe, p. 107, followed by Walsingham, i. 159).

Mowbray was summoned to the parliament of July 1321 which condemned the Despensers to exile (*Parl. Writs*, ii. ii. 163–8; *Rep. on Dignity of a Peer*, App. p. 308). He received a pardon on 20 Aug., along with Hereford and the other leaders of the triumphant party (*ib.*) But the king took up arms in the autumn, on 12 Nov. forbade Mowbray and others to assemble at Doncaster, and in January 1322 brought the Mortimers to their knees, while the northern barons still lingered over the siege of Tickhill (*ib.* p. 310). Mowbray took part in this siege, and his men did much damage in the neighbourhood (*Rot. Parl.* i. 406, 408, 410, cf. p. 406). He accompanied the Earl of Lancaster in his southward march, and in his retreat from Burton-on-Trent to Boroughbridge, where the battle was fought, on 16 March, in which Hereford was slain, and Lancaster, Mowbray, and Clifford captured by Sir Andrew Harclay (*Gesta Edwardi de Carnarvan* in *Chronicles of Edward I and Edward II*, ii. 74). On 23 March, the day after Lancaster's trial and beheading at Pontefract, Mowbray and Clifford, condemned by the same body of peers, were drawn by horses, and hung in iron chains at York (*ib.* p. 78; *Chron. de Melsa*, ii. 342; *Annales Paulini*, i. 302; MURIMUTH, p. 36; WALSINGHAM, i. 165). It was long before the king and the Despensers would suffer Mowbray's body to be taken down from the gallows (KNIGHTON, col. 2541).

Grainge, in his 'Vale of Mowbray' (p. 58), mentions a tradition still current in the vale in his time, that Mowbray was caught and hastily executed at Chophead Loaning, between Thirsk and Upsall, and his armour hung upon an oak, and that 'at midnight it may yet be heard creaking, when the east wind comes soughing up the road from the heights of Black Hambleton.'

The king took all Mowbray's lands into his own hands, his widow Alina and his son John were imprisoned in the Tower, and under pressure she divested herself of her rights in Bramber and the rest of her Sussex inheritance in favour of the elder Despenser, reserving a life interest only to her father, William de Brewes (DUGDALE, *Monast. Angl.* vi. 320; *Baronage*, i. 126; *Rot. Parl.* ii. 418, 436). She afterwards alleged that Despenser got the manor of Witham in Kent from De Brewes, at a time when he was 'frantiqe and not in good memory,' merely on a promise to release his daughter and grandson (*ib.*) The younger Despenser also secured the reversion of Mowbray's Bedfordshire manors of Stotfold, Haime, and Wilton, held for life by De Brewse (*Cal. of Ancient Deeds*, A. 98). The historian of St. Albans tells us that Mowbray, with the other lords of his party, had supported the rebellious prior of the cell of Bynham against Abbot Hugh (1308–1326), to whom they wrote letters, 'refertas non tantum precibus quantum minis implicitis,' because Despenser took the other side (*Gesta Abbatum*, ii. 141).

An inquisition post mortem of his estates was held on their restoration to his son John de Mowbray II [q. v.] in 1327 (DUGDALE, *Baronage*, i. 127; GRAINGE, pp. 363–5).

[Rolls of Parliament, vol. iii.; Lords' Rep. on the Dignity of a Peer; Parliamentary Writs; Rymer's Fœdera, Record ed.; Cal. of Ancient Deeds; Cal. of Close Rolls, 1307–1313; Trokelowe, Chronicles of Edward I and Edward II, Murimuth, Chronicon de Melsa, Walsingham's Historia Anglicana and Gesta Abbatum S. Albani, all in the Rolls Ser.; Chron. de Lanercost, Maitland Club ed.; Knighton in Twysden's Decem Scriptores; Dugdale's Baronage, i. 126, and Monasticon Anglicanum (ed. Caley, Ellis, and Bandinel), vi. 320, where the sixteenth-century account of the Mowbrays written at Newburgh Priory is printed; G. T. Clark's Cartæ de Glamorgan, i. 271, 283; Stubbs's Const. Hist. ii. 345, 350.]

J. T-T.

MOWBRAY, JOHN (II) DE, ninth BARON (*d.* 1361), son of John (I) de Mowbray [q. v.], was released from the Tower, and his father's lands were restored to him, on the deposition of Edward II in January 1327 (*Rot. Parl.* ii. 421; DUGDALE, *Monast. Angl.* vi. 320, *Baronage*, i. 127). Though still under age he was allowed livery of his lands, but his marriage was granted, for services to Queen Isabella, to Henry, earl of Lancaster, who married him to his fifth daughter, Joan (*ib.*; *Cal. of Pat. Rolls*, 1327–30, p. 26). His mother's great estates in Gower, Sussex, &c., came to him on her death in 1331 (DUGDALE, *Baronage*, i. 127). Henceforth he styled himself 'Lord of the Isle of Axholme, and of the Honours of Gower and Bramber.' The De Brewes's inheritance involved him in a protracted litigation with his mother's cousin, Thomas de Brewes, which had begun as early as 1338, and was still proceeding in 1347 (*Year-book*, 15 Edw. III, p. 266; *Rot. Parl.* ii. 195, 222; DUGDALE, *Baronage*, i. 420–1; NICOLAS, *Historic Peerage*, p. 72). Mowbray had also had a dispute before his mother's death with her second husband, Sir Richard Peshall, touching certain manors in Bedfordshire, &c., which he and his mother had granted to him for life, and in 1329 forcibly entered them (*Cal. of Pat. Rolls*, 1327–30, pp. 267, 435).

Mowbray was regularly summoned to the parliaments and 'colloquia' from 1328 to 1361, and was a member of the king's council from the former year (*Rep. on Dignity of a Peer*, App. pp. 380-625). In 1327, 1333, 1335, and again in 1337, he served against the Scots (*ib.* pp. 374, 420, 442); but there is little evidence for Dugdale's statement that he frequently served in France. In 1337, when war with France was impending, he was ordered as lord of Gower to arm his tenants; next year he had to provide ships for the king's passage to the continent, and was sent down to his Sussex estates in the prospect of a French landing (*Fœdera*, ii. 986, 1015, Record ed.) According to Froissart (i. 179, ed. Luce), he was with the king in Flanders in October 1339; but this is impossible, for he was present at the parliament held in that month, and was ordered to repair towards his Yorkshire estates to defend the Scottish marches (*Rot. Parl.* ii. 103, 106, 110). Next year he was appointed justiciar of Lothian and governor of Berwick, towards whose garrison he was to provide 120 men, including ten knights (*ib.* ii. 115). In September 1341 he was commanded to furnish Balliol with men from Yorkshire (*Fœdera*, ii. 1175). On 20 Dec. 1342 he received orders to hold himself ready to go to the assistance of the king in Brittany by 1 March 1348, and Froissart (iii. 24) makes him take part in the siege of Nantes; but the truce of Malestroit was concluded on 19 Jan., and on 6 Feb. the reinforcements were countermanded (*Fœdera*, ii. 1216, 1219; *Rep. on Dignity of a Peer*, App. p. 545).

At Neville's Cross (17 Oct. 1346) Mowbray fought in the third line, and the Lanercost chronicler (p. 351) loudly sings his praises: 'He was full of grace and kindness—the conduct both of himself and his men was such as to redound to their perpetual honour' (see also *Chron. de Melsa*, iii. 61). Froissart, nevertheless, again takes him to France with the king (iii. 130). In 1347 he was again in the Scottish marches (DUGDALE, *Baronage*, i. 127). On the expiration, in 1352, of one of the short truces which began in 1347, he was appointed chief of the commissioners charged with the defence of the Yorkshire coast against the French, and required to furnish thirty men from Gower (*ib.*) The king sent him once more to the Scottish border in 1355 (*ib.*) In December 1359 he was made a justice of the peace in the district of Holland, Lincolnshire, and in the following February a commissioner of array at Leicester for Lancashire, Nottinghamshire, Leicestershire, Derbyshire, and Rutland (*Fœdera*, iii. 463; *Rep. on Dignity of a Peer*, App. p. 621). This, taken with the fact that he was summoned on 3 April 1360 to the parliament fixed for 15 May, makes it excessively improbable that he was skirmishing before Paris in April as stated by Froissart (v. 232). It is possible, however, that the Sire de Montbrai mentioned by Froissart was Mowbray's son and heir, John.

Mowbray died at York of the plague on 4 Oct. 1361, and was buried in the Franciscan church at Bedford (WALSINGHAM, i. 296; *Cont.* of MURIMUTH, p. 195; DUGDALE, *Monast. Angl.* vi. 321). The favourable testimony which the Lanercost chronicler (p. 351) bears to the character of John de Mowbray is borne out by a piece of documentary evidence. In order to put an end to disputes between his steward and his tenants in Axholme, he executed a deed on 1 May 1359 reserving a certain part of the extensive wastes in the isle to himself, and granting the remainder *in perpetuum* to the tenants (STONEHOUSE, *Isle of Axholme*, pp. 19, 35). This deed was jealously preserved as the palladium of the commoners of Axholme in Haxey Church 'in a chest bound with iron, whose key was kept by some of the chiefest freeholders, under a window wherein was a portraiture of Mowbray, set in ancient stained glass, holding in his hand a writing, commonly reported to be an emblem of the deed' (*ib.* p. 293). This window was broken down in the 'rebellious times,' when the rights of the commoners under the deed were in large measure overridden, in spite of their protests, by the drainage scheme which was begun by Cornelius Vermuyden [q. v.] in 1626, and led to riots in 1642, and again in 1697 (*ib.* pp. 77 seq.)

Mowbray's wife was Joan, fifth daughter of Henry, third earl of Lancaster. His one son, JOHN (III) DE MOWBRAY (1328?–1368), was probably born in 1328 (DUGDALE, *Baronage*, i. 128), and succeeded as tenth baron. Before 1353 he had married Elizabeth, the only child and heiress of John, sixth lord Segrave, on whose death in that year he entered into possession of her lands, lying chiefly in Leicestershire, where the manors of Segrave, Sileby, and Mount Sorrel rounded off the Mowbray estates about Melton Mowbray, and in Warwickshire, where the castle and manor of Caludon and other lordships increased the Mowbray holding in that county (DUGDALE, *Baronage*, i. 676). The mother of Mowbray's wife, Margaret Plantagenet, was the sole heiress of Thomas of Brotherton, the second surviving son of Edward I, and she, on the death of her father in 1338, inherited the title and vast heritage in eastern England of the Bigods, earls of Norfolk, together with the great hereditary office of marshal of England, which had been conferred on her father (*ib.*) Neither her son-in-law, John de Mowbray the younger, nor his two successors were fated to enjoy her inheritance; for the countess marshal survived them, as well as a second husband, Sir Walter Manny [q. v.], and lived until May 1399 (WALSINGHAM, ii. 230). But in the fifteenth century the Mowbrays entered into actual possession of the old Bigod lands, and removed their chief place of residence from the mansion of the Vine Garths at Epworth in Axholme to Framlingham Castle in Suffolk. John III met with an untimely death at the hands of the Turks near Constantinople, on his way to the Holy Land, in 1368. His elder son, John IV, eleventh baron Mowbray of Axholme, was created Earl of Nottingham on the day of Richard II's coronation (WALSINGHAM, i. 337; MONK OF EVESHAM, p. 1); his second son, Thomas (I) de Mowbray, twelfth baron Mowbray and first duke of Norfolk, is separately noticed.

[Walsingham's Historia Anglicana, the Continuator of Adam of Murimuth, and the Chronicon de Melsa, in Rolls Series; Chronicon de Lanercost, Maitland Club ed.; Froissart, ed. Luce for Société de l'Histoire de France; the Byland and Newburgh account of the Mowbray family in Dugdale's Monasticon (see authorities for MOWBRAY, ROGER (I) DE); Rotuli Parliamentorum; Lords' Report on the Dignity of a Peer; Rymer's Fœdera, Record ed.; Calendar of Patent Rolls, 1327–30; Dugdale's Baronage; Nicolas's Historic Peerage, ed. Courthope; Stonehouse's Isle of Axholme; Grainge's Vale of Mowbray; other authorities in the text.] J. T–T.

MOWBRAY, JOHN (V), second DUKE OF NORFOLK (1389–1432), born in 1389, was the younger of the two sons of Thomas Mowbray I, first duke of Norfolk [q. v.], by his second wife, Elizabeth, sister and coheiress of Thomas, earl of Arundel (1381–1415). On the execution of his elder brother, Thomas Mowbray II [q.v.], in June 1405, John Mowbray became earl-marshal and fourth Earl of Nottingham, the ducal title having been withheld since the death of their father. In 1407 he was under the care of his great-aunt, the widow of Humphrey de Bohun, earl of Hereford (1341–1373) [q. v.], and mother-in-law of Henry IV. The latter, who was the youth's guardian, allowed her 200*l.* a year for his support, being double the provision made for him after his father's death (*Ord. Privy Council*, i. 100; WYLIE, *Henry IV*). The king took him into his own custody in March 1410, but sixteen months later transferred him to that of the powerful Yorkshire neighbour of the Mowbrays, Ralph Nevill, first earl of Westmorland [q. v.], whom he had in 1399 invested for life with the office of marshal of England, previously hereditary in the Mowbray family (*ib.*) Westmorland, who was systematically marrying his daughters to the heirs of other great houses, at once contracted the earl-marshal to Catherine, his eldest daughter by his second wife, Joan Beaufort, the king's half-sister. The marriage license bears date 13 Jan. 1412 (*Testamenta Eboracensia*, iii. 321).

Mowbray was not given livery of his lands until a fortnight before Henry's death, two days after which he was summoned to Henry V's first parliament as earl-marshal (DOYLE, *Official Baronage*). There is some reason to believe that his father-in-law then resigned the office of marshal of England into his hands (GREGORY, *Chron.*; *Rot. Parl.* iv. 270). When the king discovered the Earl of Cambridge's plot on the eve of his expedition to France in July 1415, the earl-marshal was the chief member of the judicial commission which investigated the conspiracy (*ib.* iv. 65). He was one of the peers who subsequently (5 Aug.) passed final sentence upon Cambridge and Lord le Scrope (*ib.* p. 66). A few days later he crossed to France with the king, and took part in the siege of Harfleur at the head of fifty men-at-arms and 150 horse-archers (DOYLE). But he was presently seized with illness, and was invalided home (WALSINGHAM, ii. 309). The statement in Harleian MS. 782 that he was present at Agincourt must be wrong (DOYLE). From the summer of 1417, however, he was constantly in France. He took a prominent part in the siege of Caen in August 1417, and in that of Rouen twelve months later (*Gesta Henrici V*, pp. 124, 270; *Paston Letters*, i. 10; *Historical Collections of a London Citizen*, ed. Camden Soc., pp. 7, 23; WALSINGHAM, ii. 322). At the beginning of 1419 the towns of Gournay and Neufchastel in Bray, between Dieppe and Beauvais, were placed in his charge (DOYLE). In the early spring of the following year he and the Earl of Huntingdon were covering the siege of Fresnay le Vicomte in Maine by the Earl of Salisbury, and on 16 March routed the Dauphin's forces near Le Mans, slaying five thousand men, including a hundred Scots (WALSINGHAM, ii. 331; ELMHAM, p. 244; *Gesta Henrici V*, pp. 133–4; R. TRIGER, *Fresnay le Vicomte* in *Revue Historique du Maine*, 1886, xix. 189). The author of the 'Gesta' (p. 144) says he was present at the protracted siege of Melun, which began in July. It is doubtful whether he returned to England with the king in February 1421 and bore the second sceptre at Catherine's coronation (GREGORY, p. 139; *Three Fifteenth-Century Chronicles*, p. 57; but cf. WALSINGHAM, ii. 336). Henry had appointed him governor of Pontoise before his departure, and he witnessed a document at Rouen in the middle of April (DOYLE; *Mémoires de la Société des Antiquités de Normandie*, 1858, vol. xxiii. pt. i. No. 1498). Shortly after (3 May) he was given the Garter vacated by the death of Sir John Grey (BELTZ, *Memorials of the Garter*, p. clviii).

The earl-marshal was present in the council which decided on 5 Nov. 1422 that the Duke of Gloucester should conduct the first parliament of Henry VI as royal commissioner, and not as regent, and on 9 Dec. he was nominated one of the five earls in the new council appointed to carry on the government with the protector (*Rot. Parl.* iv. 175; *Ord. Privy Council*, iii. 6, 16, iv. 101). In May 1423 he and Lord Willoughby took reinforcements to France, and, after perhaps sharing in the victory of Cravant (30 July), he assisted the Burgundian commander, John of Luxemburg, in expelling the French from the districts of Laon and Guise (*ib.* pp. 87, 101; WAVRIN, pp. 33, 70–5). With only six hundred English he scattered the Count of Toulouse's force, and, driving part of them into the fortress of La Follye, captured and destroyed it (*ib.*)

In November 1424 Mowbray joined Gloucester in his impolitic invasion of Hainault, and in the last days of the year ravaged Brabant up to the walls of Brussels (STEVENSON, *Wars of the English in France*, ii. 399, 409; LÖHER, *Jakobäa von Bayern*, ii. 154, 172). He returned with Gloucester to England in time for the parliament which met on 30 April 1425 (*Report on the Dignity of a Peer*, iv. 861). Much of his attention was devoted to endeavours to secure a recognition of his precedence over the Earl of Warwick (*Rot. Parl.* iv. 262–73; *Ord. Privy Council*, iii. 174). After the proceedings had been protracted over several weeks, a compromise suggested by the commons was accepted, by which parliament decided that the earl-marshal was by right Duke of Norfolk (*Rot. Parl.* iv. 274); on 14 July, therefore, Mowbray did homage as Duke of Norfolk. On the death of his mother a week later (8 July) her rich jointure estates, mostly lying in Norfolk and Suffolk, reverted to him, and Framlingham Castle in the latter county became his chief seat (DUGDALE, *Baronage*, i. 130; *Paston Letters*, i. 15–18).

In March 1426, Norfolk, with eight other peers, undertook to arbitrate between Gloucester and Beaufort, and two years later (3 March 1428) helped to repel Gloucester's attempt to assert 'auctorite of governance of the lond' (*Rot. Parl.* iv. 297, 327). On the night of 8 Nov. in this latter year he narrowly escaped drowning by the capsizing of his barge in passing under London Bridge (GREGORY; WILL. WORC. p. 760). He officiated as marshal of England at the coronation of Henry VI on 6 Nov. 1429, and with many other nobles accompanied him to France in the following April (GREGORY, p. 168; RAMSAY, *Lancaster and York*, i. 415; cf. *Ord. Privy Council*, iv. 36; *Rot. Parl.* v. 415). The duke accompanied Duke Philip of Burgundy when he received the surrender of Gournay en Aronde, and distinguished himself during the summer in the capture of Dammartin and other places east of Paris (WAVRIN, pp. 373, 393; MONSTRELET, iv. 398, 405; *Chron. London*, pp. 170–1).

Norfolk was in London when Gloucester effected a change of ministers at the end of February 1432, and on 7 May he, with other peers, was warned not to bring a greater retinue than usual to the approaching parliament (*Ord. Privy Council*, iv. 113, vi. 349; *Fœdera*, x. 501). He attended a council early in June, but died on 19 Oct. following at the ancient seat of his family at Epworth in the isle of Axholme, and was buried by his own direction in the neighbouring Cistercian priory which his father had founded. The alabaster tomb which Leland saw there may have been his (*Itinerary*, i. 39). One will (20 May 1429), abstracted by Dugdale, contains an injunction that his father's ashes should be brought from Venice and laid beside his own. By his last will, made on the day of his death, he left all his estates in the isle of Axholme and in Yorkshire, with the castles and honours of Bramber in Sussex and Gower in Wales, to his wife, Catherine Nevill, for her life (NICHOLS, *Royal Wills*, p. 226). Dugdale adds a list of nearly thirty manors or portions of manors in Norfolk and six other counties which were also included in her jointure (*Baronage*, i. 131; cf. *Rot. Parl.* vi. 168). But their only son, John Mowbray VI [q. v.], who succeeded his father as third Duke of Norfolk, only enjoyed a small part of his patrimony, because his mother survived him as well as two more husbands—viz. Thomas Strangeways, and John, viscount Beaumont (*d.* 1460). At the age, it is said, of nearly eighty she was moreover married by Edward IV to a youth of twenty, Sir John Wydeville, brother of the queen, a marriage which William Worcester denounces as a 'diabolic match' (*Annals*, p. 783). She was still living in January 1478 (*Rot. Parl.* vi. 169).

A portrait of Norfolk is figured in Doyle's 'Official Baronage,' after an engraving by W. Hollar, from a window in St. Mary's Hall, Coventry.

[Rotuli Parliamentorum; Lords' Report on the Dignity of a Peer; Ordinances and Proceedings of the Privy Council, ed. Palgrave; Rymer's Fœdera, original edition; Walsingham's Historia Anglicana, Wavrin's Chroniques d'Angleterre, and William Worcester's Annals (printed at the end of Stevenson's Wars of the English in France) in the Rolls Ser.; Elmham's Vita Henrici V, ed. Hearne, 1727; Gesta Henrici V, ed. Williams, for English Historical Society; Monstrelet's Chronique, ed. Douët d'Arcq; Gregory's Chronicle and Three Fifteenth-Century Chronicles, ed. Camden Soc.; Chronicle of London, ed. Harris Nicolas; Paston Letters, ed. Gairdner; Dugdale's Baronage; Ramsay's Lancaster and York; Pauli's Geschichte Englands; Wylie's Henry IV, vol. ii.; other authorities in the text.] J. T-T.

MOWBRAY, JOHN (VI), third DUKE OF NORFOLK, hereditary EARL MARSHAL OF ENGLAND, and fifth EARL OF NOTTINGHAM (1415–1461), was the only son of John Mowbray V [q. v.] and his wife, Catherine Nevill. He was born on 12 Sept. 1415 (DUGDALE, *Baronage*, i. 131). Before he was eleven years old he figured in a ceremony designed to mark the reconciliation of Humphrey, duke of Gloucester, and Bishop Beaufort. On Whitsunday (19 May) 1426 he was knighted by the infant king, Henry VI (LELAND, *Col-*

lectanea, ii. 490; *Fœdera*, x. 356; Ramsay, *Lancaster and York*, i. 368). He was still under age at his father's death in October 1432, and his estates were in the custody of Humphrey of Gloucester until 1436 (*Ord. Privy Council*, iv. 132; cf. *Rot. Parl.* iv. 433). Nevertheless, he was summoned to the council in November 1434 (*Ord. Privy Council*, iv. 287, 300). In August 1436 he served under Gloucester in the army which had been intended to relieve Calais, but arrived after the Duke of Burgundy had raised the siege, and made an inglorious raid into Flanders (Stevenson, *Wars of the English in France*, ii. p. xlix; *Three Fifteenth-Century Chronicles*, p. 61; Hardyng, p. 396). The onerous post of warden of the east march towards Scotland and captain of Berwick was in March 1437 entrusted to Norfolk for a year, and at the end of that time he was appointed a guardian of the truce concluded with Scotland (Doyle, *Official Baronage; Paston Letters*, i. 41). In 1439 he was one of the English ambassadors in the great peace conference near Oye, between Calais and Gravelines (*Fœdera*, x. 728; Wavrin [1431–47], p. 264; *Ord. Privy Council*, v. 334–407). In the summer of 1441 he was ordered to inquire into the government of Norwich, in consequence of disturbances in that city (Doyle). The disturbances were renewed in the following year, and the populace, irritated by the exactions of the prior of Christchurch, held the town against Norfolk (Will. Worc. p. 763; *Chron. of London*, ed. Nicolas, p. 131). When the riot was quelled the civic franchises were withdrawn, and Norfolk, by the royal command, installed Sir John Clifton as captain of the city (*ib.*; *Ord. Privy Council*, v. 229, 244). The council on 5 March 1443 specially thanked him for his services (*ib.* p. 235). Two years later (11 March 1445) Norfolk's ducal title, which had received parliamentary recognition in 1425, during Henry's minority, was confirmed by the king's letters patent, and precedence was assigned him next to the Duke of Exeter (*Rot. Parl.* v. 446). In October 1446 he obtained permission, then rarely sought by men of rank, to go on pilgrimage to Rome and other holy places (Doyle). He returned in time to join an embassy to France in July 1447 to treat of the surrender of Maine (*ib.*)

At the beginning of 1450 (*Paston Letters*, i. introd. p. l) popular opinion accused the Duke of Suffolk of keeping Norfolk in the background:

> The White Lion is laid to sleep
> Thorough the envy of th' Apè Clog.

Later in 1450 Richard, duke of York, came over from Ireland, after the murder of the Duke of Suffolk, and entered into a rivalry with Edmund Beaufort, duke of Somerset, for the direction of the royal policy. York's wife, Cecily Nevill, was the youngest sister of Norfolk's mother, while Norfolk's wife, Eleanor Bourchier, was sister of Viscount Bourchier, who had married York's sister. Norfolk at once became the chief supporter of York, who was thus connected with him by a double family tie. He may have been aggrieved, too, that the dukes of Somerset had been expressly given precedence over himself on the ground of 'nighness of blood and great zeal to do the king service' (*Ord. Privy Council*, v. 255). About the middle of August, before York's actual return, Norfolk went down to his chief seat, Framlingham Castle in Suffolk, whither he summoned 'certain notable knights and squires' of Norfolk, to commune with him for the 'sad rule and governance' of that county, 'which standeth right indisposed' (*Paston Letters*, i. 139, 143). In the first days of September it was rumoured in Norwich that, along with the Earl of Oxford, Lord Scales, and others, he had been entrusted with a commission of oyer and terminer to inquire into the wrongs and violences that prevailed in Norfolk (*ib.* p. 145). He met his 'uncle of York' at Bury St. Edmunds on Thursday, 15 Oct., and, after being together until nine o'clock on Friday, they settled who should be knights of the shire for Norfolk in the parliament summoned for 6 Nov. (*ib.* p. 160). Only one of their nominees, however, was returned. A week after the meeting at Bury Norfolk ordered John Paston to join him at Ipswich on 8 Nov. on his way to parliament, 'with as many cleanly people as ye may get for our worship at this time' (*ib.* p. 162). About 18 Nov. he and York arrived in London, both with a 'grete multytude of defensabylle men,' and he supported his kinsman in the fierce struggle with Somerset which ensued (Gregory, p. 195; Will. Worc. p. 770). In March 1451 he held sessions of oyer and terminer at Norwich, and in July he and York were ordered to meet the king at Canterbury (*Paston Letters*, i. 123, 216; Ramsay, *Lancaster and York*, ii. 146). He does not appear, however, to have joined York in his futile armed demonstration of February 1452 (Wavrin [1447–71], p. 265; *Paston Letters*, i. cxlviii, 232). Yet he thought it necessary to take advantage of the king's Good-Friday amnesty, and sued out a pardon on 23 June (*ib.* i. lxxxiii). At the instance of Somerset and Queen Margaret he dismissed some of his advisers 'who owed good will and service unto the Duke of York and others' (*ib.* pp. 243, 305). In Norfolk, where he declared his intention of bearing 'the principal rule and governance next the king,' and was addressed as 'your Highness' and 'Prince and Sovereign next our Sovereign Lord' (1455), his interests were in some cases opposed to those of the friends of York (*ib.* pp. 228–30, 248). On Henry's becoming insane in the autumn of 1453, Norfolk demanded an inquiry into Somerset's administration (*ib.* p. 259). But by January 1454, if not earlier, his influence with York had been overshadowed by that of the Nevills; he did not obtain any office on York's becoming protector, and was not called to the council until 16 April (*Ord. Privy Council*, vi. 174). Even after that he was rarely present. In July he was ordered to be prepared to prove his charges against Somerset on 28 Oct. following (*ib.* p. 219). He was not present at the first battle of St. Albans (22 May 1455), but is said to have come up the day after with a force of six thousand men (*Paston Letters*, i. 333). The number can hardly be correct. York having summoned a parliament for 9 July, Norfolk nominated his cousin, John Howard, afterwards Duke of Norfolk himself, and Sir Roger Chamberlain to be knights of the shire for Norfolk, and the duchess wrote in their favour to John Paston, who had again aspired to the position, urging that her lord needed in parliament 'such persons as long unto him and be of his menial servants' (*ib.* p. 337). Though some objected to Howard as having 'no livelihood or conversement' in the shire, he was duly elected (*ib.* pp. 340–1). Whether or not Norfolk was kept in the background by the Nevill influence, we hear nothing more of him until November 1456, when he made a pilgrimage on foot from Framlingham to the shrine of Our Lady at Walsingham (*ib.* p. 411). In the August of the following year he asked and obtained permission to go on pilgrimage to various holy places in Ireland, Scotland, Brittany, Picardy, and Cologne, and to the blood of our Saviour at Windesnake, as well as to Rome and Jerusalem, for the recovery of the king's health (*Fœdera*, xi. 405; Dugdale, i. 131). This seems to suggest that he was now leaning to the court party. There is no record of his having performed his vow, and he was summoned to a council in January 1458 (*Ord. Privy Council*, vi. 292). He does not appear to have figured in the 'loveday' procession of 25 March 1458, when the leaders of the rival factions were paired off with each other (cf. *ib.* vi. 297). When York, Warwick, and Salisbury again took up arms in 1459, Norfolk kept aloof from them, and in the Coventry parliament which attainted them after their flight he took (11 Dec.) the special oath to the Lancastrian succession (*Rot. Parl.* v. 351). Early in the following February he was commissioned, along with some undoubted Lancastrians, to raise forces in Norfolk and Suffolk to resist an expected landing of Warwick there (*Fœdera*, xi. 440; *Paston Letters*, i. 514). Immediately after he was appointed a guardian of the truce with Scotland.

When the Nevills returned from Calais in June 1460 and turned the tables at Northampton, Norfolk again adhered to the Yorkist cause; but he may very well have been one of the lords who in October refused to transfer the crown to the Duke of York (*Rot. Parl.* v. 375). He seems to have been left in London with Warwick, when York and Salisbury went north in December to meet their death at Wakefield, and he shared Warwick's defeat by Queen Margaret's troops at St. Albans on 17 Feb. 1461 (Will. Worc. p. 776; Gregory, pp. 211–12; *Chron.* ed. Davies, p. 107; *Three Fifteenth-Century Chronicles*, p. 155). Escaping from the battle, he was present at the meeting of Yorkist lords at Baynards Castle on 3 March, which decided that Edward, duke of York, should be king, and accompanied him next day to his enthronement at Westminster (Will. Worc. p. 777). Shortly after he went north with the new king and fought at Towton (29 March), 'like a second Ajax' says the classical Whethamstede (i. 409; Will. Worc. p. 777; *Three Fifteenth-Century Chronicles*, p. 161). A younger contemporary who wrote, however, after 1514, and was connected with the house of Norfolk, asserts that the duke brought up fresh troops whom he had been raising in Norfolk, and turned the scale at a critical point in the battle (fragment printed by Hearne ad ped. *Chron.* Sprott, and in *Chron. of the White Rose*, p. 9). The concurrence of contemporary testimony makes very doubtful Hall's statement (p. 256) that he was kept away from the battle by sickness. Apparently he returned south with the king, for on 5 June he was at Framlingham, and on the 28th officiated as earl-marshal at Edward's coronation (Doyle; *Three Fifteenth-Century Chronicles*, p. 162). He was rewarded with the offices of steward and chief justice of the royal forests south of Trent (11 July) and constable of Scarborough Castle (12 Aug.; Doyle). But Edward refused to recognise Norfolk's forcible seizure from John Paston of Sir John Fastolf's castle of Caistor near Yarmouth, to which he had no shadow of right (*Paston Letters*, ii. 14). Paston appealed to the king, and in a few months Norfolk was obliged to withdraw (*ib.* ii. xiii). He did not long survive this rebuff. He died on 6 Nov.

1461, and was buried at Thetford Priory (*Report on the Dignity of a Peer*, App. v. 326; *Paston Letters*, ii. 247; Dugdale, i. 131).

Norfolk married, before July 1437, Eleanor, daughter of William Bourchier, earl of Eu, and Anne of Gloucester, granddaughter of Edward III, a sister therefore of Viscount Bourchier and half-sister of Humphrey Stafford, first duke of Buckingham (*ib.*; *Ord. Privy Council*, v. 56). She bore him one son, John Mowbray VII (1444–1476), whom she outlived (*Paston Letters*, iii. 154). This John, fourth duke of Norfolk, was born on 18 Oct. 1444, and on 24 March 1451 the earldoms of Surrey and Warrenne were revived in his favour. They had become extinct on the death in 1415 of Thomas, earl of Arundel, whose sister, Elizabeth Fitzalan, married his great-grandfather, Thomas Mowbray I, first duke of Norfolk [q. v.] (Dugdale, i. 131; Doyle; Nicolas, *Historic Peerage*, ed. Courthope). The fourth duke makes a great figure in the 'Paston Correspondence.' Maintaining his father's baseless claim to Caistor Castle, he besieged and took it in September 1469, during the confusion of that year, and kept possession, with a short interval during the Lancastrian restoration of 1470–1, until his sudden death on 17 Jan. 1476, when it was recovered by the Pastons (*Paston Letters*, ii. 366, 383; iii. xiii, 148). He transferred his Gower and Chepstow estates to William Herbert, first earl of Pembroke (*d.* 1469), in exchange for certain manors in Norfolk and Suffolk (*Rot. Parl.* vi. 292). By his wife, Elizabeth Talbot, daughter of the great Earl of Shrewsbury, he left only a daughter, Anne Mowbray (*b.* 10 Dec. 1472), and his honours, with the exception of the baronies of Mowbray and Segrave and probably the earldom of Norfolk, became extinct (Nicolas, *Historic Peerage*). Anne Mowbray, the last of her line, was married (15 Jan. 1478) to Richard, duke of York, second son of Edward IV, who had been created Earl of Nottingham, Earl Warrenne, and Duke of Norfolk. But her husband was murdered in the Tower before the marriage was consummated, and Duchess Anne died without issue, and was buried in the chapel of St. Erasmus in Westminster Abbey (Dugdale). The Mowbray and other baronies fell into abeyance between the descendants of her great grand-aunts Margaret and Isabel, daughters of Thomas Mowbray, first duke of Norfolk [q. v.] Margaret had married Sir Robert Howard, and their son, John Howard [q. v.], 'Jockey of Norfolk,' was created Duke of Norfolk and earl marshal of England on 28 June 1483. Isabel Mowbray married James, baron Berkeley (*d.* 1462), and her son William, created Earl of Nottingham (28 June 1483) and Marquis of Berkeley (28 Jan. 1488), sold the Axholme and Yorkshire estates of the Mowbrays to Thomas Stanley, first earl of Derby (Stonehouse, *Isle of Axholme*, p. 140). His descendants, the earls of Berkeley, called themselves Barons of Mowbray, Segrave, and Breuse of Gower.

[Rotuli Parliamentorum; Lords' Report on the Dignity of a Peer; Proceedings and Ordinances of the Privy Council, ed. Palgrave; Rymer's Fœdera, original ed.; Wavrin's Chronique, Register of Abbot Whethamstede, and Annals of William Worcester (printed at the end of Stevenson's Wars of the English in France) in Rolls Series; English Chronicle, 1377–1461, ed. Davies, 'Gregory's' Chronicle (Gregory's authorship is now abandoned: see English Historical Review, viii. 565), in Collections of a London Citizen, and Three Fifteenth-Century Chronicles, all published by the Camden Society; Chronicle of London, ed. Harris Nicolas; Hardyng's Chronicle, ed. Ellis, 1812; Chronicles of the White Rose, 1845; Paston Letters, ed. Gairdner; Dugdale's Baronage; Nicolas's Historic Peerage, ed. Courthope; Doyle's Official Baronage; Stubbs's Constitutional History, vol. iii.; Ramsay's Lancaster and York; Pauli's Geschichte Englands, vol. v.] J. T-t.

MOWBRAY, ROBERT de, Earl of Northumberland (*d.* 1125?), was a son of Roger de Montbrai (in the Cotentin near St. Lô), who came over with the Conqueror, and was nephew of a far more prominent follower, Geoffrey (*d.* 1093) [q. v.], bishop of Coutances (Orderic Vitalis, ii. 223, iii. 406, ed. Prévost; Dugdale, *Baronage*, i. 56). Mowbray, a grim and turbulent baron, was, if we may believe Orderic (ii. 381), engaged in Robert's rebellion against his father in 1078. If this was so, it did not prevent his appointment between 1080 and 1082 to the earldom of Northumberland (Simeon of Durham, p. 98). In all probability he succeeded directly to Earl Aubrey, though Dugdale and Freeman, on insufficient grounds, have interposed a brief tenure of the earldom by his uncle, Bishop Geoffrey (*ib.* with Mr. Hinde's note; Dugdale, i. 56; Freeman, *Norman Conquest*, iv. 673).

In 1088 both uncle and nephew sided with Robert against his brother, William Rufus (*Chronicon Angliæ Petriburgense*, ed. J. A. Giles, s. a. 1088; Florence of Worcester, ii. 24), though Orderic (iii. 273) asserts that Mowbray remained loyal to the king. From the bishop's strong castle at Bristol the earl marched upon and burnt Bath, whence he ravaged western Wiltshire, and, making a circuit over the high ground to the south-west, besieged Ilchester, but was repulsed

(FLORENCE, ii. 24; *Proceedings of Bath Nat. Hist. and Antiquarian Club*, ii. 3, 1872; FREEMAN, *William Rufus*, i. 41–4). The rising collapsed, but the king did not feel strong enough to punish the earl.

Soon after Mowbray quarrelled with his neighbour, William of Saint Calais, bishop of Durham, over lands claimed by both, and he revenged himself upon the bishop by ordering the expulsion of Turchill, a Durham monk, from the church of St. Oswine, which belonged to the priory of Durham, but stood within the circuit of the earl's castle at Tynemouth (SIMEON OF DURHAM, *Hist. Ecclesiæ Dunelmensis*, p. 228; *Gesta Regum*, pp. 115–16). Moreover, in spite of the protests of the monks of Durham, Mowbray gave the church of St. Oswine to the Benedictines of Saint Albans to be a cell of their house, and it became the priory of Tynemouth (*ib.*; *Monasticon Anglicanum*, iii. 312; SIMEON, *Gesta Regum*, p. 116; *Hist. Translationis S. Cuthberti*, *ib.* p. 180). In the opinion, however, of the St. Albans historians the earl was divinely inspired in his gift. The foundation of Tynemouth priory is dated by Roger of Wendover (ii. 39) about 1091, the year of the return from exile of Bishop William of Durham; but according to Matthew Paris it was founded with the approval of Lanfranc, who died in 1089 (*Gesta Abb. Sti. Albani*, ed. Riley, i. 57). On the other hand, there are some grounds for believing that the earl and the bishop had not quarrelled by so early a date, and Simeon of Durham implies that the death of Abbot Paul of Saint Albans, which took place in 1093, was not long after the foundation (SIMEON, *Hist. Eccl.* p. 228; *Monasticon*, i. 249; cf. MATTHEW PARIS, *Hist. Angl.* i. 41, *Historia Major*, ii. 31, vi. 372).

Mowbray was probably prevented from taking part with the other barons of the Cotentin in the struggle between (Prince) Henry and his brothers in 1091 by the invasion of Malcolm, king of Scots, whom he seems to have driven back from Chester-le-Street in May of that year (ORDERIC, iii. 351; *Chron. Petriburgense*, 1091). When Malcolm repeated his invasion in 1093, he was surprised and slain by Mowbray near Alnwick on St. Brice's day (13 Nov.) (*ib.*; FLORENCE, ii. 31; WILLIAM OF MALMESBURY, ii. 309, 366; ORDERIC, iii. 396; MATTHEW PARIS, *Hist. Angl.* i. 47; WILLIAM OF JUMIÈGES, viii. 8; FREEMAN, *William Rufus*, ii. 595; cf. FORDUN, i. 218, ed. Skene). The earl buried Malcolm in the priory church at Tynemouth.

Elated by this success, and by the great addition to his power which had just accrued to him by the death (2 Feb. 1093) of his uncle, Bishop Geoffrey, whose 280 manors all came to him, Mowbray seems to have become a party to the conspiracy of 1095, whose object was to transfer the crown from the Conqueror's sons to their cousin, Count Stephen of Aumâle (FLORENCE, ii. 38; HENRY OF HUNTINGDON, p. 218; *Epistolæ Anselmi*, iii. 35–6). Orderic (iii. 406) says that Mowbray began the insurrection by seizing four Norwegian vessels in a Northumbrian haven, and by refusing to give satisfaction or to appear at court at the king's command. He certainly disobeyed a special summons to the Easter court at Winchester (25 March), and, though threatened with outlawry, absented himself from the Whitsun feast at Windsor, the king having refused his request for hostages and a safe-conduct (*Chron. Petriburgense*, 1095; cf. FREEMAN, ii. 41–2). Rufus then took a force of mercenaries and English militia into the North against him, captured the New Castle on the Tyne, the frontier fortress of Mowbray's earldom, containing the main body of the earl's forces, and laid siege to Tynemouth castle, which guarded the entrance of the river (FLORENCE, ii. 38; FREEMAN, ii. 47). Tynemouth, which was defended by the earl's brother, fell after a siege of two months (July?), and the king advanced to attack Mowbray himself in his great coast castle at Bamborough (*ib.*) Bamborough being virtually impregnable, Rufus built and garrisoned a tower on the land side, which he called Malveisin, or the Evil Neighbour, and went off to the Welsh war. Not long after his departure the royal garrison of the New Castle drew Mowbray into an ambush by a false promise to surrender that fortress, and took him prisoner. But in some way not explained he contrived to escape to his monastery at Tynemouth, and stood there a siege of six days, until he was wounded in the leg and dragged from the church in which he had taken refuge (FLORENCE, ii. 38; *Hist. Translationis S. Cuthberti*, in Surtees edit. of Simeon, p. 180). The Durham writers regard this as the punishment of heaven for his having robbed Saint Cuthbert of this church (*ib.* pp. 115–16, 180–1). Meanwhile Bamborough was manfully defended by his newly married wife, Mathilda de Laigle, with the assistance of his nephew, Morel, and it was not until her husband was led before the walls with a threat that, unless the castle was surrendered, his eyes should be seared out in her presence, that she gave up the keys (*Chron. Petriburgense*, 1095; FLORENCE, ii. 39; ORDERIC, iii. 410).

Mowbray was deprived of his earldom and all his possessions, and imprisoned at Windsor (*Chron. Petriburgense*; FLORENCE, ii. 39; HENRY OF HUNTINGDON, p. 218). Some authorities state or imply that he was kept in prison until his death, or at least far into the next reign (ORDERIC, iii. 199, 410; MALMESBURY, ii. 372; *Cont.* of WILLIAM OF JUMIÈGES, viii. 8; *Hist. Translationis S. Cuthberti*, p. 181). Orderic says in one place that he was imprisoned for nearly thirty years, in another for nearly thirty-four years. The story that Henry allowed him to spend his last years as a monk at Saint Albans appears in only one contemporary authority, the Magdalen manuscript of the Durham 'Libellus de Regibus Saxonicis,' printed with Simeon in the Surtees Society edition (p. 213), and deemed by its editor to have been written in 1138–9 either at Saint Albans itself or at Tynemouth. It is also found with additional details in later Saint Albans accounts of the foundation of Tynemouth priory, one of which, apparently by Matthew Paris, adds that Mowbray was blind for some years before his death, and was buried near the chapter-house where Abbot Simon afterwards built the chapel of Saint Simeon (MATTHEW PARIS, vi. 372, ed. Luard; *Hist. Angl.* iii. 175; *Monasticon*, iii. 312–13; FREEMAN, ii. 612). Mr. Doyle, accepting this version, seeks to reconcile the contradictory statements of Orderic by supposing that Mowbray became a monk in 1125 and died in 1129 (*Official Baronage*).

Mowbray had only been married three months before his capture. His wife was Mathilda, a daughter of Richer de Laigle (de Aquila) by Judith, sister of Hugh, earl of Chester (ORDERIC, iii. 406). Pope Paschal II afterwards allowed her as a widow in all but name to marry Nigel de Albini [see under MOWBRAY, ROGER I DE], a relative, probably a cousin of her husband, who founded the second house of Mowbray (*ib.* iii. 410; WILLIAM OF JUMIÈGES, viii. 8; FREEMAN, ii. 612). She apparently survived both husbands, as she was still living in 1130 (*Pipe Roll*, 31 Henry I, pp. 16, 76, ed. Hunter).

Orderic has left a graphic portrait of Mowbray: 'Powerful, rich, bold, fierce in war, haughty, he despised his equals, and, swollen with vanity, disdained to obey his superiors. He was of great stature, strong, swarthy, and hairy. Daring and crafty, stern and grim of mien, he was more given to meditation than to speech, and in conversation scarce ever smiled' (ORDERIC, iii. 406; cf. *Monasticon*, iii. 311). If he is not maligned by the Durham historians, his motives in founding Tynemouth priory scarcely entitled him to Matthew Paris's praise as 'vir quidem Deo devotus.'

[Chronicon Angliæ Petriburgense, ed. J. A. Giles; Florence of Worcester and Roger of Wendover, ed. English Historical Society; Ordericus Vitalis's Historia Ecclesiastica, ed. Le Prévost, for the Société de l'Histoire de France; Simeon of Durham's Gesta Regum, with the Historia Translationis S. Cuthberti and other Durham writings, ed. Hinde, for the Surtees Society; his Historia Ecclesiæ Dunelmensis, ed. Bedford (1732); William of Malmesbury, Henry of Huntingdon, Matthew Paris's Works, ed. Madden and Luard, and the Gesta Abbatum Sancti Albani (the earlier part of which is by Matthew Paris), all in the Rolls Series; the Continuator of William of Jumièges in Duchesne's Scriptores Normannorum. The chief incidents in Mowbray's career are exhaustively dealt with by Freeman in his William Rufus, especially Appendices CC, FF.] J. T-T.

MOWBRAY, ROGER (I) DE, second BARON (*d.* 1188?), was son of Nigel de Albini, a younger brother of that William de Albini, 'Pincerna,' whose descendants were styled 'Earls of Arundel' (NICOLAS, *Historic Peerage*, ed. Courthope, pp. 21, 27). Nigel, who at the date of Doomsday had considerable estates in Leicestershire and some manors in Warwickshire and Buckinghamshire, greatly increased them by the steady support he gave to William Rufus and Henry I, and by his marriage with Mathilde de Laigle, wife of Robert de Mowbray, earl of Northumberland [q. v.], founded the second house of Mowbray, which lasted in the direct male line for four centuries, until the death, in 1476, of the sixteenth holder of the barony. Nigel, however, subsequently put away his wife Mathilde on the ground that Mowbray, her former husband, was his relative—later pedigree makers doubtfully represent his mother as her first husband's sister—and he married Gundreda, daughter of Gerald de Gournay, who became the mother of Roger de Mowbray (ORDERIC VITALIS, ed. Le Prevost; cf. *ib.* iii. 410 *n.*) Henry I, according to a brief history of the Mowbrays written not earlier than the end of the thirteenth century (*Monast. Angl.* v. 346), had bestowed upon Nigel de Albini the whole of the vast estates of Robert de Mowbray in England and Normandy. The same authority asserts that at the time of his death, between 1127 and 1130, Nigel was on the point of taking seisin of the earldom of Northumberland. But not a single manor of the 280 which the elder Mowbrays held in England can be traced in the possession of the second house. Nigel's great acquisitions, which were not much added to until the fourteenth century, were in the midlands, where his own holding lay, or in Yorkshire. The chief of the two groups consisted of practically the whole of the lands held at the date of Doomsday by Geoffrey de Wirce in Warwickshire, Leicestershire, and Northamptonshire, with the isle of Axholme in Lincolnshire. Axholme ultimately became the centre of the Mowbray power, lying halfway between their lands in Warwickshire and Leicestershire and their Yorkshire estates. These latter, which stretched in a great crescent from Thirsk, whose valley is still called the Vale of Mowbray, to Kirkby Malzeard and the sources of the Nidd, with the outlying castle of Black Burton in Lonsdale, were forfeited by Robert de Stuteville, baron of Frontebœuf, who took the losing side at Tinchebrai, and were conferred by King Henry upon the loyal Nigel (HOVEDEN; DUGDALE, *Baronage*, i. 455). It is just possible that the former lands of Geoffrey de Wirce came into Nigel's possession as part of the Stuteville forfeiture. For when Stuteville's descendants sued for the recovery of their heritage they laid claim not only to the Yorkshire estates, but to Axholme and other lands which had undoubtedly belonged to Geoffrey de Wirce (*ib.* p. 457; *Rotuli Curiæ Regis*, ii. 231). But although there is no evidence that the second house of Mowbray was founded on the English estates of the first, it seems not improbable that they secured some of the Norman lands of the first house, including perhaps the honour of Montbrai itself (STAPLETON, *Rotuli Scaccarii Normanniæ*, ii. xcv; see pedigree in STONEHOUSE, *Isle of Axholme*, and cf. *Monast. Angl.* vi. 320).

Nigel was buried in the priory of Bec, of which he is said to have become a monk before his death (*Cont.* of WILLIAM OF JUMIÈGES, ed. Duchesne, p. 296; EYTON, *Shropshire*, viii. 212; *Pipe Roll*, 31 Hen. I, ed. Hunter, p. 138).

Roger, his young son, was probably born between 1120 and 1125 (AILRED OF RIEVAULX in *Chron. of Reigns of Stephen*, &c. iii. 184; DUGDALE, *Monast. Angl.* v. 349, 352, and *Baronage*, i. 122). His name is said to have been changed from Albini to Mowbray at the command of Henry I. He became a ward of the crown, and Ailredus, who was abbot of Rievaulx, a few miles from Roger's castle of Thirsk, relates, in illustration of the enthusiasm with which Yorkshire prepared to repel the Scots in 1138, that the barons took Roger de Mowbray, though but a boy (*adhuc puerulus*), to the battle of the Standard, but carefully avoided exposing him to danger (*Chronicles of the Reign of Stephen*, &c., iii. 183; cf. RICH. OF HEXHAM, *ib.* iii. 159). Three years later, he is said by one authority to have been taken prisoner with Stephen in the battle of Lincoln (JOHN OF HEXHAM in *Decem Scriptores*, p. 269). In these years he seems to have been at Thirsk with his mother, Gundreda, under whose guidance he became a generous benefactor to the church. In 1138 they sheltered the monks of Calder, flying before the Scots; Roger gave them a tenth of the victuals of the castle, and, on their forming themselves into a convent subordinate to Savigny in the diocese of Avranches in 1143, bestowed upon them his villa of Byland-on-the-Moors (*Monast. Angl.* v. 349–50). When the monks of Byland Abbey found their first site inconvenient and intolerably close to Rievaulx Abbey, whose bells they could hear all day long, Roger in 1147 (when the abbey became Cistercian) granted them a new site, some eight miles to the south, near Coxwold (*ib.* p. 351; cf. *English Hist. Review*, viii. 668–672). In the course of his long life he frequently made additional gifts to the abbey, including the great forest of Nidderdale. But, 'being a frugal man, and, so to speak, the standard-bearer of liberality among the magnates of the land,' Roger did not confine his generosity to a single object. As early as 1145 he joined his relative Sampson de Albini in the foundation of the great abbey of Austin canons at Newburgh, not far from the second site of Byland Abbey (*Monast. Angl.* vi. 317–21; WILLIAM OF NEWBURGH in *Chron. of the Reigns of Stephen*, &c.) He endowed Newburgh with land, and the church of Thirsk with fifteen other churches and chapels on his Yorkshire estates; while Sampson de Albini, with his consent, gave to Newburgh Abbey the churches of Masham and Kirkby Malzeard, with four in the isle of Axholme, and that of Landford in Nottinghamshire. About the same time he gave some of his land in Masham to the Earl of Richmond's infant foundation of Jervaulx in Wensleydale, which in 1150 was affiliated to Byland and the Cistercian order (*Monast. Angl.* v. 569). Mowbray was also a generous benefactor of the abbeys of Fountains, Rievaulx, and Bridlington in Yorkshire; Kenilworth in Warwickshire; and Sulby in Northamptonshire, and gave to the church of St. Mary in York the isle of Sandtoft in Axholme, and to the hospital of St. Leonards in that city the ninth sheaf of all his corn throughout England (DUGDALE, *Monast. Angl.* iii. 617, v. 282–3, 307, *Baronage*, i. 123). He doubled his father's endowment to the priory of Hurst in Axholme (*Monast. Angl.* vi. 101). In Normandy he gave all his lands in Granville to the Abbaye des Dames at Caen when his daughter became a nun there (*Neustria Pia*, p. 660). In the exaggeration of tradition he was credited with the foundation of no less than thirty-five monasteries and nunneries (*Monast. Angl.* vi. 320).

Roger was naturally drawn into the crusading movement. In 1146 or 1147 he had gone over to Normandy to defend his title to the castle of Bayeux, which Stephen had given him when he was knighted (*ib.* v. 352, but cf. p. 346), and is said to have been present in company with Odo II, duke of Burgundy, at a general chapter of the Cistercian order at Citeaux, where he was able to serve the interests of his abbey at Byland (*ib.* v. 352, 570). St. Bernard was just then preaching the second crusade, and Mowbray was apparently induced to accompany Louis VII (JOHN OF HEXHAM, ap. Twysden, p. 276). In one of his charters (*Monast. Angl.* v. 569) he alludes to a second journey to the Holy Land, which can hardly be the one he made at the very end of his life. He was probably absent from England in January 1164, for it was his son Nigel whose name was attached as a witness to the Constitutions of Clarendon; and perhaps in 1166, when his men answered for him the king's inquiries as to the number of knights' fees on his estates (*Materials for the History of Archbishop Becket*, v. 72; *Liber Niger Scaccarii*, ed. Hearne, i. 309; cf. EYTON, *Itinerary of Henry II*, p. 87). It appears from this return that in Yorkshire alone he had eighty-eight fees of the old feoffment, and eleven and three-quarters enfeoffed since the death of Henry I. Mowbray's deep interest in the crusading movement was attested by his gifts to the templars of Balshall in Warwickshire, where they placed one of their preceptories, and of Keadby-on-Trent, and other lands in Axholme and elsewhere (*Monast. Angl.* vi. 799, 800, 808, 834). The order gratefully conferred upon him and his heirs the privilege of releasing any templar whom they should find under sentence of public penance, no matter what the offence. The knights hospitallers, when they obtained most of the forfeited lands of the templars, solemnly renewed this privilege to Roger's descendant, John (I) de Mowbray [q. v.], and his heirs on 20 March 1335, with the addition that the Mowbrays should be treated in their convents beyond the seas as those to whom they were most obliged next the king himself (DUGDALE, *Baronage*, i. 123). At Burton, near Melton Mowbray in Leicestershire, Roger founded, perhaps with the assistance of a general collection, a dependency of the great Leper Hospital of St. Lazarus outside the walls of Jerusalem, 'which became the chief of all the Spittles or Lazar-houses in England' (DUGDALE, *Monast. Angl.* vi. 632; NICHOLS, *History of Leicestershire*, II. i. 272). To this day the village is called Burton Lazars.

In 1174 Mowbray appears in the new character of a rebel. Immediately after Easter he and his two sons Nigel and Robert joined the formidable coalition against the king, which had taken up arms in the previous summer. He hastily fortified his castle of Kinnardferry on the Trent in Axholme, which had been suffered to fall into disrepair, and strongly garrisoned his two Yorkshire strongholds of Thirsk and Kirkby Malzeard (BENEDICT OF PETERBOROUGH, i. 48; HOVEDEN, ii. 57; WILLIAM OF NEWBURGH, i. 180; DICETO, i. 379; WALTER OF COVENTRY, i. 216).

Mowbray's defection was one of the most dangerous elements of the situation, for his three fortresses linked the rebel earls in the midlands with the king of Scots, who was reducing the border fortresses of Northumberland and Cumberland. Thirsk and Kirkby Malzeard blocked the way through Yorkshire to any royal army sent against the Scots. The king's warlike natural son, Geoffrey, the bishop-elect of Lincoln, gathered a force in Lincolnshire, crossed the Trent, and laid siege to Kinnardferry, which was defended by Roger's younger son, Robert. The 'castle of the Island,' surrounded by the waters of the fen, was almost impregnable; but lack of water within compelled the defenders to surrender in a few days (5 May). Robert had escaped, but was captured on his way to Leicester by the rustics of Clay (Clay Cross?) (BENED. PET. i. 49; HOVEDEN, ii. 58; DICETO, i. 379; GIRALDUS CAMBRENSIS, iv. 364). After demolishing the castle, Bishop Geoffrey advanced into Yorkshire, and, reinforced by Archbishop Roger [q. v.] and a force from the shire, besieged the castle of Kirkby Malzeard, six miles north-east of Ripon. This also gave him little trouble, and was entrusted to the care of the archbishop, while he himself proceeded to attack Thirsk (BENEDICT, i. 68; HOVEDEN, ii. 58; GIRALDUS CAMBRENSIS, iv. 366–7). The castle was closely invested, and a rival fortification erected on the Percy land at Topcliffe, two and a half miles away, with a garrison under a member of the family of the Stutevilles with whom the Mowbrays had a standing feud. Mowbray, according to William of Newburgh (i. 182), now betook himself to William, king of Scots, whom he found besieging Prudhoe-on-Tyne, and secured a promise of help on condition that he assisted William in his invasion of Yorkshire, for the fulfilment of which he gave his eldest son in pledge. But, on hearing that Yorkshire was rallying round Robert Stuteville the sheriff,

William recrossed the Tyne and retreated northwards with Mowbray. Jordan Fantosme, however, gives us a different version of Mowbray's movements (ed. Surtees Soc. pp. 60, 62, 68). Mowbray, according to him, had left the defence of his castles to his sons, and, joining the Scottish king soon after his entry into Northumberland, had assisted him in the siege of Carlisle and the capture of Appleby and other towns.

However this may be, Roger was with the Scottish king when he was overtaken and captured by Stuteville and the Yorkshiremen at Alnwick on 13 July, but escaped himself into Scotland (*ib.* p. 84; NEWBURGH, i. 185). About three weeks later, when the rising in the midlands had collapsed, he came with other rebels on 31 July to King Henry at Northampton, surrendered Thirsk, and was received back into grace (BENEDICT, i. 73; HOVEDEN, ii. 65). Early in 1176 Henry ordered the demolition of the castles of Thirsk and Kirkby Malzeard, of which not a stone is now left (BENEDICT, i. 126; HOVEDEN, ii. 101; DICETO, i. 404; *Monasticon*, v. 310). The position of the Mowbrays in Yorkshire was thereby greatly weakened. Robert de Stuteville probably seized this opportunity to urge his old claim for the restoration of the lands of his ancestor, Frontebœuf, held by Mowbray, and Roger had to compromise by giving him possession of Kirkby Moorside (HOVEDEN, iv. 117, 118; *Rotuli Curiæ Regis*, ii. 231; *Monast. Angl.* v. 352). We may perhaps date from the destruction of Thirsk Castle the selection by the Mowbrays of Epworth in Axholme, with its natural defences, as their chief place of residence.

Roger witnessed Henry II's arbitration between Alfonso of Castile and Sancho of Navarre on 13 March 1177, and met Ranulf Glanvill and the five other judges sent by the king on the northern circuit in 1179 at Doncaster assizes. In 1186 he took the cross for the third time, and journeyed to the Holy Land (BENEDICT, i. 154, 239, 359; HOVEDEN, ii. 131, 316; EYTON, *Itin. of Henry II*, p. 211; *Monasticon*, v. 282; STUBBS, *Constit. Hist.* i. 487, 490). When the extension of the truce between Saladin and Guy de Lusignan allowed the crusaders to return home, he and Hugh de Beauchamp chose to remain at Jerusalem 'in the service of God' (BENEDICT, ii. 359; HOVEDEN, ii. 316). In Saladin's great victory on 6 July 1187 he was taken prisoner with King Guy, was redeemed in the following year by his protégés, the templars, but did not long survive his liberation (BENEDICT, ii. 22; HOVEDEN, ii. 325). Tradition added that he was buried at Tyre (*Monast.* v. 346). Another legendary version maintained that, wearying of these wars, he returned to England, slaying on his way a dragon which was fighting with a lion in a valley called Sarranell, whereupon the lion in his gratitude followed him to England to his castle of Hode, near Thirsk, and that fifteen years later he died at a good old age, and was buried in the abbey of Byland (*ib.* vi. 320).

By his wife Alice or Adeliza de Gant, who may very well have been related to Gilbert de Gant, earl of Lincoln (*d.* 1156), Mowbray had at least one daughter and two sons, Nigel and Robert, the former of whom succeeded him as third baron, and was father of William de Mowbray, fourth baron [q. v.] (*Monast. Angl.* v. 310, vi. 320; *Neustria Pia*, p. 660).

[The chief source for the life of Roger is the notices in the chronicles Orderic Vitalis, ed. Le Prevost, for the Société de l'Histoire de France, the Continuator of William of Jumièges (Gemeticensis) in Duchesne's Scriptores Normannorum, William of Newburgh, Ailred of Rievaulx, and Richard of Hexham in Chronicles of Stephen's Reign, &c. (Rolls Ser.), John of Hexham and Brompton of Jervaulx in Twysden's Decem Scriptores; the Gesta Henrici which go under the name of Benedict of Peterborough, Roger Hoveden, Ralph de Diceto, and Walter de Coventry, all ed. Stubbs for the Rolls Ser.; Giraldus Cambrensis's Vita Gaufridi Episcopi (Rolls Ser.) Documents relating to Byland, Newburgh, and other foundations of Roger, are printed in vols. v–vi. of Dugdale's Monasticon Anglicanum, ed. Caley, Ellis, and Bandinel, together with a brief account of the Mowbray family ('Progenies') in two versions, from the Byland register (Monast. v. 346–7), and a Newburgh manuscript at York (ib. vi. 320–1). The Byland version, which only comes down to John (I) de Mowbray, eighth baron [q. v.], seems to be the older form; the Newburgh version, which was finally revised during the lifetime of Thomas Howard, third duke of Norfolk of that line (1473–1554), and is continued to that time, adds not very trustworthy details. Some facts are derived from the Liber Niger Scaccarii, ed. Hearne; the Pipe Rolls, ed. Hunter and the Pipe Roll Society; the Rotuli Scaccarii Normanniæ, ed. Stapleton; and the Rotuli Curiæ Regis, ed. Palgrave, and Rotuli Chartarum, ed. Hardy, both for the Record Commission. See also Dugdale's Baronage, vol. i.; Hist. of Warwickshire; Nicolas's Historic Peerage, ed. Courthope; Stonehouse's Isle of Axholme; Grainge's Vale of Mowbray. Other authorities in the text.] J. T–T.

MOWBRAY, THOMAS (I), twelfth BARON MOWBRAY and first DUKE OF NORFOLK (1366?–1399), born about 1366, was the second son of John (III) de Mowbray, tenth baron Mowbray (*d.* 1368) [see under

Mowbray, John (II) de, *d.* 1361], by Elizabeth, only daughter and heiress of John, sixth lord Segrave (Doyle, *Official Baronage*). Mowbray was of the blood royal through his mother, who was daughter of Margaret, the elder daughter of the second surviving son of Edward I, Thomas of Brotherton, earl of Norfolk and earl marshal (1300–1338). Margaret married Lord Segrave before 1338, and succeeded her father as Countess of Norfolk and countess marshal in December of that year.

Mowbray's mother is said to have had him baptised Thomas, a name not previously affected by the family, to mark her special reverence for St. Thomas of Canterbury (Dugdale, *Baronage*, i. 128). The abbots of Fountains and Sawley were his sponsors. On the death without issue at the early age of nineteen, on 10 Feb. 1383, of his elder brother, John (IV) de Mowbray, eleventh baron, Thomas succeeded as twelfth Baron Mowbray of Axholme. He inherited, in addition to the great Mowbray barony, in which were merged those of Braose (Brewes) and Segrave, the expectation of the still more splendid heritage of the old Bigods, earls of Norfolk, at present enjoyed by Margaret, his grandmother. Richard at once (12 Feb.) revived, in favour of his young cousin, the title of Earl of Nottingham, which his brother had borne (Doyle). Before October he was given the garter vacant by the death of Sir John Burley (Beltz, *Memorials of the Order of the Garter*, p. 259). As Earl of Nottingham he was summoned to the parliament which met on 26 Oct. of that year (*Rep. on the Dignity of a Peer*, App. p. 705). Froissart substitutes the Earls of Northumberland and Nottingham for the Duke of Lancaster and the Earl of Buckingham as leaders of the Scottish expedition of March 1384 (cf. Monk of Evesham, p. 51; Walsingham, ii. 111). There is no doubt, however, that Nottingham was present in the expedition which Richard in person conducted against the Scots in the summer of the next year. On the eve of their departure (30 June) the king invested the earl for life with the office of earl marshal of England, which had been enjoyed by his great-grandfather, Thomas of Brotherton (Dugdale, i. 128). On the march through Yorkshire he confirmed, on 21 July, with many of the knights of the army as witnesses, his ancestor Roger's charter to Byland Abbey [see under Mowbray, Roger (I) de].

Nottingham, who was barely twenty years of age, does not appear by name among the nobles who carried out the revolution at court against the king of October to December 1386 (cf. *Continuatio Eulogii Historiarum*, iii. 361). Of nearly the same age as the king, he had been much in his company (Walsingham, ii. 156). But he had married in 1385 a sister of Arundel, who was, next to Gloucester, the chief author of the revolution, and shared with his brother-in-law the glory of his naval victory of 24 March 1387 over the French, Flemings, and Spaniards (Walsingham, ii. 153-6; *Chron. Angliæ*, pp. 374–5). He did not, however, accompany Arundel in the further expedition which he undertook for the relief of Brest (Knighton, col. 2693). Richard received Nottingham very coldly when he presented himself to report his success, and his favourite, the Duke of Ireland, refused even to speak to the two earls. They therefore retired to their estates, 'where they could live more at their ease than with the king' (Walsingham, ii. 156). Nottingham was one of those whose destruction the king and the Duke of Ireland plotted after Easter (*ib.* p. 161; Monk of Evesham, p. 84). Yet he does not seem to have taken any open part in the armed demonstration in November by which Gloucester, Arundel, and Warwick, with whom the Earl of Derby, eldest son of John of Gaunt [see Henry IV], had now ranged himself, extorted from Richard a promise that his advisers should be brought to account before parliament. It was not until after the lords in revolt had fled from court, and the Duke of Ireland was approaching with an army raised in Cheshire to relieve the king from the constraint in which he was held, that Nottingham followed Derby's example, and appeared in arms with Derby and the other three lords at Huntingdon on 12 Dec. (*Rot. Parl.* iii. 376; Monk of Evesham, p. 137). Even now, if we may trust the story which Derby and Nottingham told ten years after, when they were assisting Richard in bringing their old associates to account for these proceedings, they showed themselves more moderate than their elders. They claimed to have secured the rejection of Arundel's plan to capture and depose the king (*ib.*) The five confederates marched instead into Oxfordshire, to intercept the Duke of Ireland before he could pass the Thames. They divided their forces for the purpose on 20 Dec., and Nottingham, like some of the others, seemingly did not come up in time to take part with Derby and Gloucester in the actual fighting at Radcot Bridge, near Burford, from which the Duke of Ireland only escaped by swimming (Monk of Evesham, p. 95; Walsingham, ii. 168; Knighton, col. 2703). The victors returned through Oxford, where the chronicler Adam of Usk (p. 5) saw their army pass, with Arundel and Nottingham bringing up the rear; after spending Christmas day at St. Albans, they reached London on 26 Dec., and encamped in the fields at Clerkenwell. The London populace siding with the formidable host without, the mayor ordered the gates to be opened to the lords (Walsingham, ii. 171). They insisted on an interview with Richard in the Tower, and entered his presence with linked arms. The helpless young king consented to meet them next day at Westminster, and besought them to sup and stay the night with him, in token of goodwill. Gloucester refused, but Richard succeeded in keeping Derby and Nottingham to supper (Knighton, col. 2704; Derby only according to the Monk of Evesham, p. 100, and Walsingham, ii. 172). Next day (27 Dec.) they formally appealed his favourites of treason at Westminster, and Richard was forced to order their arrest (Knighton, col. 2705; Evesham, p. 100; Walsingham, ii. 172–3; *Fœdera*, vii. 566–8). As one of the five appellants Nottingham joined in the subsequent proscription of the king's friends in the Merciless parliament which met on 3 Feb. 1388 (*Rot. Parl.* iii. 229 seq.; Knighton, cols. 2713–26). On 10 March he was joined as marshal with Gloucester the constable to hear a suit between Matthew Gournay and Louis de Sancerre, marshal of France (*Fœdera*, vii. 570). In the early months of 1389 he is said to have been sent against the Scots, who were ravaging Northumberland; but, being entrusted with only five hundred lances, did not venture an encounter with the Scots, who numbered, if we may believe the chroniclers, thirty thousand (Walsingham, ii. 180; Monk of Evesham, p. 107).

When Richard shook off the tutelage of the appellants on 3 May, Nottingham was removed with the others from the privy council (Walsingham, ii. 182, and Monk of Evesham p. 109, mention only Gloucester and Warwick). But once his own master, Richard showed particular anxiety to conciliate the earl-marshal. He gave him the overdue livery of his lands, and a week after his emancipation (11 May) placed him on the commission appointed to negotiate a truce with Scotland (*Ord. of Privy Council*, i. 27). His great possessions in the north naturally suggested his employment in the defence of the Scottish border, as his grandfather had been employed before him. On 1 June, therefore, he was constituted warden of the east marches, captain of Berwick, and constable of Roxburgh Castle for a term of two years (Dugdale, i. 128; Doyle). By the middle of September both he and Derby had been restored to their places at the council board, which a month later (15 Oct.) was the scene of a hot dispute between the king and his new chancellor, William of Wykeham, who resisted Richard's proposal to grant a large pension to Nottingham (*Ord. of Privy Council*, i. 11, 12). Whatever may have been Richard's real feelings towards Gloucester and Arundel at this time, it was obviously to his interest to attach the younger and less prominent appellants to himself. Nottingham alone was continuously employed in the service of the state, and entrusted with the most responsible commands. On 28 June 1390 he was associated with the treasurer, John Gilbert, bishop of St. David's, and others to obtain redress from the Scots for recent infractions of the truce (*Fœdera*, vii. 678; *Ord. of Privy Council*, i. 27; Lowth, *Life of Wykeham*, p. 228). In 1391 an exchange of posts was effected between Nottingham and the Earl of Northumberland, who returned to his old office of warden of the Scottish marches, while Mowbray took the captaincy of Calais (Dugdale, i. 128; Walsingham, ii. 203). In November of the next year, this office was renewed to him for six years, in conjunction with that of lieutenant of the king in Calais and the parts of Picardy, Flanders, and Artois for the same term (Dugdale, i. 128). On 12 Jan. 1394 Richard recognised Nottingham's just and hereditary right to bear for his crest a golden leopard gorged with a silver label (Gloucester's crest), but substituted a crown for the label, on the ground that the latter would appertain to the king's son, if he had any (*Fœdera*, vii. 763; Beltz, p. 298; Doyle). In March 1394 Nottingham was appointed chief justice of North Wales, and two months later chief justice of Chester and Flint (*ib.*; Dugdale, i. 128).

Nottingham accompanied Richard to Ireland in September 1394, and on his return was commissioned, with the Earl of Rutland, son of Edmund of Langley, duke of York, and others, on 8 July, and again in October and December, to negotiate a long truce with France and a marriage for the king with Isabella, daughter of Charles VI of France (*Ann. Ricardi II*, p. 172; *Fœdera*, vii. 802). He was present at the costly wedding festivities at Calais in October 1396 (*Ann. Ricardi II*, p. 190). Nottingham thus closely identified himself with the French connection, which by its baneful influence upon Richard's character and policy, and its unpopularity in the country contributed more than anything else to hastening his misfortunes. In the parliament of January 1397 Richard gave Nottingham another signal proof of his favour by an express recognition of the earl-marshalship of England as hereditary in his house, and permission to bear a golden truncheon, enamelled in black at each end, and bearing the royal arms on the upper, and his own on the lower (*Rot. Parl.* iii. 344; Wallon, *Richard II*, i. 404–5). At the same time Nottingham secured a victory in a personal quarrel with one of Gloucester's associates, the Earl of Warwick. Warwick's father in 1352 had obtained legal recognition of his claim to the lordship of Gower, a part of the Mowbray inheritance. This judgment was now reversed in Nottingham's favour (Dugdale, pp. 236–7; *Ann. Ricardi II*, p. 201).

Nottingham was out of England from the end of February till the latter part of June on a foreign mission: his colleagues were the Earl of Rutland and Bishop Thomas Merke [q.v.], and as late as 16 June they were at Bacharach on the Rhine (*Fœdera*, vii. 850, 858). But the earl returned in time to serve as one of the instruments of Richard's revenge upon Gloucester, Arundel, and Warwick, his fellow-appellants of 1388. How far his conduct was justifiable is matter of opinion, but it was not unnatural. He was the last to join the appellants and probably the first to be reconciled to the king, and now for eight years he had been loaded by Richard with exceptional favours. He had long drifted apart from his old associates, and with one of them he was at open enmity. It must be confessed too that he was a considerable gainer by the destruction of his old friends. According to the king's story, Nottingham and seven other young courtiers, of whom all but one were related to the royal house, advised Richard to arrest Gloucester, Arundel, and Warwick on 8 and 9 July. At Nottingham on 5 Aug. they agreed to appeal them of treason in the parliament which had been summoned to meet at Westminster on 21 Sept. (*Rot. Parl.* iii. 374; *Fœdera*, viii. 7; *Ann. Ricardi II*, p. 206). Nottingham was present when Richard in person arrested Gloucester at his castle of Pleshy in Essex, and it was to his care as captain of Calais that the duke was consigned (*ib.* p. 201; Monk of Evesham, p. 130). He may have himself conducted his prisoner to Calais, though we have only Froissart's authority for this; but his presence at Nottingham on 5 Aug. proves that he did not mount guard personally over him throughout his imprisonment. He had for some time in fact been performing his duties at Calais by deputy (cf. *Rot. Parl.* iii. 377).

On Friday, 21 Sept., Nottingham and his fellow-appellants 'in red silk robes, banded with white silk, and powdered with letters of gold,' renewed in parliament the appeal they had made at Nottingham (*ib.*; Adam of Usk, p. 12; Monk of Evesham, p. 136). Arundel was forthwith tried, condemned, and beheaded on Tower Hill. A strongly Lancastrian writer asserts that Nottingham, along with Arundel's nephew, the Earl of Kent, led his brother-in-law to execution, and makes Arundel taunt them with ingratitude and prophesy time's speedy revenge (*Ann. Ricardi II*, pp. 216–17). Froissart adds that the earl-marshal bandaged Arundel's eyes and performed the execution himself.

This seems to have been the popular belief as early as 1399 (Langland, *Richard the Redeles*, Early Engl. Text Soc., 1873, Pass. iii. 105–6); but the official record states that the execution was carried out by Lord Morley, the lieutenant of the earl-marshal (*Rot. Parl.* iii. 377). Adam of Usk (p. 14) mentions the presence of Kent and others who coveted the condemned earl's lands. Nottingham was at once granted the castle and lordship of Lewes, of which he had been given the custody as early as 26 July, and all the forfeited lands of Arundel in Sussex and Surrey, except Reigate (Dugdale, i. 129). On the day of Arundel's death the king issued a writ, addressed to Nottingham as captain of Calais, or his deputy, to bring up the Duke of Gloucester before parliament to answer the charges of the appellants (*Rot. Parl.* iii. 377; *Fœdera*, viii. 15). Parliament seems to have adjourned to Monday the 24th, when Nottingham's answer was read, curtly intimating that he could not produce the duke, as he had died in his custody at Calais (*Rot. Parl.* iii. 377; Adam of Usk, p. 15). Next day a confession, purporting to have been made by Gloucester to Sir William Rickhill [q. v.], justice of the common pleas, on 8 Sept., was read in parliament, and the dead man was found guilty of treason. The whole affair is involved in mystery, and there is a strong suspicion that Richard and Nottingham were responsible for Gloucester's death. [For a full discussion of the death see art. Thomas of Woodstock.] After the accession of Henry IV a certain John Hall, a servant of Nottingham, who was by that time dead, being arrested as an accomplice in the murder of Gloucester, deposed in writing to parliament that he had been called from his bed by Nottingham one night in September 1397, had been informed that the king had ordered Gloucester to be murdered, and had been enjoined to be present with other esquires and servants of Nottingham and of the Earl of Rutland. Hall at first refused, but Nottingham struck him on the head, and said he should obey or die. He then took an oath of secrecy with eight other esquires and yeomen, whose names he gave, in the church of Notre-Dame in the presence of his master. Nottingham took them to a hostel called Prince's Inn, and there left them. Gloucester was handed over to them by John Lovetot, who was also a witness to the duke's confession made to Rickhill, and he was suffocated under a feather bed. Hall was at once condemned, without being produced, and executed; and when Serle, one of the others mentioned, was captured in 1404 he met the same fate (DUGDALE, ii. 171; *Ann. Henrici IV*, p. 390). This not altogether satisfactory evidence was adopted, with some additions of their own, by the Lancastrian chroniclers (*Ann. Ricardi II*, p. 221; *Ann. Henrici IV*, p. 309; WALSINGHAM, ii. 226, 228, 242; MONK OF EVESHAM, pp. 161–2; *Cont. Eulogii*, iii. 373). But Nottingham's guilt is not proved, though the balance of evidence is against him.

Nottingham's services, whatever their extent, were rewarded on 28 Sept. by a grant of the greater part of the Arundel estates in Sussex and Surrey, and of seventeen of the Earl of Warwick's manors in the midlands (DUGDALE, i. 129). The commons representing to the king that Derby and Nottingham had been 'innocent of malice' in their appeal of 1388, Richard vouched for their loyalty (*Rot. Parl.* iii. 355). On 29 Sept. Nottingham was created Duke of Norfolk, and his grandmother, Margaret, countess of Norfolk, was at the same time created Duchess of Norfolk for life (*ib.* iii. 355, iv. 273; MONK OF EVESHAM, p. 141; ADAM OF USK, p. 17). The statement of one authority that Richard at the same time gave him the earldom of Arundel must doubtless be referred to the grant of the estates of that earldom (*Cont. Eulogii*, iii. 377).

But new wealth and honours did not render Norfolk's position inviolable. The king was vindictive by nature, and had not forgotten that Norfolk was once his enemy; he afterwards declared that the duke had not pursued the appeal of his old friends with such zeal as those who had never turned their coats (*Rot. Parl.* iii. 383). At the same time the inner circle of the king's confidants —the Earl of Kent, now Duke of Surrey, Sir William le Scrope, now Earl of Wiltshire, and the Earl of Salisbury—were (Norfolk had reason to suspect) urging the king to rid himself of all who had ever been his enemies. Norfolk is said to have confided his fears to Hereford as they rode from Brentford to London in December 1397 (*ib.* p. 382). Richard was informed of Norfolk's language; obtained from Hereford, who probably was jealous of Norfolk's dignities and power, a written account of the interview with Norfolk, and summoned both parties to appear before the adjourned parliament, which was to meet at Shrewsbury on 30 Jan. 1398 (*ib.*; *Cont. Eulogii*, iii. 379). Hereford seems to have accompanied the king on his way to Shrewsbury, for on 25 Jan. Richard at Lilleshall gave him a full pardon for all treasons or other offences of which he might have been guilty in the past (*Fœdera*, viii. 32). Norfolk did not appear to answer the charges which Hereford, on Wednesday, 30 Jan., presented against him, and on 4 Feb. the king ordered the sheriffs to proclaim that he must appear within fifteen days (*ib.*) The story, one of several common to Adam of Usk and the French authorities, that Norfolk had laid an ambush for Hereford on his way to Shrewsbury, and which has passed into Holinshed and Shakespeare, if it is not entirely baseless, must be referred to some earlier occasion (ADAM OF USK, pp. 22, 129; *Chronique de la Trahison*; SHAKESPEARE, *Richard II*, act i. sc. i.; cf. MONK OF EVESHAM, p. 57). Meanwhile it had been settled, on 31 Jan., that the matter should be left to the king, with the advice of the committee appointed by parliament to deal with unfinished business (*Rot. Parl.* ii. 382). At Oswestry, on 23 Feb., Norfolk was present, and gave a full denial to the charges, and it was settled and confirmed by the king in council at Bristol that unless sufficient proofs of his guilt were discovered in the meantime the matter should be referred to a court of chivalry at Windsor, to be held on Sunday, 28 April (*ib.*; *Fœdera*, viii. 35–6; cf. ADAM OF USK, p. 23). The court met at Windsor on the date fixed, and next day decided that the matter should be settled by trial of battle at Coventry on 16 Sept. (*Rot. Parl.* iii. 382). The lists were prepared in a place surrounded by a ditch, outside Coventry, and on the appointed day the combatants duly appeared (ADAM OF USK, p. 23). They were both magnificently arrayed, Norfolk, we are told, having secured his armour from Germany, and Hereford's being a present from Gian Galeazzo of Milan (*Archæologia*, xx. 102; ADAM OF USK, p. 23). But Hereford was much the more splendid, having seven horses diversely equipped (*ib.*) Before they had joined issue, however, the king took the battle into his own hands, on the ground that treason was in question, and that it was undesirable that the blood royal should be dishonoured by the defeat of either (*Rot. Parl.* iii. 383). Richard then decided that inasmuch as Norfolk had confessed at Windsor to some of the charges which he had repelled at Oswestry, and was thus self-convicted of conduct which was likely to have roused great trouble in the kingdom, he should quit the realm before the octaves of St. Edward, to take up his residence in Germany, Bohemia, and Hungary, and 'pass the great sea in pilgrimage.' He was to go nowhere else in Christendom on pain of incurring the penalties of treason. Hereford was banished to France, and communication between them was expressly forbidden (*ib.* iii. 382). The same veto was laid upon all intercourse with Archbishop Arundel. Norfolk's share of the lands of Arundel and Warwick and all his offices were declared forfeited, because he had resisted the abrogation of the acts of the Merciless parliament, and failed in his duty as an appellant (*ib.*) The rest of his estates were to be taken into the king's hands, and the revenues, after paying him 1,000*l.* a year, were devoted to covering the heavy losses in which it was alleged his maladministration of his governorship of Calais had involved the king (*ib.*; MONK OF EVESHAM, p. 146). Next day his office of marshal of England was granted for the term of his (Norfolk's) life to the king's nephew, Thomas Holland, duke of Surrey (*Fœdera*, viii. 44). The captaincy of Calais had already been given by Richard to his half-brother, John Holland, duke of Exeter. Adam of Usk (p. 23) has a story that Richard stopped the battle because he thought Norfolk was likely to be beaten by Hereford, on whose destruction he was bent, and that the king banished Norfolk only as a matter of form, intending to recall him. Mr. Maunde Thompson seems inclined to accept this theory (ADAM OF USK, p. 131); but it looks rather far-fetched. A Lancastrian writer adds that Norfolk was condemned on the very day on which, a year before, he had had Gloucester suffocated (*Ann. Ricardi II*, p. 226).

On 3 Oct. the king ordered his admirals to allow free passage to Norfolk from any port between Scarborough and Orwell; licensed the duke to take with him a suite of forty persons, 1,000*l.* in money, with jewels, plate, and harness, and issued a general request to all princes and nations to allow him safe-conduct (*Fœdera*, viii. 47–8, see also p. 51). A few days later (Saturday, 19 Oct.) Norfolk took ship at the port of Kekeleyrode, a little south of Lowestoft, for Dordrecht, in the presence of the officials of Lowestoft and some of the county gentry, who testified to the fact, and added that by sunset he was six leagues and more from that port, and was favoured with 'bon vent et swef' (*Rot. Parl.* iii. 384). He perhaps now recalled the words, if they were really spoken, in which Archbishop Arundel had warned him the year before, in the presence of the king, that he and others would speedily follow him into exile (MONK OF EVESHAM, p. 203).

Of the subsequent wanderings of the 'banished Norfolk' we know no more than that he reached Venice, where on 18 Feb. 1399 the senate, at the request of King Richard, granted him (disguised in their minutes as duke of 'Gilforth') the loan of a galley for his intended visit to the Holy Sepulchre (*Cal. of State Papers*, Venetian, i. 38; *Archives de l'Orient Latin*, ii. 243). He induced some private Venetians to advance him money for the expenses of his journey, on the express undertaking, inserted in his will, that their claims should rank before all others (ELLIS, *Original Letters*, 3rd ser. i. 46, 50; *Cal. of State Papers*, Venetian, i. 47). After his death the Doge Steno pressed Henry IV to compel Norfolk's heirs to satisfy these claims (*ib.*) On the death of Norfolk's grandmother, the old duchess, Richard revoked on 18 March 1399 the letters patent by which he had empowered him to receive inheritances by attorney, and thus kept him from enjoying the revenues of the old Bigod estates (*Rot. Parl.* iii. 372). It cannot be regarded as certain that he ever made his journey to Palestine, for he died at Venice on 22 Sept. of the same year, 1399 (*Ord. of Privy Council*, i. 99). The register of Newburgh Priory says, however, that it was after his return from the Holy Land, and that he died of the plague. He was buried in Venice, and though his son John left instructions in his will that his ashes should be brought to England, nothing seems to have been done until his descendant, Thomas Howard, third duke of Norfolk, preferred a request for them to the Venetian authorities in December 1532 through the Venetian ambassador in London (*Cal. of State Papers*, Venetian, Pref. lxxxiii). Rawdon Brown identified as a part of his tomb a stone with an elaborate heraldic achievement, which was pictured, by one ignorant of the English character of its heraldry, in Casimiro Freschot's 'Li Pregi della Nobiltà Veneta abbozzati in un Giuco d'Arme,' 1682. The stone itself Brown discovered after long search in 1839; it was 'conveyed' from its place of concealment in the pavement of the terrace of the ducal palace, and was presented to Mr. Henry Howard of Corby Castle, near Carlisle, where it still remains (*ib.*; *Atlantic Monthly*, lxiii. 742). This 'Mowbray stone,' which is figured and described in 'Archæologia' (xxix. 387) and in Baines's 'Lancashire,' ed. Croston (i. 69), contains the royal banner of England and the badges of Richard II, Mowbray, and Bolingbroke in an association, which Rawdon Brown held to be emblematic of Mowbray triumphing over Bolingbroke with the assistance of Richard. Mr. Wylie, on the other hand, holds that this is a strained interpretation, and is inclined to associate it with Bolingbroke's visit to Venice in 1392–3 (*Hist. of England under Henry IV*, ii. 29).

Norfolk left lands in most counties of England and Wales, whose mere enumeration, says Mr. Wylie (ii. 29), fills eleven closely printed folio pages in the 'Inquisitiones post Mortem' (cf. DUGDALE, i. 130). Mowbray was twice married. His first wife, Elizabeth, daughter of Roger le Strange of Blackmere, died almost immediately, and in 1385 he took for his second wife Elizabeth Fitzalan, daughter of Richard, earl of Arundel, who bore him two sons: Thomas and John, who successively inherited his estates, and are separately noticed; and two daughters: Isabel, who married Sir James Berkley, and Margaret, who became wife of Sir Robert Howard, created Duke of Norfolk after the extinction of the male line of the Mowbrays (*ib.*; DOYLE, *Official Baronage*). His widow, who was allowed a large dowry in the eastern and midland counties, afterwards married Sir Gerard de Usflete and Sir Robert Goushill successively, and survived until 8 July 1425 (DUGDALE, *Baronage*, i. 130; NICHOLS, *Royal Wills*, p. 144).

It is not possible to pronounce a final verdict upon Mowbray's character while we have to suspend our judgment as to the part he had played in the mysterious death of the Duke of Gloucester. But at best he was no better than the rest of the little knot of selfish, ambitious nobles, mostly of the blood royal, into which the older baronage had now shrunk, and whose quarrels already preluded their extinction at each other's hands in the Wars of the Roses. Mowbray had some claim to be considered a benefactor of the church; for besides confirming his ancestors' grants to various monasteries (*Monast. Angl.* vi. 374), he founded and handsomely endowed in 1396 a Cistercian priory at Epworth in Axholme, dedicated to St. Mary, St. John the Evangelist, and St. Edward the Confessor, and called Domus Visitationis Beatæ Mariæ Virginis (*ib.* vi. 25–6; STONEHOUSE, *Isle of Axholme*, p. 135). To the chapel of Our Lady in this Priory-in-the-Wood, as it is sometimes designated (now Melwood Priory), Pope Boniface IX, by a bull dated 1 June 1397, granted the privileges which St. Francis had first procured for the Church of S. Maria de Angelis at Assisi (*Monast. Angl.* vi. 26).

In Weever's poem, 'The Mirror of Martyrs,' Sir John Oldcastle is said to have been a page of Mowbray, a tradition which Shakespeare transferred to Falstaff.

[Apart from the information supplied by the Rolls of Parliament, Proceedings and Ordinances of the Privy Council, Rymer's Fœdera (original edition), the Lords' Report on the Dignity of a Peer, Inquisitions post Mortem, and other printed records, the chief sources for Mowbray's life are chroniclers who wrote with an adverse Lancastrian bias. They accepted Hall's confession as establishing Norfolk's responsibility for the death of Gloucester. Walsingham's Historia Anglicana and the fuller form of its narrative from 1392, edited by Mr. Riley under the title of Annales Ricardi II et Henrici IV, with Trokelowe, are both printed in the Rolls Series. The same account is partly reproduced by the anonymous Monk of Evesham, for whose valuable Life of Richard II we have still to go to Hearne's careless edition. The very full account of the parliament of 1397 given by this authority is almost identical with that in Adam of Usk (ed. Mr. Maunde Thompson for the Royal Society of Literature), who, however, elsewhere supplies information peculiar to his chronicle. The Continuation of the Eulogium (vol. iii.) in the Rolls Series is also of value. Some not very trustworthy details may be derived from Froissart (ed. Kervyn de Lettenhove) and the Chronique de la Trahison et Mort de Richart Deux, ed. B. S. Williams for the English Historical Society. Dugdale in his Baronage (i. 128–30) has summarised the chief authorities known to him. See also his Monasticon Anglicanum; Stonehouse's History of the Isle of Axholme; Archæologia, vols. xx. xxix. xxxi.; Boutell's Heraldry; Beltz's Memorials of the Order of the Garter; Grainge's Vale of Mowbray; information from J. H. Wylie, esq., respecting the Mowbray Stone; other authorities in the text.]

J. T-T.

MOWBRAY, THOMAS (II), EARL MARSHAL and third EARL OF NOTTINGHAM (1386–1405) born in 1386, was the elder son of Thomas Mowbray I, first duke of Norfolk [q. v.], by his second wife, Elizabeth Fitzalan, sister of Thomas, earl of Arundel (1381–1415) [q. v.] His younger brother, John, second duke of Norfolk, is separately noticed. At the time of his father's death at Venice in September 1399 he was page of Richard II's child-queen, Isabella (*Ord. Privy Council*, i. 100). Young Mowbray was not allowed to assume the title of Duke of Norfolk, though it was not expressly revoked (*Rot. Parl.* iv. 274), and that of earl-marshal, which he was allowed to retain, was dissociated from the office of marshal of England, which was granted for life to the Earl of Westmoreland (*Fœdera*, viii. 89; *Chron.* ed. Giles, p. 43; WALLON, *Richard II*, i. 405). A small income was set aside from the revenue of his Gower estates for the support of Thomas and his younger brother John, and he was married towards the close of 1400 to the king's niece, Constance Holland.

whose father, John Holland, duke of Exeter [q.v.], was beheaded in the preceding January (*Ord. Privy Council*, i. 100; *Kalendars and Inventories of the Exchequer*, ii. 62).

Smarting under his exclusion from his father's honours, and perhaps urged on by his discontented Yorkshire neighbours, the Percies and Scropes, the earl-marshal joined in the treasonable movements of 1405 (*Chron.* ed. Davies, p. 31). On his own confession he was privy to the Duke of York's plot for carrying off the young Mortimers from Windsor in February of that year (*Ann. Henrici IV*, p. 399). But the king accepted his assurances that he had taken no active part in the conspiracy. Immediately afterwards he quarrelled with Richard Beauchamp, earl of Warwick. The latter claimed, in a council on 1 March, precedence of Mowbray as the holder of an earldom of elder creation (cf. *Rot. Parl.* iv. 267, 269). The king decided in Warwick's favour, and the earl-marshal withdrew in dudgeon to the north, where the Earl of Northumberland was already preparing for revolt (*Eulogium*, iii. 405; *Ord. Privy Council*, ii. 104).

Mowbray joined Archbishop Scrope of York in formulating and placarding over that city a list of grievances in English, in one form of which the king was denounced as a usurper (*Anglia Sacra*, ii. 362–8; *Ann. Henrici IV*, pp. 402–5; *Eulogium*, iii. 405; Walsingham, ii. 269; *Chron.* ed. Giles, p. 44). These articles hit most of the blots on Henry's administration, and some eight or nine thousand Yorkshiremen gathered round Scrope and Mowbray as they marched northwards from York towards Mowbray's country about Thirsk, where Sir John Fauconberg and other local knights were already in arms (*Rot. Parl.* iii. 604). They were probably aiming at a junction with Northumberland and Lord Bardolf. But the king's second son, John, afterwards Duke of Bedford, and Ralph Nevill, earl of Westmorland [q. v.], the wardens of the Scottish marches, dispersed Fauconberg's forces at Topcliffe, a Percy lordship close to Thirsk, and on 29 May intercepted the earl-marshal and Archbishop Scrope at Shipton Moor, five and a half miles north of York (*ib.*; *Eulogium*, iii. 405). It was against Mowbray's judgment that the archbishop consented to the fatal interview with Westmorland, when the latter, assuming a spirit of friendly concession, induced the archbishop to dismiss his followers (*Ann. Henrici IV*, p. 406). The leaders were then seized and hurried off to Pontefract, where the king arrived from Wales by 3 June. They were afterwards brought to the archbishop's house at Bishopthorpe, some two miles south of York. The king's wrath was fanned by his half-brother, Thomas Beaufort, and by the young Earl of Arundel, Mowbray's uncle, and he resolved that the prisoners should die where they had raised the standard of revolt (Stubbs, *Const. Hist.* iii. 30). Commissioners, among whom were Beaufort, Arundel, and Chief-justice Gascoigne, had already been appointed to try all persons concerned in the rebellion. On the morning of Monday, 8 June, the king called upon Gascoigne to pass sentence upon the archbishop and his fellow-traitors (T. Gascoigne, *Loci e Libro Veritatum*, ed. Rogers, p. 227; *Anglia Sacra*, ii. 369; *Chron.* ed. Giles, p. 45; Wylie, *Henry IV*, ii. 230–6). Gascoigne refused to sit in judgment on a prelate, and sentence of death was delivered in the name of the commissioners without form of trial by another member, Sir William Fulthorpe, a man learned in the law, though not a judge (*ib.*) He was supported by Arundel and Beaufort, who acted constable and marshal respectively (cf. *Ann. Henrici IV*, p. 409). The same day, the feast of St. William of York and a holiday in the city, the condemned men were led out to execution before a great concourse of the citizens in a cornfield under the walls of the town, which, according to one account, belonged to the nuns of Clementhorpe (*Chron.* ed. Giles, p. 46; *Ann. Henrici IV*, p. 409; cf. Murray, *Yorkshire*, p. 73). Mowbray showed some natural fear of death, but was encouraged by his companion to keep a stout heart. He was beheaded before the archbishop. His body was buried in the Grey Friars' Church (Wylie, ii. 242), but his head was placed on a stake and fixed on Bootham Bar. A legend grew up that when the king two months after permitted it to be taken down, it was found to have retained all the freshness of life (*Ann. Henrici IV*, p. 411).

[Rotuli Parliamentorum; Ordinances of the Privy Council, ed. Palgrave; Rymer's Fœdera, original edit.; Annales Henrici IV (with J. de Trokelowe), Walsingham's Historia Anglicana and the Eulogium Historiarum in the Rolls Ser.; Chronicon Angliæ incerti Scriptoris, ed. J. A. Giles, 1848; English Chronicle, 1377–1461, ed. Davies, for Camden Society; T. Gascoigne's Loci e Libro Veritatum; Anglia Sacra, ed. Wharton, 1691; Kalendars and Inventories of the Exchequer (Record Commission edit.); Dugdale's Baronage; Doyle's Official Baronage; Courthope's Historic Peerage; Ramsay's Lancaster and York, vol. i.; Pauli's Geschichte Englands, vol. v.; Wylie's Henry IV, vol. ii.] J. T-t.

MOWBRAY, WILLIAM de, fourth Baron Mowbray (*d.* 1222?), one of the executors of Magna Charta, was the eldest of four sons of Nigel de Mowbray, by Mabel, daughter of Edmund (Roger?), earl of Clare, and grandson of Roger de Mowbray, second baron [q. v.] (DUGDALE, *Monast. Angl.* vi. 320). He had livery of his lands in 1194 on payment of a relief of one hundred pounds, and was immediately called upon to pay a similar sum as his share of the scutage levied towards King Richard's ransom, for the payment of which he was one of the pledges (DUGDALE, *Baronage*, i. 124). He was a witness to the treaty with Flanders in 1197 (*Fœdera*, i. 67; STAPLETON, *Rotuli Scaccarii Normanniæ*, ii. lxxiv). When Richard I died, and John delayed to claim his crown, Mowbray was one of the barons who seized the opportunity to fortify their castles; but, like the rest, was induced to swear fealty to John by the promises which Archbishop Hubert Walter, the justiciar Geoffrey Fitz-Peter, and William Marshall made in his name (HOVEDEN, iv. 88). Apparently it was thought prudent to exempt him from the scutage which was raised early in 1200 (DUGDALE, *Baronage*, i. 124). When William de Stuteville renewed the old claim of his house to the Frontebœuf lands in the possession of the Mowbrays, thus ignoring the compromise made by his father with Roger de Mowbray [q. v.], and Mowbray supported his suit by a present of three thousand marks to the king, John and his great council dictated a new compromise. Stuteville had to accept nine knights' fees and a rent of 12*l.* in full satisfaction of his claims, and the adversaries were reconciled at a country house of the Bishop of Lincoln at Louth on 21 Jan. 1201 (HOVEDEN, iv. 117–18; *Rotuli Curiæ Regis*, ed. Palgrave, ii. 231).

In 1215 Mowbray was prominent among the opponents of John. With other north-country barons, he appeared in arms at Stamford in the last days of April. When the Great Charter had been wrung from the king, he was appointed one of the twenty-five executors, and as such was specially named among those excommunicated by Pope Innocent. The castle of York was entrusted to his care (DUGDALE, *Baronage*, i. 124). Mowbray's youngest brother, Roger, has sometimes been reckoned as one of the twenty-five, apparently by confusion with Roger de Mumbezon (*ib.* p. 618; NICOLAS, *Historic Peerage*, ed. Courthope, p. 340). Roger died without heirs about 1218, and Mowbray received his lands (DUGDALE, i. 125). Mowbray was taken prisoner in the battle of Lincoln in 1217, and his estates bestowed upon William Marshal the younger; but he redeemed them by the surrender of the lordship of Bensted in Surrey to Hubert de Burgh, before the general restoration in September of that year (MATTHEW PARIS, iii. 22; DUGDALE, *Baronage*, i. 124, and *Monast. Angl.* v. 346; *Royal Letters of the Reign of Henry III.* i. 524). Three years later, in January 1221, Mowbray assisted Hubert in driving his former colleague as one of the twenty-five executors, William of Aumâle, from his last stronghold at Biham (Bytham) in Lincolnshire (DUGDALE, *Baronage*, l.c.; STUBBS, *Const. Hist.* ii. 33).

Mowbray founded the chapel of St. Nicholas, with a chantry, at Thirsk, and was a benefactor of his grandfather's foundation at Newburgh, where, on his death in Axholme about 1222, he was buried (DUGDALE, *Monast. Angl.* vi. 320). He is said, in the sixteenth-century recension of the 'Progenies Moubraiorum' (*ib.*), to have married Agnes, a daughter of the (second?) Earl of Arundel, of the elder branch of the Albinis. By her he had two sons, Nigel and Roger. The 'Progenies' (*Monasticon*, v. 346, vi. 320) makes Nigel predecease his father, and Nicolas and Courthope accept this date; but Dugdale (*Baronage*, i. 125) adduces documentary evidence showing that he had livery of his lands in 1223, and did not die (at Nantes) until 1228. As Nigel left no issue by his wife Mathilda or Maud, daughter of Roger de Camvile, he was succeeded as sixth baron by his brother Roger II, who only came of age in 1240, and died in 1266 (*ib.* pp. 125, 628). This Roger's son, Roger III, was seventh baron (1266–1298) and father of John I de Mowbray, eighth baron [q. v.]

[Roger Hoveden and Matthew Paris and Royal Letters of Reign of Henry III in Rolls Series; Byland and Newburgh accounts of the Mowbray family in Dugdale's Monasticon (see authorities for MOWBRAY, ROGER, DE I); Dugdale's Baronage, vol. i.; Nicolas's Historic Peerage, ed. Courthope.] J. T–T.

MOWSE or **MOSSE, WILLIAM** (*d.* 1588), civilian, graduated LL.B. at Cambridge in 1538, took holy orders, and in 1552 proceeded LL.D. In the latter year, through the interest of Cranmer and Secretary Cecil, he obtained the mastership of Trinity Hall on the removal of Dr. Walter Haddon [q. v.] On the accession of Mary (6 July 1553) he took an active part in ousting Dr. Sandys [q. v.] from the vice-chancellorship, but was himself ousted from Trinity Hall to make way for the reinstatement of Bishop Gardiner [see GARDINER, STEPHEN]. The same year he was incorporated at Oxford, and in the following year was appointed regius professor of civil law there. In July 1555 he subscribed the Marian articles of religion, and on Gardiner's death, 12 Nov., the mastership of Trinity Hall was restored to him, apparently withdrawing from that office early in 1557, when he was succeeded by

Henry Harvey or Hervey (*d.* 1585) [q.v]. Cardinal Pole in 1556 made him advocate of the court of Canterbury, and on 7 Nov. 1557 he was admitted to the College of Advocates. On 12 Dec. 1558 he was instituted to the rectory of Norton or Greensnorton, Northamptonshire. Though deprived of the Oxford chair after the accession of Elizabeth, Mowse was admitted in 1559 to the prebend of Halloughton in the church of Southwell (2 May), and subsequently (19 May) was constituted vicar-general and official of the Archbishop of Canterbury, dean of the arches and peculiars, and judge of the court of audience. In 1560 he was instituted to the rectory of East Dereham, Norfolk, and on 29 Feb. 1560–1 was collated to the prebend of Botevant in the church of York. In 1564 he sat on a commission, appointed 27 April, to try admiralty causes arising from depredations alleged to have been committed by English privateers on Spanish commerce. He died in 1588. By his will, dated 30 May 1586, he was a liberal donor to Trinity Hall.

Mowse was an able lawyer and an accomplished scholar, whom Sir John Cheke [q. v.] thought worthy of his friendship. A Latin letter of thanks from him to Secretary Cecil, on occasion of his appointment to the mastership of Trinity Hall, may be read in Strype's 'Cranmer,' App. No. xci. He assisted in the compilation of the Bishop of Ross's 'Defence of the Queen of Scots' (see Leslie or Lesley, John, 1527–1596, and Murdin, *State Papers*, pp. 113, 122). It is probable that he was a Romanist without the courage of his convictions.

[Wood's Fasti Oxon. (Bliss), i. 140; Annals (Gutch), ii. 857; Baker's Northamptonshire, ii. 63; Lansd. MS. 982, f. 130; Add. MS. 5807, ff. 106–107; Strype's Cranmer, fol., i. 400; Annals, fol., i. 441; Memorials, fol., ii. 361, iii. 293; Parker, fol., i. 44; Lamb's Collection of Letters, &c., illustrative of the History of the University of Cambridge, p. 175; Newcourt's Repertorium, i. 444; Rymer's Fœdera (Sanderson), xv. 639; Sandys's Sermons (Parker Soc.), p. iv; Cranmer's Works (Parker Soc.), ii. 437; Le Neve's Fasti Eccl. Angl.; Fuller's Hist. Univ. Cambr. ed. Prickett and Wright, p. 243; Cooper's Annals of Cambridge, ii. 76, 84, 154; Cooper's Athenæ Cantabr.] J. M. R.

MOXON, EDWARD (1801–1858), publisher and verse-writer, baptised in Wakefield on 12 Dec. 1801, was son of Michael and Ann Moxon, and was educated at the Green Coat School. At the age of nine he was apprenticed to one Smith, a bookseller of Wakefield, and about 1817 proceeded to London to find similar employment. Although 'daily occupied from morning until evening,' he managed on Sundays and after midnight on week-days to educate himself, and he obtained a good knowledge of current English literature (Moxon, *Prospect*, Ded.) In 1821 he entered the service of Messrs. Longman & Co., and soon had 'the conduct of one of the four departments of the country line.' In 1826 his private study bore fruit in the publication of a volume of verse, 'The Prospect and other Poems,' which the author dedicated to Samuel Rogers. He modestly described his efforts as the work of 'a very young man unlettered and self-taught.' The verse had little merit, but Moxon's perseverance favourably impressed Rogers. He obtained introductions to other men of letters, and his pleasant manner and genuine enthusiasm for poetry gained him a welcome in literary circles. He quickly fascinated Charles Lamb, and from 1827 onwards he was a frequent visitor at Lamb's house at Enfield, dropping 'in to tea,' or supping with Lamb on bread and cheese and gin and water, and at times bringing his sisters or brother (Lamb, *Letters*, ii. 275, 281). Lamb's sister soon pined 'for Mr. Moxon's books and Mr. Moxon's society' (*ib.* p. 170), and on 30 July 1833 Moxon married Lamb's adopted daughter, Emma Isola.

Meanwhile, in the autumn of 1827 Moxon had left Longmans' to 'better himself,' and Lamb strongly recommended him to Henry Colburn as 'a young man of the highest integrity and a thorough man of business' (25 Sept. 1827; *ib.* p. 181). Finally he found employment in Hurst's publishing house in St. Paul's Churchyard, apparently as literary adviser (*ib.* pp. 198–200), and there found a useful friend in Mr. Evans, afterwards a member of the well-known printing firm of Bradbury & Evans.

In March 1829 Moxon published another volume of verse, entitled 'Christmas,' and he dedicated it to Lamb. Lamb recommended it to Bernard Barton. 'It has no pretensions and makes none, but parts are pretty' (*ib.* ii. 222). Encouraged by Lamb's sympathy and advice, Moxon soon afterwards resolved to become a publisher on his own account. Rogers, who approved the project, advanced him 500*l.*, and on that capital he began business in the spring of 1830 at 64 New Bond Street (*ib.* pp. 555, 261). In 1833 he removed to 44 Dover Street, an address long familiar to bookbuyers.

Moxon's progress as a publisher was at first slow, although he secured the support of many writers of established reputation. His earliest publication was Lamb's 'Album Verses,' which appeared in August 1830, with a genial dedication addressed to the publisher. In April 1831 he started under his own editorship the 'Englishman's Magazine,' a monthly publication, to which Lamb regularly contributed and Tennyson sent a sonnet; but Moxon deemed it prudent to abandon the venture in October (*ib.* ii. 272, 274). In 1832 he produced Allan Cunningham's 'Maid of Elvar,' Barry Cornwall's 'Songs and Ballads,' and a selection from Southey's prose works. In 1833 he issued a new edition of Lamb's 'Essays of Elia,' and a volume of 'Last Essays,' which involved him in some litigation with John Taylor, the original publisher (*ib.* pp. 287, 355). After Lamb's death in 1834 he penned a sympathetic paper of reminiscences. Lamb left his books to Moxon, who brought out a collection of his friend's prose works, with Talfourd's memoir, in 1836, and he undertook the first collection of Lamb's prose and poetry in 1840. In 1834 Wordsworth, always a steady friend, allowed him to publish a selection of his poems; next year he transferred all his works to Moxon, and in 1836 a full edition in six volumes was published. Many other works by Wordsworth proceeded at brief intervals, until the poet's death, from Moxon's publishing house. In 1838 Moxon produced the well-known illustrated edition of Rogers's 'Poems,' as well as a reissue of the illustrated edition of Rogers's 'Italy.' Many of Sheridan Knowles's dramatic works were issued between 1837 and 1847, and proved very profitable. One of Moxon's largest undertakings was Dyce's edition of Beaumont and Fletcher in eleven volumes (1843–6).

But it was as the discriminating patron of young or little known poets that Moxon deserves to be remembered. In 1833 he produced the 'Poems' of Tennyson, who, until Moxon's death, entrusted each new work to Moxon's care. In the same year he initiated a similar connection with R. Monckton Milnes, with the issue of Milnes's 'Tour in Greece.' In 1834 Moxon brought out Benjamin Disraeli's 'Revolutionary Epick;' he told Charles Greville in 1847 that Disraeli asked to enter into partnership with him, but he refused, 'not thinking that he was prudent enough to be trusted' (Greville, *Memoirs*, 2nd ser. iii. 75). Isaac D'Israeli's 'Genius of Judaism' (1833) was one of Moxon's early issues. In 1836 he privately circulated Serjeant Talfourd's 'Ion.' For Robert Browning he produced 'Sordello' in 1840, 'Bells and Pomegranates,' 8 pts., 1843–6, 'Cleon,' 1855, and 'The Statue and Bust,' 1855. Poems by Lord Hanmer appeared in 1839–40; 'Edwin the Fair' and other plays by Sir Henry Taylor in 1842; and 'Poems' by Coventry Patmore in 1844. An older writer, Landor, proved a less satisfactory client. Moxon undertook the publication of Landor's 'Poemata et Inscriptiones' in 1847, and John Mitford wrote in his copy (now in the Dyce Library): 'Moxon the publisher told me he had sold only one copy of this book—to whom?—to [Connop Thirlwall] the Bishop of St. Davids.'

Moxon's literary and social ambitions grew with his success in business. As early as 1830 he had issued a volume of sonnets by himself, which he dedicated to his brother William, a barrister. A second volume of sonnets appeared in 1835, with a dedication to Wordsworth, and reached a second edition in 1837. Croker, in a severe article in the 'Quarterly Review,' lix. 209 seq., denounced the work with much justice as a puny imitation of Wordsworth; but when he ridiculed the dandy-like care which Moxon had bestowed on the form of the book, he unfairly depreciated the neatness and delicacy in external details that characterised all Moxon's publications. Both volumes were reprinted together in 1843, and again in 1871. Croker's sneers were repeated in Thomas Powell's 'Living Authors of England,' New York, 1849, pp. 226 seq.; but, despite his defects as a writer of verse, Moxon long held an assured position in literary society. John Forster was a constant friend and adviser. Rogers proved an unswerving ally, and Moxon was a regular visitor at Rogers's breakfast parties. In 1837 he accompanied Wordsworth and Crabb Robinson to Paris, and in 1846 spent a week at Rydal Mount, when Harriet Martineau came over to see him (cf. Clayden, *Rogers and his Contemporaries*, ii. 70, 232; Crabb Robinson, *Diaries*, iii. 113, 274). Moxon maintained affectionate relations with Mary Lamb till her death in 1847, when Mrs. Moxon was appointed Mary's residuary legatee (*ib.* pp. 73, 293).

In 1840 Moxon projected a series of single-volume editions of the poets, and initiated it in April with the complete works of Shelley, edited by Mrs. Shelley. At the time Henry Hetherington [q. v.], a small publisher who was being prosecuted for issuing blasphemous publications, caused copies of Moxon's 'Shelley' to be purchased at the shops of Fraser and Otley, two well-known booksellers, and at Moxon's office in Dover Street. Hetherington then instituted a prosecution against the three men for publishing a blasphemous libel. Moxon accepted the sole responsibility, and obtained the removal of the trial to the court of queen's bench. The case was heard at Westminster before Lord-chief-justice Denman and a special jury on 23 June 1841. The crown chiefly relied on passages from Shelley's 'Queen Mab.' Moxon's friend, Serjeant Talfourd, defended him in an eloquent speech, which Moxon published. The judge summed up largely in the defendant's favour, but the jury found a verdict of guilty. Moxon was ordered to come up for judgment when called upon, and received no punishment. The prosecutions against the booksellers were allowed to drop. 'It was a prosecution instituted merely for the purpose of vexation and annoyance' (Blackburn, J., in R. *v.* Hicklin, L.R. 3, Q.B. 372). A full report of the case is in the 'State Trials,' new ser. iv. 693–722. Despite this rebuff, Moxon's series of the poets prospered. Nor did he abandon Shelley. In 1852 he purchased and published, with an introduction by Browning, some letters assigned to Shelley, but soon proved to be forgeries. Hogg's and Trelawny's lives of the poet Moxon brought out in the year of his own death. In later life he extended his business beyond the confines of pure literature, and Haydn's 'Dictionary of Dates' and nearly all the works of Samuel Sharpe the Egyptologist figured in his last lists of publications. He died at Putney Heath on 3 June 1858, and was buried in Wimbledon churchyard. His widow died at Brighton on 2 Feb. 1891, aged 82. She left one son, Arthur, and five daughters (*Illustrated London News*, 14 Feb. 1891, with portrait of Mrs. Moxon).

The publishing business did not prosper after Moxon's death. Until 1871 it was carried on in Dover Street, at first under the style of Edward Moxon & Co., and from 1869 as Edward Moxon, Son, & Co. During this period a manager, J. Bertrand Payne, conducted the concern in behalf of Moxon's relatives. Mr. Swinburne's 'Atalanta in Calydon,' 1865, his 'Chastelard,' 1866, and the original edition of his 'Poems and Ballads' appeared under the firm's auspices. In 1868 Tennyson transferred his works to Mr. Alexander Strahan. In 1871 Messrs. Ward, Lock, & Tyler purchased most of the firm's stock and copyrights, and carried on a part of their business under the style of Edward Moxon, Son, & Co. until 1878, when Edward Moxon's name finally disappeared from the list of London publishers.

[Curwen's History of Booksellers, 1873, pp. 347–62; Illustrated London News, 12 June 1858; Lupton's Wakefield Worthies (1864), pp. 229 sq.; London Directory, 1833–78; Lamb's Letters, ed. Ainger; Crabb Robinson's Diaries; English Catalogue of Books, 1835–62; Clayden's Life of Rogers; Moxon's publications; Gent. Mag. 1858, ii. 93.] S. L.

MOXON, GEORGE (1603?–1687), congregational divine, born near Wakefield, Yorkshire, about 1603, was educated at Wakefield grammar school, and at Sidney Sussex College, Cambridge, where he was reputed an excellent writer of Latin lyrics. Having been chaplain to Sir William Brereton (1604–1661) [q. v.], he obtained the perpetual curacy of St. Helen's, Lancashire, where he disused the ceremonies and got into trouble with his bishop, John Bridgeman [q. v.] Being cited for nonconformity in 1637, he left St. Helen's in disguise for Bristol, and thence sailed for New England, where he was pastor of the congregational church at Springfield, Massachusetts. He returned to England in 1653, and became colleague with John Machin (1624–1664) [q. v.] at Astbury, Cheshire, a sequestered living. Machin was a presbyterian; Moxon gathered a congregational church at Astbury, and supplied every other Sunday the perpetual curacy of Rushton-Spencer, Staffordshire. He was an assistant commissioner to the 'triers' for Cheshire. After the Restoration the rector, Thomas Hutchinson (*d.* 15 Dec. 1675), was reinstated, 21 Feb. 1661. Moxon retained his charge at Rushton till his ejection by the Uniformity Act of 1662. He seems to have preached for a time at a farmhouse near Rushton Chapel, where is still an ancient burial-ground.

In 1667 he removed to Congleton, in the parish of Astbury, and preached in his own house near Dane Bridge, which was licensed (30 April), under the indulgence of 1672, for a teacher of the congregational persuasion. Under James's declaration for liberty of conscience, a meeting-house was built for Moxon's congregation at Congleton, but he did not live to occupy it. He had been disabled by paralytic strokes and was assisted in his ministry from 1678 by Eliezer Birch (*d.* 12 May 1717). He died at Congleton on 15 Sept. 1687, 'ætat. 85.' He married a daughter of Isaac Ambrose [q. v.] The meeting-house was first used on occasion of his funeral sermon by Birch; it was destroyed by a Jacobite mob in 1712, but rebuilt. The congregation is now unitarian.

George Moxon the younger, son of the above, held after 1650 the sequestered rectory of Radwinter, Essex. At the Restoration the rector, Richard Drake, was reinstated, and Moxon became chaplain to Samuel Shute, sheriff of London (1681), who was his brother-in-law. He died at Shute's residence, Eaton Constantine, Shropshire.

[Calamy's Account, 1713, pp. 128 sq., 313; Newcome's Autobiography (Chetham Soc.), 1852, ii. 182; Urwick's Nonconformity in Cheshire, 1864, pp. 155 sq.; Pickford's Hist. of Congleton Unitarian Chapel, 1883; Head's Congleton, 1887, pp. 251 sq.; Davids's Evang. Nonconf. in Essex, 1863, pp. 445 sq.] A. G.

MOXON, JOSEPH (1627-1700), hydrographer and mathematician, was born at Wakefield, Yorkshire, on 8 Aug. 1627, and at the age of fifty had, according to his own account, been 'for many years conversant in . . . smithing, founding, drawing, joynery, turning, engraving, printing books and pictures, globe and map making, mathematical instruments, &c.' (*Mechanick Exercises*, Preface). He had also spent some time in Holland and had acquired a knowledge of the language. As early as 1657 he was settled in a shop on Cornhill, 'at the sign of Atlas,' where he published an edition of Edward Wright's 'Certain Errors in Navigation detected and corrected.' Here, too, he sold 'all manner of mathematical books or instruments and maps whatsoever,' and published 'A Tutor to Astronomie and Geographie; or an easy and speedy way to know the use of both the Globes, celestial and terrestrial,' 1659, 4to. Shortly after 1660 he was nominated 'hydrographer,' i.e. map and chart printer and seller, to the king. His shop at this time was on Ludgate Hill; afterwards, in 1683, it was 'on the west side of Fleet Ditch,' but always 'at the sign of Atlas.' In 1674 he published 'A Brief Discourse of a Passage by the North Pole to Japan, China, &c., Pleaded by Three Experiments and Answers to all Objections that can be urged against a passage that way' (London, 4to, 2nd ed. 1697). But his principal work was 'Mechanick Exercises, or the Doctrine of Handy-works. Begun 1 Jan. 1677-8, and intended to be continued monthly.' It is an interesting exposition of 'handy-works,' and though after about a year he stopped the publication on account of the Popish plot, which, he says, 'took off the minds of my few customers from buying,' he resumed it in 1683 with a detailed and technical account of type-founding and printing. It is said that he 'was the first of English letter-cutters who reduced to rule the art which before him had been practised but by guess; by nice and accurate divisions he adjusted the size, situation, and form of the several parts and members of letters and the proportion which every part bore to the whole' (TIMPERLEY, *Dictionary of Printers and Printing*, p. 567). In November 1678 he was elected a fellow of the Royal Society. He died in 1700. The fifth edition of the 'Tutor to Astronomie,' &c., referred to above, printed in 1699 'for W. Hawes at the Rose in Ludgate Street,' has a portrait with the date of his birth; and a second portrait is mentioned by Bromley.

Besides the works already named, Moxon was the author of: 1. 'A Tutor to Astronomy and Geography, or the Use of the Copernican Spheres,' 1665, 4to, a different work from that with the same first title, published in 1659. 2. 'Vignola, or the Compleat Architect,' translated from the Italian of Barozzio, 1665, 12mo. 3. 'Practical Perspective,' 1670, fol. 4. 'Regula Trium Ordinum Literarum Typographicarum, or the Rules of the Three Orders of Print Letters,' 1676, 4to. 5. 'Mathematicks made Easie, or a Mathematical Dictionary,' 1679, 8vo. Most of his works went through several editions in his lifetime, and were reprinted in the eighteenth century.

James Moxon was presumably a younger brother; his name appears on the map prefixed to Joseph Moxon's 'A Brief Discourse,' 1674, and in 1677 he was established in a shop 'neer Charing Cross in the Strand, right against King Harry the Eighth's Inne' (*Compendium Euclidis Curiosi*, translated out of the Dutch).

[Timperley's Dict. of Printers and Printing, p. 567; Wrangham's Zouch, ii. 143; Lupton's Wakefield Worthies; Moxon's writings.] J. K. L.

MOXON, WALTER, M.D. (1836-1886), physician, son of an inland revenue officer who was remotely related to Edward Jenner [q. v.], the discoverer of vaccination, was born 27 June 1836, at Midleton, co. Cork. After education in a private school he obtained a situation as a clerk in a merchant's office in London, and by work out of hours succeeded in passing the matriculation examination of the university of London. He gave up commerce and entered Guy's Hospital in 1854. While there he passed the several degree examinations with honours and graduated in the London University, M.B. 1859, M.D. 1864. He was appointed demonstrator of anatomy before he took his degree and held the office till 1866, when he was elected assistant physician to Guy's Hospital, as well as lecturer on comparative anatomy. In 1864 he read at the Linnean Society a paper on 'The Anatomy of the Rotatoria,' in 1866 published in the 'Journal of Microscopic Science' a paper on 'Peripheral Terminations of Motor Nerves,' and in 1869 one on 'The Reproduction of Infusoria' in the 'Journal of Anatomy and Physiology.' He was elected a fellow of the College of Physicians of London in 1868, and in 1869 lecturer on pathology at Guy's Hospital. He contributed many papers to the 'Transactions of the Pathological Society,' published 'Lectures on Analytical Pathology' and edited in 1875 the second edition of Dr. Wilks's 'Lectures on Pathological Anatomy.' He was next appointed lecturer on materia medica, and so great was his expository power that his lectures on this jejune subject were crowded. In 1873 he became physician to Guy's Hospital, and in 1882 lecturer on medicine. He was the author of (*Lancet*, 30 Aug. 1884) a biography of his colleague, Dr. Hilton Fagge, and wrote many papers in the 'Guy's Hospital Reports,' 'Medico-Chirurgical Review,' and 'British Medical Journal.' In 1881 he delivered the Croonian lectures at the College of Physicians 'On the Anatomical Condition of the Cerebral and Spinal Circulation.' He married in 1861, lived first at Hornsey and then at Highgate, having consulting rooms in Finsbury Circus, London. He was a fluent and emphatic speaker and always commanded attention in the College of Physicians. He died 21 July 1886, poisoned by a dose of hydrocyanic acid which he drank in his rooms at Finsbury Circus after visiting his mother's grave at Finchley and while depressed by a delusion that he was developing symptoms of an incurable illness. A medal to commemorate his attainments in clinical medicine is awarded every year by the College of Physicians.

[Memoir in British Medical Journal, 7 Aug. 1886; Lancet, 1886, vol. ii.; extract from Records at Guy's Hospital by Dr. J. C. Steele; Guy's Hospital Reports; General Index to Pathological Transactions; Medico-Chirurgical Society of London Transactions, 1887; personal knowledge.] N. M.

MOYLAN, FRANCIS (1735–1815), bishop of Cork, son of John Moylan, a well-to-do merchant in Cork, was born in that city on 17 Sept. 1735. He was educated at Paris, at Montpellier, and afterwards at the university of Toulouse, where he studied theology, and became acquainted with Henry Essex (afterwards the Abbé) Edgeworth [q. v.], then a boy, living there with his father. Edgeworth and Moylan became lifelong friends. On his ordination to the priesthood in 1761, Moylan was appointed to a curacy in Paris by the archbishop, Mgr. de Beaumont, but soon after returned to his native diocese. In 1775 he was consecrated bishop of Kerry, and was translated in 1786 to Cork, to fill the vacancy caused by the defection of Lord Dunboyne. When the French fleet appeared off the south coast of Ireland in 1796, Moylan issued a pastoral letter to his flock urging them to loyalty, and his native city, in recognition of his attitude, presented him with its freedom, an unusual mark of esteem to be bestowed on a catholic in those days. The lord-lieutenant (Earl Camden) ordered one of his pastorals to be circulated throughout the kingdom, and Pelham, the chief secretary for Ireland, wrote to congratulate Moylan on his conduct.

In 1799 Lord Castlereagh suggested to ten of the Irish bishops, who formed a board for examining into the affairs of Maynooth College, that the government would recommend catholic emancipation if the bishops in return admitted the king to have a power of veto on all future ecclesiastical appointments, and if they accepted a state endowment for the catholic clergy. The prelates, Moylan chief among them, were disposed to adopt these proposals in a modified form, but subsequently, on learning Lord Castlereagh's full intentions, repudiated them. Moylan afterwards vigorously deprecated 'any interference whatsoever' of the government in the appointment of the bishops or clergy, and took a leading part in the great 'veto' controversy.

Moylan was in favour of the legislative union of Ireland with Great Britain. He took an active part in the establishment of Maynooth College, and had some correspondence on the subject with Edmund Burke. He was a most successful administrator of his diocese, and helped materially in the establishment of the Presentation order of nuns founded by Nano Nagle [q. v.] for the education of poor girls. The Duke of Portland, whom he visited at Bulstrode, writing of him said: 'There can be, and there never has been, but one opinion of the firmness, the steadiness, and the manliness of Dr. Moylan's character, which, it was agreed by all those who had the pleasure of meeting him here [Bulstrode], was as engaging as his person, which avows and bespeaks as much goodwill as can be well imagined in a human countenance.'

He died on 10 Feb. 1815, and was buried in a vault in his cathedral.

[Short Life of Dr. Moylan, in an Appendix to Hutch's Life of Nano Nagle; Letters from the Abbé Edgeworth to his Friends, with Memoirs of his Life, including some account of Dr. Moylan, by the Rev. T. R. England; Fitzpatrick's Irish Wits and Worthies; Fitzpatrick's Secret Service under Pitt; Castlereagh Papers; S[arah] A[tkinson]'s Life of Mary Aikenhead; Husenbeth's Life of Dr. Milner; O'Renehan's Collections on Irish Church History; Caulfield's Council Book of the Corporation of the City of Cork.] P. L. N.

MOYLE, JOHN (1592?–1661), friend of Sir John Eliot, was son of Robert Moyle of Bake in St. Germans, Cornwall (buried 9 May 1604), by his wife Anne, daughter of Henry Lock of Acton, Middlesex (buried 12 April 1604). He matriculated from Exeter College, Oxford, on 10 June 1608, 'aged 16.' Among his contemporaries at Exeter was John (afterwards Sir John) Eliot, to whose father Moyle on one occasion communicated some particulars of his son's extravagance. Eliot thereupon went hastily to Moyle's house to express his resentment, and in a fit of passion drew his sword and wounded Moyle in the side. This act was unpremeditated, and Eliot expressed extreme sorrow for what he had done. The story was narrated in an erroneous form, on the authority of Dean Prideaux, by Laurence Echard (*History of England*, ed. 1718, ii. 26–7), and repeated from him by Isaac D'Israeli (*Commentaries on Charles I*, new ed., i. 319, 531–3). Its true character is set out in the 'Gentleman's Magazine' (1837, pt. ii. p. 483), by Lord Nugent in his work on 'John Hampden' (i. 152–6), and by Forster in his 'Life of Sir John Eliot' (i. 3–9, ii. 630–2). Moyle and Eliot became fast friends. The former was sheriff in 1624, and, to fill a vacancy in the Long parliament, was returned for the Cornish borough of East Looe, and ordered to be admitted on 5 July 1649. He died at Bake on 9 Oct. 1661, and was buried at St. Germans on 17 Oct. In 1612 he married Admonition, daughter of Edmond Prideaux of Netherton, Devonshire, who was buried at St. Germans on 3 Dec. 1675. Of his numerous sons, Sir Walter Moyle of Bake (1627–1701) was knighted at Whitehall 4 Feb. 1663, became sheriff of Cornwall 1671, and was father of Walter Moyle [q.v.]

Some of Moyle's correspondence with Sir John Eliot is quoted in Grosart's edition of his 'Letter-book,' pp. 109–10, 143–8, and in Forster's 'Eliot,' ii. 630–2. Papers relating to him are in the Addit. MSS. Brit. Mus. 5494, f. 79, and 5497, f. 162.

[Foster's Alumni Oxon.; Courtney's Parl. Repr. of Cornwall, p. 116; Boase and Courtney's Bibl. Cornub. i. 373; Vivian's Cornwall Visitations, p. 334.] W. P. C.

MOYLE, JOHN (*d.* 1714), naval surgeon, after serving many years at sea in merchant ships and ships of war, and having been 'in most of the sea fights that we have had with any nation in my time,' was superannuated about 1690 on a pension of apparently 40*l.* a year, and applied himself in his old age to writing his surgical experiences for the benefit of younger sea-surgeons. What he wrote was not, he said, collected out of other authors, but was his own practice, the product of real experience. He nowhere mentions any officer with whom he had served, any ship or any particular battle which he had been in, though he refers some of his experiences to 'the last Holland war,' to 'one of the last fights we had with the Hollanders'—that is in 1673; or to 'before Tripoli in Barbary, when we had wars with that place'—that is, in 1676. Similarly he speaks of having been at Newfoundland, and at many places in the Mediterranean; Alexandria, Scanderoon, Smyrna, and Constantinople are incidentally mentioned. He describes himself in 1693 as 'being grown in years and not capable to hold it longer in that employ,' as surgeon at sea. He seems to have lived for his remaining years in Westminster, where he died in February 1713–14. His published works are: 1. 'Abstractum Chirurgiæ Marinæ, or An Abstract of Sea Surgery' (12mo, 1686). 2. 'Chirurgus Marinus, or The Sea Chirurgion' (12mo, 1693). 3. 'The Experienced Chirurgion' (12mo, 1703). 4. 'Chirurgic Memoirs' (12mo, 1708). This last has a portrait in full flowing wig.

He left a widow, Mary, and three children, a son, John, and two daughters, Mary Nozet, and Susanna Willon, apparently by a former marriage. To these he bequeathed one shilling each, 'to debar them from claiming any interest in or title to any part of my real or personal estate.' To a grandson, James Willon, 'now beyond the seas,' he left 10*l.* subject to the condition of his demanding it in person within seven years. The rest of the property was left to the widow, 'sole and only executrix' (will in Somerset House, Aston, 32, dated 1 March 1702–3, proved 17 Feb. 1713–14). One of the witnesses to the will is Edward Ives, who may probably have been the father of Edward Ives [q. v.], the naval surgeon and traveller.

[His works, as named in the text; Pension list in the Public Record Office.] J. K. L.

MOYLE, MATTHEW PAUL (1788–1880), meteorologist and writer on mining, second son of John Moyle, by Julia, daughter of Jonathan Hornblower [q.v.], was born at Chacewater, Cornwall, 4 Oct. 1788, and educated at Guy's and St. Thomas's Hospitals. He became a member of the Royal College of Surgeons in 1809, and was afterwards in practice at Helston in Cornwall for the long period of sixty-nine years. A considerable portion of his practice consisted in attending the men accidentally injured in the tin and copper mines of his neighbourhood, and his attention was thus led to mining. In 1814 he sent to Thomson's 'Annals of Philosophy' 'Queries respecting the flow of Water in Chacewater Mine;' in the following years he communicated papers on 'The Temperature of Mines,' 'On Granite Veins,' and 'On the Atmosphere of Cornish Mines.' During a series of years he kept registers and made extensive and valuable observations on barometers and thermometers, and in conjunction with Robert Were Fox [q.v.] he wrote and communicated to Tilloch's 'Philosophical Magazine' in 1823, 'An Account of the Observations and Experiments on the Temperature of Mines which have recently been made in Cornwall and the North of England.' In 1841 he sent to Sturgeon's 'Annals of Electricity' a paper 'On the Formation of Electro-type Plates independently of any engraving.' He died at Cross Street, Helston, 7 Aug. 1880, leaving a large family.

[Boase and Courtney's Bibl. Cornub. 1874–82, 1890, pp. 373–4, 1289; Boase's Collect. Cornub. p. 600.] G. C. B.

MOYLE, Sir THOMAS (*d.* 1560), speaker of the House of Commons, was third son of John Moyle, who in 1488 was one of those commissioned in Cornwall to raise archers for the king's expedition to Brittany (Rymer, *Fœdera*, 1745, pt. v. vol. iii. p. 197). His mother was a daughter of Sir Robert Drury. Sir Walter Moyle [q. v.] was his grandfather. Thomas Moyle, like his grandfather, entered Gray's Inn, probably before 1522, as in that year one of his name from Gray's Inn was surety to the extent of 100*l.* for George Nevill, third baron of Abergavenny [q. v.] He became Lent reader there in 1533. In 1537 the court of augmentations was erected to manage the vast property flowing in to the treasury on the suppression of the abbeys. Of this Moyle and Thomas, father of Sir Walter Mildmay [q. v.], were appointed receivers, each having 200*l.* fee and 20*l.* diet. Moyle was afterwards promoted to the chancellorship of the same court. But the augmentation office was temporarily deprived of his services in the same year, 1537, when he was sent to Ireland on a special commission with St. Leger, Paulet, and Berners. He was also on 18 Oct. 1537 knighted. The work of the commission in Ireland was very important, as Lord Grey had made enemies of the English officials. Hence the selection of the experienced St. Leger in the work of trying to restore order (cf. Bagwell, *Ireland under the Tudors*, i. 208 et seq.)

Moyle returned to England at the end of the year, and soon made himself conspicuous as a zealous servant of Henry, rather after the manner of Audley. He enlarged his estates by securing monastic property, and soon became a rich and prominent official. In 1539 he was with Layton and Pollard in the west, and signed with them the letters from Glastonbury showing that they were trying to find hidden property in the abbey, and to collect evidence against Whiting, the abbot. The same year he was one of those appointed to receive Anne of Cleves on her arrival. Moyle was returned member for the county of Kent in 1542, and chosen speaker of the House of Commons. He addressed the king in an extraordinarily adulatory speech, but his tenure of office was made notable by the fact that he was said to be the first speaker who claimed the privilege of freedom of speech. The exact wording of his request is, however, uncertain. During his term of office the subject became prominent owing to Ferrar's case, in which Henry conciliated the commons. The king doubtless was glad to have a trusty servant in the chair, as during this session Catherine Howard and Lady Rochford were condemned. He was returned for Rochester in 1544, and in 1545 he was a commissioner for visiting Eastridge Hospital, Wiltshire. It is difficult to know the attitude he took up under Mary, but it seems that he proclaimed her queen (cf. *Cal. State Papers*, 1547–80, p. 59; Strype, *Memorials*, iii. i. 476; *Annals*, i. i. 64; and especially *Acts of the Privy Council*, 1552–6, as against Manning, *Lives of the Speakers*, and Boase, *Collect. Cornub.* p. 605), and was, like many of Henry's followers, a protestant only in a legal sense. On 20 Sept. 1553, and in March 1554, he was returned for Rochester, and on 20 Dec. 1554 was elected for both Chippenham and King's Lynn. It is hardly likely that he would have been elected so often if he had, as Manning suggests, avoided the parliaments of Mary. It is also said that a prosecution against him was actually commenced when the death of the queen intervened. Moyle died at Eastwell Court, Kent, in 1560. He left two daughters: Katherine, who married Sir Thomas Finch, ancestor of the earls of Winchelsea, and Amy, who married Sir Thomas Kempe.

[Letters and Papers of Henry VIII, passim; Maclean's Hist. of Trigg Minor, i. 278; Dixon's Hist. of the Church of England, ii. 278; Metcalfe's Knights; Trevelyan Papers (Camden Soc.), ii. 12; Chron. of Calais (Camden Soc.), p. 174; Narratives of the Reformation (Camden Soc.), p. 343; Rutland Papers (Camden Soc.), p. 75; Three Chapters of Suppression Letters (Camden Soc.), pp. 255 et seq.; Manning's Speakers of the House of Commons; Return of Members of Parliament; Strype's Memorials, iii. i. 156, 476; Annals, i. i. 64; Whitgift, iii. 352; Appendix ii. 10th Rep. Dep.-Keeper Publ. Records, p. 241; Fuller's Church Hist. of Engl., iii. 464.] W. A. J. A.

MOYLE, Sir WALTER (*d.* 1470?), judge, was third son of Thomas Moyle of Bodmin. In 1454 he was resident at Eastwell in Kent, and was commissioner for Kent to raise money for the defence of Calais (*Pro-*

ceedings of the Privy Council, vi. 239). When he was called to the bar does not appear, but he was reader at Gray's Inn, in 1443 became a serjeant-at-law, and a king's serjeant in 1454 (Wynne, *Serjeants-at-Law*, pp. 35, 36). In the same year he was the bearer of a message from the lords to the commons, refusing to interfere on behalf of the speaker, Thorpe, imprisoned by process of law, and on 9 July he was appointed a judge of the king's bench (*Cal. Pat. Rolls*, p. 296). This office he held till his death. In 1459, 1460, and 1461 he was appointed by parliament a trier of petitions from Gascony and parts abroad. He was one of those knighted in 1465 on the occasion of the coronation of Edward IV's queen, Elizabeth. He died about 1470, seised of numerous lands in Devonshire and Somerset, and his will was proved on 31 July 1480. Through his wife Margaret he acquired the manor of Stevenston in Devonshire. His son John was father of Sir Thomas Moyle [q. v.]

[Foss's Lives of the Judges; Stevenson's Letters and Papers temp. Hen. VI (Rolls Ser.), vol. ii. pt. ii. p. [284]; Rot. Parl. v. 240; Dugdale's Origines, p. 46; Hasted's Kent, vii. 392; Collins's Peerage, iii. 379, viii. 510.] J. A. H.

MOYLE, WALTER (1672–1721), politician and student, born at Bake in St. Germans, Cornwall, on 3 Nov. 1672, was the third, but eldest surviving son of Sir Walter Moyle, who died in September 1701, by his wife Thomasine, daughter of Sir William Morice [q. v.], who was buried at St. Germans on 22 March 1681–2. He was a grandson of John Moyle, the friend of Eliot. After having been well grounded in classical learning, probably at Liskeard grammar school, he matriculated from Exeter College, Oxford, on 18 March 1688–9, and a set of verses by him was inserted in the university collection of poems for William and Mary, 1689, but he left Oxford without taking a degree. About 1708 he contributed towards the erection of the new buildings at Exeter College opposite the front gate and stretching eastwards, and his second son was a fellow of the college (Boase, *Exeter Coll.*, 1893 ed., pp. viii, 90). On 26 Jan. 1690–1 he was specially admitted at the Middle Temple, and gave himself up to the study of constitutional law and history. At first Moyle frequented Maynwaring's coffee-house in Fleet Street and the Grecian near the Temple, but to be nearer the realms of fashion he removed to Covent Garden, and became a regular companion of the wits at Will's. About 1693 he translated four pieces by Lucian, which were included (i. 14–66) in the version issued in 1711 under the direction of Dryden, who, in the 'Life of Lucian,' praised Moyle's 'learning and judgment above his age.' Dryden further, in his 'Parallel of Poetry and Painting' (Scott's ed. xvii. 312), called Moyle 'a most ingenious young gentleman, conversant in all the studies of humanity much above his years,' and acknowledged his indebtedness to Moyle for the argument on the reason why imitation pleases, as well as for 'all the particular passages in Aristotle and Horace to explain the art of poetry by that of painting' (which would be used when there was time to 'retouch' the essay). Dryden again praised him in the 'Discourse on Epick Poetry' (cf. 'Memoir of the Rev. Joshua Parry,' pp. 130–2. Moyle appreciated the rising merit of Congreve. Charles Gildon [q. v.] published in 1694 a volume of 'Miscellaneous Letters and Essays' containing 'An Apology for Poetry,' in an essay directed to Moyle, and several letters between him, Congreve, and John Dennis are included in the latter's collections of 'Letters upon Several Occasions,' 1696, and 'Familiar and Courtly Letters of Voiture, with other Letters by Dryden, Wycherley, Congreve,' 1700, and reprinted in Moyle's 'Works' in 1727. So late as 1721 Dennis issued two more volumes of 'Original Letters,' containing two addressed to Moyle in 1720 in terms of warm affection, although he had been absent from London for 'twenty tedious years.'

Moyle sat in parliament for Saltash from 1695 to 1698. He was a zealous whig, with a keen desire to encourage British trade, and a strong antipathy to ecclesiastical establishments. In conjunction with John Trenchard he issued in 1697 'An Argument showing that a Standing Army is inconsistent with a Free Government, and absolutely destructive to the Constitution of the English Monarchy,' which was reprinted in 1698 and 1703, and included in the 'Pamphleteer,' x. 109–40 (1817). It caused such 'offence at court that Mr. Secretary Vernon ordered the printer to attend him to discover the author,' and it produced several other pamphlets, the most famous being Lord Somers's 'A Letter ballancing the necessity of keeping of a Land-Force in Times of Peace.'

Moyle's favourite study was history, and he speculated in his retirement from public life, in 1698, on the various forms and laws of government. He had read all the classical authors, both Greek and Latin, with the intention of compiling a history of Greece, and at a later period of life he 'launched far into ecclesiastical history.' His constant regret was that he had not travelled abroad, but to compensate for this loss he devoured every book of travel or topographical history. In the autumn of 1713 he finished a new library at Bake, and was eager to stock it with the best works and editions. He was a student of botany and ornithology, making great collections on the birds of Cornwall and Devon, helping Ray, as is acknowledged in the preface in the second edition of the 'Synopsis Methodica Stirpium Britannicarum,' and promising to send Dr. Sherard a catalogue of his specimens for insertion in the 'Philosophical Transactions,' but a lingering illness did not permit him to carry this design into effect. The books in his study were full of notes, and the margins of his copy of Willoughby's 'Ornithology' were crowded with observations. Unfortunately the whole of his library and manuscripts was destroyed by fire in 1808. Moyle died at Bake on 10 June 1721, and was buried at St. Germans on 13 June, a monument being placed to his memory at the end of the north aisle, near the chancel. He married at Bideford, Devonshire, 6 May 1700, Henrietta Maria, daughter of John Davie of that town. She died on 9 Dec. 1762, aged 85, and was buried at St. Germans on 15 Dec. They had issue two sons and one daughter.

After Moyle's death Thomas Sergeant edited the 'Works of Walter Moyle, none of which were ever before published,' 1726, 2 vols. It contained in the first volume: 1. 'Essay on the Constitution of the Roman Government.' 2. 'A Charge to the Grand Jury at Liskeard, April 1706.' 3. 'Letters to Dr. William Musgrave of Exeter.' 4. 'Dissertation on the age of Philopatris, a Dialogue commonly attributed to Lucian.' 5. 'Letters to and from Tancred Robinson, Sherard, and others.' The second volume comprised: 6. 'Remarks upon some Passages in Dr. Prideaux's Connection.' 7. 'Miracle of the Thundering Legion examin'd, in several Letters between Moyle and K——' [Richard King of Topsham, near Exeter]. This collection was followed in the subsequent year by a reprint by Curll of 'The Whole Works of Walter Moyle that were Published by Himself,' to which was prefixed some account of his life and writings by Anthony Hammond (1668–1738) [q. v.] It contained, in addition to several works already mentioned: 1. 'Xenophon's Discourse on the Revenue of Athens,' which was translated at Charles Davenant's request, and after it had been included in his 'Discourses on the Publick Revenues and the Trade of England,' 1698, was reprinted in Sir William Petty's 'Political Arithmetic,' 1751, in Davenant's 'Works' in 1771, and in the 'Works of Xenophon' translated by Ashley Cooper and others, 1831. 2. 'An Essay on Lacedæmonian Government,' which was included, with three other tracts by him, in 'A Select Collection of Tracts by W. Moyle,' printed at Dublin in 1728 and Glasgow in 1750.

The 'Essay on the Roman Government,' which was inserted in Sergeant's collection, was reprinted by John Thelwall in 1796, and, when translated into French by Bertrand Barrière, was published at Paris in 1801. The series of 'Remarks on some Passages in Dr. Prideaux's Connection' was included in the French editions of that work which were published in 1728, 1732, 1742, and 1744. Moyle's 'Examination of the Miracle of the Thundering Legion' was attacked in separate publications by the Rev. William Whiston and the Rev. Thomas Woolston, and Thomas Hearne, in his volume of 'John of Glastonbury,' referred to some of Moyle's criticisms on the 'Shield' of Dr. Woodward (*Rel. Hearnianæ*, ed. 1869, ii. 265, 290), but he was defended by Curll in 'An Apology for the Writings of Walter Moyle,' 1727. His 'Remarks on the Thundering Legion' were translated into Latin by Mosheim and published at Leipzig in 1733, discussed, with Moyle's 'Notes on Lucian,' in N. Lardner's 'Collection of Ancient Testimonies to the Truth of the Christian Religion,' ii. 229, 241–50, 355–69, and they formed the text of some letters from Charles Yorke to Warburton in 'Kilvert's Selection from the Papers of Warburton,' 1841, pp. 124 seqq.

Two letters from Moyle to Horace Walpole on the passage of the Septennial Bill are printed in Coxe's 'Sir Robert Walpole,' ii. 62–4. Several of his communications are inserted in the 'Gentleman's Magazine' for 1837, 1838, and 1839, and forty-five letters on ancient history which passed between him and two local correspondents in Devonshire are preserved in manuscript at St. John's College, Cambridge. There are frequent references to him in Sherard's correspondence (NICHOLS, *Illustrations of Literature*, i. 308–89, and DR. RICHARD RICHARDSON, *Letters*, pp. 154–250). Charles Hopkins addressed an ode to him (*Epistolary Poems*, 1694), and John Glanvill published a translation of Horace, bk. i. ode 24, which he prepared on his death (*Poems*, 1725, pp. 205–6). Moyle's friends praised his 'exactness of reasoning' and his subtle irony, and Warburton gave him the praise of great learning and acuteness (*Divine Legation*, bk. ii.; notes in *Works*, ed. 1788, i. 464). His portrait, engraved by Vertue, was prefixed to the 1726 edition of his works.

[Vivian's Visitations of Cornwall, p. 335; Foster's Alumni Oxon.; Granger and Noble's Biog. Hist. 1806; Gosse's Congreve, pp. 32–3, 40, 79–

83; Biog. Britannica; Boase and Courtney's Bibl. Cornub. i. 375–7, iii. 1289–90; Parochial Hist. of Cornwall, ii. (1868) 42, 53; Cardinal Newman's Miracles, 1870, pp. 241 sq.]

W. P. C.

MOYNE, WILLIAM DE, EARL OF SOMERSET or DORSET (*fl.* 1141). [See MOHUN.]

MOYSIE, MOISE, MOYSES, or MOSEY, DAVID (*fl.* 1590), author of the 'Memoirs of the Affairs of Scotland, 1577–1603,' was by profession a writer and notary public. The earliest record of him is his notarial attestation of a lease in 1577 (*Memoirs*, Bannatyne Club, p. xiii). From 1582 he was engaged as a crown servant, first as a clerk of the privy council, 'writing of the effairis' under the superintendence of John Andrew, and giving 'continewale attendance upon his Heines at Court' (*Treasurer's Accounts*, 1586), and afterwards, about 1596, in the office of Sir John Lindsay of Menmuir, king's secretary. On 3 Aug. 1584 he obtained a grant under the privy seal of 32*l.* Scots from the mails of certain lands of the kirk of Dunkeld for his son David, 'for his help and sustentatioun at the scolis, and education in vertew and guid lettres.' On the death of his son, soon after, he had the gift ratified in his own favour on 19 Feb. 1584–5. The only other references occur in three letters written to Sir John Lindsay the secretary in 1596—one from Moysie, the others from John Laing and George Young, secretary-deputes—from which it appears that Moysie had been complaining, but to little purpose, of the inadequacy of his annual salary of a hundred merks.

The 'Memoirs,' if devoid of literary merit, are interesting as the record of an eye witness, to whose official habit and opportunities we are indebted for many details not to be learned from the more academic historians of his time. They are extant in two manuscripts, one in the Advocates' Library, the other at Wishaw House. They were printed by Ruddiman (Edinburgh, 1755), and edited for the Bannatyne Club (Edinburgh, 1830).

[Authorities referred to above.] G. G. S.

MOYUN, REGINALD DE (*d.* 1257). [See MOHUN.]

MOZEEN, THOMAS (*d.* 1768), actor and dramatist, of French extraction, but born in England, his sponsor being Dr. Henry Sacheverell, was bred to the bar, which profession he forsook for the stage. His first traceable appearance is at Drury Lane, 20 Feb. 1745, as Pembroke in 'King John.' He played apparently the customary three years' engagement, but his name only appears to Clitander in Swiney's 'Quacks, or Love's the Physician,' 30 March 1745; Young Laroon in Fielding's 'Debauchees, or the Jesuit Caught,' 17 Oct. 1745; Charles in the 'Nonjuror,' 22 Oct. 1745; and Basil in the 'Stage Coach' of Farquhar and Motteux.

On 30 Sept. 1746 the part of Polly in the 'Beggar's Opera' was played by Mrs. Mozeen, late Miss Edwards. As Miss Edwards she was first heard at Drury Lane, when for the benefit of Mrs. Catherine Clive [q. v.], whose pupil she was, she sang, 8 March 1743, the part of Sabrina in 'Comus.' On 13 March 1744, also for Mrs. Clive's benefit, she made, as Jessica, her first appearance at Covent Garden. At Drury Lane she played Polly in the 'Beggar's Opera,' 3 Dec. 1745, and was Miranda in the 'Tempest,' 31 Jan. 1746.

In 1748–9 the Mozeens were engaged by Sheridan for Dublin as part of a musical company, concerning which it is said by Victor that 'their salaries amounted to 1,400*l.*, but the profit accruing from their performances did not amount to 150*l.*, which was paid for the writing of their music.' Chetwood asserts that Mozeen had a good person, a genteel education, judgment, voice and understanding, and was an actor of promise. The timidity of Mrs. Mozeen, who was an adept in music, and had a charming manner and voice, kept her back as an actress. Of her Tate Wilkinson says that 'at the least loose joke she blushed to such a degree as to give the beholder pain for an offence not intended.' This bashfulness was accompanied by no very keen scruples as to her conduct, which was irregular enough to induce Mrs. Clive to withdraw her support. What parts were played in Dublin is unrecorded, but Victor, as manager for Sheridan, was fortunate enough to transfer to a musical society a portion of the engagement. On 15 Sept. 1750, as Young Fashion in the 'Relapse,' Mozeen reappeared at Drury Lane. He played Benvolio in 'Romeo and Juliet,' Worthy in the 'Recruiting Officer,' and Cob in 'Every Man in his Humour.'

On 21 May 1759, for the benefit of Mozeen, Miss Barton, Miss Hippisley, and others, the 'Heiress, or Antigallican,' the solitary dramatic production of Mozeen, was given. It is a fairly written farce in two acts, in which a girl who has been brought up as a boy wins the heart of one of her own sex. It was included in a volume published for the author 1762, wholly in verse, with the exception of the play, and, curiously enough, called 'A Collection of Miscellaneous Essays by T. Mozeen.' Among its contents are many songs, epilogues, &c., delivered in Bristol and elsewhere, and at Sadler's Wells Theatre, and the introductory plan of a pantomime called 'Harlequin Deserter,' intended for Sadler's Wells. 'Frolics of May,' an interlude of singing and dancing, seems also to have been intended for the stage. 'Fables in Verse,' by T. Mozeen, 2 vols. 1765, dedicated to Richard Grenville Temple, viscount Cobham, possesses little merit. 'The Lyrical Pacquet, containing most of the Favourite Songs performed for Three Seasons past at Sadler's Wells,' &c., London, 1764, 8vo, is mentioned by Lowndes, who, however, leaves unnoticed 'Young Scarron,' London, 8vo, 1752, a rather slavish imitation of 'Le Roman Comique' of Scarron, narrating the adventures of a company of strolling players. Owen Bray, a publican, with whom he lodged at Loughlinstown, Ireland, was associated with Mozeen (to whom the well-known recitation, 'Bucks have at ye all,' has also been assigned) in writing the famous song of 'Kilruddery.' Mozeen died 28 March 1768. Mrs. Mozeen, whose career appears after a time independent of that of her husband, was for some years at the Bath Theatre.

[Genest's Account of the English Stage; Thespian Dictionary; Chetwood's General History of the Stage; Baker, Reed, and Jones's Biographia Dramatica; Tate Wilkinson's Memoirs; Penley's Bath Stage; Notes and Queries, 3rd ser. v. 502–4.] J. K.

MOZLEY, ANNE (1809–1891), author, sister of Thomas and J. B. Mozley, both of whom are separately noticed, was born at Gainsborough on 17 Sept. 1809, and in 1815 removed with the rest of the family to Derby. She took charge of her brother Thomas's house when he became curate of Buckland in 1832, and devoted herself to literary work. In 1837 she published 'Passages from the Poets,' in 1843 a volume of 'Church Poetry,' in 1845 'Days and Seasons,' and in 1849 'Poetry Past and Present.' From 1847 she reviewed books for the 'Christian Remembrancer.' In 1859 she wrote for 'Bentley's Quarterly' a review of 'Adam Bede,' which George Eliot described as 'the best review we have seen.' From 1861 to 1877 Miss Mozley contributed to the 'Saturday Review,' and two volumes of these essays, one of which reached a fourth edition, were reprinted under the title 'Essays on Social Subjects.' In 1865 she began to write for 'Blackwood's Magazine.' After the death of her mother in 1867, Anne resided with her youngest sister at Barrow-on-Trent. She subsequently returned to Derby, where she died on 27 June 1891. Like her brother Thomas, Miss Mozley suffered from partial loss of sight, which became total two years before her death. Besides the works already mentioned Miss Mozley edited 'The Letters of J. B. Mozley,' 1885, 8vo, and 'The Letters and Correspondence of Cardinal Newman,' 2 vols., 1891, 8vo. A volume of 'Essays from Blackwood' was reprinted in 1892, Edinburgh, 8vo, to which was prefixed a memoir by Dr. John Wordsworth, bishop of Salisbury

[Works in Brit. Mus. Libr.; Monthly Packet, September 1891; Memoir by Bishop Wordsworth; authorities for Thomas Mozley, and information kindly supplied by H. N. Mozley, esq., King's College, Cambridge.] A. F. P.

MOZLEY, JAMES BOWLING (1813–1878), regius professor of divinity at Oxford, was born at Gainsborough in Lincolnshire, on 15 Sept. 1813. His father, Henry Mozley, was a bookseller, and removed his family and business from Gainsborough to Derby in 1815. James was the fifth son and eighth child. An elder brother, Thomas, and a sister, Anne, are separately noticed. At nine years old he was sent to Grantham grammar school, where he remained till 1828. He was unhappy at school—a fact sufficiently explained by his mother, when she says in one of her letters to him, 'There is always much to dread when such tempers as yours and Mr. A——'s come in contact.' On his leaving Grantham, at the age of fifteen, application was made for his admission to Rugby, where Arnold had just been appointed head-master; but it was refused on the ground that he was too old. After trying for a scholarship at Corpus Christi College, Oxford, in June 1827, he was matriculated as a commoner at Oriel on 1 July 1830, and went into residence in the following October. His brother Thomas was a fellow of the college, and he consequently had the advantage of seeing much of older men. His undergraduate career was creditable, but owing to a certain mental slowness he never distinguished himself in examinations. He obtained only a third class in *literæ humaniores* in 1834, and failed in several competitions for fellowships. He was, however, successful in 1835 in gaining the prize for an English essay on 'The Influence of Ancient Oracles in Public and Private Life,' which Keble pronounced to be 'exceptionally good, and full of promise.' He continued to reside in Oxford, partly in Dr. Pusey's own house, and partly at the head of a small establishment in a house rented by Dr. Pusey for the use of theological students who had no fellowships to support them; it was called by Newman 'the Cœnobitium' (*Letters*, ii. 297), and by Mozley himself 'a reading and collating establishment to help in editing the Fathers' (*Letters*, p. 78). He proceeded M.A. in 1838, B.D. in 1846, and D.D.

in 1871, and was elected a fellow of Magdalen in 1840.

With Pusey and Newman's religious views at the date of his graduation Mozley was in complete accord, and he took an active part in the Oxford movement. For about ten years he was joint editor of the 'Christian Remembrancer,' which succeeded the 'British Critic' as the organ of the high church party. He also superintended the preparation for the press of papers on Thomas à Becket by Richard Hurrell Froude [q. v.], which were published in Froude's 'Remains.' When, however, Newman joined the Roman church in 1845, Mozley was not one of those who followed him. 'No one, of course,' he wrote on 14 May 1845, 'can prophesy the course of his own mind; but I feel at present that I could no more leave the English Church than fly' (*Letters*, p. 168).

In 1856 Mozley accepted from his college the living of Old Shoreham in Sussex, which he retained till his death. In July of the same year he married Amelia, third daughter of Dr. James A. Ogle [q. v.], regius professor of medicine, whose twin sister was the wife of his friend, Manuel John Johnson [q. v.], the Radcliffe observer.

The Gorham case, which was the occasion of Manning and the two Wilberforces leaving the English church, had on Mozley quite an opposite effect [see GORHAM, GEORGE CORNELIUS]. He says (in a letter dated 1 Jan. 1855) that, after four years of reading and considerable thought, he had 'arrived at a change of opinion, more or less modified, on some points of high church theology;' and that as to the doctrine of baptismal regeneration, he 'now entertained no doubt of the substantial justice of the Gorham decision on this point.' He therefore thought it right to withdraw from the management of the 'Christian Remembrancer;' and he also wrote three works bearing on the subject-matter of dispute: 'On the Augustinian Doctrine of Predestination,' 1855 (2nd edit. 1878); 'On the Primitive Doctrine of Baptismal Regeneration,' 1856; and 'A Review of the Baptismal Controversy,' 1862 (2nd edit. 1883). The value of these three works has been variously estimated by readers of different theological bias; he himself considered them to be some of his best, and all will acknowledge their learning and thoughtfulness. A much more valuable book was his Bampton lectures 'On Miracles,' 1865, which are devoted 'mainly to the fundamental question of the credibility of miracles, and their use; the evidences of them being only touched on subordinately and collaterally.' They were at once, on their publication, recognised as an important work, notwithstanding some controversial criticism, and reached a fifth edition in 1880. In 1869 he was appointed select university preacher, and a volume of 'University and other Sermons' was published in 1876 (4th edit 1879).

Mozley had taken a very active part in favour of Mr. Gladstone when he was elected M.P. for the university of Oxford in 1847 (cf. *Letters*, pp. 183 sq.), and Mr. Gladstone, after he became prime minister in 1868, made Mozley a canon of Worcester (1869). This preferment was exchanged in 1871 for the position of regius professor of divinity at Oxford, in succession to Dr. Payne Smith. Although his manner of delivery was somewhat lifeless and uninteresting owing to weakness of voice, the matter of his professorial lectures was excellent, and one of his best works consisted of a course delivered to graduates, mostly themselves engaged in tuition, and entitled 'Ruling Ideas in early Ages, and their relation to the Old Testament Faith,' 1877 (4th edit. 1889).

On 29 July 1872 his wife died, leaving no family. In November 1875, while at Oxford, he had a paralytic seizure, from which he partially recovered. In January 1876 the Rev. John Wordsworth (the present bishop of Salisbury) undertook to be his deputy for the delivery of his professorial lectures. Mozley passed some months at St. Leonards-on-Sea, where he employed himself in superintending the publication of his university sermons and his Old Testament lectures. In the October term of 1876 he delivered his lectures himself, but the exertion proved too great. He died at Shoreham on 4 Jan. 1878, and was buried there.

Dean Church calls Mozley, 'after Mr. Newman, the most forcible and impressive of the Oxford writers,' and speaks of him as having a 'mind of great and rare power, though only recognised for what he was much later in his life.' And in another place he speaks of the sweetness, the affectionateness, the modesty, the generosity, behind an outside that to strangers might seem impassive (*Oxford Movement*, pp. 293, 318).

Besides the works already mentioned, Mozley wrote numerous articles in the 'British Critic,' of which his brother Thomas was editor, the 'Christian Remembrancer,' and the 'Guardian' newspaper, of which he was one of the earliest supporters. Some of these, including admirable estimates of Strafford and Laud, were collected and republished after his death, in 1878, in 2 vols., entitled 'Essays, Historical and Theological' (2nd edit. 1884), with a biographical introduction by his sister Anne [q. v.] He wrote also

'Lectures, and other Theological Papers,' 1883; 'Sermons, Parochial and Occasional,' 1879, 2nd edit. 1883; 'The Theory of Development: a Criticism of Dr. Newman's Essay,' 1878, reprinted from the 'Christian Remembrancer,' January 1874. A collection of his 'Letters' was edited by his sister Anne, with a biographical introduction, in 1884.

[Foster's Alumni Oxon.; Anne Mozley's Introductions to the Essays and to the Letters; various passages in Newman's Letters and in Dean Church's Oxford Movement; a biographical notice by Church, reprinted from the Guardian in the Introduction to the Essays; see also Guardian, 13 June 1883; Spectator, 5 May 1883 and 15 Nov. 1884; Times, 27 Dec. 1884; T. Mozley's Reminiscences; Liddon's Life of Pusey; personal knowledge and recollection.] W. A. G.

MOZLEY, THOMAS (1806–1893), divine and journalist, born at Gainsborough in 1806, was third son of Henry Mozley, bookseller and publisher, who in 1815 moved his business to Derby. Anne Mozley [q. v.] was his sister, and James Bowling Mozley [q. v.] his younger brother. After spending some years at Charterhouse, Thomas matriculated on 17 Feb. 1825 from Oriel College, Oxford, where he became the pupil, and subsequently the intimate friend, of John Henry Newman [q. v.] Although evincing much literary promise, Mozley obtained only a third class in *literæ humaniores* in 1828. At Christmas he became tutor to Lord Doneraile's son at Cheltenham, and in the following April he and John F. Christie were elected to the fellowships of Oriel vacated by William Churton and Pusey. Newman remarked that Mozley would be 'one of the most surprising men we shall have numbered in our lists. He is not quick or brilliant, but deep, meditative, clear in thought, and imaginative' (*Letters*, i. 209–210). Mozley subsequently declined an offer of a tutorship. In 1831 he was ordained deacon, and in the following year priest, when he undertook the temporary charge of two parishes in Colchester. His health suffered from overwork, and after a few months he accepted the curacy of Buckland, near Oxford. Before the end of the year he received from the college the perpetual curacy of Moreton-Pinkney, Northamptonshire, and in 1835 became junior treasurer of Oriel. On 27 Sept. 1836 he married at St. Werburgh's, Derby, his first wife, Harriet Elizabeth, Newman's elder sister, and resigned his fellowship, becoming rector of the college living of Cholderton, Wiltshire. Here Mozley utilised his knowledge of architecture to rebuild the church and improve the parsonage.

From the commencement of the tractarian movement in 1833 Mozley was its enthusiastic advocate, and devoted much of his time to distributing the 'Tracts for the Times.' He soon began to contribute to the 'British Critic,' the chief organ of the movement, then edited by Newman, whom in 1841 he succeeded as editor. He signalised his first number in July by a review of Dr. Faussett's Bampton lectures, and 'was tempted to illustrate it by an apologue which soon became more famous than either the lecture or the review, and the sombre controversy . . . was lighted up by a flash of . . . merriment' (Liddon, *Life of Pusey*, ii. 218). Keble suggested that it would be well 'to put a drag on T. M.'s too Aristophanic wheels;' Pusey and Newman also objected to the apologue, and it was said to have destroyed all hope of Mozley's further preferment (*Reminiscences of Oriel*, vol. ii.) Mozley also had some difficulty in restraining the romanising zeal of his contributors, Frederick Oakeley [q. v.] and Wilfrid G. Ward [q. v.]; the latter frequently complained to Newman of Mozley's treatment of his articles.

In July 1843 Mozley and his wife visited Normandy, where he was in constant intercourse with some priests, and was favourably impressed by the Roman catholic church. On his return he was on the point of joining that church (*ib.* ii. 304–406; *The Creed*, p. xi). He wrote to the publisher Rivington resigning his editorship of the 'British Critic,' which then ceased, and also to Newman, who advised him to wait two years before taking a decisive step. But his genial undogmatic temper, sense of humour, incipient heterodoxy on the Trinity, and perhaps the influence of his wife, determined him within a much shorter period to remain a member of the Anglican church. In 1844 Mozley became connected with the 'Times,' for which he wrote leading articles almost daily for many years. In 1847 he resigned his living of Cholderton, and removed to London, where after the death of his first wife he lived with his sister Elizabeth. About 1857 he settled at Finchhampstead, Berkshire, and in 1868 he accepted the college living of Plymtree, Devon. In the following year he was sent as 'Times' correspondent to Rome to describe the proceedings of the œcumenical council. After five months his health began to suffer, and he returned home in the spring of 1870.

In 1874 he became rural dean of Plymtree, and in 1876, when his deanery was divided into two, of Ottery St. Mary. He resigned his living in 1880, and retired to Cheltenham, where he spent the remainder of his days in literary pursuits. He died quietly in his armchair on 17 June 1893. He was 'an acute thinker in a desultory sort of way, a man of vast information and versatility, and a very delightful writer.'

Mozley's works are: 1. 'Henry VII, Prince Arthur, and Cardinal Morton, from a Group representing the Adoration of the Three Kings on the Chancel Screen of Plymtree Church,' 1878, fol. 2. 'Reminiscences, chiefly of Oriel and the Oxford Movement,' 2 vols., 1882, 8vo; 2nd ed. the same year. This is a fairly complete account of Oxford during the tractarian movement: 'it is the one book to which, next to and as a corrective of the "Apologia pro Vitâ suâ," the future historian of tractarianism must resort.' 'Not even the "Apologia" will compare with it in respect of minute fulness, close personal observation, and characteristic touches' (Mark Pattison in *Academy*, xxii. 1). 3. 'Reminiscences, chiefly of Towns, Villages, and Schools,' 2 vols., 1885, 8vo. 4. 'The Word,' 1889, 8vo. 5. 'The Son,' 1891, 8vo. 6. 'Letters from Rome on the Occasion of the Œcumenical Council, 1869–1870,' 2 vols., 1891, 8vo. 7. 'The Creed, or a Philosophy,' 1893, 8vo: this contains a short autobiographical preface. Mozley also published a 'Letter to the Rev. Canon Bull,' 1882, and contributed to the 'British Critic,' and other periodicals, besides the 'Times.'

By his first wife, who died in Guilford Street, Russell Square, on 17 July 1852, Mozley had one daughter, Grace, who married in 1864 Dr. William Langford. Mrs. Mozley wrote: 1. 'The Fairy Bower,' 1841, 8vo. 2. 'The Lost Brooch,' 1841, 8vo. 3. 'Louisa, or the Bride,' 1842, 8vo. 4. 'Family Adventures,' 1852, 18mo.

In June 1861 Mozley married his second wife, who survived him. She was a daughter of George Bradshaw, esq., formerly captain in the 5th dragoon guards.

[Works of T. Mozley and Mrs. Mozley; Foster's Alumni Oxon. 1715–1886; Newman's Letters passim; J. B. Mozley's Letters passim; Crockford's Directory, 1893; Liddon's Life of Pusey, ii. 218, &c.; Edwin A. Abbott's Anglican Career of Cardinal Newman; Autobiography of Isaac Williams, pp. 120, 122; F. W. Newman's Contributions to a History of the Early Life of Cardinal Newman, pp. viii, 72–3, 113, 114; R. W. Church's Oxford Movement, pp. 115, 322; F. Oakeley's Historical Notes on the Tractarian Movement; Men and Women of the Time; Times, 20 June 1893; Athenæum, 1893, i. 798–799; Saturday Review, 24 June 1893; Allibone's Dict. of Literature (Supplement), ii. 1149–50; Gent. Mag., 1852, ii. 324; information kindly supplied by H. N. Mozley, esq., King's College, Cambridge.] A. F. P.

MUCKLOW, WILLIAM (1631–1713), quaker controversialist, born in 1631, appears to have lived at Mortlake in Surrey, and to have early attached himself to the quakers. Before 1673 he retired from the community along with a small faction who resisted the custom of removing the hat in prayer, which Mucklow considered a 'formal ceremony' [see under Perrot, John]. He published his views in 'The Spirit of the Hat, or the Government of the Quakers among themselves, as it hath been exercised of late years by George Fox, and other Leading-Men in their Monday, or Second-dayes Meeting at Devonshire-House brought to Light,' London, 1673 (edited by G. J.) This was twice reprinted, under the title of 'A Bemoaning Letter of an Ingenious *Quaker*, To a Friend of his,' &c., London, 1700. Mucklow's pamphlet was answered by William Penn [q. v.] in 'The Spirit of Alexander the Copper-Smith (lately revived; now) justly rebuked,' 1673. Mucklow and some others thereupon published 'Tyranny and Hypocrisy detected, or a further Discovery of the Tyrannical Government, Popish-Principles, and vile Practices of the now leading Quakers,' London, 1673. Penn answered this in 'Judas and the Jews, combined against Christ and his Followers,' 1673.

Mucklow next wrote 'Liberty of Conscience asserted against Imposition: Proposed in Several Sober Queries to those of the People called Quakers,' &c., London, 1673–4, to which George Whitehead [q. v.] replied with 'The Apostate Incendiary rebuked, and the People called Quakers vindicated, from Romish Hierarchy and Imposition,' 1673. Mucklow resumed his connection with the quakers some years later, and George Whitehead in a manuscript note, dated 21 July 1704, upon the title-page of a copy of the 'Apostate Incendiary,' desired that it should never be reprinted, since Mucklow had then been 'in charity with Friends for many years past.'

Mucklow died at Mortlake 18 June 1713. His wife, Priscilla, died 6 Oct. 1679. Their daughter married a son of the pamphleteer Thomas Zachary of Beaconsfield, Buckinghamshire.

[Smith's Cat. ii. 190–1, 288, 893, and Suppl. 1893, 253–4; registers at Devonshire House; Library of the Meeting for Sufferings.] C. F. S.

MUDD, THOMAS (*fl.* 1577–1590), musical composer, born about 1560, was probably son of a London mercer, and was educated at St. Paul's School. After matriculating as a sizar from Caius College, Cambridge, in June 1577, he held from 1578 to 1584 the Pauline exhibition reserved for mercers' sons, at the suit of Dean Nowell [q. v.] (Gardiner, *St. Paul's School*). He proceeded B.A. from Peterhouse 1580, M.A. 1584, and was elected fellow of Pembroke Hall. He was still living, and a fellow, in 1590. Mudd was the author of a lost comedy in which, it was complained, he 'had censured and too saucily reflected on the Mayor of Cambridge.' The vice-chancellor accordingly, on 23 Feb. 1582, committed Mudd to the Tolbooth for three days; on the 26th he, at the vice-chancellor's command, acknowledged his fault before the mayor, and asked his pardon, which was freely granted (Cooper, *Athenæ*, ii. 59).

Meres, in his 'Palladis Tamia' (1598), writes of 'M. Thomas Mudd, some time fellow of Pembroke Hall in Cambridge,' as one of sixteen excellent contemporary musicians. He was probably the composer of: 1. A series of pieces written for four viols, Ayres, Almaine, Corrantos, and Sarabands (Brit. Mus. Addit. MS. 18940-4). 2. An In Nomine in four parts (*ib.* 31390, fol. 116 *b*). 3. A full anthem in four parts, 'O God which hast prepared' (Tudway's collection, *ib.* Harl. MS. 7340, p. 79). 4. Fragments of a service in D minor or F. 5. Anthems, 'Bow down Thine Eare,' 'I will alway,' and 'We beseech Thee' (all at Ely Cathedral). Other compositions by Mudd are at Lichfield, Hereford, and Peterhouse. There is mention of Mudd's 'I will sing the Mercies' in Clifford's 'Words of Anthems.'

In the catalogue of Ely manuscripts a John or Thomas Mudd is said to have been organist at Peterborough between 1580 and 1620. But the Peterborough organist is doubtless identical, not with the Cambridge composer, but with Mudd, an unruly organist of Lincoln, who held office there in 1662 and 1663.

[Cooper's Athenæ Cantabrigienses, ii. 59; Gardiner's Registers of St. Paul's School, pp. 26, 399; Hawes and Loder's Framlingham, p. 24; Dickson's Catalogue of Ely Manuscripts; Reports of the Lincolnshire, &c., Archæological Society, xx. 42, 43; information kindly supplied by Mr. H. Davey of Brighton.]

L. M. M.

MUDFORD, WILLIAM (1782–1848), author and journalist, born in Half Moon Street, Piccadilly, London, on 8 Jan. 1782, became in 1800 assistant secretary to the Duke of Kent, whom he accompanied to Gibraltar in 1802; but he soon resigned this situation in order to devote himself to literary pursuits and to study politics, with a view to journalism. An admirer of Burke, he adopted strong conservative or old whig opinions. After a brief connection as a parliamentary reporter with the 'Morning Chronicle,' he obtained an appointment, first as assistant editor, and afterwards as editor of the 'Courier,' an evening journal which had acquired popularity and influence, and which maintained upon no unequal terms a rivalry with the 'Times.'

Mudford warmly supported Canning during the intrigues which preceded and followed his accession to the office of prime minister, and was frequently in communication with him until his death. Declining to support a change of policy on the part of the proprietors of the 'Courier,' Mudford publicly withdrew from the paper, and justified his conduct in a letter which attracted considerable attention. The 'Courier' steadily declined in circulation, and finally expired, after some unsuccessful efforts had been made to induce Mudford to resume the editorship.

A loss of his earnings during the speculative mania compelled him at forty to begin the world again, with a young wife and increasing family. He worked assiduously, and, at the invitation of the conservative party in East Kent, he became the editor, and subsequently the proprietor of the 'Kentish Observer,' and settled at Canterbury. To 'Blackwood's Magazine' he was a regular contributor, and a single number occasionally contained three articles from his pen—a tale, a review, and a political paper. His series of 'First and Last' tales and his contributions under the title of 'The Silent Member' were very popular. Mudford succeeded Theodore Hook [q. v.] in 1841 as editor of the 'John Bull,' and removed to London, but he still maintained his connection with the 'Kentish Observer.' Despite declining health he toiled incessantly. A vigorous article on the French revolution of 1848, written long after midnight, which appeared in the 'John Bull' of 5 March of that year, was the last effort of his pen. He died at 5 Harrington Square, Hampstead Road, on 10 March 1848, leaving a widow and eight children. His second son, Mr. William Heseltine Mudford, was formerly editor of the 'Standard.'

His works are: 1. 'A Critical Enquiry into the Writings of Dr. Samuel Johnson. In which it is shewn that the Pictures of Life contained in "The Rambler" and other Publications of that celebrated Writer have a dangerous tendency. To which is added an Appendix, containing a facetious Dialogue between Boz [James Boswell] and Poz [Dr. Johnson] in the Shades,' 2nd edit. London, 1803, 8vo. 2. 'Augustus and Mary, or the Maid of Buttermere, a Domestic Tale,' 1803, 12mo. 3. 'Nubilia in search of a Husband, including Sketches of Modern Society' (anon.), London, 1809, 8vo; 4th edit., with two additional chapters, in the same year. 4. 'The Contemplatist, or a Series of Essays upon Morals and Literature,' 1811, 12mo. 5. 'The Life and Adventures of Paul Plaintive, Esq., an Author. Compiled by Martin Gribaldus Swammerdam,' 2 vols. London, 1811, 12mo. 6. 'A Critical Examination of the Writings of Richard Cumberland. Also Memoirs of his Life,' 2 vols. London, 1812, and again 1814, 8vo. 7. 'An Historical Account of the Campaign in the Netherlands in 1815, under the Duke of Wellington and Prince Blucher,' London, 1817, 4to, with plates by Cruikshank, from drawings by J. Rouse. In this volume he received assistance from the Duke of Wellington, to whom it was dedicated. 8. 'The Five Nights of St. Albans' (anon.), a novel, 3 vols. London, 1829, 12mo; London [1878], 8vo. 9. 'The Premier' (anon.), a novel, 3 vols. London, 1831, 8vo. 10. 'The Canterbury Magazine. By Geoffrey Oldcastle, Gent.,' 1834, &c. 11. 'Stephen Dugard' (anon.), a novel, 3 vols. London, 1840, 12mo; reprinted in Hodgson's 'New Series of Novels,' vol. v. London [1860], 8vo. 12. 'Tales and Trifles from "Blackwood's" and other popular Magazines,' 2 vols. London, 1849, 8vo; containing the well-known story of 'The Iron Shroud,' which is reprinted in vol. i. of 'Tales from Blackwood.' 13. 'Arthur Wilson, a Study' (anon.), 3 vols. London, 1872, 8vo (a posthumous publication).

He also translated Golbéry's 'Travels in Africa,' 1803; Helvetius's 'De l'Esprit,' with a life of the author, 1807; Madame Grafigny's 'Peruvian Letters,' 1807; Cardinal de Bausset's 'Life of Fénelon,' 1810; 'Memoirs of Prince Eugene of Savoy,' 1811; and he edited Goldsmith's 'Essays on Man and Manners,' 1804, 'The British Novelists,' 1811, and Beattie's 'Beauties,' 1809, with memoir.

[Private information; Gent. Mag. June 1848, p. 665; Biog. Dict. of Living Authors, p. 245; Lowndes's Bibl. Man. (Bohn), p. 1626.] T. C.

MUDGE, HENRY (1806–1874), temperance advocate, son of Thomas Mudge, was born at Tower Hill House, Bodmin, 29 July 1806. He was educated at St. Bartholomew's Hospital, London, became a licentiate of the Society of Apothecaries 1828, and a member of the Royal College of Surgeons in the following year. He commenced practice in his native town, where he remained throughout his life. From the first he advocated strict temperance principles, never prescribing wines or spirits for his patients. In his later years he said that he had always been willing to give sick people alcohol had it been necessary for their cure, but such a necessity had not arisen in his experience. He also opposed the use of tobacco. He edited 'The Western Temperance Luminary,' 1838, twelve numbers, 'The Bodmin Temperance Luminary,' 1840–1, twelve numbers, and 'The Cornwall and Devon Temperance Journal,' 1851–8, eight volumes. Although so stern an advocate of temperance he did not approve of the Rechabites or the Oddfellows, and attacked their principles in 'Rechabitism: a Letter showing the Instability of the Independent Order of Rechabites,' 1844; 'An Exposure of Odd Fellowship, shewing that the Independent Order of Odd Fellows, Manchester Unity, is Unscriptural, and its Constitution unjust in its Finance . . . and immoral in its Practice,' 1845; and 'Caution and Testimony against Odd Fellowship,' 1846. He was twice mayor of Bodmin, and for many years a class-leader of the Wesleyan Methodist connexion. He died at Fore Street, Bodmin, 27 June 1874, leaving an only child, wife of J. S. Pethybridge, bank-manager.

Besides the works already mentioned, he wrote: 1. 'Rescued Texts or Teetotalism put under the Protection of the Gospel: being a critical Exposition of Texts of Scripture referring to Temperance. . . . With a Key to the Wine Question for the Unlearned,' 1853; 3rd edit. 1856. 2. 'Alcoholics: a Letter to Practitioners in Medicine,' 1856. 3. 'Physiology, Health and Disease demanding Abstinence from Alcoholic Drinks, and Prohibition of their common Sale. A Course of five Lectures,' 1859. 4. 'Dialogues, &c., against the Use of Tobacco,' 1861. 5. 'A Guide to the Treatment of Disease without Alcoholic Liquors,' 1863.

[Western Morning News, 29 June 1874, p. 2; Boase and Courtney's Bibl. Cornub. 1874–82, pp. 377–8, 1290.] G. C. B.

MUDGE, JOHN (1721–1793), physician, fourth and youngest son of the Rev. Zachariah Mudge [q. v.], by his first wife, Mary Fox, was born at Bideford, Devonshire, in 1721. He was educated at Bideford and Plympton grammar schools, and studied medicine at Plymouth Hospital. He soon obtained a large practice, to the success of which his family connection, his skill and winning manner, alike contributed. In 1777 he published a 'Dissertation on the Inoculated Small Pox, or an Attempt towards an Investigation of the real Causes which render the Small Pox by Inoculation so much more mild and safe then the same Disease when produced by the ordinary means of Infection' —a sensible work, which shows considerable advance upon the previous treatises by Mead and others. On 29 May 1777 Mudge was elected a fellow of the Royal Society, and in the same year was awarded the Copley medal for his 'Directions for making the best Composition for the Metals for reflecting Telescopes; together with a Description of the Process for Grinding, Polishing, and giving the great Speculum the true Parabolic Curve,' which were communicated by the author to the society, and printed in the 'Philosophical Transactions' (1777, lxvii. 296). The 'Directions' were also issued separately by Bowyer (London, 1778, 4to). Sir John Pringle [q. v.], the president, in making the presentation, remarked: 'Mr Mudge hath truly realised the expectation of Sir Isaac Newton, who, about one hundred years ago, presaged that the public would one day possess a parabolic speculum, not accomplished by mathematical rules, but by mechanical devices.' The manufacture of telescopes continued to occupy much of his spare time. He made two large ones with a magnifying power of two hundred times; one of these he gave to Count Bruhl, whence it passed to the Gotha observatory, the other descended to his son, General William Mudge (see BREWSTER, *Edinburgh Encyclopædia*, art. 'Optics,' xv. pt. ii. p. 661).

In 1778 he published 'A Radical and Expeditious Cure for recent Catarrhous Cough,' with a drawing of a remedial inhaler, which obtained wide acceptance. Some further small medical treatises were well received, and evoked several invitations to Mudge to try his fortunes in London. But he preferred to remain at Plymouth, where he practised for the remainder of his life, first as surgeon, and, after 1784, when he received the degree of M.D. from King's College, Aberdeen, as a physician.

Mudge inherited a friendship with the family of Sir Joshua Reynolds, and when in 1762 Dr. Johnson accompanied Sir Joshua on his visit to Plymouth, the pair were the guests of Dr. Mudge, 'the celebrated physician,' writes Boswell, 'who was not more distinguished for quickness of parts and variety of knowledge than loved and esteemed for his amiable manners.' Johnson became a firm friend of the family, and in 1783 he wrote very earnestly to the doctor respecting a meditated operation. 'It is doubtless painful, but,' he asks, 'is it dangerous? The pain I hope to endure with decency, but I am loth to put life into much hazard.' Another intimate friend was John Smeaton, to whom, after the storm of January 1762, Mudge wrote a letter of congratulation on the safety of the Eddystone. Above 80,000*l.* worth of damage was done in Plymouth harbour and sound, but the injury to the lighthouse was repaired with a 'gallipot of putty' (letter dated 15 Jan. in *Narrative of the Building of the Eddystone Lighthouse*, 2nd edit. p. 77). Other allies and guests of Mudge were James Ferguson, the astronomer, and James Northcote, originally a chemist's assistant, who owed his position in Reynolds's studio to the Plymouth doctor. Northcote subsequently spoke of Mudge as 'one of the most delightful persons I ever knew. Every one was enchanted with his society. It was not wit that he possessed, but such a perfect cheerfulness and good humour that it was like health coming into the room' (NORTHCOTE, *Conversations*, ed. Hazlitt, p. 89). A well-known London physician on one occasion, in sending a patient to Stonehouse for the mild air, told the lady that he was sending her to Dr. Mudge, and that if his physic did not cure her, his conversation would. He died on 26 March 1793, and was buried near his father in St. Andrew's Church, Plymouth.

Mudge was married three times, and had twenty children. By Mary Bulteel, his first wife, he had eight children. His second wife, Jane, was buried on 3 Feb. 1766 in St. Andrew's. He married thirdly, 29 May 1767, Elizabeth Garrett, who survived him, dying in 1808, aged 72. His sons, William and Zachariah, by his second and third wives respectively, are noticed separately.

A very fine portrait of Mudge as a young man by Sir Joshua Reynolds has been engraved by Grozier, W. Dickinson, and S. W. Reynolds. The original is now in the possession of Arthur Mudge, esq., of Plympton. A second portrait is by Northcote. Both are reproduced in Mr. S. R. Flint's 'Mudge Memoirs.' A portrait of his eldest son John (who died early) at the age of fifteen was presented to Dr. Mudge on his thirty-seventh birthday by Sir Joshua, who was generally chary of such gifts. A list of portraits of the family by Reynolds and other painters, is appended to the 'Mudge Memoirs.'

[Gent. Mag. 1793 pt. i. p. 376; Mr. Stamford Raffles Flint's Mudge Memoirs, pp. 79–120; Boswell's Johnson, ed. G. B. Hill, i. 378, 486, iv. 240; Nichols's Literary Anecdotes, xix. 675–6; Northcote's Life of Reynolds, p. 111; Georgian Era, iii. 485; Burke's Landed Gentry; Rees's Cyclopædia, xxxv. art. 'Telescope;' Thomson's History of the Royal Society.] T. S.

MUDGE, RICHARD ZACHARIAH (1790–1854), lieutenant-colonel royal engineers, eldest son of Major-general William Mudge [q. v.], was born at Plymouth on 6 Sept. 1790. He was educated at Blackheath and at the Royal Military Academy at Woolwich. He received a commission as second lieutenant royal engineers on 4 May

1807, and was promoted first lieutenant on 14 July the same year. In March 1809 he sailed for Lisbon, and joined the army under Sir Arthur Wellesley at Abrantes in May. He was present at the battle of Talavera, and on the enemy abandoning their position in front of Talavera he reconnoitred the river Alberche. He succeeded in reaching Escalona by the left bank, but on attempting to return to the army by the right bank in order to complete the reconnaissance, he was surprised by the enemy, who captured his attendant with his horse and baggage. He accompanied the army in the retreat from Talavera to Badajos, and was subsequently employed in the construction of the lines of Lisbon. He returned to England on 20 June 1810 in consequence of ill-health.

He was employed under his father on the ordnance survey, and was for some years in charge of the drawing department at the Tower of London. He was promoted second captain on 21 July 1813. In 1817 he was directed to assist Jean Baptiste Biot, who was sent to England as the commissioner of the Bureau des Longitudes of Paris to take pendulum observations at certain places along the great arc, and he accompanied Biot to Leith Fort, near Edinburgh, to Aberdeen, and to Unst in the Shetland islands. At Unst Mudge fell ill, and had to return to London. In 1818 he was engaged in superintending the survey of Lincolnshire.

In 1819 he went to Dunkirk in connection with the survey, and in 1821 to various places on the north coast of France. He first appears upon the list of Fellows of the Royal Society in 1823. He was promoted first captain on 23 March 1825, and regimental lieutenant-colonel on 10 Jan. 1837, remaining permanently on the ordnance survey. On the death of his uncle, Richard Rosedew of Beechwood, Devonshire, in 1837, he succeeded to the property.

About 1830 the question of the boundary between Maine and New Brunswick came prominently to the front. The United States claimed certain highlands running from the heads of the Connecticut river to within twenty miles of the St. Lawrence, which, if allowed, would have cut off the direct routes from Quebec to New Brunswick, and would have given the United States positions commanding Quebec itself. Great Britain objected that the claims were incompatible with the terms of the treaty of 1783. The question was referred to the arbitration of the king of the Netherlands, but the United States declined to abide by the compromise he proposed, and the subject assumed a more serious attitude. The British government in 1838, desiring to bring the matter to a settlement, appointed Mudge and Mr. Featherstonehaugh, who was well acquainted with America, commissioners to examine the physical character of the territory in dispute and report on the claims of the United States. In the spring of 1839 the commissioners prepared their expedition, and reached New York in July. They then went to Frederickton in New Brunswick, from whence, on 24 Aug., they commenced the journey which was the object of the expedition. The survey was completed, and the party reached Quebec on 21 Oct. From Quebec Mudge went to Niagara, and thence to New York, where he met the remainder of the expedition, and returned with them to England at the end of the year. In 1840 the commissioners carefully examined the whole history of the boundary question, and reported that the line claimed by the United States was inconsistent with the physical geography of the country and the terms of the treaty, but that they had discovered a line of highlands south of that claimed, which was in accordance with the language of the treaty. The report was laid before parliament, and the result was a compromise based on the report and settled by the treaty of Washington in 1842. Mudge retired from the army on full pay on 7 Sept. 1850, and resided at Beechwood. He died at Teignmouth, Devonshire, on 24 Sept. 1854, and was buried at Denbury.

Mudge married, on 1 Sept. 1817, Alice Watson, daughter of J. W. Hull, esq., of co. Down, Ireland, and left two daughters, Jane Rosedew, who married the Rev. William Charles Raffles Flint, and died in 1883, and Sophia Elizabeth, who married the Rev. John Richard Bogue. His portrait, painted in 1807 by James Northcote, R.A., was in the possession of his daughter, Mrs. Bogue.

Mudge wrote 'Observations on Railways, with reference to Utility, Profit, and the Obvious Necessity of a National System,' 8vo, London, 1837.

[Mudge Memoirs, by Mr. Stamford Raffles Flint, Truro, 1883; War Office Records; Records of the Corps of Royal Engineers.] R. H. V.

MUDGE, THOMAS (1717–1794), horologist, second son of Dr. Zachariah Mudge [q. v.], was born at Exeter in September 1717. Soon after his birth his father became master of the grammar school at Bideford, and there Thomas received his early education. The mechanism of watches, however, interested him much more than his school studies, and in 1731, when he was only fourteen, his father bound him apprentice to George Graham [q. v.], the successor of

Thomas Tompion, the eminent watchmaker of Water Lane, Fleet Street. Graham formed a very high estimate of his pupil's ability. On the expiration of his articles Mudge took lodgings, and continued to work privately for some years. One of the best watchmakers of the time for whom he constantly worked was Ellicot. When the latter was requested to supply Ferdinand VI of Spain with an equation watch, Mudge was entrusted with the construction of the instrument, although Ellicot's name was attached to it when finished, in accordance with the usual practice. Subsequently, when explaining the action of the watch to some men of science, Ellicot had the misfortune to injure it, and, being unable to repair the damage himself, he had to return it to Mudge. This circumstance reached the ears of the Spanish king, who had a mania for mechanical inventions, and he employed Mudge to construct for him a much more elaborate chronometer. This watch, which was made in the crutch end of a cane, struck the hours and quarters by solar time, and the motions of the wheels at the time of striking were revealed by small sliding shutters. The king constantly spoke admiringly of the maker.

Mudge had been admitted a free clockmaker on 15 Jan. 1738. In 1750 he entered into partnership with a former fellow-apprentice, William Dutton, and took the old shop at No. 67 Fleet Street, where the firm constructed for Smeaton a fine watch, with a compensation curb, and also made Dr. Johnson his first watch in 1768. In 1760 Mudge was introduced to the Count Bruhl, envoy extraordinary from the court of Saxony, who henceforth became a steady patron. During his partnership he also invented the lever escapement, the first instrument to which this improvement was applied being a watch made for Queen Charlotte in 1770.

In 1765 Mudge had published 'Thoughts on the Means of Improving Watches, and particularly those for the Use of the Sea,' and in 1771 he quitted active business and retired to Plymouth, in order to devote the whole of his time and attention to the improvement of chronometers designed to determine, with the aid of the sextant, the longitude at sea. The improvement of timekeepers for this purpose had long been an object of solicitude with the government, and a reward of 10,000*l.* had been offered by parliament in 1713 for a chronometer which should determine the longitude within sixty geographical miles; if within thirty geographical miles, twice that reward was offered. John Harrison (1693–1776) [q. v.] ultimately obtained the larger reward in 1773 for a chronometer which only erred four and a half seconds in ten weeks. Further rewards were, however, offered in the same year for a more perfect method, and Mudge felt confident that he could attain the degree of exactness required. In 1776 he was appointed king's watchmaker, and in the same year he completed his first marine chronometer. He submitted it to Dr. Hornby, Savilian professor of astronomy at Oxford, who tested it, with satisfactory results. It was then committed to Nevil Maskelyne [q. v.], the astronomer, for some more protracted tests at the observatory (1776–7). The board of longitude in the meantime gave Mudge five hundred guineas, and urged him to make another watch in order to qualify for the government's rewards, the terms of which required the construction of two watches of the specified accuracy. Mudge forthwith set about making two more timekeepers, which were known as the green and blue chronometers (one of them is still preserved in the Soane Museum, and is in going order). These were submitted to the same rigorous tests as the first, but, like it, they were described by the astronomer royal as not having satisfied the requirements of the act. A controversy ensued, in which it was stated that Maskelyne had not given the timekeepers fair trial, but that they had gone better in other hands both before and after the period during which they had been under his observation. Mudge's case was strongly urged in a pamphlet issued by his eldest son, entitled 'A Narrative of Facts relating to some Timekeepers constructed by Mr. T. Mudge for the Discovery of the Longitude at Sea, together with Observations upon the Conduct of the Astronomer Royal respecting them,' London, 1792. Maskelyne retorted in 'An Answer to a Pamphlet entitled A Narrative of Facts . . . wherein . . . the Conduct of the Astronomer Royal is vindicated from Mr. Mudge's Misrepresentations' (1792), and the controversy closed with the younger Mudge's 'Reply to the Answer . . . to which is added . . . some Remarks on some Passages in Dr. Maskelyne's Answer by his Excellency the Count de Bruhl' (1792). Mudge was supported throughout by M. de Zach, astronomer to the Duke of Saxe-Gotha, who had observed the variations of the first of Mudge's chronometers for two years, and by Admiral Campbell, who carried the chronometer on voyages to Newfoundland in 1785 and 1786 respectively. This chronometer was afterwards stated by Thomas Mudge junior to vary less than half a second per diem. It is curious that Harrison entertained similar grievances against Maskelyne, and it was currently supposed that the astronomer had a scheme of his own for finding the longitude by lunar tables which disposed him to apply ultra-rigorous tests to the chronometers.

In June 1791 Mudge's son presented to the board of longitude a memorial, stating that although his father's timekeepers during the time of the public trial had not been adjudged to go within the limits prescribed by the Act, yet as they were superior to any hitherto invented, and were constructed on such principles as would render them permanently useful, the board would be justified in exercising the powers vested in them, and giving him some reward in recognition of his labours. The memorial proving unsuccessful, he carried a petition to the same effect to the House of Commons, and a committee was appointed, on which served Pitt, Wyndham, Bathurst, and Lord Minto, to consider the value of Mudge's invention. The committee, having been assisted by Atwood and other eminent watchmakers and men of science, finally voted Mudge the sum of 2,500*l.* He died two years after receiving this reward at the house of his elder son, Thomas, at Newington Place, Surrey, on 14 Nov. 1794. He had married in 1757 Abigail Hopkins, a native of Oxford, who died in 1789, leaving two sons. The younger son, John (1763–1847), was, on the recommendation of Queen Charlotte, presented to the vicarage of Brampford-Speke, near Exeter, by the lord chancellor in 1791.

The elder son, THOMAS (1760–1843), born on 16 Dec. 1760, was called to the bar from Lincoln's Inn, practised as a barrister in London, and successfully advocated his father's claims to a government reward. For some time he conducted a manufacture of chronometers upon his father's plan, and gave some account of the enterprise in 'A Description, with Plates, of the Timekeepers invented by the late Mr. Thomas Mudge, to which is prefixed a Narrative by his Son of the Measures taken to give Effect to the Invention since the Reward bestowed upon it by the House of Commons in 1793; a Republication of a Tract by the late Mr. Mudge on the Improvement of Timekeepers; and a Series of Letters written by him to his Excellency Count Bruhl between the years 1773 and 1787,' London, 1799. He supplied some chronometers to the admiralty and also to the Spanish and Danish governments; but the venture obtained no permanent measure of success. He was also a correspondent of James Northcote [q. v.], to whom he sent a copy of verses on the 'High Rocks' at Tunbridge Wells, and other trifles. He died at Chilcompton, near Bath, on 10 Nov. 1843. By his wife, Elizabeth Kingdon, sister of Lady Brunel, the mother of the famous engineer, he had several children.

A fine portrait of Thomas Mudge the elder, belonging to Mrs. Robert Mudge, was painted for the Count de Bruhl by Nathaniel Dance, and was engraved by Charles Townley and L. Schiavonetti. It shows a face which is remarkable for its look of patient intelligence and integrity.

[S. R. Flint's Mudge Memoirs; Universal Mag., 1795, p. 311; Chalmers's Biog. Dict.; Nichols's Anecd. viii. 31, ix. 675; R. W. Worth's Three Towns Bibliography and Hist. of Plymouth, p. 470; Frodsham's Account of the Chronometer; E. J. Wood's Curiosities of Clocks and Watches; Atkins' and Overall's Clockmakers' Company, 1881, pp. 169–70; Smith's Mezzotinto Portraits, pt. i. p. 189; Georgian Era; Brit. Mus. Cat.]

T. S.

MUDGE, WILLIAM (1762–1820), major-general royal artillery, son of Dr. John Mudge [q. v.] of Plymouth, by his second wife, and grandson of the Rev. Zachariah Mudge [q. v.], was born at Plymouth on 1 Dec. 1762. He entered the Royal Military Academy at Woolwich on 17 April 1777, and while he was there his godfather, Dr. Johnson [q. v.], paid him a visit, and gave him a guinea and a book. On 9 July 1779 he received a commission as second lieutenant in the royal artillery, and was sent to South Carolina to join the army under Lord Cornwallis. He was promoted first lieutenant on 16 May 1781. On his return home he was stationed at the Tower of London, and studied the higher mathematics under Dr. Hutton, amusing himself in his spare time with the construction of clocks. He became a first-rate mathematician, and was appointed in 1791 to the ordnance trigonometrical survey, of which he was promoted to be director on the death of Colonel Williams in 1798. He was elected a fellow of the Royal Society the same year. He was promoted brevet major on 25 Sept. 1801, regimental major 14 Sept. 1803, and lieutenant-colonel 20 July 1804. While at the head of the survey he resided first, until 1808, at the Tower of London, and afterwards at 4 Holles Street, London, which he purchased; there he resided for the rest of his life. He was appointed in addition and quite unexpectedly, on 29 July 1809, by Lord Chatham, to be lieutenant-governor of the Royal Military Academy at Woolwich; and when in 1810 it was decided to move the Indian cadets to Addiscombe, Mudge was appointed public examiner to the new college. He took great pains to see that both the Woolwich and the Addiscombe cadets were well trained in surveying and topographical drawing, and for this purpose placed them before leaving college under Mr. Dawson of the ordnance survey for a course of practical study. Mudge's management of the cadets was so successful that in 1817 Lord Chatham wrote to express his high satisfaction at the result.

In 1813 it was determined to extend the meridian line into Scotland. Mudge superintended the general arrangement of the work, and in some cases took the actual measurement. It is to Mudge that Wordsworth alludes in his poem on 'Black Combe,' written in 1813. On the extension of the English arc of meridian into Scotland, the French Bureau des Longitudes applied for permission for Jean Baptiste Biot to make observations for them on that line. These observations were carried out by Biot, with the assistance of Mudge and of his son Richard Zachariah [q. v.], at Leith Fort on the Forth, and Biot assisted Mudge in extending the arc to Unst in the Shetland islands.

On 4 June 1813 Mudge was promoted brevet-colonel, and on 20 Dec. 1814 regimental colonel. In 1817 he received from the university of Edinburgh the degree of LL.D. In 1818 he travelled in France for the benefit of his health, and on his return was appointed a commissioner of the new board of longitude. In 1819 the king of Denmark visited the survey operations at Bagshot Heath, and presented Mudge with a gold chronometer. In May of this year he commenced the survey of Scotland, and on 12 Aug. he was promoted major-general. He died on 17 April 1820. With an amiable disposition and an even temper he was a careful and economical administrator.

Mudge's portrait was painted in 1804 by James Northcote, R.A., and the picture is in the possession of his granddaughter, Sophia Elizabeth, widow of the Rev. John Richard Bogue. Mudge married Margaret Jane, third daughter of Major-general Williamson, R.A., who survived him four years. He left a daughter, two sons in the royal engineers, one in the royal artillery, and one in the royal navy.

Mudge contributed to the Royal Society's 'Transactions:' 1. 'Account of the Trigonometrical Survey made in 1797, 1798, and 1799.' 2. 'Account of the Measurement of an Arc of the Meridian from Dunnose, Isle of Wight, to Clifton in Yorkshire.' 3. 'On the Measurement of Three Degrees of the Meridian conducted in England by William Mudge.'

Besides the maps of the survey published under his direction, he published: 1. 'General Survey of England and Wales,' pt. i. fol. 1805. 2. 'An Account of the Trigonometrical Survey carried on by Order of the Master-General of H.M. Ordnance in the years 1800–1809, by William Mudge and Thomas Colby.' 3. 'An Account of the Operations carried on for accomplishing a Trigonometrical Survey of England and Wales from the commencement in 1784 to the end of 1796. First published in, and now revised from, the "Philosophical Transactions," by William Mudge and Isaac Dalby. The Second Volume, continued from 1797 to the end of 1799, by William Mudge. The Third Volume, an Account of the Trigonometrical Survey in 1800, 1801, 1803 to 1809, by William Mudge and Thomas Colby,' 3 vols. 4to, London, 1799–1811. 4. 'Sailing Directions for the N.E., N., and N.W. Coasts of Ireland, partly drawn up by William Mudge, completed by G. A. Fraser,' 8vo, London, 1842.

[Survey Memoirs; Royal Artillery Proceedings; Kane's List of the Officers of the Royal Artillery; Mudge Memoirs, by Stamford Raffles Flint, Truro, 1883; Annual Biog. and Obit. for 1820; Official Records.] R. H. V.

MUDGE, WILLIAM (1796–1837), commander in the navy, born in 1796, third son of Major-general William Mudge [q. v.], was promoted to be lieutenant in the navy on 19 Feb. 1815. In August 1821 he was appointed first lieutenant of the Barracouta, with Captain Cutfield, employed on the survey of the east coast of Africa under Captain W. F. Owen [q. v.] He was afterwards moved into the Leven under the immediate command of Owen, and on 4 Oct. 1825 was promoted to the rank of commander. He was then appointed to conduct the survey of the coast of Ireland, on which he was employed till his death at Howth, on 20 July 1837. He was buried with military honours in the ground of the cathedral at Howth on 24 July.

In addition to 'Sailing Directions for Dublin Bay and for the North Coast of Ireland,' which were officially published, 1842, Mudge contributed several papers (mostly hydrographic) to the 'Nautical Magazine;' and to the Society of Antiquaries, in November 1833, an interesting account of a prehistoric village found in a Donegal bog (*Archæologia*, xxvi. 261). He married in 1827 Mary Marinda, only child of William Rae of Blackheath, by whom he had a large family. He has been confused with his father (e.g. in *Brit. Mus. Cat.*), whose work, it will be seen, was entirely geodetic.

[Flint's Mudge Memoirs; Marshall's Roy. Nav. Biog. xii. (vol. iv. pt. ii.) 175; Gent. Mag.

1837, pt. ii. p. 326; Nautical Mag. 1837, p. 616; Dawson's Memoirs of Hydrography, i. 123.]

J. K. L.

MUDGE, ZACHARIAH (1694–1769), divine, was born at Exeter, of humble parentage, in 1694. His immediate ancestry has not been traced, but the family of Mugge or Mudge, though undistinguished, was of very old standing in Devonshire. A branch migrated to New England in the seventeenth century, and has borne many vigorous offshoots (see ALFRED MUDGE, *Memorial of the Mudge Family in America*, Boston, 1868). After attending Exeter grammar school Zachary was sent in 1710 to the nonconformist academy of Joseph Hallett III [q. v.] When still among his lesson-books he fell violently in love with a certain Mary Fox, whose refusal to give serious attention to his protestations drove him in despair to take the road for London, but he returned to Exeter after three weeks of severe experiences. In 1711 one George Trosse, whose high estimate of Zachary's abilities had led him to pay for his schooling, died, and left the young man half of his library. This included a number of Hebrew works, which gave Mudge an incentive to study that language. About 1713 he left Hallett's, and became second master in the school of John Reynolds, vicar of St. Thomas the Apostle in Exeter. John Reynolds's son Samuel, master of Exeter grammar school, was the father of Sir Joshua Reynolds, and Mudge soon became the intimate friend of three generations of the family. In 1714 he married his former love, Mary Fox. In the winter of 1717–18 he left Exeter to become master of Bideford grammar school. While at Bideford he entered into a long correspondence with Bishop Weston of Exeter on the doctrines of the established church, which resulted in his relinquishing his purpose of joining the nonconformist ministry and joining the church of England. At the same time he remitted 50*l.* to the West of England Nonconformist Association to indemnify his former co-religionists for the expenses of his education. He was ordained deacon in the church of England on 21 Sept. 1729, and priest on the following day. In December of the same year he was instituted to the living of Abbotsham, near Bideford, on the presentation of Lord-chancellor King, and in August 1732 he obtained the valuable living of St. Andrew's, Plymouth. Mudge appears to have been virtually a deist, and his sound common sense and serenity of mind harmonised well with the unemotional form of religion that was dominant in his day. Boswell describes him as 'idolised in the west both for his excellence as a preacher and the uniform perfect propriety of his private conduct.' His sermons, though described by Dr. Johnson as too widely suggestive to be 'practical,' were greatly esteemed for fifty years after his death, were favourite reading with Lord Chatham, and were long prescribed for theological students at Oxford. He published a selection of them in 1739. One on 'The Origin and Obligations of Government' was reprinted by Edmund Burke in the form of a pamphlet in 1793, as being the best antidote against Jacobin principles. Another, separately published in 1731, was entitled 'Liberty: a Sermon preached in the Cathedral Church of St. Peter, Exon, on Thursday, 16 Sept. 1731, before the Gentlemen educated in the Free School at Exeter under the Rev. Mr. Reynolds.' It contained some reflections upon the nonconformists, which were answered in 'Fate and Force, or Mr. Mudge's Liberty set in a true Light,' London, 1732. According to John Fox (1693–1763) [q. v.], Mudge 'had a great measure of contempt for all our [nonconformist] great men, both divines and philosophers; he allowed them indeed to be honest, but then he said they saw but a little way.'

Mudge was made a prebendary of Exeter in 1736. In 1744 he issued a work for which he had long been preparing, 'An Essay towards a New English Version of the Book of Psalms from the original Hebrew,' London, 1744, 4to. The translation is conservative of the old phraseology, and the rendering of particular psalms is often very happy. The punctuation was novel, the notes 'more ingenious than solid;' the conjectures as to the authorship of individual psalms are for the time enlightened. In 1759, after the last mason's work had been completed on the Eddystone lighthouse, and 'Laus Deo' cut upon the last stone set over the door of the lantern, Smeaton conducted Mudge, his old friend, to the summit of his 'tower of the winds.' There in the lantern, upon Mudge's lead, the pair 'raised their voices in praise to God, and joined together in singing the grand Old Hundredth Psalm, as a thanksgiving for the successful conclusion of this arduous undertaking.'

Smeaton was only one of a number of distinguished friends by whom Mudge was greatly esteemed. Johnson was introduced to him by Reynolds in 1762. Edmund Burke, when informing Malone that it was to Mudge that Reynolds owed his disposition to generalise and 'his first rudiments of speculation,' goes on to say: 'I myself have seen Mr. Mudge at Sir Joshua's house. He was a learned and venerable old man, and, as I thought, very conversant in the Platonic philosophy, and very fond of that method of philosophising.' Sir Joshua always used to say that Mudge was the wisest man he had met in his life. It was his definition of beauty as the medium of form that Reynolds adopted in his 'Discourses,' and he often spoke of republishing Mudge's sermons, and prefixing a memoir from his own pen. Mudge's shrewdness and foresight are well illustrated by his retort to his son John, when the latter remonstrated with him for exhibiting no elation upon the news of Wolfe's victory at Quebec: 'Son, son, it will do very well whilst the Americans have the sea on one side and the French on the other; but take away the French, and they will not want our protection.' Mudge died at Coffleet, Devonshire, on the first stage of his annual pilgrimage to London, on 2 April 1769. He was buried by the communion table of St. Andrew's, Plymouth, and his funeral sermon was preached by John Gandy, his curate for many years, who also (as Mudge had desired) succeeded to the vicarage. Dr. Johnson drew his character in the 'London Chronicle' for 2 June in monumental terms. 'His principles both of thought and action were great and comprehensive. By a solicitous examination of objections and judicious comparison of opposite arguments he attained what inquiry never gives but to industry and perspicuity—a firm and unshaken settlement of conviction; but his firmness was without asperity, for knowing with how much difficulty truth was sometimes found, he did not wonder that many missed it. . . . Though studious he was popular, though argumentative he was modest, though inflexible he was candid, and though metaphysical he was orthodox.'

By his first wife, Mary, Mudge had four sons—Zachariah (1714–1753), a surgeon, who died on board an Indiaman at Canton; Thomas [q. v.]; Richard (1718–1773), who took orders, and was distinguished locally for his compositions for, and performances on, the harpsichord; and John [q. v.]—and one daughter, Mary. Mudge married, secondly, in 1762, Elizabeth Neell, who survived him many years, and died in 1782. The first Mrs. Mudge is said to have been of a parsimonious disposition. At Dr. Johnson's eighteenth cup of tea she on one occasion hazarded, 'What another, Dr. Johnson!' 'Madam, you are rude!' retorted her guest, who proceeded without interruption to his extreme limit of five and twenty.

Mudge was painted on three several occasions by Sir Joshua Reynolds, in 1761, 1762, and 1766 respectively. The third portrait is the most noteworthy, being, as Leslie says, 'a noble head, painted with great grandeur, and the most perfect truth of effect.' The chin rests on the hand, and Chantrey, who carved the whole composition in full relief for St. Andrew's, Plymouth, stated that, when the marble was placed in the right light and shadow, the shape of the light falling behind the hand and on the band and gown was exactly the same in the bust as in the picture. So great indeed was his admiration for the painting that he offered to execute the bust without charge if he might retain the picture.

[Mr. S. R. Flint's Mudge Memoirs; Boswell's Johnson, ed. G. B. Hill, i. 378, iv. 77, 79, 98; Nichols's Lit. Anecd. viii. 675, 676; Account of the Life of Reynolds by Edmund Malone, xxxiii, xcviii; Northcote's Life of Reynolds, 1818, i. 112–15; Conversations of James Northcote, 1830, pp. 85–9; J. B. Rowe's Ecclesiastical Hist. of Old Plymouth, p. 37; Chalmers's Biog. Dict. xxii. 493–4; Darling's Cycl. Bibl. col. 2131; Horne's Introduction to Critical Study of Scripture, v. 321, and Psalms, Preface; Orme's Bibl. Biblica, 1824, p. 323.] T. S.

MUDGE, ZACHARY (1770–1852), admiral, a younger son, by his third wife, of Dr. John Mudge [q. v.], and half-brother of Major-general William Mudge [q. v.], was born at Plymouth on 22 Jan. 1770. From November 1780 he was borne on the books of the Foudroyant, with Captain Jervis, afterwards Earl of St. Vincent [q. v.], and is said to have been actually on board her when she captured the Pégase on 21 April 1782. During the next seven years he served on the home and North American stations, for some time as midshipman of the Pégase; and on 24 May 1789 was promoted to the rank of lieutenant. In December 1790 he was appointed to the Discovery, with Captain George Vancouver [q. v.], then starting on his celebrated voyage of exploration on the north-west coast of America. In February 1794 he was moved into the Providence, with Commander W. R. Broughton [q. v.], and on 24 Nov. 1797 he was promoted to be commander. In November 1798 he was appointed to the Fly sloop, employed on the coast of North America. On 15 Nov. 1800 he was advanced to post rank, and in April 1801 was appointed to the Constance of 24 guns, in which he was employed convoying merchant ships or cruising with some success against the enemy's privateers.

In September 1802 he was moved into the 32-gun frigate Blanche in the West Indies. During 1803 and 1804 she effected many captures both of the enemy's merchant ships and privateers. On 19 July 1805, as she was carrying despatches from Jamaica, intended for Lord Nelson at Barbados, she fell in with a small French squadron, consisting of the 40-gun frigate Topaze, two heavy corvettes, and a brig, which brought her to action about ten in the forenoon. In a little over an hour she was reduced to a wreck and struck her colours; Mudge and the rest of the officers and crew were taken out of her, and towards evening she sank. Both at the time and afterwards it was questioned whether Mudge had made the best possible defence (James, *Naval History*, edit. of 1860, iv. 39 et seq.) The Topaze only, it was said, was actively engaged, and her loss was limited to one man killed. On the other hand, the corvettes seriously interfered with the Blanche's manœuvres; and this was the view taken by the court-martial which, on 14 Oct., acquitted Mudge of all blame, and complimented him on his 'very able and gallant conduct' against a superior force (*Naval Chronicle*, xiv. 341). On 18 Nov. he was appointed to the Phœnix, which he commanded for the next five years in the Bay of Biscay and on the coast of Portugal. In 1814 and 1815 he commanded the 74-gun ship Valiant; but had no further service. He became a rear-admiral on 22 July 1830, vice-admiral on 23 Nov. 1841, admiral on 15 Sept. 1849, and died at Plympton, on 26 Oct. 1852. He was buried at Newton Ferrers; there is a memorial window in St. Andrew's Church, Plymouth. Mudge married Jane, daughter of the Rev. Edmund Granger, rector of Sowton, Devonshire, and left issue. His eldest son, Zachary, a barrister, died, at the age of fifty-four, on 13 Dec. 1868 (*Gent. Mag.* 1868, ii. 120).

[Flint's Mudge Memoirs; O'Byrne's Nav. Biog. Dict.; Marshall's Roy. Nav. Biog. iii. (vol. ii.) 307; Gent. Mag. 1852, new ser. xxxviii. 634.]

J. K. L.

MUDIE, CHARLES EDWARD (1818–1890), founder of Mudie's Lending Library, son of Thomas Mudie, was born at Cheyne Walk, Chelsea, on 18 Oct. 1818. He assisted his father, a secondhand bookseller, newspaper agent, and lender of books at a penny a volume, until 1840, when he set up as a stationer and bookseller at 28 Upper King Street (now Southampton Row), Bloomsbury. As a publisher he was known by the production of 'Poems by James Russell Lowell,' 1844 (the first appearance of Lowell's poems in England); of R. W. Emerson's 'Man Thinking, an Oration,' 1844; and of some one-volume novels. In 1842 he commenced lending books, and in course of time this department so increased that his premises proved inadequate, and in 1852 he removed to 510 New Oxford Street. He advertised extensively, and exerted himself to procure early copies of the most popular new books, often in very great numbers. He took two thousand four hundred copies of vols. iii. and iv. of Macaulay's 'History of England,' and two thousand of Livingstone's 'Travels.' A large new hall and a library were opened in the rear of the premises on 17 Dec. 1860, and soon afterwards branches were established elsewhere in London, as well as in Birmingham and Manchester. This large extension of his undertaking was, however, more than his capital sufficed to meet, and in 1864 he made over the library to a limited company, in which he held half the shares and retained the management.

Mudie possessed excellent qualities as a business man, and his knowledge of public requirements and the tact he displayed in meeting them enabled him to establish a library which soon numbered over 25,000 subscribers, and became almost a national institution. It was also peculiarly English, the circulating library of the Mudie pattern being almost unknown on the continent or in America. On 29 Nov. 1870 Mudie was elected a member of the London School Board for the Westminster district, and served for three years. In 1872 he published 'Stray Leaves,' a volume of poems, including one or two well-known hymns, which went to a second edition in 1873. He was eminently pious and charitable, labouring in the slums of Westminster, and preaching on Sundays in a small chapel. Anxious to avoid circulating literature that would be in any way immoral, he was often attacked for his method of selecting books. He wrote to the 'Athenæum' in 1860, vindicating himself from an attack made on him on that ground in the 'Literary Gazette.' Mr. George Moore, the novelist, issued in 1885 'Literature at Nurse, or Circulating Morals,' strictures upon the selection of books in circulation at Mudie's Library. Many catalogues of the library bearing Mudie's name have been printed; the first is dated 1857. Mudie died at 31 Maresfield Gardens, Hampstead, on 28 Oct. 1890. A portrait of Mudie is given in Curwen's 'History of Booksellers.' By his wife, Mary Kingsford, daughter of the Rev. Henry Pawling of Lenham, Kent, he had eight children. Of these Charles Henry Mudie is noticed below; while Arthur Oliver Mudie, born 29 May 1854, of Magdalen College, Oxford, B.A. 1879, M.A. 1881, took, on the death of his brother, a share in conducting the business, and ultimately became the managing director.

Mudie, Charles Henry (1850–1879), philanthropist, was born at Adelaide Road, Haverstock Hill, on 26 Jan. 1850, and in early youth had the advantage of a long residence in Italy. He was educated at the London University school and, under the Rev. N. Jennings, at St. John's Wood. He is described under the name of 'Tom Holcomb' in an article by Mrs. Craik called 'A Garden Party' in a Christmas number of 'Good Words.' On coming of age he took part in the management of his father's business. He was a good musician, an amateur actor, a lecturer, and he devoted much time to the improvement of the poorer classes. He died on 13 Jan. 1879, having married, on 4 June 1874, Rebecca Jane, daughter of Edwin Lermitte of Muswell Hill, Middlesex (*Charles Henry Mudie* [by Mary Mudie, his sister], 1879, with portrait; *Athenæum*, 1879, i. 90).

[Bookseller, November 1890, p. 1232; Curwen's Booksellers, 1873, pp. 421–32, with portrait; Literary Gazette, 1860, v. 252, 285, 302, 398; Cartoon Portraits, 1873, pp. 72–3, with portrait; Illustr. London News, 3 Nov. 1890, p. 583, with portrait; Times, 30 Oct. 1890, p. 8; Athenæum, 1860 ii. 451, 594, 873, 877, 1890 ii. 588; Julian's Dict. of Hymnology, p. 774; F. Espinasse's Literary Recollections, 1893, p. 27; information from Arthur Oliver Mudie, esq.]

G. C. B.

MUDIE, ROBERT (1777–1842), miscellaneous writer, born in Forfarshire on 28 June 1777, was youngest child of John Mudie, weaver, by his wife Elizabeth Bany. After attending the village school he worked at the loom, until he was drawn for the militia. From his boyhood he devoted his scanty leisure to study. At the expiry of his militia service of four years he became master of a village school in the south of Fifeshire. In 1802 he was appointed Gaelic professor and teacher of drawing in the Inverness academy, although of Gaelic he knew little. About 1808 he acted as drawing-master to the Dundee High School, but was soon transferred to the department of arithmetic and English composition. He contributed much to the local newspaper, and conducted for some time a monthly periodical. Becoming a member of the Dundee town council, he engaged eagerly in the cause of burgh reform in conjunction with R. S. Rintoul, afterwards editor of the London 'Spectator.' In politics he was 'an ardent reformer.' In 1820 Mudie removed to London, where he was engaged as reporter to the 'Morning Chronicle,' and in that capacity went to Edinburgh on George IV's visit to that city, which he described in a volume entitled 'Modern Athens.' He was subsequently editor of the 'Sunday Times,' and also wrote largely in the periodicals of the day.

About 1838 he migrated to Winchester, where he was employed by a bookseller named Robbins in writing books, including a worthless 'History of Hampshire,' which formed the letterpress to accompany some pretentious steel engravings. The speculation failed, and Mudie returned to London, in impaired circumstances and broken health. He conducted the 'Surveyor, Engineer, and Architect,' a monthly journal, commenced in February 1840, which did not last through the year. He died at Pentonville on 29 April 1842, leaving the widow of a second marriage in destitution, one son, and four daughters.

His more important writings are: 1. 'The Maid of Griban, a Fragment,' in verse, 8vo, Dundee, 1810. 2. 'Glenfergus, a Novel,' 3 vols. 12mo, Edinburgh, 1819. 3. 'A Historical Account of His Majesty's Visit to Scotland,' 8vo, London, 1822. 4. 'Things in General, being Delineations of Persons, Places, Scenes, and Occurrences in the Metropolis, and other parts of Britain, &c., by Laurence Langshank,' 12mo, London, 1824. 5. 'Modern Athens' [a description of Edinburgh], 8vo, London, 1824. 6. 'The Complete Governess,' 12mo, London, 1824. 7. 'Session of Parliament,' 8vo, London, 1824. 8. 'Babylon the Great, a Dissection and Demonstration of Men and Things in the British Capital,' 2 vols. 12mo, London, 1825; another edit. 1828. 9. 'The Picture of India; Geographical, Historical, and Descriptive,' 2 vols. 12mo, London, 1827; 2nd edit. 1832. 10. 'Australia,' 12mo, London, 1827. 11. 'Vegetable Substances,' 18mo, London, 1828. 12. 'A Second Judgment of Babylon the Great,' 2 vols. 12mo, London, 1829. 13. 'The British Naturalist,' 8vo, London, 1830. 14. 'First Lines of Zoology,' 12mo, London, 1831. 15. 'The Emigrant's Pocket Companion,' &c., 8vo, London, 1832. 16. 'First Lines of Natural Philosophy,' 12mo, London, 1832. 17. 'A Popular Guide to the Observation of Nature' ('Constable's Miscellany,' vol. lxxvii.), 12mo, Edinburgh, 1832 (also New York, 1844, 12mo). 18. 'The Botanic Annual,' 8vo, London, 1832. 19. 'The Feathered Tribes of the British Islands,' 2 vols. 8vo, London, 1834; 2nd edit. 1835; 4th edit., by W. C. L. Martin, in Bohn's 'Illustrated Library,' 1854. 20. 'The Natural History of Birds,' 8vo, London, 1834. 21. 'The Heavens,' 12mo, 1835. 22. 'The Earth,' 12mo, London, 1835. 23. 'The Air,' 12mo, London, 1835. 24. 'The Sea,' 12mo, London, 1835. 25. 'Conversations on Moral Philosophy,' 2 vols. 8vo, London, 1835. 26. 'Astronomy,' 12mo, London, 1836. 27. 'Popular Mathematics,' 8vo, London, 1836. 28. 'Spring,' 12mo, London, 1837 (edited by A. White, 8vo, 1860). 29. 'Summer,' 12mo, London, 1837. 30. 'Autumn,' 12mo, London, 1837. 31. 'Winter,

12mo, London, 1837. 32. 'The Copyright Question and Mr. Serjeant Talfourd's Bill,' 8vo, London, 1838. 33. 'Hampshire, its Past and Present Condition and Future Prospects,' 3 vols. 8vo, Winchester [1838]. 34. 'Westley's Natural Philosophy,' re-written, 3 vols. 8vo, London, 1838. 35. 'Gleanings of Nature,' containing fifty-seven groups of animals and plants, with popular descriptions of their habits, 4to, London, 1838. 36. 'Man in his Physical Structure and Adaptations,' 12mo, London, 1838. 37. 'Domesticated Animals popularly considered,' 8vo, Winchester, 1839. 38. 'The World,' 8vo, London, 1839. 39. 'England,' 8vo, London, 1839. 40. 'Companion to Gilbert's "New Map of England and Wales,"' 8vo, London, 1839. 41. 'Winchester Arithmetic,' 8vo, London, 1839. 42. 'Man in his Intellectual Faculties and Adaptations,' 12mo, London, 1839. 43. 'Man in his Relations to Society,' 12mo, London, 1840. 44. 'Man as a Moral and Accountable Being,' 12mo, London, 1840. 45. 'Cuvier's Animal Kingdom arranged according to its Organisation. The Fishes and Radiata by R. Mudie,' 8vo, London, 1840. 46. 'Sheep, Cattle,' &c., 2 vols. 8vo, London, 1840. 47. 'China and its Resources and Peculiarities, with a View of the Opium Question, and a Notice of Assam,' 8vo, London, 1840. 48. 'Historical and Topographical Description of the Channel Islands, 8vo, London, Winchester [printed 1840]. 49. 'The Isle of Wight, its Past and Present Condition, and Future Prospects,' 8vo, London, Winchester [printed 1841]. Mudie furnished the volumes on 'Intellectual Philosophy' and 'Perspective' for improved editions of 'Pinnock's Catechisms' (1831, 1840), the greater part of the natural history section of the 'British Cyclopædia' (1834), the letterpress to 'Gilbert's Modern Atlas of the Earth' (1840), and a topographical account of Selborne prefixed to Gilbert White's 'Natural History of Selborne' (ed. 1850).

[Gent. Mag. 1842, pt. ii. 214–15; Anderson's Scottish Nation, iii. 212–13; Hannah's Life of T. Chalmers, i. 22, and Appendix.] G. G.

MUDIE, THOMAS MOLLESON (1809–1876), composer, of Scottish descent, was born at Chelsea 30 Nov. 1809, and showed much musical capacity in the first examination of candidates for admission to the Royal Academy of Music in 1823. He took for leading studies at the academy composition, pianoforte, and clarinet, on which he obtained great proficiency. He was appointed a professor of the pianoforte in the academy in 1832, and held the post till 1844. In 1834 he became organist at Gatton, Surrey, the seat of Lord Monson, who, at his death in 1840, bequeathed him an annuity of 100*l.*, but this Mudie relinquished in favour of his patron's widow. In 1844, on the death of his friend, Alfred Devaux, he went to Edinburgh to succeed him as a teacher of music. In 1863 he returned to London. He died there, unmarried, 24 July 1876, and was interred in Highgate cemetery.

As a composer Mudie's successes were mainly confined to his earlier years. While a student at the academy his song 'Lungi dal caro bene' was thought so meritorious that the committee paid the cost of its publication, an act which has been repeated only once since. Several vocal pieces, with orchestral accompaniment and symphonies in C and in B flat, were also composed while he was a student. The Society of British Musicians, founded in 1834, gave him much encouragement, and at their concerts were performed a symphony in F (1835), a symphony in D (1837), a quintet in E flat for pianoforte and strings (1843), a trio in D for pianoforte and strings (1843), and several songs and concerted vocal pieces on different occasions. While in Edinburgh he composed a number of pianoforte pieces and songs, and wrote accompaniments for a large proportion of the airs in Wood's 'Songs of Scotland.' His published music consists of forty-eight pianoforte solos, six pianoforte duets, nineteen fantasias, twenty-four sacred songs, three sacred duets, three chamber anthems for three voices, forty-two separate songs, and two duets. The existing scores of his symphonies and all his printed works are deposited in the library of the Royal Academy of Music. The drudgery of music-teaching seems to have diminished his powers of artistic conception, but some of his compositions, notably the pianoforte pieces and the symphony in B flat, are excellent.

[Grove's Dict. of Music, ii. 406; Brown's Biog. Dict. of Musicians; Musical Times, August 1876, p. 563.] J. C. H.

MUFFET, THOMAS (1553–1604), physician and author. [See MOFFETT.]

MUGGLETON, LODOWICKE (1609–1698), heresiarch, was born in Walnut Tree Yard (now New Street) off Bishopsgate Street Without, London, in July 1609, and baptised on 30 July at St. Botolph's, Bishopsgate, by Stephen Gosson [q. v.] His family came from Wilbarston, Northamptonshire, where the name still exists. His father, John Muggleton, was a farrier 'in great respect with the postmaster;' in October 1616, being then 'on the point of three score years,' he was admitted, on Gosson's recommendation, to Alleyn's Hospital at Dulwich, but removed in August 1617. His mother, Mary Muggleton, died in June 1612, aged thirty-five, when his father married again, and sent Lodowicke to be brought up 'with strangers in the country.' In 1624 Lodowicke was apprenticed to John Quick, a tailor in Walnut Tree Yard, who did a good business in livery gowns. In 1625 he had a touch of the plague which raged in that year, but soon recovered, and never had 'half a day's sickness since,' or spent 'sixpence in physic' in his life. In 1630 he was working under Richardson, a clothier and pawnbroker in Houndsditch, and became engaged to his daughter; her mother made the match, and promised 100*l.* to set them up in business. But in 1631 he went as journeyman to his cousin, William Reeve, in St. Thomas Apostle's; and Reeve, a strong puritan, convinced him of the unlawfulness of pawnbroking; his religious scruples proved fatal to his marriage prospects. He became a zealous puritan, and so remained until puritanism began to remodel the conditions of church life. Refusing to join either the 'new discipline' of presbyterianism, or the 'close fellowships' of independency, he withdrew about 1647 from all worship, fell back on 'an honest and just natural life,' and adopted an agnostic position in regard to all theology.

In 1650, by which time he had been twice a widower, he was attracted by the declarations of two 'prophets,' John Robins [q. v.], a ranter, and Thomas Tany [q. v.], a predecessor of the Anglo-israelites. Their crude pantheism took some hold of him, and he read the current English translations of Jacob Boehme. From April 1651 to January 1652 he had inward revelations, opening to him the scriptures. His cousin John Reeve (1608–1658) [q. v.], caught the infection from him. At length Reeve announced that on 3, 4, and 5 Feb. 1652 he had received personal communications 'by voice of words' from Jesus Christ, the only God, appointing Reeve the messenger of a new dispensation, and Muggleton as his 'mouth.' The two now came forward as prophets; they identified themselves with the 'two witnesses' (Rev. xi. 3), they were to declare a new system of faith, and had authority to pronounce on the eternal fate of individuals.

Reeve, a sensitive man in ailing health, who only survived his 'commission' six years, contributed to the movement its element of spirituality. He distinguished between faith and reason, as respectively the divine and demoniac elements in man. A frank anthropomorphism as regards the divine being, which they shared with the contemporary English Socinians, is common to both; so is the doctrine of the mortality of the soul, to be remedied by a physical resurrection; but the harder outlines of the system, including the rejection of prayer, belong to Muggleton. His philosophy is epicurean; having fixed the machinery of the world, and provided man with a conscience, the divine being takes, ordinarily, no notice of human affairs; the last occasion of his interference, prior to the general judgment, being his message to Reeve. In the resulting system there is a singular mixture of rationalism and literalism. The devil is a human being, witchcraft a delusion, narratives of miracle are mostly parables. On the other hand, astronomy is confuted by scripture, the sun travels round the earth, and heaven, on Reeve's calculation, is six miles off. This, however, is a pious opinion. A modest hold of the 'six principles' (formulated 1656) is enough for salvation [see Birch, James].

The 'two witnesses' made some converts of position, and printed what is known as their 'commission book,' the 'Transcendent Spirituall Treatise,' 1652. On 15 Sept. 1653 they were brought up on a warrant charging them with blasphemy in denying the Trinity, were detained in Newgate for a month, tried before the lord mayor, John Fowke [q. v.], on 17 Oct. and committed to the Old Bridewell for six months. They gained their liberty in April 1654, and pursued their mission, but Reeve's death in July 1658 left the movement entirely in Muggleton's hands.

The first to dispute his supremacy was Laurence Claxton or Clarkson [q. v.], who joined the movement about the time of Reeve's death, and aspired to become his successor. After endeavouring for a year to lead a revolt, he became Muggleton's submissive follower in 1661. Ten years later, when Muggleton was in hiding, a rebellion against his authority was led by William Medgate, a scrivener, Thomas Burton, a flaxman, Witall, a brewer, and a Scotsman named Walter Buchanan. They extracted from Muggleton's writings 'nine assertions,' which they alleged to be opposed alike to common sense and the views of Reeve. In a characteristic letter Muggleton defended the 'assertions' with vehemence, and ordered the exclusion of the ringleaders. He was at once obeyed; his faithful henchman, John Saddington [q. v.], put matters right, and only Burton was allowed to return to the fold. No other schism occurred during his lifetime.

His chief controversies were with the quakers, for whom Muggleton (differing here from Reeve) had nothing but contempt. Their 'bodiless God' was the antithesis of his own. On one of his missionary journeys he was arrested at Chesterfield, 1663, at the instance of John Coope, the vicar, on the charge of denying the Trinity. Coope had mistaken him for a quaker, and pronounced him, after examination, the 'soberest, wisest man of a fanatic that ever he talked with.' He was committed to Derby gaol, and after nine days' imprisonment was released on bail. At Derby he excited the curiosity of Gervase Bennet, a local magistrate, who had applied the term 'quaker' to Fox and his following. Bennet engaged Muggleton in discussion, but, to the delight of his brother magistrate, met his match in him.

Muggleton's books were seized in London in 1670, but he evaded arrest. In 1675 he became executor to Deborah Brunt, widow of his friend John Brunt. In this capacity he brought an action of trespass against Sir John James in respect of house property in the Postern, London Wall. In the course of the suit he had to appear in the spiritual court, and was at once arrested on the charge of blasphemous writing. His trial took place at the Old Bailey on 17 Jan. 1677 before Sir Richard Rainsford [q. v.], chief justice of the king's bench, who pelted him with abuse, and Sir Robert Atkins, justice of the common pleas, who was more lenient. It was difficult to procure a verdict against him, for he had printed nothing since 1673, and thus came within the Act of Indemnity of 1674. But his 'Neck of the Quakers Broken' bore the imprint 'Amsterdam . . . 1663;' Amsterdam was certainly a false imprint, and it was argued (incorrectly) that the book had been antedated, and really printed in 1676. Sentence was passed by the recorder, George Jeffreys (1648–1689) [q. v.] Muggleton was amerced in 500*l.*, and condemned to the pillory on three several days, his books to be burned before his face. He was duly pilloried, and thrown into Newgate in default of the fine. At length, after finding 100*l.* and two sureties for good behaviour, he was released on 19 July 1677. The anniversary of this date (reckoned 30 July since the alteration of the calendar) has ever since been kept by Muggletonians as their 'little holiday;' the other annual festival, the 'great holiday,' being 14 Feb., in commemoration of the commission to Reeve.

The rest of his life was peaceful. He printed no more books, but prepared an autobiography, and wrote an abundance of letters, more or less doctrinal, afterwards printed as collected by Alexander Delamaine [q. v.] and others. His correspondence is full of racy observations on human character, and his ethical instincts were clear and sound; he could turn a rude phrase, but was essentially a pure-minded man, of tough breed. He was a great match-maker, and ready on any emergency with shrewd and prudent counsel. No sort of approach to vice would he tolerate in his community. His puritanism lingered in his aversion to cards, which he classed with drunkenness. But he was no ascetic; he enjoyed his pipe and glass. Nothing would stir him from English soil. Scotsmen he hated; he never forgot Buchanan. In Ireland he had many followers, including Robert Phaire [q. v.], governor of Cork during the Commonwealth; but not for 'ten thousand pounds' would he 'come through that sea-gulf' which lay between Dives in hell (Ireland) and Lazarus in heaven. He forbad the bearing of arms, except for self-defence against savages. Ready enough with his sentence of posthumous damnation, he was meanwhile for a universal tolerance; 'I always,' he writes in 1668 to George Fox, 'loved the persecuted better than the persecutor.'

Swedenborg's accord with Muggleton in the primary article of the Godhead was noticed in 1800 by W. H. Reid (see White, *Swedenborg*, 1867, ii. 626). The coincidence extends to other points, and is the more remarkable as there is no reason to suppose that Swedenborg had any knowledge of the writer who has anticipated his treatment of several topics.

From the sacred canon Muggleton excluded (following Reeve) the writings assigned to Solomon. He added the 'Testaments of the Twelve Patriarchs,' which he knew in the version by Anthony Gilby [q. v.] He added also 'the books of Enoch,' though no book of Enoch was in his time known to be preserved. The translation in 1821 by Richard Laurence [q. v.] of the rediscovered 'Book of Enoch' has completed the Muggletonian canon. For his own writings and those of Reeve he claims no verbal inspiration, yet an authority equal to that of scripture.

Muggleton died at his house in the Postern on 14 March 1698, in his 89th year, after a fortnight's illness. His body lay in state on 16 March at Loriners' Hall; he was buried on 17 March in Bethlehem New churchyard; the site is in Liverpool Street, opposite the station of the North London Railway. By his first wife, Sarah (1616–1639), whom he married in 1634 or 1635, he had three daughters; Sarah, the eldest, was the first believer; she married John White; Elizabeth, the youngest, married Whitfield; both survived him. By his second wife, Mary (1626–1647), whom he married in 1640 or 1641, he had two sons and a daughter; all died in infancy, the second son, a scrofulous boy, living till 1653. In 1663 he married his third wife, Mary (*b.* 1638, *d.* 1 July 1718), daughter of John Martin, a tanner, of East Malling, Kent; with her he got some property.

Muggleton was a tall man, with aquiline nose, high cheek bones, hazel eyes, and long auburn hair. An oval portrait of him, painted in 1674, was presented to the British Museum on 26 Oct. 1758, and subsequently transferred to the National Portrait Gallery, London. A later portrait, full length, painted by William Wood, of Braintree, Essex, has belonged since 10 Dec. 1829 to the Muggletonian body, and hangs in their 'reading room,' New Street, Bishopsgate Street Without. They have also a cast of Muggleton's features, taken after death; from this a small copperplate engraving by G. V. Caffeel was executed in 1669. An engraving by J. Kennerley, 1829, half length, is from Wood's painting.

The term Muggletonian, employed by Muggleton himself, is in use among his adherents, who generally prefer to call themselves 'believers in the third commission,' or 'believers in the commission of the Spirit.' As the usual exercises of public worship are excluded from their church meetings, they do not figure in the lists of the registrar-general. They have no preachers, but they keep in print the writings of their founders, and meet to read them aloud, and sing their 'spiritual songs.' His ablest follower was Thomas Tomkinson (1631–1710?) [q. v.] In Smith's 'Bibliotheca Anti-Quakeriana,' 1873, is a bibliography (revised by the present writer) of Muggleton's works. Below are enumerated the first editions, all 4to, and all (except No. 7) without publisher's or printer's name. By Reeve and Muggleton are: 1. 'A Transcendent Spirituall Treatise,' &c. 1652 (two editions same year). 2. 'A General Epistle from the Holy Spirit,' &c., 1653. 3. 'A Letter presented unto Alderman Fouke,' &c., 1653. 4. 'A Divine Looking-Glass,' &c., 1656 (a revised edition, with omissions, was issued by Muggleton, 1661; both editions have been reprinted). Posthumous were: 5. 'A Volume of Spiritual Epistles,' &c. 1755 (written 1653–91). 6. 'A Stream from the Tree of Life,' &c. 1758 (written 1654–82). 7. 'A Supplement to the Book of Letters,' &c. 1831 (written 1656–1688). By Muggleton alone are: 8. 'A True Interpretation of the Eleventh Chapter of the Revelation,' &c. 1662. 9. 'The Neck of the Quakers Broken,' &c. 1663 (Fox replied in 1667). 10. 'A Letter sent to Thomas Taylor, Quaker,' &c. 1665. 11. 'A True Interpretation of . . . the whole Book of the Revelation,' &c. 1665. 12. 'A Looking-Glass for George Fox,' &c. 1668. 13. 'A True Interpretation of the Witch of Endor,' &c. 1669. 14. 'The Answer to William Penn, Quaker,' &c. 1673 (in reply to Penn's 'The New Witnesses proved Old Heretics,' &c. in 1672, 4to). Posthumous were: 15. 'The Acts of the Witnesses of the Spirit,' &c. 1699 (written 1677). 16. 'An Answer to Isaac Pennington,' &c. 1719 (written 1669). A few early issues of separate letters, included in the above, are not here specified.

[Muggleton's Acts of the Witnesses, 1699, is an autobiography to 1677; his later history may be traced in his letters. A modest Account of the wicked Life of . . . Muggleton, 1676, [i.e. 1677], reprinted in Harleian Miscellany, 1744, vol. i. 1810, vol. viii.; also in M. Aikin's (i.e. Edward Pugh's) Religious Imposters (*sic*), 1821, is worthless. Nathaniel Powell's True Account of the Trial, written in 1677 and printed in 1808, deserves note. See for an account of the literature of the subject, by the present writer, The Origin of the Muggletonians, and Ancient and Modern Muggletonians, in Transactions of Liverpool Literary and Philosophical Society, 1869 and 1870. In the Nineteenth Century, August 1884, is a paper on the Prophet of Walnut Tree Yard, by the Rev. Augustus Jessopp, D.D. The allusions to Muggleton by Scott and Macaulay are misleading; cf. Turner's Quakers, 1889, pp. 178–9.] A. G.

MUILMAN, RICHARD (1735?–1797), antiquary. [See CHISWELL, TRENCH.]

MUIR, JOHN (1810–1882), orientalist, born at Glasgow on 5 Feb. 1810, was the eldest son of William Muir, some time magistrate of that city. After receiving his early education at the Irvine grammar school, he attended several sessions at the Glasgow University, and thence passed to the college at Haileybury, in preparation for the service of the East India Company. In 1829 he was sent to Fort William College, Calcutta, and was subsequently appointed successively to the posts of assistant secretary to the board of revenue at Allahabad, special commissioner for a land inquiry at Meerut and Saharanpur, and collector at Azimgarh. In 1844 he filled the more congenial office of Principal of the newly established Victoria or Queen's College at Benares, and although he held the post for a year only he succeeded in that time in giving practical effect to an original educational scheme by which instruction in English and in Sanskrit was given concurrently. He next became Civil and Sessions Judge at Fatehpur. In 1853 he retired, and his services were recognised by the bestowal of the distinction of C.I.E. on the institution of the order in 1878. On 20 June 1855 he was created D.C.L. at Oxford University (Foster, *Alumni Oxon.* 1715–1886, p. 995), and in 1861 LL.D. at Edinburgh.

On leaving India Muir took up his residence in Edinburgh, and devoted himself there to the furtherance of higher education and research. He was the main originator of a society known as the Association for the better Endowment of Edinburgh University, and himself exemplified its aims by founding in 1862 the academical chair of Sanskrit and comparative philology, as well as conjointly with his brother, Sir William Muir, the Shaw fellowship for moral philosophy. He likewise instituted the Muir lectureship in comparative religion, and offered several prizes, mainly for oriental studies, both at Edinburgh and Cambridge.

Muir died unmarried, on 7 March 1882, at 10 Merchiston Avenue, Edinburgh.

Muir's earlier works were mainly addressed to the native reading public of India, and as such were chiefly written in Sanskrit with or without a vernacular rendering. The first work, 'Mataparīkshā' (Calcutta, 1839), was a missionary brochure, partly directed against Hinduism, and appears to have attracted some notice, as it was answered, likewise in Sanskrit, by a Bengal pandit. The treatise was rewritten by the author, and appeared in a new edition in 1852–4. In 1839 also appeared a somewhat mysterious work, containing 'A Description of England [on the basis of Miss Bird's] in Sanskrit' verse, which has been attributed to Muir, but of which neither author nor adapter can now with certainty be traced. In the years next following he published both in India and in London several other Sanskrit works, dealing both with Indian history and with his favourite topics of Christian apologetics and biography, the most noteworthy of the latter class being his lives of Our Lord and of St. Paul, suggested by the similar works of Dr. W. H. Mill [q. v.] But by far the greatest of Muir's works are his 'Original Sanskrit Texts on the Origin and History of the People of India' (five vols., 1858–70; 2nd ed., 1868–1873), which are still (in the words of one of the best living authorities on early Indian culture) 'eine wahre Fundgrube für Jeden, der sich über die Fragen auf dem Gebiete der älteren indischen Geschichte unterrichten will' (H. Zimmer, *Altindisches Leben*, p. xi).

In later life he was busied with translations mainly oriental and theological. To the former class belong his 'Sentiments metrically rendered from the Sanskrit' (London, 1875, 8vo) and his 'Metrical Translations from . . . Sanskrit Writers, with an Introduction, many Prose Versions and Parallel Passages from Classical Authors' (London, 1879, 8vo). To theology belong his several versions from the works of Dr. Kuenen of Leyden; 'A Brief Examination of Prevalent Opinions on the Inspiration of the Scriptures, by a Lay Member of the Church of England,' London, 1861, 8vo; and his 'Notes on Bishop Butler's Sermons,' 1867. He also published 'Notes of a Trip to Chinee in Kanawar in October 1851,' 8vo (anon); 'Notes of a Trip to Kedarnath,' 1855; and 'Hymn to Zeus from Cleanthes,' London, 1875, 8vo (a translation); and contributed eleven articles chiefly on Indian philosophy and mythology to the Journal of the Royal Asiatic Society.

[Athenæum, 1882, i. 318, 346; Academy, 1882, i. 196; Journal of Royal Asiatic Soc. new ser. vol. xiv. p. ix; Edinburgh Courant.] C. B.

MUIR, THOMAS (1765–1798), parliamentary reformer, was born at Glasgow on 24 Aug. 1765, being the only son of James Muir, a flourishing tradesman, who in 1753 published a pamphlet on England's foreign trade. He was educated at Glasgow grammar school and at the university, where he matriculated in 1777 and graduated M.A. on 24 April 1782. He intended to enter the church, but ultimately read for the bar under John Millar. In the session of 1783–1784 he was charged with writing a lampoon on professors who had quarrelled with their colleague, John Anderson (1726–1796) [q. v.], and was expelled with twelve other malcontents. Migrating to Edinburgh he completed his studies there, and on 24 Nov. 1787 was admitted into the Faculty of Advocates. He was an elder of the church at Cadder, Lanarkshire, sat in the general assembly, and had good prospects at the bar, where he sometimes pleaded gratuitously for those whom he thought oppressed. The formation of the London Society of the Friends of the People led to a meeting at Glasgow, 16 Oct. 1792, for the creation of a kindred society for obtaining parliamentary reform. Muir took part in it, and being a good speaker attended similar meetings at Kirkintilloch and Milton, as well as the convention of delegates held at Edinburgh. At one of the sittings of the latter he read an address from United Irishmen, transmitted to him by Archibald Hamilton Rowan, which expressed satisfaction at seeing that 'the spirit of freedom moves on the face of Scotland, and that light seems to break from the chaos of her internal government.' On

2 Jan. 1793 Muir was arrested on a charge of sedition, declined (as he had always advised his clients) to answer the sheriff's questions, and was liberated on bail. Shunned or insulted by his brother advocates, he immediately started for France, was entertained on the way by the London Society, and commissioned by it to remonstrate against the execution of Louis XVI, but he did not reach Paris till the day before that event. While enjoying the 'friendship of an amiable and distinguished circle' in Paris, he was outlawed at Edinburgh, his recognisances were estreated, and he was struck off the roll of the Faculty of Advocates. After some months he returned to Scotland, was arrested at Port Ettrick, and on 30 Aug. was tried before the high court of justiciary at Edinburgh. He was accused of exciting a spirit of disloyalty and disaffection, of recommending Paine's 'Rights of Man,' of distributing seditious writings, and of reading aloud a seditious writing. He had asked Erskine to defend him, but had declined Erskine's very natural stipulation that the case should be left entirely to him, and he consequently defended himself. He objected to the first five of the fifteen jurors summoned as having prejudged the case, for they belonged to the so-called Goldsmiths' Hall Association, which had offered a reward for the discovery of persons circulating Paine's works. The objection was overruled, and a naval officer who demurred to being juror in a government prosecution was required to serve. The elder Muir's maidservant and other witnesses deposed to his conversation and speeches and to his qualified approval of Paine's works, one of which he had given to an applicant. Muir called witnesses to prove that he had always deprecated violence, and he denied that he went to France on any mission but that of saving life. The trial, conducted in a tone of partisanship which shocked Romilly, a spectator, lasted till 2 A.M., and at noon on 31 Aug. Muir was convicted. He was sentenced to fourteen years' transportation. The jury were in consternation, and would have petitioned for a commutation had not one of them received a threatening anonymous letter, and a juror long afterwards told Sir J. Gibson Craig, in explanation of the verdict, 'We were all mad' (Preface to ALLEN, *Inquiry into the Prerogative*, 1830). The legality of a sentence of transportation for sedition was ineffectually disputed in both houses of parliament, and in March 1794 Muir, with T. F. Palmer, Skirving, and Margarot, was despatched to Botany Bay. He purchased a small farm, which he called Hunter's Hill, after his Scottish patrimony, and which is now a suburb of Sydney. His case excited sympathy in the United States, and the Otter, Captain Dawes, was sent out from New York to rescue him. On 11 Feb. 1796 this was effected. After a variety of adventures, shipwreck in Nootka Sound, captivity among the American Indians, hospitable treatment in Mexico, and imprisonment at Havannah, Muir was sent in a Spanish frigate to Cadiz. The frigate was attacked off Cadiz by two English vessels. Muir had one eye and part of his cheek shot off, and was lying senseless among the dead, when an old schoolfellow is said to have identified him by the inscription in the Bible clasped in his hand and to have sent him ashore with the rest of the wounded. The Cadiz authorities, though he had fought for Spain, detained him as a British subject and prisoner of war, but the French Directory obtained his release, offering him hospitality and citizenship. After a public reception at Bordeaux Muir reached Paris 4 Feb. 1798, and was welcomed by the Directory, but his wound proved incurable, and he expired at Chantilly 27 Sept. 1798. A monument to Muir and other Scottish political reformers was erected on Calton Hill, Edinburgh, in 1844.

[Life by P. Mackenzie, Glasgow, 1831; Histoire de la tyrannie exercée contre Muir, Paris, 1798; Moniteur Universel, 1797–9; Lives of Scotch Reformers, 1836; Mem. of Political Martyrs of Scotland, Edinburgh, 1837; G. B. Hill's ed. of Boswell's Johnson, i. 467, London, 1887; Lord Cockburn's Trials for Sedition, 1888; Heaton's Australian Dictionary of Dates, p. 148; Massey's Hist. of England, 1863; Adolphus's Hist. of England; Howell's State Trials and other reports of the trial.] J. G. A.

MUIR, WILLIAM (1787–1869), divine, son of William Muir, merchant, of Glasgow, was born at Glasgow on 11 Oct. 1787, and was educated there and at the divinity hall of Edinburgh. He matriculated at Glasgow University in 1800, receiving the degree of LL.D. on 1 May 1812, and subsequently that of D.D. He was licensed to preach on 7 Nov. 1810, presented to St. George's Church, Glasgow, on 9 June, and ordained on 27 Aug. 1812. In 1822 he was transferred to the New Grey Friars, Edinburgh, and thence in 1829 to St. Stephen's, Edinburgh. On 17 May 1838 he was elected moderator of the general assembly, and began to take a prominent part in the non-intrusion controversy. On 16 May 1839, in the debate on the Auchterarder case, he moved a series of abortive resolutions endeavouring to reconcile the opposing views of Cook and Chalmers; he also adopted a similar position with regard to the Strathbogie case, throughout following a middle course, which ultimately led to the passing of Lord Aberdeen's Act. At the disruption Muir threw in his lot with the established church, and, being frequently consulted by the government, is said to have exercised an unprecedented influence in the disposal of patronage. In 1845 he was appointed dean of the order of the Thistle, and chaplain in ordinary to Queen Victoria. In 1858 he was admitted a member of the university council of Glasgow. He was compelled by blindness to retire from active duties in 1867, and died at Ormelie, Murrayfield, Edinburgh, on 23 June 1869. Muir married, first, on 22 June 1813, Hannah, eldest daughter of James Black, provost of Glasgow; secondly, he married on 3 Oct. 1844 Anne, daughter of Lieutenant-general Dirom, of Mount Annan. Besides single sermons, pamphlets, and published speeches, Muir wrote: 1. 'Discourses on the Epistle of St. Jude,' London, 1822. 2. 'Discourses on the Epistles to the Seven Churches in Asia.' 3. 'Practical Sermons on the Holy Spirit,' Edinburgh, 1842. 4. 'Metrical Meditations,' Edinburgh, 1870.

[Works in Brit. Mus. Library; Hew Scott's Fasti, i. 72, 76, ii. 28, &c.; Scotsman and Edinburgh Courant, 24 June 1869; Church of Scotland Home and Foreign Missionary Record, 2 Aug. 1869, pp. 448–9; Memorial Sermon by J. C. Herdman; Bryce's Ten Years of the Church of Scotland, i. 91–2, 128, 157; Autobiography of Thomas Guthrie, pp. 166–71, 384; Memorials of R. S. Candlish; Buchanan's Ten Years' Conflict, ii. 16–19, 48–52, 126; A Letter to the Lord Chancellor by John Hope, Edinburgh, 1839; information kindly supplied by Professor Dickson, D.D., and the Rev. Robert Muir.] A. F. P.

MUIR, WILLIAM (1806–1888), engineer, second son of Andrew Muir, farmer, was born at Catrine, Ayrshire, 17 Jan. 1806. The father was a cousin of William Murdock [q. v.], the introducer of gas-lighting. After serving an apprenticeship at Kilmarnock to Thomas Morton, whose principal business was that of repairing carpet looms, Muir obtained employment at Glasgow with Girdwood & Co., makers of cotton machinery. In September 1830 he left home for Liverpool, and was present at the opening of the Liverpool and Manchester Railway. Hearing of the illness of his brother Andrew at Truro, he proceeded thither, and after working for a time at Hayle Foundry he went to London and commenced work in April 1831 at Maudslay & Field's engineering factory. During his stay there he made the acquaintance of James Nasmyth, who was Henry Maudslay's draughtsman, and Joseph Whitworth, then working as a fitter in the shop. Whitworth, it is said, cultivated Muir's acquaintance, but they never became intimate. In March 1836 Muir left Maudslay's to act as traveller for Holtzapffel, the well-known tool-maker of Long Acre and Charing Cross, but the engagement only lasted a few months, and in November he became foreman at Bramah & Robinson's foundry at Pimlico. He left in June 1840 to join Whitworth, who had then established a business at Manchester, and he assisted in working out his scheme for a universal system of screw threads, and made all the drawings and a working model of his road-sweeping machine. A strict Sabbatarian, he disagreed with Whitworth, who encouraged working on Sundays, and quitting his employ in June 1842, he started in business on his own account in Berwick Street, Manchester, his first important commission being a railway ticket-printing machine for Thomas Edmondson [q. v.] He subsequently took larger premises in Miller's Lane, Salford, Edmondson occupying the upper part as a railway-ticket printing office. His business increasing, he erected the Britannia Works at Strangeways, which have been increased from time to time, and are still carried on by his sons. He achieved a great reputation as a maker of lathes and machine tools. He supplied machinery to the royal gun factory at Woolwich and also to Enfield, for the manufacture of sights for rifles on the interchangeable principle.

Between 1853 and 1867 Muir took out eleven patents, but they are not on the whole of much importance. Some have reference to the details of the lathe, a machine in which he always took great interest. Two relate to letter-copying presses. A model of his grindstone, patented in 1853 (No. 621), may be seen at South Kensington Museum. This consists of two stones running in contact, one being caused to traverse longitudinally, with a very slow motion. In this manner each stone corrects the defects of the other, and both are maintained accurately cylindrical in form. His sugar-cutting machine, patented in 1863 (No. 1307), consists of an arrangement of circular saws by which the loaf is first cut into slices and then into cubes. This machine has come into considerable use of late years.

Muir took much interest in social questions and was a strong temperance advocate. This was manifested in a curious way in a patent which he took out in 1865 (No. 1), which consists in constructing 'the fronts of public-houses and other houses of entertainment, where men and women mix indiscriminately, of plate-glass, to enable persons outside to see those within,' while 'to impede as far as possible the entrance of females wearing steel crinolines,' the entrances were made very narrow.

He married in 1832 Eliza Wellbank Dickinson of Drypool, Hull, by whom he had five sons, most of whom became engineers. She died 5 Jan. 1882. Muir died 15 June 1888, and was buried in Brockley cemetery.

[Robert Smiles's Brief Memoir of William Muir, 1888, pp. 26, partly reprinted in The Engineer, 24 Aug. 1888.] R. B. P.

MUIRCHEARTACH (*d.* 533), king of Ireland, was son of Muireadhach, son of Eoghan, eldest son of Niall Naighiallach, and is usually spoken of in Irish writings as Muircheartach mor mac Earca. His mother's name was Eirc, daughter of Loairn (*Book of Leinster*, 183 *b*, 30), and after the death of his father she married Fergus, son of Conall Gulban, son of Niall, by whom she was mother of Feidilmid, father of Columba [q.v.], so that Muircheartach was one of the kings to whom the saint was related (*Adamnan's Life of St. Columba*, ed. Reeves, p. 8). A tract in the 'Book of Ballymote' states that in early youth he was banished from Ireland for a murder, and became acquainted in Britain with his kinsman St. Cairnech (*Leabhar Breathnach*, ed. Todd, pp. 178–93). The succeeding statement that he came from Britain to assume the kingship of Ireland, landing at the mouth of the Boyne, is contrary to the evidence of the chronicles. He is first mentioned in the 'Annals of Ulster' in 482 as fighting in the battle of Ocha in Meath, in alliance with the Dal nAraidhe and the Leinstermen against Oilill Molt, king of Ireland, who was slain, and Lughaidh [q. v.], cousin of Muircheartach made king. In 489 he led the Cinel Eoghain, of whom he was chief, against Oengus mac Nadfraich, the first Christian king of Munster, and slew him in the battle of Cellosnadh, now Kellistown, co. Carlow. Illann, son of Dunlaing, one of his allies in this battle, led the Leinstermen against him in 497, and was defeated at Indemor, co. Kildare. The brother of Duach Teangumha, king of Connaught, had put himself under the protection of Muircheartach, but was carried off by the Connaughtmen. The Cinel Eoghain were at once led by their chief into Connaught, and won a victory in 504, killing the king in the Curlieu Hills.

In 517 Lughaidh died, and Muircheartach soon after became king of Ireland. After further war with the Leinstermen, he attacked the Oirghialla, the only important neighbours with whom he had not fought, and conquered from them the northernmost part of their territory, from Glen Con to Ualraigh, both in co. Derry, a region which remained in the possession of the Cinel Eoghain till the plantation of Ulster. The Leinstermen again attacked him in 524, but he defeated them at Athsighe, a ford of the Boyne, and two years later invaded Leinster, winning battles at Eibhlinne, at Magh Ailbhe, at the Hill of Allen, and at Kinneigh, all in the co. Kildare; afterwards ravaging the district known as the Cliachs in Carlow. In the same year he fought the battle of Aidhne against the Connaughtmen. His wife was Duaibhsech, and she bore him five sons, of whom three were dead in 559, when Domhnall and Feargus became for three years joint kings of Ireland. He had a concubine, Taetan, who was of a tribe which he had dispossessed from the neighbourhood of Tara. She revenged the wrong by setting fire to the house of Cleitech, on the Boyne, where he was drunk, on Allhalloween in 533. His death is the subject of a very old bardic tale, 'Oighidh Mhuircheartaigh moir mic Earca.' His exploits were celebrated in a poem beginning 'Fillis an ri Mac Earca alleith na Neill,' by Ceannfaeladh fodhlumhtha, who died in 678. It describes how he carried off hostages from Munster, and gives some idea of the scale of great victories in his time in the expression 'Foseacht beiris noi ccairpthi' ('Seven times did he carry off nine chariots').

[Annala Rioghachta Eireann, i. 150–76; Annals of Ulster, ed. Hennessy, vol. i.; Book of Leinster, facs. fol. 24 *a* and 183 *b*, 18; Book of Ballymote, facs. fol. 48 *b*; J. O'Donovan's Battle of Magh Rath, p. 145; Leabhar Breathnach, ed. Todd; Book of Fenagh, ed. Hennessy; Lives of Saints, from Book of Lismore, ed. Stokes; Transactions of Iberno-Celtic Society, 1820, ed. O'Reilly.] N. M.

MUIRCHEARTACH (*d.* 943), king of Ailech, usually known in Irish writings as 'na gcochall gcroicionn,' of the leather cloaks, was son of Niall Glundubh [q. v.], king of Ireland, and grandson of Aedh Finnliath, king of Ailech, or Northern Ulster, and of Ireland. He is first mentioned in the chronicles in 921, the year of his father's death, as winning an important battle over Godfrey, a Dane, near the mouth of the river Bann. On 28 Dec. 926, at the head of his own clan, the Cinel Eoghain, and in alliance with the people of the lesser Ulster or Ulidia (Down and Antrim), he defeated a large force of Danes at Droichet Cluna-na-cruimhther, near Newry, co. Down, but was obliged to retire to Tyrone on the arrival of Godfrey of Dublin with a fresh force of Danes. In 927 he defeated and slew Goach, chief of the

Cianachta Glinne Gemhin (co. Derry), a rebellious vassal, and then marched south to attack Donnchadh, king of Ireland. No battle took place, as Donnchadh had sufficient notice to get his men together, but Muircheartach boasted that he had for that year prevented the holding of the great fair and games of Teltown. Some years later, in alliance with Donnchadh, he made expeditions against the Danes, and in 938 plundered their territory from Dublin to the river Greece, co. Kildare. Conghalach, son of Maelmithigh, a sarcastic poet, satirised the expedition, and an epigram of Muircheartach's in reply is preserved, beginning 'Cumba Conghalach Breagh mbuidhe ocus duine mut no got' (*Annala Rioghachta Eireann*, ii. 636). The Danes surprised Ailech in 939 and carried off the king in their fleet on Loch Swilly, but he escaped before they reached the sea. He joined the king of Ireland in 940 in expeditions against Leinster and Munster, and in 941 marched against the Deisi (co. Waterford) and Ossory. He made alliances with both. His wife Flanna, daughter of Donnchadh, the king of Ireland, died in 940, and early in 941 he married Dubhdara, daughter of Ceallach, king of Ossory, and his wife Sadbh.

Muircheartach made a sea-roving expedition to the Hebrides, plundering several Danish settlements in the same year. During his absence Ceallachan [q. v.], king of Cashel, attacked his allies, the Deisi, and this was the occasion of Muircheartach's most famous campaign, known as the 'Moirthimchell Eireann,' or great circuit of Ireland, and described in a poem written in heptasyllabic alliterative verse with vowel rhymes by Cormacan, son of Maolbrighde, his bard, who accompanied the king. The poem was written in 942, and has been printed, with notes, by John O'Donovan (Irish Archæological Society, 1841). The king, with a carefully selected force of the Cinel Eoghain, left Ailech in the beginning of the winter, crossed the river Bann near Portglenone, marched through Magh Line, and after four days in the kingdom of Uladh, during which they captured the king and Loingseach, the chief of Magh Line, reached the Boyne near Knowth. The next day they crossed Magh Breagh, then covered with snow, and surprised the Danes of Dublin, who did not expect any attack at that season. The Danes gave the king tribute of cloth, gold, meat, and cheese, and a wealthy citizen named Sitric as a hostage. The next day's march was of twenty-one miles to Dunlavin in Wicklow, and from it Aillinn, the chief fort of the king of Leinster, was attacked, and Lorcan, the king, taken as a hostage. To Ballaghmoon, in the south of Kildare, was the next day's march, and on the next day, at Gowran, co. Kilkenny, Muircheartach was hospitably received by his friends of Ossory, and spent some days receiving tribute and entertainment from the chiefs of Ossory, Ely O'Carroll, and the Deisi. He then marched on Cashel, and prepared for a pitched battle, but the Munstermen yielded up their king, Ceallachan, as a hostage and Muircheartach crossed part of the plain south of Limerick, and on the second day reached the Shannon at Killaloe. After several days in Thomond, he turned northwards through Galway and Roscommon, crossed the river Drobhaeis into Ulster, and in three days reached home by way of Bearnasmor, after a month of marching. In the spring Muircheartach sent his captives to Donnchadh, the king of Ireland, in acknowledgment of his supremacy, but the king sent them back to Ailech. His Irish cognomen, 'na gcochall gcroicionn,' was due to the leather mantles which his soldiers wore, and which are often mentioned in Cormacan's account of the circuit. In 943 he was killed in a battle against the Danes at Ardee, co. Louth. He had long yellow hair. He had a son Domhnall, whose son Muircheartach Midheach was killed by Amlaff the Dane in 975. Con Bacach O'Neill, the first earl of Tyrone [q. v.], and Hugh O'Neill, second earl of Tyrone [q. v.], who died in 1616, were directly descended from him. In the 'Book of Leinster,' a manuscript of the twelfth century, there is a poem of fifteen stanzas on his exploits by Flann Mainistrech [q. v.], beginning (f. 184, a. 29) 'assin taltin inbaid oenaig,' and ending (f. 184, a. 52), 'ar tri ced cend leis do ultaib,' with an account of the defeat by Muircheartach of the people of Ulidia, of which there is no other record.

[Book of Leinster (facsimile Royal Irish Academy), a manuscript of the twelfth century; the Circuit of Ireland, by Cormacan Eigeas, ed. J. O'Donovan, Dublin, 1841 (no earlier manuscript exists than a transcript by Cuchoicrich O'Clery of about 1620, but, though the older codices are not extant, this text bears strong internal evidence of authenticity); Annala Rioghachta Eireann, ed. O'Donovan, vol. ii.; Annals of Ulster, ed. W. M. Hennessy, vol. i.] N. M.

MUIRCHEARTACH, king of Ulster (*d.* 1166). [See O'LOCHLAINN, MUIRCHEARTACH.]

MUIRCHU MACCU MACHTHENI, SAINT (*fl.* 697), is termed in the 'Martyrology of Donegal' Mac ua Maichtene, and in the 'Lebar Brecc' Mac hui mic Teni, i.e. son of the grandson of Mac Teni. Bishop Graves suggests that the name Machtheni is a translation of Cogitosus, who mentions Muirchu as his father; the word is cognate with *machtnaigim*, 'I ponder.' Maccu Machtheni would thus mean 'of the sons of Cogitosus.' Colgan and Lanigan were disposed to identify him with Adamnan, who is known as Ua Tinne, but the resemblance of the names is only apparent. His monastery (*civitas*), according to the 'Lebar Brecc,' was in Hy Faelan, in the north of the county of Kildare, but the 'Calendar of Cashel' says Cill Murchon (Murchu's Church) was in Hy Garchon in the county of Wicklow.

Muirchu is only known as the author of the life of St. Patrick in the 'Book of Armagh,' a manuscript transcribed in 807, and now preserved in Trinity College, Dublin. This is the earliest existing life of the saint, and forms the foundation of all the later lives, which either borrow from it or enlarge on it. It was composed in obedience to the command and at the dictation of Aedh of Sletty in the south of the Queen's County, an anchorite and bishop, who appears to have been specially interested in the see of St. Patrick, and was intimately associated with Adamnan in endeavouring to introduce the Roman Easter and other foreign customs in the North. Muirchu, who was with Adamnan at the synod summoned to support the new customs over which Flann Febla, coarb of Armagh, presided, supported the innovation. He tells us that 'many had taken in hand' the life of St. Patrick, but had failed owing to the conflicting nature of the accounts then current and the many doubts of the facts expressed on all sides. He uses the 'Confession of St. Patrick' as his authority for the earlier part, and then proceeds to the traditional matter. The parts do not harmonise, but his work is of great importance, as identifying the author of the 'Confession' with the popular saint. The copy of this life in the 'Book of Armagh' was imperfect for more than two centuries owing to the loss of the first leaf, but a few years ago the Bollandist fathers found in the Royal Library of Brussels a Legendarium of the eleventh century which contained a perfect copy of the life, not taken from the Armagh codex, and in some respects more accurate. This was placed in the hands of the Rev. Edmund Hogan, S.J., by whom it was carefully edited and published in the 'Analecta Bollandiana' in 1882. Muirchu's day is 8 June.

[Vita Sancti Patricii; Analecta Bollandiana; Brussels, 1882, p. 20; Lanigan's Eccl. Hist. iii. 131; Martyrology of Donegal, p. 41; Calendar of Oengus, p. xcix; Adamnan's St. Columba, ed. Reeves, Appendix to Preface, p. 41; Goidelica, by Whitley Stokes, 2nd ed. p. 92.] T. O.

MUIRHEAD, JAMES, D.D. (1742–1808), song-writer, son of Muirhead of Logan (representing an ancient family), was born in 1742 in the parish of Buittle, Kirkcudbrightshire. After elementary training at Dumfries grammar school, he studied for the church at Edinburgh University, and was ordained minister of the parish of Urr, Kirkcudbrightshire, 28 June 1770. As a proprietor and freeholder of the county, he was one of the aristocratic victims of Burns's unsparing satire in 'Ballads on Mr. Heron's Election, 1795,' and he retaliated in a brochure, in which he quoted and liberally translated into verse Martial's 'In Vacerram' (MARTIALIS, liber, xi. ep. 66). He somewhat cleverly made out Vacerras to have been a gauger of very loose principles, and 'no publication in answer to the scurrilities of Burns ever did him so much harm in public opinion, or made Burns himself feel so sore' (manuscript of Alexander Young, quoted in CHAMBERS's *Burns*, vol. iv. Library edit.) Burns further denounced Muirhead in his election song of 1796, 'Wha will buy my Troggin?' A scholarly man, Muirhead was specially known as a mathematician and a naturalist. In 1796 he received the degree of D.D. from Edinburgh University. He died at Spottes Hall, Dumfriesshire, 16 May 1808 (*Scots Mag.* lxx. 479). He married, 21 Aug. 1777, Jean Loudon (*d.* 1826), by whom he had two sons, William, an advocate, and Charles, and a daughter, wife of Captain Skirving, of the East India Company's service.

Muirhead's one published song is the shrewd and vivid pastoral, 'Bess the Gawkie' (i.e. fool or dupe). It first appeared in Herd's 'Scottish Songs,' 1776. Burns considered it equalled by few Scottish pastorals, pronouncing it 'a beautiful song, and in the genuine Scots taste' (CROMEK, *Reliques of Burns*). Muirhead furnished particulars of the parish of Urr to Sinclair's 'Statistical Account of Scotland,' 1791–9.

[Murray's Literary Hist. of Galloway; Scots Musical Museum, ed. Laing; Rogers's Modern Scottish Minstrel; Harper's Bards of Galloway; Hew Scott's Fasti, pt. ii. pp. 608–9.] T. B.

MUIRHEAD, JAMES (1831–1889), jurist, son of Claud Muirhead of Gogan Park, Midlothian, proprietor of the 'Edinburgh Advertiser,' born in 1831, was admitted on 31 Oct. 1854 a member of the Inner Temple, where he was called to the bar on 6 June 1857, being admitted a member of the Faculty of Advocates the same year. In 1862 he was elected to the chair of civil law in the university of Edinburgh, which he held until his death. He held the post of advocate depute during Lord Beaconsfield's administration, and in 1886 was appointed sheriff of Stirling, Dumbarton, and Clackmannanshire.

Muirhead was an accomplished jurist, and besides discharging his professorial duties with eminent ability, made a European reputation by his masterly works on Roman law. In 1885 he succeeded Lord McLaren as sheriff in chancery, and the same year received from the university of Glasgow the honorary degree of LL.D. He died at his house in Drumsheugh Gardens, Edinburgh, on 8 Nov. 1889. Muirhead married, on 14 April 1857, Jemima Lock, youngest daughter of George Eastlake of Plymouth.

Muirhead edited in 1880 'The Institutes of Gaius and Rules of Ulpian. The former from Studemund's Apograph of the Verona Codex. With translation and notes critical and explanatory, and copious alphabetical digest,' Edinburgh, 8vo. His 'Historical Introduction to the Private Law of Rome,' Edinburgh, 1886, 8vo, of which an abridgment had appeared, under the title 'Roman Law,' in the ninth edition of the 'Encyclopædia Britannica,' is a work of authority, and has been translated into French and Italian. Muirhead's interesting and valuable library of law books was, after his death, purchased by subscription and presented to the Owens College, Manchester. A catalogue of it has been published by the college.

[Scotsman, 9 and 13 Nov. 1889; Times, 9 Nov. 1889; Journal of Jurisprudence, 1889, p. 639; The Student, 17 May 1889; Foster's Men at the Bar; Edinburgh Univ. Cal.] J. M. R.

MULCASTER, Sir FREDERICK WILLIAM (1772–1846), lieutenant-general, colonel-commandant royal engineers, and inspector-general of fortifications, eldest son of Major-general G. F. Mulcaster, of the royal engineers, was born at St. Augustine, East Florida, on 25 June 1772. After passing through the Royal Military Academy at Woolwich, he received a commission as second lieutenant in the royal artillery on 2 June 1792, and in June 1793 was transferred to the royal engineers. He was promoted first lieutenant in November 1793. He was sent to Portsmouth, and early in 1795 was appointed assistant quartermaster-general in the south-western district. He laid out the encampments at Weymouth, which were frequently visited by George III and the royal family. He sailed for Portugal on 1 Jan. 1797, and after making a military survey of the seat of war, he served successively as military secretary to General Hon. Sir C. Stuart and Lieutenant-General Fraser. On 11 Sept. 1798 he was promoted captain-lieutenant, and went to Minorca, where he was commanding engineer at the siege of Cindadella in that island at the end of the year. He was actively employed in the operations in the Mediterranean until 1801, and was military secretary successively to Sir C. Stuart, General Fox, and Lord Roslyn. He acted as colonial secretary of Minorca after its capture, and as judge of the vice-admiralty court in the Mediterranean. He held the latter appointment for nearly two years, and though some eight hundred prize causes came before him there were but five appeals to England, and in all these his decisions were confirmed.

In June 1801 he was appointed under-secretary to Lord Chatham, master-general of the ordnance. On 21 Sept. 1802 he was promoted captain, and in December 1803 he was appointed commanding royal engineer and inspector of the royal gunpowder factories at Faversham and Waltham Abbey. On 25 July 1810 he became brevet major, and on 1 May 1811 regimental lieutenant-colonel. In January 1812 he went to the Mauritius as commanding royal engineer of that island and of Bourbon and dependencies. He remained there until 1817, and acted as surveyor-general of the colonies and temporarily as colonial secretary, and took charge of Bourbon at a time of peculiar difficulty and delicacy, the lieutenant-governor having been superseded. He received the thanks of the governor for restoring peace in Bourbon by his judicious conduct. He was promoted colonel on 7 Feb. 1817. He returned to England in July the same year, and was placed on half-pay on reduction of the corps in August. He was made a K.C.H. for his services, and received the reward for distinguished service. He returned to full pay on 15 April 1824, and was promoted major-general on 27 May 1825. He served in various capacities on the staff at home, and on 16 July 1834 was appointed inspector-general of fortifications. He was promoted lieutenant-general 28 June 1838. He resigned the office of inspector-general of fortifications in July 1845, and died at Charlton near Canterbury on 28 Jan. 1846. Mulcaster married first, on 2 Sept. 1804, Mary Lucy, daughter of John Montrésor of Belmont, Kent, and of Portland Place, and granddaughter of James Gabriel Montrésor [q. v.], and secondly, on 10 Sept. 1822, Esther Harris of Petham, near Canterbury, and had by her one son, Frederick Montrésor.

[Royal Military Calendar, vol. v. London, 8vo, 1820; Porter's Hist. of the Corps of Royal Engineers, vol. ii. London, 8vo, 1889; Corps Records; War Office Records; Burke's Landed Gentry.] R. H. V.

MULCASTER, RICHARD (1530?–1611), schoolmaster and author, is commonly said to have been a native of Carlisle. But his most recent biographer, R. H. Quick, on evidence supplied by one of his descendants, considers his birthplace to have been 'the old border tower of Brackenhill Castle, on the river Line.' His father, William Mulcaster, was of an old border family, who traced back their history to the time of William Rufus, and had been active in repelling the incursions of the Scots. Richard, born in 1530 or 1531, was sent to Eton, where Udall was head-master from 1534 to 1543. From Udall he may have caught some tincture of the severity he afterwards himself showed as a schoolmaster, as well as his fondness for dramatic composition. In 1548 Mulcaster was elected scholar of King's College, Cambridge, but soon migrated to Christ Church, Oxford, where in 1555 he was elected a student, and proceeded M.A. in the following year. While still in residence he added to his classical studies an acquaintance with Hebrew and other oriental languages, which won from Hugh Broughton the commendation that he was one of the best Hebrew scholars of his age. In 1559 he was working as a schoolmaster in London. The date is fixed by a passage in his 'Positions,' published in 1581, in which he speaks of having been engaged in teaching twenty-two years. His reputation as a teacher became so well known that when, in 1561, the newly founded school of the Merchant Taylors was ready to be opened, Mulcaster was appointed (24 Sept.) its first head-master. In this capacity he served till 1586 with great ability and benefit to the school, though his rugged temper produced occasional friction between him and the governing body. There is good reason to believe that Spenser the poet was one of his earliest pupils. On 28 June of that year he sent in his resignation, and on the following 8 Nov. a successor was appointed. His farewell to the school was the bitter apophthegm, quoted also by Bishop Pilkington, 'Fidelis servus perpetuus asinus.'

Wilson, the historian of Merchant Taylors' School, says that immediately on leaving that school Mulcaster became surmaster of St. Paul's (p. 1177); but this is to all appearance an error (GARDINER, *Admission Registers*, p. 29). He was made vicar of Cranbrook, Kent, 1 April 1590, and prebendary of Gatesbury, Sarum, 29 April 1594. On 5 Aug. 1596, being then at least in his sixty-sixth year, he was elected high-master of St. Paul's School. He held the office for twelve years more, till his resignation in the spring of 1608. In 1598 Elizabeth, who had always shown a kindly interest in his welfare, had presented him to the rectory of Stanford Rivers in Essex. On 6 Aug. 1609 he lost his wife Katherine, with whom he had been united fifty years, and he recorded his loss in a feeling epitaph. He himself died on 15 April 1611, and was laid by his wife's side, in the chancel of Stanford Rivers Church, 26 April, but no memorial marks the spot.

Mulcaster's work as a teacher has not yet been fully appreciated. Fuller (who mistakenly calls him a Westmoreland worthy) has told us how far the 'prayers of cockering mothers prevailed with him,' which was just as far, in truth, as the 'requests of indulgent fathers, rather increasing than mitigating his severity on their offending child.' Yet his memory was revered by some of his greatest scholars. Bishop Andrewes kept his portrait over his study door, and, besides many substantial acts of friendship to him during his life, left his son, Peter Mulcaster, a legacy at his death.

In several respects Mulcaster's views on education were in advance of his age. He taught his boys music and singing, and had a hand in the 'Discantus, Cantiones, &c.,' of Tallis and Bird (cf. WHITELOCKE, *Liber Fam.* Camden Soc.) His pupils frequently performed masks, interludes, and the like before Elizabeth and the court. He insisted on the importance of physical training, and asserted the right of girls to receive as good a mental education as boys. If he would not 'set young maidens to public grammar schools,' it was only because that was 'a thing not used in my country.' He advocated a system of special training for men designed to be schoolmasters.

He wrote: **1.** 'Positions, wherein those primitive Circumstances be examined, which are necessarie for the Training up of Children, either for Skill in their Book or Health in their Bodie,' &c., London, 1581, small 4to, dedicated to Queen Elizabeth. Hazlitt and Lowndes mention editions of 1587 and 1591; it was re-edited by Quick in 1888. 2. 'The First Part of the Elementarie, which entreateth chefelie of the right Writing of our English Tung,' London, 1582, small 4to. No second part of this is known to have appeared. 3. Latin verses prefixed to Baret's 'Alvearie,' 1580; Ocland's 'Anglorum Prœlia' and 'Eirenarchia,' 1580 and 1582; Hakluyt's 'Voyages,' and others. 4. 'Catechismus Paulinus, in vsum Scholæ Paulinæ conscriptus, ad formam parui illius Anglici Catechismi qui pueris in communi precum Anglicarum libro ediscendus proponitur,' London, 1599, reprinted 1601, small 8vo; preface dated 17 Nov. 1599, in which he speaks of the great difficulties he had to contend with on first entering upon office at St. Paul's. 5. 'In Mortem Serenissimæ Reginæ Elizabethæ Nænia consolans,' London, 1603, small 4to, followed by a version in English.

[Articles in Gent. Mag. 1800 pt. i. pp. 419–21, 511–12, pt. ii. pp. 603–4, signed E. H. (the late Sir Henry Ellis?); H. B. Wilson's History of Merchant Taylors' School; Collier's Annals of the Stage, 1831, i. 205, 208–9, 248–9, and Bibliog. Account of Early English Lit.; Hunter's MS. Chorus Vatum, ii. 60–1; Wood's Athenæ; Knight's Colet (the R. Mulcaster who translated Fortescue's work was Robert Mulcaster); Warton's English Poetry; Corser's Collectanea, pt. v. p. 137; Hazlitt's Handbook to the Popular Lit. A letter from Mulcaster to Sir Philip Sydney is said to be 'among the letters at Penshurst.' To the edition of the Positions by Robert Hebert Quick [q. v.] London, 1888, was appended an account of Mulcaster and his writings; lecture by Mr. Foster Watson, in Educational Times, 1 Jan. 1893; Notes and Queries, 8th ser. vi. 142.] J. H. L.

MULGRAVE, Earls of. [See Sheffield, Edmund, first Earl, 1564?–1646; Sheffield, Edmund, second Earl, 1611?–1658; Sheffield, John, third Earl, 1648–1721; Phipps, Henry, first Earl of the second creation, 1755–1831.]

MULGRAVE, Barons. [See Phipps, Constantine John, second Baron, 1744–1792; Phipps, Henry, third Baron, 1755–1831.]

MULHOLLAND, ANDREW (1791–1866), cotton and linen manufacturer, born at Belfast in 1791, came of an old Ulster family. His father, Thomas, was in 1819 head of Messrs. Thomas Mulholland & Co., a firm of cotton manufacturers of Union Street, Belfast (cf. *Belfast Directory*, 1819, p. 52). Andrew was posted in this firm, which, on the death of his father, was carried on by himself and a brother under the title of Messrs. T. & A. Mulholland. On 10 June 1828 their cotton mill in York Street was burnt down. No machinery had yet been introduced into the manufacture of linen at Belfast, but Andrew had observed that the supply of yarns made by hand was quite insufficient to meet the demands of the Belfast spinners, and that quantities of flax were shipped across to Manchester to be spun and reimported as yarn. He accordingly determined in 1828 to set up flax-spinning machinery in a small mill in St. James's Street, and subsequently devoted the rebuilt mill in York Street to the same purpose. The first bundle of flax yarns produced by machinery in Belfast was thrown off in 1830 from the York Street mill; Messrs. Murland, however, dispute priority with the Mulhollands in the introduction of machinery. After his brother Thomas's death Andrew carried on the business single-handed. For some years he enjoyed with very profitable results almost a monopoly in the new industry which he had set on foot, and the firm still remains one of the principal concerns in Belfast. On the grant of a corporation to Belfast in 1842 Andrew became a member of it, was mayor in 1845, and presented the town with the organ in Ulster Hall at a cost of 3,000*l*. In 1860 he retired to Springvale, Ballywalter, co. Down, and subsequently became justice of the peace, deputy-lieutenant, and served as high sheriff for Down and Antrim. He died on 24 Aug. 1866 at Springvale, aged 73. He married in 1817 Eliza, daughter of Thomas McDonnell of Belfast. His eldest son, John (*b.* 1819), assisted Cobden in his negotiation of a commercial treaty with Napoleon III in 1860, entered parliament as member for co. Down in 1874, sat for Downpatrick 1880–5, and was in 1892 raised to the peerage of the United Kingdom under the title of Baron Dunleath of Ballywalter.

[Belfast Weekly News, Weekly Press, and Northern Whig for 1 Sept. 1866; J. H. Smith's Belfast and its Environs, p. 57; Belfast Directory, 1819; British Manufacturing Industries, p. 77, &c,; Charley's Flax and its Products in Ireland, pp. 36, 92, 124; Sharp's Flax, Tow, and Jute Spinning; Warden's Linen Trade, Ancient and Modern, p. 404; Foster's Peerage, 1893; information received from Baron Dunleath.] A. F. P.

MULLEN, ALLAN (*d.* 1690), anatomist. [See Molines.]

MULLENS, JOSEPH (1820–1879), missionary, born in London on 2 Sept. 1820, entered Coward College in 1837, and in 1841 graduated B.A. at the London University. In June 1842 he offered himself to the London Missionary Society (congregationalist) for service in India, and after spending one session at Edinburgh in study of mental philosophy and logic, he was ordained to the congregationalist ministry 5 Sept. at Barbican Chapel, and sailed for India in the company of the Rev. A. F. Lacroix [q. v.] Arriving in Calcutta, he entered on his work at Bhowanipore, where he married Lacroix's daughter in 1845. In 1846 he succeeded to the pastorate of the native church at the same place. He remained there twelve years. During this period he prepared a series of statistics of missions in India and Ceylon. In 1858 he returned to England, and in 1860 took a prominent part in the missionary conference in Liverpool. In 1861 he received from William College, Massachusetts, the degree of D.D., and in the same year his wife died. In 1865 Mullens became joint foreign secretary of the London Missionary Society, and in 1868 sole foreign secretary. In the earlier capacity he visited the missionary stations of the society in India and China, returning to England in 1866. In 1867 he received from the university ot Edinburgh the degree of D.D. In 1870 he attended the annual meeting of the American Board of Foreign Missions, and remained to advocate the claims of the society in Canada. In 1873 he visited Madagascar to confer with the missionaries there, and he published the results in 'Twelve Months in Madagascar' (1857). After the death of Dr. Thomson of the mission on Lake Tanganyika, Mullens left England, 24 April 1879, with Mr. Griffith and Dr. Southon, to proceed to Zanzibar for the purpose of reinforcing the mission in Central Africa. On arrival at Zanzibar, Mullens resolved to accompany the inexperienced members of the mission to the scene of operation. At Kitange, 5 July, 150 miles from Saadani, Mullens caught a severe cold, and he died on 10 July 1879 at Chakombe, eight miles beyond. He was buried at the mission station of Mpwapwa.

Mullens, by his organising power, mastery of details, and statesmanlike supervision, largely increased the efficiency of the London Missionary Society. In addition to many reports, essays, articles, and notices, he wrote: 1. 'Missions in South India visited and described,' 1854. 2. 'The Religious Aspects of Hindu Philosophy discussed,' 1860. 3. 'Brief Memorials of the Rev. Alphonse François Lacroix,' 1862. 4. 'A brief Review of Ten Years' Missionary Labour in India, between 1852 and 1861,' London, 1863. 5. 'London and Calcutta compared in their Heathenism, their Privileges, and their Prospects,' 1868. 6. 'Twelve Months in Madagascar,' 1874; 2nd edit. 1875. Mrs. Mullens wrote 'Faith and Victory: a Story of the Progress of Christianity in Bengal.'

[The Chronicle of the London Missionary Society, October 1879.] S. P. O.

MÜLLER, JOHANN SEBASTIAN (*fl.* 1715?–1790?), painter. [See MILLER, JOHN.]

MULLER, JOHN (1699–1784), mathematician, was born in Germany in 1699. His first book, a treatise on conic sections, published in London in 1736, is dated from the Tower of London, and dedicated to the master-general of the ordnance, the Duke of Argyll and Greenwich, although Muller's name does not appear in the ordnance-lists in 'Angliæ Notitiæ' at this period. In 1741 Muller was appointed head-master of the Royal Military Academy, Woolwich, at a salary of 200*l.* a year, by the new master-general [see MONTAGU, JOHN, second DUKE OF MONTAGU]. At first, the academy was a mere school, where the masters, Muller and Thomas Simpson, resented military interference, and the boys defied the masters at will (see DUNCAN, *Hist. Roy. Artillery*, vol. i.) Subsequently, matters improved, the cadet-company was formed, the academy enlarged, and Muller appointed professor of fortification and artillery, a post he held until superannuated and pensioned in September 1766 (*Records Roy. Mil. Academy*). He was 'the scholastic father of all the great engineers this country employed for forty years' (HILL, *Boswell*, i. 351). He died in April 1784, at the age of eighty-five. A portrait of Muller, painted by J. Hay, was engraved by T. Major (BROMLEY). His library was sold in 1785 (NICHOL, *Lit. Anecd.* vol. iii.)

Muller published: 1. 'A Mathematical Treatise, containing a System of Conic Sections and the Doctrine of Fluxions and Fluents applied to Various Subjects,' London, 1736, 4to. 2. 'The Attack and Defence of Fortified Places,' London, 1747. 3. 'A Treatise containing the Practical Part of Fortification, for the Use of the Royal Military Academy, Woolwich,' London, 1755, 4to. 4. 'A Treatise on Fortification, Regular and Irregular. With Remarks on the Constructions of Vauban and Coehorn,' London, 1756, 4to, 2nd edit. 5. 'The Field Engineer. Translated from the French of De Clairac, London, 1759, 8vo. 6. 'Treatise on Artillery,' a compendious work, London, 1757; with Supplement, London, 1768. 7. 'New System of Mathematics, to which is prefaced an Account of the First Principles of Algebra,' London, 1769, 8vo; another edit. London, 1771.

[Muller's writings; Watt's Bibl. Brit.; Gent. Mag. 1784, i. 475.] H. M. C.

MÜLLER, WILLIAM (*d.* 1846), writer on military and engineering science, describes himself as an officer of Electoral Hanoverian cavalry, who, about the close of last century, became the first-appointed public instructor (docent) in military science in the university of Göttingen, which conferred upon him the degrees of doctor of philosophy and master of arts (MÜLLER, *Relations of the Campaign*, 1809, Preface; *Handbuch der Groben Geschutzes*). He states that during the ten years he held that post he made a vast number of experiments in artillery, and so far as his time and pecuniary resources admitted, travelled in France, Prussia, Holland, Bohemia, Austria, &c., to inspect battlefields and engines of war (*ib.*) He adds that he had under his instruction many distinguished officers, including German and Russian princes, who served both in the German and French armies during Napoleon's subsequent campaigns (MÜLLER, *Science of War*, vol. i. Preface). After the French seized Hanover a second time in 1807, Müller came to England, and on 24 April 1809 was appointed a second lieutenant of engineers in the king's German legion, in British pay, becoming first lieutenant, 20 May 1809, and second captain, 13 Dec. 1812. He was employed in the home district; published several works in English; patented an improvement in pumps (British patent 3300, 12 Feb. 1810); and in 1813 was employed on a survey of the coast about the mouths of the Elbe, which after the peace was extended as far as Boulogne-sur-Mer. The German legion was disbanded, and Müller, with other officers, placed on half-pay from 24 Feb. 1816, when he was appointed a captain of engineers in the reformed Hanoverian army, and was much engaged on survey work. In 1828 he patented in England (British Patent 5680, 16 July 1828), an instrument he called a 'cosmosphere,' consisting of 'cosmically' (equatorially?) mounted terrestrial and celestial globes 'for the solution of problems in navigation, spherics, and other sciences.' Müller, who was a K. H., and wore the German Legion war-medal, died at Stade, in Hanover, where he had long resided, on 2 Sept. 1846.

He was author of the following works: 1. 'Analytische Trigonometrie,' Göttingen, 1807. 2. 'Anfangsgründe der reinen Mathematik,' Göttingen, 1807. 3. 'Handbuch der Verfertigung des groben Geschützes,' Göttingen, 1807. 4. 'Grundriss zu Vorlesungen der militarischen Encyclopedie,' Göttingen, 1808 (Müller states that his encyclopedia was subsequently printed in Germany, France, and Holland under the First Empire). 5. 'Handbuch der Artillerie,' Berlin, 1810 (for the preceding list see preface to MÜLLER, *Science of War*, vol. i.) 6. 'A Relation of the Military Operations of the Austrian and French Armies in the Campaign of 1809,' London, 1810, 8vo. 7. 'Elements of the Science of War,' 3 vols. 8vo, London, 1811. 8. 'A Topographical and Military Survey of Germany,' London, 1815, 12mo. 9. 'Hydroozo-chorographische General-Post- u. Wege-Carte des Königr. Hannover.' In twelve sheets and reduced, Hanover, 1823. 10. 'Special-Carte der Fürstenthums Lippe,' Hanover, 1824. 11. 'Beschreibung der Sturmfluthen an den Ofern der Nordsee u. der sich darin ergiessenden Ströme u. Flüsse, 3-4 Feb. 1825, mit Carte u. Planen,' Hanover, 1825-8. 12. 'The Cosmosphere, or Cosmographically-mounted Terrestrial and Celestial Globes, for Self-instruction and the Use of Schools,' London, 1829. With an Appendix on 'Instruments for Calculating Latitude and Longitude at Sea.' According to the British Museum Catalogue he was probably the writer of 'Versuch einer kurzen Geschichte des Königr. Hannover u. Herzogth. Braunschweig-Lüneburg,' Hanover, 1832, 8vo, a small work published under the signature 'R.'

[Hanoverian Staats-Kalendars and British Army Lists; Beamish's Hist. German Legion, vol. ii.; Müller's Writings; Neuer Nekrolog. der Deutschen, Weimar, 1846, xxiv. 1089. In the list of his works in the British Museum Catalogue Müller figures under two entries as 'Mueller, Wilhelm, officer of Hanoverian Cavalry,' and 'Mueller, Wilhelm, engineer.'] H. M. C.

MÜLLER, WILLIAM JOHN (1812–1845), landscape painter, born at Bristol on 28 June 1812, was the second son of John Samuel Müller and his wife, a Miss James of Bristol. His father, a native of Danzig, took refuge in England during the French occupation of Prussia in 1807–8, and settled at Bristol, where he married, and published 'A Natural History of the Crinoidea,' 1821, 4to. He also left a manuscript, which was lost, on 'Corals and Coralines,' and contributed several papers to the 'Transactions of the Royal Society.' He died in 1830.

Under his father's teaching Müller developed a taste for botany and natural history. He was at first intended for an engineer, but, devoting himself to art, received his first instruction from his fellow-townsman, James Barker Pyne [q. v.] He appears to have lived at Bristol till he was one-and-twenty, and was a member of the Bristol Sketching Club, which was established in 1833, his fellow-members being Samuel Jackson, J. Skinner Prout, J. B. Pyne, William West, Willis, Robert Tucker, and Evans. In the same year (1833) he exhibited for the first time at the Royal Academy, his picture being 'The Destruction of Old London Bridge—Morning.' In this or the following year he went abroad with Mr. George Fripp (still one of the members of the Royal Society of Painters in Water Colours), and spent seven months sketching in Germany, Switzerland, and Italy, after which he returned to Bristol and commenced his professional career. In 1836 he exhibited at the Royal Academy 'Peasants on the Rhine waiting for the Ferry Boat,' and sent works to the Exhibition of the Society of Artists in Suffolk Street in 1836, 1837, and 1838. In the last of these years he took a tour in Greece and Egypt, returning to Bristol with portfolios well filled with sketches. In 1839 he came to London, where his pictures found ready purchasers His dexterity in the use of both oil- and water-colour, his fine colour, and extraordinarily rapid execution, were regarded with admiration and wonder. David Cox [q. v.], his senior by nearly thirty years, who wished to improve himself in oil painting, came and watched the young genius as he painted his now famous picture of 'The Ammunition Waggon,' and procured a few of his pictures to place before him as models to work by. He again exhibited at the Royal Academy, and continued to do so yearly till his death. In 1841 he published a volume of 'Sketches illustrative of the Age of Francis I' (dedicated to Queen Adelaide), and joined the government expedition to Lycia at his own expense. During his absence he made a large number of masterly sketches, and from them he painted several pictures, like 'The Tent Scene, Xanthus,' and 'The Burial Ground, Smyrna,' which were exhibited at the Royal Academy and the British Institution during the last three years of his life.

His hands were now full of commissions, which he was unable to execute from ill-health. He returned to Bristol for rest and advice, but his heart was diseased. He painted occasionally, his last work being a sketch in water-colour of some flowers at his bedside. He died on 8 Sept. 1845, at the early age of thirty-three, and was buried in the old Lewin's Mead burial-ground, Bristol. At the sale of his works, which took place the year after his death, there was much competition for his Lycian sketches, which sold at prices varying from 20*l.* to 60*l.* apiece. A fine collection of them was left to the British Museum by John Henderson [q. v.] in 1878. His oil-pictures now sell for very large sums. The 'Chess Players' fetched 4,052*l.* at J. Heugh's sale in 1874; 'Ancient Tombs, Lycia,' 3,950*l.* at the Bolckow sale in 1888; and 'The Island of Rhodes,' 3,465*l.* at C. P. Matthews's sale in 1891. He is represented in the National Gallery by two fine but comparatively unimportant works—a 'Welsh Landscape' and an Eastern sketch (in oils), with figures. There are several of his water-colour drawings in the South Kensington Museum. Müller was one of the most original and powerful of painters from nature. He seized the characteristics of a scene with wonderful clearness and promptitude, and set it down without hesitation or difficulty. His selection and generalisation were nearly always masterly, his colour pure and strong, and he could probably suggest more, with fewer touches, than any other painter of his time. He never spoilt the freshness of his work by over-labour or detail. One of his most remarkable works, executed very rapidly, in a manner suggestive of Constable, and called 'Eel Butts at Goring,' is now in the possession of Mr. William Agnew. It is little more than a masterly sketch, and on the back of it is written in large letters by the artist himself, 'Left as a sketch for some fool to finish and ruin, W. M., Feb. 7, 1843.' It has recently been engraved in mezzotint on a large scale. Facsimiles of twenty of his Bristol sketches were published in a quarto volume under the title 'Bits of Old Bristol,' Bristol, 1883. An interesting collection of Müller's works (200) was exhibited in the Birmingham Art Gallery in 1896 (catalogue).

A portrait of Müller from a drawing by Mr. Branwhite of Bristol is prefixed to Solly's 'Life of Müller,' and a photograph of a bust in the possession of Müller's brother Edmund is given in the same work.

[Life by N. Neal Solly, London, 1875; Redgrave's Dict.; Bryan's Dict.; Graves's Dict.; Roget's Old Water-colour Society; Bates's Maclise Portrait Gallery.] C. M.

MULLINER, THOMAS (*fl.* 1550?), musician, was before 1559, according to a manuscript note in Stafford Smith's handwriting, 'master of St. Paul's school,' that is, of the school for the choristers of St. Paul's Cathedral. In 1559 Sebastian Westcott was appointed to the post. If Stafford Smith's note, which is the only evidence of Mulliner's connection with the cathedral, be correct, Mulliner was the master of Tallis and Sheppard, and deserves the credit of maintaining the St. Paul's music-school at a high level of excellence, if not of having raised it to celebrity.

Mulliner made a valuable collection of pieces for the virginals, which is now preserved in Brit. Mus. Addit. MS. 30513. The volume bears an inscription, 'Sum liber Thomæ Mullineri, Johanne Heywoode teste.' (Heywood was much employed as a musician about the court.) Most of the music in this collection is written for the virginals, in the hand, it is supposed, of Mulliner; while certain numbers, 'galliardes,' are signed T. M. The manuscript was probably written during the reign of Mary or early in that of Elizabeth; it has been judged by other authorities to belong to Henry VIII's time.

One Thomas Mulliner was scholar of Corpus Christi College, Oxford, in and before 1564, and 'organorum modulator' on 3 March 1563-4. The name of Mulliner, or Mullyner, was known in the 16th century in Suffolk (*Cal. Chanc. Proc.* ii. 398), Northamptonshire (P. C. C. Registers of wills, Dixy, 29), and Oxfordshire (Registers of wills).

[Foster's Alumni Oxon.; Sparrow Simpson's Gleanings from Old St. Paul's, p. 195; Brit. Mus. Addit. MSS. 30513.] L. M. M.

MULLINS, GEORGE (*fl.* 1760–1775), painter, was a native of Ireland, and studied painting under James Mannin [q. v.] He was employed for some time in a manufactory belonging to Mr. Wise at Waterford, where he painted trays and snuffboxes like those made at Birmingham. He obtained, however, some success as a landscape-painter, and coming to London exhibited at the early exhibitions of the Royal Academy from 1770 to 1775. He married a young woman who kept an alehouse near Temple Bar, called the Horseshoe and Magpye, a place of popular resort.

[Pasquin's Artists of Ireland; Sarsfield Taylor's Fine Arts of Great Britain and Ireland; Redgrave's Dict. of Artists.] L. C.

MULLINS, JAMES (*d.* 1639), surgeon. [See Molines.]

MULLINS, JOHN (*d.* 1591), divine. [See Molyns.]

MULOCK, DINAH MARIA, afterwards Mrs. Craik (1826–1887), authoress, daughter of Thomas Mulock and his wife Dinah, was born on 20 April 1826 at Stoke-upon-Trent, Staffordshire, where her father was then minister of a small congregation. Her childhood and early youth were much affected by his unsettled fortunes; but she obtained a good education from various quarters, and, feeling conscious of a vocation for authorship, came to London about 1846, much at the same time as two friends whose assistance was afterwards of the greatest service to her, Alexander Macmillan and Charles Edward Mudie [q. v.] Introduced by Miss Camilla Toulmin to the acquaintance of Westland Marston [q. v.], she rapidly made friends in London, and found great encouragement for the stories for the young to which she at first confined herself, of which 'Cola Monti' (1849) was the best known. In the same year she produced her first three-volume novel, 'The Ogilvies,' which obtained a great success. It was followed in 1850 by 'Olive,' perhaps the most imaginative of her fictions. 'The Head of the Family' (1851) and 'Agatha's Husband' (1853), in which the authoress used with great effect her recollections of East Dorset, were perhaps better constructed and more effective as novels, but had hardly the same charm. The delightful fairy story 'Alice Learmont' was published in 1852, and numerous short stories contributed to periodicals, some displaying great imaginative power, were published in 1853 under the title of 'Avillion and other Tales.' A similar collection, of inferior merit, appeared in 1857 under the title of 'Nothing New.' Thoroughly established in public favour as a successful authoress, Miss Mulock took a cottage at Wildwood, North End, Hampstead, and became the ornament of a very extensive social circle. Her personal attractions were at this period of her life considerable, and her simple cordiality, staunch friendliness, and thorough goodness of heart perfected the fascination. In 1857 appeared the work by which she will be principally remembered, 'John Halifax, Gentleman,' a very noble presentation of the highest ideal of English middle-class life, which after nearly forty years still stands boldly out from the works of the female writers of the period, George Eliot's excepted. In writing 'John Halifax,' however, Miss Mulock had practically delivered her message, and her next important work, 'A Life for a Life' (1859), though a very good novel—more highly remunerated, and perhaps at the time more widely read, than 'John Halifax'—was far from possessing the latter's enduring charm. 'Mistress and Maid' (1863), which originally appeared in 'Good Words,' was inferior in every respect; and, though the lapse was partly retrieved in 'Christian's Mistake' (1865), her subsequent novels were of no great account. The genuine passion which had upborne her early works of fiction had not unnaturally faded out of middle life, and had as naturally been replaced by an excess of the didactic element. This the authoress seemed to feel herself, for several of her later publications were undisguisedly didactic essays, of which 'A Woman's Thoughts about Women' and 'Sermons out of Church' obtained most notice. In her later period, however, she returned to the fanciful tale which had so frequently employed her youth, and achieved a great success with 'The Little Lame Prince' (1874), a charming story for the young. She had published poems in 1852, and in 1881 brought her pieces together under the title of 'Poems of Thirty Years, New and Old.' They are a woman's poems, tender, domestic, and sometimes enthusiastic, always genuine song, and the product of real feeling; some—such as 'Philip my King,' verses addressed to her godson, Philip Bourke Marston [q. v.], and 'Douglas, Douglas, tender and true'— achieved a wide popularity.

In 1864 Miss Mulock married George Lillie Craik, esq., a partner in the house of Macmillan & Co., and soon afterwards took up her residence at Shortlands, near Bromley, where she continued until her death. She had become very intimate with M. Guizot and his family, translated his 'Memoir of Barante' and books by his daughter, Madame De Witt, and in her latter years made tours through Cornwall and the north of Ireland, accounts of which were published, with copious illustrations, in 1884 and 1887 respectively. She died suddenly on 12 Oct. 1887 from failure of the heart's action. She had no children. Her memory, both as a woman and as an authoress, will long be preserved by the virtues of which her writings were the expression. She was not a genius, and she does not express the ideals and aspirations of women of exceptional genius; but the tender and philanthropic, and at the same time energetic and practical womanhood of ordinary life has never had a more sufficient representative.

[Miss Frances Martin in the Athenæum, 22 Oct. 1887; Wolley's Think on these Things, a sermon; Men of the Time; Miles's Poets and Poetry of the Century, vol. vii.; Griffin's Contemporary Biography in Addit. MS. 2851; personal knowledge.] R. G.

MULREADY, WILLIAM (1786–1863), *genre* painter, the son of a leather-breeches maker, was born at Ennis, co. Clare, on 1 April 1786. His father came to London before he was five years old, and settled in Old Compton Street, Soho. The child had already shown a precocious tendency towards art by copying an engraving of St. Paul's Cathedral, on the boards of the floor under the bedstead, with a piece of chalk. What are supposed to be more or less correct reproductions of some later, but still very early drawings of his, illustrate a little book called 'The Looking Glass; a true History of the Early Years of an Artist,' by Theophilus Marcliffe, which was published in 1805. It is said to be a true history of the first fifteen years of Mulready's life, written by William Godwin from information supplied by Mulready himself. A reprint of the rare original, with an appendix by F. G. Stephens, was published in 1889.

Mulready's parents were Roman catholics, and though very poor seem to have given him the best education in their power. He was first sent to a Wesleyan school, and when ten years old to a Roman catholic school in Castle Street, Long Acre. After this he passed nearly two years with an Irish chaplain, and then some time with one or two other catholic priests. From one or other he learnt some French and a little Latin, and developed a love of reading, which he gratified by taking up books at the stalls on his way to and from school. The stallman at Aldrich's in Covent Garden lent him books to take home, and gave him prints to colour. Once when he was chalking letters on a wall in imitation of the advertisements, and holding forth to an admiring group of boys as to the proper treatment of the letters, his handsome and intelligent face attracted the attention of John Graham (1754–1817) [q. v.], the historical painter, who engaged him as a model for his picture of 'Solomon receiving the blessing of his father David,' which was exhibited at the Royal Academy in 1797. He made a few pence occasionally by selling drawings and 'Turks' caps' (geometrical ornaments composed of circles and segments of circles) to his schoolfellows, and with the proceeds bought a few books and a little collection of plays. The engravings to the latter representing actors in their favourite parts he used to copy with great care. He began when about twelve years of age to draw faces and other parts of the human body from nature, and would haunt the stage door in order to obtain a near view of John Kemble, whom he drew in many of his characters. A copy by him of a figure of a harlequin attracted the notice of a young Irish painter named Neill, who recommended him to go to Mr. Baynes, a drawing master. Mr. Baynes recognised the lad's talent, but being a landscape painter would not receive him as a pupil. An application to a Mr. John Corbet, who kept a puppet-show in Norfolk Street, Strand, was more useful. This gentleman gave him drawings and a cast to copy, and recommended him to read Walker's 'Anatomy.' This he did with great diligence, using as a study the space beneath the altar of the Roman catholic chapel, near Buckingham Gate, which adjoined the house of the priest who was then instructing him. Greatly desiring to become a student at the Royal Academy, Mulready, when about thirteen, took courage, and knocked at the door of Thomas Banks [q. v.], the sculptor, with a drawing of the Apollo Belvedere in his hand. Banks received him kindly, sent him to a drawing-school in Furnival's Inn Court, and afterwards, the master having absconded, gave him tuition in his own studio, with the result that after one failure Mulready gained admission as a student of the Royal Academy in November 1800, by a drawing from a statue by Michel Angelo.

The lad was not only industrious, but independent, and from the age of fifteen contrived in some way to make his own living without trenching on the small resources of his parents. When sixteen he gained the larger silver palette of the Society of Arts for skill in painting, and about this time he made the acquaintance of John Varley [q. v.] the water-colour painter, who took him into his house (2 Harris Place, Oxford Street) as a sort of pupil-teacher. Varley and he appear to have had many tastes in common, including one for pugilism. While with Varley he improved greatly as an artist, and laid the foundation of his success as a teacher, on which his future livelihood was mainly to depend. Among those artists who benefited most by his instruction were John Linnell [q. v.] and William Henry Hunt [q. v.], who was placed under his especial care. Unfortunately he did not confine his attention to his master's pupils, but fell in love with one of Varley's sisters, and married her in 1803, when he was in his eighteenth year. The union proved a very unhappy one. Mulready's earnings were not sufficient to support a wife and the four children which she soon brought him, and dissensions arose between the young couple, which were terminated, after about six years of married life, by a separation which was deliberate, formal, and final. Mrs. Mulready, who survived her husband by a few months, declared that though they generally lived in the same neighbourhood for nearly fifty years after the separation, she had only once caught sight of him in the street. No explanation is given of this complete breakdown of sympathy, but their poverty probably did not tend to smooth the temper of Mulready, which was naturally violent. 'I remember the time,' said Mulready, 'when I had a wife, four children, nothing to do, and was 600*l.* in debt.' His want of occupation was not the result of idleness. He taught drawing, and used to say that he had 'tried his hand at everything from a miniature to a panorama.' The panorama is supposed to have been one by Sir Robert Ker Porter [q. v.] His artistic ambition is shown by the subjects of his first compositions. He painted 'Ulysses and Polyphemus,' 'The Disobedient Prophet,' and 'The Supper at Emmaus,' and made a large cartoon of 'The Judgment of Solomon.' We are told that none of these works gave any great evidence of talent, and it is probable that his intercourse with Varley moderated his ambition, and turned his attention to landscape. In 1804 he made his first appearance at the Royal Academy with two views of Kirkstall Abbey, and one of a cottage at Knaresborough, the result of a trip to Yorkshire, and he exhibited three landscapes in each of the following years. At this time he was much engaged in designing for children's books, a whole series of which were published between 1807 and 1809. The illustrations of the following are attributed to him: 'Lamb's Tales from Shakespeare,' 1807; 'The Elephant's Ball,' 1807; 'The Butterfly's Ball and the Grasshopper's Feast,' 1807; 'The Lion's Masquerade,' 1807; 'The Lioness's Ball,' 1807; 'The Peacock at Home,' 1807; 'The Lobster's Voyage to the Brazils,' 1808; 'The Cat's Concert,' 1808; 'The Fishes' Grand Gala,' 1808; 'Madame Grimalkin's Party,' 1808; 'The Jackdaw at Home,' 1808; 'The Lion's Parliament,' 1808; 'The Water-king's Levée,' 1808; and 'Think before you speak,' 1809. To these may perhaps be added 'The King and Queen of Hearts,' 'Nong Tong Paw,' 'Gaffer Gray,' and 'The Sullen Woman.' During these three years he exhibited figure subjects; in 1807, 'Old Kaspar' at the Royal Academy; in 1808, 'The Rattle' at the British Institution, and 'The Dead Hare,' and a 'Girl at Work' at the Academy. In 1809 he sent to the Academy 'Returning from the Alehouse,' since called 'Fair-time' (now in the National Gallery, with a new background painted in 1840, when it was again exhibited at the Academy), and to the British Institution 'The Carpenter's Shop.' This was his first work of any importance, a simple domestic scene, of the class of art to which he subsequently devoted himself, influenced perhaps by the success that Wilkie had just achieved by his 'Blind Fiddler.' In 1811 he improved his position by a picture of the Wilkie type called 'The Barber's Shop' (a lout brought to have his red locks cropped by the village barber), and continued this success by other humorous pictures of boy life. In 1813 he exhibited 'Punch,' 'Boys Fishing' in 1814, and in 1815 'Idle Boys.' In November 1815 he was elected an associate, and in February 1816 a Royal Academician, so that his name never appears as an associate in the catalogues. In 1816 the picture of 'The Fight interrupted,' in which we see the bully of the school severely damaged by a brave little champion of liberty, justified his rapid promotion, and greatly increased his reputation.

His style, which had hitherto shown his very careful study of the Dutch masters and a desire to rival Wilkie, now changed to one more original and peculiar to himself. In 1815 he exhibited 'Lending a Bite,' in 1820 'The Wolf and the Lamb,' in 1821 'The Careless Messenger detected,' in 1822 'The Convalescent from Waterloo,' in 1824 'The Widow,' in 1825 'The Travelling Druggist,' in 1826 'The Origin of a Painter,' in 1827 'The Cannon,' in 1828 'The Interior of an English Cottage,' in 1830 'Returning from the Hustings.' These were followed by 'Dogs of two Minds,' 1830, 'A Sailing Match,' 1831, 'Scene from St. Ronan's Well,' 1832, 'The

Forgotten Word,' 1832, 'The First Voyage,' 1833, 'The Last in,' 1835, 'Giving a Bite,' 1836, 'A Toyseller,' the first design for the picture left unfinished by the artist, 'Brother and Sister,' the first design for the picture ('The Young Brother') afterwards painted for Mr. Vernon, and now in the South Kensington Museum, 1837; 'The Seven Ages,' 1838; 'Bob-cherry,' 1839; 'The Sonnet,' 1839; and 'First Love,' 1840.

In these last two pictures he left humour for sentiment, and adopted a more brilliant palette. About this time he again turned his attention to illustration, and published a series of carefully composed and graceful designs to the 'Vicar of Wakefield,' from three of which he afterwards painted pictures. 'The Whistonian Controversy' was exhibited in 1844; 'Choosing the Wedding Gown' in 1846, and 'Sophia and Burchell Haymaking' in 1847, all of which were very popular. 'Choosing the Wedding Gown,' now at South Kensington, is celebrated for its technical merits, especially in the representation of textures. The skill of Mulready as a painter was never more fully displayed than in the imitation of the silks and brocades, the woodwork of the counter, and the coat of the little spaniel lying upon a pile of rich stuffs. It is by some considered his finest work, but Mulready himself preferred 'Train up a Child in the way he should go,' a boy giving money to some poor Lascars. This, as well as 'Crossing the Ford,' another of Mulready's most popular compositions, was exhibited before the Vicar of Wakefield series, and afterwards Mulready did no better work. His most important pictures not already recorded were 'The Bath,' 'Shooting a Cherry,' which had been many years on hand, though not exhibited till 1848, 'Women Bathing,' and 'The Bathers,' and 'The Young Brother' exhibited in 1857. His 'Mother teaching her Child to pray,' exhibited in 1859, showed a great falling off. It is in the South Kensington Museum, together with the 'Negro Toy Seller,' which was left unfinished at his death. For some time before this took place his health had been much impaired, but neither age nor ill health diminished the ardour with which he worked. He was one of the most careful and conscientious of artists, and made separate studies for every part of his pictures down to the smallest details. To the last, like Etty, he was a constant attendant at the Royal Academy Life School, drawing from the nude, and he commenced some larger pictures with life-size figures, as though his career was commencing instead of drawing to its close. 'When over seventy-five years of age he set himself to practise drawing hands and heads rapidly in pen and ink, at a little life school held by the painters in the neighbourhood of Kensington.' 'I had lost somewhat of my power in that way,' he said, 'but I have got it up again. It won't do to let these things go.'

F. G. Stephens, his biographer, who knew him well in his later life, tells us that his society was pleasant, that he was full of humour, very kind of heart, considerate and helpful to those in need, loving children, and loved by them in return. He was devoted to the Royal Academy, and his attention to its affairs was once recognised by the present of a large silver goblet by seventy-three of his brother artists. He nevertheless seems to have lived a solitary and reticent life, and had few friends. Among these were Sir John Swinburne, with whom he used to stay at his seat at Capheaton, near Newcastle, and Mr. Sheepshanks, at whose house at Blackheath he was a frequent visitor. Mr. Sheepshanks was also a constant purchaser of Mulready's pictures. His loss was severely felt by the artist, to whom was consigned the task of hanging his magnificent bequest of pictures at South Kensington. Among them are many of Mulready's finest pictures, and studies of Mr. Sheepshanks himself, his house, and a view from its windows.

Mulready resided at Kensington Gravel Pits from 1811 to 1827, but he moved to Bayswater in 1827, and lived at 1 Lindon Grove for the rest of his life. Though subject to attacks of the heart, he remained active to the end, and on the last day of his life he attended a committee meeting of the Royal Academy. He died on 7 July 1863, in the seventy-eighth year of his age, and was buried at Kensal Green.

Mulready was one of the founders and most active members of the Artist Fund, to which he gave the right of engraving his popular picture of 'The Wolf and the Lamb,' which brought that charity the sum of 1,000*l.* Among his numerous works was the first penny postage envelope issued by Rowland Hill in 1840. It was adorned with a design emblematical of Britannia sending winged messengers to all quarters of the globe. This design was the subject of a celebrated caricature by John Leech in 'Punch.' Mulready was often painted by his brother artists, and sat for 'Duncan Gray' in Wilkie's picture of that name. One of the best of his portraits was painted and engraved by John Linnell. 'The Wolf and the Lamb' belongs to the queen, but most of Mulready's best works are now at South Kensington Museum and the National Gallery, having been bequeathed to the nation by Mr. Vernon and

Mr. Sheepshanks. A large number of his drawings, including many of his carefully executed chalk studies of the nude, are also at South Kensington.

[Stephens's Masterpieces of Mulready; Stephens's Mulready, in Great Artist Series; Redgraves' Century of Painters; Redgrave's Dict.; Bryan's Dict. (Graves and Armstrong); Cunningham's Lives (Heaton); Richard Redgrave—a Memoir; Nollekens and his Times (article 'Banks'); The Looking Glass (ed. Stephens, 1805); Catalogues of National Gallery and South Kensington Museum; Life of John Linnell; Pye's Patronage of British Art, which contains engravings of some portrait sketches by Mulready; The Portfolio, 1887, pp. 86, 119; Griffin's Contemporary Biography, in Add. MS. 28511; Notes and Queries, 3rd ser. iv. 15, 324, 6th ser. xii. 428, 505; there are many other paragraphs about Leech's caricature of the envelope and other matters in 6th ser. vols. ix. x. and xi. and in 7th ser. vol. xi., but these are of no great importance.] C. M.

MULSO, HESTER (1727–1801), essayist. [See Chapone.]

MULTON or MULETON, THOMAS DE (*d.* 1240?), justiciar, was son of Lambert de Multon, and grandson of Thomas de Multon, who occur in the reigns of Henry I and Henry II as holding land in Lincolnshire. He is first mentioned as receiving the grant of a market at Flete in 1205 (*Cal. Rot. Claus.* i. 20). In 1206 he was sheriff of Lincolnshire, an office which he held till 1208, but having offended the king he was on 21 July 1208 ordered to be imprisoned in Rochester Castle till he had discharged his debt to the crown. He accompanied John to Ireland in June 1210, and on 25 Feb. 1213 was appointed to investigate the extortion of the sheriffs of Yorkshire and Lincolnshire (*Cal. Rot. Pat.* p. 97), and in 1214 to inquire into the losses of the church in the bishopric of Lincoln during the interdict (*Cal. Rot. Claus.* i. 164–6). As a northern lord he sided with the barons in 1215, and was one of the confederates at Stamford; in consequence he was one of those excommunicated by the pope in 1216. Before this Multon had been taken prisoner by the king at Rochester on 30 Nov. 1215, and placed in the custody of Peter de Mauley at Corfe. His lands were entrusted to Earl Ranulf of Chester, and, despite the efforts of his sons, he was not restored to liberty till 29 July 1217, when he made his peace with the crown (*ib.* i. 317 *b*). In 1214 he had received the custody of the daughters of Richard de Lucy of Egremont, and in 1218 married Lucy's widow, Ada, daughter of Hugh de Moreville. For this marriage he had to pay a heavy fine, but obtained in consequence the office of forester of Cumberland. In 1219 he was one of the justices-itinerant for Cumberland, Westmoreland, and Lancashire, and during the next year for Yorkshire and Northumberland (*ib.* i. 434 *b*). After 1224 he sat continually as a justice at Westminster. Fines were acknowledged before him from Easter 1224 to Easter 1236, and he was a justice-itinerant in various counties up to August 1234 (cf. *ib.* ii. 77 *b*, 151 *b*, 202, 205 *b*, 208 *b*, 213). In 1235–6 Multon occurs as 'Justiciarius de Banco,' and Dugdale, interpreting this as one of the justices of the common pleas, further suggests that he was 'capitalis.' Foss, however, does not consider that the term means more than a justice of the royal court, and rejects Dugdale's further suggestion. Multon was justice-itinerant at Dunstable in June 1224 with Henry de Braybroc [q. v.], when Falkes de Breauté, incensed at their action against him, endeavoured to seize them. Multon, more fortunate than his colleague, made good his escape. He was a witness to the confirmation of Magna Charta in 1225. In 1229 he tried a suit between the priory and town of Dunstable (*Ann. Mon.* iii. 122). From 1233 to 1236 he was sheriff of Cumberland. According to Matthew Paris (iv. 49) Multon died in 1240, but the 'Dunstable Annals' (*Ann. Mon.* iii. 144) give the date as 1236. Matthew Paris describes him as having been in his youth a bold soldier, but in his later years a very wealthy man and learned lawyer. It is implied that he was not always scrupulous in the means of acquiring wealth, for he is said to have done much injury to the abbey of Croyland, of which he was a neighbour (Matt. Paris, iv. 49). He was also defendant in a suit of novel disseisin with the abbot of Swineshead (*Cal. Rot. Claus.* ii. 124). He was, however, a benefactor of the monks of Calder and Holcotram, and of the hospital of St. Leonard, in Skirbec, Lincolnshire.

Multon married, first, a daughter of Richard Delfliet, by whom he had three sons—Alan, who was taken prisoner with him at Rochester, Lambert, and Thomas, a clerk. Lambert and Alan married Amabel and Alice de Luci, their father's wards. Lambert acquired with his wife the barony of Egremont; his grandson Thomas was summoned to parliament from 1300 to 1321, and fought at Caerlaverock in 1300; on the death of John de Multon, Thomas's son, in 1334 the title fell into abeyance. Alan's son Thomas took his mother's name, and was ancestor of the Lucies of Cockermouth. By Multon's second wife he had a daughter Julian, who married

Robert le Vavasour, and a son Thomas, who, by his marriage with Maud, daughter of Hubert de Vaux, acquired the barony of Gillesland. Thomas Multon, third baron of Gillesland, was summoned to parliament from 1297 till his death in 1313. Through his daughter Margaret the barony passed to Ralph Dacre; from this marriage sprang the titles of Baron Dacre held by Viscount Hampden, and Baron Dacre of Gillesland held by the Earl of Carlisle.

[Matthew Paris; Annales Monastici; Cal. of Close and Patent Rolls; Dugdale's Baronage, i. 567–9; Foss's Judges, ii. 415–19; Nicolas's Song of Caerlaverock, p. 109.] C. L. K.

MULVANY, CHARLES PELHAM (1835–1885), minor poet and journalist, son of Henry William Mulvany, barrister-at-law, and grandson of a captain in the royal navy who took part in the battle of Bunker Hill (17 June 1775), was born in Dublin on 20 May 1835. He entered Trinity College, Dublin, in 1850, became a scholar in 1854, and graduated B.A. at Dublin University as first-honour man in classics in June 1856. Before this date he had written verse in 'The Nation' over the signature 'C. P. M. Sch.;' he was editor of the 'College Magazine' during 1856 and 1857, and also wrote for the 'Irish Metropolitan Magazine,' 1857–8.

After a few years of service as a surgeon in the British navy Mulvany was ordained deacon of the church of England in 1868, migrated to Canada, and was ordained priest by the Bishop of Ontario in 1872. After acting for about two years as assistant professor of classics at Lenoxville, where he conducted the 'Students' Monthly,' he served as curate successively at Clarke's Mills, Huntley, Milford, and the Carrying Place, all in the province of Ontario. He became a constant contributor to Canadian newspapers and magazines, devoting the greater part of his later life to literary work. He kept up his connection with Trinity College by his brilliant contributions to the first three volumes of 'Kottabos,' issued respectively in 1874, 1877, and 1881. His latest verses, entitled 'Our Boys in the North-West Away,' appeared in the daily 'Globe,' Toronto, as late as 25 May 1885. He died at 69 Augusta Terrace, Toronto, on 31 May 1885.

Mulvany's clever verses are essentially of the imitative order. His versatility and effective use of pathos frequently suggest Hood, and he has been spoken of as an Hibernian Calverley; but neither his originality nor his rhyming power quite justifies the title. Many of his happiest parodies have not been published. These deal with local academic incidents, and are still *σποράδην ἀειδόμενα* in Trinity College.

His chief separate works are: 1. 'Lyrics of History and Life,' 1880. 2. 'Toronto, Past and Present,' 1884. 3. 'History of the North-West Rebellion of 1885.' All these were published at Toronto. At the time of his death he was preparing a 'History of Liberalism in Canada.'

[O'Donoghue's Poets of Ireland, p. 171; Cat. of Dublin Graduates; Appleton's Cyclopædia of American Biog. iv. 458; The Globe, Toronto, 1 June 1885; The Dominion Annual Register and Review for 1885, Toronto, 1886.] T. S.

MULVANY, THOMAS JAMES (*d.* 1845?), painter and keeper of the Royal Hibernian Academy, first appears as an exhibitor with the Dublin Society of Artists at the rooms of the Dublin Society in Hawkins Street, Dublin, in May 1809. When the Dublin Society in 1819 disposed of their premises and the artists were without a place of exhibition, Mulvany, with his brother, John George Mulvany, who was also a painter, was one of the most strenuous advocates for the grant of a charter of incorporation to the artists of Ireland. When at length this charter was obtained in 1823 and the Royal Hibernian Academy founded under the presidency of Francis Johnston [q. v.], Mulvany and his brother were two of the first fourteen academicians elected. He subsequently became keeper in 1841. During the last years of his life Mulvany was employed in editing 'The Life of James Gandon' [q. v.], which he did not, however, live to complete, as he died about 1845, while the book was not published until 1846. His son, George F. Mulvany (1809–1869), also practised as a painter. He succeeded his father as keeper of the Royal Hibernian Academy, and occasionally sent pictures to the Royal Academy in London. In 1854 he was elected the first director of the newly founded National Gallery of Ireland, and held the post until his death in Dublin on 6 Feb. 1869.

[Sarsfield Taylor's Fine Arts of Great Britain and Ireland; Redgrave's Dict. of Artists.] L. C.

MUMFORD, JAMES (1606–1666), jesuit, born in Norfolk in 1606, entered the Society of Jesus at Watten near St. Omer, 8 Dec. 1626, and became a professed member of the order in 1641. In 1642 he was at the English College, Liège, in the capacity of minister and consultator, and in 1645 he was confessor in the college at St. Omer. About 1647 he was rector of the college at Liège. About 1650 he was sent to the English mission, and stationed at Norwich. He was for some time rector of the 'College of the Holy Apostles,' embracing the Suffolk district. At Norwich he was seized by the parliamentary soldiers; was led round the city in his priestly vestments, amid the scoffs of the rabble, and with the sacred ornaments of the altar carried aloft on spears in a sort of triumphant procession, and was then cast into prison (SOUTHWELL, *Bibl. Scriptorum Soc. Jesu*, p. 380). He was subsequently removed to Great Yarmouth, but was remanded to Norwich, and after some months' imprisonment was discharged on bail. He died in England on 9 March 1665–6.

His works are: 1. 'A Remembrance for the Living to Pray for the Dead. Made by a Father of the Soc. of Iesus,' St. Omer, 1641, 12mo; the second part and second edit. by J. M., Lond. 1661, 12mo. Reprinted in 'St. Joseph's Ascetical Library,' Lond. 1871, 8vo, under the editorship of Father John Morris, S.J., who has added an appendix on 'The Heroic Act of Charity.' A Latin translation, under the title of 'Tractatus de misericordia fidelibus defunctis exhibenda,' was printed at Liège, 1647, 12mo; Cologne, 1649, 12mo; Strasburg, 1716, 12mo; Vienna, 1725, 16mo; Strasburg, 1762, 12mo. The work was translated into French by Father Charles Le Breton and by Father J. Brignon. Father Bouit brought out a new edition of Brignon's translation. A German translation appeared at Augsburg and Dillingen in 1695, and at Colmar, 1776. A criticism of Mumford's work by Thomas White or Albius, a secular priest, was published, under the title of 'Devotion and Reason, wherein Modern Devotion for the Dead is brought to Solid Principles and made Rational,' Paris, 1661, 12mo (DODD, *Church Hist.* iii. 288). 2. 'The Catholick Scripturist,' Ghent, 1652; 2nd edit. entitled 'The Catholic Scripturist; or the Plea of the Roman Catholics, shewing the Scriptures to hold the Roman faith in above forty of the chief Controversies now under debate,' Lond. 1686, 12mo; 3rd edit. Lond. 1687, 8vo; 4th edit. Lond. 1767, 12mo, Baltimore, 1808, 8vo, Lond. 1838 (published under the superintendence of the Catholic Institute), Lond. 1863, 8vo. It is said that Mumford wrote this book while in prison at Norwich. 3. 'The Question of Questions, which rightly solved resolveth all our Questions in Religion. This question is, Who ought to be our Judge in all these our differences? This book answereth this question; and hence sheweth a most easy, and yet most safe way, how, among so many Religions, the most unlearned and learned may find the true Religion. By Optatus Ductor,' Ghent, 1658, 4to; Lond. 1686-7, 12mo; Lond. 1767, 12mo; Lond. 1841, 12mo; and Glasgow, 1841, 12mo (revised by W. Gordon). In the 'Mémoires de Trévoux (1704, p. 1041, 1st edit.) it is stated that this work was first printed at Ghent in 1654. It was translated into French by the Capuchin father, Basile de Soissons. Basile is said to have suppressed the name of the author. 'A Vindication or Defence of St. Gregory's Dialogues' is also ascribed to Mumford.

[De Backer's Bibl. de la Compagnie de Jésus, ii. 1408; Dodd's Church Hist. iii. 321; Foley's Records, ii. 457, vii. 532; Jones's Popery Tracts, pp. 306, 317, 406, 462; Notes and Queries, 3rd ser. ix. 38; Oliver's Jesuit Collections, p. 146.]

T. C.

MUN, THOMAS (1571–1641), economic writer, was the third son of John Mun, mercer, of St. Andrew Hubbard's in the city of London, whose father, John Mun of Hackney, appears to have held the office of provost of moneyers in the Royal Mint (RUDING, *Annals of the Coinage*, i. 104), and in 1562 received a grant of arms (*Visitations of London and Middlesex*, 1633–4). William Mun, an uncle of Thomas, and also a moneyer in the mint, died at Hackney in 1610. Thomas was baptised at St. Andrew Hubbard's, 17 June 1571. His father died in 1573 (will proved in P. C. C., Peter, 12), and his mother, Margaret (*née* Barwick), married in the following year Thomas Cordell, mercer, of St. Lawrence Jewry (afterwards a director of the East India Company), by whom Mun and his brothers seem to have been carefully brought up. Mun had two elder brothers: John Mun (1564–1615), a citizen and mercer of London, who died unmarried (will, P. C. C., Rudd, 66), and according to Stow's 'Survey' (1618 edit. p. 385), had a monument in Allhallows Staining Church; the other, Edward Mun, M.A. (1568–1603), was vicar of Stepney, rector of East Barnet, and sub-almoner to Queen Elizabeth (cf. *Admin. Libr. Vic.-Gen.* fol. 110 *a*; NEWCOURT, *Repert. Eccles.* i. 740, 806; HILL and FRERE, *Memorials of Stepney Parish*, 1890, pt. i. p. 33; F. C. CASS, *East Barnet*, pt. ii. 1892, pp. 216–19).

Thomas appears to have been early engaged in mercantile affairs in the Mediterranean, especially in Italy and the Levant. In his 'England's Treasure by Forraign Trade' (pp. 44–7) he describes as within his personal observation the growth of the port of Leghorn and the encouragement of commerce by Ferdinand I, grand duke of Tuscany (1587–1609). So great was Mun's credit that Ferdinand lent him forty thousand crowns, free of interest, for transmission to Turkey, where he was about to obtain merchandise for Italy. At p. 126 of the same work he states that 'he had lived long in Italy.' In 1612 (29 Dec.) Mun married at St. Mary's Woolchurch Haw, London, Ursula, daughter of John Malcott, esq., of Bedfordshire. He settled in the parish of St. Helen's, Bishopsgate. In July 1615, as a well-known merchant, he was elected a member of the committee or a director of the East India Company, and he spent his life in actively promoting its interests.

In 1621 Mun published 'A Discourse of Trade, from England unto the East Indies; answering to diverse Objections which are usually made against the same. By T. M.' The work, which is extremely rare, contains references to the events of 1612 (at p. 47) and 1620 (pp. 20, 38). But McCulloch (*Lit. of Pol. Econ.* pp. 98–9) vaguely and erroneously suggested that the first edition appeared in 1609. A second edition, described on the title-page as 'The Second impression, corrected and amended,' is, like the first, dated 1621. It was reprinted in Purchas's 'Pilgrimes' in 1625, and again in 1856 by the Political Economy Club, in a volume of reprints of early English tracts on commerce, with a preface by McCulloch.

In his book Mun fully describes and defends the transactions of the East India Company. Complaints had been made that the carrying abroad of coin, under the company's patent, caused scarcity of it in England; but Mun argued that the exportation of specie was compatible with the due maintenance of an excess in the value of exports from this country over that of imports. The maintenance of that excess was an essential part of the currently accepted theory of the 'balance of trade.' The question of the alleged scarcity of coin was brought before parliament in 1621, and Mun appears to have submitted to the government statements entitled, in words which occur in his book, 'Reasons to prove that the trade from England unto the East Indies doth not consume, but rather increase the treasure of this kingdom' (see *Cal. State Papers*, Colon. Series, East Indies, 1617–21, 1023, pp. 431–2, and 1622–4, 155–8, pp. 68–9). In November 1621 Mun declined on private grounds a request of the court of directors of the East India Company to proceed to India to inspect their factories.

In 1622 Edward Misselden [q. v.]—who was possibly a friend of Mun, for the families of both were connected with Hackney and the East India Company—attacked in his 'Free Trade' a proposal made by Gerard Malynes [q. v.] (*Consuetudo, vel Lex Mercatoria*) to regulate compulsorily the course of exchange, as a means of controlling the 'balance of trade.' Malynes in his reply (*Maintenance of Free Trade*, 1622, p. 27) questioned the accuracy of Mun's published views. Misselden in return defended Mun in 'The Circle of Commerce,' 1623; and (pp. 36–7) remarked of him that 'his observation of the East India trade, his judgement in all trade, his diligence at home, his experience abroad, have adorn'd him with such endowments, as are rather to bee wisht in all, then easie to bee found in many Merchants of these times.' Malynes, in another treatise, 'The Centre of the Circle of Commerce,' 1623, again assailed Misselden and Mun (pp. 102–3). Mun in his posthumously published 'England's Treasure by Forraign Trade' exhaustively analysed and opposed Malynes's theories on exchanges (chaps. xii–xiv.)

In March 1624 Mun declined to serve as deputy-governor of the East India Company, but remained a member of the committee till his death (cf. 'Court Minute-books of the Company' in *Cal. State Papers*, Colonial). In 1628 the company, embarrassed by the encroachments of the Dutch on their trade, invoked the protection of the House of Commons, and for 'The Petition and Remonstrance of the Governor and Company of Merchants of London trading to the East Indies,' Mun, 'the ablest of the early advocates of the East India Company,' was mainly responsible. Many of its sentences and arguments he afterwards introduced verbatim into his 'England's Treasure.' The petition was reprinted in 1641, and was then addressed to both houses of parliament.

Mun's second book, his 'England's Treasure by Forraign Trade, or the Ballance of our Forraign Trade is the Rule of our Treasure,' was probably written about 1630, but it was not printed till 1664—some twenty-three years after his death, when it was 'published for the Common good by his son John.' In it Mun more energetically and formally than before defined the doctrine of the balance of trade. 'The ordinary means to encrease our wealth and treasure is,' he wrote (p. 11), 'by Forraign Trade, wherein wee must ever observe this rule: to sell more to strangers yearly than we consume of theirs in value.' Interesting reference is made by Mun to the customs revenue in its relation to English trade to India and other countries; and he shows much acquaintance with the operations of the mint, where his grandfather and uncle had been employed. In showing 'how the Revenues and Incomes of Princes may be justly raised,' he describes (pp. 157–9) the position of monarchs 'who have no just cause to lay extraordinary and heavy taxes upon their Subjects'—an apparent reference to the illegal exactions of Charles I. At pp. 165–6 he maintains that 'when more treasure must be raised than can be received by the ordinary taxes, it ought ever to be done with equality to avoid the hate of the people, who are never pleased except their contributions be granted by general consent: for which purpose the invention of Parliaments is an excellent policie of Government.'

In chapter xix. he deplores the neglect of the English fishing trade and the encroachments thereon by the Dutch, denounces his countrymen's habits of 'besotting themselves with pipe and pot' (p. 179), refers with approval (p. 186) to Captain Robert Hitchcock, author of 'A Political Plat for the Honour of the Prince' (1580), and to Tobias Gentleman [q. v.], author of 'England's Way to win Wealth,' (1614); and (p. 188) alludes to Grotius's 'Mare Liberum,' in questioning the right of the Dutch 'to fish in His Majesties Seas.'

Mun amassed great wealth as a merchant, and, besides inheriting lands at Mereworth, &c., in Kent, acquired the estate of Otteridge, at Bearsted, in the same county (Hasted, ii. 488). In May 1640, when a forced loan of 200,000*l.* was demanded by Charles I of the city of London, to assist him in his war in Scotland, he was reported, in the aldermen's returns to the privy council, as able to lend money to the king (cf. *Return*, ed. W. J. Harvey, 1886), but the citizens finally refused the loan. Mun died in 1641 at the age of seventy, and was buried in the chancel of his parish church, St. Helen's, Bishopsgate, on 21 July. His widow, Ursula, was buried there 11 Sept. 1655. His will was proved in P. C. C., Evelyn, 92. A stone monument mentioned in the register of St. Helen's has disappeared.

His son John, in his dedication of his father's 'Forraign Trade' (1664) to Thomas, earl of Southampton, lord high treasurer, described Mun as 'in his time famous among Merchants, and well known to most men of business, for his general Experience in Affairs, and notable Insight into Trade; neither was he less observed for his Integrity to his Prince, and Zeal to the Common-wealth.' 'England's Treasure by Forraign Trade' reached its 2nd edit. in 1669; the 3rd in 1698; the 4th in 1700, printed in one volume with Lewis Roberts's 'Merchant's Map of Commerce;' the 5th in 1713, at the time of the treaty of Utrecht; the 6th in 1755. The title of this book ('England's Treasure by Forraign Trade') became, in Adam Smith's words, 'a fundamental maxim in the political economy not of England only, but of all other commercial countries.' It gave Mun his claim to the title of founder of the mercantile system of political economy (Hallam; cf. article 'Primitive Political Economy of England' in *Edinburgh Review* for April 1847). Mun's writings are quoted in Roger Coke's 'Discourse of Trade,' 1670, p. 37, where he is called 'a man of excellent knowledge and experience in Trade;' and in the same author's 'Treatise wherein is demonstrated that the Church and State of England are in equal danger with the Trade of it,' 1671, pp. 72, 75; they are also cited in two anonymous treatises on trade, viz. England's Great Happiness, or a Dialogue beween Content and Complaint' (1677), and 'Britannia Languens' (1680), both of which were reprinted in the collection published by the Political Economy Club in 1856; as well as in Nicholas Barbon's 'Discourse of Trade,' 1690, Preface.

Mun had, besides his son John, two daughters: Anne (1613–1687), who married in 1639 Sir Robert Austen, bart., of Hall Place, Bexley, and high sheriff of Kent, on whose monument in Bexley Church the political economist is mentioned as 'Thomas Muns, Esq., Merchant' (Hasted, i. 161, and Thorpe, *Reg. Roffense*, p. 925) (their eldest son, Sir John Austen, was a commissioner of customs in 1697–9); and Mary (1618–1685), who married Edward Napper, merchant, of Allhallows, Lombard Street, London, of the ancient family of the Nappers or Napiers of Puncknoll, Dorset (Hutchins, *Dorset*, i. 560–4).

The son, John Mun (1615–1670), appears to have been admitted a member of the Mercers' Company in 1632; inherited Otteridge, in Bearsted, and in 1659 purchased Aldington Court, in the adjoining parish of Thurnham (Hasted, ii. 497); and was buried at Bearsted 30 Nov. 1670 (will, P. C. C., Duke, 146). He had by his wife Elizabeth (*d.* 1695) daughter of Walter Harlackenden of Woodchurch and Hollingborne, Kent (*Top. and Gen.*, i. 231–2, iii. 215–23), eight children. The eldest, Thomas Mun (*d.* 1692), inherited Snailham in Icklesham, Sussex (Horsfield, i. 473), was M.P. for Hastings in the last parliament of Charles II, held at Oxford in 1681, and again in the Convention parliament, 1689 (*ib.*, ii. App. pp. 60, 63; Oldfield, *Representative History*, v. 375, 380). As one of the barons of the Cinque ports he also represented Hastings at the coronations of James II, 1685, and of William and Mary, 1689 (*Sussex Arch. Coll.* xv. 193, 209). In May 1689 he, with the Hon. Sir Vere Fane, K.B. (afterwards fourth earl of Westmorland, of Mereworth Castle, Kent), and John Farthing, esq., petitioned the king for an improvement in the management of the excise (Redington, *Calendars of Treasury Papers*, 1556–7–1696, iii. 41, iv. 47, v. 69). Thomas Mun, M.P., was buried at Bearsted

15 Feb. 1691-2 (will, P. C. C., Fane, 58). He had eleven children, one of whom, Vere Mun, M.A. (1678-1736), vicar of Bodiam, Sussex, was doubtless named after the father's friend, Vere Fane (Horsfield, i. 524; will, P. C. C., Derby, 225).

[Anderson's History of Commerce, 1764 edit. ii. 3, 4, 7, 14, 41, 123-4; Postlethwayt's Dictionary of Trade and Commerce, 1766, art. 'Balance of Trade;' Adam Smith's Wealth of Nations, 1828 edit. vol. i. introd. disc. pp. xiv-xviii, xxiii, xxv, xxvii, and vol. ii. 242, 246; Macpherson's Annals of Commerce, 1805, ii. 297-300, 320, 367; Grant's Sketch of the History of the East India Company, 1813, pp. 19-20, 33, 45-7; Blanqui's Hist. de l'Économie Politique en Europe, 1837, ii. 17, 408; McCulloch's Dict. of Commerce, art. 'East India Company,' and Literature of Polit. Econ. 1845, pp. 38-9, 98-99; Hallam's Introduction to the Literature of Europe, 1847 edit. ii. 530, iii. 451-2; Edinb. Review, vol. lxxxv. April 1847, p. 426-52; Dict. de l'Écon. Polit. (Guillaumin), 1853, art. by J. Garnier, p. 258; Fox-Bourne's English Merchants, 1866, i. 297-8; Larousse's Dict. Universel du XIXme Siècle, xi. 686; W. Noel Sainsbury's Calendars of State Papers, Colonial Series (East Indies), 1513-1616, 1617-21, 1622-4, 1625-9, 1630-4; the Rev. F. Haslewood's Benenden, 1889, pp. 205, 209; Athenæum, 29 Nov. and 20 Dec. 1890, pp. 738, 853-4; Sir G. Birdwood's Report on the Old Records of the India Office, 1891, pp. 22, 213; Marshall's Principles of Economics, 1891, i. 52 *n.*; Cunningham's Growth of English Industry and Commerce in Modern Times, 1892, pp. 128, 212, 266.] A. L. H.

MUNBY, GILES (1813-1876), botanist, born at York in 1813, was the youngest son of Joseph Munby, solicitor and under-sheriff of the county, but lost both his parents when still very young. At school Munby evinced a taste for natural history, especially for botany and entomology. On leaving school he was apprenticed to a surgeon in York, named Brown, and was most assiduous in attending the poor during the cholera epidemic of 1832. Entering the medical school of the university of Edinburgh, he attended the botanical lectures and excursions held by Professor Graham, gaining the professor's gold medal for the best collection. Munby then 'walked the hospitals' in London and, in 1835, in Paris, where began a lifelong friendship with John Percy [q. v.], the metallurgist. Together they studied under Adrien de Jussieu and his assistants, Guillemin and Decaisne, and Munby passed the examinations for the degree of M.D. at Montpellier, though he never took up the diploma. They visited Dijon and, after returning to Edinburgh, started once more, in 1836, for the south of France. Notes on the botany and entomology of these trips, contributed to Loudon's and Charlesworth's 'Magazine of Natural History' (1836, ix. 113, and new ser. 1837, i. 192), were Munby's first publications. Soon after he took up his residence at St. Bertrand de Comminges, in the department of Haute-Garonne, acting as curator of the museum of a M. Boubée and giving lessons in botany; but in 1839 he accepted the offer of a free passage from Marseilles to Constantinople. Unfavourable winds landed him at Algiers, where he resolved to stay and investigate the flora. With occasional visits to England, he lived in Algiers from 1839 to 1844, collecting plants, cultivating oranges, shooting, and practising medicine among the Arabs and French soldiers. On his marriage he settled at La Senia, a small estate near Oran; but in 1859 his wife's health caused his removal to Montpellier, where she died in 1860. Munby then returned to England, settling first at Wood Green, and in 1867 at the Holt, near Farnham, Surrey. There he devoted himself to the cultivation of Algerian plants and bulbs, and there he died of inflammation of the lungs on 12 April 1876.

Munby married, first, in 1844, Jane Welsford, daughter of her majesty's consul at Oran, who died in February 1860, leaving two sons and three daughters; and, secondly, in 1862, Eliza M. A. Buckeridge, who survived him.

Munby was a skilful vegetable anatomist, as well as a most industrious collector and an acute discriminator of living plants. He distributed several centuries of 'Plantæ Algerienses exsiccatæ,' and at his death his herbarium was presented to Kew. Munby was an original member of the Botanical Society of Edinburgh, and in his later years he joined the Royal Horticultural Society, becoming a member of the scientific committee. His two principal works were the 'Flore de l'Algérie' and the 'Catalogus Plantarum in Algeriâ . . . nascentium.' The 'Flore de l'Algérie,' Paris, 1847, 8vo, contains eighteen hundred species arranged on the Linnæan system, with six plates from drawings by his sister. Two hundred of his species, belonging to thirty genera (ten of them being new to science), were unnoticed in Desfontaines's 'Flora Atlantica,' 1804. The 'Catalogus Plantarum in Algeriâ . . . nascentium,' Oran, 1859, 8vo, contained 2,600 species, of which 800 were new; and the second edition, London, 1866, 8vo, contained 364 additional. At the time of his death he was engaged upon a 'Guide du Botaniste en Algérie.'

There is an engraved portrait of Munby in

the 'Gardeners' Chronicle' (1876, ii. 260–2). The name *Munbya* has been given to two genera of plants, both now merged in others.

[Gardeners' Chronicle, 1876, ii. 260–2 (by Sir J. D. Hooker); Transactions of the Botanical Society of Edinburgh, xiii. 13.] G. S. B.

MUNCASTER, BARONS. [See PENNINGTON, SIR JOHN, first BARON, 1737–1813; PENNINGTON, SIR LOWTHER, second BARON, 1745–1818.]

MUNCASTER, RICHARD (1530?–1611), schoolmaster. [See MULCASTER.]

MUNCHENSI, WILLIAM DE (*d.* 1289), baronial leader, was son of Warine de Munchensi by his wife Dionysia. A Hubert de Munchensi occurs in the reign of Stephen; his son, Warine I, was by Agnes Fitz-John (*d.* 1224), father of Hubert, Ralph, and William. WARINE DE MUNCHENSI II (*d.* 1255) would appear to have been a younger son or nephew of the last named, who died about 1205. He had livery of the family lands in 1214. In 1223 he served in Wales, and in Poitou in 1243, when he distinguished himself by his valour in the fight at Saintes (MATT. PARIS, iv. 213). He had livery of the lands of his uncle Ralph in 1250, and died in July 1255. Matthew Paris describes him as one of the noblest and wisest of the barons of England, and a zealous defender of the peace and liberty of the realm. He left the, for that time, enormous fortune of two hundred thousand marks (*ib.* v. 504). He married, first, after 1219 Johanna, fifth daughter of William Marshal (*d.* 1219), and by her had a son, John, who predeceased him, and a daughter, Johanna, who married, 13 Aug. 1247, William de Valence [q. v.], the king's half-brother, and brought him her mother's large inheritance (*ib.* iv. 628–9; *Flores Historiarum*, ii. 339; *Chartulary of St. Mary's, Dublin*, ii. 144, 313); and secondly, Dionysia, daughter of Nicolas de Anesty, who was mother of William de Munchensi, and died in 1294, having founded Waterbeche Abbey for nuns of St. Clare in 1293.

William de Munchensi was a minor at his father's death, and was for a short time the ward of his brother-in-law, William de Valence, earl of Pembroke [q. v.] He had livery of his lands in 1256, and in 1258 was summoned to Chester for the Welsh war. Like many other young nobles who had been wards of the king's favourites, Munchensi joined the baronial party. In May 1263 he was present at the assembly of the barons in London, and was one of the barons who swore to abide by the decision of Louis IX in December. On 14 May 1264 he fought at Lewes in the division under Gilbert de Clare, earl of Gloucester. He was present in the assembly at London in June, and was one of the witnesses to the agreement for the reform of the government. Munchensi was summoned by the baronial party to the parliament held in January 1265. When the quarrel broke out between Simon de Montfort and Gilbert de Clare, he was one of the arbiters appointed to decide the dispute on 12 May. Munchensi was with the younger Simon de Montfort at Kenilworth, and was taken prisoner there by Edward on 2 Aug. He would seem to have again taken up arms as one of the disinherited in 1266, and his lands were put in the possession of William de Valence. Through the intervention of his mother, he made his submission on 13 Jan. 1267, but a little later he appears as one of the advisers of Gilbert de Clare in his occupation of London. Munchensi did not receive full pardon till 1279. He served in Wales in 1277, 1282, 1283, and 1287 (*Parl. Writs*, i. 194, 223, 246, 250), and again in 1289 under Edmund, earl of Cornwall, when he was killed at the siege of Dyryslwyan Castle by the fall of a wall which had been undermined. Munchensi is described as 'a valiant knight and wary in war' (BARTHOLOMEW COTTON, p. 168), and as 'a noble knight of great wealth in land and money' (*Ann. Mon.* iv. 310). He left by his wife Amicia an only daughter, Dionysia, who married in 1296 Hugh de Vere, son of Robert de Vere, earl of Oxford; William de Valence attempted, unsuccessfully, to have her declared illegitimate (*Rolls of Parliament*, i. 16–17). At her death without children in 1314, Munchensi's lands passed to Aymer de Valence, earl of Pembroke [q. v.], his sister's son. A younger branch of the Munchensi family, the heads of which during the thirteenth century were also called William, was settled at Edwardstone, Suffolk.

[Matthew Paris, Annales Monastici, Bartholomew Cotton (all in the Rolls Ser.); Rishanger de Bellis apud Lewes et Evesham (Camden Soc.); Dugdale's Baronage, i. 561–2; Nicolas's Historic Peerage, ed. Courthope, p. 342; Calendarium Genealogicum (the references are chiefly to the Munchensis of Edwardstone); Blomefield's History of Norfolk.] C. L. K.

MUNDAY, ANTHONY (1553–1633), poet and playwright, son of Christopher Munday, a London draper who died previous to 1576, was born in London in 1553. He claimed to be of a Staffordshire family. There were at least two contemporaries of the same names—one who was member for Penryn borough, and another, son of Henry Munday of Bidesden, who was father of John Mundy, mayor of Newbury in 1664 (*Genealogist*, 1882, vi. 65)—but to neither of these is there any evidence that the poet was related. He was, however, probably connected with William Mundy [q. v.] and John Mundy [q. v.], who were attached to the royal household. In October 1576 Munday was bound apprentice to John Allde the stationer for eight years. He was then twenty years old, and there is reason to think he had previously seen a good deal of the world, and, among other things, had been an actor. According to an unknown writer (perhaps Thomas Pound) in his 'True Reporte of the Death and Martyrdome of M. Campion, 1581,' Munday deceived his master Allde; but this charge was rebutted by Munday in his 'Breefe Aunswer' of 1582, where he inserted a certificate from John Allde to the effect that he 'dyd his duetie in all respects . . . without fraude, covin, or deceyte' during the term of his service. Nevertheless in little more than a year after the signature of his articles, probably in the spring of 1578, Munday left his master and betook himself to Rome. Although his motives are described by himself (in 'The English Romayne Lyfe,' the most entertaining of his works) as desire to see strange countries, and to learn their languages, it is more probable that, with the concurrence of Allde and one or two publisher allies, such as John Charlewood and White, he left England with the intention of making literary capital out of what he could learn to the detriment of the English catholics abroad. His enemies asserted that his object was to spy into the conduct of the English seminary at Rome, and then to betray it.

Travelling with one Thomas Nowell, Munday set sail for Boulogne, and reached Amiens on foot in a destitute condition, in consequence of having fallen into the hands of a band of marauding soldiers. At Amiens he and his companion met with an old English priest named Woodward, one of the pope's factors, who relieved their necessities, and recommended them to Dr. Allen at Rheims. They preferred to make straight for Paris, where the English ambassador gave them money to return to England. But they were persuaded by recruiting agents of the English seminaries to proceed to Rome, which they ultimately reached by way of Lyons, Milan, Bologna, Florence, and Sienna. At Rome Munday was entitled to eight days' entertainment at the English College, and he was received with more than ordinary civility by the rector, Dr. Morris, who had been a friend of his father. Munday subsequently described in 'The English Romayne Lyfe' the arrangements at the English College, the dissensions between the English and Welsh residents, the carnival at Rome, the martyrdom of Richard Atkins, and other matters calculated to excite the animosity of protestant readers. The early summer of 1578 can be with tolerable certainty assigned as the time of Munday's stay in Rome, since Captain Stukeley, whom he asseverates he saw there, perished at the battle of Alcazar on 4 Aug. 1578.

Shortly after his return home Munday 'presumed for a third time upon the clemency' of his readers with his first extant work, 'The Mirrour of Mutabilitie,' an imitation of the 'Mirrour for Magistrates,' licensed 10 Oct. 1579. The dedication to the Earl of Oxford contains some brief references to his travels. The 'Mirrour' is a work tending to edification, in which the seven deadly sins and many others are reproved by well-known personages who had suffered by committing them. A noticeable peculiarity is the employment along with rhyme of much blank-verse, printed in stanzas. The fact that the work came from Allde's press shows that a good understanding existed between the former apprentice and his master.

Munday seems about the same time to have returned to the stage as an extemporary player, and, according to the author of the 'True Reporte,' he was hissed off. Stung by this rebuff, he is stated to have written a ballad or a pamphlet against stage plays, but within the year, or at least not later than 1580, there is a strong presumption that he was again on the stage. In his 'View of Sundry Examples,' printed in that year, he subscribes an address to his readers 'servant to the right honourable the Earl of Oxenford,' the patron of a well-known theatrical company.

The popular mind was greatly occupied in 1581 by the fate of Campion and his associates, who had been captured through the treachery of George Ellyot, a co-religionist, in July. Munday thereupon turned from the stage to the more congenial work of exposing in five tracts the 'horrible and unnatural treasons' of the catholics; he narrated the circumstances of Campion's capture, and did all he could to discredit the jesuits. The second tract, purporting to be an authentic narrative of the capture of Campion, was resented by Ellyot, who retorted in 'A very true Reporte of the Apprehension . . . of Campion . . . Conteining also a Controulment of a most untrue former Booke set out by A. M.,' &c., 1581. Munday returned to the attack by bearing witness against the catholics, Bristow and Luke Kirbie, who were executed on 30 May 1582, and also against Campion, who challenged his credibility on the ground that while abroad he had feigned himself a catholic. He subsequently reported the execution of Campion in language borrowed by Holinshed and condemned by Hallam for 'a savageness and bigotry' unsurpassable by 'a scribe of the Inquisition.' The first part of this report, entitled 'A Discoverie of Edmund Campion and his Confederates,' gave a sort of official justification of the execution, and was read aloud on the scaffold when Campion suffered death. In 1582 Munday was employed by Richard Topcliffe, the leading officer engaged in the capture of priests, to guard and take bonds of recusants. Topcliffe described him to Puckering as a man 'who wants no sort of wit,' but an agent of Walsingham found it necessary on one occasion to reprove the misplaced zeal which led him to lay hands upon 40*l.*, the property of a widow, whose strong-box he had searched for Agnus Deis and hallowed grains (*Harl. MS.* 6998, f. 31; *State Papers*, Dom. 1590; undated papers, 138 A, cited in SIMPSON, *Edmund Campion*, pp. 312, 383). Nevertheless, his services were sufficiently satisfactory to secure his appointment as 'one of the messengers of her majestie's chamber' about 1584.

Political employment occupied, however, very little of Munday's life. A man of exceptional versatility, it was to literature that he chiefly devoted his career, and he tried his hand at every variety of literature that was in vogue in his day. From acting to play-writing was a natural transition. Between 1584 and 1602 he appears to have been concerned in eighteen plays, several of which were highly successful, although only four are extant. The lost pieces are: 'Fidele and Fortunio,' licensed to be printed on 12 Nov. 1584, but probably never acted; 'The Weakest goes to the Wall,' written in the same year for the Earl of Oxford's company, and erroneously ascribed to Webster; 'Mother Redcap,' a comedy, written with Michael Drayton, founded on a tract with a similar title published in 1594, and produced by Henslowe, who paid the writers 3*l.* apiece, in December 1597, the play becoming one of his stock pieces; 'Richard Cœur de Lion's Funeral,' written with Chettle, Drayton, and Wilson, produced several times in June 1598; 'Valentine and Orson,' with Hathway (1598); 'Chance Medley,' with Chettle, Drayton, and Wilson (1598); 'Owen Tudor,' with Drayton, Hathway, and Wilson (late in 1599), in earnest of which Henslowe paid the writers 4*l.*; 'The Fair Constance of Rome,' with Dekker, Drayton, and Hathway (produced in January 1600); 'The Rising of Cardinal Wolsey' (with Chettle, Drayton, and Smith), October 1601; 'Jephtha' (with Dekker), May 1602; 'Cæsar's Fall' (with Drayton, Middleton, Webster, and possibly Dekker), May 1602; 'The Two Harpes' (with Dekker, Drayton, Middleton, and Webster), May 1602; 'The Widow's Charm' (stated to be by 'Anthony the poet,' meaning in all probability the city poet or pageant writer, viz. Munday), July 1602; and 'The Set at Tennis,' December 1602 (see HENSLOWE, *Diary*, p. 228).

Of extant plays in which Munday was concerned 'John a Kent and John a Cumber' is dated December 1595, but was probably written earlier. Based upon an old ballad, it deals in humorous fashion with the grotesque and supernatural adventures of two west-country wizards. According to Mr. Fleay, it is identical with 'The Wiseman of West Chester,' produced by the Admiral's men at the Rose on 2 Dec. 1594 (see *Notes and Queries*, 1st ser. iv. 55, 83; art. KENT, JOHN). The best of Munday's extant plays, 'The Downfall of Robert Earl of Huntingdon, afterwards called Robin Hood of merrie Sherwodde,' was originally produced in February 1598–9, and reproduced, with ten shillings' worth of alterations, by Chettle for performance at court on 18 Nov. 1599. It was shortly followed by a second part, entitled 'The Death of Robert Earle of Huntingdon,' in which Munday and Chettle regularly collaborated. The British Museum possesses a black-letter quarto of the second part, dated 1601. Both parts are in the Bodleian, and are reprinted in Dodsley's 'Old Plays,' ed. Hazlitt, viii. 95–327.

Late in 1598 it seems that Munday took part in a foreign tour undertaken by Pembroke's men, who had been ousted from the Curtain theatre. According to Marston's 'Histrio-mastix' (1598–9), the exiled players were accompanied by Munday, there described as 'a pageanter,' who had been a ballad-writer, 'ought to be employed in matters of state, was great in plotting new plays that are old ones, and uses no luxury or blandishment, but plenty of old England's mother words.' In the same play Ben Jonson is introduced as Chrysoganus, 'a translating scholar,' who is refused employment by the strollers in favour of 'Posthaste Monday.' There seems no doubt that Jonson and Munday were bitter rivals, and that the former bore a very strong grudge against Munday. This feeling found expression in Jonson's earliest play, 'The Case is Altered,' 1599, in which Munday was ridiculed as Antonio Balladino, and sarcastic reference was made to his being 'in print for the best plotter,' a title which Meres had applied to him in the 'Palladis Tamia,' 1598. Before the end of 1599 Munday was back in England, and in that year he wrote, in conjunction with Drayton, Hathway, and Wilson, the 'True and Honourable History of the Life of Sir John Oldcastle, the good Lord Cobham,' in two parts, the first of which alone is extant. It was published in 1600, with the name of William Shakespeare upon the title-page; but this was promptly withdrawn. Henslowe paid 10*l.* for the play, which was so successful on the first performance that an additional two shillings and sixpence was given to each of the playwrights. Falstaff and Poins are mentioned by name, and the play seems to have been written with some view to rebutting the slur cast upon the lollard hero in Shakespeare's 'Henry IV.' It was produced in the autumn of 1599.

Munday was no less energetic as a ballad-writer. Jonson sneered at him as 'Balladino.' An ironical admonition to the ballad-singers of London, prefixed to Chettle's 'Kind-Harte's Dream,' 1592, obviously implies that Munday had complained of unprofessional ballad-mongers. Thomas Nash, in a letter to Sir Robert Cotton, written about 1597, imputes to him a popular 'ballad of Untruss,' and Kemp seems to indicate him in the 'Request to the Impudent Generation of Ballad Makers' as 'Elderton's immediate heyre' [see ELDERTON, WILLIAM]. 'Mundaie's Dreame,' a ballad, was licensed to John Allde 2 Aug. 1578 (see COLLIER, *Broadside Ballads*, 1868, p. viii). A ballad (assigned to Munday) of the 'Encouragement of an English Soldier to his Mates' was licensed to J. Charlwood 8 March 1580, and another, 'Against Plays,' 10 Nov. 1580; but neither of these is now known. In his 'Banquet of Dainty Conceits' Munday similarly tried his hand at song-writing, fitting words to well-known music by various composers (including the Mundys, his connections); but what was probably his best essay as a lyrist, the 'Sweete Sobbes and Amorous Complaintes of Sheppardes and Nymphs in a Fancye,' is not extant. It must have been this work which elicited from Webbe, in his 'Discourse of English Poetrie,' 1586, the description of Munday as 'an earnest traveller in this art,' whose poetry was to be rarely esteemed, 'especially upon nymphs and shepherds.' If Munday's lyrics really merited Webbe's praise—he credits them with an 'exquisite vaine'—it is hardly ridiculous, as has been maintained, to assign to him 'Beauty sat Bathing in a Springe,' one of two admirable lyrics subscribed by 'Shepherd Tonie' in 'England's Helicon.' The only other conjecture as to the identity of Shepherd Tonie is that he was Anthony Copley, which has far less to recommend it (see, however, *England's Helicon*, ed. Mr. A. H. Bullen, p. xvii).

Munday's lack of originality and 'plain' style, satirised by Jonson (*The Case is Altered*, Gifford, vi. 325), characterised all his dramatic work, and he wisely diversified it by excursions into a humbler branch of art—the production of the annual city pageants. The pageant for 1591, 'Descensus Astrææ,' was written by Peele. Those from 1592 to 1604 are missing, but it has been conjectured with probability that most, if not all, are by Munday (FAIRHOLT, *History of Lord Mayor's Pageants*, Percy Soc., p. 32). He certainly furnished those for 1605, 1609, 1611, 1614, 1615, 1616, 1618, and 1623, and he seems to have long been the authorised keeper of the properties of the show—dragons, giants, and the like—as his rival, Middleton, who introduced into the pageant of 1613 a virulent attack upon Munday, was compelled to apply to him to furnish 'apparel and porters' (*The Triumphs of Truth*, ad fin.) In some of these pageants Munday signs himself citizen and draper. He may have inherited the freedom of the Drapers' Company from his father. During the latter part of his life he is said to have followed the trade himself, and to have resided in Cripplegate (see also his epitaph).

But the labours which mainly commended Munday to his own generation were doubtless his voluminous translations of popular romances, the first of which, 'Palladino of England,' appeared in 1588. The two first books of 'Amadis de Gaule' were Englished by him between 1589 and 1595, and other chivalric romances of less value were transferred by him from the Spanish text. These translations lack style and fidelity, but they satisfied the half-educated public to whom they appealed (DRAKE, *Shakespeare and his Time*, i. 547).

Among Munday's literary friends was Stow, who refers to him in the 'Annales' as his authority for several facts in connection with Campion and other matters, and Munday appears to have been in a sense Stow's literary executor. Thirteen years after Stow's death, in 1605, Munday accordingly produced the 'Survay of London . . . continued, corrected, and much enlarged with many rare and worthie Notes, both of venerable Antiquity and later Memorie; such as were never published before the present year 1618,' London, 4to; dedicated to the Right Hon. George Bolles, lord mayor, and to all the knights and aldermen. This edition contains some four hundred pages of original matter; but in value it is greatly surpassed by the edition of 1633, 'completely finished by the study and labour of A. M. H[umphry] D[yson]' and others, and published four months after Munday's death (for a valuable digest of the additions made by Munday and his coadjutors, see the note by Bolton Corney in Collier's edition of *John a Kent and John a Cumber*, p. lxxi).

Munday died in 1633, and was buried on 10 Aug. in that year in the church of St. Stephen, Coleman Street. His monument, with a long inscription, was destroyed in 1666, but the inscription was printed in full in the 1633 edition of Stow's 'Survay' (p. 869). The names of Munday's children, together with the dates of their christenings, are given in the register of St. Giles, Cripplegate: Elizabeth, 28 June 1584; Roase, 17 Oct. 1585 (buried 19 Jan. 1586); Priscilla, 9 Jan. 1587; Richard, 27 Jan. 1588, perhaps Richard Munday the painter-stainer, whose heraldic labours are recorded in the Catalogue of the Harleian MSS. (1529–77); Anne, 5 Sept. 1589.

Munday was in his versatility an epitome of his age. Ready to turn his hand to any occupation, he was as a man of letters little more than a compiler, destitute of originality or style; yet, apart from such names as Shakespeare and Marlowe, there are few Elizabethan writers who occupied a greater share of public attention, or contributed more largely to popular information and amusement.

Apart from his plays which have already been enumerated, Munday's writings may be classified under three headings: (I) Translations of Romances; (II) City Pageants; (III) Miscellaneous Writings. To most of his works Munday affixes his name in full, though in some cases he uses the pseudonym Lazarus Piot, or L. P. A great number bear his motto, 'Honos alit artes;' a few another motto, 'Patere aut abstine.'

I. Romances: 1. 'The famous, pleasant, and variable Historie of Palladino of England. Discoursing of honourable Adventures of Knightly Deedes, of Armes and Chivalrie; interlaced likewise with the Love of sundrie noble Personages, &c. Translated out of French by A. M. London: printed by Edward Allde for John Perin,' 1588, 4to (see *Bridgewater Cat.* 4to, 1837, p. 203; now in Mr. Christy Miller's library at Britwell). 2. 'Palmerin d'Oliva.' Translated by A. M. John Charlwood, 1588, 4to (*ib.* p. 204; 1637, Brit. Mus.). 3. 'The famous History of Palmendos, Son to the most renowned Palmerin d'Oliva, Emperour of Constantinople, and the Heroic Queen of Tharsus,' Charlwood, 1589, 4to; 1653, 4to Brit. Mus. 4. 'Gerileon of England. The second part of his most excellent, delectable, morall and sweet contrived Historie. . . . Written in French by Estrienne de Maisonneufue, Bordelois, and translated into English by A. M.,' 1592, fol. (Britwell). 5. 'Amadis de Gaule, the first Book translated by Anthony Munday,' 1595, 4to. A copy of this work was entered at Stationers' Hall as early as January 1588–9, but no perfect copy of this date is known. The copies at the British Museum and at Britwell both want title-pages. Parts of this famous romance had been translated before, but Munday was the first to present the first book of it to English readers. 6. 'The Second Booke of Amadis de Gaule, containing the Description, Wonders, and Conquest of the Forme-Island. The Triumphs and Troubles of Amadis, his manifold Victories obtained, and sundry Services done for King Lisuart, &c. . . . Englished by L[azarus] P[iot], London, for C. Burbie,' 1595, 4to (see *Notes and Queries*, *I*, iv. 85). The first and second books were also reissued with the addition of the third and fourth in 1619, fol. 7. 'The second part of the honourable Historie of Palmerin d'Oliva . . . translated by A. M.,' 1597, 4to (Britwell). 8. 'Palmerin of England,' translated from the French, 1602. This translation, which is described by Southey as the 'Grub Street Patriarch's worst piece of work,' was entered 13 Feb. 1581, but no perfect copy earlier than 1602 is known. It contains verses by Dekker, Webster, and others, and seems to have been the work of Munday in part only. There are five editions in the Museum dated 1602, 1609, 1616, 1639, and 1664 respectively. A copy at Britwell assigned to 1596 is very imperfect. 9. 'The famous and renowned Historie of Primaleon of Greece, Sonne to the great and mighty Prince Palmerin d'Oliva, Emperor of Constantinople . . . Translated out of French and Italian into English by A. M.,' London, 1619, 8vo (Brit. Mus.) This is the first edition extant, but the work was commenced in 1589, and a complete version published in 1595.

II. Pageants: 1. 'The Triumphs of re-united Britania, performed at the Cost and Charges of the Right Worshipful Company of the Merchant Taylors, in honor of Sir Leonard Holliday,' 29 Oct. 1605, London, 4to.; reprinted in Nichols's 'Progresses of James I,' i. 564–76. 2. 'Camp-bell, or the Ironmongers Faire Field,' at the installation of Sir Thomas Campbell, 29 Oct. 1609,

4to. 3. 'Chryso-Thriambos; the Triumphs of Golde; at the Inauguration of Sir James Pemberton in the Dignity of Lord Maior of London,' 29 Oct. 1611. 4. 'Himatia-Poleos: Triumphs of Old Drapery, or the Rich Cloathing of England at the Installation of Thomas Hayes,' 1614. 5. 'Metropolis Coronata; the Triumphs of Ancient Drapery, or Rich Cloathing of England, in a second Yeere's Performance; in honour of the Advancement of Sir John Jolles . . . 30 Oct. 1615; reprinted in Nichols's 'Progresses,' iii. 107–18. 6. 'Chrysanaleia, the Golden Fishing; or the Honour of Fishmongers applauding the Advancement of Mr. John Leman to the Dignitie of Lord Maior . . . on 29 Oct. 1616,' London, 1616, 4to. Copies are in the Bodleian and Longleat Libraries. This was reproduced in a sumptuous folio, with coloured plates by Henry Shaw, by John Gough Nichols in 1844 (*ib.* iii. 195–207; cf. Nichols, *Lord Mayor's Pageants*, 1831, p. 102). 7. 'Sidero-Thriambos, or Steele and Iron Triumphing. Applauding the Advancement of Sir Sebastian Harvey . . . 29 Oct. 1618' (Hazlitt). 8. 'The Triumphs of the Golden Fleece . . . for the Enstaulment of Mr. Martin Lumley in the Maioraltie of London, 29 Oct. 1623.' The British Museum possesses all these with the exception of No. 3, which is in the Duke of Devonshire's collection.

III. Miscellaneous: 1. 'The Defence of Povertie against the Desire of Worldly Riches, dialogue-wise; collected by Anthonie Mundaye.' Licensed to John Charlwood, 18 Nov. 1577. No copy known. 2. 'The History of Galien of France.' Printed before 1579, and dedicated to the Earl of Oxford. No copy known. 3. 'The Mirrour of Mutabilite, or Principal Part of the Mirrour for Magistrates. Describing the fall of diuers famous Princes and other memorable Personages. Selected out of the Sacred Scripture by Antony Munday, and dedicated to the Right Honourable the Earle of Oxenford. Imprinted at London by John Allde, and are to be solde by Richard Ballard, at Saint Magnus Corner,' 1579, 4to, b.l. Prefixed are verses by, among others, William Hall 'in commendation of his kinsman, Antony Munday.' One of the few copies known was bequeathed to the British Museum by Tyrwhitt in 1788. Another is at Britwell. 4. 'The Paine of Pleasure. Profitable to be perused of the Wise, and necessary to be followed by the Wanton. For Henrie Car,' 1580, 4to, b.l.; in verse, and dedicated to Lady Douglas Sheffield (Pepysian Library). This work bears Munday's motto, but his authorship has been questioned. 5. 'Zelavto. The Fountaine of Fame. Erected in an Orcharde of Amorous Adventures. Containing a Delicate Disputation, gallantly discoursed betweene two noble Gentlemen of Italye. Given for a friendly Entertainment to Euphues, at his late arrival in England. By A. M., Seruant to the Right Honuorable the Earle of Oxenforde,' 1580, 4to; partly in verse (Bodleian). 6. 'A View of Sundry Examples. Reporting many straunge Murthers, sundry Persons Perjured, Signes and Tokens of God's Anger towards us. What straunge and monstrous Children have of late beene borne: And all memorable Murthers since the Murther of Maister Saunders by George Browne [the subject of 'A Warning to Fair Women,' 1599], to this present and bloody Murther of Abell Bourne, Hosyer, who dwelled in Newgate Market, 1580. Also a short Discourse of the Late Earthquake, the sixt of Aprill for William Wright,' London, 4to, b.l. (Lambeth); dedicated to William Waters and George Baker, gentlemen attendant upon the Earl of Oxford (reprinted together with Collier's 'John a Kent and John a Cumber'). 7. 'An Aduertisement and Defence for Trueth against her Backbiter, and specially against the whispring Fauourers and Colourers of Campians, and the rest of his Confederats Treasons, 1581;' no place or date, 4to (Lambeth, Britwell, and Huth Libraries; the work is believed to have been suppressed by Archbishop Grindal). 8. 'A Breefe Discourse of the taking of Edm. Campion and divers other Papists in Barkeshire,' 1581, 8vo (Lambeth). 9. 'A Covrtly Controuersie betweene Loue and Learning. Pleasauntlie passed in Disputation betweene a Ladie and a Gentleman of Scienna. Wherein is no Offence offered to the Vertuous nor any ill Motion to delight the Vicious,' 1581, sm. 8vo, b.l.; in prose (Brit. Mus.) 10. 'A Breefe and True Reporte of the Execution of Certaine Traytours at Tiborne, the xxviii and xxx. Dayes of May, 1582. Gathered by A. M., who was there Present,' 1582, 4to (British Museum, reprinted by Collier). 11. 'A Discoverie of Edmund Campion and his Confederates, their most Horrible and Traiterous Practises against her Majesties most royall Person and the Realme. Wherein may be seene how thorowe the whole Course of their Araignement; they were notably convicted in every Cause. Whereto is added the Execution of Edmund Campion, Raphe Sherwin, and Alexander Brian, executed at Tiborne the 1 of December. Published by A. M., sometime the Popes Scholler, allowed in the Seminarie at Roome amongst them, &c., January 1582, 8vo (St. John's College, Cambridge). 12. 'A Breefe Aunswer made unto two seditious Pamphlets, the one printed in

French, and the other in English. Contayning a Defence of Edmund Campion and his Complices, &c.,' 1582, b.l. 4to (Brit. Mus., Lambeth, and Britwell). 13. 'The English Romayne Lyfe; Discovering the Lives of the Englishmen at Roome, the Orders of the English Seminarie, the Dissention betweene the Englishmen and the Welshmen, the banishing of the Englishmen of out Roome, the Popes sending for them againe: a Reporte of many of the paltrie Reliques in Roome, their Vautes under the Grounde, their holy Pilgrimages, &c. Printed by John Charlewood for Nicholas Ling, at the Signe of the Maremaide,' 1582, 4to, b.l.; another edition, 1590, 4to (reprinted in 'Harleian Miscellany,' vol. vii.) 14. 'The sweete Sobbes and amorous Complaints of Sheppardes and Nymphes, in a Fancye composed by An. Munday,' 1583. No copy known. 15. 'A Watch-woord to Englande to beware of Traytours and tretcherous Practices which haue beene the ouerthrowe of many famous Kingdoms and common weales,' 1584, b.l. 4to. Dedicated to the queen, and containing also an introductory epistle to Thomas Pullison, lord-mayor elect (British Museum, Huth Library, and elsewhere). 16. 'Fidele and Fortunio, the Deceipts in Loue discoursed in a Comedie of two Italyan Gentlemen,' translated into English, 1584. It is dedicated to John Heardson, and is in rhyme. An imperfect copy is in the British Museum; no title-page appears to be extant. One of the characters, Captain Crackstone, was alluded to in Nash's 'Have with you to Saffron Walden' (1596), but the play appears never to have been acted. 17. 'Ant. Monday, his godly Exercise for Christian Families, containing an order of Praiers for Morning and Evening, with a little Cathechism betweene the Man and his Wife,' 1586, 8vo. No copy known. 18. 'A Banqvet of Daintie Conceyts. Furnyshed with verie delicate and choyse Inuentions to delight their Mindes, who take Pleasure in Musique, and there-withall to sing sweete Ditties, either to the Lute, Bandora, Virginalles, or anie other Instrument.... Written by A. M., Seruant to the Queenes most Excellent Maiestie,' 1588, b.l. 4to. In verse, with several large woodcuts (Huth Library). It is reprinted in the 'Harleian Miscellany' (vol. ix.) A sequel or 'second service of this Banquet' is announced at the end of the volume, but is not known to have appeared. 19. 'The Masque of the League and the Spanyard discovered. Wherein (1) The League is painted forth in all her Collours. (2) Is showen that it is not Lawful for a Subiect to Arme Himself against his King for what Pretence so euer it be. (3) That but few Noblemen take part with the Enemy: An Aduertisement to them cōcerning their Dutie. To my Lord the Cardinal of Burbon, from the French,' 1592, 4to. This political pamphlet reappeared in 1605, under the title 'Falsehood in Friendship, or Unions Vizard: or Wolves in Lambskins' (Huth Library). 20. 'The Defence of Contraries. Paradoxes against common Opinion . . . to exercise yong Wittes in difficult Matters,' 1593, 4to. 21. 'The Orator, handling a hundred several Discourses, by Lazarus Piot,' 1596. This is substantially an expansion of the preceding, and, like it, is based, with additions, upon 'Certen Tragicall Cases conteyninge LV Histories written in French by Alexander Vandenbush, alias Sylven, translated into English by E. A., and licensed to E. Aggas and J. Wolf 20 Aug. 1590.' This book contains the declamation of the Jew who would have his pound of flesh. 22. 'The Strangest Adventure that ever happened, either in the Ages passed or present. Containing a Discourse concerning the Successe of the King of Portugall, Dom Sebastian, from the time of his Voyage into Affricke, when he was lost in the Battell against the Infidels in the Yeare 1578, unto the sixt of January, this present 1601;' 1601, 4to. A translation from the Spanish of José Teixeira. A similar work had been licensed to J. Wolf in 1598 (British Museum, Bodleian, and Huth Libraries). 23. 'A true and admirable Historie of a Mayden of Confolens in the Prouince of Potiers, that for the space of three Yeares and more hath lived and yet doth without receiuing either Meat or Drinke,' London, 1604, 8vo, translated from the French of Nicolas Caeffeteau, bishop of Marseilles, with verses by Thomas Dekker (Britwell). 24. 'A Briefe Chronicle of the Successe of the Times from the Creation of the Worlde to this Instant,' 1611, 8vo.

Munday also translated, from the French, Thelius's 'Archaioplutus, or the Riches of Elder Ages. Prouing by manie good and learned Authors, that the Auncient Emperors and Kings, were more rich and magnificent than such as reign in these daies,' London, 1592, 4to, and, from the Low Dutch, Gabelhoner's 'Boock of Physicke,' Dort, fol. 1599. He contributed verses to 'Newes from the North,' by F. Thynne, 1579; to Hakluyt's 'Voyages,' 1589; to the 'Gorgious Gallery of Gallant Inventions,' 1578, and to Bodenham's 'Belvidere,' 1600.

[Though neither very accurate nor complete, the best basis for a biography of Munday is still afforded by J. Payne Collier's introduction to his edition of John a Kent and John a Cumber, printed for the Shakspeare Society in 1851; but this must be supplemented throughout by Joseph Hunter's Collectanea on Munday in his Chorus Vatum (Add. MS. 24488, f. 423), by Mr. Fleay's Chronicle of the English Drama 1559–1642 (ii. 110), Hazlitt's Bibliographical Collections, the Stationers' Registers in Mr. Arber's Transcripts, and, above all, by Munday's own works in the British Museum, especially The English Romayne Lyfe. Other authorities are: Ritson's Bibliographia Poetica, p. 282; Warton's English Poetry, ed. Hazlitt, iv. 427, 429; Webbe's Discourse on English Poetry, 1586; Meres's Palladis Tamia, 1598; Kempe's Nine Daies Wonder (Camden Soc.), p. 21; Baker's Biographia Dramatica, i. 504; Nichols's Progresses of James I; Corser's Collectanea Anglo-Poetica, pt. ix. vol. v. pp. 31–9; Fleay's History of the Stage and Biographical Chronicle of the English Drama; Cohn's Shakespeare in Germany, 1865, lxvii; Dunlop's Hist. of Prose Fiction, ed. Wilson, i. 379, 384, 393; Chettle's Kind-Harte's Dream (Percy Soc. 1841), p. 13; Cunningham's Extracts from Accounts of the Revels at Court (Shakspeare Soc.) passim; Anthony Copley's Wits, Fits, and Fancies, 1614, p. 134; Lowndes's Bibl. Man. (Bohn) ii. 1309; Dibdin's Library Companion, p. 709; Gifford's Jonson, 1816, vi. 325; Huth's Ancient Ballads and Broadsides, 1867, p. 370; Huth Library Catalogue; Henslowe's Diary (Shakspeare Soc.), pp. 106, 118, 158, 163, 171, 235; Collier's Memoirs of Actors (Shakspeare Soc.), p. 111; Drake's Shakespeare and his Time, i. 547, 693; Ward's English Dramatic Literature, i. 234–5, ii. 237; Simpson's Life of Campion, pp. 311–12; J. Gough Nichols's Lord Mayor's Pageants, p. 102; Fairholt's History of Lord Mayor's Pageants (Percy Soc.), p. 38; Brayley's Londiniana, 1829, iv. 92–6; Ames's Typographical Antiquities, ed. Herbert, pp. 897, 1006, 1103, 1198, 1223, 1337, 1345; Brydges's Censura Literaria and Restituta, passim; Maitland's Early English Books in Lambeth Library, p. 78; notes kindly supplied by R. E. Graves, esq.; Notes and Queries, I, iv. 55, 83, 120; II, iii. 261, xii. 203, 450; III, i. 202, iii. 65, 136, 178.]

T. S.

MUNDAY, HENRY (1623–1682), schoolmaster and physician, was the son of Henry Munday of Henley-on-Thames, and was baptised there on 21 Sept. 1623 (par. reg.) He matriculated at Corpus Christi College, Oxford, on 20 May 1642, and afterwards became postmaster or portionist of Merton College. He graduated B.A. on 2 April 1647. After enjoying, according to Wood, 'some petit employment' during the civil wars and the Commonwealth, Munday was elected head-master of the free grammar school in his native town in 1656. To his work as a teacher he added the practice of medicine, and the school suffered in consequence. His death saved him from the disgrace of dismissal. He died from a fall from his horse as he was returning home from a visit to John, third baron Lovelace [q. v.], at Hurley, on 28 June 1682, and was buried in the north chancel of Henley Church. His estate was administered for 'Alicia and Marie Mundy, minors.'

He published: 'Βιοχρηστολογία seu Commentarii de Aere Vitali, de Esculentis, de Potulentis, cum Corollario de Parergis in Victu,' Oxford, 1680, 1685; London, 1681; Frankfort, 1685; Leipzig, 1685; Leyden, 1715.

[Wood's Athenæ (Bliss), vol. iv. col. 49; Wood's Fasti (Bliss), vol. ii. col. 101; Foster's Alumni Oxon. 1500–1714; P.C.C. Administration, July 1682; Henley parish register per the Rev. J. T. Maule.]

B. P.

MUNDEFORD, OSBERT or OSBERN (*d.* 1460), treasurer of Normandy, was son of Osbert Mundeford (*d.* 1456), by Margaret Barrett. The family, whose name is sometimes spelt Mountford or Montfort, had been long seated at Hockwold in Norfolk, where they held Mundeford's Manor; they had been honourably distinguished in the French wars. Osbert went abroad probably early in Henry VI's reign, and received various offices of importance, such as bailly-general of Maine and marshal of Calais. He also served as English representative on several occasions in the conferences which were held, notably in 1447, with reference to the occupation of Le Mans. In the re-conquest of Normandy, Mundeford occupied Pont Audemer, and was taken prisoner when it fell in 1449; he was ransomed for ten thousand crowns. He afterwards wrote an account of the siege, which has been printed in the 'Chronique de Mathieu d'Escouchy,' ed. De Beaucourt, iii. 354.

Mundeford was appointed treasurer of Normandy in 1448 in succession to one Stanlawe. After the expulsion of the English he seems to have lived in Calais and about 1459 sent thence a letter in French to his relative John Paston, which has been preserved. He seems to have been a strong Lancastrian, and in June 1460 he gathered together some five hundred men in the town of Sandwich 'to fette and conduc the Duk of Somerset from Guynes in to England,' but Warwick's men came and took the town, and carrying off Mundeford to Calais beheaded him and two of his followers at the Rise Bank.

Mundeford married Elizabeth, daughter of John Berney, and a relative of the Pastons, and left a daughter, Mary, who married Sir William Tindale, K.B., and carried the estates of the family into other hands.

[De Beaucourt's Histoire de Charles VII, iv. 295, &c., v. 6, &c., 420, 441; Chronique de Mathieu d'Escouchy, ed. De Beaucourt (Soc. de l'Hist. de France), passim; De Reductione Normanniæ (Rolls Ser.), 64 *n.* &c.; Wars of the English in France, ed. Stevenson (Rolls Ser.), passim; Purton Cooper's App. to Report on Rymer's Fœdera, pp. 540–2; Paston Letters, i. 117, 439, &c.; Blomefield's Norfolk, ii. 181, &c.; Norfolk Archæology, vol. v.; Three Fifteenth-Cent. Chronicles (Camd. Soc.), p. 73; An English Chron. (Camd. Soc.), p. 85.] W. A. J. A.

MUNDEN, Sir JOHN (*d.* 1719), rear-admiral, younger brother of Sir Richard Munden [q. v.], was with him in the Mediterranean, as a lieutenant of the St. David, from 1677 to 1680. He afterwards served in the Constant Warwick, the Mary Rose, and the Charles galley; and on 23 July 1688 was promoted to be commander of the Half Moon fireship. On 14 Dec. 1688 he was promoted by Lord Dartmouth to the Edgar, from which he took post. At the battle of Barfleur, 19 May 1692, he commanded the Lennox, in the van of the red squadron, under the immediate orders of Sir Ralph Delavall. In 1693 he commanded the St. Michael, in 1695 the Monmouth, in 1696 the Albemarle, in 1697 the London. In May 1699 he was appointed to the Ranelagh, but in July was moved into the Winchester, and sent in command of a small squadron to the Mediterranean, where he negotiated a treaty with the dey of Algiers for the regulation of ships' passes, and obtained the release of the English slaves (Playfair, *Scourge of Christendom*, p. 168). He returned to England in November 1700. On 14 April 1701 he was promoted to the rank of rear-admiral, and on 30 June was appointed commander of the squadron to escort the king to Holland. On the following day he was knighted by the king on board the yacht William and Mary, 'under the standard of England' (Le Neve, *Pedigrees of the Knights*, p. 477).

On 28 Jan. 1701–2, being then rear-admiral of the red, he was ordered to wear the union flag at the mizen, as commander of a strong squadron fitting out to intercept a French squadron expected to sail from Rochelle to Corunna, and from Corunna to the West Indies, with the new Spanish viceroy of Mexico. Munden sailed from St. Helen's on 10 May 1702, and coming off Corunna, on intelligence that the French ships were daily expected there, he cruised off Cape Prior, in hopes of intercepting them. On the morning of the 28th they were seen inshore, having slipped past him, to the eastward, during the night; and before he could come up with them they reached the harbour. Unable to follow them in, owing to the heavy batteries on shore, the narrowness of the entrance, and the impossibility of going in and out with the same wind, he cruised in the Soundings for the protection of trade till 20 June, when want of provisions compelled him to return to Portsmouth. On 13 July he was tried by court-martial at Spithead on a charge of negligence, but he was fully acquitted (*Minutes of the Court-martial*). Munden accordingly rehoisted his flag 21 July; but the government, yielding apparently to popular clamour, in the queen's name, by a singular and harsh exercise of the prerogative, ordered him to be 'discharged from his post and command in the royal navy.' He lived afterwards in retirement, at Chelsea, and died there on 13 March 1718–19.

[Charnock's Biog. Nav. ii. 179, and the references there given; commission and warrant books, &c., in the Public Record Office. Copies of the documents relating to his conduct in 1702 and of the minutes of the court-martial are in Home Office Records (Admiralty), vol. ii.] J. K. L.

MUNDEN, JOSEPH SHEPHERD (1758–1832), actor, the son of a poulterer in Brook's Market, Leather Lane, Holborn, was born early in 1758, and was at the age of twelve in an apothecary's shop. Writing a good hand he was subsequently apprenticed to Mr. Druce, a law stationer in Chancery Lane. Prompted by his admiration for Garrick, he was in the habit of running away to join strolling companies, and was more than once brought home by his mother. In Liverpool he was engaged for a while at 10*s.* 6*d.* a week in the office of the town clerk, augmenting his income by appearing on the stage as a supernumerary. After playing with strollers at Rochdale, Chester, &c., and having the customary experience of hardship, he was engaged to play old men at Leatherhead. Thence he proceeded to Wallingford, Windsor, and Colnbrook, returned to London, took part in private performances at the Haymarket, and began to make his mark at Canterbury under Hurst, where in 1780 he was the original Faddle in Mrs. Burgess's comedy, 'The Oaks, or the Beauties of Canterbury.' In the company of Austin and Whitlock in Chester he held a recognised position, and he played at Brighton, Whitehaven, Newcastle, Lancaster, Preston, and Manchester. Money was then advanced to enable him to purchase the share of Austin in the management of the Chester, Newcastle, Lancaster, Preston, Warrington, and Sheffield theatres. Here he played the leading comic business, rising in reputation and fortune. A *liaison* with an actress named Mary Jones, who deserted him after having by him four children, subsequently adopted by Mrs. Munden, brought him into temporary disfavour, which was forgotten when he married, 20 Oct. 1789, at the parish church of St. Oswald, Chester, Miss Frances Butler, a lady five years his senior with some claims to social position. This lady had made her début at Lewes, 28 July 1785, as Louisa Dudley in the 'West Indian,' had joined the Chester company, and on her marriage retired from the stage. After the death in 1790 of John Edwin [q. v.], Munden was engaged at 8*l.* a week for Covent Garden. Having disposed to Stephen Kemble [q. v.] of his share in the country theatres, he came to London with his wife, living first in Portugal Street, Clare Market, and then in Catherine Street, Strand. On 2 Dec. 1790, as Sir Francis Gripe in the 'Busy Body' and Jemmy Jumps in the 'Farmer,' the latter a part created by Edwin two or three years earlier, he made his first appearance in London, and obtained a highly favourable reception.

At Covent Garden, with occasional summer appearances at the Haymarket, and frequent excursions into the country, he remained until 1811, rising gradually to the position of the most celebrated comedian of his day. In his first season he played Don Lewis in 'Love makes a Man,' Darby in the 'Poor Soldier,' Quidnunc in the 'Upholsterer,' Lazarillo in 'Two Strings to your Bow,' Lovel in 'High Life below Stairs,' Cassander in 'Alexander the Little,' Pedrillo in the 'Castle of Andalusia,' Daphne in 'Midas Reversed,' Tipple in the 'Flitch of Bacon,' and Camillo in the 'Double Falsehood.' On 4 Feb. 1791 he was the original Sir Samuel Sheepy in Holcroft's 'School for Arrogance,' an adaptation of 'Le Glorieux' of Destouches. On 14 March he was the first Frank in O'Keeffe's 'Modern Antiques,' and 16 April the earliest Ephraim Smooth in O'Keeffe's 'Wild Oats.' He presented from the first a remarkable variety of characters, and the removal of Quick and Wilson further extended his repertory. Putting on one side merely trivial parts, a list of between two and three hundred characters stands opposite his name. These include the Gentleman Usher in 'King Lear,' the Second Witch in 'Macbeth,' the First Carrier and Justice Shallow in 'King Henry IV,' Lafeu, the Tailor and Grumio in 'Katherine and Petruchio,' Autolycus, Polonius, Dromio of Syracuse, the Town Clerk and Dogberry in 'Much Ado about Nothing,' Launce, Launcelot Gobbo, Menenius in 'Coriolanus,' Malvolio and Stephano in the 'Tempest,' Sir Anthony Absolute, Hardcastle, Don Jerome in the 'Duenna,' Peachum in the 'Beggar's Opera,' Trim in 'Tristram Shandy,' Scrub in the 'Beaux Stratagem,' Robin in the 'Waterman,' Tony Lumpkin, Sir Peter Teazle, Justice Clement and Brainworm in 'Every Man in his Humour,' Marrall in 'A New Way to pay Old Debts,' Hardy in the 'Belle's Stratagem,' Croaker in the 'Good-natured Man,' Sir Fretful Plagiary in the 'Critic,' and Foresight in 'Love for Love.' Not less remarkable is his list of original characters. In countless pieces of Colman, Morton, Reynolds, and other dramatists of the day he took principal parts. His Old Dornton in Holcroft's 'Road to Ruin,' 18 Feb. 1792, sprang into immediate success, and remained a favourite to the end of his career. On 19 March 1795 he played Sir Hans Burgess in O'Keeffe's 'Life's Vagaries;' on 23 Jan. 1796 Caustic in Morton's 'Way to get Married;' 19 Nov. 1796 Old Testy in Holman's 'Abroad and at Home;' 10 Jan. 1797 Old Rapid in Morton's 'Cure for the Heart Ache;' 4 March 1797 Sir William Dorillon in Mrs. Inchbald's 'Wives as they were and Maids as they are;' 23 Nov. 1797 Solomon Single in Cumberland's 'False Impression;' and on 11 Jan. 1798 Undermine in Morton's 'Secrets worth Knowing.' These parts were all played at Covent Garden. At the Haymarket, 15 July 1797, he was the first Zekiel Homespun in the younger Colman's 'Heir-at-Law.' At Covent Garden he was, 12 Jan. 1799, Oakworth in Holman's 'Votary of Wealth;' 8 Feb. 1800 Sir Abel Handy in Morton's 'Speed the Plough,' and 1 May 1800 Dominique in Cobb's 'Paul and Virginia.' This season witnessed the dispute between the principal actors of Covent Garden and Harris the manager [see Holman, Joseph George]. Munden was one of the signatories of the appeal which Lord Salisbury, the lord chamberlain, as arbitrator, rejected in every point. Munden at the close of the season visited Dublin, Birmingham, Chester, and elsewhere.

At Covent Garden on 3 Jan. 1801, he was Old Liberal in T. Dibdin's 'School for Prejudice,' and 11 Feb. Sir Robert Bramble in the younger Colman's 'Poor Gentleman;' on 15 Jan. 1805 General Tarragon in Morton's 'School of Reform;' 16 Feb. Lord Danberry in Mrs. Inchbald's 'To marry or not to marry,' and 18 April Torrent in the younger Colman's 'Who wants a Guinea?' On 15 Nov. 1806 he was the Count of Rosenheim in Dimond's 'Adrian and Orrila,' 3 Dec. 1808 Diaper in Tobin's 'School for Authors,' and on 23 April 1811 Heartworth in Holman's 'Gazette Extraordinary.' At the close of this season Munden quarrelled with the management on financial questions, and did not again, except for a benefit, set his foot in the theatre.

At the Haymarket he played, 26 July 1811, Casimere in the 'Quadrupeds of Quedlinburgh,' taken by Colman from Canning. He was again at the Haymarket in 1812. During the two years, 1811–3, however, he was principally in the country, playing in Edinburgh (where he was introduced to Scott), Newcastle, Rochdale, Chester, Manchester, &c., obtaining large sums of money, and beginning for the first time to incur the charge of stinginess. He had hitherto been a popular and somewhat indulgent man, exercising hospitality at a house in Kentish Town, a witty companion, the secretary to the Beefsteak Club, and a martyr to gout. He now began a system of parsimony, which hardened into miserliness.

On 4 Oct. 1813, as Sir Abel Handy in 'Speed the Plough,' he made his first appearance at Drury Lane where, 11 March 1815, he created one of his greatest rôles, Dozey, an old sailor, in T. Dibdin's 'Past Ten o'Clock and a Rainy Night.' On 14 Dec. 1815 he was Vandunke in the 'Merchant of Bruges,' Kinnaird's alteration of the 'Beggar's Bush' of Beaumont and Fletcher. At Drury Lane he played few original parts of importance, the last being General Van in Knight's 'Veteran, or the Farmer's Sons,' 23 Feb. 1822. He had suffered much from illness, and took his farewell of the stage 31 May 1824, playing Sir Robert Bramble and Old Dozey, and reciting a farewell address. He was little seen after his retirement, being principally confined to the house, where he was nursed by his wife. Discontented with his receipts from his investment in government trusts, he sold out, and placing out his money at high interest experienced losses, which caused him anxieties that shortened his life. He refused many invitations to reappear, and after the death of a favourite daughter spent most of his time in bed. He died 6 Feb. 1832 in Bernard Street, Russell Square, and was buried in the vaults of St. George's, Bloomsbury. The disposition of his property, including a very inadequate provision for his wife, who died in 1836, caused unfavourable comment. He left several children. A son, Thomas Shepherd Munden, who died at Islington in July 1850, aged 50, wrote his father's biography.

There are few actors concerning whose appearance, method, and merits so much is known. Thanks to the utterances of Charles Lamb, Hazlitt, Leigh Hunt, and Talfourd, the actor still lives to the present generation. Lamb's famous criticism begins, 'There is one face of Farley, one face of Knight, one (but what a one it is!) of Liston; but Munden has none that you can properly pin down and call *his*.' Lamb calls him 'not one but legion, not so much a comedian as a company.' Elsewhere, in a letter upon Munden's death in the 'Athenæum,' Lamb says: 'He was imaginative; he could impress upon an audience an *idea*; the low one, perhaps, of a leg of mutton and turnips; but such was the grandeur and singleness of his expression, that that single impression would convey to all his auditory a notion of all the pleasures they had all received from all the *legs of muttons and turnips* they had ever eaten in their lives.' Talfourd says: 'When he fixes his wonder-working face in any of its most amazing varieties, it looks as if the picture were carved out from a rock by Nature in a sportive vein, and might last for ever. It is like what we can imagine a mask of the old Grecian comedy to have been, only that it lives, and breathes, and changes. His most fantastical gestures are the grand idea of farce.' Talfourd knew of nothing finer than his Old Dozey. Munden was altogether lacking in simplicity, and was a confirmed grimacer. Hunt compares his features to the reflection of a man's face in a ruffled stream: they undergo a perpetual undulation of grin. Much of his acting is said to consist of 'two or three ludicrous gestures and an innumerable variety of as fanciful contortions of countenance as ever threw women into hysterics.' Hazlitt holds that compared with Liston Munden was a caricaturist. Mrs. Mathews chronicles concerning him 'that his heart and soul were in his vocation.' Boaden calls his style of comedy broad and voluptuous, indicates that he was self-conscious, and charges him with unfairness to his brother actors when on the stage, adding that he 'painted remarkably high for distant effects.' The anonymous author of 'Candid and Impartial Strictures on the Performers,' &c., 1795, calls his action 'hard and deficient in variety,' his voice strong, and his figure 'vulgar and heavy.' The 'Thespian Dictionary' says that he dressed his characters with judgment. In appearance Munden was short, with large blue eyes. Leigh Hunt says that 'his profile was not good when he looked grave. There was something close, carking, and even severe in it; but it was redeemed by his front face, which was handsome for one so old, and singularly pliable about the eyes and brows.' Genest numbers among his best impersonations Sir Francis Gripe, Ephraim Smooth, Old Dornton, Polonius, Hardcastle, Nipperton, Old Rapid, Captain Bertram, King in 'Tom Thumb,' Crack in the 'Turnpike Gate,' Sir Abel Handy, Sir Robert Bramble, Marrall, Kit Sly, and Moll Flagon, to which list should be added Menenius, Obadiah Prim in 'Honest

Thieves,' Harmony in 'Every one has his Fault,' and the Witch in 'Macbeth.'

Eight portraits of Munden are in the Mathews collection in the Garrick Club. One by Zoffany shows him as Project, with Quick as Alderman Arable, and Lewis as Tanjore in 'Speculation.' De Wilde painted him as Verdun in 'Lovers' Vows,' as Peregrine Forester in 'Hartford Bridge,' as Crack in the 'Turnpike Gate,' and as Autolycus. Clint shows him as Old Brummagem in 'Lock and Key,' with Knight as Ralph, Mrs. Orger as Fanny, and Miss Cubitt as Laura. Other portraits are by John Opie, R.A., and Turmeau. An excellent sketch of Munden by George Dance, dated December 1798, was engraved by W. Daniell for 'Dance's Portraits,' London, 1808.

[The Memoir by his son, London, 1844, is the chief authority. Biographies are found in Gilliland's Dramatic Mirror, the Thespian Dictionary, and in innumerable magazines. These are even less trustworthy than usual, as Munden liked to hoax applicants for information. Genest's Account of the English Stage; Boaden's Life of Mrs. Jordan; Seilhammer's History of the American Stage, vol. iii.; Clark Russell's Representative Actors; Gilliland's Dramatic Synopsis; New Monthly Mag. vols. iii. xii.; London Mag. vol. iii.; Leigh Hunt's Critical Essays on the Performers, &c.; Hazlitt's Dramatic Essays; T. Dibdin's Reminiscences, i. 290; and manuscript information by J. Dirk Vanderpant, in a copy of the Memoir, have been consulted.] J. K.

MUNDEN, SIR RICHARD (1640–1680), captain in the navy, was the elder son of Sir Richard Munden (1602–1672) of Chelsea; the younger son was Rear-admiral Sir John Munden [q. v.] The father is described by Le Neve (*Pedigrees of the Knights*, p. 476) as 'ferryman at Chelsea,' which may mean the owner or lessee of the ferry, if, as seems probable, other well-to-do Mundens were akin to him. One John Munden was captain of a ship in the employ of the East India Company about 1620 (*Cal. State Papers*, East Indies), and towards the end of the century a William Munden was consul or agent at Alicante (*Addit. MS.* 18986, f. 399). Richard first appears as commander of the Swallow ketch in 1666, and afterwards of the Portsmouth in 1667. In 1672 he was captain of the Princess of 52 guns; and in 1673, in the Assistance, was commodore of a small squadron sent as convoy to the East India fleet. Touching at St. Helena for water, he found the island in the possession of the Dutch. After a spirited attack by sea and land he captured it on 4 May [see KEIGWIN, RICHARD], and three Dutch East Indiamen, richly laden, who anchored in the bay, were seized. With his squadron and prizes and the homeward-bound ships in convoy, Munden arrived in England in August, and on 6 Dec. was knighted by the king, 'in consideration of his eminent service.' In April 1677, in command of the St. David, he convoyed the trade to the Mediterranean, was for some time at Zante, afterwards at Scanderoon, and for fourteen months at Smyrna (*Addit. MS.* 18986, f. 433). He arrived at Plymouth with the homeward trade on 12 May 1680. On 15 June he wrote to the admiralty explaining that he had not sent home the muster-books from the Mediterranean, the postage being extremely heavy, and by no means safe (*ib.*) Ten days later, 25 June 1680, he died. He was buried in the church at Bromley, Middlesex, where the inscription on his monument still tells that 'having been (what upon public duty, and what upon merchants' accounts) successfully engaged in fourteen sea-fights . . . he died in the prime of his youth and strength, in the 40th year of his age.' Munden married Susan Gore, by whom he had five daughters and one son, Richard, born posthumously. Shortly after his death arms were granted to the widow, her children, and her husband's brother, Sir John Munden, viz. Per pale, gules and sable, on a cross engrailed argent five lozenges azure; on a chief or, three eagle's legs erased of the second; on a canton ermine, an anchor or. Crest: on a naval crown or, a leopard's head sable, bezantée (BURKE, *General Armoury*). The same arms, differing in colour, are given for Munden simply.

[Charnock's Biog. Nav. i. 243; Brooke's Hist. of St. Helena, pp. 57–63; a Relation of the retaking of the Island of St. Helena and three Dutch East India Ships, published by authority, 1673, fol., 816, m. $\frac{23}{17}$; information from the vicar, the Rev. G. A. M. How.] J. K. L.

MUNDY, SIR GEORGE RODNEY (1805–1884), admiral of the fleet, son of General Godfrey Basil Mundy (author of the 'Life of Lord Rodney') by his wife Sarah Brydges, youngest daughter of George Brydges Rodney, first lord Rodney [q. v.], was born on 19 April 1805. In February 1818 he entered the Royal Naval College at Portsmouth, and in December 1819, having gained the medal of his class, giving him two years sea-time, he was appointed to the Phaeton frigate, on the North American station. He afterwards served on the Mediterranean and South American stations; and on 4 Feb. 1826 was confirmed in the rank of lieutenant and appointed to the Éclair, which came home in September 1827. For the next twelve months he was on the coast of Portugal, in the Challenger, with Captain Adolphus FitzClarence [q. v.], and in the Pyramus with Captain G. R. Sartorius [q. v.] On 25 Aug. 1828 he was promoted to be commander. In 1832 he was on board the Donegal as confidential agent under Sir Pulteney Malcolm [q. v.] on the coast of Holland, and in 1833 was employed by the first lord of the admiralty on a special mission to Holland and Belgium. In August 1833 he was appointed to the Favourite for service in the Mediterranean. He paid her off in the early months of 1837, having been already advanced to post rank on 10 Jan. 1837.

In October 1842 he was appointed to the Iris frigate, employed during the early part of 1843 on the west coast of Africa. As the ship was very sickly she was sent home and paid off. She was then thoroughly refitted at Portsmouth, and again commissioned by Mundy, for service in India and China. She arrived at Singapore in July 1844, and for the next two years was employed in the ordinary routine of the station in Chinese or Indian waters. She was then taken by the commander-in-chief, Sir Thomas John Cochrane, to Borneo, where, in co-operation with 'Rajah' Brooke, Mundy was engaged for the next six months in a brilliant series of operations against the Borneo pirate tribes [see Brooke, Sir James], an interesting account of which, from his own and Brooke's journals, he afterwards published under the title of 'Narrative of Events in Borneo and Celebes down to the Occupation of Labuan. . . . Together with a Narrative of the Operations of H.M.S. Iris,' 2 vols. 8vo, 1848. His share in this service ended with his formally taking possession of Labuan on 24 Dec. 1846, after which he returned to Singapore, and early in April 1847 sailed for England, where he arrived on 26 July.

In July 1854 Mundy was appointed to the Nile, a screw line-of-battle ship of 91 guns, then in the Baltic. She was again in the Baltic in 1855; but, on the conclusion of peace with Russia, was sent to the West Indies. On 30 July 1857 he was promoted to the rank of rear-admiral, and was nominated a C.B. on 23 June 1859. In 1859 and 1860, with his flag in the Hannibal, as second in command in the Mediterranean, he was employed in the delicate task of protecting British interests at Palermo and at Naples, during the revolutionary civil war, and, so far as his position enabled him, in mitigating the horrors of the struggle. Afterwards, in 1861, he commanded the detached squadron on the coast of Syria, at the time of the departure of the French army of occupation. Towards the close of 1861 his health broke down, and he was compelled to return to England. His arduous services and tact during a time of very great difficulty were rewarded by a K.C.B., 10 Nov. 1862. He afterwards published 'H.M.S. Hannibal at Palermo and Naples during the Italian Revolution, with Notices of Garibaldi, Francis II, and Victor Emmanuel,' post 8vo, 1863, an intelligent history of the revolution.

On 15 Dec. 1863 he was promoted to be vice-admiral, and from 1867 to 1869 was commander-in-chief in the West Indies. On 26 May 1869 he attained the rank of admiral, and was commander-in-chief at Portsmouth 1872–5. On 2 June 1877 he was nominated a G.C.B., and on 27 Dec. 1877 was promoted to be admiral of the fleet on the retired list. He died on 23 Dec. 1884. He was not married.

Mundy was known in the navy for his strict observance of old-fashioned etiquette and for a certain pomposity of demeanour, springing partly from the high value he placed on his rank and partly from his pride of birth as the grandson of Lord Rodney. Several amusing suggestions of this will be found in his 'Hannibal at Palermo.' Some of the current stories about him when he was commander-in-chief at Portsmouth were no doubt true, but the greater number were fabrications; and, whatever his eccentricities, he was at all times courteous and considerate to those under his command.

[O'Byrne's Nav. Biog. Dict.; Morning Post, 26 Dec. 1884; Navy Lists; his own works named in the text.] J. K. L.

MUNDY, JOHN (*d.* 1630), organist and composer, the elder son of William Mundy [q. v.], was educated in music by his father, and became an able performer on the virginals and organ. He was admitted Mus.Bac. at Oxford on 9 July 1586, and proceeded Mus. Doc. on 2 July 1624, 'being in high esteem for his great knowledge in the theoretical and practical part of music' (Wood, *Fasti*, i. 236, 415). His 'Act' was a song in five or six parts (*Oxf. Univ. Register*, Oxf. Historical Soc., vol. ii. pt. i. p. 147).

Mundy is said to have become organist at Eton College (Wood; Hawkins). He was afterwards appointed organist of the free royal chapel of St. George, Windsor, probably in succession to John Marbeck [q. v.], in or before 1586—the records of the period are imperfect. Mundy held this post until about 1630. He died in that year, and was buried in the cloisters of St. George's Chapel (Wood). Mundy was survived by his only daughter, Mrs. Bennett.

He published: 1. 'Songs and Psalms, composed into three, four, and five parts, for the use and delight of all such as either loue or learn musicke,' printed by Est, 1594, and dedicated to the Earl of Essex. Burney gives 'In deep distresse' from this collection in his 'History,' iii. 55. 2. Part-song for five voices, 'Lightly she whipped o'er the dales,' in Morley's 'Triumphs of Oriana,' 1601.

Mundy is named as the composer of: 1. A Kyrie, 'In die Pasce' (*Brit. Mus. Addit. MS.* 17802). 2. Collection of Services and Psalms in English (*ib.* 29289). 3. 'Sing joyfully,' *a* 5, in a collection by Thomas Myriell, 1616 (*ib.* 29372). 4. Treble part of verse-psalms (*ib.* 15166; and cf. CLIFFORD, *Divine Services*, for the words of psalms set to music by one or other Mundy). 5. Six Services, and twelve anthems, at Durham Cathedral—including 'O God, my Strength and Fortitude;' 'Send aid;' 'Give laude unto the Lord;' 'O God, our Governour;' 'O Thou God Almighty;' 'Teach me Thy way;' 'O give thanks;' 'Almighty God, the Fountain of all wisdom;' and (for men) 'He that hath My commandments' and 'Let us now laud.' 6. Two compositions in the Oxford Music School. 7. Five pieces in Queen Elizabeth's 'Virginal Book' (Fitzwilliam Museum, Cambridge; see GROVE, *Dict.* iv. 308, iii. 35).

But among the manuscript services, psalms, and anthems ascribed to Mundy, or 'Mr. Mundy,' most of those to Latin words were probably composed by William, or by an elder John Mundy.

[Treasurers' and Precentors' Rolls of St. George's Chapel, Windsor, through the courtesy of Canon Dalton and Mr. St. John Hope, F.S.A.; Hawkins's Hist. of Music, p. 499; Burney's Hist. iii. 132; list of Mundy's music in Durham Cathedral, kindly supplied by Dr. Philip Armes.]

L. M. M.

MUNDY, PETER (*fl.* 1600–1667), traveller, came from Penryn in Cornwall. In 1609 he accompanied his father to Rouen, and was then sent into Gascony to learn French. In May 1611 he went as a cabin-boy in a merchant ship, and gradually rose in life until he became of independent circumstances. He visited Constantinople, returning thence to London overland, and afterwards made a journey to Spain. On 6 March 1627–8 he left Blackwall for Surat, where he arrived on 30 Sept. 1628. In November 1630 he was sent to Agra, and remained there until 17 Dec. 1631, when he proceeded to Puttana on the borders of Bengal. He returned again to Agra and Surat, and left the latter town in February 1633–4, arriving off Dover on 9 Sept. 1634. This portion of his travels is contained in the Harleian MS. 2286, and in the Addit. MSS. 19278–80. In the Addit. MS. 19281 is a copy of a journal which he kept on some further voyages to India, China, and Japan, when he started from the Downs on 14 April 1636. The fleet of four ships and two pinnaces were sent forth by Sir William Courten, and Mundy seems to have been employed as a factor. This copy of his journals ends somewhat abruptly, but another manuscript in the Rawlinson collection at the Bodleian Library (Rawl. A. 315) continues the narrative of his life, including journeys to Denmark, Prussia, and Russia, which lasted from 1639 to 1648. It is largely in the handwriting of a clerk, but with corrections by Mundy, who has obviously himself made all the drawings and embellishments of the volume and traced his routes in red on the maps of Hondius. It ends in 1667 after a copy of a proclamation by the king in that year, and it contains during many years notes, made after his 'last arrivall at home,' of the public events that he thought worthy of record, whether in London or Cornwall; comets, sea-fights, accidents, and political events, being equally attractive to him. The pen-and-ink drawings of various curiosities and instruments as well as scenes, which are contained in this journal, render it of great attraction. An extract from another manuscript of Mundy, then in the possession of Mr. Edwin Ley of Penzance, is printed in J. S. Courtney's 'Guide to Penzance' (pp. 15–16), and his account of the journal seems to show that it may include the narrative of some incidents not contained in the Rawlinson MS. These manuscripts of Mundy are worthy of the attention of the Hakluyt Society.

[Manuscripts referred to above; Boase and Courtney's Bibl. Cornub. i. 379; information from Mr. Falconer Madan, of Bodl. Library, and Mr. John D. Enys of Enys, near Penryn. An examination of the parish registers of Gluvias in Cornwall, within which the town of Penryn is situate, has not revealed any entry of either his baptism or burial.]

W. P. C.

MUNDY, SIR ROBERT MILLER (1813–1892), colonial governor, born in 1813, was youngest son of Edward Miller Mundy, M.P., of Shipley Hall, Derby. He entered as a cadet at Woolwich in February 1828, and became a lieutenant in the royal artillery in June 1833. In March 1841 he joined the horse artillery, and became a second captain in April 1844, and major by brevet on selling out in October 1846. After enjoying for a time a country life in Hampshire, he volunteered for service in the Turkish army on the outbreak of the Crimean war, and became a lieutenant-colonel in the Osmanli horse artillery till August 1856. He received the medal of the third class of Medjidié.

In September 1863 he was appointed lieutenant-governor of Grenada, West Indies, and embarked on a colonial career, acting temporarily as governor of the Windward Islands in 1865, of British Guiana from May 1866 to September 1867, again of the Windwards in 1868–9, and of the Leeward Islands in 1871. From Grenada he was transferred in February 1874 to the permanent appointment of lieutenant-governor of British Honduras, and retired on pension in 1877.

Created C.M.G. in 1874, and K.C.M.G. in 1877, he settled in Hampshire, and died at Hollybank, Emsworth, Hampshire, on 22 March 1892. He married in 1841 Isabella, daughter of General Popham of Littlecott, Wiltshire.

[Colonial Office List, 1889; Burke's Peerage.]
C. A. H.

MUNDY, WILLIAM (*fl.* 1563), musical composer, at one time a member of St. Paul's Cathedral choir, was sworn gentleman of the Chapel Royal on 21 Feb. 1563–4. Richard Mundaye (cf. *Revels at Court*) and John Mundaye (died about 1590), both of Queen Elizabeth's household, were probably relatives. According to the 'Old Cheque-book of the Chapel Royal,' Anthony Anderson was 'sworn, 12 Oct. 1591, in Mr. Mundaie's room.' Rimbault assumed here a reference to William's death; but John Mundy the elder, who described himself in his will as yeoman and servant to the queen, is doubtless intended. (One of the overseers of and witnesses to John's will was William Hunnis [q. v.] the musician, *Registers P. C. C.*, Sainberbe, 9.)

A pedigree compiled by his grandson, Stephen Mundy, in the seventeenth century (Harl. MS. 5800) states that William married Mary Alcock and had two sons, John [q. v.], and Stephen, gentleman of the household to James I and Charles I. The family bore the arms and crest of Mundy of London. The descent of John from William Munday, questioned by Hawkins, is here confirmed, thus bearing out the general interpretation of the lines by Baldwin, lay-clerk of Windsor, and contemporary with John Mundy—

Mundye th'oulde one of the Quene's pallis;
Mundie yonge, th'oulde man's son
(cf. HAWKINS, *Hist. of Music*, p. 469).

On the other hand, the statement of the pedigree, that William was sub-dean of the chapel, is unsupported. Some complimentary office or title may have been conferred upon him by the dean and chapter; for in 1573 or 1574 they received from a William Mundy a fee in acknowledgment for 'litt. testimonialibus' (*Treasurer's Rolls*).

Mundy was esteemed by Morley and other English musicians as inferior to none of their contemporaries abroad, and so correct as to deem it 'no greater sacrilege to spurn against the image of a saint than to make two perfect cords of one kind together.' There are printed in Barnard's 'Selected Church Music,' 1641, a service by Mundy for four, five, and six voices in D minor, and anthems. Barnard, like Clifford and an early seventeenth-century manuscript (Brit. Mus. Addit. MS. 29289, fol. 83), also assigns to him 'O Lord, the Maker of all things,' *a* 4; but Dr. Philip Armes has discovered among the Durham Cathedral manuscripts many seventeenth-century voice-parts of this anthem under the name of John Shepherd, while the old tradition ascribing the music to Henry VIII has the support of no less an authority than Dean Aldrich. 'O Lord, the world's Saviour,' *a* 4; 'O Lord, I bow the knees of my heart,' *a* 5; and 'Ah! helpless wretch,' for counter-tenor with chorus, are also printed as Mundy's by Barnard.

In manuscript there are, besides many transcriptions of the above: 1. A second Service. 2. Anthem, 'O give thanks;' 3. Eleven Latin motets in a set of parts, all at the Royal College of Music. 4. Seven Latin motets, &c.; and 5, 6, two Masses 'upon the square,' at the British Museum (Addit. MSS. 17802–5). 7. Four part-songs, &c. (*ib.* 31390). 8. Three pieces in lute notation, by W. or J. Mundy (*ib.* 29246). 9. Song, 'Prepare you, time wereth away' (Harl. MS. 7578). 10. Seventeen motets at Christ Church, Oxford. Other music in manuscript by Mundy is in the libraries of York and Lambeth.

[Grove's Dict. of Music, ii. 409, 422; Chappell's Popular Music, i. 53; Rimbault's Old Cheque-book, pp. 1, 5, 181; Cunningham's Revels at Court, p. 12; Morley's Introduction to Practicall Musicke, p. 151; information kindly given by Alfred James Monday, esq., Taunton; authorities cited.]
L. M. M.

MUNGO, SAINT (518?–603). [See KENTIGERN.]

MUNN, PAUL SANDBY (1773–1845), water-colour painter, born at Thornton Row, Greenwich, on 8 Feb. 1773, was son of James Munn, carriage decorator and landscape-painter, and Charlotte Mills, his wife. His father was an occasional exhibitor at the Old Society of Painters in Water-colours and at the Society of Artists from 1764 to 1774. Munn was named after his godfather, Paul Sandby [q. v.], who gave him his first instructions in water-colour painting. He first exhibited at the Royal Academy in 1798, sending some views in the Isle of Wight, and was subsequently a frequent contributor of topographical drawings to that and other exhibitions. He was elected an associate exhibitor of the old Society of Painters in Water-colours in 1806, and was for some years a contributor to their exhibitions. He was an intimate friend of John Sell Cotman [q. v.], and they made several sketching tours together at home and abroad. He drew some of the views in Britton's 'Beauties of England and Wales.' Munn's drawings are delicately and carefully executed, usually in pale and thin colours, resembling the tinted drawings of the early school of water-colour painting. There are examples in the South Kensington Museum and the print room, British Museum. Munn painted little after 1832, when he devoted himself chiefly to music. He married Cecilia, daughter of Captain Timothy Essex, but died without issue at Margate on 17 Feb. 1845.

[Roget's Hist. of the Old Society of Painters in Water Colours; Redgrave's Dict. of Artists; information from the Rev. C. J. Rowland Berkeley and Major-general Emeric Berkeley.]

L. C.

MUNNU, Saint (*d.* 634). [See Fintan.]

MUNRO. [See also Monro.]

MUNRO, ALEXANDER (1825–1871), sculptor, born in 1825, was son of a stonemason in Sutherlandshire. His artistic abilities were discovered by the Duchess of Sutherland, the wife of the second duke, who assisted him in his art and general education [cf. Leveson-Gower, Harriet Elizabeth Georgiana]. Among the works which he executed for her were 'The Four Seasons' on the terrace at Cliveden. Munro came to London in 1848, and was employed for some time on the stone carving for the new Houses of Parliament. He exhibited for the first time at the Royal Academy in 1849, sending two busts, and was a regular annual contributor during the remainder of his life. His main work was portrait-sculpture, especially in relief, though he occasionally executed subject groups, such as 'Paolo e Francesca' (Royal Academy, 1852), 'Undine' (Royal Academy, 1858), and the statue of a nymph, which forms the drinking fountain erected by the Marquis of Lansdowne in Berkeley Square. Among his larger works were a statue of Queen Mary for the Houses of Parliament, a colossal statue of James Watt for Birmingham, and a colossal bust of Sir Robert Peel for the memorial at Oldham. Among the many notable people of whom he exhibited portrait-busts or medallions at the Royal Academy were Lady Constance Grosvenor (1853), Sir John Millais, Lady Alwyne Compton, and Baron Bunsen (1854), Right Hon. W. E. Gladstone (1855), Adelaide Ristori (1858), Mrs. George Murray Smith (1859), William Hunt, the water-colour painter (1862), Sir James Stephen (1866), and the Duchess of Vallombrosa (1869). All Munro's work was sketchy and wanting in strength, but full of refinement and true feeling. He was by nature small and delicate, and before reaching middle age was attacked by lung disease, which slowly undermined his constitution. He lived for some time at 152 Buckingham Palace Road; but being compelled to reside most of the year at Cannes, he built himself a house and studio there, where he continued to work at his profession till his death, on 1 Jan. 1871.

Munro married a daughter of Robert Carruthers [q. v.], editor of the 'Inverness Courier.' She died in 1872 at Cannes, and was buried with her husband. By her Munro had two sons.

Munro was popular in cultivated and artistic society. Among his friends were John Ruskin—who stood godfather to one of his sons—Louis Blanc, and Giuseppe Mazzini.

[Redgrave's Dict. of Artists; Times, 13 Jan. 1871; Royal Academy Catalogues; private information.]

L. C.

MUNRO, Sir HECTOR (1726–1805), general, born in 1726, was son of Hugh Munro of Novar, Cromartyshire, and his wife Isobel Gordon, who died in 1799, aged 92. The Novar family was an ancient branch of Munro of Foulis, from which it separated in the fifteenth century. According to family tradition, Hector, when quite a lad, saved the life of a lady whose horses had run away with her, and she subsequently obtained a commission for him in the army. His name first appears in the military records, on appointment as ensign in the company commanded by Sir Harry Munro of Foulis in Lord Loudoun's highlanders, 28 May 1747 (*Home Office Military Entry Book*, vol. xix. f. 461). This was an unnumbered highland regiment, raised by John Campbell, fourth earl of Loudoun [q. v.], the greater part of which was taken by the clans on 30 March 1746, and sent to Prince Charles's headquarters at Inverness (cf. Fraser, *Earls of Cromartie*, ii. 397). The officers' commissions were dated June 1745. Among them was a George

Munro of Novar. There is a local tradition that Hector Munro was of the number taken by the clans, and that he escaped from his escort by the way. At the date of his commission, the regiment was embarking for the Low Countries, where, with some regiments of Scots-Dutch, it distinguished itself at the defence of Bergen-op-Zoom, July–September 1747. It was disbanded at Perth in June 1748 (see STEWART, *Scottish Highlanders*, vol. ii.)

Munro was reappointed to the army as ensign in the 48th foot (Lord H. Beauclerk's) 4 Feb. 1749 (*Home Office Military Entry Book*, vol. xxii. f. 94); was promoted lieutenant in the 31st foot, in Ireland, 5 Jan. 1754; and in August 1756 obtained his company in the newly raised second battalion of that regiment, which was formed into the 70th foot in April 1758. The year after, Major (afterwards General) Staates Long Morris, who had been a captain in the 31st, and had married the widowed mother of the young Duke of Gordon [see under GORDON, ALEXANDER, fourth DUKE], raised a regiment of highlanders on the Gordon estates. Hector Munro, on 14 Oct. 1759, was appointed junior major of the new corps, which assembled at Gordon Castle in December 1759, and was numbered as the 89th foot. Under Munro's command the regiment embarked at Portsmouth for India in December 1760, and arrived at Bombay in November 1761. During the next four years the corps did good service in various parts of India. The greater part of the regiment was brought home and disbanded in 1765, and it was remarked that during its five years' service there was only one change among its officers, and not a single desertion from its ranks. In the eight companies originally raised not a single man was ever flogged (STEWART, vol. ii.) Early in 1764 Munro was ordered to Patna to replace Major John Carnac [q. v.] in command of the company's forces. The time was extremely critical, and Carnac's sepoys in a state of mutiny. Taking with him the men of the 89th and 96th regiments who were willing to extend their service in India, Munro proceeded to Calcutta, where, at the request of the council, he remained a short time, to acquaint himself with the views of individual members and the general position of affairs. On 13 Aug. he repaired to Patna, and by stern measures effectually stamped out the mutiny. On 27 Oct. 1764, with a force of seven thousand men, including some fifteen hundred European details, and twenty guns, he utterly routed the confederated princes of Hindostan in a great battle at Buxar in Behar. The enemy, who had fifty thousand men, left six thousand men and 133 guns on the field. The victory saved Bengal, and placed Hindostan at the feet of the conquerors. The battle ranks among the most decisive ever fought (MALLESON, *Decisive Battles of India*, p. 208). The prize-money of the victors amounted to the enormous sum of twelve lacs of rupees. Munro resigned the command of the company's troops soon afterwards, and returned home, where he spent some years on half-pay as lieutenant-colonel, a rank he attained on 8 Oct. 1765. In 1768 he was returned to parliament for the burghs of Inverness, Nairn, Forres, and Fortrose, which he represented for many years. He became a brevet-colonel in 1777.

Unfortunate disputes in the Madras government led the court of directors, in June 1777, to appoint a temporary council, consisting of Sir Thomas Rumbold [q.v.] as president, John Whitehill as second, and Munro, who was to command the troops, with the local rank of major-general, as third, without power of further advancement (see MILL, *Hist. of India*, ed. Wilson, iv. 118 et seq.) Munro landed with Rumbold at Madras in February 1778 and assumed command of the army. In the same year he captured Pondicherry from the French. He was made K.B. in 1779. But his administrative action did not satisfy the directors. In their letter of 10 Jan. 1781 the court of directors dismissed Rumbold and other members of the council, and severely censured Munro for the council's treatment of the zemindars of the northern circars, and of other questions of native policy (*ib.*) In the meantime the military situation grew serious. In July 1780 Hyder Ali swept over the Carnatic with an immense army. Munro, in opposition to the advice of his second in command, Lord Macleod [see MACKENZIE, JOHN, LORD MACLEOD], marched to Conjeveram, to meet a detachment under Colonel William Baillie (*d.* 1782) [q. v.], ordered down from Guntoor. Baillie's detachment was destroyed, between Pollilore and Conjeveram, on the morning of 10 Sept. 1780. Munro then fell back to Chingleput, and subsequently moved his forces to St. Thomas Mount. There he was encamped when Sir Eyre Coote (1726–1783) [q. v.] landed on 5 Nov. 1780, and assumed the command-in-chief. Munro commanded the right division of Coote's army, which carried the day at the great victory of Porto Novo on 1 July 1781. At Pollilore, on 27 Aug. following, a harsh reply to a suggestion from Munro caused an estrangement between him and Coote, and Munro, who was in wretched health, remained for a time unemployed at Madras. At the request of the new governor, Lord Macartney, he took command of the expedition against the Dutch settlements, which captured Negapatam, after a four weeks' siege, on 12 Nov. 1781, and afterwards returned home. He became a major-general on the English establishment from 26 Nov. 1782. After his return he received the sinecure appointment of barrack-master-general in North Britain. He was appointed colonel of the 42nd highlanders (Black Watch) on 1 June 1787, became a lieutenant-general in 1793, and general on 1 Jan. 1798.

Munro spent his latter years in enlarging and improving his estate at Novar. He was returned again and again for the Inverness burghs, which he represented altogether for thirty-four years, and he was during that time a steady supporter of the government of the day. He was more than once provost of Inverness and other towns. In his prime Munro was a robust, handsome man, a firm but humane disciplinarian, and, although not a great tactician, a brave, enterprising, and successful soldier. In his later years he proved himself a beneficent and public-spirited country gentleman. He accepted the Chiltern Hundreds in 1801. He was defeated for Inverness at the general election of 1802, and petitioned, but the petition was withdrawn. Munro died at Novar on 27 Dec. 1805, aged 79 (inscription on tombstone at Novar). He was married and had a daughter, Jean, who died in 1803, having married in 1798 Lieutenant-colonel (afterwards Sir Ronald) Craufurd Ferguson [q. v.]

Munro was succeeded in the Novar property by his brother, Sir Alexander Munro, kt., many years consul-general at Madrid, and afterwards a commissioner of excise, who died at Ramsgate on 26 Aug. 1809, aged 83 (see *Scots Mag.* 1809, p. 416). Alexander Munro's official correspondence in Spain is among the British Museum Add. MSS. (period 1771–8, 24167–72; period 1785–7, 28060–2). He was succeeded by his son, by whom the collection of pictures now at Novar was formed. At his death in 1865 Novar passed into the female line, now represented by the Munro-Fergusons of Raith, Kirkcaldy, Fifeshire (see BURKE, *Landed Gentry*, 1888 ed. vol. ii.)

[Information from private sources; Stewart's Sketches of the Scottish Highlanders (Edinburgh, 1823), vol. ii., under 'Loudoun's Highlanders' and '89th Gordon Highlanders;' Wilks's Hist. Sketches of S. India, vol. ii.; Mill's Hist. of India, vol. iv., and particularly footnotes and references by H. Wilson; Barrow's Life of Lord Macartney; Malleson's Decisive Battles of India, under 'Baksah' (Buxar) and 'Porto Novo;' Cannon's Hist. Rec. 42nd Royal Highlanders—'Succession of Colonels;' Brit. Mus. Addit. MSS.; Munro's letters to Warren Hastings and Lord Macartney; Hist. MSS. Comm. 3rd Rep.] H. M. C.

MUNRO, HUGH ANDREW JOHNSTONE (1819–1885), classical scholar and critic, born at Elgin 19 Oct. 1819, was the natural son of Penelope Forbes and H. A. J. Munro of Novar, Ross-shire, the owner of a famous collection of pictures. His early youth was spent at Elgin. He was sent to Shrewsbury school in August 1833, and took a good place from the first. In 1836 Dr. Benjamin Hall Kennedy [q. v.] succeeded Dr. Samuel Butler [q. v.] as headmaster of Shrewsbury; and Munro himself has put on record (in his memoir of Edward Meredith Cope [q. v.], prefixed to the latter's posthumous edition of Aristotle's 'Rhetoric') the powerful influence which the enthusiasm and scholarship of their teacher exercised upon the sixth form. In October 1838 he entered at Trinity College, Cambridge, as a pensioner, was elected scholar in 1840, and university Craven scholar in 1841. In 1842 he graduated as second classic, and gained the first chancellor's medal. He was elected a fellow of his college in 1843, and after some residence in Paris, Florence, and Berlin, took holy orders and began to lecture on classical subjects at Trinity. From this time until his death, Trinity College was his permanent home, though he paid many visits to the continent, and generally spent some part of the summer in Scotland.

He first attracted attention in Cambridge by his lectures on Aristotle; and his first publication was a paper, read before the Philosophical Society 11 Feb. 1850, in which he reviewed with remarkable power and no less remarkable frankness Whewell's interpretation of Aristotle's account of inductive reasoning. Five years later, in the 'Journal of Sacred and Classical Philology,' he published an important paper on the same author, in which he maintained the Eudemian authorship of the fifth, sixth, and seventh books of the Nicomachean ethics. The theory was adopted by Grant in his edition; and most English scholars are now agreed that Munro proved his point. But the main work of his life was to be done in other fields.

Early in life he turned his attention to the poem of Lucretius: between 1849 and 1851 he collated all the Lucretian manuscripts in the Vatican and Laurentian libraries, and examined those at Leyden. It was known on what subject he was working; and his friends supposed, when Lachmann's critical edition appeared in 1850, that Munro would find nothing left for him to do. But he himself knew better. When the 'Journal of Sacred and Classical Philology' began to appear in 1854, he contributed a number of papers, chiefly on Lucretius. In 1860 he edited a text with a critical introduction; and in 1864 he published a revision of his text, with introductions, a prose translation, and a full commentary, both critical and explanatory. The book was at once recognised by competent judges as the most valuable contribution to Latin scholarship that any Englishman had made during the century. In the three subsequent editions he tended more and more to defend the traditional text in passages where he had originally followed Lachmann in emendation.

In 1867 he published a text of the Latin poem known as 'Aetna.' He was led to do so by the accidental discovery in the university library of a much better manuscript than any previously known. In 1868 he published a text of Horace, adorned with woodcuts of antique gems selected by a brother-fellow, Charles William King [q. v.] A remarkable introduction from his pen is prefixed, in which the soundness of his judgment is perhaps even more conspicuous than elsewhere, the question of Horace's text being one of the most difficult problems of philology.

In 1869 a professorship of Latin was founded at Cambridge in honour of Dr. Kennedy, and Munro was elected to fill the chair at once and without competition. Shilleto expressed the general feeling when he wrote

Esto professor carus editor Cari,
Carus Sabrinæ, carior suæ Grantæ.

This position he resigned (1872) after three years. His manner of lecturing was not calculated to attract large audiences under the present system of instruction for the purpose of examination. He had no flow of language and always spoke with a measured deliberation which most men reserve for their written works, and he was at times absent-minded: so that, if an attractive train of thought suggested itself, he was apt to follow it up without due regard to the original topic from which he had digressed.

The 'Criticisms and Elucidations of Catullus'—Munro's last book—appeared in 1878. Much of it had already been printed in the form of papers in the 'Journal of Philology,' to which he was a constant contributor from its first appearance in 1864. As there was no necessity here for extreme compression, this book contains the strongest evidence of his knowledge and appreciation of literature, both ancient and modern.

Munro's strong constitution and temperate habits gave every promise of a very long life; but in the spring of 1885 he suffered from sleeplessness, and, going abroad for change and rest, he was attacked at Rome by an inflammation of the mucous membrane, and, when this was abating, a malignant abscess, which proved fatal, appeared on the neck. He died on 30 March 1885, in his sixty-sixth year. He was buried in the protestant cemetery at Rome, where his college has erected a marble cross in his memory. Memorial brasses have also been placed in Trinity College chapel and in the Elgin Academy.

Throughout his whole life Munro had a great fondness for composing in Greek and especially in Latin verse, and many specimens may be seen in the 'Sabrinæ Corolla' and 'Arundines Cami.' Though all his published Latin verses are translations, he often expressed his own thoughts in this form in private letters or in books given to friends. His verses have been attacked on the ground that they are not Ovidian. Against such a charge on one occasion Munro defended himself with characteristic vigour ('Modern Latin Verse,' *Macmillan's Magazine*, February 1875). The charge is, perhaps, true; but if his verses are not Ovidian, they are certainly Latin. Just before his death Munro printed a collection of these translations privately, and gave copies to his friends.

Munro will always hold a high position among English scholars. Though his knowledge was great and his memory retentive, in these points others may have surpassed him; but he had an unusual soundness of judgment, which seemed instinctively to dismiss the false and grasp the true, and a noble love of all great literature, which gives freshness and interest to every page of his writing. Homer and Lucretius were hardly more familiar to him than Shakespeare, Goethe, and Dante. The last he considered the greatest poet of any age or nation. He spoke French, German, and Italian, deliberately, indeed, as he did English, but with correct idiom and good accent.

His character, like his intellect, was strong. Generally reserved, and sometimes absent-minded, he united dignity and courteousness of manner with a very marked simplicity, and a strongly expressed antipathy for anything which he considered false or mean. He had not many intimate friends: to such as he had his attachment was extraordinarily strong.

He was of middle height and strongly built. His forehead was remarkably broad and massive, with thick nut-brown hair growing close to the head. The lines round the mouth were strongly marked and the lips tightly compressed. The general expression of his face was that of strength and benignity. No adequate idea of his living presence can be gained from the two posthumous busts at Cambridge.

Munro's published books are: 1. 'Lucretius' (text), 1860. 2. 'Lucretius' (text, commentary, and translation), 2 vols. 1864; 4th and final edition, 3 vols. 1886. 3. 'Ætna' (text and commentary), 1867. 4. 'Horace' (text, with introduction), 1869. 5. 'The Pronunciation of Latin,' a pamphlet, 1871. 6. 'Criticisms and Elucidations of Catullus,' 1878, 2nd edit. 1905 (with preface by J. D. Duff). 7. 'Translations into Latin and Greek Verse,' privately printed 1884, published 1906 with portrait and preface by J. D. Duff.

His chief papers in learned journals are: 1. 'Cambridge Philosophical Society's Transactions,' x. 374–408, a Latin inscription at Cirta. 2. 'Journal of Sacred and Classical Philology,' i. 21–46, 252–8, 372–8, 'Lucretius;' ii. 58–81, 'Aristotle;' iv. 121–45, 'Lucretius.' 3. 'Journal of Philology,' i. 113–45, 'Lucretius;' ii. 1–33, 'Catullus;' iii. 115–28, 'Lucretius;' iv. 120–6, and 243–251, 'Lucretius;' pp. 231–43, 'Catullus;' v. 301–7, 'Catullus;' vi. 28–70, 'Propertius;' vii. 293–314, and viii. 201–26, 'Lucilius;' x. 233–53, 'Fragments of Euripides.'

[Athenæum, 4 April 1885; personal knowledge; private information.] J. D. D.

MUNRO, INNES (*d.* 1827) of Poyntzfield, Cromarty, N.B., lieutenant-colonel and author, was related to Sir Hector Munro ot Novar [q. v.] He was appointed on 29 Dec. 1777 to a lieutenancy in the 73rd, afterwards 71st, highlanders, then raised by Lord Macleod [see Mackenzie, John, Lord Macleod]. As lieutenant and captain in the first battalion of that regiment he made the campaigns of 1780–4 against Hyder Ali, which he afterwards described, and at the close was placed on half-pay as a captain of the disbanded second battalion of the regiment. On 8 July 1793 he was brought on full pay as captain in the Scottish brigade (disbanded as the 94th foot in 1818). He belonged to that regiment until 1808, when he left the army as major and brevet lieutenant-colonel. He had served for many years as paymaster of a recruiting district. Munro, who had married Ann, daughter of George Gordon, minister of Clyne, died at Poyntzfield in 1827. He published 'A Narrative of the Military Operations in the Carnatic in 1780–4,' London, 1789, 4to, and 'A System of Farm Bookkeeping based on Act ual Practice,' Edinburgh, 1821. Donaldson says of the latter: 'It is the most complex idea that has ever been published. It may amuse the gentleman, but would never suit the farmer' (*Agricultural Biog.* p. 113).

[Army Lists; Donaldson's Agricultural Biog.; Munro's Works.] H. M. C.

MUNRO, Sir THOMAS (1761–1827), major-general, baronet, K.C.B., governor of Madras, was the son of Alexander Munro, a Glasgow merchant trading with Virginia. He was born on 27 May 1761, and educated at the grammar school and at the university of Glasgow. He appears not to have been particularly studious at school, but was an adept at all athletic sports, a good swimmer and boxer. At the university he developed a taste for reading, history—especially military history—mathematics, and chemistry being his favourite subjects. He also studied political economy, and the French, Italian, and Spanish languages. He began the business of life in a mercantile firm at Glasgow, but, owing to family reverses, was compelled to accept an appointment in the mercantile marine service of the East India Company, which, however, he never joined, having been appointed a cadet of infantry at Madras, where he arrived on 15 Jan. 1780. A few months after his arrival in India the regiment to which he was attached formed part of the force sent against Hyder Ali, and he was present at all the operations under Sir Hector Munro [q. v.] and Sir Eyre Coote [q. v.] in 1780 and the three following years. He early attracted the notice of Coote, who appointed him quartermaster of a brigade when he was still an officer of less than two years' service. In August 1788 he was appointed to the intelligence department under Captain Read, and served in most of the operations under Lord Cornwallis, including the siege and capture of Bangalore. Some of the letters which he wrote during these years to his father, describing the military operations, are quoted by Wilson in his annotations to Mill's 'History of British India' as embodying the most accurate accounts available of some of the engagements with Hyder Ali. He also in those early days formed very clear views on the political situation, recognising the paramount importance of subverting the powerful and dangerous government which Hyder had founded in Mysore, the strength of which he deemed to be far more formidable than that of the Mahrattas. He was also an attentive observer of European affairs and of the French revolution, which he regarded as fraught with danger to the maintenance of British superiority. He strongly held the opinion that the territorial possessions of the East India Company must be extended if the company was to continue to exist as a territorial power. After the peace with Tippoo in 1792 Munro was employed for some years under Captain Read in forming and conducting the civil administration of the Baramahal, one of the districts ceded by Tippoo. It was there that he gained his first insight into civil duties, and especially into those connected with the land revenue, and it was there that he formed the opinions in favour of the system of landed tenures which, under the designation of the ryotwár system, has always been identified with his name. His employment in the Baramahal terminated in 1799, when, on the renewal of the war with Tippoo, he rejoined the army, and after the fall of Seringapatam was employed as one of the secretaries to a commission appointed by Lord Wellesley to arrange for the future administration of Mysore, Captain (afterwards Sir John) Malcolm being the other secretary. While serving on this commission Munro was brought into close intercourse with the future Duke of Wellington, then Colonel Wellesley, with whom he contracted a lasting friendship. Munro appears to have been much opposed to the resolution of the governor-general to set up another native dynasty, differing on this point from Colonel Wellesley, who supported his brother's policy, and regarded Munro's views respecting the political expediency of increasing the company's territories as somewhat hazardous. In one of his letters to Munro about this time he wrote: 'I fancy that you will have the pleasure of seeing some of your grand plans carried into execution' (*Wellington Despatches*, i. 254); and in another: 'This is expensive, but if you are determined to conquer all India at the same moment, you must pay for it' (*Selections from the Minutes and other Official Writings of Sir T. Munro*, Introductory Memoir, p. lxix). In the 'Wellington Despatches,' ii. 338, there is an interesting letter written by General Wellesley to Munro after the battle of Assye, explaining his tactics, and commencing with the remark: 'As you are a judge of a military operation, and as I am desirous of having your opinion on my side,' &c. Munro's reply is characteristic, modest, cordial, and friendly, but frank in its criticism, and affording evidence of considerable strategic ability on the part of the writer (*ib.* p. cxi).

Munro's employment upon the commission at Seringapatam was followed by his appointment to the administrative charge of Canara, a district on the western coast of India, which, like the Baramahal, had been brought under the company's rule in 1792, but which from various causes had given a good deal of trouble. Owing to the unruly character of the inhabitants the duty was an arduous one, but in a very few months Munro, by his firm and wise rule, put down crime and rebellion, and substituted settled government for anarchy and disorder. He was then transferred to a still more important charge, viz., that of the districts south of the Tungabhadra, comprising an area little short of twenty-seven thousand square miles, and including the present districts of Ballári, Cuddapah, and Karnúl, and also the Palnád. This large tract of country had been a scene of excessive misrule for upwards of two centuries. It was full of turbulent petty chiefs, called poligárs, some of whom had to be expelled, while those who remained were forced to disband their armed retainers, and to abstain from unauthorised exactions from the cultivators of the soil. Munro spent seven years in the ceded districts. It was probably the most important period in his long official life. In the Baramahal his position had been a subordinate one. In Canara, where for the first time he was invested with an independent charge, his tenure of office had been too short to admit of his doing more than to suppress disorder, and to lay down principles of administration which his successors could work out. In the ceded districts he remained long enough to guide and direct the development of the system which he introduced, and to habituate the people to the spectacle of a ruler who, with inflexible firmness in securing the just rights of the state and in maintaining law and order, combined a patient and benevolent attention to the well-being of all classes. To this day it is considered by the natives in the ceded districts a sufficient answer to inquiries regarding the reason for any revenue rule that it was laid down by the 'Colonel Dora,' the rank which Munro held during the greater part of his service in those districts. It was while holding this charge that Munro thoroughly worked out the ryotwár system of land tenure and land revenue which prevails throughout the greater part of the Madras presidency and also in Bombay. This may be described as a system of peasant proprietors paying a land tax direct to the state, as distinguished from the system of large proprietors, called Zemindars, which obtains in Bengal and in parts of Madras. In introducing the ryotwár system Munro was cordially supported by the governor of Madras, Lord William Cavendish Bentinck [q.v.], but encountered serious opposition from the authorities in Bengal and from some of the higher officials at Madras, an opposition which so far prevailed that shortly after Munro left the ceded districts the ryotwár method of settlement was superseded by a system, first of triennial, and subsequently of decennial leases, under which the revenue of an entire village was farmed to the principal ryot, or, in the event of his refusing to accept the lease, to a stranger; but under both there were heavy losses of revenue to the state and much damage to the prosperity of the country, and, after eight years' trial of the plan of leases to middlemen, a recurrence to the ryotwár system was ordered by the court of directors.

Munro left India in October 1807, carrying away with him warm encomiums from the government of Madras, and much regretted by the natives of the districts which had been for seven years under his charge, and by the officers who had served under him. He remained in England for upwards of six years, during which time he was much consulted by the government and the court of directors on the various administrative questions which came under discussion in connection with the passing of the Company's Charter Act of 1813. The evidence given by him before the House of Commons produced a most favourable impression. It was mainly through his influence that the plan of applying the zemindári system of land tenure to the whole of India was finally abandoned, and that the ryotwár system was authorised for those districts in the Madras and Bombay presidencies which had not been already permanently settled, and his views on the judicial system and on the police were so highly approved that in 1814 he was sent back to Madras on a special commission for the purpose of preparing on the spot a scheme for giving effect to them.

It was not, however, exclusively upon questions of internal Indian administration that Munro's opinion was sought at this time by the home authorities. On the question of the company's trade, which it was then proposed to throw open, and especially upon the question of extending it to the outports, as well as to London; on the question of the demand in India for European manufactures, as to the probable extent of the import trade from India, as to the policy of withdrawing the restrictions then in force upon the admission into India of Europeans not in the service of the company, and on the question of the military organisation best adapted for India—on all these questions Munro's opinion was sought, and was given in language so clear and straightforward as to compel the admiration even of those who on some points held different views. He evinced little sympathy with the outcry raised against the company's monopoly, which in his opinion had been the source of many great national advantages, enabling it to acquire the extensive dominions then under British rule in India. His views on the organisation of the Indian army were very similar to those which have been acted on since the mutiny of 1857. He regarded the establishment of English officers provided by the organisation of 1796 to be excessive, and he disapproved of the plan of appointing young officers to native regiments on first obtaining their commissions. His opinion was that every officer on first entering the service should be employed one or two years with a European regiment until he had learnt his duty, and, by making himself in some degree acquainted with the character of the natives, had become qualified to command and to act with sepoys. He deprecated a proposal to abolish the company's European regiments, and, on the contrary, like Lord Canning fifty years later, was in favour of adding to their number both in infantry and cavalry.

Before returning to India Munro married Jane, daughter of Richard Campbell of Craige House, Ayrshire, a beautiful and accomplished woman, whose picture, by Sir Thomas Lawrence, hangs in the drawing-room of Government House at Madras. Accompanied by his wife, he returned to Madras early in the autumn of 1814, and at once entered upon the duties of his commission. Mr. Stratton, one of the judges of the chief court of appeal of the presidency, was associated with him on the commission. At the outset it encountered many obstacles from the local authorities, but after a time Munro's patience and firmness triumphed, and in 1816 a series of regulations was passed involving organic changes in the judicial and police departments of the administration. The new regulations transferred the superintendence of the police, and also the functions of magistrate of the district, from the judge to the collector. They expressly recognised the employment of the village officials in the performance of police duties, and empowered the head men of villages to hear and determine petty suits. They extended the powers of native judges, they simplified the rules of practice in the courts, and legalised a system of village and district pancháyats, or courts of arbitration, to which, as being adapted to native habits and usages, Munro attached special importance.

The work of framing these regulations had not been fully completed when the outbreak of the second Mahratta war led to Munro's re-employment for a time in a military capacity. Although he had been employed for a good many years upon civil duties, his military ability, as evinced in the earlier part of his Indian career, was well known and fully recognised by the highest military authorities, and before the war began he had been placed in military as well as civil command of certain districts recently ceded to the Peshwa. As soon as hostilities commenced he was invested with the rank of brigadier-general and with the command of the reserve division, formed to reduce the southern Mahratta country and to oppose the forces of the Peshwa, who, after his unsuccessful attack upon the Poona residency, had moved southwards. The campaign which followed, conducted with an extremely small force and attended with brilliant success, at once established Munro's capacity as a military commander, and subsequently drew forth from Mr. Canning the panegyric that 'Europe had never produced a more accomplished statesman, nor India, so fertile in heroes, a more skilful soldier.'

On the termination of the war Munro, whose eyesight had suffered from the work and exposure he had gone through, returned to England. But shortly after his arrival he was nominated to succeed Mr. Elliot as governor of Madras, and re-embarked for India in the latter part of 1819. He had previously been created a knight commander of the Bath. Munro's government of Madras, which lasted seven years, more than maintained the reputation which he had previously achieved. His thorough knowledge of Indian district administration, and his command of the native languages, were great advantages. He made frequent tours throughout the country, travelling by short stages, and making himself thoroughly accessible to the people. At the end of each tour he embodied the results of his observations in a minute, which formed the basis of the orders subsequently issued. With his colleagues in council he was always on the best of terms, treating them with invariable frankness; and, while there never was an Indian government in which there was less friction between the governor and the council, it may be affirmed that there never was a government which was more essentially the government of the governor than the Madras government was while Munro presided over it. His minutes on the tenure of land, on the assessment of the revenue, on the condition of the people, on the training of civil servants, on the advancement of the natives in the public service, on the military system, on the press, are state papers which are still often referred to as containing lucid expositions of the true principles of administration. He entertained and expressed very strong opinions in favour of the policy of more largely utilising native agency, and of fitting the natives of India by education for situations of trust and emolument in the public service. But on this, as on all other subjects, his views were eminently practical. He was entirely opposed to any measures which might endanger British supremacy in India. He was altogether opposed to the establishment of a free press in that country, and was responsible for the famous dictum that 'the tenure with which we hold our power never has been and never can be the liberties of the people.' The first war with Burmah occurred while Munro was governor of Madras, and, although the operations were carried on under the direct orders of the governor-general, Lord Amherst [see Amherst, William Pitt, Earl Amherst of Arracan], the success of the war was much facilitated by the assistance rendered by Munro, who was created a baronet for his services in connection with it. Munro died of cholera on 6 July 1827, when making a farewell tour through the ceded districts on the eve of his retirement from the government. His death was mourned as a public calamity by all classes of the community. By the English members of the civil and military services, as well as by non-official Englishmen in India, he was regarded as a man who by his great and commanding talents, by the force of his character, by his extraordinary capacity for work, and by the justness and liberality of his views, had done more than any man in India to raise the reputation of the East India Company's service. By the natives he was venerated as the protector of their rights, familiar with their customs, and tolerant of their prejudices, ever ready to redress their grievances, but firm in maintaining order and obedience to the law. In a gazette extraordinary issued by his colleagues, on the receipt of the intelligence of his death, testimony was borne in language of more than ordinary eulogy to his public services and personal character, and to the universal regret which was felt at his death. An equestrian statue by Chantrey stands in a conspicuous position on the road from Fort St. George to Government House, and an excellent portrait by Sir Martin Archer Shee is in the Madras Banqueting Hall; another by Sir Henry Raeburn was in the third loan collection of national portraits, the property of Campbell Munro, esq.

[The Rev. G. R. Gleig's Life of Major-general Sir Thomas Munro, Bart., K.C.B., 1830; Selections from the Minutes and other Official Writings of Major-general Sir Thomas Munro, Bart., K.C.B., Governor of Madras, with an Introductory Memoir and Notes by the writer of this article, 1881; the introductory memoir in the last work was issued separately, with a new preface and some revision, under the title of 'Major-general Sir Thomas Munro, Bart., K.C.B., Governor of Madras: a Memoir,' 1889. A biography of Munro by John Bradshaw appeared in the 'Rulers of India' series in 1894.] A. J. A.

MUNRO, WILLIAM (1818–1880), general and botanist, eldest son of William Munro of Druids Stoke, Gloucestershire, entered the army as ensign 39th foot 20 Jan. 1834. His subsequent steps in the regiment, all by purchase, were lieutenant April 1836, captain 2 July 1844, major 7 May 1852, and lieutenant-colonel 11 Nov. 1853. He served with his regiment many years in India, and as adjutant was severely wounded at the battle of Maharajpore, 24 Dec. 1843, where the regiment suffered heavy loss (Maharajpore Star). He commanded the regiment at the siege of Sebastopol, and commanded the supports of the 3rd division in the attack on the Redan, 18 June 1855 (C.B., Legion of Honour and Medjidié, and English and Turkish Crimean medals). He commanded the 39th during its subsequent service in Canada and at Bermuda, retiring on half-pay in 1865.

Munro became a major-general 6 March 1868, commanded the troops in the West Indies 1870–6, was made a lieutenant-general 10 Feb. 1876, was appointed honorary colonel 93rd highlanders 11 Oct. the same year, and became a full general 25 June 1878. He died at Taunton, 29 Jan. 1880.

Munro was a 'learned botanist' (*Nature*, 12 Feb. 1880, p. 357). He contrived to combine with his military duties 'so close a study of the characters, nomenclature, affinities, and classification of grasses as to have been for many years the most trustworthy referee on that difficult order.' A 'Monograph on the Bamboos' in the 'Transactions of the Linnean Society' proves 'his industry and profound knowledge of his subject' (*Gardener's Chron.* 5 Feb. 1880). When Munro retired from active service and established himself at Taunton, he commenced a general monograph of the whole order of Gramineæ, in continuation of the 'Prodromus' of A. de Candolle. To the abiding loss of science, the monograph was not completed.

Munro was author of the following papers: 'Discovery [by Lieutenant W. Munro] of Fossil Plants at Kamptee,' 'Proceedings of Agricultural Society of India,' 1842, pp. 22–23; 'On Antidotes to Snake-bites,' 'Journal of Agricultural Society of India,' 1848, vi. 1–23; 'Report on Timber Trees of Bengal,' 'Edinburgh New Philosophical Journal,' 1849, xlvi. 84–94; 'Froriep Notizen,' 1849, x. 81–7, 'Characters of some New Grasses collected at Hong Kong and in the vicinity by Mr. Charles Wright in the North Pacific Exploring Expedition,' 'American Academy Proceedings,' 1857–60, vi. 362–8; 'An Identification of the Grasses of Linnæus's Herbarium, now in possession of the Linnean Society of London,' 'Linnean Society's Journal,' 1862, vi. 33–55.

[Hart's Army Lists; Kinglake's Crimea, cab. ed.; Cat. Scientific Papers, under 'Munro, William;' Broad Arrow, February 1880.] H. M. C.

MUNSON, LIONEL (*d.* 1680), Roman catholic priest. [See ANDERSON.]

MUNSTER, kings of. [See O'BRIEN, DONOUGH, *d.* 1064; O'BRIEN, TURLOUGH, 1009–1086; O'BRIEN, MURTOGH, *d.* 1119; O'BRIEN, DOMHNALL, *d.* 1194; O'BRIEN, DONOGH CAIRBRECH, *d.* 1242; O'BRIEN, CONCHOBHAR, *d.* 1267; O'BRIEN, BRIAN RUADH, *d.* 1276.]

MUNSTER, EARL OF. [See FITZCLARENCE, GEORGE AUGUSTUS FREDERICK, first EARL, 1794–1842.]

MUNTZ, GEORGE FREDERICK (1794–1857), political reformer, eldest son of Philip Frederick Muntz, was born in Birmingham on 26 November 1794 in a house in Great Charles Street, then a country residence. His ancestors were Poles, whom persecution drove to France. Muntz's grandfather, born in a country château near Soulz sur la Forêt, was a landowner of very aristocratic position. During the French revolution the family was broken up, and Philip Frederick Muntz, the father, travelled extensively, and after spending some time as a merchant at Amsterdam removed to England, and finally to Birmingham, where, partly owing to the advice of Matthew Boulton, he bought a share for 500*l.* in the firm of Mynors & Robert Purden, merchants. The firm was afterwards widely known as Muntz & Purden. He married Catherine, Purden's daughter, on 6 March 1793, and resided at Selly Hall, Worcestershire.

George Frederick was educated at home till his twelfth year, when he was sent to Dr. Currie's school at Small Heath, and after a twelvemonth went into business. He spoke French and German well. On the death of his father in 1811 he managed the metal works which the elder Muntz had established in Water Street (now pulled down). To their development Muntz devoted much of his energies, and realised a large fortune by the manufacture and extended application of what is known as 'Muntz metal.' The invention closely resembled that of James Keir [q. v.], who patented in 1779 'a compound metal, capable of being forged when red hot or when cold, more fit for the making of bolts, nails, and sheathing for ships than any metals heretofore used or applied for those purposes.' The similarity of the Keir to the Muntz metal was first noticed in 1866 in the 'Birmingham and Midland Hardware District' volume of Reports, and in the discussions which followed it was shown that in the autumn of 1779 Matthew Boulton brought the invention to the notice of the Admiralty. Whether Muntz knew of Keir's efforts is uncertain, but he first introduced the metal into universal use. In 1837 he became a partner with the copper smelters, Pascoe, Grenfell, & Sons of London and Swansea, but his principal metal works were at French Walls, near Birmingham. In 1832 he took out two patents (Nos. 6325 and 6347), one for 'Muntz's metal,' and one for 'ships' bolts of Muntz's metal,' and in 1846 a patent for an 'alloy for sheathing ships' (cf. R. B. Prosser, *Birmingham Inventors and Inventions*, privately printed, 1881).

From his youth upwards Muntz interested himself in public affairs, adopting liberal opinions. He studied specially the 'currency question,' and was an ardent disciple of the 'Birmingham school.' In 1829 he wrote letters on currency to the Duke of Wellington, which aroused attention, and was associated with Thomas Attwood and others in helping to repeal the Test and Corporation Acts, and in advocating catholic emancipation and reform of parliament. In 1829, in conjunction with Attwood and Joshua Scholefield, he founded the 'Political Union for the Protection of Public Rights,' and sought to alleviate the distress of the poorer population. On 5 Jan. 1830 he signed a memorial to the high bailiff of Birmingham (William Chance) asking him to call a meeting to consider the 'general distress,' and 'to form a general political union between the lower and the middle classes of the people,' for the 'further redress of public wrongs and grievances' by 'an effectual reform in the Commons House of Parliament.' The high bailiff refused, but a meeting of fifteen thousand persons was held, and approved Muntz's principles. Muntz was chairman. Numerous meetings followed on 'Newhall Hill' till the Reform Bill was passed. Muntz's 'burly form, rough and ready oratory, his thorough contempt for all conventionalities, the heartiness of his objurgations, all made him a favourite with the population, and an acceptable speaker at all their gatherings.' When the Duke of Wellington was especially unpopular, Muntz 'thundered to the ears of thousands' 'To stop the duke, go for gold,' and dangerous 'runs' on the banks followed just before the duke resigned (November 1830). Warrants for the arrest of Attwood, Scholefield, and Muntz were found in the home office, filled up, but unsigned.

On 24 May 1840 Muntz was elected M.P. for Birmingham in succession to Attwood, and he retained the seat, despite serious opposition, till his death. Although a radical, and almost a republican, he gloried in being 'independent,' and often offended his best friends and colleagues. 'As a speaker he was not notable. He often spoke obscurely and enigmatically, and was frequently charged with speaking one way and voting another. He uttered strong, rugged sentences in a deep diapason.' His legislative achievements included only an Act for the Prevention of Explosions on Steamers, but he induced a reluctant minister to adopt the system of perforated postage stamps, and to give a substantial sum to the inventor. In local politics he was a determined enemy to church rates. At one of the Easter vestry meetings in St. Martin's Church, Birmingham, he demanded to see the books, and was refused access to them. He proposed that the rector should be removed from the chair, and a riot ensued. An application was made to the court of queen's bench against him and three others, and the case was tried at Warwick on 30 March 1838 before Mr. Justice Parke for 'unlawful and riotous assembly.' After three days' trial they were virtually acquitted, but Muntz was found guilty of 'an affray,' and acquitted on twelve other counts. The proceedings were appealed against, and the court decided that 'the proceedings were illegal, and that the prosecution should never have been instituted.' 'The costs were 2,500*l.*, but Muntz refused any aid in paying them.'

Early in May 1857 signs of internal disease appeared. The death of a daughter greatly distressed him in his last years. Muntz's mother, who survived him, had a presentiment that he would die on the same day as his father, 31 July, and he himself held the same opinion. He 'died within a few hours of the dreaded day,' 30 July 1857, in his sixty-third year. He resided latterly at Umberslade Hall, Warwickshire. He married Eliza, daughter of John Pryce, and had six sons and two daughters. His manly figure and handsome face, with its huge black beard, his swinging walk, sonorous voice, and frank speech made his personality impressive. His son Philip Albert Muntz (1839–1908), who was conservative M.P. for Warwickshire (Tamworth division) from 1884 till death, was created a baronet in 1902.

[Birmingham and Midland Hardware Dist. 1866; R. B. Prosser's Birmingham Inventors, 1881; Aris's Birmingham Gazette, 1857; Gent. Mag. 1867, ii. 339; Birmingham Journal, 1857; Dent's Old and New Birmingham, 1880; personal knowledge; Percy's Metallurgy, p. 619.] S. T.

MÜNTZ, JOHN HENRY (*fl.* 1755–1775), painter, was of Swiss origin, and originally served in the French army. After the disbandment of his regiment he was found in the island of Jersey by Richard Bentley (1708–1782) [q. v.], who brought him to England, and introduced him to Horace Walpole at Strawberry Hill. Walpole employed him for some time as a painter and engraver. He also recommended him to his friends William Chute and others, and Müntz worked for some time at Chute's residence, The Vyne, near Basingstoke, where some of his paintings remain. Müntz painted chiefly Italian landscapes in a hard, cold manner, of which there were several examples at Strawberry Hill. He also copied pictures for Walpole. Together with Walpole he practised the art of encaustic painting, as revived by Caylus, and they projected a joint publication on the subject. This was checked, however, by a quarrel arising from an intrigue of Müntz with one of Walpole's servants, whom he subsequently married. The incident led to his dismissal from Walpole's service. He then came to London, where in 1760 he published 'Encaustic, or Count Caylus's Method of Painting in the Manner of the Ancients,' with an etching on the title-page by himself. In 1762 he exhibited a painting in encaustic at the Society of Artists, and again in 1763. After that there are no traces of him, but he may have gone to Holland, and is probably identical with J. H. Müntz, engineer and architect, who in 1772 compiled a work with drawings on ancient vases, which remains in manuscript in the South Kensington Art Library.

[Walpole's Letters, ed. P. Cunningham, vols. i. and iii.; Edwards's Anecdotes of Painters; Chute's Hist. of The Vyne; Cat. of Books on Art (South Kensington Museum).] L. C.

MURA (*d.* 645?), Irish saint, called by Irish writers Múra Othaine or Múra Fhothaine, and in Latin Murus or Muranus, was son of Feradach, who was fifth in descent from Niall Naighiallaigh, king of Ireland, and was born in Tireoghain, in the north of Ulster. Derinill was his mother's name. She is called in Irish Cethirchicheach, a cognomen expressing the not uncommon variety of structure in which a pair of supplementary mammæ are present, and was also the mother by another husband of St. Domangurt. Mura founded the abbey of Fahan, on the eastern shore of Lough Swilly, and was the first of a succession of learned abbots [see Maelmura]. He received a grant of lands from Aodh Uairidhneach, king of Ireland (605–12), who had made a pilgrimage to Fahan before his accession, and when the king was dying in 612 he sent for Mura to receive his confession. The saint reproved him for desiring to enslave the Leinstermen, the countrymen of so holy a person as St. Brigit, and administered the last sacraments to him (*Fragment of Annals, copied by MacFirbis from a manuscript of Gillananaemh MacÆdhagain*, Irish Archæological Society, 1860, ed. O'Donovan, pp. 12–16). A poem on the life of St. Columcille, of which only a few lines are extant, beginning 'Rugadh i ngartan da dheoin,' is attributed to Mura. No early authority for this exists, but it is quoted by Maghnus O'Donnell [q. v.] in 1532 as universally accepted in his time, and Colgan in 1645 states that it had been preserved till modern times with other compositions of the saint (*Acta Sanctorum Hiberniæ*, p. 587) at Fahan. The staff and the bell of the saint were also preserved there, and both still exist—the staff in the museum of the Royal Irish Academy, and the bell in the collection of Lord Otho Fitzgerald (*Ulster Journal of Archæology*, vol. i.; *Proceedings of Royal Irish Academy*, vol. v.) He died about 645, and 12 March was the day observed at Fahan as that of his death. He became the patron saint of the Cinel Eoghain and the O'Neills, and MacLochlainns used to take solemn oaths upon his staff. The foundation of the church of Banagher, co. Londonderry, was also his, and the present very ancient church is probably the immediate successor of the one built by him. His tomb, a sandstone structure of great antiquity, with a rude vertical effigy, stands on the same hill as the church in the townland of Magheramore, and a handful of the sand near it is believed in the country to insure the holder from drowning. At Banagher the identity of the saint has been lost, and Reeves (*Primate Colton's Visitation*, p. 107) prints his name Muriedach O'Heney, which is an attempt to represent the native pronunciation. The guttural is a modern addition, often made to terminal vowels in Ulster, and O'Heney is not a patronymic, but the genitive case with aspirated initial sound of the name of the saint's abbey of Fathan. The identity of the founder of Fahan with the founder of Banagher has not been determined before. The abbot of Fahan is always spoken of in Irish writings as 'comharba Mura,' successor of Mura.

[Annala Rioghachta Eireann, ed. O'Donovan, ii. 906; Colgan's Acta Sanct. Hiberniæ, i. 587; Bollandists' Acta Sanctorum, March 12; W. Reeves's Adamnan's Life of St. Columba; W. Reeves's Acts of Archbishop Colton, 1850, note, p. 106; Martyrology of Donegal, p. 74; J. O'Donovan's Three Fragments of Irish Annals, 1860, p. 10; J. H. Todd's Irish Version of the Historia Britonum, 1848; Petrie's Ecclesiastical Architecture of Ireland, 1845, p. 454, and Dunraven's Notes on Irish Architecture, for Drawings of the saint's tomb and church of Banagher; Ulster Journal of Archæology, i. 270, and Proc. of Royal Irish Academy, v. 206, as to bell and staff; local inquiries by the writer at Banagher and Inishowen.] N. M.

MURCHISON, CHARLES (1830–1879), physician, born in Jamaica on 26 July 1830, was younger son of the Hon. Alexander Murchison, M.D., cousin of Sir Roderick Impey Murchison [q. v.]. When Murchison was three years old the family returned to Scotland and settled at Elgin, where he received his first education. At the age of fifteen he entered the university of Aberdeen as a student of arts, and two years later commenced the study of medicine in the university of Edinburgh. Here he distinguished himself in natural history, botany, and chemistry, and later in more distinctly professional subjects, obtaining a large number of medals and prizes. He especially excelled in surgery, and passed the examination of the College of Surgeons of Edinburgh when little over twenty years of age, in 1850, and in the same year became house surgeon to James Syme [q. v.] In 1851 he graduated M.D. with a dissertation on the 'Structure of Tumours' (Edinburgh, 1852, 8vo), based on his own experience, which obtained the honour of a gold medal. He then spent a short time as physician to the British embassy at Turin, and, returning to Edinburgh, was for a short time resident physician in the Royal Infirmary.

After further study at Dublin and Paris Murchison entered the Bengal army of the East India Company on 17 Jan. 1853. On reaching India he was almost immediately made professor of chemistry at the Medical College, Calcutta. Later on he served with the expedition to Burmah in 1854, and his experience there furnished the materials for two papers in the 'Edinburgh Medical Journal' for January and April 1855 on the 'Climate and Diseases of Burmah.' But in October 1855 Murchison left the service and settled in London as a physician, commencing the long series of his medical appointments by becoming physician to the Westminster General Dispensary. Shortly afterwards he was connected with St. Mary's Hospital as lecturer on botany and curator of the museum, of which he prepared in a remarkably short time an excellent catalogue. In 1856 he was appointed assistant physician to King's College Hospital, but had to resign, in conformity with the rules of the hospital, in 1860. Murchison had no difficulty in obtaining a like position (combined with that of lecturer on pathology) at the Middlesex Hospital in the same year, and, being promoted to the post of full physician in 1866, retained his connection with that hospital till 1871. He also acted as assistant physician to the London Fever Hospital from 1856; and was promoted to be physician in 1861, an appointment which gave a definite bias to his medical researches. On his retirement in 1870 a testimonial was presented to him by public subscription. In 1871, when the staff of St. Thomas's Hospital was enlarged, consequent on the opening of its new buildings, Murchison accepted the posts of physician and lecturer on medicine, which he held till his death, with increase of reputation to himself and his school. In the autumn of 1873 he traced the origin of an epidemic of typhoid fever to polluted milk supply, and the residents in West London presented him with a testimonial. In 1866 he was elected fellow of the Royal Society. He became member of the Royal College of Physicians in 1855, was elected fellow in 1859, and gave the Croonian lectures in 1873. In 1870 he received the honorary degree of LL.D from the university of Edinburgh. In 1875 he was examiner in medicine to the university of London. His only court appointment was that of physician to the Duke and Duchess of Connaught. As a clinical teacher Murchison acquired a high reputation; his method was chiefly catechetical, and was impressive through his earnest and forcible manner. In exposition he was clear and positive, stating the subject in broad outlines, and inclining to be rather dogmatic, so that the attentive student carried away valuable and precise rules for practice. He was a man of high character and resolute integrity. With an unpretentious manner he possessed great kindness of heart and warm family affections.

Murchison's consulting practice was based at first on his special knowledge of fevers, but extended to other branches of medicine, and before his death was very considerable. His opinion was highly valued for his accuracy and prompt decision. In the forenoon of 23 April 1879, while seeing patients in his consulting room, he died suddenly of heart disease affecting the aortic valves. He had suffered from the ailment for nine years, but had resolutely declined the advice of medical friends to retire from practice. He was buried in Norwood cemetery. Murchison married in July 1859 Clara Elizabeth, third daughter of Robert Bickersteth, surgeon, of Liverpool, and had nine children; his wife, two sons and four daughters survived him. To his memory was founded a Murchison scholarship in medicine, to be awarded in alternate years in London by the Royal College of Physicians, and in Edinburgh by the university. A marble portrait bust was also placed in St. Thomas's Hospital. The great characteristic of his literary work was its solidity and accuracy of detail. He had the genius of thoroughness, and at the same time a happy fluency which enabled him to complete large masses of work with rapidity and precision. His own views were very positive, and he was a keen controversialist on some important questions, especially the relation of bacteria to disease. The side which he warmly defended has not been the winning side, and his views are fundamentally opposed to those now accepted; but the value of the materials which he contributed to the discussion is still great.

Murchison's most important contribution to medical science was 'A Treatise on the Continued Fevers of Great Britain,' London, 1862; 2nd ed. 1873; 3rd ed. (by Cayley), 1884. A German translation by W. Zuelzer appeared at Brunswick in 1867, 8vo, and a French translation of one part by Lutaud at Paris in 1878. This work became at once a standard authority. He treated the same subject in the 'Annual Reports of the London Fever Hospital,' 1861–9, and in medical journals. Another subject to which he gave special attention was that of diseases of the liver. After translating Frerichs's work on that subject for the New Sydenham Society in 1861, he published in 1868 'Clinical Lectures on Diseases of the Liver, Jaundice, and Abdominal Dropsy,' London, 8vo, and in 1874 took as the subject of his Croonian lectures at the College of Physicians 'Functional Derangements of the Liver,' London, 1874, 8vo; republished with 'Clinical Lectures on Diseases of the Liver,' 2nd ed. 1877; 3rd ed. (by Brunton) 1885. A French translation by Jules Cyr appeared at Paris in 1878. His regard for the memory of his friend, Dr. Hugh Falconer [q. v.], induced him to take great pains in bringing out the latter's 'Palæontological Memoirs' in 1868; geology was a favourite pursuit with Murchison.

Murchison took an active part in scientific societies, more especially the Pathological Society, of which he became a member in 1855; was secretary 1865–8; treasurer 1869–76, and president 1877–81. To the 'Transactions' of the society he contributed in all 143 papers and reports, some of them of considerable importance. He was also a member of the Royal Medical and Chirurgical, the Clinical, and the Epidemiological Societies, and contributed, though less frequently, to their transactions. Murchison also contributed to the 'Edinburgh Medical Journal,' the 'British and Foreign Medico-Chirurgical Review,' Beale's 'Archives of Medicine,' 'St. Thomas's Hospital Reports,' the 'British Medical Journal,' and other medical papers. The total number of his published works, memoirs, lectures, &c., was, according to a list in his own handwriting, 311.

[Lancet, 3 May 1879; British Medical Journal, 26 April 1879; Med. Times and Gazette, 10 May 1879; personal knowledge and private information.] J. F. P.

MURCHISON, Sir RODERICK IMPEY (1792–1871), geologist, born on 19 Feb. 1792 at Tarradale in Eastern Ross, was the eldest son of Kenneth Murchison by his wife, the daughter of Roderick Mackenzie of Fairburn. The Murchisons were a highland sept, living near Kintail and Lochalsh, the members of which were active in the rebellion of 1715. Kenneth Murchison was educated for the medical profession, went out to India, and held a lucrative appointment at Lucknow. After an absence of seventeen years he returned to Scotland with his savings, purchased Tarradale, and married in 1791. But about four years afterwards his health began to fail; he left Tarradale for the south of England, where he died in 1796. His widow settled in Edinburgh with her two boys, and before long married Colonel Robert Macgregor Murray, an old friend of her late husband. In 1799 Roderick was placed at the grammar school, Durham, where he led in mischief more often than in his class. In 1805 he was removed to the military college, Great Marlow, where he kept up his Durham reputation, but was attentive to work distinctly professional. In 1807 he was gazetted ensign in the 36th regiment, but did not join till the following winter, though even then he was under sixteen. The regiment—a smart and distinguished one—was then quartered at Cork, but during the summer it was hurried off to

Portugal, where it fought with distinction at Vimeiro, and afterwards shared in Sir John Moore's Spanish campaign and his disastrous retreat to Corunna. The regiment embarked safely during the night of 16 Jan. 1809, but narrowly escaped shipwreck on the Cornish coast. It remained in England, but in the autumn Murchison went out to Sicily as aide-de-camp to his uncle, General Mackenzie, returning in 1811. The latter was then appointed to a command in Ireland, and took Murchison with him. But the peace of 1814 placed him on half-pay. As it happened, he was in Paris when the news of Napoleon's landing arrived. Murchison then, in hope of seeing active service, and against his uncle's advice, exchanged into a cavalry regiment to no purpose, for his troop remained in England. But as a consolation he met in the Isle of Wight Charlotte, daughter of General and Mrs. Hugonin, whom he married on 29 Aug., and shortly afterwards retired from the army.

This was the turning-point of Murchison's life. 'From this time he came under the influence of a thoughtful, cultivated, and affectionate woman . . . to his wife he owed his fame, as he never failed gracefully to record' (GEIKIE). It was, however, still some years before he settled down to scientific work. For a brief time he thought of being ordained, but soon gave up the idea, and started with his wife in the spring of 1816 for a leisurely tour on the continent. Here they remained till the summer of 1818, chiefly at Rome and Naples, where Murchison plunged enthusiastically into the study of art and antiquities. On his return to England he sold Tarradale, to the benefit of his income, and settled down at Barnard Castle, devoting himself to field-sports. But about five years afterwards he became acquainted with Sir Humphry Davy, and determined to remove to London in order to pursue science instead of the fox. In the autumn of 1824 he began to attend lectures diligently at the Royal Institution. He was admitted on 7 Jan. 1825 a fellow of the Geological Society, and that science quickly kindled his enthusiasm. The following summer was devoted to field-work around Nursted, Kent (where General Hugonin resided), and to a tour westwards as far as Cornwall. Murchison's first paper, a 'Geological Sketch of the North-western extremity of Sussex and the adjoining parts of Hants and Surrey,' was read to the Geological Society at the end of 1825. In 1826 he was elected F.R.S., an honour which at that time indicated social position more than scientific distinction, and spent the summer examining the Jurassic rocks of Yorkshire and on both coasts of Scotland. This was the first of a series of summer journeys for the study of geology, and of a number of papers which quickly made him 'one of the most prominent members of the Geological Society.' In 1827 he travelled with Sedgwick in the highlands; in 1828, accompanied by his wife, with C. Lyell in Auvergne and Northern Italy, the Murchisons returning from Venice across the Tyrol to the Lake of Constance. In 1829 Murchison and Sedgwick wandered through Rhine-Prussia and Germany to Trieste, whence they worked their way through the Eastern Alps to the Salzkammergut, and so back by Constance across France. In 1830 Murchison with his wife revisited the Eastern Alps to continue the last year's work.

After five years of service as secretary of the Geological Society he was elected president in 1831, and almost simultaneously quitted the secondary rocks, hitherto the chief subject of his studies, for those older masses, underlying the carboniferous or the old red sandstone, which were called by Weiner the transition, by some greywacke. These, geologically speaking, were an almost unknown land. In the summer of 1831 Sedgwick attacked the northern part of Wales from Anglesey, Murchison the more southern district from the eastern borderland. At one time a joint tour had been suggested; but the intention was unfortunately never realised. Murchison devoted the next two summers to similar work, and in the autumn of 1833 determined that his researches should result in a book. In the summer of 1834 the two friends spent some days together in Wales, endeavouring to fit their separate work, but unluckily they parted without discovering that the lower part of Murchison's system of strata (to which in 1835 he assigned the name Silurian) was identical with the upper part of that worked out and called Cambrian by Sedgwick. The preparation of Murchison's book took a long time, but field-work went on in the summer, and in 1836 he made the first of three journeys to Devonshire to unravel another 'greywacke' district. At last, at the end of 1838, 'The Silurian System,' a thick quarto book, with a coloured map and an atlas of plates, of fossils, and sections, was published. It embodied and systematised the results obtained by Murchison himself, or supplied to him by others, which had been already communicated to geologists in numerous papers.

The researches of Sedgwick and Murchison in the west of England were followed by papers in which was proposed the establishment of a Devonian system intermediate between the carboniferous and Silurian, and so equivalent to the old red sandstone, and the two friends in 1839 visited Germany and the Boulonnais to obtain further confirmation of their views.

In this year Murchison's social influence was increased by an augmentation of fortune, which enabled him to move to a house in Belgrave Square, his residence for the rest of his life, which became a meeting-place for workers of science with those otherwise distinguished. He also planned a visit to Russia, in which country the palæozoic rocks were comparatively undisturbed, and so presented fewer difficulties than they did in Britain. Accompanied by De Verneuil, and greatly aided by the officials and savants of Russia, Murchison crossed the northern part of that country to the shores of the White Sea, and thence up the Dwina to Nijni Novgorod, Moscow, and back to St. Petersburg. In the following summer the two travellers returned to Moscow, and, after examining the carboniferous rocks in the neighbourhood, struck off for the Ural Mountains, followed them southwards to Orsk, thence westward to the Sea of Azof, and so back to Moscow. After a third visit to St. Petersburg by way of Scandinavia and Finland, besides travel at home as usual, the important work on 'The Geology of Russia and the Ural Mountains,' by Murchison, Von Keyserling, and De Verneuil, was published in April 1845.

Honours other than scientific now began to come in. From the emperor of Russia he had already received the orders of St. Anne and of Stanislaus, and in February 1846 he was knighted. In 1843 he was elected president of the Geographical Society, an office which henceforth somewhat diverted his attention from geology. Still the old love was not forgotten. His summer journeys consinued, and from July 1847 to September 1848 Sir Roderick and Lady Murchison, partly on account of her health, were on the continent, revisiting Rome, Naples, and the Eastern Alps. This journey had for its result an important paper on the geological structure of the Alps, Apennines, and Carpathians (*Quarterly Journal Geological Society*, v. 157). Auvergne also was revisited in 1850. Murchison for some time had been occupied in recasting the 'Silurian System' into a more convenient form, and the new book, under the title 'Siluria,' appeared in 1854.

The following year brought an important change in Murchison's life, for on the death Sir H. De la Beche [q. v.] he was appointed director-general of the geological survey. The same summer also witnessed the beginning of a new piece of work, the attempt to unravel the complicated structure of the Scottish highlands. A journey undertaken in 1858 with C. Peach [q. v.] made it clear that the Torridon sandstone of the north-western highlands was much less ancient than a great series of coarse gneissose rocks, to which Murchison gave the name of fundamental gneiss, afterwards identifying it with the Laurentian gneiss of North America. The Torridon sandstone afforded no traces of life, but it was followed by quartzites and limestones, then supposed to be, from their fossils, of lower Silurian age, but now placed low in the Cambrian, and above these, in apparent sequence, came a series of crystalline schists less coarse grained, and with a more stratified aspect than the 'fundamental gneiss.' Of these schists much of the central highlands and the southern part of the north-western were evidently composed. Murchison, then, regarded these as Silurian strata altered by metamorphism. Professor J. Nicol [q. v.], who had been at first associated with Murchison, dissented from this view, maintaining these schists to be really part of the fundamental gneiss, brought up by faulting. Murchison accordingly revisited the highlands in 1859 with Professor Alexander Ramsay [q. v.], and in 1860 with Mr. A. Geikie, and returned more than ever convinced of the accuracy of his view, which was maintained in a joint paper read to the Geological Society early in 1861. But Professor Nicol, as time has shown, in the main was right.

This highland tour closed the more active part of Murchison's life. Afterwards he made no lengthy journey, though he visited various localities in Britain, and even went to Germany in order to investigate questions which arose out of his former work. Much time also was occupied by his official labours at Jermyn Street, and by other duties arising from his position and his general interest in scientific affairs. After 1864 he wrote few more papers, but continued president of the Geographical Society, and gave an annual address till 1871. Early in 1869 Lady Murchison died, after an illness of some duration, In November 1870 he was struck by paralysis. From this he partially recovered, but during the later part of the following summer the malady began to make marked progress, and his life was closed by an attack of bronchitis on 22 Oct. 1871. Four days afterwards he was laid in Brompton cemetery by his wife's side.

Murchison could not complain that his merits were unrecognised. Besides the distinctions mentioned above, and valuable presents from the czar of Russia, he was made a K.C.B. in 1863, and a baronet in 1866. He received the degree of D.C.L. from Oxford, that of LL.D. from Cambridge and from Dublin, and was an honorary member of numerous societies in all parts of the world, including the Academy of Sciences in the French Institute. He was president of the geographical and the geological sections of the British Association more than once, and of the association itself (which he helped to found) in 1846. He was for fifteen years president of the Geographical Society, and twice president of the Geological Society, for which he received the Wollaston medal. He was also awarded the Copley medal of the Royal Society, the Brisbane medal of the Royal Society of Edinburgh, and the *Prix Cuvier*.

In person Murchison was tall, wiry, muscular, of a commanding presence and dignified manner. A portrait was painted by Pickersgill, which has been engraved, and there are marble busts at the Geological Society and in the Museum of Economic Geology.

Murchison was fortunate not only in the society of a wife who saved him from becoming a mere idler, but also in the possession of means which from the first placed him above want, and in later life were very ample. He was not insensible to the advantages of aristocratic friends and royal favour. His social influence was considerable, and it was exercised for the benefit of science and its workers. One of his last acts was to contribute half the endowment to a chair of geology at Edinburgh. He was a hospitable host, a firm and generous friend, though perhaps, especially in his later years, somewhat too self-appreciative and intolerant of opposition. He was a man of indomitable energy and great powers of work, blessed with an excellent constitution, very methodical and punctual in his habits. His contributions to scientific literature were very numerous, for, in addition to the books already mentioned, a list of above 180 papers (several of them written in conjunction with others), notes, and addresses is appended to the memoir of his life, nearly all on geographical or geological subjects. Of the value of his work it is still difficult to speak, for the dispute as to the limits of the Cambrian and Silurian systems which arose between him and Sedgwick unfortunately created some bitterness which extended beyond the principals. Into its details we need not enter, but we must admit that in the 'Silurian System' Murchison made at least two grave mistakes, that of confusing the Llandovery rocks with the Caradoc sandstone, and of mistaking the position of the Llandilo beds in the typical area near that town. Murchison's strength lay in rapidly apprehending the dominant features in the geology of a district. His knowledge of palæontology was limited, but here generally he was able to avail himself of the assistance of others; of petrology he knew less, and his errors on the subject of metamorphism, particularly in regard to the Scottish highlands, most seriously impeded, both directly and indirectly, the progress of that branch of geology in Britain. In short, as his biographer candidly states, 'he was not gifted with the philosophic spirit which evolves broad laws and principles in science. He had hardly any imaginative power. He wanted, therefore, the genius for dealing with questions of theory, even when they had reference to branches of science the detailed facts of which were familiar to him. . . . But he will ever hold a high place among the pioneers by whose patient and sagacious power of gathering new facts new kingdoms of knowledge are added to the intellectual domain of man. He was not a profound thinker, but his contemporaries could hardly find a clearer, more keen-eyed and careful observer.'

[Archibald Geikie's Life of Sir Roderick I. Murchison, 2 vols. 1875; Griffin's Contemporary Biography in Addit. MS. 28511.] T. G. B.

MURCOT, JOHN (1625–1654), puritan divine, born at Warwick in 1625, son of Job Murcot and his wife Joan Townshend, was educated at the King's school, Warwick, and in 1641 entered Merton College, Oxford, his tutor being Ralph Button [q. v.], a strict presbyterian. He temporarily quitted Oxford when it was garrisoned for the king, and went to 'table' with John Ley [q. v.], presbyterian minister of Budworth in Cheshire. On the permanent defeat of Charles, after graduating B.A. at Oxford 30 March 1647, he again retired to Cheshire; while there he received a 'call' to the church of Astbury in the hundred of Northwich, and received ordination from the Manchester classis on 9 Feb. 1647–1648. No trace of his name appears in the register at Astbury, and he appears very shortly after to have removed to Eastham, in the hundred of Wirral, Cheshire (there is a gap in the Eastham registers from 1644–54). But before 30 June 1648 he was succeeded at Eastham by Richard Banner, and was himself presented to the rectory of West Kirby by the Committee for Plundered Ministers in place of his deceased father-in-law, Ralph Marsden. From West Kirby he was 'motioned' to Chester, but without any result. He did not 'remove' thither, the cause of his refusal being doubtless his growing leaning towards independency. In 1651 he crossed to Dublin with his family, at the invitation of Sir Robert King, whose guest he became. He was appointed one of the preachers in ordinary to Lord-deputy Fleetwood and the council of Ireland, and attached himself to the independent congregation of Dr. Samuel Winter, provost of Trinity College, Dublin, which met in the church of St. Michan's Within. At the request of the congregation he undertook the work of 'teaching' among them, the pastorate being left to Dr. Winter. Murcot subsequently became pastor. The vestry book, under date 29 Aug. 1651, mentions the engagement of Mr. Thomas Serle as preacher 'before Mr. Moorecot was settled in this parish.' But in 1653 he describes himself as 'preacher of the Gospel at St. Owen's' (St. Audoens) He died on 26 Nov. 1654, and was buried in Christ Church Cathedral, Dublin, where a monument, not now existing, was erected to his memory. His funeral was attended by Lord-deputy Fleetwood, the council, the lord mayor of Dublin, and others. His youth and erudition provoked extravagant eulogy from his acquaintances.

His publications comprise a sermon preached at Dublin (1656), and a volume entitled 'Several Works' all on religious topics (London, 1657, 4to), with a life attributed to various friends, among them Samuel Eaton the independent and Dr. Samuel Winter. A portrait, engraved by Faithorne, is prefixed to his collected 'works.'

[Wood's Athenæ Oxon.; Granger's Biog. Hist.; Urwick's Nonconformity in Cheshire; Minutes of the Manchester Classis (Chetham Soc.); Dr. W. Reynell in the Irish Builder for 1 Aug. 1888; Dr. William Urwick's Independency in Dublin in the Olden Times; Colvile's Warwickshire Worthies; Hunter's Oliver Heywood, p. 81; O. Heywood's Diaries, iv. 10; Newcome's Autobiography (Chetham Soc.); Lancashire and Cheshire Record Soc. i. 255; Watt's Bibl. Brit.; Plundered Ministers' MSS. in the writer's possession; manuscripts of the late J. E. Bailey (Chetham Library, Manchester); information from the rectors of Astbury and Eastham and from the Rev. W. Reynell, B.D.] W. A. S.

MURDAC, HENRY (*d.* 1153), archbishop of York, a member of a wealthy and important family of Yorkshire, was given a place among the clergy of the church of York by Archbishop Thurstan. Having received a letter from St. Bernard of Clairvaux, eloquently exhorting him to adopt the monastic life, he became a monk, and entered the Cistercian monastery of Clairvaux. From this letter it may be inferred that he was a learned man; in its address he is styled 'magister,' exhorted to become a member of the 'school of piety,' to take Jesus as his master, and to leave his books for the solitude of the woods, and the address ends with a postscript by two of the monks of Clairvaux, who appear to have been his pupils (S. BERNARD, *Ep.* 106, ap. *Opp.* i. cols. 110, 111). After remaining at Clairvaux for some time he was sent by Bernard in 1135 with twelve companions to found a monastery at Vauclair, in the diocese of Laon, and was the first abbot of the new house. While there he was engaged in a sharp dispute with Luke, abbot of the neighbouring Præmonstratensian house at Cuissi (*Gallia Christiana*, ix. 633). On the death, at Clairvaux in 1143, of Richard, second abbot of Fountains, in Yorkshire, Bernard wrote to the prior and convent telling them that he was about to send Abbot Henry to them, and bidding them take his advice as to the election of abbot, and obey him in all things (*Ep.* 320, *Opp.* i. col. 299). At the same time he wrote to Murdac bidding him, if he should be elected abbot of Fountains, by no means to refuse, and promising in that case to watch over the interests of Vauclair (*Ep.* 321, *Opp.* i. col. 300). Murdac went to Fountains, was elected abbot, and accepted the office.

It was a time of extraordinary energy at Fountains, as many as five daughter houses, Woburn in Bedfordshire, Lisa in Norway, Kirkstall in Yorkshire, Vaudy in Lincolnshire, and Meaux in Yorkshire, being founded from it during Murdac's abbacy. He made reforms in his own house, and brought it into full accord with the severe life observed at Clairvaux; its possessions were increased under his rule (DUGDALE, *Monasticon*, v. 301, 302). Relying on the help that he was certain to receive from Pope Eugenius III, the friend of Bernard, he took a prominent part in the opposition to William Fitzherbert [q. v.], archbishop of York (JOHN OF HEXHAM, ii. 318). In 1146 some of the knights of the archbishop's party, in revenge for his suspension by the pope, armed themselves and broke into Fountains. They sacked the house, and finding little spoil, set the buildings on fire. Meanwhile Murdac was stretched at the foot of the altar in the oratory. Part of the oratory was burnt, but the invaders did not see him. He escaped, and at once set about rebuilding, in a more comely style, his monastery, which they had reduced to a ruin (*Monasticon*, v. 302). Murdac attended the council of Paris held by the pope in the spring of 1147, and there Fitzherbert was deprived (GERVASE, i. 134; BARONIUS, *Annales*, ed. Pagi, xix. 7, 8; NORGATE, *Angevin Kings*, i. 366). On 24 July the chapter of York, together with the suffragan bishops, William of Durham and Aldulf of Carlisle, met in St. Martin's Priory at Richmond to choose an archbishop in place of Fitzherbert. Robert of Gaunt, the dean of York, and Hugh of Puiset, the treasurer, King Stephen's nephew, both of them Fitzherbert's supporters, were in favour of Hilary [q. v.], afterwards bishop of Chichester, while the two bishops, the archdeacon, and others voted for Henry Murdac (John of Hexham, ii. 321); the election seems to have been referred to the pope for decision. Murdac crossed to France and paid a visit to Bernard, and then went to meet the pope at Trèves. Eugenius received him with honour, confirmed his election, consecrated him at Trèves on 7 Dec., and gave him the pall (*ib.*; William of Newburgh, i. 48).

On his return to England in 1148 to take possession of his see he found the king highly incensed against him, for both Stephen and Henry of Blois [q. v.], bishop of Winchester, upheld the cause of their nephew, Fitzherbert. The prebends of his church were confiscated and the tenants oppressed, the citizens of York refused to allow him to enter the city, and no one who went out to him was allowed to return. Murdac excommunicated Hugh of Puiset, the head of the opposition to him, and laid an interdict on York. In return Hugh excommunicated him and forced the clergy to perform the services as usual. Murdac took up his residence at Ripon, where he seems, though no longer abbot, to have continued to watch over the affairs of Fountains (S. Bernard, *Ep.* 206, *Opp.* i. 288). He visited the Bishop of Durham, and was received by him as his metropolitan, and also went to meet David of Scotland [q. v.] at Carlisle, and was honourably received by Bishop Adelulf. This visit to Carlisle very probably took place at Whitsuntide 1148, when David received Henry, duke of Normandy, afterwards Henry II [q.v.], there; for immediately afterwards Stephen went to York, and thence proceeded to Beverley, where he laid a fine upon the people for having received Murdac. After the king's departure Murdac's interdict was, at least to some extent, observed at York. On hearing this, Eustace, the king's son, compelled the clergy to conduct the services without omissions, and drove out of the city those who refused, the senior archdeacon being slain by Eustace's party. Whereupon Murdac wrote a pressing complaint to the pope. Stephen at last found that it was dangerous to provoke the pope further, and Eustace mediated between him and Murdac. Eustace was reconciled to Murdac, and succeeded in making peace between him and the king, both agreeing to forgive all causes of complaint, one against the other.

Murdac was magnificently received at York, and was enthroned on 25 Jan. 1151. He absolved Hugh of Puiset from excommunication, and having promised to use his influence with the pope on Stephen's behalf, and if possible secure the pope's recognition of Eustace as heir to the throne, he went to Rome and spent Easter there. A large part of the summer of 1152 he spent at Hexham, where he endeavoured to introduce a stricter manner of life among the canons. He made a complaint to David of Scotland that the king's men engaged in mining for silver wasted his forest there. In 1153 he substituted canons regular in the place of the prebendaries in the church of St. Oswald at Gloucester, and placed them under the rule of a monk from Lanthony. He designed to make a like change at Beverley, but was prevented by death. He was much displeased at the election of Hugh of Puiset to the see of Durham, and refused to recognise it both on the ground of Hugh's youth and character, and because he had not been consulted. He excommunicated the prior and archdeacons of Durham and the prior of Brinkburn. On Ash Wednesday they came to York to request that the sentence might be recalled, but as they maintained that the election was legal, he refused. The citizens of York took their part, rose against the archbishop, abused him, and called him a traitor to the king. He fled in haste, and did not return to York alive. He went to Beverley. There Eustace came to him, and on his own account and his father's prayed him to yield, but he would not. Finally Theobald, archbishop of Canterbury, persuaded him to absolve the offenders, but he did not do so until after they had appeared before him and had submitted to a scourging (*Historiæ Dunelmensis Tres Scriptores*, pp. 4, 5; John of Hexham, ii. 329; William of Newburgh, i. 70). Murdac died at Sherburn on 14 Oct. in that year, very shortly after the deaths of the other two great Cistercians, Pope Eugenius and St. Bernard, with whom he was closely allied in mutual affection. He was buried in York Minster. He loved righteousness, and was perhaps too unbending in his opposition to all that he disapproved. Working as he did in unison with St. Bernard, and being of like mind with him, he did much to bring the Cistercian order in England to its greatest height, and the chronicler of Fountains classes him with Eugenius and Bernard, speaking of the three as 'guardians of the Lord's flock, columns of the Lord's house, and lights of the world' (*Monasticon*, v. 303). He was austere in his own life, and continually wore a hair-shirt. In the story of 'The Nun of Watton' he is represented as appearing to the nun after his death and bringing her help (AILRED ap. *Decem Scriptores*, col. 419). The foundation of Watton in Yorkshire had been confirmed by him as archbishop (*Monasticon*, vi. 955).

[Raine's Fasti Ebor. pp. 310–20, contains a life of Murdac, with copious references; S. Bernardi Epp. 106, 206, 320, 321, ap. Opp. i. cols. 110, 111, 288, 299, 300, ed. Mabillon; Symeon of Durham Cont. and John of Hexham ap. Symeon of Durham, i. 167, 169, ii. 317, 320–5, 331 (Rolls Ser.); Dugdale's Monasticon, v. 301–303, vi. 955; Hist. Dunelm. Tres Scriptt. pp. 4, 5 (Surtees Soc.); Gervase of Cant. i. 155, 157, ii. 386 (Rolls Ser.); William of Newburgh, i. 48, 70 (Engl. Hist. Soc.); Gallia Christiana, ix. 633; Norgate's Angevin Kings, i. 365–7, 378, 380.] W. H.

MURDAC or MURDOCH, second DUKE OF ALBANY (*d.* 1425). [See STEWART.]

MURDOCH, JOHN (1747–1824), miscellaneous writer and friend of Burns, was born at Ayr in 1747. He received a liberal education in that town, and finished his studies at Edinburgh. For some time he was assistant at a private academy, and was afterwards appointed master of Ayr school. Among his pupils was Burns, who is described by Murdoch as being 'very apt,' but his ear was 'remarkably dull and his voice untuneable.' Desiring to extend his knowledge of the world, he left Ayr for London, and spent the night before his departure at the house of Burns's father, reading aloud part of the tragedy of 'Titus Andronicus,' by which the poet was much affected. Several letters subsequently passed between Burns and Murdoch. After a short stay in London Murdoch went on to Paris, where he formed a lifelong intimacy with Colonel Fullarton, secretary to the British embassy. On his return to London Murdoch taught the French and English languages with much success, both at pupils' houses and at his own house in Staple Inn. Talleyrand during his residence as an emigrant in this country was taught English by him. Murdoch fell into much distress in old age, and was obliged to appeal to the public for support. The 'Gentleman's Magazine' inserted a notice begging for aid for him (1824, pt. i. p. 165). He died on 20 April 1824. His wife, whom he married in 1780, survived him.

Murdoch edited the stereotyped edition of 'Walker's Pronouncing Dictionary.' His own works consist of: 1. 'An Essay on the Revolutions of Literature,' translated from the Italian of Signor C. Denina, 1771. 2. 'A Radical Vocabulary of the French Language,' 1782. 3. 'Pictures of the Hearts,' 1783, a collection of essays, tales, and a drama. 4. 'The Pronunciation and Orthography of the French Language,' 1788. 5. 'The Dictionary of Distinctions,' 1811, to facilitate spelling and pronunciation. In this book 'The Tears of Sensibility' was announced as preparing for publication. It was to contain novels from the French of D'Arnaud, but no copy is to be found in the British Museum Library.

[European Mag., 1783, iii. 130; Notes and Queries, 2nd ser. xii. 419; Dict. of Living Authors, 1816, p. 245; Gent. Mag., 1824, pt. ii. p. 186; R. Chambers's Life and Works of Burns, 1891, i. 9, 11, 14, 17, ii. 161, iii. 111, 125.] M. G. W.

MURDOCH, PATRICK (*d.* 1774), author, a native of Dumfries, was educated at the university of Edinburgh, where he distinguished himself in mathematics, and was the pupil and friend of Colin Maclaurin [q. v.] In 1729 he was appointed tutor to John Forbes, only son of Lord-president Duncan Forbes of Culloden, and visited with him Orleans, Montauban, Rome, and other continental cities. Forbes subsequently paid Murdoch long and frequent visits at Stradishall rectory, Suffolk, and placed his eldest son, Duncan, under his tuition (BURTON, *Lives of Lord Lovat and Duncan Forbes*, pp. 344–6). Murdoch was likewise travelling tutor to the younger sons of James Vernon, ambassador to the court of Denmark. He was presented by James Vernon to the rectory of Stradishall in 1738, when his friend, James Thomson, addressed to him some pleasing lines (*Works*, ed. 1762, i. 457). On 20 March 1745 he was elected F.R.S. (THOMSON, *Hist. of Royal Soc.* App. iv. p. xliv), and in 1748 was admitted M.A. at Cambridge *per literas regias*. William Leman gave him the rectory of Kettlebaston, Suffolk, in 1749, which he resigned in 1760 on being presented by Edward Vernon to the vicarage of Great Thurlow; but he still continued to reside at Stradishall. In 1756 he accompanied his friend Andrew (afterwards Sir Andrew) Mitchell (1695?–1771) [q. v.], to Berlin, where he remained until 1757, conducting part of the correspondence, while Mitchell and his secretary, Burnet, were with the army (BISSET, *Memoirs of Sir A. Mitchell*, i. 37–41). Shortly after his return home he received the degree of D.D., presumably from the university of Edinburgh. Murdoch died in October 1774 in St. Clement Danes, London (NICHOLS, *Lit. Anecd.* viii. 465; *Probate Act Book*, P. C. C. 1774). He appears to have been amiable and simple-hearted, and a good scholar. Though he speaks of his engagement to a lady whom he met in Paris in 1742 (*Culloden Papers*, p. 177), he died a bachelor (see will, P. C. C. 402, Bargrave). His library was sold in 1776 (NICHOLS, iii. 656).

Murdoch, having written the 68th stanza in canto i. of Thomson's 'Castle of Indolence,' in which he portrayed the poet, Thomson gave the next stanza as descriptive of Murdoch, referring to him as 'a little, round, fat, oily man of God.' Murdoch also wrote a short but clear and lively memoir of Thomson prefixed to the memorial edition of the poet's 'Works,' 2 vols. 4to, 1762, and to nearly all the later editions of 'The Seasons.'

To Colin Maclaurin's 'Account of Sir Isaac Newton's Philosophical Discoveries,' 4to, London, 1748, which he saw through the press for the benefit of the author's children, he prefixed an account of his life. Another edition was issued in 1750, 8vo. He also edited the illustrations of perspective from conic sections, entitled 'Neutoni Genesis Curvarum per Umbras,' &c., 8vo, London, 1746. He contemplated a complete edition of Newton's works, and by 1766 had found a publisher in Andrew Millar [q.v.], but increasing infirmities obliged him to abandon the undertaking.

Murdoch was author of 'Mercator's Sailing, applied to the true Figure of the Earth; with an Introduction,' &c., 4to, London, 1741. To the 'Philosophical Transactions' he communicated eight papers, two of which 'Trigonometry abridged,' 1758, and 'On Geographical Maps,' 1758, exist in the original manuscript among the Additional MSS. in the British Museum (No. 4440, arts. 564 and 565). He translated from the German the portion of Anton Friedrich Buesching's 'New System of Geography,' which relates to the European states, 6 vols. 4to, London, 1762, and prefixed three explanatory essays.

Murdoch's letters to Dr. Thomas Birch, 1756–9, are in Additional MS. 4315; those to Sir Andrew Mitchell, 1756–70, are contained in Additional MS. 6840; while twelve letters by him are printed in the 'Culloden Papers,' 4to, 1815. His letterbook, when acting for Mitchell at Berlin, 1756–7, is Additional MS. 6841 (cf. *Add. MSS.* 6805, f. 48, 6839, f. 105).

[Davy's Suffolk Collections (Addit. MS. 19103, under Stradishall); Suffolk Garland, pp. 25–6.] G. G.

MURDOCH, SIR THOMAS WILLIAM CLINTON (1809–1891), civil servant, born on 22 March 1809 in London, was son of Thomas Murdoch, F.R.S., of Portland Place, and Charlotte, daughter of John Leacock of Madeira. He was educated at the Charterhouse, and entered the colonial office as a junior clerk in 1826. In September 1839 he went out under Sir George Arthur to Canada to act as chief secretary, and, after acting also during part of 1841 as provincial secretary for Lower Canada, returned to the colonial office in September 1842. He became a senior clerk there in May 1846.

In November 1847 Murdoch was appointed to the important position of chairman of the Colonial Land and Emigration Commissioners, and it is in connection with the regulation of emigration and colonisation during the succeeding years that his name is best known. In 1870 he visited Canada on a mission connected with free grants to settlers. At the same time he carried important instructions on the Red River matter; and he went on to the United States to discuss the question of offences on British passenger ships plying to the States.

Murdoch was created a K.C.M.G. in 1870, and retired on pension in December 1876. He was a great reader, and spent his later years chiefly among his books. He died on 30 Nov. 1891, at 88 St. George's Square, London. He married in 1836 Isabella Anne, daughter of Robert Lukin of the war office, and left issue; the eldest son, C. S. Murdoch, C.B., was assistant under-secretary of the home office 1896–1903.

[Private information; Colonial Office List and Records; Dod's Peerage.] C. A. H.

MURDOCK, WILLIAM (1754–1839), engineer, and inventor of coal-gas lighting, second son of John Murdock, millwright, was born at Bellow Mill, near Old Cumnock, Ayrshire, on 21 Aug. 1754. His father and grandfather had been gunners in the royal artillery, and pay-sheets bearing their signatures are still preserved in the royal artillery records at Woolwich. He altered the spelling of his name after his arrival in England, on account of the inability of the Englishmen to give it the true guttural pronunciation, and this practice is continued by his descendants. Brought up to his father's trade, he obtained in 1777 employment under Boulton & Watt at Soho. According to a well-known story, Boulton was struck on his first interview with Murdock by the peculiar hat which he was wearing, and Murdock stated, in answer to Boulton's questions, that it was made of wood, and that he had turned it on a lathe of his own making. It appears that Murdock in his nervousness let the hat fall on the floor, and it was the unusual noise produced that attracted Boulton's attention. He was engaged by Boulton, and about 1779 he was sent to Cornwall to look after the numerous pumping-engines erected by the firm in that county. He proved an invaluable help to Watt, and the references to him in the Soho correspondence are very numerous. He lived at Redruth, and is stated by Smiles to have returned to Soho in 1798; but in a patent which he took out on 25 Aug. 1799 he is described as 'of Redruth.' The specification of this patent, which was executed a month afterwards, was witnessed by Gregory Watt, James Watt's son, the declaration being made before a master-extraordinary in chancery who carried on business in Birmingham. According to documents at Soho, he signed an agreement on 30 March 1800 to act as an engineer and superintendent of the Soho foundry for a period of five years. He was, however, constantly despatched to different parts of the country, and he frequently visited Cornwall after he ceased to reside there permanently. His connection with Boulton & Watt's firm continued until 1830, when he practically retired, and died on 15 Nov. 1839, within sight of the Soho foundry, at his house at Sycamore Hill, which he built for himself in 1816. He was buried in Handsworth Church, where there is a bust of him by Chantrey.

Murdock married Miss Paynter, daughter of a mine captain residing at Redruth, and had two sons, William (1788–1831) and John (1790–1862); the former was employed by Boulton & Watt. Mrs. Murdock died in 1790, at the early age of twenty-four.

Murdock's unambitious career was entirely devoted to the interests of his employers, and his fame has been somewhat overshadowed by the great names of Boulton & Watt. About 1792, while residing at Redruth, he commenced making experiments on the illuminating properties of gases produced by distilling coal, wood, peat, &c. (*Phil. Trans.* 1808, p. 124). He lighted up his house at Redruth, and Mr. Francis Trevithick wrote in 1872: 'Those still live who saw the gas-pipes conveying gas from the retort in the little yard to near the ceiling of the room, just over the table. A hole for the pipe was made in the window-frame' (*Life of Trevithick*, i. 64). The house is still standing, and a commemorative tablet was recently placed upon it by Mr. Richard Tangye of Birmingham. The year 1792 has been fixed upon as the date when gas-lighting was first introduced, and the centenary of that event was celebrated in 1892, but it seems certain that 1792 is much too early. Among the documents preserved at Soho are two letters from Thomas Wilson (Boulton & Watt's agent in Cornwall), dated 27 Jan. and 29 Jan. 1808, in which he gives the results of his attempts to obtain evidence for the purpose of opposing the Gas Light and Coke Company's Bill before the House of Commons. Murdock's mother-in-law, then still resident at Redruth, told Wilson that 'the gas was never set fire to' at Murdock's house 'at a greater distance than the length of a gun-barrel fixed to the retort.' The only certain piece of evidence which Wilson could obtain was that Murdock had shown some experiments at Neath Abbey Iron Works in November 1795 and February 1796, when gas was made in 'an iron retort with an iron tube of from three to four feet in length, and through which the gas from coal then used in the retort issued, and at the end thereof was set fire to, and gave a strong and beautiful light, which continued burning a considerable time.' This date agrees very closely with a statement made by James Watt the younger in his evidence before a parliamentary committee in 1809, when he said that Murdock commnnicated to him in 1794 or 1795 the results of some experiments with coal-gas. In his letter of 29 Jan. Wilson says: 'It is strange how all who have seen it disagree on one point or the other ... On the whole I am afraid we shall be able to do little satisfactory.' These facts, now published for the first time, show that up to the date when he left Cornwall Murdock had done much less to advance the art of gas-lighting than is generally supposed.

Upon his return to Soho about 1799 he put up an apparatus, which was, however, only of an experimental character, for the purpose of demonstrating the capabilities of the new method of obtaining light. James Watt was doubtless interested in Murdock's experiments, as he had been at work for some time, in conjunction with Dr. Beddoes, the founder of the Pneumatic Institution at Bristol, in investigating the curative properties of oxygen and hydrogen gases when inhaled. In 1795 Watt issued a tract, illustrated with plates, describing the various retorts and purifiers manufactured by Boulton & Watt for preparing oxygen and hydrogen (cf. *Considerations on the Medicinal Use and on the Production of Factitious Airs*, pt. i. by Thomas Beddoes, M.D.; pt. ii. by James Watt, engineer. Bristol, 1795). The question of taking out a patent was then considered; but it was decided to await the result of certain litigation then pending, as it was somewhat doubtful whether a valid patent could be obtained. The experiments were accordingly suspended until about the end of 1801, when Gregory Watt wrote to his father from

Paris, giving an account of Lebon's experiments, and urging that if anything was to be done about the patent it must be done at once. The matter was taken up again, and on the occasion of the rejoicings at the peace of Amiens, in March 1802, gas was used to a small extent in the extensive illuminations at Soho, but not in a manner to attract much attention. The earliest reference to the use of gas at Soho in 1802 is contained in an editorial postscript to an article by Professor Henry in Nicholson's 'Journal of Natural Philosophy,' June 1805, xi. 74.

Samuel Clegg [q. v.], who was then an apprentice at Soho, and who assisted Murdock in his experiments, states in his son's book on 'Coal-gas,' 1841, p. 6: 'In March 1802 . . . Mr. Murdock first publicly exhibited the gas-light by placing at each end of the Soho manufactory what was termed a Bengal light. The operation was simply effected by fixing a retort in the fireplace of the house below, and then conducting the gas issuing from thence into a copper vase. This was the only gas used on that occasion.' As some misconception has arisen, it should be explained that there were at that time two buildings, situated at some distance apart: one was the Soho factory, now destroyed, and the other, the Soho foundry which still exists. It was the factory which was illuminated.

In 1803 apparatus was erected by which a part of the Soho foundry was regularly lighted with gas, and the manufacture of gas-making plant seems to have been commenced about this period, in connection no doubt with the business of supplying apparatus for producing oxygen and hydrogen for medical purposes. In 1804 George Augustus Lee, of the firm of Phillips & Lee, cotton-spinners, of Manchester, ordered an apparatus for lighting his house with gas [see under Lee, John, *d.* 1781]. About the end of the year Messrs. Phillips & Lee decided to light their mills with gas, and on 1 Jan. 1806 Murdock wrote informing Boulton & Watt that 'fifty lamps of the different kinds' were lighted that night, with satisfactory results. There was, Murdock stated, 'no Soho stink'—an expression which seems to show that the method of purification in use at Soho was of a somewhat primitive nature. The work was not finished for some time afterwards, as the Soho books contain entries of charges to Phillips & Lee extending over the next year, and even later. From 30 Sept. 1805 to 1807 3,674*l.* was charged to Phillips & Lee's account. The early forms of gas apparatus made at Soho are fully described in the supplement to the fourth and fifth editions of the 'Encyclopædia Britannica,' article 'Gas,' which was written by Creighton, one of the Soho managers.

In February 1808 Murdock read a paper before the Royal Society (*Phil. Trans.* xcviii. 124), in which he gave a full account of his investigations, and also of the saving effected by the adoption of gas-lighting at Phillips & Lee's mill. This paper is the earliest practical essay on the subject. The Rumford gold medal, bearing the inscription 'ex fumo dare lucem,' was awarded to Murdock for this paper, which concludes with these words: 'I believe I may, without presuming too much, claim both the first idea of applying and the first actual application of this gas to economical purposes.' As to the justice of this claim there can be no doubt.

By this time gas-lighting had fallen into the hands of the company promoters, and in 1809 application was made to parliament for a bill to incorporate the Gas Light and Coke Company. It was opposed by James Watt the younger on behalf of Boulton & Watt, who feared that their trade might be interfered with. The evidence given by James Watt and George Lee (of Phillips & Lee) before the committee to which the bill was referred contains valuable information concerning the history of Murdock's early efforts. Boulton & Watt were represented before the committee by Henry Brougham, and his speech was printed separately. It has been incorrectly stated that Murdock himself gave evidence. In answer to a statement put forth by the promoters of the bill, charging Murdock with plagiarism, he issued on 4 May 1809 'A Letter to a Member of Parliament . . . in Vindication of his Character and Claims.' This tract and the paper in the 'Philosophical Transactions' comprise the whole of Murdock's literary efforts. Only two or three copies of the tract seem to have survived, but it was reprinted for private distribution by the writer of this notice on the occasion of the Murdock centenary in 1892. Murdock's connection with gas-lighting seems to have come to an end in 1809. The 'Monthly Magazine' for November 1814, p. 357, refers to a gas company established in Water Lane, Fleet Street, by Messrs. Grant, Knight, & Murdoch, but the relationship (if any) of the Murdoch there named to the subject of this notice has not been established. Murdock lighted up the house which he built for himself in 1816 at Sycamore Hill, Handsworth, by gas supplied from the Soho foundry, probably when he first went to reside there. Some remains of the apparatus are still in existence (cf. *Birmingham Faces and Places*, December 1889, p. 125).

Claims have been put forward by various writers that Murdock ought to be regarded as one of the inventors of the locomotive; but from a strictly practical point of view this can hardly be conceded, as his experiments led to no results, and those who followed him worked on different lines. His attention seems to have been directed to the subject of locomotion by steam in 1784 (cf. MUIRHEAD, *Life of Watt*, pp. 443–5). On 9 Aug. 1786 Thomas Wilson, Boulton & Watt's agent in Cornwall, wrote to Soho: 'Wm. Murdock desires me to inform you that he has made a small engine of ¾ dia. and 1½-inch stroke, that he has apply'd to a small carriage, which answers amazingly.' In all probability this is the well-known model which was purchased a few years ago from the Murdock family by Messrs. Tangye Brothers, and by them presented to the Birmingham Art Gallery, where it is now exhibited, although the dimensions do not quite correspond with those given by Wilson. The true date of its construction is probably 1786. An exact reproduction of the Birmingham model may be seen in the machinery and inventions department of the South Kensington Museum. A section of the engine, carefully drawn to scale, appeared in 'The Engineer,' 10 June 1881, p. 432.

Writing to Watt from Truro on 2 Sept. 1786, Boulton stated that near Exeter he had met a coach in which was William Murdock. 'He got out, and we had a parley for some time. He said he was going to London to get men; but I soon found he was going there with his steam carriage to show it, and take out a patent, he having been told by Mr. Wm. Wilkinson what Sadler has said, and he has likewise read in the newspaper Symington's puff, which has rekindled all Wm.'s fire and impatience to make steam carriages. However, I prevailed upon him to return to Cornwall by the next day's diligence, and he accordingly arrived here this day at noon, since which he hath unpacked his carriage and made travil a mile or two in Rivers's great room, making it carry the fire-shovel, poker, and tongs. I think it fortunate that I met him, as I am persuaded I can either cure him of the disorder or turn the evil to good. At least I shall prevent a mischief that would have been the consequence of his journey to London.' On the 8th of the same month Boulton again writes to Watt: 'Murdock seems in good spirits and good humour, and has neither thought upon nor done anything about the wheel carriage since his return, because he hath so much to do about the mines.' On the 17th he writes: 'Send all the engines as soon as possible, and he will be better employed than about wheel carriages. He hath made a very pretty working model, which keeps him in good humour, and that is a matter of great consequence to us. He says he has contrived, or rather is contriving, to save the power ariseing from the descent of the carriage when going down hill, and applying that power to assist it in its ascent up hill, and thus balance y[e] acct. up and down. How he means to accomplish it I know not . . . Wm. uses no separate valves, but uses y[e] valve piston, something like the 12-inch little engine at Soho, but not quite.'

The originals of these letters—hitherto unnoticed—are at Soho. They are of considerable importance, as they not only fix the date of the model, but they also go to prove that Murdock made another and larger engine, the Birmingham locomotive being quite incapable of carrying the weight of a set of fire-irons. There is a passage in Trevithick's 'Life of Trevithick,' i. 150, which may possibly refer to the larger model, or perhaps even to a third engine. Writing to Davies Giddy, under date 10 Oct. 1803, Trevithick says: 'I have desired Captain A. Vivian to wait on you to give you every information respecting Murdock's carriage, whether the large one at Mr. Budge's foundry [at Tuckingmill] was to be a condensing engine or not.' As Mr. Trevithick observes, 'this opens up a curious question in the history of the locomotive,' and there appears to be good ground for believing that Murdock made three locomotives: (1) the model now at Birmingham; (2) the model mentioned by Boulton in his letter of 2 Sept. 1786; and (3) the engine referred to in Trevithick's 'Life,' which, as the context shows, was certainly of considerable size. No. 2 is in all probability the engine which alarmed the vicar of Redruth when Murdock was trying it one night on the path leading to the church (SMILES, *Lives of Boulton and Watt*, 1874, p. 367). Both Watt and Boulton did all they could to discourage and hinder Murdock from pursuing his experiments, and in a letter from Watt to his partner, dated 12 Sept. 1786, probably in answer to one of those just referred to, he says: 'I am extremely sorry that W. M. still busies himself with the steam carriage. . . . I wish W. could be brought to do as we do, to mind the business in hand and let such as Symington and Sadler throw away their time and money hunting shadows' (MUIRHEAD, *Life of Watt*, 2nd ed. p. 445; *Mechanical Inventions of Watt*, ii. 210).

Apart from the locomotive, Murdock was the author of several improvements in the steam-engine, many of which, however, probably became merged in the general work of the establishment, and cannot now be identified. The well-known 'sun and planet motion,' which is included in Watt's patent of 1781, was contrived by Murdock, as Smiles indubitably shows (*Lives of Boulton and Watt*, 1874, p. 245). In 1784 or 1785 he made a wooden model of an oscillating engine (now exhibited at South Kensington on loan from its owner, the inventor's great grandson, William Murdock of Govilon, near Abergavenny), and it is figured and described in Muirhead's 'Mechanical Inventions of Watt,' vol. i. p. ccxvii, and vol. iii. plate 34; and also in the same author's 'Life of Watt,' 2nd ed. p. 438. He does not appear to have proceeded any further in the matter, but he is entitled to the credit of the first suggestion of this form of engine. His patent of 1799 (No. 2340) includes a method of driving machines for boring cylinders, a method of casting jacketed cylinders in one piece, and a 'sliding eduction pipe,' which was afterwards modified and became the long D slide-valve, eventually displacing the complicated gear of Watt's earlier engines. A particular form of rotary engine is also described in the specification; but, like many other similar projects, it was not a practical success, though Murdock used it in his experimental workshop for many years. In conjunction with John Southern, another of Watt's assistants at Soho, he designed what was probably the earliest form of independent or self-contained engine, adapted to stand on the ground without requiring support from the walls of a building. From the shape of one of the parts it was called a 'bell-crank engine,' and, according to Farey (*Steam Engine*, p. 677, and plate 16), it was brought out in 1802. These engines were well adapted for purposes where a small power only was required, and where space was an object. Some engines of this type were still at work in Birmingham until within the last thirty years. In the later form of these engines the valve was worked by an eccentric, the invention of which Farey (op. cit.) attributes to Murdock.

Murdock's miscellaneous inventions comprise a method of treating mundic to obtain paint for protecting ships' bottoms, for which he obtained a patent in 1791 (No. 1802). In 1810 he took out a patent (No. 3292) for making stone pipes, which he sold to the Manchester Stone Pipe Company, a company established in Manchester for the purpose of supplying that city with water. He also devised apparatus for utilising the force of compressed air; the bells in his house at Sycamore Hill were rung by that method, and it was afterwards adopted by Sir Walter Scott at Abbotsford (Lockhart, *Life of Scott*, p. 500). As early as 1803 he made a steam gun, which was tried at Soho. The invention of 'iron cement,' which consists of a mixture of sal-ammoniac and iron filings, largely used by engineers to this day, is also attributed to him.

In 1883 a proposal, which came to nothing, was made to purchase Murdock's house at Handsworth, and to convert it into an international gas museum. On 29 July 1892 the centenary of gas-lighting was celebrated, and Lord Kelvin unveiled a bust of Murdock, by D. W. Stevenson, in the Wallace Monument at Stirling. In 1882 the National Gas Institute founded the Murdock medal, which is awarded periodically to the authors of useful inventions connected with gas-making.

A portrait of Murdock in oil, by John Graham-Gilbert, is in the possession of the Royal Society of Edinburgh, and there is another by the same artist in the Art Gallery, Birmingham. The bust by Chantrey in Handsworth Church is said to be an admirable likeness. A copy of this bust, by Papworth, is in the Art Gallery, Birmingham. It has been frequently engraved.

[Muirhead's Mechanical Inventions of Watt, vol. i. pp. ccxiv–ccxviii; Buckle's memoir in Proceedings of the Institution of Mechanical Engineers, 23 Oct. 1850, p. 16, written from personal knowledge; Smiles's Lives of Boulton and Watt, ed. 1874; lecture by M. Macfie in Gas Engineer, 1 Oct. 1883, p. 461; Times, 11 and 15 Sept. 1883; A. Murdock's Light without a Wick, Glasgow, 1892. A view of Murdock's birthplace is given in the Pictorial World, 28 July 1883.] R. B. P.

MURE, Sir WILLIAM (1594–1657), poet, was the third successive owner of Rowallan, Ayrshire, with the same name and title. Sir William, his grandfather, a man 'of a meik and gentle spirit,' who 'delyted much in the study of phisick,' died in 1616; and Sir William, his father, who was 'ane strong man of bodie, and delyted much in hounting and halking,' died in 1639 (*Hist. and Descent of the House of Rowallane*, pp. 92–4). Mure's mother was Elizabeth Montgomerie, sister of Alexander Montgomerie (*fl.* 1590) [q. v.], author of the 'Cherrie and the Slae.' To this relationship Muir makes reference in a set of verses addressed to Charles, prince of Wales, afterwards Charles I. His muse, he says, can make but little boast,

Save from Montgomery she her birth doth claim

(Lyle, *Ancient Ballads and Songs*, 1827). Mure was liberally educated, being probably an alumnus of Glasgow University, like his brother Hugh, who was trained there for the church. With a correct and educated taste Mure 'delyted much in building and planting,' and he 'reformed the whole house [at Rowallan] exceidingly.' Previous to his father's death he gave much time to literature, but subsequently he was drawn into active life, when he showed an excellent public spirit. In 1643 he was a member of parliament at Edinburgh, and he was on the 'Committee of Warre' for the sheriffdom of Ayr in 1644. In the same year he engaged in England in several of the encounters between the royalist and the parliamentary forces. On 2 July he was wounded at Marston Moor, and in August he was at Newcastle, where for a time he commanded his regiment. Of his last ten years there is no record, but the book of his 'House' (in a paragraph supplementing his own story) shows that he was 'pious and learned, and had an excellent vaine in poyesie,' and that he 'lived Religiouslie and died Christianlie' in 1657. Before 1615 he married Anna Dundas, daughter of Dundas of Newliston, by whom he had eleven children; and he married, secondly, Jane Hamilton, lady Duntreath, who bore two sons and two daughters. He was succeeded by his son, Sir William, a well-known covenanter, upon the death of whose son in 1700, without a male heir, the title became extinct.

Mure left numerous manuscript verses, including a Latin tribute to his grandfather, an English 'Dido and Æneas' from the 'Æneid,' and two religious poems, 'The Joy of Tears' and 'The Challenge and Reply.' In the 'Muses' Welcome,' 1617, there is a poetical address by Mure to King James when at Hamilton. In 1628 he translated —'invected in English Sapphics'—Boyd of Trochrig's Latin 'Hecatombe Christiana,' to which he appended a poem on 'Doomsday.' In 1629 appeared his 'True Crucifixe for True Catholikes,' 12mo, Edinburgh. This poem, Mure's most ambitious effort, is ingenious and interesting, but unquestionably heavy. About 1639 he cleverly paraphrased the Psalms, of which Principal Baillie of Edinburgh highly approved (letter from Westminster Assembly, 1 Jan. 1644, quoted by Lyle). The general assembly of the church of Scotland commended Mure's Psalms to the attention of that committee which chose the version of Rous for congregational use. In his latter days Mure wrote the quaint and valuable 'Historie and Descent of the House of Rowallane,' edited by the Rev. W. Mure, 1825. In T. Lyle's 'Ancient Ballads and Songs, chiefly from Tradition, MSS., and Scarce Works,' a number of Mure's miscellaneous poems occur, including examples in heroic couplet, two addresses to his wife, and several sonnets excellent in sentiment and creditable in structure.

[Historie and Descent of the House of Rowallane; Memoir in Lyle's Ancient Ballads and Songs; Anderson's Scottish Nation.] T. B.

MURE, WILLIAM (1718–1776), baron of the Scots exchequer, was eldest son and successor to William Mure of Caldwell in Ayr and Renfrewshire, by his wife Anne, daughter of Sir James Stewart of Coltness, lord advocate, and widow of James Maxwell of Blawarthill. He was born late in 1718. His father dying in April 1722, he was brought up at home by his mother, under the tutorship of Rev. William Leechman, afterwards professor of divinity in, and eventually by his influence promoted to be principal of, Glasgow University. He then studied law at Edinburgh and Leyden, and travelled during 1741 in France and Holland. Returning to Scotland in November 1742, he was elected member of parliament for Renfrewshire, a seat which he held without opposition during three parliaments till 1761, when he was appointed a baron of the Scots exchequer. He spoke rarely, and attended irregularly, his principal interest lying in the direction of agricultural improvements, upon which he became an acknowledged authority. He is principally known as the friend of Lord Bute [see Stuart, John, third Earl of Bute], and of David Hume. Through the services that he rendered to the former in connection with the management of the Bute estates he became his intimate friend and trusted adviser, and rising with his fortunes was eventually one of the most influential men in Scotland in regard to the management of its local affairs and distribution of Scottish patronage. Of Hume he was at the same time one of the oldest and most valued friends, and from 1742 onwards their letters are numerous. Mure's house at Abbey hill, near Holyrood, was one of Hume's favourite resorts. Apropos of his history Hume wrote Mure in 1756: 'If you do not say that I have done both parties justice, and if Mrs. Mure be not sorry for poor King Charles, I shall burn all my papers and return to philosophy.' Mure was well known in Scottish literary society, and published privately a couple of tracts on political economy. In 1764 and 1765 he was lord rector of Glasgow University, and was again put in nomination for that post in 1776, but was defeated. He died at Caldwell on 25 March 1776 of gout in the stomach. He married Anne, daughter of James Graham, lord Easdale, a judge of the court of session, by whom he had two sons and four daughters. Many of the letters addressed to him and other papers are published with a portrait in the 'Caldwell Papers,' vols. ii. and iii.

[Caldwell Papers (Maitland Club); Hill Burton's Life of Hume; Anderson's Scottish Nation.]

J. A. H.

MURE, WILLIAM (1799–1860), classical scholar, born at Caldwell, Ayrshire, on 9 July 1799, was the eldest son of William Mure of Caldwell, colonel of the Renfrew militia, and lord rector of Glasgow University 1793–1794, by his wife Anne, eldest daughter of Sir James Hunter Blair, bart., of Dunskey, Wigtownshire, and was thus grandson of William Mure [q. v.], baron of exchequer, and a descendant of the Mures of Rowallan (*Caldwell Papers*, i. 45, 46, &c.) He was educated at Westminster School (WELCH, *Queen's Scholars*, p. 474), at the university of Edinburgh, and afterwards in Germany at the university of Bonn. When he was about twenty-two he contributed to the 'Edinburgh Review' an article on Spanish literature (T. MOORE, *Diary*, v. 11). His first independent publication was 'Brief Remarks on the Chronology of the Egyptian Dynasties' (against Champollion), issued in 1829 (London, 8vo). It was followed in 1832 by 'A Dissertation on the Calendar and Zodiac of Ancient Egypt' (Edinburgh, 8vo). In 1838 Mure began a tour in Greece, leaving Ancona for Corfu on 17 Feb. He studied the topography of Ithaca, and visited Acarnania, Delphi, Bœotia, Attica, and the Peloponnese. He published an interesting 'Journal of a Tour in Greece and the Ionian Islands' in 1842 (Edinburgh, 8vo). His principal work, 'A Critical History of the Language and Literature of Ancient Greece,' was issued 1850–7, London, 8vo; 2nd edit. 1859, 8vo; it consists of five volumes, but deals only with a part of the subject, viz. the early history of writing, Homer, Hesiod, the early lyric poets and historians Herodotus, Thucydides, and Xenophon. It contains no account of the dramatists, orators, or any literature subsequent to 380 B.C. Mure also published 'The Commercial Policy of Pitt and Peel,' 1847, 8vo; 'Selections from the Family Papers [of the Mures] preserved at Caldwell,' Maitland Club, 1854, 8vo; 'Remarks on the Appendices to the second vol. 3rd edit. of Mr. Grote's History of Greece,' London, 1851, 8vo; and 'National Criticism in 1858' (on a criticism of Mure's 'History of the Literature of Greece'), London, 1858, 8vo.

Mure had succeeded to the Caldwell estates on his father's death, 9 Feb. 1831. He was, like his father, for many years colonel of the Renfrewshire militia, and was lord rector of Glasgow University in 1847–8. He was M.P. for Renfrewshire from 1846 to 1855 in the conservative interest, but seldom spoke in the house. He was created D.C.L. by Oxford University on 9 June 1833. He was a man of commanding presence, winning manners, and kindly disposition. He died at Kensington Park Gardens, London, on 1 April 1860, aged 60 (*Gent. Mag.* 1860, pt. i. p. 532).

Mure married, on 7 Feb. 1825, Laura, second daughter of William Markham of Becca Hall, Yorkshire, and granddaughter of Dr. Markham, archbishop of York, and had issue three sons and three daughters. The second son, Charles Reginald, became an officer in the 43rd light infantry. The eldest son, William, was lieutenant-colonel in the Scots fusilier guards, M.P. for Renfrewshire 1874–80, and died in 1880, leaving an only son William.

[Burke's Landed Gentry, 'Mure of Caldwell;' Gent. Mag. 1860, pt. i. pp. 634–5; Caldwell Papers; Brit. Mus. Cat.]

W. W.

MURFORD, NICHOLAS (*fl.* 1650), poet, belonged to a Norfolk family. One Peter Murford was in 1629 lieutenant of the military company of Norwich (BLOMEFIELD, *Norfolk*, iii. 374), and was described in 1639 as a leading citizen of Yarmouth (cf. *Cal. State Papers*, 1639, p. 412). According to Nicholas's account, his father spent 13,000*l.* 'for the good of the Commonwealth Anº 1632' (*Memoria Sacra*, Ded.) Nicholas appears to have settled as a merchant at Lynn, and to have travelled largely for business purposes in Germany, France, and the Netherlands. Salt was one of the commodities in which he dealt, and he invented a new method of manufacture, which he described in 'A most humble declaration . . . concerning the making of salt here in England' (manuscript in All Souls Coll. Oxf. 276, No. 101). The Company or Corporation of Saltworkers was formed by royal letters patent about 1638 near Great Yarmouth to work the invention (*Cal. State Papers*, Dom. 1639, pp. 153–4). But the enterprise was not successful. On 1 Oct. 1638 Murford petitioned Charles I to prohibit the importation of foreign salt (cf. *ib.* 1638–9, p. 45); he complained that the saltworkers of North and South Shields had infringed his patent, and asked the government to arrange so that he could obtain coal from Newcastle at the same cost as it was supplied to the saltworkers at Newcastle or Hartlepool (*ib.* 1639–1640, p. 236). Murford sought to direct the attention of the Short parliament to his grievances (cf. *A Draught of the Contract about Salt on the behalf of Nicholas Murford, also a Proposition made by Thomas Horth, Merchant, and other Owners of Salt Pans at North and South Shields, and another Petition in the behalf of the Town of Yarmouth. The consideration whereof is humbly presented to the Houses of Parliament*, 1640?). But he only succeeded in obtaining a respite for the payment of some arrears of salt duty (*Cal. State Papers*, 1640, p. 15). On like grounds he involved himself in a dispute with the corporation of Southampton (*Hist. MSS. Comm.* 11th Rep. iii. 133). In 1652 Murford was a prisoner for debt in the Fleet, and petitioned Cromwell for the repayment of the 13,000*l.* which his father had devoted to public objects in 1632, and which Charles I, he said, had undertaken to repay (*Mem. Sacra*, Ded.) He wrote an elegy on a daughter Amy (*Fragmenta Poetica*, C_2.)

Murford dabbled in literature, and produced two volumes of pedestrian verse. The earlier, 'Fragmenta Poetica, or Miscelanies of Poetical Musings, Moral and Divine,' printed for Humphrey Moseley in 1650, is a rare book (Brit. Mus.) Among the writers of commendatory verse, prefixed to it, are Thomas Parker, M.D., and Nicholas Toll, pastor at Lynn. A 'satyre' is addressed to Martin Holbeach, the traveller. One song was 'made at my last coming out of Germany,' another is dated from Embden. A portrait of the author was inserted, and was afterwards altered and made to serve as a portrait of James Forbes, (1629?–1712) [q. v.] Murford's second work was not printed; it is extant among the British Museum manuscripts (Addit MS. 28602). Its title runs: 'Memoria sacra: or Offertures unto the Fragrant Memory of the Right Honourable Henry Ireton (late) Lord Deputy of Ireland. Intended to have been humbly presented at his Funerall. By a Nurschild of Maro. Anagr. *Fui Ireton*.' The dedication 'to his excellency (my noblist patron, the Lord General Cromwell)' is dated 8 Feb. 1651–2. The elegy is poor doggerel. In the opening verses, called 'The Sigh,' passing allusion is made to James Howell and Sir Philip Sidney. Some verses addressed by Murford to William Lilly, the astrologer, are among the Ashmolean MSS. at Oxford.

[Hunter's Chorus Vatum in Addit. MS. 24491, f. 99; Brydges's Restituta Lit. iv. 479; Corser's Collectanea (Chetham Soc.), pt. ix. pp. 39–44.]

S. L.

MURGATROID, MICHAEL (1551–1608), author, born in Yorkshire in November 1551, was educated at the expense of his kinsman (probably uncle), Richard Gascoigne, a gentleman of that county. He matriculated as a pensioner of Jesus College, Cambridge, in June 1573, graduated B.A. in 1576–7, was fellow from 1577 until 1600, and commenced M.A. in 1580. He was Greek reader of his college, and subsequently became secretary to Archbishop Whitgift, then comptroller, and ultimately steward of his household, and commissary of the faculties. He died on 3 April 1608 at Waddon, near Croydon, Surrey, where he leased a farm from George and John Whitgift (*Probate Act Book*, P.C.C. 1605–1609), and was buried on the 12th in the chancel of Croydon Church, as near Archbishop Whitgift as possible. On the east wall of the chantry of St. Nicholas in the old church was his monument, having under a recessed arch his statue clad in a black gown, and kneeling at a desk, with inscriptions over his head and under his feet. By his marriage on 26 April 1602 to Anne, widow of a Mr. Yeomans and sister of Robert Bickerstaffe, he left a daughter, Mary. Another child was born posthumously (NICHOLS, *Collectanea*, ii. 294). A son-in-law, George Yeomans, he set up as a yeoman at Waddon. One of the witnesses to his will (P.C.C. 44, Windebanck) was his 'cousin,' George Gascoigne.

Murgatroid was author of: 1. 'Michaelis Murgertod de Græcarum disciplinarum laudibus oratio: cum epistolis 2; et versibus Johanni Bell, Collegii Jesus Cantab. præfecto, inscriptis; et Oratione cum Aristotelis Meteorologica exponeret habita;' it is Harleian MS. 4159. The first oration was delivered at college. 2. 'Memoirs of affairs in Church and State in Archbishop Whitgift's time,' among the Lambeth MSS. (No. 178, f. 1). 3. 'Ad Domini Richardi Cosini tumulum,' Latin verses in the university collection on the death of Dr. Cosin, 1598.

[Cooper's Athenæ Cantabr. ii. 480–1.]

G. G.

MURIMUTH, ADAM (1275?–1347), historian, was born between Michaelmas 1274 and Michaelmas 1275. His family apparently belonged to Fifield, Oxfordshire, where a John de Muremuth occurs as lord of the manor in 1316; of other members of the family, Richard de Murimuth occurs as one of the royal clerks in 1328–9 (*Cal. Pat. Rolls Edward III*, 1327–30, pp. 329, 360), as dean of Wimborne in 1338, and held the prebends of Oxgate, at St. Paul's, 1340–54, and Banbury, Lincoln, in 1352. An Adam Murimuth, junior, probably held the prebend of Harleston, St. Paul's; he was rector of Thurgarton, Norfolk, 1327–8, and was prebend of Exeter, dying in 1370; the last named at least was, from the similarity of his preferments, most likely a relative of the historian. Murimuth was educated at Oxford, where he had graduated as doctor of civil law before 14 June 1312. At that date he was appointed one of the proctors of the university at the court of Rome in a complaint against the Black Friars (*Chron. Edw. I and II*, pp. lxi, *n.* 1, lxviii). About the same time he was appointed by Archbishop Winchelsey to represent him at Avignon in his cause against Walter Langton [q. v.] (*Continuatio Chronicarum*, p. 18). Next year he was apparently acting at Avignon, as agent for the chapter of Canterbury, to secure the confirmation of Thomas Cobham in the archbishopric. In 1314 he was employed by the king to secure the preferment of John Sandale to the deanery of St. Paul's (*Fœdera*, ii. 243), and on 22 Nov. was appointed to the rectory of Hayes, Middlesex. In 1315 he received the rectory of Lyminge, Kent, and on 15 March of that year had letters dimissory from Archbishop Walter Reynolds permitting him to receive deacon's or priest's orders. On 20 Oct. 1318 Reynolds presented him, being now a priest, to the living of Cliffe at Hoo. Murimuth was still acting at Avignon for the king (*Fœdera*, ii. 305, 339), for the chapter of Canterbury, and perhaps for the university of Oxford in 1316 and 1317. In August of the former year he received a pension of 60*s.* from the chapter for his faithful counsel (cf. *Litt. Cant.* ii. 59–70). Murimuth must have returned home in 1318, and in May 1319 was proctor for the chapter of Canterbury in the parliament held at York (*Parl. Writs*, II. i. 199). In a letter dated 28 May 1319 William de Melton [q. v.] alludes to information with which Murimuth had furnished him (*Letters from the Northern Registers*, p. 288, Rolls Ser.) In 1319 Murimuth was sent on another mission by the king to obtain the pope's assent to a grant from the clergy (*Cont. Chron.* p. 30). From 1 April 1320 to February 1321 he held the prebend of Bullinghope, Hereford (Le Neve, *Fasti*, i. 496), and during 1321 and 1322 was official and vicar-general for Stephen de Gravesend, bishop of London. In August 1323, when he is still styled canon of Hereford, he was sent on a mission to King Robert of Sicily concerning Edward's claims to lands in Provence (*Fœdera*, ii. 531). This same year he was also employed in the king's behalf against the Scots at Avignon and to represent Edward's complaints against his late envoy, John Stratford [q. v.] (*ib.* ii. 531–2; *Cont. Chron.* p. 41). On 16 May 1325 he received the prebend of Ealdstreet St. Paul's, which he exchanged for that of Neasden on 2 Feb. 1328; the Adam Murimuth who at a later date held the prebend of Harleston was probably not the historian. In 1325 he was vicar-general for Archbishop Reynolds, and on 21 Aug. had letters of protection as intending to go with the king to France (*Fœdera*, ii. 604). In 1328 Murimuth appears as precentor of Exeter, a post which he may have received as early as 1319; he was certainly connected with that cathedral in 1327, when he was one of the deputation from the chapter to the king on the death of Bishop Berkeley. On 21 March 1330 his precentorship was confirmed to him for life (*Cal. Pat. Rolls Edward III*, 1327–30, pp. 378, 380), but he exchanged it for the rectory of Wyradisbury or Wraysbury, Buckinghamshire, in 1337. In 1334 he had a dispute with the chapter of Canterbury as to his pension (*Litt. Cant.* ii. 59, 70), and in 1335 appears as commissary for the archbishop. He is mentioned on 5 June 1338 as receiving a lease of the manor of Barnes from the chapter of St. Paul's; references to him occur in the 'Literæ Cantuarienses' under date 27 Oct. 1338 and 2 Feb. 1340 (ii. 196, 219). From 1338 onwards Murimuth records his age in his chronicle year by year; the last entry is in 1347, when he was seventy-two. He probably died before 26 June 1347, when his successor at Wyradisbury was instituted.

Murimuth was the author of a work which he styles 'Continuatio Chronicarum,' and which covers the period from 1303 to 1347. According to his own account in his preface, he found that the chronicles at Exeter did not proceed beyond 1302, nor those at Westminster beyond 1305. Down to the latter date he uses the Westminster chronicles, and after this, when he was of an age to judge for himself, and write in his own manner 'ex libro dierum meorum,' his history is based on what he had himself heard and seen. Since Murimuth describes himself as canon of St. Paul's, he clearly wrote after 1325. In its first form the history was brought down to 1337, a second edition carries it on to 1341, and in its final form the work ends with the year of the author's death, 1347. An anonymous continuation extends to 1380. The earlier portion of the history is very meagre, and was 'probably made up from scanty notes and from personal recollections.' While, however, the notices of English history are slight, the record of ecclesiastical affairs and the relations of England with the court of Rome have a peculiar value. But for the last nine years 'the chronicle is much fuller, and is of particular value for the history of the campaigns in France' and of the negotiations connected with them. For this portion Murimuth's position at St. Paul's gave him the advantage of easy access to documents and private information. The 'Continuatio Chronicarum' is somewhat confused by Murimuth's perverse adoption of Michaelmas as the beginning of the year. It was first edited by Anthony Hall, Oxford, 1722, in which edition we have the true chronicle to 1337 from Queen's College, Oxford MS. 304, with the continuation to 1380. In an edition for the English Historical Society in 1846 Mr. Thomas Hog published the true text to 1346, with the continuation to 1380. The full text down to 1347 was for the first time edited for the Rolls Series by Dr. Maunde Thompson in 1889. An account of the extant manuscripts will be found in the last edition, pp. xvii–xxii.

There seems no reason to suppose that Murimuth's reference to the 'Liber dierum meorum' is anything more than a rhetorical expression. Henry Wharton [q. v.], however, ascribes to him the authorship of the continuation of the 'Flores Historiarum,' which has been published under the title of 'Annales Paulini' in 'Chronicles of Edward I and Edward II' in the Rolls Series. These annals undoubtedly show a close connection with Murimuth's work, and Dr. Thompson (*Pref.* p. xv) considers that their author was indebted to a copy of the first edition of the 'Continuatio Chronicarum.' Bishop Stubbs discusses the question of the connection of the two works in the preface to 'Chronicles of Edward I and Edward II,' vol. i. pp. lxvii–lxxiv; he concludes that the internal evidence is against Murimuth's authorship, but suggests that 'Adam may have contributed the material which is in common in the two chronicles.' In the 'Flores Historiarum' (iii. 232, Rolls Series), Murimuth is said to have written a history from 1313 to 1347; and the brief narrative of 1325 and 1328 there printed, is in the main extracted from his chronicle.

[Tanner's Bibl. Brit.-Hib. pp. 8–9; Maunde Thompson's Preface to Chronica A. Murimuth et R. Avesbury, pp. xx–xxxii.; Bishop Stubbs's Pref. to Chronicles of Edward I and Edward II, vol. i. pp. lix–lxxiv; Archæologia Cantiana, xv. 225–7, 261; Oliver's Bishops of Exeter, pp. 278, 315, 318; other authorities quoted.] C. L. K.

MURLIN, JOHN (1722–1799), methodist preacher, was born at St. Stephen in Brannell, Cornwall, in the early part of August 1722, being the second son of Richard and Elizabeth Murlin or Morlen. His father, who died in 1735, was a farmer in that parish, and until his death he was assisted by his son. At Michaelmas 1735 the boy was bound apprentice as a carpenter for seven years, and for several years after the expiration of his articles he served another master in the same trade. In February 1749 he was converted to methodism, soon became a local preacher, and on the invitation of John Wesley travelled in West Cornwall as an itinerant preacher from 12 Oct. 1754 to August 1755. After that date he visited many parts of England and Ireland, his stay in any town being usually limited to a few weeks. He was stationed in London in 1755, 1766, 1768, 1770, 1776, 1779, and 1782; he was at Bristol during several years, and in 1784 he was resident at Manchester. In 1787, when no longer able to keep a circuit, he retired to High Wycombe, Buckinghamshire, but he preached in Great Queen Street Chapel, London, in the winter of 1798–9. He died at High Wycombe, 7 July 1799, and was buried in the same vault with John Wesley in the City Road Chapel, London, when his executors erected a plain white marble tablet to his memory. On 11 Feb. 1762 he married in London Elizabeth, second daughter of John Walker, a tradesman, and the widow of John Berrisford, a cashier in the Bank of England. She was born in May 1710 and died at Bristol 18 Jan. 1786, being buried at Temple. Her funeral sermon was preached by Jeremiah Brettell on 24 Jan., and a memoir by her husband, appeared in the 'Arminian Magazine,' ix. 422–8.

Murlin was a methodist of the primitive stamp of character, but of great independence. In 1760 he and two other preachers at Norwich began, 'without Wesley's permission and without consulting any of their coadjutors,' to administer the sacrament. Through his marriage he came into considerable property, and in 1770 Wesley wrote with much bitterness of tone that many of his preachers would go where they liked. 'Mr. Murlin says he must be in London. 'Tis certain he has a mind to be there; therefore so it must be, for you know a man of fortune is master of his own motions.' When 'an angel blowing a trumpet was placed on the sounding-board over the pulpit' at Halifax in 1779, Murlin refused to preach under it, and when a majority of one voted for its removal he 'hewed it in pieces.' In the pulpit he was always in tears and was known, like James Nalton [q. v.], as the 'weeping prophet.'

Murlin wrote: 1. 'A Letter to Richard Hill on that gentleman's five Letters to the Rev. J. Fletcher. By J. M.,' Bristol, 1775. 2. 'Sacred Hymns on various subjects,' Leeds, 1781; 2nd edit. Bristol, 1782. 3. 'Elegy on Mrs. Fletcher and other Poems,' 3rd edit.,

High Wycombe, 1788. 4. 'Letter to Rev. Joseph Benson on the Administration of the Sacraments in Methodist Chapels by Unordained Ministers.' This he printed and circulated among the preachers towards the close of 1794. 'A Short Account of Mr. John Murlin, written by himself,' an expansion of a memoir in the 'Arminian Magazine,' ii. 530–6, was printed in 1780 (cf. THOMAS JACKSON, *Early Methodist Preachers*, ii. 415–28). His portrait at the age of seventy-five was engraved by Ridley, and inserted in the 'Methodist Magazine,' April 1798.

[Osborn's Wesleyan Bibliography, pp. 145–6; Blanshard's Samuel Bradburn, 2nd edit. p. 109; Almore's Methodist Memorial, 1871 ed., pp. 156–8; Tyerman's John Wesley, ii. 381–3, iii. 70, 292; G. Smith's Wesleyan Methodism, 2nd ed., ii. 117, 311; Stevenson's City Road Chapel, pp. 246, 352, 369–76.] W. P. C.

MURPHY, ARTHUR (1727–1805), author and actor, the son of Richard Murphy, a Dublin merchant, and his wife Jane French, was born 27 Dec. 1727 at Clomquin, Roscommon, the house of his maternal uncle, Arthur French. After the death in 1729 of his father—lost at sea—Arthur Murphy and his elder brother James [see below] lived with their mother at St. George's Quay, Dublin, until in 1735 the family removed to London. In 1736 he was at Boulogne with his aunt, Mrs. Arthur Plunkett, and was sent in 1738, under the name of Arthur French, to the English College at St. Omer, which he quitted after a residence of six years, returning to his mother in London in July 1744. In August 1747 he was sent by his uncle, Jeffery French, M.P., to serve as clerk with Edmund Harold, a merchant in Cork, where he stayed until April 1749. Shortly afterwards, having offended his uncle by refusing to go to Jamaica, he transferred himself to the banking-house of Ironside & Belchier in Lombard Street, where he stayed until the end of 1751. Frequenting the theatre and the coffee-houses he conceived literary aspirations, made friends with Samuel Foote [q. v.] and others, and on 21 Oct. 1752 published the first number of the 'Gray's Inn Journal,' a weekly periodical on the lines of the 'Spectator' or the 'Rambler,' dealing to some extent with the drama and stage, and giving occasionally essays in the shape of dialogues. This publication, which concluded 12 Oct. 1754, occupies two volumes of his collected works. On the death of his uncle he found himself disappointed of an expected legacy, and being 300*l.* in debt he took, at Foote's advice, to the stage. On 18 Oct. 1754, as Othello, to the Iago of Ryan and the Desdemona of George Anne Bellamy [q. v.], he made at Covent Garden his first appearance as an actor. Mrs. Hamilton, the Emilia, spoke a prologue by Murphy in which he said of himself,

He copies no man—of what Shakespeare drew
His humble sense he offers to your view.

This performance was received with favour and repeated on the 19th and 21st, and for the fifth time on 5 Dec. According to Tate Wilkinson, he had good judgment, but wanted powers for great effect. For Mrs. Bellamy's benefit, 18 March 1755, he played Zamor in 'Alzira,' assumably Aaron Hill's adaptation from Voltaire, in which, at Mrs. Bellamy's request, Murphy made some alterations. Young Bevil in the 'Conscious Lovers' and Archer, both for benefits, followed, and on 4 April, for his own benefit, he appeared as Hamlet. Richard III, Biron in the 'Fatal Marriage,' and Macbeth were given during the season. His first appearance at Drury Lane took place under Garrick, 20 Sept. 1755, as Osmyn in the 'Mourning Bride.' Essex in the 'Earl of Essex,' Bajazet in 'Tamerlane,' Richard III, Barbarossa, and Horatio followed.

On 2 Jan. 1756 Murphy's first farce, the 'Apprentice' (8vo, 1756), was given at Drury Lana. It is in two acts, and derides the ambition to act of the uneducated. A prologue written by Garrick was spoken by Woodward, and an epilogue was given by Mrs. Clive. Woodward obtained much reputation as Dick, a part subsequently played by Bannister and Lewis. Murphy also published anonymously, 8vo, 1756, with the connivance of Garrick, 'The Spouter, or the Triple Revenge,' a two-act farce (not included in his collected works), the characters in which include, under transparent disguises, Garrick, Rich, Theophilus Cibber, Foote, and John Hill. The latter three were satirised with some coarseness under the names of Slender, Squint-eyed Pistol, and Dapperwit. Garrick was called Patent. For Murphy's attack on Foote some justification was afforded. In the summer of 1755 he had conceived a farce, 'The Englishman from Paris,' in avowed continuation of Foote's 'Englishman in Paris.' Proud of his idea, he had incautiously communicated it, with the development of his whole plot, characters, &c., to Foote, who approved it and hastily turned it into 'The Englishman returned from Paris,' which he gave 3 Feb. 1756 at Covent Garden, thus taking the wind out of the sails of Murphy's play, which could not be produced until 3 April (the author's benefit), and was given only once. At the close of this season Murphy, who had lived economically and had made a considerable sum by his 'Apprentice' and his benefit, retired from the stage the owner of 100*l.* after his debts had been paid. On 30 March 1757, for Mossop's benefit, was played at Drury Lane the 'Upholsterer, or What News?' a two-act farce by Murphy, avowedly taken from the 'Tatler,' but owing more to Fielding's 'Coffee-house Politician.' Superbly acted by Garrick, Yates, Woodward, Palmer, Mrs. Clive, and Mrs. Yates, the piece long held possession of the stage. In 1763 Murphy made alterations in it, and in 1807 an additional scene by Joseph Moser [q. v.], printed in the 'European Magazine,' vol. lii., was supplied. It shows a number of meddling tradesmen neglecting their own business to discuss political issues, and is a fairly clever caricature. Meanwhile, in 1757 he applied for admission as a student to the Middle Temple, and was refused by the benchers on the ground that he was an actor. He then began, in opposition to the 'Contest' of Owen Ruffhead, the 'Test,' a weekly paper, in which he supported Henry Fox, afterwards Lord Holland [q. v.], by whom Lord Mansfield was induced to take up the cause of Murphy, and secure his admission at Lincoln's Inn. In opposition to the 'North Briton' he also edited a weekly paper called 'The Auditor.'

Murphy's first tragedy, 'The Orphan of China,' 8vo, 1759, was produced at Drury Lane 21 April 1759, and played nine times. It was built upon the 'Orphelin de la Chine' of Voltaire, produced 20 Aug. 1755 at the Théâtre Français. Reshaped by Murphy it was played with indifferent success at Covent Garden, 6 Nov. 1777, and was acted in Dublin so recently as 1810. On 24 Jan. 1759 two pieces by Murphy were produced at Drury Lane. 'The Desert Island,' 8vo, 1760, is a dull dramatic poem in three acts, imitated from Metastasio. 'The Way to keep him,' a comedy, 8vo, 1760, was played and printed originally in three acts. On 10 Jan. 1761 it was produced in five acts, the characters of Sir Bashful and Lady Constant being added and other changes made. Garrick on both occasions played Lovemore. The piece, which had a considerable success, was reprinted in its enlarged form, 8vo, 1761. It satirises with some cleverness women who after marriage are at no pains to retain their husbands. 'All in the Wrong,' 8vo, 1761, an adaptation of Molière's 'Cocu Imaginaire,' was brought out by Foote and Murphy in partnership during a summer season at Drury Lane, 15 June 1761. On 2 July 'The Citizen,' 8vo, 1763, printed as a farce but acted as a comedy, and 'The Old Maid,' 8vo, 1761, a comedy, both by Murphy, were played under the same joint-management. The earlier piece owes something to the 'Fausse Agnès' of Destouches, produced two years earlier in Paris; the second, a two-act comedy, is indebted to 'L'Étourderie' of Fagan. 'No one's Enemy but his own,' 8vo, 1764, a three-act comedy, subsequently shortened to two acts, given at Drury Lane 9 Jan. 1764, a version of 'L'Indiscret' of Voltaire, was unsuccessful, as was a second piece by Murphy, taken from the 'Guardian,' No. 173, and called at first 'What we must all come to,' 8vo, 1764. This was hissed from the stage before the performance was completed. Revived 30 March 1776 it was successful, and has since been frequently played as 'Three Weeks after Marriage.' 'The Choice,' not printed apparently until 1786, was played at Drury Lane 23 Feb. 1764. 'The School for Guardians,' 8vo, 1767, was given at Covent Garden 10 Jan. 1667. It is founded on three plays of Molière, 'L'École des Femmes' being principally used, and was subsequently at the same house turned into a three-act opera called 'Love finds the Way.' Murphy's tragedy 'Zenobia,' 8vo, 1768, 1786, was given at Drury Lane 27 Feb. 1768, and is a translation from Crébillon. It was followed, 26 Feb. 1772, at the same theatre by 'The Grecian Daughter,' 8vo, 1772, Murphy's best-known tragedy. 'Alzuma,' 8vo, 1773, a tragedy, 23 Feb. 1773, saw the light at Covent Garden. It is an unsuccessful compilation from many plays. 'News from Parnassus,' a rather sparkling satire on actors, critics, &c., printed only in the collection of Murphy's works, was given at Covent Garden 23 Sept. 1776. 'Know your own Mind,' 8vo, 1778, a rendering of the 'Irrésolu' of Destouches, was played for Woodward's benefit at Covent Garden, 10 April 1777. 'The Rival Sisters,' 8vo, 1786, was not acted until 18 March 1793, when for her benefit Mrs. Siddons produced it and played Ariadne. Another tragedy, 'Arminius,' included in the 1786 collection, was not seen on the stage.

Murphy retired from the bar in 1788. He had made very considerable sums by his dramas, and had inherited a bequest of West Indian slaves, which he sold for 1,000*l.*, but remained in straitened circumstances, and was appointed by Lord Loughborough a commissioner of bankrupts. At the recommendation of Addington he was granted a pension of 200*l.* a year by George III, beginning 5 Jan. 1803. He involved himself in considerable debt, however, in his attempts to publish his translations, and was compelled to sell his residence, the westernmost house in Hammersmith Terrace, and a portion of his library. It is stated that he ate himself out of every tavern from the other end of Temple Bar to the West End. He afterwards lived in Brompton, and was in the habit, when writing, of staying at an hotel at Richmond. It was only in his later years, when his health and mind had begun to fail, that he was free from pecuniary embarrassments. He was a favourite in society, a guest at noble houses, and a man much respected and courted. According to his friend Samuel Rogers, whom he introduced to the Piozzis, Murphy used at one time to walk arm in arm with Lord Loughborough. Rogers, who had bills of his for over 200*l.*, received an assignment of his 'Tacitus' and other works, and found that they had already been assigned to a bookseller. For this conduct Murphy offered an abject apology. On other occasions the honourable conduct of Murphy is praised. He was in 1784 a member of the Essex Head Club, and Johnson, according to the 'Collectanea' of Dr. Maxwell, 'very much loved him.' His correspondence with Garrick shows him, however, suspicious and irascible, if soon appeased. Rogers says that when any of his plays encountered opposition he took a walk to cool himself in Covent Garden.

Murphy died 18 June 1805 at his residence, 14 Queen's Row, Knightsbridge. He was buried at his own request in Hammersmith Church in a grave he had previously bought for his mother. An epitaph was placed there by his executor and biographer, Jesse Foot [q. v.] He was fairly well built, narrow-shouldered, had an oval face with a fair complexion and full light eyes, and was marked with the small-pox. Two portraits of him appear in the 'Life' by Foot, and one, painted by Nathaniel Dance, was engraved by W. Ward. Murphy brought on the stage and lived with a Miss Ann Elliot, an uneducated girl of natural abilities, who was his original Maria in the 'Citizen.' He took great interest in her and wrote her biography (1769, 12mo). She died young and left him her money, which he transferred to her relatives.

The comedies of Murphy have not in all cases lost the spirit of the originals from which he took them. Several of them were acted early in the present century. His tragedies are among the worst that have obtained any reputation. 'Zenobia,' however, was played so late as 1815, and the 'Grecian Daughter' many years later. Totally devoid of invention, Murphy invariably took his plots from previous writers. He showed, however, facility and skill in adapting them to English tastes. His collected works appeared in 1786 in 7 vols. 8vo, with a portrait by Cook after Dance. These consist of the plays and the 'Gray's Inn Journal.' Many of his plays figure in Bell's, Inchbald's, and other collections.

Murphy edited in 1762 an edition in 12 vols. of the 'Works' of Henry Fielding, with a life, giving facts with very slight attention to chronological sequence. In 1801 he issued in 2 vols. a 'Life of David Garrick,' which is clumsy and ill-digested and largely occupied with his own relations, seldom too amiable, to Garrick. It was abridged and translated into French. He published an 'Essay on the Life and Genius of Samuel Johnson, LL.D.,' 8vo, 1792, and collected materials for a life of Foote. He translated 'Tacitus' in 4 vols. 4to, 1793, described as an 'elegant but too paraphrastic version;' Sallust, 8vo, 1807; Vaniere's 'The Bees,' from the 14th Book of the 'Prædium Rusticum,' and Vida's 'Game of Chess.' Other works by him are: 'A Letter to Mons. de Voltaire on the "Desert Island," by Arthur Murphy,' London, 1760, 8vo; 'The Examiner [originally called 'The Expostulation']: a Satire by Arthur Murphy,' London, 1761, 4to, directed against Lloyd, Churchill, &c., an answer to 'The Murphiad, a Mock-heroic Poem,' London, 1761, 4to; the 'Meretriciad,' and other satires; an 'Ode to the Naiads of Fleet Ditch, by Arthur Murphy,' London, 1761, 4to, a furious attack on Churchill, who in his 'Apology' had derided Murphy and his 'Desert Island;' 'Beauties of Magazines, consisting of Essays by . . . Murphy,' 12mo, 1772; 'Anecdotes by Murphy,' added to Boswell's 'Johnson,' 1835, 8vo; 'A Letter from a Right Honourable Personage, translated into Verse by A. Murphy,' 4to, 1761; 'A Letter from the anonymous Author of the "Letters Versified" to the anonymous Writer of the "Monitor,"' 4to, 1761; 'Seventeen Hundred and Ninety-One: an Imitation of the 13th Satire of Juvenal,' 1791, 4to.

'A Letter from Mons. de Voltaire to the Author of the "Orphan of China,"' London, 8vo, was published in 1759.

The actor's elder brother, JAMES MURPHY (1725–1759), dramatic writer, was born on St. George's Quay, Dublin, in September 1725, and was educated at Westminster School. He studied law in the Middle Temple, and was called to the bar. He soon adopted the surname of French, from his uncle Jeffery French, M.P. for Milbourne Port, and was generally known as James Murphy French. When his brother started the 'Gray's Inn Journal' he joined him, and wrote for it occasionally. He made the acquaintance of Samuel Foote and David Garrick, and wrote two plays, 'The Brothers,' a comedy adapted from Terence's 'Adelphi,' and a farce entitled 'The Conjuror, or the Enchanted Garden,' neither of which was apparently printed or performed, but a correspondence respecting them is given in Foot's life of Arthur Murphy. He wrote fugitive verse of a passable kind, and some specimens will be found in his brother's biography. In 1758 he went to Jamaica, where his uncle owned some property, intending to practise his profession there, but he died soon after his arrival at Kingston on 5 Jan. 1759 (FOOT, *Life of Arthur Murphy*, p. 114). The manuscripts of his two plays were sold at the sale of Arthur Murphy's library.

[The principal source of information is the biography by Foot (4to, 1811), founded on papers, including portions of an autobiography, left by Murphy. The Garrick Correspondence overflows with letters from him. His stage career is extracted from Genest, who gives a summary of his performances. See also Nichols's Anecdotes; Boswell's Johnson, ed. Hill; Dibdin's Hist. of the Stage; Davies's Dramatic Miscellanies and Life of Garrick; Cumberland's Memoirs; Rogers's Table Talk; Georgian Era; Clark Russell's Representative Actors; Chalmers's Biog. Dict.; Baker's Biographia Dramatica.] J. K.

MURPHY, DENIS BROWNELL (*d.* 1842), miniature-painter, was a native of Dublin. He was a patriot and strong sympathiser with the cause of United Ireland in 1798, but in that year removed for professional reasons to Whitehaven in England with his wife and family. In 1802 they removed to Newcastle-on-Tyne, but in 1803 came to London, settling first at Hanwell. Murphy had considerable practice as a miniature-painter, and was in that capacity attached to the household of Princess Charlotte, being in 1810 appointed painter in ordinary to her royal highness. He copied one or two of Lely's famous 'Beauties,' then at Windsor Castle (now at Hampton Court), and by command of the princess completed a series of miniature copies of these, adding some from pictures not at Windsor. Murphy had apartments assigned him at Windsor during the progress of this work, which was from time to time inspected and approved by the royal family. The set was not completed at the time of the princess's death, which put an end to the work and to Murphy's connection with the court. The paintings were sent in to Prince Leopold, with a claim for payment, but to the painter's great disappointment were declined and returned. The set were, however, purchased by a friend, Sir Gerard Noel, and it was suggested that use should be made of them by having them engraved as a series, with illustrative text from the pen of Murphy's daughter, Mrs. Anna Brownell Jameson [q.v.] This work was successfully completed and published in 1833 under the title of 'The Beauties of the Court of King Charles the Second.' Murphy occasionally exhibited miniatures in enamel or on ivory at the Royal Academy from 1800 to 1827, but his work did not attain any great distinction. The latter part of his life was very closely connected with that of his more famous daughter, Mrs. Jameson.

Murphy died in March 1842, leaving by his wife, who survived him, five daughters, of whom the eldest, Anna Brownell, married Robert Jameson, and was the well-known writer on art [see JAMESON, ANNA BROWNELL]. Of the others, Camilla became Mrs. Sherwin, and died on 28 May 1886, at Brighton, aged 87, and Louisa became Mrs. Bate, while Eliza and Charlotte Alicia died unmarried, the former at Brighton on 31 March 1874 in her seventy-ninth year, the latter at Ealing on 13 June 1876, aged 71.

[Redgrave's Dict. of Artists; Mrs. Macpherson's Memoirs of the Life of Anna Jameson; private information.] L. C.

MURPHY or MORPHY, EDWARD or DOMINIC EDWARD (*d.* 1728), Roman catholic archbishop of Dublin, belonged to a family settled in Carlow county. He was appointed bishop of Kildare and Leighlin on 11 Sept. 1715, and was consecrated on 18 Dec. by Edmund Byrne, archbishop of Dublin. He was translated to the archiepiscopal see of Dublin by a papal brief dated September 1724. He was consecrated before 5 Jan. 1725, and the dispensation to perform all the archiepiscopal acts without the pallium was demanded in the congregation of 5 April.

On 25 Nov. 1728 he applied for a coadjutor, and he died on 22 Dec. in the same year. His death was announced in the propaganda congregation of 13 Feb. 1729. The historian of Kildare in his dedication to the Rev. Dr. Magee of Stradbally, a descendant of Murphy, speaks of the latter as 'one of the noblest bishops elect that Kildare and Leighlin had just reason to be proud of.'

[O'Byrne's Eccles. Hist. of the Bishops of Kildare and Leighlin, p. 58; W. M. Brady's Episcopal Succession, i. 340, 356; Gams's Series Episcop. Eccles. Hibern. p. 219.] G. LE G. N.

MURPHY, FRANCIS (1795–1858), first Roman catholic bishop of Adelaide, was born at Navan, county Meath, on 20 May 1795, and received his preparatory education in the diocesan seminary of his native town. In his twentieth year he entered St. Patrick's College, Maynooth, and in 1826 was ordained a priest by Dr. Daniel Murray, archbishop of Dublin. After serving as missioner at Bradford in Yorkshire for three years, he in 1829 took charge of St. Anne's, Toxteth Park, Liverpool. In 1838 he went out to New South Wales with Dr. Ullathorne (afterwards bishop of Birmingham), and on the latter's recall to England in the same year succeeded him as vicar general of Australia. On 8 Sept. 1844 he was consecrated in St. Mary's Cathedral, Sydney, bishop of the newly established suffragan see of Adelaide, being the first bishop consecrated in Australia. His diocese at this period contained only fifteen hundred Roman catholics, and he came to it with only 150*l.* which had been subscribed in Sydney. He held service in a store in Pirie Street, Adelaide, until his sole assistant, Michael Ryan, obtained a site and erected a church in West Terrace. The discovery of gold in 1851 caused the dispersion of a large portion of his congregations, and his churches were only kept open by Mr. Ryan visiting the gold fields, and there collecting money from the Adelaide diggers. When the excitement had somewhat subsided, he commenced erecting a cathedral in Victoria Street, but did not live to see it finished. He, however, succeeded in establishing twenty-one churches, served by thirteen priests, and in the management of his diocese won general esteem. He died of consumption at West Terrace, Adelaide, on 26 April 1858, and was buried within the precincts of his cathedral.

[South Australian Register, 27 April 1858; Tablet, 24 July 1858, p. 467; Heaton's Australian Dict. of Dates, 1879, p. 149.] G. C. B.

MURPHY, SIR FRANCIS (1809–1891), first speaker of the legislative assembly of Victoria, son of Francis D. Murphy, superintendent of the transportation of convicts from Ireland, was born at Cork in 1809, and educated in that city. Proceeding to Trinity College, Dublin, he studied medicine, and eventually took his diploma from the Royal College of Surgeons in London.

In June 1836 he arrived at Sydney, and was on 1 Jan. 1837 placed on the staff of colonial surgeons as district surgeon for Bungonia, Argyle county. Becoming interested in agricultural operations, he resigned his appointment in 1840, and settled at Goulburn on a large station, where he became the chief grain grower in the county. He was a magistrate for the district. In 1847 he removed to Port Phillip, and took up land on the Ovens River in the Beechworth district, farming about fifty thousand acres at Tarawingi.

On the separation of Victoria from New South Wales in 1851, Murphy entered public life as member for Murray in the legislative council. In November 1851 he was appointed chairman of committees. In 1852 he sold his properties, and, going to reside at Melbourne, devoted himself to politics. He was active in promoting improvements; the Scab in Sheep Prevention Act was due to him, and he pressed in 1852–3 a reform of the state-aided education, which was adopted much later. In March 1853, under the new road act he was appointed chairman of the central road board, but was at once re-elected for the Murray district, and for short periods during 1853 and 1854 acted first as chairman of committees and again as speaker. In the same year he was a member of the commission on internal communication in the colony. In the debates on the Constitution Bill he showed marked judgment and moderation, and when in 1856 an elective legislature was inaugurated, he entered the assembly as member for the Murray district, resigning his post on the road board. He was at once elected speaker of the assembly by a considerable majority. In 1859 he was unanimously re-elected speaker for the second session, and in four subsequent sessions he held the post through the stormy times of McCulloch's contests with the upper chamber [see MCCULLOCH, SIR JAMES]. He was knighted in 1860. Different estimates have been formed of his tenure of the chair during this critical period. Rusden is unfavourable, viewing him as too pliable in the hands of the government; the general contemporary opinion seems to have credited him with firmness and tact.

In the election of 1871 Murphy was defeated in the contest for Grenville, which he had represented since 1865. In the ensuing session, after considerable debate, the house passed an act to present him with a sum of 3,000*l.* in consideration of his services as speaker during fourteen years. In 1872 Murphy was elected by the eastern province to a seat in the upper house, which he retained for four years without taking a very active part in its discussions. In 1877 he retired into private life, and visited England, where he resided some years.

Murphy was in 1861 a member of the commission on the Burke and Wills expedition, and in 1863 chairman of the league directed against further transportation. He was chairman of the National Bank of Australasia and director of other companies.

Murphy died on 30 March 1891, at his residence, St. Kilda Road, Melbourne, and was buried in Boroondara cemetery. In 1840 he married the daughter of Lieutenant Reid, R.N., a settler in his neighbourhood. He left six daughters and three sons, one of whom was a member of the legislative assembly of Queensland.

[Melbourne Argus, 31 March 1891; Mennell's Dict. Austral. Biog.; Victorian Parliamentary Debates, passim.] C. A. H.

MURPHY, FRANCIS STACK (1810?–1860), serjeant-at-law, born in Cork about 1810, was son of Jeremiah Murphy, a rich merchant, whose brother John was catholic bishop of Cork from 1815 to 1847. He was educated at Clongoweswood College, co. Kildare, and was one of the pupils of Francis Sylvester Mahony [q. v.], 'Father Prout.' Proceeding to Trinity College, Dublin, he graduated B.A. in 1829 and M.A. in 1832. He studied law in London, and in 1833 was called to the English bar. In 1834 he became connected with 'Fraser's Magazine' as an occasional contributor, assisting 'Father Prout' in his famous 'Reliques.' He was an excellent classical scholar, and was responsible for some of Mahony's Greek and Latin verses (see Bates, *Maclise Portrait Gallery*, 1883, pp. 464, 466–7). Mahony introduces him in his 'Prout Papers' as 'Frank Cresswell of Furnival's Inn.' In 1837 Murphy became M.P. for co. Cork, and retained the seat for sixteen years. On 25 Feb. 1842 he was made serjeant-at-law, and resigned his place in parliament in September 1853, when appointed one of the commissioners of bankruptcy in Dublin. He died on 17 June 1860. His portrait figures in Maclise's well-known group of 'The Fraserians.' He was a clever lawyer, and was noted for his wit; many of his repartees are recorded in Duffy's 'League of North and South' (1886, pp. 211, 227) and in Serjeant Robinson's 'Bench and Bar' (1891). Only one work bears his name on the title-page, 'Reports of Cases argued and determined in the Court of Exchequer, 1836–1837,' which was written in conjunction with Edwin T. Hurlstone, 8vo, London, 1838.

A first cousin, Jeremiah Daniel Murphy (1806–1824), born at Cork in 1806, developed as a boy rare linguistic faculties, mastering Greek, Latin, French, Portuguese, Spanish, German, and Irish. He contributed to 'Blackwood's Magazine' some excellent Latin verse: 'Adventus Regis' (December 1821), and an English poem, 'The Rising of the North' (November 1822). He died of disease of heart on 5 Jan. 1824, and his precocity was commemorated in English and Latin verse in 'Blackwood's' next month (cf. Bates, *Maclise Gallery*, pp. 41, 489).

[Annual Register, 1860; Gent. Mag. 1860; authorities cited in text.] D. J. O'D.

MURPHY, JAMES CAVANAH (1760–1814), architect and antiquary, was born in 1760 of obscure parents at Blackrock, near Cork, and was originally a bricklayer. He showed early talent for drawing, and made his way to Dublin to study. His name appears in a list of the pupils of the drawing school of the Dublin Society about 1775, as working in miniature, chalk, and crayons (Herbert, *Irish Varieties*, p. 56). Afterwards he practised in Dublin, and in 1786 was one of seven architects who were consulted as to the additions to the House of Commons. To him and another was entrusted the execution of James Gandon's design for the work (Mulvany, *Life of Gandon*, pp. 116, 144). In December 1788 William Burton Conyngham commissioned him to make drawings for him of the great Dominican church and monastery of Batalha, and he accordingly proceeded to Portugal. He was back in Dublin in 1790, and was in England at the end of the year. In 1802 he went to Cadiz, where he remained for seven years studying Moorish architecture and occasionally performing some diplomatic duties. Settling in England in 1809, he spent his time in preparing his notes on Arabian architecture for the press, but died on 12 Sept. 1814 in Edward Street, Cavendish Square (now Lower Seymour Street), when only a portion of his book had been published. T. Hartwell Horne [q. v.] superintended the completion of the publication. T. C. Croker (*Researches in the South of Ireland*, p. 204) mentions that he left a large collection of notes and drawings. In the library of the Royal Institute of British Architects is a large folio volume of his drawings of arabesque ornaments. He was unmarried, and his estate (5,000*l.*) was administered in November 1814 by his sister, Hannah, wife of Bernard McNamara.

His published works are: 1. 'Plans, Elevations, Sections, and Views of the Church of Batalha. . . . To which is prefixed an Introductory Discourse on the Principles of Gothic Architecture,' twenty-seven plates, London, 1795, 1836. A history and description of the church by Manoel de Sousa Coutinho (translated by Murphy) occupies pp. 27–57. One drawing, Murphy's design for the completion of the monument of King Emmanuel, is in the print room of the British Museum, and a volume of studies and copies of Murphy's letters in the library of the Society of Antiquaries. A German translation of the 'Discourse on Gothic Architecture,' by J. D. E. W. Engelhard, was published in Darmstadt in 1828. 2. 'Travels in Portugal,' London, 1795, with portrait, after a painting by Sir Martin Archer Shee. A German translation by M. C. Sprengel was published at Halle in 1796 as vol. vi. of an 'Auswahl der besten ausländischen . . . Nachrichten,' and a French translation by Lallemant (2 vols. 8vo, 1 vol. 4to) in Paris, in 1797. 3. 'General View of the State of Portugal,' London, 1798 (see *Gent. Mag.* 1798, pp. 960–3). 4. 'Arabian Antiquities of Spain,' London, 1813–16, embellished with 110 plates from drawings by Murphy (cf. T. F. DIBDIN, *Library Companion*, p. 310). The work was edited and the descriptions written by T. Hartwell Horne. A 'History of the Mahometan Empire,' by John Shakespear, T. H. Horne, and John Gillies, and designed as an introduction to Murphy's book, was published in London in 1816. Murphy took out a patent in 1813 for a method of preserving timber and other substances from decay.

[Dict. of Architecture; Murphy's works; Manuscript Diary, 1790, in Libr. of R.I.B.A. (with sketches of building in Liverpool, Chester, Manchester, York, Cambridge, and Ely); Univ. Cat. of Books on Art; Keyser's Bücher-Lexicon; Cat. of Libr. of Sir John Soane's Museum; Admon. Act Book, November 1814 (in Somerset House); Annual Register (App. to Chronicle), 1814, p. 335.] B. P.

MURPHY, JOHN (1753?–1798), Irish rebel, the son of a small farmer, was born at Tincurry, in the parish of Ferns, in co. Wexford, about 1753. After receiving some instruction at a neighbouring hedge-school he proceeded to Seville, where he completed his education. Having taken orders, and apparently graduated D.D., he returned to Ireland in 1785, and was appointed coadjutor, or assistant priest, of the parish of Boulavogue, in the diocese of Ferns. His simple piety and upright life soon obtained for him considerable influence in the district. In November 1797, when the government proclaimed a number of parishes in the county, he was one of the first to take the oath of allegiance, and when in April 1798 the whole county was proclaimed he was very active in inducing the catholic peasantry to surrender their arms. Whether his motives were, as Musgrave insinuates, insincere, or whether, as seems more likely, he was driven into rebellious courses by the outrages practised on himself and his parishioners by the military (PLOWDEN, *Historical Register*, ii. 716; BYRNE, *Memoirs*, i. 46), he was the first to raise the standard of revolt in the county of Wexford at Boulavogue on 26 May 1798. Having routed a small body of yeomanry that tried to withstand him, he proceeded to the hill of Oulart. The inhabitants, animated by his success, flocked to his standard, and on the following day he defeated and almost exterminated a picked body of the North Cork militia. He displayed considerable military ability, and having captured Camolin and Ferns, he marched directly on Enniscorthy. Here he met with a stubborn resistance, but, having taken the place on 28 May, he established a permanent camp on Vinegar Hill. His followers, the majority a mere rabble of half-starved peasants, of whom a great number were women, armed with whatever weapons they could procure, now amounted to several thousands, and it required all his influence to prevent them dispersing in order to plunder and murder those who were personally obnoxious to them. After some hesitation as to what course to pursue, Murphy's opinion carried the day, and that night the rebels under his leadership marched in the direction of Wexford, as far as a place called Three Rocks. The following day Wexford surrendered, and the rebels, having appointed Matthew Keugh [q. v.] governor of the town, retired. They then divided into three bodies, and with one of these Murphy directed his march towards Arklow. On 4 June he encountered Colonel Walpole in the neighbourhood of Ballymore Hill, and having defeated and slain that officer, he advanced as far as Gorey. Here he imprudently, as the event proved, lingered several days accumulating provisions, and it was not till 9 June that he advanced on Arklow. After a desperate attempt to capture the town he was repulsed with heavy loss by General Needham. Discouraged by his failure he appears to have divided his forces, and, while the larger division penetrated into Wicklow as far as Tinahely, he himself retreated with the other in the direction of Wexford. He took part in the battle of Vinegar Hill on 21 June, and, managing to escape to Wexford, he joined the main body of the rebels under Philip Roche [q. v.] at Three Rocks. He disapproved of Roche's plan of capitulation, and when the arrest of that general placed him at the head of the rebels, he resolved to make an effort to extend the rebellion into Carlow and Kilkenny. Accordingly, early on 22 June, he quitted Three Rocks, and, proceeding through Scollogh Gap, he made his way through Carlow towards Castlecomer, the centre of the coal district in the north of co. Kilkenny. Castlecomer was reached on 24 June, and a few miners were induced to join the rebels, but the inhabitants generally were apathetic, and, after plundering the town, Murphy and his followers, now greatly diminished in number, retraced their steps towards Wexford. At

Kilcomney Hill, on the borders of Carlow and Wexford, they were attacked and routed by General Sir Charles Asgill [q. v.] on 26 June. Some uncertainty attaches to the fate of Murphy. He was missed by his followers during the fight, but it is credibly stated that he was captured by some yeomen, and taken to Tullow, where, after being grossly insulted and whipped, he was on the same day (26 June) hanged and beheaded, and his body burnt (PLOWDEN, *Historical Register*, ii. 717, 752, note). Nearly a year afterwards subscriptions were solicited in Dublin to enable a person claiming to be Murphy to escape from Ireland, but the man was declared by Byrne (*Memoirs*, i. 230) to be an impostor.

Father Murphy, as he was generally called, was a well-built, agile man, about five feet nine inches high, of a fair complexion, and rather bald. He was regarded even by members of his own creed as somewhat of a religious fanatic. He was personally very brave, and in the management of the rebellion he displayed considerable military skill. He was not naturally of a cruel disposition, but where religion was concerned he appears to have been indifferent to shedding blood, and was directly responsible for some of those outrages on life and property that marked the course of the insurrection.

[Sir R. Musgrave's Memoirs of the different Rebellions in Ireland; Edward Hay's Hist. of the Insurrection in the County of Wexford, A.D. 1798; Thomas Cloney's Personal Narrative of those Transactions in County Wexford in which the Author was engaged during the awful period of 1798; the Rev. J. Gordon's Hist. of the Rebellion in Ireland; Miles Byrne's Memoirs; Plowden's Historical Register; the Rev. George Taylor's Hist. of the Rebellion in the County of Wexford; Castlereagh Correspondence; Webb's Compendium of Irish Biography; Froude's English in Ireland; Lecky's England in the Eighteenth Century; De Quincey's Works, 1863, xiv. 248.] R. D.

MURPHY, JOHN (*fl.* 1780–1820), engraver, was born in Ireland about 1748, and came to London, where he practised as an engraver, chiefly in mezzotint. His plates are not numerous, but some of them are singularly brilliant and masterly in treatment. He engraved historical subjects after contemporary English painters and the old masters, and also portraits. Murphy's plates include: 'A Tyger,' after Northcote; 'A Tigress,' after G. Stubbs; 'Jael and Sisera,' after Northcote; 'Mark Antony's Oration,' after West; 'George III and his Family,' after T. Stothard; 'Portrait of the Duke of Portland,' after Reynolds; two subjects from the history of Joseph, after Guercino; 'Titian's Son and Nurse,' after Titian; 'Christ appearing to the Magdalen,' after P. da Cortona; 'Sacrifice of Abraham,' after Rembrandt; and 'The Cyclops at their Forge,' after L. Giordano. The last four were done for Boydell's 'Houghton Gallery.' Murphy was also a portrait draughtsman. Several of his plates are from his own designs, and a portrait of Arthur O'Leary [q.v.], drawn by him, has been engraved by G. Keating. The latest date on Murphy's prints is 1809, but, according to a list of living artists published in 1820, he was then residing in Howland Street, Fitzroy Square.

[Redgrave's Dict. of Artists; J. Chaloner Smith's British Mezzotinto Portraits; Huber and Rost's Manuel des Curieux et des Amateurs de l'Art, 1804; Annals of the Fine Arts, iv. 665.] F. M. O'D.

MURPHY, MARIE LOUISE (1737–1814), mistress of Louis XV, was born at Rouen 21 Oct. 1737, being the fifth daughter of Daniel Murphy, an Irishman who had served in the French army, but had become a shoemaker. Her mother's name was Margaret Hickey. Her parents removed to Paris, where her mother, after her father's death, became a secondhand clothes dealer near the Palais Royal. The daughters, all handsome, were disposed of by the mother as soon as they became marketable. Two are said to have been actresses. The eldest was a model at the Academy of Painting, and Marie Louise, to whom the reversion of that post had been promised, sat to Boucher, and in this way fell under the notice of Madame de Pompadour, who contrived that she should pose for the Virgin in a Holy Family painted for the queen's oratory. The king, as was expected, was smitten with the portrait, and in March 1753 Marie Louise was lodged, as its first occupant, in the small house at Versailles, styled the Parc aux Cerfs, round which so many legends have gathered. There on 21 May 1754 she gave birth to a child, described by some contemporaries as a girl, but probably a boy. Witty as well as handsome, 'la petite Morfi' is said to have aimed at supplanting Madame de Pompadour, but was dismissed in disgrace, and was married, on 25 Nov. 1755, to Major Beaufranchet d'Ayat, a man of good connections but poor. She retired with him on a pension to Ayat in Auvergne, being forbidden to reappear at Versailles. According to Argenson, her sister, Marie Brigitte, succeeded her in the Parc aux Cerfs. Her husband, promoted general, was killed at Rossbach in 1757, shortly after which she married François-Nicolas Le Normant, a revenue official at Riom. Valfons alleges (*Souvenirs*, Paris, 1860) that Louis XV, after giving his consent to this marriage, revoked it, the revocation, however, arriving too late. Le Normant, probably after the king's death, when his wife's banishment would no longer be insisted upon, obtained the treasurership of the Marc d'Or, a Paris office which levied first-fruits on fresh appointments. Marie Louise again became a widow in 1783, and was accorded a pension of twelve thousand francs. During the Reign of Terror she was imprisoned as a 'suspect,' under the name of O'Murphy, at Sainte-Pélagie and at the English Benedictine convent in Paris. On her release she married Louis Philippe Dumont, a Calvados deputy in the convention, nearly thirty years her junior. He obtained a divorce in January 1799. Marie Louise died at Paris 11 Dec. 1814. Her son, General Beaufranchet, has been taken by some writers (*Revue Bleue*, 13 Sept. 1890; *Notes and Queries*, 7th ser. xi. 302, 429) for her child by Louis XV, but that child was probably brought up under an assumed name, and Beaufranchet was most likely the issue of her first marriage. He was a royal page in 1771, lieutenant of infantry in 1774, was probably present as chief of Berruyer's staff at Louis XVI's execution, and served as brigadier-general in Vendée. Suspended as a *ci-devant* in July 1793, he addressed remonstrances to the minister of war, excusing himself for having been born in a class justly disliked, and mentioning his mother, then at Havre with her grandchildren, but making no reference to his father. Through the influence of Desaix, his cousin, he was in 1798 allowed a retiring pension; he sat in the Corps Législatif in 1803, and died at Paris 2 July 1812.

[Journal du Marquis d'Argenson, Paris, 1859–1867; Goncourt's and Vatel's Lives of Madame de Pompadour; Livre Rouge, Paris, 1790; Soulavie's Anecdotes de la Cour de France (untrustworthy); Casanova's Memoirs, chap. xiv.; Alger's Englishmen in French Revolution, London, 1889; Revue Historique, 1887, xxxv. 294; Revue Rétrospective, October 1892, which throws doubt on the commonly received version of her introduction to Louis XV.] J. G. A.

MURPHY, MICHAEL (1767?–1798), Irish rebel, the son of a peasant, was born at Kilnew, co. Wexford, about 1767. Having acquired some learning at a hedge-school at Oulart, he was ordained a priest at Whitsuntide 1785, and sent to complete his education at the Irish College at Bordeaux. On his return to Ireland he was appointed officiating priest of the parish of Ballycanew in the diocese of Ferns. He is described by an unexceptionable witness (Taylor, *Hist. of the Rebellion*, p. 17) as a man of exemplary life, and much esteemed by persons of all persuasions. In 1798 he was still a young man, strongly built, and of a dark complexion. When the government early in that year began to take extraordinary measures for the preservation of the peace of the county, Murphy displayed great zeal in inducing his parishioners to surrender their arms and to take the oath of allegiance. On the outbreak of the rebellion he was reluctantly compelled to take up arms for his own safety (Hay, *Hist. of the Insurrection*, p. 88). He joined the rebels at Oulart under Father John Murphy [q. v.], whose fortunes he shared till his death at the battle of Arklow on 9 June 1798. He greatly distinguished himself by his intrepid conduct on that occasion. He was shot while leading the attack on the barricade, and his death greatly discomfited his followers, whose ardour he had inflamed by the belief that he was invulnerable. His head was struck off and his body burnt by the order of Lord Mountnorris.

[The Rev. George Taylor's Hist. of the Rebellion in the County of Wexford; Sir R. Musgrave's Memoirs of the different Rebellions in Ireland; Miles Byrne's Memoirs; E. Hay's Hist. of the Insurrection in the county of Wexford, A.D. 1798; Froude's English in Ireland; Lecky's England in the Eighteenth Century.] R. D.

MURPHY, PATRICK (1782–1847), weather prophet, was born in 1782. His name was very prominent in 1838 as the author of 'The Weather Almanack (on Scientific Principles, showing the State of the Weather for every Day of the Year 1838). By P. Murphy, Esq., M.N.S.,' i.e. member of no society. Under the date of 20 Jan. he said, 'Fair, prob. lowest deg. of winter temp.' By a happy chance this proved to be a remarkably cold day, the thermometer at sunrise standing at four degrees below zero. This circumstance raised his celebrity to a great height as a weather prophet, and the shop of his publishers, Messrs. Whittaker & Co., was besieged with customers, while the winter of 1837–8 became known as Murphy's winter. The 1838 almanac ran to forty-five editions, and the prophet made 3,000*l.*, which he almost immediately lost in an unsuccessful speculation in corn. There was nothing very remarkable about the prediction, as the coldest day generally falls about 20 Jan. In the predictions throughout the year the forecasts were partly right on 168 days and decidedly wrong on 197 days. A popular song of the day, a parody on 'Lesbia has a beaming eye,' commenced 'Murphy has a weather eye.' The almanack was afterwards occasionally published, but its sale very much fell off after the 'nine days' wonder' was past, and ultimately it had a very limited circulation. Murphy, however, persevered in his pursuit, and was about bringing out an almanac for 1848, when he died at his lodgings, 108 Dorset Street, St. Bride's, London, on 1 Dec. 1847, aged 65.

His other works were: 1. 'An Inquiry into the Nature and Cause of Miasmata, more particularly illustrated in the former and present state of the Campagna di Roma,' 1825. 2. 'Rudiments of the Primary Forces of Gravity, Magnetism, and Electricity in their Agency on the Heavenly Bodies,' 1830. 3. 'The Anatomy of the Seasons, Weather Guide Book, and Perpetual Companion to the Almanack,' 1834. 4. 'Meteorology considered in its connection with Astronomy, Climate, and the Geological Distribution of Animals and Plants, equally as with the Seasons and Changes of the Weather,' 1836. 5. 'Observation on the Laws and Cosmical Dispositions of Nature in the Solar System. With two Papers on Meteorology and Climate,' 1843. The two papers were written for meetings of the Society of Scienziati Italiani at Padua, of which Murphy was elected a member. 6. 'Weather Tables for the Year 1845,' 1844. 7. 'Astronomical Aphorisms or Theory of Nature, founded on the Immutable Basis of Meteoric Action,' 1847, 2nd edit. 1847.

[Times, 7 Dec. 1847, p. 8; Illustr. London News, 11 Dec. 1847, p. 383; Gent. Mag. April 1848, p. 443; Chambers's Book of Days, 1864, i. 137; Notes and Queries, 1886, 7th ser. i. 70, 117; Fraser's Mag. 1838, xvii. 378–84.]

G. C. B.

MURPHY, ROBERT (1806–1843), mathematician, born in 1806, was the third of the seven children of a shoemaker, parish clerk of Mallow, co. Cork. When eleven years of age he was run over by a cart, and for twelve months he lay on his bed with a fractured thigh-bone. During this confinement he studied Euclid and algebra, and before attaining the age of thirteen was an extraordinarily efficient mathematician. Subsequently he continued his studies in a classical school kept by Mr. Hopley at Mallow. At the age of eighteen he published a remarkable 'Refutation of a Pamphlet written by the Rev. John Mackey, R[oman] C[atholic] P[riest], entitled "A Method of making a Cube double of a Cube, founded on the principles of elementary geometry," wherein his principles are proved erroneous, and the required solution not yet obtained,' Mallow, 1824, 12mo.

His friends raised a subscription to send him to the university, and he began his residence in Gonville and Caius College, Cambridge, in October 1825. In 1829 he graduated B.A. and came out third wrangler. In May 1829 he was elected a fellow of his college, and shortly afterwards he was admitted to deacon's orders in the church of England. In May 1831 he was appointed dean of his college—an office which involved the regulation of chapel discipline. Unfortunately he fell into dissipated habits, and in December 1832 he left Cambridge, with his fellowship under sequestration for the benefit of his creditors. After living for some time among his friends in Ireland, he came to London in 1836 to begin life again as a teacher and writer; and in October 1838 he was appointed examiner in mathematics and natural philosophy in the university of London. He died on 12 March 1843.

His friend, Augustus De Morgan [q. v.], remarks that 'he had a true genius for mathematical invention;' and that 'his works on the theory of equations and on electricity, and his papers in the "Cambridge Transactions," are all of high genius.'

To the 'Cambridge Philosophical Transactions' his contributions were: vol. iii. pt. iii., 'General Properties of Definite Integrals;' vol. iv. pt. i., 'On the Resolution of Algebraic Equations;' pt. iii. 'On the Inverse Method of Definite Integrals, with Physical Applications,' with two further memoirs on the same (v., ii. and iii.); vol. v. pt. i., 'On Elimination between an Indefinite Number of Unknown Quantities;' vol. vi. pt. i., 'On the Resolution of Equations in Finite Differences.'

To the 'Philosophical Transactions' he contributed: 1837, pt. i., 'Analysis of the Roots of Equations;' pt. i., 'First Memoir on the Theory of Analytical Operations.'

His separate works are: 1. 'Elementary Principles of Electricity, Heat, and Molecular Actions, part i. On Electricity,' Cambridge, 1833, 8vo. 2. 'Theory of Algebraical Equations,' in 'Library of Useful Knowledge,' London, 1839, 8vo; reprinted 1847.

[Athenæum, 6 Aug. 1864, p. 181; De Morgan's Budget of Paradoxes, p. 214; Gent. Mag. May 1843, p. 545; Penny Cycl. 1st. Suppl. p. 337 (by Augustus De Morgan); Cat. of Library of Trin. Coll. Dublin.]

T. C.

MURRAY or MORAY, Earls of. [See Randolph, Thomas, first Earl of the Randolph family, *d.* 1332; Randolph, John, third Earl, *d.* 1346; Stewart, James, first Earl of the Stewart family, 1499?–1544; Stewart, James, first Earl of a new creation, 1531?–1570; Stewart, James, second Earl, *d.* 1592; Stewart, Alexander, fifth Earl, *d.* 1701.]

MURRAY, ADAM (*d.* 1700), defender of Londonderry, was descended from the Murrays of Philiphaugh in Selkirkshire. His father, Gideon Murray, came to Ireland in 1648, settled at Ling on the Faughan Water, nine miles from Londonderry, and held some of the lands planted by the London Skinners' Company. When the protestants of Ulster armed against Tyrconnel at the end of 1688, Adam Murray raised a troop of horse among his neighbours. Robert Lundy [q. v.] sent him on 15 April 1689 with thirty men, as part of the force destined to hold the ford over the Finn at Clady, near Strabane, but neglected to provide the necessary supplies. Having only three rounds of ammunition apiece, the defenders were dispersed, and Rosen passed the river. On the 18th James himself appeared under the walls of Londonderry, but was driven away by the fire of the enraged citizens. Murray at the same time approached with his horse, and was admitted by James Morrison, captain of the city guard, who acted in defiance of Lundy, and by so doing saved the town. Walker had offered to take in Murray without his men, but he indignantly refused (Mackenzie). Murray was followed about by the anxious people, and he promised to stand by them. Afterwards, at a meeting of officers, he taxed Lundy with cowardice or treason at Clady and elsewhere. Murray was thenceforth the soul of the no-surrender party, and was chosen to command the horse. On 19 April the people wished to make him governor, but he refused, and Major Baker was chosen. Next day Claude Hamilton, lord Strabane, came into the town with a flag of truce, and offered Murray a colonel's commission and 1,000*l.* on King James's part. He declined both, and saw his lordship through the lines. As the siege went on, says the author of the 'Londerias,'

> The name of Murray grew so terrible
> That he alone was thought invincible:
> Where'er he came, the Irish fled away.

In the sally to Pennyburn Mill on 21 April he had a horse shot under him, and, according to two local authorities, slew the French general, Maumont, with his own hand (Mackenzie, chap. v.; *Londerias*). The identical sword is still shown, but Avaux reported to his government that Maumont was killed by a musket-shot in the head (Macaulay). About the middle of May General Richard Hamilton [q. v.] sent Murray's father, who was living near, to persuade his son that the town must be yielded. According to the author of the 'Londerias,' who likens him to Hamilcar and Regulus, the old man counselled unflinching resistance, and then returned to the besiegers' camp. To his credit, Hamilton allowed him to live unmolested. On 18 June Murray was badly hurt in the head. In the fight at the Windmill on 16 July he was shot through both thighs, and did not fully recover until the end of October.

When Kirke entered the relieved city at the beginning of August, he proposed to amalgamate the disabled hero's regiment with another, but nearly all the men 'refused, and went off into the country with their carbines and pistols, and the major-general seized the saddles, as he also did Colonel Murray's horse, which he had preserved with great care during all the siege' (Mackenzie, chap. vi.)

Murray died probably in 1700, and, it is believed, at Ling. He was buried in Glendermot churchyard, near the spot where Governor Mitchelburn [q. v.] was laid more than twenty years later. He married Isabella Shaw, by whom he had a son, whose descendants exist in the female line, and a daughter, who enjoyed a pension from the crown for life. Murray did not himself seek any reward, but William III presented him with a watch. He has been claimed both by the presbyterians and episcopalians, but there is no conclusive evidence either way (Witherow, p. 325; Hempton, pp. vi–xii). His name has been locally perpetuated by the Murray Club.

Besides his sword and watch, Murray's snuff box is in possession of his descendant, Mr. Alexander of Caw House, Londonderry.

[There are three contemporary accounts of the siege of Londonderry, besides subsidiary pamphlets on controverted points, viz. George Walker's True Account, and the narratives of the Rev. John Mackenzie and Captain Thomas Ash. The curious Londerias, in halting heroic verse, by Joseph Aickin, was published in 1699. See also Hempton's Siege and Hist. of Londonderry; the Rev. John Graham's Ireland Preserved; Walter Harris's Life of William III; Witherow's Derry and Enniskillen, 3rd ed. 1885; Reid's Presbyterian Church of Ireland, ed. Killen, vol. ii.; Macaulay's Hist. chap. xii.; Cat. of Industrial and Loan Exhibition, Londonderry, 1890.] R. B-l.

MURRAY, ALEXANDER (*d.* 1777), Jacobite, was the fourth son of Alexander, fourth lord Elibank, by Elizabeth, daughter of George Stirling, surgeon, Edinburgh. He served for some time in the army, having received an ensigncy in the 26th regiment of foot, or Cameronians, 11 Aug. 1737. Horace Walpole wrote of him and his brother, the fifth Lord Elibank [see Murray, Patrick], that they were 'both such active Jacobites, that if the Pretender had succeeded they would have produced many witnesses to testify their great zeal for him; both so cautious that no witnesses of active treason could be produced by the government against them' (*Journal of George II*, p. 17). At the famous Westminster election of 1750 Murray took a very active part in favour of Sir George Vandeput, the anti-ministerial candidate. A complaint was preferred against him to the House of Commons by Peter Leigh, high bailiff of Westminster, on 20 Jan. 1751, to the effect that on 15 May 1750 he was the ringleader of a mob, whom he encouraged to acts of violence by shouting, 'Will no one have courage enough to knock the dog down?' On 1 Feb. 1751 he was called before the house, and after being taken into the custody of the sergeant-at-arms was admitted to bail, but on 6 Feb., by a majority of 169 to 52, he was ordered to be committed a close prisoner to Newgate. Thereafter, by a majority of 166 to 40, it was resolved that he should be brought to receive admonition on his knees, but to the speaker's request that he should kneel he answered, 'Sir, I beg to be excused; I never kneel but to God' (*ib.* p. 29). It was thereupon carried that since he had 'absolutely refused to be on his knees,' he was 'guilty of a high and most dangerous contempt of the authority of the House of Commons,' and he was ordered to be recommitted to Newgate, the use of paper and pens being forbidden him, and no person to be admitted to him without the leave of the house. On the report of the doctor that his life was endangered by the gaol distemper he was ordered to be discharged from Newgate, and committed to the custody of the sergeant-at-arms, with the same restrictions as formerly; but he declined to accept the relief offered him, and elected to remain in Newgate. On 27 April he was again brought before the house, when a motion was made to admit him to bail, which, however, was refused. In May he caused himself to be brought before the court of queen's bench on a writ of habeas corpus, but the judges unanimously refused to discharge him, deciding that the commons had power to judge their own privileges (Hallam, *Const. Hist.* iii. 274, 280). After the prorogation of parliament on 25 June he was released by the sheriffs of London; and in a coach, accompanied by Lord Carpenter and Sir George Vandeput, with the sheriffs in attendance in a chariot, went in procession from Newgate to the house of his brother, Lord Elibank, in Henrietta Street, with a banner carried before him inscribed 'Murray and Liberty.' His portrait in mezzotint was engraved, and a pamphlet on the case was circulated entitled 'The Case of the Hon. Alexander Murray, Esq., in an Appeal to the People of Great Britain, more particularly the Inhabitants of the City and Liberty of Westminster,' 1751 According to Horace Walpole, the author of the pamphlet was Paul Whitehead (*Letters*, ii. 201). Search was made for the pamphlet by the high bailiff of Westminster, and on 2 July Pugh the printer and Owen the publisher, after examination at the secretary's office, were detained in custody. Before the meeting of parliament in November Murray passed over to France, where he was known as Count Murray. On 25 Nov. a motion was carried in the House of Commons for his recommittal to Newgate, and a reward of five hundred pounds was offered for his apprehension. In 1763 he was concerned in the quarrel at Paris between his friend Captain Forbes and the notorious John Wilkes. In the 'Great Douglas cause' against James George, fourth duke of Hamilton, he displayed much zeal on behalf of the pursuer [see under Douglas, Archibald James Edward, first Baron Douglas]. In April 1771 he was recalled from exile by letter under the king's privy seal. He died unmarried in 1777. Murray was a correspondent of David Hume, for whom he had a high admiration. A portrait by Allan Ramsay is in the Scottish National Gallery, and was engraved by J. Faber.

[Case of Honourable Alexander Murray, 1751; Orders of the House of Commons, to which are added Proceedings of the House against the Hon. Mr. Murray, 2nd edit. 1756; Horace Walpole's George II; Horace Walpole's Letters; Burton's Life of Hume; Gent. Mag.; 1751; Douglas's Scots' Peerage (ed. Wood, rev. by Paul), 1904; Mahon's Hist. of England, iv. 29–30.] T. F. H.

MURRAY, ALEXANDER, Lord Henderland (1736–1795), Scottish judge, born in Edinburgh in 1736, was the son of Archibald Murray of Murrayfield, near Edinburgh, advocate. He was called to the Scottish bar on 7 March 1758, and succeeded his father as sheriff-depute of the shire of Peebles in 1761, and as one of the commissaries of Edinburgh in 1765. On 24 May 1775 he was appointed solicitor-general for Scotland, and at the general election in September 1780 was returned to the House of Commons for Peeblesshire. The only speech he is recorded to have made in parliament was in opposition to Sir George Savile's motion relating to the petition of the delegated counties for a redress of grievances (*Parl. Hist.* xxii. 161–164). He succeeded Henry Home, lord Kames [q. v.], as an ordinary lord of session and a commissioner of the court of justiciary, and took his seat on the bench with the title of Lord Henderland on 6 March 1783.

He took part in the trials for sedition at Edinburgh in 1793 (see HOWELL, *State Trials*, 1817, xxiii. 11 et seq.), and died of cholera at Murrayfield on 16 March 1795.

He married, on 15 March 1773, Katherine, daughter of Sir Alexander Lindsay of Evelick, Perthshire, bart., by whom he had, with other issue, Sir John Archibald Murray, lord Murray [q.v.] Henderland was joint clerk of the pipe in the court of exchequer, an office which, through the influence of Lord Melville, was subsequently conferred on his two sons. His 'Disputatio Juridica . . . de Divortiis et Repudiis,' &c., was published in 1758 (Edinburgh, 4to).

There is a small etching of Henderland in Kay's 'Original Portraits,' vol. i. (No. 99).

[Brunton and Haig's Senators of the College of Justice, 1832, p. 537; Kay's Original Portraits and Caricature Etchings, 1877, i. 243–4, 302, 307, 418, ii. 90, 346; Grant's Old and New Edinburgh, ii. 81, 255, 270, iii. 103–4; Foster's Members of Parliament, Scotland, 1882, p. 262; Burke's Landed Gentry; Scots Mag. xxiii. 224, xxvii. 448, xxxv. 222, lvii. 206.] G. F. R. B.

MURRAY, ALEXANDER, D.D. (1775–1813), linguist, was born on 22 Oct. 1775 at Dunkitterick, Kirkcudbrightshire, where his father was a shepherd. Up to 1792 he had little more than thirteen months of school education, but he had learnt the alphabet in a crude way from his father, and by his own efforts he had mastered English and the rudiments of Latin, Greek, and Hebrew, knew something of French and German, and had begun the study of Abyssinian. Meanwhile he had been engaged, partly as a shepherd and partly as a tutor to children remote from school like himself, and the small funds accruing from these sources helped his literary needs. He translated Drackenburg's German lectures on Roman authors, and when he visited Dumfries with his version in 1794, after unsuccessfully offering it to two separate publishers, he met Burns, who gave him wise advice (autobiographical sketch prefixed to *History of European Languages*). The father of Robert Heron (1764–1807) [q. v.] lent him useful books, and James M'Harg, a literary pedlar from Edinburgh, proposed that Murray should visit the university authorities. His parish minister, J. G. Maitland of Minnigaff, gave him an introductory letter to Principal Baird, which led to an examination, in which Murray agreeably surprised his examiners by his knowledge of Homer, Horace, the Hebrew psalms, and French. Admitted to Edinburgh University as a deserving student, he won his way by class distinctions and the help of private teaching. Lord Cockburn remembered him as a fellow-student, 'a little shivering creature, gentle, studious, timid, and reserved' (*Memorials of his Time*, p. 276). He completed a brilliant career by becoming a licentiate of the church of Scotland.

Murray early formed the acquaintance of John Leyden (LEYDEN, *Poetical Remains*, p. xvii), and among his friends were Dr. Anderson, editor of 'The British Poets,' Brougham, Jeffrey, Thomas Brown, Campbell, and others. Through Leyden he became a contributor to the 'Scots Magazine,' and he edited the seven numbers of that periodical from February 1802, inserting verses of his own under one of the signatures 'B,' 'X,' or 'Z.' He was meanwhile diligently studying languages. From the spoken tongues of Europe he advanced about this time to those of Western Asia and North-east Africa. His latter studies led him to contribute to three successive numbers of the 'Scots Magazine' a biography of Bruce, the Abyssinian traveller, which he afterwards expanded into a volume (1808). Constable the publisher, struck with his knowledge and thoroughness, engaged him in September 1802 to prepare a new edition of 'Bruce's Travels' (7 vols. 1805, new edit. 1813), to which he did ample justice, despite hindrances due to the stupid jealousy of the traveller's son, James Bruce, and his family (*Archibald Constable and his Literary Correspondents*, i. 222). At the same time (1802–5) he worked for the 'Edinburgh Review,' and his letters to Constable mark a writer with an easy, humorous, incisive style, and keenly alive to the importance of literary excellence and a wide and generous culture. Almost from the outset, as De Quincey says, he had before him 'a theory, and distinct purpose' (DE QUINCEY, *Works*, x. 34, ed. Masson).

In 1806 Murray was appointed assistant to Dr. James Muirhead (1742–1808) [q. v.], parish minister of Urr, Kirkcudbrightshire, whom he fully succeeded at his death in 1808. He married, 9 Dec. 1808, Henrietta Affleck, daughter of a parishioner. He soon became popular both as a man and a preacher. His interesting, frank, and sometimes sprightly letters to Constable mark steady social development, patriotic spirit, and literary and philosophical earnestness. He hailed with enthusiasm Chalmers's 'Caledonia,' and Scott's 'Minstrel' and 'Marmion.' Among his own literary projects for a time were, an edition of the classics, suggested by Constable, and a history of Galloway, which he seriously contemplated, and about which he had some correspondence with Scott (*Constable and his Literary Correspondents*, i.

267). His chief interest, however, centred in comparative language. He thought of writing a philosophical history of the European languages (*ib.* p. 289). In 1811 he translated, with approbation, an Ethiopic letter for George III, brought home by Salt, the Abyssinian envoy, whose familiarity with the revised edition of Bruce's 'Travels' prompted his suggestion of Murray to the Marquis of Wellesley as the only capable translator 'in the British dominions.' On 13 Aug. 1811 Murray wrote to Constable that he had mastered the Lappish tongue, that he saw 'light through the extent of Europe in every direction,' and that he trusted to unite the histories of Europe and Asia by aid of their respective languages. He added his conviction that the day would come when 'no monarch, however great and virtuous, would be ashamed of knowing him.'

In July 1812, after a keen contest involving some bitterness of feeling, Murray was appointed professor of oriental languages in Edinburgh University. His interests were materially served by the advocacy of Salt, and the active help of Constable (*Scots Mag.* August 1812; *Constable*, ut supra). He received from the university on 17 July the degree of doctor of divinity. He entered on his work at the end of October, publishing at the same date 'Outlines of Oriental Philology' (1812), for the use of his students. He lectured through the winter, against his strength, attracting both students and literary men to his room. His health completely gave way in the spring, and he died of consumption at Edinburgh 15 April 1813, leaving his widow and a son and daughter. Mrs. Murray survived about twelve years, supported by a government pension of 80*l.*, which had been granted to her in return for Murray's translation of the Abyssinian letter. The daughter died of consumption in 1821, and the son, who was practically adopted by Archibald Constable, qualified for a ship surgeon, and was drowned on his first voyage (*ib.* p. 336). A monument to Murray was erected near his birthplace in 1834, and it received a suitable inscription in 1877. A portrait by Andrew Geddes, formerly in the possession of Constable, is now in the National Portrait Gallery, Edinburgh.

Murray's wonderful promise was not equalled by his performance. But he proved himself an ideal editor and biographer, and his impulse, method, and style had a permanent influence. To the 'Edinburgh Review' of 1803 Murray contributed a review of Vallancey's 'Prospectus of an Irish Dictionary;' to the number for January 1804 he furnished an article on Clarke's 'Progress of Maritime Discovery;' and in January 1805 he discussed Maurice's 'History of Hindostan.' His 'Letters to Charles Stuart, M.D.,' appeared in 1813. His great work, the 'History of the European Languages, or Researches into the Affinities of the Teutonic, Greek, Celtic, Slavonic, and Indian Nations,' was edited by Dr. Scott, and published, with a life, by Sir H. W. Moncreiff, in 2 vols. 8vo, 1823. The Life includes a minute autobiographical sketch of Murray's boyhood, addressed to the minister of Minnigaff, Kirkcudbrightshire. He figures as a lyrist on his 'Native Vale' in Harper's 'Bards of Galloway.'

[Life prefixed to European Languages; Archibald Constable and his Literary Correspondents; Murray's Literary History of Galloway; John Reith's Life and Writings of Rev. Alex. Murray, Dumfries, 1903.] T. B.

MURRAY, AMELIA MATILDA (1795–1884), writer, born in 1795, was fourth daughter of Lord George Murray [q. v.], bishop of St. Davids, by Anne Charlotte (*d.* 1844), second daughter of Lieutenant-general Francis Ludovick Grant, M.P. (Burke, *Peerage*, 1891, p. 69). In 1805, when staying at Weymouth, she became known to George III and the royal family, and on her mother being appointed in 1808 a lady in waiting upon the Princesses Augusta and Elizabeth, she was frequently at court, where her brightness attracted much notice. One of the most intimate friends of her earlier years was Lady Byron. She became an excellent botanist and artist, and interested herself in the education of destitute and delinquent children, being an original member of the Children's Friend Society, which was established in 1830, and of kindred institutions. In 1837 she was chosen maid of honour to Queen Victoria. In July 1854 she started on a tour through the United States, Cuba, and Canada, returning home in October 1855 a zealous advocate for the abolition of slavery. Upon her proposing to print an account of her travels she was reminded that court officials were not allowed to publish anything savouring of politics. Rather than suppress her opinions, Miss Murray resigned her post in 1856, but was subsequently made extra woman of the bedchamber. She died on 7 June 1884 at Glenberrow, Herefordshire.

Miss Murray published: 1. 'Remarks on Education in 1847,' 16mo, London, 1847. 2. 'Letters from the United States, Cuba, and Canada,' 2 vols. 8vo, London, 1856. She had prepared, but did not publish, a series of sketches to accompany these volumes. 3. 'Recollections from 1803 to 1837, with a Conclusion in 1868,' 8vo, London, 1868. 4. 'Pictorial and Descriptive Sketches of the Odenwald,' 2 pts. oblong 4to, London, 1869.

[Miss Murray's Recollections; Times, 11 June 1884, p. 12.] G. G.

MURRAY or **MORAY**, **Sir ANDREW** (*d.* 1338), of Bothwell, warden of Scotland, was the son of Sir Andrew Moray of Bothwell, the companion of Wallace, who fell at Stirling on 11 Sept. 1297 (Wyntoun, ii. 344). He is first mentioned as the leader of a serious rising (*non modicus*) in Moray in the late summer of 1297 (*Doc. Illust. of Hist. of Scotland*, ed. Stevenson, ii. 210). On 28 Aug. he received letters of safe-conduct to visit his father, then a prisoner in the Tower of London (*ib.* p. 228). In the same year he was, though still a young man, joined in command with Wallace in the Scottish advance into Northumberland (Hemingford, i. 131), and in the succeeding raids into Cumberland and Annandale. On 8 Nov. he and Wallace appear as the grantors of a charter of protection to the monastery of Hexham, which had suffered at the hands of their wild soldiery (*ib.* i. 135). In 1326 he married Christian, sister of Robert I, widow of (1) Gratney, earl of Mar, and (2) Sir Christopher Seton. He appears to have been in receipt of an annuity in 1329–1330 (*Exchequer Rolls*, i. 218, 287, 341). Shortly after Edward Baliol was crowned, in 1332, Moray was elected warden or regent by the Scots who adhered to the young king, David II, but he had no opportunity of attempting anything till the following year, when he attacked Baliol at Roxburgh. While endeavouring to rescue Ralph Golding he was taken, and, refusing to be the prisoner of any one but the king of England, was carried to Durham, April 1333 (Wyntoun, ii. 396; iii. 292). No sooner was he set at liberty, in 1334, than he raised armed opposition to the English. With Alexander de Mowbray he marched into Buchan, and besieged Henry de Beaumont in his castle of Dundarg, on the Moray Firth (August–November). By cutting the waterpipes he compelled his foe to surrender, but he permitted him to return to England. Moray was present at the futile parliament convened at Dairsie in April 1335 by the steward of Scotland and the returned Earl of Moray, the regents. In the subsequent surrender to Edward, and in the making of the treaty of Perth (18 Aug. 1335), Moray had no part, but chose to go into hiding with the Earl of March and William Douglas of Liddesdale. When the Earl of Athole laid siege to the castle of Kildrummie, in which Moray's wife and children had been placed, the three fugitives came from their fastnesses, and marched against Kildrummie with eleven hundred men. They surprised and slew Athole in the forest of Kilblain or Culbleen. Thereupon Moray assembled a parliament at Dunfermline, and was again made warden. Edward marched into Scotland, and vainly endeavoured to bring him to action (see the anecdote of Moray's delays in the wood of Stronkaltere, as told to Wyntoun by men who were present—ii. 429–30). During the winter, 1335–6, Moray kept an army in the field, and laid siege to the castles of Cupar-Fife and Lochindorb in Cromdale, in the latter of which was Catherine, Athole's widow. He retired from Lochindorb on the approach of Edward, who had been summoned by the disconsolate lady. No sooner had Edward returned to England than he assumed the offensive, captured the castles of Dunnottar, Lauriston, and Kinclevin, and laid waste the lands of Kincardine and Angus. Early in 1337, having received the support of the Earls of March and Fife and William Douglas, he marched through Fife, destroyed the tower of Falkland, took the castle of Leuchars, and, after three weeks' siege, captured and sacked the castle of St. Andrews (28 Feb.) Cupar still held out, under the ecclesiastic, William Bullock (Wyntoun, ii. 436). In March the castle of Bothwell was reduced, and the way to England cleared. Moray led his troops as far as Carlisle, then wheeled about on Edinburgh, which he proceeded to invest. The English Marchers rushed to its relief, and met the Scots at Crichton. In the combat Douglas was wounded, and Sir Andrew, though claiming the victory, saw fit to raise the siege. From this time till his death, in 1338, we have but scanty record of him. Fordun states, on the authority of 'sum cornykill,' that he appeared before Stirling in October 1336, and was forced to retire on the approach of Edward, but the chronology seems to be faulty (see Fordun, ii. 437; Hailes, ii. 234; and Tytler, ii. 49). In 1337 he is referred to as having been keeper of Berwick Castle (*Exchequer Rolls*, i. 450). From the same source we have details of some moneys paid to him as warden in 1337 (pp. 428, 435, 451, 461, 468), of sums received at Kildrummy (p. 445), and of his expenses at Rothes (p. 445). He retired in 1338 to his castle of Avoch in Ross, and there died. He was buried in the chapel of Rosemarkie (Rosmarkyne), but his remains were afterwards removed to Dunfermline Abbey. Wyntoun gives an interesting character-sketch of the Scottish Fabius (ii. 439), for the most part panegyrical, but with a criticism of his destruction of castles and his wasting of his native land. Andrew de Moray had, however, to meet Edward with his own strategics, and the smallness of his force compelled him, as in the case of St. Andrews, to cast down what could be of use only to foes.

[Chronicles of Wyntoun, Fordun, and Hemingford; Exchequer Rolls, vol. i.; Hailes's Annals, vols. i. ii.; Historical Documents illustrative of the History of Scotland, ed. Stevenson, 1870, vol. ii.; Tytler, vols. i. ii.] G. G. S.

MURRAY, Sir ANDREW, first Baron Balvaird (1597?–1644), minister of Abdie, Fifeshire, was second son of David Murray of Balgonie, Fifeshire, by Agnes, daughter of Moncrieff of Moncrieff. He was educated at the university of St. Andrews, where he graduated M.A. in 1618. In 1622 he was presented by his grandfather, Sir David Murray, first viscount Stormont [q. v.], to the church of Abdie, to which he was admitted on 1 Oct. On the death of his grandfather in 1631 he succeeded to the baronies of Arngask and Kippo in Fifeshire. During the visit of Charles I to Scotland for his coronation in 1633 he was, on 15 June, dubbed a knight at Seton 'after dinner' (Sir James Balfour, *Annals*, iv. 367). He was the second of those who, in February 1638, signed the covenant in Greyfriars Church, Edinburgh (Gordon, *Scots Affairs*, i. 43); but, although his name was also inserted as supporting the libel against the bishops in the same year, he told Gordon of Rothiemay 'that he never concurred with the libel, and that some others there named knew not of it' (*ib.* p. 127). At a meeting of the assembly of the kirk in the same year, he, although not a member of it, exerted his influence to modify the attitude of the extremists towards the king's proposals; and his conduct was so favourably reported to the king by the high commissioner, the Marquis of Hamilton, that on 17 Nov. 1641 he was created a peer by the title of Lord Balvaird. He is the only minister of the church of Scotland on whom a knighthood or peerage was ever conferred. As a peer he attended a meeting of the convention of estates; but on 10 Aug. 1643 it was, 'after much reasoning,' decided by the assembly of the kirk 'that my Lord Balvaird should keep his ministry, and give over voicing in parliament, under pain of deposition and further censure' (Robert Baillie, *Letters and Journals*, ii. 91). On the death of the second Viscount Stormont in March 1642, Lord Balvaird succeeded to the lands, lordship, and barony of Stormont, but not to the title. He died on 24 Sept. 1644, aged about 47. By his wife Lady Elizabeth Carnegie, daughter of David, first earl of Southesk, he had five sons and three daughters. The sons were David, second lord Balvaird, who on the death of James, earl of Annandale, in 1658, succeeded to the titles of Viscount Stormont and Lord Scone; Sir Andrew Murray of Pitlochrie; the Hon. James Murray, M.D., a physician of some eminence; Sir John Murray of Drumcairne, who was appointed a lord of session in October 1681, and a lord of justiciary in July 1687, but at the revolution was deprived of all his offices; and the Hon. William Murray, an advocate at the Scottish bar. The daughters were: Catherine; Marjory, married to Sir Alexander Gibson of Durie, a lord of session; and Barbara, married to Patrick, lord Gray.

[Sir James Balfour's Annals; Gordon's Scots Affairs (Spalding Club); Robert Baillie's Letters and Journals (Bannatyne Club); Hew Scott's Fasti Eccles. Scot. ii. 467; Douglas's Scots' Peerage (ed. Wood, rev. by Paul), 1904.] T. F. H.

MURRAY, ANDREW (1812–1878), naturalist, born in Edinburgh, 19 Feb. 1812, was son of William Murray of Conland, Perthshire. Murray was educated for the law, became a writer to the signet, joined the firm of Murray & Rhind, and for some time practised in Edinburgh. His earliest scientific papers were entomological, and did not appear until he was forty. On the death of the Rev. John Fleming, professor of natural science in New College, Edinburgh, in 1857, Murray took up his work for one session, and in the same year he became a fellow of the Royal Society of Edinburgh. On the foundation of the Oregon Exploration Society he became its secretary, and this apparently first aroused his interest in Western North America and in the Coniferæ. In 1858–9 Murray acted as president of the Botanical Society of Edinburgh, and in 1860, abandoning the legal profession, he came to London and became assistant secretary to the Royal Horticultural Society; in the following year he was elected fellow of the Linnean Society. In 1868 he joined the scientific committee of the Royal Horticultural Society, and in 1877 was appointed its scientific director. In 1868 he began the collection of economic entomology for the Science and Art Department, now at the Bethnal Green Museum. In the following year he went to St. Petersburg as one of the delegates to the botanical congress, and in 1873 to Utah and California to report on some mining concessions. This latter journey seems to have permanently injured his health. He died at Bedford Gardens, Campden Hill, Kensington, 10 Jan. 1878. His chief contributions to entomology deal with Coleoptera, the unfinished monograph of the Nitidulariæ, in the Linnean 'Transactions' (vol. xxiv. 1863–4), undertaken at the suggestion of Dr. J. E. Gray, being perhaps the most important. His chief work on the Coniferæ was to have been published by the Ray Society, but was never completed.

Among his independent works were: 1. 'Catalogue of the Coleoptera of Scotland,' in conjunction with the Rev. W. Little and others, Edinburgh, 1853, 8vo. 2. 'Letter to the Secretary of State . . . on the Proper Treatment of Criminals,' Edinburgh, 1856, 8vo. 3. 'The Skipjack or Wireworm and the Slug, with notices of the Microscope, Barometer, and Thermometer, for the use of Parish Schools' (anon.), 1858, 8vo. 4. 'On the Disguises of Nature, being an Enquiry into the Laws which regulate External Form and Colour in Plants and Animals,' Edinburgh, 1859, 8vo. 5. 'The Pines and Firs of Japan,' London, 1863, 8vo. 6. The letterpress to Peter Lawson's 'Pinetum Britannicum,' 1866, fol. 7. 'The Geographical Distribution of Mammals,' London, 1866, 4to. 8. 'Catalogue of the Doubleday Collection of Lepidoptera,' South Kensington, 1876, 8vo. 9. 'Economic Entomology,' South Kensington, 1876, 8vo. 10. 'List of the Collection of Economic Entomology,' South Kensington, 1876, 8vo. 11. 'List of Coleoptera from Old Calabar,' London, 1878, 8vo. He also edited 'The Book of the Royal Horticultural Society,' 1863, 4to; 'Journal of Travel and Natural History,' vol. i. London, 1868–9; and 'Paxton's Flower Garden,' 1873, 4to.

[Transactions of Botanical Society of Edinburgh, xiii. 379; Entomologists' Monthly Magazine, xiv. 215; Gardener's Chronicle, 1878, i. 86.] G. S. B.

MURRAY, Lord CHARLES, first Earl of Dunmore (1661–1710), second son of John, second earl and first marquis of Atholl [q. v.], by Lady Amelia Sophia Stanley, daughter of the seventh Earl of Derby, was born 28 Feb. 1660–1. On the enrolment in 1681 of General Thomas Dalyell's regiment of horse, now the Scots greys, Lord Charles Murray was appointed its lieutenant-colonel. He was also master of horse to Princess Anne. After the death of Dalyell he on 6 Nov. 1685 obtained the command of the regiment, and he was also about the same time appointed master of the horse to Mary of Modena, queen consort of James II. During 1684 he was engaged in the campaign in Flanders, and was present at the siege of Luxemburg (*Hist. MSS. Comm.* 12th Rep. App. pt. viii. p. 35). On 6 Aug. 1686 he was created by James II Earl of Dunmore, Viscount Fincastle, and Lord Murray of Blair, Moulin, and Tulliemet. At the revolution he was deprived of all his offices. According to the Earl of Balcarres, the supporters of King James at the revolution depended chiefly on Lord Dunmore to influence his father, the Marquis of Atholl, against the convention (Balcarres, *Memoirs*, p. 35); and he states that Dunmore 'used all endeavours to keep him to his duty,' and also to further the cause of King James (*ib.*) Being suspected of intrigues against the government he was arrested about the same time as Balcarres (*ib.*), but on 16 Jan. 1690 was admitted to bail (*Leven and Melville Papers*, p. 372). On 16 May 1692 he was apprehended along with the Earl of Middleton [see Middleton, Charles, second Earl] in disguise at a quaker's in Goodman's Fields, near the Tower, and after examination was committed to the Tower (Luttrell, *Short Relation*, ii. 453).

After the accession of Queen Anne, Dunmore was sworn a privy councillor 4 Feb. 1703, and in the parliament of 21 May his patent was read and ordered to be recorded, whereupon he took his seat. Lockhart, who denounces him and Balcarres as 'wretches of the greatest ingratitude,' states that from the accession of Anne he remained a firm supporter of the court party (*Papers*, i. 64). He also declares the conduct of Dunmore especially to have been 'inexcusable,' since he had 'above five hundred pounds a year of his own, and yet sold his honour for a present which the queen had yearly given his lady since the late revolution' (*ib.*) He further affirms that he and Balcarres 'had no further ambition than how to get as much money as to make themselves drunk once or twice a day, so no party was much a gainer or loser by having or wanting such a couple' (*ib.* p. 65). In 1704 Dunmore was appointed one of a committee of parliament for examining the public accounts, and in September 1705 his services were rewarded by a gratuity. He gave constant support to the union with England. In 1707 he was appointed governor of Blackness Castle. He died in 1710.

In 1682 he married Catherine, daughter of Richard Watts, of Great Munden, Herts. Of his seven sons and three daughters, James, viscount Fincastle, died without issue in 1704; John and William became successively second and third earls of Dunmore; Robert (*d.* 1738), was colonel 38th foot and brigadier-general; Thomas, lieutenant-general; Henriet was married to Patrick, third lord Kinnaird; Anne, to John, fourth earl of Dundonald; and Catherine, to her cousin John, third lord Nairn. The second son, John, second earl of Dunmore, fought at Blenheim as ensign, 13 Aug. 1704, and as a lieutenant-general under the Earl of Stair at Dettingen in June 1743, was on 22 June 1745 appointed governor of Plymouth, and raised to the rank of full general. William, the third son, who became third Earl of Dunmore on the death of his brother in 1752, was concerned in the rebellion of 1745, and sent prisoner to London, but pleading guilty was pardoned.

[Balcarres's Memoirs and Leven and Melville Papers (both in the Bannatyne Club); Lockhart Papers; Luttrell's Short Relation; Douglas's Scots' Peerage (Wood, rev. Paul), 1904.] T. F. H.

MURRAY, Lord CHARLES (1691–1720), Jacobite, born 24 Sept. 1691, was fourth son of John, second marquis and first duke of Atholl [q. v.], by Lady Katherine, eldest daughter of William Douglas, third duke of Hamilton [q. v.] He became a cornet in the 5th dragoons in 1712, and served in Flanders during that and the next year (cf. Patten, *History of the Rebellion*, pt. i. p. 57). With his brothers, William, marquis of Tullibardine [q. v.], and Lord George Murray [q. v.], he, in opposition to the wish of his father, took part in the rising; and he held command of a regiment in the army, raised in Atholl, which crossed the Forth from Fife and marched into England. Like his brother Lord George he won the strong affection of his men by his readiness to share their hardships as well as their perils. While on the march he never could be persuaded to ride on horseback, but kept at the head of his regiment on foot in the highland dress (*ib.*) At the battle of Preston, Lancashire, 12–13 Nov. 1715, he commanded at a barrier, at the end of a lane leading into the fields, and maintained his position with such determination that the enemy were driven off. Being taken prisoner after the defeat, he was treated as a deserter—on the ground that he was an officer—and being found guilty was condemned to be shot. He ultimately, through the intercession of his father, obtained a pardon (*Hist. MSS. Comm.* 12th Rep. App. pt. viii. p. 70). He was gazetted out of the 5th dragoons (then known as Sidney's regiment) on 23 Dec. 1715 (*London Gazette*). He died without issue in 1720.

[Patten's History of the Rebellion; Hist. MSS. Comm. 12th Rep. App. pt. viii.; Douglas's Scots' Peerage (ed. Wood, rev. by Paul), 1904.] T. F. H.

MURRAY, CHARLES (1754–1821), actor and dramatist, the son of Sir John Murray of Broughton [q. v.], was born in 1754 at Cheshunt, Hertfordshire, stayed for some time in France, studied pharmacy and surgery in London, and took as surgeon's mate some voyages to the Mediterranean. After playing as an amateur in Liverpool he went, with an introduction from Younger, the Liverpool manager, to Tate Wilkinson of the York circuit, making, under the name of Raymur, at York his first professional appearance on the stage as Carlos in 'Love makes a Man, or the Fop's Fortune,' by Colley Cibber, an important part which he took at short notice. Attending assiduously to his profession, he made steady progress. A quarrel in a tavern in Wakefield in September 1776, in which he resented some contemptuous treatment on the part of a man of position, led to a scene in the theatre, renewed on the following evening, when an apology was demanded from Murray and refused. A large portion of the audience took his part, compelled him to go in private dress through a character he had resigned, and escorted him in triumph to Doncaster. After one or two further trips to sea he acted in his own name with Griffiths at Norwich, where he is believed to have produced a poor farce entitled 'The Experiment,' 8vo, 1779. This Genest classes among unacted plays. Murray is also credited in the 'Dramatic Mirror' with the 'New Maid of the Oaks,' said also to have been acted in Norwich, 8vo, 1778. This wretched tragedy is in the 'Biographia Dramatica' assigned to Ahab Salem, and is said to have been acted near Saratoga. On 8 Oct. 1785, as Sir Giles Overreach in 'A New Way to pay Old Debts,' he made his first appearance in Bath, where he played Joseph Surface, and was the original Albert in Reynolds's 'Werter' on 3 Dec. 1785. Here or at Bristol he played in his first season Macbeth, Clifford in the 'Heiress,' Evander in the 'Grecian Daughter,' Shylock, Iago, Iachimo, Pierre, Lord Davenant, Mr. Oakly, several French characters, and other parts, appearing for his benefit as Gibbet in the 'Beaux Stratagem,' with his wife as Cherry. Genest chronicles that they did not sell a single ticket. Here he remained until 1796, playing a great variety of parts, including King John, Osmyn, Adam in 'As you like it,' Sir Peter Teazle, Old Dornton in the 'Road to Ruin.' Mrs. Murray was occasionally seen, and on 1 July 1793, for the benefit of her father and of her mother, who played Queen Elinor, his daughter, subsequently Mrs. H. Siddons, made as Prince Arthur her first appearance on any stage. She subsequently played Titania, and on Mrs. Murray's final benefit in Bath on 19 May 1796, Fine Lady in Garrick's 'Lethe.' On this occasion Murray spoke a farewell address. The occasion only produced 64*l.*, while the average receipts were 150*l.*

Murray came to Covent Garden with a good reputation, though Genest holds his coming to have been too long delayed. His first appearance in London took place on 30 Sept. as Shylock, with, it is said, Bagatelle in the 'Poor Soldier.' He was found interesting rather than great, and suited for secondary parts rather than primary. Murray had a good presence and bad tricks of pronunciation, and never attained a foremost position. Alcanor in 'Mahomet,' King in 'First Part of King Henry IV,' King Henry in 'King Richard III,' the King in 'Philaster,' Heartley in the 'Guardian,' Cassio, Lusignan, Strickland in the 'Suspicious Husband,' Dr. Caius, Manly in the 'Provoked Husband,' and many other parts were played in his first season. For his benefit, on 12 May 1798, he was Polixenes, Miss Murray making, as Perdita, her first appearance in London. He was on 11 Oct. 1798 the original Baron Wildenhaim in Mrs. Inchbald's 'Lovers' Vows.' On 10 May 1799 he was, for his benefit, Friar Lawrence to the Juliet of his daughter, Mrs. Murray making, as the Nurse, her first appearance at Covent Garden. From this time Miss Murray played ingénue parts, and on 13 Sept. 1802 appeared as Mrs. H. Siddons [q. v.] Murray's last appearance at Covent Garden appears to have been on 17 July 1817 as Brabantio to the Othello of Young, the Iago of Booth, and the Desdemona of Miss O'Neill. During this season he had been on 3 May 1817 the original Alvarez in Shiel's 'Apostate,' and took part in John Philip Kemble's retiring performances, ending 23 June with Coriolanus. The 'Theatrical Inquisitor' of February 1817, x. 147, speaks of Murray as a veteran, and makes ungracious reference to his infirmities. Threatened with paralysis he withdrew to Edinburgh to be near his children, Mrs. Henry Siddons and William Henry Murray [q. v.], and died there on 8 Nov. 1821. The 'Georgian Era' credits him, in error, with being the manager of the Edinburgh Theatre, a post held by his son.

Murray was especially commended for the dignity of his old men. Portraits of him by Dupont as Baron Wildenhaim in 'Lovers' Vows,' and by De Wilde as Tobias in the 'Stranger,' are in the Mathews collection at the Garrick Club.

[Books cited; Genest's Account of the English Stage; Gilliland's Dramatic Mirror; Thespian Dict.; Georgian Era; Dibdin's Edinburgh Stage; Penley's Bath Stage; Notes and Queries, 8th ser. ii. 391.] J. K.

MURRAY, DANIEL (1768–1852), archbishop of Dublin, born on 18 April 1768 at Sheepwalk, near Arklow, co. Wicklow, was the son of a farmer. He studied at Dublin and Salamanca, and on receiving ordination as a priest of the Roman catholic church, he was employed as a curate at Dublin and Arklow. Apprehensive of violence from disorderly troops in the latter district, he removed to Dublin, and acquired the esteem of the archbishop of that see, John Thomas Troy. Murray was consecrated in 1809 Troy's coadjutor, under the title of archbishop of Hierapolis 'in partibus infidelium.' Murray acted for a time as president of the Roman catholic college at Maynooth, and earnestly opposed the projected arrangement with government designated the 'veto.' On the death of Archbishop Troy in 1823 Murray succeeded to the see of Dublin. He enjoyed the confidence of successive popes, and was held in high respect by the British government. Pusey had an interview with him in 1841, and bore testimony to his moderation, and Newman had some correspondence with him before 1845 (LIDDON, *Life of Pusey*, ii. 246–7; J. B. MOZLEY, *Letters*, p. 122). A seat in the privy council at Dublin, officially offered to him in 1846, was not accepted. His life was mainly devoted to ecclesiastical affairs, the establishment and organisation of religious associations for the education and relief of the poor. Among these was the order of the 'Sisters of Charity,' for the constitution of which he obtained papal confirmation. As a preacher Murray is stated to have been 'pre-eminently captivating and effective,' especially in appeals for charitable objects. Murray took part in the synod of the Roman catholic clergy at Thurles in 1850, and died at Dublin on 26 Feb. 1852. He was interred in the pro-cathedral, Dublin, where a marble statue of him has been erected in connection with a monument to his memory, executed by James Farrell, president of the Royal Hibernian Academy of Fine Arts. The only published works of Murray are pastoral letters, sermons, and religious discourses. Two volumes of his sermons appeared at Dublin in 1859, extending to nearly fourteen hundred pages, 8vo, with his portrait prefixed from a painting by Crowley in 1844. A marble bust of Archbishop Murray is in the National Gallery of Ireland, Dublin.

[Notices of Archbishop Murray, by the Rev. W. Meagher, Dublin, 1853; Dalton's Archbishops of Dublin, 1838; Madden's United Irishmen, 1858; Brady's Episcopal Succession, 1876; Life of M. Aikenhead, by S. Atkinson, Dublin, 1882.]

J. T. G.

MURRAY, SIR DAVID (1567–1629), of Gorthy, poet, born in 1567, was the second son of Robert Murray of Abercairny, Perthshire, by a daughter of Murray of Tullibardine, Perthshire. In August 1600 he appears to have been comptroller of the household to James VI (DALYEL, *Fragments of Scottish Hist.* p. 50). Very learned and accomplished, he became gentleman of the bedchamber to Prince Henry, with whom he was a special favourite, and after 1610 was successively his groom of the stole and gentleman of the robes (BIRCH, *Life of Henry, Prince of Wales*, 1760, p. 218). A free gift of 2,000*l.* was bestowed upon him in 1613, and in 1615 he received 5,200*l.* to promote discharge of his debts (NICHOLS, *Progresses of King James*, ii. 374). From Charles I he obtained a charter under the great seal, bestowing upon him the estate of Gorthy, Perthshire. He died without an heir in 1629. A portrait by an unknown hand is in the National Portrait Gallery, Edinburgh; it has an inscription, '1603, Æ. 36, Sir David Murray.' A line engraving is given in David Laing's 'Specimen of a proposed Catalogue of a portion of the Library at Britwell House,' Edinburgh, 1852, and also in Laing's 'Adversaria' (Bannatyne Club). Another portrait is at Abercairny, Perthshire.

In 1611 Murray published in London an octavo volume containing (1) 'The Tragicall Death of Sophonisba,' a long poem in seven-line stanzas, to which are prefixed two sonnets addressed to Prince Henry, and (2) 'Cœlia,' in which are included twenty-six respectable sonnets, a pastoral ballad, 'The Complaint of the Shepheard Harpalus,' and an 'Epitaph on the Death of his Deare Cousin M. Dauid Moray.' The 'Complaint' was published separately in single sheet folio [1620?]. In 'Sophonisba' Murray displays numerous irregularities, while occasionally bursting into genuine verse. Of three introductory sonnets to the piece, one is by Drayton, who praises his friend's 'strong muse.' Other complimentary verses in the volume are by Simon Grahame [q. v.], and by John Murray (1575–1632) [q. v.] His 'Psalm CIV.' was printed in 4to by Andro Hart, Edinburgh, 1615, and of this the only extant copy is believed to be in the Drummond Collection in the Edinburgh University Library. Murray's 'Poems' were reprinted by the Bannatyne Club in 1823.

[Irving's History of Scotish Poetry; A. Campbell's Hist. of Poetry in Scotland, p. 130; Brydges's Censura, x. 373–6; Poems by Sir D. Murray of Gorthy, No. 2 of Bannatyne Club Series; Douglas's Baronetage of Scotland.] T. B.

MURRAY, SIR DAVID, of Gospertie, BARON SCONE, and afterwards VISCOUNT STORMONT (*d.* 1631), comptroller of Scotland and captain of the king's guard, was the second son of Sir Andrew Murray of Arngask and Balvaird, brother of Sir William Murray of Tullibardine [q. v.], by his second wife, Janet Graham, fourth daughter of William, second earl of Montrose. He was brought up at the court of James VI, who made him his cupbearer and master of the horse. On 12 Dec. 1588 he presented a complaint against the inhabitants of Auchtermuchty, Fifeshire, who, when he went to take possession of the lands of Auchtermuchty, of which he had obtained a heritable infeftment, attacked him and the gentlemen of his company, wounding him in various parts of the body, and cutting off one of the fingers of his right hand (*Reg. P. C. Scotl.* iv. 336). He is mentioned by Calderwood as one of the 'cubicular courtiers' who, 'finding themselves prejudged by the Octavians,' endeavoured to 'kindle a fire betwixt them and the kirk' (*Hist.* v. 510). After he had been knighted by James VI—at what date is uncertain—he was, on 26 April 1599, admitted on the privy council as comptroller of the royal revenues, in room of George Hume, laird of Wedderburn (*Reg. P. C. Scotl.* v. 552). He was also made steward of the stewartry of Fife, and on 6 Dec. 1599, while holding a court at Falkland, was attacked by the neighbouring lairds and their servants to the number of thirty (*ib.* vi. 62; cf. SCOT OF SCOTSTARVET, *Staggering State*, ed. 1872, p. 114).

Murray was at Perth at the time of the Gowrie conspiracy, 5 Aug. 1600, and was subsequently credited with having been privy to the concoction of an artificial semblance of a plot with a view to the overthrow of the Earl of Gowrie. He took a prominent part in allaying the excitement of the inhabitants of Perth when they knew that their provost, the Earl of Gowrie, was slain, and with others succeeded in bringing the king in safety to Falkland. Murray succeeded Gowrie as provost of Perth, and also obtained a grant of the barony of Ruthven, and of the lands belonging to the abbacy of Scone, of which Gowrie was commendator. In May 1601 he was appointed by the assembly of the kirk one of a commission to treat as to the best means of advancing the 'work of the constant platt,' or proposed plan for a permanent method of adequately supporting the kirk and clergy in all the districts of Scotland (CALDERWOOD, vi. 119). On 31 July he was named a componitor to the treasurer 'of all signatures and other casualties concerning the treasury' (*Reg. P. C. Scotl.* vi. 276), and on 17 Nov. he was named one of a commission to perfect an agreement between the bailies of Edinburgh and the strangers imported for making cloth (*ib.* p. 309). On 10 Nov. he obtained from the king the castle land of Falkland, with the office of ranger of the Lomonds and forester of the woods.

Murray was one of the retinue who attended King James in 1603 when he went to take possession of the English throne. On his return to Scotland on 11 Aug. he obtained a commission for raising a guard or police of forty horsemen to be at the service of the privy council in repressing disorder and apprehending criminals who had been placed at the horn (*ib.* p. 581). He was one of the Scottish commissioners named by the parliament of Perth in 1604 to treat concerning a union with England (Calderwood, vi. 263). On 1 April 1605 the barony of Ruthven and the lands belonging to the abbacy of Scone were erected into the temporal lordship of Scone, with a seat and vote in parliament, with which he was invested; on 30 May 1606 he had charter of the barony of Segie, erected into the lordship of Segie; and on 18 Aug. 1608 of the lands and barony which belonged to the abbacy of Scone, united into the temporal lordship of Scone.

In June 1605 Scone, as comptroller and captain of the guards, was appointed to proceed to Cantyre in Argyllshire to receive the obedience of the chiefs of the clans of the southern Hebrides, and payment of the king's rents and duties (*Reg. P. C. Scotl.* vii. 59). He was one of the assessors for the trial at Linlithgow in January 1606 of the ministers concerned in the contumacious Aberdeen assembly of 1605. In March 1607 he was appointed one of the commissioners to represent the king in the synods of Perth and Fife, in connection with the scheme for the appointment of perpetual moderators. The synod of Perth having resisted his proposal for the appointment of Alexander Lindsay as perpetual moderator, he, in the king's name, dissolved the assembly, and as the members of the assembly resolved to proceed to the choice of their own moderator, a violent scene ensued. Scone, being asked by the moderator in the name of Christ to desist troubling the meeting, replied, 'The devil a Jesus is here.' After attempting by force to prevent the elected moderator taking the chair, Scone sent for the bailies of the town, and commanded them to ring the common bell and remove the rebels. On pretence of consulting the council of the city the bailies withdrew, but did not return, and avoided interference in the dispute. After the close of the sitting Scone locked the doors, whereupon the assembly met in the open air and proceeded with their business (Calderwood, vi. 644–52; James Melville, *Diary*). Probably it was, as Calderwood states (*Hist.* vi. 658), on account of Scone's contest with the synod of Perth that the synod of Fife, which should have met at Dysart on 28 April, was on the 23rd prorogued on pretence of the prevalence of the pestilence in the burgh. When it did meet, on 18 Aug., it also proved contumacious (*ib.* pp. 674–7).

In November 1607 Scone was censured by the privy council for negligence in his duty as captain of the guard in not securing the arrest of the Earl of Crawford and the laird of Edzell (*Reg. P. C. Scotl.* viii. 485–6), and he was also, on 2 Feb. 1608, urged to adopt more energetic measures for the arrest of Lord Maxwell (*ib.* p. 491). Some time before March 1608 he was succeeded in the comptrollership by Sir James Hay of Fingask, but he still continued to hold the office of captain of the guard. In June he resigned his office of componitor to the treasurer (*ib.* p. 127). As commissioner from the king he took part in the ecclesiastical conference at Falkland on 4 May 1609, in regard to the discipline of the kirk (Calderwood, vii. 27–38), and he was one of the lords of the articles for the parliament which met at Edinburgh in the following June. On 8 March 1609 he was appointed one of a commission for preventing the dilapidation of the bishoprics (*Reg. P. C. Scotl.* viii. 600), and on the 23rd he was appointed, along with the Archbishop of St. Andrews, to examine into the charge against John Fairfull, minister of Dunfermline, of having prayed for the restoration of the banished ministers (*ib.* p. 602), with the result that Fairfull was found guilty (Calderwood, vii. 53). Scone was chosen one of the members of the privy council on its reconstruction, 20 Jan. 1609–10, when it was limited to thirty-five members (*Reg. P. C. Scotl.* viii. 815). On the institution of the office of justice of the peace in June 1610, he was appointed justice for the counties of Fife, Kinross, and Perth (*ib.* ix. 78). On 15 Nov. he was appointed one of the assessors to aid the Earl of Dunbar as treasurer (*ib.* p. 85). On 25 April 1611 an act was passed by the privy council disbanding the king's guard, as being now of 'no grite use or necessite' (*ib.* p. 161), but Scone was still to receive his pay as captain, and on 11 June he was authorised to retain nine of the guard for the apprehension of persons at the horn for the non-payment of taxes (*ib.* pp. 189–90). Subsequently the guard was placed under the command of Sir Robert Ker of Ancrum, and Scone had an act exonerating him for all he had done while holding the office of captain (*ib.* p. 367).

Scone was one of the three commissioners

appointed by the king to the general assembly at Perth on 5 Aug. 1618, when sanction was given to the obnoxious 'five articles' introducing various ceremonial and episcopal observances (CALDERWOOD, vii. 304). He was also the king's commissioner to a conference between the bishops and presbyterian ministers at St. Andrews in August 1619 (*ib.* p. 397). At the parliament held at Edinburgh in July 1621 he was chosen by the bishops one of the lords of the articles (*ib.* p. 490); and after the sanction by parliament of the five articles of the Perth assembly he the same night hastened to London with the news (*ib.* p. 506). Chiefly on account of his zeal in carrying out the ecclesiastical policy of the king, he was, by patent of 16 Aug., raised to the dignity of Viscount Stormont, to him and heirs male of his body. On 19 May 1623 he was named one of a commission to sit in Edinburgh twice a week for the hearing of grievances (*ib.* p. 576). He died 27 Aug. 1631, and was buried at Scone, where a sumptuous monument was erected to his memory. Scot of Scotstarvet says that 'albeit an ignorant man, yet he was bold, and got great business effectuated' (*Staggering State*, p. 114).

Stormont had, on 20 July 1625, been served heir male and entire of Sir Andrew Murray of Balvaird, the son of his brother, and on 26 Oct. of the same year made a settlement of the lordship of Scone and other estates to certain relatives of the name of Murray. As by his wife Elizabeth, daughter of David Beton or Bethune of Creich, Fifeshire, he had no issue, he secured the succession of his titles to Sir Mungo Murray, son of the Earl of Tullibardine, who had married his niece Anne, eldest daughter of Sir Andrew Murray of Arngask, and to the heirs male of his body, failing whom to John, first earl of Annandale, and his heirs male, with remainder to his own heirs male. To preserve his family of Balvaird in the line of heirs male he adopted his cousin-german's son, Sir Andrew Murray (afterwards created Lord Balvaird), minister of Abdie, Fifeshire, son of David Murray of Balgonie, and settled on him the fee of the estate of Balvaird.

[Calderwood's History of the Kirk of Scotland; James Melville's Diary (Bannatyne Club or Wodrow Society); Scot's Staggering State of Scottish Statesmen; Reg. P. C. Scotl.; Cal. State Papers, Dom. Ser. reign of James I; Douglas's Scots' Peerage (ed. Wood, rev. by Paul), 1904.] T. F. H.

MURRAY, DAVID, second EARL OF MANSFIELD (1727–1796), diplomatist and statesman, was eldest son of David, sixth viscount Stormont, by Anne, only daughter of John Stewart of Innernylie. Born on 9 Oct. 1727, he was educated at Westminster School and Christ Church, Oxford, where he matriculated 28 May 1744 and graduated B.A. in 1748. In the latter year, by the death of his father, 23 July, he succeeded to the viscounty of Stormont. He entered the diplomatic service, and was attaché at the British embassy, Paris, in 1751, when he contributed to the 'Epicedia Oxoniensia, in obitum Celsissimi et Desideratissimi Frederici Principis Walliæ' (Oxford, fol.), an English elegy of more than ordinary merit (cf. *English Poems on the Death of his Royal Highness Frederick Prince of Wales*, Edinburgh, 1751, 12mo).

Accredited envoy extraordinary to the court of Saxony, Stormont arrived at Dresden early in 1756. On the invasion of the electorate by Frederic the Great in the following September, he made of his own initiative a fruitless attempt to mediate between the belligerents. The elector took refuge in his Polish kingdom, and during the rest of the war Stormont resided with the court at Warsaw, where on 16 Aug. 1759 he married Henrietta Frederica, daughter of Henry Count Bunau of the elector's privy council. On 28 April 1761 he was nominated plenipotentiary at the intended congress of Augsburg. On the failure of that project he was recalled to the United Kingdom, was elected a representative peer of Scotland, and on 20 July 1763 was sworn of the privy council. During the next nine years Stormont was envoy extraordinary at the imperial court, where he enjoyed much of the confidence of Maria Theresa and the Emperor Joseph. The death of Lady Stormont in the prime of life, 16 March 1766, weighed so heavily on his mind that, after burying her heart in the family vault at Scone, he sought relief in Italian travel. At Rome, in the spring of 1768, he became intimate with Winckelmann, who calls him (*Briefe*, ed. Forster, zweiter Band, S. 326) 'the most learned person of his rank whom I have yet known,' and praises his unusual accomplishment in Greek. On his return to Vienna the same year he was invested (30 Nov.) with the order of the Thistle. Transferred to the French court in August 1772, he remained at Paris until March 1778, when, hostilities being imminent, he was recalled. The same year he was appointed lord-justice general of Scotland. Notwithstanding his absence from the kingdom, he had retained his seat in the House of Lords at the general elections of 1768 and 1774, and he was re-elected in 1780, 1784, and 1790. On 27 Oct. 1779 he entered the cabinet as secretary of state for the southern department, but went out of office with Lord North in July 1782. In the debate of 17 Feb. 1783 he severely censured the preliminary articles of peace, and on 2 April following accepted the office of president of the council in the Duke of Portland's coalition ministry. On its dismissal, after the rejection by the House of Lords of Fox's East India bill, 19 Dec. the same year, he attached himself for a time to the whigs, and made himself formidable to the government by his trenchant criticism of Pitt's East India bill, motion for reform, and the Irish commercial propositions (1784–1785). He also took an active part in the debates on the Regency bill (1788). His long and varied diplomatic experience lent weight to his censure of the policy of intervention in the war between Russia and the Porte (1791–2), and to the support which he at once gave to ministers when, in answer to the French declaration of war on 1 Feb. 1793, they declared war against France on 11 Feb. In 1794 he returned to office as president of the council in succession to Lord FitzWilliam. He died at Brighton on 1 Sept. 1796. Stormont had succeeded, 20 March 1793, to the earldom of Mansfield of Caen Wood, Middlesex, on the death of his uncle, William Murray, first earl of Mansfield [q. v.], by whose side he was buried in the North Cross, Westminster Abbey, on 9 Sept. 1796.

Mansfield was an eminently able and honourable diplomatist and statesman, and, though no orator, a ready and powerful speaker. He retained his scholarly tastes to the end. On 3 July 1793 the university of Oxford conferred upon him the degree of D.C.L., and the same year he was made chancellor of Marischal College, Aberdeen. After the death of his first wife, by whom he had issue two daughters only, he married, 5 May 1776, the Hon. Louisa Cathcart, third daughter of Charles, ninth lord Cathcart, by whom he had issue three sons and a daughter. On the death of the first Earl of Mansfield, Lady Stormont became Countess of Mansfield in the county of Nottingham in her own right by reason of the peculiar form of the original patent creating the earldom of Mansfield. She survived Mansfield, and married, secondly, 19 Oct. 1797, her cousin-german, Robert Fulke Greville, third son of Francis, first earl of Warwick; she died on 11 July 1843.

[Alumni Westmonast.; Foster's Alumni Oxon.; Douglas's Peerage of Scotland, 'Stormont;' Gent. Mag. 1761 p. 504, 1796 p. 795; Horace Walpole's Letters, ed. Cunningham; Polit. Corresp. Friedrichs des Grossen, Bände xi–xiv. and xviii–xix.; Lord Chesterfield's Letters, ed. Lord Mahon, ii. 81; Wraxall's Hist. and Posth. Mem., ed. Wheatley; Parl. Hist. 1778–95; Mrs. Delany's Autobiogr., ed. Lord Llanover, iii. 553; Grenville Papers, iii. 373; Add. MSS. 24159, 24162–5; Nicolas's British Knighthood, vol. iii. Chron. List. p. xxx; Haydn's Book of Dignities, ed. Ockerby; Chester's Westminster Abbey Registers; Carlyle's Frederick the Great, passim.]

J. M. R.

MURRAY, ELIZABETH, Countess of Dysart, and afterwards Duchess of Lauderdale (*d.* 1697), was the elder daughter of William Murray, first earl of Dysart [q. v.], by his wife, Catharine Bruce of Clackmannan. As the earldom was conferred with remainder to heirs male and female, and the earl had no son, the succession to the title fell to Elizabeth, who became Countess of Dysart in 1650. On 5 Dec. 1670 she obtained from Charles II a charter confirming her title, and allowing her to name any of her issue as heir to the honours.

In 1647 Elizabeth married her first husband, Sir Lionel Tollemache, third baronet, the descendant of an ancient Suffolk family, and by him she had three sons and two daughters. Sir Lionel died in 1668. Scandal had already made very free with Elizabeth's reputation. The improbable rumour was long current that she was the mistress of Oliver Cromwell when he was in Scotland, and that she secured immunity to her relatives from the Protector's exactions through her personal influence. Sir John Reresby, nearly thirty years later, after Cromwell's death, writing of an interview with her, described her as having 'been a beautiful woman, the supposed mistress of Oliver Cromwell, and at that time a lady of great parts' (*Memoirs*, p. 49). It is more certain that in her first husband's lifetime she had formed a *liaison* with John Maitland, duke of Lauderdale [q. v.], which scandalised even the court of Charles II. After the death of his first wife Lauderdale married Lady Elizabeth in February 1671–2. As both mistress and wife of the duke a vast amount of patronage lay within her power, and, sharing her husband's unpopularity, she was the subject of many lampoons. But she had her parasites. Bishop Burnet, in 1677, had hopes of securing some advantage for himself at her hands, and addressed her in poetical strains of the most fulsome flattery. After describing the 'deep extasie' into which her appearance had thrown him, he wrote—

Cherub I doubt's too low a name for thee,
For thou alone a whole rank seems to be:
The onelie individual of thy kynd,
No mate can fitlie suit so great a mind.

Soured by the disappointment of his hopes, he afterwards became one of her most inveterate enemies.

Even in advanced years she held a prominent place among the ladies of the court of Charles II, and was usually mentioned along with Lady Cleveland, Lady Portsmouth, and the numerous beauties of doubtful character who were then the leaders of fashion. But a love of litigation and insatiable greed characterised her as much as her passion for gallantry. Before the death of her husband, the duke of Lauderdale, she prevailed upon him to settle all his estate upon her; and when his brother succeeded, on the duke's death, to the earldom of Lauderdale, in 1682, she at once began a series of law-pleas against the earl which brought him to the verge of ruin. She directed that the duke should have a most extravagant funeral, and that the whole of the expense should be borne by the Lauderdale estates. The duke had purchased Duddingston, near Edinburgh, and presented it to her, but for the purpose raised 7,000*l.* with her consent on her estate of Ham. Though she retained possession of Duddingston after the duke's death, she compelled the Earl of Lauderdale to repay the money borrowed for its purchase. In this case, through lack of documentary evidence, the earl incautiously referred the matter to her oath, and Fountainhall distinctly charges her with perjury. That Fountainhall was not alone in this opinion is shown by a letter to Lord Preston on 16 Oct. 1684, now in the collection of Sir Frederick Graham, bart., of Netherby. At that time the duchess was suspected of having furnished funds to the Earl of Argyll (whose son was married to her daughter), to assist in Monmouth's rebellion. The writer says: 'It will be hard to prove that she sent money to my Lord Argyll; for no doubt she did it cunningly enough, and can for a shift turn it over on [her daughter] my Lady Lorne, who can hardly be troubled for it. Thus they will be necessitated to refer all to the duchess's oath, in which case, one would think, she is in no great danger. Shall an estate acquired without conscience be lost by it? But she is as mean-spirited in adversity as she was insolent in prosperity.' It is supposed that when Wycherley wrote his comedy of the 'Plain Dealer,' the character of the Widow Blackacre was intended as a portrait of the duchess, whom the dramatist must have met at court. In a late pasquil the ghosts of her two husbands, Sir Lionel Tollemache and the Duke of Lauderdale, discuss her character and conduct in painfully free language. The duchess died on 24 Aug. 1697, and was succeeded in the earldom of Dysart by her eldest son, Sir Lionel Tollemache, from whom the present Earl of Dysart is descended. She had no children by the duke.

A portrait, by Lely, is at Ham House.

[Douglas's Scots' Peerage (ed. Wood, rev. Paul), 1904; Burnet's Hist. of my own Time; Maidment's Scottish Pasquils; Hist. MSS. Comm. 7th Rep. p. 378; Fountainhall's Decisions.] A. H. M.

MURRAY, GASTON (1826–1889), actor. [See under MURRAY, HENRY LEIGH.]

MURRAY, Lord GEORGE (1694–1760), Jacobite general, was the fifth son of John, second marquis and first duke of Atholl [q. v.], by Lady Catherine Hamilton, eldest daughter of Anne, duchess of Hamilton in her own right, and William Douglas, third duke of Hamilton. He was born at Huntingtower, near Perth, 4 Oct. 1694. In 1709 he was studying Horace at the school at Perth. On 16 March 1710 he sent to his father a complaint against his schoolmaster for not allowing him, in accordance with a privilege conferred at Candlemas, to protect a boy who was whipped, and strongly urged that on account of the 'affront' he might be permitted to leave school. In Dec. 1710 he entered at Glasgow University, but next June went to Flanders as ensign of the 1st regiment, the Royals. He gambled freely and contracted debt. At the peace of Utrecht in 1713 the Royals returned to England. In July 1715 Murray was at Dunkeld with his father.

During the rebellion of 1715 Murray served with the Jacobites under his brother, the Marquis of Tullibardine [see MURRAY, WILLIAM], and at Sheriffmuir held command of a battalion (PATTEN, *Hist. of the Rebellion*, pt. ii. p. 59). Along with Tullibardine he, after Sheriffmuir, in reply to a representation from the Duke of Atholl, intimated his willingness to forsake Mar provided he had full assurance of an indemnity (*Hist. MSS. Comm.* 6th Rep. pp. 702–3), but the negotiation came to nothing, and after the collapse of the rebellion he escaped to the continent. In June 1716 he was at Avignon with the Earl of Mar, who states that he had not 'been well almost ever since he came' (Letter, 16 June, THORNTON, *Stuart Dynasty*, 2nd ed. p. 276). In 1718 a bill for treason was found against him at a court of oyer and terminer held at Cupar Fife. Throughout that year he was living in poverty at Bordeaux. In 1719 he accompanied the expedition under Marischal and Tullibardine to the north-western highlands, and was wounded at the battle of Glenshiels on 10 June, but made his escape, and is said to have lurked in Highland mountains for many months, studying the Bible. On

19 April 1720 he sailed from Methil in Fife and landed in Rotterdam; thence he passed to France. His father sought a pardon for him from the English government, and he secretly returned to Scotland in Aug. 1724 while the negotiations were in progress. In November his father died, but a year later Murray's pardon passed the Great Seal. Marrying in 1728 he settled down to a country life at Tullibardine at Strathearn, where he leased the house from his brother the new duke. He took no part at this period in political intrigue, and in 1745 was nominated deputy sheriff to his brother the duke, who was sheriff of Perthshire.

Through the influence of his brother, the Marquis of Tullibardine, Murray was induced, after some hesitation, in Aug. 1745 to join the standard of Prince Charles. Arriving in Perth on 26 Aug. with a number of the Atholl men, he was made lieutenant-general by the prince, who had entered the city on the previous day. Almost from the beginning Murray was, says Scott, 'the soul of the undertaking.' But for his enthusiasm and skill it would have collapsed at least before the battle of Falkirk. He won the attachment and confidence of the clansmen as completely as did Montrose or Dundee, and had he been left untrammelled might have gained a reputation equal to theirs. His thorough knowledge of highland habits and modes of warfare enabled him to utilise the fighting power of his forces to the best advantage. Nor was he less prudent and practical than courageous. His pride and high temper led him more than once almost into altercations with the prince, but in the matter of his contentions he was unquestionably in the right. The Chevalier Johnstone plausibly asserted that 'had Prince Charles slept during the whole of the expedition, and allowed Lord George Murray to act for him according to his own judgment, he would have found the crown of Great Britain on his head when he awoke' (*Memoirs*, ed. 1822, p. 27).

The army of the prince, after receiving large accessions from the highlands, began its march southwards from Perth on 11 Sept., and, proceeding by Stirling and Falkirk, obtained possession of Edinburgh without opposition. After resting there for three days, it advanced eastwards against Sir John Cope, who had disembarked his troops at Dunbar. Cope resolved to await the attack in a strong but cramped position at the village of Prestonpans. Murray seized the higher eminences and drew up his men on ground sloping towards the village of Tranent. He soon, however, discovered that this position would be of no advantage to the highlanders in executing their impetuous charge, since Cope's position was defended not only by houses and enclosures, but by a morass, which was almost impassable. He therefore resolved to defer the attack till Cope could be taken by surprise. In the early morning of the 21st the highlanders, crossing the morass in the darkness, with noiseless celerity, made their attack almost before Cope was able to draw up his line of battle. The right of the highlanders was led by the Duke of Perth and the left by Murray, to whose men belongs the chief credit of the victory. 'Lord George,' says the Chevalier Johnstone, 'at the head of the first line, did not give the enemy time to recover from their panic. . . . The highlanders rushed upon them sword in hand, and the cavalry was instantly thrown into confusion' (*ib.* p. 35). After the victory the insurgents remained for six weeks quartered round Edinburgh, partly to receive reinforcements, but chiefly because they were at a loss as to their future course of action. Ultimately the prince announced his intention to march into England, and on 30 Oct. appointed his principal officers for the expedition, the Duke of Perth to be general and Murray lieutenant-general. The march commenced on the 31st, the division under Murray proceeding by Peebles and Moffat, and the other by Lauder and Kelso. After their union at Reddings in Cumberland, Carlisle was invested, the siege being conducted by the Duke of Perth. On account of the prominence assigned to the duke during the siege, Murray resigned his command, intimating his desire henceforth to serve as a volunteer. Perth thereupon also resigned, and his resignation was accepted, it being understood that Murray, whose skill was necessary to the continuance of the enterprise, should act as general under the prince.

At a council of war, held shortly after the surrender of Carlisle (18 Nov.), the prince intimated his preference for a march on London, and appealed to Murray for his opinion. Murray stated that if the prince chose to make the experiment he was persuaded that the army, small as it was (about 4,500), would follow him. The whole proposal, however, emanated from the prince, Murray simply acquiescing in what he was probably powerless to prevent. Finding on reaching Derby on 4 Dec. that they were threatened by a powerful force under the Duke of Cumberland, the hopelessness of the enterprise, in the almost total absence of recruits from England, became apparent to all except the prince. On Murray's advice they determined to retreat northwards until they could effect a junction with additional recruits from Scotland. Murray, who had previously led the advance, now undertook the charge of the rear, and it was chiefly owing to his courage and alertness that the retreat was conducted with perfect order and complete success. So silently and swiftly was it begun that the Duke of Cumberland was unaware of the movement before the highlanders were two days' march from Derby. The highlanders, by their method of marching, were almost beyond pursuit even by cavalry, when Murray, with the rear-guard, was on the 17th detained at Clifton in Cumberland by the breaking down of some baggage wagons. Next morning the advanced guard of the duke appeared on the adjoining heights, and, desiring to check the pursuit, Murray despatched a message to the prince for a reinforcement of a thousand men, his purpose being, by a midnight march, to gain the flank of the pursuers, and, according to the method adopted at Prestonpans, take them by surprise in the early morning. The prince replied by ordering him, without risking any engagement, to join the main body with all speed at Penrith. But Murray, probably deeming retreat more hazardous than attack, disregarded the order, and posted his men strongly at the village of Clifton to await the approach of the dragoons. The sun had set, but the dragoons continued their march by moonlight, and the semi-obscurity favoured the highlanders, who, led by Murray, and disregarding the enemies' fire, rushed upon them with their claymores and drove them back with great loss. Murray thereupon hastened to obey the prince's orders, and joined the main body. The check thus given to the pursuit delivered the insurgents from further danger or annoyance. The duke dared not venture into the broken and hilly country beyond Carlisle, which he contented himself with investing, and the highlanders entering Scotland on the 20th, and marching in two divisions to Glasgow, where they levied a heavy subsidy, proceeded to besiege the castle of Stirling. It was probably the refusal of the prince to send a reinforcement to Murray while in difficulties at Clifton that led Murray on 6 Jan. 1746 to present to him a memorial that he should from time to time call a council of war, and that upon sudden emergencies a discretionary power should be vested in those who had commands. To the memorial the prince replied on the 7th, refusing to adopt the advice proposed, and complaining at length of the attempt to limit his prerogative (*Hist. MSS. Comm.* 7th Rep. p. 704, 12th Rep. App. pt. viii. p. 73).

At Stirling the insurgents were joined by reinforcements from France and the highlands, which with their lowland allies brought up their numbers to about nine thousand. On learning of the approach towards Falkirk of the English army under General Hawley, they advanced to more favourable ground, and drew up on the Plean Moor. The battle of Falkirk took place on 17 Jan. As usual the highlanders determined to make the attack before Hawley completed his dispositions. His men had also to contend with a storm of wind and rain which beat in their faces. The right wing was led by Murray, who fought on foot, sword in hand, at the head of the Macdonalds of Keppoch. He gave orders that they should reserve their fire till within twelve paces of the enemy. This so broke the charge of the dragoons that the highlanders were able to mingle in their ranks, and engage in a hand-to-hand struggle, where their peculiar mode of fighting at once gave them the advantage. In a few seconds the dragoons were in headlong flight, and breaking through the infantry assisted to complete the confusion caused by the furious attack of the highlanders in other parts of the line. So completely panic-stricken were the English soldiers that, had the pursuit been followed up with sufficient vigour, the highland victory might have been as signal as at Prestonpans; but the slightness of the resistance made to their onset caused the highlanders to discredit their good fortune. Dreading that the retreat might be but a feint, they hesitated to pursue until Hawley was able to withdraw safely towards Edinburgh. After his retirement the siege of Stirling was resumed, but they were unable to effect its capture before the approach of a powerful force under Cumberland compelled them—after blowing up their powder stored in the church of St. Ninians—to retreat northwards towards Inverness, where reinforcements were expected from France. Murray deemed such a precipitate retreat decidedly imprudent, as tending seriously to discourage the supporters of the prince in other parts of the country (*Jacobite Correspondence of the Atholl Family*, p. 184). He also urged that a stand should be made in Atholl, and offered to do so with two thousand men (*ib.* p. 185). His counsels were, however, overruled, and on reaching Crieff on 2 Feb. the army was formed in two divisions, the highlanders under the prince marching to Inverness by the direct mountain route, while the lowland regiments, led by Murray, proceeded along the eastern coast by Angus and Aberdeen. Murray joined the prince while he was investing Fort George. A small garrison had been left in it by Lord Loudoun, who for greater safety withdrew into Ross; but Murray cleverly surmounted the difficulty of attacking him there by collecting a fleet of fishing boats, with which he crossed the Dornoch Firth. The outposts of Lord Loudoun were surprised, and he himself was compelled to retreat westwards, and finally disbanded his forces. Some time afterwards Murray learned that the Atholl country was in the hands of the government, Blair Castle, as well as the houses of the fencers, being occupied by detachments of the royal troops. To free it from the indignity he set out in March with a picked force of seven hundred men, and, on reaching Dalnaspidal on the 10th, divided them into separate detachments, assigning to each the task of capturing one of the posts of the enemy before daybreak, after which they were to rendezvous at the Bridge of Bruar, near Blair. The contrivance was attended with complete success, except in the case of Blair Inn, the party there making their escape to Blair Castle. The commander, Sir Andrew Agnew, thereupon sent out a strong force from the castle to reconnoitre, and Murray, the first at the rendezvous, accompanied with but twenty-four men, was all but surprised. His readiness of resource was, however, equal to the occasion. Placing his men at wide intervals behind a turf wall, and ordering the banners to be displayed at still wider distances, and the pipes to strike up a defiant pibroch, he so alarmed the royal soldiers that they beat a hasty retreat towards the castle. On the arrival of the different detachments of his men he proceeded to invest the castle, but when the garrison were nearly at the last extremity he was on 31 March called northwards to Inverness, owing to the approach of the Duke of Cumberland.

Murray was entirely opposed to making a stand against Cumberland at Culloden, for the simple reason that the ground, which was favourable both for cavalry and artillery, afforded no opportunity for utilising to the best advantage the highland mode of attack. He therefore advised that meanwhile a retreat should be made to the hills to await reinforcements, and when overruled in this, stipulated for a night attack as affording the only possible chance of victory. On the afternoon of 15 April 1746 the insurgents commenced their march towards the army of the duke, encamped about ten miles distant round Nairn, but their progress was so slow that Murray, who commanded the first line, took upon him during the night to discontinue the march, on finding that it would be impossible to reach the duke's camp before daylight. Convinced that it would be 'perfect madness' to attack 'what was near double their number in daylight, where they would be prepared to receive them' (Letter in *Lockhart Papers*, ii. 2), he advised that they should at least retire to strong ground on the other side of the water of Nairn; but the prince reverted to his original purpose, and resolved to await the attack at Culloden. Murray led the right wing, and, fighting at the head of the Atholl men, broke the Duke of Cumberland's line, and captured two pieces of cannon. While advancing towards the second line he was thrown from his horse, which had become unmanageable, but ran to the rear to bring up other regiments to support the attack. So deadly, however, was the fire of the duke's forces that their second line was never reached, and in a short time the highlanders were in full retreat.

The Duke of Cumberland inflicted on Murray's name a gratuitous injury by representing next day that orders issued by Murray before the battle contained an injunction to the Jacobites to refuse quarter to the English forces. Copies of Murray's orders to his troops at Culloden are extant at Blair Castle, among Cumberland's papers at Windsor, and among the Hardwicke MSS. at the British Museum. None contain any reference to the alleged denial of quarter, and all contain the sentence 'No body on Pain of Death to Strip the Slain or Plunder till the Battle be over.' Cumberland clearly invented the so-called 'no quarter' order, so as to justify his ruthless pursuit of his broken foe.

After the battle Murray, with a number of the highland chiefs, retired to Ruthven and Badenoch, where they had soon a force of three thousand men. On 17 April he sent a letter to the prince, in which, while regretting that the royal standard had been set up without more definite assurances of assistance from the king of France, and also 'the fatal error that had been made in the situation chosen for the battle,' he resigned his command (*Hist. MSS. Comm.* 12th Rep. App. pt. viii. p. 74). On learning, however, that the prince had determined to give up the contest and withdraw to France, he earnestly entreated him to remain, asserting that the highlanders 'would have made a summer's campaign without the risk of any misfortune.' As these representations failed to move the prince's resolution, Murray disbanded his forces and retired to France. According to Douglas he arrived at Rome on 27 March 1747, where he was received with great splendour by the Pretender, who fitted up an apartment in his palace for his reception, and introduced him to the pope (*Scottish Peerage*, ed. Wood, i. 153). He also proposed to allow him four hundred livres per month, and endeavoured to secure for him a pension from the French court (*Hist. MSS. Comm.* 12th Rep. pt. viii. p. 75). There was, however, a current rumour that the prince deeply resented the terms in which he had resigned his command, and although the prince himself always professed his full approval of the manner in which Lord George had conducted himself, it would appear that for some time at least he was seriously estranged from him. This view is confirmed by the Chevalier's refusal to receive Lord George at Paris in July 1747 (*ib.* p. 74). Between December 1746 and August 1748 Murray journeyed through Germany, Silesia, Poland, Prussia, and other countries (*ib.* p. 75). He lived for some years at Emmerich. He died at Medemblik in Holland on 2 Oct. 1760. By his wife Amelia, only daughter of James Murray of Glencarse and Strowan, whom he married in 1728, he had three sons and two daughters: John, third duke of Atholl; James Murray of Strowan, colonel of the Atholl highlanders, and ultimately major-general, who while serving under Prince Ferdinand was wounded by a musket-ball, which prevented him ever afterwards lying in a recumbent position; George Murray of Pitkeathly, who became vice-admiral of the white; Amelia, married first to John, eighth lord Sinclair, and secondly to James Farquharson of Invercauld; and Charlotte, who died unmarried. Various letters and journals of Murray belong, with an anonymous portrait, to the Duke of Atholl.

[Chevalier Johnstone's Memoirs; Histories of the Rebellion by Patten, Rae, Ray, Home, and Chambers; Hist. MSS. Comm. 12th Rep. App. pt. viii.; Jacobite Correspondence of the Atholl Family (Bannatyne Club); Culloden Papers; Burton's Hist. of Scotland, viii. 444; Douglas's Scots' Peerage (ed. Wood, rev. by Paul), 1904; A Military History of Perthshire, 1908; Elcho's Short Account of the Affairs of Scotland, 1744–6, ed. Charteris, Edinburgh, 1907.] T. F. H.

MURRAY, Lord GEORGE (1761–1803), bishop of St. David's, born on 30 Jan. 1761, was the fourth son of John, third duke of Atholl [q. v.], by his wife and cousin, Lady Charlotte Murray, daughter of James, second duke of Atholl [q. v.] He matriculated from New College, Oxford, on 28 June 1779, graduating B.A. in 1782, and D.D. by diploma on 27 Nov. 1800. On 5 Nov. 1787 he was made archdeacon of Man, was also rector of Hurston, Kent, and dean of Bocking, Essex. 'Applying his scientific skill and philosophical knowledge to that curious mechanical invention, the telegraph, he made many improvements in that machine' (Douglas, *Peerage*, ed. Wood, i. 154), and was granted the management of the telegraphs (i.e. a species of semaphore) at various seaports, and on Wimbledon Common. On 18 Dec. 1795 he was introduced to the king, and in March 1796 the direction of the telegraph at the admiralty was committed to him (see Nichols, *Lit. Illustrations*, v. 701). In 1798 he was eager to take part in recruiting forces to oppose the threatened French invasion, but a meeting of prelates at Lambeth checked the 'arming influenza of their inferior brethren' (*ib.* v. 732). On 19 Nov. 1800 Murray was nominated bishop of St. David's. He was elected on 6 Dec., confirmed on 7 and consecrated on 11 Feb. 1801. He caught a chill waiting for his carriage on leaving the House of Lords, and died at Cavendish Square on 3 June 1803, aged 42. One published sermon of his is in the British Museum Library. Murray married at Farnborough, Hampshire, on 18 Dec. 1780, Anne Charlotte, daughter of Lieutenant-general Francis Ludovic Grant, M.P., by whom he had nine children, of whom John (*b.* 1786) became a commander in the royal navy, and died in the West Indies in December 1803. Amelia Matilda Murray [q. v.], was the fourth daughter.

The second son, George Murray (1784–1860), born at Farnham on 12 Jan. 1784, matriculated from Christ Church, Oxford, on 22 Dec. 1801, graduating B.A. in 1806, M.A. in 1810, and D.D. by diploma on 13 March 1814. On 29 Sept. 1808 he was installed, like his father, archdeacon of Man; on 22 May 1813 he was nominated bishop of Sodor and Man by the Duke of Atholl, and consecrated 6 March 1814. On 24 Nov. 1827 he was elected bishop of Rochester, receiving back the temporalities on 14 Dec. 1827, and on 19 March 1828 was nominated dean of Worcester, being succeeded in 1845 by John Peel. While commending the character of the leaders of the Oxford movement, Murray mildly attacked the 'Tracts for the Times,' especially Nos. 81 and 93, in his episcopal charge of October 1843. Several of his sermons and charges were published. He died, after a protracted illness, at his town residence in Chester Square, London, on 16 Feb. 1860, aged 76, and was buried in the family vault at Kensal Green. He married, on 5 May 1811, Lady Sarah Hay-Drummond, second daughter of Robert, ninth earl of Kinnoull, by whom he had five sons and six daughters.

[Douglas's Scots' Peerage, ed. Wood, rev. by Paul, 1904; Foster's Peerage; Foster's Alumni Oxon. 1715–1886; Jones and Freeman's St. David's, p. 356; Le Neve's Fasti, passim; Nichols's Lit. Illustr. v. 701, 732; Gent. Mag. 1803, i. 601; Times, 17 and 23 Feb. 1860.] A. F. P.

MURRAY, Sir GEORGE (1759–1819), vice-admiral, of a younger branch of the Elibank family [see Murray, Sir Gideon, and Murray, Patrick, fifth Baron Elibank], settled at Chichester, was the son of Gideon Murray, for many years a magistrate and alderman of that city. In 1770, being then eleven years of age, his name was entered on the books of the Niger with Captain Francis Banks in the Mediterranean. His actual service in the navy probably began in 1772, when he joined the Panther, carrying the broad pennant of Commodore Shuldham on the Newfoundland station. He was afterwards in the Romney, the flagship of Rear-admiral John Montagu, on the same station; and in the Bristol, with Captain Morris and Sir Peter Parker (1721–1811) [q. v.], at the bloody but unsuccessful attack on Sullivan's Island on 28 June 1776. In September he followed Parker to the Chatham, and in her was at the reduction of Rhode Island in December 1776. In the beginning of 1778 he was taken by Lord Howe into the Eagle, in which he engaged in the operations of the summer campaign against the French fleet under D'Estaing. On his return to England he passed his examination, 19 Nov. 1778, and on 31 Dec. was promoted to be lieutenant of the Arethusa frigate, with Captain Everitt. A few weeks later, the Arethusa, in chasing a French frigate in-shore, was lost on the Breton coast, and Murray became a prisoner. He devoted his enforced leisure to the study of French and of the organisation of the French navy, and after two years was released on parole, consequent, it is said, on M. de Sartine's approval of his spirited conduct in chastising an American privateer's-man, who had the insolence to appear in public wearing the English naval uniform and the royal cockade (*Naval Chronicle*, xviii. 181).

Murray was a free man by the beginning of 1781, and was appointed to the Monmouth, commanded by his fellow-townsman, Captain James Alms [q. v.] In her he took part in the action at Port Praya, and in the capture of the Dutch merchant-ships in Saldanha Bay [see Johnstone, George], and afterwards in the East Indies, in the first two actions between Sir Edward Hughes [q. v.] and the Bailli de Suffren. He was then moved into the flagship, the Superb; was wounded in the action of 3 Sept. 1782; on 9 Oct. was promoted to the command of the Combustion; and on 12 Oct. was posted to the San Carlos frigate. After the fifth action with Suffren he was moved into the Inflexible of 74 guns, in which he returned to England. He is said to have devoted the following years to study, and to have resided for some time in France in order to perfect his knowledge of the language and its literature. In 1793 he was appointed to the Triton frigate, and afterwards to the Nymphe, just captured from the French [see Pellew, Edward, Viscount Exmouth]. In her he was with the squadron under Sir John Borlase Warren [q. v.] when, on 23 April 1794, it fell in with four French frigates off Guernsey, captured three of them, and chased the fourth into Morlaix. The Nymphe, however, was some distance astern and had little part in the action (James, i. 222; Troude, ii. 323). In June 1795 she was attached to the fleet under Lord Bridport, and was present at the action off Lorient, on the 23rd.

In the following year Murray was appointed to the Colossus of 74 guns, in which he joined Sir John Jervis in the Mediterranean, and on 14 Feb. 1797 took part in the battle off Cape St. Vincent (James, ii. 40). In September 1798 the Colossus, having convoyed some store-ships up the Mediterranean, joined Nelson at Naples, and, being then under orders for home, Sir William Hamilton (1730–1803) [q. v.] took the opportunity of sending by her a large part of his valuable collection. Unfortunately, as she drew near England she was wrecked on a ledge of rocks among the Scilly Islands, 7 Dec. 1798, with no loss of life, but with the total loss of her valuable freight. The circumstances of the wreck were inquired into by a court-martial on 19 Jan. 1799, when Murray was acquitted of all blame. He was immediately afterwards appointed to the Achilles, and in the next year was moved into the Edgar, which in 1801 was one of the fleet sent to the Baltic under Sir Hyde Parker. As a small 74, the Edgar was one of the ships chosen by Nelson in forming his squadron for the attack on the sea defences of Copenhagen, and on 2 April 1801 led the way in and had a brilliant share in the battle [see Nelson, Horatio, Viscount]. He then commanded a squadron of seven line-of-battle ships off Bornholm, subsequently rejoining the fleet under Nelson.

On the renewal of hostilities in 1803, Murray was appointed to the Spartiate, but at the same time Nelson invited him to go with him as captain of the fleet in the Mediterranean. Murray hesitated, on the ground that such a service often led to a disagreement between an admiral and his first captain, and he valued Nelson's friendship too highly to risk the danger of an estrangement. This objection was overcome, and Murray accepted the post, which he held during the long watch off Toulon, 1803–5, and the voyage to the West Indies in 1805, being meantime promoted to be rear-admiral on 23 April 1804. On his return to England, in August 1805, he found himself, by the death of his father-in-law, to whom he was executor, involved in private business, which prevented him accompanying Nelson in his last voyage. In 1807 he was appointed commander-in-chief of the naval operations against Buenos Ayres, but the share of the navy in those operations was limited to convoying and landing the troops (James, iv. 281), and again embarking them when the evacuation of the place had been agreed on. On 25 Oct. 1809 he was promoted to be vice-admiral, was nominated a K.C.B. on 2 Jan. 1815, and died suddenly at Chichester on 28 Feb. 1819, in his sixtieth year (*Gent. Mag.* 1819, i. 281).

[Naval Chronicle (with a portrait), xviii. 177; Nicolas's Despatches and Letters of Lord Nelson, freq. (see index); official letters of Sir Edward Hughes, 1782–3, in the Public Record Office, and information kindly supplied by Mr. D. O. Murray.] J. K. L.

MURRAY, Sir **GEORGE** (1772–1846), general and statesman, second son of Sir William Murray, bart., and Lady Augusta Mackenzie, seventh and youngest daughter of George, third earl of Cromarty, was born at the family seat, Ochtertyre, Crieff, Perthshire, on 6 Feb. 1772. He was educated at the High School and at the university of Edinburgh, and received an ensign's commission in the 71st regiment on 12 March 1789. He was transferred to the 34th regiment soon after, and in June 1790 to the 3rd footguards. He served the campaign of 1793 in Flanders, was present at the affair of St. Amand, battle of Famars, siege of Valenciennes, attack of Lincelles, investment of Dunkirk, and attack of Lannoy. On 16 Jan. 1794 he was promoted to a lieutenancy with the rank of captain, and in April returned to England. He rejoined the army in Flanders in the summer of the same year, and was in the retreat of the allies through Holland and Germany. In the summer of 1795 he was appointed aide-de-camp to Major-general Alexander Campbell, on the staff of Lord Moira's army in the expedition for Quiberon, and in the autumn on that for the West Indies under Sir Ralph Abercromby, but returned in February 1796 on account of ill-health. In 1797 and 1798 he served as aide-de-camp to Major-general Campbell on the staff in England and Ireland. On 5 Aug. 1799 he obtained a company in the 3rd guards with the rank of lieutenant-colonel. He was employed on the staff of the quartermaster-general in the expedition to Holland, and wounded at the action near the Helder. He returned to Cork, whence in the autumn of 1800 he sailed for Gibraltar, was appointed to the staff of the quartermaster-general, and sent upon a special mission. In 1801 he was employed in the expedition to Egypt, was present at the landing, was engaged in the battles of 13 and 21 March at Marmorici and Aboukir, at Rosetta, and Rhamanie, and at the investments of Cairo and Alexandria. In 1802 he was appointed adjutant-general to the forces in the West Indies. The following year he returned to England and was appointed assistant quartermaster-general at the horse guards. In 1804 he was made deputy quartermaster-general in Ireland. In 1805 he served in the expedition to Hanover under Lieutenant-general Sir George Don [q. v.] In 1806 he returned to his staff appointment in Ireland. In 1807 he was placed at the head of the quartermaster-general's department in the expedition to Stralsund, and afterwards in that to Copenhagen under Sir William Schaw, afterwards Earl Cathcart [q. v.] In the spring of 1808 he was quartermaster-general in the expedition to the Baltic under Sir John Moore, and in the autumn he went in the same capacity to Portugal. He was present at the battle of Vimiera, the affairs at Lago and Villa Franca, and at the battle of Corunna. His services on the staff were particularly commended in Lieutenant-general Hope's despatch containing the account of that battle.

On 9 March 1809 he received the brevet of colonel, and was appointed quartermaster-general to the forces in Spain and Portugal under Lord Wellington. He was present in the affairs on the advance to Oporto and the passage of the Douro. He was engaged in the battles of Talavera, Busaco, Fuentes d'Onoro, and Vittoria. He returned home in 1811, and in May 1812 was appointed quartermaster-general in Ireland. There he remained until September 1813, when he again joined the army in the Peninsula, and took part in the battles of the Pyrenees, Nivelle, Nive, Orthes, and Toulouse, and in the subsequent operations until the termination of hostilities in 1814. He had been promoted major-general on 1 Jan. 1812, and on 9 Aug. 1813 he was made colonel of the 7th battalion of the 60th regiment. He was made a K.C.B. on 11 Sept. 1813, before the enlargement of the order. On his return home in 1814 he was appointed adjutant-general to the forces in Ireland, and at the end of the year was sent to govern the Canadas, with the local rank of lieutenant-general.

On the escape of Napoleon from Elba, Murray obtained leave to join the army of Flanders, but various delays prevented him reaching it until Waterloo had been fought and Paris occupied. He remained with the army of occupation for three years as chief of the staff, with the local rank of lieutenant-general. In 1817 he was transferred from the colonelcy of the 7th battalion of the 60th regiment to that of the 72nd foot. On his return home in 1818 he was appointed governor of Edinburgh Castle. In August 1819 he was made governor of the Royal Military College at Sandhurst, a post he held until 1824. On 14 June 1820, the university of Oxford conferred upon him the degree of D.C.L. In September 1823 he was transferred to the colonelcy of the 42nd royal highlanders, and the same year was returned to parliament in the tory interest as member for Perth county. In January 1824 he was elected a fellow of the Royal Society, and the following March was appointed lieutenant-general of the ordnance. In March 1825 he went to Ireland as commander-in-chief of the forces, and was promoted lieutenant-general on 27 May. He held the Irish command until May 1828, when he was made a privy councillor on taking office as secretary of state for the colonies in the Duke of Wellington's administration. He held the post until November 1830. In September 1829 he was appointed governor of Fort George, North Britain.

At the general election of 1832 he was defeated at Perth, but regained the seat at a by-election in 1834. On his appointment as master-general of the ordnance he again lost the election, and did not again sit in parliament, although he contested Westminster in 1837, and Manchester in 1838 and 1841. He, however, continued to hold office as master-general of the ordnance until 1846. He was promoted general on 23 Nov. 1841, and was transferred to the colonelcy of the 1st royals in December 1843. He died at his residence, 5 Belgrave Square, London, on 28 July 1846, and was buried beside his wife in Kensal Green cemetery on 5 Aug.

He married, in 1826, Lady Louisa Erskine, sister of the Marquis of Anglesea, and widow of Sir James Erskine, by whom he had one daughter, who married his aide-de-camp, Captain Boyce, of the 2nd life guards. His wife died 23 Jan. 1842.

Murray was a successful soldier, an able minister, and a skilful and fluent debater. For his distinguished military services he received the gold cross with five clasps for the Peninsula, the orders of knight grand cross of the Bath, besides Austrian, Russian, Portuguese, and Turkish orders.

He was the author of: 1. 'Speech on the Roman Catholic Disabilities Relief Bill,' 8vo, London, 1829. 2. 'Special Instructions for the Offices of the Quartermaster-general's Department,' 12mo, London, and 3. edited 'The Letters and Despatches of John Churchill, first Duke of Marlborough, from 1702 to 1712,' 8vo, London, 5 vols. 1845. These letters were accidentally discovered in October 1842, on the removal to the newly built muniment room at Blenheim of a chest which had long been lying at the steward's house at Hensington, near Woodstock.

[Chambers's Dict. of Eminent Scotsmen; Royal Military Calendar, vol. iii. 1820; Records of the 1st Royal Regiment; Gent. Mag. 1846 pt. ii.; Despatches and War Office Records.] R. H. V.

MURRAY, Sir GIDEON, Lord Elibank (*d.* 1621), of Elibank, deputy treasurer and lord of session, was third son of Sir John Murray of Blackbarony, Peeblesshire, by Griselda, daughter of Sir John Bethune of Creich, Fifeshire, and relict of William Scott younger of Branxholm, Roxburghshire, ancestor of the Scotts, dukes of Buccleuch. The Murrays of Blackbarony claim an origin distinct from the other great families of the name of Murray, and trace their descent from Johan de Morreff, who in 1296 swore allegiance to Edward I of England. His supposed great-grandson, John de Moravia, or Moray, is mentioned in a charter of 14 March 1409–10 as possessing the lands of Halton-Murray, or Blackbarony, and from him the Murrays of Blackbarony descend in a direct line.

Sir Gideon of Elibank was originally designated of Glenpoyt or Glenpottie. He studied for the church, and in an act of the privy council of 25 April 1583 is mentioned as chanter of Aberdeen (*Reg. P. C. Scotl.* p. 564). According to Scot of Scotstarvet, he gave up thoughts of the church because he killed in a quarrel a man named Aichison. For this he was imprisoned in the castle of Edinburgh, but through the interposition of the wife of the chancellor Arran he was pardoned and set at liberty (*Staggering State*, ed. 1872, p. 65). Afterwards he became chamberlain to his nephew, Sir Walter Scott of Buccleugh, and had charge of his affairs during his absence in Italy (*ib.* p. 66). On 14 Oct. 1592–3 he became surety for William Scott of Hartwoodmyres and other borderers (*Reg. P. C. Scotl.* v. 733). On 15 March 1593–4 he had a charter of the lands of Elibank, Selkirkshire, with a salmon fishing in the Tweed (*Reg. Mag. Sig. Scot.* 1593–1608, entry 235). In the fray of Dryfe Sands on 7 Dec. 1593 between the Scotts and the Johnstones, in which John, seventh or eighth lord Maxwell [q. v.], was slain, Murray was present with five hundred of the Scotts, and carried their laird's standard (*Staggering State*, p. 66). Along with other border chiefs he in October 1602 signed the general band against border thieves (*Reg. P. C. Scotl.* vi. 828).

After the accession of James to the English throne Murray was appointed one of a commission of justiciary for the borders (*ib.* vii. 702). On 14 March 1605 he received the honour of knighthood, and on the 14th he was appointed one of a conjunct commission for the borders consisting of Englishmen and Scotsmen (*ib.* p. 707). Along with his brother, the laird of Blackbarony, he was nominated in June 1607 commissioner to the presbytery of Peebles, to secure there the inauguration of the scheme for the appointment of perpetual moderators (*ib.* p. 376). On 3 Aug. he was appointed with other commissioners to assist the Earls of Dunbar and Cumberland in establishing peace and obedience in the middle shires (borders) (*ib.* p. 729), for which he received a fee of 800*l.* (*ib.* viii. 16). On 19 Jan. 1607–8 the privy council passed an order of approbation of his services and that of the other commissioners (*ib.* p. 38), and on 1 March 1610 the king's special approbation of his individual services was ratified by the council (*ib.* p. 432). On 20 Feb. he also obtained a pension of 1,200*l.* Scots from the Earl of Dunbar, which was subsequently ratified by the states.

During 1610 the quarrels of Murray's second son, Walter, and a son of Lord Cranstoun, who had challenged each other to single combat, occupied much of the attention of the council, and on 4 Aug. Murray had to give caution in five thousand marks for his son to remain in Edinburgh until freed by the council (*ib.* ix. 653). On 28 Aug. 1610 he was admitted a member of the privy council in place of Sir James Hay of Fingask (*ib.* p. 76). On 15 Nov. he was named a member of the royal commission of the exchequer (*ib.* p. 85). He was one of the 'new Octavians' appointed in April 1611 for the management of the king's affairs in Scotland, and on 15 June he was named a member of a royal commission for the borders (*ib.* p. 194). As a token of his special regard for him the king also in this year made over to him a number of presentation cups given to him by various Scottish burghs.

On 30 July 1611 Elibank had a commission for managing the affairs of the king's favourite, Robert Car (or Ker), viscount Rochester, in Scotland, and through his influence he was in December 1612 appointed treasurer depute. In the parliament which met at Edinburgh in October 1612 he sat as member for Selkirkshire (Foster, *Members of the Scottish Parliament*, 2nd edit. p. 265). On 28 April 1613 he was named one of a commission for exacting fines on the Macgregors (*Reg. P. C. Scotl.* x. 51–5). On 2 Nov. he was appointed a lord of session, with the title of Lord Elibank, and he was at the same time named a commissioner for the middle shires, with a salary of 500*l.* (*ib.* p. 164). He was one of the commission who in December 1614 examined John Ogilvie, the jesuit, with torture. In December 1615 he was appointed a commissioner in the new court of high commission, and on 30 July 1616 one of a commission of justiciary for the north. The same year his pension was increased to 2,400*l.* Scots, and extended to the lifetime of his two sons. His management of the revenue of Scotland fully justified this recognition of his services, for it had been so prudent and able as to enable him not only to carry out extensive repairs on the royal residences of Holyrood, Dunfermline, Linlithgow, and Falkland, and the castles of Edinburgh, Stirling, and Dumbarton, but also to have in the treasury a surplus sufficient to defray the expenses of King James and his court during the royal visit to Scotland in 1617 (*Staggering State*, p. 60). Elibank was appointed one of a commission to the diocesan assembly at St. Andrews in October of this year, to take the place of the king's commissioner, the Earl of Montrose, who was ill (Calderwood, vii. 284), and he was one of the courtiers who on Easter day 1618 took the communion kneeling in the royal chapel (*ib.* p. 297). At the assembly held at Perth on 25 Aug. 1618 he was one of the assessors of the king's commissioners (*ib.* p. 304). As a proof of the high esteem in which Elibank was held by the king, Scot of Scotstarvet states that when on one occasion in the bedchamber, with none present but the king, Elibank, and Scot, Elibank happened to drop his chevron, the king, though both old and stiff, stooped to pick it up, and gave it him, saying, 'My predecessor, Queen Elizabeth, thought she did a favour to any man who was speaking with her when she let her glove fall, that he might take it up and give it to her; but, sir, you may say a king lifted your glove' (*Staggering State*, p. 66). Nevertheless, when in 1621 Elibank was accused by James Stewart, lord Ochiltree, of malversations as treasurer depute, the king ordered a day for his trial. The accusation, however, upset his reason, and being haunted by the delusion that he had no money to obtain for himself bread or drink, he refused to take food, and died on 28 June, after an illness of twenty days (*ib.*; Calderwood, vii. 462). By his wife Margaret Pentland he had two sons and a daughter: Sir Patrick, who was created a baronet of Nova Scotia on 6 May 1628, was raised to the peerage by the title Lord Elibank on 18 March 1643, consistently supported Charles I during the civil war, and died on 12 Nov. 1649;

Walter of Livingstone; and Agnes, married to Sir William Scott of Harden.

[Calderwood's Hist. of the Kirk of Scotland; Scot's Staggering State of Scottish Statesmen; Reg. Mag. Sig. Scot.; Reg. P. C. Scotl.; Brunton and Haig's Senators of the College of Justice; Douglas's Scots' Peerage (ed. Wood, rev. by Paul), 1904.] T. F. H.

MURRAY, GRENVILLE (1824–1881), whose full name was Eustace Clare Grenville Murray, journalist, was natural son of Richard Grenville, second duke of Buckingham and Chandos. Born in 1824, he matriculated from Magdalen Hall, Oxford, on 1 March 1848, and was entered a student of the Inner Temple in 1850. He attracted at an early age the notice of Lord Palmerston, at his instigation entered the diplomatic service, and was on 14 July 1851 sent as an attaché to the embassy at Vienna. Murray entered at the same time into an agreement with the 'Morning Post,' by which he undertook to act as Vienna correspondent. Such a contravention of the usages of the foreign office was by an accident brought to the notice of the British ambassador, Lord Westmorland, by whom Murray, though protected against dismissal by the interest of Palmerston, was ostracised from the British chancery. On 7 April 1852 he was temporarily transferred to Hanover, and on 19 Oct. of the same year he was appointed fifth paid attaché at Constantinople, where his relations with Lord Stratford de Redclyffe (then Sir Stratford Canning) were from the first the reverse of cordial, and resulted in his being banished as vice-consul to Mitylene. In 1854 appeared his admirably written 'Roving Englishman,' a series of desultory chapters on travel, in which the Turkish ambassador was satirised as Sir Hector Stubble. Palmerston was unwilling to recall Murray, but in 1855 he was transferred to Odessa as consul-general. He returned to England, after thirteen years of discord with the British residents in Odessa, in 1868, contributed to the first numbers of 'Vanity Fair,' and in the following year started a weekly journal of the most mordant type, entitled 'The Queen's Messenger,' a prototype of the later 'Society papers.' On 22 June 1869 Murray was horsewhipped by Lord Carrington, at the door of the Conservative Club in St. James's Street, for a slander upon his father, Robert John, second lord Carrington. The assault was made under strong provocation. Lord Carrington was prosecuted by Murray, and was found guilty at the Middlesex sessions on 22 July, but was only ordered to appear for judgment when called upon. Meanwhile, on 17 July, Murray had been charged at Bow Street with perjury in denying the authorship of the article in dispute. He was remanded on bail until the 29th, but before that date he withdrew to Paris, and practically exiled himself from this country. He became well known in the French capital as the Comte de Rethel d'Aragon, taking the title of the Spanish lady whom he had married. He produced several novels, but was more at home in short satirical pieces, and wrote innumerable essays and sketches, caustic in matter and incisive in style, for the English and American press. He was Paris correspondent of the 'Daily News' and the 'Pall Mall Gazette,' was one of the early writers in the 'Cornhill Magazine' and in the 'World,' of which he was for a short time joint proprietor, and contributed character sketches to the 'Illustrated London News,' and 'Queer Stories' to 'Truth.' He was certainly one of the most accomplished journalists of his day. He probably did more than any single person to initiate the modern type of journal, which is characterised by a tone of candour with regard to public affairs, but owes its chief attraction to the circulation of private gossip, largely by means of hint and innuendo. He died at Passy on 20 Dec., and was buried in Paris on 24 Dec. 1881.

Murray's chief works were: 1. 'Droits et Devoirs des Envoyés Diplomatiques,' London, 1853, 12mo: the nucleus of 'Embassies and Foreign Courts,' published two years later. 2. 'The Roving Englishman' (reprinted from 'Household Words'), 1854, 8vo. 3. 'Pictures from the Battlefields,' 1856, 8vo, à propos of the Crimean campaigns. 4. 'Sport and its Pleasures,' 1859, 8vo. 5. 'The Oyster: where, how, and when to find, breed, cook, and eat it,' 1861, London, 12mo. 6. 'The Member for Paris: a Tale of the Second Empire,' 1871, 8vo (French translation, 1876). 7. 'Men of the Second Empire,' 1872, 8vo. 8. 'Men of the Third Republic,' 1873, 8vo (two French editions). 9. 'Young Brown; or the Law of Inheritance,' 1874, 8vo. This first appeared in the 'Cornhill Magazine,' and is partly autobiographical (French translation, 1875). 10. 'The Boudoir Cabal,' 1875, 8vo (French translation, 1876). 11. 'Turkey: being Sketches from Life,' 1877, 8vo. 12. 'The Russians of To-day,' 1878, 8vo (French translation, 1878). 13. 'Round about France,' 1878, 8vo: a series of interesting papers which originally appeared in the 'Daily News.' 14. 'Lucullus, or Palatable Essays,' 1878, 8vo. 15. 'Side Lights on English Society; or Sketches from Life, Social and Satirical,' 1881, 2 vols. 8vo: a series of gross satires upon social and political personages in England, with an ironical dedication to the queen; illustrated by Frank Barnard. 16. 'High Life in France under the Republic' (posthumous), 1884, 8vo. 17. 'Under the Lens: Social Photographs,' 1885, 2 vols. 8vo, containing some sketches reprinted from the 'Pall Mall Gazette' in a vein somewhat resembling that of the 'Snob Papers.'

[Foster's Alumni Oxon. 1715–1886; Irving's Annals of Our Times, pp. 876, 881; Edmund Yates's Recollections and Experiences, 1885, p. 448 sq.; Fox Bourne's English Newspapers, ii. 301–11; Vizetelly's Glances back through Fifty Years, ii. 432; Daily News, 24 Dec. 1881; Times, 24 Dec. 1881; Truth, 29 Dec. 1881; Annual Register, 1881, p. 154; Athenæum, 1881, ii. 902; Foreign Office Lists, 1853–6; Men of the Reign, p. 655; Murray's works.] T. S.

MURRAY, HENRY LEIGH (1820–1870), actor, whose name was originally Wilson, was born in Sloane Street, London, 19 Oct. 1820. While clerk in a merchant's office he joined some amateurs in a small theatre in Catherine Street, Strand, making his first appearance about 1838 as Buckingham in 'King Richard III.' Cassio, Macduff, Faulconbridge, Iago, &c., followed, and on 2 Dec. 1839, under Hooper, manager of the York circuit, he made at Hull his début as an actor, playing Ludovico in 'Othello.' On 17 Sept. 1840, as Leigh, perhaps to avoid confusion with his manager, he appeared at the Adelphi Theatre, Edinburgh, under William Henry Murray [q. v.], as Lieutenant Morton in the 'Middy Ashore.' While occasionally visiting Dundee, Perth, and other towns, he remained in Edinburgh, at the Theatre Royal or the Adelphi, till the spring of 1845, marrying in 1841 Miss Elizabeth Lee, a member of the company. Among the characters he played were Dr. Caius, Jan Dousterswyvel in the 'Lost Ship,' Hotspur, and Mark Antony, in which character he took his farewell of the Edinburgh stage. His salary in Edinburgh in 1842 was 1*l.* 10*s.* weekly, his wife receiving 2*l.* 15*s.* Murray's first appearance in London took place at the Princess's under Maddox on 19 April 1845, as Sir Thomas Clifford in the 'Hunchback,' with Lester Wallack, by whom he had been brought from Edinburgh, as the Hunchback, Miss Cushman being the Julia, Mr. Walter Lacy Lord Tinsel, Mr. Compton Modus, and Mrs. Stirling Helen. He played Bassanio, Orlando, Leonardo Gonzaga, &c., and was the original Herman Lindorf in Kenney's 'Infatuation,' and Malcolm Young in White's 'King of the Commons.' He was also Icilius to Macready's Virginius and De Mauprat to his Richelieu. With Macready he went, in the autumn of 1846, to the Surrey, where he played secondary characters in Shakespeare and Loveless in the 'Relapse.' On the recommendation of Dickens he was chosen to play at the Lyceum Alfred Heathfield in Albert Smith's adaptation of the 'Battle of Life.' At the Lyceum he remained under the Keeley and the Mathews managements. His Marquis de Volange in the 'Pride of the Market' won special recognition. In Dublin in 1848 he supported Miss Faucit (Lady Martin), playing Romeo, Jaffier, Biron, Leonatus, Beverley, Claude Melnotte, Charles Surface, &c. Quitting the Lyceum for the Olympic he became stage-manager under Stocqueler, and afterwards under Spicer and Davidson. Here he played character parts in pieces then in vogue, such as 'Time tries all,' 'His First Champagne,' &c. In the representations given during 1848 and 1849 at Windsor Castle he played Lorenzo in the 'Merchant of Venice,' Laertes, Octavius in 'Julius Cæsar,' and Gustavus in 'Charles XII.' Accompanying William Farren [q. v.], whose stage-manager he became, to the Strand and back to the Olympic, he played at the former house Joseph Surface, Falkland, Harry Dornton, Mr. Oakly, &c. His original characters at this time included Herbert Clavering in 'Patronage,' Fouché in 'Secret Service,' Captain Wagstaff in 'Hearts are Trumps,' Count Tristan in 'King René's Daughter,' the Comte de Saxe in an adaptation of 'Adrienne Lecouvreur,' Stephen Plum in 'All that glitters is not Gold,' and many others. He supported Gustavus Vaughan Brooke [q. v.] as Iago and Wellborn in 'A New Way to pay Old Debts.' Murray accompanied B. Webster [q. v.] to the Adelphi, where on 1 April 1853 he played in Mark Lemon's farce 'Mr. Webster at the Adelphi,' and made, 10 Oct. 1853, a high mark in Webster's 'Discarded Son,' the first of many adaptations of 'Un Fils de Famille.' On 20 March 1854 he was Sir Gervase Rokewode in 'Two Loves and a Life,' by Tom Taylor and Charles Reade, and on 31 May was first Raphael Duchatelet in the 'Marble Heart,' Selby's adaptation of 'Les Filles de Marbre.' In September he quitted the Adelphi, and in the next year was at Sadler's Wells. On 4 Nov. 1856 he reappeared at the Adelphi as Sir Walter Raeburn in the 'Border Marriage' ('Un Mariage à l'Arquebuse'). On 8 March 1858 he was, at Drury Lane, the first M. Bernard in Stirling Coyne's 'Love Knot.' As John Mildmay in 'Still Waters run deep' he reappeared at the Lyceum on 7 Aug. 1859, and played subsequently M. Tourbillon in 'Parents and Guardians,' and Claude Melnotte. On 9 Nov. he enacted at the St. James's the original

Harrington in James Kenney's 'London Pride, or Living for Appearances.' A benefit was given him at Drury Lane on 27 June 1865, with a view of aiding him in a trip to the south, rendered necessary by failing health. Representations were given by various London actors, the share of Leigh Murray and his wife consisting in the delivery of a duologue written by Shirley Brooks. Murray died 17 Jan. 1870 and was buried in Brompton cemetery.

He played a large range of characters, and was in his time unequalled as Maurice de Saxe, Harry Dornton, Gustave de Grignon in the 'Ladies' Battle,' Captain Damer in the 'Camp at Chobham,' Sir Charles Pomander in 'Masks and Faces,' and Birchall in the 'Vicar of Wakefield.' He also approached excellence as Captain Absolute and Charles Surface. A painstaking and competent actor, but wanting in robustness, he owed his reputation in part to the naturalness and ease of his style, to his avoidance of artifice and convention, and to the absence of mannerism. He was a member of the Garrick Club, and his popularity there, with its attendant temptations, did something to sap his health.

Mrs. Elizabeth Leigh Murray (*d.* 1892), the second daughter of Henry Lee (1765–1836) [q. v.], dramatist and manager for fifty years of the Taunton circuit, appeared at the age of five in 'Little Pickle,' and played a round of characters in her father's theatres, and in York, Leeds, Hull, &c. She appeared in London at the Olympic under Mme. Vestris, playing Cupid in an extravaganza of that name, and accompanied her manager to Covent Garden, taking part in the opening performance of 'Love's Labour's Lost,' 30 Sept. 1839. She then went to Sadler's Wells, and, after playing in various country towns, reached Edinburgh, where she appeared, under the name of Miss E. Lee, as Lady Staunton in the 'Whistler of the Glen, or the Fate of the Lily of St. Leonards,' an adaptation of the 'Heart of Midlothian,' and in 1841 as Mrs. Leigh. Returning to London, she reappeared at the Lyceum as The Lady in 'A Perplexing Predicament.' As a singer, and in drawing-room or domestic comedy, she won high reputation. Among numerous original parts, in many of which she supported her husband, she was seen as Apollo in Frank Talfourd's 'Diogenes and his Lantern,' Strand, 7 Feb. 1850; Mme. Duchatelet in the 'Marble Heart;' Lady Lavender in Stirling Coyne's 'Love Knot,' Drury Lane, 8 March 1858; Mrs. Burr in the 'Porter's Knot,' Olympic 2 Dec. 1858; Patty in the 'Chimney Corner,' Olympic, 21 Feb. 1861; Mrs. Kinpeck in Robertson's 'Play,' Prince of Wales's, 15 Feb. 1868; Lady Lundie in Wilkie Collins's 'Man and Wife,' Prince of Wales's, 22 Feb. 1873; Mrs. Crumbley in Burnand's 'Proof Positive,' Opera Comique, 16 Oct. 1875; Mrs. Foley in 'Forget me not,' Lyceum, 21 Aug. 1879; Mrs. McTartan in Byron's 'Courtship,' Court, 16 Oct. 1879; Lady Tompkins in Burnand's 'Colonel,' Prince of Wales's, 2 Feb. 1881. She also played in her later years Mrs. Candour and many similar parts. She died 25 May 1892.

Murray's younger brother, Gaston Murray (1826–1889), born in 1826, whose real name was Garstin Parker Wilson, first appeared in London at the Lyceum on 2 March 1855 as Tom Saville in 'Used up,' played in various theatres, and essayed some of his brother's parts. He died 8 Aug. 1889. His wife, Mary Frances (*d.* 1891), known as Mrs. Gaston Murray, daughter of Henry Hughes, of the Adelphi Theatre, was a capable actress and played intelligently many parts at the Globe, the Court, and St. James's, including Mrs. Penguin in the 'Scrap of Paper.' Her Mrs. Primrose in the 'Vicar of Wakefield' at the Lyceum was excellent. On 24 May 1889, at the opening of the Garrick Theatre by Mr. Hare, she was the original Mrs. Stonehay in Mr. Pinero's 'Profligate.' She died on 15 Jan. 1891.

[Personal knowledge and private information; Tallis's Dramatic Magazine; Theatrical Times, vols. i. and iii.; Scott and Howard's Life and Reminiscences of E. L. Blanchard; Westland Marston's Our Recent Actors; Mr. and Mrs. Bancroft's On and Off the Stage; Dickens's Life of Charles J. Mathews; Pascoe's Dramatic List; Era Almanack, various years; Sunday Times, various years; Era newspaper, 23 Jan. 1870.] J. K.

MURRAY, HUGH (1779–1846), geographer, born in 1779, was the younger son of Matthew Murray (1735–1791), minister of North Berwick, and grandson of George Murray (*d.* 1757), who had held the same benefice. His elder brother, George (1772–1822), was also minister of North Berwick from 1795 till his death (Hew Scott, *Fasti Eccl. Scot.* pt. i. 345). His mother was daughter of John Hill, minister of St. Andrews, and sister of Henry David Hill, professor at St. Andrews. Hugh entered the Edinburgh excise office as a clerk, but from the first devoted his leisure to literary pursuits, publishing 'The Swiss Emigrants,' a tale (anon.), in 1804; two philosophical treatises ('The Morality of Fiction,' 1805, and 'Enquiries respecting the Character of Nations,' 1808); and another romance, 'Corasmin, or the Minister,' in 1814. On 22 Jan. 1816 he was elected a fellow of the Royal Society of Edinburgh, to whose 'Transactions' he contributed, among other papers, one, in 1818, 'On the Ancient Geography of Central and Eastern Asia, with Illustrations derived from Recent Discoveries in the North of India' (*Trans.* viii. 171–203). In 1817 he enlarged and completed Dr. Leyden's 'Historical Account of Discoveries and Travels in Africa.' Similar works by him on Asia and North America followed; the former being published in three volumes at Edinburgh in 1820 (cf. *Quarterly Review*, xxiv. 311–41), and the latter in London in 1829.

Murray's *magnum opus* was the 'Encyclopædia of Geography, a Description of the Earth, physical, statistical, civil, and political' (London, 1834), of which the purely geographical part was written by himself, while Sir W. Hooker undertook the zoological, Professor W. Wallace the geological, and W. W. Swainston the astronomical departments. A supplement was published in 1843. The work contained eighty-two maps and over a thousand woodcuts. It was well received, and an American edition (1843) in three volumes, edited by Thos. G. Bradford, had a large sale. Murray also contributed largely to the press, and in the Edinburgh Cabinet Library there appeared compilations by him on the history or geography of the 'Southern Seas' (1826), the 'Polar Seas' (1830), 'British India' (1832), 'China' (1836), 'British America' (1839), 'Africa' (1830), 'The United States' (1844). Many of these volumes had the advantage of contributions on natural history by Jameson, Traill, J. Nicol, and others. Murray was for a time editor of the 'Scots Magazine,' and was a fellow of the Royal Geographical Society of London. His connection with Constable's 'Edinburgh Gazetteer' caused him to figure in the celebrated tory squib, written by Hogg and others, called 'Translation from an Ancient Chaldee MS.' (ch. iii. 47–8), which appeared in 'Blackwood's Magazine' for October 1817. He died, after a short illness, while on a visit to London, in Wardrobe Place, Doctors' Commons, on 4 March 1846. T. Constable refers to him as 'an eminent geographer, whose extreme modesty prevented his being known and honoured as he deserved to be' (*Arch. Constable and his Friends*, ii. 381).

Besides the works mentioned Murray's chief publications were: 1. 'A Catechism of Geography,' 4th ed. enlarged, Edinb. 1833, 12mo, 7th ed. 1842. 2. 'Travels of Marco Polo,' amended and enlarged, with notes,' 1844 8vo, 1845 12mo. Posthumously: 3. 'The African Continent: a Narrative of Discovery and Invention . . . with an Account of recent exploring expeditions by J. M. Wilson,' 1853, 8vo. 4. 'Pictorial History of the United States of America to the close of Pres. Taylor's Admin. . . . with Additions and Corrections by H. C. Watson,' illustrated, Boston, Massachusetts, 1861, 8vo.

[Literary Gazette, 7 March and 11 April 1846; Ann. Reg. 1846, App. to Chron. pp. 243, 244; Irving's Book of Scotsmen; Cat. of Living Authors, 1816; Men of the Reign; Journ. Roy. Geog. Soc. vol. xvi. p. xl.] G. Le G. N.

MURRAY, JAMES (*d.* 1592), of Pardewis, author of the placards against Bothwell, was third son of Sir William Murray of Tullibardine, by Katherine, daughter of Sir Duncan Campbell of Glenurchy. He was a younger brother of Sir William Murray of Tullibardine [q. v.], comptroller. On 24 Aug. 1564 Mary queen of Scots wrote to Elizabeth for a passport for him to trade with England for the space of one year (*Cal. State Papers*, For. Ser. 1564–5, entry 632). The real purpose of the pass seems, however, to have been to permit him to proceed on a private embassy of the queen of Scots to France. In February 1565 he returned from France as a messenger from Bothwell to the queen in regard to the conditions of Bothwell's return to Scotland (*ib.* entry 1017), and on 30 May a pass was obtained for him to go back again through England to France (*ib.* entry 1207).

Notwithstanding his previous relations with Bothwell, Murray, after the murder of Darnley, became his determined enemy. When the privy council on 12 Feb. published a proclamation announcing a reward of two thousand merks Scots for the discovery of the perpetrators of the crime, placards were on the 16th affixed on the Tolbooth declaring the murderers to be Bothwell, Sir James Balfour, and others. On the proclamation of a reward for the name of the person who had issued the placards, another was affixed in which the author expressed his willingness to disclose himself and to make good his accusation, provided the money were placed in an honest man's hands. In March Murray announced that he was the author of the placards (Drury to Cecil, 21 March 1567, *ib.* entry 1034), and on 14 March an order was issued by the privy council to prevent him leaving the country (*Reg. P. C. Scotl.* i. 500). Nevertheless Murray succeeded in escaping arrest, and even offered to furnish proofs at the trial of Bothwell of the guilt of Bothwell and his accomplices, provided his own safety were guaranteed, but the queen declined to agree to these conditions (Drury to Cecil, 27 March and 2 April, *Cal. State Papers*, For. Ser. 1566–8, entries 1052 and

1060). Murray also expressed his readiness to accept Bothwell's challenge after the trial, placards being affixed to the Tolbooth to this effect in his name. Should Bothwell decline to meet him on the ground of his rank, he further declared his readiness, with other five gentlemen, to 'prove by the law of arms that six of his followers were with him at that foul and barbarous murder' (Kirkcaldy to Bedford, entry 1034; BUCHANAN, *History of Scotland*, bk. xviii.) Murray also renewed at Carberry Hill his challenge to fight Bothwell [see under MURRAY, SIR WILLIAM, of Tullibardine].

In 1572 Murray married his first wife, Maria, daughter of Sir Simon Preston. On 20 Dec. 1574 he had a grant of the lands of Dowald in Strathearn, Perthshire (*Reg. Mag. Sig.* 1546–80, entry 2342), and on 17 April 1582 he and his second wife Agnes Lindsay had a grant of the lands of Tunygask, Fifeshire (*ib.* 1580–93, entry 392). During the ascendency of Arran he was summoned before the council, and declining to appear he was on 12 May 1584 denounced a rebel (*Reg. P. C. Scotl.* iii. 665), and at a parliament held the ensuing August sentence of forfeiture was passed against him (CALDERWOOD, *History*, iv. 198), his lands of Dowald being on 8 Oct. conferred on David Beton (*Reg. Mag. Sig.* 1580–93, entry 742). On account, however, of the return of the banished lords from England, and the consequent fall of Arran, the sentence remained inoperative. Murray died in September 1592, and left by his second wife Agnes Lindsay, besides other children, a son John, who succeeded him (*ib.* 1593–1608, entry 418).

[Reg. Mag. Sig. Scot.; Reg. P. C. Scotl.; Cal. State Papers, For. Ser. reign of Elizabeth; Hists. of Calderwood and Buchanan; Douglas's Scots' Peerage (ed. Wood, rev. by Paul), 1904.] T. F. H.

MURRAY, SIR JAMES, LORD PHILIPHAUGH (1655–1708), of Philiphaugh, lord clerk register of Scotland, eldest son of Sir John Murray of Philiphaugh, by Anne, daughter of Sir Archibald Douglas of Cavers, was born in 1655. As member for Selkirkshire he sat in the convention of estates which assembled at Edinburgh 26 June 1678, and he was chosen member for the same county in 1681. He was also sheriff of Selkirk in succession to his father. On 18 Nov. 1680 he and Urquhart of Meldrum, a commander of the king's troops, brought complaints against each other before the privy council. Murray asserted that Urquhart had sought to interfere with his jurisdiction as sheriff and had threatened him with imprisonment, while Urquhart accused Murray of remissness in taking proceedings against the covenanters, and of declining to supply him with a list of those concerned in the rebellion. As power had only been granted to Urquhart to act as justice of the peace, and not to sit alone as magistrate, he had exceeded his prerogatives in interfering with the duties of Murray as sheriff, but the council declined to affirm that he had acted beyond his powers (LAUDER OF FOUNTAINHALL, *Historical Notices*, p. 277). On 21 Jan. 1681 the case was again brought before the council, and finally, on 6 Oct., the council found that Murray had 'malversed and been remiss in punishing conventicles,' and therefore they simply deprived him of his right of sheriffship of Selkirk, it not being heritable, but bought by King Charles from his father, and declared it was devolved in the king's hands to give it to any other (*ib.* p. 331). According to Lauder some said that 'seeing the Duchess of Lauderdale's courtship, by which he had stood, was now dried up, he came well off that he was not likewise fined' (*ib.*)

After the discovery of the Rye House plot Murray was, in September 1684, committed to prison. Being brought before the council on the 6th, and threatened with the boots, he made a confession and threw himself on the mercy of Queensberry (*ib.* p. 556), and on 1 Oct. he was liberated on bail of 1,000*l.* to appear when called (*ib.* p. 561). Subsequently, on application to the king, he and others received pardon, with the view of their testimony being used against the chief contrivers of the Rye House plot. He was a witness against Robert Baillie of Jerviswood [q. v.] on 23 Dec. 1684, and also against the Earl of Tarras on 5 and 6 Jan. 1685. His evidence was also adduced against Patrick Hume, first earl of Marchmont [q. v.], Pringle of Torwoodlie, and others, against whom sentence of forfeiture was passed in their absence.

After the revolution Murray was, on 28 Oct. 1689, made an ordinary lord of session, with the title Lord Philiphaugh, and he took his seat on 1 Nov. Subsequently he became the close political associate of James Douglas, second duke of Queensberry [q. v.], and he is described by George Lockhart as 'by very far the most sufficient and best man he trusted and advised with' (*Papers*, i. 61; cf. CARSTARES, *State Papers*, pp. 381–4). On 3 Oct. 1698 Queensberry wrote to William Carstares expressing a wish that 'when his Majesty shall think to dispose of the other places now vacant' Philiphaugh might be made lord justice clerk, adding that 'besides being well qualified for the office' he had placed him under such obligation as he could 'in no other wise requite than by using his interest for his advancement' (*ib.*

p. 452). The application was, however, unsuccessful. In 1700 Philiphaugh wrote several letters to Carstares in regard to the state of political feeling in Scotland, and urging the advisability of the king paying Scotland a visit in order to tranquillise matters (*ib.* passim). On 17 July 1701 the Duke of Argyll in a letter to Carstares, recounting his difficulties in persuading Queensberry to adopt measures for gaining over Lord Whitelaw, wrote: 'But alas! still Philiphaugh is the burden of his song, and, to speak in Jocky terms, he is his dead weight' (*ib.* p. 697).

After the accession of Queen Anne Philiphaugh was appointed clerk-register, in succession to the Earl of Seafield, 21 Nov. 1702. According to George Lockhart, when Queensberry in 1703 informed Philiphaugh of the difficulties which his agreement with the Jacobites had brought him into with Argyll and others, Philiphaugh informed him that he had brought them upon himself by having 'dealings with such a pack' [Argyll and his friends] (*Papers*, i. 62). It is quite clear that Philiphaugh exerted all his influence to induce Queensberry to join the cavalier party, a fact which sufficiently explains the encomiums passed on him by Lockhart. The removal of Queensberry from office, on account of his imprudent negotiations with Simon Fraser, twelfth lord Lovat [q. v.], which resulted in the so-called Queensberry plot, led to Philiphaugh being superseded as clerk-register in June 1704 by James Johnston [q. v.] Lockhart, however, states that Philiphaugh was one of the agents in negotiating that 'the examination of the plot should not be pushed to any length,' provided the Duke of Queensberry's friends would join the cavaliers in opposing the succession and other measures of the court (*ib.* p. 98). When Queensberry was restored to office in 1705 Philiphaugh was on 1 June also restored to his office of clerk-register. He died at Inch 1 July 1708.

By his first wife, Anne, daughter of Hepburn of Blackcastle, he had no issue. By his second wife, Margaret, daughter of Sir Alexander Don of Newton, he had three sons and five daughters. He was succeeded by his eldest son, John. Macky describes Philiphaugh as of 'fair complexion, fat, middle-sized.' He also states that he was of 'clever natural parts,' and 'notwithstanding of that unhappy step of being an evidence to save his life,' he 'continued still a great countryman.'

[Lauder of Fountainhall's Historical Notices; Carstares's State Papers; Lockhart Papers; Macky's Memoirs; Brunton and Haig's Senators of the College of Justice; Douglas's Scots' Peerage; Brown's Hist. of Selkirkshire.] T. F. H.

MURRAY, JAMES (1702–1758), dissenting divine, born at Dunkeld, Perthshire, in 1702, was educated at Marischal College, Aberdeen, and having obtained presbyterian ordination removed to London, and for some years was assistant minister at Swallow Field Presbyterian Church, Piccadilly. He was not popular, and eventually retired, but found a patron in the Duke of Atholl, with whom he resided until his death in 1758. He published 'Aletheia; or a System of Moral Truths,' London, 1747, 2 vols. 12mo.

[New and Gen. Biog. Dict. 1798, xi. 142; Wilson's Hist. and Antiq. Dissenting Churches, iv. 48.] J. M. R.

MURRAY, JAMES, second Duke of Atholl (1690–1764), lord privy seal, born 28 Sept. 1690, was third son of John, second marquis and first duke of Atholl [q. v.], by Lady Katherine Hamilton. On 1 Jan. 1711–2 he was made captain-lieutenant of the 1st footguards (king's company) and on 14 June 1714 captain and lieutenant-colonel. On the attainder in 1716 of his elder brother, William, marquis of Tullibardine [q. v.], for taking part in the rebellion, an act was passed by parliament vesting the family honours and estates in him as the next heir. Lord James joined the Duke of Argyll at Perth in January - February 1716, and marched with him in pursuit of the Jacobites to Aberdeen. He then went to London (cf. *Hist. MSS. Comm.* 12th Rep. App. pt. viii. pp. 70–1). At the election of 1715 he had been chosen M.P. for Perthshire, and he was rechosen in 1722. He succeeded to the peerage on the death of his father in 1724; and in 1733 an act of parliament was passed to explain and extend the act of 1716, by providing that the attainder of William, marquis of Tullibardine, should not extend to prevent any descent of honour and estate to James, duke of Atholl, and his issue, or to any of the issue or heirs male of John, late duke of Atholl, other than the said William Murray and his issue. In June of the same year he was made lord privy seal in room of Lord Islay, and on 21 Sept. he was chosen a representative peer. He was rechosen in 1734, when he was invested with the order of the Thistle. As maternal great-grandson of James Stanley, seventh earl of Derby [q. v.], Atholl, on the death of James, tenth earl of Derby, in 1736, succeeded to the sovereignty of the Isle of Man, and to the ancient barony of Strange of Knockyn, Wotton, Mohun, Burnel, Basset, and Lacy. From 1737 to the general election of 1741 he sat in parliament both as an English baron and as a Scottish representative peer.

On the approach of the highland army after the landing of the prince in 1745, Atholl fled southwards, and his elder brother, the Marquis of Tullibardine, took possession of the castle of Blair. Atholl, however, joined the army of the Duke of Cumberland in England, and, arriving with him in Edinburgh on 30 Jan. 1746, went northwards. On 9 Feb. he sent a summons to his vassals to attend at Dunkeld and Kirkmichael and join the king's troops (*ib.* p. 72). On 6 April 1763 Atholl resigned the office of privy seal on being appointed keeper of the great seal in room of Charles Douglas (1698–1778), duke of Queensberry and Dover. He was also at the same time made lord justice general. He died at Dunkeld on 8 Jan. 1764, in his seventy-fourth year.

By his first wife, Jean, widow of James Lannoy of Hammersmith, youngest daughter of Thomas Frederick, son and heir-apparent of Sir John Frederick, knight, alderman of London, he had two sons and two daughters. The sons died in infancy. Of the daughters, Jean married John, first earl of Crawford; and Charlotte, who survived her sister, and inherited on her father's death in 1764 the barony of Strange and the sovereignty of the Isle of Man, married in 1753 John Murray, third duke of Atholl [q. v.], eldest son of Lord George Murray [q. v.] By his second wife, Jane, daughter of John Drummond of Megginch, the second duke had no issue. This lady was the heroine of Dr. Austin's song 'For lack of gold she left me, oh!' She had jilted the doctor for the duke.

[Histories of the Rebellions in 1715 and 1745; Hist. MSS. Comm. 12th Rep. App. pt. viii.; Douglas's Scots' Peerage (ed. Wood, rev. by Paul), 1904.] T. F. H.

MURRAY, JAMES (1732–1782), author of 'Sermons to Asses,' was descended from a respectable family at Fans, near Earlstown, Berwickshire, where it is believed he was born in 1732. He studied at the university of Edinburgh, and his certificate from Dr. Hamilton, the professor of divinity, is dated 28 April 1760. Shortly afterwards he went to Mouson, near Belford, Northumberland, as private tutor to the family of William Weddell, esq., and in 1761 he became assistant to John Sayers, minister of the Bondgate meeting-house at Alnwick. Disagreements arose, and he was dismissed, but a large proportion of the congregation formed themselves into a separate community, built a chapel in Bailiffgate Square, and ordained him their minister. He was not ordained to the pastoral charge by any presbytery, as he held that every congregation was at liberty to adopt such modes of government as seemed most conducive to their religious improvement. In early life he was presented with the freedom of Kelso, for some services he had rendered to that town.

In 1764 Murray removed to Newcastle-on-Tyne, where he had numerous friends, many of whom belonged to the Silver Street meeting-house. His followers chose him to be their pastor, and built the High Bridge Chapel. There Murray laboured with great zeal during the remainder of his life. He was extremely active in opposing Sir George Saville's bill for the removal of certain catholic disabilities, and published 'News from the Pope to the Devil,' 1781, and 'Popery not Christianity,' an evening lecture, besides attacking the catholics in several papers which appeared in the 'Protestant Packet.' He was also strongly opposed to the American war, and delivered many political lectures condemnatory of the administration of Lord North. He died at Newcastle on 28 Jan. 1782. He married Sarah Weddell of Mouson (she died 1798), and left several children.

Thomas Bewick, the engraver, says Murray was 'a most cheerful, facetious, sensible, pleasant man—a most agreeable companion, full of anecdote and information; keen in his remarks, though he carefully refrained from hurting the feelings of any of the company.' His best known work was 'Sermons to Asses' (anon.), London, 1768, 8vo. This satirical work he dedicated to 'the very excellent and reverend Messrs. G. W., J. W., W. R., and M. M.,' observing that 'there are no persons in Britain so worthy of a dedication of a work of this kind as yourselves.' The initials referred to George Whitfield, John Wesley, William Romaine, and Martin Madan [q. v.] To a similar category belongs 'Sermons to Doctors in Divinity,' being the second volume of 'Sermons to Asses;' 'Sermons to Men, Women, and Children, by the author of "Sermons to Asses,"' Newcastle, 1768, 8vo; and 'New Sermons to Asses,' London, 1773, 8vo, reprinted as 'Seven New Sermons to Asses,' 1796.

Murray's other works are: 1. 'The History of Religion, particularly of the different Denominations of Christians. By an Impartial Hand.' 2nd edit. 4 vols, London, 1764, 8vo. 2. 'Select Discourses upon several important Subjects,' Newcastle, 1765, 8vo, 2nd edit. 1768. 3. 'An Essay on Redemption by Jesus Christ,' Newcastle, 1768, 8vo. 4. 'Rudiments of the English Tongue, or the Principles of English Grammar,' 2nd edit. Newcastle, 1771, 12mo. 5. 'A History of the Churches in England and Scotland, from the Reformation to the present Time. By a Clergyman,' 3 vols., Newcastle, 1771–2, 8vo. 6. 'The Travels of the Imagination, a true Journey from Newcastle to London in a Stage Coach, with Observations upon the Metropolis. By J. M.,' London, 1773, 8vo; 2nd edit., London, 1828, 8vo. 7. 'ΕΙΚΩΝ ΒΑΣΙΛΙΚΗ, or the Character of Eglon, King of Moab, and his Ministry, wherein is demonstrated the Advantage of Christianity in the exercise of Civil Government,' Newcastle, 1773. 8. 'Lectures to Lords Spiritual, or an Advice to the Bishops concerning Religious Articles, Tithes, and Church Power. With a Discourse on Ridicule,' London, 1774, 12mo. 9. 'A grave Answer to Mr. [John] Wesley's calm Address to our American Colonies. By a Gentleman of Northumberland,' 1775. 10. 'Lectures upon the most remarkable Characters and Transactions recorded in the Book of Genesis,' 2 vols. Newcastle, 1777, 12mo. 11. 'The Magazine of Ants, or Pismire Journal,' Newcastle, 1777, 8vo. 12. 'Lectures on Genius,' 2 vols. 1777, 8vo. 13. 'Lectures upon the Book of the Revelation of John the Divine,' 2 vols. Newcastle, 1778, 12mo. 14. 'The New Maid of the Oaks, a Tragedy, as lately acted near Saratoga . . . By Ahab Salem,' London, 1778, 8vo (cf. Baker, *Biog. Dram.* 1812, iii. 79). 15. 'An Impartial History of the present War in America,' 2 vols., Newcastle [1778], 8vo, and again [1780], 8vo. 16. 'Sermons to Ministers of State,' Newcastle, 1781, 12mo. 17. 'Sermons for the General Fast Day,' London, 1781, 8vo. 18. 'The Fast, a Poem.' 19. 'A Course of Lectures on the Philosophy of the Human Mind.' This and the three following works were left in manuscript. 20. 'Lectures on the Book of Job.' 21. 'A Journey through Cumberland and the Lakes.' 22. 'A Journey to Glasgow.'

In 1798 R. Smith, bookseller of Paisley, republished his 'Sermons to Doctors in Divinity,' 'Lectures to Lords Spiritual,' 'An Evening Lecture delivered in 1780,' and 'An Address to the Archbishops and Bishops.' William Hone republished the 'Sermons to Asses,' 1817, 'Sermons to Doctors in Divinity,' 1817, 'Sermons to Ministers of State,' 1817, 'New Sermons to Asses,' 1817, and 'Lectures to Lords Spiritual,' 1818. These he collected together in one volume, with a portrait of the author and an original sketch of his life. Murray was one of the principal editors of the 'Freeman's Magazine, or the Constitutional Repository,' Newcastle, 1774.

His portrait, prefixed to the 'History of the American War,' was painted by Van Cook, and engraved by Pollard. Though not a very good likeness, it is better than that given by Hone. There is also an engraved portrait prefixed to the second edition of 'Travels of the Imagination.'

[Memoir prefixed to Travels of the Imagination, 1828; Evans's Cat. of Engraved Portraits, No. 7538; Lowndes's Bibl. Man. (Bohn), p. 1636; Mackenzie's Hist. of Newcastle-upon-Tyne, i. 387; Notes and Queries, 2nd ser. xii. 292, 3rd ser. vii. 479; Scots Mag. 1782, p. 111; Watt's Bibl. Brit.] T. C.

MURRAY, JAMES (1719?–1794), general, governor of Quebec and of Minorca, born about 1719, was fifth son of Alexander, fourth lord Elibank, and his wife Elizabeth, daughter of George Stirling, surgeon, and M.P. for Edinburgh city. He was brother of Henry Murray, fifth lord Elibank, and of Alexander Murray (1723–1777) [q. v.] There is some ambiguity in the date of his first commission, as there are several officers of the name undistinguishable in the entry and commission books. Probably he was the James Murray who, on 2 Feb. 1740, was appointed second lieutenant in Wynyard's marines (*Home Office Military Entry Book*, xviii. 12). Henry Murray was lieutenant-colonel of that regiment. In a memorial to Ligonier in 1758 James Murray states that he had then served nearly twenty years as a commissioned officer, and had been present with the 15th foot throughout all its service in the West Indies, Flanders, and Brittany during the last war (*Addit. MS.* 21628, f. 302). These services included the Carthagena expedition and subsequent operations in the east of Cuba, the defence of Ostend in 1745 by a mixed force of British and Austrians under Count Chanclos, and the L'Orient expedition of 1748 (Cannon, *Hist. Rec. 15th Foot*). At L'Orient Murray was captain of the grenadier company of the 15th, which attacked the French with great gallantry when many of the other troops shamefully misbehaved. Murray became major in the 15th in Ireland in the following year, and on 5 Jan. 1751 purchased the lieutenant-colonelcy. He commanded the regiment in the Rochfort expedition of 1757, and was a witness for the defence at the ensuing trial of Sir John Mordaunt (1697–1780) [q. v.] He took the regiment out to America in 1757, and commanded a brigade at the siege of Louisburg, Cape Breton, in 1758. Wolfe wrote to Lord George Sackville, afterwards Germain, from Louisburg: 'Murray, my old antagonist, has acted with infinite spirit. The public is much indebted to him for great services in advancing . . . this siege' (*Hist. MSS. Comm.* 9th Rep. pt. iii. p. 76 *a*). Murray was one of the three brigadiers (Monckton and Townshend were the other two) under Wolfe in the expedition against Quebec. Wolfe appears to have had a high opinion of Murray, and singled him out for the most hazardous exploits of the campaign (Wright, *Life of Wolfe*, p. 501). Murray commanded the left wing of the army in the battle on the Plain of Abraham, 13 Sept. 1759, where Wolfe fell. The city surrendered on 18 Sept., when a council of war decided on its retention. Murray was left there with four thousand troops, while the rest of the army sailed away with the fleet, before the navigation of the St. Lawrence should be closed for the season. Murray spent the winter of 1759–1760 in active preparations for an expected siege, and his difficulties were numerous (cf. his manuscript journal from September 1759 to May 1760, printed by the Historical Society of Quebec in 1870). He was without funds, which had to be raised at 5 per cent. on the note of hand of the two senior officers; drunkenness and thieving were rife among the soldiers, and had to be met by special measures; sickness was very prevalent. Knox, who was one of the garrison, says that during the first nine months of the occupation they buried a thousand men, and had a daily average of an equal number sick, chiefly of scurvy (Knox, *Hist. Account*, vol. ii.) Murray established a number of outposts round the city, repaired the defences, and mounted 132 pieces of cannon of all sorts upon them. On 26 April 1760 the French commander, De Levis, landed in the vicinity with a very superior force, and was menacing the outposts at Lorette and St. Foix. On 28 April Murray marched out with two thousand men and twenty guns, and attacked the French at Sillery with great vigour, driving their first line in upon the second, and inflicting very heavy loss. The audacity of the attack with a force so inferior surprised the French; but the British were outnumbered three to one, and after losing one-third of their number were driven back into the city, which was forthwith besieged by an army of fifteen thousand men. A plan of the battle, showing the country round about Quebec, is in the British Museum (*Addit. MS.* 21686, ff. 61, 81). Walpole repeats the version of the affair current in London—that Murray 'got into a mistake and a morass, and was enclosed, embogged, and defeated' (Walpole, *Letters*, iii. 317). The French batteries did not open upon the city until 11 May, and on 15 May De Levis, disheartened by the arrival in the St. Lawrence of a naval squadron under Lord Colville, and the destruction of the French ships by some of the advanced frigates, raised the siege and retired precipitately to Montreal, where he joined the troops under De Vaudreuil. In accordance with orders from General Amherst [see Amherst, Jeffrey, Lord Amherst], Murray embarked on 10 June 1760 with all his remaining effective troops, 2,500 in all, for Montreal, the only place of importance in Canada remaining in the hands of the French, whither columns from New York under Amherst, and from Crown Point under Colonel William Haviland [q. v.], were converging. After a tedious voyage Murray landed on the island of Montreal on 7 Sept., Haviland arrived the same evening, and Amherst the next day. On 13 Sept. 1760 De Vaudreuil's troops, which included all the French troops remaining in the country, laid down their arms, and the dominion of Canada passed to the victors.

Murray was appointed governor of Quebec 27 Oct. 1760 (*War Office, Privy Council*, p. 21). He had been made colonel-commandant of a battalion of the 60th royal Americans 18 Oct. 1759, and was promoted to major-general 10 July 1762. He was accused of harshness in his government, and his severity was contrasted with the conduct of General Thomas Gage (1721–1787) [q. v.], in command at Montreal. A report of his government by Murray in 1762 is in the British Museum (Addit. MS. 21667). When Canada was finally ceded to Great Britain on the peace of 1763, Murray was appointed on 21 Nov. that year governor of Canada, a position he held till 1766. In September of the same year he suppressed, without resorting to extreme measures, a dangerous mutiny of the troops at Quebec, who, in consequence of a stoppage of supplies, threatened to march to New York and lay down their arms to General Amherst. During Murray's administration the forms of government and the laws to be observed in the new colony were promulgated; but his efforts to alleviate the discontent of the conquered population met with only partial success. Representatives of the people were summoned to Quebec by the government in 1765; but the attempt to form a representative assembly failed, owing, it is said, to the objection of the Roman catholics to the test-oath imposed by statute. Murray's efforts to conciliate the French Canadians incensed the British settlers, who accused him of sacrificing their interests to French prejudices, and petitioned for his recall. An inquiry in the House of Lords after his return home in 1766 fully absolved Murray from these charges. His last years in Canada were troubled by the uprising of the Indian tribes in the west, known as the Conspiracy of Pontiac.

After his retirement from Canada in 1766, Murray was for a time on the Irish staff. He was transferred from the royal Americans to the colonelcy of the 13th foot in 1767, became a lieutenant-general 25 May 1772, and in 1774 was appointed governor of Minorca, in succession to Sir George Howard [q. v.] When war broke out with Spain, in 1779, a lieutenant-governor was added to the establishment of the island, in the person of Sir William Draper, K.B. [q. v.], between whom and Murray there was want of accord from the first, and afterwards open rupture. In 1781 Minorca was threatened with a siege. Murray sent off his wife and family to Leghorn, and, shutting himself up in Fort St. Philip, prepared for a vigorous defence. On 20 Aug. he was blockaded by a force of sixteen thousand French and Spaniards under the Duc de Crillon. Murray's garrison consisted of 2,016 regular troops, four hundred of them being invalids ('worn-out soldiers'), and all the troops more or less unhealthy, and two hundred seamen from the Minorca sloop of war, which had been scuttled and sunk at the mouth of the harbour to bar the entrance. Despairing of reducing the place, which had very extensive bomb-proof cover, De Crillon secretly offered Murray a bribe of a million sterling to surrender. Murray spurned the insult. 'When your brave ancestor,' he wrote back to De Crillon under date 16 Oct. 1781, 'was desired by his sovereign to assassinate the Duc de Guise, he returned the answer that you should have done when you were charged to assassinate the character of a man whose birth is as illustrious as your own or that of the Duc de Guise. I can have no further communication with you except in arms. If you have any humanity, pray send clothing for your unfortunate prisoners in my possession. Leave it at a distance to be taken for them, as I will admit of no contact for the future but such as is hostile to the most inveterate degree.' De Crillon replied: 'Your letter restores each of us to our place; it confirms the high opinion I always had of you. I accept your last proposal with pleasure.' On 5 Feb. 1782 Murray's garrison was so reduced by the ravages of scurvy that only six hundred men remained fit for duty, and of these five hundred were tainted with the disease. 'Such was the uncommon spirit of the king's troops that they concealed their disorder and inability rather than go into hospital; several men died on guard after having stood on sentry, their fate not being discovered till called upon for the relief' (Murray's despatch, see *Ann. Reg.* 1782, chap. x.) A capitulation was arranged, and the remnant of the garrison, six hundred old and decrepit soldiers, two hundred seamen, a hundred and twenty artillerymen, and forty-five Corsicans, Greeks, Turks, Moors, and Jews marched out between two lines of fourteen thousand French and Spanish troops, and laid down their arms on the glacis of George Town, declaring 'they surrendered to God alone, as the victors could not plume themselves on taking a hospital' (*ib.*) After the return home of the troops Sir William Draper preferred a number of miscellaneous charges against Murray—twenty-nine in all—alleging waste of public money and stores, extortion, rapacity, cruelty, &c. Murray was tried by a general court-martial presided over by Sir George Howard, which sat at the Horse Guards in November–December 1782 and January 1783. Contemporary accounts of the trial describe Murray—'Old Minorca' he was nicknamed—as 'looking very broken, but with all the remains of a very stout man, and quite the old soldier.' The court fully and honourably acquitted Murray of all the charges preferred against him except two of trivial import—some interference with auction-dues in the island, and the issue of an order derogatory to his lieutenant-governor—for which it sentenced him to be reprimanded. On the proceedings being submitted to him, the king 'was pleased to approve of the zeal, courage, and firmness with which General Murray had conducted himself in the defence of Fort St. Philip, as well as of his former long and approved services.' The reprimand was dispensed with, and the king further expressed 'his concern that an officer like Sir William Draper should have allowed his judgment to become so perverted as to bring such charges against his superior. Lest some intemperate expressions of Draper should lead to a duel, the court dictated an apology to be signed by Draper, which, after some difficulty, was acquiesced in by Murray. Immediately afterwards a Mr. Sutherland brought an action against Murray for illegal suspension from the office of judge of the vice-admiralty court in Minorca. Murray had offered to reinstate Sutherland on his making a certain apology. The matter had been referred home, and the king had approved Murray's action; but a jury, the king's approval notwithstanding, found that Murray had acted arbitrarily and unreasonably, and gave damages against him to the amount of 5,000*l.* Baron Eyre declared that it never occurred to any lawyer to question the verdict (*Term Reports*, p. 538). On 6 May

1785, on a division by 57 ayes against 22 noes, the House of Commons decided that the damages and Murray's costs be paid out of the public money.

Murray, who was made a full general 19 Feb. 1783, and colonel of the 21st fusiliers 5 June 1789, and was governor of Hull, died at his residence, Beauport House, near Battle, Sussex, 18 June 1794, 'aged 75.' A portrait, engraved by J. S. Weele, is mentioned by Bromley.

A namesake predeceased him by a few weeks, Major-general James Murray, M.P., colonel 72nd foot and governor of Fort William, who died 19 April 1794 (see obituary notice in *Gent. Mag.* 1794, pt. i. p. 384, in which he is wrongly entitled the 'Honble.' James Murray).

Murray was twice married: first, to Cordelia, eldest daughter of John Collier of Hastings (*d.* at Beauport House, in 1779, without issue); secondly, to Anne, daughter of Abraham Witham, consul-general of Majorca, by whom he had three daughters and one son, Major-general James Patrick Murray, C.B., sometime M.P. for Yarmouth, who, born in 1782, was disabled by a wound at the passage of the Douro in 1809, and died at Killineure, near Athlone, Ireland, 5 Dec. 1834 (*Nav. and Mil. Gaz.* 13 Dec. 1834).

[Foster's Peerage under 'Elibank;' biographies in Douglas's Scots' Peerage (ed. Wood, rev. by Paul), 1904, and Appleton's Encycl. Amer. Biog. Also Cannon's Hist. Rec. 15th Cambridgeshire Reg., Beatson's Naval and Military Memoirs, Knox's Hist. Account of the Campaign in America (London, 1769), Wright's Life of Wolfe, Parkman's Montcalm and Wolfe (London, 1884), Parkman's Conspiracy of Pontiac (London, 1851), Ann. Registers under dates, Calendars of State Papers, Home Office, 1760–6 and 1766–9, Proceedings of Court-martial, printed from Gurney's shorthand notes, and Draper's reply, printed separately, Walpole's Letters, chiefly vol. viii. Many papers relating to Murray's administration of Canada and of Minorca are in the Public Record Office, London. Murray's general orders, instructions, correspondence with the ministers, &c., when in America, are among the British Museum Addit. MSS., chiefly in the Haldimand and Newcastle Papers; but the indexing under Murray's name in the Haldimand collection is somewhat misleading. His papers are bound up with those of other general officers, covering the period 1758–78, but do not extend beyond the period of his own American command, which ended in 1766. Later material must be sought in the Public Record Office. Numerous extracts from Murray's letters in the Marquis Townshend's MSS. are given in Hist. MSS. Comm. 11th Rep. pt. iv.; and the existence of a number of his letters among the Marquis of Landsdowne's MSS. is noted in the 5th Report.] H. M. C.

MURRAY (afterwards **MURRAY PULTENEY**), Sir **JAMES** (1751?–1811), seventh baronet of Clermont, Fifeshire, general, was only son of Sir Robert Murray, sixth baronet, by his first wife, Janet, daughter of the fourth Lord Elibank, and half-brother of Sir John Murray, afterwards eighth baronet of Clermont [q. v.] James was gazetted on 30 April 1771 to a company in the 57th foot, then in Ireland, and succeeded his father in the baronetcy in the same year. He went with his regiment to America, as part of the reinforcements under Lord Cornwallis, in December 1775; took part in the unsuccessful attempt on Charleston, South Carolina, in the following year, and was afterwards engaged in various minor expeditions about New York. On 19 May 1778 Murray was promoted to a majority in the 4th king's own foot. He accompanied that regiment to the West Indies, and commanded a provisional battalion of light companies at the capture of St. Lucia the same year. The 4th returned home from Antigua in 1780, and Murray, who became a brevet lieutenant-colonel 6 Feb., was on 2 March appointed lieutenant-colonel of the 94th foot (second of the five regiments which in succession bore their number). When the 94th was disbanded on the peace of 1783, Murray was placed on half-pay. In 1789 he was made aide-de-camp to the king, and in 1790 became a major-general. He was adjutant-general to the Duke of York in Flanders in 1793–4, and was repeatedly sent on diplomatic missions.

Murray assumed the name of Pulteney on his marriage, July 1794, with Henrietta Laura Pulteney, baroness Bath. The lady was daughter of Sir William Johnstone, afterwards Johnstone-Pulteney, baronet of Westerhall, Dumfriesshire, by his first wife, the daughter and sole heir of Daniel Pulteney, first cousin of the first Earl of Bath. As Miss Pulteney, Pulteney's wife is said to have been at one time engaged to Charles James Fox. On succeeding after her mother's death to the Bath estates, she was created Baroness Bath in her own right, 26 July 1792, and 26 Oct. 1803 was advanced to the dignity of countess in her own right. Her father, who was M.P. for Weymouth, and is described in the journals of the day as the richest commoner and the greatest holder of American stock ever known, died intestate in 1805, and the countess paid 6,000*l.* in stamp duties, the largest sum then on record, and took the bulk of his property (*Gent. Mag.* 1805, pt. i. p. 587). In the year of his marriage (1794) Pulteney was appointed colonel of the 18th royal Irish foot. He held a major-general's command in Ireland in 1798, became a lieutenant-general in 1799, and accompanied Sir Ralph Abercromby with the advance of the Duke of York's army to North Holland, where he was shot through the arm at the landing. He had odd ways, and Bunbury describes him as chuckling at having now been shot through both arms and both legs (Bunbury, *Narrative*, p. 47). Abercromby wrote of him, 'Sir James Pulteney surprised me. He showed ardour and intelligence, and did himself honour' (Dunfermline, *Life of Abercromby*, p. 174). In August 1800 Pulteney was sent with a body of troops against Ferrol. The troops were landed, the Spanish outposts driven in, and the heights above the port occupied; but Pulteney considered the place too strong to be taken except by a regular siege, which would afford time for the Spanish armies to move to its relief. Accordingly he re-embarked his troops. This gave great dissatisfaction, the naval officers of Sir John Borlase Warren's squadron holding that the place could easily have been carried. Sir John Moore afterwards told Bunbury that during a hasty reconnaissance in 1804 he saw enough to convince him that the place could not have been carried by a coup de main (Bunbury, *Narrative*, p. 73). Reinforced by additional troops, Pulteney then sailed away to Gibraltar with twenty thousand men. He was second in command under Sir Ralph Abercromby in the demonstration against Cadiz in October the same year; after which he proceeded to Lisbon with the troops enlisted for European service only. Most of these subsequently went to Malta, and Pulteney returned home. He stood proxy for Sir William Medows at an installation of the Bath in 1803. He held a lieutenant-general's command in Sussex, with his headquarters at Eastbourne, during the invasion alarms of 1803–4. His plans in the event of an invasion are given by Bunbury (*ib.* pp. 178-9).

Pulteney represented the combined boroughs of Weymouth and Melcombe Regis in successive parliaments from November 1790 until his death. A petition was lodged against his return in 1802, and referred to a committee, which reported that the petition was not frivolous and vexatious, although Murray was duly elected. He was secretary at war under the Grenville administration in 1806–7. In April 1811 a powder-flask burst in his hands and destroyed one of his eyes. No danger was at first apprehended, and his calm, unruffled temperament favoured recovery, but inflammation supervened and proved fatal. He died at Buckenham, a seat he rented in Norfolk, on 26 April 1811. He is stated to have left 600,000*l.* to his half-brother, Sir John Murray, who succeeded him as eighth baronet, and 200,000*l.* to another half-brother, the Rev. William Murray, who ultimately became ninth baronet (*Gent. Mag.* 1811, pt. i. p. 499). The Pulteney estates passed under the will of his wife, who had died at Brighton, 14 Aug. 1808, and had been buried beside her father in Westminster Abbey, to the children of Mrs. E. Markham, a daughter of Sir Richard Sutton, bart., and the divorced wife of a son of William Markham, D.C.L., archbishop of York.

Bunbury writes of Pulteney: 'He was a very odd man. In point of natural abilities he took high rank. He had seen a great deal of the world and of military service; he had read much and variously, and possessed a great fund of knowledge and considerable science. Remarkably good-tempered and unpretending, he was utterly indifferent to danger and to hardship.' He was, however, inclined to indecisive argument, and lacked confidence in his own opinion, while his awkward manners and 'a grotesque and rather repulsive exterior' concealed the best points in his character (Bunbury, *Narrative*, pp. 46–7).

[Foster's Baronetage, under 'Murray of Clermont;' Army Lists and London Gazettes; Jones's Hist. of the Campaigns in Flanders, also War Office Records in the Public Record Office, 'Correspondence with the Army on the Continent,' 1793–4; Bunbury's Narrative of Passages in the late War with France, London, 1854. A few notices of Murray will be found in the Journal and Correspondence of the first Lord Auckland.]

H. M. C.

MURRAY, JAMES (1831–1863), architect, born in Armagh on 9 Dec. 1831, was articled to W. Scott, architect, of Liverpool, in 1845, and afterwards practised there in partnership with T. D. Barry. He was for a time in Coventry, and subsequently settled in London, where and on the continent he executed several works in connection with E. Welby Pugin [q. v.] At the dissolution of this partnership he returned to Coventry, and resided there until his death, which took place on 24 Oct. 1863. Among his most important works are the Justice Rooms, Coventry, and the Corn Exchange of that town, 1856, of Banbury, 1857, and St. Albans, 1853, besides churches at Warwick, Boulton, Sunderland, Newcastle, St. James's, Stratford-on-Avon, Emscote, Birmingham, and Stortford; and a Gothic warehouse for Messrs. Bennoch in Silver Street, London (1857–8). He published 'Modern Architecture, Ecclesiastic, Civil, and Domestic;' 'Gothic and Classic Buildings erected since 1850,' pt. i. 4to, Coventry, 1862.

[The Builder, 1863, xxi. 780, 807; The Dictionary of Architecture, v. 146.]

A. N.

MURRAY, Sir JAMES (1788–1871), discoverer of fluid magnesia, born in co. Londonderry in 1788, was son of Edward Murray of that county. He studied medicine in Edinburgh and Dublin, and in 1807 became a licentiate of the College of Surgeons in Edinburgh, and in the following year was admitted a member of the Dublin college. In 1809 he married a Miss Sharrock, and seems to have settled down as a practising physician in Belfast. In 1817 he published a paper on 'The Danger of using Solid Magnesia, and on its great value in a Fluid State for internal use.' He gave much time and attention to the dissemination of his views on this subject, and is said to have taken out a patent, although it is not noticed in Woodcroft's 'Index of Patents.' In 1829 he graduated M.D. at Edinburgh University, and in the same year published his treatise on 'Heat and Humidity.' The success of this work led the Marquis of Anglesey, then lord-lieutenant of Ireland, to appoint him his resident physician and to knight him. In 1832 Murray was presented with the honorary degree of M.D. Dublin University. He secured an extensive practice in Dublin, and was continued in his post of resident physician by the Marquis of Normanby and Viscount Ebrington, and received the appointment of inspector of anatomy in Dublin, a post which he held nearly forty years. In 1834 he accompanied Lord Anglesey to Rome, and returned in the following year. He established a manufactory for fluid magnesia, which still benefits his descendants, and successfully prosecuted several firms for infringements of his patent. He formulated various theories, such as a system of dry cupping, a proposal for the prevention of cholera by the insertion of a layer of non-conducting material beneath the ground floors of dwelling-houses, and was probably the first to suggest electricity as a curative agent, in which he strongly believed. He also suggested the utilisation of atmospheric pressure in air-baths. His work on 'Cholera,' published in 1844, was translated into Italian. His death took place in Upper Temple Street, Dublin, on 8 Dec. 1871, at the age of eighty-four, and he was buried at Glasnevin. His son, John Fisher Murray [q. v.], predeceased him.

The following are Murray's most important works: 1. 'Dissertation on the Influence of Heat and Humidity, with Practical Observations on the Inhalation of Iodine,' 8vo, London, 1829. 2. 'Four Letters on the Relief of the Sick Poor in Ireland,' 8vo, Dublin, 1837. 3. 'Abstract of a Popular Lecture on Artificial Respiration,' 8vo, Dublin, 1838. 4. 'Observations on Fluid Magnesia,' 8vo, London, 1840. 5. 'Electricity as a Cause of Cholera or other Epidemics, and the Relation of Galvanism to the Action of Remedies,' 12mo, Dublin, 1849.

[Lancet, 16 Dec. 1871; Northern Whig, 13 Dec. 1871; Irish Times, 12 Dec. 1871; Brit. Mus. Cat.; private information.] D. J. O'D.

MURRAY, JOHN (*d.* 1510), laird of Falahill, the so-called 'outlaw' of the old border ballad, was the son of Patrick Murray, sixth of Falahill. The family trace their descent from Archibald de Moravia, who is mentioned in a chartulary of Newbottle in 1280, and swore fealty to Edward I in 1296, and whose son, Roger de Moravia, obtained in 1321 a charter of the lands of Falahill from James, lord Douglas, his superior. The so-called outlaw was included in 1484 in his father's lease of Lewinshop and Hangandschaw (*Exchequer Rolls of Scotland*, ix. 272). He was undoubtedly for many years on friendly terms with the Scottish kings. In 1489 he received from James II the gift of a horse of twenty angels value (*Accounts of the Lord High Treasurer*, i. 121), and on 9 Feb. 1488–9 the king conceded to him the lands of Greviston in Peebles (*Reg. Mag. Sig.* i. 1927). In a grant to him of the lands of Cranston Riddle on 5 Nov. 1497 he is called the king's 'familiaris armigerus' (*ib.* entry 2379). In 1501 he was made sheriff of Selkirk under Lord Erskine. On 29 Jan. 1508–9 he is mentioned as viscount deputy of Selkirkshire (*ib.* entry 3295), and on 30 Nov. 1509 he obtained a grant of the hereditary sheriffdom of Selkirk (*ib.* entry 3388). Besides his estates in Selkirkshire and the Lothians, he possessed a town house in Edinburgh, which he inherited from his uncle, who was rector of Hawick.

According to the ballad Murray had taken possession of Ettrick Forest in Selkirkshire with five hundred men, and declared his intention to hold it 'contrair all kings of Christentie.' When James IV set out against him with a large force, he called to his aid his kinsmen, Murray of Cockpool and Murray of Traquair; but on the approach of the royal force he expressed his willingness to own fealty to the king, on condition that he was made hereditary sheriff of the forest. Although there is no historical record of any expedition against him, not improbably the ballad commemorates some action taken by him to make good his claims to the sheriffdom. 'The tradition of Ettrick Forest,' says Sir Walter Scott, 'bears that the outlaw was a man of prodigious strength, possessing a baton or club, with which he laid lee the country for many miles round, and that he was at length slain by Buccleugh, or some of his clan, at a little mount covered with fir trees, adjoining Newark Castle, and said to have been part of a garden.' As a matter of fact Murray was slain in 1510 by Andrew Ker of Gateschaw and Thomas Scott, brother of Philip Scott of Aidschaw. By his wife Janet Forrester (*Exchequer Rolls*, x. 732, 757), widow of Schaw of Knockhill (*ib.* p. 727), he had, besides other children, four sons; John, who succeeded him; James, who succeeded John; William, ancestor of the Murrays of Romano; and Patrick, who became laird of Broadmeadows. It was his son John—not he, as usually stated—who was married to Lady Margaret Hepburn, daughter of the first Earl of Bothwell. The grandson of the 'outlaw,' Patrick Murray of Falahill, obtained on 28 Jan. 1528 the lands of Philiphaugh.

[Reg. Mag. Sig. Scot.; Exchequer Rolls of Scotland; Accounts of the Lord High Treasurer of Scotland; Sir Walter Scott's Minstrelsy of the Scottish Border; Brown's Hist. of Selkirkshire; Douglas's Scots' Peerage (ed. Wood, rev. by Paul), 1904.] T. F. H.

MURRAY or **MORAY, JOHN** (1575?–1632), Scottish divine, was the fourth son of Robert Moray of Abercairney, Perthshire, by his wife Catherine, daughter of William Murray of Tullibardine. He was a younger brother of Sir David Murray of Gorthy [q. v.] He studied at the university of Edinburgh, where he took the degree of M.A. on 10 Aug. 1595. On 15 Dec. 1597 he was presented to the parish of Borthwick, Midlothian, and in 1603 he was translated to South Leith second charge. When, in 1607, the act regarding the appointment of a permanent moderator was read in the presbytery of Edinburgh, Moray, according to Calderwood, 'proved so evidently that the said act was the overthrow of the liberty of the kirk, that none could confute his reasoning' (*History*, vi. 628). He was also a strong opponent of episcopacy, and sympathised with the ministers condemned to banishment at Linlithgow; he entertained them at Leith before they sailed to England, and thus incurred the special hostility of the bishops. A synodal sermon preached by him in 1607 on Galatians ii. 1 (*ib.* p. 690) brought matters to a crisis. Copies of this sermon had been given by him to David Hume (1560?–1630?) [q. v.] and others, and it was printed at London in 1608 without his knowledge or authority. A copy of the printed sermon was given by Bancroft, bishop of London, to the king, who ordered the secretary, Elphinstone, to inquire into the matter. On 25 Feb. 1608 Moray was brought before the council at the instance of the bishops, who presented certain articles of accusation against him (*ib.* pp. 691–9), but in the end the council 'favourably dismissed him, and sent him to his charge' (*ib.* p. 701). On 10 March the council sent a favourable presentation of his case to the king (*Reg. P. C. Scotl.* viii. 493); but on the 7th the king had expressed the desire that he should be 'exemplarily punished' (*ib.* p. 492), and on the 20th he sent them a severe rebuke for their leniency, and ordered them to forward him with speed 'some advertisement of the punishment of Mr. John Moray' (*ib.* p. 496). Orders were therefore given on 12 April for his apprehension, on account of his 'impertinent sermon' (*ib.* p. 72), and he was confined in the castle of Edinburgh, where he remained a prisoner for a year. On 5 March 1609 the king sent a letter to the council authorising his release, but ordering him to be sent to New Abbey in Nithsdale, and to confine himself within five miles of that town (*ib.* p. 563). At the instance of the bishops, his charge at Leith was also declared vacant, and David Lindsay (1566?–1627) [q. v.] inducted in his stead (Calderwood, vii. 18–20). Moray took up his residence at Dumfries, about four miles from New Abbey, where he stayed about a year and a half, preaching either in Dumfries or the church of Traquair (*ib.* p. 20), and afterwards, without license from the king or council, he settled with his family at Dysart. Six months afterwards he removed to Salt Preston (Prestonpans), Midlothian, where he preached every Sunday without challenge from the bishops (*ib.*) In 1614 he was admitted to the second charge of Dunfermline, and as he refused to acknowledge episcopacy or submit to the Articles of Perth, he, until 1618, fulfilled the duties of the charge without remuneration. About 1620 he was removed to the first charge, but on 12 Dec. 1621 he was summoned to answer before the Bishop of St. Andrews for nonconformity to the Articles of Perth (*ib.* p. 516), and as he failed to appear then or on 3 Jan. he was removed from his charge at Dunfermline, and ordered to confine himself within two miles of Fowlis Wester, his native parish in Strathearn (*ib.* p. 520). On 24 June 1624 he was summoned to appear before the privy council, but excused his attendance on account of an injury received by a fall from his horse, whereupon he was ordered to confine himself more strictly within the parish of Fowlis (*ib.* p. 614). His residence at Fowlis was Gorthy, which belonged to his elder brother Sir David. On Sir David's death in 1629 he again removed to Prestonpans. He died there in

January 1632. By his first wife, Margaret Leslie, daughter of John, master of Rothes, he had two children, who both died young. By his second wife, Mary Melville, he had a daughter Jean. Besides the sermon above alluded to, Moray was the author of 'A Dialogue between Cosmophilus and Theophilus anent the Urging of New Ceremonials upon the Church of Scotland,' 1620.

[Histories of Row and Calderwood; Livingstone's Remarkable Observations (Wodrow Society); Reg. P. C. Scotl.; Hew Scott's Fasti Eccles. Scot. i. 104, 266, ii. 566–7, 571; Douglas's Baronage.] T. F. H.

MURRAY, JOHN, first EARL OF ANNANDALE (*d.* 1640), was the seventh and youngest son of Sir Charles Murray of Cockpool, Dumfriesshire, and Margaret, eldest daughter of Hugh, fifth Lord Somerville. In early life he was introduced to the Scottish court by the Earl of Morton, and was appointed groom of the bedchamber to James VI, whom he accompanied to London in 1603 (*Register of the Privy Council*, vi. 773, viii. 594). He became one of James's most confidential servants, was made keeper of the privy purse, and after the king was disabled by a sore hand from signing documents, he had the custody of the 'cachet' or signature stamp used by the king. Among many other marks of the royal favour he received in 1605 a lease of the estate of Plumpton Park in the debateable lands. In the following year, and again in 1612, the abbacy of Dundrennan and other lands, with the castle of Lochmaben, were erected in his favour into the lordship of Lochmaben. On 28 June 1622 he was created Lord Murray of Lochmaben and Viscount Annand, and on 13 March 1624 Earl of Annandale, Viscount Annand, Lord Murray of Lochmaben and Tynninghame, while on 13 July 1625 his lands in Scotland were erected into the earldom of Annandale. In the patents King James makes grateful mention of the faithful services which John Murray of Renpatrick rendered him, even from his childhood, including 'arduous,' almost incredible labours' (*Annandale Peerage Minutes of Evidence*, 1877, pp. 293, 294). Gifts of English estates were also conferred upon him. He was, on 17 Sept. 1605, appointed keeper of Guildford Park for life, and it was at his residence there that Prince Charles (afterwards Charles I) slept on the night of his return from Spain in 1623 (*State Papers*, Dom. 1623–5 p. 93, 1625 p. 58). Annandale also received the escheats of Sir John Musgrave of Catterlen, Cumberland, in 1608, and of Sir Robert Dudley in 1610, and was lord of the barony of Langley, bearing the style of Baron of Langley (*ib.* 1622 p. 365, 1623–5 p. 22).

After the death of James VI in 1625, Annandale was continued in his office as groom of the bedchamber to Charles I, but complained of neglect. He was sent to Scotland in 1626 to explain Charles's delay in going thither to be crowned (*Hist. MSS. Comm.* 11th Rep. pt. i. p. 82). When Charles went to Scotland in 1633 he accompanied him, and at the meeting of the Scottish parliament was appointed constable of the palace, hill, and Lomonds of Falkland, with the moor adjacent called the Newpark. In 1636 he succeeded to the paternal estates of Cockpool, all his brothers having died before him without leaving lawful issue. Owing to his prominent position as a Scottish border peer, he was frequently engaged on commissions and judicial service in connection with the borders (FRASER, *Douglas Book*, iv. 376; *Book of Carlaverok*, ii. 3–129, passim). In 1638 he was sent to Scotland to assist Charles's party against the covenanters, and was one of the noblemen who swore the 'king's covenant' (GORDON, *Scots Affairs*, i. 108); but returning to London, he died there in September 1640. His body was embalmed, and was buried at Hoddam in Dumfriesshire.

Annandale married Elizabeth, daughter of Sir John Shaw, who was in the service of Queen Anne (*Hist. MSS. Comm.* 4th Rep., Appendix, p. 299), and by her he had a son, James, whose baptism in the chapel royal at Holyrood, on 19 Aug. 1617, is described by Calderwood (*History*, Wodrow Society edit. vii. 277). He succeeded his father as second Earl of Annandale in 1640, and two years later succeeded his cousin as third Viscount of Stormont. He died in 1658 without issue.

[Douglas's Scots' Peerage (ed. Wood, rev. by Paul), 1904; Acts of the Parliaments of Scotland, vols. iv. and v. passim; Works of Sir James Balfour, ii. 101–408; State Papers, Dom. 1603–40, passim.] H. P.

MURRAY, JOHN, second EARL and first MARQUIS OF ATHOLL (1631–1703), eldest son of John, first earl of Atholl of the Murray line, by Jean, youngest daughter of Sir Duncan Campbell of Glenurchy, was born 2 May 1631. The first earl was royalist in his sympathies, and in 1640 his territories were invaded by Argyll, who brought him a prisoner to Edinburgh. He was released on payment of 10,000*l.* (Scots) and an engagement to take south to the covenanting army a regiment of five hundred men under his own command (BALFOUR, *Annals*, ii. 380). Subsequently, along with Montrose, he signed the band of Cumbernauld in defence of the king. He died in June 1642. The son was also a strong loyalist, and in 1650 took up arms with his followers to rescue Charles II from covenanters' tyranny. The attempt proved, however, abortive, the king deeming it advisable to return to Perth, and shortly afterwards a letter was written to Atholl in the name of the king and the estates asking him to give in his submission, on pain of high treason (*ib.* iv. 117). On 16 Oct. he presented a supplication that the word 'rebellion' be deleted out of his pardon, and a more favourable term inserted, that pardon should be granted to one of his followers for the slaughter of a lieutenant, and that he shonld have the keeping of his own house of Blair on promise of fidelity. Only the first of his requests was granted (*ib.* p. 126). On 20 Dec. he was, however, appointed one of the colonels of foot for Perth (*ib.* p. 211), and on the 23rd the castle of Blair was restored to him upon sufficient security that he would be forthcoming for the king and parliament's service (*ib.* p. 215). Atholl was the main support of the highland rising under Middleton and Glencairn in 1653, joining the royalists with two thousand men. He was excepted from Cromwell's Act of Grace, 12 April 1654.

At the Restoration, in 1660, Atholl was sworn of the privy council, and on 28 Aug. he was nominated sheriff of Fifeshire. From 1661 to 1675 he was justice-general of Scotland. Captain of a troop of horse 1666–7, he was present at the battle of Pentland Hill 28 Nov. 1666. He was captain of the Highland Watch 1667–9 and colonel of a regiment of foot-militia in 1668. He became in 1670 captain of the king's life-guards, in 1672 keeper of the privy seal, and on 14 Jan. 1672–3 an extraordinary lord of session. He succeeded to the earldom of Tullibardine on the death of James, fourth earl, in 1670, and on 7 Feb. 1676 he was created Marquis of Atholl, Earl of Tullibardine, Viscount Balquhidder, Lord Murray, Balvenie, and Gask.

Atholl was at first a strong supporter of the policy of Lauderdale, and endeavoured to win over Hamilton into 'an entire confidence with him' (Burnet, *Own Time*, 1838 ed. p. 224), promising him the chief direction under Lauderdale of 'all affairs in Scotland.' He also represented to him the 'great advantages that Scotland, more particularly the great nobility, might find' by making the king absolute in England (*ib.* p. 225). In the prosecution of conventicles he was likewise for some time extremely active, raising in one week no less than 1,900*l.* sterling by arbitrary fines (*ib.* p. 226). In 1678, at the head of some 2,400 men, he accompanied the 'highland host' in their raid on the western shires, and was at the battle of Bothwell Brig in 1679, but on account of the excesses then committed he severed himself from Lauderdale, and joined the deputation which shortly afterwards went to the king to plead for a mitigation of the severities against the covenanters (*ib.* p. 278; Wodrow, ii. 449). On this account he was denounced by the Bishop of Galloway as a sympathiser with conventicles (*ib.*) Owing to his opposition to Lauderdale, he lost his troop of life-guards and keepership of the privy seal (1678). He was appointed, however, vice-admiral of Scotland in 1680 and in 1681, on the death of the chancellor, John Leslie, first duke of Rothes [q. v.], he acted as president of the parliament, but he was disappointed of succeeding to the chancellorship, which, after delay, was conferred on George Gordon, first earl of Aberdeen [q. v.] On 5 March a commission was given Atholl to execute the laws against conventicles (*ib.* iii. 372), and on 5 May he was appointed on a committee to inquire into charges against Lord Halton (Lauder of Fountainhall, p. 355). The fall of the Maitlands led to his restoration to favour. On 5 Aug. 1684 he was appointed lord-lieutenant and sheriff of Argyll and Tarbat. This, according to Lauder of Fountainhall, was 'to please him, seeing he lost the chancellor's place, and to perfect Argyll's ruin' (*ib.* p. 547). Argyll had fled to Holland, and Atholl having entered Argyllshire with some 1,000 men, apprehended Lord Neill Campbell, Campbell of Ardkinglass, and others, disarmed the inhabitants, brought their arms to Inverary, and prohibited the 'indulged' ministers from officiating from that time forth (*Hist. MSS. Comm.* 12th Rep. App. pt. viii. pp. 12–13). On learning of the landing of Argyll in Kintyre in May 1685 [see Campbell, Archibald, ninth Earl of Argyll], Atholl left Edinburgh on the 18th, and on the 30th reached Inverary, where he was joined by the Earl of Breadalbane. The energetic measures undertaken by him against Argyll, and the closeness with which he dogged his movements, caused the gradual dispersion of his followers, and on 18 June Argyll was captured at Inchinnan (for various particulars see *ib.* pp. 17–24). After Argyll's capture Atholl was reported to have harassed and plundered his territories (Wodrow, iii. 310). In July he captured Argyll's second son, Charles, who had sent round the fiery cross to raise the clan, and had also garrisoned a house in Argyll. Atholl, in virtue of his justiciary power, is said to have purposed hanging his prisoner at his father's gate at

Inverary, had the privy council not interfered (LAUDER OF FOUNTAINHALL, p. 655); but Atholl's character was not vindictive. On 29 May 1687 he was made a knight of the Thistle, on that order's revival.

At the revolution the part played by Atholl was very equivocal, and the weakness and irresolution that characterised his conduct lost him the confidence of both parties. He was one of the secret committee of King James which met in September 1688 to plan measures in opposition to the threatened expedition of the Prince of Orange (BALCARRES, *Memoirs*, p. 6), but in January 1689 went to wait on the prince in London. His readiness to acknowledge the prince is assigned to the influence of his eldest son and of his wife, a daughter of the seventh Earl of Derby, who was related to the house of Orange by her mother, a descendant of the family of Tremouille in France. In any case his conduct seems to have been chiefly regulated by personal interests, for being disappointed at his reception by the prince he again attached himself after a fashion to the party of King James. At the convention of the Scottish estates on 14 March 1689 he was proposed by the Jacobites in opposition to the Duke of Hamilton, who, however, had a majority of fifteen. After James II by his imprudent message had fatally ruined his prospects with the convention, Atholl consented to the proposal of Dundee and Balcarres to hold a convention of Jacobites in the name of James at Stirling (*ib.* p. 16), but his fatal irresolution at the last moment, and his stipulation for a day's delay, caused the frustration of the scheme (*ib.* pp. 27, 30). Subsequently he proposed that the Duke of Gordon, who held the castle of Edinburgh, should fire on the city, to intimidate the convention (*ib.* p. 31). He remained in Edinburgh after the withdrawal of Dundee. When the vote was taken in the convention as to the dethroning of James II, he and Queensberry withdrew from the meeting, but after the resolution was carried they returned, and explained that since the estates had declared the throne vacant they were convinced that none were so well fitted to fill it as the Prince and Princess of Orange (*ib.* p. 36). On 13 April Atholl wrote a letter to King William, professing sincere loyalty, but hoping that the king would not assent to the abolition of episcopacy in Scotland (*Leven and Melville Papers*, p. 12). To avoid entangling himself in the contest inaugurated by Dundee he withdrew from Atholl to the south of England, explaining to King William's government that he had 'to go to the baths for his health, being troubled with violent pains' (*ib.* p. 22). He was undoubtedly ill, and he gave his eldest son strictest orders to dissuade his followers from joining Dundee. But it seems that personally he had no desire to further the interests of the Prince of Orange, or to do more than was necessary to save himself from prosecution. Macaulay rhetorically calls him 'the falsest, the most fickle, the most pusillanimous of mankind,' but, he adds with truth, a word from him 'would have sent two thousand claymores to the Jacobite side;' but while 'all Scotland was waiting with impatience and anxiety to see in which army his numerous retainers would be arrayed he stole away to Bath and pretended to drink the waters' (*History*, 1885, ii. 53). None of Atholl's 'men' took part in Killiecrankie, but a few under Atholl's bailie, Stewart of Ballechin, drove, at Dundee's orders, Lord Murray's garrison from Blair Castle and seized it. After Killiecrankie, the Atholl men joined in pursuit of the routed government forces. On news reaching the government of the disaster, Atholl was brought up from Bath to London in custody of a messenger (LUTTRELL, *Short Relation*, i. 567), but he does not appear to have been detained after his examination. In 1690 he was concerned in intrigues against the Prince of Orange, and he was in the secret of the Montgomery plot (BALCARRES, *Memoirs*, p. 61; see MONTGOMERY, SIR JAMES, *fl.* 1690). In a Jacobite memorial of October 1691 it is stated that Arran answers 'body for body for Argyll and Atholl' (FERGUSON, *Ferguson the Plotter*, p. 290), and it was proposed that he should act as one of the lieutenant-generals in an intended Jacobite rising (*ib.*) Afterwards, with the Marquis of Breadalbane, he was appointed by the government to conduct negotiations for the pacification of the highlands.

Atholl died 6 May 1703, and was buried in the church of Dunkeld. By his wife Lady Amelia Sophia, fourth daughter of James Stanley, seventh earl of Derby, he had eight sons and four daughters. Two sons and two daughters died young. The other children were: John, first duke [q. v.]; Lord Charles, first earl of Dunmore [q. v.]; Lord James of Dowally, who joined the Highland army in 1689 after Killiecrankie, but on making submission received a free pardon; Lord William, who became Lord Nairn; Lord Mungo; Lord Edward, captain in the royal Scots; Lady Charlotte, who married Thomas Cooper; Lady Amelia, married to Hugh, tenth lord Lovat, and after his death carried off by Simon Fraser, twelfth lord Lovat [q. v.]

[Hist. MSS. Comm. 7th Rep. and 12th Rep. App. pt. viii.; Balfour's Annals of Scotl.; Burnet's Own Time; Wodrow's Hist. of the Kirk of Scotl.; Lauder of Fountainhall's Historical Notices, Balcarres's Memoirs, and Leven and Melville Papers (all in the Bannatyne Club); Luttrell's Brief Relation; General Mackay's Memoirs; Napier's Memorials of Dundee; Douglas's Scots' Peerage (Wood, revised by Paul), 1904.] T. F. H.

MURRAY, JOHN, second MARQUIS and first DUKE of ATHOLL (1660–1724), eldest son of John, second earl and first marquis [q. v.], by his wife Lady Amelia Sophia Stanley, fourth daughter of James, seventh earl of Derby, was born at Knowsley, Lancashire, on 24 Feb. 1659–60. During the lifetime of his father he was first known as Lord Murray, until on 27 July 1696 he was created Earl of Tullibardine. He accompanied his father with the 'highland host' to the western shires in 1678 (Letter in *Hist. MSS. Comm.* 12th Rep. App. pt. viii. p. 34). On the arrival of the Prince of Orange he went to visit him in London. A convinced whig, he, with clearer purpose than his father, seems to have done his best to further the interests of William in Atholl. When his father left 'his principality' for the south, he undertook to act as his delegate, and was at any rate desirous to prevent the clan joining Dundee. That he should prevent this was all that the government dared hope from his 'father's son;' but even in this he was unsuccessful. Dundee repeatedly wrote him urging him to hold the castle of Blair for King James, but receiving no answer, he induced Stewart of Ballechin, Atholl's bailie, to seize the castle. Lord Murray then formally assembled fifteen hundred of the clan, with a view to blockade the castle and induce or compel Stewart to deliver it up. Many of his followers withdrew to protect their cattle from Dundee's advancing army. Others, on learning that Murray purposed to support William of Orange, left the ranks, and after drinking success to King James from the water of the neighbouring river, returned to their homes. Murray thereupon endeavoured to dissuade General Mackay from his purposed march into Atholl, but in a despatch from Dunkeld on 26 July Mackay declared that if the castle was not in Murray's hands by the time he reached it he would have it, cost what it might, and would hang Ballechin over the highest wall (*ib.* p. 40), and that if Murray in any way countenanced Stewart in holding out, he would burn it from end to end (*ib.*) In a later despatch on the same day Mackay ordered Murray to post himself in the entry of the pass on the side towards Blair (*ib.*) This order he obeyed, but was unable to muster under his command more than two hundred men, while large numbers of the clan afterwards joined the rebels under the command of his brother, Lord James Murray. The attitude of the clan roused serious doubts as to Lord Murray's sincerity, and Mackay wrote him: 'I can say little or nothing to your lordship's vindication, and as little to accuse you, except it bee by the practis of the kingdom who make the chiefs answerable for their clans and followers' (*ib.* p. 42). There can, however, be no doubt that Murray was entirely opposed to his brother's conduct, and was greatly embarrassed by it (*ib.* p. 43).

In 1693 Murray was appointed a commissioner to inquire into the massacre of Glencoe, and displayed great activity in securing evidence to bring its perpetrators to justice, affirming that it concerned 'the whole nation to have that barbarous action . . . laied on to the true author and contriver of it' (*ib.* p. 45). In 1694 he was given the command of a regiment, to be raised in Scotland, and in 1695 was made sheriff of Perthshire for life. After the fall of Dalrymple, he was in 1696 appointed to succeed him as secretary of state for Scotland; and by patent, 27 July 1696, he was created Earl of Tullibardine, Viscount Glenalmond, and Lord Murray for life. From 1696 to 1698 he acted as lord high commissioner to parliament. Being, however, disappointed that Sir Hugh Dalrymple was made president of the session in preference to Sir William Hamilton of Whitelaw, to whom he practically promised the office 'for a considerable service he was to do in the Scots parliament,' he in 1698 threw up the secretaryship on the ground that 'he could not justify his word given to him in any other way' (MACKY, *Secret Memoirs*, p. 104). He showed little sympathy with the government during the rest of William's reign, opposing the laying on of cess, and proposing a reduction of the land forces. He was also a warm supporter of the Darien colonisation scheme. After the accession of Queen Anne he was sworn a privy councillor, and in April 1703 appointed lord privy seal. On 30 June of the same year he was created Duke of Atholl, Marquis of Tullibardine, Earl of Strathtay and Strathardle, Viscount of Balquhidder, Glenalmond, and Glenlyon, and Lord Murray, Balvenie, and Gask; and on 5 Feb. 1703–4 he was made a knight of the Thistle.

According to Lockhart, Atholl, in the parliament of 1703, 'trimmed between court and cavaliers, and probably would have continued to do so' but for the Queensberry plot (*Papers*, i. 73; see DOUGLAS, JAMES, second

Duke of Queensberry, and Fraser, Simon, twelfth Lord Lovat). The fact that Lovat owed his outlawry to the Atholl family was almost sufficient to discredit his story that he had been entrusted with confidential communications to Atholl, and in any case his known enmity against Atholl ought to have put Queensberry on his guard. The only adequate explanation seems to be that Queensberry was so irritated at Atholl's support of the act of security as to be ready to welcome any feasible means of securing his expulsion from office. Lovat's statement of the current opinion that Atholl was 'notoriously the incorrigible enemy of King James' may be exaggerated, but it is unlikely that he was then engaged in secret intrigues with St. Germains. Having been informed of Lovat's machinations by Ferguson the plotter [see Ferguson, Robert], Atholl presented a memorial to the queen, which was considered at a meeting of the Scots privy council at St. James's on 18 Feb. 1704–5 (see *Caldwell Papers*, i. 197–203). Although it was clear that Queensberry had, as regards the particular incident, been made the dupe of Lovat, Atholl found it impossible to clear himself from all suspicion, and consequently resigned his office. There seem to have been other reasons for doubting his loyalty. According to Burnet, he was not averse to a proposal that the 'Prince of Wales' should be recognised as the successor of Queen Anne (*Own Time*, ed. 1838, p. 746). But whatever may have been his previous sympathies, his treatment by the whigs did, according to Lockhart, 'so exasperate him against the court' that he 'became a violent Jacobite,' used all means to 'gain the confidence of the cavaliers,' and 'affected to be the head of that party and outrival Hamilton' (*Papers*, i. 73). He strongly opposed the union in 1705, and on 1 Sept. proposed a clause prohibiting the commissioner from leaving Scotland until the repeal of the act of the English parliament declaring the subjects of Scotland aliens. On the rejection of the clause he, with eighty members, entered his protest, and he also protested against the clause leaving the nomination of the commissioners with the queen. He continued his strenuous opposition to the union throughout all the subsequent discussions. Burnet states that 'he was believed to be in foreign correspondence and was strongly set on violent methods' to oppose it (*Own Time*, p. 800), and this is confirmed by Lockhart (*Papers*, i. 73). Through John Ker of Kersland [q. v.] negotiations were begun with the Cameronians to induce them to co-operate with the Jacobites in resisting the union by force, and the Duke of Atholl had undertaken to hold Stirling, when, according to Ker's account, Ker himself was induced by the arguments of Queensberry to dissuade the Cameronians from proceeding further (Ker, *Memoirs*, pp. 30–4). Atholl continued his opposition to the union, in spite of some vague offer to pay off arrears of salaries or pensions, which was made him through his brother, Lord Dunmore, one of the duke's creditors.

Nathaniel Hooke (1664–1738) [q. v.], during his subsequent dealings with the Scottish Jacobites, found it impossible to obtain any definite promises from Atholl (see *Negotiations*, passim). At the time of the Jacobite expedition of 1708 Atholl was attacked by illness either real or feigned. On the failure of the enterprise he was summoned to appear before the council at Edinburgh, but sent a physician to swear that he was so ill as to be unable to obey the summons (Luttrell, *Brief Relation*, vi. 298). Thereupon the dragoons were ordered to seize his castle of Blair, but the order was countermanded upon 'just certificate of his dangerous illness' (*ib.* p. 300), and he was not further proceeded against. On the return of the tories to power in 1710, Atholl was chosen one of the Scots representative peers, and he was again chosen in 1713. On 7 Nov. 1712 he was named an extraordinary lord of session, and in 1713 he was rechosen keeper of the privy seal. In 1712, 1713, and 1714 he acted as lord high commissioner to the general assembly of the kirk of Scotland. On the death of Queen Anne he proclaimed King George at Perth, and although deprived of the office of lord privy seal, was made lord-lieutenant of Perthshire (Aug. 1715). As at the revolution, so at the rebellion of 1715, the house of Atholl was divided. Atholl and his son Lord James were with the government, but his sons, William, marquis of Tullibardine [q. v.], Lord George [q. v.], and Lord Charles [q. v.], followed the Chevalier.

On 27 July 1715 Atholl sent a letter to the provost of Perth offering to supply, if required, two or three hundred men to guard the burgh at the town's charge (*Hist. MSS. Comm.* 12th Rep. App. pt. viii. p. 67). He also on 7 Sept. sent to Argyll information of Mar's movements, informing him at the same time that he would stop Mar's passage through his territory, and would guard the fords and boats on the Tay between Dunkeld and Loch Tay (*ib.* p. 67). Moreover, on 9 Oct. he wrote to the Earl of Sutherland beseeching him to come with all expedition to Atholl with what men he could collect, and assuring him that if he could bring between two and three thousand men he would soon recover the north side of the Forth (*ib.* p. 68), but to this letter he received no reply (*ib.* p. 69). After the battle of Sheriffmuir he intimated his intention of marching as soon as possible to Perth to recover the town from the rebels (*ib.* p. 70). This purpose was not carried out; but after the retreat and dispersion of the rebels he displayed great activity in collecting arms from those who had been in rebellion, and also endeavoured still further to ingratiate himself with the government by capturing, 4 June 1717, Rob Roy (Robert Macgregor), with whom he had for years been on friendly terms (*ib.* p. 71). Atholl died at Huntingtower, Perthshire, on 14 Nov. 1724, and was buried on the 26th at Dunkeld. By his first wife, Lady Katherine Hamilton, eldest daughter of Anne, duchess, and William Douglas, third duke of Hamilton, he had six sons and one daughter who survived childhood: John, marquis of Tullibardine, matriculated at Leyden University 22 Jan. 1706, became colonel of a regiment in the service of Holland, and was killed at the battle of Malplaquet, 31 Aug. 1709; William, marquis of Tullibardine [q. v.]; James [q. v.], to whom, on account of the rebellion of his brother William in 1715, the heirship of the estates and titles was conveyed by act of parliament, and who succeeded his father as second duke; Lord Charles [q. v.]; Lord George [q. v.]; Lord Basil, died young; and Lady Susan, married to William Gordon, second earl of Aberdeen. By his second wife, Mary, second daughter of William, twelfth lord Ross [q. v.], whom he married in 1710, he had three sons who survived childhood: Lord John, Lord Edward, Lord Frederick, and a daughter, Lady Mary, married to James Ogilvie, sixth earl of Findlater and Seafield.

Lockhart states that Atholl was 'endowed with good natural parts, tho' by reason of his proud, imperious, haughty, passionate temper he was noways capable to be the leading man of a party which he aimed at' (*Papers*, i. 73). This estimate is corroborated by Macky: 'He is of a very proud, fiery, partial disposition; does not want sense, but cloaks himself with passion, which he is easily wound up to when he speaks in public assemblies' (*Secret Memoirs*, p. 184). Lockhart also adds that 'tho' no scholar nor orator' he 'yet expressed himself very handsomely on public occasions.'

[Burnet's Own Time; Macpherson's Original Papers; Lockhart's Papers; Macky's Secret Memoirs; Ker of Kersland's Memoirs; Carstares's State Papers; Luttrell's Brief Relation; General Mackay's Memoirs; Leven and Melville Papers (Bannatyne Club); Nathaniel Hooke's Negotiations (Bannatyne Club); Napier's Memoirs of Viscount Dundee; Hist. MSS. Comm. 3rd Rep. and 12th Rep. App. pt. viii.; Douglas's Scots' Peerage (Wood and Paul), 1904.] T. F. H.

MURRAY, JOHN, third DUKE OF ATHOLL (1729–1774), eldest son of Lord George Murray [q. v.], by his wife Amelia, only surviving child and heiress of James Murray of Glencarse and Strowan, was born 6 May 1729. While a boy, he held (1745–6) a captain's commission in Lord Loudoun's regiment of foot, but never served. At the general election of 1761 he was chosen M.P. for Perth. On the death of his uncle James, second duke of Atholl, 8 Jan. 1764, Murray, who besides being nearest male heir, had married Lady Charlotte Murray, the duke's only surviving child, laid claim to the dukedom of Atholl. As, however, his father, Lord George Murray, had been forfeited, he deemed it advisable to petition the king that his claim to the dukedom might be allowed. The petition was referred by the king to the House of Lords, who on 7 Feb. 1764 resolved that he had a right to the title. His wife, on the death of her father, the second duke, succeeded to the sovereignty of the Isle of Man, and to the ancient English barony of Strange of Knockyn, Wotton, Mohun, Burnel, Basset, and Lacy. For some time negotiations had been in progress with the English government for the union of the sovereignty to the English crown; and in 1765 an act of parliament was passed to give effect to a contract between the lords of the treasury and the Duke and Duchess of Atholl for the purchase of the sovereignty of Man and its dependencies for 70,000*l.*, the duke and duchess retaining their landed property on payment of a yearly sum to the crown, the patronage of the bishopric and other ecclesiastical benefices, the fisheries, minerals, &c. The arrangement is reported to have rendered them very unpopular in Man. The duke and duchess had also a grant of an annuity of 2,000*l.* for their lives.

Atholl was chosen a representative peer in succession to the Earl of Sutherland, who died 21 Aug. 1764, and he was rechosen in 1768. In 1767 he was invested with the order of the Thistle. He died at Dunkeld on 5 Nov. 1774. By Lady Charlotte Murray he had seven sons and four daughters: John, fourth duke of Atholl (*b.* 30 June 1755, *d.* 29 Sept. 1830), who in 1786 was created Earl Strange and Baron Murray of Stanley in the United Kingdom, raised as lord-lieutenant of Perthshire (1794–1830) a large number of volunteers and militia during the Napoleonic wars, was deeply interested in afforestation, is believed to have first planted larch on a large scale in Scotland, and was the author of 'Observations on Larch,' London,

1810; Lord James Murray; George, died an infant; Lord George [q. v.], who became bishop of St. Davids; Lord William; Lord Henry; Lord Charles, dean of Bocking, Essex; Lady Charlotte, died unmarried; Lady Amelia, married first to Thomas Ivie Cooke, an officer of the army, and secondly to Sir Richard Gamon 'of Minchenden, Middlesex'; Jane, to John Groset Muirhead of Breadisholme, Lanarkshire; and Mary, to the Rev. George Martin.

[Train's History of the Isle of Man; Douglas's Scottish Peerage (Wood), i. 153.] T. F. H.

MURRAY, Sir JOHN (1718–1777), of Broughton, secretary to Prince Charles during the rebellion of 1745, born in 1718, was the second son of Sir David Murray of Stanhope, Peeblesshire, by his second wife, Margaret, daughter of Sir John Scot of Ancrum. The father is mentioned in a letter of George Lockhart of 29 July 1726 to the Old Pretender as 'eminently zealous' in his service, and as a fit agent for carrying on a correspondence with the highland clans, more especially since he had a residence in the highlands (*Papers*, ii. 299); but on being sounded as to his willingness to undertake such duties, the elder Murray declined, partly because he wished meanwhile to devote all his attention to the development of his estate, and partly because when he 'got his life after the last affair' (in 1715) he entered into engagements which made it impossible for him to take an active part in plots against the government (*ib.* p. 302). He nevertheless joined in the rebellion of 1745, for which he was sentenced to death at York, and was subsequently pardoned on condition that he left the country, his estates also being forfeited.

The son was educated at the university of Edinburgh. He was possessed of the small estate of Broughton, Peeblesshire, and has on this account been erroneously regarded as one of the Murrays of Broughton in Galloway. In February 1741–2 the highland Jacobites employed him and Drummond of Balhaldie to go to Rome to assure the Pretender of their zeal for his service (*State Trials*, xviii. 651). He paid a second visit to Paris in 1743, and returned in 1745 with information of the prince's intended expedition. The general feeling of the highland Jacobites was against the proposed rising (*ib.* p. 662), the promises of aid from France being regarded as unsatisfactory. An attempt, however, to prevent the prince setting sail miscarried; nor was the project of sending Murray to watch for his arrival in the west highlands and warn him off the coast more successful. Murray remained at his post during the whole of June, when, supposing the project to have been deferred, he returned to his house at Broughton. But on the arrival of the prince he joined him at Kinlochmoidart, Inverness-shire, and during the campaign he acted as his secretary. In the discharge of his duties he manifested great activity and energy, but is supposed to have been the chief cause of the prince's difficulties with Lord George Murray, of whom he was extremely jealous. Murray strongly represented the prestige that would accrue to the cause of the prince by the occupation of Edinburgh; and from his accurate local knowledge he was chosen to guide the movements of the rebel army on approaching it. When James VIII was proclaimed king at the cross of Edinburgh, Murray's wife, who was one of the beauties of the Edinburgh society of the period, appeared at the ceremony on horseback decorated with ribbons, and having a drawn sword in her hand.

Some time before Culloden Murray had become so seriously unwell as to be unable to discharge his duties as secretary. On the eve of the battle he was sent in a litter to Foyers on Loch Ness, whence he was carried across to Glenmoriston. Here he was informed of the result of the battle. After it was decided to discontinue the contest, he went to the house of Cameron of Lochiel, where he seems to have recovered his health. From French ships that had arrived at Borrodale he secured six casks of gold, the greater part of which, according to his own account, he buried in secret places: 15,000*l.* in a mound near Loch Arkaig and 12,000*l.* near the foot of the same lake, and retained only about 5,000*l.* to meet current expenses (manuscript memoirs of Murray quoted in Chambers, *Hist. of the Rebellion*, ed. 1869, p. 326). When, however, the prince sent a messenger, Donald Macleod, to ask for a supply of money from Murray, who was found along with Lochiel at the head of Loch Arkaig, he 'got no money at all from Murray, who said he had none to give, having only about sixty louis d'or to himself, which it was not worth the trouble to send' (Forbes, *Jacobite Memoirs*, p. 397). Macleod adds that the prince looked on Murray as 'one of the honestest, finest men in the whole world' (*ib.*) Subsequently Murray made his way south through the passes, but was taken prisoner at the house of his brother-in-law, Mr. Hunter of Polmood, Peeblesshire. Thence he was sent up to London, where he turned king's evidence against the Jacobites. When Sir John Douglas of Kelhead was brought before the privy council at St. James's, and asked, in reference to Murray, 'Do you know this witness?' 'Not I,' he answered; 'I once knew a person who bore the designation of Murray of Broughton, but that was a gentleman and a man of honour, and one that could hold up his head' (LOCKHART, *Life of Scott*, edit. 1842, p. 49). Murray was one of the principal witnesses against Simon Fraser, twelfth lord Lovat. On his appearance Lord Lovat objected that Murray was attainted by act of parliament made in the previous session, and that 'he did not surrender himself before 12 July last' (*State Trials*, xviii. 607), but the attorney-general replied that he had surrendered on the 20th to the lord justice clerk in Edinburgh (*ib.* p. 610). That Murray wished to surrender is corroborated by the author of 'Ascanius,' who states that when a party was in search for him at Broughton a boy was sent to them from Murray with the message that he was at Polmood. He, however, adds that at Edinburgh Murray 'was so drunk that he could not speak to the justice clerk till after a few hours' sleep' (edit. 1779, p. 142). Murray was discharged about Christmas 1747 (*ib.*)

In 1764 Murray disposed of the estate of Broughton to Dickson of Havana. After the death of Sir David Murray of Stanhope, at Leghorn, without issue, 19 Oct. 1770, he succeeded to the baronetcy. He died 6 Dec. 1777. By his wife Margaret, daughter of Colonel Robert Ferguson, brother of William Ferguson of Cailloch, Nithsdale, he had three sons: David, his heir, who became a naval officer; Robert, who succeeded on the death of his brother David in 1791 without issue; and Thomas, who became a lieutenant-general. His first wife was unfaithful to him, and he married as second wife a young quaker lady named Webb, whom he found in a provincial boarding-school in England. By this lady he had six children, the eldest being Charles Murray [q. v.], the comedian (note to CHAMBERS, *History of the Rebellion in* 1745, edit. 1869, p. 331).

Murray was a client of Sir Walter Scott's father, a W.S. in Edinburgh, and used to visit him in the evening, arriving in a sedan-chair carefully muffled up in a mantle. Curious as to who the visitor might be, Mrs. Scott on one occasion entered as he was about to leave with a salver and a dish of tea. He accepted it, but the moment he left, 'Mr. Scott, lifting up the window-sash, took the cup and tossed it out upon the pavement. The lady exclaimed for her china, but was put to silence by her husband's saying, "I can forgive your little curiosity, madam, but you must pay the penalty. I may admit into my house, on a piece of business, persons wholly unworthy to be treated as guests by my wife. Neither lip of me nor of mine comes after Murray of Broughton's"' (LOCKHART, *Life of Scott*).

[Memorials of John Murray of Broughton (Scot. Hist.Soc.), 1895; State Trials, vol. xviii.; Forbes's Jacobite Memoirs; Histories of the Rebellion, especially that by Robert Chambers, which quotes the MS. memoirs, now fully printed by Scot. Hist. Soc.; Ascanius, or the Young Adventurer; Memoirs of John Murray, Esq., 1747; Douglas's Scots' Peerage, ed. Wood and Paul; Notes and Queries, 4th ser. xi. 414, 491, 531, xii. 16, 97.] T. F. H.

MURRAY, LORD JOHN (1711–1787), of Banner Cross, Yorkshire, general, born 14 April 1711, was eldest son by his second wife of John Murray, second marquis and first duke of Atholl [q. v.], and was half-brother of the Jacobite leaders, William Murray, marquis of Tullibardine [q. v.], and Lord George Murray (1705–1760) [q. v.] He was appointed ensign in the 3rd foot-guards 7 Oct. 1727, on the recommendation of General Wade (*Hist. MSS. Comm.* 11th Rep. pt. iv. p. 199), and lieutenant and captain 3rd foot-guards (Scots guards) in 1733, in which regiment he became captain-lieutenant in 1737, and captain and lieutenant-colonel in 1738. On 25 April 1745 he was appointed to the colonelcy of the 42nd highlanders or Black Watch, which he held for forty-two years. He served with his regiment in Flanders in 1745, although he was absent from Fontenoy. In 1747 he was at the attempted relief of Hulst and the defence of Fort Sandberg, and commanded the British troops in the retreat to Welshorden, as well as at the defence of Bergen-op-Zoom. He was especially devoted to his regiment, and did more to foster the national character of the corps than any other officer. Papers of the day speak of him as marching down in full regimentals at the head of the many highlanders disabled at Ticonderoga in 1758, to plead their claims before the Chelsea board, with the result that every man received a pension. He offered every man who liked to accept it a cottage and garden on his estate rent free. Murray became a major-general in 1755, a lieutenant-general in 1758, and general in 1770. He was elected M.P. for Perth in 1734, 1741, 1747, and 1754. In 1779–80 Lord John raised at his own expense a second battalion to the 42nd, which in 1786 became the 73rd foot, and in 1881 was re-linked to the 42nd as second battalion. He married, at Sheffield, on 13 Sept. 1758, Miss Dalton of Bannercross, a Yorkshire lady of property. He died in Paris on 26 May 1787, the senior general in the army.

He left a daughter, Mary, married to Captain, afterwards Lieutenant-general, William Foxlowe, who took the name of Murray in 1782.

[Foster's Peerage, under 'Atholl;' Douglas's Peerage of Scotland, i. 151; Cannon's Hist. Rec. 42nd Royal Highlanders; Stewart's Scottish Highlanders, vol. i.; Keltie's Hist. Scottish Highlanders, ii. 358.] H. M. C.

MURRAY, JOHN, fourth Earl of Dunmore (1732–1809), eldest son of William, the third earl, by the Hon. Catherine Nairn, third daughter of William, second lord Nairn, was born in 1732. He succeeded to the peerage in 1756, and sat in the House of Lords as a representative peer of Scotland in the twelfth and first two sessions of the thirteenth parliament of Great Britain (1761–9). In 1770 he was appointed governor of the colony of New York, to which was subsequently added that of Virginia. He arrived in New York in October 1770, and met the House of Assembly at Williamsburg, Virginia, in the spring of 1772. After a brief session he prorogued the assembly, and did not again convene it until March 1773, when he dissolved it upon its adoption of resolutions for the appointment of a committee of correspondence to concert common action on the part of the colonies in the struggle with the mother country (12 March). A vote for a public fast upon occasion of the passing of the Boston Port Act led to another dissolution in May 1774. In the following autumn Dunmore aggravated the disaffection of the colonists by concluding a disadvantageous peace with the Ohio Indians. They appointed a convention to meet in May 1775, and Dunmore prohibited it by proclamation. He also, on the night of 20 April, had part of the powder removed from the Williamsburg magazine to the Magdalen man-of-war in James River. The people thereupon armed, volunteers by thousands flocked into the town, and peace was only preserved by payment of the value of the powder. On 1 June Dunmore convened the assembly to consider Lord North's conciliatory propositions. While they were under discussion a riot occurred (5 June), and Dunmore shifted the seat of government to the Fowey man-of-war lying off Yorktown twelve miles off. The assembly continued its deliberations and forwarded to him various bills to which he refused to give his assent without the attendance of the burgesses on board the ship. This the burgesses voted a high breach of their privileges, resolved that the governor had abdicated, and constituted themselves a convention, and vested the executive in a committee of safety. Meanwhile Dunmore collected and manned a small flotilla, and began a series of desultory operations on the river banks. An attack on Hampton was repulsed with loss on 25 Oct. On 7 Nov. he proclaimed freedom to all negroes who should rally to his standard. On 9 Dec. he was severely beaten in an encounter with the colonists at Great Bridge, about twenty miles from Norfolk. On 1 Jan. 1776 he reduced Norfolk to ashes. On 1 June he occupied Gwynn's Island in the Chesapeake, whence he was dislodged with loss by Andrew Lewis on 8 July. He thereupon disbanded his troops and returned to England, where he had already, January 1776, been elected to the seat in the House of Lords left vacant by the death of the Earl of Cassilis. He was rechosen at the general elections of October 1780 and May 1784. From 1787 to 1796 he was governor of the Bahama Islands. He died at Ramsgate in May 1809.

Dunmore married at Edinburgh on 21 Feb. 1759 Lady Charlotte Stewart, sixth daughter of Alexander, sixth earl of Galloway, by whom he had issue five sons and four daughters.

[Hist. Journ. Amer. War (Mass. Hist. Soc.), 1795, pp. 5, 20, 32; Douglas's Peerage, i. 485; Proceedings of the House of Burgesses of Virginia, 1 June 1775, Williamsburg; Campbell's Virginia, 1860, pp. 569 et seq.; Coll. Mass. Hist. Soc. 2nd ser. ii. 223; Winsor's Hist. Amer. 1888, vi. 167–8, 238, 611, 618, 713–14; Virginia State Papers, ed. Palmer, 1652–1781, p. 265; Lords' Journ. xxx. 103, xxxii. 146, xxxiv. 546, xxxvi. 178, xxxvii. 73; Parl. Hist. xviii. 137–8; Ann. Reg. 1776; Gent. Mag. 1809, pt. i. p. 587; Add. MSS. 21730 f. 147, 22900 ff. 176, 210, 24322 ff. 122, 129, 133–9; Horace Walpole's Journ. Reign of Geo. III, i. 492, 497, ii. 19.] J. M. R.

MURRAY, JOHN (*d.* 1820), chemist and physicist, a native of Scotland, was educated at Edinburgh, where he rose to eminence as a lecturer on natural philosophy, chemistry, materia medica, and pharmacy. He became M.D. of St. Andrews on 17 Oct. 1814, and was elected fellow of the Royal College of Physicians, Edinburgh, on 7 Nov. 1815. He was a fellow of the Royal Society of Edinburgh and of the Geological Society of London. To the 'Transactions' of the former body (vol. viii.) he contributed four papers. Twenty-eight papers are assigned him in the Royal Society's 'Catalogue of Scientific Papers,' but those numbered 19 to 22, relative to the safety-lamp and explosions of firedamp, are by another John Murray (*d.* 1851) [q. v.] The two John Murrays had a discussion about the safety-lamp in the 'Philosophical Magazine.' Murray died in Nicolson Street, Edinburgh, on 22 July 1820.

His works comprise: 1. 'Elements of Chemistry,' 2 vols. 8vo, Edinburgh, 1801; 6th ed. 1828. 2. 'A Comparative View of the Huttonian and Neptunian Systems of Geology' (anon.), 8vo, Edinburgh, 1802. 3. 'Elements of Materia Medica and Pharmacy,' 2 vols. 8vo, Edinburgh, 1804; 6th ed. 1832. 4. 'A System of Chemistry,' 4 vols. 8vo, Edinburgh, 1806–7; 6th ed. 1832.

His son, John Murray (1798–1873), who edited the later editions of his father's works, was born on 19 April 1798, graduated M.D. of St. Andrews in 1815, and became a fellow of the Royal College of Surgeons, Edinburgh, in November 1826. He afterwards emigrated to Melbourne, where he died on 4 June 1873.

[Gent. Mag. 1820, pt. ii. p. 185; Watt's Bibl. Brit.; Royal Soc. List of Papers; information kindly supplied by Dr. G. A. Gibson, secretary Roy. Coll. Phys. Edinb., and J. Robertson, esq., secretary Roy. Coll. Surg. Edinb.]

B. B. W.

MURRAY, Sir JOHN (1768?–1827), eighth baronet of Clermont, Fifeshire, general, born about 1768, was eldest son by his second wife, Susan, daughter of John Renton of Lamerton, of Sir Robert Murray, sixth baronet, and was half-brother of Sir James Murray, afterwards Pulteney [q. v.] He was appointed ensign 3rd footguards (Scots guards) 24 Oct. 1788, and became lieutenant and captain in that regiment 25 April 1793. He served in Flanders in 1793–1794, as aide-de-camp first to the Hanoverian field-marshal Freytag, and afterwards to the Duke of York [see Frederick Augustus], and was present at St. Amand, Famars, the sieges of Valenciennes and Dunkirk, Tournay, &c., and in the winter retreat through Holland to Bremen. On 15 Nov. 1794 he was appointed lieutenant-colonel 2nd battalion 84th foot (now 2nd York and Lancaster regiment). He commanded the 84th at the capture of the Cape of Good Hope in 1796, and took it on to India. In 1798 he was sent into the Red Sea with a small force, which, on the urgent solicitations of the Ottoman government to the sultan of Sana, then sovereign of the peninsula of Aden, was allowed to remain awhile in that stronghold. In 1799 Murray was appointed British commissioner in the Red Sea, and was sent with three hundred men to occupy Perim in the straits of Bab el Mandeb, so as to intercept all communication with India by way of the Red Sea. The troops landed 3 May 1799, and remained until 1 Sept. Finding, after every practicable exertion, that the island yielded not a drop of fresh water, and that the shore batteries could not command the straits, Murray withdrew his detachment to Aden, where they were most hospitably entertained, and remained till March 1800 (the Rev. G. P. Badger in the *Times*, 31 May 1858). Early in the following year Murray was appointed quartermaster-general of the Indian army proceeding to Egypt under Major-general David Baird [q. v.], which, after many delays in the Red Sea, arrived at Kosseir in June 1801, crossed the desert to Cairo, and descended the Nile. Returning to India with Baird's troops, Murray commanded the Bombay division, which joined Major-general Arthur Wellesley's force at Poona in May 1803, and commanded in Guzerat during the subsequent operations against the Mahrattas. From Guzerat he moved into Malwa, and on 24 Aug. 1804 seized and occupied Holkar's capital (see Gurwood, *Well. Desp.* vols. i. and ii. passim). Wellesley disapproved of many of Murray's proceedings, and in September 1804 recommended that he should be relieved from the command in Malwa (*ib.* i. 462). Murray advanced to Kota, where his force was in a dangerous position, in January 1805 (*ib.*) On notification of his promotion to major-general from 1 Jan. 1805 he returned home. He commanded a brigade in the eastern counties in 1806–7, and the troops of the king's German legion with Sir John Moore in the expedition to Sweden in 1808, and afterwards in Portugal. He joined Sir Arthur Wellesley's army in Portugal in 1809, and distinguished himself at the passage of the Douro in May that year (*ib.* iii. 227). When Beresford was made a local lieutenant-general, Murray, who was his senior, was indisposed to serve under him, and returned home.

In 1811 Murray succeeded his elder half-brother, Sir James Murray Pulteney, in the baronetcy and a fortune of over half a million, and also as member for the boroughs of Weymouth and Melcombe Regis, which he represented until the dissolution of 1818. Murray appears to have applied for employment in the Peninsular army. But in a letter in February 1811 Lord Wellington recommended that his application should be passed over: 'He is a very able officer, but when he was here before he was disposed not to avoid questions of precedence, but to bring them unnecessarily to discussion and decision' (*ib.* iv. 588). Murray became a lieutenant-general 1 Jan. 1812, and later was appointed to the army in Sicily under command of Lord William Bentinck [q. v.] On 26 Feb. 1813 he arrived at Alicante, and took command of a motley force of Anglo-Sicilians there, of which Major-general John Mackenzie had been in command since the retirement of General Frederick Maitland [q. v.] in the previous November. Wellington suggested the recapture of Tarragona, 'which with the means at your command should not be a difficult operation (*ib.* vi. 389, letter dated 29 March 1813). The French under Suchet attacked Murray in a strong position at Castalla, whither he had advanced, and were defeated by him on 13 April 1813. On 31 May 1813 Murray sailed from Alicante, and on 3 June disembarked before Tarragona. He had then at his disposal, including Spaniards, a force of twelve thousand men, of whom only 4,500 were British and Germans. On the approach of Suchet to raise the siege, Murray, whose movements had been marked by great indecision, hastily re-embarked his troops on 12 June, leaving his guns and stores behind him (see Napier, *Hist. Peninsular War*, rev. edit. vol. v. bk. xxi. chap. i.; cf. Gurwood, vi. 565–9). Instead of obeying his instructions to proceed to Valencia (*ib.* vi. 426–9), to support the Spaniards there in case of withdrawal from Tarragona, Murray landed a part of his troops at the Col de Balaguer, where Lord William Bentinck arrived and assumed command four days later. Wellington condemned Murray's disregard of his instructions and his ready sacrifice of his guns and stores, which Murray defended on principle as having been resorted to successfully by French strategists. 'I have a very high opinion of . . . talents,' Wellington wrote in a passage which is anonymous in his published despatches, but evidently applies to Murray, 'but he always appeared to me to want what is better than abilities, viz. sound sense' (*ib.* vi. 665–7). Wellington recommended that Murray should be tried by court-martial, and as it would not be fair to take the officers from the Peninsular army, officers to form the court should be sent from England and Gibraltar to some Mediterranean port, where the witnesses could readily be assembled. After long delay Murray was arraigned at Winchester on 16 Jan. 1815, before a general court-martial, of which Sir Alured Clarke [q. v.] was president, and General George, afterwards first lord Harris [q. v.], Sir Samuel Auchmuty [q. v.], Sir George Beckwith [q. v.], Sir Edward Paget, and other distinguished officers were members. The three charges were very verbose; the first alleged unmilitary conduct, the second neglect of duty and disobedience of the Marquis of Wellington's written instructions, and the third, neglect of proper preparations and arrangements for re-embarking his troops, 'to the prejudice of the service and the detriment of the British military character.' After sitting for fifteen days the court acquitted Murray, except so much of the first part of the third charge as amounted to an error in judgment, for which they sentenced him to be admonished. The prince regent dispensed with the admonition, and Murray was afterwards made a G.C.H., and in 1818 was transferred from the colonelcy 3rd West India regiment to that of 56th foot. He became a full general in 1825. He had the decorations of the Red Eagle of Prussia, and St. Januarius of Naples.

He died at Frankfort-on-Maine 15 Oct. 1827. Murray married, 25 Aug. 1807, the Hon. Anne Elizabeth Cholmley Phipps, only daughter of Constantine John, lord Mulgrave. She died 10 April 1848; she had no issue.

Murray was a liberal patron of art, and collected some good pictures. His portrait appears in the first of a set of four pictures of patrons and lovers of art, painted by Pieter Christoph Wonder. The pictures were commissioned by Murray about 1826, and are now in the National Portrait Gallery (see *Catalogue*, 1881, p. 516).

[Foster's Baronetage, under 'Murray of Clermont;' Philippart's Roy. Military Calendar, 1820, ii. 227–8; Letter of the Rev. G. P. Badger in Times, 31 May 1858, on Perim; Mill's Hist. of India, vol. vi.; Napier's Hist. Peninsular War, rev. edit.; Gurwood's Wellington Desp. vols. i. ii. iii. vi.; Shorthand Notes of Trial of Sir John Murray; Gent. Mag. 1827, ii. 560.] H. M. C.

MURRAY, JOHN (1778–1843), publisher, born at 32 Fleet Street, London on 27 Nov. 1778, was son of John Mac Murray, a descendant of the Murrays of Athol. The father was born in Edinburgh in 1745, and, after serving as lieutenant of marines from 1762, retired on half-pay in 1768, and commenced business as a London bookseller and publisher, purchasing, in November 1768, the business of William Sandby, at the sign of the 'Ship,' 32 Fleet Street, and discontinuing the prefix 'Mac' before his surname. He advanced slowly, publishing many important works, and meeting with alternate gains and losses. He also wrote several pamphlets, and edited an annual register, successively entitled 'The London Mercury' and 'The English Review.' A half-length portrait is in the possession of John Murray, Esq. His first wife having died childless, he married again, and had three sons, the two elder of whom died in infancy. John, the third, was educated successively at private schools in Edinburgh, Margate, Gosport, and Kennington. While at Gosport, under Dr. Burney, he lost the sight of his right eye from an accident occasioned by the carelessness of a writing master. His father died on 6 Nov. 1793, and during young Murray's minority the business was conducted by the principal assistant, Samuel Highley, who became a partner. Murray, however, was dissatisfied with Highley's want of enterprise, and, although he attempted no change on coming of age in 1799, he procured a dissolution of partnership on 25 March 1803, retaining the house in Fleet Street, while Highley took the medical publications of the firm. He commenced business on his own account with the same spirit which he continued to display throughout; his first step, even before the dissolution was completed, being to offer Colman 300*l.* for the copyright of his comedy of 'John Bull,' just produced at Covent Garden.

Murray's first publication of importance was 'The Revolutionary Plutarch,' December 1803. Before this he had opened up a correspondence with Archibald Constable [q. v.], the Edinburgh publisher, which had important consequences. Murray became London agent for Constable's publications, had a share in 'Marmion' and other important works jointly brought out by them, and acted for a while as London agent for the 'Edinburgh Review,' of which he was part publisher from April 1807 to October 1808. Murray paid three visits to Scotland, partly on Constable's affairs and partly on a more interesting errand, that of wooing Anne, daughter of the deceased Charles Elliot, publisher, a constant correspondent of his father. The marriage took place at Edinburgh on 6 March 1807. Shortly afterwards relations with Constable became unsatisfactory, chiefly owing to the Edinburgh publisher's habit of drawing accommodation bills. Business relations were broken off in 1808, and, though resumed in 1810, were finally terminated in 1813. A personal reconciliation between Murray and Constable, however, took place shortly before the death of the latter.

The breach with Constable enabled Murray to carry out a scheme which he had for some time contemplated. While still one of the publishers of the 'Edinburgh Review,' and therefore in a peculiarly favourable position for appreciating its iniquities, he had denounced them in a letter to Canning (25 Sept. 1807), and had suggested the establishment of an opposition review on tory principles. Negotiations in this quarter were greatly facilitated by a service Murray had previously rendered to Stratford Canning, Canning's cousin, and other young Etonians by relieving them of risk in connection with 'The Miniature,' an Etonian magazine for which they had become liable. The conjuncture was favourable. Scott, estranged by political differences and the treatment accorded to his 'Marmion' by Jeffrey, had ceased to write in the 'Edinburgh.' Murray visited him in November 1808, and secured his co-operation. Southey, who had always refused to contribute to the 'Edinburgh,' promised his assistance. Gifford was appointed editor, and after busy arrangements and discussions, in which George Ellis [q. v.] bore an important part, the first number appeared in February 1809. 'It did not entirely realise the sanguine views of its promoters,' writes Dr. Smiles, 'or burst like a thunderclap on the reading public,' but it soon reached a second edition. 'Although,' Murray wrote, 'I am considerably out of pocket by the adventure at present, yet I hope that in the course of next year it will at least pay its expenses.' Yet in August 1810 he still had to write to Gifford, 'I cannot yet manage to make the "Review" pay its expenses.' One great hindrance to its success was the unpunctuality of its appearance, due partly to the lack of business qualifications on the part of Gifford—an excellent editor in all literary respects—and partly to the liberties which leading contributors permitted themselves. One article, to which Murray himself strongly objected, had to be inserted 'from the utter impossibility of filling our number without it' when the number was already six weeks late. 'This was enough,' remarks Dr. Smiles, 'to have killed any publication which was not redeemed by the excellence of its contents.' Gradually greater punctuality was attained, although many years elapsed before the publication of the 'Review' could be effected with the undeviating regularity which would now be regarded as a matter of course. From 1811 onwards Southey became a regular and copious contributor; his essays raised the general tone and character of the 'Review,' and he was for many years paid at the rate of 100*l.* per article. He was, however, exceedingly restive under Gifford's excisions. In December 1811 Murray sent Gifford a present of 500*l.*, which may be considered evidence that the periodical had begun to pay. Gifford's services were entirely editorial, and no article wholly from his own pen ever appeared in the 'Quarterly.' The overthrow of Napoleon and the disappointment of the whigs' expectations under the regency were favourable circumstances for the 'Quarterly,' which went on prospering, until in 1817 Southey could write of Murray, 'The "Review" is the greatest of all works, and it is all his own creation; he prints ten thousand, and fifty times ten thousand read its contents.'

While the 'Quarterly' was still struggling two of the most important incidents in Murray's life occurred—his purchase in May 1812 of the historic house No. 50 Albemarle Street, and his acquaintance with Byron. The house was bought from William Miller (1769–1844) [q. v.], a retiring publisher, along with his copyrights. The price paid for the whole was 3,822*l.* 12*s.* 6*d.*, which was not finally liquidated until 1821, and for which Miller received as security the copyrights of the 'Quarterly Review' and Mrs. Rundell's 'Cookery' (one of Murray's most successful speculations). Murray's acquaintance with Byron had been made the preceding year by his agreement to publish the first and second cantos of 'Childe Harold' on account of Mr. Dallas, to whom Byron had given them in one of his fits of whimsical generosity. After Byron 'awoke and found himself famous,' Murray purchased the copyright from Dallas for six hundred guineas, contrary to the advice of Gifford. Rogers, however, assured him that he would never repent it, and this judgment was soon verified. For several years Murray's relations with Byron continued to be a singular inversion of those usually existing between author and publisher, the publisher continually striving to force money upon the author, which the latter long rejected. Byron probably could not forget that he had himself most unreasonably denounced Scott for making money out of 'Marmion;' but at length his consistency and his pride gave way to his necessities, though he magnanimously refused the relief which Murray with equal generosity pressed upon him when his affairs had become hopelessly deranged about the time of his separation from Lady Byron. The alliance subsisted long after Byron's retirement to the continent, and only broke down under the strain of 'Don Juan;' Murray produced cantos i. to v., however, before his tory principles compelled him to desist. The mutual regard of the two was never impaired, and, notwithstanding much caprice on Byron's part and some self-interest on Murray's, this episode in their lives must be pronounced equally honourable to both. Murray did not shine equally in his relations with Coleridge, to whom he offered no more than 100*l.* for a translation of 'Faust.' It is probable, however, that he had a very imperfect idea what 'Faust' was like, and doubtless believed that Coleridge, who accepted his terms and never produced a line of the translation, would have followed the same course if the terms had been ten times as liberal. Murray made one great mistake when he declined to buy the copyright of the 'Rejected Addresses' for 20*l.* He wished to obtain a share of the 'Waverley Novels,' but Scott was bound hand and foot to his Edinburgh publishers. He had himself made an excursion into Scotland by becoming a joint publisher of 'Blackwood's Magazine,' but relinquished it after a while from disapprobation of its personalities. The list of important books published by him at this time would be a very long one, but not many have maintained a permanent place in literature. The more remarkable exceptions were perhaps the novels of Jane Austen, which afterwards passed into the hands of Bentley, and the poems of Crabbe, for whose 'Tales of the Hall' Murray gave three times as much as was offered by Longman. A noticeable feature of his business was the number of books of travel, in the selection of which he derived much assistance from Sir John Barrow [q. v.], who had become one of the most extensive contributors to the 'Quarterly.'

The year 1824 produced two events of importance to Murray—first, the controversy relating to Lord Byron's 'Memoirs,' resulting in their destruction. (The history of this transaction is fully related under Byron. Murray's view of it is fully presented in Dr. Smiles's 'Biography,' chap. xvii.) Towards the close of the year Gifford's health compelled him to retire from the editorship of the 'Quarterly.' He was succeeded by Mr. (afterwards Sir) John Taylor Coleridge, who withdrew after a year in consequence of increasing practice at the bar. He may not have been a very strong editor, and his views on the catholic question were too liberal for Southey and others of Murray's allies. He was succeeded by Lockhart, a rather surprising choice when Lockhart's share in the personalities that had driven Murray away from 'Blackwood' is considered. Lockhart, however, had been brought into intimate connection with Murray through his having been selected by Disraeli for the editorship of a proposed newspaper called 'The Representative,' and although Scott disapproved of his son-in-law's connection with a newspaper, he was most willing to see him editor of the 'Quarterly.' His influence carried the day, and Lockhart soon proved himself one of the greatest of editors, far more efficient than Gifford in business matters, and, unlike Gifford, able to enrich the 'Review' with a series of brilliant contributions from his own pen. He entered upon his office with an unfriendly feeling towards Croker, but they were soon reconciled, and during Lockhart's editorship Croker continued to be more intimately identified with the periodical in the public mind than Lockhart himself, not entirely to its advantage.

The project suggested about this time to Murray by Benjamin Disraeli for starting a daily newspaper, to be entitled 'The Representative,' was perhaps the only one of Murray's important enterprises which brought him nothing but mortification and loss, and the only one in which his usual excellent judgment failed to be displayed. Nothing can more forcibly evince the extraordinary talent of Disraeli than the spell which at the age of twenty he threw over this sagacious and experienced man of the world. At the same time it is sufficiently evident that the secret of his fascination lay in his own intense belief in his own project, and that the measures he took to further it were judicious as well as energetic; while it is by no means certain that the scheme might not have been a success after all if Murray had not trusted his confederate only by halves. When Disraeli, not from his own default, but from that of the person on whom he had relied, proved unable to advance his share of the capital, Murray immediately broke with him, and in so doing 'took the post-horses from his carriage,' as Brougham said on another occasion. It is strange that all the resources of his house should have produced nothing more creditable, but so it was: 'The Representative' was an unmitigated failure from first to last, and its discontinuance in July 1826, after an ignominious existence of six months, left Murray no other cause for self-congratulation than the fortitude with which he had shown himself capable of bearing a loss of 26,000*l*. The affair naturally led to the interruption of his old friendship with the elder Disraeli, and sowed the seeds of the enmity between Disraeli and Croker which bore literary fruit in 'Coningsby.' It also inspired 'Vivian Grey,' long supposed to have been derived from actual experience of party cabals, but now seen to be neither more nor less than the history of 'The Representative' transported into the sphere of politics. Murray and Disraeli were afterwards coldly reconciled, and the latter's 'Contarini Fleming' and 'Gallomania' were published in Albemarle Street. Another reconciliation, prompted by the strongest mutual interest, produced Moore's 'Life of Byron' and his edition of Byron's works, Murray buying up all the copyrights not already in his possession for more than 3,000*l*.

Murray's latter years were unmarked by striking incidents. He published many of the most important books of his day, among which may be particularly mentioned the first volume of Napier's 'Peninsular War,' by which he lost heavily; Croker's 'Boswell,' so lashed by Macaulay and slighted by Carlyle; Borrow's 'Bible in Spain,' Lyell's 'Geology,' and Mrs. Somerville's 'Connection of the Physical Sciences;' and he narrowly escaped publishing 'Sartor Resartus' and Mill's 'Logic.' He deferred so far to the growing taste for cheap literature as to bring out 'The Family Library,' a most admirable collection of popular treatises by Scott, Southey, Milman, Palgrave, and other first-class writers, which ran to forty-seven volumes, but does not appear to have been exceedingly profitable. Another very important undertaking was that of the world-famous handbooks, which originated in the publication by him of Mrs. Mariana Starke's 'Guide for Travellers on the Continent' in 1820, but received their present form as a consequence of the continental travels of his son, the third John Murray [q. v.] He depended much on his own judgment; his principal literary advisers seem to have been Lockhart, Milman, Barrow, and Lady Calcott.

Murray's health began to decline in the autumn of 1842, and he died on 27 June 1843. His character was that of a consummate man of business, who had caught from his pursuits much of the urbanity that should characterise the man of letters, and possessed moreover an innate generosity and magnanimity which continually streams forth in his transactions with individuals, and inspired this general maxim: 'The business of a publishing bookseller is not in his shop, or even in his connections, but in his brains.' These qualities were evinced not merely by his frequently munificent dealings with individual authors, but by his steady confidence in the success of the best literature, and his pride in being himself the medium for giving it to the world. His own interest was indeed the polestar of his life, nor could he otherwise have obtained his extraordinary success; but he was always ready to devote time, trouble, and money to the service of others. If some instances of his liberality to the most conspicuous writers (who not unfrequently repaid him in kind) may have been the effect of calculation, he was also liberal to some, like Maturin and Foscolo, from whom he could expect little return. He did more than any man of his time to dignify the profession of bookselling, and was amiable and estimable in every private relation.

A portrait of Murray by Pickersgill was lent by his son to the third loan exhibition of national portraits.

[Smiles's A Publisher and his Friends, 1891. The more important books from which information about Murray may be obtained are Moore's Life of Byron and his Diary, and Thomas Constable's memoir of his father, 1873.] R. G.

MURRAY, JOHN (1786?–1851), scientific writer and lecturer, son of James Murray, sea-captain, and of Grace, his wife, was born at Stranraer about 1786. He seems to have early directed his attention to scientific matters, and in 1815 he published at Saffron Walden 'The Elements of Chemical Science,' describing himself as 'Lecturer on the Philosophy of Physics and of Chemistry.' In 1816 he published at Dumfries a volume entitled 'Minor Poems,' which was dedicated to Capell Lofft (1751–1824) [q. v.] In the same year he lectured at the Surrey Institution established in the early part of the century in the Blackfriars Road, on the model of the Royal Institution. He gave an annual course there for many years, and became well known as a lecturer at mechanics' institutions in various parts of the kingdom. In an address at the Leeds Philosophical Society Lord Brougham referred to him as 'one of the best lecturers in the world.' He was industrious and wrote with facility and clearness, but the wide range of subjects to which he gave attention prevented him from attaining eminence in any. He was much interested in the safety lamp, and took part in the discussion which arose about 1816 consequent on the publication of Sir H. Davy's memoirs in the 'Philosophical Transactions.' In that year he published papers in the 'Philosophical Magazine' (xlvii. 411, xlviii. 453), in which he showed that a sieve of hair or whalebone, or a sheet of perforated cardboard, formed an effectual barrier to the passage of flame. He also exhibited at his lectures an experimental safety lamp, the body of which consisted of muslin rendered incombustible by steeping it in a solution of phosphate of ammonia, and which was quite effective. From these experiments Murray deduced a theory of the efficiency of the safety-lamp which was opposed to that propounded by Davy. A *résumé* of his researches on this subject is given in his 'Observations on Flame and Safety Lamps,' 1833. Among his opponents was John Murray (*d.* 1820) [q. v.], with whom he has been frequently confused. The papers in the 'Philosophical Magazine,' xlviii. 286, 360, 451, and xlix. 47, are by the subject of this notice, and not by Dr. John Murray (cf. *Royal Society's Catalogue of Scientific Papers*). In 1835 he gave evidence on the safety lamp and ventilation before the select committee of the House of Commons on accidents in mines (*Reports*, pp. 237–49).

Murray was a fellow of the Society of Antiquaries (1822) and of the Geological (1823), Linnean (1819), and Horticultural Societies (1824), and he is also described on his tombstone as 'Ph.D.' and 'M.A.' He is sometimes referred to by contemporary writers as Dr. Murray, or Professor Murray.

He seems to have settled in Hull about 1842, and at the end of 1850 he removed to Broadstone House, near Stranraer, where he died on 28 June 1851, aged 65, his death having been accelerated by the pressure of pecuniary difficulties (*Mining Journal*, 14 June 1851, p. 288). He was buried in Inch churchyard, where there is a tombstone commemorating several members of his family.

Besides the works already mentioned, Murray wrote: 1. 'Remarks on the Cultivation of the Silkworm,' Glasgow, 1825. 2. 'Experiments illustrative of Chemical Science,' 2nd edit. 1828; 5th edit. 1839. 3. 'Remarks on Modern Paper,' Edinburgh, 1829. 4. 'Treatise on Atmospherical Electricity,' London, 1830, which was translated into French as one of the 'Manuels-Roret.' 5. 'Pulmonary Consumption,' London, 1830. 6. 'Remarks on Hydrophobia,' London, 1830. 7. 'Memoir on the Diamond,' 1831. 8. 'A Method for forming an Instantaneous Connection with the Shore in Shipwreck,' London, 1832. 9. 'Description of a new Lightning Conductor,' London, 1833. 10. 'Account of the Palo de Vacca, or Cow Tree,' London, 1837. 11. 'Considerations on the Vital Principle,' 1837. 12. 'The Truth of Revelation,' 2nd edit. London, 1840; the first edition seems to have been published anonymously in 1831. In a letter in the 'Mining Journal' of 10 May 1851 Murray claims to have written twenty-eight separate works; upwards of twenty are mentioned in the 'British Museum Catalogue.' His contributions to scientific journals and periodicals cover a wide field, and relate to chemistry, physics, medicine, geology, natural history, and manufactures. The Royal Society's 'Catalogue' enumerates about sixty; but Murray wrote much in the 'Mechanics' Magazine' from 1831 to 1844, and also in the 'Mining Journal,' of which he was a very steady correspondent for about the last ten years of his life.

[Obituary notice in Galloway Advertiser, 3 July 1851 (copied in Mining Journal, 12 July 1851, p. 336); tombstone in Inch churchyard and private information.] R. B. P.

MURRAY, JOHN (1808–1892), publisher, eldest son of John Murray (1778–1843) [q. v.], by Anne, daughter of Charles Elliot, publisher, of Edinburgh, was born on 16 April 1808, the year before the foundation of the 'Quarterly Review.' When he was barely four years old his father moved to the present home of the firm at 50 Albemarle

Street, a house which became famous as a meeting-place of eminent men of letters. He was educated at Charterhouse and at Edinburgh University, whence he graduated in 1827. In January of that year the young Murray breakfasted with Sir Walter Scott, who observes in his journal under that date: 'English boys have this advantage—that they are well bred and can converse, when ours are regular-built cubs.' He completed his education by a long course of foreign travel, his father giving him carte blanche as to ways, means, and plans. 'It was in 1829,' Murray himself writes (in 'Murray's Magazine,' November 1889), 'that I first set foot on the continent at Rotterdam. . . . I set forth unprovided with any guide excepting a few manuscript notes about towns and inns furnished me by my good friend Dr. Somerville.' His difficulties impressed on his mind the value of practical information gathered upon the spot, and he set to work to collect for himself all the facts, information, statistics, &c., which an English tourist would be likely to require. The result was the first of the world-familiar red 'handbooks' (so christened by Murray's father, though the idea of their origin was entirely his own). Murray continued his travels over three years, visited Weimar, and delivered the dedication of Byron's 'Marino Faliero' to Goethe in person, was admitted to an interview with Metternich at Vienna, and in 1836 saw through the press the first of the handbooks, his own 'Holland, Belgium, and the Rhine.' This was followed by 'France,' 'South Germany,' and 'Switzerland,' all of which were written by himself. Subsequently he enlisted the services of such specialists as Richard Ford (Spain), Sir Gardner Wilkinson (Egypt), and Sir Francis Palgrave (North Italy).

From 1830 to 1843 Murray ably seconded his father in the general conduct of the business of the firm. Henceforth the chief events of his life are closely connected with the books which he published for a succession of great writers. One of the last works issued by his father was Borrow's 'Bible in Spain' (1843); he maintained his father's cordial friendship with the author, and produced Borrow's later works, including 'Lavengro' (1851) and 'Wild Wales' (1862). He also inherited a close connection with Croker, Lyell, Lockhart, Hallam, Sir Francis Head, and Lord Stanhope. Among the earliest of his own publishing exploits were 'Nineveh and its Remains' (1848), giving the first news to the public of Layard's great discoveries in Syria; Lord Campbell's 'Lives of the Chancellors' (1845–48), and 'Lives of the Chief Justices' (1849); Grote's 'History of Greece' (1846–55); Murray's British Classics, including annotated library editions of Byron, Gibbon, Goldsmith, and other writers; and the series of valuable dictionaries connected with the name of Dr. (afterwards Sir William) Smith, a constant friend and adviser of the firm, who became editor of the 'Quarterly' in 1867. The numerous volumes of Milman's 'Latin Christianity' appeared rapidly between 1854 and 1856; Livingstone's 'Travels' in 1857; Darwin's 'Origin of Species' in 1859. Murray's later publications include Maine's 'Ancient Law,' Elwin's edition of Pope, Schliemann's 'Archæological Researches,' the architectural volumes of Fergusson and Street, Kugler's 'History of Painting,' and the various works of Dean Stanley, John Lothrop Motley, and Dr. Smiles; while quite a recent speculation was the monumental 'Dictionary of Hymnology' by Dr. Julian. Another great enterprise was 'The Speaker's Commentary' (1871–81), so called as having been originally set on foot by John Evelyn Denison, viscount Ossington [q. v.], speaker of the House of Commons. In 1887 he started 'Murray's Magazine,' in fulfilment of a project formed by his father as long ago as 1816; but the magazine ceased in 1891. On the other hand the 'Quarterly,' in spite of change and competition, fully sustained under Murray's auspices its reputation as an organ of the highest criticism. But perhaps the greatest glory of the firm under the third Murray's direction consists in the admirable series of illustrated books of travels, associated with the names of Miss Bird (Mrs. Bishop), Dr. Lumholtz, Du Chaillu, Bates, and Yule, whose edition of 'Marco Polo' was largely due to Murray's enlightened enterprise. One of the last books the production of which he superintended was Mr. Whymper's work on 'The High Andes;' this appeared almost simultaneously with Murray's death, which took place at 50 Albemarle Street on 2 April 1892. After a preliminary service in St. James's, Piccadilly, he was buried on 6 April in the parish church at Wimbledon, where he had resided for nearly fifty years. He had married in 1847 Marion, youngest daughter of Alexander Smith, banker, of Edinburgh, and sister of David Smith, a well-known writer to the signet, and left two sons, John and Hallam, who now conduct the business, and two daughters.

Murray was a survivor of the patriarchal age of English publishing, when the publisher endeavoured to associate with the functions of the capitalist the eighteenth-century traditions of literary patronage. He was well served by a retentive memory. He had spoken with Moore and Campbell, Rogers and Hazlitt, Crabbe and Southey; and remembered conducting the two lame poets Scott and Byron as they went stumping arm in arm down the staircase in Albemarle Street. This was in 1815, and shortly afterwards he was present at an interesting after-dinner conversation between Byron and Sir John Malcolm. As heir-presumptive of the house, he had also been present at the historic burning of Byron's manuscript 'Memoirs' in 1824, after a heated discussion in his father's drawing-room. But his most fortunate reminiscence was of the Theatrical Fund banquet in 1827 at Edinburgh, when Scott formally avowed himself author of the 'Waverley Novels.' He inherited intimacies with the Disraelis and with Mr. Gladstone, and he made for himself a host of friends among men of eminence. He was a magistrate for Surrey, a fellow of the Society of Antiquaries, and a well-known member of the Athenæum Club.

From the days when he attended Dr. Jamieson's classes at Edinburgh University, Murray was an ardent student of geology, and he published anonymously in 1877 (2nd edit. 1878) a book on the subject entitled 'Scepticism in Geology.'

Two portraits of the publisher, by Sir George Reid and Mr. C. W. Furse, are in the possession of his sons John and Hallam respectively.

[Smiles's A Publisher and his Friends, vol. ii. passim; Academy, 9 April 1892; Athenæum, Saturday Review, Graphic, and Illustrated London News (with portraits) of the same date; Times, Daily Chronicle, and Daily News, 4 April 1892; Blaikie's Life of Livingstone; Scott's Journals, ii. 440; Murray's Magazine, November 1887; private information.] T. S.

MURRAY, Sir JOHN ARCHIBALD, Lord Murray (1779–1859), Scottish judge, was the second son of Alexander Murray, lord Henderland [q. v.], lord of session and justiciary. His mother was Katherine, daughter of Sir Alexander Lindsay of Evelick, Perthshire, and a niece of the first Lord Mansfield. Born in Midlothian in 1779, he was educated successively at the Edinburgh High School, at Westminster School, and at the university of Edinburgh. At Edinburgh he was a member of the Juvenile Literary Society, of which Henry Brougham and Francis Horner were the leading spirits, and of the Speculative Society. He constantly corresponded with Horner till the latter's death in 1817, and his letters form a chief part of the 'Memoirs of Horner,' 1843. In 1799 Murray passed to the Scottish bar. On the establishment of the 'Edinburgh Review,' Sydney Smith, F. Horner, Francis Jeffrey, Dr. Thomas Brown, and he, met for a time as joint editors in Jeffrey's house, and he long continued a frequent contributor. His early career at the bar was distinguished, but being in easy circumstances he latterly relaxed his efforts. In 1826 he married Mary, the eldest daughter of William Rigby of Oldfield Hall, Cheshire.

An ardent liberal, Murray threw in his lot with the brilliant band of young Edinburgh whig lawyers, and took a prominent part in the agitation which led to the passing of the Reform Bill of 1832. In December of that year he was returned unopposed for Leith, which had been enfranchised under the bill, and was appointed recorder of the great roll and clerk of the pipe, a sinecure in the Scottish exchequer which he did not long hold. On the elevation of Jeffrey to the bench in 1835, Murray succeeded him as lord advocate. He introduced a large number of bills into the House of Commons, including measures for the reform of the universities, for giving popular magistracies to small towns, for enabling sheriffs to hold small-debt circuits, for the reform of the court of session, and for amending the bankruptcy law, but only succeeded in carrying a few minor reforms. In 1839 he was savagely attacked in parliament by his old friend Brougham for his conduct in the case of five cotton-spinners who were tried on a charge of murder arising out of a trade-union dispute, but he answered the charges to the complete satisfaction of the house. Murray seemed to feel himself unfitted for political life, and in 1839 he left parliament for the court of session. He was knighted and took his seat on the bench as Lord Murray. He remained on the bench till his death at Edinburgh in March 1859. His only son died in boyhood.

Murray's early manhood was the most brilliant portion of his career, but, though he never occupied that position in public life which might have been predicted for him from his early distinction, his connection with the past, his generous patronage of art and letters, his geniality and interest in the welfare of his fellow-citizens, gave him in his later years a peculiar position in Edinburgh society. His hospitality was profuse and famous. Scott in his 'Diary' records many pleasant evenings spent at Murray's house, and Harriet Martineau celebrates his tea-parties at St. Stephen's when he was lord advocate. In Edinburgh and in his country residence at Strachur on Loch Fyne, and afterwards in Jura, he gathered his friends round him, while Lady Murray, an accomplished musician, ably helped him to entertain them.

[Memoirs and Correspondence of Francis Horner, M.P., London, 1843; Journal of Henry Cockburn, Edinburgh, 1874; Biographical Sketches by Harriet Martineau, London, 1869; Scotsman, 18 March 1859; Journal of Sir Walter Scott, Edinburgh, 1890.] J. F–Y.

MURRAY, JOHN FISHER (1811–1865), Irish poet and humorist, eldest son of Dr. (afterwards Sir) James Murray [q. v.], was born in Belfast on 11 Feb. 1811, and after being educated in that town proceeded to Trinity College, Dublin, where he graduated B.A. in 1830 and M.A. in 1832. His earliest productions apparently were published in 'Blackwood's Magazine,' to which he was for some years a constant contributor. There he wrote many amusing sketches of London life, afterwards reprinted separately, and also some stories and a series of papers in 1840, entitled 'Some Account of Himself, by the Irish Oyster Eater,' which have been attributed to William Maginn [q. v.] He also wrote for the 'Belfast Vindicator,' previous to 1840, and when the 'Nation' was started in 1842 contributed occasionally in its columns. His article entitled 'War with Everybody,' in its third number, was reprinted in 'The Voice of the Nation,' a collection of articles from the paper published in 1844. After a long interval he also wrote some poems for it over the signature of 'Maire,' one or two of which are still remembered. To the 'United Irishman' of 1848 Murray contributed a few characteristic pieces, and the 'Dublin University Magazine' contains a good many of his productions. His last years were spent in retirement, and his death took place in Dublin on 20 Oct. 1865. He was buried in Glasnevin. Murray's writings exhibit great satirical power, and were in their day widely popular. His 'Viceroy' is a scathing description of life in fashionable Dublin at the beginning of the century. His published volumes are: 1. 'The Court Doctor Dissected,' a severe pamphlet on the case of Lady Flora Hastings [q. v.], 8vo, London, 1839; fourth edition, 1839. 2. 'The Chinese and the Ministry,' 8vo, London, 1840. 3. 'The Viceroy,' a three-volume novel, 12mo, London, 1841. 4. 'The Environs of London—Western Division,' 8vo, Edinburgh, 1842. 5. 'The World of London,' 2 vols. 8vo, Edinburgh, 1843; second series, 2 vols. 12mo, London, 1845.

[Duffy's Young Ireland, and Four Years of Irish History, 1880–1883; Northern Whig, 27 Oct. 1875; Brit. Mus. Cat.] D. J. O'D.

MURRAY, Mrs. LEIGH (*d.* 1892), actress. [See under Murray, Henry Leigh.]

MURRAY, LINDLEY (1745–1826), grammarian, was born at Swatara, Pennsylvania, on 22 April 1745. His father, Robert Murray, a member of an old quaker family, was one of the leading New York merchants. Murray was the eldest of twelve children, all of whom he survived, although he was puny and delicate in childhood. When six years old, he was sent to school in Philadelphia, but soon left to accompany his parents to North Carolina, where they lived until 1753. They then removed to New York, where Murray was sent to a good school, but proved a 'heedless boy' (*Autobiography*). Contrary to his inclinations, he was placed when only fourteen in his father's counting-house. In spite of endeavours to foster in him the commercial spirit, the lad's interests were mainly concentrated in science and literature. Collecting his books, he escaped to Burlington, New Jersey, entered a boarding-school, and commenced to study French. His retreat was discovered, he was brought back to New York, and allowed a private tutor. His father still desired him to apply himself to commerce, but he stated arguments in favour of a literary profession so ably in writing that his father's lawyer advised him to let the lad study law.

Four years later Murray was called to the bar, and practised as counsel and attorney in the province of New York. At the age of twenty-two he married, and in 1770 came to England, whither his father had preceded him, but Lindley returned in 1771 to New York. Here his practice became both large and lucrative, in spite of his conscientious care to 'discourage litigation, and to recommend a peaceable settlement of differences.' On the outbreak of hostilities in America, Murray went with his wife to Long Island, where four years were spent in fishing, sailing, and shooting. On the declaration of independence he returned to New York, and was so successful that he retired in 1783 to a beautiful place on the Hudson. His health failing, he decided to try the English climate. In 1784 he left America and never returned. The remainder of his life was spent in literary pursuits at Holgate, near York. His library became noted for its theological and philological treasures. He studied botany, and his garden was said to exceed in variety the Royal Gardens at Kew. The summer-house in which his grammars were composed still remains.

Murray's first published work, 'The Power

of Religion on the Mind,' York, 1787, 20th edit. 1842, was twice translated into French. To the 8th edit. (1795) was added 'Extracts from the Writings of divers Eminent Men representing the Evils of Stage Plays, &c.,' published separately 1789 and 1799. His attention was then drawn to the want of suitable lesson-books for a Friends' school for girls in York, and in 1795 he published his 'English Grammar.' The manuscript petition from the teachers requesting him to prepare it has been religiously preserved. The work became rapidly popular; it went through nearly fifty editions, was edited, abridged, simplified, and enlarged in England and America, and for a long time was used in schools to the exclusion of all other grammar-books. In 1816 an edition corrected by the author was issued in 2 vols. 8vo. An 'Abridgment' of this version by Murray, issued two years later, went through more than 120 editions of ten thousand each. It was printed at the New England Institution for the Blind in embossed characters, Boston, 1835, and translated into Maráthi, Bombay, 1837. 'English Exercises' followed (1797), with 'A Key' (27th edit. London, 1847), and both works were in large demand. Murray's 'English Reader,' 'Sequel,' and 'Introduction,' issued respectively 1799, 1800, and 1801 (31st edit. 1836), were equally successful, as well as the 'Lecteur Français,' 1802, and 'Introduction to the Lecteur Français,' 1807. 'An English Spelling Book,' 1804, reached forty-four editions, and was translated into Spanish (Cadiz, 1841). Of a 'First Book for Children' the 150th thousand, with portrait and woodcuts, was issued in 1859. The sales of the 'Grammar,' 'Exercises,' 'Key,' and 'Lecteur Français' brought Murray in each case 700*l.*, and he devoted the whole sum to philanthropic objects. The copyright of his religious works he presented to his publishers. By his will, a sum of money for the purchase and distribution of religious literature was vested in trustees in America. When the Retreat for the Insane was founded at York by William Tuke [q. v.] in 1792, Murray did his utmost to second Tuke's efforts to introduce a humane system of treatment.

He was a recorded minister of the York 'monthly meeting' for eleven years, when his voice failed and he asked permission to resign. For the last sixteen years of his life he never left the house. He died on 16 Jan. 1826, aged 81. Westoby, a miniature-painter who first saw him after death, produced an excellent portrait, which was engraved by Dean. Murray married, on 22 June 1767, Hannah Dobson, who died 25 Sept. 1834. They had no children.

Besides the works mentioned Murray was author of 'Some Account of the Life of Sarah Grubb,' Dublin, 1792; a 'Selection from Bishop Horne's Commentary on the Psalms,' 1812; 'A Biographical Sketch of Henry Tuke,' York, 1815; 'A Compendium of Religious Faith and Practice,' 1815; 'The Duty and Benefit of a daily perusal of the Holy Scriptures in Families,' York, 1817. In 1795 he also assisted the Friends confined in York Castle to prepare and publish 'The Prisoners' Defence' and the 'Prisoners' Defence supported.'

Murray was tall, slender, and of a ruddy complexion. In spite of bad health he was always cheerful, and his manner was conspicuously modest. He has been styled the father of English grammar, and his work, although not free from error and soon superseded, undoubtedly helped more efficiently than any contemporary manual to teach the Englishmen of his day to speak and write their language correctly. He introduced system into the study of grammar where chaos had existed before, but it is noticeable that his own style of writing frequently illustrates the defects which he warns his readers to avoid. There may have been some truth in the jest of his friend John Dalton [q. v.] the chemist, 'that of all the contrivances invented by human ingenuity for puzzling the brains of the young, Lindley Murray's grammar was the worst.'

[Memoir of the Life and Writings of Lindley Murray (partly autobiographical), by Elizabeth Frank, York, 1826; Life of Murray, by W. H. Egle, New York, 1885; Journal of Travels in England, &c., by B. Silliman of Yale College, Newhaven, 1820, iii. 156–8; Appleton's Cyclopædia of American Biog. iv. 470; Gent. Mag. 1826, pt. i. pp. 182–3; European Mag. 1803, pp. 35–6; The Bad English of Lindley Murray and other Writers, by G. Washington Moon, London, 1869; Annual Monitor, 1827 pp. 28–34, 1835 pp. 51–6; Smith's Cat. pp. 192–208, and Suppl. 1893, pp. 254–5; Dr. Hack Tuke's Reform in the Treatment of the Insane, 1892.] C. F. S.

MURRAY, MATTHEW (1765–1826), engineer, born in 1765 near Newcastle-on-Tyne, was apprenticed to a blacksmith, and on the expiration of his indentures found work, about 1789, at Marshall's, the great flax spinners, at Leeds. He introduced the use of 'sponge weights' for damping the front rollers of flax-spinning machines, which ultimately led to the important innovation of wet spinning, flax having previously been spun dry. In 1790 he took out a patent (No. 1752) for spinning and drawing-frames, and in 1793 another patent (No. 1971) for preparing and spinning flax, hemp, tow, wool, and silk, in which a carding engine is described. In the specification of these patents he describes himself as a 'whitesmith' and as a 'whitesmith and mechanic.' He was awarded a gold medal by the Society of Arts in 1809 for a machine for heckling flax (*Trans. Soc. Arts*, xxvii. 148).

He quitted Marshall's service in 1795, and started in business at Leeds, in partnership with James Fenton and David Wood, who found the necessary capital. The style of the firm was Fenton, Murray, & Wood, and subsequently Fenton, Murray, & Jackson. Their place of business was known as the Round Foundry, now in the occupation of Messrs. Smith, Beacock, & Tannett. In addition to the manufacture of flax machinery, Murray turned his attention to the steam-engine, and the firm became a formidable rival to Boulton & Watt, who went the length of surreptitiously purchasing the adjacent land, to prevent the extension of the foundry (Smiles, *Industrial Biography*, p. 262). He was one of the first to study the external form of the steam-engine, endeavouring to improve the general design of the machine, as well as to secure compactness of arrangement, solidity, and accessibility of parts. Views of Murray's engines may be found in Stuart's 'Anecdotes of Steam Engines' (ii. 441–4); Farey's 'Steam Engine' (pp. 682, 688, 691); Nicholson's 'Journal of Science' (1805, ix. 93). He took out patents for improvements in various details of the steam-engine in 1799 (No. 2327), 1801 (No. 2531), and 1802 (No. 2632). The patent of 1801 was set aside by *scire facias*, at the instance of Boulton & Watt, on the ground that certain portions of it infringed their rights (*Repertory of Arts*, 1803, 2nd ser. iii. 235). Murray is generally credited with the invention of the 'short D-slide valve' for controlling the supply of steam to the cylinder, and an approach to that form may be seen in his patent of 1802. It is described by Farey (p. 692) as forming part of one of Murray's engines built in 1810. As a proof of the soundness of Murray's work it may be mentioned that one of his engines, put up at Water Hall Mills, Leeds, about 1813, is still in good condition, and was regularly running until 1885.

In 1812 Murray was employed by Blenkinsop to build locomotives to run on his rack railway from Middleton collieries to Leeds, a distance of about three miles and a half. The 'Salamanca' and the 'Prince Regent' were put upon the road in 1812, and the 'Lord Wellington' and 'Marquis Wellington' in the following year. This was the first instance of the regular employment of locomotives for commercial purposes, and the engines ran for at least twenty years (Wood, *Railroads*, 1831, 2nd ed. p. 128). They were fitted with two double-acting cylinders, no fly-wheel being required. This was an important improvement. Murray was also a builder of boat engines, and the 'Leeds Mercury' of 24 June 1813 states that a steamboat to ply between Yarmouth and Norwich was then being fitted up in the canal basin at Leeds. This boat ran regularly until April 1817, when the boiler exploded, and several persons were killed (see *Society of Arts Journal*, 30 March 1877, p. 446, 7 Sept. 1877, p. 943). He is one of the numerous claimants to the invention of the planing-machine, which seems to have been in use in his shop in 1814.

Murray died at Holbeck, Leeds, 20 Feb. 1826, and was buried in Holbeck churchyard.

[Smiles's Industrial Biography, pp. 260–4; Meysey-Thompson in Proceedings of the Institution of Mechanical Engineers, 1882, p. 266; information communicated by Murray's grandson, Mr. George March of Leeds.] R. B. P.

MURRAY, MUNGO (*d.* 1770), writer on shipbuilding, published in 1754 a 'Treatise on Shipbuilding and Navigation,' 4to. On the title-page he describes himself as 'Shipwright in his Majesty's yard, Deptford;' and in an advertisement it is stated that in the evenings, from six to eight, except Wednesdays and Saturdays, he taught 'the several branches of mathematics treated of in the book,' and sold mathematical instruments. In May 1758 he was appointed to the Magnanime, with Lord Howe, in the rating of midshipman, but in reality, it would seem, as a teacher of mathematics and navigation; and on 9 Jan. 1760 he received a warrant as schoolmaster. In June 1762 he was turned over, with Howe, to the Princess Amelia, which was paid off at the peace (*Pay-book of Magnanime and Princess Amelia*). During his service in the Magnanime, which embraced the date of the battle of Quiberon Bay, he published 'The Rudiments of Navigation . . . compiled for the use of the Young Gentlemen on board the Magnanime,' 1760, 8vo (there is a copy in the library of the Royal Society). In 1764 he wrote a short note on an eclipse of the sun, which was printed in the 'Philosophical Transactions' (liv. 171). In 1765 he issued a new and enlarged edition of his 'Treatise on Shipbuilding,' and at some later date 'Four Prints (with references and explanations), exhibiting the different Views of a Sixty-gun Ship.' The prints, but not the explanations, are in the British Museum. These last are in the library of the Royal

United Service Institution. He describes himself on the title-page as then carpenter of the Weymouth. He also published 'Forty Plates of Elevations, Sections, and Plans of different Vessels.' The copy in the British Museum wants the title-page. He died 19 Oct. 1770. When in the Magnanime his wages were paid to Christian Murray, presumably his wife.

[Gent. Mag. 1770, p. 487.] J. K. L.

MURRAY, PATRICK, fifth Baron Elibank (1703–1778), born in 1703, was son of Patrick Murray, fourth lord Elibank (1677–1736), by his wife Elizabeth (*d.* 1756), daughter of George Stirling of Keir, and an eminent surgeon in Edinburgh. General James Murray (1720–1794) [q. v.] was his younger brother. Although admitted a member of the Faculty of Advocates in 1722, he soon turned from legal to military pursuits, becoming an ensign in the army, and subsequently major in Ponsonby's foot and lieutenant-colonel in Wynyard's marines. With the latter regiment he served at the siege of Carthagena in 1740.

After the failure of that expedition Murray quitted the army. He had married in 1735, and had succeeded his father as Lord Elibank the next year. Returning to Scotland, he associated chiefly with the members of the legal profession, among whom he had been brought up, and seems to have been very popular; but his chief interests were literary. He was long in intimate relations with Lord Kames and David Hume, and the three were regarded in Edinburgh as a committee of taste in literary matters, from whose judgment there was no appeal. He was the early patron of Dr. Robertson the historian, and of Home the tragic poet, both of whom were at one time ministers of country parishes near his seat in East Lothian.

Upon the accession of George III Elibank, like many other Jacobites, rallied to the house of Hanover; and when Lord Bute came into power it was determined to bring him into the House of Lords. This plan was, however, foiled by a severely sarcastic article by Wilkes in the 'North Briton' on his presumed services to the Pretender. Wilkes had been an unsuccessful candidate for the governorship of Canada when that office was conferred on Elibank's brother, General James Murray.

When in Scotland in 1773 Dr. Johnson paid Elibank a visit at his house of Ballencrieff, Haddingtonshire, and is said to have told him, when taking leave, that he was 'one of the few Scotchmen whom he met with pleasure and parted from with regret.' To Elibank is ascribed the reply made to Dr Johnson, when the latter remarked that 'oatmeal was food for horses in England and for men in Scotland:' 'And where would you see such horses and such men?' The doctor also on one occasion observed that he was never in Elibank's company without learning something. 'Lord Elibank,' he remarked to Boswell, 'has read a great deal. It is true I can find in books all that he has read; but he has a great deal of what is in books, proved by the test of real life.' Smollett in his 'Humphry Clinker' (Letter of 18 July) described him as a nobleman whom he had 'long revered for his humanity and universal intelligence, over and above the entertainment arising from the originality of his character' (cf. Alexander Carlyle's *Autobiog.* p. 266).

Elibank died at Ballencrieff on 3 Aug. 1778. He was married in 1735 to Maria Margaretta, daughter of Cornelius de Yonge, lord of Elmeet in Holland, receiver-general of the United Provinces, and widow of William, lord North and Grey; but there was no issue of the marriage. Lady Elibank's jointure-house was Kirtling Park, Cambridgeshire, the ancient seat of the North family, now pulled down, and there she and Elibank often resided. She died in 1762.

Elibank's works were: 1. 'Thoughts on Money Circulation and Paper Currency,' Edinburgh, 1758. 2. 'Queries relating to the proposed Plan of altering the Entails in Scotland,' Edinburgh, 1765. 3. 'Letter to Lord Hailes on his Remarks on the History of Scotland,' Edinburgh, 1773. 4. 'Considerations on the present State of the Peerage of Scotland,' Edinburgh, 1774, in which he attacked with much warmth the mode of electing Scottish peers to the House of Lords.

[Douglas's Scottish Peerage, ed. Wood; Manuscripts of John Ramsay of Ochtertyre; Boswell's Life of Johnson, ed. Dr. Birkbeck Hill; John Wilkes' The North Briton.] D. O. M.

MURRAY, PATRICK ALOYSIUS (1811–1882), catholic theologian, was born at Clones, co. Monaghan, on 18 Nov. 1811. He entered Maynooth on 25 Aug. 1829. After his six years' course he became a curate, and in the summer of 1838 was appointed professor of belles-lettres in the college. In 1841 he was appointed to the chair of theology, and held the post for forty-one years. Nearly two thousand priests passed through his classes. Personally he was held in reverence, but Carlyle, who saw him in Ireland during his tour, was not favourably impressed by him. He died in the college on 15 Nov. 1882, and was buried within its precincts. His greatest work was the 'Tractatus de Ecclesia Christi' (Dublin, 3 vols. 1860-6). Dr. Healy, a distinguished scholar, now bishop of Clonfert, who wrote the obituary notice of Dr. Murray for the 'Freeman's Journal' (17 Nov. 1882), declares that this 'great treatise is now universally recognised as the most complete and exhaustive work in that wide branch of theological science. It is admitted to be the highest authority even in the French and Roman schools.' A compendium of it, in one volume, was published for Maynooth students. Murray was for many years one of the leading contributors to the 'Dublin Review,' and was a poet of ability.

His other works are: 1. 'The Irish Annual Miscellany,' 1850, &c. 2. 'Essays, chiefly Theological,' 1851. 3. 'Sponsa Mater et Christi,' a poem, with notes and illustrations, 8vo, Dublin, 1858. 4. 'Prose and Verse,' 8vo, Dublin and London, 1867. 5. 'Tractatus de Gratia,' 8vo, Dublin, 1877.

[Irish Monthly, xix. 337–46; Freeman's Journ. 17 Nov. 1882; Brit. Mus. Cat.] D. J. O'D.

MURRAY or **MORAY**, **Sir ROBERT** (*d.* 1673), one of the founders of the Royal Society, was a grandson of Robert Moray of Abercairney, and son of Sir Mungo Moray of Craigie in Perthshire, by his wife, a daughter of George Halket of Pitfirran, Perthshire. His brother, Sir William Moray of Dreghorn, was master of the works to Charles II. Robert was born about the beginning of the seventeenth century, was educated at the university of St. Andrews and in France, and took military service under Louis XIII. Richelieu favoured him highly, and he attained the rank of lieutenant-colonel, probably of the Scots guard. He returned, however, to Britain soon after the civil troubles began, and was knighted by Charles I at Oxford on 10 Jan. 1643. He left England immediately afterwards to take up his command in France, came to be on good terms with Mazarin, and fought with his regiment in Germany. With a brother and another fellow-officer of the Scots regiment he was made a prisoner of war in Bavaria in 1645. In the same year James Campbell, earl of Irvine, colonel of the Scots regiment, died, and Moray was appointed in Irvine's place. He was also nominated by the Scots as a secret envoy to negotiate a treaty between France and Scotland by which it was proposed to attempt the restoration of Charles I. His release from Bavaria was therefore obtained, and, arriving in London, he was in constant communication with the French envoy, De Montereul. He revisited Paris in 1646 in order to bring the negotiation to a conclusion. Subsequently he recommended the king's surrender to the Scots, and was with Charles both at Newark and Newcastle. In December 1646 he concerted with William Murray, later Earl of Dysart [q. v.], at Newcastle, a plan for the king's escape from Scottish custody, which was barely frustrated by the royal captive's timidity (cf. Gardiner, *Great Civil War*, and *Hamilton Papers*, Camden Soc., i. 106–46, where, in addition to numerous references to Moray, are a number of his letters). Moray left Newcastle just before the king was delivered by the Scots to the army. De Montereul complained that Moray deceived him as to the Scots' intentions through this critical period. Clarendon mentions him as 'a cunning and a dexterous man,' employed by the Scots in 1645 in a futile negotiation for the establishment of presbyterian government in England (*Hist. of the Rebellion*, iv. 163, Macray's edit.)

Moray resumed his career in France after the downfall of monarchy in England, and the Scottish parliament sent cargoes of prisoners to recruit his corps. He continued at the same time in the confidence of Charles II, and seems to have been with him in Scotland in 1651, when he received the nominal appointments of justice-clerk and lord of session, and was nominated privy councillor. In 1653 he took arms in the highlands under William Cunningham, ninth earl of Glencairn [q. v.], but the collapse of the rising, and perhaps the disclosure of a plot to destroy his credit with the army, induced him, in May 1654, to join the king in Paris, with his brother-in-law, Alexander Lindsay, earl of Balcarres [q. v.], and Lady Balcarres (Lady Anna Mackenzie), whom he called his 'gossip' and 'cummer.' They were subsequently joined by Alexander Bruce, afterwards second Earl of Kincardine [q. v.], Moray's correspondence with whom is of singular interest. Between 1657 and 1660 Murray was at Maestricht, Bruce at Bremen. His life, he tells Bruce, was that of a recluse, most of his time being devoted to chemical pursuits. The cultivation of music, although 'three fiddles' were 'hanging by his side on the wall' as he wrote, was relegated to better times. The letters show literary cultivation, wide knowledge, strong common sense, as well as nobility of mind and tenderness of heart.

Moray repaired to London shortly after the Restoration, having first successfully conducted a negotiation with the presbyterians regarding the introduction of episcopacy into Scotland, a measure which he, however, desired to postpone. He was reappointed lord of session and justice-clerk in

1661, but never sat on the bench. He was also a lord of exchequer for Scotland, and became deputy-secretary on 5 June 1663. Thenceforward, down to 1670, the government of that country was mainly carried on by Lauderdale, the king, and himself [see MAITLAND, JOHN, second EARL and first DUKE OF LAUDERDALE]. Charles had great confidence in him, and his counsels were uniformly for prudence and moderation. Despatched to Scotland by Lauderdale in May 1667, he executed with firmness and skill his difficult task of breaking up the cabal between the church and the military party. His tour of inspection through the western counties included a visit to James Hamilton, third marquis and first duke [q. v.] Until Lauderdale finally broke with him in 1670, Moray was his zealous coadjutor, sparing no pains to maintain him in the royal favour. Yet the disinterestedness and elevation of his aims were universally admitted. He was devoid of ambition; indeed, as he said, he 'had no stomach for public employments.'

Moray took an active share in the foundation of the Royal Society, and presided almost continuously over its meetings from March 1661 to July 1662. He watched assiduously over its interests, and was described by Huygens as its 'soul.' He imparted to it his observations of the comet of December 1664 (BIRCH, *Hist. of the Royal Society*, i. 508, 510), and his communications on points connected with geology and natural history were numerous.

Moray mixed largely in London society. Burnet regarded him as 'another father,' and extols him as 'the wisest and worthiest man of the age' (*Hist. of his own Time*, ii. 20). His genius he considered to be much like that of Peiresc, and his knowledge of nature unsurpassed. 'He had a most diffused love of mankind, and he delighted in every occasion of doing good, which he managed with great discretion and zeal' (*ib.* i. 101–2). His temper and principles were stoical, but religion was the mainspring of his life, and amidst courts and camps he spent many hours a day in devotion. Wood calls him 'a renowned chymist, a great patron of the Rosicrucians, and an excellent mathematician,' and asserts that 'though presbyterianly inclined, he had the king's ear as much as any other person, and was indefatigable in his undertakings' (*Athenæ Oxon.* ed. Bliss, ii. 725). Charles II, indeed, thoroughly esteemed him, and often visited him privately in his laboratory at Whitehall. The king used to say, in illustration of Moray's independence of character, that he 'was head of his own church.' Evelyn styled him his 'dear and excellent friend' (*Diary*, ii. 84, 1850 edit.) Pepys speaks of him as 'a most excellent man of reason and learning, and understands the doctrine of musique and everything else I could discourse of, very finely' (*Diary*, 16 Feb. 1667). Yet his brilliant gifts left no lasting impress on his time. Many of his letters to Huygens, whom he kept informed of the progress of science in London, have been recently published at the Hague (*Œuvres Complètes de C. Huygens*, iii. iv. 1890–1).

He died suddenly on 4 July 1673, in his pavilion in the gardens of Whitehall, and was buried at the king's expense in Westminster Abbey, near the monument to Sir William D'Avenant [q. v.] About 1647 Moray married Sophia, daughter of David Lindsay, first lord Balcarres. She died at Edinburgh on 2 Jan. 1653, and was buried at Balcarres. They had no children.

[Correspondence of Sir Robert Moray with Alexander Bruce, 1657–1660, by Osmund Airy, Scottish Review, v. 22 (the materials for which were furnished by a manuscript copy of the letters in question lent by Mr. David Douglas of Edinburgh, the originals being in the possession of the Earl of Elgin); notes from the archives of the French foreign office (despatches of De Montereul to Mazarin 1645–8) kindly supplied by Mr. J. G. Fotheringham of Paris; the Lauderdale Papers, vols. i. ii., published by the Camden Soc., 1884–5, ed. O. Airy; Phil. Trans. Abridged, ii. 106 (Hutton); Birch's Hist. of the Royal Society, iii. 113, and passim; Chambers's Biog. Dict. of Eminent Scotsmen (Thomson); Burke's Hist. of the Landed Gentry, i. 540, 7th edit.; Douglas's Peerage of Scotland, i. 168; Lord Lindsay's Memoir of Lady Anna Mackenzie, p. 32, 1868 edit.; Chester's Registers of Westminster, 1876; Stanley's Hist. Memorials of Westminster Abbey, p. 297; Biog. Brit. (Kippis), art. 'Brouncker;' Thomson's Hist. of the Royal Soc.; Poggendorff's Biog.-lit. Handwörterbuch.]
A. M. C.

MURRAY, ROBERT (1635–1725?), writer on trade, born in 1635 in the Strand, London, was son of Robert Murray, 'civis et scissor Londini.' In 1649 he was entered as an apprentice on the books of the Clothworkers' Company, and took up his freedom in 1660. He is subsequently spoken of as 'milliner,' and again as 'uphosterer,' but describes himself in his publications as 'gent.,' possibly having retired from the trade.

For several years from 1676 he wrote on matters of banking and national revenue. He was the inventor of ruled copybooks for children, and in 1681 or, according to Wood, in 1679, he is said to have originated the idea of the penny post in London, 'but to Dockwra belongs the credit of giving it practical shape' (JOYCE, *History of the Post Office*, p. 36). The earliest instance of a stamped penny letter is dated 9 Dec. 1681. Two years later he assigned his interest in this to William Docwra [q. v.], merchant, of London, but in 1690 it was adjudged to pertain to the Duke of York as a branch of the general post office (cf. WOOD, *Athenæ Oxon.* ed. Bliss, iii. 726). He is questionably identified by Wood with the Robert Murray who was 'afterwards clerk to the general commissioners for the revenue of Ireland, and clerk to the commissioners of the grand excise of England.' In August 1697 he had been active in the 'malt and other' proposals in parliament, and was then in custody in a sponging house near St. Clement's Church. In 1703 he offered to the Lord High Treasurer 'a scheme for tin,' and asked for the royal bounty. Some time before July 1720 he succeeded George Murray as 'comptroller and paymaster of the standing orders of the lottery of 1714,' and in this capacity had transactions with the South Sea Company. By the act 10 & 11 Will. III c. 17 lotteries had been prohibited, but from 1709 onwards the government resorted to them as a means of raising money. In 1714 exchequer bills had been issued to the amount of 1,400,000*l.*, but lottery prizes were offered in addition to interest in the shape of terminable or perpetual annuities. In 1721, after a memorial from Murray, the South Sea Company proposed to discharge the unsubscribed orders into their own capital stock (for Murray's part in this transaction see *Treasury Papers*, vol. ccxxxiii. passim).

Murray was superseded as paymaster of this lottery in 1724, and in February 1726 is spoken of as the 'late Robert Murray, Esq.' His will is not in the prerogative court.

He published: 1. 'A Proposal for the Advancement of Trade, &c.,' London, 1676 (a proposal for the establishment of a combined bank and Lombard or *mont de piété* for the issue of credit against 'dead stock' deposited at 6 per cent. interest). 2. 'Composition Credit, or a Bank of Credit made Current by Common Consent in London more Useful than Money,' London, 1682. 3. 'An Account of the Constitution and Security of the General Bank of Credit,' London, 1683. 4. 'A Proposal for the more easy advancing to the Crown any fixed Sum of Money to carry on the War against France,' &c. (a noticeable proposal to establish negotiable bills of credit upon security of some branch of the royal revenue; Murray's credit bank proposals presage the greater scheme of Law, but it does not show the remarkable grasp of theory which characterises Law). 5. 'A Proposal for the better securing our Wool against Exportation by working up and manufacturing such' (a proposal to revive the law of the staple, and to establish a royal company of staplers). 6. 'A Proposal for translating the Duty of Excise from Malt Drinks to Mast, whereby may be advanced to the Crown 15 Millions for the War against France.' 7. 'An Advertisement for the more Easy and Speedy Collecting of Debts.' The last four publications are without place or date.

[Wood's Athenæ Oxon. iii. 726, 1264; Haydn's Dict. of Dates; Cal. of Treasury Papers, vols. i. ii. and iii.; Lascelles's Liber Mun. Publ. Hib.; Commons' Journals, ix. 331 seq.; Hist. MSS. Comm. 10th Rep. iv. 125; Brit. Mus. MS. 5755; Harl. MS. 1898; information from Sir Owen Roberts, clerk to the Clothworkers' Company.]

W. A. S.

MURRAY, the HON. MRS. SARAH (1744–1811), topographical writer. [See AUST.]

MURRAY, SIR TERENCE AUBREY (1810–1873), Australian politician, son of Captain Terence Murray of the 48th foot, by Ellen, daughter of James Fitzgerald of Movida, co. Limerick, was born at Limerick in 1810, and educated in Dublin. In 1827 he went to New South Wales with his father, and spent four years on his father's sheep station at Lake George. In 1833 he was gazetted a magistrate, and in connection with the mounted police helped to repress bushranging. From 1843 to 1856 he represented Murray, King, and Georgiana in the legislature of New South Wales, and after a fully responsible government was granted to the colony in 1856, Murray sat in the legislative assembly for Argyle from that date until 1862, when he was appointed a member of the legislative council or upper house. From 26 Aug. 1856 to 2 Oct. 1856 he was secretary for lands and works in the Cowper ministry, also acting as auditor-general from 26 Aug. to 16 Sept.; he was again secretary for lands and public works in the second Cowper ministry from 7 Sept. 1857 to 12 Jan. 1858. On 31 Jan. 1860 he was elected speaker of the legislative assembly, and on 14 Oct. 1862 president of the legislative council, an office which he held till 22 June 1873. He was knighted by letters patent on 4 May 1869. He died at Sydney on 22 June 1873.

He married, first, in 1843, Mary, second daughter of Colonel Gibbes, the collector of customs at Sydney (she died in 1857); and, secondly, Agnes, third daughter of John

Edwards of Fairlawn House, Hammersmith, London. She died February 1890. The second son by the second marriage, George Gilbert Aimé Murray, born at Sydney in 1866, became Regius Professor of Greek at Oxford in 1908.

[Times, 28 July 1873, 4 Sept.; Dod's Peerage, 1873, p. 483; Melbourne Argus, 24 June 1873; Heaton's Australian Dict.] G. C. B.

MURRAY, THOMAS (1564–1623), provost of Eton, born in 1564, was the son of Murray of Woodend, and uncle of William Murray, first earl of Dysart [q. v.] He was early attached to the court of James VI of Scotland, and soon after James's accession to the English throne was appointed tutor to Charles, then duke of York. On 26 June 1605 he was granted a pension of two hundred marks for life, and in July was presented, through the intervention of the Bishop of Durham, to the mastership of Christ's Hospital, Sherburn, near Durham. From that time he received numerous grants, and was in constant communication with the Earl of Salisbury, Sir Albertus Morton, Sir Dudley Carleton, and others, many of his letters being preserved among the state papers (cf. *Cal. State Papers*, Dom. Ser. 1603–23, passim). He was 'much courted, but his honesty' made 'him well esteemed.' Andrew Melville [q. v.], when he sought his liberty in November 1610, placed the management of his case in the hands of Murray, to whom he refers as his special friend. In 1615 George Gladstanes [q. v.], archbishop of St. Andrews, made an unsuccessful attempt to get Murray removed from the tutorship of Prince Charles as 'ill-affected to the estate of the kirk.' In August 1617 the king promised him the provostship of Eton, but his appointment was opposed on suspicion of his puritanism, and he received the post of secretary to Prince Charles instead. In October 1621 he was confined to his house for opposing the Spanish marriage. In February 1621–2 he was elected provost of Eton, but fell seriously ill in February 1622–3, and died on 9 April, aged 59. He left behind him five sons and two daughters, one of whom became the wife of Sir Henry Newton, afterwards Puckering [q. v.], while the other was Lady Anne Halkett [q. v.] His widow, Jane, and a son received a pension of 500*l.* for their lives.

Murray was author of some Latin poems, which have been printed in the 'Delitiæ Poetarum Scotorum,' ed. 1637, ii. 180–200. He has been eulogised by John Leech [q. v.] in his 'Epigrammata,' ed. 1623, p. 19, and by Arthur Johnston [q. v.] in his 'Poemata,' ed. 1642, p. 381.

[Cal. State Papers, Dom. Ser. 1603–23, passim; McCrie's Life of Melville, ii. 269, 528; Harwood's Alumni Etonenses; Douglas's Peerage, ed. Wood, i. 486; Birch's Life of Henry, Prince of Wales, p. 295, note; Le Neve's Fasti, iii. 243.] A. F. P.

MURRAY, SIR THOMAS (1630?–1684), of Glendoick, clerk-register, was descended from a junior branch of the Murrays of Tullibardine, now represented by the Duke of Atholl. Born about 1630, he was the younger son of Thomas Murray of Cassochie and Woodend, advocate, who was sheriff-depute of Perthshire in 1649, and died in 1666. Having adopted the law as his profession, he was admitted advocate on 14 Dec. 1661. A second cousin of Lady Elizabeth Murray, countess of Dysart [q. v.], her patronage speedily brought preferment. In 1662 he was appointed lord-clerk-register, and on 14 June 1674 he became a senator of the College of Justice, with the title of Lord Glendoick, a designation taken from the estate in the Carse of Gowrie, which he had purchased, and which was ratified to him by parliament in February 1672. On 2 July 1676 he was created a baronet of Nova Scotia. In 1679 a royal license was granted to him to 'reprint the whole acts, laws, constitutions, and ordinances of the parliament of the kingdom of Scotland, both old and new.' The license was granted for nineteen years, and Murray farmed it to David Lindsay, merchant, and John Cairnes, printer, both of Edinburgh. He does not seem to have taken much share in the preparation of the volumes that still are quoted under his name, and certainly did not avail himself of the special facilities for executing the work which his position as lord-clerk-register gave him. His edition of the statutes is copied directly from Skene's edition of 1597, with the subsequent laws printed from sessional publications to bring up the work to 1681. 'This is the more unpardonable,' writes Professor Cosmo Innes, 'since he professes to have extracted the work from the original records of parliament; whereas, in fact, even the more accurate and ample edition of 1566 does not appear to have been consulted.' Two editions were printed in 1681, one of them in duodecimo and the other in folio. The former, though most frequently quoted, is the less accurate, and reproduces even the typographical errors of Skene's edition. But Murray's edition of the statutes, with all its imperfections, was habitually quoted in the Scottish courts as an authority until the beginning of this century.

The marriage of Lady Dysart with the

Duke of Lauderdale secured Murray for a time in his public offices, and it was supposed that he shared his emoluments with the duchess. When the power of the duke was overthrown Murray was superseded. His name was not included in the commission for the administration of justice appointed in 1681, and his office of lord-clerk-register was given to Sir George Mackenzie [q. v.] of Tarbat, afterwards Earl of Cromarty. Murray spent the remainder of his life in retirement. His death took place in 1684, not 1687 as usually stated; his eldest son was served heir to him in February 1685. By his marriage with Barbara, daughter of Thomas Hepburn of Blackcastle, he had five sons and four daughters. The two eldest sons succeeded each other in the baronetcy, but the title expired with Sir Alexander Murray of Balmanno and Glendoick, fifth baronet and great-grandson of Sir Thomas, who was killed in the American war of independence in 1776.

[Brunton and Haig's Senators of the College of Justice; Cosmo Innes's edition of the Acts of the Parliaments of Scotland; Millar's Roll of Eminent Burgesses of Dundee; Ross and Grant's Nisbet's Heraldic Plates.] A. H. M.

MURRAY or MURREY, THOMAS (1663–1734), portrait-painter, born in 1663, was of Scottish origin, and received his first lessons in art from one of the De Critz family [see under De Critz, John]. Subsequently he became a pupil of the eminent portrait-painter, John Riley [q. v.] Like his master, Murrey was nothing more than a face-painter, leaving the rest of the picture to be completed by others. He had a delicate and expressive method of painting, which is much obscured by the dull heaviness of the accessories in his portraits. Murrey was handsome in appearance, as appears from his portrait by himself in the gallery of painters in the Uffizi Gallery at Florence, which has been engraved several times. He amassed a great deal of money, which he increased by usury and extremely parsimonious habits. He died in June 1734, leaving no children, and bequeathed his money to a nephew, with instructions that his monument, with a bust, should be erected in Westminster Abbey, provided that it did not cost too much. His nephew, however, taking him at his word, buried him in St. Paul's, Covent Garden, and found the monument too expensive to erect. Murrey's portraits are frequently to be met with, and many of them were engraved, especially by the mezzotint engravers of the day. Among them may be noted Captain William Dampier and Sir John Pratt at the National Portrait Gallery, Sir Hans Sloane at the Royal College of Physicians, Edmund Halley at the Royal Society, Bishop Buckeridge at St. John's College, Oxford, Queen Anne (full length, seated) in the townhall at Stratford-on-Avon, King William and Queen Mary in Fishmongers' Hall, London, Christopher, duke of Albemarle (an early work), Henry St. John, viscount Bolingbroke, George, landgrave of Hesse, Bishop Edmund Gibson, Philip Frowde (1732), and many others.

[Vertue's Notebooks (Brit. Mus. Add. MS. 23076); Redgrave's Dict. of Artists; information from George Scharf, esq., C.B.] L. C.

MURRAY, THOMAS (1792–1872), printer and miscellaneous writer, was born of working-class parents in 1792, in the parish of Girthon, Kirkcudbrightshire. He was educated at the parish school, and at Edinburgh University, which he entered in 1810. Thomas Carlyle, Alexander Murray [q. v.], the oriental scholar, and he were early friends, and walked together from Galloway to Edinburgh each session during their college career. A regular correspondence passed between Carlyle and Murray for some years afterwards. One of Murray's letters appears in Froude's 'Carlyle.' Murray was destined for the ministry of the established church, but, after obtaining license and preaching for some time, he took to literary pursuits. He became connected with Sir David Brewster and a staff of writers on 'Brewster's Cyclopædia,' and formed the acquaintance of Leonard Horner [q. v.] and John Ramsay McCulloch [q. v.], who imbued him with his free-trade principles and a taste for political economy. In 1843 he was one of the founders, and for many years afterwards (1843–72) secretary, of the Edinburgh Galloway Association, the prototype of numerous county associations now flourishing in Edinburgh. In 1846 he was one of the founders and original members of the Edinburgh Philosophical Institution (of which Thomas Carlyle was president till his death), and acted for about thirty years as secretary of the Edinburgh School of Arts (1844–72). For six years (1854–60) he was a member of the Edinburgh town council, where he acted with the whig or moderate liberal party. In 1841 Murray established in Edinburgh the printing business of Murray & Gibb, the firm afterwards becoming her majesty's printers for Scotland. This business proved most successful, and still flourishes under the name of Morrison & Gibb. He died at Elm Bank, near Lasswade on 15 April 1872. He left a widow (Janet, daughter of Alexander Murray of Wigton) and two daughters, one of whom married Sir William Wilson Hunter, K.C.S.I. Murray was sagacious and kindly, and made many friends. He was a patient, if not profound, scholar of the old Scottish type, and had commenced the study of Gaelic at the time of his death.

His works, apart from pamphlets, are: 1. 'The Literary History of Galloway: from the Earliest Period to the Present Time,' Edinburgh, 1822, 8vo. 2. 'The Life of Samuel Rutherford,' Edinburgh, 1828, 12mo. 3. 'The Life of Robert Leighton, D.D., archbishop of Glasgow,' Edinburgh, 1828, 12mo. 4. 'The Life of John Wycliffe,' Edinburgh, 1829, 12mo. 5. 'Biographical Annals of the Parish of Colinton,' Edinburgh, 1863, 8vo. Murray also edited Samuel Rutherford's 'Last Speeches of John, Viscount Kenmure,' Edinburgh, 1827, 12mo; and 'Letters of David Hume,' Edinburgh, 1841, 8vo.

[Obituary notice in the Scotsman, 16 April 1872; information supplied by Lady Hunter.]

G. S-H.

MURRAY, Sir WILLIAM (*d.* 1583), of Tullibardine, comptroller of Scotland, was the eldest son of Sir William Murray of Tullibardine, by Catherine, daughter of Sir Duncan Campbell of Glenurchy. The family was descended from Sir William de Moravia, who in 1284 acquired the lands of Tullibardine, Perthshire, by marriage with Adda, daughter of Malise of Strathern. This Sir William represented a younger branch of the Murrays, having as their common ancestor a Flemish settler of the name of Freskin, who in 1130 obtained a large grant of land in the district of Moray. Of the elder branch were the Morays, lords of Bothwell, and the Morays of Abercairny. Among the more notable of the lairds of Tullibardine was Andrew, the son of the first Sir William, who in August 1332 by guiding the English to a ford across the Earn, which he had marked with a large stake, was the chief means of the Scottish defeat at Dupplin. For his treason he was shortly afterwards executed at Perth. The father of the comptroller was a supporter of the lords of the congregation against the queen-regent, and signed the instructions to the commissioners for the treaty at Berwick-on-Tweed in February 1559-60 (Knox, *Works*, ii. 56). He died in January 1562. The son was a supporter of the Darnley marriage, and was present at St. Andrews when the band of the men of Fife was received (*Reg. P. C. Scotl.* i. 367). From 1566 to his death he was comptroller, and was named a member of the privy council 5 Nov. 1565 (*ib.* p. 389). He was lodged in the palace of Holyrood at the time of the murder of Rizzio, but that same night was permitted by the conspirators to retire from the palace (Sir James Melville, *Memoirs*, p. 149). After the queen's marriage to Bothwell he joined the confederate lords, and he was one of the principal leaders of the army that assembled against her at Carberry. When Bothwell refused on the ground of his rank the challenge of Tullibardine's brother, James Murray of Pardewis [q. v.], Tullibardine himself took it up, asserting that his house was more ancient than Bothwell's (Knox, ii. 561). During the queen's journey to Edinburgh after her surrender the followers of Tullibardine were among the most prominent in raising cries of execration against her (Drury to Cecil, 20 June, *Cal. State Papers*, For. Ser. 1566-8, entry 1324). Tullibardine is mentioned by Morton as present at the 'sichting' of the Casket letters on 21 June (Henderson, *Casket Letters*, p. 115). He attended the coronation of the young king at Stirling on 29 July (*Reg. P. C. Scotl.* i. 537-8). On 9 Aug. in a conference with Throckmorton, he revealed to him a proposal of the Hamiltons for the execution of the queen, on account of her connection with the murder, as the best method of reconciling all parties (*Cal. State Papers*, Scott. Ser. i. 255, and more at length in Tytler's *History of Scotland*, ed. 1864, iii. 270). Shortly afterwards Tullibardine and Sir William Kirkcaldy of Grange [q. v.] were sent in command of three armed ships to the northern isles in pursuit of Bothwell (*Reg. P. C. Scotl.* i. 544-6), but did not succeed in capturing him.

Notwithstanding his strong hostility to Bothwell, Tullibardine was always inclined to treat the queen with gentleness, and her continued confinement in Lochleven after the flight of Bothwell was distasteful to him. He signed the band for her deliverance, and with George Douglas and nine horsemen waited in Kinross to be ready to receive her on landing when she made her escape (Calderwood, *History*, ii. 404). After her flight to England he is said to have 'enterprised,' with the consent of the Hamiltons, a scheme for the assassination of the regent Murray (Drury to Cecil, 31 July, *Cal. State Papers*, For. Ser. 1566-8, entry 1387). If he did propose such a scheme, nothing was done to punish him; and his name appears as one of the privy council at a meeting on 5 April 1569 (*Reg. P. C. Scotl.* i. 653). He attended the convention at Perth on 27 July 1569, and voted for the queen's divorce from Bothwell (*ib.* ii. 8). In July 1572 he was employed by the regent's party in negotiations with Kirkcaldy of Grange for a surrender of the castle of Edinburgh (*Cal. State Papers*, For. Ser. 1569–71, entry 1081). After the death of the regent Mar on 28 Oct. he was appointed joint governor, along with Alexander Erskine, of the young king, but Morton is stated to have induced him to renounce his share in the charge of the young king by renewing to him the office of comptroller (*Hist. of James the Sext*, p. 120). Tullibardine joined the conspiracy in 1578 for ousting Morton from the regency, and after his retirement was chosen one of the new privy councillors in 1579 (Moysie, *Memoirs*, p. 5). According to Calderwood, however, it was through insinuating himself into Tullibardine's favour, and persuading him to influence the young Earl of Mar, that Morton subsequently obtained admittance into the castle of Stirling and resumed his authority over the young king (*History*, iii. 409). After the death of Robert Stewart, earl of Lennox, Tullibardine was on 20 May 1579 appointed one of a commission for 'sichting' the Lennox papers (*Reg. P. C. Scotl.* iii. 163). In October 1581 he protested against the infeftment of William, lord Ruthven, in the earldom of Gowrie in so far as it might prejudice his interests (*ib.* 427). In the quarrel between Arran and the Duke of Lennox in December, Tullibardine supported the former (Calderwood, iii. 593). He also supported the Earl of Gowrie against Lennox in July 1582 (*ib.* p. 632). After the expulsion of Arran from court in February 1582–3, Tullibardine resigned his office of comptroller, which was given to John Fenton, who had been clerk to the office (*ib.* viii. 238). Tullibardine died on 16 March 1582–3. By his wife Lady Agnes Graham, third daughter of William, second earl of Montrose, he had four sons: Sir John, who succeeded him, and was made Lord Murray of Tullibardine in 1604 and Earl of Tullibardine in 1606; Captain William of Pitcairly; Colonel Alexander of Drumdewan; and Sir Mungo of Denork.

[Reg. P. C. Scotl. vols. i–iii.; Cal. State Papers, For. Ser. reign of Elizabeth; Cal. State Papers, Scott. Ser.; Knox's Works; Calderwood's History of the Kirk of Scotland; Moysie's Memoirs, Sir James Melville's Memoirs, and History of James the Sext (all in Bannatyne Club); Hist. MSS. Comm. 12th Rep. App. pt. viii.; Douglas's Scots' Peerage (Wood and Paul), 1904.]

T. F. H.

MURRAY, WILLIAM, first Earl of Dysart (1600?–1651), born about 1600, was son of William Murray (1561?–1616), minister of Dysart, Fifeshire, by his wife Margaret. The father was a younger brother of Murray of Woodend, and was descended from a younger son of the family of Dollarie, which was a branch of the house of Tullibardine. William's uncle, Thomas Murray (1564–1623) [q. v.], took his nephew to court when a boy, and educated him along with Prince Charles. The latter and Murray were about the same age, and became very intimate. In 1626 Charles appointed him one of the gentlemen of the bedchamber, and retained him in his service ever afterwards. Murray had great influence with him, both as an adviser and in procuring favours for others. He was closely related to some of the leading covenanters—the Rev. Robert Murray, minister of Methven from 1615 to 1648, whose daughter married George Gillespie, being his uncle—and was a medium of private negotiations betwixt them and the king. Montrose affirmed that Murray had sent to the Scots at Newcastle in October 1640 copies of private letters which he had written to the king, then at York. He accompanied Charles to Scotland in 1641, and having got access to Montrose, who was then a prisoner in Edinburgh Castle, by order of the covenanters, he carried communications from one to the other. After encouraging the impeachment of Hamilton and Argyll, it is said that Murray informed them of their danger, and hence their flight. At this time Murray stood high in favour with the Scottish church, for soon after the king's return to England the commission of assembly besought Charles to 'lay on him the agenting of the affairs of the church about his majesty.'

It was generally believed that Murray told his friend, Lord Digby, of the king's intention to arrest the five members of the House of Commons, and that Digby betrayed the secret. On the outbreak of the civil war he was sent by the king to Montrose to inform him and other friends in Scotland of the state of his affairs, and to procure their advice and help. In 1645 Murray was with the queen in Paris, and was employed by her in her negotiations on the king's behalf with foreign powers, and with the pope. On his return to England in February 1646 he was seized as a spy in passing through Canterbury, and was sent as a prisoner to the Tower of London, where he remained till summer, when he was released through the influence of the Scots commissioners in London, who urged 'that he had done good offices to many of the best ministers in Scotland.' He was allowed to go to the king, then at Newcastle, on the assurance of his countrymen that he would do all in his power to induce his master to yield to the conditions of the parliament. In September Charles wrote to the queen: 'William Murray is let loose upon me from London.' 'As for religion, he and

I are consulting for the best means how to accommodate it without going directly against my conscience.' 'We are consulting to find such a present compliance as may stand with conscience and policy.' In October Murray was sent back to London on a secret mission, which he undertook at some risk of 'putting his neck to a new hazard,' but on his return he informed the king 'that the Scots commissioners hindered him to do anything therein for the little hope he could give them of his ratifying the covenant.' Soon after he and Sir Robert Murray [q. v.] made arrangements for the king's flight, but when the critical moment came Charles changed his mind. After the king was given up to the English, Murray was forbidden his presence, and returned to the continent. In 1648 the queen sent him to Scotland to further 'the engagement,' and to persuade his countrymen to receive the Prince of Wales, whom she wished to take part in the effort for the deliverance of the king. He first tried to induce Argyll and the dominant party in the church to support the resolutions of the Scottish estates, but, failing in this, he took counsel with the Duke of Hamilton and his friends, and in May he returned to the continent with letters from them formally inviting the prince to Scotland.

Among those who gathered round Charles II at the Hague immediately after his father's death Lord Byron mentions 'old William Murray, employed here by Argyll.' After the Scots commissioners returned unsatisfied in June 1649 from their visit to Holland, Charles sent over William Murray with private letters to Argyll and Loudoun. It is to this period apparently that John Livingston refers in his 'Autobiography' when he says that William Murray and Sir Robert Moray, who had long been very intimate with Argyll, 'put him in hopes that the king might marry his daughter.' In 1650, when the Scots commissioners were treating with Charles at Breda, Murray was sent with instructions to them, and in May of that year Sir William Fleming, who carried letters from Charles to Montrose, with whom he was still in correspondence, was directed to advise with William Murray and others as to whether Montrose should still keep the field or not. This goes to show that Murray abetted and shared in the king's duplicity. Burnet says that Murray was 'very insinuating, but very false, and of so revengeful a temper that rather than any of the counsels given by his enemies should succeed he would have revealed them and betrayed both the king and them. It was generally believed that he had betrayed the most important of all his [the king's] secrets to his enemies. He had one particular quality, that when he was drunk, which was very often, he was upon a most exact reserve, though he was pretty open at all other times.' The last statement does not seem very credible, but the attempt to please both his royal master and the extreme covenanters was not compatible with straightforwardness. He received his earldom from Charles I at Oxford in 1643, or, as Burnet says, at Newcastle in 1646, when he persuaded the king to antedate it by three years. As the patent did not pass the great seal, he ranked as a commoner till 1651, when, according to Lamont's 'Diary,' several of the gentry were ennobled by Charles II, and among them 'William Murray of the bedchamber, who was made Lord Dysart.' He died early in the same year.

He married Catherine Bruce, grand-daughter of Sir Robert Bruce of Clackmannan and Margaret Murray of the Tullibardine family, and had four daughters. The first, Elizabeth Murray, countess of Dysart and afterwards duchess of Lauderdale, is separately noticed. Murray's second daughter, Margaret, married William, second lord Maynard.

[Douglas's Peerage; Complete Peerage, by G. E. C.; Clarendon's History; Gardiner's History of the Civil War; Balfour's Annals; Baillie's Letters; Burnet's History of my own Time, and Memoirs of the Dukes of Hamilton; Letters of Charles I in 1646 (Camden Society, 1855); Disraeli's Charles I; Denham's Poems, 1684, p. 70; Masson's Life of Milton; Napier's Life of Montrose.] G. W. S.

MURRAY, Lord WILLIAM, second Baron Nairne (*d.* 1724). [See under Nairne, John, third Baron, 1691–1770.]

MURRAY, WILLIAM, Marquis of Tullibardine (1689–1746), born 14 April 1689, was second and eldest surviving son of John, second marquis and first duke of Atholl [q. v.], by Lady Katherine Hamilton. He entered the navy early in 1708; in a letter dated at Spithead, 29 Aug. 1708, he gives his father an account of an unsuccessful attempt at landing on the coast of France in which his ship took part (*Hist. MSS. Comm.* 12th Rep. pt. viii. p. 64). At first he was known as Lord William Murray, but became Marquis of Tullibardine on the death of his elder brother John at Malplaquet 31 Aug. 1709.

Tullibardine was one of the first to join the standard of Mar and the Chevalier in 1715, and although his father remained faithful to the government some 1,400 of the Atholl men accompanied him (Patten, *Rebellion*, pt. ii. p. 91). The Earl of Nottingham intimated to the duke on 13 Sept. that he had hopes of his son's returning 'to his duty' providing he were assured of pardon; but although this offer was practically made, it proved unavailing (*Hist. MSS. Comm.* 12th Rep. pt. viii. p. 68). At the battle of Sheriffmuir his forces formed part of the left wing, which was routed and fled northwards, the marquis reaching Perth the same night with only a few horse (*ib.* p. 70). It was the intention of the prince, when after the retreat from Perth he embarked at Montrose for France, to have taken Tullibardine with him, but he was then at Brechin with a part of the foot (Mar's Journal in Patten, pt. ii. p. 109). He, however, managed to shift from place to place till he found an opportunity to escape (Patten, p. 89). On 21 Jan. 1717 he was created by the exiled prince Duke of Rannoch, which proved a mere nominal dignity. On account of his share in the rebellion he was attainted, and the titles and estates of the family conferred on a younger brother, Lord James Murray [q. v.]

Tullibardine was in chief command on land, aided by the Earl Marischal [see Keith, George, tenth Earl Marischal], in the expedition to the north-west highlands in 1719. There seems no genuine foundation for the allegation that Tullibardine and his brother Lord George [q. v.] induced Atholl men and the Macgregors under Rob Roy to co-operate with the Spanish forces. Lockhart asserts that Tullibardine and Marischal were soon at variance about the command (*Papers*, ii. 19), and to their divided counsels is generally attributed the defeat at Glenshiel on 10 June. A reward of 2,000*l.* was offered for Tullibardine's capture, but he succeeded in again making his escape to the continent. In October 1736 he had for some time been a prisoner for debt in Paris, but on appeal to the parliament of Paris he was set at liberty, on the ground that one of his rank was not liable to confinement for debt (*Notes and Queries*, 4th ser. x. 161; cf. *Jacobite Corresp. of the Atholl Family*, p. 227). After the death of his father in 1724 he was recognised by the Jacobites as Duke of Atholl.

Tullibardine was one of the seven followers of Prince Charles who on 22 June 1745 embarked with him at Nantes on the Loire for Scotland, and on 25 July landed with him at Borrodale. On account of his strong and consistent Jacobitism, and as representative of the powerful house of Atholl, he was chosen to unfurl the standard at Glenfinnan on 16 Aug., when he also read a manifesto in the name of James VIII, dated Rome, December 1743, proclaiming a regency in favour of his son, Prince Charles. As Tullibardine hoped to gain the Atholl men before his brother the duke should have time to bring his influence to bear on them, the insurgents, instead of making any attempt to pursue General Cope, who evaded them at Corryarrick, marched southwards into Atholl. On their approach the duke fled from his castle of Blair, which was immediately taken possession of by Tullibardine, who as the rightful possessor here entertained the prince. The prince then proceeded to Perth, and the day on which he reached it, 4 Sept., was joined by Tullibardine's brother, Lord George Murray [q. v.], who was made lieutenant-general. Tullibardine was not present at the battle of Prestonpans, having remained at Blair to collect men and arms and to rally the highland clans to the standard of the prince (see *Correspondence of the Atholl Family*, passim). On 22 Sept. he was named commander-in-chief of the forces north of the Forth (*ib.* p. 227). After bringing large reinforcements to the prince at Edinburgh he accompanied the expedition into England. On the defeat of the insurgents at Culloden on 16 April 1746, Tullibardine, accompanied by an Italian, fled south-westwards, with the intention of gaining the seacoast; but their horses tiring, and Tullibardine, on account of bad health, being unable to proceed on foot, they went on 27 April to the house on Loch Lomond of Archibald Buchanan, whose son William was a justice of the peace. William's wife was Tullibardine's cousin, but William treacherously betrayed his guests to the garrison at Dumbarton. Tullibardine and his companions were taken to Dumbarton Castle, whence the marquis was sent by way of Edinburgh to the Tower of London, where he died without issue on the 9th of the following July, in his fifty-eighth year.

[Histories of the Rebellions of 1715 and 1745; Hist. MSS. Comm. 12th Rep. pt. viii.; Jacobite Corresp. of the Atholl Family (Bannatyne Club); Douglas's Scots' Peerage (Wood & Paul), 1904; Letters of Mrs. Grant of Laggan.] T. F. H.

MURRAY, WILLIAM, first Earl of Mansfield (1705–1793), judge, fourth son of David, fifth viscount Stormont, by Margery, only child of David Scott of Scotstarvet, was born at the Abbey of Scone on 2 March 1704–5, and educated successively at Perth grammar school, at Westminster School, where he was king's scholar in 1719, and at Christ Church, Oxford, where he matriculated on 18 June 1723, and was elected to a studentship. Among his contemporaries and friends at Westminster were Thomas Newton [q. v.], afterwards bishop of

Bristol, James Johnson [q. v.], afterwards bishop of Worcester, and Thomas Foley, afterwards second Baron Foley, who furnished him with the means to adopt the law as a profession instead of the church, for which, as the younger son of a poor Scottish peer, he had been intended (Seward, *Biographiana*, ii. 577). His family was Jacobite, and the high ideas of the royal prerogative with which Murray was in after life identified were doubtless due to his early training. A remarkable talent for declamation evinced at school he improved at Oxford by assiduous study of the classical models, particularly the orations of Cicero, some of which he translated into English and back again into Latin. An extant fragment of one of his academic exercises, a declamation in praise of Demosthenes, attests the purity and elegance of his latinity, and an 'Outline of a Course of Legal Study' which he made for the heir to the dukedom of Portland about 1730 proves the width of his reading. In 1727 he graduated B.A., and began a lifelong rivalry with William Pitt, afterwards Earl of Chatham, by defeating him in the competition for the prize offered by the university for a Latin poem on the death of George I. He proceeded M.A. in 1730, and on 23 Nov. of the same year was called to the bar at Lincoln's Inn, of which he was made a bencher in 1743. Murray was initiated into the mysteries of special pleading and conveyancing by Thomas Denison, afterwards justice of the king's bench, and James Booth (*d.* 1778) [q. v.] He frequented a debating club where mootpoints of law were discussed in solemn form, 'drank champagne with the wits,' and practised elocution and the airs and graces of the advocate in the seclusion of his chambers at 5 King's Bench Walk, with the aid of a looking-glass and his friend Alexander Pope. Bolingbroke, Warburton, and Hurd were also among his friends (Seward, *Anecdotes*, ii. 388; Charles Butler, *Reminiscences*, 1824, pp. 120 et seq.; Boswell, *Johnson*, ed. Hill, ii. 37, 158).

Aided by his Scottish connection Murray got rapidly into practice, and argued before the House of Lords in the case of Paterson *v.* Graham on 12 March 1732–3. Other Scottish briefs followed; he gained popularity by his eloquent speech before the House of Commons in support of the merchants' petition concerning the Spanish depredations (30 March 1737–8), and after Walpole's fall he was made king's counsel and solicitor-general to Lord Wilmington's government, 27 Nov. 1742, entering parliament as member for Boroughbridge, Yorkshire, which he continued to represent until his elevation to the bench (Coxe, *Memoirs of Sir Robert Walpole*, i. 580). He was continued in office on Pelham's accession to power, 25 Aug. 1743, and by his speeches against the disbandment of the Hanoverian mercenaries, 6 Dec. 1743, and in support of the Habeas Corpus Suspension Bill, introduced in view of the threatened Jacobite insurrection, 28 Feb. 1743–4, proved himself the ablest defender of the government in the House of Commons. In September 1743 he was presented with the freedom of Edinburgh, in recognition of his professional services to that city when threatened with disfranchisement for its behaviour in the affair of the Porteous riots (cf. *Comm. Journ.* xxii. 896; Boyse, *Hist. Rev. Trans. of Europe*, i. 463; Maitland, *Hist. of Edinburgh*, i. 123; Coxe, *Walpole*). The prosecution of the rebel lords occupied him during the summer of 1746 and spring of 1747, and so well did he play his part that Lovat claimed kinship with him, and complimented him on his speech. A free-trader before Adam Smith, Murray made Lord Hardwicke's bill for prohibiting the insurance of French ships the occasion of an indictment of the policy of commercial restrictions pursued by the country during the previous half-century (18 Dec. 1747). He was now the acknowledged leader of the house, and by his defence of the treaty of Aix-la-Chapelle (1748), of the Bavarian subsidiary treaties, and of the Regency Bill (1750–1), rendered the government yeoman's service. To discredit him a musty story was raked up of his toasting the Pretender in old days at the house of a Jacobite mercer in Ludgate (see Johnson, James, 1705–1774, bishop of Worcester, and *Add. MS.* 33050, ff. 200–368). His denial of the charge was accepted by the cabinet (26 Feb. 1752–3), but the Duke of Bedford moving for papers on the subject in the House of Lords, the oath of secrecy was dispensed with, and the whole affair rediscussed, the motion being eventually negatived without a division. On more than one subsequent occasion Pitt in the House of Commons threw out dark hints of Jacobitism in high places, which were generally understood to refer to Murray, and the charge was revived by Churchill in the fourth book of his 'Ghost.' While this miserable business was pending Murray was engaged in vindicating, as far as learning and logic could vindicate, the rights of his country and the authority of the law of nations against the high-handed procedures of the king of Prussia, who had made the arrest by English cruisers of some Prussian merchant ships suspected of carrying contraband of war to French ports during the war with France a pretext for withholding payment of money due to English subjects on account of the Silesian loan. A report on the subject (printed in Martens's 'Causes Célèbres du Droit des Gens,' ii. 46 et seq.) drafted by Murray and communicated to the Prussian minister in 1753 amply justified the arrest by the law of nations. The king of Prussia, however, by continuing the lien on the loan, eventually succeeded in extorting 20,000*l.* from the British government.

On the death of Pelham, Murray became, 9 April 1754, attorney-general to the Duke of Newcastle's administration, which for two years he defended almost single-handed against the incessant attacks of Pitt. On the death of Sir Dudley Rider [q. v.] he claimed the vacant chief-justiceship and a peerage, and though offered the Duchy of Lancaster for life and a pension of 6,000*l.* to remain in the House of Commons, refused to waive his claim, and on 8 Nov. 1756 was called to the degree of serjeant-at-law, sworn in as lord chief justice of the king's bench, and created Baron Mansfield of Mansfield in the county of Nottingham. He celebrated the event the same evening by a splendid banquet in Lincoln's Inn Hall. On 11 Nov. he took his seat in the court of king's bench, and in acknowledging a purse of gold presented to him by the Hon. Charles Yorke [q. v.], treasurer of Lincoln's Inn, on behalf of that society, paid an eloquent tribute to Lord Hardwicke (Holliday, p. 106).

On the formation of the Duke of Devonshire's administration (November 1756) Murray was sworn of the privy council and offered but declined the great seal. He took his seat in the House of Lords on 2 Dec. following, and made his maiden speech against the bill for releasing the court-martial on Admiral Byng from their oath of secrecy. During the interval between the dismissal of Legge (5 April 1757) and his return to the exchequer (30 June) Murray held the seals of that office. In Newcastle's new administration, formed at the latter date, he accepted a seat without office, but with the disposal of Scottish patronage in lieu of the great seal, which was again pressed upon him. In May 1758 he opposed the bill for the extension of the Habeas Corpus Act to civil cases. He attached himself to Lord Bute when that nobleman became prime minister (1762), and supported him throughout his administration. He retired on the formation of the Grenville administration in April 1763, but gave some support to Lord Rockingham's government (July 1766), although he opposed its repeal of the Stamp Act, arguing with perverse ingenuity that the American colonists were 'virtually' represented in parliament. With the Duke of Grafton's administration, formed under Pitt's guidance in July 1766, he was not much in sympathy. He attacked ministers for the technical breach of the constitution involved in the prohibition by order in council of the exportation of corn during the scarcity of the autumn of 1766. But he again held the seals of the exchequer during the interval between the death of Townshend and the appointment of Lord North (September–December 1767) (*Add. MS.* 32985, f. 53).

In May 1765 he had given his general support to Pratt in the case of Leach *v.* Three King's Messengers, in which general warrants were affirmed to be illegal, as they were declared to be by a resolution in the House of Commons in the following year. In 1767, however, he incurred some popular odium by discountenancing some prosecutions under the penal law of 1700 (11 & 12 William III, c. 4), which made celebration of mass by a Roman catholic priest punishable by imprisonment for life (Barnard, *Life of Challoner*, ed. 1784, pp. 165 et seq.) He evinced the same enlightened spirit in the case of the Chamberlain of London *v.* Evans. The defendant, a protestant dissenter, had been fined by the corporation of London, under one of their by-laws, for refusing to serve the office of sheriff, to which he had been elected, though ineligible by reason of not having taken the communion according to the rites of the church of England within a year before the election. He refused to pay the fine, and after prolonged litigation the case came before the House of Lords on writ of error from the court of delegates, and their unanimous judgment in favour of the defendant was delivered by Mansfield, in a speech of classic eloquence, on 4 Feb. 1767 (Furneaux, *Letters to the Hon. Mr. Justice Blackstone*, App. ii.) At a somewhat later date Mansfield made a precedent of far-reaching consequence by suffering a member of the Society of Friends to give evidence on affirmation in lieu of oath (Cowper, *Reports*, i. 382). Mansfield increased his unpopularity by his conduct in the case of Wilkes. A technical flaw in the informations filed in respect of the publication of No. 45 of the 'North Briton' and the 'Essay on Woman' he allowed to be amended during Wilkes's absence abroad. Wilkes accordingly, on his return to England after his outlawry, denounced Mansfield as a subverter of the laws, and took proceedings in the king's bench to reverse the outlawry. The case thus came before Mansfield himself, and during its progress persistent attempts were made to intimidate him by threatening letters. He is said to have been constitutionally timid, and some colour is given to the charge by the solicitude which his judgment evinced to vindicate himself from all suspicion of being influenced by any considerations but those of abstract justice. The question was intricate and obscure, and after careful argument and much scrutiny of precedents, Mansfield decided against Wilkes on all the points raised by his counsel. He then proceeded to reverse the outlawry on a technical flaw discovered by himself, and substituted a sentence of fine and imprisonment (8 June 1768).

Mansfield acted as speaker of the House of Lords in the interval between the death of Charles Yorke [q. v.] (20 Jan. 1770) and the creation of Lord-chancellor Bathurst. He defeated Lord Chatham's attempt to involve the lords in the struggle between Wilkes and the House of Commons (May 1770), and carried a measure (10 Geo. III, c. 50) rendering the servants of members of either house of parliament liable to civil process during prorogation. By the committal of Bingley, the printer of Nos. 50 and 51 of the 'North Briton,' to the Marshalsea for refusing to answer interrogatories (7 Nov. 1768), and by his directions to the jury in three cases of seditious libel arising out of the publication and sale of Junius's 'Letter to the King,' he aggravated the ill-odour in which he already stood. The cases were tried in the summer of 1770, and Mansfield in each instance directed the jury that if they were satisfied of the fact of publication or sale they ought to find for the crown, as the question of libel or no libel was a matter of law for the court to decide. He thus secured a verdict in one case; in one of the other two the jury acquitted the defendant; in the third, that of Rex *v.* Woodfall, they found a special verdict of 'guilty of printing and publishing only.' This verdict being ambiguous, a motion was made on the part of the crown to enter it 'according to its legal import,' i.e. omitting the word 'only,' upon which Mansfield, after consultation with his colleagues, reaffirmed, with their unanimous concurrence, his original ruling, and directed a venire de novo (Howell, *State Trials*, xvii. 671). This decision elicited from Junius a letter (No. 41) of unusual acerbity, charging Mansfield with a design to subvert the constitution by form of law, and was made the occasion of an animated debate in the House of Commons (6 Dec.) In answer to some animadversions on the subject in the House of Lords, Mansfield laid a copy of the judgment in Rex *v.* Woodfall on the table of the house, but evaded Lord Camden's challenge for a formal discussion of the matter.

In July 1777 Mansfield presided at the trial of John Horne, afterwards Horne-Tooke [q. v.], for seditious libel. His statement of the law did not materially vary from that which he had previously given, and was accepted by the jury. In the case of the Dean of St. Asaph [see Shipley, William Davies], which came before him on motion for a new trial in Michaelmas term 1784, Mansfield reaffirmed his doctrine of the respective functions of judge and jury in cases of libel. That the doctrine itself was strictly in accordance with precedent admits of no doubt [cf. Lee, Sir William]; but the feeling of the country was strongly against it (cf. W. Davy's *England's Alarm*, London, 1785), and a few years later (1792) it was swept away by Fox's Libel Act.

While thus, according to his enemies, forging fetters for his countrymen, Mansfield struck a blow for the emancipation of the slave. In December 1771 James Somersett, a negro confined in irons on board a ship in the Thames, was produced before him on habeas corpus in the court of king's bench. The return was that he had been purchased in Virginia, brought to England, had run away, and, having been retaken, had been shipped for export to Jamaica. The case raised the broad question whether slaves could lawfully be kept in England, on which there was no direct authority, though Francis Hargrave [q. v.] based a learned argument on the extinction of villenage. In the end, Mansfield decided the case on the simple ground that slavery was 'so odious' that nothing could 'be suffered to support it but positive law,' and released the negro. In the following year he was attacked by Junius, for his supposed partiality to the Scots, with even more bitterness and brilliance than before (Letter lxviii.), and in 1773 by Andrew Stuart for the part he had taken in deciding the great Douglas cause (see Douglas, Lady Jane, supra, and *Letters to the Right Hon. Lord Mansfield from Andrew Stuart, Esq.*) In 1774–5 Mansfield decided two cases of great constitutional importance. The first, that of Campbell *v.* Hall, decided 28 Nov. 1774, is the Magna Charta of countries annexed by conquest to the British crown. The action was by a landowner of Grenada against a customs officer to recover the amount of a duty levied under royal letters patent, issued after the cession of the island by France (1763), and its provision with a constitutional government—the whole question being whether the letters patent were valid or not. The jury having returned a special verdict, the question of law was thrice argued before Mansfield, who, on 28 Nov. 1774, decided it in the negative, on the ground that the sovereign cannot by his prerogative so legislate for conquered countries as to contravene the fundamental principles of the constitution. The second case was that of Fabrigas *v.* Mostyn, an action for false imprisonment by a native of Minorca against the late governor of that island, removed by writ of error from the common pleas, where the plaintiff had obtained a verdict, to the king's bench. The question raised by the writ of error was whether an English court had jurisdiction to try an action founded on a wrong done in Minorca, where English law had not been introduced. After hearing the case twice argued, Mansfield, by means of a legal fiction by which Minorca was considered 'the parish of St. Mary-le-Bow, in the ward of Cheap,' affirmed the jurisdiction and the judgment of the court below (27 Jan. 1775).

The long vacation of 1774 was spent by Mansfield at Paris as the guest of his nephew, Lord Stormont, British ambassador at the French court. He travelled incognito, and was thought to be charged with a secret mission (Walpole, *George III*, i. 394). In regard to American affairs Mansfield was credited with being the author of the Quebec bill of 1775. He strongly supported the prohibitory bill of the same year, and throughout the subsequent history of the struggle never wavered in his firm adhesion to the policy of coercion. Though not in Lord North's cabinet, it is probable that he was in the confidence of ministers, and privy to most of their measures (*ib.* ii. 196).

On 31 Oct. 1776 he was advanced to an earldom, by the title of Earl of Mansfield in the county of Nottingham, with remainder, in default of male issue, to Louisa, viscountess Stormont, and her heirs by his nephew Viscount Stormont in tail male. The peculiar limitation of the remainder was made in consequence of the mistaken idea then prevalent, that a Scottish peer could not take an English peerage otherwise than by inheritance. When the contrary was decided, a new patent was issued, 1 Aug. 1792, by which Mansfield was created Earl of Mansfield of Caen Wood in the county of Middlesex, with remainder, in default of male issue, to his brother's son, Viscount Stormont. His nephew David Murray [q. v.] accordingly succeeded him as second earl.

On occasion of Lord Chatham's final scene in the House of Lords, on 7 April 1778, Mansfield disgraced himself by exhibiting an ostentatious indifference; nor did he attend the great patriot's funeral, or pay his tribute of respect to his memory in the debate on the bill for pensioning his posterity. On 25 Nov. 1779 he proposed a coalition of all parties for the purpose of grappling with the now desperate situation of American affairs. His advice was rejected, and he took little further part in politics. The Roman Catholic Relief Bill of 1778 was, however, known to have had his approval, and on the outbreak of the Gordon riots (2 June 1780) he experienced the vengeance of the mob. His carriage windows were broken, and he was hustled as he passed to the House of Lords, of which he was then speaker *pro tempore*, and on the night of 7 June his house in Bloomsbury Square was sacked and burned. With Lady Mansfield he made his escape by a back door shortly before the mob effected an entrance. His books, manuscripts, pictures, and furniture were entirely destroyed or dispersed. Apparently stunned by the blow, he took no part in quelling the riot, and was not even consulted as to the lawfulness of firing on the mob, though he afterwards justified the ministers in the House of Lords. Cowper lamented in some pretty verses the loss of his library and manuscripts.

In presiding at the subsequent trial of Lord George Gordon, Mansfield exhibited as much judicial impartiality as if he had himself sustained no injury by the riots. As speaker of the House of Lords while the great seal was in commission (February to December 1783) he presided during the animated debates on the Receipt Tax and Fox's India Bill. He closed his political career by a speech on a corrupt practices bill on 23 March 1784.

Ill-health, which visits to Tunbridge Wells failed to restore, compelled Mansfield to resign office on 4 June 1788. He retired to his house, Caen Wood, Highgate, and devoted his declining days to horticulture, the study of the classics, society, and religious meditation. Still interested in public affairs, he lived to see the outbreak of the French revolution, of which he took from the first a very gloomy view. He died peacefully of old age on 20 March 1793. He was buried on the 28th in the North Cross, Westminster Abbey, in accordance with a desire expressed in his will that his bones might rest near the place of his early education. The funeral by his express direction was private. His monument by Flaxman, on the west side of the north transept, was placed there in 1801. His bust by Nollekens is at Trinity Hall, Cambridge. Portraits of him by Allan Ramsay and Copley are in the National Portrait Gallery. His portrait by Reynolds, painted in 1785–6 and engraved in stipple by Bartolozzi, is in the possession of the present Earl of Mansfield. Another by David Martin hangs in the hall of Christ Church, Oxford.

Mansfield's fine person, elegant manners, and sprightly wit rendered him a great favourite with ladies. Pope celebrates his charms in 'Imitations of Horace,' Carm. iv. i. He married, on 20 Sept. 1738, Lady Elizabeth Finch, seventh daughter of Daniel, second earl of Nottingham, and sixth earl of Winchilsea, by whom he had no issue. She died on 10 April 1784, and was also buried in the North Cross, Westminster Abbey.

As a parliamentary debater Mansfield was second, if second, only to Chatham, to whose stormy invective and theatrical tones and gestures, his 'silver-tongued' enunciation, graceful action, and cogent argument formed a singular contrast. 'In all debates of consequence,' wrote Lord Waldegrave in 1755 (*Memoirs*, p. 53), 'Murray, the attorney-general, had greatly the advantage over Pitt in point of argument; and, abuse only excepted, was not much his inferior in any part of oratory;' and Horace Walpole, one of his bitterest enemies, confessed, in reference to his speech on the Habeas Corpus Extension Bill of 1758, that he 'never heard so much argument, so much sense, so much oratory united' (*Memoirs of the Reign of George II*, ed. Lord Holland, iii. 120). On the other hand, he was conspicuously lacking in the 'præfervidum ingenium' usually characteristic of his countrymen, and was charged by his enemies with pusillanimity. His spiritless conduct in the debate on Wilkes's exclusion from the House of Commons (1 May 1770), and his subsequent evasion of Lord Camden's challenge in regard to the law of libel, severely damaged his reputation. At the bar his mere statement of a case, by its extreme lucidity, was supposed to be worth the argument of any other man. As a statesman his fame is tarnished by his blind adhesion to the policy of coercing America, nor is his name associated with any statute of first-rate importance. Macaulay terms him, however, 'the father of modern toryism, of toryism modified to suit an order of things in which the House of Commons is the most powerful body in the state.'

As a judge, by his perfect impartiality, inexhaustible patience, and the strength and acumen of his understanding, he ranks among the greatest who have ever administered justice. Such was his ascendency over his colleagues, that during the first twelve years of his tenure of office they invariably, though by no means insignificant lawyers, concurred in his judgment. The first case of a final and irreconcilable difference of opinion occurred in 1769, on the question whether literary copyright in published works existed at common law, or was a mere creation of statute. Mansfield held the former alternative, but the latter was eventually affirmed by the House of Lords (cf. BURROW, *Reports*, iv. 2395; *Pamphleteer*, ii. 194; *Parl. Hist.* xvii. 971 et seq.) A scholar and well read in the civil law, Mansfield was charged by Junius (Letter xli.) with the black offence of corrupting the ancient simplicity of the common law with principles drawn from the corpus juris, and his preference of reason to routine offended the pedants of Westminster Hall. The silly technicality which required a deed to be indented he abrogated by holding any deed an indenture which had not its edges mathematically straight. In the once famous case of Perrin *v.* Blake he startled the profession by deviating from the narrow way of the rule in Shelley's case (SIR WILLIAM BLACKSTONE, *Reports*, i. 672). His decision, however, was reversed by the exchequer chamber, and sharply criticised by Charles Fearne [q. v.] in his classical treatise on 'Contingent Remainders.' By reversing the decision of the court of session in the case of Edmondstone *v.* Edmonstone (PATON, *Scotch Appeal Cases*, ii. 255) he 'struck off,' says Lord Campbell, 'the fetters of half the entailed estates in Scotland.' At Guildhall, where he trained and attached to himself a select body of special jurors who were regularly impanelled for mercantile causes, and taught him the usages of trade, he did much, by the unerring instinct with which he grasped, and the lucidity with which he formulated, the general principle underlying each particular case, to forward the work, already begun by Sir John Holt [q. v.], of moulding the law into accordance with the needs of a rapidly expanding commerce and manufacture. He thus converted our mercantile law from something bordering upon chaos into what was almost equivalent to a code. He also improved the law of evidence and the procedure of the courts. His humorous maxim, 'No case, abuse plaintiff's attorney,' and his advice to a colonial governor ignorant of law, on no account to give reasons for his judgments, have often been quoted.

Mansfield was a sincere Christian, but so careless of times and seasons that he once proposed to try a case on Good Friday, and only abandoned the idea in deference to the protest of one of the leading counsel against following a precedent set by Pontius Pilate. A sense of justice and regard for the memory of an old friend induced him to protest against Warburton's treatment of Bolingbroke (1754) in an anonymous letter (WARBURTON, *Works*, ed. 1787, vii. 555). A thanksgiving sermon, preached by his friend Bishop Johnson in Westminster Abbey 29 Nov. 1759, is said to have been written at Mansfield's dictation (cf. HOLLIDAY, *Addenda*).

Mansfield's decisions are reported by Burrow, Cowper, Sir William Blackstone, Douglas (Lord Glenbervie), and Durnford and East. A selection from them, entitled 'A General View of the Decisions of Lord Mansfield in Civil Causes,' was edited by William David Evans in 1803, London, 2 vols. 4to. A few of his speeches in parliament and judgments have been reprinted in pamphlet form. His 'Outline of a Course of Legal Study' is printed in the 'European Magazine,' March 1791 – May 1792, in his life by Holliday, and in 'A Treatise on the Study of the Law,' London, 1797, 8vo. A manuscript poem by him, entitled 'Ædes Blenhamianæ,' is in the possession of Lord Monboddo (*Hist. MSS. Comm.* 6th Rep. App. p. 680). 'The Thistle, a Dispassionate Examine of the Prejudice of Englishmen in General to the Scotch Nation, and particularly of a late arrogant Insult offered to all Scotchmen by a Modern English Journalist,' in a letter to the author of 'Old England' of 27 Dec. 1746, London, 8vo, has been attributed to Mansfield [cf. WILLES, SIR JOHN]. Letters from him to Warburton, Warren Hastings, the Dukes of Newcastle, and others are in the British Museum.

[The principal authorities are the Life of William, late Earl of Mansfield, by Holliday, 1797, with those in the Law Magazine, vols. iv. and v. 1830–1; Welsby's Eminent English Judges, 1846; Lardner's Cabinet Cyclopædia; Lord Campbell's Chief Justices; and Foss's Judges. See also Gent. Mag. 1738 p. 490, 1742 p. 603, 1784 pt. i. p. 317; Collins's Peerage (Brydges), iii. 402, v. 144–50; Douglas's Peerage, 'Stormont;' Alumni Westmonast.; Foster's Alumni Oxon.; Warburton's Works, ed. Hurd, 1811, i. 36; Lords' Journ. xxix. 209, 553, xxxv. 5; Law Review, ii. 314–15; Bubb Dodington's Diary, pp. 228 et seq.; Jenkinson's Collection of Treaties, iii. 59; Coxe's Memoirs of Sir Robert Walpole, p. 580; Bedford Corresp. iii. 129; Lord Charlemont's Corresp. p. 22; Chatham Corresp. i. 159; Harris's Life of Lord Hardwicke, iii. 93; Grenville Papers; Horace Walpole's Letters, ed. Cunningham, Memoirs of George II, ed. Holland, Memoirs of George III, ed. Le Marchant, and Journal of George III, ed. Doran; Parl. Hist.; Royal and Noble Authors, ed. Park, iv. 35; Howell's State Trials; Nichols's Lit. Anecd. and Illustr. of Lit.; Rockingham Memoirs, ed. Earl of Albemarle, i. 160, ii. 257; Works of Thomas Newton, Bishop of Bristol, 1782, i. 102, 127; Wraxall's Memoirs, ed. Wheatley; Ann. Reg. 1780, Chron. App.; Northcote's Life of Reynolds, ii. 98; Autobiography and Corresp. of Mrs. Delany, ed. Lady Llanover; Brougham's Historical Sketches; Notes and Queries, 5th ser. iv. 500, 6th ser. iv. 165, v. 486; Chester's Westminster Abbey Registers (Harl. Soc.); Pope's Works, ed. Elwin and Courthope.] J. M. R.

MURRAY, WILLIAM HENRY (1790–1852), actor and manager, son of Charles Murray [q. v.], was born in 1790 at Bath, where as an infant he appeared as Puck, probably on 11 March 1794, when, for his father's benefit, 'A Midsummer-Night's Dream' was played, with his sister as Titania. This sister, Maria, subsequently married Joseph Leathley Cowell [q. v.], and was mother of Samuel Houghton Cowell [q. v.] Another sister married Henry Siddons [q. v.] William accompanied his father to London, and played various small parts at Covent Garden under the Kemble management, beginning in 1803–4. To Charles Farley, the stage-manager at Covent Garden, Murray afterwards stated that he owed his training in stage management and the manipulation of theatrical spectacle. On 20 Nov. 1809 (not the 10th as in his own account) he made his first appearance in Edinburgh, with which he was subsequently associated for forty-two years. His brother-in-law, Henry Siddons, had secured the royal letters patent, and leaving the theatre in Shakspere Square, Edinburgh, had fitted up as a playhouse the Circus in Leith Walk. There until 1811 Murray filled many small parts, at first, according to his own confession, with very little success. His first part was Count Cassel in 'Lovers' Vows,' 20 Nov. 1809, and on 29 Nov. he was Sanguine in Dimond's 'Foundling of the Forest.' On 8 Jan. 1810 he produced, as stage-manager, the 'Tempest.' Murray was the original Red Murdoch, 15 Jan. 1811, in Eyres's dramatisation of the 'Lady of the Lake,' a part he resigned when on 18 March the play was replaced by the 'Knight of Snowdoun,' Morton's adaptation of the same poem. Murray had now removed with the company to the theatre in Shakspere Square. On 12 April 1815 Henry Siddons died, and Murray, on behalf of the widow, his sister, and her children, entered on the management, then in a crippled condition, beginning, according to a statement he put forth, with a debt of 3,100*l.*, and a weekly expenditure of 230*l.* From the first he displayed much energy, and a summer engagement of Miss O'Neill was a great success. On the opening of the season 1815–16 Mrs. Siddons, who had retired, reappeared. On 6 Jan. Murray played Sebastian to his sister's Viola in 'Twelfth Night.' Engagements of Kemble and Charles Mathews followed, and were succeeded by the appearance of Kean. Murray's own parts, which were subordinate, included Osric and Dirk Hatterick in the production, 25 Feb. 1817, of Terry's adaptation of 'Guy Mannering,' the first of the Waverley dramas given in Edinburgh. Murray played, on the last night of Kemble's appearance in Edinburgh, Rosse to Kemble's Macbeth, and, for his own benefit, Tony Lumpkin. After taking his company to Glasgow he enacted the Manager in the 'Actor of All Work' and Charles in the 'Jealous Wife.' Yates and many good actors had been seen, but the fortunes of the house continued to decline until 15 Feb. 1819, when 'Rob Roy MacGregor, or Auld Langsyne,' was produced, and proved the greatest and most enduring success probably ever known in Scotland. Murray was Captain Thornton. The great feature in the cast was the Bailie Nicol Jarvie of Mackay, then a recent acquisition to the theatre. Scott, through the Ballantynes, under the signature 'Jedediah Cleishbotham,' sent Mackay a letter of thanks and advice. The piece ran forty-one consecutive nights, and even yet, when revived, draws well. Murray was then seen as Flutter in the 'Belle's Stratagem,' Horatio, one of the Dromios, and other parts. He also directed the pantomime, and showed ability as a pantomimist. In the 'Heart of Midlothian' (February 1820), another success, Murray was Black Frank and his wife Effie Deans. In the production of the 'Antiquary' (December 1820), Murray was Jonathan Oldbuck, and was Craigengelt in the 'Bride of Lammermoor' (May 1822). On the famous visit of George IV to the Edinburgh Theatre, 27 Aug. 1822, he resumed his part of Captain Thornton. Murray was George Heriot in the 'Fortunes of Nigel,' and Lance Outram in 'Peveril of the Peak.' He was Wamba in a version of 'Ivanhoe' compiled by himself, and produced 24 Nov. 1823, and the Laird of Balmawhapple in a version of 'Waverley' (May 1824). In Planché's adaptation of 'St. Ronan's Well' Murray was Peregrine Touchwood. He played Figaro in the 'Barber of Seville,' was Old Adam of Teviot in the 'Rose of Ettrick Dale,' Joshua Geddes in a version of 'Redgauntlet' attributed to himself, Sir Kenneth of Scotland in the 'Talisman,' and Roland in 'Mary Stuart,' his own adaptation of the 'Abbot.' In the season of 1825–6 he played Zabouc in Abou Hassan, and made a great hit as Paul Pry (November 1825). In 'Woodstock, or the Cavalier,' 17 June 1826, Murray was Colonel Everard. His farce 'No,' produced 10 Feb. 1827, had much success, and was followed, 25 June, by his drama of 'Gilderoy.' In 'Charles Edward, or the Last of the Stuarts,' he was Lieutenant Standard. In Planché's 'Charles XII' he played Liston's part of Adam Brock (6 Feb. 1829). A piece of unpardonable sharp practice in obtaining a manuscript copy of this piece is commented on by Planché in 'Recollections and Reflections,' i. 148, and led to the passing of the first Dramatic Authors' Act. Scott's 'House of Aspen' was produced on 17 Dec. 1829. On the expiration of the patent of H. Siddons the theatre became the property of Mrs. Siddons, who had paid up the purchase-money, 42,000*l.* In course of a dispute with the 'Edinburgh Dramatic Review' it came out that Murray's salary had been 46*l.* a week, with 100*l.* annually for his expenses as manager.

Refusing an offer to act at Covent Garden, Murray remained at Edinburgh, and secured the lease not only of the Theatre Royal, but also, in conjunction with Yates, of the playhouse in Leith Walk which had been known during the previous ten years as the Pantheon and latterly as the Caledonian, but was now renamed the Adelphi. The partnership with Yates lasted only one year. The Theatre Royal opened for the first time under Murray's direct management 17 Nov. 1830, with the 'Honeymoon,' in which Murray played Jaques. Among other parts in which Murray was seen were Modus in the 'Hunchback,' Sir Benjamin Backbite, Bob Acres, Caliban, Falstaff, Figaro, and Dick Luckless in the 'Highland Widow,' taken from Scott's 'Chronicles of the Canongate.' A version of Harrison Ainsworth's 'Jack Sheppard' is attributed to Murray, who appeared in it as Hogarth. Newman Noggs in 'Nicholas Nickleby' and Bumble in 'Oliver Twist' belong to this period. For his benefit, 29 May 1843, he played Shylock. On 2 Nov. 1844 Murray had to deplore the death of his sister, Mrs. H. Siddons, long a mainstay of the theatre. His management of both the Theatre Royal and the Adelphi had been an unbroken success. On 17 July 1845, at the Adelphi, he played Goldthumb in 'Time Works wonders,' and 31 July Caudle in 'Mr. and Mrs. Caudle.' Caleb Plummer in the 'Cricket on the Hearth' followed at the other house. Cox in 'Box and Cox' was another favourite part.

In 1848, through age, he resigned his function of stage manager. He still played some new parts, including Christopher Sly. On 22 Oct. 1851, at the Adelphi, Murray, as Sir Anthony Absolute, made, for his benefit, his last appearance on the Edinburgh stage. He was said to be in bad health, and so tired of his profession as to have destroyed his diary and all books connected with his stage life, and to have given away his stage wardrobe. He acted, however, more than once subsequently in Aberdeen and Dundee. He retired with a competency to live in St. Andrews, and returning from a party at Professor Playfair's, 5 May 1852, he was taken ill, and shortly afterwards died. Murray was twice married. His first wife was a Miss Dyke, sister of Mrs. Thomas Moore; the second a Miss Gray, a member of his company. She survived until 1888. He left several children. More than one daughter played occasionally at the Theatre Royal, and a son, Henry Murray, in middle life became an actor.

An excellent actor in juvenile parts where no deep emotion or pathos had to be displayed, Murray was good also in comedy, and in what are known as 'character' parts he excelled. He wrote many dramas intended to serve a temporary purpose, and without literary aim. 'Diamond cut Diamond,' an interlude, from 'How to die for Love,' a translation from Kotzebue; 'Cramond Brig,' assigned by error to Lockhart, and depreciated by Scott; 'Mary Stuart,' 'Gilderoy,' and a burlesque of 'Romeo and Juliet,' were among his successes. His management was judicious and resolute, but did not escape the charge of being penurious; his relations with dramatists were not always satisfactory, or even creditable; and he suffered in later years from depression, uncertain temper, and an unreasonable fear of bankruptcy. About 1819 he helped to found the Edinburgh Theatrical Fund, and became a director. A special feature in Murray's management was the addresses he spoke at the beginning and close of a season, and on other occasions. These are both in verse and prose, are well written, effective, and not wanting in humour. A collection of them was published in 1851, and is now scarce. He was in the main a worthy man, staid, formal, and a trifle pedantic. Scott often makes friendly reference to him, and records how, in 'High Life below Stairs' (2 March 1827), Murray, answering the question 'Who wrote Shakespeare?' after one had answered Ben Jonson and another Finis, said 'No, it is Sir Walter Scott; he confessed it at a public meeting the other day.'

A portrait of Murray by his friend, Sir William Allan, P.R.S.A., is in the Scottish National Portrait Gallery.

[Private information, in part kindly forwarded by James C. Dibdin, esq.; Dibdin's Annals of the Edinburgh Stage; Genest's Account of the English Stage; the Farewell and Occasional Addresses delivered by W. H. Murray, Esq., Edinburgh, 1851; The Theatre, Edinburgh, 1851–2; Theatrical Inquisitor, vol. iv. London, 1814; Lockhart's Life of Scott; Journal of Sir Walter Scott; Memoirs of Charles Mathews, by Mrs. Mathews; Tallis's Dramatic Magazine.] J. K.

MURRELL, JOHN (*fl.* 1630), writer on cookery, was a native of London and by profession a cook. He had travelled in France, Italy, and the Low Countries, and his foreign experiences greatly improved his knowledge of his art. With the methods of both French and Dutch cookery he was intimately acquainted. He was author of a popular treatise on his art, which was licensed for the press to John Browne on 29 April 1617, under the title 'The Ladies' Practise, or plaine and easie Directions for Ladies and Gentlewomen.' It was first published in 1621 as 'A Delightfull Daily Exercise for Ladies and Gentlewomen, whereby is set foorth the secrete Misteries of the purest Preservings in Glasse and other Confrictionaries, as making of Breads, Pastes, Preserves, Suckets, Marmalates, Tart Stuffes, Rough Candies, with many other Things never before in print, whereto is added a Booke of Cookery by John Murrell, professor thereof' (12mo, Brit. Mus.) In an address to 'all ladies and gentlemen and others whatsoever,' Murrell speaks of the favour previously extended to other books by him, none of which seem extant. Thomas Dewe, the publisher, advertises his readiness to sell the 'moulds' described by Murrell in the text. About 1630 Murrell published another volume called 'A new Booke of Cookerie, with the newest art of Carving and Serving.' The first edition of 'Murrels Two Books of Cookerie and Carving'—a compilation from earlier works—appeared in the same year. A long title-page describes the recipes as 'all set forth according to the now new English and French fashion.' The first book on cookery is dedicated, under date 20 July 1630, to Martha, daughter of Sir Thomas Hayes, lord mayor; the second book to the wife of Sir John Brown. A fifth edition 'with new additions' is dated 1638 (Brit. Mus.) Another edition was issued in 1641 (Bodl. Libr.), and a seventh in 1650. Murrell's writings—especially his first volume which deals mainly with ornamental cookery—give an attractive picture of the culinary art of his day. But they have their barbarous episodes. Murrell strongly recommended for invalids 'an excellent and much approved' beverage, of which the chief ingredients were white snails.

[Murrell's Works; Quart. Rev. January 1894; Arber's Stationers' Registers, iii. 608.] S. L.

MUSCHAMP, GEOFFREY DE (*d.* 1208), bishop of Lichfield and Coventry. [See Geoffrey.]

MUSGRAVE, Sir ANTHONY (1828–1888), colonial administrator, son of Anthony Musgrave, M.D., of the island of Antigua, was born in 1828. He acted as private secretary to Mr. Mackenzie when governor-in-chief of the Leeward Islands in 1850–1. In the latter year he entered as a student at the Inner Temple, but was never called to the bar. He was appointed treasury accountant at Antigua in 1852, and colonial secretary there in 1854; administrator at Nevis in October 1860 and at St. Vincent's in April 1861, and lieutenant-governor of St. Vincent's in May 1862; governor of Newfoundland in April 1864, of British Columbia in January 1869, lieutenant-governor of Natal in May 1872, governor of South Australia in June 1873, governor-in-chief and captain-general in Jamaica in January 1877, and governor and commander-in-chief in Queensland in 1888.

Musgrave was made C.M.G. in 1871 and K.C.M.G. in 1875, and died at Brisbane, Queensland, in October 1888. He was twice married: first in 1854 to Christiana Elizabeth, daughter of the Hon. Sir William Byam of Antigua (she died in 1859); secondly, to Jeannie Lucinda, daughter of David Dudley Field of New York.

Musgrave was author of 'Studies in Political Economy,' London, 1875, 8vo, and of some pamphlets.

[Dod's Knightage, 1888; Colonial List, 1888; Times, 6 Oct. 1888.] H. M. C.

MUSGRAVE, Sir CHRISTOPHER (1632?–1704), statesman, third son of Sir Philip Musgrave [q.v.], bart., of Edenhall, and of Musgrave and Hartley Castle, Westmoreland, was born at Edenhall in 1631 or 1632. He matriculated from Queen's College, Oxford, on 10 July 1651, and graduated B.A. the same day. In 1654 he entered as a student of Gray's Inn. He suffered imprisonment in the Tower and other places for his adherence to the royal cause, and was concerned in the unsuccessful rising of Sir George Booth at Chester in 1659. After the Restoration he was given a commission as captain of a foot company in Carlisle garrison, and in 1663 made clerk of the robes to Queen Catherine. This post he nearly lost by non-attendance and through failure to have his accounts properly audited, but pleaded that he had been detained in the north by the disturbed state of the country due to Atkinson's rising. His company at Carlisle was disbanded in 1668, and in 1669 he was made a captain in the king's guards. In 1671 he was knighted, in 1672 served as mayor of Carlisle, and in 1677 became governor of Carlisle Castle on the death of his father. In 1681 he was nominated lieutenant-general of the ordnance, and in 1687 he succeeded as fourth baronet to the family honours on the death of his elder brother, Sir Richard.

Musgrave sat in parliament for forty-three years, from 1661 to his death, being M.P. for Carlisle 1661–90, Westmoreland 1690–5, Appleby 1695–8, Oxford University 1698–1700, Westmoreland 1700–1, Totnes 1701–2, Westmoreland 1702–4. He was a staunch supporter of the crown, and in the 'List of Court Pensioners in Parliament,' published in 1677 (said to be by Andrew Marvell), he appears as receiving 200*l.* a year. He strongly opposed the Exclusion Bill, and appears to have assisted in 1684 in the surrender of the charters of Carlisle and Appleby to the king (Lowther, *Memoirs of the Reign of James II*). But in 1687 he lost his post as lieutenant-general of the ordnance for refusing to support James II in repealing the test and penal laws. In the Convention parliament he was one of the few who opposed the resolution declaring the throne vacant, and became the leader of the high tories and the country gentlemen. In this position he carried on a fierce warfare with Sir John Lowther [q. v.], M.P. for Westmoreland, who had been made first lord of the treasury and leader of the House of Commons. Sir Christopher carried a proposal that the revenue of the king should be settled for only four years against Lowther, who wished it to be settled for life. In the parliament of 1692–3 Musgrave supported the Triennial Bill, thus joining the whigs out of office, but still opposing Lowther, who objected to the bill. After 1695 Musgrave played a less prominent part in parliament. But in 1696 he refused to sign the association formed by the commons for the defence of the king after the discovery of Barclay's assassination plot. In 1696 he also supported the resolution for the removal of Somers. When that motion was lost he argued for the resolution prohibiting foreigners from sitting in the privy council. In 1698, when a new grant had to be made to the king, Lowther proposed one million pounds, and Musgrave rose in indignation and proposed 700,000*l.*, which was granted. This, says Onslow, was a prearrangement between the king and Musgrave, and had it not been for the latter's intervention the king would have only obtained 500,000*l.* Musgrave received a large sum of money for his action, but as he was coming away from the king's closet one of the bags of guineas burst and revealed what he had been there for. It is to this that Pope alludes in the lines:

Once, we confess, beneath the patriot's cloak,
From the cracked bag the dropping guinea spoke,
And jingling down the backstairs, told the crew,
'Old Cato is as great a rogue as you.'

(*Epistle III. to Lord Bathurst*, ll. 35–9; Elwin, *Pope*, iii. 131.) Burnet states that Musgrave had 12,000*l.* from the king at different times for yielding points of importance.

Under Anne he obtained some favour at court, becoming upon her accession one of the tellers of the exchequer. He died of apoplexy in London on 29 July 1704, and was buried in the church of Holy Trinity in the Minories, London.

He married for the first time, on 31 May 1660, Mary, daughter and coheiress of Sir Andrew Cogan of Greenwich, bart., by whom he had two sons and a daughter. She died at Carlisle Castle on 11 July 1664. In 1671 he married his second wife, Elizabeth, daughter of Sir John Franklin of Willesden, by whom he had six sons and six daughters. She died on 11 April 1701.

His elder son by his first wife, Philip (1661–1689), was M.P. for Appleby 1685–7 and 1689, and clerk of the council and of the deliveries in the ordnance under James II. He was succeeded as clerk of the council by his younger brother, Christopher (*d.* 1718). He married in 1685 Mary, daughter of George Legge, lord Dartmouth, and left a son Christopher (*d.* 1735), who succeeded his grandfather as fifth baronet, and was M.P. for Carlisle and clerk of the council from 1710.

Of Musgrave's sons by his second wife, Joseph (1676–1757) was elected bencher of Gray's Inn in 1724, and was M.P. for Cockermouth in 1713, while George (1683–1751), a graduate of Christ Church, Oxford, was storekeeper of Chatham dockyard and was great-grandfather of George Musgrave Musgrave, who is noticed separately below.

[Foster's Alumni Oxon. (1500–1714); Boyer's Annals of Queen Anne; Betham's Baronetage; Luttrell's Brief Hist. Relation; Foster's Gray's Inn Reg.; Burnet's History of his own Time; Cobbett's Parl. Hist.; Lowther's Memoirs of the Reign of James II; Ferguson's Cumberland and Westmoreland M.P.s; Burton's Life of Sir Philip Musgrave; Le Neve's Mon. Angl.; Cal. State Papers, Charles II; History of Carlisle; Burn and Nicolson's Hist. of Cumberland.]

C. O.

MUSGRAVE, GEORGE MUSGRAVE (1798–1883), divine and topographer, born in the parish of St. Marylebone, London, 1 July 1798, was the eldest son of George Musgrave (*d.* 1861) of Marylebone and Shillington Manor, Bedfordshire, who married, 19 Aug. 1790, Margaret (*d.* 1859), only daughter of Edmund Kennedy. The son George was one of the earliest pupils of Charles Parr Burney, and on 17 Feb. 1816 he matriculated from Brasenose College, Oxford. He graduated B.A. 1819, when he took a second class in classics, and M.A. 1822, and he was ordained deacon 1822, and priest 1823. In 1824 he held the curacy of All Souls, Marylebone, and from 1826 to 1829 he served in the same position at the parish church of Marylebone. During the years 1835–8 he filled the rectory of Bexwell, near Downham, Norfolk, and he was vicar of Borden, Kent, from 1838 to 1854, when he resigned in favour of his son-in-law. Musgrave was lord of the manor of Borden as well as one of its chief landowners, and while vicar he filled the east and west windows of the church with stained glass to the memory of his relations. After 1854 he lived in retirement, first at Withycome-Raleigh, near Exmouth, Devonshire, then near Hyde Park, London, and lastly at Bath. During these years he travelled much in France, and he frequently lectured at local institutes on his tours or his antiquarian studies. Two prizes were founded by him at the Clergy Orphan Corporation School for Boys, St. Thomas's Mount, Canterbury, and three at its school for girls, St. John's Wood, London. He died at 13 Grosvenor Place, Bath, 26 Dec. 1883. His first wife, whom he married on 4 July 1827, was Charlotte Emily, youngest daughter of Thomas Oakes, formerly senior member of council and president of the board of revenue, Madras, and they had issue two sons and three daughters. He married, secondly, 24 July 1877, Charlotte Matilda, elder daughter of the Rev. William Stamer, rector of St. Saviour's, Bath, and widow of Richard Hall Appleyard, barrister-at-law. She died at Paignton 20 April 1893, and was buried at Bath.

Musgrave was an assiduous traveller, and probably knew the surface of France better than any Englishman since Arthur Young's day. He also explored the recesses of Sicily and wandered on the coasts of the Adriatic, among the Apennines and the Alps, and by the Elbe and the Danube. In 1863 he issued, under the veil of 'Viator Verax, M.A.,' a pamphlet called 'Continental Excursions. Cautions for the First Tour,' which passed through four impressions in that year, and in 1866 passed into a fifth edition as 'Foreign Travel, or Cautions for the First Tour.' This brochure exposed, with some exaggeration, the impositions and indecencies of continental travelling. He published, moreover, seven books, narrating his leisurely and gossipping rambles in his favourite country of France. Their titles were: 1. 'Parson, Pen, and Pencil,' 1848, 3 vols., reissued in 1849 with the more exact description of 'Excursions to Paris, Tours, and Rouen.' 2. 'Ramble through Normandy, or Scenes, Characters, and Incidents in Calvados,' 1855. 3. 'Pilgrimage into Dauphiné, with a Visit to the Grand Chartreuse,' 1857, 2 vols. 4. 'Byroads and Battle-fields in Picardy,' 1861. 5. 'Ten Days in a French Parsonage in the Summer of 1863,' 1864, 2 vols. 6. 'Nooks and Corners in Old France,' 1867, 2 vols. 7. 'Ramble into Brittany,' 1870, 2 vols.

When vicar of Borden, a living in an agricultural district, Musgrave published several useful works for the benefit of his parishioners, both young and old. Among them were: 1. 'Nine and Two, or School Hours; a Book of Plain and Simple Instruction,' 1843. 2. An appendix thereto entitled 'A Vocabulary of Explanations, or List of Words and certain difficult Sentences in the Gospels,' 1843. 3. 'The Crow-keeper, or Thoughts in the Field,' 1846. 4. A new and improved edition called 'The Farm-boy's Friend, or Thoughts in the Field and Plantation,' 1847. 5. 'Plain and Simple Hymns for Public Worship in Agricultural Parishes,' 3rd edit., Sittingbourne, 1852. In his retirement he compiled: 6. 'A Manual of Plain, Short, and Intelligible Family Prayers,' 1865. 7. 'Psalter for Private Commune,' 1872. 8. 'Readings for Lent,' 1877.

Musgrave also published 'Translations from Tasso and Petrarch,' 1822, 'The Psalms of David in English blank verse,' 1833, and 'The Odyssey of Homer, rendered into English blank verse,' 1865, 2 vols.; 2nd edit. revised and corrected, 1869, 2 vols.

[Foster's Alumni Oxon.; Burke's Landed Gentry, 1886 ed.; Men of the Time, 11th ed.; Crockford, 1882 ed.; Academy, 5 Jan. 1884, p. 9; Gent. Mag. 1861 pt. ii. p. 215.] W. P. C.

MUSGRAVE, JOHN (*fl.* 1654), pamphleteer, was youngest son of John Musgrave, by Isabel, daughter of Thomas Musgrave of Hayton, Cumberland, and grandson of Sir Simon Musgrave, bart., of Edenhall in the same county. He himself resided at Milnerigg, Cumberland (Jefferson, *Cumberland*, i. 416). Upon the outbreak of the civil war he allied himself with the parliamentarians, greatly to the displeasure of his family, and was made a captain in their army. Owing, however, to his quarrelsome disposition, he proved of little service to his new friends. He wished, too, to become a quaker, but was refused admission to the society. Along with a kindred spirit, Captain Richard Crackenthorpe, of Little Strickland, Westmoreland, Musgrave was imprisoned in 1642 for six months in Carlisle gaol by the justices and commissioners of array in Cumberland for maintaining, as he asserted, the 'parliamentary protestations' and opposing the 'arbitrary and tyrannical government of the corrupt magistracy and ministry there.' On being removed by habeas corpus to London, the pair petitioned parliament for their release, and they were ordered to be discharged on 13 Dec. (*Commons' Journals*, ii. 886). At his return home Musgrave again refused to submit to the commission of array, and spent the best part of the next two years in Scotland. Coming back to Cumberland in 1644, he found the militia and authorities settled in the hands of 'such as were the sworn and professed enemies of the kingdom.' Accordingly with some other 'exiles for the parliament's cause' Musgrave represented the state of things to the parliamentary commissioners, but on failing to obtain redress went to London in company with John Osmotherley, to petition parliament in behalf of the 'well affected' of Cumberland and Westmoreland. In particular he charged Richard Barwis, M.P., with having betrayed his trust by placing disaffected persons in office. The house referred the matter to a committee, and finally sent Musgrave to the Fleet on 28 Oct. 1645 for contempt, on his refusal to answer certain interrogatories. About the same time his colleague, Osmotherley, was lodged in Wood Street compter for debt. Musgrave beguiled his imprisonment by writing three virulent pamphlets, full of reckless charges against those in power, which the house took notice of (*ib.* iv. 419, 451, 682). On being released in January 1647, he and his friend Crackenthorpe presented a petition to the House of Lords setting forth the great losses they had sustained by adhering to the cause of the parliament (*Lords' Journals*, ix. 670, 676). Their petition was referred to the commons, who declined to grant them any recompense. In July he was again a prisoner by order of the house (*Commons' Journals*, v. 245). In September Musgrave attempted to force parliament to redress his alleged grievances by convening a meeting of the London apprentices at Guildhall, though he afterwards denied having been there at all (*Cal. State Papers*, Dom. 1645–7, p. 601). Some bloodshed was the result, and on 25 Sept. the house resolved to indict him at the King's Bench bar for high treason, and ordered him to be confined in Newgate (*Commons' Journals*, v. 316–17). Proceedings against him were ultimately dropped, and on 3 June 1648 he was allowed to be released on bail (*ib.* v. 584). He now devoted his energies to 'discovering' delinquents and seeing that they compounded for their estates to the utmost value (*Proc. of Comm. for Advance of Money*, p. 87). He boasted that in this way he brought a yearly revenue of 13,000*l.* into the state. On 27 Aug. 1649 Musgrave, with Crackenthorpe and others, complained to the council of state that the Cumberland and Westmoreland militia was not placed in trusty hands (*Cal. State Papers*, Dom. 1649–50, p. 291), and in consequence was challenged by Charles Howard, afterwards first earl of Carlisle [q. v.], to make good his accusation (*ib.* p. 455). He next took exception to the persons nominated by Sir Arthur Hesilrige [q. v.] to be commissioners for the northern counties, and was ordered to formulate his charges against them (*ib.* pp. 461, 499). Thereupon he attempted to create a diversion by laying, on 19 June 1650, an information against six prominent Cumberland gentlemen, including Howard and Sir Wilfrid Lawson, for delinquency (*Cal. of Committee for Advance*, &c., p. 1237). Hesilrige, having been ordered to investigate the matter, reported that there was no truth in the charge. Musgrave attacked him in a pamphlet, which the council of state, on 19 Dec., ordered to be seized (*Cal. State Papers*, Dom. 1650, pp. 473, 568). In the event Musgrave's imputations upon Howard and Hesilrige were declared by the council of state, in January 1651, to be 'false and scandalous,' and Hesilrige was recommended to institute proceedings against him (*ib.* 1651, pp. 21, 23). He was now mistrusted by all parties. On 3 Feb. the committee for advance of money obliged him to enter into a bond in 1,000*l.* to prosecute several Cumberland men for alleged undervaluations in their composition at Goldsmiths' Hall (*Cal. of Proc.* p. 1238). Musgrave made a last attempt to gain the ear of the public, by describing himself in a pamphlet as an 'innocent Abel,' Cain being represented by his two brothers and sister-in-law. It appears that his mother having married for her second husband John Vaux, a violent quarrel over some property between Musgrave and the Vaux family ensued, and in the end recourse was had to the court of chancery.

Musgrave wrote: 1. 'A Word to the Wise, displaying great augmented grievances and heavie pressures of dangerous consequence,' 4to [London], 1646, in which he complains of illegal imprisonment. 2. 'Another Word to the Wise, shewing that the Delay of Justice is great Injustice,' 4to [London], 1646. 3. 'Yet another Word to the Wise, shewing that the grievances in Cumberland and Westmoreland are unredressed,' 4to [London], 1646. 4. 'A Fourth Word to the Wise; or, a Plaine Discovery of Englands Misery,' 4to [London, 1647], addressed to Ireton. 5. 'A Declaration of Captaine J. Musgrave . . . vindicating him against the misprisians and imputed reasons of his sad imprisonment for High Treason,' &c., 4to, London, 1647. 6. 'A True and Exact Relation of the great and heavy Pressures and Grievances the well-affected of the Northern Bordering Counties lye under by Sir Arthur Haslerigs misgovernment,' &c., 4to, London, 1650. A reply, entitled 'Musgrave Muzl'd,' appeared in 1651, which was answered by Musgrave in 7. 'Musgraves Musle Broken . . . wherein is Discovered how the Commonwealth is abused by Sub-Commissioners for Sequestrations,' &c., 4to, London, 1651. 8. 'A Cry of Blood of an Innocent Abel against two Bloody Cains,' &c., 4to, London, 1654, addressed to General Lambert. Musgrave also published a letter signed T. G. entitled 'A Plain Discovery how the Enemy and Popish Faction in the North upholds their Interest,' 4to, London, 1649. An extract attributed to François Balduin, from Edward Grimstone's 'History of the Netherlands,' 1608, p. 356, which he read in prison, he published under the title of 'Good Counsel in Bad Times,' 4to, London, 1647, and prefixed to it a characteristic 'Epistle.'

[Musgrave's pamphlets; Cal. of Committee for Compounding; Cal. State Papers, Dom. 1651, p. 266.] G. G.

MUSGRAVE, SIR PHILIP (1607–1678), royalist, born on 21 May 1607, and descended from Thomas, baron Musgrave (*d.* 1384) [q. v.], was the son of Sir Richard Musgrave, bart., of Hartley, Westmoreland (*d.* 1611), by Frances, daughter of Philip, lord Wharton. He was educated at Peterhouse, Cambridge, and at Trinity College, Oxford, where he became a commoner in 1624, and was admitted to Gray's Inn on 2 Feb. 1626–7. He represented the county of Westmoreland in the two parliaments elected in 1640, declared for the king at the outbreak of the civil war, and became governor of Carlisle and commander-in-chief of the royalist forces in the counties of Cumberland and Westmoreland. Musgrave joined Montrose in his first attempt to penetrate into Scotland, and was with him at the capture of Dumfries (*Mercurius Aulicus*, 28 April 1644). After the surrender of Carlisle he joined the king at Cardiff, and was taken prisoner in September at the battle of Rowton Heath (WALKER,

Historical Discourses, p. 140; BURTON, *Life of Musgrave*, pp. 6–10).

Musgrave took an active part in the intrigues which led to the second civil war, and came to Edinburgh in March 1648 to negotiate with the Scottish royalists. On 31 March the commissioners of the English parliament demanded that he should be surrendered to them, to be dealt with by parliament as an 'incendiary betwixt the nations' (*Old Parliamentary History*, xvii. 91, 106, 114, 133). But the Scottish government refused to surrender him, and on 29 April Musgrave seized Carlisle and declared for the king. Before long the advance of General Lambert drove most of the northern royalists to take shelter in Carlisle. They were relieved by the march of Hamilton [see HAMILTON, JAMES, third MARQUIS and first DUKE OF HAMILTON] into England; but Musgrave was obliged to hand over Carlisle to the Scots to garrison. Musgrave was not personally present at the defeat of Preston, as his forces had been united with the Scottish division of Sir George Munro [q. v.], and formed the rear of the invading army. After the defeat he and Monro separated, and Musgrave, who had thrown himself into Appleby, capitulated on 9 Oct. 1648. He wrote a narrative of the campaign for the assistance of Clarendon, which shows how much the dissensions between the English and Scottish royalists were responsible for their joint failure (CLARENDON, *Rebellion*, xi. 14, 43–50; *Clarendon MS.* 2867; RUSHWORTH, vii. 1106, 1114, 1157, 1294; GARDINER, *Great Civil War*, iii. 435, 487; ORMEROD, *Lancashire Civil War Tracts*, p. 274; *Hamilton Papers*, i. 210, 218; BURTON, pp. 12–15). Musgrave left England immediately after the king's death. Parliament, on 14 March 1649, voted that Musgrave and eleven others named should be 'proscribed and banished as enemies and traitors, and die without mercy, wheresoever they shall be found within the limits of this nation, and their estates be confiscated' (*Commons' Journals*, vi. 164). In the summer of 1650 he accompanied Charles II to Scotland, but was immediately expelled by the Scottish government, and joined the Earl of Derby [see STANLEY, JAMES, seventh EARL OF DERBY] in the Isle of Man (WALKER, *Historical Discourses*, p. 161; CARTE, *Original Letters*, ii. 28). In August 1651, however, the king sent for him to take part in the expedition into England (CARY, *Memorials of the Civil War*, ii. 321). He missed the king in Lancashire, was nearly taken prisoner, returned to the Isle of Man, and was governor of that island when it surrendered to Colonel Duckenfield (BURTON, pp. 19–29; *Mercurius Politicus*, 6–13 Nov. 1651). Musgrave was allowed to return to England under the protectorate, and was engaged in several royalist conspiracies against the Protector (*Cal. Clarendon Papers*, ii. 335, 383, 395, iii. 130). He was arrested in September 1653, imprisoned again as concerned in the attempted rising of 1655, and summoned before the council in the summer of 1659 (*Cal. State Papers*, Dom. 1653–4 pp. 157, 276, 1655 p. 215, 1659–60 p. 35; BURTON, pp. 30–5, 53).

At the Restoration Musgrave presented a petition recounting his services, and was rewarded by the government of Carlisle and a grant of the farm of the tolls in Cumberland and Westmoreland (*Cal. State Papers*, Dom. 1660–1, pp. 280, 431). He represented the county of Westmoreland in the Long parliament of Charles II, and was very active in the suppression of recusants, nonconformists, and plotters against the government (*Hist. MSS. Comm.* 12th Rep. pt. vi. pp. 31, 69, 109). Musgrave was granted on 25 March 1650 a warrant creating him a peer, by the title of Baron Musgrave of Hartley Castle, but the patent was never issued (BURTON, p. 55). He died on 7 Feb. 1677–8, and was buried in the church of St. Cuthbert at Edenhall in Cumberland. His epitaph and that of his wife Julian, daughter of Sir Richard Hutton of Goldsborough, Yorkshire, are printed by Le Neve (*Monumenta Anglicana*, ii. 71, 181; *Fairfax Correspondence*, iii. 205–208). Her portrait belonged to the Rev. George Musgrave in 1866 (*Cat. First Nat. Portrait Exhibition*, South Kensington, No. 693). Musgrave was succeeded in the baronetcy by his eldest son Richard. His third son, Christopher, is separately noticed.

[The chief authority for Musgrave's life is the contemporary Life of Sir Philip Musgrave, by Gilbert Burton, vicar of Edenhall, edited by Samuel Jefferson, Carlisle, 1840. For pedigrees see Foster's Cumberland and Westmoreland Visitation Pedigrees, 1615 and 1666, and Foster's Baronetage. On Musgrave's connection with the siege of Carlisle, see A Narrative of the Siege of Carlisle, by Isaac Tullie, ed. by S. Jefferson, and Transactions of the Cumberland and Westmoreland Archæological Society, vii. 48, xi. 104. Jefferson's Hist. of Cumberland, Leath Ward, p. 416; Nicolson and Burn's Hist. of Westmoreland and Cumberland, 1777, i. 590–9. Many letters of Musgrave's are among the Dom. State Papers, Restoration Ser., and in the manuscripts of S. H. Le Fleming, esq., 12th Rep. of Hist. MSS. Comm. pt. vii.] C. H. F.

MUSGRAVE, SIR RICHARD (1757?–1818), Irish political writer, eldest son of Christopher Musgrave of Tourin, co. Waterford, by Susannah, daughter of James Usher of Ballintaylor, near Dungarvan, in the same county, was born about 1757. In 1778 he entered the Irish parliament as member for Lismore, which he continued to represent until the union. A strong protestant and loyalist he was rewarded with a baronetcy on 2 Dec. 1782, and on the union received the lucrative post of collector of the Dublin city excise. During the previous troubles he had displayed great zeal and energy in enforcing the law. On one occasion, while high sheriff of co. Waterford (September 1786), he had flogged a Whiteboy with his own hand, as no one else could be found to execute the sentence. He gave warning of the approaching rebellion in 'A Letter on the Present Situation of Public Affairs,' dedicated to the Duke of Portland, London, 1794 and 1795, 8vo, and 'Considerations on the Present State of England and France' in 1796. On the suppression of the rebellion he published, under the pseudonym 'Camillus,' an address 'To the Magistrates, the Military, and the Yeomanry of Ireland,' Dublin, 1798, 8vo, in which he exonerated the executive from the charge of having provoked it by arbitrary measures. In 1801 appeared his 'Short View of the Political Situation of the Northern Powers,' 8vo, and 'Memoirs of the different Rebellions in Ireland from the Arrival of the English, with a Particular Detail of that which broke out the 23rd of May, 1798; the History of the Conspiracy which preceded it, and the Characters of the Principal Actors in it,' Dublin, 4to, 3rd edit. 1802, 2 vols. 8vo, a work so steeped in anti-catholic prejudice as to be almost worthless historically. It elicited a sober and dignified 'Reply' from Dr. Caulfield, Roman catholic bishop of Ferns, to which Musgrave rejoined in 'Observations on the Reply,' Dublin, 1802, 8vo. In 1804 Musgrave published 'Strictures upon an "Historical Review of the State of Ireland," by Francis Plowden, Esq., or a Justification of the Conduct of the English Governments in that Country,' to which Plowden replied in an 'Historical Letter,' London, 1805, 8vo (cf. also the *British Critic*, November and December 1803, and the *Anti-Jacobin*, December 1804, and September 1805).

Musgrave was a man of considerable talent, warped by blind prejudice and savage party spirit. Though strongly attached to the English connection, he was no less strongly opposed to the Act of Union, and never sat in the imperial parliament. He died at his house in Holles Street, Dublin, on 7 April 1818. Musgrave married, on 10 Nov. 1780, Deborah, daughter of Sir Henry Cavendish, bart., of Doveridge Hall, Derbyshire, by whom he had no issue. The title devolved upon his brother, Sir Christopher Frederick Musgrave. Besides the works mentioned above, Musgrave published in 1814 'Observations on Dr. Drumgoole's Speech at the Catholic Board,' 8 Dec. 1813, 8vo.

[Ann. Biog. 1819 p. 507, 1820 pp. 34 et seq.; Gent. Mag. 1818, pt. i. p. 381; Burke's Peerage; Froude's English in Ireland, ii. 473; Gordon's Hist. of the Rebellion in Ireland, 1803, Preface; Hay's Hist. of the Insurrection of the County of Wexford, 1803, Appendix; Sir Jonah Barrington's Personal Sketches, i. 75; The Treble Almanack, 1801; Cornwallis Corresp. (Ross), iii. 150; Notes and Queries, 6th ser. ii. 170; Fitzgerald's Secret Service under Pitt; Lecky's Hist. of Engl. in Eighteenth Cent.] J. M. R.

MUSGRAVE, SAMUEL (1732–1780), physician and classical scholar, son of Richard Musgrave, gentleman, of Washfield, Devonshire, was born at Washfield on 29 Sept. 1732. He was educated at Barnstaple grammar school, and matriculated at Queen's College, Oxford, on 11 May 1749. After his appointment on 27 Feb. 1749–50 to a scholarship at Corpus Christi College, Oxford, he was entered on its books as a commoner, and graduated B.A. 27 Feb. 1753–4, M.A. 5 March 1756. About 1754 he was elected Radcliffe travelling fellow of University College, and spent many years on the continent, chiefly in Holland and France. He became fellow of the Royal Society on 12 July 1760, and took the degree of M.D. at Leyden in 1763, when he revisited Paris, and was elected a corresponding member of the Royal Academy of Inscriptions and Belles-Lettres. He afterwards alleged that during this residence at Paris in 1764 he received trustworthy information that the peace signed the previous year had been sold to the French by some persons of high rank. These persons, it subsequently appeared, were the princess dowager, Lord Bute, and Lord Holland. On 10 May 1765, on his return to England, he saw Lord Halifax, then secretary of state, on the subject, who required some corroborative evidence of the facts, and, when none was forthcoming, declined to make any movement. Musgrave then applied to the speaker, but he was again met by a refusal to take any action in the matter.

Musgrave's tenure of the Radcliffe fellowship had now expired, and he settled about 1766 at Exeter, where he was elected on 24 July in that year physician to the Devon and Exeter Hospital. As he did not succeed in obtaining sufficient practice at Exeter, he resigned this post in the latter part of 1768, and removed to Plymouth. An advertisement by him in the 'St. James's Evening Chronicle' in October 1766, that he was preparing for the press a volume of papers on the late peace, attracted little attention. But a printed 'Address to the Gentlemen, Clergy, and Freeholders of Devon,' which he issued on 12 Aug. 1769, as a preliminary to a general meeting in Exeter Castle on the subsequent 5 Oct., excited universal astonishment. He admitted that he could not himself prove the charges, but he regarded the action of Halifax as 'a wilful obstruction of national justice.' Among the pieces published by Musgrave was one entitled 'An Account of the Chevalier d'Éon's Overtures to Impeach three persons, by name, of selling the Peace to the French.' D'Éon, who had been French plenipotentiary in England in 1763, was alleged to have been restrained from taking any open steps by the machinations of the parties accused. Many pamphlets appeared for and against Musgrave, and among them was one from D'Éon himself, repudiating all knowledge of him and of the circumstances which he alleged to have occurred. After a full and patient hearing in the House of Commons, Musgrave's accusations were voted 'frivolous and unworthy of credit,' 29 Jan. 1770 (*Gent. Mag.* 1770, passim; *European Mag.* 1791, i. 336).

These proceedings ruined Musgrave's chances of professional advancement at Plymouth, and he determined on living in London. He took the degree of M.D. at Oxford on 8 Dec. 1775, and settled at Hart Street, Bloomsbury. On 30 Sept. 1776 he was admitted a candidate of the College of Physicians, London, proceeded fellow on 30 Sept. 1777, and was appointed Gulstonian lecturer and censor in 1779. He was harassed by pecuniary difficulties, and, when he found that his practice did not improve, was forced to eke out his income by his pen. As a Greek scholar he had few superiors, and his great delight was the study and annotation of the works of Euripides, but through want he was unable to carry out his design of publishing an edition of that author, and he was forced to sell his collections to the university of Oxford for 200*l.* He died in very reduced circumstances at Hart Street, Bloomsbury, on 4 July 1780, and was buried, with a short inscription, in the burial-ground of St. George, Bloomsbury.

Musgrave's library was sold by James Robson of New Bond Street, London, in 1780, and, mainly through the exertions of Thomas Tyrwhitt, who is said to have surrendered to the widow a bond for several hundred pounds advanced by him to Musgrave, a very liberal subscription was obtained for the publication, in 1782, of 'Two Dissertations' for the benefit of his family.

Musgrave's works were: 1. 'Euripidis Hippolytus. Variis lectionibus et Notis Editoris. Accessere Jeremiæ Markland emendationes,' 1756. For the production of this volume he visited Paris, and collated several editions in its libraries. The notes of Markland were obtained through a friend, and his name was prefixed without his knowledge, 'and very much against his inclination.' This text was adopted in the Eton editions of the play in 1792 and 1799. 2. 'Remarks on Boerhaave's Theory of the Attrition of the Blood in the Lungs,' 1759. 3. 'Exercitationum in Euripidem libri duo,' Leyden, 1762. 4. 'Dissertatio Medica inauguralis sive Apologia pro Medicina Empirica,' Leyden, 1763. 5. 'Address to the Gentlemen, Clergy, and Freeholders of Devon,' dated Plymouth, 12 Aug. 1769. 6. 'True Intention of Dr. Musgrave's Address to the Freeholders of Devon,' 1769. 7. 'Dr. Musgrave's Reply to a Letter published in the Newspapers by the Chevalier d'Éon,' 1769. The 'Gentleman's Magazine' and the 'Oxford Magazine' for that year are full of comments on this controversy. 8. 'Speculations and Conjectures on the Qualities of the Nerves,' 1776. 9. 'Essay on Nature and Cure of Worm Fever,' 1776. 10. 'Euripidis quæ extant omnia,' Oxford, 1778, 4 vols.; another edition, Glasgow, 1797. Musgrave's collections, embodied in this edition, consisted of collations of the text, fragments of the lost plays, various readings, notes, and a revision of the Latin translation. His notes were included in the Leipzig edition of 1778–88 and the Oxford edition of 1821. The British Museum possesses two copies of the 1778 edition, with manuscript notes by Charles Burney. 11. 'Gulstonian Lectures on Pleurisy and Pulmonary Consumption,' 1779. 12. 'Two Dissertations: i. On the Græcian Mythology. ii. An Examination of Sir Isaac Newton's Objections to the Chronology of the Olympiads,' 1782. They were prepared for the press by Musgrave, and were handed by him shortly before his death to Tyrwhitt.

His notes on Euripides were included in the following editions: 1. 'The Alcestis,' published at Leipzig by C. T. Kuinoel in 1789. 2. 'The Medea,' published at Eton, 1785, 1792, and 1795. 3. 'The Electra,' for Westminster School, 1806, and a Glasgow issue in 1820. 4. 'Hecuba, Orestes et Phœnissæ,' 1809. 5. 'Hecuba, Orestes, Phœnissæ et Medea,' 1823. Selections from his notes were included in editions of 'Iphigenia in Aulis' and 'Iphigenia in Tauris,' published at Oxford in 1810. A letter from him to

Joseph Warton (15 Dec. 1771) on a projected edition by the delegates of the Clarendon Press, under his editorship, of the plays of Euripides, is in Wooll's 'Warton,' pp. 387–8.

Musgrave's notes on Sophocles were bought by the Oxford University after his death, and were inserted in an edition of the tragedies printed at Oxford in two volumes in 1800. A volume of the tragedies of Æschylus printed at Glasgow in two volumes in 1746, and now at the British Museum, contains manuscript notes which are said to be in his handwriting. He edited in 1776 the treatise of Dr. William Musgrave [q. v.], 'De Arthritide primogenia et regulari,' and he translated into Latin Ducarel's letter to Meerman on the dispute concerning Corcellis as the first printer in England.

[Munk's Coll. of Phys. ed. 1878, ii. 312–16; Western Antiq. vii. 33–5, 86; Telfer's D'Éon, pp. 199–205; Leyden Students (Index Soc.), p. 72; Letters of Radcliffe and James (Oxford Hist. Soc. vol. ix.), p. 91; Walpole's George III, iii. 384–5; Letters of Junius, xxxix.; Cavendish Debates, i. 623–4; Journ. House of Commons, 1770; Foster's Alumni Oxon.; Gent. Mag. 1780, p. 347; Nichols's Lit. Anecd. iii. 149–50, 663, iv. 285, 288, vi. 387, viii. 119, ix. 685.] W. P. C.

MUSGRAVE, THOMAS, Baron Musgrave (*d.* 1384), was son of Thomas Musgrave. He represented Westmoreland in parliament from 1341 to 1344 (*Return of Members of Parliament*, i. 135–40), and was present at the battle of Nevill's Cross on 17 Oct. 1346. In January 1347 he gave an indenture for the custody of Berwick (*Cal. of Documents relating to Scotland*, iii. 1477). On 20 July 1352 he was directed to arrest robbers in the marches of Scotland. On 4 Oct. 1353 he had a license to crenellate Harcla (or Hartley), which had been often destroyed by the Scots, and on 3 March 1359 was appointed to arrest Maria, daughter of William Douglas (*ib.* iii. 1564, 1572, iv. 45). In 1359 he was sheriff of Yorkshire and custos of York Castle, and in 1368 and subsequent years escheator for Yorkshire, Northumberland, Cumberland, and Westmoreland. In November 1373 he was appointed warden of Berwick for one year, with an allowance of four hundred marks, an appointment that was afterwards extended to November 1378. In the early part of 1377 Berwick was captured by the Scots. Musgrave took part in the operations for its recovery under Henry Percy, earl of Northumberland. On the conclusion of the siege the English invaded Scotland, and the Earls of Northumberland and Nottingham detached a body of three hundred lances and as many archers under the command of Musgrave to occupy Melrose. Two squires, whom Musgrave sent out to reconnoitre, were taken by the Scots, who then endeavoured to surprise him at Melrose. Bad weather prevented their purpose; but Musgrave, on learning of their approach through his foragers, rode out to meet them on 27 Aug. The Scots were three to one, and after a hard fight the English were defeated, and Musgrave and his son taken prisoners. This is the account given by Froissart; the St. Albans chronicler simply states that Musgrave, during a raid into Scotland, fell into an ambush and was taken prisoner (*Chron. Angliæ*, 1328–88, pp. 165–6). Musgrave was released under security in January 1378, but on failing to surrender the Earl of March in May forfeited his bail. Eventually a thousand marks was advanced by John Neville for his ransom and that of his son; this sum was still unpaid on 5 March 1382, when a distress was levied on the Musgraves in consequence. Musgrave was summoned to parliament from 25 Nov. 1350 to 4 Oct. 1373, but the summons was not continued to his descendants. He died in 1384 (Foster, *Visitation Pedigrees of Cumberland and Westmoreland*). He married Isabella, daughter of Thomas, lord Berkeley, and widow of Robert Clifford. His son Thomas was knighted by him before the fight with the Scots in 1377. Musgrave was ancestor of the Musgraves of Edenhall, Cumberland [see under Musgrave, Sir Philip], Hayton, and Tourin, co. Waterford, on which families baronetcies were conferred in 1611, 1638, and 1782 respectively.

[Froissart, vii. 37–58, ed. Buchon; Calendar of Documents relating to Scotland, vols. iii. and iv.; Dugdale's Baronage, ii. 153; Burke's Dormant and Extinct Peerage, p. 390; Nicolson and Burn's Westmoreland and Cumberland, i. 590–9, ii. 155 sqq.; Visitation Pedigrees of Cumberland and Westmoreland.] C. L. K.

MUSGRAVE, Sir THOMAS (1737–1812), general, sixth son of Sir Richard Musgrave, bart., of Hayton Castle, Cumberland (*d.* 1739), by his wife, the second daughter of John Hylton of Hylton Castle, Durham, was born in 1737, and entered the army in 1754 as ensign in the 3rd buffs. He became lieutenant 21 June 1756, and captain in the 64th 20 Aug. 1759; a brevet-major 22 July 1772; major, 40th foot, December 1775; and lieutenant-colonel, 27 Aug. 1776, on the death of Lieutenant-colonel James Grant at Brooklyn (Flat Bush). He commanded his regiment (40th foot) in the expedition to Philadelphia, and greatly distinguished himself at Germantown, one of Lord Cornwallis's outposts in front of Philadelphia, when the American army in great force attacked the village on the morning of 4 Oct. 1777. Musgrave, with six companies of his regiment, threw himself into a large stone house, belonging to a Mr. Chew, which he defended with great resolution against repeated attacks, until he was reinforced and the Americans repulsed. The action was commemorated by a silver medal, which was at one time worn as a regimental order of merit (see Hastings, Irwin, and Tancred, works on medals). Chew's house is represented on the medal, and is the background of one of the engraved portraits of Musgrave in the British Museum Prints.

Musgrave went in 1778 to the West Indies as quartermaster-general of the troops sent from New York under Major-general James Grant (1720–1806) [q. v.], of Ballindalloch, to capture and defend St. Lucia. He left the West Indies sick, but afterwards returned as brigadier-general to America, and was the last British commandant of New York. He became a brevet-colonel in 1781, and on his return home at the peace was made aide-de-camp to the king, and lieutenant-general of Stirling Castle. Cornwallis mentions him as at the reviews at Berlin in 1785 with Ralph Abercromby and David Dundas (1735–1820) [q. v.] (*Cornwallis Corresp.* vol. i.) On 12 Oct. 1787 Musgrave was appointed colonel of the new 76th or 'Hindoostan' regiment (now 2nd West Riding), which then was raised for service in India, where it became famous. The rendezvous was at Chatham, and the recruits were chiefly from the Musgrave family estates in the north of England. Musgrave went out to India with it, and served on the staff at Madras for several years. He became a major-general, 28 April 1790. His hopes of a command against Tippoo Sultân were disappointed by Lord Cornwallis, who appears to have thought that Musgrave did not work harmoniously with the civil government of Madras (*ib.* i. 473–9). Musgrave's plan of operations is published in 'Cornwallis's Correspondence' (ii. 8, 50). On his return Musgrave received many marks of attention from royalty. He was appointed lieutenant-general of Chelsea Hospital, but exchanged with David Dundas for that of Tilbury Fort, which did not require residence. He became a lieutenant-general 26 June 1797, and general 29 April 1802. He died in London on 31 Dec. 1812, aged 75, and was buried in the churchyard of St. George's, Hanover Square, in which parish he had long resided.

A portrait of Musgrave, painted by J. Abbott in 1786, was engraved and appeared in the 'British Military Panorama' in 1813 (*Notes and Queries*, 8th ser. v. 148).

[Foster's and Burke's Baronetages; Army Lists and London Gazettes; Beatson's Nav. and Mil. Memoirs, vols. iv–vi.; Cornwallis's Corresp. vols. i–ii.; Biography of Musgrave in British Military Panorama, vol. iii. London, 1813.] H. M. C.

MUSGRAVE, THOMAS (1788–1860), successively bishop of Hereford and archbishop of York, the son of W. Peet Musgrave, a wealthy tailor and woollendraper of Cambridge, by Sarah his wife, was born in Slaughter House Lane on 30 March 1788, and baptised at the parish church of Great St. Mary's on 25 April. He and his two brothers—the elder of whom, Charles Musgrave, became eventually archdeacon of Craven—were educated at the grammar school, Richmond, Yorkshire, then in the zenith of its reputation under Dr. Tate. He was admitted pensioner of Trinity College, Cambridge, in 1804, was elected scholar in 1807, graduated B.A. as fourteenth wrangler in 1810, when William (afterwards Sir William) Henry Maule [q. v.] was senior wrangler, and Thomas Shaw Brandreth [q. v.] second. Musgrave proceeded M.A. in 1813. In 1811 he was members' prizeman. He was elected junior fellow in 1812, and senior fellow in 1832. In 1821, though his knowledge of oriental tongues was by no means profound, he was appointed lord almoner's professor of Arabic. In 1831 he served the office of senior proctor. He took holy orders, and filled in succession the college livings of Over (1823), St. Mary's, Cambridge (1825–1833), and Bottisham (1837). He became senior bursar of his college in 1825, and during a long tenure of the office—only resigning it on his finally quitting Cambridge in 1837—his sound judgment and practical knowledge of business proved of great service. He was also an active and judicious county magistrate. In politics he was a decided liberal, but without any admixture of party spirit. He was a warm advocate for the relaxation of all religious tests on admission to university degrees. The petition which, in March 1834, was presented to both houses of parliament with that object lay at his rooms for signature (Clark, *Life of Sedgwick*, p. 419; Lamb, *Collection of Documents*, pp. lvi–lxv). In May of the same year the pressure put upon Connop Thirlwall [q. v.], afterwards bishop of St. David's, by the master, Dr. Christopher Wordsworth [q. v.], which led Thirlwall to resign his tutorship, excited the indignation of Musgrave. He and Sedgwick drew up a paper addressed to the master, which was signed by George Peacock [q. v.], afterwards dean of Ely, Romilly, and others, calling upon him to summon a meeting of the seniority to take the matter into consideration (Clark, u.s. p. 427 *n.*)

Musgrave's university distinction and liberal politics marked him out for preferment from the whig government. In 1837 he was appointed dean of Bristol, when he finally left Cambridge. His friend Sedgwick wrote on his departure: 'A friend of thirty years' standing, with whom an unkind word or an unkind thought never passed, is not to be replaced' (*ib.* p. 431). He held the deanery of Bristol only a few months, being nominated to the see of Hereford, vacated by the death of Bishop Edward Grey, brother to Earl Grey, the premier. He was consecrated by Archbishop Howley at Lambeth 1 Oct. 1837. At Hereford he revived the office of rural dean, and was instrumental in setting on foot the Diocesan Church Building Society (Phillott, *Diocesan Histories,* 'Hereford'). On the death of Archbishop Edward Harcourt [q. v.] in 1847, he was translated to the primatial see of York. His enthronisation in York Minster took place 15 Jan. 1848. His episcopate, although characterised by much practical ability, was marked by no considerable reforms. His motto was 'Quieta non movere,' and he had a great dread of changes and changers. The revival of the deliberative action of the church seemed to him fraught with danger, and during his archiepiscopate the northern house of convocation was allowed to meet *pro forma* only. A large portion of the estates of Trinity College lay in Yorkshire; his position as bursar had given him an intimate acquaintance with many parts of his diocese, and he acquired an accurate knowledge of the requirements of the many large towns of the diocese. Naturally fond of retirement, he did not appear much in public, especially after a severe illness he had in 1854; but he was always ready of access to his clergy. Although abrupt in manner, he is described as 'the kindest of men, generous and unostentatious, his gifts free and liberal.' He was warmly attached to evangelical principles. He died 4 May 1860 at 41 Belgrave Square, and was buried at Kensal Green cemetery.

He married in 1839 Catherine, daughter of Richard Cavendish, second lord Waterpark. His widow died 16 May 1863. There is a portrait of him in the dining-room at Bishopthorpe. He printed nothing besides charges and occasional sermons. A contemporary, Thomas Moore Musgrave, who published in 1826 (London, 8vo) a blank verse translation of the 'Lusiad' of Camoens, with elaborate notes, does not appear to have been related either to the bishop's family or to that of General Sir Thomas Musgrave [q. v.]

[Gent. Mag. 1860, i. 625–6; private information.] E. V.

MUSGRAVE, WILLIAM (1655?–1721), physician and antiquary, was third son of Richard Musgrave of Nettlecombe, Somerset. The date of his birth is given in Munk's 'College of Physicians' as 4 Nov. 1655, but according to Collinson it occurred at Charlton Musgrove in 1657. He was educated at Winchester College, being elected to a scholarship in 1669, and at New College, Oxford, where he matriculated 17 July 1675, was admitted scholar on 7 Aug. 1675, and held a fellowship from 7 Aug. 1677 to September 1692. Ten years later he contributed 55*l.* towards the new buildings at his college. He passed one session at the university of Leyden, his name being entered in its books on 29 March 1680, but he soon returned to Oxford, and took the degree of B.C.L. on 14 June 1682. For his distinction in natural philosophy and physic he was elected F.R.S. on 19 March 1683–4, and admitted on 1 Dec. 1684. During 1685 he acted as secretary of the Royal Society, edited the 'Philosophical Transactions' from numbers 167 to 178 (vol. xv.), and on his retirement from office was presented with a service of plate, sixty ounces in weight. Musgrave took the degree of M.B. at Oxford, by decree of convocation, on 8 Dec. 1685, and proceeded M.D. on 6 July 1689. He was one of the little set of enthusiasts who in the autumn of 1685 formed themselves into a scientific body at Oxford, and for some years he practised in that city. On 30 Sept. 1692 he was elected a fellow of the College of Physicians at London. In the previous year he settled at Exeter, and there he practised with great success until his death. His house was in St. Lawrence parish, at the head of Trinity Lane, afterwards called Musgrave Alley in recognition of his restoration and enlargement in 1694 and 1711 of the chapel of Holy Trinity. Musgrave died in December 1721, and was buried on 23 Dec. in a vault in St. Leonard's churchyard, Exeter, outside the city, as he believed that intramural burial in cities was unwholesome for the living. His wife was Philippa, third daughter of William Speke of Jordans, White Lackington, Somerset, by his wife, Anne Roynon. She died 14 Nov. 1715, aged 55, and was buried at St. Leonard's, Exeter, on 21 Nov. A handsome altar-tomb which was erected to their memory has now been removed. A portrait of Musgrave is mentioned by Bromley. Their son, William Musgrave, M.B., of King's College, Cambridge, was buried at St. Leonard's on 28 Nov. 1724. Their daughter married Thomas Brown of King's Kerswell, Devonshire.

Musgrave published at Exeter in 1703 a treatise, 'De Arthritide Symptomatica,' and in 1707 a further dissertation 'De Arthritide Anomala.' A second edition of the latter, with a treatise by Mead, was issued at Amsterdam in 1710, and new editions of both of them were included in Sydenham's 'Opera Medica,' 1716, vol. ii. At his death he left in manuscript a treatise, 'De Arthritide primogenia et regulari,' which his son committed to the press, but did not live to see published. It remained in sheets at the Clarendon Press until 1776, when it was published by Samuel Musgrave [q. v.] Numerous articles by him, many of which are on medical points, are inserted in the 'Philosophical Transactions.'

His antiquarian investigations are described in three volumes, issued at Exeter in 1719, with the general title-page of 'Antiquitates Britanno-Belgicæ, præcipue Romanæ figuris illustratæ . . . quorum I de Belgio Britannico II de Geta Britannico III de Julii Vitalis epitaphio cum Notis criticis H. Dodwelli;' but the second volume originally appeared in 1716, and the third in 1711. His portrait, painted by G. Gandy in 1718, and engraved by Vandergucht, was prefixed. A fourth volume, 'quod tribus ante editis est appendix,' came out in 1720. Belga consisted, in the opinion of Musgrave, of the district from the Solent to near Henley-on-Thames and from Cirencester to Bath and Porlock, returning by Ilchester to the border of Hampshire, and his volumes contained particulars of numerous Roman remains which had been found within its borders.

For these researches Musgrave was presented by George I, or his son, the Prince of Wales, with a diamond ring (6 Aug. 1720). His account of the Roman legions, addressed to Sir Hans Sloane, and a portion of his letter to Gisbert Cuper, burgomaster of Deventer, on the Roman eagles, written to prove that they were made of some light substance and plated over, are in the 'Philosophical Transactions,' xxviii. 80–90, and 145–50 (cf. *Letters of Gisbert Cuper*, pp. 291, 371). Some Roman curiosities procured by Musgrave from Bath were set up by him at Exeter (LYSONS, *Devon*, p. cccx). Numerous communications on such topics passed between him and Walter Moyle [q. v.] Further manuscript letters by him are in the Ballard collection at the Bodleian Library, xxiv. 75–85.

[Munk's Coll. of Phys. (2nd edit.), i. 486–90; Dymond's St. Leonard's, Exeter, pp. 29–30; Kirby's Winchester Scholars, p. 196; Weld's Royal Society, i. 305; Collinson's Somerset, iii. 37; Burke's Commoners, iv. 539; Foster's Alumni Oxon.; Wood's Fasti, ii. 383, 396, 407; Wood's Athenæ Oxon. (Bliss), iv. 556–7, 776; information from the Rev. Dr. Sewell, New College, Oxford; Hearne's Collections, ed. Doble, i. 266, ii. 198, 206–8, 213, 217, 220, 347, iii. 141, 149, 182, 262, 277–9, 330; information from the Rev. J. F. Sheldon, St. Leonard's, Exeter.] W. P. C.

MUSH, JOHN (1552–1617), Roman catholic divine, was born in Yorkshire in 1552. When twenty-five years of age he passed over to the English seminary at Douay, and in the October following was sent with a few select students to join the English College at Rome, in the first year of its foundation. After spending seven years there he was sent upon the mission, carrying with him a reputation for learning and scholarship. Mush was highly esteemed by Cardinal Allen, who at one time thought of appointing him vice-president of the Rheims seminary in the place of Dr. Richard Barret [q. v.], who intended to go into England. In England Mush's character and abilities marked him out as the leader of the northern clergy. He came forward prominently at the crisis in the affairs of the clergy, when the grave dissensions among the priests confined in Wisbech Castle threatened to bring ruin or disgrace upon the mission. In company with Dr. Dudley he visited the prisoners as a chosen arbitrator in the dispute. Failing to bring about a reconciliation, he with his friend John Colleton [q. v.] projected the 'association' which was intended in the absence of episcopal government to supply the secular clergy with some system of voluntary organisation. Thwarted in this scheme by the opposition of the jesuit party, and by the unexpected appointment of George Blackwell [q. v.], said to be a creature of Father Parsons, as archpriest, Mush threw himself earnestly, though never with violence or misrepresentation, on the side of the appellant priests, who denied the legality of the appointment until it was confirmed by the pope, and finally appealed to Rome against the tyranny of Blackwell and the political scheming of the jesuits. Mush was one of the thirty-three priests who signed this appeal, 17 Nov. 1600, and was later on, 3 Jan. 1603, one of the thirteen who signed the protestation of allegiance to Queen Elizabeth.

For his conduct in the prosecution of the appeal Mush was more than once suspended by the archpriest. In 1602 he was one of the four deputies who, with the connivance of the English government, were sent to Rome to lay the grievances of the anti-jesuit and loyal section of the clergy before Clement VIII. Mush has left a record of these negotiations, which were protracted at Rome for nine months, in a 'Diary,' which is preserved among the Petyt MSS. in the Inner Temple (No. 538, vol. liv. ff. 190-9). Soon after the settlement of the dispute Mush became an assistant to the archpriest—in accordance with the terms of the papal brief, which directed that three of the appellants should be so appointed on the first vacancies—and he continued for many years to take a leading part in the government of the clergy.

Mush resided chiefly in Yorkshire, and was there the spiritual director of Mrs. Margaret Clitherow [q. v.] the martyr, whose life he wrote. Bishop Challoner, who writes with respect of Mush's missionary labours, says (i. 189) that 'after having suffered prisons and chains, and received even the sentence of death, for his faith, he died at length in his bed in a good old age in 1617.'

Mush was author of 'The Life and Death of Mistris Margaret Clitherow, who for the Profession of the Catholike Faith was Martyred at York in the Eight and Twentith Yeare of the Raine of Qu. Elizabeth in the yeare of our Lord God, 1586. Written presently after her death by her Spiritual Father, upon Certaine Knowledge of her Life and the Processes, Condemnation, and Death.' It was edited from the original manuscript by William Nicholson of Thelwall Hall, Cheshire, and printed by Richardson & Son, Derby, in 1849. Mush also wrote, according to Dodd, an account of the sufferings of the catholics in the northern parts of England, and a treatise against Thomas Bell, formerly a fellow-student at Rome and missionary in Yorkshire, who joined the church of England and wrote several books of controversy. But neither of these works of Mush appears to be extant.

A work of more historical importance was his well-written treatise, which he dedicated to the pope, in defence of his brethren of the secular clergy in their conflicts with the jesuits and Blackwell, giving the text of the appeal and ending with a letter of an earlier date, 1598, written by himself to Monsignor Morro, reviewing the causes of the dissensions at the English College at Rome. It is entitled 'Declaratio Motuum ac Turbationum quæ ex controversiis inter jesuitas iisq. in omnibus faventem D. Georg. Blackwellum, Archipresbyterum et Sacerdotes Seminariorum in Anglia, ab obitu ill^mi Card^lis Alani piæ Memoriæ ad annum usque 1601. Ad S. D. N. Clementem octavum exhibita ab ipsis sacerdotibus qui schismatis, aliorumq. criminum sunt insimulati. Rhotomagi apud Jacobum Molæum' [but probably London], 1601.

[A brief notice of Mush will be found in Dodd's Church Hist. ii. 115. See also Douay Diaries, pp. 101, 111, 297; Letters and Memorials of Allen, pp. 197, 356; Foley's Records, vi. 134; and Dr. Bagshaw's True Relation of the Faction begun at Wisbich (1601), printed in the Historical Sketch of the Conflicts between Jesuits and Seculars in the Reign of Elizabeth, by T. G. Law (London, 1889), pp. 52, 93, and Introduction.] T. G. L.

MUSHET, DAVID (1772–1847), metallurgist, eldest son of William Mushet and Margaret Cochrane, was born at Dalkeith, near Edinburgh, on 2 Oct. 1772, and brought up as an ironfounder. In February 1792 he was engaged as accountant at the Clyde Iron Works, where he soon became so interested in the processes of the manufacture that when in 1793 a reduction was made in the staff, and he was left almost sole occupant of the office, he began a series of experimental researches on his own account. In this he was at first encouraged by his employers, and was allowed to teach assaying to the manager's son; but later on, without cause assigned, he was prohibited, and his studies had to be prosecuted after office hours. By dint of sheer hard work, frequently labouring into the early morning, he became in a few years one of the first authorities at home and abroad upon all points connected with the manufacture of iron and steel. His employers becoming jealous of him, he was dismissed from the Clyde Iron Works in 1800. The following year, when engaged with partners in erecting the Calder Iron Works, he discovered the 'Black-band Ironstone,' and showed that this so-called 'wild coal' was capable of being used economically. Though it brought nothing to Mushet, this discovery was of immense value to others, owing to the extent of the deposit.

A series of some thirty papers by Mushet in the 'Philosophical Magazine' shows that he was at the Calder Iron Works till 1805, when he came to England. In 1808 he dates from the Alfreton Iron Works, Derbyshire, while from 1812 to 1823 he is described as 'of Coleford, Forest of Dean,' and he is said to have possessed extensive property in that district. In 1843 he gave valuable evidence in the hot-blast patent case tried at Edinburgh (*Report of Trial—Neilson* v. *Baird & Co.*, Edinburgh, 1843, pp. 48, 312).

The chief of Mushet's inventions, all of which relate to improvements in the methods of manufacturing iron and steel, was perhaps the one patented in 1800 for the preparation of steel from bar-iron by a direct process. Although the method cannot be distinguished in principle from that followed by the Hindoos in the preparation of wootz, the patent was sold to a Sheffield firm for 3,000*l.* (PERCY, *Iron and Steel*, pp. 670, 672). His other patents relate to the extraction of iron from cinder and to improvements in the process of puddling iron.

Mushet's communications to the 'Philosophical Magazine' were in 1840 collected by him into a volume entitled 'Papers on Iron and Steel, &c.,' 8vo, London. He also wrote 'The Wrongs of the Animal World,' 8vo, London, 1839, in which he denounced the use of dogs as draught-animals. He was the author of the articles 'Blast Furnace' and 'Blowing Machine' in Rees's 'Cyclopædia' and 'Iron' in the 'Encyclopædia Britannica' Supplement.

Mushet died at Monmouth on 13 June 1847 (*Gent. Mag.* 1847, p. 220). By his wife Agnes Wilson he was father of Robert Forester Mushet, who is noticed separately. An older son, David (cf. MUSHET, *Papers on Iron and Steel*, Pref.), was a metallurgist and took out several patents.

[Preface to Papers on Iron and Steel; Imp. Dict. of Univ. Biog.; Engl. Encyclopædia; Brit. Mus. Cat.; Roy. Soc. Cat.; Phillips's Elements of Metallurgy, 2nd edit. 1887, pp. 325 and 332.]

B. B. W.

MUSHET, ROBERT (1782–1828), of the royal mint, sixth son of William Mushet and Margaret Cochrane, his wife, was born at Dalkeith on 10 Nov. 1782. He was a brother of David Mushet [q. v.] According to a statement contained in his evidence before the House of Lords' committee on the resumption of cash payments in 1819, he entered the service of the royal mint about 1804, but his name does not occur in the 'Royal Kalendar' until 1808, when he appears as third clerk to the master. Subsequently he held the post of first clerk to the master, melter, and refiner. He paid particular attention to the currency question, and gave evidence before the committee above mentioned on 29 March and 7 April 1819. He was also examined before Peel's committee in the House of Commons on the same subject on 19 March. He stated that he had made out tables of the exchanges and prices of gold from 1760 to 1810 (see the printed reports of those committees). In 1823 he took out a patent (No. 4802) for preparing copper for sheathing ships by alloying it with small quantities of zinc, tin, antimony, and arsenic. He died at Millfield House, Edmonton, on 1 Feb. 1828, having married Henrietta, daughter of John Hunter (1745–1837) [q. v.] of St. Andrews, by whom he had issue.

Mushet wrote: 1. 'An Enquiry into the Effect produced on the National Currency and Rates of Exchange by the Bank Restriction Bill,' 2nd ed., 1810; 3rd ed., 1811. This was noticed in the 'Edinburgh Review,' 1810, xvii. 340. 2. 'Tables exhibiting the Gain and Loss to the Fundholder arising from the Fluctuations of the Value of the Currency from 1800 to 1821,' 2nd ed., corrected, 1821. 3. 'An Attempt to explain from Facts the Effect of the Issues of the Bank of England upon its own Interests, Public Credit, and Country Banks,' 1826. This was noticed in the 'Quarterly Review,' 1829, xxxix. 451.

[Gent. Mag. 1828 pt. i. p. 275, and private information.]

R. B. P.

MUSHET, ROBERT (1811–1871), of the royal mint, born at Dalkeith in 1811, was second son of Richard Mushet—a brother of David Mushet [q. v.] and of Robert Mushet (1782–1828) [q. v.] His mother was Marion Walker. He came up to London to assist his uncle Robert Mushet in the mint, and in 1833 his name appears for the first time in the 'Royal Kalendar' as 'second clerk and probationer melter.' Upon the reorganisation of the mint in 1851, when the 'moneyers,' as they were called, were abolished, Mushet was appointed senior clerk and melter with a residence at the mint. That office he held until his death. He died on 4 Sept. 1871 at Hayward's Heath, and was buried there.

He was the author of: 1. 'The Trinities of the Ancients,' London, 1837. 2. 'The Book of Symbols,' London, 1844; 2nd ed., 1847. 3. The article 'Coinage' in the eighth edition of the 'Encyclopædia Britannica;' reprinted in 'The Coin Book,' Philadelphia, 1873.

[Authorities cited and private information.]

R. B. P.

MUSHET, ROBERT FORESTER (1811–1891), metallurgist, born at Coleford, Forest of Dean, on 8 April 1811, was the youngest son of David Mushet [q. v.] He received the name 'Forester' from the place of his birth, but he never seems to have used it until 1874 in a patent which he took out in that year. He was always known as Robert Mushet.

His early years seem to have been spent at Coleford, assisting his father in his metallurgical researches and experiments. In that way he became familiar with the value of manganese in steel-making, and in 1848 his attention was accidentally directed to a sample of 'spiegeleisen,' an alloy of iron and manganese, manufactured in Rhenish Prussia from a double carbonate of iron and manganese known as spathose iron-ore. Mushet immediately commenced making experiments with this metal, and, although the results were of no immediate practical value, they ultimately became of great importance in connection with the Bessemer process. He found that spiegeleisen possessed the property of restoring the quality of 'burnt iron,' i.e. of wrought iron which had been injured by long exposure to heat. Bessemer's celebrated process of refining iron by blowing air through it when in a molten condition was made public in a paper read before the British Association at Cheltenham in August 1856, and a sample of the refined metal fell into Mushet's hands shortly afterwards. It appeared to him to be in a condition analogous to that of 'burnt' wrought iron, and he found by experiment that the addition of molten spiegeleisen produced a substance which 'was, in fact, cast steel, worth 42*s.* per cwt. I saw then,' says Mushet, 'that the Bessemer process was perfected, and that, with fair play, untold wealth would reward Mr. Bessemer and myself' (*The Bessemer-Mushet Process*; *or, Manufacture of Cheap Steel*, 1883, p. 11). On 16 Sept. 1856 he took out three patents for improving the quality of iron, refined by blowing air through it when in a molten condition, and two other patents were entered on the 22nd of the same month; but none of the specifications contain any direct reference to Bessemer's process, the method being stated to be applicable to an abortive patent taken out by Martien in 1855. Mushet bases his claim to the invention upon his patent of 22 Sept. (No. 2219), in which he specifies 'the addition of a triple compound or material of or containing iron, carbon, and manganese, to cast iron which has been purified and decarbonised by the action of air whilst in a molten or fluid state.' Mushet took out several other patents for modifications of the process, but by an unfortunate accident (so he asserts) he omitted to pay the stamp duty on the patent of 1856, which became due in 1859, so that all his patent rights in this country and abroad were at once extinguished.

Much discussion has taken place as to the originality and value of Mushet's invention. There was an admitted difficulty in ascertaining with certainty when the decarbonising action of the blast of air in the Bessemer process had proceeded to the right extent, and therefore when it should be stopped. Mushet's plan was to decarbonise completely or nearly so, and then add a given proportion of carbon in the state in which it exists in molten spiegeleisen, the precise composition of which should, of course, be known. Mr. J. S. Jeans states in the 'Engineering Review' for 20 July 1893, p. 7, that, 'as a matter of fact, Bessemer had actually gone so far with his experiments on manganese that he had virtually solved the problem before the Mushet patents were published,' and this fact will, it is believed, be made clear by Sir Henry Bessemer's 'Autobiography.' Mushet says: 'I by no means arrogate to myself the idea that, if I had not invented my spiegeleisen process, no one else would ever have found it out. On the other hand, I have frankly and publicly said that Mr. Bessemer would, in all probability, sooner or later have made the discovery. I, however, was fortunate enough to anticipate him' (*The Bessemer-Mushet Process*, Preface). In 1876 the Bessemer Medal of the Iron and Steel Institute was awarded to Mushet, with the full approval of the founder. In making the presentation, the president, Mr. Menelaus, said that the application of spiegeleisen was one of the most elegant, as it was one of the most beautiful, processes in metallurgy, and that it was worthy of being associated with Mr. Bessemer's process. But the reticence of both parties has rendered it difficult to determine the degree of validity to be allotted to all Mushet's pretensions. In 1883 Mushet published his version of the matter, but Sir Henry Bessemer has not yet put his entire case forward. Although he paid Mushet an annuity of 300*l.* for some years before his death, he invariably refused to pay him royalty; and he intimated his readiness to allow Mushet and his legal advisers to see the whole process carried out, and challenged him to bring an action for infringement. This challenge Mushet declined (cf. Jeans, *Creators of the Age of Steel*, p. 61; and Jeans, *Steel*, p. 78).

Between 1859 and 1861 Mushet took out about twenty patents for the manufacture of alloys of iron and steel with titanium, tungsten, and chromium. A summary of these patents is given in Percy's 'Iron and Steel,' pp. 165, 188, 194. His experiments with tungsten alloys led to the invention about 1870 of what is known as 'special steel,' which possesses the remarkable quality of self-hardening. It is forged at a low red heat, and allowed to cool gradually, acquiring a degree of hardness which renders it of great value for engineers' tools, for which it is now very largely used (*Engineering*, April 1870, pp. 223, 236; Jeans, *Steel*, p. 532). The precise mode of preparation is a secret, but, from an analysis by Gruner (*Bulletin de la Société d'Encouragement*, 1873, p. 84), it appears to owe its properties to the presence of about 8 per cent. of tungsten.

Mushet was of a very self-contained and reliant disposition. 'I was never inside any steel works but my own,' he says, 'and never even saw the outside of one except that of the Avonside Steel Works in Bristol;' nor did he ever visit Sheffield, the centre of the steel industry. From about 1848 and onwards he was a very constant correspondent of the 'Mining Journal.' In 1857-8 he wrote a series of letters to that paper on the Bessemer process under the signature 'Sideros' while carrying on a correspondence under his own name. In 1856 he read a paper before the British Association 'On an Ancient Miner's Axe discovered in the Forest of Dean' (*Reports*, p. 71). His work on 'The Bessemer-Mushet Process' (1883) was put forth in 1883 in order 'that there may no longer be any doubt regarding the relation, the nature, and the value of the two processes which constitute the Bessemer-Mushet combined or binary processes of manufacturing cheap steel.'

He died on 19 Jan. 1891 at Cheltenham, aged 79, after many years of enfeebled health, leaving a widow and two sons, Henry Charles Brooklyn Mushet and Edward Maxwell Mushet, who were engaged as managers to a firm of steel-makers at Sheffield. There is a portrait from a photograph in the possession of the Iron and Steel Institute in the 'Engineering Review' 20 July 1893, p. 7.

[Mushet's Bessemer-Mushet Process, 1883; Jeans's Creators of the Age of Steel, 1884, pp. 60-5; Journal of the Iron and Steel Institute, 1876, pp. 1-4; private information.] R. B. P.

MUSHET, WILLIAM (1716-1792), physician, was born in 1716 at Dublin of a Jacobite family, who had fled thither from Stirling. He is supposed to have been educated at Trinity College, Dublin, and was entered at Leyden on 26 Aug. 1745 (PEACOCK, *Index*, p. 72). Mushet was also a member of King's College, Cambridge, and proceeded M.D. there in 1746, becoming a candidate of the College of Physicians on 4 April 1748 and a fellow on 20 March 1749. He delivered in 1751 the Gulstonian lectures. He was made physician in chief to the forces, and served at the battle of Minden (1759), but declined an offer of a baronetcy for his services in that campaign.

Mushet was intimately connected with the Duke of Rutland, and had apartments for eleven years at Belvoir Castle. He died at York on 11 Dec. 1792. A monument was erected to his memory by his daughter Mary in the church of St. Mary Castlegate, York, with a long inscription written by Sir Robert Sinclair, recorder of York.

[Munk's Coll. of Phys.] L. M. M. S.

MUSKERRY, ROBERT MACCARTHY, VISCOUNT (*d.* 1769). [See under MACCARTHY, DONOUGH, fourth EARL OF CLANCARTY.]

MUSKERRY, LORD OF. [See MACCARTHY, CORMAC LAIDHIR OGE, *d.* 1536.]

MUSKET, *alias* FISHER, GEORGE (1583-1645), catholic divine, son of Thomas Fisher and Magdalene Ashton, was born in 1583 at Barton, Northamptonshire. His father was of the middle class, and his mother of high family. After being educated at Barton and at Stilton, he was for half a year in Wisbech Castle, in attendance on the incarcerated priests as a volunteer, and where in 1597 he was converted to the catholic religion (MORRIS, *Troubles of our Catholic Forefathers*, ii. 266, 267). Two of his brothers were also converted about the same time, viz. Richard, who ultimately joined the Society of Jesus, and Thomas, who became a secular priest. George proceeded to the English College of Douay, and was formally reconciled to the Roman catholic church. He continued his studies there for four years, and was then sent to the English College at Rome, where he was admitted 21 Oct. 1601. He took the college oath 3 Nov. 1602, was ordained priest 11 March 1605-6, and was sent to England in May 1607, but he appears to have been detained at Douay, where he was engaged for upwards of a year in teaching theology.

On 9 Sept. 1608 he left Douay for the English mission. He resided for the most part in London, and Dodd says it was the general belief that 'no missioner ever took greater pains, or reconciled more persons to the Catholic church' (*Church History*, iii. 98). He was very dexterous in managing conferences between representatives of his own co-religionists and protestants, and gave a remarkable instance of his polemical capacity on 21 and 22 April 1621, when he and John Fisher [q. v.] the jesuit held a disputation with Dr. Daniel Featley [q. v.] and Dr. Thomas Goad [q. v.] In the reign of Charles I he was in confinement for many years. On 6 Jan. 1626-7 secretaries Conway and Coke issued a warrant for the apprehension of him and of Dr. Smith, bishop of Chalcedon, and there is a list, dated 22 March 1626-7, of 'Popish books and other things belonging to Popery,' taken in the house of William Sharples in Queen's Street, St. Giles's-in-the-Fields, presumed to belong to 'Mr. Fisher, otherwise Mr. Muskett.' A memorandum, conjecturally dated 1627, states that Musket had several years before broken out of Wisbech Castle, had since been banished, and, having returned, had again been taken prisoner. On 6 Oct. 1628 he was in confinement at the Gatehouse. Subsequently he was brought to trial, and, as one of the witnesses swore positively to his saying mass, he was condemned to death. He remained for twenty years under sentence, 'during which time he found means to exercise his functions with the same success as if he had enjoy'd his liberty' (Dodd, iii. 98). At the intercession of Queen Henrietta Maria he was reprieved and afterwards pardoned, but only on the condition of his remaining in confinement during the king's pleasure. When a proposal was made in 1635 for the appointment of a catholic bishop for England, Musket's name was in the list of persons proposed to the holy see. He was still a prisoner when he was chosen president of the English College of Douay in succession to Dr. Matthew Kellison [q. v.], who died on 21 Jan. 1640–1; but through the queen's intercession he was released and banished. He arrived at Douay on 14 Nov. 1641. Though he governed the college in the worst of times, he contrived to extinguish a debt of twenty-five thousand florins. He died on 24 Dec. 1645, and was succeeded in the presidency by Dr. William Hyde [q. v.]

Dodd says that 'as to his person he was of the lowest size, but perfectly well shaped and proportioned. . . . His eyes were black and large, and his countenance both awful and engaging.' The Italians styled him 'Flos Cleri Anglicani.'

He is believed to be the author of an anonymous book, entitled 'The Bishop of London, his Legacy; or Certaine Motiues of D. King, late Bishop of London, for his change of Religion and dying in the Catholike and Roman Church. With a Conclusion to his Brethren, the LL. Bishops of England. Permissa Superiorum' [St. Omer], 1624, 4to, pp. 174. In this polemical work the author only personates Bishop John King [q. v.], as he himself declares (cf. Brydges, *British Bibliographer*, i. 506). Dodd says of this work, 'Some Protestant writers ascribe it to Mr. Musket, a learned clergyman, but how truly I will not say' (*Church Hist.* i. 491).

[Foley's Records, vi. 207, 211, 221; Gee's Foot out of the Snare, 1624, pp. 78–80, 99; Panzani's Memoirs, p. 226; Cal. State Papers, Dom. 1627–1628 pp. 7, 105, 480, 486, 1628–9 pp. 345, 365.]

T. C.

MUSPRATT, JAMES (1793–1886), founder of the alkali industry in Lancashire, was born in Dublin, 12 Aug. 1793, of English parents, Evan and Sarah Muspratt. His mother belonged to the Cheshire family of Mainwarings. He was educated at a commercial school in Dublin, and at the age of fourteen was apprenticed to a wholesale chemist and druggist there, named Mitcheltree, with whom he remained between three and four years. He lost his father in 1810, and his mother in the following year. Failing to obtain a cavalry commission in order to serve in the Peninsular war, and refusing to accept a commission in the infantry, he went to Spain and followed in the wake of the British troops. After the temporary abandonment of Madrid by General Hill in 1812 he was left in that city prostrated by fever; but, in order not to fall into the hands of the French, he rose from his sick bed, and managed to walk one hundred miles in two days on the way to Lisbon. He has left a record of the journey in a diary. Muspratt then enlisted as midshipman on the Impétueux, took part in the blockade of Brest, and was promoted second officer on another vessel. But the harsh discipline of his superiors proved intolerable to him, and, with a comrade, he deserted by night in the Mumbles roadstead off Swansea. He returned to Dublin about 1814, and became the intimate friend of Samuel Lover [q. v.], James Sheridan Knowles [q. v.], and the actress Eliza O'Neill, whom he was able to help in her profession.

A little later his inheritance, much diminished by a long chancery suit, came into his hands, and in 1818, at the age of twenty-five, after starting the manufacture of certain chemicals in a small way by himself, he set up, with a friend named Abbott, as a manufacturer of prussiate of potash. In 1823 the duty of 30*l.* per ton was taken off salt, and Muspratt at once took advantage of the opportunity of introducing into this country the manufacture of soda on a large scale by the Leblanc process. Losh had preceded him on the Tyne in 1814, and Charles Tennant [q. v.] on the Clyde in 1816, but only a beginning had been made. Muspratt saw that the valley of the Mersey, with its coalfields, salt-mines, and seaport, offered advantages of the first order for alkali works, and he set up his first plant at Liverpool. At first he was actually obliged to give away his soda-ash to the soap-boilers (who were prejudiced in favour of potash), and to teach them how to use it; but soon the demand for his products increased so much that the works outgrew the land at his disposal, and Muspratt joined an Irishman, Josias Christopher Gamble, in building new works at St. Helens in 1828. Two years later he left Gamble and set up another manufactory at Newton. At this time the means for condensing the hydrochloric acid produced in the Leblanc process were quite inadequate, and the Liverpool corporation and the landowners near Newton, on account of the damage done to vegetation by the acid fumes, began litigation against Muspratt, which lasted from 1832 to 1850. Finally Muspratt closed his works and opened new and successful ones in Widnes and Flint, which he left in 1857 to his sons on retiring from business. Muspratt was the first to build a Leblanc soda-works in England on a large scale, and it is as the chief founder of the alkali manufacture in this country that he will be remembered. In the towns of St. Helens and Widnes thousands of workmen are now employed in the manufacture.

Muspratt took in his later years a keen interest in educational matters, and helped to found the Liverpool Institute. He passed much of his time in foreign travel, and paid long visits to the chemist Liebig at Giessen and Munich. He died on 4 May 1886 at Seaforth Hall, near Liverpool, and was buried in the parish churchyard of Walton.

Muspratt married Julia Connor, in Dublin, on 6 Oct. 1819. He had ten children, four of whom, James Sheridan [q. v.], Richard, Frederick (of whom see obituary in the *Journ. Chem. Soc.* xxvi. 780), and Edmund Knowles, became chemists, and succeeded him in his business.

A woodcut engraving of Muspratt is prefixed to the memoir quoted below.

[Memoir of James Muspratt, by J. F. Allen; Chemical Trade Journal, v. 240 (1889); Obituary, Journ. Soc. Chemical Industry, v. 314; J. S. Muspratt's Chemistry, ii. 920 (1st edit.); First Annual Report under the Alkali Act, by R. Angus Smith, p. 14 (1865); private information from his son, E. K. Muspratt, esq.] P. J. H.

MUSPRATT, JAMES SHERIDAN (1821–1871), chemist, son of James Muspratt [q. v.], was born at Dublin on 8 March 1821. He first studied chemistry under T. Graham [q. v.] at the Andersonian University, Glasgow, and at University College, London. Before the age of seventeen he was entrusted with the chemical department at Peel Thompson's manufactory in Manchester. A little later he went to America, and entered into a business partnership which proved a failure. He returned to Europe, and in 1843 entered the laboratory of Liebig at Giessen, where he did his best work. He published in 1845 an important research on the sulphites, which served as his inaugural thesis for the degree of Ph.D., and also investigations on toluidine and nitraniline, which were first prepared by himself and A. W. Hofmann. After travelling for some years in Germany, he returned to England, and in 1848 founded the Liverpool College of Chemistry, a private institution for the training of chemists. In 1857 Muspratt succeeded to a share in his father's business. From 1854 to 1860 he was engaged in editing a large and readable dictionary of 'Chemistry . . . as applied to the Arts and Manufactures,' of which several editions have been published in English, and in German and Russian translations. He also translated Plattner's classical treatise on the 'Blowpipe' (London, 8vo, 1845), and published 'Outlines of Analysis' (1849), and works on 'The Chemistry of Vegetation' and the 'Influence of Chemistry in the Animal, Vegetal, and Mineral Kingdoms.' The 'Royal Society's Catalogue' contains a list of thirty-five papers published independently, three in collaboration with Hofmann, and one with Danson.

In 1848 Muspratt married the American actress Susan Cushman, who died in 1859. Muspratt died on 3 April 1871 at West Derby, Liverpool.

A steel engraving from a photograph is prefixed to the first volume of Muspratt's 'Chemistry.'

[Besides the sources cited, see Biography of Sheridan Muspratt, by a London Barrister-at-Law, 1852; Biography by W. White, London, 1869; Men of the Time, 1868; Chem. News, xxiii. 82; Journ. Chem. Soc. xxiv. 620; H. Carrington Bolton's Bibliography of Chemistry, 1893.] P. J. H.

MUSS, CHARLES (1779–1824), enamel- and glass-painter, born in 1779, was son of Boniface Muss (or Musso), an Italian artist, who exhibited a drawing at the Society of Artists' exhibition in 1790, and is stated to have practised at Newcastle-on-Tyne. Muss was principally employed on glass-painting, and as such became one of the principal artists in Collins's glass-works near Temple Bar. He obtained some eminence in this art, and executed among others a copy of Rubens's 'Descent from the Cross' on glass for St. Bride's Church, Fleet Street. He devoted much time to the art of painting in enamel, and after some vicissitudes of fortune brought it to great perfection. He copied in this manner a number of important works by the old masters, some in an unusually large size, such as the 'Holy Family,' after Parmegiano. He was appointed enamel-painter to the king, and received many commissions from him. He had, however, barely secured success and a recognised position in his arts when his career was cut short by his death, which happened about August 1824. He had been an occasional exhibitor of enamels at the Royal Academy from 1800 to 1823. Muss was a personal friend of John Martin [q. v.] the painter, who undertook to direct the completion as far as possible of Muss's unfinished works on glass and in enamel. Muss had also prepared for publication a set of thirty-three original outline illustrations to Gay's 'Fables,' and a few copies were worked off for inspection before his death, which stopped their publication. He left a widow, and on 29 and 30 Nov. 1824 his collections of prints, drawings, &c., and completed works were sold by auction for her benefit.

[Gent. Mag. 1824, pt. ii. p. 186; Redgrave's Dict. of Artists; Graves's Dict. of Artists, 1760–1880.] L. C.

MUSTERS, GEORGE CHAWORTH (1841–1879), 'King of Patagonia,' commander, royal navy, was the son of John George Musters of Wiverton Hall, Nottinghamshire, formerly of the 10th royal hussars, by his wife Emily, daughter of Philip Hammond, of Westacre, Norfolk. His grandfather, John Musters of Colwick Hall, Nottinghamshire, 'the king of gentlemen huntsmen,' married in 1805 Mary Ann Chaworth, sole heiress of Chaworth of Annesley, Nottinghamshire, the 'Mary' of Byron's poem, 'The Dream.'

George Chaworth Musters was born at Naples, while his parents were travelling, 13 Feb. 1841. He was one of three children. His father dying in 1842, and his mother in 1845, he was brought up chiefly by his mother's brothers; one of whom, Robert Hammond, had sailed with Admiral Robert Fitzroy [q. v.] in H.M.S. Beagle. George went to school at Saxby's in the Isle of Wight, and Green's at Sandgate, and thence to Burney's academy at Gosport, to prepare for the navy. He was entered on board the Algiers, 74 guns, in 1854, and served in her in the Black Sea, receiving the English and Turkish Crimean medals by the time he was fifteen. In October 1856 he was transferred to the Gorgon, and served in 1857–8 in the Chesapeake, and in 1859–61 in the Marlborough. In 1861 he passed in the first class in his examination; was posted to the Victoria and Albert royal yacht; promoted to lieutenant 4 Sept. 1861, and appointed to the Stromboli sloop of war, Captain Philips, serving in her on the coast of South America from December 1861 until she was paid off in June 1866. When at Rio in 1862 he and a midshipman of the Stromboli, in a youthful freak, climbed the well-known Sugar Loaf mountain, and planted the British ensign on the summit, where for some years it defied all efforts to dislodge it. While on the South American station he bought land, and started sheep-farming at Montevideo.

After he was placed on half-pay, he carried out a long-cherished project of travelling over South America. The journey is described in his 'At Home with the Patagonians, a Year's Wanderings on Untrodden Ground from the Straits of Magellan to the Rio Negro,' London, 1871, 2nd ed. 1873. In this bold and adventurous undertaking, which occupied 1869–70, Musters lived on the most friendly terms with the Patagonian aborigines, by whom he was treated as a king, travelling with one of the hordes from Magellan Straits to the Rio Negro, and afterwards traversing the northern part of Patagonia from east to west, a distance of fourteen hundred miles. The results were a considerable addition to geographical knowledge—particularly of the south-eastern slopes of the Andes—full particulars of the character and customs of the Tehuelche tribes, and many interesting observations on the climate. The Royal Geographical Society of London presented him with a gold watch in 1872. The open-air habits acquired in this sort of life had a singular effect on his constitution. After his return to England he often preferred to sleep in the garden wrapped in a blanket, although as a rule he was susceptible to cold. Musters subsequently visited Vancouver's Island, and had some adventures with the Indians of British Columbia, of which a narrative was promised, but never published. Returning to South America, he set out to traverse Chili and Patagonia from west to east, but was obliged to return to Venezuela. He came home to England in 1873, married, and went out to South America with his wife to reside in Bolivia. From February 1874 to September 1876 he travelled much in Bolivia and the countries adjacent, gathering a large amount of geographical information, which is published in the Royal Geographical Society's 'Proceedings,' vol. xlvii. After his return home Musters resided chiefly with his brother at Wiverton, an old seat of the Chaworth family. In October 1878 he repaired to London in order to prepare himself for the Mozambique, where he had been appointed consul. He died on 25 Jan. 1879. He was a fearless explorer, and a man of unfailing tact and winning manners.

Musters's wife, Herminia, daughter of George Williams of Sucre, Bolivia, was authoress of 'A Book of Hunting Songs and Sport,' London, 1888, 12mo (Allibone).

[Burke's Landed Gentry, 1886 ed., under 'Musters;' Musters's At Home with the Patagonians, 2nd ed. 1873; Proceedings Royal Geographical Soc. London, vol. xlvii., and obituary notice in Proceedings, new ser. vol. i. (1879), pp. 397–8; Allibone's Dict., Suppl.] H. M. C.

MUTFORD, JOHN DE (*d.* 1329), judge, a member of a knightly family that took its name from Mutford in Suffolk, was engaged for Edward I in 1294 (Foss), and, a petition having been presented in parliament by one Isabella de Beverley in 1306, was called upon to inform the treasurer and barons of the exchequer as to the king's right to interfere in the matter (*Rolls of Parliament*, i. 197). In that year he was appointed one of four justices in trailbaston for ten counties (*ib.* p. 218). In common with other justices and members of the council he was summoned to attend parliament in 1307. He received a summons in January 1308 to attend the coronation of Edward II (*Fœdera*, II. i. 27), and acted as an itinerant justice at various times during the reign. In 1310 he was ordered to be ready to go to Gascony on the king's business. Having receded from parliament in 1311 he was ordered to return to it, and in October was appointed a commissioner for the settlement of discontent in Ireland (*ib.* II. i. 143, 144). On 30 April 1316 he was appointed a justice of common pleas, and held that office until 1329, when he died, and was buried in Norwich Cathedral.

[Foss's Judges, iii. 467; Suckling's Hist. of Suffolk, p. 274; Blomefield's Norfolk, iv. 39; Rolls of Parl. i. 197, 218; Parl. Writs, I. ii. passim; Rymer's Fœdera, II. i. 27, 143, 144 (Record ed.)] W. H.

MUTRIE, MARTHA DARLEY (1824–1885), flower-painter, elder daughter of Robert Mutrie, a native of Rothesay in Bute, who had settled in Manchester in the cotton trade, was born at Ardwick, then a suburb of Manchester, on 26 Aug. 1824. She studied from 1844 to 1846 in the private classes of the Manchester School of Design, then under the direction of George Wallis, and afterwards in his private art school. She exhibited for some years at the Royal Manchester Institution, and in 1853 sent her first contribution, 'Fruit,' to the exhibition of the Royal Academy. In 1854 she settled in London, and sent a picture of 'Spring Flowers' to the Royal Academy, where she afterwards exhibited annually until 1878. Her pictures of 'Geraniums' and 'Primulas' in the exhibition of 1856 attracted the notice of John Ruskin, who mentioned them with praise in his 'Notes on some of the Principal Pictures in the Royal Academy.' She also contributed to the Art Treasures Exhibition held at Manchester in 1857, and to several international exhibitions, both at home and abroad. A 'Group of Camellias' is in the South Kensington Museum. She died at 36 Palace Gardens Terrace, Kensington, on 30 Dec. 1885, and was buried in Brompton cemetery.

ANNIE FERAY MUTRIE (1826–1893), younger sister of the above, was born at Ardwick on 6 March 1826, and also studied at the Manchester School of Design and under George Wallis. She first exhibited at the Royal Academy in 1851, when she sent a picture of 'Fruit,' which was followed in 1852 by two pictures of 'Fruit and Flowers,' and in 1853 by 'Flowers.' She removed with her sister to London in 1854, and in 1855 exhibited at the Royal Academy 'Azaleas' and 'Orchids,' which were highly praised by John Ruskin for their 'very lovely, pure, and yet unobtrusive colour.' She continued to exhibit almost annually until 1882, some of her best works being 'Roses' and 'Orchids' in 1856, 'Autumn Flowers' in 1857, 'Reynard's Glove' in 1858, 'Where the Bee sucks' in 1860, 'York and Lancaster' in 1861, 'Autumn' in 1863, 'The Balcony' in 1871, 'My First Bouquet' in 1874, 'Farewell, Summer,' in 1875, 'The Evening Primrose' in 1876, and 'Wild Flowers of South America' in 1877. She also exhibited at the Manchester Art Treasures Exhibition of 1857, at the British Institution, and elsewhere. A 'Group of Cactus, &c.,' is in the South Kensington Museum. She died at 26 Lower Rock Gardens, Brighton, on 28 Sept. 1893, and was interred in Brompton cemetery.

[Athenæum, 1886 i. 75, 1893 ii. 496; Royal Academy Exhibition Catalogues, 1851–82; Catalogue of the National Gallery of British Art at South Kensington, 1893; information from Frederick Bower, esq.] R. E. G.

MWYNFAWR (*d.* 665?), king of Glamorgan. [See MORGAN.]

MYCHELBOURNE. [See MICHELBORNE.]

MYCHELL, JOHN (*fl.* 1556), printer. [See MITCHELL.]

MYDDELTON. [See also MIDDLETON.]

MYDDELTON or MIDDLETON, SIR HUGH (1560?–1631), projector of the New River, born at Galch Hill in the parish of Hênllan, Denbigh, North Wales, in 1559 or 1560, was sixth son of Richard Myddelton, M.P., governor of Denbigh Castle, by Jane, daughter of Hugh or Richard Dryhurst, alderman of Denbigh (BURKE, *Extinct Baronetage*, p. 351). Sir Thomas Myddelton [q. v.], lord mayor of London, and William Myddelton [q. v.] were brothers. He was sent up to London to learn the trade of a goldsmith, which then embraced banking; and he carried on business successfully in Bassishaw or Basinghall Street through life. He also embarked in ventures of trade by sea, being probably encouraged thereto by his intimacy with Sir Walter Raleigh and other sea captains, including his brother, William Myddelton [q. v.], who made profitable speculations on the Spanish main (Williams, *Ancient and Modern Denbigh*, p. 105). There is a tradition that Myddelton and Raleigh used to sit together at the door of the former's shop and smoke the newly introduced weed tobacco, greatly to the amazement of the passers-by. He likewise entered into the new trade of clothmaking with great energy, and followed it with so much success, that in a speech delivered by him in the House of Commons between 1614 and 1617 on the proposed cloth patent, he stated that he and his partner employed several hundred families.

Myddelton continued to keep up a friendly connection with Denbigh, and he seems to have been mainly instrumental in obtaining for the borough its charter of incorporation in 1596. In recognition of this service the burgesses elected him their first alderman, and in that capacity he signed the first by-laws of the borough in 1597. About the same date he made an abortive attempt to sink for coal in the neighbourhood. He was subsequently appointed recorder of Denbigh, and in 1603 he was elected M.P. for the borough, and again in 1614, 1620, 1623, 1625, and 1628. He was frequently associated with his brother Robert on parliamentary committees of inquiry into matters connected with trade and finance.

London had now far outgrown its existing means of water supply, but although complaints had been constantly made, and even acts of parliament had been obtained in 1605 and 1606, authorising the corporation to remedy the want by bringing in a stream from the springs at Chadwell and Amwell, Hertfordshire, no steps had been taken to carry them out. At length Myddelton, who had already paid considerable attention to the subject as a member of the committees of the House of Commons, before whom the recent acts had been discussed, offered to execute the work. The corporation readily agreed to transfer to him their powers on condition of his finishing the work within four years from the spring of 1609. The first sod upon the works of the proposed New River was turned on 21 April 1609. With untiring energy Myddelton persevered in his undertaking, despite the opposition of the landowners through whose property the stream was to pass, and who complained that their land was likely to suffer in consequence by the overflow of water. In 1610 his opponents carried their complaints before the House of Commons, and a committee was directed to make a report upon their case as soon as the house reassembled in October.

When that date arrived, the members had more important matters to attend to, and Myddelton's hands were soon set free by the dissolution of parliament. The opposition of the landlords was so annoying, and the demands which were made on his purse were in all probability increased so largely thereby, that Myddelton in 1611 was compelled to apply to the corporation for an extension of the stipulated time, which was granted by indenture dated 28 March, and to the king for assistance in raising the capital. James had already had dealings with Myddelton as a jeweller. Moreover he had become interested in the works from observing their progress at Theobalds, and he now agreed, by document dated 2 May 1612, to pay half the cost of the work, both past and future, upon condition of receiving half the profit, and without reserving to the crown any share in the management of the work, except that of appointing a commissioner to examine the accounts, and receive payment of the royal share of the profit. On Michaelmas day 1613 the work was complete; and the entrance of the New River water into London was celebrated at the new cistern at Clerkenwell by a public ceremony, presided over by the lord mayor, Sir Thomas Myddelton, the projector's elder brother. A large print was afterwards published by George Bickham in commemoration of the event, entitled 'Sir Hugh Myddelton's Glory.' The statement that Myddelton was knighted on the occasion is erroneous.

The New River, as originally executed, was a canal of ten feet wide, and probably about four feet deep. It drew its supply of water from the Chadwell and Amwell springs, near Ware, and followed a very winding course of about thirty-eight miles and three-quarters, with a slight fall, to Islington, where it discharged its water into a reservoir called the New River Head. In more recent times its channel has been widened, shortened, and otherwise improved; larger reservoirs have been constructed, and a great additional supply of water has been obtained from the river Lea, and from numerous wells in the chalk; but the general course and site of the works are nearly the same as in the time of Myddelton. While superintending the works Myddelton lived at a house at Bush Hill, near Edmonton, which he afterwards made his country residence (Robinson, *Edmonton*, p. 32). Monumental pedestals have been erected to his memory at the sources of the New River at Chadwell and Amwell. There are also statues to him at Islington Green, on the Holborn Viaduct, and in the Royal Exchange.

In 1614 Myddelton, who had involved himself in difficulties by locking up his capital in this costly undertaking, was obliged to solicit the loan of 3,000*l.* from the corporation, which was granted him in 'consideration of the benefit likely to accrue to the city from his New River.' Of the thirty-six shares owned by him he sold as many as twenty-eight, but appears to have repurchased some before his death, when he held thirteen (*Wills from Doctors' Commons*, Camd. Soc.) The shareholders were incorporated by letters patent on 21 June 1619, under the title of 'The Governor and Company of the New River brought from Chadwell and Amwell to London,' and at the first court of proprietors held on 2 Nov. Myddelton was appointed governor. No dividend was paid until 1633—two years after Myddelton's death—when it only amounted to 15*l.* 3*s.* 3*d.* a share; but after 1640 the prosperity of the company steadily kept pace with the growth of the metropolis in population and wealth.

In 1617 Myddelton took from the governor and company of mines royal in Cardiganshire a lease of some lead and silver mines in the district about Plynlimmon, between the Dovey and the Ystwith, which had been unsuccessfully worked by former adventurers, and were flooded with water. He succeeded in partially clearing the mines of water, and obtained a large profit by working them. While conducting operations he resided at Lodge, now called Lodge Park, in the immediate neighbourhood of the mines. Two cups manufactured by him out of the Welsh silver were presented by him to the corporations of Denbigh and Ruthin, of which towns he was a burgess, and a gold one to the head of his family at Gwaynynog, near Denbigh, all of which are still preserved (Newcome, *Denbigh*, p. 48). In 1620 Myddelton began the work of reclaiming from the sea a flooded district at the eastern extremity of the Isle of Wight, called Brading Harbour (*Cal. State Papers*, Dom. 1619–23, p. 172). He employed Dutch workmen and some invention of his own for draining land, which he patented in 1621. This undertaking was for a time successful; but in 1624 Myddelton's connection with it ceased, and the works fell into neglect, and were destroyed by the sea. The scheme was revived a few years ago, and completed in 1882.

On 19 Oct. 1622 James created Myddelton a baronet with the remission of the customary fees in recognition of his enterprise and engineering skill (*ib.* 1619–23, p. 455; *Harl. MS.* 1507, art. 40; *Addit. Birch MS.* 4177, art. 220). The king likewise confirmed to him the lease of the mines royal, and exempted him from the payment of royalty for whatever precious metals he might discover.

In these ways Myddelton, though never a rich man, and much impoverished by his work on the New River, was enabled to end his days in comfort, and leave a respectable patrimony to his children. He died in Basinghall Street on 10 Dec. 1631, aged 71 (*Probate Act Book, P. C. C.*, 1631), and was buried in accordance with his desire in St. Matthew, Friday Street, where he had often officiated as churchwarden (will registered in P. C. C. 137, St. John, and printed in *Wills from Doctors' Commons*, Camd. Soc.) He was twice married, first to Anne, daughter of a Mr. Collins of Lichfield, and widow of Richard Edwards of London, who died childless; and secondly to Elizabeth, daughter and heiress of John Olmested of Ingatestone, Essex, by whom he had ten sons and six daughters. His eldest surviving son, William, married Eleanor, daughter of Sir Thomas Harris, bart., of Shrewsbury. To the Goldsmiths' Company Myddelton bequeathed a share in the New River Company for the benefit of the more necessitous brethren of that guild, 'especially to such as should be of his name, kindred, and country,' a fund that contributed to the support of several of his more improvident descendants.

On 24 June 1632 Lady Myddelton memorialised the common council of London with reference to the loan of 3,000*l.* advanced to Myddelton, which does not seem to have been repaid; and on 10 Oct. 1634 the corporation re-allowed 1,000*l.* of the amount, in consideration of the public benefit conferred on the city by Myddelton through the formation of the New River. Lady Myddelton died at Bush Hill on 19 July 1643, aged 63, and was buried in the chancel of Edmonton Church.

Portraits of Myddelton and his second wife, painted by Cornelius Jansen, belonged in 1866 to the Rev. J. M. St. Clere Raymond (*Catalogue of Portraits at South Kensington*, pp. 81–2, Nos. 478 and 483). Another portrait of Myddelton by Jansen hangs in Goldsmiths' Hall; it was engraved by George Vertue in 1722, and again by Phillibrown for Lodge's 'Portraits.'

[Smiles's Lives of the Engineers (new edit. 1874), section i.; Biographia Britannica under 'Middleton;' Lewis's Hist. of Islington, pp. 424–30; Stow's London (Strype), bk. i. p. 25, bk. v. p. 60; Lodge's Portraits (Bohn), iii. 267–273; Fuller's Worthies (ed. 1662), 'Wales,' p. 36; Gardiner's Hist. of England, ii. 215; Cal. State Papers, Dom. 1605–31; Granger's Biog.

Hist. of England (2nd edit.), i. 400; Waller's Imperial Dict.; London Society, vi. 455-66; Penny Mag. viii. 36-8; Overall's Remembrancia. The will of Lady Myddelton, which was proved in September 1643, is among the Oxford wills at Somerset House.] G. G.

MYDDELTON or **MIDDLETON, JANE** (1645-1692), 'the great beauty of the time of Charles II,' daughter of Sir Robert Needham (*d.* 1661) by his second wife, Jane, daughter of William Cockayne of Clapham, was born at Lambeth during the latter part of 1645, and baptised in Lambeth Church on 23 Jan. 1645-6. Her father's first wife, Elizabeth Hartop, was a relative of John Evelyn the diarist. Jane was married at Lambeth Church on 18 June 1660 to Charles Myddelton of Ruabon, third surviving son of Sir Thomas Myddelton of Chirk. By her husband she had two daughters, of whom the elder, Jane, was baptised 21 Dec. 1661, married a Mr. May, and died in 1740. Myddelton and his wife lived in London and appear to have subsisted for a time upon the bounty of relatives. A legacy from Lady Needham fell in upon that lady's death in 1666, and another upon Sir Thomas Myddelton's death in the same year; but from 1663, at least, the family's finances must have been mainly dependent upon the generosity of the lady's lovers. The first of these may have been the Chevalier de Grammont, who was enthralled almost immediately upon his arrival in London, but found 'la belle Myddelton' more than coy. 'Lettres et présens trottèrent,' wrote Hamilton, but the lover 'en restait là.' Comminges hints, however, in explanation that the chevalier's love-tokens were intercepted by the lady's-maid (Jusserand, *French Ambassador at the Court of Charles II*, p. 93). Before the year was out De Grammont fell under the sway of his future wife, and the road was clear for Richard Jones, viscount Ranelagh [q. v.] From neither this gallant nor from Ralph (afterwards Duke of) Montagu did Mrs. Myddelton ever incur the reproach of obduracy. To them succeeded William Russell, son of the Hon. Edward Russell, and standard-bearer in the first regiment of foot-guards. In 1665 Mrs. Myddelton's beauty attracted the attention of the king (*Addit. MS.* 5810, f. 299), and proved for the time a serious menace to the Countess of Castlemaine's supremacy. Pepys states that at this time Edmund Waller the poet was already dangling after her. On 22 Sept. 1665 Evelyn, who elsewhere speaks of her as 'that famous and indeed incomparable beauty' (*Diary*, ii. 183), told Pepys that 'in painting the beautiful Mrs. Myddelton is rare.' On 23 June 1667 Pepys heard from another authority that the Duke of York's advances were not encouraged by Mrs. Myddelton. During the next year Myddelton and his wife fixed their abode on the north side of Charles Street at the extreme west end of the town. Mrs. Myddelton had besides a country retreat at Greenwich, and she was constantly a guest of George Villiers, second duke of Buckingham, at Clevedon, where during her visits Edmund Waller was a frequent caller (Letter from Waller, *Eg. MS.* 922). The *liaison* with the poet seems to have terminated by 1686, when Sacharissa wrote (8 July), 'Mrs. Myddelton and I have lost old Waller—he has gone away frightened' (Miss Berry, *Life of Lady Russell*, 1819, p. 130). St. Evrémond, the Earl of Rochester, and the Hon. Francis Russell seem to have been in the train of her lovers, and Andrew Marvell, in his 'Instructions to a Painter about the Dutch Wars' (*Works*, 1776, iii. 392), appears to allude to an intimacy between 'sweet Middleton' and Archbishop Sheldon.

That Mrs. Myddelton was a peerless beauty of the languorous type seems to be unquestioned. The popular enthusiasm was evinced not only at the play and in the park, but also at church, where the beauty was regular in her attendance. In 1680 Courtin, the predecessor of Barillon, had to take the Duc de Nevers and suite (then on a special mission at the English court) in two coaches to see the fair celebrity; Louvois was so impressed by the account they took home that he sent over for a portrait. Her literary attainments were considerable, but she seems to have been prone to platitudinising, and Hamilton accuses her of sending her lovers to sleep with irreproachable sentiments. By St. Evrémond, who also contributed an epitaph upon her, she is introduced into a 'Scène de Bassette,' playing cards with the Duchesse de Mazarin and the Hon. Francis Villiers, and talking affectedly to the latter, to the vast irritation of the duchess, who is losing.

After the accession of her old lover, James II, she enjoyed an annual pension of 500*l.* from the secret service money (Ackerman, pp. 152, 165, 183). The husband, who had for some years held a place of about 400*l.* a year in the prize office, died insolvent in 1691. Mrs. Myddelton died in the following year, and was buried beside her husband in Lambeth Church.

The most notable of the numerous portraits of Mrs. Myddelton are the three-quarter length by Lely at Hampton Court, formerly at Windsor, and painted in 1663 for Anne, duchess of York (engraved in stipple by

Wright for Mrs. Jameson's 'Beauties'); another by the same artist, at Althorp (also engraved by Wright for Dibdin's 'Ædes Althorpianæ,' 1822); and a third by an artist unknown, which has been engraved by Van den Berghe. These three paintings agree in representing a soft and slightly torpid type of blonde loveliness, with voluptuous figure, full lips, auburn hair, and dark hazel eyes.

Jane's younger sister, Eleanor, was mistress for several years to the Duke of Monmouth and mother by him of four children, who bore the name of Crofts (SANDFORD, *Genealogical History of Kings and Queens of England*, 1707, f. 645); one of the daughters, Henrietta (*d.* 1730), married in 1697 Charles Paulet, second duke of Bolton [q. v.] (cf. *Treasury Papers*, 1683; *Post-Boy*, 23 Jan. 1722).

[G. S. Steinman's monograph Memoir of Mrs. Myddelton, the great Beauty of the time of Charles II, 1864, which contains a full pedigree, and the same writer's Althorp Memoirs, 1869. See also Mrs. Jameson's Beauties of the Court of Charles II, 1833; Law's Hampton Court, ii. 242; Forneron's Louise de Keroualle; Œuvres de Saint Evrémond, v. 284–5, 316–20, vi. 62–4; Poems on Affairs of State, 1716, i. 132; Granger's Biog. Hist. of England, 1775, iv. 181; Waller's Poems, ed. Thorn Drury; Pepys's Diary, and Hamilton's Memoirs of Grammont, 1889, passim; Julia Cartwright's Sacharissa, 1893, pp. 277–8, 293.] T. S.

MYDDELTON or **MIDDLETON**, SIR THOMAS (1550–1631), lord mayor of London, fourth son of Richard Myddelton of Denbigh and Jane, daughter of Hugh Dryhurst, was born in 1550 at Denbigh, probably at Denbigh Castle, of which his father was governor. William Myddelton [q. v.] and Sir Hugh Myddelton [q. v.] were younger brothers. In his youth he visited foreign countries, and the experience of trade thus gained greatly contributed to his subsequent mercantile success. He was apprenticed to Ferdinando Pointz, citizen and grocer, and was admitted to the freedom of the Grocers' Company on 14 Jan. 1582, to the livery on 21 March 1592, and to the office of assistant in 1611. On 17 Feb. 1591–2 he and three others were appointed surveyors of the customs in all ports of England except London (deed at Chirk Castle). He was largely indebted for his advancement to his intimacy with Sir Francis Walsingham.

Myddelton was a parishioner of St. Mary Aldermary, and carried on business in a house in the churchyard of that parish (funeral certificate in College of Arms). He entered parliament in 1597–8 as member for Merionethshire, and was appointed lord-lieutenant and custos rotulorum of the same county in 1599. In 1598 he paid 20*l.* as his share of the loan to Queen Elizabeth. He was an adventurer in the East India voyage of 1599, and is mentioned as a member of the East India Company in its charter of incorporation granted in 1600.

Myddelton in 1595 purchased the estate of Chirk Castle in his native county, and in 1615 he also purchased the manor of Stansted Mountfichet in Essex, which he made his principal residence. He was, against his will, elected alderman for Queenhithe ward on 24 May 1603, and on refusing to take the oath of office was committed to Newgate on 10 June. This brought a sharp letter of reprimand from the king to the lord mayor and aldermen, directing them to release Myddelton immediately, as he was employed in an important service for the state, which privileged him from municipal duties (*Remembrancia*, p. 3). The city, nevertheless, won the day, and Myddelton was sworn into office on 21 June. Three days later he was elected sheriff, and was knighted by the king at Whitehall on 26 July. He now became very active in civic affairs, and was appointed a commissioner or referee on various occasions, both by the council and the court of aldermen (cf. *ib.* p. 555).

Myddelton was elected lord mayor on Michaelmas day 1613, this day being chosen by his brother Hugh for opening the New River Head. A pageant was devised for the occasion in honour of the newly elected lord mayor by his namesake, Thomas Myddelton the dramatist [q. v.], and entitled 'The Manner of his Lordship's Entertainment on Michaelmas Day last,' &c. Another pageant was prepared by the same writer, under the title of 'The Triumphs of Truth,' for Myddelton's mayoralty inauguration on 29 Oct. A copy of each of these pageants is in the Guildhall Library. Myddelton was elected, during the year of his mayoralty, president of Bridewell and Bethlehem hospitals. On 22 March 1613 he was translated to the aldermanship of Coleman Street ward by right of his prerogative as lord mayor. He continued to represent this ward until his death, and was for many years senior alderman or father of the city. In August 1621 'Yt pleased the Right Worshipful Knight Sir Thomas Middleton to make a very religious speach and exhortation to the whole assemblie of the Misterie of the Grocerie of London.'

Myddelton was one of the original chartered adventurers in the New River Company, and also an adventurer in 1623 in the Virginia Company, to which he subscribed 37*l.* 10*s.*, but paid 62*l.* 10*s.* He was a representative of the city of London in parliament in 1624–5, 1625, and 1626, and was a colonel of the city militia. In 1630, in conjunction with Rowland Heylyn [q. v.], Myddelton caused to be published the first popular edition of the Bible in Welsh, small 4to; it was produced at great expense (T. R. Phillips, *Memoirs of the Civil War in Wales*, p. 60). A pamphlet called 'A Discourse of Trade from England unto the East Indies' is also attributed to Myddelton. Towards the close of his life Myddelton resided at Stansted Mountfichet, where he died on 12 Aug. 1631, and was buried in the church on 8 Sept. following, aged 81, 'or thereabouts.' His monument was on the south side of the chancel, of sumptuous workmanship, with a life-sized effigy under a decorated arch. It bore two Latin inscriptions in prose and verse, followed by a short rhyming inscription in English (Muilman, *Essex*, iii. 29).

Myddelton was four times married: first, about 1586, to Hester, daughter of Sir Richard Saltonstall of South Ockendon, Essex, lord mayor of London in 1597–8; secondly, about 1590, to Elizabeth, widow of John Olmested of Ingatestone, Essex; thirdly, to Elizabeth, widow of Miles Hobart, clothworker of London; and fourthly, to Anne, widow of Jacob Wittewronge, brewer, of London, who survived him. On the occasion of this last marriage, according to Pennant, she being a young wife and he an old man, the famous song of 'Room for Cuckolds, here comes my Lord Mayor,' was composed. Myddelton had issue by his first two wives only; by the first wife two sons: Richard, who died young, and Sir Thomas Myddelton [q. v.], his heir, of Chirk Castle, the parliamentarian general; by his second wife he had two sons and two daughters: Henry, who died young; Timothy, who succeeded to the estate of Stansted Mountfichet; Hester, married to Henry Salisbury of Llewenny, Denbighshire, afterwards created a baronet; and Mary, married to Sir John Maynard, K.B. By Middleton's will, dated 20 Nov. 1630, and proved in the P. C. C. on 15 Aug. 1631 (94, St. John), he left property of the annual value of 7*l.* to the Grocers' Company for the benefit of their poor members. The company also received valuable bequests under the will of his widow, who died on 7 Jan. 1646.

[Notes on the Middleton family by William Duncombe Pink, reprinted from The Cheshire Sheaf, 1891, pp. 6, 12–15; Account of Sir Thomas Middleton by G. E. Cockayne, in London and Middlesex Note-book, pp. 252–7; Grocers' Company's Records; authorities above cited; information kindly supplied by W. M. Myddelton, esq.] C. W-h.

MYDDELTON, Sir THOMAS (1586–1666), parliamentarian, born in 1586, was the eldest son of Sir Thomas Myddelton [q. v.], and nephew of William Myddelton [q. v.] and of Sir Hugh Myddelton [q. v.] Thomas matriculated from Queen's College, Oxford, on 22 Feb. 1604–5, and became a student of Gray's Inn in 1607; he was knighted on 10 Feb. 1617, and was M.P. for Weymouth and Melcombe Regis, 1624–5, and for the county of Denbigh in 1625 and 1640–8. He showed from the first a strong puritan temperament. In the summer of 1642 he was sent to his constituency to exercise his influence on behalf of the parliament, and accordingly, in December 1642, he addressed to his countrymen a 'menacing' letter to submit to and assist parliament. Thereupon, by the king's order, Colonel Ellis of Gwesnewydd, near Wrexham, seized Myddelton's residence, Chirk Castle, in his absence in January 1642–3. A garrison was placed there under Sir John Watts.

By a parliamentary ordinance, dated 11 June 1643, Myddelton, who had by that time returned to London, was appointed sergeant-major-general for North Wales. On 10 Aug. he reached Nantwich in Cheshire, where he was joined by Sir William Brereton (1604–1661) [q. v.] They proceeded on 4 Sept. to Drayton, and on 11 Sept. to Wem, which they seized, garrisoned, and made their Shropshire headquarters. While they were still engaged in fortifying Wem, Lord Capel, with reinforcements from Staffordshire, marched on Nantwich, but was signally defeated outside Wem in two separate conflicts, on 17 and 18 Oct. (*ib.* i. 176–8, ii. 86–8). After this victory 'Brereton the general, and Myddelton, his sub-general,' as they were styled by the royalists (see Carte, *Life of Ormonde*, v. 514), left Nantwich on 7 Nov., were joined at Stretton by Sir George Booth with troops from Lancashire, and crossing the Dee at Holt, entered North Wales, where Wrexham, Hawarden, Flint, Mostyn Mold, and Holywell were taken in quick succession. But all were abandoned precipitately after the landing at Mostyn on 18 Nov. of some 2,500 royalist soldiers from Ireland (Phillips, ii. 101–2). This hasty retreat was condemned by writers of their own party: 'they made such haste as not to relieve Hawarden Castle,' and 'so many good friends who had come to them were left to the mercy of the enemy' (Burghall, *Providence Improved*, quoted by Phillips, i. 186). Myddelton's troops were raw militiamen, while his opponents were trained soldiers.

In February 1643–4 Myddelton's command in North Wales was confirmed by a fresh commission 'vesting him with almost unlimited power as to levying contributions and sequestrating estates of delinquents' (PHILLIPS, i. 219). He left London about the end of May 1644, and marched to Nantwich, and thence to Knutsford, where a muster of all the Cheshire forces was intended, so as to carry out a 'great design' of 'going against Prince Rupert into Lancashire' (*ib.* ii. 175; *Hist. MSS. Comm.* iv. 268). But the royalists, to the number of about four thousand, laid siege to Oswestry, recently won by the parliamentarians, and Myddelton, hurrying to the scene before the arrival of his colleagues, raised the siege by a brilliant action on 2 July (*ib.* ii. 179–88). Returning to Nantwich, Myddelton for some time watched Prince Rupert's movements, making occasional raids into Montgomeryshire. On 4 Sept. he captured the garrison at Newtown, and the same day advanced to Montgomery, and without any resistance the castle there was surrendered to him by its owner, Edward, first lord Herbert of Cherbury [q. v.] (*Hist. MSS. Comm.* vi. 28; *Archæologia Cambrensis*, 4th ser. xii. 325). Thereupon Sir Michael Ernely, who was in command of the royalist forces at Shrewsbury, marched upon Montgomery to recover it—a manœuvre anticipated by Myddelton, who sallied out to collect provisions in the neighbourhood so as to victual his men in case of a siege. Ernely, however, intercepted his return, and defeated him outside the town. Myddelton's foot-soldiers, under Colonel Mytton, succeeded in re-entering the castle, which Ernely at once besieged; but Myddelton retired to Oswestry, and after obtaining reinforcements from Lancashire returned, accompanied by Brereton and Sir William Fairfax. They arrived on 17 Sept. in sight of Montgomery, where the whole strength of both parties in North Wales and the borders was now assembled. After a desperate conflict, in which the issue long remained doubtful, and Fairfax was mortally wounded, the parliamentarians completely routed their opponents. The royalists regarded their defeat as the deathblow to their power in North Wales (see the despatches of Myddelton and others in PHILLIPS, ii. 201–9; *Autobiography of Lord Herbert of Cherbury*, ed. Lee, pp. 281–91). Myddelton was left for a time in command at Montgomery, but after capturing Powis Castle on 3 Oct. (PHILLIPS, ii. 212–13) the county generally declared for parliament, and Myddelton was therefore able to turn to Shrewsbury, where he captured most of the outposts, and blocked the passages to the town (*ib.* i. 266–7). Intending to keep Christmas in one of his own houses, Myddelton appeared on 21 Dec. 1644 before his own castle of Chirk, still held by Sir John Watts, who after a three days' siege was able to write on Christmas day to Prince Rupert that he had beaten Myddelton off (the original letter is now preserved at Chirk Castle, see *Memorials of Chirk Castle*).

By the self-denying ordinance Myddelton was superseded and the command was transferred to his brother-in-law, Colonel Thomas Mytton [q. v.] When, however, there was a general reaction in the county in favour of the king in 1648, Myddelton was one of the persons to whom the principal inhabitants of Flintshire and Denbighshire, in their fidelity to parliament, entrusted the management of their county affairs (PHILLIPS, i. 409, ii. 371, cf. pp. 399–401). On 14 May 1651 Myddelton was ordered by the council of state to enter into a bond of 10,000*l.* for his general good behaviour, and having received the security it was further ordered on 16 May that the garrison should be withdrawn from his house.

In 1659 Myddelton joined Sir George Booth's rising in favour of the recall of Charles II, and went to meet Booth and others at Chester. Issuing a declaration 'in vindication of the freedom of parliament,' Myddelton marched back into Wales. After defeating Booth, General Lambert besieged Chirk Castle and compelled Myddelton to surrender on 24 Aug. 1659 (Lambert's despatch on the surrender and articles of capitulation are printed in the *Public Intelligencer*, 22–9 Aug. 1659). One side of the castle was demolished, and the trees in the park were cut and sold (YORKE, *Royal Tribes in Wales*, pp. 94–6). Charles II is said to have subsequently shown his gratitude towards Myddelton by bestowing on him 'a cabinet of great beauty, said to have cost 10,000*l.*,' and still preserved at Chirk Castle, where there are also a large collection of muskets used in the civil war, and other relics of the period (*Gossiping Guide to Wales*, large ed. p. 123). Myddelton died in 1666.

Myddelton's religious character is strongly impressed on all his despatches, in which he freely bestows the credit for his own successes on other officers, or ascribes them to the bravery of his own men, for whose safety he shows the greatest solicitude. His peaceable disposition and his aversion from unnecessary bloodshed are revealed in the 'friendly summons' to surrender which he addressed to the governor of Denbigh Castle, a former acquaintance of his (his letter, dated Wrexham, 14 Nov. 1643, is printed in *Memorials of the Bagot Family*, App. i., and in PARRY, *Royal Progresses*, p. 350). The almost unlimited powers of sequestering estates which he possessed as major-general for North

Wales he exercised with very great moderation, and the most serious charge brought against him by his enemies consisted of such alleged acts of vandalism as breaking up the fine organ of Wrexham Church for the sake of supplying his men with bullets.

He married, first, Margaret, daughter and heiress of George Savile of Wakefield in Yorkshire, by whom he had no issue; and secondly, Mary, daughter of Sir Robert Napier, bart., of Luton Hoo, Bedfordshire, by whom he had seven sons and six daughters. The eldest, Thomas Myddelton (*d.* 1663), who was created a baronet in 1660, and was besieged by Lambert in Chirk Castle in August 1659, left two sons, Thomas (*d.* 1684), M.P. for Denbigh, and Richard Myddelton (*d.*1716), M.P. for Denbigh 1685–1716, both of whom succeeded in turn to the baronetcy. Sir Richard's son, William Myddelton, fourth baronet, died unmarried in 1718, when the baronetcy became extinct and the estates reverted to Robert Myddelton of Llysvassi, a son of the parliamentary general's third son Richard, from whom Mr. Myddelton-Biddulph, the present owner of Chirk Castle, traces descent. A daughter of Myddelton, Ann, married Edward, third lord Herbert of Cherbury, grandson of the first lord.

[The chief authority is J. Roland Phillips's Civil War in Wales and the Marches, vol. ii. Among the collections of private pedigrees in the possession of the Heralds' College are several illustrative of the Myddelton family; see also Dwnn's Heraldic Visitations, ii. 334–5; Foster's Alumni Oxon.; Gray's Inn Register.]

D. Ll. T.

MYDDELTON, WILLIAM (1556?–1621), Welsh poet and seaman, was the third son of Richard Myddelton, governor of Denbigh Castle, by Jane, daughter of Hugh Dryhurst, also of Denbigh. Richard Myddelton was the fourth son of Foulk Myddelton, who claimed descent from Ririd Flaidd; on Richard's death in 1575 his elegy was written by Rhys Cain, and he was buried at Whitchurch, the parish church of Denbigh, where there is a brass effigy showing Richard kneeling at an altar with his nine sons behind him, while round the figure of his wife, who had predeceased him in 1565, are grouped their seven daughters. Among the sons were Sir Hugh Myddelton [q. v.] and Sir Thomas Myddelton [q. v.], lord mayor of London, the father of Sir Thomas Myddelton (1587–1666) [q. v.], the parliamentarian. William was, according to Wood, educated at Oxford, but he must be distinguished from the 'William Myddelton of co. Denbigh, gent.,' who matriculated from Gloucester Hall on 23 Oct. 1584, aged 15 (Foster, *Alumni Oxon.*), and was of Gwaynynog; no other Oxford student of the name appears in the university register at a possible date. Myddelton, while young, certainly became a seaman, and may have been the 'Captain Middleton' mentioned in a letter to Lord Burghley of 6 Nov. 1590 as 'returning with a prize of pepper' (*Cal. State Papers*, Dom. Ser.); though possibly this refers to John Middleton [see under Middleton, Sir Henry]. In 1591, when the English squadron, under the command of Lord Thomas Howard, had been sent to the Azores, with the view of intercepting the homeward-bound treasure-ships of Spain, George Clifford, earl of Cumberland, who was then on the coast of Portugal, sent off a pinnace, under Myddelton's command, to warn Howard of a powerful fleet that was on the point of sailing from Spain to attack him. The pinnace being 'a good sailer' Myddelton was able to keep company with the Spanish ships for three days, 'both to discover their forces as also to give advice of their approach,' and on 31 Aug. (1591) he delivered the news to Howard scarcely before the Spaniards were in sight. Howard forthwith retired, but Sir Richard Grenville (1541?–1591) [q. v.], in spite of Myddelton's eloquent entreaties, remained behind in the Revenge (cf. *The Last Fight of the Revenge at Sea*, ed. Professor Arber, London, 1871).

Previous to this Myddelton was a recognised authority on Welsh prosody; Dr. John David Rhys speaks eulogistically of him in his 'Welsh Grammar' (London, 1592, fol.), and inserts therein an appendix contributed by Myddelton, under his bardic name of Gwilym Ganoldref—a Welsh translation of William Middle town—together with two original poems intended to illustrate Welsh metres (*Cambrytannicæ . . . Linguæ Institutiones*, &c., pp. 235–49). But finding that Rhys's 'Grammar,' owing to its being in Latin, was of little use to his fellow-countrymen, Myddelton, in 1593, published a work of his own, entitled 'Bardhoniaeth neu Brydydhiaeth, y Lhyfr Kyntaf' (London, 8vo), which was reprinted in 1710 as a part of a work called 'Flores Poetarum Britannicorum, sef Blodeuog Waith y Prydyddion Brytanaidd' (Shrewsbury, 12mo; 2nd edit., London, 1864; 3rd edit., undated, Llanrwst), and has been laid under contribution by almost every subsequent writer on Welsh prosody. Myddelton's chief work was his metrical version of the Psalms, published in 1603 (after the author's death) by Thomas Salesbury, under the title 'Psalmae y Brenhinol Brophwyd Dafydh, gwedi i cynghaneddu mewn mesurau cymreig,' London, 4to. This work was finished, according to a note at the end, on 24 Jan. 1595, in the West Indies, 'apud Scutum insulam occidentalium Indorum.' A second edition, edited by the Rev. Walter Davies [q. v.], was published at Llanfair Caereinion in 1827. Being written in strict Welsh metres, this version never became popular, and was superseded by the free metrical version of Edmund Prys [q. v.] Myddelton died on 27 March 1621, probably at Antwerp, where he was buried. From his brother's account-book, which is extant at Chirk Castle, it appears that he was a Roman catholic.

Pennant (*Tours in Wales*, ed. 1883, ii. 146) and several other writers (e.g. Yorke, *Royal Tribes of Wales*, ed. 1799, p. 107) state that Myddelton, with Captain Thomas Price of Plas iolyn and a Captain Koet, was the first who smoked tobacco publicly in the streets of London. A similar story is told of his brother Hugh.

[For the pedigrees of the Myddeltons, see Dwnn's Heraldic Visitations, ii. 334–5, and Llyfr Silin, printed in Archæologia Cambrensis, 5th ser. v. 107–12. See also Wood's Athenæ Oxon.; Williams's Eminent Welshmen, p. 353; Rowlands's Cambrian Bibliography; a Memoir of Chirk Castle, Chester, 1859. An excellent Welsh biography, by the Rev. Walter Davies, was published in Y Gwyliedydd for March 1827, and reprinted in Davies's Works (Gwaith Gwallter Mechain), pp. 431–40.] D. Ll. T.

MYERS, FREDERIC (1811–1851), author and divine, was born at Blackheath 20 Sept. 1811. After being carefully educated by his father, Thomas Myers [q. v.], then on the staff of the Royal Military Academy at Woolwich, he entered Clare Hall, Cambridge, as a scholar in 1829. The following year he gained the Hulsean essay prize, and he became in 1833 Crosse scholar and graduated B.A. Shortly afterwards he was elected a fellow of his college, and in 1836 gained the Tyrwhitt Hebrew scholarship. He was ordained in 1835 to the curacy of Ancaster in Lincolnshire. In 1838 he was appointed perpetual curate of the newly formed district parish of St. John's, Keswick, and in this, his sole preferment, he remained till his death. Besides the charm of scenery and the attraction of congenial neighbours —Wordsworth was still living at Rydal Mount—the new incumbent found a satisfaction in being able, in a recently constituted parish, to form his own methods of spiritual oversight. The thoroughness with which he devoted himself to the work may be judged from the fact that his 'Lectures on Great Men,' which have repeatedly issued from the press, were prepared as simple parish lectures. In the spring of 1850 his health failed, and he died at Clifton 20 July 1851.

Myers married, firstly, in Oct. 1839, Fanny, youngest daughter of J. C. Lucas Calcraft, esq.; she died in Jan. following. In 1842 Myers married, secondly, Susan Harriet, youngest daughter of John Marshall, esq., of Hallsteads, Cumberland, M.P. for Yorkshire before 1832. By her Myers left a family. The eldest son, Frederic William Henry Myers, is noticed in the Supplement. The youngest son, Arthur Thomas Myers, M.D., died in London on 8 Jan. 1894, aged 42; he was the author of the article 'James Esdaile' in this 'Dictionary.'

The most important of Myers's published works was 'Catholic Thoughts,' in four books, on the church of Christ, the church of England, the Bible, and theology. The first part was privately printed in 1834, and the whole, after being reprinted at intervals in 1841 and 1848, still for private circulation, was published in a collected form in 1873, with the author's name, in the series of 'Latter-Day Papers' edited by Bishop Ewing; it was again issued in 1883, with an introduction by the author's son, F. W. H. Myers. In the preface Myers states his conviction 'that the primary Idea of the Church of Christ is that of a Brotherhood of men worshipping Christ as their revelation of the Highest; and that equality of spiritual privileges is so characteristic of its constitution, that the existence of any priestly Caste in it is destructive of it; and also that the faith which it should make obligatory on its members is emphatically faith in Christ Himself, . . . and very subordinately only in any definite theoretic creed.' The book had a fate unusual in theological controversy, in that the demand for its publication came most strongly thirty or forty years after it was written. As a literary work it is characterised by singular grace and lucidity of style.

Myers also published: 1. The Hulsean prize essay for 1830, on 'Miracles,' printed in 1831. 2. 'An Ordination Sermon, preached at Buckden,' 1835. 3. 'Four Sermons, preached before the University of Cambridge,' Keswick, 1846; reprinted, with two others, 1852. 4. 'Lectures on Great Men,' 1848, of which eight editions have since appeared.

[Introduction to Catholic Thoughts, by F. W. H. Myers, 1883; Funeral Sermons in St. John's Church, Kendal, 27 July 1851, by the Revs. T. D. H. Battersby and H. V. Elliott; Gent. Mag. 1851 pt. ii. p. 327; Contributions to the Religious Thought &c., by J. M. Wilson, 1888, p. 32; information from members of the family.]

J. H. L.

MYERS, THOMAS (1774–1834), mathematician and geographer, was born 13 Feb. 1774, at Hovingham, near York, of a family long settled in the county. In 1806 he was appointed professor of mathematics at the Royal Military Academy, Woolwich. He died 21 April 1834, at his residence in Lee Park, Blackheath. In 1807 he married Anna Maria, youngest daughter of John Hale, esq., by whom he had issue. His son Frederic Myers is separately noticed.

Myers wrote: 1. 'A Compendious System of Modern Geography, with Maps,' 1812, London, 8vo; re-edited ten years later in 2 vols. 4to. 2. 'A Statistical Chart of Europe,' 1813. 3. 'An Essay on Improving the Condition of the Poor, . . . with Hints on the Means of Employing those who are now Discharged from His Majesty's Service,' 1814. 4. 'A Practical Treatise on finding the Latitude and Longitude at Sea, with Tables, &c., translated from the French of M. de Rossel' [1815]. 5. 'Remarks on a Course of Education designed to prepare the Youthful Mind for a career of Honour, Patriotism, and Philanthropy,' 1818. In this the author, described as honorary member of the London Philosophical Society, recommends the study of mathematics, and especially of geometry, 'not only for checking the wanderings of a volatile disposition, . . . but for inspiring the mind with a love of truth.' The work was reprinted in the twelfth volume of the 'Pamphleteer.' Myers also wrote essays, chiefly on astronomical subjects, in various of the annual numbers of 'Time's Telescope' from 1811 onwards. The memoir of Captain Parry, in one of these, and an 'Essay on Man' are praised in the 'Gentleman's Magazine,' 1823 p. 524, 1825 p. 541.

[Myers's Works; Gent. Mag. 1834, pt. i. p. 108; information from the family.] J. H. L.

MYKELFELD, MAKELSFELD, MACLESFELD, or MASSET, WILLIAM (*d.* 1304), cardinal, was born, according to the 'Dictionnaire des Cardinaux,' at Coventry, during the pontificate of Innocent IV, that is to say, between 1243 and 1254. He is said by some to have been born at Canterbury; there is no evidence to show that he belonged either to the family of Macclesfield of Macclesfield in Cheshire (cf. *Ancient Parish of Prestbury*, Chetham Society, pp. 168 sq.), or to that of Watford (cf. *Gesta Abbatum Monasterii Sancti Albani*, Rolls Ser. i. 480). He became a friar-preacher at Coventry and completed his education in the 'gymnasium sanjacobeum' (the seminary of the Jacobins, or dominican friar-preachers) at Paris, where he proceeded B.D. Returning to England he was elected fellow of Merton College, Oxford, in 1291, and proceeded D.D. He lectured in Oxford and was a great authority on the Bible; mingling also in the controversies of the time and confuting the heresies of William Delamere. In clerical politics he was a disciplinarian, and probably was no friend to the laxity which prevailed under Boniface VIII. In 1303 he represented his order on the nomination, it is supposed, of Edward I, at the synod of Besançon. Benedict XI nominated him cardinal priest with the title of St. Sabina on 18 Dec. 1303, but it is doubtful whether the news reached him, as he died while on his way to England early in 1304 (Migne cannot be right in dating the appointment of his successor 1303). Walter Winterburn (*d.* 1305), confessor to the king and also a friar-preacher, was at once made cardinal of St. Sabina in his stead. The following works are attributed to Mykelfeld by Echard: 1. 'Postillæ in sacra Biblia.' 2. 'In Evangelium de decem Virginibus.' 3. 'Questiones de Angelis.' 4. 'Questiones Ordinariæ.' 5. 'Contra Henricum de Gandavo, in quibus impugnat S. Thomam de Aquino.' 6. 'Contra Corruptorem S. Thomæ.' 7. 'De Unitate Formarum.' 8. 'De Comparatione Statuum.' 9. 'Orationes ad Clerum.' 10. 'Varia Problemata.'

[Echard's Scriptores Ord. Præd. i. 493–4; Brodrick's Memorials of Merton (Oxf. Hist. Soc. p. 182; Folkestone Williams's Lives of the English Cardinals, i. 432–3; Migne's Dictionnaire des Cardinaux; Tanner's Bibl. Brit. (s.v. 'Massetus,' 518); Rishanger's Chron. (Rolls Ser.), p. 221.] W. A. J. A.

MYLES or MILES, JOHN (1621–1684), founder of Welsh baptist churches, son of Walter Myles of Newton-Welsh, Herefordshire, was born in 1621. On 11 March 1636 he matriculated at Brasenose College, Oxford; nothing further is known of his university career. He seems to have begun to preach in Wales in 1644 or 1645, probably as an independent. In the spring of 1649 he went to London with Thomas Proud; they joined a baptist church at the Glasshouse, Broad Street, under William Consett and Edward Draper. Returning to Wales, Myles and Proud formed on 1 Oct. 1649 the first baptist church in Wales, at Ilston, Glamorganshire. The rector of Ilston, William Houghton, was sequestered, and Myles obtained the rectory. His name appears in the act (22 Feb. 1650) 'for the better propagation and preaching of the Gospel in Wales' among the twenty-five ministers on whose recommendation and approval the seventy-one lay commissioners were to act [see Powell Vavasor]. He soon found himself at the head of sixteen baptist preachers, by whose efforts five churches were formed by 1652. These churches did not all make adult baptism a term of communion, though Myles's own church did. They differed also about imposition of hands at baptism, and the use of conjoint singing in public worship. These differences did not hinder their union in a common association. Myles in 1651 was this association's delegate to a meeting of baptists in London.

At the Restoration Houghton recovered the rectory of Ilston, and Myles soon afterwards emigrated to New England. In 1663 he formed a baptist church at Rehoboth, Massachusetts. But on 2 July 1667 Thomas Prince, governor of Massachusetts, fined Myles and James Brown, his coadjutor, 5*l.* apiece for 'breach of order in setting up a public meeting without the knowledge and approbation of the court.' It was decided that 'their continuance at Rehoboth' could not be allowed, as 'being very prejudicial to the peace of that church and that town;' but on their desisting from their meeting within a month, and removing elsewhere, they were to be tolerated. Myles removed to Barrington, Rhode Island, where he built a house; to this day a bridge there, over the river, is known as Myles's Bridge. On 30 Oct. 1667 the court of Massachusetts granted a tract of land, on which a town named Swansea was built. Among the incorporators was Captain Willetts, the first mayor of New York city. Myles was the town's minister. In 1673 a school was built, of which Myles was master. His church at Swansea was scattered during the Indian war, and he removed to Boston, Massachusetts, where he preached to a baptist church, and lived in good accord with the congregational divines, and modified his opinion of the necessity of adult baptism for communion. He returned to Swansea, Massachusetts, in 1678, and preached there till his death on 3 Feb. 1683-4. His son returned to England. His grandson, Samuel Myles (1664-1728), graduated B.A. at Harvard in 1684, and was incorporated M.A. at Oxford on 15 July 1693; he was the first rector (from 29 June 1689) of King's Chapel, Boston, Massachusetts.

[Mather's Magnalia Christi Americana, 1702, iii. 7, iv. 138; Calamy's Account, 1713, p. 731; Calamy's Continuation, 1727, ii. 847; Walker's Sufferings of the Clergy, 1714, ii. 278; Hutchinson's Hist. of the Colony of Massachuset's Bay, 1765, p. 228; Backus's Hist. of New England, 1777, pp. 350 seq., as cited in Rees's Hist. Prot. Nonconformity in Wales, 1883, pp. 90 seq., 114 seq.; Appleton's Cyclopædia of American Biography, 1888, iv. 474; Foster's Alumni Oxon. 1500-1714, iii. 1012.] A. G.

ed the band of sixteen baptist preachers by whose efforts five churches were formed by 1663. These churches did not admit adults to communion, though Myles's own church did. They differed also about the imposition of hands at baptism, and the use of conjoint singing in public worship. These differences did not hinder their union in a common association. Myles in 1651 was this association's delegate to a meeting of baptists in London.

At the restoration Houghton recovered the rectory of Ilston, and Myles soon afterwards emigrated to New England. In 1663 he formed a baptist church at Rehoboth, Mass.; but on 2 July 1667 Thomas Prince, governor of Massachusetts, fined Myles and James Brown, his coadjutor, 5*l.* apiece for "breach of order in setting up a public meeting without the knowledge and approbation of the court." It was decided that their continuance at Rehoboth could not be allowed as "being very prejudicial to the peace of that church and that town;" but on their removing their meeting within about a mile of Rehoboth, they are to be tolerated. He removed to Barrington, Rhode Island, where he built a house; and the bridge over the river is known as Myles's Bridge. On 30 Oct. 1667 the court granted a tract of land, on which many married two persons built. Among the incorporators was Captain Willett, the first mayor of New York city. Myles was the town's minister. In 1673 a school was built, of which Myles was master. His church at Swansea was scattered during the Indian war, and he removed to Boston, Massachusetts, where he preached to a baptist church, and lived in good accord with the congregational divines, and modified his opinion of the necessity of adult baptism for communion. He returned to Swansea, Massachusetts, in 1679, and preached there till his death on 3 Feb. 1683-4. His son returned to England. His grandson, Samuel Myles (1664-1728), graduated B.A. at Harvard in 1684, and was incorporated M.A. at Oxford on 16 July 1693; he was the first rector (from 29 June 1689) of King's Chapel, Boston, Massachusetts.

[Mather's Magnalia Christi Americana, 1702, ii. 189; Calamy's Account, 1713, ii. 734; Calamy's Continuation, 1727, ii. 847; Walker's Sufferings of the Clergy, 1714, ii. 27; Hutchinson's Hist. of the Colony of Massachusetts Bay, 1765, i. 226; Backus's Hist. of New England, 1777, pp. 350 seq.; Rees's Hist. Prot. Nonconformity in Wales, 1883, pp. 80 seq.; Appleton's Cyclopaedia of American Biography, 1888, iv. 475; Foster's Alumni Oxon. 1500-1714, iii. 1049.] A. G.

INDEX

TO

THE THIRTEENTH VOLUME.

Lives in Supplement, Vol. XXII

Massie, T. L. p. 1023.

X X

Lives in Supplement, Vol. XXII

Lives in Supplement, Vol. XXII

Lives in Supplement, Vol. XXII

Lives in Supplement, Vol. XXII

Lives in Supplement, Vol. XXII

Lives in Supplement, Vol. XXII

END OF THE THIRTEENTH VOLUME.

PRINTED IN GREAT BRITAIN AT THE UNIVERSITY PRESS, OXFORD
BY CHARLES BATEY, PRINTER TO THE UNIVERSITY